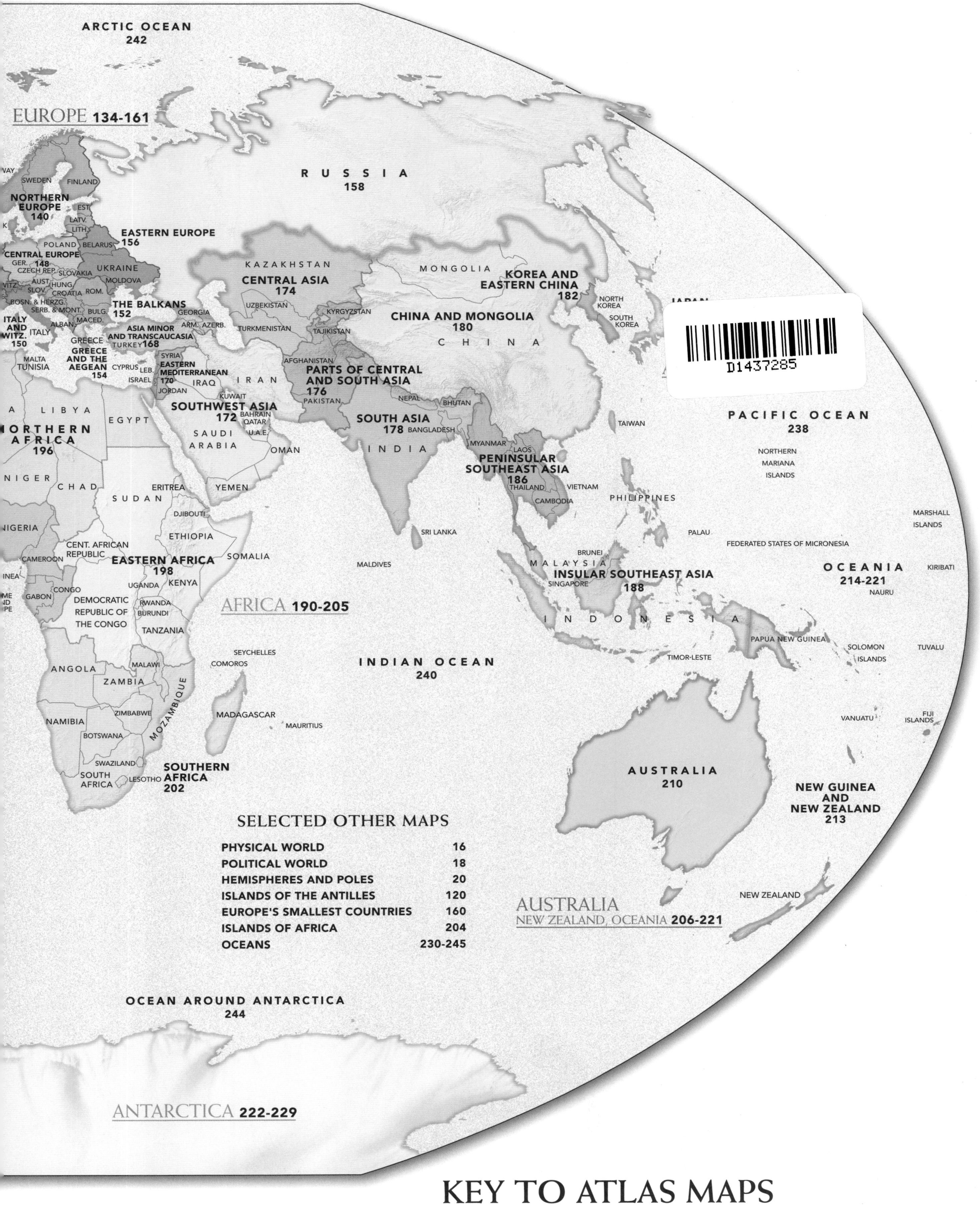

ARCTIC OCEAN 242
EUROPE 134-161
RUSSIA 158
SWEDEN
FINLAND
NORTHERN EUROPE 140
EST.
LATV.
LITH.
EASTERN EUROPE 156
POLAND
BELARUS
CENTRAL EUROPE
GER. 148
CZECH REP.
SLOVAKIA
AUST.
HUNG.
SLOV.
CROATIA
ROM.
UKRAINE
MOLDOVA
BOSN. & HERZG.
SERB. & MONT.
BULG.
MACED.
ALBAN.
THE BALKANS 152
ITALY AND SWITZ. 150
ITALY
GREECE
GREECE AND THE AEGEAN 154
MALTA
TUNISIA
GEORGIA
ARM.
AZERB.
ASIA MINOR AND TRANSCAUCASIA
TURKEY 168
CYPRUS
SYRIA
LEB.
ISRAEL
JORDAN
EASTERN MEDITERRANEAN 170
IRAQ
IRAN
KUWAIT
SOUTHWEST ASIA 172
BAHRAIN
QATAR
U.A.E.
SAUDI ARABIA
OMAN
YEMEN
KAZAKHSTAN
CENTRAL ASIA 174
UZBEKISTAN
TURKMENISTAN
KYRGYZSTAN
TAJIKISTAN
AFGHANISTAN
PARTS OF CENTRAL AND SOUTH ASIA 176
PAKISTAN
NEPAL
BHUTAN
SOUTH ASIA 178
BANGLADESH
INDIA
SRI LANKA
MALDIVES
MONGOLIA
CHINA AND MONGOLIA 180
CHINA
KOREA AND EASTERN CHINA 182
NORTH KOREA
SOUTH KOREA
TAIWAN
MYANMAR
LAOS
PENINSULAR SOUTHEAST ASIA 186
THAILAND
VIETNAM
CAMBODIA
PHILIPPINES
BRUNEI
MALAYSIA
INSULAR SOUTHEAST ASIA 188
SINGAPORE
INDONESIA
PAPUA NEW GUINEA
TIMOR-LESTE
PACIFIC OCEAN 238
NORTHERN MARIANA ISLANDS
PALAU
FEDERATED STATES OF MICRONESIA
MARSHALL ISLANDS
OCEANIA 214-221
KIRIBATI
NAURU
SOLOMON ISLANDS
TUVALU
VANUATU
FIJI ISLANDS
NEW GUINEA AND NEW ZEALAND 213
AUSTRALIA 210
NEW ZEALAND
AUSTRALIA
NEW ZEALAND, OCEANIA 206-221
LIBYA
EGYPT
NORTHERN AFRICA 196
NIGER
CHAD
SUDAN
ERITREA
DJIBOUTI
ETHIOPIA
NIGERIA
CENT. AFRICAN REPUBLIC
CAMEROON
EASTERN AFRICA 198
SOMALIA
UGANDA
KENYA
CONGO
GABON
DEMOCRATIC REPUBLIC OF THE CONGO
RWANDA
BURUNDI
TANZANIA
AFRICA 190-205
SEYCHELLES
COMOROS
MALAWI
ANGOLA
ZAMBIA
MOZAMBIQUE
ZIMBABWE
NAMIBIA
BOTSWANA
MADAGASCAR
MAURITIUS
SWAZILAND
SOUTH AFRICA
LESOTHO
SOUTHERN AFRICA 202
INDIAN OCEAN 240
SELECTED OTHER MAPS
PHYSICAL WORLD 16
POLITICAL WORLD 18
HEMISPHERES AND POLES 20
ISLANDS OF THE ANTILLES 120
EUROPE'S SMALLEST COUNTRIES 160
ISLANDS OF AFRICA 204
OCEANS 230-245
OCEAN AROUND ANTARCTICA 244
ANTARCTICA 222-229

KEY TO ATLAS MAPS

NATIONAL GEOGRAPHIC

Family Reference Atlas of the World

SECOND EDITION

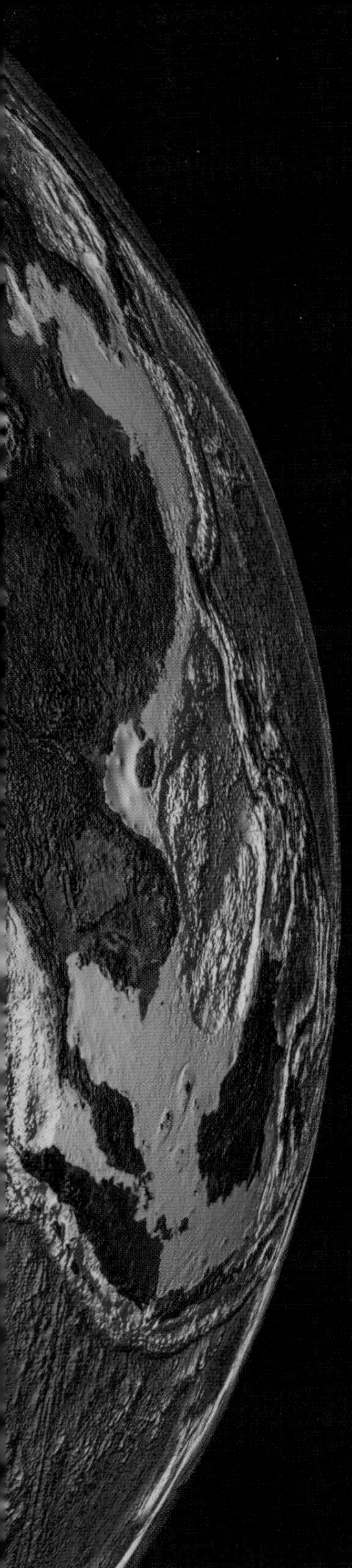

NATIONAL GEOGRAPHIC

Family Reference Atlas of the World

SECOND EDITION

NATIONAL GEOGRAPHIC
WASHINGTON, D.C.

Founded in 1888, the National Geographic Society is one of the largest nonprofit scientific and educational organizations in the world. It reaches more than 285 million people worldwide each month through its official journal, NATIONAL GEOGRAPHIC, and its four other magazines; the National Geographic Channel; television documentaries; radio programs; films; books; videos and DVDs; maps; and interactive media. National Geographic has funded more than 8,000 scientific research projects and supports an education program combating geographic illiteracy.

For more information, please call
1-800-NGS LINE (647-5463)
or write to the following address:

National Geographic Society
1145 17th Street N.W.
Washington, D.C. 20036-4688 U.S.A.

Log on to nationalgeographic.com;
AOL Keyword: NatGeo.

For information about special discounts
for bulk purchases, please contact
National Geographic Books Special Sales:
ngspecsales@ngs.org

Library of Congress Cataloging in Publication data is available upon request.

ISBN-13: 978-1-4262-0248-3

This atlas was made possible by the contributions of numerous experts and organizations around the world, including the following:

Center for International Earth Science Information Network (CIESIN), Columbia University

Central Intelligence Agency (CIA)

Conservation International (CI)

Cooperative Association for Internet Data Analysis (CAIDA)

Earth Science System Education Program, Michigan State University

Global Land Cover Group, University of Maryland

International Monetary Fund (IMF)

International Union for the Conservation of Nature and Natural Resources (IUCN)

Lunar and Planetary Institute (LPI)

National Aeronautics and Space Administration (NASA)
NASA Ames Research Center, NASA Goddard Space Flight Center, NASA Jet Propulsion Laboratory (JPL), NASA Marshall Space Flight Center

National Geospatial-Intelligence Agency (NGA)

National Oceanic and Atmospheric Administration (NOAA)
National Climatic Data Center (NCDC), National Environmental Satellite, Data, and Information Service (NESDIS), National Geophysical Data Center (NGDC), National Ocean Service (NOS)

National Science Foundation (NSF)

Population Reference Bureau (PRB)

Scripps Institution of Oceanography

Smithsonian Institution

United Nations (UN)
UN Conference on Trade and Development (UNCTAD), UN Development Programme (UNDP), UN Educational, Scientific, and Cultural Organization (UNESCO), UN Environment Programme (UNEP), UN Millennium Project, UN Population Division, UN Refugee Agency (UNHCR), UN Statistics Division (UNSD), Food and Agriculture Organization of the United Nations (FAO), International Telecommunication Union (ITU), World Conservation Monitoring Centre (WCMC)

U.S. Board on Geographic Names (BGN)

U.S. Bureau of the Census

U.S. Department of Agriculture (USDA)

U.S. Department of Energy (DOE)

U.S. Department of the Interior
Bureau of Land Management (BLM), National Park Service (NPS), U.S. Geological Survey (USGS)

U.S. Department of State: Office of the Geographer

World Bank

World Health Organization (WHO)
Pan American Health Organization (PAHO)

World Resources Institute (WRI)

World Trade Organization (WTO)

Worldwatch Institute

World Wildlife Fund (WWF)

For a complete listing of contributors, see page 380.

Introduction

WHY GEOGRAPHY? Today as never before, geographic information provides a powerful key to understanding an increasingly complicated world. While maps still record political boundaries and landforms, they now do far more than record country borders and mountains and seas: They track the more elusive boundaries that result in cultural divides, religious divides, and the borderless, global community created by communication and technological advances. In this second edition of the *Family Reference Atlas,* maps become pictures that tell stories of natural phenomena and of human hopes, desires, disasters, and successes.

National Geographic has been at the forefront of cartographic innovation for nearly a century, but the mapmaking technologies we now use surpass the wildest imaginings of our predecessors. Those master craftsmen made maps by the time-honored pen-and-ink method; today, satellites and computer systems allow us to acquire, combine, and overlay data in moments. By marrying the artistry of mapmaking with science and technology, we can track how a change in ocean temperatures in one region can give rise to superstorms in another; how the growing trend toward urbanization in many countries is depleting resources, affecting weather patterns, and encouraging poverty and diseases; and how shrinking populations in other countries are impacting economic growth and future opportunity. In this single volume you can quickly gain an understanding of these and other changes and their implications for regions, continents, the planet, and humankind.

In order to bring you a more detailed picture of certain parts of the globe, we've expanded the European and Caribbean sections. And we've added or enhanced world thematic maps on globalization, technology and communication, hot spots of conflict and terror, even the Internet and Internet-spread viruses. We've also included maps of our planetary neighbor Mars, based on data sent back by rovers Spirit and Opportunity and more recently, by the Mars Reconnaissance Orbiter (MRO).

Ours has never been a static planet, but the pace of change on Earth has accelerated with the explosion of the human population and the proliferation of human technologies. Large questions loom for the future—what will the continued growth of India and China mean for the planet; how will melting glaciers, rising sea levels, and an ever more volatile climate impact us all? Can we, in our daily lives, help improve life on Earth? When people "discover that they must be part of the solutions," Wangari Maathai, the Kenyan activist and environmentalist said in accepting her Nobel Peace Prize, "they realize their hidden potential and are empowered to overcome inertia and take action." We hope this atlas will serve to empower you, giving you and your family the knowledge you need to be engaged global citizens.

JOHN M. FAHEY, JR.

PRESIDENT AND
CHIEF EXECUTIVE OFFICER

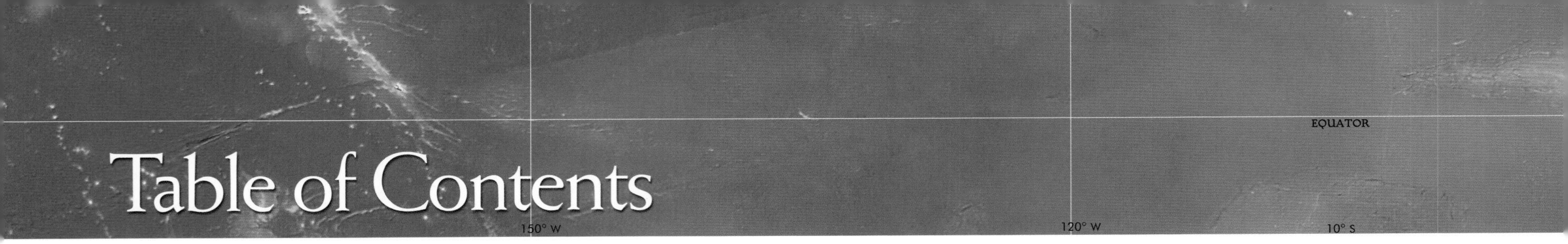

Table of Contents

10 USING THIS ATLAS MAP POLICIES • PHYSICAL MAPS • POLITICAL MAPS WORLD THEMATIC MAPS • REGIONAL MAPS • MAP SYMBOLS

14 WORLD

14 Introduction

16 Physical World

18 Political World

20 Hemispheres and Poles

22 Structure of the Earth
Continents Adrift in Time • Geologic Time • Geologic Forces Change the Face of the Planet • Plate Tectonics

24 Earth's Rocky Exterior
Rock Classes • The Rock Cycle • Global Distribution of Rock Types • Reading Earth History from Rocks

26 Landforms
Major Landform Types • Endogenic Landforms • Exogenic Landforms • Other Landforms • Landforms Created by Wind • Landforms Created by Water • Landforms Created by Ice

30 Surface of the Earth
Distribution of Earth's Elevations and Depths (Hypsometry) • Surface by the Numbers • A Slice of Earth • Earth Surface Elevations and Depths

32 Land Cover
Global Land Cover Composition

34 Climate
January and July: Solar Energy, Average Temperature, Cloud Cover, Precipitation • Major Factors that Influence Climate • Temperature Change over Time • Climate Zones • Climographs

38 Weather
Major Factors that Influence Weather • Cloud Types • Tropical Cyclones • Lightning • El Niño and La Niña

40 Biosphere
The Biosphere from Space • Biosphere Dynamics • Earth System Dynamics • Size of the Biosphere • The Biosphere over Time

42 Biodiversity
The Natural World • Species Diversity • Threatened Ecoregions • Threatened Species • Projected Biodiversity Status

44 Population
Lights of the World • Population Pyramids • Population Growth • Population Density • Regional Population Growth Disparities • Fertility • Urban Population Densities • Urban Population Growth • Life Expectancy • Migration • Most Populous Places • Most Crowded Places • Demographic Extremes

48 Languages
Voices of the World • Vanishing Languages • Evolution of Languages • How Many Speak What? • Major Language Families Today

50 Religions
Major Religions • Sacred Places • Adherents Worldwide • Adherents by Continent • Adherents by Country

52 Health and Education
Health-Care Availability • Income Levels: Indicators of Health and Literacy • Access to Improved Sanitation • Nutrition • HIV • Global Disease Burden • Causes of Death • Under-Five Mortality • Maternal Mortality • Education and Literacy • School Enrollment for Girls • Developing Human Capital

54 Conflict and Terror
Political Violence • Peace-Building Capacities • Change in Magnitude of Ongoing Conflicts • Global Regimes by Type • Genocides and Politicides Since 1955 • Refugees • Terrorist Attacks • Weapons Possessions

56 Economy
Global Economic Activity • Labor Migration • Top GDP Growth Rates • The World's Richest and Poorest Countries • Gross Domestic Product • Gross Domestic Product: Purchasing Power Parity (PPP) • Major Manufacturers

58 Trade
World Merchandise Trade • Growth of World Trade • Merchandise Exports • Main Trading Nations • World Debt • Trade Blocs • Trade Flow: Fuels • Trade Flow: Agricultural Products • Top Merchandise Exporters and Importers • Top Commercial Services Exporters and Importers

60 Food
Land Use and Commercial Agriculture • Fishing and Aquaculture • World Agricultural Production • Undernourishment in the Developing World • Caloric Supply • World Grain Production

62 Energy
Annual Energy Consumption • Energy Production • Fossil Fuel Extraction • Biomass, Hydroelectric, and Geothermal Power • Wind and Solar Power • Renewable Resources

64 Minerals
World Mineral Production • World Minerals by Economic Value

66 Environmental Stresses
Global Climate Change • Depletion of the Ozone Layer • Pollution • Water Scarcity • Soil Degradation and Desertification • Deforestation

68 Protected Areas
World Heritage Sites • Designated Protected Areas • The World Heritage Site System • Endemism

70 Globalization
Globalization Status • Transnational Corporations • Extremes of Globalization • Economic Integration • Personal Contact • Technological Connectivity • Political Engagement • International Outsourcing

72 Technology and Communication
Centers of Technological Innovation • Milestones in Technology • The Digital Divide

74 Internet
Mapping the Spread of a Computer Virus • Internet Users Worldwide (estimated), 1995-2005 • Global Internet Connectivity • Worldwide Distribution of Internet Resources

76 NORTH AMERICA

76 Introduction

80 North America: Physical and Political

82 Canada
Canada • Greenland • St.-Pierre and Miquelon

84 United States: Physical

86 United States: Political

88 United States
Temperature and Precipitation • Land Use, Agriculture, and Fishing • Population • Industry and Mining

90 United States: Major Highways

92 United States: Federal Lands

NORTHEAST **94**
Connecticut • Maine • Massachusetts • New Hampshire • New Jersey • New York • Pennsylvania • Rhode Island • Vermont

SOUTH ATLANTIC **96**
Delaware • District of Columbia • Florida • Georgia • Maryland • North Carolina • South Carolina • Virginia • West Virginia

GREAT LAKES **98**
Illinois • Indiana • Michigan • Ohio • Wisconsin

MIDDLE SOUTH **100**
Alabama • Arkansas • Kentucky • Louisiana • Mississippi • Tennessee

TEXAS AND OKLAHOMA **102**

NORTHERN PLAINS **104**
Iowa • Kansas • Minnesota • Missouri • Nebraska • North Dakota • South Dakota

ROCKY MOUNTAINS **106**
Arizona • Colorado • Idaho • Montana • New Mexico • Utah • Wyoming

WEST COAST **108**
California • Nevada • Oregon • Washington

ALASKA **110**

HAWAI'I **112**

114 Mexico and Central America
Belize • Costa Rica • El Salvador • Guatemala • Honduras • Mexico • Nicaragua • Panama

116 Bahamas and Greater Antilles
Bahamas • Bermuda • Cayman Islands • Cuba • Dominican Republic • Haiti • Jamaica • Puerto Rico • Turks and Caicos Islands

118 Lesser Antilles
Anguilla • Antigua and Barbuda • Aruba • Barbados • British Virgin Islands • Dominica • Grenada • Guadeloupe • Martinique • Montserrat • Netherlands Antilles • St. Kitts and Nevis • St. Lucia • St. Vincent and the Grenadines • Trinidad and Tobago • U.S. Virgin Islands

120 Islands of the Antilles
Abaco Islands • Anguilla • Antigua • Aruba • Barbados • Bermuda Islands • Bimini Islands • Bonaire • Curacao • Dominica • Eleuthera • Exuma • Grand Bahama Island • Grand Cayman • Grenada • Guadeloupe • Jamaica • Martinique • Montserrat • New Providence • Puerto Rico • San Salvador • St. Croix • St. Kitts and Nevis • St. Lucia • St. Martin (St. Maarten) • St. Thomas and St. John • St. Vincent • Tobago • Tortola • Trinidad • Virgin Gorda

122 SOUTH AMERICA

122 Introduction

126 South America: Physical and Political

128 Northern South America
Colombia • Ecuador • French Guiana • Guyana • Suriname • Venezuela

130 Central South America
Bolivia • Brazil • Paraguay • Peru

132 Southern South America
Argentina • Chile • Falkland Islands • Uruguay

134 EUROPE

134 Introduction

138 Europe: Physical and Political

140 Northern Europe
Denmark • Estonia • Finland • Iceland • Latvia • Lithuania • Norway • Sweden • Faroe Islands

142 Britain and Ireland
Ireland • United Kingdom

144 Iberian Peninsula
Portugal • Spain

146 France and the Low Countries
Belgium • France • Luxembourg • Netherlands

148 Central Europe
Austria • Czech Republic • Germany • Hungary • Poland • Slovakia

150 Italy and Switzerland

152 The Balkans
Albania • Bosnia and Herzegovina • Bulgaria • Croatia • Macedonia • Romania • Serbia and Montenegro • Slovenia

154 Greece and the Aegean

156 Eastern Europe
Belarus • Moldova • Ukraine • Western Russia

158 Russia

160 Europe's Smallest Countries
Andorra • Cyprus • Liechtenstein • Luxembourg • Malta • Monaco • San Marino • Vatican City • Gibraltar

CONTINUES NEXT PAGE >

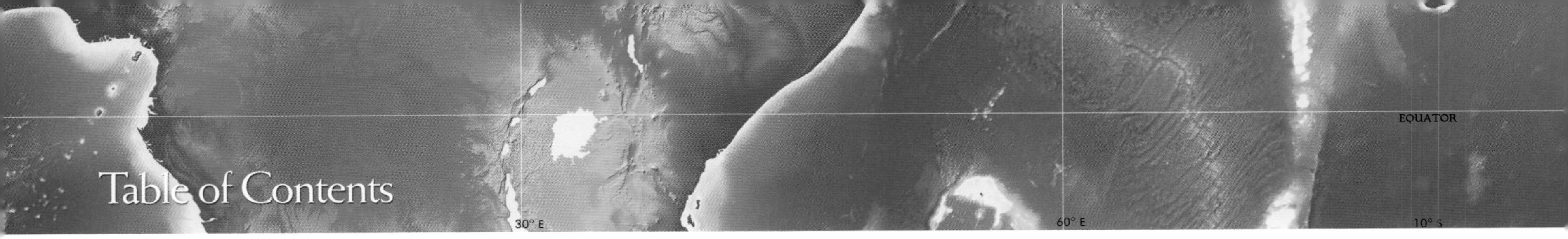

Table of Contents

162 ASIA

162 Introduction

166 Asia: Physical and Political

168 Asia Minor and Transcaucasia
Armenia • Azerbaijan • Georgia • Turkey

170 Eastern Mediterranean
Israel • Jordan • Lebanon • Syria

172 Southwest Asia
Bahrain • Iran • Iraq • Kuwait • Oman • Qatar • Saudi Arabia • United Arab Emirates • Yemen

174 Central Asia
Kazakhstan • Turkmenistan • Uzbekistan

176 Parts of Central and South Asia
Afghanistan • Kyrgyzstan • Pakistan • Tajikistan

178 South Asia
Bangladesh • Bhutan • India • Maldives • Nepal • Sri Lanka

180 China and Mongolia

182 Korea and Eastern China
Eastern China • North Korea • South Korea

184 Japan

186 Peninsular Southeast Asia
Cambodia • Laos • Myanmar • Thailand • Vietnam

188 Insular Southeast Asia
Brunei • Indonesia • Malaysia • Philippines • Singapore • Timor-Leste

190 AFRICA

190 Introduction

194 Africa: Physical and Political

196 Northern Africa
Algeria • Chad • Egypt • Gambia • Libya • Mali • Mauritania • Morocco • Niger • Senegal • Tunisia • Western Sahara

198 Eastern Africa
Burundi • Central African Republic • Democratic Republic of the Congo • Djibouti • Eritrea • Ethiopia • Kenya • Rwanda • Somalia • Sudan • Tanzania • Uganda

200 West-Central Africa
Benin • Burkina Faso • Cameroon • Congo • Côte d'Ivoire • Equatorial Guinea • Gabon • Ghana • Guinea • Guinea-Bissau • Liberia • Nigeria • Sao Tome and Principe • Sierra Leone • Togo

202 Southern Africa
Angola • Botswana • Cabinda • Comoros • Lesotho • Madagascar • Malawi • Mozambique • Namibia • Seychelles • South Africa • Swaziland • Zambia • Zimbabwe

204 Islands of Africa
Bioko • Canary Islands • Cape Verde • Comoros • Madiera Islands • Mauritius • Mayotte • Réunion • Rodrigues • Sao Tome and Principe • Seychelles

206 AUSTRALIA • NEW ZEALAND • OCEANIA

206 Introduction

210 Australia: Physical and Political

212 Australia
Temperature and Precipitation • Land Use, Agriculture, and Fishing • Population • Industry and Mining

213 New Guinea and New Zealand
New Zealand • Papua New Guinea

214 Islands of Oceania

216 Oceania
Inset Maps • Flags and Facts

222 ANTARCTICA

222 Introduction

226 Antarctica: Physical

228 Antarctica
Elevation of the Ice Sheet • Measurements of a Paradox • Ice on the Move • Ultimate Winds • Antarctic Treaty • Antarctic Convergence

230 OCEANS

230 World Bathymetry

232 Oceanography
The Ocean Floor • Major Surface Currents • Ocean Conveyor Belt

234 Limits of the Oceans and Seas

236 Atlantic Ocean

238 Pacific Ocean

240 Indian Ocean

242 Arctic Ocean

244 Ocean Around Antarctica

246 SPACE

246 Introduction

248 The Moon: Near Side

250 The Moon: Far Side

252 Mars

254 The Solar System

256 The Planets
Sun • Mercury • Venus • Earth • Mars • Jupiter • Saturn • Uranus • Neptune • Pluto

258 The Universe

260 Space Exploration Time Line

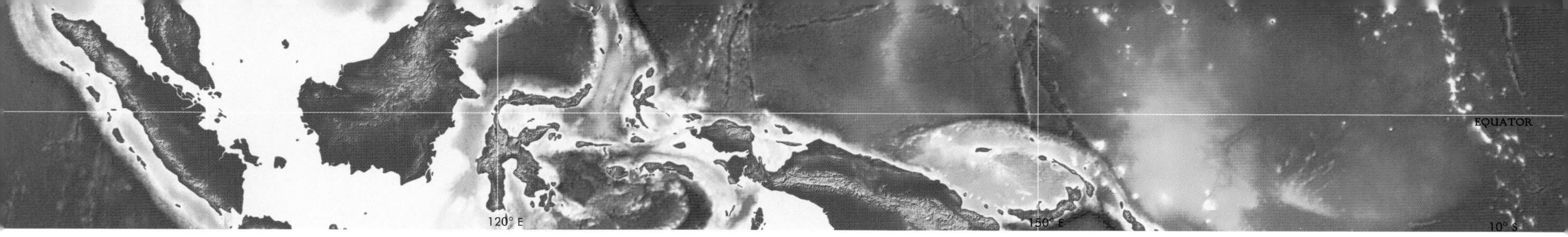

262 APPENDIX

262 Airline Distances, Abbreviations, Metric Conversions

264 Geographic Comparisons

266 Political Entities and Status
Independent States of the World • Dependencies of the World • Areas of Special Status • Areas Geographically Separated from Mainland Countries

270 Special Flags
Development of the Stars and Stripes • International Flags • Regional Flags • Religious Flags • Ethnic Flags • Specialized Flags

272 Foreign Terms

274 World Time Zones

276 Major Cities of the World

278 World Temperature and Rainfall

282 Glossary of Geographic Terms

285 INDEX

285 Place-name Index

378 Moon Index

380 Acknowledgments
Consultants • Physical and Political Maps • Principal Reference Sources • Satellite Images • Photographs • Key to Flags and Facts

A long belt of land and mostly sea—reaching ten degrees north and ten degrees south of the Equator—wraps around the globe to form a complete circle of elevation coverage (top and previous spread).

The round—azimuthal—projection (bottom) represents a view from atop the world. The geographic North Pole at 90 degrees latitude is located at the center of the image. Shown in its entirety, the Northern Hemisphere radiates from the Pole to the periphery of the map, aligning with the Equator at zero degrees latitude.

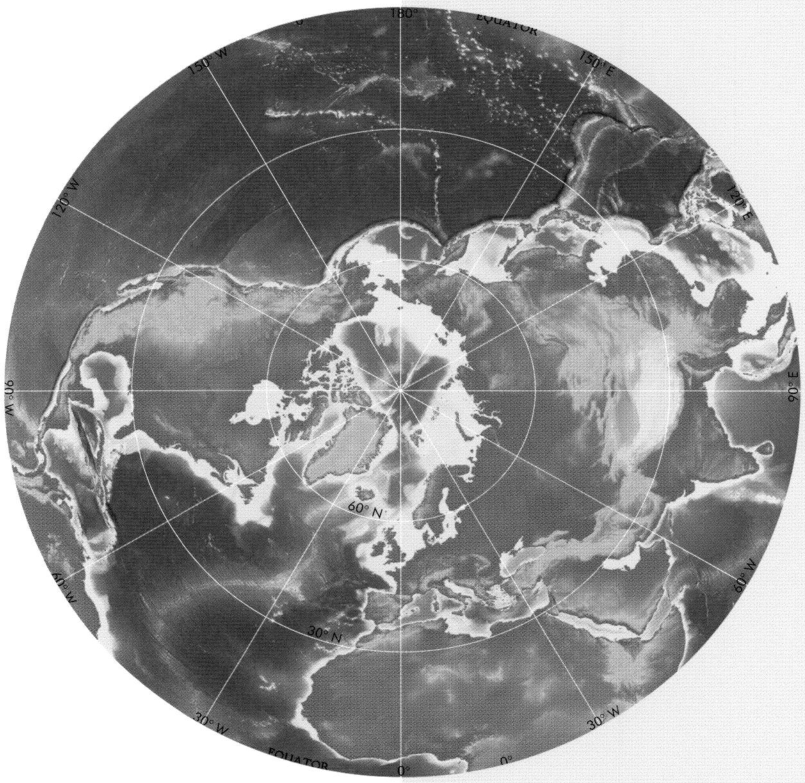

Using this Atlas

MAP POLICIES Maps are a rich, useful, and—to the extent humanly possible—accurate means of depicting the world. Yet maps inevitably make the world seem a little simpler than it really is. A neatly drawn boundary may in reality be a hotly contested war zone. The government-sanctioned, "official" name of a provincial city in an ethnically diverse region may bear little resemblance to the name its citizens routinely use. These cartographic issues often seem obscure and academic. But maps arouse passions. Despite our carefully reasoned map policies, users of National Geographic maps write us strongly worded letters when our maps are at odds with their worldviews.

How do National Geographic cartographers deal with these realities? With constant scrutiny, considerable discussion, and help from many outside experts. Examples:

Nations: Issues of national sovereignty and contested borders often boil down to "de facto versus de jure" discussions. Governments and international agencies frequently make official rulings about contested regions. These de jure decisions, no matter how legitimate, are often at odds with the wishes of individuals and groups, and they often stand in stark contrast to real-world situations. The inevitable conclusion: It is simplest and best to show the world as it is—de facto—rather than as we or others wish it to be.

Africa's Western Sahara, for example, was divided by Morocco and Mauritania after the Spanish government withdrew in 1976. Although Morocco now controls the entire territory, the United Nations does not recognize Morocco's sovereignty over this still-disputed area. This atlas shows the de facto Moroccan rule but includes an explanatory note.

Place-names: Ride a barge down the Danube, and you'll hear the river called *Donau, Duna, Dunaj, Dunărea, Dunav, Dunay*. These are local names. This atlas uses the conventional name, "Danube," on physical maps. On political maps, local names are used, with the conventional name in parentheses where space permits. Usage conventions for both foreign and domestic place-names are established by the U.S. Board on Geographic Names, a group with representatives from several federal agencies.

Physical Maps

Physical maps of the world, the continents, and the ocean floor reveal landforms and vegetation in stunning detail. Painted by relief artists John Bonner and Tibor Tóth, the maps have been edited for accuracy. Although painted maps are human interpretations, these depictions can emphasize subtle features that are sometimes invisible in satellite imagery.

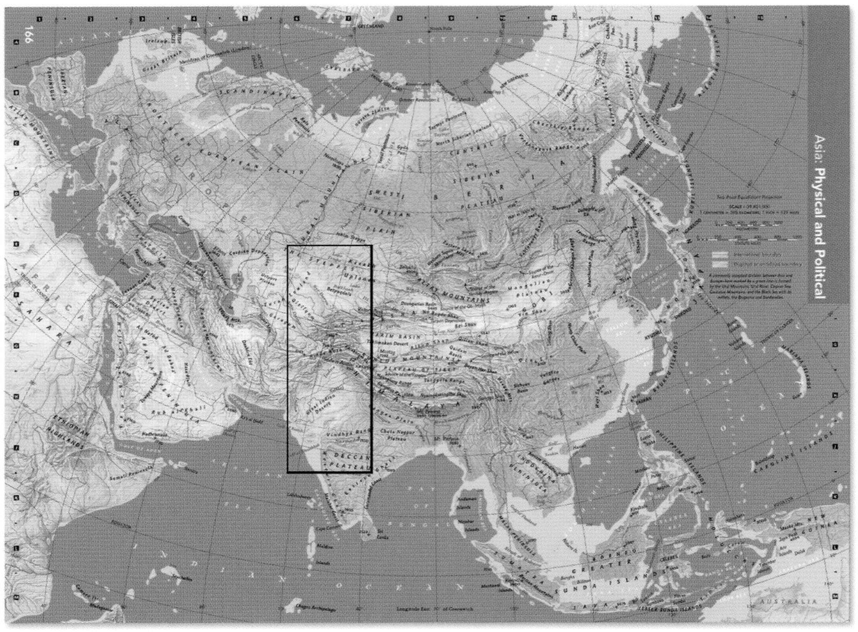

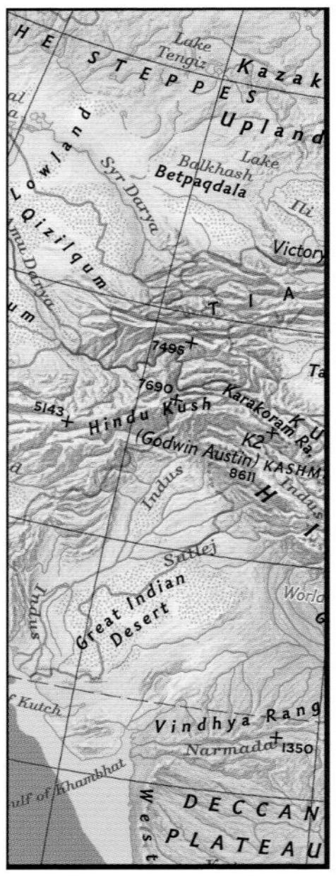

PHYSICAL FEATURES: Colors and shading illustrate variations in elevation, landforms, and vegetation. Patterns indicate specific landscape features, such as sand, glaciers, and swamps.

WATER FEATURES: Blue lines indicate rivers; other water bodies are shown as areas of blue. Lighter shading reflects the limits of the Continental Shelf.

BOUNDARIES AND POLITICAL DIVISIONS are shown in red. Dotted lines indicate disputed or uncertain boundaries.

Political Maps

Political maps portray features such as international boundaries, the locations of cities, road networks, and other important elements of the world's human geography. Most index entries are keyed to the political maps, listing the page numbers and then the specific locations on the pages. (See page 285 for details on how to use the index.)

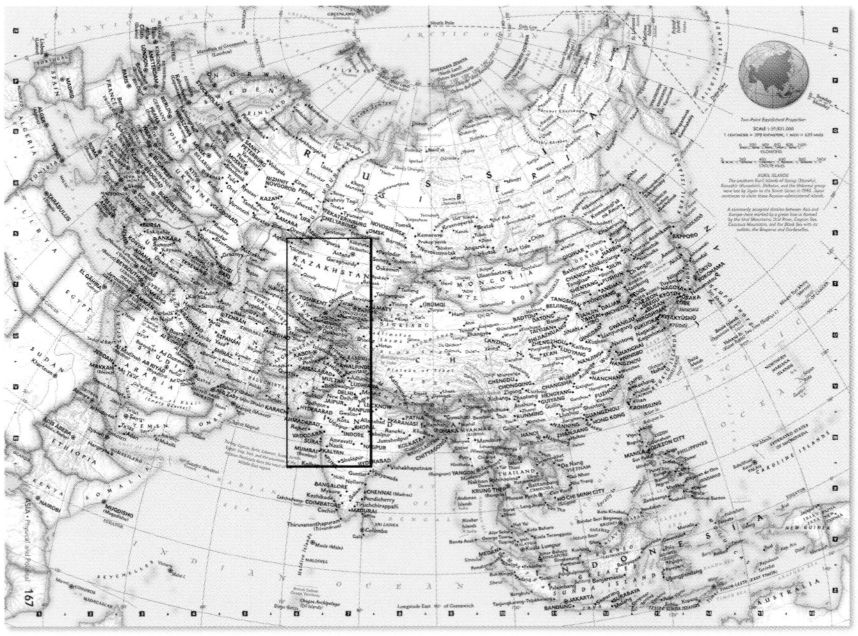

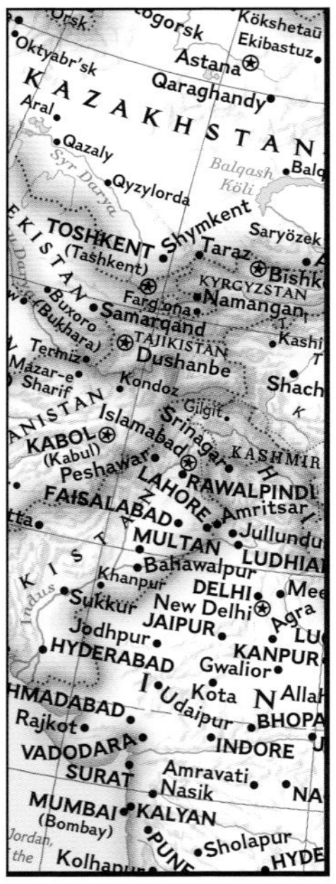

PHYSICAL FEATURES: Gray relief shading depicts surface features such as mountains, hills, and valleys.

WATER FEATURES are shown in blue. Solid lines and filled-in areas indicate perennial water features; dashed lines and patterns indicate intermittent features.

BOUNDARIES AND POLITICAL DIVISIONS are defined with both lines and colored bands; they vary according to whether a boundary is internal or international (for details, see map symbols key at right).

CITIES: The regional political maps that form the bulk of this atlas depict four categories of cities or towns. The largest cities are shown in all capital letters (e.g., LONDON).

World Thematic Maps

Thematic maps reveal the rich patchwork and infinite interrelationships of our changing planet. The thematic section at the beginning of the atlas focuses on physical and biological topics such as geology, landforms, land cover, and biodiversity. It also charts human patterns, with information on population, languages, religions, and the world economy. Two-page spreads on energy and minerals illustrate how people have learned to use Earth's resources, while spreads devoted to environmental stresses and protected lands focus on the far-reaching effects of human activities and the need for resource conservation. Throughout this section of the atlas, maps are coupled with satellite imagery, charts, diagrams, photographs, and tabular information; together, they create a very useful framework for studying geographic patterns.

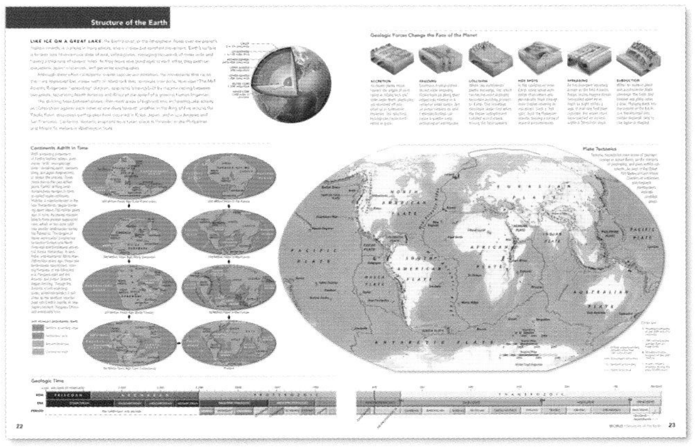

Structure of the Earth

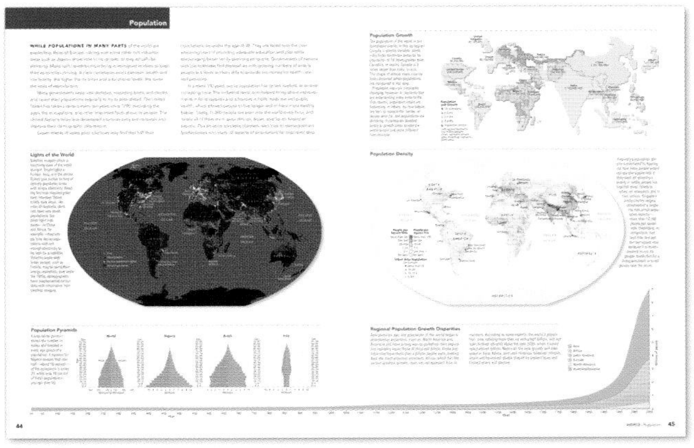

World Population

Regional Maps

This atlas divides the continents into several subregions, each displayed on a two-page spread. Large-scale maps capture the political divisions and major surface features, whereas accompanying regional thematic maps lend insight into natural and human factors that give character to a region. Fact boxes, which include flag designs and information on populations, languages, religions, and economies, appear alongside the maps as practical reference tools.

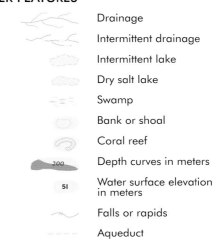

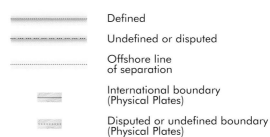

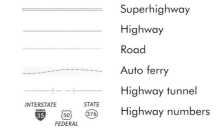

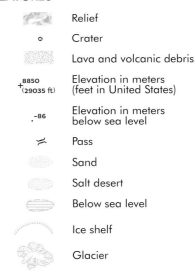

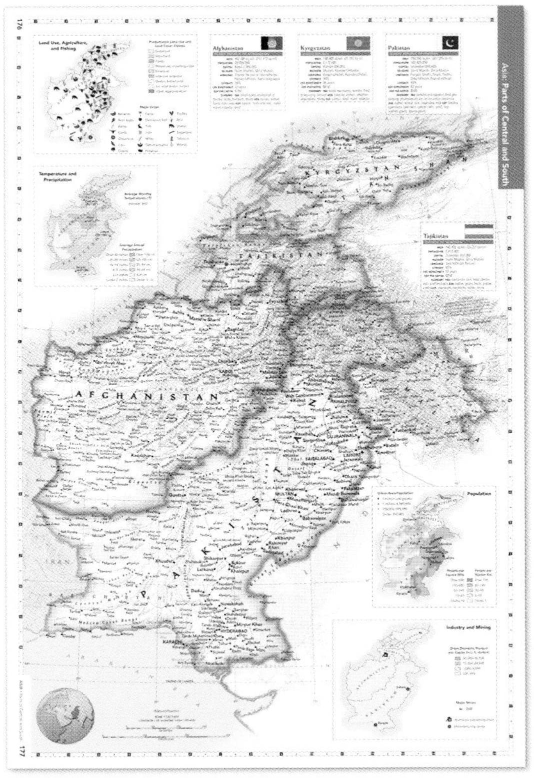

For more details on the regional map spreads, see pages 12–13.

Map Symbols

BOUNDARIES

- Defined
- Undefined or disputed
- Offshore line of separation
- International boundary (Physical Plates)
- Disputed or undefined boundary (Physical Plates)

CITIES

- Capitals
- Towns

TRANSPORTATION

- Superhighway
- Highway
- Road
- Auto ferry
- Highway tunnel
- INTERSTATE 35 FEDERAL 50 STATE 376 — Highway numbers

WATER FEATURES

- Drainage
- Intermittent drainage
- Intermittent lake
- Dry salt lake
- Swamp
- Bank or shoal
- Coral reef
- 200 — Depth curves in meters
- 51 — Water surface elevation in meters
- Falls or rapids
- Aqueduct

PHYSICAL FEATURES

- Relief
- Crater
- Lava and volcanic debris
- 8850 (29035 ft) — Elevation in meters (feet in United States)
- -86 — Elevation in meters below sea level
- Pass
- Sand
- Salt desert
- Below sea level
- Ice shelf
- Glacier

CULTURAL FEATURES

- Oil field
- Canal
- Dam
- Wall
- U.S. National Park
- Site
- Ruin

Using this Atlas

LOCATORS:

Each regional spread contains a locator map showing where the featured region lies within a continent. The region of interest is highlighted in the continental section's color (in this case, purple, for Europe). Surrounding areas on the same continent appear in gray; other land areas are brown.

Spain

KINGDOM OF SPAIN

AREA	505,988 sq km (195,363 sq mi)
POPULATION	43,484,000
CAPITAL	Madrid 5,103,000
RELIGION	Roman Catholic
LANGUAGE	Castilian Spanish (official), Catalan, Galician, Basque
LITERACY	98%
LIFE EXPECTANCY	80 years
GDP PER CAPITA	$24,386
ECONOMY	IND: textiles and apparel, food and beverages, metals and metal manufactures, chemicals AGR: grain, vegetables, olives, wine grapes; beef; fish EXP: machinery, motor vehicles, foodstuffs, pharmaceuticals

FLAGS AND FACTS:

This atlas recognizes 192 independent nations. All of these countries, along with dependencies and U.S. states, are profiled in the continental regional sections of the atlas. Accompanying each entry are highlights of geographic, demographic, and economic data. These details provide a brief overview of each country, state, or territory; they are not intended to be comprehensive. A detailed description of the sources and policies used in compiling the listings is included in the Key to Flags and Facts on page 383.

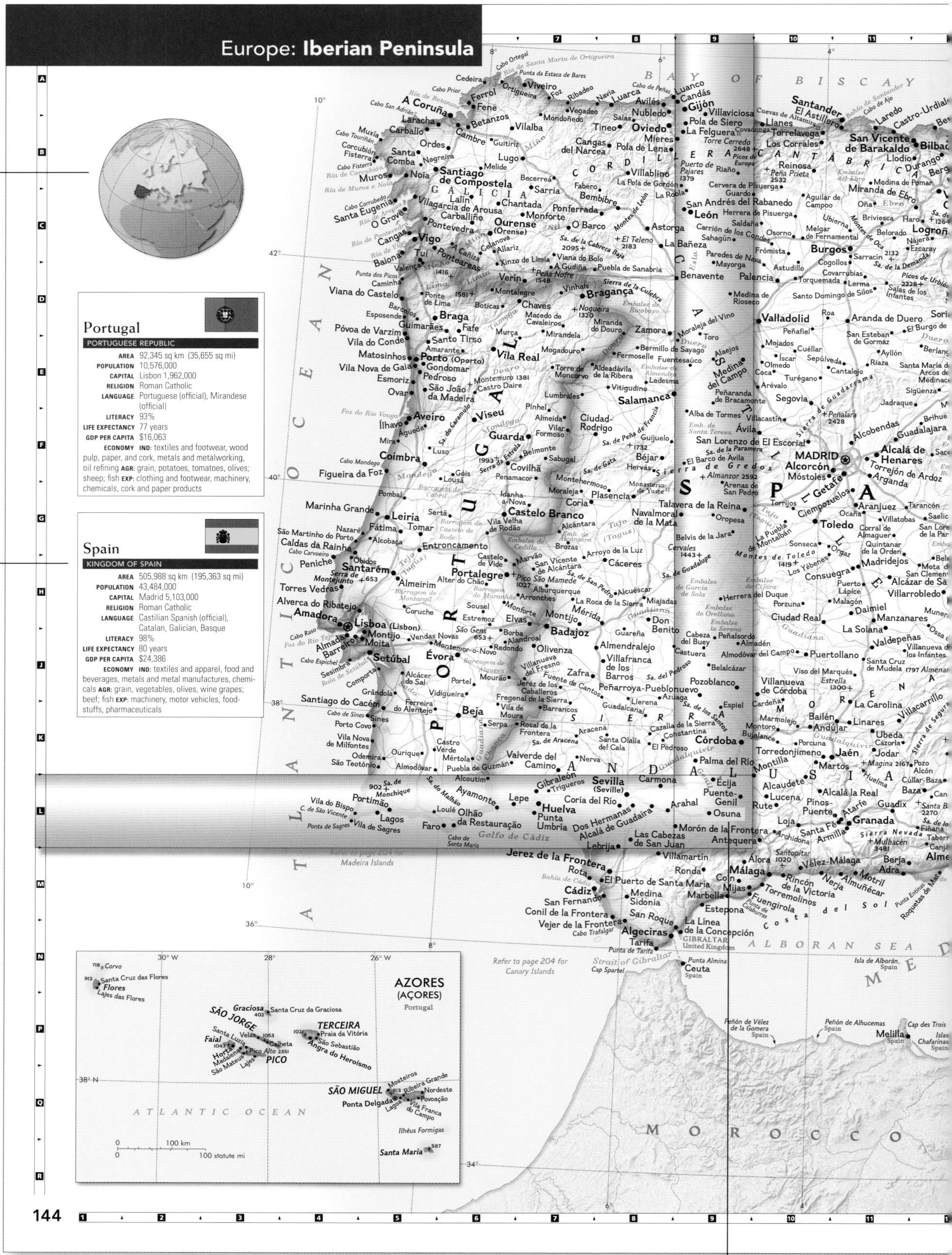

INDEX AND GRID:

Beginning on page 285 is a full index of place-names found in this atlas. The edge of each map is marked with letters (in rows) and numbers (in columns), to which the index entries are referenced. As an example, "Osuna, *Sp.* **144** L9" (see inset section, right) refers to the grid section on page 144 where row L and column 9 meet. More examples and additional details about the index are included on page 285.

Ostrów Wielkopolski, *Pol.* **149** E14
O'Sullivan Dam, *Wash., U.S.* **108** D7
Osŭm, river, *Bulg.* **153** H14
Ōsumi Kaikyō, *Japan* **185** U4
Ōsumi Shotō, *Japan* **185** U4
Osuna, *Sp.* **144** L9
Oswego, *N.Y., U.S.* **94** H8
Oswestry, *Eng., U.K.* **143** T10
Ōta, *Japan* **185** N12
Otaki, *N.Z.* **213** M19
Otar, *Kaz.* **175** H16

MAP PROJECTIONS:
Map projections determine how land shapes are distorted when transferred from a sphere (the Earth) to a flat piece of paper. Many different projections are used in this atlas—each carefully chosen for a map's particular coverage area and purpose.

MAP SCALES:
Scale information indicates the distance on Earth represented by a given length on the map. Here, map scale is expressed in three ways: 1) as a representative fraction where scale is shown as a fraction or ratio as in 1:3,290,000. This means that one centimeter or one inch on the map represents 3,290,000 centimeters or inches on Earth's surface. 2) as a verbal statement: one centimeter equals 118 kilometers or one inch equals 187 miles and 3) as a bar scale, a linear graph symbol subdivided to show map lengths in kilometers and miles in the real world.

THEMATIC MAPS:
In combination, the four thematic maps on each regional spread—Temperature and Precipitation; Population; Land Use, Agriculture, and Fishing; and Industry and Mining—provide a fascinating overview of the area's physical and cultural geography. Temperature and Precipitation maps show which areas receive the most rain, and what the average temperatures are at different times during the year. Population maps allow one to see, at a glance, which areas are the least and most crowded, and where the major urban centers are located. Land Use, Agriculture, and Fishing maps paint a general picture of the ways humans use land resources. And Industry and Mining maps indicate the relative economic well-being of countries (expressed in GDP per capita) and show major centers of mining, mineral processing, and manufacturing. Interesting relationships can be observed: For example, although mines can be located anywhere that mineral deposits occur, processing centers are only feasible in areas with inexpensive electricity and adequate access to transportation.

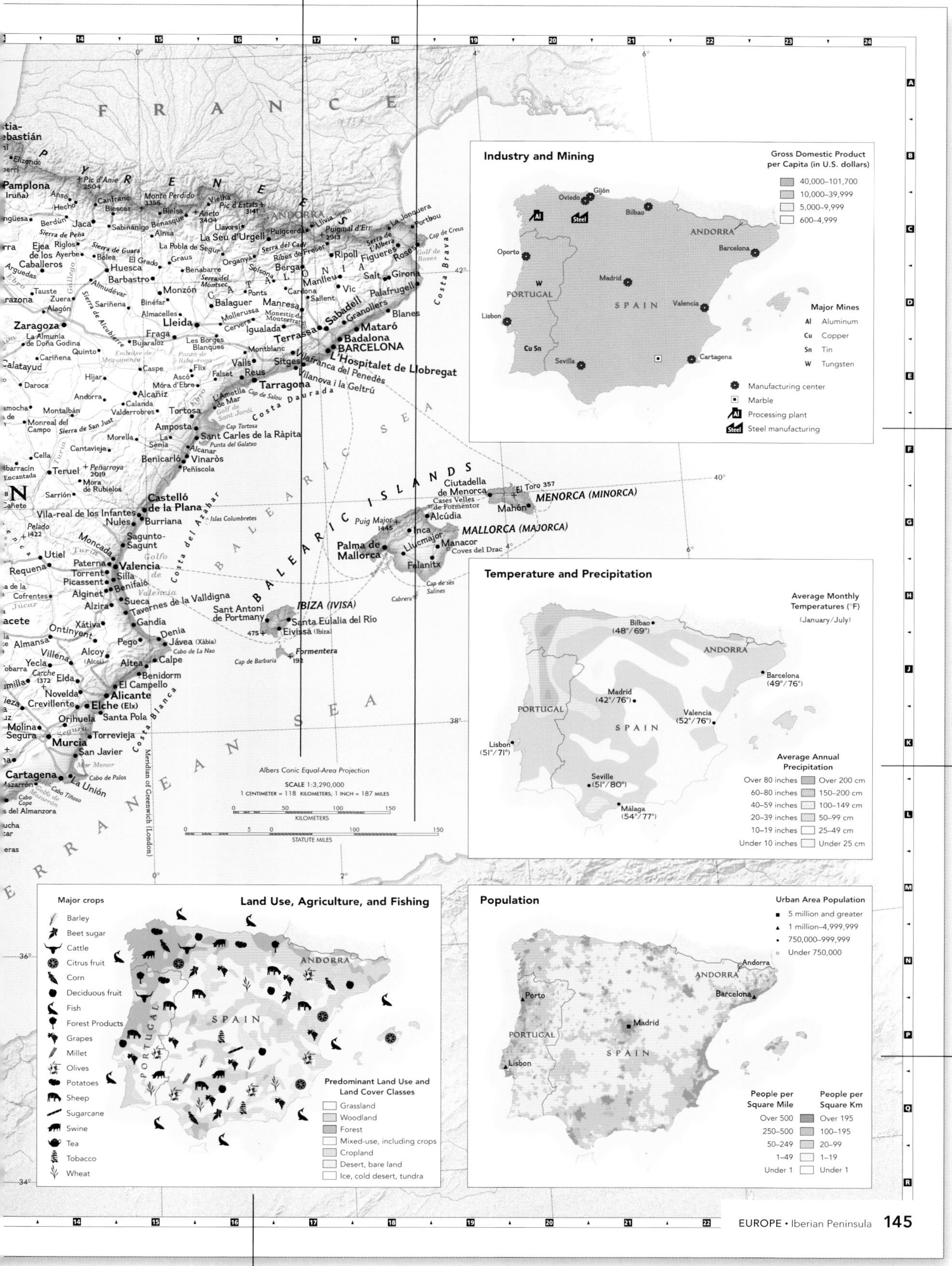

INDUSTRY AND MINING MAPS:
On these maps, major manufacturing centers, mines, and processing plants are shown with symbols; countries are colored according to gross domestic product (GDP) per capita. The GDP per-capita key breakdowns are consistent among all regions of a continent. For example, Northern Europe, Britain and Ireland, and the remaining regional maps of Europe match this key for the Iberian Peninsula.

TEMPERATURE AND PRECIPITATION MAPS:
These maps show climatic averages over time. Colors represent precipitation information; point symbols show average January and July temperatures for selected cities and towns.

POPULATION MAPS:
Colors indicate relative population density, with the most crowded areas shown in the darkest red-orange color. Geometric point symbols indicate the sizes of selected major cities and national capitals and their urban areas.

LAND USE, AGRICULTURE, AND FISHING MAPS:
The colors on these maps indicate predominant land use and land-cover types—showing, for example, whether an area comprises mainly cropland or forest. Symbols for major crops give a general picture of each region's agricultural activity.

The rapid worldwide decline in the diversity of plant and animal life ("bio-diversity"), an unfortunate result of human activity, is catching the growing attention of scientists. Increasingly, conservationists realize that to protect the planet's biodiversity they must look past political boundaries to work with nature's own organization. The many hundreds of terrestrial and coastal marine areas shown on this map represent ecoregions defined by the World Wildlife Fund (WWF) and The Nature Conservancy. Each ecoregion has unique species and communities, many found nowhere else on Earth. For detailed information on each region, see the online maps at: www.worldwildlife.org/wildworld/terrestrial.html and www.worldwildlife.org/MEOW.

The World

Some 93 million miles from the sun, Earth whirls in space, its exact origins shrouded in time. According to scientists, our planet and every other object in the solar system descend from a great cloud of interstellar gas and dust that condensed to form the sun about 4.6 billion years ago. Life is known to have found a foothold only on Earth—more than 3.5 billion years ago—but in recent years researchers have made intriguing discoveries about potential habitats for life on other planets or their moons.

Scientists continue to study habitats here at home as well. Using the very latest technologies, they are gaining a much better understanding of the natural processes that support life, shape landscapes, and keep the currents of the air and sea always in motion. They are learning, too, how we humans, relative newcomers among life-forms, are affecting our world, for better or worse.

The image at left represents one way to see and understand the diversity of life on Earth. It portrays more than a thousand "ecoregions," charted according to climate, oceanography, plant and animal communities, and other ecological features, rather than political boundaries. Maps such as this can be an invaluable learning tool for scientists and laypeople alike.

The following pages present a wide array of other maps, tables, graphs, images, and text, covering all aspects of physical and cultural geography. Together, they reveal the state of our world, this complex, dynamic realm we call Earth.

180°
160°
140°
120°
100°
80°
60°
40°
20°
90°
80°
70°
60°
50°
40°
30°
20°
10°
0°
LOMONOSOV RIDGE
MAKAROV BASIN
ARCTIC
CANADA BASIN
CHUKCHI PLAIN
CHUKCHI PLATEAU
MENDELEYEV PLAIN
NORTHWIND ESCARPMENT
CONTINENTAL SHELF
CANADA PLAIN
North Magnetic Pole 2006
North Geomagnetic Pole 2005
QUEEN ELIZABETH ISLANDS
Axel Heiberg Island
Ellesmere Island
Lincoln Sea
Knud Rasmussen Land
GREENLAND
Prince Patrick Island
Melville I.
Banks Island
Victoria Island
Devon I.
Beaufort Sea
Wrangel I.
SIBERIA
Chukchi Sea
Chukchi Pen.
Point Barrow
North Slope
Brooks Range
ARCTIC CIRCLE
ALASKA
Seward Pen.
BERING SEA
Mt. McKinley (Denali)
6194
Alaska Range
Mt. Logan
5959
Gulf of Alaska
Aleutian Islands
ALEUTIAN TRENCH
Alexander Archipelago
Queen Charlotte Is.
Vancouver Island
Boothia Pen.
Melville Pen.
Foxe Basin
Baffin Bay
Baffin Island
Southampton Island
Hudson Bay
Hudson Strait
Ungava Bay
LABRADOR SEA
Davis Strait
Denmark Strait
Gunnbjørn
ICELAND PLATEAU
Iceland
CONTINENTAL SLOPE
Cape Farewell
NORTHWEST ATLANTIC MID-OCEAN CANYON
REYKJANES RIDGE
CHARLIE-GIBBS FRACTURE ZONE
FARADAY FRACTURE ZONE
ROCKALL TROUGH
Great Slave Lake
Great Bear Lake
Lake Winnipeg
James Bay
Canadian Shield
NORTH AMERICA
ROCKY MOUNTAINS
Great Plains
Missouri
Source of the Mississippi
L. Superior
L. Michigan
L. Huron
Lake Ontario
L. Erie
St. Lawrence
Gulf of St. Lawrence
Anticosti I.
Island of Newfoundland
Grand Banks of Newfoundland
Flemish Cap
Nova Scotia
Bay of Fundy
Gulf of Maine
Cape Cod
Long Island
Laurentian Fan
Appalachian Mountains
Ozark Plateau
Mt. Mitchell
2037
Cape Hatteras
Chesapeake Bay
Kelvin Seamount
SOHM PLAIN
Bermuda Islands
BERMUDA RISE
NORTH AMERICAN BASIN
HATTERAS PLAIN
BLAKE PLATEAU
Florida
Coastal Plain
Mississippi Fan
GULF OF MEXICO
MEXICO BASIN
Campeche Bank
Yucatán Peninsula
Great Basin
Great Salt Lake
Mt. Whitney
4418
Mt. Elbert
4399
Sierra Nevada
Cascade Range
Death Valley
Cape Mendocino
CASCADIA BASIN
TUFTS PLAIN
Harris Seamount
MENDOCINO FRACTURE ZONE
PIONEER FRACTURE ZONE
MURRAY FRACTURE ZONE
MOLOKAI FRACTURE ZONE
CLARION FRACTURE ZONE
CLIPPERTON FRACTURE ZONE
GALÁPAGOS FRACTURE ZONE
MARQUESAS FRACTURE ZONE
CHALLENGER FRACTURE ZONE
AGASSIZ FRACTURE ZONE
VALDIVIA FRACTURE ZONE
MENARD FRACTURE ZONE
HEEZEN FRACTURE ZONE
ELTANIN FRACTURE ZONE
THARP FRACTURE ZONE
UDINTSEV FRACTURE ZONE
NORTH PACIFIC OCEAN
NORTHEAST PACIFIC BASIN
NORTHWEST HAWAIIAN RIDGE
Musicians Seamounts
Midway Is.
Hawaiian Islands
TROPIC OF CANCER
NECKER RIDGE
Kaua'i
O'ahu
Maui
Hawai'i
Mendelssohn Seamount
Fieberling Tablemount
Moonless Mts.
Guadalupe I.
Henderson Seamount
Baja California
Sierra Madre Occidental
Sierra Madre Oriental
Gulf of California
CEDROS TRENCH
PATTON ESCARPMENT
Johnston Atoll
Mathematicians Seamounts
CENTRAL PACIFIC BASIN
MAGELLAN RISE
Palmyra Atoll
Kiritimati (Christmas I.)
Howland I.
Baker I.
EQUATOR
Jarvis I.
Phoenix Islands
Atafu
Tokelau
Swains I.
Wallis Islands
Samoa
Upolu
Savai'i
Nassau
Cook Islands
Rose Atoll
Niue
Rarotonga
Mangaia
Caroline I.
Flint I.
Marquesas Islands
Pukapuka
Mataiva
Tuamotu Archipelago
Scilly
Tahiti
Society Islands
Maria
Morane
Îles Gambier
President Thiers Bank
Rapa
Marotiri
Austral Islands
Pitcairn I.
Isla Sala y Gómez
Easter Island
TONGA TRENCH
LAU BASIN
Tonga Islands
Fiji Is.
TROPIC OF CAPRICORN
Kermadec Islands
KERMADEC TRENCH
LOUISVILLE RIDGE
Chatham Islands
CHATHAM RISE
SOUTH PACIFIC OCEAN
SOUTHWEST PACIFIC BASIN
EAST PACIFIC RISE
PERU BASIN
GALÁPAGOS RISE
CHILE RISE
SOUTHEAST PACIFIC BASIN
HUMBOLDT PLAIN
BELLINGSHAUSEN PLAIN
De Gerlache Seamounts
PACIFIC-ANTARCTIC RIDGE
AMUNDSEN PLAIN
ANTARCTIC CIRCLE
AMUNDSEN RIDGE
Marie Byrd Seamount
Peter I I.
Thurston I.
Scott Island
Siple Island
Carney I.
Amundsen Sea
Bellingshausen Sea
Ellsworth Land
Mt. Sidley
4181
Vinson Massif
4897
Ellsworth Mountains
Ronne Ice Shelf
Berkner Island
Filchner Ice Shelf
Marie Byrd Land
Bentley Subglacial Trench
Ice thickness
Sulzberger Bay
Edward VII Pen.
Ross Sea
Roosevelt I.
Ross Ice Shelf
TRANSANTARCTIC MOUNTAINS
ANTARCTICA
Longitude West of Greenwich
GUATEMALA BASIN
Cocos Island
COCOS RIDGE
COLON RIDGE
PANAMA BASIN
Galápagos Islands
Carnegie Ridge
Gulf of Guayaquil
Pariñas Point
MIDDLE AMERICA TRENCH
CENTRAL AMERICA
Clipperton
Pico de Orizaba
5747
CAYMAN TRENCH
Cuba
Jamaica
Hispaniola
Puerto Rico
PUERTO RICO TRENCH
Greater Antilles
Bahama Is.
WEST INDIES
CARIBBEAN SEA
COLOMBIAN BASIN
AVES RIDGE
Lesser Antilles
Trinidad
Isthmus of Panama
Maracaibo
Llanos
Orinoco
Angel Falls
Mt. Roraima
Guiana Highlands
Pico da Neblina
Amazon Basin
Amazon
Marajó I.
Amazon Fan
DEMERARA PLAIN
CEARA PLAIN
Point Calcanhar
Point Coqueiros
PERNAMBUCO PLAIN
Nevado Huascarán
6768
ANDES
La Montaña
PERU-CHILE TRENCH
Source of the Amazon
Lake Titicaca
SOUTH AMERICA
Brazilian Highlands
Pantanal
Gran Chaco
Atacama Desert
Salar de Uyuni
NAZCA RIDGE
CHILE BASIN
San Félix I.
San Ambrosio I.
Iguazú Falls
Paraná
Salinas Grandes
Cerro Aconcagua
6960
Pampas
Juan Fernández Islands
Cape Frio
Santos Plateau
RIO GRANDE RISE
Isla Grande de Chiloé
Corcovado Gulf
Taitao Peninsula
Wellington I.
Valdés Peninsula
Gulf of San Jorge
ARGENTINE PLAIN
FALKLAND ESCARPMENT
FALKLAND PLATEAU
Falkland Islands
Strait of Magellan
Tierra del Fuego
Cape Horn
Drake Passage
Scotia Sea
South Georgia
SOUTH GEORGIA RIDGE
SOUTH SANDWICH TRENCH
South Sandwich Islands
South Orkney Islands
South Shetland Islands
Adelaide Island
ANTARCTIC PENINSULA
Alexander Island
WEDDELL SEA
WEDDELL PLAIN
Cape Norvegia
NORTH ATLANTIC OCEAN
MID-ATLANTIC RIDGE
OCEANOGRAPHER FRACTURE ZONE
ATLANTIS FRACTURE ZONE
Azores
Josephine Seamount
Madeira Is.
Canary Islands
Great Meteor Tablemount
CAPE VERDE PLAIN
Corner Seamounts
Krylov Seamount
Cape Verde Islands
Cape Verde
GAMBIA PLAIN
Senegal
VEMA FRACTURE ZONE
DOLDRUMS FRACTURE ZONE
SIERRA LEONE RISE
SIERRA LEONE BASIN
ROMANCHE FRACTURE ZONE
Romanche Gap
CHAIN FRACTURE ZONE
ASCENSION FRACTURE ZONE
Ascension
Stocks Seamount
BRAZIL BASIN
Hotspur Seamount
Martin Vaz Islands
Columbia Seamount
Vitória Seamount
ST. HELENA FRACTURE ZONE
MARTIN VAZ FRACTURE ZONE
SOUTH ATLANTIC OCEAN
RIO GRANDE FRACTURE ZONE
TRISTAN DA CUNHA FRACTURE ZONE
GOUGH FRACTURE ZONE
ISLAS ORCADAS RISE
Cape Finisterre
Flemish Cap
Faroe Is.
Rockall Rise
Wandel Sea
Oodaaq I.
Hayes Peninsula
Cape Farewell

ARCTIC OCEAN
NANSEN RIDGE
NANSEN BASIN
POLE PLAIN
MAKAROV BASIN
North East Land
Spitsbergen
Edge Island
Svalbard
Bear Island
George Land
Franz Josef Land
Graham Bell Island
Vize I.
Komsomolets Island
October Revolution Island
Bol'shevik Island
Cape Chelyuskin
North Land
935
CONTINENTAL SLOPE
CONTINENTAL SHELF
New Siberian Islands
374
EAST SIBERIAN SEA
Wrangel I.
LAPTEV SEA
Taymyr Peninsula
Lake Taymyr
KARA SEA
Novaya Zemlya
BARENTS SEA
NORWEGIAN SEA
North Cape
Kolguyev I.
Gyda Peninsula
Yamal Pen.
Gulf of Ob
North Siberian Lowland
Chukchi Range
ARCTIC CIRCLE
Kolyma
Kolyma Range
Koryak Range
Cherskiy Range
Verkhoyansk Range
Lena
SIBERIA
Central Siberian Plateau
1701
Angara
Scandinavia
Kola Pen.
White Sea
Timan Ridge
G. of Bothnia
Lake Onega
Lake Ladoga
Gulf of Finland
Ural Mountains
1895
Ob
West Siberian Plain
Yenisey
Irtysh
Baltic Sea
Jutland
Source of the Volga
Volga
EUROPE
Northern European Plain
Pinsk Marshes
Central Russian Upland
Carpathian Mts.
Danube
Alps
Apennines
Adriatic Sea
Balkan Peninsula
Crimea
Sea of Azov
Don
Black Sea
Bosporus
Caucasus Mts.
El'brus 5642
Caspian Depression
-28
Caspian Sea
Aral Sea -56
Ustyurt Plateau
Ural
The Steppes
Kazakh Uplands
Lake Balkhash
Belukha 4506
Altay Mountains
Dzungarian Basin
Syr Darya
Kyzylkum
Turan Lowland
Amu Darya
Garagum
Tian Shan
Victory Peak 7439
Turpan Depression -154
TARIM BASIN
Taklimakan Desert
Altun Shan
Kunlun Mountains
Muztag 6987
K2 8611
Hindu Kush
Source of the Yangtze
Plateau of Tibet
Mongolian Plateau
GOBI
Yellow
Qinghai Hu
Qin Ling
Eastern Sayan Mts.
Lake Baikal
Yablonovyy Range
Stanovoy Range
Amur
Greater Khingan Range
Manchurian Plain
Sikhote Alin Range
North China Plain
Yangtze
ASIA
Kamchatka Peninsula
SEA OF OKHOTSK
Sakhalin
1397
Central Range
BERING SEA
ALEUTIAN BASIN
4750
Attu
Aleutian Is.
ALEUTIAN TRENCH
Detroit Tablemount 1857
EMPEROR TROUGH
EMPEROR SEAMOUNTS
NORTHWEST PACIFIC BASIN
HESS RISE
2194
Kuril Islands
KURIL TRENCH
Hokkaido
SEA OF JAPAN (EAST SEA)
Korea
Honshu
JAPAN TRENCH
Fuji 3776
Shikoku
Kyushu
Yellow Sea
CONTINENTAL SHELF
EAST CHINA SEA
NORTH PACIFIC BASIN
6416
SHATSKIY RISE
3510
Isakov Seamount 3105
PACIFIC OCEAN
Makarov Seamount 1471
Grosvenor Seamount 2712
MAPMAKER SEAMOUNTS
5831
TROPIC OF CANCER
9695
IZU TRENCH
Nampo Shoto
RYUKYU TRENCH
Ryukyu Islands
KYUSHU PALAU RIDGE
Taiwan
Taiwan Str.
Luzon Strait
Luzon
PHILIPPINE SEA
BONIN TRENCH
MARIANA TROUGH
Mariana Islands
MARIANA TRENCH
9018
MID-PACIFIC MOUNTAINS
Wake I.
1550
MAGELLAN SEAMOUNTS
1330
WEST MARIANA BASIN
PHILIPPINE BASIN
Guam
Challenger Deep 10920
EAST MARIANA BASIN
Bikini Atoll
Enewetak Atoll
Kwajalein Atoll
Taongi Atoll
Marshall Islands
CENTRAL PACIFIC BASIN
1975
Pohnpei (Ponape)
5225
Chuuk
MICRONESIA
Caroline Islands
EAST CAROLINE BASIN
WEST CAROLINE BASIN
7248
YAP TRENCH
PALAU TRENCH
8527
Gilbert Islands
EQUATOR
Nauru
Banaba
Beru
Admiralty Is.
New Ireland
Bismarck Archipelago
New Britain
Bougainville
Solomon Islands
Solomon Sea
Nanumea
Tuvalu
Guadalcanal
VITYAZ TRENCH
8322
9175
NORTH NEW HEBRIDES TRENCH
Vanuatu
NORTH FIJI BASIN
Fiji Islands
3250
New Caledonia
NEW HEBRIDES TRENCH
TROPIC OF CAPRICORN
SOUTH FIJI BASIN
NEW CALEDONIA BASIN
LORD HOWE RISE
Lord Howe I.
2194
SOUTH PACIFIC OCEAN
CORAL SEA BASIN
CORAL SEA
Great Barrier Reef
HIMALAYA
Brahmaputra
Mt. Everest 8850 (29035 ft)
Ganges
Indus
Great Indian Desert
INDIA
Deccan Plateau
Western Ghats
Eastern Ghats
BAY OF BENGAL
Ganges Fan
Andaman Islands
4267
3601
Sri Lanka (Ceylon)
Nicobar Islands
Andaman Sea
Mekong
G. of Tonkin
Hainan
Indochina Peninsula
Gulf of Thailand
Malay Pen.
Strait of Malacca
SOUTH CHINA SEA
1902
Mt. Pinatubo 1486
PALAWAN TROUGH
SULU BASIN
Philippine Islands
PHILIPPINE TRENCH
10057
Mindanao
Kinabalu 4101
CELEBES BASIN
5722
Borneo
Celebes
INDONESIA
Sumatra
Kerinci 3800
Java Sea
Greater Sunda Islands
Java
Banda Sea
Buru
Flores
Moluccas
New Guinea
Jaya Peak 4884
7258
Arafura Sea
Timor
Timor Sea
Lesser Sunda Islands
JAVA TRENCH
JAVA RIDGE
7125
Christmas I.
CONTINENTAL SHELF
Cape York Pen.
Gulf of Carpentaria
NORTH AUSTRALIAN BASIN
Kimberley Plateau
Great Sandy Desert
Western Macdonnell Ranges
AUSTRALIA
Great Artesian Basin
Central Lowlands
Great Dividing Range
Lake Eyre -16
Great Victoria Desert
Nullarbor Plain
Great Australian Bight
Murray
Darling
Mt. Kosciuszko 2228
CONTINENTAL SLOPE
Bass Strait
Tasmania
TASMAN PLAIN
TASMAN SEA
Gascoyne Tablemount 93
North Island
NEW ZEALAND
South Island
Mt. Cook 3754
4956
Stewart Island
EAST TASMAN PLATEAU
SOUTH TASMAN RISE
CAMPBELL PLATEAU
Auckland Is.
MACQUARIE RIDGE
Macquarie I.
Wallaby Plateau
2540
North West Cape
EXMOUTH PLATEAU
5678
WHARTON BASIN
Cape Inscription
PERTH BASIN
Cape Naturaliste
BROKEN RIDGE
936
DIAMANTINA FRACTURE ZONE
6602
SOUTH AUSTRALIAN BASIN
INVESTIGATOR RIDGE
NINETYEAST RIDGE
COCOS BASIN
Cocos Islands
OSBORN PLATEAU
CEYLON PLAIN
Nikitin Seamount 1549
1842
927
MID-INDIAN BASIN
MID-INDIAN RIDGE
CHAGOS TRENCH
Chagos Archipelago
Diego Garcia 6402
5406
CHAGOS-LACCADIVE PLATEAU
Maldive Islands
CARLSBERG RIDGE
ARABIAN SEA
ARABIAN BASIN
Indus Fan
OWEN FRACTURE ZONE
Socotra
Gulf of Aden
SOMALI BASIN
Coco-de-Mer Seamounts
Seychelles
Amirante Isles 5273
MASCARENE PLATEAU
MASCARENE BASIN
Maromokotro 2876
MASCARENE PLAIN
Mascarene Islands
Rodrigues
Mauritius
Réunion
1922
MADAGASCAR BASIN
INDIAN OCEAN
SOUTHWEST INDIAN RIDGE
NATAL BASIN
MADAGASCAR PLATEAU
MOZAMBIQUE PLATEAU
Madagascar
Mozambique Channel
Comoro Is.
Aldabra Is.
Zanzibar I.
6291
6810
CROZET BASIN
Amsterdam
St. Paul
Crozet Islands
Prince Edward Islands
PRINCE EDWARD FRACTURE ZONE
Kerguélen Islands
KERGUÉLEN PLATEAU
Heard Island
Ob Tablemount 247
Lena Tablemount 254
SOUTHEAST INDIAN RIDGE
SOUTH INDIAN BASIN
ENDERBY PLAIN
Cosmonaut Sea
Riiser-Larsen Peninsula
Cape Ann
Enderby Land
Prydz Bay
Cape Poinsett
South Magnetic Pole 2006
ANTARCTIC CIRCLE
Queen Maud Land
ANTARCTICA
Balleny Is.
2435
Ice thickness 4776
Transantarctic Mountains
Victoria Land
Ross Sea
Ross Ice Shelf
AGULHAS BASIN
AGULHAS RIDGE
AGULHAS PLATEAU
Meteor Seamount
5372
ATLANTIC-INDIAN RIDGE
Wyandot Seamount 1637
Cape of Good Hope
Cape Agulhas
Great Karroo
Drakensberg
Thabana Ntlenyana 3482
Vema Seamount
4958
Kalahari Desert
Namib Desert
Victoria Falls
Lake Kariba
Lake Malawi
Zambezi
Katanga Plateau
Congo Canyon
Lower Guinea
Mitumba Mts.
Lake Tanganyika
Sources of the Nile
Lake Victoria
Kilimanjaro 5895
Congo Basin
Congo
Ruwenzori 5109
Lake Albert
Lake Turkana (L. Rudolf)
Somali Peninsula
Cameroon Mt. 4100
Bioko
Ethiopian Highlands
Danakil -156
4533
Blue Nile
White Nile
Marra Mts. 3088
Lake Chad
SAHEL
SAHARA
Tibesti Mts. 3415
Mt. Tahat 3003
Aïr Massif 2022
Libyan Desert
Western Desert
Qattara Depression -133
Nubian Desert
Eastern Desert
Nile
Red Sea
Sinai
Nile Fan
Great Eastern Dunes
Rub al Khali (Empty Quarter)
ARABIAN PENINSULA
An Nafūd
Syrian Desert
Dead Sea -416 (-1365 ft)
Mesopotamia
Tigris
Euphrates
Zagros Mountains
Persian Gulf
G. of Oman
Elburz Mts. 5671
Mt. Ararat 5137
ANATOLIA (ASIA MINOR)
Cyprus
Crete
Sicily
Ionian Sea
Aegean Sea
MEDITERRANEAN SEA
Winkel Tripel Projection, Central Meridian 0°
SCALE 1:80,470,600
1 CENTIMETER = 805 KILOMETERS; 1 INCH = 1270 MILES AT THE EQUATOR
0 500 1000 1500 2000 2500
KILOMETERS
0 500 1000 1500 2000 2500
STATUTE MILES
Longitude East of Greenwich
20° 40° 60° 80° 100° 120° 140° 160° 180°
90° 80° 70° 60° 50° 40° 30° 20° 10° 0° 10° 20° 30° 40° 50° 60° 70° 80° 90°

Longitude West of Greenwich
ARCTIC
QUEEN ELIZABETH ISLANDS
GREENLAND
(KALAALLIT NUNAAT)
Denmark
BEAUFORT SEA
BAFFIN BAY
CANADA
HUDSON BAY
LABRADOR SEA
ALASKA
ARCTIC CIRCLE
BERING SEA
Aleutian Islands
RUSSIA
Brooks Range
NORTH
UNITED STATES
ROCKY MOUNTAINS
Vancouver
Seattle
Portland
San Francisco
Los Angeles
San Diego
Phoenix
Denver
Dallas
Houston
Chicago
Detroit
Toronto
Montréal
Ottawa
New York
Philadelphia
Washington
Boston
Atlanta
Miami
Winnipeg
Calgary
Edmonton
ATLANTIC
PACIFIC
OCEAN
TROPIC OF CANCER
GULF OF MEXICO
MEXICO
Mexico
Guadalajara
Monterrey
CUBA
Havana
BAHAMAS
CARIBBEAN SEA
HAITI
DOMINICAN REP.
PUERTO RICO
JAMAICA
GUATEMALA
HONDURAS
EL SALVADOR
NICARAGUA
COSTA RICA
PANAMA
HAWAII
Honolulu
EQUATOR
VENEZUELA
Caracas
COLOMBIA
Bogotá
ECUADOR
Quito
GUYANA
SURINAME
FRENCH GUIANA
BRAZIL
Brasília
São Paulo
Rio de Janeiro
Salvador
Recife
Fortaleza
Manaus
Belém
PERU
Lima
BOLIVIA
La Paz
Sucre
PARAGUAY
Asunción
CHILE
Santiago
ARGENTINA
Buenos Aires
URUGUAY
Montevideo
PATAGONIA
TIERRA DEL FUEGO
FALKLAND ISLANDS
(ISLAS MALVINAS)
U.K.
GALÁPAGOS ISLANDS
(ARCHIPIÉLAGO DE COLÓN)
Ecuador
KIRIBATI
LINE ISLANDS
PHOENIX ISLANDS
SAMOA
AMERICAN SAMOA
TONGA
COOK ISLANDS
FRENCH POLYNESIA
TUAMOTU ARCHIPELAGO
TROPIC OF CAPRICORN
SOUTH
Easter Island
(Isla de Pascua)
Chile
Date Line
SCOTIA SEA
Drake Passage
ANTARCTIC PENINSULA
ANTARCTIC CIRCLE
WEDDELL SEA
ELLSWORTH LAND
MARIE BYRD LAND
ROSS SEA
Vinson Massif
4897
(16067 ft)
TRANSANTARCTIC MOUNTAINS
ANTARCTICA
PORTUGAL
MAURITANIA
SENEGAL
CAPE VERDE
ICELAND
Reykjavík

Longitude East of Greenwich
ARCTIC OCEAN
RUSSIA
KAZAKHSTAN
MONGOLIA
CHINA
INDIA
PAKISTAN
AFGHANISTAN
IRAN
IRAQ
SAUDI ARABIA
TURKEY
UKRAINE
EGYPT
LIBYA
SUDAN
ETHIOPIA
KENYA
SOMALIA
TANZANIA
ANGOLA
ZAMBIA
NAMIBIA
BOTSWANA
SOUTH AFRICA
MADAGASCAR
INDONESIA
MALAYSIA
PHILIPPINES
JAPAN
AUSTRALIA
NEW ZEALAND
PAPUA NEW GUINEA
SOLOMON ISLANDS
FEDERATED STATES OF MICRONESIA
NORTH PACIFIC OCEAN
SOUTH PACIFIC OCEAN
INDIAN OCEAN
ARABIAN SEA
BAY OF BENGAL
SOUTH CHINA SEA
PHILIPPINE SEA
TASMAN SEA
CORAL SEA
TROPIC OF CANCER
EQUATOR
TROPIC OF CAPRICORN
ARCTIC CIRCLE
ANTARCTIC CIRCLE
ANTARCTICA
ENDERBY LAND
WILKES LAND
Transantarctic Mountains
ROSS SEA
Moscow
St. Petersburg
Istanbul
Tehran
Karachi
Delhi
Mumbai (Bombay)
Kolkata (Calcutta)
Dhaka
Bangkok
Beijing
Shanghai
Hong Kong
Seoul
Tokyo
Manila
Jakarta
Singapore
Sydney
Melbourne
Perth
Cairo
Nairobi
Cape Town
Winkel Tripel Projection, Central Meridian 0°
SCALE 1:80,470,600
1 CENTIMETER = 805 KILOMETERS; 1 INCH = 1270 MILES AT THE EQUATOR
0 500 1000 1500 2000 2500
KILOMETERS
0 500 1000 1500 2000 2500
STATUTE MILES
International boundaries and disputed territories, where scale permits, reflect de facto status at the time of publication.

Western Hemisphere
EQUATOR
0 km 3000
0 mi 2000
Azimuthal Equidistant Projection
Eastern Hemisphere
EQUATOR
0 km 3000
0 mi 2000
Azimuthal Equidistant Projection

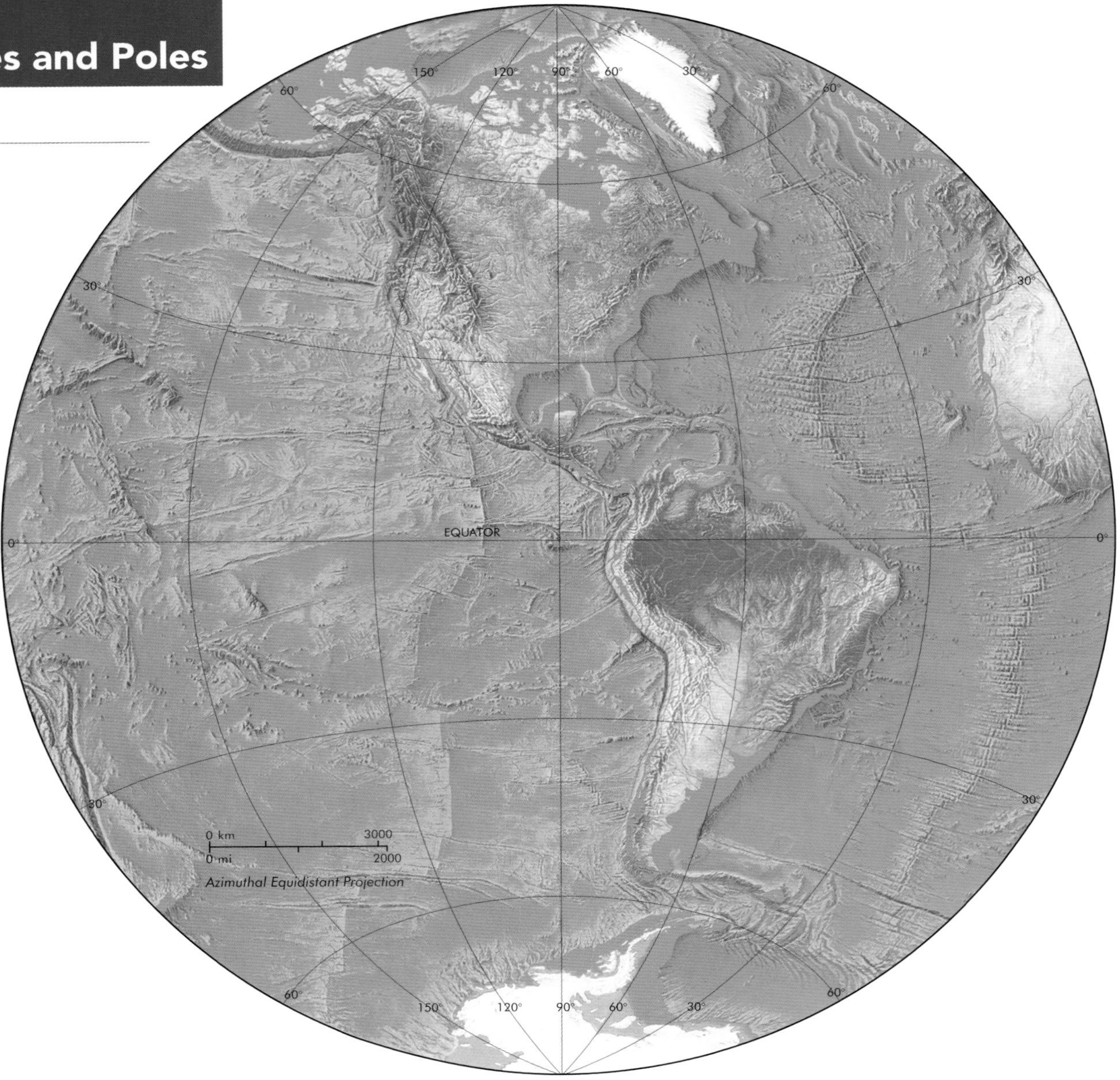

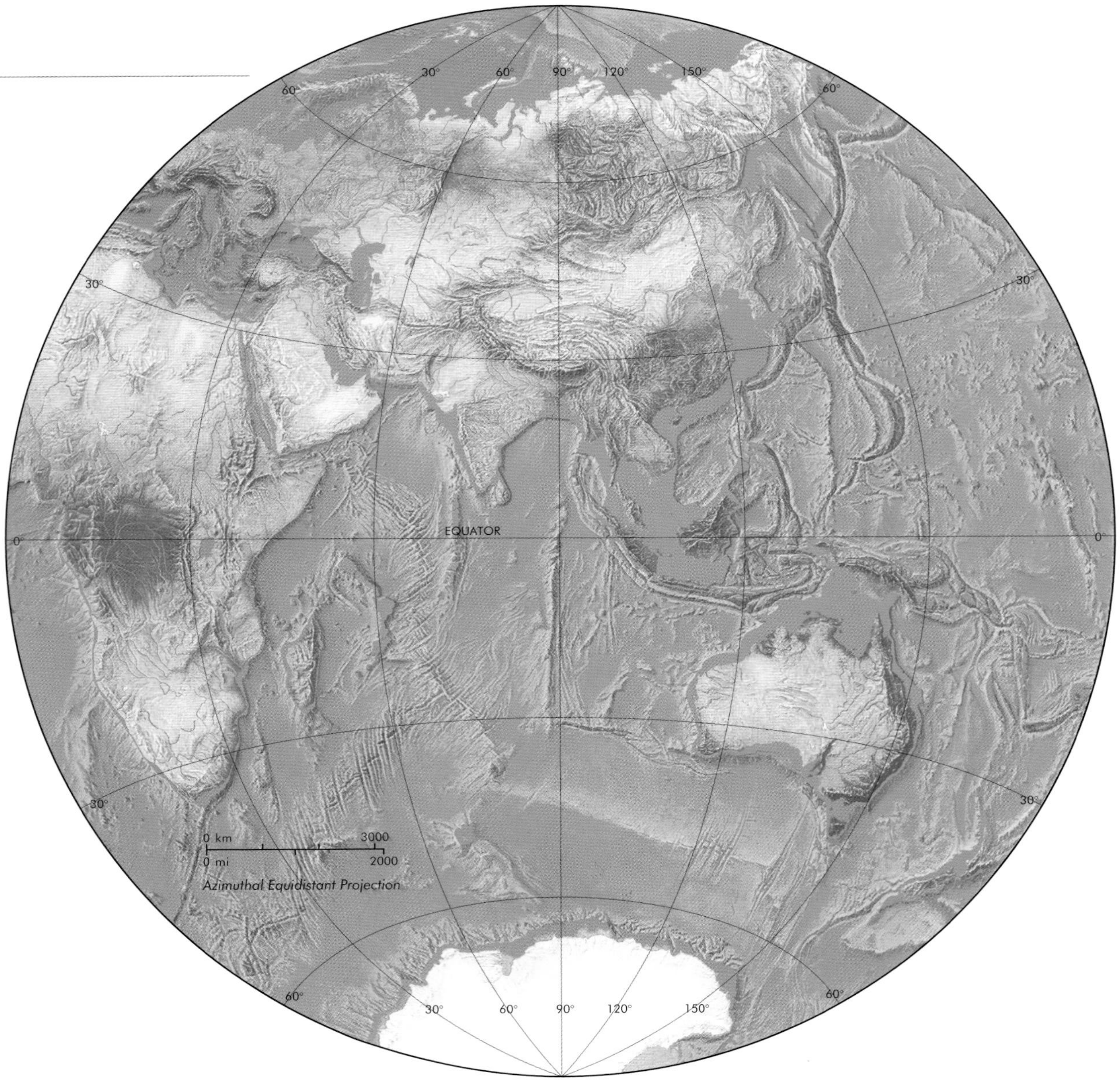

North Pole

Bering Sea
180°
165°
Anchorage
Nome
Anadyr'
Kolyma
150°
ALASKA
United States
Fairbanks
ARCTIC CIRCLE
135°
Yukon
Chukchi Sea
Wrangel Island
East Siberian Sea
Indigirka
Yakutsk
Barrow
Mackenzie
Beaufort Sea
120°
Great Slave L.
Great Bear Lake
Yellowknife
New Siberian Islands
Tiksi
Lena
Banks Island
ARCTIC
Laptev Sea
105°
Victoria Island
North Magnetic Pole 2006
CANADA
OCEAN
North Land
RUSSIA
Queen Elizabeth Islands
North Pole
90°
Ellesmere Island
Noril'sk
Yenisey
Limit of Multiyear Ice
North Geomagnetic Pole 2005
Kara Sea
Franz Josef Land
Russia
Baffin Island
Baffin Bay
Novaya Zemlya
75°
Vorkuta
Ob'
Svalbard
Norway
Spitsbergen
Longyearbyen
Davis Strait
Barents Sea
GREENLAND
Denmark
60°
Nuuk (Godthåb)
0 km 600
0 mi 600
Azimuthal Equidistant Projection
Greenland Sea
Murmansk
Winter Extent of Sea Ice
Arkhangel'sk
45°
Norwegian Sea
Reykjavík
ICELAND
ARCTIC CIRCLE
FINLAND
30°
ATLANTIC OCEAN
SWEDEN
Helsinki
15°
0°
NORWAY

South Pole

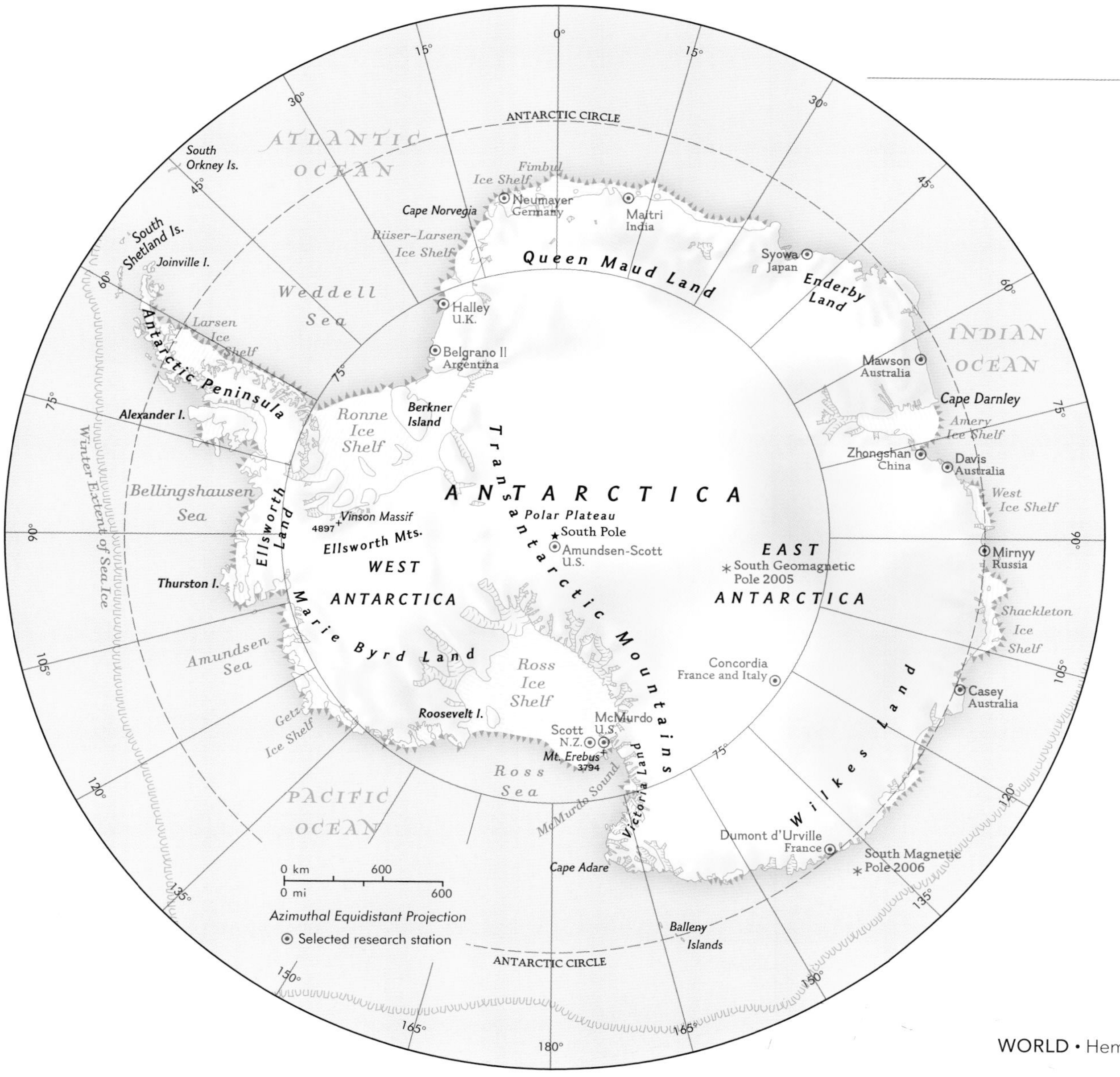
0°
15°
30°
ANTARCTIC CIRCLE
ATLANTIC OCEAN
South Orkney Is.
Fimbul Ice Shelf
Neumayer Germany
Maitri India
45°
Cape Norvegia
Riiser-Larsen Ice Shelf
South Shetland Is.
Joinville I.
Syowa Japan
Queen Maud Land
Enderby Land
60°
Weddell Sea
Halley U.K.
Larsen Ice Shelf
INDIAN OCEAN
Antarctic Peninsula
Belgrano II Argentina
Mawson Australia
75°
Alexander I.
Berkner Island
Ronne Ice Shelf
Cape Darnley
Amery Ice Shelf
Zhongshan China
Davis Australia
Transantarctic Mountains
Bellingshausen Sea
Ellsworth Land
ANTARCTICA
West Ice Shelf
Vinson Massif
4897
Polar Plateau
South Pole
Ellsworth Mts.
Amundsen-Scott U.S.
90°
WEST
EAST
Mirnyy Russia
South Geomagnetic Pole 2005
Thurston I.
ANTARCTICA
ANTARCTICA
Winter Extent of Sea Ice
Shackleton Ice Shelf
Marie Byrd Land
Amundsen Sea
Ross Ice Shelf
Concordia France and Italy
105°
Casey Australia
Getz Ice Shelf
Roosevelt I.
Scott N.Z.
McMurdo U.S.
Mt. Erebus 3794
Wilkes Land
120°
Ross Sea
Victoria Land
PACIFIC OCEAN
McMurdo Sound
Dumont d'Urville France
South Magnetic Pole 2006
0 km 600
0 mi 600
Cape Adare
135°
Azimuthal Equidistant Projection
Selected research station
Balleny Islands
ANTARCTIC CIRCLE
150°
165°
180°

LIKE ICE ON A GREAT LAKE, the Earth's crust, or the lithosphere, floats over the planet's molten innards, is cracked in many places, and is in slow but constant movement. Earth's surface is broken into 16 enormous slabs of rock, called plates, averaging thousands of miles wide and having a thickness of several miles. As they move and grind against each other, they push up mountains, spawn volcanoes, and generate earthquakes.

Although these often cataclysmic events capture our attention, the movements that cause them are imperceptible, a slow waltz of rafted rock that continues over eons. How slow? The Mid-Atlantic Ridge (see "spreading" diagram, opposite) is being built by magma oozing between two plates, separating North America and Africa at the speed of a growing human fingernail.

The dividing lines between plates often mark areas of high volcanic and earthquake activity as plates strain against each other or one dives beneath another. In the Ring of Fire around the Pacific Basin, disastrous earthquakes have occurred in Kobe, Japan, and in Los Angeles and San Francisco, California. Volcanic eruptions have taken place at Pinatubo in the Philippines and Mount St. Helens in Washington State.

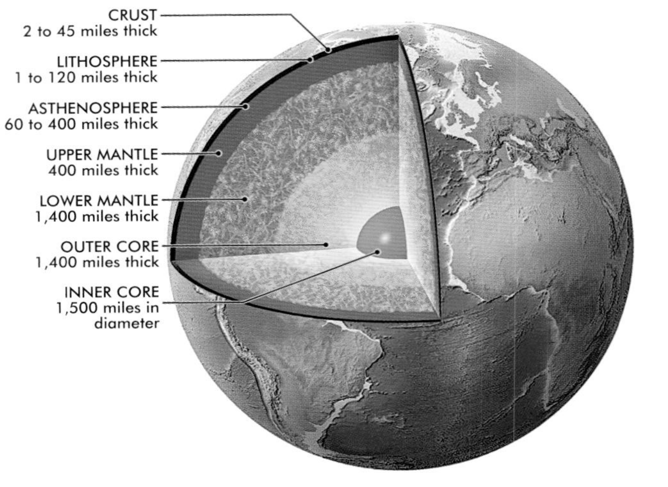

Continents Adrift in Time

With unceasing movement of Earth's tectonic plates, continents "drift" over geologic time—breaking apart, reassembling, and again fragmenting to repeat the process. Three times during the past billion years, Earth's drifting landmasses have merged to form so-called supercontinents. Rodinia, a supercontinent in the late Precambrian, began breaking apart about 750 million years ago. In time, its pieces reassembled to form another supercontinent, which in turn later split into smaller landmasses during the Paleozoic. The largest of these were called Euramerica (ancestral Europe and North America) and Gondwana (ancestral Africa, Antarctica, Arabia, India, and Australia). More than 250 million years ago, these two landmasses recombined, forming Pangaea. In the Mesozoic era, Pangaea split and the Atlantic and Indian Oceans began forming. Though the Atlantic is still widening today, scientists predict it will close as the seafloor recycles back into Earth's mantle. A new supercontinent, Pangaea Ultima, will eventually form.

KEY TO PALEO-GEOGRAPHIC MAPS

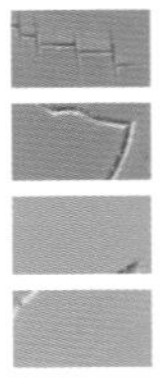

- Seafloor spreading ridge
- Subduction zone
- Ancient landmass
- Continental shelf

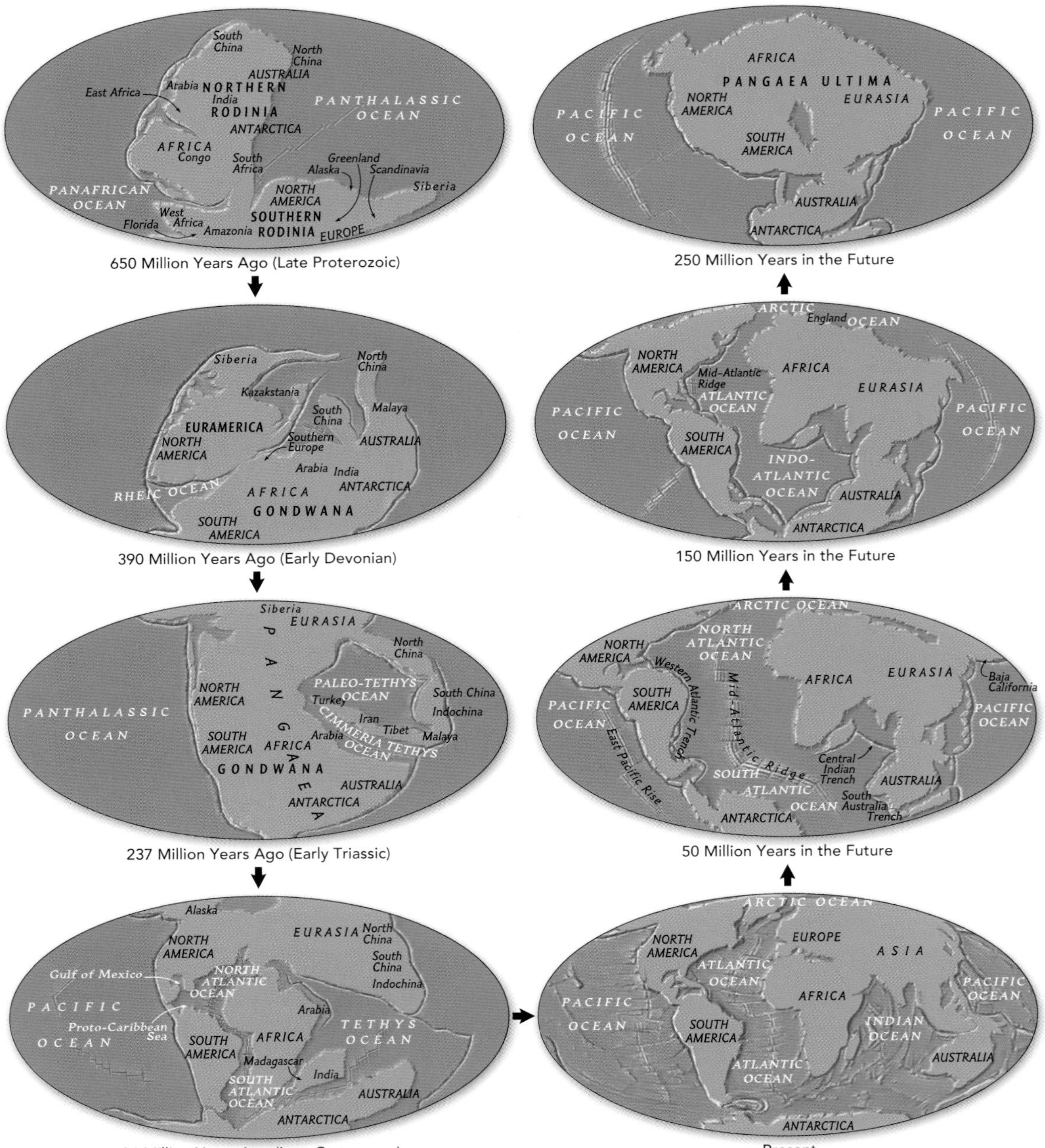

650 Million Years Ago (Late Proterozoic)

390 Million Years Ago (Early Devonian)

237 Million Years Ago (Early Triassic)

94 Million Years Ago (Late Cretaceous)

Present

50 Million Years in the Future

150 Million Years in the Future

250 Million Years in the Future

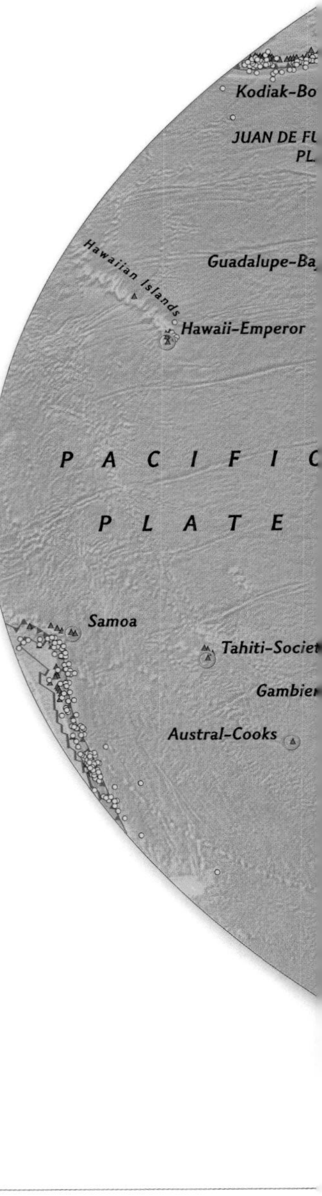

Geologic Time

MILLIONS OF YEARS AGO	4,500	3,500	3,000	2,500	2000	1500	1000
EON	PRISCOAN	ARCHAEAN			PROTEROZOIC		
ERA	EOARCHEAN	PALEOARCHEAN	MESOARCHEAN	NEOARCHEAN	PALEOPROTEROZOIC	MESOPROTEROZOIC	
PERIOD	No subdivision into periods				SIDERIAN, RHYACIAN, OROSIRIAN, STATHERIAN	CALYMMIAN, ECTASIAN, STENIAN	TONIAN

Geologic Forces Change the Face of the Planet

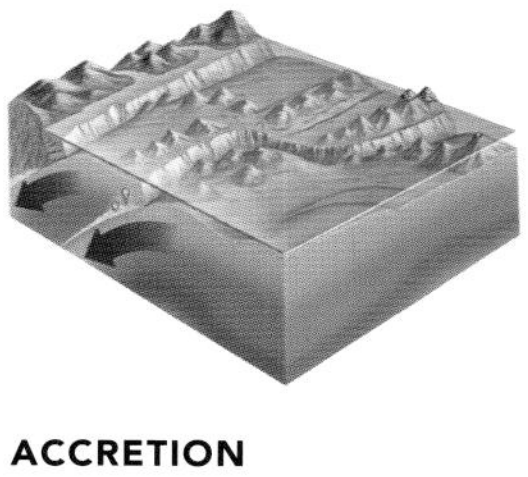

ACCRETION
As ocean plates move toward the edges of continents or island arcs and slide under them, seamounts are skimmed off and piled up in submarine trenches. The resulting buildup can cause continents to grow.

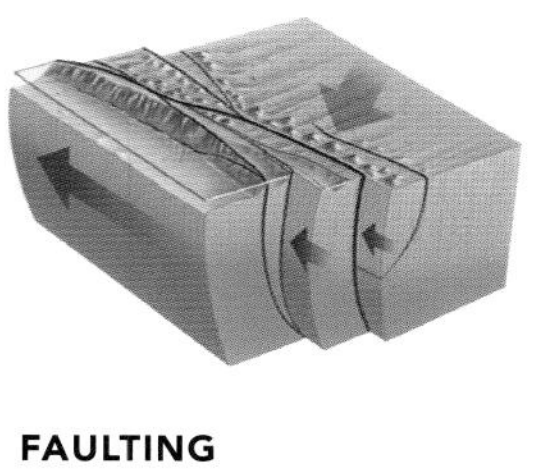

FAULTING
Enormous crustal plates do not slide smoothly. Strain built up along their edges may release in a series of small jumps, felt as minor tremors on land. Extended buildup can cause a sudden jump, producing an earthquake.

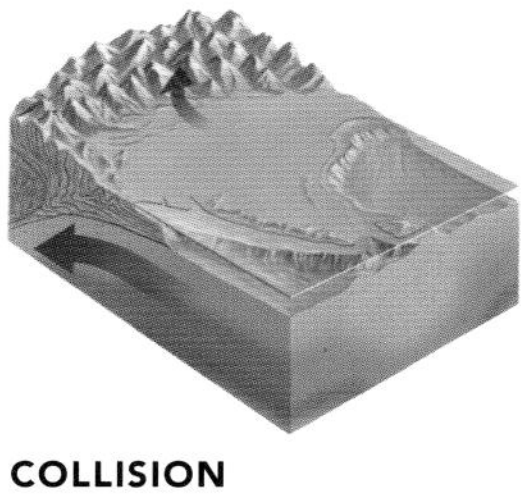

COLLISION
When two continental plates converge, the result can be the most dramatic mountain-building process on Earth. The Himalaya mountain range rose when the Indian subcontinent collided with Eurasia, driving the land upward.

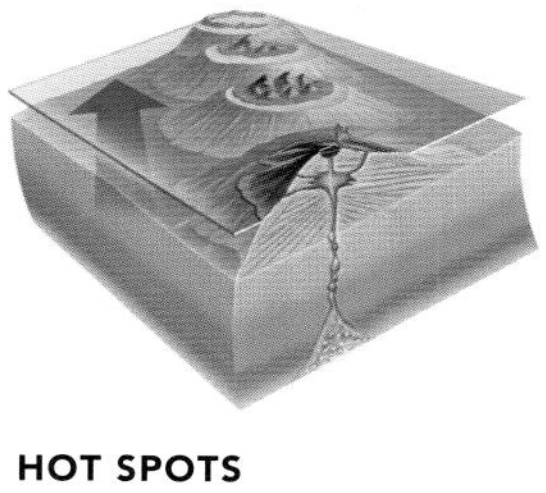

HOT SPOTS
In the cauldron of inner Earth, some areas burn hotter than others and periodically blast through their crustal covering as volcanoes. Such a "hot spot" built the Hawaiian Islands, leaving a string of oceanic protuberances.

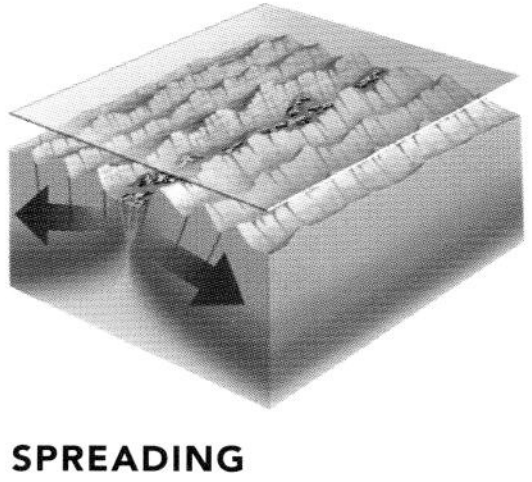

SPREADING
At the divergent boundary known as the Mid-Atlantic Ridge, oozing magma forces two plates apart by as much as eight inches a year. If that rate had been constant, the ocean could have reached its current width in 30 million years.

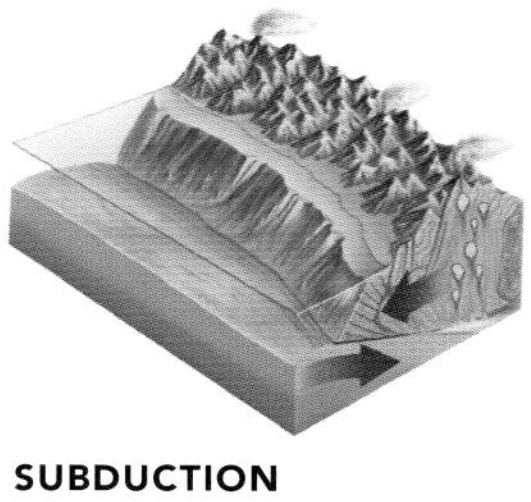

SUBDUCTION
When an oceanic plate and a continental plate converge, the older and heavier sea plate takes a dive. Plunging back into the interior of the Earth, it is transformed into molten material, only to rise again as magma.

Plate Tectonics

Tectonic boundaries mark areas of geologic change in ocean floors, on the margins of continents, and even within continents, as seen in the Great Rift Valley of East Africa. Clusters of volcanoes and frequent earthquakes indicate unstable areas.

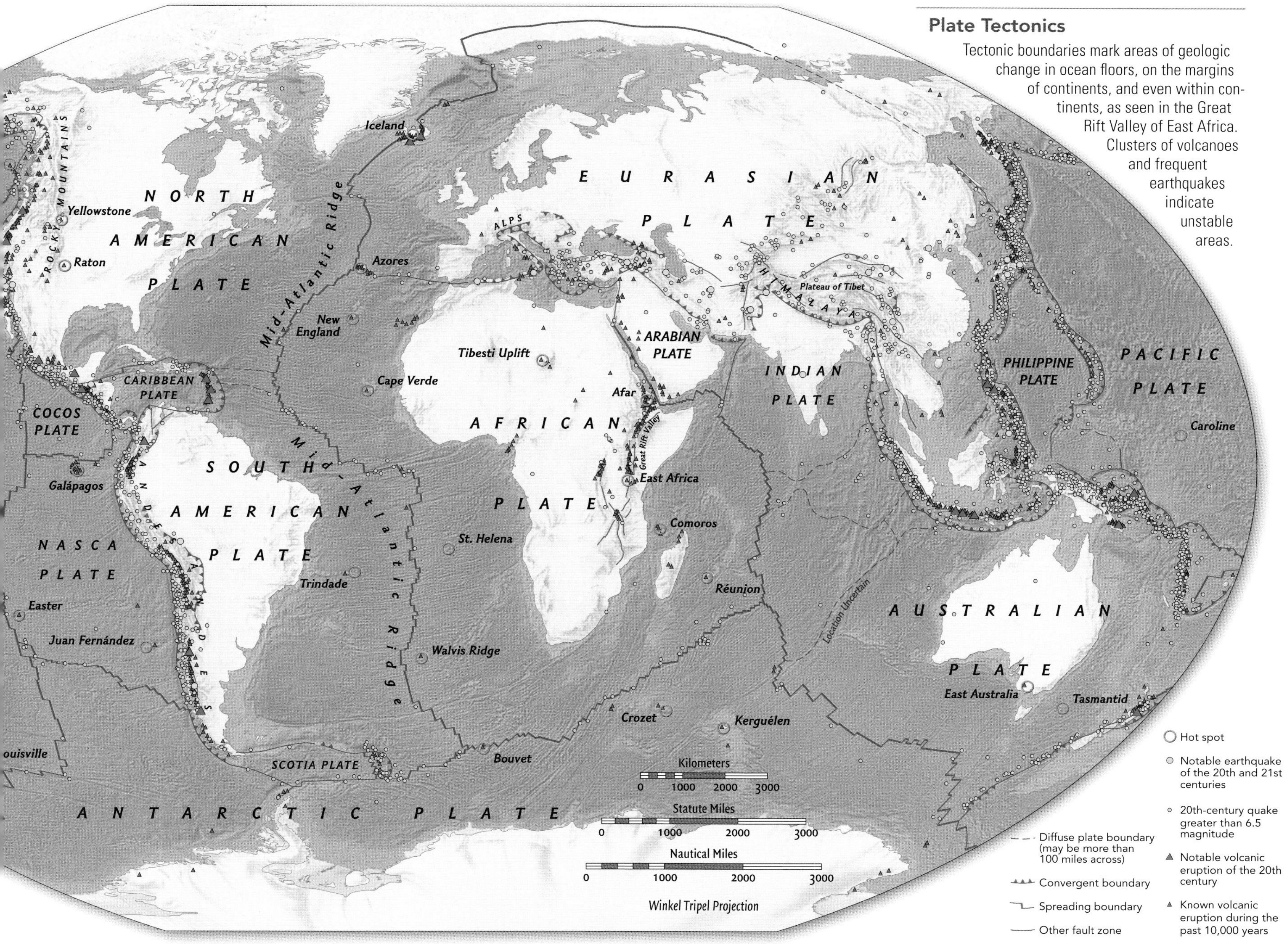

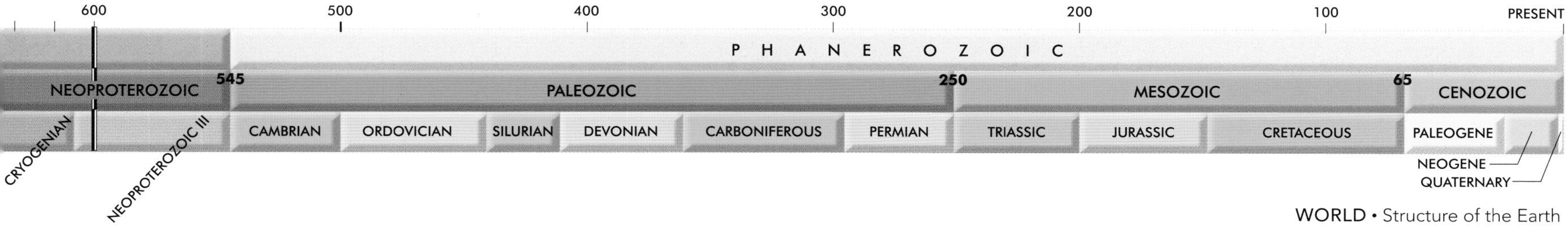

EARTH'S OUTERMOST LAYER, the crust, ranges from 2 to 45 miles (3 to 70 km) thick and comprises a large variety of rocks that are aggregates of one or more types of minerals.

Scientists recognize three main classes of rock. Igneous rock forms when molten material cools and solidifies, either rapidly at the Earth's surface—as perhaps a lava flow—or more slowly underground, as an intrusion. Sedimentary rocks form from mineral or rock fragments, or from organic material that is eroded or dissolved, then deposited at Earth's surface. Metamorphic rocks form when rocks of any origin (igneous, sedimentary, or metamorphic) are subjected to very high temperature and pressure; this type also forms as rocks react with fluids deep within the crust. Igneous and metamorphic rocks make up 95 percent of the crust's volume. Sedimentary rocks make up only about 5 percent; even so, they cover a large percentage of Earth's surface.

As a result of plate tectonics, the crust is in constant slow motion; thus, rocks change positions over time. Their compositions also change as they are gradually modified by metamorphism and melting. Rocks form and re-form in a sequence known as the rock cycle (see below). Understanding their nature and origin is important because rocks contain materials that sustain modern civilization. For example, steel requires the processing of iron—mainly from ancient sedimentary rocks; copper is mined principally from slowly cooled igneous rocks called plutons; and fossil fuels (e.g., coal, oil, natural gas) derive from organic material trapped ages ago in relatively young sedimentary rocks.

Rock Classes

IGNEOUS

Igneous rocks form when molten rock (magma) originating from deep within the Earth solidifies. The chemical composition of the magma and its cooling rate determine the final rock type.

Type	Description	Examples
Intrusive (Plutonic)	Intrusive igneous rocks are formed from magma that cools and solidifies deep beneath the Earth's surface. The insulating effect of the surrounding rock allows the magma to solidify very slowly. Slow cooling means the individual mineral grains have a long time to grow, so they grow to a relatively large size. Intrusive rocks typically are coarser grained than volcanic rocks.	Examples: gabbro, diorite, granite
Extrusive (Volcanic)	Extrusive igneous rocks are formed from magma that cools and solidifies at or near the Earth's surface. Exposure to the relatively cool temperature of the atmosphere or water makes the erupted magma solidify very quickly. Rapid cooling means the individual mineral grains have only a short time to grow, so their final size is very tiny, or fine-grained. Sometimes the magma is quenched so rapidly that individual minerals have no time to grow. This is how volcanic glass forms.	Examples: basalt, andesite, and rhyolite

SEDIMENTARY

Sedimentary rocks are formed from preexisting rocks or pieces of once living organisms. They form deposits that accumulate on the Earth's surface, generally with distinctive layering or bedding.

Type	Description	Examples
Clastic	Clastic sedimentary rocks are made up of pieces (clasts) of preexisting rocks. Pieces of rock are loosened by weathering, then transported to a basin or depression where sediment is trapped. If the sediment is buried deeply, it becomes compacted and cemented, forming sedimentary rock. Clastic sedimentary rocks may have particles ranging in size from microscopic clay to huge boulders. Their names are based on their grain size.	Examples: sandstone, mudstone, conglomerate
Chemical	Chemical sedimentary rocks are formed by chemical precipitation. This process begins when water traveling through rock dissolves some of the minerals, carrying them away from their source. Eventually these minerals are redeposited when the water evaporates.	Examples: evaporite, dolomite
Biologic	Biologic sedimentary rocks form from once living organisms. They may comprise accumulated carbon-rich plant material or deposits of animal shells.	Examples: coal, chalk, limestone, chert

METAMORPHIC

Metamorphic rocks are those rocks that have been substantially changed from their original igneous, sedimentary, or earlier metamorphic form. They form when rocks are subjected to high heat; high pressure; hot, mineral-rich fluids; or, more commonly, some combination of these.

Type	Description	Examples
Foliated	Foliated rocks form when pressure deforms tabular minerals within a rock so they become aligned. These rocks develop a platy or sheetlike structure that reflects the directions from which pressure was applied.	Examples: schist, gneiss, slate
Massive (Nonfoliated)	Nonfoliated metamorphic rocks do not have a platy or sheetlike structure. There are several ways that nonfoliated rocks can be produced. Some rocks, such as limestone, are made of minerals that are not flat or elongated; no matter how much pressure is applied, the grains will not align despite recrystallization. Contact metamorphism occurs when hot igneous rock intrudes into preexisting rock. The preexisting rock is essentially baked by the heat, which changes mineral composition and texture primarily from heating rather than pressure effects.	Examples: marble, quartzite, hornfels

The Rock Cycle

To learn the origin and history of rocks, geologists study their mineralogy, texture, and fabric—characteristics that result from dynamic Earth-shaping processes driven by internal and external energy.

Internal energy is heat contained within the Earth. This intense heat creates convection currents in the mantle, which in turn cause tectonic plate movements and volcanism. External energy comes from the sun, which drives atmospheric processes that produce rain, snow, ice, and wind—powerful agents of weathering and erosion.

As internal energy builds and rebuilds Earth's rocky exterior, the forces of weathering and erosion break down surface materials and wear them away.

Ultimately, soil particles and rock fragments, called sediments, are carried by rivers into the oceans, where they may lithify, or harden into solid rock. In time, these sedimentary rocks may be subjected to heat and pressure at great depth. Mineral and structural changes occur as the rocks break and fold; they are transformed into metamorphic rocks.

Solid rocks subject to high heat and pressure during metamorphism can melt to form magma, which later can form igneous rocks, either intrusive or extrusive. The subsurface intrusive rocks (i.e., plutons) can later be uplifted by tectonic forces and (or) exposed by erosion. At the surface, the cycle continues as weathering and erosion break it down and wear it away.

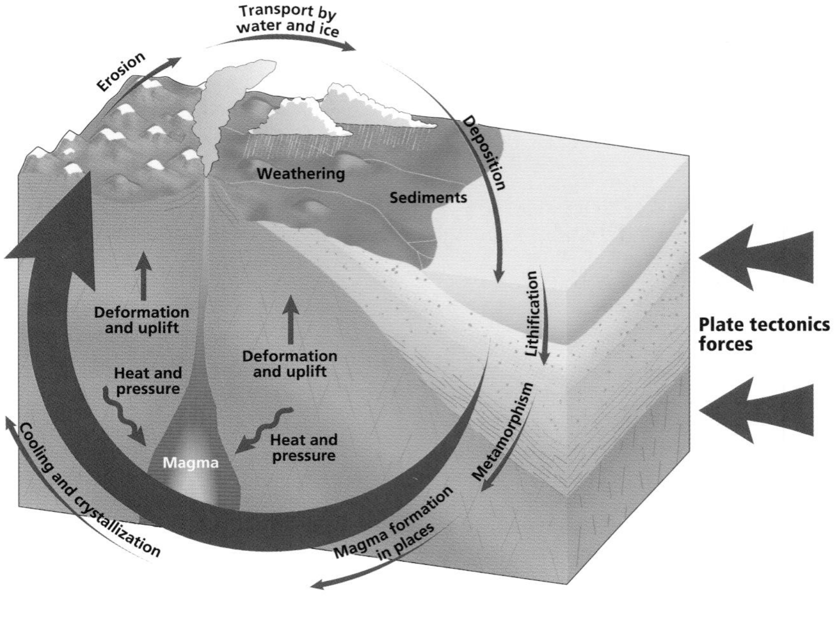

Global Distribution of Rock Types

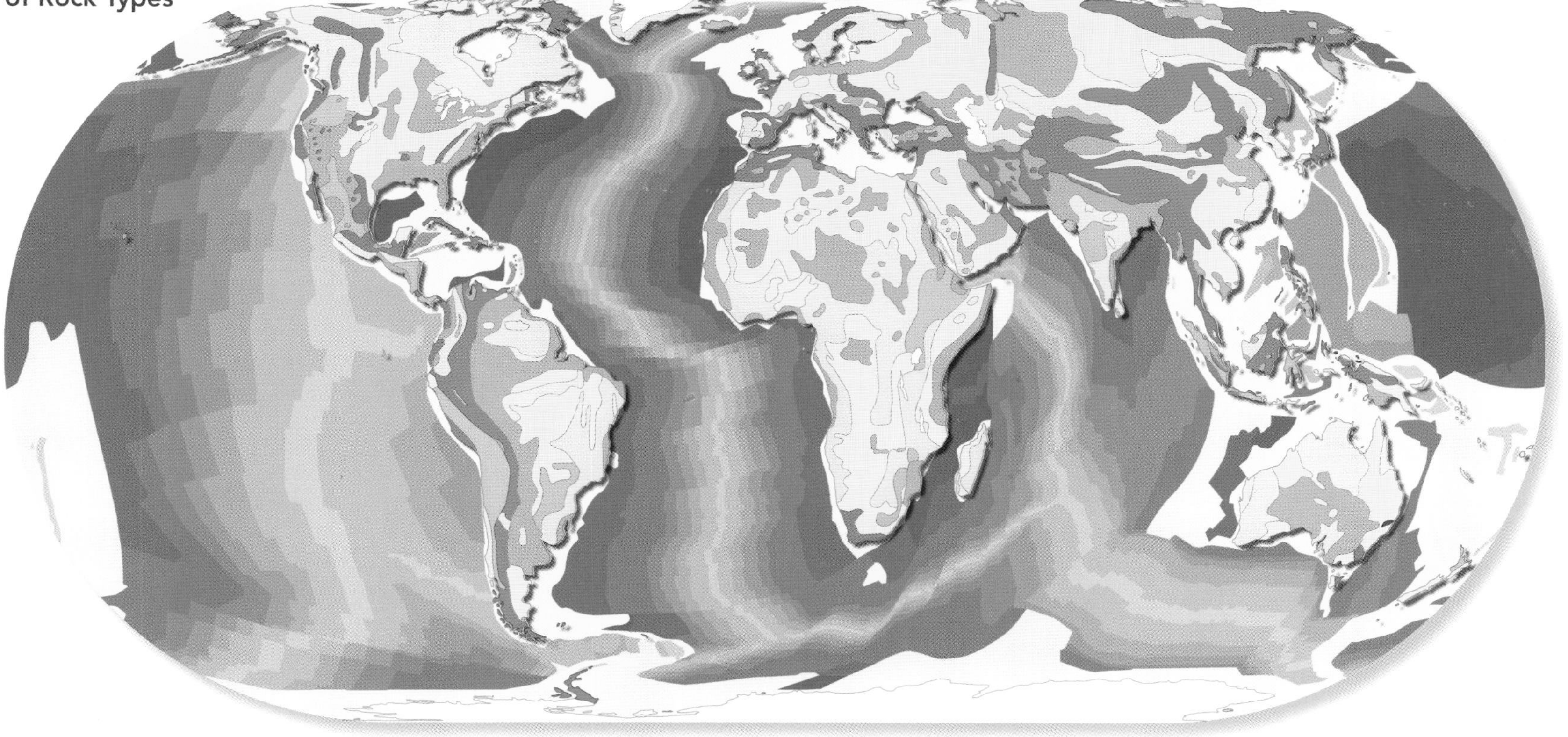

Age of Oceanic Crust

Million years ago (Ma)

0 5.3 23.8 33.7 53 65 98.9 144.2 170

Holocene Miocene Oligocene Eocene Paleocene Upper Cretaceous Lower Cretaceous Upper to Middle Jurassic

Geologic period

In general, oceanic crust is much younger than surface rock.

- Continental shelf (primarily 550–170 Ma)
- Age uncertain

Global Distribution of Surface Rock

- Unconsolidated sediments
- Intrusive igneous or metamorphic rocks
- Extrusive igneous rocks
- Highly faulted or folded sedimentary, metamorphic, and igneous rocks
- Flat or gently dipping sedimentary rocks

Reading Earth History from Rocks

The Earth is 4.6 billion years old, with a long, complex history written in layers of rock.* By reading sequences of sedimentary rock, we can discover information about past environments and processes. The principle of superposition states that, provided rocks are not turned upside down by deformation, the oldest rocks are at the bottom of a sequence and younger rocks are found at the top. Unconformities tell us that uplift and erosion occurred before the deposition of younger sediments resumed. As an example, the rock sequence exposed in the Grand Canyon of Arizona indicates from oldest to youngest, the following major events:

DURING PRECAMBRIAN TIME:

1. Deposition of Vishnu sediment (about 2 billion years ago)
2. Mountain building, metamorphism of Vishnu sediment into Vishnu schist, and intrusion of Zoroaster granite (1.8 to 1.4 billion years ago)
3. Uplift and erosion resulting in an unconformity (1.4 to 1.2 billion years ago)
4. Deposition of Unkar Group sediments (1.2 to 1 billion years ago)
5. Tilting (1 billion years ago)
6. Erosion resulting in angular unconformity (1 billion to 543 million years ago)

DURING THE PHANEROZOIC (CAMBRIAN-RECENT) EON:

7. Deposition of Cambrian to Permian (and younger rocks not shown) sediments (543 to 520 million years ago), with disconformities indicating erosion and "missing" time where noted
8. Uplift and erosion of the Grand Canyon (20 million years ago to present)

The ages for these events are broadly defined by the radioisotopic dating of minerals in the metamorphic and igneous rocks, and by fossils and correlation to other rocks for the sedimentary rocks that are younger than the Precambrian-Cambrian boundary (543 million years ago).

Yavapai Point, Grand Canyon

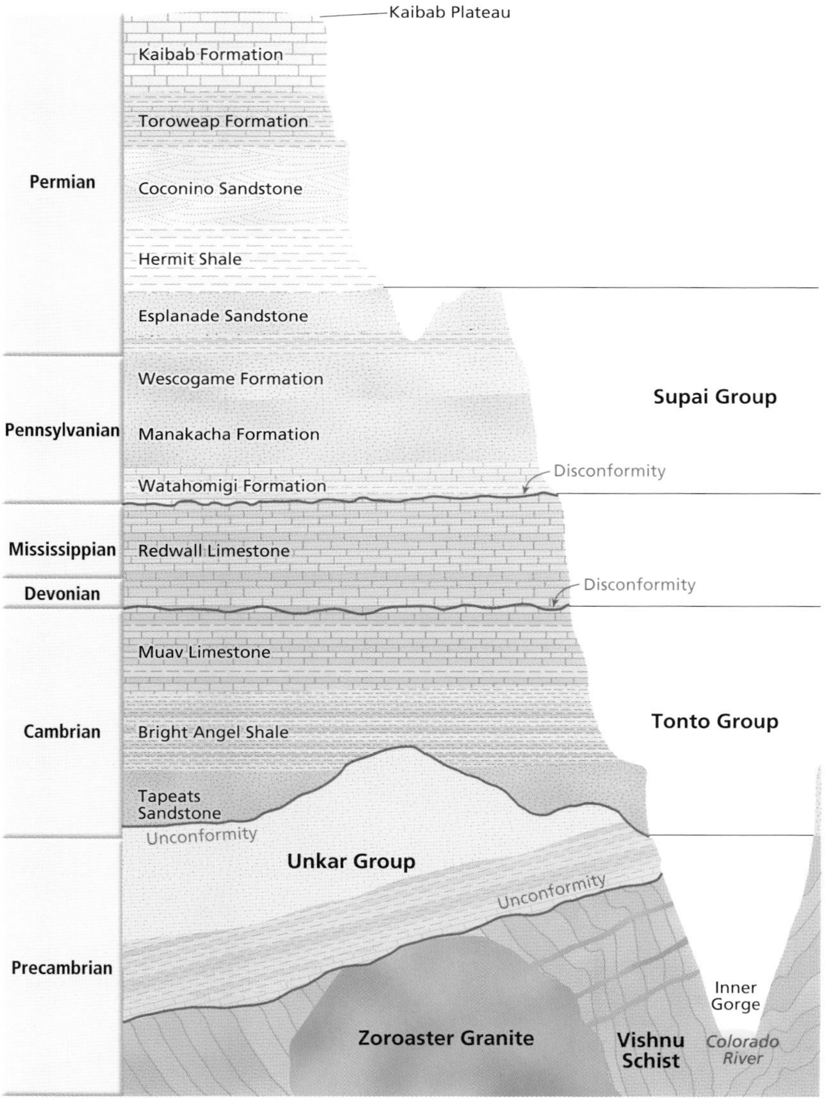

The oldest known, dated rocks on Earth go back to 4 billion years ago; geologic records of older rocks have been destroyed by more recent geologic events.

SEVEN MAJOR LANDFORM types are found on Earth's surface (see map); except for ice caps, all result from tectonic movements and denudational forces.

The loftiest landforms, mountains, often define the edges of tectonic plates. In places where continental plates converge, Earth's crust crumples into high ranges such as the Himalaya. Where oceanic plates dive beneath continental ones, volcanic mountains can rise. Volcanoes are common along the west coast of South America, which is part of the so-called Pacific Ring of Fire, the world's most active mountain-building zone.

Widely spaced mountains are another type, and examples of this landform are seen in the Basin and Range province of the western United States. These features are actually the tops of heavily eroded, faulted mountains. The eroded material filled adjacent valleys, giving these old summits the look of widely spaced mountains.

Extensive, relatively flat lands that are higher than surrounding areas are called plateaus. Formed by uplift, they include the Guiana Highlands of South America. Hills and low plateaus are rounded natural elevations of land with some local relief. The Canadian Shield and Ozarks of North America provide good examples. Depressions are large basins delimited by higher lands, an example of which is the Tarim Basin in western China. Plains are extensive areas of level or rolling treeless country. Examples include the steppes of Russia, the Ganges River plains, and the outback of Australia.

Endogenic Landforms

LANDFORMS THAT RESULT FROM "INTERNAL" PROCESSES

Forces deep within the Earth give rise to mountains and other endogenic landforms. Some mountains (e.g., the Himalaya) were born when continental plates collided. Others rose in the form of volcanoes (the Cascades of North America, Mount Fuji of Japan) as sea plates subducted beneath continental plates or as plates moved over hot spots in Earth's mantle (Hawai'i). Still others were thrust up by tectonic uplift (parts of the western United States). Rifting and faulting, which occur along plate boundaries and sometimes within the plates themselves, also generate vertical tectonic landforms; these can be seen in Africa's Rift Valley and along the San Andreas Fault of California.

Clockwise from above: The Wasatch Range in Utah, uplifted by tectonic forces; the San Andreas Fault in California, a fracture in Earth's crust marking a plate boundary; Mount Fuji in Japan, a volcanic peak; Crater Lake in Oregon, a deep lake inside the caldera of Mount Mazama.

Exogenic Landforms

LANDFORMS THAT RESULT FROM "EXTERNAL" PROCESSES

External agents create exogenic landforms. Weathering by rain, groundwater, and other natural elements slowly breaks down rocks, such as the limestone in karst landscapes or the granite in an exfoliation dome (Yosemite's Half Dome). Erosion removes weathered material and transports it from place to place. In the American Southwest, erosion continues to shape the spires of Bryce Canyon and the walls of slot canyons.

Clockwise from above: tower karst in Thailand, weathered limestone in humid climate; Bryce Canyon in Utah, eroded sedimentary rocks in arid climate; slot canyon in the American Southwest, sedimentary rock eroded by water; Half Dome in Yosemite, California, weathered granite batholith.

Other Landforms

Some landforms are the impact sites (or craters) of asteroids, comets, and meteorites. The most readily observable are Meteor Crater in Arizona and New Quebec Crater in eastern Canada. Other landforms include man-made dams and open-pit mines, as well as biogenic features such as coral reefs made by coral polyps and giant mounds built by termites.

Meteor Crater, Arizona

Termite mound, Cape York Peninsula, Australia

All of Earth's features are created and continually reshaped by such factors as wind, water, ice, tectonics, and humans. This painting brings together 34 natural and man-made features to show typical locations and relationships of landforms; it does not depict an actual region. Definitions of most landforms can be found in the glossary.

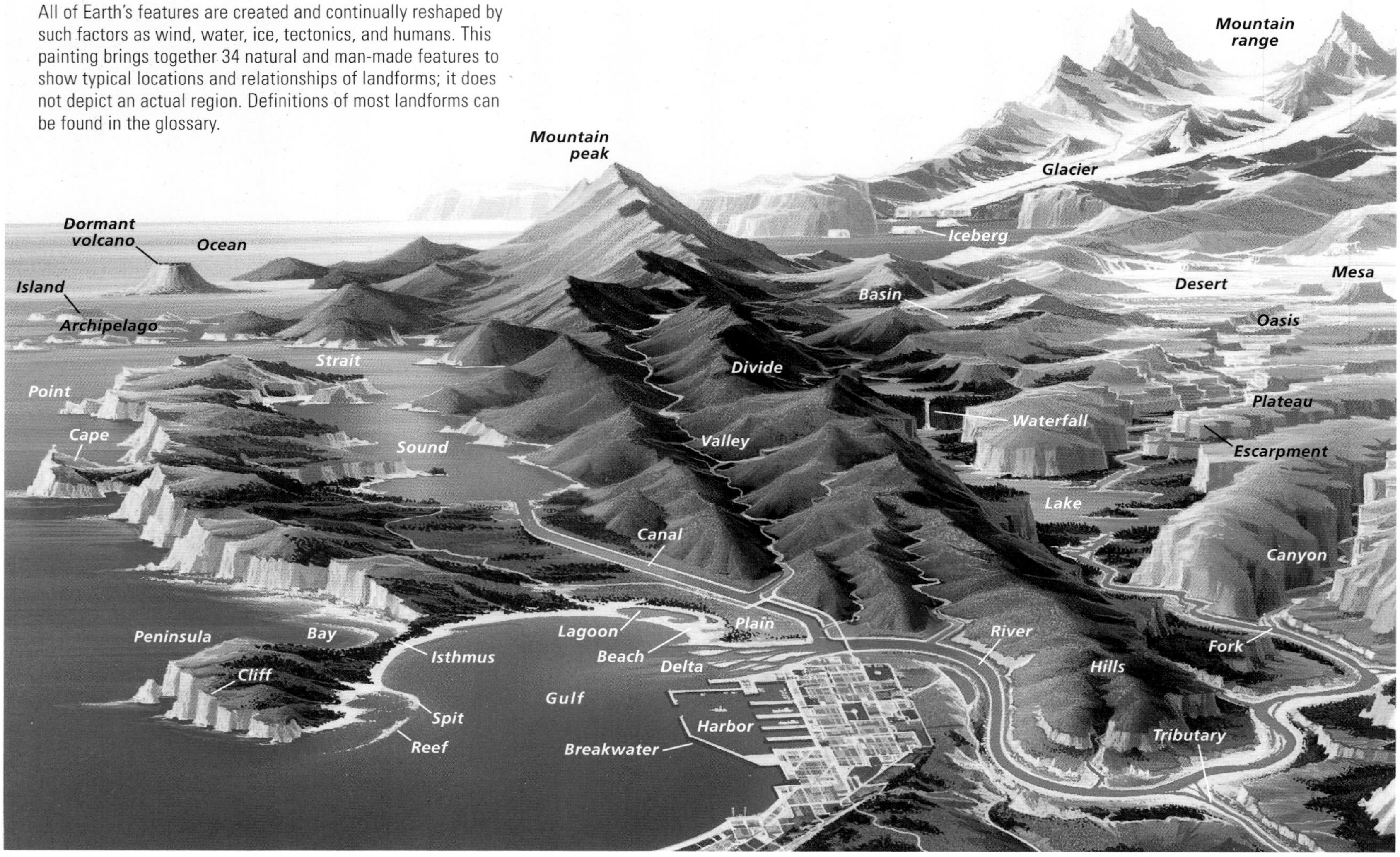

Landforms Created by Wind

The term "eolian" (from Aeolus, the Greek god of the winds) describes landforms shaped by the wind. The erosive action of wind is characterized by deflation, or the removal of dust and sand from dry soil; sandblasting, the erosion of rock by wind-borne sand; and deposition, the laying down of sediments. The effects of wind erosion are evident in many parts of the world (see map), particularly where there are large deposits of sand or loess (dust and silt dropped by wind). Among desert landforms, sand dunes may be the most spectacular. They come in several types (below): **Barchan dunes** are crescents with arms pointing downwind; **transverse dunes** are "waves," with crests perpendicular to the wind; **star dunes** have curving ridges radiating from their centers; **parabolic dunes** are crescents with arms that point upwind; and **longitudinal dunes** lie parallel to the wind.

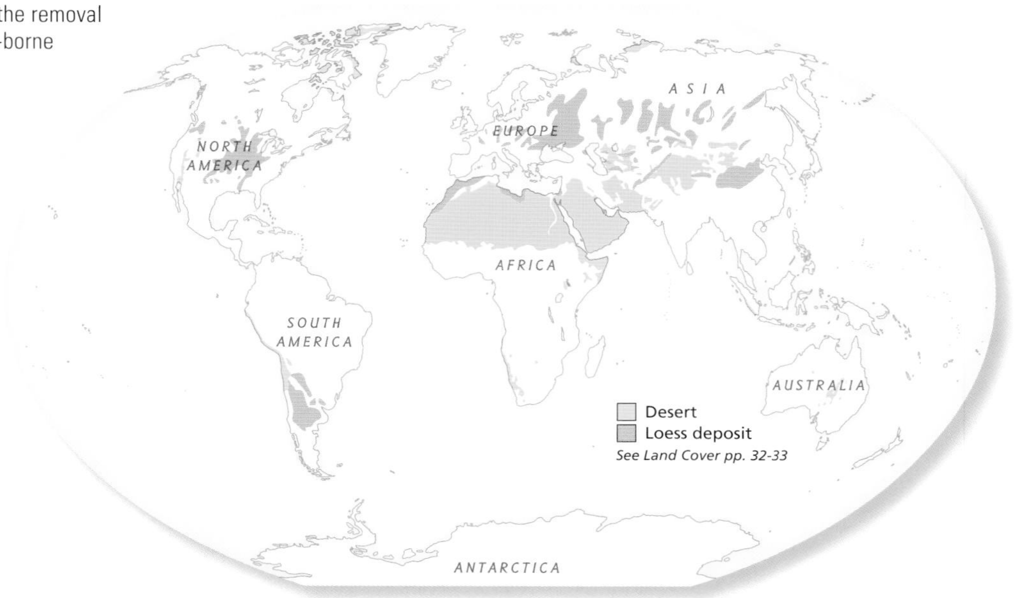

Wind direction

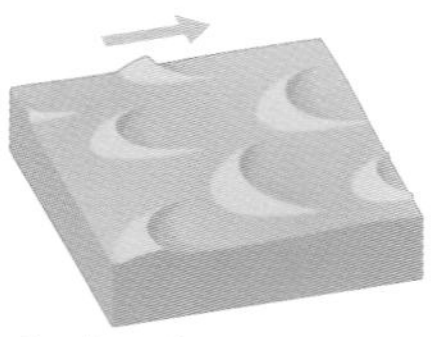
Barchan dunes

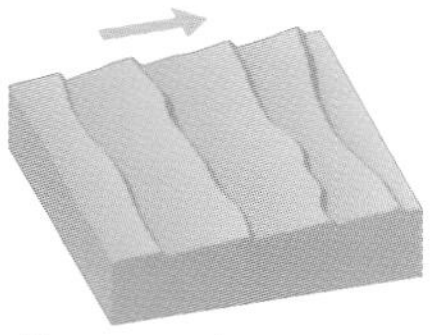
Transverse dunes

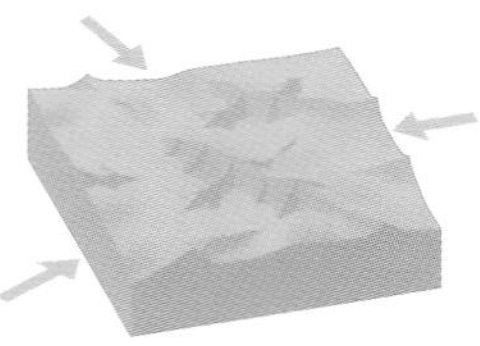
Star dunes

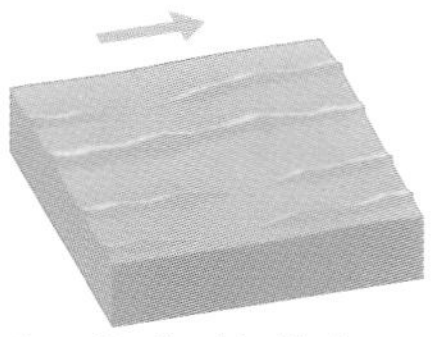
Longitudinal (seif) dunes

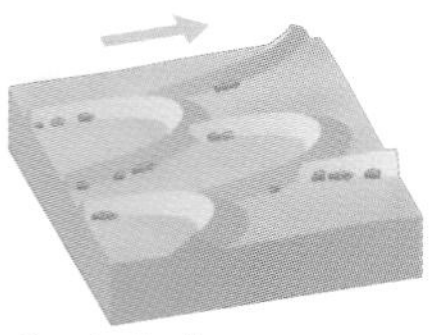
Parabolic dunes

EOLIAN LANDFORMS

Desert dunes, which actually cover only a small portion of desert areas, range in height from just a few feet to more than a thousand feet. Coastal dunes form when wind and waves deposit sediments along the shores of oceans and other large bodies of water. Loess hills are large deposits of wind-borne silt, the most extensive of which are found in North America and Asia.

Desert dunes: Death Valley National Park, California

Coastal dunes: Dune du Nord, Quebec

Loess deposits: Palouse Hills, Washington

Landforms Created by Water

Highlighted on the map at right are Earth's major watersheds. These are drainage basins for rivers, which create fluvial (from a Latin word meaning "river") landforms. Wave action and groundwater also produce characteristic landforms.

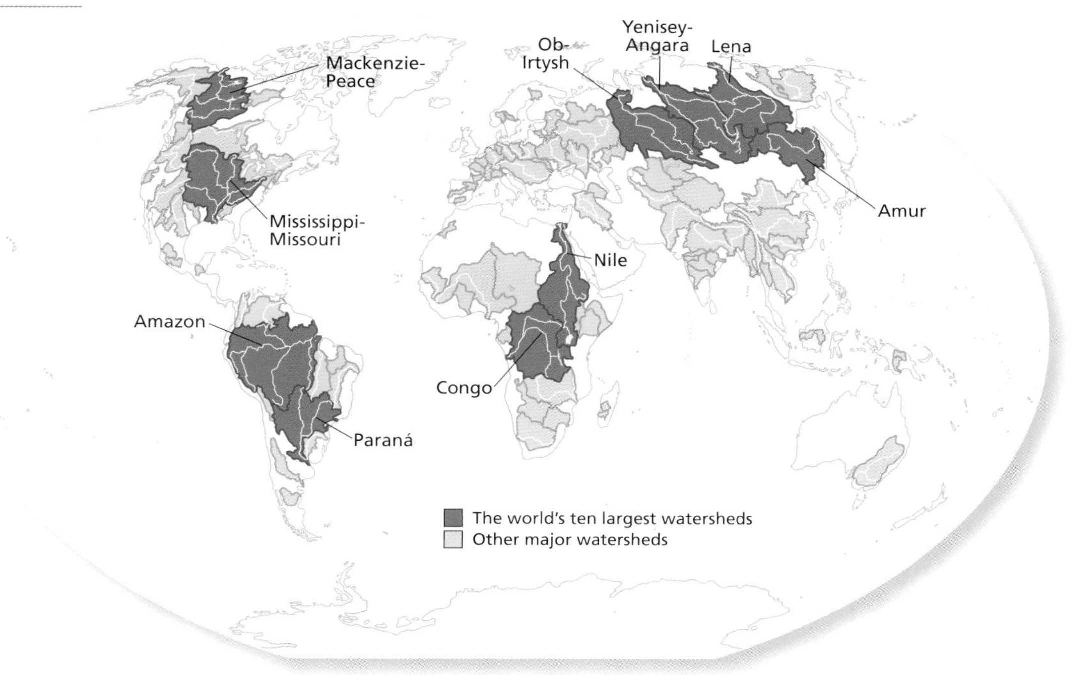

RIVERS

Some rivers form broad loops called meanders (below) as faster currents erode their outer banks and slower currents deposit materials along inner banks. When a river breaks through the narrow neck of a meander, the abandoned curve becomes an oxbow lake.

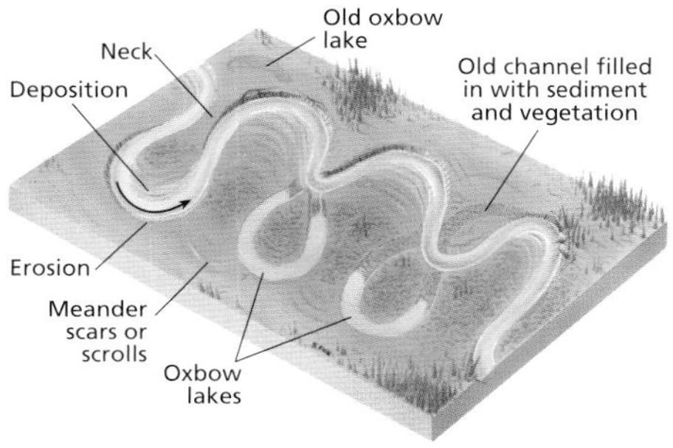

RIVER DELTAS

Sediment deposited at a river's mouth builds a delta, a term first used by the ancient Greeks to describe the Nile Delta; its triangular shape resembles the fourth letter of the Greek alphabet. Not all deltas have that classic shape: The Mississippi River forms a bird's-foot delta.

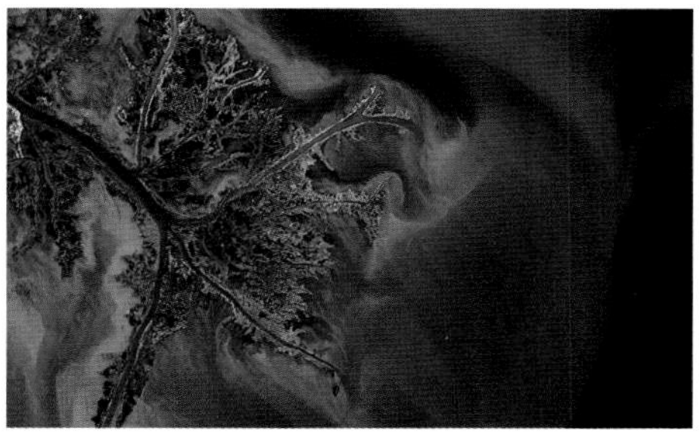

Mississippi River Delta

COASTAL AREAS

Through erosion and deposition, tides and wave action continually reshape the coastlines of the world. Ocean currents transport sand and gravel from one part of a shore to another, sometimes building beach extensions called spits, long ridges that project into open water. Relentless waves undercut coastal cliffs, eroding volumes of material and leaving behind sea stacks and sea arches, remnants made of more resistant rock. As ocean levels rise, narrow arms of the sea (fjords) may reach inland for miles, filling deep valleys once occupied by glaciers flowing to the sea.

Sea stacks: Victoria, Australia

GROUNDWATER

Water in the ground slowly dissolves limestone, a highly soluble rock. Over time, caves form and underground streams flow through the rock; sinkholes develop at the surface as underlying rock gives way. Karst landscapes, named for the rugged Karst region of the former Yugoslavia, are large areas of unusual landforms created by weathered and eroded limestone.

Karst cave: Kickapoo Cave, Texas

Landforms Created by Ice

Among the legacies of Earth's most recent ice age (see map) are landforms shaped by glaciers. There are two kinds of glaciers: valley, or alpine, and continental ice sheets. These large, slow-moving masses of ice can crush or topple anything in their paths; they even stop rivers in their tracks, creating ice-dammed lakes. Glaciers are also powerful agents of erosion, grinding against the ground and picking up and carrying huge amounts of rock and soil, which they deposit at their margins when they begin to melt; these deposits are called lateral and terminal moraines. The paintings below show how an ice sheet (upper) leaves a lasting imprint on the land (lower).

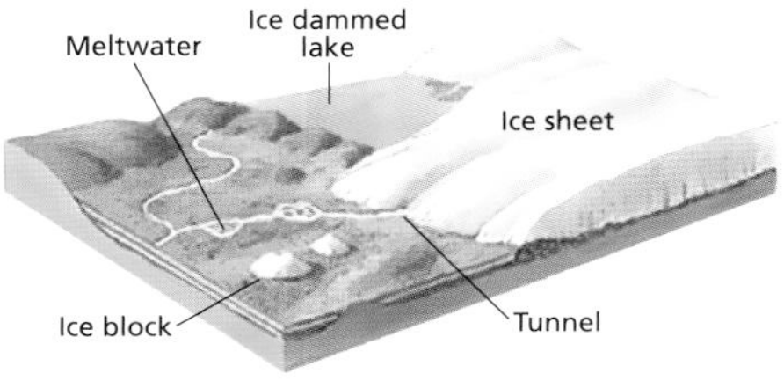

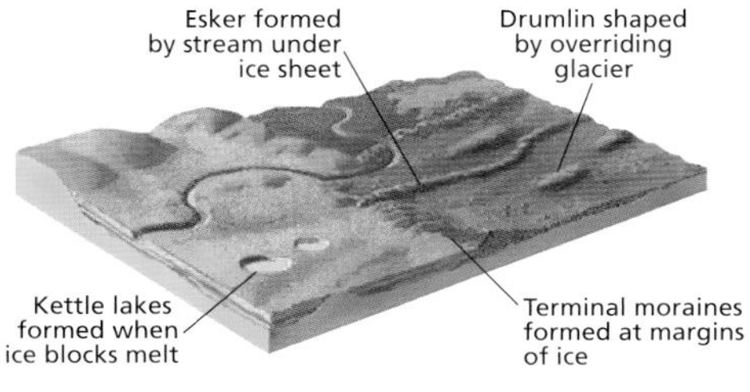

BEFORE AND AFTER (LEFT)

Meltwater deposits material in long, narrow ridges (eskers). Ice embedded in the ground melts and forms lakes (kettles). Ice overruns unconsolidated materials and shapes them into hills (drumlins).

Glacial valley: Sierra Nevada, California

POSTGLACIAL LANDFORMS

As they move, alpine glaciers widen their V-shaped valleys, often leaving behind U-shaped ones when they withdraw (left). Ice sheets leave an even larger legacy simply because they cover more territory. Among their creations are drumlin fields (right) and lake basins, including the ones now filled by the Great Lakes of North America.

Drumlins: Kejimkujik Lake, Nova Scotia

Surface of the Earth

EARTH'S LARGEST FEATURES—oceans and continents—can be seen from thousands of miles out in space. So can some of its relatively smaller ones: vast plains and long mountain chains, huge lakes and great ice sheets. The sizes, shapes, locations, and interrelationships of these and innumerable other features, large and small, give Earth its unique appearance.

Mountains, plateaus, and plains give texture to the land. In North and South America, the Rockies and Andes rise above great basins and plains, while in Asia the Himalaya and Plateau of Tibet form the rugged core of Earth's largest continent. All are the result of powerful forces within the planet pushing up the land. Other features, such as valleys and canyons, were created when weathering and erosion wore down parts of the surface. Landmasses are not the only places with dramatic features: Lying beneath the oceans are enormous mountains and towering volcanoes, high plateaus and seemingly bottomless trenches.

Around most continents are shallow seas concealing gently sloping continental shelves. From the margins of these shelves, steeper continental slopes lead ever deeper into the abyss. Although scientists use different terms to describe their studies of the ocean depths (bathymetry) and the lay of the land (topography), Earth's surface is a continuum, with similar features giving texture to lands both above and below the sea level.

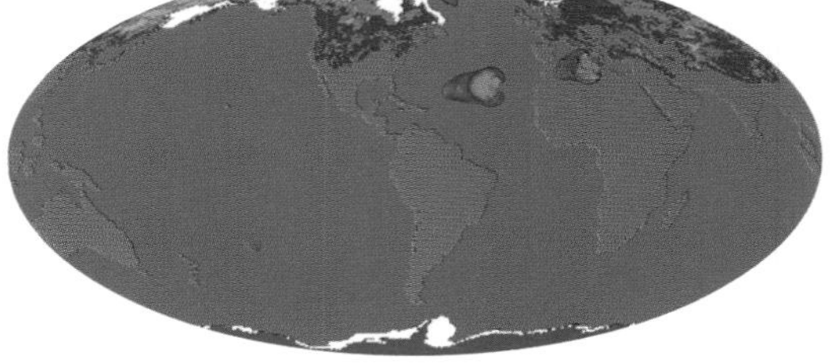

SNOW AND ICE Just over 2 percent of Earth's water is locked in ice, snow, and glaciers. Ice and snow reflect solar energy back into space, thus regulating the temperature. Ocean levels can also be affected, rising or falling as polar ice sheets shrink or grow.

Distribution of Earth's Elevations and Depths (Hypsometry)

Hypsometry measures the distribution of elevation and depth as a function of the area covered. At right, the "Raw %" curve shows two concentrations of average elevation: about 4,000 meters (13,000 ft) below sea level and about 800 meters (2,600 ft) above sea level. The "peaks" in the curve reflect the large, nearly flat areas of ocean floor, and vast land areas of Asia, Greenland, and Antarctica. The "Cumulative %" curve shows that about 72 percent of Earth's surface is below sea level, based on a worldwide two-minute (latitude-longitude) grid and a 200-meter (650-ft) grouping of vertical data.

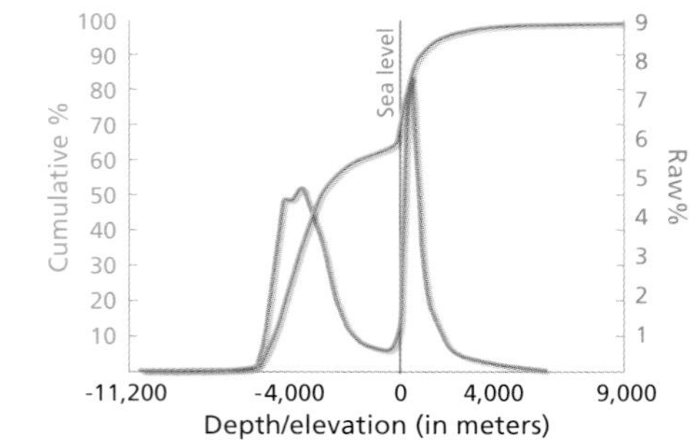

Earth Surface Elevations and Depths

WORLD IMAGE
Using gradations of color and exaggerated vertical relief, the above image depicts variations in elevation. Mountain ranges and ice caps stand out in shades of red; lowlands appear in green. Pale aqua marks shallow seas along continental margins and over peaks and ridges rising from the ocean floor.

Surface by the Numbers

AREA

TOTAL SURFACE AREA: 196,938,000 square miles (510,066,000 sq km)

LAND AREA: 57,393,000 square miles (148,647,000 sq km), 29.1 percent of total surface area

WATER AREA: 139,545,000 square miles (361,419,000 sq km), 70.9 percent of total surface area

SURFACE FEATURES

HIGHEST LAND: Mount Everest, 29,035 feet (8,850 m) above sea level

LOWEST LAND: shore of Dead Sea, 1,365 feet (416 m) below sea level

OCEAN DEPTHS

DEEPEST PART OF OCEAN: Challenger Deep, in the Pacific Ocean southwest of Guam, 35,827 feet (10,920 m) below the surface

AVERAGE OCEAN DEPTH: 12,205 feet (3,720 m)

CHEMICAL MAKEUP OF EARTH'S CRUST

As a percentage of the crust's weight: oxygen 46.6, silicon 27.7, aluminum 8.1, iron 5.0, calcium 3.6, sodium 2.8, potassium 2.6, magnesium 2.1, and other elements totaling 1.5.

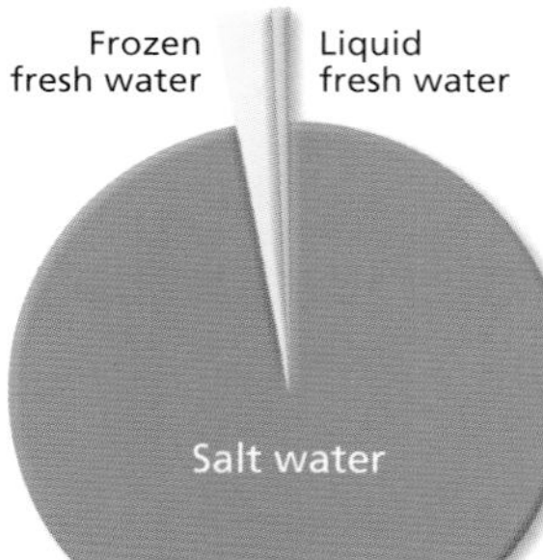

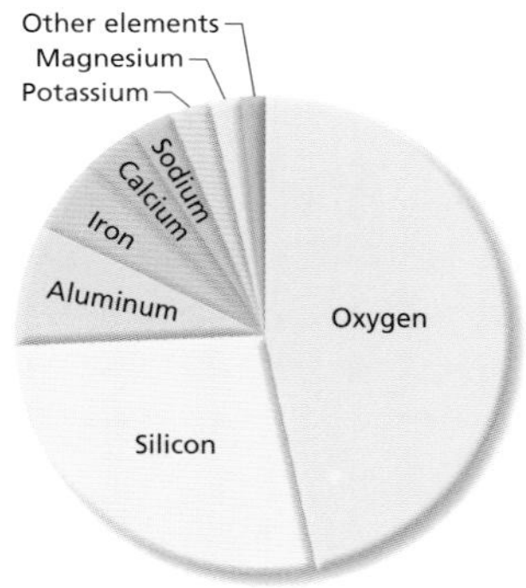

A Slice of Earth

Combining bathymetric and topographic data, this profile shows details of the Earth's crust—from the western Pacific Basin (A) to the Atlantic Basin; across Africa, the Himalaya, and the Japan Trench; then back to the western Pacific margin (B).

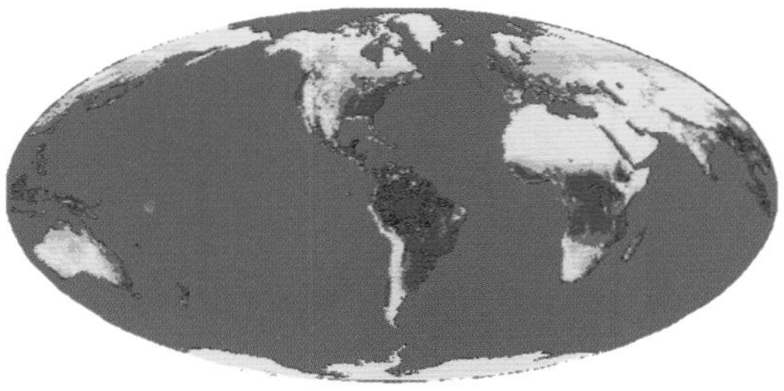

VEGETATIVE COVER Forests and woodlands cover 28 percent of Earth's land areas, helping those regions retain heat and thus playing a major role in the shaping of climate. Vast grasslands hold grains that are an important element in the world food supply.

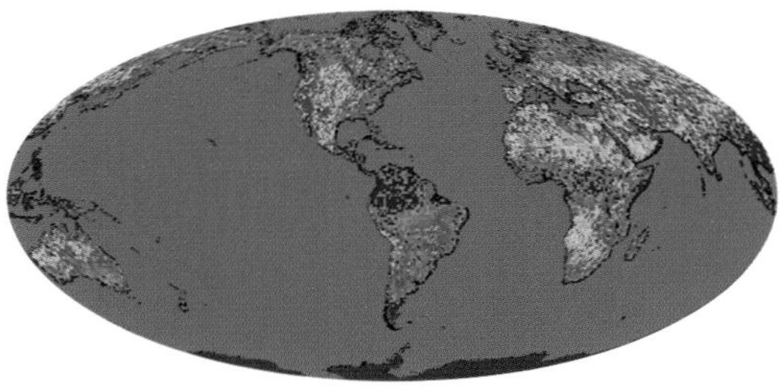

DAY AND NIGHT TEMPERATURE DIFFERENCES Vegetative cover influences variations between day and night temperatures in an area. Rain forests and other heavily vegetated regions retain heat well and experience relatively small changes, whereas deserts (in red) are subject to extreme variations.

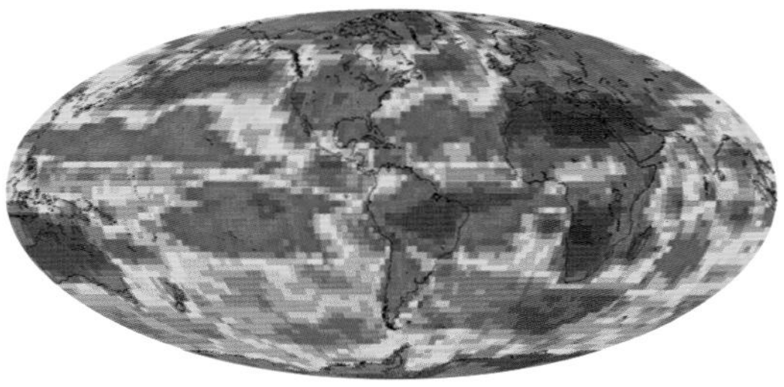

CLOUD COVER This composite image shows the regions with the heaviest cloud cover (red) on a typical June day. The gradation to blue signifies decreasing cover. Clouds contain moisture, affect temperatures, and on any given day cover 50 to 70 percent of Earth's surface.

Note: On these artistic representations, the vertical scale of the relief has been exaggerated so that individual features show up clearly.

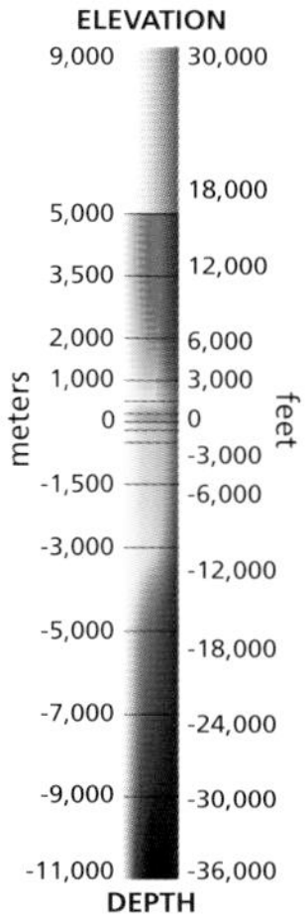

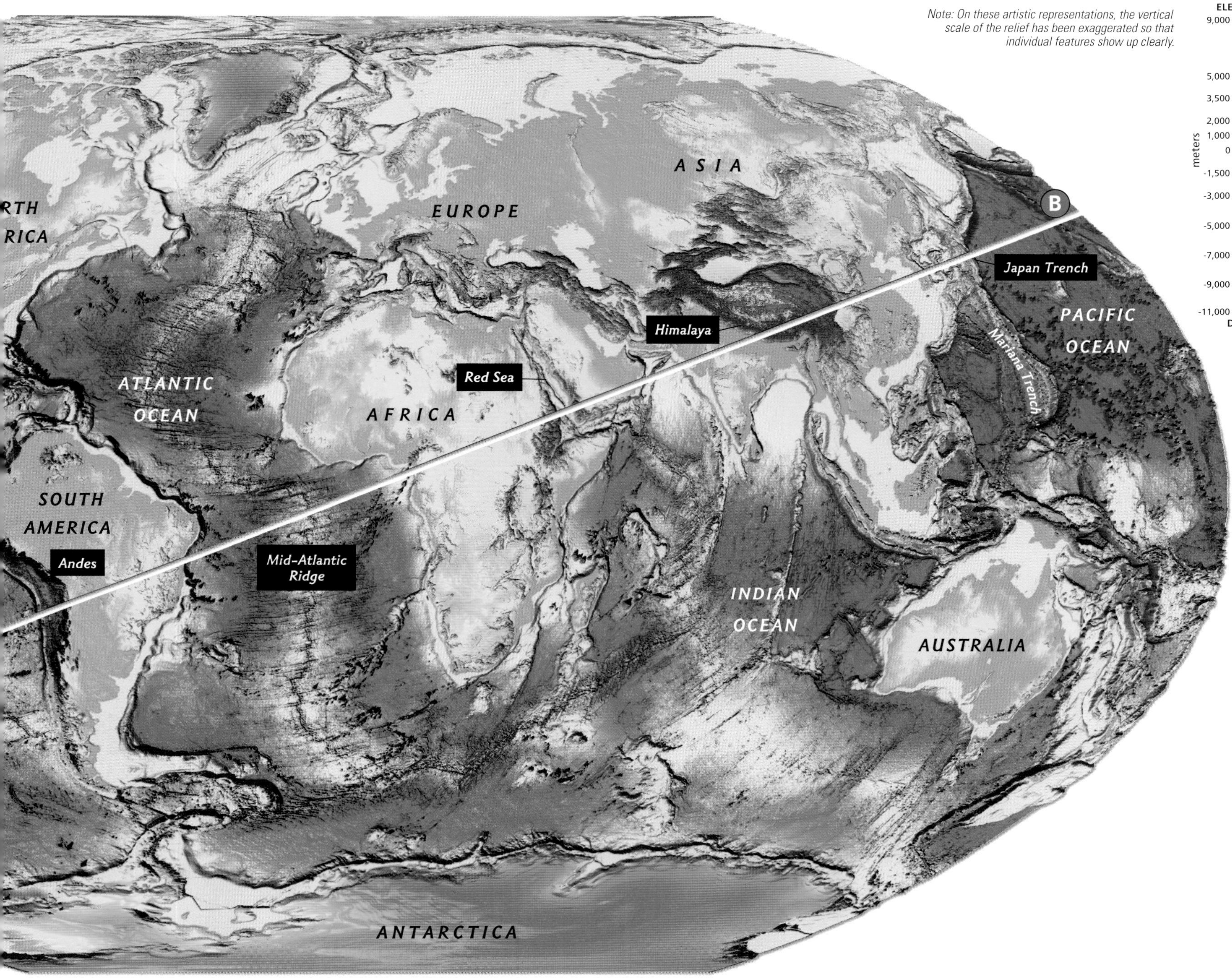

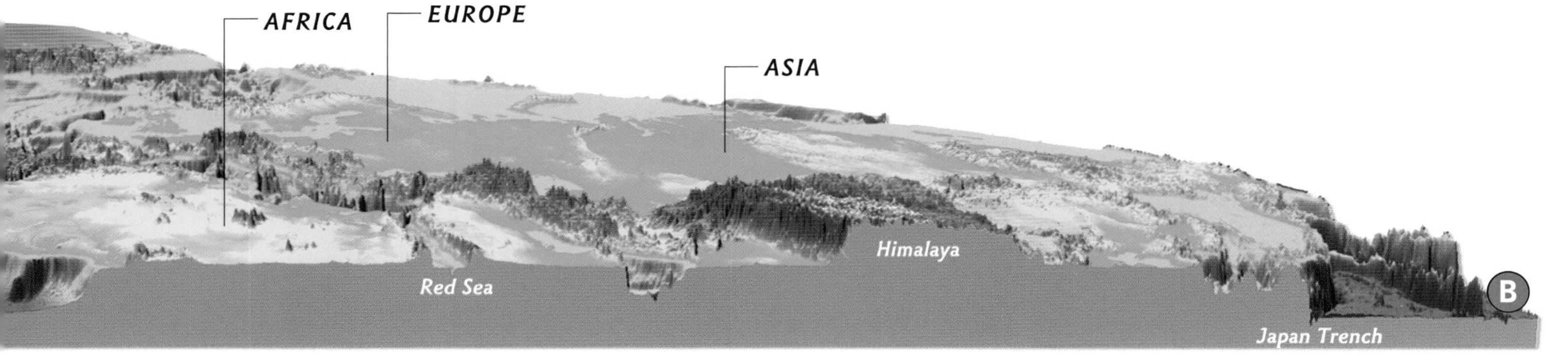

RELIABLE INFORMATION on global vegetative cover is an important requirement for many Earth-system studies, and the best source for an overall view of the planet is satellite data. Such data allow for the creation of internally consistent, reproducible, and accurate land cover maps like the one at right, which is based on a year of global satellite imagery from the Advanced Very High Resolution Radiometer (AVHRR) at a spatial resolution of one kilometer.

The change of vegetation through time, or its phenology, is captured in the satellite record and used to differentiate classes of vegetative cover. By recording the data at different wavelengths of the electromagnetic spectrum, scientists can derive land cover types through spectral variation. Maps made from this information help identify places undergoing changes. Descriptions of the various land cover types are provided below.

Global Land Cover Composition

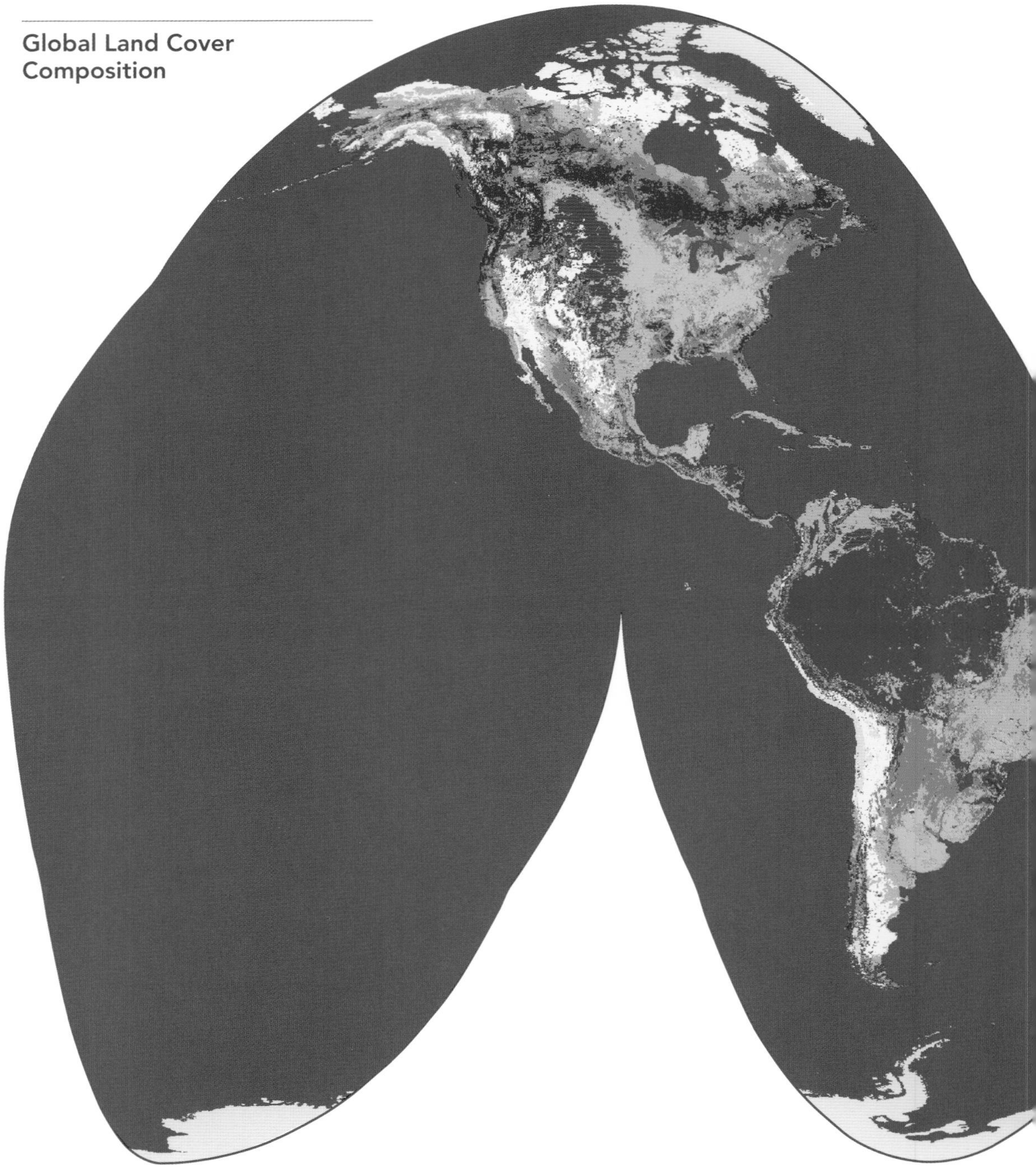

Evergreen needleleaf forest | Evergreen broadleaf forest | Deciduous needleleaf forest | Deciduous broadleaf forest | Mixed forest | Woodland | Wooded grassland | Closed shrubland | Open shrubland | Grassland | Cropland | Barren (desert and polar ice) | Built-up

EVERGREEN NEEDLE-LEAF FOREST
In this land cover type, more than 60 percent of the land is covered by a forest canopy; tree height exceeds 5 meters. Evergreen needleleaf forests are typical of the boreal (northern subarctic) region. In many of these areas, trees are grown on plantations and logged for the making of paper and building products.

EVERGREEN BROAD-LEAF FOREST
More than 60 percent of the land is covered by a forest canopy; tree height exceeds 5 meters. Such forests, which include tropical rain forests, dominate in the tropics and contain the greatest concentrations of biodiversity.
In many areas, mechanized farms, ranches, and tree plantations are replacing this land cover.

DECIDUOUS NEEDLE-LEAF FOREST
More than 60 percent of the land is covered by a forest canopy; tree height exceeds 5 meters. Trees respond to cold seasons by shedding their leaves simultaneously. This class is dominant only in Siberia, taking the form of larch forests with a short June-to-August growing season.

DECIDUOUS BROAD-LEAF FOREST
More than 60 percent of the land is covered by a forest canopy; tree height exceeds 5 meters. In dry or cold seasons, trees shed their leaves simultaneously. Much of this forest has been converted to cropland in temperate regions, with large remnants found only on steep slopes.

MIXED FOREST
More than 60 percent of the land is covered by a forest canopy; tree height exceeds 5 meters. Both needleleaf and deciduous types appear, with neither having coverage of less than 25 percent or more than 75 percent. This type is largely found between temperate deciduous and boreal evergreen forests.

WOODLAND
Land has herbaceous or woody understories and tree canopy cover of 40 to 60 percent; trees exceed 5 meters and may be evergreen or deciduous. This type is common in the tropics and is most highly degraded in areas with long histories of human habitation, such as West Africa.

WOODED GRASSLAND
Land has herbaceous or woody understories and tree canopy cover of 10 to 40 percent; trees exceed 5 meters and may be evergreen or deciduous. This type includes classic African savanna, as well as open boreal woodlands that demarcate tree lines and the beginning of tundra ecosystems.

CLOSED SHRUBLAND
Bushes or shrubs dominate, with a canopy coverage of more than 40 percent. Bushes do not exceed 5 meters in height; shrubs or bushes can be evergreen or deciduous. Tree canopy is less than 10 percent. This land cover can be found where prolonged cold or dry seasons limit plant growth.

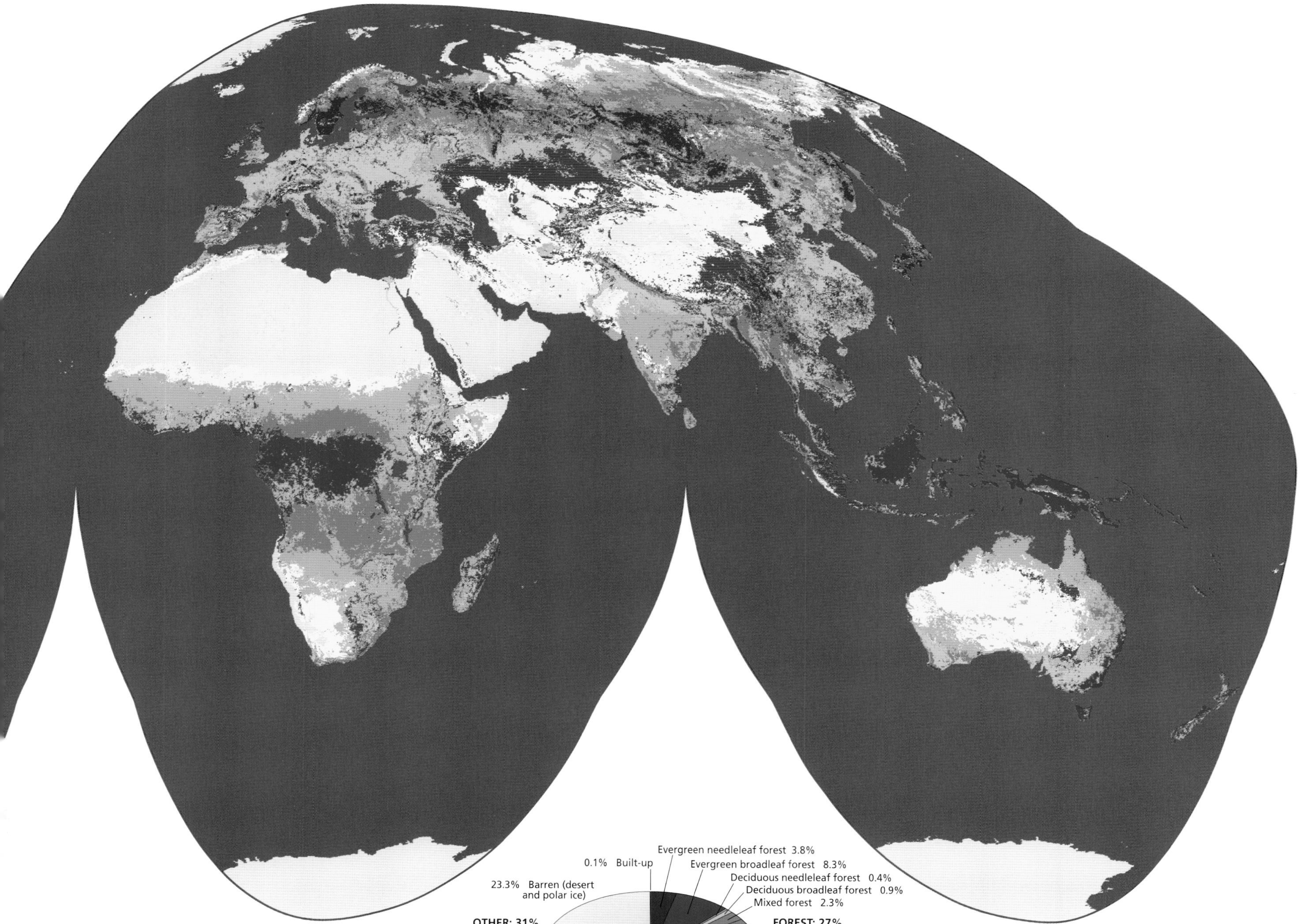

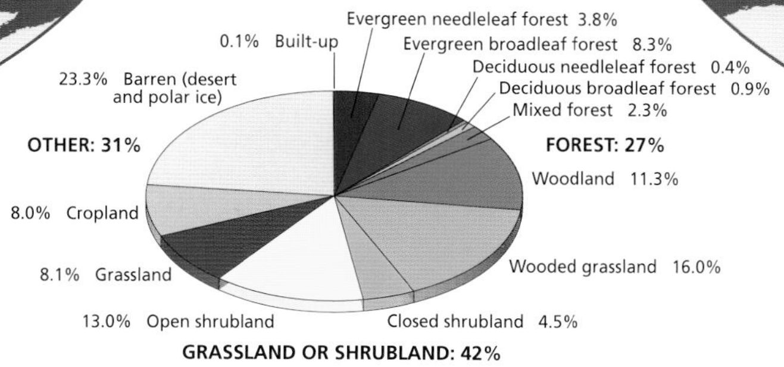

OPEN SHRUBLAND
Shrubs are dominant, with a canopy cover between 10 and 40 percent; they do not exceed 2 meters in height and can be evergreen or deciduous. The remaining land is either barren or characterized by annual herbaceous cover. This land cover type occurs in semiarid or severely cold regions.

GRASSLAND
Land has continuous herbaceous cover and less than 10 percent tree or shrub canopy cover. This type occurs in a wide range of habitats. Perennial grasslands in the central United States and Russia, for example, are the most extensive and mark a line of decreased precipitation that limits agriculture.

CROPLAND
Crop-producing fields make up more than 80 percent of the landscape. Areas of high-intensity agriculture, including mechanized farming, stretch across temperate regions. Much agriculture in the developing world is fragmented, however, and occurs on small plots of land.

BARREN AND DESERT
Exposed soil, sand, or rocks are typical; the land never has more than 10 percent vegetated cover during any time of year. This class includes true deserts, such as the Sahara in Africa. Desertification, the expansion of deserts due to land degradation or climate change, is a problem in areas.

URBAN AND BUILT-UP
Land cover includes buildings and other man-made structures. This class was mapped using the populated places layer that is part of the "Digital Chart of the World" (Danko, 1992). Urban and built-up cover represents the most densely developed areas of human habitation.

SNOW AND ICE
Land has permanent snow and ice; it never has more than 10 percent vegetated cover at any time of year. The greatest expanses of this class can be seen in Greenland, on other Arctic islands, and in Antarctica. Glaciers at high elevations form significant examples in Alaska, the Himalaya, and Iceland.

THE TERM "CLIMATE" describes the average "weather" conditions, as measured over many years, that prevail at any given point around the world at a given time of the year. Daily weather may differ dramatically from that expected on the basis of climatic statistics.

Energy from the sun drives the global climate system. Much of this incoming energy is absorbed in the tropics. Outgoing heat radiation, much of which exits at high latitudes, balances the absorbed incoming solar energy. To achieve a balance across the globe, huge amounts of heat are moved from the tropics to polar regions by both the atmosphere and the oceans.

The tilt of Earth's axis leads to shifting patterns of incoming solar energy throughout the year. More energy is transported to higher latitudes in winter than in summer, and hence the contrast in temperatures between the tropics and polar regions is greatest at this time of year—especially in the Northern Hemisphere.

Scientists present this data in many ways, using climographs (see page 36), which show information about specific places. Alternatively, they produce maps, which show regional and worldwide data.

The effects of the climatic contrasts are seen in the distribution of Earth's life-forms. Temperature, precipitation, and the amount of sunlight all determine what plants can grow in a region and the animals that live there. People are more adaptable, but climate exerts powerful constraints on where we live.

Climatic conditions define planning decisions, such as how much heating oil we need for the winter, and the necessary rainfall for agriculture in the summer. Fluctuations from year to year (e.g., cold winters or summer droughts) make planning more difficult.

In the longer term, continued global warming may change climatic conditions around the world, which could dramatically alter temperature and precipitation patterns and lead to more frequent heat waves, floods, and droughts.

JANUARY SOLAR ENERGY

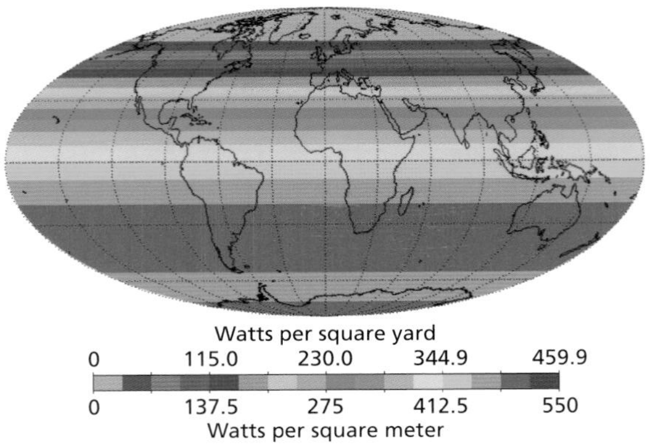

JULY SOLAR ENERGY

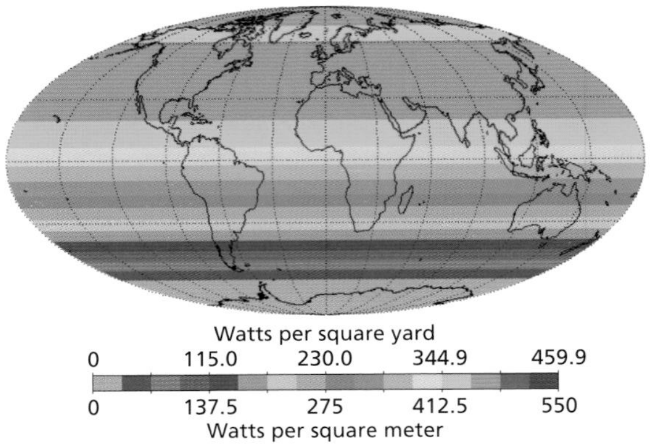

JANUARY AVERAGE TEMPERATURE

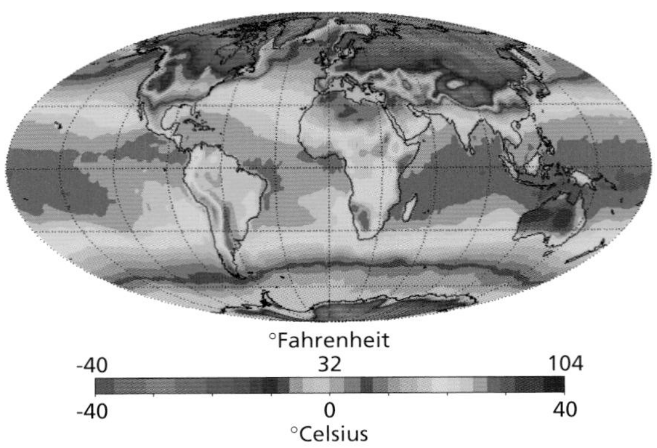

JULY AVERAGE TEMPERATURE

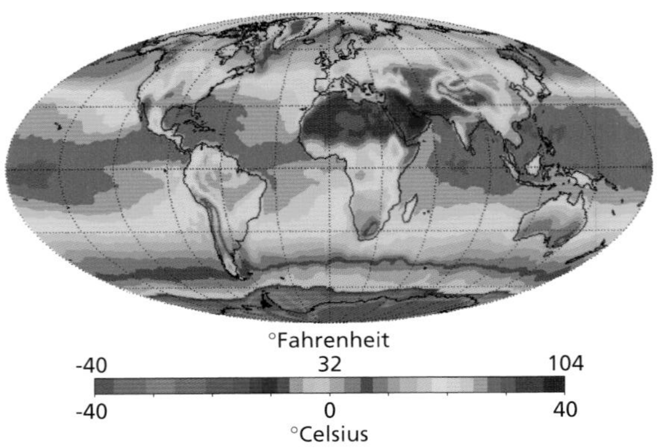

JANUARY CLOUD COVER

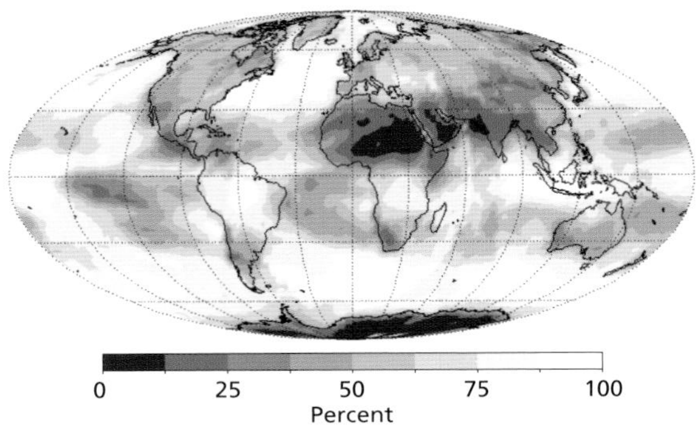

JULY CLOUD COVER

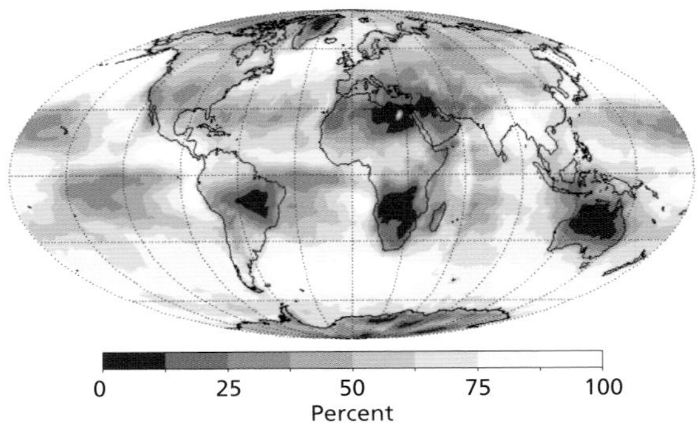

JANUARY PRECIPITATION

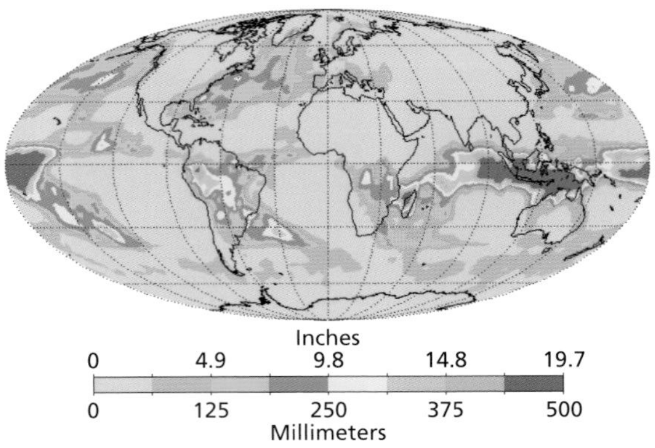

JULY PRECIPITATION

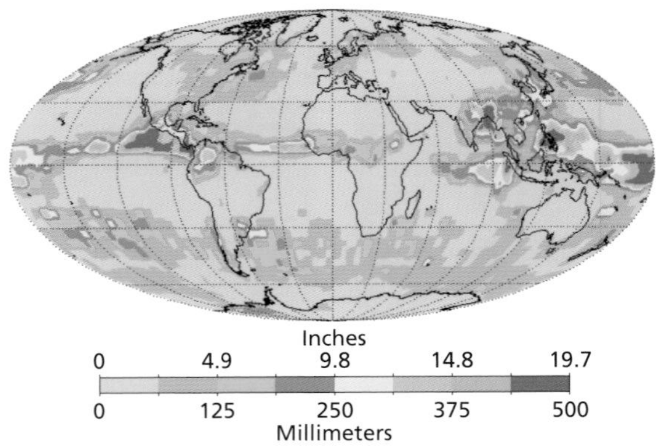

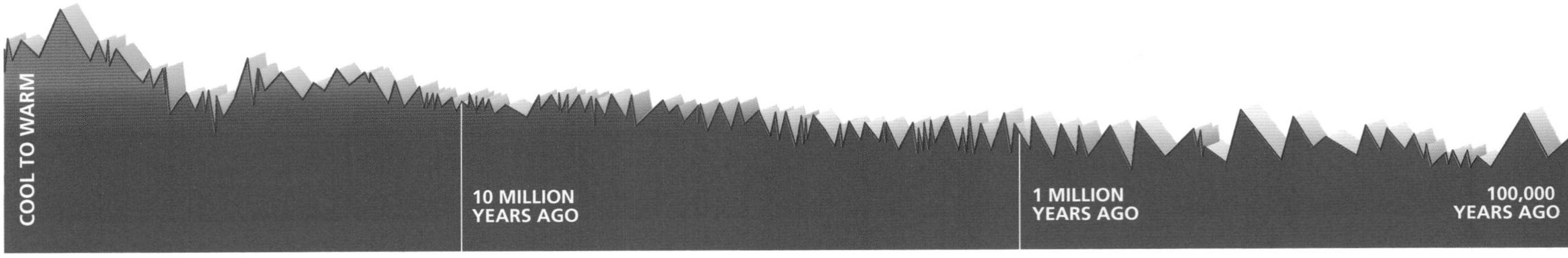

Major Factors that Influence Climate

LATITUDE AND ANGLE OF THE SUN'S RAYS

As Earth circles the sun, the tilt of its axis causes changes in the angle of the sun's rays and in the periods of daylight at different latitudes. Polar regions experience the greatest variation, with long periods of limited or no sunlight in winter and sometimes 24 hours of daylight in the summer.

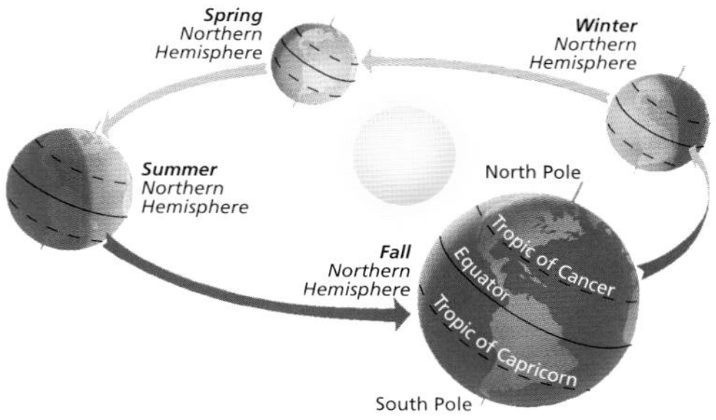

ELEVATION (ALTITUDE)

In general, climatic conditions become colder as elevation increases, just as they do when latitude increases. "Life zones" on a high mountain reflect the changes: Plants at the base are the same as those in surrounding countryside. Farther up, treed vegetation distinctly ends at the tree line; at the highest elevations, snow covers the mountain.

Mount Shasta, California

TOPOGRAPHY

Mountain ranges are natural barriers to air movement. In California (see diagram at right), winds off the Pacific carry moisture-laden air toward the coast. The Coast Ranges allow for some condensation and light precipitation. Inland, the taller Sierra Nevada range wrings more significant precipitation from the air. On the leeward slopes of the Sierra Nevada, sinking air warms from compression, clouds evaporate, and dry conditions prevail.

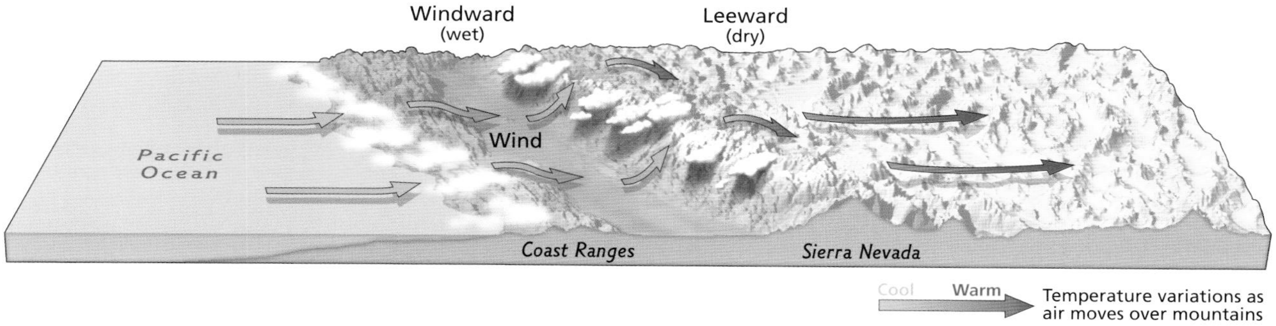

EFFECTS OF GEOGRAPHY

The location of a place and its distance from mountains and bodies of water help determine its prevailing wind patterns and what types of air masses affect it. Coastal areas may enjoy refreshing breezes in summer, when cooler ocean air moves ashore. Places south and east of the Great Lakes can expect "lake effect" snow in winter, when cold air travels over relatively warmer waters. In spring and summer, people living in "Tornado Alley" in the central United States watch for thunderstorms. Here, three types of air masses often converge: cold and dry from the north, warm and dry from the southwest, and warm and moist from the Gulf of Mexico. The colliding air masses often spawn tornadic storms.

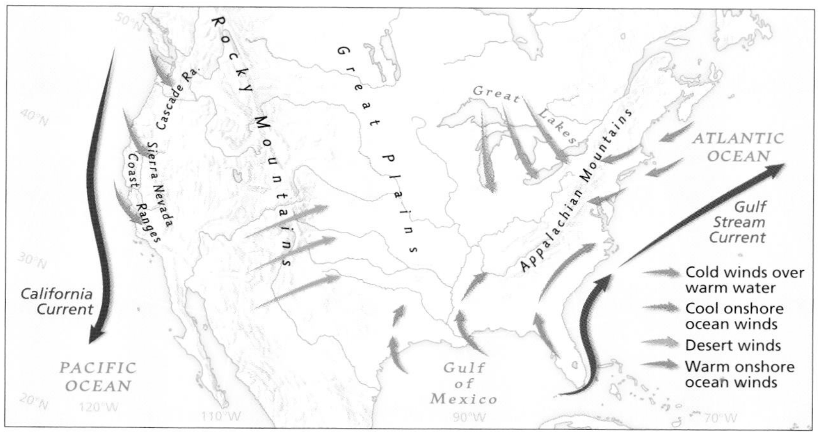

PREVAILING GLOBAL WIND PATTERNS

As shown at right, three large-scale wind patterns are found in the Northern Hemisphere and three are found in the Southern Hemisphere. These are average conditions and do not necessarily reflect conditions on a particular day. As seasons change, the wind patterns shift north or south. So does the intertropical convergence zone, which moves back and forth across the Equator. Sailors called this zone the doldrums because its winds are typically weak.

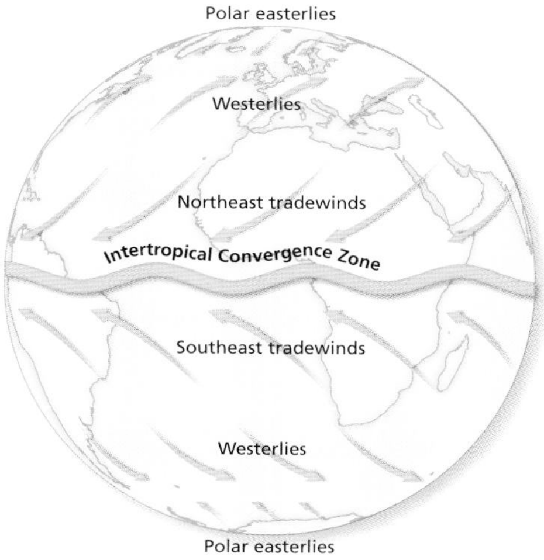

SURFACE OF THE EARTH

Just look at any globe or a world map showing land cover, and you will see another important influence on climate: Earth's surface. The amount of sunlight that is absorbed or reflected by the surface determines how much atmospheric heating occurs. Darker areas, such as heavily vegetated regions, tend to be good absorbers; lighter areas, such as snow- and ice-covered regions, tend to be good reflectors. Oceans absorb a high proportion of the solar energy falling upon them, but release it more slowly. Both the oceans and the atmosphere distribute heat around the globe.

Temperature Change over Time

Cold and warm periods punctuate Earth's long history. Some were fairly short (perhaps hundreds of years); others spanned hundreds of thousands of years. In some cold periods, glaciers grew and spread over large regions. In subsequent warm periods, the ice retreated. Each period profoundly affected plant and animal life. The most recent cool period, often called the little ice age, ended in western Europe around the year 1850.

Since the turn of the 20th century, temperatures have been rising steadily throughout the world. But it is not yet clear how much of this warming is due to natural causes and how much derives from human activities, such as the burning of fossil fuels and the clearing of forests.

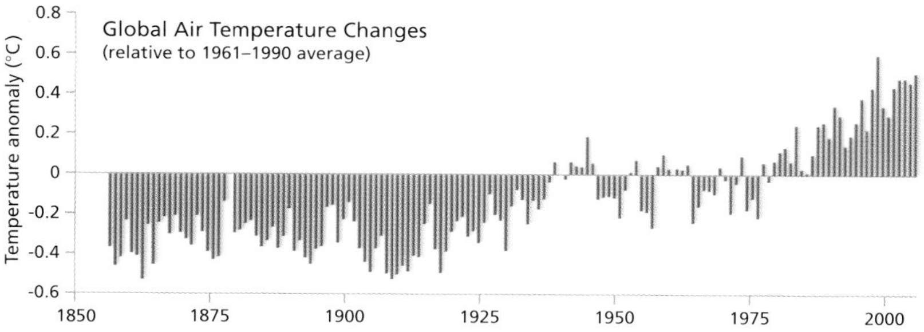

CLIMATE ZONES ARE PRIMARILY CONTROLLED by latitude—which governs the prevailing winds, the angle of the sun's rays, and the length of day throughout the year—and by geographical location with respect to mountains and oceans. Elevation, surface attributes, and other variables modify the primary controlling factors. Latitudinal banding of climate zones is most pronounced over Africa and Asia, where fewer north-south mountain ranges mean less disruption of prevailing winds. In the Western Hemisphere, the high, almost continuous mountain range that extends from western Canada to southern South America helps create dry regions on its leeward slopes. Over the United States, where westerly winds prevail, areas to the east of the range lie in a "rain shadow" and are therefore drier. In northern parts of South America, where easterly trade winds prevail, the rain shadow lies west of the mountains. Ocean effects dominate much of western Europe and southern parts of Australia.

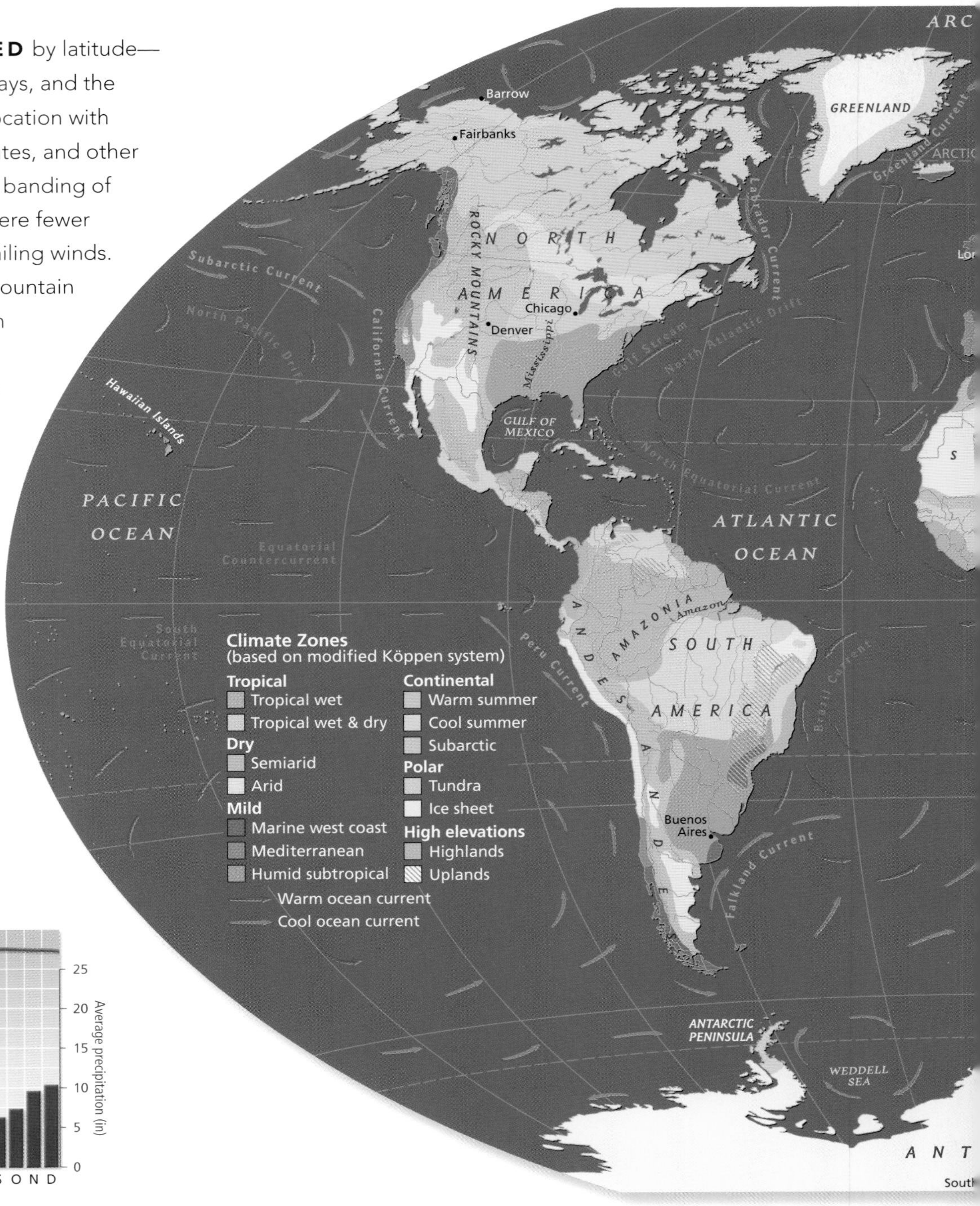

Climographs

The map at right shows the global distribution of climate zones, while the following 12 climographs (graphs of monthly temperature and precipitation) provide snapshots of the climate at specific places. Each place has a different climate type, which is described in general terms. Rainfall is shown in a bar graph format (scale on right side of the graph); temperature is expressed with a line graph (scale on left side). Places with highland and upland climates were not included because local changes in elevation can produce significant variations in local conditions.

TROPICAL WET

This climate type has the most predictable conditions. Warm and rainy year-round, regions with a tropical wet climate experience little variation from month to month. This type is mainly found within a zone extending about 10 degrees on either side of the Equator. With as much as 60 inches (152 cm) of rain each year, the tropical wet climate supports lush vegetation.

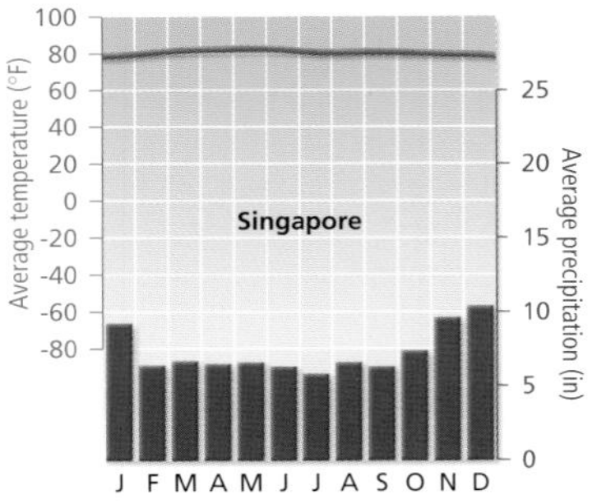

TROPICAL WET AND DRY

Because of seasonal reversals in wind direction (monsoons), this climate type is characterized by a slightly cooler dry season and a warmer, very moist wet season. The highest temperatures usually occur just before the wet season. Although average annual conditions may be similar to a tropical wet climate, the rainy season brings much more rain.

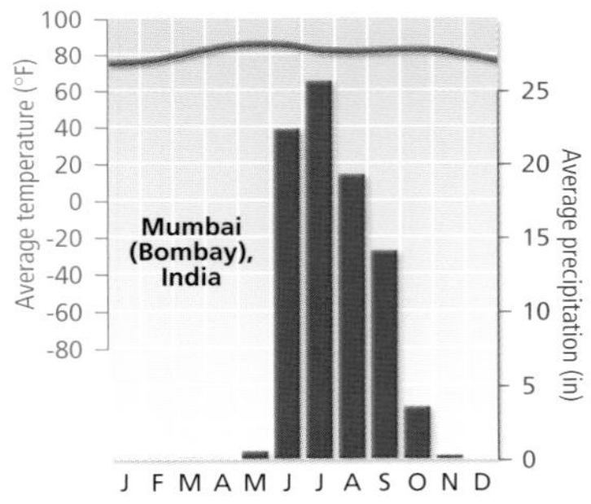

ARID

Centered between 20° and 30° north and south latitude, this climate type is the result of a persistent high-pressure area and, along the western margins of continents, a cold ocean current. Rainfall amounts in regions with this climate type are negligible, and there is some seasonal variation in temperature. Desert vegetation is typically sparse.

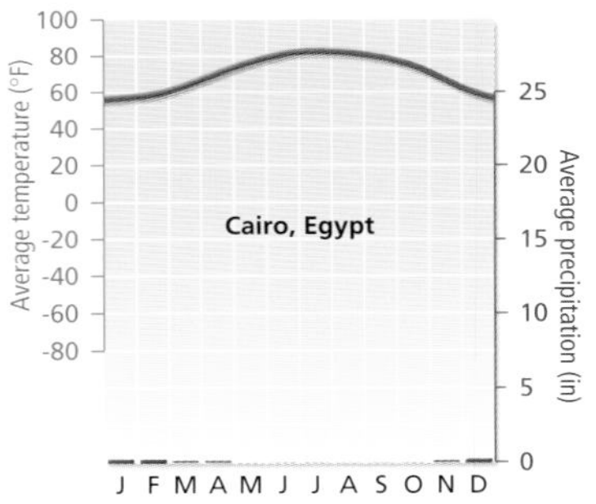

SEMIARID

Regions with a semiarid climate lie poleward of areas with a desert (arid) climate; they have a much greater range in monthly temperatures and receive significantly more rainfall than deserts. This climate type is often found in inland regions, in the rain shadow of mountain ranges. Annual rainfall amounts support mainly grasses and small shrubs.

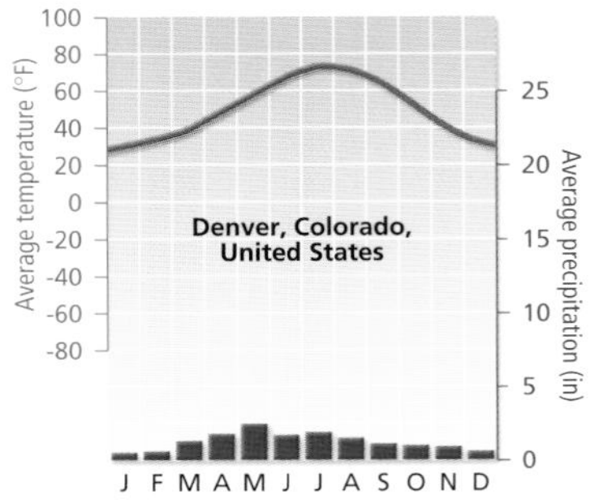

MARINE WEST COAST

This climate type is primarily found between 40 and 60 degrees latitude; it occurs on the west coasts of continents and across much of Europe. Prevailing westerly winds bring milder ocean air ashore, but sunny days are limited and precipitation is frequent. Except in the highest elevations, most precipitation falls as rain. This climate supports extensive forests.

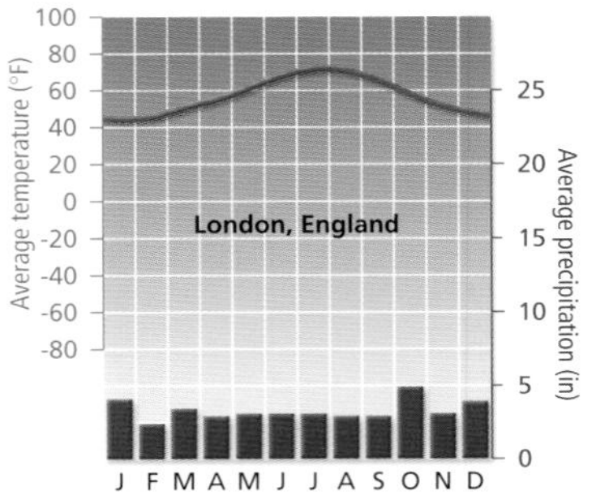

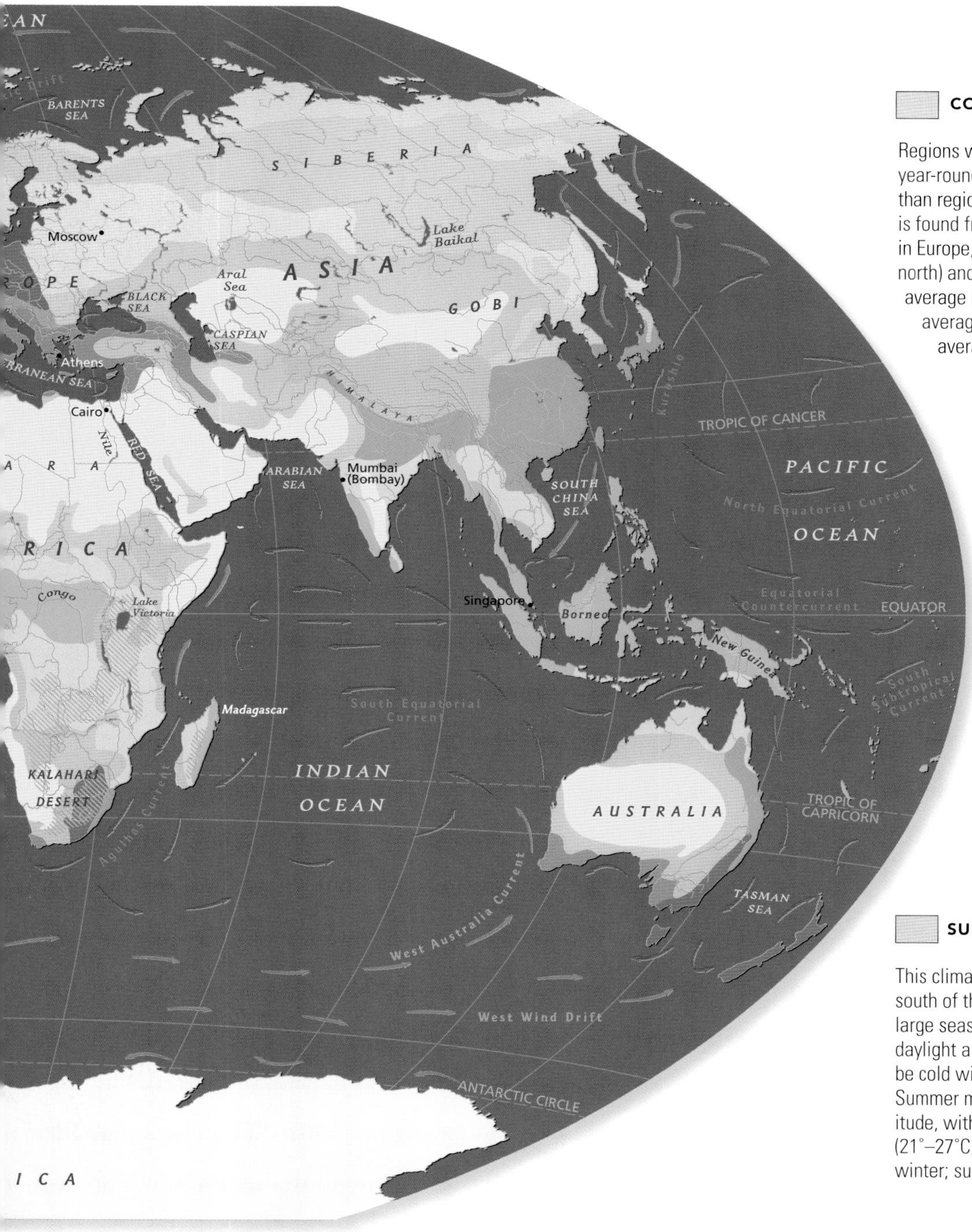

CONTINENTAL WARM SUMMER

Regions with this climate type have warmer year-round temperatures and more rainfall than regions with cool summers. This type is found from about 40° to 50° north (except in Europe, where it extends to about 60° north) and is marked by large variations in average monthly temperature. Summer averages can exceed 70°F (21°C); winter averages can be in the 20s (-7°C).

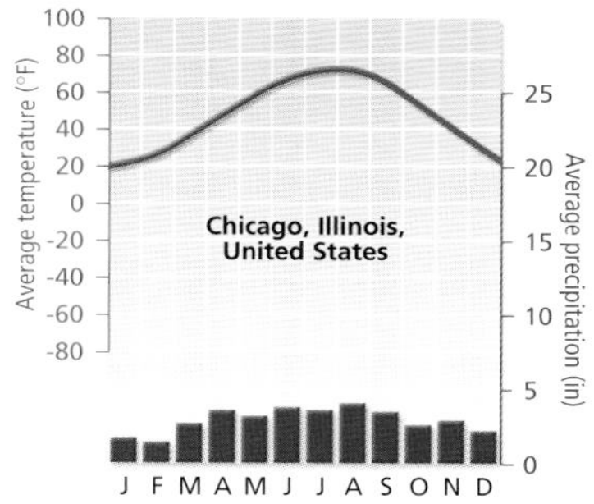

CONTINENTAL COOL SUMMER

Found only from about 40° to 60° north, this type is marked by temperature extremes. Summers are cool (around 60°F/15°C as a monthly average); winter months may have below-freezing average temperatures. Rainfall is moderate to abundant.

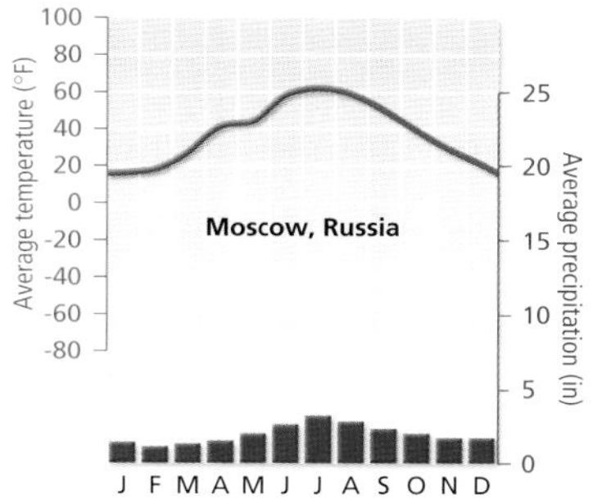

SUBARCTIC

This climate type is found along and just south of the Arctic Circle; it is driven by large seasonal swings in the amount of daylight a region receives. Winter tends to be cold with light snow and little melting. Summer months are quite warm for the latitude, with temperatures 70 or 80 degrees (21°–27°C) higher than monthly averages in winter; summer has significant rainfall.

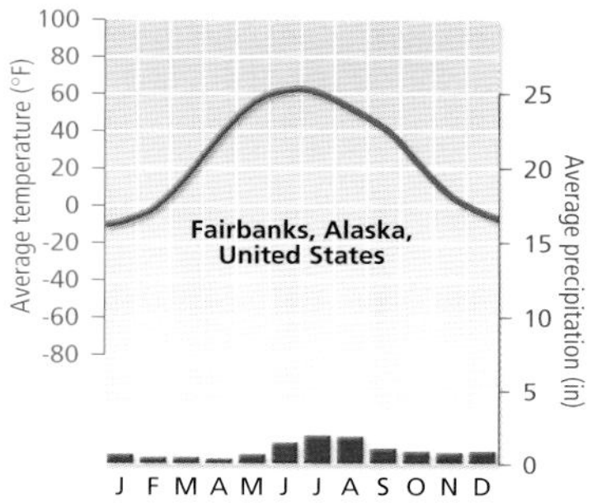

MEDITERRANEAN

This term describes the climate of much of the Mediterranean region. Such a climate is also found in narrow bands along the west coasts of continents that lie around 30 to 35 degrees poleward from the Equator. Summer months are typically warm to hot with dry conditions, while winter months are cool (but not cold) and provide modest precipitation.

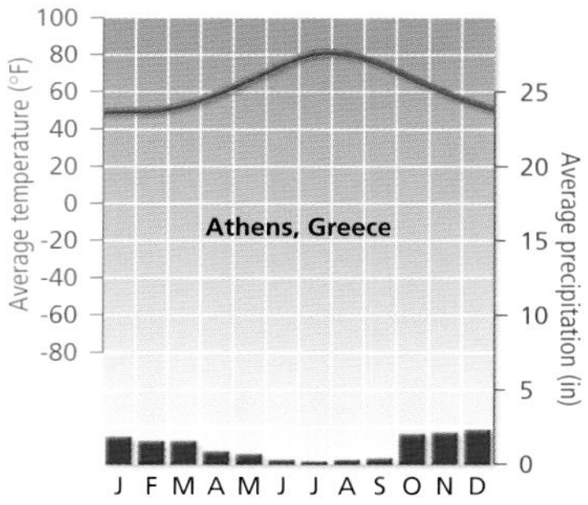

TUNDRA

Along the southern boundary of this climatic zone, ground-hugging plants meet the northernmost trees (the tree line). Here, the warmest average monthly temperature is below 50°F (10°C), with only one to four months having an average monthly temperature that is above freezing. Precipitation amounts are low, typically about 10 inches (25 cm) or less annually.

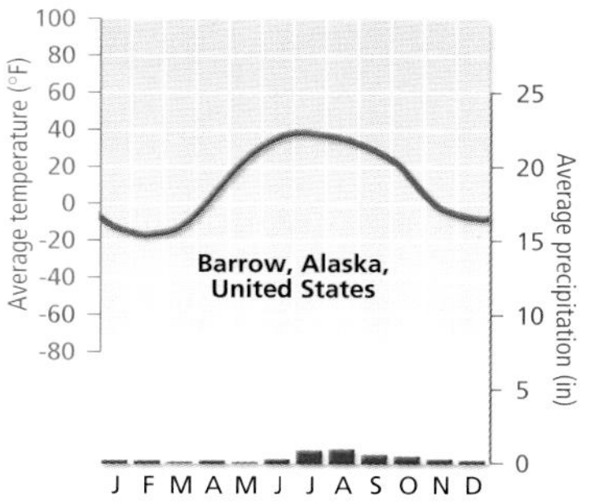

HUMID SUBTROPICAL

This climate type dominates eastern regions of continents at 30 to 35 degrees latitude. Here, warm ocean waters lead to warm and humid summers. Rainfall is greatest near the coast, supporting forest growth; precipitation is less farther west, supporting grasslands. Winter can bring cold waves and snowy periods, except in areas right on the coast.

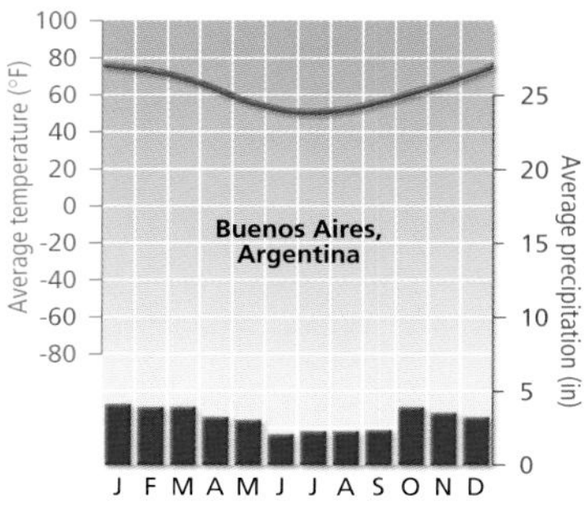

ICE SHEET

This climate type is found at high latitudes in interior Greenland and across most of Antarctica; average monthly temperatures are around zero degrees Fahrenheit (-18°C) and below. Snow defines the landscape, but precipitation is only about 5 inches (13 cm) or less annually. The combined effects of cold and dryness produce desert-like conditions.

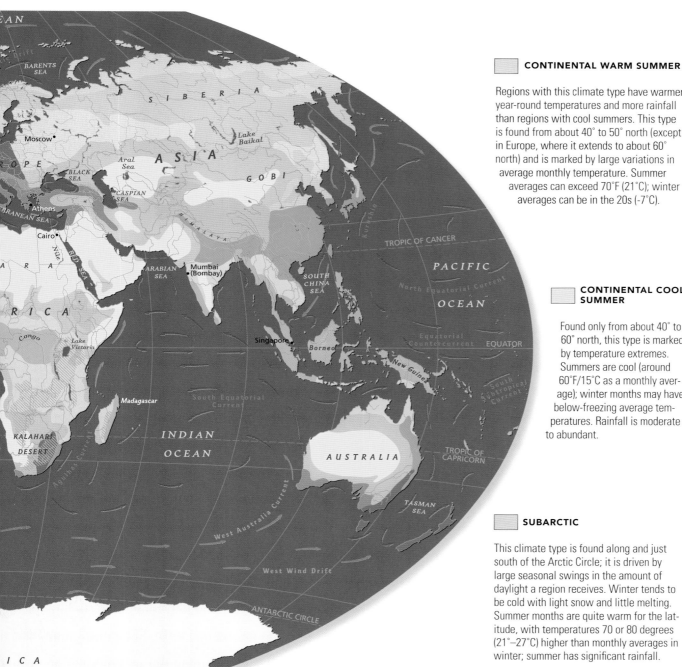

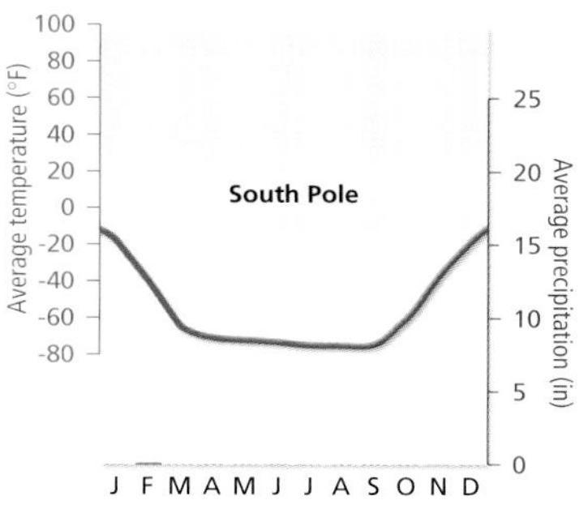

STEP OUTSIDE AND YOU EXPERIENCE many facets of weather. Humidity, air temperature and pressure, wind speed and direction, cloud cover and type, and the amount and form of precipitation are all atmospheric characteristics of the momentary conditions we call weather.

The sun is ultimately responsible for the weather. Its rays are absorbed differently by land and water surfaces (equal amounts of solar radiation heat the ground more quickly than they heat water). Differential warming, in turn, causes variations in the temperature and pressure of overlying air masses.

As an air mass warms, it becomes lighter and rises higher into the atmosphere. As an air mass cools, it becomes heavier and sinks. Pressure differences between masses of air generate winds, which tend to blow from high-pressure areas to areas of low pressure. Fast-moving, upper-atmosphere winds known as jet streams help move weather systems around the world.

Large weather systems called cyclones rotate counterclockwise in the Northern Hemisphere (clockwise in the Southern Hemisphere); they are also called "lows," because their centers are low-pressure areas. Clouds and precipitation are usually associated with these systems. Anti-cyclones, or "highs," rotate in the opposite direction and are high-pressure areas. They usually bring clearer skies and more settled weather.

The boundary between two air masses is called a front. Here, wind, temperature, and humidity change abruptly, producing atmospheric instability. When things get "out of balance" in the atmosphere, storms may develop, bringing rain or snow and sometimes thunder and lightning as well. Storms are among nature's great equalizers.

The weather you experience is influenced by many factors, including your location's latitude, elevation, and proximity to water bodies. Even the degree of urban development, which creates "heat islands," and the amount of snow cover, which chills an overlying air mass, play important roles. The next time you watch a weather report on television, think about the many factors, some thousands of miles away, that help make the weather what it is.

The swirling cloud pattern and well-formed eye of Hurricane Katrina stand out in this NOAA satellite image from late morning on August 29, 2005. At the time, Katrina was making its third landfall near the Louisiana-Mississippi border, and was by now a weakening Category Two storm. (The other two landfalls were near Miami, Florida, as a strong tropical storm, and just south of New Orleans as a hurricane.) Its storm surge, flooding, and high winds caused incredible destruction from Louisiana eastward to Alabama, and Katrina ranks as the costliest—and also one of the deadliest—hurricanes ever to strike the U.S.

Hurricanes (defined as tropical low-pressure systems with sustained winds of at least 74 miles an hour) can also be prolific rainmakers. In 1972, Agnes dropped torrents of rain on the northeast U.S., causing severe flooding in several states. Despite the dramatic rainfall sometimes brought by hurricanes, nontropical (or extratropical) low-pressure systems actually bring most of the precipitation that falls in the middle latitudes (30° to 60° latitude).

Major Factors that Influence Weather

THE WATER CYCLE

As the sun warms the surface of Earth, water rises in the form of water vapor from lakes, rivers, oceans, plants, the ground, and other sources. This process is called evaporation. Water vapor provides the moisture that forms clouds; it eventually returns to Earth in the form of precipitation, and the cycle continues.

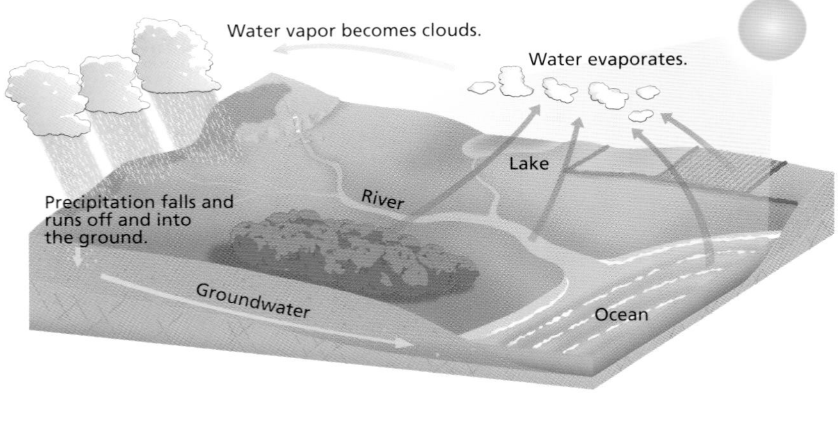

AIR MASSES

When air hovers for a while over a surface area with uniform humidity and temperature, it takes on the characteristics of the area below. For example, an air mass over the tropical Atlantic Ocean would become warm and humid; an air mass over the winter snow and ice of northern Canada would become cold and dry. These massive volumes of air often cover thousands of miles and reach to the stratosphere. Over time, mid-latitude cyclonic storms and global wind patterns move them to locations far from their source regions.

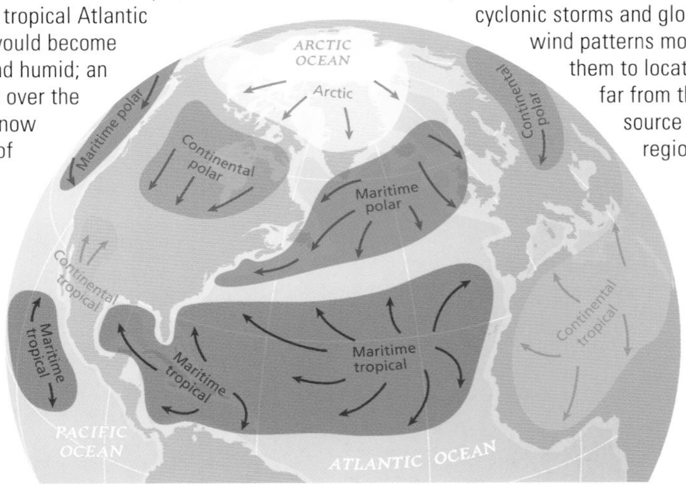

JET STREAM

A meandering current of high-speed wind, a jet stream is usually found around five to ten miles above Earth's surface. It generally flows west to east, often in a noncontinuous wavy fashion, with cold, Equatorward dips (called troughs) and warm, Poleward bulges (called ridges). The polar jet separates cold and warm masses of air; the subtropical jet is less likely to be related to temperature differences. Fronts and low-pressure areas are typically located near a jet stream.

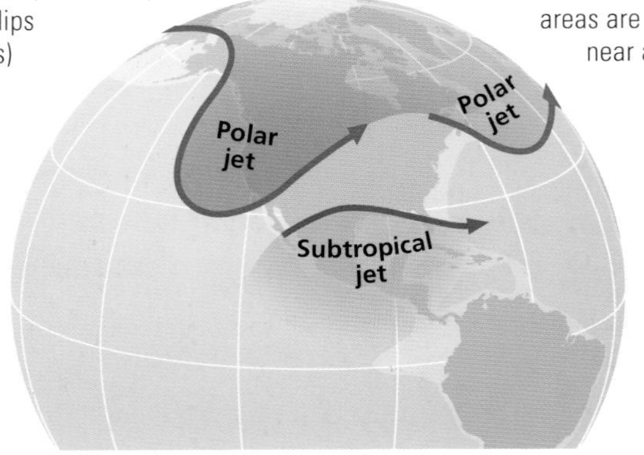

WEATHER FRONTS

The transition zone between two air masses of different humidity and temperature is called a front. Along a cold front, cold air displaces warm air; along a warm front, warm air displaces cold air. When neither air mass displaces the other, a stationary front develops. Towering clouds and intense storms may form along cold fronts, while widespread clouds and rain, snow, sleet, or drizzle may accompany warm fronts.

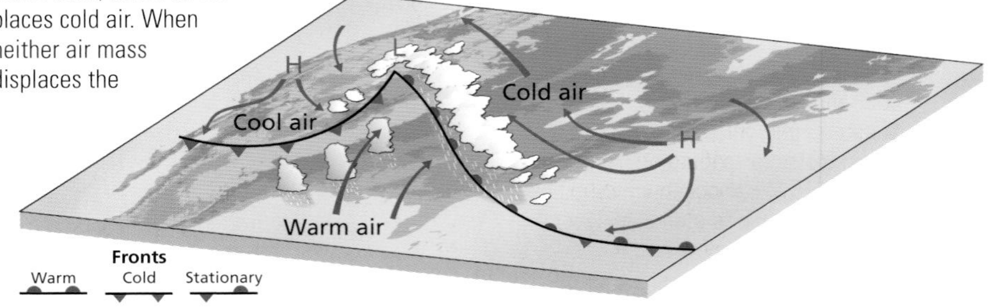

Cloud Types

Clouds are the visible collections of water droplets or ice particles in the atmosphere. Meteorologists classify them according to shape and altitude.

Stratus are low-level clouds that are flat or layered; they are much longer and wider than they are tall. Fog is a stratus cloud that touches the ground. Altostratus (alto means "high") is a stratus cloud about two miles above Earth. When these clouds rain or snow, they are called nimbostratus. Cirrostratus clouds lie at an altitude of about four miles.

Cumulus clouds have flat bottoms and puffy tops. The flat bottoms mark the altitude at which rising air reaches its condensation level (typically about a mile above Earth's surface); the puffy tops show how the cloud "bubbles up." Cumulus often develop as sunlight heats the ground and the ground, in turn, heats the air. If cumulus tower, they can transform into cumulonimbus (thunderstorm) clouds, with their tops reaching an altitude of seven miles or more.

Cumulus clouds can also develop in layers. Stratocumulus is a layered cumulus cloud about a mile above the ground. Altocumulus is a similar cloud at an altitude of two miles. Its greater distance from the ground makes the cumulus puffs appear smaller than those of stratocumulus clouds. The cirrocumulus type (with still smaller puffs) is found about four to five miles higher.

Cirrus clouds occur at an altitude of four miles or more, where the temperature is always below freezing; hence, these clouds are always filled with ice crystals.

As a general forecasting rule, dry weather is most likely when cumulus clouds remain flat and/or when mid-level (altocumulus) clouds are not present. Precipitation is most likely when two or more clouds occur at the same time, and/or when cumulus clouds tower to great heights or turn into cumulonimbus clouds.

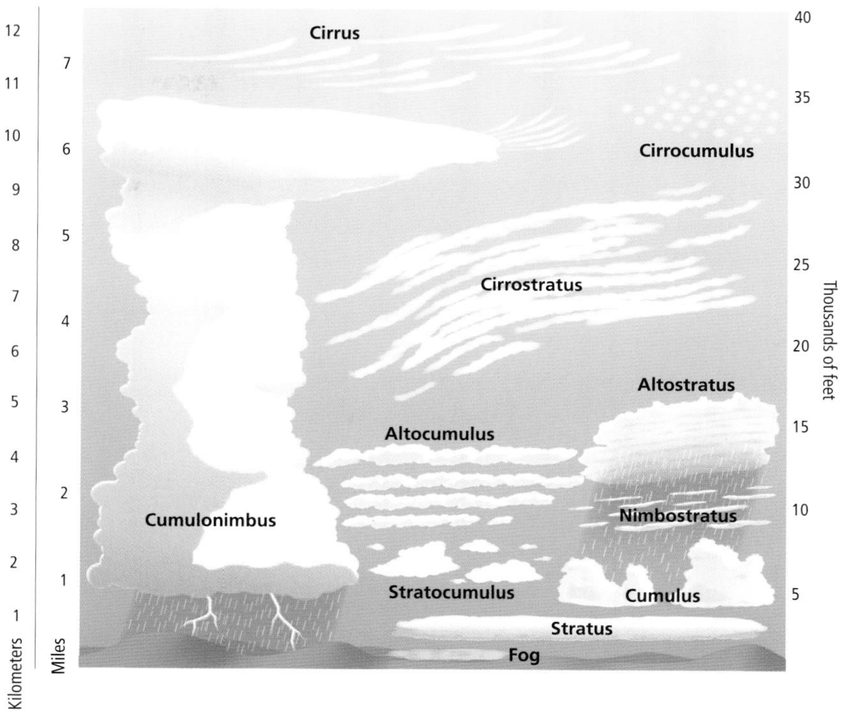

Tropical Cyclones

Hurricanes and their counterparts in other places (typhoons near Japan and cyclones off India and Australia) are moderately large low-pressure systems that form most often during the warmer months of the year. They occur mainly near the Equator, in regions with prevailing easterly winds. These systems develop winds between 75 and 150 miles an hour and, on some rare occasions, even stronger winds. As the storms move toward the middle latitudes, where the prevailing winds are mainly westerly, they can "recurve" (move toward the east). Some hurricanes have stayed nearly stationary at times, while others have made loops and spirals along their paths.

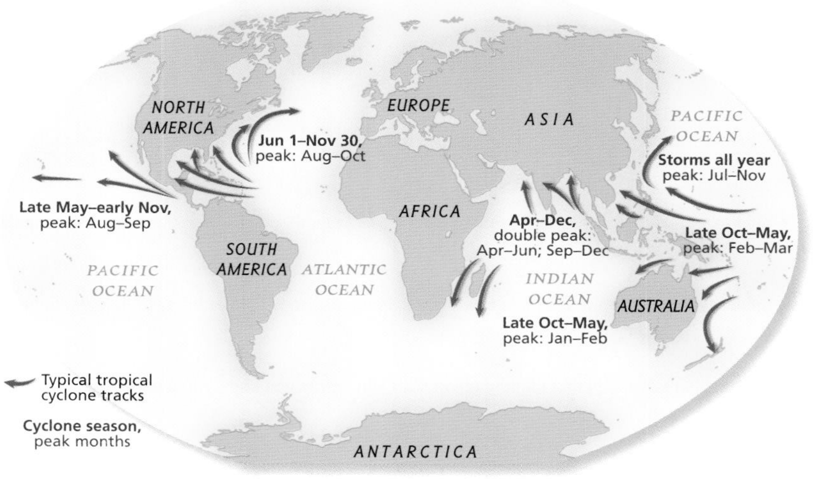

Lightning

In order to estimate the mean annual distribution of lightning (more than 1.2 billion intracloud and cloud-to-ground flashes), NASA scientists used five years of data taken from a satellite orbiting 460 miles above Earth. Lightning distribution is directly linked to climate, with maximal occurrence in areas that see frequent thunderstorms (the red areas on the map below).

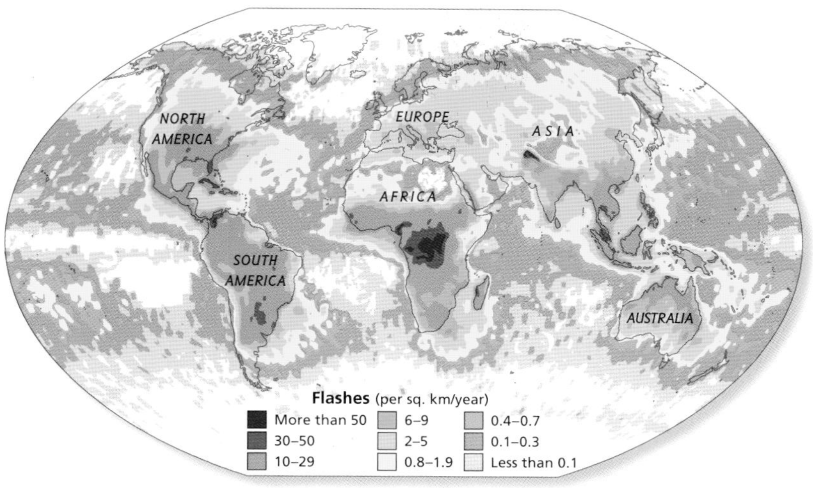

El Niño and La Niña

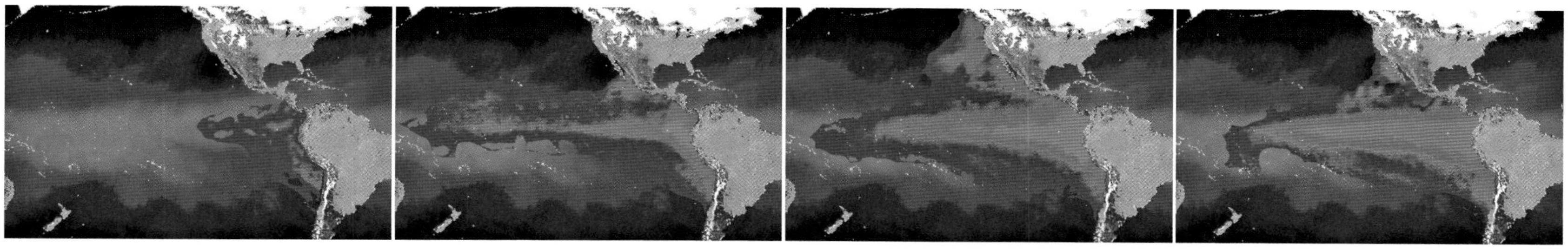

Periodic shifts in wind speed and direction in the tropical eastern Pacific can lead to changes in sea-surface temperatures. In what scientists call El Niño events, prevailing easterly winds weaken or give way to westerly winds, and the normal upwelling process, which brings cool, nutrient-rich waters up from lower levels of the ocean, stops. This stoppage causes sea-surface temperatures to rise, providing an unfavorable habitat for many fish. The warmer ocean conditions can also lead to more rainfall and floods along the west coast of the Americas. A stronger easterly wind flow, on the other hand, can increase upwelling and make the sea-surface temperatures even colder, producing La Niña. Both phenomena can have far-reaching weather effects. For example, strong El Niño events often result in a weak Atlantic Ocean hurricane season but produce plentiful precipitation in the normally dry southwestern United States. La Niña events favor more Atlantic hurricanes, but can spell drought in the southwestern U.S., even for normally dry southern California.

From left to right, the above image sequence shows how temperatures in the Pacific Ocean changed as the 1997 to 1998 El Niño event evolved. The first image, from March 10, 1997, shows a mostly cool ocean (blue shades). By mid-June, sea-surface temperatures (red shades) were above average from South America across much of the tropical Pacific. By mid-September, the warmth had extended from California southward to Chile and westward across most of the tropical Pacific. The final image, from late December 1997, shows a major El Niño, with sea-surface temperatures measuring six to eight degrees above average on the Fahrenheit scale.

To learn about weather extremes, see Geographic Comparisons on page 264.

HOME TO ALL LIVING THINGS, the biosphere is an intricate system made up of constantly interacting realms that support life: parts of the atmosphere (air), lithosphere (land), and hydrosphere (water in the ground, at the surface, and in the air).

As a result of the interaction between realms of the biosphere and changes in the distance of Earth's rotation around the sun, Earth's flora and fauna have changed over the eons, sometimes slowly and sometimes rapidly. Some species have continued to evolve; others, like the dinosaurs, have become extinct.

Life, of course, interacts with the land, water, and air, playing a significant role in shaping Earth's face and influencing its natural processes. Billions of years ago one of the smallest life-forms, photosynthetic bacteria (organisms that produce oxygen as a by-product of their metabolism), helped provide the oxygen in the air we breathe.

Human beings are currently Earth's dominant life-form. Through the ages, we have evolved the means to affect the planet in ways both positive and negative. At present, we are introducing changes to the biosphere at greater rates than natural processes may be able to accommodate, as societies make ever increasing demands on Earth's resources.

It is now clear that human beings are able to greatly influence the fate of the biosphere. It is also clear that developing a better understanding of how the biosphere functions, and how its realms interact, is fundamental to sustaining it. This requires a multi- and interdisciplinary perspective that brings together different worldviews from each of the physical, biological, and social sciences.

The Biosphere from Space

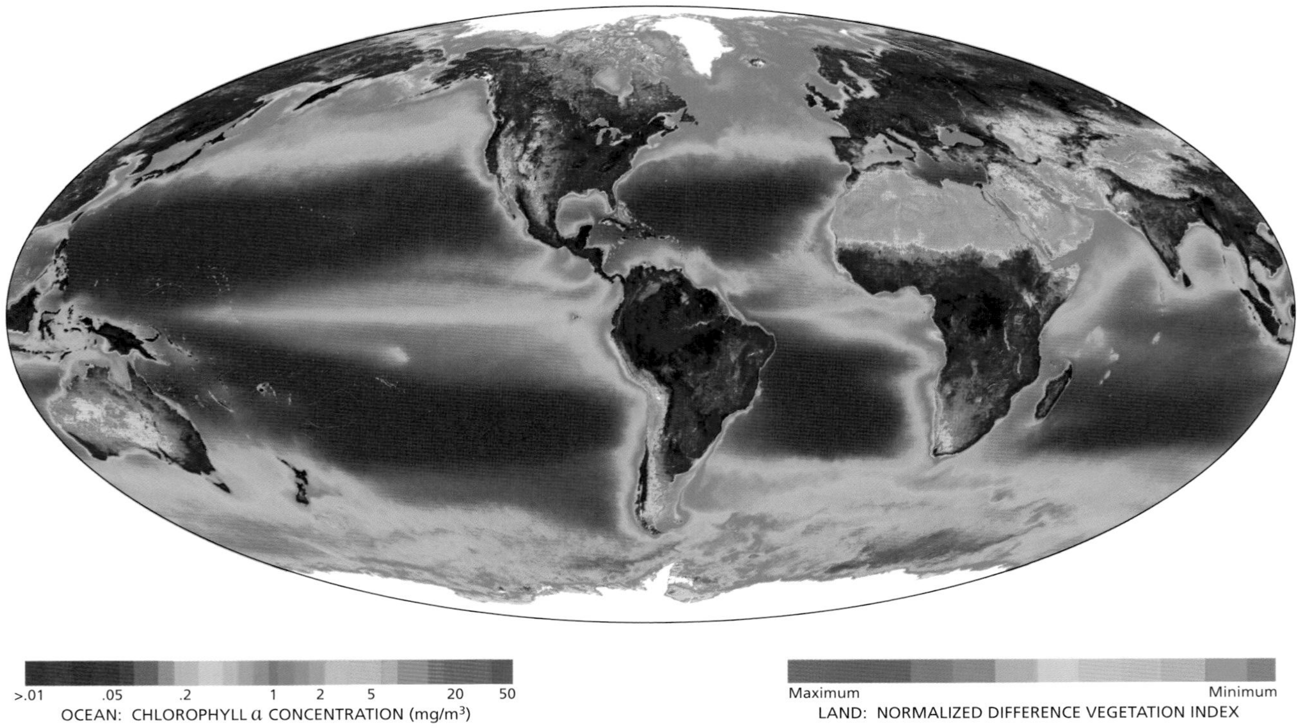

Satellite technology enables us to monitor life on Earth. For example, satellite sensors help us measure the amount of chlorophyll—the green pigment used by plants during photosynthesis—on land and in masses of water. Satellite measurements can also provide an estimate of the distribution and abundance of both terrestrial vegetation and aquatic phytoplankton. By color-coding data (see the color scales for the world map), we can actually quantify changes in vegetation on land and in the oceans from season to season and from year to year. The map reveals an unequal distribution of life for the June-to-August period. Most of the Northern Hemisphere has become green, except in areas of low rainfall or poor soil. Spectacular phytoplankton blooms are evident in the equatorial Pacific. Vegetation has lightened in the southern winter, as the rays of the sun provide less energy.

Biosphere Dynamics

A fundamental characteristic of the biosphere is the interconnectivity among all of its components. Known as holoceonosis, this interrelationship means that when one part of the biosphere changes, so will others. The biosphere is a dynamic system where interactions are occurring all the time between and within living and nonliving components.

The main fuel that keeps the biosphere dynamic is the sun's energy, which is captured by Earth's surface and later harvested by plants and other photosynthetic organisms. The energy flows from these organisms through a living web that includes herbivores (plant feeders), carnivores (flesh feeders), and decomposers (detritus feeders). Energy from the sun also drives the recycling of water and all chemical elements necessary for life. The flow of energy and the continuous recycling of matter are two key processes of the biosphere.

Humans are part of this web of life. We have evolved, we interact with other living organisms, and we may become extinct. We have also developed large-scale organizations (societies, for example) that constitute the "sociosphere." Human interactions within this sphere occur through a diverse array of technologies and cultural frameworks and include activities such as fishing, agriculture, forestry, mining, and urban development. All are resource-utilization processes that can affect the biosphere on a global scale.

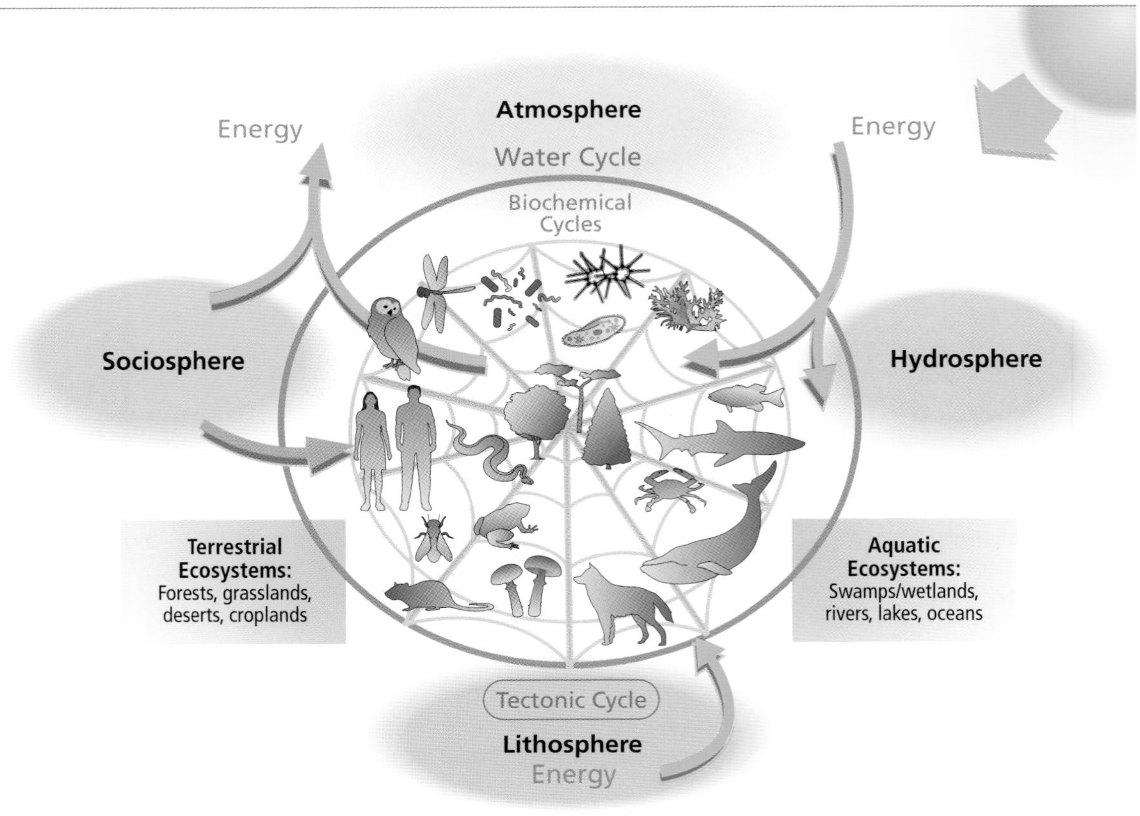

Earth System Dynamics

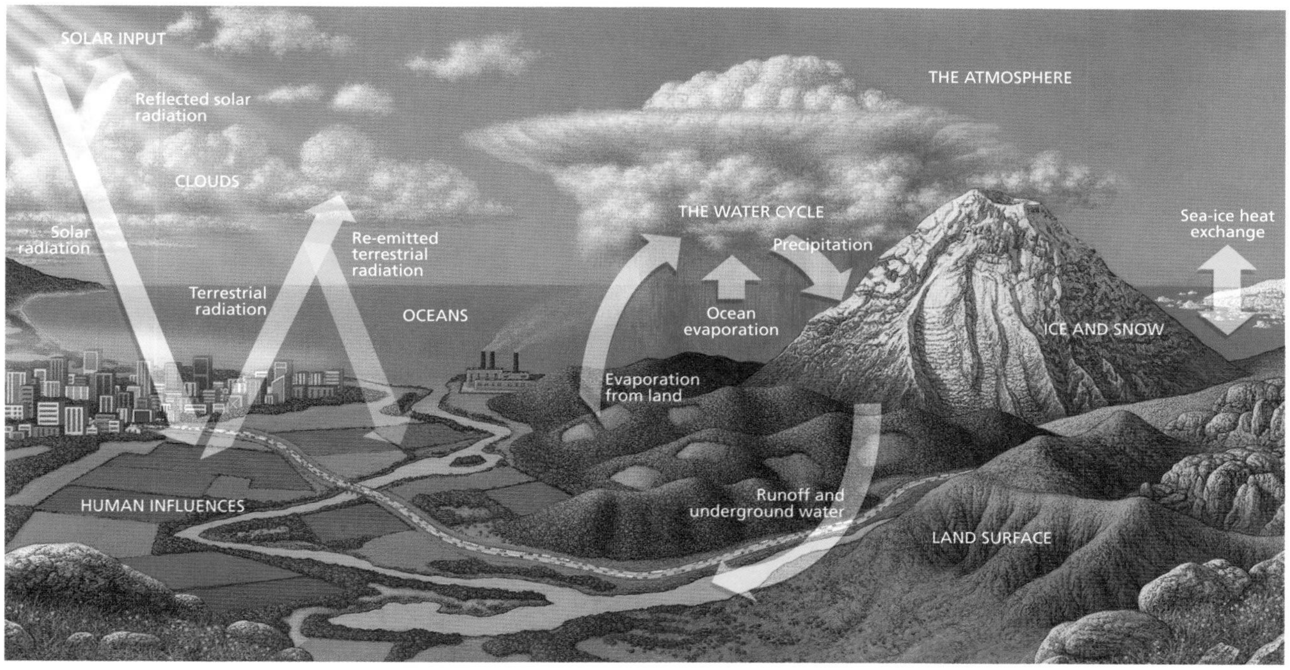

Earth is a dynamic system driven by energy flow from the sun and the planet's interior. Electromagnetic energy from the sun is converted to heat energy in the atmosphere (the greenhouse effect). Energy imbalances cause atmospheric and oceanic currents and drive the water cycle—a result of which is the wearing down of landscapes. Energy flow from Earth's interior drives the tectonic cycle, which builds landscapes. The cycles vary because they derive from independent forces that operate on different time scales and with changing intensities. Variations in these cycles keep the complex interactions among the biosphere, lithosphere, hydrosphere, and atmosphere from reaching a balance; the tendency of Earth processes to reach a balance causes natural global change. People can influence these interactions: By modifying the chemical composition of the atmosphere, for example, humans can cause changes in the greenhouse effect.

Size of the Biosphere

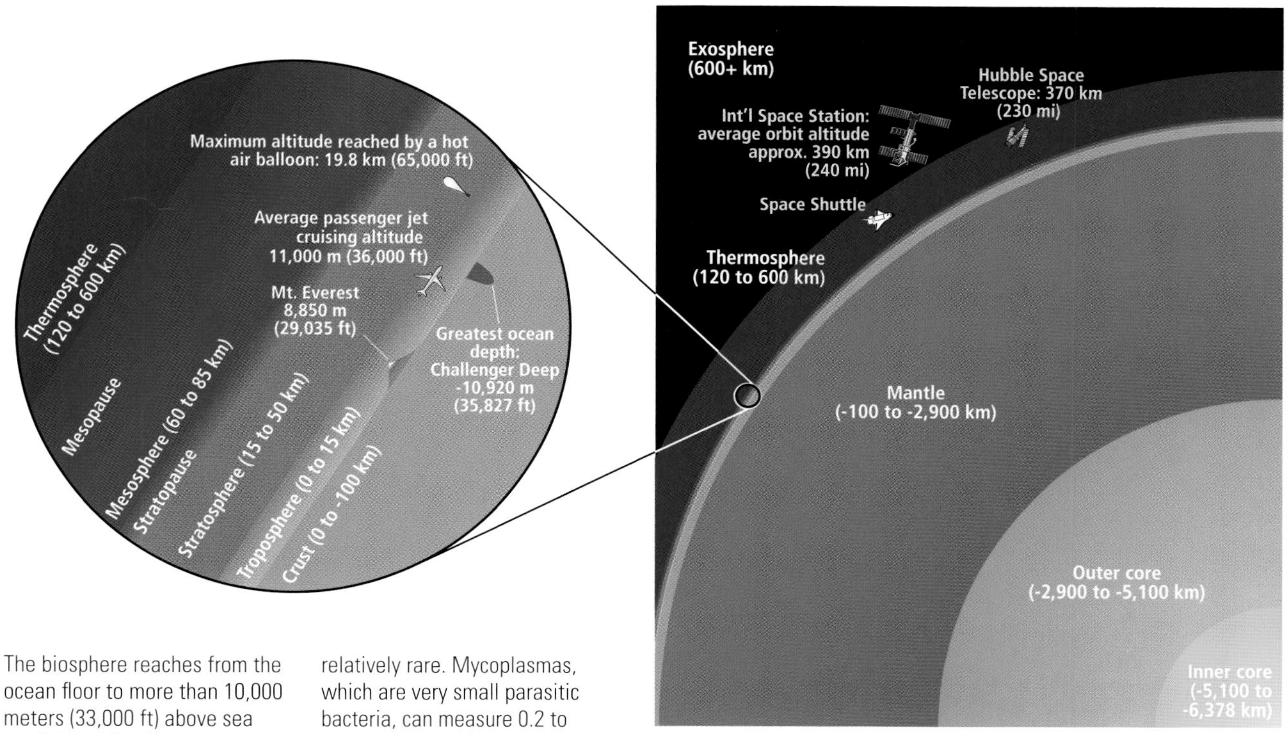

The biosphere reaches from the ocean floor to more than 10,000 meters (33,000 ft) above sea level. Most life, however, occurs in a zone extending from about 200 meters (650 ft) below the surface of the ocean to 6,000 meters (20,000 ft) above sea level. Humans can occupy much of the biosphere and exert influence on all of its regions.

Organisms that make up the biosphere vary greatly in size and number. Small life-forms generally reach very high numbers, while large ones may be relatively rare. Mycoplasmas, which are very small parasitic bacteria, can measure 0.2 to 0.3 micrometers (one micrometer is one-millionth of a meter, or three-millionths of a foot). Other organisms can be very large: Blue whales weigh about 110,000 kilograms (240,000 lbs) and reach a length of more than 25 meters (80 ft); they are the largest animals on Earth. Dinosaurs weighed as much as 80,000 kilograms (175,000 lbs) and measured up to 33 meters (108 ft) long.

The Biosphere over Time

Ever since life arose on Earth more than three billion years ago, the biosphere has gone through many changes (see time line at right). These have been driven, in part, by drifting continents, ice ages, shifting sea levels, and the consequences of activities in the biosphere itself.

Over millions of years, the addition of oxygen to the atmosphere allowed for the development of terrestrial ecosystems. But in fairly rapid fashion, humans have had a significant effect on the world's ecosystems; our ability to modify species through gene manipulation will further increase our impact.

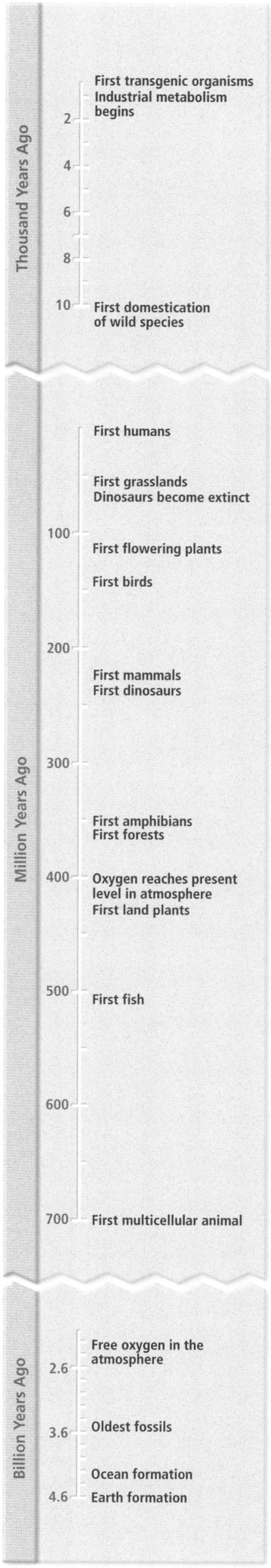

BIODIVERSITY REFERS TO THREE MEASURES of Earth's intricate web of life: the number of different species, the genetic diversity within a species, and the variety of ecosystems in which species live. Greatest in the wet tropics, biodiversity is important for many reasons, including helping to provide food and medicine, breathable air, drinkable water, livable climates, protection from pests and diseases, and ecosystem stability.

Humankind is only one species in a vast array of life-forms. It is, however, an especially influential and increasingly disruptive actor in the huge cast of characters on the stage of planet Earth. Estimates of the total number of plant and animal species range from ten million to a hundred million; of these, fewer than two million have been described. Yet a substantial number of those species may be gone before we even have a chance to understand their value.

For most of human history, people have often looked at plants and animals simply as resources for meeting their own basic needs. Scientists today count more than a quarter million plant species, of which just nine provide three-quarters of all our food; in that respect, biodiversity has been an unimaginable luxury. It is ironic that as humankind's power to destroy other species grows, so does our ingenuity in finding new and beneficial uses for them.

Sometimes the benefits of preserving a species may have nothing to do with food or medicine. Before a worldwide ban on exports of elephant ivory, the estimated value of such exports was 40 million dollars a year for all of Africa. Now, in Kenya alone, the viewing value of elephants by tourists is thought to be 25 million dollars a year.

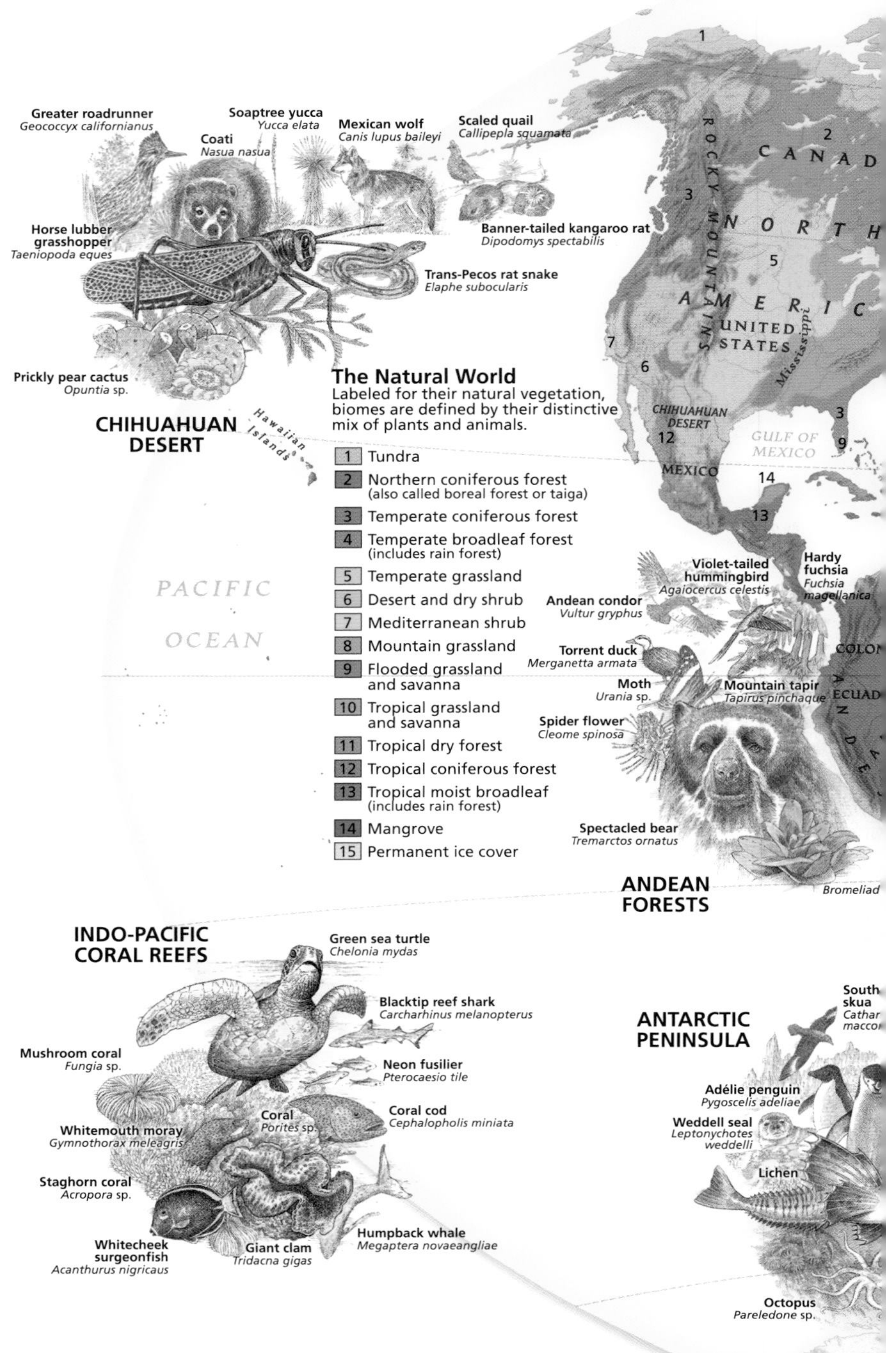

Species Diversity

Among fauna and flora, insects make up the largest classification in terms of sheer number of species, with fungi ranked a distant second. At the other extreme, the categories with the smallest numbers—mammals, birds, and mollusks—also happen to be the classes with the greatest percentage of threatened species (see middle graph, below). This is not just a matter of proportion: These groups include the most at-risk species in terms of absolute numbers as well.

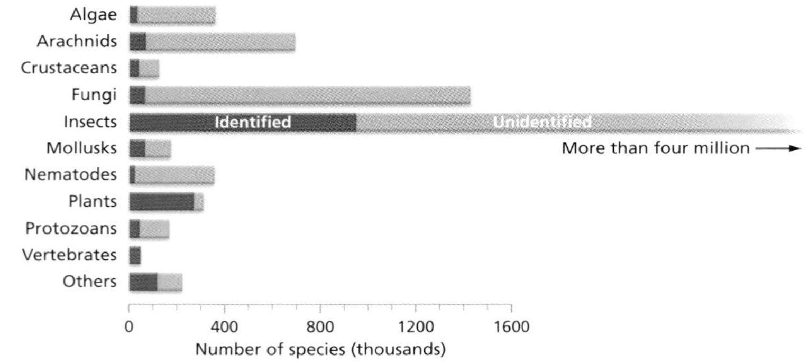

Threatened Ecoregions

British ecologist Norman Myers defined the "biodiversity hotspot" concept in 1988 to help address the dilemma of identifying conservation priorities. The biodiversity hotspots hold especially high numbers of endemic species, yet their combined area of remaining habitat covers only 2.3 percent of the Earth's land surface. Each hotspot faces extreme threats and has already lost at least 70 percent of its original natural vegetation. Of particular concern to scientists is that 75 percent of all threatened terrestrial vertebrates occur only in the hotspots.

Threatened Species

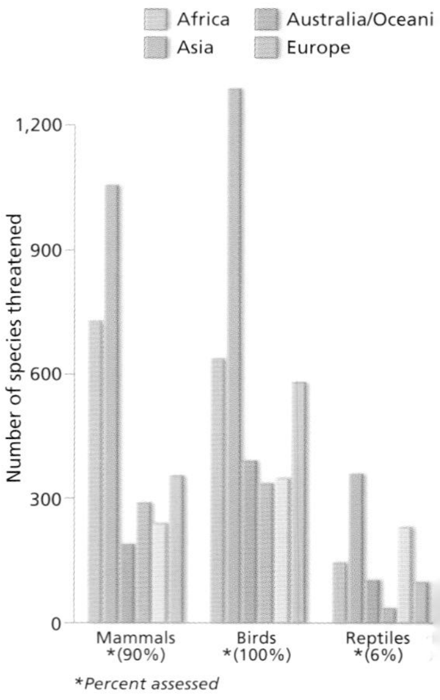

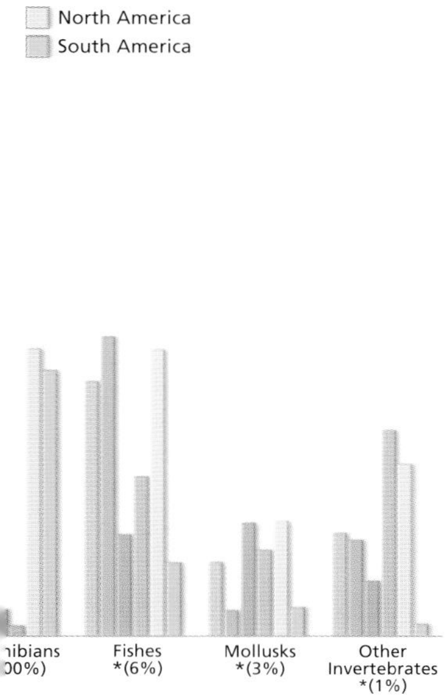

Projected Biodiversity Status

Biodiversity is decreasing at a rapidly increasing rate. According to scientists, current extinction rates are a hundred to a thousand times greater than the normal rate of extinction; furthermore, the number of species threatened with extinction continues to increase (with, for example, one in three amphibians and one in four mammals at risk in the wild). Species are not being killed off directly: The two leading causes of extinction are loss of habitats and the impact of invasive species, although other threats include overexploitation, pollution, disease, and climate change.

WHILE POPULATIONS IN MANY PARTS of the world are expanding, those of Europe—along with some other rich industrial areas such as Japan—show little to no growth, or may actually be shrinking. Many such countries must bring in immigrant workers to keep their economies thriving. A clear correlation exists between wealth and low fertility: the higher the incomes and educational levels, the lower the rates of reproduction.

Many governments keep vital statistics, recording births and deaths, and count their populations regularly to try to plan ahead. The United States has taken a census every ten years since 1790, recording the ages, the occupations, and other important facts about its people. The United Nations helps less developed countries carry out censuses and improve their demographic information.

Governments of some poor countries may find that half their populations are under the age of 20. They are faced with the overwhelming tasks of providing adequate education and jobs while encouraging better family-planning programs. Governments of nations with low birthrates find themselves with growing numbers of elderly people but fewer workers able to provide tax money for health care and pensions.

In a mere 150 years, world population has grown fivefold, at an ever increasing pace. The industrial revolution helped bring about improvements in food supplies and advances in both medicine and public health, which allowed people to live longer and to have more healthy babies. Today, 15,000 people are born into the world every hour, and nearly all of them are in poor African, Asian, and South American nations. This situation concerns planners, who look to demographers (professionals who study all aspects of population) for important data.

Lights of the World

Satellite imagery offers a surprising view of the world at night. Bright lights in Europe, Asia, and the United States give a clear picture of densely populated areas with ample electricity. Reading this map requires great care, however. Some totally dark areas, like most of Australia, do in fact have very small populations, but other light-free areas—in China and Africa, for example—may simply hide dense populations with not enough electricity to be seen by a satellite. Wealthy areas with fewer people, such as Florida, may be using their energy wastefully. Ever since the 1970s, demographers have supplemented census data with information from satellite imagery.

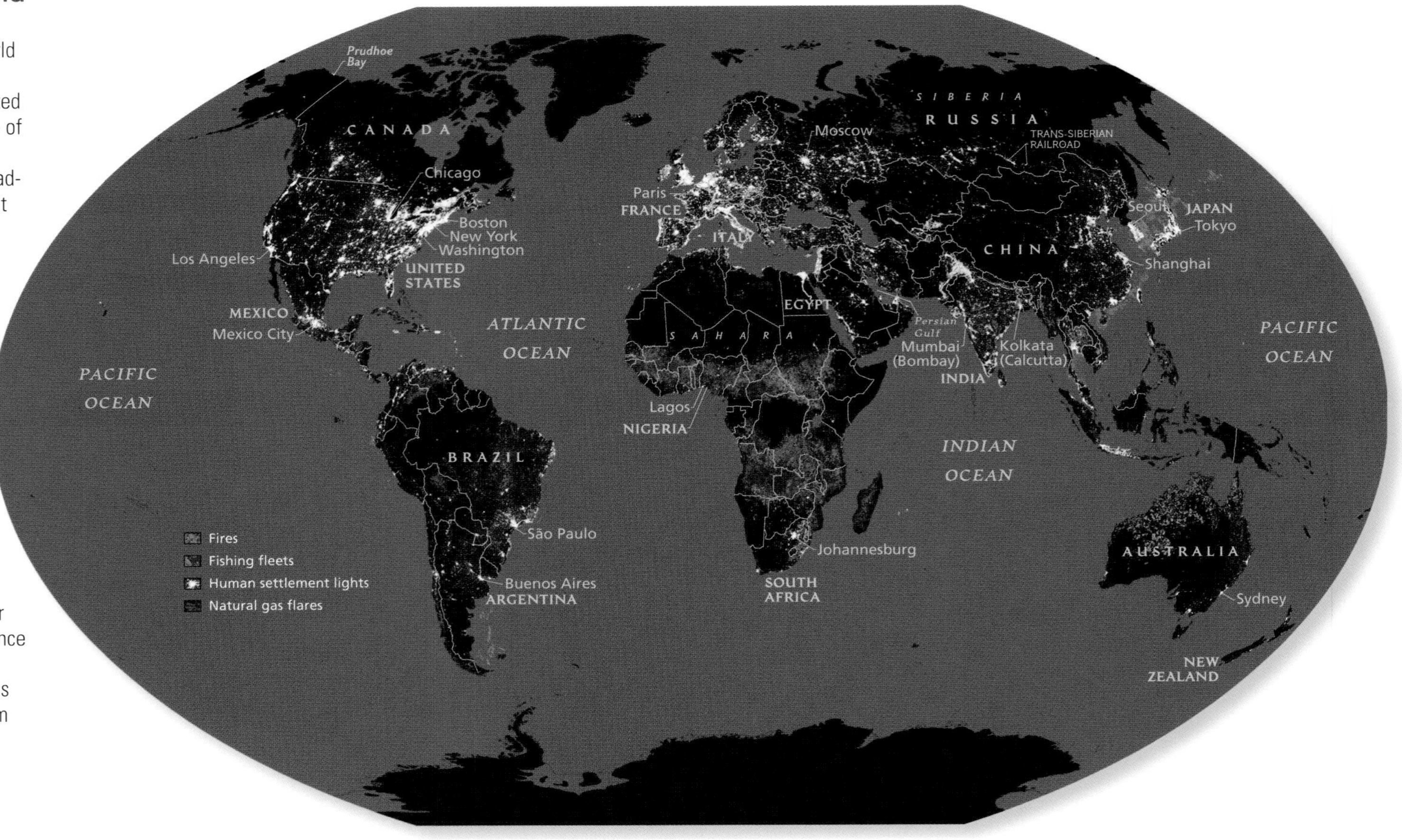

Population Pyramids

A population pyramid shows the number of males and females in every age group of a population. A pyramid for Nigeria reveals that over half—about 55 percent—of the population is under 20, while only 19 percent of Italy's population is younger than 20.

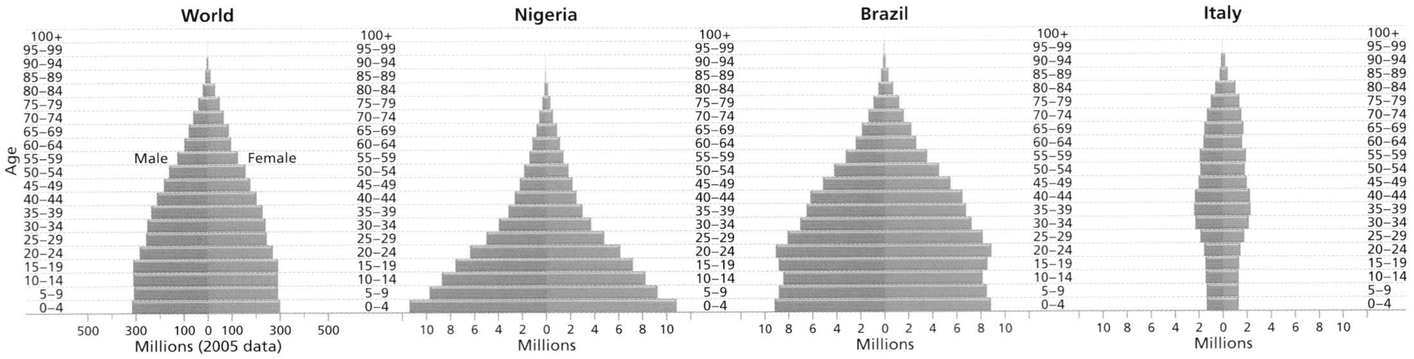

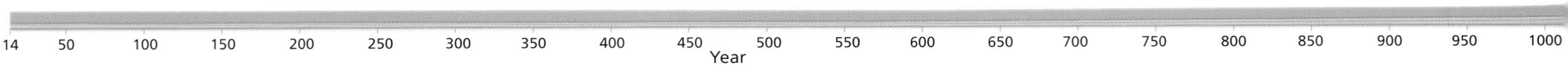

Population Growth

The population of the world is not distributed evenly. In this cartogram Canada is almost invisible, while India looks enormous because its population is 34 times greater than Canada's. In reality, Canada is 3 times larger than India, in size. The shape of almost every country looks distorted when populations are compared in this way.

Population sizes are constantly changing, however. In countries that are experiencing many more births than deaths, population totals are ballooning. In others, too few babies are born to replace the number of people who die, and populations are shrinking. A cartogram devoted solely to growth rates around the world would look quite different from this one.

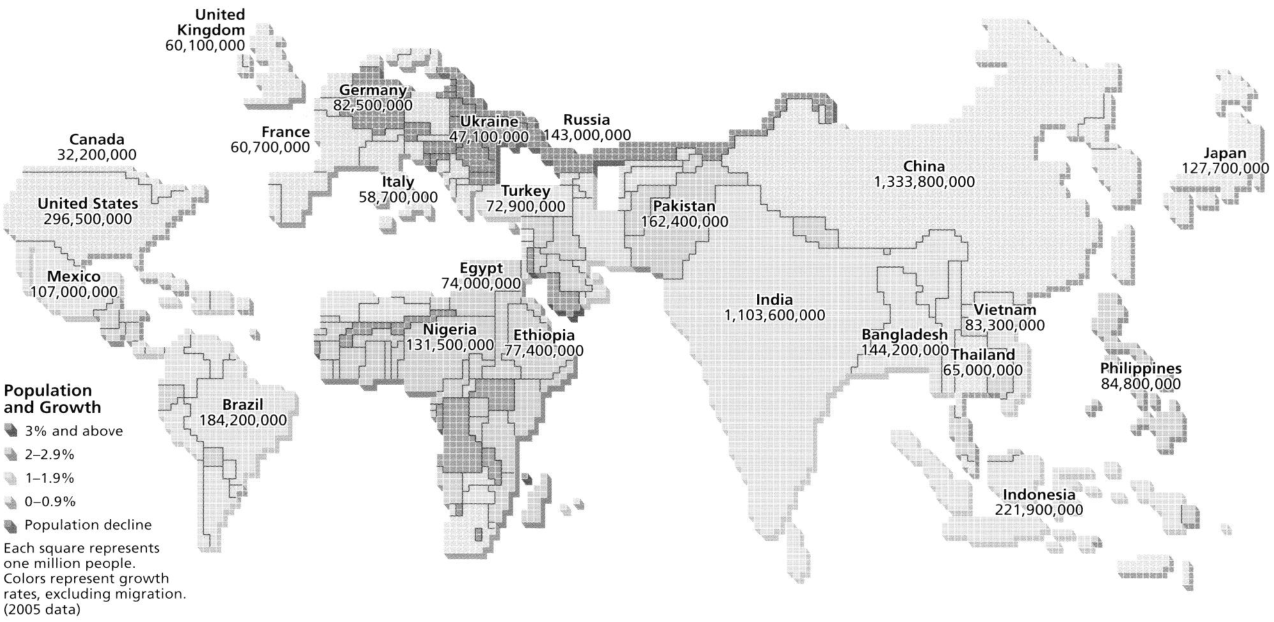

Population Density

A country's population density is estimated by figuring out how many people would occupy one square mile if they were all spread out evenly. In reality, people live together most closely in cities, on seacoasts, and in river valleys. Singapore, a tiny country largely composed of a single city, has a high population density—more than 17,000 people per square mile. Greenland, by comparison, has less than one person per square mile because it is mostly covered by ice. Its people mainly fish for a living and dwell in small groups near the shore.

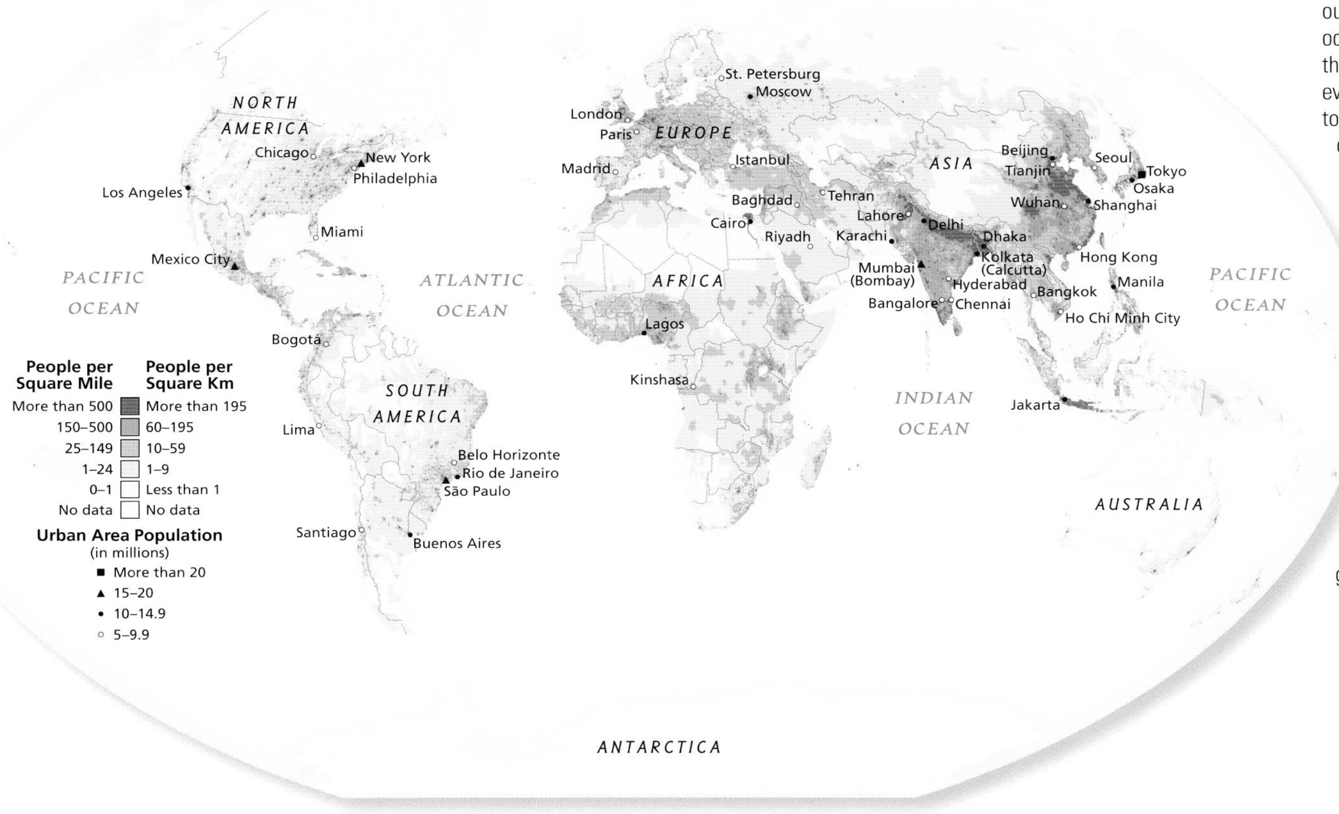

Regional Population Growth Disparities

Two centuries ago, the population of the world began a phenomenal expansion. Even so, North America and Australia still have a long way to go before their population numbers equal those of Asia and Africa. China and India now have more than a billion people each, making Asia the most populous continent. Africa, which has the second greatest growth, does not yet approach Asia in numbers. According to some experts, the world's population, now totaling more than six and a half billion, will not start to level off until about the year 2200, when it could reach eleven billion. Nearly all the new growth will take place in Asia, Africa, and Latin America; however, Africa's share will be almost double that of its present level and China's share will decline.

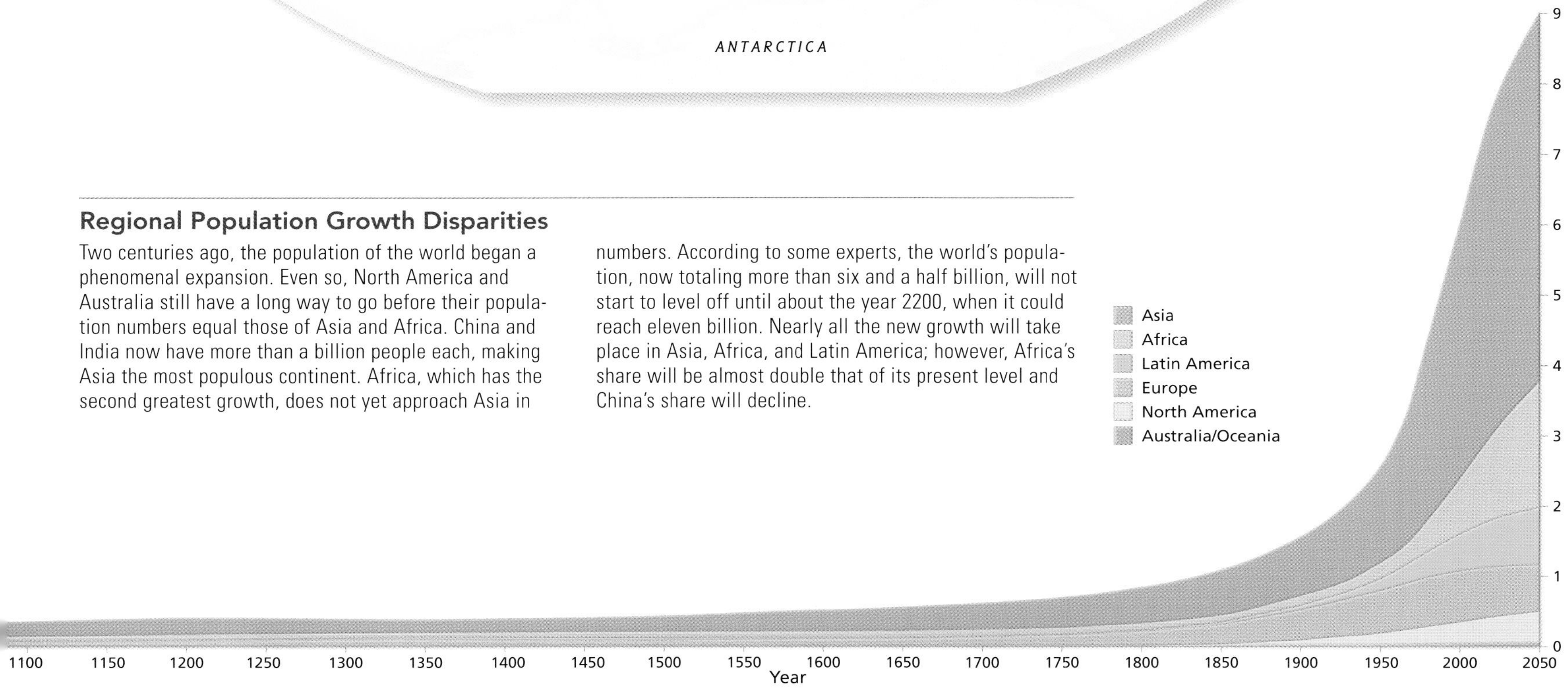

Fertility

Fertility, or birthrate, measures the average number of children born to women in a given population. It can also be expressed as the number of live births per thousand people in a population per year. In low-income countries with limited educational opportunities for girls and women, birthrates reach their highest levels.

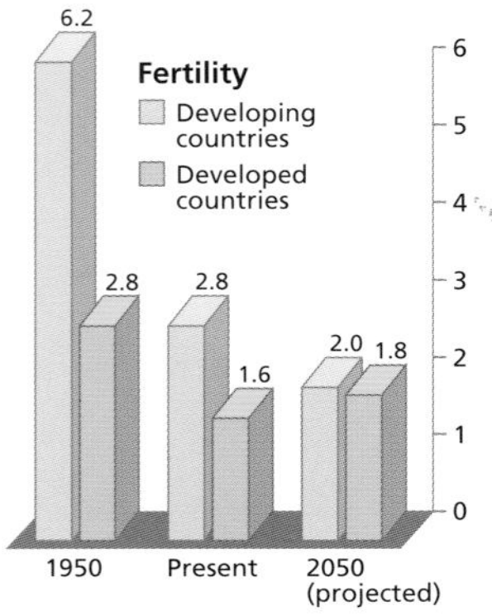

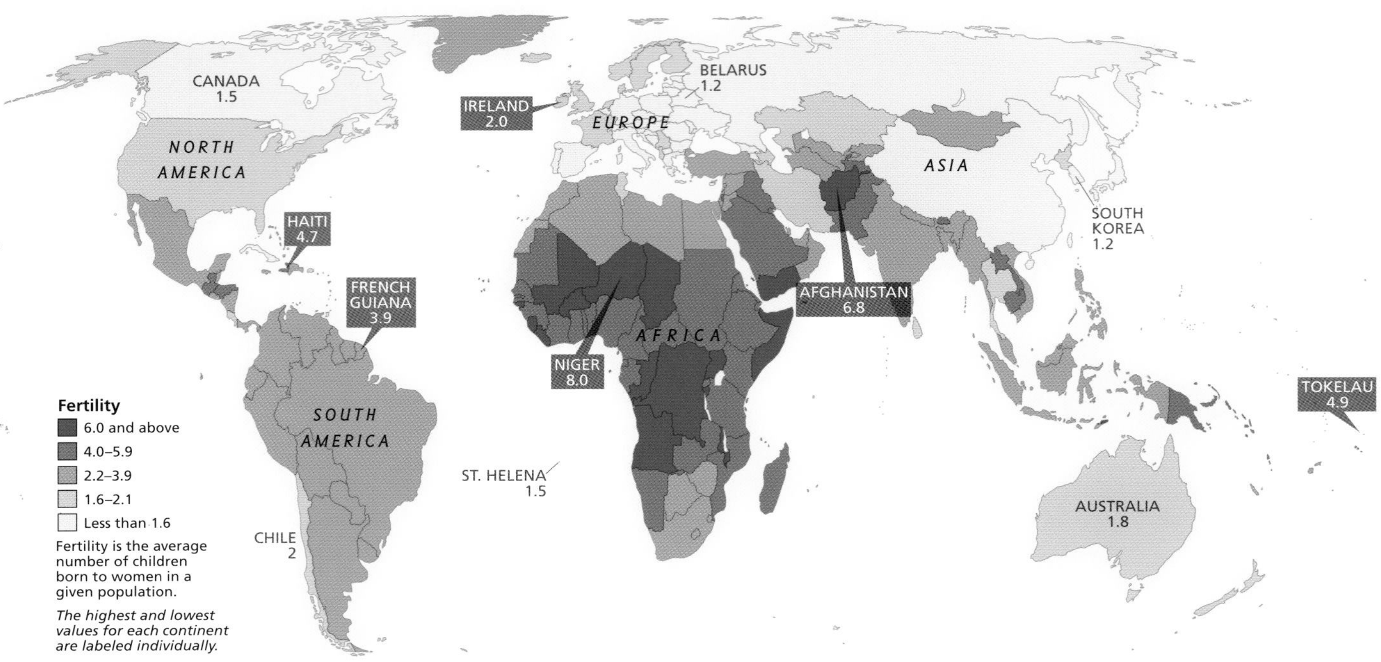

Urban Population Densities

People around the world are leaving farms and moving to cities, where jobs and opportunities are better. In 2000 almost half the world's people lived in towns or cities. The shift of population from the countryside to urban centers will probably continue in less developed countries for many years to come.

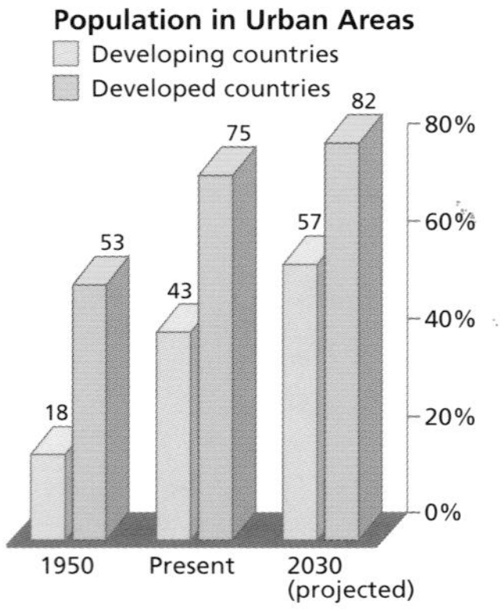

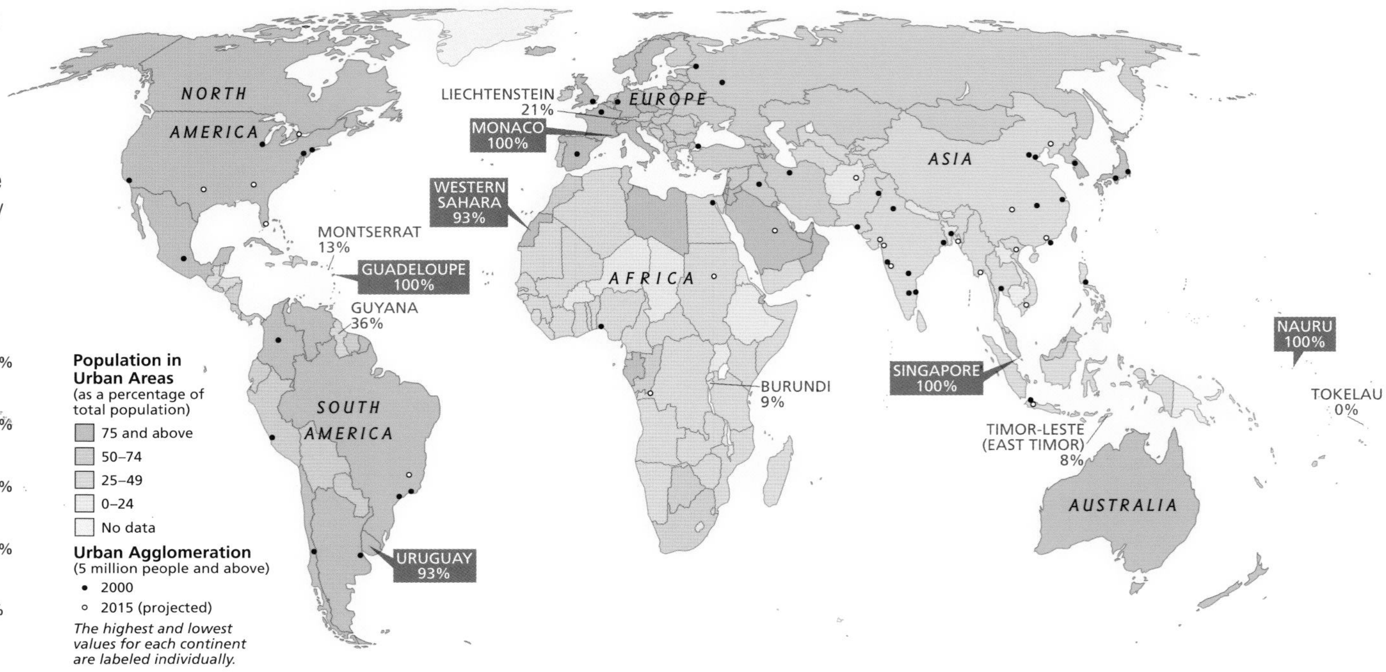

Urban Population Growth

Urban populations are growing more than twice as fast as populations as a whole. Soon, the world's city dwellers will outnumber its rural inhabitants as towns become cities and cities merge into megacities with more than ten million people. Globalization speeds the process. Although cities generate wealth and provide better health care along with electricity, clean water, sewage treatment, and other benefits, they can also cause great ecological damage. Squatter settlements and slums may develop if cities cannot keep up with millions of new arrivals. Smog, congestion, pollution, and crime are other dangers. Good city management is a key to future prosperity.

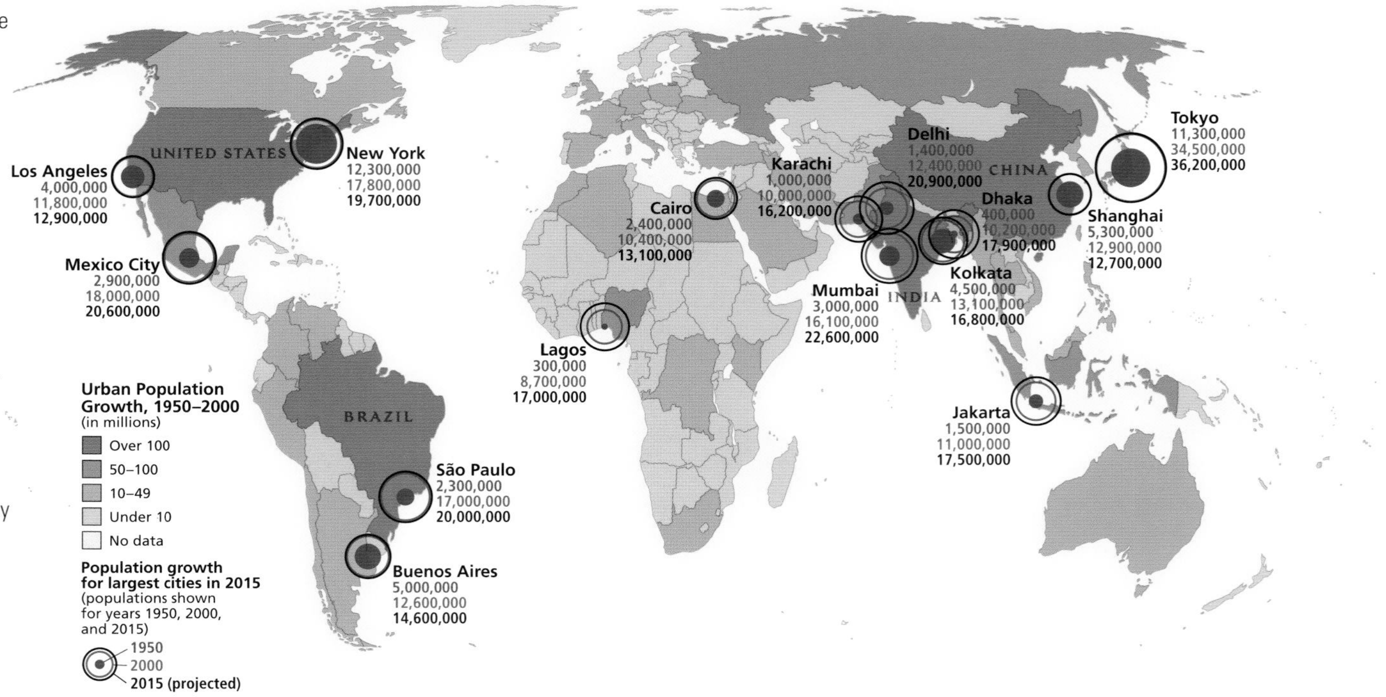

Life Expectancy

Life expectancy for population groups does not mean that all people die by a certain age. It is an average of death statistics. High infant mortality results in low life expectancy: People who live to adulthood will probably reach old age; there are just fewer of them.

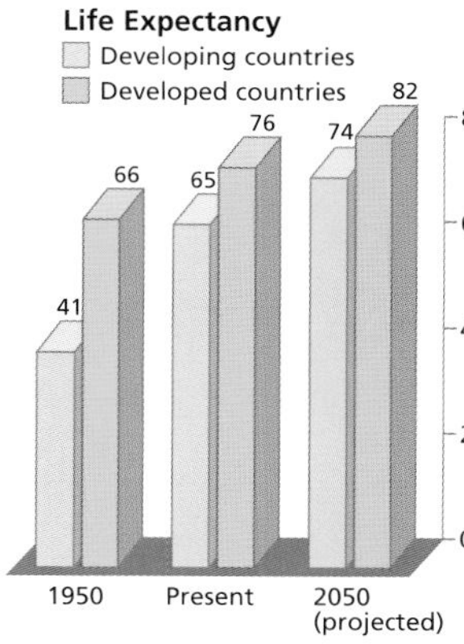

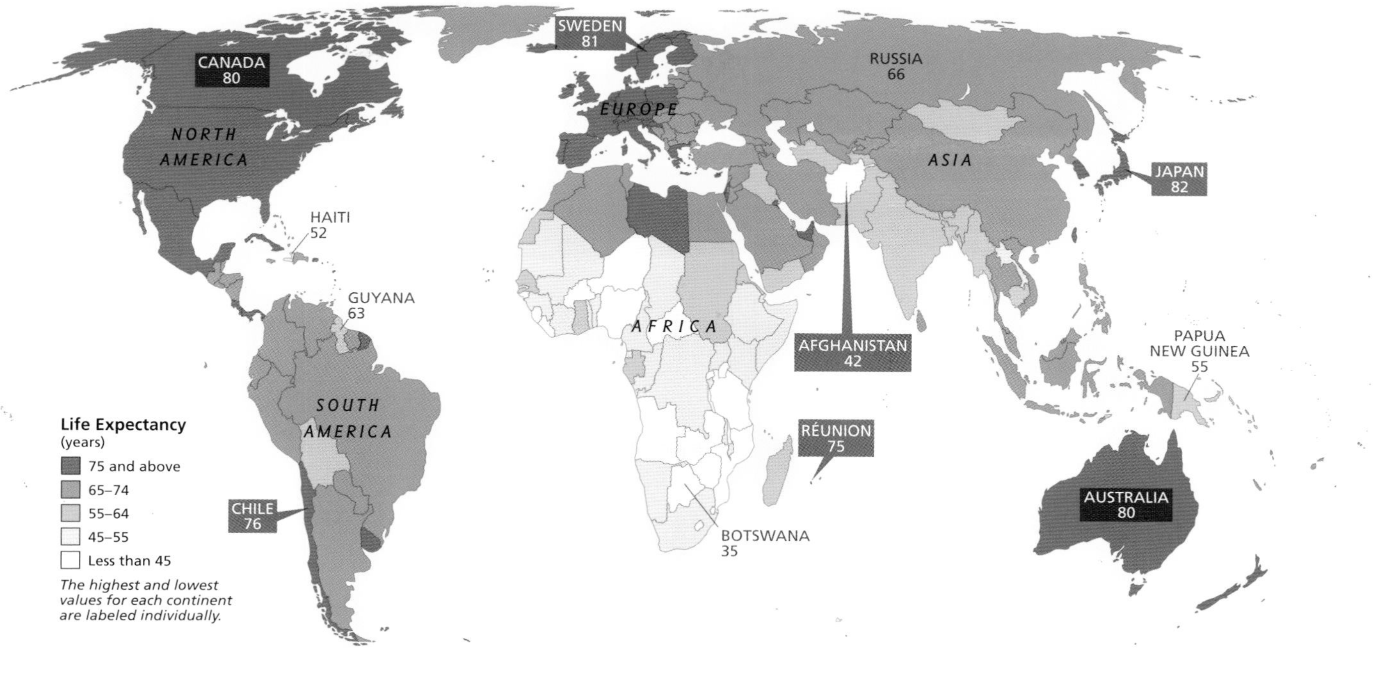

Migration

International migration has reached its highest level, with foreign workers now providing the labor in several Middle Eastern nations and immigrant workers proving essential to rich countries with low birthrates. Refugees continue to escape grim political and environmental conditions, while businesspeople and tourists keep many economies spinning.

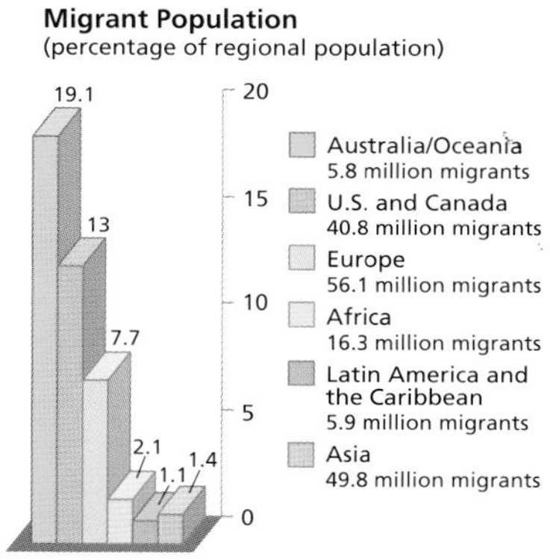

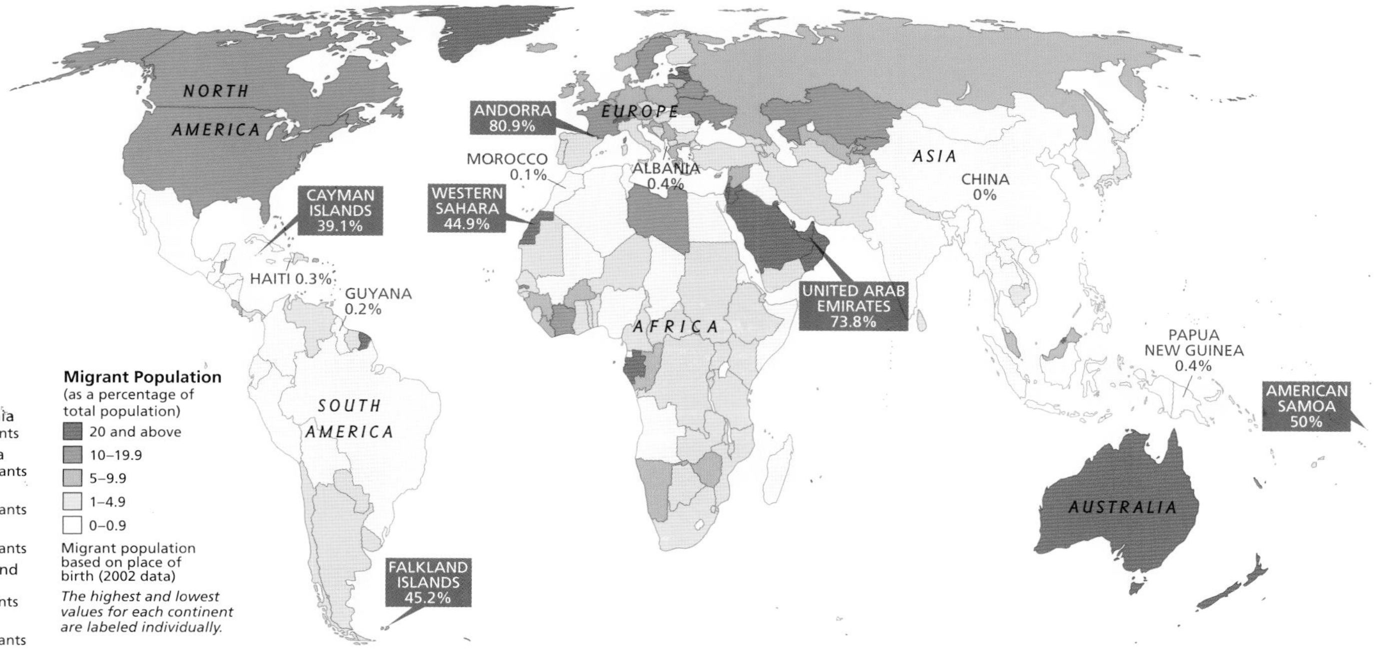

Most Populous Places

(MID-2005 DATA)

1. China 1,333,827,000
2. India 1,103,596,000
3. United States 296,483,000
4. Indonesia 221,932,000
5. Brazil 184,184,000
6. Pakistan 162,420,000
7. Bangladesh 144,233,000
8. Russia 143,025,000
9. Nigeria 131,530,000
10. Japan 127,728,000
11. Mexico 107,029,000
12. Philippines 84,765,000
13. Vietnam 83,305,000
14. Germany 82,490,000
15. Ethiopia 77,431,000
16. Egypt 74,033,000
17. Turkey 72,907,000
18. Iran 69,515,000
19. Thailand 65,002,000
20. Dem. Rep. of Congo 60,764,000

Most Crowded Places

POPULATION DENSITY (POP/SQ. MI.)

1. Monaco 41,250
2. Singapore 17,946
3. Gibraltar (U.K.) 7,511
4. Malta 3,278
5. Bermuda (U.K.) 3,212
6. Bahrain 2,744
7. Bangladesh 2,594
8. Maldives 2,538
9. Channel Islands 1,987
10. Taiwan 1,627
11. Mauritius 1,578
12. Palestinian Areas 1,556
13. Barbados 1,554
14. Nauru 1,529
15. Aruba 1,322
16. San Marino 1,295
17. South Korea 1,260
18. Mayotte (Fr.) 1,249
19. Puerto Rico (U.S.) 1,132
20. Netherlands 1,033

Demographic Extremes

LIFE EXPECTANCY

LOWEST (FEMALE, IN YEARS):

35 Botswana, Lesotho
37 Swaziland, Zambia
41 Zimbabwe
42 Afghanistan, Angola, Sierra Leone

LOWEST (MALE, IN YEARS):

34 Botswana, Swaziland
36 Lesotho
38 Zambia
39 Angola, Sierra Leone

HIGHEST (FEMALE, IN YEARS):

85 Japan
84 France, San Marino, Spain
83 Australia, Iceland, Italy, Sweden, Switzerland

HIGHEST (MALE, IN YEARS):

79 Iceland, Liechtenstein
78 Anguilla , Australia, Israel, Japan, Norway, San Marino, Sweden, Switzerland
77 Canada, Cayman Islands (U.K.), Faroe Islands (Den.), France, Italy, Kuwait, Singapore, Spain

POPULATION AGE STRUCTURE

HIGHEST % POPULATION UNDER AGE 15

51% Uganda
48% Chad, Dem. Rep. of Congo , Niger
47% Burundi, Mali
46% Angola, Burkina Faso, Congo, Guinea-Bissau, Liberia, Malawi, Palestinian Areas, Yemen

HIGHEST % POPULATION OVER AGE 65

22% Monaco
20% Japan
19% Italy
18% Germany, Greece

A PERSON'S NATIONALITY AND LANGUAGE are often assumed to be the same: A German speaks German, for example. The ability to use a specific language has often been viewed as a defining characteristic of a citizen. But there are only about 200 countries, while there are some 5,000 living languages. In a quarter of all nations, no single language is spoken by a majority of the inhabitants. Canada is legally bilingual; India has 22 official languages; and French, Spanish, English, Portuguese, and German are each the official language of at least two nations.

Most languages are spoken by only a few hundred or a few thousand people. Over 200 languages are spoken by more than a million people; 23 languages have 50 million or more speakers.

How we define language makes it difficult to determine the exact number of languages. A dialect, for instance, is a variety of language used by a specific group of persons, with its own rules of grammar or pronunciation. Other linguistic systems that fail to attain the full status of languages are pidgins (contact languages used by groups with different native languages to communicate) and creoles (what pidgins are called when they are adopted as native languages).

Voices of the World

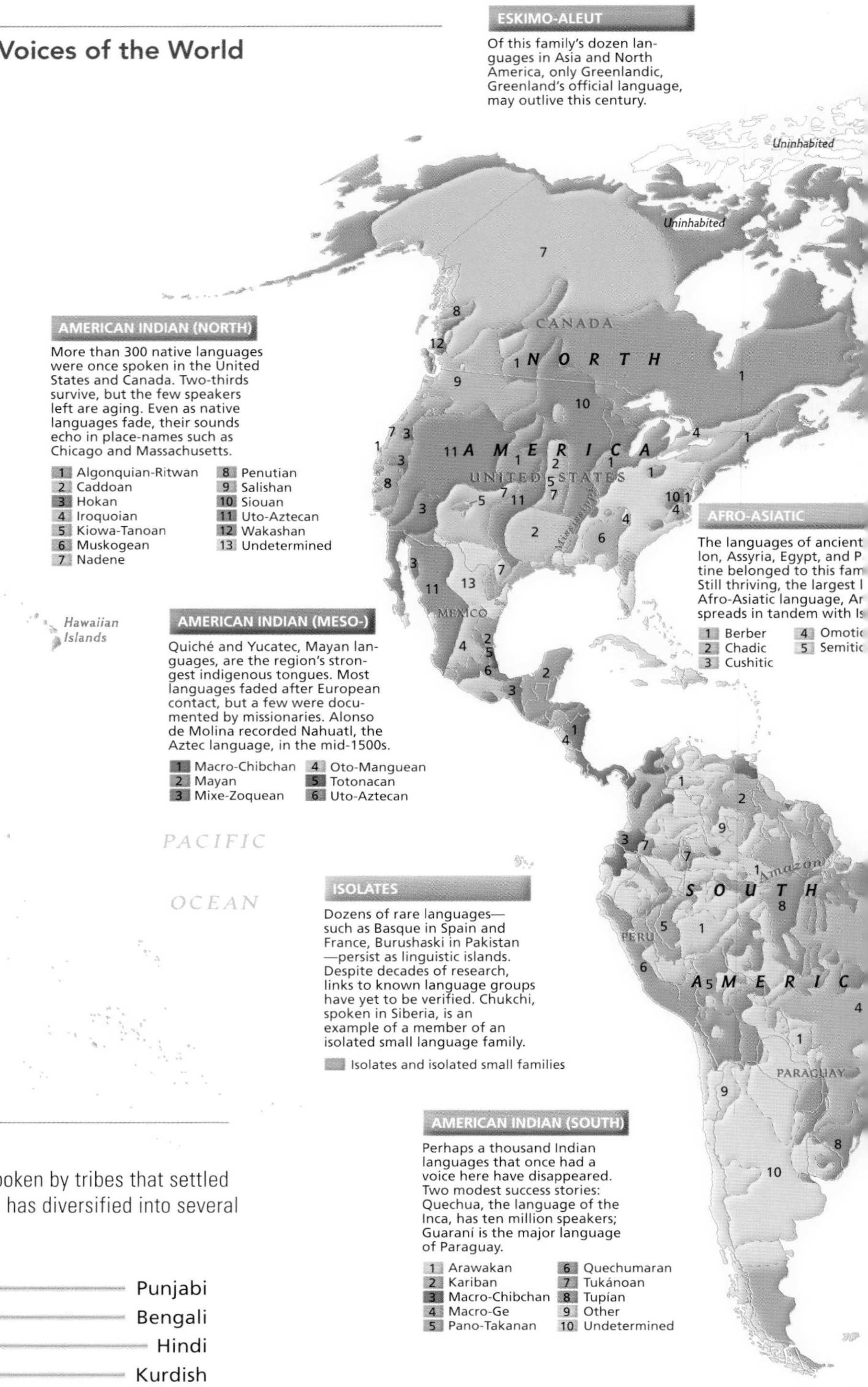
ESKIMO-ALEUT
Of this family's dozen languages in Asia and North America, only Greenlandic, Greenland's official language, may outlive this century.
Uninhabited
Uninhabited
CANADA
NORTH AMERICA
UNITED STATES
MEXICO
AMERICAN INDIAN (NORTH)
More than 300 native languages were once spoken in the United States and Canada. Two-thirds survive, but the few speakers left are aging. Even as native languages fade, their sounds echo in place-names such as Chicago and Massachusetts.
1 Algonquian-Ritwan
2 Caddoan
3 Hokan
4 Iroquoian
5 Kiowa-Tanoan
6 Muskogean
7 Nadene
8 Penutian
9 Salishan
10 Siouan
11 Uto-Aztecan
12 Wakashan
13 Undetermined
Hawaiian Islands
AMERICAN INDIAN (MESO-)
Quiché and Yucatec, Mayan languages, are the region's strongest indigenous tongues. Most languages faded after European contact, but a few were documented by missionaries. Alonso de Molina recorded Nahuatl, the Aztec language, in the mid-1500s.
1 Macro-Chibchan
2 Mayan
3 Mixe-Zoquean
4 Oto-Manguean
5 Totonacan
6 Uto-Aztecan
AFRO-ASIATIC
The languages of ancient
lon, Assyria, Egypt, and P
tine belonged to this fam
Still thriving, the largest l
Afro-Asiatic language, Ar
spreads in tandem with Is
1 Berber
2 Chadic
3 Cushitic
4 Omotic
5 Semitic
PACIFIC
OCEAN
ISOLATES
Dozens of rare languages—such as Basque in Spain and France, Burushaski in Pakistan—persist as linguistic islands. Despite decades of research, links to known language groups have yet to be verified. Chukchi, spoken in Siberia, is an example of a member of an isolated small language family.
Isolates and isolated small families
SOUTH AMERICA
PERU
PARAGUAY
Amazon
AMERICAN INDIAN (SOUTH)
Perhaps a thousand Indian languages that once had a voice here have disappeared. Two modest success stories: Quechua, the language of the Inca, has ten million speakers; Guarani is the major language of Paraguay.
1 Arawakan
2 Kariban
3 Macro-Chibchan
4 Macro-Ge
5 Pano-Takanan
6 Quechumaran
7 Tukánoan
8 Tupian
9 Other
10 Undetermined

Vanishing Languages

Some 10,000 languages—or more—are thought to have once existed (see graph at right). This is an estimate; unlike extinct animals, dead languages rarely left traces, as most lacked a written form. About 5,000 still exist, but linguists fear that the rate of loss is quickening.

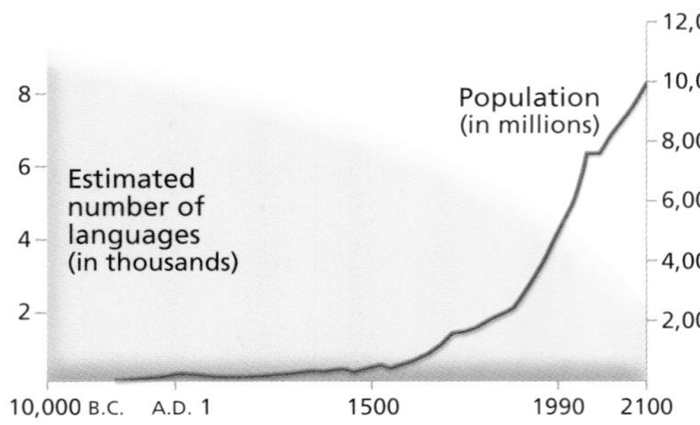
8
6
4
2
Estimated number of languages (in thousands)
Population (in millions)
12,000
10,000
8,000
6,000
4,000
2,000
10,000 B.C.
A.D. 1
1500
1990
2100

Evolution of Languages

Even as many languages have disappeared, a few dominant linguistic groups have spawned numerous related tongues. Thus, the Germanic language, which derived from Proto-Indo-European and was spoken by tribes that settled in northern and western Europe, has diversified into several major languages today.

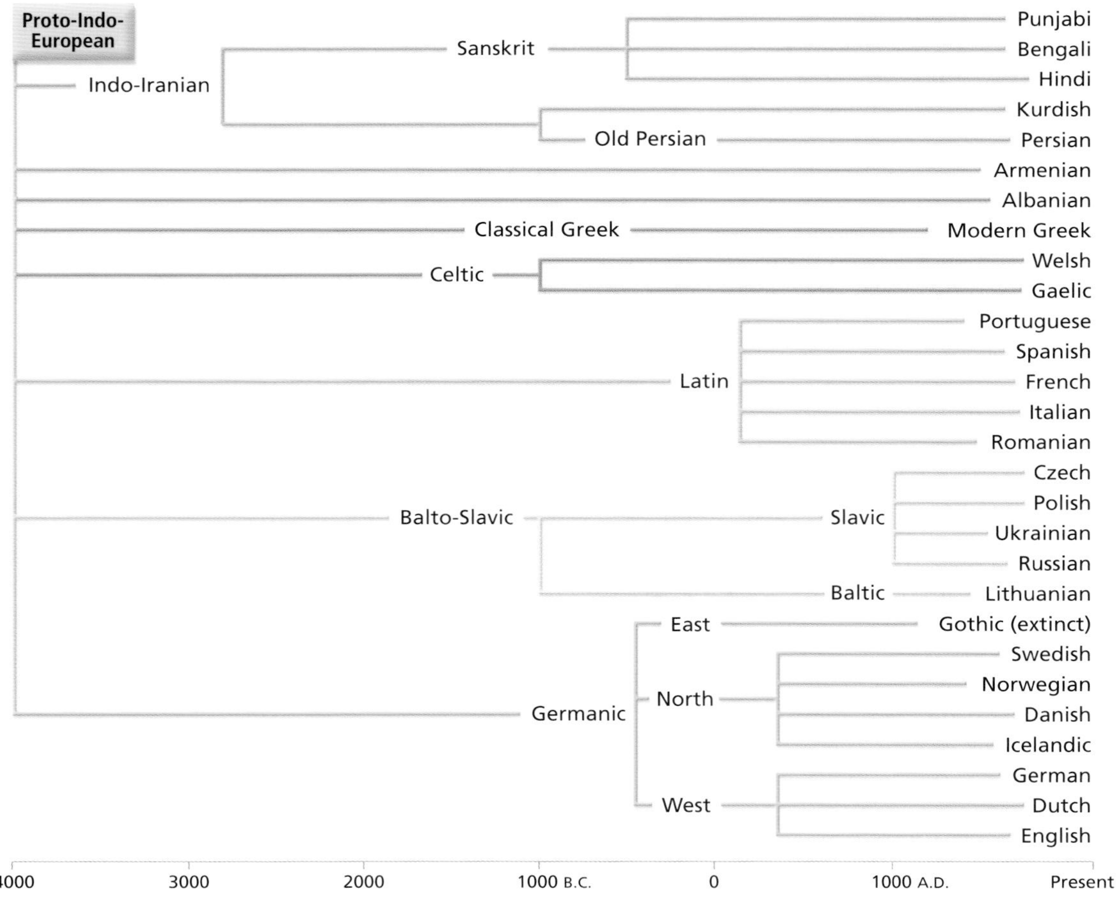
Proto-Indo-European
Indo-Iranian
Sanskrit
Punjabi
Bengali
Hindi
Kurdish
Old Persian
Persian
Armenian
Albanian
Classical Greek
Modern Greek
Celtic
Welsh
Gaelic
Latin
Portuguese
Spanish
French
Italian
Romanian
Balto-Slavic
Slavic
Czech
Polish
Ukrainian
Russian
Baltic
Lithuanian
Germanic
East
Gothic (extinct)
North
Swedish
Norwegian
Danish
Icelandic
West
German
Dutch
English
4000
3000
2000
1000 B.C.
0
1000 A.D.
Present

How Many Speak What?

Languages can paint vivid historical pictures of migration and colonization. English, Spanish, and Portuguese, for example, originated in parts of Europe with only a tenth of China's population and area; yet they rival Mandarin Chinese in total number of speakers. They spread because England, Spain, and Portugal built large overseas empires. India, which has been a part of several empires, currently has 22 official languages (in addition to English) and a population of one billion; only a fifth of its people speak Hindi.

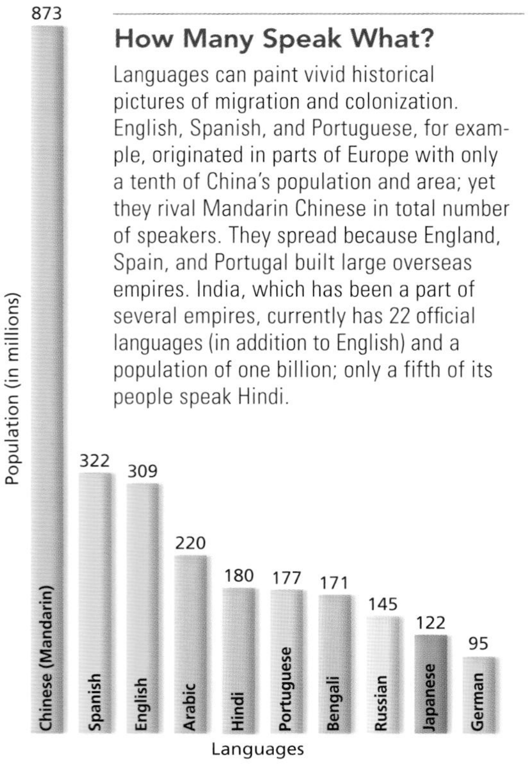
Population (in millions)
873
Chinese (Mandarin)
322
Spanish
309
English
220
Arabic
180
Hindi
177
Portuguese
171
Bengali
145
Russian
122
Japanese
95
German
Languages

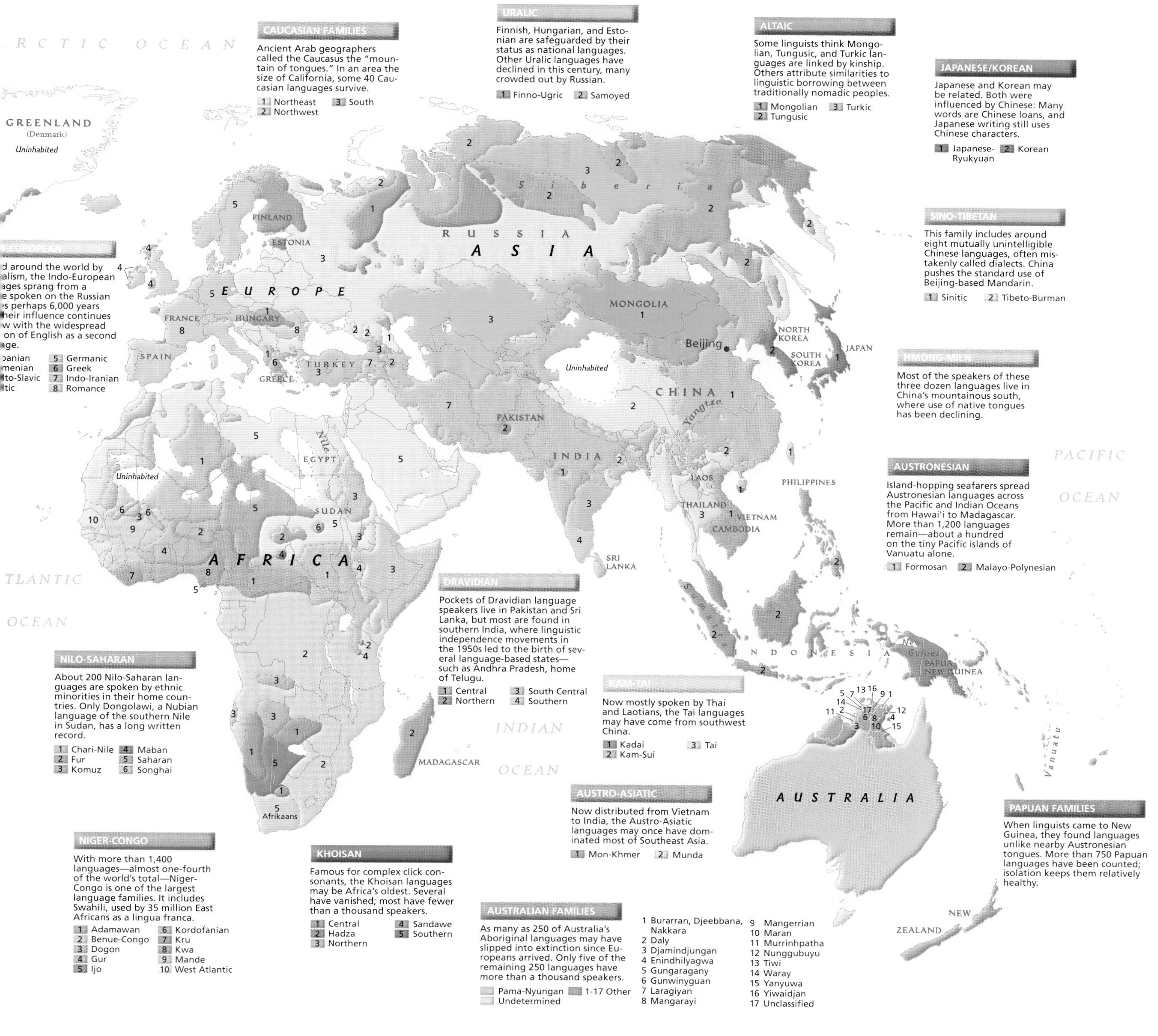
CAUCASIAN FAMILIES
Ancient Arab geographers called the Caucasus the "mountain of tongues." In an area the size of California, some 40 Caucasian languages survive.
1 Northeast 3 South
2 Northwest
URALIC
Finnish, Hungarian, and Estonian are safeguarded by their status as national languages. Other Uralic languages have declined in this century, many crowded out by Russian.
1 Finno-Ugric 2 Samoyed
ALTAIC
Some linguists think Mongolian, Tungusic, and Turkic languages are linked by kinship. Others attribute similarities to linguistic borrowing between traditionally nomadic peoples.
1 Mongolian 3 Turkic
2 Tungusic
JAPANESE/KOREAN
Japanese and Korean may be related. Both were influenced by Chinese: Many words are Chinese loans, and Japanese writing still uses Chinese characters.
1 Japanese-Ryukyuan 2 Korean
SINO-TIBETAN
This family includes around eight mutually unintelligible Chinese languages, often mistakenly called dialects. China pushes the standard use of Beijing-based Mandarin.
1 Sinitic 2 Tibeto-Burman
HMONG-MIEN
Most of the speakers of these three dozen languages live in China's mountainous south, where use of native tongues has been declining.
AUSTRONESIAN
Island-hopping seafarers spread Austronesian languages across the Pacific and Indian Oceans from Hawai'i to Madagascar. More than 1,200 languages remain—about a hundred on the tiny Pacific islands of Vanuatu alone.
1 Formosan 2 Malayo-Polynesian
-EUROPEAN
d around the world by alism, the Indo-European ages sprang from a e spoken on the Russian s perhaps 6,000 years heir influence continues w with the widespread on of English as a second ge.
banian 5 Germanic
menian 6 Greek
to-Slavic 7 Indo-Iranian
tic 8 Romance
DRAVIDIAN
Pockets of Dravidian language speakers live in Pakistan and Sri Lanka, but most are found in southern India, where linguistic independence movements in the 1950s led to the birth of several language-based states—such as Andhra Pradesh, home of Telugu.
1 Central 3 South Central
2 Northern 4 Southern
KAM-TAI
Now mostly spoken by Thai and Laotians, the Tai languages may have come from southwest China.
1 Kadai 3 Tai
2 Kam-Sui
NILO-SAHARAN
About 200 Nilo-Saharan languages are spoken by ethnic minorities in their home countries. Only Dongolawi, a Nubian language of the southern Nile in Sudan, has a long written record.
1 Chari-Nile 4 Maban
2 Fur 5 Saharan
3 Komuz 6 Songhai
NIGER-CONGO
With more than 1,400 languages—almost one-fourth of the world's total—Niger-Congo is one of the largest language families. It includes Swahili, used by 35 million East Africans as a lingua franca.
1 Adamawan 6 Kordofanian
2 Benue-Congo 7 Kru
3 Dogon 8 Kwa
4 Gur 9 Mande
5 Ijo 10 West Atlantic
KHOISAN
Famous for complex click consonants, the Khoisan languages may be Africa's oldest. Several have vanished; most have fewer than a thousand speakers.
1 Central 4 Sandawe
2 Hadza 5 Southern
3 Northern
AUSTRO-ASIATIC
Now distributed from Vietnam to India, the Austro-Asiatic languages may once have dominated most of Southeast Asia.
1 Mon-Khmer 2 Munda
AUSTRALIAN FAMILIES
As many as 250 of Australia's Aboriginal languages may have slipped into extinction since Europeans arrived. Only five of the remaining 250 languages have more than a thousand speakers.
Pama-Nyungan 1-17 Other
Undetermined
1 Burarran, Djeebbana, Nakkara
2 Daly
3 Djamindjungan
4 Enindhilyagwa
5 Gungaragany
6 Gunwinyguan
7 Laragiyan
8 Mangarayi
9 Mangerrian
10 Maran
11 Murrinhpatha
12 Nunggubuyu
13 Tiwi
14 Waray
15 Yanyuwa
16 Yiwaidjan
17 Unclassified
PAPUAN FAMILIES
When linguists came to New Guinea, they found languages unlike nearby Austronesian tongues. More than 750 Papuan languages have been counted; isolation keeps them relatively healthy.
GREENLAND (Denmark)
Uninhabited
RCTIC OCEAN
FINLAND
ESTONIA
RUSSIA
ASIA
Siberia
EUROPE
FRANCE
HUNGARY
SPAIN
TURKEY
GREECE
MONGOLIA
NORTH KOREA
SOUTH KOREA
JAPAN
Beijing
CHINA
Yangtze
Uninhabited
PAKISTAN
INDIA
LAOS
THAILAND
VIETNAM
CAMBODIA
PHILIPPINES
SRI LANKA
EGYPT
Nile
SUDAN
AFRICA
TLANTIC OCEAN
PACIFIC OCEAN
INDIAN OCEAN
MADAGASCAR
Sumatra
INDONESIA
New Guinea
PAPUA NEW GUINEA
AUSTRALIA
Vanuatu
NEW ZEALAND
Afrikaans

Major Language Families Today

Many of the world's languages belong to the Indo-European language group, which is thought to have ancient roots in the Russian Steppes. The map at right illustrates how far members of this group—and others—have spread over the millennia. The map locates languages by territory; it does not indicate the number of speakers. For example, the Altaic group covers a vast area, but it has only about 145 million speakers. Austronesian, on the other hand, is spoken within a much smaller area, but it has 312 million speakers.

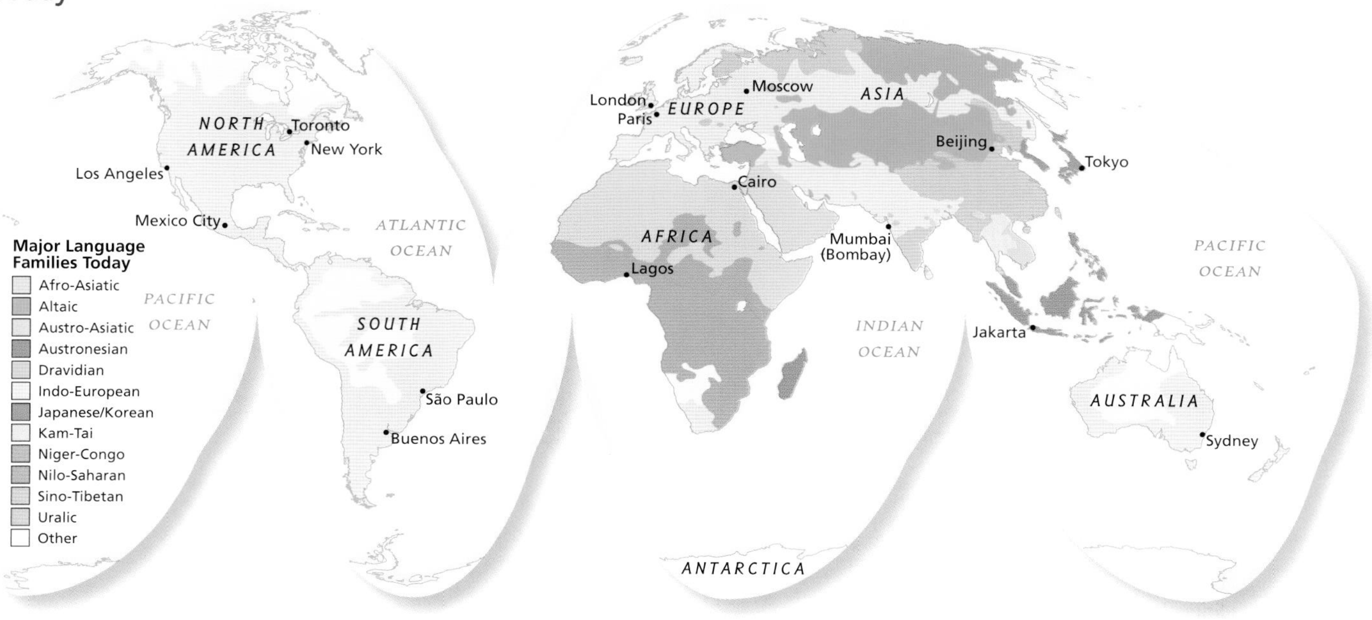

THE GREAT POWER OF RELIGION comes from its ability to speak to the heart of individuals and societies. Since earliest human times, honoring nature spirits or the belief in a supreme being has brought comfort and security in the face of fundamental questions of life and death.

Billions of people are now adherents of Hinduism, Buddhism, Judaism, Christianity, and Islam, all of which began in Asia. Universal elements of these faiths include ritual and prayer, sacred sites and pilgrimage, saints and martyrs, ritual clothing and implements, dietary laws and fasting, festivals and holy days, and special ceremonies for life's major moments. Sometimes otherworldly, most religions have moral and ethical guidelines that attempt to make life better on Earth as well. Their tenets and goals are taught not only at the church, synagogue, mosque, or temple but also through schools, storytelling, parables, painting, sculpture, and even dance and drama.

The world's major religions blossomed from the teachings and revelations of individuals who heeded and transmitted the voice of God or discovered a way to salvation that could be understood by others. Abraham and Moses for Jews, the Buddha for Buddhists, Jesus Christ for Christians, and Muhammad for Muslims fulfilled the roles of divine teachers who experienced essential truths of existence.

Throughout history, priests, rabbis, clergymen, and imams have recited, interpreted, and preached the holy words of sacred texts and writings to the faithful. Today the world's religions, with their guidance here on Earth and hopes and promises for the afterlife, continue to exert an extraordinary force on billions of people.

BUDDHISM
Founded about 2,500 years ago by Shakyamuni Buddha (or Gautama Buddha), Buddhism teaches liberation from suffering through the threefold cultivation of morality, meditation, and wisdom. Buddhists revere the Three Jewels: Buddha (the Awakened One), Dharma (the Truth), and Sangha (the community of monks and nuns).

CHRISTIANITY
Christian belief in eternal life is based on the example of Jesus Christ, a Jew born some 2,000 years ago. The New Testament tells of his teaching, persecution, crucifixion, and resurrection. Today Christianity is found around the world in three main forms: Roman Catholicism, Eastern Orthodox, and Protestantism.

HINDUISM
Hinduism began in India more than 4,000 years ago and is still flourishing. Sacred texts known as the Vedas form the basis of Hindu faith and ritual.

Adherents Worldwide

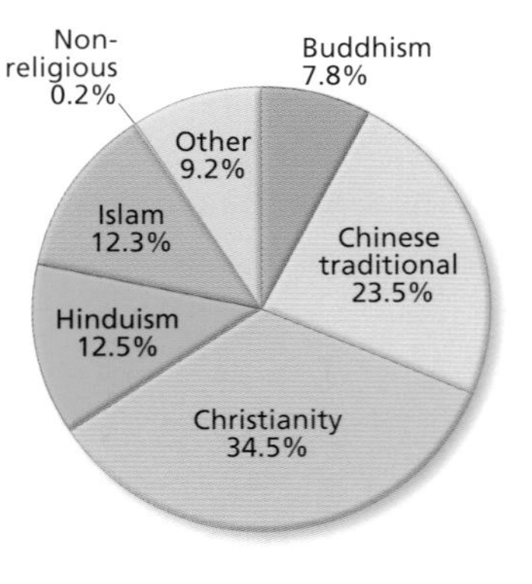

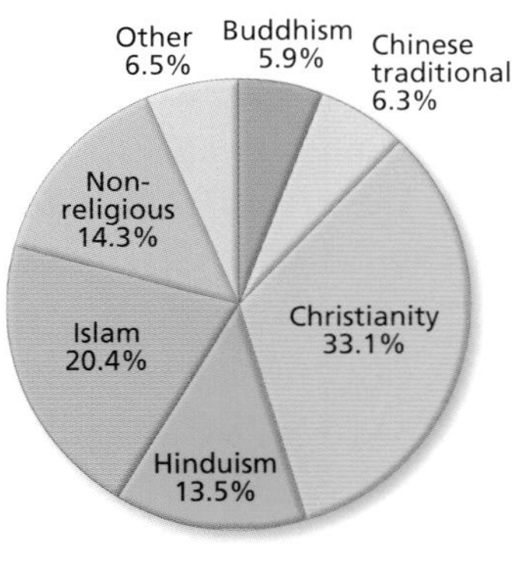

The growth of Islam and the decline of Chinese traditional religion stand out as significant changes over the past hundred years. Christianity, the largest of the world's main faiths, has remained fairly stable in its number of adherents. Today more than one in six people claim to be atheistic or nonreligious.

Adherents by Continent

In terms of the total number of religious adherents, Asia ranks first. This is not only because half the world's people live on that continent, but also because three of the five major faiths are practiced there: Hinduism in South Asia; Buddhism in East and Southeast Asia; and Islam from Indonesia to the Central Asian republics to Turkey. Oceania, Europe, North America, and South America are overwhelmingly Christian. Africa, with many millions of Muslims and Christians,also retains large numbers of animists.

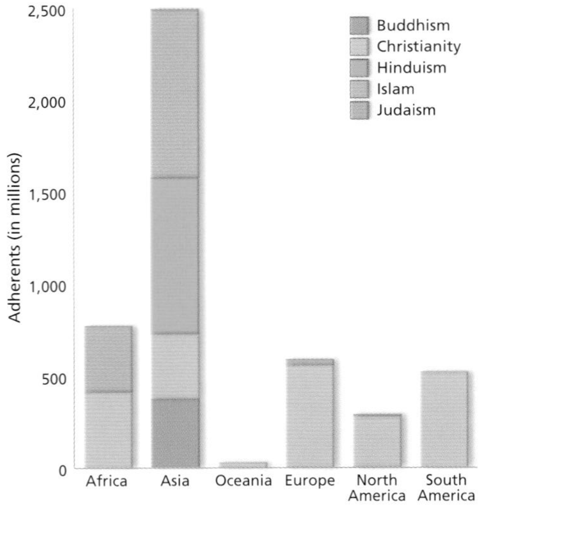

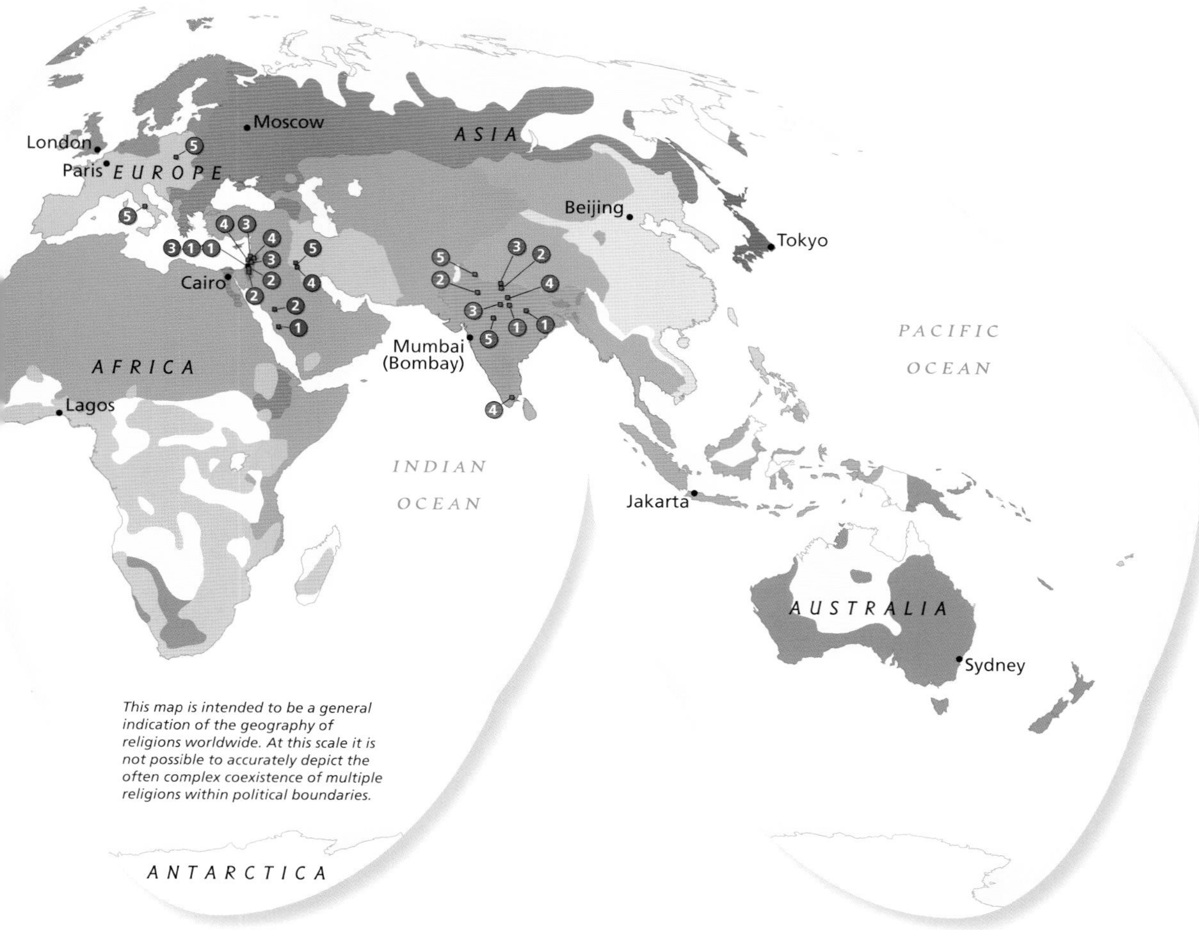

Sacred Places

BUDDHISM
1. Bodhgaya: Where Buddha attained awakening
2. Kusinagara: Where Buddha entered nirvana
3. Lumbini: Place of Buddha's last human birth
4. Sarnath: Place where Buddha delivered his first sermon
5. Sanchi: Location of famous stupa containing relics of Buddha

CHRISTIANITY
1. Jerusalem: Church of the Holy Sepulchre, Jesus's crucifixion
2. Bethlehem: Jesus's birthplace
3. Nazareth: Where Jesus grew up
4. Shore of the Sea of Galilee: Where Jesus gave the Sermon on the Mount
5. Rome and the Vatican: Tombs of St. Peter and St. Paul

HINDUISM
1. Varanasi (Banaras): Most holy Hindu site, home of Shiva
2. Vrindavan: Krishna's birthplace
3. Allahabad: At confluence of Ganges and Yamuna rivers, purest place to bathe
4. Madurai: Temple of Minakshi, great goddess of the south
5. Badrinath: Vishnu's shrine

ISLAM
1. Mecca: Muhammad's birthplace
2. Medina: City of Muhammad's flight, or hegira
3. Jerusalem: Dome of the Rock, Muhammad's stepping-stone to heaven
4. Najaf (Shiite): Tomb of Imam Ali
5. Kerbala (Shiite): Tomb of Imam Hoseyn

JUDAISM
1. Jerusalem: Location of the Western Wall and first and second temples
2. Hebron: Tomb of the patriarchs and their wives
3. Safed: Where Kabbalah (Jewish mysticism) flourished
4. Tiberias: Where Talmud (source of Jewish law) first composed
5. Auschwitz: Symbol of six million Jews who perished in the Holocaust

he main trinity of gods com-
rises Brahma the creator,
ishnu the preserver, and
hiva the destroyer. Hindus
elieve in reincarnation.

ISLAM
Muslims believe that the Koran, Islam's sacred book, accurately records the spoken word of God (Allah) as revealed to the Prophet Muhammad, born in Mecca around A.D. 570. Strict adherents pray five times a day, fast during the holy month of Ramadan, and make at least one pilgrimage to Mecca, Islam's holiest city.

JUDAISM
The 4,000-year-old religion of the Jews stands as the oldest of the major faiths that believe in a single god. Judaism's traditions, customs, laws, and beliefs date back to Abraham, the founder, and to the Torah, the first five books of the Old Testament, believed to have been handed down to Moses on Mount Sinai.

Adherents by Country

COUNTRIES WITH THE MOST BUDDHISTS

COUNTRY	BUDDHISTS
1. China	111,359,000
2. Japan	70,723,000
3. Thailand	53,294,000
4. Vietnam	40,781,000
5. Myanmar	37,152,000
6. Sri Lanka	13,235,000
7. Cambodia	12,698,000
8. India	7,597,000
9. South Korea	7,281,000
10. Taiwan*	4,823,000

COUNTRIES WITH THE MOST CHRISTIANS

COUNTRY	CHRISTIANS
1. United States	252,394,000
2. Brazil	166,847,000
3. China	110,956,000
4. Mexico	102,012,000
5. Russia	84,495,000
6. Philippines	73,987,000
7. India	68,190,000
8. Germany	61,833,000
9. Nigeria	61,438,000
10. Congo, Dem. Rep.	53,371,000

COUNTRIES WITH THE MOST HINDUS

COUNTRY	HINDUS
1. India	810,387,000
2. Nepal	19,020,000
3. Bangladesh	17,029,000
4. Indonesia	7,633,000
5. Sri Lanka	2,173,000
6. Pakistan	2,100,000
7. Malaysia	1,855,000
8. United States	1,144,000
9. South Africa	1,079,000
10. Myanmar	1,007,000

COUNTRIES WITH THE MOST MUSLIMS

COUNTRY	MUSLIMS
1. Indonesia	171,569,000
2. Pakistan	154,563,000
3. India	134,150,000
4. Bangladesh	132,868,000
5. Turkey	71,323,000
6. Iran	67,724,000
7. Egypt	63,503,000
8. Nigeria	54,666,000
9. Algeria	31,859,000
10. Morocco	31,001,000

COUNTRIES WITH THE MOST JEWS

COUNTRY	JEWS
1. United States	5,764,000
2. Israel	4,772,000
3. France	607,000
4. Argentina	520,000
5. Palestine*	451,000
6. Canada	414,000
7. Brazil	384,000
8. United Kingdom	312,000
9. Russia	245,000
10. Germany	226,000

*Non-sovereign nation

All figures are estimates based on data for the year 2005.
Countries with the highest reported nonreligious populations include China, Russia, United States, Germany, India, Japan, North Korea, Vietnam, France, and Italy.

IN THE PAST 50 YEARS, health conditions have improved dramatically. With better economic and living conditions and access to immunization and other basic health services, global life expectancy has risen from 40 to 65 years; the death rate for children under five years old has fallen by half; and diseases that once killed and disabled millions have been eradicated, eliminated, or greatly reduced in impact. Today, fully three-quarters of the world's children benefit from protection against six infectious diseases that were responsible in the past for many millions of infant and child deaths.

Current efforts to improve health face new and daunting challenges, however. Infant and child mortality from infectious diseases remains relatively high in many poor countries. Each year, more than ten million children under five years old die—41 percent of them in sub-Saharan Africa and 34 percent in South Asia. Improvement in children's health has slowed dramatically in the past 20 years, particularly where child death rates have historically been highest.

The HIV/AIDS pandemic has erased decades of steady improvements in sub-Saharan Africa. An estimated 25 million people are HIV-positive in Africa alone—and AIDS is taking a toll in India, China, and Eastern Europe. The death toll in Africa is contributing to reversals in life expectancy—just 47 years instead of the estimated 62 years without AIDS. An estimated 15 million children have lost one or both their parents to the disease.

Vast gaps in health outcomes between rich and poor persist. About 99 percent of global childhood deaths occur in poor countries, with the poorest within those countries having the highest child-mortality rates. In Indonesia, for example, a child born in a poor household is four times as likely to die by her fifth birthday than a child born to a well-off family.

In many high- and middle-income countries, chronic, lifestyle-related diseases such as cardiovascular disease, diabetes, and others are becoming the predominant cause of disability and death. Because the focus of policymakers has been on treatment rather than prevention, the costs of dealing with these ailments contributes to high (and rapidly increasing) health-care spending. Tobacco-related illnesses are major problems worldwide. In developed countries, smoking is the cause of more than one-third of male deaths in middle age, and about one in eight female deaths. It is estimated that due to trends of increasing tobacco use, of all the people aged under 20 alive today in China, 50 million will die prematurely from tobacco.

Health-Care Availability

Regional differences in health-care resources are striking. While countries in Europe and the Americas have relatively large numbers of physicians and nurses, nations with far higher burdens of disease (particularly African countries) are experiencing severe deficits in both health workers and health facilities.

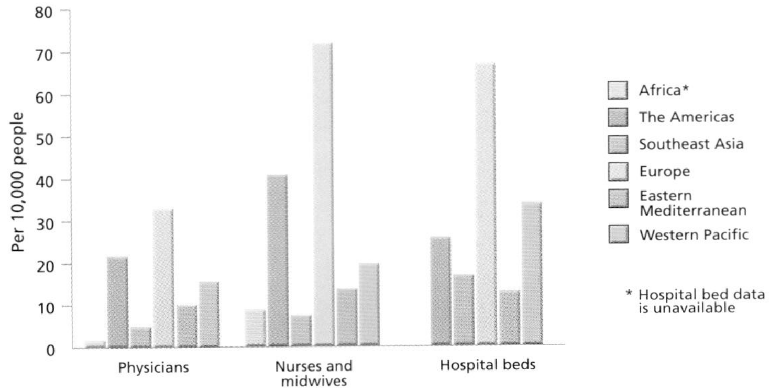

Income Levels: Indicators of Health and Literacy

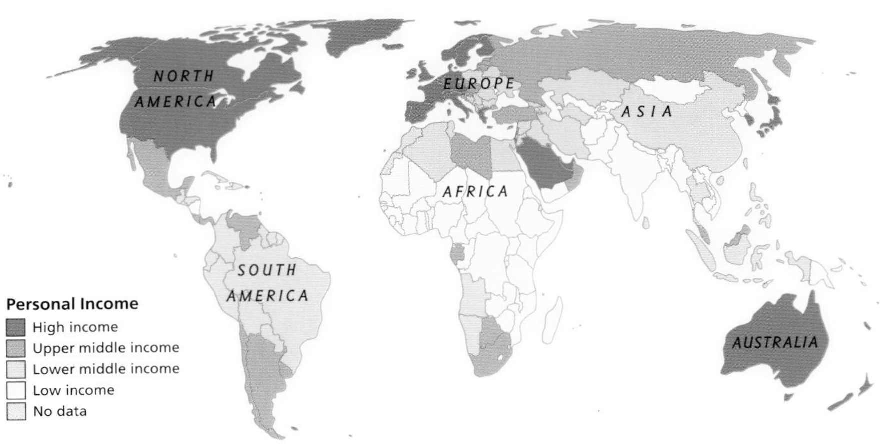

Access to Improved Sanitation

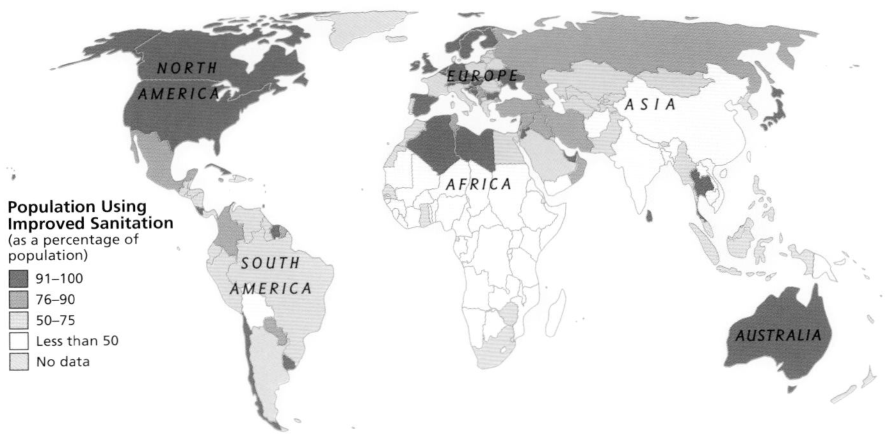

Nutrition

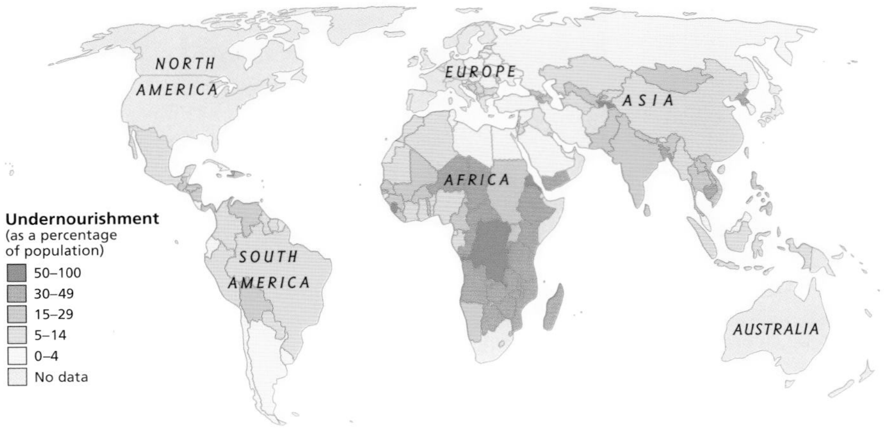

HIV

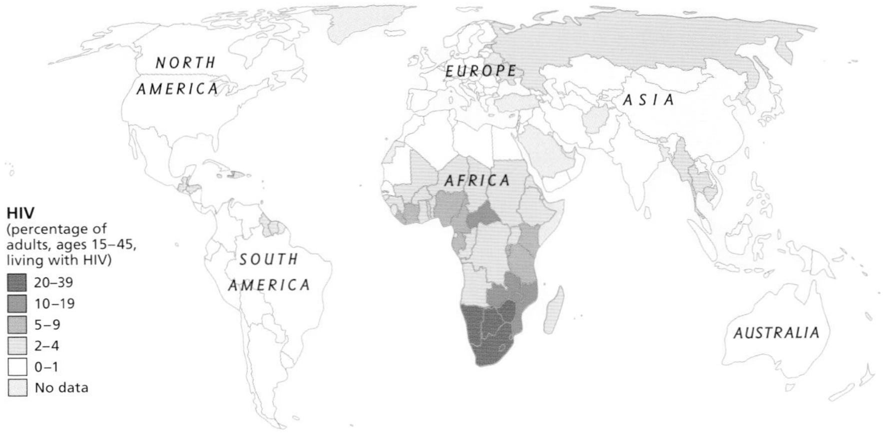

Global Disease Burden

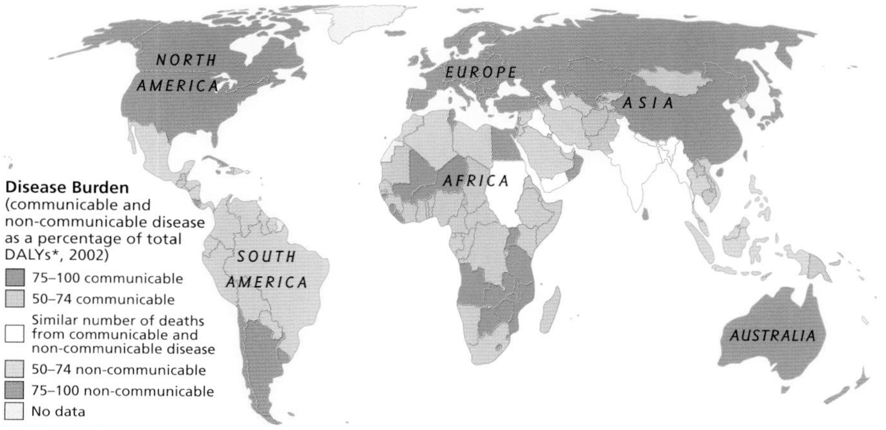

DALYs (disability adjusted life years) are a health gap measure used to quantify potential years of life lost to illness or premature death. One DALY can be thought of as one lost year of "healthy" life.

While infectious and parasitic diseases account for nearly one-quarter of total deaths in developing countries, they result in relatively few deaths in wealthier nations. In contrast, cardiovascular diseases and cancer are more significant causes of death in industrialized countries. Over time, as fertility rates fall, social and living conditions improve, the population ages, and further advances are made against infectious diseases in poorer countries, the distribution of causes of death between developed and developing nations may converge.

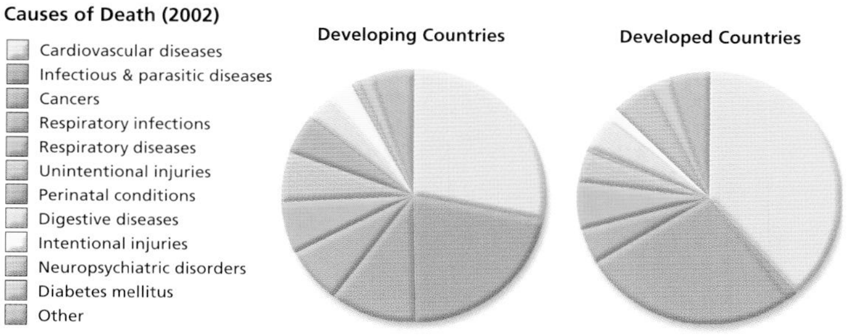

Under-Five Mortality

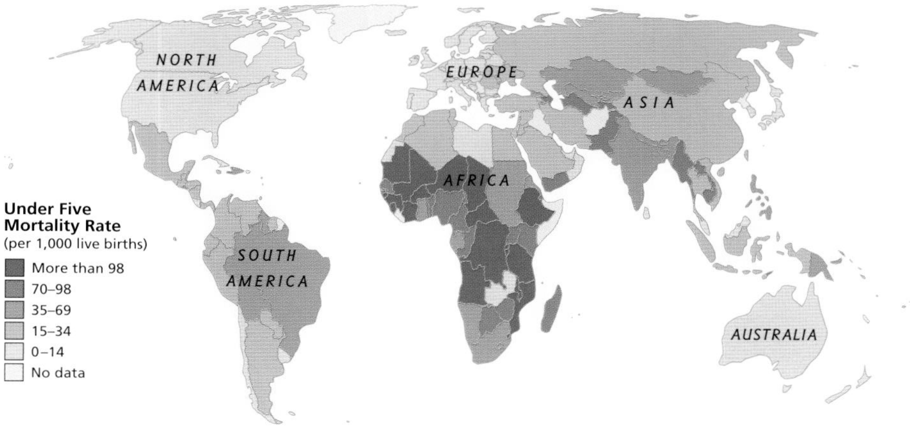

Maternal Mortality

MATERNAL MORTALITY RATIO PER 100,000 LIVE BIRTHS*

COUNTRIES WITH THE HIGHEST MATERNAL MORTALITY RATES:	
1. Sierra Leone	2,000
2. Malawi	1,800
3. Angola	1,700
4. Niger	1,600
5. Tanzania	1,500
6. Rwanda	1,400
7. Mali	1,200
8. Zimbabwe	1,100
9. Central African Republic	1,100
10. Guinea-Bissau	1,100

COUNTRIES WITH THE LOWEST MATERNAL MORTALITY RATES:	
1. Iceland	0
2. Sweden	2
3. Slovakia	3
4. Spain	4
5. Austria	4
6. Kuwait	5
7. Portugal	5
8. Italy	5
9. Denmark	5
10. Ireland	5

**Adjusted for underreporting and misclassification*

Education and Literacy

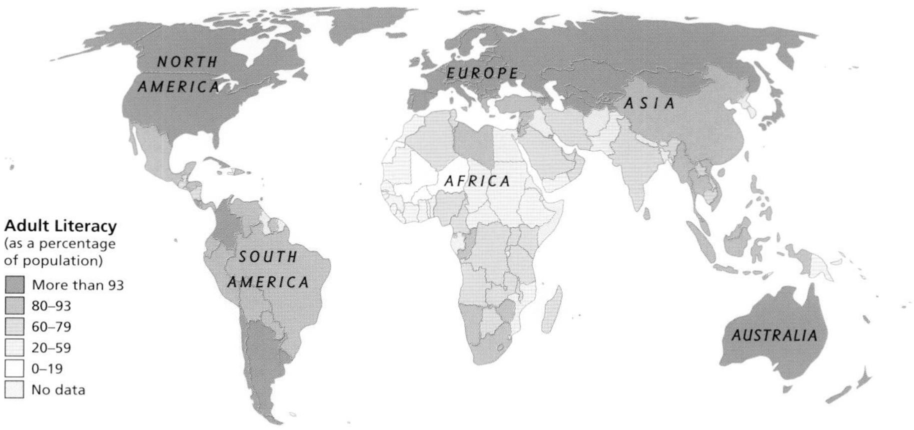

Basic education is an investment for the long-term prosperity of a nation, generating individual, household, and social benefits. Some countries (e.g., Eastern and Western Europe, the U.S.) have long traditions of high educational attainment among both genders, and now have well-educated populations of all ages. In contrast, many low-income countries have only recently expanded access to primary education; girls still lag behind boys in enrollment and completion of primary school, and then in making the transition to secondary school. These countries will have to wait many years before most individuals in the productive ages have even minimal levels of reading, writing, and basic arithmetic skills.

The expansion of secondary schooling tends to lag even further behind, so countries with low educational attainment will likely be at a disadvantage for at least a generation. Although no one doubts that the key to long-term economic growth and poverty reduction lies in greater education opportunities for all, many poor countries face the tremendous challenge of paying for schools and teachers today, while having to wait 20 years for the economic returns to those investments.

School Enrollment for Girls

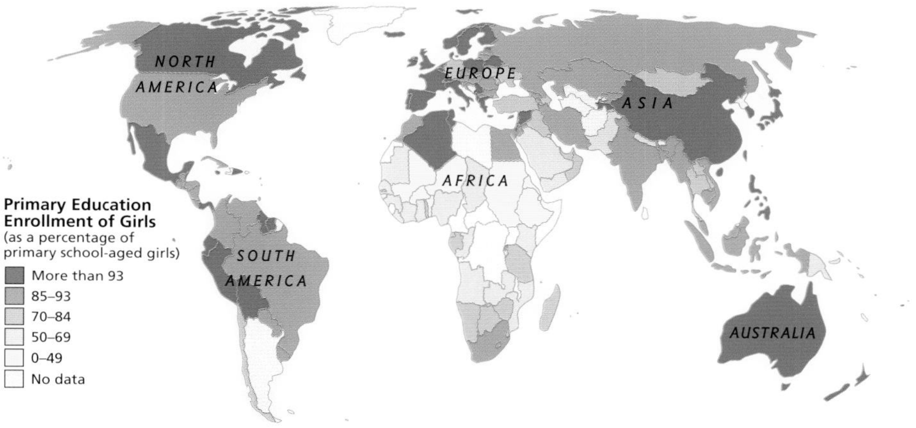

Developing Human Capital

In the pyramids below, more red and blue in the bars indicates a higher level of educational attainment, or "human capital," which contributes greatly to a country's ability for future economic growth. These two countries are similar in population size, but their human capital measures are significantly different.

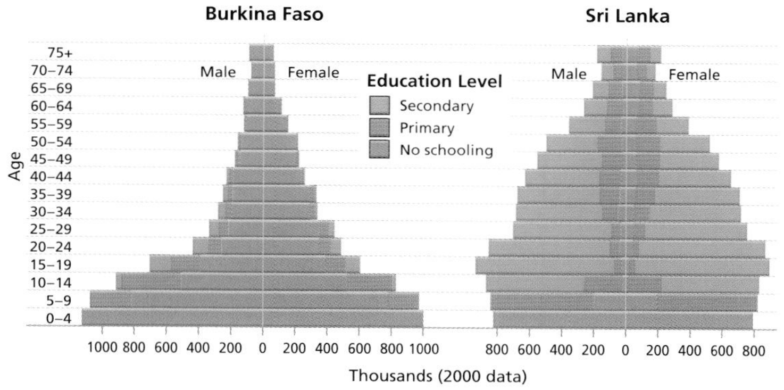

POLITICAL VIOLENCE, WAR, AND TERROR continue to plague many areas of the world in the early 21st century, despite dramatic decreases in major armed conflict since 1991. The 20th century is often described as the century of "total war" as modern weapons technologies made every facet of society a potential target in warfare. The globe was rocked by two world wars, self-determination wars in developing countries, and the threat of nuclear annihilation during the Cold War. Whereas the first half of the century was torn by interstate wars among the most powerful states, the latter half was consumed by protracted civil wars in the weakest states. The end of the Cold War emboldened international engagement, and concerted efforts toward peace had reduced armed conflicts more than half by early 2006.

While long-standing wars still smolder in Africa and Asia in the early 21st century, global apprehension is riveted on super-powerful states, super-empowered individuals, and the proliferation of "weapons of mass disruption." Globalization is both bringing people closer together and making us ever more vulnerable. Though violence is generally subsiding and democracy spreading, tensions appear to be increasing across the world's oil-producing regions. A little-understood "war on terror" punctuates the hard-won peace and prods us toward an uncertain future. Prospects for an ever more peaceful world are good, yet much work remains.

Political Violence

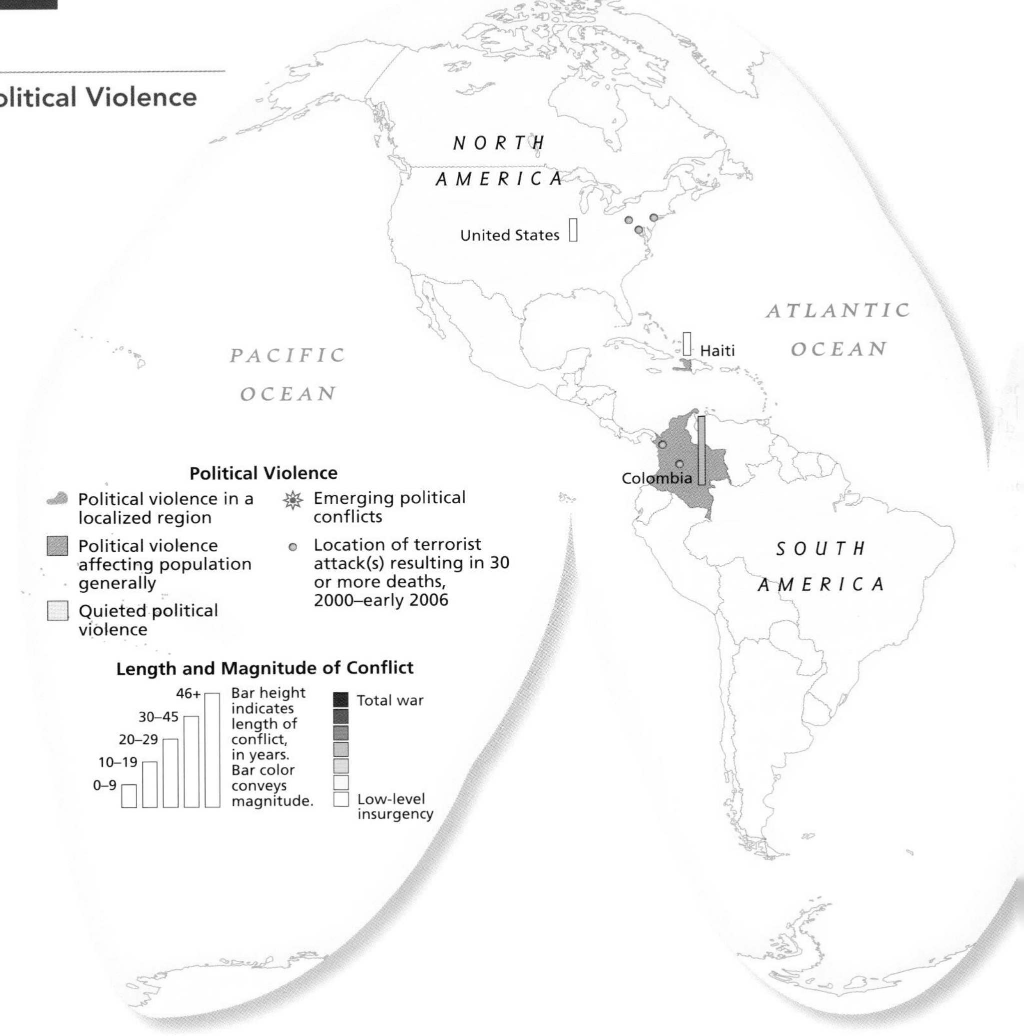

Peace-Building Capacities

The quality of a government's response to rising tensions is the most crucial factor in the management of political conflict. "Peace-building capacity" gauges a country's ability to manage emerging conflicts successfully and avoid outbreaks of serious violence. This capacity is greatest when a government provides reasonable levels of human security; does not condone policies of political or economic discrimination; has a successful track record of managing self-determination movements; maintains stable, democratic institutions; has attained substantial human and material resources; and is free of serious threats from neighboring countries. Peace-building capacities have generally improved since the end of the Cold War; they remain weakest in African and Muslim countries.

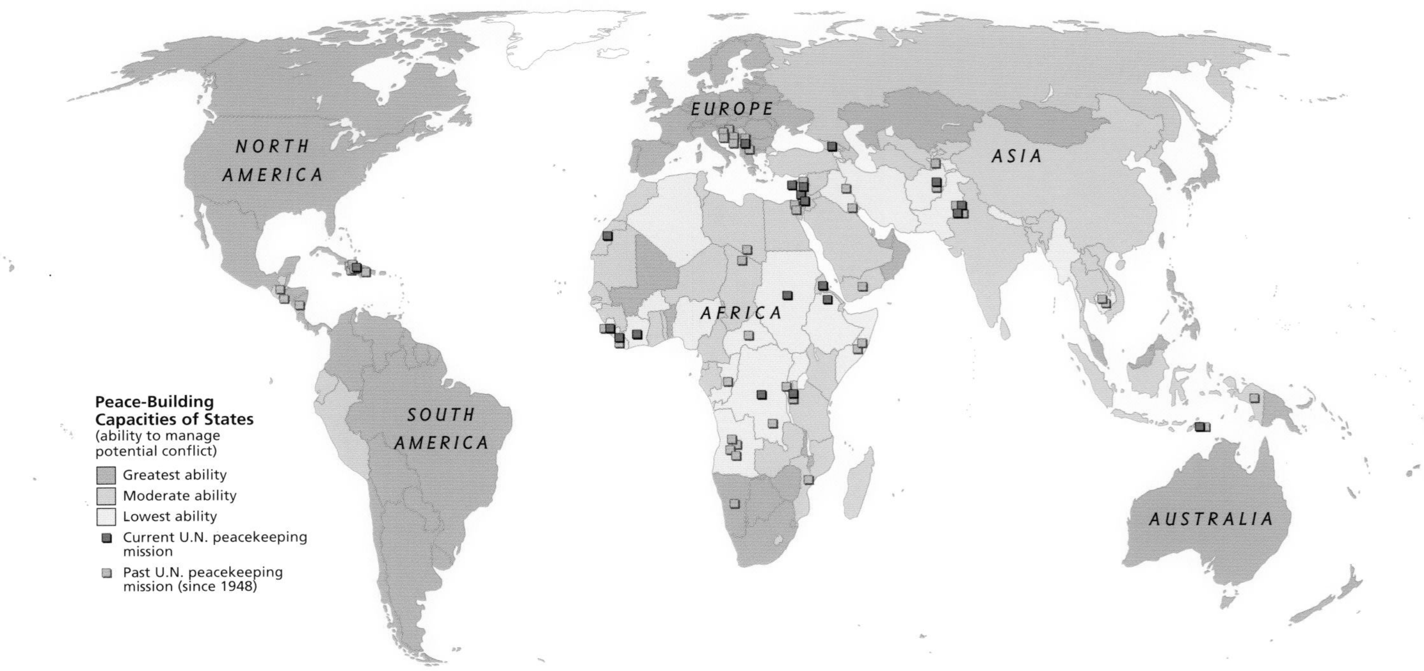

Change in Magnitude of Ongoing Conflicts

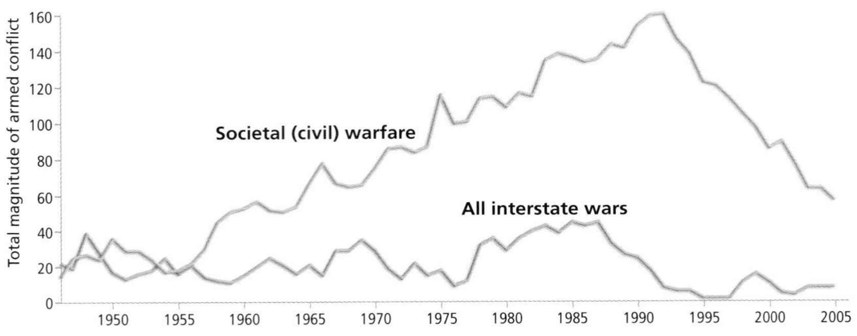

Global Regimes by Type

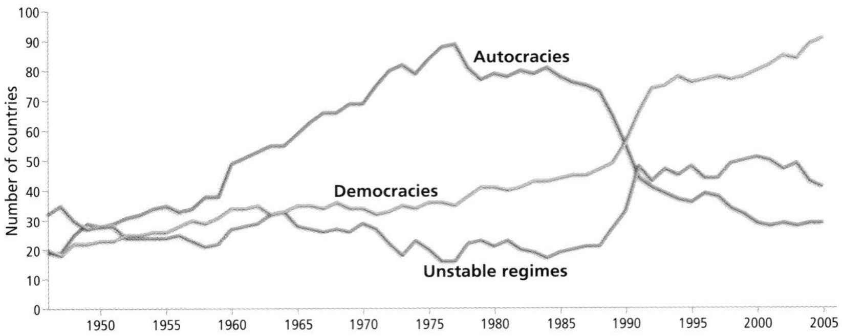

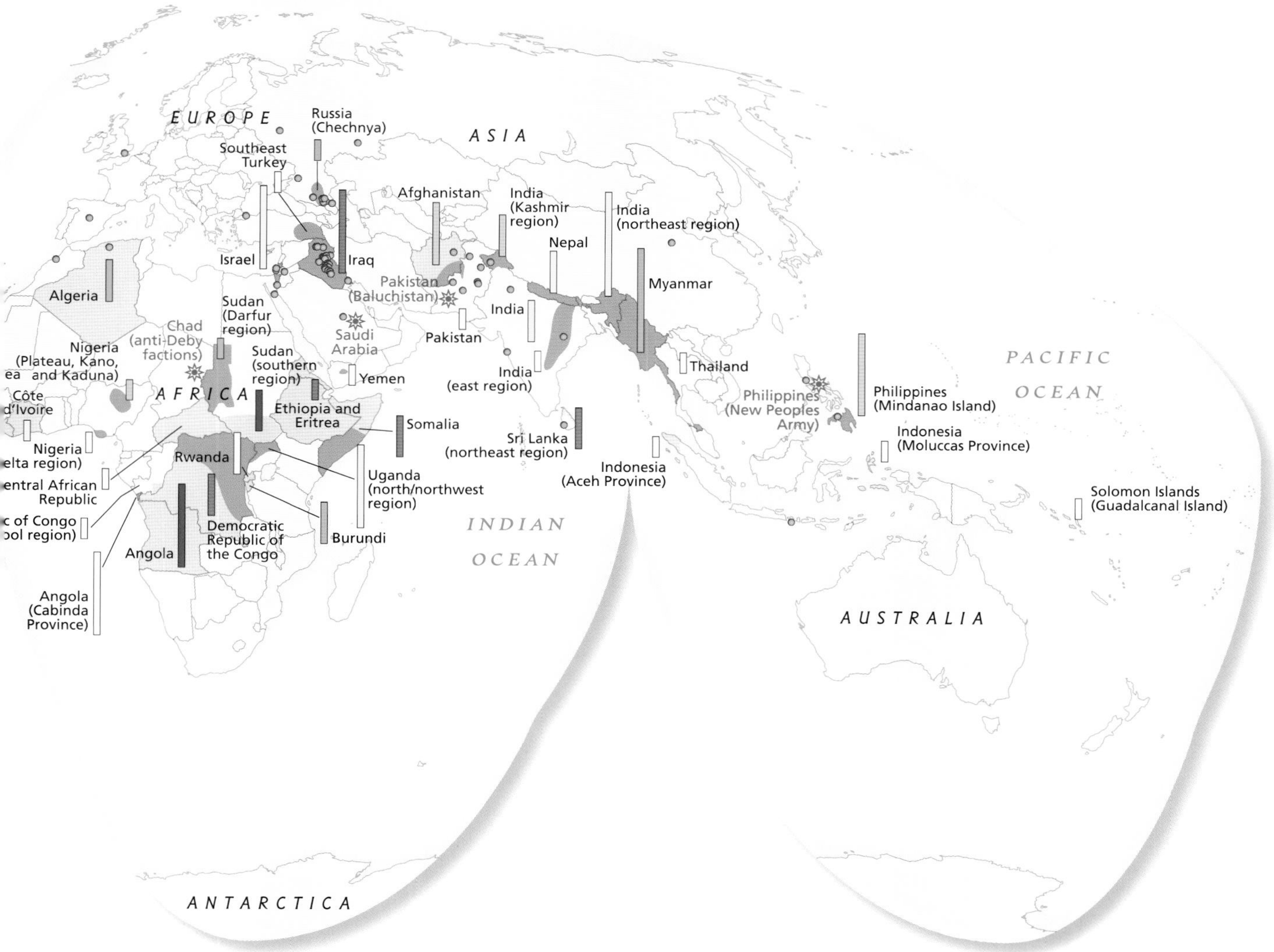

Terrorist Attacks

"Terrorism" has a special connotation with violent attacks on civilians. The vast majority of such attacks are domestic. "International terrorism" is a special subset of attacks linked to globalization in which militants go abroad to strike their targets, select domestic targets linked to a foreign state, or attack international transports such as planes or ships. The numbers of victims are quite low compared with other forms of violence and terrorism but have doubled since the dramatic 9/11 attacks on the United States.

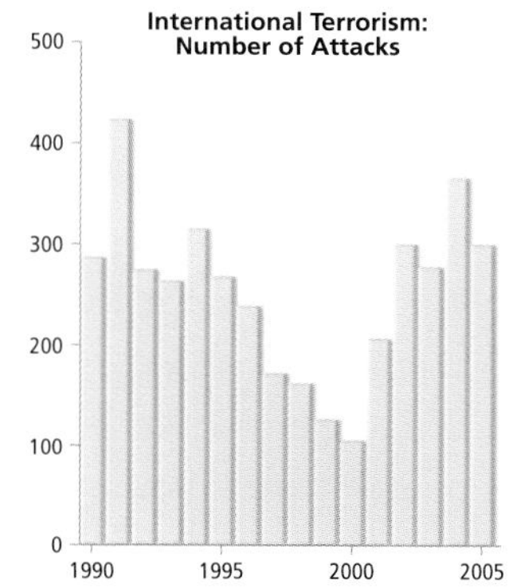

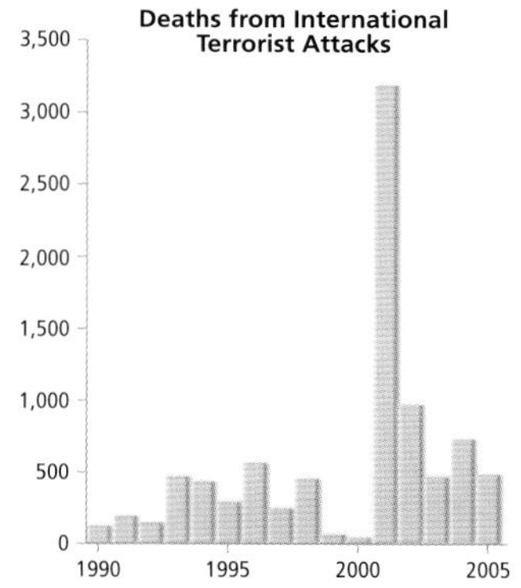

Genocides and Politicides Since 1955

Our worst fears are realized when governments are directly involved in killing their own, unarmed citizens. Lethal repression is most often associated with autocratic regimes; its most extreme forms are termed genocide and politicide. These policies involve the intentional destruction, in whole or in part, of a communal or ethnic group (genocide) or opposition group (politicide). "Death squads" and "ethnic cleansing" have brutalized populations in 29 countries at various times since 1955.

Weapons Possessions

	Nuclear: Declared stockpile	Nuclear: Suspected or undeclared program	Chemical: Declared stockpile now being destroyed	Chemical: Undeclared stockpile or development program	Biological: Suspected offensive development program
Albania			●		
China	●			●	●
Egypt				●	●
France	●				
India	●		●		
Iran		●		●	●
Israel	●			●	●
Libya			●		
North Korea		●		●	●
Pakistan	●				
Russia	●		●		●
South Korea			●		
Syria				●	●
United Kingdom	●				
United States	●		●		

The proliferation of weapons of mass destruction (WMD) is a principal concern in the 21st century. State weakness and official corruption increase the possibilities that these modern technologies might fall into the wrong hands and be a source of terror, extortion, or war.

Refugees

Refugees are persons who have fled their country of origin due to fear of persecution for reasons of, for example, race, religion, or political opinion. IDPs (internally displaced persons) are often displaced for the same reasons as refugees, but they still reside in their country of origin. By the end of 2004, the global number of refugees was 9.2 million persons. The most recent estimate of IDPs worldwide (December 2005) was just under 24 million.

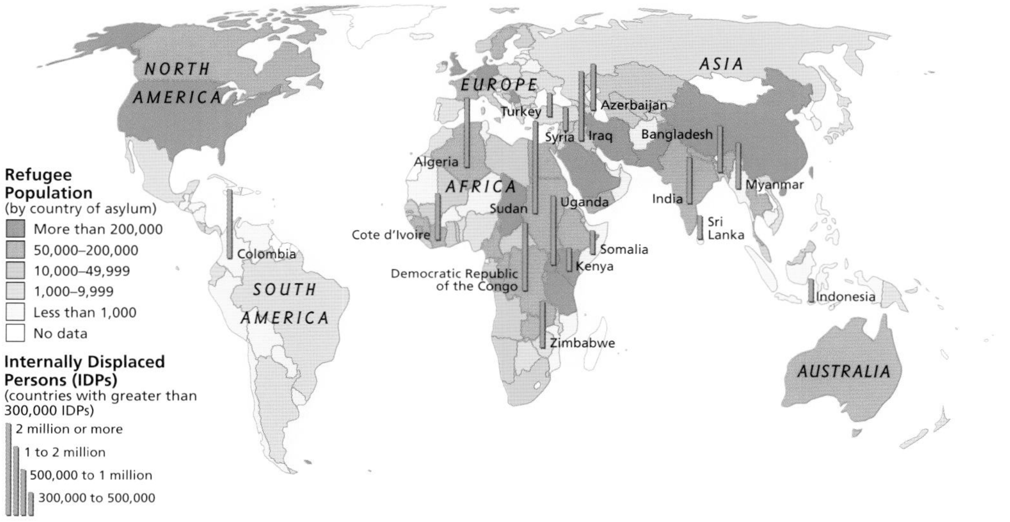

A GLOBAL ECONOMIC ACTIVITY MAP (right) reveals striking differences in the composition of output in advanced economies (such as the United States, Japan, and western Europe) compared with less developed countries (such as Nigeria and China). Advanced economies tend to have high proportions of their GDP in services, while developing economies have relatively high proportions in agriculture and industry.

There are different ways of looking at the distribution of manufacturing industry activity. When examined by country, the United States leads in production in many industries, but Western European countries are also a major manufacturing force. Western Europe outpaces the U.S. in the production of cars, chemicals, and food.

The world's sixth largest economy is found in China, and it has been growing quite rapidly. Chinese workers take home only a fraction of the cash pocketed each week by their economic rivals in the West, but are quickly catching up to the global economy with their purchase of cell phones and motor vehicles—two basic consumer products of the modern age.

The Middle East—a number of whose countries enjoy relatively high per-capita GDP values—produces more fuel than any other region, but it has virtually no other economic output besides that single commodity.

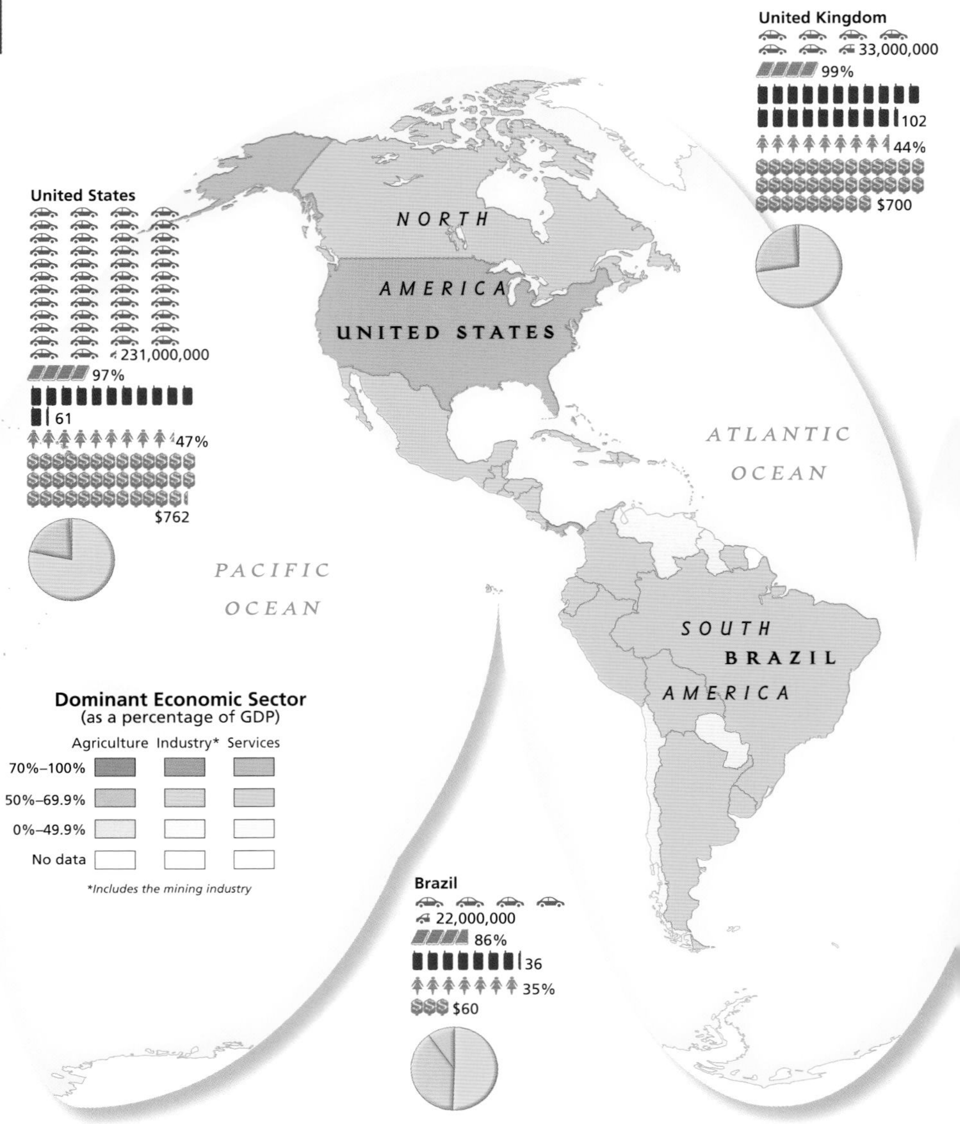

Labor Migration

People in search of jobs gravitate toward the higher-income economies, unless immigration policies prevent them from doing so. Japan, for instance, has one of the world's most restrictive immigration policies and a population that is more than 99 percent Japanese. Some nations are "labor importers," while others are "labor exporters." In the mid-1990s, Malaysia was the largest Asian importer (close to a million workers) and the Philippines was the largest Asian exporter (4.2 million). The largest share of foreign workers in domestic employment is found in the Persian Gulf and Singapore.

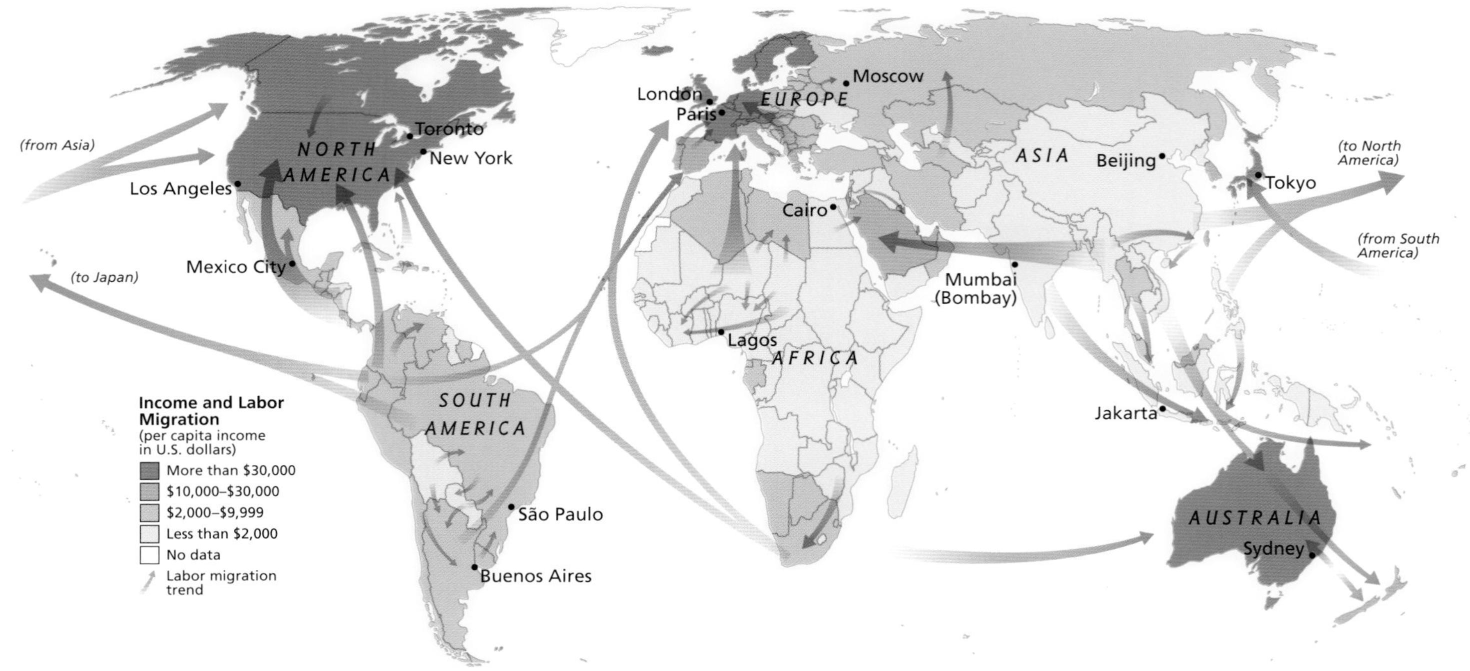

Top GDP Growth Rates
(based on PPP, or purchasing power parity)*

(2000–2005 AVERAGE)		
1.	Equatorial Guinea	13%
2.	Turkmenistan	12%
3.	Sierra Leone	12%
4.	Chad	12%
5.	Armenia	11%
6.	Azerbaijan	11%
7.	Kazakhstan	11%
8.	Tajikistan	11%
9.	China	11%
10.	Myanmar	11%

The World's Richest and Poorest Countries

RICHEST		GDP PER CAPITA (PPP) (2005)
1.	Luxembourg	$64,900
2.	Norway	$40,800
3.	United States	$39,700
4.	Ireland	$38,200
5.	Qatar	$33,800
6.	Denmark	$33,300
7.	Canada	$33,000
8.	Iceland	$32,800
9.	Austria	$32,100
10.	Equatorial Guinea	$30,800

POOREST		GDP PER CAPITA (PPP) (2005)
1.	Sierra Leone	$630
2.	Democratic Rep. of the Congo	$640
3.	Tanzania	$670
4.	Malawi	$680
5.	Yemen	$700
6.	Ethiopia	$750
7.	Burundi	$760
8.	Guinea-Bissau	$820
9.	Madagascar	$850
10.	Niger	$860

*For more information on PPP, please see map on page 57.

Figures are listed in U.S. dollars.

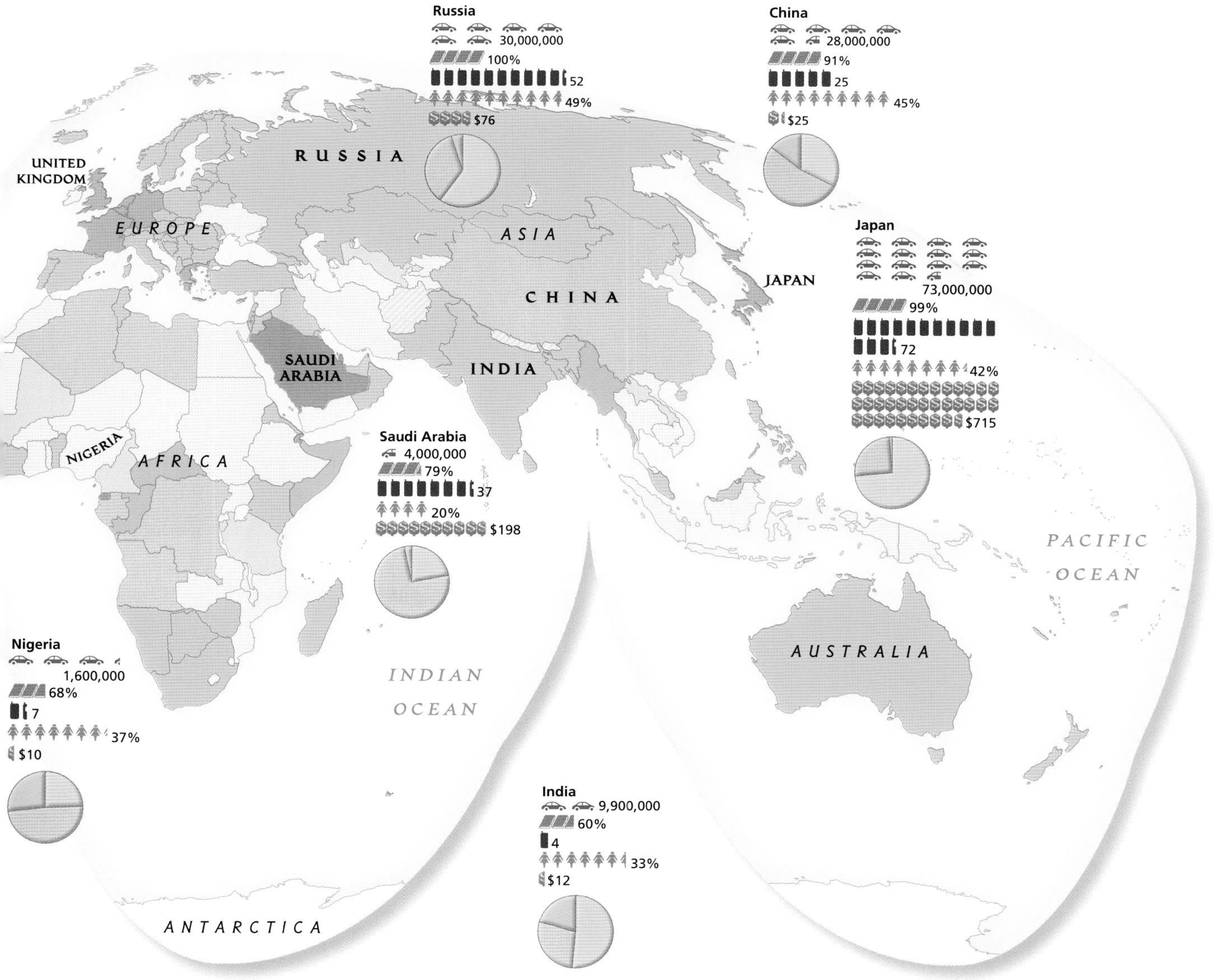

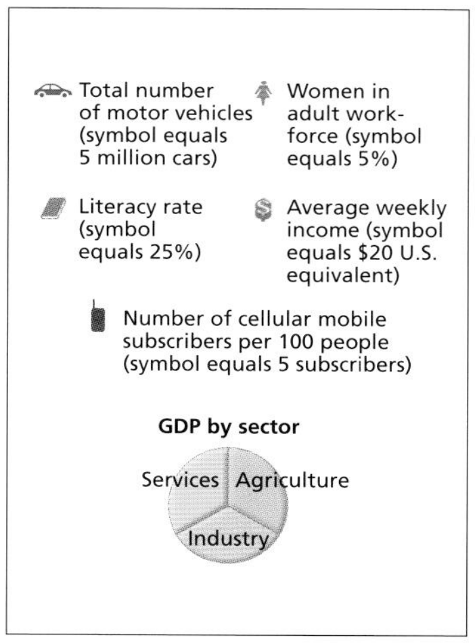

Major Manufacturers

(All figures in billions of U.S. dollars, 2004)

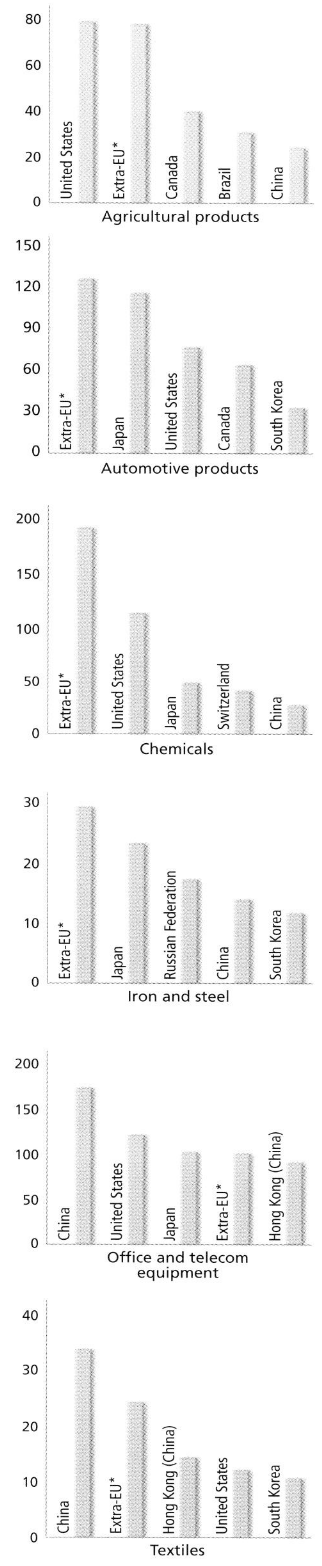

*Extra-EU trade statistics record goods imported and exported between European Union members and non-European Union members.

Gross Domestic Product

The gross domestic product (GDP) is the total market value of goods and services produced by a nation's economy in a given year using global currency exchange rates. It is a convenient way of calculating the level of a nation's international purchasing power and economic strength, but it does not show average wealth of individuals or measure standard of living. For example, a country could have high exports in products, but still have a low standard of living.

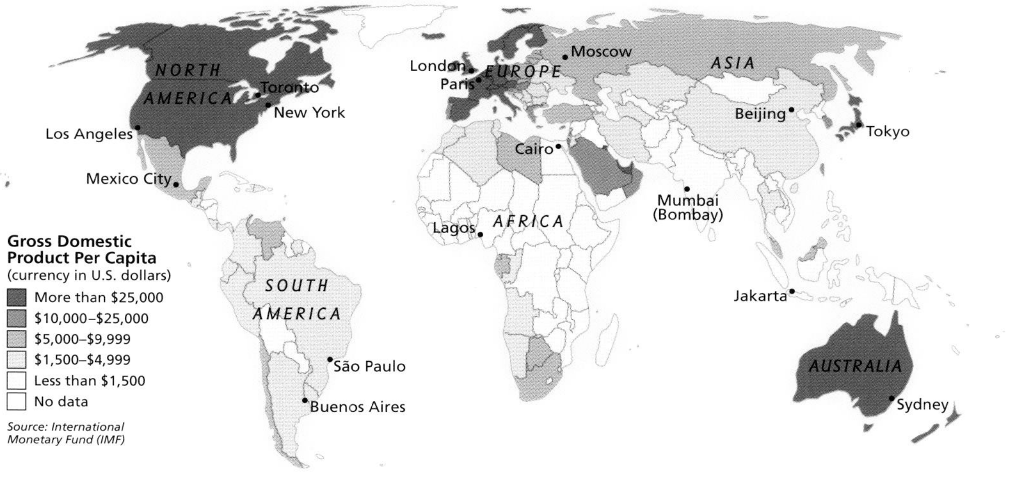

Gross Domestic Product: Purchasing Power Parity (PPP)

The PPP method calculates the relative value of currencies based on what each currency will buy in its country of origin–providing a good comparison between national economies. Per capita GDP at PPP is a very good but not perfect indicator of living standards. For instance, although workers in China earn only a fraction of the wage of American workers, (measured at current dollar rates) they also spend it in a lower-cost environment.

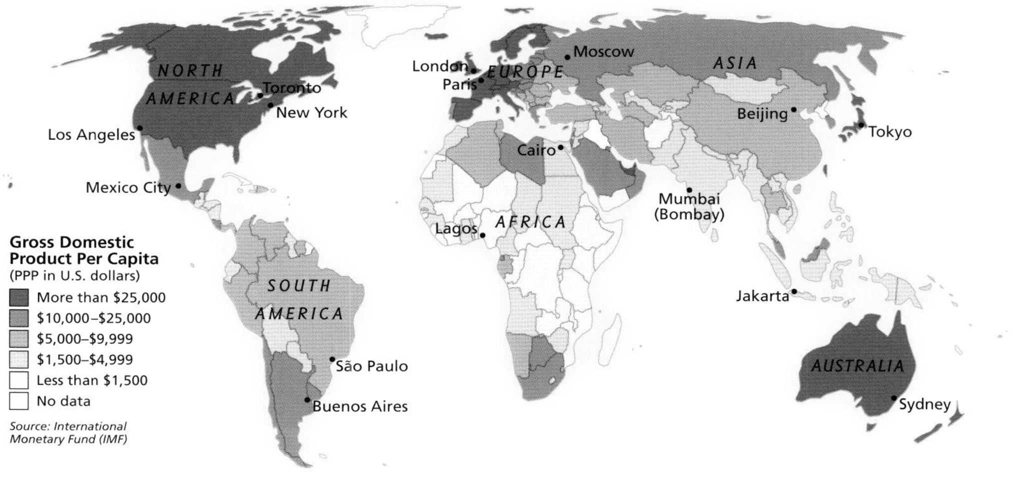

WORLD TRADE HAS EXPANDED at a dizzying pace in the decades following World War II. The dollar value of world merchandise exports rose from $61 billion in 1950 to $10.1 trillion in 2005. Adjusted for price changes, world trade grew 30 times over the last 55 years, much faster than world output. Trade in manufactures expanded much faster than that of mining products (including fuels) and agricultural products. In the last decades many developing countries have become important exporters of manufactures (e.g. China, South Korea, Mexico). However, there are still many less-developed countries—primarily in Africa and the Middle East—that are dependent on a few primary commodities for their export earnings. Commercial services exports have expanded rapidly over the past two decades, and amounted to $2.4 trillion in 2005. While developed countries account for more than two-thirds of world services trade, some developing countries now gain most of their export earnings from services exports. Earnings from tourism in the Caribbean and that from software exports in India are prominent examples of developing countries' dynamic services exports.

Capital flows and worker remittances have gained in importance worldwide and are another important aspect of globalization. The stock of worldwide foreign direct investment was estimated to be close to $9 trillion at the end of 2004, $2.2 trillion of which was invested in developing countries. Capital markets in many developing countries remain small, fragile, and underdeveloped, which hampers household savings and the funding of local enterprises.

Growth of World Trade

After World War II the export growth of manufactured goods greatly outstripped other exports. This graph shows the volume growth on a semi-log scale (a straight line represents constant growth) rather than a standard scale (a straight line indicates a constant increase in the absolute values in each year).

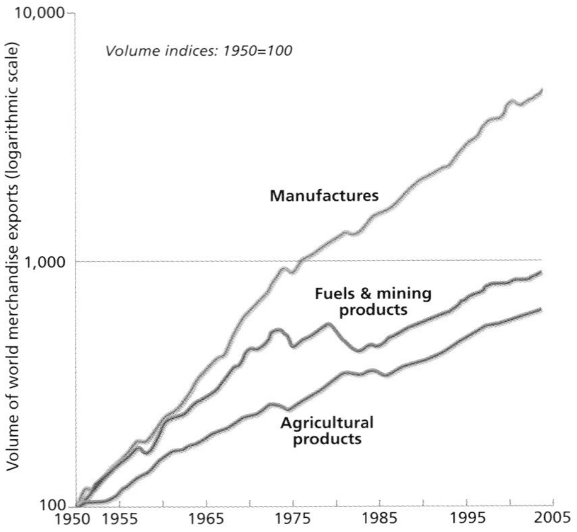

Merchandise Exports

Manufactured goods account for three-quarters of world merchandise exports. Export values of two subtypes—machinery and office/telecom equipment—exceed the total export value of mining products; world exports in chemicals and automotive products exceed the export value of all agricultural products.

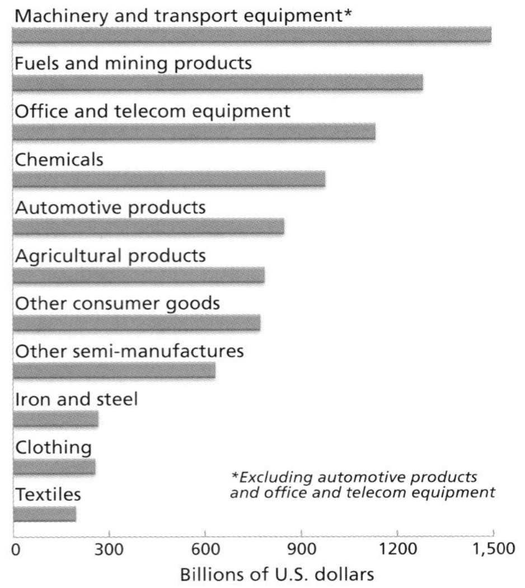

Main Trading Nations

The U.S., Germany, and Japan account for nearly 30 percent of total world merchandise trade. Ongoing negotiations among the 144 member nations of the World Trade Organization are tackling market-access barriers in agriculture, textiles, and clothing—areas where many developing countries hope to compete.

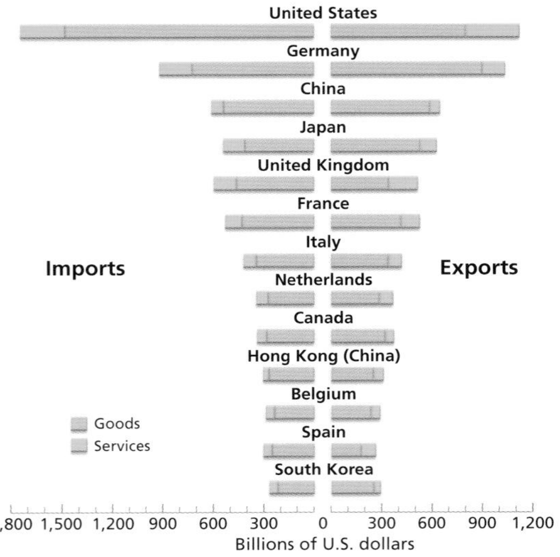

World Debt

Measuring a nation's outstanding foreign debt in relation to its GDP indicates the size of future income needed to pay back the debt; it also shows how much a nation has relied in the past on foreign savings to finance investment and consumption expenditures. A high external debt ratio can pose a financial risk if debt service payments are not assured.

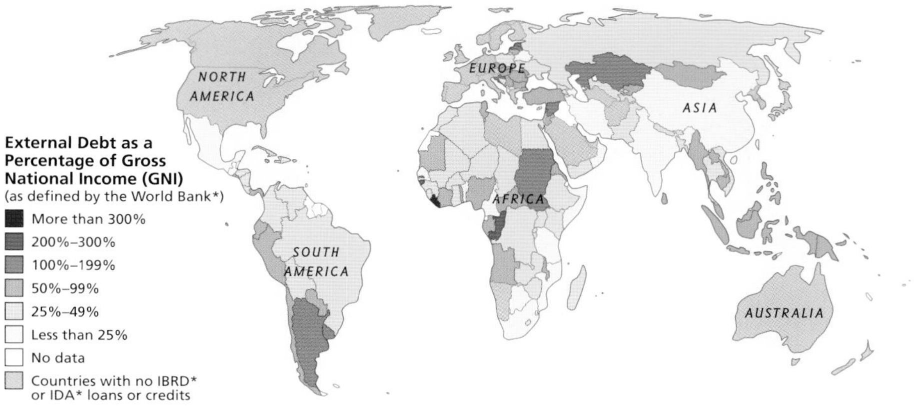

*The World Bank–International Bank for Reconstruction and Development (IBRD) and the International Development Association (IDA)–provide low-interest loans, interest-free credit, and grants to developing countries.

Trade Blocs

Regional trade is on the rise. Agreements between neighboring countries to offer each other trade benefits can create larger markets and improve the economy of the region as a whole. But they can also lead to discrimination, especially when more efficient suppliers outside the regional agreements are prevented from supplying their goods and services.

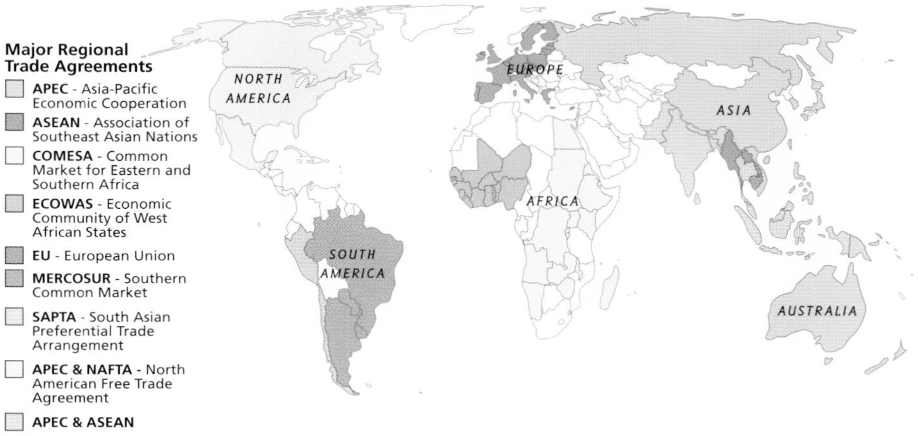

Trade Flow: Fuels

The leading exporters of fuel products are countries in the Middle East, Africa, Russia, and central and western Asia; all export more fuel than they consume. But intraregional energy trade is growing, with some of the key producers—Canada, Indonesia, Norway, and the United Kingdom, for example—located in regions that are net energy importers.

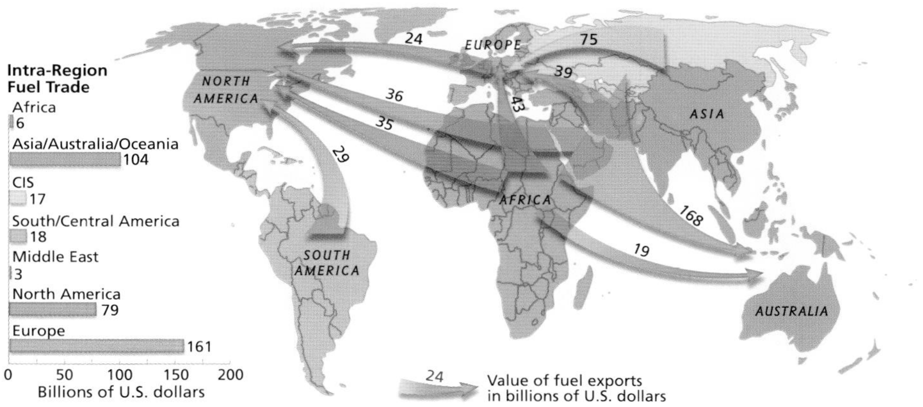

Trade Flow: Agricultural Products

The world trade in agricultural products is less concentrated than trade in fuels, with processed goods making up the majority. Agricultural products encounter high export barriers, which limit the opportunities for some exporters to expand into foreign markets. Reducing such barriers is a major challenge for governments that are engaged in agricultural trade negotiations.

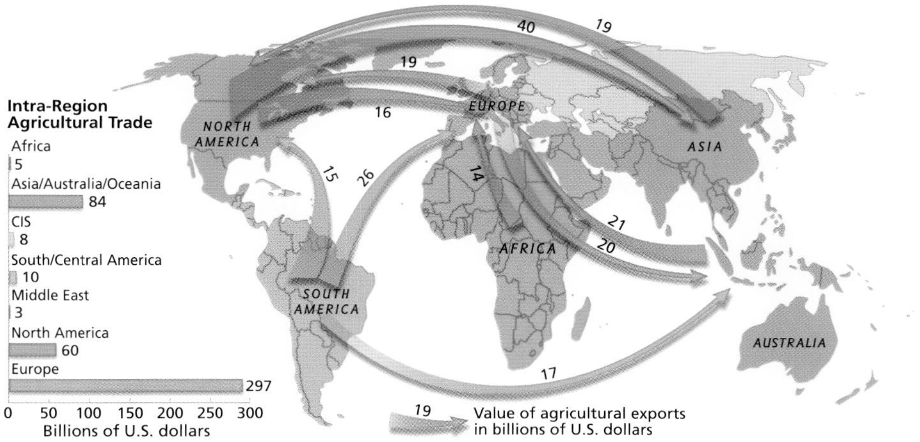

Top Merchandise Exporters and Importers

	PERCENTAGE OF WORLD TOTAL	VALUE (BILLIONS)
TOP EXPORTERS		
Germany	9.3	$971
United States	8.7	$904
China	7.3	$762
Japan	5.7	$596
France	4.4	$459
Netherlands	3.9	$401
United Kingdom	3.6	$378
Italy	3.5	$367
Canada	3.5	$360
Belgium	3.2	$330
Hong Kong (China)	2.8	$292
South Korea	2.7	$285
Russia	2.4	$245
Singapore	2.2	$230
Mexico	2.1	$214
TOP IMPORTERS		
United States	16.1	$1,733
Germany	7.2	$774
China	6.1	$660
Japan	4.8	$516
United Kingdom	4.7	$501
France	4.6	$496
Italy	3.5	$380
Netherlands	3.3	$358
Belgium	3.0	$320
Canada	3.0	$320
Hong Kong (China)	2.8	$301
Spain	2.6	$278
South Korea	2.4	$261
Mexico	2.2	$232
Singapore	1.9	$200

Top Commercial Services Exporters and Importers

(includes transportation, travel, and other services)

	PERCENTAGE OF WORLD TOTAL	VALUE (BILLIONS)
TOP EXPORTERS		
United States	14.6	$353
United Kingdom	7.6	$183
Germany	5.9	$143
France	4.7	$114
Japan	4.4	$107
Italy	3.9	$93
Spain	3.8	$91
China	3.4	$81
Netherlands	3.1	$75
India	2.8	$68
Hong Kong (China)	2.5	$60
Ireland	2.3	$55
Austria	2.2	$54
Belgium	2.2	$53
Canada	2.1	$51
TOP IMPORTERS		
United States	12.2	$289
Germany	8.4	$199
United Kingdom	6.4	$150
Japan	5.8	$136
France	4.4	$103
Italy	3.9	$92
China	3.6	$85
Netherlands	2.9	$69
Ireland	2.9	$68
India	2.9	$67
Spain	2.8	$65
Canada	2.6	$62
South Korea	2.5	$58
Austria	2.2	$52
Belgium	2.2	$51

THE POPULATION OF THE PLANET, which nearly tops six and a half billion, continues to increase by 230,000 new mouths a day. What will they eat? Where will the additional food come from?

Worldwide, agricultural production also continues to grow, but the food-producing regions are unevenly distributed around the globe. And though efforts to raise the levels of production even more (while relying less on chemical applications that damage the environment) are vitally important, they can go only so far in solving a great dilemma: How can we get more food to the millions of people who do not have enough to eat? Invariably, it is the economic situation of nations—which ones have food surpluses to sell; which ones need food and have or don't have enough money to buy it—that determines who goes hungry.

For people in the world's poorest regions, the situation is grim. The United Nations Food and Agriculture Organization reports that every night 815 million people in the developing world go to bed hungry and that malnourishment contributes to at least one-third of all child deaths. It also says that 13 million people in southern Africa face famine. Most cases of malnutrition are found in the developing countries of the tropics, where rapid population growth and other factors are depleting agricultural and financial resources.

Land Use and Commercial Agriculture

At various times and in various places, people began to till the land. The beginning of agriculture—cultivating soil, producing crops, and raising livestock—created a generally reliable food supply. Many historians believe that the planting and tending of crops also led to the first fixed settlements. Over thousands of years, the human population has grown in number, occupying more land and producing more food. Today most of the world's potential cropland is being cultivated. The challenge now is to balance population and land use. Human occupation, commercial agriculture, and Earth's ecosystems (including woodlands, forests, and deserts, which feed far fewer people per acre than croplands) all have to be sustained. People must eat, but they also need viable ecosystems in which to live.

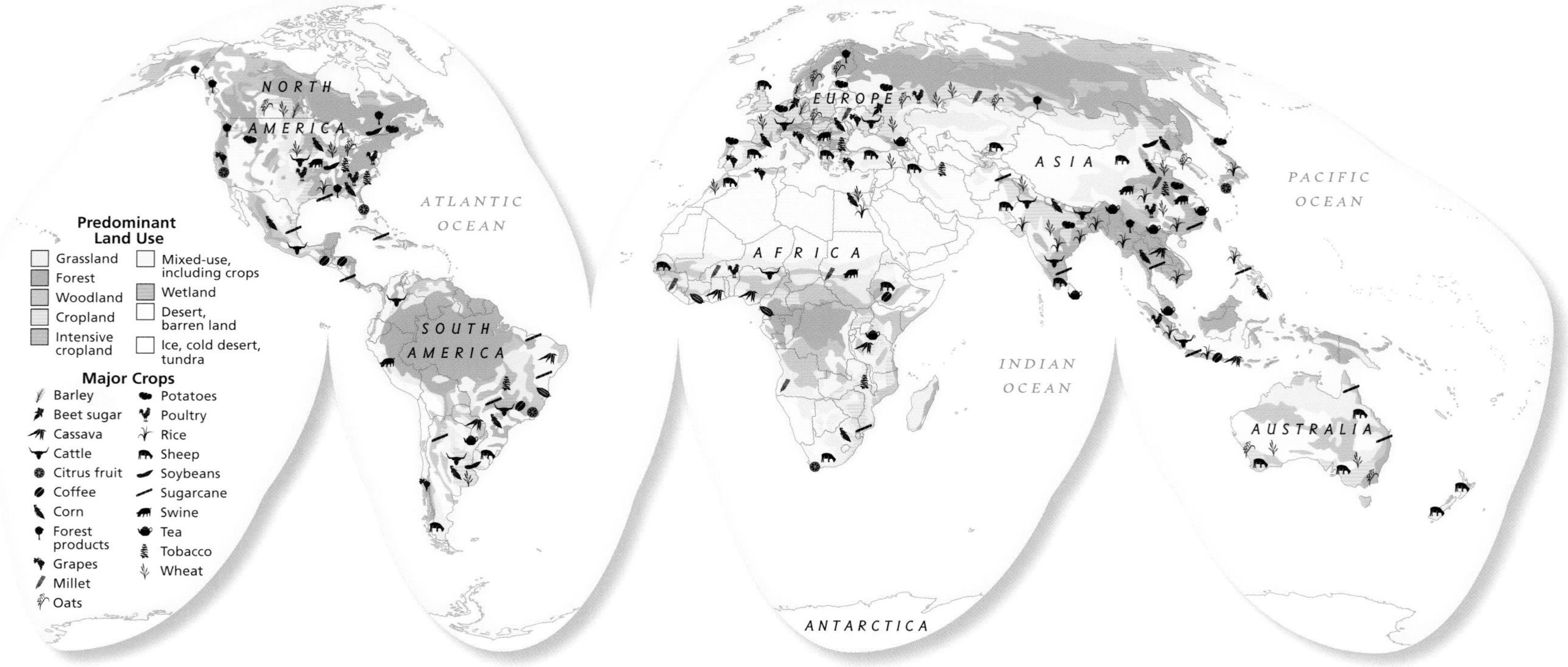

Fishing and Aquaculture

Fish, a low-cost source of protein, is assuming a more central role in the human diet. Since 1950, the world's yearly catch of ocean fish has more than quadrupled. And an increase in fish-farming ponds and commercial production of seaweed, collectively called aquaculture, has spawned one of the fastest-growing areas of food production; it now accounts for 40 percent of the fish people eat. About 90 percent of aquaculture occurs in developing countries, with China (where the technique began some 4,000 years ago) accounting for a bit more than two-thirds of total output. Experts project that by 2010, fish farming may overtake cattle ranching as a world food source.

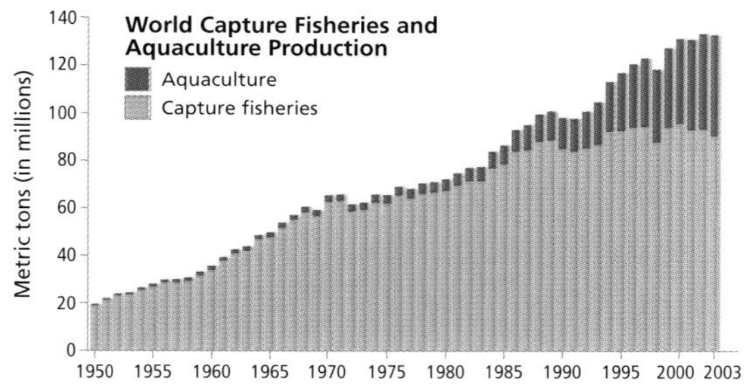

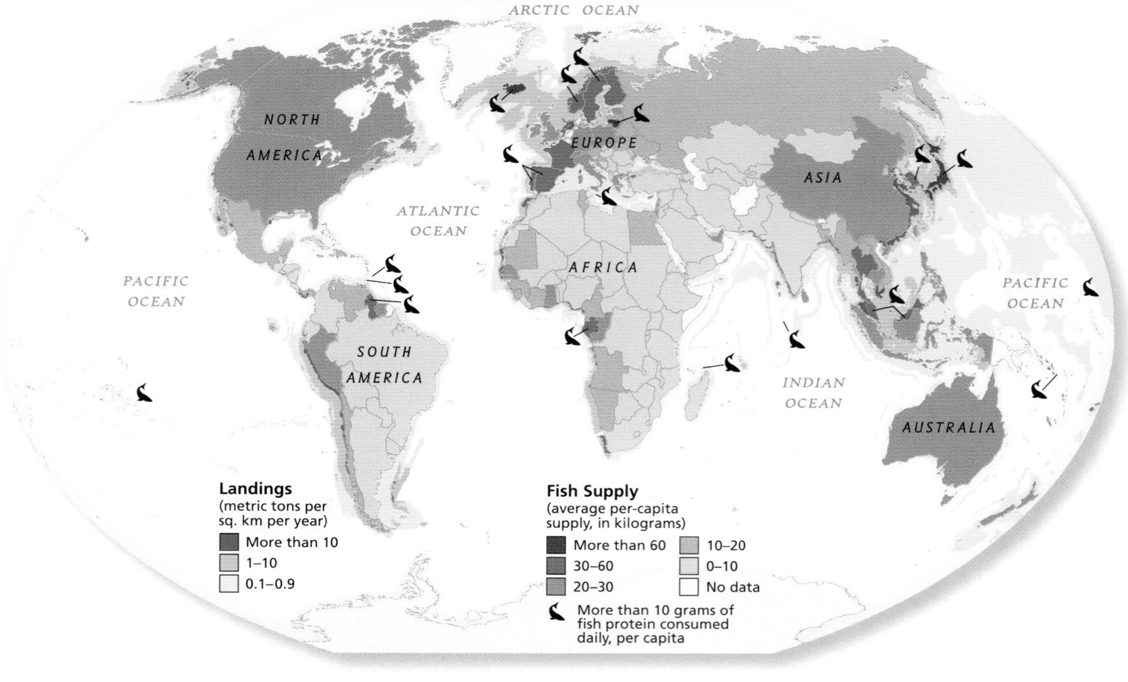

World Agricultural Production

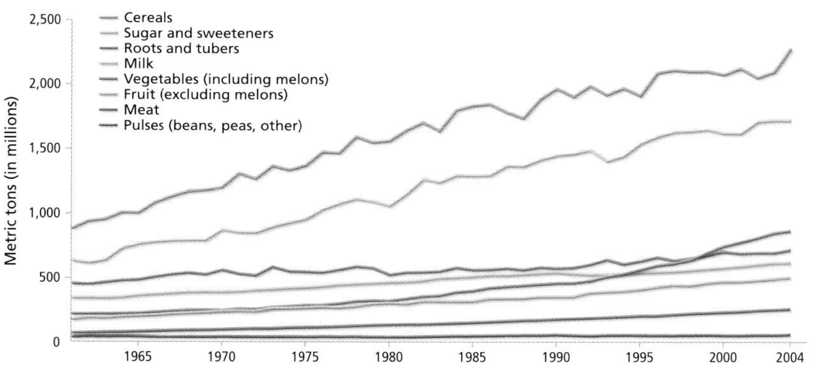

In the past few decades, world food production has more than kept pace with the burgeoning global population. Meat and cereals account for the most dramatic increases. New high-yield crops, additional irrigated land, and fertilizers have contributed to the rise in production. But there are related problems: Scientists warn that overuse of fertilizers causes nitrogen overload in Earth's waters. Insufficient use, in particular in Africa, has long-term adverse consequences for food security.

Undernourishment in the Developing World

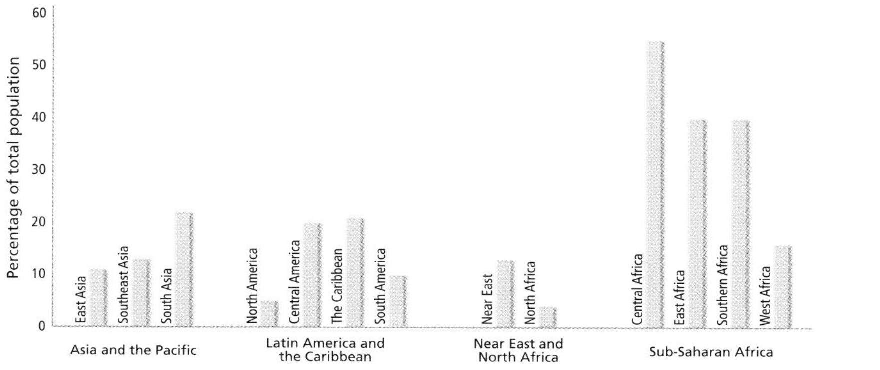

More food than ever is produced, but its distribution is uneven. Africa, in particular, is a continent of contrasts: Almost half the people in central, eastern, and southern Africa are undernourished, while a much lower percentage of people in the north and west are undernourished. The United Nations estimates that more than three-quarters of a billion people suffer from persistent malnourishment. Without access to adequate food, these populations cannot lead healthy, productive lives.

Caloric Supply

As shown at right, cereals (grains) dominate the caloric supply of people in Africa and Asia. Sugars, oils, and proteins comprise a much higher portion in other parts of the world, and the increasing consumption rates of these foods leads to obesity problems in many countries.

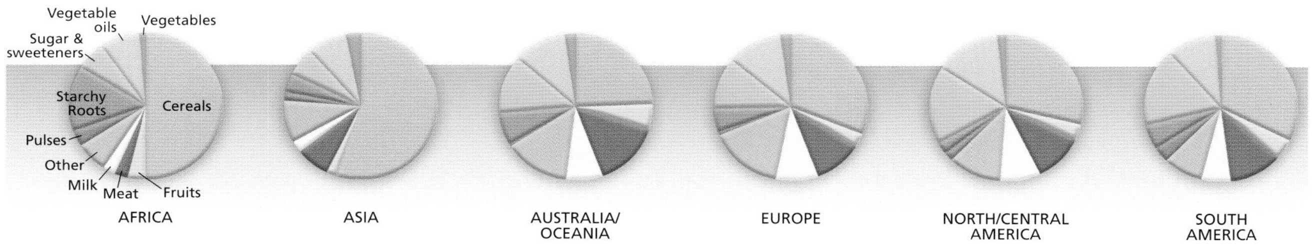

Indicates breakdown of per-capita calorie supply

World Grain Production

Humans rely on plant sources for carbohydrates, with grains (the edible parts of cereal plants) providing 80 percent of the food energy (calorie) supply. This means that the major grains—corn, wheat, and rice—are the foods that fuel humanity. Most cereal grains are grown in the Northern Hemisphere (see map), with the United States and France producing enough to be the largest exporters. Many parts of the world cannot grow cereal grains because they do not have productive farmland or the needed technology. Again and again throughout history, the actions of nations have been shaped by disparities in the supply and demand of grains, and by the knowledge that grains equal survival. Waverley Root, a food historian, once wrote: "[p]ossession of wheat or lack of it sways the destinies of nations; nor is it rare to find wheat being used as a political weapon.... [I]t is difficult to foresee any future in which it will not still exert a powerful influence on human history."

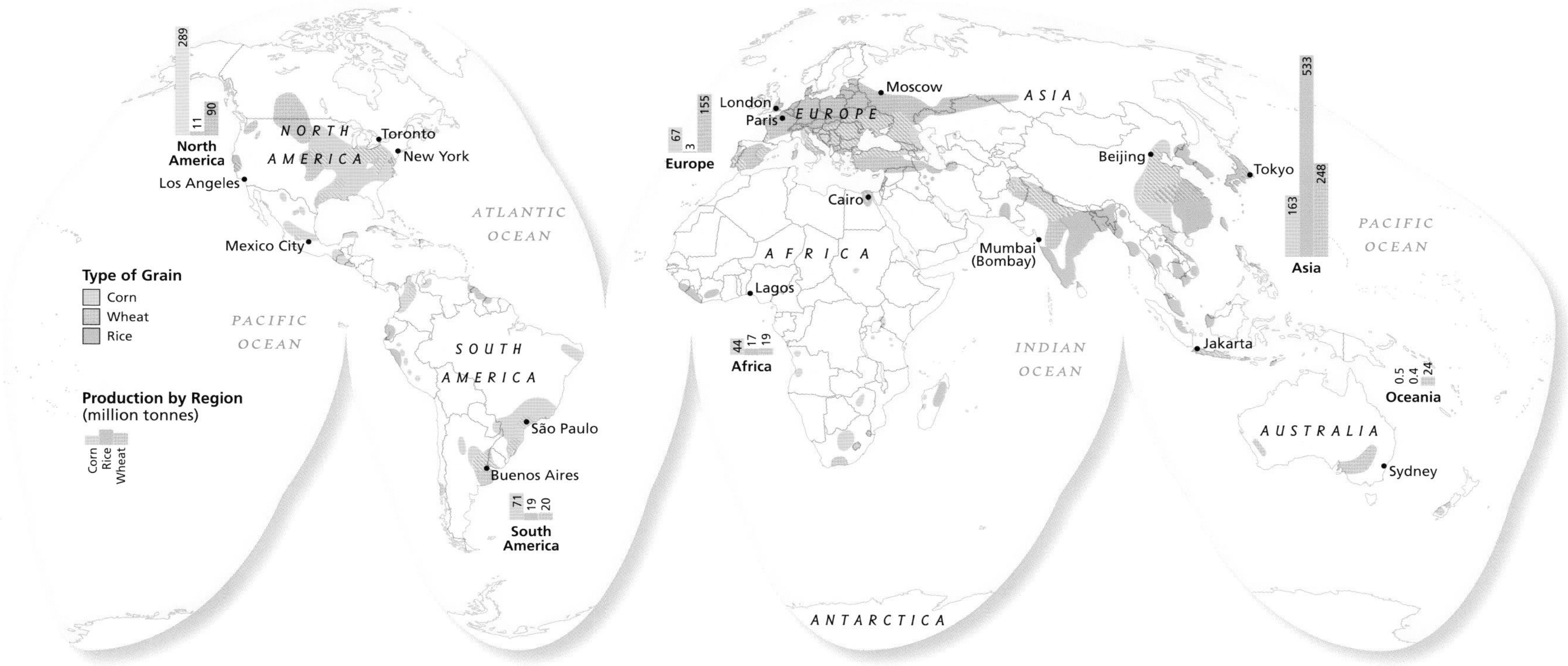

CORN
A staple in prehistoric Mexico and Peru, corn (or maize) is native to the New World. By the time Columbus's crew first tasted it, corn already was a hardy crop in much of North and South America.

WHEAT
Among the two oldest foods (barley is the other), wheat was important in ancient Mediterranean civilizations; today it is the most widely cultivated grain. Wheat grows best in temperate climates.

RICE
Originating in Asia many millennia ago, rice is the staple grain for about half the world's people. It is a labor-intensive plant that grows primarily in paddies (wet land) and thrives in the hot, humid tropics.

PRIMARY ENERGY comes in many different forms. Some fuels, such as animal dung and fuelwood, have a low energy content, while coal, natural gas, and oil contain much more. By adopting a common measurement that takes these differences into account, we can compare energy usage around the world. Today, the international standard is the "metric ton of oil equivalent" (toe), which translates all forms of energy (solid, liquid, or gas) to a common baseline. On this basis, global energy consumption is currently about 10.2 billion tons of oil equivalent a year.

The world's chief sources of energy are oil, natural gas, and coal, in that order. In each case, however, the major consuming countries are becoming increasingly dependent on imports. While oil has been shipped from producing countries to consumers for many years, increasing amounts of coal—mainly used for generating electricity—are on the move. Western Europe and countries like the United States and Japan are also beginning to import liquified natural gas, adding to their reliance on energy from elsewhere.

Production and consumption patterns show major differences worldwide. North America, with less than one-tenth of the world's population, uses about one-quarter of its energy. Countries with rapidly developing economies, like China and India, need more. As demand for energy grows, prices rise and alternative sources become more attractive.

Energy Production

WORLD ENERGY PRODUCTION BY TYPE

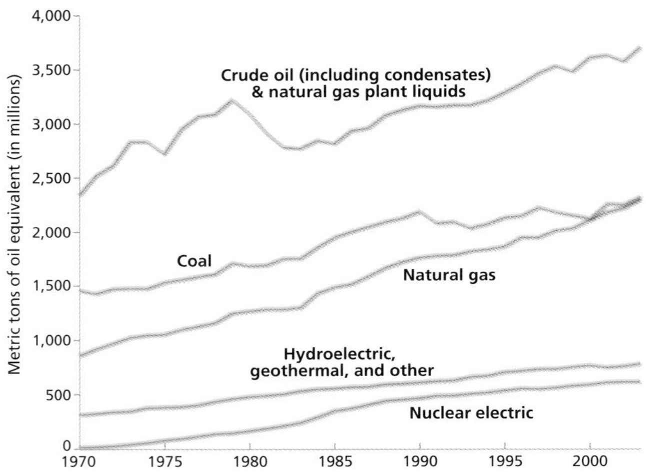

WORLD ENERGY PRODUCTION BY REGION

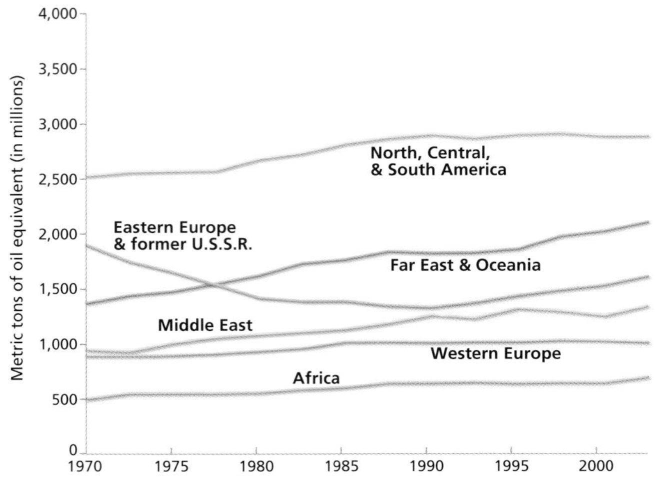

Fossil Fuel Extraction

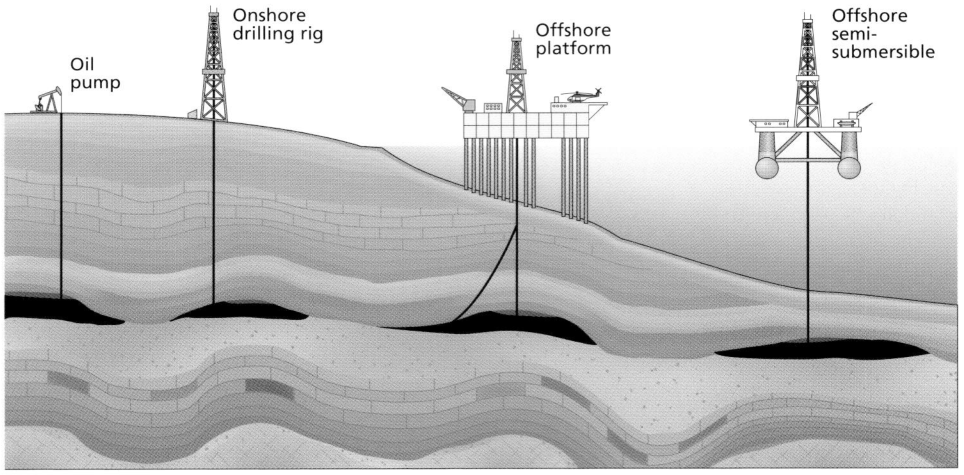

OIL EXTRACTION
Drilling-operation types depend on whether oil is in the ground or under the ocean. An onshore drilling rig uses a basic derrick; off-shore drilling is done with platform or semisubmersible designs (as shown above).

GAS EXTRACTION
Natural gas occurs in many of the same types of geologic structures as oil, and it is generally thought to have the same organic origins as oil. Gas-drilling and oil-drilling operations are essentially the same.

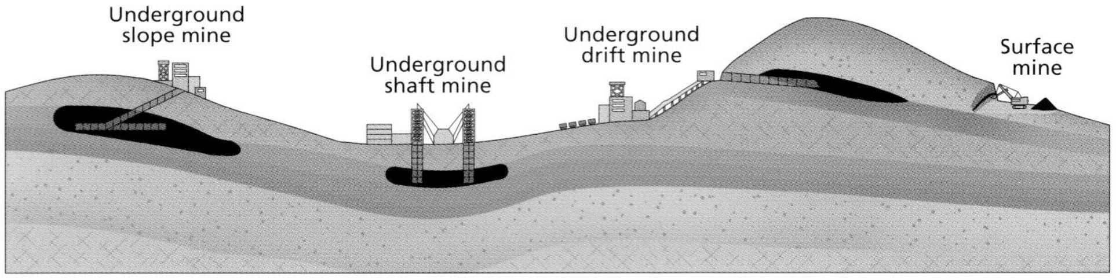

COAL MINING
The mining of coal made the industrial revolution possible, and coal still provides a major energy source. Once a labor-intensive process, coal mining is now heavily mechanized. An underground slope mine allows coal to be transported to the surface by a conveyor rather than an elevator. Underground drift mines and surface mines allow the easiest use of coal-cutting machinery.

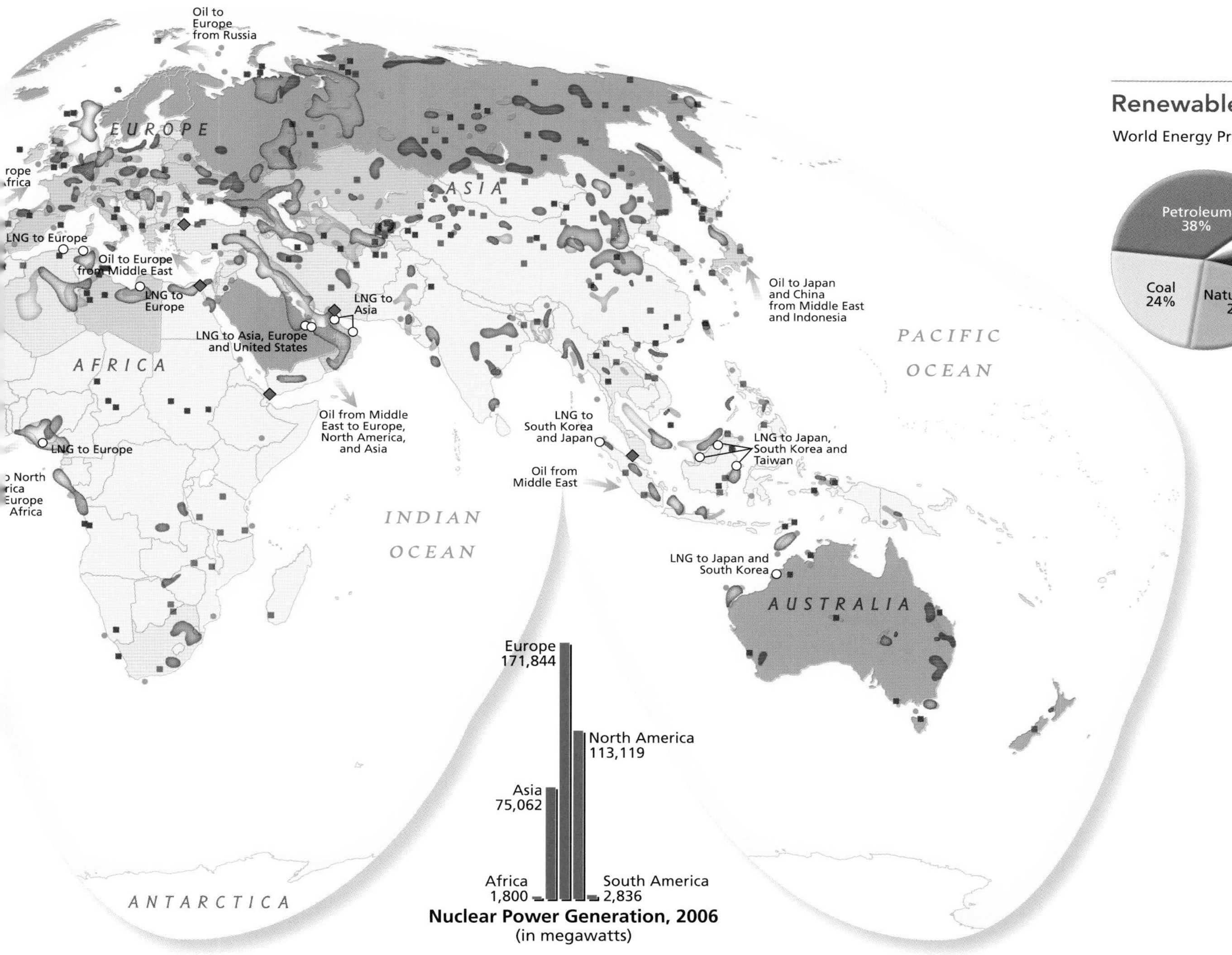

Renewable Resources

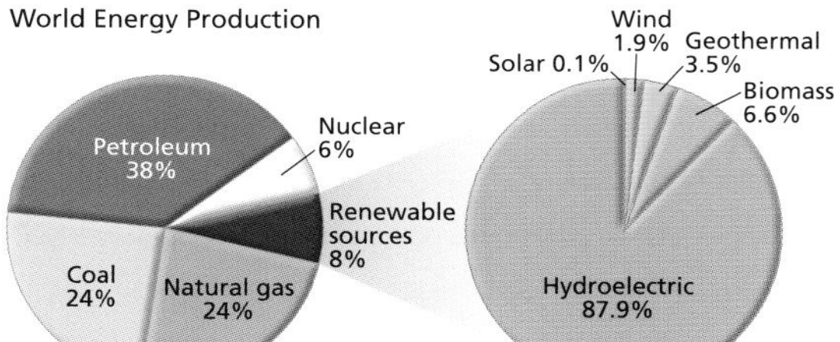

HYDROELECTRIC POWER
Hydroelectric plants in South America and the United States (Grand Coulee, in Washington State) are among the largest in the world. China has the greatest hydroelectric potential.

GEOTHERMAL POWER
Geothermal power plants pipe steam and hot water from the ground to make electricity. The world's largest installation—The Geysers—is in California.

SOLAR POWER
California holds the Earth's largest solar power arrays, one of which helps provide 160 megawatts of electric power.

WIND POWER
Harnessing the wind is the goal of the fastest-growing energy technology. In the U.S., the wind industry generates enough power each year to meet the electricity needs of one million people.

Biomass, Hydroelectric, and Geothermal Power

Burning biomass to release energy is a carbon-neutral process (i.e., it does not cause a net increase in carbon dioxide); the carbon is already part of the cycle. Biomass would require extensive conversion, however. Hydroelectric power is potentially the major renewable energy source, and more than 30 percent of the potential sites around the world have not yet been developed. In many geothermal sites it is possible to drill wells for a steady supply of steam, which can then be used to run turbines to generate electricity.

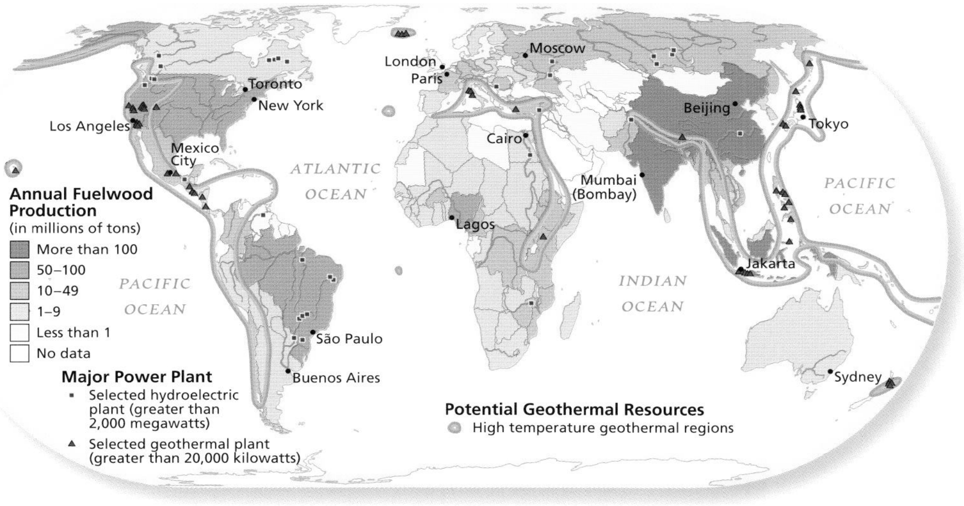

Wind and Solar Power

Wind, solar, tidal, wave, and other technologies are promising sources of natural, renewable energy. As the technology and economics of wind power improve, certain regions of the world could become "Saudi Arabias of wind." Solar radiation received on Earth each year corresponds to 3,000 times global energy consumption, but the problem with solar energy, just as with many other renewable energy resources, is their intermittent nature and the lack of storage technologies.

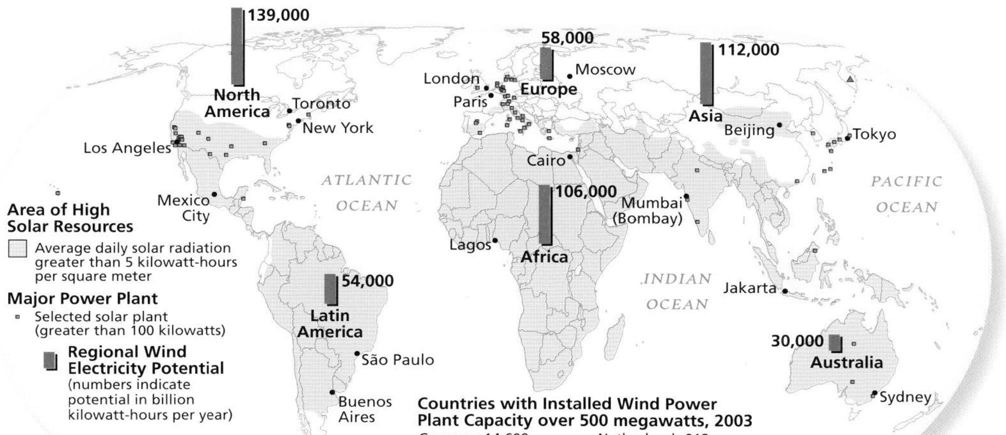

Countries with Installed Wind Power Plant Capacity over 500 megawatts, 2003

Germany 14,609	Netherlands 912
United States 6,374	Italy 904
Spain 6,202	Japan 686
Denmark 3,110	United Kingdom 649
India 2,110	China 568

Minerals

THE SPATIAL PATTERN of world mineral production is the result of several factors: geology, climate, economic systems, and social preferences. This pattern can be seen on the map at right, which locates major production and processing sites for various mineral commodities (see below for profiles on 18 important minerals).

Plate movements, volcanism, and sedimentation are geologic processes that form valuable concentrations of minerals. The same geologic forces that formed the Andes, for example, are responsible for the porphyry copper deposits along South America's Pacific coast. Other processes concentrate copper in sedimentary basins and in volcanic arcs. Climatic factors, such as the tropical conditions that contribute to bauxite formation, are also important.

Mineral consumption by industries is positively correlated with income and differs greatly among countries. Developed nations use larger volumes of materials and a wider variety of mineral commodities than less developed countries. In developed nations, annual copper use is typically 5 to 10 kilograms per person; for less developed ones, usage is only a few kilograms per person. Recent economic growth has led to greater demand for many mineral resources. Meeting that need without causing harm to the environment will be one of the major challenges for societies in the 21st century.

World Mineral Production

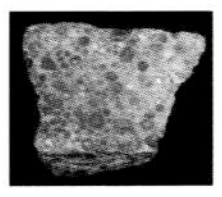

Aluminum (Al) Bauxite, the principal ore of aluminum, is an aggregate of millimeter- to centimeter-size oval structures, composed of aluminum hydroxide, that form in areas of deep and prolonged tropical weathering of aluminum-rich parent materials. World production of bauxite was 156 million tons in 2004. Australia was the largest producer (56 million), followed by Brazil, Guinea, and China. Alumina (Al_2O_3), an intermediate product, is made by refining bauxite and then smelting to make aluminum metal; both of these steps are very energy intensive. China, the United States, and Russia have the largest aluminum smelting capacities. In 2004, the world production of aluminum was estimated at 28.9 million tons.

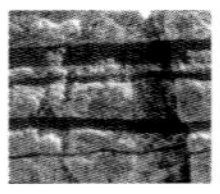

Chromium (Cr) Chromite ($FeCr_2O_4$) is the principal ore mineral of chromium. Black chromite forms in layered, iron- and magnesium-rich igneous deposits (as in this photo), which contributed nearly half the world's 2004 production, estimated at more than 17 million tons. South Africa has long been the largest producer on the planet. Kazakhstan and India together produced another 33 percent. The main use of chromium is in the manufacture of stainless and heat-resistant steels. Chromite is also used in the production of chromium chemicals and in acid-resistant refractories.

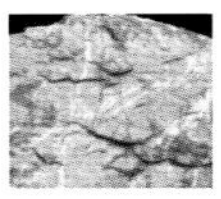

Copper (Cu) Chalcopyrite ($CuFeS_2$), the principal ore of copper, occurs as veins and disseminations in igneous and sedimentary host rocks. Copper is also mined as other sulfides, the native metal, and oxides. In 2004, world mine production of copper metal was 14.5 million tons. Chile was the leading producer (5.4 million tons), followed by the U.S. (1.2 million), and Peru (1 million). Copper is used for electric and electronic products, in construction of buildings, and as an alloy metal.

Diamond (gem and industrial) Diamonds are used both as gems and as materials to increase the hardness of cutting tools. Natural diamonds are generally brought to the Earth's surface by unusual volcanic eruptions, gas-charged igneous melts that originate at depths of 150+ km in the Earth. The map locates the major producers of natural gems and industrial diamonds. Diamonds can also be produced synthetically, and about 88 percent of industrial diamonds now have this origin. Industrial diamond mining produced 70 million carats in 2004, more than 90 percent of which came from the Congo, Australia, Russia, Botswana, and South Africa.

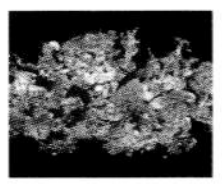

Gold (Au) Native gold and electrum, an alloy with silver, are the most common forms and precipitate from hot, water-rich fluids in the Earth. Historically, gold was used as money or as a backup for paper money. Today, no major country backs its currency with gold, but private investors may hold gold as a hedge against economic uncertainty. Gold is also used in jewelry, as a dental material, and in electronic equipment. South Africa was the largest producer of mined gold in 2004 (344 tons), followed by the U.S., Australia, and China. Total world production in 2004 was estimated at 2,470 tons.

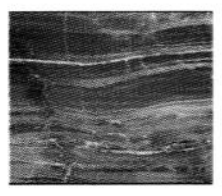

Iron Ore and Steel Iron (Fe) is the 4th most abundant element in the Earth's crust and occurs in a wide variety of oxide (magnetite and hematite), hydroxide (goethite), sulfide (pyrite, pyrrhotite), carbonate (siderite), and silicate minerals found in sedimentary rocks. Nearly all the 2004 world production of 1.25 billion tons came from iron oxide and hydroxide deposits. The largest producers were China, Brazil, and Australia. In 2004, world crude steel production was over one billion tons. China, the EU countries, and Japan were the main producers.

Lead (Pb) Galena (PbS) is the principal ore mineral of lead. In 2004, world mine production of lead was 3.1 million tons. China was the largest producer (950,000 tons), followed by Australia and the United States. Due to lead's toxicity, the number of lead-containing products has been reduced in recent years, and automobile lead-acid batteries are effectively recycled. This effort has reduced the consumption of primary (new) lead in the United States and Europe, but China's use continues to expand. Lead is also used in ammunition, solder, in television glass, and in the radiation shields for x-ray equipment.

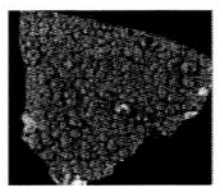

Manganese (Mn) This element is essential to steel making as an additive to remove sulfur and excess oxygen. It is also employed as an alloying element and is used in dry-cell batteries. Mn geochemistry is similar to iron's; however, it is never mined from the same deposits. World production was 11 million tons in 2004. The largest producers are South Africa and Gabon. Australia comes in third, followed by Brazil, Ghana, and India. China does not produce much, and must import manganese.

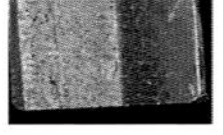

Nickel (Ni) Two very different types of deposits are the sources for nickel. In sulfide deposits found in ultramafic rock complexes, nickel occurs primarily in the mineral pentlandite ($(Fe,Ni)_9S_8$). It is also produced from oxide and silicate minerals in thick soils that form over certain rock types in tropical environments. World mine production was 1.4 million tons in 2004. Russia (the top producer, at 315,000 tons) and Canada produce nickel from sulfide ores; Australia, Indonesia, and New Caledonia rely on the deeply weathered soils. Nickel is used to make stainless steel and in electroplating.

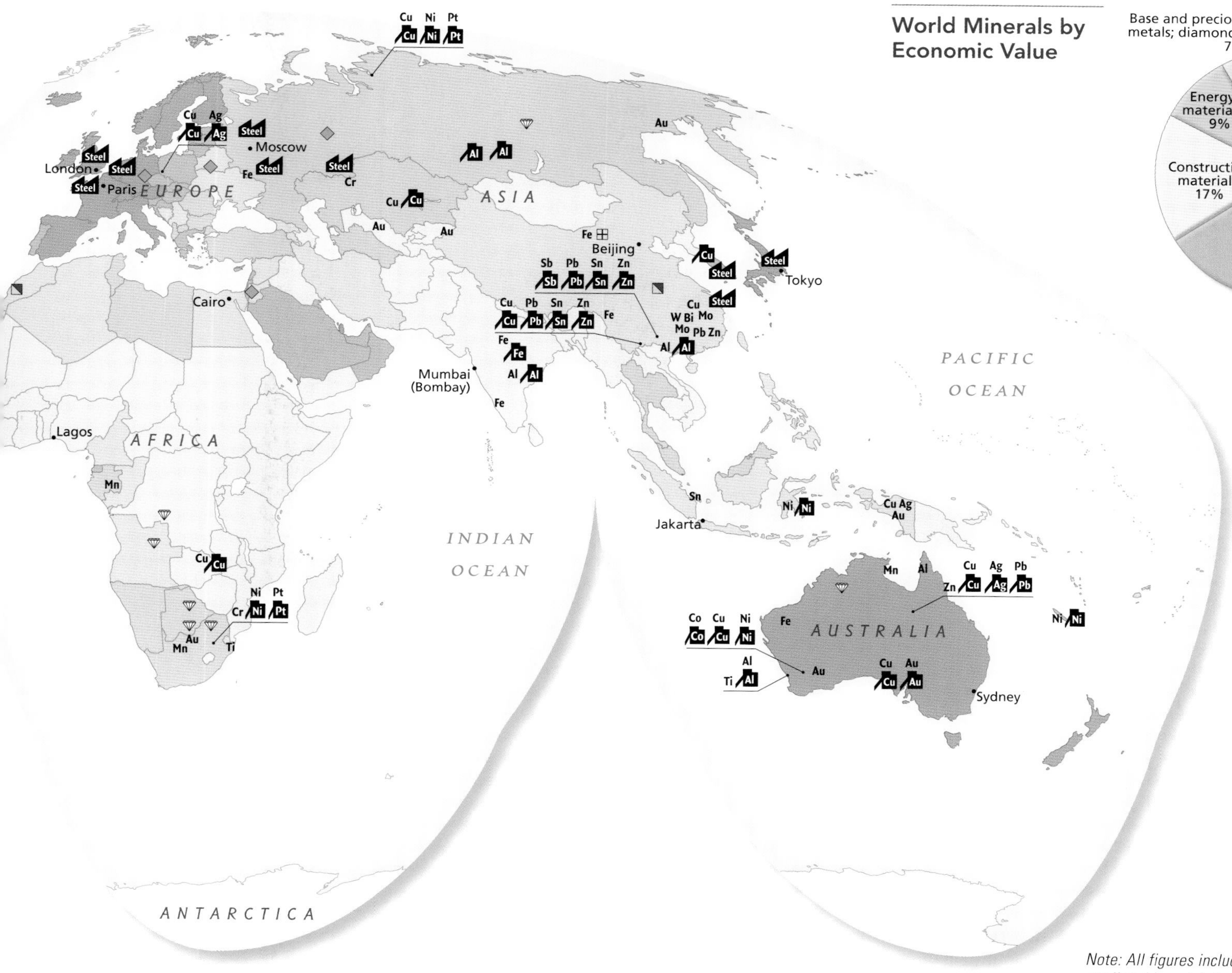

World Minerals by Economic Value

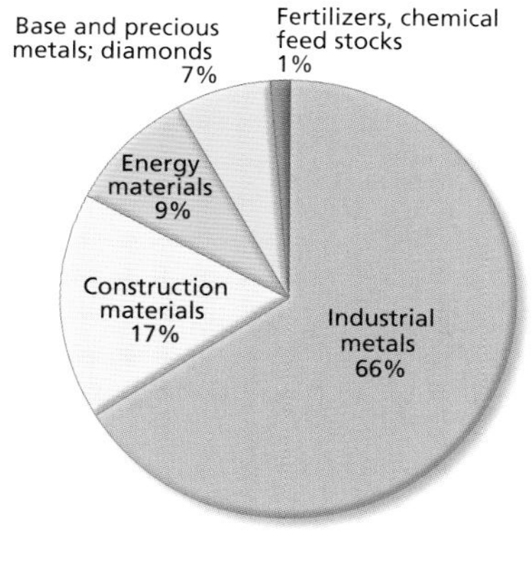

Note: All figures included in descriptions below are listed in metric tons.

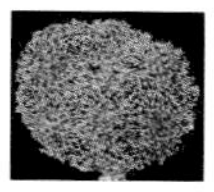

Phosphate Rock (P) This substance is the primary ore needed to make phosphoric acid, which is used in the production of certain fertilizers. Most phosphate deposits initially formed when phosphorus-rich deep-ocean waters upwelled onto tropical continental shelves, and phosphate-rich sediments were deposited through biologic activity. In 2004, the world production of phosphate rock was 138 million tons; the United States was the leading producer (37 million tons). China (25 million) was second, while Morocco and Western Sahara together accounted for 23 million tons.

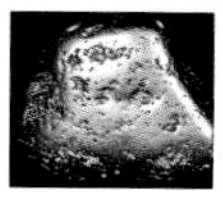

Platinum-Group Metals (Pt, Pd, Ru, Rh, Ir, Os) These substances are used in catalytic converters that clean the exhaust from cars; they are also used in jewelry and in chemotherapy for cancer. World mine production of platinum and palladium in 2004 was 218 tons and 190 tons, respectively, and came from mafic igneous rock complexes, usually of Precambrian age. South Africa was the leading producer of platinum (163 tons), followed by Russia (36 tons). Russia produced 74 tons of palladium, while South Africa mined 78 tons. Other important producers of platinum-group metals are the U.S. and Canada.

Potash (K) This term is the industrial name for a group of water-soluble salts that contain potassium. The main sources are deposits that include mixtures of the minerals halite ($NaCl$), sylvite (KCl), and carnallite ($KMgCl_3 \bullet 6H_2O$), along with other potassium-, magnesium-, and bromine-bearing minerals and saline brines. Most is used in fertilizer, while the remainder is employed in the production of chemicals. Total 2004 production of 30 million tons came mainly from Canada (9.5), Russia (4.7), Belarus (4.65), and Germany (3.67 million). Israel and Jordan produce significant amounts of potash from the Dead Sea.

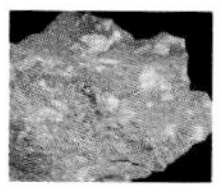

Rare Earths (REE) This group of 17 metals ranges from lanthanum (La) to lutetium (Lu) in the periodic table of elements. Rare earth metals are used in the making of a wide variety of products, including chemical catalysts for petroleum refining, rechargeable batteries, phosphors for TV and computer screens, and superalloys. These elements are indeed "rare," and concentrated only in unusual igneous bodies. World mine production of rare earth oxides was 102,000 tons in 2004 with China producing the great majority (95,000) of these.

Silver (Ag) This substance has the highest electrical conductivity of all elements. It occurs in native form; mixed with native gold in electrum; as simple sulfides (argentite, Ag_2S); as complex antimony- and arsenic-bearing minerals; and as a trace constituent in galena. Silver is used for coins, electrical and electronic components, jewelry, tableware, and in film photography (digital cameras are causing a reduced demand). In 2004, world mine production was 19,500 tons. Mexico, which mined 2,850 tons of silver, was the largest producer; it was followed by Peru (2,800 tons) and China (2,600 tons).

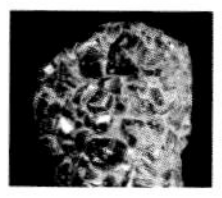

Tin (Sn) The most common use of tin is as a coating to prevent oxidation of a covered metal, such as steel in "tin cans." When alloyed with other metals, tin makes solder, pewter, and bronze. Window glass is manufactured by floating molten glass on molten tin. Organo-tin chemicals are used as pesticides, fungicides, and wood preservatives. The major ore mineral of tin is cassiterite (SnO_2). China, which mined 100,000 tons in 2004, was the world's largest producer that year. Indonesia (70,000 tons) and Peru (40,000 tons) were the second and third largest producers. Total world production in 2004 was 250,000 tons.

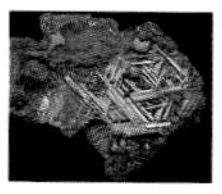

Titanium (Ti) More than 95 percent of titanium is consumed as TiO_2 pigment; the rest is processed to make titanium metal or sponge. Because titanium metal is light, has high strength, and resists corrosion, it is used in aerospace, marine, medical, and military applications. Russia, Japan, and Kazakhstan were the largest makers of titanium sponge in 2004. The titanium-bearing minerals ilmenite ($FeTiO_3$) and rutile (TiO_2), originally formed in igneous rocks, are common components in beach and dune sands and are processed into TiO_2 pigment used in paints and plastics. Australia (1.1 million tons) and South Africa (also 1.1 million) were the largest producers of titanium-bearing mineral concentrates in 2004.

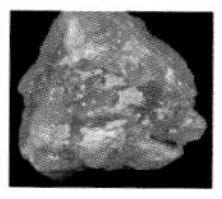

Tungsten (formerly wolfram) (W) The main use of tungsten is in tungsten-carbide cutting tools. Because of its high melting point, this substance is added to certain steels to give them strength at high temperatures. It is also used in light-bulb filaments. Tungsten mainly occurs in two types of deposits—either in skarns than contain scheelite ($CaWO4$), or in veins that contain wolframite ($Fe,Mn(WO_4)$. In 2004, China produced 53,000 tons of tungsten, followed by Russia, with 3,500 tons. World production was 60,000 tons.

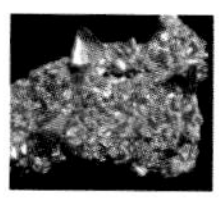

Zinc (Zn) The largest use of zinc is as a coating for steel; zinc-coated, "galvanized" steel resists rust and corrosion. Zinc is also used to make brass, solder, and batteries, and it is added to soil, rubber, and cosmetics. In 2004, world mine production was 9.1 million tons. The largest producers were China (2 million), Peru (1.4 million), and Australia (1.3 million). Canada and the United States were also significant producers, with 90 percent of U.S. production coming from a single mine in Alaska. Sphalerite (ZnS) is the principal ore mineral of zinc.

MOST ENVIRONMENTAL DAMAGE is due to human activity. Some harmful actions are inadvertent—the release, for example, of chlorofluorocarbons (CFCs), once thought to be inert gases, into the atmosphere. Others are deliberate and include such acts as the disposal of sewage into rivers.

Among the root causes of human-induced damage are excessive consumption (mainly in industrialized countries) and rapid population growth (primarily in the developing nations). So, even though scientists may develop products and technologies that have no adverse effects on the environment, their efforts will be muted if both population and consumption continue to increase worldwide.

Socioeconomic and environmental indicators can reveal much about long-term trends; unfortunately, such data are not collected routinely in many countries. With respect to urban environmental quality, suitable indicators would include electricity consumption, numbers of automobiles, and rates of land conversion from rural to urban. The rapid conversion of countryside to built-up areas during the last 25 to 50 years is a strong indicator that change is occurring at an ever-quickening pace.

Many types of environmental stress are interrelated and may have far-reaching consequences. Global warming, for one, will likely increase water scarcity, desertification, deforestation, and coastal flooding (due to rising sea level)—all of which can have a significant impact on human populations.

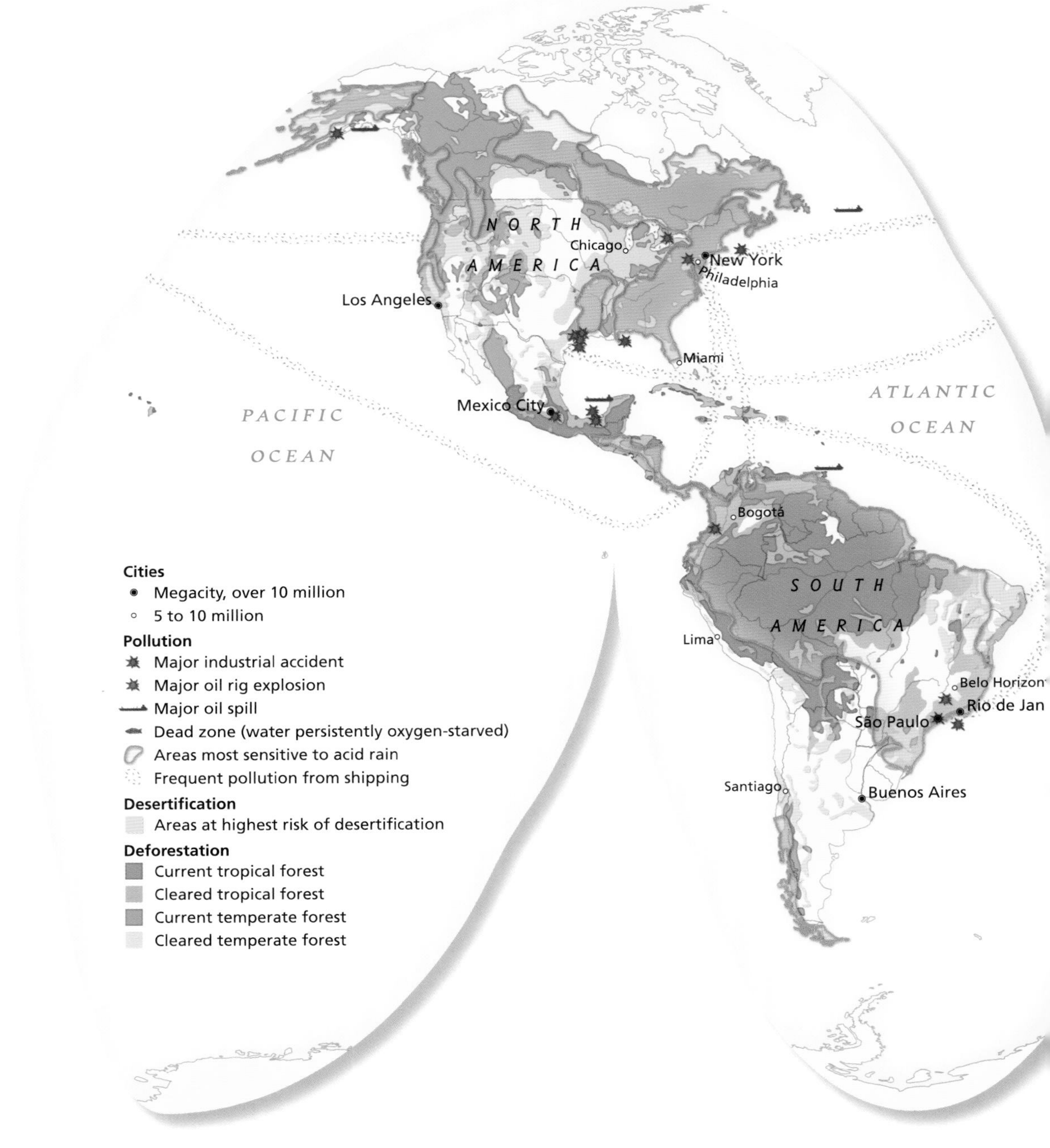

Global Climate Change

The world's climate is constantly changing—over decades, centuries, and millennia. Currently, several lines of reasoning support the idea that humans are likely to live in a much warmer world before the end of this century. Atmospheric concentrations of carbon dioxide and other "greenhouse gases" are now well above historical levels, and simulation models predict that these gases will result in a warming of the lower atmosphere (particularly in polar regions) but a cooling of the stratosphere. Experimental evidence supports these predictions.

Indeed, throughout the last decade the globally averaged annual surface temperature was higher than the hundred-year mean. Model simulations of the impacts of this warming—and studies indicating significant reductions already occurring in polar permafrost and sea ice cover—are so alarming that most scientists and many policy people believe that immediate action must be taken to slow the changes.

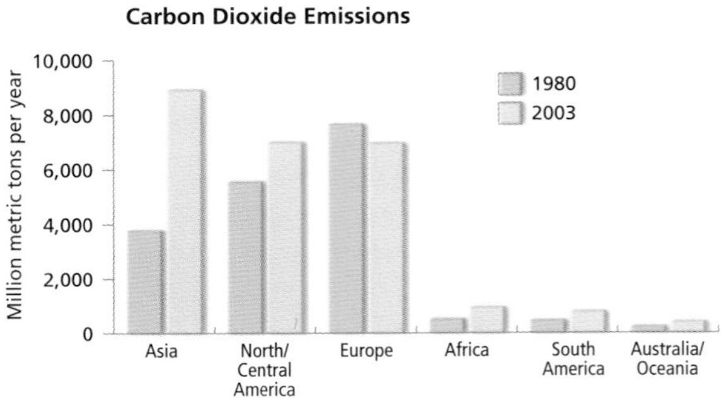

Depletion of the Ozone Layer

The ozone layer in the stratosphere has long shielded the biosphere from harmful solar ultraviolet radiation. Since the 1970s, however, the layer has been thinning over Antarctica—and more recently elsewhere. If the process continues, there will be significant effects on human health, including more cases of skin cancer and eye cataracts, and on biological systems. Fortunately, scientific understanding of the phenomenon came rather quickly.

Beginning in the 1950s, increasing amounts of CFCs (and other gases with similar properties) were released into the atmosphere. CFCs are chemically inert in the lower atmosphere but decompose in the stratosphere, subsequently destroying ozone. This understanding provided the basis for successful United Nations actions (Vienna Convention, 1985; Montréal Protocol, 1987) to phase out these gases.

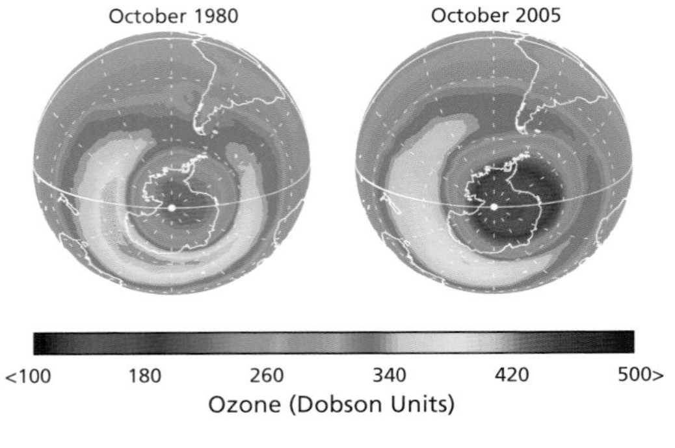

Pollution

People know that water is not always pure and that beaches may be closed to bathers due to raw sewage. An example of serious contamination is the Minamata, Japan, disaster of the 1950s. More than a hundred people died and thousands were paralyzed after they ate fish containing mercury discharged from a local factory. Examples of water and soil pollution also include the contamination of groundwater, salinization of irrigated lands in semiarid regions, and the so-called chemical time bomb issue, where accumulated toxins are suddenly mobilized following a change in external conditions. Preventing and mitigating such problems requires the modernization of industrial plants, additional staff training, a better understanding of the problems, the development of more effective policies, and greater public support.

Urban air quality remains a serious problem, particularly in developing countries. In some developed countries, successful control measures have improved air quality over the past 50 years; in others, trends have actually reversed, with brown haze often hanging over metropolitan areas.

Solid and hazardous waste disposal is a universal urban problem, and the issue is on many political agendas. In the world's poorest countries, "garbage pickers" (usually women and children) are symbols of abject poverty. In North America, toxic wastes are frequently transported long distances. But transport introduces the risk of highway and rail accidents, causing serious local contamination.

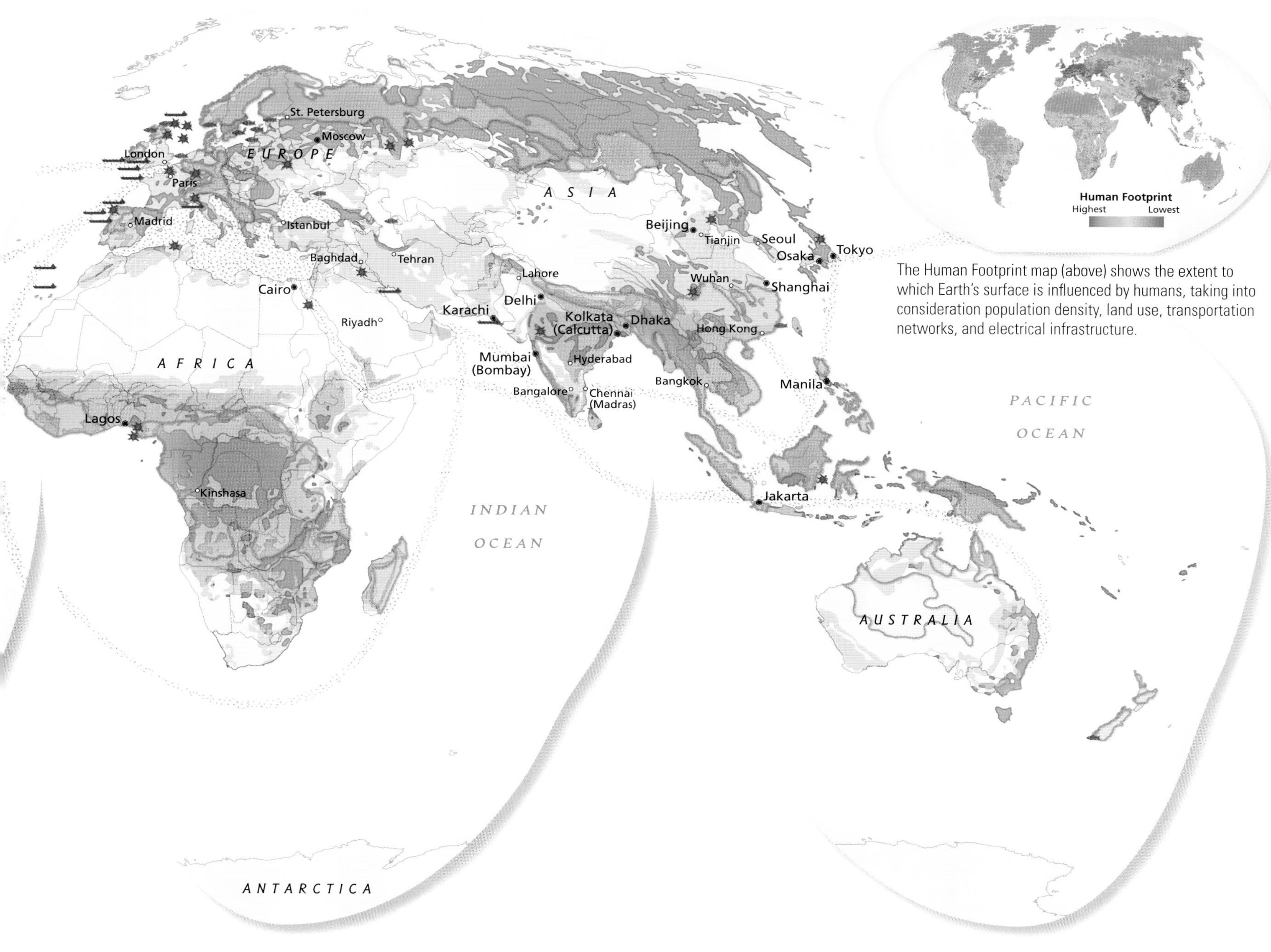

The Human Footprint map (above) shows the extent to which Earth's surface is influenced by humans, taking into consideration population density, land use, transportation networks, and electrical infrastructure.

Water Scarcity

Shortages of drinking water are increasing in many parts of the world, and studies indicate that by the year 2025, one billion people in northern China, Afghanistan, Pakistan, Iraq, Egypt, Tunisia, and other areas will face "absolute drinking water scarcity." But water is also needed by industry and agriculture, in hydroelectric-power production, and for transport. With increasing population, industrialization, and global warming, the situation can only worsen.

Water scarcity has already become a major brake on development in many countries, including Poland, Singapore, and parts of North America. In countries where artesian wells are pumping groundwater more rapidly than it can be replaced, water is actually being mined. In river basins where water is shared by several jurisdictions, social tensions will increase. This is particularly so in the Middle East, North Africa, and East Africa, where the availability of fresh water is less than 1,300 cubic yards (1,000 cu m) per capita per annum; water-rich countries such as Iceland, New Zealand, and Canada enjoy more than a hundred times as much.

Irrigation can be a particularly wasteful use of water. Some citrus-growing nations, for example, are exporting not only fruit but also so-called virtual water, which includes the water inside the fruit as well as the wasted irrigation water that drains away from the orchards. Many individuals and organizations believe that water scarcity is the major environmental issue of the 21st century.

Soil Degradation and Desertification

Deserts exist where rainfall is too little and too erratic to support life except in a few favored localities. Even in these "oases," occasional sandstorms may inhibit agricultural activity. In semiarid zones, lands can easily become degraded or desert-like if they are overused or subject to long or frequent drought. The Sahel of Africa faced this situation in the 1970s and early 1980s, but rainfall subsequently returned to normal, and some of the land recovered.

Often, an extended drought over a wide area can trigger desertification if the land has already been degraded by human actions. Causes of degradation include overgrazing, overcultivation, deforestation, soil erosion, overconsumption of groundwater, and the salinization/waterlogging of irrigated lands.

An emerging issue is the effect of climate warming on desertification. Warming will probably lead to more drought in more parts of the world. Glaciers would begin to disappear, and the meltwater flowing through semiarid downstream areas would diminish.

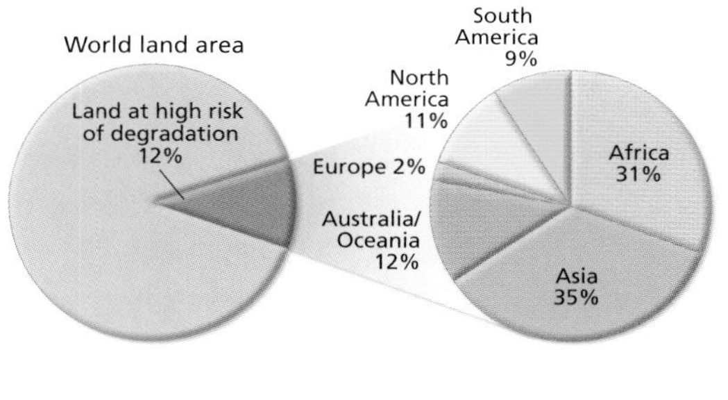

Deforestation

Widespread deforestation in the wet tropics is largely the result of short-term and unsustainable uses. In Mexico, Brazil, and Peru, only 30, 42, and 45 percent (respectively) of the total land still has a closed forest cover. International agencies such as FAO, UNEP, UNESCO, WWF/IUCN, and others are working to improve the situation through education, restoration, and land protection. Venezuela enjoys a very high level of forest protection (63 percent); by comparison, Russia protects just 2 percent.

The loss of forests has contributed to the atmospheric buildup of carbon dioxide (a greenhouse gas), changes in rainfall patterns (in Brazil at least), soil erosion, and soil nutrient losses. Deforestation in the wet tropics, where more than half of the world's species live, is the main cause of biodiversity loss.

In contrast to the tropics, the forest cover in the temperate zones has increased slightly in the last 50 years because of the adoption of conservation practices and because abandoned farmland has been replaced by forest.

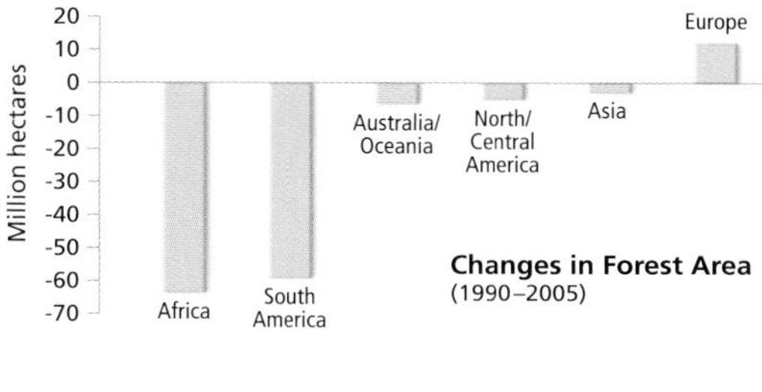

Protected Areas

IN RECENT YEARS, environmental groups and world organizations have identified certain sites and land areas whose value is so great, and status so critical, that they require special protection.

This protection takes various forms. UNESCO's World Heritage Committee has identified more than 800 sites that are of great cultural or natural value. Some are very famous: Stonehenge, the Great Wall of China, the Taj Mahal, the Great Barrier Reef, and the Grand Canyon, for example. Others are monuments to important and sometimes tragic chapters in history: Auschwitz in Poland and the Senegalese island of Gorée, which was for 400 years the largest slaving station on the African coast. Some sites are threatened natural features of great value: the Danube Delta in Romania, for instance, and Lake Baikal in Russia.

Conservationists have identified 34 "biodiversity hotspots" (see World Biodiversity, pp. 42-43) that make up less than 2.5 percent of Earth's land surface but are the only remaining habitats for 50 percent of all plant species and 42 percent of all nonfish vertebrates. Currently, the average protected area coverage of hotspots is 10 percent of their original extent.

Though "protected areas" vary greatly in their objectives, the extent to which they are integrated into the wider landscape, and the effectiveness with which they are managed, provide powerful evidence of a nation's commitment to conservation.

Designated Protected Areas

An array of overlapping conventions designed to preserve everything from wetlands, seas, and wilderness to birds and biogenetic reserves protects approximately 11.5 percent of Earth's land area. In contrast, less than one percent of the total ocean area is protected.

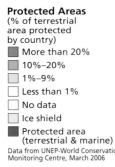

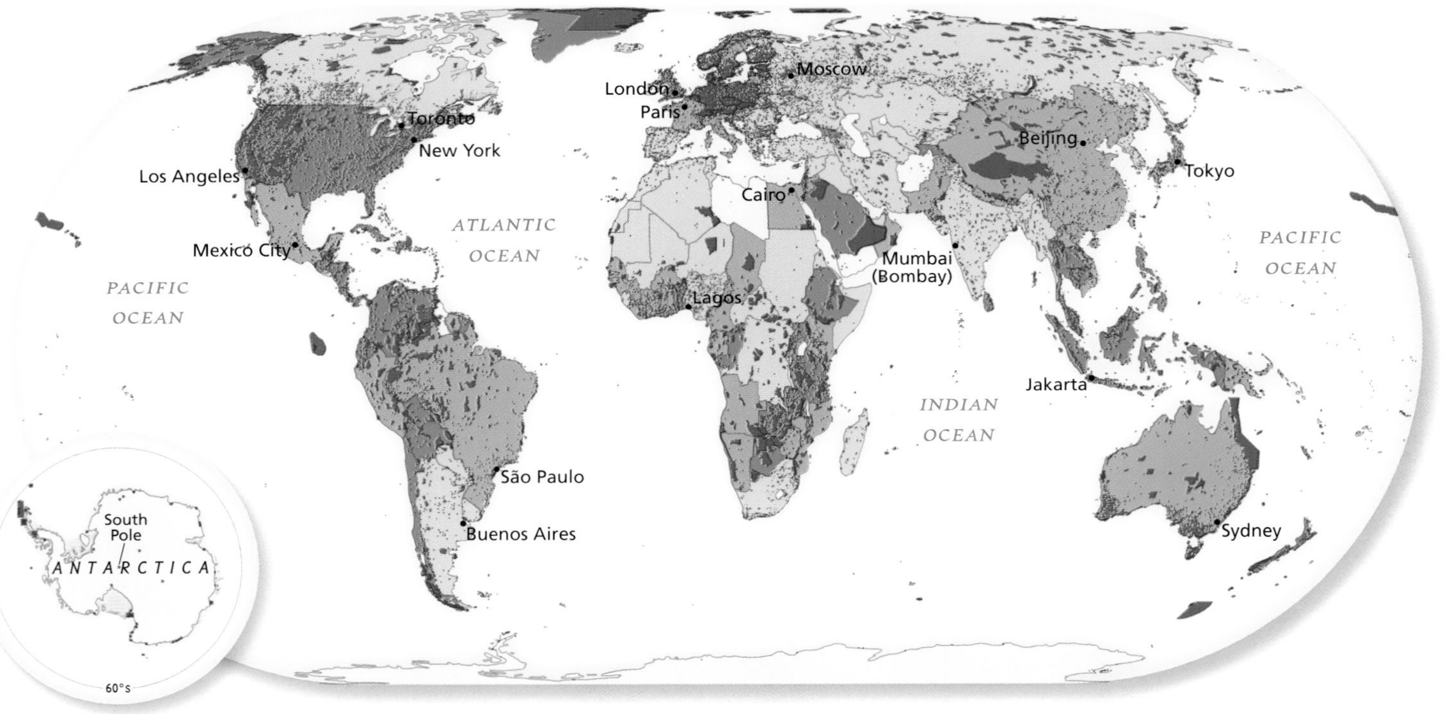

Protected Areas
(% of terrestrial area protected by country)
- More than 20%
- 10%–20%
- 1%–9%
- Less than 1%
- No data
- Ice shield
- Protected area (terrestrial & marine)

Data from UNEP-World Conservation Monitoring Centre, March 2006

COUNTRIES WITH HIGHEST % PROTECTED AREA

COUNTRY (WITH TOTAL AREA >11,000 SQ. MI.)	PERCENTAGE OF LAND PROTECTED	GDP PER CAPITA (U.S. $)	POP. DENSITY (SQ. MI.)
Venezuela	70.3	4,260	76
Zambia	41.5	460	39
Tanzania	39.7	300	100
Saudi Arabia	38.5	10,200	30
Panama	37.2	4,270	111
Guatemala	32.6	2,160	302
Colombia	32.6	2,130	105
New Zealand	32.1	24,500	39
Germany	31.5	33,160	598
Estonia	31.4	8,230	77

COUNTRIES WITH LOWEST % PROTECTED AREA

COUNTRY (WITH TOTAL AREA >11,000 SQ. MI.)	PERCENTAGE OF LAND PROTECTED	GDP PER CAPITA (U.S. $)	POP. DENSITY (SQ. MI.)
Iraq	0.0	950	170
Yemen	0.0	640	102
Libya	0.1	3,400	8
Lesotho	0.2	760	154
Haiti	0.3	470	774
Afghanistan	0.3	180	119
Uruguay	0.4	3,840	50
Bosnia and Herzegovina	0.5	2,020	185
Somalia	0.8	260	35
Mauritania	1.1	420	8

PROTECTED LAND AREAS BY REGION

CONTINENT OR REGION	SQUARE MILES PROTECTED	AS PERCENTAGE OF TOTAL LAND AREA
North America	1,249,049	16.5
South America	1,370,046	19.8
Europe	877,583	9.0
Africa	1,187,394	10.2
Asia	1,193,905	12.0
Australia/Oceania	382,786	12.3
Antarctica	1,749	0.03
WORLD	**6,653,720**	**11.5**

Endemism

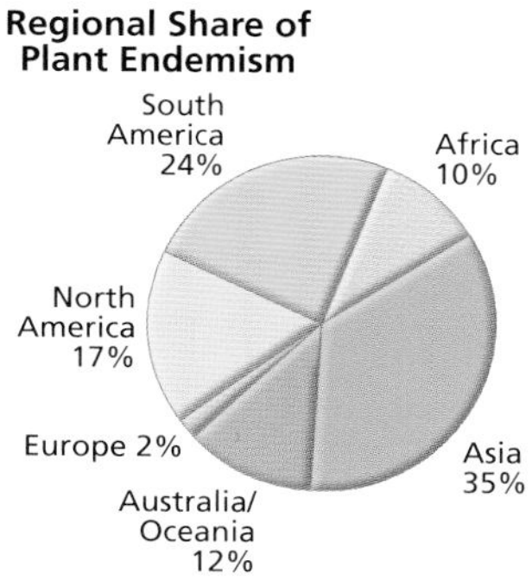

Endemism—the presence of species found nowhere else—is a key criterion for determining conservation priorities, as areas with high levels of endemism are the most vulnerable to biodiversity loss. The highest levels of endemism occur on oceanic islands and in montane regions.

Ouratea dependens is one of thousands of plants unique to Madagascar.

The World Heritage Site System

NATURAL HERITAGE SITE
Canada's Tatshenshini-Alsek Provincial Wilderness holds a portion of the largest nonpolar ice cap and hundreds of valley glaciers; it is the last major stronghold for North America's grizzly bears. The park designation averted what would have been an enormous open-pit mine.

CULTURAL HERITAGE SITE
Site of some of the most important monuments of ancient Greece, the Acropolis illustrates the civilizations, myths, and religions that flourished there for a period of over a thousand years. Europe claims about half of the world's cultural heritage sites, with over 300.

MIXED HERITAGE SITE
The town of Ohrid, on the shores of Lake Ohrid in the former Yugoslav Republic of Macedonia, exemplifies a mixed heritage site. The ten-million-year-old lake may be the oldest in Europe, and the town is one of the continent's oldest continuously inhabited sites.

WORLD HERITAGE LIST
The World Heritage List was established under the terms of the 1972 UNESCO "Convention Concerning the Protection of the World Cultural and Natural Heritage."

The first 12 World Heritage Sites were named in 1978; among them were L'Anse aux Meadows in Canada, the site of the first Viking settlement in North America; the Galápagos Islands; the cathedral of Aachen, Germany; the historic city center of Krakow, Poland; the island of Gorée, off Senegal; and Mesa Verde and Yellowstone National Parks in the United States.

New sites are added annually. In December 2005, the list comprised 812 sites, with 628 cultural, 160 natural, and 24 mixed sites, located in 137 countries. On average, 30 newly designated sites are added to the list each year, but 2000 must have been considered an auspicious time for listings; 61 sites were added that year, the largest number ever.

MOST VISITED NATURAL HERITAGE SITES

NAME	SIZE OF SITE (SQ. MI.)	COUNTRY	VISITORS PER YEAR
Great Smoky Mountains National Park	805	United States	9,205,037
Wet Tropics of Queensland	3,453	Australia	5,000,000
Canadian Rocky Mountain Parks	8,907	Canada	6,017,221
Grand Canyon National Park	1,880	United States	4,308,549
Yosemite National Park	1,176	United States	3,272,155
Olympic National Park	1,425	United States	3,047,234
Yellowstone National Park	3,428	United States	2,866,785
Glacier/Waterton National Park	1,767	U.S./Canada	2,399,161
Great Barrier Reef	134,633	Australia	1,971,945

THERE IS A GROWING CONSENSUS that globalization is defined by increasing levels of interdependence over vast distances, not just in the economic dimension, but along the lines of person-to-person contact, technological connectivity, and political ties. In many important ways, global integration is continuing to deepen over the years, and ties between countries have continued to strengthen despite deterrents such as acts of terror, stalling of trade talks, and divisions over international peace and security issues.

The A.T. Kearney/Foreign Policy magazine Globalization Index "reverse-engineers" the globalization phenomenon and quantifies its most important component indicators—spanning trade, finance, political engagement, information technology, and personal contact—to determine the rankings of 62 countries. These countries together account for 96 percent of the world's gross domestic product (GDP) and 85 percent of the world's population. The index measures 12 variables, which are divided into four "baskets": economic integration, technological connectivity, personal contact, and political engagement.

In years past, Western European countries have claimed many of the top spots as engaged participants in the international system. Small trading nations like Singapore and Ireland have tended to take top places in the index due in part to their particular reliance on other countries for trade, investment, and tourism.

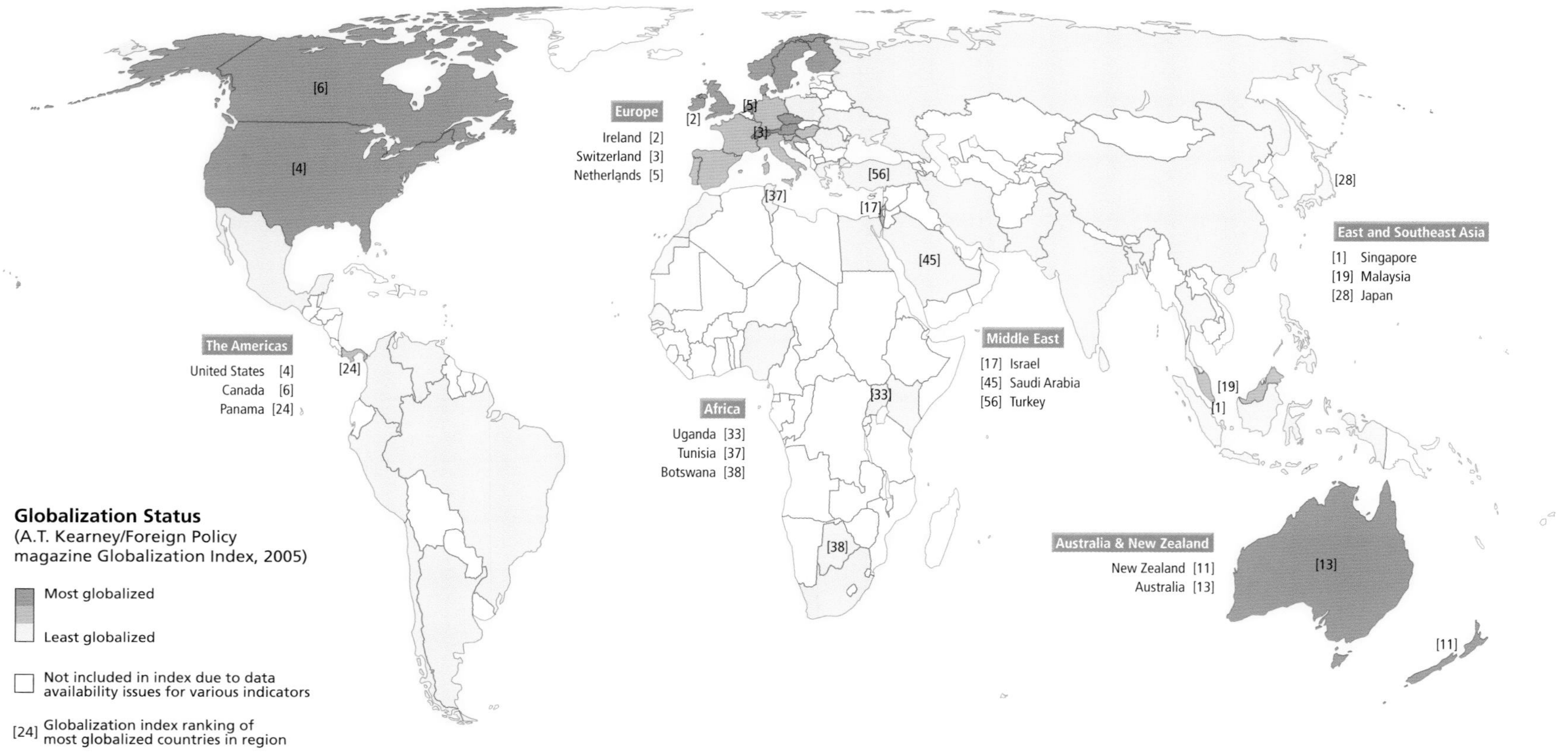

Transnational Corporations

Transnational corporations have played an important role in global economic integration, through sales, investments, and operations in countries around the world. In fact, a number of them have assets equivalent to or larger than the nominal GDPs of some nations. Many of these companies have also made their non-economic influence felt as their products and services shape consumption habits, business practices, and local cultures.

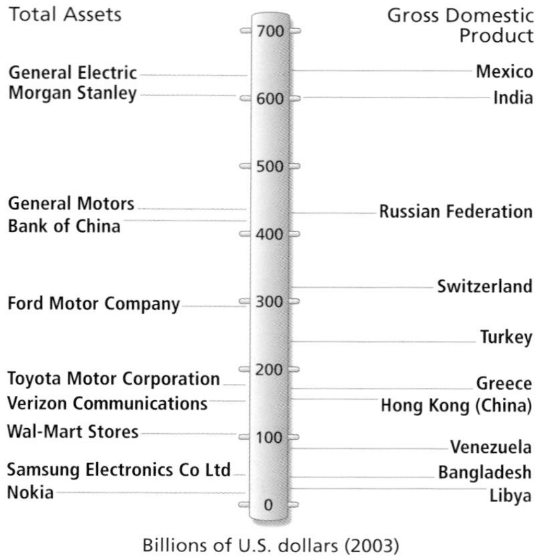

Extremes of Globalization

In the 2005 Globalization Index, Singapore took the top spot on the strength of its foreign trade ties and increased political engagement. Ireland came second, with moderate gains in investment inflows and services trade, as well as an increase in non-economic ties such as international travel and continued participation in the United Nations' peacekeeping efforts. The strong United States showing is primarily a result of its remarkable technological prowess, evidenced by the growth in Internet hosts and secure servers, which are enabling factors for continued technological integration.

Yet a glance at this year's index suggests that those who seek to expand globalization's benefits have their work cut out for them. The bottom ten countries in the index account for more than 50 percent of the world's population. As many indicators are measured on a per-capita basis, gains from globalization may be slow to reach the massive populations of these nations.

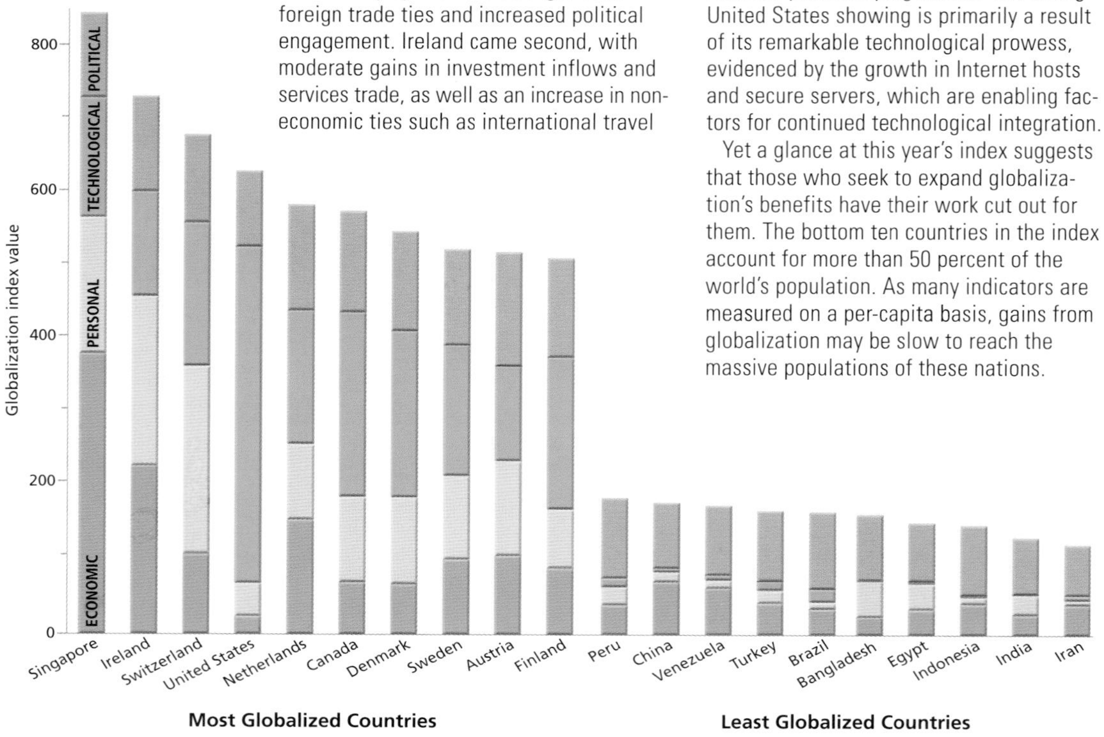

Economic Integration

Economic integration combines data on trade and foreign direct investment. Measured as a percentage of gross domestic product (GDP), foreign direct investment flows include investments in physical assets, such as plant and equipment, both into and out of a country. These measures reflect a country's dependence on global trade and investment; however, they do not necessarily reflect economic strength.

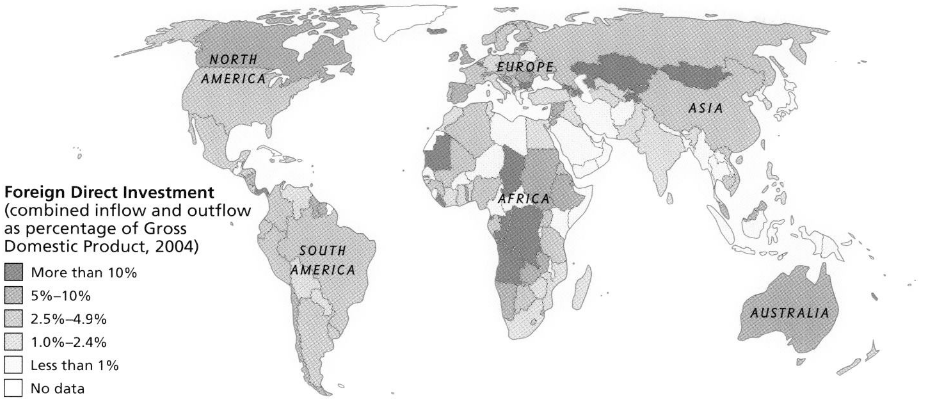

Personal Contact

Personal contact tracks international travel and tourism, international telephone traffic, and cross-border remittances and personal transfers (including worker remittances, compensation to employees, and other person-to-person and nongovernmental transfers). International telephone calls sum up the total number of minutes of telephone traffic into and out of a country on a per-capita basis.

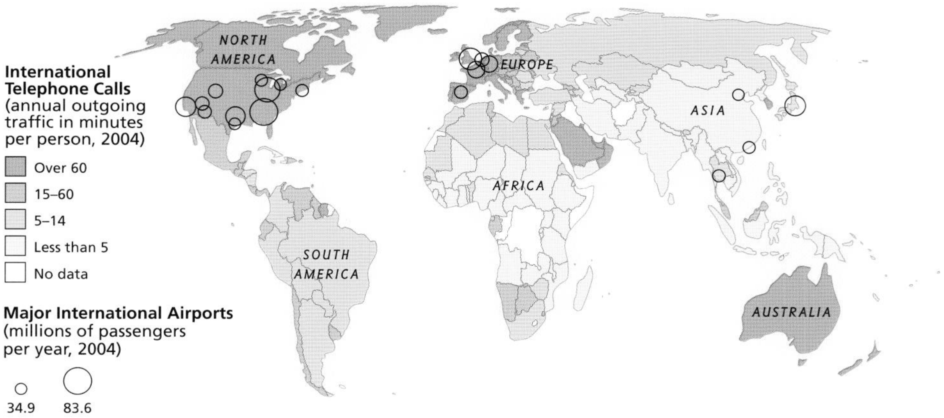

Technological Connectivity

Technological connectivity counts the number of Internet users, hosts, and secure servers through which transactions are carried out. These indicators measure penetration—that is, how many users there are, as well as how widespread the infrastructure is, for each country. The Internet has broken down physical borders, bridging continents and multiplying networks between businesses, governments, and citizens at a faster pace than ever.

Political Engagement

Political engagement includes each country's memberships in a variety of representative international organizations, personnel and financial contributions to UN peacekeeping missions, ratification of selected multilateral treaties, and amounts of governmental transfer payments and receipts. The measures provide an indication of how various countries rank as participants of international arrangements relative to their economic and population sizes.

International Outsourcing

Improvements in communication technologies, such as the Internet and digital telephone lines, are making it increasingly possible for firms to source their service inputs from suppliers abroad. Recent examples include call centers and computer software development services provided by India to the rest of the world. Until recently, global production networks mostly involved the offshoring of manufactured intermediate inputs, whereas now many services, as well, can be produced in one country and utilized in another.

TRENDS IN OUTSOURCING

International outsourcing of services has been steadily increasing but it is still at relatively low levels. Although U.S. business service imports have roughly doubled in each of the past several decades, they remained at less than one-half of one percent of total GDP in 2003. India, reported to be the recipient of significant outsourcing, itself outsources a large amount of services.

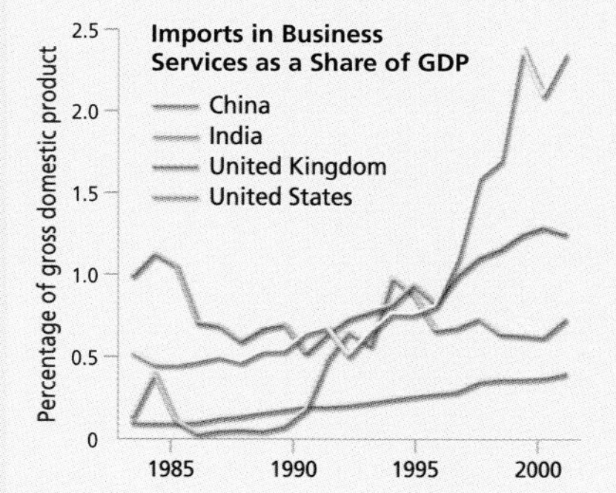

As shown in the graph below, the U.K. and the U.S. have the largest net surpluses in business services. But this is not true for all industrialized countries. The data reveal no clear pattern of developing or industrial countries either being net exporters or net importers. For example, in addition to the U.K. and the U.S. having a net surplus in business services, India also does. Yet, Indonesia has a large net deficit in business services, as do Germany and Ireland.

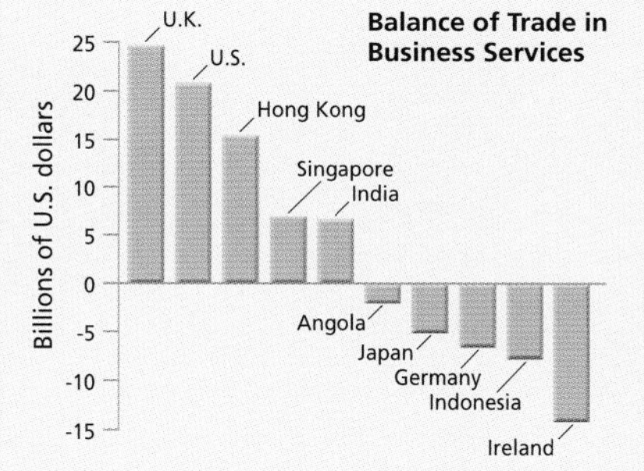

TOP OUTSOURCERS OF BUSINESS SERVICES

VALUE (BILLIONS OF U.S. DOLLARS)	
United States	44
Germany	40
Italy	24
Netherlands	24
France	23
Japan	23
United Kingdom	22
Ireland	22

In dollar value terms, the U.S. ranks highest in outsourcing of business services, but as a share of the country's overall GDP, its value is comparatively low (0.4 percent at the end of 2003). In smaller countries, trade generally accounts for a larger percentage of GDP. Among the top relative outsourcers of business services are several small developing countries, such as Angola (16 percent of GDP), Lebanon (12 percent), Congo (10 percent), Azerbaijan (9 percent), and Seychelles (8 percent).

THE TECHNOLOGICAL REVOLUTION that began in the 1950s has given rise to a new Information Age in which global communications networks underpin virtually every facet of modern life. Each day, trillions of dollars worth of goods and services are traded worldwide in the form of bits and bytes, zipping through space, under the seas, beneath our feet, and in the air around us. Information has never been so plentiful, or so cheap. The first mass-produced book, the Gutenberg Bible, took up to two years to print and was beyond the means of all but a wealthy few. Today, a copy of the Bible can be downloaded over the Internet for free in seconds.

The Net itself has quickly evolved into a ubiquitous "network of networks" carrying everything from financial data to phone calls, entertainment to e-shopping, messaging to multimedia. Now the stage is set for a paradigm shift that will see inanimate objects around us become part of an intelligent "Internet of things," exchanging information spontaneously without the need for human intervention.

Already, tiny radio-frequency tags track goods from manufacturer to consumer; soon they could be providing information about a person's identity, buying habits, medical history, and more. Work is also underway on networks of miniscule wireless sensors capable of measuring a huge range of environmental variables, from temperature, pressure, and movement to whether a refrigerator needs restocking.

Centers of Technological Innovation

With access to information technology (IT) now a major determinant of economic growth and social development, researchers are working on ways to measure and map the distribution of technology.

The Technological Achievement Index aims to provide a country-by-country snapshot of IT penetration by measuring local levels of innovation, access to newer technologies like the Internet, the availability of old technology (e.g., telephones and electricity), and the potential for future skills development via schools and training.

The Technological Innovation Index, meanwhile, shines a spotlight on the centers of innovation that are driving today's technological revolution. Each country is assigned an innovation score based on the number of patents generated by its residents, which is then weighted against national population figures to provide a global perspective. The results can be surprising, with some of the world's smaller nations easily outstripping the industrial giants.

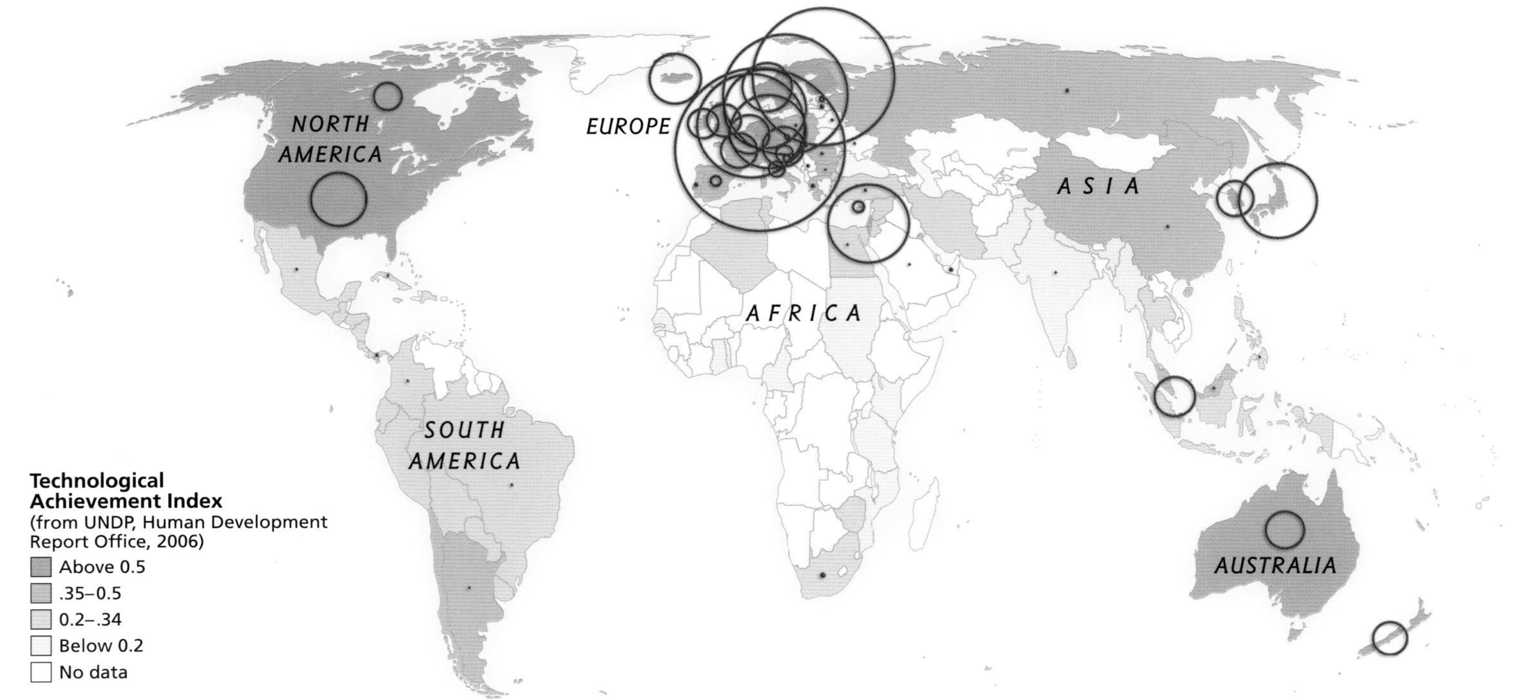
NORTH AMERICA
EUROPE
ASIA
AFRICA
SOUTH AMERICA
AUSTRALIA

Technological Achievement Index
(from UNDP, Human Development Report Office, 2006)

- Above 0.5
- .35–0.5
- 0.2–.34
- Below 0.2
- No data

Technological Innovation Index
(international patent applications per 1 million people)

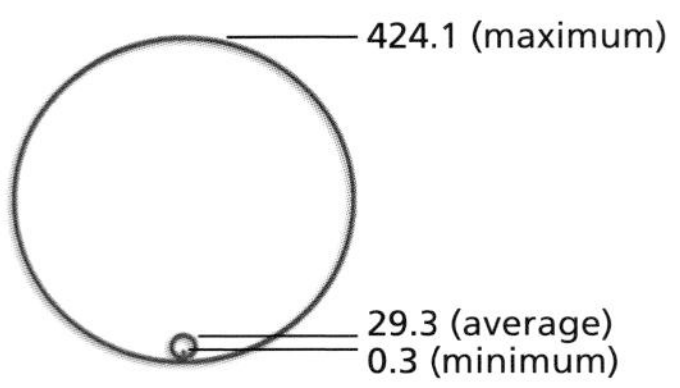
424.1 (maximum)
29.3 (average)
0.3 (minimum)

Data from World Intellectual Property Organization, 2006

424.1	Switzerland	100.9	Belgium	10.5	Czech Republic	2.3	Belarus
354.4	Finland	95.8	Australia	9.7	Estonia	1.9	China
311.4	Sweden	90.9	South Korea	7.6	South Africa	1.4	Malaysia
269.6	Netherlands	90.9	France	6.5	Latvia	1.4	Brazil
229.8	Luxembourg	85.0	New Zealand	5.9	Slovakia	1.3	Saudi Arabia
204.9	Denmark	84.4	United Kingdom	5.0	Portugal	1.3	Mexico
202.1	Israel	76.6	Ireland	5.0	Greece	1.1	Ukraine
193.7	Japan	70.1	Canada	5.0	United Arab Emirates	1.0	Cuba
191.6	Germany	43.0	Slovenia	4.0	Panama	0.7	Egypt
138.4	United States	39.4	Italy	3.8	Russia	0.6	Romania
128.8	Iceland	28.0	Cyprus	3.3	Serbia & Montenegro	0.6	India
124.5	Norway	25.4	Spain	2.7	Bulgaria	0.5	Colombia
103.8	Austria	16.0	Croatia	2.5	Poland	0.5	Argentina
101.0	Singapore	15.6	Hungary	2.3	Turkey	0.3	Philippines

Milestones in Technology

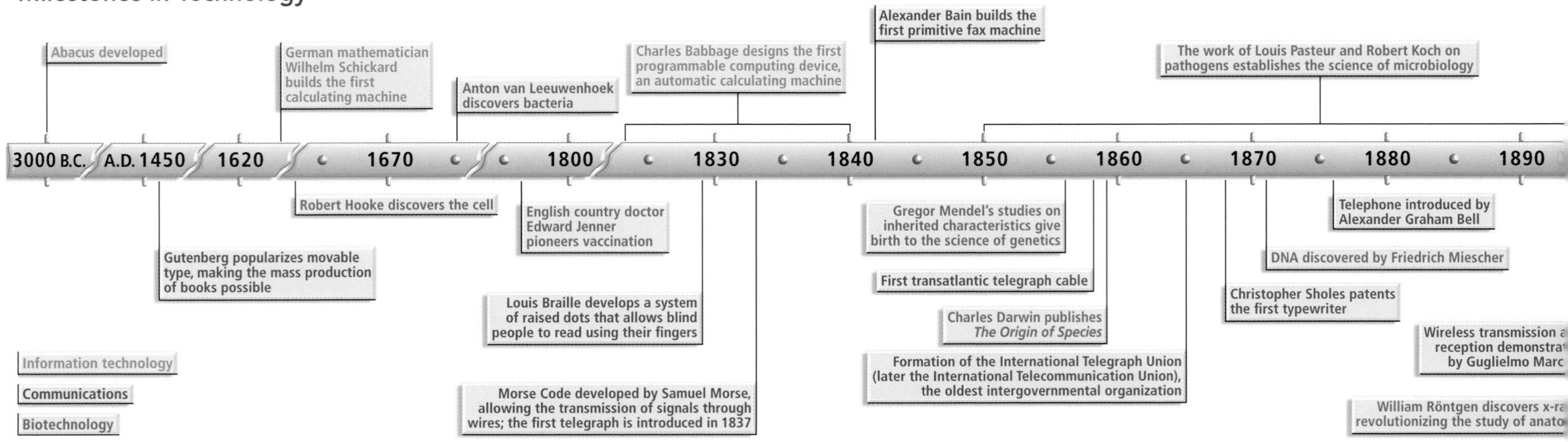
Abacus developed
German mathematician Wilhelm Schickard builds the first calculating machine
Anton van Leeuwenhoek discovers bacteria
Charles Babbage designs the first programmable computing device, an automatic calculating machine
Alexander Bain builds the first primitive fax machine
The work of Louis Pasteur and Robert Koch on pathogens establishes the science of microbiology
3000 B.C.
A.D. 1450
1620
1670
1800
1830
1840
1850
1860
1870
1880
1890
Robert Hooke discovers the cell
English country doctor Edward Jenner pioneers vaccination
Gutenberg popularizes movable type, making the mass production of books possible
Louis Braille develops a system of raised dots that allows blind people to read using their fingers
Morse Code developed by Samuel Morse, allowing the transmission of signals through wires; the first telegraph is introduced in 1837
Gregor Mendel's studies on inherited characteristics give birth to the science of genetics
First transatlantic telegraph cable
Charles Darwin publishes The Origin of Species
Formation of the International Telegraph Union (later the International Telecommunication Union), the oldest intergovernmental organization
Telephone introduced by Alexander Graham Bell
DNA discovered by Friedrich Miescher
Christopher Sholes patents the first typewriter
Wireless transmission a
reception demonstra
by Guglielmo Marc
William Röntgen discovers x-ra
revolutionizing the study of anato
Information technology
Communications
Biotechnology

The Digital Divide

If access to digital information is taken for granted in industrialized nations, information and communication technologies (ICTs) remain far out of reach for millions living in the developing world. The result of widespread poverty and geographical challenges like mountainous terrain or widely dispersed, isolated communities, this "digital divide" threatens to further entrench global economic imbalances. Connecting the estimated one billion still unconnected means finding ways to measure differences in ICT access within and between economies worldwide. The International Telecommunication Union's Digital Opportunity Index is a composite model based on 11 different indicators of opportunity, infrastructure, and utilization. Among the information-rich, South Korea, Japan, and Denmark score the highest; at the thin end of the scale, sub-Saharan Africa fares the worst. The fastest improvement is taking place in the Asia-Pacific region—especially China, which now has the world's largest number of mobile cellular subscribers.

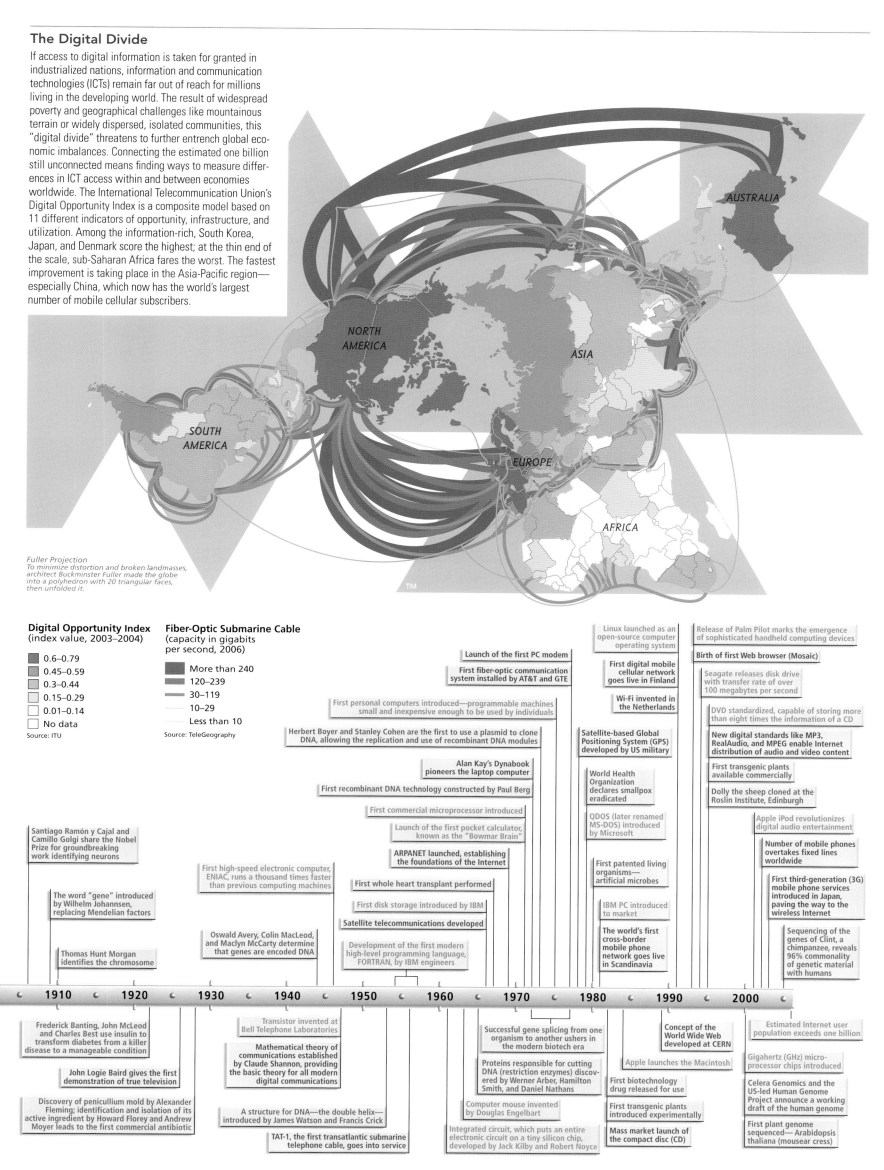

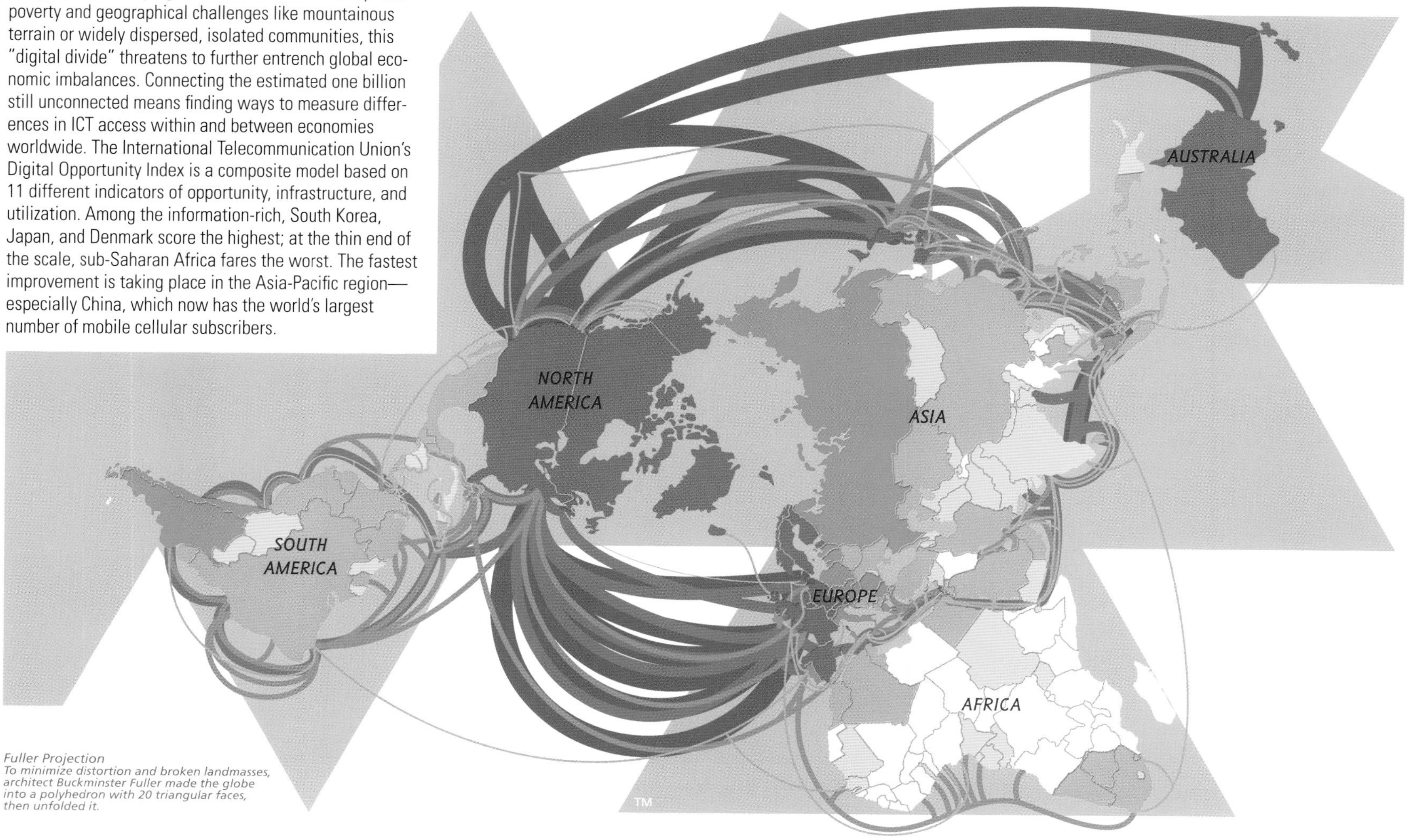

Fuller Projection
To minimize distortion and broken landmasses, architect Buckminster Fuller made the globe into a polyhedron with 20 triangular faces, then unfolded it.

Digital Opportunity Index (index value, 2003–2004)

- 0.6–0.79
- 0.45–0.59
- 0.3–0.44
- 0.15–0.29
- 0.01–0.14
- No data

Source: ITU

Fiber-Optic Submarine Cable (capacity in gigabits per second, 2006)

- More than 240
- 120–239
- 30–119
- 10–29
- Less than 10

Source: TeleGeography

1910 · 1920 · 1930 · 1940 · 1950 · 1960 · 1970 · 1980 · 1990 · 2000

- Santiago Ramón y Cajal and Camillo Golgi share the Nobel Prize for groundbreaking work identifying neurons
- The word "gene" introduced by Wilhelm Johannsen, replacing Mendelian factors
- Thomas Hunt Morgan identifies the chromosome
- Frederick Banting, John McLeod and Charles Best use insulin to transform diabetes from a killer disease to a manageable condition
- John Logie Baird gives the first demonstration of true television
- Discovery of penicullium mold by Alexander Fleming; identification and isolation of its active ingredient by Howard Florey and Andrew Moyer leads to the first commercial antibiotic
- Oswald Avery, Colin MacLeod, and Maclyn McCarty determine that genes are encoded DNA
- First high-speed electronic computer, ENIAC, runs a thousand times faster than previous computing machines
- Transistor invented at Bell Telephone Laboratories
- Mathematical theory of communications established by Claude Shannon, providing the basic theory for all modern digital communications
- Development of the first modern high-level programming language, FORTRAN, by IBM engineers
- A structure for DNA—the double helix—introduced by James Watson and Francis Crick
- TAT-1, the first transatlantic submarine telephone cable, goes into service
- Satellite telecommunications developed
- First disk storage introduced by IBM
- First whole heart transplant performed
- Integrated circuit, which puts an entire electronic circuit on a tiny silicon chip, developed by Jack Kilby and Robert Noyce
- Computer mouse invented by Douglas Engelbart
- ARPANET launched, establishing the foundations of the Internet
- Launch of the first pocket calculator, known as the "Bowmar Brain"
- First commercial microprocessor introduced
- First recombinant DNA technology constructed by Paul Berg
- Alan Kay's Dynabook pioneers the laptop computer
- Herbert Boyer and Stanley Cohen are the first to use a plasmid to clone DNA, allowing the replication and use of recombinant DNA modules
- First personal computers introduced—programmable machines small and inexpensive enough to be used by individuals
- First fiber-optic communication system installed by AT&T and GTE
- Launch of the first PC modem
- Proteins responsible for cutting DNA (restriction enzymes) discovered by Werner Arber, Hamilton Smith, and Daniel Nathans
- Successful gene splicing from one organism to another ushers in the modern biotech era
- World Health Organization declares smallpox eradicated
- QDOS (later renamed MS-DOS) introduced by Microsoft
- First patented living organisms—artificial microbes
- IBM PC introduced to market
- The world's first cross-border mobile phone network goes live in Scandinavia
- First biotechnology drug released for use
- First transgenic plants introduced experimentally
- Mass market launch of the compact disc (CD)
- Apple launches the Macintosh
- Satellite-based Global Positioning System (GPS) developed by US military
- Wi-Fi invented in the Netherlands
- First digital mobile cellular network goes live in Finland
- Linux launched as an open-source computer operating system
- Concept of the World Wide Web developed at CERN
- Release of Palm Pilot marks the emergence of sophisticated handheld computing devices
- Birth of first Web browser (Mosaic)
- Seagate releases disk drive with transfer rate of over 100 megabytes per second
- DVD standardized, capable of storing more than eight times the information of a CD
- New digital standards like MP3, RealAudio, and MPEG enable Internet distribution of audio and video content
- First transgenic plants available commercially
- Dolly the sheep cloned at the Roslin Institute, Edinburgh
- Apple iPod revolutionizes digital audio entertainment
- Number of mobile phones overtakes fixed lines worldwide
- First third-generation (3G) mobile phone services introduced in Japan, paving the way to the wireless Internet
- Sequencing of the genes of Clint, a chimpanzee, reveals 96% commonality of genetic material with humans
- Estimated Internet user population exceeds one billion
- Gigahertz (GHz) microprocessor chips introduced
- Celera Genomics and the US-led Human Genome Project announce a working draft of the human genome
- First plant genome sequenced— Arabidopsis thaliana (mousear cress)

THE "COOPERATIVE ANARCHY" of the global Internet, a vast collection of interconnected computer networks communicating through specific protocols (information exchange rules), defies easy characterization or measurement of its behavior. Still, a lack of understanding has not stalled development of technologies that enable and support Internet growth.

Old behavior models for telephone networks no longer apply to packet delivery (data sent over a network) and to application support over multiple links, routers, and Internet Service Providers (ISPs). The sheer volume of traffic and the high capacity of electronic pathways have made Internet monitoring and analysis a more challenging endeavor. Users and providers both benefit from measurements that detect and isolate problems, but watching every link is not practical or particularly effective.

Each ISP monitors its own infrastructure and quality of service; however, business and policy concerns often keep ISPs from sharing such information. Common sense supports creation of a measurement infrastructure that would yield maximal Internet coverage for a reasonable price. But dynamically changing network configurations, as well as complex business and geopolitical concerns, make it difficult to acquire a worldwide view of the Internet.

A BRIEF HISTORY

1960s: ARPANET, a system designed to promote the sharing of supercomputers by researchers in the United States, is commissioned by the Department of Defense.

1970s: People begin to use ARPANET to collaborate on research projects and discuss common interests. In **1974**, a commercial version goes online for the first time.

1980s: Corporations begin to use the Internet for e-mail. As the Internet grows in importance, viruses start to create concerns about online privacy and security. New terms such as "hacker" come into use.

1990s: After the introduction of browsers for navigating the World Wide Web, Internet use expands rapidly (see graph below). By the late 1990s, 200 million people are connected, with online consumer spending totaling in the tens of billions of dollars. During this time, Internet-related companies attract enormous amounts of money from investors.

EARLY 2000s: Internet stock values take a deep plunge following the "dotcom" crash of April 2000. But rapid Internet growth continues, with more than 100 million new users each year. Satellite communications technology allows people to easily access the Internet with handheld devices.

Mapping the Spread of a Computer Virus

The graphics below detail the spread of the Nyxem E-mail Virus during early 2006. This virus operates in much the same way other viruses do, running as an e-mail attachment that attempts to disable antivirus software and harvest e-mail addresses to automatically spread itself. However, the Nyxem virus stands out because it exhibits the rare behavior of reporting its progress to a single web site, thus allowing researchers to undertake a detailed analysis of its activity.

These images, generated with a geographic visualization tool called Cuttlefish, highlight the correlation between human activity at certain times of the day (e.g., booting computers and reading e-mail), the spread of the virus, and the corresponding geographical locations of the infected computers.

The image at upper left includes a key that maps colors to the number of infected hosts. Circles of varying diameter and color depict the number of infected hosts in each region. At top right is a histogram showing the number of infected hosts over the roughly two-week period of analysis.

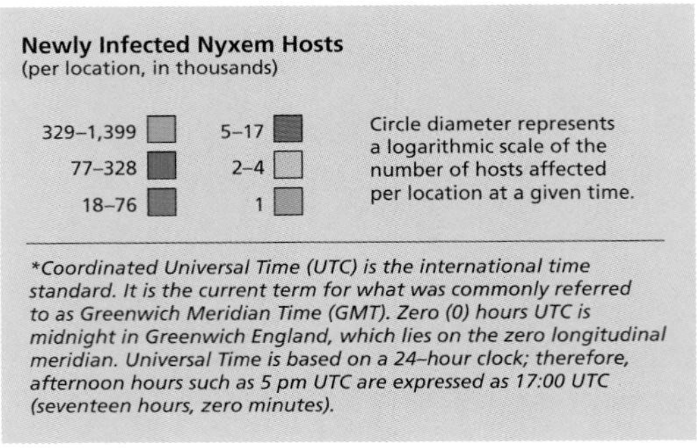
Newly Infected Nyxem Hosts
(per location, in thousands)
329–1,399
77–328
18–76
5–17
2–4
1
Circle diameter represents a logarithmic scale of the number of hosts affected per location at a given time.
*Coordinated Universal Time (UTC) is the international time standard. It is the current term for what was commonly referred to as Greenwich Meridian Time (GMT). Zero (0) hours UTC is midnight in Greenwich England, which lies on the zero longitudinal meridian. Universal Time is based on a 24-hour clock; therefore, afternoon hours such as 5 pm UTC are expressed as 17:00 UTC (seventeen hours, zero minutes).

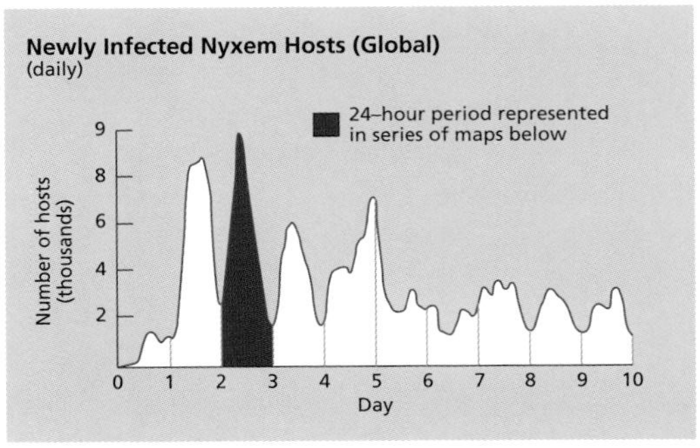
Newly Infected Nyxem Hosts (Global)
(daily)
24-hour period represented in series of maps below
Number of hosts (thousands)
9
8
6
4
2
0
1
2
3
4
5
6
7
8
9
10
Day

00:00 UTC

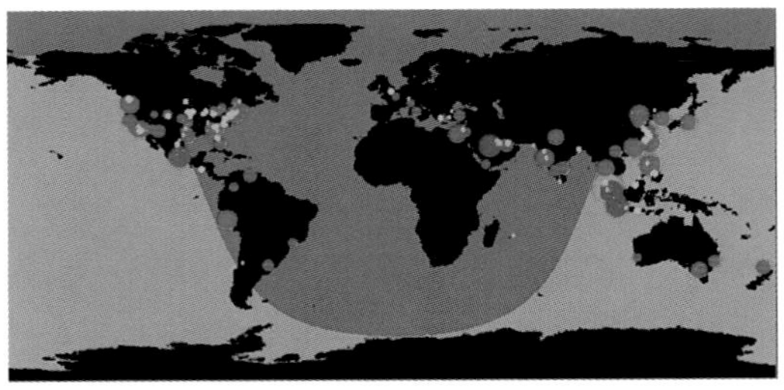

12:00 UTC

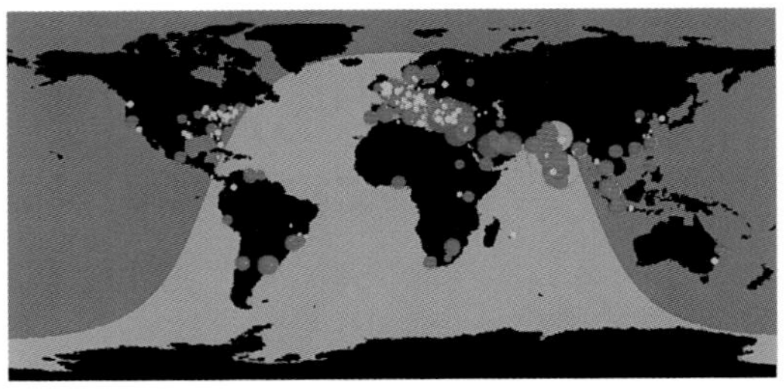

03:00 UTC

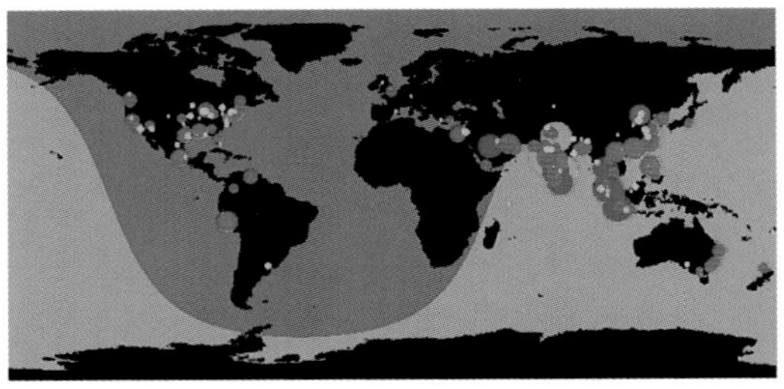

15:00 UTC

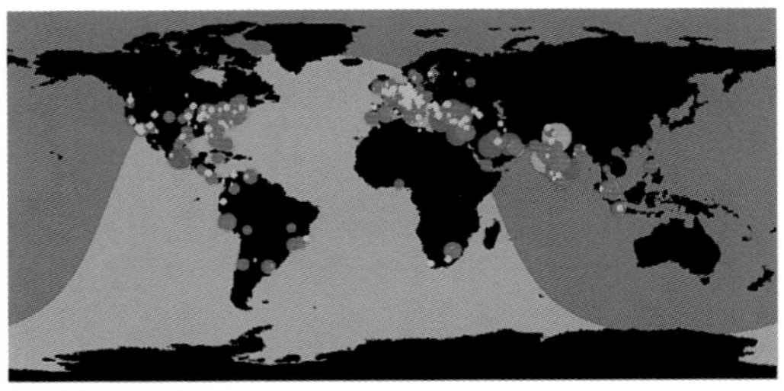

06:00 UTC

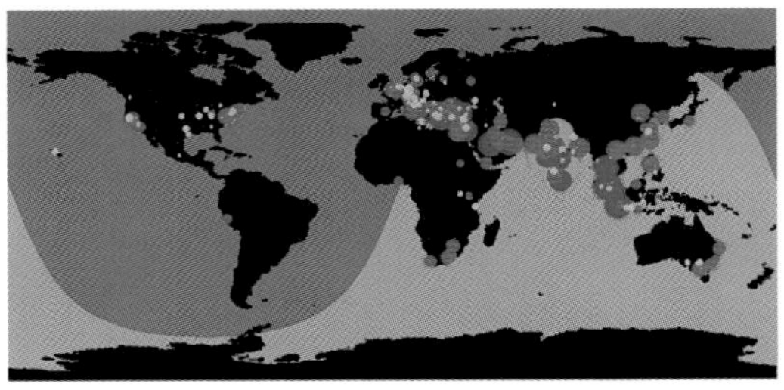

18:00 UTC

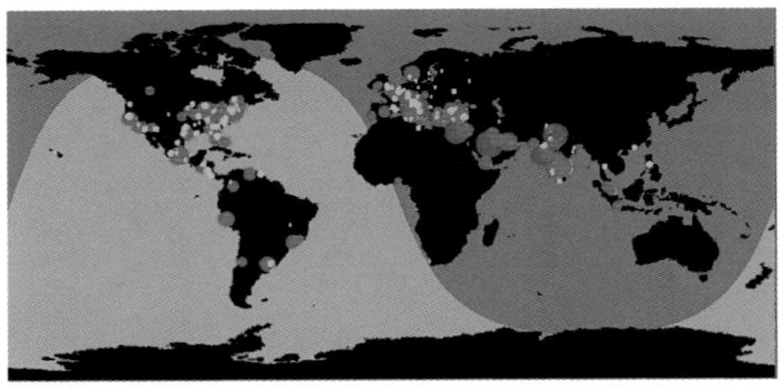

09:00 UTC

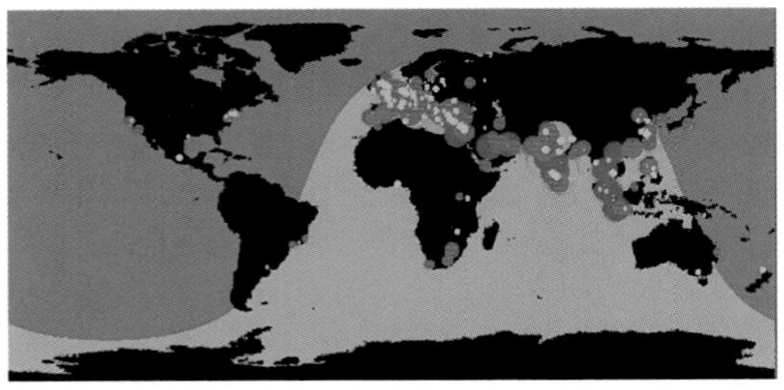

21:00 UTC

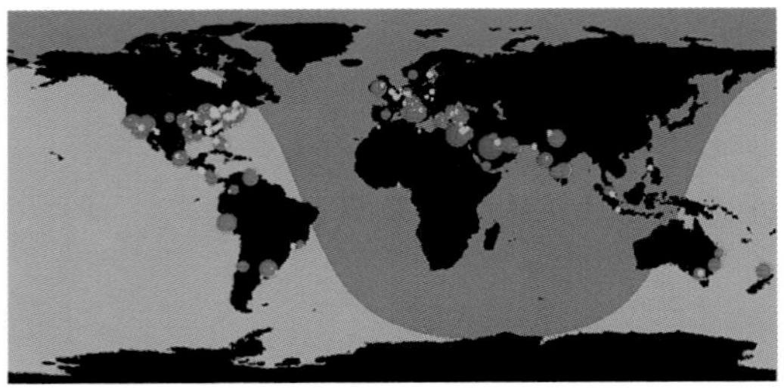

Internet Users Worldwide (estimated), 1995–2005

December 1995: 40 million
December 2000: 400 million

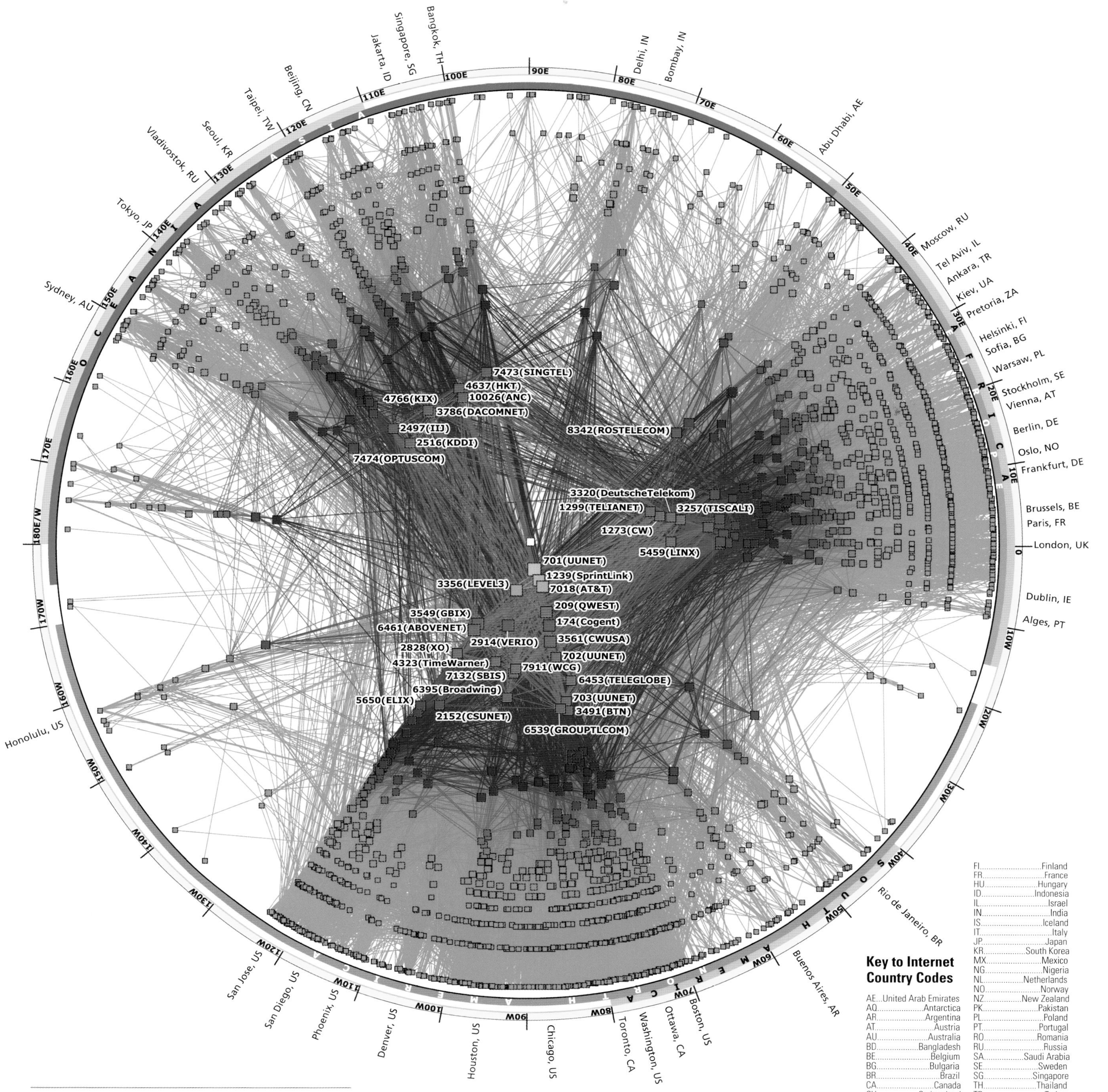

Key to Internet Country Codes

AE	United Arab Emirates
AQ	Antarctica
AR	Argentina
AT	Austria
AU	Australia
BD	Bangladesh
BE	Belgium
BG	Bulgaria
BR	Brazil
CA	Canada
CH	Switzerland
CN	China
DE	Germany
DK	Denmark
EG	Egypt
ES	Spain
FI	Finland
FR	France
HU	Hungary
ID	Indonesia
IL	Israel
IN	India
IS	Iceland
IT	Italy
JP	Japan
KR	South Korea
MX	Mexico
NG	Nigeria
NL	Netherlands
NO	Norway
NZ	New Zealand
PK	Pakistan
PL	Poland
PT	Portugal
RO	Romania
RU	Russia
SA	Saudi Arabia
SE	Sweden
SG	Singapore
TH	Thailand
TR	Turkey
TW	Taiwan
UA	Ukraine
UK	United Kingdom
US	United States
ZA	South Africa

Global Internet Connectivity

The above graph is a macroscopic snapshot of the Internet core, based on data collected from April 4 to April 17, 2005. Internet Service Providers (ISPs) are represented by squares, with better-connected ISPs found toward the center. The colors indicate "outdegree" (the number of "next-hop" systems that were observed accepting traffic from a link), from lowest (blue) to highest (yellow).

The top 11 network nodes observed in this data set are based in the United States, and one of the European ISPs in the top 15 observed networks is the European branch of an American company. While ISPs in Europe and Asia have many links with ISPs in the United States, there are few direct links between ISPs in Asia and Europe. Both technical (cabling and router placement and management) and policy factors (business and cost models, geopolitical considerations) contribute to the ISP associations represented in this graph.

Worldwide Distribution of Internet Resources

The worldwide distribution of Internet resources—ISPs, Autonomous System (AS) routers, address space—is highly nonuniform and is unrelated to a region's size or population. For this graph, Internet addresses of routable paths announced on March 21, 2006, were mapped to physical locations and compared with public demographic data.

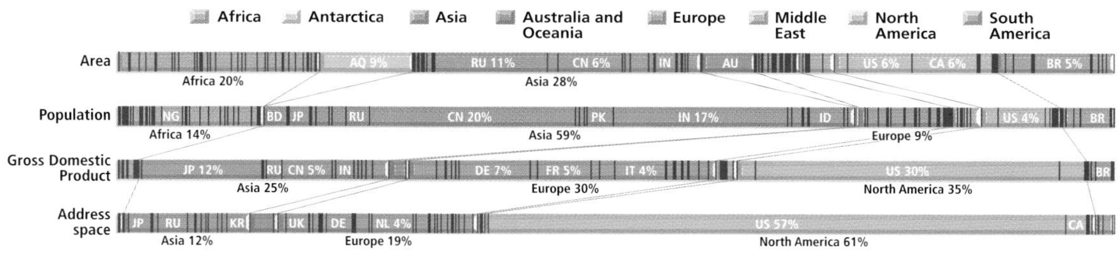

December 2005: 940 million

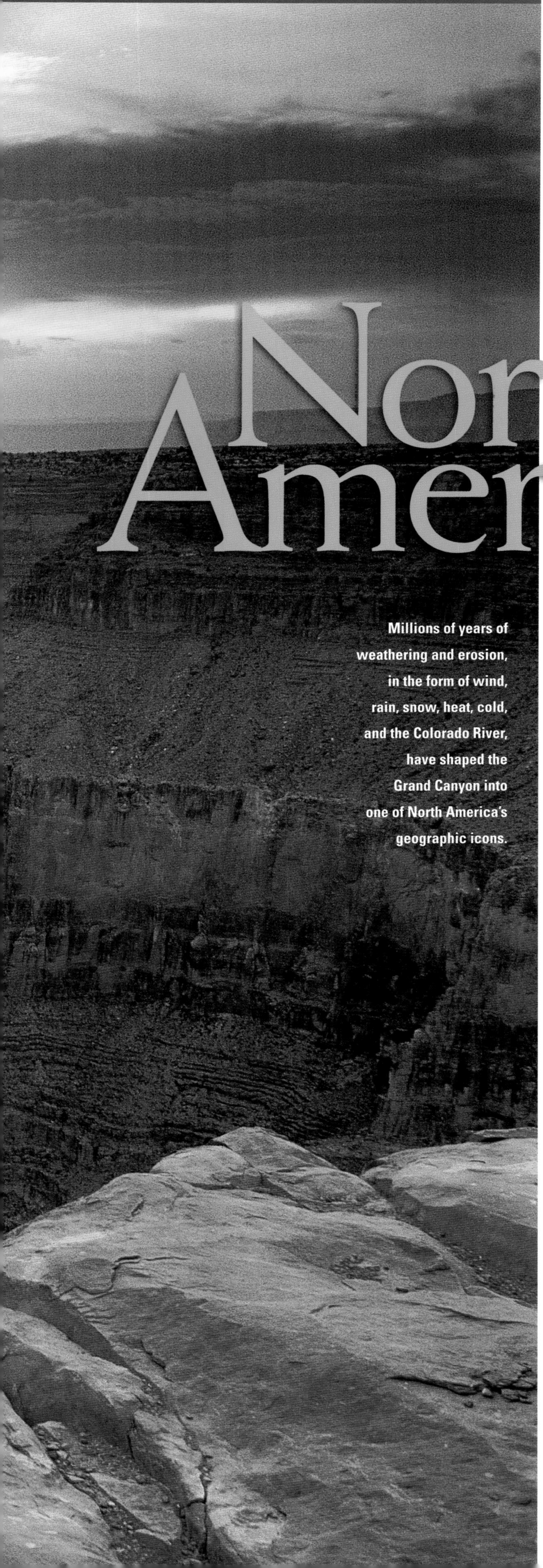

Millions of years of weathering and erosion, in the form of wind, rain, snow, heat, cold, and the Colorado River, have shaped the Grand Canyon into one of North America's geographic icons.

North America

North America is both incredibly old, geologically speaking, and relatively young, when viewed in terms of its human history.

About 200 million years ago, North America separated from Africa when the supercontinent Pangaea began to break apart. For a while, it was attached to Europe, but in time that connection was broken and the North American landmass began roughly assuming its current shape and size. Meanwhile, the other continents were still separating from one another and jockeying for position on the face of the planet.

Some of the oldest stones in the world are found in North America. Dating from nearly four billion years ago, they form the stout underbelly of Canada's frozen tundra. In the east, an ancient mountain system—the Appalachians—runs from the United States into Canada. But not everything is so utterly ancient: North America's human history is only thousands of years old, while that of Africa, the birthplace of humankind, dates back millions of years. Just in the past couple of centuries, North America has experienced dramatic changes in its population, landscapes, and environment, an incredible transformation brought about by waves of immigration, booming economies, and relentless development.

PHYSICAL GEOGRAPHY From the world's largest island (Greenland) and greatest concentration of fresh water (the Great Lakes) to such spectacular features as the Grand Canyon and Niagara Falls, North America holds a wealth of superlatives. It is also home to Earth's largest and tallest trees (the redwoods of California) and many of its biggest animals (grizzly bears, moose, and bison). The continent is known as well for dramatic extremes of climate—from the sauna-like 134°F (57°C) recorded in California's Death Valley to the brutally cold minus 87°F (-66°C) logged on Greenland's windswept ice cap.

Third largest of the continents, after Asia and Africa, North America encompasses 9.45 million square miles (24.5 million sq km); its northernmost tip is in Greenland (Cape Morris Jesup), and its southernmost point is in Panama (Península de Azuero).

Deeply indented with inlets and bays, North America claims the longest coastline when compared with other continents. Its land is surrounded by vast oceans and sizable seas: the Atlantic in the east, the Pacific in the west, the Arctic in the north, and the Gulf of Mexico and Caribbean Sea in the south. This geographic circumstance kept the continent isolated for millions of years, greatly influencing the development of its flora and fauna, as well as its human history. Into North America's coastal waters pour a number of mighty rivers, including the Saint Lawrence, Rio Grande, Yukon, Columbia, and Mississippi.

Three significant geologic features dominate the continental landmass: the Canadian (Laurentian) Shield; the great Western Cordillera, which includes the Rocky Mountains, Sierra Nevada, and Sierra Madre; and a colossal flatland that embraces the Great Plains, the Mississippi-Missouri River basin, and most of the Great Lakes region. Other major components include the ancient Appalachian Mountains and the predominantly volcanic islands of the Caribbean Sea. The continent peaks out at 20,320 feet (6,194 m) on the summit of Mount McKinley (Denali), in Alaska, and drops to 282 feet (86 m) below sea level in Death Valley.

The climates of North America range from the frigid conditions of the Arctic ice cap to the steamy tropics of Central America (considered part of North America) and the Caribbean; in between are variations of dry, mild, and continental climes.

The continent has an equally diverse biological heritage, ranging from seemingly endless tundra and coniferous forests in the north to vast deserts and dense rain forests in the south. North America once held huge herds of bison, antelope, elk, and other large wildlife, but such populations declined as the human population grew and spread across the continent.

HISTORY Although the exact date will probably never be determined, North America's human history began sometime between 12,000 and 30,000 years ago, when Asiatic nomads crossed the Bering Strait into Alaska. The descendants of these people spread throughout the continent, evolving into distinct tribes with their own lifestyles and more than 550 different languages.

Most of these original Americans were still hunting and gathering when Europeans arrived in North America; however, several groups had already developed sophisticated cultures. By 1200 B.C., the Olmec of Mexico had created what is generally deemed the first "civilization" in the Western Hemisphere; theirs was a highly advanced society with a calendar, writing system, and stonework architecture. About a hundred years later, the Maya took root in Mexico and Central America, reaching an apex around A.D. 700 with the creation of an elaborate religion and sprawling temple cities. In central Mexico, the highly militaristic Toltec and Aztec forged sprawling empires that drew cultural inspiration from both the Olmec and Maya.

One of the most significant moments for North America—indeed, it was among the most influential events in world history—came in 1492, when a Spanish expedition under Christopher Columbus set foot on an island in the Bahamas. This initial landing ushered in an era of European exploration and settlement that would alter the social fabric of the entire continent. In the next few decades, Hernán Cortés vanquished the Aztec, and Spain claimed virtually the whole Caribbean region and Central America. Other Europeans soon followed—English, French, Dutch, Russians, and even Danes—the leading edge of a migration that would become one of the greatest in human history (more than 70 million people and still counting).

The Native American cultures were unable to compete: They were plagued by European diseases, against which they had little or no resistance; unable to counter the superior firepower of the invaders; and relentlessly driven from their lands. The continent's rich tribal mosaic gradually melted away, replaced by myriad European colonies. By the end of the 19th century, these colonies had been superseded by autonomous nation-states, such as Canada, Mexico, and the United States. Since 1960, many of the Caribbean isles have gained independence, yet quite a few remain colonial possessions under the British, French, Dutch, and U.S. flags.

During the past century, both the U.S. and Canada managed to propel themselves into the ranks of the world's richest nations. But the rest of the continent failed to keep pace, plagued by poverty, despotic governments, and social unrest. In the decades since World War II, many of the Spanish-speaking nations—Cuba, the Dominican

Republic, Nicaragua, El Salvador, and Guatemala—have been racked by bloody revolution. The U.S., on the other hand, ended the 20th century as the only true superpower, with a military presence and political, economic, and cultural influences that extend around the globe.

CULTURE North America's cultural landscape has changed profoundly over the past 500 years. Before the 16th century, the continent was fragmented into hundreds of different cultures developed along tribal lines. From the Inuit people of the Arctic to the Cuña Indians of the Panama jungle, a majority of North America's people had barely risen above Stone Age cultural levels. Noteworthy exceptions included the great civilizations of Mexico and Central America, the pueblo builders of the southwestern U.S., and the highly organized cultivators of the Great Lakes region and the Mississippi Valley. But for the most part, the average North American was migratory, had no concept of written language, and used stone or wooden tools.

The arrival of the Europeans brought permanent settlements, metal tools (and weapons), and written languages. The newcomers founded towns based on Old World models, some of which would evolve into world-class cities—New York, Los Angeles, Chicago, Toronto, and Mexico City among them. Native tongues gave way to a trio of European languages—English, Spanish, and French—now spoken by most of North America's 515 million people. And ancient beliefs yielded to new religions, like Roman Catholicism and Protestantism, which now dominate the continent's spiritual life. The Europeans brought ideas—concepts like democracy, capitalism, religious choice, and free speech—that continue to shape political, intellectual, and economic life.

Despite common historical threads, the coat that comprises today's North America is one of many colors. Mexico and Central America are dominated by Hispano-Indian culture and tend to have more in common with South America than with their neighbors north of the Rio Grande. Although Anglo-Saxon ways still hold sway in the U.S. and Canada, a surge of immigration from Latin America, Asia, and Pacific islands has introduced new cultural traditions. From the Rastafarians of Jamaica to the Creoles of Martinique, the Caribbean islands have fostered myriad microcultures that blend European, African, and Latin traditions.

ECONOMY When it comes to business and industry, North America—and especially the U.S.—is the envy of the world. No other continent produces such an abundance of merchandise or profusion of crops, and no other major region comes close to North America's per capita resource and product consumption. From the high-tech citadels of Silicon Valley to the dream factories of Hollywood, the continent is a world leader in dozens of fields and industries, including computers, entertainment, aerospace, finance, medicine, defense, and agriculture.

The quest for monetary and material success can be traced all the way back to early European immigrants and the tireless work ethic they brought with them. These people, and their cultural descendants, sought to improve their standard of living by exploiting the natural wealth of the land. North America's forests, minerals, and farmlands stoked an industrial revolution that by the end of the 19th century had propelled the U.S. into the ranks of the richest and most powerful nations. Indeed, the continent has an abundance of natural resources: vast petroleum reserves in Alaska and around the Gulf of Mexico, huge coal deposits in the Appalachian and Rocky Mountains, swift-flowing rivers to produce hydropower, and fertile soils that lead to copious harvests.

But the most important product has always been ideas—the ability of its inhabitants to imagine. Next is the ability to transform those ideas into reality through experimentation and hard work. Many of the innovations that revolutionized modern life—the telephone, electric lighting, motor vehicles, airplanes, computers, shopping malls, television, the Internet—were either invented or first mass-produced in the U.S.

Globalization has spread U.S. goods—and by extension, American ideas and culture—around the planet. To a large extent the U.S. dollar has become the world currency, and the financial wizards of New York's Wall Street now control a lion's share of global investment funds. The creation of the North American Free Trade Association (NAFTA) in 1994 drew Canada and Mexico into the same economic web. But success has brought a host of concerns, not the least of which involves the continued exploitation of natural resources. North America is home to only roughly 8 percent of the planet's people, yet its per capita consumption of energy is almost six times as great as the average for all other continents. Its appetite for timber, metals, and water resources is just as voracious.

Other parts of the continent continue to lag in terms of economic vitality. Most Caribbean nations—along with Costa Rica and Belize—now rely on the tourist industry to generate the bulk of their gross national product, while most Central American countries continue to bank on agricultural commodities such as bananas and coffee. Poverty has spurred millions of Mexicans, Central Americans, and Caribbean islanders to migrate northward (legally and illegally) in search of better lives. Finding ways to integrate these disenfranchised masses into the continent's economic miracle is one of the greatest challenges facing North America in the 21st century.

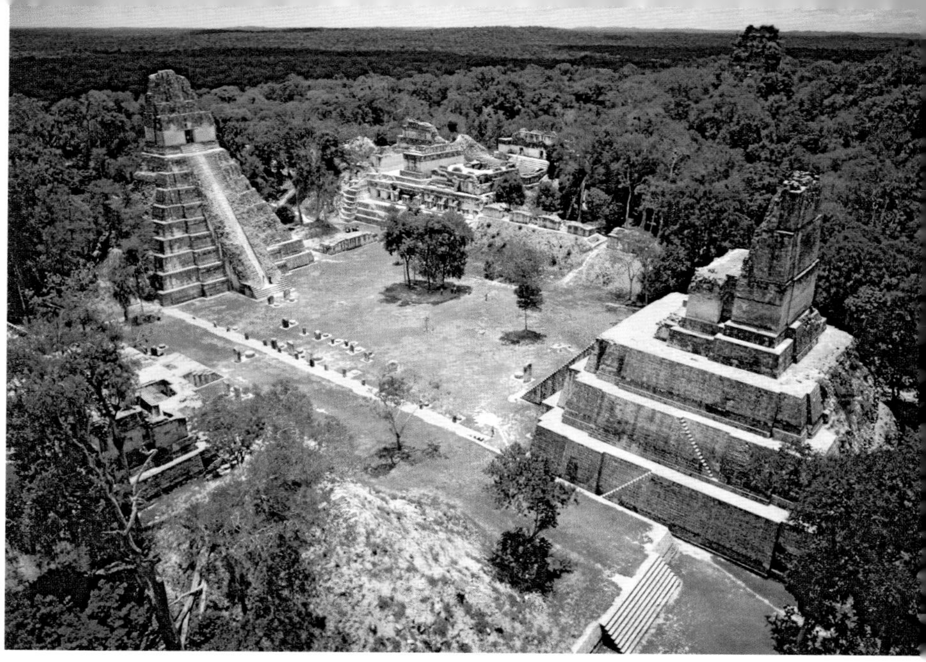

The ceremonial core of Tikal, a major Maya cultural and population center in Guatemala's Petén region, covers approximately one square mile (2.5 sq km). From its early beginnings as a small village (900–300 B.C.), Tikal grew in stature and size to house some 50,000 people at its peak (A.D. 600–800). Even in ruins, its massive Temple I (left) and Temple II (right) remain impressive structures amid myriad palaces, plazas, and ball courts.

North America: Physical and Political
ARCTIC OCEAN
North Magnetic Pole 2006
QUEEN ELIZABETH ISLANDS
Ellesmere Island
Axel Heiberg Island
Cape Morris Jesup
Peary Land
Lincoln Sea
GREENLAND SEA
NORWEGIAN SEA
Meridian of Greenwich (London)
Jan Mayen
King Frederik VIII Land
King Wilhelm Land
King Christian X Land
KNUD RASMUSSEN LAND
GREENLAND
North Geomagnetic Pole 2005
Hayes Pen.
Cape York
Melville Bay
King Christian IX Land
Gunnbjørn 3700
Mont Forel 3360
King Frederik VI Coast
Cape Farewell
Denmark Strait
ICELAND
Faroe Islands
ARCTIC CIRCLE
BAFFIN BAY
Davis Strait
Qeqertarsuaq
Bering Sea
Bering Str.
ASIA
St. Lawrence Island
Seward Peninsula
Norton Sound
Nunivak I.
Point Barrow
North Slope
Brooks Range
Baird Mts.
BEAUFORT SEA
Prince Patrick Island
Cape Prince Alfred
PARRY ISLANDS
Melville I.
Bathurst I.
Cornwallis I.
Devon I.
Banks Island
Victoria Island
Somerset Island
Prince of Wales I.
Bylot Island
Borden Pen.
Brodeur Pen.
Baffin Island
Boothia Peninsula
Gulf of Boothia
Wollaston Peninsula
Collinson Peninsula
Queen Maud Gulf
Melville Hills
Kuskokwim Mts.
Mt. McKinley (Denali) 6194 (20320 ft)
Highest point in North America
Alaska Range
White Mts.
Davidson Mts.
Richardson Mts.
Ogilvie Mountains
YUKON PLATEAU
Selwyn Mts.
Mackenzie Mts.
Franklin Mts.
Cook Inlet
Kenai Peninsula
Kodiak Island
Chugach Mts.
Mt. Logan 5959
GULF OF ALASKA
Great Bear Lake
ARCTIC CIRCLE
Source of the Yukon
Coast Mts.
Alexander Archipelago
Queen Charlotte Is.
Great Slave Lake
Caribou Mts.
Birch Mts.
Lake Athabasca
Source of the Mackenzie-Peace
ROCKY MOUNTAINS
COAST MOUNTAINS
Vancouver I.
Cape Flattery
Columbia Mts.
Selkirk Mts.
Mt. Rainier 4392
Mt. St. Helens 2550
CASCADE RANGE
CANADIAN SHIELD
Melville Pen.
Foxe Basin
Prince Charles I.
Cumberland Peninsula
Cape Dobbs
Southampton Island
Foxe Pen.
Meta Incognita Peninsula
Hudson Strait
Coats I.
Mansel I.
Ungava Peninsula
Killiniq Island
LABRADOR SEA
HUDSON BAY
Cape Churchill
Cape Tatnam
Belcher Islands
Wollaston Lake
Reindeer Lake
Lac la Ronge
GREAT PLAINS
Lake Winnipeg
Lake Winnipegosis
Lake Manitoba
Trout Lake
Lake St. Joseph
James Bay
Akimiski I.
Torngat Mts.
Labrador
Cape Harrison
Mts. Otish 1135
Smallwood Reservoir
Réservoir Caniapiscau
Laurentide Scarp
Anticosti I.
Gulf of St. Lawrence
Long Range Mts.
ISLAND OF NEWFOUNDLAND
Avalon Peninsula
Cabot Str.
Cape Breton Island
Gaspé Pen.
Prince Edward I.
Mt. Katahdin 1606
NOVA SCOTIA
Sable I.
Cape Sable
Bay of Fundy
Gulf of Maine
Cape Cod
Long Island
Lake Nipigon
Lake Superior
Lake of the Woods
Mt. Tremblant 968
Laurentian Scarp
Upper Pen.
Lake Michigan
Lower Peninsula
L. Huron
L. Ontario
L. Erie
Niagara Falls
Adirondack Mts.
White Mts.
Mt. Washington 1917
Georgian Bay
Source of the Missouri-Red Rock
Source of the Mississippi (Lake Itasca)
Lake Sakakawea
Lake Oahe
Badlands
Black Hills 2207
Bighorn Mts.
Grand Teton 4197
Bitterroot Ra.
Columbia Plateau
Snake River Plain
Great Sandy Desert
Cape Blanco
Cape Mendocino
Mt. Shasta 4317
Sierra Nevada
Sacramento Valley
San Joaquin Valley
Great Basin
Great Salt Lake
Wasatch Ra.
Farallon Islands
Monterey Bay
Point Conception
Channel Islands
Lowest point in North America
-86 (-282 ft)
Death Valley
Mojave Desert
Colorado Plateau
Grand Canyon
Painted Desert
Source of the Rio Grande
Lake Powell
Lake Mead
Pikes Peak 4301
Front Range
Sangre de Cristo Mountains
Geographical Center of the 48 Contiguous United States
CENTRAL LOWLAND
Ozark Plateau 540
Ouachita Mts. 811
Wichita Mts. 756
Llano Estacado (Staked Plain)
Edwards Plateau
Appalachian Plateau
Allegheny Mts.
APPALACHIAN MOUNTAINS
Piedmont
Chesapeake Bay
Cape Charles
Great Dismal Swamp
Cape Hatteras
Cape Fear
Sea Islands
Okefenokee Swamp
ATLANTIC OCEAN
PACIFIC OCEAN
Bermuda Is.
Azimuthal Equidistant Projection
SCALE 1:28,768,000
1 CENTIMETER = 288 KILOMETERS; 1 INCH = 454 MILES
KILOMETERS
STATUTE MILES
International boundary
Elevations in meters
COASTAL PLAIN
Sonoran Desert
Altar Desert
BAJA CALIFORNIA
GULF OF CALIFORNIA
Guadalupe I.
Vizcaíno Bay
Eugenia Point
TROPIC OF CANCER
Alijos Rocks
Magdalena Bay
False Cape
Revillagigedo Islands
San Benedicto I.
Clarión I.
Roca Partida I.
Socorro I.
Marías Islands
Banderas Bay
Cape Corrientes
SIERRA MADRE OCCIDENTAL
SIERRA MADRE ORIENTAL
Bolsón de Mapimí
2626
Galveston Bay
Mississippi River Delta
Florida
Cape Canaveral (Cape Kennedy)
Lake Okeechobee
Everglades
Florida Keys
Strs. of Florida
GULF OF MEXICO
Madre Lagoon
BAHAMAS
Andros I.
San Salvador
Rum Cay
Great Inagua I.
Caicos Islands
Turks Islands
CUBA
Cape San Antonio
Cape Catoche
Yucatan Channel
Isle of Youth
Yucatan Peninsula 250
Cozumel Island
Cape Rojo
Popocatépetl 5426
Pico de Orizaba 5747
Isthmus of Tehuantepec
Sierra Madre del Sur
Gulf of Tehuantepec
Sierra Madre
CENTRAL AMERICA
Gulf of Fonseca
Lake Managua
Lake Nicaragua
Mosquito Coast
Cape Gracias a Dios
Cape Camarón
Bay Islands
Gulf of Honduras
Chetumal Bay
Grand Cayman
JAMAICA
Pedro Cays
Roncador Cay
Mono Point (Monkey Point)
Nicoya Peninsula
Coronado Bay
Cord. de Talamanca
Isthmus of Panama
Gulf of Panama
Burica Point
Coiba I.
Azuero Pen.
Cocos I.
GREATER ANTILLES
HISPANIOLA
PUERTO RICO
Virgin Islands
Windward Pass.
Mona Pass.
CARIBBEAN SEA
WEST INDIES
LESSER ANTILLES
Leeward Islands
Aruba
Curaçao
Bonaire
Lake Maracaibo
ANDES
SOUTH AMERICA
Longitude West 90° of Greenwich
EQUATOR
BERING SEA AND THE ALEUTIAN ISLANDS
Same Scale as Main Map
Longitude East of Greenwich
Longitude West of Greenwich
SIBERIA
Koryak Range
Kamchatka Peninsula
Karaginskiy I.
Gulf of Anadyr
Chukchi Pen.
Cape Navarin
St. Lawrence Island
Norton Sound
Cape Romanzof
St. Matthew I.
ALASKA
Kuskokwim Mts.
Kilbuck Mts.
Nunivak Island
Kuskokwim Bay
Commander Islands
BERING SEA
Pribilof Is.
Hagemeister Island
Bristol Bay
Alaska Peninsula
ALEUTIAN ISLANDS
Attu
Near Islands
Agattu
Rat Islands
Andreanof Islands
Fox Islands
Shumagin Is.

ARCTIC OCEAN
North Magnetic Pole 2006
QUEEN ELIZABETH ISLANDS
GREENLAND (KALAALLIT NUNAAT)
Denmark
NORWEGIAN SEA
GREENLAND SEA
ICELAND
UNITED KINGDOM
BAFFIN BAY
BEAUFORT SEA
ALASKA
United States
YUKON
NORTHWEST TERRITORIES
NUNAVUT
ARCTIC CIRCLE
CANADA
HUDSON BAY
Hudson Strait
LABRADOR SEA
NEWFOUNDLAND AND LABRADOR
NOUVEAU QUÉBEC
QUEBEC
ONTARIO
MANITOBA
SASKATCHEWAN
ALBERTA
BRITISH COLUMBIA
GULF OF ALASKA
PACIFIC OCEAN
ATLANTIC OCEAN
UNITED STATES
GULF OF MEXICO
MEXICO
TROPIC OF CANCER
CARIBBEAN SEA
GREATER ANTILLES
LESSER ANTILLES
BAHAMAS
CUBA
VENEZUELA
COLOMBIA
SOUTH AMERICA
Bermuda Is.
U.K.
Azimuthal Equidistant Projection
SCALE 1:28,768,000
1 CENTIMETER = 288 KILOMETERS; 1 INCH = 454 MILES
KILOMETERS
STATUTE MILES
BERING SEA AND THE ALEUTIAN ISLANDS
Same Scale as Main Map
Longitude West 90° of Greenwich

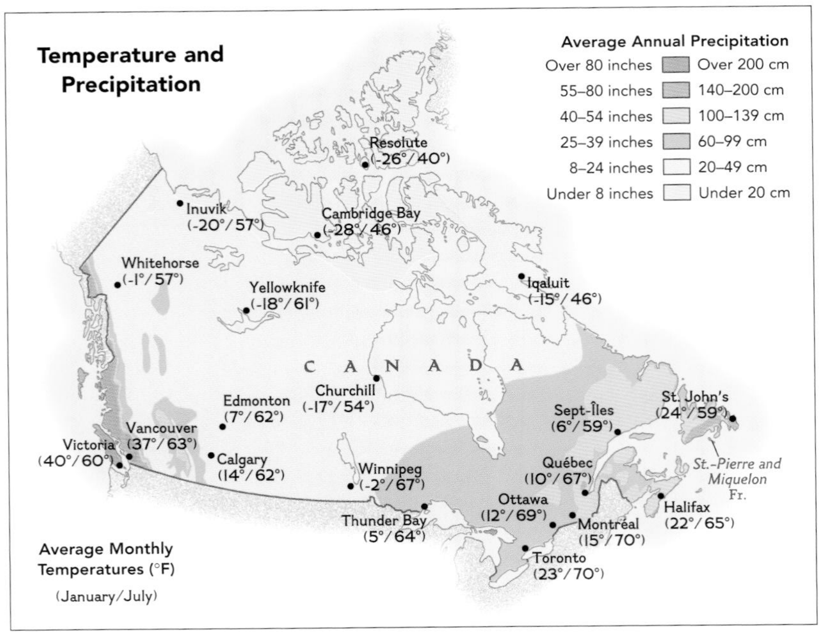

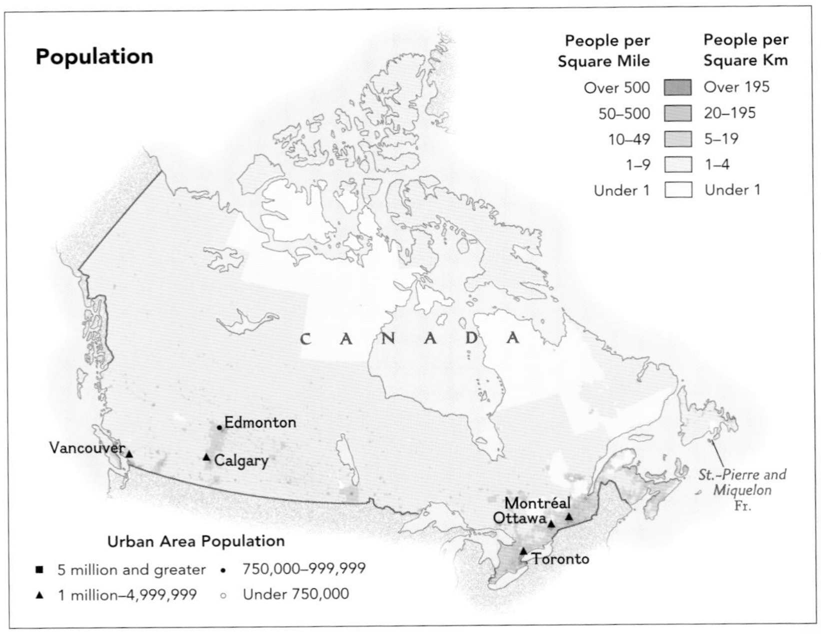

Azimuthal Equidistant Projection

SCALE 1:14,903,000

1 CENTIMETER = 149 KILOMETERS; 1 INCH = 235 MILES

0 200 400 600 800 KILOMETERS

0 200 400 600 800 STATUTE MILES

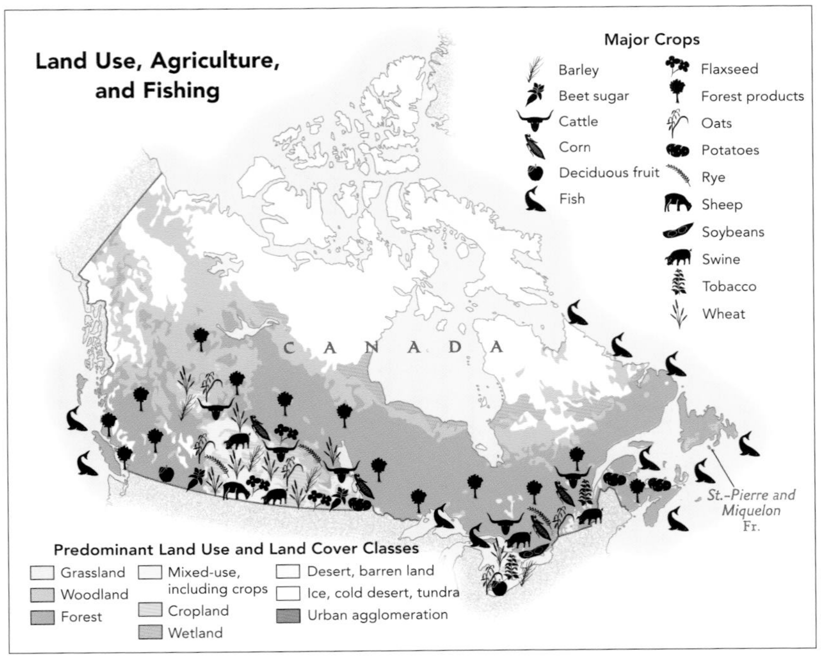

Canada

CANADA

AREA 9,984,670 sq km (3,855,101 sq mi)
POPULATION 32,225,000
CAPITAL Ottawa 1,093,000
RELIGION Roman Catholic, Protestant
LANGUAGE English (official), French (official)
LITERACY 97%
LIFE EXPECTANCY 80 years
GDP PER CAPITA $31,031
ECONOMY **IND:** transportation equipment, chemicals, processed and unprocessed minerals, food products **AGR:** wheat, barley, oilseed, tobacco; dairy products; forest products; fish **EXP:** motor vehicles and parts, industrial machinery, aircraft, telecommunications equipment

SOVEREIGN LOCAL

Greenland (Denmark)

GREENLAND

AREA 2,166,086 sq km (836,086 sq mi)
POPULATION 57,000
CAPITAL Nuuk (Godthåb) 14,000
RELIGION Evangelical Lutheran
LANGUAGE Greenlandic, Danish, English
LITERACY NA
LIFE EXPECTANCY 67 years
GDP PER CAPITA $20,000
ECONOMY **IND:** fish processing (shrimp, halibut), mining, handicrafts, hides and skins **AGR:** forage crops, garden and greenhouse vegetables; sheep; fish **EXP:** fish and fish products

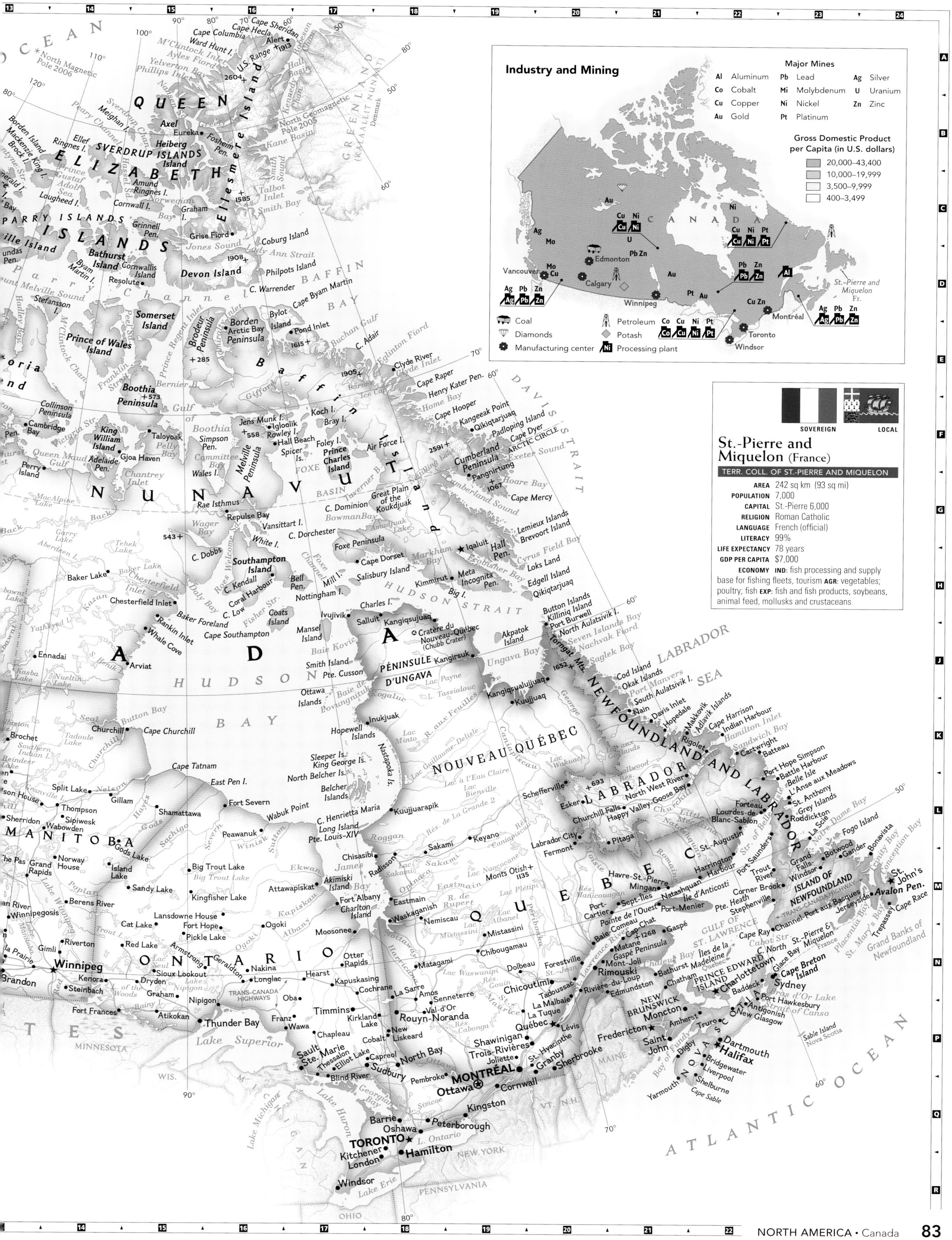

St.-Pierre and Miquelon (France)

SOVEREIGN LOCAL

TERR. COLL. OF ST.-PIERRE AND MIQUELON

AREA	242 sq km (93 sq mi)
POPULATION	7,000
CAPITAL	St.-Pierre 6,000
RELIGION	Roman Catholic
LANGUAGE	French (official)
LITERACY	99%
LIFE EXPECTANCY	78 years
GDP PER CAPITA	$7,000

ECONOMY **IND:** fish processing and supply base for fishing fleets, tourism **AGR:** vegetables; poultry; fish **EXP:** fish and fish products, soybeans, animal feed, mollusks and crustaceans

PACIFIC OCEAN
CANADA
ROCKY MOUNTAINS
GREAT PLAINS
CASCADE RANGE
COAST RANGES
SIERRA NEVADA
GREAT BASIN
COLORADO PLATEAU
Columbia Plateau
Mojave Desert
Sonoran Desert
Great Sandy Desert
Klamath Mountains
Salmon River Mountains
Bitterroot Range
Blue Mountains
Wallowa Mts.
Clearwater Mts.
Absaroka Range
Wind River Ra.
Bighorn Mts.
Uinta Mts.
Wasatch Ra.
Bear River Ra.
Front Range
Laramie Mts.
Medicine Bow Mts.
Sangre de Cristo Mts.
San Juan Mts.
Black Hills
Sand Hills
Llano Estacado
Edwards Plateau
Great Divide Basin
Snake River Plain
Harney Basin
Black Rock Desert
Great Salt Lake Desert
Painted Desert
Grand Canyon
Mogollon Rim
Imperial Valley
Sacramento Valley
San Joaquin Valley
Death Valley
Continental Divide
Mt. Baker 10778
Mt. Olympus 7980
Mt. Rainier 14411
Mt. St. Helens 8366
Mt. Adams 12307
Mt. Hood 11239
Mt. Shasta 14162
Lassen Peak 10457
Mt. Whitney 14494 (4418 m)
-282 (-86 m)
Boundary Peak 13140
Borah Pk. 12662
Granite Pk. 12799
Grand Teton 13770
Gannett Pk. 13804
Kings Pk. 13528
Mt. Elbert 14433
Pikes Peak 14110
Longs Peak 14255
Blanca Pk. 14345
Wheeler Pk. 13161
Wheeler Pk. 13063
Guadalupe Pk. 8749
Harney Pk. 7242
Cape Flattery
Cape Disappointment
Cape Blanco
Cape Mendocino
Point Arena
Point Reyes
San Francisco Bay
Monterey Bay
Point Conception
Channel Islands
Great Salt Lake
Lake Mead
Lake Powell
Salton Sea
Lake Sakakawea
Lake Oahe
Fort Peck Lake
Missouri
Yellowstone
Snake
Colorado
Rio Grande
Columbia
Geographical Center of the 50 United States
Geographical Center of the 48 Contiguous United States
MEXICO
ALASKA
BEAUFORT SEA
CHUKCHI SEA
BERING SEA
GULF OF ALASKA
ARCTIC CIRCLE
RUSSIA
North Slope
BROOKS RANGE
ALASKA RANGE
Mt. McKinley (Denali) 20320 (6194 m)
Kuskokwim Mountains
Chugach Mountains
St. Elias Mountains
COAST MOUNTAINS
ALASKA PENINSULA
ALEUTIAN RANGE
SEWARD PENINSULA
KENAI PENINSULA
ALEXANDER ARCHIPELAGO
Kodiak Island
Mt. St. Elias 18008
Mt. Fairweather 15300
Wrangell Mts.
Yukon
0 100 200 300 km
0 50 100 150 statute mi

ATLANTIC OCEAN
GULF OF MEXICO
GULF OF MAINE
CENTRAL LOWLAND
APPALACHIAN MOUNTAINS
Appalachian Plateau
Allegheny Mountains
Blue Ridge
Piedmont
Cumberland Plateau
Ozark Plateau
Black Belt
Lake Superior
Lake Michigan
Lake Huron
Lake Erie
Lake Ontario
Upper Peninsula
Lower Peninsula
Isle Royale
Keweenaw Peninsula
Eagle Mt. 2301
Mt. Arvon 1979
Timms Hill 1951
Charles Mound 1235
Campbell Hill 1550
Taum Sauk Mt. 1772
Magazine Mt. 2753
Woodall Mt. 806
Cheaha Mt. 2407
Britton Hill 345
Driskill Mt. 535
Mt. Katahdin 5268
Mt. Washington 6288
Mt. Mansfield 4393
Mt. Marcy 5344
Mt. Greylock 3491
Mt. Frissell 2380
Jerimoth Hill 812
Slide Mt. 4180
High Pt. 1803
3213 Mt. Davis
Backbone Mt. 3360
4863 Spruce Knob
Black Mt. 4145
Mt. Rogers 5729
Clingmans Dome 6643
Mt. Mitchell 6684
Sassafras Mt. 3560
Brasstown Bald 4784
Adirondack Mts.
Catskill Mts.
Green Mts.
White Mts.
Great Smoky Mts.
Boston Mts.
Ouachita Mts.
Mesabi Ra.
Gogebic Ra.
Cape Cod
Cape Ann
Cape May
Cape Charles
Cape Hatteras
Cape Lookout
Cape Fear
Cape Canaveral
Cape Romano
Cape Sable
Cape San Blas
Chesapeake Bay
Delaware Bay
Albemarle Sound
Pamlico Sd.
Long Island Sd.
Long I.
Martha's Vineyard
Nantucket I.
Mt. Desert I.
Bay of Fundy
Sea Islands
Okefenokee Swamp
Great Dismal Swamp
Lake Okeechobee
The Everglades
Florida Keys
Straits of Florida
Tampa Bay
Charlotte Harbor
Mississippi River Delta
Lake Pontchartrain
Galveston Bay
TROPIC OF CANCER
CUBA
BAHAMAS
HAITI
elevations in feet
10,000
9,000
8,000
7,000
6,000
5,000
4,000
3,000
2,000
1,000
250
0 (sea level)
Albers Conic Equal-Area Projection
SCALE 1:10,824,000
1 CENTIMETER = 108 KILOMETERS; 1 INCH = 171 MILES
KILOMETERS
STATUTE MILES
Longitude West 90° of Greenwich
Longitude West 159° of Greenwich
PACIFIC OCEAN
PRINCIPAL HAWAIIAN ISLANDS
KAUA'I
Kawaikini 5243
NI'IHAU
O'AHU
4019
MOLOKA'I
Kamakou 4970
LĀNA'I 3370
MAUI
10023
Kaho'olawe
HAWAI'I
Mauna Kea 13796
Mauna Loa 13679
Kilauea 4077
Ka Lae (South Cape)
100 km
100 statute mi

PACIFIC OCEAN
BRITISH COLUMBIA
ALBERTA
SASKATCHEWAN
MANITOBA
CANADA
Str. of Juan de Fuca
WASHINGTON
Bellingham
Everett
Seattle
Bremerton
Mt. Olympus 7980
Olympia
Tacoma
Aberdeen
Centralia
Longview
Astoria
Kelso
Vancouver
Mt. Rainier 14411
Mt. St. Helens 8366
Wenatchee
Colville
Sandpoint
Coeur d'Alene
Spokane
Yakima
Richland
Pullman
Walla Walla
Columbia
OREGON
Portland
Newport
Salem
Albany
Corvallis
Eugene
Springfield
North Bend
Coos Bay
Roseburg
Grants Pass
Medford
Ashland
Klamath Falls
Crescent City
Mt. Hood 11239
The Dalles
Pendleton
La Grande
Baker City
John Day
Burns
Ontario
Crane
Goose L.
IDAHO
Bonners Ferry
Lewiston
Wallace
Salmon
Payette
Caldwell
Boise
Nampa
Mountain Home
Sun Valley
Borah Pk. 12662
Idaho Falls
Blackfoot
Pocatello
Jerome
Twin Falls
Burley
Rupert
Montpelier
Preston
Snake
MONTANA
ROCKY MOUNTAINS
Kalispell
Cut Bank
Shelby
Havre
Turner
Polson
Malta
Glasgow
Fort Peck Lake
Fort Benton
Great Falls
Missoula
Deer Lodge
Helena
Lewistown
Wolf Point
Sidney
Williston
Missouri
Glendive
Roundup
Butte
Bozeman
Livingston
Miles City
Billings
Laurel
Forsyth
Dillon
Hardin
Baker
WYOMING
Powell
Cody
Sheridan
Buffalo
Worland
Gillette
Newcastle
Thermopolis
Grand Teton 13770
Gannett Pk. 13804
Riverton
Lander
Casper
Douglas
Lusk
Kemmerer
Green River
Rock Springs
Rawlins
Evanston
Laramie
Cheyenne
NORTH DAKOTA
Portal
St. John
Stanley
Minot
Rugby
Grafton
Devils Lake
Thief River
Lake Sakakawea
Harvey
Grand Forks
Dickinson
Mandan
Bismarck
Jamestown
Fargo
Valley City
Moorhead
Mott
Fort Yates
Ashley
Oakes
Lemmon
SOUTH DAKOTA
Mobridge
Aberdeen
Lake Oahe
Faith
Watertown
Belle Fourche
Lead
Rapid City
Pierre
Huron
Brookings
Hot Springs
Martin
Lake Francis Case
Mitchell
Sioux Falls
Yankton
NEBRASKA
Chadron
Valentine
Ainsworth
Alliance
Norfolk
Scottsbluff
Sidney
North Platte
Grand Island
Columbus
Kearney
Hastings
Lincoln
Platte
McCook
Beatrice
CALIFORNIA
Crescent City
Yreka
Mt. Shasta 14162
Eureka
Redding
Red Bluff
Susanville
Fort Bragg
Ukiah
Yuba City
Sacramento
Santa Rosa
Vallejo
San Francisco
Oakland
San Mateo
Stockton
Palo Alto
Modesto
Santa Cruz
San Jose
Monterey
Salinas
Coalinga
Fresno
Visalia
Paso Robles
Delano
San Luis Obispo
Bakersfield
Santa Maria
Lompoc
Santa Barbara
Ridgecrest
Mojave
Glendale
LOS ANGELES
Pasadena
Long Beach
San Bernardino
Santa Ana
Riverside
Palm Springs
Salton Sea
SAN DIEGO
National City
El Centro
Bishop
Death Valley -282
Needles
SIERRA NEVADA
NEVADA
GREAT BASIN
Denio
McDermitt
Winnemucca
Lovelock
Carlin
Elko
Wells
Reno
Carson City
Ely
McGill
Hawthorne
Mt. Jefferson 11949
Tonopah
Goldfield
Pioche
Caliente
Beatty
Las Vegas
Boulder City
Lake Mead
UTAH
Great Salt Lake
Logan
Ogden
Salt Lake City
Tooele
Provo
Utah L.
Kings Pk. 13528
Vernal
Nephi
Price
Sevier Lake
Fillmore
Manti
Richfield
Moab
Parowan
Panguitch
Cedar City
St. George
Kanab
Monticello
Lake Powell
COLORADO
Craig
Fort Collins
Greeley
Longmont
Boulder
Fort Morgan
Denver
Aurora
Glenwood Springs
Grand Junction
Colorado
Delta
Gunnison
Montrose
Pikes Pk. 14110
Colorado Springs
Pueblo
Salida
Canon City
Silverton
Cortez
Durango
Alamosa
Walsenburg
Trinidad
La Junta
Lamar
COLORADO PLATEAU
ARIZONA
Grand Canyon
Kingman
Williams
Flagstaff
Prescott
Winslow
Holbrook
Wickenburg
PHOENIX
Scottsdale
Mesa
Globe
Baldy Peak 11403
Gila Bend
Casa Grande
Morenci
Safford
Ajo
Eloy
Tucson
Willcox
Benson
Tombstone
Nogales
Bisbee
Douglas
Yuma
NEW MEXICO
Farmington
Wheeler Peak 13161
Raton
Clayton
Springer
Los Alamos
Santa Fe
Las Vegas
Gallup
Grants
Albuquerque
Tucumcari
Belen
Vaughn
Fort Sumner
Clovis
Magdalena
Socorro
Truth or Consequences
Roswell
Alamogordo
Silver City
Artesia
Lordsburg
Deming
Las Cruces
Hobbs
Carlsbad
El Paso
KANSAS
Norton
Colby
Goodland
Russell
Hays
Salina
Manhattan
Great Bend
Garden City
Hutchinson
Arkansas
Dodge City
Wichita
Arkansas City
Liberal
OKLAHOMA
Guymon
Woodward
Ponca City
Enid
Stillwater
Shawnee
Oklahoma City
Chickasha
Lawton
Ardmore
Red
TEXAS
Dalhart
Dumas
Borger
Pampa
Amarillo
Hereford
Childress
Vernon
Wichita Falls
Plainview
Lubbock
Brownfield
Lamesa
Snyder
Sweetwater
Abilene
Fort Worth
Dallas
Midland
Big Spring
Odessa
Brownwood
Waco
Temple
Austin
Pecos
Van Horn
San Angelo
Ozona
Sonora
Fort Stockton
Marfa
Alpine
Sanderson
Amistad Reservoir
Rio Grande
Del Rio
New Braunfels
SAN ANTONIO
Uvalde
Eagle Pass
Victoria
Beeville
Aransas Pass
Alice
Laredo
Kingsville
Falfurrias
Raymondville
Edinburg
McAllen
Brownsville
MEXICO
ALASKA
ARCTIC OCEAN
BEAUFORT SEA
CHUKCHI SEA
ARCTIC CIRCLE
RUSSIA
BERING SEA
Bering Str.
Barrow
Wainwright
Atqasuk
Point Lay
Prudhoe Bay
Kaktovik
Point Hope
Umiat
North Slope
BROOKS RANGE
Kivalina
Noatak
Kotzebue
Shishmaref
Selawik
Kiana
Shungnak
Kobuk
Wiseman
Fort Yukon
Wales
Teller
Deering
Allakaket
Beaver
Hughes
Circle
Yukon
Nome
Koyuk
Galena
Nulato
Rampart
Tanana
Fairbanks
Eagle
Gambell
Savoonga
St. Lawrence Island
Golovin
Kaltag
Ruby
Unalakleet
Lake Minchumina
Nenana
Big Delta
ALASKA RANGE
Tanacross
Alakanuk
Kotlik
St. Michael
Cantwell
Mountain Village
Anvik
McGrath
Mt. McKinley (Denali) 20320
Northway
Hooper Bay
Flat
Farewell
Gulkana
Holy Cross
Aniak
Red Devil
Skwentna
Palmer
Tununak
Mekoryuk
Bethel
Nyac
Kashegelok
Anchorage
Whittier
Valdez
Cordova
Nunivak Island
Quinhagak
Kenai
Goodnews Bay
Newhalen
Homer
Seward
Cape Yakataga
Yakutat
Iliamna Lake
Togiak
Seldovia
Dillingham
Naknek
King Salmon
GULF OF ALASKA
Egegik
Kodiak
Kodiak Island
Pilot Point
Karluk
Chignik
Sand Point
Cold Bay
PACIFIC OCEAN
CANADA
U.S.
YUKON
NORTHWEST TERRITORIES
BRITISH COLUMBIA
Skagway
Haines
Juneau
Gustavus
Hoonah
Sitka
Petersburg
Wrangell
Ketchikan
Hydaburg
0 100 200 300 km
0 50 100 150 statute mi

United States
UNITED STATES OF AMERICA
AREA 9,826,630 sq km (3,794,083 sq mi)
POPULATION 296,483,000
CAPITAL Washington, D.C. 4,098,000
RELIGION Protestant, Roman Catholic
LANGUAGE English, Spanish
LITERACY 97%
LIFE EXPECTANCY 78 years
GDP PER CAPITA $39,650
ECONOMY IND: petroleum, steel, motor vehicles, aerospace AGR: wheat, corn, other grains, fruits; beef; forest products; fish EXP: capital goods, industrial supplies, consumer goods, agricultural products
Albers Conic Equal-Area Projection
SCALE 1:10,824,000
1 CENTIMETER = 108 KILOMETERS; 1 INCH = 171 MILES
0 100 200 300 400 500
KILOMETERS
0 100 200 300 400 500
STATUTE MILES
ONTARIO
QUEBEC
NEW BRUNSWICK
PRINCE EDWARD ISLAND
NOVA SCOTIA
Lake of the Woods
Lake Superior
Lake Michigan
Lake Huron
Georgian Bay
Lake Ontario
Lake Erie
St. Lawrence
Bay of Fundy
GULF OF MAINE
ATLANTIC OCEAN
GULF OF MEXICO
Straits of Florida
BAHAMAS
CUBA
HAITI
TROPIC OF CANCER
MINNESOTA
WISCONSIN
MICHIGAN
IOWA
ILLINOIS
INDIANA
OHIO
MISSOURI
KENTUCKY
TENNESSEE
ARKANSAS
MISSISSIPPI
ALABAMA
GEORGIA
LOUISIANA
FLORIDA
SOUTH CAROLINA
NORTH CAROLINA
VIRGINIA
WEST VIRGINIA
PENNSYLVANIA
NEW YORK
NEW JERSEY
DELAWARE
MARYLAND
CONN.
RHODE ISLAND
MASSACHUSETTS
VERMONT
NEW HAMPSHIRE
MAINE
APPALACHIAN MOUNTAINS
Washington, D.C.
NEW YORK
PHILADELPHIA
CHICAGO
Boston
Baltimore
Detroit
Cleveland
Pittsburgh
Atlanta
Miami
Jacksonville
Memphis
Nashville
Louisville
Indianapolis
Columbus
Cincinnati
Milwaukee
St. Louis
Kansas City
New Orleans
Baton Rouge
Richmond
Raleigh
Charlotte
Tallahassee
Orlando
Tampa
St. Petersburg
Fort Lauderdale
Hollywood
Key West
Florida Keys
PRINCIPAL HAWAIIAN ISLANDS
PACIFIC OCEAN
Longitude West 159° of Greenwich
KAUA'I
NI'IHAU
O'AHU
MOLOKA'I
LĀNA'I
MAUI
HAWAI'I
Honolulu
Hilo
Mauna Loa 13679
Kīlauea 4077
0 100 km
0 100 statute mi
Longitude West 90° of Greenwich

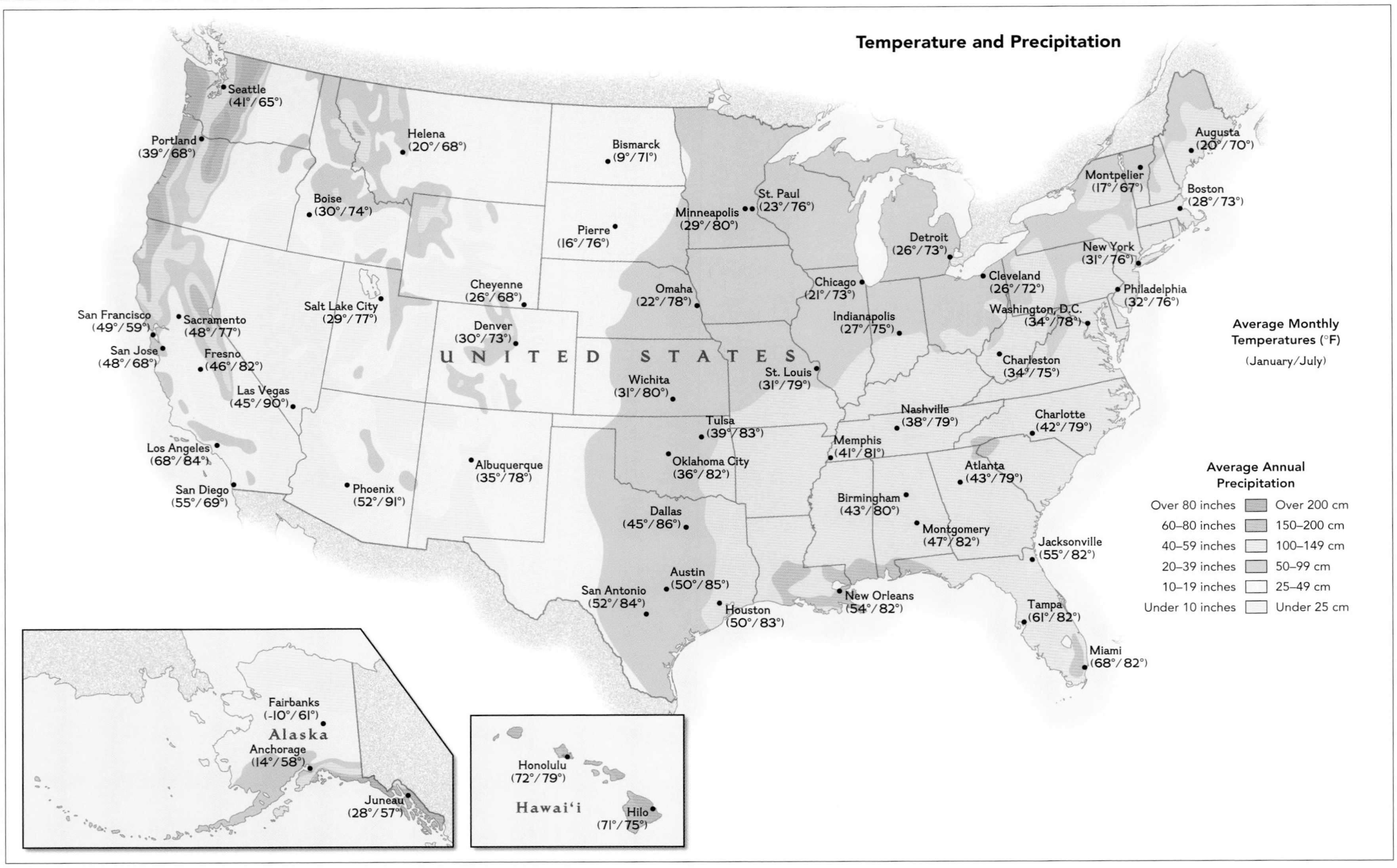
Temperature and Precipitation
Seattle (41°/65°)
Portland (39°/68°)
Helena (20°/68°)
Bismarck (9°/71°)
Boise (30°/74°)
Pierre (16°/76°)
Minneapolis (29°/80°)
St. Paul (23°/76°)
Detroit (26°/73°)
Montpelier (17°/67°)
Augusta (20°/70°)
Boston (28°/73°)
New York (31°/76°)
Philadelphia (32°/76°)
Cleveland (26°/72°)
Washington, D.C. (34°/78°)
Chicago (21°/73°)
Indianapolis (27°/75°)
Omaha (22°/78°)
Cheyenne (26°/68°)
Salt Lake City (29°/77°)
San Francisco (49°/59°)
Sacramento (48°/77°)
San Jose (48°/68°)
Fresno (46°/82°)
Denver (30°/73°)
UNITED STATES
Wichita (31°/80°)
St. Louis (31°/79°)
Charleston (34°/75°)
Las Vegas (45°/90°)
Nashville (38°/79°)
Charlotte (42°/79°)
Tulsa (39°/83°)
Memphis (41°/81°)
Los Angeles (68°/84°)
Albuquerque (35°/78°)
Oklahoma City (36°/82°)
Atlanta (43°/79°)
San Diego (55°/69°)
Phoenix (52°/91°)
Birmingham (43°/80°)
Dallas (45°/86°)
Montgomery (47°/82°)
Jacksonville (55°/82°)
Austin (50°/85°)
San Antonio (52°/84°)
Houston (50°/83°)
New Orleans (54°/82°)
Tampa (61°/82°)
Miami (68°/82°)
Fairbanks (-10°/61°)
Alaska
Anchorage (14°/58°)
Juneau (28°/57°)
Honolulu (72°/79°)
Hawai'i
Hilo (71°/75°)
Average Monthly Temperatures (°F)
(January/July)
Average Annual Precipitation
Over 80 inches Over 200 cm
60–80 inches 150–200 cm
40–59 inches 100–149 cm
20–39 inches 50–99 cm
10–19 inches 25–49 cm
Under 10 inches Under 25 cm

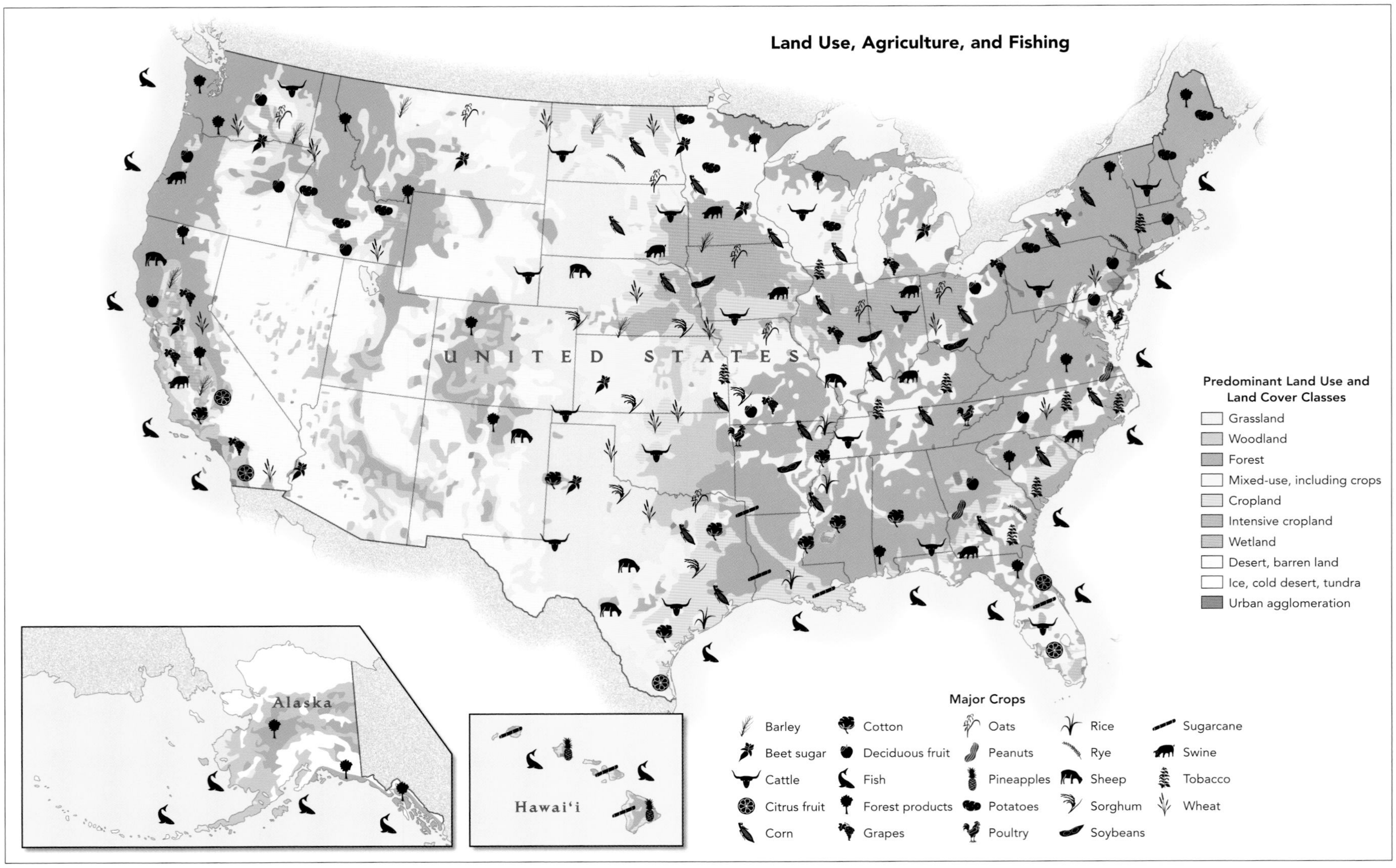
Land Use, Agriculture, and Fishing
UNITED STATES
Alaska
Hawai'i
Predominant Land Use and Land Cover Classes
Grassland
Woodland
Forest
Mixed-use, including crops
Cropland
Intensive cropland
Wetland
Desert, barren land
Ice, cold desert, tundra
Urban agglomeration
Major Crops
Barley
Beet sugar
Cattle
Citrus fruit
Corn
Cotton
Deciduous fruit
Fish
Forest products
Grapes
Oats
Peanuts
Pineapples
Potatoes
Poultry
Rice
Rye
Sheep
Sorghum
Soybeans
Sugarcane
Swine
Tobacco
Wheat

Population

Seattle
Portland
Minneapolis-St. Paul
Milwaukee
Detroit
Buffalo
Boston
Providence
Hartford
Bridgeport-Stamford
New York-Newark
Philadelphia
Chicago
Cleveland
Pittsburgh
Salt Lake City
San Francisco-Oakland
Sacramento
San Jose
Denver-Aurora
Columbus
Baltimore
Indianapolis
Washington, D.C.
Cincinnati
Richmond
Kansas City
St. Louis
Louisville
Virginia Beach
Las Vegas
UNITED STATES
Los Angeles-Long Beach-Santa Ana
Riverside-San Bernardino
Nashville-Davidson
Charlotte
Memphis
Phoenix-Mesa
San Diego
Atlanta
Dallas-Fort Worth
Jacksonville
Austin
San Antonio
New Orleans
Houston
Orlando
Tampa-St. Petersburg
Miami
Alaska
Hawai'i

Urban Area Population

- ■ 5 million and greater
- ▲ 1 million–4,999,999
- • 750,000–999,999
- ○ Under 750,000

People per Square Mile	People per Square Km
Over 250	Over 100
100–250	40–100
10–99	5–39
1–9	1–4
Under 1	Under 1

Industry and Mining

Al
Seattle
Pb Zn Ag
Portland
Pt
Fe
Fe
Minneapolis
St. Paul
Boston
Rochester
Buffalo
Flint
Steel
Milwaukee
Cu Au Mo Ag
Au
UNITED STATES
Detroit
Toledo
Cleveland
Steel
Allentown
Newark
Nassau-Suffolk counties
New York
Philadelphia
Chicago
Steel
Gary
Pittsburgh
San Francisco
San Jose
Au Ag
Be
Mo
Denver
Au
Indianapolis
Dayton
Columbus
Baltimore
Kansas City
St. Louis
Cincinnati
Al
Louisville
He
Pb
Pb Zn
Greensboro
Charlotte
Los Angeles
Anaheim
San Diego
Cu Au Mo Ag
I
Greenville
Atlanta
Birmingham
Fort Worth
Dallas
Al
Houston
Pb Zn Ag
Au
Alaska
Hawai'i

Gross Domestic Product per Capita (in U.S. dollars)

- 20,000–43,400
- 10,000–19,999
- 3,500–9,999
- 400–3,499

Major Mines

Be	Beryllium
Cu	Copper
Au	Gold
He	Helium
I	Iodine
Fe	Iron
Pb	Lead
Mo	Molybdenum
Pt	Platinum
Ag	Silver
Zn	Zinc

- Borates
- Coal
- Heavy mineral sands
- Kaolin
- Manufacturing center
- Petroleum
- Phosphate
- Potash
- Processing plant
- Rare earth elements
- Soda ash
- Steel manufacturing

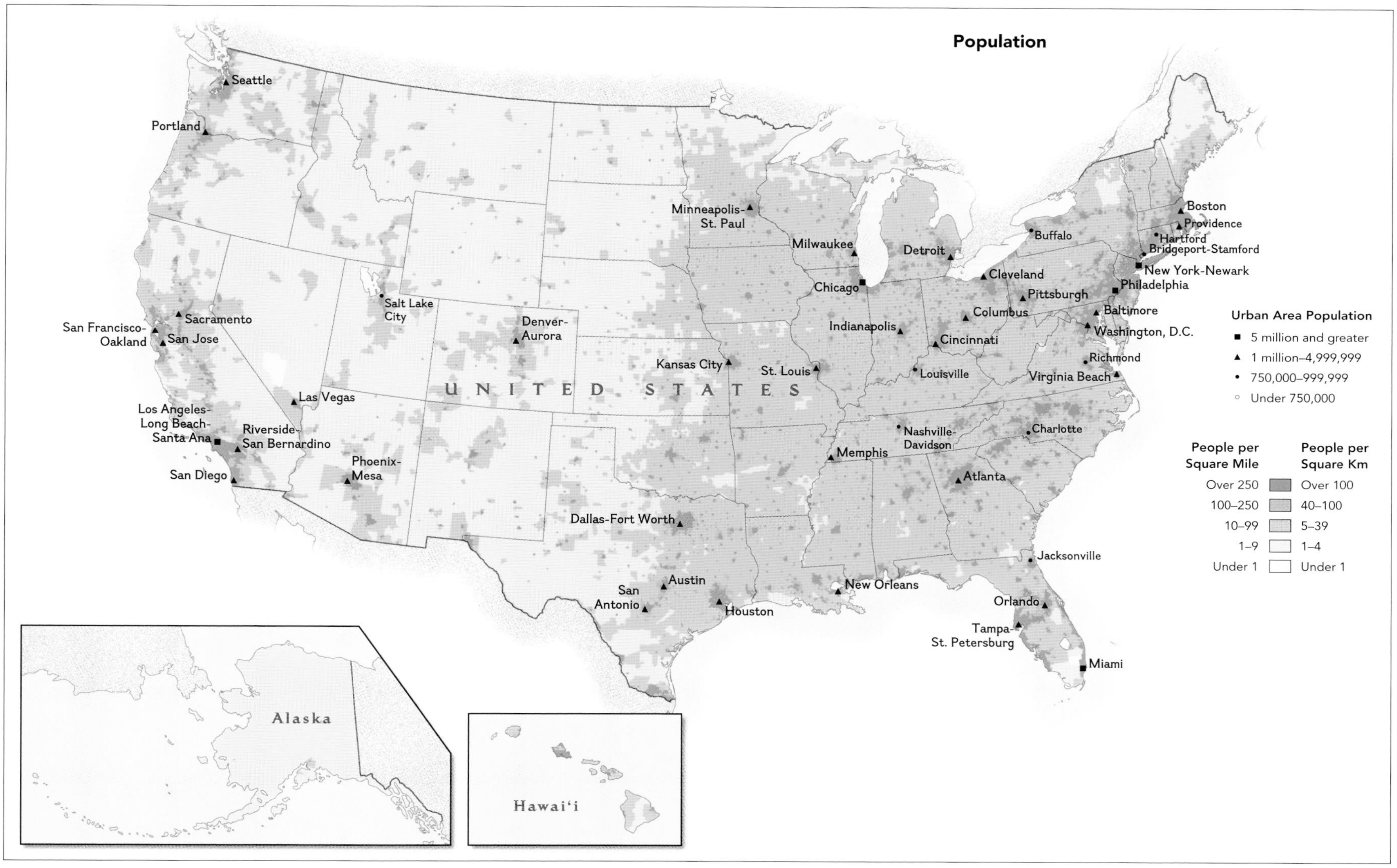

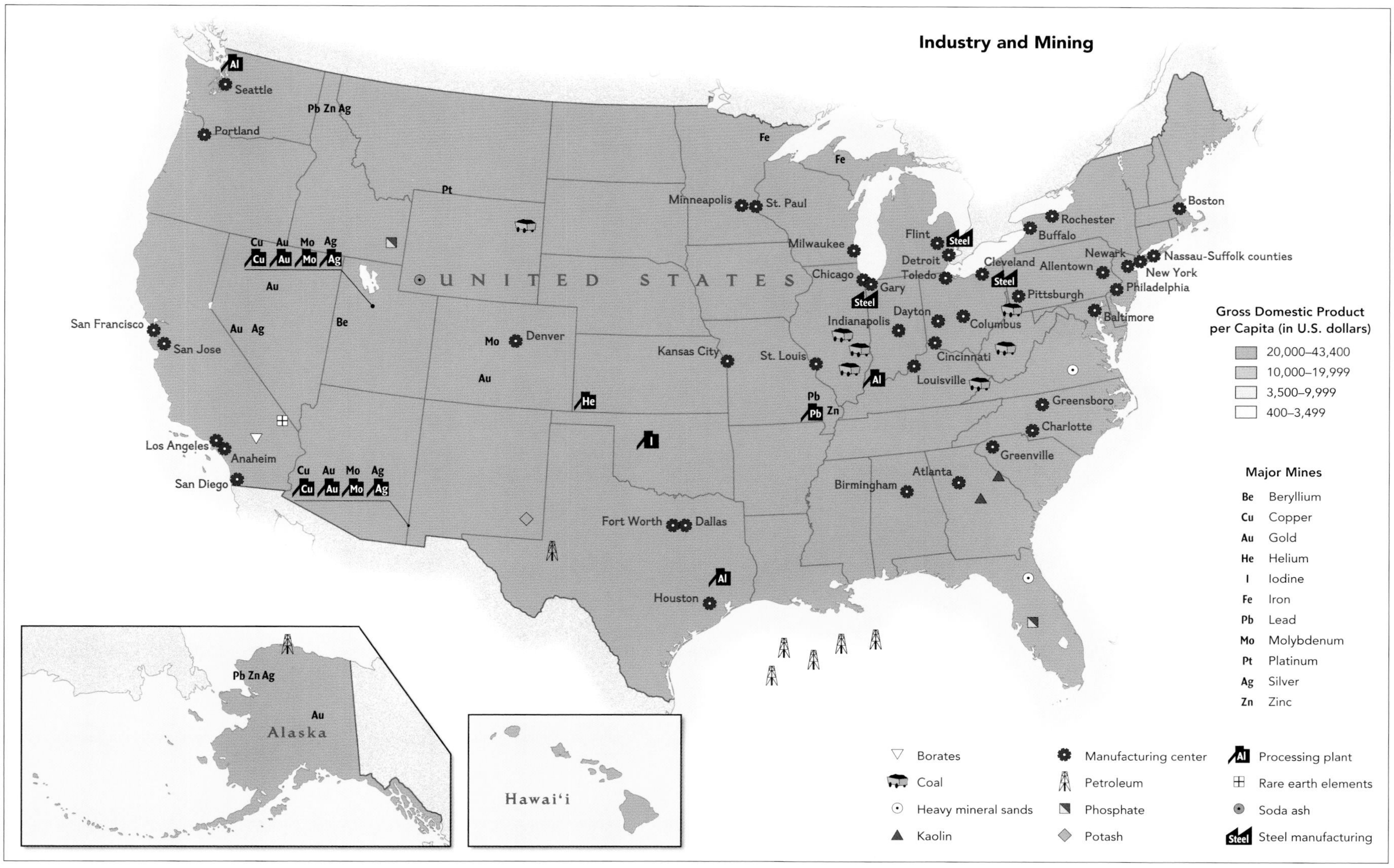

PACIFIC OCEAN
WASHINGTON
OREGON
CALIFORNIA
NEVADA
IDAHO
MONTANA
WYOMING
UTAH
COLORADO
ARIZONA
NEW MEXICO
TEXAS
NORTH DAKOTA
SOUTH DAKOTA
NEBRASKA
KANSAS
MEXICO
ALBERTA
SASKATCHEWAN
MANITOBA
BRITISH COLUMBIA
GREAT BASIN
COLORADO PLATEAU
SIERRA NEVADA
COAST RANGES
CASCADE RANGE
Seattle
Olympia
Bellingham
Aberdeen
Spokane
Yakima
Richland
Coeur d'Alene
Portland
Salem
Newport
Burns
Crescent City
Klamath Falls
Eureka
Reno
Carson City
Sacramento
Oakland
San Francisco
San Jose
Bakersfield
LOS ANGELES
San Bernardino
SAN DIEGO
Winnemucca
Elko
Ely
Tonopah
Pioche
Las Vegas
Lewiston
Boise
Idaho Falls
Pocatello
Missoula
Kalispell
Helena
Butte
Bozeman
Great Falls
Havre
Billings
Miles City
Glendive
Hardin
Salt Lake City
Provo
Cedar City
Montpelier
Rock Springs
Laramie
Cheyenne
Casper
Buffalo
Gillette
Denver
Grand Junction
Colorado Springs
Pueblo
Durango
Farmington
Gallup
Santa Fe
Taos
Albuquerque
Kingman
Flagstaff
PHOENIX
Yuma
Tucson
Safford
Nogales
Douglas
Alamogordo
Las Cruces
El Paso
Roswell
Carlsbad
Clovis
Amarillo
Lubbock
Abilene
Wichita Falls
Fort Worth
Odessa
Midland
San Angelo
Van Horn
Pecos
Fort Stockton
Del Rio
Austin
SAN ANTONIO
Laredo
Corpus Christi
McAllen
Brownsville
Oklahoma City
Enid
Wichita
Salina
Garden City
North Platte
Grand Island
Valentine
Rapid City
Pierre
Aberdeen
Bismarck
Minot
Williston
Bowman
Grand Forks
ALASKA
ARCTIC OCEAN
BEAUFORT SEA
CHUKCHI SEA
BERING SEA
GULF OF ALASKA
PACIFIC OCEAN
ARCTIC CIRCLE
RUSSIA
CANADA
U.S.
North Slope
BROOKS RANGE
ALASKA RANGE
YUKON
NORTHWEST TERRITORIES
BRITISH COLUMBIA
Prudhoe Bay
Circle
Manley Hot Springs
Fairbanks
Eagle
Nenana
Big Delta
Tok
Cantwell
Gulkana
Palmer
Anchorage
Valdez
Whittier
Seward
Homer
Haines
Skagway
Juneau
St. Lawrence Island
Nunivak Island
Kodiak Island
0 100 200 300 km
0 50 100 150 statute mi

CANADA
ONTARIO
QUEBEC
NEW BRUNSWICK
PRINCE EDWARD ISLAND
NOVA SCOTIA
St. Lawrence
Lake of the Woods
International Falls
Isle Royale
Lake Superior
Bemidji
Duluth
Ironwood
Marquette
MINNESOTA
St. Paul
Minneapolis
Rochester
La Crosse
Eau Claire
Wausau
WISCONSIN
Green Bay
Appleton
Madison
Milwaukee
MICHIGAN
L. Michigan
Georgian Bay
Lake Huron
Saginaw
Flint
Grand Rapids
Lansing
Ann Arbor
Detroit
Toledo
Lake Erie
L. Ontario
Rochester
Niagara Falls
Buffalo
Syracuse
Watertown
NEW YORK
Albany
Binghamton
L. Champlain
Burlington
Montpelier
VERMONT
NEW HAMPSHIRE
Concord
MAINE
Ft. Kent
Houlton
Bangor
Augusta
Portland
Bay of Fundy
GULF OF MAINE
Boston
MASSACHUSETTS
Cape Cod
Nantucket I.
Martha's Vineyard
Providence
R.I.
Hartford
CONN.
New Haven
Long Island
NEW YORK
NEW JERSEY
Trenton
PHILADELPHIA
Atlantic City
Wilmington
Dover
DEL.
MD.
Baltimore
Annapolis
Washington, D.C.
Erie
Williamsport
Scranton
PENNSYLVANIA
Harrisburg
Pittsburgh
Youngstown
Cleveland
Akron
OHIO
Columbus
Dayton
Cincinnati
Lima
Fort Wayne
INDIANA
Indianapolis
IOWA
Waterloo
Dubuque
Rockford
CHICAGO
Davenport
Des Moines
Burlington
Bloomington
ILLINOIS
Quincy
Springfield
Kansas City
Jefferson City
St. Louis
MISSOURI
Springfield
Mississippi
Ohio
Louisville
Frankfort
Lexington
Evansville
KENTUCKY
Paducah
Bowling Green
Parkersburg
Clarksburg
W. VA.
Charleston
Beckley
Charlottesville
Richmond
Chesapeake Bay
Norfolk
Virginia Beach
VIRGINIA
Roanoke
Kitty Hawk
Cape Hatteras
Durham
Raleigh
Greensboro
NORTH CAROLINA
New Bern
Wilmington
Bristol
Knoxville
Nashville
TENNESSEE
Dyersburg
Jackson
Memphis
Chattanooga
Asheville
APPALACHIAN MOUNTAINS
Charlotte
Spartanburg
SOUTH CAROLINA
Columbia
Florence
Orangeburg
Charleston
Fayetteville
ARKANSAS
Little Rock
Pine Bluff
Texarkana
Huntsville
Tupelo
Birmingham
Tuscaloosa
ALABAMA
Montgomery
Atlanta
Augusta
Macon
GEORGIA
Columbus
Savannah
Albany
Waycross
Valdosta
Jacksonville
Dothan
Tallahassee
Greenville
Jackson
MISSISSIPPI
Meridian
Hattiesburg
Shreveport
Monroe
LOUISIANA
Natchez
Alexandria
Baton Rouge
Lafayette
Lake Charles
New Orleans
Gulfport
Pascagoula
Mobile
Pensacola
Panama City
Beaumont
HOUSTON
Galveston
FLORIDA
Ocala
Daytona Beach
Orlando
Tampa
St. Petersburg
Tampa Bay
Fort Pierce
L. Okeechobee
Fort Lauderdale
Miami
Florida Keys
Key West
Straits of Florida
GULF OF MEXICO
ATLANTIC OCEAN
BAHAMAS
CUBA
HAITI
TROPIC OF CANCER
Albers Conic Equal-Area Projection
SCALE 1:10,824,000
1 CENTIMETER = 108 KILOMETERS; 1 INCH = 171 MILES
KILOMETERS
STATUTE MILES
90°
80°
70°
50°
40°
30°
20°
Longitude West 90° of Greenwich
PRINCIPAL HAWAIIAN ISLANDS
Longitude West 159° of Greenwich
156°
21°
PACIFIC OCEAN
KAUA'I
Kīlauea
Waimea
Ni'ihau
Līhu'e
Ka'ula
O'AHU
Waipahu
Kāne'ohe
Honolulu
MOLOKA'I
Kaunakakai
Maunaloa
Lahaina
LĀNA'I
Wailuku
Hāna
MAUI
Kaho'olawe
Hāwī
Honoka'a
Waimea (Kamuela)
Hilo
Kailua
HAWAI'I
Pāhoa
Pāhala
Nā'ālehu
Kalae
100 km
100 statute mi

United States: Federal Lands

OLYMPIC COAST NATIONAL MARINE SANCTUARY
NORTH CASCADES N.P.
OLYMPIC N.P.
WASHINGTON
MT. RAINIER N.P.
GLACIER N.P.
PACIFIC OCEAN
Columbia
Snake
IDAHO
MONTANA
Missouri
NORTH DAKOTA
THEODORE ROOSEVELT N.P.
Yellowstone
OREGON
CRATER LAKE N.P.
REDWOOD N.P.
YELLOWSTONE N.P.
GRAND TETON N.P.
SOUTH DAKOTA
WIND CAVE N.P.
BADLANDS N.P.
WYOMING
LASSEN VOLCANIC N.P.
NEVADA
Great Salt Lake
NEBRASKA
Platte
CORDELL BANK N.M.S.
CALIFORNIA
ROCKY MOUNTAIN N.P.
GULF OF THE FARALLONES N.M.S.
YOSEMITE N.P.
GREAT BASIN N.P.
UTAH
ARCHES N.P.
COLORADO
KINGS CANYON N.P.
CAPITOL REEF N.P.
BRYCE CANYON N.P.
CANYONLANDS N.P.
BLACK CANYON OF THE GUNNISON N.P.
KANSAS
MONTEREY BAY N.M.S.
SEQUOIA N.P.
DEATH VALLEY N.P.
ZION N.P.
MESA VERDE N.P.
GREAT SAND DUNES N.P.
Arkansas
Colorado
GRAND CANYON N.P.
CHANNEL ISLANDS N.M.S.
CHANNEL ISLANDS N.P.
ARIZONA
PETRIFIED FOREST N.P.
NEW MEXICO
OK
JOSHUA TREE N.P.
Red
SAGUARO N.P.
CARLSBAD CAVERNS N.P.
GUADALUPE MOUNTAINS N.P.
TEXAS
Rio Grande
Pecos
MEXICO
BIG BEND N.P.
ARCTIC OCEAN
RUSSIA
GATES OF THE ARCTIC N.P. AND PRESERVE
KOBUK VALLEY N.P.
Noatak
ALASKA
CANADA
BERING SEA
Yukon
DENALI N.P. AND PRESERVE
WRANGELL-ST. ELIAS N.P. AND PRESERVE
LAKE CLARK N.P. AND PRESERVE
KATMAI N.P. AND PRESERVE
KENAI FJORDS N.P.
GLACIER BAY N.P. AND PRESERVE
GULF OF ALASKA
ALASKA
0 200 km
0 200 statute mi
MAP KEY
National Park System
National Forest
National Wildlife Refuge
National Grassland
Bureau of Land Management
Indian Reservation
Military Reservation
Department of Energy
National Marine Sanctuary
Only national parks and marine sanctuaries are labeled.

MINNESOTA
WISCONSIN
MICHIGAN
IOWA
ILLINOIS
INDIANA
OHIO
PENNSYLVANIA
NEW YORK
VERMONT
NEW HAMPSHIRE
MAINE
MASSACHUSETTS
CONN.
RHODE ISLAND
NEW JERSEY
DELAWARE
MARYLAND
Washington, D.C.
WEST VIRGINIA
VIRGINIA
KENTUCKY
MISSOURI
ARKANSAS
TENNESSEE
NORTH CAROLINA
SOUTH CAROLINA
GEORGIA
ALABAMA
MISSISSIPPI
LOUISIANA
FLORIDA
ATLANTIC OCEAN
GULF OF MEXICO
BAHAMAS
CUBA
Lake of the Woods
Lake Superior
Lake Michigan
Lake Huron
Georgian Bay
Lake Erie
Lake Ontario
Lake Champlain
St. Lawrence
Hudson
Mississippi
Missouri
Ohio
Savannah
Lake Okeechobee
VOYAGEURS N.P.
ISLE ROYALE N.P.
THUNDER BAY N.M.S.
CUYAHOGA VALLEY N.P.
ACADIA N.P.
STELLWAGEN BANK N.M.S.
SHENANDOAH N.P.
MAMMOTH CAVE N.P.
GREAT SMOKY MOUNTAINS N.P.
MONITOR N.M.S.
CONGAREE N.P.
HOT SPRINGS N.P.
GRAY'S REEF N.M.S.
FLOWER GARDEN BANKS N.M.S.
EVERGLADES N.P.
BISCAYNE N.P.
DRY TORTUGAS N.P.
FLORIDA KEYS N.M.S.
Albers Conic Projection
SCALE 1:9,683,000
1 CENTIMETER = 97 KILOMETERS; 1 INCH = 153 MILES
0 100 200 300 400
KILOMETERS
0 100 200 300 400
STATUTE MILES
Longitude West 90° of Greenwich
Longitude West 159° of Greenwich
PACIFIC OCEAN
KAUA'I
O'AHU
MOLOKA'I
MAUI
LĀNA'I
HAWAI'I
HAWAIIAN ISLANDS HUMPBACK WHALE NATIONAL MARINE SANCTUARY
HALEAKALĀ N.P.
HAWAI'I VOLCANOES NATIONAL PARK
PRINCIPAL HAWAIIAN ISLANDS
0 100 km
0 100 statute mi

Lambert Conformal Conic Projection, Standard Parallels 33° And 45°

SCALE 1:3,102,000
1 CENTIMETER = 31 KILOMETERS; 1 INCH = 49 MILES

KILOMETERS 0 50 100 150

STATUTE MILES 0 50 100 150

Elevations in feet

LAKE ONTARIO

75°

45°

ONTARIO

St. Lawrence

ST. LAWRENCE
ISLANDS N.P.

Rouses Point

• Massena
Norwood • Malone Plattsburgh •
• Potsdam Dannemora Lake
Canton Champlain
Ogdensburg Burlington
Morristown
Gouverneur Mt. Mar
Alexandria Saranac Saranac Lake
Bay Lakes • Lake Placid
Clayton Tupper Lake ADIRONDACK
Cape Mt. Marcy VE
Vincent Carthage Cranberry 5344 Port Henry
Sackets Lake Ticonderoga
Harbor Watertown Raquette L. MOUNTAINS
Ellisburg Lowville Snowy Mt. Lake
Port Ontario Boonville Great Sacandaga Whitehall Fair
Lycoming Pulaski 3899 Lake Hav
Oswego Camden FT. STANWIX Glens Falls
Fulton Rome NAT. MON. Corinth Granville
Wolcott Canastota Saratoga
Medina Albion Kendall Baldwinsville Oneida Utica Gloversville Springs
Lockport Greece Brockport Lyons Little Falls Johnstown Amsterdam
Niagara Falls N. Tonawanda Rochester Palmyra Newark Ilion Herkimer
Grand ERIE CANAL Batavia Fairport Solvay Mohawk Schenectady
Island Le Roy Auburn Syracuse Cohoes
Buffalo Amherst Canandaigua Seneca Falls Geneva Hamilton Cooperstown Albany Troy
Lackawanna Cheektowaga Geneseo Oneida Mt. Greylock
E. Aurora Penn Geneva Ravena
Hamburg NEW Yan Finger L. Homer YORK Oneonta Stamford Chatham
Farnham Dansville Cortland Norwich Delhi Catskill Hudson
Dunkirk Gowanda Watkins Glen Ithaca Cayuga L. Sidney CATSKILL
Fredonia Springville Hornell Bath Johnson City Walton Saugerties
North East Franklinville Canisteo Corning Endicott Binghamton MTS. Kingston
Westfield Salamanca Wellsville Horseheads Owego Deposit Slide Mt. Hyde Park
Erie Wesleyville Jamestown Olean Elmira Chemung Susquehanna 4180 Poughkeepsie CON
N. Springfield Girard Waverly Sayre Mt. Frissel Waterbury
Corry Warren Bradford Sayre Liberty 2380 Torrington
Cambridge Springs Union Port Allegany Elkland Tioga Towanda Monticello West Point Danbury
City Smethport Coudersport Galeton Mansfield Carbondale Newburgh
Meadville Titusville Kane Mt. Austin Wellsboro Canton Archbald Port Jervis Middletown Waterbury
Jewett Elk Mt. Dickson City High Point Peekskill Bri
Greenville Oil City Johnsonburg Emporium Scranton 2693 DELAWARE 1803 New City
Franklin Ridgway St. Marys Renovo Williamsport Old Forge Dunmore WATER GAP White Plains Stamford
Sharon Polk Brookville Brockway Jersey Shore Kingston Pittston N.R.A. Paterson Yonkers New Rochelle
Farrell Clarion Du Bois Lock Haven Muncy Plymouth Wilkes- Stroudsburg Morristown Mount Vernon
Slippery Rock Grove City Clearfield Milton Nanticoke Barre Pocono Mts. E. Orange
New Brookville PENNSYLVANIA Bloomsburg Hazleton Easton Elizabeth NEW
Castle Butler Philipsburg Bellefonte Sunbury Shenandoah Bethlehem Plainfield YORK
Aliquippa Kittanning State College Shamokin Pottsville Allentown New Brunswick Jersey City
McKees Rocks Indiana Tyrone Mt. Carmel Emmaus Quakertown Princeton Staten Long Branch
Pittsburgh Penn Hills Altoona Huntingdon Lewistown Reading Doylestown Freehold Asbury Park
Upper St. Clair Duquesne Johnstown Hollidaysburg Mechanicsburg Lebanon Pottstown Lansdale Trenton Levittown
Washington Clairton McKeesport Windber Carlisle Harrisburg Norristown PHILADELPHIA Point Pleasant
Monessen Greensburg FLIGHT 93 3136 Steelton Lancaster W. Chester Camden NEW Lakewood
Waynesburg Connellsville NAT. MEM. Shippensburg Columbia Bristol Levittown JERSEY Seaside Park
Somerset Bedford Breezewood York Upper Darby Woodbury
Uniontown Chambersburg Hanover Oxford Chester Glassboro Barnegat Barnegat Light
Masontown Gettysburg Woodstown Hammonton Beach Haven
Mt. Davis Greencastle Waynesboro Vineland Pleasantville Tuckerton
3213 Bridgeton Millville Atlantic City
WEST Port Norris Ventnor City
VIRGINIA ALLEGHENY MARYLAND DELAWARE Ocean City
Delaware
Bay Wildwood
39° Cape May 39°
75°

New Jersey
GARDEN STATE

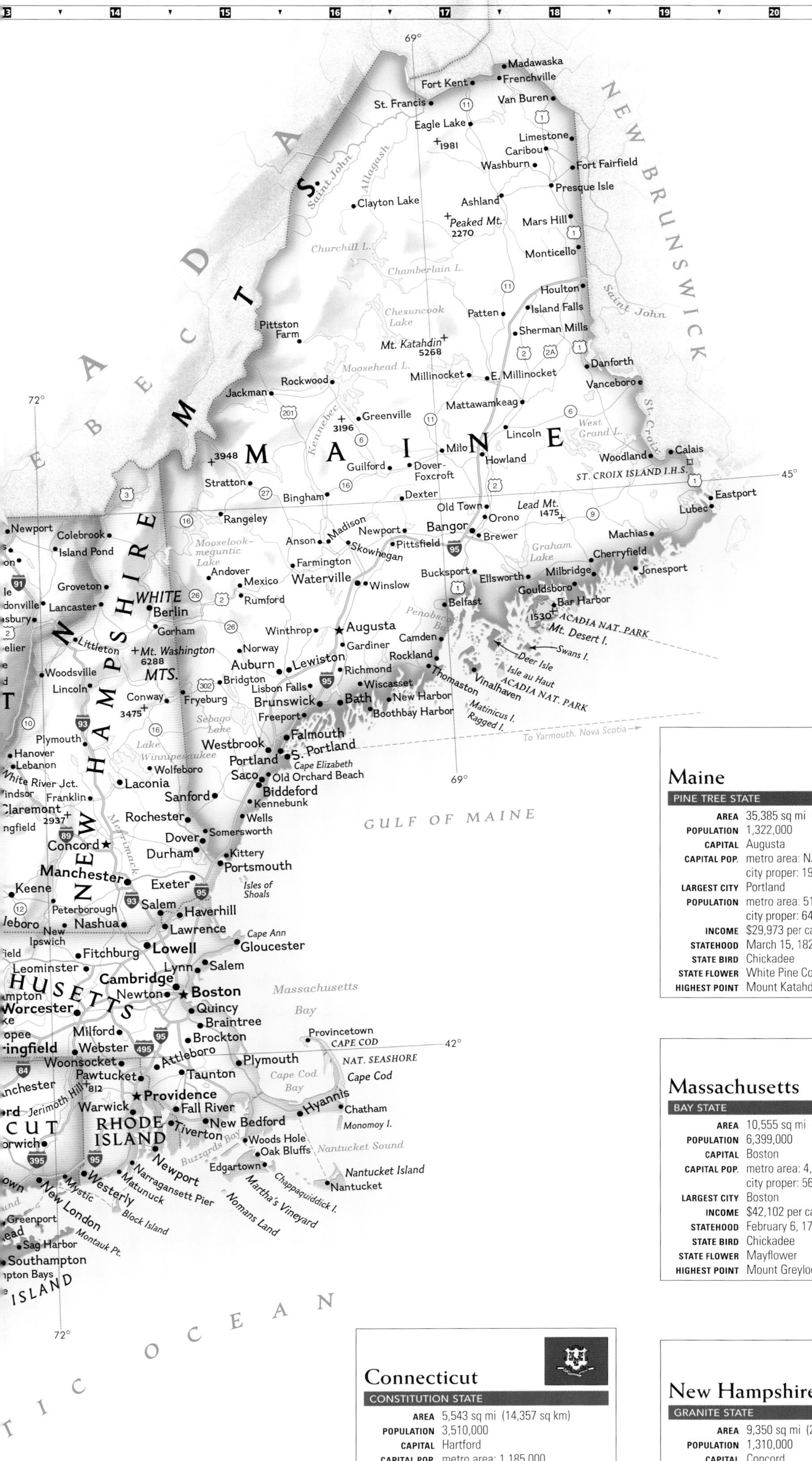

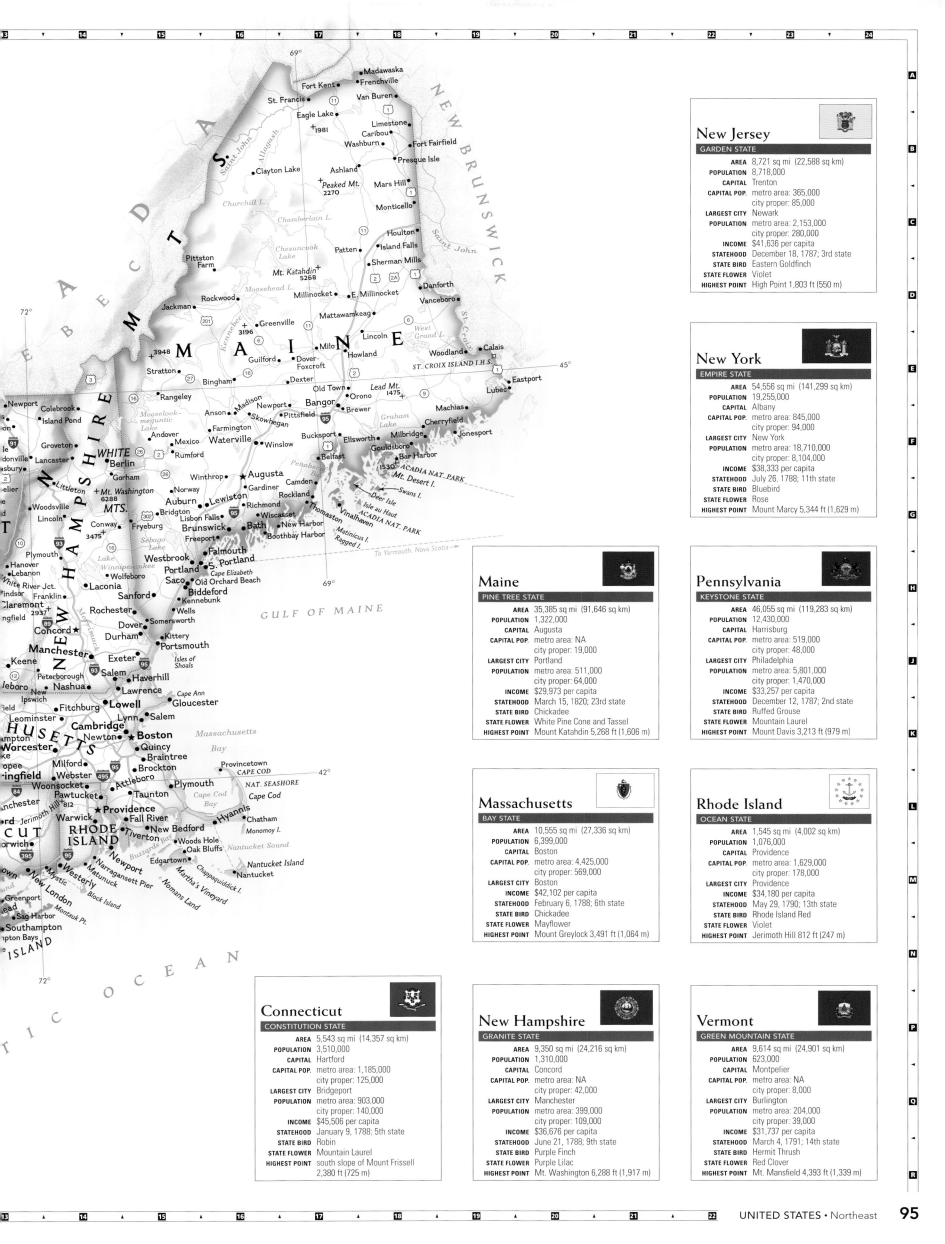

AREA	8,721 sq mi (22,588 sq km)
POPULATION	8,718,000
CAPITAL	Trenton
CAPITAL POP.	metro area: 365,000
	city proper: 85,000
LARGEST CITY	Newark
POPULATION	metro area: 2,153,000
	city proper: 280,000
INCOME	$41,636 per capita
STATEHOOD	December 18, 1787; 3rd state
STATE BIRD	Eastern Goldfinch
STATE FLOWER	Violet
HIGHEST POINT	High Point 1,803 ft (550 m)

New York
EMPIRE STATE

AREA	54,556 sq mi (141,299 sq km)
POPULATION	19,255,000
CAPITAL	Albany
CAPITAL POP.	metro area: 845,000
	city proper: 94,000
LARGEST CITY	New York
POPULATION	metro area: 18,710,000
	city proper: 8,104,000
INCOME	$38,333 per capita
STATEHOOD	July 26, 1788; 11th state
STATE BIRD	Bluebird
STATE FLOWER	Rose
HIGHEST POINT	Mount Marcy 5,344 ft (1,629 m)

Maine
PINE TREE STATE

AREA	35,385 sq mi (91,646 sq km)
POPULATION	1,322,000
CAPITAL	Augusta
CAPITAL POP.	metro area: NA
	city proper: 19,000
LARGEST CITY	Portland
POPULATION	metro area: 511,000
	city proper: 64,000
INCOME	$29,973 per capita
STATEHOOD	March 15, 1820; 23rd state
STATE BIRD	Chickadee
STATE FLOWER	White Pine Cone and Tassel
HIGHEST POINT	Mount Katahdin 5,268 ft (1,606 m)

Pennsylvania
KEYSTONE STATE

AREA	46,055 sq mi (119,283 sq km)
POPULATION	12,430,000
CAPITAL	Harrisburg
CAPITAL POP.	metro area: 519,000
	city proper: 48,000
LARGEST CITY	Philadelphia
POPULATION	metro area: 5,801,000
	city proper: 1,470,000
INCOME	$33,257 per capita
STATEHOOD	December 12, 1787; 2nd state
STATE BIRD	Ruffed Grouse
STATE FLOWER	Mountain Laurel
HIGHEST POINT	Mount Davis 3,213 ft (979 m)

Massachusetts
BAY STATE

AREA	10,555 sq mi (27,336 sq km)
POPULATION	6,399,000
CAPITAL	Boston
CAPITAL POP.	metro area: 4,425,000
	city proper: 569,000
LARGEST CITY	Boston
INCOME	$42,102 per capita
STATEHOOD	February 6, 1788; 6th state
STATE BIRD	Chickadee
STATE FLOWER	Mayflower
HIGHEST POINT	Mount Greylock 3,491 ft (1,064 m)

Rhode Island
OCEAN STATE

AREA	1,545 sq mi (4,002 sq km)
POPULATION	1,076,000
CAPITAL	Providence
CAPITAL POP.	metro area: 1,629,000
	city proper: 178,000
LARGEST CITY	Providence
INCOME	$34,180 per capita
STATEHOOD	May 29, 1790; 13th state
STATE BIRD	Rhode Island Red
STATE FLOWER	Violet
HIGHEST POINT	Jerimoth Hill 812 ft (247 m)

Connecticut
CONSTITUTION STATE

AREA	5,543 sq mi (14,357 sq km)
POPULATION	3,510,000
CAPITAL	Hartford
CAPITAL POP.	metro area: 1,185,000
	city proper: 125,000
LARGEST CITY	Bridgeport
POPULATION	metro area: 903,000
	city proper: 140,000
INCOME	$45,506 per capita
STATEHOOD	January 9, 1788; 5th state
STATE BIRD	Robin
STATE FLOWER	Mountain Laurel
HIGHEST POINT	south slope of Mount Frissell 2,380 ft (725 m)

New Hampshire
GRANITE STATE

AREA	9,350 sq mi (24,216 sq km)
POPULATION	1,310,000
CAPITAL	Concord
CAPITAL POP.	metro area: NA
	city proper: 42,000
LARGEST CITY	Manchester
POPULATION	metro area: 399,000
	city proper: 109,000
INCOME	$36,676 per capita
STATEHOOD	June 21, 1788; 9th state
STATE BIRD	Purple Finch
STATE FLOWER	Purple Lilac
HIGHEST POINT	Mt. Washington 6,288 ft (1,917 m)

Vermont
GREEN MOUNTAIN STATE

AREA	9,614 sq mi (24,901 sq km)
POPULATION	623,000
CAPITAL	Montpelier
CAPITAL POP.	metro area: NA
	city proper: 8,000
LARGEST CITY	Burlington
POPULATION	metro area: 204,000
	city proper: 39,000
INCOME	$31,737 per capita
STATEHOOD	March 4, 1791; 14th state
STATE BIRD	Hermit Thrush
STATE FLOWER	Red Clover
HIGHEST POINT	Mt. Mansfield 4,393 ft (1,339 m)

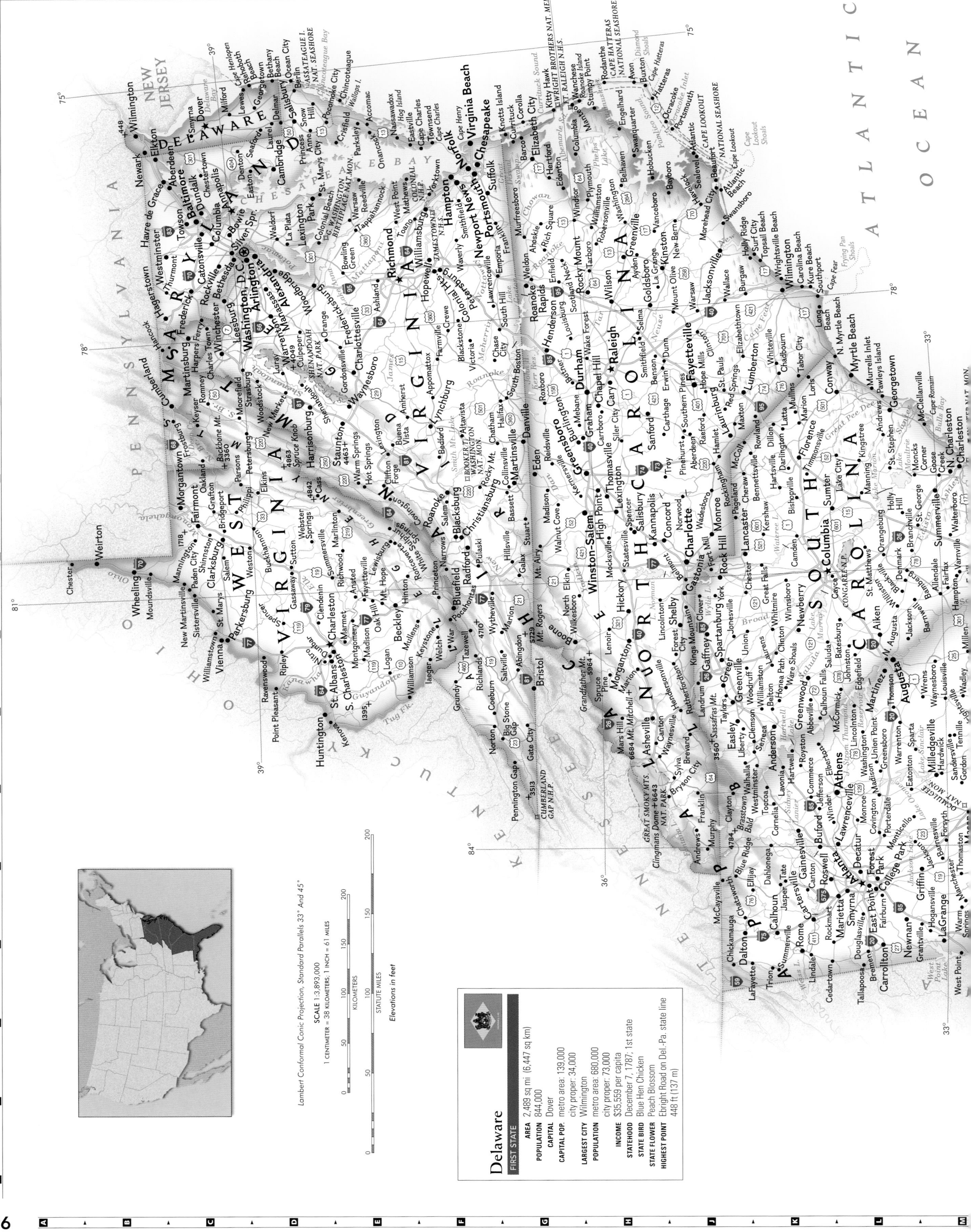

Lambert Conformal Conic Projection, Standard Parallels 33° And 45°

SCALE 1:3,893,000

1 CENTIMETER = 38 KILOMETERS; 1 INCH = 61 MILES

Elevations in feet

Delaware

FIRST STATE

AREA 2,489 sq mi (6,447 sq km)
POPULATION 844,000
CAPITAL Dover
CAPITAL POP. metro area: 139,000; city proper: 34,000
LARGEST CITY Wilmington
POPULATION metro area: 680,000; city proper: 73,000
INCOME $35,559 per capita
STATEHOOD December 7, 1787; 1st state
STATE BIRD Blue Hen Chicken
STATE FLOWER Peach Blossom
HIGHEST POINT Ebright Road on Del.-Pa. state line 448 ft (137 m)

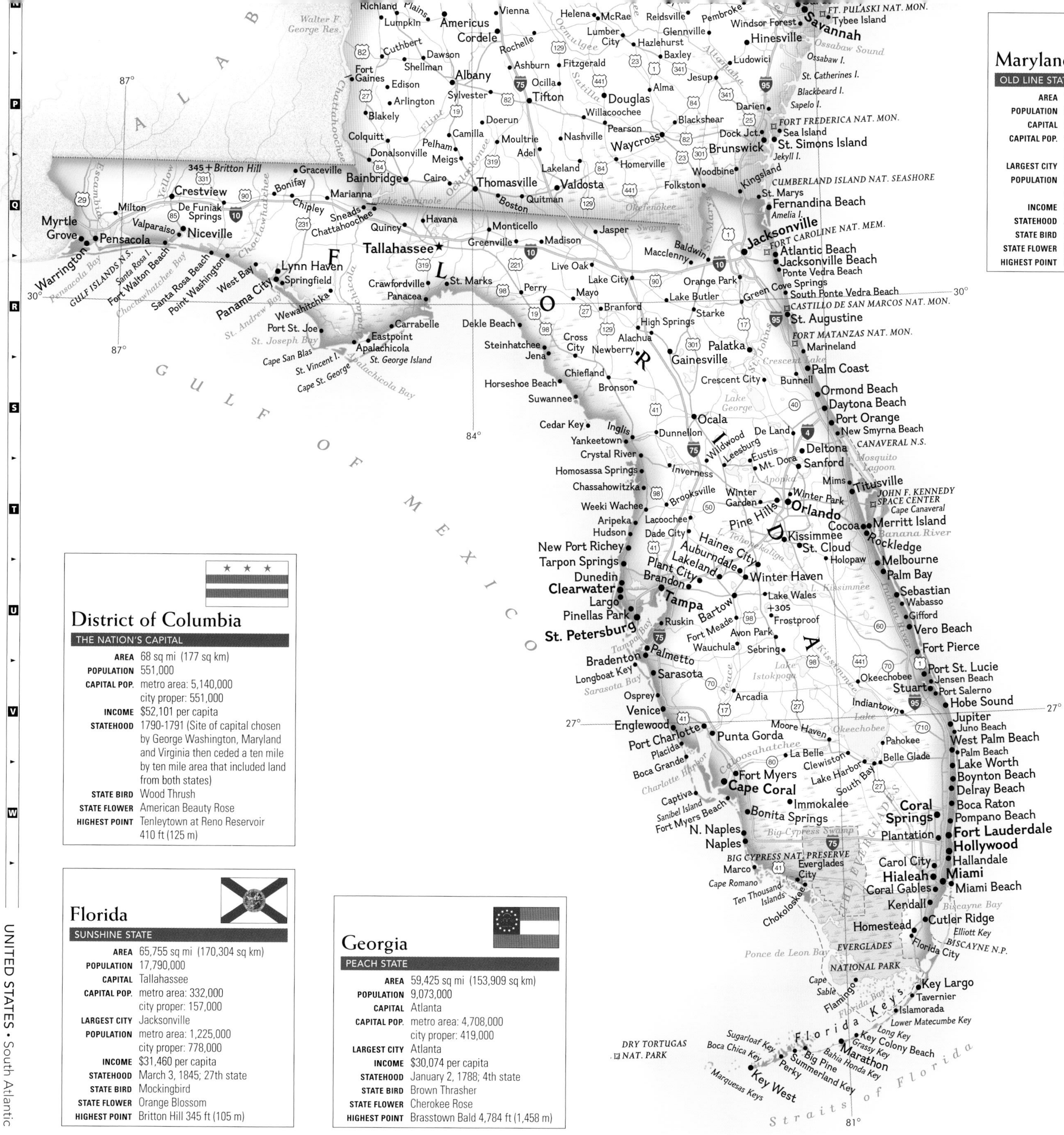

Maryland
OLD LINE STATE

AREA 12,407 sq mi (32,133 sq km)
POPULATION 5,600,000
CAPITAL Annapolis
CAPITAL POP. metro area: 2,639,000; city proper: 36,000
LARGEST CITY Baltimore
POPULATION metro area: 2,639,000; city proper: 636,000
INCOME $39,629 per capita
STATEHOOD April 28, 1788; 7th state
STATE BIRD Baltimore Oriole
STATE FLOWER Black-eyed Susan
HIGHEST POINT Backbone Mt. 3,360 ft (1,024 m)

North Carolina
TAR HEEL STATE

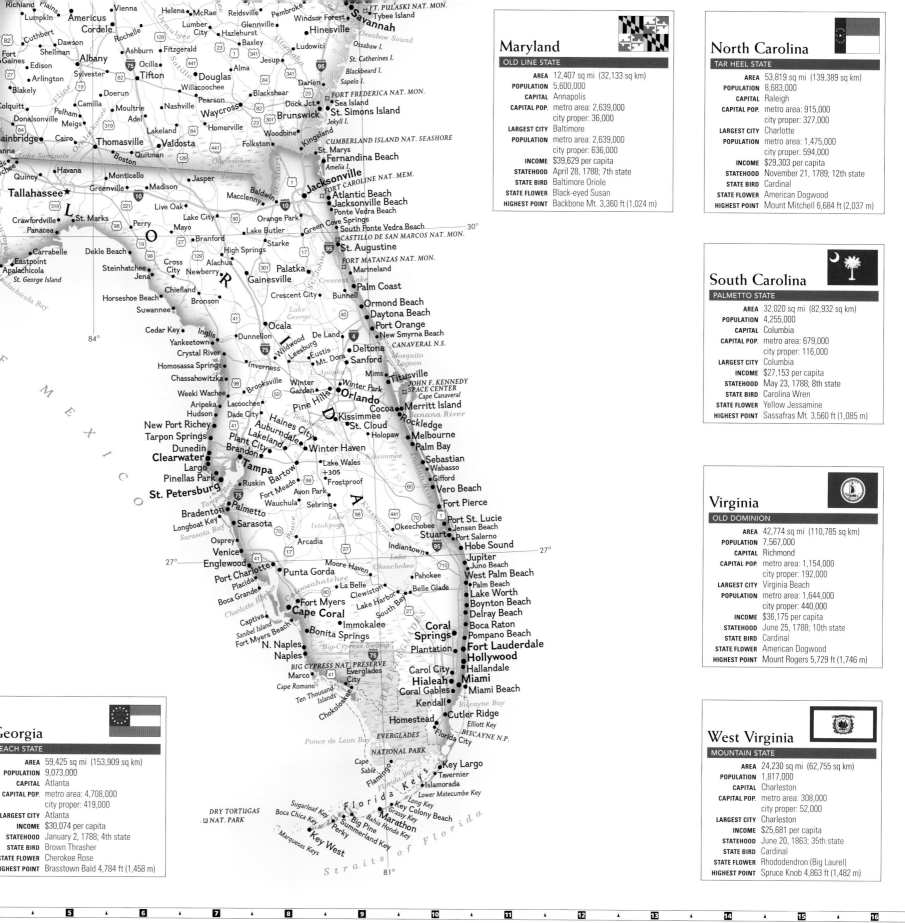

AREA 53,819 sq mi (139,389 sq km)
POPULATION 8,683,000
CAPITAL Raleigh
CAPITAL POP. metro area: 915,000; city proper: 327,000
LARGEST CITY Charlotte
POPULATION metro area: 1,475,000; city proper: 594,000
INCOME $29,303 per capita
STATEHOOD November 21, 1789; 12th state
STATE BIRD Cardinal
STATE FLOWER American Dogwood
HIGHEST POINT Mount Mitchell 6,684 ft (2,037 m)

South Carolina
PALMETTO STATE

AREA 32,020 sq mi (82,932 sq km)
POPULATION 4,255,000
CAPITAL Columbia
CAPITAL POP. metro area: 679,000; city proper: 116,000
LARGEST CITY Columbia
INCOME $27,153 per capita
STATEHOOD May 23, 1788; 8th state
STATE BIRD Carolina Wren
STATE FLOWER Yellow Jessamine
HIGHEST POINT Sassafras Mt. 3,560 ft (1,085 m)

Virginia
OLD DOMINION

AREA 42,774 sq mi (110,785 sq km)
POPULATION 7,567,000
CAPITAL Richmond
CAPITAL POP. metro area: 1,154,000; city proper: 192,000
LARGEST CITY Virginia Beach
POPULATION metro area: 1,644,000; city proper: 440,000
INCOME $36,175 per capita
STATEHOOD June 25, 1788; 10th state
STATE BIRD Cardinal
STATE FLOWER American Dogwood
HIGHEST POINT Mount Rogers 5,729 ft (1,746 m)

West Virginia
MOUNTAIN STATE

AREA 24,230 sq mi (62,755 sq km)
POPULATION 1,817,000
CAPITAL Charleston
CAPITAL POP. metro area: 308,000; city proper: 52,000
LARGEST CITY Charleston
INCOME $25,681 per capita
STATEHOOD June 20, 1863; 35th state
STATE BIRD Cardinal
STATE FLOWER Rhododendron (Big Laurel)
HIGHEST POINT Spruce Knob 4,863 ft (1,482 m)

District of Columbia
THE NATION'S CAPITAL

AREA 68 sq mi (177 sq km)
POPULATION 551,000
CAPITAL POP. metro area: 5,140,000; city proper: 551,000
INCOME $52,101 per capita
STATEHOOD 1790-1791 (Site of capital chosen by George Washington, Maryland and Virginia then ceded a ten mile by ten mile area that included land from both states)
STATE BIRD Wood Thrush
STATE FLOWER American Beauty Rose
HIGHEST POINT Tenleytown at Reno Reservoir 410 ft (125 m)

Florida
SUNSHINE STATE

AREA 65,755 sq mi (170,304 sq km)
POPULATION 17,790,000
CAPITAL Tallahassee
CAPITAL POP. metro area: 332,000; city proper: 157,000
LARGEST CITY Jacksonville
POPULATION metro area: 1,225,000; city proper: 778,000
INCOME $31,460 per capita
STATEHOOD March 3, 1845; 27th state
STATE BIRD Mockingbird
STATE FLOWER Orange Blossom
HIGHEST POINT Britton Hill 345 ft (105 m)

Georgia
PEACH STATE

AREA 59,425 sq mi (153,909 sq km)
POPULATION 9,073,000
CAPITAL Atlanta
CAPITAL POP. metro area: 4,708,000; city proper: 419,000
LARGEST CITY Atlanta
INCOME $30,074 per capita
STATEHOOD January 2, 1788; 4th state
STATE BIRD Brown Thrasher
STATE FLOWER Cherokee Rose
HIGHEST POINT Brasstown Bald 4,784 ft (1,458 m)

C A N A D A
ONTARIO
LAKE SUPERIOR
LAKE HURON
LAKE MICHIGAN
MICHIGAN
UPPER PENINSULA
WISCONSIN
MINNESOTA
ONTARIO
Isle Royale
ISLE ROYALE NATIONAL PARK
Keweenaw Peninsula
APOSTLE ISLANDS NAT. LAKESHORE
PICTURED ROCKS NAT. LAKESHORE
SLEEPING BEAR DUNES NAT. LAKESHORE
ST. CROIX NAT. SCENIC RIVERWAY
Green Bay
Saginaw Bay
Grand Traverse Bay
Thunder Bay
Door Pen.
Sault Ste. Marie
Marquette
Escanaba
Alpena
Superior
Eau Claire
Wausau
Green Bay
Appleton
Oshkosh
Milwaukee
Madison
La Crosse
Racine
Kenosha
Traverse City
Grand Rapids
Muskegon
Lansing
Flint
Saginaw
Port Huron
Warren
Sterling Hts.

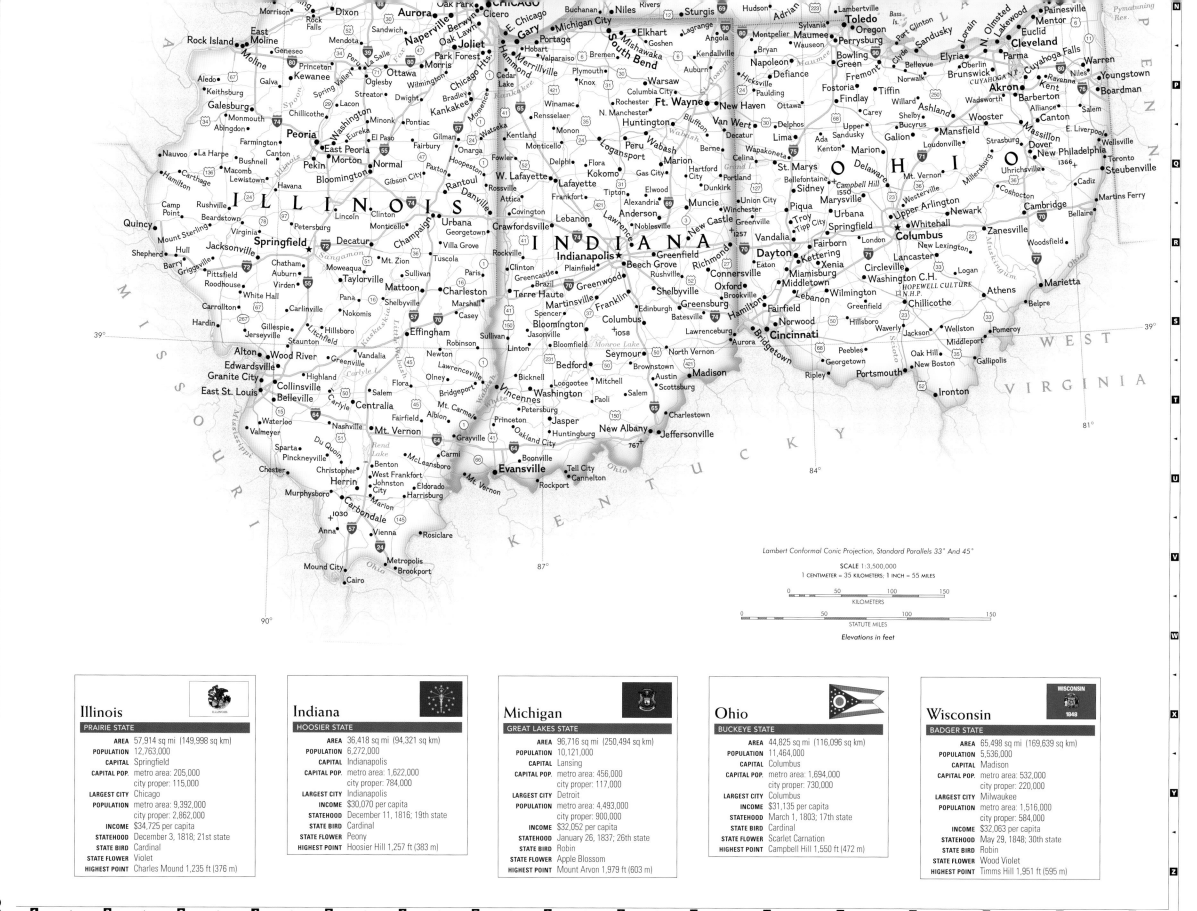

Illinois
PRAIRIE STATE

AREA	57,914 sq mi (149,998 sq km)
POPULATION	12,763,000
CAPITAL	Springfield
CAPITAL POP.	metro area: 205,000 city proper: 115,000
LARGEST CITY	Chicago
POPULATION	metro area: 9,392,000 city proper: 2,862,000
INCOME	$34,725 per capita
STATEHOOD	December 3, 1818; 21st state
STATE BIRD	Cardinal
STATE FLOWER	Violet
HIGHEST POINT	Charles Mound 1,235 ft (376 m)

Indiana
HOOSIER STATE

AREA	36,418 sq mi (94,321 sq km)
POPULATION	6,272,000
CAPITAL	Indianapolis
CAPITAL POP.	metro area: 1,622,000 city proper: 784,000
LARGEST CITY	Indianapolis
INCOME	$30,070 per capita
STATEHOOD	December 11, 1816; 19th state
STATE BIRD	Cardinal
STATE FLOWER	Peony
HIGHEST POINT	Hoosier Hill 1,257 ft (383 m)

Michigan
GREAT LAKES STATE

AREA	96,716 sq mi (250,494 sq km)
POPULATION	10,121,000
CAPITAL	Lansing
CAPITAL POP.	metro area: 456,000 city proper: 117,000
LARGEST CITY	Detroit
POPULATION	metro area: 4,493,000 city proper: 900,000
INCOME	$32,052 per capita
STATEHOOD	January 26, 1837; 26th state
STATE BIRD	Robin
STATE FLOWER	Apple Blossom
HIGHEST POINT	Mount Arvon 1,979 ft (603 m)

Ohio
BUCKEYE STATE

AREA	44,825 sq mi (116,096 sq km)
POPULATION	11,464,000
CAPITAL	Columbus
CAPITAL POP.	metro area: 1,694,000 city proper: 730,000
LARGEST CITY	Columbus
INCOME	$31,135 per capita
STATEHOOD	March 1, 1803; 17th state
STATE BIRD	Cardinal
STATE FLOWER	Scarlet Carnation
HIGHEST POINT	Campbell Hill 1,550 ft (472 m)

Wisconsin
BADGER STATE

AREA	65,498 sq mi (169,639 sq km)
POPULATION	5,536,000
CAPITAL	Madison
CAPITAL POP.	metro area: 532,000 city proper: 220,000
LARGEST CITY	Milwaukee
POPULATION	metro area: 1,516,000 city proper: 584,000
INCOME	$32,063 per capita
STATEHOOD	May 29, 1848; 30th state
STATE BIRD	Robin
STATE FLOWER	Wood Violet
HIGHEST POINT	Timms Hill 1,951 ft (595 m)

Alabama

HEART OF DIXIE

AREA	52,419 sq mi (135,765 sq km)
POPULATION	4,558,000
CAPITAL	Montgomery
CAPITAL POP.	metro area: 355,000 city proper: 201,000
LARGEST CITY	Birmingham
POPULATION	metro area: 1,082,000 city proper: 233,000
INCOME	$27,630 per capita
STATEHOOD	December 14, 1819; 22nd state
STATE BIRD	Northern Flicker (Yellowhammer)
STATE FLOWER	Camellia
HIGHEST POINT	Cheaha Mountain 2,407 ft (734 m)

Arkansas

NATURAL STATE

AREA	53,179 sq mi (137,732 sq km)
POPULATION	2,779,000
CAPITAL	Little Rock
CAPITAL POP.	metro area: 637,000 city proper: 184,000
LARGEST CITY	Little Rock
INCOME	$25,724 per capita
STATEHOOD	June 15, 1836; 25th state
STATE BIRD	Mockingbird
STATE FLOWER	Apple Blossom
HIGHEST POINT	Magazine Mt. 2,753 ft (839 m)

Kentucky

BLUEGRASS STATE

AREA	40,409 sq mi (104,659 sq km)
POPULATION	4,173,000
CAPITAL	Frankfort
CAPITAL POP.	metro area: NA city proper: 27,000
LARGEST CITY	Louisville
POPULATION	metro area: 1,201,000 city proper: 556,000
INCOME	$27,151 per capita
STATEHOOD	June 1, 1792; 15th state
STATE BIRD	Cardinal
STATE FLOWER	Goldenrod
HIGHEST POINT	Black Mountain 4,145 ft (1,263 m)

Louisiana

PELICAN STATE

AREA	51,840 sq mi (134,264 sq km)
POPULATION	4,524,000
CAPITAL	Baton Rouge
CAPITAL POP.	metro area: 729,000 city proper: 224,000
LARGEST CITY	New Orleans*
POPULATION	metro area: 1,320,000 city proper: 462,000
INCOME	$27,219 per capita
STATEHOOD	April 30, 1812; 18th state
STATE BIRD	Brown Pelican
STATE FLOWER	Magnolia
HIGHEST POINT	Driskill Mountain 535 ft (163 m)

*Due to the devastation of Hurricane Katrina, the city's Emergency Operations Center in January 2006, estimated the city population at between 160,000 and 202,000.

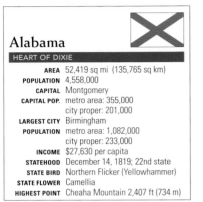

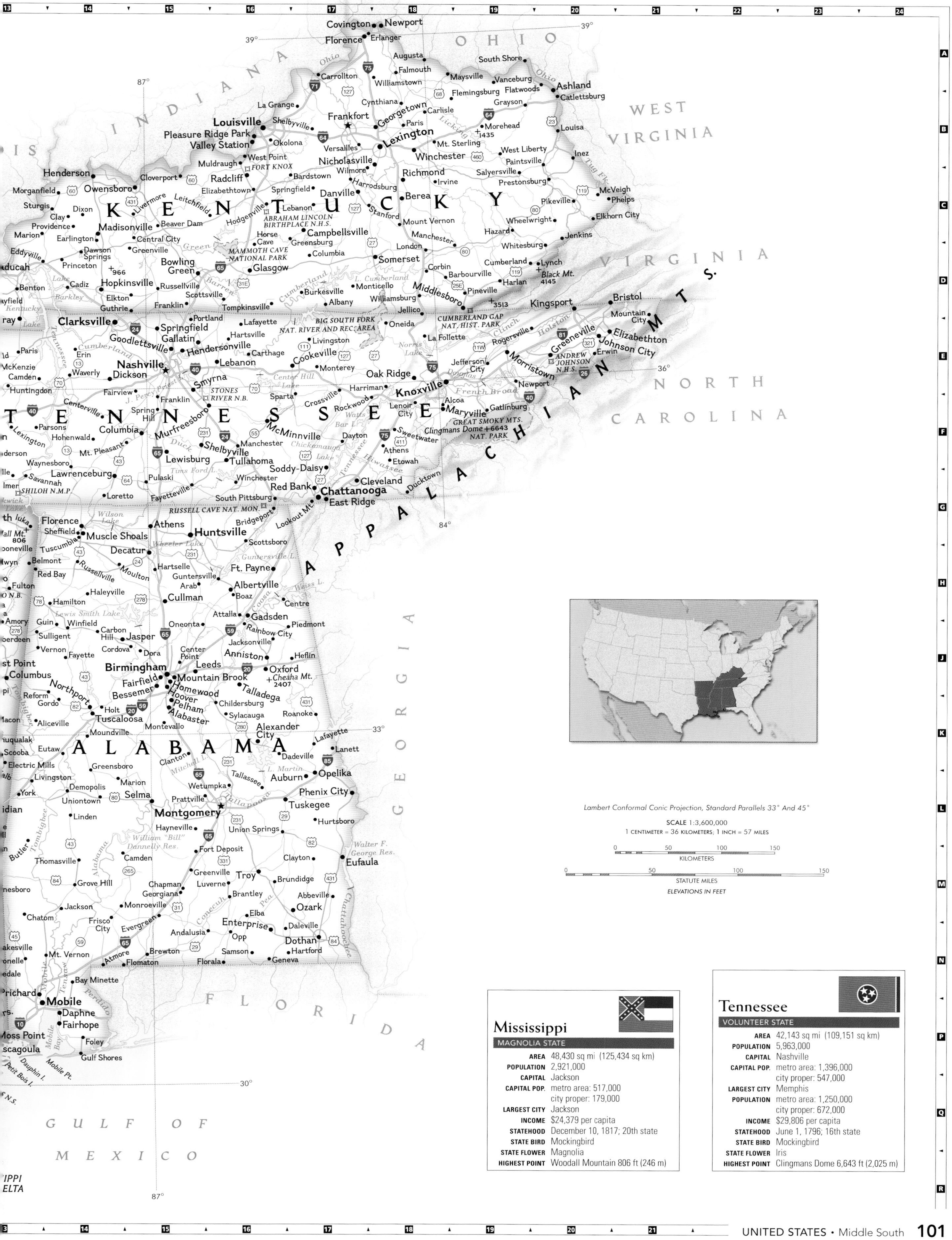

Mississippi

MAGNOLIA STATE

AREA	48,430 sq mi (125,434 sq km)
POPULATION	2,921,000
CAPITAL	Jackson
CAPITAL POP.	metro area: 517,000 city proper: 179,000
LARGEST CITY	Jackson
INCOME	$24,379 per capita
STATEHOOD	December 10, 1817; 20th state
STATE BIRD	Mockingbird
STATE FLOWER	Magnolia
HIGHEST POINT	Woodall Mountain 806 ft (246 m)

Tennessee

VOLUNTEER STATE

AREA	42,143 sq mi (109,151 sq km)
POPULATION	5,963,000
CAPITAL	Nashville
CAPITAL POP.	metro area: 1,396,000 city proper: 547,000
LARGEST CITY POPULATION	Memphis metro area: 1,250,000 city proper: 672,000
INCOME	$29,806 per capita
STATEHOOD	June 1, 1796; 16th state
STATE BIRD	Mockingbird
STATE FLOWER	Iris
HIGHEST POINT	Clingmans Dome 6,643 ft (2,025 m)

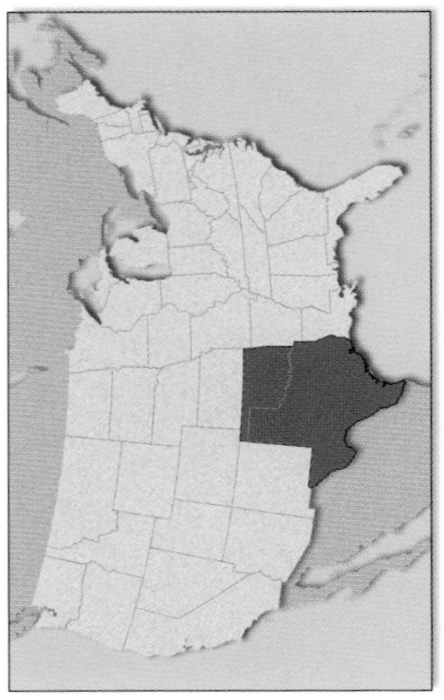

Lambert Conformal Conic Projection, Standard Parallels 33° And 45°

SCALE 1:3,500,000

1 CENTIMETER = 35 KILOMETERS; 1 INCH = 55 MILES

Elevations in feet

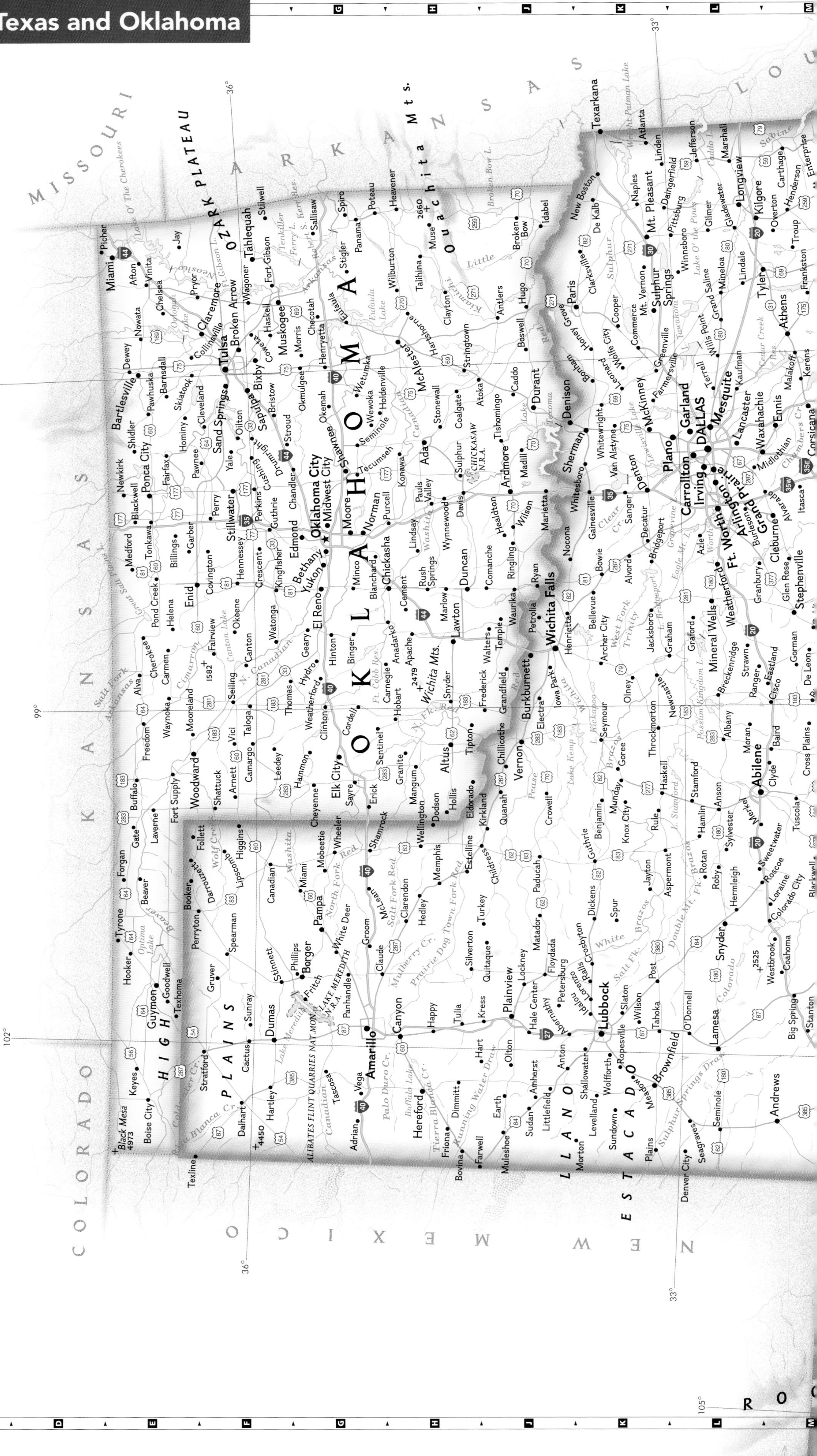

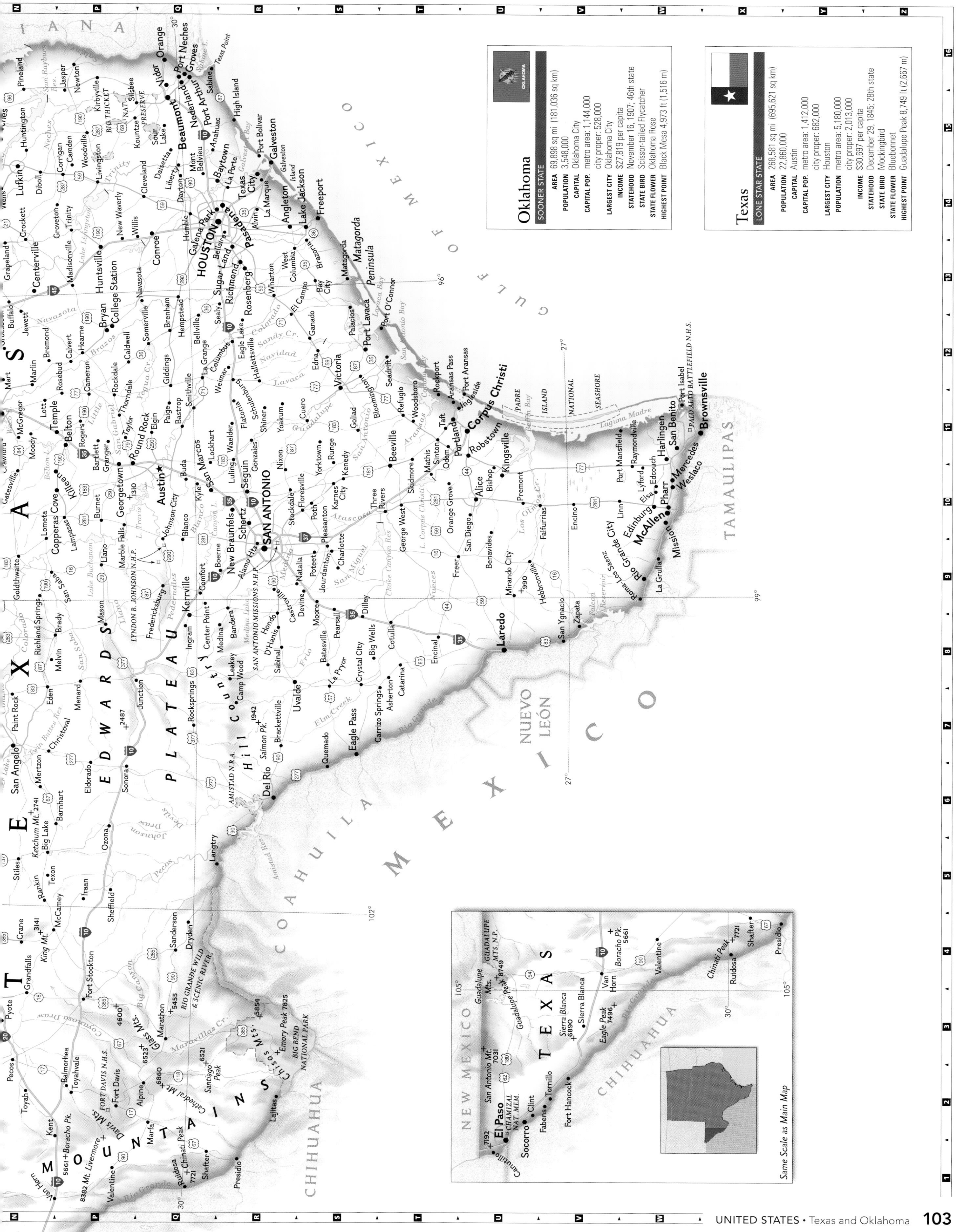

Oklahoma

SOONER STATE

AREA	69,898 sq mi (181,036 sq km)
POPULATION	3,548,000
CAPITAL	Oklahoma City
CAPITAL POP.	metro area: 1,144,000 city proper: 528,000
LARGEST CITY	Oklahoma City
INCOME	$27,819 per capita
STATEHOOD	November 16, 1907; 46th state
STATE BIRD	Scissor-tailed Flycatcher
STATE FLOWER	Oklahoma Rose
HIGHEST POINT	Black Mesa 4,973 ft (1,516 m)

Texas

LONE STAR STATE

AREA	268,581 sq mi (695,621 sq km)
POPULATION	22,860,000
CAPITAL	Austin
CAPITAL POP.	metro area: 1,412,000 city proper: 682,000
LARGEST CITY	Houston
POPULATION	metro area: 5,180,000 city proper: 2,013,000
INCOME	$30,697 per capita
STATEHOOD	December 29, 1845; 28th state
STATE BIRD	Mockingbird
STATE FLOWER	Bluebonnet
HIGHEST POINT	Guadalupe Peak 8,749 ft (2,667 m)

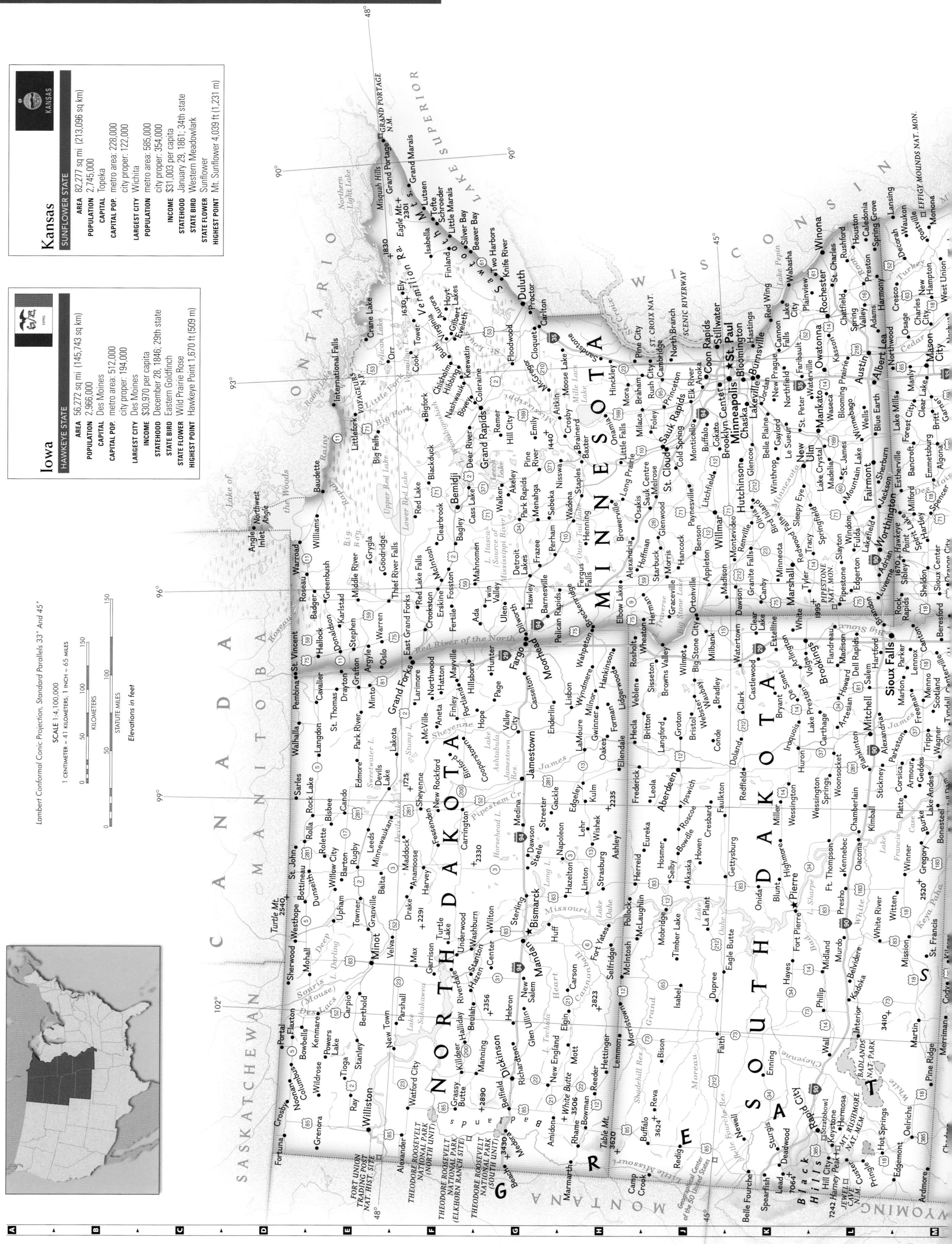

Iowa

HAWKEYE STATE

AREA	56,272 sq mi (145,743 sq km)
POPULATION	2,966,000
CAPITAL	Des Moines
CAPITAL POP.	metro area: 512,000 city proper: 194,000
LARGEST CITY	Des Moines
INCOME	$30,970 per capita
STATEHOOD	December 28, 1846; 29th state
STATE BIRD	Eastern Goldfinch
STATE FLOWER	Wild Prairie Rose
HIGHEST POINT	Hawkeye Point 1,670 ft (509 m)

Kansas

SUNFLOWER STATE

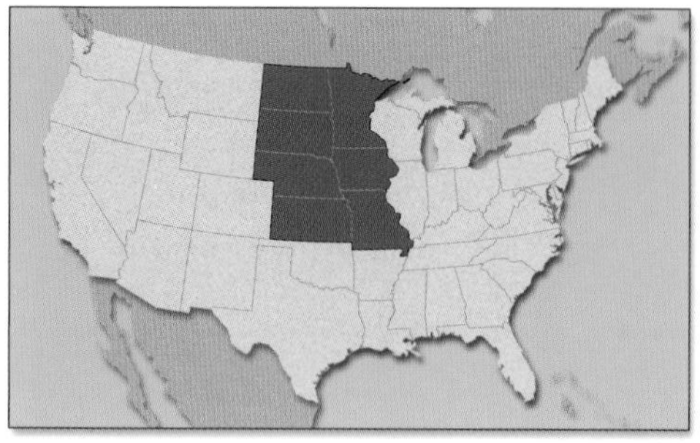

AREA	82,277 sq mi (213,096 sq km)
POPULATION	2,745,000
CAPITAL	Topeka
CAPITAL POP.	metro area: 228,000 city proper: 122,000
LARGEST CITY	Wichita
POPULATION	metro area: 585,000 city proper: 354,000
INCOME	$31,003 per capita
STATEHOOD	January 29, 1861; 34th state
STATE BIRD	Western Meadowlark
STATE FLOWER	Sunflower
HIGHEST POINT	Mt. Sunflower 4,039 ft (1,231 m)

Minnesota

GOPHER STATE

AREA	86,939 sq mi (225,171 sq km)
POPULATION	5,133,000
CAPITAL	St. Paul
CAPITAL POP.	metro area: 3,116,000 city proper: 277,000
LARGEST CITY	Minneapolis
POPULATION	metro area: 3,116,000 city proper: 374,000
INCOME	$36,173 per capita
STATEHOOD	May 11, 1858; 32nd state
STATE BIRD	Common Loon
STATE FLOWER	Pink and White Lady's Slipper
HIGHEST POINT	Eagle Mountain 2,301 ft (701 m)

Missouri

SHOW ME STATE

AREA	69,704 sq mi (180,533 sq km)
POPULATION	5,800,000
CAPITAL	Jefferson City
CAPITAL POP.	metro area: 142,000 city proper: 39,000
LARGEST CITY	Kansas City
POPULATION	metro area: 1,925,000 city proper: 444,000
INCOME	$30,516 per capita
STATEHOOD	August 10, 1821; 24th state
STATE BIRD	Bluebird
STATE FLOWER	Hawthorn Blossom
HIGHEST POINT	Taum Sauk Mt. 1,772 ft (540 m)

Nebraska

CORNHUSKER STATE

AREA	77,354 sq mi (200,345 sq km)
POPULATION	1,759,000
CAPITAL	Lincoln
CAPITAL POP.	metro area: 278,000 city proper: 236,000
LARGEST CITY	Omaha
POPULATION	metro area: 804,000 city proper: 409,000
INCOME	$32,276 per capita
STATEHOOD	March 1, 1867; 37th state
STATE BIRD	Western Meadowlark
STATE FLOWER	Goldenrod
HIGHEST POINT	Panorama Point 5,424 ft (1,654 m)

North Dakota

PEACE GARDEN STATE

AREA	70,700 sq mi (183,112 sq km)
POPULATION	637,000
CAPITAL	Bismarck
CAPITAL POP.	metro area: 98,000 city proper: 57,000
LARGEST CITY	Fargo
POPULATION	metro area: 182,000 city proper: 91,000
INCOME	$29,247 per capita
STATEHOOD	November 2, 1889; 39th state
STATE BIRD	Western Meadowlark
STATE FLOWER	Wild Prairie Rose
HIGHEST POINT	White Butte 3,506 ft (1,069 m)

South Dakota

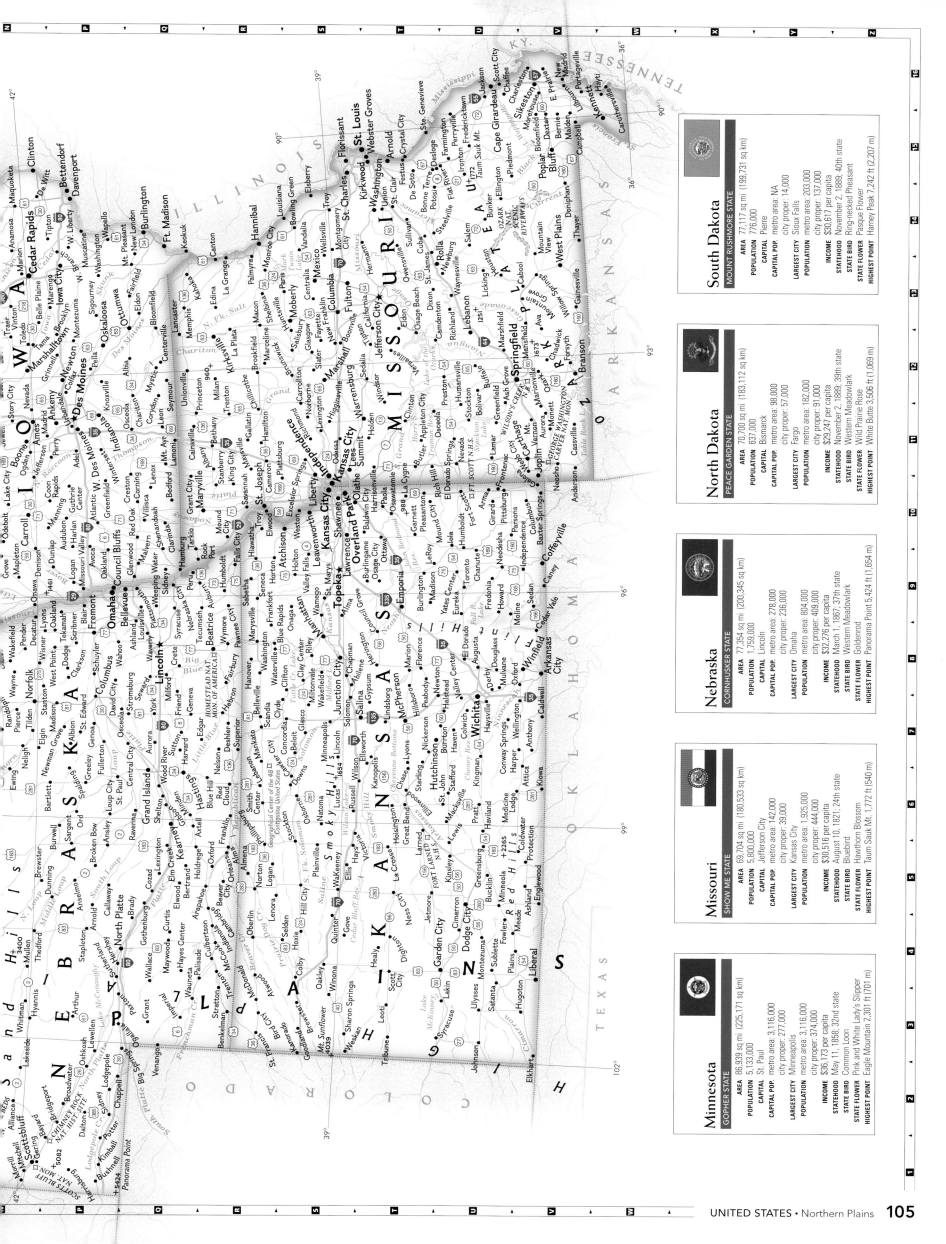

MOUNT RUSHMORE STATE

AREA	77,117 sq mi (199,731 sq km)
POPULATION	776,000
CAPITAL	Pierre
CAPITAL POP.	metro area: NA city proper: 14,000
LARGEST CITY	Sioux Falls
POPULATION	metro area: 203,000 city proper: 137,000
INCOME	$30,617 per capita
STATEHOOD	November 2, 1889; 40th state
STATE BIRD	Ring-necked Pheasant
STATE FLOWER	Pasque Flower
HIGHEST POINT	Harney Peak 7,242 ft (2,207 m)

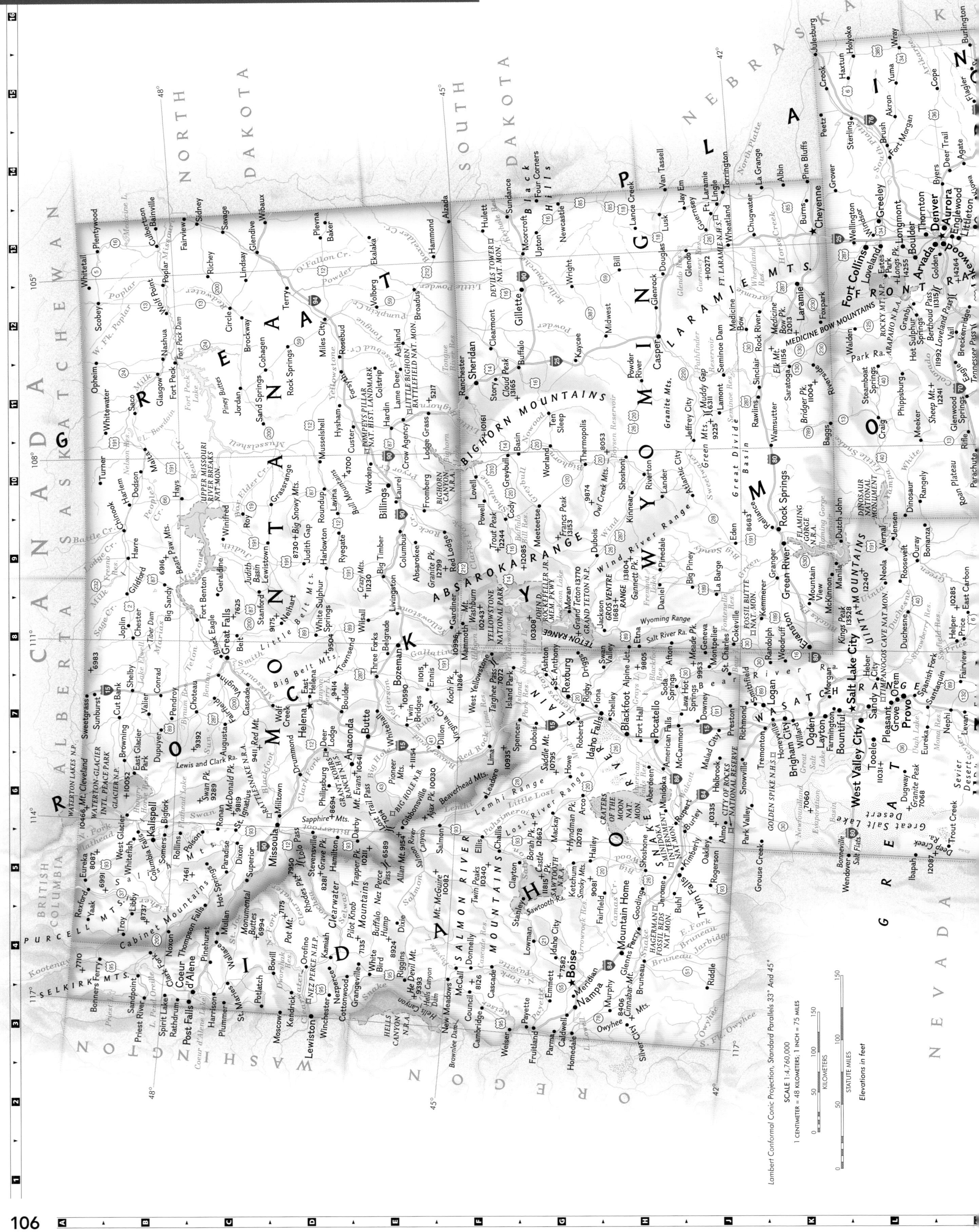

CANADA
ALBERTA
SASKATCHEWAN
BRITISH COLUMBIA
NORTH DAKOTA
SOUTH DAKOTA
NEBRASKA
WASHINGTON
OREGON
NEVADA
MONTANA
IDAHO
WYOMING
GREAT PLAINS
SNAKE RIVER PLAIN
GREAT BASIN
BIGHORN MOUNTAINS
ABSAROKA RANGE
LARAMIE MTS.
MEDICINE BOW MOUNTAINS
UINTA MOUNTAINS
WASATCH RANGE
SALMON RIVER MOUNTAINS
BLACK HILLS
Wind River Range
Cabinet Mountains
PURCELL MTS.
SELKIRK MTS.
Big Belt Mts.
Little Belt Mts.
Beaverhead Mts.
Lemhi Range
Lost River Range
Great Divide Basin
Great Salt Lake
Great Salt Lake Desert
Yellowstone National Park
Grand Teton N.P.
Glacier N.P.
Helena
Boise
Cheyenne
Salt Lake City
Denver
Billings
Missoula
Great Falls
Butte
Bozeman
Casper
Sheridan
Laramie
Rock Springs
Idaho Falls
Pocatello
Twin Falls
Ogden
Provo
Fort Collins
Lewiston
Coeur d'Alene
Kalispell
Lambert Conformal Conic Projection, Standard Parallels 33° And 45°
SCALE 1:4,760,000
1 CENTIMETER = 48 KILOMETERS; 1 INCH = 75 MILES
KILOMETERS
STATUTE MILES
Elevations in feet

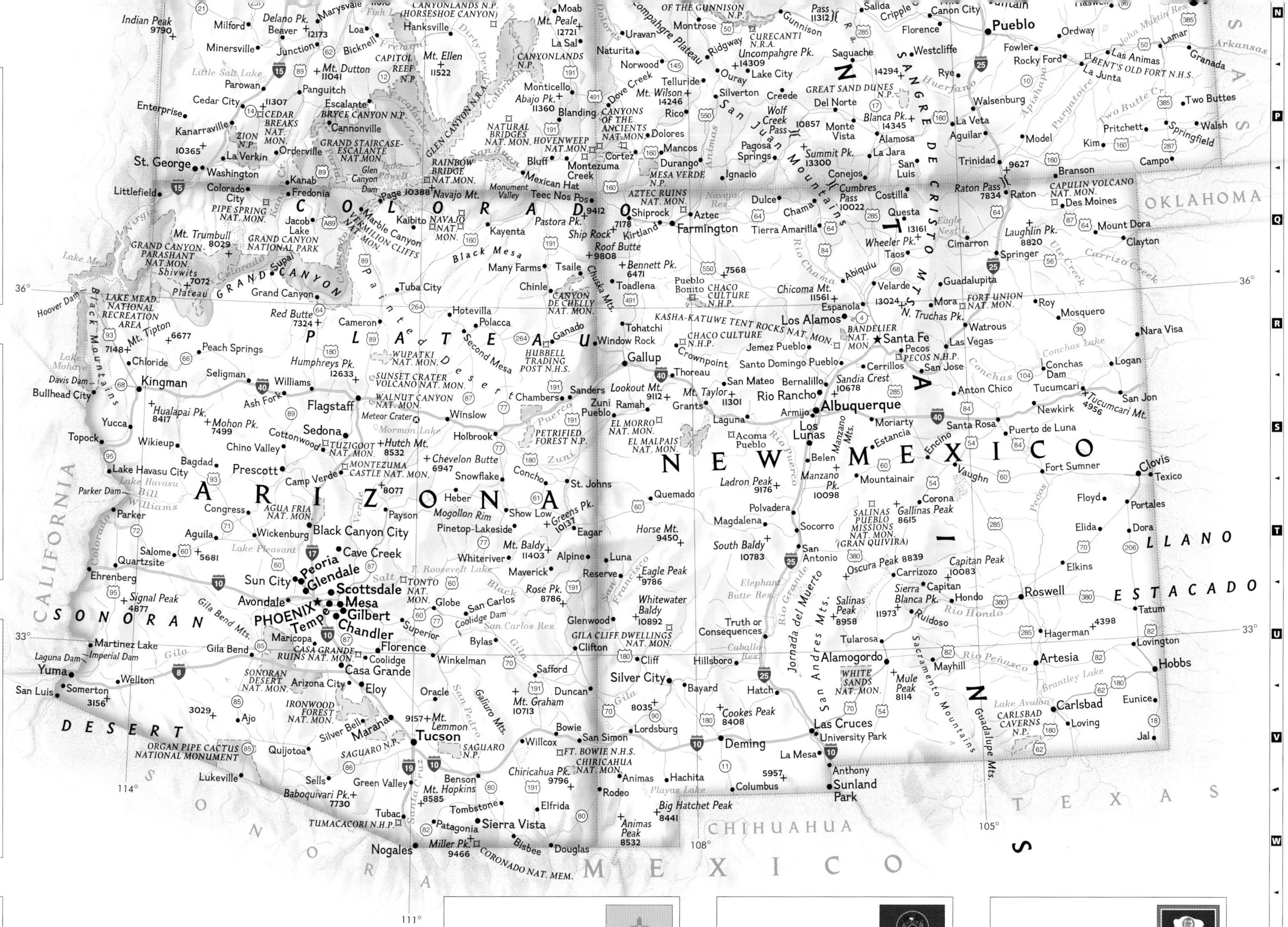

Arizona
GRAND CANYON STATE

AREA	113,998 sq mi (295,254 sq km)
POPULATION	5,939,000
CAPITAL	Phoenix
CAPITAL POP.	metro area: 3,715,000 city proper: 1,418,000
LARGEST CITY	Phoenix
INCOME	$28,609 per capita
STATEHOOD	February 14, 1912; 48th state
STATE BIRD	Cactus Wren
STATE FLOWER	Saguaro Cactus Blossom
HIGHEST POINT	Humphreys Pk. 12,633 ft (3,851 m)

Colorado
CENTENNIAL STATE

AREA	104,094 sq mi (269,601 sq km)
POPULATION	4,665,000
CAPITAL	Denver
CAPITAL POP.	metro area: 2,330,000 city proper: 557,000
LARGEST CITY	Denver
INCOME	$36,109 per capita
STATEHOOD	August 1, 1876; 38th state
STATE BIRD	Lark Bunting
STATE FLOWER	White and Lavender Columbine
HIGHEST POINT	Mount Elbert 14,433 ft (4,399 m)

Idaho
GEM STATE

AREA	83,570 sq mi (216,446 sq km)
POPULATION	1,429,000
CAPITAL	Boise
CAPITAL POP.	metro area: 525,000 city proper: 190,000
LARGEST CITY	Boise
INCOME	$26,839 per capita
STATEHOOD	July 3, 1890; 43rd state
STATE BIRD	Mountain Bluebird
STATE FLOWER	Syringa
HIGHEST POINT	Borah Peak 12,662 ft (3,859 m)

Montana
TREASURE STATE

AREA	147,042 sq mi (380,838 sq km)
POPULATION	936,000
CAPITAL	Helena
CAPITAL POP.	metro area: NA city proper: 27,000
LARGEST CITY	Billings
POPULATION	metro area: 144,000 city proper: 97,000
INCOME	$27,666 per capita
STATEHOOD	November 8, 1889; 41st state
STATE BIRD	Western Meadowlark
STATE FLOWER	Bitterroot
HIGHEST POINT	Granite Peak 12,799 ft (3,901 m)

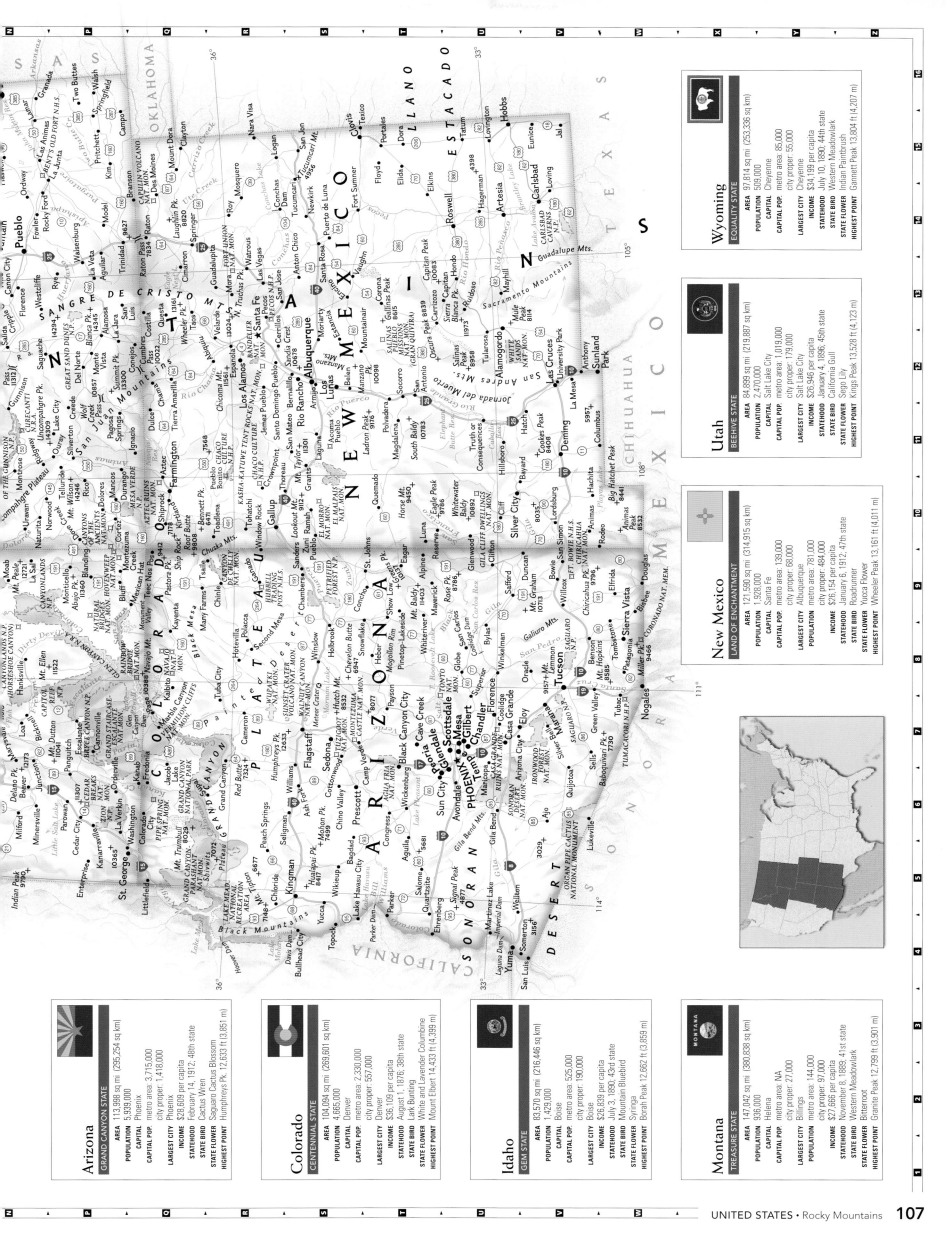

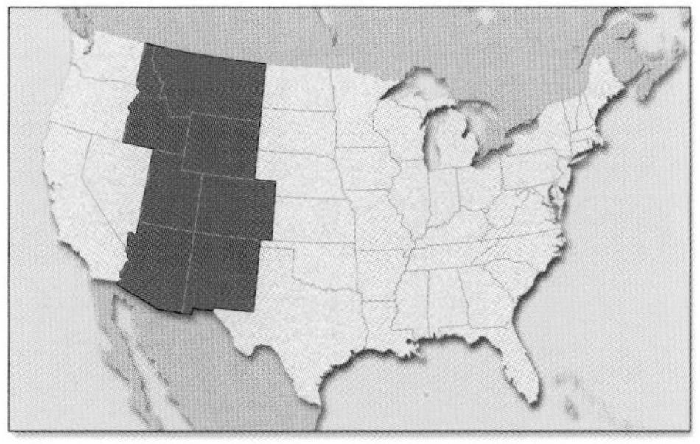

New Mexico
LAND OF ENCHANTMENT

AREA	121,590 sq mi (314,915 sq km)
POPULATION	1,928,000
CAPITAL	Santa Fe
CAPITAL POP.	metro area: 139,000 city proper: 68,000
LARGEST CITY	Albuquerque
POPULATION	metro area: 781,000 city proper: 484,000
INCOME	$26,154 per capita
STATEHOOD	January 6, 1912; 47th state
STATE BIRD	Roadrunner
STATE FLOWER	Yucca Flower
HIGHEST POINT	Wheeler Peak 13,161 ft (4,011 m)

Utah
BEEHIVE STATE

AREA	84,899 sq mi (219,887 sq km)
POPULATION	2,470,000
CAPITAL	Salt Lake City
CAPITAL POP.	metro area: 1,019,000 city proper: 179,000
LARGEST CITY	Salt Lake City
INCOME	$26,946 per capita
STATEHOOD	January 4, 1896; 45th state
STATE BIRD	California Gull
STATE FLOWER	Sego Lily
HIGHEST POINT	Kings Peak 13,528 ft (4,123 m)

Wyoming
EQUALITY STATE

AREA	97,814 sq mi (253,336 sq km)
POPULATION	509,000
CAPITAL	Cheyenne
CAPITAL POP.	metro area: 85,000 city proper: 55,000
LARGEST CITY	Cheyenne
INCOME	$34,199 per capita
STATEHOOD	July 10, 1890; 44th state
STATE BIRD	Western Meadowlark
STATE FLOWER	Indian Paintbrush
HIGHEST POINT	Gannett Peak 13,804 ft (4,207 m)

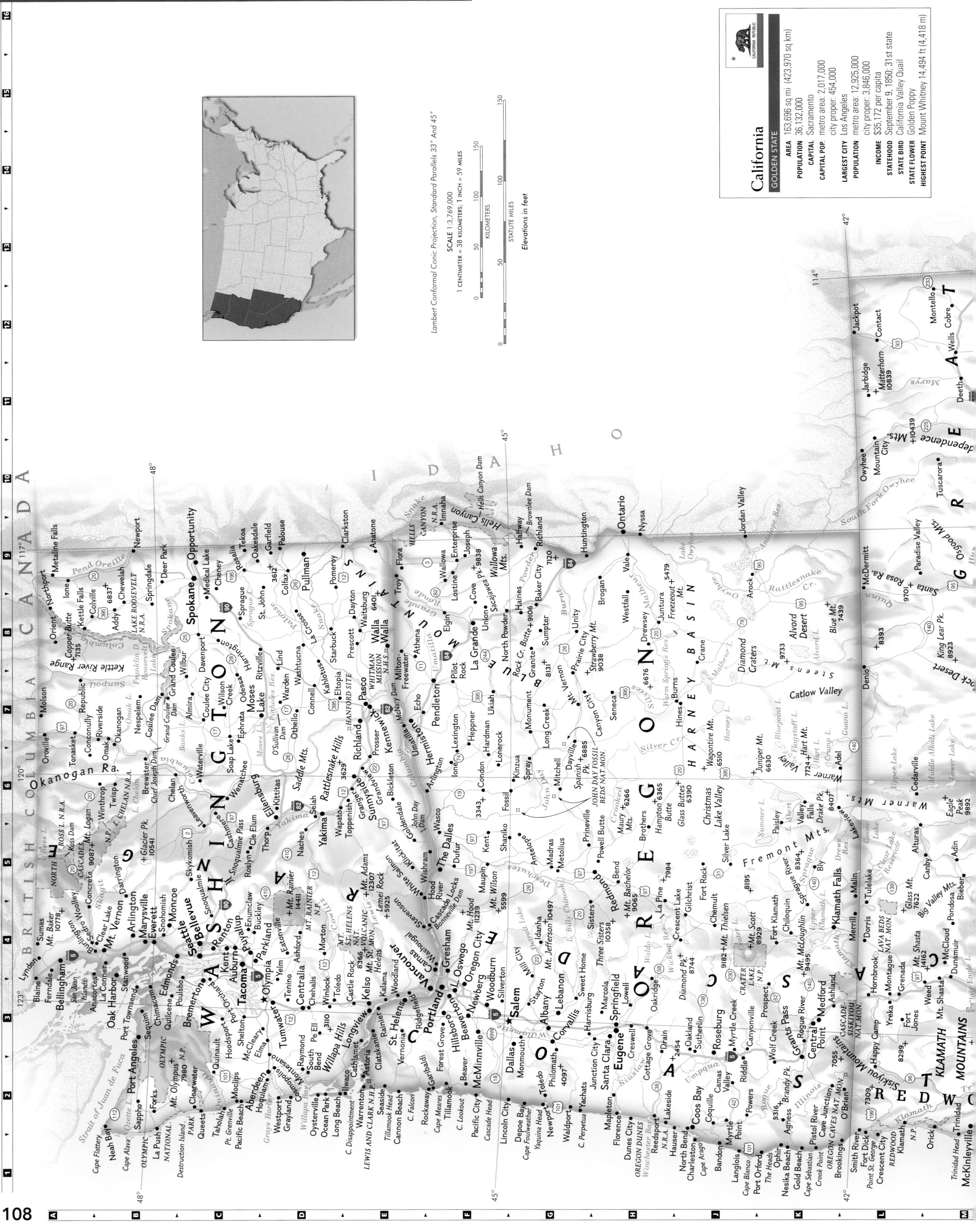
Lambert Conformal Conic Projection, Standard Parallels 33° And 45°
SCALE 1:3,769,000
1 CENTIMETER = 38 KILOMETERS; 1 INCH = 59 MILES
KILOMETERS
STATUTE MILES
Elevations in feet
California
GOLDEN STATE
AREA 163,696 sq mi (423,970 sq km)
POPULATION 36,132,000
CAPITAL Sacramento
CAPITAL POP. metro area: 2,017,000
city proper: 454,000
LARGEST CITY Los Angeles
POPULATION metro area: 12,925,000
city proper: 3,846,000
INCOME $35,172 per capita
STATEHOOD September 9, 1850; 31st state
STATE BIRD California Valley Quail
STATE FLOWER Golden Poppy
HIGHEST POINT Mount Whitney 14,494 ft (4,418 m)
BRITISH COLUMBIA
CANADA
WASHINGTON
OREGON
IDAHO
NEVADA

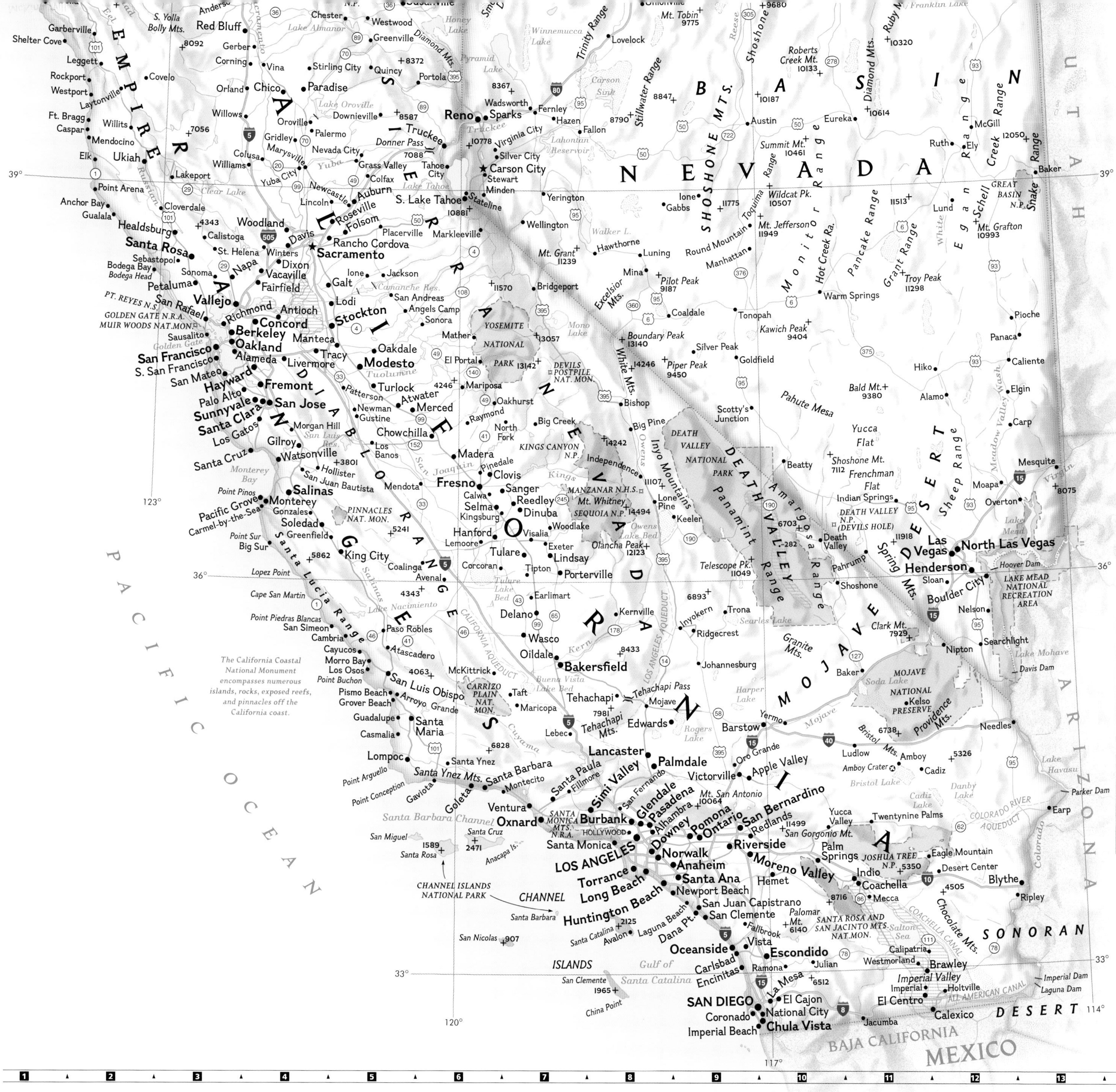

Nevada

SILVER STATE

AREA	110,561 sq mi (286,351 sq km)
POPULATION	2,415,000
CAPITAL	Carson City
CAPITAL POP.	metro area: NA city proper: 56,000
LARGEST CITY	Las Vegas
POPULATION	metro area: 1,651,000 city proper: 535,000
INCOME	$33,783 per capita
STATEHOOD	October 31, 1864; 36th state
STATE BIRD	Mountain Bluebird
STATE FLOWER	Sagebrush
HIGHEST POINT	Boundary Peak 13,140 ft (4,005 m)

Oregon

STATE OF OREGON 1859

OBVERSE REVERSE

BEAVER STATE

AREA	98,381 sq mi (254,805 sq km)
POPULATION	3,641,000
CAPITAL	Salem
CAPITAL POP.	metro area: 369,000 city proper: 146,000
LARGEST CITY	Portland
POPULATION	metro area: 2,064,000 city proper: 533,000
INCOME	$30,584 per capita
STATEHOOD	February 14, 1859; 33rd state
STATE BIRD	Western Meadowlark
STATE FLOWER	Oregon Grape
HIGHEST POINT	Mount Hood 11,239 ft (3,426 m)

Washington

EVERGREEN STATE

AREA	71,300 sq mi (184,665 sq km)
POPULATION	6,288,000
CAPITAL	Olympia
CAPITAL POP.	metro area: 225,000 city proper: 44,000
LARGEST CITY	Seattle
POPULATION	metro area: 3,167,000 city proper: 571,000
INCOME	$35,017 per capita
STATEHOOD	November 11, 1889; 42nd state
STATE BIRD	Willow Goldfinch
STATE FLOWER	Coast Rhododendron
HIGHEST POINT	Mount Rainier 14,411 ft (4,392 m)

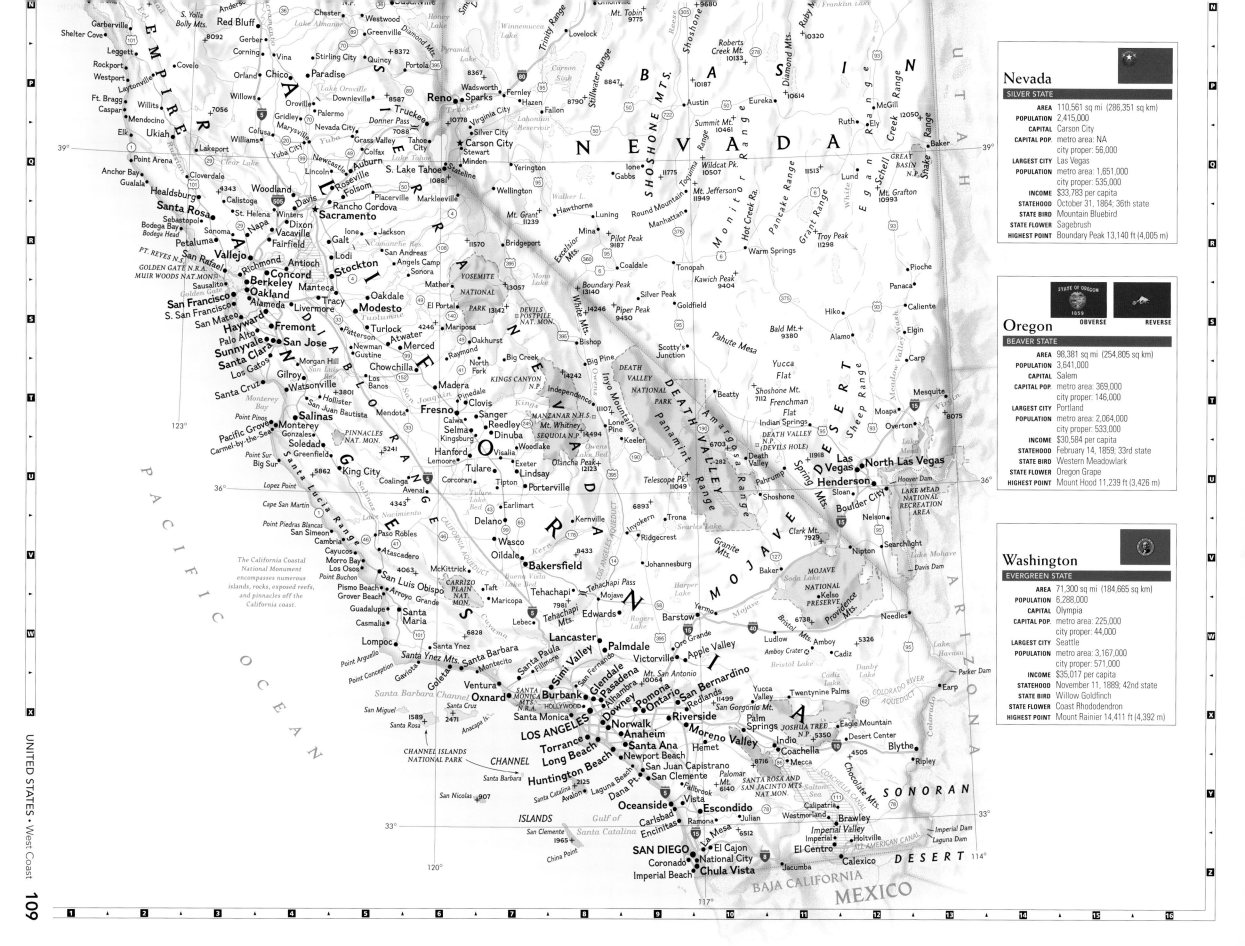

C A N A D A
WASH.
MONTANA
N. DAK.
MINN.
ME.
OREG.
IDAHO
S. DAK.
WIS.
VT.
N.H.
MASS.
WYO.
MICH.
N.Y.
R.I.
CONN.
NEVADA
IOWA
PA.
N.J.
NEBR.
San Francisco
UTAH
ILL.
IND.
OHIO
MD.
DEL.
COLO.
W.VA.
D.C.
VA.
MO.
KANS.
KY.
CALIF.
N.C.
TENN.
ARIZ.
OKLA.
N. MEX.
ARK.
S.C.
GA.
MISS.
ALA.
TEXAS
LA.
Jacksonville
FLA.
MEXICO
KILOMETERS
0 250 500 750
STATUTE MILES
0 250 500 750
RELATIVE SIZE OF
ALASKA AND THE
CONTIGUOUS U.S.

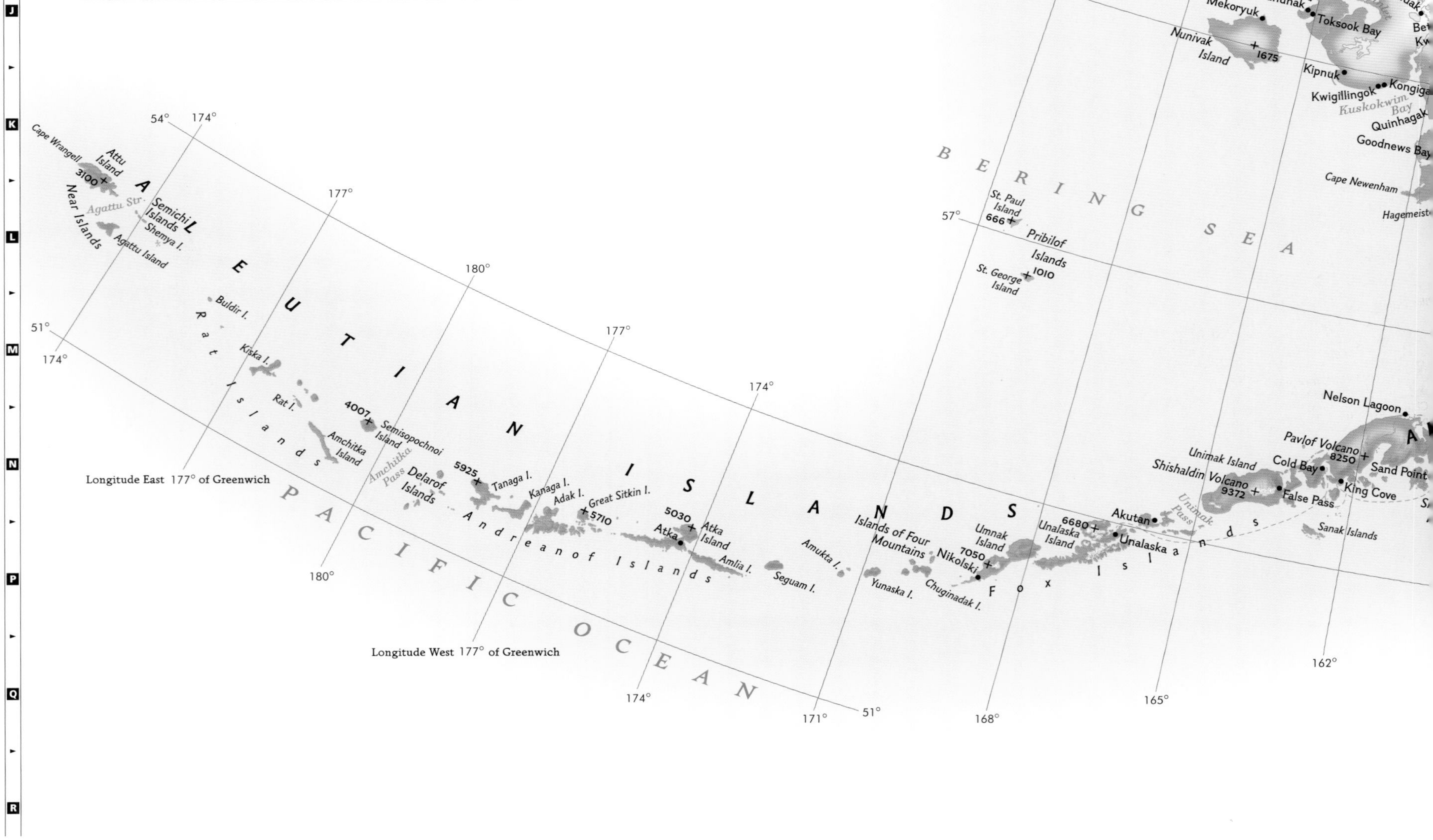

177°
174°
171°
180°
69°
CHUKCHI
SEA
Monday
Sunday
Cape Lisburne
Point Hope
ARCTIC CIRCLE
66°
180°
RUSSIA
Date Line
CAPE KRUSENSTERN
Shishmaref
Diomede Is.
Bering Strait
Cape Prince of Wales
Wales
King I.
Teller
Seward Peninsula
4714
White Mountain
Nome
63°
177°
Gambell
Savoonga
Kookooligit Mts.
2207
St. Lawrence Island
Yukon Delta
Alakanuk
Emmonak
Sheldon Point
Mountain Village
Scammon Bay
Pilot Station
Hooper Bay
Chevak
Russian
St. Matthew Island
1506
60°
174°
Nelson Island
Tununak
Atmautluak
Mekoryuk
Toksook Bay
Nunivak Island
1675
Kipnuk
Kwigillingok
Kongiganak
Kuskokwim Bay
Quinhagak
Goodnews Bay
Cape Newenham
Hagemeister
BERING SEA
St. Paul Island
666
57°
Pribilof Islands
St. George Island
1010
54°
174°
Cape Wrangell
Attu Island
3100
Near Islands
Agattu Str.
Semichi Islands
Shemya I.
Agattu Island
177°
180°
ALEUTIAN ISLANDS
Buldir I.
Rat Islands
Kiska I.
Rat I.
51°
174°
4007
Semisopochnoi Island
Amchitka Island
Amchitka Pass
Delarof Islands
5925
Tanaga I.
Kanaga I.
Adak I.
Great Sitkin I.
5710
Andreanof Islands
5030
Atka Island
Atka
Amlia I.
Seguam I.
Amukta I.
Islands of Four Mountains
Yunaska I.
Chuginadak I.
Umnak Island
7050
Nikolski
Unalaska Island
6680
Akutan
Unalaska
Fox Islands
Unimak Pass
Unimak Island
Shishaldin Volcano
9372
False Pass
Pavlof Volcano
8250
Cold Bay
Sand Point
King Cove
Sanak Islands
Nelson Lagoon
Longitude East 177° of Greenwich
Longitude West 177° of Greenwich
PACIFIC OCEAN
180°
174°
171°
51°
168°
165°
162°

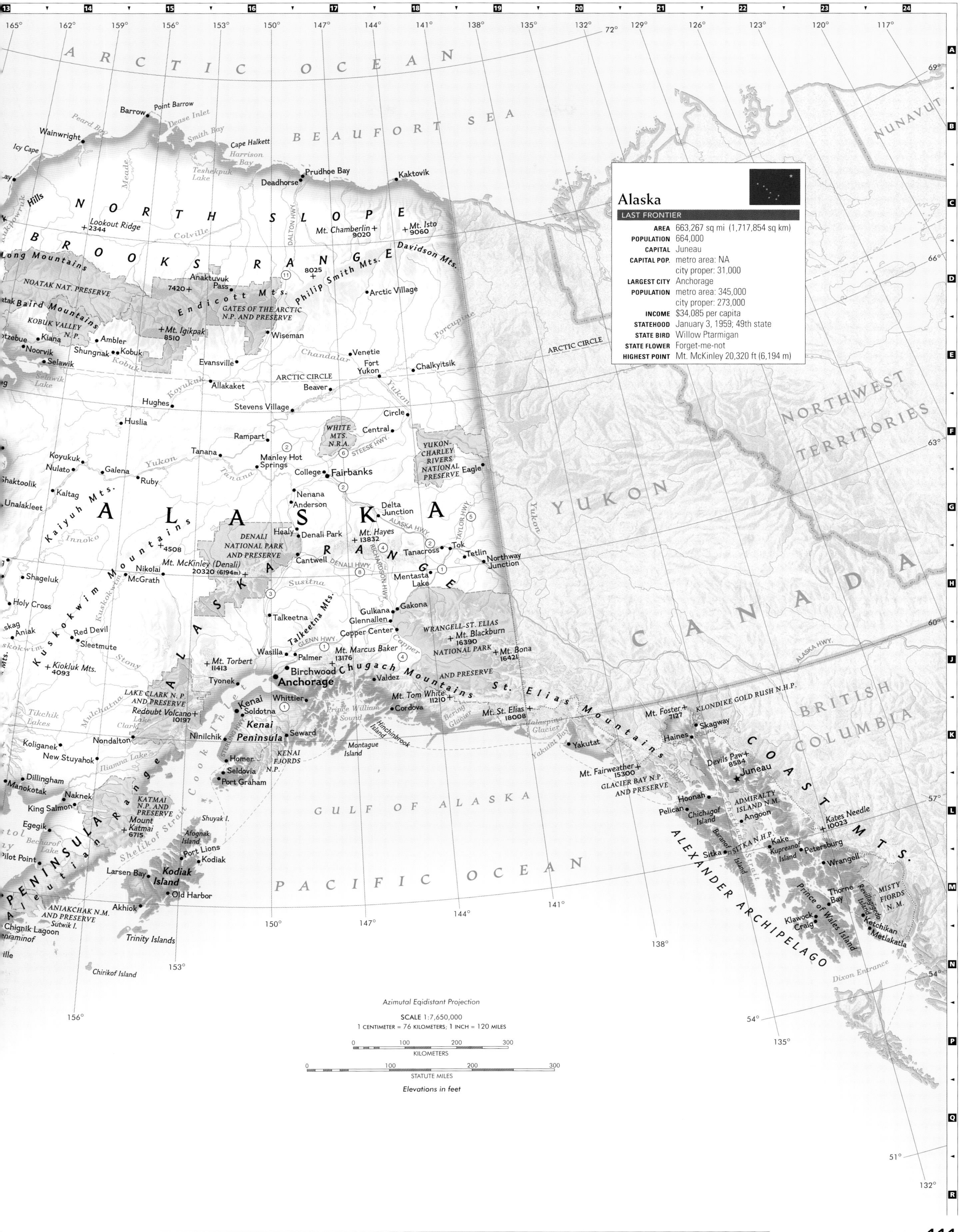

Alaska

LAST FRONTIER

AREA	663,267 sq mi (1,717,854 sq km)
POPULATION	664,000
CAPITAL	Juneau
CAPITAL POP.	metro area: NA city proper: 31,000
LARGEST CITY	Anchorage
POPULATION	metro area: 345,000 city proper: 273,000
INCOME	$34,085 per capita
STATEHOOD	January 3, 1959; 49th state
STATE BIRD	Willow Ptarmigan
STATE FLOWER	Forget-me-not
HIGHEST POINT	Mt. McKinley 20,320 ft (6,194 m)

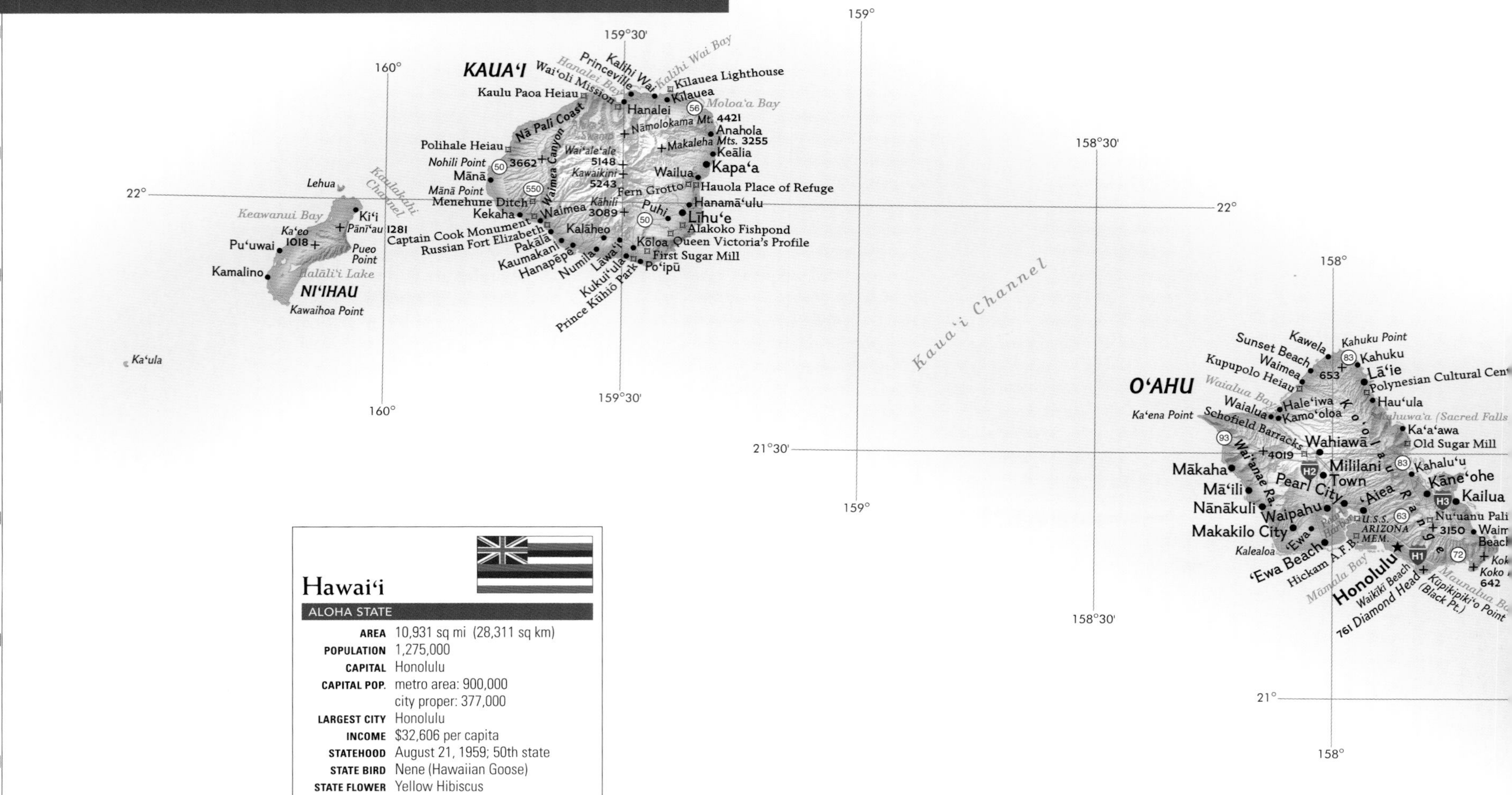

Hawai'i	
ALOHA STATE	
AREA	10,931 sq mi (28,311 sq km)
POPULATION	1,275,000
CAPITAL	Honolulu
CAPITAL POP.	metro area: 900,000 city proper: 377,000
LARGEST CITY	Honolulu
INCOME	$32,606 per capita
STATEHOOD	August 21, 1959; 50th state
STATE BIRD	Nene (Hawaiian Goose)
STATE FLOWER	Yellow Hibiscus
HIGHEST POINT	Mauna Kea (Pu'u Wekiu) 13,796 ft (4,205 m)

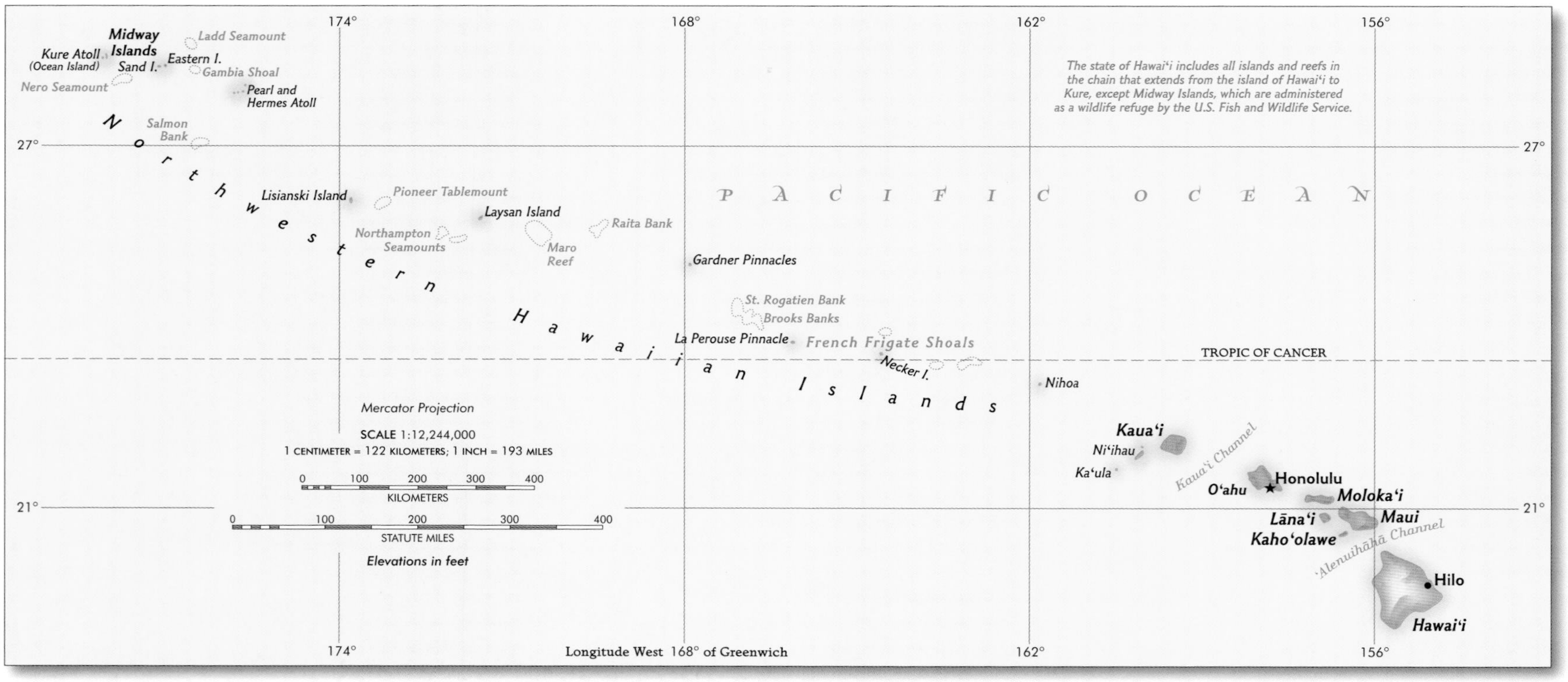

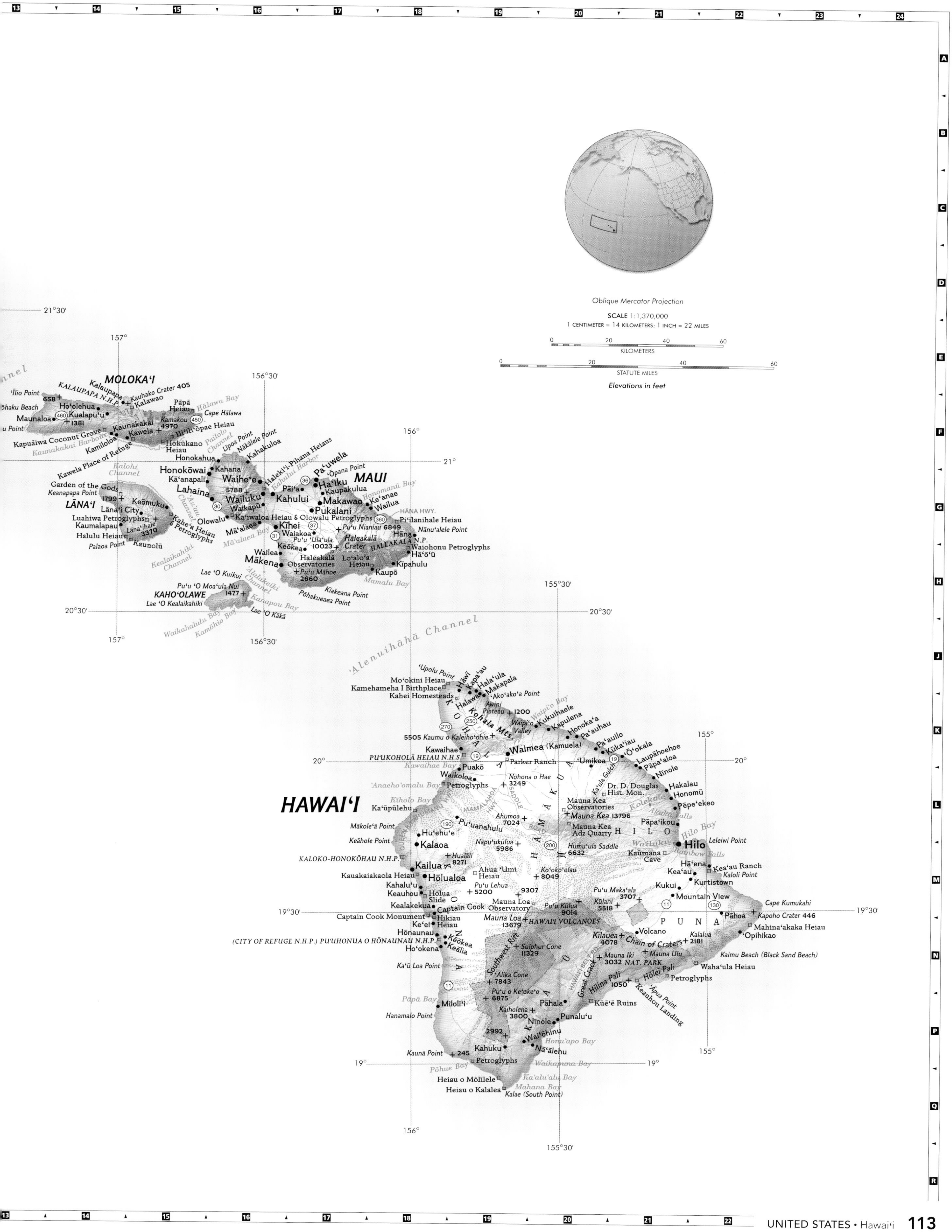
HAWAI‘I
MAUI
MOLOKA‘I
LĀNA‘I
KAHO‘OLAWE
Oblique Mercator Projection
SCALE 1:1,370,000
1 CENTIMETER = 14 KILOMETERS; 1 INCH = 22 MILES
KILOMETERS
STATUTE MILES
Elevations in feet
‘Alenuihāhā Channel
Kalaupapa
KALAUPAPA N.H.P.
Kauhako Crater 405
Kalawao
‘Īlio Point
Kualapu‘u
Ho‘olehua
Maunaloa
Kaunakakai
Kawela
Kamakou 4970
Kapuāiwa Coconut Grove
Kamiloloa
Kawela Place of Refuge
Pāpā Heiau
Cape Hālawa
Hālawa Bay
‘Ili‘ili‘ōpae Heiau
Hōkūkano Heiau
Pailolo Channel
Lipoa Point
Nākālele Point
Kahakuloa
Honokahua
Kalohi Channel
Honokōwai
Kahana
Kā‘anapali
Lahaina
Waihe‘e
Wailuku
Waikapū
Kahului
Pā‘ia
Ha‘ikū
Pa‘uwela
‘Ōpana Point
Makawao
Pukalani
Kaupakulua
Ke‘anae
Wailua
Haleki‘i-Pihana Heiaus
Kahului Harbor
Garden of the Gods
Keanapapa Point
Keōmuku
Lāna‘i City
Lāna‘ihale 3370
Luahiwa Petroglyphs
Kaumalapau
Halulu Heiau
Palaoa Point
Kaunolū
Kahe‘a Heiau & Petroglyphs
‘Au‘au Channel
Olowalu
Ka‘iwaloa Heiau & Olowalu Petroglyphs
Mā‘alaea
Mā‘alaea Bay
Kīhei
Waiakoa
Kēōkea
Wailea
Mākena
Haleakalā Observatories
Pu‘u Māhoe 2660
Pu‘u ‘Ula‘ula 10023
Haleakalā Crater
HALEAKALĀ N.P.
Pu‘u Nianiau 6849
Lo‘alo‘a Heiau
Kaupō
Kīpahulu
Hāna
Hā‘ō‘ū
Waiohonu Petroglyphs
Pi‘ilanihale Heiau
Nānu‘alele Point
HĀNA HWY.
Honomanū Bay
Kealaikahiki Channel
Lae ‘O Kuikui
Pu‘u ‘O Moa‘ula Nui 1477
Lae ‘O Kealaikahiki
Lae ‘O Kākā
Kanapou Bay
Waikahalulu Bay
Kamōhio Bay
‘Alalākeiki Channel
Kīakeana Point
Pōhakueaea Point
Mamalu Bay
‘Upolu Point
Hāwī
Kapa‘au
Hala‘ula
Makapala
Halawa
Mo‘okini Heiau
Kamehameha I Birthplace
Kahei Homesteads
‘Ako‘ako‘a Point
Awini Plateau 1200
Kohala Mts.
KOHALA
Waipi‘o Bay
Waipi‘o Valley
Kukuihaele
Kapulena
Honoka‘a
Pa‘auhau
Pa‘auilo
Kūka‘iau
‘Ō‘ōkala
Laupāhoehoe
Pāpa‘aloa
Nīnole
Hakalau
Honomū
Pepe‘ekeo
Pāpa‘ikou
Hilo
Hilo Bay
Leleiwi Point
5505 Kaumu o Kaleiho‘ohie
Kawaihae
PU‘UKOHOLĀ HEIAU N.H.S.
Kawaihae Bay
Waimea (Kamuela)
Parker Ranch
‘Umikoa
Puakō
Waikoloa
Petroglyphs
‘Anaeho‘omalu Bay
Nohona o Hae 3249
Ka‘ula Gulch
Dr. D. Douglas Hist. Mon.
Mauna Kea Observatories
Mauna Kea 13796
Mauna Kea Adz Quarry
HĀMĀKUA
HILO
Kīholo Bay
Ka‘ūpūlehu
MAMALAHOA HWY.
SADDLE ROAD
Ahumoa 7024
Mākole‘ā Point
Pu‘uanahulu
Keāhole Point
Hu‘ehu‘e
Kalaoa
Nāpu‘ukūlua 5986
Humu‘ula Saddle 6632
Wailuku
Rainbow Falls
Kaūmana Cave
KALOKO-HONOKŌHAU N.H.P.
Hualālai 8271
Kailua
KONA
Kauakaiakaola Heiau
Hōlualoa
Ahua ‘Umi Heiau
Ko‘oko‘olau 8049
Hā‘ena
Kea‘au
Kea‘au Ranch
Kaloli Point
Kurtistown
Kukui
Mountain View
Kahalu‘u
Keauhou
Hōlua Slide
Pu‘u Lehua 5200
9307
Pu‘u Maka‘ala 3707
Kealakekua
Captain Cook
Mauna Loa Observatory
Pu‘u Kūlua 9014
Kūlani 5518
Cape Kumukahi
Kapoho Crater 446
Pāhoa
Mahina‘akaka Heiau
‘Ōpihikao
PUNA
Captain Cook Monument
Hikiau Heiau
Ke‘ei
Mauna Loa 13679
HAWAI‘I VOLCANOES
Volcano
Hōnaunau
(CITY OF REFUGE N.H.P.) PU‘UHONUA O HŌNAUNAU N.H.P.
Kēōkea
Ho‘okena
Kealia
Sulphur Cone 11329
Kīlauea 4078
Chain of Craters
Kalalua 2181
Mauna Iki 3032
Mauna Ulu
NAT. PARK
Kaimu Beach (Black Sand Beach)
Waha‘ula Heiau
Ka‘ū Loa Point
Southwest Rift
‘Alika Cone 7843
Great Crack
Hilina Pali
Hōlei Pali
Petroglyphs
‘Āpua Point
Keauhou Landing
Pu‘u o Ke‘oke‘o 6875
Pāpā Bay
Miloli‘i
Pāhala
Kū‘ē‘ē Ruins
Hanamalo Point
Kaiholena 3800
Nīnole
Punalu‘u
KA‘Ū
2992
Wai‘ōhinu
Honu‘apo Bay
Nā‘ālehu
Kaunā Point
245
Kahuku
Petroglyphs
Pōhue Bay
Waikapuna Bay
Heiau o Mōlilele
Ka‘alu‘alu Bay
Heiau o Kalalea
Mahana Bay
Kalae (South Point)
21°30′
21°
20°30′
20°
19°30′
19°
157°
156°30′
156°
155°30′
155°

Belize

BELIZE

AREA 22,965 sq km (8,867 sq mi)
POPULATION 292,000
CAPITAL Belmopan 9,000
RELIGION Roman Catholic, Protestant
LANGUAGE English (official), Spanish, Mayan, Garifuna (Carib), Creole
LITERACY 94%
LIFE EXPECTANCY 70 years
GDP PER CAPITA $3,594
ECONOMY **IND:** garment production, food processing, tourism, construction **AGR:** bananas, coca, citrus, sugar; lumber; fish **EXP:** sugar, bananas, citrus, clothing

Costa Rica

REPUBLIC OF COSTA RICA

AREA 51,100 sq km (19,730 sq mi)
POPULATION 4,331,000
CAPITAL San José 1,085,000
RELIGION Roman Catholic, Evangelical
LANGUAGE Spanish (official), English
LITERACY 96%
LIFE EXPECTANCY 79 years
GDP PER CAPITA $4,325
ECONOMY **IND:** microprocessors, food processing, textiles and clothing, construction materials **AGR:** coffee, pineapples, bananas, sugar; beef; timber **EXP:** coffee, bananas, sugar, pineapples

El Salvador

REPUBLIC OF EL SALVADOR

AREA 21,041 sq km (8,124 sq mi)
POPULATION 6,881,000
CAPITAL San Salvador 1,424,000
RELIGION Roman Catholic, Protestant
LANGUAGE Spanish, Nahua
LITERACY 80%
LIFE EXPECTANCY 70 years
GDP PER CAPITA $2,301
ECONOMY **IND:** food processing, beverages, petroleum, chemicals **AGR:** coffee, sugar, corn, rice; beef; shrimp **EXP:** offshore assembly exports, coffee, sugar, shrimp

Guatemala

REPUBLIC OF GUATEMALA

AREA 108,889 sq km (42,042 sq mi)
POPULATION 12,701,000
CAPITAL Guatemala City 951,000
RELIGION Roman Catholic, Protestant, indigenous Mayan beliefs
LANGUAGE Spanish, 23 officially recognized Amerindian languages
LITERACY 71%
LIFE EXPECTANCY 66 years
GDP PER CAPITA $2,157
ECONOMY **IND:** sugar, textiles and clothing, furniture, chemicals **AGR:** sugarcane, corn, bananas, coffee; cattle **EXP:** coffee, sugar, petroleum, apparel

Honduras

REPUBLIC OF HONDURAS

AREA 112,492 sq km (43,433 sq mi)
POPULATION 7,212,000
CAPITAL Tegucigalpa 1,007,000
RELIGION Roman Catholic
LANGUAGE Spanish, Amerindian dialects
LITERACY 76%
LIFE EXPECTANCY 71 years
GDP PER CAPITA $1,046
ECONOMY **IND:** sugar, coffee, textiles, clothing **AGR:** bananas, coffee, citrus; beef; timber; shrimp **EXP:** coffee, shrimp, bananas, gold

Mexico

UNITED MEXICAN STATES

AREA 1,964,375 sq km (758,449 sq mi)
POPULATION 107,029,000
CAPITAL Mexico City 18,660,000
RELIGION Roman Catholic, Protestant
LANGUAGE Spanish, various Mayan, Nahuatl, and other indigenous languages
LITERACY 92%
LIFE EXPECTANCY 75 years
GDP PER CAPITA $6,397
ECONOMY **IND:** food and beverages, tobacco, chemicals, iron and steel **AGR:** corn, wheat, soybeans, rice; beef; wood products **EXP:** manufactured goods, oil and oil products, silver, fruits

Nicaragua

REPUBLIC OF NICARAGUA

AREA 130,000 sq km (50,193 sq mi)
POPULATION 5,774,000
CAPITAL Managua 1,098,000
RELIGION Roman Catholic, Evangelical
LANGUAGE Spanish (official), English, indigenous languages
LITERACY 68%
LIFE EXPECTANCY 69 years
GDP PER CAPITA $820
ECONOMY **IND:** food processing, chemicals, machinery and metal products, textiles **AGR:** coffee, bananas, sugarcane, cotton; beef **EXP:** coffee, beef, shrimp and lobster, tobacco

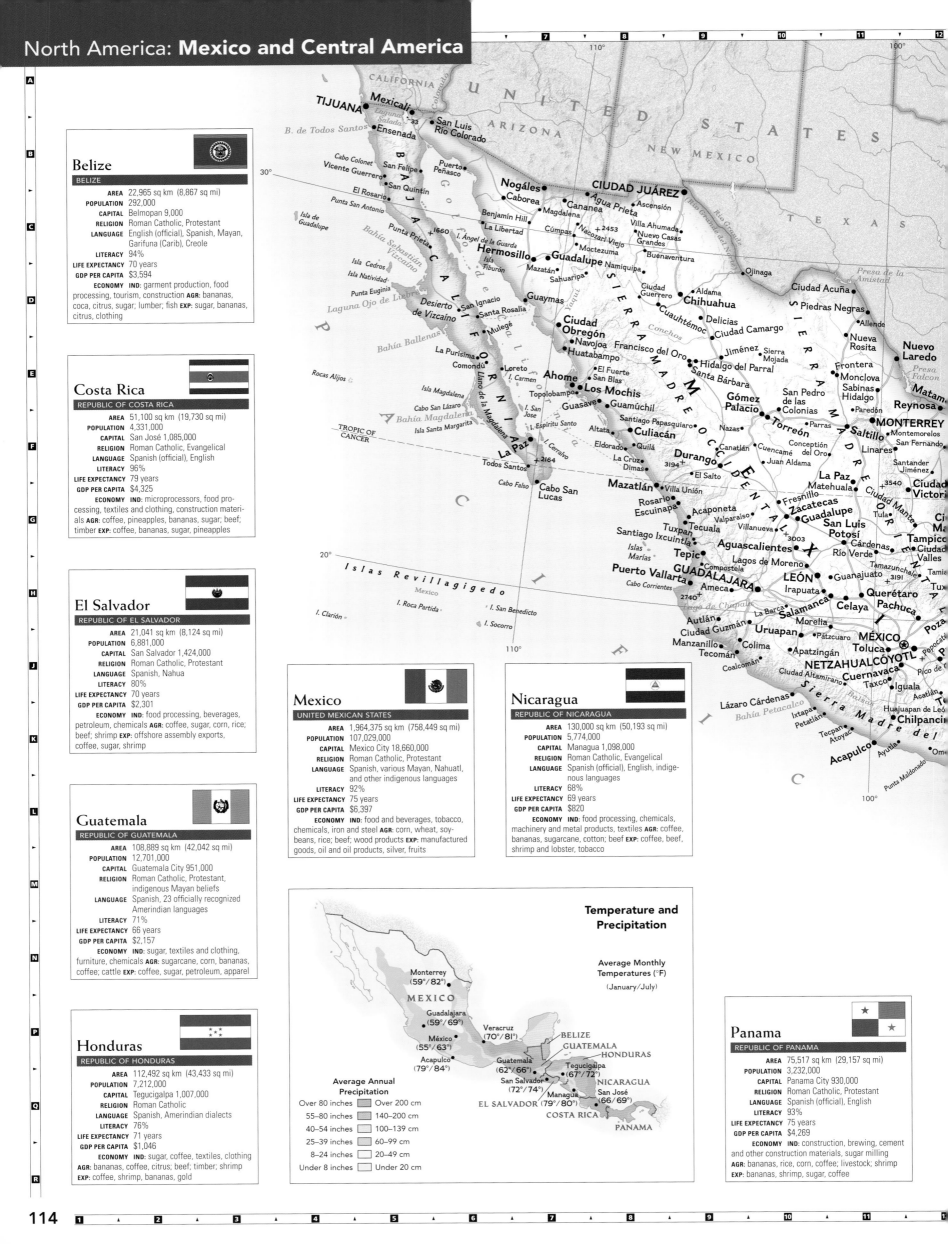

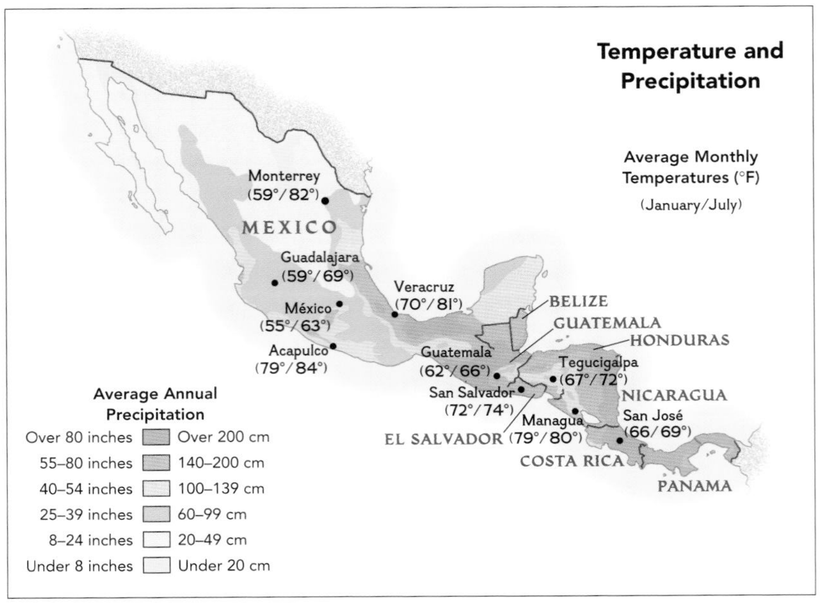

Panama

REPUBLIC OF PANAMA

AREA 75,517 sq km (29,157 sq mi)
POPULATION 3,232,000
CAPITAL Panama City 930,000
RELIGION Roman Catholic, Protestant
LANGUAGE Spanish (official), English
LITERACY 93%
LIFE EXPECTANCY 75 years
GDP PER CAPITA $4,269
ECONOMY **IND:** construction, brewing, cement and other construction materials, sugar milling **AGR:** bananas, rice, corn, coffee; livestock; shrimp **EXP:** bananas, shrimp, sugar, coffee

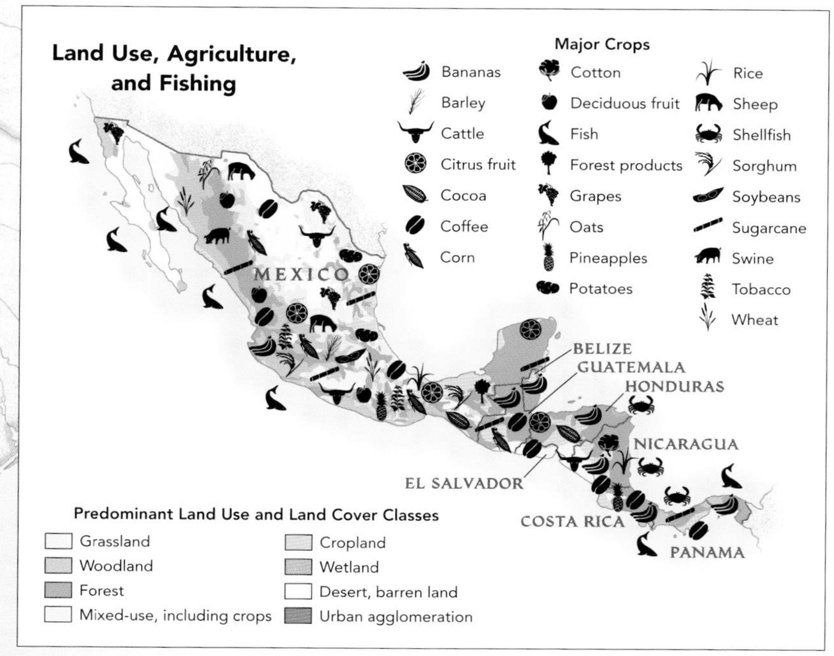

Land Use, Agriculture, and Fishing
Major Crops
Bananas
Barley
Cattle
Citrus fruit
Cocoa
Coffee
Corn
Cotton
Deciduous fruit
Fish
Forest products
Grapes
Oats
Pineapples
Potatoes
Rice
Sheep
Shellfish
Sorghum
Soybeans
Sugarcane
Swine
Tobacco
Wheat
MEXICO
BELIZE
GUATEMALA
HONDURAS
NICARAGUA
EL SALVADOR
COSTA RICA
PANAMA
Predominant Land Use and Land Cover Classes
Grassland
Woodland
Forest
Mixed-use, including crops
Cropland
Wetland
Desert, barren land
Urban agglomeration

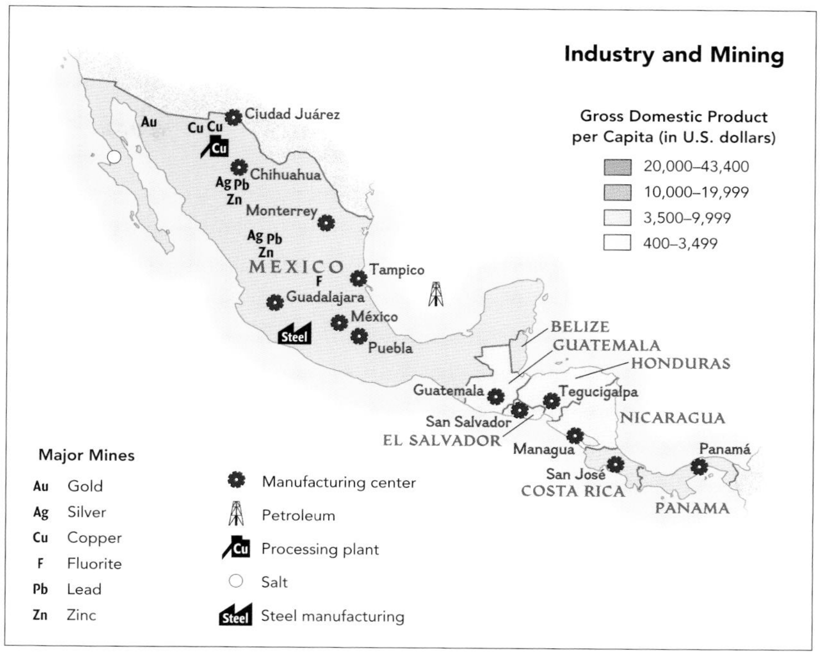

Industry and Mining
Gross Domestic Product per Capita (in U.S. dollars)
20,000–43,400
10,000–19,999
3,500–9,999
400–3,499
Ciudad Juárez
Chihuahua
Monterrey
MEXICO
Tampico
Guadalajara
México
Puebla
BELIZE
GUATEMALA
HONDURAS
Guatemala
Tegucigalpa
San Salvador
EL SALVADOR
NICARAGUA
Managua
San José
COSTA RICA
Panamá
PANAMA
Major Mines
Au Gold
Ag Silver
Cu Copper
F Fluorite
Pb Lead
Zn Zinc
Manufacturing center
Petroleum
Processing plant
Salt
Steel manufacturing

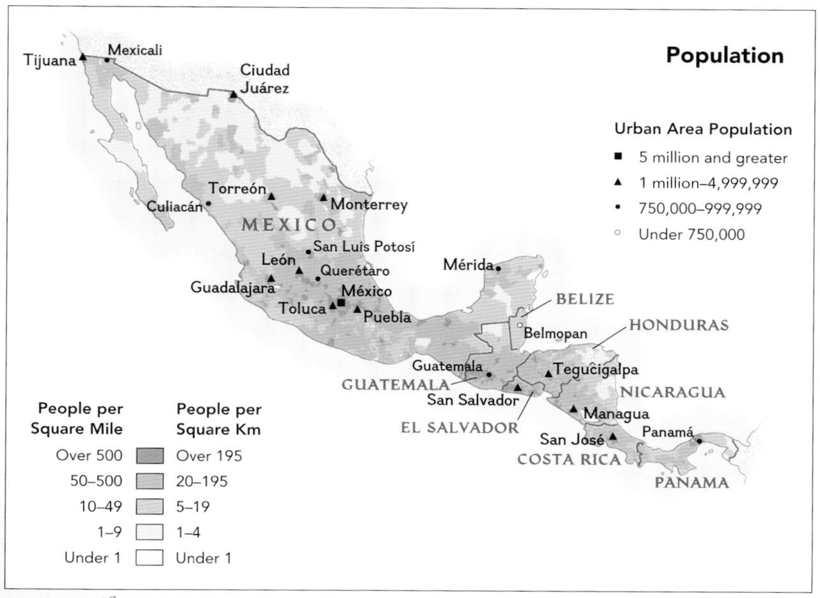

Population
Tijuana
Mexicali
Ciudad Juárez
Urban Area Population
5 million and greater
1 million–4,999,999
750,000–999,999
Under 750,000
Torreón
Monterrey
Culiacán
MEXICO
San Luis Potosí
León
Querétaro
Mérida
Guadalajara
México
Toluca
Puebla
BELIZE
Belmopan
HONDURAS
Guatemala
Tegucigalpa
GUATEMALA
NICARAGUA
San Salvador
Managua
EL SALVADOR
San José
Panamá
COSTA RICA
PANAMA
People per Square Mile
Over 500
50–500
10–49
1–9
Under 1
People per Square Km
Over 195
20–195
5–19
1–4
Under 1

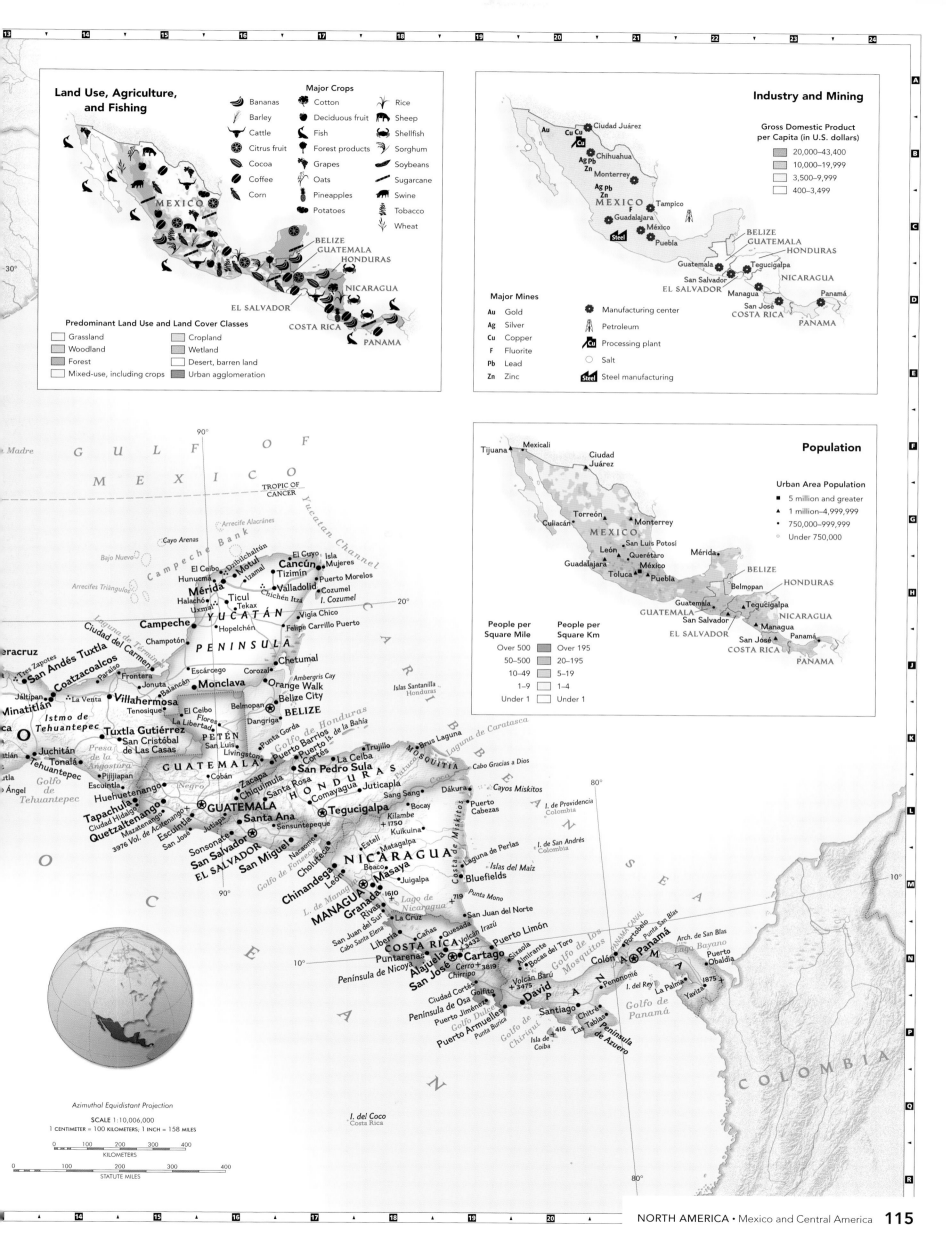

GULF OF MEXICO
TROPIC OF CANCER
Yucatan Channel
Campeche Bank
Arrecife Alacránes
Cayo Arenas
Bajo Nuevo
Arrecifes Triángulos
Mérida
Campeche
Cancún
Valladolid
Chichén Itzá
I. Cozumel
YUCATÁN PENINSULA
Ciudad del Carmen
Chetumal
Belmopan
BELIZE
Belize City
Villahermosa
Coatzacoalcos
San Andrés Tuxtla
Minatitlán
Istmo de Tehuantepec
Tuxtla Gutiérrez
San Cristóbal de Las Casas
PETÉN
GUATEMALA
GUATEMALA
Quetzaltenango
Tapachula
Golfo de Tehuantepec
Golfo de Honduras
San Pedro Sula
La Ceiba
HONDURAS
Tegucigalpa
MOSQUITIA
Laguna de Caratasca
Cabo Gracias a Dios
Cayos Miskitos
Santa Ana
San Salvador
EL SALVADOR
San Miguel
Golfo de Fonseca
NICARAGUA
MANAGUA
Masaya
Granada
Lago de Nicaragua
Bluefields
Islas del Maíz
I. de San Andrés Colombia
I. de Providencia Colombia
CARIBBEAN SEA
COSTA RICA
San José
Cartago
Puerto Limón
Península de Nicoya
Península de Osa
Golfo de los Mosquitos
PANAMA CANAL
Colón
Panamá
PANAMA
David
Santiago
Golfo de Panamá
Península de Azuero
Golfo de Chiriquí
Isla de Coiba
I. del Coco Costa Rica
COLOMBIA
PACIFIC OCEAN
Azimuthal Equidistant Projection
SCALE 1:10,006,000
1 CENTIMETER = 100 KILOMETERS; 1 INCH = 158 MILES
0 100 200 300 400
KILOMETERS
0 100 200 300 400
STATUTE MILES

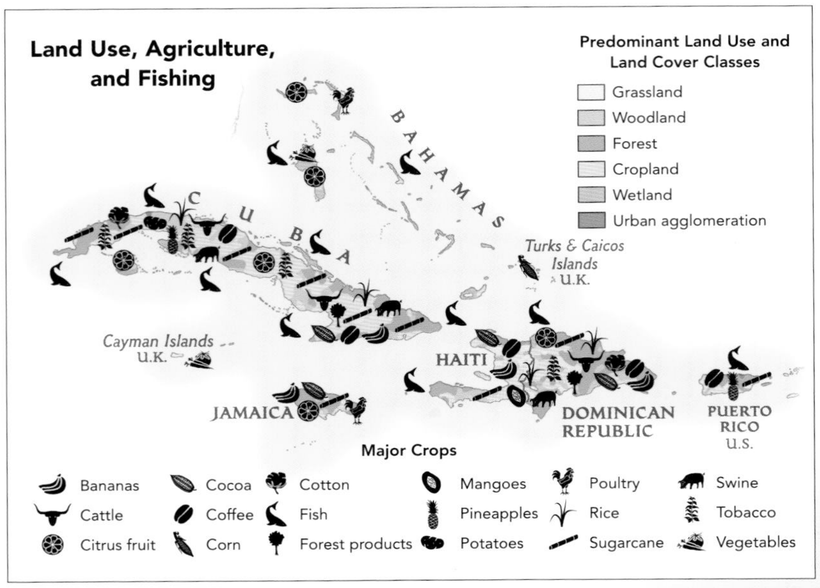

Bahamas

COMMONWEALTH OF THE BAHAMAS

AREA 13,939 sq km (5,382 sq mi)
POPULATION 319,000
CAPITAL Nassau 222,000
RELIGION Baptist, Anglican, Roman Catholic, Pentecostal
LANGUAGE English (official), Creole
LITERACY 96%
LIFE EXPECTANCY 70 years
GDP PER CAPITA $15,099
ECONOMY **IND:** tourism, banking, cement, oil transshipment **AGR:** citrus, vegetables; poultry **EXP:** mineral products and salt, animal products, rum, chemicals

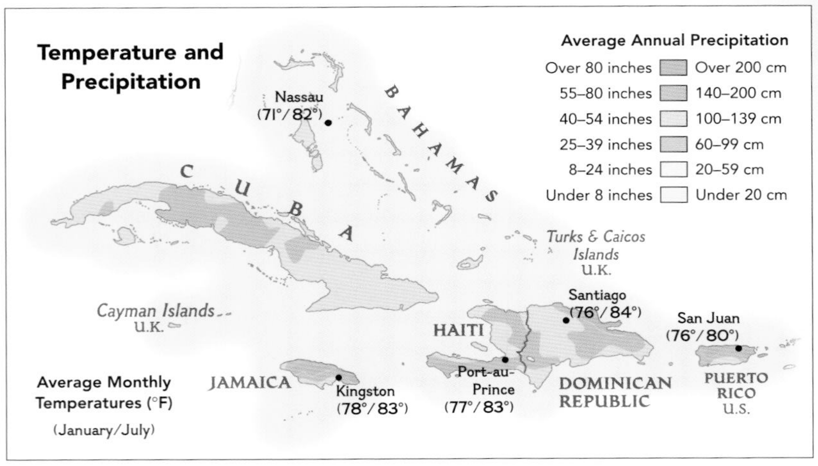

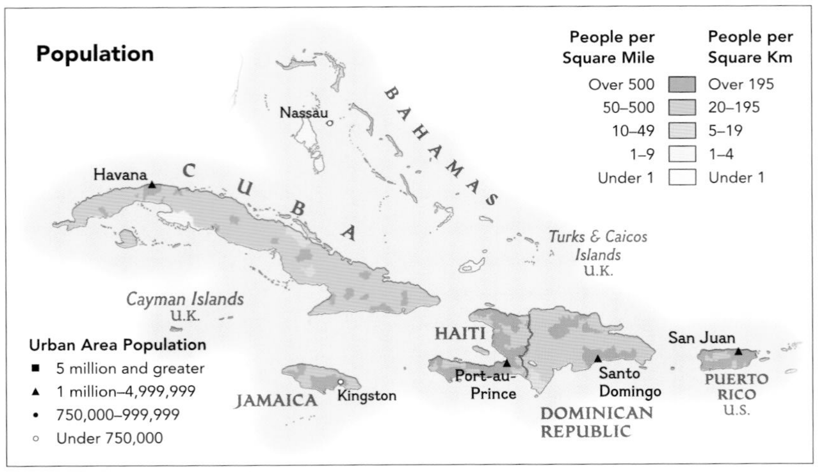

SOVEREIGN LOCAL

Bermuda (U.K.)

BERMUDA

AREA 53 sq km (21 sq mi)
POPULATION 62,000
CAPITAL Hamilton 1,000
RELIGION Anglican, Roman Catholic, African Methodist Episcopal
LANGUAGE English (official), Portuguese
LITERACY 98%
LIFE EXPECTANCY 77 years
GDP PER CAPITA $64,749
ECONOMY **IND:** tourism, international business, light manufacturing **AGR:** bananas, vegetables, citrus, flowers; dairy products **EXP:** reexports of pharmaceuticals

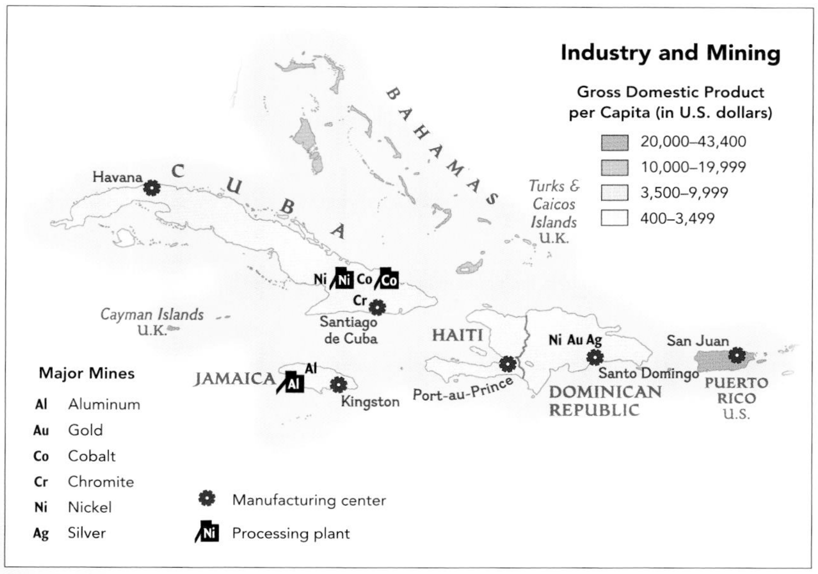

Cayman Islands (U.K.)

SOVEREIGN LOCAL

CAYMAN ISLANDS

AREA 262 sq km (101 sq mi)
POPULATION 44,000
CAPITAL George Town 24,000
RELIGION United Church, Anglican, Baptist, Church of God
LANGUAGE English
LITERACY 98%
LIFE EXPECTANCY 79 years
GDP PER CAPITA $38,594
ECONOMY **IND:** tourism, banking, insurance and finance, construction **AGR:** vegetables, fruit; livestock **EXP:** turtle products, manufactured consumer goods

Haiti

REPUBLIC OF HAITI

AREA 27,750 sq km (10,714 sq mi)
POPULATION 8,288,000
CAPITAL Port-au-Prince 1,961,000
RELIGION Roman Catholic, Protestant, Voodoo
LANGUAGE French (official), Creole (official)
LITERACY 53%
LIFE EXPECTANCY 52 years
GDP PER CAPITA $471
ECONOMY **IND:** sugar refining, flour milling, textiles, cement **AGR:** coffee, mangoes, sugarcane, rice; wood **EXP:** manufactures, coffee, oils, cocoa

Cuba

REPUBLIC OF CUBA

AREA 110,860 sq km (42,803 sq mi)
POPULATION 11,275,000
CAPITAL Havana 2,189,000
RELIGION Roman Catholic, Protestants, Jehovah's Witnesses, Jews, Santeria
LANGUAGE Spanish
LITERACY 97%
LIFE EXPECTANCY 77 years
GDP PER CAPITA $3,059
ECONOMY **IND:** sugar, petroleum, tobacco, construction **AGR:** sugar, tobacco, citrus, coffee; livestock **EXP:** sugar, nickel, tobacco, fish

Jamaica

JAMAICA

AREA 10,991 sq km (4,244 sq mi)
POPULATION 2,666,000
CAPITAL Kingston 575,000
RELIGION Church of God, Seventh-Day Adventist, Baptist, Pentecostal
LANGUAGE English, patois English
LITERACY 88%
LIFE EXPECTANCY 73 years
GDP PER CAPITA $3,225
ECONOMY **IND:** tourism, bauxite/alumina, textiles, agro processing **AGR:** sugarcane, bananas, coffee, citrus; poultry; crustaceans **EXP:** alumina, bauxite, sugar, bananas

Dominican Republic

DOMINICAN REPUBLIC

AREA 48,442 sq km (18,704 sq mi)
POPULATION 8,862,000
CAPITAL Santo Domingo 1,865,000
RELIGION Roman Catholic
LANGUAGE Spanish
LITERACY 85%
LIFE EXPECTANCY 68 years
GDP PER CAPITA $2,706
ECONOMY **IND:** tourism, sugar processing, ferronickel and gold mining, textiles **AGR:** sugarcane, coffee, cotton, cocoa; cattle **EXP:** ferronickel, sugar, gold, silver

SOVEREIGN LOCAL

Puerto Rico (U.S.)

COMMONWEALTH OF PUERTO RICO

AREA 9,086 sq km (3,508 sq mi)
POPULATION 3,912,000
CAPITAL San Juan 2,332,000
RELIGION Roman Catholic, Protestant
LANGUAGE Spanish, English
LITERACY 94%
LIFE EXPECTANCY 77 years
GDP PER CAPITA $21,481
ECONOMY **IND:** pharmaceuticals, electronics, apparel, food products **AGR:** sugarcane, coffee, pineapples, plantains; livestock products **EXP:** chemicals, electronics, apparel, canned tuna

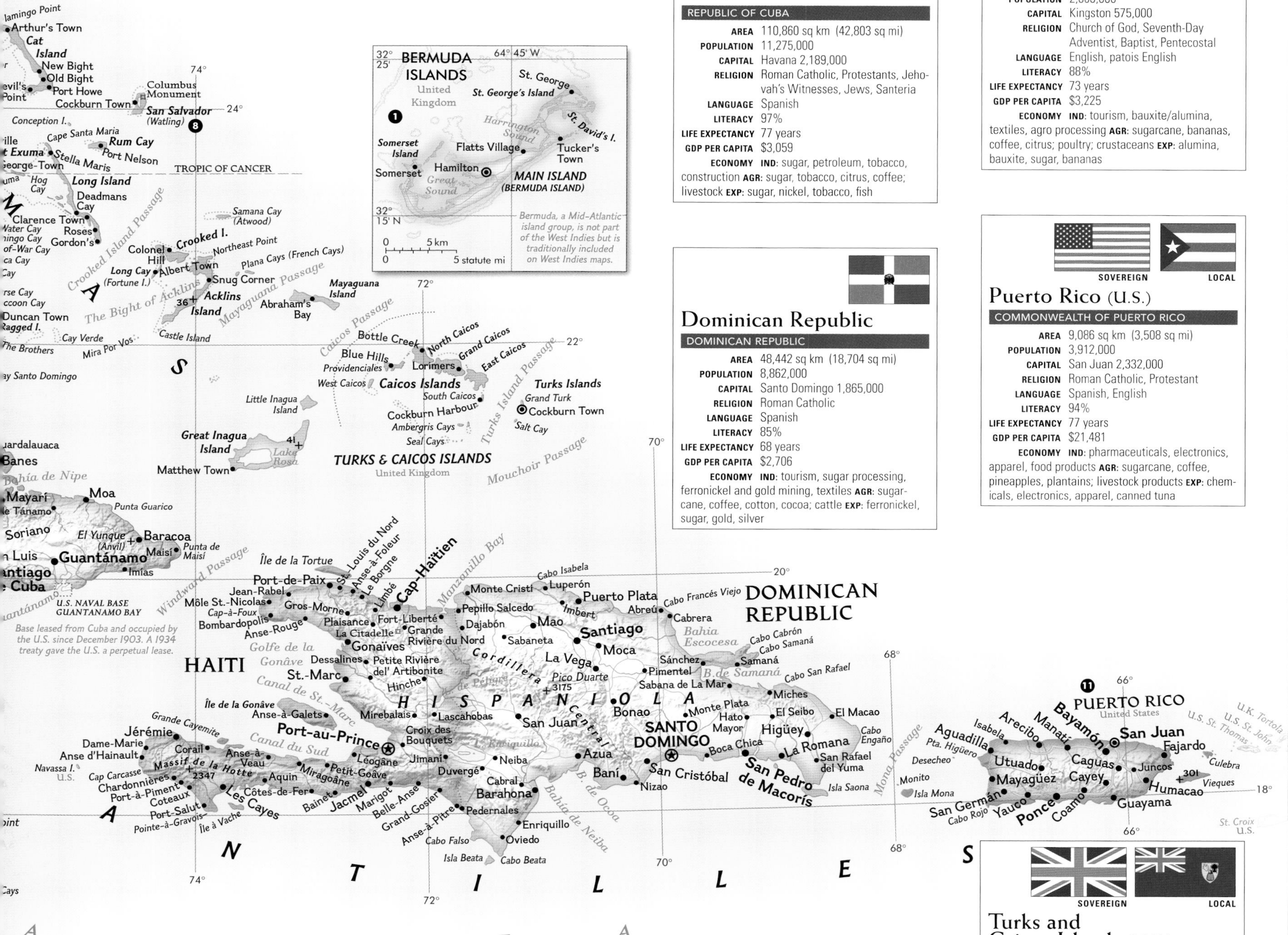

Turks and Caicos Islands (U.K.)

SOVEREIGN LOCAL

TURKS AND CAICOS ISLANDS

AREA 430 sq km (166 sq mi)
POPULATION 21,000
CAPITAL Cockburn Town (on Grand Turk Island) 6,000
RELIGION Baptist, Anglican, Methodist, Church of God
LANGUAGE English (official)
LITERACY 98%
LIFE EXPECTANCY 74 years
GDP PER CAPITA $9,924
ECONOMY **IND:** tourism, offshore financial services **AGR:** corn, beans, cassava, citrus fruits; fish **EXP:** lobster, dried and fresh conch, conch shells

Oblique Mercator Projection

SCALE 1:4,869,000
1 CENTIMETER = 49 KILOMETERS; 1 INCH = 77 MILES

0 50 100 150 200 KILOMETERS
0 50 100 150 200 STATUTE MILES

Numbered islands correspond to larger-scale maps on pages 120–121.

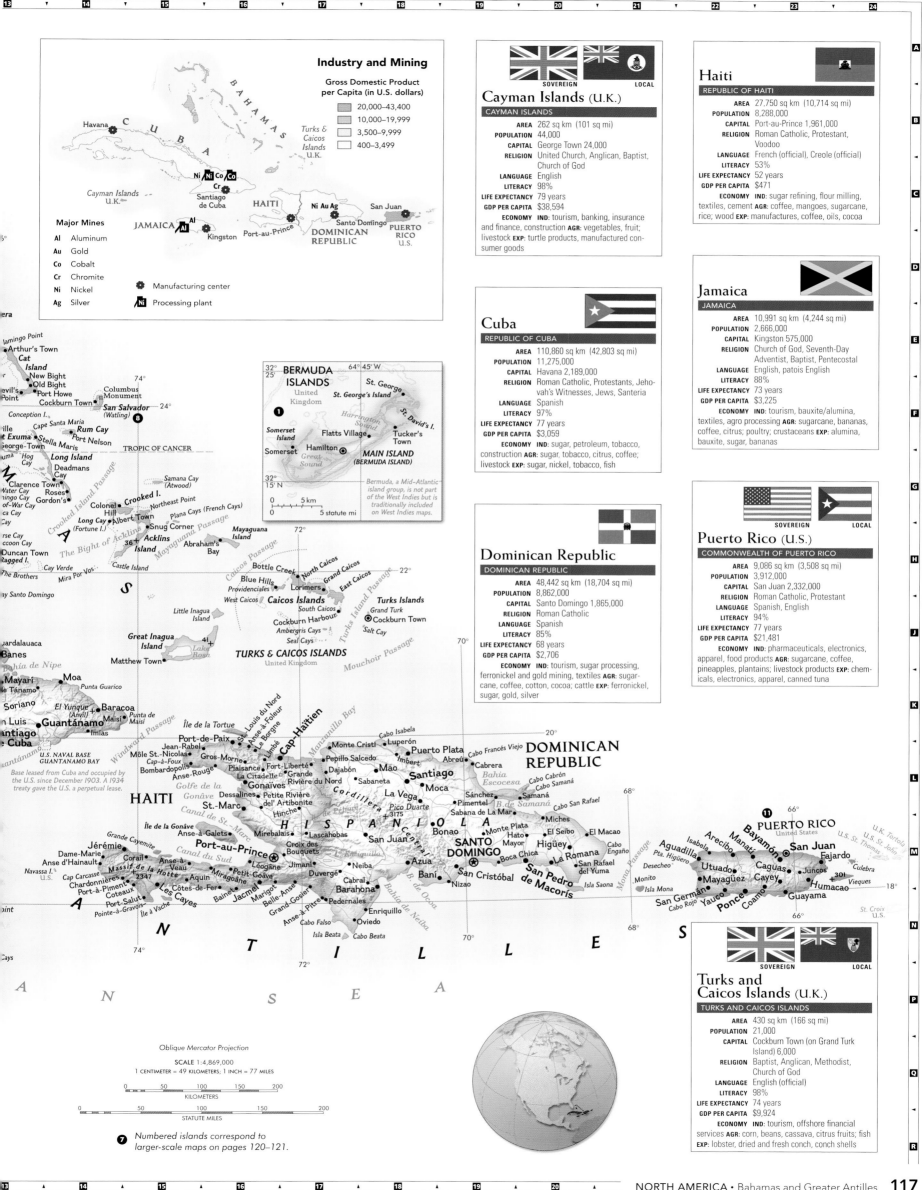

Anguilla (U.K.)

ANGUILLA

AREA 96 sq km (37 sq mi)
POPULATION 13,000
CAPITAL The Valley 1,000
RELIGION Anglican, Methodist, other Protestant, Roman Catholic
LANGUAGE English (official)
LITERACY 95%
LIFE EXPECTANCY 78 years
GDP PER CAPITA $10,811
ECONOMY **IND:** tourism, boat building, offshore financial services **AGR:** small quantities of tobacco, vegetables; cattle raising **EXP:** lobster, fish, livestock, salt

Antigua and Barbuda

ANTIGUA AND BARBUDA

AREA 442 sq km (171 sq mi)
POPULATION 80,000
CAPITAL St. John's 28,000
RELIGION Anglican, other Protestant, Roman Catholic
LANGUAGE English (official), local dialects
LITERACY 89%
LIFE EXPECTANCY 71 years
GDP PER CAPITA $8,595
ECONOMY **IND:** tourism, construction, light manufacturing (clothing, alcohol, household appliances) **AGR:** cotton, fruits, vegetables, bananas; livestock **EXP:** petroleum products, manufactures, machinery and transport equipment, food and live animals

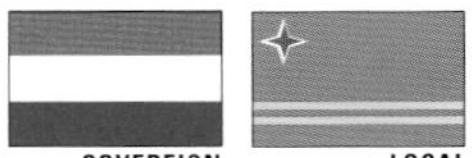

Aruba (Netherlands)

ARUBA

AREA 193 sq km (75 sq mi)
POPULATION 97,000
CAPITAL Oranjestad 29,000
RELIGION Roman Catholic, Protestant
LANGUAGE Dutch (official), Papiamento, English, Spanish
LITERACY 97%
LIFE EXPECTANCY 79 years
GDP PER CAPITA $21,131
ECONOMY **IND:** tourism, transshipment facilities, oil refining **AGR:** aloes; livestock; fish **EXP:** live animals and animal products, art and collectibles, machinery and electrical equipment, transport equipment

Barbados

BARBADOS

AREA 430 sq km (166 sq mi)
POPULATION 258,000
CAPITAL Bridgetown 140,000
RELIGION Anglican, Pentecostal, Methodist
LANGUAGE English
LITERACY 100%
LIFE EXPECTANCY 72 years
GDP PER CAPITA $10,538
ECONOMY **IND:** tourism, sugar, light manufacturing, component assembly for export **AGR:** sugarcane, vegetables, cotton **EXP:** sugar and molasses, rum, other foods and beverages, chemicals

British Virgin Islands (U.K.)

BRITISH VIRGIN ISLANDS

AREA 153 sq km (59 sq mi)
POPULATION 22,000
CAPITAL Road Town 12,000
RELIGION Protestant, Roman Catholic
LANGUAGE English (official)
LITERACY 98%
LIFE EXPECTANCY 74 years
GDP PER CAPITA $43,366
ECONOMY **IND:** tourism, light industry, construction, rum **AGR:** fruits, vegetables; livestock; fish **EXP:** rum, fresh fish, fruits, animals

Dominica

COMMONWEALTH OF DOMINICA

AREA 751 sq km (290 sq mi)
POPULATION 70,000
CAPITAL Roseau 27,000
RELIGION Roman Catholic, Protestant
LANGUAGE English (official), French patois
LITERACY 94%
LIFE EXPECTANCY 74 years
GDP PER CAPITA $3,466
ECONOMY **IND:** soap, coconut oil, tourism, copra **AGR:** bananas, citrus, mangoes, root crops; forest and fishery potential not exploited **EXP:** bananas, soap, bay oil, vegetables

Grenada

GRENADA

AREA 344 sq km (133 sq mi)
POPULATION 101,000
CAPITAL St. George's 33,000
RELIGION Roman Catholic, Anglican, other Protestant
LANGUAGE English (official), French patois
LITERACY 98%
LIFE EXPECTANCY 71 years
GDP PER CAPITA $3,872
ECONOMY **IND:** food and beverages, textiles, light assembly operations, tourism **AGR:** bananas, cocoa, nutmeg, mace **EXP:** bananas, cocoa, nutmeg, fruit and vegetables

Guadeloupe (France)

OVERSEAS DEPARTMENT OF FRANCE

AREA 1,705 sq km (658 sq mi)
POPULATION 450,000
CAPITAL Basse-Terre 11,000
RELIGION Roman Catholic
LANGUAGE French (official)
LITERACY 90%
LIFE EXPECTANCY 78 years
GDP PER CAPITA $7,900
ECONOMY **IND:** construction, cement, rum, sugar **AGR:** bananas, sugarcane, tropical fruits and vegetables; cattle **EXP:** bananas, sugar, rum

Martinique (France)

OVERSEAS DEPARTMENT OF FRANCE

AREA 1,100 sq km (425 sq mi)
POPULATION 397,000
CAPITAL Fort-de-France 93,000
RELIGION Roman Catholic, Protestant
LANGUAGE French, Creole patois
LITERACY 98%
LIFE EXPECTANCY 79 years
GDP PER CAPITA $14,400
ECONOMY **IND:** construction, rum, cement, oil refining **AGR:** pineapples, avocados, bananas, flowers **EXP:** refined petroleum products, bananas, rum, pineapples

Montserrat (U.K.)

MONTSERRAT

AREA 102 sq km (39 sq mi)
POPULATION 5,000
CAPITAL Plymouth (abandoned)
RELIGION Anglican, Methodist, Roman Catholic, Pentecostal, Seventh-Day Adventist, other Christian denominations
LANGUAGE English
LITERACY 97%
LIFE EXPECTANCY 79 years
GDP PER CAPITA $12,067
ECONOMY **IND:** tourism, rum, textiles, electronic appliances **AGR:** cabbages, carrots, cucumbers, tomatoes; livestock products **EXP:** electronic components, plastic bags, apparel, hot peppers

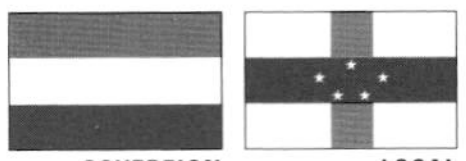

Netherlands Antilles (Neth.)

NETHERLANDS ANTILLES

AREA 800 sq km (309 sq mi)
POPULATION 187,000
CAPITAL Willemstad 134,000
RELIGION Roman Catholic
LANGUAGE Papiamento, English, Dutch (official), Spanish
LITERACY 97%
LIFE EXPECTANCY 76 years
GDP PER CAPITA $17,164
ECONOMY **IND:** tourism, petroleum refining, petroleum transshipment facilities, light manufacturing **AGR:** aloes, sorghum, peanuts, vegetables **EXP:** petroleum products

St. Kitts and Nevis

FEDERATION OF SAINT KITTS AND NEVIS

AREA 269 sq km (104 sq mi)
POPULATION 48,000
CAPITAL Basseterre 13,000
RELIGION Anglican, other Protestant, Roman Catholic
LANGUAGE English
LITERACY 97%
LIFE EXPECTANCY 70 years
GDP PER CAPITA $9,269
ECONOMY **IND:** sugar processing, tourism, cotton, salt **AGR:** sugarcane, rice, yams, vegetables; fish **EXP:** machinery, food, electronics, beverages

St. Lucia

SAINT LUCIA

AREA 616 sq km (238 sq mi)
POPULATION 163,000
CAPITAL Castries 14,000
RELIGION Roman Catholic, Seventh-Day Adventist, Pentecostal
LANGUAGE English (official), French patois
LITERACY 90%
LIFE EXPECTANCY 74 years
GDP PER CAPITA $4,506
ECONOMY **IND:** clothing, assembly of electronic components, beverages, corrugated cardboard boxes **AGR:** bananas, coconuts, vegetables, citrus **EXP:** bananas, clothing, cocoa, vegetables

St. Vincent and the Grenadines

SAINT VINCENT AND THE GRENADINES

AREA 389 sq km (150 sq mi)
POPULATION 111,000
CAPITAL Kingstown 29,000
RELIGION Anglican, Methodist, Roman Catholic
LANGUAGE English, French patois
LITERACY 96%
LIFE EXPECTANCY 72 years
GDP PER CAPITA $3,357
ECONOMY **IND:** food processing, cement, furniture, clothing **AGR:** bananas, coconuts, sweet potatoes, spices; cattle; fish **EXP:** bananas, eddoes and dasheen (taro), arrowroot starch, tennis racquets

Trinidad and Tobago

REPUBLIC OF TRINIDAD AND TOBAGO

AREA 5,128 sq km (1,980 sq mi)
POPULATION 1,305,000
CAPITAL Port-of-Spain 55,000
RELIGION Roman Catholic, Hindu, Anglican, Baptist, Pentecostal, Muslim
LANGUAGE English (official), Hindi, French, Spanish, Chinese
LITERACY 99%
LIFE EXPECTANCY 71 years
GDP PER CAPITA $8,772
ECONOMY **IND:** petroleum, chemicals, tourism, food processing **AGR:** cocoa, rice, citrus, coffee; poultry **EXP:** petroleum and petroleum products, chemicals, steel products, fertilizer

Virgin Islands (U.S.)

UNITED STATES VIRGIN ISLANDS

AREA 386 sq km (149 sq mi)
POPULATION 109,000
CAPITAL Charlotte Amalie 51,000
RELIGION Baptist, Roman Catholic, Episcopalian
LANGUAGE English, Spanish or Spanish Creole, French or French Creole
LITERACY NA
LIFE EXPECTANCY 79 years
GDP PER CAPITA $17,200
ECONOMY **IND:** tourism, petroleum refining, watch assembly, rum distilling **AGR:** fruit, vegetables, sorghum; Senepol cattle **EXP:** refined petroleum products

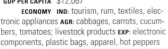

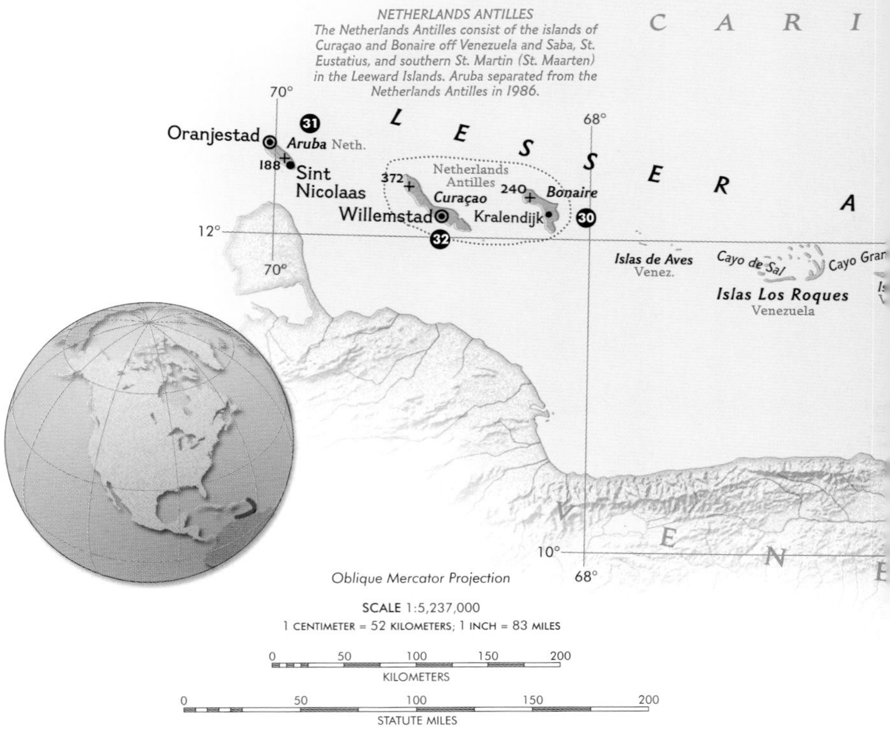

Numbered islands correspond to larger-scale maps on pages 120–121.

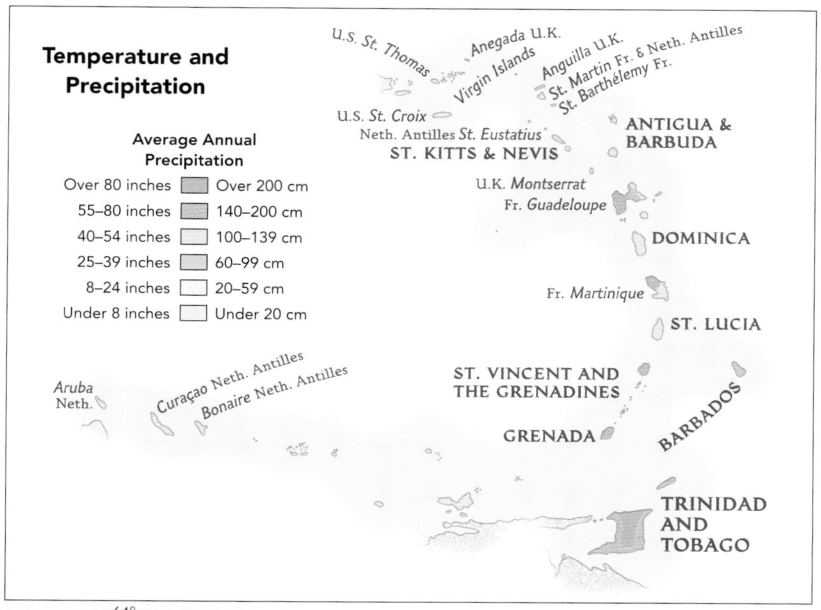

Temperature and Precipitation
Average Annual Precipitation
Over 80 inches Over 200 cm
55–80 inches 140–200 cm
40–54 inches 100–139 cm
25–39 inches 60–99 cm
8–24 inches 20–59 cm
Under 8 inches Under 20 cm
U.S. St. Thomas
Anegada U.K.
Virgin Islands
Anguilla U.K.
St. Martin Fr. & Neth. Antilles
St. Barthélemy Fr.
U.S. St. Croix
Neth. Antilles St. Eustatius
ST. KITTS & NEVIS
ANTIGUA & BARBUDA
U.K. Montserrat
Fr. Guadeloupe
DOMINICA
Fr. Martinique
ST. LUCIA
ST. VINCENT AND THE GRENADINES
BARBADOS
GRENADA
TRINIDAD AND TOBAGO
Aruba Neth.
Curaçao Neth. Antilles
Bonaire Neth. Antilles

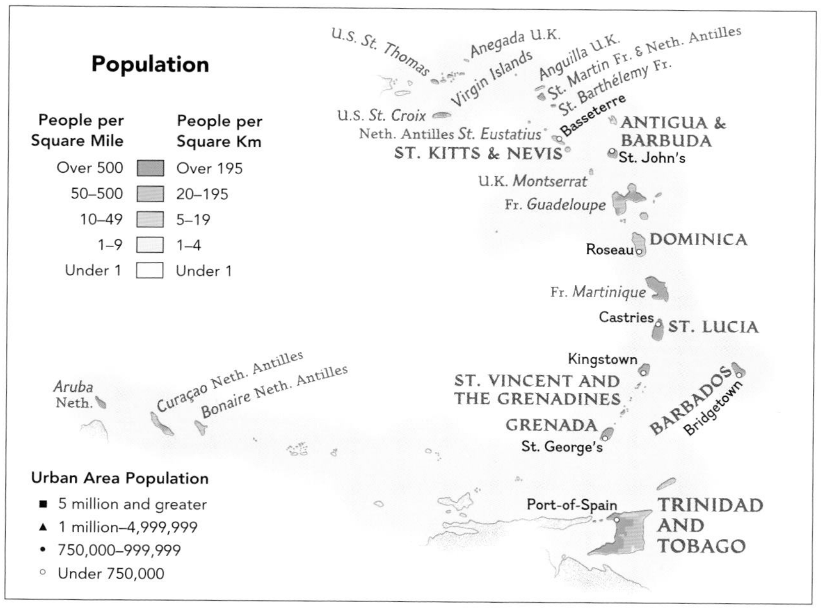

Population
People per Square Mile
People per Square Km
Over 500 Over 195
50–500 20–195
10–49 5–19
1–9 1–4
Under 1 Under 1
Urban Area Population
5 million and greater
1 million–4,999,999
750,000–999,999
Under 750,000
U.S. St. Thomas
Anegada U.K.
Virgin Islands
Anguilla U.K.
St. Martin Fr. & Neth. Antilles
St. Barthélemy Fr.
Basseterre
U.S. St. Croix
Neth. Antilles St. Eustatius
ST. KITTS & NEVIS
ANTIGUA & BARBUDA
St. John's
U.K. Montserrat
Fr. Guadeloupe
Roseau
DOMINICA
Fr. Martinique
Castries
ST. LUCIA
Kingstown
ST. VINCENT AND THE GRENADINES
BARBADOS
Bridgetown
GRENADA
St. George's
Port-of-Spain
TRINIDAD AND TOBAGO
Aruba Neth.
Curaçao Neth. Antilles
Bonaire Neth. Antilles

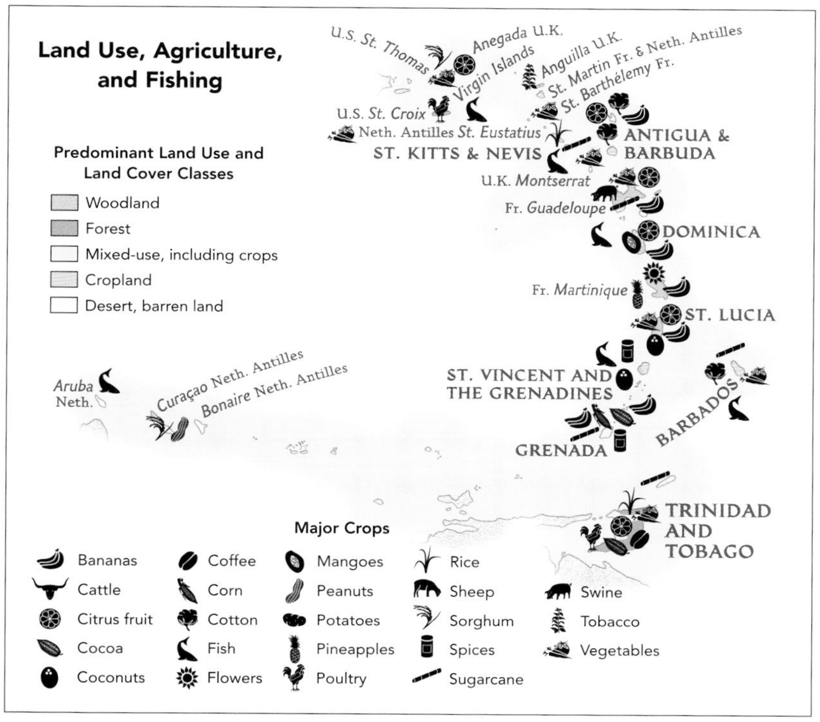

Land Use, Agriculture, and Fishing
Predominant Land Use and Land Cover Classes
Woodland
Forest
Mixed-use, including crops
Cropland
Desert, barren land
Major Crops
Bananas
Cattle
Citrus fruit
Cocoa
Coconuts
Coffee
Corn
Cotton
Fish
Flowers
Mangoes
Peanuts
Potatoes
Pineapples
Poultry
Rice
Sheep
Sorghum
Spices
Sugarcane
Swine
Tobacco
Vegetables
U.S. St. Thomas
Anegada U.K.
Virgin Islands
Anguilla U.K.
St. Martin Fr. & Neth. Antilles
St. Barthélemy Fr.
U.S. St. Croix
Neth. Antilles St. Eustatius
ST. KITTS & NEVIS
ANTIGUA & BARBUDA
U.K. Montserrat
Fr. Guadeloupe
DOMINICA
Fr. Martinique
ST. LUCIA
ST. VINCENT AND THE GRENADINES
BARBADOS
GRENADA
TRINIDAD AND TOBAGO
Aruba Neth.
Curaçao Neth. Antilles
Bonaire Neth. Antilles

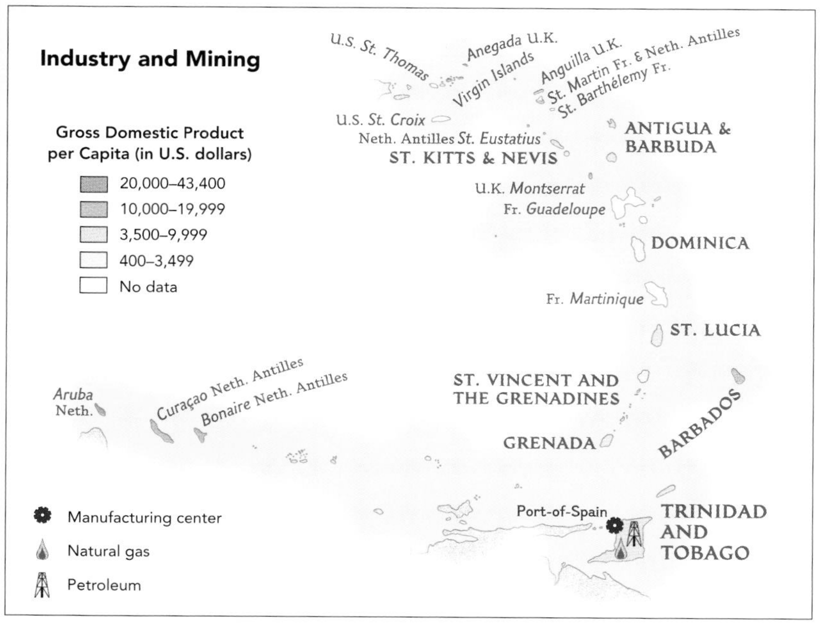

Industry and Mining
Gross Domestic Product per Capita (in U.S. dollars)
20,000–43,400
10,000–19,999
3,500–9,999
400–3,499
No data
Manufacturing center
Natural gas
Petroleum
U.S. St. Thomas
Anegada U.K.
Virgin Islands
Anguilla U.K.
St. Martin Fr. & Neth. Antilles
St. Barthélemy Fr.
U.S. St. Croix
Neth. Antilles St. Eustatius
ST. KITTS & NEVIS
ANTIGUA & BARBUDA
U.K. Montserrat
Fr. Guadeloupe
DOMINICA
Fr. Martinique
ST. LUCIA
ST. VINCENT AND THE GRENADINES
BARBADOS
GRENADA
Port-of-Spain
TRINIDAD AND TOBAGO
Aruba Neth.
Curaçao Neth. Antilles
Bonaire Neth. Antilles

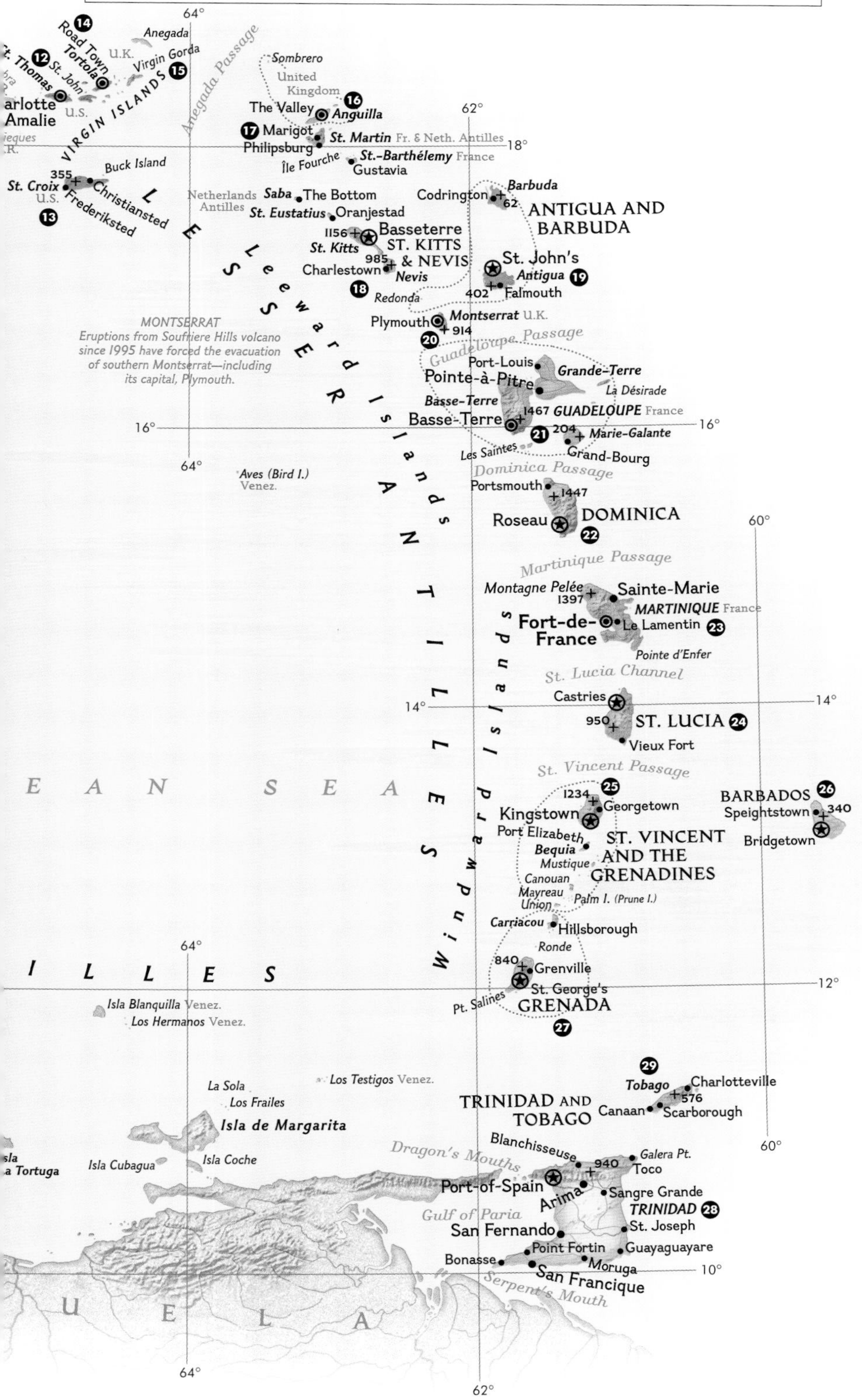

Road Town
Tortola
St. John
Anegada
U.K.
Virgin Gorda
VIRGIN ISLANDS
Anegada Passage
Sombrero
United Kingdom
The Valley
Anguilla
Marigot
Philipsburg
St. Martin Fr. & Neth. Antilles
Île Fourche
St.-Barthélemy France
Gustavia
Buck Island
St. Croix
U.S.
Christiansted
Frederiksted
Netherlands Antilles
Saba
The Bottom
St. Eustatius
Oranjestad
Codrington
Barbuda
ANTIGUA AND BARBUDA
Basseterre
ST. KITTS & NEVIS
St. Kitts
Charlestown
Nevis
Redonda
St. John's
Antigua
Falmouth
LEEWARD ISLANDS
MONTSERRAT
Eruptions from Soufriere Hills volcano since 1995 have forced the evacuation of southern Montserrat—including its capital, Plymouth.
Plymouth
Montserrat U.K.
Guadeloupe Passage
Port-Louis
Pointe-à-Pitre
Grande-Terre
La Désirade
Basse-Terre
GUADELOUPE France
Marie-Galante
Les Saintes
Grand-Bourg
Aves (Bird I.) Venez.
Dominica Passage
Portsmouth
Roseau
DOMINICA
Martinique Passage
Montagne Pelée
Sainte-Marie
MARTINIQUE France
Fort-de-France
Le Lamentin
Pointe d'Enfer
St. Lucia Channel
Castries
ST. LUCIA
Vieux Fort
LESSER ANTILLES
WINDWARD ISLANDS
St. Vincent Passage
Kingstown
Georgetown
Port Elizabeth
Bequia
Mustique
ST. VINCENT AND THE GRENADINES
Canouan
Mayreau
Union
Palm I. (Prune I.)
BARBADOS
Speightstown
Bridgetown
Carriacou
Hillsborough
Ronde
Grenville
St. George's
Pt. Salines
GRENADA
Isla Blanquilla Venez.
Los Hermanos Venez.
CARIBBEAN SEA
La Sola
Los Testigos Venez.
Los Frailes
Isla de Margarita
Isla Cubagua
Isla Coche
La Tortuga
Tobago
Charlotteville
TRINIDAD AND TOBAGO
Canaan
Scarborough
Blanchisseuse
Galera Pt.
Dragon's Mouths
Toco
Port-of-Spain
Arima
Sangre Grande
TRINIDAD
Gulf of Paria
San Fernando
St. Joseph
Point Fortin
Guayaguayare
Bonasse
Moruga
San Francique
Serpent's Mouth
VENEZUELA

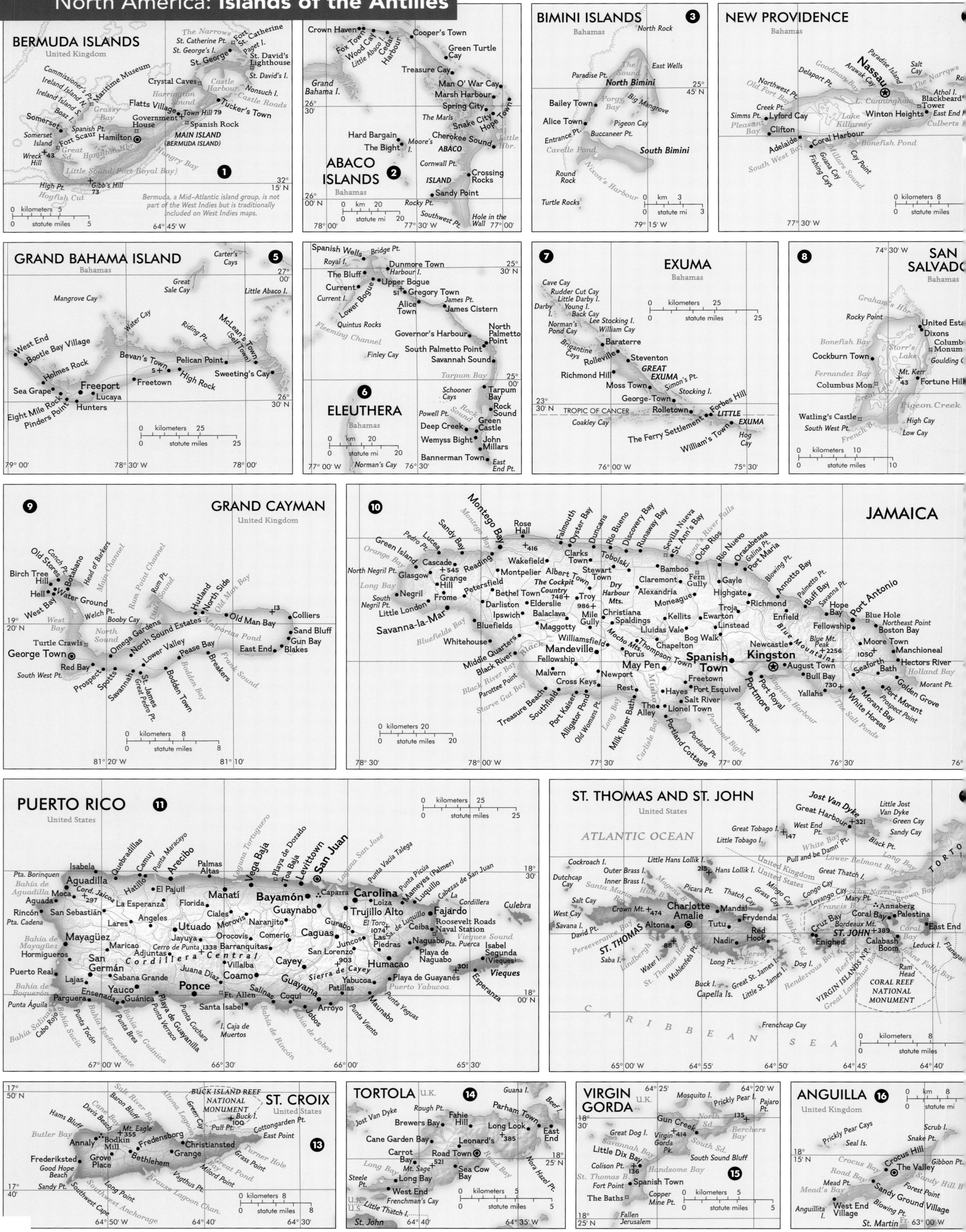
BERMUDA ISLANDS
United Kingdom
St. George's I.
St. George
St. David's I.
Hamilton
MAIN ISLAND (BERMUDA ISLAND)
Somerset
Bermuda, a Mid-Atlantic island group, is not part of the West Indies but is traditionally included on West Indies maps.
ABACO ISLANDS
Bahamas
Marsh Harbour
Hope Town
Cherokee Sound
Sandy Point
BIMINI ISLANDS
Bahamas
North Bimini
South Bimini
Alice Town
Bailey Town
NEW PROVIDENCE
Bahamas
Nassau
Lyford Cay
Coral Harbour
GRAND BAHAMA ISLAND
Bahamas
Freeport
Lucaya
West End
Eight Mile Rock
ELEUTHERA
Bahamas
Governor's Harbour
Dunmore Town
Rock Sound
EXUMA
Bahamas
George Town
GREAT EXUMA
LITTLE EXUMA
TROPIC OF CANCER
SAN SALVADOR
Bahamas
Cockburn Town
GRAND CAYMAN
United Kingdom
George Town
Bodden Town
East End
North Side
West Bay
JAMAICA
Kingston
Spanish Town
Montego Bay
Mandeville
May Pen
Savanna-la-Mar
Port Antonio
Ocho Rios
Negril
Blue Mountain Peak
PUERTO RICO
United States
San Juan
Bayamón
Carolina
Caguas
Ponce
Mayagüez
Arecibo
Aguadilla
Humacao
Fajardo
Guayama
Cordillera Central
Vieques
Culebra
ST. THOMAS AND ST. JOHN
United States
ATLANTIC OCEAN
CARIBBEAN SEA
Charlotte Amalie
ST. THOMAS
ST. JOHN
VIRGIN ISLANDS N.P.
CORAL REEF NATIONAL MONUMENT
ST. CROIX
United States
BUCK ISLAND REEF NATIONAL MONUMENT
Christiansted
Frederiksted
TORTOLA
U.K.
Road Town
VIRGIN GORDA
U.K.
Spanish Town
ANGUILLA
United Kingdom
The Valley

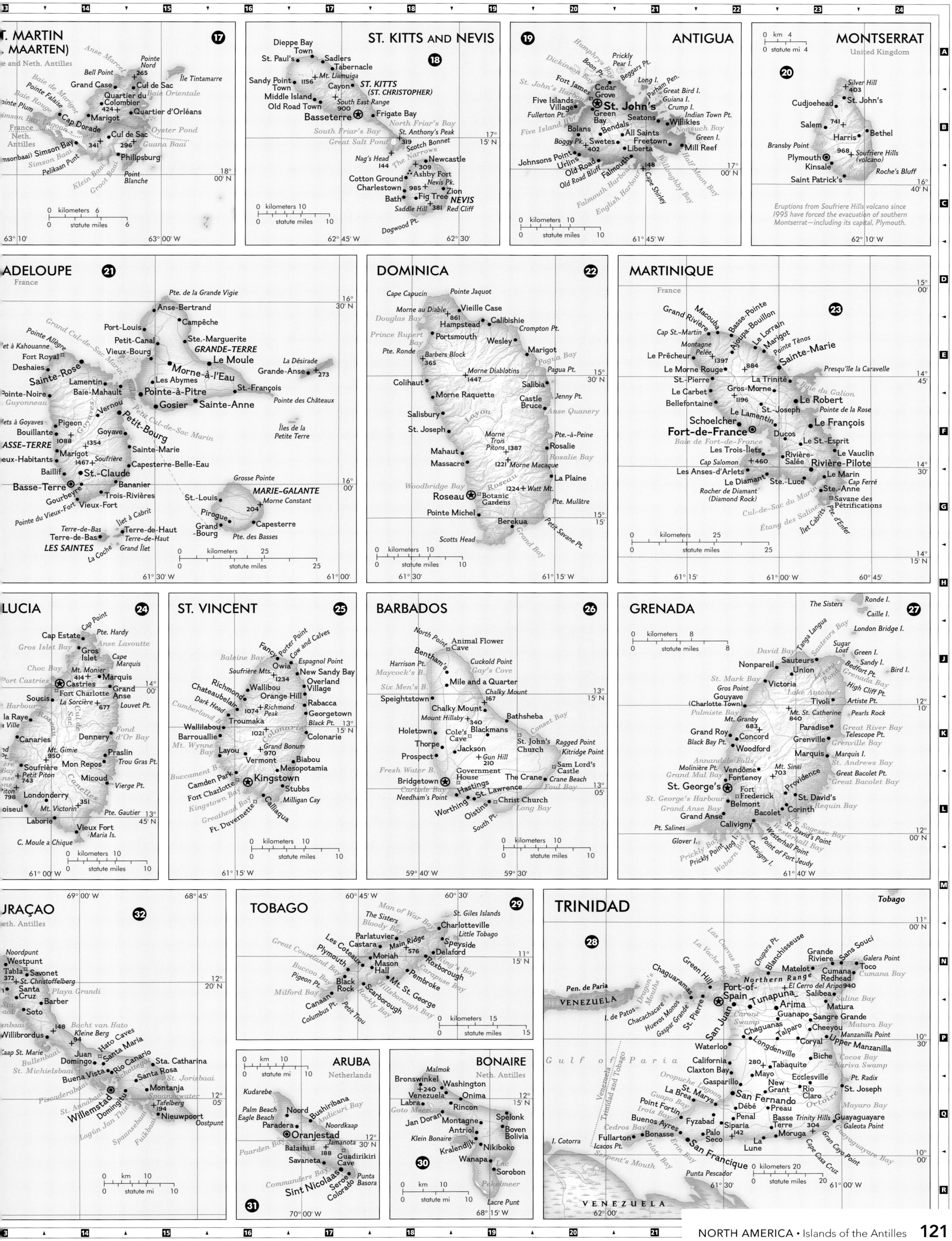

ST. MARTIN (ST. MAARTEN)
Fr. and Neth. Antilles
17
Anse Marcel
Pointe Nord
265
Bell Point
Île Tintamarre
Grand Case
Cul de Sac
Baie Orientale
Quartier du Colombier
424
Quartier d'Orléans
Marigot
Baie de Marigot
Pointe Falaise
Baie Rouge
Pointe Plum
Cap Dorade
France
Neth. Antilles
Cul de Sac
Oyster Pond
Guana Baai
341
296
Simson Bay
Simson Baai
Pelikaan Punt
Philipsburg
Point Blanche
Klein Baai
Groot Baai
18° 00' N
63° 10'
63° 00' W
ST. KITTS AND NEVIS
18
Dieppe Bay Town
St. Paul's
Sadlers
Tabernacle
Sandy Point Town
1156
Mt. Liamuiga
Cayon
ST. KITTS (ST. CHRISTOPHER)
Middle Island
Old Road Town
900
South East Range
Basseterre
Frigate Bay
North Friar's Bay
South Friar's Bay
St. Anthony's Peak
Great Salt Pond
319
Scotch Bonnet
The Narrows
Nag's Head
144
Newcastle
309
Ashby Fort
Nevis Pk.
Cotton Ground
Charlestown
985
Zion
Fig Tree
NEVIS
Bath
Saddle Hill
381
Red Cliff
Dogwood Pt.
17° 15' N
62° 45' W
62° 30'
ANTIGUA
19
Humphreys Bay
Dickinson Bay
Boon Pt.
Prickly Pear I.
Beggars Pt.
St. John's Harbour
Fort James
Cedar Grove
Long I.
Parham Pen.
Great Bird I.
Guiana I.
Crump I.
Five Islands Village
St. John's
Fullerton Pt.
Green Bay
Seatons
Indian Town Pt.
Willikies
Five Island Hbr.
Bolans
Bendals
All Saints
Nonsuch Bay
Green I.
Boggy Pk.
402
Swetes
Freetown
Mill Reef
Liberta
Johnsons Point
Urlins
Old Road
Old Road Bluff
Falmouth
148
Falmouth Harbour
English Harbour
Cape Shirley
Willoughby Bay
Half Moon Bay
17° 00' N
61° 45' W
MONTSERRAT
United Kingdom
20
Silver Hill
403
St. John's
Cudjoehead
Salem
741
Harris
Bethel
Bransby Point
968
Soufriere Hills (volcano)
Plymouth
Kinsale
Roche's Bluff
Saint Patrick's
16° 40' N
Eruptions from Soufriere Hills volcano since 1995 have forced the evacuation of southern Montserrat—including its capital, Plymouth.
62° 10' W
GUADELOUPE
France
21
Pte. de la Grande Vigie
Anse-Bertrand
16° 30' N
Campêche
Grand Cul-de-Sac Marin
Port-Louis
Pointe Allègre
Petit-Canal
Ste.-Marguerite
GRANDE-TERRE
Anse à Kahouanne
Vieux-Bourg
Le Moule
Fort Royal
La Désirade
Deshaies
Morne-à-l'Eau
Grande-Anse
273
Sainte-Rose
Lamentin
Les Abymes
Baie-Mahault
Pointe-à-Pitre
St.-François
Pointe-Noire
Guyonneau
Gosier
Sainte-Anne
Pointe des Châteaux
Vernou
Goyaves
Petit-Bourg
Petit Cul-de-Sac Marin
Îles de la Petite Terre
Îlets à Goyaves
Pigeon
Goyave
Bouillante
1088
1354
BASSE-TERRE
Sainte-Marie
Vieux-Habitants
Marigot
1467
Soufrière
Capesterre-Belle-Eau
Baillif
St.-Claude
Grosse Pointe
Basse-Terre
Banannier
MARIE-GALANTE
Trois-Rivières
St.-Louis
Morne Constant
Gourbeyre
Vieux-Fort
204
Pointe du Vieux-Fort
Îlet à Cabrit
Pirogue
Capesterre
Terre-de-Bas
Terre-de-Haut
Grand-Bourg
Pte. des Basses
LES SAINTES
La Coche
Grand Îlet
16° 00'
61° 30' W
61° 00'
DOMINICA
22
Cape Capucin
Pointe Jaquot
Morne au Diable
861
Vieille Case
Douglas Bay
Hampstead
Calibishie
Crompton Pt.
Prince Rupert Bay
Portsmouth
Wesley
Pte. Ronde
Marigot
Barbers Block
365
Pagua Bay
Morne Diablotins
1447
Pagua Pt.
Colihaut
Salibia
Morne Raquette
Castle Bruce
Jenny Pt.
Anse Quanery
Layou
Salisbury
St. Joseph
Pte.-à-Peine
Morne Trois Pitons
1387
Rosalie
Mahaut
Rosalie Bay
Massacre
1221
Morne Macaque
La Plaine
Woodbridge Bay
1224
Watt Mt.
Roseau
Botanic Gardens
Pte. Mulâtre
Pointe Michel
Berekua
Scotts Head
Grand Bay
Petite Savane Pt.
15° 30' N
15° 15'
61° 30'
61° 15' W
MARTINIQUE
France
23
Grand Rivière
Macouba
Basse-Pointe
Ajoupa-Bouillon
Cap St.-Martin
Le Lorrain
Marigot
Montagne Pelée
1397
Pointe Ténos
Le Prêcheur
Sainte-Marie
Le Morne Rouge
884
Presqu'île la Caravelle
St.-Pierre
La Trinité
Le Carbet
Gros-Morne
1196
Baie du Galion
Bellefontaine
Le Robert
Le Lamentin
St.-Joseph
Pointe de la Rose
Schoelcher
Fort-de-France
Le François
Baie de Fort-de-France
Ducos
Le St.-Esprit
Les Trois-Îlets
Le Vauclin
Cap Salomon
Rivière-Salée
460
Rivière-Pilote
Les Anses-d'Arlets
Le Marin
Le Diamant
Ste.-Luce
Cap Ferré
Rocher de Diamant (Diamond Rock)
Ste.-Anne
Savane des Pétrifications
Cul-de-Sac du Marin
Étang des Salines
Îlet Cabrits
Pte. d'Enfer
15° 00'
14° 45'
14° 30'
14° 15' N
61° 15'
61° 00' W
60° 45'
ST. LUCIA
24
Cap Point
Cap Estate
Pte. Hardy
Anse Lavoutte
Gros Islet Bay
Gros Islet
Cape Marquis
Choc Bay
Mt. Monier
Marquis
Port Castries
414
Castries
Grand Anse
Fort Charlotte
La Sorcière
677
Louvet Pt.
Soucis
Harbour
La Raye
Anse la Ville
Cul de Sac
Canaries
Dennery
Fond d'Or Bay
Mt. Gimie
950
Praslin
Soufrière
Mon Repos
Trou Gras Pt.
Petit Piton
743
Micoud
Gros Piton
798
Vierge Pt.
Londonderry
351
Choiseul
Mt. Victorin
Pte. Gautier
Laborie
Vieux Fort
Maria Is.
C. Moule a Chique
14° 00'
13° 45' N
61° 00' W
ST. VINCENT
25
Porter Point
Cow and Calves
Fancy
Baleine Bay
Owia
Espagnol Point
Soufrière Mts.
1234
New Sandy Bay
Overland Village
Wallibou
Richmond
Orange Hill
Chateaubelair
Rabacca
Dark Head
1074
Richmond Peak
Georgetown
Cumberland B.
Troumaka
Black Pt.
Wallilabou
1021
Colonarie
Barrouallie
Grand Bonum
970
Mt. Wynne Bay
Layou
Biabou
Vermont
Mesopotamia
Buccament B.
Camden Park
Kingstown
Fort Charlotte
Stubbs
Kingstown Bay
Milligan Cay
Greathead Bay
Calliaqua
Ft. Duvernette
13° 15' N
61° 15' W
BARBADOS
26
North Point
Animal Flower Cave
Bentham's
Harrison Pt.
Cuckold Point
Maycock's B.
Gay's Cove
Six Men's B.
Mile and a Quarter
Chalky Mount
Speightstown
167
Chalky Mount
Mount Hillaby
340
Bathsheba
Conset Bay
Holetown
Cole's Cave
Blackmans
St. John's Church
Ragged Point
Thorpe
Kitridge Point
Jackson
Prospect
Gun Hill
210
Sam Lord's Castle
Fresh Water B.
Government House
The Crane
Bridgetown
Crane Beach
Carlisle Bay
Hastings
Foul Bay
Needham's Point
St. Lawrence
Christ Church
Worthing
Oistins
Long Bay
South Pt.
13° 15' N
13° 05'
59° 40' W
59° 30'
GRENADA
27
The Sisters
Ronde I.
Caille I.
London Bridge I.
Tanga Langua
Sauteurs Bay
Sugar Loaf
Green I.
David Bay
Sauteurs
Sandy I.
Nonpareil
Union
Bedford Pt.
Bird I.
St. Mark Bay
Levera Pond
Grenada Bay
Victoria
High Cliff Pt.
Gros Point
Lake Antoine
Gouyave (Charlotte Town)
Tivoli
Artiste Pt.
Palmiste Bay
Mt. St. Catherine
840
Pearls Rock
Mt. Granby
683
Paradise
Great River Bay
Grand Roy
Concord
Telescope Pt.
Black Bay Pt.
Grenville
Grenville Bay
Woodford
Marquis
Marquis I.
Annandale Falls
St. Andrews Bay
Molinière Pt.
Vendôme
Mt. Sinai
703
Great Bacolet Pt.
Grand Mal Bay
Fontenoy
Providence
Great Bacolet Bay
St. George's
Fort Frederick
St. George's Harbour
St. David's
Belmont
Requin Bay
Grand Anse Bay
Corinth
Grand Anse
Bacolet
Calivigny
La Sagesse Bay
Pt. Salines
St. David's Point
Westerhall Bay
Glover I.
Westerhall Point
Prickly Bay
Point of Fort Jeudy
Prickly Point
Hog I.
Woburn Bay
Calivigny I.
12° 10'
12° 00' N
61° 40' W
CURAÇAO
Neth. Antilles
32
69° 00' W
68° 45'
Noordpunt
Westpunt
Tabla
372
Savonet
St. Christoffelberg
Playa Grandi
Santa Cruz
Barber
Soto
Bacht van Hato
Willibrordus
148
Kleine Berg
94
Hato Caves
Kaap St. Marie
Juan Domingo
Santa Maria
Bullenbaai
St. Michielsbaai
Rio Canario
Sta. Catharina
Buena Vista
Santa Rosa
St. Jorisbaai
Piscaderabaai
Montanja
Willemstad
Domingitu
Spanish Water
St. Annabaai
Tafelberg
194
Nieuwpoort
Lagún Jan Thiel
Oostpunt
Spaansbaai
Fuikbaai
12° 20' N
12° 05'
TOBAGO
29
60° 45' W
60° 30'
Man of War Bay
The Sisters
St. Giles Islands
Bloody Bay
Charlotteville
Little Tobago
Parlatuvier
Castara
Main Ridge
Speyside
576
Great Courland Bay
Les Coteaux
Delaford
Plymouth
Moriah
King's Bay
Mason Hall
Roxborough
Buccoo Bay
Black Rock
Pembroke
Pigeon Pt.
Milford Bay
Hillsborough Bay
Canaan
Mt. St. George
Columbus Pt.
Scarborough
Rockly Bay
Petit Trou
11° 15' N
TRINIDAD
Tobago
28
Las Cuevas Bay
Chupara Pt.
Blanchisseuse
Grande Riviere
Sans Souci
Galera Point
La Vache Bay
Green Hill
Matelot
Cumana
Toco
Cumana Bay
Chaguaramas
Northern Range
Redhead
Pen. de Paria
Dragon's Mouths
El Cerro del Aripo
940
Port-of-Spain
Tunapuna
Salibea
VENEZUELA
Arima
Saline Bay
Chacachacare
Huevos
Monos
Gaspar Grande
St. Pierre
San Juan
Caroni Swamp
Matura
I. de Patos
Guanapo
Sangre Grande
Talparo
Matura Bay
Chaguanas
Cheeyou
Manzanilla Point
Longdenville
Coryal
Upper Manzanilla
Waterloo
Biche
California
280
Tabaquite
Cocos Bay
Gulf of Paria
Nariva Swamp
Claxton Bay
Mayo
Ecclesville
Pt. Radix
Oropuche Lagoon
Gasparillo
New Grant
Rio Claro
St. Joseph
Venezuela
Trinidad and Tobago
San Fernando
La Brea
St. Marys
Guapo Bay
Débé
Ortoire
Mayaro Bay
Point Fortin
Irois Bay
Penal
Basse Terre
Trinity Hills
Guayaguayare
Fyzabad
304
Galeota Point
Buenos Ayres
Siparia
188
Moruga
142
Cedros Bay
Bonasse
Palo Seco
Guayaguayare Bay
Grand Cayo Point
Fullarton
I. Cotorra
Icacos Pt.
Erin Bay
Lune
Cape Casa Cruz
Serpent's Mouth
Islote Bay
San Francique
Punta Pescador
VENEZUELA
11° 00' N
10° 30'
10° 00'
61° 30'
61° 00' W
62° 00'
ARUBA
Netherlands
31
Kudarebe
Palm Beach
Noord
Bushiribana
Eagle Beach
Andicuri Bay
Paradera
Noordkaap
Oranjestad
Jamanota
188
Paarden Bay
Balashi
Guadirikiri Cave
Savaneta
Commanders Bay
Sint Nicolaas
Seroe Colorado
Punta Basora
12° 30' N
70° 00' W
BONAIRE
Neth. Antilles
30
Malmok
Bronswinkel
Washington
240
Venezuela
Onima
Labra
Goto Meer
Rincon
Jan Doran
Montagne
Spelonk
Antriol
Boven Bolivia
Klein Bonaire
Kralendijk
Nikiboko
Wanapa
Lac
Sorobon
Pekelmeer
Lacre Punt
12° 15' N
68° 15' W
kilometers
statute miles
km
statute mi

South America

South America is a place of remarkable extremes—sweltering jungle heat and face-numbing cold, endless towering mountains and dense tropical forests that seem to stretch forever, the world's mightiest river and the planet's driest spot. While the region's coastal areas are highly developed, the heart of the continent remains largely vacant, a rugged expanse of mountains, desert, grassland, and forest that constitutes one of the world's last great wilderness treasures.

Although much of the continent remains wild and untamed, South America has its refined side. It provided a cradle for several ancient civilizations and in modern times has given birth to some of the world's biggest metropolises. Yet indigenous communities, though only a small percentage of the population, still exist—high in the mountains of Ecuador, deep in the Amazon jungle of Brazil, scattered in the forested hinterlands of Suriname, and elsewhere.

The ice-shrouded Torres del Paine Mountains take pride of place in Chile's harsh Patagonia region. Home to indigenous populations and endemic flora and fauna, Patagonia, which also encompasses a large swath of Argentina, has often been described as "the last place on Earth."

South America has also afforded us some of the great cultural highlights of the past hundred years—the astonishing discovery of the lost city of Machu Picchu in the Peruvian Andes, Evita Perón rousing crowds in Argentina, the alluring "Girl from Ipanema" on the beach in Brazil, and Pele's magic with a soccer ball.

PHYSICAL GEOGRAPHY With a base along the Caribbean coast and an apex at Cape Horn, South America is shaped rather like an elongated triangle. Embracing a total area of nearly 6.9 million square miles (17.8 million sq km), it's the fourth largest continent, bounded by the Atlantic Ocean in the east, the Pacific Ocean in the west, and the Caribbean Sea in the north. Its only connection to another landmass (North America) is the narrow Isthmus of Panama between Colombia and Panama. In the deep south, only the stormy Drake Passage separates South America from the Antarctic continent.

Despite its hefty size, South America has a relatively short coastline and few islands. However its offshore elements are distinctive: frigid Tierra del Fuego, the battle-torn Falklands (Malvinas), the biologically wondrous Galápagos, the spectacular fiord country of southern Chile, and untamed Marajó Island in the Amazon delta.

Three huge physical features dominate the South American mainland: the Andes mountains, the Amazon Basin, and a wide southern plain that encompasses the Pampas, the Gran Chaco, and much of Patagonia. The Andes cordillera, which runs all the way from northern Colombia to southern Chile and Argentina, is the world's longest mountain range. It's also one of the highest—more than 50 peaks over 20,000 feet (6,100 m)—and one of the most active in terms of volcanism and earthquakes.

South America's hydrology is perhaps the most astounding of any continent. Rainwater spilling off the Andes creates the mighty Amazon River and its thousand-plus tributaries, which in turn sustain the world's largest rain forest and greatest diversity of flora and fauna. Although the Amazon itself is not the planet's longest watercourse, it carries more liquid than the next ten biggest rivers combined. Spilling off a tabletop mountain in the northern Amazon is Angel Falls, the world's highest cascade at 3,212 feet (979 m), and tumbling off an ancient lava cliff between Brazil and Argentina is thunderous Iguazú Falls.

Among the continent's other geographic oddities are windswept Patagonia at the continent's southern tip and the extremely arid Atacama Desert, which often goes without rain for hundreds of years. The endless Pampas prairie of Argentina and Uruguay was the birthplace of gaucho culture, while the Pantanal region of southern Brazil is among the Earth's great wetlands.

HISTORY Like its continental cousin to the north, South America was first inhabited by nomads whose Asiatic ancestors crossed the Bering Strait during the last great ice age, sometime between 12,000 and 30,000 years ago. After crossing the Isthmus of Panama, they diffused throughout the continent and evolved into hundreds of different tribal groups with their own languages, customs, and traditions.

Starting around 3000 B.C., Amerindians living in the Andes region began to cultivate beans, squash, cotton, and potatoes. By 1000 B.C., villages along Peru's northern coastal plain had evolved into the Chavin culture, the continent's first true civilization. With a religion based on worship of the jaguar god, the Chavin built great ceremonial centers with mud-brick temples and pyramids. They also developed polychrome pottery, intricate weaving, and South America's first metallurgy. By the sixth century A.D., the Chavin had been eclipsed by other sophisticated Peruvian cultures such as the Moche, Nasca, and Tiwanaku. The last of the region's great Amerindian cultures was the Inca; master stonemasons and soldiers, the Inca forged an empire that stretched from present-day southern Colombia to northern Chile and Argentina.

Christopher Columbus "discovered" South America in 1498 on his third voyage to the New World, but the landmass (and adjacent North America) didn't receive its current name until Italian mariner Amerigo Vespucci explored its coast (1499–1502) and first postulated that it was a continent unto itself rather than part of Asia. In their quest for riches, the Spanish conquistadors came into violent contact with local Amerindian groups, climaxing in Francisco Pizarro's invasion of the Andes and bloody triumph over the Inca Empire in the 1530s. While the Spaniards were busy conquering the west coast, the Portuguese were claiming the continent's eastern shore, an area they called Brazil after a local dyewood tree. Driven off their land, decimated by disease, and pressed into slavery, South America's native population quickly declined in all but the most remote regions. Within half a century of first contact, European hegemony over the entire continent was assured.

Three distinct groups—the military, wealthy families, and the Roman Catholic Church—came to dominate South America's new Iberian colonies by the end of the 16th century. Using Indian labor and millions of slaves imported from Africa, they developed a society based on sprawling ranches and European-style cities such as Lima and Bogotá. Missions under the direction of the Jesuits and Franciscans were used to convert and control Indians in frontier areas. By the dawn of the 19th century—inspired by popular uprisings in the United States and France—South America's colonies had hatched their own revolutions. Between 1810 and 1824, Simón Bolívar and José de San Martín liberated all of the region's Spanish-speaking lands. Brazil declared its independence from Portugal in 1822.

Despite impressive economic gains in some countries—most notably Argentina—most of South America's independent states were stagnant by the early 20th century, struggling beneath a twin yoke of brutal military rule and neocolonial economic exploitation. This status quo endured until the late 1990s, when democracy flowered across the continent.

One of the most dramatic ruins in South America, the Inca ceremonial center of Machu Picchu hovers 2,000 feet (610 m) above the Urubamba River in the Peruvian Andes. It was built in the mid- to late 1400s at the behest of Pachacuti, the ruler who greatly enlarged the Inca Empire through conquest and colonization.

CULTURE A rich blend of Iberian, African, and Amerindian traditions, South America has some of the world's most lively and distinctive cultures. These cultures are also among the most urban. Despite romantic images of the Amazon and Machu Picchu, the vast majority of South Americans live in cities rather than the rain forest or mountains. A massive rural exodus since the 1950s has transformed South America into the most urbanized continent after Australia, a region that now boasts three of the world's 15 largest cities: São Paulo (18 million), Buenos Aires (13 million), and Rio de Janeiro (11 million). Ninety percent of these people live within 200 miles (320 km) of the coast, leaving huge expanses of the interior virtually unpopulated.

Several common threads bind the continent's more than 370 million people. Iberian languages dominate, with about half speaking Spanish and the other half Portuguese. There are several linguistic anomalies—French, Dutch, and English in the Guianas, and Amerindian dialects in the remote Amazon and Andes—but most South Americans don't need a translator when talking to one another. And despite recent inroads by Protestant missionaries—especially among remote Indian tribes and the urban poor—nearly 90 percent of South Americans adhere to the Roman Catholic faith.

Yet the continent also flaunts an amazing ethnic diversity. Although the majority of people can still trace their ancestors back to Spain or Portugal, waves of immigration have transformed South America into an ethnic smorgasbord. Amerindians and mixed-blood mestizos make up more than 80 percent of the population in Bolivia, Ecuador, and Peru. More than one-third of Argentines can boast Italian roots. Blond-haired, blue-eyed Germans populate many parts of Chile, Uruguay, and southern Brazil. Almost 40 percent of Brazilians and a high percentage of the residents of coastal Colombia and Venezuela are the descendants of African slaves. Asian Indians comprise the largest ethnic groups in both Suriname and Guyana.

This blend has produced a vibrant modern culture with influence far beyond the bounds of its South American cradle. Argentina's beloved tango—music, lyrics, and dance steps born of the Buenos Aires ghettos—is now an icon of romance all around the world. Brazil's steamy port cities hatched sensual Afro-Latino rhythms such as samba and bossa nova, Peruvian pipe music has become synonymous with the Andes, while Colombia has produced a rousing Latino rock. South America's rich literary map includes everything from the magical realism of Gabriel García Márquez and Mario Vargas Llosa to the sensual poems of Pablo Neruda and the poignant prose of Jorge Luis Borges. A similar passion flows through soccer, the region's favorite game, where the likes of Pele and Maradona have led their respective national teams (Brazil and Argentina) to multiple World Cup titles.

ECONOMICS Even though South America's colonies gained their independence at a relatively early stage, they were not able to achieve economic autonomy to any large extent. By the early 20th century, nearly all of them were dependent on commodity exports to Europe or the United States: bananas, rubber, sugar, coffee, timber, emeralds, copper, oil, and beef. In the short term some countries did very well with exports, especially Argentina, which counted itself among the world's richest nations until the 1950s. But failure to make a full transition from resource extraction into modern business and industry spelled economic doom for the entire continent.

By the 1960s, most of South America was mired in negative or neutral economic growth, increasingly dependent on overseas aid, and plagued by unemployment and poverty. Corruption, military rule, and mismanagement augmented an already dire situation. Hyperinflation of several hundred percent per annum battered Brazil and Argentina in the 1980s, nearly crippling the continent's two largest economies. During the same era, narcotics became one of South America's most important money spinners—cocaine exported in great quantities from Colombia, Bolivia, and Peru. Yet by the 1990s, most countries saw light at the end of their dim economic tunnels. In the early years of the 21st century, although fundamental problems remain—like huge foreign debt—the region's nouvelle democracy spurred an era of relative prosperity, raising the GDP per capita in many countries.

South America still relies, to a large extent, on commodity exports: oil from Venezuela, coffee from Colombia, and copper from Chile. But recent decades have seen a dramatic shift toward manufacturing and niche agriculture. Brazil now earns more money from making automobiles and aircraft than from shipping rubber overseas. Chile has earned a worldwide market for its wine, fruit, and salmon.

Despite protests from indigenous tribes and environmental groups, South American governments have tried to spur even more growth by opening up the Amazon region to economic exploitation—the extraction of oil and timber and the transformation of rain forest into cattle ranches. But this practice is already wreaking widespread ecological havoc. The Amazon could very well be the key to the region's economic future—not by the decimation of the world's richest forest, but by the sustainable management and commercial development of its largely untapped biodiversity into medical, chemical, and nutritional products. Many researchers believe that potential treatments for cancer and other ailments may lie hidden in South America's shadowy rain forest.

South America: Physical and Political
CARIBBEAN SEA
Guajira Peninsula
Gulf of Venezuela
Paraguaná Pen.
LESSER ANTILLES
Margarita I.
Paria Pen.
Tobago
Trinidad
Tortuga I.
Serra Nevada de Santa Marta 5775
Lake Maracaibo
L. Valencia
Coast Range 2660
Gulf of Morrosquillo
Gulf of Urabá
PANAMA CANAL
Isthmus of Panama
Gulf of Panama
Maracaibo Basin
5007
Cordillera de Mérida
Magdalena
Apure
Orinoco
Orinoco River Delta
LLANOS
Longitude West 55° of Greenwich
Shell Beach
Serranía de Baudó
Cordillera Central
Cordillera Oriental
Cordillera Occidental
4080
5493
Tomo
Angel Falls
Total drop 979 meters
World's highest waterfall
Mt. Roraima 2772
Pakaraima Mts.
GUIANA HIGHLANDS
Sierra Pacaraima
Wilhelmina Mts.
Kanuku Mts.
854
Serra de Tumucumaque
Devil's Island
Cape Orange
Malpelo Island
Buenaventura Bay
Guaviare
Source of the Orinoco
Cerro Otare 910
Pico da Neblina 3014
Maracá Island
Mouths of the Amazon
Galera Point
Balbina Reservoir
Gurupá I.
Marajó Island
Marajó Bay
Cape Gurupi
EQUATOR
Chimborazo 6310
AMAZON
Amazon
Napo
Amazon (Solimões)
Negro
Tapajós
Xingu
Iriri
Tocantins
Serra do Tiracambu
São Marcos Bay
Pt. Jericoacoara
Santa Elena Peninsula
Gulf of Guayaquil
Pongo de Manseriche
Juruá
Purus
Madeira
Selvas
Caatinga
Parnaíba
Sa. da Ibiapaba
725
Atol das Rocas
Cape São Roque
Marañón
Aguja Point
Sechura Desert
Lobos Islands
BASIN
LA MONTAÑA
Cordillera Oriental
Cordillera Central
Araguaia
Teles Pires
Sa. do Uruçuí
Sobradinho Reservoir
Borborema Plateau 1123
São Francisco
Sertão
Nevado Huascarán 6768
Beni
Mamoré
Jiparaná
Serra dos Parecis
640
Juruena
Serra do Tombador
Serra Formosa
BRAZILIAN HIGHLANDS
670
Sa. do Roncador
Serra Dourada
Espigão Mestre
Campos
Manguinho Point
Guaporé
Chincha Is.
Paracas Peninsula
Source of the Amazon
Lake Titicaca 3810
Illampu 6362
Illimani 6462
Yungas
Secure
Cord. Oriental
Cordillera Central
Altiplano
5453
Grande
Bañados del Izozog
1349
2040
Serra do Espinhaço
Todos os Santos Bay
Baleia Point
Madrid Point
Salar de Uyuni
Chaco Boreal
Pantanal
Paraguai
Serra de Maracaju 558
Paranaíba
Grande
Pico de la Bandeira 2890
Source of the Paraná
Serra da Mantiqueira
Cape São Tomé
Cape Frio
Angamos Point
Atacama Desert
Puna de Atacama
Cerro Galan 6600
Pilcomayo
Sete Quedas Falls
Iguaçu Falls
Serra Geral
Serra do Mar
São Sebastião I.
TROPIC OF CAPRICORN
Gran Chaco
Chaco Austral
Salado
Paraná
Uruguay
1340
Paranaguá Bay
Isla San Félix
Isla San Ambrosio
Cerro Bonete 6872
Cape Bascuñán
Salinas Grandes
Salinas de Ambargasta
Cape Santa Marta Grande
Laguna Mar Chiquita
Lengua de Vaca Pt.
Patos Lagoon
Entre Ríos
Cerro Mercedario 6770
2790
Sierras de Córdoba
Lake Rincón del Bonete
Negro
299
Cuchilla Grande
Highest point in South America
Cerro Aconcagua 6960 (22834 ft)
Cerro Tupungato 6800
Maipo Volcano 5323
Islas Juan Fernández
Isla Róbinson Crusoe
River Plate
Punta del Este
Samborombón Bay
Cape San Antonio
PAMPAS
Arauco Gulf
Colorado
Sierra del Tandil 524
Copulhue Pass 2101
Llaima Volcano 3060
Arco Pass 1401
Mogotes Point
Embalse Ezequiela Ramos Mexia
Blanca Bay
Rasa Point
San Matías Gulf
Meseta de Somuncurá
Valdés Peninsula -40
Isla Grande de Chiloé
Chubut
Meseta de Montemayor
Chonos Archipelago
Lake Buenos Aires
Gulf of San Jorge
Cape Tres Puntas
Tres Montes Peninsula
Deseado
Cerro Puntudo 1000
San Julián Bay
Lake Viedma
Laguna del Carbón
Lowest point in South America
-105 (-344 ft)
Wellington Island
Lake Argentino
Grande Bay
PATAGONIA
ANDES
FALKLAND ISLANDS
West Falkland
East Falkland
Cape Virgenes
Queen Adelaida Archipelago
Strait of Magellan
TIERRA DEL FUEGO
Staten Island
Cape Horn
Shag Rocks
Black Rock
South Georgia
PACIFIC OCEAN
ATLANTIC OCEAN
Azimuthal Equidistant Projection
SCALE 1:22,838,000
1 CENTIMETER = 228 KILOMETERS; 1 INCH = 360 MILES
KILOMETERS
STATUTE MILES
International boundary

Longitude West 55° of Greenwich
TRINIDAD AND TOBAGO
Port-of-Spain
CARACAS
VALENCIA
MARACAIBO
BARRANQUILLA
CARTAGENA
Santa Marta
Barquisimeto
Ciudad Bolívar
Ciudad Guayana
Maturín
Barcelona
Cumaná
Georgetown
Paramaribo
Cayenne
GUYANA
SURINAME
FRENCH GUIANA
VENEZUELA
COLOMBIA
BOGOTÁ
MEDELLÍN
CALI
Bucaramanga
Cúcuta
Panamá
ECUADOR
QUITO
GUAYAQUIL
Cuenca
PERU
LIMA
Trujillo
Chiclayo
Piura
Arequipa
Cusco
Iquitos
BOLIVIA
La Paz
Sucre
Cochabamba
Santa Cruz
BRAZIL
MANAUS
BELÉM
FORTALEZA
RECIFE
SALVADOR (Bahia)
BRASÍLIA
GOIÂNIA
BELO HORIZONTE
RIO DE JANEIRO
SÃO PAULO
CURITIBA
PORTO ALEGRE
Porto Velho
Cuiabá
Campo Grande
Teresina
São Luís
Natal
João Pessoa
Maceió
Aracaju
Florianópolis
Vitória
PARAGUAY
Asunción
URUGUAY
MONTEVIDEO
ARGENTINA
BUENOS AIRES
SAN JUSTO
CÓRDOBA
ROSARIO
San Miguel de Tucumán
Mendoza
Mar del Plata
Bahía Blanca
CHILE
SANTIAGO
Valparaíso
Antofagasta
Concepción
Puerto Montt
Punta Arenas
ANDES
EQUATOR
TROPIC OF CAPRICORN
PACIFIC OCEAN
ATLANTIC OCEAN
FALKLAND ISLANDS (ISLAS MALVINAS) U.K.
Administered by United Kingdom (claimed by Argentina)
West Falkland
East Falkland
Stanley
South Georgia U.K.
ISLA GRANDE DE TIERRA DEL FUEGO
Isla de los Estados (Staten Island)
Cabo de Hornos (Cape Horn)
Islas Juan Fernández Chile
Isla San Félix
Isla San Ambrosio Chile
Isla de Malpelo Colombia
Arquipélago de Fernando de Noronha Brazil
Azimuthal Equidistant Projection
SCALE 1:22,838,000
1 CENTIMETER = 228 KILOMETERS; 1 INCH = 360 MILES
0 200 400 600 800
KILOMETERS
0 200 400 600 800
STATUTE MILES

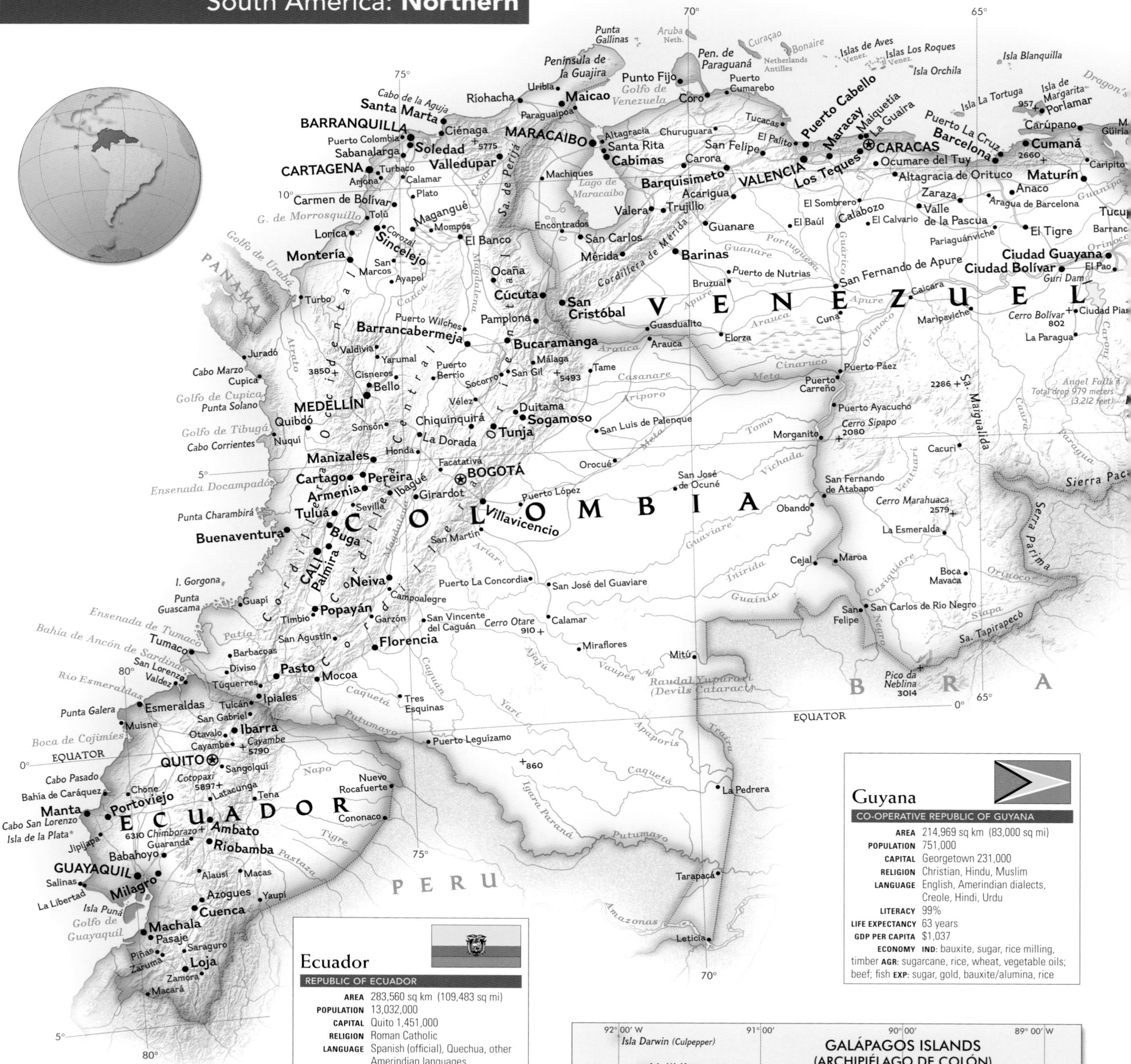

Guyana

CO-OPERATIVE REPUBLIC OF GUYANA

AREA 214,969 sq km (83,000 sq mi)
POPULATION 751,000
CAPITAL Georgetown 231,000
RELIGION Christian, Hindu, Muslim
LANGUAGE English, Amerindian dialects, Creole, Hindi, Urdu
LITERACY 99%
LIFE EXPECTANCY 63 years
GDP PER CAPITA $1,037
ECONOMY **IND:** bauxite, sugar, rice milling, timber **AGR:** sugarcane, rice, wheat, vegetable oils; beef; fish **EXP:** sugar, gold, bauxite/alumina, rice

Ecuador

REPUBLIC OF ECUADOR

AREA 283,560 sq km (109,483 sq mi)
POPULATION 13,032,000
CAPITAL Quito 1,451,000
RELIGION Roman Catholic
LANGUAGE Spanish (official), Quechua, other Amerindian languages
LITERACY 93%
LIFE EXPECTANCY 74 years
GDP PER CAPITA $2,302
ECONOMY **IND:** petroleum, food processing, textiles, wood products **AGR:** bananas, coffee, cocoa, rice; cattle; balsa wood; fish **EXP:** petroleum, bananas, cut flowers, shrimp

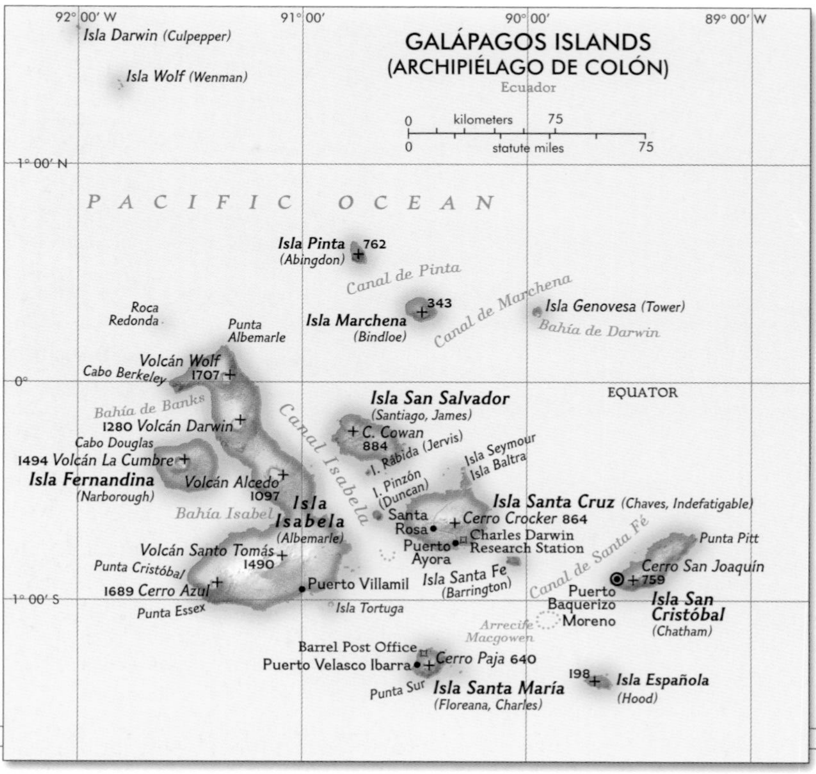

Colombia

REPUBLIC OF COLOMBIA

AREA 1,141,748 sq km (440,831 sq mi)
POPULATION 46,039,000
CAPITAL Bogotá 7,290,000
RELIGION Roman Catholic
LANGUAGE Spanish
LITERACY 93%
LIFE EXPECTANCY 72 years
GDP PER CAPITA $2,130
ECONOMY **IND:** textiles, food processing, oil, clothing and footwear **AGR:** coffee, cut flowers, bananas, rice; forest products; shrimp **EXP:** petroleum, coffee, coal, apparel

French Guiana (France)

OVERSEAS DEPARTMENT OF FRANCE

AREA 86,504 sq km (33,400 sq mi)
POPULATION 195,000
CAPITAL Cayenne 56,000
RELIGION Roman Catholic
LANGUAGE French
LITERACY 83%
LIFE EXPECTANCY 75 years
GDP PER CAPITA $8,300
ECONOMY **IND:** construction, shrimp processing, forestry products, rum **AGR:** corn, rice, manioc (tapioca), sugar; cattle **EXP:** shrimp, timber, gold, rum

Suriname

REPUBLIC OF SURINAME

AREA 163,265 sq km (63,037 sq mi)
POPULATION 447,000
CAPITAL Paramaribo 253,000
RELIGION Hindu, Protestant, Roman Catholic, Muslim
LANGUAGE Dutch (official), English, Sranang Tongo, Hindustani, Javanese
LITERACY 88%
LIFE EXPECTANCY 69 years
GDP PER CAPITA $2,475
ECONOMY **IND:** bauxite and gold mining, alumina production, oil, lumbering **AGR:** paddy rice, bananas, palm kernels, coconuts; beef; forest products; shrimp **EXP:** alumina, crude oil, lumber, shrimp and fish

Venezuela

BOLIVARIAN REPUBLIC OF VENEZUELA

AREA 912,050 sq km (352,144 sq mi)
POPULATION 26,749,000
CAPITAL Caracas 3,226,000
RELIGION Roman Catholic
LANGUAGE Spanish (official), numerous indigenous dialects
LITERACY 93%
LIFE EXPECTANCY 73 years
GDP PER CAPITA $4,260
ECONOMY **IND:** petroleum, iron ore mining, construction materials, food processing **AGR:** corn, sorghum, sugarcane, rice; beef; fish **EXP:** petroleum, bauxite and aluminum, steel, chemicals

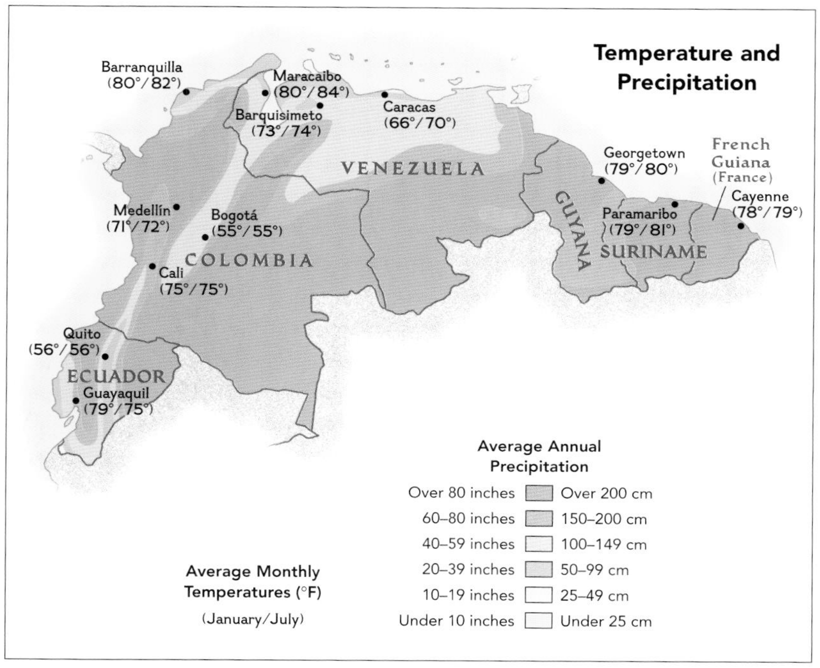

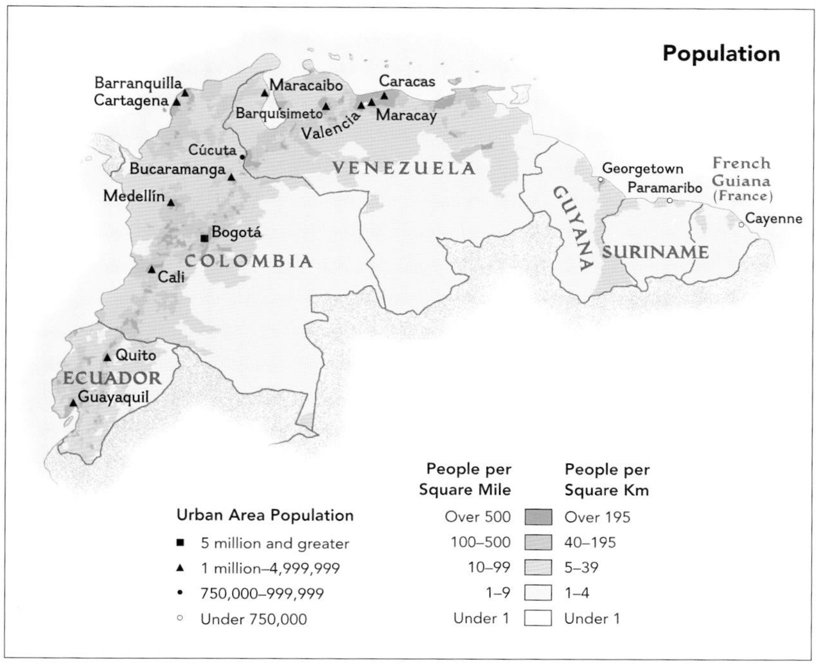

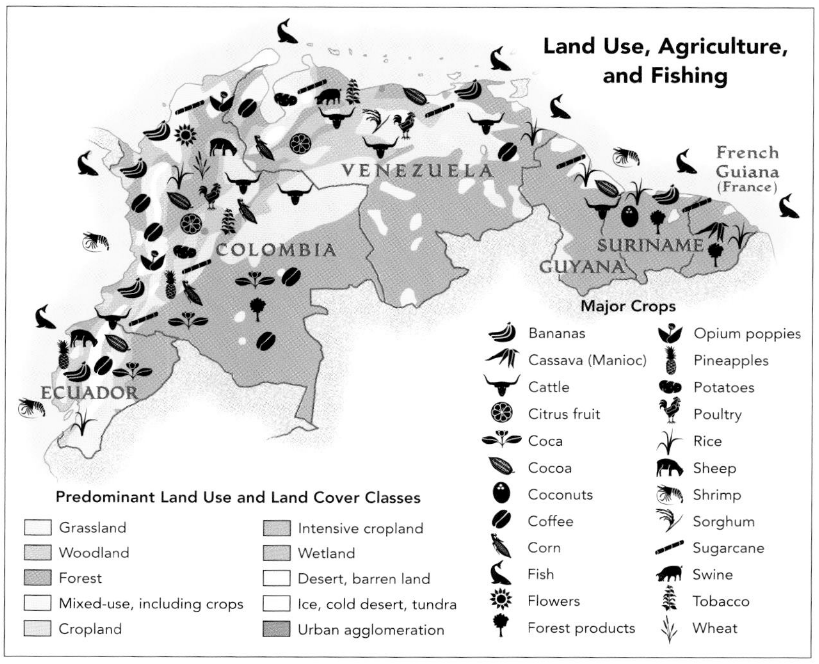

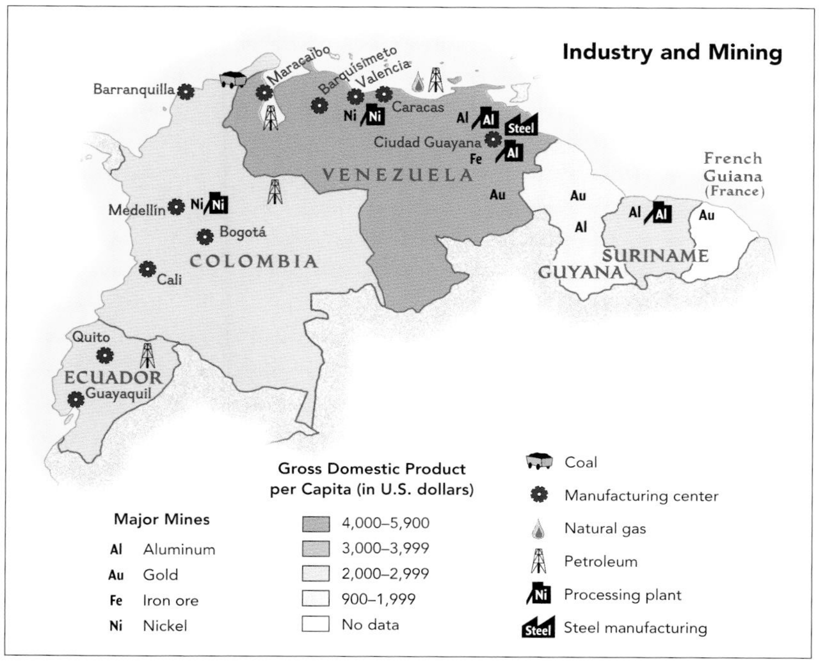

Bolivia

REPUBLIC OF BOLIVIA

AREA	1,098,581 sq km (424,164 sq mi)
POPULATION	8,922,000
CAPITAL	La Paz (administrative) 1,477,000; Sucre (constitutional) 212,000
RELIGION	Roman Catholic
LANGUAGE	Spanish (official), Quechua (official), Aymara (official)
LITERACY	87%
LIFE EXPECTANCY	64 years
GDP PER CAPITA	$935

ECONOMY IND: mining, smelting, petroleum, food and beverages AGR: soybeans, coffee, coca, cotton; timber EXP: natural gas, soybeans and soy products, crude petroleum, zinc ore

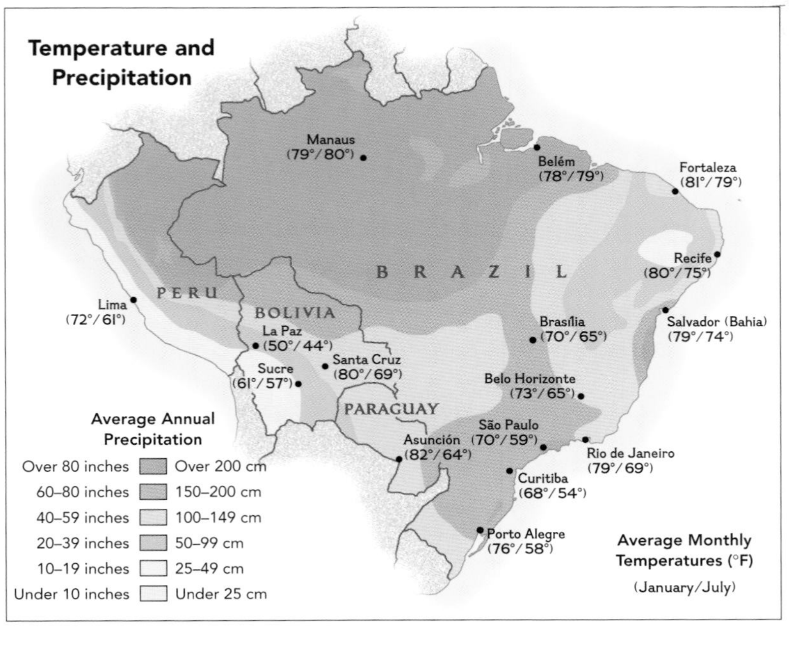

Brazil

FEDERATIVE REPUBLIC OF BRAZIL

AREA	8,547,403 sq km (3,300,169 sq mi)
POPULATION	184,184,000
CAPITAL	Brasília 3,099,000
RELIGION	Roman Catholic, Protestant
LANGUAGE	Portuguese (official)
LITERACY	86%
LIFE EXPECTANCY	71 years
GDP PER CAPITA	$3,225

ECONOMY IND: textiles, shoes, chemicals, cement AGR: coffee, soybeans, wheat, rice; beef EXP: transport equipment, iron ore, soybeans, footwear

Azimuthal Equidistant Projection

SCALE 1:15,025,000

1 CENTIMETER = 150 KILOMETERS; 1 INCH = 237 MILES

0 200 400 600 KILOMETERS

0 200 400 600 STATUTE MILES

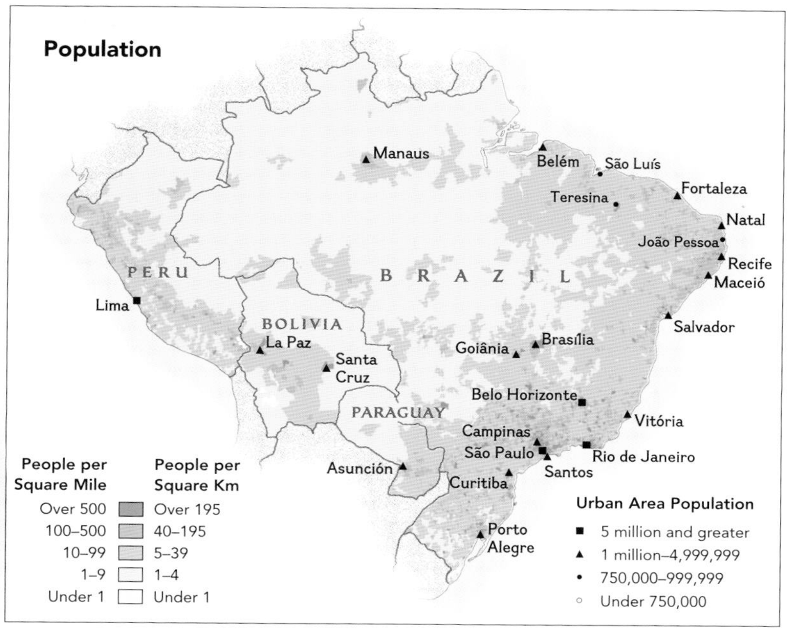

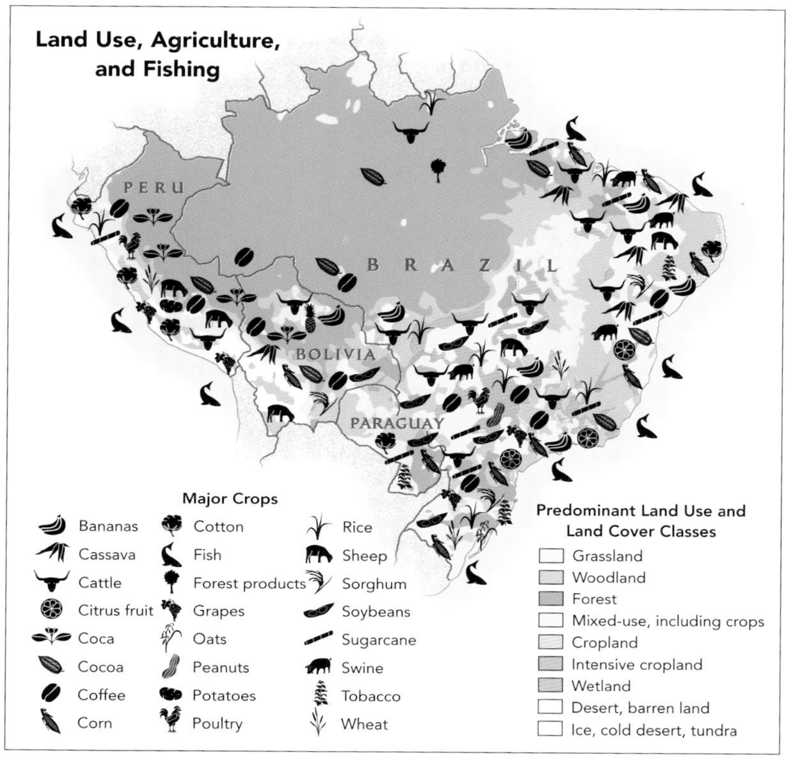

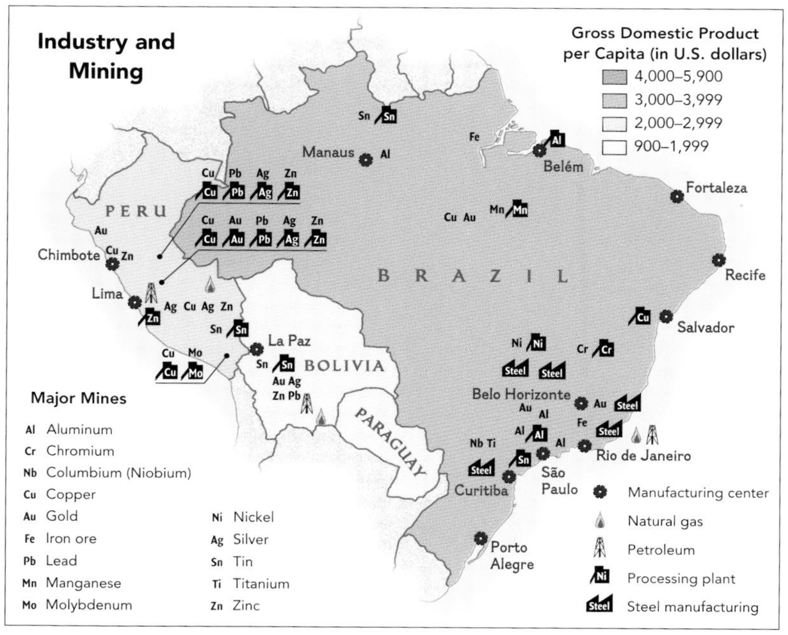

OBVERSE REVERSE

Paraguay

REPUBLIC OF PARAGUAY

AREA 406,752 sq km (157,048 sq mi)
POPULATION 6,158,000
CAPITAL Asunción 1,639,000
RELIGION Roman Catholic, Protestant
LANGUAGE Spanish (official), Guarani (official)
LITERACY 94%
LIFE EXPECTANCY 71 years
GDP PER CAPITA $1,168
ECONOMY **IND:** sugar, cement, textiles, beverages **AGR:** cotton, sugarcane, soybeans, corn; beef; timber **EXP:** soybeans, feed, cotton, meat

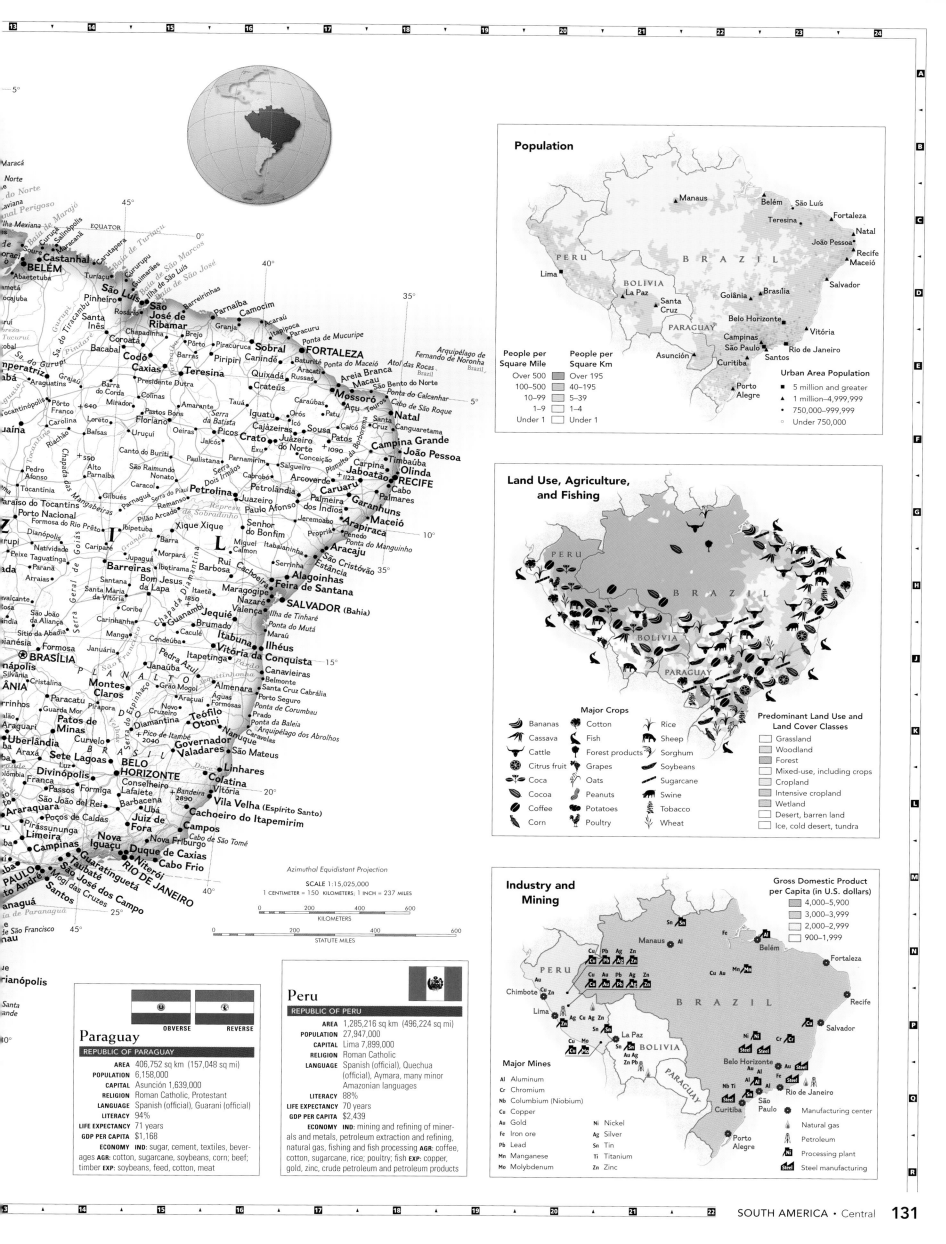

Peru

REPUBLIC OF PERU

AREA 1,285,216 sq km (496,224 sq mi)
POPULATION 27,947,000
CAPITAL Lima 7,899,000
RELIGION Roman Catholic
LANGUAGE Spanish (official), Quechua (official), Aymara, many minor Amazonian languages
LITERACY 88%
LIFE EXPECTANCY 70 years
GDP PER CAPITA $2,439
ECONOMY **IND:** mining and refining of minerals and metals, petroleum extraction and refining, natural gas, fishing and fish processing **AGR:** coffee, cotton, sugarcane, rice; poultry; fish **EXP:** copper, gold, zinc, crude petroleum and petroleum products

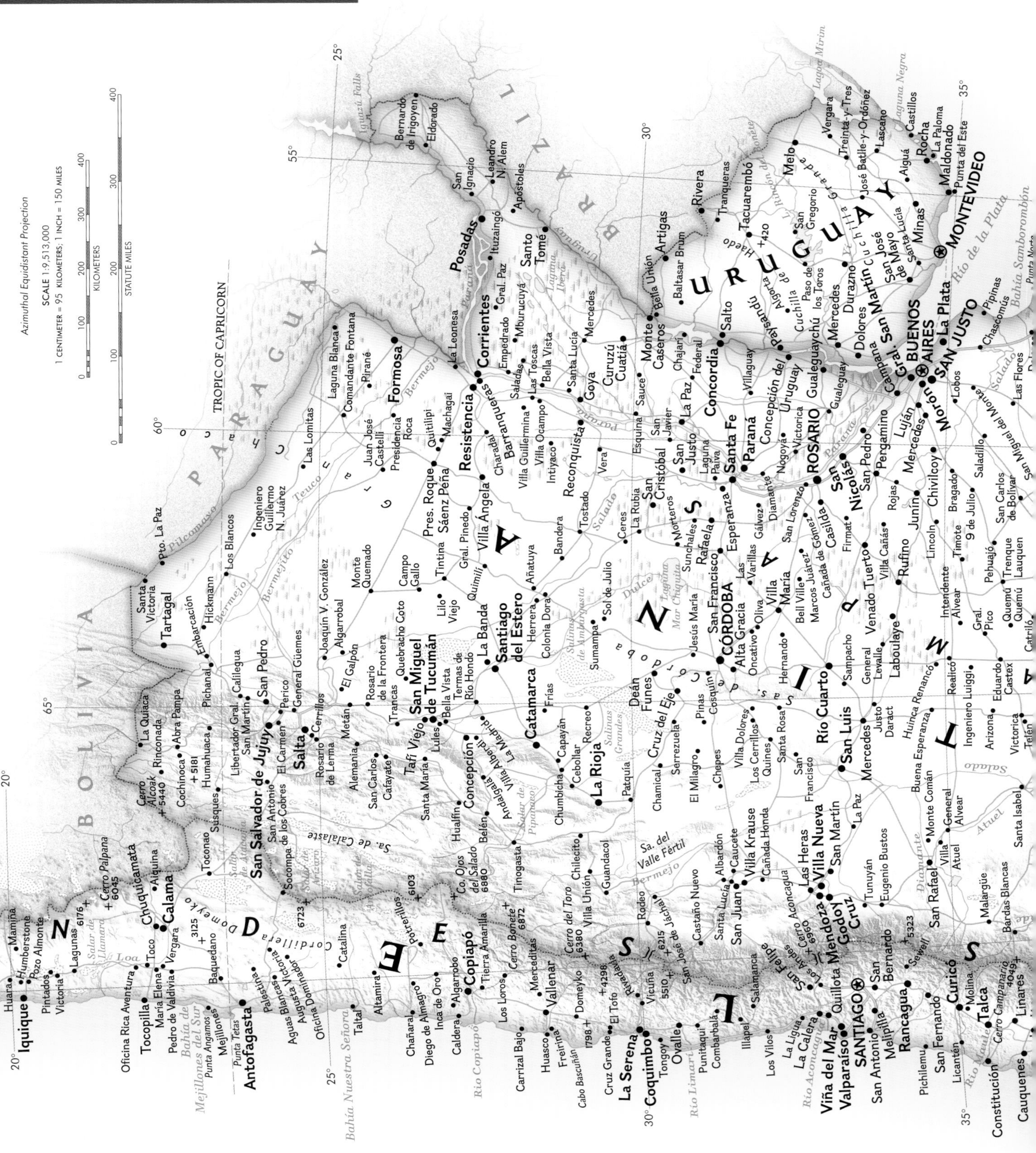

Land Use, Agriculture, and Fishing

Predominant Land Use and Land Cover Classes
- Grassland
- Woodland
- Forest
- Mixed-use, including crops
- Cropland
- Intensive cropland
- Wetland
- Desert, barren land
- Ice, cold desert, tundra
- Urban agglomeration

Major Crops
- Bananas
- Barley
- Beet sugar
- Cattle
- Citrus fruit
- Corn
- Cotton
- Fish
- Flaxseed
- Forest products
- Grapes
- Oats
- Peanuts
- Potatoes
- Poultry
- Rice
- Sheep
- Sorghum
- Soybeans
- Sugarcane
- Sunflower seeds
- Swine
- Tobacco
- Wheat

Temperature and Precipitation

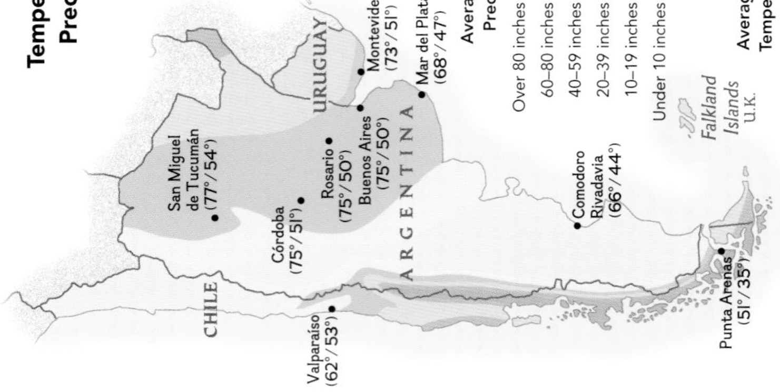

Average Annual Precipitation
- Over 80 inches / Over 200 cm
- 60–80 inches / 150–200 cm
- 40–59 inches / 100–149 cm
- 20–39 inches / 50–99 cm
- 10–19 inches / 25–49 cm
- Under 10 inches / Under 25 cm

Average Monthly Temperatures (°F) (January/July)

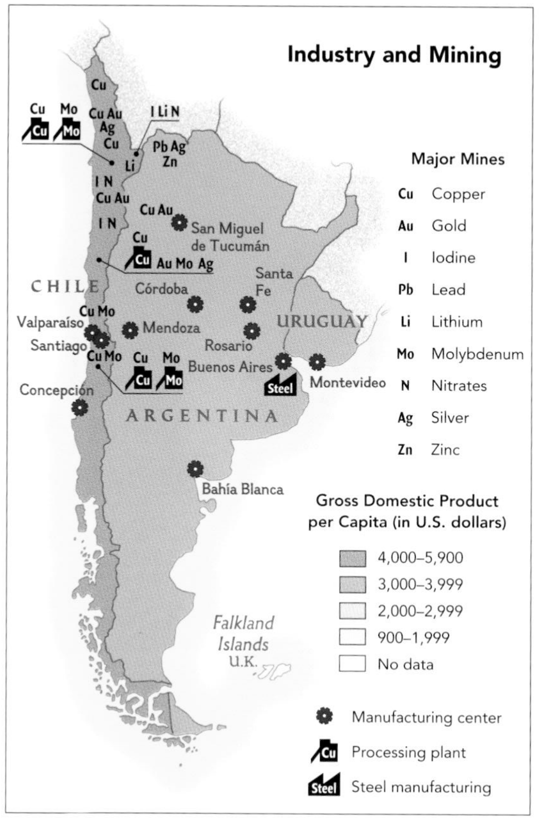

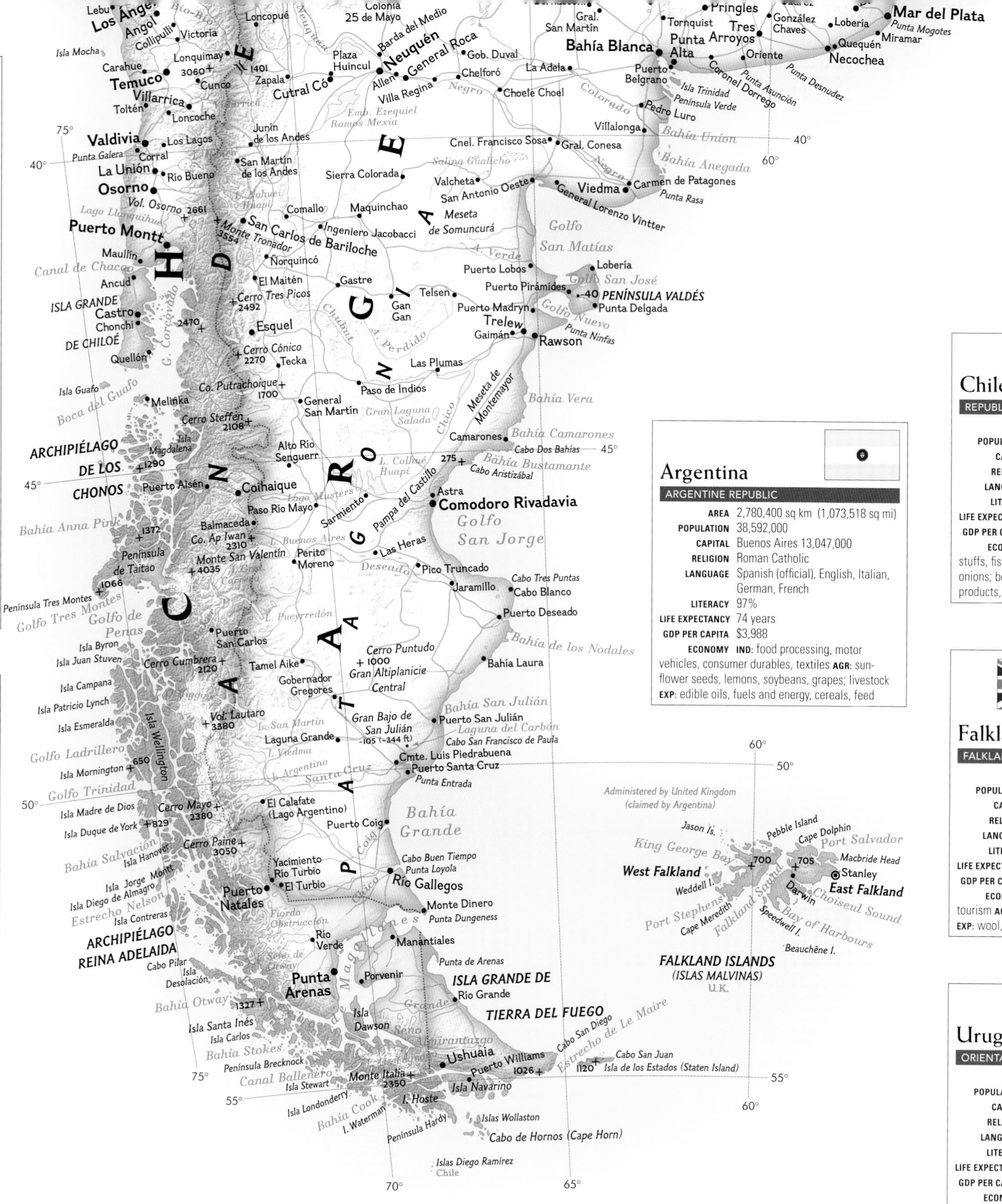

Argentina

ARGENTINE REPUBLIC

AREA 2,780,400 sq km (1,073,518 sq mi)
POPULATION 38,592,000
CAPITAL Buenos Aires 13,047,000
RELIGION Roman Catholic
LANGUAGE Spanish (official), English, Italian, German, French
LITERACY 97%
LIFE EXPECTANCY 74 years
GDP PER CAPITA $3,988
ECONOMY **IND:** food processing, motor vehicles, consumer durables, textiles **AGR:** sunflower seeds, lemons, soybeans, grapes; livestock **EXP:** edible oils, fuels and energy, cereals, feed

Chile

REPUBLIC OF CHILE

AREA 756,096 sq km (291,930 sq mi)
POPULATION 16,136,000
CAPITAL Santiago 5,478,000
RELIGION Roman Catholic, Protestant
LANGUAGE Spanish
LITERACY 96%
LIFE EXPECTANCY 76 years
GDP PER CAPITA $5,838
ECONOMY **IND:** copper, other minerals, foodstuffs, fish processing **AGR:** grapes, apples, pears, onions; beef; timber; fish **EXP:** copper, fruit, fish products, paper and pulp

Falkland Islands (U.K.)

SOVEREIGN LOCAL

FALKLAND ISLANDS

AREA 12,173 sq km (4,700 sq mi)
POPULATION 3,000
CAPITAL Stanley 2,000
RELIGION Protestant, Roman Catholic
LANGUAGE English
LITERACY NA
LIFE EXPECTANCY NA
GDP PER CAPITA $25,000
ECONOMY **IND:** fish and wool processing, tourism **AGR:** fodder and vegetable crops; sheep **EXP:** wool, hides, meat

Uruguay

ORIENTAL REPUBLIC OF URUGUAY

AREA 176,215 sq km (68,037 sq mi)
POPULATION 3,419,000
CAPITAL Montevideo 1,341,000
RELIGION Roman Catholic
LANGUAGE Spanish, Portunol, Brazilero
LITERACY 98%
LIFE EXPECTANCY 75 years
GDP PER CAPITA $3,842
ECONOMY **IND:** food processing, electrical machinery, transportation equipment, petroleum products **AGR:** rice, wheat, corn, barley; livestock; fish **EXP:** meat, rice, leather products, wool

The fantastical Neuschwanstein Castle, built in the late 1800s and later the model for Disneyland's iconic fairy-tale castle, sits high above the Alpsee in the Bavarian Alps. Although "Mad King Ludwig" intended his creation to be a paean to medieval architecture, he actually incorporated running water, automatic flush toilets, and other revolutionary conveniences of the day.

Europe

Europe is the world's second smallest continent, after Australia. A cluster of peninsulas and islands extending from northwestern Asia, Europe comprises more than 40 countries. Despite its northern location, most of its population enjoys a mild climate tempered by warm ocean currents such as the Gulf Stream.

Europe has been inhabited for some 40,000 years. During the past millennium Europeans explored the planet and established far-flung empires. Europe led the world in science and invention, and launched the industrial revolution. By the end of the 19th century, it dominated world commerce, spreading European ideas, languages, legal systems, and political patterns around the globe.

The 20th century brought unprecedented changes. Germany and its neighbors ignited two world wars. The Russian Revolution introduced communism. And Europe, weakened by war, lost its dominant position in the world along with its empires.

In 1947, the United States and the Soviet Union entered into a Cold War, pitting capitalism and democracy against communism and state control. Western Europe, backed by the U.S., prospered with market economies, democracy, and free speech; Eastern and Central European countries, their centrally planned economies closely tied to the Soviet Union's, fell behind and, despite full employment and social benefits, people suffered the lack of personal freedom.

In Western Europe, age-old enemies started cooperating. In 1952 six countries founded a common market for coal and steel; it soon included more countries and more commodities until, in 1991, the European Union was formed. Border controls were eliminated between 15 member countries (in 1999, 12 members introduced a common European currency). Also in 1991, the Soviet Union collapsed. Germany, which had been split by the Cold War, was reunified. Eastern and Central Europe started the difficult transition toward Western-style democracy and privatization.

When chaos overtook the Balkans, Yugoslavia shattered into five countries. But other forces are working toward a cohesive Europe. People move freely throughout the continent; they share the same pop culture, pursue similar urban lifestyles, and rely heavily on cell phones and the Internet.

Environmental problems are often international. Acid rain from England kills life in Swedish lakes. A nuclear accident in Ukraine damages dozens of countries. The Danube and Rhine Rivers spread industrial pollution downstream. Wherever possible, regional solutions hold the most promise, like the projected cleanup of the Baltic Sea involving nine surrounding countries.

Although the European Union enforces strict environmental laws, Eastern Europe understood little about the environment until the 1990s. Some countries still contain toxic waste dumps, untreated sewage, and other hazards, but they have insufficient funds to meet the high costs of cleanup.

A political United States of Europe will probably never happen, but the economic advantages of the European Union have greatly benefitted its member countries (currently numbering 25, with 4 more waiting for membership) as they enter a new era of history.

PHYSICAL GEOGRAPHY Europe is bounded by the Arctic Ocean in the north, the Atlantic Ocean in the west, the Mediterranean and Black Seas in the south, and the Caspian Sea in the southeast. The traditional land boundary is a line following the Ural Mountains south across Russia from the Arctic Ocean, via the Ural River to the Caspian Sea. The line then continues west along the crest of the Caucasus Mountains between the Caspian and Black Seas, making Mount El'brus (18,510 ft; 5,642 m), on the northern side, the highest mountain in Europe. Waterways linking the Black Sea to the Mediterranean place a small part of Turkey in Europe.

Two mountain systems lie between icy tundra and boreal forest in the far north and the warm, dry, hilly Mediterranean coast in the south. Ancient, rugged highlands, worn down by successive Ice Age glaciers, arc southwestward from Scandinavia, through the British Isles, to the Iberian Peninsula, while an active Alpine system spreads east to west across southern Europe. Still rising from a collision of tectonic plates, these mountains include the Carpathians, the Alps, the Pyrenees, and their many spurs. The high point is Mont Blanc (15,781 ft; 4,810 m), shared by France and Italy. Three major navigable rivers—the Danube, the Rhine, and the Rhône—rise in the Alps. Europe's longest river, however, is the Volga, flowing southeast across Russia to the Caspian Sea. Movements in Earth's crust cause earthquakes and volcanic eruptions in southern Europe and in Iceland. The best known volcanoes are Vesuvius, Etna, and Stromboli, all three in Italy.

Between Europe's two mountain systems, a rolling, fertile plain stretches across the continent from the Pyrenees to the Urals, well drained by several rivers. Some of the world's greatest cities are located here, including Paris, Berlin, and Moscow. Huge industrial areas on this plain are home to much of Europe's dense population.

HISTORY Named for King Minos, the first civilization in Europe appeared in Crete about 2000 B.C. Minoans traded with Egypt and western Asia, produced impressive art and architecture, and developed a unique form of writing. Around 1450 B.C., their culture disappeared, probably after a major volcanic eruption or an invasion by warlike Mycenaeans. Homer's *Iliad* and *Odyssey* describe the Mycenaean era that followed.

Classical Greek civilization began in the eighth century B.C. The great achievements of the Greeks in philosophy, mathematics, natural sciences, political thought, and the arts have influenced European civilization ever since. Greece bequeathed its legacy to Rome, known for its builders, engineers, military strategists, and lawmakers. The Roman Empire eventually reached from Britain to Persia and lasted roughly 500 years, until invasions by Germanic tribes from the north destroyed it.

During Roman times a new religion, Christianity, entered Europe from western Asia. As Rome declined, the Christian Church became the common thread binding Europeans together. It maintained schools and learning in its monasteries through the Middle Ages. In the 11th century, theological differences split Christianity into Orthodoxy in the east, led by patriarchs, and Roman Catholicism in the west, under popes.

Ottoman Turks introduced Islam to the Balkans through conquest during the 14th and 15th centuries. A hundred years later, the Protestant Reformation in northern Europe broke the unity of the Roman Catholic Church and provoked a century of wars.

Rome's greatest landmark, the Colosseum, was completed in A.D. 80; it held 50,000 spectators during gladiator fights and other events. Four stories high, this structure combines Greek esthetics with Roman building techniques.

In the 15th and 16th centuries, the Renaissance—a rebirth of arts, science, and culture—spread northward throughout the continent. Political power shifted to Western Europe, where strong nations emerged, notably England, France, Spain, and Portugal. Under powerful kings, worldwide explorations created mercantile empires, even as ideas of democracy and equality started circulating.

In the 18th century, Britain's American colonies became independent and, in the wake of the French Revolution that toppled the monarchy, Napoleon tried, but failed, to seize all of Europe. In 1815, a balance of power was reestablished among European countries until the forces of nationalism, socialism, and democracy exploded into two world wars a century later.

Following World War II, the Cold War between the U.S. and the Soviet Union replaced the old balance of power with a deadly balance of nuclear armaments, reducing Europe to lesser status. But by the time the Cold War came to an end in the 1990s, Western Europe had coalesced into the European Union. A large number of countries were also allied with the North Atlantic Treaty Organization (NATO), and Europe was embarking on a new era of economic and military cooperation.

CULTURE Next to Asia, Europe has the world's densest population. Scores of distinct ethnic groups, speaking some 40 languages, inhabit more than 40 countries, which vary in size from vast European Russia to tiny Vatican City, each with its own history and traditions. Yet Europe has a more uniform culture than any other continent. Its population is overwhelmingly of one race, Caucasian, despite the recent arrival of immigrants from Africa and Asia. Most of its languages fall into three groups with Indo-European roots: Germanic, Romance, or Slavic. One religion, Christianity, predominates in various forms, and social structures nearly everywhere are based on economic classes.

Great periods of creativity in the arts have occurred at various times all over the continent and shape its collective culture. Classical Greek sculpture and architecture are widely seen as paradigms of beauty. Gothic cathedrals of medieval France still inspire awe. Renaissance works of art, from paintings by Leonardo da Vinci in Florence to plays by Shakespeare in England, are famous worldwide. Music composed by Mozart of Austria, Beethoven of Germany, and Tchaikovsky of Russia has passed far beyond Europe. Spanish artist Pablo Picasso transformed the Western world's concept of art. By the 20th century, European culture had penetrated everywhere.

The success of America's multibillion-dollar entertainment industry makes some Europeans feel culturally threatened. American movies flood the continent; American products and lifestyles are aggressively marketed. English is becoming the preferred second language for students all over Europe. Others see the blending of cultures as an inevitable aspect of globalization and a chance to export their own pop music, plays, architecture, fashions, and gourmet foods to other countries. A more imminent worry focuses on immigrant groups established as legitimate and illegal workers, refugees, and asylum seekers, who cling to their own habits, religions, and languages. Every European society is becoming multicultural, with political as well as cultural consequences.

ECONOMY Europe is fortunate in having fertile soil, a temperate climate, ample natural resources, and a long, irregular coastline that gives most countries access to the sea and foreign trade. Navigable rivers often help the 13 landlocked countries.

Europe is currently undertaking two of the most far-reaching economic experiments in its history. While some countries in Eastern and Central Europe are still converting centrally planned, communist-style economies to the democratic market system, 25 highly developed European nations have created a powerful "eurozone" by replacing their national money with the euro, a shared currency.

The progress of many ex-Soviet bloc countries has been slower than anticipated due, in part, to a need for laws preventing corruption and abuse of the new system, and for institutions to assure sound financial management. Poland and Slovenia have been among the most successful. Russia and Belarus, on the other hand, have slipped into worsening poverty, causing some people to clamor for a return to the safety nets of communism.

The eurozone countries did not have a totally smooth transition to the single currency. The new European Central Bank could not keep the euro from losing a quarter of its value against the U.S. dollar in its first three years; however, in recent years, the euro has strengthened considerably and the advantages of a shared currency are increasingly tangible: Banking has become faster and easier, and the newly enlarged bond market has led to many corporate reforms and important mergers. A majority of voters in Britain, Sweden, and Denmark, called "euroskeptics," refused to adopt the euro in 1999 like other European Union members. But they will probably vote to do so as the eurozone grows in strength and influence.

Meanwhile, the advantages offered by the European Union encourage outside countries to practice the tough economic and fiscal policies that are prerequisites for membership. Ten countries were admitted in 2004: Estonia, Latvia, Lithuania, Cyprus, Malta, the Czech Republic, Hungary, Poland, Slovakia, and Slovenia. With the anticipated addition of Bulgaria and Romania in 2007, the European Union will have a population of nearly half a billion, firmly cementing it as one of the largest economies in the world. Many Europeans speculate that in time the euro may rival the U.S. dollar as the principal global currency.

Europe: Physical and Political
A commonly accepted division between Asia and Europe–here marked by a green line–is formed by the Ural Mountains, Ural River, Caspian Sea, Caucasus Mountains, and the Black Sea with its outlets, the Bosporus and Dardanelles.
Azimuthal Equidistant Projection
SCALE 1:18,036,000
1 CENTIMETER = 180 KILOMETERS; 1 INCH = 284 MILES
KILOMETERS
STATUTE MILES
International boundary
ARCTIC CIRCLE
NORWEGIAN SEA
ATLANTIC OCEAN
NORTH SEA
BARENTS SEA
BALTIC SEA
GULF OF BOTHNIA
BLACK SEA
CASPIAN SEA
Caspian Sea: Surface elevation -28 m (-92 ft) Lowest point in Europe
SEA OF AZOV
MEDITERRANEAN SEA
TYRRHENIAN SEA
IONIAN SEA
ADRIATIC SEA
AEGEAN SEA
SEA OF CRETE
LIGURIAN SEA
BALEARIC SEA
ALBORAN SEA
BAY OF BISCAY
English Channel
Strait of Gibraltar
Gulf of Sidra
PERSIAN GULF
ARAL SEA
ICELAND
Reykjanes
Hekla
Surtsey
Vestmannaeyjar
Faroe Islands
Shetland Islands
Orkney Islands
BRITISH ISLES
IRELAND
GREAT BRITAIN
Grampian Mts.
The Pennines
Snowdon
Cambrian Mts.
Carrantuohill
Land's End
Channel Islands
Normandy
Armorican Massif
PARIS BASIN
AQUITAINE BASIN
MASSIF CENTRAL
PYRENEES
IBERIAN PENINSULA
Cantabrian Mountains
Sierra Morena
Baetic Mountains
Mulhacén
Cape Finisterre
Cape St. Vincent
BALEARIC ISLANDS
CORSICA
SARDINIA
SICILY
Etna
Vesuvius
MALTESE ISLANDS
APENNINES
ALPS
Mont Blanc
Matterhorn
Grossglockner
Jura Mts.
Vosges
Black Forest
Ardennes
Frisian Islands
JUTLAND
Kattegat
Skagerrak
SCANDINAVIA
Kebnekaise
Lofoten
North Cape
Finnmark Plateau
KOLA PENINSULA
Murman Coast
Kanin Pen.
Gotland
Öland
Åland Is.
Hiiumaa
Saaremaa
Gulf of Riga
Lake Ladoga
Lake Onega
NORTHERN EUROPEAN PLAIN
CARPATHIAN MOUNTAINS
Great Hungarian Plain
Transylvanian Alps
DINARIC ALPS
BALKAN PENINSULA
Balkan Mountains
Rhodope Mts.
Olympus
Pindus Mts.
PELOPONNESUS
CRETE
RHODES
CYPRUS
Dodecanese
Cyclades
IONIAN ISLANDS
Sea of Marmara
Bosporus
ANATOLIA
CRIMEA
Crimean Mts.
Danube River Delta
Volyn-Podolian Upland
Dnieper Upland
Dnieper Lowland
Central Russian Upland
Valdai Hills
Source of the Volga
Volga Upland
Donets Ridge
Kuban Lowland
Stavropol' Plateau
Yergeni Hills
CAUCASUS MOUNTAINS
El'brus
Highest point in Europe
Lesser Caucasus
Mount Ararat
MESOPOTAMIA
SYRIAN DESERT
Dead Sea
World's lowest point
Levant Coast
SUEZ CANAL
Caspian Depression
Absheron Pen.
Volga River Delta
Obshchiy Syrt
Mugodzhar Hills
URAL MOUNTAINS
WEST SIBERIAN PLAIN
Timan Ridge
Northern Uvals
Upper Kama Upland
Malozemel'skaya Tundra
Bol'shezemel'skaya Tundra
ATLAS MOUNTAINS
SAHARA
AFRICA
ASIA
ARABIAN PENINSULA

Azimuthal Equidistant Projection
SCALE 1:18,036,000
1 CENTIMETER = 180 KILOMETERS; 1 INCH = 284 MILES
KILOMETERS
STATUTE MILES
Small country
A commonly accepted division between Asia and Europe—here marked by a green line—is formed by the Ural Mountains, Ural River, Caspian Sea, Caucasus Mountains, and the Black Sea with its outlets, the Bosporus and Dardanelles.
Meridian of Greenwich (London)
Longitude East 5° of Greenwich
5° Longitude West of Greenwich
ARCTIC CIRCLE
NORWEGIAN SEA
ATLANTIC OCEAN
NORTH SEA
BLACK SEA
CASPIAN SEA
MEDITERRANEAN SEA
ICELAND
NORWAY
SWEDEN
FINLAND
RUSSIA
ESTONIA
LATVIA
LITHUANIA
BELARUS
UKRAINE
POLAND
GERMANY
FRANCE
SPAIN
PORTUGAL
ITALY
UNITED KINGDOM
IRELAND
GREECE
TURKEY
KAZAKHSTAN
UZBEKISTAN
TURKMENISTAN
IRAN
IRAQ
SYRIA
SAUDI ARABIA
EGYPT
LIBYA
TUNISIA
ALGERIA
MOROCCO
ASIA
AFRICA
MOSKVA (Moscow)
LONDON
PARIS
BERLIN
ROMA
MADRID

Denmark

KINGDOM OF DENMARK

AREA 43,098 sq km (16,640 sq mi)
POPULATION 5,418,000
CAPITAL Copenhagen 1,066,000
RELIGION Evangelical Lutheran
LANGUAGE Danish, Faroese, Greenlandic, German
LITERACY 100%
LIFE EXPECTANCY 77 years
GDP PER CAPITA $44,593
ECONOMY **IND:** iron, steel, nonferrous metals, chemicals **AGR:** barley, wheat, potatoes, sugar beets; pork; fish **EXP:** machinery and instruments, meat and meat products, dairy products, fish

Latvia

REPUBLIC OF LATVIA

AREA 64,589 sq km (24,938 sq mi)
POPULATION 2,300,000
CAPITAL Riga 733,000
RELIGION Lutheran, Roman Catholic, Russian Orthodox
LANGUAGE Latvian (official), Russian
LITERACY 100%
LIFE EXPECTANCY 72 years
GDP PER CAPITA $5,876
ECONOMY **IND:** buses, vans, street and railroad cars, synthetic fibers **AGR:** grain, sugar beets, potatoes, vegetables; beef; fish **EXP:** wood and wood products, machinery and equipment, metals, textiles

Norway

KINGDOM OF NORWAY

AREA 323,758 sq km (125,004 sq mi)
POPULATION 4,620,000
CAPITAL Oslo 795,000
RELIGION Church of Norway (Lutheran)
LANGUAGE Norwegian (official)
LITERACY 100%
LIFE EXPECTANCY 80 years
GDP PER CAPITA $54,383
ECONOMY **IND:** petroleum and gas, food processing, shipbuilding, pulp and paper products **AGR:** barley, wheat, potatoes; pork; fish **EXP:** petroleum and petroleum products, machinery and equipment, metals, chemicals

Sweden

KINGDOM OF SWEDEN

AREA 449,964 sq km (173,732 sq mi)
POPULATION 9,029,000
CAPITAL Stockholm 1,697,000
RELIGION Lutheran
LANGUAGE Swedish
LITERACY 99%
LIFE EXPECTANCY 81 years
GDP PER CAPITA $38,457
ECONOMY **IND:** iron and steel, precision equipment, wood pulp and paper products, processed foods **AGR:** barley, wheat, sugar beets; meat **EXP:** machinery, motor vehicles, paper products, pulp and wood

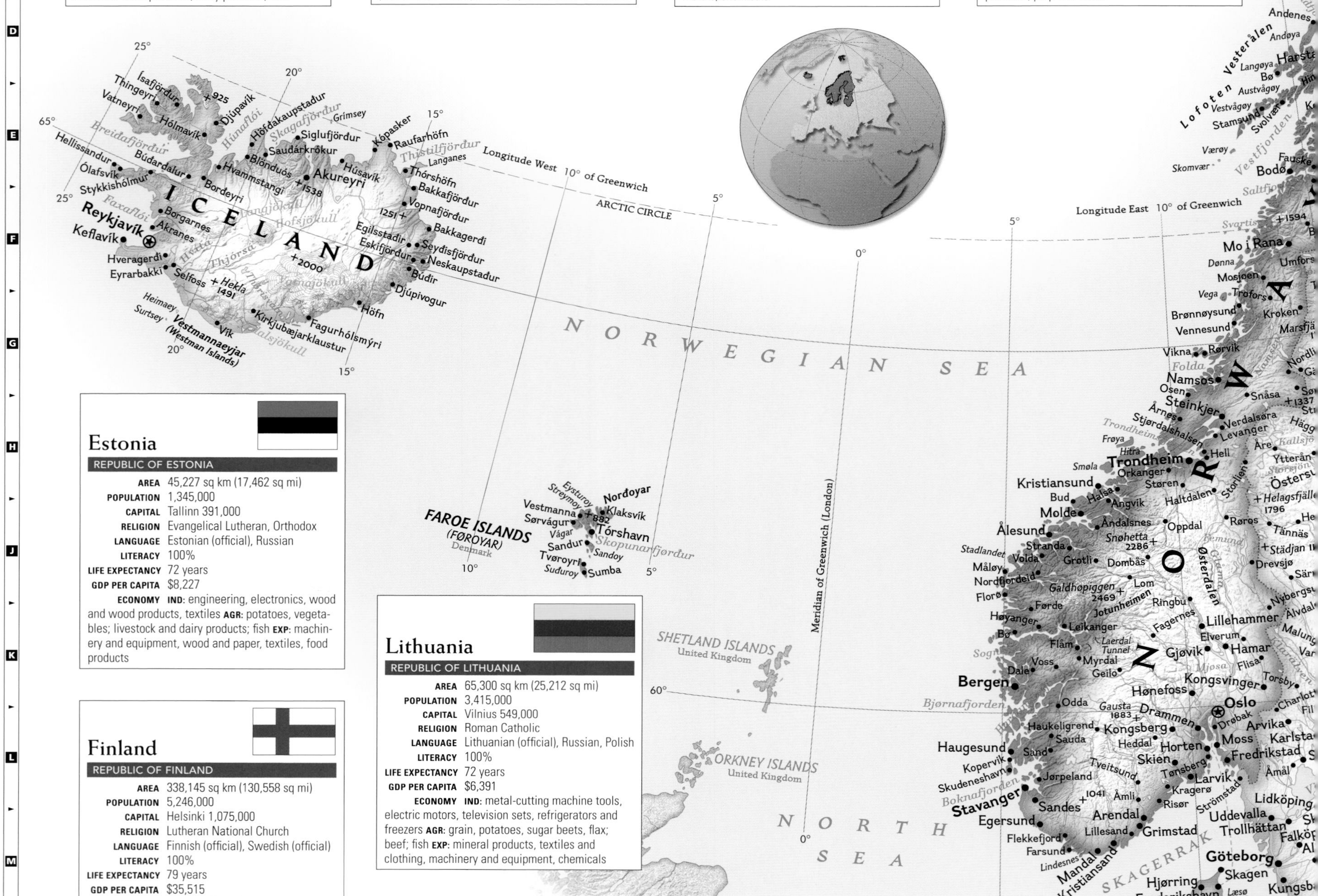

Estonia

REPUBLIC OF ESTONIA

AREA 45,227 sq km (17,462 sq mi)
POPULATION 1,345,000
CAPITAL Tallinn 391,000
RELIGION Evangelical Lutheran, Orthodox
LANGUAGE Estonian (official), Russian
LITERACY 100%
LIFE EXPECTANCY 72 years
GDP PER CAPITA $8,227
ECONOMY **IND:** engineering, electronics, wood and wood products, textiles **AGR:** potatoes, vegetables; livestock and dairy products; fish **EXP:** machinery and equipment, wood and paper, textiles, food products

Lithuania

REPUBLIC OF LITHUANIA

AREA 65,300 sq km (25,212 sq mi)
POPULATION 3,415,000
CAPITAL Vilnius 549,000
RELIGION Roman Catholic
LANGUAGE Lithuanian (official), Russian, Polish
LITERACY 100%
LIFE EXPECTANCY 72 years
GDP PER CAPITA $6,391
ECONOMY **IND:** metal-cutting machine tools, electric motors, television sets, refrigerators and freezers **AGR:** grain, potatoes, sugar beets, flax; beef; fish **EXP:** mineral products, textiles and clothing, machinery and equipment, chemicals

Finland

REPUBLIC OF FINLAND

AREA 338,145 sq km (130,558 sq mi)
POPULATION 5,246,000
CAPITAL Helsinki 1,075,000
RELIGION Lutheran National Church
LANGUAGE Finnish (official), Swedish (official)
LITERACY 100%
LIFE EXPECTANCY 79 years
GDP PER CAPITA $35,515
ECONOMY **IND:** metals and metal products, electronics, machinery and scientific instruments, shipbuilding **AGR:** barley, wheat, sugar beets, potatoes; dairy cattle; fish **EXP:** machinery and equipment, chemicals, metals, timber

Iceland

REPUBLIC OF ICELAND

AREA 103,000 sq km (39,769 sq mi)
POPULATION 295,000
CAPITAL Reykjavík 184,000
RELIGION Lutheran Church of Iceland
LANGUAGE Icelandic, English, Nordic languages
LITERACY 100%
LIFE EXPECTANCY 81 years
GDP PER CAPITA $41,913
ECONOMY **IND:** fish processing, aluminum smelting, ferrosilicon production, geothermal power **AGR:** potatoes, green vegetables; mutton; fish **EXP:** fish and fish products, aluminum, animal products, ferrosilicon

Temperature and Precipitation

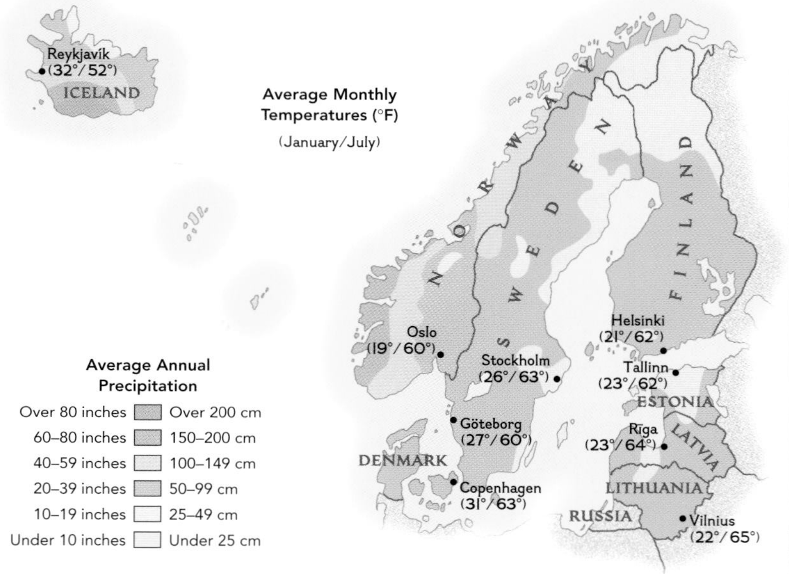

Faroe Islands (Denmark)

SOVEREIGN LOCAL

FAROE ISLANDS

AREA 1,399 sq km (540 sq mi)
POPULATION 50,000
CAPITAL Tórshavn 18,000
RELIGION Evangelical Lutheran
LANGUAGE Faroese (derived from Old Norse), Danish
LITERACY NA
LIFE EXPECTANCY 79 years
GDP PER CAPITA $22,000
ECONOMY **IND:** fishing, fish processing, small ship repair and refurbishment, handicrafts **AGR:** milk, potatoes, vegetables; sheep; salmon **EXP:** fish and fish products, stamps, ships

Azimuthal Equidistant Projection

SCALE 1:8,024,000
1 CENTIMETER = 80 KILOMETERS; 1 INCH = 127 MILES

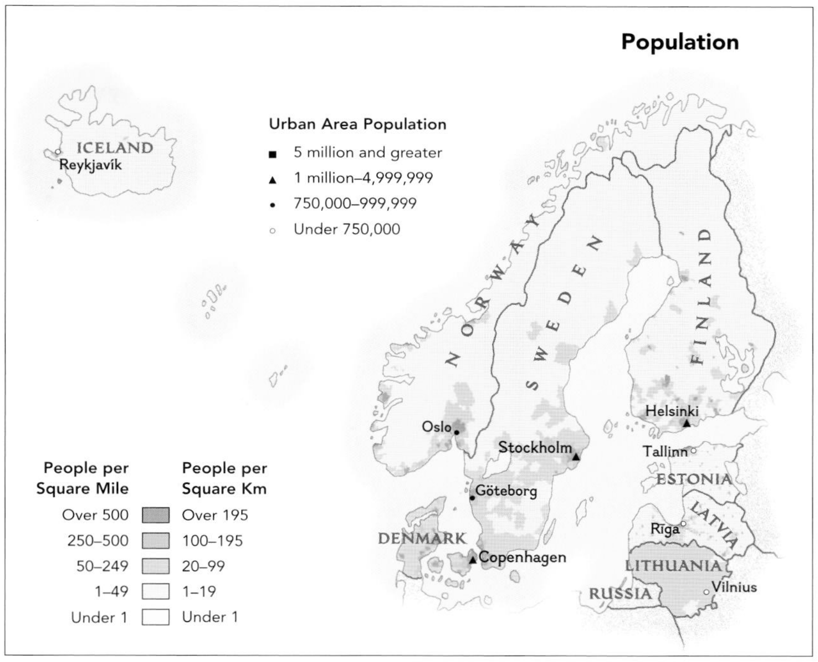

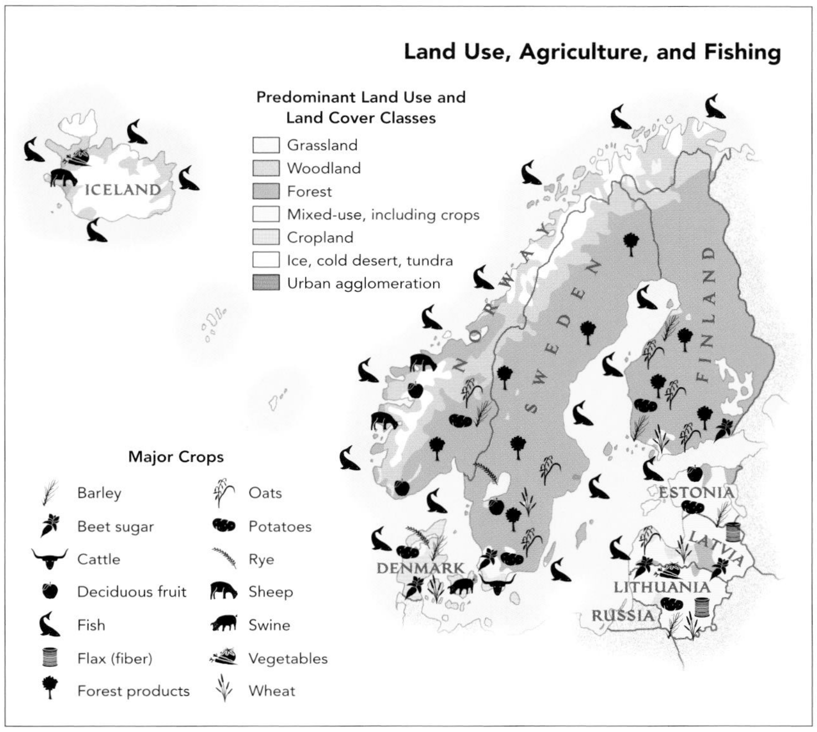

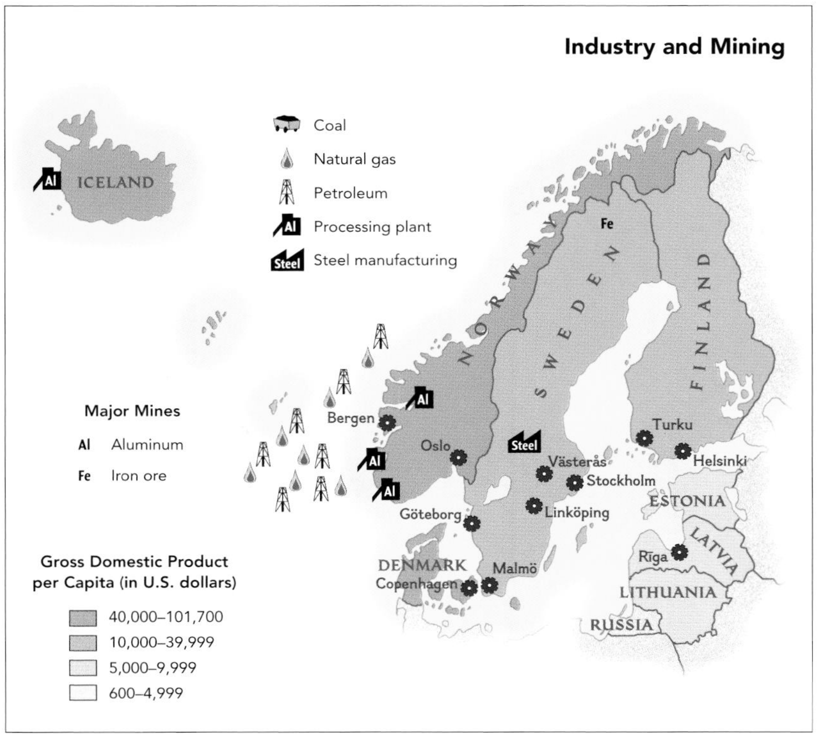

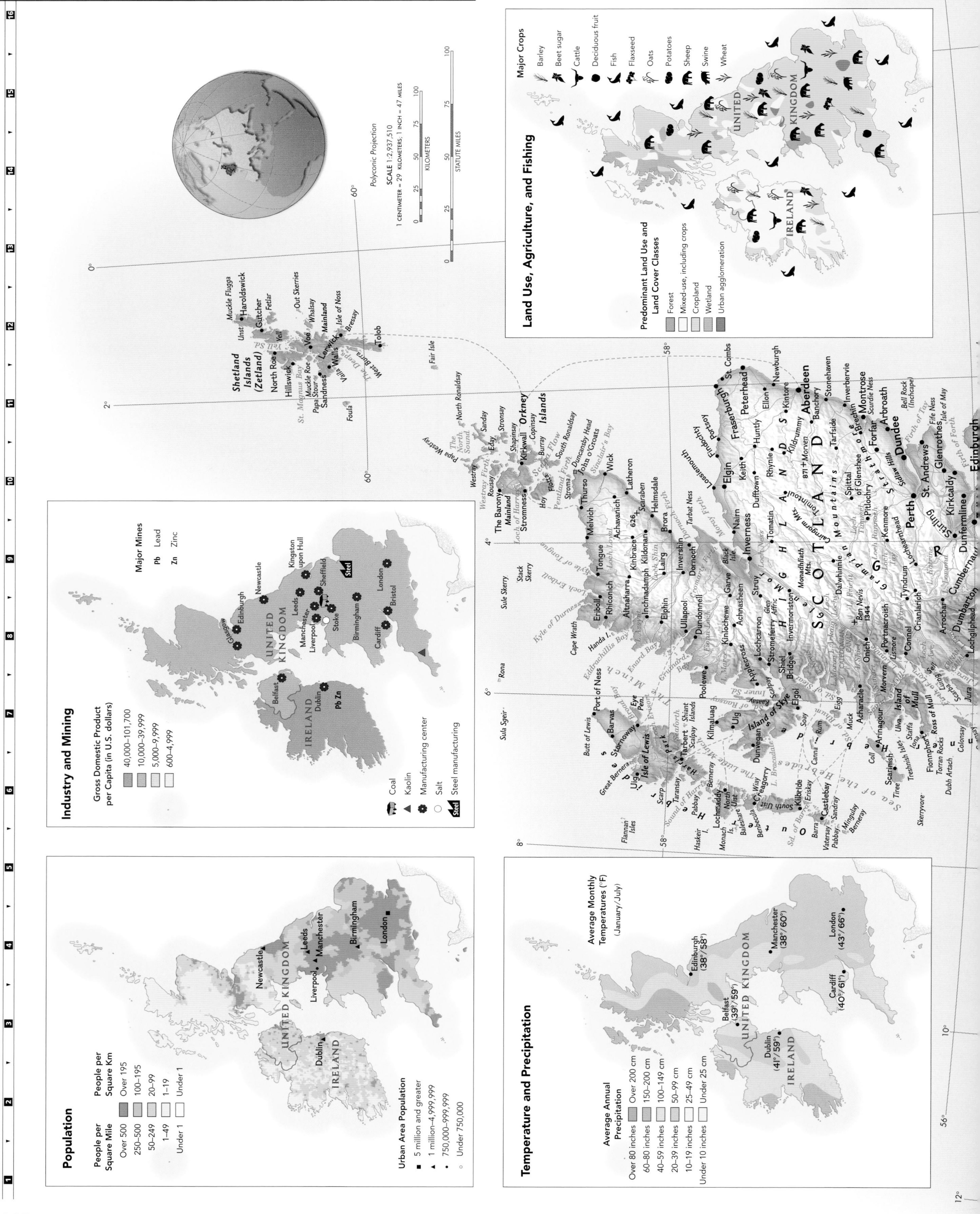
Population
People per Square Mile
Over 500
250–500
50–249
1–49
Under 1
People per Square Km
Over 195
100–195
20–99
1–19
Under 1
Urban Area Population
5 million and greater
1 million–4,999,999
750,000–999,999
Under 750,000
Industry and Mining
Gross Domestic Product per Capita (in U.S. dollars)
40,000–101,700
10,000–39,999
5,000–9,999
600–4,999
Coal
Kaolin
Manufacturing center
Salt
Steel manufacturing
Major Mines
Pb Lead
Zn Zinc
Temperature and Precipitation
Average Annual Precipitation
Over 80 inches Over 200 cm
60–80 inches 150–200 cm
40–59 inches 100–149 cm
20–39 inches 50–99 cm
10–19 inches 25–49 cm
Under 10 inches Under 25 cm
Average Monthly Temperatures (°F) (January/July)
Edinburgh (38°/58°)
Belfast (39°/59°)
Dublin (41°/59°)
Manchester (38°/60°)
Cardiff (40°/61°)
London (43°/66°)
Land Use, Agriculture, and Fishing
Predominant Land Use and Land Cover Classes
Forest
Mixed-use, including crops
Cropland
Wetland
Urban agglomeration
Major Crops
Barley
Beet sugar
Cattle
Deciduous fruit
Fish
Flaxseed
Oats
Potatoes
Sheep
Swine
Wheat
Polyconic Projection
SCALE 1:2,937,510
1 CENTIMETER = 29 KILOMETERS; 1 INCH = 47 MILES
KILOMETERS
STATUTE MILES
UNITED KINGDOM
IRELAND
SCOTLAND
HIGHLANDS
Shetland Islands (Zetland)
Orkney Islands
Outer Hebrides
Isle of Lewis
Island of Skye
Aberdeen
Dundee
Perth
Inverness
Edinburgh
Glasgow
Newcastle
Leeds
Manchester
Liverpool
Sheffield
Birmingham
London
Bristol
Cardiff
Belfast
Dublin

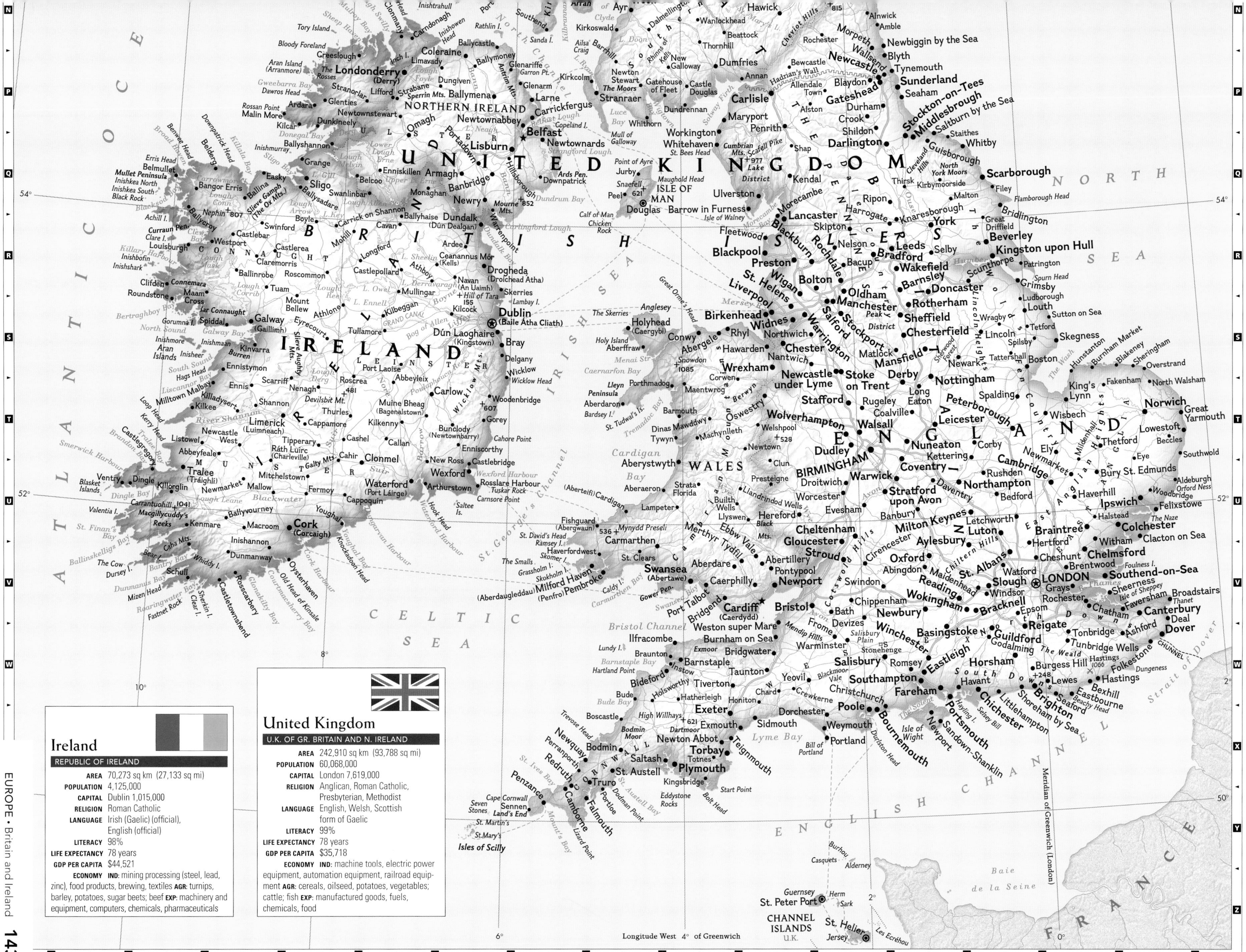

Ireland

REPUBLIC OF IRELAND

AREA 70,273 sq km (27,133 sq mi)
POPULATION 4,125,000
CAPITAL Dublin 1,015,000
RELIGION Roman Catholic
LANGUAGE Irish (Gaelic) (official), English (official)
LITERACY 98%
LIFE EXPECTANCY 78 years
GDP PER CAPITA $44,521
ECONOMY **IND:** mining processing (steel, lead, zinc), food products, brewing, textiles **AGR:** turnips, barley, potatoes, sugar beets; beef **EXP:** machinery and equipment, computers, chemicals, pharmaceuticals

United Kingdom

U.K. OF GR. BRITAIN AND N. IRELAND

AREA 242,910 sq km (93,788 sq mi)
POPULATION 60,068,000
CAPITAL London 7,619,000
RELIGION Anglican, Roman Catholic, Presbyterian, Methodist
LANGUAGE English, Welsh, Scottish form of Gaelic
LITERACY 99%
LIFE EXPECTANCY 78 years
GDP PER CAPITA $35,718
ECONOMY **IND:** machine tools, electric power equipment, automation equipment, railroad equipment **AGR:** cereals, oilseed, potatoes, vegetables; cattle; fish **EXP:** manufactured goods, fuels, chemicals, food

Portugal

PORTUGUESE REPUBLIC

AREA 92,345 sq km (35,655 sq mi)
POPULATION 10,576,000
CAPITAL Lisbon 1,962,000
RELIGION Roman Catholic
LANGUAGE Portuguese (official), Mirandese (official)
LITERACY 93%
LIFE EXPECTANCY 77 years
GDP PER CAPITA $16,063
ECONOMY **IND:** textiles and footwear, wood pulp, paper, and cork, metals and metalworking, oil refining **AGR:** grain, potatoes, tomatoes, olives; sheep; fish **EXP:** clothing and footwear, machinery, chemicals, cork and paper products

Spain

KINGDOM OF SPAIN

AREA 505,988 sq km (195,363 sq mi)
POPULATION 43,484,000
CAPITAL Madrid 5,103,000
RELIGION Roman Catholic
LANGUAGE Castilian Spanish (official), Catalan, Galician, Basque
LITERACY 98%
LIFE EXPECTANCY 80 years
GDP PER CAPITA $24,386
ECONOMY **IND:** textiles and apparel, food and beverages, metals and metal manufactures, chemicals **AGR:** grain, vegetables, olives, wine grapes; beef; fish **EXP:** machinery, motor vehicles, foodstuffs, pharmaceuticals

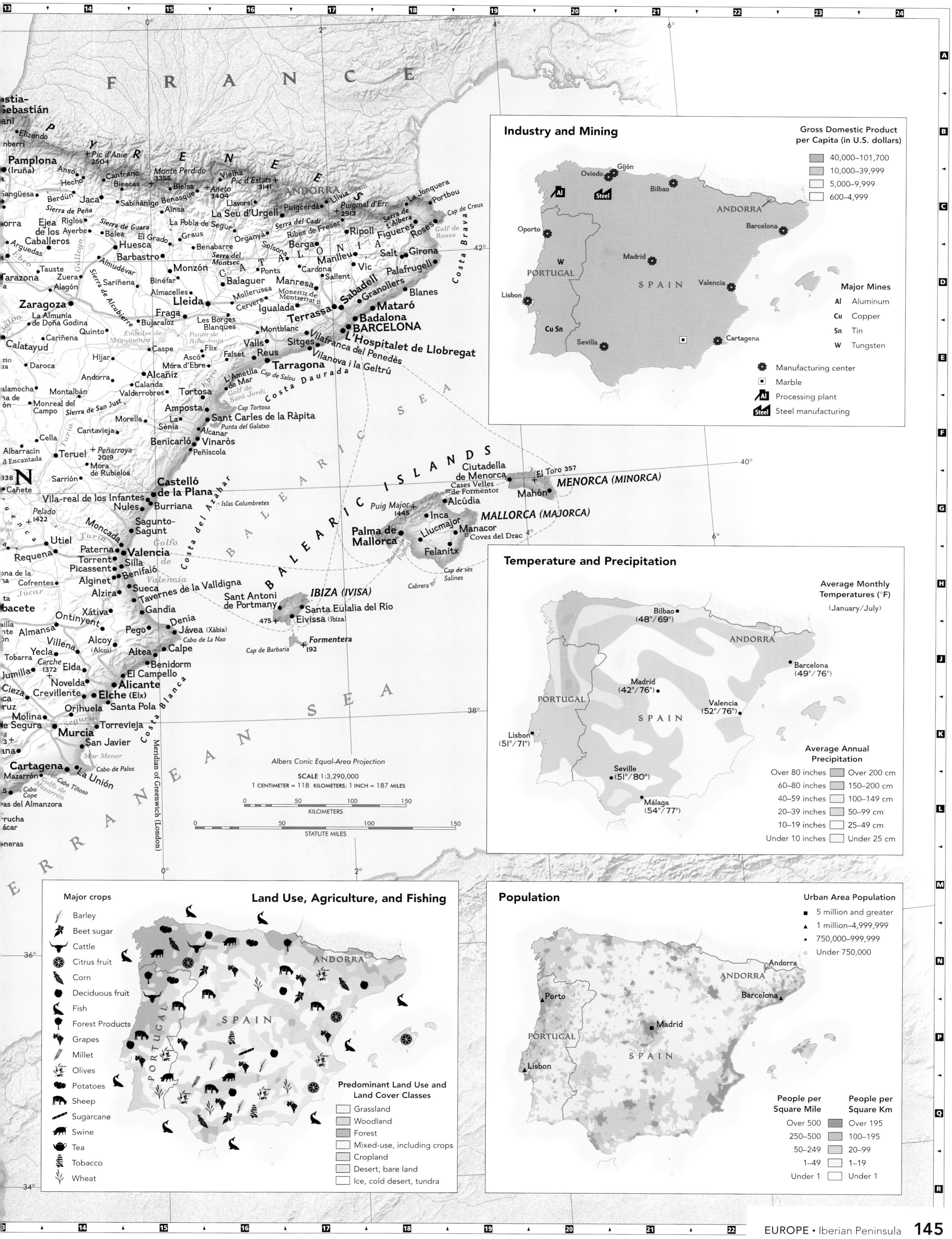
FRANCE
PYRENEES
Pamplona (Iruña)
Pic d'Anie 2504
Monte Perdido 3355
Aneto 3404
Pic d'Estats 3141
ANDORRA
La Seu d'Urgell
Puigcerdà
Puigmal d'Err 2913
Jaca
Huesca
Barbastro
Monzón
Ejea de los Caballeros
Tarazona
Zaragoza
La Almunia de Doña Godina
Cariñena
Calatayud
Daroca
Lleida
Fraga
Caspe
Alcañiz
Balaguer
Manresa
Terrassa
Sabadell
Granollers
Mataró
Badalona
BARCELONA
L'Hospitalet de Llobregat
Vilafranca del Penedès
Vilanova i la Geltrú
Sitges
Valls
Reus
Tarragona
Cambrils
Costa Daurada
Tortosa
Amposta
Sant Carles de la Ràpita
Vinaròs
Benicarló
Peñíscola
Girona
Figueres
Roses
Costa Brava
Vic
Ripoll
Olot
Palafrugell
Blanes
Teruel
Peñarroya 2019
Castelló de la Plana
Vila-real de los Infantes
Nules
Burriana
Sagunto-Sagunt
Costa del Azahar
Islas Columbretes
Valencia
Paterna
Torrent
Picassent
Silla
Alginet
Sueca
Alzira
Tavernes de la Valldigna
Gandia
Xàtiva
Ontinyent
Almansa
Villena
Alcoy (Alcoi)
Denia
Jávea (Xàbia)
Cabo de La Nao
Calpe
Altea
Benidorm
El Campello
Alicante
Elche (Elx)
Santa Pola
Costa Blanca
Novelda
Elda
Yecla
Jumilla
Crevillente
Orihuela
Torrevieja
Molina de Segura
Murcia
San Javier
Mar Menor
Cabo de Palos
Cartagena
La Unión
Mazarrón
Requena
Utiel
Moncada
Golfo de Valencia
BALEARIC ISLANDS
MENORCA (MINORCA)
Ciutadella de Menorca
Mahón
El Toro 357
MALLORCA (MAJORCA)
Palma de Mallorca
Puig Major 1445
Alcúdia
Inca
Llucmajor
Manacor
Felanitx
Cabrera
IBIZA (IVISA)
Sant Antoni de Portmany
Santa Eulalia del Río
Eivissa (Ibiza)
Formentera
BALEARIC SEA
MEDITERRANEAN SEA
Meridian of Greenwich (London)
Albers Conic Equal-Area Projection
SCALE 1:3,290,000
1 CENTIMETER = 118 KILOMETERS; 1 INCH = 187 MILES
KILOMETERS
STATUTE MILES
Industry and Mining
Gross Domestic Product per Capita (in U.S. dollars)
40,000–101,700
10,000–39,999
5,000–9,999
600–4,999
Major Mines
Al Aluminum
Cu Copper
Sn Tin
W Tungsten
Manufacturing center
Marble
Processing plant
Steel manufacturing
Oviedo
Gijón
Bilbao
Oporto
Madrid
Barcelona
Valencia
Lisbon
Sevilla
Cartagena
PORTUGAL
SPAIN
Temperature and Precipitation
Average Monthly Temperatures (°F) (January/July)
Bilbao (48°/69°)
Barcelona (49°/76°)
Madrid (42°/76°)
Valencia (52°/76°)
Lisbon (51°/71°)
Seville (51°/80°)
Málaga (54°/77°)
Average Annual Precipitation
Over 80 inches | Over 200 cm
60–80 inches | 150–200 cm
40–59 inches | 100–149 cm
20–39 inches | 50–99 cm
10–19 inches | 25–49 cm
Under 10 inches | Under 25 cm
Land Use, Agriculture, and Fishing
Major crops
Barley
Beet sugar
Cattle
Citrus fruit
Corn
Deciduous fruit
Fish
Forest Products
Grapes
Millet
Olives
Potatoes
Sheep
Sugarcane
Swine
Tea
Tobacco
Wheat
Predominant Land Use and Land Cover Classes
Grassland
Woodland
Forest
Mixed-use, including crops
Cropland
Desert, bare land
Ice, cold desert, tundra
Population
Urban Area Population
5 million and greater
1 million–4,999,999
750,000–999,999
Under 750,000
Andorra
Porto
Barcelona
Madrid
Lisbon
People per Square Mile | People per Square Km
Over 500 | Over 195
250–500 | 100–195
50–249 | 20–99
1–49 | 1–19
Under 1 | Under 1

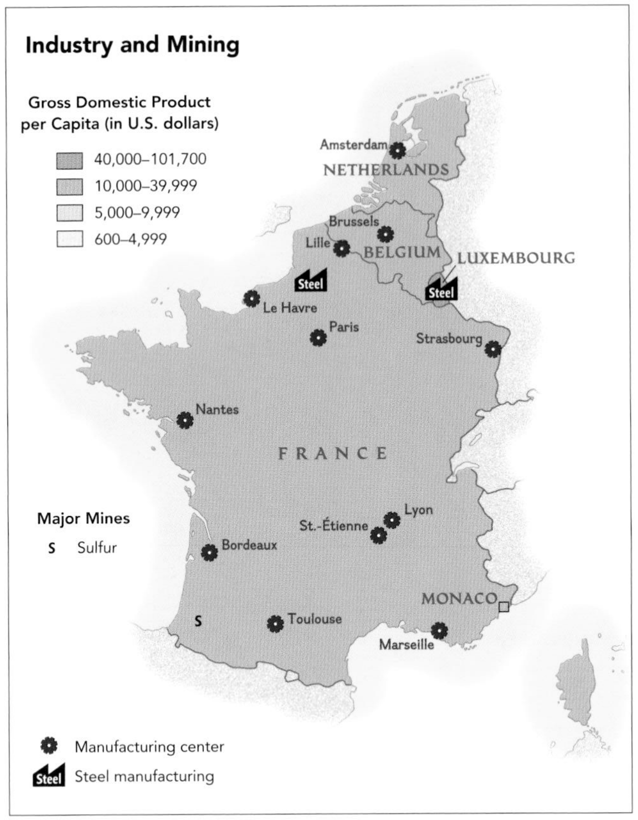

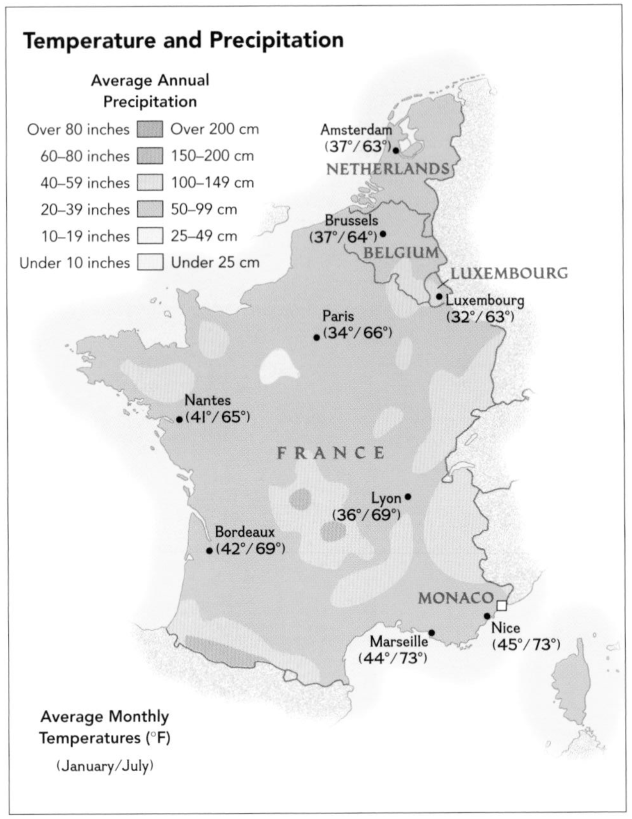

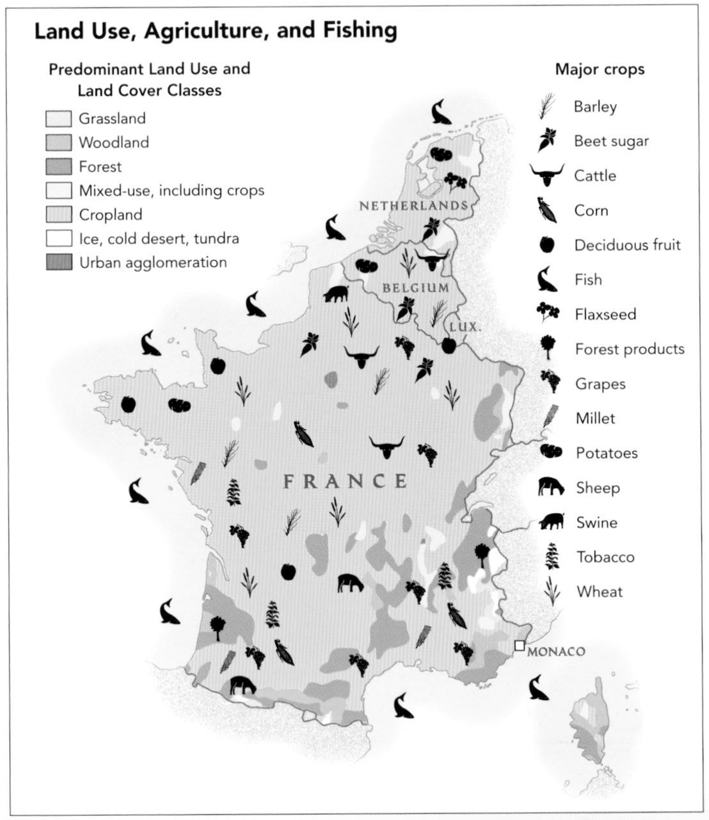

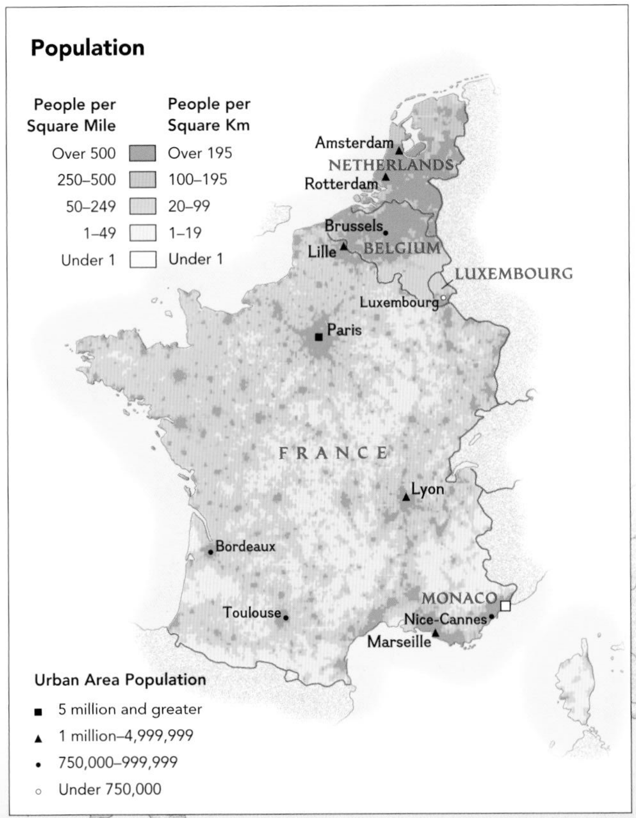

Belgium

KINGDOM OF BELGIUM

AREA 30,528 sq km (11,787 sq mi)
POPULATION 10,458,000
CAPITAL Brussels 998,000
RELIGION Roman Catholic, Protestant
LANGUAGE Dutch (official), French (official), German (official)
LITERACY 98%
LIFE EXPECTANCY 79 years
GDP PER CAPITA $33,879
ECONOMY **IND:** engineering and metal products, motor vehicle assembly, transportation equipment, scientific instruments **AGR:** sugar beets, fresh vegetables, fruits, grain; beef **EXP:** machinery and equipment, chemicals, diamonds, metals and metal products

France

FRENCH REPUBLIC

AREA 543,965 sq km (210,026 sq mi)
POPULATION 60,742,000
CAPITAL Paris 9,794,000
RELIGION Roman Catholic, Muslim
LANGUAGE French
LITERACY 99%
LIFE EXPECTANCY 80 years
GDP PER CAPITA $32,984
ECONOMY **IND:** machinery, chemicals, automobiles, metallurgy **AGR:** wheat, cereals, sugar beets, potatoes; beef; fish **EXP:** machinery and transportation equipment, aircraft, plastics, chemicals

Luxembourg

GRAND DUCHY OF LUXEMBOURG

AREA 2,586 sq km (998 sq mi)
POPULATION 457,000
CAPITAL Luxembourg 77,000
RELIGION Roman Catholic
LANGUAGE Luxembourgish, German, French
LITERACY 100%
LIFE EXPECTANCY 78 years
GDP PER CAPITA $69,423
ECONOMY **IND:** banking, iron and steel, food processing **AGR:** barley, oats, potatoes; livestock products **EXP:** machinery, steel products, chemicals

Netherlands

KINGDOM OF THE NETHERLANDS

AREA 41,528 sq km (16,034 sq mi)
POPULATION 16,296,000
CAPITAL Amsterdam 1,145,000
RELIGION Roman Catholic, Dutch Reformed, Calvinist, Muslim
LANGUAGE Dutch (official), Frisian (official)
LITERACY 99%
LIFE EXPECTANCY 79 years
GDP PER CAPITA $35,683
ECONOMY **IND:** agro-industries, metal and engineering products, electrical machinery and equipment, chemicals **AGR:** grains, potatoes, sugar beets, fruits; livestock **EXP:** machinery and equipment, chemicals, fuels, foodstuffs

Austria

REPUBLIC OF AUSTRIA

AREA 83,858 sq km (32,378 sq mi)
POPULATION 8,151,000
CAPITAL Vienna 2,179,000
RELIGION Roman Catholic
LANGUAGE German (official), Slovene, Croatian, Hungarian
LITERACY 98%
LIFE EXPECTANCY 79 years
GDP PER CAPITA $35,777
ECONOMY **IND:** construction, machinery, vehicles and parts, food **AGR:** grains, potatoes, sugar beets, wine; dairy products; lumber **EXP:** machinery and equipment, motor vehicles and parts, paper and paperboard, metal goods

Czech Republic

CZECH REPUBLIC

AREA 78,866 sq km (30,450 sq mi)
POPULATION 10,212,000
CAPITAL Prague 1,170,000
RELIGION Roman Catholic
LANGUAGE Czech
LITERACY 100%
LIFE EXPECTANCY 75 years
GDP PER CAPITA $10,462
ECONOMY **IND:** metallurgy, machinery and equipment, motor vehicles, glass **AGR:** wheat, potatoes, sugar beets, hops; pigs **EXP:** machinery and transport equipment, chemicals, raw materials and fuel

Germany

FEDERAL REPUBLIC OF GERMANY

AREA 357,022 sq km (137,847 sq mi)
POPULATION 82,490,000
CAPITAL Berlin 3,327,000
RELIGION Protestant, Roman Catholic
LANGUAGE German
LITERACY 99%
LIFE EXPECTANCY 79 years
GDP PER CAPITA $33,162
ECONOMY **IND:** iron, steel, coal, cement **AGR:** potatoes, wheat, barley, sugar beets; cattle **EXP:** machinery, vehicles, chemicals, metals and manufactures

Land Use, Agriculture, and Fishing

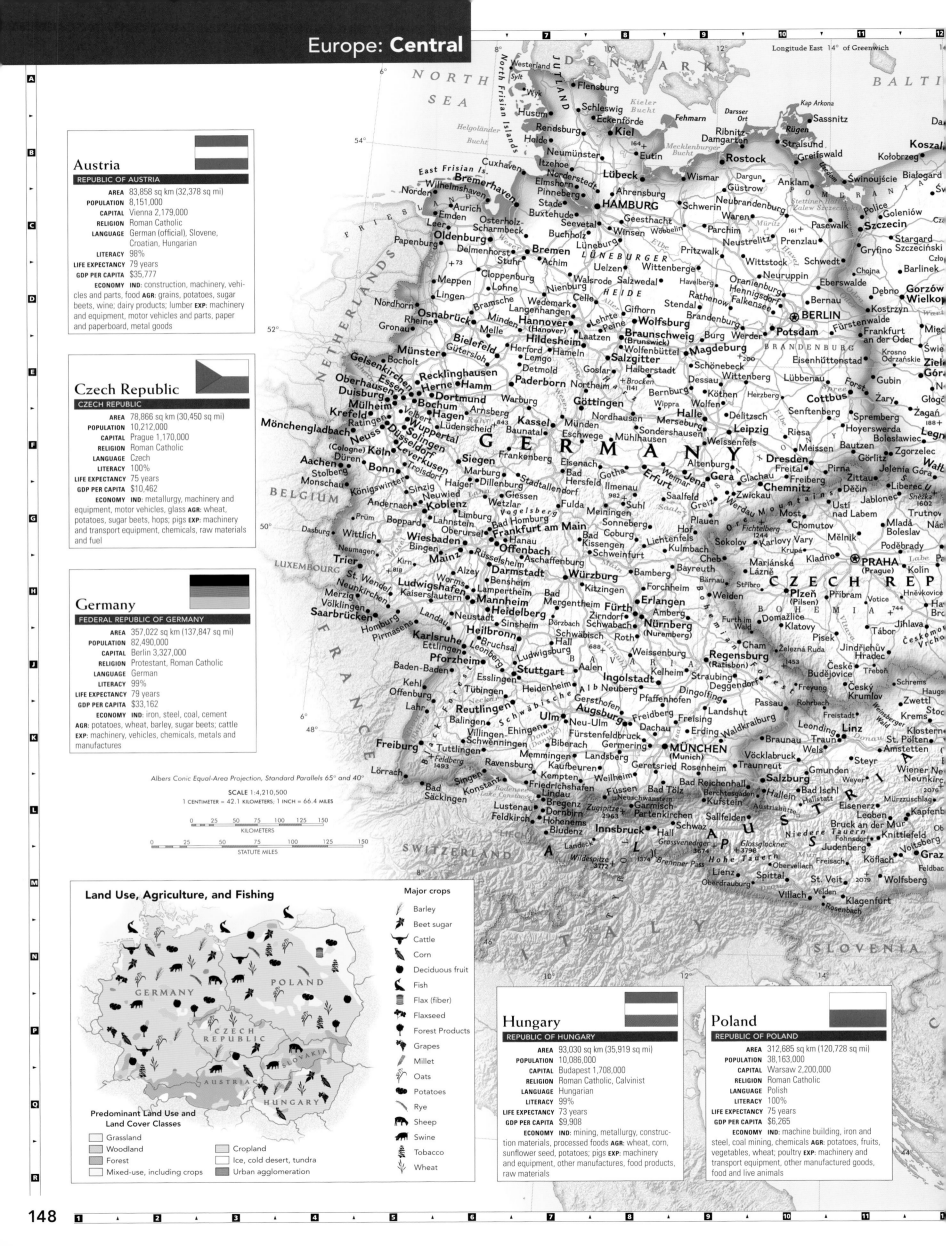

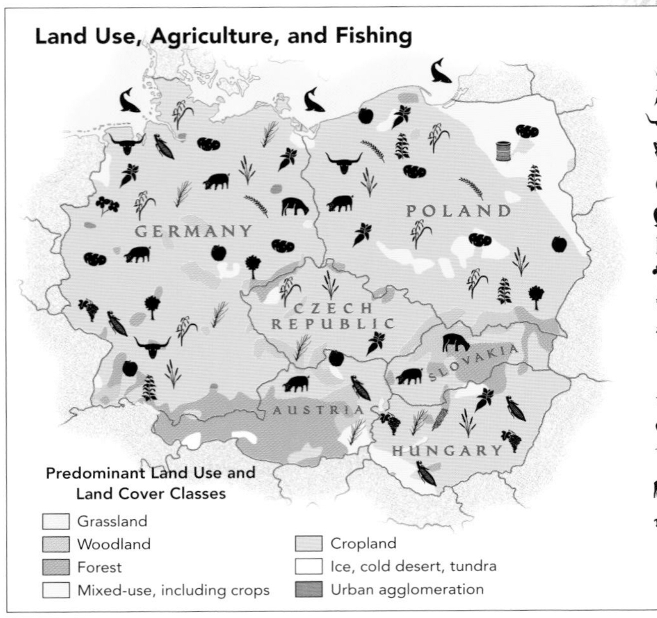

Hungary

REPUBLIC OF HUNGARY

AREA 93,030 sq km (35,919 sq mi)
POPULATION 10,086,000
CAPITAL Budapest 1,708,000
RELIGION Roman Catholic, Calvinist
LANGUAGE Hungarian
LITERACY 99%
LIFE EXPECTANCY 73 years
GDP PER CAPITA $9,908
ECONOMY **IND:** mining, metallurgy, construction materials, processed foods **AGR:** wheat, corn, sunflower seed, potatoes; pigs **EXP:** machinery and equipment, other manufactures, food products, raw materials

Poland

REPUBLIC OF POLAND

AREA 312,685 sq km (120,728 sq mi)
POPULATION 38,163,000
CAPITAL Warsaw 2,200,000
RELIGION Roman Catholic
LANGUAGE Polish
LITERACY 100%
LIFE EXPECTANCY 75 years
GDP PER CAPITA $6,265
ECONOMY **IND:** machine building, iron and steel, coal mining, chemicals **AGR:** potatoes, fruits, vegetables, wheat; poultry **EXP:** machinery and transport equipment, other manufactured goods, food and live animals

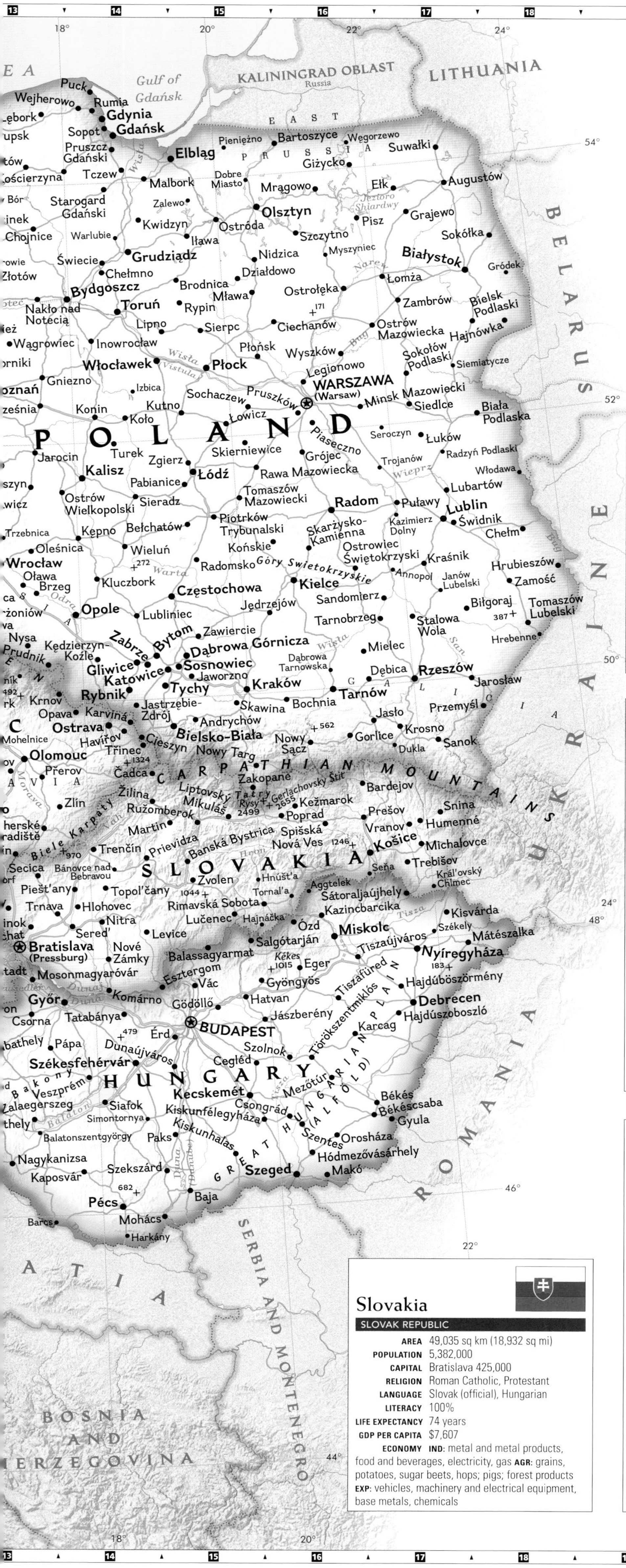

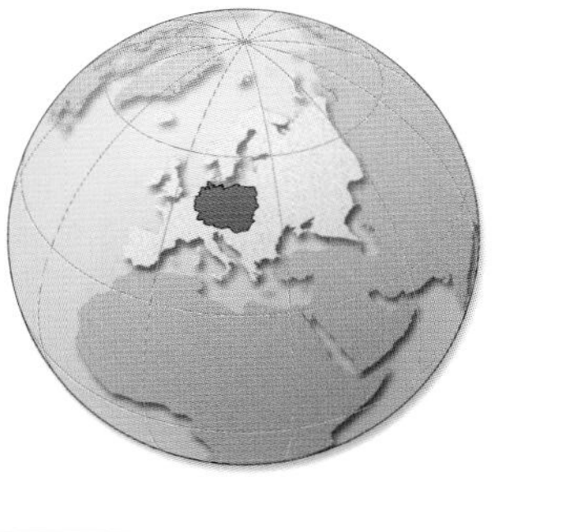

Industry and Mining

Gross Domestic Product per Capita (in U.S. dollars)

- 40,000–101,700
- 10,000–39,999
- 5,000–9,999
- 600–4,999

Major Mines

- Al Aluminum
- Cu Copper
- W Tungsten

- Coal
- Kaolin
- Manufacturing center
- Potash
- Processing plant
- Salt
- Steel manufacturing

Temperature and Precipitation

Average Monthly Temperatures (°F)
(January/July)

Average Annual Precipitation

Over 80 inches	Over 200 cm
60–80 inches	150–200 cm
40–59 inches	100–149 cm
20–39 inches	50–99 cm
10–19 inches	25–49 cm
Under 10 inches	Under 25 cm

Population

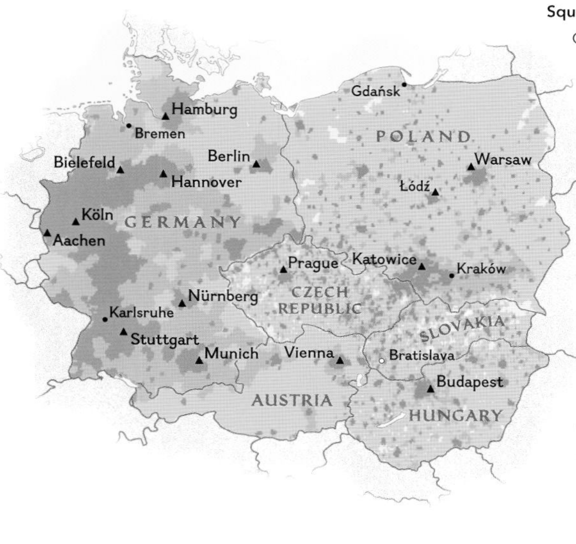

People per Square Mile	People per Square Km
Over 500	Over 195
250–500	100–195
50–249	20–99
1–49	1–19
Under 1	Under 1

Urban Area Population

- 5 million and greater
- 1 million–4,999,999
- 750,000–999,999
- Under 750,000

Slovakia

SLOVAK REPUBLIC

AREA 49,035 sq km (18,932 sq mi)
POPULATION 5,382,000
CAPITAL Bratislava 425,000
RELIGION Roman Catholic, Protestant
LANGUAGE Slovak (official), Hungarian
LITERACY 100%
LIFE EXPECTANCY 74 years
GDP PER CAPITA $7,607
ECONOMY **IND:** metal and metal products, food and beverages, electricity, gas **AGR:** grains, potatoes, sugar beets, hops; pigs; forest products **EXP:** vehicles, machinery and electrical equipment, base metals, chemicals

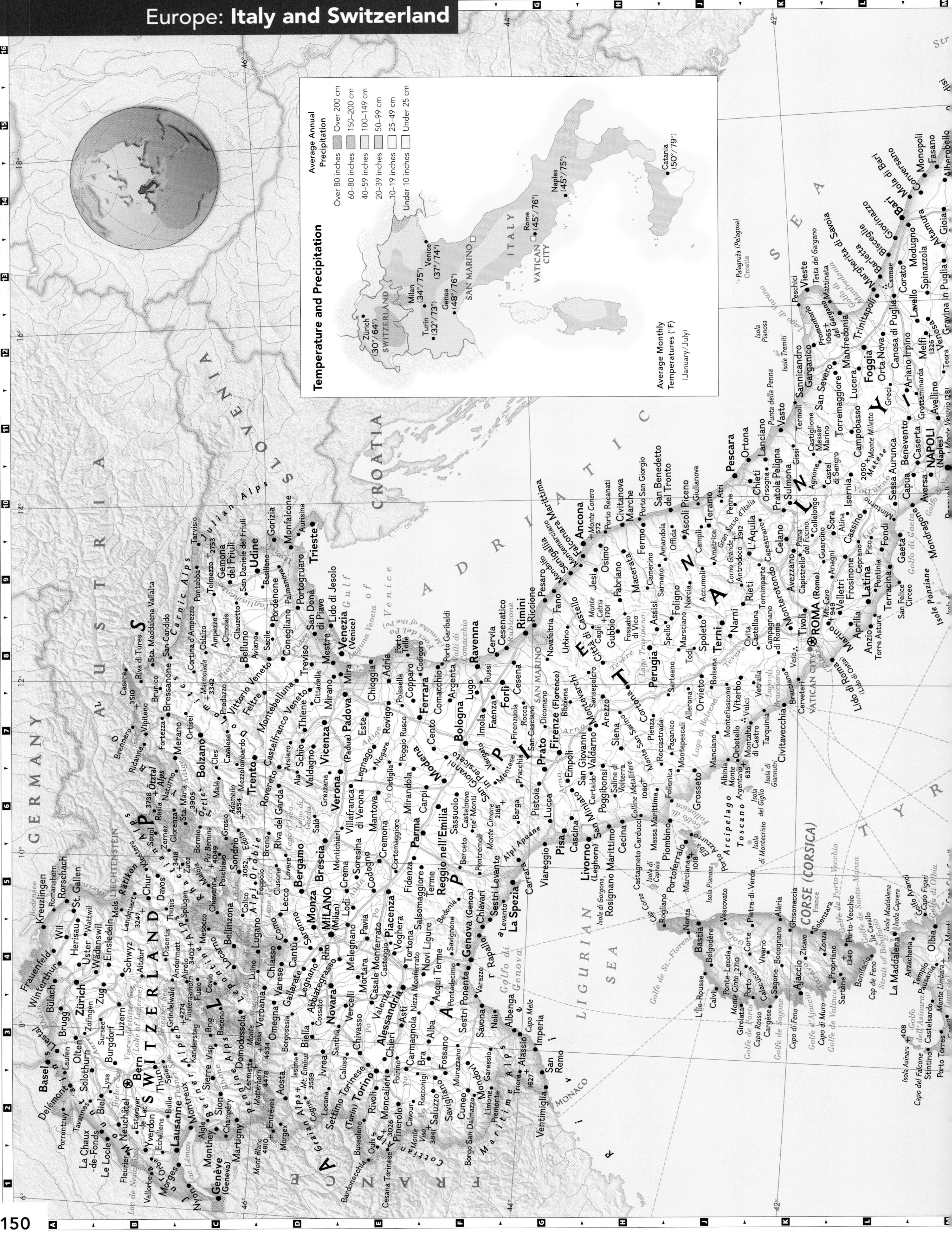
Temperature and Precipitation
Average Annual Precipitation
Over 80 inches Over 200 cm
60–80 inches 150–200 cm
40–59 inches 100–149 cm
20–39 inches 50–99 cm
10–19 inches 25–49 cm
Under 10 inches Under 25 cm
Average Monthly Temperatures (°F) (January/July)
Zürich (30°/64°)
SWITZERLAND
Milan (34°/75°)
Turin (32°/73°)
Genoa (48°/76°)
Venice (37°/74°)
SAN MARINO
ITALY
Rome (45°/76°)
VATICAN CITY
Naples (45°/75°)
Catania (50°/79°)
GERMANY
AUSTRIA
LIECHTENSTEIN
SLOVENIA
CROATIA
FRANCE
MONACO
SWITZERLAND
ITALY
CORSE (CORSICA)
LIGURIAN SEA
ADRIATIC SEA
TYRRHENIAN SEA
Gulf of Venice
Bern
Genève (Geneva)
Lausanne
Zürich
Basel
Luzern
MILANO (Milan)
Torino (Turin)
Genova (Genoa)
Venezia (Venice)
Bologna
Firenze (Florence)
ROMA (Rome)
NAPOLI (Naples)
Bari
Pescara
Ancona
Trieste
Bastia
Ajaccio

Italy

ITALIAN REPUBLIC

AREA 301,333 sq km (116,345 sq mi)
POPULATION 58,742,000
CAPITAL Rome 2,665,000
RELIGION Roman Catholic
LANGUAGE Italian (official), German, French, Slovene
LITERACY 99%
LIFE EXPECTANCY 80 years
GDP PER CAPITA $28,913
ECONOMY **IND:** tourism, machinery, iron and steel, chemicals **AGR:** fruits, vegetables, grapes, potatoes; beef; fish **EXP:** engineering products, textiles and clothing, production machinery, motor vehicles

Switzerland

SWISS CONFEDERATION

AREA 41,284 sq km (15,940 sq mi)
POPULATION 7,446,000
CAPITAL Bern 320,000
RELIGION Roman Catholic, Protestant
LANGUAGE German (official), French (official), Italian (official)
LITERACY 99%
LIFE EXPECTANCY 80 years
GDP PER CAPITA $49,367
ECONOMY **IND:** machinery, chemicals, watches, textiles **AGR:** grains, fruits, vegetables; meat **EXP:** machinery, chemicals, metals, watches

Population

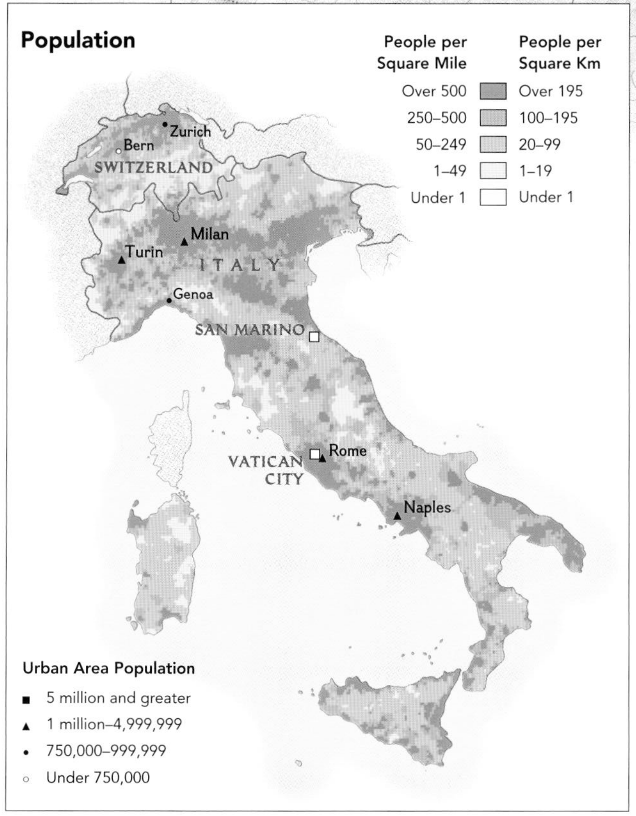

Industry and Mining

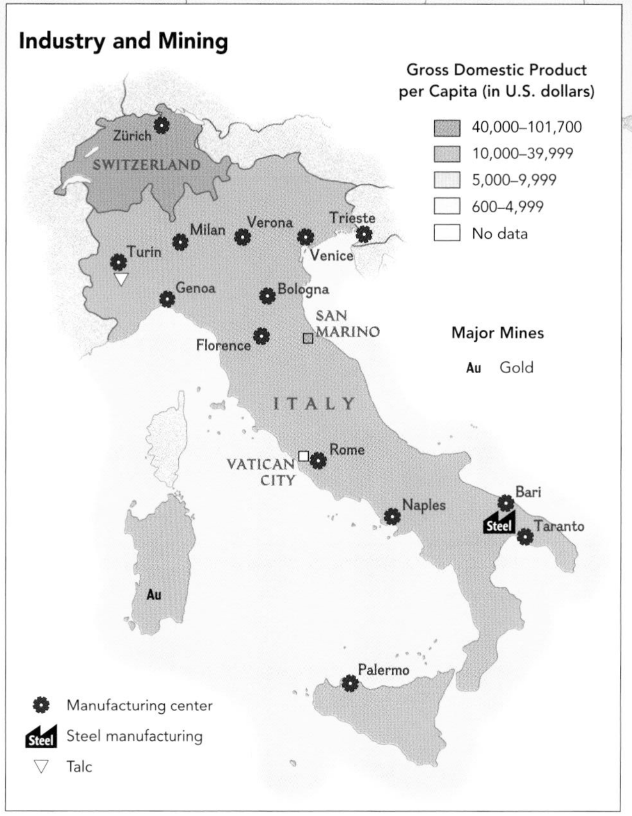

Land Use, Agriculture, and Fishing

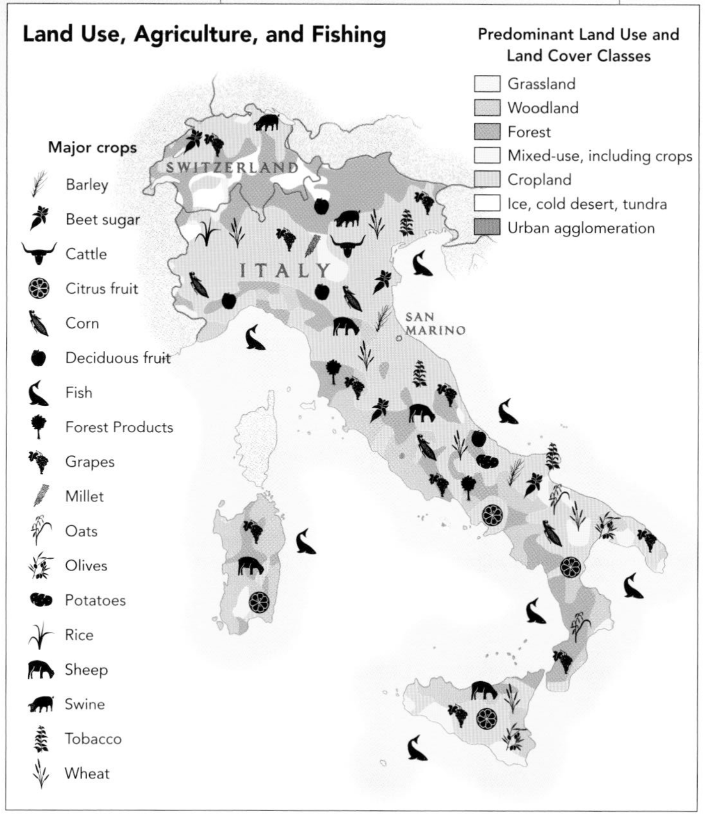

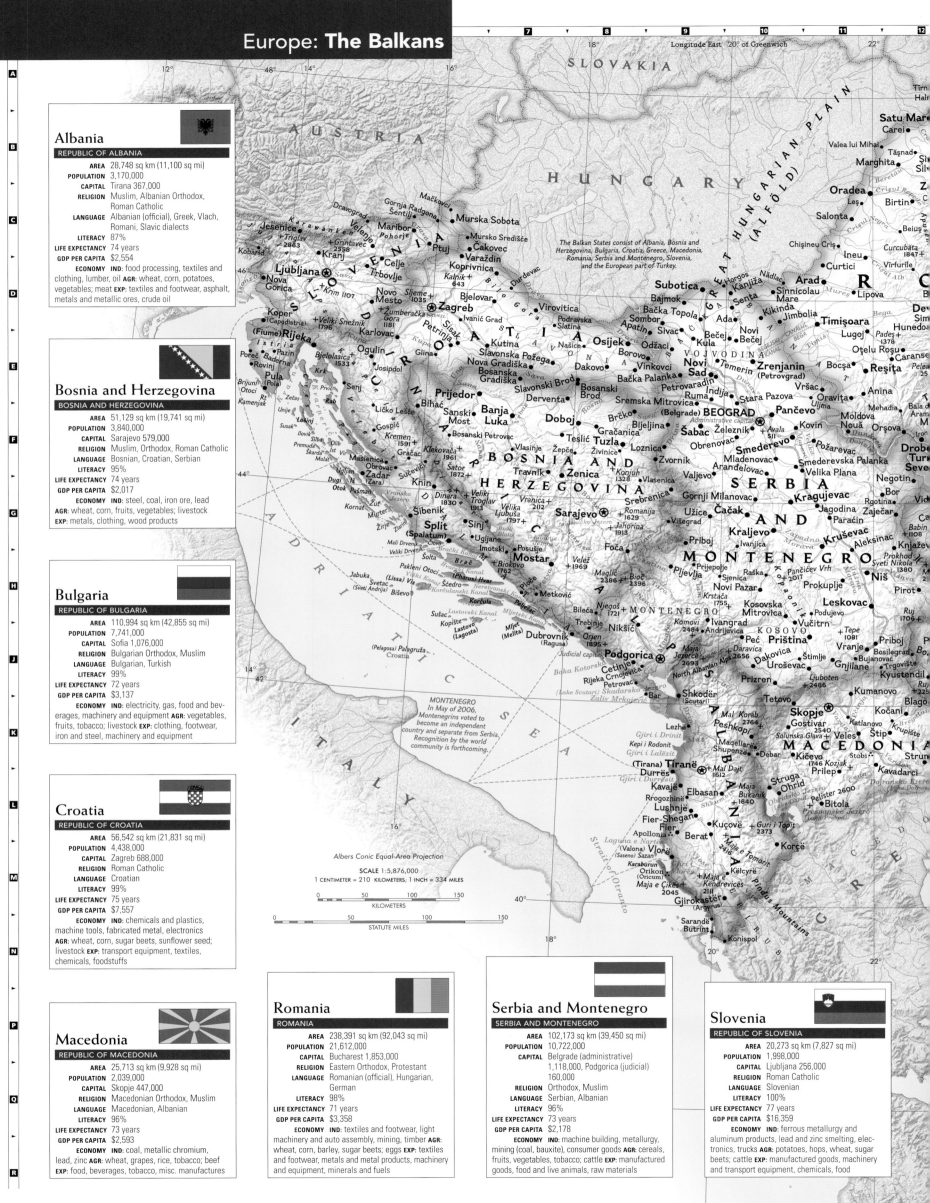

Albania
REPUBLIC OF ALBANIA
AREA 28,748 sq km (11,100 sq mi)
POPULATION 3,170,000
CAPITAL Tirana 367,000
RELIGION Muslim, Albanian Orthodox, Roman Catholic
LANGUAGE Albanian (official), Greek, Vlach, Romani, Slavic dialects
LITERACY 87%
LIFE EXPECTANCY 74 years
GDP PER CAPITA $2,554
ECONOMY IND: food processing, textiles and clothing, lumber, oil **AGR:** wheat, corn, potatoes, vegetables; meat **EXP:** textiles and footwear, asphalt, metals and metallic ores, crude oil

Bosnia and Herzegovina
BOSNIA AND HERZEGOVINA
AREA 51,129 sq km (19,741 sq mi)
POPULATION 3,840,000
CAPITAL Sarajevo 579,000
RELIGION Muslim, Orthodox, Roman Catholic
LANGUAGE Bosnian, Croatian, Serbian
LITERACY 95%
LIFE EXPECTANCY 74 years
GDP PER CAPITA $2,017
ECONOMY IND: steel, coal, iron ore, lead **AGR:** wheat, corn, fruits, vegetables; livestock **EXP:** metals, clothing, wood products

Bulgaria
REPUBLIC OF BULGARIA
AREA 110,994 sq km (42,855 sq mi)
POPULATION 7,741,000
CAPITAL Sofia 1,076,000
RELIGION Bulgarian Orthodox, Muslim
LANGUAGE Bulgarian, Turkish
LITERACY 99%
LIFE EXPECTANCY 72 years
GDP PER CAPITA $3,137
ECONOMY IND: electricity, gas, food and beverages, machinery and equipment **AGR:** vegetables, fruits, tobacco; livestock **EXP:** clothing, footwear, iron and steel, machinery and equipment

Croatia
REPUBLIC OF CROATIA
AREA 56,542 sq km (21,831 sq mi)
POPULATION 4,438,000
CAPITAL Zagreb 688,000
RELIGION Roman Catholic
LANGUAGE Croatian
LITERACY 99%
LIFE EXPECTANCY 75 years
GDP PER CAPITA $7,557
ECONOMY IND: chemicals and plastics, machine tools, fabricated metal, electronics **AGR:** wheat, corn, sugar beets, sunflower seed; livestock **EXP:** transport equipment, textiles, chemicals, foodstuffs

Macedonia
REPUBLIC OF MACEDONIA
AREA 25,713 sq km (9,928 sq mi)
POPULATION 2,039,000
CAPITAL Skopje 447,000
RELIGION Macedonian Orthodox, Muslim
LANGUAGE Macedonian, Albanian
LITERACY 96%
LIFE EXPECTANCY 73 years
GDP PER CAPITA $2,593
ECONOMY IND: coal, metallic chromium, lead, zinc **AGR:** wheat, grapes, rice, tobacco; beef **EXP:** food, beverages, tobacco, misc. manufactures

Romania
ROMANIA
AREA 238,391 sq km (92,043 sq mi)
POPULATION 21,612,000
CAPITAL Bucharest 1,853,000
RELIGION Eastern Orthodox, Protestant
LANGUAGE Romanian (official), Hungarian, German
LITERACY 98%
LIFE EXPECTANCY 71 years
GDP PER CAPITA $3,358
ECONOMY IND: textiles and footwear, light machinery and auto assembly, mining, timber **AGR:** wheat, corn, barley, sugar beets; eggs **EXP:** textiles and footwear, metals and metal products, machinery and equipment, minerals and fuels

Serbia and Montenegro
SERBIA AND MONTENEGRO
AREA 102,173 sq km (39,450 sq mi)
POPULATION 10,722,000
CAPITAL Belgrade (administrative) 1,118,000, Podgorica (judicial) 160,000
RELIGION Orthodox, Muslim
LANGUAGE Serbian, Albanian
LITERACY 96%
LIFE EXPECTANCY 73 years
GDP PER CAPITA $2,178
ECONOMY IND: machine building, metallurgy, mining (coal, bauxite), consumer goods **AGR:** cereals, fruits, vegetables, tobacco; cattle **EXP:** manufactured goods, food and live animals, raw materials

Slovenia
REPUBLIC OF SLOVENIA
AREA 20,273 sq km (7,827 sq mi)
POPULATION 1,998,000
CAPITAL Ljubljana 256,000
RELIGION Roman Catholic
LANGUAGE Slovenian
LITERACY 100%
LIFE EXPECTANCY 77 years
GDP PER CAPITA $16,359
ECONOMY IND: ferrous metallurgy and aluminum products, lead and zinc smelting, electronics, trucks **AGR:** potatoes, hops, wheat, sugar beets; cattle **EXP:** manufactured goods, machinery and transport equipment, chemicals, food

The Balkan States consist of Albania, Bosnia and Herzegovina, Bulgaria, Croatia, Greece, Macedonia, Romania, Serbia and Montenegro, Slovenia, and the European part of Turkey.

MONTENEGRO
In May of 2006, Montenegrins voted to become an independent country and separate from Serbia. Recognition by the world community is forthcoming.

Albers Conic Equal-Area Projection

SCALE 1:5,876,000
1 CENTIMETER = 210 KILOMETERS; 1 INCH = 334 MILES

KILOMETERS

STATUTE MILES

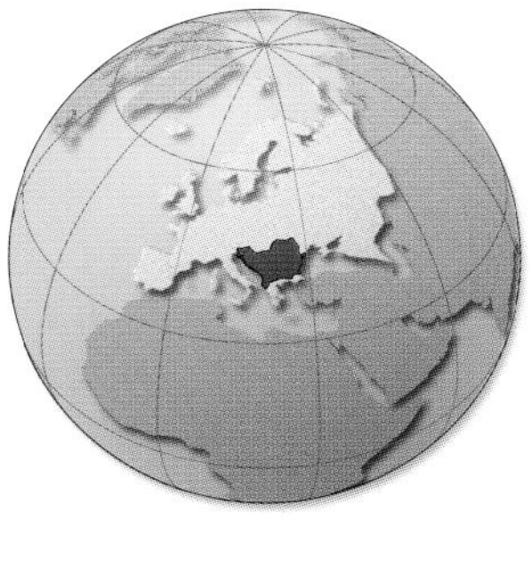

UKRAINE
MOLDOVA
TRANSDNIESTRIA
ROMANIA
BULGARIA
TURKEY
BLACK SEA
CARPATHIAN MOUNTAINS
BALKAN MOUNTAINS
Rhodope Mountains
Ludogorsko Plato
BUCUREŞTI (Bucharest)
Cluj-Napoca
Iaşi
Suceava
Botoşani
Piatra Neamţ
Bacău
Galaţi
Brăila
Tulcea
Constanţa
Ploieşti
Braşov
Sibiu
Piteşti
Buzău
Ruse
Dobrich
Varna
Shumen (Kolarovgrad)
Pleven
Veliko Tŭrnovo
Sliven
Burgas
Stara Zagora
Plovdiv (Philippopolis)
Kŭrdzhali
Smolyan
Svilengrad
KOSOVO
In 1999 ethnic persecution of Kosovo's Albanian majority by Serbian forces led to NATO intervention in Serbia and Montenegro.
Industry and Mining
SLOVENIA
CROATIA
BOSNIA AND HERZEGOVINA
SERBIA AND MONTENEGRO
MACEDONIA
ALBANIA
ROMANIA
BULGARIA
Zagreb
Belgrade
Sofia
Ploieşti
Bucharest
Gross Domestic Product per Capita (in U.S. dollars)
40,000–101,700
10,000–39,999
5,000–9,999
600–4,999
Major Mines
Cu Copper
Manufacturing center
Processing plant
Temperature and Precipitation
Ljubljana (30°/67°)
Zagreb (32°/71°)
Belgrade (33°/71°)
Sarajevo (30°/66°)
Varna (36°/72°)
Sofia (30°/68°)
Skopje (32°/74°)
Tirana (44°/76°)
Average Annual Precipitation
Over 80 inches — Over 200 cm
60–80 inches — 150–200 cm
40–59 inches — 100–149 cm
20–39 inches — 50–99 cm
10–19 inches — 25–49 cm
Under 10 inches — Under 25 cm
Average Monthly Temperatures (°F) (January/July)
Land Use, Agriculture, and Fishing
Major Crops
Barley
Beet sugar
Cattle
Corn
Deciduous fruit
Fish
Forest products
Grapes
Millet
Oats
Olives
Potatoes
Sheep
Swine
Tobacco
Wheat
Predominant Land Use and Land Cover Classes
Grassland
Woodland
Forest
Mixed-use, including crops
Cropland
Ice, cold desert, tundra
Urban agglomeration
Population
Urban Area Population
5 million and greater
1 million–4,999,999
750,000–999,999
Under 750,000
Ljubljana
Zagreb
Belgrade
Bucharest
Sarajevo
Sofia
Skopje
Tirana
People per Square Mile — People per Square Km
Over 500 — Over 195
250–500 — 100–195
50–249 — 20–99
1–49 — 1–19
Under 1 — Under 1

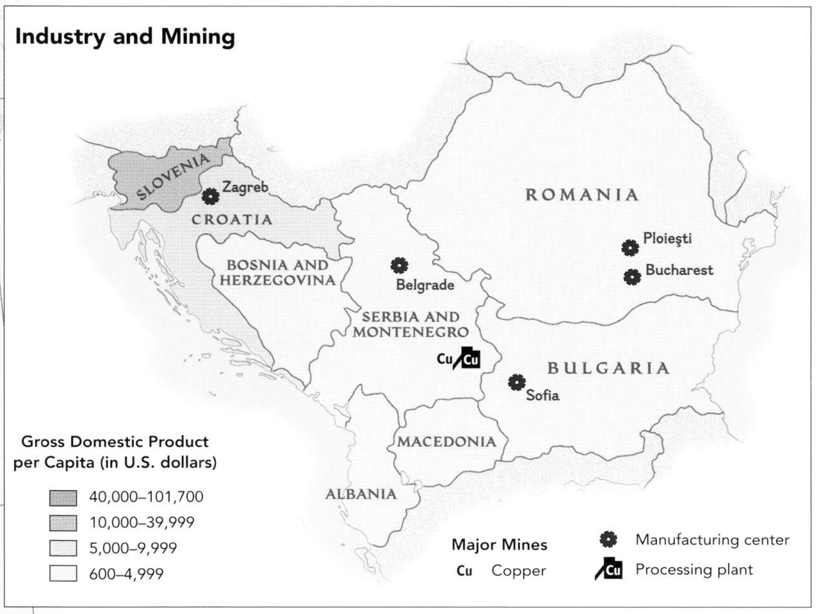

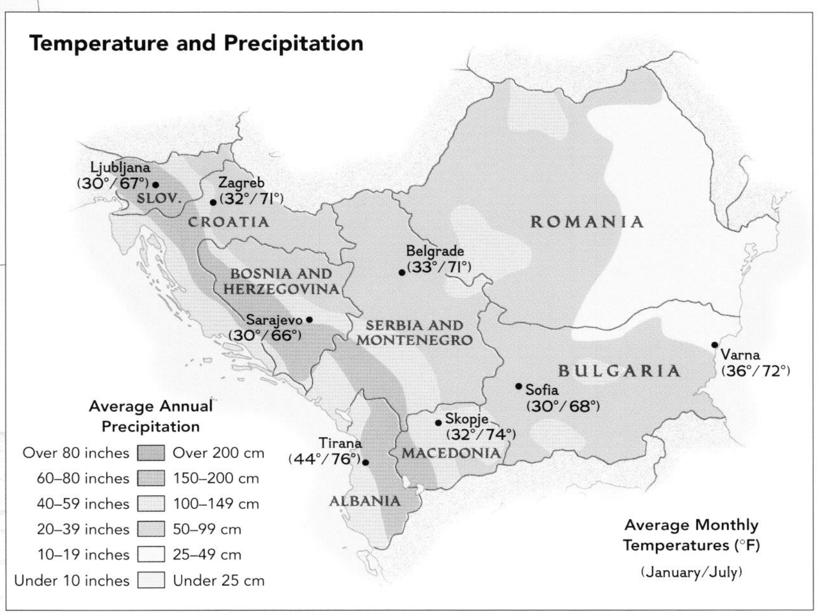

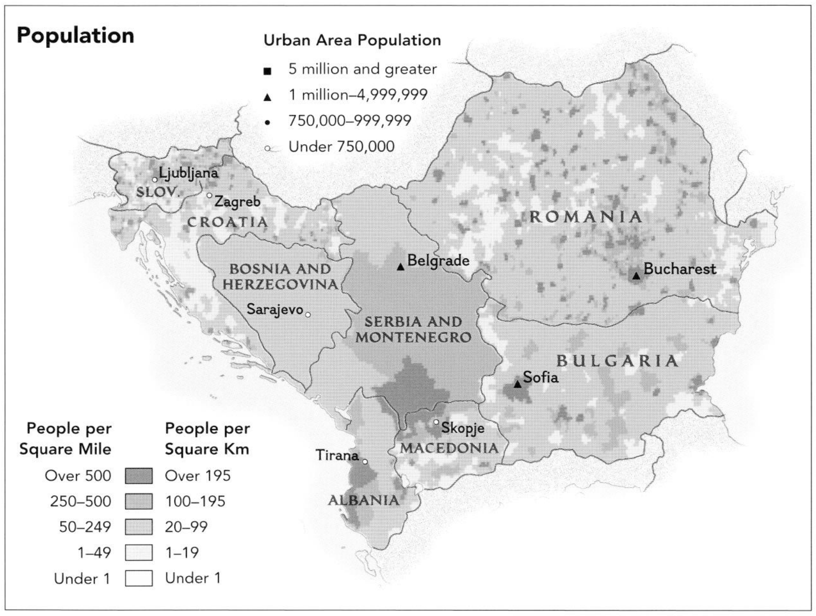

Population

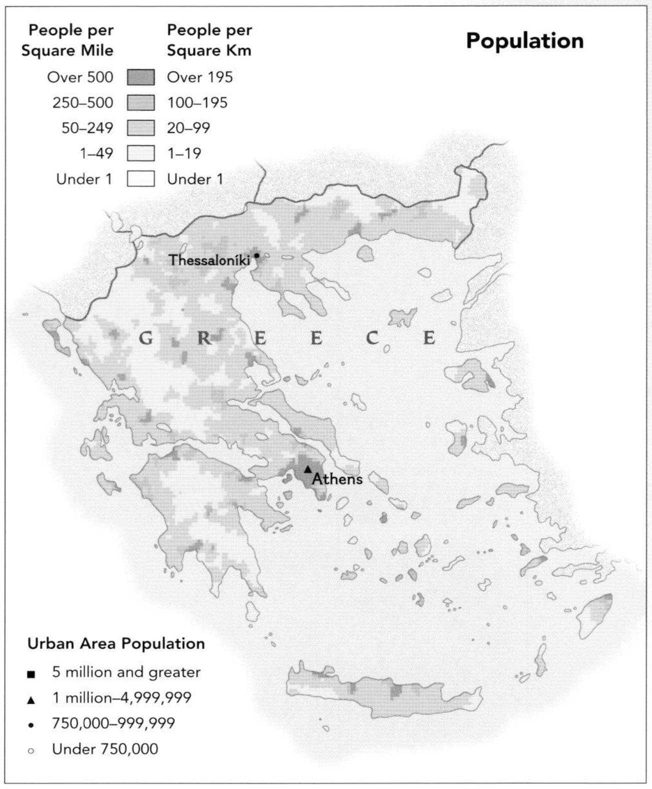

Industry and Mining

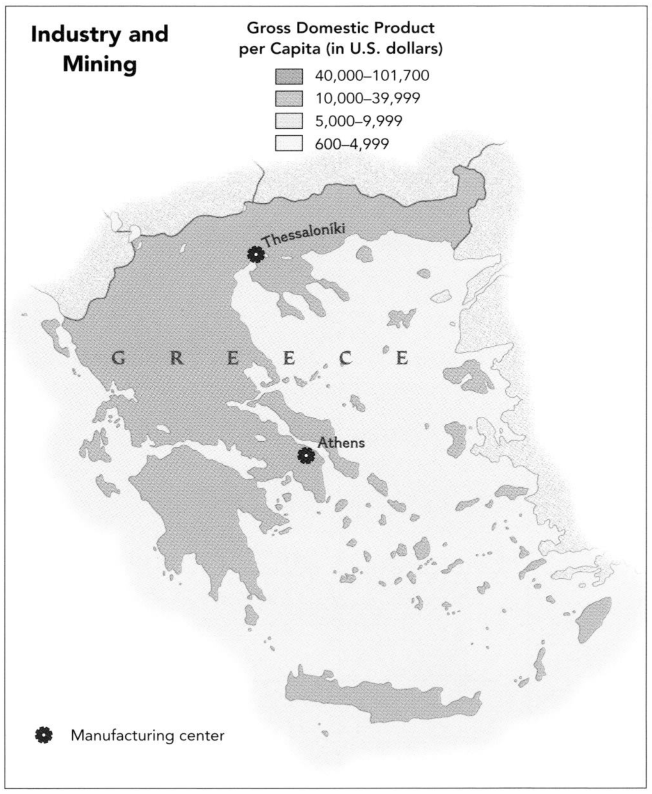

Greece

HELLENIC REPUBLIC

AREA	131,957 sq km (50,949 sq mi)
POPULATION	11,100,000
CAPITAL	Athens 3,215,000
RELIGION	Greek Orthodox
LANGUAGE	Greek (official)
LITERACY	98%
LIFE EXPECTANCY	79 years
GDP PER CAPITA	$18,492

ECONOMY **IND:** tourism, food and tobacco processing, textiles, chemicals **AGR:** wheat, corn, barley, sugar beets; beef **EXP:** food and beverages, manufactured goods, petroleum products, chemicals

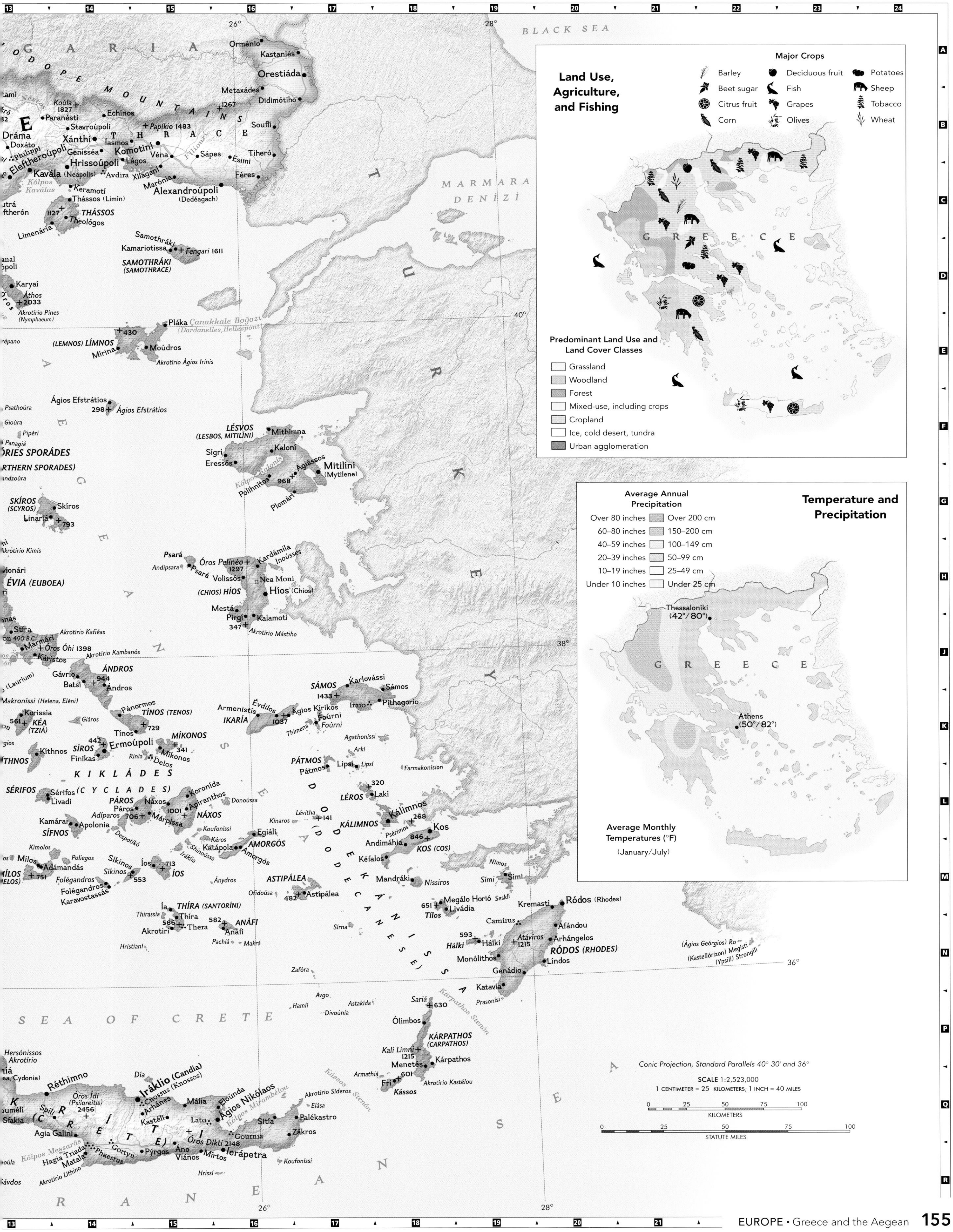
BLACK SEA
Land Use, Agriculture, and Fishing
Major Crops
Barley
Beet sugar
Citrus fruit
Corn
Deciduous fruit
Fish
Grapes
Olives
Potatoes
Sheep
Tobacco
Wheat
Predominant Land Use and Land Cover Classes
Grassland
Woodland
Forest
Mixed-use, including crops
Cropland
Ice, cold desert, tundra
Urban agglomeration
G R E E C E
Temperature and Precipitation
Average Annual Precipitation
Over 80 inches
Over 200 cm
60–80 inches
150–200 cm
40–59 inches
100–149 cm
20–39 inches
50–99 cm
10–19 inches
25–49 cm
Under 10 inches
Under 25 cm
Thessaloníki (42°/80°)
Athens (50°/82°)
G R E E C E
Average Monthly Temperatures (°F)
(January/July)
RODOPE MOUNTAINS
THRACE
Orménio
Kastaniés
Orestiáda
Metaxádes
Didimótiho
Soufli
Tiheró
Féres
Alexandroúpoli (Dedéagach)
Komotiní
Xánthi
Dráma
Kavála (Neapolis)
Kólpos Kaválas
THÁSSOS
Thássos (Limín)
Limenária
Theológos
SAMOTHRÁKI (SAMOTHRACE)
Kamariotissa
Samothráki
Fengari 1611
MARMARA DENİZİ
TURKEY
Çanakkale Boğazı (Dardanelles, Hellespont)
(LEMNOS) LÍMNOS
Mírina
Moúdros
Akrotírio Áyios Irínis
Ágios Efstrátios
LÉSVOS (LESBOS, MITILÍNI)
Míthimna
Kaloní
Sígri
Eressós
Mitilíni (Mytilene)
Plomári
Polihnítos
SKÍROS (SCYROS)
Skíros
Linariá
Psará
(CHIOS) HÍOS
Híos (Chios)
Volissós
Kardámila
Nea Moni
Mestá
Pirgí
Kalamotí
Akrotírio Mástiho
ÉVIA (EUBOEA)
Kárístos
Óros Óhi 1398
ÁNDROS
Ándros
Gávrio
Batsí
SÁMOS
Sámos
Karlovássi
Pithagorio
IKARÍA
Évdilos
Ágios Kírikos
Armenistís
Foúrni
TÍNOS (TENOS)
Tínos
MÍKONOS
Míkonos
Delos
KÉA (TZIÁ)
Kíthnos
SÍROS
Ermoúpoli
Fínikas
KIKLÁDES (CYCLADES)
SÉRIFOS
Livadi
PÁROS
Páros
NÁXOS
Náxos
SÍFNOS
Apolonia
Kamárai
Mílos
Adámandas
Folégandros
Síkinos
Íos
ÍOS
AMORGÓS
Egiáli
Katápola
PÁTMOS
Pátmos
Lipsí
LÉROS
Lakí
KÁLIMNOS
Kálimnos
KOS (COS)
Kos
Kéfalos
Nísiros
ASTIPÁLEA
Astipálea
THÍRA (SANTORÍNI)
Thíra
Ía
Akrotiri
ANÁFI
Anáfi
DODEKÁNISSA (DODECANESE)
Tílos
Sími
Hálki
RÓDOS (RHODES)
Ródos (Rhodes)
Líndos
Kremastí
Afándou
Arhángelos
Camirus
Monólithos
Genádio
Katavía
Prasonísi
(Ágios Geórgios) Ro
(Kastellórizon) Megísti
(Ypsili) Strongilí
KÁRPATHOS (CARPATHOS)
Kárpathos
Ólimbos
Sariá
Menetés
Kárpathos Stenón
Kássos
Frí
Kássos Stenón
SEA OF CRETE
KRÍTI (CRETE)
Iráklio (Candia)
Cnossus (Knossos)
Réthimno
Mália
Elounda
Ágios Nikólaos
Kólpos Mirabéllou
Sitía
Palékastro
Zákros
Ierápetra
Óros Ídi (Psiloreítis) 2456
Óros Díkti 2148
Phaestus
Gortyn
Mátala
Agia Galini
Kólpos Messarás
Akrotírio Síderos
Koufonísi
AEGEAN SEA
26°
28°
40°
38°
36°
Conic Projection, Standard Parallels 40° 30′ and 36°
SCALE 1:2,523,000
1 CENTIMETER = 25 KILOMETERS; 1 INCH = 40 MILES
KILOMETERS
STATUTE MILES

Population

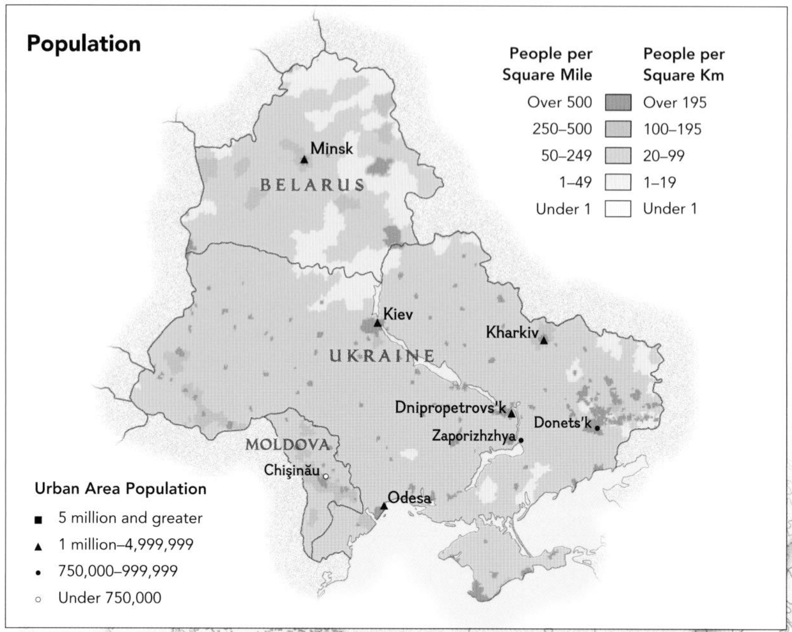

Industry and Mining

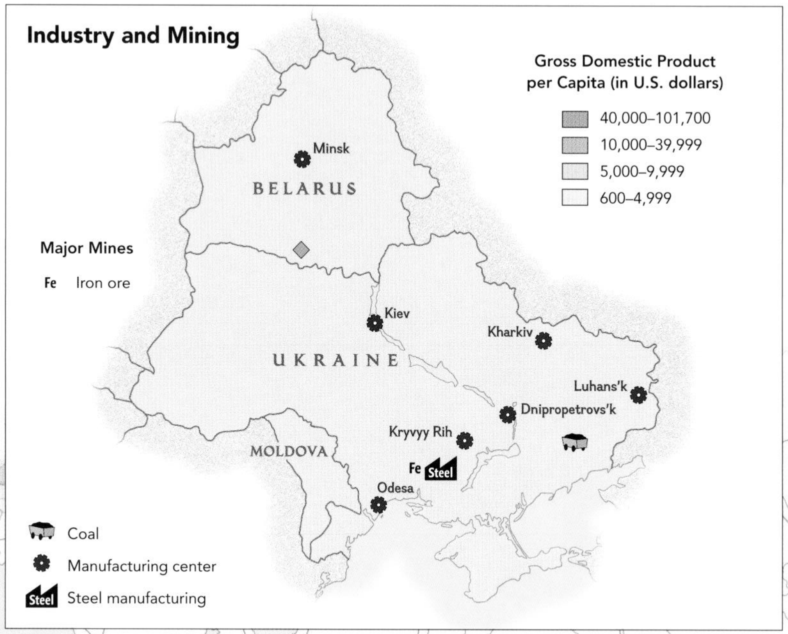

Belarus

REPUBLIC OF BELARUS

AREA 207,595 sq km (80,153 sq mi)
POPULATION 9,776,000
CAPITAL Minsk 1,705,000
RELIGION Eastern Orthodox, Roman Catholic, Protestant, Jewish, Muslim
LANGUAGE Belarusian, Russian
LITERACY 100%
LIFE EXPECTANCY 69 years
GDP PER CAPITA $2,335
ECONOMY **IND:** metal-cutting machine tools, tractors, trucks, earthmovers **AGR:** grain, potatoes, vegetables, sugar beets; beef **EXP:** machinery and equipment, mineral products, chemicals, metals

Moldova

REPUBLIC OF MOLDOVA

AREA 33,800 sq km (13,050 sq mi)
POPULATION 4,206,000
CAPITAL Chişinău 662,000
RELIGION Eastern Orthodox
LANGUAGE Moldovan (official), Russian, Gagauz
LITERACY 99%
LIFE EXPECTANCY 68 years
GDP PER CAPITA $615
ECONOMY **IND:** food processing, agricultural machinery, foundry equipment, refrigerators and freezers **AGR:** vegetables, fruits, wine, grain; beef **EXP:** foodstuffs, textiles, machinery

Ukraine

UKRAINE

AREA 603,700 sq km (233,090 sq mi)
POPULATION 47,110,000
CAPITAL Kiev 2,618,000
RELIGION Ukrainian Orthodox, Orthodox, Ukrainian Greek Catholic
LANGUAGE Ukrainian (official), Russian
LITERACY 100%
LIFE EXPECTANCY 68 years
GDP PER CAPITA $1,384
ECONOMY **IND:** coal, electric power, ferrous and nonferrous metals, machinery and transport equipment **AGR:** grain, sugar beets, sunflower seeds, vegetables; beef **EXP:** ferrous and nonferrous metals, fuel and petroleum products, chemicals, machinery and transport equipment

Temperature and Precipitation

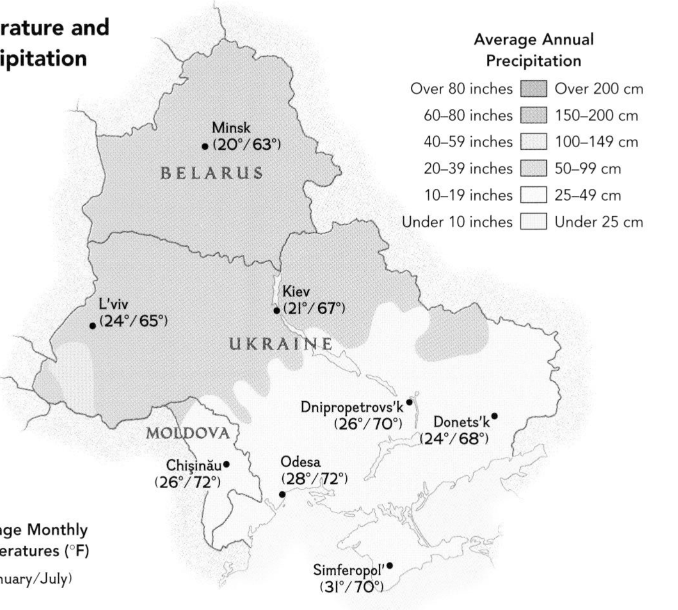

Land Use, Agriculture, and Fishing

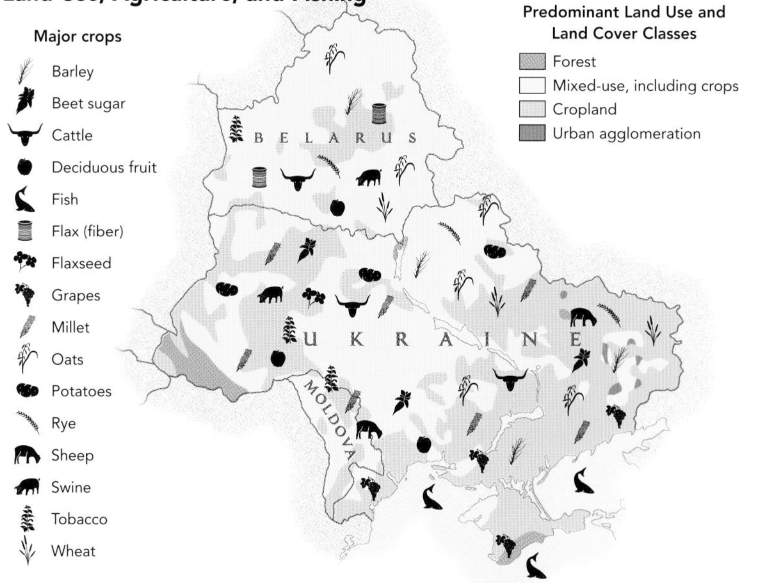

Europe – Asia Boundary

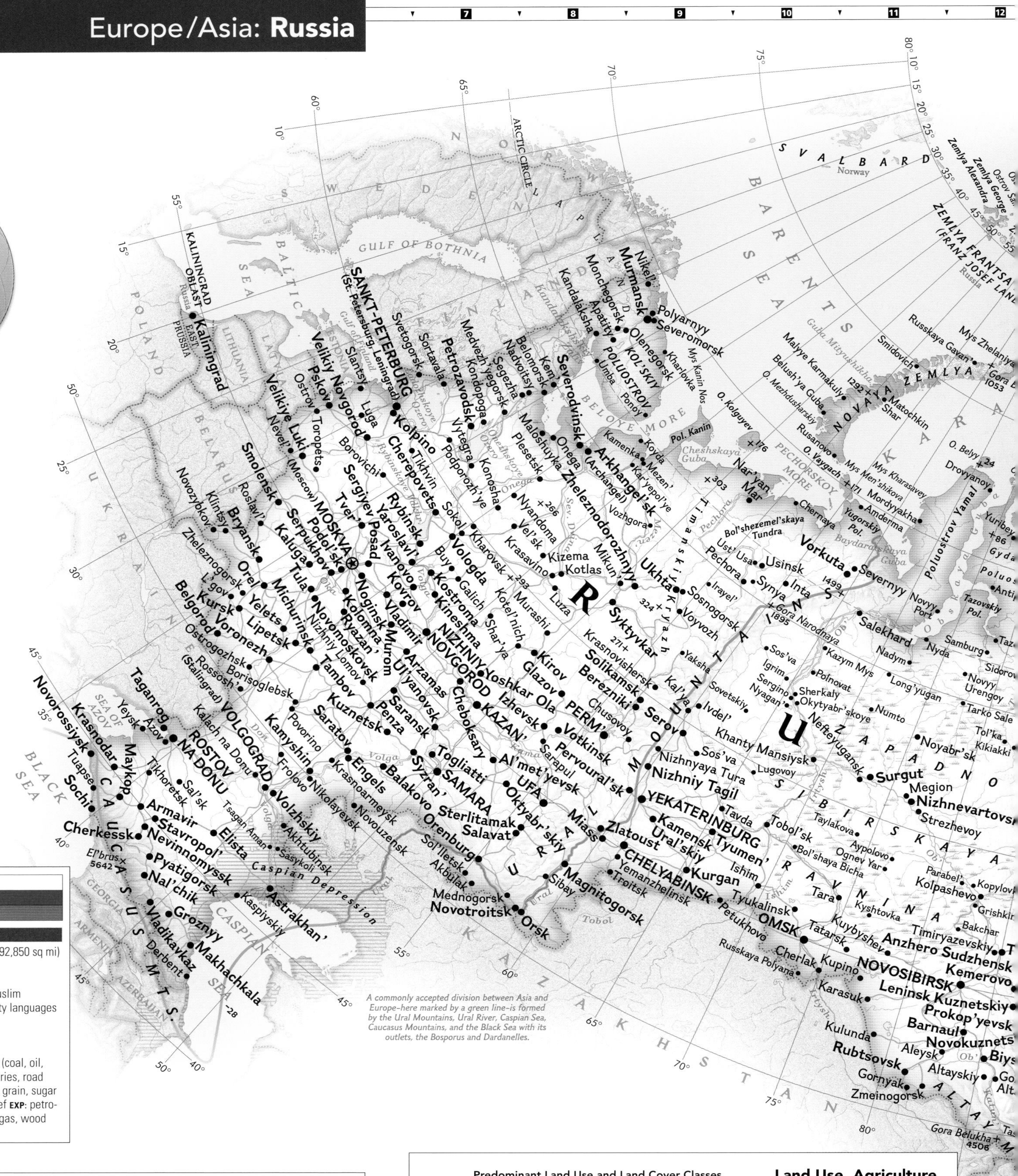

Russia
RUSSIAN FEDERATION

AREA 17,075,400 sq km (6,592,850 sq mi)
POPULATION 143,025,000
CAPITAL Moscow 10,469,000
RELIGION Russian Orthodox, Muslim
LANGUAGE Russian, many minority languages
LITERACY 100%
LIFE EXPECTANCY 66 years
GDP PER CAPITA $4,047
ECONOMY **IND:** mining industries (coal, oil, gas), machine building, defense industries, road and rail transportation equipment **AGR:** grain, sugar beets, sunflower seed, vegetables; beef **EXP:** petroleum and petroleum products, natural gas, wood and wood products, metals

A commonly accepted division between Asia and Europe–here marked by a green line–is formed by the Ural Mountains, Ural River, Caspian Sea, Caucasus Mountains, and the Black Sea with its outlets, the Bosporus and Dardanelles.

Industry and Mining

Gross Domestic Product Per Capita (in U.S. Dollars)
- 40,000–101,700
- 10,000–39,999
- 5,000–9,999
- 600–4,999

Major Mines
Al	Aluminum	**Mo**	Molybdenum	
Asb	Asbestos	**Ni**	Nickel	
Co	Cobalt	**Pt**	Platinum	
Cu	Copper	**Sn**	Tin	
Au	Gold	**Ti**	Titanium	
Fe	Iron ore	**W**	Tungsten	

- Coal
- Diamond mine
- Manufacturing center
- Natural gas
- Petroleum
- Phosphate
- Potash
- Processing plant **Al**
- Steel manufacturing **Steel**

Land Use, Agriculture, and Fishing

Predominant Land Use and Land Cover Classes
- Grassland
- Woodland
- Forest
- Mixed-use, including crops
- Cropland
- Intensive cropland
- Desert, barren land
- Ice, cold desert, tundra
- Urban agglomeration

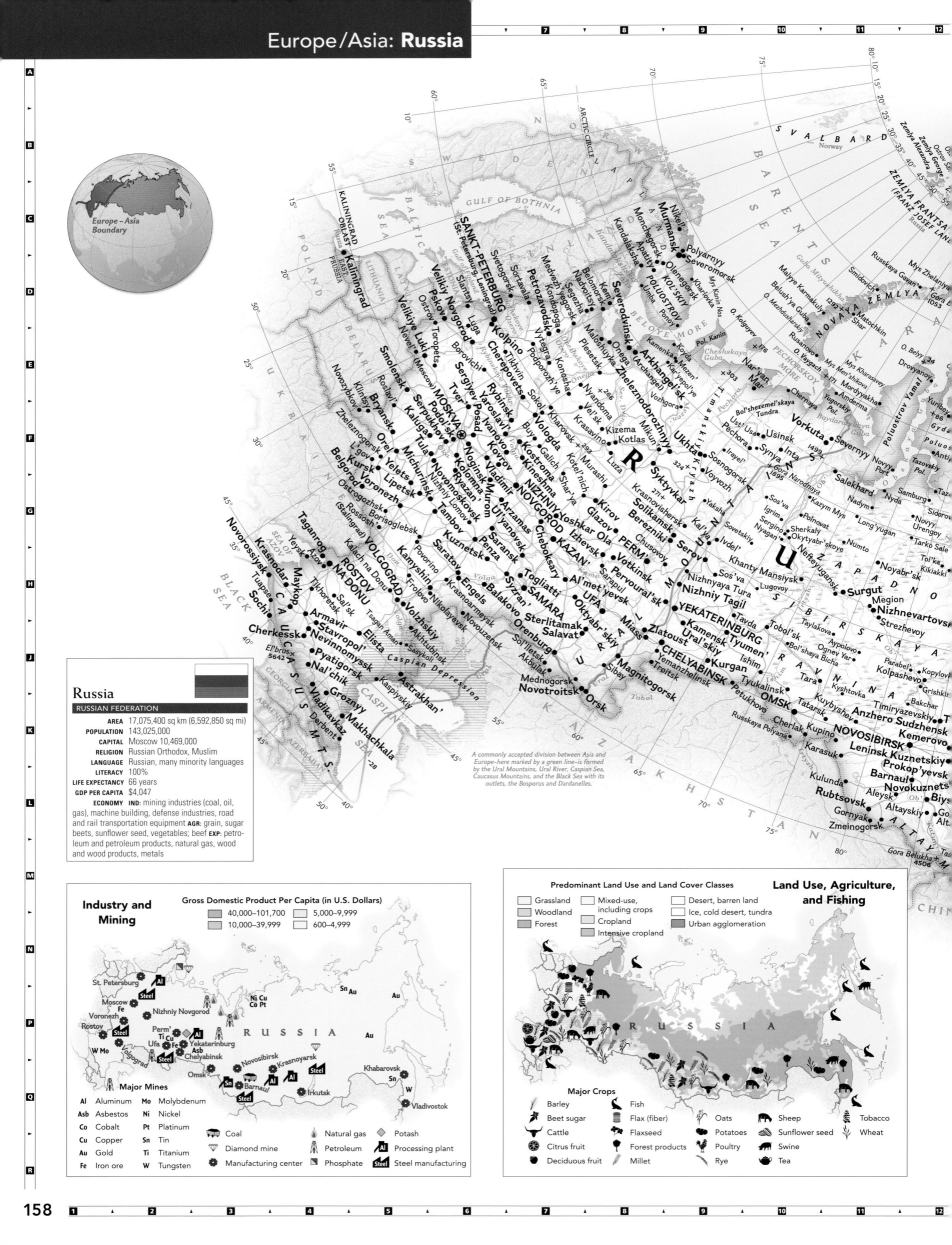

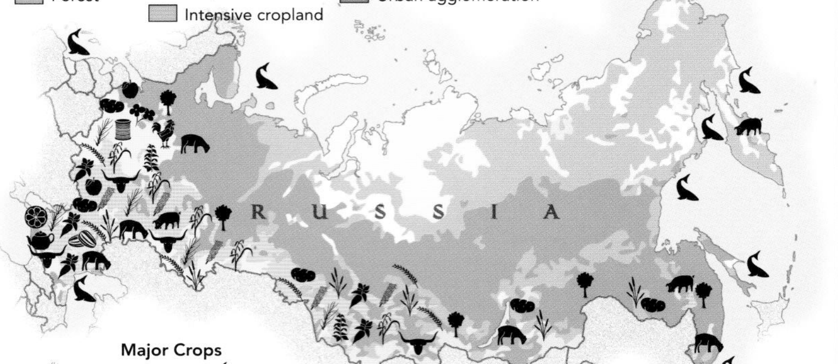

Major Crops
- Barley
- Beet sugar
- Cattle
- Citrus fruit
- Deciduous fruit
- Fish
- Flax (fiber)
- Flaxseed
- Forest products
- Millet
- Oats
- Potatoes
- Poultry
- Rye
- Sheep
- Sunflower seed
- Swine
- Tea
- Tobacco
- Wheat

Two-Point Equidistant Projection
SCALE 1:19,775,000
1 CENTIMETER = 198 KILOMETERS; 1 INCH = 312 MILES
KILOMETERS
STATUTE MILES
ARCTIC OCEAN
LAPTEV SEA
EAST SIBERIAN SEA
CHUKCHI SEA
BERING SEA
SEA OF OKHOTSK
PACIFIC OCEAN
SEA OF JAPAN (EAST SEA)
ALASKA
United States
SIBERIA
CHINA
MONGOLIA
KOREA
JAPAN
KURIL ISLANDS
The southern Kuril Islands of Iturup (Etorofu), Kunashir (Kunashiri), Shikotan, and the Habomai group were lost by Japan to the Soviet Union in 1945. Japan continues to claim these Russian-administered islands.
Longitude East 120° of Greenwich
Date Line
ARCTIC CIRCLE
Sunday
Monday
Temperature and Precipitation
Average Annual Precipitation
Over 80 inches
Over 200 cm
60–80 inches
150–200 cm
40–59 inches
100–149 cm
20–39 inches
50–99 cm
10–19 inches
25–49 cm
Under 10 inches
Under 25 cm
Average Monthly Temperatures (°F)
(January/July)
Moscow (14°/65°)
Perm' (5°/65°)
Ufa (6°/67°)
Rostov (23°/73°)
Omsk (-1°/67°)
Novosibirsk (6°/66°)
Irkutsk (-4°/64°)
Ulan Ude (-13°/67°)
Vladivostok (7°/64°)
Magadan (1°/52°)
Anadyr' (-5°/51°)
RUSSIA
Urban Area Population
5 million and greater
1 million–4,999,999
750,000–999,999
Under 750,000
People per Square Mile
Over 150
25–150
5–24
1–4
Under 1
People per Square Km
Over 60
10–60
2–9
1
Under 1
St. Petersburg
Moscow
Nizhniy Novgorod
Voronezh
Kazan'
Perm'
Rostov
Saratov
Samara
Yekaterinburg
Volgograd
Ufa
Chelyabinsk
Omsk
Novosibirsk
Krasnoyarsk
Population

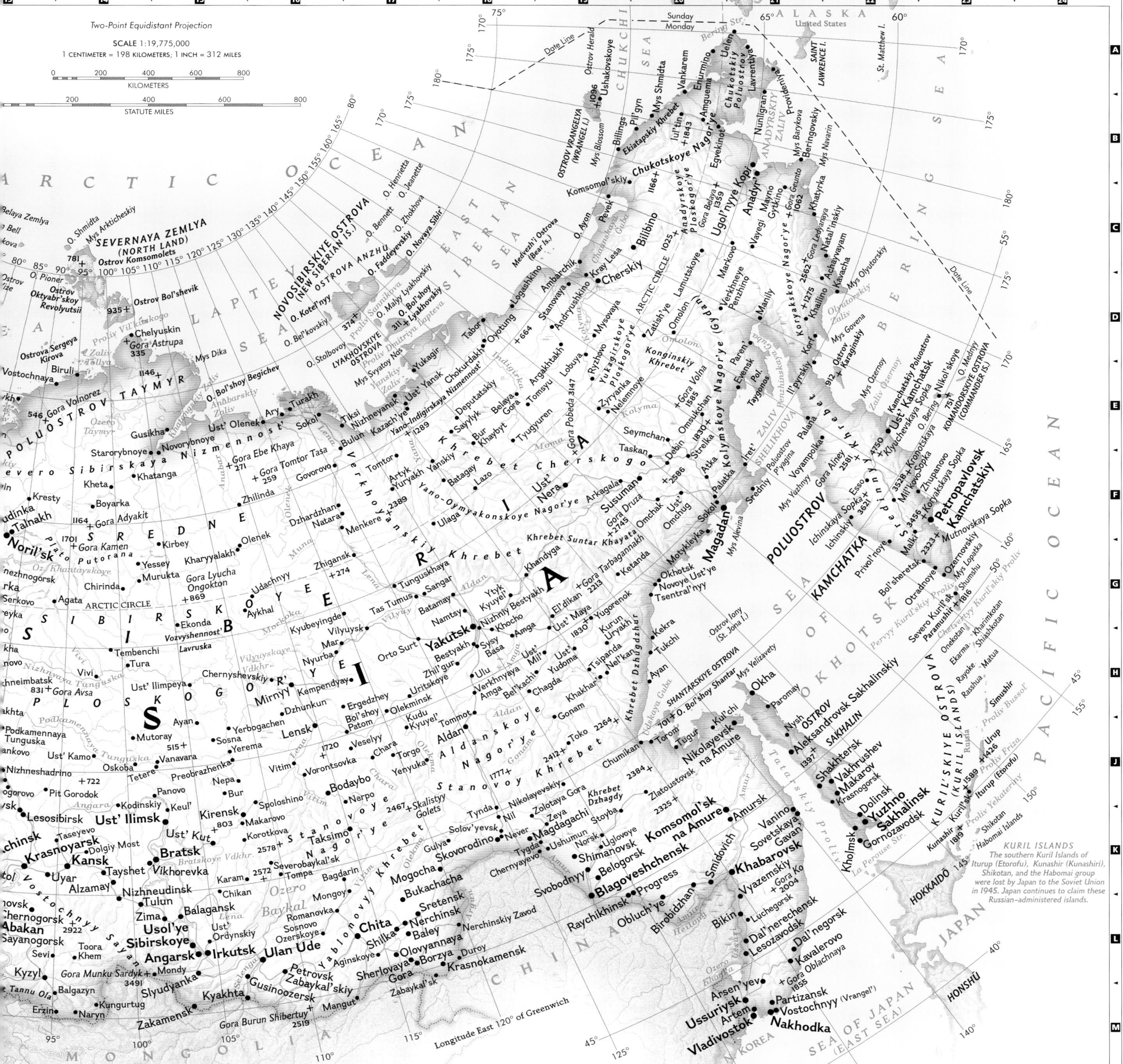

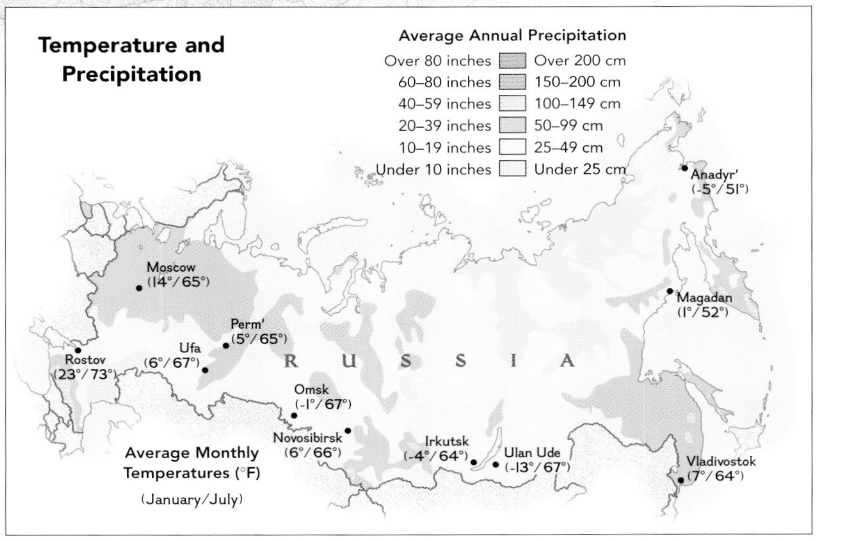

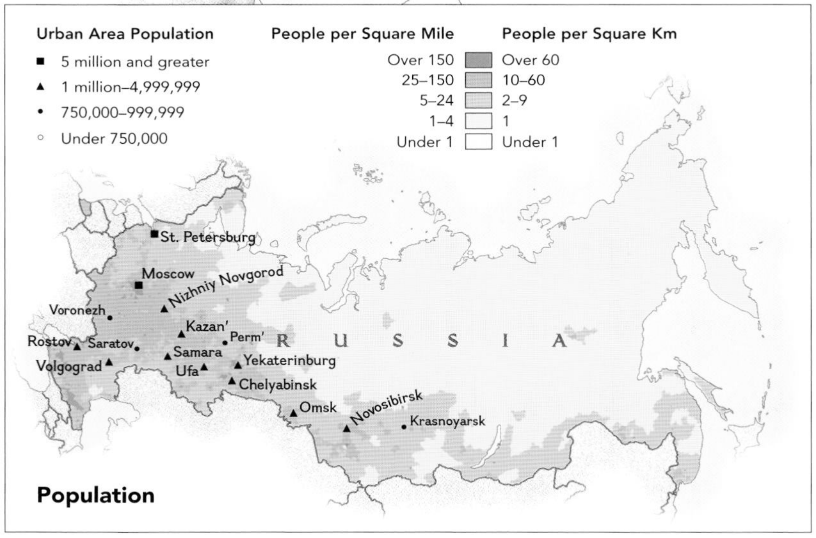

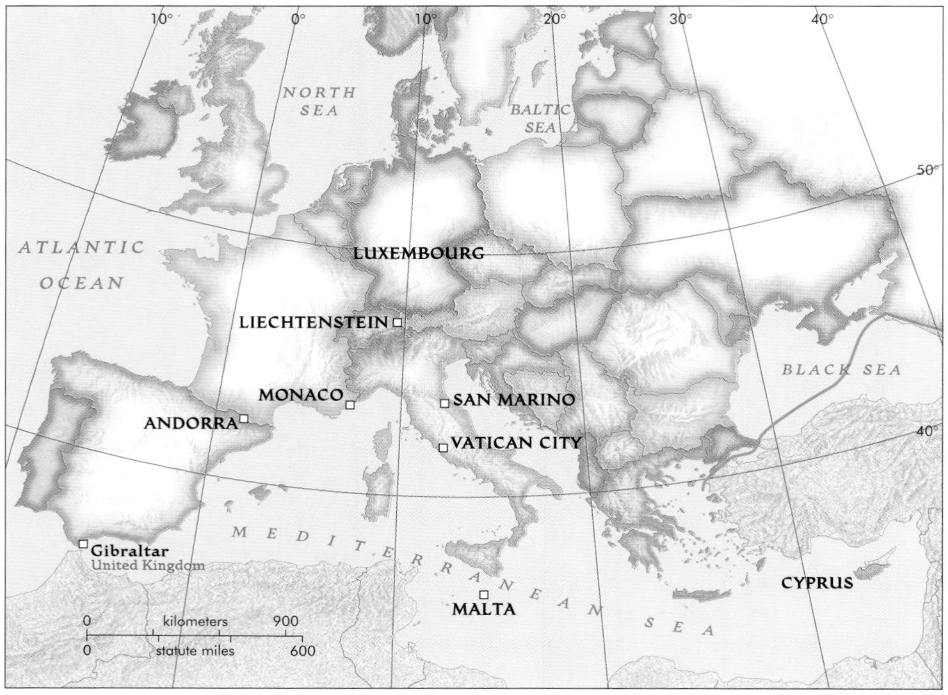

Independent Nations

Andorra

PRINCIPALITY OF ANDORRA

AREA 468 sq km (181 sq mi)
POPULATION 74,000
CAPITAL Andorra la Vella 21,000
RELIGION Roman Catholic
LANGUAGE Catalan (official), French, Castilian, Portuguese
LITERACY 100%
LIFE EXPECTANCY 84 years
GDP PER CAPITA $33,335
ECONOMY **IND:** tourism (particularly skiing), cattle raising, timber, banking **AGR:** rye, wheat, barley, oats; sheep **EXP:** tobacco products, furniture

Cyprus

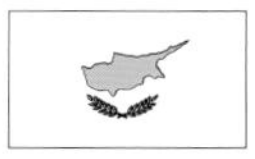

REPUBLIC OF CYPRUS

AREA 9,251 sq km (3,572 sq mi)
POPULATION 965,000
CAPITAL Nicosia 205,000
RELIGION Greek Orthodox, Muslim
LANGUAGE Greek, Turkish, English
LITERACY 98%
LIFE EXPECTANCY 77 years
GDP PER CAPITA $18,562
ECONOMY **IND:** tourism, food and beverage processing, cement and gypsum production, ship repair **AGR:** citrus, vegetables, barley, grapes; poultry **EXP:** citrus, potatoes, pharmaceuticals, cement

Liechtenstein

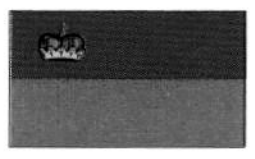

PRINCIPALITY OF LIECHTENSTEIN

AREA 160 sq km (62 sq mi)
POPULATION 35,000
CAPITAL Vaduz 5,000
RELIGION Roman Catholic, Protestant
LANGUAGE German (official)
LITERACY 100%
LIFE EXPECTANCY 80 years
GDP PER CAPITA $101,654
ECONOMY **IND:** electronics, metal manufacturing, dental products **AGR:** wheat, barley, corn; livestock **EXP:** small machinery, audio/video connectors

Luxembourg

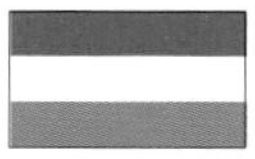

GRAND DUCHY OF LUXEMBOURG

AREA 2,586 sq km (998 sq mi)
POPULATION 457,000
CAPITAL Luxembourg 77,000
RELIGION Roman Catholic
LANGUAGE Luxembourgish, German, French
LITERACY 100%
LIFE EXPECTANCY 78 years
GDP PER CAPITA $69,423
ECONOMY **IND:** banking, iron and steel, food processing **AGR:** barley, oats, potatoes; livestock **EXP:** machinery, steel products, chemicals

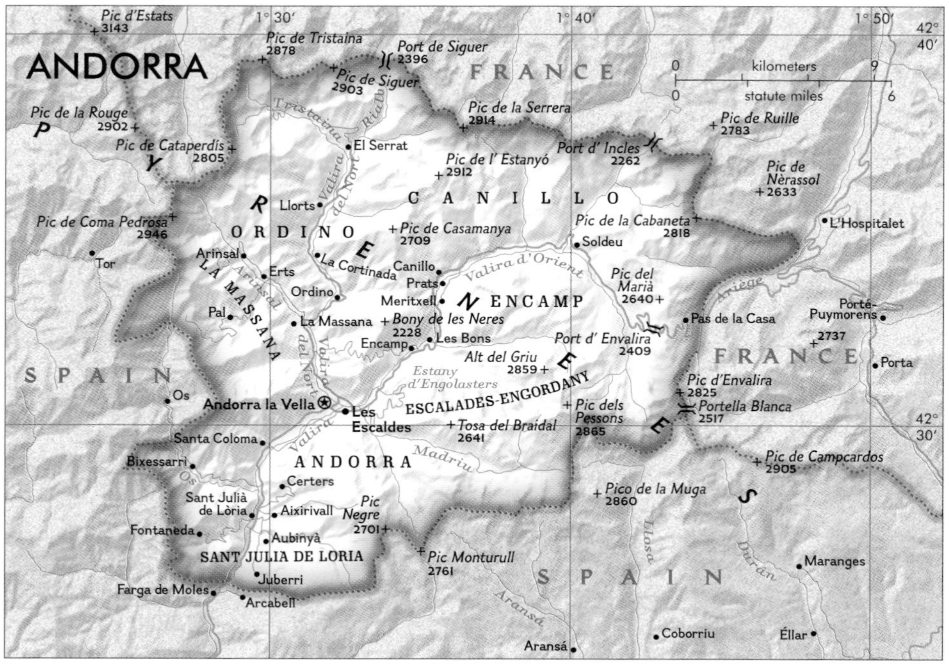

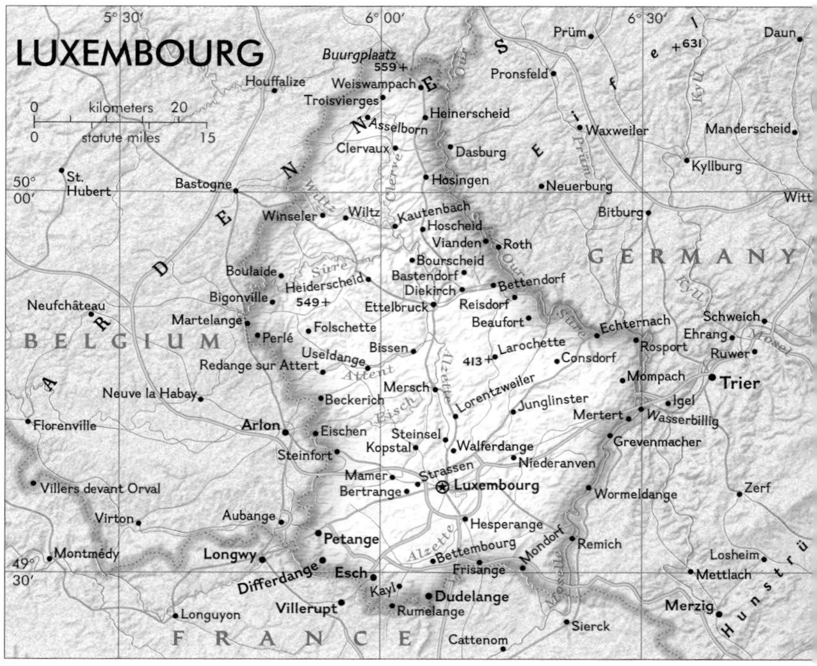

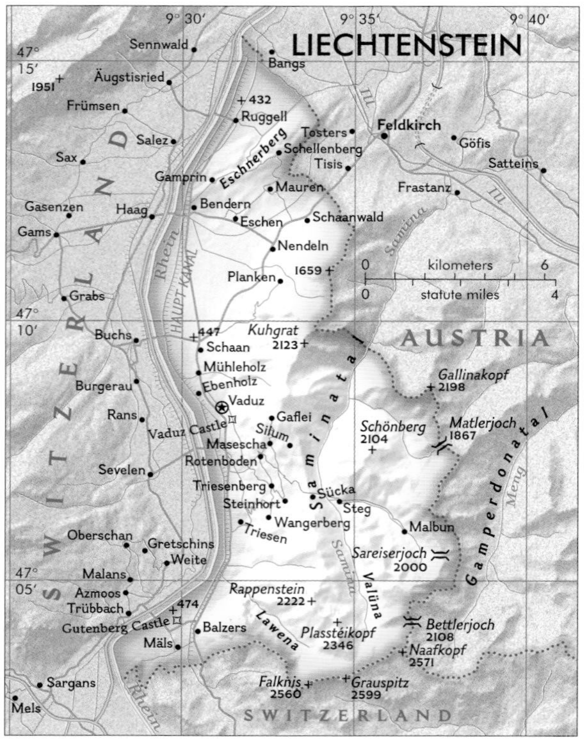

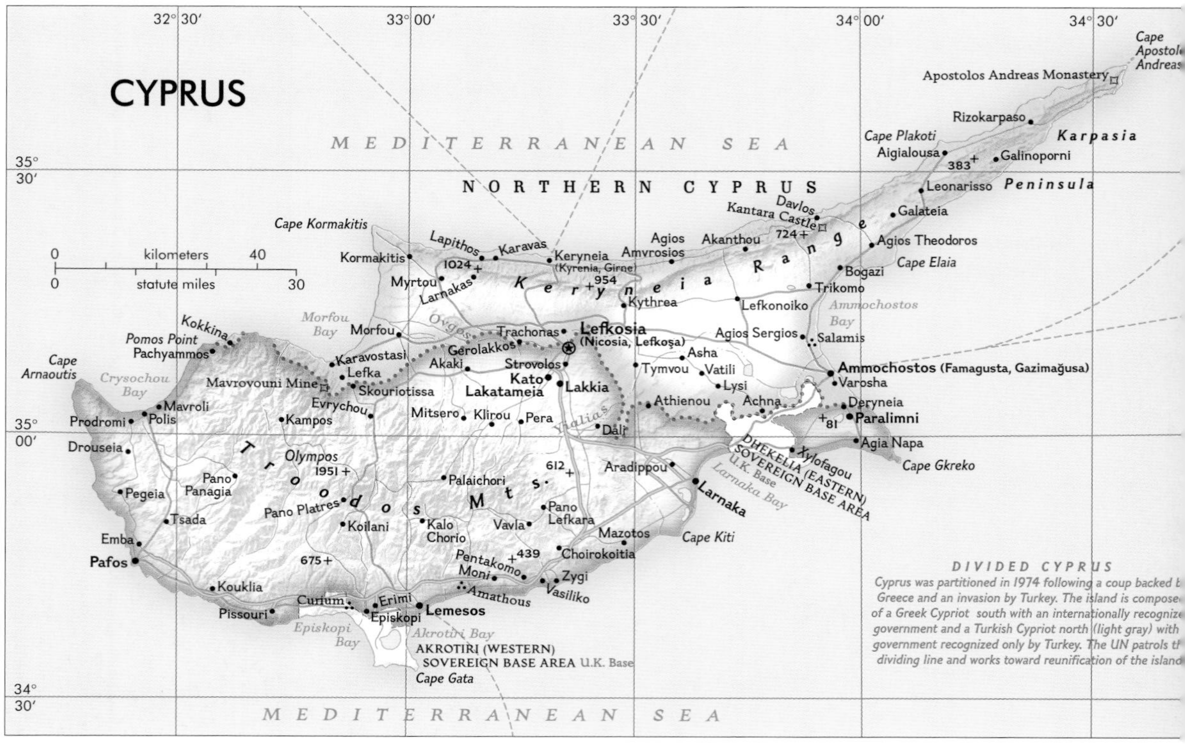

Malta

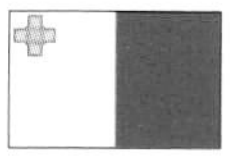

REPUBLIC OF MALTA

AREA 316 sq km (122 sq mi)
POPULATION 405,000
CAPITAL Valletta 83,000
RELIGION Roman Catholic
LANGUAGE Maltese (official), English (official)
LITERACY 93%
LIFE EXPECTANCY 78 years
GDP PER CAPITA $14,074
ECONOMY **IND:** tourism, electronics, ship building and repair, construction **AGR:** potatoes, cauliflower, grapes, wheat; pork **EXP:** machinery and transport equipment, manufactures

Monaco

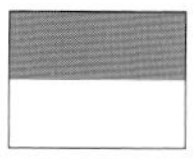

PRINCIPALITY OF MONACO

AREA 2 sq km (1 sq mi)
POPULATION 33,000
CAPITAL Monaco 34,000
RELIGION Roman Catholic
LANGUAGE French (official), English, Italian, Monegasque
LITERACY 99%
LIFE EXPECTANCY 80 years
GDP PER CAPITA $32,984
ECONOMY **IND:** tourism, construction, small-scale industrial and consumer products **AGR:** NA **EXP:** Full customs integration with France

San Marino

REPUBLIC OF SAN MARINO

AREA 61 sq km (24 sq mi)
POPULATION 30,000
CAPITAL San Marino 5,000
RELIGION Roman Catholic
LANGUAGE Italian
LITERACY 96%
LIFE EXPECTANCY 81 years
GDP PER CAPITA $44,607
ECONOMY **IND:** tourism, banking, textiles, electronics **AGR:** wheat, grapes, corn, olives; cattle **EXP:** building stone, lime, wood, chestnuts

Vatican City

THE HOLY SEE (STATE OF THE VATICAN CITY)

AREA 0.4 sq km (0.2 sq mi)
POPULATION 1,000
RELIGION Roman Catholic
LANGUAGE Italian, Latin, French
LITERACY 100%
LIFE EXPECTANCY NA
GDP PER CAPITA NA
ECONOMY **IND:** printing, production of coins, medals, and postage stamps, a small amount of mosaics and staff uniforms, worldwide banking and financial activities **AGR:** NA **EXP:** NA

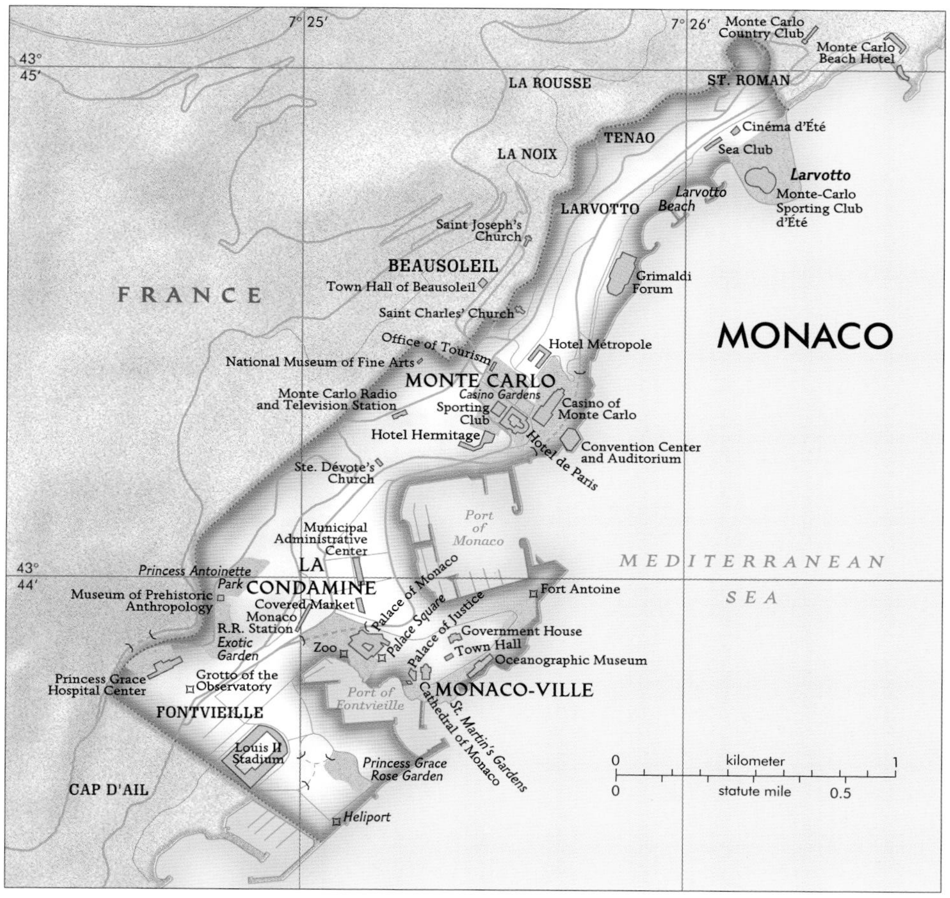

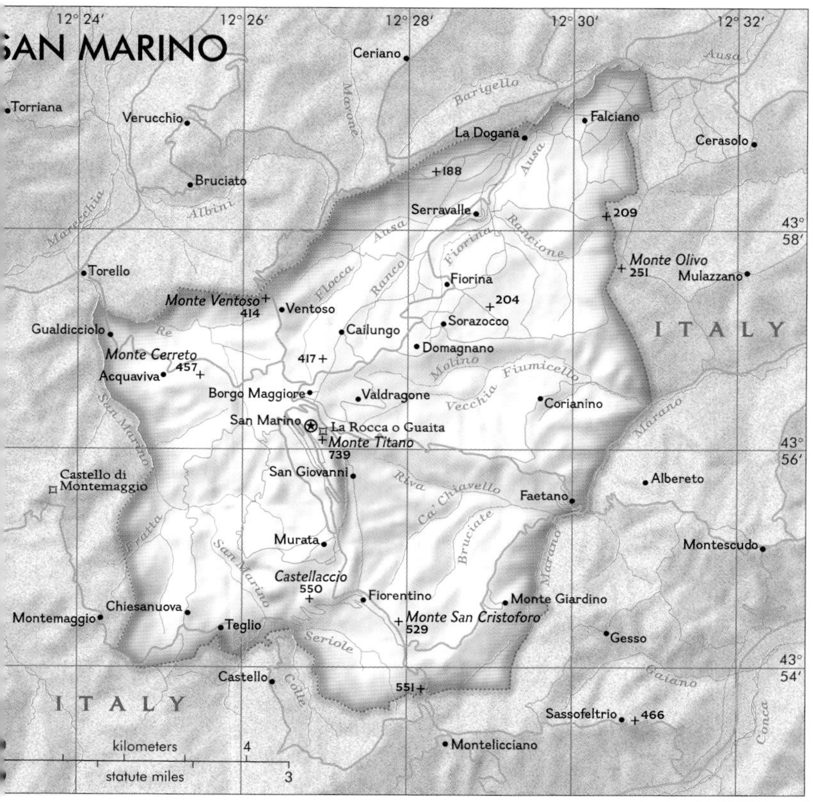

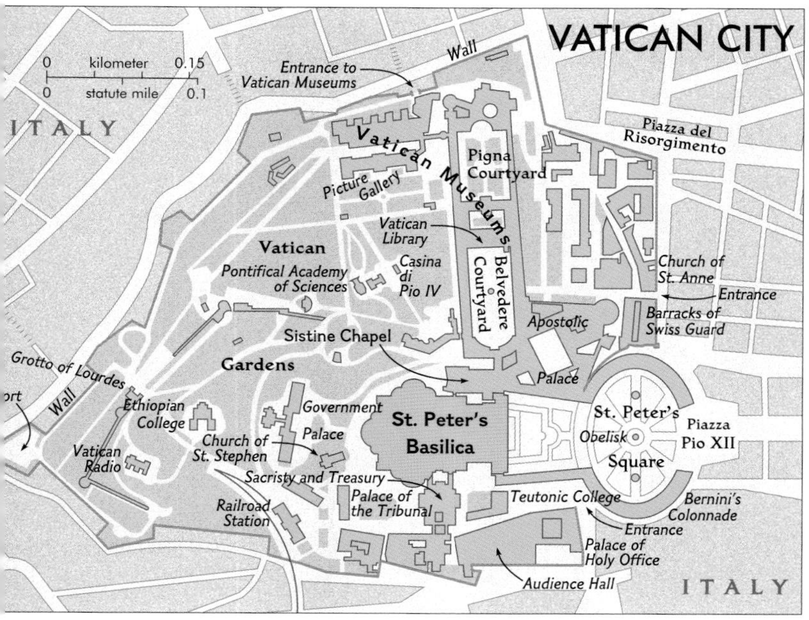

Dependency

SOVEREIGN

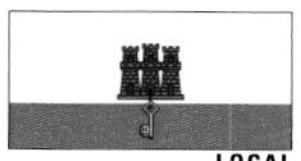
LOCAL

Gibraltar (U.K.)

GIBRALTAR

AREA 7 sq km (3 sq mi)
POPULATION 29,000
CAPITAL Gibraltar 27,000
RELIGION Roman Catholic, Church of England
LANGUAGE English, Spanish, Italian, Portuguese
LITERACY NA
LIFE EXPECTANCY 80 years
GDP PER CAPITA $27,900
ECONOMY **IND:** tourism, banking and finance, ship repairing, tobacco **AGR:** NA **EXP:** petroleum, manufactured goods

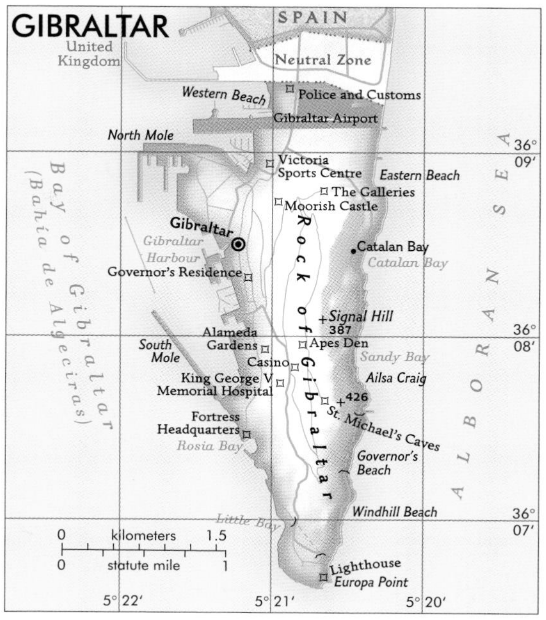

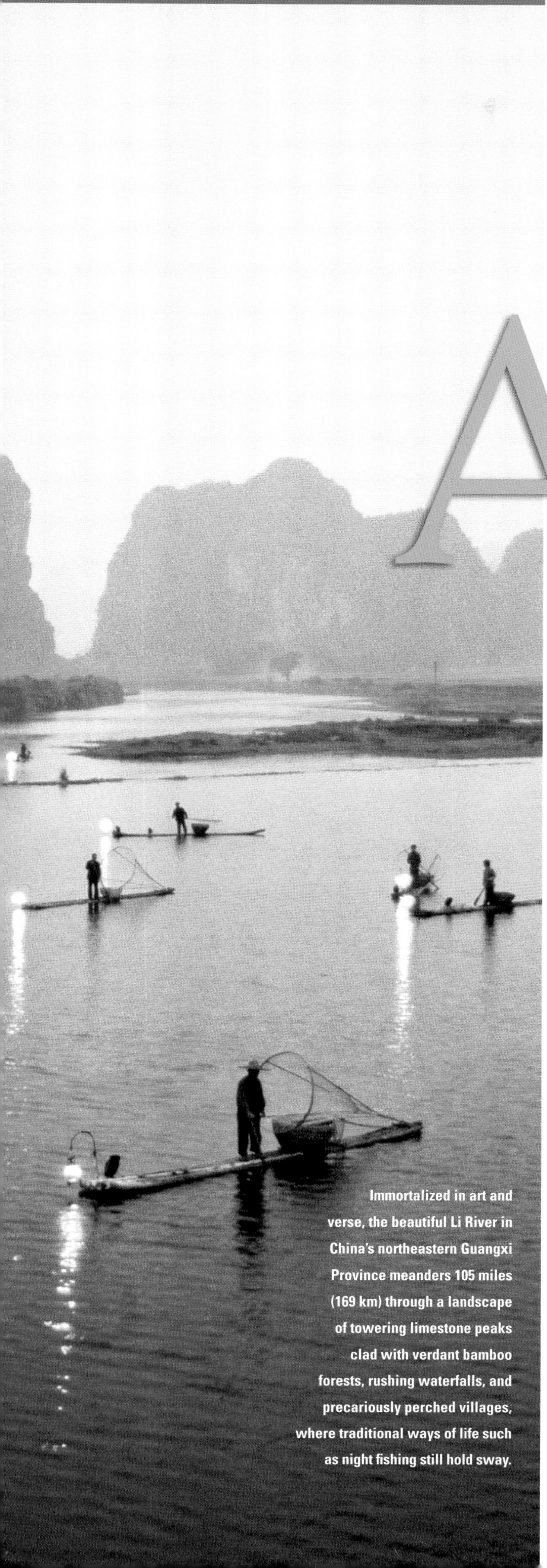

Immortalized in art and verse, the beautiful Li River in China's northeastern Guangxi Province meanders 105 miles (169 km) through a landscape of towering limestone peaks clad with verdant bamboo forests, rushing waterfalls, and precariously perched villages, where traditional ways of life such as night fishing still hold sway.

Asia

The continent of Asia, occupying four-fifths of the giant Eurasian landmass, stretches across ten time zones from the Pacific Ocean in the east to the Ural Mountains and Black Sea in the west. It is the largest of continents, with dazzling geographic diversity and 30 percent of the Earth's land surface. Asia includes numerous island nations, such as Japan, the Philippines, Indonesia, and Sri Lanka, as well as many of the world's major islands: Borneo, Sumatra, Honshu, Celebes, Java, and half of New Guinea.

Siberia, the huge Asian section of Russia, reaches deep inside the Arctic Circle and fills the continent's northern quarter. To its south lie the large countries of Kazakhstan, Mongolia, and China. In all, Asia contains 46 nations, accounting for 60 percent of the Earth's population—more than 3.9 billion people—yet deserts, mountains, jungles, and other inhospitable zones render much of Asia empty or underpopulated.

For millennia, people have lived near the seas and along great rivers. Early civilizations arose in China along the Yellow River, in South Asia on the Indus, and in the Middle East along the Tigris and Euphrates. Today, Asia's large populations continue to thrive near inland waterways and coastal regions.

India and China, historically isolated from each other by the Himalaya Mountains and Myanmar's jungles, developed rich, vibrant cultures with art, literature, and philosophy of the highest order. China's 1.3 billion people and India's billion make up nearly two-thirds of Asia's population. These countries stand as rivals, each trying to modernize and assert itself while struggling with formidable problems of poverty, pollution, urbanization, and illiteracy.

Breakup of the Soviet Union in 1991 allowed for the creation of eight new Asian countries, five in Central Asia—Kazakhstan, Kyrgyzstan, Uzbekistan, Turkmenistan, and Tajikistan—and three in the Caucasus region—Georgia, Armenia, and Azerbaijan.

Asia's few democracies, including Israel, India, and Japan, contrast with much more authoritarian governments or military regimes, which are numerous and widespread. Monarchies in Bhutan, Nepal, Jordan, Saudi Arabia, and Brunei (a sultanate) pass rulership through family lines.

Events at the start of the 21st century have put new focus on the Middle East, the role of Islam, and control of religious extremism. More than half of Asia's countries are Muslim, yet they possess very different languages, climates, economies, and ethnic groups. But all share emotional links with their co-religionists and care deeply about the development of Islam in the decades ahead.

PHYSICAL GEOGRAPHY Asia, the planet's youngest continent, displays continuing geologic activity. Volcanoes form a chain known as the Ring of Fire along the entire Pacific edge, from Siberia's Kamchatka Peninsula to the islands of the Philippines and Indonesia. The Indian subcontinent pushes into the heart of Asia, raising and contorting the towering Karakoram and Himalaya ranges. Earthquakes rattle China, Japan, and West Asia.

Geographic extremes allow Asia to claim many world records. Mount Everest, monarch of the Himalaya, is the planet's highest point at 29,035 feet (8,850 m). The super-salty Dead Sea lies 1,365 feet (416 m) below sea level—the lowest point. A site in Assam, India, receives an astonishing 39 feet (12 m) of rain each year, making it the wettest spot on Earth, and Siberia's ancient Lake Baikal, arcing 395 miles (636 km), plunges over a mile (5,371 ft; 1,637 m) as the world's deepest lake. It harbors many unique plant and animal species, including tens of thousands of freshwater seals.

The Caspian Sea, salty and isolated on the border of Europe and Asia, is the largest lake, measuring more than four times the area of Lake Superior. A 39,000-mile (62,800 km) coastline, longest of any continent's, allows all but 12 Asian nations direct access to the sea.

These landlocked countries, mostly in Central Asia (excepting Laos), form part of a great band across the middle latitudes comprised of deserts, mountains, and arid plateaus. The vast Tibetan Plateau, home to the yak, snow leopard, wild ass, and migrating antelope, gives rise to Asia's vital rivers: the Yellow, Yangtze, Indus, Ganges, Salween, and Mekong. At the heart of the continent exists a convergence of the world's mighty mountains: Himalaya, Karakoram, Hindu Kush, Pamir, and Kunlun.

Flowing sand dunes of the Arabian Peninsula contrast with steppes that extend for thousands of grassy miles from Europe to Mongolia. To the north, girdling Asia's northern latitudes, grow boreal forests made up of conifers—the taiga—largest unbroken woodlands in the world. Beyond the taiga lie frozen expanses of tundra.

Far to the south, monsoon winds bring annual rains to thickly populated regions of South and Southeast Asia. These wet, green domains support some of the world's last rain forests and amazing numbers of plants. Human impact through agriculture, animal grazing, and forestry has altered much of Asia's landscape and continues to threaten the natural realm.

HISTORY Asia's great historical breadth encompasses thousands of years, vast distances, and a kaleidoscope of peoples. From China to Lebanon, from Siberia to Sri Lanka, Asia has more ethnic and national groups than any other continent. Their histories have evolved through peaceful growth and migration, but more often through military conquest.

The Fertile Crescent region of the Middle East saw the emergence of agriculture and early settlements some 10,000 years ago. Later, successful irrigation helped bring forth the first civilization in Sumer, today's southern Iraq; Sumerians invented the first wheeled vehicles, the potter's wheel, the first system of writing—cuneiform—and codes of law.

During the second millennium B.C., a pastoral people called Aryans, or Indo-Iranians, pushed into present-day Afghanistan and eastern Iran, then steadily occupied much of India, Western, and Central Asia.

Central Asia has always been a historic melting pot of flourishing cultures. More than 2,000 years ago a braid of ancient caravan tracks—the Silk Road—carried precious goods between East Asia and the rest of the world: sleek horses, exotic foods, medicines, jewels, birds, and perfume. More practical were gunpowder, the magnetic compass, the printing press, mathematics, ceramics, and silk. Trade flourished especially during China's Han dynasty (206 B.C.–A.D. 220), Tang dynasty (A.D. 618–907), and the Mongol period (13th and 14th centuries). Mongols at their height came closer than any other people to conquering all of Asia, threatening Europe in the west and twice trying to invade Japan.

Another great expansion was the conquest and settlement of Siberia and Central Asia by Russians. The Trans-Siberian Railway, built between 1891 and 1905, opened up Siberia for settlement. During the 19th century, Russian armies and colonizers spread through Central

Asia as well, claiming the khanates for an expanding Russian empire. Great Britain, France, and other European countries also laid claim to parts of Asia.

Today, colonial empires have ended and a seemingly stable community of nations with defined borders exists in Asia. Yet rivalries, threats, and war dominate many regions. Indochina is only now healing after decades of violence. The Korean Peninsula remains divided. Nuclear-armed India and Pakistan have fought three wars since independence in 1947. Religious and ethnic hostilities inflame many areas, nowhere more so than in the Middle East. Troubled Afghanistan, victim of almost continuous warfare since 1979, saw a U.S.-led invasion in 2001 to oust the Taliban government and destroy terrorist groups. Many claim peace will come to these areas only after economic stability, steps towards democracy, and recognition of human rights are achieved.

CULTURE Numerous cultural forces, each linked to broad geographic areas, have formed and influenced Asia's rich civilizations and hundreds of ethnic groups. The two oldest are the cultural milieus of India and China.

India's culture still reverberates throughout countries as varied as Sri Lanka, Pakistan, Afghanistan, Nepal, Bangladesh, Myanmar (Burma), and across seas to Thailand, Cambodia, Singapore, and Indonesia. The world religions of Hinduism and Buddhism originated in India and spread as traders, scholars, and priests sought distant footholds. The island of Bali in predominantly Muslim Indonesia remains Hindu today. Many regions of Asia first encountered writing in the form of Sanskrit, the holy script of Hinduism.

China's civilization, more than four thousand years old, has profoundly influenced the development of all of East Asia, much of Southeast Asia, and parts of Central Asia. Chinese institutions such as government, warfare, architecture, the arts and sciences, and even chopsticks reached to the heart of other lands and peoples. Most important of all were the Chinese written language, a complex script with thousands of characters, and Confucianism, an ethical world view that affected philosophy, politics, and relations within society. Japan, Korea, and Vietnam especially absorbed these cultural gifts.

Today, most Chinese call themselves "Han," a term that embraces more than 90 percent of the population—a billion people—and thus makes them the world's largest ethnic group. In addition, China's government recognizes 55 other ethnic minorities within its borders.

Islam, a third great cultural influence in Asia, proved formidable in its energy and creative genius. Arabs from the seventh century onward, spurred on by faith, moved rapidly into Southwest Asia. Their religion and culture, particularly Arabic writing, spread through Iran and Afghanistan to the Indian subcontinent. In time, shipping, commerce, and missionaries carried Islam on to the Malay Peninsula and Indonesian archipelago. Indonesia, the largest Muslim country with more than 200 million believers, and Pakistan and Bangladesh, each with more than 100 million Muslims, attest to Islam's success.

Europeans, too, have affected Asia's cultures, from the conquests of Alexander the Great to today's multinational corporations. Colonial powers, especially Britain in India, France in Indochina, Holland in the Indonesian archipelago, and numerous countries in China, left a lasting mark even after nationalist movements forced them out in the late 1940s and early 1950s.

In 1791, King Bodawapaya of Myanmar commissioned an enormous Buddhist pagoda in Mingun. Although construction stopped upon the king's death in 1819, the building still measures an astounding 256 feet square (78 m sq) at its base and is 150 feet (45.7 m) tall. Subsequent earthquakes cracked the structure.

ECONOMY Blessed with resources and teeming with energetic people, Asia still suffers from great disparities between rich and poor. The livelihood of most Asians rests on agriculture and age-old methods of production. Vietnamese women turn waterwheels by foot-power. Iranian farmers plow using buffaloes. Indian villagers, bent at the waist, plant rice seedlings by hand. Bangladeshi fishermen cast circular nets, hoping for a few small fish. Burmese lacquerwork, Chinese embroidery, Middle Eastern brassware, and Indonesian batik cloth represent local crafts.

Wet-rice cultivation from Japan southward has shaped life for hundreds of millions of Asians. To the west, across north China, Central Asia, and beyond to the Middle East, wheat growing has dominated. Plantation and cash crops, too, such as rubber, tea, palm oil, coconuts, sugarcane, and tobacco continue to sustain regional economies.

Across Asia, country dwellers have flocked in the millions to the cities, seeking jobs and a better life. From Jakarta to Baghdad, the growth of megacities represents a dramatic change over the past 50 years. In China, as many as 100 million people form a floating population, seeking work wherever it can be found.

The emergence of postwar Japan as Asia's strongest economy set a model for newly industrialized centers such as South Korea, Hong Kong, Singapore, and Taiwan. Japan, with few natural resources, imports oil, foodstuffs, and textiles, but succeeds by exporting cars, chemicals, and electronics. Central Asian nations of the former Soviet Union have industrialized but require further diversification to rise above poverty. Lands in the Persian Gulf region have flourished from petroleum, and many countries now use light industry as a motor for growth. Tourism, too, plays its part and has helped Thailand, Nepal, and parts of Indonesia and China, including Hong Kong.

India's liberalized economy has encouraged a large, growing middle class, and China—an economic dynamo with plentiful resources—may become the world's largest economy in 25 years.

Yet hunger for minerals, water, agricultural land, fuelwood, housing, and animal products poses great challenges for Asia as every nation tries to raise the standard of living of its people.

Asia: Physical and Political

Two-Point Equidistant Projection
SCALE 1:39,821,000
1 CENTIMETER = 398 KILOMETERS; 1 INCH = 629 MILES
KILOMETERS
STATUTE MILES
International boundary
Disputed or undefined boundary
A commonly accepted division between Asia and Europe–here marked by a green line–is formed by the Ural Mountains, Ural River, Caspian Sea, Caucasus Mountains, and the Black Sea with its outlets, the Bosporus and Dardanelles.
ATLANTIC OCEAN
ARCTIC OCEAN
North Pole
GREENLAND
SVALBARD
FRANZ JOSEF LAND
NOVAYA ZEMLYA
BARENTS SEA
KARA SEA
GREENLAND SEA
NORWEGIAN SEA
ARCTIC CIRCLE
NORTH SEA
BALTIC SEA
BRITISH ISLES
Ireland
Great Britain
Meridian of Greenwich (London)
SCANDINAVIA
Gulf of Bothnia
Kola Peninsula
White Sea
Lake Onega
Lake Ladoga
NORTHERN EUROPEAN PLAIN
EUROPE
ALPS
IBERIAN PENINSULA
BALKAN PENINSULA
ATLAS MOUNTAINS
MEDITERRANEAN SEA
BLACK SEA
Crimea
ANATOLIA (ASIA MINOR)
Taurus Mts.
Cyprus
Caucasus Mountains
El'brus 5642
Mt. Ararat
CASPIAN SEA
Caspian Depression
URAL MOUNTAINS
Narodnaya 1895
Yamal Peninsula
Gyda Pen.
WEST SIBERIAN PLAIN
Ishim Steppe
THE STEPPES
Kazakh Uplands
Aral Sea
Ustyurt Plateau
Turan Lowland
Qizilqum
Garagum
Kopet Mts.
Elburz Mts.
Dasht-e Lut
Zagros Mountains
Mesopotamia
Syrian Desert
An Nafud
Ad Dahna'
ARABIAN PENINSULA
Rub' al Khali
Hasa Plain
PERSIAN GULF
GULF OF OMAN
Ra's al Hadd
Hadhramaut
GULF OF ADEN
Socotra
RED SEA
Hejaz
Tihamah
SINAI
AFRICA
SAHARA
TROPIC OF CANCER
ETHIOPIAN HIGHLANDS
Somali Peninsula
EQUATOR
Seychelles
Comoro Is.
ARABIAN SEA
LACCADIVE SEA
Lakshadweep
Maldive Islands
INDIAN OCEAN
Great Indian Desert
Indus
Gulf of Kutch
DECCAN PLATEAU
Western Ghats
Eastern Ghats
Malabar Coast
Coromandel Coast
Cape Comorin
Sri Lanka
Vindhya Range
Chota Nagpur Plateau
Ganges Plain
BAY OF BENGAL
Andaman Islands
Nicobar Islands
ANDAMAN SEA
Hindu Kush
Karakoram Ra.
K2 (Godwin Austin) 8611
KASHMIR
HIMALAYA
Mt. Everest 8850 (29035 ft)
PLATEAU OF TIBET
KUNLUN MOUNTAINS
Taklimakan Desert
TARIM BASIN
TIAN SHAN
Victory Peak 7439
Dzungarian Basin
Turpan Depression
Bogda Shan
Altun Shan
Qaidam Basin
Qilian Shan
Bei Shan
Lop Nur
ALTAY MOUNTAINS
Belukha 4506
Western Sayan Mts.
Eastern Sayan Mts.
CENTRAL SIBERIAN PLATEAU
SIBERIA
North Siberian Lowland
Taymyr Peninsula
October Revolution I.
Komsomolets I.
Bol'shevik I.
SEVERNAYA ZEMLYA
NEW SIBERIAN IS.
Kotel'nyy I.
EAST SIBERIAN SEA
Wrangel I.
CHUKCHI SEA
Chukchi Pen.
Bering Str.
East Cape
Verkhoyansk Range
Cherskiy Range
Kolyma Range
Kolyma Lowland
Koryak Range
Gulf of Anadyr
Cape Navarin
Cape Olyutorskiy
BERING SEA
Commander Islands
ALEUTIAN ISLANDS
KAMCHATKA PENINSULA
Klyuchevskaya Sopka 4750
Central Range
Cape Lopatka
SEA OF OKHOTSK
KURIL ISLANDS
Shantar Islands
Dzhugdzhur Range
Stanovoy Range
Yablonovyy Range
Lake Baikal
World's deepest lake 1637 m (5371 ft)
Source of the Amur-Onon
Source of the Yenisey-Angara
Source of the Ob-Irtysh
MONGOLIAN PLATEAU
GOBI
Yin Shan
Greater Khingan Range
Lesser Khingan Range
Manchurian Plain
SAKHALIN
Tatar Strait
Sikhote Alin' Range
Korea
SEA OF JAPAN (EAST SEA)
HOKKAIDO
HONSHU
JAPAN
SHIKOKU
KYUSHU
Fuji
Izu Islands
Bonin Islands
Volcano Islands
PACIFIC OCEAN
TROPIC OF CANCER
MARIANA ISLANDS
Guam
CAROLINE ISLANDS
PHILIPPINE SEA
RYUKYU ISLANDS
Okinawa
EAST CHINA SEA
YELLOW SEA
Bo Hai
North China Plain
Lüliang Shan
Qin Ling
Sichuan Basin
Yangtze Gorges
Wuyi Shan
TAIWAN
Taiwan Strait
Hainan
Gulf of Tonkin
SOUTH CHINA SEA
Daxue Mts.
Gongga Shan 7556
Bayan Har Shan
Tanggula Range
Nyainqentanglha Shan
Mt. Victoria 3053
INDOCHINA PENINSULA
Annam Cordillera
Gulf of Thailand
MALAY PENINSULA
Strait of Malacca
SUMATRA
Barisan Mountains
Kerinci 3800
Mentawai Islands
Nias
Natuna Is.
Bangka
Billiton
BORNEO
Kinabalu 4101
PHILIPPINE ISLANDS
Luzon
Mindoro
Palawan
Panay
Negros
Samar
Mindanao
SULU SEA
CELEBES SEA
CELEBES
Makassar Strait
MOLUCCAS
Halmahera
Ceram
Buru
BANDA SEA
GREATER SUNDA ISLANDS
JAVA SEA
Flores
Timor
TIMOR SEA
ARAFURA SEA
Tanimbar Islands
Aru Islands
NEW GUINEA
Maoke Mts.
Jaya Peak 4884
Dolak
Babelthuap
AUSTRALIA

Two-Point Equidistant Projection
SCALE 1:39,821,000
1 CENTIMETER = 398 KILOMETERS; 1 INCH = 629 MILES
KILOMETERS
STATUTE MILES
KURIL ISLANDS
The southern Kuril Islands of Iturup (Etorofu), Kunashir (Kunashiri), Shikotan, and the Habomai group were lost by Japan to the Soviet Union in 1945. Japan continues to claim these Russian-administered islands.
A commonly accepted division between Asia and Europe—here marked by a green line—is formed by the Ural Mountains, Ural River, Caspian Sea, Caucasus Mountains, and the Black Sea with its outlets, the Bosporus and Dardanelles.

Conic Projection

SCALE 1:4,628,000

1 CENTIMETER = 46.3 KILOMETERS; 1 INCH = 73.1 MILES

0 100 200 KILOMETERS

0 100 200 STATUTE MILES

Temperature and Precipitation

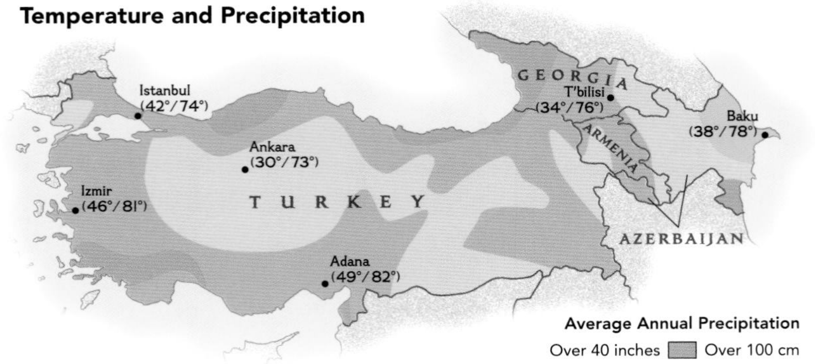

Average Annual Precipitation

Over 40 inches	Over 100 cm
20–40 inches	50–100 cm
10–19 inches	25–49 cm
4–9 inches	10–24 cm
2–3 inches	5–9 cm
Under 2 inches	Under 5 cm

Average Monthly Temperatures (°F)
(January/July)

Population

Urban Area Population

- ■ 5 million and greater
- ▲ 1 million–4,999,999
- • 750,000–999,999
- ○ Under 750,000

People per Square Mile	People per Square Km
Over 500	Over 195
100–500	40–195
10–99	5–39
1–9	1–4
Under 1	Under 1

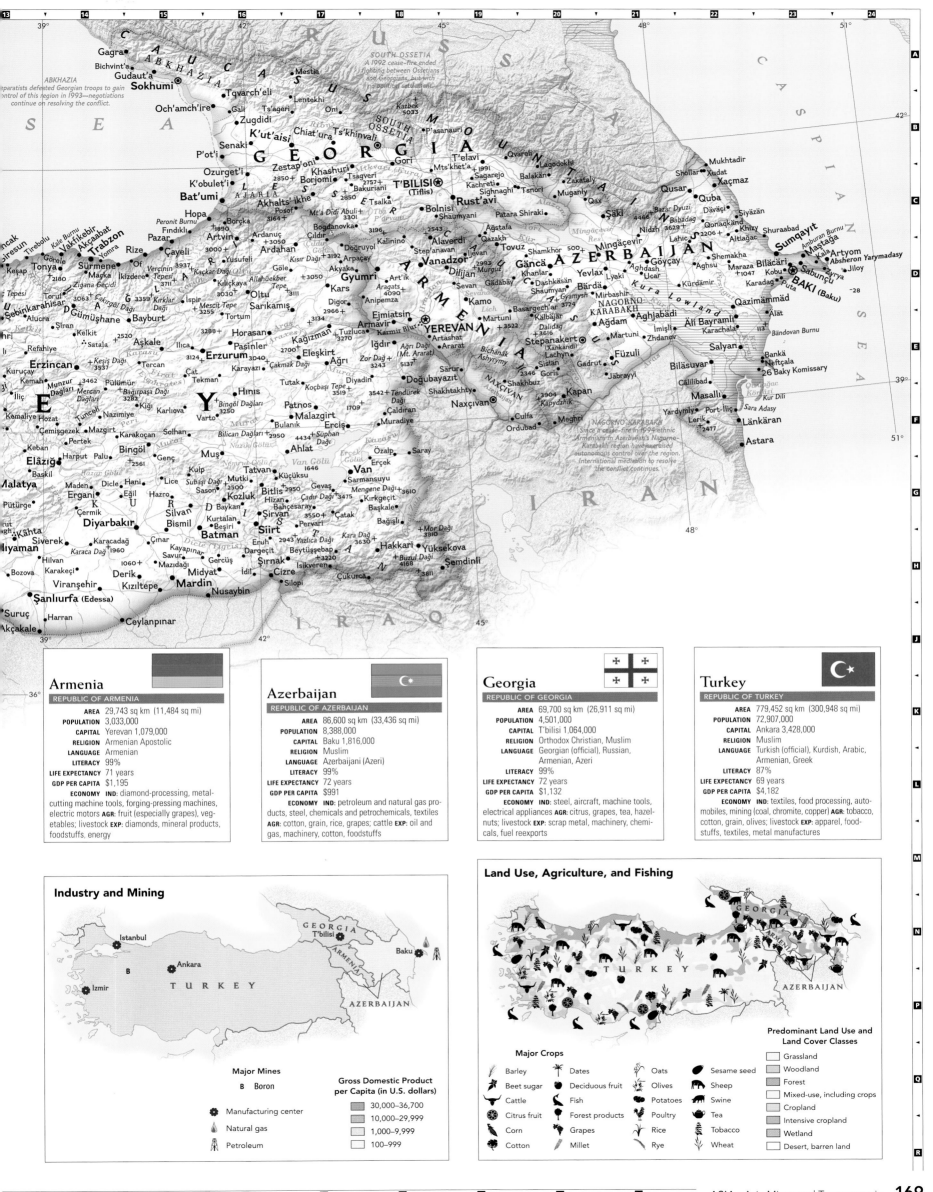

Armenia

REPUBLIC OF ARMENIA

AREA 29,743 sq km (11,484 sq mi)
POPULATION 3,033,000
CAPITAL Yerevan 1,079,000
RELIGION Armenian Apostolic
LANGUAGE Armenian
LITERACY 99%
LIFE EXPECTANCY 71 years
GDP PER CAPITA $1,195
ECONOMY **IND:** diamond-processing, metal-cutting machine tools, forging-pressing machines, electric motors **AGR:** fruit (especially grapes), vegetables; livestock **EXP:** diamonds, mineral products, foodstuffs, energy

Azerbaijan

REPUBLIC OF AZERBAIJAN

AREA 86,600 sq km (33,436 sq mi)
POPULATION 8,388,000
CAPITAL Baku 1,816,000
RELIGION Muslim
LANGUAGE Azerbaijani (Azeri)
LITERACY 99%
LIFE EXPECTANCY 72 years
GDP PER CAPITA $991
ECONOMY **IND:** petroleum and natural gas products, steel, chemicals and petrochemicals, textiles **AGR:** cotton, grain, rice, grapes; cattle **EXP:** oil and gas, machinery, cotton, foodstuffs

Georgia

REPUBLIC OF GEORGIA

AREA 69,700 sq km (26,911 sq mi)
POPULATION 4,501,000
CAPITAL T'bilisi 1,064,000
RELIGION Orthodox Christian, Muslim
LANGUAGE Georgian (official), Russian, Armenian, Azeri
LITERACY 99%
LIFE EXPECTANCY 72 years
GDP PER CAPITA $1,132
ECONOMY **IND:** steel, aircraft, machine tools, electrical appliances **AGR:** citrus, grapes, tea, hazelnuts; livestock **EXP:** scrap metal, machinery, chemicals, fuel reexports

Turkey

REPUBLIC OF TURKEY

AREA 779,452 sq km (300,948 sq mi)
POPULATION 72,907,000
CAPITAL Ankara 3,428,000
RELIGION Muslim
LANGUAGE Turkish (official), Kurdish, Arabic, Armenian, Greek
LITERACY 87%
LIFE EXPECTANCY 69 years
GDP PER CAPITA $4,182
ECONOMY **IND:** textiles, food processing, automobiles, mining (coal, chromite, copper) **AGR:** tobacco, cotton, grain, olives; livestock **EXP:** apparel, foodstuffs, textiles, metal manufactures

Industry and Mining

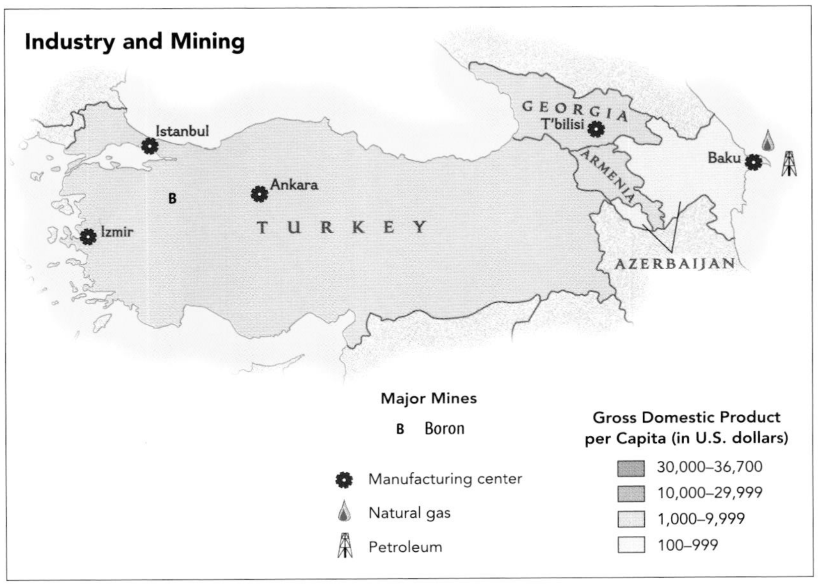

Land Use, Agriculture, and Fishing

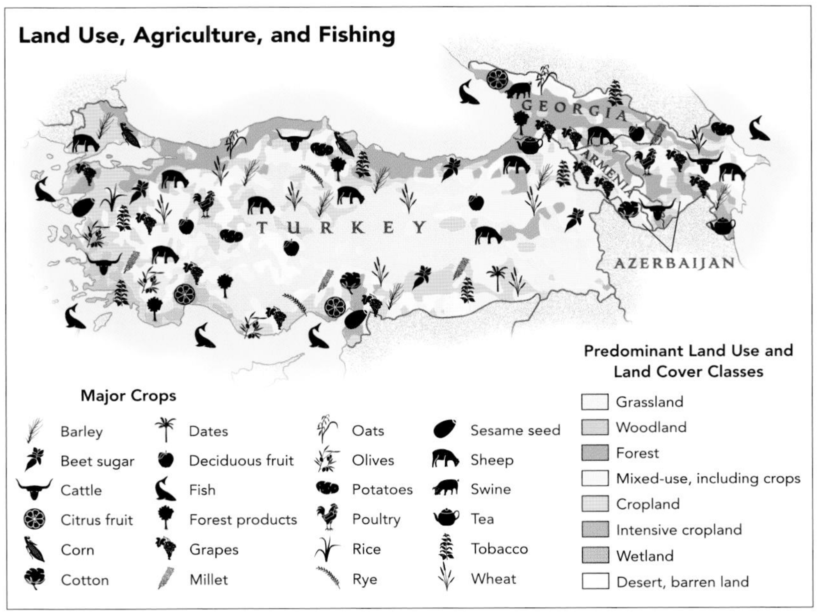

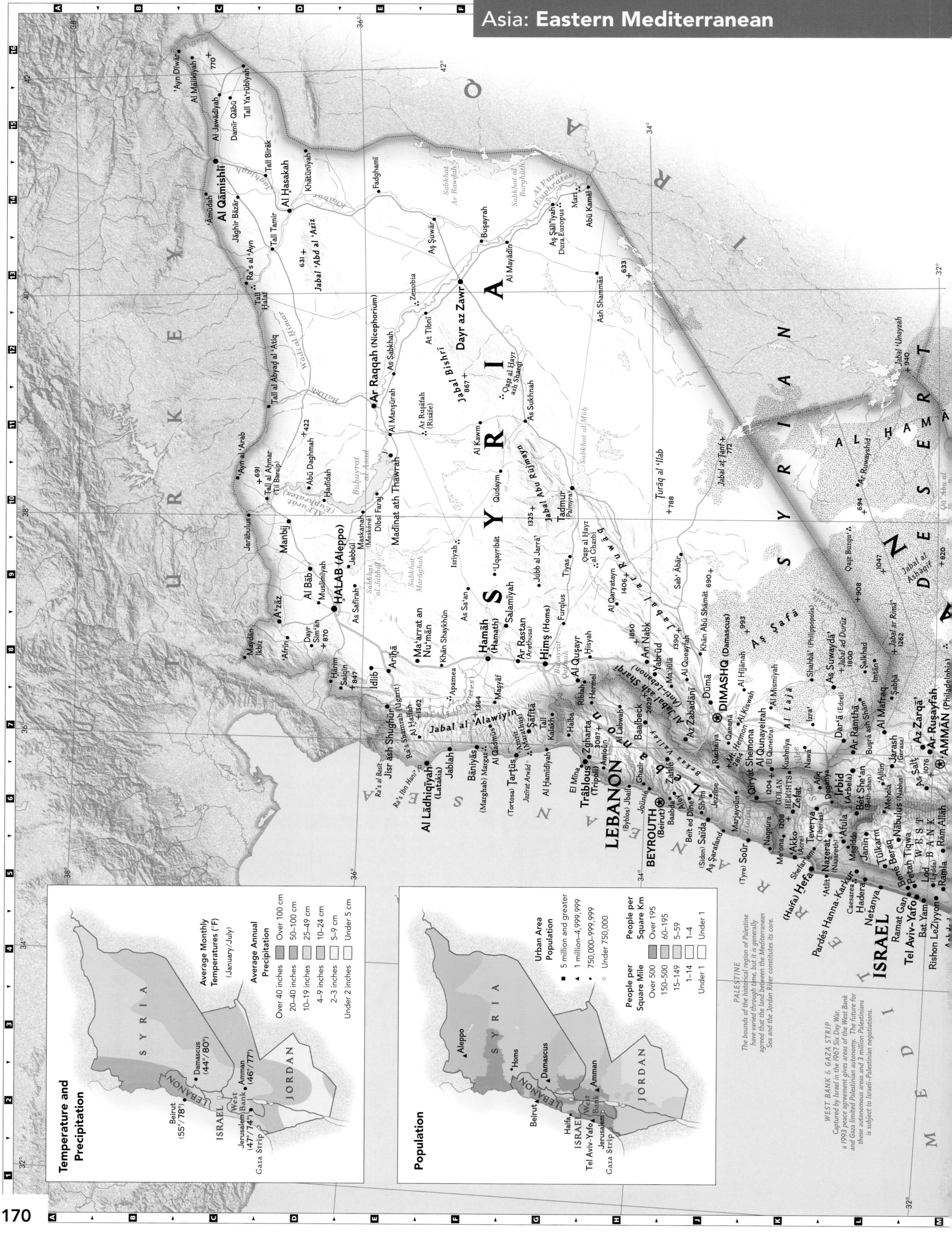
TURKEY
SYRIA
IRAQ
LEBANON
ISRAEL
JORDAN
SYRIAN DESERT
MEDITERRANEAN SEA
AL ḤAMĀD
WEST BANK
GOLAN HEIGHTS
HALAB (Aleppo)
DIMASHQ (Damascus)
BEYROUTH (Beirut)
'AMMĀN (Philadelphia)
Ḥimṣ (Homs)
Ḥamāh (Hamath)
Al Lādhiqīyah (Latakia)
Ar Raqqah (Nicephorium)
Dayr az Zawr
Al Qāmishlī
Al Ḥasakah
Tadmur (Palmyra)
Ţarābulus (Tripoli)
Ṣaydā (Sidon)
Ṣoûr (Tyre)
Ḥefa (Haifa)
Tel Aviv-Yafo
Irbid
Az Zarqā'
Jabal Bishrī
Jabal 'Abd al 'Azīz
Jabal al 'Alawīyīn
Jabal Abū Rujmayn
Jabal ad Durūz
Jabal ash Sharqī (Anti-Lebanon)
Buḥayrat al Asad
Al Furāt (Euphrates)
Bekaa Valley
Mt. Hermon 2814
Zenobia
Dura Europus
Mari
Ṭurāq al 'Ilab
As Ṣafā
Al Lajā

Temperature and Precipitation
Average Monthly Temperatures (°F) (January/July)
Beirut (55°/78°)
Damascus (44°/80°)
Amman (46°/77°)
Jerusalem (47°/74°)
Average Annual Precipitation
Over 40 inches | Over 100 cm
20–40 inches | 50–100 cm
10–19 inches | 25–49 cm
4–9 inches | 10–24 cm
2–3 inches | 5–9 cm
Under 2 inches | Under 5 cm

Population
Urban Area Population
5 million and greater
1 million–4,999,999
750,000–999,999
Under 750,000
People per Square Mile | People per Square Km
Over 500 | Over 195
150–500 | 60–195
15–149 | 5–59
1–14 | 1–4
Under 1 | Under 1

PALESTINE
The bounds of the historical region of Palestine have varied through time, but it is generally agreed that the land between the Mediterranean Sea and the Jordan River constitutes its core.

WEST BANK & GAZA STRIP
Captured by Israel in the 1967 Six Day War, a 1993 peace agreement gives areas of the West Bank and Gaza limited Palestinian autonomy. The future for these autonomous areas and 3 million Palestinians is subject to Israeli-Palestinian negotiations.

Conic Projection

SCALE 1:3,000,000

1 CENTIMETER = 30 KILOMETERS; 1 INCH = 47 MILES

KILOMETERS 0 50 100 150

STATUTE MILES 0 50 100 150

Israel

STATE OF ISRAEL

AREA 22,145 sq km (8,550 sq mi)
POPULATION 7,105,000
CAPITAL Jerusalem 686,000
RELIGION Jewish, Muslim
LANGUAGE Hebrew (official), Arabic, English
LITERACY 95%
LIFE EXPECTANCY 80 years
GDP PER CAPITA $18,651
ECONOMY **IND:** high-technology projects (aviation, communications), wood and paper products, potash and phosphates, food **AGR:** citrus, vegetables, cotton; beef **EXP:** machinery and equipment, software, cut diamonds, agricultural products

Jordan

HASHEMITE KINGDOM OF JORDAN

AREA 89,342 sq km (34,495 sq mi)
POPULATION 5,795,000
CAPITAL Amman 1,237,000
RELIGION Sunni Muslim, Christian
LANGUAGE Arabic (official), English
LITERACY 91%
LIFE EXPECTANCY 72 years
GDP PER CAPITA $1,945
ECONOMY **IND:** phosphate mining, pharmaceuticals, petroleum refining, cement **AGR:** wheat, barley, citrus, tomatoes; sheep **EXP:** clothing, phosphates, fertilizers, potash

Lebanon

LEBANESE REPUBLIC

AREA 10,452 sq km (4,036 sq mi)
POPULATION 3,779,000
CAPITAL Beirut 1,792,000
RELIGION Muslim, Christian
LANGUAGE Arabic (official), French, English, Armenian
LITERACY 87%
LIFE EXPECTANCY 74 years
GDP PER CAPITA $5,634
ECONOMY **IND:** banking, tourism, food processing, jewelry **AGR:** citrus, grapes, tomatoes, apples; sheep **EXP:** authentic jewelry, inorganic chemicals, miscellaneous consumer goods, fruit

Syria

SYRIAN ARAB REPUBLIC

AREA 185,180 sq km (71,498 sq mi)
POPULATION 18,389,000
CAPITAL Damascus 2,228,000
RELIGION Sunni Muslim, Alawite, Druze, other Muslim sects, Christian
LANGUAGE Arabic (official), Kurdish, Armenian, Aramaic, Circassian
LITERACY 77%
LIFE EXPECTANCY 72 years
GDP PER CAPITA $1,261
ECONOMY **IND:** petroleum, textiles, food processing, beverages **AGR:** wheat, barley, cotton, lentils; beef **EXP:** crude oil, petroleum products, fruits and vegetables, cotton fiber

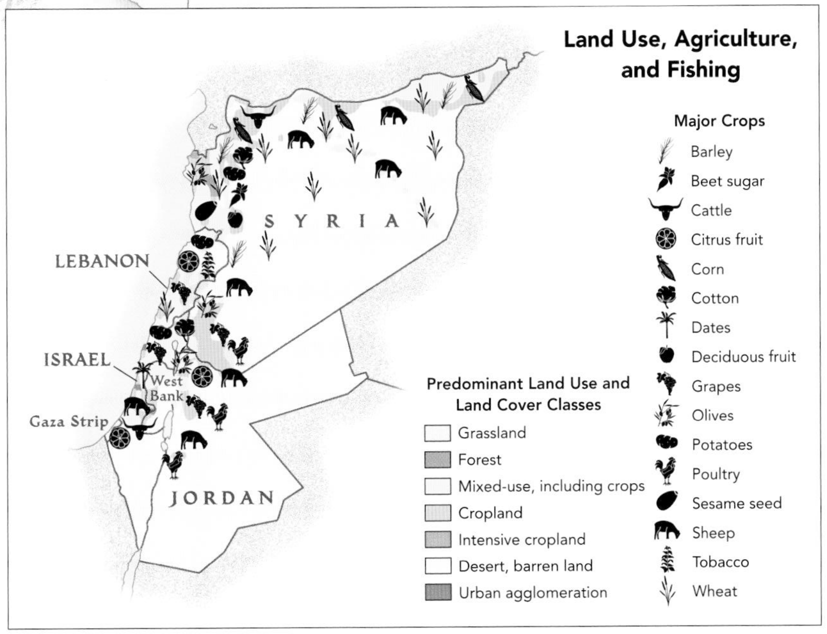

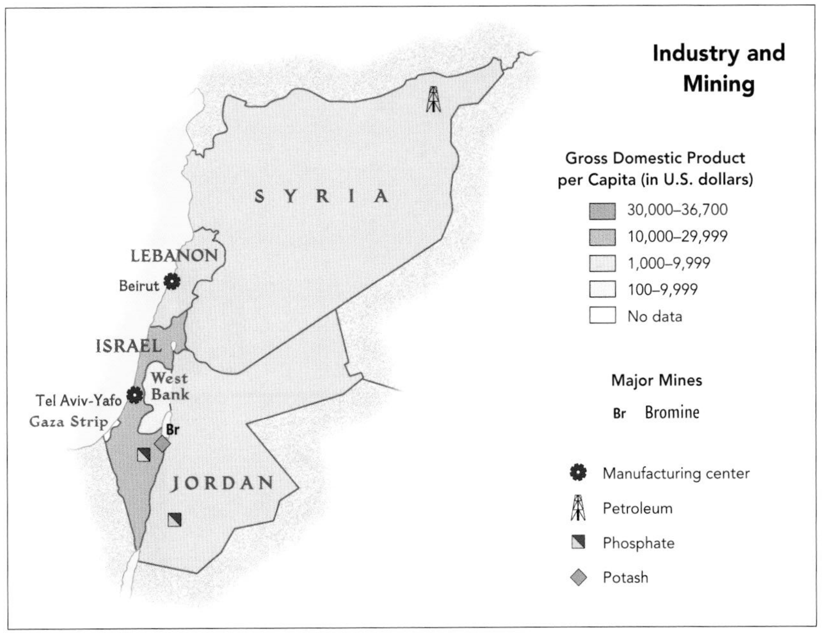

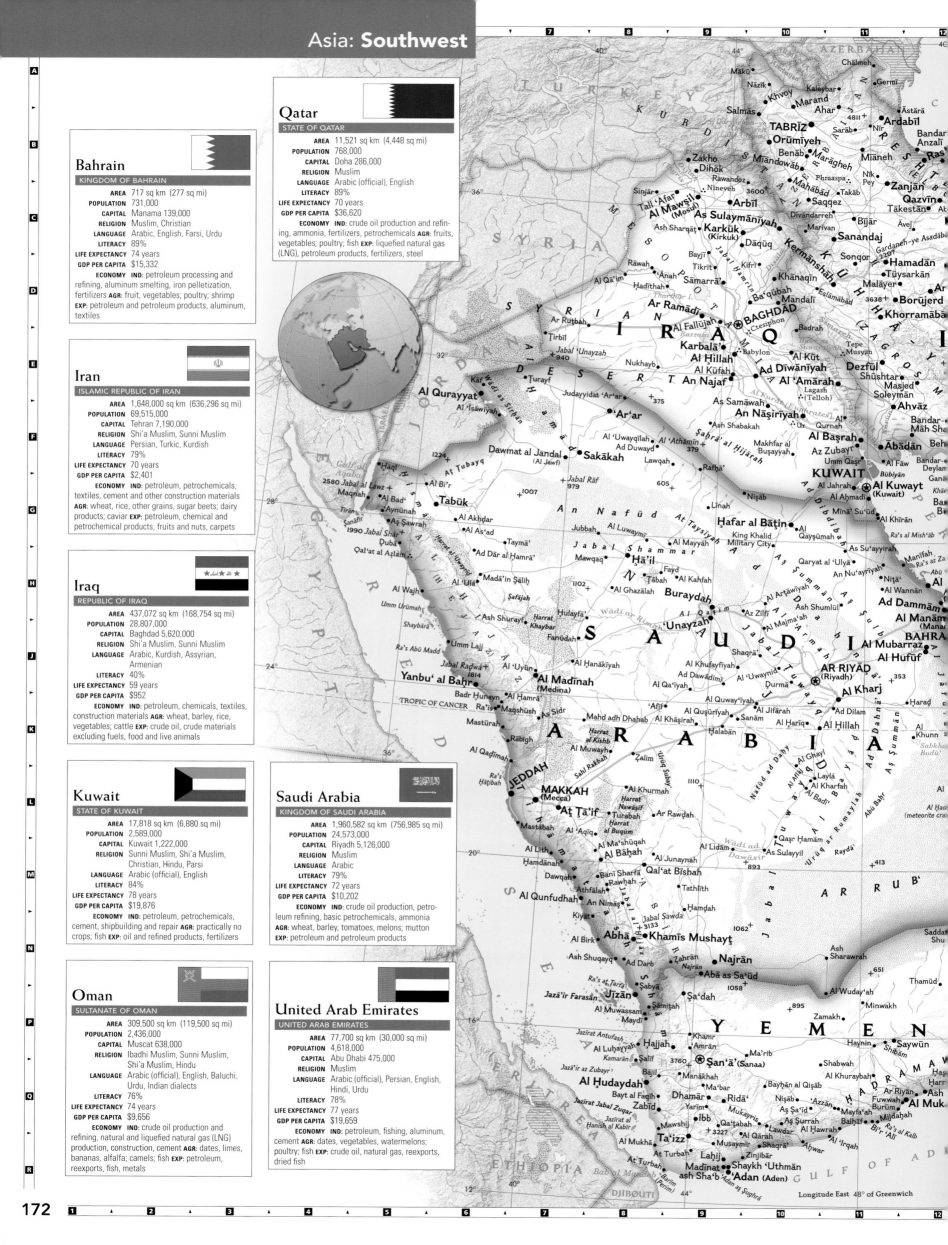

Bahrain

KINGDOM OF BAHRAIN

AREA 717 sq km (277 sq mi)
POPULATION 731,000
CAPITAL Manama 139,000
RELIGION Muslim, Christian
LANGUAGE Arabic, English, Farsi, Urdu
LITERACY 89%
LIFE EXPECTANCY 74 years
GDP PER CAPITA $15,332
ECONOMY **IND:** petroleum processing and refining, aluminum smelting, iron pelletization, fertilizers **AGR:** fruit, vegetables; poultry; shrimp **EXP:** petroleum and petroleum products, aluminum, textiles

Iran

ISLAMIC REPUBLIC OF IRAN

AREA 1,648,000 sq km (636,296 sq mi)
POPULATION 69,515,000
CAPITAL Tehran 7,190,000
RELIGION Shi'a Muslim, Sunni Muslim
LANGUAGE Persian, Turkic, Kurdish
LITERACY 79%
LIFE EXPECTANCY 70 years
GDP PER CAPITA $2,401
ECONOMY **IND:** petroleum, petrochemicals, textiles, cement and other construction materials **AGR:** wheat, rice, other grains, sugar beets; dairy products; caviar **EXP:** petroleum, chemical and petrochemical products, fruits and nuts, carpets

Iraq

REPUBLIC OF IRAQ

AREA 437,072 sq km (168,754 sq mi)
POPULATION 28,807,000
CAPITAL Baghdad 5,620,000
RELIGION Shi'a Muslim, Sunni Muslim
LANGUAGE Arabic, Kurdish, Assyrian, Armenian
LITERACY 40%
LIFE EXPECTANCY 59 years
GDP PER CAPITA $952
ECONOMY **IND:** petroleum, chemicals, textiles, construction materials **AGR:** wheat, barley, rice, vegetables; cattle **EXP:** crude oil, crude materials excluding fuels, food and live animals

Kuwait

STATE OF KUWAIT

AREA 17,818 sq km (6,880 sq mi)
POPULATION 2,589,000
CAPITAL Kuwait 1,222,000
RELIGION Sunni Muslim, Shi'a Muslim, Christian, Hindu, Parsi
LANGUAGE Arabic (official), English
LITERACY 84%
LIFE EXPECTANCY 78 years
GDP PER CAPITA $19,876
ECONOMY **IND:** petroleum, petrochemicals, cement, shipbuilding and repair **AGR:** practically no crops; fish **EXP:** oil and refined products, fertilizers

Oman

SULTANATE OF OMAN

AREA 309,500 sq km (119,500 sq mi)
POPULATION 2,436,000
CAPITAL Muscat 638,000
RELIGION Ibadhi Muslim, Sunni Muslim, Shi'a Muslim, Hindu
LANGUAGE Arabic (official), English, Baluchi, Urdu, Indian dialects
LITERACY 76%
LIFE EXPECTANCY 74 years
GDP PER CAPITA $9,656
ECONOMY **IND:** crude oil production and refining, natural and liquefied natural gas (LNG) production, construction, cement **AGR:** dates, limes, bananas, alfalfa; camels; fish **EXP:** petroleum, reexports, fish, metals

Qatar

STATE OF QATAR

AREA 11,521 sq km (4,448 sq mi)
POPULATION 768,000
CAPITAL Doha 286,000
RELIGION Muslim
LANGUAGE Arabic (official), English
LITERACY 89%
LIFE EXPECTANCY 70 years
GDP PER CAPITA $36,620
ECONOMY **IND:** crude oil production and refining, ammonia, fertilizers, petrochemicals **AGR:** fruits, vegetables; poultry; fish **EXP:** liquefied natural gas (LNG), petroleum products, fertilizers, steel

Saudi Arabia

KINGDOM OF SAUDI ARABIA

AREA 1,960,582 sq km (756,985 sq mi)
POPULATION 24,573,000
CAPITAL Riyadh 5,126,000
RELIGION Muslim
LANGUAGE Arabic
LITERACY 79%
LIFE EXPECTANCY 72 years
GDP PER CAPITA $10,202
ECONOMY **IND:** crude oil production, petroleum refining, basic petrochemicals, ammonia **AGR:** wheat, barley, tomatoes, melons; mutton **EXP:** petroleum and petroleum products

United Arab Emirates

UNITED ARAB EMIRATES

AREA 77,700 sq km (30,000 sq mi)
POPULATION 4,618,000
CAPITAL Abu Dhabi 475,000
RELIGION Muslim
LANGUAGE Arabic (official), Persian, English, Hindi, Urdu
LITERACY 78%
LIFE EXPECTANCY 77 years
GDP PER CAPITA $19,659
ECONOMY **IND:** petroleum, fishing, aluminum, cement **AGR:** dates, vegetables, watermelons; poultry; fish **EXP:** crude oil, natural gas, reexports, dried fish

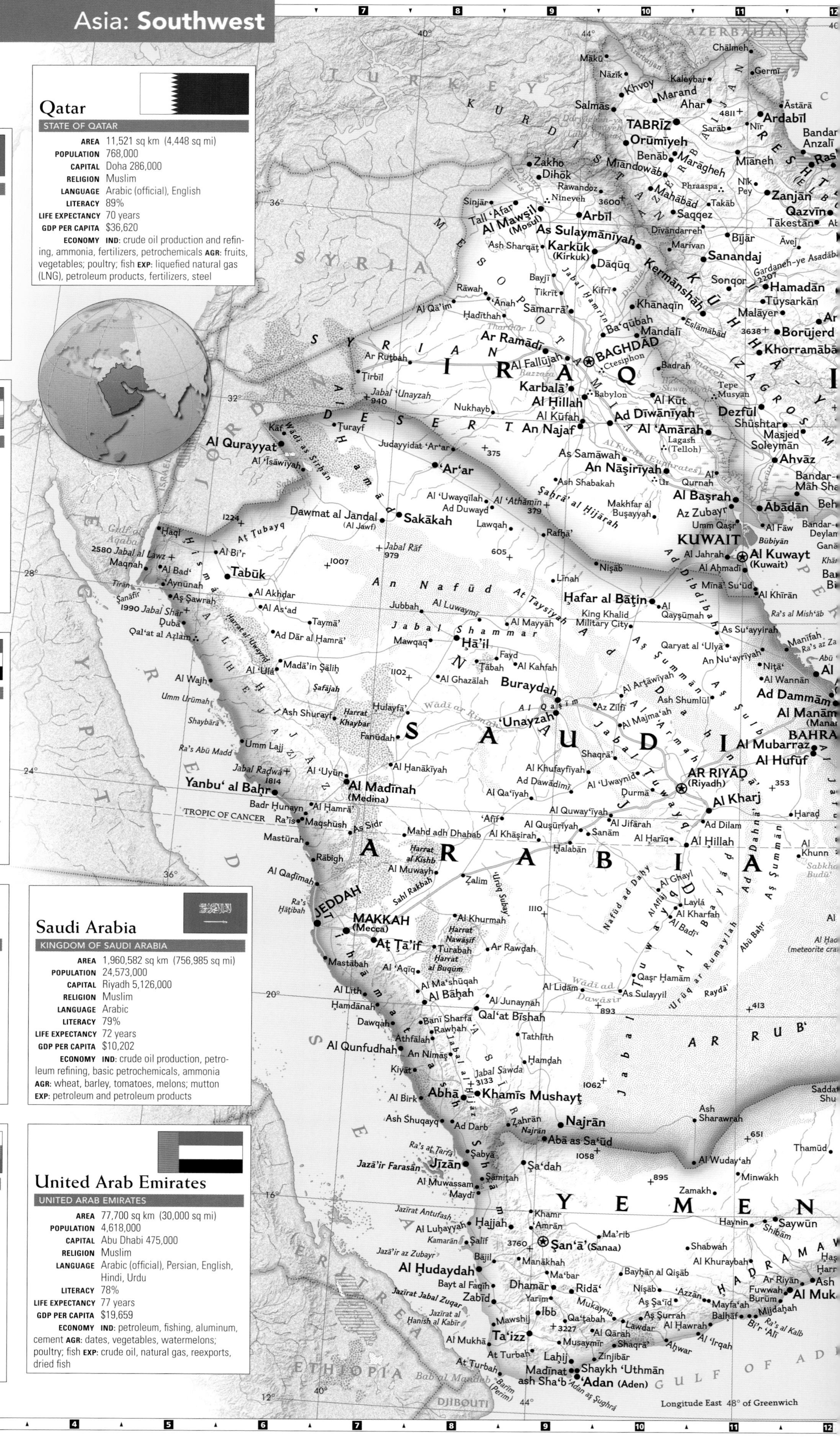

Yemen

REPUBLIC OF YEMEN

AREA 536,869 sq km (207,286 sq mi)
POPULATION 20,727,000
CAPITAL Sanaa 1,469,000
RELIGION Muslim
LANGUAGE Arabic
LITERACY 50%
LIFE EXPECTANCY 61 years
GDP PER CAPITA $643
ECONOMY **IND:** crude oil production and petroleum refining, small-scale production of cotton textiles and leather goods, food processing, handicrafts **AGR:** grain, fruits, vegetables, pulses; dairy products; fish **EXP:** crude oil, coffee, dried and salted fish

Temperature and Precipitation

Population

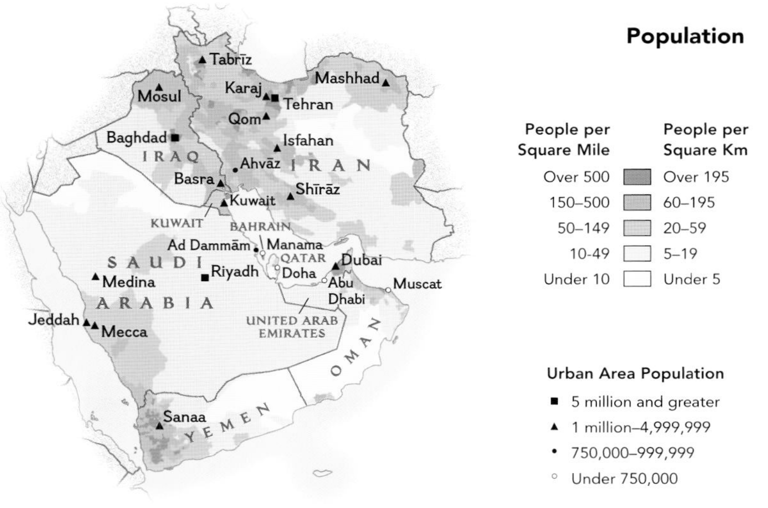

Land Use, Agriculture, and Fishing

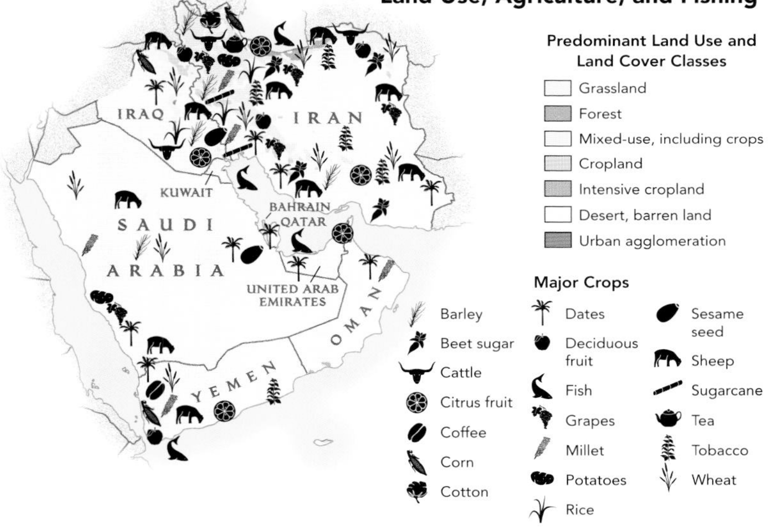

Industry and Mining

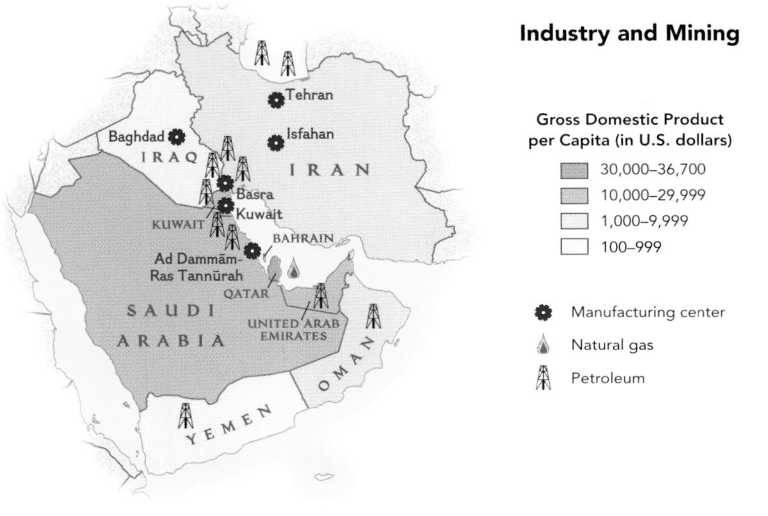

![Kazakhstan flag]

Kazakhstan

REPUBLIC OF KAZAKHSTAN

AREA 2,717,300 sq km (1,049,155 sq mi)
POPULATION 15,079,000
CAPITAL Astana 332,000
RELIGION Muslim, Russian Orthodox
LANGUAGE Kazakh (Qazaq), Russian (official)
LITERACY 98%
LIFE EXPECTANCY 66 years
GDP PER CAPITA $2,746
ECONOMY **IND:** oil, coal, iron ore, manganese **AGR:** grain (mostly spring wheat), cotton; livestock **EXP:** oil and oil products, ferrous metals, chemicals, machinery

Turkmenistan

TURKMENISTAN

AREA 488,100 sq km (188,456 sq mi)
POPULATION 5,240,000
CAPITAL Ashgabat 574,000
RELIGION Muslim, Eastern Orthodox
LANGUAGE Turkmen, Russian, Uzbek
LITERACY 99%
LIFE EXPECTANCY 63 years
GDP PER CAPITA $2,596
ECONOMY **IND:** natural gas, oil, petroleum products, textiles **AGR:** cotton, grain; livestock **EXP:** gas, crude oil, petrochemicals, cotton fiber

Uzbekistan

REPUBLIC OF UZBEKISTAN

AREA 447,400 sq km (172,742 sq mi)
POPULATION 26,444,000
CAPITAL Tashkent 2,155,000
RELIGION Muslim, Eastern Orthodox
LANGUAGE Uzbek, Russian
LITERACY 99%
LIFE EXPECTANCY 67 years
GDP PER CAPITA $450
ECONOMY **IND:** textiles, food processing, machine building, metallurgy **AGR:** cotton, vegetables, fruits, grain; livestock **EXP:** cotton, gold, energy products, mineral fertilizers

Temperature and Precipitation

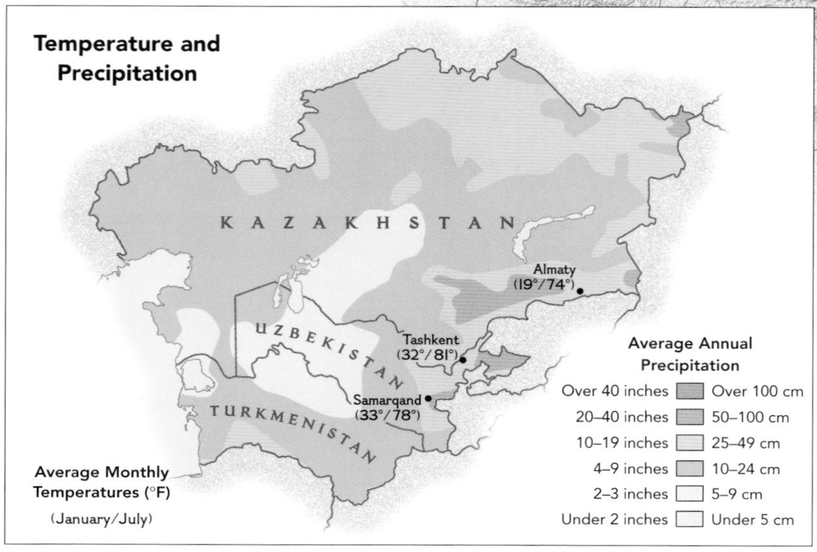

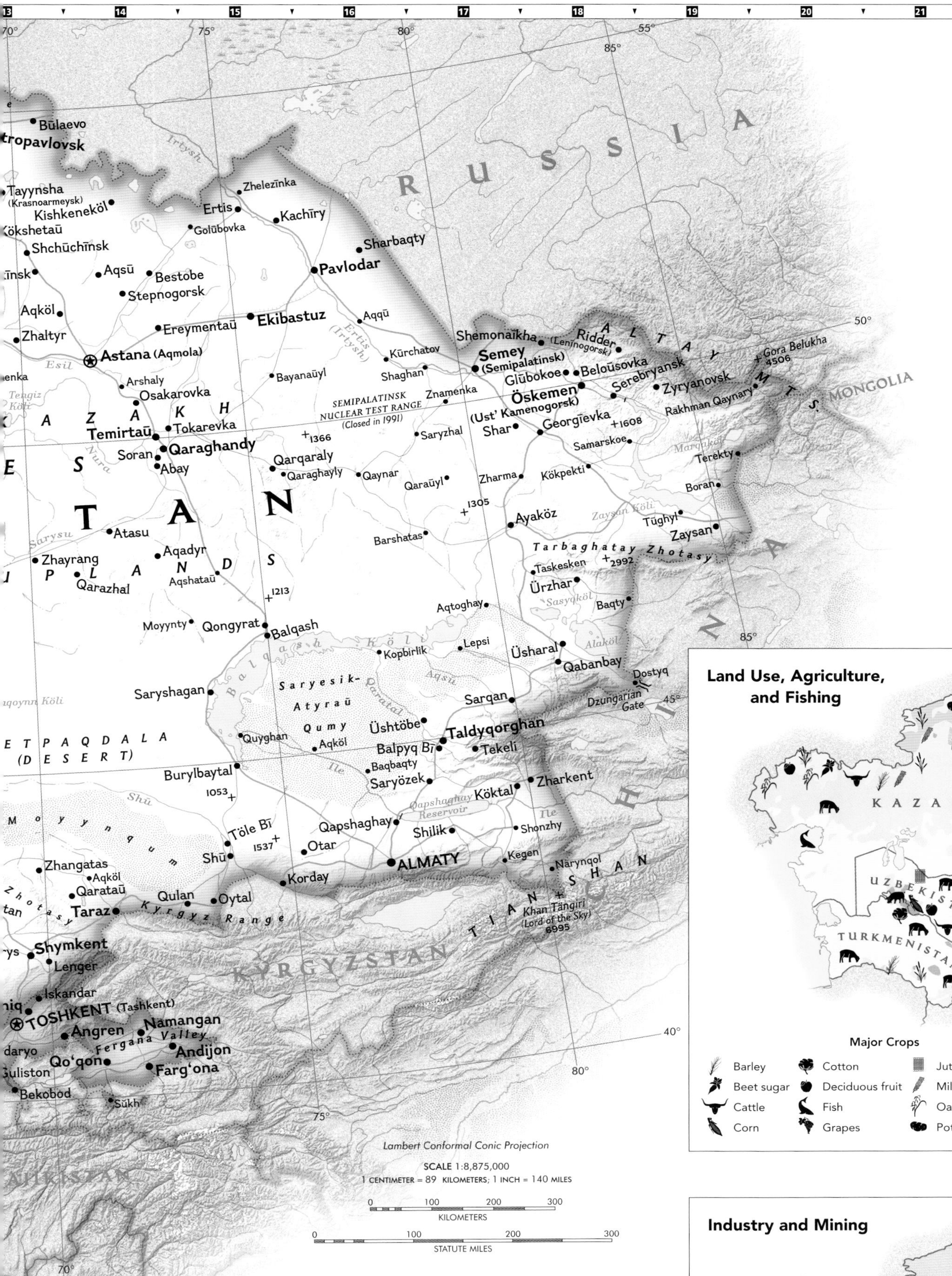
R U S S I A
Būlaevo
Petropavlovsk
Irtysh
Tayynsha (Krasnoarmeysk)
Kishkeneköl
Zhelezīnka
Ertis
Kachīry
Golūbovka
Kökshetaū
Shchūchīnsk
Sharbaqty
Pavlodar
Aqsū
Bestobe
Stepnogorsk
Aqköl
Ereymentaū
Ekibastuz
Aqqū
Zhaltyr
Astana (Aqmola)
Esil
Kūrchatov
Shemonaīkha
Ridder (Leninogorsk)
A L T A Y M T S.
Gora Belukha 4506
Semey (Semipalatinsk)
Glūbokoe
Beloūsovka
Serebryansk
Zyryanovsk
Rakhman Qaynary
MONGOLIA
Shaghan
Bayanaūyl
Arshaly
Osakarovka
Tengiz Köli
SEMIPALATINSK NUCLEAR TEST RANGE (Closed in 1991)
Znamenka
Öskemen (Ust' Kamenogorsk)
K A Z A K H S T A N
Temirtaū
Tokarevka
Saryzhal
Shar
Georgīevka
1608
1366
Samarskoe
Soran
Qaraghandy
Abay
Qarqaraly
Qaraghayly
Qaynar
Qaraūyl
Zharma
Kökpekti
Terekty
Boran
1305
Ayaköz
Zaysan Köli
Tūghyl
Zaysan
Atasu
Sarysu
Barshatas
Zhayrang
Aqadyr
Aqshataū
Qarazhal
U P L A N D S
Tarbaghatay Zhotasy
Taskesken
2992
Ürzhar
Sasyqköl
Baqty
1213
Aqtoghay
Moyynty
Qongyrat
Balqash
Balqash Köli
Kopbirlik
Lepsi
Alaköl
Üsharal
Qabanbay
Dostyq
Saryshagan
Saryesik-Atyraū Qumy
Aqsū
Dzungarian Gate
Sarqan
Üshtöbe
Taldyqorghan
Tekeli
Quyghan
Aqköl
Balpyq Bī
Baqbaqty
BETPAQDALA (DESERT)
Burylbaytal
1053
Saryözek
Ile
Zharkent
Köktal
Shū
Moyynqum
Qapshaghay Reservoir
Qapshaghay
Shilik
Shonzhy
Töle Bī
1537
Otar
Shū
Zhangatas
Aqköl
Qarataū
Kegen
Narynqol
ALMATY
Korday
Qulan
Oytal
Taraz
Kyrgyz Range
Zhotasy
TIAN SHAN
Khan Tängiri (Lord of the Sky) 6995
KYRGYZSTAN
Shymkent
Lenger
Iskandar
TOSHKENT (Tashkent)
Angren
Namangan
Fergana Valley
Andijon
Qo'qon
Farg'ona
Guliston
Bekobod
Sūkh
AFGHANISTAN
CHINA
Lambert Conformal Conic Projection
SCALE 1:8,875,000
1 CENTIMETER = 89 KILOMETERS; 1 INCH = 140 MILES
KILOMETERS
STATUTE MILES

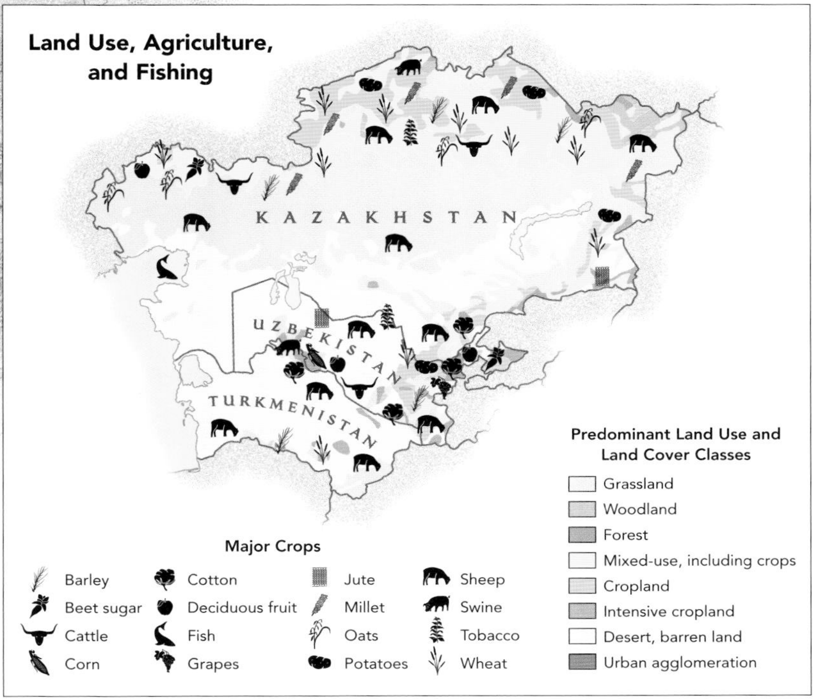
Land Use, Agriculture, and Fishing
KAZAKHSTAN
UZBEKISTAN
TURKMENISTAN
Major Crops
Barley
Beet sugar
Cattle
Corn
Cotton
Deciduous fruit
Fish
Grapes
Jute
Millet
Oats
Potatoes
Sheep
Swine
Tobacco
Wheat
Predominant Land Use and Land Cover Classes
Grassland
Woodland
Forest
Mixed-use, including crops
Cropland
Intensive cropland
Desert, barren land
Urban agglomeration

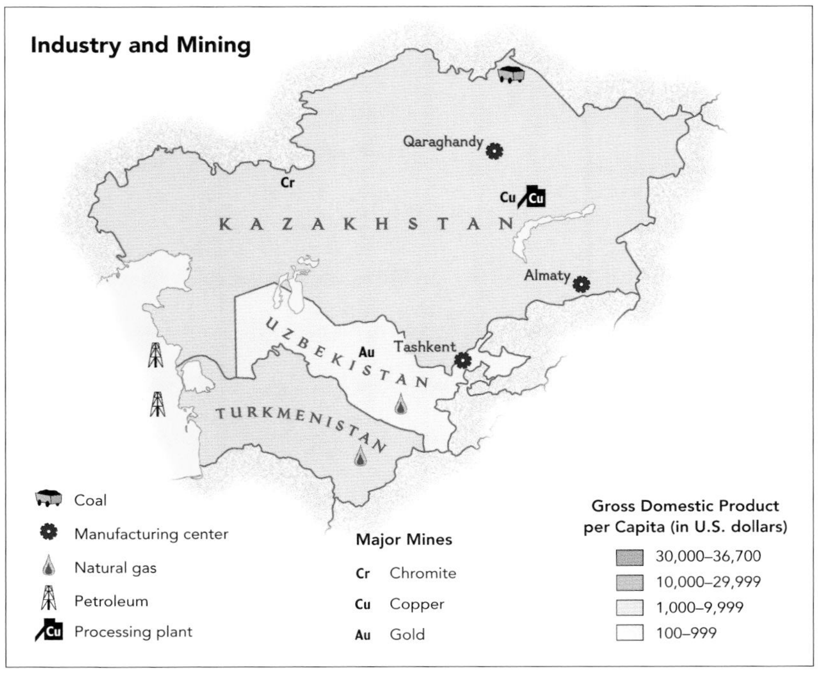
Industry and Mining
Qaraghandy
Cr
Cu
KAZAKHSTAN
Almaty
UZBEKISTAN
Au
Tashkent
TURKMENISTAN
Coal
Manufacturing center
Natural gas
Petroleum
Processing plant
Major Mines
Cr Chromite
Cu Copper
Au Gold
Gross Domestic Product per Capita (in U.S. dollars)
30,000–36,700
10,000–29,999
1,000–9,999
100–999

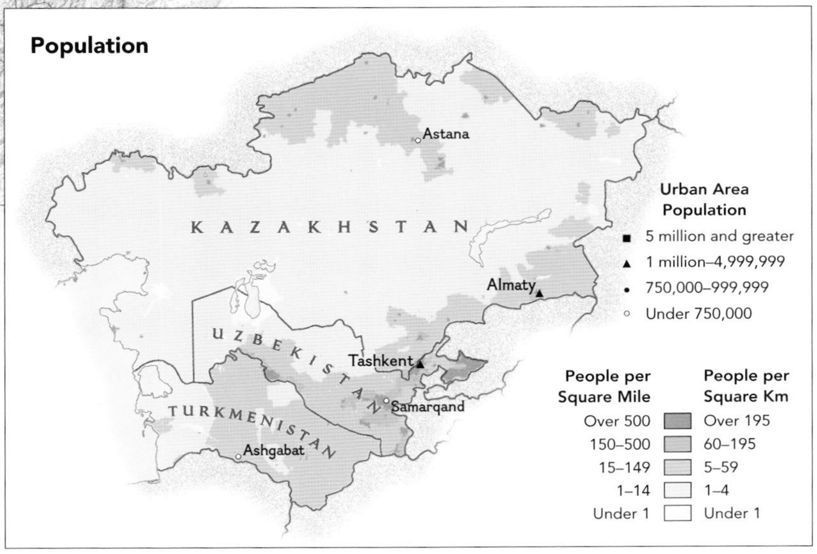
Population
Astana
KAZAKHSTAN
Almaty
UZBEKISTAN
Tashkent
Samarqand
TURKMENISTAN
Ashgabat
Urban Area Population
5 million and greater
1 million–4,999,999
750,000–999,999
Under 750,000
People per Square Mile
Over 500
150–500
15–149
1–14
Under 1
People per Square Km
Over 195
60–195
5–59
1–4
Under 1

Land Use, Agriculture, and Fishing

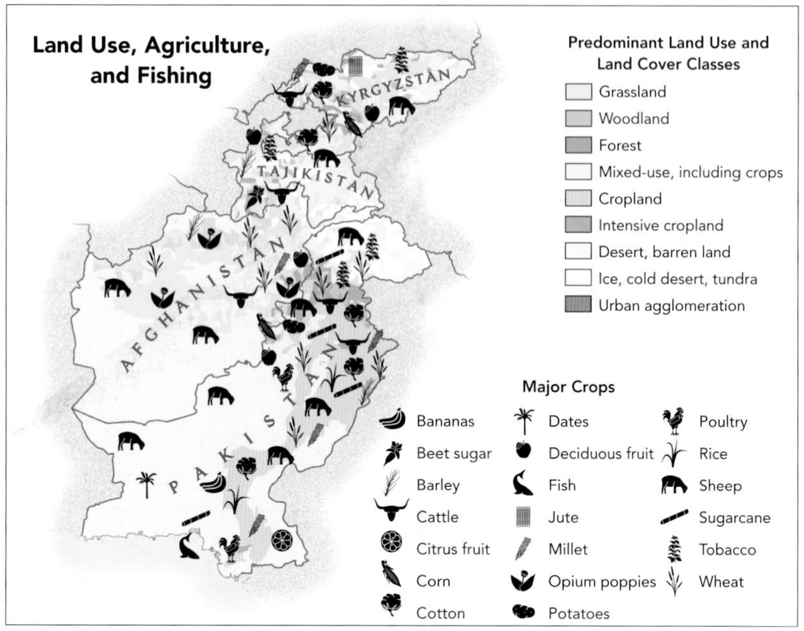

Temperature and Precipitation

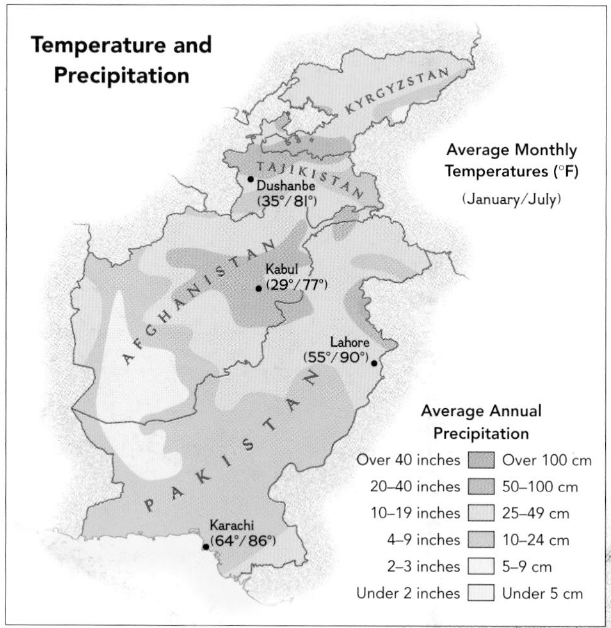

Afghanistan

ISLAMIC REPUBLIC OF AFGHANISTAN

AREA 652,090 sq km (251,773 sq mi)
POPULATION 29,929,000
CAPITAL Kabul 2,956,000
RELIGION Sunni Muslim, Shi'a Muslim
LANGUAGE Afghan Persian or Dari (official), Pashtu (official), Turkic languages
LITERACY 36%
LIFE EXPECTANCY 42 years
GDP PER CAPITA $184
ECONOMY **IND:** small-scale production of textiles, soap, furniture, shoes **AGR:** opium, wheat, fruits, nuts; wool **EXP:** opium, fruits and nuts, hand-woven carpets, wool

Kyrgyzstan

KYRGYZ REPUBLIC

AREA 199,900 sq km (77,182 sq mi)
POPULATION 5,172,000
CAPITAL Bishkek 806,000
RELIGION Muslim, Russian Orthodox
LANGUAGE Kyrgyz (official), Russian (official)
LITERACY 99%
LIFE EXPECTANCY 68 years
GDP PER CAPITA $416
ECONOMY **IND:** small machinery, textiles, food processing, cement **AGR:** tobacco, cotton, potatoes, vegetables; sheep **EXP:** cotton, wool, meat, tobacco

Pakistan

ISLAMIC REPUBLIC OF PAKISTAN

AREA 796,095 sq km (307,374 sq mi)
POPULATION 162,420,000
CAPITAL Islamabad 698,000
RELIGION Sunni Muslim, Shi'a Muslim
LANGUAGE Punjabi, Sindhi, Siraiki, Pashtu, Urdu (official), English (official)
LITERACY 49%
LIFE EXPECTANCY 62 years
GDP PER CAPITA $605
ECONOMY **IND:** textiles and apparel, food processing, pharmaceuticals, construction materials **AGR:** cotton, wheat, rice, sugarcane; milk **EXP:** textiles (garments, bed linen, cotton cloth, yarn), rice, leather goods, sports goods

Tajikistan

REPUBLIC OF TAJIKISTAN

AREA 143,100 sq km (55,251 sq mi)
POPULATION 6,813,000
CAPITAL Dushanbe 554,000
RELIGION Sunni Muslim, Shi'a Muslim
LANGUAGE Tajik (official), Russian
LITERACY 99%
LIFE EXPECTANCY 63 years
GDP PER CAPITA $297
ECONOMY **IND:** aluminum, zinc, lead, chemicals and fertilizers **AGR:** cotton, grain, fruits, grapes; cattle **EXP:** aluminum, electricity, cotton, fruits

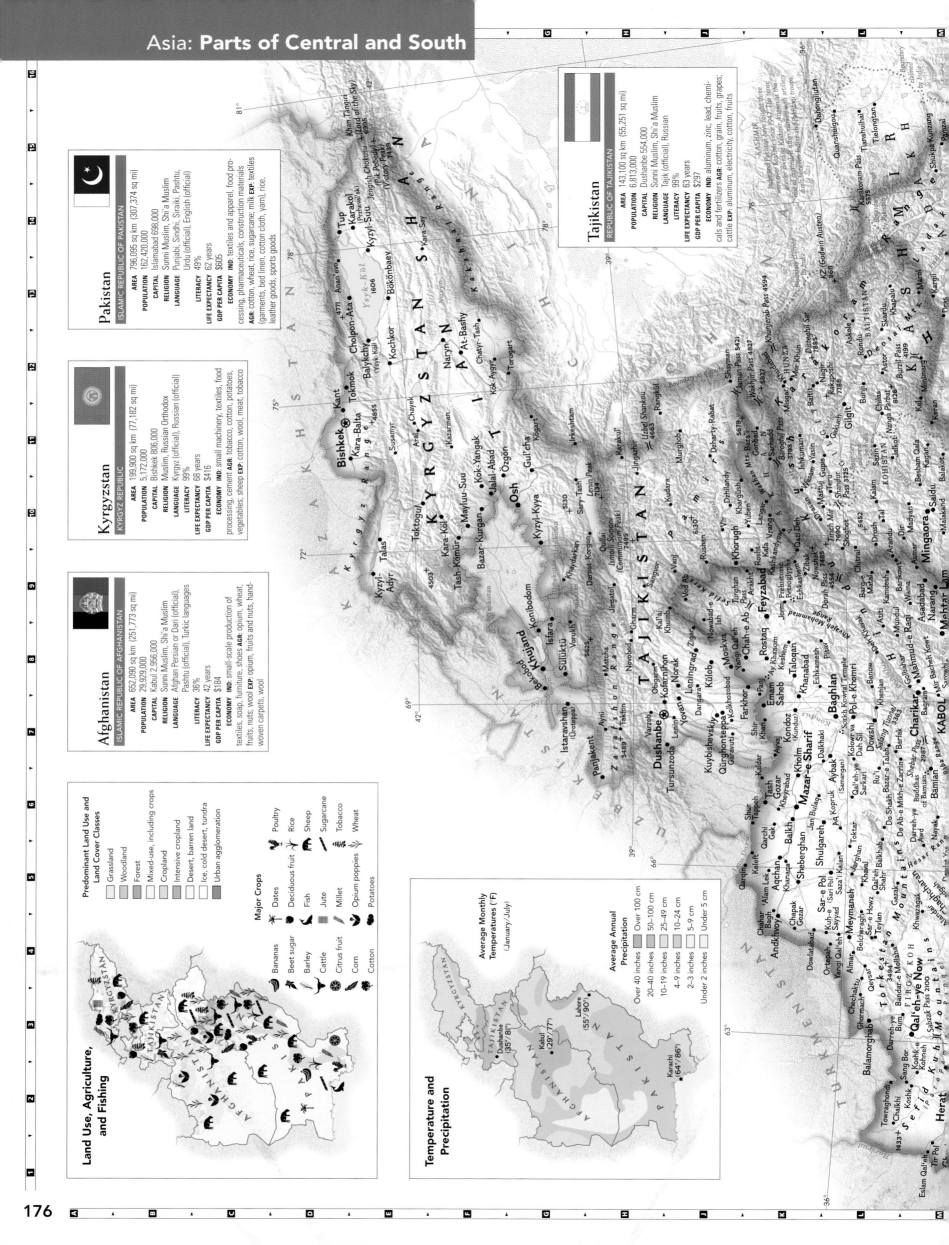

Nepal

KINGDOM OF NEPAL

AREA	147,181 sq km (56,827 sq mi)
POPULATION	25,371,000
CAPITAL	Kathmandu 741,000
RELIGION	Hindu, Buddhist
LANGUAGE	Nepali, Maithali, Bhojpuri, Tharu, Tamang, English
LITERACY	45%
LIFE EXPECTANCY	62 years
GDP PER CAPITA	$245

ECONOMY **IND:** tourism, carpet, textiles, small rice, jute, sugar, and oilseed mills **AGR:** rice, corn, wheat, sugarcane; milk **EXP:** carpets, clothing, leather goods, jute goods

Sri Lanka

DEMOCRATIC SOCIALIST REP. OF SRI LANKA

AREA	65,525 sq km (25,299 sq mi)
POPULATION	19,722,000
CAPITAL	Colombo 648,000
RELIGION	Buddhist, Muslim, Hindu, Christian
LANGUAGE	Sinhala (official), Tamil, English
LITERACY	92%
LIFE EXPECTANCY	73 years
GDP PER CAPITA	$935

ECONOMY **IND:** rubber processing, tea, coconuts, other agricultural commodities **AGR:** rice, sugarcane, grains, pulses; milk **EXP:** textiles and apparel, tea and spices, diamonds, emeralds

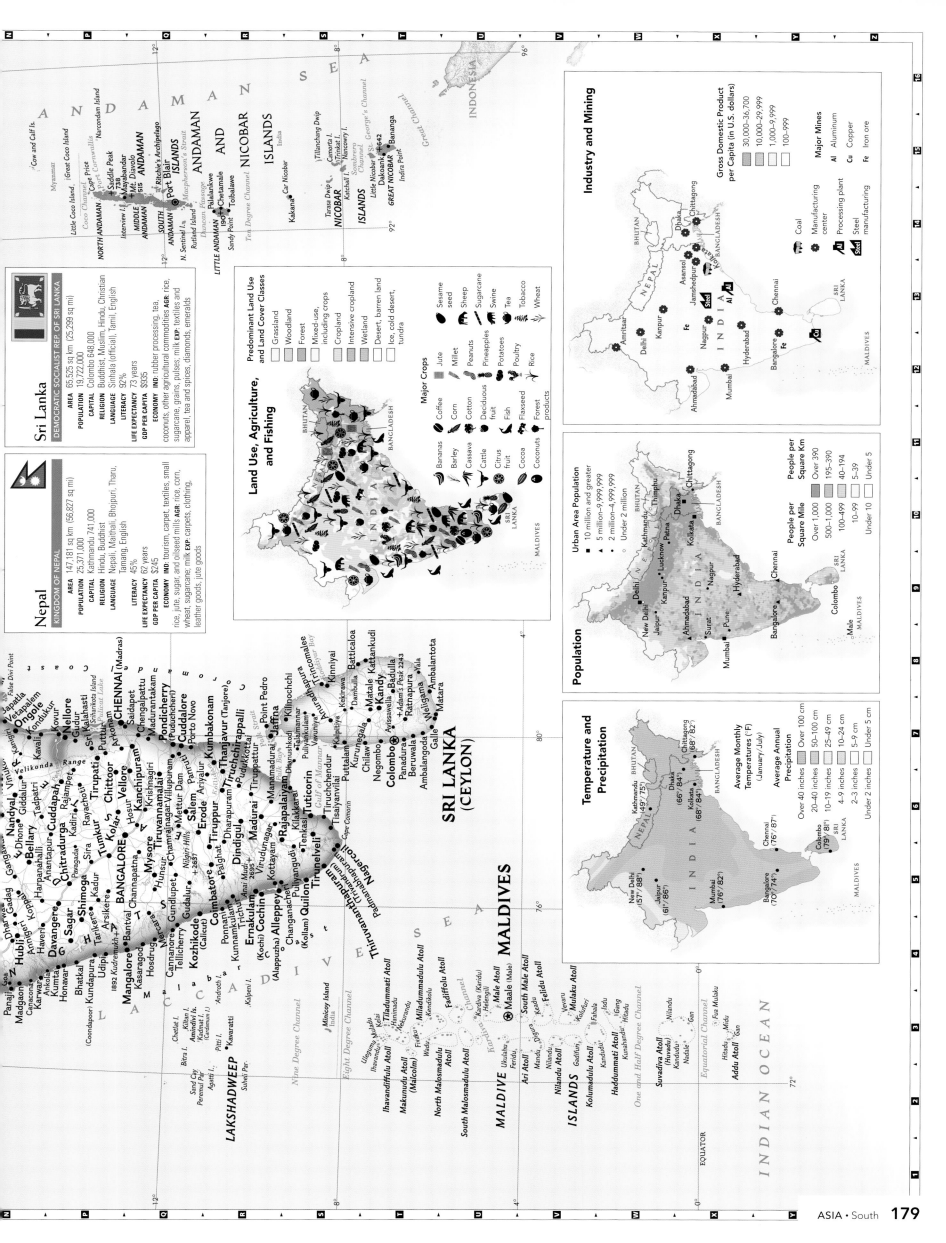

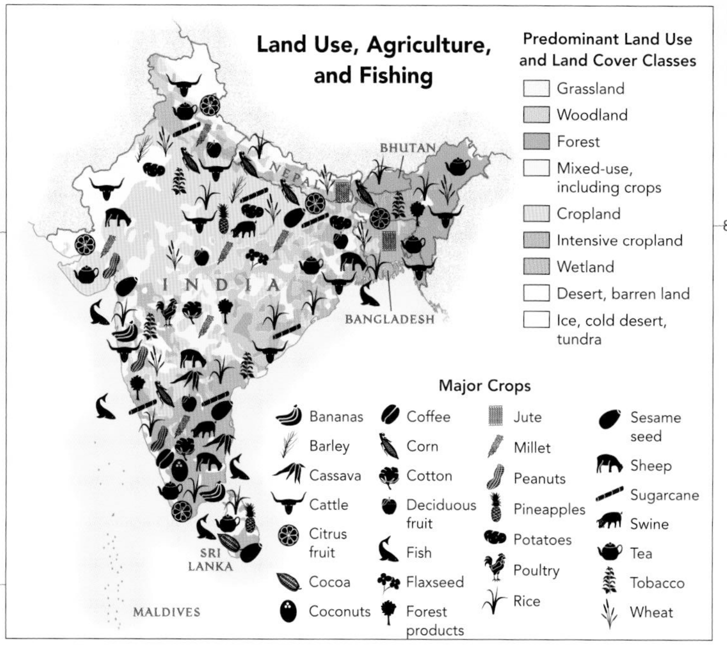

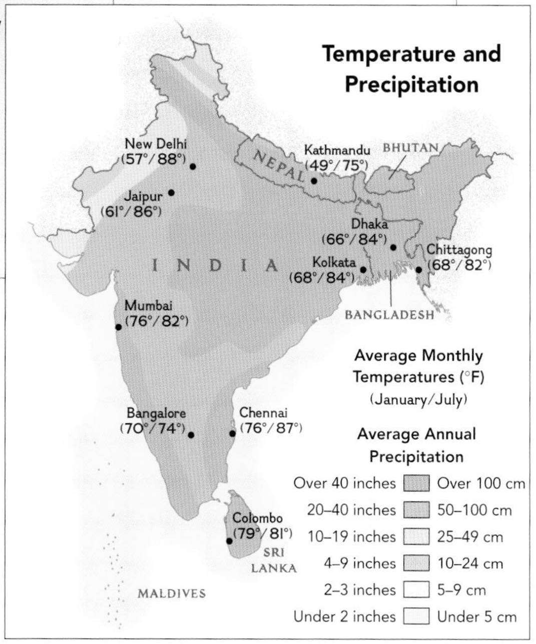

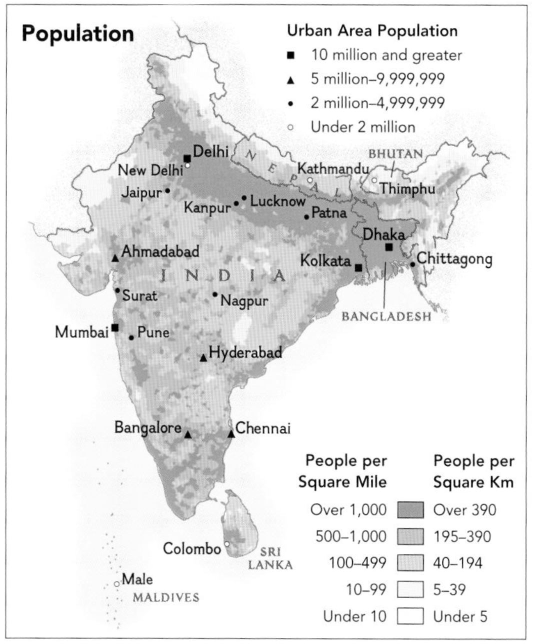

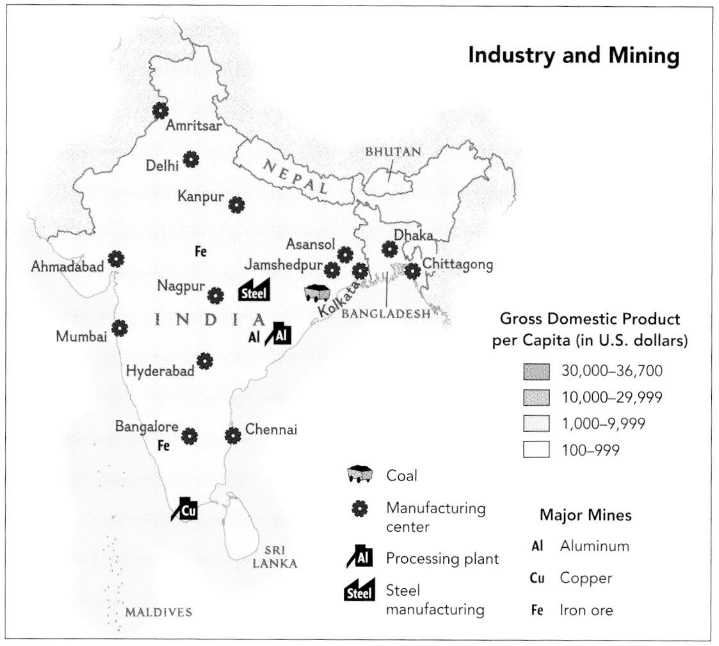

Mongolia

MONGOLIA

AREA	1,564,116 sq km (603,909 sq mi)
POPULATION	2,646,000
CAPITAL	Ulaanbaatar 812,000
RELIGION	Lamaistic Buddhist
LANGUAGE	Khalkha Mongol, Turkic, Russian
LITERACY	98%
LIFE EXPECTANCY	64 years
GDP PER CAPITA	$486
ECONOMY	IND: construction and construction materials, mining (coal, copper), oil, food and beverages AGR: wheat, barley, vegetables, forage crops; sheep EXP: copper, apparel, livestock, animal products

China

PEOPLE'S REPUBLIC OF CHINA

AREA	9,596,960 sq km (3,705,405 sq mi)
POPULATION	1,333,827,000
CAPITAL	Beijing 10,848,000
RELIGION	Daoist, Buddhist
LANGUAGE	Standard Chinese or Mandarin, Yue, Wu, Minbei, local dialects and languages
LITERACY	91%
LIFE EXPECTANCY	72 years
GDP PER CAPITA	$1,283
ECONOMY	IND: mining and ore processing (iron, steel, aluminum), coal, machine building, armaments AGR: rice, wheat, potatoes, corn; pork; fish EXP: machinery and equipment, plastics, optical and medical equipment, iron and steel

Temperature and Precipitation

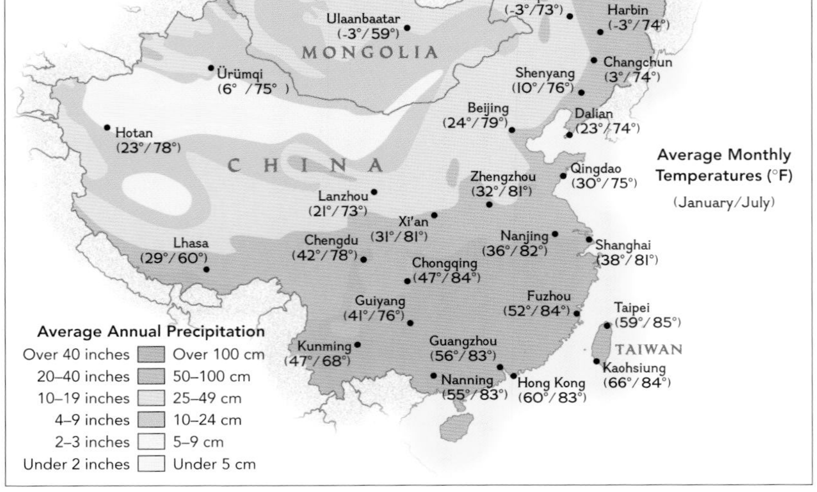

Average Annual Precipitation

Over 40 inches	Over 100 cm
20–40 inches	50–100 cm
10–19 inches	25–49 cm
4–9 inches	10–24 cm
2–3 inches	5–9 cm
Under 2 inches	Under 5 cm

Urban Area Population
10 million and greater
4 million–9,999,999
2 million–3,999,999
Under 2 million
MONGOLIA
CHINA
TAIWAN
People per Square Mile
Over 1000
250–1000
25–249
1–24
Under 1
People per Square Km
Over 390
100–390
10–99
1–9
Under 1
Population
Land Use, Agriculture, and Fishing
Predominant Land Use and Land Cover Classes
Grassland
Woodland
Forest
Mixed-use, including crops
Cropland
Intensive cropland
Wetland
Desert, barren land
Ice, cold desert, tundra
Major Crops
Bananas
Barley
Beet sugar
Cassava
Cattle
Citrus fruit
Corn
Cotton
Deciduous fruit
Fish
Flax
Forest products
Jute
Millet
Oats
Peanuts
Potatoes
Poultry
Rice
Rye
Sheep
Sorghum
Soybeans
Sugarcane
Swine
Tea
Tobacco
Wheat
Industry and Mining
Major Mines
Al Aluminum
Sb Antimony
Bi Bismuth
Co Cobalt
Cu Copper
F Fluorite
Au Gold
Fe Iron ore
Pb Lead
Mo Molybdenum
Ni Nickel
Sn Tin
Ti Titanium
V Vanadium
W Tungsten
Zn Zinc
Gross Domestic Product per Capita (in U.S. dollars)
30,000–36,700
10,000–29,999
1,000–9,999
100–999
Coal
Manufacturing center
Natural gas
Petroleum
Phosphate
Processing plant
Rare earth elements
Steel manufacturing
TAIWAN
The People's Republic of China claims Taiwan as its 23rd province. Taiwan's government (Republic of China) maintains that there are two political entities. The islands of Matsu, Pescadores, Pratas, and Quemoy are administered by Taiwan.
BEIJING (Peking)
TIANJIN
SHANGHAI
HARBIN
CHANGCHUN
SHENYANG
DALIAN (Dairen)
QINGDAO
NANJING
WUHAN
GUANGZHOU (Canton)
HONG KONG
TAIPEI
YELLOW SEA
EAST CHINA SEA
SOUTH KOREA
NORTH KOREA
Bo Hai
Korea Bay
TROPIC OF CANCER
Tungsha Tao (Pratas Island)

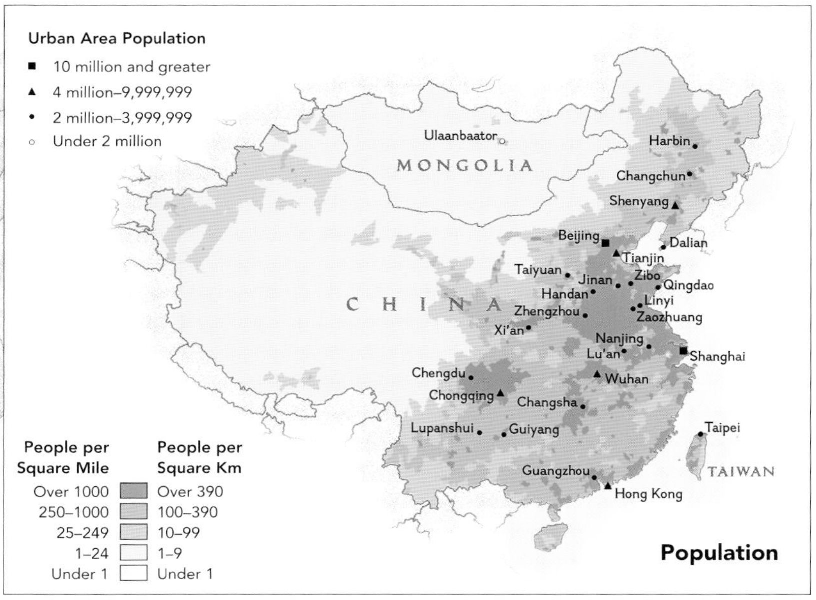

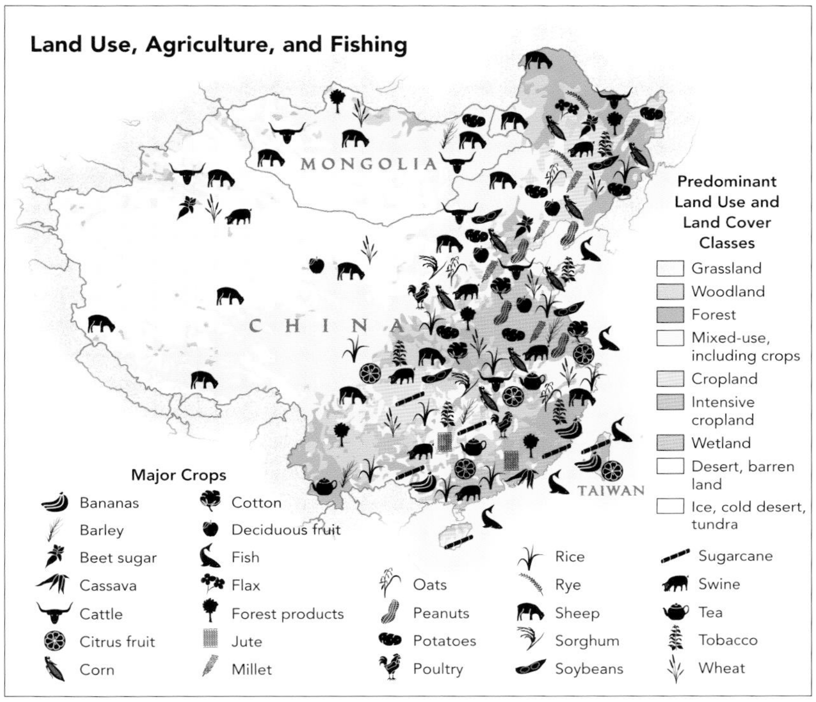

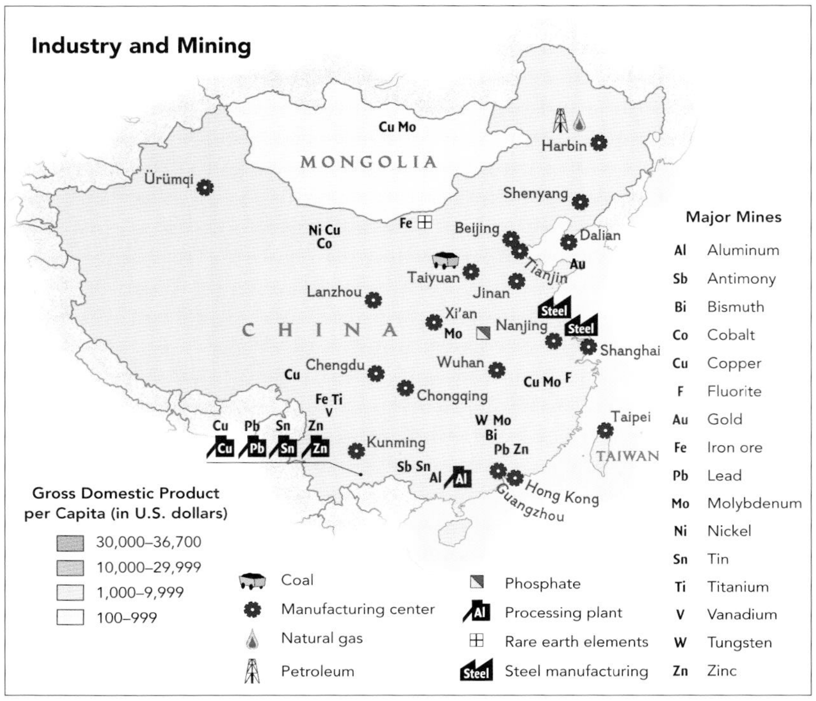

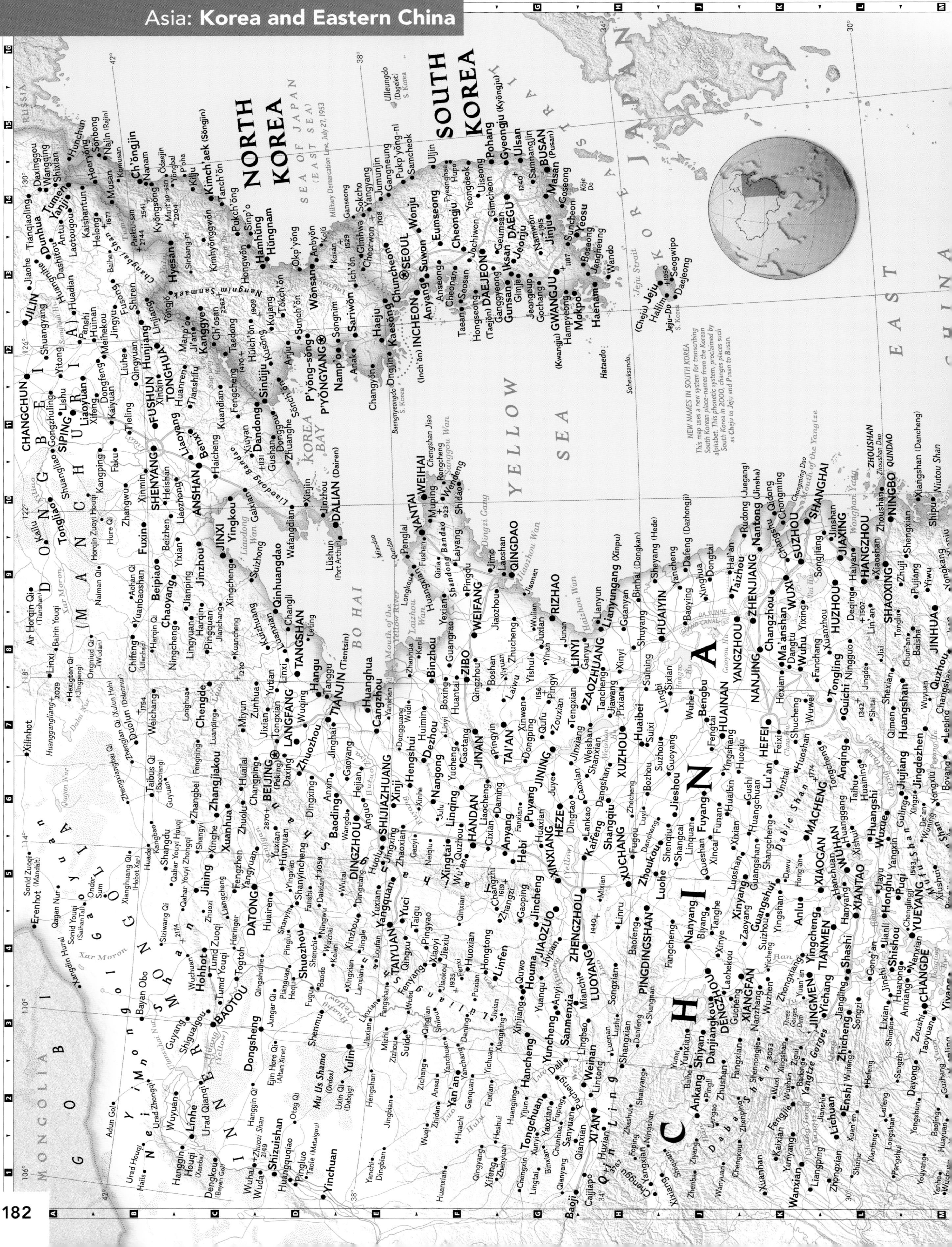
NORTH KOREA
SOUTH KOREA
JAPAN
RUSSIA
MONGOLIA
CHINA
SEA OF JAPAN (EAST SEA)
YELLOW SEA
EAST CHINA SEA
BO HAI
KOREA BAY
KOREA STRAIT
Military Demarcation Line, July 27, 1953
NEW NAMES IN SOUTH KOREA
This map uses a new system for transcribing South Korean place-names from the Korean alphabet. This phonetic system, proclaimed by South Korea in 2000, changes places such as Cheju to Jeju and Pusan to Busan.
P'YŎNGYANG
SEOUL
BUSAN (Pusan)
INCHEON (Inch'ŏn)
DAEGU
DAEJEON (Taejŏn)
GWANGJU (Kwangju)
BEIJING (Peking)
TIANJIN (Tientsin)
SHENYANG
DALIAN (Dairen)
QINGDAO
SHANGHAI
NANJING
HANGZHOU
ZHENGZHOU
XI'AN
TAIYUAN
SHIJIAZHUANG
JINAN
HEFEI
WUHAN
CHANGCHUN
JILIN
HOHHOT
BAOTOU
NEI MONGOL (INNER MONGOLIA)
MANCHURIA (DONGBEI)
Yangtze Gorges
Mouth of the Yangtze

North Korea

DEMOCRATIC PEOPLE'S REPUBLIC OF KOREA

AREA 120,538 sq km (46,540 sq mi)
POPULATION 22,912,000
CAPITAL Pyongyang 3,228,000
RELIGION Buddhist, Confucianist
LANGUAGE Korean
LITERACY 99%
LIFE EXPECTANCY 71 years
GDP PER CAPITA $612
ECONOMY **IND:** military products, machine building, electric power, chemicals **AGR:** rice, corn, potatoes, soybeans; cattle **EXP:** minerals, metallurgical products, manufactures (including armaments), textiles and fishery products

South Korea

REPUBLIC OF KOREA

AREA 99,250 sq km (38,321 sq mi)
POPULATION 48,294,000
CAPITAL Seoul 9,714,000
RELIGION Christian, Buddhist
LANGUAGE Korean, English widely taught
LITERACY 98%
LIFE EXPECTANCY 77 years
GDP PER CAPITA $14,266
ECONOMY **IND:** electronics, telecommunications, automobile production, chemicals **AGR:** rice, root crops, barley, vegetables; cattle; fish **EXP:** semiconductors, wireless telecommunications equipment, motor vehicles, computers

Population

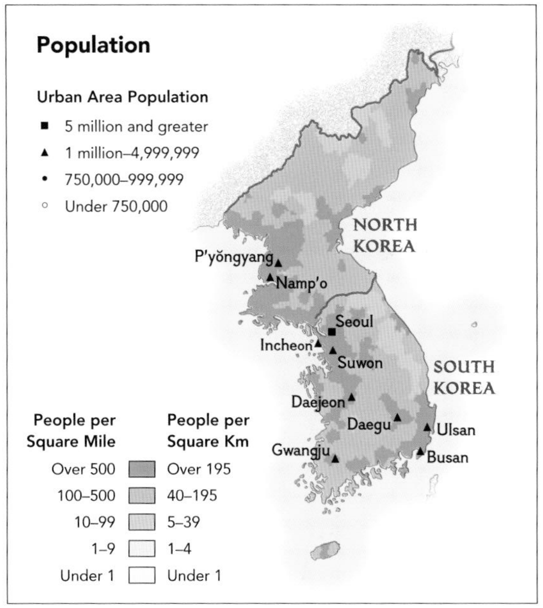

Temperature and Precipitation

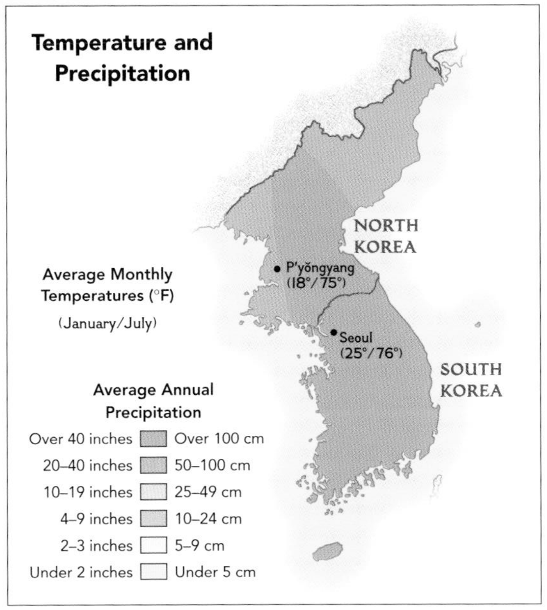

Land Use, Agriculture, and Fishing

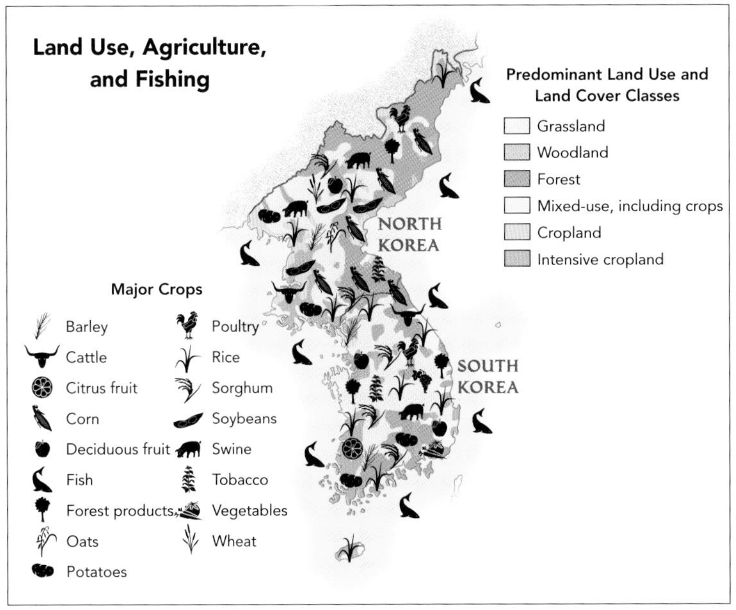

Industry and Mining

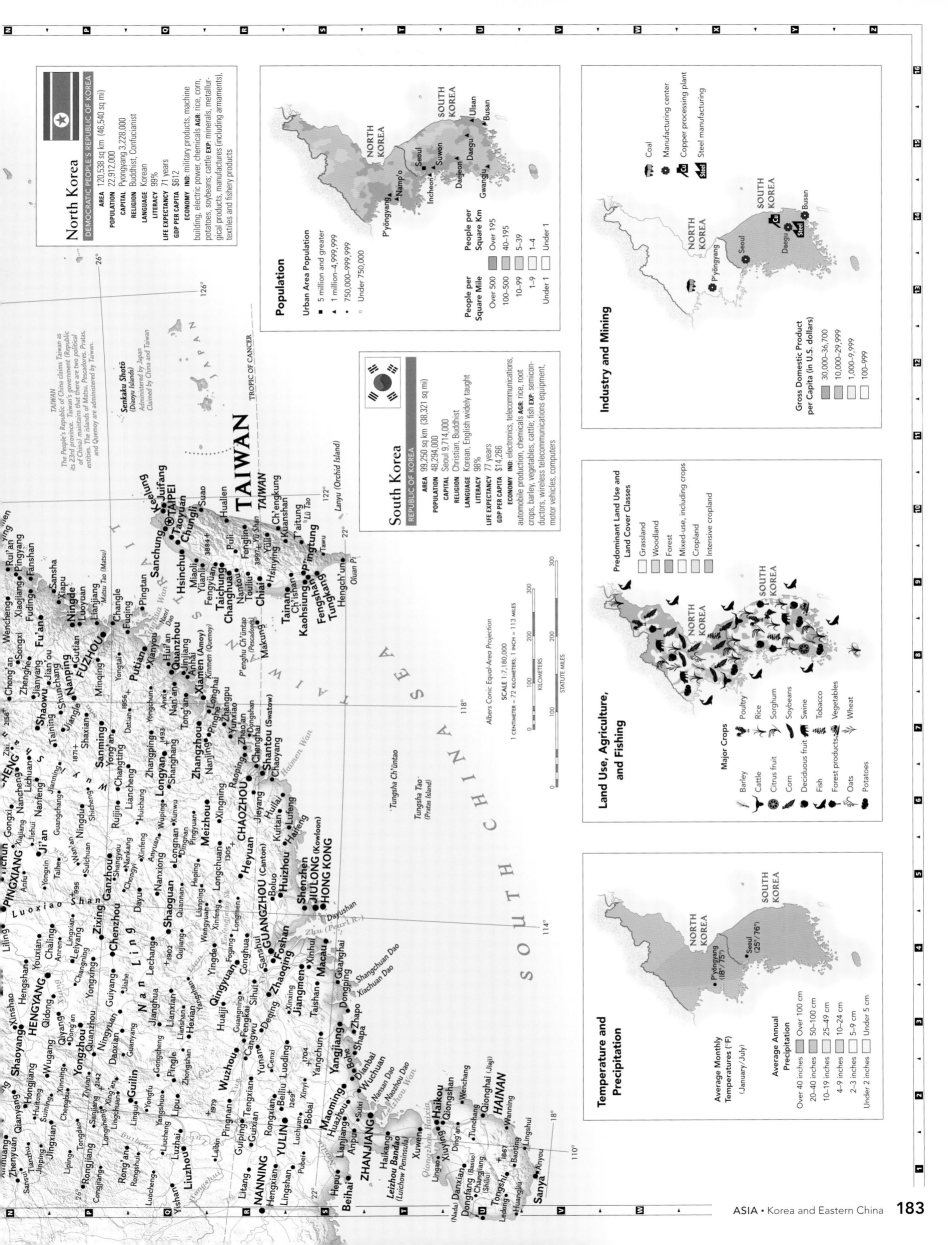

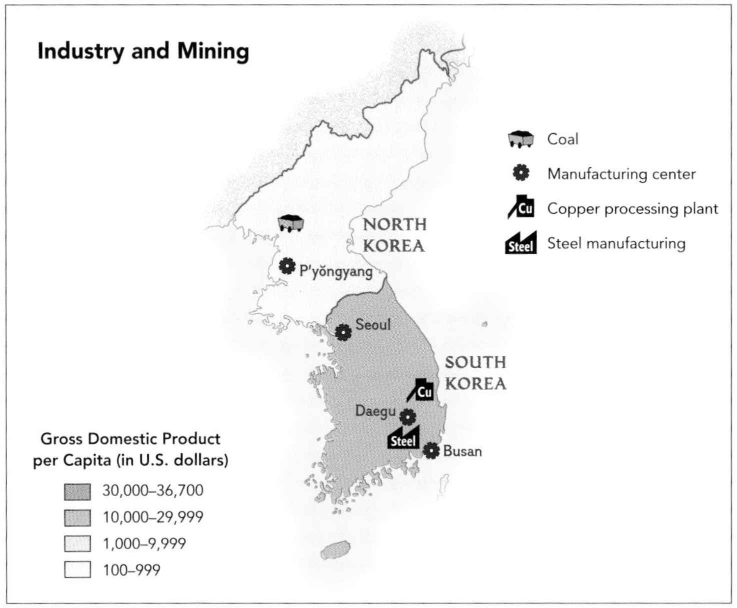

Temperature and Precipitation

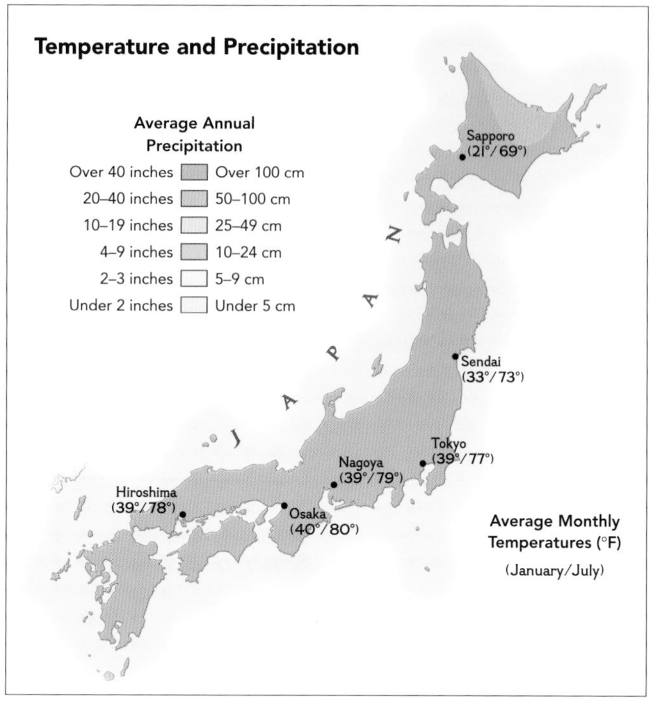

Population

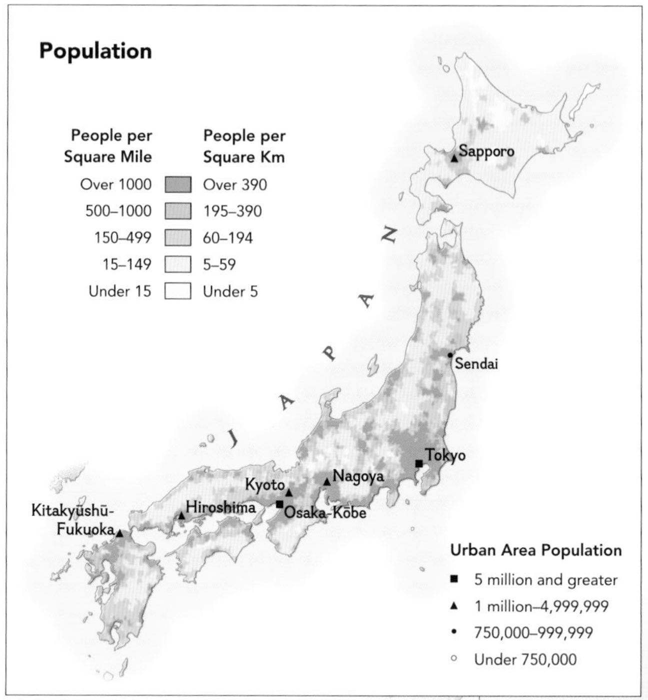

Japan

JAPAN

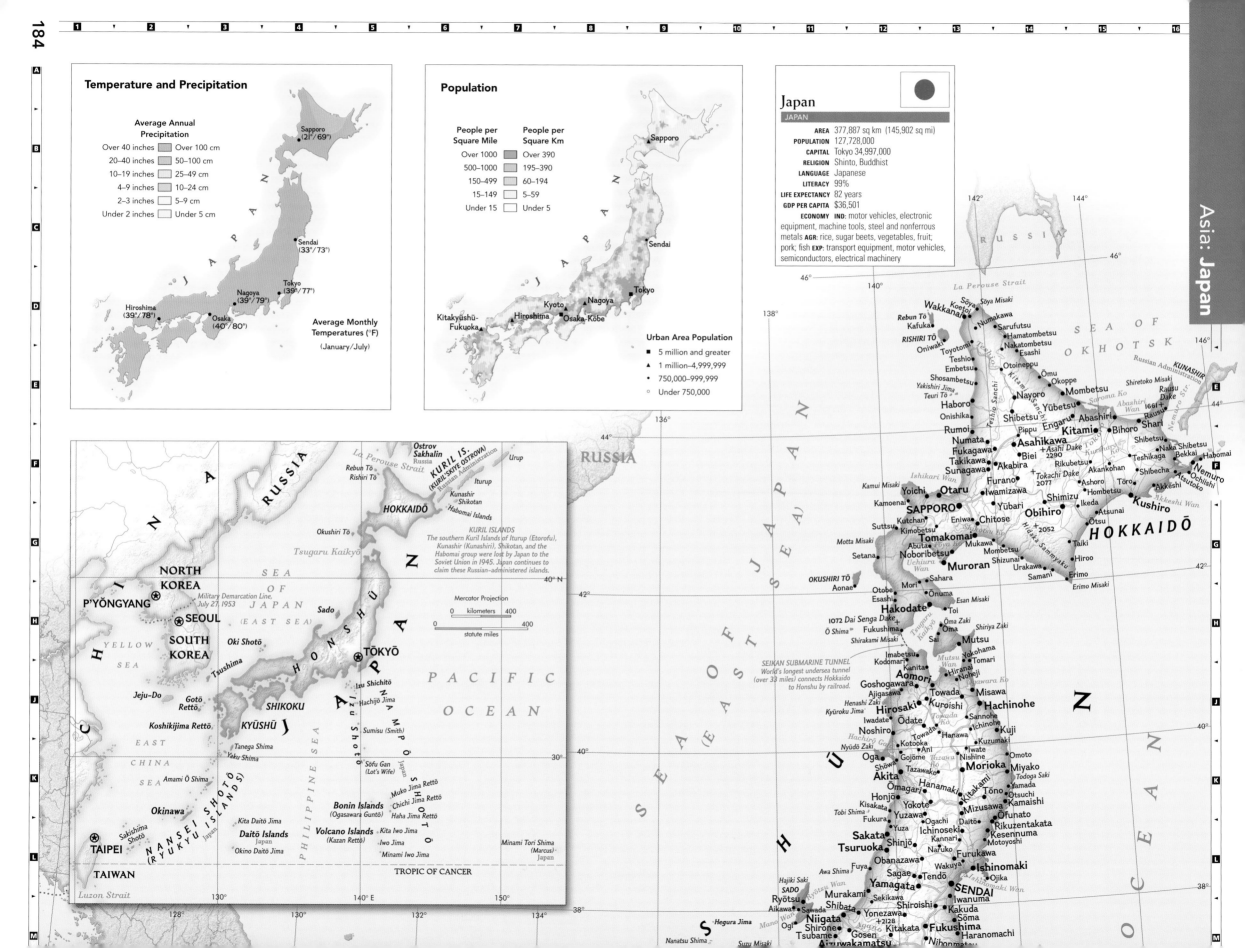

AREA	377,887 sq km (145,902 sq mi)
POPULATION	127,728,000
CAPITAL	Tokyo 34,997,000
RELIGION	Shinto, Buddhist
LANGUAGE	Japanese
LITERACY	99%
LIFE EXPECTANCY	82 years
GDP PER CAPITA	$36,501
ECONOMY	**IND:** motor vehicles, electronic equipment, machine tools, steel and nonferrous metals **AGR:** rice, sugar beets, vegetables, fruit; pork; fish **EXP:** transport equipment, motor vehicles, semiconductors, electrical machinery

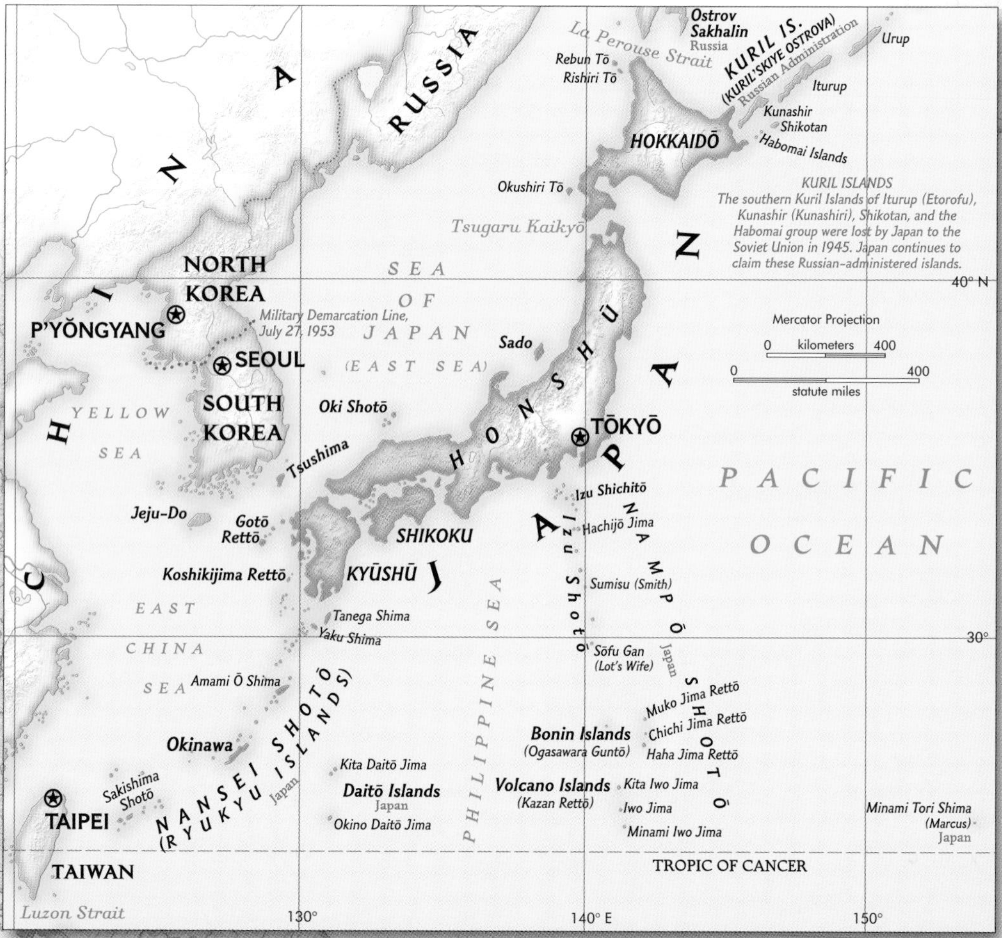

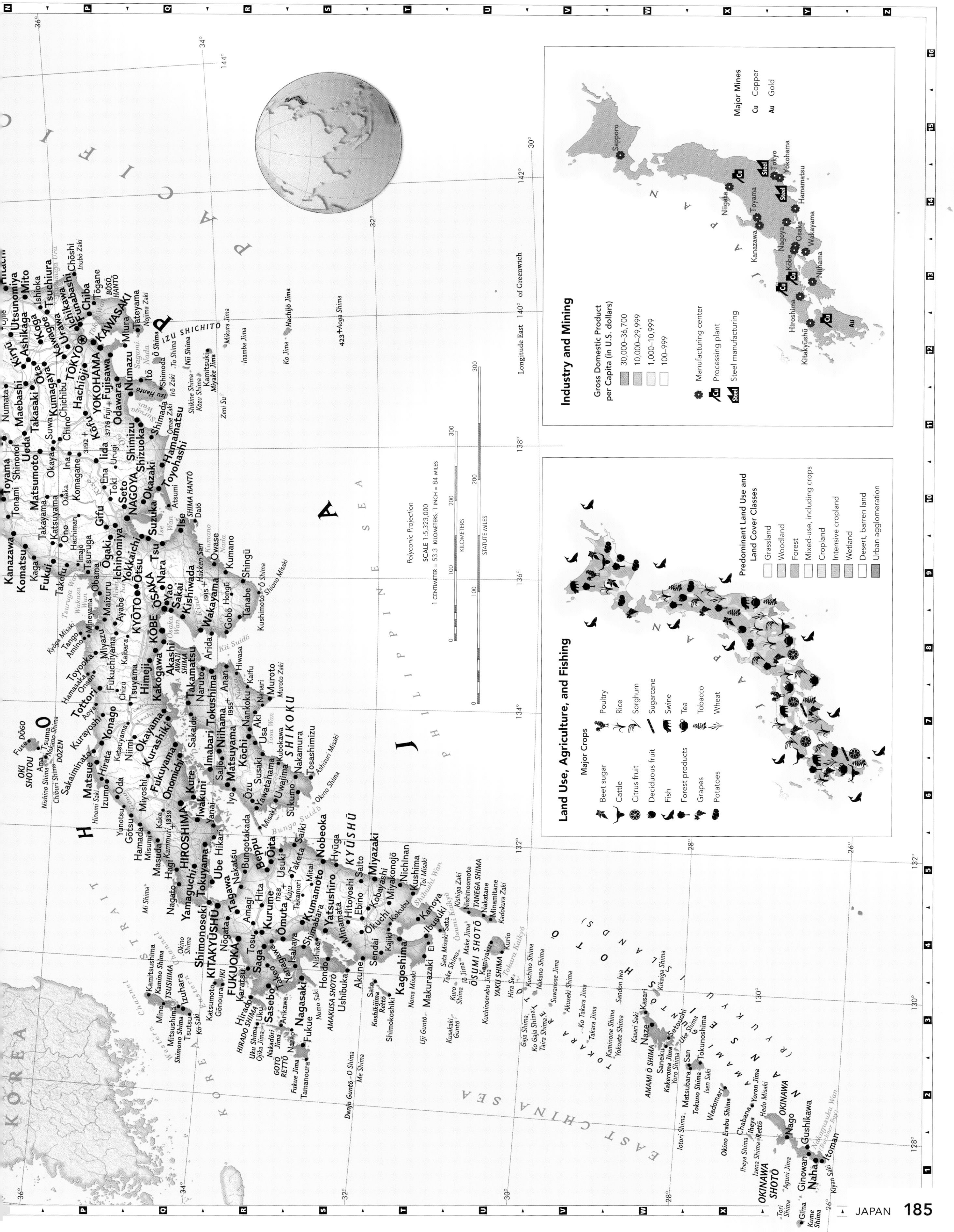

Land Use, Agriculture, and Fishing
Major Crops
Beet sugar
Cattle
Citrus fruit
Deciduous fruit
Fish
Forest products
Grapes
Potatoes
Poultry
Rice
Sorghum
Sugarcane
Swine
Tea
Tobacco
Wheat
Predominant Land Use and Land Cover Classes
Grassland
Woodland
Forest
Mixed-use, including crops
Cropland
Intensive cropland
Wetland
Desert, barren land
Urban agglomeration
Industry and Mining
Gross Domestic Product per Capita (in U.S. dollars)
30,000–36,700
10,000–29,999
1,000–10,999
100–999
Manufacturing center
Processing plant
Steel manufacturing
Major Mines
Cu Copper
Au Gold
Polyconic Projection
SCALE 1:5,323,000
1 CENTIMETER = 53.3 KILOMETERS; 1 INCH = 84 MILES
KILOMETERS
STATUTE MILES
Longitude East 140° of Greenwich
PACIFIC OCEAN
PHILIPPINE SEA
EAST CHINA SEA
KOREA
KOREA STRAIT
JAPAN
HONSHU
SHIKOKU
KYŪSHŪ
TŌKYŌ
YOKOHAMA
NAGOYA
ŌSAKA
KYŌTO
KŌBE
HIROSHIMA
FUKUOKA
KITAKYŪSHŪ
NANSEI SHOTŌ (RYUKYU ISLANDS)
OKINAWA

Cambodia

KINGDOM OF CAMBODIA

AREA 181,035 sq km (69,898 sq mi)
POPULATION 13,329,000
CAPITAL Phnom Penh 1,157,000
RELIGION Theravada Buddhist
LANGUAGE Khmer (official)
LITERACY 74%
LIFE EXPECTANCY 56 years
GDP PER CAPITA $316
ECONOMY **IND:** tourism, garments, rice milling, fishing **AGR:** rice, rubber, corn, vegetables **EXP:** clothing, timber, rubber, rice

Myanmar (Burma)

UNION OF MYANMAR

AREA 676,552 sq km (261,218 sq mi)
POPULATION 50,519,000
CAPITAL Yangon (Rangoon) 3,874,000
RELIGION Buddhist
LANGUAGE Burmese and minority ethnic
LITERACY 85%
LIFE EXPECTANCY 60 years
GDP PER CAPITA $219
ECONOMY **IND:** agricultural processing, knit and woven apparel, wood and wood products, copper **AGR:** rice, pulses, beans, sesame; hardwood; fish and fish products **EXP:** clothing, gas, wood products, pulses

Thailand

KINGDOM OF THAILAND

AREA 513,115 sq km (198,115 sq mi)
POPULATION 65,002,000
CAPITAL Bangkok 6,486,000
RELIGION Buddhist
LANGUAGE Thai, English, ethnic and regional dialects
LITERACY 93%
LIFE EXPECTANCY 71 years
GDP PER CAPITA $2,519
ECONOMY **IND:** tourism, textiles and garments, agricultural processing, beverages **AGR:** rice, cassava (tapioca), rubber, corn **EXP:** textiles and footwear, fishery products, rice, rubber

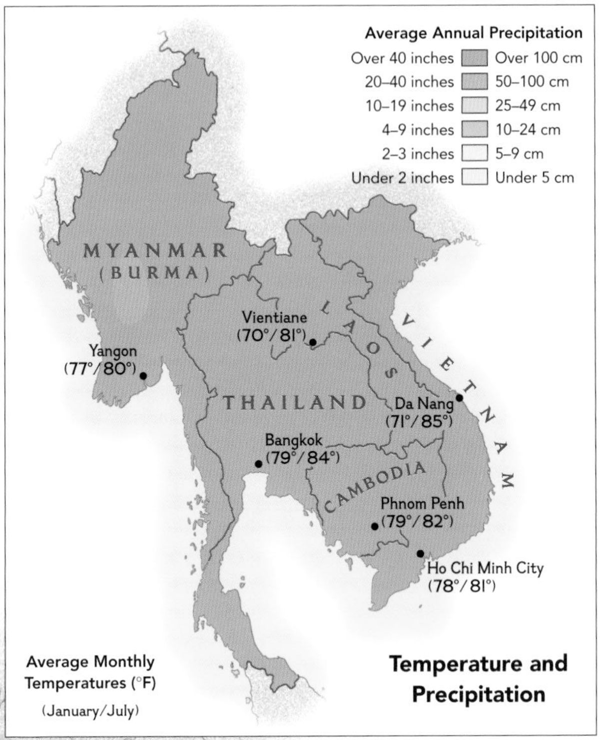

Temperature and Precipitation

Laos

LAO PEOPLE'S DEMOCRATIC REPUBLIC

AREA 236,800 sq km (91,429 sq mi)
POPULATION 5,924,000
CAPITAL Vientiane 716,000
RELIGION Buddhist, animist
LANGUAGE Lao (official), French, English, various ethnic languages
LITERACY 66%
LIFE EXPECTANCY 54 years
GDP PER CAPITA $419
ECONOMY **IND:** copper, tin, and gypsum mining, timber, electric power, agricultural processing **AGR:** sweet potatoes, vegetables, corn, coffee; water buffalo **EXP:** garments, wood products, coffee, electricity

Vietnam

SOCIALIST REPUBLIC OF VIETNAM

AREA 331,114 sq km (127,844 sq mi)
POPULATION 83,305,000
CAPITAL Hanoi 3,977,000
RELIGION Buddhist, Catholic
LANGUAGE Vietnamese (official), English, French, Chinese, Khmer
LITERACY 90%
LIFE EXPECTANCY 72 years
GDP PER CAPITA $551
ECONOMY **IND:** food processing, garments, shoes, machine-building **AGR:** paddy rice, coffee, rubber, cotton; poultry; fish and seafood **EXP:** crude oil, marine products, rice, coffee

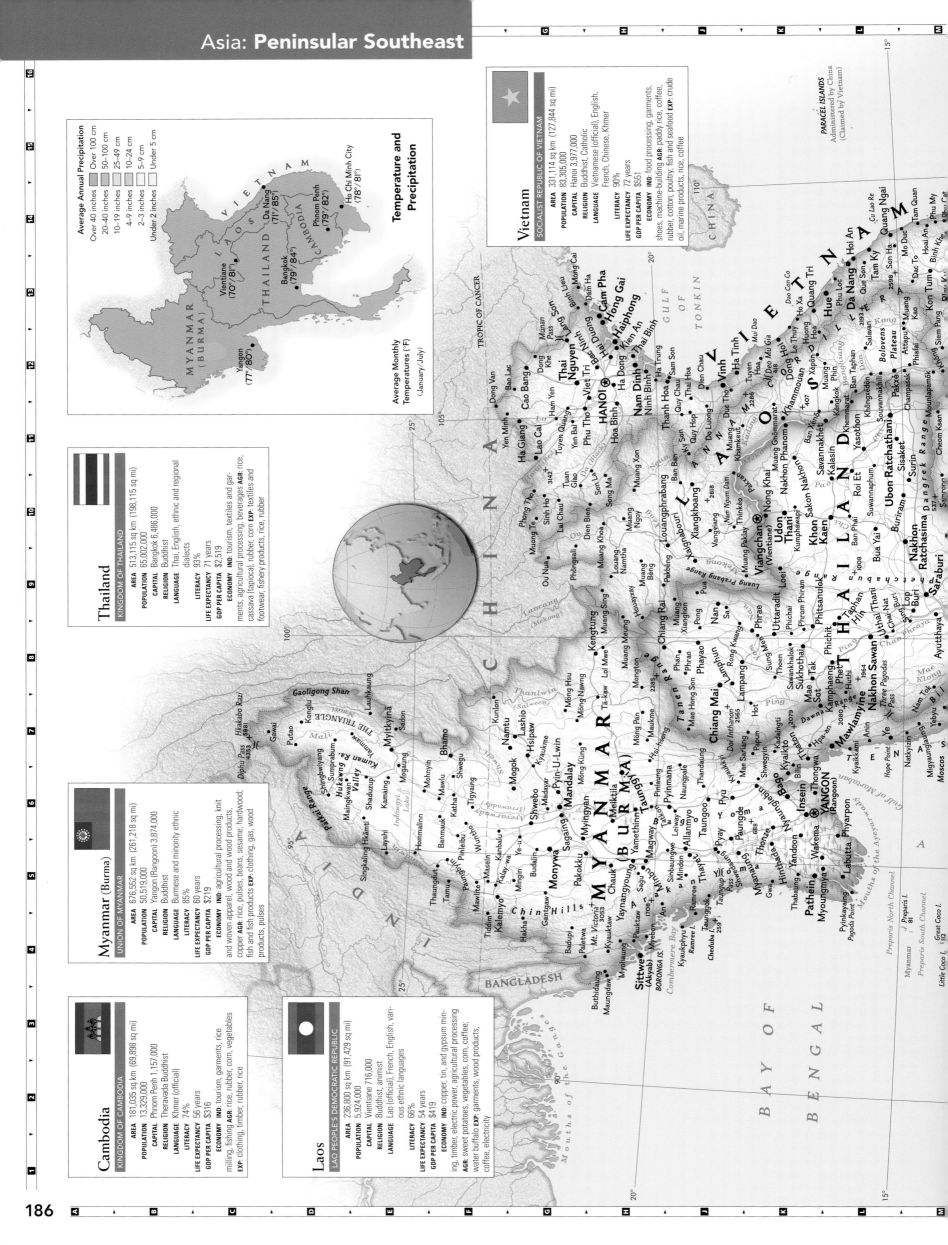

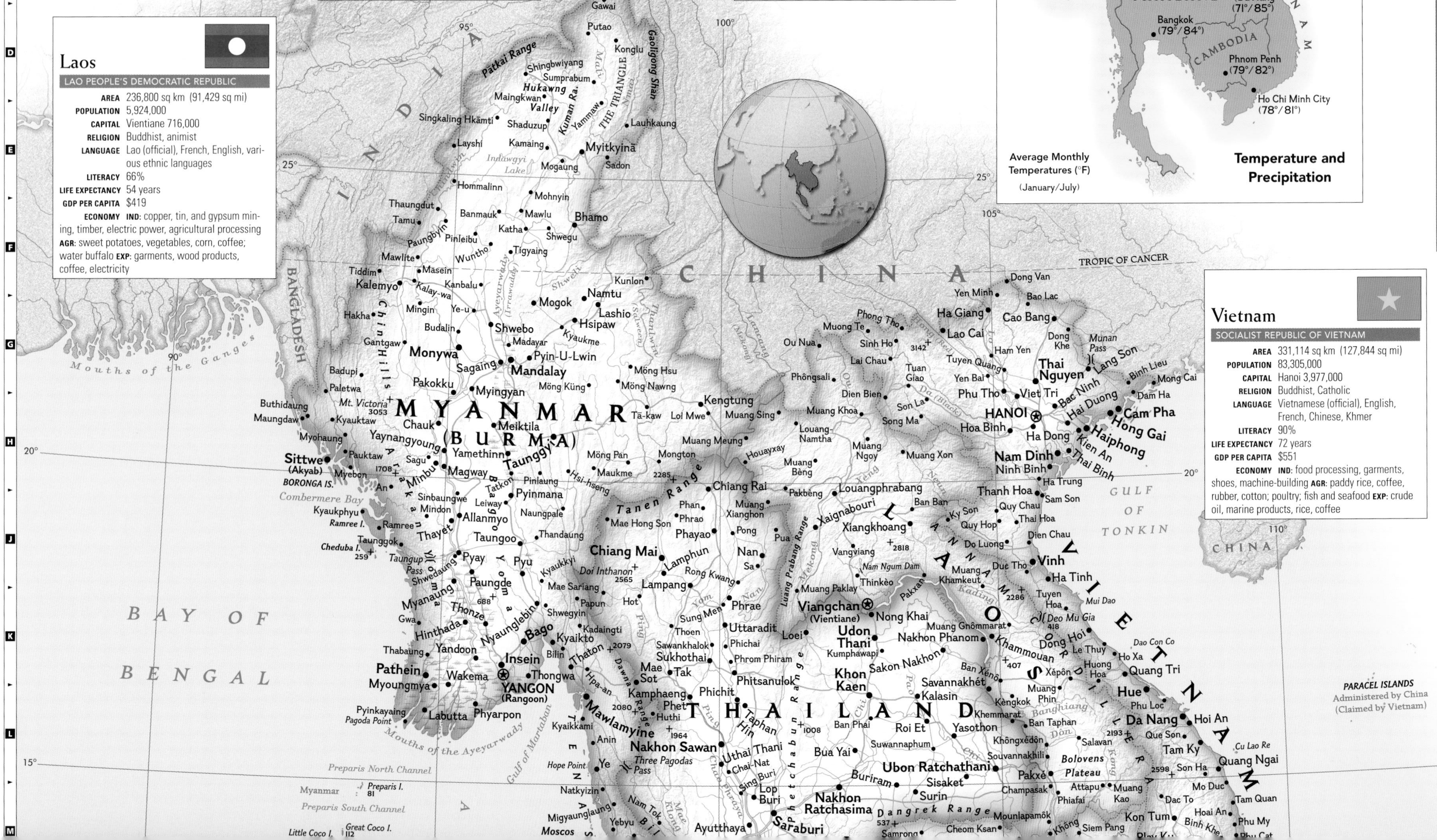

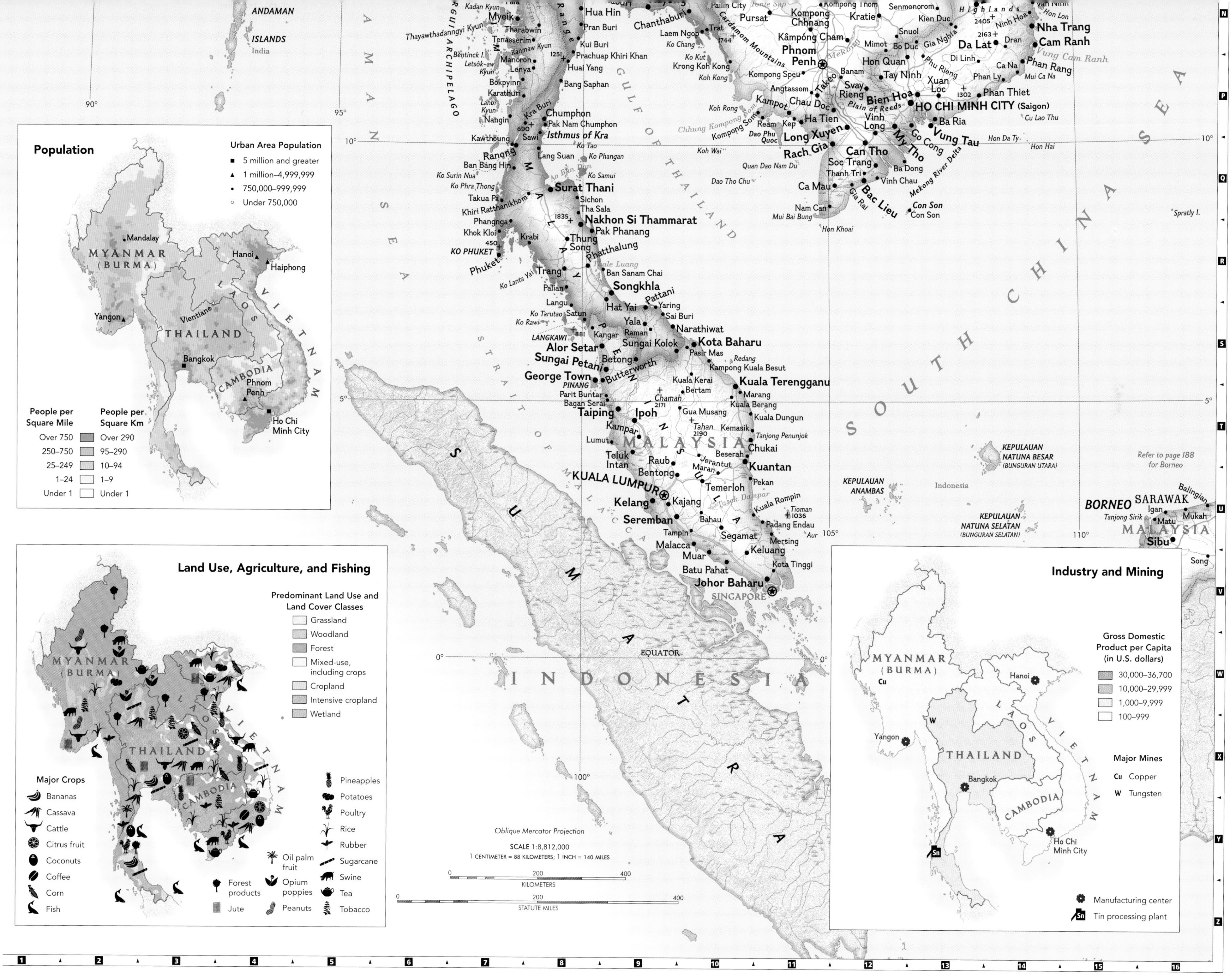

Population
Urban Area Population
5 million and greater
1 million–4,999,999
750,000–999,999
Under 750,000
People per Square Mile
Over 750
250–750
25–249
1–24
Under 1
People per Square Km
Over 290
95–290
10–94
1–9
Under 1
MYANMAR (BURMA)
THAILAND
LAOS
VIETNAM
CAMBODIA
Mandalay
Yangon
Bangkok
Vientiane
Hanoi
Haiphong
Phnom Penh
Ho Chi Minh City
Land Use, Agriculture, and Fishing
Predominant Land Use and Land Cover Classes
Grassland
Woodland
Forest
Mixed-use, including crops
Cropland
Intensive cropland
Wetland
Major Crops
Bananas
Cassava
Cattle
Citrus fruit
Coconuts
Coffee
Corn
Fish
Forest products
Jute
Oil palm fruit
Opium poppies
Peanuts
Pineapples
Potatoes
Poultry
Rice
Rubber
Sugarcane
Swine
Tea
Tobacco
Industry and Mining
Gross Domestic Product per Capita (in U.S. dollars)
30,000–36,700
10,000–29,999
1,000–9,999
100–999
Major Mines
Cu Copper
W Tungsten
Manufacturing center
Tin processing plant
SOUTH CHINA SEA
GULF OF THAILAND
ANDAMAN SEA
STRAIT OF MALACCA
MALAY PENINSULA
MALAYSIA
INDONESIA
SUMATRA
SINGAPORE
BORNEO
SARAWAK
ANDAMAN ISLANDS
India
MERGUI ARCHIPELAGO
Isthmus of Kra
KUALA LUMPUR
HO CHI MINH CITY (Saigon)
Phnom Penh
Johor Baharu
George Town
Ipoh
Kota Baharu
Kuala Terengganu
Kuantan
Songkhla
Nakhon Si Thammarat
Surat Thani
Phuket
Nha Trang
Cam Ranh
Da Lat
Can Tho
Vung Tau
KEPULAUAN NATUNA BESAR (BUNGURAN UTARA)
KEPULAUAN ANAMBAS
KEPULAUAN NATUNA SELATAN (BUNGURAN SELATAN)
Refer to page 188 for Borneo
EQUATOR
Oblique Mercator Projection
SCALE 1:8,812,000
1 CENTIMETER = 88 KILOMETERS; 1 INCH = 140 MILES
KILOMETERS
STATUTE MILES

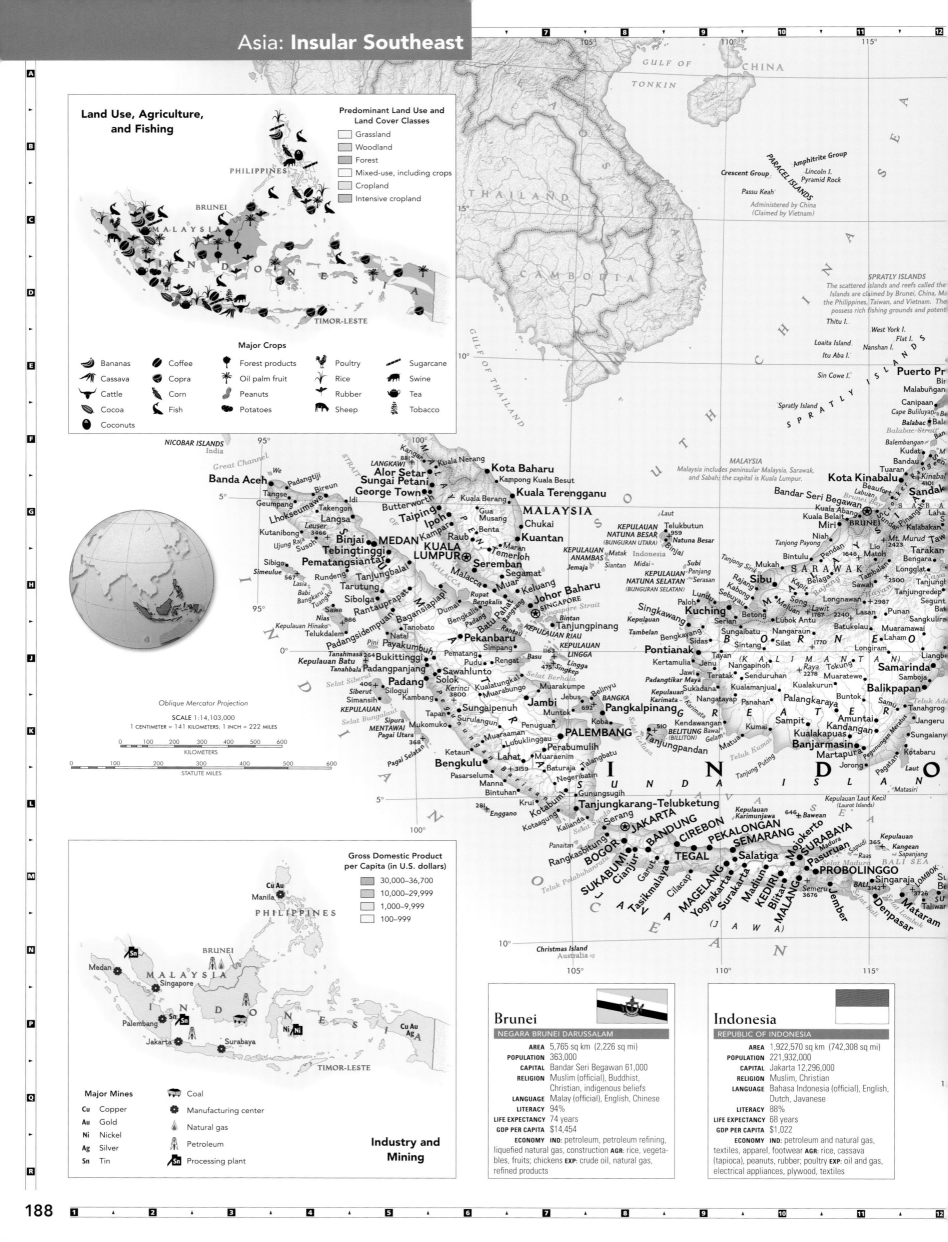

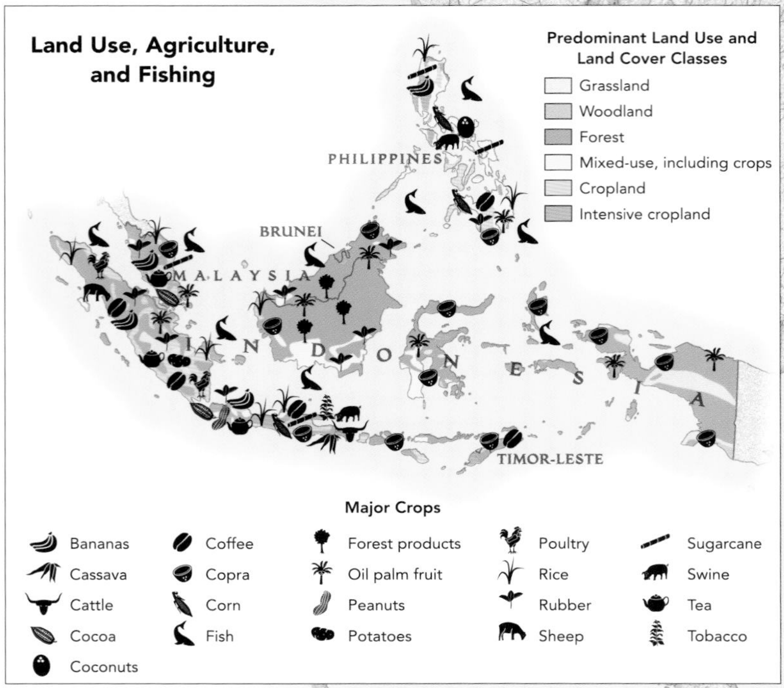

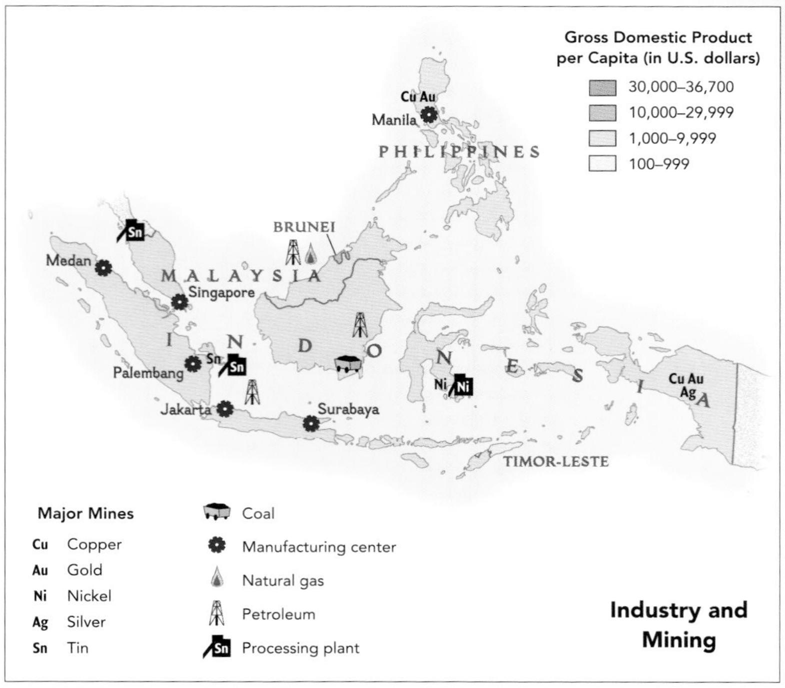

Brunei

NEGARA BRUNEI DARUSSALAM

AREA 5,765 sq km (2,226 sq mi)
POPULATION 363,000
CAPITAL Bandar Seri Begawan 61,000
RELIGION Muslim (official), Buddhist, Christian, indigenous beliefs
LANGUAGE Malay (official), English, Chinese
LITERACY 94%
LIFE EXPECTANCY 74 years
GDP PER CAPITA $14,454
ECONOMY **IND:** petroleum, petroleum refining, liquefied natural gas, construction **AGR:** rice, vegetables, fruits; chickens **EXP:** crude oil, natural gas, refined products

Indonesia

REPUBLIC OF INDONESIA

AREA 1,922,570 sq km (742,308 sq mi)
POPULATION 221,932,000
CAPITAL Jakarta 12,296,000
RELIGION Muslim, Christian
LANGUAGE Bahasa Indonesia (official), English, Dutch, Javanese
LITERACY 88%
LIFE EXPECTANCY 68 years
GDP PER CAPITA $1,022
ECONOMY **IND:** petroleum and natural gas, textiles, apparel, footwear **AGR:** rice, cassava (tapioca), peanuts, rubber; poultry **EXP:** oil and gas, electrical appliances, plywood, textiles

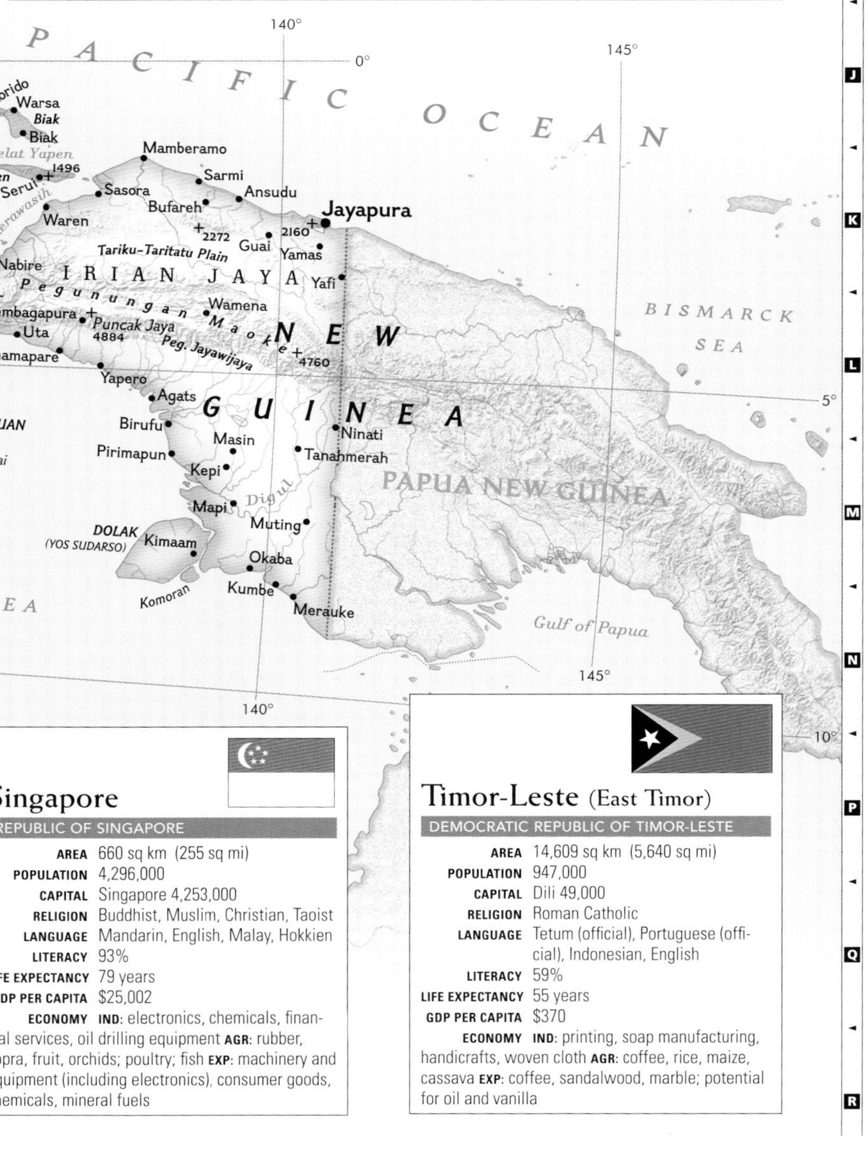

Philippines

REPUBLIC OF THE PHILIPPINES

AREA 300,000 sq km (115,831 sq mi)
POPULATION 84,765,000
CAPITAL Manila 10,352,000
RELIGION Roman Catholic, other Christian, Muslim
LANGUAGE Filipino (based on Tagalog) (official), English (official), eight major dialects
LITERACY 93%
LIFE EXPECTANCY 70 years
GDP PER CAPITA $1,059
ECONOMY **IND:** electronics assembly, garments, footwear, pharmaceuticals **AGR:** sugarcane, coconuts, rice, corn; pork; fish **EXP:** electronic equipment, machinery and transport equipment, garments, optical instruments

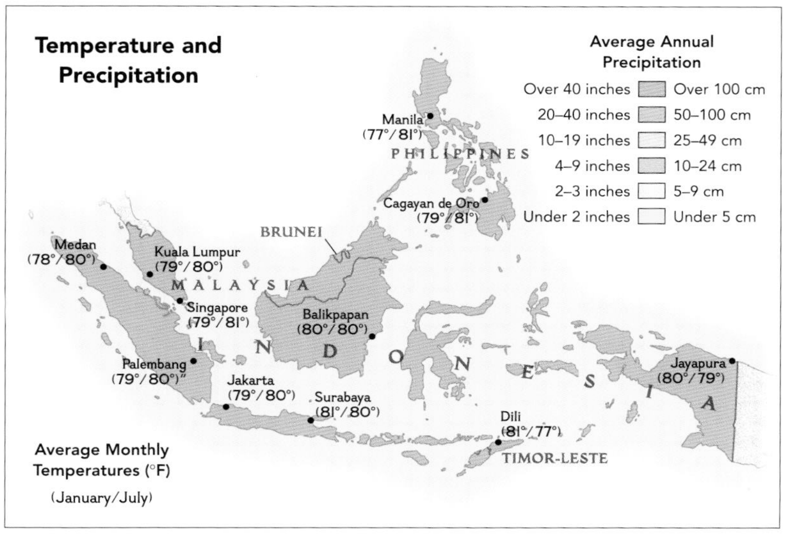

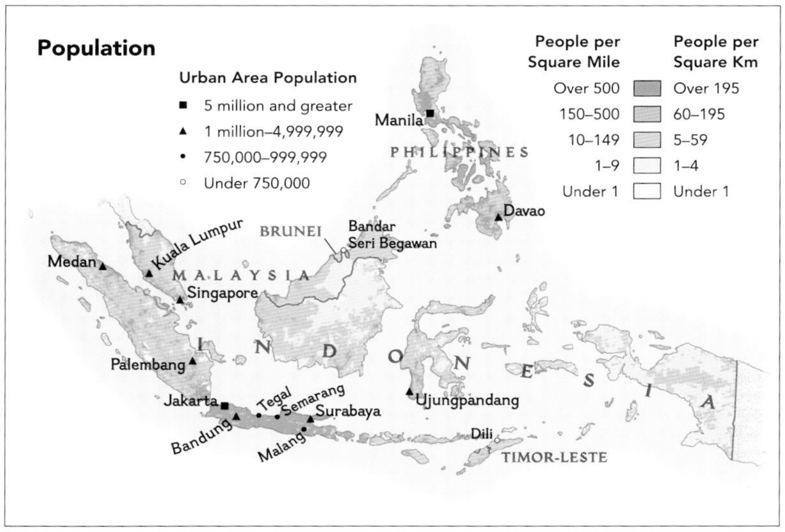

Malaysia

MALAYSIA

AREA 329,847 sq km (127,355 sq mi)
POPULATION 26,121,000
CAPITAL Kuala Lumpur 1,352,000
RELIGION Muslim, Buddhist, Daoist, Hindu, Christian, Sikh, Shamanist
LANGUAGE Bahasa Melayu (official), English, Chinese dialects, Tamil, Telugu, indigenous languages
LITERACY 89%
LIFE EXPECTANCY 73 years
GDP PER CAPITA $4,731
ECONOMY **IND:** rubber and palm oil processing and manufacturing, light manufacturing industry, logging, petroleum production **AGR:** rubber, palm oil, subsistence crops, rice; timber **EXP:** electronic equipment, petroleum and liquefied natural gas, wood and wood products, palm oil

Singapore

REPUBLIC OF SINGAPORE

AREA 660 sq km (255 sq mi)
POPULATION 4,296,000
CAPITAL Singapore 4,253,000
RELIGION Buddhist, Muslim, Christian, Taoist
LANGUAGE Mandarin, English, Malay, Hokkien
LITERACY 93%
LIFE EXPECTANCY 79 years
GDP PER CAPITA $25,002
ECONOMY **IND:** electronics, chemicals, financial services, oil drilling equipment **AGR:** rubber, copra, fruit, orchids; poultry; fish **EXP:** machinery and equipment (including electronics), consumer goods, chemicals, mineral fuels

Timor-Leste (East Timor)

DEMOCRATIC REPUBLIC OF TIMOR-LESTE

AREA 14,609 sq km (5,640 sq mi)
POPULATION 947,000
CAPITAL Dili 49,000
RELIGION Roman Catholic
LANGUAGE Tetum (official), Portuguese (official), Indonesian, English
LITERACY 59%
LIFE EXPECTANCY 55 years
GDP PER CAPITA $370
ECONOMY **IND:** printing, soap manufacturing, handicrafts, woven cloth **AGR:** coffee, rice, maize, cassava **EXP:** coffee, sandalwood, marble; potential for oil and vanilla

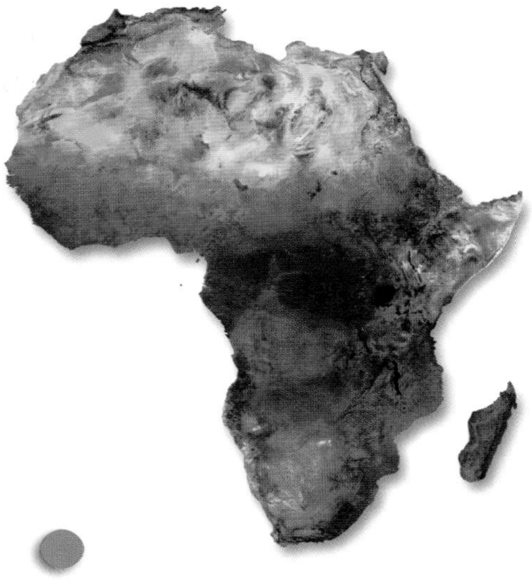

Africa

A lone African elephant drinks at a water hole in Chobe National Park, Botswana, where protected enclaves help support some 120,000 of the continent's 400,000 to 660,000 elephants. In the late 1970s, there were 1.3 million elephants in Africa; poaching and habitat loss contributed to the decline.

Africa is often called the continent of beginnings. Fossil and bone records of the earliest humans go back more than 4 million years, and perhaps 1.8 million years ago our early upright ancestor, *Homo erectus*, departed Africa on the long journey that eventually peopled the Earth. It now seems likely that every person today comes from a lineage that leads back to an ancient African. Innumerable cave paintings and petroglyphs, from the Sahara to South Africa, provide clues to the beliefs and way of life of these age-old hominids.

Second largest continent after Asia, Africa accounts for a fifth of the world's land surface. Its unforgettable form, bulging to the west, lies surrounded by oceans and seas and can be considered underpopulated because only slightly more than 13.5 percent of the world's population lives here. Yet Africa's 53 countries now contain more than 905 million people, two-thirds living in the countryside, mostly in coastal regions, near lakes, and along river courses.

The mighty Sahara, largest hot desert in the world, covers more than a quarter of Africa's surface and divides the continent. Desert zones—Sahara, Kalahari, Namib—contrast with immense tropical rain forests. Watered regions of lakes and rivers lie beyond the Sahel, a vast semiarid zone of short grasses that spans the continent south of the Sahara. Most of Africa is made up of savanna—high, rolling, grassy plains.

These savannas have been home since earliest times to people often called Bantu, a reference to both social groupings and their languages. Other distinct physical types exist around the continent as well: BaMbuti (Pygmies), San (Bushmen), Nilo-Saharans, and Hamito-Semitics (Berbers and Cushites). Africa's astonishing number of spoken languages—1,600, more than any other continent—reflect the great diversity of ethnic and social groups.

Near the Equator, perpetual ice and snow crown Mount Kilimanjaro, the continent's highest point at 19,340 feet (5,895 m). The Nile, longest river in the world at 4,241 miles (6,825 km), originates in mountains south of the Equator and flows north-northeast before finally delivering its life-giving waters into the Mediterranean Sea.

Africa, blessed with wondrous deserts, rivers, grasslands, forests, and multihued earth, and possessing huge reserves of mineral wealth and biodiversity, waits expectantly for a prosperous future.

Many obstacles, however, complicate the way forward. African countries experience great gaps in wealth between city and country, such as between Lagos and Nigeria and Cairo and Egypt.

Nearly 40 other African cities have populations numbering more than a million. Lack of clean water and the spread of diseases—malaria, tuberculosis, cholera, and AIDS among them—undermine people's health. In addition, war and huge concentrations of refugees displaced by fighting, persecution, and famine deter any chance of growth and stability. Africa today seems to stand between hope and hopelessness.

PHYSICAL Africa stretches an astounding 5,000 miles (8,047 km) from north to south and 4,600 miles (7,403 km) from east to west. The continent rises from generally narrow coastal strips to form a gigantic plateau, with portions over 2,000 feet (610 m) in height. It has limited harbors and a coastline with few bays and inlets. Though formed by a series of expansive uplands, Africa has few true mountain chains. Main ranges in the north are the Atlas in Morocco and the Ahaggar in the Sahara. To the southeast, the Ethiopian Highlands form a broad area of high topography. The massive volcanic peaks of Mount Kilimanjaro and Mount Kenya rise in dramatic isolation from surrounding plains. Between Uganda and Democratic Republic of the Congo, the Ruwenzori Range runs north to south and falls steeply in the west to the Rift Valley.

The East African Rift System is the continent's most dramatic geologic feature. This great rent actually begins in the Red Sea, then cuts southward to form the stunning landscape of lakes, volcanoes, and deep valleys that finally ends near the mouth of the Zambezi River. The Rift Valley, a region of active plate tectonics, marks the divide where East Africa is steadily being pulled away, eventually to become a mini-continent.

The Great Escarpment in southern Africa, a plateau edge that falls off to the coastal strip, is best represented by the stark, highly eroded Drakensberg Range, which reaches altitudes over 11,400 feet (3,482 m).

Madagascar, fourth largest island in the world, lies east of the main continent and is remarkable for its flora and fauna, including medicinal plants and lemur species.

Africa's great rivers include the Niger, Congo, and Zambezi, each regionally important for internal transport and fishing. The Nile drains 6 percent of the continent; its two main branches, the Blue Nile and the White Nile, meet at Khartoum, in Sudan.

Wildlife still abounds in eastern and southern Africa and supports ecotourism, but hundreds of plant and animal species live precariously close to extinction.

HISTORY After millions of years of human evolution, there arose along the Nile River the brilliant civilization of Egypt. Mastery of agriculture and the river's annual flooding led to a series of dynasties that lasted for some 3,000 years, creating an astounding legacy of tombs, statuary, pyramids, temples, and hieroglyphic writing.

The long-standing power of Carthage ruled the western Mediterranean, but was conquered by the Roman Empire in 146 B.C. Rome and Byzantium henceforth controlled all of North Africa's coastal strip until the Arab influx from the seventh century onward. The Arabs quickly took all of North Africa and spread their language and religion. Arabic and Islam have been unifying forces ever since. Trans-Sahara trade and contact converted many sub-Saharan people, such as the Hausa of Nigeria, to Islam.

Indigenous kingdoms have punctuated Africa's history. Finds from Great Zimbabwe, a massive fortress-city and inland empire that flourished from the 11th to 15th centuries, show contacts with places as far away as India and China.

Along the Niger River, regional empires rose and fell between A.D. 800 and 1600. Slaves, ivory, gold, and kola nuts, used for flavoring and medicine, formed the basis of trade. In the Niger Delta area, Yoruba, Ashanti, and Hausa states also had their periods of grandness. Longest lasting of all was Benin, a major African kingdom that survived from the 13th to 19th centuries.

The Swahili (literally, "coastal plain") culture arose from a mix of Arabs, local people, and others who from A.D. 900 onward spread to towns and cities of the east coast, along the Indian Ocean, from Somalia to Zanzibar. The Swahili language remains a major lingua franca in east, central, and southern Africa.

Colonialism's long period of domination, during which Portugal, Great Britain, France, Belgium, Germany, and Italy ruled the continent, spans from the mid-1500s to the mid-1900s. The Portuguese arrived first in search of riches and the sea route to India. In time, commerce and Christianity pushed Europe into Africa.

The terrible slave trade shipped millions of Africans to North and South America and Arab regions. European presence encouraged exploration to find the sources of Africa's main rivers and to fill in blank spots on the map.

In the late 19th century, Europe's powers embarked on a "scramble for Africa," which led to a partitioning of the entire continent by 1914. After the two World Wars colonialism weakened. Independence for some countries began in the 1950s and came to most in the 1960s, in power transfers ranging from peaceful (Ghana, Senegal) to bloody (Kenya, Algeria). Freedom arrived in Rhodesia, with the new name Zimbabwe, in 1980, and in Namibia in 1990. The end of white rule in South Africa culminated with the election of Nelson Mandela in 1994.

CULTURE Hunting, fishing, and gathering supported Africa's early humans. In time, agriculture led to permanent settlements and diversity in society, first along the Nile River and then in the south.

Village-based communities, resilient and lasting in their institutions, have formed the core of African life for thousands of years. With crop cultivation came domestication of animals—cattle, sheep, and goats. Ironworking reached sub-Saharan Africa from the north by about the fourth century B.C., allowing for new tools and weapons that accelerated change.

Kingdoms grew from the soil of village life. Kings and their courts resembled village elders in their roles as judges, mediators of disputes, and masters of trade. Early kingdoms in Mali, Ghana, and elsewhere conducted long-distance trade in gold, ivory, hides, jewels, feathers, and salt.

In some places, religious leaders became kings. Seen as divine, they assumed rights over land and cattle herds and in return took responsibility for the people's well-being.

Settled life allowed time and energy for arts, crafts, and other creative activities. In West Africa, artists, carvers, and bronze casters of the Ife (12th and 13th centuries) and Benin (16th and 17th centuries) kingdoms produced masterpieces in different mediums, culminating in terra-cotta heads and bronze statues and bas-reliefs of exquisite craftsmanship and naturalism. African art, especially sculpture, continues to hold a high place in world culture.

Rich traditions of oral narrative survive to preserve the history and collective memories of different tribes and groups. Bards known as griots tell tales and sing epic songs while accompanied by their instruments.

Traditional religion and ritual still have a powerful place in Africa, for health, wealth, good harvests, and to honor the forces of nature. The Dogon people retain a complex cosmology and perform a great ceremony every 60 years to mark the appearance of the star Sirius between two mountains.

Most major world religions are represented in Africa: Islam, Christianity, Judaism, even Hinduism. Islam predominates in the north, and south of the Sahara Christianity claims multitudes of followers—Islam and Christianity claim respectively 350 million and 400 million followers.

The magnificent Temple of Ramses II (circa 1279–1213 B.C.) at Abu Simbel is so revered that when the damming of the Nile at Aswan promised to submerge it, both it and the Temple of Nefertari (not shown) were meticulously dismantled and reassembled (1964–68) on higher ground 600 feet (184 m) to the west.

European languages and schooling, legacies of colonialism, have had lasting effects on modern Africa. Yet far from the cities one can still find blue-turbanned Tuareg wandering the Sahara, slender Masai on the savannas of East Africa, Pygmies in the rain forests, and San (Bushmen) adapted to the Kalahari Desert's harsh conditions. Color, exuberance, and diversity manage to shine through the clouds of trouble that beset the nations of Africa.

ECONOMY Africa ranks among the richest regions in the world in natural resources; it contains vast reserves of fossil fuels, precious metals, ores, and gems, including almost all of the world's chromium, much uranium, copper, tremendous underground gold reserves, and diamonds. West Africa exports major amounts of iron ore.

Yet Africa, the poorest continent, accounts for a mere one percent of world economic output. South Africa's economy alone nearly equals that of all other sub-Saharan countries combined.

With little history of refining and manufacturing (limited to parts of North and South Africa), small-scale agriculture dominates the activities of more than 60 percent of Africans: Main crops are corn, wheat, rice, yams, potatoes, and cassava. Economic life revolves around farmsteads and village markets. Important cash crops include cacao, coffee, tea, fruit, and palm and vegetable oils.

Even though food production is increasing, agriculture takes place on only 6 percent of Africa's land and fails to keep pace with population growth—six children is the average for every woman, and in many countries nearly half the people are under 15. Most countries rely on imported food and loans. A cycle of crushing debt repayment, unemployment, and instability repels much-needed foreign investment.

Tourism, while offering hope to numerous countries, mostly in north, east, and southern Africa, highlights the need for conservation and interdependence between humans and the varied ecosystems that support Africa's plants and wildlife. Stresses today include poaching, overgrazing, and deforestation.

The African Union (AU)—formerly the Organization of African Unity (OAU)—and numerous regional trading blocks try to encourage economic cooperation and political stability, essential for sustained growth. After decades of corruption, ruinous to many economies, Africans now realize that any hope for development lies with themselves and their leaders.

Africa: Physical and Political

Longitude West 20° of Greenwich
Longitude East 30° of Greenwich
E U R O P E
A S I A
IBERIAN PENINSULA
BALKAN PENINSULA
ANATOLIA (ASIA MINOR)
BLACK SEA
CASPIAN SEA
AZORES
Corsica
Sardinia
Balearic Is.
Sicily
Peloponnesus
Crete
Rhodes
Cyprus
MEDITERRANEAN SEA
Strait of Gibraltar
Cape Blanc
G. of Tunis
G. of Hammamet
G. of Gabes
Jerba I.
Chott Melrhir
Shott el Jerid
Er Rif 2456
2308 Atlas
2326
Tell Atlas
ATLAS MOUNTAINS
Saharan Atlas
High Atlas
Jebel Toubkal 4165
Oued Drâa
Hamada du Drâa
Madeira
MADEIRA ISLANDS
C. Beddouza
Salvage Islands
Cape Rhir
CANARY ISLANDS
La Palma
Tenerife
Gomera
Ferro
Gran Canaria
Lanzarote
Fuerteventura
C. Boujdour
Great Western Dunes
Great Eastern Dunes
Tademaït Plateau
Hamada de Tinrhert
Jabal Nafūsah
Gefara
Cape Misurata
Gulf of Sidra
Jabal al Akhḑar
Ras al Hilāl
G. of Bomba
G. of Salûm
Arabs Gulf
Nile River Delta
SUEZ CANAL
SINAI
Mt. Sinai 2285
Gulf of Aqaba
G. of Suez
Rās Muhammad
Libyan Plateau 264
-133 Qattara Depression
Sand Sea of Calanscio
Sarīr Calanscio
Western Desert
Eastern Desert
Jabal as Sawdā'
Al Harūj al Aswad
Şaḩrā' Awbārī
Sebkha Mekerrhane
Sebkha Azzel Matti
Tassili-n-Ajjer
Şaḩrā' Marzūq
1200
Erg Iguid
Erg Chech
'Erg
Zednes 460
TROPIC OF CANCER
Tanezrouft
Mount Tahat 3003
Ahaggar Mts.
Rebiana Sand Sea 701
Kufra Oasis
Abu Ballâs 467
Gilf Kebîr Plateau
Toshka Lakes
Lake Nasser
Rās Banās
Cape Elba (Ras Hadarba)
ARABIAN PENINSULA
RED SEA
C. Blanc
C. Timiris
Akchâr
El Djouf
SAHARA
1000
Adrar des Iforas
Tassili Oua -n- Ahaggar
Djado Plateau
Pic Touside 3315
Tibesti Mts.
Emi Koussi 3415
Jebel 'Uweinat 1893
Libyan Desert
Gebel Siri 420
Lake Nubia
Nubian Desert
Jabal Abyad Plateau
Nile
Jebel Sabidana 1907
Suakin Archipelago
Ras Kasar
Trarza
Tagant
El Mreyyé
Tarazit Massif
Aïr Massif
Mt. Bagzane 2022
Ténéré
Lake Faguibine
Hodh
Bodele Depression
Ennedi
1310
Dahlak Archipelago
C. Verde
Senegal
Gambia
Falémé
Lake Débo
Inland Niger Delta
Bani
Niger
Manga
Lake Chad
Jebel Teljo 1954
Atbara
Blue Nile
Lowest point in Africa
Ras Dejen 4533
Danakil Desert
Lake Assal -156 (-512 ft)
Bab al Mandab
GULF OF ADEN
G. of Tadjoura
2408
Bissagos Is.
Fouta Djallon
1116
765
White Volta
Black Volta
Komoé
SAHEL
Hadejia
Yobe
Gana
Guéra Massif 1613
3088
Marra Mts.
Jebel ed Dair 1412
Nuba Mts. 1325
El Gezira
White Nile
Lake Tana
ETHIOPIAN HIGHLANDS
Loma Mts. 1948
Source of the Niger
Nimba Mts.
UPPER GUINEA
Lake Volta
Kainji Res.
Jos Plateau 1781
Chari
Logone
Dar Rounga 1400
Chaîne des Bongos
Bahr el Arab
Tondou Massif
Sudd
Gurage 3719
GREAT RIFT VALLEY
Mendebo Mts.
Batu 4307
Ogadēn
Haud
SOMALI PENINSULA
Grain Coast
Ivory Coast
Gold Coast
Slave Coast
Bight of Benin
Cape Palmas
Cavally
Benue
1213
Mbang Mts.
Karre Mts.
Mountain Nile
Lake Abaya
Dawa
L. Chew Bahir
Shebele
Niger Delta
Cameroon Mt. 4100
Sanaga
Lobaye
Kotto
Bomu
Uele
Lake Turkana (L. Rudolf)
Chalbi Desert
GULF OF GUINEA
Bioko
Principe
São Tomé
Annobón
Cape Lopez
Ntem
Ngoko
Ubangi
Congo
Itimbiri
Aruwimi
Albert
Lake Albert
Mt. Elgon 4321
Lorian Swamp
Juba
Benadir
EQUATOR
Meridian of Greenwich (London)
CONGO BASIN
Lulonga
Boyoma Falls
Ruwenzori 5109
Lake Edward
KENYA HIGHLANDS
Mt. Kenya 5199
Tshuapa
Lac Ntomba
Crystal Mountains
1190
Lake Victoria 1133
Serengeti Plain
Olduvai Gorge
Kilimanjaro 5895 (19340 ft)
Highest point in Africa
Ungama Bay
Tana
Raas Kaambooni
Lomami
Lake Kivu
Lukenie
Kasai
Sankuru
Sources of the Nile
Iwembere Steppe
Masai Steppe
Pemba Island
Zanzibar Island
LOWER GUINEA
Kwango
Lulua
Mitumba Mountains
1006
2460
Lake Tanganyika
L. Rukwa
Great Ruaha
Rufiji
Mafia Island
Ascension 875
Bengo Bay
Palmeirinhas Pt.
Kwanza
Chicapa
L. Upemba
Lake Mweru
Lake Bangweulu
Kilombero
Ruvuma
Cape Delgado
Aldabra Is.
Comoro Group
COMORO IS.
Source of the Zambezi
KATANGA PLATEAU
Source of the Congo
Chambeshi
Muchinga Mountains
Luangwa
Lake Malawi
Lugenda
Lúrio
Pemba Bay
Maromokotro 2876
Mahajamba Bay
2620
Bié Plateau
1554
1893
1610
Lungwebungu
Busanga Swamp
Kafue
Lago de Cahora Bassa
L. Chilwa
Namuli 2419
Cap St. André
Saint Helena 823
Albina Point
Tiger Bay
Cunene
Huila Plateau
Cubango
Cuando
Zambezi
Lake Kariba
Shire
Mozambique Channel
Kaokoland
Ovamboland
Okavango
Chobe
Victoria Falls
Sa. da Gorongosa 1863
Zambezi River Delta
Barren Is.
Bemaraha Plat.
Bongo Lava
MADAGASCAR
CANAL DES PANGALANES
Etosha Pan
Okavango Delta
Skeleton Coast
Namib Desert
Brandberg 2573
Makgadikgadi Pans
Matopo Hills 1549
Shashe
Save
Cape São Sebastião
Bassas da India
C. St. Vincent
Europa I.
Boby Peak 2658
Pelican Point
Auas Mts. 2484
KALAHARI DESERT
1024
Limpopo
Blouberg 2046
Barra Point
St. Augustin Bay
Salapaly Bay
Cape Ste. Marie
TROPIC OF CAPRICORN
Nosob
Molopo
Lebombo Mts.
414
Baía de Maputo
Azimuthal Equidistant Projection
SCALE 1:30,268,000
1 CENTIMETER = 303 KILOMETERS; 1 INCH = 478 MILES
0 200 400 600 800 1000 KILOMETERS
0 200 400 600 800 1000 STATUTE MILES
Huns Mts. 1655
Karas Mts. 2202
Kaap Plat.
Vaal
Tugela Falls Total drop 948 meters
Drakensberg
Wreck Point
Orange
Thabana Ntlenyana 3482
Northern Karroo
Sneeuberg 2504
St. Helena Bay
Cape Columbine
Great Karroo
Seweweekspoortpiek 2325
Cape of Good Hope
False Bay
Cape Agulhas
Mossel Bay
Algoa Bay
Cape Recife
St. Francis Bay
International boundary
Disputed or undefined boundary
Tristan da Cunha Group
Tristan da Cunha I.
Inaccessible I.
Nightingale I.
ATLANTIC OCEAN
INDIAN OCEAN
PERSIAN GULF

Longitude West 20° of Greenwich
Longitude East 20° of Greenwich
Meridian of Greenwich (London)
EQUATOR
TROPIC OF CANCER
TROPIC OF CAPRICORN
Azimuthal Equidistant Projection
SCALE 1:30,268,000
1 CENTIMETER = 303 KILOMETERS; 1 INCH = 478 MILES
KILOMETERS
STATUTE MILES
A T L A N T I C O C E A N
I N D I A N O C E A N
M E D I T E R R A N E A N S E A
B L A C K S E A
GULF OF GUINEA
GULF OF ADEN
Mozambique Channel
S A H A R A
MOROCCO
ALGERIA
TUNISIA
LIBYA
EGYPT
WESTERN SAHARA
MAURITANIA
MALI
NIGER
CHAD
SUDAN
ETHIOPIA
SOMALIA
KENYA
TANZANIA
DEMOCRATIC REPUBLIC OF THE CONGO
CENTRAL AFRICAN REPUBLIC
CAMEROON
NIGERIA
GABON
CONGO
ANGOLA
ZAMBIA
ZIMBABWE
MOZAMBIQUE
MALAWI
BOTSWANA
NAMIBIA
SOUTH AFRICA
MADAGASCAR
SAUDI ARABIA
TURKEY
IRAN
RUSSIA
UKRAINE
KAZAKHSTAN
FRANCE
SPAIN
ITALY
ALGER (Algiers)
TUNIS
TARĀBULUS (Tripoli)
EL QĀHIRA (Cairo)
KHARTOUM
ĀDĪS ĀBEBA (Addis Ababa)
NAIROBI
KINSHASA
LUANDA
LUSAKA
HARARE
PRETORIA (Tshwane)
CAPE TOWN
ANTANANARIVO
DAR ES SALAAM
MUQDISHO (Mogadishu)
Tristan da Cunha Group
Ascension U.K.
Saint Helena U.K.

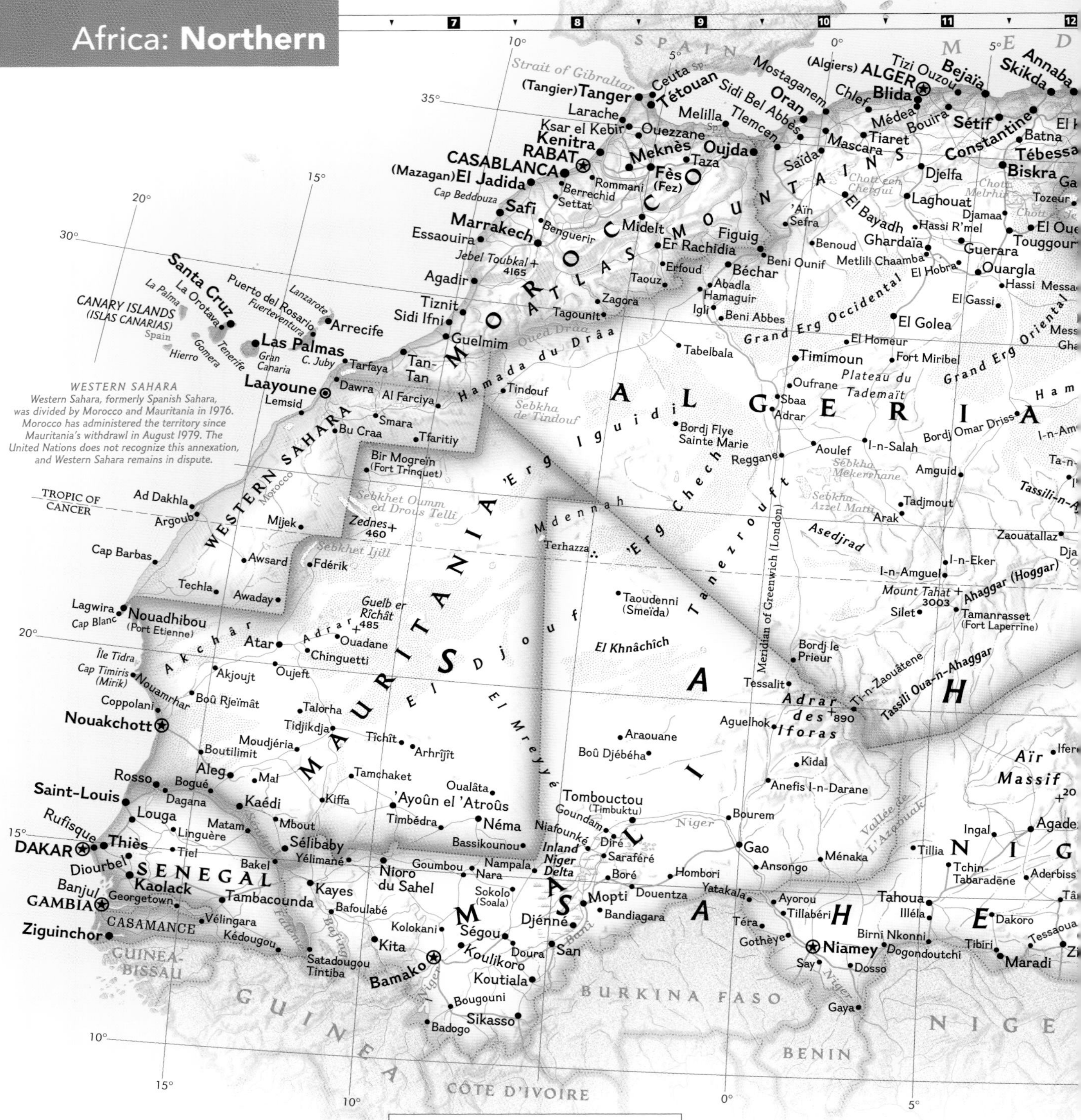

Algeria

PEOPLE'S DEMOCRATIC REP. OF ALGERIA

AREA 2,381,741 sq km (919,595 sq mi)
POPULATION 32,814,000
CAPITAL Algiers 3,060,000
RELIGION Sunni Muslim
LANGUAGE Arabic (official), French, Berber dialects
LITERACY 70%
LIFE EXPECTANCY 73 years
GDP PER CAPITA $2,497
ECONOMY **IND:** petroleum, natural gas, light industries, mining **AGR:** wheat, barley, oats, grapes; sheep **EXP:** petroleum, natural gas, petroleum products

Chad

REPUBLIC OF CHAD

AREA 1,284,000 sq km (495,755 sq mi)
POPULATION 9,657,000
CAPITAL N'Djamena 797,000
RELIGION Muslim, Christian, animist
LANGUAGE French (official), Arabic (official), Sara, over 120 different languages and dialects
LITERACY 48%
LIFE EXPECTANCY 47 years
GDP PER CAPITA $426
ECONOMY **IND:** oil, cotton textiles, meatpacking, beer brewing **AGR:** cotton, sorghum, millet, peanuts; cattle **EXP:** cotton, cattle, gum arabic

Egypt

ARAB REPUBLIC OF EGYPT

AREA 1,002,000 sq km (386,874 sq mi)
POPULATION 74,033,000
CAPITAL Cairo 10,834,000
RELIGION Sunni Muslim, Coptic Christian
LANGUAGE Arabic (official), English, French
LITERACY 58%
LIFE EXPECTANCY 70 years
GDP PER CAPITA $1,222
ECONOMY **IND:** textiles, food processing, tourism, chemicals **AGR:** cotton, rice, corn, wheat; cattle **EXP:** crude oil and petroleum products, cotton, textiles, metal products

Gambia

REPUBLIC OF THE GAMBIA

AREA 11,295 sq km (4,361 sq mi)
POPULATION 1,595,000
CAPITAL Banjul 372,000
RELIGION Muslim, Christian
LANGUAGE English (official), Mandinka, Wolof, Fula
LITERACY 40%
LIFE EXPECTANCY 53 years
GDP PER CAPITA $281
ECONOMY **IND:** peanut, fish, and hide processing, tourism, beverages, agricultural machinery assembly **AGR:** rice, millet, sorghum, peanuts; cattle **EXP:** peanut products, fish, cotton lint, palm kernels

Libya

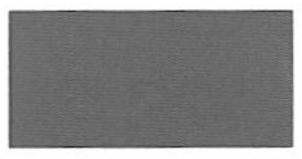

GR. SOC. PEOPLE'S LIBYAN ARAB JAMAHIRIYA

AREA 1,759,540 sq km (679,362 sq mi)
POPULATION 5,766,000
CAPITAL Tripoli 2,006,000
RELIGION Sunni Muslim
LANGUAGE Arabic, Italian, English
LITERACY 83%
LIFE EXPECTANCY 76 years
GDP PER CAPITA $3,403
ECONOMY **IND:** petroleum, iron and steel, food processing, textiles **AGR:** wheat, barley, olives, dates; cattle **EXP:** crude oil, refined petroleum products, natural gas

Mali

REPUBLIC OF MALI

AREA 1,240,192 sq km (478,841 sq mi)
POPULATION 13,518,000
CAPITAL Bamako 1,264,000
RELIGION Muslim, indigenous beliefs
LANGUAGE French (official), Bambara, numerous African languages
LITERACY 46%
LIFE EXPECTANCY 48 years
GDP PER CAPITA $377
ECONOMY **IND:** food processing, construction, phosphate and gold mining **AGR:** cotton, millet, rice, corn; cattle **EXP:** cotton, gold, livestock

Mauritania

ISLAMIC REPUBLIC OF MAURITANIA

AREA 1,030,700 sq km (397,955 sq mi)
POPULATION 3,069,000
CAPITAL Nouakchott 600,000
RELIGION Muslim
LANGUAGE Arabic (official), Pulaar, Soninke, French, Hassaniya, Wolof
LITERACY 42%
LIFE EXPECTANCY 52 years
GDP PER CAPITA $416
ECONOMY **IND:** fish processing, mining of iron ore and gypsum **AGR:** dates, millet, sorghum, rice; cattle **EXP:** iron ore, fish and fish products, gold

Morocco

KINGDOM OF MOROCCO

AREA 710,850 sq km (274,461 sq mi)
POPULATION 30,704,000
CAPITAL Rabat 1,759,000
RELIGION Muslim
LANGUAGE Arabic (official), Berber dialects, French
LITERACY 52%
LIFE EXPECTANCY 70 years
GDP PER CAPITA $1,589
ECONOMY **IND:** phosphate rock mining and processing, food processing, leather goods, textiles **AGR:** barley, wheat, citrus, wine; livestock **EXP:** clothing, fish, inorganic chemicals, transistors

Niger

REPUBLIC OF NIGER

AREA 1,267,000 sq km (489,191 sq mi)
POPULATION 13,957,000
CAPITAL Niamey 890,000
RELIGION Muslim, indigenous beliefs, Christian
LANGUAGE French (official), Hausa, Djerma
LITERACY 18%
LIFE EXPECTANCY 43 years
GDP PER CAPITA $199
ECONOMY **IND:** uranium mining, cement, brick, soap **AGR:** cowpeas, cotton, peanuts, millet; cattle **EXP:** uranium ore, livestock, cowpeas, onions

Temperature and Precipitation

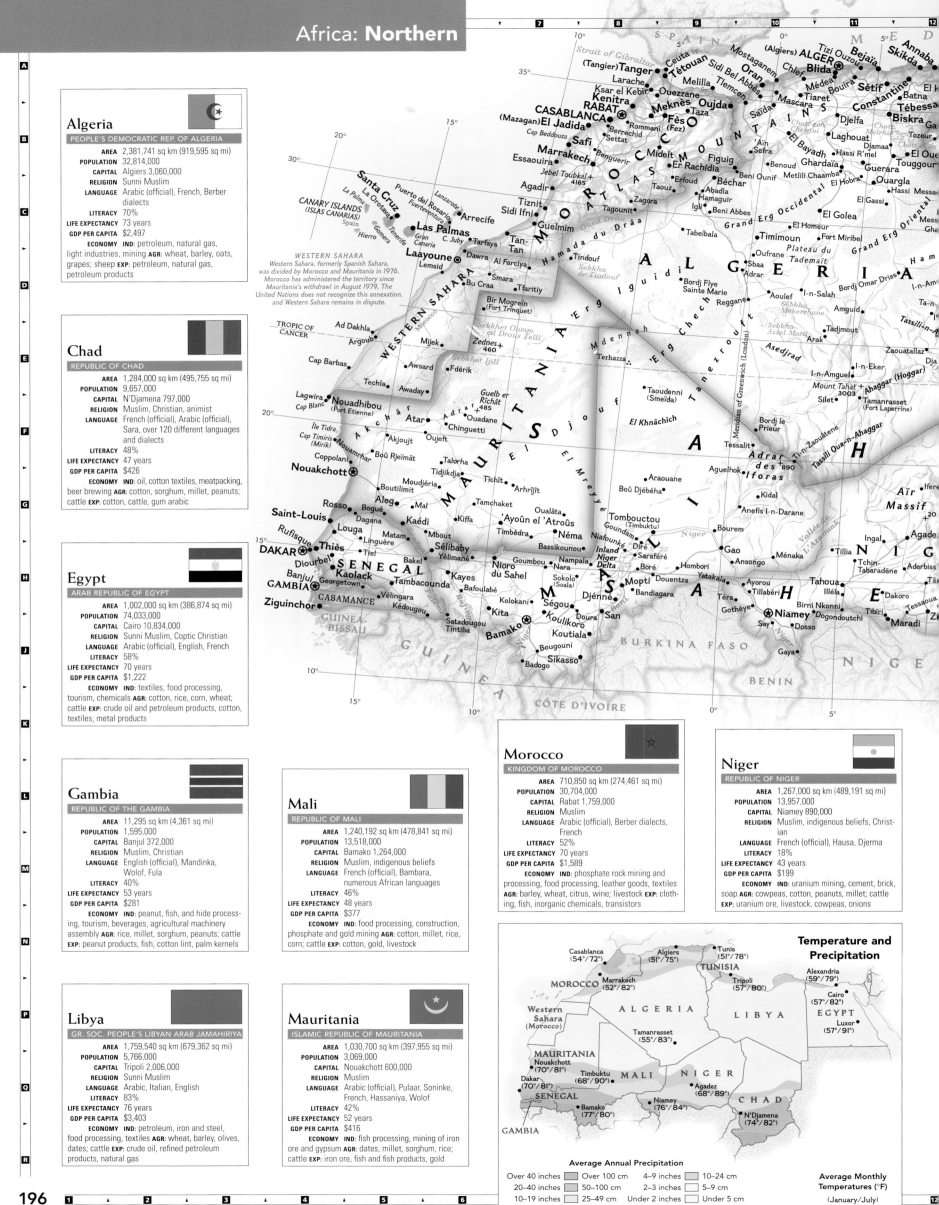

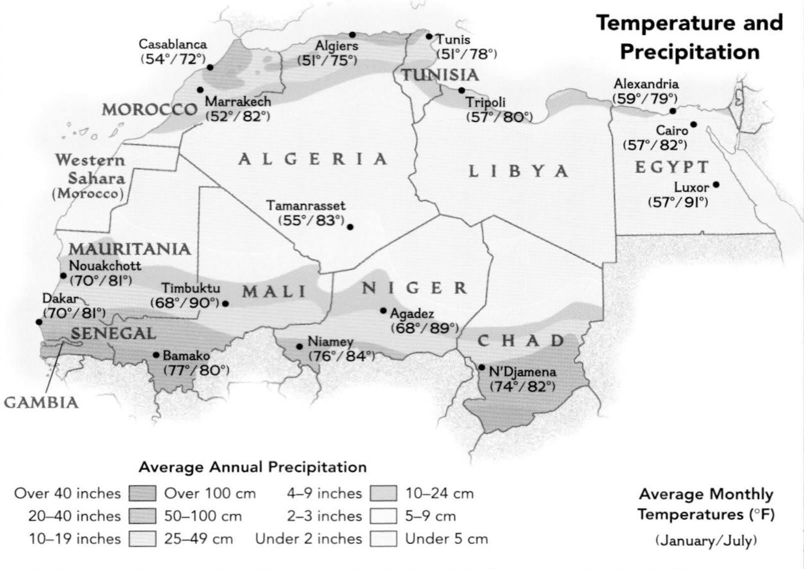

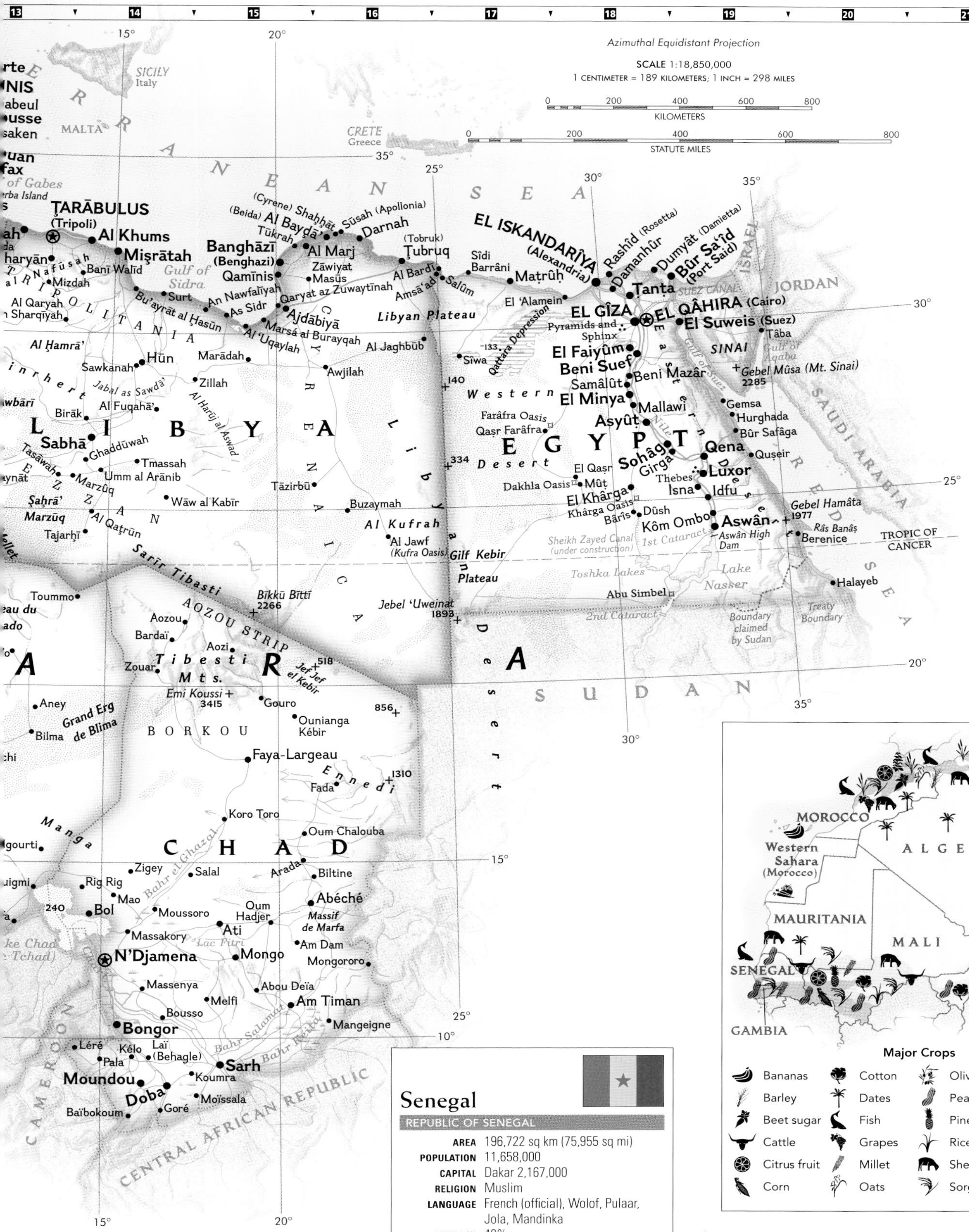

Tunisia

TUNISIAN REPUBLIC

AREA 163,610 sq km (63,170 sq mi)
POPULATION 10,043,000
CAPITAL Tunis 1,996,000
RELIGION Muslim
LANGUAGE Arabic (official), French
LITERACY 74%
LIFE EXPECTANCY 73 years
GDP PER CAPITA $2,815
ECONOMY **IND:** petroleum, mining (particularly phosphate and iron ore), tourism, textiles **AGR:** olives, olive oil, grain; dairy products **EXP:** textiles, mechanical goods, phosphates and chemicals, agricultural products

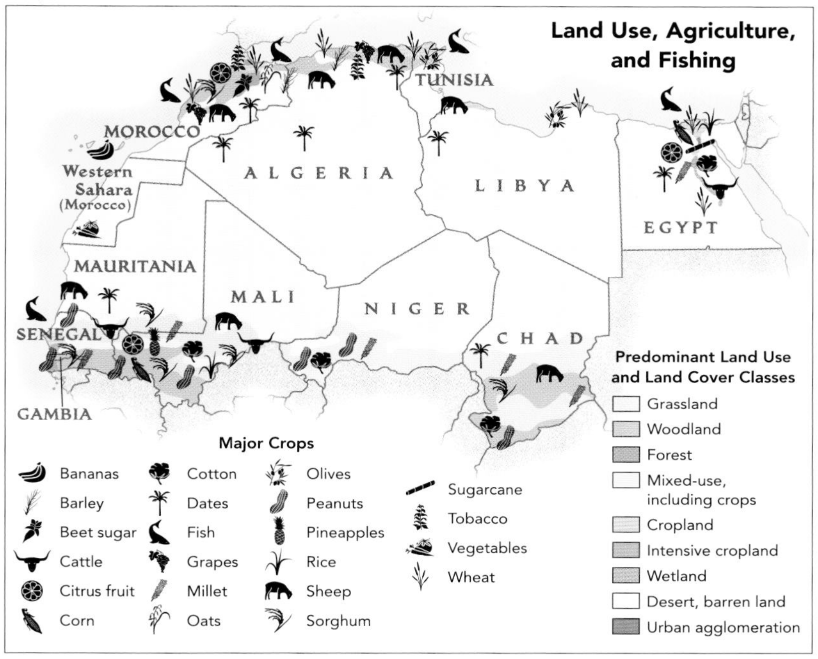

Senegal

REPUBLIC OF SENEGAL

AREA 196,722 sq km (75,955 sq mi)
POPULATION 11,658,000
CAPITAL Dakar 2,167,000
RELIGION Muslim
LANGUAGE French (official), Wolof, Pulaar, Jola, Mandinka
LITERACY 40%
LIFE EXPECTANCY 56 years
GDP PER CAPITA $672
ECONOMY **IND:** agricultural and fish processing, phosphate mining, fertilizer production, petroleum refining **AGR:** peanuts, millet, corn, sorghum; cattle; fish **EXP:** fish, groundnuts (peanuts), petroleum products, phosphates

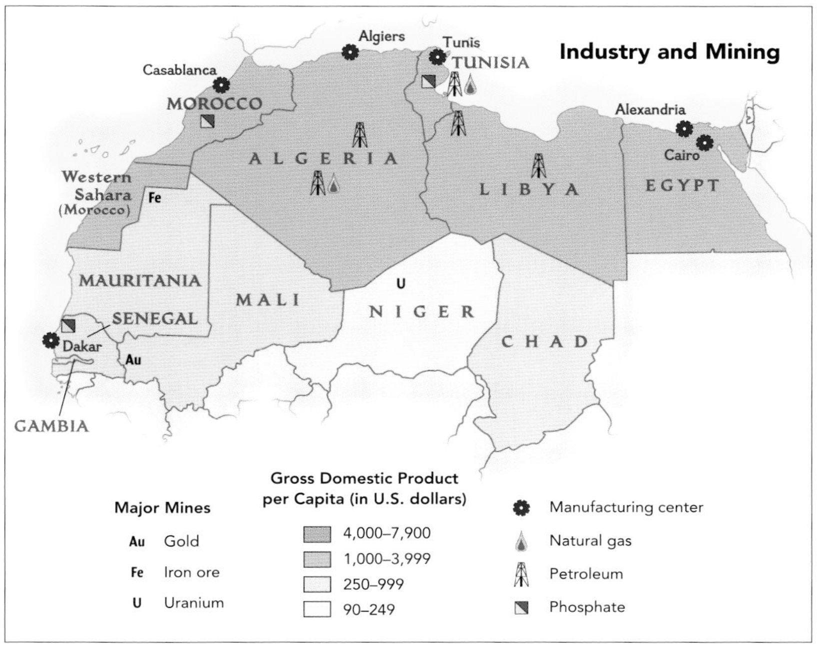

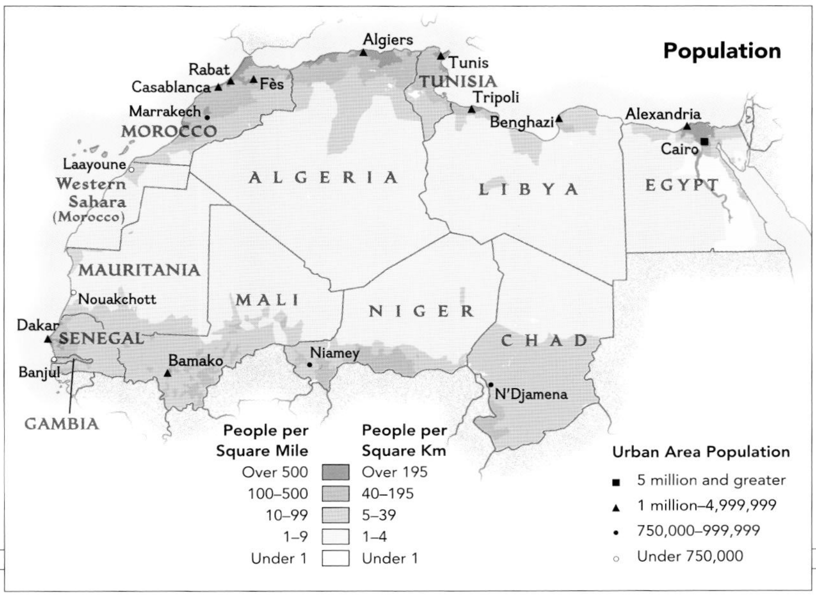

Burundi

REPUBLIC OF BURUNDI

AREA 27,834 sq km (10,747 sq mi)
POPULATION 7,795,000
CAPITAL Bujumbura 378,000
RELIGION Roman Catholic, indigenous beliefs, Muslim, Protestant
LANGUAGE Kirundi (official), French (official), Swahili
LITERACY 52%
LIFE EXPECTANCY 49 years
GDP PER CAPITA $93
ECONOMY **IND:** light consumer goods, assembly of imported components, public works construction, food processing **AGR:** coffee, cotton, tea, corn; beef **EXP:** coffee, tea, sugar, cotton

Central African Republic

CENTRAL AFRICAN REPUBLIC

AREA 622,984 sq km (240,535 sq mi)
POPULATION 4,238,000
CAPITAL Bangui 698,000
RELIGION indigenous beliefs, Protestant, Roman Catholic, Muslim
LANGUAGE French (official), Sangho, tribal languages
LITERACY 51%
LIFE EXPECTANCY 44 years
GDP PER CAPITA $330
ECONOMY **IND:** gold and diamond mining, logging, brewing, textiles **AGR:** cotton, coffee, tobacco, manioc (tapioca); timber **EXP:** diamonds, timber, cotton, coffee

Congo, Democratic Republic of the

DEMOCRATIC REPUBLIC OF THE CONGO

AREA 2,344,885 sq km (905,365 sq mi)
POPULATION 60,764,000
CAPITAL Kinshasa 5,277,000
RELIGION Roman Catholic, Protestant, Kimbanguist, Muslim
LANGUAGE French (official), Lingala, Kingwana, Kikongo, Tshiluba
LITERACY 66%
LIFE EXPECTANCY 50 years
GDP PER CAPITA $115
ECONOMY **IND:** mining (diamonds, copper, zinc), mineral processing, consumer products, cement **AGR:** coffee, sugar, palm oil, rubber; wood products **EXP:** diamonds, copper, crude oil, coffee

Djibouti

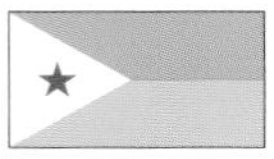

REPUBLIC OF DJIBOUTI

AREA 23,200 sq km (8,958 sq mi)
POPULATION 793,000
CAPITAL Djibouti 502,000
RELIGION Muslim, Christian
LANGUAGE French (official), Arabic (official), Somali, Afar
LITERACY 68%
LIFE EXPECTANCY 52 years
GDP PER CAPITA $852
ECONOMY **IND:** construction, agricultural processing, salt **AGR:** fruits, vegetables; goats **EXP:** reexports, hides and skins, coffee (in transit)

Eritrea

STATE OF ERITREA

AREA 121,144 sq km (46,774 sq mi)
POPULATION 4,670,000
CAPITAL Asmara 556,000
RELIGION Muslim, Coptic Christian, Roman Catholic, Protestant
LANGUAGE Afar, Arabic, Tigre, Kunama, Tigrinya, other Cushitic languages
LITERACY 59%
LIFE EXPECTANCY 58 years
GDP PER CAPITA $187
ECONOMY **IND:** food processing, beverages, clothing and textiles, salt **AGR:** sorghum, lentils, vegetables, corn; livestock; fish **EXP:** livestock, sorghum, textiles, food

Ethiopia

FEDERAL DEMOCRATIC REP. OF ETHIOPIA

AREA 1,133,380 sq km (437,600 sq mi)
POPULATION 77,431,000
CAPITAL Addis Ababa 2,723,000
RELIGION Muslim, Ethiopian Orthodox, animist
LANGUAGE Amharic, Oromigna, Tigrinya, Guaragigna, Somali
LITERACY 43%
LIFE EXPECTANCY 48 years
GDP PER CAPITA $106
ECONOMY **IND:** food processing, beverages, textiles, chemicals **AGR:** cereals, pulses, coffee, oilseed; hides **EXP:** coffee, qat, gold, leather products

Kenya

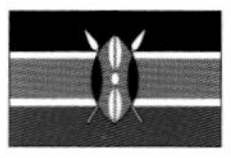

REPUBLIC OF KENYA

AREA 580,367 sq km (224,081 sq mi)
POPULATION 33,830,000
CAPITAL Nairobi 2,575,000
RELIGION Protestant, Roman Catholic, indigenous beliefs, Muslim
LANGUAGE English (official), Kiswahili (official), many indigenous languages
LITERACY 85%
LIFE EXPECTANCY 47 years
GDP PER CAPITA $443
ECONOMY **IND:** small-scale consumer goods (plastic, furniture), agricultural products, oil refining, aluminum **AGR:** tea, coffee, corn, wheat; dairy products **EXP:** tea, horticultural products, coffee, petroleum products

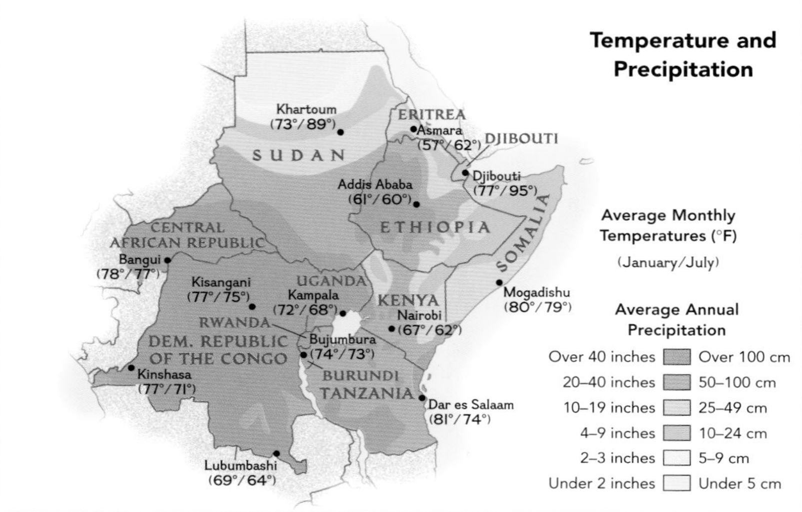

Rwanda

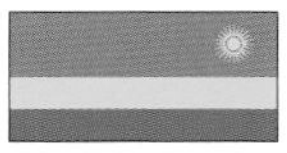

REPUBLIC OF RWANDA

AREA 26,338 sq km (10,169 sq mi)
POPULATION 8,722,000
CAPITAL Kigali 656,000
RELIGION Roman Catholic, Protestant, Adventist
LANGUAGE Kinyarwanda (official), French (official), English (official), Kiswahili
LITERACY 70%
LIFE EXPECTANCY 44 years
GDP PER CAPITA $205
ECONOMY **IND:** cement, agricultural products, small-scale beverages, soap **AGR:** coffee, tea, pyrethrum, bananas; livestock **EXP:** coffee, tea, hides, tin ore

Tanzania

UNITED REPUBLIC OF TANZANIA

AREA 945,087 sq km (364,900 sq mi)
POPULATION 36,481,000
CAPITAL Dar es Salaam (administrative) 2,441,000; Dodoma (legislative) 155,000
RELIGION Muslim, indigenous beliefs, Christian
LANGUAGE Swahili (official), English (official), Arabic, local languages
LITERACY 78%
LIFE EXPECTANCY 44 years
GDP PER CAPITA $297
ECONOMY **IND:** agricultural processing, diamond, gold and iron mining, soda ash, oil refining **AGR:** coffee, sisal, tea, cotton; cattle **EXP:** gold, coffee, cashew nuts, manufactures

Uganda

REPUBLIC OF UGANDA

AREA 241,139 sq km (93,104 sq mi)
POPULATION 26,907,000
CAPITAL Kampala 1,246,000
RELIGION Roman Catholic, Protestant, indigenous beliefs, Muslim
LANGUAGE English (official), Ganda or Luganda, many local languages
LITERACY 70%
LIFE EXPECTANCY 48 years
GDP PER CAPITA $280
ECONOMY **IND:** sugar, brewing, tobacco, cotton textiles **AGR:** coffee, tea, cotton, tobacco; beef **EXP:** coffee, fish and fish products, tea, gold

Population

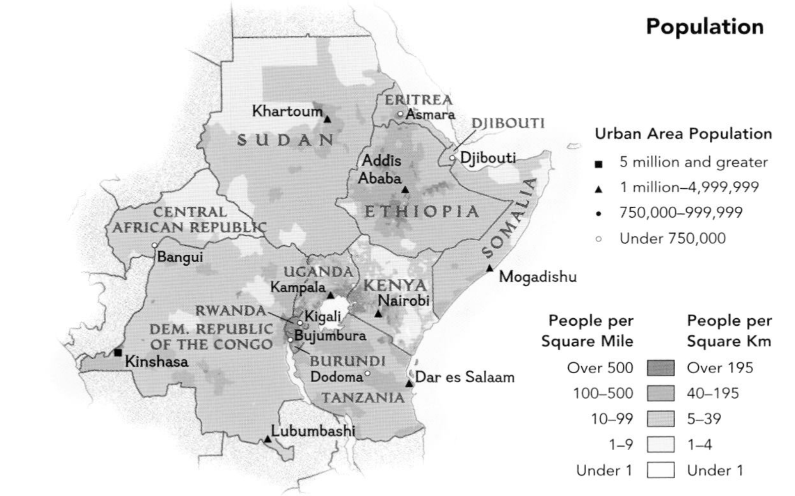

Industry and Mining

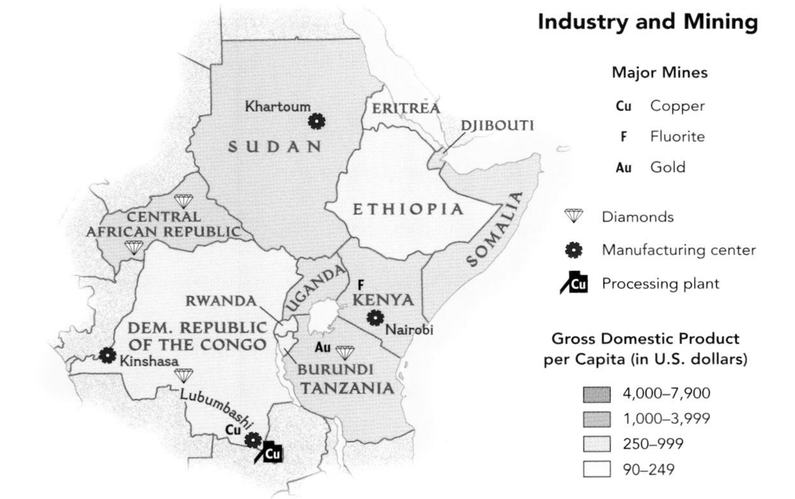

Land Use, Agriculture, and Fishing

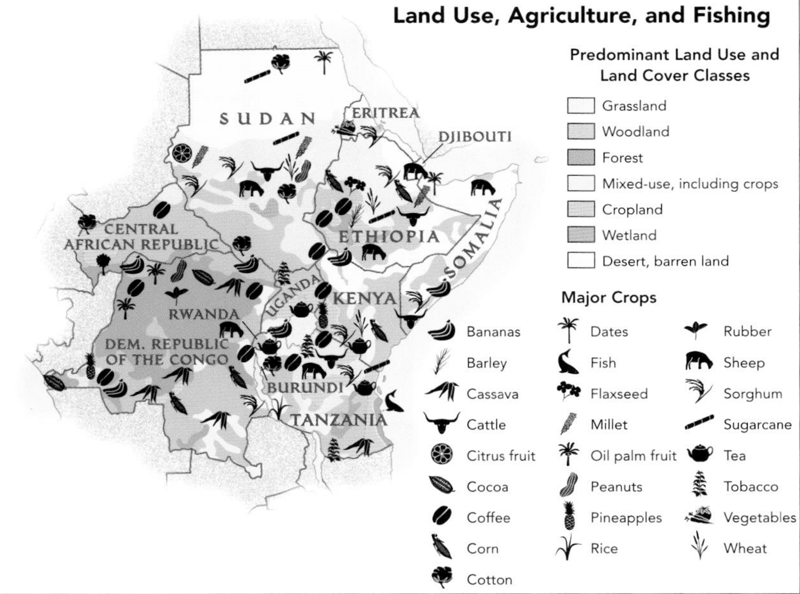

Somalia

SOMALIA

AREA 637,657 sq km (246,201 sq mi)
POPULATION 8,592,000
CAPITAL Mogadishu 1,175,000
RELIGION Sunni Muslim
LANGUAGE Somali (official), Arabic, Italian, English
LITERACY 38%
LIFE EXPECTANCY 47 years
GDP PER CAPITA $262
ECONOMY **IND:** sugar refining, textiles, wireless communication **AGR:** bananas, sorghum, corn, coconuts; cattle; fish **EXP:** livestock, bananas, hides, fish

Sudan

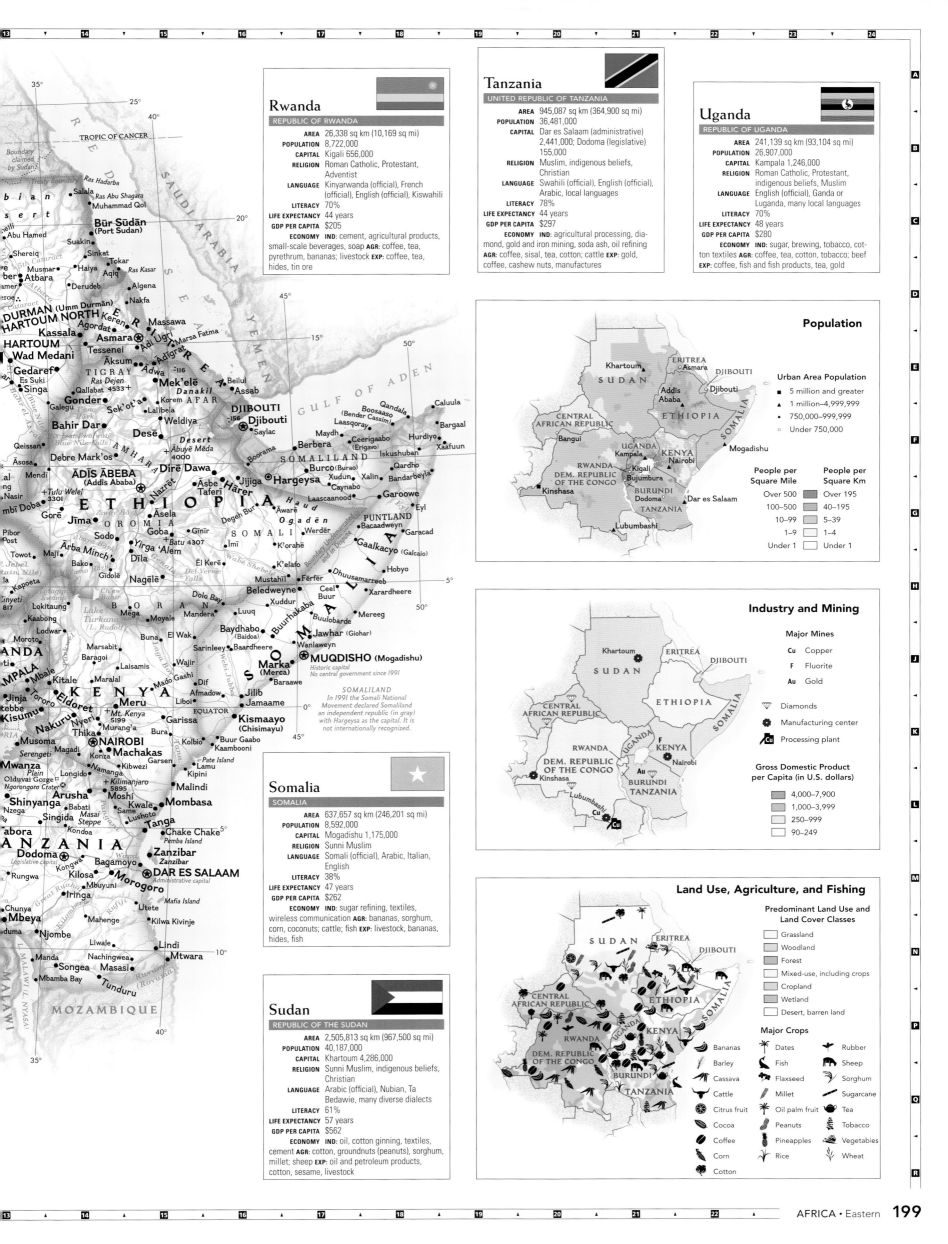

REPUBLIC OF THE SUDAN

AREA 2,505,813 sq km (967,500 sq mi)
POPULATION 40,187,000
CAPITAL Khartoum 4,286,000
RELIGION Sunni Muslim, indigenous beliefs, Christian
LANGUAGE Arabic (official), Nubian, Ta Bedawie, many diverse dialects
LITERACY 61%
LIFE EXPECTANCY 57 years
GDP PER CAPITA $562
ECONOMY **IND:** oil, cotton ginning, textiles, cement **AGR:** cotton, groundnuts (peanuts), sorghum, millet; sheep **EXP:** oil and petroleum products, cotton, sesame, livestock

Azimuthal Equidistant Projection

SCALE 1:13,485,000
1 CENTIMETER = 135 KILOMETERS; 1 INCH = 213 MILES

0 200 400 600
KILOMETERS

0 200 400 600
STATUTE MILES

Benin
REPUBLIC OF BENIN

AREA 112,622 sq km (43,484 sq mi)
POPULATION 8,439,000
CAPITAL Porto-Novo (constitutional) 238,000; Cotonou (seat of government) 828,000
RELIGION indigenous beliefs, Christian, Muslim
LANGUAGE French (official), Fon, Yoruba, tribal languages
LITERACY 34%
LIFE EXPECTANCY 54 years
GDP PER CAPITA $500
ECONOMY **IND:** textiles, food processing, construction materials, cement **AGR:** cotton, corn, cassava (tapioca), yams; livestock **EXP:** cotton, crude oil, palm products, cocoa

Burkina Faso
BURKINA FASO

AREA 274,200 sq km (105,869 sq mi)
POPULATION 13,925,000
CAPITAL Ouagadougou 821,000
RELIGION Muslim, indigenous beliefs, Christian
LANGUAGE French (official), native African languages
LITERACY 27%
LIFE EXPECTANCY 44 years
GDP PER CAPITA $348
ECONOMY **IND:** cotton lint, beverages, agricultural processing, soap **AGR:** cotton, peanuts, shea nuts, sesame; livestock **EXP:** cotton, livestock, gold

Cameroon
REPUBLIC OF CAMEROON

AREA 475,442 sq km (183,569 sq mi)
POPULATION 16,380,000
CAPITAL Yaoundé 1,616,000
RELIGION indigenous beliefs, Christian, Muslim
LANGUAGE 24 major African language groups, English (official), French (official)
LITERACY 79%
LIFE EXPECTANCY 48 years
GDP PER CAPITA $1,007
ECONOMY **IND:** petroleum production and refining, aluminum production, food processing, light consumer goods **AGR:** coffee, cocoa, cotton, rubber; livestock; timber **EXP:** crude oil and petroleum products, lumber, cocoa beans, aluminum

Côte d'Ivoire (Ivory Coast)
REPUBLIC OF CÔTE D'IVOIRE

AREA 322,462 sq km (124,503 sq mi)
POPULATION 18,154,000
CAPITAL Abidjan (administrative) 3,337,000; Yamoussoukro 416,000
RELIGION Muslim, indigenous beliefs, Christian
LANGUAGE French (official), Dioula, 60 native dialects
LITERACY 51%
LIFE EXPECTANCY 47 years
GDP PER CAPITA $908
ECONOMY **IND:** foodstuffs, beverages, wood products, oil refining **AGR:** coffee, cocoa beans, bananas, palm kernels; timber **EXP:** cocoa, coffee, timber, petroleum

Gabon
GABONESE REPUBLIC

AREA 267,667 sq km (103,347 sq mi)
POPULATION 1,384,000
CAPITAL Libreville 611,000
RELIGION Christian, animist
LANGUAGE French (official), Fang, Myene, Nzebi, Bapounou/Eschira
LITERACY 63%
LIFE EXPECTANCY 56 years
GDP PER CAPITA $4,710
ECONOMY **IND:** petroleum extraction and refining, manganese and gold mining, chemicals, ship repair **AGR:** cocoa, coffee, sugar, palm oil; okoume (a tropical softwood); fish **EXP:** crude oil, timber, manganese, uranium

Guinea
REPUBLIC OF GUINEA

AREA 245,857 sq km (94,926 sq mi)
POPULATION 9,453,000
CAPITAL Conakry 1,366,000
RELIGION Muslim, Christian, indigenous beliefs
LANGUAGE French (official), ethnic languages
LITERACY 36%
LIFE EXPECTANCY 49 years
GDP PER CAPITA $421
ECONOMY **IND:** bauxite, gold, diamonds, alumina refining **AGR:** rice, coffee, pineapples, palm kernels; cattle; timber **EXP:** bauxite, alumina, gold, diamonds

Congo
REPUBLIC OF THE CONGO

AREA 342,000 sq km (132,047 sq mi)
POPULATION 3,999,000
CAPITAL Brazzaville 1,080,000
RELIGION Christian, animist
LANGUAGE French (official), Lingala, Monokutuba, local languages
LITERACY 84%
LIFE EXPECTANCY 52 years
GDP PER CAPITA $1,129
ECONOMY **IND:** petroleum extraction, cement, lumber, brewing **AGR:** cassava (tapioca), sugar, rice, corn; forest products **EXP:** petroleum, lumber, plywood, sugar

Equatorial Guinea
REPUBLIC OF EQUATORIAL GUINEA

AREA 28,051 sq km (10,831 sq mi)
POPULATION 504,000
CAPITAL Malabo 95,000
RELIGION Roman Catholic, pagan practices
LANGUAGE Spanish (official), French (official), pidgin English, Fang, Bubi, Ibo
LITERACY 86%
LIFE EXPECTANCY 45 years
GDP PER CAPITA $7,845
ECONOMY **IND:** petroleum, fishing, sawmilling, natural gas **AGR:** coffee, cocoa, rice, yams; livestock; timber **EXP:** petroleum, methanol, timber, cocoa

Ghana
REPUBLIC OF GHANA

AREA 238,537 sq km (92,100 sq mi)
POPULATION 22,019,000
CAPITAL Accra 1,847,000
RELIGION Christian, indigenous beliefs, Muslim
LANGUAGE English (official), Akan, Moshi-Dagomba, Ewe, Ga
LITERACY 75%
LIFE EXPECTANCY 58 years
GDP PER CAPITA $403
ECONOMY **IND:** mining, lumbering, light manufacturing, aluminum smelting **AGR:** cocoa, rice, coffee, cassava (tapioca); timber **EXP:** gold, cocoa, timber, tuna

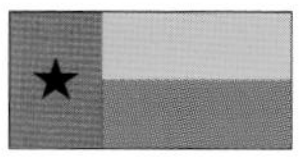

Guinea-Bissau
REPUBLIC OF GUINEA-BISSAU

AREA 36,125 sq km (13,948 sq mi)
POPULATION 1,586,000
CAPITAL Bissau 336,000
RELIGION indigenous beliefs, Muslim
LANGUAGE Portuguese (official), Crioulo, African languages
LITERACY 42%
LIFE EXPECTANCY 44 years
GDP PER CAPITA $176
ECONOMY **IND:** agricultural products processing, beer, soft drinks **AGR:** rice, corn, beans, cassava (tapioca); timber; fish **EXP:** cashew nuts, shrimp, peanuts, palm kernels

Liberia

REPUBLIC OF LIBERIA

AREA 111,370 sq km (43,000 sq mi)
POPULATION 3,283,000
CAPITAL Monrovia 572,000
RELIGION indigenous beliefs, Christian, Muslim
LANGUAGE English (official), some 20 ethnic group languages
LITERACY 58%
LIFE EXPECTANCY 42 years
GDP PER CAPITA $146
ECONOMY **IND:** rubber processing, palm oil processing, timber, diamonds **AGR:** rubber, coffee, cocoa, rice; sheep; timber **EXP:** rubber, timber, iron, diamonds

Sierra Leone

REPUBLIC OF SIERRA LEONE

AREA 71,740 sq km (27,699 sq mi)
POPULATION 5,525,000
CAPITAL Freetown 921,000
RELIGION Muslim, indigenous beliefs, Christian
LANGUAGE English (official), Mende, Temne, Krio
LITERACY 30%
LIFE EXPECTANCY 40 years
GDP PER CAPITA $196
ECONOMY **IND:** diamond mining, small-scale manufacturing (beverages, textiles), petroleum refining **AGR:** rice, coffee, cocoa, palm kernels; poultry; fish **EXP:** diamonds, rutile, cocoa, coffee

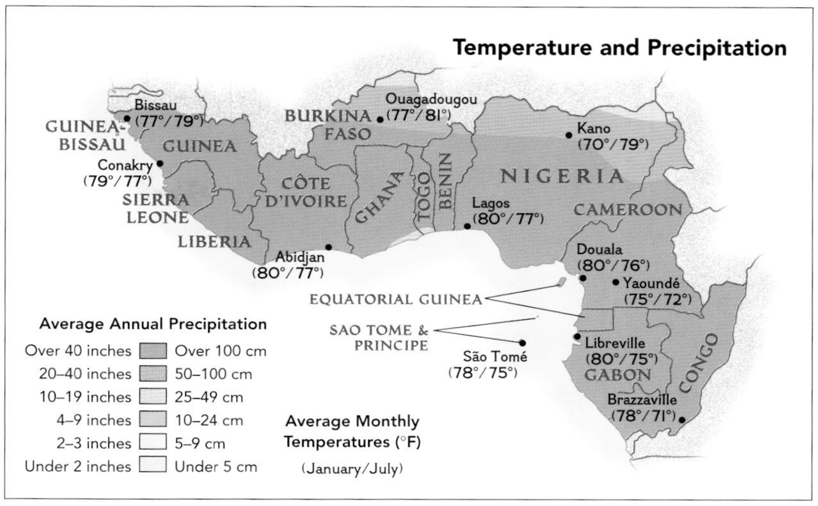

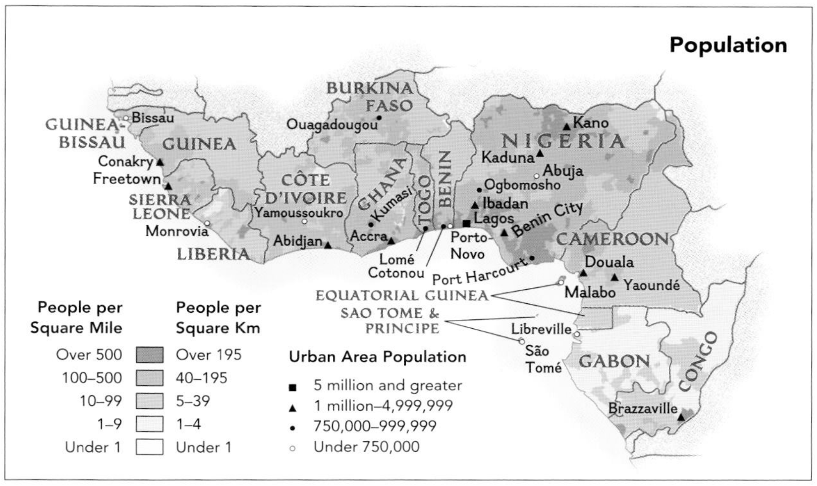

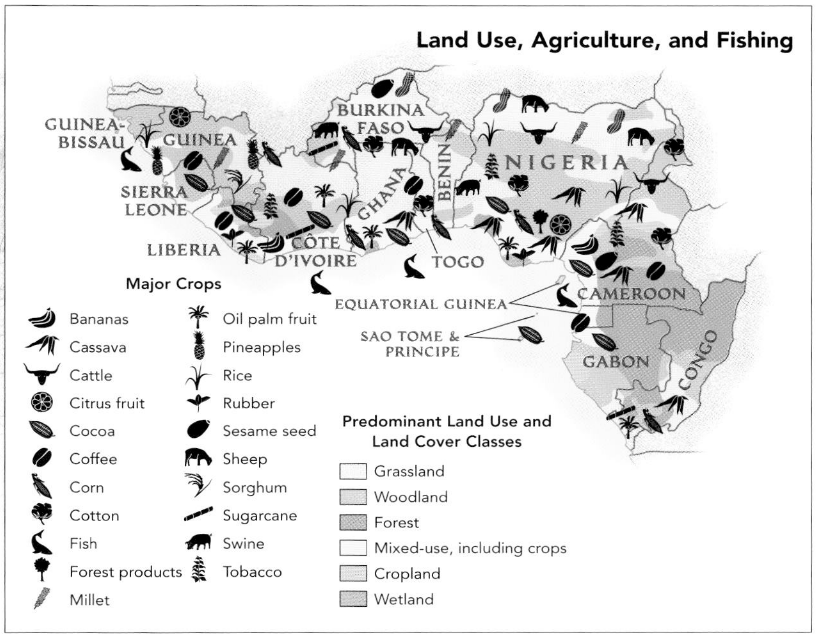

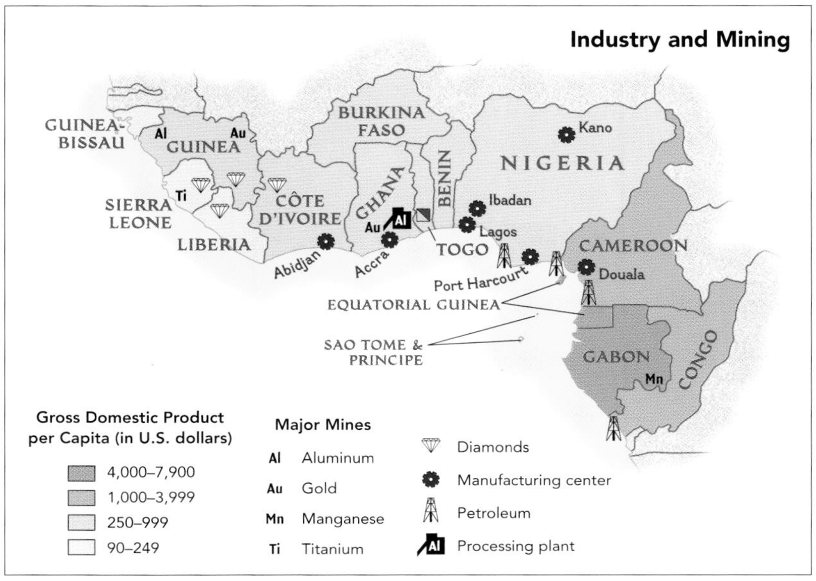

Nigeria

FEDERAL REPUBLIC OF NIGERIA

AREA 923,768 sq km (356,669 sq mi)
POPULATION 131,530,000
CAPITAL Abuja 452,000
RELIGION Muslim, Christian, indigenous beliefs
LANGUAGE English (official), Hausa, Yoruba, Igbo (Ibo), Fulani
LITERACY 68%
LIFE EXPECTANCY 44 years
GDP PER CAPITA $1,000
ECONOMY **IND:** crude oil, coal, tin, columbite **AGR:** cocoa, peanuts, palm oil, corn; cattle; timber; fish **EXP:** petroleum and petroleum products, cocoa, rubber

Togo

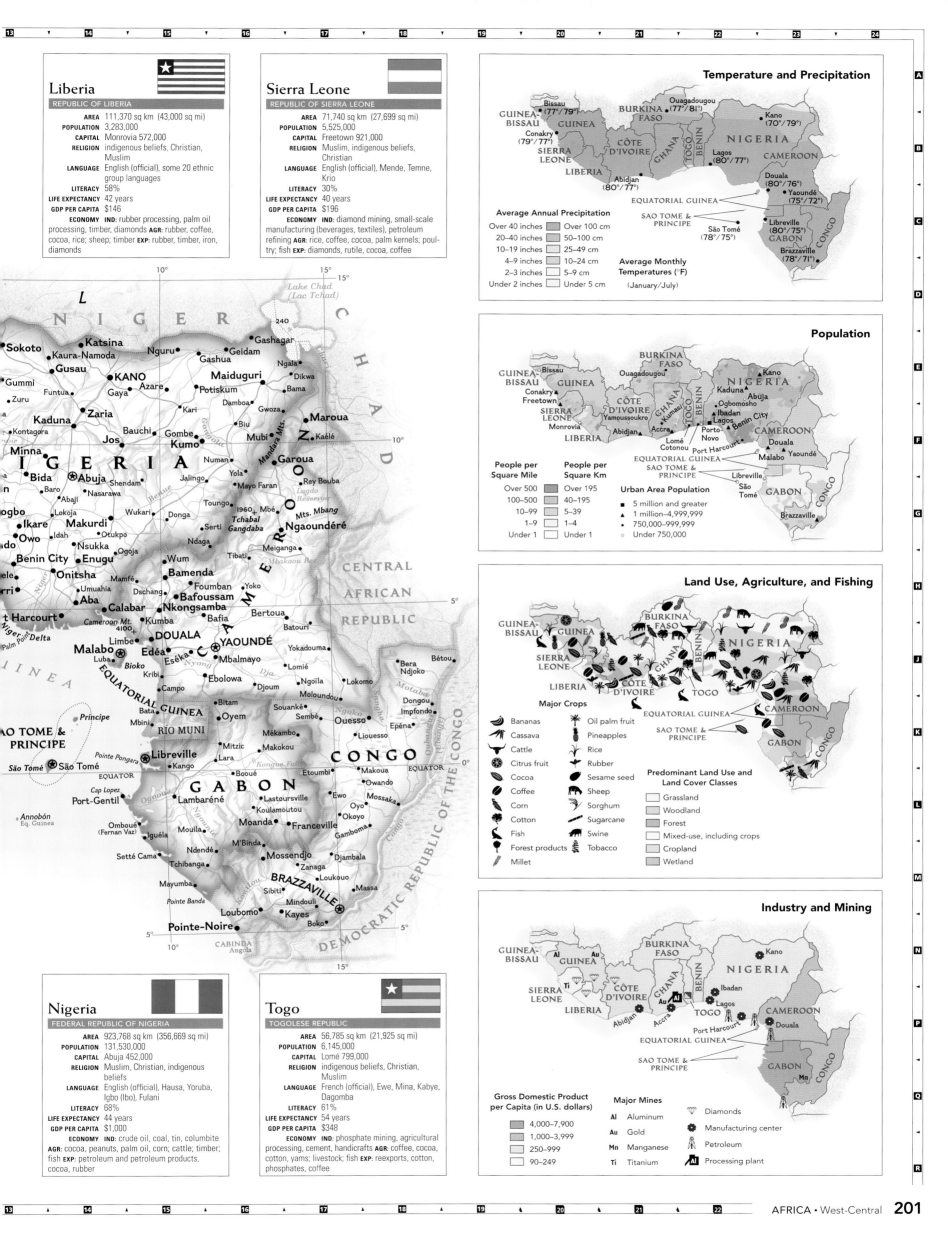

TOGOLESE REPUBLIC

AREA 56,785 sq km (21,925 sq mi)
POPULATION 6,145,000
CAPITAL Lomé 799,000
RELIGION indigenous beliefs, Christian, Muslim
LANGUAGE French (official), Ewe, Mina, Kabye, Dagomba
LITERACY 61%
LIFE EXPECTANCY 54 years
GDP PER CAPITA $348
ECONOMY **IND:** phosphate mining, agricultural processing, cement, handicrafts **AGR:** coffee, cocoa, cotton, yams; livestock; fish **EXP:** reexports, cotton, phosphates, coffee

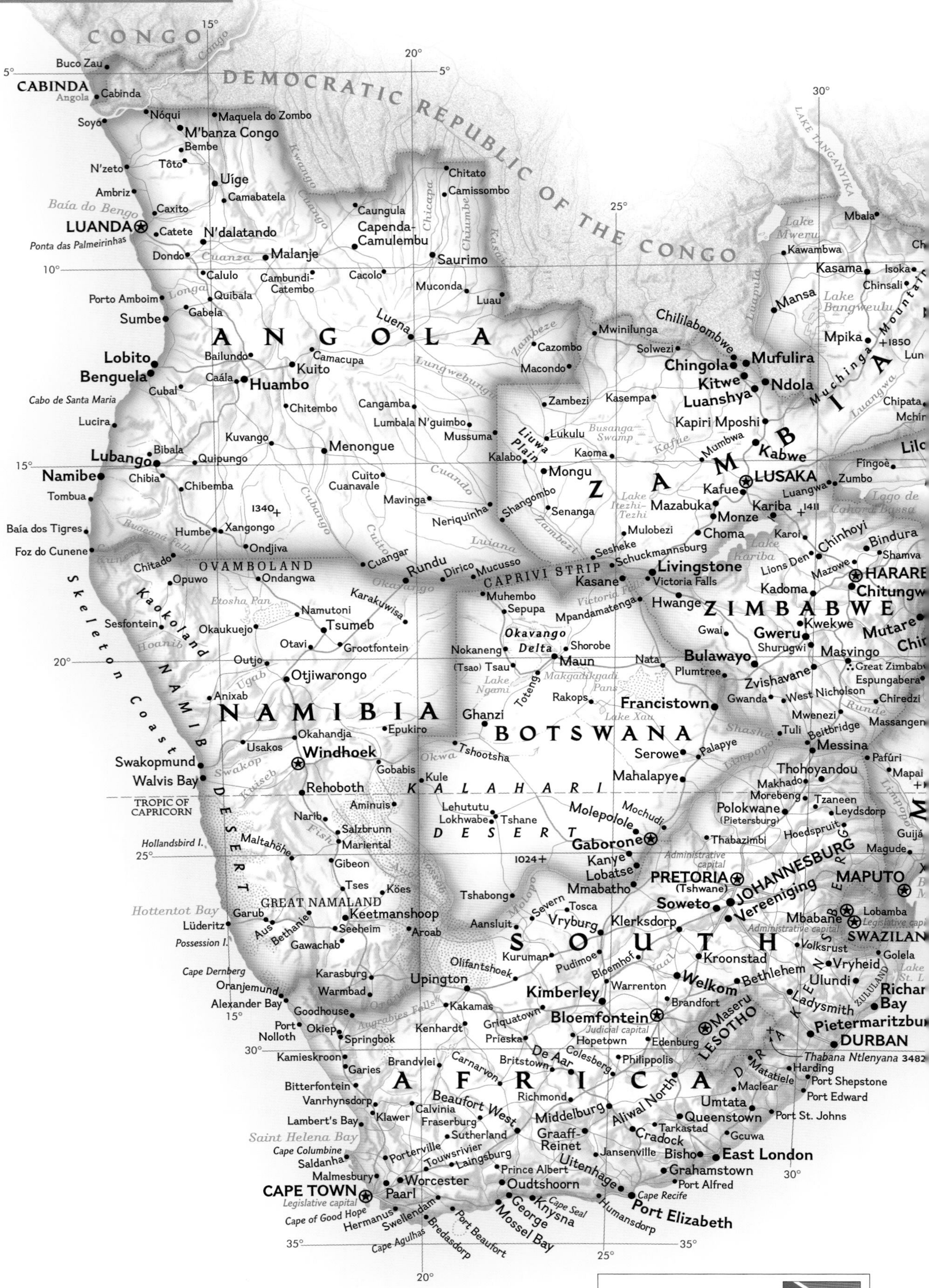

Angola
REPUBLIC OF ANGOLA

AREA 1,246,700 sq km (481,354 sq mi)
POPULATION 15,375,000
CAPITAL Luanda 2,623,000
RELIGION indigenous beliefs, Roman Catholic, Protestant
LANGUAGE Portuguese (official), Bantu and other African languages
LITERACY 67%
LIFE EXPECTANCY 40 years
GDP PER CAPITA $1,309
ECONOMY **IND:** petroleum, diamonds, iron ore, phosphates **AGR:** bananas, sugarcane, coffee, sisal; livestock; forest products; fish **EXP:** crude oil, diamonds, refined petroleum products, gas

Botswana
REPUBLIC OF BOTSWANA

AREA 581,730 sq km (224,607 sq mi)
POPULATION 1,640,000
CAPITAL Gaborone 199,000
RELIGION Christian, Badimo
LANGUAGE Setswana, Kalanga, Sekgalagadi, English (official)
LITERACY 80%
LIFE EXPECTANCY 35 years
GDP PER CAPITA $4,771
ECONOMY **IND:** diamonds, copper, nickel, salt **AGR:** livestock, sorghum, maize, millet **EXP:** diamonds, copper, nickel, soda ash

Lesotho
KINGDOM OF LESOTHO

AREA 30,355 sq km (11,720 sq mi)
POPULATION 1,804,000
CAPITAL Maseru 170,000
RELIGION Christian, indigenous beliefs
LANGUAGE Sesotho, English (official), Zulu, Xhosa
LITERACY 85%
LIFE EXPECTANCY 35 years
GDP PER CAPITA $764
ECONOMY **IND:** food, beverages, textiles, apparel assembly **AGR:** corn, wheat, pulses, sorghum; livestock **EXP:** clothing, footwear, road vehicles, wool and mohair

Madagascar
REPUBLIC OF MADAGASCAR

AREA 587,041 sq km (226,658 sq mi)
POPULATION 17,308,000
CAPITAL Antananarivo 1,678,000
RELIGION indigenous beliefs, Christian, Muslim
LANGUAGE French (official), Malagasy (official)
LITERACY 69%
LIFE EXPECTANCY 55 years
GDP PER CAPITA $222
ECONOMY **IND:** meat processing, soap, breweries, tanneries **AGR:** coffee, vanilla, sugarcane, cloves; livestock products **EXP:** coffee, vanilla, shellfish, sugar

Malawi
REPUBLIC OF MALAWI

AREA 118,484 sq km (45,747 sq mi)
POPULATION 12,341,000
CAPITAL Lilongwe 587,000
RELIGION Christian, Muslim
LANGUAGE Chichewa (official), Chinyanja, Chiyao, Chitumbuka
LITERACY 63%
LIFE EXPECTANCY 45 years
GDP PER CAPITA $165
ECONOMY **IND:** tobacco, tea, sugar, sawmill products **AGR:** tobacco, sugarcane, cotton, tea; cattle **EXP:** tobacco, tea, sugar, cotton

Mozambique
REPUBLIC OF MOZAMBIQUE

AREA 799,380 sq km (308,642 sq mi)
POPULATION 19,420,000
CAPITAL Maputo 1,221,000
RELIGION Catholic, Zionist Christian, Muslim
LANGUAGE Emakhuwa, Xichangana, Portuguese (official), Elomwe, Cisena, Echuwabo
LITERACY 48%
LIFE EXPECTANCY 42 years
GDP PER CAPITA $328
ECONOMY **IND:** food, beverages, chemicals (fertilizer, soap, paints), aluminum **AGR:** cotton, cashew nuts, sugarcane, tea; beef **EXP:** aluminum, prawns, cashews, cotton

Namibia
REPUBLIC OF NAMIBIA

AREA 824,292 sq km (318,261 sq mi)
POPULATION 2,031,000
CAPITAL Windhoek 237,000
RELIGION Lutheran, other Christian, indigenous beliefs
LANGUAGE Afrikaans, German, English (official), indigenous languages
LITERACY 84%
LIFE EXPECTANCY 46 years
GDP PER CAPITA $2,661
ECONOMY **IND:** meatpacking, fish processing, dairy products, mining (diamonds, lead, zinc) **AGR:** millet, sorghum, peanuts; livestock; fish **EXP:** diamonds, copper, gold, zinc

South Africa
REPUBLIC OF SOUTH AFRICA

AREA 1,219,090 sq km (470,693 sq mi)
POPULATION 46,923,000
CAPITAL Pretoria (administrative) 1,209,000; Bloemfontein (judicial) 381,000; Cape Town (legislative) 2,967,000
RELIGION Zion Christian, Pentecostal, Catholic, Methodist, Dutch Reformed
LANGUAGE IsiZulu, IsiXhosa, Afrikaans, Sepedi, English, Setswana
LITERACY 86%
LIFE EXPECTANCY 52 years
GDP PER CAPITA $4,507
ECONOMY **IND:** mining (platinum, gold, chromium), automobile assembly, metalworking, machinery **AGR:** corn, wheat, sugarcane, fruits; beef **EXP:** gold, diamonds, platinum, other metals and minerals

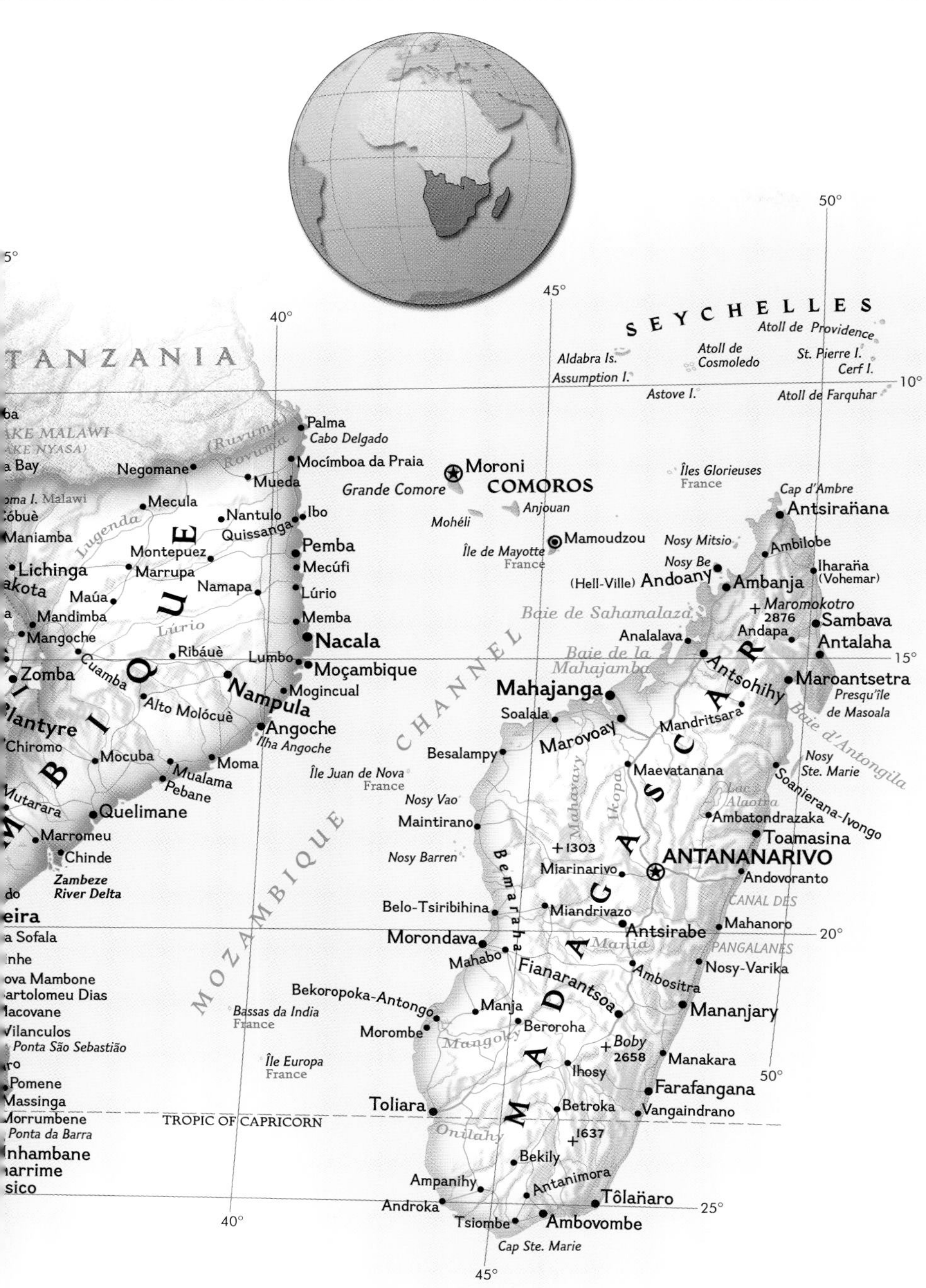

Azimuthal Equidistant Projection

SCALE 1:16,384,000
1 CENTIMETER = 164 KILOMETERS; 1 INCH = 259 MILES

KILOMETERS 0 200 400 600

STATUTE MILES 200 400 600

Zambia

REPUBLIC OF ZAMBIA

AREA 752,614 sq km (290,586 sq mi)
POPULATION 11,227,000
CAPITAL Lusaka 1,394,000
RELIGION Christian, Muslim, Hindu
LANGUAGE English (official), about 75 indigenous languages
LITERACY 81%
LIFE EXPECTANCY 37 years
GDP PER CAPITA $463
ECONOMY **IND:** copper mining and processing, construction, foodstuffs, beverages **AGR:** corn, sorghum, rice, peanuts; cattle **EXP:** copper, cobalt, electricity, tobacco

Zimbabwe

REPUBLIC OF ZIMBABWE

AREA 390,757 sq km (150,872 sq mi)
POPULATION 13,010,000
CAPITAL Harare 1,469,000
RELIGION Syncretic (part Christian, part indigenous beliefs), Christian, indigenous beliefs
LANGUAGE English (official), Shona, Sindebele
LITERACY 91%
LIFE EXPECTANCY 41 years
GDP PER CAPITA $351
ECONOMY **IND:** mining (coal, gold, platinum), steel, wood products, cement **AGR:** corn, cotton, tobacco, wheat; sheep **EXP:** cotton, tobacco, gold, ferroalloys

Swaziland

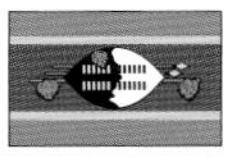

KINGDOM OF SWAZILAND

AREA 17,363 sq km (6,704 sq mi)
POPULATION 1,138,000
CAPITAL Mbabane (administrative) 70,000; Lobamba (legislative and royal) 5,000
RELIGION Zionist, Roman Catholic, Muslim
LANGUAGE English (official), siSwati (official)
LITERACY 82%
LIFE EXPECTANCY 35 years
GDP PER CAPITA $2,231
ECONOMY **IND:** mining (coal, raw asbestos), wood pulp, sugar, soft drink concentrates **AGR:** sugarcane, cotton, corn, tobacco; cattle **EXP:** soft drink concentrates, sugar, wood pulp, cotton yarn

Land Use, Agriculture, and Fishing

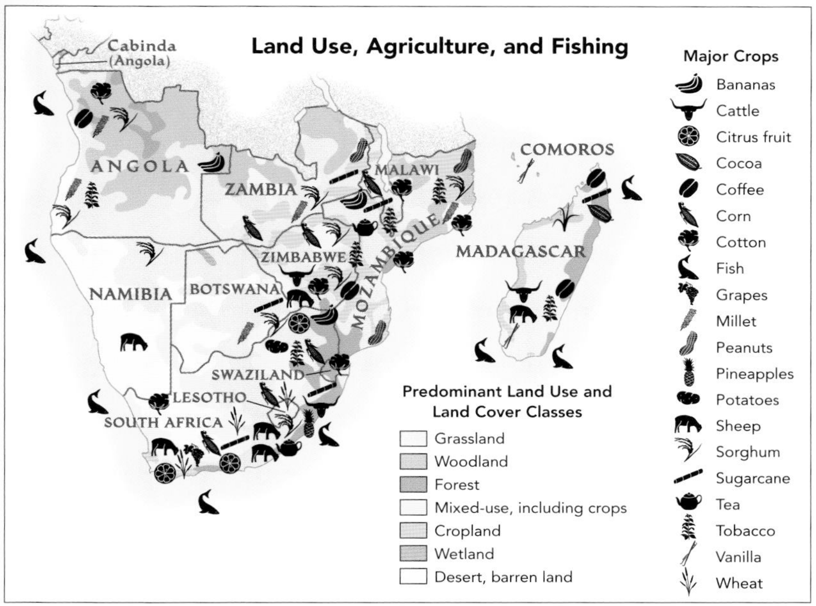

Population

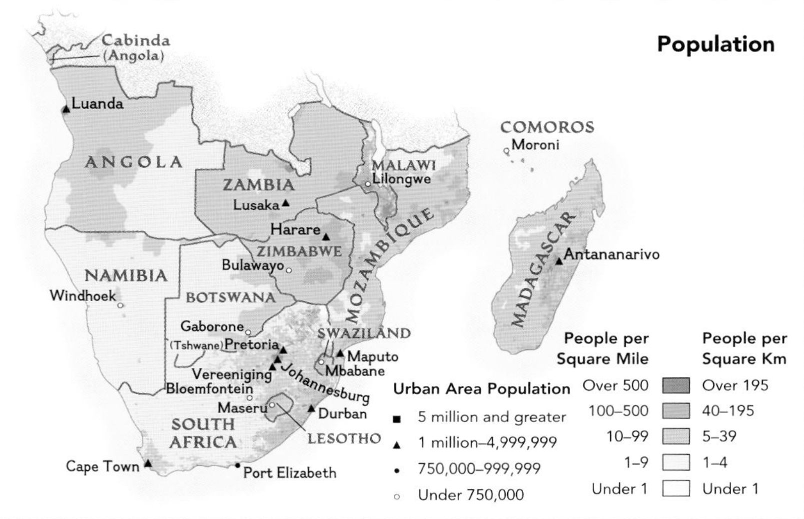

Temperature and Precipitation

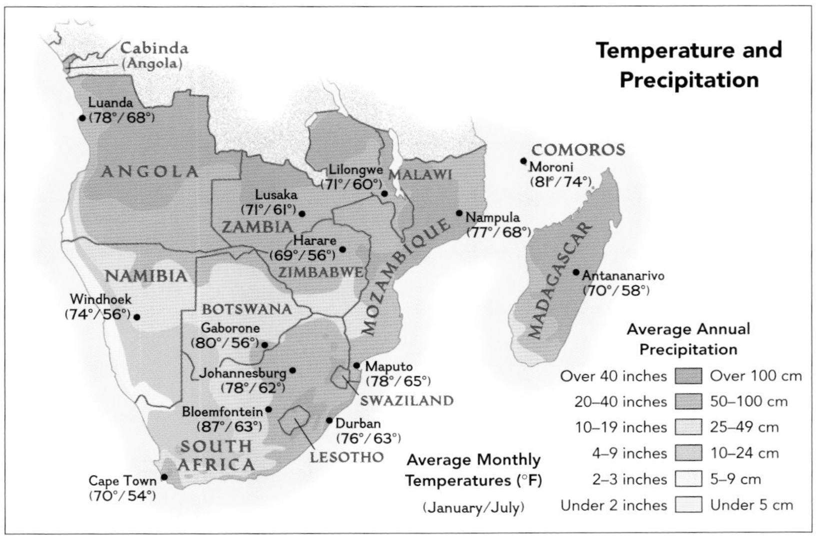

Industry and Mining

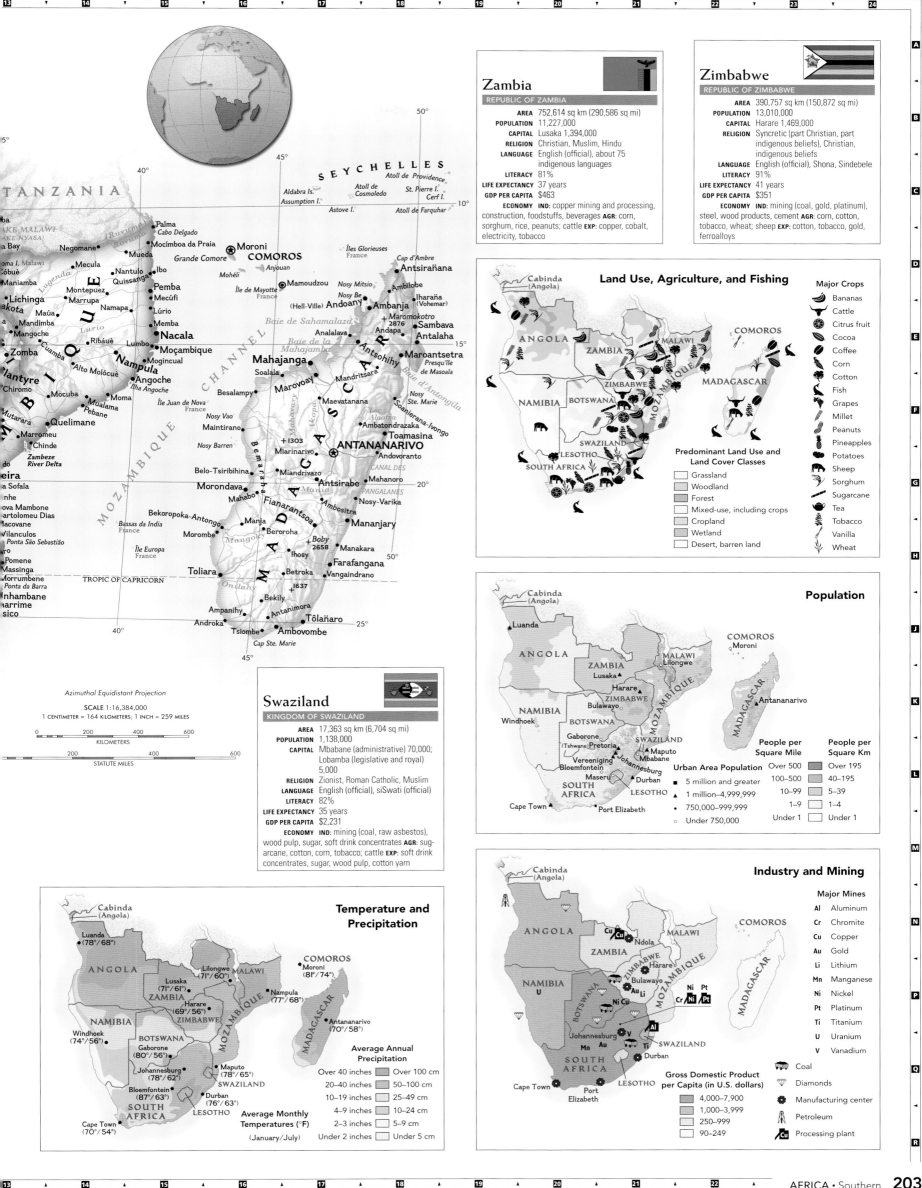

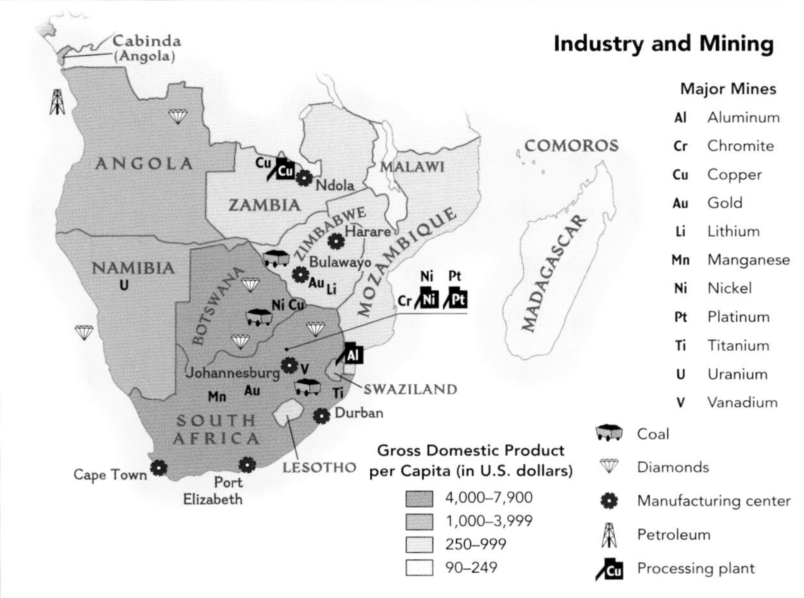

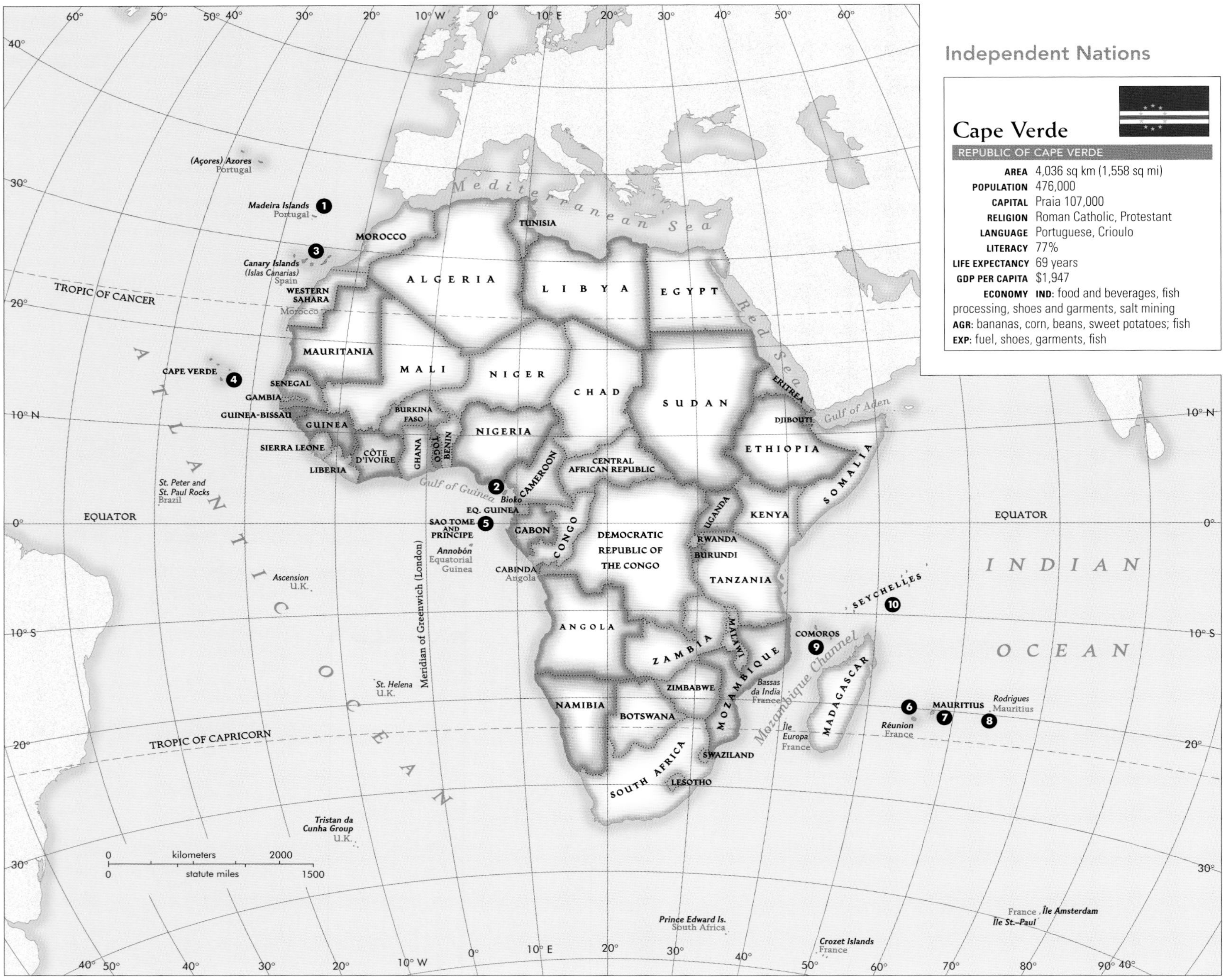

Independent Nations

Cape Verde

REPUBLIC OF CAPE VERDE

AREA 4,036 sq km (1,558 sq mi)
POPULATION 476,000
CAPITAL Praia 107,000
RELIGION Roman Catholic, Protestant
LANGUAGE Portuguese, Crioulo
LITERACY 77%
LIFE EXPECTANCY 69 years
GDP PER CAPITA $1,947
ECONOMY **IND:** food and beverages, fish processing, shoes and garments, salt mining **AGR:** bananas, corn, beans, sweet potatoes; fish **EXP:** fuel, shoes, garments, fish

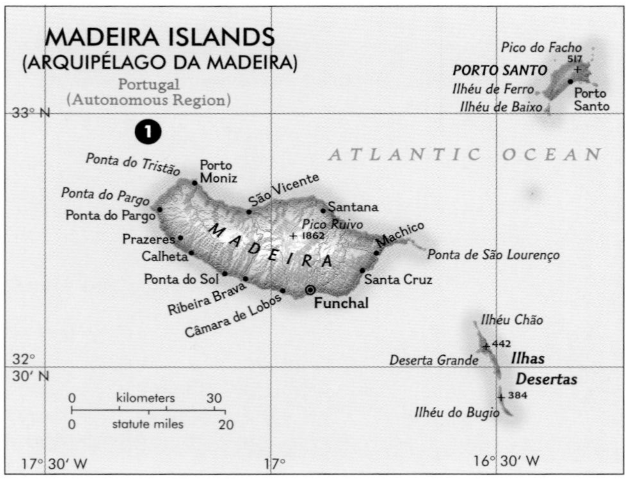

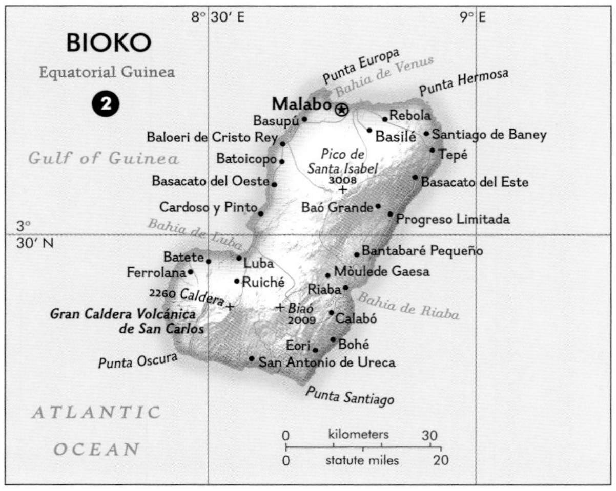

Comoros

UNION OF THE COMOROS

AREA 1,862 sq km (719 sq mi)
POPULATION 671,000
CAPITAL Moroni 53,000
RELIGION Sunni Muslim
LANGUAGE Arabic (official), French (official), Shikomoro
LITERACY 57%
LIFE EXPECTANCY 60 years
GDP PER CAPITA $427
ECONOMY **IND:** tourism, perfume distillation **AGR:** vanilla, cloves, perfume essences, copra **EXP:** vanilla, ylang-ylang, cloves, perfume oil

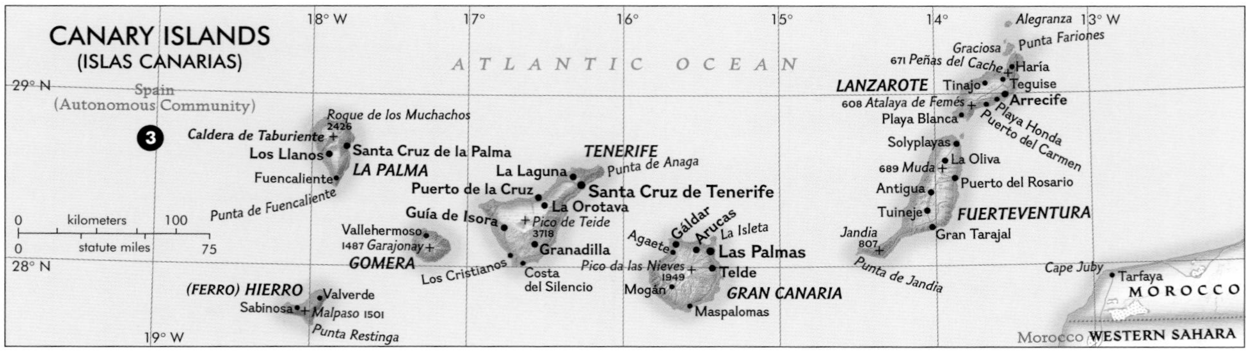

Mauritius

REPUBLIC OF MAURITIUS

AREA 2,040 sq km (788 sq mi)
POPULATION 1,243,000
CAPITAL Port Louis 143,000
RELIGION Hindu, Roman Catholic, Muslim, other Christian
LANGUAGE Creole, Bhojpuri, French (official)
LITERACY 86%
LIFE EXPECTANCY 72 years
GDP PER CAPITA $5,123
ECONOMY **IND:** food processing (largely sugar milling), textiles, clothing, chemicals **AGR:** sugarcane, tea, corn, potatoes; cattle; fish **EXP:** clothing and textiles, sugar, cut flowers, molasses

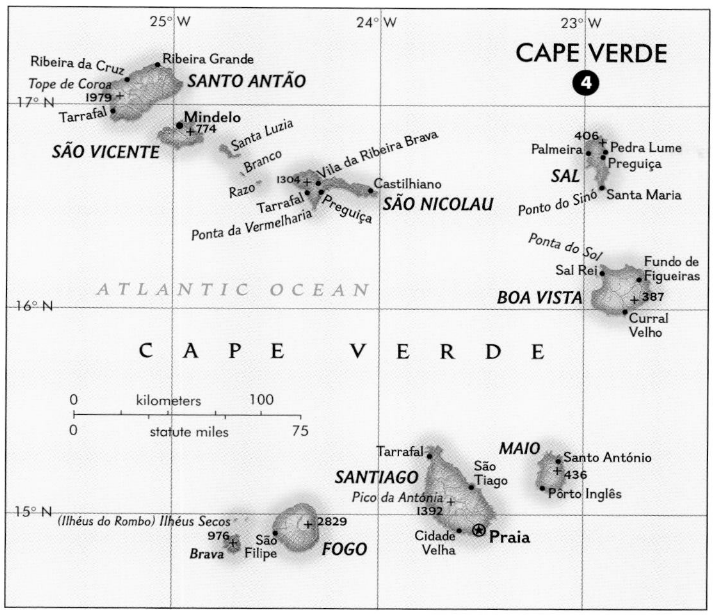

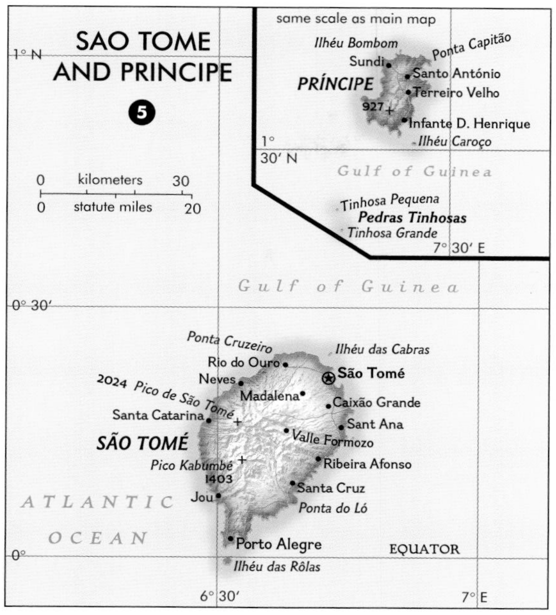

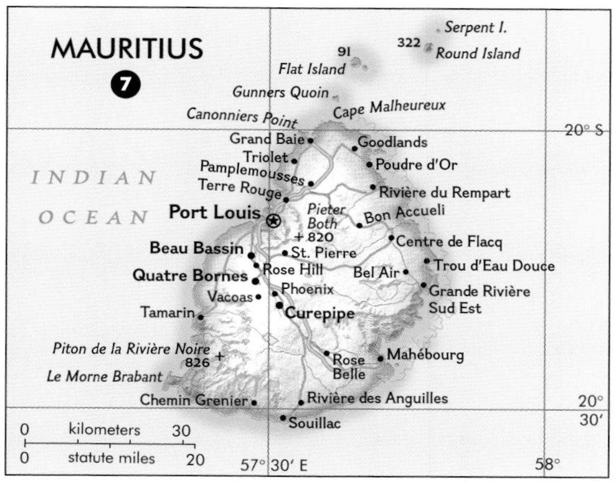

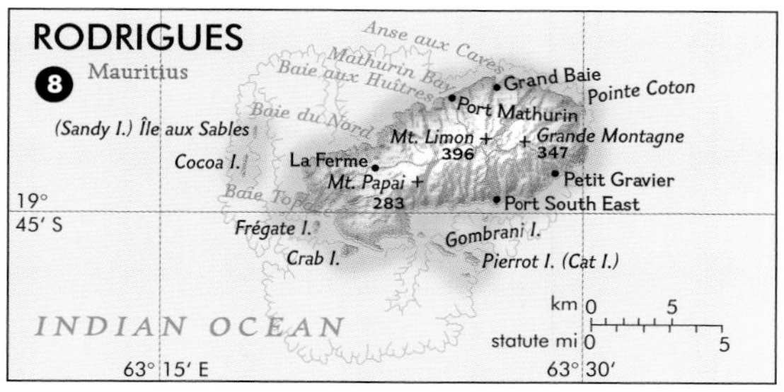

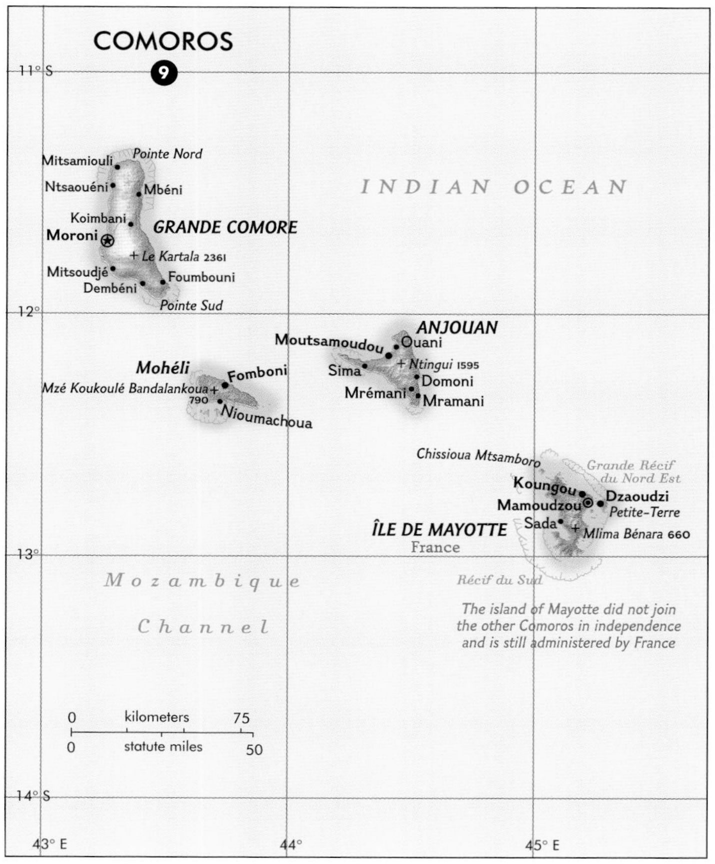

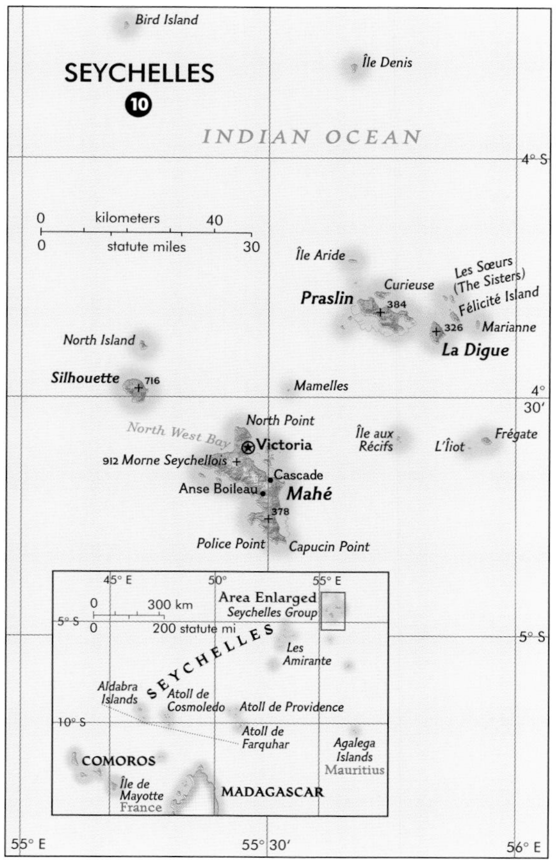

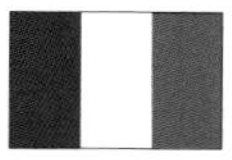

Réunion (France)

OVERSEAS DEPARTMENT OF FRANCE

AREA 2,507 sq km (968 sq mi)
POPULATION 782,000
CAPITAL St.-Denis 178,000
RELIGION Roman Catholic, Hindu, Muslim, Buddhist
LANGUAGE French (official), Creole
LITERACY 89%
LIFE EXPECTANCY 75 years
GDP PER CAPITA $6,200
ECONOMY **IND:** sugar, rum, cigarettes, handicraft items **AGR:** sugarcane, vanilla, tobacco, tropical fruits **EXP:** sugar, rum and molasses, perfume essences, lobster

Sao Tome and Principe

DEM. REP. OF SAO TOME AND PRINCIPE

AREA 1,001 sq km (386 sq mi)
POPULATION 153,000
CAPITAL São Tomé 54,000
RELIGION Roman Catholic, Protestant
LANGUAGE Portuguese (official)
LITERACY 79%
LIFE EXPECTANCY 63 years
GDP PER CAPITA $447
ECONOMY **IND:** light construction, textiles, soap, beer **AGR:** cocoa, coconuts, palm kernels, copra; poultry; fish **EXP:** cocoa, copra, coffee, palm oil

Seychelles

REPUBLIC OF SEYCHELLES

AREA 455 sq km (176 sq mi)
POPULATION 81,000
CAPITAL Victoria 25,000
RELIGION Roman Catholic, Anglican
LANGUAGE Creole, English (official)
LITERACY 92%
LIFE EXPECTANCY 71 years
GDP PER CAPITA $8,874
ECONOMY **IND:** fishing, tourism, processing of coconuts and vanilla, coir (coconut fiber) rope **AGR:** coconuts, cinnamon, vanilla, sweet potatoes; broiler chickens; tuna fish **EXP:** canned tuna, frozen fish, cinnamon bark, copra

Dependencies

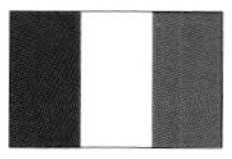

Mayotte (France)

TERRITORIAL COLLECTIVITY OF MAYOTTE

AREA 374 sq km (144 sq mi)
POPULATION 181,000
CAPITAL Mamoudzou 58,000
RELIGION Muslim
LANGUAGE Mahorian (a Swahili dialect), French (official)
LITERACY NA
LIFE EXPECTANCY 60 years
GDP PER CAPITA $2,600
ECONOMY **IND:** newly created lobster and shrimp industry, construction **AGR:** vanilla, ylang-ylang (perfume essence), coffee, copra **EXP:** ylang-ylang (perfume essence), vanilla, copra, coconuts

SOVEREIGN

LOCAL

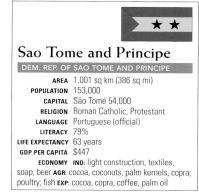

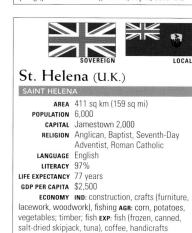

St. Helena (U.K.)

SAINT HELENA

AREA 411 sq km (159 sq mi)
POPULATION 6,000
CAPITAL Jamestown 2,000
RELIGION Anglican, Baptist, Seventh-Day Adventist, Roman Catholic
LANGUAGE English
LITERACY 97%
LIFE EXPECTANCY 77 years
GDP PER CAPITA $2,500
ECONOMY **IND:** construction, crafts (furniture, lacework, woodwork), fishing **AGR:** corn, potatoes, vegetables; timber; fish **EXP:** fish (frozen, canned, salt-dried skipjack, tuna), coffee, handicrafts

The largest structure ever built by living creatures, the Great Barrier Reef lies off Australia's northeast coast. Some 400 coral species and 1,500 species of fish inhabit its warm, shallow waters.

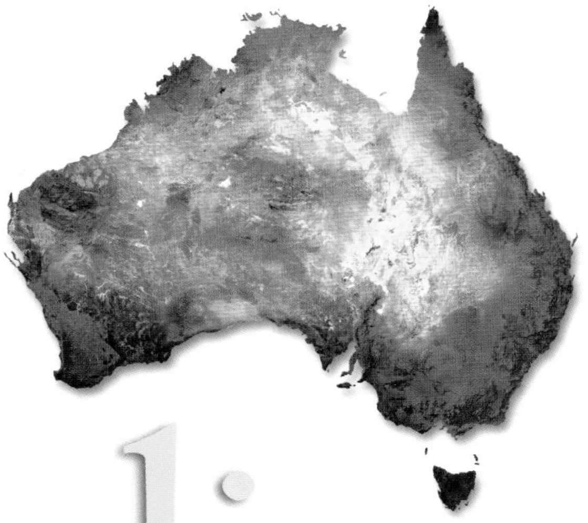

Australia
New Zealand and Oceania

Smallest of continents and sixth largest country in the world, Australia is the lowest, flattest, and, apart from Antarctica, the driest continent.

The Australian landmass is relatively arid, but varied climatic zones give it surprising diversity and a rich ecology. Unlike Europe and North America, where much of the landscape dates back 20,000 years to when great ice sheets retreated, Australia's land is many millions of years old; it retains an ancient feeling and distinctive geography and endures extremes of droughts, floods, tropical cyclones, severe storms, and bushfires.

Off the coast of northeast Queensland lies the Great Barrier Reef, the world's largest coral reef, which extends about 1,429 miles (2,300 km). The reef was formed and expanded over millions of years as tiny marine animals deposited their skeletons. Coral reefs, and the Great Barrier Reef especially, are considered the rain forests of the ocean for their complex life forms and multilayered biodiversity.

The island of Tasmania lies off Australia's southeast coast. East from there, across the Tasman Sea, is the island nation of New Zealand, composed of South Island and North Island, respectively the 12th and 14th largest islands on Earth. North Island, unlike its southern neighbor, is riddled with geothermic activity.

Extending into the massive Pacific Ocean north and east of Australia and New Zealand are the thousands of islands—which include 12 independent nations and more than 20 territories—that make up greater Oceania. The term Oceania normally designates all the islands of the Central and South Pacific, including Australia, New Zealand, and specifically the islands of Melanesia, Micronesia, and Polynesia, including Hawai'i. Eons of isolation have allowed outstanding and bizarre life-forms to evolve, such as the duck-billed platypus—a monotreme, or egg-laying mammal native to Australia and Tasmania—and New Zealand's kiwi, a timid, nocturnal, wingless bird.

Oceania has many ethnic groups and layers and types of society, from sophisticated cosmopolitan cities to near-Stone Age people in the New Guinea highlands. Many became Christian converts in the 19th century; as a result, Christianity is widespread and dominant in many countries today. Excluding Australia, some 13 million people live in Oceania, three-fourths of whom are found in Papua New Guinea and New Zealand.

Polynesia, which means "many islands," is the most extensive of the ocean realms. It can be seen as a huge triangle in the central-south Pacific, with the points being New Zealand in the southwest, Easter Island in the southeast, and Hawai'i as the northern point. Other island groups include Tuvalu, Tokelau, Wallis and Futuna, Samoa, Tonga, Cook Islands, and French Polynesia.

Micronesia, north and west of Polynesia, includes the islands and island groups of Nauru, Marshall Islands, Palau, Mariana Islands, Kiribati, and Guam.

Melanesia, one of the three main divisions of Oceania, includes the Solomon Islands, Vanuatu, New Caledonia, the Bismarck Archipelago, and Fiji, and sometimes takes in Papua New Guinea, where more than 700 of the giant region's 1,200 languages are spoken.

PHYSICAL GEOGRAPHY The continent of Australia can be divided into three parts: the Western Plateau, Central Lowlands, and Eastern Highlands. The Western Plateau consists of very old rocks, some more than three billion years old. Much of the center of Australia is flat, but some ranges and the famous landmark Ayers Rock (Uluru) still rise up, everything around them having eroded away.

Much variety exists within the general context of a red, dusty, dry, flat continent, of which a third is desert and a third scrub and steppe. Sand dunes, mostly fixed and running north to south, and stony deserts mark the great tableland.

Many of Australia's rivers drain inland; though they erode their valleys near the highland sources, their lower courses are filling up with alluvium, and the rivers often end in salt lakes, dry for much of each year, when they become beds of salt and caked mud. Yet occasional spring rains in the outback can bring spectacular wildflowers.

Sparsely populated, Australia has nearly all its 20 million people along the east and southeast coasts, and of these about 40 percent live in the two cities of Sydney and Melbourne. Along the coasts are some fine harbors and long beaches and rocky headlands.

The Eastern Highlands rise gently from central Australia toward a series of high plateaus, the highest part around Mount Kosciuszko (7,310 ft; 2,228 m). The Great Escarpment runs from northern Queensland to the Victoria border in the south. Australia's highest waterfalls occur where rivers flow over the Great Escarpment.

The longest of all Australian river systems, the Murray River and its tributaries, including the long Darling River, drain part of Queensland, the major part of New South Wales, and a large part of Victoria before finally flowing into the Indian Ocean just east of Adelaide.

Most of the Great Dividing Range that separates rivers flowing to Central Australia from those flowing to the Pacific runs across remarkably flat country dotted with lakes and airstrips. In ancient times volcanoes erupted in eastern Australia, and lava plains covered large areas.

Australia is blessed with a fascinating mix of native flora and fauna. Its distinctive plants include the ubiquitous eucalyptus, sometimes called a gum tree, and acacia, which Australians call wattle, each with several hundred species. Other common plants include bottlebrushes, paperbarks, and tea trees. Animals include the iconic kangaroo, koala, wallaby, wombat, and dog-like dingo, also the echidna—a spiny anteater—and numerous beloved birds, such as parrots, cockatoos, and kookaburras, and the emu, second largest of all birds after the ostrich.

Foreign animals have been introduced. The rabbit and fox have proven to be particularly noxious pests, overgrazing the land and killing and driving out native species. A fence built in 1907, still maintained, runs a thousand miles from the north coast to the south to prevent rabbits from invading Western Australia.

New Zealand is mountainous compared to Australia; it has peaks over 10,000 feet in the Southern Alps and considerably more rain, making the climate cooler and more temperate. Among New Zealand's oddities is a fossil lizard species, the tuatara; individuals can live up to a hundred years.

The atolls, mountains, volcanoes, and sandy isles of greater Oceania, with limited land and small populations, have for most of history been isolated from the more settled parts of the world.

Peaks and promontories of the many islands of Polynesia form clouds and capture rain, making these islands very wet.

HISTORY Australia's first inhabitants, the Aborigines, migrated there some 50,000 or more years ago from Asia. Until the arrival of Europeans, the Aborigines had remained isolated from outside influences except for occasional trading in the north with Indonesian islanders.

Aboriginal pictographs, some repainted generation upon generation, grace the rock shelters and escarpment walls of Kakadu National Park in Australia's Northern Territory. Some paintings are considered *andjamun,* sacred and dangerous, and only may be viewed by tribal elders, while others may be looked upon by everyone.

In 1688 Englishman William Dampier landed on the northwest coast. Little interest was aroused, however, until Capt. James Cook noted the fertile east coast during his 1770 voyage, which stopped at Botany Bay, just south of today's Sydney. He claimed the entire continent for the British Empire and named it New South Wales.

Australia's formative moment came when Britain began colonizing the east coast in 1788 as a penal colony, so as to relieve overcrowded prisons in England. Altogether, 161,000 English, Irish, and other convicts were forced to settle there. Prison transports ended in 1868, and by that time regular emigrants had already begun settling down under, as Australia was called for being so far south of the Equator. By the mid-1800s systematic, permanent colonization had completely replaced the old penal settlements.

Introduction of sheep proved vital, and the wool industry flourished. A gold strike in Victoria in 1851 attracted prospectors from all over the world. Other strikes followed, and with minerals, sheep, and grain forming the base of the economy, Australia developed rapidly, expanding across the whole continent.

By 1861, Australians had established the straight-line boundaries between the colonies, and the Commonwealth of Australia was born January 1, 1901, relying on British parliamentary and U.S. federal traditions. Australia and New Zealand share a common British heritage and many similar characteristics, and both are democracies that continue to honor the British monarch.

The great seafaring navigators of Polynesia and Micronesia took part in the last phase of mankind's settlement of the globe, into the widely dispersed islands of the great Pacific. Their particular genius and contribution was the development of seafaring and navigation skills and canoe technology, which let them sail back and forth among islands across great distances. The more diverse, land-based Melanesians fished along the coasts and practiced horticulture farther inland.

CULTURE Australia's Aborigines were hunters and gatherers moving with the seasons, taking with them only those possessions necessary for hunting and preparing food. Perhaps 500 or more tribes lived in Australia at the time of Captain Cook in 1770.

Aboriginal society was based on a complex network of intricate kinship relationships. No formal government or authority existed, but social control was maintained by a system of beliefs called the Dreaming. These beliefs found expression in song, art, and dance. A rich oral tradition existed in which stories of the Dreamtime, the time of creation, or recent history were passed down. Aboriginal rock carvings and paintings date back at least 30,000 years.

Australia's Aborigines have faced two centuries and more of lost land, brutalization, and discrimination. In the 1960s an Aboriginal movement grew to press for full citizenship and improved education. Modern Aboriginal art has undergone a revival as Aboriginal artists have preserved their ancient values while learning from the contemporary world.

Most Australians are of British and Irish ancestry and the majority live in urban areas. The population has more than doubled since the end of World War II, spurred by an ambitious postwar immigration program, with many coming from Greece, Turkey, Italy, and Lebanon. In the 1970s Australia officially ended discriminatory immigration policies, and substantial Asian immigration followed. Today Asians make up some 7 percent of the population.

The largest church groups are the Anglican and Roman Catholic, though some say sport is the national religion; Australians are famous in cricket, rugby, and swimming.

The Maori—indigenous Polynesian people of New Zealand—arrived in different migrations starting around 1150, and a "great fleet" arrived in the 14th century, probably from Tahiti. Maori art is characterized by beautiful wood carvings that adorn houses and fish hooks carved out of whale bone. In the 1840 Treaty of Waitangi, the Maori gave formal control of their land to the British, though they kept all other rights of livelihood.

ECONOMY Australia dominates all of Oceania economically. Its connection to Asia grows more important as a supplier of raw material to other Pacific Rim countries and an importer of finished manufactured products. Japan is Australia's leading trade partner and thousands of children learn Japanese in Australian schools. The standard of living is high and people have considerable leisure time, a sign for Australians of a good life.

Most of the rich farmland and good ports are in the east, particularly the southeast, and the areas around Perth, in Western Australia. Melbourne, Sydney, Brisbane, and Adelaide are the leading industrial and commercial cities.

Australia is highly industrialized. Its chief industries include mining, food processing, and the manufacture of industrial and transportation equipment, chemicals, iron and steel, textiles, machinery, and motor vehicles. Some lumbering is done in the east and southeast. Tropical and subtropical produce are also important, as are vineyards, dairy farms, and tobacco farms.

Chief export commodities are coal, gold, beef, mutton, wool, minerals, cereals, and manufactured products. Australia's economic ties with Asia and the Pacific Rim are increasingly important. Air transport and modern communications have shrunk distances, with landing strips on isolated atolls, in the desert outback, and in Papuan jungles.

Australia: Physical and Political

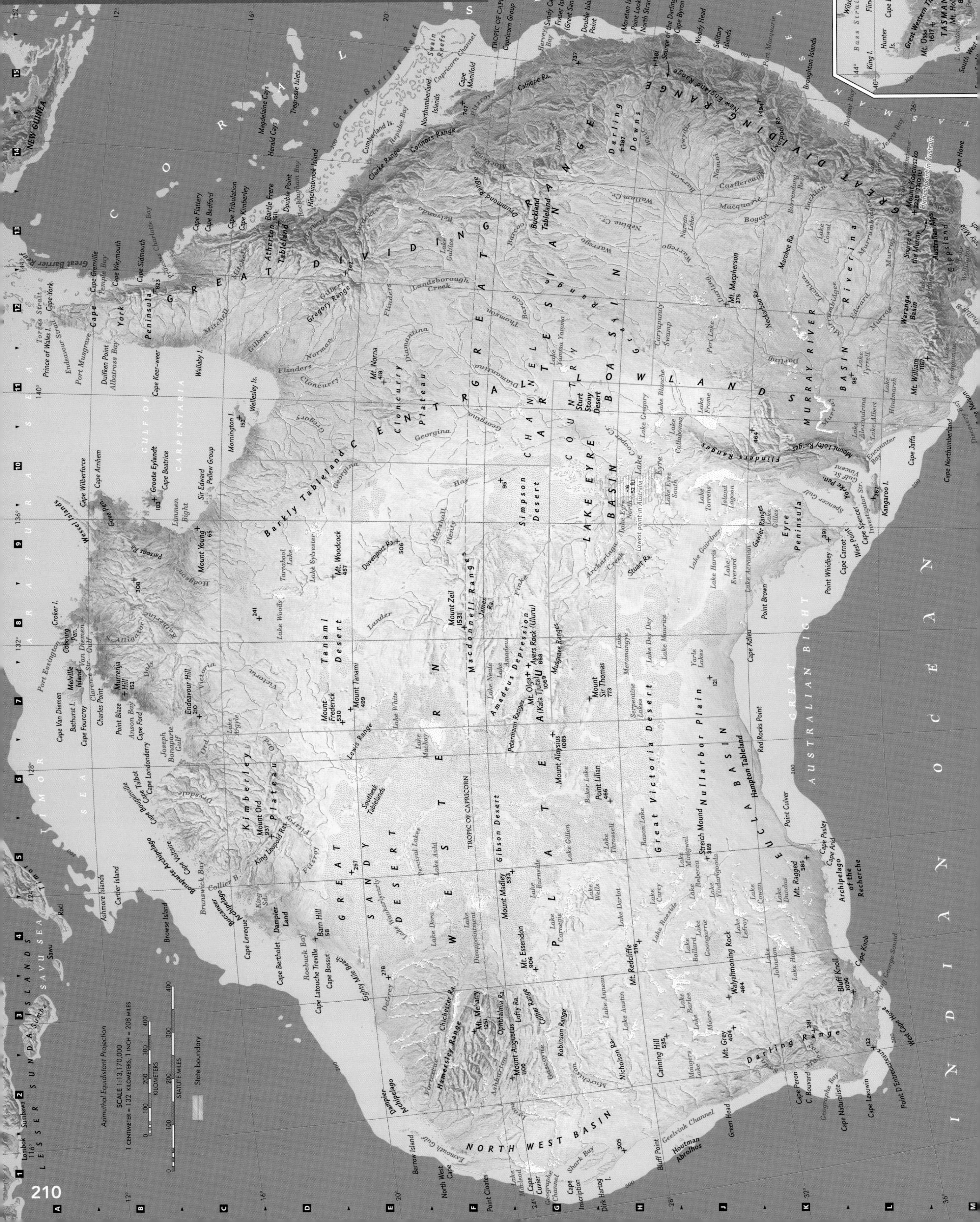

Azimuthal Equidistant Projection
SCALE 1:13,170,000
1 CENTIMETER = 132 KILOMETERS; 1 INCH = 208 MILES
KILOMETERS
STATUTE MILES
State boundary
CORAL SEA
ARAFURA SEA
TIMOR SEA
GULF OF CARPENTARIA
INDIAN OCEAN
GREAT AUSTRALIAN BIGHT
TASMAN SEA
LESSER SUNDA ISLANDS
SAVU SEA
NEW GUINEA
Great Barrier Reef
GREAT DIVIDING RANGE
CENTRAL LOWLANDS
GREAT ARTESIAN BASIN
LAKE EYRE BASIN
MURRAY RIVER BASIN
WESTERN PLATEAU
GREAT SANDY DESERT
Gibson Desert
Great Victoria Desert
Tanami Desert
Simpson Desert
Sturt Stony Desert
Nullarbor Plain
EUCLA BASIN
NORTH WEST BASIN
Kimberley Plateau
Barkly Tableland
Cloncurry Plateau
Macdonnell Ranges
Musgrave Ranges
Amadeus Depression
Hamersley Range
Darling Range
Flinders Ranges
Mount Lofty Ranges
Australian Alps
Riverina
Darling Downs
New England Range
Cape York Peninsula
Eyre Peninsula
Ayers Rock (Uluru) 868
Mt. Olga (Kata Tjuta) 1069
Mount Zeil 1531
Mt. Meharry 1251
Mount Kosciuszko 2228 (7310 ft) Highest point in Australia
Lake Eyre North -16 (-52 ft) Lowest point in Australia
Lake Torrens
Lake Gairdner
Lake Frome
Lake Mackay
Lake Amadeus
Lake Carnegie
Lake Disappointment
TROPIC OF CAPRICORN
Darling
Murray
Murrumbidgee
Lachlan
Cooper Cr.
Diamantina
Georgina
Flinders
Fitzroy
Victoria
Kangaroo I.
Melville Island
Bathurst I.
Groote Eylandt
Fraser Island (Great Sandy I.)
TASMANIA
Bass Strait
FURNEAUX GROUP
Flinders I.
King I.
Mt. Ossa 1617
Wilsons Promontory
Cape York
Cape Leeuwin

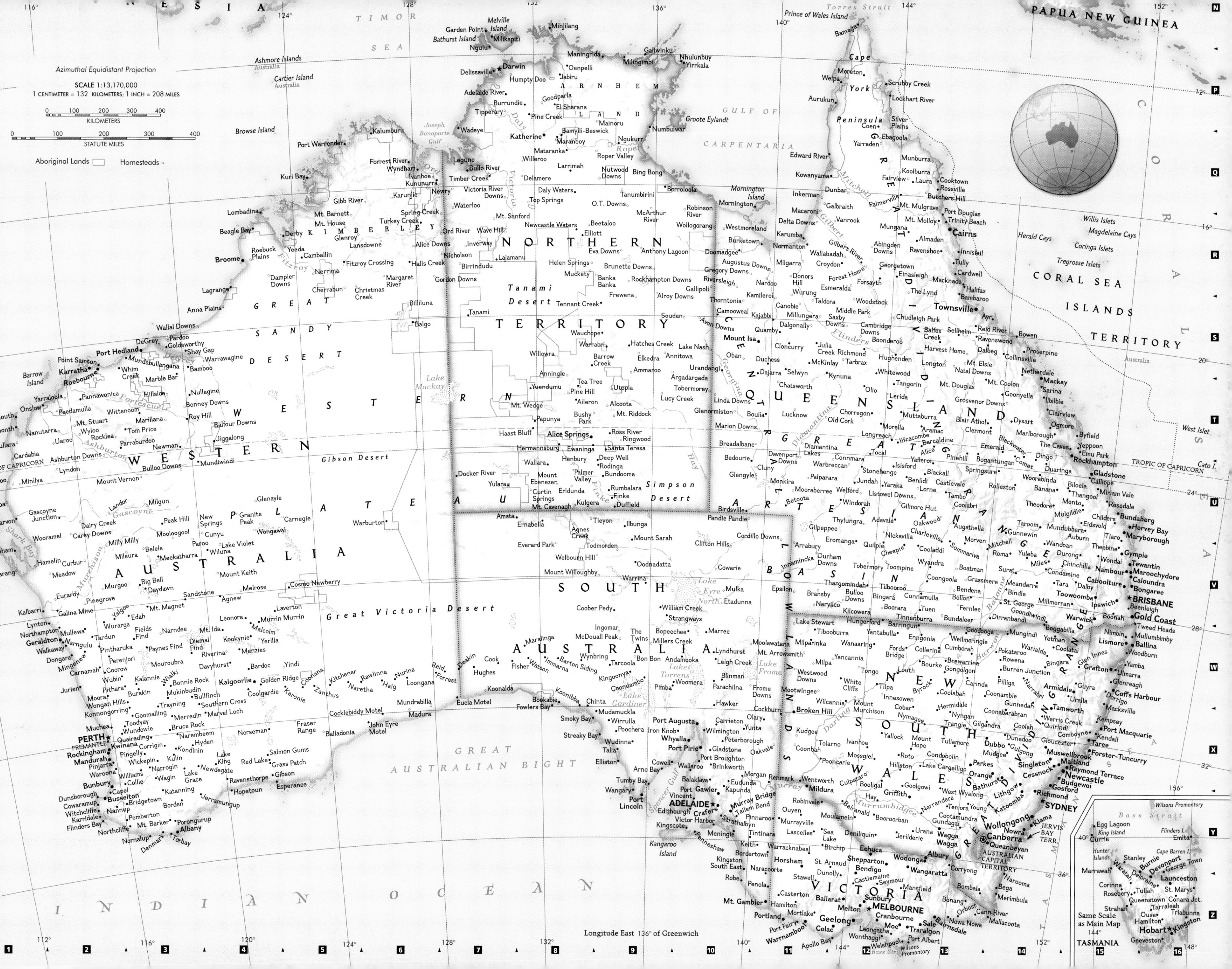
Azimuthal Equidistant Projection
SCALE 1:13,170,000
1 CENTIMETER = 132 KILOMETERS; 1 INCH = 208 MILES
KILOMETERS
STATUTE MILES
Aboriginal Lands
Homesteads
PAPUA NEW GUINEA
TIMOR SEA
GULF OF CARPENTARIA
CORAL SEA ISLANDS TERRITORY
CORAL SEA
TROPIC OF CAPRICORN
NORTHERN TERRITORY
WESTERN AUSTRALIA
SOUTH AUSTRALIA
QUEENSLAND
NEW SOUTH WALES
VICTORIA
TASMANIA
AUSTRALIAN CAPITAL TERRITORY
GREAT SANDY DESERT
Gibson Desert
Great Victoria Desert
Tanami Desert
Simpson Desert
GREAT ARTESIAN BASIN
GREAT DIVIDING RANGE
ARNHEM LAND
KIMBERLEY
WESTERN PLATEAU
CAPE YORK PENINSULA
GREAT AUSTRALIAN BIGHT
INDIAN OCEAN
Bass Strait
Torres Strait
Darwin
Alice Springs
Perth
Adelaide
Melbourne
Sydney
Canberra
Brisbane
Hobart
Cairns
Townsville
Rockhampton
Gold Coast
Newcastle
Wollongong
Geelong
Launceston
Kalgoorlie
Broome
Port Hedland
Mount Isa
Katherine
Same Scale as Main Map
Longitude East 136° of Greenwich

Temperature and Precipitation

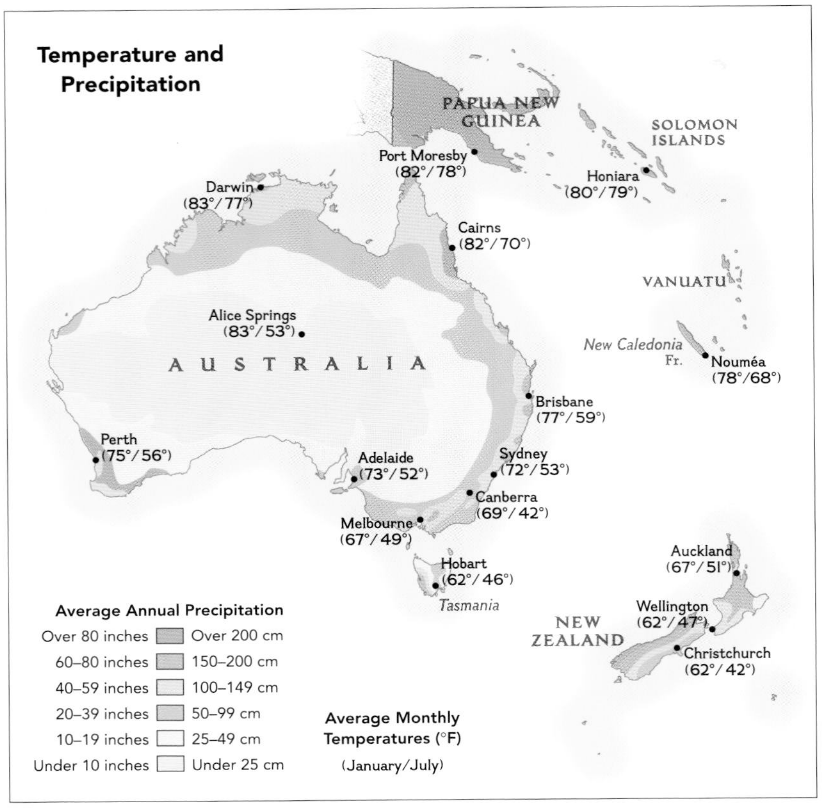

Population

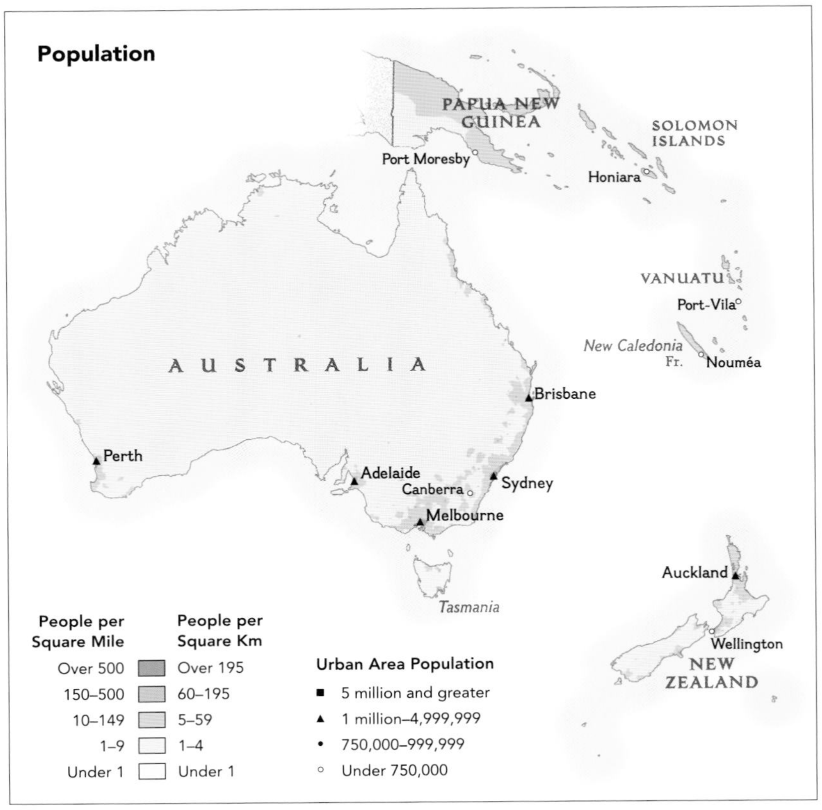

Land Use, Agriculture, and Fishing

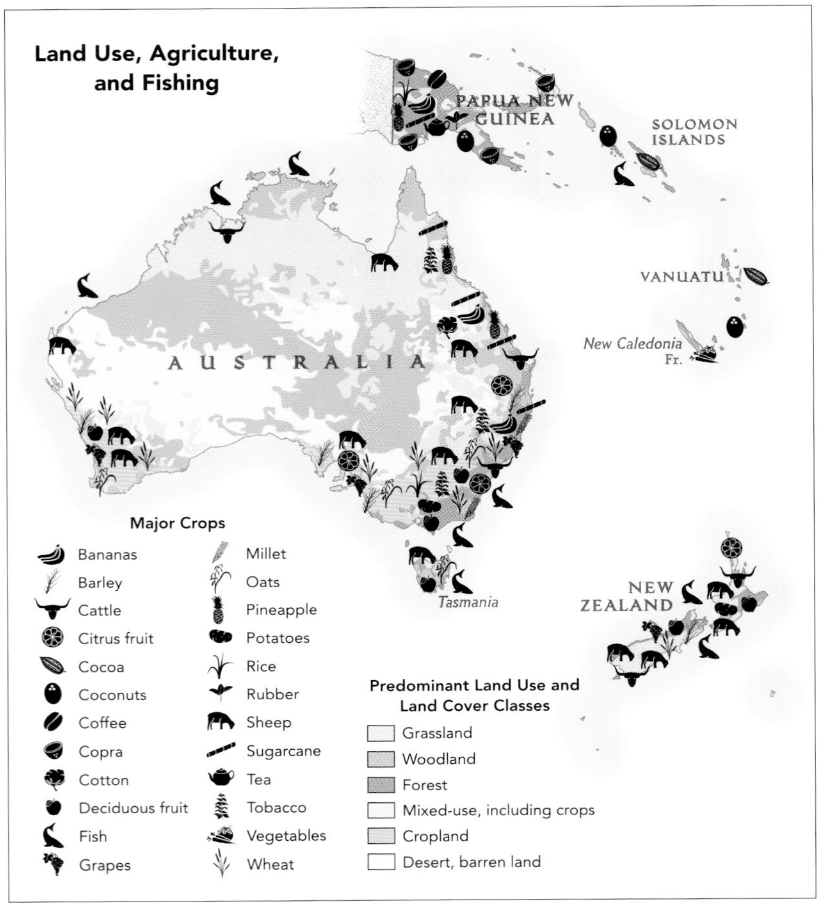

Industry and Mining

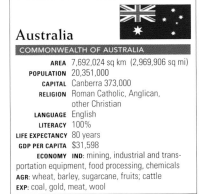

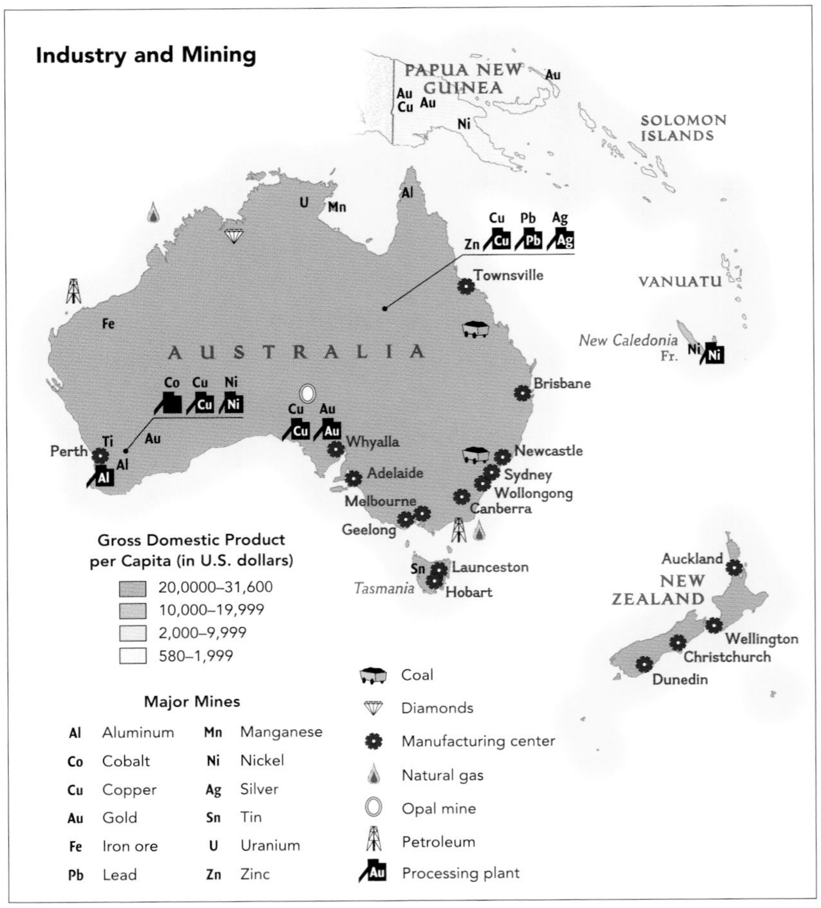

Australia

COMMONWEALTH OF AUSTRALIA

AREA 7,692,024 sq km (2,969,906 sq mi)
POPULATION 20,351,000
CAPITAL Canberra 373,000
RELIGION Roman Catholic, Anglican, other Christian
LANGUAGE English
LITERACY 100%
LIFE EXPECTANCY 80 years
GDP PER CAPITA $31,598
ECONOMY **IND:** mining, industrial and transportation equipment, food processing, chemicals
AGR: wheat, barley, sugarcane, fruits; cattle
EXP: coal, gold, meat, wool

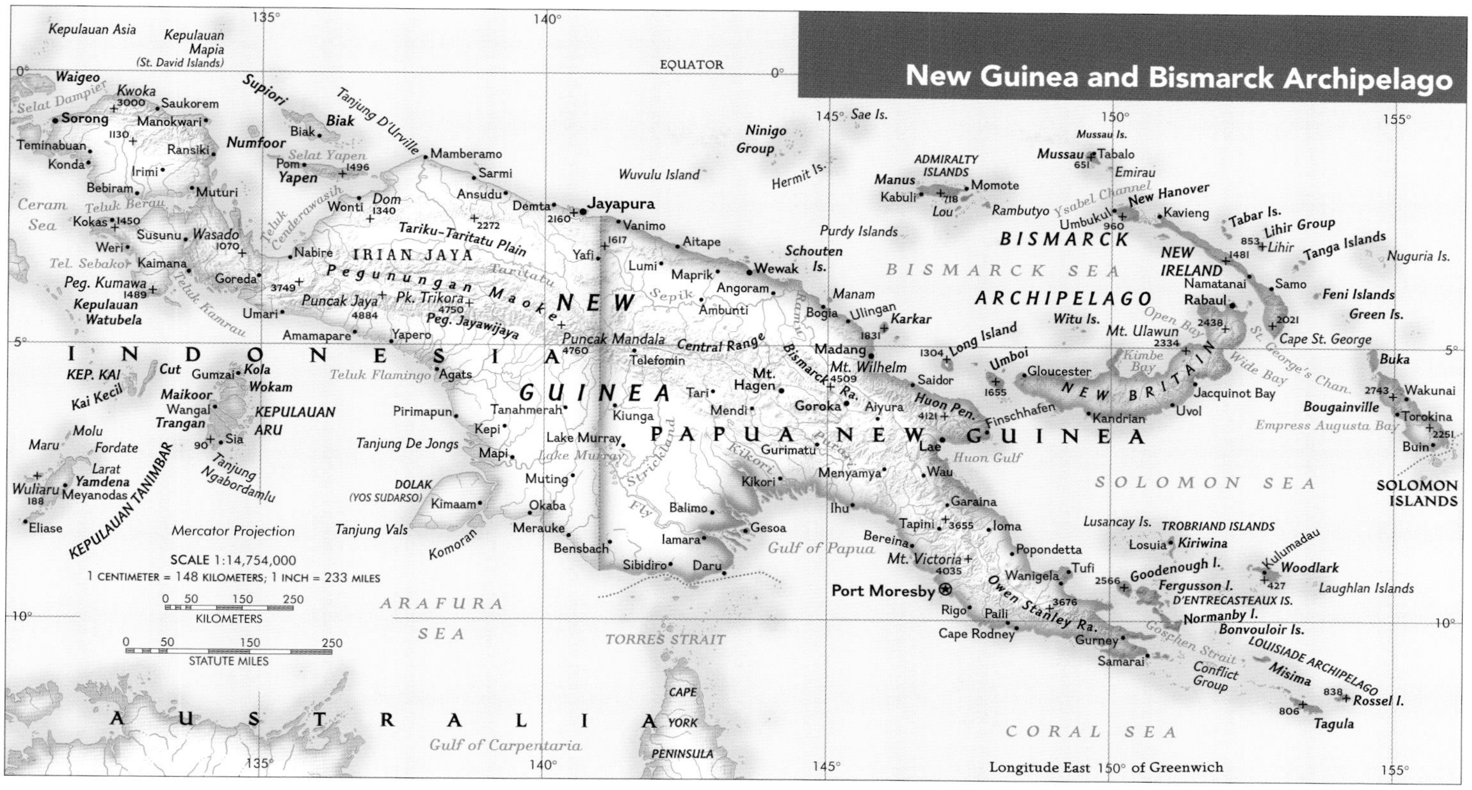

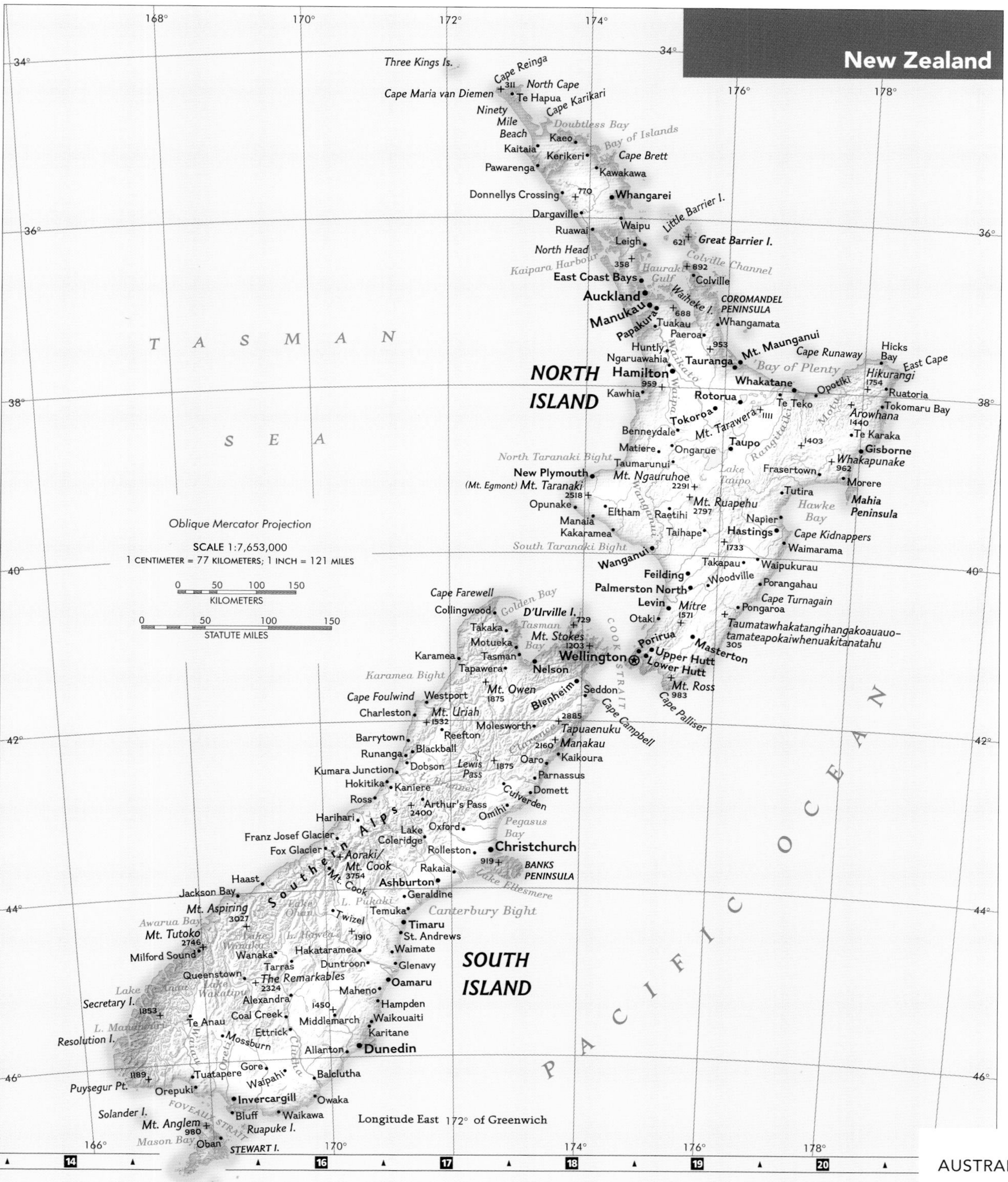

New Zealand

NEW ZEALAND

AREA 270,534 sq km (104,454 sq mi)
POPULATION 4,107,000
CAPITAL Wellington 343,000
RELIGION Anglican, Roman Catholic, Presbyterian
LANGUAGE English (official), Maori (official)
LITERACY 99%
LIFE EXPECTANCY 79 years
GDP PER CAPITA $24,499
ECONOMY **IND:** food processing, wood and paper products, textiles, machinery **AGR:** wheat, barley, potatoes, pulses; wool; fish **EXP:** dairy products, meat, wood and wood products, fish

Papua New Guinea

IND. STATE OF PAPUA NEW GUINEA

AREA 462,840 sq km (178,703 sq mi)
POPULATION 5,887,000
CAPITAL Port Moresby 275,000
RELIGION indigenous beliefs, Roman Catholic, Lutheran, other Protestant
LANGUAGE Melanesian Pidgin, 715 indigenous languages
LITERACY 65%
LIFE EXPECTANCY 55 years
GDP PER CAPITA $824
ECONOMY **IND:** copra crushing, palm oil processing, plywood production, wood chip production **AGR:** coffee, cocoa, coconuts, palm kernels; poultry **EXP:** oil, gold, copper ore, logs

NORTH KOREA
P'YŎNGYANG
DALIAN
SEA OF JAPAN (EAST SEA)
SEOUL
SOUTH KOREA
BUSAN
QINGDAO
YELLOW SEA
JAPAN
Akita
SENDAI
TŌKYŌ
YOKOHAMA
NAGOYA
HONSHŪ
KŌBE
ŌSAKA
SHIKOKU
KYŪSHŪ
Jeju-Do
CHINA
SHANGHAI
EAST CHINA SEA
Yaku Shima
Tanega Shima
Hachijō Jima
Izu Shotō Japan
Sumisu (Smith)
Sōfu Gan (Lot's Wife)
NAMPŌ SHOTŌ
Amami Ō Shima
Okinawa
NANSEI SHOTŌ
Sakishima Shotō
Japan
Kita Daitō Jima
Daitō Islands
Japan
Okino Daitō Jima
Bonin Islands (Ogasawara Guntō)
Muko Jima Rettō
Chichi Jima Rettō
Haha Jima Rettō
Volcano Islands (Kazan Rettō)
Japan
Kita Iwo Jima
Iwo Jima
Minami Iwo Jima
TAIPEI
TAIWAN
KAOHSIUNG
Luzon Strait
Batan Is.
Babuyan Is.
Parece Vela Japan
Farallon de Pajaros
Minami Tori Shima (Marcus) Japan
TROPIC OF CANCER
NORTH PACIFIC
Monday Sunday
Kure Atoll
Midway Islands
Pearl and Hermes Atoll
Lisianski I.
Laysan I.
United States
Gardner Pinnacles
La Perouse Pinnacle
Necker I.
Refer to pages 112-113 for large-scale map of Hawai'i
HAWAI'I
Nihoa
Ni'ihau
Ka'ula
Kaua'i
O'ahu
Honolulu
Lāna'i
Kaho'olawe
Hawai'i
PHILIPPINE SEA
Asuncion
Agrihan
Pagan
Alamagan
Sarigan
Anatahan
NORTHERN MARIANA ISLANDS U.S.
Tinian
Saipan
Rota
Guam U.S.
Wake Island U.S.
Johnston Atoll U.S.
Taongi Atoll
LUZON
MANILA
PHILIPPINES
Mindoro
Samar
Panay
Leyte
Negros
Sulu Sea
MINDANAO
DAVAO
Sulu Archipelago
Celebes Sea
MICRONESIA
Bikini Atoll
Enewetak Atoll
Rongelap Atoll
Utirik Atoll
Ailuk Atoll
Wotje Atoll
MARSHALL ISLANDS
Maloelap Atoll
Majuro
Arno Atoll
Mili Atoll
Ralik Chain
Ratak Chain
Jaluit Atoll
Kili I.
Ujelang Atoll
Kwajalein Atoll
Ailinglapalap Atoll
Namorik Atoll
Ebon Atoll
Date Line
Ulithi Atoll
Yap Islands
Fais
Gaferut
Ifalik Atoll
Satawal
Namonuito Atoll
Hall Is.
Chuuk (Truk Is.)
Oroluk Atoll
Senyavin Is.
Pohnpei (Ponape)
Palikir
Kosrae (Kusaie)
PALAU
Koror
Ngulu Atoll
Woleai Atoll
Eauripik Atoll
Puluwat Atoll
Pulap Atoll
Pulusuk
Mortlock Is.
Ngatik Atoll
CAROLINE ISLANDS
FEDERATED STATES OF MICRONESIA
Sonsorol Is.
Pulo Anna
Merir
Helen I.
Tobi
Nukuoro Atoll
Kepulauan Talaud
Morotai
Halmahera
Molucca Sea
Kep. Mapia
Kapingamarangi Atoll
EQUATOR
Butaritari
Abaiang
Marakei
GILBERT ISLANDS
Tarawa (Bairiki)
Abemama
Nonouti
Tabiteuea
Beru
Tamana
Arorae
Banaba (Ocean I.)
NAURU
Howland Island
Baker Island
U.S.
Jarvis Island
KIRIBATI
Kanton
Enderbury I.
McKean Island
Birnie I.
Rawaki
Nikumaroro
Orona
Manra
PHOENIX ISLANDS
Palmyra Atoll U.S.
Teraina (Washington I.)
Tabuaeran (Fanning I.)
Kiribati
Kiritimati (Christmas I.)
Malden I.
Starbuck Island
LINE ISLANDS
POLYNESIA
Teluk Tomini
SULAWESI (Celebes)
Peleng
Kep. Sula
Waigeo
Biak
Teluk Cenderawasih
Buru
Ceram
INDONESIA
Banda Sea
Buton
Muna
Kep. Kai
Kep. Aru
NEW GUINEA
Admiralty Islands
Manus
Mussau Is.
New Hanover
BISMARCK ARCHIPELAGO
New Ireland
Bismarck Sea
Rabaul
Green Islands
New Britain
Bougainville
Nukumanu Islands
SOLOMON ISLANDS
Choiseul
Huon G.
Trobriand Is.
Solomon Sea
Woodlark
New Georgia
Santa Isabel
Malaita
Honiara
Guadalcanal
San Cristobal
Rennell
PAPUA NEW GUINEA
Port Moresby
Flores
Lomblen
Alor
Wetar
Moa
Dili
TIMOR-LESTE
Timor
Babar
Kep. Tanimbar
Savu Sea
Roti
Timor Sea
Arafura Sea
Lesser Sunda Islands
Torres Str.
Cape York
D'Entrecasteaux Islands
Louisiade Archipelago
Duff Islands
Santa Cruz Islands
Nupani
Nendo (Ndeni)
Utupua
Vanikolo Is.
Tikopia
Anuta (Cherry I.)
Fataka (Mitre I.)
Torres Islands
Banks Islands
Espiritu Santo
Maéwo
Malakula
Port-Vila
Éfaté
VANUATU
Erromango
Tanna
Futuna
Anatom
Nanumea
Niutao
Nanumanga
Nui
Vaitupu
Nukufetau
Funafuti
Nukulaelae
Niulakita
TUVALU
Rotuma Fiji
Îles Wallis
Uvea
France
Îles de Horne
Niuafo'ou
Vanua Levu
FIJI ISLANDS
Taveuni
Viti Levu
Suva
Kadavu
Lau Group
Vatoa
Ono-i-Lau
Atafu
Nukunono
Fakaofu
TOKELAU
Swains I.
SAMOA
Savai'i
Apia
Upolu
AMERICAN SAMOA U.S.
Pago Pago
Tutuila
Manua Is.
Rose Atoll
SAMOA ISLANDS
Tafahi
Niuatoputapu
TONGA ISLANDS
Vava'u Group
Ha'apai Group
TONGA
Nuku'alofa
Tongatapu Group
'Eua
'Ata
Niue
Pukapuka Atoll (Danger Is.)
Nassau
Suwarrow Atoll
New Zealand
Palmerston Atoll
COOK ISLANDS
Rakahanga Atoll
(Tongareva) Penrhyn Atoll
Manihiki Atoll
Aitutaki Atoll
Hervey Is.
Mitiaro
Atiu
Maupihaa
Rarotonga
Mangaia
Gulf of Carpentaria
Cairns
Great Dividing Range
Willis Islets
CORAL SEA ISLANDS TERRITORY Australia
CORAL SEA
Îles Chesterfield
Île Huon
Îles Bélep
Ouvéa
Lifou
Loyalty Is.
Maré
NEW CALEDONIA France
Nouméa
Île des Pins (Kunié)
Matthew
Hunter
TROPIC OF CAPRICORN
AUSTRALIA
Fraser Island
BRISBANE
Norfolk Island Australia
Phillip Island
Raoul I. (Sunday)
Macauley I.
Curtis I.
Kermadec Islands N.Z.
L'Esperance Rock
Lord Howe I.
Ball's Pyramid Australia
GREAT AUSTRALIAN BIGHT
ADELAIDE
SYDNEY
Canberra
Kangaroo I.
MELBOURNE
Wilsons Promontory
Bass Strait
King I.
Furneaux Group
TASMANIA
Hobart
South East Cape
TASMAN SEA
Three Kings Islands
Cape Maria van Diemen
North Cape
Great Barrier Island
Auckland
Bay of Plenty
NORTH ISLAND
East Cape
Cook Str.
Cape Farewell
Wellington
SOUTH ISLAND
NEW ZEALAND
Chatham Islands
Chatham Is. N.Z.
Pitt Island
Puysegur Point
Foveaux Strait
Stewart Island
The Snares
Bounty Islands N.Z.
Antipodes Islands N.Z.
Auckland Islands N.Z.
Campbell I. N.Z.
Macquarie I. Australia
SOUTH
INDIAN OCEAN
Longitude East 150° of Greenwich

UNITED STATES
Washington
San Francisco
Cape Mendocino
Sierra Nevada
LOS ANGELES
SAN DIEGO
TIJUANA
OCEAN
ATLANTIC OCEAN
Baja California
Golfo de California
Isla de Guadalupe
Mexico
Isla Cedros
Punta Eugenia
Rocas Alijos
Mexico
MEXICO
GULF OF MEXICO
BAHAMAS
CUBA
TROPIC OF CANCER
Cabo Falso
Mazatlán
Islas Revillagigedo
Mexico
Isla San Benedicto
Isla Socorro
Isla Clarión
Isla Roca Partida
MÉXICO
HAITI
JAMAICA
DOMINICAN REPUBLIC
Belmopan
BELIZE
Acapulco
GUATEMALA
GUATEMALA
HONDURAS
Tegucigalpa
CARIBBEAN SEA
San Salvador
EL SALVADOR
NICARAGUA
MANAGUA
Clipperton
France
San José
PANAMA
CARACAS
COSTA RICA
Panamá
VENEZUELA
Golfo de Panamá
Isla del Coco
Costa Rica
BOGOTÁ
Isla de Malpelo
Colombia
COLOMBIA
Isla Darwin
Ecuador
Galápagos Islands
(Archipiélago de Colón)
Isla San Salvador
Isla Santa Cruz
Isla Fernandina
Isla San Cristóbal
Isla Isabela
Isla Santa María
EQUATOR
QUITO
ECUADOR
GUAYAQUIL
Refer to page 120 for large-scale map of the Galápagos Islands
MARQUESAS ISLANDS
France
Eiao
Hatutu
Nuku Hiva
Ua Huka
Ua Pu
Hiva Oa
Tahuata
Mohotani (Motane)
Fatu Hiva
Caroline Island
BRAZIL
Trujillo
PERU
LIMA
TUAMOTU ARCHIPELAGO
Napuka
Manihi
Takaroa
Pukapuka
Mataiva
Makatea
Rangiroa
Tikei
Makemo
Moorea
Papeete
Anaa
Tatakoto
Tahiti
Hikueru
Hao
FRENCH POLYNESIA
France
BOLIVIA
La Paz
Hereheretue
Îles Duc de Gloucester
Tureia
Tematagi
Moruroa
Marutea
Tubuai
Morane
Mangareva
United Kingdom
Raivavae (Vavitu)
Îles Gambier
Temoe
Oeno Island
Henderson Island
Ducie Island
Pitcairn Island
TROPIC OF CAPRICORN
Sala-y-Gómez
Chile
Isla de Pascua
(Easter Island)
Chile
Isla San Félix
Isla San Ambrosio
Chile
Rapa
Marotiri
(Îlots de Bass)
ANDES
Chile
Islas Juan Fernández
Valparaíso
Isla Santa Clara
Isla Alejandro Selkirk
Isla Róbinson Crusoe
SANTIAGO
PACIFIC OCEAN
Concepción
ARGENTINA
CHILE
Isla Grande de Chiloé
Archipiélago de los Chonos
Golfo de Penas
Isla Campana
Isla Wellington
Isla Madre de Dios
Archipiélago Reina Adelaida
Isla Santa Inés
Mercator Projection
SCALE 1:39,295,000 AT THE EQUATOR
1 CENTIMETER = 392 KILOMETERS; 1 INCH = 620 MILES
0 500 1000 1500 2000
KILOMETERS
0 500 1000 1500 2000
STATUTE MILES
20 Numbered islands correspond to larger-scale maps on the following pages.
Major Pacific Island Groups
Mariana Islands
Marshall Islands
Caroline Islands
Society Islands and Tuamotu Archipelago
Other island
Longitude West of Greenwich
150° 140° 130° 120° 110° 100° 90° 80° 70°
40° 30° 20° 10° 0° 10° 20° 30° 40° 50°

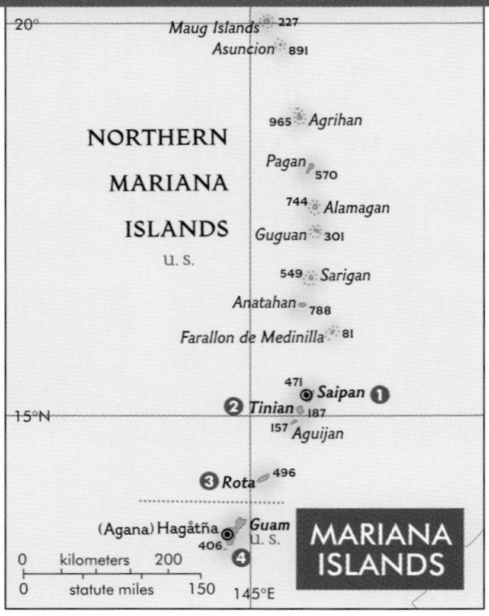
NORTHERN MARIANA ISLANDS
U.S.
MARIANA ISLANDS
Maug Islands
Asuncion
Agrihan
Pagan
Alamagan
Guguan
Sarigan
Anatahan
Farallon de Medinilla
Saipan
Tinian
Aguijan
Rota
(Agana) Hagåtña
Guam
U.S.
20°
15°N
145°E
kilometers 200
statute miles 150

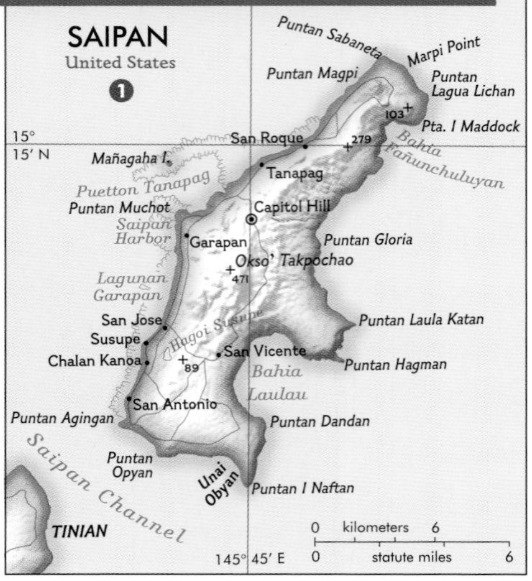
SAIPAN
United States
Puntan Sabaneta
Marpi Point
Puntan Lagua Lichan
Pta. I Maddock
Puntan Magpi
San Roque
Mañagaha I.
Tanapag
Puetton Tanapag
Puntan Muchot
Saipan Harbor
Capitol Hill
Garapan
Okso' Takpochao
Puntan Gloria
Lagunan Garapan
San Jose
Susupe
Chalan Kanoa
San Vicente
Puntan Laula Katan
Puntan Hagman
Bahia Laulau
San Antonio
Puntan Agingan
Puntan Dandan
Puntan Opyan
Unai Obyan
Puntan I Naftan
Saipan Channel
TINIAN
Bahia Fanunchuluyan
145° 45′ E
15° 15′ N
kilometers 6
statute miles 6

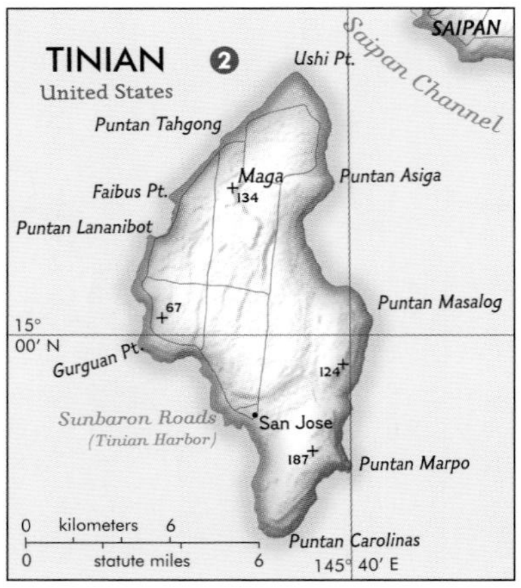
TINIAN
United States
SAIPAN
Ushi Pt.
Saipan Channel
Puntan Tahgong
Maga
Puntan Asiga
Faibus Pt.
Puntan Lananibot
Puntan Masalog
Gurguan Pt.
Sunharon Roads (Tinian Harbor)
San Jose
Puntan Marpo
Puntan Carolinas
15° 00′ N
145° 40′ E
kilometers 6
statute miles 6

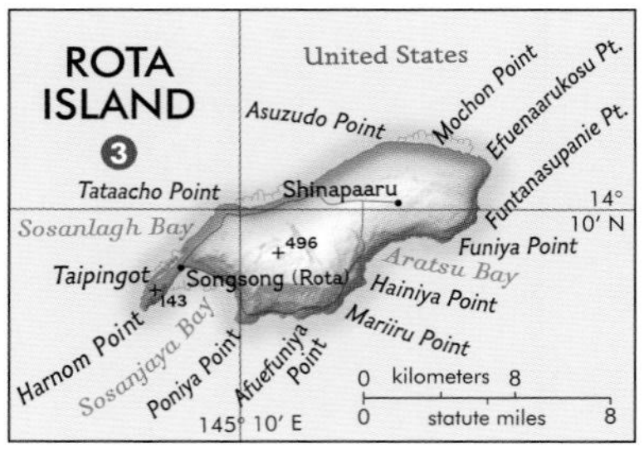
ROTA ISLAND
United States
Asuzudo Point
Mochon Point
Efuenaarukosu Pt.
Funtanasupanie Pt.
Tataacho Point
Shinapaaru
Sosanlagh Bay
Taipingot
Songsong (Rota)
Funiya Point
Aratsu Bay
Hainiya Point
Mariiru Point
Harnom Point
Sosanjaya Bay
Poniya Point
Afuefuniya Point
14° 10′ N
145° 10′ E
kilometers 8
statute miles 8

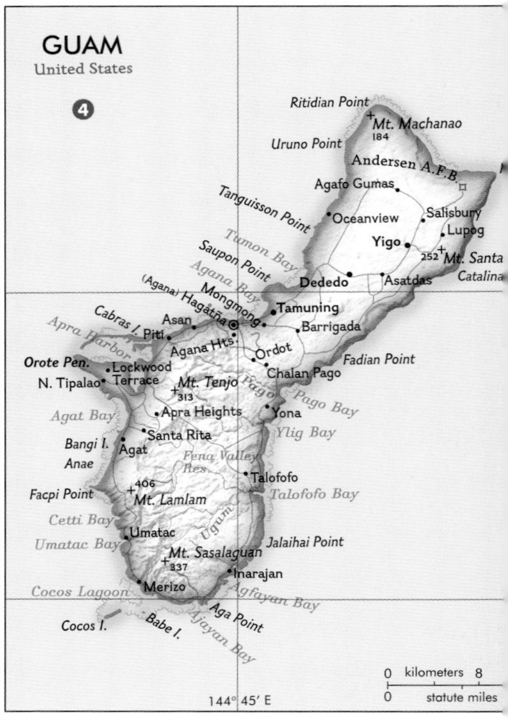
GUAM
United States
Ritidian Point
Mt. Machanao
Uruno Point
Andersen A.F.B.
Agafo Gumas
Tanguisson Point
Oceanview
Salisbury
Lupog
Yigo
Mt. Santa Catalina
Tumon Bay
Saupon Point
Agana Bay
Dededo
Asatdas
(Agana) Hagåtña
Mongmong
Tamuning
Barrigada
Cabras I.
Piti
Asan
Apra Harbor
Agana Hts.
Ordot
Fadian Point
Orote Pen.
N. Tipalao
Lockwood Terrace
Mt. Tenjo
Chalan Pago
Pago Bay
Agat Bay
Apra Heights
Yona
Ylig Bay
Santa Rita
Bangi I.
Agat
Anae
Talofofo
Talofofo Bay
Facpi Point
Mt. Lamlam
Cetti Bay
Umatac
Jalaihai Point
Umatac Bay
Mt. Sasalaguan
Inarajan
Merizo
Cocos Lagoon
Cocos I.
Babe I.
Aga Point
Ajayan Bay
Achang Bay
144° 45′ E
kilometers 8
statute miles 8

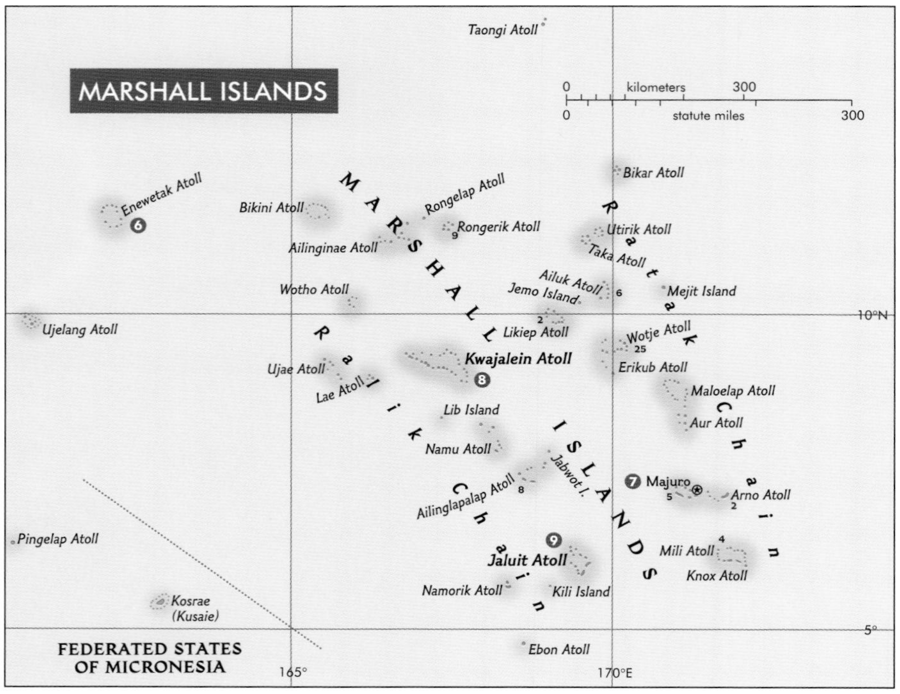
MARSHALL ISLANDS
Taongi Atoll
kilometers 300
statute miles 300
Enewetak Atoll
Bikini Atoll
Rongelap Atoll
Rongerik Atoll
Ailinginae Atoll
Bikar Atoll
Utirik Atoll
Taka Atoll
Wotho Atoll
Ailuk Atoll
Jemo Island
Mejit Island
Ujelang Atoll
Likiep Atoll
Wotje Atoll
Erikub Atoll
Kwajalein Atoll
Ujae Atoll
Lae Atoll
Maloelap Atoll
Aur Atoll
Lib Island
Namu Atoll
Ailinglapalap Atoll
Jabwot I.
Majuro
Arno Atoll
Pingelap Atoll
Jaluit Atoll
Mili Atoll
Knox Atoll
Namorik Atoll
Kili Island
Kosrae (Kusaie)
Ebon Atoll
FEDERATED STATES OF MICRONESIA
RATAK CHAIN
RALIK CHAIN
MARSHALL ISLANDS
10°N
5°
165°
170°E

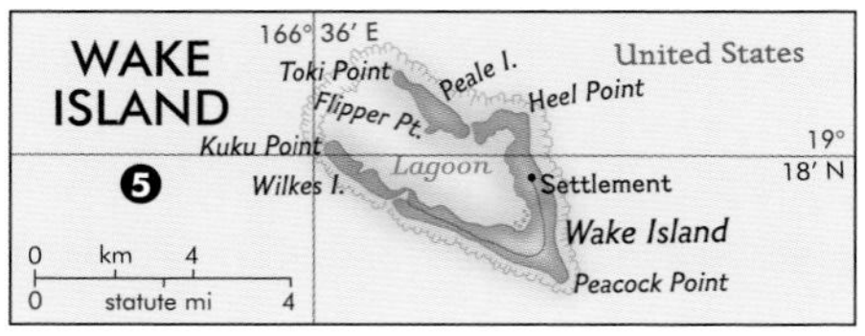
WAKE ISLAND
166° 36′ E
United States
Toki Point
Peale I.
Heel Point
Flipper Pt.
Kuku Point
Wilkes I.
Lagoon
Settlement
Wake Island
Peacock Point
19° 18′ N
km 4
statute mi 4

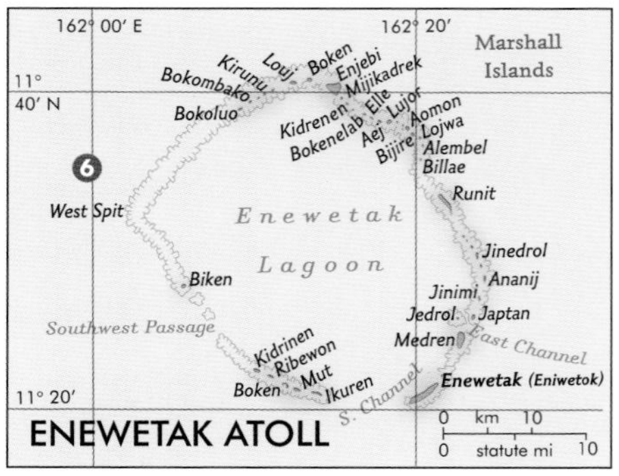
ENEWETAK ATOLL
162° 00′ E
162° 20′
Marshall Islands
11° 40′ N
Bokombako
Kirunu
Louj
Boken
Enjebi
Mijikadrek
Bokoluo
Kidrenen
Bokenelab
Elle
Aej
Lujor
Aomon
Bijire
Lojwa
Alembel
Billae
Runit
West Spit
Enewetak Lagoon
Jinedrol
Ananij
Biken
Jimini
Jedrol
Japtan
Southwest Passage
Medren
Kidrinen
Ribewon
Boken
Mut
Ikuren
Enewetak (Eniwetok)
Deep Channel
East Channel
11° 20′
km 10
statute mi 10

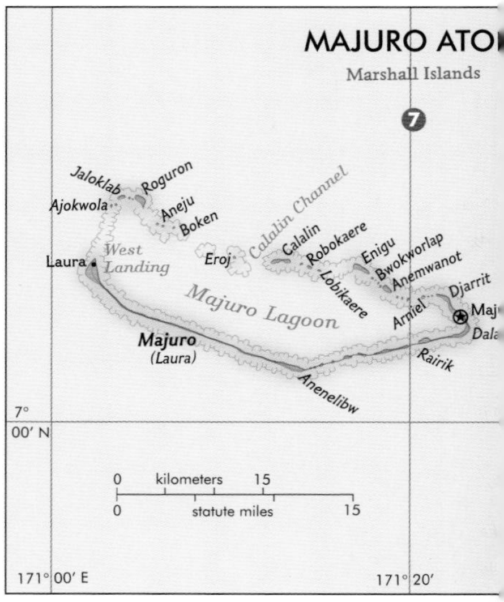
MAJURO ATOLL
Marshall Islands
Jaloklab
Rogruon
Ajokwola
Aneju
Boken
Calalin Channel
Calalin
Robokaere
Laura
West Landing
Eroj
Enigu
Bwokworlap
Anemwanot
Lobikaere
Djarrit
Majuro Lagoon
Arniel
Majuro (Laura)
Rairik
Aneneliibw
7° 00′ N
171° 00′ E
171° 20′
kilometers 15
statute miles 15

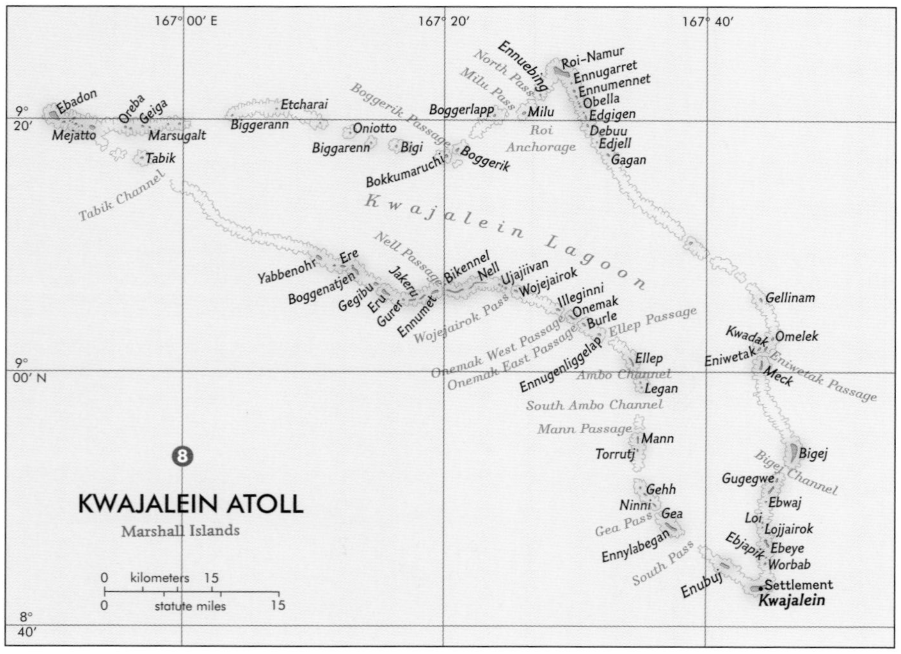
KWAJALEIN ATOLL
Marshall Islands
167° 00′ E
167° 20′
167° 40′
9° 20′
9° 00′ N
8° 40′
Ebadon
Oreba
Geiga
Mejatto
Marsugalt
Tabik
Etcharai
Biggerann
Oniotto
Bigi
Boggerlapp
Milu
Enneubing
Roi-Namur
Ennugarret
Ennumennet
Obella
Edgigen
Debuu
Edjell
Gagan
Boggerik
Bokkumaruch
Roi Anchorage
Tabik Channel
Kwajalein Lagoon
Yabbenohr
Ere
Boggenatjen
Gegibu
Eru
Gurer
Ennumet
Jakeru
Nell
Bikennel
Ujajiivan
Wojejairok
Illeginni
Onemak
Burle
Ellep Passage
Gellinam
Kwadak
Omelek
Eniwetak
Meck
Ellep
Legan
Ennugenliggelap
South Ambo Channel
Mann Passage
Mann
Torrutj
Bigej
Bigej Channel
Gugegwe
Gehh
Ninni
Gea
Gea Pass
Loi
Lojjairok
Ebeye
Ebjadik
Ennylabegan
Worbab
South Pass
Enubuj
Settlement
Kwajalein
kilometers 15
statute miles 15

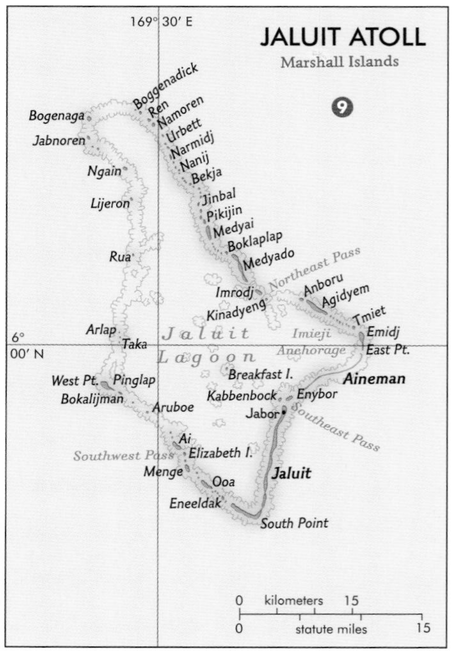
JALUIT ATOLL
Marshall Islands
169° 30′ E
Bogenaga
Boggenadick
Ren
Jabnoren
Namoren
Urbett
Narmidj
Nanij
Ngain
Bekja
Lijeron
Jinbal
Pikijin
Medyai
Boklaplap
Medyado
Rua
Northeast Pass
Imrodj
Anboru
Kinadyeng
Agidyem
Arlap
Taka
Jaluit Lagoon
Imieji
Tmiet
Emidj
Anchorage
East Pt.
West Pt.
Pinglap
Breakfast I.
Aineman
Bokalijman
Kabbenbock
Enybor
Aruboe
Jabor
Southeast Pass
Southwest Pass
Ai
Elizabeth I.
Menge
Ooa
Jaluit
Eneeldak
South Point
6° 00′ N
kilometers 15
statute miles 15

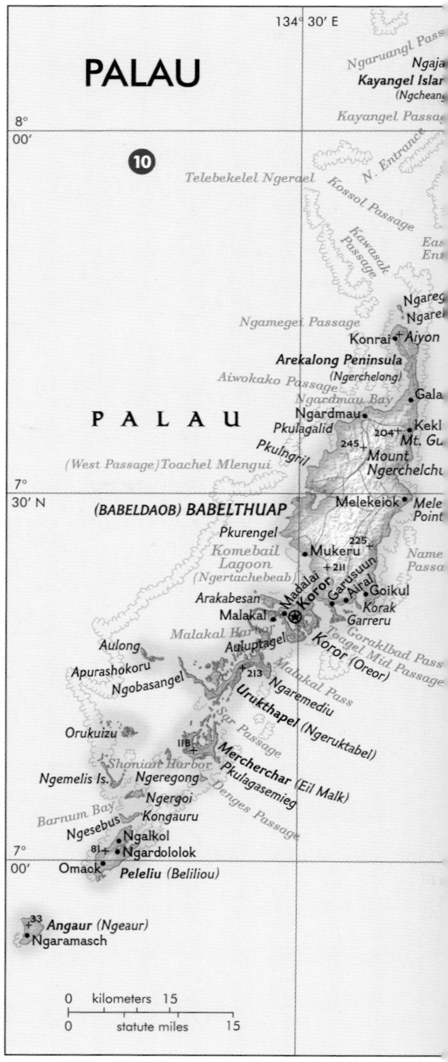
PALAU
134° 30′ E
Ngaruangl Passage
Kayangel Islands
Kayangel Passage
8° 00′
Telebekelel Ngeruangel
Kossol Passage
Kawasak Passage
Ngameget Passage
Konrai
Aiyon
Arekalong Peninsula (Ngerchelong)
Aiwokako Passage
Ngardmau Bay
Ngardmau
Pkulagalid
Mt. Ngerchelchuus
(West Passage) Toachel Mlengui
Pkulngril
(BABELDAOB) BABELTHUAP
Melekeiok
Pkurengel
Komebail Lagoon (Ngertachebeab)
Mukeru
Arakabesan
Malakal
Melekeok
Goikul
Korak
Garreru
Malakal Harbor
Airai
Aulong
Apurashokoru
Ngobasangel
Koror (Oreor)
Aguptagel
Urukthapel (Ngeruktabel)
Orukuizu
Eil Malk
Mercherchar
Shonian Harbor
Ngemelis Is.
Ngeregong
Ngergoi
Barnum Bay
Kongauru
Ngesebus
Ngarkol
Ngardololok
Omekang
Peleliu (Beliliou)
Angaur (Ngeaur)
Ngaramasch
7° 30′ N
7° 00′
kilometers 15
statute miles 15

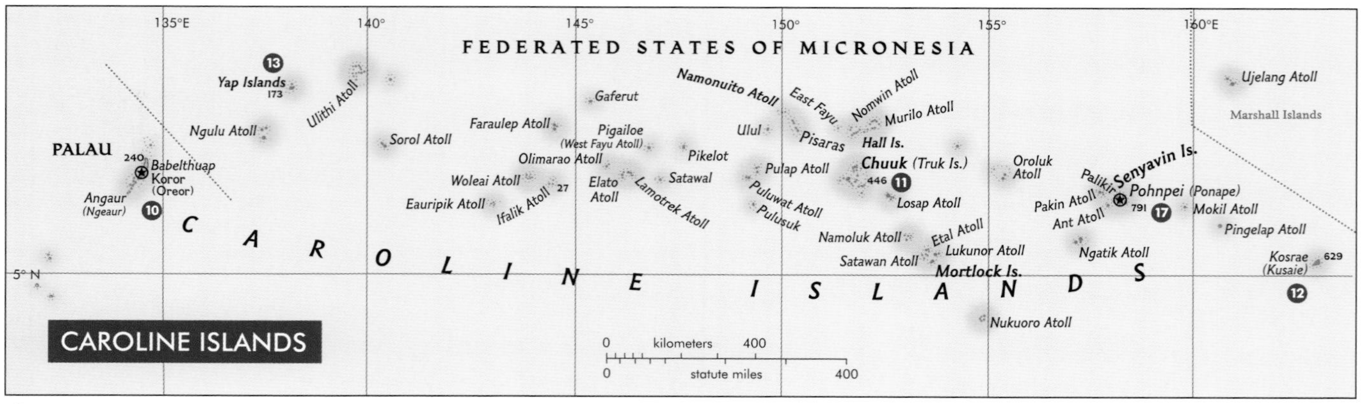
FEDERATED STATES OF MICRONESIA
CAROLINE ISLANDS
Yap Islands
Ulithi Atoll
Ngulu Atoll
PALAU
Babelthuap
Koror (Oreor)
Angaur (Ngeaur)
Sorol Atoll
Faraulep Atoll
Gaferut
Pigailoe (West Fayu Atoll)
Olimarao Atoll
Woleai Atoll
Eauripik Atoll
Ifalik Atoll
Elato Atoll
Lamotrek Atoll
Satawal
Pikelot
Namonuito Atoll
East Fayu
Nomwin Atoll
Murilo Atoll
Hall Is.
Pisaras
Ulul
Pulap Atoll
Puluwat Atoll
Pulusuk
Chuuk (Truk Is.)
Losap Atoll
Namoluk Atoll
Satawan Atoll
Etal Atoll
Lukunor Atoll
Mortlock Is.
Nukuoro Atoll
Oroluk Atoll
Pakin Atoll
Ant Atoll
Palikir
Senyavin Is.
Pohnpei (Ponape)
Mokil Atoll
Pingelap Atoll
Ngatik Atoll
Ujelang Atoll
Marshall Islands
Kosrae (Kusaie)
135°E
140°
145°
150°
155°
160°E
5°N
kilometers 400
statute miles 400

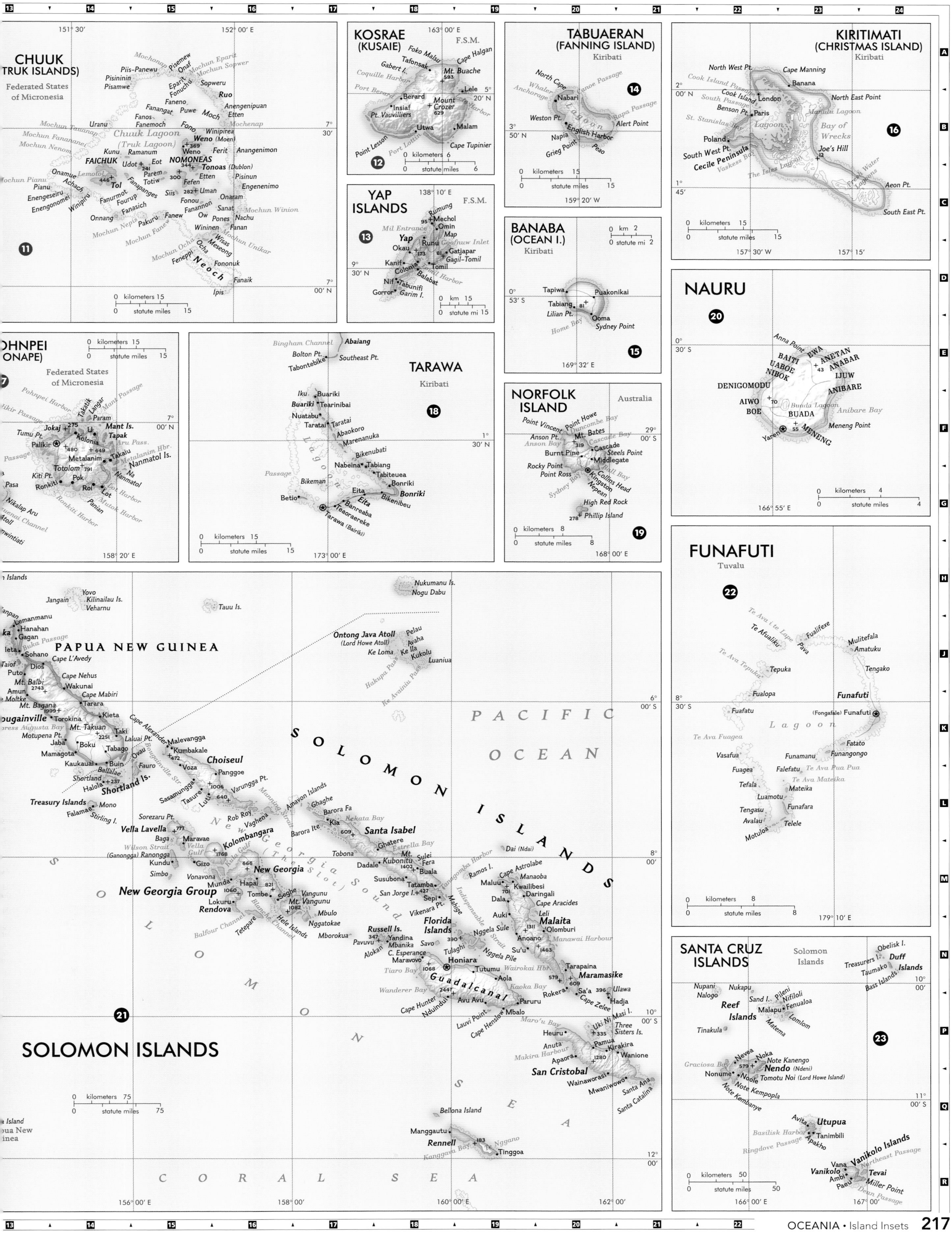
CHUUK
(TRUK ISLANDS)
Federated States of Micronesia
Chuuk Lagoon
(Truk Lagoon)
Weno (Moen)
Tonoas (Dublon)
FAICHUK
Tol
NOMONEAS
Fefen
Uman
Udot
Neoch
Ruo
Piis-Panewu
Pisininin
Pisamwe
Sopweru
Uranu
Fanangat
Faneno
Fanos
Fanemoch
Fono
Winipirea
Anengenipuan
Etten
Kunu
Ramanum
Ferit
Anangenimon
Eot
Parem
Totiw
Pisinun
Engenenimo
Onamue
Pianu
Enengeseiru
Enengonomei
Winipiru
Fanurmot
Fourup
Fanasich
Onnang
Pakuru
Fanew
Siis
Fonou
Fanannon
Ow
Onaram
Sanat
Nachu
Pones
Fanan
Wininen
Wisas
Meseong
Ocha
Feneppi
Fononuk
Fanaik
Ipis
KOSRAE
(KUSAIE)
F.S.M.
Cape Halgan
Mt. Buache
Foko Malsu
Tafonsak
Gabert I.
Coquille Harbor
Port Berard
Berard
Insiaf
Pt. Vauvilliers
Mount Crozer
Lele
Utwa
Malam
Cape Tupinier
Point Lesson
Port Lottin
YAP
ISLANDS
Mil Entrance
Rumung
Mechol
Omin
Map
Yap
Runu
Goofnuw Inlet
Okau
Gatjapar
Gagil-Tomil
Kanif
Colonia
Tomil
Tomil Harbor
Nif
Balabat
Gorror
Tabunifi
Garim I.
TABUAERAN
(FANNING ISLAND)
Kiribati
North Cape
Whaler Anchorage
Canoe Passage
Nabari
Rapa Passage
Weston Pt.
Alert Point
Lagoon
English Harbor
Napia
Grieg Point
Peao
BANABA
(OCEAN I.)
Kiribati
Tapiwa
Buakonikai
Tabiang
Lilian Pt.
Ooma
Home Bay
Sydney Point
NORFOLK
ISLAND
Australia
Point Vincent
Point Howe
Duncombe Bay
Anson Pt.
Anson Bay
Mt. Bates
Cascade Bay
Cascade
Burnt Pine
Steels Point
Middlegate
Rocky Point
Point Ross
Ball Bay
Kingston
Collins Head
Sydney Bay
Nepean
High Red Rock
Phillip Island
KIRITIMATI
(CHRISTMAS ISLAND)
Kiribati
North West Pt.
Cape Manning
Banana
Cook Island Passage
Cook Island
South Passage
London
Benson Pt.
Paris
North East Point
Manulu Lagoon
St. Stanislas Bay
Lagoon
Bay of Wrecks
Poland
South West Pt.
Cecile Peninsula
Vaskess Bay
Joe's Hill
The Isles Lagoon
Fresh Water Lagoons
Aeon Pt.
South East Pt.
NAURU
Anna Point
EWA
ANETAN
BAITI
ANABAR
UABOE
NIBOK
IJUW
DENIGOMODU
ANIBARE
AIWO
BOE
Buada Lagoon
BUADA
Anibare Bay
Yaren
MENENG
Meneng Point
POHNPEI
(PONAPE)
Federated States of Micronesia
Pohnpei Harbor
Takatik
Langar
Mant Passage
Param
Jokaj
Mant Is.
Tapak
Kolonia
Tumu Pt.
Palikir
Aru Pass.
Metalanim Hbr.
Metalanim
Takaiu
Nanmatol Is.
Totolom
Kiti Pt.
Pok
Ronkiti
Roi
Lot
Na
Nanmatol
Pasa
Lot Harbor
Panian
Mutok Harbor
Ronkiti Harbor
Nikalap Aru
TARAWA
Kiribati
Bingham Channel
Abaiang
Bolton Pt.
Southeast Pt.
Tabontebike
Iku
Buariki
Tearinibai
Nuatabu
Taratai
Abaokoro
Marenanuka
Lagoon
Bikenubati
Nabeina
Tabiang
Tabiteuea
Bonriki
Passage
Bikeman
Eita
Betio
Banreaba
Teaoraereke
Tarawa (Bairiki)
Bikenibeu
FUNAFUTI
Tuvalu
Te Ava i te Lape
Te Afualiku
Fualifexe
Mulitefala
Amatuku
Te Ava Tepuka
Tepuka
Tengako
Fualopa
Funafuti
Fuafatu
(Fongafale) Funafuti
Lagoon
Te Ava Fuagea
Fatato
Vasafua
Funamanu
Funangongo
Fuagea
Falefatu
Te Ava Pua Pua
Te Ava Mateika
Tefala
Mateika
Luamotu
Tengasu
Funafara
Avalau
Telele
Motuloa
SANTA CRUZ
ISLANDS
Solomon Islands
Obelisk I.
Duff Islands
Treasurers I.
Taumako
Bass Islands
Nupani
Nukapu
Nalogo
Pileni
Nifiloli
Reef Islands
Sand I.
Fenualoa
Malapu
Lomlom
Matema
Tinakula
Graciosa Bay
Nevea
Noka
Note Kanengo
Nendo (Ndeni)
Nonume
Noole
Tomotu Noi (Lord Howe Island)
Note Kempola
Note Kambanye
Avita
Utupua
Tanimbili
Basilisk Harbor
Apakho
Ringdove Passage
Vanikolo Islands
Northeast Passage
Vana
Vanikolo
Tevai
Ambi
Paeu
Miller Point
Dean Passage
PAPUA NEW GUINEA
SOLOMON ISLANDS
PACIFIC OCEAN
SOLOMON SEA
CORAL SEA
Nukumanu Is.
Nogu Dabu
Yovo
Kilinailau Is.
Jangain
Veharnu
Tauu Is.
Ontong Java Atoll
(Lord Howe Atoll)
Pelau
Avaha
Ke Loma
Ke Ila
Kukolu
Luaniua
Hakupu Pass
Ke Avainiu Pass
Hanahan
Gagen
Buka Passage
Sohano
Cape L'Avedy
Dios
Cape Nehus
Puto
Mt. Balbi
Wakunai
Amun
Cape Mabiri
Mt. Bagana
Tarara
Bougainville
Torokina
Kieta
Mt. Takuan
Empress Augusta Bay
Taki
Motupena Pt.
Jaba
Boku
Tabago
Mamagota
Kaukauai
Buin
Ballalae
Shortland
Shortland Is.
Halola
Fauro
Treasury Islands
Mono
Falamae
Stirling I.
Cape Alexander
Lauiai Pt.
Malevangga
Kumbakale
Choiseul
Bougainville Str.
Voza
Panggoe
Sasamungga
Tasure
Luti
Varungga Pt.
Manning Strait
Arnavon Islands
Ghaghe
Barora Fa
Kia
Barora Ite
Rekata Bay
Santa Isabel
Rob Roy
Vaghena
Sorezaru Pt.
Vella Lavella
Baga
Maravae
Kolombangara
Wilson Strait
Vella Gulf
Kula Gulf
(Ganongga) Ranongga
Kundu
Gizo
Simbo
New Georgia
New Georgia Group
Vonavona
Munda
Hapai
Tombe
Seghe
Vangunu
Mt. Vangunu
Lokuru
Rendova
Mbulo
Nggatokae
Blanche Channel
Hele Islands
Balfour Channel
Tetepare
Mborokua
New Georgia Sound (The Slot)
Tobona
Ghatere
Estrella Bay
Mt. Sulei
Dadale
Kubonitu
Fera
Buala
Susubona
Tatamba
San Jorge I.
Sepi
Vikenara Pt.
Florida Islands
Mahige
Tunggomba Harbor
Indispensable Strait
Russell Is.
Yandina
Pavuvu
Mbanika
Alokan
C. Esperance
Savo
Maravovo
Tulaghi
Honiara
Nggela Sule
Nggela Pile
Tiaro Bay
Guadalcanal
Tutumu
Wairokai Hbr.
Aola
Wanderer Bay
Avu Avu
Paruru
Cape Hunter
Nduindui
Mbalo
Lauvi Point
Cape Henslow
Dai (Ndai)
Ramos I.
Cape Astrolabe
Maluu
Manaoba
Kwailibesi
Dala
Daringali
Cape Aracides
Auki
Leli
Malaita
Olomburi
Anoano
Manawai Harbour
Su'u
Kaoka Bay
Tarapaina
Maramasike
Rokera
Sa'a
Ulawa
Hadja
Cape Zelee
Maro'u Bay
Uki Ni Masi I.
Three Sisters Is.
Heuru
Pamua
Kirakira
Anuta
Makira Harbour
Apaora
Wanione
San Cristobal
Wainaworasi
Mwaniwowo
Santa Ana
Santa Catalina
Bellona Island
Manggautu
Rennell
Nggano
Kanggava Bay
Tinggoa
kilometers
statute miles
km
statute mi

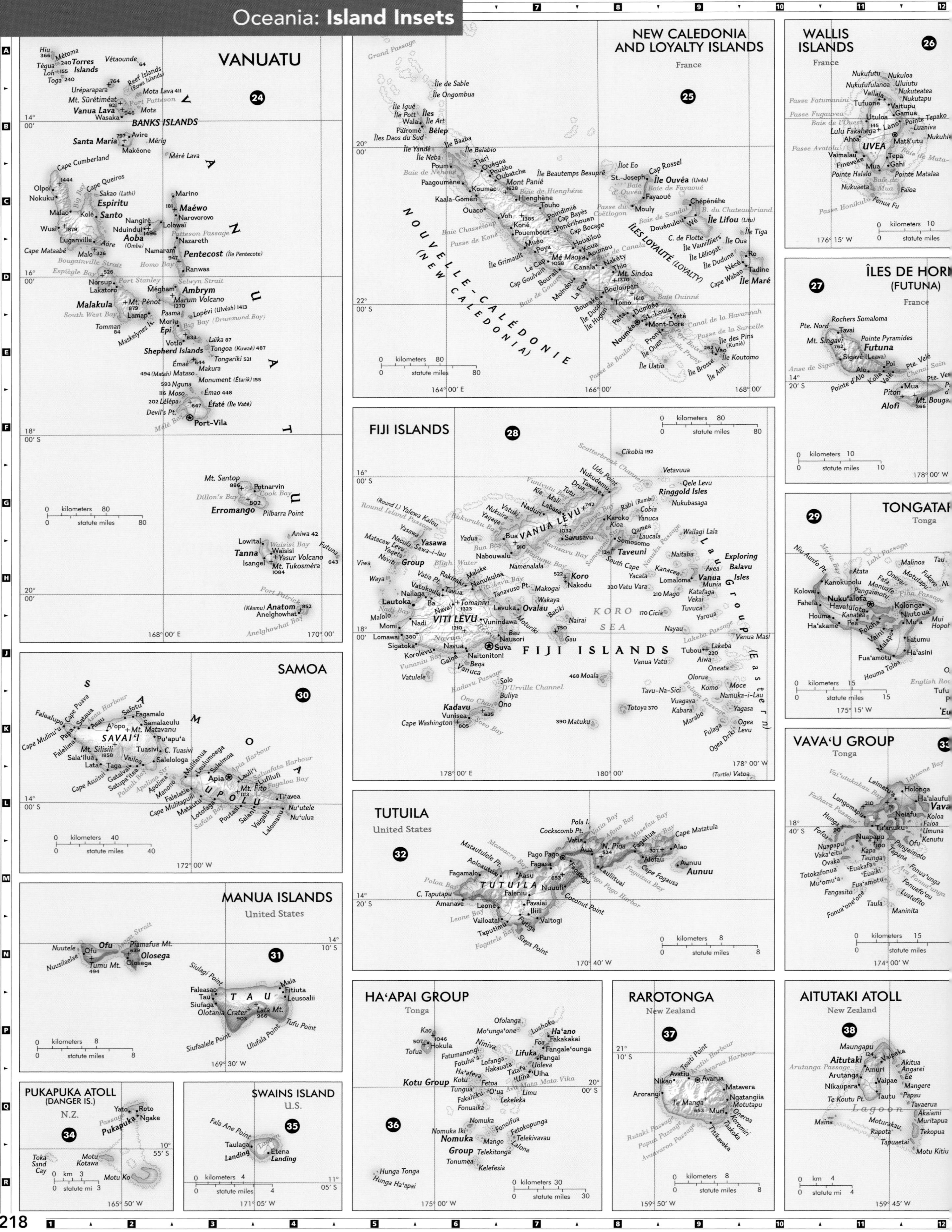
VANUATU
24
BANKS ISLANDS
Espiritu Santo
Malakula
Ambrym
Pentecost (Île Pentecote)
Maéwo
Aoba (Omba)
Epi
Shepherd Islands
Éfaté (Île Vaté)
Port-Vila
Erromango
Tanna
Anatom
VANUATU
NEW CALEDONIA AND LOYALTY ISLANDS
France
25
NOUVELLE-CALÉDONIE (NEW CALEDONIA)
ÎLES LOYAUTÉ (LOYALTY)
Île Ouvéa (Uvéa)
Île Lifou (Lifu)
Île Maré
Nouméa
Île des Pins (Kunié)
WALLIS ISLANDS
France
26
UVEA
ÎLES DE HORN (FUTUNA)
France
27
Futuna
Alofi
FIJI ISLANDS
28
VITI LEVU
VANUA LEVU
Taveuni
Kadavu
Suva
Lau Group (Eastern)
KORO SEA
FIJI ISLANDS
TONGATAPU
Tonga
29
Nuku'alofa
SAMOA
30
SAVAI'I
UPOLU
Apia
MANUA ISLANDS
United States
31
Ofu
Olosega
TAU
TUTUILA
United States
32
Pago Pago
Aunuu
VAVA'U GROUP
Tonga
33
Neiafu
PUKAPUKA ATOLL (DANGER IS.)
N.Z.
34
Pukapuka
SWAINS ISLAND
U.S.
35
HA'APAI GROUP
Tonga
36
Lifuka
Kotu Group
Nomuka Group
RAROTONGA
New Zealand
37
Avarua
AITUTAKI ATOLL
New Zealand
38
Aitutaki
Lagoon

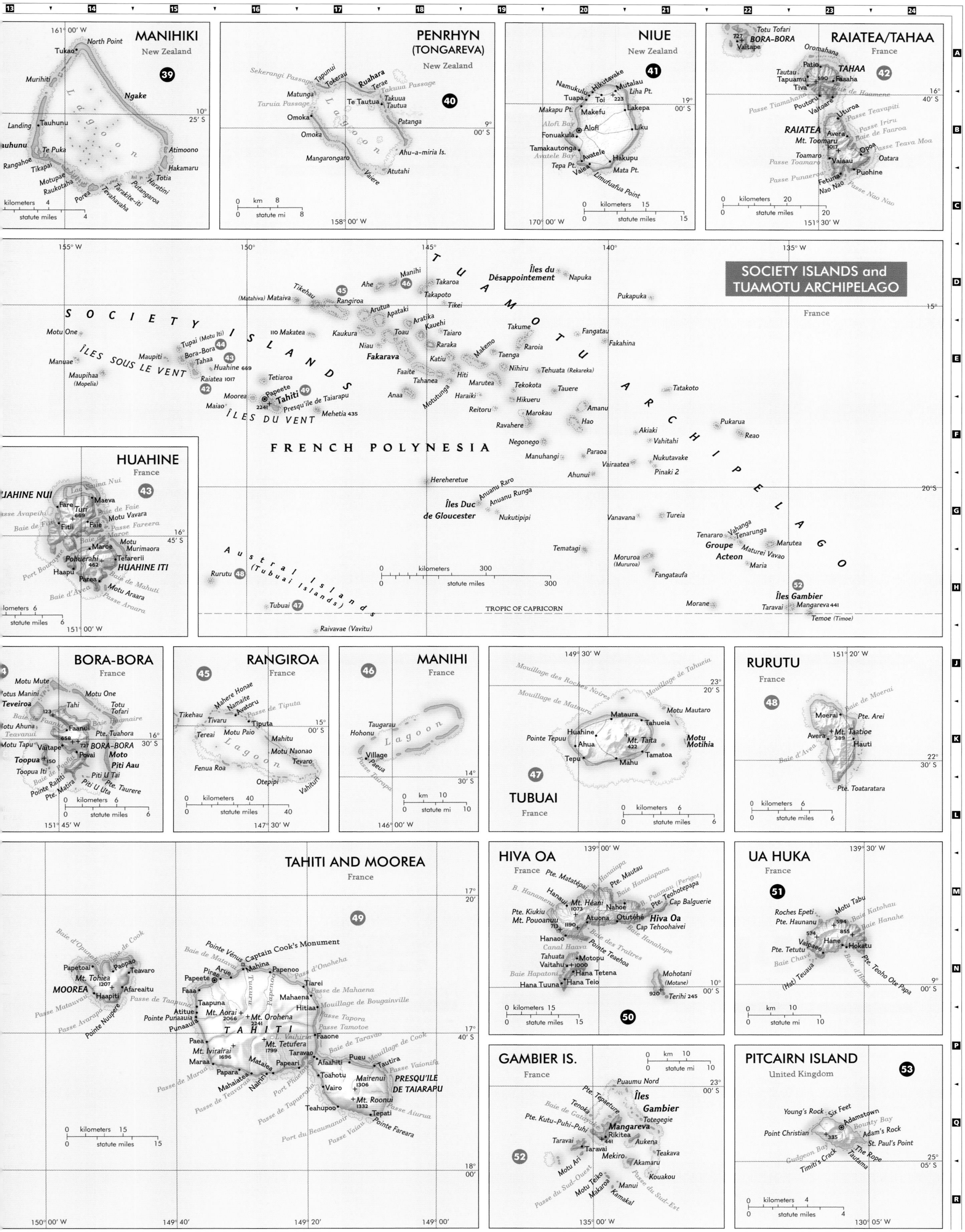

MANIHIKI
New Zealand
39
161° 00' W
North Point
Tukao
Murihiti
Ngake
Lagoon
10° 25' S
Landing
Tauhunu
Te Puka
Atimoono
Rangahoe
Tikapai
Hakamaru
Motupae
Raukotaha
Totia
Haratini
Porea
Tevahavaha
Tarakite-iti
Putangaroa
kilometers 4
statute miles 4
PENRHYN (TONGAREVA)
New Zealand
40
Sekerangi Passage
Tapunui
Tokerau
Ruahara
Terae
Takuua Passage
Matunga
Taruia Passage
Te Tautua
Takuua
Tautua
Omoka
Lagoon
Patanga
9° 00' S
Omoka
Mangarongaro
Ahu-a-miria Is.
Atutahi
Vaiere
0 km 8
0 statute mi 8
158° 00' W
NIUE
New Zealand
41
Namukulu
Hikutavake
Mutalau
Liha Pt.
Tuapa
Toi
223
19° 00' S
Makapu Pt.
Makefu
Lakepa
Alofi Bay
Alofi
Liku
Fonuakula
Tamakautonga
Avatele Bay
Avatele
Hakupu
Tepa Pt.
Vaiea
Mata Pt.
Limufuafua Point
0 kilometers 15
0 statute miles 15
170° 00' W
RAIATEA/TAHAA
France
42
Totu Tofari
727
BORA-BORA
Vaitape
Oromahana
Patio
TAHAA
Tautau
Tapuamu
590
Faaaha
Tiva
Baie de Haamene
16° 40' S
Passe Tiamahana
Poutoru
Vaitoare
Passe Teavapiti
Uturoa
Passe Iriru
RAIATEA
Avera
Baie de Faaroa
Mt. Toomaru
1017
Opoa
Passe Teava Moa
Toamaro
Passe Toamaro
Vaiaau
Oatara
Puohine
Passe Punaeroa
Fetuna
Nao Nao
Passe Nao Nao
0 kilometers 20
0 statute miles 20
151° 30' W
SOCIETY ISLANDS and TUAMOTU ARCHIPELAGO
France
155° W
150°
145°
140°
135° W
15°
20°S
TUAMOTU ARCHIPELAGO
SOCIETY ISLANDS
ÎLES SOUS LE VENT
ÎLES DU VENT
FRENCH POLYNESIA
Îles du Désappointement
Napuka
Manihi
46
Takaroa
Tikehau
45
Ahe
(Matahiva) Mataiva
Rangiroa
Takapoto
Tikei
Pukapuka
Arutua
Apataki
Motu One
110 Makatea
Kaukura
Aratika
Kauehi
Takume
Fangatau
Tupai (Motu Iti)
Toau
Taiaro
Fakahina
Bora-Bora
44
Niau
Raraka
Maupiti
Tahaa
43
Fakarava
Makemo
Raroia
Manuae
Huahine 669
Katiu
Taenga
Maupihaa (Mopelia)
Raiatea 1017
Tetiaroa
Faaite
Hiti
Nihiru
Tehuata (Rekareka)
42
Tahanea
Marutea
Tekokota
Tauere
Tatakoto
Papeete
Moorea
Tahiti
49
Motutunga
Haraiki
Hikueru
Maiao
2241
Presqu'île de Taiarapu
Anaa
Reitoru
Marokau
Amanu
Mehetia 435
Ravahere
Hao
Pukarua
Akiaki
Reao
Negonego
Vahitahi
Manuhangi
Paraoa
Nukutavake
Vairaatea
Ahunui
Pinaki 2
Hereheretue
Anuanu Raro
Îles Duc de Gloucester
Anuanu Runga
Nukutipipi
Vanavana
Tureia
Tenararo
Vahanga
Tenarunga
Groupe Acteon
Maturei Vavao
Marutea
Maria
Tematagi
Moruroa (Mururoa)
Fangataufa
Austral Islands (Tubuai Islands)
Rurutu
48
0 kilometers 300
0 statute miles 300
52
Îles Gambier
Morane
Mangareva 441
Taravai
Tubuai
47
TROPIC OF CAPRICORN
Temoe (Timoe)
Raivavae (Vavitu)
HUAHINE
France
43
Lac Fauna Nui
HUAHINE NUI
Maeva
Fare
Turi
Passe Avapeihi
669
Baie de Faie
Fitii
Motu Vavara
Faie
Baie de Fitii
Passe Fareera
Baie de Maroe
16° 45' S
Maroe
Motu Murimaora
Port Bourayne
Fitii
Tefarerii
Pohuerahi
462
HUAHINE ITI
Haapu
Parea
Baie de Mahuti
Baie d'Avea
Motu Araara
Passe Araara
kilometers 6
statute miles 6
151° 00' W
BORA-BORA
France
44
Motu Mute
Motu Manini
Motu One
Teveiroa
Tahi
Totu Tofari
Motu Ahuna
123
Baie Faanui
Baie Haamaire
Teavanui
Faanui
Pte. Tuahora
16° 30' S
Motu Tapu
Vaitape
658
727
BORA-BORA
Povai
Moto
Toopua
Iso
Baie de Povai
Piti Aau
Toopua Iti
Piti U Tai
Pointe Raititi
Pte. Matira
Piti U Uta
Pte. Taurere
0 kilometers 6
0 statute miles 6
151° 45' W
RANGIROA
France
45
Mahere Honae
Namaite
Avatoru
Passe de Tiputa
Tikehau
Tivaru
Tiputa
15° 00' S
Tereai
Motu Paio
Mahitu
Lagoon
Motu Naonao
Tevaro
Fenua Roa
Otepipi
Vahituri
0 kilometers 40
0 statute miles 40
147° 30' W
MANIHI
France
46
Taugarau
Hohonu
Lagoon
Village
Paeua
Passe Tairapa
14° 30' S
0 km 10
0 statute mi 10
146° 00' W
149° 30' W
Mouillage des Roches Noires
Mouillage de Tahueia
Mouillage de Mataura
23° 20' S
Mataura
Motu Mautaro
Tahueia
Huahine
Pointe Tepuu
Ahua
Mt. Taita
422
Motu Motihia
Tepu
Tamatoa
Mahu
47
TUBUAI
France
0 kilometers 6
0 statute miles 6
RURUTU
France
151° 20' W
48
Baie de Moerai
Moerai
Pte. Arei
Avera
Mt. Taatioe
389
Hauti
Baie d'Avea
22° 30' S
Pte. Toataratara
0 kilometers 6
0 statute miles 6
TAHITI AND MOOREA
France
17° 20'
49
Baie d'Opunohu
Baie de Cook
Papetoai
Paopao
Teavaro
Mt. Tohiea
1207
MOOREA
Afareaitu
Haapiti
Passe Matauvau
Passe Avaroa
Pointe Nuupere
Pointe Vénus
Captain Cook's Monument
Baie de Matavai
Mahina
Papenoo
Arue
Pirae
Papeete
Tuauru
Papenoo
Passe d'Onoheha
Tiarei
Faaa
Passe de Mahaena
Mahaena
Passe de Taapuna
Taapuna
Hitiaa
Mouillage de Bougainville
Atitue
Mt. Aorai
2066
Mt. Orohena
2241
Passe Tapora
Pointe Punaauia
Punaauia
TAHITI
Passe Tamotoe
17° 40' S
L. Vaihiria
Faaone
Paea
Mt. Tetufera
1799
Baie de Taravao
Mouillage de Cook
Mt. Ivirairai
1696
Taravao
Maraa
Mataiea
Papeari
Afaahiti
Pueu
Tautira
Papara
Passe Vaionifa
Passe de Maraa
Mahaiatea
Nanu
Toahotu
Mairenui
1306
PRESQU'ILE DE TAIARAPU
Port Phaeton
Vairo
Passe de Teavaraa
Mt. Roonui
1332
Passe de Tapuaeraha
Teahupoo
Tepati
Passe Aiurua
Port du Beaumanoir
Passe Vaiau
Pointe Fareara
0 kilometers 15
0 statute miles 15
18° 00'
150° 00' W
149° 40'
149° 20'
149° 00'
HIVA OA
France
139° 00' W
Pte. Matatepai
Hanaiapa
Pte. Mautau
Baie Hanaiapaoa
B. Hanamenu
Hanaui
Mt. Heani
1073
Puamau (Perigot)
Pte. Teohotepapa
Cap Balguerie
Nahoe
Pte. Kiukiu
Atuona
Mt. Pouoanuu
713
1190
Otutého
Hiva Oa
Cap Tehoohaivei
Baie des Traitres
Baie Hanahupe
Hanaoo
Canal Haava
Pointe Teaehoa
Tahuata
Motopu
Vaitahu
1000
Baie Hapatoni
Hana Tetena
Mohotani (Motane)
Hana Tuuna
Hana Teio
920
Terihi 245
10° 00' S
0 kilometers 15
0 statute miles 15
50
UA HUKA
France
139° 30' W
51
Motu Tabu
Baie Katohau
Roches Epeti
Pte. Haunanu
594
Baie Hanahe
574
855
Pte. Tetutu
Vaipaee
Hane
Hokatu
Baie Chave
Baie d'Haavei
Pte. Teoho Ote Papa
(Hat) Teuaua
9° 00' S
0 km 10
0 statute mi 10
GAMBIER IS.
France
0 km 10
0 statute mi 10
Puaumu Nord
23° 00' S
Pte. Tepapature
Îles Gambier
Baie de Gatavake
Tenoka
Totegegie
Pte. Kutu-Puhi-Puhi
Mangareva
Rikitea
441
Taravai
Aukena
Taravai
Teakava
52
Mekiro
Akamaru
Motu Ari
Passe du Sud-Est
Kouakou
Passe du Sud-Ouest
Motu Teiko
Makaroa
Manui
Kamaka
135° 00' W
PITCAIRN ISLAND
United Kingdom
53
Young's Rock
Six Feet
Adamstown
Bounty Bay
Point Christian
335
Adam's Rock
St. Paul's Point
Gudgeon Bay
Timiti's Crack
The Rope
Tautama
25° 05' S
0 kilometers 4
0 statute miles 4
130° 05' W

Independent Nations

Fiji Islands

REPUBLIC OF THE FIJI ISLANDS

AREA 18,376 sq km (7,095 sq mi)
POPULATION 842,000
CAPITAL Suva 210,000
RELIGION Christian, Hindu, Muslim
LANGUAGE English (official), Fijian, Hindustani
LITERACY 94%
LIFE EXPECTANCY 68 years
GDP PER CAPITA $3,229
ECONOMY **IND:** tourism, sugar, clothing, copra **AGR:** sugarcane, coconuts, cassava (tapioca), rice; cattle; fish **EXP:** sugar, garments, gold, timber

Kiribati

REPUBLIC OF KIRIBATI

AREA 811 sq km (313 sq mi)
POPULATION 92,000
CAPITAL Tarawa 42,000
RELIGION Roman Catholic, Protestant
LANGUAGE I-Kiribati, English (official)
LITERACY NA
LIFE EXPECTANCY 63 years
GDP PER CAPITA $815
ECONOMY **IND:** fishing, handicrafts **AGR:** copra, taro, breadfruit, sweet potatoes; fish **EXP:** copra, coconuts, seaweed, fish

Marshall Islands

REPUBLIC OF THE MARSHALL ISLANDS

AREA 181 sq km (70 sq mi)
POPULATION 59,000
CAPITAL Majuro 25,000
RELIGION Protestant, Assembly of God, Roman Catholic
LANGUAGE Marshallese (official), English (official)
LITERACY 94%
LIFE EXPECTANCY 68 years
GDP PER CAPITA $1,797
ECONOMY **IND:** copra, tuna processing, tourism, craft items from shell, wood, and pearls **AGR:** coconuts, tomatoes, melons, taro; pigs **EXP:** copra cake, coconut oil, handicrafts, fish

Micronesia

FEDERATED STATES OF MICRONESIA

AREA 702 sq km (271 sq mi)
POPULATION 108,000
CAPITAL Palikir 7,000
RELIGION Roman Catholic, Protestant
LANGUAGE English (official), Trukese, Pohnpeian, Yapese, Kosrean
LITERACY 89%
LIFE EXPECTANCY 67 years
GDP PER CAPITA $2,072
ECONOMY **IND:** tourism, construction, fish processing, specialized aquaculture **AGR:** black pepper, tropical fruits and vegetables, coconuts, cassava (tapioca); pigs **EXP:** fish, garments, bananas, black pepper

Nauru

REPUBLIC OF NAURU

AREA 21 sq km (8 sq mi)
POPULATION 13,000
CAPITAL Yaren 5,000
RELIGION Protestant, Roman Catholic
LANGUAGE Nauruan (official), English
LITERACY NA
LIFE EXPECTANCY 61 years
GDP PER CAPITA $4,322
ECONOMY **IND:** phosphate mining, offshore banking, coconut products **AGR:** coconuts **EXP:** phosphates

Solomon Islands

SOLOMON ISLANDS

AREA 28,370 sq km (10,954 sq mi)
POPULATION 472,000
CAPITAL Honiara 56,000
RELIGION Protestant, Roman Catholic
LANGUAGE Melanesian pidgin, English (official), 120 indigenous languages
LITERACY NA
LIFE EXPECTANCY 62 years
GDP PER CAPITA $585
ECONOMY **IND:** fish (tuna), mining, timber **AGR:** cocoa beans, coconuts, palm kernels, rice; cattle; timber; fish **EXP:** timber, fish, copra, palm oil

Palau

REPUBLIC OF PALAU

AREA 489 sq km (189 sq mi)
POPULATION 21,000
CAPITAL Koror 14,000
RELIGION Roman Catholic, Protestant, Modekngei, Seventh-Day Adventist
LANGUAGE Palauan, Filipino, English, Chinese
LITERACY 92%
LIFE EXPECTANCY 70 years
GDP PER CAPITA $6,717
ECONOMY **IND:** tourism, craft items (from shell, wood, pearls), construction, garment making **AGR:** coconuts, copra, cassava (tapioca), sweet potatoes **EXP:** shellfish, tuna, copra, garments

Samoa

INDEPENDENT STATE OF SAMOA

AREA 2,831 sq km (1,093 sq mi)
POPULATION 188,000
CAPITAL Apia 40,000
RELIGION Congregationalist, Roman Catholic, Methodist, Latter-Day Saints, Assembly of God
LANGUAGE Samoan (Polynesian), English
LITERACY 100%
LIFE EXPECTANCY 73 years
GDP PER CAPITA $1,968
ECONOMY **IND:** food processing, building materials, auto parts **AGR:** coconuts, bananas, taro, yams **EXP:** fish, coconut oil and cream, copra, taro

Tonga

KINGDOM OF TONGA

AREA 748 sq km (289 sq mi)
POPULATION 102,000
CAPITAL Nuku'alofa 35,000
RELIGION Christian
LANGUAGE Tongan, English
LITERACY 99%
LIFE EXPECTANCY 71 years
GDP PER CAPITA $1,930
ECONOMY **IND:** tourism, fishing **AGR:** squash, coconuts, copra, bananas; fish **EXP:** squash, fish, vanilla beans, root crops

Tuvalu

TUVALU

AREA 26 sq km (10 sq mi)
POPULATION 10,000
CAPITAL Funafuti 6,000
RELIGION Church of Tuvalu (Congregationalist)
LANGUAGE Tuvaluan, English, Samoan, Kiribati
LITERACY NA
LIFE EXPECTANCY 64 years
GDP PER CAPITA $2,141
ECONOMY **IND:** fishing, tourism, copra **AGR:** coconuts; fish **EXP:** copra, fish

Vanuatu

REPUBLIC OF VANUATU

AREA 12,190 sq km (4,707 sq mi)
POPULATION 218,000
CAPITAL Port-Vila 34,000
RELIGION Presbyterian, Anglican, Roman Catholic, Seventh-Day Adventist, indigenous beliefs
LANGUAGE over 100 local languages, pidgin (known as Bislama or Bichelama)
LITERACY 74%
LIFE EXPECTANCY 67 years
GDP PER CAPITA $1,405
ECONOMY **IND:** food and fish freezing, wood processing, meat canning **AGR:** copra, coconuts, cocoa, coffee; beef; fish **EXP:** copra, beef, cocoa, timber

Dependencies

AUSTRALIA

SOVEREIGN LOCAL

Norfolk Island

TERRITORY OF NORFOLK ISLAND

AREA 35 sq km (14 sq mi)
POPULATION 2,000
CAPITAL Kingston 900
RELIGION Anglican, Roman Catholic, Uniting Church in Australia
LANGUAGE English (official), Norfolk
LITERACY NA
LIFE EXPECTANCY 78 years
GDP PER CAPITA NA
ECONOMY **IND:** tourism, light industry, ready mixed concrete **AGR:** pine and palm seed, cereals, vegetables, fruit; cattle **EXP:** postage stamps, pine and palm seed, avocados

Coral Sea Islands

CORAL SEA ISLANDS TERRITORY

AREA Less than 3 sq km (1 sq mi)
POPULATION none

UNITED KINGDOM

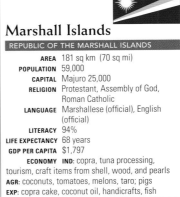

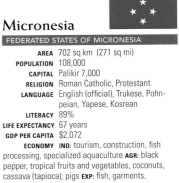

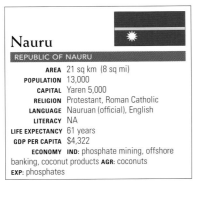

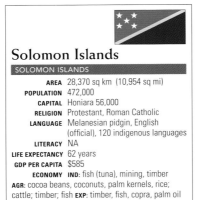

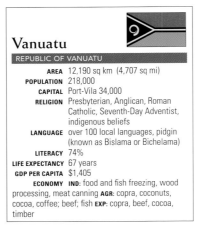

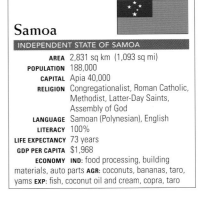

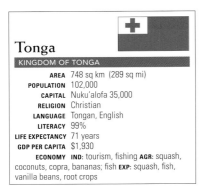

SOVEREIGN LOCAL

Pitcairn Islands

PITCAIRN, HENDERSON, DUCIE, & OENO IS.

AREA 47 sq km (18 sq mi)
POPULATION 45
CAPITAL Adamstown 50
RELIGION Seventh-Day Adventist
LANGUAGE English (official), Pitcairnese
LITERACY NA
LIFE EXPECTANCY NA
GDP PER CAPITA NA
ECONOMY **IND:** postage stamps, handicrafts, beekeeping, honey **AGR:** fruits and vegetables; goats **EXP:** fruits, vegetables, curios, stamps

Dependencies

FRANCE

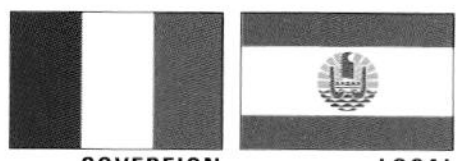
SOVEREIGN LOCAL

French Polynesia

OVERSEAS LANDS OF FRENCH POLYNESIA

AREA 4,167 sq km (1,608 sq mi)
POPULATION 255,000
CAPITAL Papeete 126,000
RELIGION Protestant, Roman Catholic
LANGUAGE French (official), Polynesian (official)
LITERACY 98%
LIFE EXPECTANCY 68 years
GDP PER CAPITA $19,605
ECONOMY **IND:** tourism, pearls, agricultural processing, handicrafts **AGR:** coconuts, vanilla, vegetables, fruits; poultry **EXP:** cultured pearls, coconut products, mother-of-pearl, vanilla

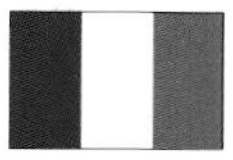

New Caledonia

TERR. OF NEW CALED. AND DEPENDENCIES

AREA 19,060 sq km (7,359 sq mi)
POPULATION 227,000
CAPITAL Nouméa 140,000
RELIGION Roman Catholic, Protestant
LANGUAGE French (official), 33 Melanesian-Polynesian dialects
LITERACY 91%
LIFE EXPECTANCY 73 years
GDP PER CAPITA $17,538
ECONOMY **IND:** nickel mining and smelting **AGR:** vegetables; beef **EXP:** ferronickels, nickel ore, fish

SOVEREIGN LOCAL

Wallis and Futuna

TERR. OF THE WALLIS AND FUTUNA ISLANDS

AREA 161 sq km (62 sq mi)
POPULATION 15,000
CAPITAL Matâ'utu 1,000
RELIGION Roman Catholic
LANGUAGE Wallisian (indigenous Polynesian language), Futunian, French
LITERACY 50%
LIFE EXPECTANCY 74 years
GDP PER CAPITA $3,800
ECONOMY **IND:** copra, handicrafts, fishing, lumber **AGR:** breadfruit, yams, taro, bananas; pigs **EXP:** copra, chemicals, construction materials

Clipperton Island

CLIPPERTON ISLAND

AREA 7 sq km (3 sq mi)
POPULATION None

NEW ZEALAND

SOVEREIGN LOCAL

Cook Islands

COOK ISLANDS

AREA 240 sq km (93 sq mi)
POPULATION 13,000
CAPITAL Avarua 13,000
RELIGION Cook Islands Christian Church, Roman Catholic, Seventh-Day Adventists
LANGUAGE English (official), Maori
LITERACY 95%
LIFE EXPECTANCY 70 years
GDP PER CAPITA $8,945
ECONOMY **IND:** fruit processing, tourism, fishing, clothing **AGR:** copra, citrus, pineapples, tomatoes; pigs **EXP:** copra, papayas, fresh and canned citrus fruit, coffee

SOVEREIGN LOCAL

Niue

NIUE

AREA 263 sq km (102 sq mi)
POPULATION 2,000
CAPITAL Alofi 1,000
RELIGION Ekalesia Niue, Latter-Day Saints, Roman Catholic
LANGUAGE Niuean, English
LITERACY 95%
LIFE EXPECTANCY 70 years
GDP PER CAPITA $3,600
ECONOMY **IND:** tourism, handicrafts, food processing **AGR:** coconuts, passion fruit, honey, limes; pigs **EXP:** canned coconut cream, copra, honey, vanilla

SOVEREIGN LOCAL

Tokelau

TOKELAU

AREA 12 sq km (5 sq mi)
POPULATION 2,000
CAPITAL none
RELIGION Congregational Christian Church, Roman Catholic
LANGUAGE Tokelauan (a Polynesian language), English
LITERACY NA
LIFE EXPECTANCY 69 years
GDP PER CAPITA $1,000
ECONOMY **IND:** copra production, woodworking, plaited craft goods, stamps **AGR:** coconuts, copra, breadfruit, papayas; pigs **EXP:** stamps, copra, handicrafts

UNITED STATES

SOVEREIGN LOCAL

American Samoa

TERRITORY OF AMERICAN SAMOA

AREA 199 sq km (77 sq mi)
POPULATION 63,000
CAPITAL Pago Pago 52,000
RELIGION Christian Congregationalist, Roman Catholic, Protestant
LANGUAGE Samoan, English
LITERACY 97%
LIFE EXPECTANCY 75 years
GDP PER CAPITA $8,000
ECONOMY **IND:** tuna canneries (largely supplied by foreign fishing vessels), handicrafts **AGR:** bananas, coconuts, vegetables, taro; dairy products **EXP:** canned tuna

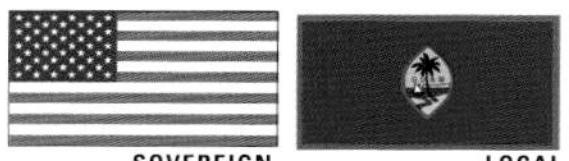
SOVEREIGN LOCAL

Guam

TERRITORY OF GUAM

AREA 561 sq km (217 sq mi)
POPULATION 169,000
CAPITAL Hagåtña (Agana) 140,000
RELIGION Roman Catholic
LANGUAGE English, Chamorro, Philippine languages
LITERACY 99%
LIFE EXPECTANCY 78 years
GDP PER CAPITA $15,000
ECONOMY **IND:** US military, tourism, construction, transshipment services **AGR:** fruits, copra, vegetables; eggs **EXP:** transshipments of refined petroleum products, construction materials, fish, food and beverage products

SOVEREIGN LOCAL

Northern Mariana Islands

COMMONWEALTH OF THE N. MARIANA IS.

AREA 477 sq km (184 sq mi)
POPULATION 80,000
CAPITAL Saipan 71,000
RELIGION Christian, traditional beliefs
LANGUAGE Philippine languages, Chinese, Chamorro, English
LITERACY 97%
LIFE EXPECTANCY 75 years
GDP PER CAPITA $12,500
ECONOMY **IND:** tourism, construction, garments, handicrafts **AGR:** coconuts, fruits, vegetables; cattle **EXP:** garments

Baker Island

BAKER ISLAND

AREA 1.4 sq km (0.5 sq mi)
POPULATION None

Howland Island

HOWLAND ISLAND

AREA 1.6 sq km (0.6 sq mi)
POPULATION None

Jarvis Island

JARVIS ISLAND

AREA 4.5 sq km (1.7 sq mi)
POPULATION None

Johnston Atoll

JOHNSTON ATOLL

AREA 2.8 sq km (1.1 sq mi)
POPULATION None

Kingman Reef

KINGMAN REEF

AREA 1 sq km (0.4 sq mi)
POPULATION None

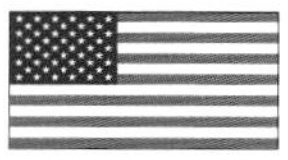

Midway Islands

MIDWAY ISLANDS

AREA 6.2 sq km (2.4 sq mi)
POPULATION None

Palmyra Atoll

PALMYRA ATOLL

AREA 11.9 sq km (4.6 sq mi)
POPULATION None

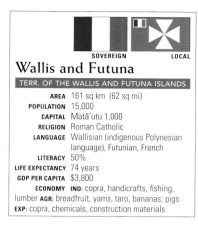

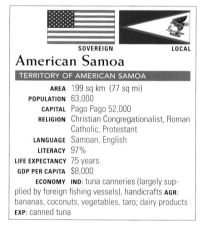

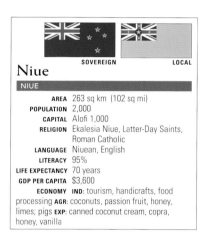

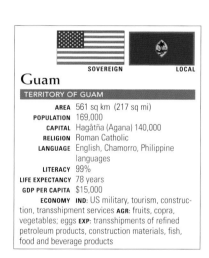

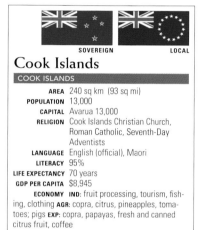

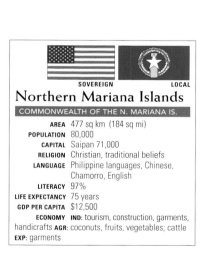

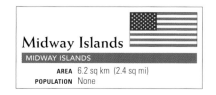

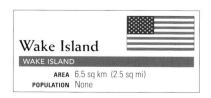

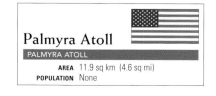

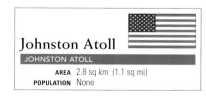

Wake Island

WAKE ISLAND

AREA 6.5 sq km (2.5 sq mi)
POPULATION None

A tabular iceberg drifts in the Bransfield Strait near the tip of the Antarctic Peninsula. These types of icebergs, which break off of ice shelves, can be very large. B-15, which calved from the Ross Ice Shelf in March 2000, measured nearly 4,244 square miles (10,990 sq km), the size of Jamaica, before it broke into relatively smaller bergs.

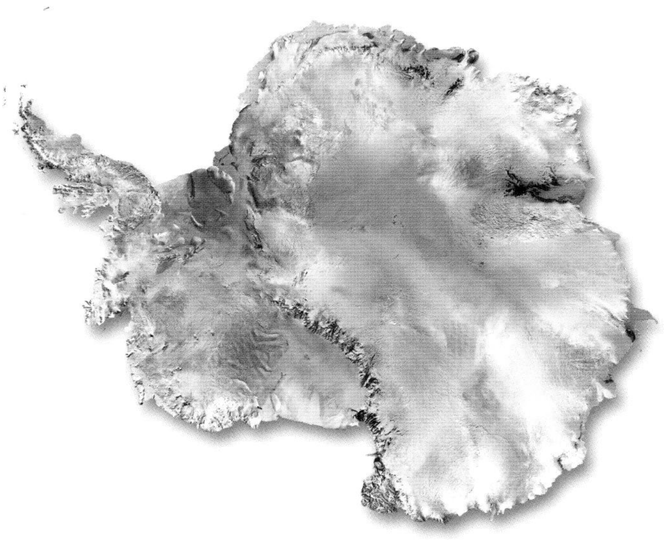

Antarctica

Often called the last wilderness on Earth, Antarctica's unspoiled expanses of austere frozen beauty remain largely untouched by humans. Antarctica is the driest, coldest, windiest, and least populated of Earth's seven continents, and an average elevation of 8,000 ft (2,438 m) makes it the highest as well. It is larger than Europe or Australia; its 5.1 million square miles (13.2 million sq km) of ice-shrouded land sit at the bottom of the world.

Antarctica's ice cap, the greatest body of ice in the world, holds some 70 percent of Earth's fresh water. Yet despite all this ice and water, the Antarctic interior averages only two inches of precipitation per year, making it the largest ice desert in the world; the little snow that does fall, however, almost never melts.

The immensely heavy ice sheet, averaging over a mile (1.6 km) thick and reaching almost three miles (4.8 km) thick in places, compresses much of the continent's surface to below sea level. The weight actually deforms the South Pole, creating a slightly pear-shaped Earth.

Beneath the ice exists a continent of valleys, lakes, islands, and mountains, little dreamed of until the compilation of more than 2.5 million ice-thickness measurements revealed startling topography below. Less than 2 percent of Antarctica actually breaks through the ice cover to reveal stretches of coastline, islands, and features such as the outstanding Transantarctic Mountains, which extend for 1,800 miles (2,898 km) and separate East and West Antarctica.

In spite of perpetual light during the Antarctic summer (December to March), little heat accumulates because the white, snowy landscape reflects as much as 90 percent of the sun's incoming rays. During the half year of darkness, terrible cold and storms buffet the continent. The winter of 1983 saw the lowest temperature ever recorded on Earth—minus 128.6°F (-89.2°C).

Annual winter temperatures over the elevated central plateau average minus 80°F (-62.2°C), and this cold season causes the ice around Antarctica to grow quickly. Sea ice averaging six feet (2 m) deep more than doubles the size of the continent, extending outward to create a belt ranging from 300 miles to more than 1,000 miles (483–1,610 km) wide.

In spring, melting ice coincides with calving of huge white and blue-green icebergs from the Antarctic glaciers. The largest iceberg ever spotted, in 1956, measured 208 miles (335 km) long by 60 miles (97 km) wide, slightly larger than Belgium.

Antarctica's Southern Ocean, which holds 10 percent of the world's seawater, swirls in rhythm with the Antarctic Circumpolar Current, the largest, fastest current in the world, which sweeps clockwise around the globe unimpeded by any land. These high southern latitudes experience extremes of wind and weather. At around 60° south latitude, a remarkable interface of relatively warm waters from the southern Atlantic, Indian, and Pacific Oceans and the cold Southern Ocean creates conditions for an eruption of rich nutrients, phytoplankton, and zooplankton. These form the base for a flourishing marine ecosystem. Though limited in numbers of species—for example, only about 120 kinds of the world's 20,000 fish swim here—Antarctica's animal life has adapted extremely well to so harsh a climate. Seasonal feeding and energy storage in fats exemplify this specialization. Well-known animals of the far south include seals, whales, and distinctive birds such as flightless penguins, albatrosses, terns, and petrels.

PHYSICAL GEOGRAPHY Every summer thousands of scientists travel to Antarctica to obtain vital information about Earth's weather and ecology and the state of the southernmost continent. This interest attests to the region's role as a pristine laboratory, where measurements and rates of change in numerous scientific fields can point to larger issues of the world's environmental health.

Antarctica's oceanic and atmospheric system—indicator and element of climate change—is a main area of focus. Oceanographers attempt to understand more fully the global exchange of heat, sea-ice dynamics, salt and trace elements, and the entire marine biosphere. Other important research has included the 1985 discovery of a hole in Earth's protective ozone layer by scientists at the British Halley research station. This find brought to prominence a major ecological threat.

Ice and sediment cores provide insight into the world's ancient climate and allow for comparison with conditions today. Studies of the Antarctic ice sheet help predict future sea levels, important news for the three billion people who live in coastal areas. If the Antarctic ice sheet were to melt, global seas would rise by an estimated 200 feet, inundating many oceanic islands and gravely altering the world's coastlines.

Three basic water masses comprise the Southern Ocean: Antarctic Surface Water, Circumpolar Deep Water, and Antarctic Bottom Water. Sharp boundaries separate the water masses, each with its own characteristics. These differences drive circulation around the continent and contribute to the global heat engine and overall transfer of energy around the world.

Prominent physical features include the Vinson Massif, Antarctica's highest mountain at 16,067 feet (4,897 m). Discovered only in 1958 by U.S. Navy aircraft, it was first climbed by an American team in 1966.

The Antarctic Peninsula, reaching like a long arm 800 miles (1,288 km) into the Southern Ocean toward the tip of South America, is made up of a mountain range and many islands linked together by ice. Seals, penguins, and other sea birds find it particularly suitable, and the peninsula's relative accessibility makes it the Antarctic area most visited by humans.

The continent's only sizable river, the Onyx, arises from a coastal glacier near McMurdo Sound. Every summer its waters flow inland for some 20 miles (32 km), replenishing and raising the surface level of Lake Vanda, one of several lakes in the Dry Valleys. These valleys, free of snow and ice unlike the rest of Antarctica, were created by ancient glaciers. They stretch to the coast from the Transantarctic Mountains, a range high enough here to prevent the great Polar Plateau ice sheet from flowing down to the sea through the Dry Valleys, perhaps the driest places on Earth.

Immense ice shelves, produced by the main plateau disgorging masses of ice, rim much of the continent's coast and extend far into the sea. Largest are the Ross Ice Shelf, the size of France, and the Ronne Ice Shelf.

Special names exist for the many different types of ice: frazil ice, an early stage of sea-ice growth in which crystals below the surface form an unstructured slush; nilas, a thin sheen of ice on the sea surface that bends but does not break with wave action; pancake ice, named for its flattened circular shape; pack ice, frozen sea water and floating ice driven together to form a continuous mass; and fast ice, that part of the sea-ice cover attached to land.

Scientists seeking to understand sea ice are suspended above the icescape. Pancake ice forms when a thin surface film of ice crystals breaks up and thickens into irregular disks. These disks can measure from 1 to 10 feet (0.3–3 m) in diameter. Constant battering of the disks against one another causes the turned-up rims.

CULTURE, HISTORY, AND EXPLORATION The search for Antarctica represented the last great adventure of global exploration. British Capt. James Cook crossed three times into Antarctic waters between 1772 and 1775 and was probably the first to cross the Antarctic Circle. Though he never saw the continent, he believed in "a tract of land at the Pole that is the source of all the ice that is spread over this vast Southern Ocean."

His observations of marine mammals in great numbers lured whalers and sealers into the freezing southern waters in search of skins and oil. First sightings of the continent then followed in 1820.

Scientists seeking the south magnetic pole included British naval officer James Clark Ross, who between 1839–43 charted unknown territory, including a giant ice shelf later named after him, and located the approximate position of the south magnetic pole—the point toward which a compass needle points from any direction throughout surrounding areas.

In 1895 Norwegian whalers landed on the continent beyond the Antarctic Peninsula for the first time, and in 1898 a major Belgian scientific expedition overwintered in the Antarctic when their ship became stuck in pack ice for almost 13 months.

Douglas Mawson reached the south magnetic pole as part of Ernest Shackleton's 1907 Nimrod expedition. Later, Mawson led the Australasian Antarctic Expedition (1911–14), which produced observations in magnetism, geology, biology, and meteorology.

A race to reach the South Geographic Pole came to a climax in 1911–12. Norwegian Roald Amundsen's expedition reached the South Pole on December 14, 1911, after 97 days on the move, relying on husky dogs to pull their sleds. Simultaneously, the British team of Robert Falcon Scott and four companions set off unaware of Amundsen's swifter, better-managed effort. Scott's use of Manchurian ponies proved a mistake; his team reached the Pole 34 days later, only to find the Norwegian flag flying. The five men began the bitter return trip, but succumbed to cold, hunger, exhaustion, and bad weather, just 11 miles (18 km) from supplies. All died.

Another epic adventure involved Ernest Shackleton, whose British expedition aimed to traverse the entire continent. In 1915 Shackleton's main party of 28 men became stranded when sea ice trapped and crushed their ship. After more than a year on drifting ice, they sailed in lifeboats to Elephant Island at the tip of the Antarctic Peninsula. Shackleton and five others then embarked on an astonishing 800-mile (1,288 km) journey in a small boat to South Georgia, from where he eventually rescued his other men.

In 1935 Caroline Mikkelsen, wife of a Norwegian whaling captain, became the first woman to stand on Antarctica. Almost a dozen years later the U.S. Navy brought 4,700 men, 13 ships, and 23 aircraft to the continent, using icebreakers for the first time. The vast enterprise mapped large areas of the coastline and interior and took 70,000 aerial photographs.

The modern scientific era arrived with the 18-month-long International Geophysical Year (IGY, 1957–58), when many nations advanced knowledge of the continent. The Antarctic Treaty, signed in 1959 by 12 leading IGY participants, has done much to protect Antarctica.

Today about 50 research stations stand at many sites around Antarctica, and an ever shifting population, including tourists, can reach as high as 23,000 people in the summer. Tourism brings its own troubles. Recently, species of non-native grasses, presumably carried on visitors' clothing, have been found on the continent. Further unintentional aliens, such as algae, crustaceans, and parasites arrive on floating plastic bottles and other man-made debris.

MINERALS AND ECONOMY Many believe Antarctica has great resource wealth, but the harsh climate, short work season, and need to drill through thick ice make the recovery of these resources difficult.

Minerals under the ice include gold, uranium, cobalt, chromium, nickel, copper, iron, and platinum, as well as potentially large deposits of diamonds. Oil probably exists below the ocean floor, and coal deposits have been detected along the coast and throughout the Transantarctic Mountains.

A pressing reason to limit mineral exploration and drilling is Antarctica's extreme fragility. Sensitive plants, including rare moss beds on the Antarctic Peninsula, take three to four hundred years to grow, and a single human boot can cause tremendous damage.

In January 1998 an addition to the Antarctic Treaty, known as the Madrid Protocol, went into force, deeming Antarctica a natural reserve devoted to peace and science. It specifically banned mining and mineral exploitation of any kind until 2048.

But pressure builds yearly to find new mineral and petroleum deposits. Despite the ban, Russia and other countries appear to be actively exploring Antarctic oil, gas, and mineral resources. Also significant is the growing commercialization of Southern Ocean fisheries. Particularly vulnerable are the tiny shrimp-like krill that form a vital part of Antarctica's food chain. The collapse of fish and krill species might be analogous to the wholesale slaughter of fur seal populations in the late 1700s and early 1800s and the near destruction of the Southern Ocean's whales in the 20th century.

Antarctica already witnesses vehicle pollution; dumping of plastics, solid wastes, food, and batteries; burning of fossil fuels; and construction of roads and airstrips at the many scientific bases.

Even the most obvious resource of all—ice—may one day serve to relieve thirsty nations. Ships towing icebergs from Antarctica to all parts of the world could deliver this huge potential of fresh water, but at present such a project is simply too expensive.

Antarctica: Physical

Laurie I.
Orcadas Argentina
Coronation Island
S. ORKNEY ISLANDS
ANTARCTIC PENINSULA AREA STATIONS
Argentina
1 Esperanza.....C4
2 Jubany.....C3
3 Marambio.....C4
4 San Martín.....E5
Brazil
5 Comandante Ferraz.....C3
Chile
6 Escudero.....C3
7 General Bernardo O'Higgins.....C4
8 Presidente Eduardo Frei.....C3
China
9 Great Wall.....C3
Korea, South
10 King Sejong.....C3
Poland
11 Arctowski.....C3
Russia
12 Bellingshausen.....C3
Ukraine
13 Vernadsky.....D4
United Kingdom
14 Rothera.....E4
United States
15 Palmer.....D4
Uruguay
16 Artigas.....C3
Contributions from the following organizations are gratefully acknowledged: National Science Foundation, Washington, D.C.; Norwegian Polar Institute, Tromsø, Norway; British Antarctic Survey, Cambridge, United Kingdom; University of Cambridge, Scott Polar Institute, Cambridge, United Kingdom; U.S. Navy/NOAA Joint Ice Center, Washington, D.C.; U.S. Geological Survey; Lamont-Doherty Earth Observatory of Columbia University, Palisades, New York; National Aeronautics and Space Administration. Special thanks to Richard S. Williams, Jr., John Smellie, George E. Watson, and Guy Gutheridge.
F. G. von Bellingshausen, a Russian, sighted what may have been the mainland during his circumnavigation in 1820.
DECEPTION ISLAND
Deception Island is the horseshoe-shaped summit of a largely submerged volcano with a flooded caldera. It was particularly active in the 19th century and late 18th centuries, and saw eruptions during two episodes in the 20th century (1906-12 and 1967-70), resulting in the destruction of scientific stations on the island. Now it is a popular destination for tourists, many of whom swim in the volcanically-heated waters.
Edward Bransfield charted this region in 1820, establishing the British claim to discovery of Antarctica. The following year members of a sealing expedition led by John Davis, an American, went ashore at Hughes Bay, the first known landing on the continent.
This was the location of Shackleton Base, point of departure for the Commonwealth Trans-Antarctic Expedition, which crossed the continent by tractor in 1957-58. Led by Sir Vivian Fuchs, the expedition traveled 3,472 kilometers (2,157 mi) to Scott Base in 99 days. A major calving event in 1986 removed more than 11,500 sq km of ice from the Filchner Ice Shelf.
LARSEN ICE SHELF
During the past few decades, the Larsen Ice Shelf has been disintegrating on the north and along its eastern margin to the south. In recent years, the break up appears to have accelerated.
ANTARCTIC PENINSULA
A mountain range welded to clusters of islands by a relatively thin coat of ice, this 1,300-kilometer-long (800 mi) peninsula is popular with penguins and other seabirds, including gulls, skuas, and petrels and provides important habitat for several species of seals.
MINERALS
The mineral-resource potential of Antarctica is unknown. Geologists have located copper, lead, zinc, gold, and silver on the Antarctic Peninsula. Chromium and platinum may exist in the Pensacola Mountains, and low-grade coal lies in the Transantarctic Mountains. East Antarctica contains iron ore. Oil and natural gas are almost certainly present in sedimentary basins as deep as 14,000 m (46,000 ft) near Prydz Bay, the Ross Sea, and the Weddell Sea, but exploitation has been banned for at least 50 years. In 1991, Antarctic Treaty parties signed an agreement to prohibit "any activity relating to mineral resources other than scientific research." In 1998, Antarctic Treaty parties signed an agreement to establish the Committee for Environmental Protection (CEP). The CEP will help preserve the continent's immeasurable value as an archive of the world's climatic past and will enable it to continue to be a sensitive barometer of the planet's future.
HIGHEST POINT
At 4,897 m (16,067 ft) Vinson Massif is the highest elevation on Antarctica. It was climbed first by a U.S. team in 1966.
In 1898, Adrien de Gerlache de Gomery, a Belgian, led the first expedition to endure the Antarctic winter, after his ship froze in pack ice.
ELEVATION OF THE ICE SHEET
Many mountaintops rise higher than Antarctica's highest point—Vinson Massif, 16,067 feet—but with an average elevation of 8,000 feet, the continent ranks as Earth's highest. Asia, its closest competitor, averages 3,000 feet. Roughly dome shaped, the ice sheet conceals much of the bedrock relief below. The 1,800-mile-long Transantarctic Mountains rival the Rockies in height, but only the peaks break through the ice.
CLIMATE
The southern polar region is substantially colder than its northern counterpart. The lofty ice sheet reflects as much as 90 percent of solar radiation back to space, whereas in the Arctic Ocean ice partly melts in summer and the dark waters absorb heat. The temperature difference between the equatorial and polar regions drives atmospheric circulation. Because the South Pole is colder than the North, winds are stronger in the Southern Hemisphere. The ice sheet contains a climate record that extends back at least 200,000 years at some locations. Ice cores preserve a record of past atmospheric composition, volcanic eruptions, and other environmental information.
Bentley Subglacial Trench
Lowest known point in Antarctica -2555 m (-8383 ft) (Ice covered)
ICE SHELVES
Large areas of floating glacier ice fringe the coast of Antarctica. The two largest ice shelves are the Ross Ice Shelf and the Ronne Ice Shelf, both separated by glacier ice that is grounded below sea level. Large tabular icebergs periodically calve from ice shelves.
KATABATIC WINDS
Upper-level air circulates toward Antarctica from the tropics. By the time it reaches the continent, most moisture has been lost. Intensely chilled, the air descends over the central polar plateau, where winds are typically light. Then, like cold air spilling out of an open refrigerator, the air pours downhill with increasing speed until it blasts the coast at as much as 300 km (180 mi) an hour.
In 1841 Sir James Clark Ross penetrated the pack ice to the ice shelf now named f
Rear Adm. Richard E. Byrd, USN, established five scientific stations (named Little America I through V) on Ross Ice Shelf near the Bay of Whales, the first in 1928, the last in 1956. As the ice shelf flowed forward and calved off, the stations were carried out to sea.
METEORITES
More than 16,000 meteorite fragments have been recovered from blue-ice areas of the Antarctic ice sheet. Found in almost pristine condition and representing most classes of meteorites described previously from finds in Earth's other continents, they yield information about the origin and evolution of the solar system. Some meteorites found are thought to have their origin on Mars or the Earth's moon because of their unique geochemical composition.
Azimuthal Equidistant Projection
SCALE 1:13,759,000
1 CENTIMETER = 137 KILOMETERS; 1 INCH = 217 MILES
KILOMETERS
STATUTE MILES
Year-round research station
Blue figures on the continent indicate thickness of the ice in meters.
MOUNT EREBUS
Almost always observed with a vapor cloud issuing from its large summit crater, 3,794-meter-tall (12,488 ft) Erebus is an active volcano. A deep inner crater discovered in 1972 holds a bubbling lava lake.
In 1899, C. E. Borchgrevink led a British expedition that was the first to winter on the continent.
WEDDELL SEA
RONNE ICE SHELF
BELLINGSHAUSEN SEA
AMUNDSEN SEA
ROSS SEA
ROSS ICE SHELF
WEST ANTARCTICA
ANTARCTIC PENINSULA
GRAHAM LAND
PALMER LAND
ELLSWORTH LAND
MARIE BYRD LAND
ELLSWORTH MTS.
Vinson Massif (16067 ft) 4897
Sentinel Range
Heritage Range
HOLLICK-KENYON PLATEAU
ROCKEFELLER PLATEAU
TRANSANTARCTIC MOUNTAINS
QUEEN MAUD MTS.
PENSACOLA MOUNTAINS
BERKNER ISLAND
ALEXANDER ISLAND
THURSTON ISLAND
SOUTH SHETLAND ISLANDS
PALMER ARCHIPELAGO
BISCOE ISLANDS
Longitude West 170° of Greenwich

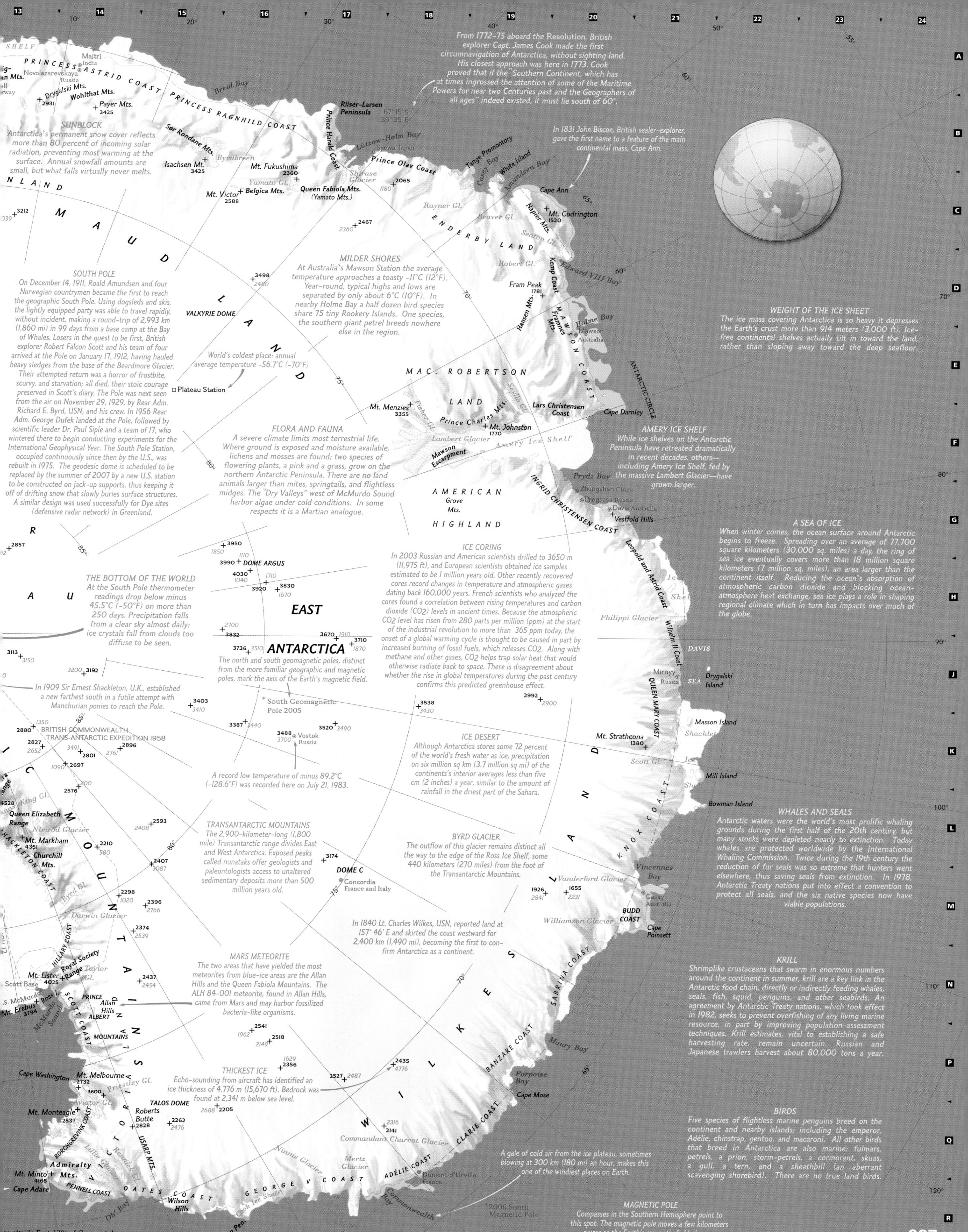
From 1772-75 aboard the Resolution, British explorer Capt. James Cook made the first circumnavigation of Antarctica, without sighting land. His closest approach was here in 1773. Cook proved that if the "Southern Continent, which has at times ingrossed the attention of some of the Maritime Powers for near two Centuries past and the Geographers of all ages" indeed existed, it must lie south of 60°.
In 1831 John Biscoe, British sealer-explorer, gave the first name to a feature of the main continental mass, Cape Ann.
SUNBLOCK
Antarctica's permanent snow cover reflects more than 80 percent of incoming solar radiation, preventing most warming at the surface. Annual snowfall amounts are small, but what falls virtually never melts.
MILDER SHORES
At Australia's Mawson Station the average temperature approaches a toasty -11°C (12°F). Year-round, typical highs and lows are separated by only about 6°C (10°F). In nearby Holme Bay a half dozen bird species share 75 tiny Rookery Islands. One species, the southern giant petrel breeds nowhere else in the region.
SOUTH POLE
On December 14, 1911, Roald Amundsen and four Norwegian countrymen became the first to reach the geographic South Pole. Using dogsleds and skis, the lightly equipped party was able to travel rapidly, without incident, making a round-trip of 2,993 km (1,860 mi) in 99 days from a base camp at the Bay of Whales. Losers in the quest to be first, British explorer Robert Falcon Scott and his team of four arrived at the Pole on January 17, 1912, having hauled heavy sledges from the base of the Beardmore Glacier. Their attempted return was a horror of frostbite, scurvy, and starvation; all died, their stoic courage preserved in Scott's diary. The Pole was next seen from the air on November 29, 1929, by Rear Adm. Richard E. Byrd, USN, and his crew. In 1956 Rear Adm. George Dufek landed at the Pole, followed by scientific leader Dr. Paul Siple and a team of 17, who wintered there to begin conducting experiments for the International Geophysical Year. The South Pole Station, occupied continuously since then by the U.S., was rebuilt in 1975. The geodesic dome is scheduled to be replaced by the summer of 2007 by a new U.S. station to be constructed on jack-up supports, thus keeping it off of drifting snow that slowly buries surface structures. A similar design was used successfully for Dye sites (defensive radar network) in Greenland.
World's coldest place: annual average temperature -56.7°C (-70°F)
WEIGHT OF THE ICE SHEET
The ice mass covering Antarctica is so heavy it depresses the Earth's crust more than 914 meters (3,000 ft). Ice-free continental shelves actually tilt in toward the land, rather than sloping away toward the deep seafloor.
AMERY ICE SHELF
While ice shelves on the Antarctic Peninsula have retreated dramatically in recent decades, others—including Amery Ice Shelf, fed by the massive Lambert Glacier—have grown larger.
FLORA AND FAUNA
A severe climate limits most terrestrial life. Where ground is exposed and moisture available, lichens and mosses are found; two species of flowering plants, a pink and a grass, grow on the northern Antarctic Peninsula. There are no land animals larger than mites, springtails, and flightless midges. The "Dry Valleys" west of McMurdo Sound harbor algae under cold conditions. In some respects it is a Martian analogue.
A SEA OF ICE
When winter comes, the ocean surface around Antarctica begins to freeze. Spreading over an average of 77,700 square kilometers (30,000 sq. miles) a day, the ring of sea ice eventually covers more than 18 million square kilometers (7 million sq. miles), an area larger than the continent itself. Reducing the ocean's absorption of atmospheric carbon dioxide and blocking ocean-atmosphere heat exchange, sea ice plays a role in shaping regional climate which in turn has impacts over much of the globe.
ICE CORING
In 2003 Russian and American scientists drilled to 3650 m (11,975 ft), and European scientists obtained ice samples estimated to be 1 million years old. Other recently recovered cores record changes in temperature and atmospheric gases dating back 160,000 years. French scientists who analyzed the cores found a correlation between rising temperatures and carbon dioxide (CO2) levels in ancient times. Because the atmospheric CO2 level has risen from 280 parts per million (ppm) at the start of the industrial revolution to more than 365 ppm today, the onset of a global warming cycle is thought to be caused in part by increased burning of fossil fuels, which releases CO2. Along with methane and other gases, CO2 helps trap solar heat that would otherwise radiate back to space. There is disagreement about whether the rise in global temperatures during the past century confirms this predicted greenhouse effect.
THE BOTTOM OF THE WORLD
At the South Pole thermometer readings drop below minus 45.5°C (-50°F) on more than 250 days. Precipitation falls from a clear sky almost daily; ice crystals fall from clouds too diffuse to be seen.
EAST ANTARCTICA
The north and south geomagnetic poles, distinct from the more familiar geographic and magnetic poles, mark the axis of the Earth's magnetic field.
South Geomagnetic Pole 2005
In 1909 Sir Ernest Shackleton, U.K., established a new farthest south in a futile attempt with Manchurian ponies to reach the Pole.
BRITISH COMMONWEALTH TRANS-ANTARCTIC EXPEDITION 1958
Vostok Russia
ICE DESERT
Although Antarctica stores some 72 percent of the world's fresh water as ice, precipitation on six million sq km (3.7 million sq mi) of the continent's interior averages less than five cm (2 inches) a year, similar to the amount of rainfall in the driest part of the Sahara.
A record low temperature of minus 89.2°C (-128.6°F) was recorded here on July 21, 1983.
WHALES AND SEALS
Antarctic waters were the world's most prolific whaling grounds during the first half of the 20th century, but many stocks were depleted nearly to extinction. Today whales are protected worldwide by the International Whaling Commission. Twice during the 19th century the reduction of fur seals was so extreme that hunters went elsewhere, thus saving seals from extinction. In 1978, Antarctic Treaty nations put into effect a convention to protect all seals, and the six native species now have viable populations.
TRANSANTARCTIC MOUNTAINS
The 2,900-kilometer-long (1,800 mile) Transantarctic range divides East and West Antarctica. Exposed peaks called nunataks offer geologists and paleontologists access to unaltered sedimentary deposits more than 500 million years old.
BYRD GLACIER
The outflow of this glacier remains distinct all the way to the edge of the Ross Ice Shelf, some 440 kilometers (270 miles) from the foot of the Transantarctic Mountains.
DOME C
Concordia France and Italy
In 1840 Lt. Charles Wilkes, USN, reported land at 157° 46′ E and skirted the coast westward for 2,400 km (1,490 mi), becoming the first to confirm Antarctica as a continent.
MARS METEORITE
The two areas that have yielded the most meteorites from blue-ice areas are the Allan Hills and the Queen Fabiola Mountains. The ALH 84-001 meteorite, found in Allan Hills, came from Mars and may harbor fossilized bacteria-like organisms.
KRILL
Shrimplike crustaceans that swarm in enormous numbers around the continent in summer, krill are a key link in the Antarctic food chain, directly or indirectly feeding whales, seals, fish, squid, penguins, and other seabirds. An agreement by Antarctic Treaty nations, which took effect in 1982, seeks to prevent overfishing of any living marine resource, in part by improving population-assessment techniques. Krill estimates, vital to establishing a safe harvesting rate, remain uncertain. Russian and Japanese trawlers harvest about 80,000 tons a year.
THICKEST ICE
Echo-sounding from aircraft has identified an ice thickness of 4,776 m (15,670 ft). Bedrock was found at 2,341 m below sea level.
BIRDS
Five species of flightless marine penguins breed on the continent and nearby islands; including the emperor, Adélie, chinstrap, gentoo, and macaroni. All other birds that breed in Antarctica are also marine: fulmars, petrels, a prion, storm-petrels, a cormorant, skuas, a gull, a tern, and a sheathbill (an aberrant scavenging shorebird). There are no true land birds.
A gale of cold air from the ice plateau, sometimes blowing at 300 km (180 mi) an hour, makes this one of the windiest places on Earth.
MAGNETIC POLE
Compasses in the Southern Hemisphere point to this spot. The magnetic pole moves a few kilometers a year as the Earth's magnetic field changes.
2006 South Magnetic Pole
Longitude East 170° of Greenwich

Elevation of the Ice Sheet

Antarctica is Earth's coldest, driest, and on average highest continent (about 8,000 ft; 2,438 m). The continent is covered by a vast ice sheet that blankets over 96 percent of the land mass. The highest point, located in East Antarctica, rises to 13,222 feet (4,030 m). The ice sheet is interrupted only by occasional mountain peaks that pierce the ice. One such peak is the Vinson Massif, Antarctica's highest point, which reaches an elevation of 16,067 feet (4,897 m) and is located in West Antarctica. Otherwise the icy surface is smooth (surface slopes rarely exceed more than 1 or 2 degrees). The shape of the ice sheet is determined in part by the weight of the ice itself, which causes the ice to flow outward. It is also determined in part by forces acting at the base of the ice sheet that tend to restrain it. The balance of these forces leads to a characteristically parabola-like shape. Departures from this simple shape occur as the ice from the interior domes spreads slowly over hills and valleys in the rocky base and where coastal mountain ranges channel the flow into outlet glaciers. Ice shelves form where there is sufficient ice to spread over the ocean. Ice shelves are the lowest and flattest parts of the ice sheet and are the source of the huge tabular icebergs that intermittently calve into the coastal ocean.

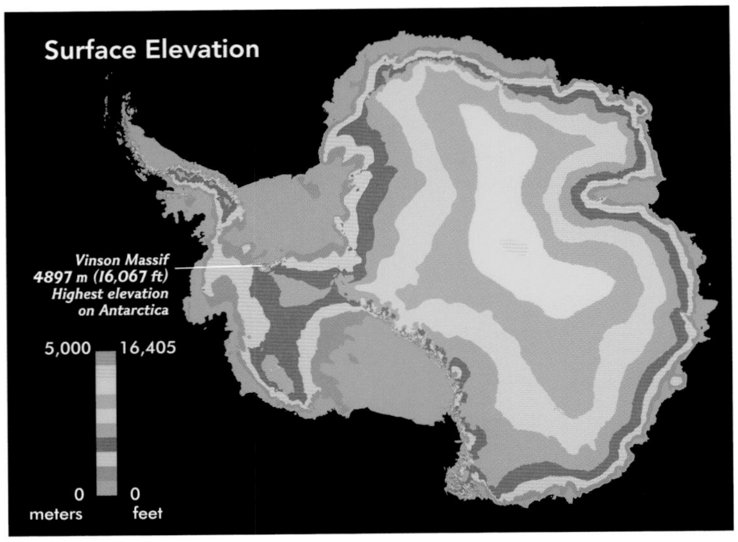

Measurements of a Paradox

Ninety percent of the world's ice and 70 percent of the world's fresh water are found here, yet most of Antarctica is truly a desert. The snow equivalent of less than three inches of rain falls over the high interior of the continent each year. But snow and ice have been slowly accumulating on Antarctica for millions of years. More than 15,600 feet (4,755 m) deep at its thickest, the mean depth of the ice exceeds 6,600 feet (2,012 m). Ice is generally much thicker on the interior of the ice sheet than at edges. This is because ice flows from the interior to edges, where it eventually returns to the ocean either in the form of icebergs or by melting directly into the ocean. The few areas of thin ice on the interior lie over chains of subglacial mountains. Glaciologists measure ice thickness with either a downward-pointing radar or by seismic sounding, which records the echo from an explosive shot buried just beneath the surface of the ice sheet. The thickness measurements used for this map were collected by scientists from 15 nations over the last 50 years. Although in theory the amount of ice in the ice sheet is sufficient to raise global sea levels by approximately 187 feet (57 m), it is extremely unlikely that the entire ice sheet could be lost in the foreseeable future.

Ice on the Move

Glaciologists once thought that ice motion in Antarctica's interior was slow and relatively uniform, with just a few fast-moving outlet glaciers and some ice streams (in West Antarctica) drawing ice from the interior down to the ice shelves and the sea. A computer model of ice flow, based on new satellite elevation measurements, suggests a more intricate ice-movement pattern. Like rivers, coastal ice flows appear to be fed by complex systems of tributaries that penetrate hundreds of miles into major drainage basins, and the major streams identified in East Antarctica dwarf those of the West. New satellite-based radar images agree with this more dynamic view. Ice velocities in the streams can be ten times greater than the flow of the adjacent slow-moving ice, and the resulting stream boundaries are often heavily crevassed and detectable from space. The computer model combines measurements of surface elevation, ice sheet thickness, and snowfall to calculate the pattern of ice flow that would keep Antarctica in balance at its present shape. The resulting continent-wide baseline picture of this "balanced" flow generally resembles the actual situation, and detailed observations can be compared against it to uncover any changes occurring in the size and shape of the ice sheet.

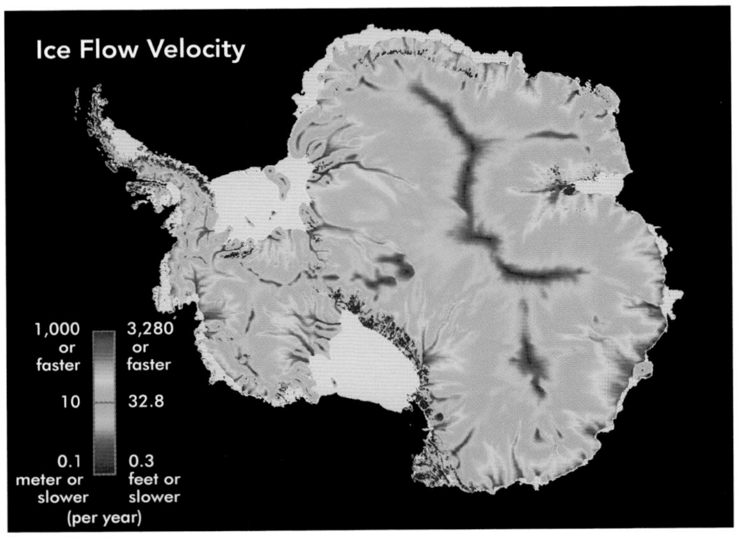

Ultimate Winds

Katabatic winds—cold air pouring down glacial slopes—often blow at 80 miles (129 km) per hour and can exceed 180 miles (290 km) per hour. These winds, which drain cold air masses from central Antarctica under the influence of gravity, are funnelled down valleys outward towards the coast, as indicated by the streamline arrows (right) on the white background of the Antarctic continent. When katabatic winds reach the coastline they often turn westward to blow counterclockwise around the continent. Offshore, circumpolar winds and currents push against the sea ice that grows to surround Antarctica each winter, leading to drift distances of up to several miles per day. The resulting near-shore movement of the sea ice is known as the East Wind drift, due to the dominant winds from the east. In some locations, such as the Weddell Sea, the drift is forced northward along the Antarctic Peninsula. In this case, and in the Bellingshausen, Amundsen, and Ross Seas, the combination of winds, currents, bathymetry, and topography leads to clockwise circulations known as gyres. In this image, the average sea-ice drift was determined from meteorological satellites. It illustrates the monthly average drift during the austral mid-winter, when sea-ice cover is at its maximum extent.

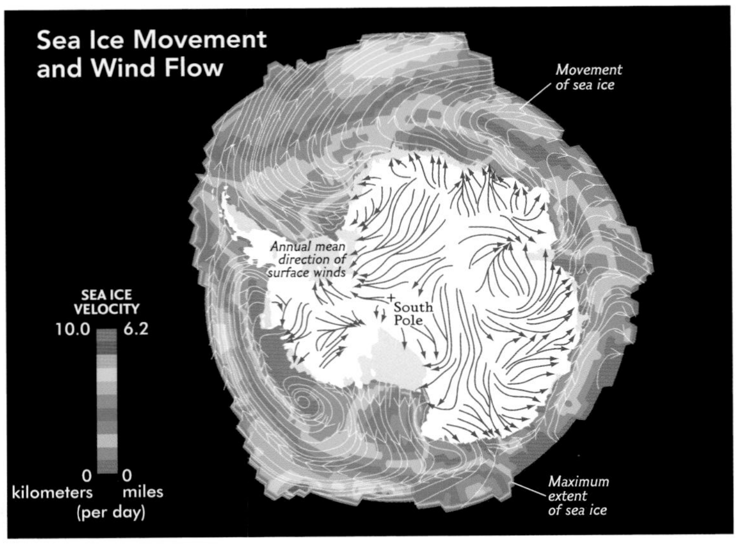

Antarctic Treaty

On December 1, 1959, after a decade of secret meetings, 12 nations—Argentina, Australia, Belgium, Chile, France, Japan, New Zealand, Norway, South Africa, the Soviet Union (Russia), the United Kingdom, and the United States—signed the Antarctic Treaty to preserve the frozen continent for peaceful scientific use only, a major feat during the height of Cold War rivalries. Since then, 32 other nations have joined.

The treaty includes all land, islands, and ice shelves south of 60° south latitude and enshrines the principles of peace, freedom of scientific research and exchange, and total banning of all military activity, nuclear testing, or disposal of radioactive waste. In addition, research stations are fully open to inspection, scientists may travel anywhere on the continent at any time, and countries can carry out aerial observations over any area.

A 1991 meeting prohibited mining in Antarctica. Other gatherings have asserted the importance of protecting wildlife, such as the Ross and fur seals, conserving unique biological habitats, and limiting human impact on sensitive ecological zones. The Antarctic Treaty made static all territorial claims held by 7 of the original 12 countries and prohibits any new claims. The treaty affirms that no country "rules the continent." For more than four decades it has proven to be an unprecedented example of international cooperation.

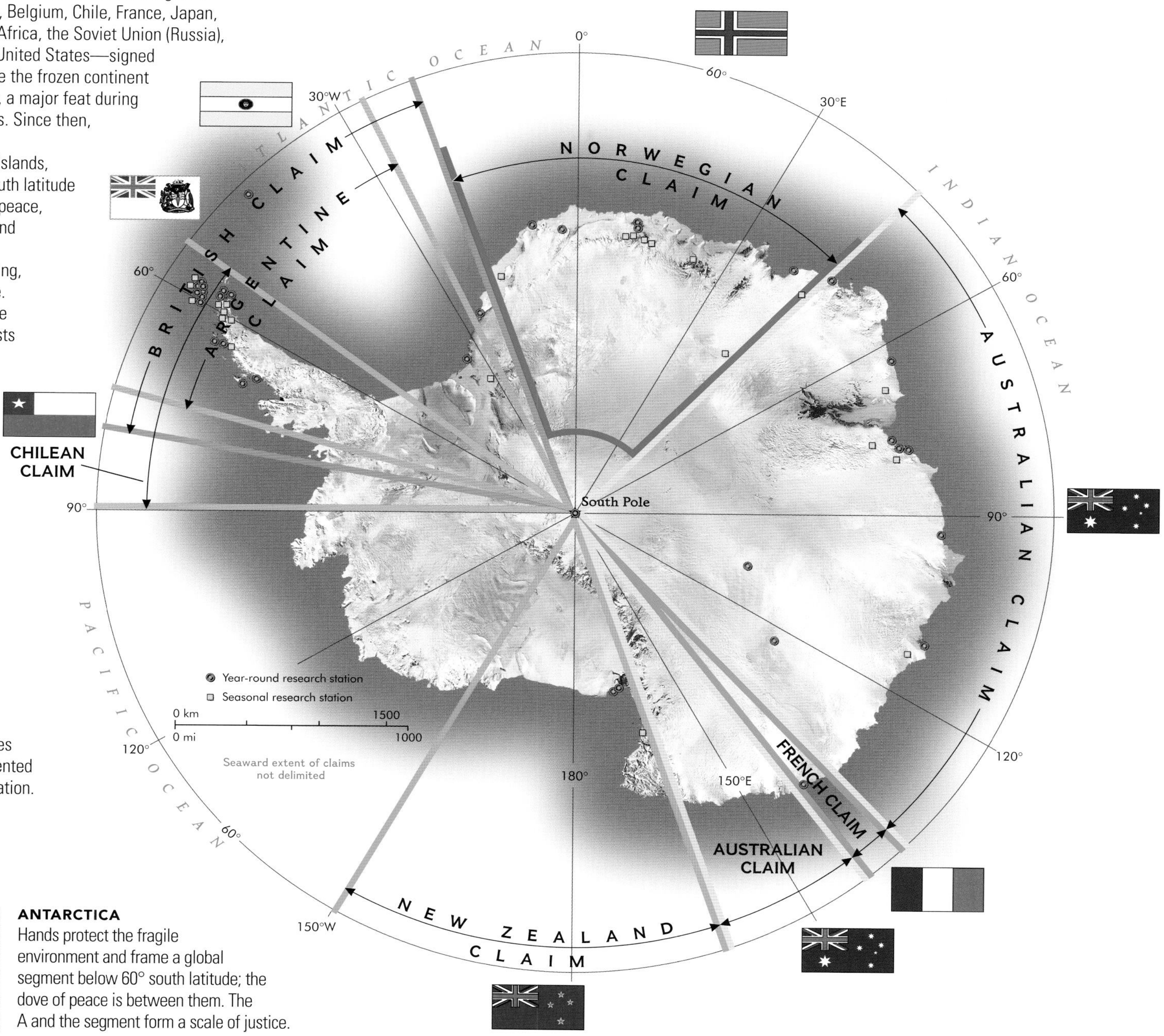

ANTARCTICA
Hands protect the fragile environment and frame a global segment below 60° south latitude; the dove of peace is between them. The A and the segment form a scale of justice.

Antarctic Convergence

The Antarctic Convergence refers to an undulating boundary in the seas that rings Antarctica roughly 950 miles (1,529 km) off the continental coast, between 50° and 60° south latitude. This narrow zone marks the meeting place of relatively warm waters from the southern Atlantic, Indian, and Pacific Oceans and the cold Antarctic Circumpolar Current. Because cold water sinks, it slips under the more buoyant warmer water and acts to power the great oceanic conveyor belt that affects life and weather around the world. The Antarctic Convergence also generates one of Earth's richest marine ecosystems. Mist and fog often rise at the interface of blended warm and cold waters. Immediately air becomes brisker and marine life alters. Water temperatures can plummet a dozen degrees (Fahrenheit) or more upon entering the Southern Ocean. The Antarctic Convergence functions as a barrier and forms Antarctica's biological extent. It delimits the Southern Ocean, which holds 10 percent of the world's seawater, and thus creates a largely closed ecosystem and isolates the continent from warmer waters. Deep, cold waters permit the proliferation of diatoms—single-celled algae—that in turn support krill, shrimp-like organisms that exist in enormous numbers. Krill form a vital part of the food chain, directly or indirectly providing nutrition for Antarctica's amazing wildlife, particularly fish, seals, whales, and birds, including five species of flightless penguins. Losses of this food source through over-harvesting by humans would seriously affect marine life.

As one travels north into warmer regions beyond the Antarctic Convergence, krill—the basis of Antarctica's life—perish and disappear. The Southern Ocean's rich waters, full of plant and animal life, stand apart from the continent itself, frozen and incredibly harsh, where vegetation is limited to lichens, mosses, and a mere two species of flowering plants. A small insect known as the wingless midge represents the largest land animal. In contrast, large body size and slow growth mark many marine animals, all of which have adapted magnificently to the cold environment.

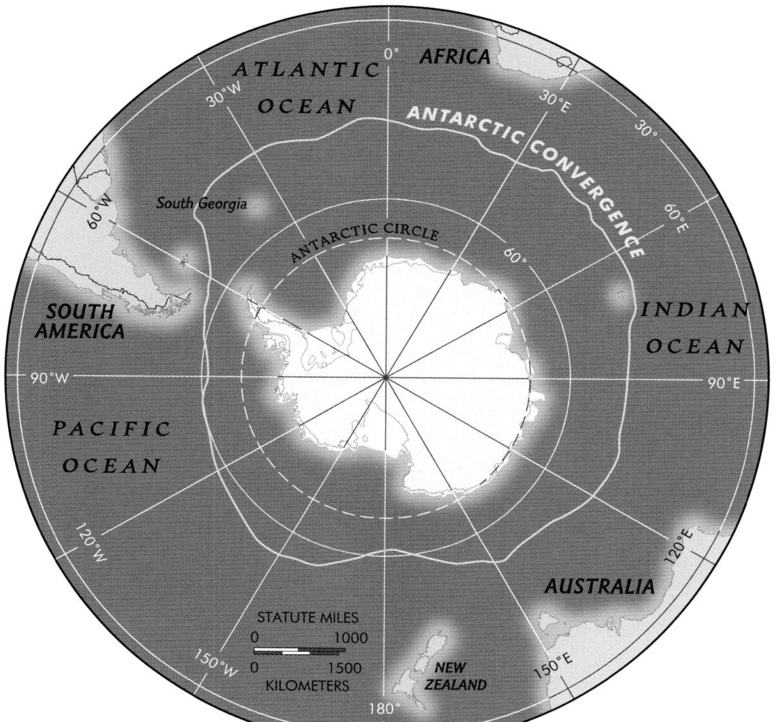

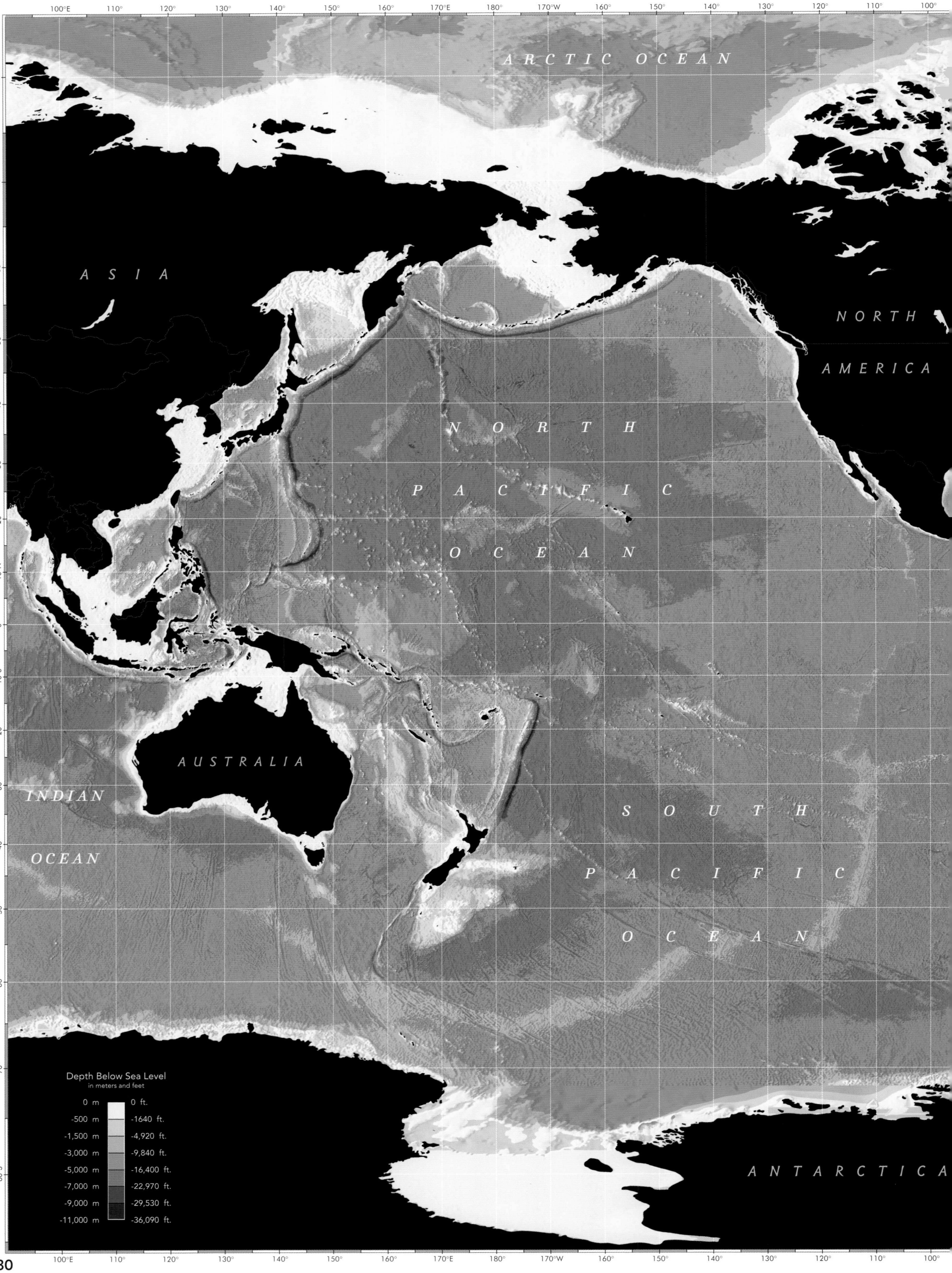

ARCTIC OCEAN
ASIA
NORTH AMERICA
NORTH PACIFIC OCEAN
AUSTRALIA
INDIAN OCEAN
SOUTH PACIFIC OCEAN
ANTARCTICA
100°E
110°
120°
130°
140°
150°
160°
170°E
180°
170°W
160°
150°
140°
130°
120°
110°
100°
80°N
70°
60°
50°
40°
30°
20°
10°N
0°
10°S
20°
30°
40°
50°
60°
70°
80°S
Depth Below Sea Level
in meters and feet
0 m 0 ft.
-500 m -1640 ft.
-1,500 m -4,920 ft.
-3,000 m -9,840 ft.
-5,000 m -16,400 ft.
-7,000 m -22,970 ft.
-9,000 m -29,530 ft.
-11,000 m -36,090 ft.

Oceans
ARCTIC OCEAN
Greenland
EUROPE
ASIA
NORTH
ATLANTIC
OCEAN
AFRICA
SOUTH
AMERICA
SOUTH
ATLANTIC
OCEAN
INDIAN
OCEAN
World Bathymetry
Kilometers
0 1,000 2,000 3,000
Statute Miles
0 1,000 2,000 3,000
Nautical Miles
0 1,000 2,000 3,000
Scale at the Equator
Miller Cylindrical Projection

EARTH IS A WATERY PLANET: More than 70 percent of its surface is covered by interconnected bodies of salt water that together make up a continuous, global ocean. Over the centuries, people have created artificial boundaries that divide this great water body into smaller oceans with numerous seas, gulfs, bays, straits, and channels.

The global ocean is a dynamic participant in Earth's physical, chemical, and biological processes. Millions of years ago, life itself most likely evolved in its waters. These are restless waters, always in motion. Tidal movement—the regular rise and fall of the ocean surface—results from gravitational forces exerted by the sun and the moon. The spin of Earth on its axis, coupled with wind, generates surface currents that redistribute warm and cold water around the planet. Variations in the temperature and salinity of water keep the thermohaline circulation system moving; this enormous system of interconnected currents, at the surface and deep in the ocean, influences climate patterns and circulates nutrients.

Where marine and terrestrial realms meet, one may find reefs built by tiny coral polyps or see cliffs and sea stacks shaped by countless waves. Many coastal zones are threatened, however, by overdevelopment, pollution, and overfishing. Farther out, in the deep ocean, lie vast untouched plains, high mountains and ridges, and valleys with floors lying as much as seven miles (11 km) below the sea surface. Teeming with life, the ocean includes "rain forests of the sea" and a host of marine species—even creatures who dwell in superhot waters near hydrothermal vents.

New technology is helping scientists to explore ever deeper and farther and to create more accurate maps of the ocean. Some of this underwater world has been explored with diving vessels and satellite imagery, but so much more remains to be discovered.

The Ocean Floor

The ocean floor is dynamic and varied. From the edge of the continental shelf (the shelf break), the continental slope plunges to the continental rise, which reaches to the abyssal plain. Periodically, terrestrial rocks and sediment flow through submarine canyons and form alluvial fans. The Mid-Ocean Ridge builds new seafloor; erosion and subsidence create atolls and guyots; and subducting tectonic plates form deep trenches in the ocean floor.

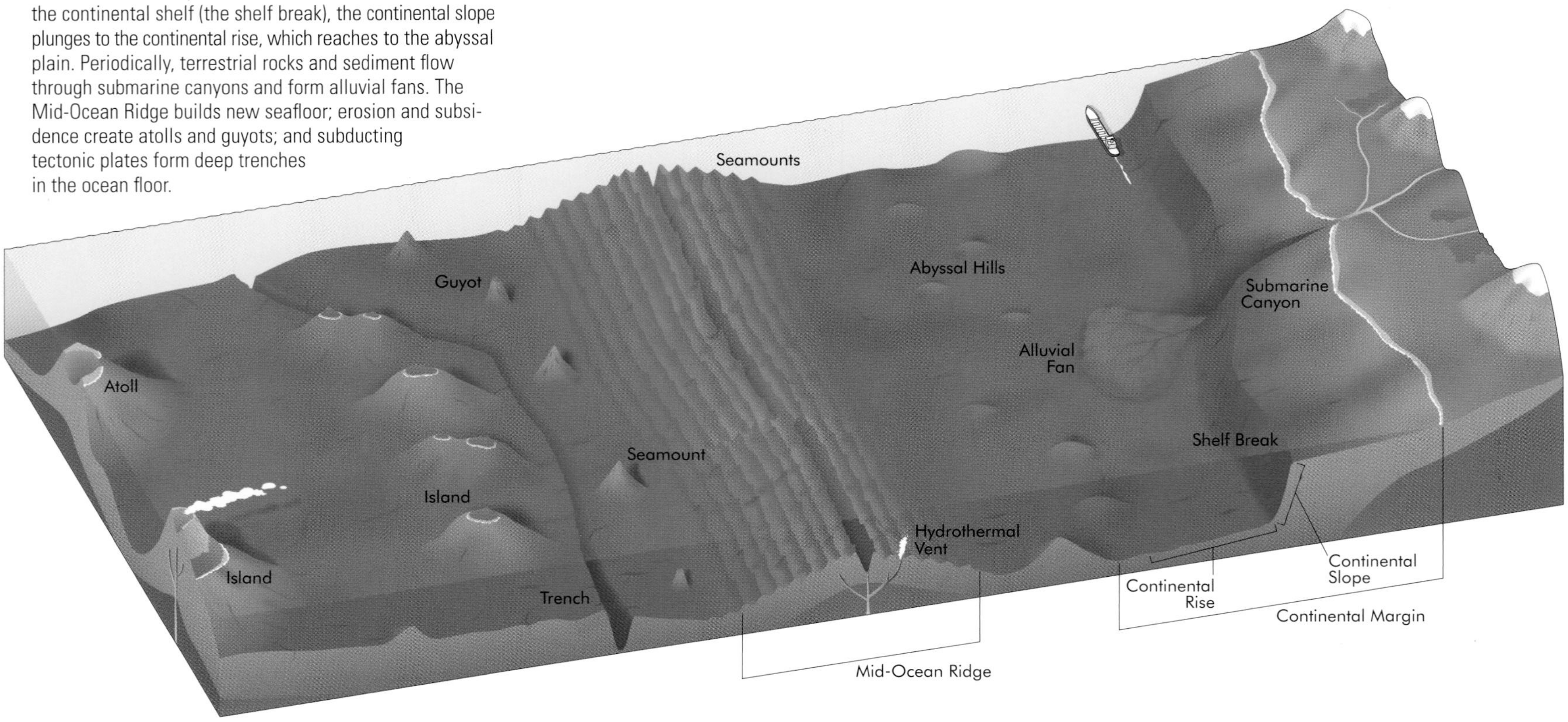

OCEAN WAVES

Waves may be born thousands of miles from shore, a result of large storms churning over the ocean. Wind pushing on the sea surface forms unorganized groups of waves that travel in all directions. In time, they organize into swell—groups of waves that can carry energy over thousands of miles of ocean. As the waves approach a surf zone, they steepen until their crests curl forward and break upon the beach.

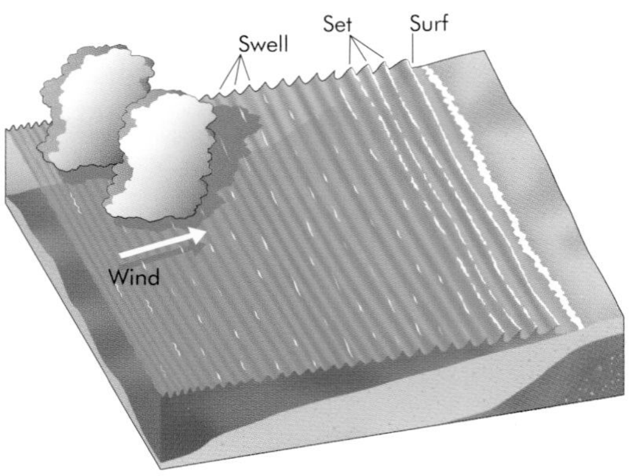

CORAL MORPHOLOGY

Coral reefs—Earth's largest structures with biological origins—form primarily in the tropics, where water is clear and warm. They begin as fringing reefs, colonies built along coastlines by tiny organisms known as coral polyps. As a coastal area subsides, a fringing reef becomes a barrier reef enclosing a protected lagoon. Corals on a reef's seaward side rely on spur and groove formations to withstand powerful waves.

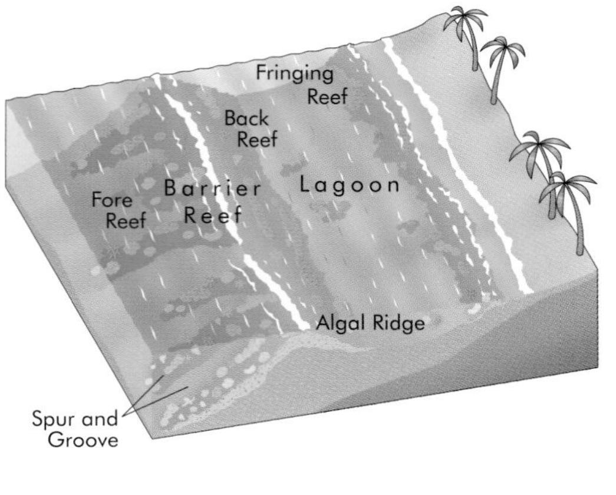

COASTAL MORPHOLOGY

The contours of a coast determine how approaching ocean waves release their energy. In bays, wave energy is dispersed; at headlands, it is concentrated. Waves approaching at an angle produce longshore currents, which flow parallel to shore and transport sediment. Rip currents, generated by wind and the return flow of water, move outward. Over time, waves and currents reshape the coastlines of the world.

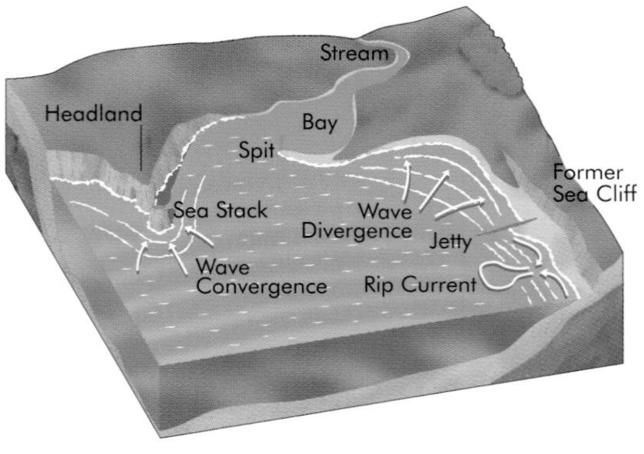

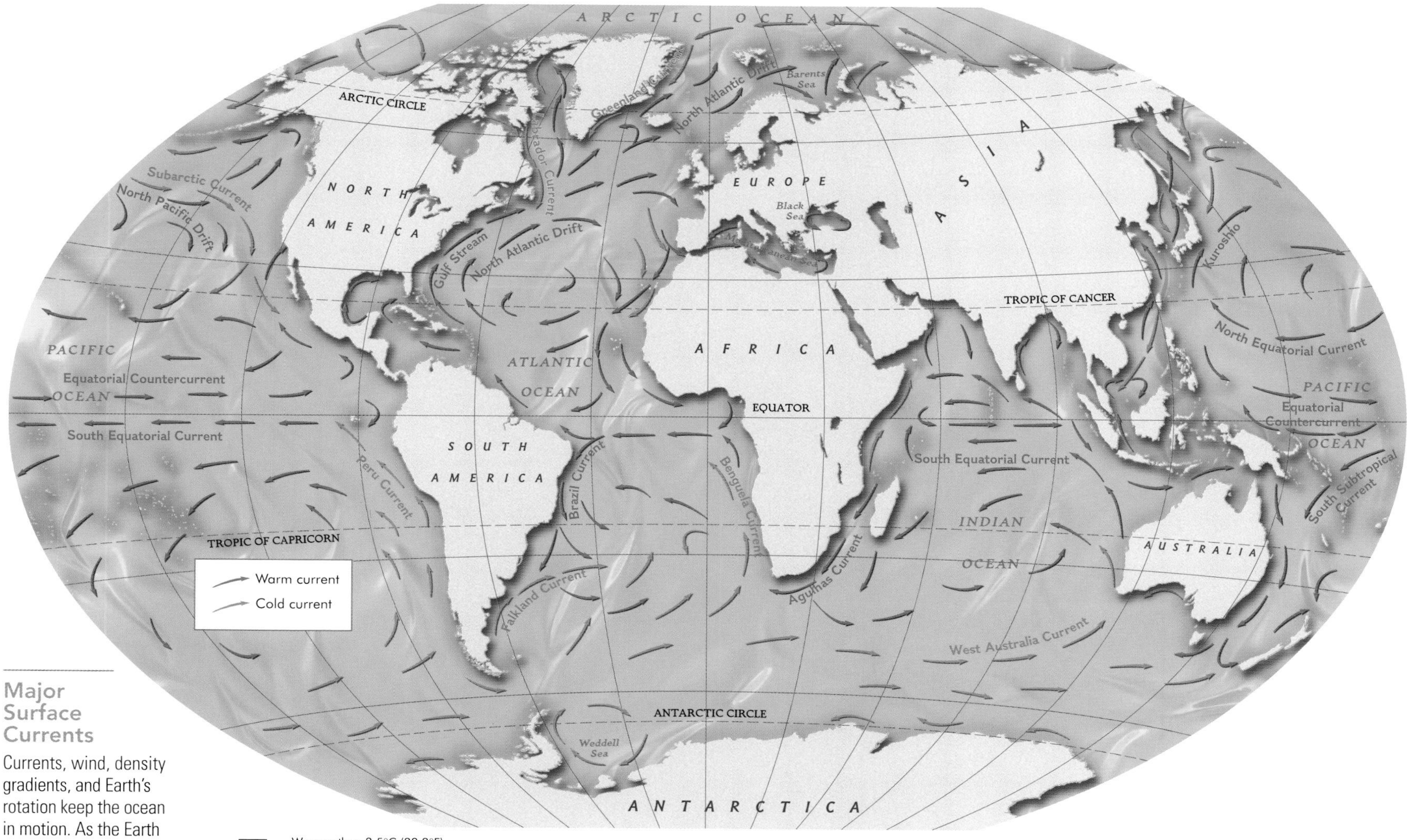

Major Surface Currents

Currents, wind, density gradients, and Earth's rotation keep the ocean in motion. As the Earth spins, wind and surface currents are deflected to the right in the Northern Hemisphere and to the left in the Southern Hemisphere. This effect creates enormous gyres that transport warm water from equatorial regions into the much colder polar regions. El Niño events in the Pacific, as well as the monsoon season in the Indian Ocean, alter surface currents.

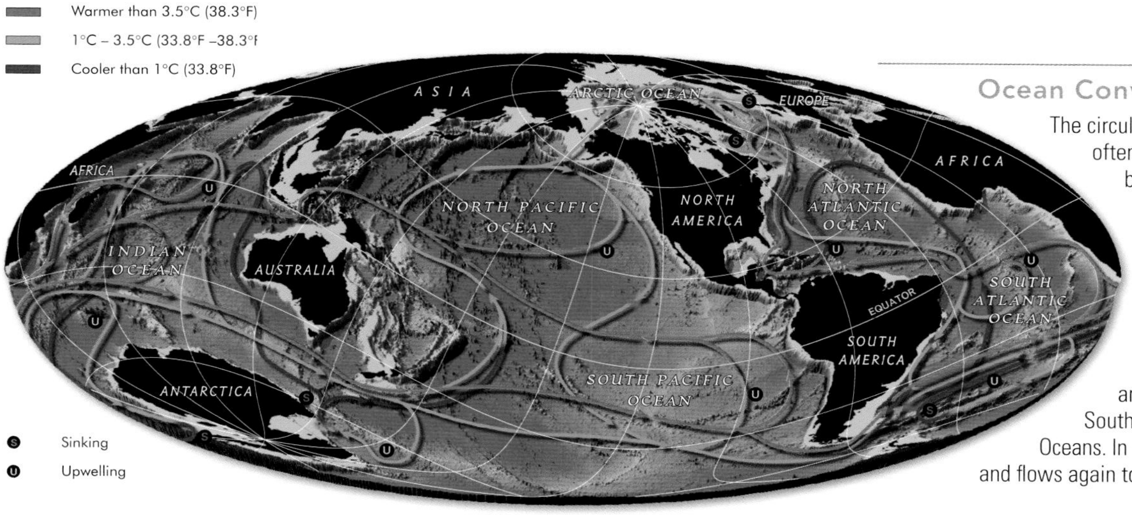

Ocean Conveyor Belt

The circulation of ocean water is often compared to a conveyor belt. Warm water flows into the North Atlantic, cools, becomes saltier (due to evaporation), and sinks because its density has increased. Then it flows south along the seafloor to Antarctica, chills further, and flows outward into the South Atlantic, Indian, and Pacific Oceans. In these warm waters, it rises and flows again toward the North Atlantic.

TIDES

Both the sun and moon exert gravitational force on the Earth's ocean, creating tides. But because the moon is closer, its tug is much greater. During spring tides, when the moon is new or full, the combined pull of the sun and moon causes very high and low tides. Neap tides occur during the first and third quarters of the moon; at those times, the difference between tides is much smaller.

MAPPING THE OCEAN

Mapping the ocean requires myriad devices. In space, some satellites carry microwave radars to record data on wind speed and sea height; others use visible and infrared radiometers to collect biological productivity data. Radar altimetry and scatterometry are also used to record wind speed and direction. Out in the ocean, profiling floats collect temperature and salinity data. Ships use acoustics to map the sea floor.

THERMOHALINE CIRCULATION SYSTEM

Differences in the relative densities of volumes of water—determined by temperature (thermo) and salinity (haline)—drive thermohaline circulation. In polar regions, density increases as water cools and as evaporation makes it saltier; the mass of water sinks and flows along the ocean floor. Near the Equator, water warms and rises to the surface. If this system shut down, significant climate effects could occur.

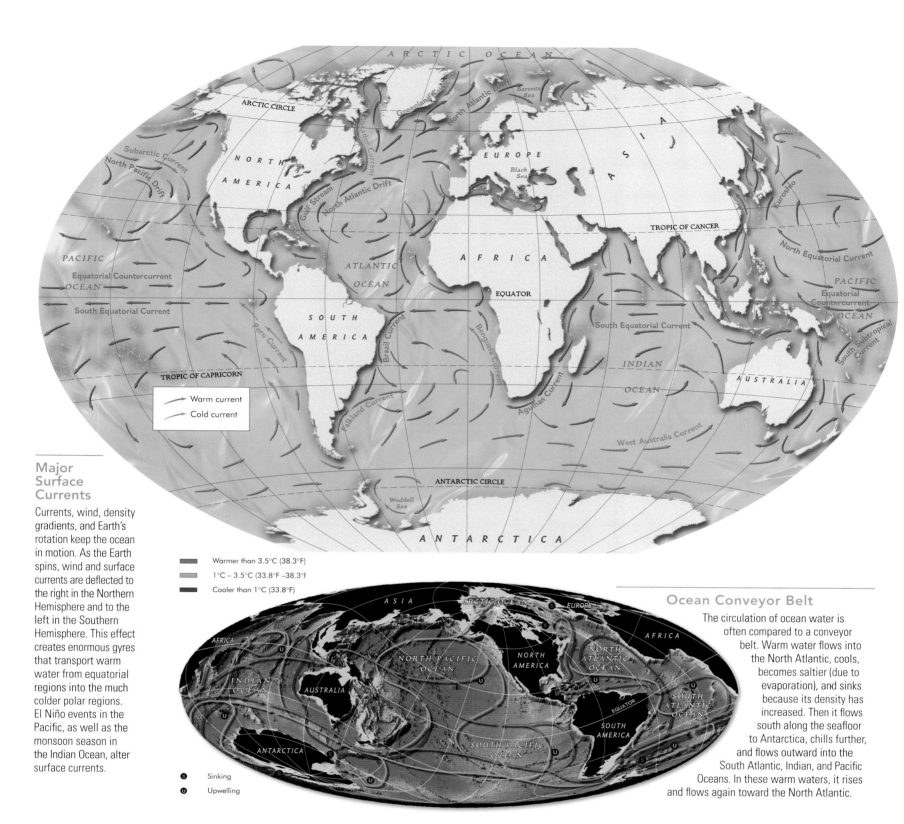

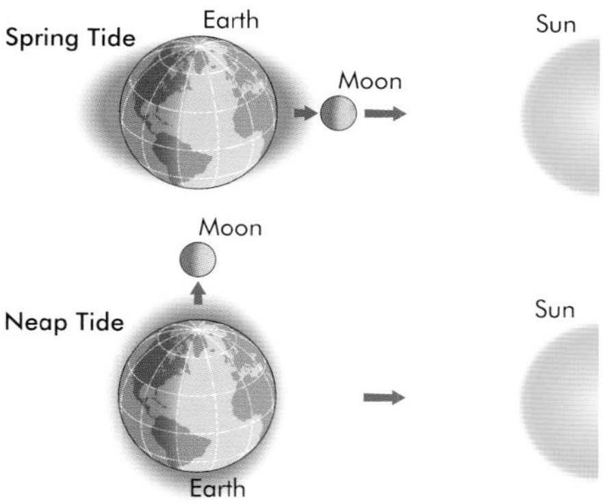

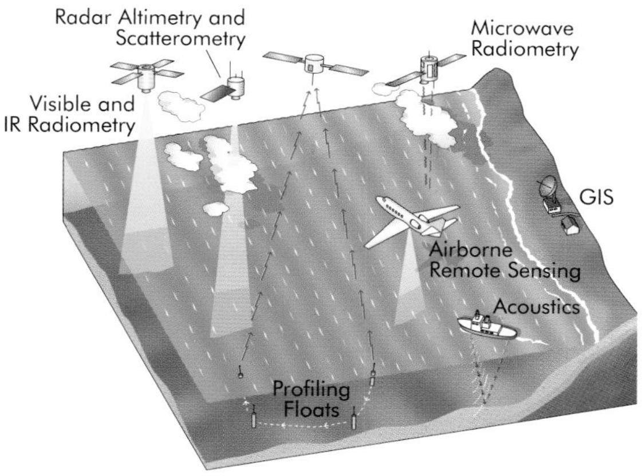

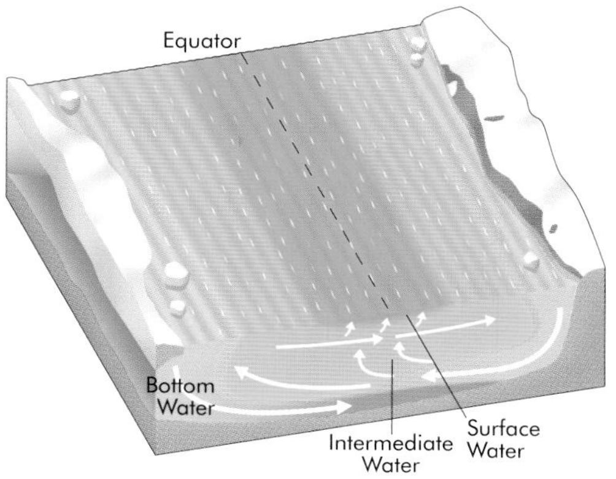

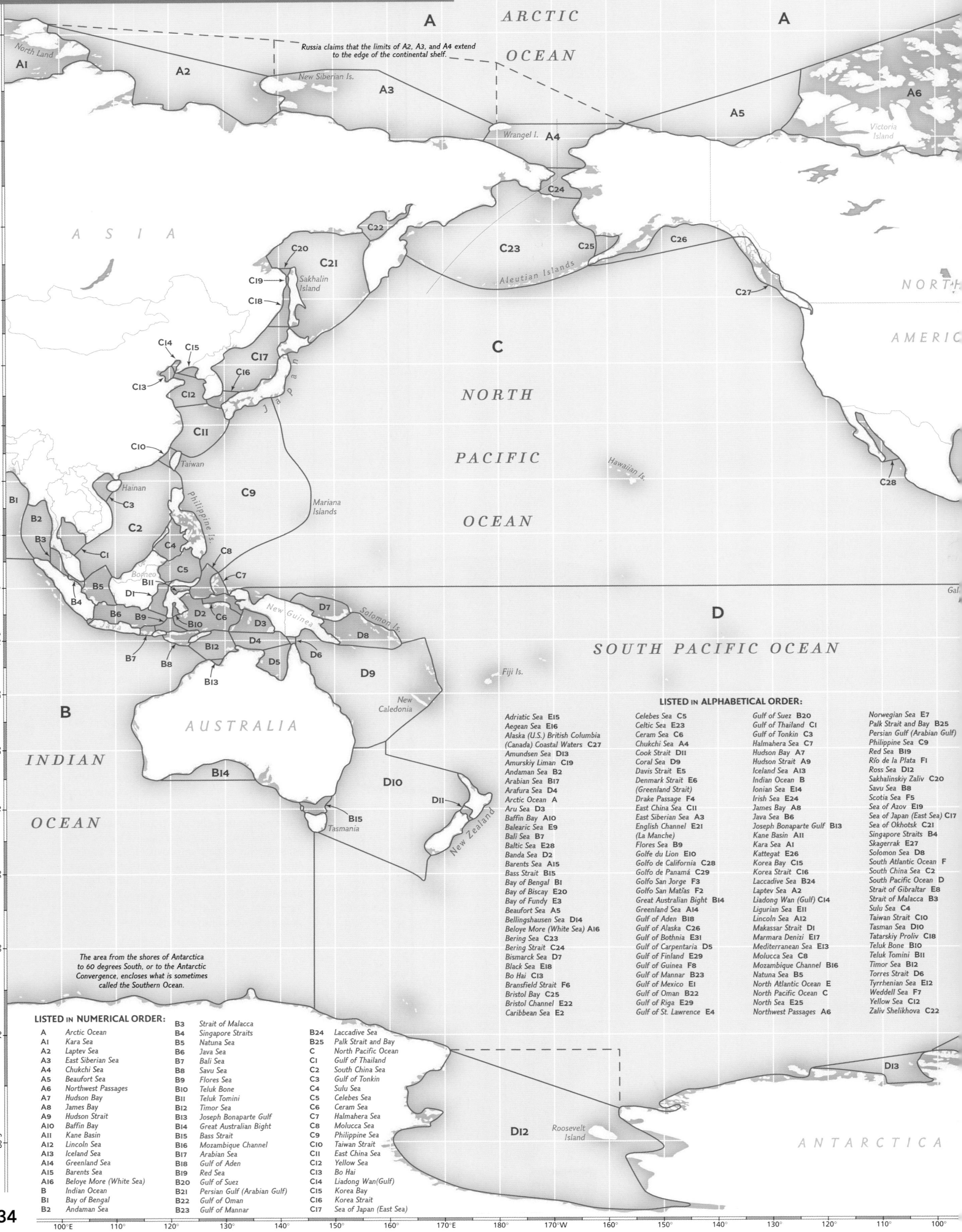

LISTED IN ALPHABETICAL ORDER:

Adriatic Sea **E15**
Aegean Sea **E16**
Alaska (U.S.) British Columbia (Canada) Coastal Waters **C27**
Amundsen Sea **D13**
Amurskiy Liman **C19**
Andaman Sea **B2**
Arabian Sea **B17**
Arafura Sea **D4**
Arctic Ocean **A**
Aru Sea **D3**
Baffin Bay **A10**
Balearic Sea **E9**
Bali Sea **B7**
Baltic Sea **E28**
Banda Sea **D2**
Barents Sea **A15**
Bass Strait **B15**
Bay of Bengal **B1**
Bay of Biscay **E20**
Bay of Fundy **E3**
Beaufort Sea **A5**
Bellingshausen Sea **D14**
Beloye More (White Sea) **A16**
Bering Sea **C23**
Bering Strait **C24**
Bismarck Sea **D7**
Black Sea **E18**
Bo Hai **C13**
Bransfield Strait **F6**
Bristol Bay **C25**
Bristol Channel **E22**
Caribbean Sea **E2**
Celebes Sea **C5**
Celtic Sea **E23**
Ceram Sea **C6**
Chukchi Sea **A4**
Cook Strait **D11**
Coral Sea **D9**
Davis Strait **E5**
Denmark Strait **E6** *(Greenland Strait)*
Drake Passage **F4**
East China Sea **C11**
East Siberian Sea **A3**
English Channel **E21** *(La Manche)*
Flores Sea **B9**
Golfe du Lion **E10**
Golfo de California **C28**
Golfo de Panamá **C29**
Golfo San Jorge **F3**
Golfo San Matías **F2**
Great Australian Bight **B14**
Greenland Sea **A14**
Gulf of Aden **B18**
Gulf of Alaska **C26**
Gulf of Bothnia **E31**
Gulf of Carpentaria **D5**
Gulf of Finland **E29**
Gulf of Guinea **F8**
Gulf of Mannar **B23**
Gulf of Mexico **E1**
Gulf of Oman **B22**
Gulf of Riga **E29**
Gulf of St. Lawrence **E4**
Gulf of Suez **B20**
Gulf of Thailand **C1**
Gulf of Tonkin **C3**
Halmahera Sea **C7**
Hudson Bay **A7**
Hudson Strait **A9**
Iceland Sea **A13**
Indian Ocean **B**
Ionian Sea **E14**
Irish Sea **E24**
James Bay **A8**
Java Sea **B6**
Joseph Bonaparte Gulf **B13**
Kane Basin **A11**
Kara Sea **A1**
Kattegat **E26**
Korea Bay **C15**
Korea Strait **C16**
Laccadive Sea **B24**
Laptev Sea **A2**
Liadong Wan (Gulf) **C14**
Ligurian Sea **E11**
Lincoln Sea **A12**
Makassar Strait **D1**
Marmara Denizi **E17**
Mediterranean Sea **E13**
Molucca Sea **C8**
Mozambique Channel **B16**
Natuna Sea **B5**
North Atlantic Ocean **E**
North Pacific Ocean **C**
North Sea **E25**
Northwest Passages **A6**
Norwegian Sea **E7**
Palk Strait and Bay **B25**
Persian Gulf (Arabian Gulf)
Philippine Sea **C9**
Red Sea **B19**
Río de la Plata **F1**
Ross Sea **D12**
Sakhalinskiy Zaliv **C20**
Savu Sea **B8**
Scotia Sea **F5**
Sea of Azov **E19**
Sea of Japan (East Sea) **C17**
Sea of Okhotsk **C21**
Singapore Straits **B4**
Skagerrak **E27**
Solomon Sea **D8**
South Atlantic Ocean **F**
South China Sea **C2**
South Pacific Ocean **D**
Strait of Gibraltar **E8**
Strait of Malacca **B3**
Sulu Sea **C4**
Taiwan Strait **C10**
Tasman Sea **D10**
Tatarskiy Proliv **C18**
Teluk Bone **B10**
Teluk Tomini **B11**
Timor Sea **B12**
Torres Strait **D6**
Tyrrhenian Sea **E12**
Weddell Sea **F7**
Yellow Sea **C12**
Zaliv Shelikhova **C22**

LISTED IN NUMERICAL ORDER:

A	*Arctic Ocean*
A1	*Kara Sea*
A2	*Laptev Sea*
A3	*East Siberian Sea*
A4	*Chukchi Sea*
A5	*Beaufort Sea*
A6	*Northwest Passages*
A7	*Hudson Bay*
A8	*James Bay*
A9	*Hudson Strait*
A10	*Baffin Bay*
A11	*Kane Basin*
A12	*Lincoln Sea*
A13	*Iceland Sea*
A14	*Greenland Sea*
A15	*Barents Sea*
A16	*Beloye More (White Sea)*
B	*Indian Ocean*
B1	*Bay of Bengal*
B2	*Andaman Sea*
B3	*Strait of Malacca*
B4	*Singapore Straits*
B5	*Natuna Sea*
B6	*Java Sea*
B7	*Bali Sea*
B8	*Savu Sea*
B9	*Flores Sea*
B10	*Teluk Bone*
B11	*Teluk Tomini*
B12	*Timor Sea*
B13	*Joseph Bonaparte Gulf*
B14	*Great Australian Bight*
B15	*Bass Strait*
B16	*Mozambique Channel*
B17	*Arabian Sea*
B18	*Gulf of Aden*
B19	*Red Sea*
B20	*Gulf of Suez*
B21	*Persian Gulf (Arabian Gulf)*
B22	*Gulf of Oman*
B23	*Gulf of Mannar*
B24	*Laccadive Sea*
B25	*Palk Strait and Bay*
C	*North Pacific Ocean*
C1	*Gulf of Thailand*
C2	*South China Sea*
C3	*Gulf of Tonkin*
C4	*Sulu Sea*
C5	*Celebes Sea*
C6	*Ceram Sea*
C7	*Halmahera Sea*
C8	*Molucca Sea*
C9	*Philippine Sea*
C10	*Taiwan Strait*
C11	*East China Sea*
C12	*Yellow Sea*
C13	*Bo Hai*
C14	*Liadong Wan(Gulf)*
C15	*Korea Bay*
C16	*Korea Strait*
C17	*Sea of Japan (East Sea)*

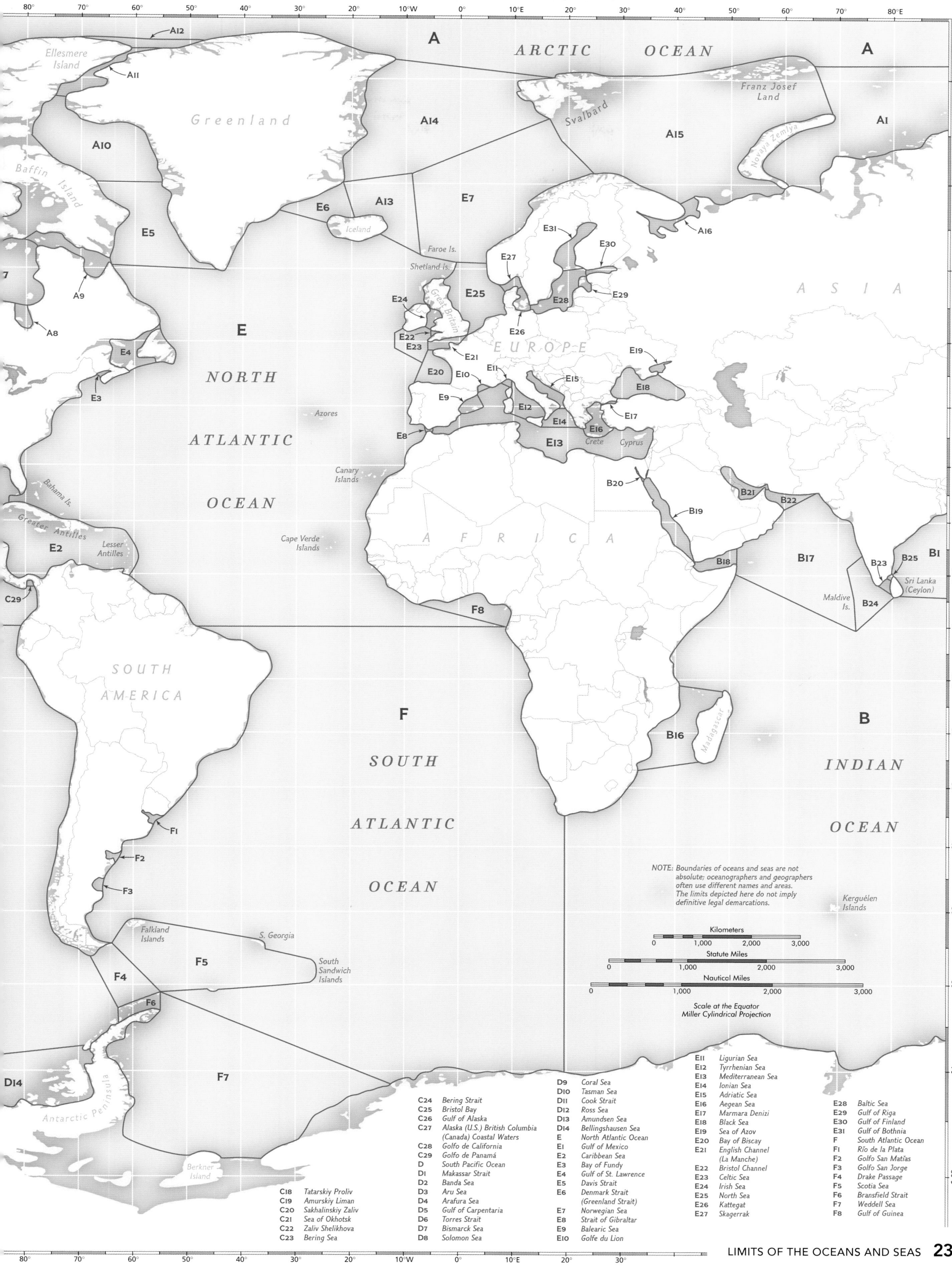
ARCTIC OCEAN
NORTH ATLANTIC OCEAN
SOUTH ATLANTIC OCEAN
INDIAN OCEAN
Greenland
EUROPE
ASIA
AFRICA
SOUTH AMERICA
Ellesmere Island
Baffin Island
Iceland
Faroe Is.
Shetland Is.
Great Britain
Svalbard
Franz Josef Land
Novaya Zemlya
Azores
Canary Islands
Cape Verde Islands
Bahama Is.
Greater Antilles
Lesser Antilles
Crete
Cyprus
Madagascar
Maldive Is.
Sri Lanka (Ceylon)
Kerguélen Islands
Falkland Islands
S. Georgia
South Sandwich Islands
Antarctic Peninsula
Berkner Island
NOTE: Boundaries of oceans and seas are not absolute; oceanographers and geographers often use different names and areas. The limits depicted here do not imply definitive legal demarcations.
Kilometers 0 1,000 2,000 3,000
Statute Miles 0 1,000 2,000 3,000
Nautical Miles 0 1,000 2,000 3,000
Scale at the Equator
Miller Cylindrical Projection
C18 Tatarskiy Proliv
C19 Amurskiy Liman
C20 Sakhalinskiy Zaliv
C21 Sea of Okhotsk
C22 Zaliv Shelikhova
C23 Bering Sea
C24 Bering Strait
C25 Bristol Bay
C26 Gulf of Alaska
C27 Alaska (U.S.) British Columbia (Canada) Coastal Waters
C28 Golfo de California
C29 Golfo de Panamá
D South Pacific Ocean
D1 Makassar Strait
D2 Banda Sea
D3 Aru Sea
D4 Arafura Sea
D5 Gulf of Carpentaria
D6 Torres Strait
D7 Bismarck Sea
D8 Solomon Sea
D9 Coral Sea
D10 Tasman Sea
D11 Cook Strait
D12 Ross Sea
D13 Amundsen Sea
D14 Bellingshausen Sea
E North Atlantic Ocean
E1 Gulf of Mexico
E2 Caribbean Sea
E3 Bay of Fundy
E4 Gulf of St. Lawrence
E5 Davis Strait
E6 Denmark Strait (Greenland Strait)
E7 Norwegian Sea
E8 Strait of Gibraltar
E9 Balearic Sea
E10 Golfe du Lion
E11 Ligurian Sea
E12 Tyrrhenian Sea
E13 Mediterranean Sea
E14 Ionian Sea
E15 Adriatic Sea
E16 Aegean Sea
E17 Marmara Denizi
E18 Black Sea
E19 Sea of Azov
E20 Bay of Biscay
E21 English Channel (La Manche)
E22 Bristol Channel
E23 Celtic Sea
E24 Irish Sea
E25 North Sea
E26 Kattegat
E27 Skagerrak
E28 Baltic Sea
E29 Gulf of Riga
E30 Gulf of Finland
E31 Gulf of Bothnia
F South Atlantic Ocean
F1 Río de la Plata
F2 Golfo San Matías
F3 Golfo San Jorge
F4 Drake Passage
F5 Scotia Sea
F6 Bransfield Strait
F7 Weddell Sea
F8 Gulf of Guinea

Atlantic Ocean Floor

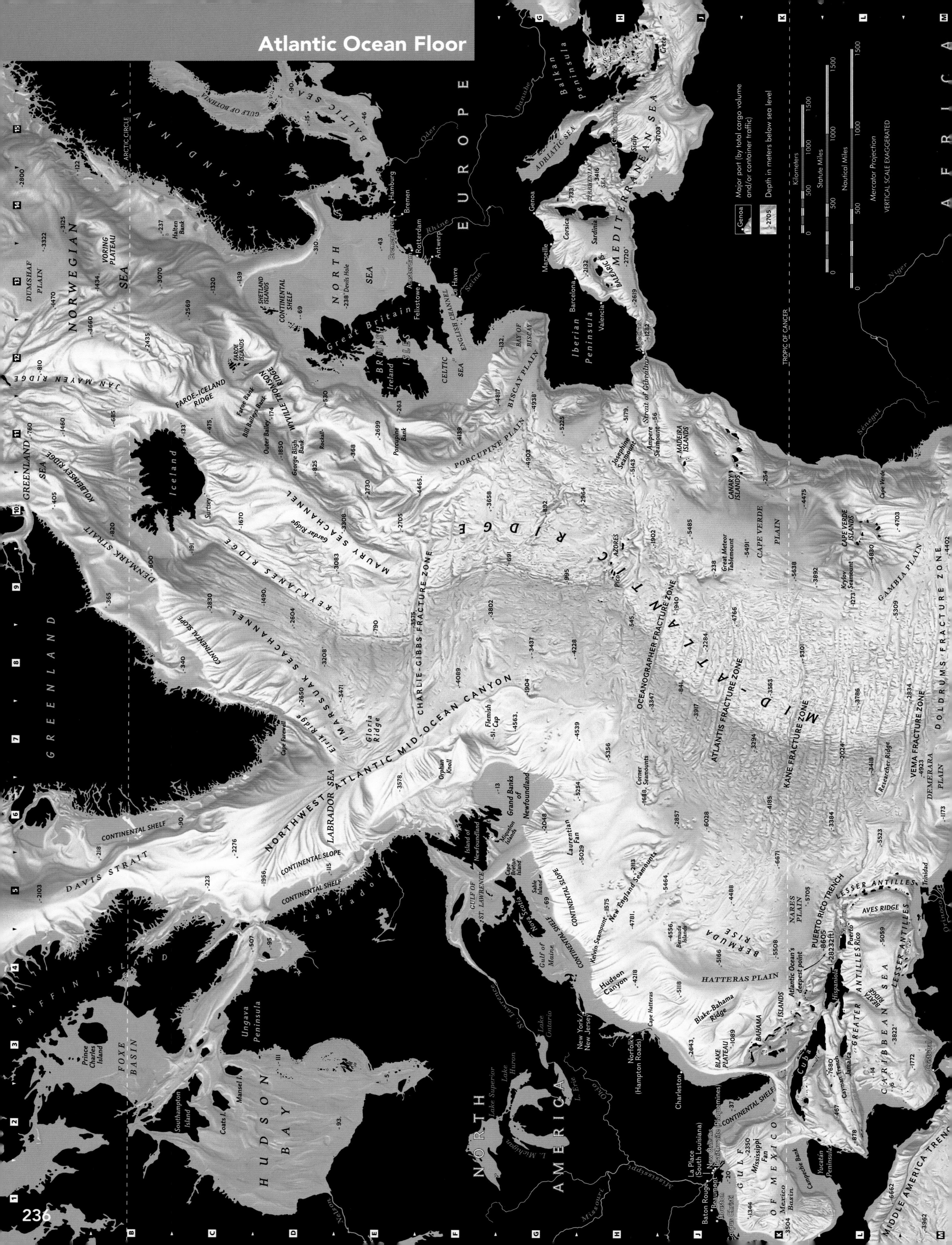

Atlantic Ocean Floor
Genoa Major port (by total cargo volume and/or container traffic)
-2705 Depth in meters below sea level
Kilometers
Statute Miles
Nautical Miles
Mercator Projection
VERTICAL SCALE EXAGGERATED
NORTH AMERICA
EUROPE
AFRICA
GREENLAND
SCANDINAVIA
Iceland
BRITISH ISLES
Iberian Peninsula
Balkan Peninsula
NORWEGIAN SEA
NORTH SEA
BALTIC SEA
MEDITERRANEAN SEA
LABRADOR SEA
HUDSON BAY
CARIBBEAN SEA
GULF OF MEXICO
MID-ATLANTIC RIDGE
REYKJANES RIDGE
NORTHWEST ATLANTIC MID-OCEAN CANYON
CHARLIE-GIBBS FRACTURE ZONE
OCEANOGRAPHER FRACTURE ZONE
ATLANTIS FRACTURE ZONE
KANE FRACTURE ZONE
VEMA FRACTURE ZONE
DOLDRUMS FRACTURE ZONE
PORCUPINE PLAIN
BISCAY PLAIN
HATTERAS PLAIN
NARES PLAIN
CAPE VERDE PLAIN
GAMBIA PLAIN
DEMERARA PLAIN
BERMUDA RISE
PUERTO RICO TRENCH
-8605 (-28232 ft)
Atlantic Ocean's deepest point
DAVIS STRAIT
DENMARK STRAIT
ARCTIC CIRCLE
TROPIC OF CANCER

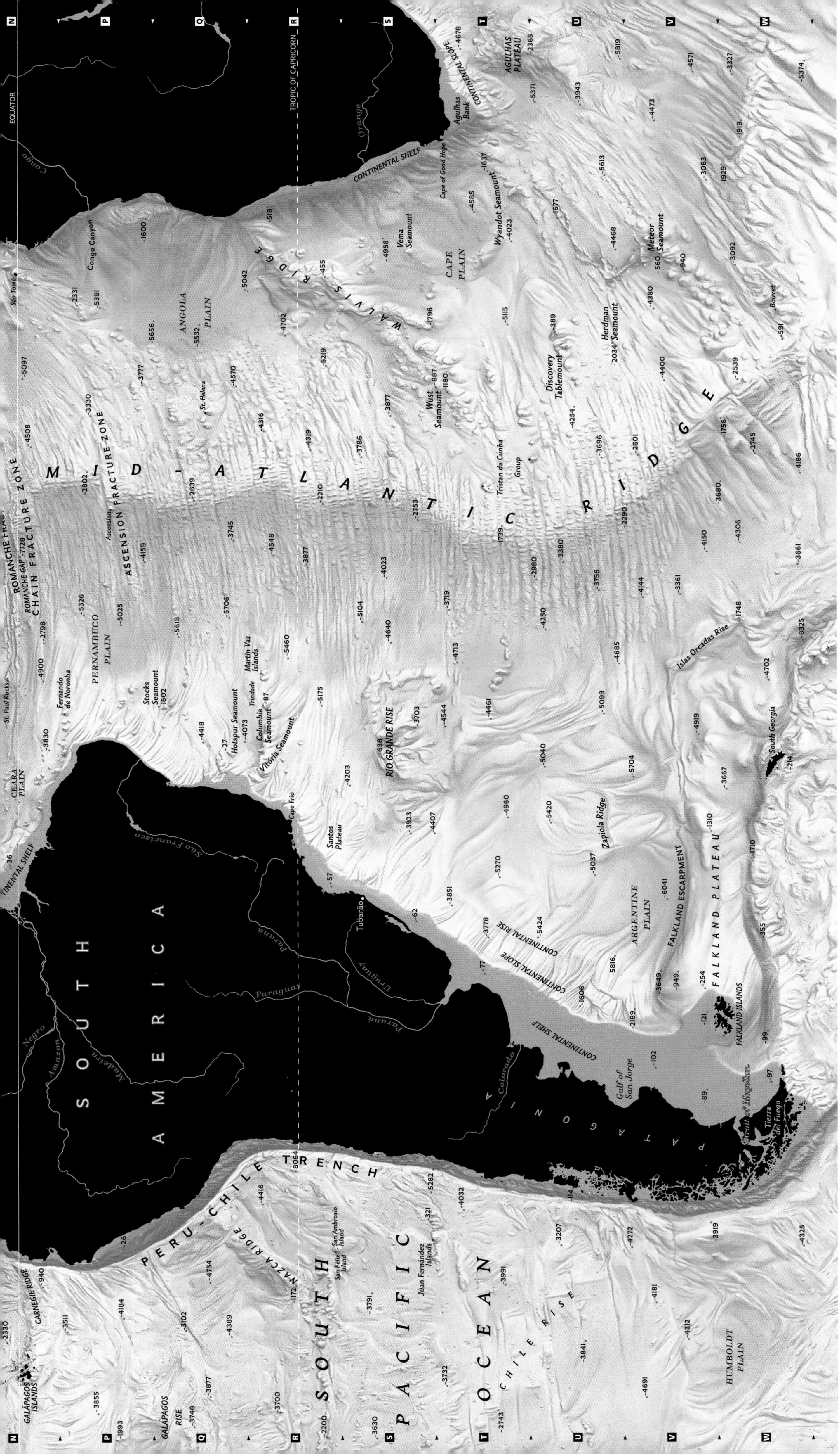

The ragged spine of the Mid-Atlantic Ridge fills the center of the Atlantic Ocean Basin from north to south. This prominent spreading ridge was not discovered until the middle of the 20th century.

Pacific Ocean Floor

ASIA
SEA OF OKHOTSK
Sakhalin
Kamchatka Peninsula
BERING SEA
St. Lawrence I.
CONTINENTAL SHELF
Nunivak I.
Pribilof Islands
ALASKA
SHIRSHOV RIDGE
ALEUTIAN BASIN
BOWERS RIDGE
ALEUTIAN ISLANDS
ALEUTIAN TRENCH
Detroit Seamount
EMPEROR SEAMOUNTS
EMPEROR TROUGH
CHINOOK TROUGH
Comstock Seamount
Harris Seamount
NORTHEAST
MENDOCINO
KURIL BASIN
KURIL TRENCH
Hokkaido
Honshu
SEA OF JAPAN (East Sea)
JAPAN
JAPAN TRENCH
Xingang
Dalian
Incheon
Qingdao
YELLOW SEA
Busan
Ulsan
Nagoya
Tokyo
Chiba
Yokohama
Kobe
Osaka
Kitakyushu
Kyushu
Guangyang
EAST CHINA SEA
Shanghai
Yangtze
Yellow
Amur
NORTHWEST PACIFIC BASIN
SHATSKY RISE
HESS RISE
NORTHWEST HAWAIIAN RIDGE
Judge Seamount
Ferguson Seamount
Grosvenor Seamount
Isakov Seamount
Makarov Seamount
Midway Is.
Lisianski I.
HAWAIIAN RIDGE
HAWAIIAN ISLANDS
NECKER RIDGE
O'ahu
Hawai'i
Musicians Seamounts
Mendelssohn Seamount
MURRAY
Mapmaker Seamounts
MID-PACIFIC MOUNTAINS
Johnston Atoll
IZU TRENCH
BONIN TRENCH
Bonin Is.
RYUKYU ISLANDS
RYUKYU TRENCH
Daito Is.
Taichung
Keelung
Taiwan
Kaohsiung
TROPIC OF CANCER
Hong Kong
Yantian
Hainan
PHILIPPINE SEA
KYUSHU-PALAU RIDGE
WEST MARIANA BASIN
MARIANA TROUGH
Mariana Islands
MARIANA TRENCH
Guam
Magellan Seamounts
EAST MARIANA BASIN
Challenger Deep -10920 (-35827ft) World's greatest ocean depth
YAP TRENCH
PALAU TRENCH
Palau
Wake I.
Taongi Atoll
Bikini Atoll
Enewetak Atoll
Kwajalein Atoll
MARSHALL ISLANDS
Majuro Atoll
CENTRAL PACIFIC BASIN
MAGELLAN RISE
Palmyra Atoll
LINE ISLANDS
Kiritimati (Christmas I.)
Jarvis I.
Howland I.
Baker I.
Butaritari
Tarawa
Gilbert Islands
Banaba
Nauru
Beru
INDOCHINA PENINSULA
Mekong
Laem Chabang
SOUTH CHINA SEA
Luzon
Manila
PHILIPPINE ISLANDS
PHILIPPINE TRENCH
PALAWAN TROUGH
SULU BASIN
Mindanao
ANDAMAN BASIN
Nicobar
CONTINENTAL SHELF
CELEBES BASIN
CAROLINE ISLANDS
Chuuk
Pohnpei (Ponape)
WEST CAROLINE BASIN
EAURIPIK RISE
EAST CAROLINE BASIN
Singapore
EQUATOR
Sumatra
Borneo
Celebes
INDONESIA
GREATER SUNDA ISLANDS
LESSER SUNDA ISLANDS
BANDA SEA
WEBER BASIN
Java
Bali
JAVA TRENCH
JAVA RIDGE
-7125 (-23376ft) Indian Ocean's deepest point
Christmas I.
Cocos Is.
INVESTIGATOR RIDGE
New Guinea
BISMARCK ARCHIPELAGO
SOLOMON ISLANDS
Nukumanu
Tuvalu
Funafuti
Nikumaroro
Phoenix Islands
Atafu
Tokelau
Swains I.
Rawaki
VITYAZ TRENCH
Wallis Is.
Savai'i
Upolu
Samoa Islands
Rose Atoll
MANIHIKI PLATEAU
Manihiki Atoll
Nassau
COOK ISLANDS
NORTH AUSTRALIAN BASIN
WHARTON BASIN
EXMOUTH PLATEAU
WALLABY PLATEAU
CUVIER PLATEAU
PERTH BASIN
BROKEN RIDGE
NATURALISTE PLATEAU
DIAMANTINA FRACTURE ZONE
CONTINENTAL SLOPE
CONTINENTAL SHELF
Great Barrier Reef
CORAL SEA BASIN
CORAL SEA
VANUATU
NORTH NEW HEBRIDES TRENCH
NEW HEBRIDES TRENCH
NORTH FIJI BASIN
FIJI
Fiji Islands
FIJI PLATEAU
LAU BASIN
Tonga Islands
Ata
TONGA TRENCH
New Caledonia
TROPIC OF CAPRICORN
AUSTRALIA
NORFOLK RIDGE
NEW CALEDONIA BASIN
LORD HOWE RISE
SOUTH FIJI BASIN
LAU RIDGE
Kermadec Islands
KERMADEC TRENCH
LOUISVILLE RIDGE
SOUTHWEST
Îles Maria
Mangaia
Newcastle
Lord Howe I.
Ball's Pyramid
Taupo Tablemount
Gascoyne Tablemount
TASMAN PLAIN
TASMAN BASIN
TASMAN SEA
SOUTH AUSTRALIAN BASIN
NEW ZEALAND
North Island
South Island
CHATHAM RISE
Chatham Is.
BOUNTY TROUGH
Bounty Is.
Tasmania
EAST TASMAN PLATEAU
SOUTH TASMAN RISE
INDIAN OCEAN
SOUTHEAST INDIAN RIDGE
CAMPBELL PLATEAU
Antipodes Is.
Bollons Tablemount
Auckland Is.
Campbell I.
MACQUARIE RIDGE
EMERALD BASIN
UDINTSEV FRACTURE ZONE

The Pacific Ocean Basin is shrinking as it is subsumed under surrounding continents on all sides.

Indian Ocean Floor

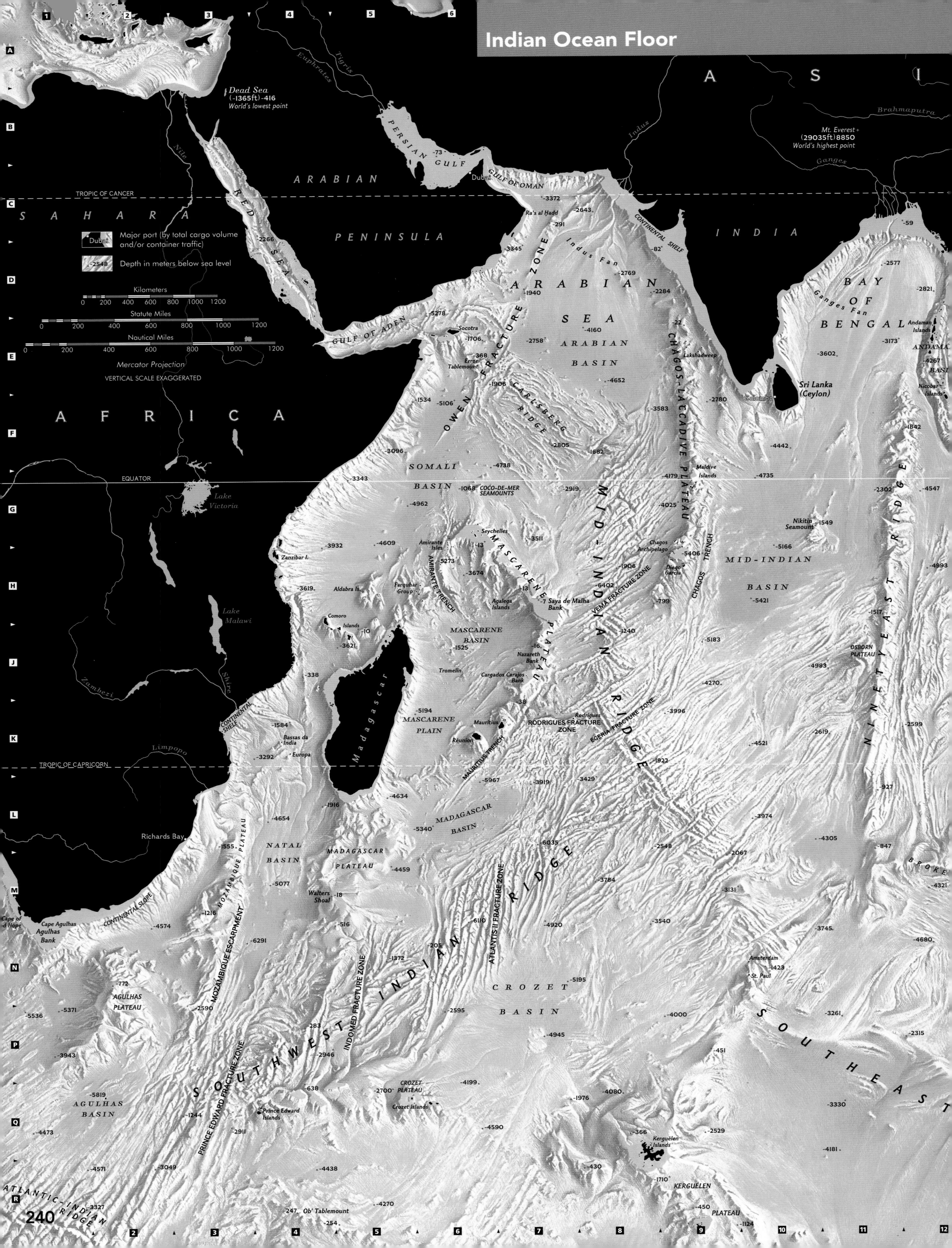

Dead Sea
(-1365ft) -416
World's lowest point
Mt. Everest
(29035ft) 8850
World's highest point
Major port (by total cargo volume and/or container traffic)
Depth in meters below sea level
Kilometers
0 200 400 600 800 1000 1200
Statute Miles
0 200 400 600 800 1000 1200
Nautical Miles
0 200 400 600 800 1000 1200
Mercator Projection
VERTICAL SCALE EXAGGERATED
TROPIC OF CANCER
EQUATOR
TROPIC OF CAPRICORN
A S I A
S A H A R A
A F R I C A
ARABIAN PENINSULA
I N D I A
Euphrates
Tigris
Nile
Indus
Brahmaputra
Ganges
Zambezi
Limpopo
Shire
RED SEA
PERSIAN GULF
GULF OF OMAN
GULF OF ADEN
Dubai
Ra's al Hadd
Lake Victoria
Lake Malawi
Madagascar
Sri Lanka (Ceylon)
Colombo
Richards Bay
Cape of Good Hope
Cape Agulhas
Agulhas Bank
CONTINENTAL SHELF
CONTINENTAL SLOPE
ARABIAN SEA
ARABIAN BASIN
Indus Fan
BAY OF BENGAL
Ganges Fan
Andaman Islands
Nicobar Islands
Lakshadweep
Maldive Islands
Chagos Archipelago
Diego Garcia
CHAGOS TRENCH
CHAGOS-LACCADIVE PLATEAU
OWEN FRACTURE ZONE
CARLSBERG RIDGE
Socotra
Error Tablemount
SOMALI BASIN
COCO-DE-MER SEAMOUNTS
Seychelles
Amirante Isles
AMIRANTE TRENCH
MASCARENE PLATEAU
Saya de Malha Bank
Nazareth Bank
Cargados Carajos Bank
Agalega Islands
Farquhar Group
Aldabra Is.
Comoro Islands
Zanzibar I.
MASCARENE BASIN
Tromelin
MASCARENE PLAIN
Mauritius
Réunion
MAURITIUS TRENCH
Rodrigues
RODRIGUES FRACTURE ZONE
EGERIA FRACTURE ZONE
VEMA FRACTURE ZONE
MID-INDIAN RIDGE
MID-INDIAN BASIN
Nikitin Seamount
NINETYEAST RIDGE
OSBORN PLATEAU
BROKEN
Bassas da India
Europa
MADAGASCAR BASIN
MADAGASCAR PLATEAU
NATAL BASIN
MOZAMBIQUE PLATEAU
MOZAMBIQUE ESCARPMENT
Walters Shoal
SOUTHWEST INDIAN RIDGE
ATLANTIS II FRACTURE ZONE
INDOMED FRACTURE ZONE
PRINCE EDWARD FRACTURE ZONE
Prince Edward Islands
AGULHAS PLATEAU
AGULHAS BASIN
CROZET BASIN
CROZET PLATEAU
Crozet Islands
Amsterdam
St. Paul
SOUTHEAST
Kerguelen Islands
KERGUELEN PLATEAU
Ob' Tablemount
ATLANTIC-INDIAN RIDGE

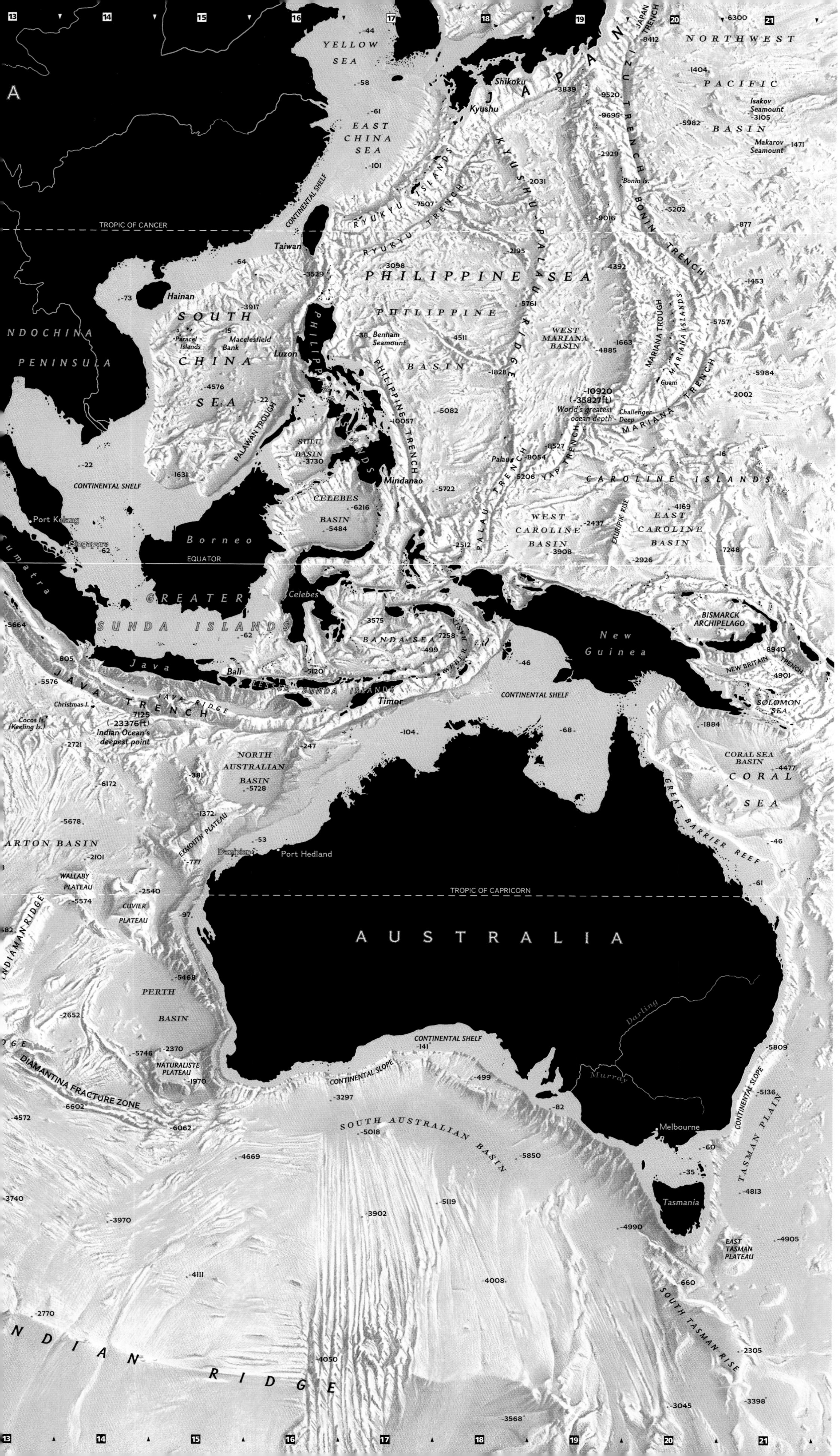

The Ninety East Ridge, the longest linear feature in the world, formed as ocean crust moved north over a hot spot deep in the Earth.

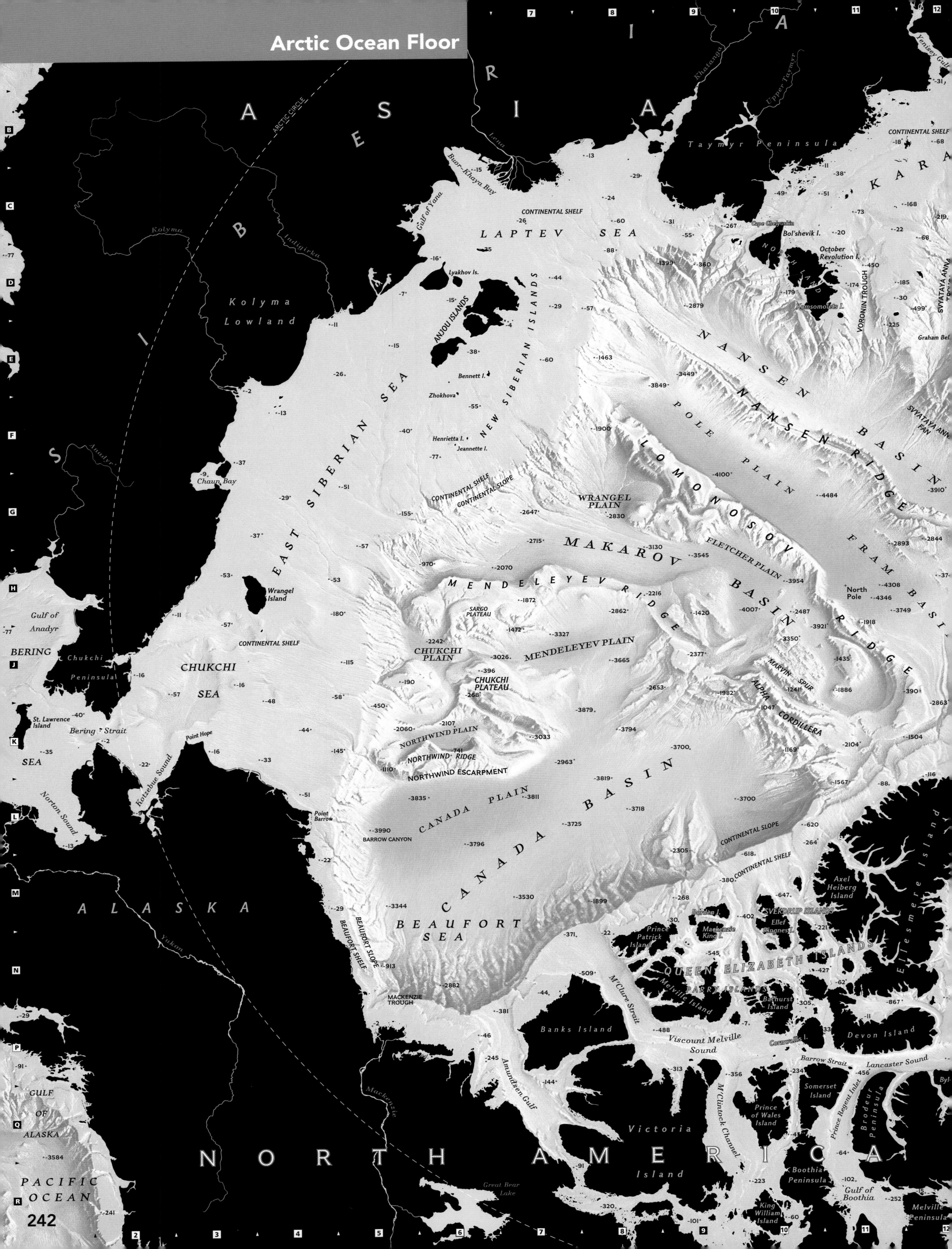
S I B E R I A
ARCTIC CIRCLE
Kolyma
Indigirka
Kolyma Lowland
Anadyr
Lena
Khatanga
Upper Taymyr
Yenisey Gulf
Taymyr Peninsula
KARA
CONTINENTAL SHELF
Buor-Khaya Bay
Gulf of Yana
LAPTEV SEA
Cape Chelyuskin
Bol'shevik I.
October Revolution I.
Komsomolets I.
VORONIN TROUGH
SVYATAYA ANNA TROUGH
Graham Bell
Lyakhov Is.
ANJOU ISLANDS
NEW SIBERIAN ISLANDS
Bennett I.
Zhokhova
Henrietta I.
Jeannette I.
EAST SIBERIAN SEA
Chaun Bay
NANSEN BASIN
NANSEN RIDGE
POLE PLAIN
LOMONOSOV RIDGE
FRAM BASIN
SVYATAYA ANNA FAN
CONTINENTAL SHELF
CONTINENTAL SLOPE
WRANGEL PLAIN
MAKAROV BASIN
FLETCHER PLAIN
North Pole
MENDELEYEV RIDGE
SARGO PLATEAU
Wrangel Island
Gulf of Anadyr
BERING
Chukchi Peninsula
CHUKCHI SEA
CHUKCHI PLAIN
MENDELEYEV PLAIN
CHUKCHI PLATEAU
MARVIN SPUR
ALPHA CORDILLERA
St. Lawrence Island
Bering Strait
SEA
Point Hope
Kotzebue Sound
Norton Sound
NORTHWIND PLAIN
NORTHWIND RIDGE
NORTHWIND ESCARPMENT
CANADA PLAIN
CANADA BASIN
Point Barrow
BARROW CANYON
CONTINENTAL SLOPE
CONTINENTAL SHELF
Axel Heiberg Island
Ellesmere Island
ALASKA
Yukon
BEAUFORT SEA
BEAUFORT SLOPE
BEAUFORT SHELF
Borden I.
SVERDRUP ISLANDS
Prince Patrick Island
Mackenzie King I.
Ellef Ringnes I.
QUEEN ELIZABETH ISLANDS
PARRY ISLANDS
Melville Island
Bathurst Island
MACKENZIE TROUGH
M'Clure Strait
Banks Island
Viscount Melville Sound
Cornwallis I.
Devon Island
Barrow Strait
Lancaster Sound
Amundsen Gulf
Mackenzie
M'Clintock Channel
Somerset Island
Prince of Wales Island
Prince Regent Inlet
Brodeur Peninsula
Victoria Island
GULF OF ALASKA
PACIFIC OCEAN
NORTH AMERICA
Great Bear Lake
Boothia Peninsula
Gulf of Boothia
King William Island
Melville Peninsula

Water depths in the Arctic Ocean must often be measured from submarines under the ice. They discovered three almost parallel ridges crossing the Arctic Basin.

Ocean Floor Around Antarctica

Major port (by total cargo volume and/or container traffic)
Dampier
Depth in meters below sea level
-2203
Kilometers
0 200 400 600 800 1000
Statute Miles
0 200 400 600 800 1000
Nautical Miles
0 200 400 600 800 1000
Azimuthal Equidistant Projection
VERTICAL SCALE EXAGGERATED
SOUTH AMERICA
Tubarão
Paraná
Uruguay
Colorado
Patagonia
Tierra del Fuego
Cape Horn
Falkland Islands
ARGENTINE PLAIN
CONTINENTAL SLOPE
CONTINENTAL SHELF
FALKLAND PLATEAU
MID-ATLANTIC RIDGE
FALKLAND FRACTURE ZONE
Discovery Tablemount
Herdman Seamount
Merz Seamount
Bouvet I.
Spiess Seamount
ATLANTIC
AMERICA-ANTARCTIC RIDGE
SOUTH SANDWICH TRENCH
South Georgia
South Sandwich Islands
SCOTIA SEA
South Orkney Is.
WEDDELL PLAIN
MAUD RISE
ANTARCTIC CIRCLE
Queen Maud Land
S. Shetland Is.
WEDDELL SEA
CONTINENTAL SHELF
Antarctic Peninsula
Berkner I.
RONNE ICE SHELF
Alexander I.
BELLINGSHAUSEN SEA
Peter I Island
Thurston I.
ANTARCTICA
BELLINGSHAUSEN PLAIN
AMUNDSEN SEA
Marie Byrd Land
ROSS ICE SHELF
Ross I.
ROSS SEA
ANTARCTIC CIRCLE
Scott I.
Balleny Is.
PACIFIC-ANTARCTIC RIDGE
PERU-CHILE TRENCH
NAZCA RIDGE
San Ambrosio I.
San Félix I.
Juan Fernández Islands
CHILE RISE
SALA-Y-GÓMEZ RIDGE
Sala-y-Gómez I.
CHALLENGER FRACTURE ZONE
EAST PACIFIC RISE
MENARD FRACTURE ZONE
ELTANIN FRACTURE ZONE
UDINTSEV FRACTURE ZONE
Ducie I.
Henderson I.
Oeno I.
Pitcairn I.
Îles Gambier
TUAMOTU ARCHIPELAGO
Marotiri
Rapa
Neilson Reef
LOUISVILLE RIDGE
CAMPBELL PLATEAU
Campbell I.
Auckland
Bounty Is.
Chatham Is.
CHATHAM RISE
NEW ZEALAND
South Island
North Island

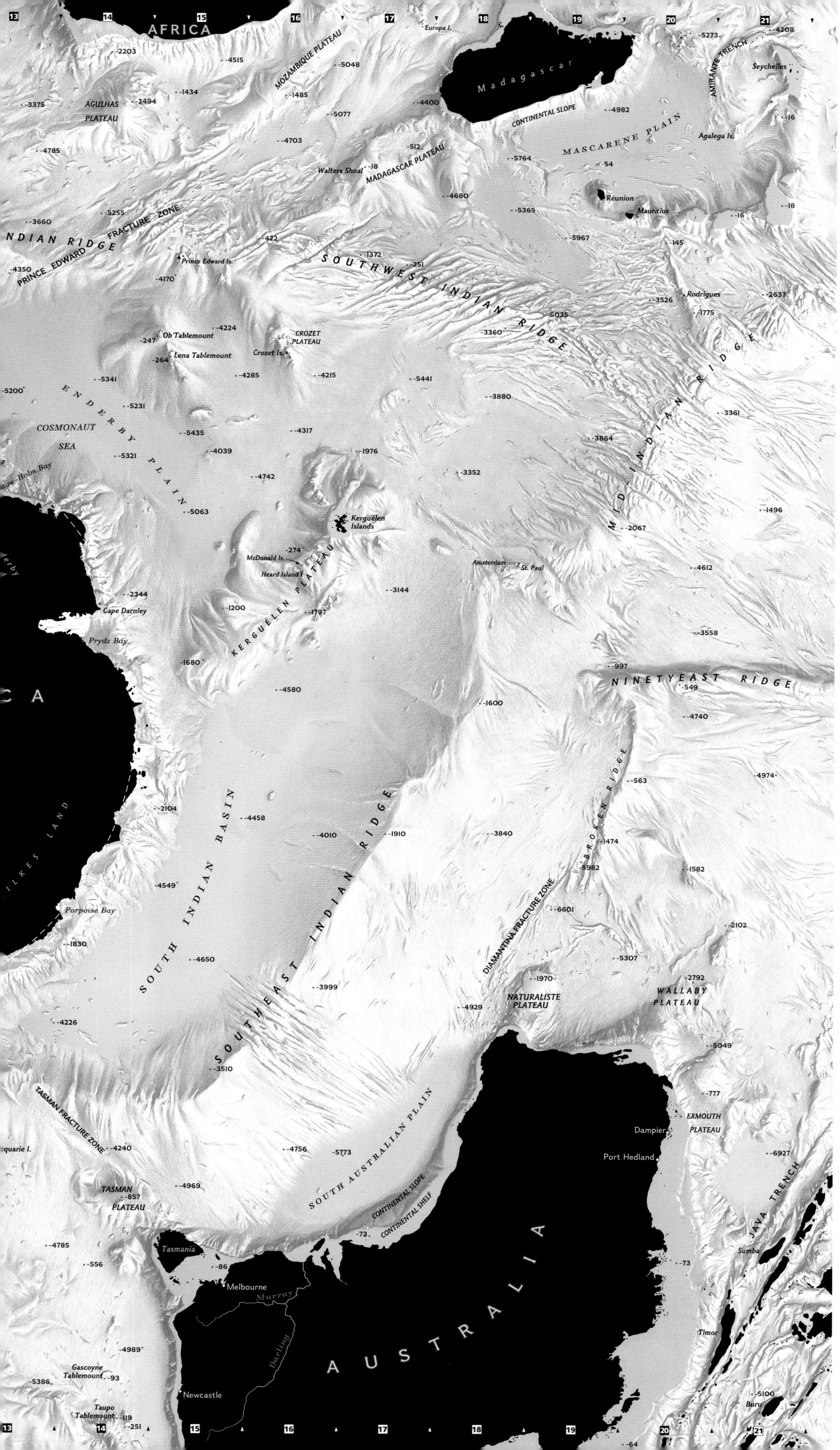

The ice-covered Antarctic continent is surrounded by deep, fairly flat underwater plains.

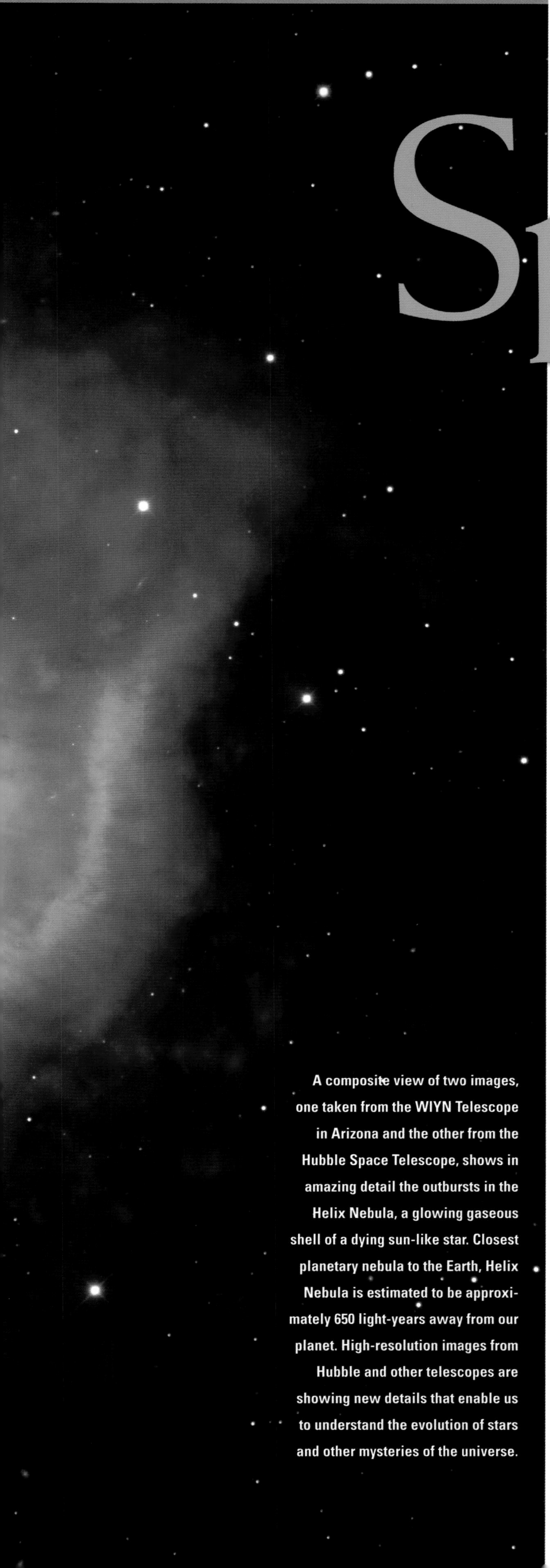

A composite view of two images, one taken from the WIYN Telescope in Arizona and the other from the Hubble Space Telescope, shows in amazing detail the outbursts in the Helix Nebula, a glowing gaseous shell of a dying sun-like star. Closest planetary nebula to the Earth, Helix Nebula is estimated to be approximately 650 light-years away from our planet. High-resolution images from Hubble and other telescopes are showing new details that enable us to understand the evolution of stars and other mysteries of the universe.

Space

In the first decade of the new millennium, astronomers are conducting extensive surveys of new frontiers in space, registering millions of galaxies, each composed of billions of stars. New orbiters and surface rovers explored Mars, confirming the presence of liquid water in its distant past and detecting methane in its atmosphere. A probe descended through the atmosphere of Titan, a moon of Saturn, and returned the first pictures from its surface, showing a strange, cold new world. A capsule traveling through space returned samples of the sun, and another spacecraft is now en route to Pluto. Meanwhile, a copper "cannonball" deployed from a spacecraft created the first man-made impact crater on a comet while another returned comet dust to Earth.

Wherever we look, we see evidence of cataclysmic events, indicating that we live in a 13-billion-year-old universe that is still evolving. Some suns, their atmospheres curiously enriched with telltale elements, may be "death stars" that swallowed whole planets long ago. Our own Milky Way is gradually devouring a small galaxy in the constellation Sagittarius, and elsewhere larger galaxies collide and distort each other. The universe began with a big bang and has been expanding ever since. A mysterious "dark energy" that exceeds all known forms of energy is thought to cause this expansion; space is also pervaded by unseen "dark matter," the dominant component of the universe. In laboratories on Earth and on the drawing boards of aerospace engineers, we are preparing to explore the next frontier of astronomical observation, looking for gravitational waves that may disturb the very fabric of space and time.

THE YOUNG EARTH HAD NO MOON. At some point in Earth's early history, an object larger than Mars struck Earth a great, glancing blow. Instantly, most of the rogue body and a sizable chunk of Earth were vaporized. The ensuing cloud rose to above 14,000 miles (22,500 km) altitude, where it condensed into innumerable solid particles that orbited Earth as they aggregated into ever larger moonlets, eventually combining to form the moon. This "giant impact" hypothesis of the moon's origin is based on computer simulations and on laboratory analyses of lunar rocks gathered by six teams of Apollo astronauts. It also fits with data on the lunar topography and environment recorded by the United States' Clementine and Lunar Prospector spacecraft.

The airless lunar surface bakes in the sun at up to 243°F (117°C) for two weeks at a time. All the while, it is sprayed with the solar wind of subatomic particles. Then, for an equal period, the same spot is in the dark, cooling to about minus 272°F (-169°C) when the sun sets. Day and night, the moon is bombarded by micrometeoroids and larger space rocks. The moon's rotation is synchronized with Earth's in such a way that it always shows the same face to Earth. One hemisphere, the near side, always faces us, while the other, the far side, always faces away. The far side has been photographed only from spacecraft. *(Continued on page 250)*

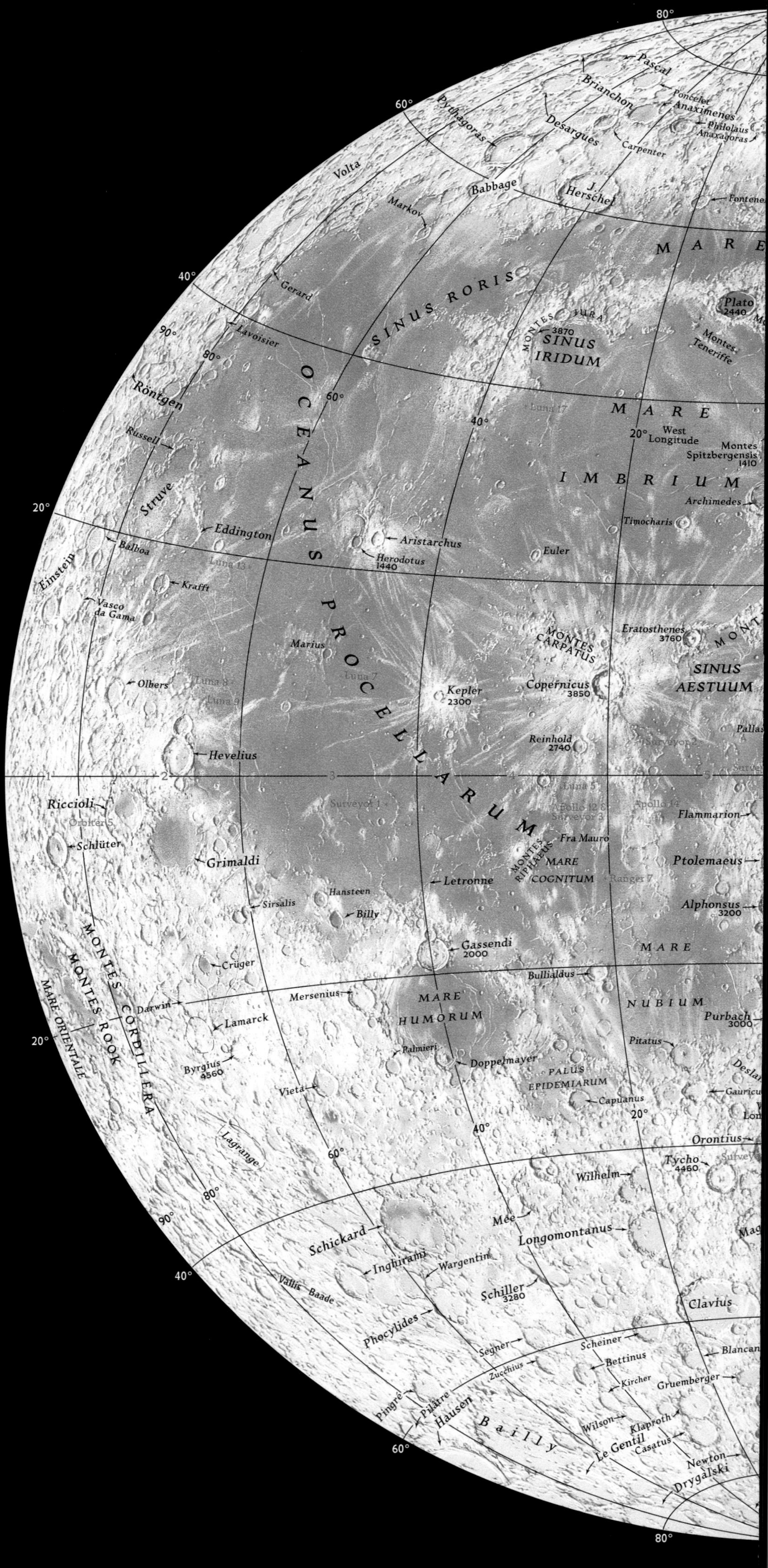

One square centimeter on this Lambert Azimuthal Equal-Area projection equals 28,700 square kilometers on the moon; elevations of prominent features are stated in meters. Impact craters, including those (labeled in blue) commemorating the seven *Challenger* astronauts, predominate on the far side. Landing site labels are in red.

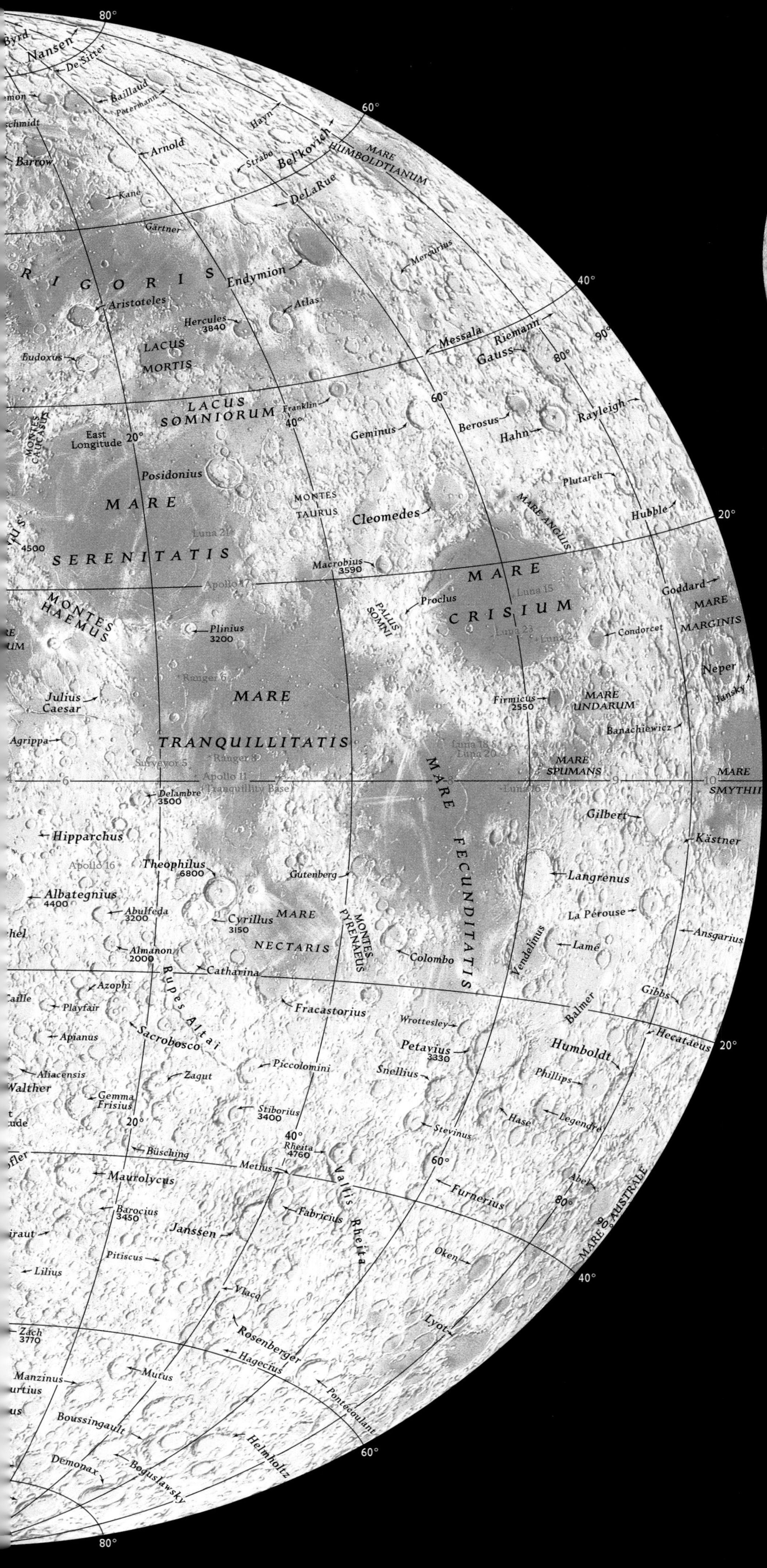

Clementine Digital Elevation Map

The digital elevation map of the near side of the moon was made from data provided by the Clementine mission in 1994. For middle latitudes (+70° to -70°), elevations were determined by laser ranging, which measures the altitude of surface features to within ± 130 feet (± 40 m). Horizontal resolution is fixed by the spacing of orbital ground tracks, about 40 miles (64 km). For the polar regions (latitudes greater than 70°), overlapping Clementine images were used to generate a stereo model of topography, with a vertical uncertainty of ± 330 feet (± 100 m) and a horizontal resolution of less than a mile (1.6 km). Most of the dark, lowland maria of the moon are on the near side. These plains were created when volcanic lava flooded depressions; thus, the near side is relatively smooth, showing relief of only about 3 to 4 miles (5 to 6 km).

(Continued from page 248)

The rocks and materials brought back by the Apollo missions are extremely dry; the moon has no indigenous water. However, it is bombarded by water-rich comets and meteoroids. Most of this water is lost to space, but some is trapped in permanently shadowed areas near the moon's poles.

To the unaided eye, the bright lunar highlands and the dark maria (Latin for "seas") make up the "man in the moon." A telescope shows that they consist of a great variety of round impact features, scars left by objects that struck the moon long ago. In the highlands, craters are closely packed together. In the maria, they are fewer. The largest scars are the impact basins, ranging up to about 1,500 miles (2,400 km) across. The basin floors were flooded with lava some time after the titanic collisions that formed them. The dark lava flows are what the eye discerns as maria. Wrinkled ridges, domed hills, and fissures mark the maria, all familiar aspects of volcanic landscapes. Young craters are centers of radial patterns of bright ejecta, material thrown from the impacts that made them. Because the force of gravity is weaker on the moon, blocks of rock hurled from impacts travel farther than they would on Earth.

The moon has no mountains like the Himalaya, produced by one tectonic plate bumping into another. There is no continental drift. Everywhere, the lunar surface is sheathed in regolith, a rocky rubble created by the constant bombardment by meteoroids, asteroids, and comets. Lunar mountains consist of volcanic domes and the central peaks and rims of impact craters.

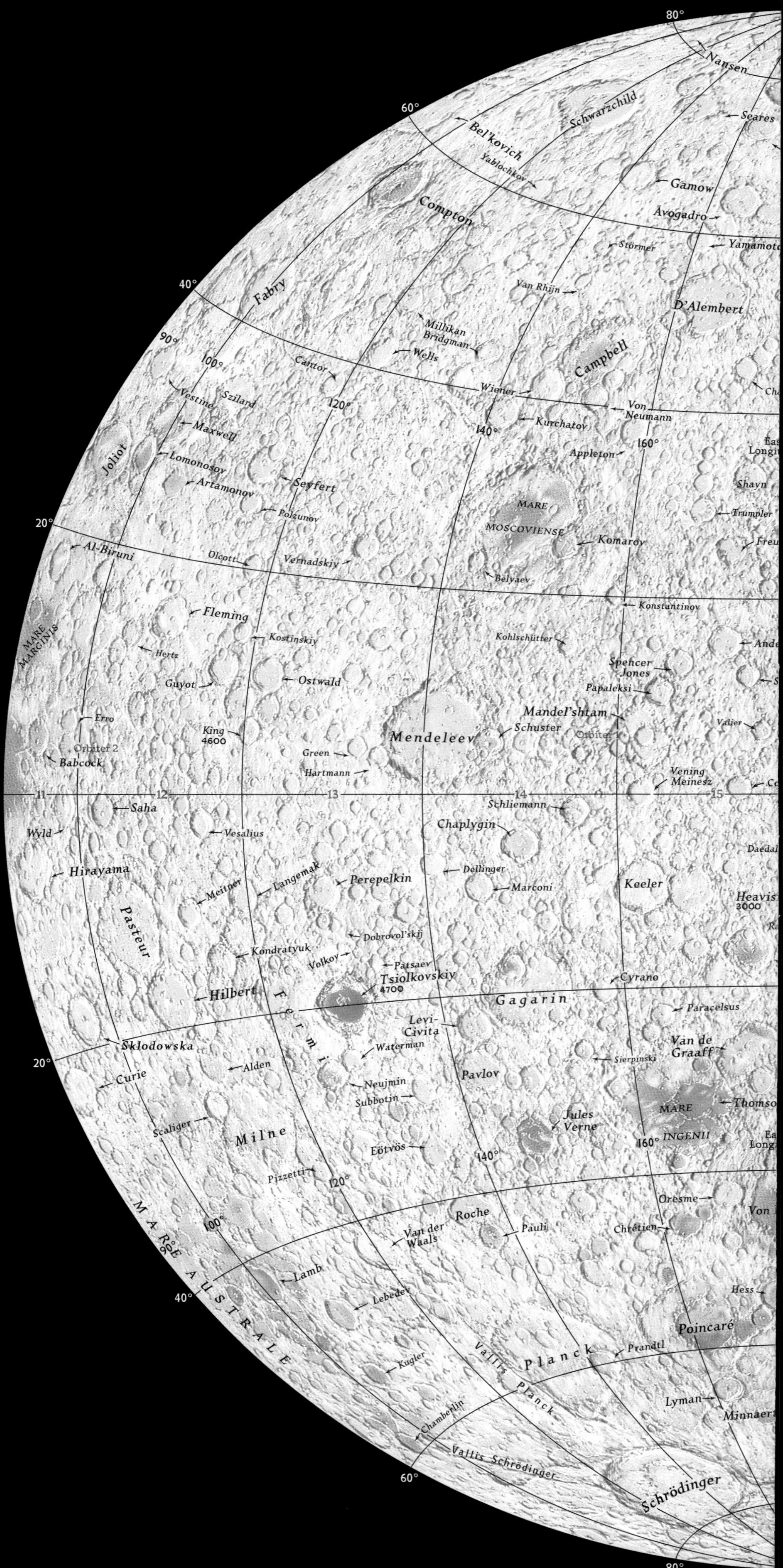

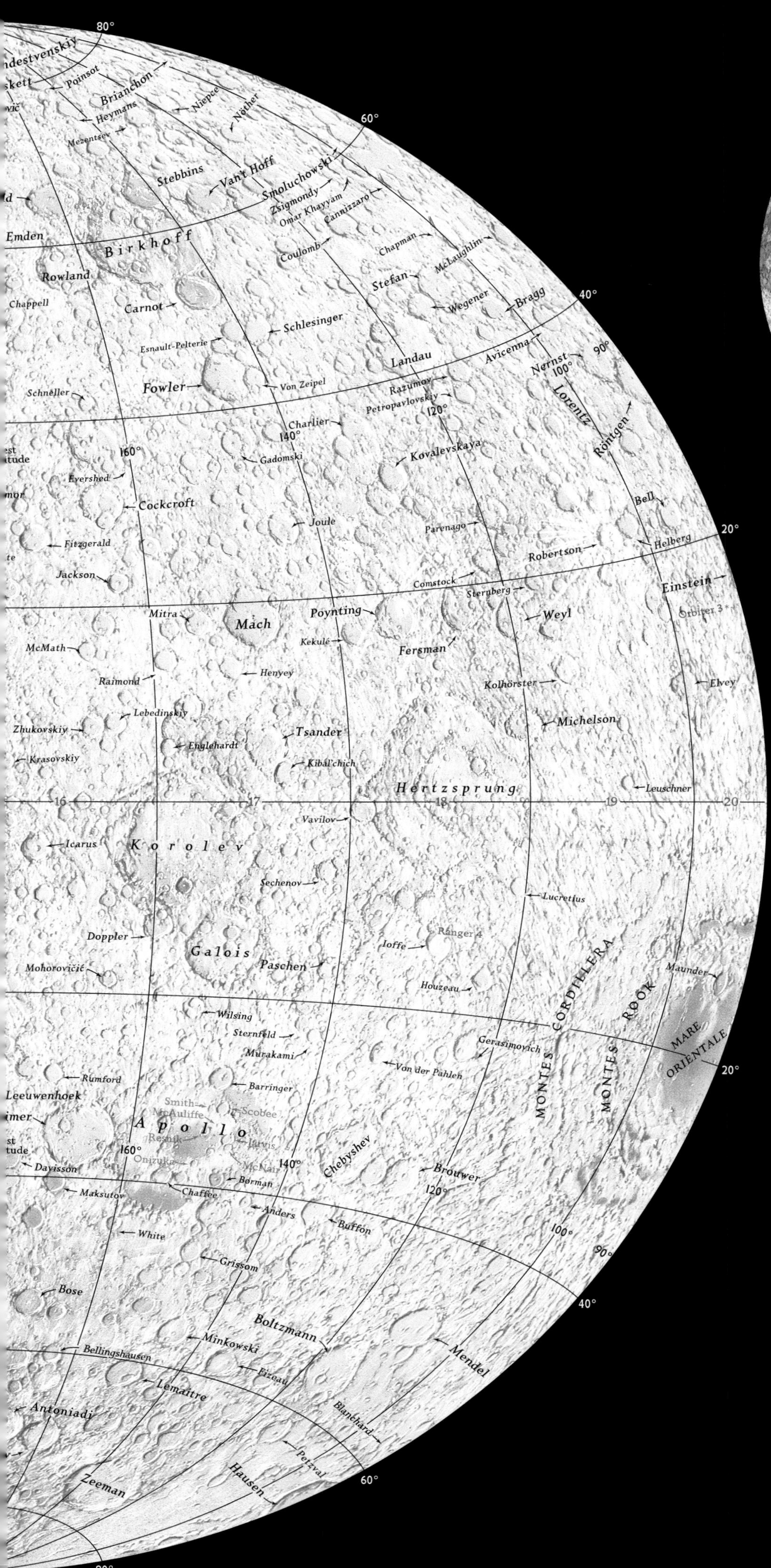

Clementine Digital Elevation Map

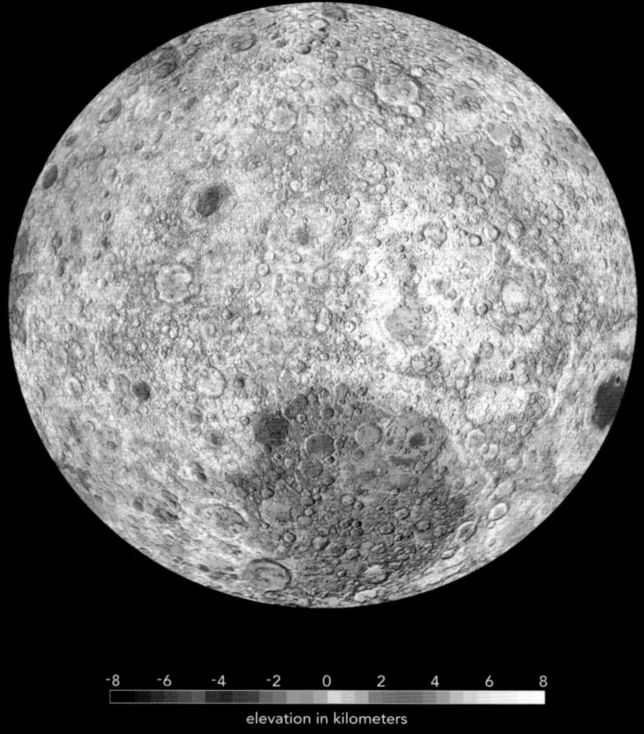

The digital elevation map shows the far side of the moon. This side, which we can never see from Earth, displays the full range of elevations found on the moon, from more than 5 miles deep to more than 5 miles high (-8 km to +8 km). The ruggedness of the far side is mostly caused by a lack of flooding by dark volcanic lava. The reasons for this hemispheric difference are not fully clear, but they are probably related to the near side having a thinner crust than the far side; thus, lava can more easily reach the surface on the near side. Note the large, circular depression at the center of the far side; this is the South Pole-Aitken basin. At 1,600 miles (2,600 km) in diameter and more than 8 miles (13 km) deep, it is one of the largest known impact craters in the solar system.

THE MARTIAN LANDSCAPE is both familiar and alien. All of its features, from rugged riverbeds to shifting sand dunes, are also found on Earth. Yet Mars, with its lower gravity and thinner atmosphere, imprints its own character on these features: The volcanoes are taller, the canyons wider, the ice caps more ephemeral than on Earth.

Compiled from NASA spacecraft data, the map at right depicts the remarkable terrain of the red planet. Mars's polar caps have frozen water, like our Arctic and Antarctic, but during the winters frozen carbon dioxide also coats the poles. The huge crater at far left is a caldera atop Olympus Mons, a Missouri-size volcano three times the height of Mount Everest. Three more large calderas, to the right of Olympus Mons, mark the peaks of three other volcanoes along the Tharsis rise. To the right of Tharsis, the dark canyons of the Valles Marineris (Mariner Valleys) extend more than 4,000 kilometers (2,500 mi). To the right of center, the dark patch running north-south is Syrtis Major, often the easiest feature to spot with a small telescope.

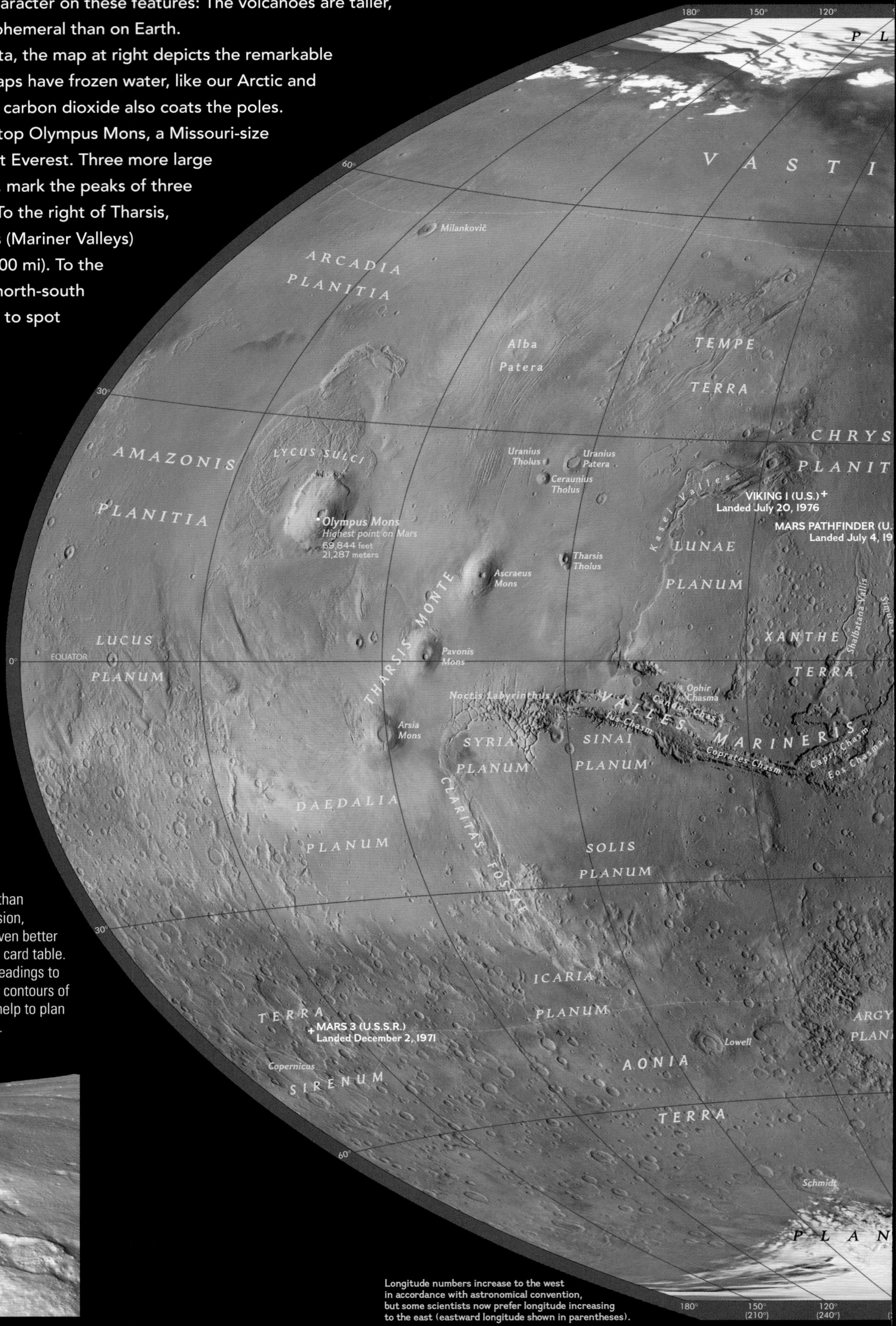

Longitude numbers increase to the west in accordance with astronomical convention, but some scientists now prefer longitude increasing to the east (eastward longitude shown in parentheses).

MARS RECONNAISSANCE ORBITER
The best maps of Mars already show greater detail than maps of some regions of Earth. The latest Mars mission, Mars Reconnaissance Orbiter, will make the maps even better by snapping pictures that show details as small as a card table. Scientists will combine the pictures with elevation readings to produce perspective views like this one showing the contours of Martian mountains and canyons. Images like these help to plan future missions that will search for signs of past life.

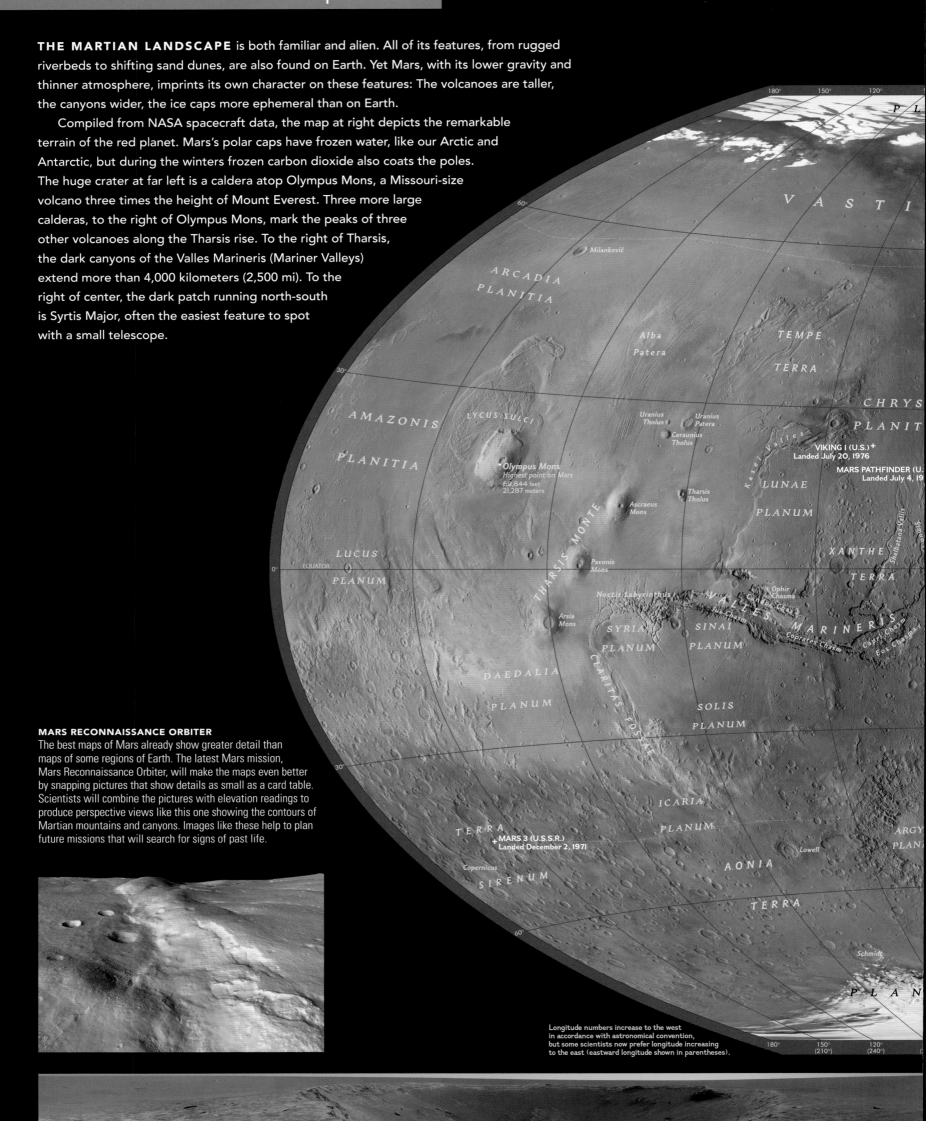

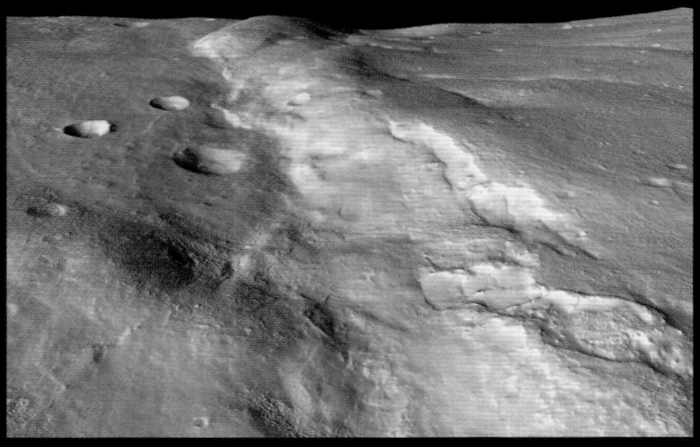

SPIRIT PANORAMA
NASA's Spirit rover surveys the Columbia Hills from the summit of Husband Hill, one of the tallest points in the range of hills that it began exploring in 2004. The rover's twisting tracks reveal light-colored soil, some of which is salty, beneath the powdery orange dust that coats much of Mars.

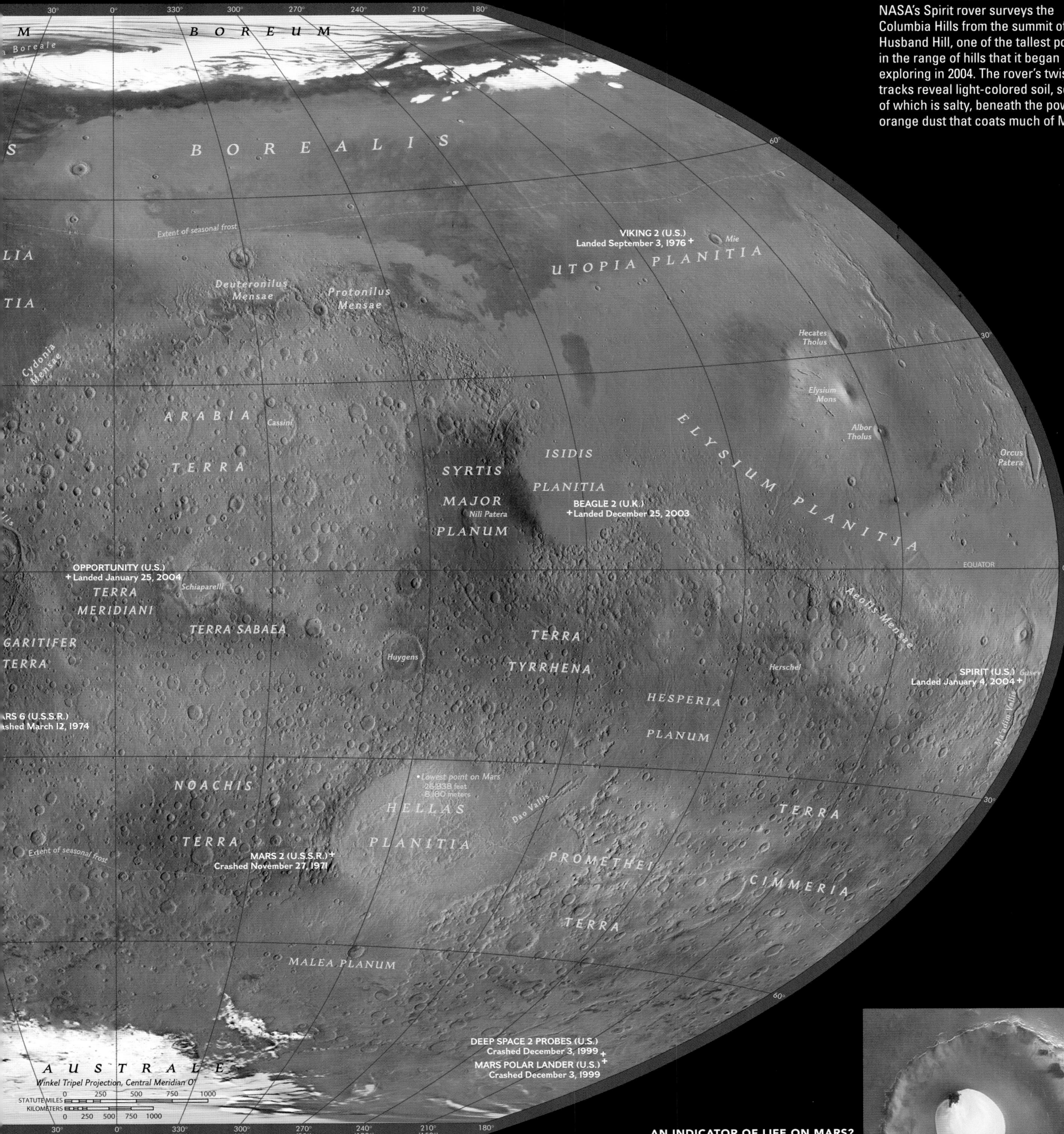

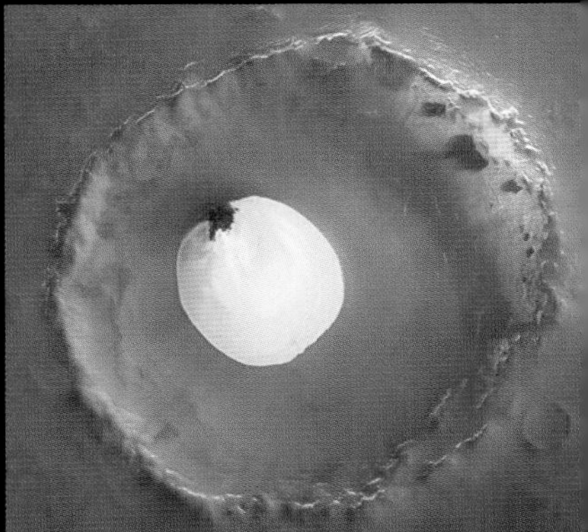

AN INDICATOR OF LIFE ON MARS?
A possible "pond" of frozen water pools at the bottom of an impact crater in Vastitas Borealis, a far-northern plain, in this image from the European Space Agency's Mars Express. Frost covers much of the crater's rim. Because water is an essential ingredient for life, such features are of great scientific interest.

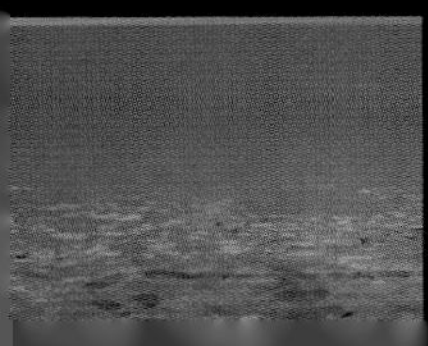

OPPORTUNITY PANORAMA
This 360-degree panorama shows an impact crater known as Endurance, along with the surrounding plains of Meridiani Planum. During six months inside the crater, the Opportunity rover

INNER SOLAR SYSTEM

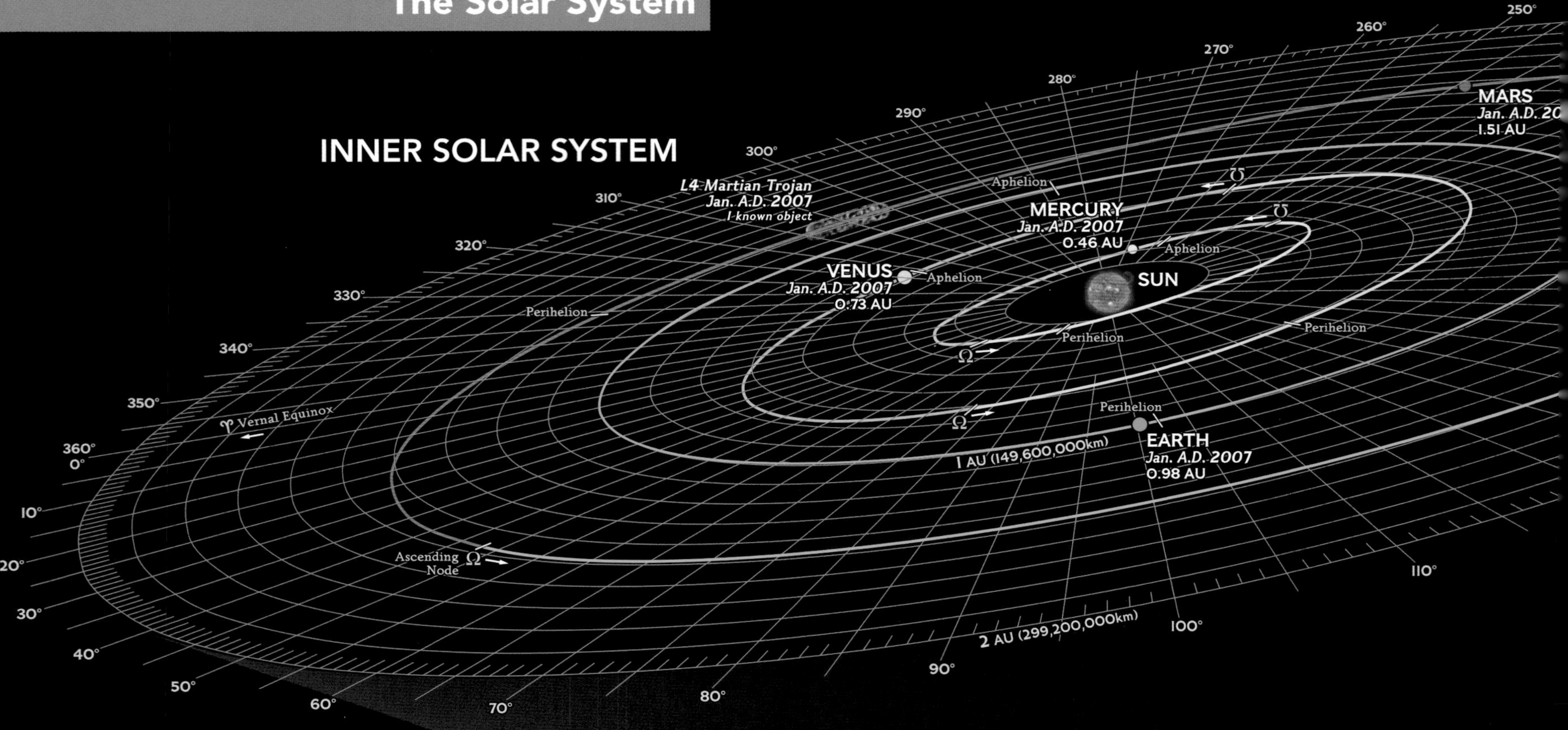

MAPPING THE SOLAR SYSTEM
The orbits of the planets and the path of Halley's comet appear on grids marked in astronomical units (1 AU = about 150 million kilometers). The inner four planets' orbits (above) are barely distinguishable in the chart of the solar system (right). All planets move counterclockwise as seen from above and north; Halley's comet travels oppositely.

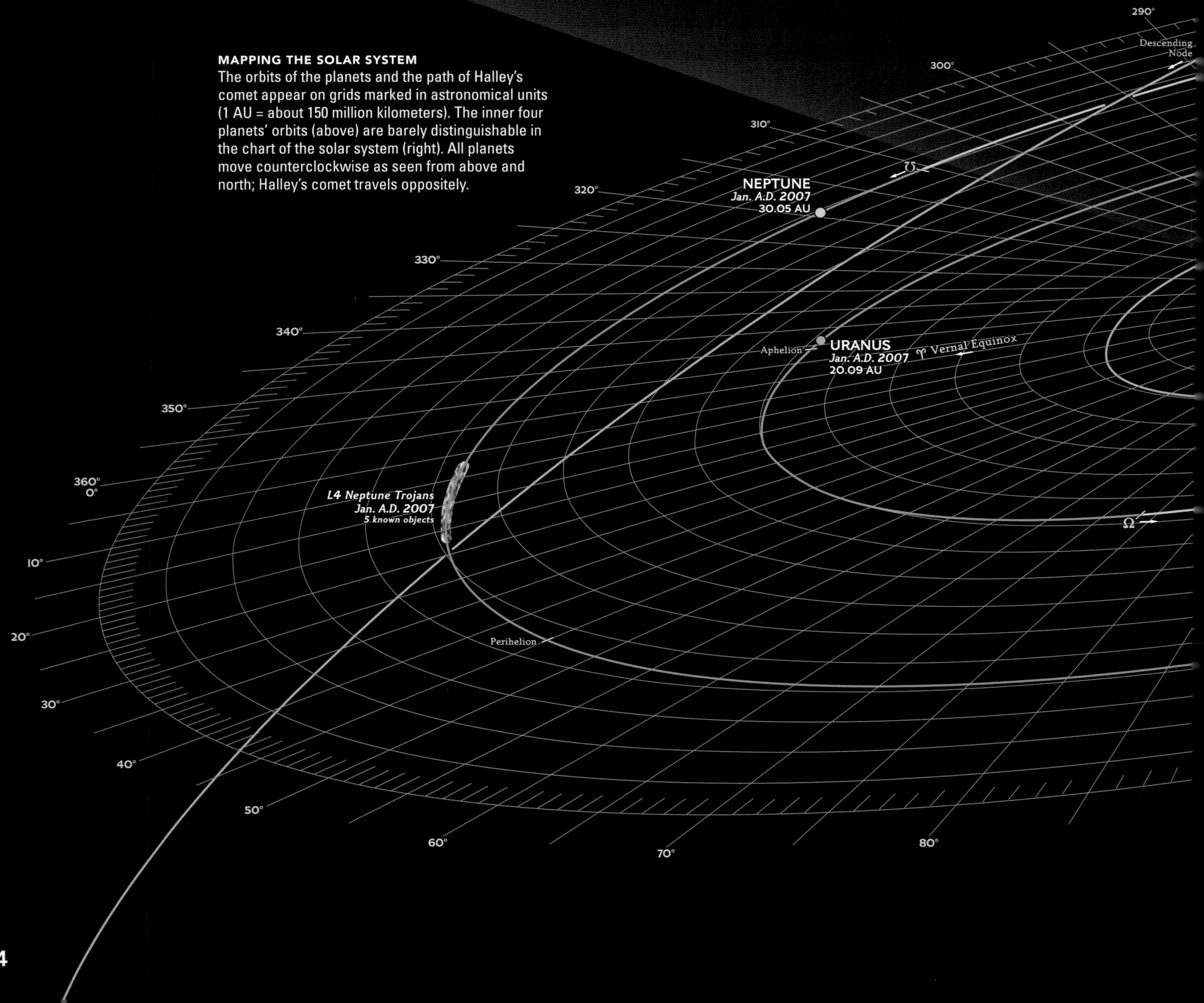

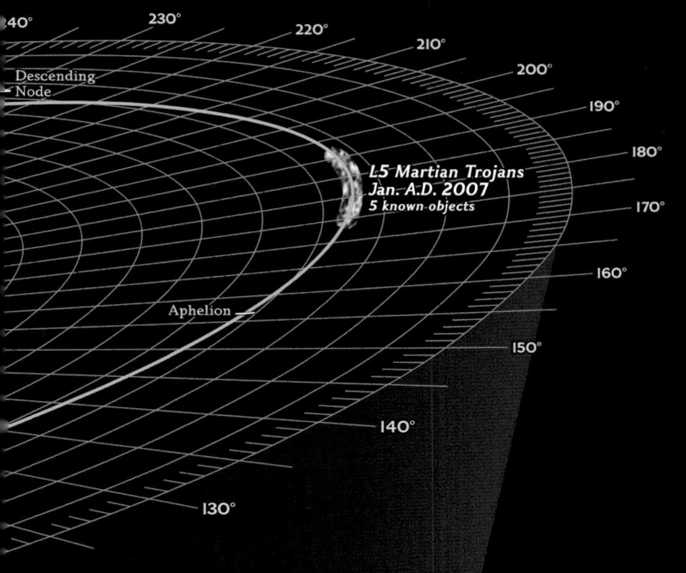

ASTEROIDS
Remnants from the age of planetary formation, the largest asteroids are spherical, like planets, but most others have irregular shapes, like potatoes. They sometimes collide and break up. A few are known to have tiny moons.

COMETS
Comets are composed of ice and other frozen substances, mixed in with interplanetary dust. As they approach the sun, the ices vaporize and the coma, or atmosphere, grows. Then, a long tail or tails sweep back in the antisolar direction.

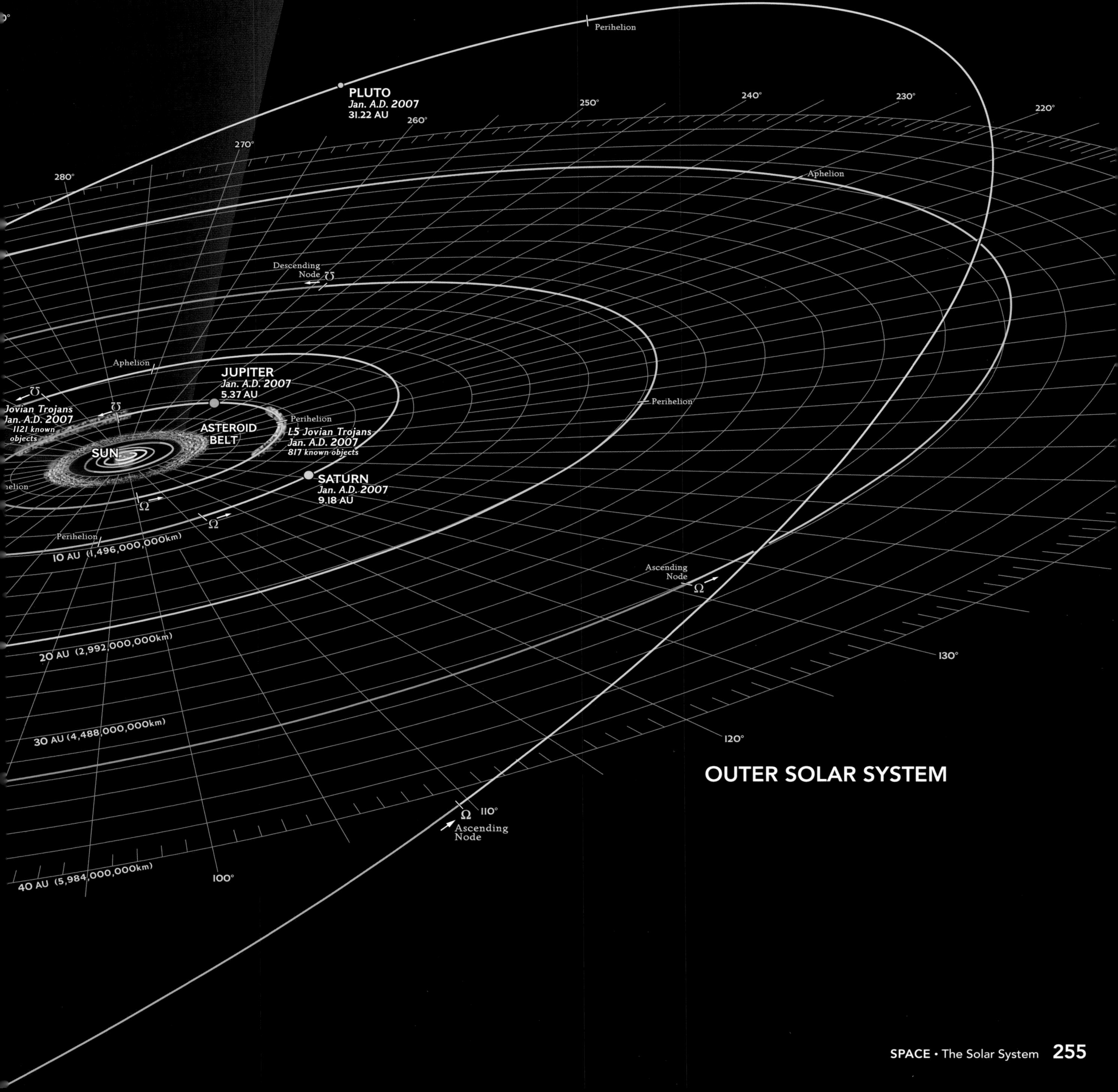

OUTER SOLAR SYSTEM

WHAT IS A PLANET?

Due to improvements in telescopic observation, we're continually learning more about our solar system, its planets and planet-like objects, and their evolution. Yet even as scientists learn and discover more, there is not yet uniform agreement among them about what actually defines a planet. In the last decade or so, observatories around the Earth have detected evidence of large bodies orbiting other stars. Are they also planets? The question is difficult to answer because beyond tradition, there is currently no universally accepted definition.

The solar system has two classes of planets whose origins can be partially explained or understood. The Inner planets (Mercury, Venus, Earth, and Mars) have solid surfaces and mean densities that suggest a rocky core. The Outer planets, called gas giants (Jupiter, Saturn, Uranus, and Neptune), are primarily hydrogen and helium gas and thus have much lower mean densities. Planets within our solar system vary widely in other ways as well: for example, in overall size, and in whether they have moons, rings, irregular shapes, and/or internal heat sources.

The discovery of yet another planet-like object, Xena, in 2005 has once again raised the question of "What is a planet?" The International Astronomical Union (IAU), an organization of professional astronomers, is at work on addressing this issue.

Mass and gravity data for each planet are expressed in proportional relation to Earth. Approximate values for Earth are given in both categories, allowing comparison between planets.

MERCURY	
Average distance from the sun:	57,900,000 km
Perihelion:	46,000,000 km
Aphelion:	69,820,000 km
Revolution period:	88 days
Average orbital speed:	47.9 km/s
Average temperature:	167°C
Rotation period:	58.9 days
Equatorial diameter:	4,879 km
Mass (Earth=1):	0.055
Density:	5.43 g/cm^3
Surface gravity (Earth=1):	0.38
Known satellites:	none

Image by: Mariner 10

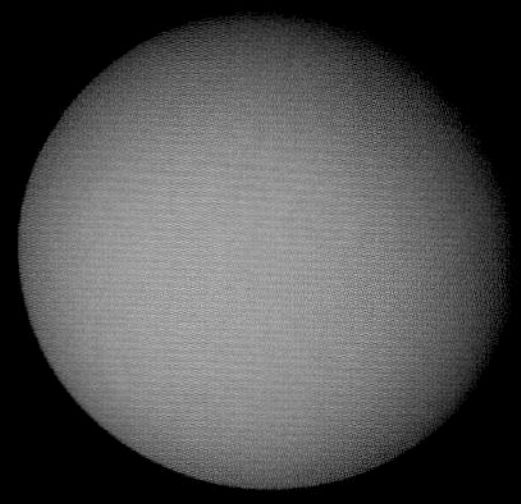

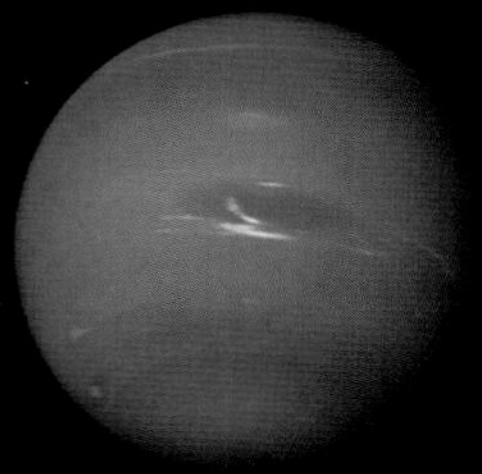

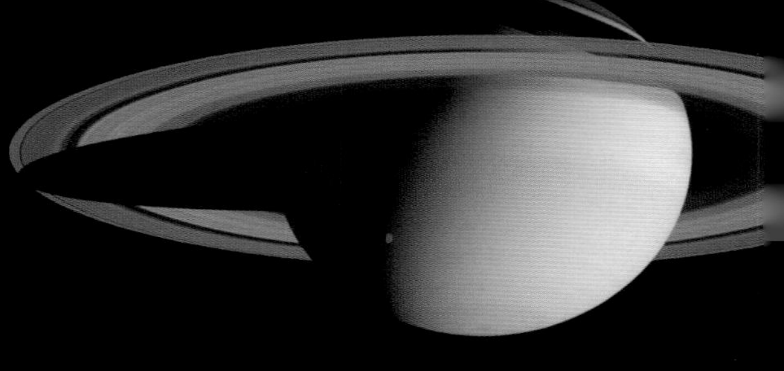

JUPITER	
Average distance from the sun:	778,600,000 km
Perihelion:	740,520,000 km
Aphelion:	816,620,000 km
Revolution period:	11.87 years
Average orbital speed:	13.1 km/s
Average temperature:	-110°C
Rotation period:	9.9 hours
Equatorial diameter:	142,984 km
Mass (Earth=1):	317.8
Density:	1.33 g/cm^3
Surface gravity (Earth=1):	2.36
Known satellites:	63
Largest satellites:	Ganymede, Callisto, Io, Europa

Image by: Cassini Orbiter

SATURN	
Average distance from the sun:	1,433,500,000 km
Perihelion:	1,352,550,000 km
Aphelion:	1,514,500,000 km
Revolution period:	29.44 years
Average orbital speed:	9.7 km/s
Average temperature:	-140°C
Rotation period:	10.7 hours
Equatorial diameter:	120,536 km
Mass (Earth=1):	95.2
Density:	0.69 g/cm^3
Surface gravity (Earth=1):	0.92
Known satellites:	47
Largest satellites:	Titan, Rhea, Iapetus, Dione, Tethys

Image by: Cassini Orbiter

RELATIVE SCALE

The planets are shown here in proportionate size to one another. See the Planetary Orbits diagram in the upper right of this plate for their proper relationship to the Sun.

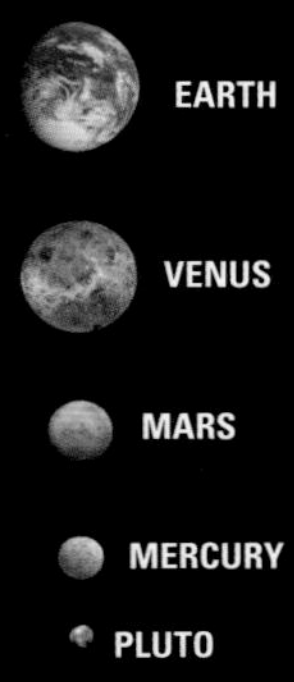

SUN

Average surface temperature:	5,505°C
Average core temperature	16,000,000°C
Rotation period:	25 days
Equatorial diameter:	1,392,000 km
Mass (Earth=1):	332,950
Density:	1.41 g/cm^3
Surface gravity (Earth=1):	28.0

PLANETARY ORBITS

(see also page 259)

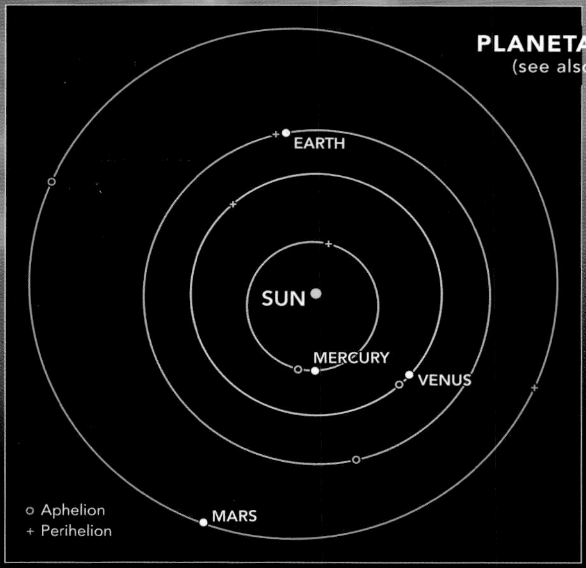

INNER SOLAR SYSTEM

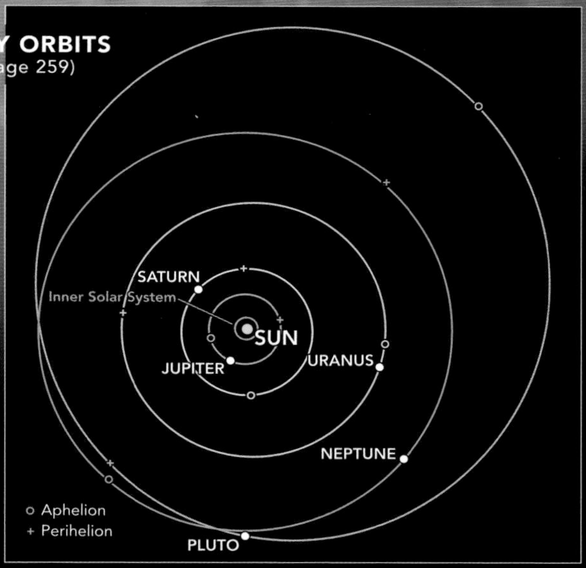

OUTER SOLAR SYSTEM

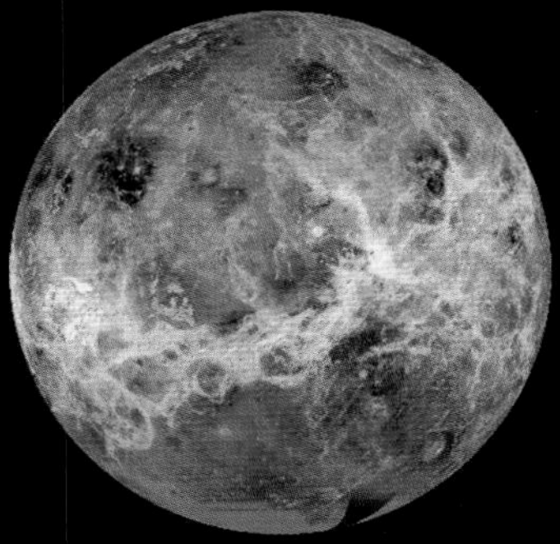

VENUS

Average distance from the sun:	108,200,000 km
Perihelion:	107,480,000 km
Aphelion:	108,940,000 km
Revolution period:	224.7 days
Average orbital speed:	35 km/s
Average temperature:	464°C
Rotation period:	244 days
Equatorial diameter:	12,104 km
Mass (Earth=1):	0.816
Density:	5.24 g/cm^3
Surface gravity (Earth=1):	0.91
Known satellites:	none

Image by: Magellan

EARTH

Average distance from the sun:	149,600,000 km
Perihelion:	147,090,000 km
Aphelion:	152,100,000 km
Revolution period:	365.2 days
Average orbital speed:	29.8 km/s
Average temperature:	15°C
Rotation period:	23.9 hours
Equatorial diameter:	12,756 km
Mass :	5,974,000,000,000,000,000,000 metric tons
Density:	5.52 g/cm^3
Surface gravity	9.81 m/s^2
Known satellites:	1
Largest satellite:	Earth's Moon

Image by: Galileo Orbiter

MARS

Average distance from the sun:	227,900,000 km
Perihelion:	206,620,000 km
Aphelion:	249,230,000 km
Revolution period:	687 days
Average orbital speed:	24.1 km/s
Average temperature:	-65°C
Rotation period:	24.6 hours
Equatorial diameter:	6,794 km
Mass (Earth=1):	0.107
Density:	3.93 g/cm^3
Surface gravity (Earth=1):	0.38
Known satellites:	2
Largest satellites:	Phobos, Deimos

Image by: Mars Global Surveyor

URANUS

Average distance from the sun:	2,872,500,000 km
Perihelion:	2,741,300,000 km
Aphelion:	3,003,620,000 km
Revolution period:	83.81 years
Average orbital speed:	6.8 km/s
Average temperature:	-195°C
Rotation period:	17.2 hours
Equatorial diameter:	51,118 km
Mass (Earth=1):	14.5
Density:	1.27 g/cm^3
Surface gravity (Earth=1):	0.89
Known satellites:	27
Largest satellites:	Titania, Oberon, Umbriel, Ariel

Image by: Hubble Space Telescope

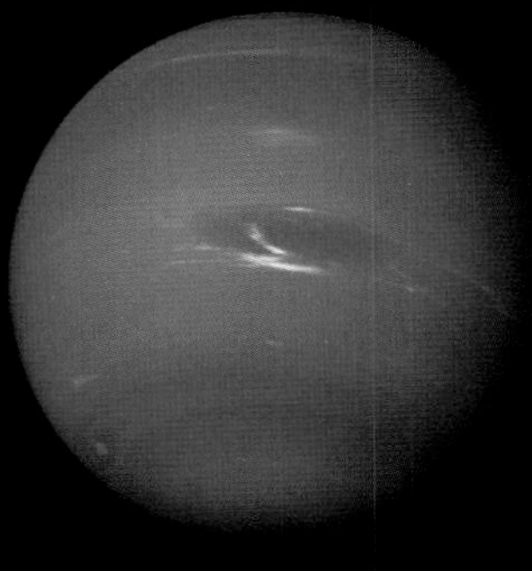

NEPTUNE

Average distance from the sun:	4,495,100,000 km
Perihelion:	4,444,450,000 km
Aphelion:	4,545,670,000 km
Revolution period:	163.84 years
Average orbital speed:	5.4 km/s
Average temperature:	-200°C
Rotation period:	16.1 hours
Equatorial diameter:	49,528 km
Mass (Earth=1):	17.1
Density:	1.64 g/cm^3
Surface gravity (Earth=1):	1.12
Known satellites:	13
Largest satellite:	Triton

Image by: Voyager II

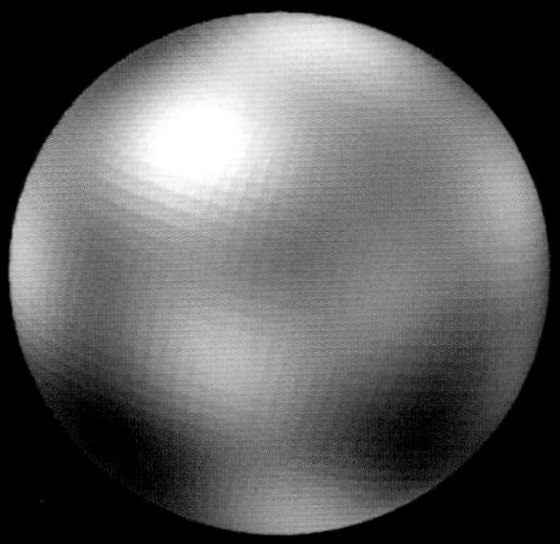

PLUTO

Average distance from the sun:	5,870,000,000 km
Perihelion:	4,436,820,000 km
Aphelion:	7,375,930,000 km
Revolution period:	248.19 years
Average orbital speed:	4.7 km/s
Average temperature:	-225°C
Rotation period:	6.4 days
Equatorial diameter:	2,390 km
Mass (Earth=1):	0.002
Density:	1.75 g/cm^3
Surface gravity (Earth=1):	0.06
Known satellites:	1
Largest satellite:	Charon

Image by: Hubble Space Telescope

LOOKING BACK IN TIME FOR ORIGINS
Supercomputer calculations simulate the structure of the early universe. Great chains of protogalaxies may have been stimulated by seed concentrations of as yet unidentified dark matter or shock waves from titanic explosions of the first stars. Only 500 to 800 million years elapsed from the dawn of time until the first galaxies formed. Hydrogen and helium from the big bang were transformed by nuclear reactions in stars and supernova explosions into all the other chemical elements found on Earth.

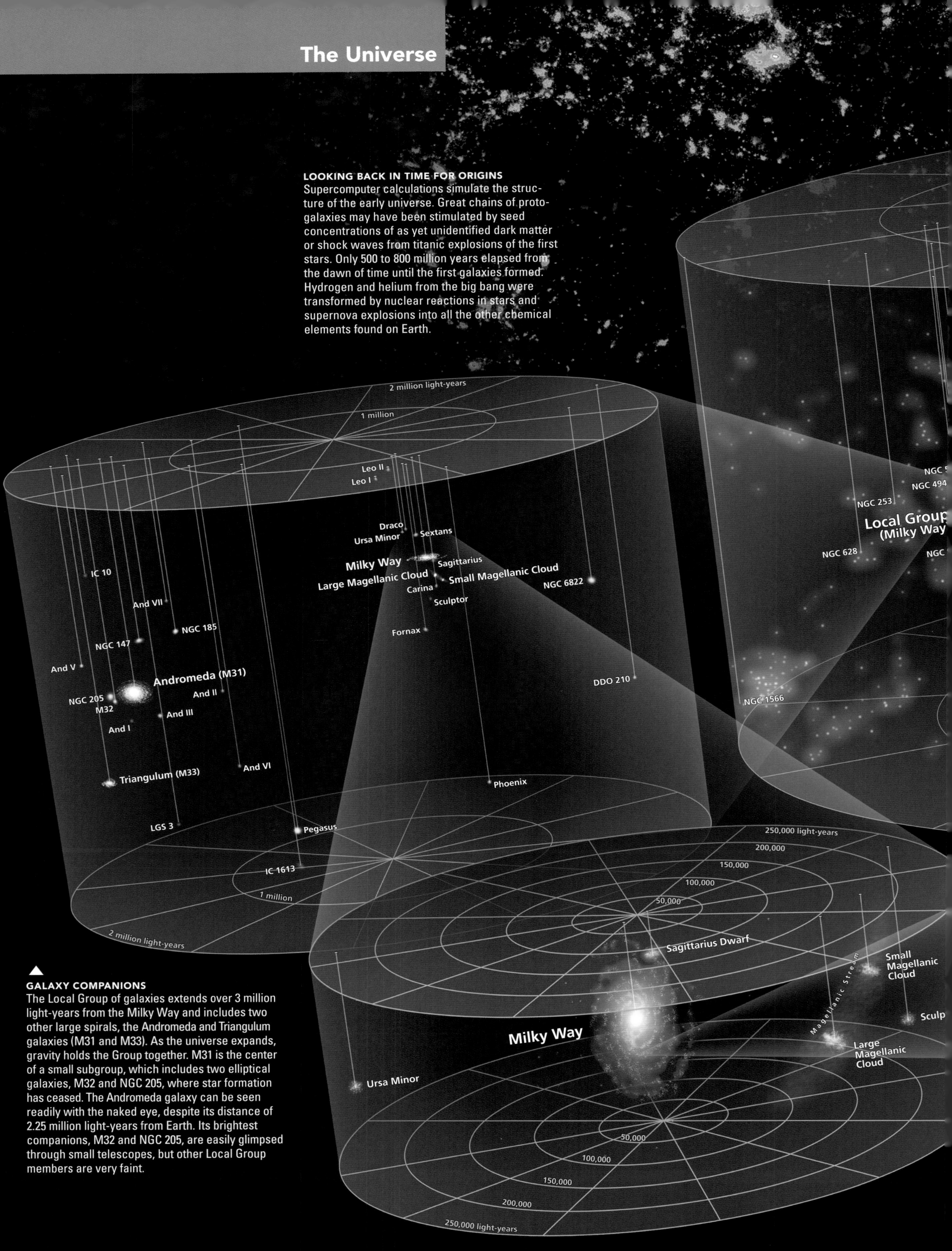

GALAXY COMPANIONS
The Local Group of galaxies extends over 3 million light-years from the Milky Way and includes two other large spirals, the Andromeda and Triangulum galaxies (M31 and M33). As the universe expands, gravity holds the Group together. M31 is the center of a small subgroup, which includes two elliptical galaxies, M32 and NGC 205, where star formation has ceased. The Andromeda galaxy can be seen readily with the naked eye, despite its distance of 2.25 million light-years from Earth. Its brightest companions, M32 and NGC 205, are easily glimpsed through small telescopes, but other Local Group members are very faint.

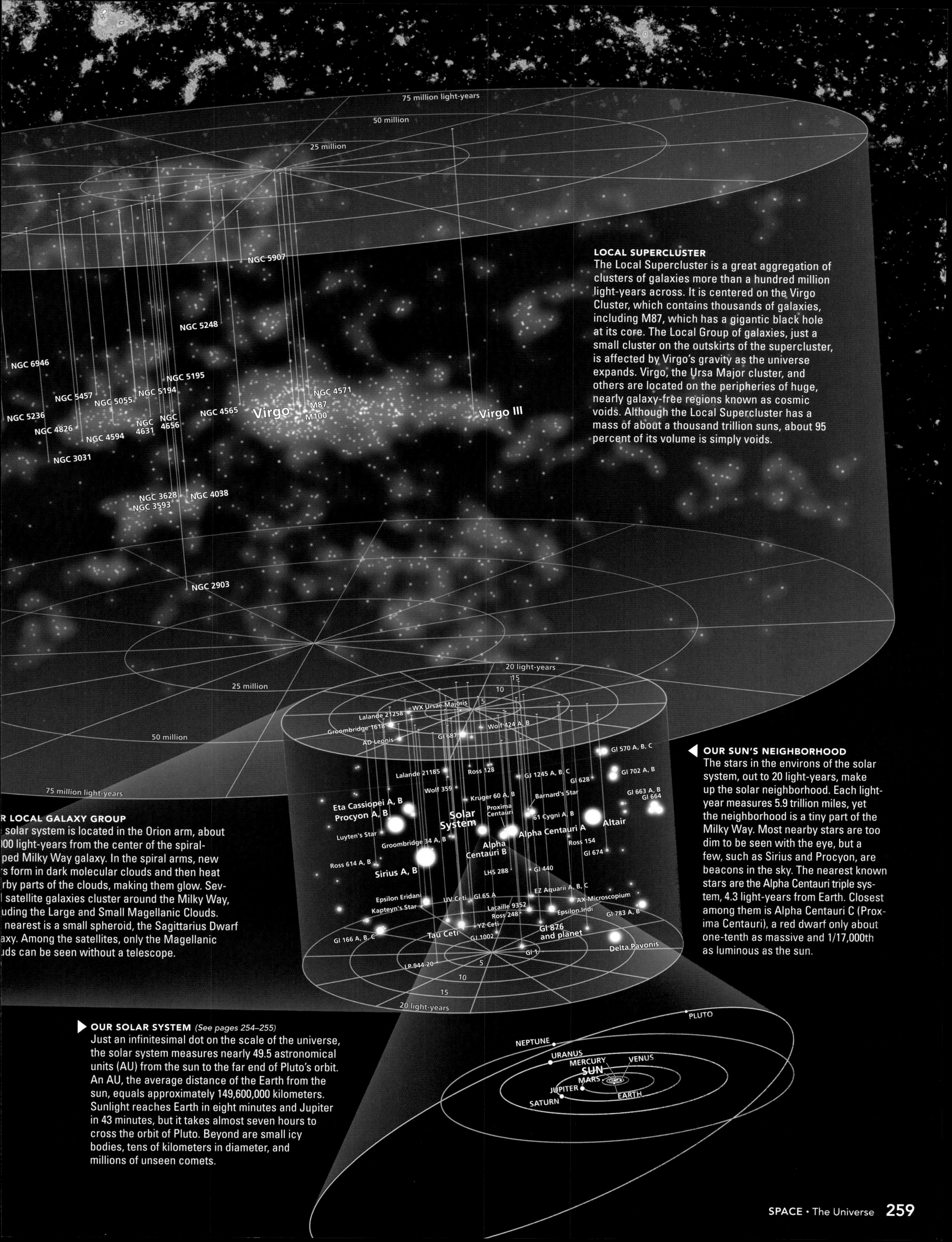

LOCAL SUPERCLUSTER
The Local Supercluster is a great aggregation of clusters of galaxies more than a hundred million light-years across. It is centered on the Virgo Cluster, which contains thousands of galaxies, including M87, which has a gigantic black hole at its core. The Local Group of galaxies, just a small cluster on the outskirts of the supercluster, is affected by Virgo's gravity as the universe expands. Virgo, the Ursa Major cluster, and others are located on the peripheries of huge, nearly galaxy-free regions known as cosmic voids. Although the Local Supercluster has a mass of about a thousand trillion suns, about 95 percent of its volume is simply voids.

R LOCAL GALAXY GROUP
solar system is located in the Orion arm, about 00 light-years from the center of the spiral-ped Milky Way galaxy. In the spiral arms, new s form in dark molecular clouds and then heat rby parts of the clouds, making them glow. Sev- l satellite galaxies cluster around the Milky Way, uding the Large and Small Magellanic Clouds. nearest is a small spheroid, the Sagittarius Dwarf axy. Among the satellites, only the Magellanic uds can be seen without a telescope.

OUR SUN'S NEIGHBORHOOD
The stars in the environs of the solar system, out to 20 light-years, make up the solar neighborhood. Each light-year measures 5.9 trillion miles, yet the neighborhood is a tiny part of the Milky Way. Most nearby stars are too dim to be seen with the eye, but a few, such as Sirius and Procyon, are beacons in the sky. The nearest known stars are the Alpha Centauri triple system, 4.3 light-years from Earth. Closest among them is Alpha Centauri C (Proxima Centauri), a red dwarf only about one-tenth as massive and 1/17,000th as luminous as the sun.

OUR SOLAR SYSTEM *(See pages 254–255)*
Just an infinitesimal dot on the scale of the universe, the solar system measures nearly 49.5 astronomical units (AU) from the sun to the far end of Pluto's orbit. An AU, the average distance of the Earth from the sun, equals approximately 149,600,000 kilometers. Sunlight reaches Earth in eight minutes and Jupiter in 43 minutes, but it takes almost seven hours to cross the orbit of Pluto. Beyond are small icy bodies, tens of kilometers in diameter, and millions of unseen comets.

Space Exploration Timeline

1957

First Artificial Satellite
U.S.S.R.
Oct. 4, 1957
Sputnik I was launched; it transmitted radio signals back to Earth for a short time.

First Live Animal in Space
U.S.S.R.
Nov. 3, 1957
Dog named Laika lived eight days in space aboard Sputnik 2.

1958

First American Satellite
U.S.
Jan. 31, 1958
Explorer I discovered radiation belts around the Earth.

Creation of NASA
U.S.
Oct. 1, 1958
National Aeronautics and Space Administration (NASA) was established.

1959

First Man-made Object to Achieve Solar Orbit
U.S.S.R.
Jan. 4, 1959
Luna 1

First Spacecraft to Impact on The Moon
U.S.S.R.
Sept. 14, 1959
Luna 2

First View of Moon's Far Side
U.S.S.R.
Oct. 7, 1959
Luna 3 photographed 70 percent of the far side.

1960

First Weather Satellite
U.S.
Apr. 1, 1960
Tiros 1 established satellites as a useful tool for studying weather conditions.

1961

First Man in Space
U.S.S.R.
Apr. 12, 1961
Yuri Gagarin orbited Earth once in Vostok I, completing the trip in 108 minutes.

First American in Space
U.S.
May 5, 1961
Alan Shepard's Freedom 7 flight lasted 15 minutes and did not reach orbit.

President John F. Kennedy's Historic Speech
U.S.
May 25, 1961
Kennedy challenged nation to land man on moon by end of decade.

1967

First U.S. Space Tragedy
U.S.
Jan. 27, 1967
Three astronauts were killed in a fire during a test.

First Spaceflight Casualty
U.S.S.R.
Apr. 24, 1967
Soyuz 1 crashed, killing one.

First Venus Probe Launched
U.S.S.R.
June 12, 1967
Venera 4 compiled data on Venusian atmosphere.

1968

First Moon Orbit
U.S.S.R.
Sept. 15, 1968
Zond 5

First Manned Apollo Mission
U.S.
Oct. 11, 1968
Apollo 7 orbited Earth once.

1969

First Manned Moon Orbit
U.S.
Dec. 24, 1968
Apollo 8 made ten orbits on six-day mission.

First Manned Moon Landing
U.S.
July 20, 1969
Neil Armstrong and Edwin Aldrin Jr. were first to set foot on the moon.

1970

Apollo 13 Launch
U.S.
Apr. 11, 1970
After oxygen tanks exploded three astronauts were nearly killed; mission control coordinated their dramatic rescue.

First Automated Return of Lunar Soil
U.S.S.R.
Sept. 12, 1970
Luna 16, an automated spacecraft, returned lunar soil samples.

1971

First Robotic Lunar Mission
U.S.S.R.
Nov. 10, 1970
Robot controlled from Earth

First Landing on Venus
U.S.S.R.
Dec. 15, 1970
Venera 7 transmitted from Venus' surface for 23 minutes.

1977

Launch of Voyager Missions
U.S.
Aug.–Sept. 1977
Voyager I and II traveled to Jupiter and Saturn; they were the first spacecraft sent to explore these planets.

1978

Arrival of U.S. Probes at Venus
U.S.
Dec. 1978
U.S. probes obtained data on the atmosphere and mapped the surface.

1979

Arrival of Voyager 1 at Jupiter
U.S.
Mar. 5, 1979
Voyager 1 transmitted pictures of the planet and its moons.

Arrival of Voyager 2 at Jupiter
U.S.
July 9, 1979
Voyager 2 transmitted images of the planet and its moons.

First Images of Saturn
U.S.
Sept. 1, 1979
Space probe Pioneer 11

1980

Arrival of Voyager 1 at Saturn
U.S.
Nov. 12, 1980
Probe transmitted images of the planet and its moons.

1981

First Space Shuttle Launch
U.S.
Apr. 12, 1981
First mission of the Space Transportation System (STS-1)

Arrival of Voyager 2 at Saturn
U.S.
Aug. 25, 1981
Probe transmitted images of the planet and its moons.

1987

1988

New Space Endurance Record
U.S.S.R.
Dec. 29, 1987
Yuri Romanenko inhabited Mir for 326 days.

1989

Arrival of Voyager 2 at Neptune
U.S.
Aug. 25, 1989
First close-up images of Neptune and its moons were transmitted.

1990

Launch of Hubble Space Telescope
U.S.
Apr. 24, 1990
Telescope was successfully deployed, but a flawed mirror resulted in fuzzy images.

Arrival of Magellan at Venus
U.S.
Aug. 10, 1990
Magellan used radar to map the Venusian surface.

1991

1997

Landing of Mars Pathfinder on Mars
U.S.
July 4, 1997
Spacecraft examined terrain and returned images of the planet's surface.

1998

Return of John Glenn to Space
U.S.
Oct. 29, 1998
Glenn returned to space for first time in 36 years.

Launch of First Module of I.S.S. (International Space Station)
Russia
Nov. 20, 1998
Russian rocket carried first component of I.S.S.

1999

First American I.S.S. Module
U.S.
Dec. 4, 1998
New module was attached to Russian module.

2000

100th Space Shuttle Mission
U.S.
Oct. 11, 2000
The 28th *Discovery* mission

First Landing on an Asteroid
U.S.
Feb. 12, 2001
NEAR spacecraft landed on asteroid Eros and sent back images.

2001

100th U.S. Space Walk
U.S.
Feb. 14, 2001
Space walk was necessary to install a new module for the I.S.S.

New Space Walk Record
U.S.
Mar. 11, 2001
Susan Helms and Jim Voss spent 8 hours, 56 minutes installing new I.S.S. module.

First Tourist in Space
U.S.- Russia
Apr. 28, 2001
Dennis Tito paid 20 million dollars to fly in a Russian Soyuz space capsule and board the I.S.S.

1962

First American in Orbit
U.S.
Feb. 20, 1962
John Glenn orbited the Earth three times on Friendship 7.

1963

First Woman in Space
U.S.S.R.
June 16, 1963
Valentina Tereshkova

1964

1965

First Space Walk
U.S.S.R.
Mar. 18, 1965
Alexei Leonov's tethered space walk lasted 12 minutes.

First Images of Mars
U.S.
July 14, 1965
Pictures from Mariner 4 showed no evidence of life on Mars.

First Spacecraft to Land on the Moon
U.S.S.R.
Feb. 3, 1966
Luna 9 demonstrated the moon's surface strong enough to support large spacecraft.

1966

First American Spacecraft on the Moon
U.S.
June 2, 1966
Surveyor I soft-landed on the moon and transmitted photographs.

1972

First Space Station
U.S.S.R.
Apr. 19, 1971
Salyut I orbited for more than two years.

First Occupation of Space Station
U.S.S.R.
June 7, 1971
Three cosmonauts occupied Salyut 1 for several weeks.

First Lunar Rover Mission
U.S.
July 30, 1971
Astronauts explored the moon's surface with a rover.

1973

First Spacecraft to Orbit Another Planet
U.S.
Nov. 13, 1971
Mariner 9 orbited Mars and mapped the surface.

1974

First Black Hole Candidate
U.S.
Dec. 1972
Cignus X-1 was designated as first probable black hole.

First U.S. Space Station
U.S.
May 14, 1973
Skylab was launched for science experiments.

1975

First Skylab Crew
U.S.
May 25, 1973
Crew repaired damage to Skylab sustained during launch.

First Inter-National Space Rendezvous
U.S. - U.S.S.R.
July 17, 1975
American Apollo 18 and Soviet Soyuz 19 docked together.

First Surface Images of Venus
U.S.S.R.
Oct. 1975
Venera 9 and 10

1976

First Surface Images of Mars
U.S.
July 20, 1976
Viking 1 represented first U.S. attempt at landing on another planet.

Discovery of Water Frost on Mars
U.S.
Sept. 1976
Viking 2 found water frost on Utopia Planitia.

1982

First Venus Soil Samples
U.S.S.R.
Mar. 1, 1982
Venera 13

First Operational Space Shuttle Mission
U.S.
Nov. 11, 1982
Space shuttle *Columbia* deployed two satellites.

1983

New Space Endurance Record
U.S.S.R.
Dec. 11, 1982
Two Soviet cosmonauts inhabited space station Salyut 7 for 211 days.

Maiden Voyage of *Challenger*
U.S.
Apr. 4, 1983
America's second space shuttle

1984

First American Woman in Space
U.S.
June 18, 1983
Sally Ride traveled on *Challenger* mission STS-7.

First Untethered Space Walk
U.S.
Feb. 3, 1984
Astronaut Bruce McCandless used the new Manned Maneuvering Unit.

1985

Maiden Voyage of *Discovery*
U.S.
Aug. 30, 1984
America's third space shuttle

Maiden Voyage of *Atlantis*
U.S.
Oct. 3, 1985
America's fourth space shuttle

Arrival of Voyager 2 at Uranus
U.S.
Jan. 24, 1986
Captured the first close-up views of Uranus and its moons

1986

***Challenger* Tragedy**
U.S.
Jan. 28, 1986
Shuttle's crew of seven were killed in an explosion when a leak ignited the fuel tank shortly after liftoff.

Launch of *Mir* Space Station
U.S.S.R.
Feb. 20, 1986
First module successfully launched into orbit.

1992

Maiden Voyage of *Endeavour*
U.S.
May 7, 1992
Launch brought the number of orbiters in the shuttle fleet back to four.

50th Space Shuttle Mission
U.S.
Sept. 12, 1992
The second *Endeavour* mission

1993

First H.S.T. Servicing Mission
U.S.
Dec. 2, 1993
Endeavour began the first servicing mission of the Hubble Space Telescope.

1994

First Russian Cosmonaut Aboard Shuttle
U.S.- Russia
Feb. 3, 1994
Sergei Krikalev flew aboard *Discovery.*

First Female Shuttle Pilot
U.S.
Feb. 3, 1995
Eileen M. Collins piloted *Discovery* on mission STS-63.

1995

New Space Endurance Record
Russia
Mar. 22, 1995
Valeriy Polyakov spent 438 days aboard *Mir.*

First Shuttle Docking with *Mir*
U.S.- Russia
June 29, 1995
American space shuttle *Atlantis* rendezvoused with the Russian space station.

Arrival of Galileo at Jupiter
U.S.
Dec. 7, 1995
Studies were made of the planet and its atmosphere.

1996

75th Space Shuttle Mission
U.S.
Feb. 22, 1996
The 19th *Columbia* mission

Return of Shannon Lucid From *Mir*
U.S.- Russia
Sept. 26, 1996
Lucid set U.S. space endurance record of 188 days aboard *Mir.*

2002

Launch of Shenzhou IV
China
Dec. 30, 2002
China launched its Shenzhou IV spacecraft in a test launch to prepare for manned space voyages.

Space Shuttle *Columbia* Mission
U.S.
Feb. 1, 2003
The shuttle *Columbia* broke up during its return descent, killing all seven crew members.

2003

Successful Chinese Orbit
China
Oct. 15, 2003
China launched a human into space, who returned safely after orbiting Earth for two days.

Spirit Rover on Mars
U.S.
Jan. 15, 2004
The NASA Rover Spirit rolled onto the surface of Mars after bouncing to a landing nearly two weeks earlier.

2004

Data From Titan
U.S.
Jan. 14, 2005
Huygens made a parachute-assisted descent through the atmosphere of Titan (a moon of Saturn), collecting data.

First Probe into a Comet
U.S.
Jul. 4, 2005
In a planned collision, Deep Impact became the first space mission to probe inside the surface of a comet.

2005

Mission to Pluto
U.S.
Jan. 15–19, 2006
Stardust Capsule returned to Earth, bringing samples of Comet Wild. A few days later, a mission was launched to explore Pluto.

Discovery of Ice Volcanoes
U.S.
Mar. 9, 2006
NASA announced discovery of ice volcanoes on Enceladus.

2006

E.S.A. Venus Express
Europe
Apr. 11, 2006
European Space Agency's (ESA) Venus Express went into orbit around Venus.

FUTURE

In 2007, India will launch its first mission to the moon. In 2008, NASA plans to launch the Lunar Reconnaissance Orbiter for making detailed maps of the moon to be used in future manned missions. A few years later, NASA's second New Frontiers Mission, Juno, is expected to be launched. Juno will become the first solar-powered spacecraft to orbit Jupiter, collect information about its interior, and reveal new information about the formation and evolution of the solar system.

Appendix

Airline Distances in Kilometers

	BEIJING	CAIRO	CAPE TOWN	CARACAS	HONG KONG	HONOLULU	LONDON	MELBOURNE	MÉXICO	MONTRÉAL	MOSCOW	NEW DELHI	NEW YORK	PARIS	RIO DE JANEIRO	ROME	SAN FRANCISCO	SINGAPORE	STOCKHOLM	TOKYO
BEIJING		7557	12947	14411	1972	8171	8160	9093	12478	10490	5809	3788	11012	8236	17325	8144	9524	4465	6725	2104
CAIRO	7557		7208	10209	8158	14239	3513	13966	12392	8733	2899	4436	9042	3215	9882	2135	12015	8270	3404	9587
CAPE TOWN	12947	7208		10232	11867	18562	9635	10338	13703	12744	10101	9284	12551	9307	6075	8417	16487	9671	10334	14737
CARACAS	14411	10209	10232		16380	9694	7500	15624	3598	3932	9940	14221	3419	7621	4508	8363	6286	18361	8724	14179
HONG KONG	1972	8158	11867	16380		8945	9646	7392	14155	12462	7158	3770	12984	9650	17710	9300	11121	2575	8243	2893
HONOLULU	8171	14239	18562	9694	8945		11653	8862	6098	7915	11342	11930	7996	11988	13343	12936	3857	10824	11059	6208
LONDON	8160	3513	9635	7500	9646	11653		16902	8947	5240	2506	6724	5586	341	9254	1434	8640	10860	1436	9585
MELBOURNE	9093	13966	10338	15624	7392	8862	16902		13557	16730	14418	10192	16671	16793	13227	15987	12644	6050	15593	8159
MÉXICO	12478	12392	13703	3598	14155	6098	8947	13557		3728	10740	14679	3362	9213	7669	10260	3038	16623	9603	11319
MONTRÉAL	10490	8733	12744	3932	12462	7915	5240	16730	3728		7077	11286	533	5522	8175	6601	4092	14816	5900	10409
MOSCOW	5809	2899	10101	9940	7158	11342	2506	14418	10740	7077		4349	7530	2492	11529	2378	9469	8426	1231	7502
NEW DELHI	3788	4436	9284	14221	3770	11930	6724	10192	14679	11286	4349		11779	6601	14080	5929	12380	4142	5579	5857
NEW YORK	11012	9042	12551	3419	12984	7996	5586	16671	3362	533	7530	11779		5851	7729	6907	4140	15349	6336	10870
PARIS	8236	3215	9307	7621	9650	11988	341	16793	9213	5522	2492	6601	5851		9146	1108	8975	10743	1546	9738
RIO DE JANEIRO	17325	9882	6075	4508	17710	13343	9254	13227	7669	8175	11529	14080	7729	9146		9181	10647	15740	10682	18557
ROME	8144	2135	8417	8363	9300	12936	1434	15987	10260	6601	2378	5929	6907	1108	9181		10071	10030	1977	9881
SAN FRANCISCO	9524	12015	16487	6286	11121	3857	8640	12644	3038	4092	9469	12380	4140	8975	10647	10071		13598	8644	8284
SINGAPORE	4465	8270	9671	18361	2575	10824	10860	6050	16623	14816	8426	4142	15349	10743	15740	10030	13598		9646	5317
STOCKHOLM	6725	3404	10334	8724	8243	11059	1436	15593	9603	5900	1231	5579	6336	1546	10682	1977	8644	9646		8193
TOKYO	2104	9587	14737	14179	2893	6208	9585	8159	11319	10409	7502	5857	10870	9738	18557	9881	8284	5317	8193	

Abbreviations

Adm.	*Administrative*
Af.	*Africa*
Afghan.	*Afghanistan*
Agr.	*Agriculture*
Ala.	*Alabama*
Alas.	*Alaska*
Alban.	*Albania*
Alg.	*Algeria*
Alta.	*Alberta*
Arch.	*Archipelago, Archipiélago*
Arg.	*Argentina*
Ariz.	*Arizona*
Ark.	*Arkansas*
Arm.	*Armenia*
Atl. Oc.	*Atlantic Ocean*
Aust.	*Austria*
Austral.	*Australia*
Azerb.	*Azerbaijan*
B.	*Baai, Baía, Baie, Bahía, Bay, Buḩayrat*
B.C.	*British Columbia*
Belg.	*Belgium*
Bol.	*Bolivia*
Bosn. & Herzg.	*Bosnia and Herzegovina*
Braz.	*Brazil*
Bulg.	*Bulgaria*
C.	*Cabo, Cap, Cape, Capo*
Calif.	*California*
Can.	*Canada*
Cen. Af. Rep.	*Central African Republic*
C.H.	*Court House*
Chan.	*Channel*
Chap.	*Chapada*
Cmte.	*Comandante*
Cnel.	*Coronel*
Co.-s.	*Cerro-s*
Col.	*Colombia*
Colo.	*Colorado*
Conn.	*Connecticut*
Cord.	*Cordillera*
C.R.	*Costa Rica*
Cr.	*Creek, Crique*
C.S.I. Terr.	*Coral Sea Islands Territory*
D.C.	*District of Columbia*
Del.	*Delaware*
Den.	*Denmark*
Dom. Rep.	*Dominican Republic*
D.R.C.	*Democratic Republic of the Congo*
E.	*East-ern*
Ecua.	*Ecuador*
El Salv.	*El Salvador*
Eng.	*England*
Ens.	*Ensenada*
Eq.	*Equatorial*
Est.	*Estonia*
Eth.	*Ethiopia*
Exp.	*Exports*
Falk. Is.	*Falkland Islands*
Fd.	*Fiord, Fiordo, Fjord*
Fin.	*Finland*
Fk.	*Fork*
Fla.	*Florida*
Fn.	*Fortín*
Fr.	*France, French*
F.S.M.	*Federated States of Micronesia*
ft	*feet*
Ft.	*Fort*
G.	*Golfe, Golfo, Gulf*
Ga.	*Georgia*
Ger.	*Germany*
Gl.	*Glacier*
Gr.	*Greece*
Gral.	*General*
Hbr.	*Harbor, Harbour*
Hist.	*Historic, -al*
Hond.	*Honduras*
Hts.	*Heights*
Hung.	*Hungary*
Hwy.	*Highway*
I.-s.	*Île-s, Ilha-s, Isla-s, Island-s, Isle, Isol-a, -e*
Ice.	*Iceland*
I.H.S.	*International Historic Site*
Ill.	*Illinois*
Ind.	*Indiana*
Ind.	*Industry*
Ind. Oc.	*Indian Ocean*
Intl.	*International*
Ire.	*Ireland*
It.	*Italy*
Jap.	*Japan*
Jct.	*Jonction, Junction*
Kans.	*Kansas*
Kaz.	*Kazakhstan*
Kep.	*Kepulauan*
Ky.	*Kentucky*
Kyrg.	*Kyrgyzstan*
L.	*Lac, Lago, Lake, Límni Loch, Lough*
La.	*Louisiana*
Lab.	*Labrador*
Lag.	*Laguna*
Latv.	*Latvia*
Leb.	*Lebanon*
Lib.	*Libya*
Liech.	*Liechtenstein*
Lith.	*Lithuania*
Lux.	*Luxembourg*
m	*meters*
Maced.	*Macedonia*
Madag.	*Madagascar*
Maurit.	*Mauritius*
Mass.	*Massachusetts*
Md.	*Maryland*
Me.	*Maine*
Medit. Sea	*Mediterranean Sea*
Mex.	*Mexico*
Mgne.	*Montagne*
Mich.	*Michigan*
Minn.	*Minnesota*
Miss.	*Mississippi*
Mo.	*Missouri*
Mon.	*Monument*
Mont.	*Montana*
Mor.	*Morocco*
Mt.-s.	*Mont-s, Mount-ain-s*
N.	*North-ern*
Nat.	*National*
Nat. Mem.	*National Memorial*
Nat. Mon.	*National Monument*
N.B.	*National Battlefield*
N.B.	*New Brunswick*
N.C.	*North Carolina*
N. Dak.	*North Dakota*
N.E.	*Northeast*
Nebr.	*Nebraska*
Neth.	*Netherlands*
Nev.	*Nevada*
Nfld.	*Newfoundland*
N.H.	*New Hampshire*
Nicar.	*Nicaragua*
Nig.	*Nigeria*
N. Ire.	*Northern Ireland*
N.J.	*New Jersey*
N. Mex.	*New Mexico*
N.M.P.	*National Military Park*
N.M.S.	*National Marine Sanctuary*
Nor.	*Norway*
N.P.	*National Park*
N.S.	*Nova Scotia*
N.S.W.	*New South Wales*
N.V.M.	*National Volcanic Monument*
N.W.T.	*Northwest Territories*
N.Y.	*New York*
N.Z.	*New Zealand*
O.	*Ostrov, Oued*
Oc.	*Ocean*
Okla.	*Oklahoma*
Ont.	*Ontario*
Oreg.	*Oregon*
Oz.	*Ozero*
Pa.	*Pennsylvania*
Pac. Oc.	*Pacific Ocean*
Pak.	*Pakistan*
Pan.	*Panama*
Para.	*Paraguay*
Pass.	*Passage*
Peg.	*Pegunungan*
P.E.I.	*Prince Edward Island*
Pen.	*Peninsula, Péninsule*
Pk.	*Peak*
P.N.G.	*Papua New Guinea*
Pol.	*Poland*
Pol.	*Poluostrov*
Port.	*Portugal, Portuguese*
P.R.	*Puerto Rico*
Prov.	*Province, Provincial*
Pt.-e.	*Point-e*
Pta.	*Ponta, Punta*
Qnsld.	*Queensland*
Que.	*Quebec*
R.	*Río, River, Rivière*
Ra.-s.	*Range-s*
Rec.	*Recreation*
Rep.	*Republic*
Res.	*Reservoir, Reserve, Reservatório*
R.I.	*Rhode Island*
Rom.	*Romania*
Russ.	*Russia*
S.	*South-ern*
Sa.-s.	*Serra, Sierra-s*
S. Af.	*South Africa*
Sask.	*Saskatchewan*
S.C.	*South Carolina*
Scot.	*Scotland*
Sd.	*Sound*
S. Dak.	*South Dakota*
Serb. & Mont.	*Serbia and Montenegro*
Sev.	*Severn-yy, -aya, -oye*
Sk.	*Shankou*
Slov.	*Slovenia*
Sp.	*Spain, Spanish*
Spr.-s.	*Spring-s*
Sta.	*Santa*
St.-e.	*Saint-e, Sankt, Sint*
Str.-s.	*Straat, Strait-s*
Switz.	*Switzerland*
Syr.	*Syria*
Taj.	*Tajikistan*
Tas.	*Tasmania*
Tenn.	*Tennessee*
Terr.	*Territory*
Tex.	*Texas*
Tg.	*Tanjung*
Thai.	*Thailand*
Trin.	*Trinidad*
Tun.	*Tunisia*
Turk.	*Turkey*
Turkm.	*Turkmenistan*
U.A.E.	*United Arab Emirates*
U.K.	*United Kingdom*
Ukr.	*Ukraine*
U.N.	*United Nations*
Uru.	*Uruguay*
U.S.	*United States*
Uzb.	*Uzbekistan*
Va.	*Virginia*
Vdkhr.	*Vodokhranilishche*
Vdskh.	*Vodoskhovyshche*
Venez.	*Venezuela*
V.I.	*Virgin Islands*
Vic.	*Victoria*
Viet.	*Vietnam*
Vol.	*Volcán, Volcano*
Vt.	*Vermont*
W.	*Wadi, Wādī, Webi*
W.	*West-ern*
Wash.	*Washington*
Wis.	*Wisconsin*
W. Va.	*West Virginia*
Wyo.	*Wyoming*
Yug.	*Yugoslavia*
Zakh.	*Zakhod-ni, -nyaya, -nye*
Zimb.	*Zimbabwe*

QUICK REFERENCE CHART FOR METRIC TO ENGLISH CONVERSION

1 METER	1 METER = 100 CENTIMETERS
1 FOOT	1 FOOT = 12 INCHES
1 KILOMETER	1 KILOMETER = 1,000 METERS
1 MILE	1 MILE = 5,280 FEET

METERS	1	10	20	50	100	200	500	1,000	2,000	5,000	10,000
FEET	3.281	32.81	65.62	164.05	328.1	656.2	1,640.5	3,281.0	6,562.0	16,405.0	32,810.0
KILOMETERS	1	10	20	50	100	200	500	1,000	2,000	5,000	10,000
MILES	0.621	6.21	12.42	31.05	62.1	124.2	310.5	621.0	1,242.0	3,105.0	6,210.0

CONVERSION FROM METRIC MEASURES

SYMBOL	WHEN YOU KNOW	MULTIPLY BY	TO FIND	SYMBOL
		LENGTH		
cm	centimeters	0.39	inches	in
m	meters	3.28	feet	ft
m	meters	1.09	yards	yd
km	kilometers	0.62	miles	mi
		AREA		
cm^2	square centimeters	0.16	square inches	in^2
m^2	square meters	10.76	square feet	ft^2
m^2	square meters	1.20	square yards	yd^2
km^2	square kilometers	0.39	square miles	mi^2
ha	hectares	2.47	acres	—
		MASS		
g	grams	0.04	ounces	oz
kg	kilograms	2.20	pounds	lb
t	metric tons	1.10	short tons	—
		VOLUME		
mL	milliliters	0.06	cubic inches	in^3
mL	milliliters	0.03	liquid ounces	liq oz
L	liters	2.11	pints	pt
L	liters	1.06	quarts	qt
L	liters	0.26	gallons	gal
m^3	cubic meters	35.31	cubic feet	ft^3
m^3	cubic meters	1.31	cubic yards	yd^3
		TEMPERATURE		
°C	degrees Celsius (centigrade)	9/5 then add 32	degrees Fahrenheit	°F

CONVERSION TO METRIC MEASURES

SYMBOL	WHEN YOU KNOW	MULTIPLY BY	TO FIND	SYMBOL
		LENGTH		
in	inches	2.54	centimeters	cm
ft	feet	0.30	meters	m
yd	yards	0.91	meters	m
mi	miles	1.61	kilometers	km
		AREA		
in^2	square inches	6.45	square centimeters	cm^2
ft^2	square feet	0.09	square meters	m^2
yd^2	square yards	0.84	square meters	m^2
mi^2	square miles	2.59	square kilometers	km^2
—	acres	0.40	hectares	ha
		MASS		
oz	ounces	28.35	grams	g
lb	pounds	0.45	kilograms	kg
—	short tons	0.91	metric tons	t
		VOLUME		
in^3	cubic inches	16.39	milliliters	mL
liq oz	liquid ounces	29.57	milliliters	mL
pt	pints	0.47	liters	L
qt	quarts	0.95	liters	L
gal	gallons	3.79	liters	L
ft^3	cubic feet	0.03	cubic meters	m^3
yd^3	cubic yards	0.76	cubic meters	m^3
		TEMPERATURE		
°F	degrees Fahrenheit	5/9 after subtracting 32	degrees Celsius (centigrade)	°C

THE EARTH

Mass: 5,974,000,000,000,000,000,000 (5.974 sextillion) metric tons

Total Area: 510,066,000 sq km (196,938,000 sq mi)

Land Area: 148,647,000 sq km (57,393,000 sq mi), 29.1% of total

Water Area: 361,419,000 sq km (139,545,000 sq mi), 70.9% of total

Population: 6,477,451,000

THE EARTH'S EXTREMES

Hottest Place: Dalol, Danakil Depression, Ethiopia, annual average temperature 34°C (93°F)

Coldest Place: Plateau Station, Antarctica, annual average temperature -56.7°C (-70°F)

Hottest Recorded Temperature: Al Aziziyah, Libya 58°C (136.4°F), September 3, 1922

Coldest Recorded Temperature: Vostok, Antarctica -89.2°C (-128.6°F), July 21, 1983

Wettest Place: Mawsynram, Assam, India, annual average rainfall 1,187 cm (467 in)

Driest Place: Arica, Atacama Desert, Chile, rainfall barely measurable

Highest Waterfall: Angel Falls, Venezuela 979 m (3,212 ft)

Largest Hot Desert: Sahara, Africa 9,000,000 sq km (3,475,000 sq mi)

Largest Ice Desert: Antarctica 13,209,000 sq km (5,100,000 sq mi)

Largest Canyon: Grand Canyon, Colorado River, Arizona 446 km (277 mi) long along river, 180 m (600 ft) to 29 km (18 mi) wide, about 1.8 km (1.1 mi) deep

Largest Cave Chamber: Sarawak Cave, Gunung Mulu National Park, Malaysia 16 hectares and 79 meters high (40.2 acres and 260 feet)

Largest Cave System: Mammoth Cave, Kentucky, over 530 km (330 mi) of passageways mapped

Most Predictable Geyser: Old Faithful, Wyoming, annual average interval 66 to 80 minutes

Longest Reef: Great Barrier Reef, Australia 2,300 km (1,429 mi)

Greatest Tidal Range: Bay of Fundy, Canadian Atlantic Coast 16 m (52 ft)

AREA OF EACH CONTINENT

	SQ KM	SQ MI	PERCENT OF EARTH'S LAND
Asia	44,579,000	17,212,000	30.0
Africa	30,065,000	11,608,000	20.2
North America	24,474,000	9,449,000	16.5
South America	17,819,000	6,880,000	12.0
Antarctica	13,209,000	5,100,000	8.9
Europe	9,938,000	3,837,000	6.7
Australia	7,687,000	2,968,000	5.2

HIGHEST POINT ON EACH CONTINENT

	METERS	FEET
Mount Everest, Asia	8,850	29,035
Cerro Aconcagua, South America	6,960	22,834
Mount McKinley (Denali), N. America	6,194	20,320
Kilimanjaro, Africa	5,895	19,340
El'brus, Europe	5,642	18,510
Vinson Massif, Antarctica	4,897	16,067
Mount Kosciuszko, Australia	2,228	7,310

LOWEST SURFACE POINT ON EACH CONTINENT

	METERS	FEET
Dead Sea, Asia	-416	-1,365
Lake Assal, Africa	-156	-512
Laguna del Carbón, South America	-105	-344
Death Valley, North America	-86	-282
Caspian Sea, Europe	-28	-92
Lake Eyre, Australia	-16	-52
Bentley Subglacial Trench, Antarctica	-2,555	-8,383

LARGEST ISLANDS

	AREA SQ KM	AREA SQ MI
1 Greenland	2,166,000	836,000
2 New Guinea	792,500	306,000
3 Borneo	725,500	280,100
4 Madagascar	587,000	226,600
5 Baffin Island	507,500	196,000
6 Sumatra	427,300	165,000
7 Honshu	227,400	87,800
8 Great Britain	218,100	84,200
9 Victoria Island	217,300	83,900
10 Ellesmere Island	196,200	75,800
11 Sulawesi (Celebes)	178,700	69,000
12 South Island (New Zealand)	150,400	58,100
13 Java	126,700	48,900
14 North Island (New Zealand)	113,700	43,900
15 Island of Newfoundland	108,900	42,000

LARGEST DRAINAGE BASINS

	AREA SQ KM	AREA SQ MI
1 Amazon, South America	7,050,000	2,721,000
2 Congo, Africa	3,700,000	1,428,000
3 Mississippi-Missouri, North America	3,250,000	1,255,000
4 Paraná, South America	3,100,000	1,197,000
5 Yenisey-Angara, Asia	2,700,000	1,042,000
6 Ob-Irtysh, Asia	2,430,000	938,000
7 Lena, Asia	2,420,000	934,000
8 Nile, Africa	1,900,000	733,400
9 Amur, Asia	1,840,000	710,000
10 Mackenzie-Peace, North America	1,765,000	681,000
11 Ganges-Brahmaputra, Asia	1,730,000	668,000
12 Volga, Europe	1,380,000	533,000
13 Zambezi, Africa	1,330,000	513,000
14 Niger, Africa	1,200,000	463,000
15 Chang Jiang (Yangtze), Asia	1,175,000	454,000

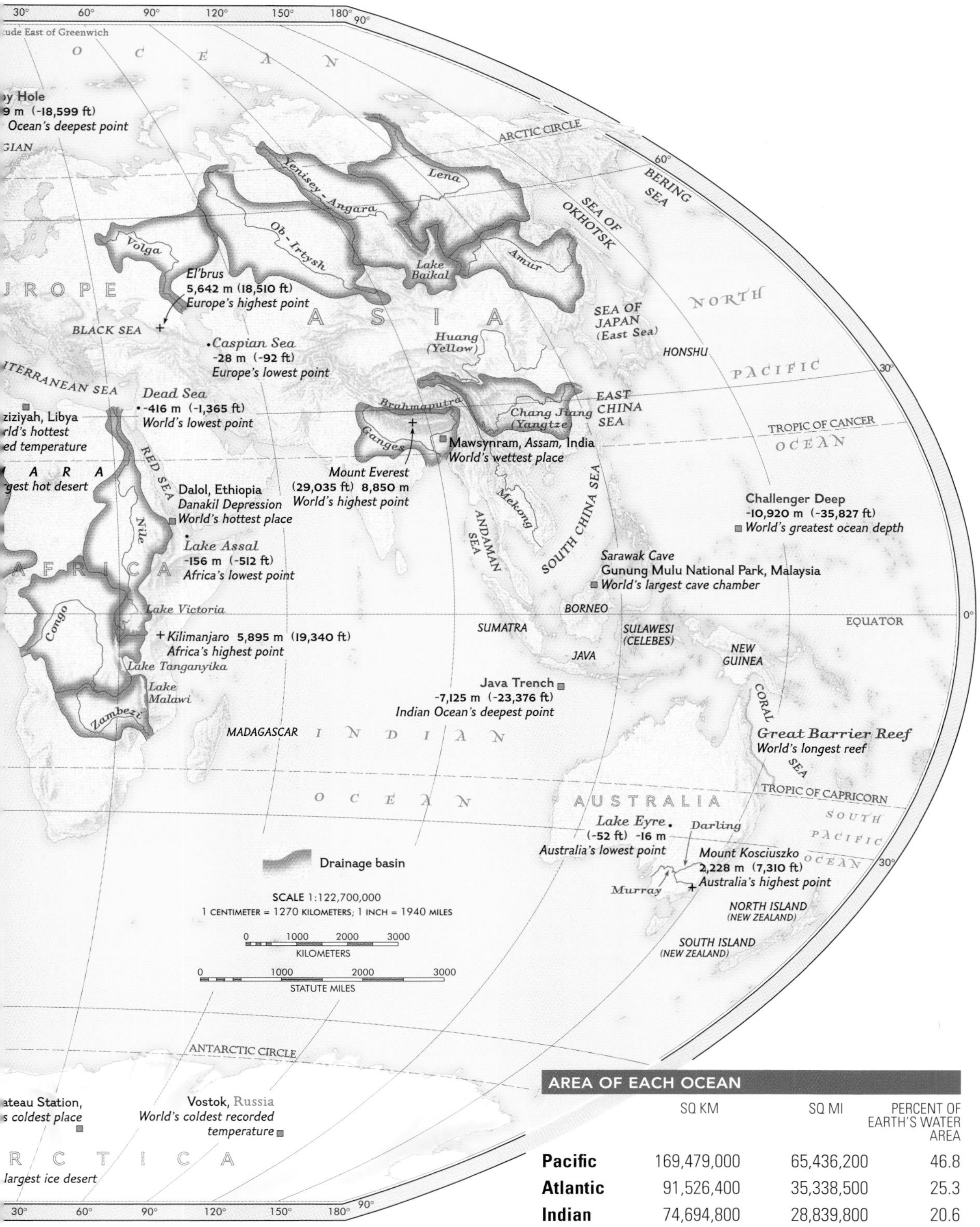

AREA OF EACH OCEAN

	SQ KM	SQ MI	PERCENT OF EARTH'S WATER AREA
Pacific	169,479,000	65,436,200	46.8
Atlantic	91,526,400	35,338,500	25.3
Indian	74,694,800	28,839,800	20.6
Arctic	13,960,100	5,390,000	3.9

LONGEST RIVERS

		KM	MI
1	**Nile, Africa**	6,825	4,241
2	**Amazon, South America**	6,437	4,000
3	**Chang Jiang (Yangtze), Asia**	6,380	3,964
4	**Mississippi-Missouri, North America**	5,971	3,710
5	**Yenisey-Angara, Asia**	5,536	3,440
6	**Huang (Yellow), Asia**	5,464	3,395
7	**Ob-Irtysh, Asia**	5,410	3,362
8	**Amur, Asia**	4,416	2,744
9	**Lena, Asia**	4,400	2,734
10	**Congo, Africa**	4,370	2,715
11	**Mackenzie-Peace, North America**	4,241	2,635
12	**Mekong, Asia**	4,184	2,600
13	**Niger, Africa**	4,170	2,591
14	**Paraná-Río de la Plata, S. America**	4,000	2,485
15	**Murray-Darling, Australia**	3,718	2,310
16	**Volga, Europe**	3,685	2,290
17	**Purus, South America**	3,380	2,100

DEEPEST POINT IN EACH OCEAN

	METERS	FEET
Challenger Deep, Pacific Ocean	-10,920	-35,827
Puerto Rico Trench, Atlantic Ocean	-8,605	-28,232
Java Trench, Indian Ocean	-7,125	-23,376
Molloy Hole, Arctic Ocean	-5,669	-18,599

LARGEST LAKES BY AREA

		AREA SQ KM	AREA SQ MI	MAXIMUM DEPTH METERS	MAXIMUM DEPTH FEET
1	**Caspian Sea**	371,000	143,200	1,025	3,363
2	**Lake Superior**	82,100	31,700	406	1,332
3	**Lake Victoria**	69,500	26,800	82	269
4	**Lake Huron**	59,600	23,000	229	751
5	**Lake Michigan**	57,800	22,300	281	922
6	**Lake Tanganyika**	32,600	12,600	1,470	4,823
7	**Lake Baikal**	31,500	12,200	1,637	5,371
8	**Great Bear Lake**	31,300	12,100	446	1,463
9	**Lake Malawi**	28,900	11,200	695	2,280
10	**Great Slave Lake**	28,600	11,000	614	2,014

GEOPOLITICAL EXTREMES

Largest Country: Russia 17,075,400 sq km (6,592,850 sq mi)

Smallest Country: Vatican City 0.4 sq km (0.2 sq mi)

Most Populous Country: China 1,333,827,000 people

Least Populous Country: Vatican City 1,000 people

Most Crowded Country: Monaco 16,500 per sq km (41,250 per sq mi)

Least Crowded Country: Mongolia 1.7 per sq km (4.4 per sq mi)

Largest Metropolitan Area: Tokyo 34,997,000 people

Country with the Greatest Number of Bordering Countries: China 14, Russia 14

ENGINEERING WONDERS

Tallest Office Building: Taipei 101, Taipei, Taiwan 508 m (1,667 ft)

Tallest Tower (Freestanding): CN Tower, Toronto, Canada 553 m (1,815 ft)

Tallest Manmade Structure: KVLY TV tower, near Fargo, North Dakota 629 m (2,063 ft)

Longest Wall: Great Wall of China, approx. 3,460 km (2,150 mi)

Longest Road: Pan-American highway (not including gap in Panama and Colombia), more than 24,140 km (15,000 mi)

Longest Railroad: Trans-Siberian Railroad, Russia 9,288 km (5,772 mi)

Longest Road Tunnel: Laerdal Tunnel, Laerdal, Norway 24.5 km (15.2 mi)

Longest Rail Tunnel: Seikan submarine rail tunnel, Honshu to Hokkaido, Japan 53.9 km (33.5 mi)

Highest Bridge (over water): Royal Gorge Bridge, Colorado 321 m (1,053 ft) above water

Longest Highway Bridge: Lake Pontchartrain Causeway, Louisiana 38.4 km (23.9 mi)

Longest Suspension Bridge: Akashi-Kaikyo Bridge, Japan 3,911 m (12,831 ft)

Longest Boat Canal: Grand Canal, China, over 1,770 km (1,100 mi)

Longest Irrigation Canal: Garagum Canal, Turkmenistan, nearly 1,100 km (700 mi)

Largest Artificial Lake: Lake Volta, Volta River, Ghana 9,065 sq km (3,500 sq mi)

Tallest Dam: Rogun Dam, Vakhsh River, Tajikistan 335 m (1,099 ft)

Tallest Pyramid: Great Pyramid of Khufu, Egypt 137 m (450 ft)

Deepest Mine: Savuka Mine, South Africa approx. 4 km (2.5 mi) deep

Longest Submarine Cable: Sea-Me-We 3 cable, connects 33 countries on four continents, 39,000 km (24,200 mi) long

LARGEST SEAS BY AREA

		AREA SQ KM	AREA SQ MI	AVGERAGE DEPTH METERS	AVGERAGE DEPTH FEET
1	**Coral Sea**	4,183,510	1,615,260	2,471	8,107
2	**South China Sea**	3,596,390	1,388,570	1,180	3,871
3	**Caribbean Sea**	2,834,290	1,094,330	2,596	8,517
4	**Bering Sea**	2,519,580	972,810	1,832	6,010
5	**Mediterranean Sea**	2,469,100	953,320	1,572	5,157
6	**Sea of Okhotsk**	1,625,190	627,490	814	2,671
7	**Gulf of Mexico**	1,531,810	591,430	1,544	5,066
8	**Norwegian Sea**	1,425,280	550,300	1,768	5,801
9	**Greenland Sea**	1,157,850	447,050	1,443	4,734
10	**Sea of Japan**	1,008,260	389,290	1,647	5,404
11	**Hudson Bay**	1,005,510	388,230	119	390
12	**East China Sea**	785,990	303,470	374	1,227
13	**Andaman Sea**	605,760	233,890	1,061	3,481
14	**Red Sea**	436,280	168,450	494	1,621
15	**Black Sea**	410,150	158,360	1,336	4,383

ALL OF THE EARTH'S LANDS are grouped into four categories on pages 266 through 269: independent states, dependencies, areas of special status, and areas geographically separated from their mainland countries. At right, a world map uses different colors to show the distribution of lands within each category.

Each of the 192 countries listed in the independent states category (below) is a recognized territory whose government is the highest legal authority over the land and people within its boundaries.

A dependency, on the other hand, is a region whose territory is controlled by another, often very distant, country; it is not, however, considered an inherent part of the controlling country. Most dependencies are inhabited and have some form of local government with limited autonomy.

An area of special status is a region of ambiguous political status. Most of these areas can be described as disputed territory, territory not recognized as independent by other countries, or territory leased by one government to another. In the fourth category are populated lands considered integral parts of independent states, but they are separated from the rest of their countries by a significant distance.

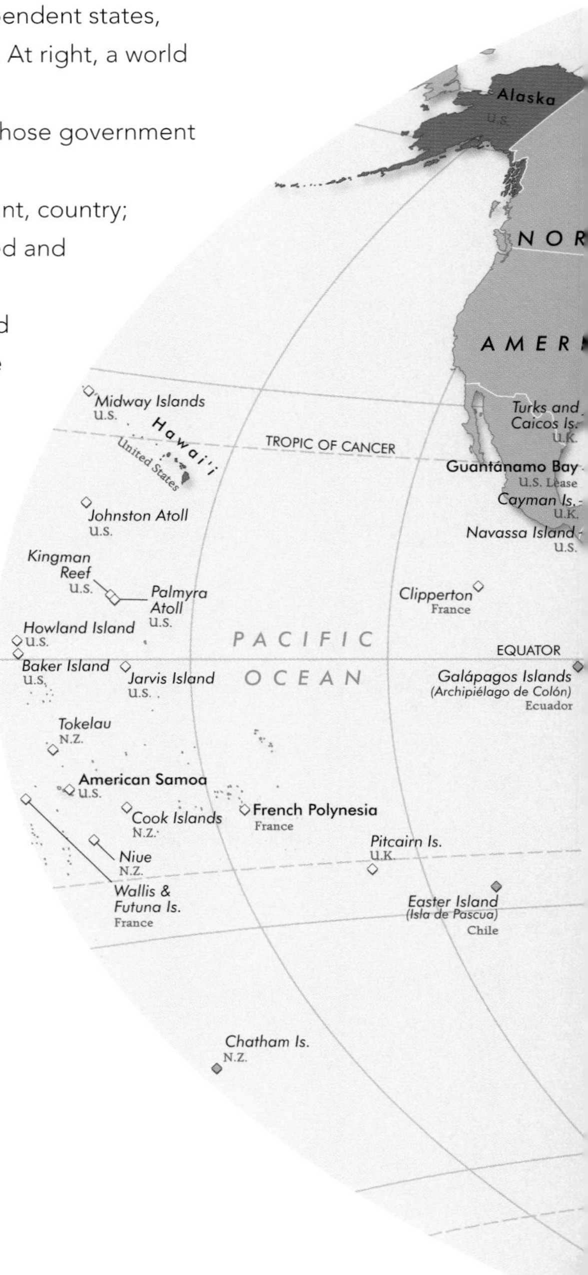

INDEPENDENT STATES OF THE WORLD

COUNTRY	CAPITAL	2005 POPULATION	DATE OF INDEPENDENCE
AFGHANISTAN	Kabul	29,929,000	Aug. 19, 1919
ALBANIA	Tirana	3,170,000	Nov. 28, 1912
ALGERIA	Algiers	32,814,000	July 5, 1962
ANDORRA	Andorra la Vella	74,000	1278
ANGOLA	Luanda	15,375,000	Nov. 11, 1975
ANTIGUA AND BARBUDA	St. John's	80,000	Nov. 1, 1981
ARGENTINA	Buenos Aires	38,592,000	July 9, 1816
ARMENIA	Yerevan	3,033,000	Sept. 21, 1991
AUSTRALIA	Canberra	20,351,000	Jan. 1, 1901
AUSTRIA	Vienna	8,151,000	1156
AZERBAIJAN	Baku	8,388,000	Aug. 30, 1991
BAHAMAS	Nassau	319,000	July 10, 1973
BAHRAIN	Manama	731,000	Aug. 15, 1971
BANGLADESH	Dhaka	144,233,000	Dec. 16, 1971
BARBADOS	Bridgetown	258,000	Nov. 30, 1966
BELARUS	Minsk	9,776,000	Aug. 25, 1991
BELGIUM	Brussels	10,458,000	July 21, 1831
BELIZE	Belmopan	292,000	Sept. 21, 1981
BENIN	Porto-Novo, Cotonou	8,439,000	Aug. 1, 1960
BHUTAN	Thimphu	970,000	Aug. 8, 1949
BOLIVIA	La Paz, Sucre	8,922,000	Aug. 6, 1825
BOSNIA AND HERZEGOVINA	Sarajevo	3,840,000	Mar. 1, 1992
BOTSWANA	Gaborone	1,640,000	Sept. 30, 1966
BRAZIL	Brasília	184,184,000	Sept. 7, 1822
BRUNEI	Bandar Seri Begawan	363,000	Jan. 1, 1984
BULGARIA	Sofia	7,741,000	Mar. 3, 1878
BURKINA FASO	Ouagadougou	13,925,000	Aug. 5, 1960
BURUNDI	Bujumbura	7,795,000	July 1, 1962
CAMBODIA	Phnom Penh	13,329,000	Nov. 9, 1953
CAMEROON	Yaoundé	16,380,000	Jan. 1, 1960
CANADA	Ottawa	32,225,000	Dec. 11, 1931
CAPE VERDE	Praia	476,000	July 5, 1975
CENTRAL AFRICAN REPUBLIC	Bangui	4,238,000	Aug. 13, 1960
CHAD	N'Djamena	9,657,000	Aug. 11, 1960
CHILE	Santiago	16,136,000	Sept. 18, 1810
CHINA	Beijing	1,303,701,000	221 B.C.
COLOMBIA	Bogotá	46,039,000	July 20, 1810
COMOROS	Moroni	671,000	July 6, 1975
CONGO	Brazzaville	3,999,000	Aug. 15, 1960
CONGO, DEMOCRATIC REPUBLIC OF THE	Kinshasa	60,764,000	June 30, 1960
COSTA RICA	San José	4,331,000	Sept. 15, 1821
CÔTE D'IVOIRE	Yamoussoukro, Abidjan	18,154,000	Aug. 7, 1960
CROATIA	Zagreb	4,438,000	June 25, 1991
CUBA	Havana	11,275,000	May 20, 1902
CYPRUS	Nicosia	965,000	Aug. 16, 1960
CZECH REPUBLIC	Prague	10,212,000	Jan. 1, 1993
DENMARK	Copenhagen	5,418,000	10th century
DJIBOUTI	Djibouti	793,000	June 27, 1977
DOMINICA	Roseau	70,000	Nov. 3, 1978
DOMINICAN REPUBLIC	Santo Domingo	8,862,000	Feb. 27, 1844
ECUADOR	Quito	13,032,000	May 24, 1822
EGYPT	Cairo	74,033,000	Feb. 28, 1922
EL SALVADOR	San Salvador	6,881,000	Sept. 15, 1821
EQUATORIAL GUINEA	Malabo	504,000	Oct. 12, 1968
ERITREA	Asmara	4,670,000	May 24, 1993
ESTONIA	Tallinn	1,345,000	May 1919
ETHIOPIA	Addis Ababa	77,431,000	circa 1 A.D.
FIJI ISLANDS	Suva	842,000	Oct. 10, 1970
FINLAND	Helsinki	5,246,000	Dec. 6, 1917
FRANCE	Paris	60,742,000	486
GABON	Libreville	1,384,000	Aug. 17, 1960
GAMBIA	Banjul	1,595,000	Feb. 18, 1965
GEORGIA	T'bilisi	4,501,000	April 9, 1991
GERMANY	Berlin	82,490,000	Jan. 18, 1871
GHANA	Accra	22,019,000	Mar. 6, 1957
GREECE	Athens	11,100,000	1829
GRENADA	St. George's	101,000	Feb. 7, 1974
GUATEMALA	Guatemala	12,701,000	Sept. 15, 1821
GUINEA	Conakry	9,453,000	Oct. 2, 1958
GUINEA-BISSAU	Bissau	1,586,000	Sept. 24, 1973
GUYANA	Georgetown	751,000	May 26, 1966
HAITI	Port-au-Prince	8,288,000	Jan. 1, 1804
HONDURAS	Tegucigalpa	7,212,000	Sept. 15, 1821
HUNGARY	Budapest	10,086,000	1001
ICELAND	Reykjavík	295,000	June 17, 1944
INDIA	New Delhi	1,103,596,000	Aug. 15, 1947
INDONESIA	Jakarta	221,932,000	Aug. 17, 1945
IRAN	Tehran	69,515,000	Apr. 1, 1979
IRAQ	Baghdad	28,807,000	Oct. 3, 1932
IRELAND	Dublin	4,125,000	Dec. 6, 1921
ISRAEL	Jerusalem	7,105,000	May 14, 1948
ITALY	Rome	58,742,000	Mar. 17, 1861
JAMAICA	Kingston	2,666,000	Aug. 6, 1962
JAPAN	Tokyo	127,728,000	660 B.C.
JORDAN	Amman	5,795,000	May 25, 1946
KAZAKHSTAN	Astana	15,079,000	Dec. 16, 1991
KENYA	Nairobi	33,830,000	Dec. 12, 1963
KIRIBATI	Tarawa	92,000	July 12, 1979
KOREA, NORTH	Pyongyang	22,912,000	Aug. 15, 1945
KOREA, SOUTH	Seoul	48,294,000	Aug. 15, 1945
KUWAIT	Kuwait	2,589,000	June 19, 1961
KYRGYZSTAN	Bishkek	5,172,000	Aug. 31, 1991
LAOS	Vientiane	5,924,000	July 19, 1949
LATVIA	Riga	2,300,000	Dec. 1919
LEBANON	Beirut	3,779,000	Nov. 22, 1943
LESOTHO	Maseru	1,804,000	Oct. 4, 1966
LIBERIA	Monrovia	3,283,000	July 26, 1847
LIBYA	Tripoli	5,766,000	Dec. 24, 1951
LIECHTENSTEIN	Vaduz	35,000	Jan. 23, 1719
LITHUANIA	Vilnius	3,415,000	April 1919
LUXEMBOURG	Luxembourg	457,000	1839
MACEDONIA	Skopje	2,039,000	Sept. 17, 1991
MADAGASCAR	Antananarivo	17,308,000	June 26, 1960
MALAWI	Lilongwe	12,341,000	July 6, 1964
MALAYSIA	Kuala Lumpur	26,121,000	Aug. 31, 1957
MALDIVES	Male	294,000	July 26, 1965
MALI	Bamako	13,518,000	Sept. 22, 1960
MALTA	Valletta	405,000	Sept. 21, 1964
MARSHALL ISLANDS	Majuro	59,000	Oct. 21, 1986
MAURITANIA	Nouakchott	3,069,000	Nov. 28, 1960
MAURITIUS	Port Louis	1,243,000	Mar. 12, 1968
MEXICO	Mexico	107,029,000	Sept. 16, 1810
MICRONESIA, FEDERATED STATES OF	Palikir	108,000	Nov. 3, 1986
MOLDOVA	Chisinau	4,206,000	Aug. 27, 1991
MONACO	Monaco	33,000	1419
MONGOLIA	Ulaanbaatar	2,646,000	July 11, 1921
MOROCCO	Rabat	30,704,000	Mar. 2, 1956
MOZAMBIQUE	Maputo	19,420,000	June 25, 1975
MYANMAR (BURMA)	Yangon (Rangoon)	50,519,000	Jan. 4, 1948
NAMIBIA	Windhoek	2,031,000	Mar. 21, 1990
NAURU	Yaren	13,000	Jan. 31, 1968
NEPAL	Kathmandu	25,371,000	1768
NETHERLANDS	Amsterdam	16,296,000	1579
NEW ZEALAND	Wellington	4,107,000	Sept. 26, 1907
NICARAGUA	Managua	5,774,000	Sept. 15, 1821
NIGER	Niamey	13,957,000	Aug. 3, 1960

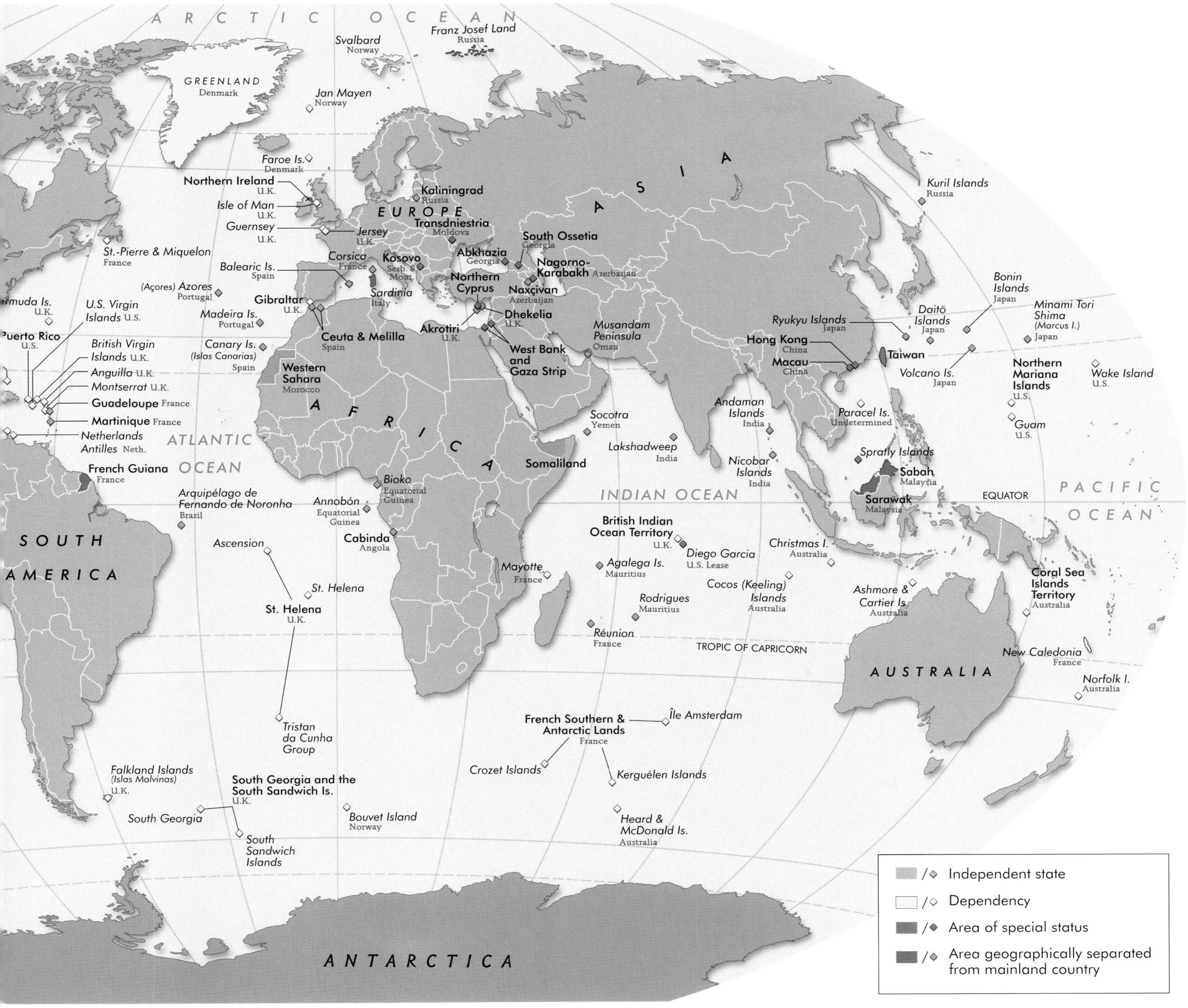

COUNTRY	CAPITAL	2005 POPULATION	DATE OF INDEPENDENCE
NIGERIA	Abuja	131,530,000	Oct. 1, 1960
NORWAY	Oslo	4,620,000	June 7, 1905
OMAN	Muscat	2,436,000	1650
PAKISTAN	Islamabad	162,420,000	Aug. 14, 1947
PALAU	Koror	21,000	Oct. 1, 1994
PANAMA	Panama	3,232,000	Nov. 3, 1903
PAPUA NEW GUINEA	Port Moresby	5,887,000	Sept. 16, 1975
PARAGUAY	Asunción	6,158,000	May 14, 1811
PERU	Lima	27,947,000	July 28, 1821
PHILIPPINES	Manila	84,765,000	July 4, 1946
POLAND	Warsaw	38,163,000	Nov. 11, 1918
PORTUGAL	Lisbon	10,576,000	1140
QATAR	Doha	768,000	Sept. 3, 1971
ROMANIA	Bucharest	21,612,000	Mar. 26, 1881
RUSSIA	Moscow	143,025,000	Aug. 24, 1991
RWANDA	Kigali	8,722,000	July 1, 1962
ST. KITTS AND NEVIS	Basseterre	48,000	Sept. 19, 1983
ST. LUCIA	Castries	163,000	Feb. 22, 1979
ST. VINCENT AND THE GRENADINES	Kingstown	111,000	Oct. 27, 1979
SAMOA	Apia	188,000	Jan. 1, 1962
SAN MARINO	San Marino	30,000	Sept. 3, 301
SAO TOME AND PRINCIPE	São Tomé	153,000	July 12, 1975

COUNTRY	CAPITAL	2005 POPULATION	DATE OF INDEPENDENCE
SAUDI ARABIA	Riyadh	24,573,000	Sept. 23, 1932
SENEGAL	Dakar	11,658,000	Aug. 20, 1960
SERBIA AND MONTENEGRO	Belgrade, Podgorica	10,722,000	Apr. 27, 1992
SEYCHELLES	Victoria	81,000	June 29, 1976
SIERRA LEONE	Freetown	5,525,000	Apr. 27, 1961
SINGAPORE	Singapore	4,296,000	Aug. 9, 1965
SLOVAKIA	Bratislava	5,382,000	Jan. 1, 1993
SLOVENIA	Ljubljana	1,998,000	June 25, 1991
SOLOMON ISLANDS	Honiara	472,000	July 7, 1978
SOMALIA	Mogadishu	8,592,000	July 1, 1960
SOUTH AFRICA	Pretoria, Cape Town, Bloemfontein	46,923,000	May 31, 1910
SPAIN	Madrid	43,484,000	1492
SRI LANKA	Colombo	19,722,000	Feb. 4, 1948
SUDAN	Khartoum	40,187,000	Jan. 1, 1956
SURINAME	Paramaribo	447,000	Nov. 25, 1975
SWAZILAND	Mbabane, Lobamba	1,138,000	Sept. 6, 1968
SWEDEN	Stockholm	9,029,000	June 6, 1523
SWITZERLAND	Bern	7,446,000	Aug. 1, 1291
SYRIA	Damascus	18,389,000	Apr. 17, 1946
TAJIKISTAN	Dushanbe	6,813,000	Sept. 9, 1991
TANZANIA	Dar es Salaam, Dodoma	36,481,000	Apr. 26, 1964
THAILAND	Bangkok	65,002,000	1238

COUNTRY	CAPITAL	2005 POPULATION	DATE OF INDEPENDENCE
TIMOR-LESTE (EAST TIMOR)	Dili	947,000	May 20, 2002
TOGO	Lomé	6,145,000	Apr. 27, 1960
TONGA	Nuku'alofa	102,000	June 4, 1970
TRINIDAD AND TOBAGO	Port-of-Spain	1,305,000	Aug. 31, 1962
TUNISIA	Tunis	10,043,000	Mar. 20, 1956
TURKEY	Ankara	72,907,000	Oct. 29, 1923
TURKMENISTAN	Ashgabat	5,240,000	Oct. 27, 1991
TUVALU	Funafuti	10,000	Oct. 1, 1978
UGANDA	Kampala	26,907,000	Oct. 9, 1962
UKRAINE	Kiev	47,110,000	Aug. 24, 1991
UNITED ARAB EMIRATES	Abu Dhabi	4,618,000	Dec. 2, 1971
UNITED KINGDOM	London	60,068,000	10th century
UNITED STATES	Washington, D.C.	296,483,000	July 4, 1776
URUGUAY	Montevideo	3,419,000	Aug. 25, 1825
UZBEKISTAN	Tashkent	26,444,000	Sept. 1, 1991
VANUATU	Port-Vila	218,000	July 30, 1980
VATICAN CITY	Vatican City	1,000	Feb. 11, 1929
VENEZUELA	Caracas	26,749,000	July 5, 1811
VIETNAM	Hanoi	83,305,000	Sept. 2, 1945
YEMEN	Sanaa	20,727,000	May 22, 1990
ZAMBIA	Lusaka	11,227,000	Oct. 24, 1964
ZIMBABWE	Harare	13,010,000	Apr. 18, 1980

DEPENDENCIES OF THE WORLD

DEPENDENCY	POPULATION	LOCATION	CAPITAL OR CHIEF CITY	DEPENDENCY OF	POLITICAL STATUS (SYSTEM)*
AMERICAN SAMOA	63,000	South Pacific Ocean	Pago Pago	United States	Unincorporated territory
ANGUILLA	13,000	Caribbean Sea	The Valley	United Kingdom	Overseas territory
ARUBA	97,000	Caribbean Sea	Oranjestad	Netherlands	Part of the Netherlands (parliamentary democracy)
ASHMORE AND CARTIER ISLANDS	no indigenous inhabitants	Indian Ocean	Administered from Canberra	Australia	Territory
BAKER ISLAND	uninhabited	North Pacific Ocean	Administered from Washington, D.C.	United States	Unincorporated territory
BERMUDA	62,000	North Atlantic Ocean	Hamilton	United Kingdom	Overseas territory (parliamentary government)
BOUVET ISLAND	uninhabited	South Atlantic Ocean	Administered from Oslo	Norway	Territory
BRITISH INDIAN OCEAN TERRITORY[1]	no indigenous inhabitants	Indian Ocean	Administered from London	United Kingdom	Overseas territory
BRITISH VIRGIN ISLANDS	22,000	Caribbean Sea	Road Town	United Kingdom	Overseas territory
CAYMAN ISLANDS	44,000	Caribbean Sea	George Town	United Kingdom	Overseas territory (British crown colony)
CHRISTMAS ISLAND	500	Indian Ocean	The Settlement	Australia	Territory
CLIPPERTON	uninhabited	North Pacific Ocean	Administered from French Polynesia	France	Possession of France
COCOS (KEELING) ISLANDS	600	Indian Ocean	West Island	Australia	Territory
COOK ISLANDS	13,000	South Pacific Ocean	Avarua	New Zealand	Free association with New Zealand (parliamentary democracy)
CORAL SEA ISLANDS TERRITORY	no indigenous inhabitants	South Pacific Ocean	Administered from Canberra	Australia	Territory
FALKLAND ISLANDS[2]	3,000	South Atlantic Ocean	Stanley	United Kingdom	Overseas territory
FAROE ISLANDS	50,000	North Atlantic Ocean	Tórshavn	Denmark	Part of Denmark (self-governing overseas division)
FRENCH POLYNESIA	255,000	South Pacific Ocean	Papeete	France	Overseas territory
FRENCH SOUTHERN AND ANTARCTIC LANDS[3]	no indigenous inhabitants	Indian Ocean	Administered from Paris	France	Overseas territory
GIBRALTAR	29,000	Europe	Gibraltar	United Kingdom	Overseas territory
GREENLAND (KALAALLIT NUNAAT)	57,000	North Atlantic Ocean	Nuuk (Godthåb)	Denmark	Part of Denmark (self-governing overseas division)
GUAM	169,000	North Pacific Ocean	Hagåtña (Agana)	United States	Unincorporated territory
GUERNSEY (Channel Islands)[4]	65,000	English Channel	St. Peter Port	United Kingdom	British crown dependency
HEARD AND MCDONALD ISLANDS	uninhabited	Indian Ocean	Administered from Canberra	Australia	Territory
HOWLAND ISLAND	uninhabited	North Pacific Ocean	Administered from Washington, D.C.	United States	Unincorporated territory
ISLE OF MAN	78,000	Irish Sea	Douglas	United Kingdom	British crown dependency (parliamentary democracy)
JAN MAYEN[5]	no indigenous inhabitants	Norwegian Sea	Administered from Oslo	Norway	Territory
JARVIS ISLAND	uninhabited	South Pacific Ocean	Administered from Washington, D.C.	United States	Unincorporated territory
JERSEY (Channel Islands)	91,000	English Channel	St. Helier	United Kingdom	British crown dependency
JOHNSTON ATOLL	uninhabited	North Pacific Ocean	Administered from Washington, D.C.	United States	Unincorporated territory
KINGMAN REEF	uninhabited	North Pacific Ocean	Administered from Washington, D.C.	United States	Unincorporated territory
MAYOTTE	181,000	Mozambique Channel	Mamoudzou	France	Territorial collectivity
MIDWAY ISLANDS	no indigenous inhabitants	North Pacific Ocean	Administered from Washington, D.C.	United States	Unincorporated territory
MONTSERRAT	5,000	Caribbean Sea	Plymouth (abandoned)	United Kingdom	Overseas territory
NAVASSA ISLAND	uninhabited	Caribbean Sea	Administered from Washington, D.C.	United States	Unincorporated territory
NETHERLANDS ANTILLES[6]	187,000	Caribbean Sea	Willemstad	Netherlands	Part of the Netherlands (parliamentary government)
NEW CALEDONIA	227,000	South Pacific Ocean	Nouméa	France	Overseas territory
NIUE	1,600	South Pacific Ocean	Alofi	New Zealand	Free association with New Zealand (parliamentary democracy)
NORFOLK ISLAND	2,000	South Pacific Ocean	Kingston	Australia	Territory
NORTHERN MARIANA ISLANDS	80,000	North Pacific Ocean	Saipan	United States	Commonwealth in political union with the U.S. (commonwealth government)
PALMYRA ATOLL	no indigenous inhabitants	North Pacific Ocean	Administered from Washington, D.C.	United States	Incorporated territory
PARACEL ISLANDS[7]	no indigenous inhabitants	South China Sea	Administered from China	undetermined	NA
PITCAIRN ISLANDS	45	South Pacific Ocean	Adamstown	United Kingdom	Overseas territory
PUERTO RICO	3,912,000	Caribbean Sea	San Juan	United States	Commonwealth associated with the U.S. (commonwealth government)
ST. HELENA[8]	6,000	South Atlantic Ocean	Jamestown	United Kingdom	Overseas territory
SAINT-PIERRE AND MIQUELON	7,000	North Atlantic Ocean	Saint-Pierre	France	Self-governing territorial collectivity
SOUTH GEORGIA AND THE SOUTH SANDWICH ISLANDS[2]	no indigenous inhabitants	South Atlantic Ocean	Administered from Stanley	United Kingdom	Overseas territory
SVALBARD	2,700	Arctic Ocean	Longyearbyen	Norway	Territory
TOKELAU	1,500	South Pacific Ocean	Administered from Wellington	New Zealand	Territory
TURKS AND CAICOS ISLANDS	21,000	North Atlantic Ocean	Cockburn Town (on Grand Turk Island)	United Kingdom	Overseas territory
U.S. VIRGIN ISLANDS	109,000	Caribbean Sea	Charlotte Amalie	United States	Unincorporated territory
WAKE ISLAND	no indigenous inhabitants	North Pacific Ocean	Administered from Washington	United States	Unincorporated territory
WALLIS AND FUTUNA ISLANDS	15,000	South Pacific Ocean	Matâ'utu	France	Overseas territory

NOTES TO DEPENDENCIES OF THE WORLD

* *The political status of dependencies is based on the designation provided by the administering country. The variety of political designations reflects the diverse nature of the relationship dependencies have with their controlling countries.*

1 Chagos Archipelago

2 Dependent territory of the United Kingdom (also claimed by Argentina).

3 The French Southern and Antarctic Lands dependency includes Île Amsterdam, Île Saint-Paul, the Crozet Islands, and the Kerguélen Islands in the southern Indian Ocean. It also includes Terre Adélie, the French-claimed sector of Antarctica; the French claim to this region is not internationally recognized, however (see "Areas of Special Status," opposite, for information on claims to Antarctica).

4 The Bailiwick of Guernsey includes the islands of Alderney, Guernsey, Herm, and Sark, as well as smaller islands nearby.

5 Jan Mayen is administered from Oslo, Norway, through a governor resident in Longyearbyen, Svalbard.

6 Netherlands Antilles comprises two groupings of islands: Curaçao and Bonaire are located off the coast of Venezuela; Saba, Sint Eustatius, and Sint Maarten (the Dutch two-fifths of the island of Saint Martin) lie 500 miles (800 km) to the northeast.

7 South China Sea islands are occupied by China but claimed by Vietnam.

8 The territory of Saint Helena includes the island group of Tristan da Cunha, far to the southwest Saint Helena also administers Ascension Island, lying to the northwest.

AREAS OF SPECIAL STATUS

AREA	POPULATION	LOCATION
ABKHAZIA	**537,500**	**Part of Georgia**

Following the collapse of the Soviet Union in 1991 and Georgia's subsequent independence, the Abkhazian parliament declared its sovereignty and restoration of its 1925 constitution. In 1992 Georgian troops invaded, but by 1993 the Georgian government lost control of the entire area of Abkhazia. Years of negotiations have not resulted in movement toward a settlement.

ANTARCTICA **no indigenous inhabitants** **Territory south of 60 degrees south latitude**

Seven countries claim Antarctic territory, but these claims are not legally recognized by the Antarctic Treaty of 1959. This treaty prohibits military activities and dedicates Antarctica to peaceful use and free exchange of scientific information. Individual nations maintain bases, and the research projects they support typically involve collaborators from many countries.

DIEGO GARCIA **military base** **Indian Ocean**

Diego Garcia constitutes the southernmost island of the British Indian Ocean Territory, a dependency of Great Britain. In 1966, the United States leased Diego Garcia for 50 years and established a joint military base with Great Britain on the island. The U.S. lease will expire in 2016. Diego Garcia, along with the Chagos Archipelago, is claimed by Mauritius.

GUANTÁNAMO BAY **military base** **Cuba**

After helping Cuba gain independence in 1902, the United States leased 45 square miles (116 sq km) of territory around Guantánamo Bay. This lease was reaffirmed in a 1934 treaty stipulating that the return of Guantánamo Bay to Cuba could only be arranged through the mutual consent of the U.S. and Cuba. Though Guantánamo Bay remains sovereign Cuban territory, the American lease does not have a termination date.

HONG KONG **6,921,000** **Part of China**

Hong Kong became a Special Administrative Region (SAR) of China on July 1, 1997. China has promised that under its "one country, two systems" formula, China's socialist economic system will not be practiced in Hong Kong and that Hong Kong will enjoy a high degree of autonomy in all matters, except foreign and defense affairs, for the next 50 years.

KOSOVO **2,473,000** **Part of Serbia and Montenegro**

Hostilities broke out in Kosovo in 1998. Ethnic Albanians, who make up 90 percent of the local population, sought an independent state, while Serbs fought to keep Kosovo part of Serbia and Montenegro. NATO air strikes helped bring about an agreement to end the fighting, and the UN began administering Kosovo in June 1999.

MACAU **474,000** **Part of China**

After more than 400 years as a Portuguese outpost, Macau reverted to China in December 1999 as a Special Administrative Region, a status it will maintain for 50 years. Like Hong Kong, it enjoys a high degree of autonomy in all matters except foreign and defense affairs.

NAGORNO-KARABAKH **192,400** **Part of Azerbaijan**

A predominantly ethnic Armenian enclave within Azerbaijan, Nagorno-Karabakh sought to unite with Armenia in 1988. Azerbaijani forces attempted to reestablish control in 1992, but were met with fierce resistance. More than 30,000 have died and over a million people have been displaced as a result of the fighting. A cease-fire was signed in 1994, and international efforts to resolve the conflict are ongoing.

NORTHERN CYPRUS **200,000** **Eastern Mediterranean Sea**

Following a Greek-led coup and the landing of Turkish forces on the island in 1974, Cyprus split into two hostile territories. The internationally recognized Greek Cypriot government controls the southern portion of the island whereas Turkish Cypriots, bolstered by a Turkish military force, control the northern portion. Turkish Cypriots unilaterally declared independence in 1983, but their claims have not been recognized by any nation other than Turkey.

SOMALILAND **3,500,000** **Horn of Africa**

The government of Somalia collapsed in 1991, after a bloody civil war. Somaliland claims independence and governs some three million people in the north—an area that roughly corresponds to the former British Somaliland. The United Nations does not recognize Somaliland as an independent state.

SOUTH OSSETIA **99,800** **Part of Georgia**

In 1990 South Ossetia, wishing to unite with North Ossetia in the Russian Federation, declared independence from Georgia. Armed clashes resulted between Georgian forces and separatists. A cease-fire was signed in 1992, but peace remains fragile.

SPRATLY ISLANDS **no indigenous inhabitants** **South China Sea**

The scattered islands and reefs known as the Spratly Islands are claimed in part by Brunei, Malaysia, the Philippines, and entirely by China, Taiwan, and Vietnam.

TAIWAN **22,731,000** **Southeast of China**

The People's Republic of China claims the island of Taiwan as its 23rd province. The government of Taiwan (Republic of China) maintains that there is one China—but two political entities.

TRANSDNIESTRIA **634,000** **Part of Moldova**

In 1992 separatist forces, made up largely of Ukrainian and Russian minorities, declared a "Dniester Republic" between the east bank of the Dniester River and the Ukrainian border. Armed conflict occurred between Moldovan government forces and Transdniestrian separatists. Negotiations to resolve the conflict continue, and a cease-fire is still in effect.

WEST BANK AND GAZA STRIP **3,762,000** **Adjacent to Israel**

The West Bank and Gaza Strip were captured by Israel in the 1967 Six Day War. A peace agreement was signed in 1993, which gave areas of the West Bank and Gaza Strip limited Palestinian autonomy. In August of 2005 Israel evacuated the Gaza Strip, removing settlers and military personnel. The future of the autonomous regions, and more than 3.7 million Palestinians, are subject to Israeli-Palestinian negotiations.

WESTERN SAHARA **341,000** **Southwest of Morocco**

Formerly Spanish Sahara, Western Sahara was annexed by Morocco in the late 1970s and brought under Moroccan administration. The Polisario Front, a resistance group that repudiated Moroccan sovereignty, fought a guerrilla war that ended in a 1991 cease-fire administered by the United Nations. A referendum on the final status of Western Sahara has repeatedly been postponed.

AREAS GEOGRAPHICALLY SEPARATED FROM MAINLAND COUNTRIES

REGION	POPULATION	COUNTRY	LOCATION
AGALEGA ISLANDS	300	Mauritius	Indian Ocean
AKROTIRI	military base	United Kingdom	Cyprus
ALASKA	664,000	United States	North America
ANDAMAN ISLANDS	314,000	India	Indian Ocean
ANNOBÓN	5,000	Equatorial Guinea	Gulf of Guinea
ARQUIPÉLAGO DE FERNANDO DE NORONHA	2,100	Brazil	South Atlantic Ocean
AZORES	241,000	Portugal	North Atlantic Ocean
BALEARIC ISLANDS	982,000	Spain	Mediterranean Sea
BIOKO	260,000	Equatorial Guinea	Gulf of Guinea
BONIN ISLANDS	2,800	Japan	North Pacific Ocean
CABINDA	100,000	Angola	Africa
CANARY ISLANDS	1,938,000	Spain	North Atlantic Ocean
CEUTA AND MELILLA	138,000	Spain	North Africa
CHATHAM ISLANDS	700	New Zealand	South Pacific Ocean
CORSICA	268,000	France	Mediterranean Sea
DAITO ISLANDS	2,100	Japan	North Pacific Ocean
DHEKELIA	military base	United Kingdom	Cyprus
EASTER ISLAND	4,000	Chile	South Pacific Ocean
FRANZ JOSEF LAND	not permanently inhabited	Russia	Arctic Ocean
FRENCH GUIANA	195,000	France	South America
GALÁPAGOS ISLANDS	19,000	Ecuador	Pacific Ocean
GUADELOUPE	450,000	France	Caribbean Sea
HAWAI'I	1,275,000	United States	North Pacific Ocean
KALININGRAD	955,000	Russia	Europe
KURIL ISLANDS	30,000	Russia	North Pacific Ocean
LAKSHADWEEP	61,000	India	Indian Ocean
MADEIRA ISLANDS	244,000	Portugal	North Atlantic Ocean
MARTINIQUE	397,000	France	Caribbean Sea
MUSANDAM PENINSULA	28,000	Oman	Arabian Peninsula
NAXÇIVAN	370,000	Azerbaijan	Asia
NICOBAR ISLANDS	42,000	India	Indian Ocean
NORTHERN IRELAND	1,710,000	United Kingdom	Ireland
RÉUNION	782,000	France	Indian Ocean
RODRIGUES	36,000	Mauritius	Indian Ocean
RYUKYU ISLANDS	1,492,000	Japan	North Pacific Ocean
SABAH AND SARAWAK	4,675,000	Malaysia	Borneo
SARDINIA	1,650,000	Italy	Mediterranean Sea
SOCOTRA	44,000	Yemen	Indian Ocean
VOLCANO ISLANDS	no indigenous inhabitants	Japan	North Pacific Ocean

DISCLAIMER

The list of geographically separate areas includes places that do not fit conveniently into any of the three previous categories. Politically, these areas are integral parts of independent countries; thus, they are not dependencies. Nor are they areas of special status. They warrant inclusion in this category simply because they lie a significant distance, across either land or water, from the rest of their countries' land areas. In compiling this list, we chose to include only the areas that are populated at least part of the year. This means that we have not listed myriad uninhabited islands. Determining exactly what constitutes sufficient geographical separation to justify inclusion involves a certain degree of subjectivity. For this reason, the fourth category of Earth's lands should not be considered an official grouping. Instead, it should be viewed only as one way of classifying areas that do not fall neatly into the three other categories—but which are significant enough to deserve special attention.

Special Flags

IF WE COULD BRING A SNAPSHOT back from the future, few images would tell us more about what lies ahead than a flag chart showing the banners of all countries. The independence of new nations, the breakup of empires, even changing political and religious currents—all would be reflected in the symbols and colors of the national flags. This is dramatically evident in the changing flag of the United States (below), but similar visual statements could be made for most countries.

Germany provides another example. In the Middle Ages a gold banner with a black eagle proclaimed its Holy Roman Emperor a successor to the Caesars. A united 19th-century German Empire adopted a black-white-red tricolor for Bismarck's "blood and iron" policies. The liberal Weimar and Federal Republics (1919-1933 and since 1949) hailed a black-red-gold tricolor. The dark years from 1933 to 1945 were under the swastika flag of the Nazi regime. These and similar flags in other countries are more than visual aids to history: Their development and use are a fundamental part of the political and social life of a community.

Like maps, flags are ways to communicate information in condensed form. The study of geography is paralleled by the study of flags, known as vexillology (from the Latin word vexillum, for "small sail" or flag). Books, journals, Web sites, and other sources convey information on vexillology; there are also organizations and institutions around the world linked by the International Federation of Vexillological Associations. Even very young students can gain understanding of countries, populations, political changes, religious movements, and historical events by learning about flags.

All flags embody myths and historical facts, whether they are displayed at the Olympic Games, carried by protesters, placed at a roadside shrine, or arrayed at a ceremony of national significance, such as a presidential inauguration. Flags are powerful symbols, attractive to groups of all kinds; hence their once prominent display by Nazis and Communists to manipulate the masses, their waving by the East Timorese after a successful struggle for independence, and their spontaneous use by people in the United States after September 11, 2001.

Flags of nations may be the most significant flags today, but they are far from the only ones. Sport teams, business enterprises, religious groups, ethnic groups, schools, and international organizations frequently rally, reward, and inspire people through the use of flags. An observant person will also notice advertising banners, nautical signals, warning flags, decorative pennants, the rank flags of important individuals, and many related symbols such as coats of arms and logos. Examples of flags, as presented on these two pages, only hint at the rich possibilities of design, usage, and symbolism. The vexillophile (flag hobbyist) can easily and inexpensively acquire a substantial collection of flags and flag-related items. The vexillographer (flag designer) can create flags for self or family, club or team, or even for a city or county. The vexillologist (flag scholar) will find endless connections between flags and history, political science, communications theory, social behavior, and other areas. As with geography, the knowledge gained by a study of flags can be a richly rewarding personal experience.

Development of the Stars and Stripes

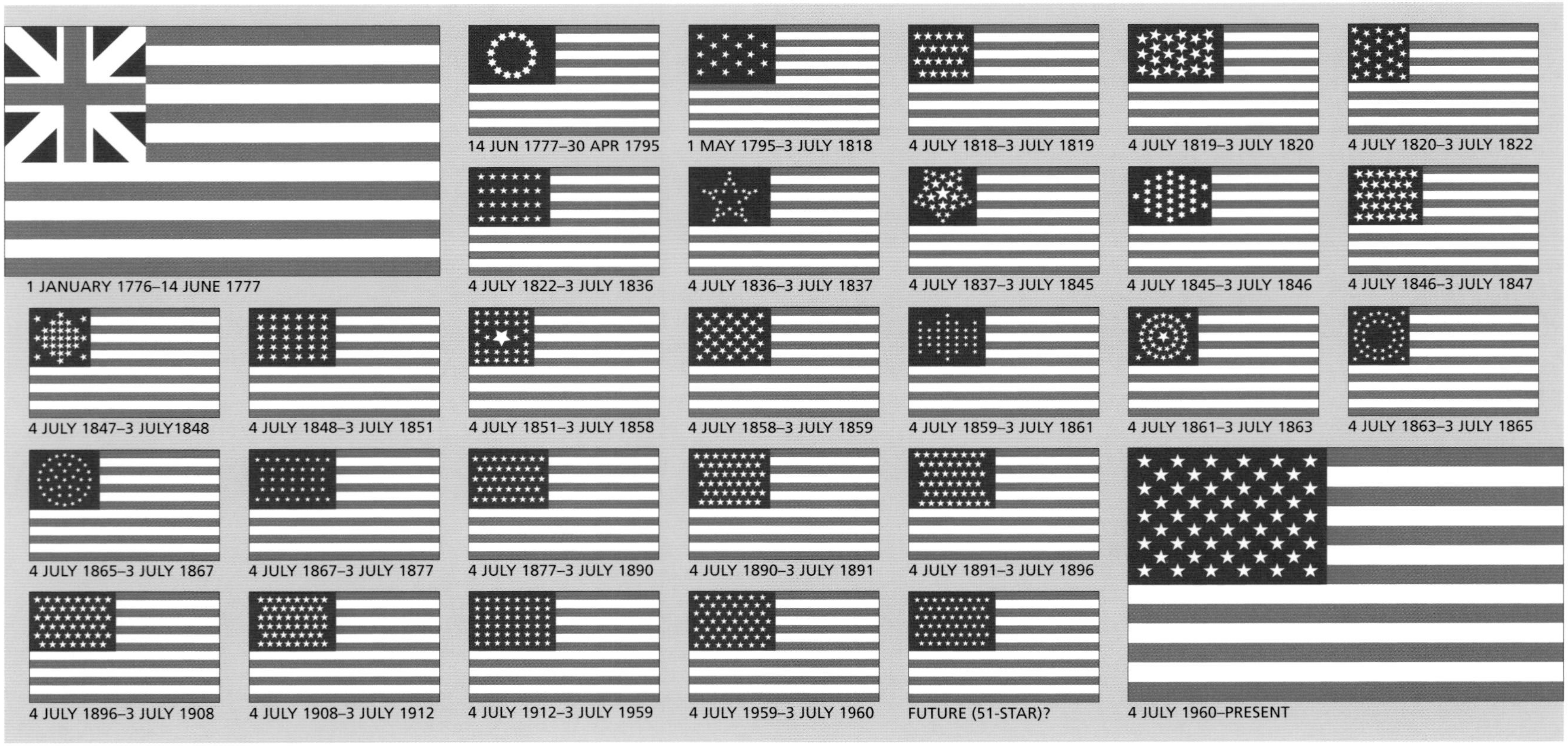

No country has changed its flag as frequently as the United States. The Continental Colors (top left) represented the Colonies during the early years of the American Revolution. Its British Union Jack, which signified loyalty to the crown, was replaced on June 14, 1777, by "13 stars...representing a new constellation." Congressman Francis Hopkinson was the designer.

The number of stars and stripes was increased to 15 in 1795. In 1817 Congressman Peter Wendover wrote the current flag law. The number of stripes was permanently limited to 13; the stars were to correspond to the number of states, with new stars added to the flag the following Fourth of July.

Star arrangement was not specified, however, and throughout the 19th century a variety of exuberant star designs—"great luminaries," rings, ovals, and diamonds—were actually used. With the increasing number of states, the modern alternating rows of stars became standard. Finally, in 1912, President Taft set forth exact regulations for all flag details.

If a new state joins the Union, a 51-star flag will be needed. There is a logical design for it: alternating rows of nine and eight stars, as shown above.

International Flags

MOURNING
The black flag signals death, piracy, protest, and danger. It is also a symbol of mourning for the dead.

OLYMPIC GAMES
The colors refer to those in the national flags of participating countries. The Olympic flag was created in 1913.

RED CRESCENT
In Muslim nations, Geneva Convention organizations rejected the red cross in favor of a red crescent, officially recognized in 1906.

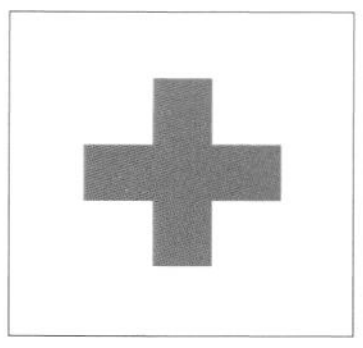

RED CROSS
The Geneva Convention chose its symbol and flag in 1864 to identify people, vehicles, and buildings protected during wartime.

TRUCE/PEACE
For a thousand years a white flag has served as a symbol of truce, surrender, noncombatant status, neutrality, and peace.

UNITED NATIONS
Olive branches of peace and a world map form the symbol adopted by the United Nations in 1946. The flag dates from 1947.

Regional Flags

ARAB LEAGUE
The color green and the crescent are often symbols in member countries of the League of Arab States, founded in 1945.

ASEAN
A stylized bundle of rice, the principal local crop, appears on the flag of the Association of South East Asian Nations (ASEAN).

COMMONWEALTH
Once the British Empire, the modern Commonwealth under this flag informally links countries with common goals.

EUROPEAN UNION
The number of stars for this flag, adopted in 1955, is permanently set at 12. The ring is a symbol for unity.

OAS
Flags of member nations appear on the flag of the Organization of American States; each new member prompts a flag change.

PACIFIC COMMISSION
The palm tree, surf, and sailboat are found in all of the member nations; each star on the flag represents a country.

Religious Flags

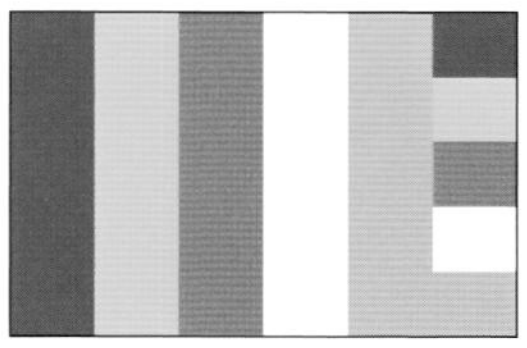

BUDDHISM
Designed in 1885 by Henry Olcott of the United States, the Buddhist flag features the auras associated with the Buddha.

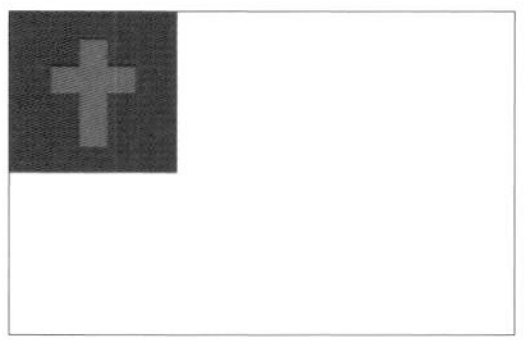

CHRISTIANITY
The sacrifice of Christ on the Cross is heralded in this 1897 flag, which features a white field for purity.

ISLAM
"There Is No God But Allah and Muhammad Is the Prophet of Allah" is written on this widely used but unofficial flag.

Ethnic Flags

LA RAZA
Crosses for the ships of Columbus and a golden Inca sun recall the Spanish and Indian heritage of Latin Americans.

PALESTINIANS
Since 1922 Palestinians have used this flag, with traditional Arab dynastic colors, as a symbol of the statehood they desire.

ROMA (GYPSIES)
Against a background of blue sky and green grass, a wheel represents the vehicles (and homes) of the nomadic Roma people.

Specialized Flags

ANARCHISTS
Opposition to all forms of authority is hinted at in the "hand-drawn" rendition of an encircled A in the anarchist flag.

BLUE FLAG
The campaign for the improvement of the environment presents this flag as an award for success.

BOY SCOUTS
Created in 1961, this flag shows the traditional Boy Scout fleur-de-lis within a rope tied with a reef knot.

CIRCLE CROSS
This ancient religious symbol, related to the swastika, is widely used as a neo-Nazi symbol in Europe and North America.

CONFEDERATE BATTLE FLAG
In many countries this flag represents protest against established authority in culture, politics, and lifestyle.

DIVERS FLAG
As a warning signal to other boats, this flag flies wherever divers are underwater nearby—and at divers' clubhouses.

ESPERANTO
On the flag promoting Esperanto as a world language, a star signifies unity; green, traditionally, is a symbol of hope.

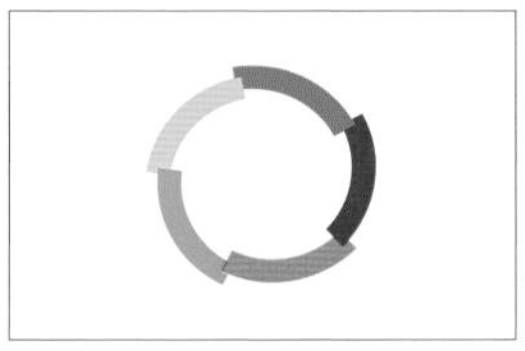

FRANCOPHONIE
French speakers share their common language and culture in periodic conferences and activities held under this flag.

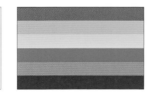

GAY PRIDE
The Rainbow Flag, in various configurations, has been flown since 1978 by the gay and lesbian community and their families.

GIRL SCOUTS
The trefoil with a compass needle adorns the World Flag of Girl Guides and Girl Scouts, which was adopted in May 1991.

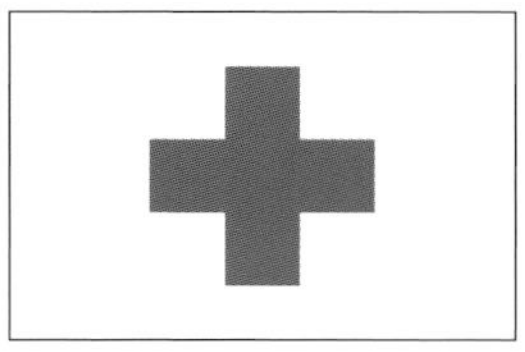

GREEN CROSS
Organizations that display this flag promote public safety in natural disasters, transportation, and the workplace.

MASONS
The unofficial flag of the Masons displays their traditional logo with symbolic square and compass.

Aaglet *well*
Aain *spring*
Aauinat *spring*
Āb *river, water*
Ache *stream*
Açude *reservoir*
Ada,-si *island*
Adrar *mountain-s, plateau*
Aguada *dry lake bed*
Aguelt *water hole, well*
'Ain, Aïn *spring, well*
Aïoun-et *spring-s, well*
Aivi *mountain*
Ákra, Akrotírion *cape, promontory*
Alb *mountain, ridge*
Alföld *plain*
Alin' *mountain range*
Alpe-n *mountain-s*
Altiplanicie *high-plain, plateau*
Alto *hill-s, mountain-s, ridge*
Älv-en *river*
Āmba *hill, mountain*
Anou *well*
Anse *bay, inlet*
Ao *bay, cove, estuary*
Ap *cape, point*
Archipel, Archipiélago *archipelago*
Arcipelago, Arkhipelag *archipelago*
Arquipélago *archipelago*
Arrecife-s *reef-s*
Arroio, Arroyo *brook, gully, rivulet, stream*
Ås *ridge*
Ava *channel*
Aylagy *gulf*
'Ayn *spring, well*

Ba *intermittent stream, river*
Baai *bay, cove, lagoon*
Bāb *gate, strait*
Badia *bay*
Bælt *strait*
Bagh *bay*
Bahar *drainage basin*
Bahía *bay*
Bahr, Baḩr *bay, lake, river, sea, wadi*
Baía, Baie *bay*
Bajo-s *shoal-s*
Ban *village*
Bañado-s *flooded area, swamp-s*
Banc, Banco-s *bank-s, sandbank-s, shoal-s*
Band *lake*
Bandao *peninsula*
Baño-s *hot spring-s, spa*
Baraj-ı *dam, reservoir*
Barra *bar, sandbank*
Barrage, Barragem *dam, lake, reservoir*
Barranca *gorge, ravine*
Bazar *marketplace*
Ben, Benin *mountain*
Belt *strait*
Bereg *bank, coast, shore*
Berg-e *mountain-s*
Bil *lake*
Biq'at *plain, valley*
Bir, Bîr, Bi'r *spring, well*
Birket *lake, pool, swamp*
Bjerg-e *mountain-s, range*
Boca, Bocca *channel, river, mouth*
Bocht *bay*
Bodden *bay*
Boğaz, -i *strait*
Bögeni *reservoir*
Boka *gulf, mouth*
Bol'sh-oy, -aya, -oye *big*
Bolsón *inland basin*
Boubairet *lagoon, lake*
Bras *arm, branch of a stream*
Braţ, -ul *arm, branch of a stream*
Bre, -en *glacier, ice cap*
Bredning *bay, broad water*
Bruch *marsh*
Bucht *bay*
Bugt-en *bay*
Buḩayrat, Buheirat *lagoon, lake, marsh*
Bukhta, Bukta, Bukt-en *bay*
Bulak, Bulaq *spring*
Bum *hill, mountain*
Burnu, Burun *cape, point*
Busen *gulf*
Buuraha *hill-s, mountain-s*
Buyuk *big, large*

Cabeza-s *head-s, summit-s*
Cabo *cape*
Cachoeira *rapids, waterfall*
Cal *hill, peak*
Caleta *cove, inlet*
Campo-s *field-s, flat country*
Canal *canal, channel, strait*
Caño *channel, stream*
Cao Nguyen *mountain, plateau*
Cap, Capo *cape*
Capitán *captain*
Càrn *mountain*
Castillo *castle, fort*
Catarata-s *cataract-s, waterfall-s*
Causse *upland*
Çay *brook, stream*
Cay-s, Cayo-s *island-s, key-s, shoal-s*
Cerro-s *hill-s, peak-s*
Chaîne, Chaînons *mountain chain, range*
Chapada-s *plateau, upland-s*
Chedo *archipelago*
Chenal *river channel*
Chersónisos *peninsula*
Chhung *bay*
Chi *lake*
Chiang *bay*
Chiao *cape, point, rock*
Ch'ih *lake*
Chink *escarpment*
Chott *intermittent salt lake, salt marsh*
Chou *island*
Ch'ü *canal*
Ch'üntao *archipelago, islands*
Chute-s *cataract-s, waterfall-s*
Chyrvony *red*
Cima *mountain, peak, summit*
Ciudad *city*
Co *lake*
Col *pass*
Collina, Colline *hill, mountains*
Con *island*
Cordillera *mountain chain*
Corno *mountain, peak*
Coronel *colonel*
Corredeira *cascade, rapids*
Costa *coast*
Côte *coast, slope*
Coxilha, Cuchilla *range of low hills*
Crique *creek, stream*
Csatorna *canal, channel*
Cul de Sac *bay, inlet*

Da *great, greater*
Daban *pass*
Dağ, -ı, Dagh *mountain*
Dağlar, -ı *mountains*
Dahr *cliff, mesa*
Dake *mountain, peak*
Dal-en *valley*
Dala *steppe*
Dan *cape, point*
Danau *lake*
Dao *island*
Dar'ya *lake, river*
Daryācheh *lake, marshy lake*
Dasht *desert, plain*
Dawan *pass*
Dawḩat *bay, cove, inlet*
Deniz, -i *sea*
Dent-s *peak-s*
Deo *pass*
Desēt *hummock, island, land-tied island*
Desierto *desert*
Détroit *channel, strait*
Dhar *hills, ridge, tableland*
Ding *mountain*
Distrito *district*
Djebel *mountain, range*
Do *island-s, rock-s*
Doi *hill, mountain*
Dome *ice dome*
Dong *village*
Dooxo *floodplain*
Dzong *castle, fortress*

Eiland-en *island-s*
Eilean *island*
Ejland *island*
Elv *river*
Embalse *lake, reservoir*
Emi *mountain, rock*
Enseada, Ensenada *bay, cove*
Ér *rivulet, stream*
Erg *sand dune region*
Est *east*
Estación *railroad station*
Estany *lagoon, lake*
Estero *estuary, inlet, lagoon, marsh*
Estrecho *strait*
Étang *lake, pond*
Eylandt *island*
Ežeras *lake*
Ezers *lake*

Falaise *cliff, escarpment*
Farvand-et *channel, sound*
Fell *mountain*
Feng *mount, peak*
Fiord-o *inlet, sound*
Fiume *river*
Fjäll-et *mountain*
Fjällen *mountains*
Fjärd-en *fjord*
Fjarðar, Fjörður *fjord*
Fjeld *mountain*
Fjell-ene *mountain-s*
Fjöll *mountain-s*
Fjord-en *inlet, fjord*
Fleuve *river*
Fljót *large river*
Flói *bay, marshland*
Foci *river mouths*
Főcsatorna *principal canal*
Förde *fjord, gulf, inlet*
Forsen *rapids, waterfall*
Fortaleza *fort, fortress*
Fortín *fortified post*
Foss-en *waterfall*
Foum *pass, passage*
Foz *mouth of a river*
Fuerte *fort, fortress*
Fwafwate *waterfalls*

Gacan-ka *hill, peak*
Gal *pond, spring, waterhole, well*
Gang *harbor*
Gangri *peak, range*
Gaoyuan *plateau*
Garaet, Gara'et *lake, lake bed, salt lake*
Gardaneh *pass*
Garet *hill, mountain*
Gat *channel*
Gata *bay, inlet, lake*
Gattet *channel, strait*
Gaud *depression, saline tract*
Gave *mountain stream*
Gebel *mountain-s, range*
Gebergte *mountain range*
Gebirge *mountains, range*
Geçidi *mountain pass, passage*
Geçit *mountain pass, passage*
Gezâir *islands*
Gezîra-t, Gezîret *island, peninsula*
Ghats *mountain range*
Ghubb-at, -et *bay, gulf*
Giri *mountain*
Gletscher *glacier*
Gobernador *governor*
Gobi *desert*
Gol *river, stream*
Göl, -ü *lake*
Golets *mountain, peak*
Golf, -e, -o *gulf*
Gor-a, -y, Gór-a, -y *mountain,-s*
Got *point*
Gowd *depression*
Goz *sand ridge*
Gran, -de *great, large*
Gryada *mountains, ridge*
Guan *pass*
Guba *bay, gulf*
Guelta *well*
Guntō *archipelago*
Gunung *mountain*
Gura *mouth, passage*
Guyot *table mount*

Haḍabat *plateau*
Haehyŏp *strait*
Haff *lagoon*
Hai *lake, sea*
Haihsia *strait*
Haixia *channel, strait*
Hakau *reef, rock*
Hakuchi *anchorage*
Halvø, Halvøy-a *peninsula*
Hama *beach*
Hamada, Ḩammādah *rocky desert*
Hamn *harbor, port*
Hāmūn, Hamun *depression, lake*
Hana *cape, point*
Hantō *peninsula*
Har *hill, mound, mountain*
Ḩarrat *lava field*
Hasi, Hassi *spring, well*
Hauteur *elevation, height*
Hav-et *sea*
Havn, Havre *harbor, port*
Hawr *lake, marsh*
Häyk' *lake, reservoir*
Hegy, -ség *mountain, -s, range*
Heiau *temple*
Ho *canal, lake, river*
Hoek *hook, point*
Hög-en *high, hill*
Höhe, -n *height, high*
Høj *height, hill*
Holm, -e, Holmene *island-s, islet -s*
Ḩolot *dunes*
Hon *island-s*
Hor-a, -y *mountain, -s*
Horn *horn, peak*
Houma *point*
Hoved *headland, peninsula, point*
Hraun *lava field*
Hsü *island*
Hu *lake, reservoir*
Huk *cape, point*
Hüyük *hill, mound*

Idehan *sand dunes*
Île-s, Ilha-s, Illa-s, Îlot-s *island-s, islet-s*
Îlet, Ilhéu-s *islet, -s*
Irhil *mountain-s*
'Irq *sand dune-s*
Isblink *glacier, ice field*
Is-en *glacier*
Isla-s, Islote *island-s, islet*
Isol-a, -e *island, -s*
Istmo *isthmus*
Iwa *island, islet, rock*

Jabal, Jebel *mountain-s, range*
Järv, -i, Jaure, Javrre *lake*
Jazā'ir, Jazīrat, Jazīreh *island-s*
Jehīl *lake*
Jezero, Jezioro *lake*
Jiang *river, stream*
Jiao *cape*
Jibāl *hill, mountain, ridge*
Jima *island-s, rock-s*
Jøkel, Jökull *glacier, ice cap*
Joki, Jokka *river*
Jökulsá *river from a glacier*
Jūn *bay*

Kaap *cape*
Kafr *village*
Kaikyō *channel, strait*
Kaise *mountain*
Kaiwan *bay, gulf, sea*
Kanal *canal, channel*
Kangri *mountain, peak*
Kap, Kapp *cape*
Kavīr *salt desert*
Kefar *village*
Kënet' *lagoon, lake*
Kep *cape, point*
Kepulauan *archipelago, islands*
Khalîg, Khalīj *bay, gulf*
Khirb-at, -et *ancient site, ruins*
Khrebet *mountain range*
Kinh *canal*
Klint *bluff, cliff*
Kō *bay, cove, harbor*
Ko *island, lake*
Koh *island, mountain, range*
Köl-i *lake*
Kólpos *gulf*
Kong *mountain*
Körfez, -i *bay, gulf*
Kosa *spit of land*
Kou *estuary, river mouth*
Kowtal-e *pass*
Krasn-yy, -aya, -oye *red*
Kryazh *mountain range, ridge*
Kuala *estuary, river mouth*
Kuan *mountain pass*
Kūh, Kūhhā *mountain-s, range*
Kul', Kuli *lake*
Kum *sandy desert*
Kundo *archipelago*
Kuppe *hill-s, mountain-s*
Kust *coast, shore*
Kyst *coast*
Kyun *island*

La *pass*
Lac, Lac-ul, -us *lake*
Lae *cape, point*
Lago, -a *lagoon, lake*
Lagoen, Lagune *lagoon*
Laguna-s *lagoon-s, lake-s*
Laht *bay, gulf, harbor*
Laje *reef, rock ledge*
Laut *sea*
Lednik *glacier*
Leida *channel*
Lhari *mountain*
Li *village*
Liedao *archipelago, islands*
Liehtao *archipelago, islands*
Liman-ı *bay, estuary*
Límni *lake*
Ling *mountain-s, range*
Linn *pool, waterfall*
Lintasan *passage*
Liqen *lake*
Llano-s *plain-s*
Loch, Lough *lake, arm of the sea*
Loma-s *hill-s, knoll-s*

Mal	*mountain, range*
Mal-yy, -aya, -oye	*little, small*
Mamarr	*pass, path*
Man	*bay*
Mar, Mare	*large lake, sea*
Marsa, Marsá	*bay, inlet*
Masabb	*mouth of river*
Massif	*massif, mountain-s*
Mauna	*mountain*
Mēda	*plain*
Meer	*lake, sea*
Melkosopochnik	*undulating plain*
Mesa, Meseta	*plateau, tableland*
Mierzeja	*sandspit*
Minami	*south*
Mios	*island*
Misaki	*cape, peninsula, point*
Mochun	*passage*
Mong	*town, village*
Mont-e, -i, -s	*mount, -ain, -s*
Montagne, -s	*mount, -ain, -s*
Montaña, -s	*mountain, -s*
More	*sea*
Morne	*hill, peak*
Morro	*bluff, headland, hill*
Motu, -s	*islands*
Mouïet	*well*
Mouillage	*anchorage*
Muang	*town, village*
Mui	*cape, point*
Mull	*headland, promontory*
Munkhafad	*depression*
Munte	*mountain*
Munţi-i	*mountains*
Muong	*town, village*
Mynydd	*mountain*
Mys	*cape*
Nacional	*national*
Nada	*gulf, sea*
Næs, Näs	*cape, point*
Nafūd	*area of dunes, desert*
Nagor'ye	*mountain range, plateau*
Nahar, Nahr	*river, stream*
Nakhon	*town*
Namakzār	*salt waste*
Ne	*island, reef, rock-s*
Neem	*cape, point, promontory*
Nes, Ness	*peninsula, point*
Nevado-s	*snow-capped mountain-s*
Nez	*cape, promontory*
Ni	*village*
Nísi, Nísia, Nisís, Nísoi	*island-s, islet-s*
Nisídhes	*islets*
Nizhn-iy, -yaya, -eye	*lower*
Nizmennost'	*low country*
Noord	*north*
Nord-re	*north-ern*
Nørre	*north-ern*
Nos	*cape, nose, point*
Nosy	*island, reef, rock*
Nov-yy, -aya, -oye	*new*
Nudo	*mountain*
Numa	*lake*
Nunatak, -s, -ker	*peak-s surrounded by ice cap*
Nur	*lake, salt lake*
Nuruu	*mountain range, ridge*
Nut-en	*peak*
Nuur	*lake*
Ö-n, Ø-er	*island-s*
Oblast'	*administrative division, province, region*
Oceanus	*ocean*
Odde-n	*cape, point*
Øer-ne	*islands*
Oglat	*group of wells*
Oguilet	*well*
Ór-os, -i	*mountain, -s*
Órmos	*bay, port*
Ort	*place, point*
Øst-er	*east*
Ostrov, -a, Ostrv-o, -a	*island, -s*
Otoci, Otok	*islands, island*
Ouadi, Oued	*river, watercourse*
Øy-a	*island*
Øyane	*islands*
Ozer-o, -a	*lake, -s*
Pää	*mountain, point*
Palus	*marsh*
Pampa-s	*grassy plain-s*
Pantà	*lake, reservoir*
Pantanal	*marsh, swamp*
Pao, P'ao	*lake*
Parbat	*mountain*
Parque	*park*
Pas, -ul	*pass*
Paso, Passo	*pass*
Passe	*channel, pass*
Pasul	*pass*
Pedra	*rock*
Pegunungan	*mountain range*
Pellg	*bay, bight*
Peña	*cliff, rock*
Pendi	*basin*
Penedo-s	*rock-s*
Péninsule	*peninsula*
Peñón	*point, rock*
Pereval	*mountain pass*
Pertuis	*strait*
Peski	*sands, sandy region*
Phnom	*hill, mountain, range*
Phou	*mountain range*
Phu	*mountain*
Piana-o	*plain*
Pic, Pik, Piz	*peak*
Picacho	*mountain, peak*
Pico-s	*peak-s*
Pistyll	*waterfall*
Piton-s	*peak-s*
Pivdennyy	*southern*
Plaja, Playa	*beach, inlet, shore*
Planalto, Plato	*plateau*
Planina	*mountain, plateau*
Plassen	*lake*
Ploskogor'ye	*plateau, upland*
Pointe	*point*
Polder	*reclaimed land*
Poluostrov	*peninsula*
Pongo	*water gap*
Ponta, -l	*cape, point*
Ponte	*bridge*
Poolsaar	*peninsula*
Portezuelo	*pass*
Porto	*port*
Poulo	*island*
Praia	*beach, seashore*
Presa	*reservoir*
Presidente	*president*
Presqu'île	*peninsula*
Prokhod	*pass*
Proliv	*strait*
Promontorio	*promontory*
Průsmyk	*mountain pass*
Przylądek	*cape*
Puerto	*bay, pass, port*
Pulao	*island-s*
Pulau, Pulo	*island*
Puncak	*peak, summit, top*
Punt, Punta, -n	*point, -s*
Pun	*peak*
Puu	*hill, mountain*
Puy	*peak*
Qal'eh	*castle, fort*
Qā'	*depression, marsh, mud flat*
Qal'at	*fort*
Qanâ	*canal*
Qārat	*hill-s, mountain-s*
Qaşr	*castle, fort, hill*
Qila	*fort*
Qiryat	*settlement, suburb*
Qolleh	*peak*
Qooriga	*anchorage, bay*
Qoz	*dunes, sand ridge*
Qu	*canal*
Quebrada	*ravine, stream*
Qullai	*peak, summit*
Qum	*desert, sand*
Qundao	*archipelago, islands*
Qurayyāt	*hills*
Raas	*cape, point*
Rabt	*hill*
Rada	*roadstead*
Rade	*anchorage, roadstead*
Rags	*point*
Ramat	*hill, mountain*
Rand	*ridge of hills*
Rann	*swamp*
Raqaba	*wadi, watercourse*
Ras, Râs, Ra's	*cape*
Ravnina	*plain*
Récif-s	*reef-s*
Regreg	*marsh*
Represa	*reservoir*
Reservatório	*reservoir*
Restinga	*barrier, sand area*
Rettō	*chain of islands*
Ri	*mountain range, village*
Ría	*estuary*
Ribeirão	*stream*
Río, Rio	*river*
Rivière	*river*
Roca-s	*cliff, rock-s*
Roche-r, -s	*rock-s*
Rosh	*mountain, point*
Rt	*cape, point*
Rubha	*headland*
Rupes	*scarp*
Saar	*island*
Saari, Sar	*island*
Sabkha-t, Sabkhet	*lagoon, marsh, salt lake*
Sagar	*lake, sea*
Sahara, Şaḩrā'	*desert*
Sahl	*plain*
Saki	*cape, point*
Salar	*salt flat*
Salina	*salt pan*
Salin-as, -es	*salt flat-s, salt marsh-es*
Salto	*waterfall*
Sammyaku	*mountain range*
San	*hill, mountain*
San, -ta, -to	*saint*
Sandur	*sandy area*
Sankt	*saint*
Sanmaek	*mountain range*
São	*saint*
Sarīr	*gravel desert*
Sasso	*mountain, stone*
Savane	*savanna*
Scoglio	*reef, rock*
Se	*reef, rock-s, shoal-s*
Sebjet	*salt lake, salt marsh*
Sebkha	*salt lake, salt marsh*
Sebkhet	*lagoon, salt lake*
See	*lake, sea*
Selat	*strait*
Selkä	*lake, ridge*
Semenanjung	*peninsula*
Sen	*mountain*
Seno	*bay, gulf*
Serra, Serranía	*range of hills or mountains*
Severn-yy, -aya, -oye	*northern*
Sgùrr	*peak*
Sha	*island, shoal*
Sha'ib	*ravine, watercourse*
Shamo	*desert*
Shan	*island-s, mountain-s, range*
Shankou	*mountain pass*
Shanmo	*mountain range*
Sharm	*cove, creek, harbor*
Shaţţ	*large river*
Shi	*administrative division, municipality*
Shima	*island-s, rock-s*
Shō	*island, reef, rock*
Shotō	*archipelago*
Shott	*intermittent salt lake*
Shuiku	*reservoir*
Shuitao	*channel*
Shyghanaghy	*bay, gulf*
Sierra	*mountain range*
Silsilesi	*mountain chain, ridge*
Sint	*saint*
Sinus	*bay, sea*
Sjö-n	*lake*
Skarv-et	*barren mountain*
Skerry	*rock*
Slieve	*mountain*
Sø	*lake*
Sønder, Søndre	*south-ern*
Sopka	*conical mountain, volcano*
Sor	*lake, salt lake*
Sør, Sör	*south-ern*
Sory	*salt lake, salt marsh*
Spitz-e	*peak, point, top*
Sredn-iy, -yaya, -eye	*central, middle*
Stagno	*lake, pond*
Stantsiya	*station*
Stausee	*reservoir*
Stenón	*channel, strait*
Step'-i	*steppe-s*
Štít	*summit, top*
Stor-e	*big, great*
Straat	*strait*
Straum-en	*current-s*
Strelka	*spit of land*
Stretet, Stretto	*strait*
Su	*reef, river, rock, stream*
Sud	*south*
Sudo	*channel, strait*
Suidō	*channel, strait*
Şummān	*rocky desert*
Sund	*sound, strait*
Sunden	*channel, inlet, sound*
Svyat-oy, -aya, -oye	*holy, saint*
Sziget	*island*
Tagh	*mountain-s*
Tall	*hill, mound*
T'an	*lake*
Tanezrouft	*desert*
Tang	*plain, steppe*
Tangi	*peninsula, point*
Tanjong, Tanjung	*cape, point*
Tao	*island-s*
Tarso	*hill-s, mountain-s*
Tassili	*plateau, upland*
Tau	*mountain-s, range*
Taūy	*hills, mountains*
Tchabal	*mountain-s*
Te Ava	*tidal flat*
Tel-l	*hill, mound*
Telok, Teluk	*bay*
Tepe, -si	*hill, peak*
Tepuí	*mesa, mountain*
Terara	*hill, mountain, peak*
Testa	*bluff, head*
Thale	*lake*
Thang	*plain, steppe*
Tien	*lake*
Tierra	*land, region*
Ting	*hill, mountain*
Tir'at	*canal*
Tó	*lake, pool*
To, Tō	*island-s, rock-s*
Tonle	*lake*
Tope	*hill, mountain, peak*
Top-pen	*peak-s*
Träsk	*bog, lake*
Tso	*lake*
Tsui	*cape, point*
Tübegi	*peninsula*
Tulu	*hill, mountain*
Tunturi-t	*hill-s, mountain-s*
Uad	*wadi, watercourse*
Udde-m	*point*
Ujong, Ujung	*cape, point*
Umi	*bay, lagoon, lake*
Ura	*bay, inlet, lake*
'Urūq	*dune area*
Uul, Uula	*mountain, range*
'Uyûn	*springs*
Vaara	*mountain*
Vaart	*canal*
Vær	*fishing station*
Vaïn	*channel, strait*
Valle, Vallée	*valley, wadi*
Vallen	*waterfall*
Valli	*lagoon, lake*
Vallis	*valley*
Vanua	*land*
Varre	*mountain*
Vatn, Vatten, Vatnet	*lake, water*
Veld	*grassland, plain*
Verkhn-iy, -yaya, -eye	*higher, upper*
Vesi	*lake, water*
Vest-er	*west*
Via	*road*
Vidda	*plateau*
Vig, Vík, Vik, -en	*bay, cove*
Vinh	*bay, gulf*
Vodokhranilishche	*reservoir*
Vodoskhovyshche	*reservoir*
Volcan, Volcán	*volcano*
Vostochn-yy, -aya, -oye	*eastern*
Vötn	*stream*
Vozvyshennost'	*plateau, upland*
Vozyera	*lake-s*
Vrchovina	*mountains*
Vrch-y	*mountain-s*
Vrh	*hill, mountain*
Vrŭkh	*mountain*
Vyaliki	*big, large*
Vysočina	*highland*
Wabē	*stream*
Wadi, Wâdi, Wādī	*valley, watercourse*
Wâhât, Wāḩat	*oasis*
Wald	*forest, wood*
Wan	*bay, gulf*
Water	*harbor*
Webi	*stream*
Wiek	*cove, inlet*
Xia	*gorge, strait*
Xiao	*lesser, little*
Yanchi	*salt lake*
Yang	*ocean*
Yarymadasy	*peninsula*
Yazovir	*reservoir*
Yŏlto	*island group*
Yoma	*mountain range*
Yü	*island*
Yumco	*lake*
Yunhe	*canal*
Yuzhn-yy, -aya, -oye	*southern*
Zaki	*cape, point*
Zaliv	*bay, gulf*
Zan	*mountain, ridge*
Zangbo	*river, stream*
Zapadn-yy, -aya, -oye	*western*
Zatoka	*bay, gulf*
Zee	*bay, sea*
Zemlya	*land*

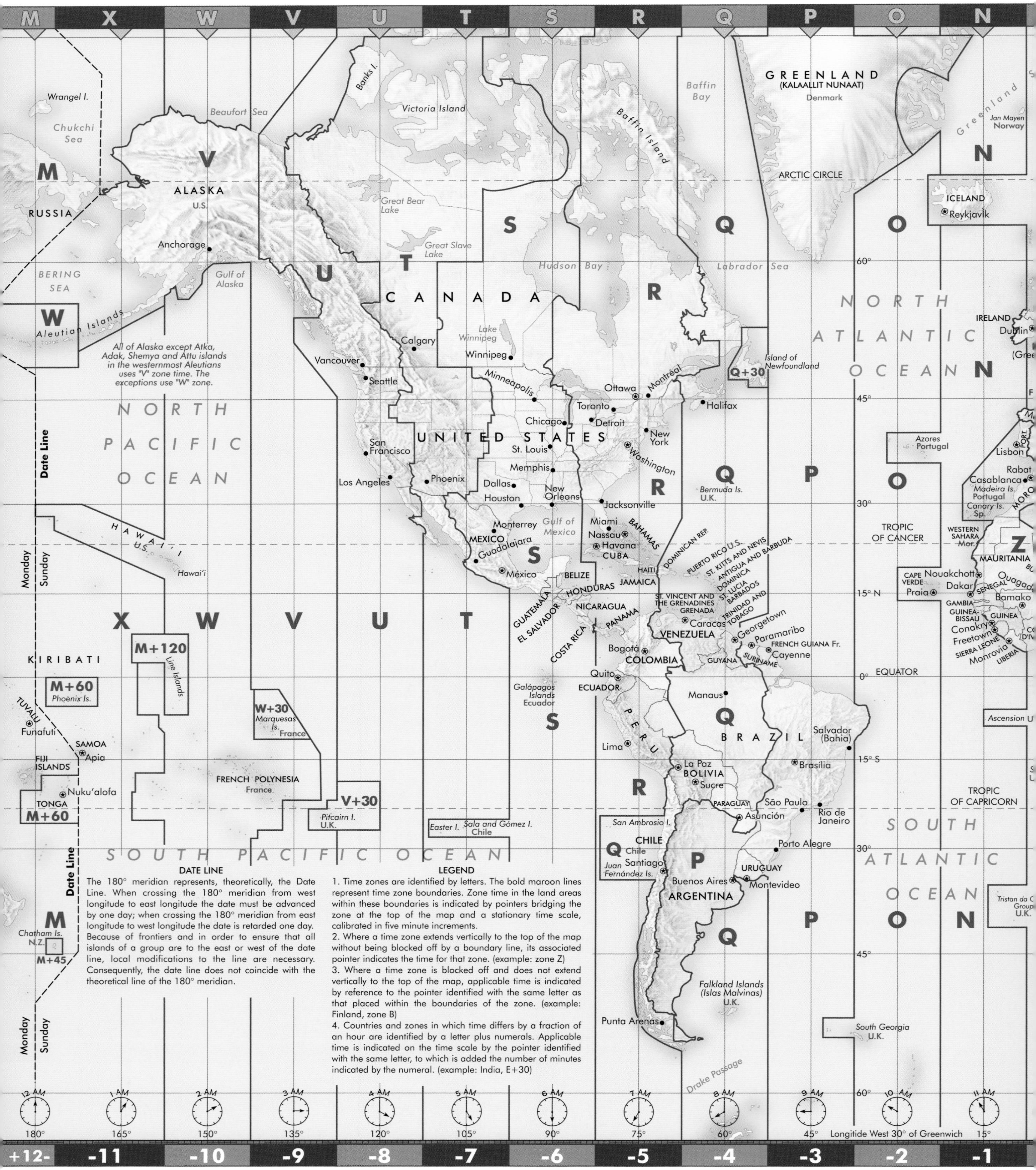

DATE LINE

The 180° meridian represents, theoretically, the Date Line. When crossing the 180° meridian from west longitude to east longitude the date must be advanced by one day; when crossing the 180° meridian from east longitude to west longitude the date is retarded one day. Because of frontiers and in order to ensure that all islands of a group are to the east or west of the date line, local modifications to the line are necessary. Consequently, the date line does not coincide with the theoretical line of the 180° meridian.

LEGEND

1. Time zones are identified by letters. The bold maroon lines represent time zone boundaries. Zone time in the land areas within these boundaries is indicated by pointers bridging the zone at the top of the map and a stationary time scale, calibrated in five minute increments.
2. Where a time zone extends vertically to the top of the map without being blocked off by a boundary line, its associated pointer indicates the time for that zone. (example: zone Z)
3. Where a time zone is blocked off and does not extend vertically to the top of the map, applicable time is indicated by reference to the pointer identified with the same letter as that placed within the boundaries of the zone. (example: Finland, zone B)
4. Countries and zones in which time differs by a fraction of an hour are identified by a letter plus numerals. Applicable time is indicated on the time scale by the pointer identified with the same letter, to which is added the number of minutes indicated by the numeral. (example: India, E+30)

The numeral in each tab directly above shows the number of hours to be added to, or subtracted from, Coordinated Universal Time (UTC), formerly Greenwich Mean Time (GMT).

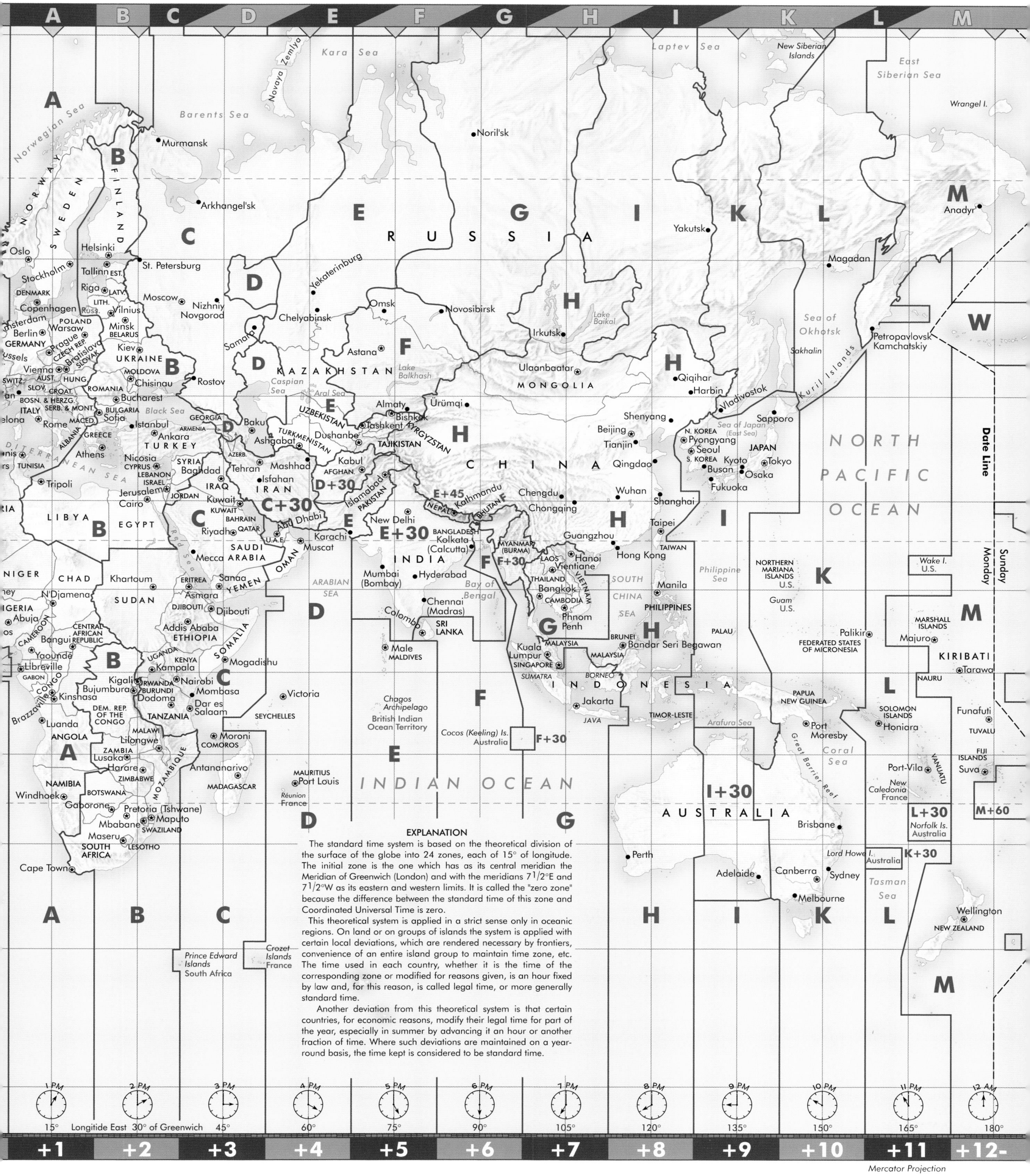

EXPLANATION

The standard time system is based on the theoretical division of the surface of the globe into 24 zones, each of 15° of longitude. The initial zone is the one which has as its central meridian the Meridian of Greenwich (London) and with the meridians $7^1/2$°E and $7^1/2$°W as its eastern and western limits. It is called the "zero zone" because the difference between the standard time of this zone and Coordinated Universal Time is zero.

This theoretical system is applied in a strict sense only in oceanic regions. On land or on groups of islands the system is applied with certain local deviations, which are rendered necessary by frontiers, convenience of an entire island group to maintain time zone, etc. The time used in each country, whether it is the time of the corresponding zone or modified for reasons given, is an hour fixed by law and, for this reason, is called legal time, or more generally standard time.

Another deviation from this theoretical system is that certain countries, for economic reasons, modify their legal time for part of the year, especially in summer by advancing it an hour or another fraction of time. Where such deviations are maintained on a year-round basis, the time kept is considered to be standard time.

NOTES ON MAJOR CITY DATA

The population figures in the following list are from *World Urbanization Prospects: the 2003 Revision,* prepared by the United Nations. The list shows urban agglomerations with at least 1,000,000 inhabitants in the year 2003. An "urban agglomeration" is a contiguous territory with an urban level of population density; it includes one or more cities or towns and adjacent thickly settled areas. Thus, its geographic extent roughly coincides with the limits of a built-up urban area as seen from on high. Because an urban agglomeration is basically a metropolitan area, the population figure given for each area on the list will naturally be greater than the city-proper population figure cited in many other publications.

It is difficult to compare city populations because definitions of cities and metropolitan areas, as well as the availability of statistics, vary widely among countries. Also, the names given to metropolitan areas and the regions that comprise them may vary. As a result, some of the urban agglomeration names and population figures used in this atlas differ from names and figures given for the same general areas included on lists in other publications.

Spellings may vary, too. The UN list sometimes uses spellings that do not agree with ones used on National Geographic maps. In such cases, we have listed the place-names as they appear in the *Family Reference Atlas.* We did not change a UN spelling if we included it in the atlas as a parenthetical name or used it as a conventional name on world or physical maps.

Some of the names on the following list do not appear at all on maps in the atlas because they are regions rather than cities (Germany's Rhein-Ruhr South, for example). Others (some cities in China, for instance) were not included because of space limitations due to map scale.

CITY	COUNTRY	POPULATION
AACHEN	Germany	1,071,000
ABIDJAN	Côte d'Ivoire	3,337,000
ACCRA	Ghana	1,847,000
ADANA	Turkey	1,199,000
ADDIS ABABA	Ethiopia	2,723,000
ADELAIDE	Australia	1,124,000
AGRA	India	1,431,000
AHMADABAD	India	4,869,000
ALEXANDRIA	Egypt	3,653,000
ALGIERS	Algeria	3,060,000
ALLAHABAD	India	1,106,000
ALMATY	Kazakhstan	1,115,000
AMMAN	Jordan	1,237,000
AMRITSAR	India	1,092,000
AMSTERDAM	Netherlands	1,145,000
ANKARA	Turkey	3,428,000
ANSHAN	China	1,457,000
ANTANANARIVO	Madagascar	1,678,000
ASANSOL	India	1,187,000
ASUNCIÓN	Paraguay	1,639,000
ATHENS	Greece	3,215,000
ATLANTA	United States	3,999,000
AUCKLAND	New Zealand	1,117,000
AUSTIN	United States	1,028,000
BAGHDAD	Iraq	5,620,000
BAKU	Azerbaijan	1,816,000
BALTIMORE	United States	2,141,000
BAMAKO	Mali	1,264,000
BANDUNG	Indonesia	3,765,000
BANGALORE	India	6,141,000
BANGKOK	Thailand	6,486,000
BAOTOU	China	1,348,000
BARCELONA	Spain	4,406,000
BARRANQUILLA	Colombia	1,830,000
BASRA	Iraq	1,150,000
BEIHEI	China	1,026,000
BEIJING (PEKING)	China	10,848,000
BEIRUT	Lebanon	1,792,000
BELÉM	Brazil	1,956,000
BELGRADE	Serb. & Mont.	1,118,000
BELO HORIZONTE	Brazil	5,048,000
BERLIN	Germany	3,327,000
BHOPAL	India	1,563,000
BIELEFELD	Germany	1,309,000
BIRMINGHAM	U. K.	2,224,000
BOGOTÁ	Colombia	7,290,000
BOSTON	United States	4,212,000
BRASÍLIA	Brazil	3,099,000
BRAZZAVILLE	Congo	1,080,000
BRISBANE	Australia	1,712,000
BUCARAMANGA	Colombia	1,019,000
BUCHAREST	Romania	1,853,000
BUDAPEST	Hungary	1,708,000
BUENOS AIRES	Argentina	13,047,000
BURSA	Turkey	1,320,000
BUSAN (PUSAN)	South Korea	3,579,000
CAIRO	Egypt	10,834,000
CALGARY	Canada	1,014,000
CALI	Colombia	2,452,000
CAMPINAS	Brazil	2,488,000
CAPE TOWN	South Africa	2,967,000
CARACAS	Venezuela	3,226,000
CASABLANCA	Morocco	3,578,000
CHANGCHUN	China	3,010,000
CHANGDE	China	1,438,000
CHANGSHA	China	1,935,000
CHELYABINSK	Russia	1,077,000
CHENGDU	China	3,404,000
CHENNAI (MADRAS)	India	6,691,000
CHICAGO	United States	8,568,000
CHIFENG (ULANHAD)	China	1,119,000
CHITTAGONG	Bangladesh	3,794,000
CHONGQING	China	4,848,000
CINCINNATI	United States	1,552,000
CIUDAD JUÁREZ	Mexico	1,381,000
CLEVELAND	United States	1,814,000
COCHIN (KOCHI)	India	1,412,000
COIMBATORE	India	1,544,000
COLUMBUS	United States	1,190,000
CONAKRY	Guinea	1,366,000
COPENHAGEN	Denmark	1,066,000
CÓRDOBA	Argentina	1,533,000
CURITIBA	Brazil	2,721,000
DAEGU	South Korea	2,502,000
DAEJEON (TAEJON)	South Korea	1,426,000
DAKAR	Senegal	2,167,000
DALIAN (DAIREN)	China	2,677,000
DALLAS-FORT WORTH	United States	4,446,000
DAMASCUS	Syria	2,228,000
DAQING	China	1,101,000
DAR ES SALAM	Tanzania	2,441,000
DATONG	China	1,134,000
DAVAO	Philippines	1,254,000
DELHI	India	14,146,000
DENVER	United States	2,135,000
DETROIT	United States	3,951,000
DHAKA	Bangladesh	11,560,000
DHANBAD	India	1,135,000
DNIPROPETROVSK	Ukraine	1,052,000
DONETSK	Ukraine	1,005,000
DONGGUAN	China	1,217,000
DOUALA	Cameroon	1,858,000
DUBLIN	Ireland	1,015,000
DURBAN	South Africa	2,551,000
EAST RAND	South Africa	2,808,000
ESFAHAN	Iran	1,480,000
FAISALABAD	Pakistan	2,370,000
FARIDABAD	India	1,200,000
FORTALEZA	Brazil	3,107,000
FUSHUN	China	1,420,000
FUYU	China	1,051,000
FUZHOU	China	1,398,000
GHAZIABAD	India	1,129,000
GOIÂNIA	Brazil	1,770,000
GRANDE VITÓRIA	Brazil	1,521,000
GUADALAJARA	Mexico	3,825,000
GUANGZHOU (CANTON)	China	3,887,000
GUAYAQUIL	Ecuador	2,262,000
GUIYANG	China	2,402,000
GUJRANWALA	Pakistan	1,366,000
GWANGJU (KWANGJU)	South Korea	1,410,000
HAIPHONG	Vietnam	1,755,000
HALAB (ALEPPO)	Syria	2,379,000
HAMBURG	Germany	2,681,000
HANDAN	China	2,070,000
HANGZHOU	China	1,883,000
HANNOVER	Germany	1,293,000
HANOI	Vietnam	3,977,000
HARARE	Zimbabwe	1,469,000
HARBIN	China	2,911,000
HAVANA	Cuba	2,189,000
HEFEI	China	1,288,000
HELSINKI	Finland	1,075,000
HEZE	China	1,743,000
HO CHI MINH CITY (SAIGON)	Vietnam	4,851,000
HONG KONG	China	7,049,000
HOUSTON	United States	4,118,000
HUAINAN	China	1,394,000
HUAIYIN	China	1,271,000
HUZHOU	China	1,092,000
HYDERABAD	India	5,864,000
HYDERABAD	Pakistan	1,319,000
IBADAN	Nigeria	2,284,000
INCHEON	South Korea	2,575,000
INDIANAPOLIS	United States	1,318,000
INDORE	India	1,800,000
ISTANBUL	Turkey	9,371,000
IZMIR	Turkey	2,388,000
JABALPUR	India	1,180,000
JAIPUR	India	2,575,000
JAKARTA	Indonesia	12,296,000
JAMSHEDPUR	India	1,179,000
JEDDAH	Saudi Arabia	3,557,000
JILIN	China	1,471,000
JINAN	China	2,619,000
JINGMEN	China	1,197,000
JINING	China	1,068,000
JINXI	China	1,800,000
JOHANNESBURG	South Africa	3,084,000
KABUL	Afghanistan	2,956,000
KADUNA	Nigeria	1,273,000
KAMPALA	Uganda	1,246,000
KANO	Nigeria	2,763,000
KANPUR	India	2,879,000
KANSAS CITY	United States	1,398,000
KAOHSIUNG	China	1,489,000
KARACHI	Pakistan	11,078,000
KARAJ	Iran	1,165,000
KATOWICE	Poland	2,962,000
KAZAN	Russia	1,108,000
KHARKIV	Ukraine	1,455,000
KHARTOUM	Sudan	4,286,000
KHULNA	Bangladesh	1,401,000
KIEV	Ukraine	2,618,000
KINSHASA	D. R. C.	5,277,000
KITAKYUSHU	Japan	2,777,000
KOLKATA (CALCUTTA)	India	13,806,000
KUALA LUMPUR	Malaysia	1,352,000
KUNMING	China	1,729,000
KUWAIT CITY	Kuwait	1,222,000
KYOTO	Japan	1,806,000
LA PAZ	Bolivia	1,477,000
LAGOS	Nigeria	10,103,000
LAHORE	Pakistan	5,989,000
LANZHOU	China	1,765,000
LAS VEGAS	United States	1,568,000

CITY	COUNTRY	POPULATION
LEEDS	U.K.	1,406,000
LEÓN	Mexico	1,383,000
LESHAN	China	1,158,000
LILLE	France	1,021,000
LIMA	Peru	7,899,000
LINYI	China	1,993,000
LISBON	Portugal	1,962,000
LONDON	U.K.	7,619,000
LOS ANGELES	United States	12,018,000
LUAN	China	1,934,000
LUANDA	Angola	2,623,000
LUBUMBASHI	D. R. C.	1,012,000
LUCKNOW	India	2,439,000
LUDHIANA	India	1,496,000
LUOYANG	China	1,535,000
LUPANSHUI	China	2,080,000
LUSAKA	Zambia	1,394,000
LYON	France	1,391,000
MACEIÓ	Brazil	1,062,000
MADRID	Spain	5,103,000
MADURAI	India	1,222,000
MANAGUA	Nicaragua	1,098,000
MANAUS	Brazil	1,559,000
MANCHESTER	U.K.	2,203,000
MANILA	Philippines	10,352,000
MAPUTO	Mozambique	1,221,000
MARACAIBO	Venezuela	2,073,000
MARACAY	Venezuela	1,090,000
MARSEILLE	France	1,373,000
MASHHAD	Iran	2,080,000
MECCA	Saudi Arabia	1,446,000
MEDAN	Indonesia	2,010,000
MEDELLÍN	Colombia	3,099,000
MEERUT	India	1,260,000
MELBOURNE	Australia	3,577,000
MEMPHIS	United States	1,016,000
MENDOZA	Argentina	1,025,000
MEXICO CITY	Mexico	18,660,000
MIAMI	United States	5,216,000
MIANYANG	China	1,129,000
MILAN	Italy	4,064,000
MILWAUKEE	United States	1,330,000
MINNEAPOLIS-ST. PAUL	United States	2,476,000
MINSK	Belarus	1,705,000
MOGADISHU	Somalia	1,175,000
MONTERREY	Mexico	3,422,000
MONTEVIDEO	Uruguay	1,341,000
MONTRÉAL	Canada	3,471,000
MOSCOW	Russia	10,469,000
MOSUL	Iraq	1,163,000
MULTAN	Pakistan	1,376,000
MUMBAI (BOMBAY)	India	17,431,000
MUNICH	Germany	2,312,000
NAGOYA	Japan	3,164,000
NAGPUR	India	2,251,000
NAIROBI	Kenya	2,575,000
NAMPO	North Korea	1,124,000
NANCHANG	China	1,696,000
NANCHONG	China	1,045,000
NANJING	China	2,780,000
NANNING	China	1,361,000
NAPLES	Italy	2,934,000
NASIK	India	1,287,000
NEIJIANG	China	1,427,000
NEWCASTLE	U.K.	1,031,000
NEW ORLEANS	United States	1,005,000
NEW YORK	United States	18,252,000
NINGBO	China	1,182,000
NIZHNIY NOVGOROD	Russia	1,306,000
NORFOLK-VIRGINIA BEACH-NEWPORT NEWS	United States	1,424,000
NOVOSIBIRSK	Russia	1,430,000
NÜRNBERG	Germany	1,203,000
ODESA	Ukraine	1,021,000
OMSK	Russia	1,137,000
ORLANDO	United States	1,244,000
OSAKA	Japan	11,244,000
OTTAWA	Canada	1,093,000

CITY	COUNTRY	POPULATION
PALEMBANG	Indonesia	1,569,000
PARIS	France	9,794,000
PATNA	India	1,898,000
PERTH	Australia	1,442,000
PESHAWAR	Pakistan	1,176,000
PHILADELPHIA	United States	5,261,000
PHNOM PENH	Cambodia	1,157,000
PHOENIX	United States	3,218,000
PINGXIANG	China	1,538,000
PITTSBURGH	United States	1,770,000
PORT-AU-PRINCE	Haiti	1,961,000
PORTLAND-VANCOUVER	United States	1,718,000
PORTO	Portugal	1,283,000
PORTO ALEGRE	Brazil	3,682,000
PRAGUE	Czech Republic	1,170,000
PRETORIA	South Africa	1,209,000
PROVIDENCE-PAWTUCKET	United States	1,211,000
PUEBLA	Mexico	1,876,000
PUNE	India	4,144,000
P'YONGYANG	North Korea	3,228,000
QINGDAO	China	2,385,000
QIQIHAR	China	1,445,000
QUITO	Ecuador	1,451,000
RABAT	Morocco	1,759,000
RAJKOT	India	1,110,000
RAWALPINDI	Pakistan	1,680,000
RECIFE	Brazil	3,411,000
RHEIN-MAIN	Germany	3,712,000
RHEIN-NECKAR	Germany	1,620,000
RHEIN-RUHR MIDDLE	Germany	3,301,000
RHEIN-RUHR NORTH	Germany	6,560,000
RHEIN-RUHR SOUTH	Germany	3,076,000
RIO DE JANEIRO	Brazil	11,214,000
RIVERSIDE-SAN BERNARDINO	United States	1,614,000
RIYADH	Saudi Arabia	5,126,000
ROME	Italy	2,665,000
ROSARIO	Argentina	1,280,000
ROSTOV NA DONU	Russia	1,075,000
ROTTERDAM	Netherlands	1,104,000
SACRAMENTO	United States	1,487,000
SALVADOR	Brazil	3,187,000
SAMARA	Russia	1,155,000
SAN ANTONIO	United States	1,386,000
SAN DIEGO	United States	2,766,000
SAN FRANCISCO-OAKLAND	United States	3,300,000
SAN JOSE	United States	1,584,000
SAN JOSÉ	Costa Rica	1,085,000
SAN JUAN	Puerto Rico	2,332,000
SAN SALVADOR	El Salvador	1,424,000
SANAA	Yemen	1,469,000
SANTA CRUZ	Bolivia	1,231,000
SANTIAGO	Chile	5,478,000
SANTO DOMINGO	Dominican Republic	1,865,000
SANTOS	Brazil	1,569,000
SÃO PAULO	Brazil	17,857,000
SAPPORO	Japan	1,800,000
SEATTLE	United States	2,870,000
SEOUL	South Korea	9,714,000
SHANGHAI	China	12,759,000
SHANTOU (SWATOW)	China	1,281,000
SHENYANG	China	4,882,000
SHENZHEN	China	1,221,000
SHIJIAZHUANG	China	1,680,000
SHIRAZ	Iran	1,186,000
SINGAPORE	Singapore	4,253,000
SOFIA	Bulgaria	1,076,000
SRINAGAR	India	1,037,000
ST. LOUIS	United States	2,110,000
ST. PETERSBURG	Russia	5,286,000
STOCKHOLM	Sweden	1,697,000
STUTTGART	Germany	2,697,000
SUINING	China	1,483,000
SUQIAN	China	1,230,000
SURABAYA	Indonesia	2,616,000

CITY	COUNTRY	POPULATION
SURAT	India	3,261,000
SUWON	South Korea	1,073,000
SUZHOU	China	1,168,000
SYDNEY	Australia	4,274,000
TABRIZ	Iran	1,346,000
TAIAN	China	1,531,000
TAICHUNG	China	1,018,000
TAIPEI	China	2,505,000
TAIYUAN	China	2,476,000
TAMPA-ST. PETERSBURG-CLEARWATER	United States	2,168,000
TANGSHAN	China	1,732,000
TASHKENT	Uzbekistan	2,155,000
TBILISI	Georgia	1,064,000
TEGUCIGALPA	Honduras	1,007,000
TEHRAN	Iran	7,190,000
TEL AVIV-YAFO	Israel	2,917,000
TIANJIN (TIENTSIN)	China	9,271,000
TIANMEN	China	1,878,000
TIANSHUI	China	1,236,000
TIJUANA	Mexico	1,465,000
TOKYO	Japan	34,997,000
TOLUCA	Mexico	1,778,000
TORONTO	Canada	4,880,000
TORREÓN	Mexico	1,039,000
TRIPOLI	Libya	2,006,000
TUNIS	Tunisia	1,996,000
TURIN	Italy	1,203,000
UFA	Russia	1,043,000
UJUNGPANDANG	Indonesia	1,140,000
ULSAN	South Korea	1,042,000
URUMQI	China	1,501,000
VADODARA	India	1,596,000
VALENCIA	Venezuela	2,160,000
VANCOUVER	Canada	2,059,000
VARANASI (BENARES)	India	1,259,000
VIENNA	Austria	2,179,000
VIJAYAWADA	India	1,055,000
VISHAKHAPATNAM	India	1,404,000
VOLGOGRAD	Russia	1,016,000
WANXIAN	China	1,879,000
WARSAW	Poland	2,200,000
WASHINGTON, D.C.	United States	4,098,000
WEIFANG	China	1,331,000
WENZHOU	China	1,394,000
WUHAN	China	5,653,000
WUXI	China	1,166,000
XIAN	China	3,203,000
XIANTAO	China	1,699,000
XIAOSHAN	China	1,128,000
XINGHUA	China	1,575,000
XINTAI	China	1,330,000
XINYI	China	1,002,000
XUZHOU	China	1,621,000
YANCHENG	China	1,631,000
YANGON (RANGOON)	Myanmar	3,874,000
YANTAI	China	1,667,000
YAOUNDÉ	Cameroon	1,616,000
YEKATERINBURG	Russia	1,292,000
YEREVAN	Armenia	1,079,000
YIXING	China	1,121,000
YIYANG	China	1,441,000
YONGZHOU	China	1,148,000
YUEYANG	China	1,256,000
YULIN	China	1,637,000
YUZHOU	China	1,205,000
ZAOYANG	China	1,174,000
ZAOZHUANG	China	2,131,000
ZHANJIANG	China	1,481,000
ZHENGZHOU (CHENGCHOW)	China	2,176,000
ZIBO	China	2,735,000
ZIGONG	China	1,102,000

Average daily high and low temperatures and monthly rainfall for selected world locations:

CANADA	JAN.			FEB.			MARCH			APRIL			MAY			JUNE			JULY			AUG.			SEPT.			OCT.			NOV.			DEC.		
CALGARY, *Alberta*	-4	-16	14	-2	-14	15	3	-9	20	11	-3	27	17	3	54	20	7	82	24	9	65	23	8	57	18	3	40	12	-1	18	3	-9	16	-2	-13	14
CHARLOTTETOWN, *P.E.I.*	-3	-11	100	-3	-12	83	1	-7	83	7	-1	77	14	4	79	20	10	75	24	14	78	23	14	86	18	10	91	13	5	106	6	0	106	0	-7	111
CHURCHILL, *Manitoba*	-23	-31	15	-22	-30	12	-15	-25	18	-6	-15	23	2	-5	27	11	1	43	17	7	55	16	7	62	9	2	53	2	-4	44	-9	-16	31	-18	-26	18
EDMONTON, *Alberta*	-9	-18	23	-5	-15	18	0	-9	19	10	-1	24	17	5	45	21	9	79	23	12	87	22	10	64	17	5	36	11	0	20	0	-8	18	-6	-15	22
FORT NELSON, *B.C.*	-18	-27	23	-11	-23	21	-2	-15	21	8	-4	20	16	3	44	21	8	65	23	10	76	21	8	58	15	3	39	6	-4	28	-9	-17	26	-16	-24	23
GOOSE BAY, *Nfld.*	-12	-22	1	-10	-21	4	-4	-15	4	3	-7	15	10	0	46	17	5	97	21	10	119	19	9	98	14	4	87	6	-2	58	0	-8	21	-9	-18	7
HALIFAX, *Nova Scotia*	0	-8	139	0	-9	121	3	-5	123	8	0	109	14	5	110	18	9	96	22	13	93	22	14	103	19	10	93	13	5	127	8	1	142	2	-5	141
MONTRÉAL, *Quebec*	-6	-15	71	-4	-13	66	2	-7	71	11	1	74	18	8	69	24	13	84	26	16	87	25	14	91	20	10	84	13	4	76	5	-2	90	-3	-11	85
MOOSONEE, *Ontario*	-14	-27	39	-12	-25	32	-5	-19	37	3	-8	36	11	0	55	18	5	72	22	9	79	20	8	78	15	5	77	8	0	66	-1	-9	53	-11	-21	41
OTTAWA, *Ontario*	-6	-16	67	-5	-15	59	1	-8	67	11	0	60	19	7	72	24	12	82	27	15	86	25	13	80	20	9	77	13	3	69	4	-3	70	-4	-12	74
PRINCE RUPERT, *B.C.*	4	-3	237	6	-1	198	7	0	202	9	2	179	12	5	133	14	8	110	16	10	115	16	10	149	15	8	218	11	5	345	7	1	297	5	-1	275
QUÉBEC, *Quebec*	-7	-17	85	-6	-16	75	0	-9	79	8	-1	76	17	5	93	22	10	108	25	13	112	23	12	109	18	7	113	11	2	89	3	-4	100	-5	-13	104
REGINA, *Saskatchewan*	-12	-23	17	-9	-21	13	-2	-13	18	10	-3	20	18	3	45	23	9	77	26	11	59	25	10	44	19	4	35	11	-2	20	0	-11	16	-8	-19	14
SAINT JOHN, *N.B.*	-3	-14	141	-2	-14	115	3	-7	111	10	-1	111	17	4	116	22	9	103	25	12	100	24	11	100	19	7	108	14	2	118	6	-3	149	-1	-10	157
ST. JOHN'S, *Nfld.*	-1	-8	69	-1	-9	69	1	-6	74	5	-2	80	10	1	91	16	6	95	20	11	78	20	11	122	16	8	125	11	3	147	6	0	122	2	-5	91
TORONTO, *Ontario*	-1	-8	68	-1	-9	60	3	-4	66	11	2	65	17	7	71	23	13	68	26	16	77	25	15	70	21	11	73	14	5	62	7	0	70	1	-6	67
VANCOUVER, *B.C.*	5	0	146	8	1	121	10	2	102	13	5	69	17	8	56	19	11	47	22	13	31	22	13	37	19	10	60	14	6	116	9	3	155	6	1	172
WHITEHORSE, *Yukon*	-14	-23	17	-9	-18	13	-2	-13	13	5	-5	9	13	1	14	18	5	30	20	8	37	18	6	39	12	3	31	4	-3	21	-6	-13	20	-12	-20	19
WINNIPEG, *Manitoba*	-13	-23	21	-10	-21	19	-2	-13	26	9	-2	34	18	5	55	23	10	81	26	14	74	25	12	66	19	6	55	12	1	35	-1	-9	26	-9	-18	22
YELLOWKNIFE, *N.W.T.*	-24	-32	14	-20	-30	12	-12	-24	11	-1	-13	10	10	0	16	18	8	20	21	12	35	18	10	39	10	4	29	1	-4	32	-10	-18	23	-20	-28	17
UNITED STATES																																				
ALBANY, *New York*	-1	-12	61	1	-10	59	7	-4	76	14	2	77	21	7	86	26	13	83	29	15	80	27	14	87	23	10	78	17	4	77	9	-1	80	2	-8	74
AMARILLO, *Texas*	9	-6	13	12	-4	14	16	0	23	22	6	28	26	11	71	31	16	88	33	19	70	32	18	74	28	14	50	23	7	35	15	0	15	10	-5	15
ANCHORAGE, *Alaska*	-6	-13	20	-3	-11	21	1	-8	17	6	-2	15	12	4	17	16	8	26	18	11	47	17	10	62	13	5	66	5	-2	47	-3	-9	29	-5	-12	28
ASPEN, *Colorado*	0	-18	32	2	-16	26	5	-11	35	10	-6	28	16	-2	39	22	1	34	26	5	44	25	4	45	21	0	34	15	-5	36	6	-10	31	1	-15	32
ATLANTA, *Georgia*	10	0	117	13	1	117	18	6	139	23	10	103	26	15	100	30	19	92	31	21	134	31	21	93	28	18	91	23	11	77	17	6	95	12	2	105
ATLANTIC CITY, *N.J.*	5	-6	83	6	-5	78	11	0	98	16	4	86	22	10	82	27	15	63	29	18	103	29	18	103	25	13	78	19	7	72	13	2	84	7	-3	81
AUGUSTA, *Maine*	-2	-11	76	0	-10	71	4	-5	84	11	1	92	19	7	95	23	12	85	26	16	85	25	15	84	20	10	80	14	4	92	7	-1	114	0	-8	93
BIRMINGHAM, *Alabama*	11	0	128	14	1	114	19	6	150	24	10	114	27	14	112	31	18	97	32	21	132	32	20	95	29	17	105	24	10	75	18	5	103	13	2	120
BISMARCK, *N. Dak.*	-7	-19	12	-3	-15	11	4	-8	20	13	-1	37	20	6	56	25	11	74	29	14	59	28	12	44	22	6	38	15	0	21	4	-8	14	-4	-16	12
BOISE, *Idaho*	2	-6	38	7	-3	28	12	0	32	16	3	31	22	7	31	27	11	22	32	14	8	31	14	9	25	9	16	18	4	18	9	-1	35	3	-5	35
BOSTON, *Massachusetts*	2	-6	95	3	-5	91	8	0	100	13	5	93	19	10	84	25	15	79	28	18	73	27	18	92	23	14	82	17	8	87	11	4	110	5	-3	105
BROWNSVILLE, *Texas*	21	10	37	22	11	36	26	15	16	29	19	41	31	22	64	33	24	74	34	24	39	34	24	69	32	23	134	30	19	89	26	15	41	22	11	30
BURLINGTON, *Vermont*	-4	-14	46	-3	-13	44	4	-6	55	12	1	71	20	7	78	24	13	85	27	15	90	26	14	101	21	9	85	14	4	77	7	-1	76	-1	-9	59
CHARLESTON, *S.C.*	14	3	88	16	4	80	20	9	114	24	12	71	28	17	97	31	21	155	32	23	180	32	22	176	29	20	135	25	14	77	21	8	63	16	5	82
CHARLESTON, *W. Va.*	5	-5	87	7	-4	82	14	2	100	19	6	85	24	11	99	28	15	92	30	18	126	29	17	102	26	14	81	20	7	67	14	2	85	8	-2	85
CHEYENNE, *Wyoming*	3	-9	10	5	-8	11	7	-6	26	13	-1	35	18	4	64	24	9	56	28	13	51	27	12	42	22	7	31	16	1	19	8	-5	15	4	-9	10
CHICAGO, *Illinois*	-1	-10	48	1	-7	42	8	-1	72	15	5	97	22	10	83	27	16	103	29	19	103	28	18	89	24	14	79	18	7	70	9	1	73	2	-6	65
CINCINNATI, *Ohio*	3	-6	89	5	-4	67	12	1	97	18	7	94	24	12	101	28	17	99	30	19	102	30	18	86	26	14	75	19	8	62	12	3	81	5	-3	75
CLEVELAND, *Ohio*	1	-7	62	2	-6	58	8	-2	78	15	4	85	21	9	90	26	14	89	28	17	88	27	16	86	23	12	80	17	7	65	10	2	80	3	-4	70
DALLAS, *Texas*	13	1	47	15	4	58	20	8	74	25	13	105	29	18	125	33	22	86	35	24	56	35	24	60	31	20	82	26	14	100	19	8	64	14	3	60
DENVER, *Colorado*	6	-9	14	8	-7	16	11	-3	34	17	1	45	22	6	63	27	11	43	31	15	47	30	14	38	25	9	28	19	2	26	11	-4	23	7	-8	15
DES MOINES, *Iowa*	-2	-12	26	1	-9	30	8	-2	57	17	4	85	23	11	103	28	16	108	30	19	97	29	18	105	24	13	80	18	6	58	9	-1	46	0	-9	31
DETROIT, *Michigan*	-1	-7	42	1	-7	43	7	-2	62	14	4	75	21	10	69	26	15	85	29	18	86	27	18	87	23	14	78	16	7	55	9	2	67	2	-4	67
DULUTH, *Minnesota*	-9	-19	31	-6	-16	21	1	-9	44	9	-2	59	17	4	84	22	9	105	25	13	102	23	12	101	18	7	95	11	2	62	2	-6	48	-6	-15	32
EL PASO, *Texas*	13	-1	11	17	1	11	21	5	8	26	9	7	31	14	9	36	18	17	36	20	38	34	19	39	31	16	34	26	10	20	19	4	11	14	-1	14
FAIRBANKS, *Alaska*	-19	-28	14	-14	-26	11	-5	-19	9	5	-6	7	15	3	15	21	10	35	22	11	45	19	8	46	13	2	28	0	-8	21	-12	-21	18	-17	-26	19
HARTFORD, *Connecticut*	1	-9	83	2	-7	79	8	-2	97	16	3	97	22	9	95	27	14	85	29	17	86	28	16	104	24	11	101	18	5	96	11	0	105	3	-6	99
HELENA, *Montana*	-1	-12	15	3	-9	12	7	-5	18	13	-1	24	19	4	45	24	9	53	29	12	28	28	11	27	21	5	28	15	0	19	6	-6	14	0	-12	16
HONOLULU, *Hawai'i*	27	19	80	27	19	68	28	20	72	28	20	32	29	21	25	30	22	10	31	23	15	32	23	14	31	23	18	31	22	53	29	21	67	27	19	89
HOUSTON, *Texas*	16	4	98	19	6	75	22	10	88	26	15	91	29	18	142	32	21	133	34	22	85	34	22	95	31	20	106	28	14	120	22	10	97	18	6	91
INDIANAPOLIS, *Indiana*	1	-8	69	4	-6	61	11	0	92	17	5	94	23	11	98	28	16	98	30	18	111	29	17	88	25	13	74	19	6	69	11	1	89	4	-5	77
JACKSONVILLE, *Florida*	18	5	83	19	6	89	23	10	100	26	13	77	29	17	92	32	21	140	33	22	164	33	22	186	31	21	199	27	15	99	23	10	52	19	6	65
JUNEAU, *Alaska*	-1	-7	139	1	-5	116	4	-3	113	8	0	105	13	4	109	16	7	88	18	9	120	17	8	160	13	6	217	8	3	255	3	-2	186	0	-5	153
KANSAS CITY, *Missouri*	2	-9	30	5	-6	32	12	0	67	18	7	88	24	12	138	29	17	102	32	20	115	30	19	99	26	14	120	20	8	83	11	1	56	4	-6	43
LAS VEGAS, *Nevada*	14	0	14	17	4	12	20	7	13	25	10	5	31	16	5	38	21	3	41	25	9	40	23	13	35	19	7	28	12	6	20	6	11	14	1	10
LITTLE ROCK, *Arkansas*	9	-1	85	12	1	88	17	6	120	23	11	134	26	15	141	31	20	84	33	22	83	32	21	80	28	18	85	23	11	102	16	6	153	10	1	123
LOS ANGELES, *California*	19	9	70	19	10	61	19	10	51	20	12	20	21	14	3	22	15	1	24	17	1	25	18	2	25	17	5	24	15	7	21	12	38	19	9	43
LOUISVILLE, *Kentucky*	5	-5	85	7	-3	88	14	2	113	20	7	101	24	13	114	29	17	90	31	20	106	30	19	84	27	15	76	21	8	68	14	3	92	7	-2	89
MEMPHIS, *Tennessee*	9	-1	118	12	2	114	17	6	136	23	11	142	27	16	126	32	21	98	34	23	101	33	22	87	29	18	83	24	11	74	17	6	124	11	2	135
MIAMI, *Florida*	24	15	52	25	16	53	26	18	63	28	20	82	30	22	150	31	24	227	32	25	152	32	25	198	31	24	215	29	22	178	27	19	80	25	16	47
MILWAUKEE, *Wisconsin*	-3	-11	32	-1	-8	31	5	-3	54	12	2	87	18	7	73	24	13	87	27	17	85	26	16	94	22	12	95	15	6	66	7	-1	65	0	-7	53
MINNEAPOLIS, *Minnesota*	-6	-16	21	-3	-13	22	4	-5	45	14	2	58	21	9	80	26	14	103	29	17	97	27	16	95	22	10	70	15	4	49	5	-4	37	-4	-12	24
NASHVILLE, *Tennessee*	8	-3	108	10	-1	100	16	4	127	22	9	104	26	14	118	30	18	99	32	21	99	31	20	85	28	16	89	23	9	67	16	4	101	10	-1	112
NEW ORLEANS, *Louisiana*	16	5	136	18	7	147	22	11	124	26	15	119	29	18	135	32	22	147	33	23	167	32	23	157	30	21	138	26	15	76	22	11	101	18	7	132
NEW YORK, *New York*	3	-4	80	4	-3	76	9	1	99	15	7	94	21	12	93	26	17	80	29	21	101	28	20	107	24	16	85	18	10	81	12	5	96	6	-1	90
OKLAHOMA CITY, *Okla.*	8	-4	28	11	-1	36	17	4	61	22	9	76	26	14	145	31	19	107	34	21	74	34	21	65	29	17	97	23	10	80	16	4	43	10	-2	37
OMAHA, *Nebraska*	-1	-12	18	2	-9	21	9	-2	61	17	5	73	23	11	118	28	16	105	30	19	96	29	18	95	24	13	90	18	6	60	9	-1	35	1	-9	23
PENSACOLA, *Florida*	15	5	109	17	7	126	21	11	150	25	15	112	28	19	105	32	22	168	32	23	187	32	23	176	30	21	166	26	15	102	21	11	91	17	7	105
PHILADELPHIA, *Pa.*	3	-5	82	5	-4	70	11	1	95	17	6	88	23	12	94	28	17	87	30	20	108	29	19	97	25	15	86	19	8	67	13	3	85	6	-2	86
PHOENIX, *Arizona*	19	3	21	22	5	21	25	7	30	29	9	7	33	13	5	38	18	3	39	23	21	38	22	30	36	18	23	30	12	14	23	7	18	19	3	28
PITTSBURGH, *Pa.*	1	-8	66	3	-7	60	9	-1	85	16	4	80	21	9	92	26	14	91	28	16	98	27	16	83	24	12	74	17	6	61	10	1	69	4	-4	71
PORTLAND, *Oregon*	7	1	133	11	2	105	13	4	92	16	5	61	20	8	53	23	12	38	27	14	15	27	14	23	24	11	41	18	7	76	11	4	135	8	2	149
PROVIDENCE, *R.I.*	3	-7	101	4	-6	91	8	-2	111	14	3	102	20	9	89	25	14	77	28	17	77	27	17	102	24	12	88	18	6	93	12	2	117	5	-4	110
RALEIGH, *N.C.*	9	-2	89	11	0	88	17	4	94	22	8	70	26	13	96	29	18	91	31	20	111	30	20	110	27	16	79	22	9	77	17	4	76	12	0	79
RAPID CITY, *S. Dak.*	2	-12	10	4	-10	12	8	-6	26	14	0	52	20	6	84	25	12	89	30	15	63	29	13	43	23	7	32	17	1	26	8	-5	12	3	-11	10
RENO, *Nevada*	7	-6	28	11	-4	24	14	-2	20	18	1	11	23	5	17	28	8	11	33	11	7	32	10	6	26	5	9	20	1	10	12	-3	19	8	-7	27
ST. LOUIS, *Missouri*	3	-6	50	6	-4	54	13	2	84	19	8	97	25	13	100	30	19	103	32	21	92	31	20	76	27	16	73	20	9	70	13	3	78	5	-3	64
SALT LAKE CITY, *Utah*	2	-7	32	6	-4	30	11	0	45	16	3	52	22	8	46	28	13	23	33	18	18	32	17	21	26	11	27	19	5	34	10	-1	34	3	-6	34
SAN DIEGO, *California*	19	9	56	19	10	41	19	12	50	20	13	20	21	15	5	22	17	2	25	19	1	25	20	2	25	19	5	24	16	9	21	12	30	19	9	35
SAN FRANCISCO, *Calif.*	14	8	112	16	9	77	16	9	78	17	10	34	17	10	10	18	11	4	18	12	1	19	13	2	20	13	7	20	13	28	17	11	73	14	8	91

RED FIGURES: Average daily high temperature (°C) **BLUE FIGURES:** Average daily low temperature (°C) **BLACK FIGURES:** Average monthly rainfall (mm)
1 millimeter = 0.039 inches

	JAN.			FEB.			MARCH			APRIL			MAY			JUNE			JULY			AUG.			SEPT.			OCT.			NOV.			DEC.		
UNITED STATES																																				
SANTA FE, *New Mexico*	6	-10	11	9	-7	9	13	-5	12	18	-1	13	24	4	23	29	9	31	31	12	52	29	11	64	25	7	38	20	1	32	13	-5	14	7	-9	12
SEATTLE, *Washington*	7	2	141	10	3	107	12	4	94	14	5	64	18	8	42	21	11	38	24	13	20	24	13	27	21	11	47	15	8	89	10	5	149	7	2	149
SPOKANE, *Washington*	1	-6	52	5	-3	39	9	-1	37	14	2	28	19	6	35	24	10	33	28	12	15	28	12	16	22	8	20	15	2	31	5	-2	51	1	-6	57
TAMPA, *Florida*	21	10	54	22	11	73	25	14	90	28	16	44	31	20	76	32	23	143	32	24	189	32	24	196	32	23	160	29	18	60	25	14	46	22	11	54
VICKSBURG, *Mississippi*	14	2	155	16	3	131	21	8	160	25	12	147	29	16	130	32	20	88	33	22	106	33	21	80	30	18	85	26	12	106	20	8	126	16	4	168
WASHINGTON, *D.C.*	6	-3	71	8	-2	66	14	3	90	19	8	72	25	14	94	29	19	80	31	22	97	31	21	104	27	17	84	21	10	78	15	5	76	8	0	79
WICHITA, *Kansas*	4	-7	19	8	-5	23	14	1	57	20	7	57	25	12	99	30	18	105	34	21	82	33	20	78	27	15	85	21	8	62	13	1	37	6	-5	29
MIDDLE AMERICA																																				
ACAPULCO, *Mexico*	29	21	8	31	21	1	31	21	0	31	22	1	32	23	36	32	24	325	32	24	231	32	24	236	31	24	353	31	23	170	31	22	30	31	21	10
BALBOA, *Panama*	31	22	34	32	22	16	32	22	14	32	23	73	31	23	198	30	23	203	31	23	176	31	23	200	30	23	197	29	23	271	29	23	260	31	23	133
CHARLOTTE AMALIE, *V.I.*	28	23	50	27	22	41	28	23	49	28	23	63	29	24	105	30	25	67	31	26	71	31	26	112	31	26	132	31	25	139	29	24	131	28	23	69
GUATEMALA, *Guatemala*	23	12	4	25	12	5	27	14	10	28	14	32	29	16	110	27	16	257	26	16	197	26	16	193	26	16	235	24	16	98	23	14	33	22	13	13
GUAYMAS, *Mexico*	23	13	17	24	14	6	26	16	5	29	18	1	31	21	2	34	24	1	34	27	46	35	27	71	35	26	28	32	22	17	28	18	8	23	13	18
HAVANA, *Cuba*	26	18	71	26	18	46	27	19	46	29	21	58	30	22	119	31	23	165	32	24	124	32	24	135	31	24	150	29	23	173	27	21	79	26	19	58
KINGSTON, *Jamaica*	30	19	29	30	19	24	30	20	23	31	21	39	31	22	104	32	23	96	32	23	46	32	23	107	32	23	127	31	23	181	31	22	95	31	21	41
MANAGUA, *Nicaragua*	33	21	2	33	21	3	35	22	4	36	23	3	35	24	136	32	23	237	32	23	132	32	23	121	33	23	213	32	23	315	32	22	42	32	22	10
MÉRIDA, *Mexico*	28	17	30	29	17	23	32	19	18	33	21	20	34	22	81	33	23	142	33	23	132	33	23	142	32	23	173	31	22	97	29	19	33	28	18	33
MEXICO, *Mexico*	19	6	8	21	6	5	24	8	11	25	11	19	26	12	49	24	13	106	23	12	129	23	12	121	23	12	110	21	10	44	20	8	15	19	6	7
MONTERREY, *Mexico*	20	9	18	22	11	23	24	14	16	29	17	29	31	20	40	33	22	68	32	22	62	33	22	76	30	21	151	27	18	78	22	13	26	18	10	20
NASSAU, *Bahamas*	25	18	48	25	18	43	26	19	41	27	21	65	29	22	132	31	23	178	31	24	153	32	24	170	31	24	180	29	23	171	27	21	71	26	19	43
PORT-AU-PRINCE, *Haiti*	31	20	32	31	20	50	32	21	79	32	22	156	32	22	218	33	23	96	34	23	73	34	23	139	33	23	166	32	22	164	31	22	84	31	21	35
PORT-OF-SPAIN, *Trinidad*	29	19	69	30	19	41	31	19	46	31	21	53	32	21	94	31	22	193	31	21	218	31	22	246	31	22	193	31	22	170	31	21	183	30	21	124
SAN JOSÉ, *Costa Rica*	24	14	11	24	14	5	26	15	14	26	17	46	27	17	224	26	17	276	25	17	215	26	16	243	26	16	326	25	16	323	25	16	148	24	14	42
SAN JUAN, *Puerto Rico*	27	21	75	27	21	56	27	21	59	28	22	95	29	23	156	29	24	112	29	24	115	29	24	133	30	24	136	29	24	140	29	23	148	27	22	118
SAN SALVADOR, *El Salv.*	32	16	7	33	16	7	34	17	13	34	18	53	33	19	179	31	19	315	32	18	312	32	19	307	31	19	317	31	18	230	31	17	40	32	16	12
SANTO DOMINGO, *Dom. Rep.*	29	19	57	29	19	43	29	19	49	29	21	77	30	22	179	31	22	154	31	22	155	31	23	162	31	22	173	31	22	164	30	21	111	29	19	63
TEGUCIGALPA, *Honduras*	25	13	9	27	14	4	29	14	8	30	17	32	29	18	151	28	18	159	28	17	82	28	17	87	28	17	185	27	17	135	26	16	38	25	15	12
SOUTH AMERICA																																				
ANTOFAGASTA, *Chile*	24	17	0	24	17	0	23	16	0	21	14	0	19	13	0	18	11	1	17	11	1	17	11	1	18	12	0	19	13	0	21	14	0	22	16	0
ASUNCIÓN, *Paraguay*	35	22	150	34	22	133	33	21	142	29	18	145	25	14	120	22	12	73	23	12	51	26	14	48	28	16	83	30	17	136	32	18	144	34	21	142
BELÉM, *Brazil*	31	22	351	30	22	412	31	23	441	31	23	370	31	23	282	31	22	164	31	22	154	31	22	122	32	22	129	32	22	105	32	22	101	32	22	202
BOGOTÁ, *Colombia*	19	9	48	20	9	52	19	10	81	19	11	119	19	11	103	18	11	61	18	10	47	18	10	48	19	9	58	19	10	142	19	10	115	19	9	67
BRASÍLIA, *Brazil*	27	18	262	27	18	213	28	18	202	28	17	103	26	13	20	25	11	4	26	11	4	28	13	6	31	16	35	28	18	140	28	19	238	26	18	329
BUENOS AIRES, *Arg.*	29	17	93	28	17	81	26	16	117	22	12	90	18	8	77	14	5	64	14	6	59	16	6	65	18	8	78	21	10	97	24	13	89	28	16	96
CARACAS, *Venezuela*	24	13	41	25	13	27	26	14	22	27	16	20	27	17	36	26	17	52	26	16	53	26	16	53	27	16	48	26	16	47	25	16	50	26	14	58
COM. RIVADAVIA, *Arg.*	26	13	16	25	13	11	22	11	21	18	8	21	13	6	34	11	3	21	11	3	25	12	3	22	14	5	13	19	9	13	22	10	13	24	12	15
CÓRDOBA, *Argentina*	31	16	110	30	16	102	28	14	96	24	11	45	21	7	25	18	3	10	18	3	10	21	4	13	23	7	27	25	11	69	28	13	97	30	16	118
GUAYAQUIL, *Ecuador*	31	21	224	31	22	278	31	22	287	32	22	180	31	20	53	31	20	17	29	19	2	30	18	0	31	19	2	30	20	3	31	20	3	31	21	30
LA PAZ, *Bolivia*	17	6	130	17	6	105	18	6	72	18	4	47	18	3	13	17	1	6	17	1	9	17	2	14	18	3	29	19	4	40	19	6	50	18	6	93
LIMA, *Peru*	28	19	1	28	19	1	28	19	1	27	17	0	23	16	1	20	14	2	19	14	4	19	13	3	20	14	3	22	14	2	23	16	1	26	17	1
MANAUS, *Brazil*	31	24	264	31	24	262	31	24	298	31	24	283	31	24	204	31	24	103	32	24	67	33	24	46	33	24	63	33	24	111	33	24	161	32	24	220
MARACAIBO, *Venezuela*	32	23	5	32	23	5	33	23	6	33	24	39	33	25	65	34	25	55	34	24	25	34	25	53	34	25	76	33	24	119	33	24	55	33	24	22
MONTEVIDEO, *Uruguay*	28	17	95	28	16	100	26	15	111	22	12	83	18	9	76	15	6	74	14	6	86	15	6	84	17	8	90	20	9	98	23	12	78	26	15	84
PARAMARIBO, *Suriname*	29	22	209	29	22	149	29	22	168	30	23	219	30	23	307	30	23	302	31	23	227	32	23	163	33	23	80	33	23	82	32	23	117	30	22	204
PUNTA ARENAS, *Chile*	14	7	35	14	7	28	12	5	39	10	4	41	7	2	42	5	1	32	4	-1	34	6	1	33	8	2	28	11	3	24	12	4	29	14	6	32
QUITO, *Ecuador*	22	8	113	22	8	128	22	8	154	21	8	176	21	8	124	22	7	48	22	7	20	23	7	24	23	7	78	22	8	127	22	7	109	22	8	103
RECIFE, *Brazil*	30	25	62	30	25	102	30	24	197	29	24	252	28	23	301	28	23	302	27	22	254	27	22	156	28	23	78	29	24	36	29	24	29	29	25	40
RIO DE JANEIRO, *Brazil*	29	23	135	29	23	124	28	22	134	27	21	109	25	19	78	24	18	52	24	17	45	24	18	46	24	18	62	25	19	82	26	20	100	28	22	137
SANTIAGO, *Chile*	29	12	3	29	11	3	27	9	5	23	7	13	18	5	64	14	3	84	15	3	76	17	4	56	19	6	30	22	7	15	26	9	8	28	11	5
SÃO PAULO, *Brazil*	27	17	225	28	18	208	27	17	160	26	14	71	23	12	67	22	11	54	22	9	35	23	11	48	23	12	77	24	14	117	26	15	139	27	16	185
VALPARAÍSO, *Chile*	22	13	0	22	13	0	21	12	0	19	11	22	17	10	38	16	9	100	16	8	111	16	8	42	17	9	27	18	10	15	21	11	15	22	12	1
EUROPE																																				
AJACCIO, *Corsica*	13	3	76	14	4	58	16	5	66	18	7	56	21	10	41	25	14	23	27	16	71	28	16	18	26	15	43	22	11	97	18	7	112	15	4	79
AMSTERDAM, *Neth.*	4	1	79	5	1	44	8	3	89	11	6	39	16	10	50	18	13	60	21	15	73	20	15	60	18	13	80	13	9	104	8	5	76	5	2	72
ATHENS, *Greece*	13	6	48	14	7	41	16	8	41	20	11	23	25	16	18	30	20	7	33	23	5	33	23	8	29	19	10	24	15	53	19	12	55	15	8	62
BARCELONA, *Spain*	13	6	38	14	7	38	16	9	47	18	11	47	21	14	44	25	18	38	28	21	28	28	21	44	25	19	76	21	15	96	16	11	51	13	8	44
BELFAST, *N. Ireland*	6	2	83	7	2	55	9	3	59	12	4	51	15	6	56	18	9	65	18	11	79	18	11	78	16	9	82	13	7	85	9	4	75	7	3	84
BELGRADE, *Serb. & Mont.*	3	-3	42	5	-2	39	11	2	43	18	7	57	23	12	73	26	15	84	28	17	63	28	17	53	24	13	47	18	8	50	11	4	55	5	0	52
BERLIN, *Germany*	2	-3	43	3	-3	38	8	0	38	13	4	41	19	8	49	22	12	64	24	14	71	23	13	62	20	10	44	13	6	44	7	2	46	3	-1	48
BIARRITZ, *France*	11	4	106	12	4	93	15	6	92	16	8	95	18	11	97	22	14	93	23	16	64	24	16	74	22	15	102	19	11	129	15	7	135	12	5	134
BORDEAUX, *France*	9	2	76	11	2	65	15	4	66	17	6	65	20	9	71	24	12	65	25	14	52	26	14	59	23	12	70	18	8	87	13	5	88	9	3	86
BRINDISI, *Italy*	12	6	57	13	7	61	15	8	67	18	11	35	22	14	26	26	18	20	29	21	9	29	21	25	26	18	47	22	15	71	18	11	72	14	8	65
BRUSSELS, *Belgium*	4	-1	82	7	0	51	10	2	81	14	5	53	18	8	74	22	11	74	23	12	58	22	12	42	21	11	69	15	7	85	9	3	61	6	0	68
BUCHAREST, *Romania*	1	-7	44	4	-5	37	10	-1	35	18	5	46	23	10	65	27	14	86	30	16	56	30	15	56	25	11	35	18	6	28	10	2	45	4	-3	42
BUDAPEST, *Hungary*	1	-4	41	4	-2	36	10	2	41	17	7	49	22	11	69	26	15	71	28	16	53	27	16	53	23	12	45	16	7	52	8	3	58	4	-1	49
CAGLIARI, *Sardinia*	14	7	53	15	7	52	17	9	45	19	11	35	23	14	27	27	18	10	30	21	3	30	21	10	27	19	29	23	15	57	19	11	56	16	9	55
CANDIA, *Crete*	16	9	94	16	9	76	17	10	41	20	12	23	23	15	18	27	19	3	29	21	1	29	22	3	27	19	18	24	17	43	21	14	69	18	11	102
COPENHAGEN, *Denmark*	2	-2	42	2	-3	25	5	-1	35	10	3	40	16	8	42	19	11	52	22	14	67	21	14	75	18	11	51	12	7	53	7	3	52	4	1	51
DUBLIN, *Ireland*	7	2	64	8	2	51	10	3	52	12	5	49	14	7	56	18	9	55	19	11	65	19	11	77	17	10	62	14	7	73	10	4	69	8	3	69
DURAZZO, *Albania*	11	6	76	12	6	84	13	8	99	17	13	56	22	17	41	25	21	48	28	23	13	28	22	48	24	18	43	20	14	180	14	11	216	12	8	185
EDINBURGH, *Scotland*	6	1	55	6	1	41	8	2	47	11	4	39	14	6	50	17	9	50	18	11	64	18	11	69	16	9	63	12	7	62	9	4	63	7	2	61
FLORENCE, *Italy*	9	2	64	11	3	62	14	5	69	19	8	71	23	12	73	27	15	56	30	18	34	30	17	47	26	15	83	20	11	99	14	7	103	11	4	79
GENEVA, *Switzerland*	4	-2	55	6	-1	53	10	2	60	15	5	63	19	9	76	23	13	81	25	15	72	24	14	90	21	12	90	14	7	91	8	3	81	4	0	66
HAMBURG, *Germany*	2	-2	61	3	-2	40	7	-1	52	13	3	47	18	7	55	21	11	74	22	13	81	22	12	79	19	10	68	13	6	62	7	3	65	4	0	71
HELSINKI, *Finland*	-3	-9	46	-4	-9	37	0	-7	35	6	-1	37	14	4	42	19	9	46	22	13	62	20	12	75	15	8	67	8	3	69	3	-1	66	-1	-5	55
LISBON, *Portugal*	14	8	95	15	8	87	17	10	85	20	12	60	21	13	44	25	15	18	27	17	4	28	17	5	26	17	33	22	14	75	17	11	100	15	9	97
LIVERPOOL, *England*	7	2	69	7	2	48	9	3	38	11	5	41	14	8	56	17	11	51	19	13	71	18	13	79	16	11	66	13	8	76	9	5	76	7	3	64
LONDON, *England*	7	2	62	7	2	36	11	8	50	13	4	43	17	7	45	21	11	46	23	13	46	22	12	44	19	11	43	14	7	73	9	4	45	7	2	59
LUXEMBOURG, *Lux.*	3	-1	66	4	-1	54	10	1	55	14	4	53	18	8	66	21	11	65	23	13	70	22	12	69	19	10	62	13	6	70	7	3	71	4	0	74
MADRID, *Spain*	9	2	45	11	2	43	15	5	37	18	7	45	21	10	40	27	15	25	31	17	9	30	17	10	25	14	29	19	10	46	13	5	64	9	2	47
MARSEILLE, *France*	10	2	49	12	2	40	15	5	45	18	8	46	22	11	46	26	15	26	29	17	15	28	17	24	25	15	63	20	10	94	15	6	76	11	3	59

APPENDIX • Temperature and Rainfall 279

World Temperature and Rainfall

Average daily high and low temperatures and monthly rainfall for selected world locations:

	JAN.			FEB.			MARCH			APRIL			MAY			JUNE			JULY			AUG.			SEPT.			OCT.			NOV.			DEC.		
EUROPE																																				
MILAN, *Italy*	5	0	61	8	2	58	13	6	72	18	10	85	23	14	98	27	17	81	29	20	68	28	19	81	24	16	82	17	11	116	10	6	106	6	2	75
MUNICH, *Germany*	1	-5	49	3	-5	43	9	-1	52	14	3	70	18	7	101	21	11	123	23	13	127	23	12	112	20	9	83	13	4	62	7	0	54	2	-4	51
NANTES, *France*	8	2	79	9	2	62	13	4	62	15	6	54	19	9	61	22	12	55	24	14	50	24	13	54	21	12	70	16	8	89	11	5	91	8	3	86
NAPLES, *Italy*	12	4	94	13	5	81	15	6	76	18	9	66	22	12	46	26	16	46	29	18	15	29	18	18	26	16	71	22	12	130	17	9	114	14	6	137
NICE, *France*	13	4	77	13	5	73	15	7	73	17	9	64	20	13	49	24	16	37	27	18	19	27	18	32	25	16	65	21	12	111	17	8	117	13	5	88
OSLO, *Norway*	-2	-7	41	-1	-7	31	4	-4	34	10	1	36	16	6	45	20	10	59	22	13	75	21	12	86	16	8	72	9	3	71	3	-1	57	0	-4	49
PALERMO, *Italy*	16	8	44	16	8	35	17	9	30	20	11	29	24	14	14	27	18	9	30	21	2	30	21	8	28	19	28	25	16	59	21	12	66	18	10	68
PALMA DE MALLORCA, *Spain*	14	6	39	15	6	35	17	8	37	19	10	35	22	13	34	26	17	20	29	20	8	29	20	18	27	18	52	23	14	77	18	10	54	15	8	54
PARIS, *France*	6	1	46	7	1	39	12	4	41	16	6	44	20	10	56	23	13	57	25	15	57	24	14	55	21	12	53	16	8	57	10	5	54	7	2	49
PRAGUE, *Czech. Rep.*	1	-4	21	3	-2	19	7	1	26	13	4	36	18	9	59	22	13	68	23	14	67	23	14	62	18	11	41	12	7	30	5	2	27	1	-2	23
RIGA, *Latvia*	-4	-10	32	-3	-10	24	2	-7	26	10	1	35	16	6	42	21	9	58	22	11	72	21	11	68	17	8	66	11	4	54	4	-1	52	-2	-7	39
ROME, *Italy*	11	5	80	13	5	71	15	7	69	19	10	67	23	13	52	28	17	34	30	20	16	30	19	24	26	17	69	22	13	113	16	9	111	13	6	97
SEVILLE, *Spain*	15	6	56	17	7	74	20	9	84	24	11	58	27	13	33	32	17	23	36	20	3	36	20	3	32	18	28	26	14	66	20	10	94	16	7	71
SOFIA, *Bulgaria*	2	-4	34	4	-3	34	10	1	38	16	5	54	21	10	69	24	14	78	27	16	56	26	15	43	22	11	40	17	8	35	9	3	52	4	-2	44
SPLIT, *Croatia*	10	5	80	11	5	65	14	7	65	18	11	62	23	16	62	27	19	48	30	22	28	30	22	43	26	19	66	20	14	87	15	10	111	12	7	113
STOCKHOLM, *Sweden*	-1	-5	31	-1	-5	25	3	-4	26	8	1	29	14	6	34	19	11	44	22	14	64	20	13	66	15	9	49	9	5	51	5	1	44	2	-2	39
VALENCIA, *Spain*	15	6	23	16	6	38	18	8	23	20	10	30	23	13	28	26	17	33	29	20	10	29	20	13	27	18	56	23	13	41	19	10	64	16	7	33
VALETTA, *Malta*	14	10	84	15	10	58	16	11	38	18	13	20	22	16	10	26	19	3	29	22	1	29	23	5	27	22	33	24	19	69	20	16	91	16	12	99
VENICE, *Italy*	6	1	51	8	2	53	12	5	61	17	10	71	21	14	81	25	17	84	27	19	66	27	18	66	24	16	66	19	11	94	12	7	89	8	3	66
VIENNA, *Austria*	1	-4	38	3	-3	36	8	1	46	15	6	51	19	10	71	23	14	69	25	15	76	24	15	69	20	11	51	14	7	25	7	3	48	3	-1	46
WARSAW, *Poland*	0	-6	28	0	-6	26	6	-2	31	12	3	37	20	9	50	23	12	66	24	15	77	23	14	72	19	10	47	13	5	41	6	1	38	2	-3	35
ZÜRICH, *Switzerland*	2	-3	61	5	-2	61	10	1	68	15	4	85	19	8	101	23	12	127	25	14	128	24	13	124	20	11	98	14	6	83	7	2	71	3	-2	72
ASIA																																				
ADEN, *Yemen*	27	23	8	27	23	7	29	24	8	31	26	4	34	28	3	35	29	1	34	28	2	33	27	3	34	28	4	32	26	2	29	24	2	27	23	4
ALMATY, *Kazakhstan*	-5	-14	33	-3	13	23	4	-6	56	13	3	102	20	10	94	24	14	66	27	16	36	27	14	30	22	8	25	13	2	51	4	-5	48	-2	-9	33
ANKARA, *Turkey*	4	-4	49	6	-3	52	11	-1	45	17	4	44	23	9	56	26	12	37	30	15	13	31	15	8	26	11	28	21	7	21	14	3	28	6	-2	63
ARKHANGEL'SK, *Russia*	-12	-20	30	-10	-18	28	-4	-13	28	5	-4	18	12	2	33	17	6	48	20	10	66	19	10	69	12	5	56	4	-1	48	-2	-7	41	-8	-15	33
BAGHDAD, *Iraq*	16	4	27	18	6	28	22	9	27	29	14	19	36	19	7	41	23	0	43	24	0	43	24	0	40	21	0	33	16	3	25	11	20	18	6	26
BALIKPAPAN, *Indonesia*	29	23	243	30	23	221	30	23	249	29	23	226	29	23	258	29	23	252	28	23	259	29	23	257	29	23	201	29	23	186	29	23	176	29	23	245
BANGKOK, *Thailand*	32	20	11	33	22	28	34	24	31	35	25	72	34	25	189	33	24	152	32	24	158	32	24	187	32	24	320	31	24	231	31	22	57	31	20	9
BEIJING, *China*	2	-9	4	5	-7	5	12	-1	8	20	7	18	27	13	33	31	18	78	32	22	224	31	21	170	27	14	58	21	7	18	10	-1	9	3	-7	3
BEIRUT, *Lebanon*	17	11	187	17	11	151	19	12	96	22	14	51	26	18	19	28	21	2	31	23	0	32	23	0	30	23	6	27	21	48	23	16	119	18	13	176
BRUNEI	30	24	371	30	24	193	31	24	198	32	24	249	32	24	277	31	24	241	31	25	229	31	24	185	31	24	300	31	24	368	31	24	386	30	24	330
CHENNAI (MADRAS), *India*	29	19	29	31	20	9	33	22	9	35	26	17	38	28	44	38	27	52	36	26	99	35	26	124	34	25	125	32	24	285	29	22	345	29	21	138
CHONGQING, *China*	9	5	18	13	7	21	18	11	38	23	16	94	27	19	148	29	22	174	34	24	151	35	25	128	28	22	144	22	16	103	16	12	49	13	8	23
COLOMBO, *Sri Lanka*	30	22	84	31	22	64	31	23	114	31	24	255	31	26	335	29	25	190	29	25	129	29	25	96	29	25	158	29	24	353	29	23	308	29	22	152
DAMASCUS, *Syria*	12	2	39	14	4	32	18	6	23	24	9	13	29	13	5	33	16	1	36	18	0	37	18	0	33	16	0	27	12	9	19	8	26	13	4	42
DAVAO, *Philippines*	31	22	117	32	22	110	32	22	109	33	22	149	32	23	223	31	23	205	31	22	171	31	22	161	32	22	177	32	22	184	32	22	139	31	22	139
DHAKA, *Bangladesh*	26	13	8	28	15	21	32	20	58	33	23	116	33	24	267	32	26	358	31	26	399	31	26	317	32	26	256	31	24	164	29	19	30	26	14	6
HANOI, *Vietnam*	20	13	20	21	14	30	23	17	64	28	21	91	32	23	104	33	26	284	33	26	302	32	26	386	31	24	254	29	22	89	26	18	66	22	15	71
HO CHI MINH CITY, *Viet.*	32	21	14	33	22	4	34	23	9	35	24	51	33	24	213	32	24	309	31	24	295	31	24	271	31	23	342	31	23	261	31	23	119	31	22	47
HONG KONG, *China*	18	13	27	17	13	44	19	16	75	24	19	140	28	23	298	29	26	399	31	26	371	31	26	377	29	25	297	27	23	119	23	18	38	20	15	25
IRKUTSK, *Russia*	-16	-26	13	-12	-25	10	-4	-17	8	6	-7	15	13	1	33	20	7	56	21	10	79	20	9	71	14	2	43	5	-6	18	-7	-17	15	-16	-24	15
ISTANBUL, *Turkey*	8	3	91	9	2	69	11	3	62	16	7	42	21	12	30	25	16	28	28	18	24	28	19	31	24	16	48	20	13	66	15	9	92	11	5	114
JAKARTA, *Indonesia*	29	23	342	29	23	302	30	23	210	31	24	135	31	24	108	31	23	90	31	23	59	31	23	48	31	23	69	31	23	106	30	23	139	29	23	208
JEDDAH, *Saudi Arabia*	29	19	5	29	18	1	29	19	1	33	21	1	35	23	1	36	24	0	37	23	1	37	27	1	36	25	1	35	23	1	33	22	25	30	19	30
JERUSALEM, *Israel*	13	5	140	13	6	111	18	8	116	23	10	17	27	14	6	29	16	0	31	17	0	31	18	0	29	17	0	27	15	11	21	12	68	15	7	129
KABUL, *Afghanistan*	2	-8	33	4	-6	54	12	1	70	19	6	66	26	11	21	31	13	1	33	16	5	33	15	1	29	11	2	23	6	4	17	1	11	8	-3	21
KARACHI, *Pakistan*	25	13	7	26	14	10	29	19	10	32	23	3	34	26	0	34	28	10	33	27	90	31	26	58	31	25	27	33	22	3	31	18	3	27	14	5
KATHMANDU, *Nepal*	18	2	17	19	4	15	25	7	30	28	12	37	30	16	102	29	19	201	29	20	375	28	20	325	28	19	189	27	13	56	23	7	2	19	3	10
KOLKATA (CALCUTTA), *India*	27	13	12	29	15	25	34	21	32	36	24	53	36	25	129	33	26	291	32	26	329	32	26	338	32	26	266	32	23	131	29	18	21	26	13	7
KUNMING, *China*	16	3	11	18	4	14	21	7	17	24	11	20	26	14	90	25	17	175	25	17	205	25	17	203	24	15	126	21	12	78	18	7	40	17	3	13
LAHORE, *Pakistan*	21	4	25	22	7	24	28	12	27	35	17	15	40	22	17	41	26	39	38	27	155	36	26	135	36	23	63	35	15	10	28	8	3	23	4	14
LHASA, *China*	7	-10	0	9	-7	3	12	-2	4	16	1	6	19	5	24	24	9	72	23	9	132	22	9	128	21	7	58	17	1	9	13	-5	1	9	-9	1
MANAMA, *Bahrain*	30	14	14	21	15	16	24	17	11	29	21	8	33	26	1	36	28	0	37	29	0	38	29	0	36	27	0	32	24	0	28	21	7	22	16	17
MANDALAY, *Myanmar*	28	13	2	31	15	13	36	19	7	38	25	35	37	26	142	34	26	124	34	26	83	33	25	113	33	24	155	32	23	125	29	19	45	27	14	10
MANILA, *Philippines*	30	21	21	31	21	10	33	22	15	34	23	30	34	24	123	33	24	262	31	24	423	31	24	421	31	24	353	31	23	197	31	22	135	30	21	65
MOSCOW, *Russia*	-9	-16	38	-6	-14	36	0	-8	28	10	1	46	19	8	56	21	11	74	23	13	76	22	12	74	16	7	48	9	3	69	2	-3	43	-5	-10	41
MUMBAI (BOMBAY), *India*	28	19	3	28	19	1	30	22	1	32	24	2	33	27	14	32	26	518	29	25	647	29	24	384	29	24	276	32	24	55	32	23	15	31	21	2
MUSCAT, *Oman*	25	19	28	25	19	18	28	22	10	32	26	10	37	30	1	38	31	3	36	31	1	33	29	1	34	28	0	34	27	3	30	23	10	26	20	18
NAGASAKI, *Japan*	9	2	75	10	2	87	14	5	124	19	10	190	23	14	191	26	18	326	29	23	284	31	23	187	27	20	236	22	14	108	17	9	89	12	4	80
NEW DELHI, *India*	21	7	23	24	9	20	31	14	15	36	20	10	41	26	15	39	28	68	36	27	200	34	26	200	34	24	123	34	18	19	29	11	3	23	8	10
NICOSIA, *Cyprus*	15	5	70	16	5	50	19	7	35	24	10	21	29	14	26	34	18	9	37	21	1	37	21	2	33	18	6	28	14	23	22	10	41	17	7	74
ODESA, *Ukraine*	0	-6	25	2	-4	18	5	-1	18	12	6	28	19	12	28	23	16	48	26	18	41	26	18	36	21	14	28	16	9	36	10	4	28	4	-2	28
PHNOM PENH, *Cambodia*	31	21	7	32	22	9	34	23	32	34	24	73	33	24	149	33	24	149	32	24	151	32	24	157	31	24	231	31	24	259	30	23	129	30	22	38
PONTIANAK, *Indonesia*	31	23	275	32	23	213	32	23	242	33	23	280	33	23	279	32	23	228	32	23	178	32	23	206	32	23	245	32	23	356	31	23	385	31	23	321
RIYADH, *Saudi Arabia*	21	8	14	23	9	10	28	13	30	32	18	30	38	22	13	42	25	0	42	26	0	42	24	0	39	22	0	34	16	1	29	13	5	21	9	11
ST. PETERSBURG, *Russia*	-7	-13	25	-5	-12	23	0	-8	23	8	4	25	15	6	41	20	11	51	21	13	64	20	13	71	15	9	53	9	4	46	2	-2	36	-3	-8	30
SANDAKAN, *Malaysia*	29	23	454	29	23	271	30	23	200	31	23	118	32	23	153	32	23	196	32	23	185	32	23	205	32	23	240	31	23	263	31	23	356	30	23	470
SAPPORO, *Japan*	-2	-12	100	-1	-11	79	2	-7	70	11	0	61	16	4	59	21	10	65	24	14	86	26	16	117	22	11	136	16	4	114	8	-2	106	1	-8	102
SEOUL, *South Korea*	0	-9	21	3	-7	28	8	-2	49	17	5	105	22	11	88	27	16	151	29	21	384	31	22	263	26	15	160	19	7	49	11	0	43	3	-7	24
SHANGHAI, *China*	8	1	47	8	1	61	13	4	85	19	10	95	25	15	104	28	19	174	32	23	145	32	23	137	28	19	138	23	14	69	17	7	52	12	2	37
SINGAPORE, *Singapore*	30	23	239	31	23	165	31	24	174	31	24	166	32	24	171	31	24	163	31	24	150	31	24	171	31	24	164	31	23	191	31	23	250	31	23	269
TAIPEI, *China*	19	12	95	18	12	141	21	14	162	25	17	167	28	21	209	32	23	280	33	24	248	33	24	277	31	23	201	27	19	112	24	17	76	21	14	76
T'BILISI, *Georgia*	6	-2	16	7	-1	21	12	2	30	18	7	52	23	12	83	27	16	73	31	19	49	31	19	40	26	15	44	20	9	39	13	4	32	8	0	21
TEHRAN, *Iran*	7	-3	42	10	0	37	15	4	39	22	9	33	28	14	15	34	19	3	37	22	2	36	22	2	32	18	2	24	12	9	17	6	24	11	1	32
TEL AVIV-YAFO, *Israel*	17	9	165	18	9	64	19	10	58	23	12	13	27	16	3	29	18	0	31	21	0	31	21	0	30	20	1	29	18	14	25	15	85	19	11	144
TOKYO, *Japan*	8	-2	50	9	-1	72	12	2	106	17	8	129	22	12	144	24	17	176	28	21	136	30	22	149	26	19	216	21	13	194	16	6	96	11	1	54
ULAANBAATAR, *Mongolia*	-19	-32	1	-13	-29	1	-4	-22	3	7	-8	5	13	-2	8	21	7	25	22	11	74	21	8	48	14	2	20	6	-8	5	-6	-20	5	-16	-28	3
VIENTIANE, *Laos*	28	14	7	30	17	18	33	19	41	34	23	88	32	23	212	32	24	216	31	24	209	31	24	254	31	24	244	31	21	81	29	18	16	28	16	5
VLADIVOSTOK, *Russia*	-11	-18	8	-6	-14	10	1	-7	18	8	1	30	13	6	53	17	11	74	22	16	84	24	18	119	20	13	109	13	5	48	2	-4	30	-7	-13	15

50
CELSIUS
40
30
20
10
0
-10
-20
-30
-40
CELSIUS
-50

RED FIGURES: Average daily high temperature (°C) **BLUE FIGURES:** Average daily low temperature (°C) **BLACK FIGURES:** Average monthly rainfall (mm) 1 millimeter = 0.039 inches

FAHRENHEIT 120° 110° 100° 90° 80° 70° 60° 50° 40° 30° 20° 10° 0° 10° 20° 30° 40° 50° 60° FAHRENHEIT

	JAN.			FEB.			MARCH			APRIL			MAY			JUNE			JULY			AUG.			SEPT.			OCT.			NOV.			DEC.		
ASIA																																				
WUHAN, *China*	8	1	41	9	2	57	14	6	92	21	13	136	26	18	165	31	23	212	34	26	165	34	26	114	29	21	73	23	16	74	17	9	49	11	3	30
YAKUTSK, *Russia*	-43	-47	8	-33	-40	5	-18	-29	3	-3	-14	8	9	-1	10	19	9	28	23	12	41	19	9	33	10	1	28	-5	-12	13	-26	-31	10	-39	-43	8
YANGON (RANGOON), *Myanmar*	32	18	4	33	19	4	36	22	17	36	24	47	33	25	307	30	24	478	29	24	535	29	24	511	30	24	368	31	24	183	31	23	62	31	19	11
YEKATERINBURG, *Russia*	-14	-21	8	-10	-17	10	-4	-12	5	6	-3	8	14	4	15	18	9	48	21	12	38	18	10	53	12	5	46	3	-2	23	-7	-12	10	-12	-18	8
AFRICA																																				
ABIDJAN, *Côte d'Ivoire*	31	23	22	32	24	47	32	24	110	32	24	142	31	24	309	29	23	543	28	23	238	28	22	36	28	23	74	29	23	172	31	23	168	31	23	85
ACCRA, *Ghana*	31	23	15	31	24	29	31	24	57	31	24	90	31	24	136	29	23	199	27	23	50	27	22	19	27	23	43	29	23	64	31	24	34	31	24	20
ADDIS ABABA, *Ethiopia*	24	6	17	24	8	38	25	9	68	25	10	86	25	10	86	23	9	132	21	10	268	21	10	281	22	9	186	24	7	28	23	6	11	23	5	10
ALEXANDRIA, *Egypt*	18	11	52	19	11	28	21	13	13	23	15	4	26	18	1	28	21	0	29	23	0	31	23	0	30	23	1	28	20	8	25	17	35	21	13	55
ALGIERS, *Algeria*	15	9	93	16	9	73	17	11	67	20	13	52	23	15	34	26	18	14	28	21	2	29	22	5	27	21	33	23	17	77	19	13	96	16	11	114
ANTANANARIVO, *Madag.*	26	16	287	26	16	262	26	16	194	24	14	57	23	12	18	21	10	9	20	9	8	21	9	10	23	11	16	27	12	61	27	14	153	27	16	290
ASMARA, *Eritrea*	23	7	0	24	8	0	25	9	1	26	11	7	26	12	23	26	12	48	22	12	114	22	12	123	23	13	49	22	12	4	22	10	3	22	9	0
BAMAKO, *Mali*	33	16	0	36	19	0	39	22	3	39	24	19	39	24	59	34	23	131	32	22	229	31	22	307	32	22	198	34	22	63	34	18	7	33	17	0
BANGUI, *Cen. Af. Rep.*	32	20	20	34	21	39	33	22	107	33	22	133	32	21	163	31	21	143	29	21	181	29	21	225	31	21	190	31	21	202	31	20	93	32	19	29
BEIRA, *Mozambique*	32	24	267	32	24	259	31	23	263	30	22	117	28	18	67	26	16	40	25	16	34	26	17	33	28	18	25	31	22	34	31	22	121	31	23	243
BENGHAZI, *Libya*	17	10	66	18	11	41	21	12	20	23	14	5	26	17	3	28	20	1	29	22	1	29	22	1	28	21	3	27	19	18	23	16	46	19	12	66
BUJUMBURA, *Burundi*	29	20	97	29	20	97	29	20	126	29	20	129	29	20	64	29	19	11	30	19	3	30	19	17	31	20	43	31	20	62	29	20	98	29	20	100
CAIRO, *Egypt*	18	8	5	21	9	4	24	11	4	28	14	2	33	17	1	35	20	0	36	21	0	35	22	0	32	20	0	30	18	1	26	14	3	20	10	6
CAPE TOWN, *S. Africa*	26	16	16	26	16	15	25	14	22	22	12	50	19	9	92	18	8	105	17	7	91	18	8	83	18	9	54	21	11	40	23	13	24	24	14	19
CASABLANCA, *Morocco*	17	7	57	18	8	53	19	9	51	21	11	38	22	13	21	24	16	6	26	18	0	27	19	1	26	17	6	24	14	34	21	11	65	18	8	73
CONAKRY, *Guinea*	31	22	1	31	23	1	32	23	6	32	23	21	32	24	141	30	23	503	28	22	1210	28	22	1016	29	23	664	31	23	318	31	24	106	31	23	14
DAKAR, *Senegal*	26	18	1	27	17	1	27	18	0	27	18	0	29	20	1	31	23	15	31	24	75	31	24	215	32	24	146	32	24	42	30	23	3	27	19	4
DAR ES SALAAM, *Tanzania*	31	25	66	31	25	66	31	24	130	30	23	290	29	22	188	29	20	33	28	19	31	28	19	30	28	19	30	29	21	41	30	22	74	31	24	91
DURBAN, *S. Africa*	27	21	119	27	21	126	27	20	132	26	18	84	24	14	56	23	12	34	22	11	35	22	13	49	23	15	73	24	17	110	25	18	118	26	19	120
HARARE, *Zimbabwe*	26	16	190	26	16	177	26	14	107	26	13	33	23	9	10	21	7	3	21	7	1	23	8	2	26	12	7	28	14	32	27	16	93	26	16	173
JOHANNESBURG, *S. Africa*	26	14	150	25	14	129	24	13	110	22	10	48	19	6	24	17	4	6	17	4	10	20	6	10	23	9	25	25	12	65	25	13	126	26	14	141
KAMPALA, *Uganda*	28	18	58	28	18	68	27	18	128	26	18	185	26	17	134	25	17	71	25	17	55	26	16	87	27	17	100	27	17	119	27	17	142	27	17	95
KHARTOUM, *Sudan*	32	15	0	34	16	0	38	19	0	41	22	0	42	25	4	41	26	7	38	25	49	37	24	69	39	25	21	40	24	5	36	20	0	33	17	0
KINSHASA, *D.R.C.*	31	21	138	31	22	148	32	22	184	32	22	220	31	22	145	29	19	5	27	18	3	29	18	4	31	20	40	31	21	133	31	22	235	30	21	156
KISANGANI, *D.R.C.*	31	21	97	31	21	107	31	21	172	31	21	190	31	21	162	30	21	128	29	19	114	28	20	178	29	20	164	30	20	233	29	20	207	30	20	105
LAGOS, *Nigeria*	31	23	27	32	25	44	32	26	98	32	25	146	31	24	252	29	23	414	28	23	253	28	23	69	28	23	153	29	23	197	31	24	66	31	24	25
LIBREVILLE, *Gabon*	31	23	164	31	22	137	32	23	248	32	23	232	31	22	181	29	21	24	28	20	3	29	21	6	29	22	69	30	22	332	30	22	378	31	22	197
LIVINGSTONE, *Zambia*	29	19	175	29	19	160	29	18	95	30	15	25	28	11	5	25	7	1	25	7	0	28	10	0	32	15	2	34	19	26	33	19	78	31	19	176
LUANDA, *Angola*	28	23	34	29	24	35	30	24	90	29	24	127	28	23	18	25	20	0	23	18	0	23	18	1	24	19	2	26	22	6	28	23	32	28	23	23
LUBUMBASHI, *D.R.C.*	28	16	253	28	17	256	28	16	210	28	14	51	27	10	4	26	7	1	26	6	0	28	8	0	32	11	6	33	14	31	31	16	150	28	17	272
LUSAKA, *Zambia*	26	17	213	26	17	172	26	17	104	26	15	22	25	12	3	23	10	0	23	9	0	25	12	0	29	15	1	31	18	14	29	18	86	27	17	200
LUXOR, *Egypt*	23	6	0	26	7	0	30	10	0	35	15	0	40	21	0	41	21	0	42	23	0	41	23	0	39	22	0	37	18	1	31	12	0	26	7	0
MAPUTO, *Mozambique*	30	22	153	31	22	134	29	21	99	28	19	52	27	16	29	25	13	18	24	13	15	26	14	13	27	16	32	28	18	51	28	19	78	29	21	94
MARRAKECH, *Morocco*	18	4	27	20	6	31	23	9	36	26	11	32	29	14	17	33	17	7	38	19	2	38	20	3	33	17	7	28	14	20	23	9	37	19	6	28
MOGADISHU, *Somalia*	30	23	0	30	23	0	31	24	8	32	26	58	32	25	59	29	23	78	28	23	67	28	23	42	29	23	21	30	24	38	31	24	40	30	24	9
MONROVIA, *Liberia*	30	23	5	29	23	3	31	23	112	31	23	297	30	22	340	27	23	917	27	22	615	27	23	472	27	22	759	28	22	640	29	23	208	30	23	74
NAIROBI, *Kenya*	25	12	45	26	13	43	25	14	73	24	14	160	22	13	119	21	12	30	21	11	13	21	11	13	24	11	26	24	13	42	23	13	121	23	13	77
N'DJAMENA, *Chad*	34	14	0	37	16	0	40	21	0	42	23	8	40	25	31	38	24	62	33	22	150	31	22	215	33	22	91	36	21	22	36	17	0	33	14	0
NIAMEY, *Niger*	34	14	0	37	18	0	41	22	3	42	25	6	41	27	35	38	25	75	34	23	143	32	23	187	34	23	90	38	23	16	38	18	1	34	15	0
NOUAKCHOTT, *Maurit.*	29	14	1	31	15	3	32	17	1	32	18	1	34	21	1	33	23	3	32	23	13	32	24	104	34	24	23	33	22	10	32	18	3	28	13	1
TIMBUKTU, *Mali*	31	13	0	34	14	0	38	19	0	42	22	1	43	26	4	43	27	19	39	25	62	36	24	79	39	24	33	40	23	3	37	18	0	32	13	0
TRIPOLI, *Libya*	16	8	69	17	9	40	19	11	27	22	14	13	24	16	5	27	19	1	29	22	0	30	22	1	29	22	11	27	18	38	23	14	60	18	9	81
TUNIS, *Tunisia*	14	6	62	16	7	52	18	8	46	21	11	38	24	13	22	29	17	10	32	20	3	33	21	7	31	19	32	25	15	55	20	11	54	16	7	63
WADI HALFA, *Sudan*	24	9	0	27	10	0	31	14	0	36	18	0	40	22	1	41	24	0	41	25	1	41	25	0	40	24	0	37	21	0	30	15	0	25	11	0
YAOUNDÉ, *Cameroon*	29	19	26	29	19	55	29	19	140	29	19	193	28	19	216	27	19	163	27	19	62	27	18	80	27	19	216	27	18	292	28	19	120	28	19	28
ZANZIBAR, *Tanzania*	32	24	75	33	24	61	33	25	150	30	25	350	29	24	251	28	23	54	28	22	44	28	22	39	29	22	48	30	23	86	32	24	201	32	24	145
ZOMBA, *Malawi*	27	18	299	27	18	269	26	18	230	26	17	85	24	14	23	22	12	13	22	12	8	24	13	8	27	15	8	29	18	29	29	19	124	27	18	281
ATLANTIC ISLANDS																																				
ASCENSION ISLAND	29	23	4	31	23	8	31	24	23	31	24	27	31	23	10	29	23	14	29	22	12	28	22	10	28	22	8	28	22	7	28	22	4	29	22	3
FALKLAND ISLANDS	13	6	71	13	5	58	12	4	64	9	3	66	7	1	66	5	-1	53	4	-1	51	5	-1	51	7	1	38	9	2	41	11	3	51	12	4	71
FUNCHAL, *Madeira Is.*	19	13	87	18	13	88	19	13	79	19	14	43	21	16	22	22	17	9	24	19	2	24	19	3	24	19	27	23	18	85	22	16	106	19	14	87
HAMILTON, *Bermuda Is.*	20	14	112	20	14	119	20	14	122	22	15	104	24	18	117	27	21	112	29	23	114	30	23	137	29	22	132	26	21	147	23	17	127	21	16	119
LAS PALMAS, *Canary Is.*	21	14	28	22	14	21	22	15	15	22	16	10	23	17	3	24	18	1	25	19	1	26	21	0	26	21	6	26	19	18	24	18	37	22	16	32
NUUK, *Greenland*	-7	-12	36	-7	-13	43	-4	-11	41	-1	-7	30	4	-2	43	8	1	36	11	3	56	11	3	79	6	1	84	2	-3	64	-2	-7	48	-5	-10	38
PONTA DELGADA, *Azores*	17	12	105	17	11	91	17	12	87	18	12	62	20	13	57	22	15	36	25	17	25	26	18	34	25	17	75	22	16	97	20	14	108	18	12	98
PRAIA, *Cape Verde*	25	20	1	25	19	2	26	20	0	26	21	0	27	21	0	28	22	0	28	24	7	29	24	63	29	25	88	29	24	44	28	23	15	26	22	5
REYKJAVÍK, *Iceland*	2	-2	86	3	-2	75	4	-1	76	6	1	56	10	4	42	12	7	45	14	9	51	14	8	62	11	6	71	7	3	88	4	0	83	2	-2	84
THULE, *Greenland*	-17	-27	7	-20	-29	8	-19	-28	4	-13	-23	4	-2	-9	5	5	-1	6	8	2	14	6	1	17	1	-6	13	-5	-13	11	-11	-19	11	-18	-27	5
TRISTAN DA CUNHA	19	15	103	20	16	110	19	14	133	18	14	137	16	12	153	14	11	153	14	10	54	13	9	162	13	9	157	15	11	148	16	12	124	18	14	131
PACIFIC ISLANDS																																				
APIA, *Samoa*	30	24	437	29	24	360	30	23	356	30	24	236	29	23	174	29	23	135	29	23	100	29	24	111	29	23	144	29	24	206	30	23	259	29	23	374
AUCKLAND, *New Zealand*	23	16	70	23	16	86	22	15	77	19	13	96	17	11	115	14	9	126	13	8	131	14	8	112	16	9	94	17	11	93	19	12	82	21	14	78
DARWIN, *Australia*	32	25	396	32	25	331	33	25	282	33	24	97	33	23	18	31	21	3	31	19	1	32	21	4	33	23	15	34	25	60	34	26	130	33	26	239
DUNEDIN, *New Zealand*	19	10	81	19	10	70	17	9	78	15	7	75	12	5	78	9	4	78	9	3	70	11	3	61	13	5	61	15	6	70	17	7	79	18	9	81
GALÁPAGOS IS., *Ecuador*	30	22	20	30	24	36	31	24	28	31	24	18	30	23	1	28	22	1	27	21	1	27	19	1	27	19	1	27	19	1	27	20	1	28	21	1
GUAM, *Mariana Is.*	29	24	138	29	23	116	29	24	121	31	24	108	31	25	164	31	25	150	30	24	274	30	24	368	30	24	374	30	24	334	30	25	231	29	24	160
HOBART, *Tasmania*	22	12	51	22	12	38	20	11	46	17	9	51	14	7	46	12	5	51	11	4	51	13	5	49	15	6	47	17	8	60	19	9	52	21	11	57
MELBOURNE, *Australia*	26	14	48	26	14	47	24	13	52	20	11	57	17	8	58	14	7	49	13	6	49	15	6	50	17	8	59	19	9	67	22	11	60	24	12	59
NAHA, *Okinawa*	19	13	125	19	13	126	21	15	159	24	18	165	27	20	252	29	24	280	32	25	178	31	25	270	31	24	175	27	21	165	24	18	133	21	14	111
NOUMÉA, *N. Caledonia*	30	22	111	29	23	130	29	22	155	28	21	121	26	19	106	25	18	107	24	17	91	24	16	73	26	17	56	27	18	53	28	20	55	30	21	77
PAPEETE, *Tahiti*	32	22	335	32	22	292	32	22	165	32	22	173	31	21	124	30	21	81	30	20	66	30	20	48	30	21	58	31	21	86	31	22	165	31	22	302
PERTH, *Australia*	29	17	9	29	17	13	27	16	19	24	14	45	21	12	122	18	10	182	17	9	174	18	9	136	19	10	80	21	12	53	24	14	21	27	16	13
PORT MORESBY, *P.N.G.*	32	24	179	31	24	196	31	24	190	31	24	120	30	24	65	29	23	39	28	23	27	28	23	26	29	23	33	30	24	35	31	24	56	32	24	121
SUVA, *Fiji Islands*	30	23	305	30	23	293	30	23	367	29	23	342	28	22	261	27	21	166	26	20	142	26	20	184	27	21	200	27	21	217	28	22	266	29	23	296
SYDNEY, *Australia*	26	18	103	26	18	111	24	17	131	22	14	130	19	11	123	16	9	129	16	8	103	17	9	80	19	11	69	22	13	83	23	16	81	25	17	78
WELLINGTON, *N.Z.*	21	13	79	21	13	80	19	12	85	17	11	98	14	8	121	13	7	124	12	6	139	12	6	121	14	8	99	16	9	105	17	10	88	19	12	90

A

abyssal plain a flat, relatively featureless region of the deep ocean floor extending from the mid-ocean ridge to a continental rise or deep-sea trench

acculturation the process of losing the traits of one cultural group while assimilating with another cultural group

alloy a substance that is a mixture of two metals or a metal and a nonmetal

alluvial fan a depositional, fan-shaped feature found where a stream or channel gradient levels out at the base of a mountain

antipode a point that lies diametrically opposite any given point on the surface of the Earth

Archaean (Archean) eon the second eon of Earth's geologic history, ending around 2,500 million years ago

archipelago an associated group of scattered islands in a large body of water

asthenosphere the uppermost zone of Earth's mantle; it consists of rocks in a "plastic" state, immediately below the lithosphere

atmosphere the thin envelope of gases surrounding the solid Earth and comprising mostly nitrogen, oxygen, and various trace gases

atoll a circular coral reef enclosing a lagoon

B

barrier island a low-lying, sandy island parallel to a shoreline but separated from the mainland by a lagoon

basin a low-lying depression in the Earth's surface; some basins are filled with water and sediment, while others are dry most of the time

bathymetry the measurement of depth within bodies of water or the information gathered from such measurements

bay an area of a sea or other body of water bordered on three sides by a curved stretch of coastline but usually smaller than a gulf

biodiversity a broad concept that refers to the variety and range of species (flora and fauna) present in an ecosystem

biogeography the study of the distribution patterns of plants and animals and the processes that produce those patterns

biological weapon a weapon that uses an organism or toxin, such as a bacteria or virus, to harm individuals

biome a very large ecosystem made up of specific plant and animal communities interacting with the physical environment (climate and soil)

biosphere the realm of Earth that includes all plant and animal life-forms

bluff a steep slope or wall of consolidated sediment adjacent to a river or its floodplain

bog soft, spongy, waterlogged ground consisting chiefly of partially decayed plant matter (peat)

breakwater a stone or concrete structure built near a shore to prevent damage to watercraft or construction

butte a tall, steep-sided, flat-topped tower of rock that is a remnant of extensive erosional processes

C

caldera a large, crater-like feature with steep, circular walls and a central depression resulting from the explosion and collapse of a volcano

canal an artificially made channel of water used for navigation or irrigation

canopy the ceiling-like layer of branches and leaves that forms the uppermost layer of a forest

capitalism an economic system characterized by resource allocation primarily through market mechanisms; means of production are privately owned (by either individuals or corporations), and production is organized around profit maximization

capture fishery all of the variables involved in the activities to harvest a given fish (e.g., location, target resource, technology used, social characteristic, purpose, season)

carbon cycle one of the several geochemical cycles by which matter is recirculated through the lithosphere, hydrosphere, atmosphere, and biosphere

carbon neutral process a process resulting in zero net change in the balance between emission and absorption of carbon

carrying capacity the maximum number of animals and/or people a given area can support at a given time under specified levels of consumption

cartogram a map designed to present statistical information in a diagrammatic way, usually not to scale

cartographer a person who interprets, designs, and creates maps and other modes of geographic representation

chemical weapon a weapon that uses toxic properties of chemical substances to harm individuals

chlorofluorocarbon a molecule of industrial origin containing chlorine, fluorine, and carbon atoms; causes severe ozone destruction

civilization a cultural concept suggesting substantial development in the form of agriculture, cities, food and labor surplus, labor specialization, social stratification, and state organization

climate the long-term behavior of the atmosphere; it includes measures of average weather conditions (e.g., temperature, humidity, precipitation, and pressure), as well as trends, cycles, and extremes

colonialism the political, social, or economic domination of a state over another state or people

commodity an economic good or product that can be traded, bought, or sold

composite image a product of combining two or more images

coniferous trees and shrubs with thin leaves and producing cones; also a forest or wood composed of these trees

continental drift a theory that suggests the continents were at one time all part of a prehistoric supercontinent that broke apart; according to the theory, the continents slowly "drifted" across the Earth's surface to their present positions

continental shelf the submerged, offshore extension of a continent

continental slope the steeply graded sea floor connecting the edge of the continental shelf to the deep-ocean floor

convection the transfer of heat within a gas or solid of nonuniform temperature from mass movement or circulatory motion due to gravity and uneven density within the substance

convergent boundary where tectonic plates move toward each other along their common boundary, causing subduction

core the dense, innermost layer of Earth; the outer core is liquid, while the inner core is solid

Coriolis effect the deflection of wind systems and ocean currents (as well as freely moving objects not in contact with the solid Earth) to the right in the Northern Hemisphere and to the left in the Southern Hemisphere as a consequence of the Earth's rotation

crust the rocky, relatively low density, outermost layer of Earth

cultural diffusion the spread of cultural elements from one group to another

culture the "way of life" for a group; it is transmitted from generation to generation and involves a shared system of meanings, beliefs, values, and social relations; it also includes language, religion, clothing, music, laws, and entertainment

D

dead zone oxygen-starved areas in oceans and lakes where marine life cannot be supported, often linked to runoff of excess nutrients

deciduous trees and shrubs that shed their leaves seasonally; also a forest or wood mostly composed of these trees

deformation general term for folding and faulting of rocks due to natural shearing, compression, and extension forces

delta a flat, low-lying, often fan-shaped region at the mouth of a river; it is composed of sediment deposited by a river entering a lake, an ocean, or another large body of water

demography the study of population statistics, changes, and trends based on various measures of fertility, mortality, and migration

denudation the overall effect of weathering, mass wasting, and erosion, which ultimately wears down and lowers the continental surface

desert a region that has little or no vegetation and averages less than 10 inches of precipitation a year

desertification the spread of desert conditions in arid and semiarid regions; desertification results from a combination of climatic changes and increasing human pressures in the form of overgrazing, removal of natural vegetation, and cultivation of marginal land

developed country general term for an industrialized country with a diversified and self-sustaining economy, strong infrastructure, and high standard of living

developing country general term for a non-industrialized country with a weak economy, little modern infrastructure, and low standard of living

dialect a regional variation of one language, with differences in vocabulary, accent, pronunciation, and syntax

diffuse plate boundary a zone of faulting and earthquakes extending to either side of a plate boundary

digital elevation model (DEM) a digital representation of Earth's topography in which data points representing altitude are assigned coordinates and viewed spatially; sometimes called a digital terrain model (DTM)

disconformity a discontinuity in sedimentary rocks in which the rock beds remain parallel

divide a ridge separating watersheds

dormant volcano an active volcano that is temporarily in repose, but expected to erupt in the future

E

earthquake vibrations and shock waves caused by volcanic eruptions or the sudden movement of Earth's crustal rocks along fracture zones called faults

easterlies a regular wind that blows from the east

ecosystem a group of organisms and the environment with which they interact

elevation the height of a point or place above an established datum, sometimes mean sea level

El Niño a pronounced warming of the surface waters along the coast of Peru and the equatorial region of the east Pacific Ocean; it is caused by weakening (sometimes reversal) of the trade winds, with accompanying changes in ocean circulation (including cessation of upwelling in coastal waters)

emigrant a person migrating away from a country or area; an out-migrant

endangered species a species at immediate risk of extinction

endemic typical to or native of a particular area, people, or environment

endogeneous introduced from or originating within a given organism or system

environment the sum of the conditions and stimuli that influence an organism

eon the largest time unit on the geologic time scale; consists of several shorter units called eras

Equator latitude 0°; an imaginary line running east and west around Earth and dividing it into two equal parts known as the Northern and Southern Hemispheres; the Equator always has approximately 12 hours of daylight and 12 hours of darkness

equinox the time of year (usually September 22-23 and March 21-22) when the length of night and day are about equal, and the sun is directly overhead at the Equator

era a major subdivision of time on the geologic time scale; consists of several shorter units called periods

erosion the general term for the removal of surface rocks and sediment by the action of water, air, ice, or gravity

escarpment a cliff or steep rock face that separates two comparatively level land surfaces

estuary a broadened seaward end or extension of a river (usually a drowned river mouth), characterized by tidal influences and the mixing of fresh and saline water

ethnic group minority group with a collective self-identity within a larger host population

ethnocentrism a belief in the inherent superiority of one's own ethnic group and culture; a tendency to view all other groups or cultures in terms of one's own

eutrophication the process that occurs when large amounts of nutrients from fertilizers or animal wastes enter a water body and bacteria break down the nutrients; the bacterial action causes depletion of dissolved oxygen

Exclusive Economic Zone (EEZ) an oceanic zone extending up to 200 nautical miles (370 km) from a shoreline, within which a coastal state claims jurisdiction over fishing, mineral exploration, and other economically important activities

exogenous introduced from or originating outside a given organism or system

external debt debt owed to non-residents; repayable in foreign currency, goods, or services

F

fault a fracture or break in rock where the opposite sides are displaced relative to each other

fjord a coastal inlet that is narrow and deep and reaches far inland; it is usually formed by the sea filling in a glacially scoured valley or trough

flood basalt a huge lava flow that produces thick accumulations of basalt layers over a large area

floodplain a wide, relatively flat area adjacent to a stream or river and subject to flooding and sedimentation; it is the most preferred land area for human settlement and agriculture

food chain the feeding pattern of organisms in an ecosystem, through which energy from food passes from one level to the next in a sequence

fork the place where a river separates into branches; also may refer to one of those branches

fossil fuel fuel in the form of coal, petroleum, or natural gas derived from the remains of ancient plants and animals trapped and preserved in sedimentary rocks

G

galaxy a collection of stars, gas, and dust bound together by gravity; there are billions of galaxies in the universe, and the Earth is in the Milky Way galaxy

genocide the intentional destruction, in whole or in part, of a national, ethnic, racial, or religious group

genome the complete set of genetic material of an organism

geochemistry a branch of geology focusing on the chemical composition of earth materials

geographic information system (GIS) an integrated hardware-software system used to store, organize, analyze, manipulate, model, and display geographic information or data

geography literally means "Earth description"; as a modern academic discipline, geography is concerned with the explanation of the physical and human characteristics and patterns of Earth's surface

geomorphology the study of planetary surface features, especially the processes of landform evolution on Earth

geopolitics the study of how factors such as geography, economics, and demography affect the power and foreign policy of a state

glaciation a period of glacial advancement through the growth of continental ice sheets and/or mountain glaciers

glacier a large, natural accumulation of ice that spreads outward on the land or moves slowly down a slope or valley

global positioning system (GPS) a system of artificial satellites that provides information on three-dimensional position and velocity to users at or near the Earth's surface

global warming the warming of Earth's average global temperature due to a buildup of "greenhouse gases" (e.g., carbon dioxide and methane) released by human activities; increased levels of these gases cause enhanced heat absorption by the atmosphere

globe a scale model of the Earth that correctly represents not only the area, relative size, and shape of physical features but also the distance between points and true compass directions

great circle the largest circle that can be drawn around a sphere such as a globe; a great circle route is the shortest route between two points on the surface of a sphere

greenhouse effect an enhanced near-surface warming that is due to certain atmospheric gases absorbing and re-radiating long-wave radiation that might otherwise have escaped to space had those gases not been present in the atmosphere

gross domestic product (GDP) the total market value of goods and services produced by a nation's economy in a given year using global currency exchange rates

gross national income (GNI) the income derived from the capital and income belonging to nationals employed domestically or abroad

gravitational waves ripples in the fabric of space and time, usually caused by the interaction of two or more large masses

gulf a very large area of an ocean or a sea bordered by coastline on three sides

gyre a large, semicontinuous system of major ocean currents flowing around the outer margins of every major ocean basin

H

habitat the natural environment (including controlling physical factors) in which a plant or animal is usually found or prefers to exist

hemisphere half a sphere; cartographers and geographers, by convention, divide the Earth into the Northern and Southern Hemispheres at the Equator and the Eastern and Western Hemispheres at the prime meridian (longitude 0°) and 180° meridian

herbaceous a type of plant lacking woody tissue, and usually with a life of just one growing season

hot spot a localized and intensely hot region or mantle plume beneath the lithosphere; it tends to stay relatively fixed geographically as a lithospheric plate migrates over it

human geography one of the two major divisions of systematic geography; it is concerned with the spatial analysis of human population, cultures, and social, political, and economic activities

hurricane a large, rotating storm system that forms over tropical waters, with very low atmospheric pressure in the central region and winds in excess of 74 mph (119km/h); it is called a typhoon over the western Pacific Ocean and a cyclone over the northern Indian Ocean

hydrologic cycle the continuous recirculation of water from the oceans, through the atmosphere, to the continents, through the biosphere and lithosphere, and back to the sea

hydrosphere all of the water found on, under, or over Earth's surface

hypsometry the measurement of contours and elevation of land above sea level

I

ice age a period of pronounced glaciation usually associated with worldwide cooling, a greater proportion of global precipitation falling as snow, and a shorter snowmelt period

igneous the rock type formed from solidified molten rock (magma) that originates deep within Earth; the chemical composition of the magma and its cooling rate determine the final rock type

immigrant a person migrating into a particular country or area; an in-migrant

impact crater a circular depression on the surface of a planet or moon caused by the collision of another body, such as an asteroid or comet

indigenous native to or occurring naturally in a specific area or environment

industrial metabolism a concept that describes the process of converting raw materials into a final product and waste through energy and labor

infrastructure transportation and communications networks that allow goods, people, and information to flow across space

inorganic not relating to or being derived from living things

interdependence mutual reliance among beings or processes

internally displaced person a person who flees his/her home, to escape danger or persecution, but does not leave the country

International Date Line an imaginary line that roughly follows the 180° meridian in the Pacific Ocean; immediately west of the date line the calendar date is one day ahead of the calendar date east of the line; people crossing the date line in a westward direction lose one calendar day, while those crossing eastward gain one calendar day

intertropical convergence zone (ITCZ) a zone of low atmospheric pressure created by intense solar heating, thereby leading to rising air and horizontal convergence of northeast and southeast trade winds; over the oceans, the ITCZ is usually found between 10° N and 10° S, and over continents the seasonal excursion of the ITCZ is much greater

isthmus a relatively narrow strip of land with water on both sides and connecting two larger land areas

J

jet stream a high-speed west-to-east wind current; jet streams flow in narrow corridors within upper-air westerlies, usually at the interface of polar and tropical air

K

karst a region underlain by limestone and characterized by extensive solution features such as sinkholes, underground streams, and caves

L

lagoon a shallow, narrow water body located between a barrier island and the mainland, with freshwater contributions from streams and saltwater exchange through tidal inlets or breaches throughout the barrier system

La Niña the pronounced cooling of equatorial waters in the eastern Pacific Ocean

latitude the distance north or south of the Equator; lines of latitude, called parallels, are evenly spaced from the Equator to the North and South Poles (from 0° to 90° N and S latitude); latitude and longitude (see below) are measured in terms of the 360 degrees of a circle and are expressed in degrees, minutes, and seconds

leeward the side away from or sheltered by the wind

lingua franca a language used beyond its native speaker population as a common or commercial language

lithosphere the rigid outer layer of the Earth, located above the asthenosphere and comprising the outer crust and the upper, rigid portion of the mantle

longitude the distance measured in degrees east or west of the prime meridian (0° longitude) up to 180°; lines of longitude are called meridians (compare with latitude, above)

M

macroscopic concerned with or considered in large units

magma molten, pressurized rock in the mantle that is occasionally intruded into the lithosphere or extruded to the surface of the Earth by volcanic activity

magnetic pole the points at Earth's surface at which the geomagnetic field is vertical; the location of these points constantly changes

mantle the dense layer of Earth below the crust; the upper mantle is solid and with the crust, forms the lithosphere, the zone containing tectonic plates; the lower mantle is partially molten, making it the pliable base upon which the lithosphere "floats"

map projection the geometric system of transferring information about a round object, such as a globe, to a flat piece of paper or other surface for the purpose of producing a map with known properties and quantifiable distortion

maria volcanic plains on the moon's surface that appear to the naked eye as smooth, dark areas

meridian a north-south line of longitude used to reference distance east or west of the prime meridian (longitude 0°)

mesa a broad, flat-topped hill or mountain with marginal cliffs and/or steep slopes formed by progressive erosion of horizontally bedded sedimentary rocks

metamorphic the rock type formed from preexisting rocks that have been substantially changed from their original igneous, sedimentary, or earlier metamorphic form; catalysts of this change include high heat, high pressure, hot and mineral-rich fluids, or, more commonly, some combination of these

metric ton (tonne) unit of weight equal to 1,000 kilograms or 2,205 pounds

micrometeoroids a tiny particle of rock or dust in space, usually weighing less than a gram

microscopic considered in or concerned with small units

migration the movement of people across a specified boundary for the purpose of establishing a new place of residence

mineral an inorganic solid with a distinctive chemical composition and a specific crystal structure that affect its physical characteristics

moment magnitude scale a measure of the total energy released by an earthquake; preferred to the Richter scale because it more accurately measures strong earthquakes and can be used with data for distant earthquakes

monsoon a seasonal reversal of prevailing wind patterns, often associated with pronounced changes in moisture

N

nation a cultural concept for a group of people bound together by a strong sense of shared values and cultural characteristics, including language, religion, and common history

nebula a cloud of interstellar gas and dust

node a point where distinct lines or objects intersect

Normalized Difference Vegetation Index (NDVI) a measurement of plant growth density over the Earth's surface, measured on a scale of 0.1 to 0.8 (low to high vegetation)

North Pole the most northerly geographic point on the Earth; the northern end of the Earth's axis of rotation; 90° N

nuclear weapon a weapon which uses nuclear reactions to derive destructive force

O

oasis a fertile area with water and vegetation in a desert

ocean current the regular and persistent flow of water in the oceans, usually driven by atmospheric wind and pressure systems or by regional differences in water density (temperature, salinity)

offshoring relocating business processes to another country, where they are performed by either another branch of the parent company or an external contractor (international outsourcing)

organic relating to or derived from living things

oxbow lake a crescent-shaped lake or swamp occupying a channel abandoned by a meandering river

outsourcing delegating non-core processes from within a business to an external entity such as a subcontractor

ozone a bluish gas composed of three oxygen atoms and harmful to breathe

ozone layer region of Earth's atmosphere where ozone concentration is relatively high; the ozone layer absorbs harmful ultraviolet rays from the sun

P

paleo-geographic map a map depicting the past positions of the continents, developed from historic magnetic, biological, climatological, and geologic evidence

Pangaea the supercontinent from which today's continents are thought to have originated

peninsula a long piece of land jutting out from a larger piece of land into a body of water

period a basic unit of time on the geologic time scale, generally 35 to 70 million years in duration; a subdivision of an era

Phanerozoic eon an eon of Earth's geologic history that comprises the Paleozoic, Mesozoic, and Cenozoic eras

photosynthesis process by which plants convert carbon dioxide and water to oxygen and carbohydrates

physical geography one of the two major divisions of systematic geography; the spatial analysis of the structure, process, and location of Earth's natural phenomena, such as climate, soil, plants, animals, water, and topography

pilgrimage a typically long and difficult journey to a special place, often of religious importance

plain an extensive, flat-lying area characterized generally by the absence of local relief features

planetary nebula an interstellar cloud of gas and dust formed when a star runs out of central nuclear fuel, finally ejecting its outer layers in a gaseous shell

plate tectonics the theory that Earth's lithospheric plates slide or shift slowly over the asthenosphere and that their interactions cause earthquakes, volcanic eruptions, movement of landmasses, and other geologic events

plateau a landform feature characterized by high elevation and gentle upland slopes

politicide the intentional destruction, in whole or in part, of a group of people based on their political or ideological beliefs

point a sharp prominence or headland on the coast that juts out into a body of water

pollution a direct or indirect process resulting from human activity; part of the environment is made potentially or actually unsafe or hazardous to the welfare of the organisms that live in it

porphyry an igneous rock characterized by large crystals within a matrix of much finer crystals

primary energy energy sources as they are found naturally—i.e., before they have been processed or transformed into secondary sources

prime meridian the line of 0° longitude that runs through Greenwich, England, and separates the Eastern and Western Hemispheres

Priscoan eon the earliest eon of Earth's geologic history; also known as the Hadean eon

proliferation the process of growing rapidly and suddenly

Proterozoic eon the eon of geologic time that includes the interval between the Archean and Phanerozoic eons and is marked by rocks that contain fossils indicating the first appearance of eukaryotic organisms (as algae)

protogalaxy a cloud of gas, possibly consisting of dark matter, hydrogen, and helium, that is forming into a galaxy

purchasing power parity (PPP) a method of measuring gross domestic product that compares the relative value of currencies based on what each currency will buy in its country of origin; PPP provides a good comparison between national economies and is a decent indicator of living standards

R

rain shadow the dry region on the downwind (leeward) side of a mountain range

raster data spatial data represented as a unified grid of equal-area cells, each with a single numerical value; best-suited for contiguous data such as elevation

red dwarf a relatively small, cool, and faint star with a very long estimated lifespan; the most common type of star

reef a strip of rocks or sand either at or just below the surface of water

refugee a person who flees his/her country of origin to escape danger or persecution for reasons of, for example, race, religion, or political opinion

regolith a layer of disintegrated or partly decomposed rock overlying unweathered parent materials; regolith is usually found in areas of low relief where the physical transport of debris is weak

remote sensing the measurement of some property of an object by means other than direct contact, usually from aircraft or satellites

renewable resource a resource that can be regenerated or maintained if used at rates that do not exceed natural replenishment

Richter scale a logarithmic scale devised to represent the relative amount of energy released by an earthquake; moment magnitude has superceded the Richter scale as the preferred measurement of earthquake magnitude

rift a long, narrow trough created by plate movement at a divergent boundary

rift valley a long, structural valley formed by the lowering of a block between two parallel faults

Ring of Fire (also Rim of Fire) an arc of volcanoes and tectonic activity along the perimeter of the Pacific Ocean

S

salinization the accumulation of salts in soil

satellite data information collected by a vehicle orbiting a celestial body

savanna a tropical grassland with widely spaced trees; it experiences distinct wet and dry seasons

seamount a submerged volcano rising from the ocean floor

sedimentary the rock type formed from preexisting rocks or pieces of once-living organisms; deposits accumulate on Earth's surface, generally with distinctive layering or bedding

solar radiation energy emitted by the sun

solar wind the stream of atoms and ions moving outward from the solar corona at 300 to 500 kilometers per second

solstice a celestial event that occurs twice a year (usually June 20-21 and December 21-22), when the sun appears directly overhead to observers at the Tropic of Cancer or the Tropic of Capricorn

sound a broad channel or passage of water connecting two larger bodies of water or separating an island from the mainland

South Pole the most southerly geographic point on the Earth; the southern end of the Earth's axis of rotation; 90° S

spatial resolution a measure of the smallest distinguishable separation between two objects

spectral resolution a measure of the ability of a sensing system to distinguish electromagnetic radiation of different frequencies

spit beach extension that forms along a shoreline with bays and other indentations

spreading boundary where plates move apart along their common boundary, creating a crack in the Earth's crust (typically at the mid-ocean ridge), which is then filled with upwelling molten rock; also called a divergent boundary

steppe semiarid, relatively flat, treeless region that receives between 10 and 20 inches of precipitation yearly

state an area with defined and internationally acknowledged boundaries; a political unit

strait a narrow passage of water that connects two larger bodies of water

subduction the tectonic process by which the down-bent edge of one lithospheric plate is forced underneath another plate

subatomic particle a part of an atom, such as a proton, neutron, or electron

T

tariff a surcharge on imports levied by a state; a form of protectionism designed to increase imports' market price and thus inhibit their consumption

tectonic plate (also lithospheric or crustal plate) a section of the Earth's rigid outer layer that moves as a distinct unit upon the plastic-like mantle materials in the asthenosphere

temperate mild or moderate

temporal resolution a measure of the frequency with which a sensing system gathers data

terrestrial radiation natural sources of radiation found in earth materials

threatened species species at some, but not immediate, risk of extinction

tide the regular rise and fall of the ocean, caused by the mutual gravitational attraction between the Earth, moon, and sun, as well as the rotation of the Earth-moon system around its center of gravity

ton a unit of weight equal to 2,000 pounds in the U.S. or 2,240 pounds in the U.K.

tonne (see metric ton)

topography the relief features that are evident on a planetary surface

tornado a violently rotating, funnel-shaped column of air characterized by extremely low atmospheric pressures and exceptional wind speeds generated within intense thunderstorms

tradewind a wind blowing persistently from the same direction; particularly from the subtropical high-pressure centers toward the equatorial low-pressure zone

transgenic an organism artificially or naturally containing one or more genes from a different type of organism

tributary a river or stream flowing into a larger river or stream

tropical warm and moist; occuring in or characteristic of the Tropics

Tropic of Cancer latitude 23.5° N; the farthest northerly excursion of the sun when it is directly overhead

Tropic of Capricorn latitude 23.5° S; the farthest southerly excursion of the sun when it is directly overhead

tsunami a series of ocean waves, often very destructive along coasts, caused by the vertical displacement of the seafloor during an earthquake, submarine landslide, or volcanic eruption

tundra a zone in cold, polar regions (mostly in the Northern Hemisphere) that is transitional between the zone of polar ice and the limit of tree growth; it is usually characterized by low-lying vegetation, with extensive permafrost and waterlogged soils

U

unconformity a discontinuity in sedimentary rocks caused by erosion or nondeposition

uplift the slow, upward movement of Earth's crust

upwelling the process by which water rich in nutrients rises from depth toward the ocean surface; it is usually the result of diverging surface waters

urban agglomeration a group of several cities and/or towns and their suburbs

urbanization a process in which there is an increase in the percentage of people living and working in urban places as compared to rural places; a process of change from a rural to urban lifestyle

V

vector data spatial data represented as as nodes and connectors identified by geographic coordinates, and related to one another to symbolize geographic features; best-suited for geographic features that can be represented as points, lines, or polygons

volcanism the upward movement and expulsion of molten (melted) material and gases from within the Earth's mantle onto the surface where it cools and hardens, producing characteristic terrain

W

watershed the drainage area of a river and its tributaries

weathering the processes or actions that cause the physical disintegration and chemical decomposition of rock and minerals

westerlies a regular wind that blows from the west

wetland an area of land covered by water or saturated by water sufficiently enough to support vegetation adapted to wet conditions

wilderness a natural environment that has remained essentially undisturbed by human activities and, increasingly, is protected by government or nongovernment organizations

windward the side toward or unsheltered from the wind

X

xerophyte a plant that thrives in a dry environment

Y

yazoo a tributary stream that runs parallel to the main river for some distance

Z

zenith the point in the sky that is immediately overhead; also the highest point above the observer's horizon obtained by a celestial body

zoning the process of subdividing urban areas as a basis for land-use planning and policy

Place-Name Index

THE FOLLOWING SYSTEM is used to locate a place on a map in the National Geographic Family Reference Atlas of the World. The boldface type after an entry refers to the plate on which the map is found. The letter-number combination refers to the grid on which the particular place-name is located. The edge of each map is marked horizontally with numbers and vertically with letters. In between, at equally spaced intervals, are index ticks (▲). If these ticks were connected with lines, each page would be divided into a 12- by 16-square grid. Take Abilene, Kansas, for example. The index entry reads "**Abilene, *Kans., U.S.* 105 S8.**" On page 105, Abilene is located within the grid square where row S and column 8 intersect.

A place-name may appear on several maps, but the index lists only the best presentation. Usually, this means that a feature is indexed to the largest-scale map on which it appears in its entirety. (Note: Rivers are often labeled multiple times even on a single map. In such cases, the rivers are indexed to labels that are closest to their mouths.) The name of the country or continent in which a feature lies is shown in italic type and is usually abbreviated. (A full list of abbreviations appears on page 262.)

The index lists more than proper names. Some entries include a description, as in "**Elba, island, *It.* 150 J5**" and "**Urubamba, river, *Peru* 130 H5.**" In languages other than English, the description of a physical feature may be part of the name; e.g., the "Berg" in "**Kleine Berg, *Neth. Antilles, Neth.* 121 P14**" means "mountain." The Glossary of Foreign Terms on page 272 translates such terms into English.

When a feature or place can be referred to by more than one name, both may appear in the index with cross-references. These are especially useful for finding major cities in China, where the phonetic Pinyin system has replaced the Wade-Giles system for the romanization of the Chinese language. For example, the entry for Canton reads "**Canton *see* Guangzhou, *China* 183 R4.**" That entry is "**Guangzhou (Canton), *China* 183 R4.**"

A

Aachen, *Ger.* **148** F4
Aalen, *Ger.* **148** J7
Aalsmeer, *Neth.* **146** J12
Aalst, *Belg.* **146** L11
Aansluit, *S. Af.* **202** J9
Aare, river, *Switz.* **150** A3
Aarschot, *Belg.* **146** L12
Aasu, *Amer. Samoa, U.S.* **218** M7
Aba, *China* **180** K11
Aba, *Dem. Rep. of the Congo* **198** H12
Aba, *Nigeria* **201** H14
Abā as Saʻūd, *Saudi Arabia* **172** N9
Abaco Island, *Bahamas* **120** C6
Ābādān, *Iran* **172** F11
Ābādeh, *Iran* **173** F13
Abadla, *Alg.* **196** C9
Abaetetuba, *Braz.* **131** D13
Abaiang, island, *Kiribati* **214** G8
Abaji, *Nigeria* **201** G14
Abajo Peak, *Utah, U.S.* **107** P9
Abakan, *Russ.* **159** L13
Abancay, *Peru* **130** H5
Abaokoro, island, *Kiribati* **217** F17
Abashiri, *Japan* **184** E15
Abashiri Wan, *Japan* **184** E15
Abay, *Kaz.* **175** E14
Ābaya Hāyk', *Eth.* **199** H14
Abbaye, Point, *Mich., U.S.* **98** E7
Abbeville, *Ala., U.S.* **101** M17
Abbeville, *Fr.* **146** M9
Abbeville, *La., U.S.* **100** Q8
Abbeville, *S.C., U.S.* **96** K7
Abbeyfeale, *Ire.* **143** T3
Abbeyleix, *Ire.* **143** T5
Abbiategrasso, *It.* **150** E4
Abbot Ice Shelf, *Antarctica* **226** J6
Abbotsford, *B.C., Can.* **82** M8
Abbotsford, *Wis., U.S.* **98** H4
Abbottabad, *Pak.* **176** M11
ʻAbda (Eboda), ruin, *Israel* **171** P5
ʻAbd al ʻAzīz, Jabal, *Syr.* **170** D13
ʻAbd al Kūrī, island, *Yemen* **173** R13
Abéché, *Chad* **197** H16
Ab-e Istadeh-ye Moqor, lake, *Afghan.* **177** P7
Abemama, island, *Kiribati* **214** G8
Abengourou, *Côte d'Ivoire* **200** H9
Åbenrå, *Den.* **140** P11
Abeokuta, *Nigeria* **200** G12
Aberaeron, *Wales, U.K.* **143** U9
Aberdare, *Wales, U.K.* **143** V10
Aberdaron, *Wales, U.K.* **143** T8
Aberdaugleddau *see* Milford Haven, *Wales, U.K.* **143** V8
Aberdeen, *Idaho, U.S.* **106** H6
Aberdeen, *Md., U.S.* **96** C14
Aberdeen, *Miss., U.S.* **101** J13
Aberdeen, *N.C., U.S.* **96** J11
Aberdeen, *S. Dak., U.S.* **104** J6
Aberdeen, *Scot., U.K.* **142** K11
Aberdeen, *Wash., U.S.* **108** D2
Aberdeen Lake, *Nunavut, Can.* **83** H14
Aberffraw, *Wales, U.K.* **143** S9
Abergele, *Wales, U.K.* **143** S10
Abergwaun *see* Fishguard, *Wales, U.K.* **143** U8
Abernathy, *Tex., U.S.* **102** J5
Abert, Lake, *Oreg., U.S.* **108** K6
Abertawe *see* Swansea, *Wales, U.K.* **143** V9
Aberteifi *see* Cardigan, *Wales, U.K.* **143** U9
Abertillery, *Wales, U.K.* **143** V10
Aberystwyth, *Wales, U.K.* **143** U9
Abhā, *Saudi Arabia* **172** N8
Abidjan, *Côte d'Ivoire* **200** H9
Abilene, *Kans., U.S.* **105** S8
Abilene, *Tex., U.S.* **102** L8
Abingden Downs, *Qnsld., Austral.* **211** R12
Abingdon *see* Pinta, Isla, island, *Ecua.* **128** N9
Abingdon, *Eng., U.K.* **143** V12
Abingdon, *Ill., U.S.* **99** Q4
Abingdon, *Va., U.S.* **96** G8
Abiquiu, *N. Mex., U.S.* **107** R12
Abisko, *Sw.* **141** D13
Abitibi, river, *N. Amer.* **80** H8
Abitibi, Lake, *N. Amer.* **80** H8
Abkhazia, *Rep. of Georgia* **169** A15
Åbo *see* Turku, *Fin.* **141** K15
Abohar, *India* **178** E4
Abomey, *Benin* **200** G11
Abraham Lincoln Birthplace National Historic Site, *Ky., U.S.* **101** C16
Abraham's Bay, *Bahamas* **117** H16
Abra Pampa, *Arg.* **132** D9
Abreú, *Dom. Rep.* **117** L19
Abrolhos, Arquipélago dos, *Braz.* **131** K16
Absalom, Mount, *Antarctica* **226** E11
Absaroka Range, *Wyo., U.S.* **106** F9
Absarokee, *Mont., U.S.* **106** E9
Absheron Yarymadasy, peninsula, *Azerb.* **169** D23
Abū al Abyaḑ, island, *U.A.E.* **173** J14
Abu al Ḩuşayn, Qāʻ, *Jordan* **170** M10
Abū ʻAlī, island, *Saudi Arabia* **172** H12
Abū Baḩr, plain, *Saudi Arabia* **172** L11
Abu Ballâs, peak, *Egypt* **194** E8
Abū Daghmah, *Syr.* **170** D10
Abu Dhabi *see* Abū Z̧aby, *U.A.E.* **173** J14
Abu Durba, *Egypt* **171** T2
Abu Hamed, *Sudan* **199** C13
Abuja, *Nigeria* **201** F14
Abū Kamāl, *Syr.* **170** H14
Abū Madd, Ra's, *Saudi Arabia* **172** J6
Abu Matariq, *Sudan* **198** F11
Abunã, river, *Bol., Braz.* **130** G7
Abunã, *Braz.* **130** G7
Abū Qumayyiş, Ra's, *Saudi Arabia* **173** J13
Abu Rudeis, *Egypt* **171** S2
Abu Rūjmayn, Jabal, *Syr.* **170** G10
Abu Shagara, Ras, *Sudan* **199** C14
Abu Simbel, site, *Egypt* **197** F19
Abuta, *Japan* **184** G13
Ābuyē Mēda, peak, *Eth.* **199** F15
Abu Zabad, *Sudan* **198** F12
Abū Z̧aby (Abu Dhabi), *U.A.E.* **173** J14
Abu Zenîma, *Egypt* **171** S2
Abwong, *Sudan* **199** G13
Abyad, El Bahr el (White Nile), *Sudan* **199** F13
Abyek, *Iran* **172** C12
Academy Glacier, *Antarctica* **226** H10
Acadia National Park, *Me., U.S.* **95** F18
A Cañiza, *Sp.* **144** C6
Acaponeta, *Mex.* **114** G9
Acapulco, *Mex.* **114** K11
Acaraú, *Braz.* **131** D16
Acarigua, *Venez.* **128** C8
Acatenango, Volcán de, *Guatemala* **115** L15
Acatlán, *Mex.* **114** J12
Accomac, *Va., U.S.* **96** E15
Accra, *Ghana* **200** H11
Accumoli, *It.* **150** J9
Achach, island, *F.S.M.* **217** C14
Acharacle, *Scot., U.K.* **142** L7
Achavanich, *Scot., U.K.* **142** H10
Achayvayam, *Russ.* **159** D21
Achill Island, *Ire.* **143** R3
Achim, *Ger.* **148** C7
Achinsk, *Russ.* **159** K13
Achna, *Cyprus* **160** P9
Achnasheen, *Scot., U.K.* **142** J8
Acıgöl, lake, *Turk.* **168** G5
Acıpayam, *Turk.* **168** H5
Ackerman, *Miss., U.S.* **100** K12
Ackley, *Iowa, U.S.* **105** N12
Acklins, The Bight of, *Bahamas* **117** H15
Acklins Island, *Bahamas* **117** H15
Acoma Pueblo, *N. Mex., U.S.* **107** S11
Aconcagua, Cerro, *Arg.* **132** K7
Aconcagua, Río, *Chile* **132** K6
Açores *see* Azores, islands, *Atl. Oc.* **204** C3
A Coruña, *Sp.* **144** A6
Acquaviva, *San Marino* **161** J14
Acqui Terme, *It.* **150** F3
Acraman, Lake, *Austral.* **210** J9
Acre, river, *Braz., Peru* **130** G6
Acre *see* ʻAkko, *Israel* **170** K5
Acteon, Groupe, *Fr. Polynesia, Fr.* **219** G22
Actium, battle, *Gr.* **154** G7
Açu, *Braz.* **131** F17
Ada, *Ghana* **200** H11
Ada, *Minn., U.S.* **104** G8
Ada, *Ohio, U.S.* **99** Q12
Ada, *Okla., U.S.* **102** H12
Ada, *Serb. & Mont.* **152** D10
Adair, Cape, *Nunavut, Can.* **83** E17
Adak Island, *Alas., U.S.* **110** N5
Adalia *see* Antalya, *Turk.* **168** H6
Adam, *Oman* **173** K16
Adámandás, *Gr.* **155** M13
Adamello, peak, *It.* **150** C6
Adams, *Minn., U.S.* **104** L12
Adams, *Wis., U.S.* **98** K5
Adams, Mount, *Wash., U.S.* **108** E5
Adam's Peak, *Sri Lanka* **179** T7
Adam's Rock, *Pitcairn I., U.K.* **219** Q23
Adamstown, *Pitcairn I., U.K.* **219** Q23
Adamsville, *Tenn., U.S.* **101** G13
ʻAdan (Aden), *Yemen* **172** R9
Adana, *Turk.* **168** J10
ʻAdan aş Şughrá, cape, *Yemen* **172** R9
Adang, Teluk, *Indonesia* **188** K12
Adare, Cape, *Antarctica* **227** R13
Adavale, *Qnsld., Austral.* **211** U12
Adda, river, *It.* **150** E5
Ad Dahnā', desert, *Saudi Arabia* **172** H10
Ad Dakhla, *W. Sahara, Mor.* **196** E5
Ad Dammām, *Saudi Arabia* **172** H12
Ad Dār al Ḩamrā', *Saudi Arabia* **172** H6
Ad Darb, *Saudi Arabia* **172** N8
Ad Dawādimī, *Saudi Arabia* **172** J9
Ad Dawḩah (Doha), *Qatar* **173** J13
Ad Dibdibah, region, *Iraq, Kuwait, Saudi Arabia* **172** G10
Ad Dilam, *Saudi Arabia* **172** K11
Addis Ababa *see* Ādīs Ābeba, *Eth.* **199** G15
Ad Dīwānīyah, *Iraq* **172** E10
Addu Atoll, *Maldives* **179** X3
Ad Duwayd, *Saudi Arabia* **172** F8
Addy, *Wash., U.S.* **108** B8
Adel, *Ga., U.S.* **97** P6
Adel, *Iowa, U.S.* **105** P11
Adel, *Oreg., U.S.* **108** L6
Adelaide, *Bahamas* **120** B10
Adelaide, *S. Aust., Austral.* **211** Y10
Adelaide Island, *Antarctica* **226** E4
Adelaide Peninsula, *Nunavut, Can.* **83** F14
Adelaide River, *N. Terr., Austral.* **211** P7
Adelfi, island, *Gr.* **155** G13
Adélie Coast, *Antarctica* **227** Q18
Aden *see* ʻAdan, *Yemen* **172** R9
Aden, Gulf of, *Ind. Oc.* **240** E5
Aderbissinat, *Niger* **196** H12
Adieu, Cape, *Austral.* **210** J8
Adige, river, *It.* **150** E7
Ādīgrat, *Eth.* **199** E15
Adilabad, *India* **178** L6
Adímilos, island, *Gr.* **155** M13
Adin, *Calif., U.S.* **108** M5
Adinkerke, *Belg.* **146** L10
Adíparos, island, *Gr.* **155** L14
Adirondack Mountains, *N.Y., U.S.* **94** G11
Ādīs Ābeba (Addis Ababa), *Eth.* **199** G15
Adi Ugri, *Eritrea* **199** E15
Adıyaman, *Turk.* **169** H13
Adjud, *Rom.* **153** D16
Adjuntas, *P.R., U.S.* **120** N3
Adlavik Islands, *Nfld. & Lab., Can.* **83** K22
Adler, *Russ.* **157** U11
Admiralty Inlet, *Nunavut, Can.* **83** E16
Admiralty Inlet, *Wash., U.S.* **108** B4
Admiralty Island, *Alas., U.S.* **84** Q7
Admiralty Island National Monument, *Alas., U.S.* **111** L22
Admiralty Islands, *P.N.G.* **213** B19
Admiralty Mountains, *Antarctica* **227** Q14
Abou Deïa, *Chad* **197** J15
Adour, river, *Fr.* **147** X7
Adra, *Sp.* **144** M11
Adrano, *It.* **151** S11
Adrar, *Alg.* **196** D10
Adrar, region, *Mauritania* **196** F6
Adrar des Iforas, range, *Mali* **196** F10
Adraskan, *Afghan.* **177** N2
Adria, *It.* **150** E8
Adrian, *Mich., U.S.* **99** N11
Adrian, *Minn., U.S.* **104** L9
Adrian, *Tex., U.S.* **102** G4
Adrianople *see* Edirne, *Turk.* **168** B3
Adriatic Sea, *Eur.* **138** J7
Adun Gol, *China* **182** B2
Ādwa, *Eth.* **199** E15
Adyakit, Gora, *Russ.* **159** F14
Aegean Sea, *Eur.* **138** K9
Aegina *see* Égina, island, *Gr.* **154** K12
Aegir Ridge, *Arctic Oc.* **243** J20
Aej, island, *Marshall Is.* **216** G8
Aeon Point, *Kiribati* **217** C24
Afaahiti, *Fr. Polynesia, Fr.* **219** P17
Afándou, *Gr.* **155** N20
Afar, region, *Eth.* **199** E16
Afareaitu, *Fr. Polynesia, Fr.* **219** N14
Affric, Glen, *Scot., U.K.* **142** K8
Afghanistan, *Asia* **167** U6
ʻAfīf, *Saudi Arabia* **172** K8
Afiq, *Israel* **170** K6
Afitos, *Gr.* **154** D12
Afmadow, *Somalia* **199** J16
Afobaka, *Suriname* **129** E16
Afognak Island, *Alas., U.S.* **111** L15
Afono Bay, *Amer. Samoa, U.S.* **218** L8
ʻAfrīn, *Syr.* **170** D8
Afşin, *Turk.* **168** G12

Afton, Okla., U.S. 102 E14
Afton, Wyo., U.S. 106 H8
Afuefuniya Point, N. Mariana Is., U.S. 216 E8
'Afula, Israel 170 L5
Afyon, Turk. 168 F6
Agadez, Niger 196 G12
Agadir, Mor. 196 C7
Agaete, Canary Is. 204 Q5
Agafo Gumas, Guam, U.S. 216 B11
Agalega Islands, Seychelles 205 Q20
Agana see Hagåtña, Guam, U.S. 216 C10
Agana Bay, Guam, U.S. 216 C10
Agana Heights, Guam, U.S. 216 C10
Agano, river, Japan 184 M12
Aga Point, Guam, U.S. 216 E10
Agar, India 178 H5
Agartala, India 178 H13
Agassiz Fracture Zone, Pac. Oc. 239 P14
Agat, Guam, U.S. 216 D10
Agata, Russ. 159 G14
Agat Bay, Guam, U.S. 216 C10
Agate, Colo., U.S. 106 M14
Agate Fossile Beds National Monument, Nebr., U.S. 105 N1
Agathoníssi, island, Gr. 155 K18
Agats, Indonesia 189 L20
Agatti Island, India 179 R2
Agattu Island, Alas., U.S. 110 L1
Agattu Strait, Alas., U.S. 110 L1
Agboville, Côte d'Ivoire 200 H9
Ağdam, Azerb. 169 E20
Agde, Fr. 147 Y11
Agde, Cap d', Fr. 147 Y11
Agen, Fr. 147 W8
Agfayan Bay, Guam, U.S. 216 E10
Aggtelek, Hung. 149 K16
Aghdash, Azerb. 169 D21
Aghjabädi, Azerb. 169 E21
Aghsu, Azerb. 169 D22
Agiá, Gr. 154 E11
Agia Galini, Gr. 155 Q14
Agia Napa, Cyprus 160 P10
Agía Pelagía, Gr. 154 N11
Agía Rouméli, Gr. 155 Q13
Agiássos, Gr. 155 G17
Agidyem, island, Marshall Is. 216 L8
Agingan, Puntan, N. Mariana Is., U.S. 216 C4
Aginskoye, Russ. 159 L17
Ágio Óros, peninsula, Gr. 155 D13
Agios Amvrosios, Cyprus 160 N9
Agios Efstrátios, Gr. 155 F14
Ágios Irínis, Akrotírio, Gr. 155 E15
Ágios Kírikos, Gr. 155 K16
Ágios Nikólaos, Gr. 155 Q16
Agios Sergios, Cyprus 160 N10
Agios Theodoros, Cyprus 160 N10
Agiou Orous, Kólpos, Gr. 154 D12
Agnes Creek, S. Aust., Austral. 211 U8
Agness, Oreg., U.S. 108 K2
Agnew, W. Aust., Austral. 211 V4
Agnita, Rom. 153 D14
Agnone, It. 150 K11
Agordat, Eritrea 199 D14
Agra, India 178 G6
Agrakhanskiy Poluostrov, Russ. 157 T15
Agrakhanskiy Zaliv, Russ. 157 T15
Ágreda, Sp. 145 D13
Ağrı, Turk. 169 E17
Agría Gramvoúsa, Gr. 154 P12
Ağrı Dağı (Mount Ararat), Turk. 169 E18
Agrigento, It. 151 T10
Agrihan, island, N. Mariana Is., U.S. 216 A2
Agropoli, It. 151 N11
Agrínio, Gr. 154 H8
Agryz, Russ. 156 H16
Ağstafa, Azerb. 169 C19
Aguada, P.R., U.S. 120 M1
Aguada de Pasajeros, Cuba 116 H8
Aguadilla, P.R., U.S. 120 M1
Aguadilla, Bahía de, P.R., U.S. 120 M1
Agua Fria National Monument, Ariz., U.S. 107 T7
Aguán, river, N. Amer. 80 P7
Aguapeí, Braz. 130 J9
Agua Prieta, Mex. 114 C8
Aguas Blancas, Chile 132 E7
Aguascalientes, Mex. 114 G10
Águas Formosas, Braz. 131 K16
A Gudiña, Sp. 144 D7
Águeda, Port. 144 F5
Aguelhok, Mali 196 G10
Aguijan, island, N. Mariana Is., U.S. 216 C2
Águila, Punta, P.R., U.S. 120 P1
Aguila, Ariz., U.S. 107 T6
Aguilar, Colo., U.S. 107 P14
Aguilar de Campoo, Sp. 144 C10
Aguilas, Sp. 145 L13
Aguja, Cabo de la, Col. 128 B5
Agulhas, Cape, S. Af. 202 M8
Agulhas Bank, Ind. Oc. 240 N1
Agulhas Basin, Ind. Oc. 240 Q1
Agulhas Plateau, Ind. Oc. 240 N2
Aguni Jima, Japan 185 Y1
Ahaggar (Hoggar), range, Alg. 196 E11
Ahar, Iran 172 A11
Aharnés, Gr. 154 J12
Ahe, island, Fr. Polynesia, Fr. 219 D17
Ahelóos, river, Gr. 154 H8
Ahiri, India 178 L7
Ahlat, Turk. 169 F17
Ahlatlıbel, ruin, Turk. 168 E8
Ahmadabad, India 178 J3
Ahmadnagar, India 178 L4
Ahmadpur East, Pak. 177 S9
Ahmad Wal, Pak. 177 S5
Ahoa, Wallis & Futuna, Fr. 218 B11
Ahome, Mex. 114 E7
Ahoskie, N.C., U.S. 96 G13
Ahram, Iran 173 G13
Ahrax Point, Malta 161 J21
Ahrensburg, Ger. 148 C8
Ahtme, Est. 141 K17
Ahua, Fr. Polynesia, Fr. 219 K20
Ahu-a-miria Islands, Cook Is., N.Z. 219 B18
Ahua 'Umi Heiau, Hawaii, U.S. 113 M19
Ahumoa, peak, Hawaii, U.S. 113 L19
Ahuna, Motu, Fr. Polynesia, Fr. 219 K13
Ahunui, island, Fr. Polynesia, Fr. 219 G20
Ahvāz, Iran 172 F11
Ahvenanmaa see Åland, island, Fin. 141 K14
Aḩwar, Yemen 172 R10
Ai, island, Marshall Is. 216 M7
'Aiea, Hawai'i, U.S. 112 E11
Aigialousa, Cyprus 160 M11
Aigle, Switz. 150 C2
Aigoual, Mont, Fr. 147 W11
Aiguá, Uru. 132 L14
Aigurande, Fr. 147 T9
Aikawa, Japan 184 M11
Aiken, S.C., U.S. 96 L8
Aileron, N. Terr., Austral. 211 T8
Ailinginae Atoll, Marshall Is. 216 F3
Ailinglapalap Atoll, Marshall Is. 216 H4
Ailsa Craig, Gibraltar, U.K. 161 Q23
Ailsa Craig, island, Scot., U.K. 143 N8
Ailuk Atoll, Marshall Is. 216 F4
Aimere, Indonesia 189 M13
Ainaži, Latv. 141 L16
Aineman, island, Marshall Is. 216 M9
Aïnhoa, Fr. 147 Y5
Aínsa, Sp. 145 C15
'Aïn Sefra, Alg. 196 B10
Ainsworth, Nebr., U.S. 105 N5
Aiquile, Bol. 130 K7
Aiquina, Chile 132 D8
Airai, Palau 216 N12
Airão, Braz. 130 D9
Air Force Island, Nunavut, Can. 83 F17
Aïr Massif, Niger 196 G12
Airolo, Switz. 150 C4
Aisey, Fr. 147 R12
Aitape, P.N.G. 213 C18
Aitkin, Minn., U.S. 104 G11
Aitutaki, island, Cook Is., N.Z. 218 P11
Aitutaki Atoll, Cook Is., N.Z. 214 K12
Aiud, Rom. 153 D13
Aiurua, Passe, Fr. Polynesia, Fr. 219 Q18
Aiwa, island, Fiji Is. 218 J9
Aiwo, region, Nauru 217 F22
Aiwokako Passage, Palau 216 M11
Aix, Île d', Fr. 147 T6
Aix-en-Provence, Fr. 147 X13
Aixirivall, Andorra 160 K2
Aix-les-Bains, Fr. 147 U14
Aiyon Mountain, Palau 216 L12
Aiyura, P.N.G. 213 D19
Aizawl, India 178 H14
Aizenay, Fr. 147 S5
Aizpute, Latv. 141 M15
Aizuwakamatsu, Japan 184 M12
Ajaccio, Fr. 150 K3
Ajaccio, Golfe d', Fr. 150 K3
Ajajú, river, Col. 128 H6
Ajaria, Rep. of Georgia 169 C16
Ajax Peak, Idaho, U.S. 106 E6
Ajayan Bay, Guam, U.S. 216 E10
Ajdābiyā, Lib. 197 C15
Ajigasawa, Japan 184 J12
Ajjer, Tassili-n-, Alg. 196 E12
'Ajlūn, Jordan 170 L6
'Ajmān, U.A.E. 173 J15
Ajmer, India 178 G4
Ajo, Ariz., U.S. 107 V6
Ajo, Cabo de, Sp. 144 B11
Ajokwola, island, Marshall Is. 216 G10
Ajoupa-Bouillon, Martinique, Fr. 121 E22
Ajrestan, Afghan. 177 N6
Akabira, Japan 184 F14
Akaiami, island, Cook Is., N.Z. 218 Q12
Akaka Falls, Hawai'i, U.S. 113 L21
Akaki, Cyprus 160 P8
Akamaru, island, Fr. Polynesia, Fr. 219 R21
Akankohan, Japan 184 F15
Akanthou, Cyprus 160 N9
Akashi, Japan 185 Q8
Akaska, S. Dak., U.S. 104 J5
Akbulak, Russ. 158 J7
Akçaabat, Turk. 169 D14
Akçadağ, Turk. 169 G13
Akçakale, Turk. 169 J13
Akçakışla, Turk. 168 E11
Akçakoca, Turk. 168 C7
Akçay, Turk. 168 E3
Akçay, Turk. 168 J5
Akchâr, region, Mauritania 196 F5
Akdağ, peak, Turk. 168 F2
Akdağ, peak, Turk. 168 J7
Ak Dağlar, Turk. 168 J5
Akdağmadeni, Turk. 168 E11
Akeley, Minn., U.S. 104 G10
Akera, river, Azerb. 169 E20
Aketi, Dem. Rep. of the Congo 198 J10
Akhalts'ikhe, Rep. of Georgia 169 C17
Akhḑar, Jabal al, Lib. 194 D7
Akhiok, Alas., U.S. 111 M15
Akhisar, Turk. 168 F3
Akhnur, India 177 N12
Akhtuba, river, Russ. 174 E4
Akhtubinsk, Russ. 157 Q14
Aki, Japan 185 R7
Akiachak, Alas., U.S. 110 J12
Akiaki, island, Fr. Polynesia, Fr. 219 F21
Akimiski Island, Nunavut, Can. 83 M17
Akita, Japan 184 K12
Akitua, island, Cook Is., N.Z. 218 P11
Akjoujt, Mauritania 196 F5
Akkeshi, Japan 184 F16
Akkeshi Wan, Japan 184 F16
'Akko (Acre), Israel 170 K5
Akkuş, Turk. 168 D12
Aklavik, N.W.T., Can. 82 E9
Aklera, India 178 H5
'Ako'ako'a Point, Hawai'i, U.S. 113 K19
Akobo, Sudan 199 G13
Ākobo, river, Eth. 199 G13
Akola, India 178 K5
Akosombo Dam, Ghana 200 H11
Akpatok Island, Nunavut, Can. 83 J19
Akqi, China 180 F5
Akranes, Ice. 140 F2
Akráta, Gr. 154 J10
Akron, Colo., U.S. 106 L15
Akron, Iowa, U.S. 104 M8
Akron, Ohio, U.S. 99 P14
Akrotiri, Gr. 155 N15
Akrotiri Bay, Cyprus 160 Q7
Akrotiri (Western) Sovereign Base Area, Cyprus 160 Q7
Aksai Chin, China 180 H4
Aksaray, Turk. 168 G9
Aksay, China 180 G9
Aksay, Russ. 157 Q13
Akşehir, Turk. 168 G7
Akşehir Gölü, Turk. 168 G7
Akseki, Turk. 168 H7
Aksu, China 180 F5
Aksu, Kaz. 174 J6
Aksu, river, Turk. 168 H6
Āksum, Eth. 199 E15
Aktag, peak, China 180 H6
Akto, China 180 F4
Akune, Japan 185 S4
Akureyri, Ice. 140 E3
Akuse, Ghana 200 H11
Akuseki Shima, Japan 185 V3
Akutan, Alas., U.S. 110 N10
Akyab see Sittwe, Myanmar 186 H4
Akyaka, Turk. 169 D17
Akyazı, Turk. 168 D6
Alà, Monti di, It. 150 M4
Ala, It. 150 D6
Alabama, river, Ala., U.S. 101 M14
Alabama, U.S. 101 K14
Alabaster, Ala., U.S. 101 K15
Alaca, Turk. 168 E10
Alaca Dağ, Turk. 168 H7
Alacahöyük, ruin, Turk. 168 E10
Alaçam, Turk. 168 C11
Alachua, Fla., U.S. 97 R7
Alacránes, Arrecife, Mex. 115 G16
Aladağ, peak, Turk. 168 G7
Aladağ, peak, Turk. 168 H10
Alaejos, Sp. 144 E9
Al Aflāj, region, Saudi Arabia 172 L10
Alagir, Russ. 157 U13
Alagoinhas, Braz. 131 H17
Alagón, Sp. 145 D14
Al Aḩmadī, Kuwait 172 G11
Alaja, Turkm. 174 L6
Alajuela, Costa Rica 115 N19
Alaka'i Swamp, Hawai'i, U.S. 112 B5
Alakanuk, Alas., U.S. 110 H12
Al Akhḑar, Saudi Arabia 172 G6
Alakoko Fishpond, Hawai'i, U.S. 112 C6
Alaköl, lake, Kaz. 175 F18
'Alalakeiki Channel, Hawai'i, U.S. 113 H16
Alalakh, ruin, Turk. 168 J11
Alamagan, island, N. Mariana Is., U.S. 216 B2
Al 'Amārah, Iraq 172 E11
Alameda, Calif., U.S. 109 S3
Alameda Gardens, Gibraltar, U.K. 161 P22
'Alam Lek, Afghan. 176 K5
Alamo, Nev., U.S. 109 S12
Alamo, Tenn., U.S. 100 F12
Alamogordo, N. Mex., U.S. 107 U13
Alamo Heights, Tex., U.S. 103 R9
Alamosa, Colo., U.S. 107 P12
Åland (Ahvenanmaa), island, Fin. 141 K14
Alandar, Afghan. 176 M4
Alandroal, Port. 144 J6
Alanya, Turk. 168 J7
Alao, Amer. Samoa, U.S. 218 M9
Alaotra, Lac, Madagascar 203 F18
Alappuzha see Alleppey, India 179 R5
Al 'Aqabah (Aqaba), Jordan 171 R5
Al 'Aqīq, Saudi Arabia 172 L8
Alara, river, Turk. 168 J7
Alarcón, Embalse de, Sp. 144 G12
Al 'Armah, plateau, Saudi Arabia 172 H10
Al Arṭāwīyah, Saudi Arabia 172 H10
Al 'Āṣ (Orontes), river, Syr. 170 F7
Al As'ad, Saudi Arabia 172 G6
Alaşehir, Turk. 168 F4
Al Ashkharah, Oman 173 L17
Alaska, U.S. 111 G14
Alaska, Gulf of, Alas., U.S. 111 L18
Alaska Highway, Alas., U.S. 111 G18
Alaska Peninsula, Alas., U.S. 110 M13
Alaska Range, Alas., U.S. 111 J15
Alassio, It. 150 G3
Alät, Azerb. 169 E23
Al 'Athāmīn, peak, Iraq 172 F9
Alatyr', Russ. 156 K13
Alausí, Ecua. 128 K3
Alava, Cape, Wash., U.S. 108 B1
Alaverdi, Arm. 169 D18
'Alawīyīn, Jabal al, Syr. 170 F7
Alāyat Samā'il, Oman 173 K16
Al 'Ayn, U.A.E. 173 J15
Alazani, river, Azerb., Rep. of Georgia 169 C20
Alba, It. 150 F3
Al Bāb, Syr. 170 D9
Albac, Rom. 152 C12
Albacete, Sp. 145 H13
Al Bad', Saudi Arabia 172 G5
Alba de Tormes, Sp. 144 F9
Al Badī', Saudi Arabia 172 L10
Al Bāḩah, Saudi Arabia 172 M8
Alba Iulia, Rom. 153 D13
Albanel, Lac, Que., Can. 83 M19
Albania, Eur. 139 X8
Albany, Ga., U.S. 97 P5
Albany, Ky., U.S. 101 D17
Albany, Mo., U.S. 105 R11
Albany, N.Y., U.S. 94 K11
Albany, river, Ont., Can. 83 N17
Albany, Oreg., U.S. 108 G3
Albany, Tex., U.S. 102 L8
Albany, W. Aust., Austral. 211 Y3
Al Bardī, Lib. 197 C17
Albardón, Arg. 132 J8
Albarracín, Sp. 145 F13
Al Başrah, Iraq 172 F11
Albatross Bay, Austral. 210 B12
Al Bayāḑ, plain, Saudi Arabia 172 L11
Al Bayḑā' (Beida), Lib. 197 B16
Albemarle see Isabela, Isla, island, Ecua. 128 Q8
Albemarle, Punta, Ecua. 128 P8
Albemarle Sound, N.C., U.S. 96 G14
Albenga, It. 150 G3
Albera, Serra de l', Fr. 147 Z10
Albereto, It. 161 K17
Alberobello, It. 150 M14
Albert, Lake, Austral. 210 L10
Albert, Lake, Dem. Rep. of the Congo, Uganda 198 J12
Alberta, Can. 82 L10
Albert Lea, Minn., U.S. 104 L11
Albert Nile, river, Uganda 199 J13
Albert Town, Bahamas 117 G14
Albert Town, Jam. 120 H8
Albertville, Ala., U.S. 101 H16
Albertville, Fr. 147 U14
Albi, Fr. 147 X10
Albia, Iowa, U.S. 105 Q12
Albin, Wyo., U.S. 106 K14
Albina Point, Angola 194 M6
Albini, river, It. 161 H14
Albinia, It. 150 J7
Albion, Ill., U.S. 99 T7
Albion, Mich., U.S. 98 M11
Albion, N.Y., U.S. 94 H6
Albion, Nebr., U.S. 105 P7
Al Bi'r, Saudi Arabia 172 G5
Al Birk, Saudi Arabia 172 N8
Alborán, Isla de, Sp. 144 N11
Alboran Sea, Sp. 144 N10
Ålborg, Den. 140 N11
Alborz, Reshteh-ye (Elburz Mountains), Iran 172 B11
Albox, Sp. 144 L12
Albuquerque, N. Mex., U.S. 107 S12
Alburquerque, Sp. 144 H7
Albury, N.S.W., Austral. 211 Y13
Alby, Fr. 147 U14
Alcácer do Sal, Port. 144 J5
Alcalá de Guadaira, Sp. 144 L8
Alcalá de Henares, Sp. 144 F11
Alcalá la Real, Sp. 144 L10
Alcamo, It. 151 S9
Alcanar, Sp. 145 F15
Alcañiz, Sp. 145 E15
Alcántara, Sp. 144 G7
Alcántara, Embalse de, Sp. 144 G7
Alcaraz, Sp. 144 J12
Alcaudete, Sp. 144 L10
Alcázar de San Juan, Sp. 144 H11
Alcedo, Volcán, Ecua. 128 Q8
Alchevs'k, Ukr. 157 Q10
Alcoa, Tenn., U.S. 101 F18
Alcoak, Cerro, Arg. 132 D8
Alcobaça, Port. 144 G5
Alcobendas, Sp. 144 F11
Alcoi see Alcoy, Sp. 145 J14
Alcoota, N. Terr., Austral. 211 T9
Alcorcón, Sp. 144 F11
Alcoutim, Port. 144 L6
Alcoy (Alcoi), Sp. 145 J14
Alcubierre, Sierra de, Sp. 145 D14
Alcúdia, Sp. 145 G18
Alcuéscar, Sp. 144 H8
Aldabra Islands, Seychelles 203 C17
Aldama, Mex. 114 D9
Aldan, river, Russ. 159 G18
Aldan, Russ. 159 J18
Aldanskoye Nagor'ye, Russ. 159 J18
Aldeadávila de la Ribera, Sp. 144 E7
Aldeburgh, Eng., U.K. 143 U16
Alderney, island, Ch. Is. 143 Y11
Aledo, Ill., U.S. 99 P3
Aleg, Mauritania 196 G5
Alegranza, island, Canary Is. 204 P8
Alegrete, Braz. 130 P10
Aleksandrov Gay, Russ. 157 N15
Aleksandrovsk Sakhalinskiy, Russ. 159 J21

Alekseyevka, Russ. 156 L14
Alekseyevka, Russ. 156 L16
Alekseyevka, Russ. 157 N10
Aleksin, Russ. 156 K9
Aleksinac, Serb. & Mont. 152 H11
Alemania, Arg. 132 F9
Alembel, island, Marshall Is. 216 H8
Alençon, Fr. 147 Q7
Alenquer, Braz. 130 D11
ʻAlenuihāhā Channel, Hawaiʻi, U.S. 113 J18
Aleppo see Ḩalab, Syr. 170 D9
Aléria, Fr. 150 K4
Alert, Nunavut, Can. 83 A16
Alert Point, Kiribati 217 B20
Alès, Fr. 147 W12
Ales, It. 151 P3
Alessandria, It. 150 E4
Ålesund, Nor. 140 J10
Aleutian Basin, Pac. Oc. 238 B9
Aleutian Islands, Alas., U.S. 111 L2
Aleutian Range, Alas., U.S. 111 M13
Aleutian Trench, Pac. Oc. 238 C9
Alevina, Mys, Russ. 159 F21
Alexander, N. Dak., U.S. 104 F2
Alexander, Cape, Solomon Is. 217 K15
Alexander Archipelago, Alas., U.S. 111 M22
Alexander Bay, S. Af. 202 K6
Alexander City, Ala., U.S. 101 K16
Alexander Island, Antarctica 226 F5
Alexandra, N.Z. 213 Q16
Alexandra, Zemlya, Russ. 158 B12
Alexándria, Gr. 154 C10
Alexandria see El Iskandarîya, Egypt 197 C18
Alexandria, Ind., U.S. 99 Q9
Alexandria, Jam. 120 H8
Alexandria, La., U.S. 100 N8
Alexandria, Minn., U.S. 104 H9
Alexandria, Rom. 153 G15
Alexandria, S. Dak., U.S. 104 L7
Alexandria, Va., U.S. 96 D13
Alexandria Bay, N.Y., U.S. 94 G9
Alexandrina, Lake, Austral. 210 L10
Alexandroúpoli (Dedéagach), Gr. 155 C16
Aley, Leb. 170 J6
Aleysk, Russ. 158 L11
Al Fallūjah, Iraq 172 D9
Al Farciya, W. Sahara, Mor. 196 D7
Alfaro, Sp. 145 D13
Alfatar, Bulg. 153 G16
Al Fāw, Iraq 172 F11
Alföld see Great Hungarian Plain, plain, Hung., Serb. & Mont. 149 M16
Al Fujayrah, U.A.E. 173 J15
Al Fuqahā', Lib. 197 D14
Al Furāt (Euphrates), river, Iraq 172 F10
Algarrobal, Arg. 132 F10
Algarrobo, Chile 132 G7
Algeciras, Sp. 144 N8
Algeciras, Bahía de see Gibraltar, Bay of, Gibraltar, U.K. 161 P21
Algena, Eritrea 199 D15
Alger (Algiers), Alg. 196 A11
Algeria, Af. 195 E16
Algha, Kaz. 174 D8
Alghabas, Kaz. 174 D6
Al Ghayḑah, Yemen 173 P13
Al Ghayl, Saudi Arabia 172 K10
Al Ghazālah, Saudi Arabia 172 H8
Alghero, It. 150 M3
Algiers see Alger, Alg. 196 A11
Alginet, Sp. 145 H14
Algoa Bay, S. Af. 194 R8
Algoma, Wis., U.S. 98 J7
Algona, Iowa, U.S. 104 M11
Algorta, Uru. 132 K13
Al Ḩadīdah, crater, Saudi Arabia 172 L12
Al Ḩaffah, Syr. 170 F7
Al Ḩamād, desert, Jordan, Saudi Arabia 172 E7
Alhambra, Calif., U.S. 109 X8
Al Ḩamīdīyah, Syr. 170 G7
Al Ḩamrā', Saudi Arabia 172 K6
Al Ḩamrā', region, Lib. 197 C13
Al Ḩanākīyah, Saudi Arabia 172 J7
Al Ḩarīq, Saudi Arabia 172 K10
Al Harūj al Aswad, range, Lib. 197 D15
Al Ḩasakah, Syr. 170 D14
Al Ḩawrah, Yemen 172 Q11
Al Hījānah, Syr. 170 K7
Al Ḩijāz (Hejaz), region, Saudi Arabia 172 H6
Al Ḩillah, Iraq 172 E9
Al Ḩillah, Saudi Arabia 172 K10
Alhucemas, Peñón de, Sp. 144 P10
Al Ḩudaydah, Yemen 172 Q8
Al Hufūf, Saudi Arabia 172 J12
Alì, It. 151 S12
Aliabad, Iran 173 G15
Aliákmonas, river, Gr. 154 D10
Alibates Flint Quarries National Monument, Tex., U.S. 102 G5
Äli Bayramlı, Azerb. 169 E22
Alicante, Sp. 145 J14
Alice, Qnsld., Austral. 211 T13
Alice, Tex., U.S. 103 U10
Alice, Punta, It. 151 P14
Alice Downs, W. Aust., Austral. 211 R6
Alice Springs, N. Terr., Austral. 211 T8
Alice Town, Bahamas 120 B8
Alice Town, Bahamas 120 D6
Aliceville, Ala., U.S. 101 K13
Alicudi, Isola, It. 151 R11
Aligarh, India 178 F6
Alijos, Rocas, Mex. 114 E4
Alijos Rocks see Alijos, Rocas, N. Amer. 80 M2
ʻĀlika Cone, Hawaiʻi, U.S. 113 N19
Al Ikhwān (The Brothers), islands, Yemen 173 R14
Alindau, Indonesia 189 J13
Alingsås, Sw. 140 M12
Alipur, Pak. 177 S9
Alipur Duar, India 178 G12
Aliquippa, Pa., U.S. 94 N3
Al ʻIrqah, Yemen 172 R11
Alişar Hüyük, ruin, Turk. 168 E10
Al ʻĪsāwīyah, Saudi Arabia 172 F6
Alissós, Gr. 154 J9
Alistráti, Gr. 155 B13
Alivéri, Gr. 155 H13
Aliwal North, S. Af. 202 L10
Alizai, Pak. 177 N9
Al Jafr, Jordan 171 Q7
Al Jāfūrah, desert, Saudi Arabia 172 J12
Al Jaghbūb, Lib. 197 C16
Al Jahrah, Kuwait 172 G11
Al Jawādīyah, Syr. 170 C15
Al Jawf see Dawmat al Jandal, Saudi Arabia 172 F7
Al Jawf (Kufra Oasis), Lib. 197 E16
Al Jifārah, Saudi Arabia 172 K10
Al Jīzah, Jordan 170 M7
Al Jubayl, Saudi Arabia 172 H12
Al Jumaylīyah, Qatar 173 J13
Al Junaynah, Saudi Arabia 172 M8
Al Junaynah see Geneina, Sudan 198 E10
Al Kahfah, Saudi Arabia 172 H9
Al Karak, Jordan 171 N6
Al Kawm, Syr. 170 F11
Al Khābūrah, Oman 173 K16
Al Khalīl (Hebron), W. Bank 171 N5
Al Kharfah, Saudi Arabia 172 L10
Al Kharj, Saudi Arabia 172 K11
Al Khāṣirah, Saudi Arabia 172 K9
Al Khawr, Qatar 173 J13
Al Khīrān, Kuwait 172 G11
Al Khufayfīyah, Saudi Arabia 172 J9
Al Khums, Lib. 197 B14
Al Khunn, Saudi Arabia 172 K12
Al Khuraybah, Yemen 172 Q11
Al Khurmah, Saudi Arabia 172 L8
Al Kiswah, Syr. 170 J7
Al Kūfah, Iraq 172 E9
Al Kufrah, region, Lib. 197 E16
Al Kūt, Iraq 172 E10
Al Kuwayt (Kuwait), Kuwait 172 G11
Al Labwah, Leb. 170 H7
Al Lādhiqīyah (Latakia), Syr. 170 F6
Allagash, river, Me., U.S. 95 B16
Allahüekber Tepe, Turk. 169 D17
Allahabad, India 178 H8
Al Lajā, desert, Syr. 170 K7
Allakaket, Alas., U.S. 111 E16
All American Canal, Calif., U.S. 109 Z12
Allan Hills, Antarctica 227 N14
Allan Mountain, Idaho, U.S. 106 E5
Allanmyo, Myanmar 186 J5
Allanton, N.Z. 213 R16
Allariz, Sp. 144 C6
Allegan, Mich., U.S. 98 M9
Allegheny, river, Pa., U.S. 94 N4
Allegheny Mountains, U.S. 85 H18
Allegheny Reservoir, Pa., U.S. 94 L5
Allègre, Pointe, Guadeloupe, Fr. 121 E14
Allen, Arg. 133 P8
Allen, Bog of, Ire. 143 S6
Allen, Lough, Ire. 143 Q5
Allendale, S.C., U.S. 96 M8
Allendale Town, Eng., U.K. 143 P11
Allende, Mex. 114 D11
Allentown, Pa., U.S. 94 N9
Alleppey (Alappuzha), India 179 R5
Aller, river, Ger. 148 D8
Allerona, It. 150 J8
Alliance, Nebr., U.S. 105 N2
Alliance, Ohio, U.S. 99 P15
Al Lidām, Saudi Arabia 172 M9
Alligator Pond, Jam. 120 J8
Allinge, Den. 141 P13
Allison Peninsula, Antarctica 226 H6
Al Līth, Saudi Arabia 172 M7
All Saints, Antigua & Barbuda 121 B21
Al Luḩayyah, Yemen 172 P8
Al Luwaymī, Saudi Arabia 172 G8
Alma, Ark., U.S. 100 F6
Alma, Ga., U.S. 97 P7
Alma, Kans., U.S. 105 S9
Alma, Mich., U.S. 98 L11
Alma, Nebr., U.S. 105 R5
Almacelles, Sp. 145 D15
Almada, Port. 144 J4
Almadén, Sp. 144 J9
Almaden, Qnsld., Austral. 211 R13
Al Madīnah (Medina), Saudi Arabia 172 J7
Al Mafraq, Jordan 170 L7
Al Majmaʻah, Saudi Arabia 172 J10
Al Mālikīyah, Syr. 170 C16
Al Manāmah (Manama), Bahrain 172 H12
Almanor, Lake, Calif., U.S. 109 N5
Almansa, Sp. 145 J14
Al Manşūrah, Syr. 170 E11
Almanzor, peak, Sp. 144 F9
Almar, Afghan. 176 L4
Al Marj, Lib. 197 C15
Al Maʻshūqah, Saudi Arabia 172 M8
Almaty, Kaz. 175 H16
Al Mawşil (Mosul), Iraq 172 C9
Al Mayādīn, Syr. 170 G13
Al Mayyāh, Saudi Arabia 172 G9
Almazán, Sp. 144 E12
Almeida, Port. 144 F7
Almeirim, Port. 144 H5
Almeirim, Braz. 130 D12
Almelo, Neth. 146 H14
Almena, Kans., U.S. 105 R5
Almenara, peak, Sp. 144 J12
Almenara, Braz. 131 J16
Almendra, Embalse de, Sp. 144 E8
Almendralejo, Sp. 144 J8
Almere, Neth. 146 J12
Almería, Sp. 144 M12
Almería, Golfo de, Sp. 144 M12
Al'met'yevsk, Russ. 156 J16
Almina, Punta, Sp. 144 N9
Al Mintirib, Oman 173 K16
Almira, Wash., U.S. 108 C7
Almirantazgo, Seno, Chile 133 X8
Almirante, Pan. 115 N20
Almirí, Gr. 154 J11
Almirós, Gr. 154 F11
Al Mismīyah, Syr. 170 K7
Almo, Idaho, U.S. 106 J6
Almodôvar, Port. 144 K5
Almodóvar del Campo, Sp. 144 J10
Al Mubarraz, Saudi Arabia 172 J12
Al Mudawwarah, Jordan 171 S7
Almudévar, Sp. 145 D14
Al Mughayrā', U.A.E. 173 K14
Al Mukallā, Yemen 172 Q12
Al Mukhā, Yemen 172 R8
Almuñécar, Sp. 144 M11
Almus, Turk. 168 D12
Almus Barajı, Turk. 168 D12
Al Muwassam, Saudi Arabia 172 P8
Al Muwayh, Saudi Arabia 172 K8
Alney, Gora, Russ. 159 F22
Alnwick, Eng., U.K. 143 N12
Alo, Wallis & Futuna, Fr. 218 E11
Alo, Pointe d', Wallis & Futuna, Fr. 218 E11
Alofau, Amer. Samoa, U.S. 218 M8
Alofi, island, Wallis & Futuna, Fr. 218 F11
Alofi, Niue, N.Z. 219 B20
Alofi Bay, Niue, N.Z. 219 B20
Alokan, island, Solomon Is. 217 N18
Along, India 178 F15
Alónissos, island, Gr. 154 F12
Alónissos, Gr. 154 G12
Alor, island, Indonesia 189 M15
Alor, Kepulauan, Indonesia 189 M15
Alora, Sp. 144 M9
Alor Setar, Malaysia 187 S8
Aloysius, Mount, Austral. 210 G7
Alpena, Mich., U.S. 98 H12
Alpha Cordillera, Arctic Oc. 242 K10
Alpine, Ariz., U.S. 107 T9
Alpine, Tex., U.S. 103 Q2
Alpine Junction, Wyo., U.S. 106 H8
Alps, range, Eur. 138 H6
Al Qābil, Oman 173 K15
Al Qaḑīmah, Saudi Arabia 172 K7
Al Qadmūs, Syr. 170 F7
Al Qā'im, Iraq 172 D8
Al Qaʻīyah, Saudi Arabia 172 J9
Al Qāmishlī, Syr. 170 C15
Al Qārah, Yemen 172 Q10
Al Qaryah ash Sharqīyah, Lib. 197 C13
Al Qaryatayn, Syr. 170 H9
Al Qaşīm, region, Saudi Arabia 172 H9
Al Qaţīf, Saudi Arabia 172 H12
Al Qaţrānah, Jordan 171 N7
Al Qaţrūn, Lib. 197 E14
Al Qayşūmah, Saudi Arabia 172 G10
Al Queayfah, Syr. 170 J8
Alqueva, Barragem de, Port. 144 J6
Al Qunayeirah (El Quneitra), Syr. 170 K6
Al Qunfudhah, Saudi Arabia 172 M7
Al Qurayyat, Saudi Arabia 172 E6
Al Qurnah, Iraq 172 F11
Al Quşayr, Syr. 170 G8
Al Quşūrīyah, Saudi Arabia 172 K9
Al Quwayʻīyah, Saudi Arabia 172 K10
Al Quwayrah, Jordan 171 R5
Alroy Downs, N. Terr., Austral. 211 R9
Alsace, region, Fr. 147 Q15
Alsask, Sask., Can. 82 M11
Alsasua, Sp. 144 B12
Alston, Eng., U.K. 143 P11
Alta, Iowa, U.S. 105 N9
Alta, Nor. 141 C14
Alta Floresta, Braz. 130 G10
Alta Gracia, Arg. 132 J10
Altagracia, Venez. 128 B7
Altagracia de Orituco, Venez. 128 B10
Altamaha, river, Ga., U.S. 97 P8
Altamira, Chile 132 F7
Altamira, Braz. 130 D12
Altamura, It. 150 M13
Altan Xiret see Ejin Horo Qi, China 182 D3
Altar Desert, N. Amer. 80 L3
Altata, Mex. 114 F8
Altavista, Va., U.S. 96 F11
Altay, China 180 D8
Altay, Mongolia 180 D10
Altay Mountains, Russ. 158 M12
Altayskiy, Russ. 158 L12
Alt del Griu, Andorra 160 J4
Altdorf, Switz. 150 B4
Altea, Sp. 145 J15
Altenburg, Ger. 148 F9
Alter do Chão, Port. 144 H6
Altıağac, Azerb. 169 C22
Altinekin, Turk. 168 G8
Altınhisar, Turk. 168 G9
Altıntaş, Turk. 168 F6
Altınyayla, Turk. 168 H5
Altiplano, region, S. Amer. 126 H4
Altmühl, river, Ger. 148 J8
Altnaharra, Scot., U.K. 142 H9
Alto, Tex., U.S. 103 N14
Alto, Pico, Azores 144 P3
Alto Araguaia, Braz. 130 J11
Alto Garças, Braz. 130 J11
Alto Molócuè, Mozambique 203 E14
Alton, Ill., U.S. 99 S4
Altona, Virgin Islands, U.S. 120 N9
Altona Lagoon, Virgin Islands, U.S. 120 Q3
Altoona, Pa., U.S. 94 N5
Alto Paraguai, Braz. 130 H10
Alto Parnaíba, Braz. 131 G14
Alto Purús, river, Peru 130 G5
Alto Río Senguerr, Arg. 133 S7
Altun Shan, China 180 G7
Alturas, Calif., U.S. 108 L5
Altus, Okla., U.S. 102 H8
Al ʻUbaylah, Saudi Arabia 172 L12
Al Ubayyiḑ see El Obeid, Sudan 198 E12
Alucra, Turk. 169 E13
Al ʻUlá, Saudi Arabia 172 H6
Al ʻUnnāb, site, Jordan 171 R8
Al Uqaylah, Lib. 197 C15
Alushta, Ukr. 157 T8
Aluta, Dem. Rep. of the Congo 198 K11
Al ʻUwaynāt, Lib. 197 E13
Al ʻUwaynid, Saudi Arabia 172 J10
Al ʻUwayqīlah, Saudi Arabia 172 F8
Al ʻUyūn, Saudi Arabia 172 J7
Alva, Okla., U.S. 102 E9
Alvarado, Tex., U.S. 102 M11
Älvdalen, Sw. 140 J12
Alverca do Ribatejo, Port. 144 H4
Alvesta, Sw. 141 M13
Alvin, Tex., U.S. 103 R14
Älvkarleby, Sw. 141 K13
Alvorada, Braz. 131 H13
Alvord, Tex., U.S. 102 K10
Alvord Desert, Oreg., U.S. 108 K8
Alvord Lake, Oreg., U.S. 108 K8
Al Wajh, Saudi Arabia 172 H5
Al Wannān, Saudi Arabia 172 H11
Alwar, India 178 F5
Al Wudayʻah, Saudi Arabia 172 P11
Alxa Zuoqi, China 180 H12
Alytus, Lith. 141 N17
Alzada, Mont., U.S. 106 F13
Alzamay, Russ. 159 K14
Alzette, river, Lux. 160 J10
Alzey, Ger. 148 H6
Alzira, Sp. 145 H14
Ama, Japan 185 P6
Amadeus, Lake, Austral. 210 F7
Amadeus Depression, Austral. 210 F7
Amadi, Sudan 198 H12
Amadjuak Lake, Nunavut, Can. 83 G18
Amadora, Port. 144 H4
Amagi, Japan 185 R4
Amahai, Indonesia 189 K16
Amakusa Shotō, Japan 185 S4
Åmål, Sw. 140 L12
Amalfi, It. 150 M11
Amaliáda, Gr. 154 J8
Amamapare, Indonesia 189 L20
Amambaí, Braz. 130 M11
Amami Guntō, Japan 185 X3
Amami Ō Shima, Japan 185 W3
Amamula, Dem. Rep. of the Congo 198 K11
Amanave, Amer. Samoa, U.S. 218 M6
Amandola, It. 150 J9
Amangeldi, Kaz. 174 D11
Amantea, It. 151 Q13
Amanu, island, Fr. Polynesia, Fr. 219 F20
Amapá, Braz. 130 B12
Amarante, Port. 144 E6
Amarante, Braz. 131 F15
Amargosa Range, Calif., U.S. 109 U10
Amarillo, Tex., U.S. 102 G5
Amarkantak, India 178 J8
Amarwara, India 178 J7
Amasa, Mich., U.S. 98 F6
Amasra, Turk. 168 C8
Amasya, Turk. 168 D11
Amata, S. Aust., Austral. 211 U7
Amatari, Braz. 130 D9
Amathous, ruin, Cyprus 160 Q8
Amatrice, It. 150 J9
Amatuku, island, Tuvalu 217 J23
Amatusuk Hills, Alas., U.S. 111 C13
Amavon Islands, Solomon Is. 217 L16
Amazon (Solimões), river, S. Amer. 126 D8
Amazon, Mouths of the, S. Amer. 126 C8
Amazon, Source of the, S. Amer. 126 G3
Amazonas, river, S. Amer. 126 D8
Amazon Basin, S. Amer. 126 D4
Ambajogai, India 178 L5
Ambala, India 178 E6
Ambalangoda, Sri Lanka 179 T7
Ambalantota, Sri Lanka 179 T8
Ambanja, Madagascar 203 E18
Ambarchik, Russ. 159 C19
Ambargasta, Salinas de, Arg. 132 H10
Ambato, Ecua. 128 J3
Ambatondrazaka, Madagascar 203 F18
Ambelákia, Gr. 154 E10
Ambelau, island, Indonesia 189 K16
Amberg, Ger. 148 H9
Ambergris Cay, Belize 115 J17
Ambergris Cays, Turks & Caicos Is., U.K. 117 J17
Ambi, Solomon Is. 217 R23

Ambikapur, India 178 J9
Ambilobe, Madagascar 203 D18
Amble, Eng., U.K. 143 N12
Ambler, Alas., U.S. 111 E14
Ambo, Peru 130 G3
Ambo Channel, Marshall Is. 216 M5
Amboise, Fr. 147 R8
Ambon, island, Indonesia 189 K16
Ambon, Indonesia 189 K16
Ambositra, Madagascar 203 G17
Ambovombe, Madagascar 203 J16
Amboy, Calif., U.S. 109 W11
Amboy Crater, Calif., U.S. 109 W11
Ambre, Cap d', Madagascar 203 D18
Ambriz, Angola 202 C5
Ambrym, island, Vanuatu 218 D3
Ambunti, P.N.G. 213 C18
Amburan Burnu, Azerb. 169 D23
Amchitka Island, Alas., U.S. 110 N3
Amchitka Pass, Alas., U.S. 110 N4
Am Dam, Chad 197 J15
Amderma, Russ. 158 E11
Amdi, India 178 H8
Ameca, Mex. 114 H9
Ameland, island, Neth. 146 G13
Amelia Island, Fla., U.S. 97 Q8
America-Antarctica Ridge, Antarctic Oc. 244 D10
American Falls, Idaho, U.S. 106 H6
American Falls Reservoir, Idaho, U.S. 106 H6
American Highland, Antarctica 227 G19
American Samoa, U.S., Pac. Oc. 214 J10
Americus, Ga., U.S. 97 N5
Amersfoort, Neth. 146 J13
Amery, Wis., U.S. 98 H2
Amery Ice Shelf, Antarctica 227 F19
Ames, Iowa, U.S. 105 N11
Amfilohía, Gr. 154 G8
Amfípoli, Gr. 154 C12
Amfissa, Gr. 154 H10
Amga, river, Russ. 159 H18
Amga, Russ. 159 H18
Amguema, Russ. 159 B20
Amguid, Alg. 196 D11
Amhara, region, Eth. 199 F15
Amherst, N.S., Can. 83 P22
Amherst, N.Y., U.S. 94 J5
Amherst, Tex., U.S. 102 J4
Amherst, Va., U.S. 96 E11
Ami, Île, New Caledonia, Fr. 218 E9
Amidon, N. Dak., U.S. 104 G2
Amiens, Fr. 146 M10
Amik Gölü, Turk. 168 J11
Amíndeo, Gr. 154 C9
Amindivi Islands, India 179 Q3
Amino, Japan 185 P8
Aminuis, Namibia 202 H7
Amioûn, Leb. 170 H6
Amir, river, Afghan. 176 L6
Amirante Trench, Ind. Oc. 240 H6
Amir Chah, Pak. 177 S2
Amistad, Presa de la, Mex. 114 D11
Amistad National Recreation Area, Tex., U.S. 103 R6
Amistad Reservoir, Tex., U.S. 103 R5
Amite, La., U.S. 100 N10
Amity, Ark., U.S. 100 H7
Åmli, Nor. 140 L11
Amlia Island, Alas., U.S. 110 P6
'Ammān (Philadelphia), Jordan 170 M7
Ammaroo, N. Terr., Austral. 211 S9
Ammochostos (Famagusta, Gazimağusa), Cyprus 160 P10
Ammochostos Bay, Cyprus 160 N10
'Amol, Iran 173 C13
Amolar, Braz. 130 K10
Amorgós, island, Gr. 155 M16
Amorgós, Gr. 155 M16
Amory, Miss., U.S. 101 J13
Amos, Que., Can. 83 P18
Amoy see Xiamen, China 183 Q7
Ampani, India 178 L8
Ampanihy, Madagascar 203 J16
Ampere Seamount, Atl. Oc. 236 H11
Ampezzo, It. 150 C9
Amphitrite Group, China 188 B10
Amplepuis, Fr. 147 T12
Amposta, Sp. 145 F15
'Amrān, Yemen 172 P9
Amravati, India 178 K6
Amreli, India 178 J2
'Amrīt (Marathus), ruin, Syr. 170 G7
Amritsar, India 177 Q12
Amsā'ad, Lib. 197 C17
Amsterdam, island, Ind. Oc. 240 N10
Amsterdam, N.Y., U.S. 94 J11
Amsterdam, Neth. 146 J12
Amsterdam, Île, Ind. Oc. 204 J10
Amstetten, Aust. 148 K11
Am Timan, Chad 197 J15
'Āmūdah, Syr. 170 C14
Amu Darya (Oxus), river, Turkm. 174 M11
Amuderýa, Turkm. 174 M11
Amukta Island, Alas., U.S. 110 P7
Amun, P.N.G. 217 K13
Amund Ringnes Island, Nunavut, Can. 83 C15
Amundsen Bay, Antarctica 227 C19
Amundsen Gulf, N.W.T., Can. 82 E11
Amundsen-Scott South Pole, station, Antarctica 226 J12
Amundsen Sea, Antarctica 226 L6
Amuntai, Indonesia 188 K11
Amur, river, Asia 166 D12
Amurang, Indonesia 189 H15
Amuri, Cook Is., N.Z. 218 P11
Amur-Onon, Source of the, Mongolia 166 F10
Amursk, Russ. 159 K21
Amvrakía see Árta, Gr. 154 F8
Amvrakikós Kolpos, Gr. 154 G8
Amvrosiyivka, Ukr. 157 Q10
An, Myanmar 186 H5
Anaa, island, Fr. Polynesia, Fr. 219 E18
Anabar, region, Nauru 217 E23
Anabar, river, Russ. 159 F15
Anabarskiy Zaliv, Russ. 159 E15
Anacapa Islands, Calif., U.S. 109 X7
Anaco, Venez. 128 C11
Anacoco, La., U.S. 100 N7
Anaconda, Mont., U.S. 106 E6
Anacortes, Wash., U.S. 108 B4
Anadarko, Okla., U.S. 102 H10
Anadyr, Gulf of, Russ. 166 A12
Anadyr', river, Russ. 166 B12
Anadyr', Russ. 159 B21
Anadyrskiy Zaliv, Russ. 159 B21
Anadyrskoye Ploskogor'ye, Russ. 159 C20
Anae, island, Guam, U.S. 216 D10
'Anaeho'omalu Bay, Hawaii, U.S. 113 L18
Anáfi, island, Gr. 155 N16
Anáfi, Gr. 155 N16
Anaga, Punta de, Canary Is. 204 Q5
Anagni, It. 150 L9
'Ānah, Iraq 172 D8
Anaheim, Calif., U.S. 109 X9
Anahola, Hawaii, U.S. 112 B6
Anahuac, Tex., U.S. 103 Q15
Anai Mudi, peak, India 179 R5
Anak, N. Korea 182 E12
Anakapalle, India 178 M9
Anaktuvuk Pass, Alas., U.S. 111 D16
Analalava, Madagascar 203 E17
Anamã, Braz. 130 D8
Ana María, Cayos, Cuba 116 J10
Ana María, Golfo de, Cuba 116 J10
Anambas, Kepulauan, Indonesia 188 H8
Anamoose, N. Dak., U.S. 104 F5
Anamosa, Iowa, U.S. 105 N14
Anamur, Turk. 168 J8
Anamur Burnu, Turk. 168 K8
Anan, Japan 185 R8
Anand, India 178 J3
Anan'evo, Kyrg. 176 D13
Anangenimon, island, F.S.M. 217 B16
Ananij, island, Marshall Is. 216 H9
Anantapur, India 179 P6
Anantnag (Islamabad), India 177 N12
Anapa, Russ. 157 T9
Anápolis, Braz. 131 J13
Anār, Iran 173 F14
Anārak, Iran 173 D14
Anar Darreh, Afghan. 177 P2
Anatahan, island, N. Mariana Is., U.S. 216 C2
Anatolia (Asia Minor), region, Turk. 168 F5
Anatom (Kéamu), island, Vanuatu 218 H4
Anatone, Wash., U.S. 108 E9
Añatuya, Arg. 132 H11
Anboru, island, Marshall Is. 216 L8
Anbyŏn, N. Korea 182 D13
Ancenis, Fr. 147 R6
Anchorage, Alas., U.S. 111 J16
Anchor Bay, Calif., U.S. 109 Q2
Anclitas, Cayo, Cuba 116 K10
Ancona, It. 150 H9
Ancón de Sardinas, Bahía de, Col., Ecua. 128 H3
Ancud, Chile 133 Q6
Andacollo, Arg. 133 N7
Andalgalá, Arg. 132 G9
Åndalsnes, Nor. 140 J10
Andalusia, Ala., U.S. 101 N16
Andalusia, region, Sp. 144 K9
Andaman and Nicobar Islands, India 179 Q15
Andaman Basin, Ind. Oc. 240 E12
Andaman Islands, India 179 Q15
Andaman Sea, Ind. Oc. 166 K10
Andamooka, S. Aust., Austral. 211 W10
Andapa, Madagascar 203 E18
Andelot-Blancheville, Fr. 147 Q13
Andenes, Nor. 140 D12
Andermatt, Switz. 150 B4
Andernach, Ger. 148 G5
Andersen Air Force Base, Guam, U.S. 216 B12
Anderson, Alas., U.S. 111 G16
Anderson, Calif., U.S. 109 N3
Anderson, Ind., U.S. 99 R9
Anderson, Mo., U.S. 105 V11
Anderson, river, N.W.T., Can. 82 E11
Anderson, S.C., U.S. 96 K7
Andes, range, S. Amer. 126 D2
Andfjorden, bay, Nor. 140 D12
Andicuri Bay, Aruba, Neth. 121 Q17
Andijon, Uzb. 175 K14
Andikíthira, island, Gr. 154 P11
Andimáhia, Gr. 155 M18
Andípaxi, island, Gr. 154 F6
Andipsara, island, Gr. 155 H15
Andırın, Turk. 168 H11
Andkhvoy, Afghan. 176 K4
Andoany (Hell-Ville), Madagascar 203 D18
Andoas, Peru 130 D3
Andorra, region, Andorra 160 K3
Andorra, Eur. 160 D2
Andorra, Sp. 145 E14
Andorra la Vella, Andorra 160 J3
Andover, Me., U.S. 95 F15
Andovoranto, Madagascar 203 G18
Andøya, island, Nor. 140 D12
Andradina, Braz. 130 L12
Andreanof Islands, Alas., U.S. 110 P5
Andreapol', Russ. 156 H7
Andrew Johnson National Historic Site, Tenn., U.S. 101 E20
Andrews, N.C., U.S. 96 J5
Andrews, S.C., U.S. 96 L11
Andrews, Tex., U.S. 102 M4
Andrijevica, Serb. & Mont. 152 J9
Androka, Madagascar 203 J16
Ándros, island, Gr. 155 J14
Andros, Gr. 155 J14
Andros Island, Bahamas 116 E11
Andros Town, Bahamas 116 E11
Androth Island, India 179 R3
Andrychów, Pol. 149 H15
Andryushkino, Russ. 159 D19
Andselv, Nor. 141 D13
Andújar, Sp. 144 K10
Anefis I-n-Darane, Mali 196 G10
Anegada, island, Virgin Islands, U.K. 119 E14
Anegada, Bahía, Arg. 133 P11
Anegada Passage, Lesser Antilles 119 F14
Anécho, Togo 200 H11
Aneju, island, Marshall Is. 216 G10
Anelghowhat, Vanuatu 218 H4
Anelghowhat Bay, Vanuatu 218 H4
Anemwanot, island, Marshall Is. 216 G11
Anenelibw, island, Marshall Is. 216 H11
Anengenipuan, island, F.S.M. 217 B16
Aneta, N. Dak., U.S. 104 F7
Anetan, region, Nauru 217 E23
Aneto, peak, Sp. 145 C15
Aney, Niger 197 G13
Anfu, China 183 N5
Angamos, Punta, Chile 132 E6
Angara, river, Russ. 166 E9
Angarei, island, Cook Is., N.Z. 218 Q11
Angarsk, Russ. 159 L15
Angaur (Ngeaur), island, Palau 216 R10
Ånge, Sw. 141 J13
Ángel de la Guarda, Isla, Mex. 114 C6
Angeles, P.R., U.S. 120 N2
Angeles, Philippines 189 C13
Angel Falls, Venez. 128 E12
Angelina, river, Tex., U.S. 103 N14
Angels Camp, Calif., U.S. 109 R5
Ångermanälven, river, Sw. 141 G13
Angers, Fr. 147 R7
Angerville, Fr. 147 Q9
Angkor, ruin, Cambodia 186 M11
Angle Inlet, Minn., U.S. 104 D9
Anglem, Mount, N.Z. 213 R15
Anglesey, island, Wales, U.K. 143 S9
Anglet, Fr. 147 X5
Angleton, Tex., U.S. 103 R14
Anglure, Fr. 147 P11
Ango, Dem. Rep. of the Congo 198 H11
Angoche, Mozambique 203 F15
Angoche, Ilha, Mozambique 203 F15
Angohrān, Iran 173 H16
Angol, Chile 133 N6
Angola, Af. 195 M19
Angola, Ind., U.S. 99 N10
Angola Plain, Atl. Oc. 237 Q13
Angoon, Alas., U.S. 111 L22
Angora see Ankara, Turk. 168 E8
Angoram, P.N.G. 213 C18
Angostura, Presa de la, Mex. 115 K14
Angoulême, Fr. 147 U7
Angra do Heroísmo, Azores 144 P4
Angren, Uzb. 175 K14
Angtassom, Cambodia 187 P11
Anguilla, island, U.K., Lesser Antilles 119 F15
Anguilla Cays, Bahamas 116 F9
Anguillita Island, Anguilla, U.K. 120 R10
Angul, India 178 K10
Anguo, China 182 E6
Angvik, Nor. 140 J10
Anhai, China 183 Q8
Anholt, island, Den. 140 N12
Anhua, China 182 M3
Ani, Japan 184 K12
Aniak, Alas., U.S. 111 J13
Aniakchak National Monument and Preserve, Alas., U.S. 111 M13
Anibare, region, Nauru 217 F23
Anibare Bay, Nauru 217 F23
Anie, Pic d', Fr., Sp. 145 B14
Animal Flower Cave, Barbados 121 J18
Animas, river, Colo., U.S. 107 P11
Animas, N. Mex., U.S. 107 V10
Animas Peak, N. Mex., U.S. 107 W10
Anin, Myanmar 186 L7
Anina, Rom. 152 E11
Anipemza, Arm. 169 D18
Aniwa, island, Vanuatu 218 G4
Anixab, Namibia 202 G6
Anjar, India 178 J2
Anjira, Pak. 177 T5
Anjouan, island, Comoros 205 N16
Anjou Islands, Russ. 242 E6
Anju, N. Korea 182 D12
Ankang, China 182 J2
Ankara, river, Turk. 168 E7
Ankara (Angora), Turk. 168 E8
Ankeny, Iowa, U.S. 105 P11
An Khe, Vietnam 186 M14
Anklam, Ger. 148 C10
Ankola, India 179 P4
Anlu, China 182 K5
Ann, Cape, Antarctica 227 C19
Ann, Cape, Mass., U.S. 95 J15
Anna, Ill., U.S. 99 V5
Anna, Lake, Va., U.S. 96 E12
Annaba, Alg. 196 A12
Annaberg, ruin, Virgin Islands, U.S. 120 M11
An Nabk, Syr. 170 H8
An Nafūd, desert, Saudi Arabia 172 G7
An Najaf, Iraq 172 E9
Annaly, Virgin Islands, U.S. 120 Q2
Annam Cordillera, Laos, Vietnam 186 K12
Annan, Scot., U.K. 143 P10
Annandale Falls, Grenada 121 K22
Anna Pink, Bahía, Chile 133 T6
Anna Plains, W. Aust., Austral. 211 S4
Anna Point, Nauru 217 E23
Annapolis, Md., U.S. 96 C13
Annapurna, peak, Nepal 178 F9
Ann Arbor, Mich., U.S. 98 M12
An Nashshāsh, U.A.E. 173 K14
An Nāşirīyah, Iraq 172 F10
An Nawfalīyah, Lib. 197 C15
Annean, Lake, Austral. 210 H3
Annecy, Fr. 147 T14
Annecy, Lac d', Fr. 147 U14
Annemasse, Fr. 147 T14
Annenskiy Most, Russ. 156 E9
Annigeri, India 179 N4
An Nimāş, Saudi Arabia 172 M8
Anningie, N. Terr., Austral. 211 S8
Anniston, Ala., U.S. 101 J16
Annitowa, N. Terr., Austral. 211 S9
Annobón, island, Eq. Guinea 201 L13
Annonay, Fr. 147 V12
Annopol, Pol. 149 F17
Annotto Bay, Jam. 120 H10
An Nu'ayrīyah, Saudi Arabia 172 H11
Annunziata, It. 150 M11
Anoano, Solomon Is. 217 N19
Anoka, Minn., U.S. 104 J11
Ano Viános, Gr. 155 R15
Anpu, China 183 S2
Anqing, China 182 L7
Anren, China 183 P4
Ansai, China 182 F2
Anse-à-Foleur, Haiti 117 L16
Anse-à-Galets, Haiti 117 M16
Anse-à-Pitre, Haiti 117 N17
Anse-à-Veau, Haiti 117 M15
Anse-Bertrand, Guadeloupe, Fr. 121 D15
Anse Boileau, Seychelles 205 P20
Anse d'Hainault, Haiti 117 M14
Anse la Raye, St. Lucia 121 K13
Anselmo, Nebr., U.S. 105 P5
Anseong, S. Korea 182 F13
Anse-Rouge, Haiti 117 L16
Anshan, China 182 C10
Ansley, Nebr., U.S. 105 P5
Ansó, Sp. 145 C14
Anson, Me., U.S. 95 F16
Anson, Tex., U.S. 102 L7
Anson Bay, Austral. 210 B7
Anson Bay, Norfolk I., Austral. 217 F20
Ansongo, Mali 196 H9
Anson Point, Norfolk I., Austral. 217 F20
Ansted, W. Va., U.S. 96 E8
Ansudu, Indonesia 189 K21
Antalaha, Madagascar 203 E18
Antalya (Adalia), Turk. 168 H6
Antalya Körfezi, Turk. 168 J6
Antananarivo, Madagascar 203 G17
Antanimora, Madagascar 203 J16
Antarctic Peninsula, Antarctica 226 D5
Ant Atoll, F.S.M. 216 Q8
Antelope, Oreg., U.S. 108 G5
Antelope Reservoir, Oreg., U.S. 108 K9
Antequera, Sp. 144 L10
Anthony, Kans., U.S. 105 V7
Anthony, N. Mex., U.S. 107 V12
Anthony Lagoon, N. Terr., Austral. 211 R9
Antibes, Fr. 147 X15
Anticosti, Île d', Que., Can. 83 M21
Anticosti Island, N. Amer. 80 G10
Antifer, Cap d', Fr. 147 N7
Antigo, Wis., U.S. 98 H6
Antigonish, N.S., Can. 83 P22
Antigua, island, Antigua & Barbuda 119 G16
Antigua, Canary Is. 204 Q7
Antigua and Barbuda, N. Amer. 81 N24
Anti-Lebanon see Sharqī, Al Jabal ash, range, Leb., Syr. 170 H7
Antilla, Cuba 117 J13
Antioch, Calif., U.S. 109 R4
Antioch see Hatay, Turk. 168 J11
Antioche, Pertuis d', Fr. 147 T5
Antipayuta, Russ. 158 F12
Antipodes Islands, N.Z. 214 Q9
Antlers, Okla., U.S. 102 J13
Antofagasta, Chile 132 E7
Antofalla, Salar de, Arg. 132 F8
Antoine, Lake, Grenada 121 J23
Anton, Tex., U.S. 102 J4
Anton Chico, N. Mex., U.S. 107 S13
Antongila, Baie d', Madagascar 203 E18
Antónia, Pico da, Cape Verde 205 D16
Antrain, Fr. 147 Q6
Antrim Mountains, N. Ire., U.K. 143 P7
Antriol, Neth. Antilles, Neth. 121 Q19
Antrodoco, It. 150 J9
Antropovo, Russ. 156 G12
Antsirabe, Madagascar 203 G17
Antsirañana, Madagascar 203 D18
Antsohihy, Madagascar 203 E17
Antu, China 182 A14
Antufash, Jazīrat, Yemen 172 P8
Antwerp see Antwerpen, Belg. 146 K12
Antwerpen (Antwerp), Belg. 146 K12
An Uaimh see Navan, Ire. 143 R6
Anuanu Raro, island, Fr. Polynesia, Fr. 219 G19
Anuanu Runga, island, Fr. Polynesia, Fr. 219 G19
Anupgarh, India 178 E4

Anuradhapura, Sri Lanka 179 S7
Anuta, island, Solomon Is. 217 P20
Anuta (Cherry Island), island, Solomon Is. 214 J7
Anvers Island, Antarctica 226 D4
Anvik, Alas., U.S. 111 H13
Anvil see El Yunque, peak, Cuba 117 K14
Anxi, China 183 Q8
Anxi, China 180 G9
Anxiang, China 182 M4
Anxin, China 182 D6
Anyang, China 182 G5
Anyang, S. Korea 182 F13
Ánydros, island, Gr. 155 M15
A'nyêmaqên Shan, China 180 J10
Anyi, China 182 G3
Anyi, China 182 M6
Anyou, China 183 V1
Anyuan, China 183 Q6
Anzhero Sudzhensk, Russ. 158 K12
Anzhu, Ostrova, Russ. 159 D17
Anzio, It. 150 L8
Aoa Bay, Amer. Samoa, U.S. 218 M8
Aoba (Omba), island, Vanuatu 218 C2
Ao Ban Don, bay, Thai. 187 Q8
Aoga Shima, Japan 185 S12
Aohan Qi, China 182 B9
Aojing, China 181 M17
Aola, Solomon Is. 217 N19
Aoloautuai, Amer. Samoa, U.S. 218 M7
Aomon, island, Marshall Is. 216 G8
Aomori, Japan 184 J13
Aonae, Japan 184 H12
Aóös, river, Gr. 154 E8
A'opo, Samoa 218 K2
Aorai, Mont, Fr. Polynesia, Fr. 219 P16
Aoraki, peak, N.Z. 213 P16
Aóre, island, Vanuatu 218 D2
Aosta, It. 150 D2
Aoulef, Alg. 196 D10
Aoumou, New Caledonia, Fr. 218 D8
Aoya, Japan 185 P7
Aozi, Chad 197 F15
Aozou, Chad 197 F14
Aozou Strip, region, Chad 197 F15
Apa, river, Braz., Parag. 130 L10
Apache, Okla., U.S. 102 H9
Apakho, Solomon Is. 217 Q23
Apalachee Bay, Fla., U.S. 85 M18
Apalachicola, river, Fla., U.S. 97 R4
Apalachicola, Fla., U.S. 97 R4
Apalachicola Bay, Fla., U.S. 97 R4
Apamea, ruin, Syr. 170 F7
Apaora, Solomon Is. 217 P20
Apaporis, river, Col. 128 H7
Aparri, Philippines 189 B14
Apataki, island, Fr. Polynesia, Fr. 219 D18
Apatin, Serb. & Mont. 152 E9
Apatity, Russ. 158 D8
Apatzingán, Mex. 114 J10
Apeldoorn, Neth. 146 J13
A. Perdido, river, Arg. 133 R8
Apes Den, Gibraltar, U.K. 161 P23
Áphaea, ruin, Gr. 154 K12
Apia, Samoa 218 L3
Apia, Samoa 214 J10
Apia Harbour, Samoa 218 L3
Apíranthos, Gr. 155 L15
Apishapa, river, Colo., U.S. 107 P14
Ap Iwan, Cerro, Arg., Chile 133 T7
Apolima, island, Samoa 218 L2
Apolima Strait, Samoa 218 L2
Apollo Bay, Vic., Austral. 211 Z12
Apollonia, ruin, Albania 152 L9
Apollonia see Sūsah, Lib. 197 B16
Apolo, Bol. 130 J6
Apolonia, Gr. 155 L14
Apopka, Lake, Fla., U.S. 97 T8
Aporema, Braz. 130 C12
Apostle Islands, Wis., U.S. 98 E4
Apostle Islands National Lakeshore, Wis., U.S. 98 E4
Apóstoles, Arg. 132 G14
Apostolic Palace, Vatican City 161 P16
Apostolos Andreas, Cape, Cyprus 160 L12
Apostolos Andreas Monastery, Cyprus 160 M12
Apoteri, Guyana 129 F14
Appalachian Mountains, U.S. 85 J17
Appalachian Plateau, U.S. 85 J17
Appennini, It. 150 F3
Applecross, Scot., U.K. 142 J7
Appleton, Minn., U.S. 104 J9
Appleton, Wis., U.S. 98 J6
Appleton City, Mo., U.S. 105 T11
Apple Valley, Calif., U.S. 109 W9
Appomattox, Va., U.S. 96 F11
Apra Harbor, Guam, U.S. 216 C10
Apra Heights, Guam, U.S. 216 C10
Aprilia, It. 150 L8
Apsheronsk, Russ. 157 T11
Apuane, Alpi, It. 150 G5
'Āpua Point, Hawai'i, U.S. 113 N21
Apucarana, Braz. 130 M12
Apurashokoru, island, Palau 216 P10
Apure, river, Venez. 128 D9
Apurímac, river, Peru 130 H4
Apuseni Mountains, Rom. 152 C12
Aqaba see Al 'Aqabah, Jordan 171 R5
Aqaba, Gulf of, Asia 166 F2
Aqadyr, Kaz. 175 F14
Aqchan, Afghan. 176 K5
Aqiq, Sudan 199 D14
Aqköl, Kaz. 175 C13
Aqköl, Kaz. 175 G16
Aqköl, Kaz. 175 J14
Aq Kopruk, Afghan. 176 L6
Aqmola see Astana, Kaz. 175 D14
Aqqikkol Hu, China 180 H7
Aqqū, Kaz. 175 C16
Aqqystaū, Kaz. 174 F6
Aqsay, Kaz. 174 C7
Aqshataū, Kaz. 175 F15
Aqsū, river, Kaz. 175 G17
Aqsū, Kaz. 175 C14
Aqtaū, Kaz. 174 H5
Aqtöbe, Kaz. 174 D8
Aqtoghay, Kaz. 175 F17
Aquidauana, Braz. 130 L10
Aquin, Haiti 117 M15
Aquitaine Basin, Fr. 138 H4
Ara, India 178 G9
Araara, Motu, Fr. Polynesia, Fr. 219 H14
Araara, Passe, Fr. Polynesia, Fr. 219 H14
Arab, Ala., U.S. 101 H15
'Arab, Bahr al, Sudan 194 H8
'Arabah, Wādī al, Israel, Jordan 171 Q5
Arabian Basin, Ind. Oc. 240 E8
Arabian Peninsula, Asia 166 G3
Arabian Sea, Ind. Oc. 166 J5
Arabs Gulf, Egypt 194 D8
Araç, river, Turk. 168 C9
Araç, Turk. 168 C9
Aracaju, Braz. 131 H17
Aracati, Braz. 131 E17
Araçatuba, Braz. 130 L12
Aracena, Sp. 144 K7
Aracena, Sierra de, Sp. 144 K7
Aracides, Cape, Solomon Is. 217 M20
Araçuaí, Braz. 131 K15
Arad, Rom. 152 D11
Arada, Chad 197 H15
Aradippou, Cyprus 160 P9
Arafura Sea, Asia, Austral. 166 L16
Aragarças, Braz. 130 J12
Aragats, peak, Arm. 169 D18
Arago, Cape, Oreg., U.S. 108 J1
Araguacema, Braz. 131 F13
Aragua de Barcelona, Venez. 128 C11
Araguaia, river, Braz. 131 E13
Araguaína, Braz. 131 F13
Araguari, Braz. 131 K13
Araguatins, Braz. 131 E13
Arahal, Sp. 144 L8
Árahthos, river, Gr. 154 F8
Arai, Japan 185 N11
Arak, Alg. 196 E11
Arāk, Iran 172 D12
Arakabesan, island, Palau 216 N11
Arakan Yoma, range, Myanmar 186 J5
Arakht, Afghan. 176 K9
Aral, Kaz. 174 F10
Aral, Kyrg. 176 E11
Aral Mangy Qaraqumy, desert, Kaz. 174 F10
Aral Sea, Kaz., Uzb. 174 G9
Aralsor, Lake, Kaz. 138 F13
Aralsor Köli, Kaz. 174 D5
Aralsul'fat, Kaz. 174 F10
Araltobe, Kaz. 174 D9
Aramac, Qnsld., Austral. 211 T13
Aramits, Fr. 147 Y6
Ārān, Iran 173 D13
Aranda de Duero, Sp. 144 D11
Aranđelovac, Serb. & Mont. 152 F10
Arandu, Pak. 176 L9
Aran Island (Arranmore), Ire. 143 P4
Aran Islands, Ire. 143 S3
Aranjuez, Sp. 144 G11
Aransá, river, Sp. 160 K4
Aransá, Sp. 160 L4
Aransas, river, Tex., U.S. 103 T11
Aransas Pass, Tex., U.S. 103 T11
Araouane, Mali 196 G8
Arapahoe, Nebr., U.S. 105 R5
Arapaho National Recreation Area, Colo., U.S. 106 L12
Arapiraca, Braz. 131 G17
Arapkir, Turk. 169 F13
'Ar'ar, Saudi Arabia 172 F8
Araraquara, Braz. 131 L13
Ararat, Arm. 169 E19
Ararat, Mount see Ağrı Dağı, Turk. 169 E18
Araria, India 178 G11
Aras (Araxes), river, Turk. 169 E17
Aratika, island, Fr. Polynesia, Fr. 219 E18
Aratsu Bay, N. Mariana Is., U.S. 216 E8
Arauá, river, Braz. 130 E7
Arauca, Col. 128 D7
Arauca, river, Col., Venez. 128 D8
Arauco Gulf, S. Amer. 126 M3
Aravalli Range, India 178 G4
Arawak Cay, Bahamas 120 B11
Araxá, Braz. 131 K13
Araxes see Aras, river, Turk. 169 E17
Arayit Dağı, Turk. 168 F7
Ārba Minch', Eth. 199 H14
Arbatax, It. 151 N5
Arbazh, Russ. 156 G14
Arbela see Irbid, Jordan 170 L6
Arbīl, Iraq 172 C9
Arbroath, Scot., U.K. 142 L11
Arcabell, Sp. 160 K2
Arcachon, Fr. 147 V6
Arcachon, Bassin d', Fr. 147 V6
Arcadia, Fla., U.S. 97 V8
Arcadia, La., U.S. 100 L7
Arcadia, Mich., U.S. 98 J9
Arcadia, Wis., U.S. 98 J3
Arcata, Calif., U.S. 108 M2
Archangel see Arkhangel'sk, Russ. 158 E8
Archbald, Pa., U.S. 94 M9
Archer City, Tex., U.S. 102 K9
Arches National Park, Utah, U.S. 107 N9
Archiac, Fr. 147 U7
Archialus see Pomorie, Bulg. 153 J17
Archidona, Sp. 144 L10
Archman, Turkm. 174 L7
Arcis, Fr. 147 P12
Arckaringa Creek, Austral. 210 H9
Arco, Idaho, U.S. 106 G6
Arco Pass, S. Amer. 126 N4
Arcos de Jalón, Sp. 144 E12
Arcoverde, Braz. 131 G17
Arctic Bay, Nunavut, Can. 83 E16
Arctic Red, river, N.W.T., Can. 82 E9
Arctic Village, Alas., U.S. 111 D17
Arctowski, station, Antarctica 226 C3
Arda, river, Bulg. 153 K15
Ardabīl, Iran 172 B11
Ardahan, Turk. 169 D17
Ardakān, Iran 173 E14
Ardanuç, Turk. 169 D16
Ardara, Ire. 143 P4
Arḑ aş Şawwān, region, Jordan 171 P8
Ardee, Ire. 143 R6
Ardennes, region, Belg., Fr. 146 M13
Ardennes, Canal des, Fr. 147 N12
Ardestān, Iran 173 D13
Ardmore, Okla., U.S. 102 J11
Ardmore, S. Dak., U.S. 104 M1
Ardres, Fr. 146 L9
Ards Peninsula, N. Ire., U.K. 143 Q8
Åre, Sw. 140 H12
Arecibo, P.R., U.S. 120 M3
Arei, Pointe, Fr. Polynesia, Fr. 219 K23
Areia Branca, Braz. 131 E17
Arekalong Peninsula (Ngerchelong), Palau 216 M12
Arena, Point, Calif., U.S. 84 F2
Arenápolis, Braz. 130 H10
Arenas, Cayo, Mex. 115 G15
Arenas, Punta de, Arg. 133 W9
Arenas de San Pedro, Sp. 144 G9
Arendal, Nor. 140 M11
Areópoli, Gr. 154 M10
Arequipa, Peru 130 J5
Arès, Fr. 147 V6
Arethusa see Ar Rastan, Syr. 170 G8
Arévalo, Sp. 144 E10
Arezzo, It. 150 H7
Argadargada, N. Terr., Austral. 211 S10
Argakhtakh, Russ. 159 D19
Arganda, Sp. 144 F11
Argelès-Gazost, Fr. 147 Y7
Argent, Fr. 147 R10
Argenta, It. 150 F7
Argentan, Fr. 147 P7
Argentario, Monte, It. 150 J7
Argentat, Fr. 147 V9
Argenteuil, Fr. 147 P10
Argentiera, Capo dell', It. 150 M3
Argentina, S. Amer. 127 P17
Argentina Range, Antarctica 226 F10
Argentine Plain, Atl. Oc. 237 V6
Argentino, Lago, Arg. 133 V7
Argenton, Fr. 147 T9
Argenton-Château, Fr. 147 S7
Argeş, river, Rom. 153 F15
Arghandab, river, Afghan. 177 P6
Arghandab, Band-e, Afghan. 177 Q5
Arghastan, river, Afghan. 177 Q5
Arghestan, Afghan. 177 Q6
Argo, Sudan 198 C12
Argolikós Kólpos, Gr. 154 K11
Argonne, range, Fr. 147 N13
Argos, Gr. 154 K10
Argos Orestikó, Gr. 154 D8
Argostóli, Gr. 154 J7
Argoub, W. Sahara, Mor. 196 E5
Arguedas, Sp. 145 D13
Arguello, Point, Calif., U.S. 109 W5
Argun, river, China, Russ. 166 E11
Argus, Dome, Antarctica 227 H16
Arguut, Mongolia 180 E11
Argyle, Minn., U.S. 104 E8
Argyle, Lake, Austral. 210 C7
Argyrus see Gjirokastër, Albania 152 M9
Arhánes, Gr. 155 Q15
Arhángelos, Gr. 155 N20
Ar Horqin Qi (Tianshan), China 182 A9
Arhrîjît, Mauritania 196 G7
Århus, Den. 140 N11
Ari, Motu, Fr. Polynesia, Fr. 219 Q20
Ariano Irpino, It. 150 M11
Ariari, river, Col. 128 F6
Ari Atoll, Maldives 179 V3
Arica, Chile 132 B6
Arid, Cape, Austral. 210 K5
Arida, Japan 185 R8
Aride, Île, Seychelles 205 M20
Aridéa, Gr. 154 B10
Ariège, river, Fr. 160 H5
Arifwala, Pak. 177 R11
Arīḩā, Syr. 170 E8
Arīḩā (Jericho), W. Bank 170 M6
Arikaree, river, Colo., U.S. 106 L15
Arikawa, Japan 185 R3
Arimã, Braz. 130 E8
Arima, Trinidad & Tobago 121 P22
Arinagour, Scot., U.K. 142 L7
Arinos, river, Braz. 130 H10
Arinsal, river, Andorra 160 H2
Arinsal, Andorra 160 H2
Aripeka, Fla., U.S. 97 T7
Aripo, El Cerro del, Trinidad & Tobago 121 N23
Ariporo, river, Col. 128 E7
Aripuanã, river, Braz. 130 F9
Aripuanã, Braz. 130 G9
Ariquemes, Braz. 130 G8
'Arîsh, Wâdi el, Egypt 171 Q3
Aristizábal, Cabo, Arg. 133 S9
Ariyalur, India 179 R6
Arizaro, Salar de, Arg. 132 F8
Arizona, Arg. 132 M9
Arizona, U.S. 107 T5
Arizona City, Ariz., U.S. 107 U7
Arjeplog, Sw. 141 F13
Arjona, Col. 128 B5
Arkadak, Russ. 156 M12
Arkadelphia, Ark., U.S. 100 H7
Arkagala, Russ. 159 F19
Arkaig, Loch, Scot., U.K. 142 K8
Arkansas, river, U.S. 85 K14
Arkansas, U.S. 100 G7
Arkansas City, Ark., U.S. 100 J10
Arkansas City, Kans., U.S. 105 V8
Arkansas Post National Memorial, Ark., U.S. 100 H9
Arkhangel'sk (Archangel), Russ. 158 E8
Arkhangel'skoye, Russ. 156 M11
Arkí, island, Gr. 155 K17
Arkítsa, Gr. 154 G11
Arkona, Kap, Ger. 148 A10
Arkonam, India 179 P7
Arkticheskiy, Mys, Russ. 159 C14
Arlanc, Fr. 147 U11
Arlap, island, Marshall Is. 216 L7
Arles, Fr. 147 X12
Arlington, Ga., U.S. 97 P4
Arlington, Oreg., U.S. 108 F6
Arlington, S. Dak., U.S. 104 K8
Arlington, Tex., U.S. 102 L11
Arlington, Va., U.S. 96 C13
Arlington, Wash., U.S. 108 B4
Arlington Heights, Ill., U.S. 99 N7
Arlon, Belg. 147 N13
Arma, Kans., U.S. 105 U10
Armagh, N. Ire., U.K. 143 Q6
Armathiá, island, Gr. 155 Q18
Armavir, Arm. 169 E18
Armavir, Russ. 157 S11
Armenia, Asia 167 T4
Armenia, Col. 128 F4
Armenistís, Gr. 155 K16
Armidale, N.S.W., Austral. 211 W15
Armijo, N. Mex., U.S. 107 S12
Armilla, Sp. 144 L11
Armorican Massif, Fr. 138 G4
Armour, S. Dak., U.S. 104 M6
Armstrong, Ont., Can. 83 N15
Armur, India 178 L6
Arnaoutis, Cape, Cyprus 160 P5
Arnay-le-Duc, Fr. 147 S12
Arnéa, Gr. 154 D12
Arnedo, Sp. 144 C12
Årnes, Nor. 140 H11
Arnett, Okla., U.S. 102 F8
Arnhem, Neth. 146 J13
Arnhem, Cape, Austral. 210 B10
Arnhem Land, N. Terr., Austral. 211 P9
Arniel, island, Marshall Is. 216 G12
Árnissa, Gr. 154 C9
Arno, river, It. 150 G6
Arno Atoll, Marshall Is. 216 H5
Arno Bay, S. Aust., Austral. 211 X9
Arnold, Mo., U.S. 105 T15
Arnold, Nebr., U.S. 105 P5
Arnøy, island, Nor. 141 C13
Arnsberg, Ger. 148 F6
Aroab, Namibia 202 K8
Arock, Oreg., U.S. 108 J9
Arorae, island, Kiribati 214 G8
Arorangi, Cook Is., N.Z. 218 Q9
Arousa, Ría de, Sp. 144 C5
Arowhana, peak, N.Z. 213 K20
Arpa, river, Arm., Turk. 169 D18
Arpaçay, Turk. 169 D17
Arqalyq, Kaz. 174 D12
Ar Rabbah, Jordan 171 N6
Arrabury, Qnsld., Austral. 211 V11
Arraias, Braz. 131 H14
Ar Ramādī, Iraq 172 D9
Ar Ramlah, Jordan 171 R6
Ar Ramthā, Jordan 170 L7
Arran, Island of, Scot., U.K. 143 N8
Arranmore see Aran Island, island, Ire. 143 P4
Ar Raqqah (Nicephorium), Syr. 170 E11
Arras, Fr. 146 M10
Ar Rashādīyah, Jordan 171 P6
Ar Rastan (Arethusa), Syr. 170 G8
Ar Rawḑah, Saudi Arabia 172 L8
Ar Rawḑah, Sabkhat, Syr. 170 F14
Arreau, Fr. 147 Y7
Arrecife, Canary Is. 204 P7
Arrée, Montagnes d', Fr. 147 Q3
Ar Riyaḑ (Riyadh), Saudi Arabia 172 J10
Ar Riyān, Yemen 172 Q12
Arrochar, Scot., U.K. 142 M8
Arromanches, Fr. 147 N7
Arronches, Port. 144 H7
Arrou, Fr. 147 Q8
Arrow, Lough, Ire. 143 Q4
Arrowrock Reservoir, Idaho, U.S. 106 G4
Arroyo, P.R., U.S. 120 P5
Arroyo de la Luz, Sp. 144 H7
Arroyo Grande, Calif., U.S. 109 V5
Arroyos de Mantua, Cuba 116 H4
Arroyos y Esteros, Parag. 130 M10
Ar Rub' Al Khālī, desert, Saudi Arabia 172 M12
Ar Ruşāfah (Risāfe), ruin, Syr. 170 F11
Ar Ruşayfah, Jordan 170 M7
Ar Ruţbah, Iraq 172 D7
Ar Ruwayshid, Jordan 170 L10
Ars-en-Ré, Fr. 147 T5
Arsen'yev, Russ. 159 L21
Arshaly, Kaz. 175 D14
Arsiero, It. 150 D7
Arsikere, India 179 P5
Arsuk, Greenland, Den. 81 D22
Art, Île, New Caledonia, Fr. 218 B6

Árta (Amvrakía), Gr. 154 F8
Artashat, Arm. 169 E18
Artem, Russ. 159 M21
Artemisa, Cuba 116 G6
Artemivs'k, Ukr. 157 Q10
Artemovsk, Russ. 159 L13
Artesia, N. Mex., U.S. 107 U14
Artesian, S. Dak., U.S. 104 L7
Arthur, Nebr., U.S. 105 P3
Arthur's Pass, N.Z. 213 N17
Arthur's Town, Bahamas 117 E13
Arthurstown, Ire. 143 U6
Artigas, station, Antarctica 226 C3
Artigas, Uru. 132 J14
Art'ik, Arm. 169 D18
Artiste Point, Grenada 121 K23
Artova, Turk. 168 E11
Artux, China 180 F4
Artvin, Turk. 169 D16
Artyk, Turkm. 174 M8
Artyk Yuryakh, Russ. 159 F17
Artyom, Azerb. 169 D23
Aru, Kepulauan, Indonesia 213 D15
Arua, Uganda 198 J12
Aruanã, Braz. 130 J12
Aruba, island, Neth., Lesser Antilles 118 M8
Aruboe, island, Marshall Is. 216 M7
Arucas, Canary Is. 204 Q6
Arue, Fr. Polynesia, Fr. 219 N16
Aru Islands, Indonesia 166 L15
Arumã, Braz. 130 E8
Aru Passage, F.S.M. 217 F14
Arusha, Tanzania 199 L14
Arutanga, Cook Is., N.Z. 218 Q11
Arutanga Passage, Cook Is., N.Z. 218 Q11
Arutua, island, Fr. Polynesia, Fr. 219 D17
Aruwimi, river, Dem. Rep. of the Congo 198 J11
Arvada, Colo., U.S. 106 M13
Arvayheer, Mongolia 180 E11
Arviat, Nunavut, Can. 83 J15
Arvidsjaur, Sw. 141 F13
Arvika, Sw. 140 L12
Arvon, Mount, Mich., U.S. 98 F7
Arwād, Jazīrat, Syr. 170 G7
Arxan, China 181 D15
Ary, Russ. 159 E16
Arys, Kaz. 175 J13
Arys Köli, Kaz. 174 G12
Arzachena, It. 150 M4
Arzamas, Russ. 156 J12
Arzgir, Russ. 157 S13
Asad, Afghan. 177 P5
Asad, Buḩayrat al, Syr. 170 E10
Asadabad, Afghan. 176 M9
Asadābād, Gardaneh-ye, Iran 172 D11
Asaga Strait, Amer. Samoa, U.S. 218 N2
Aşağıpınarbaşı, Turk. 168 G8
Asahi, river, Japan 185 Q7
Asahi Dake, Japan 184 F14
Asahikawa, Japan 184 F14
Asan, Guam, U.S. 216 C10
Asansol, India 178 J11
Asatdas, Guam, U.S. 216 B11
Asau, Samoa 218 K1
Asau Harbour, Samoa 218 K1
Āsbe Taferī, Eth. 199 G15
Asbury Park, N.J., U.S. 94 P11
Ascención, Bol. 130 J8
Ascensión, Mex. 114 C8
Ascension, island, Atl. Oc. 204 G4
Ascension Fracture Zone, Atl. Oc. 237 P11
Aschaffenburg, Ger. 148 H7
Ascó, Sp. 145 E15
Ascoli Piceno, It. 150 J10
Asedjrad, range, Alg. 196 E10
Āsela, Eth. 199 G15
Asenovgrad, Bulg. 153 K14
Aşgabat (Ashgabat), Turkm. 174 M8
Asha, Cyprus 160 N9
Ashāqif, Jabal al, Jordan 170 M9
Ashburn, Ga., U.S. 97 P6
Ashburton, N.Z. 213 P17
Ashburton, river, W. Aust., Austral. 211 T2
Ashburton Downs, W. Aust., Austral. 211 T2
Ashby Fort, ruin, St. Kitts & Nevis 121 C18
Ashchyköl, lake, Kaz. 174 H12
Ashdod, Israel 170 M5
Ashdown, Ark., U.S. 100 J6
Asherton, Tex., U.S. 103 T8
Asheville, N.C., U.S. 96 H7
Ashford, Eng., U.K. 143 W15
Ashford, Wash., U.S. 108 D4
Ash Fork, Ariz., U.S. 107 S6
Ashgabat see Aşgabat, Turkm. 174 M8
Ash Grove, Mo., U.S. 105 U11
Ashikaga, Japan 185 N12
Ashizuri Misaki, Japan 185 S6
Ashland, Kans., U.S. 105 V5
Ashland, Ky., U.S. 101 A20
Ashland, Me., U.S. 95 B18
Ashland, Mont., U.S. 106 E12
Ashland, Nebr., U.S. 105 Q8
Ashland, Ohio, U.S. 99 P14
Ashland, Oreg., U.S. 108 K3
Ashland, Va., U.S. 96 E13
Ashland, Wis., U.S. 98 F4
Ashley, N. Dak., U.S. 104 H6
Ashley, river, S.C., U.S. 96 M10
Ashmore Islands, W. Aust., Austral. 211 P4
Ashmyany, Belarus 156 K4
Ashoro, Japan 184 F15
Ashqelon, Israel 170 M4
Ash Shabakah, Iraq 172 F9
Ash Shammās, Syr. 170 H13
Ash Sharawrah, Saudi Arabia 172 N11
Ash Sharqāţ, Iraq 172 C9
Ash Shawbak, Jordan 171 P6
Ash Shīdīyah, Jordan 171 R6
Ash Shiḩr, Yemen 172 Q12
Ash Shişar, Oman 173 N14
Ash Shumlūl, Saudi Arabia 172 H11
Ash Shuqayq, Saudi Arabia 172 N8
Ash Shurayf, Saudi Arabia 172 J7
Ashtabula, Ohio, U.S. 99 N15
Ashtabula, Lake, N. Dak., U.S. 104 G7
Ashton, Idaho, U.S. 106 G7
Asia, Kepulauan, Indonesia 213 A14
Asia Minor see Anatolia, region, Turk. 168 F6
Asifabad, India 178 L7
Asiga, Puntan, N. Mariana Is., U.S. 216 B8
Asika, India 178 L10
Asinara, Golfo dell', It. 150 M3
Asinara, Isola, It. 150 M3
Asipovichy, Belarus 156 L5
'Asīr, region, Saudi Arabia 172 M8
Asiros, Gr. 154 C11
Aşkale, Turk. 169 E15
Askenderun Körfezi, Turk. 168 J11
Askole, Pak. 176 L13
Asl, Egypt 171 R1
Asmar, Afghan. 176 M9
Asmara, Eritrea 199 E15
Āsosa, Eth. 199 F13
Aspen, Colo., U.S. 106 M11
Aspermont, Tex., U.S. 102 K7
Aspiring, Mount, N.Z. 213 P15
Aspres, Fr. 147 W14
Aspromonte, range, It. 151 R13
Asprovália, Gr. 154 C12
As Sa'an, Syr. 170 F9
Assab, Eritrea 199 E16
As Sabkhah, Syr. 170 E12
Aş Şafā, desert, Syr. 170 K8
As Safīrah, Syr. 170 E9
Aş Şa'īd, Yemen 172 Q10
Assal, Lake, Djibouti 199 F16
Aş Şāli'īyah, Syr. 170 G14
As Salţ, Jordan 170 M6
As Samāwah, Iraq 172 F10
As Sanām, desert, Saudi Arabia 173 K13
Aş Şarafand, Leb. 170 J6
Assateague Island National Seashore, Md., U.S. 96 D15
Aş Şawrah, Saudi Arabia 172 G5
Asselborn, Lux. 160 G9
Assen, Neth. 146 G14
As Sidr, Lib. 197 C15
As Sidr, Saudi Arabia 172 K7
Assis, Braz. 130 L12
Assisi, It. 150 H8
Assos, ruin, Turk. 168 E2
As Su'ayyirah, Saudi Arabia 172 H11
As Sukhnah, Syr. 170 G11
As Sulaymānīyah, Iraq 172 C10
As Sulayyil, Saudi Arabia 172 M10
Aş Şulb, region, Saudi Arabia 172 H11
Aş Şummān, plateau, Saudi Arabia 172 H10
Assumption Island, Seychelles 203 C17
Aş Şurrah, Yemen 172 Q10
Aş Şuwār, Syr. 170 F14
As Suwaydā', Syr. 170 L8
As Suwayḩ, Oman 173 K17
Assynt, Loch, Scot., U.K. 142 H8
Astakída, island, Gr. 155 P17
Astakós, Gr. 154 H8
Astana (Aqmola), Kaz. 175 D14
Astara, Azerb. 169 F22
Āstārā, Iran 172 B11
Asti, It. 150 E3
Astipálea, island, Gr. 155 M17
Astipálea, Gr. 155 M17
Astola Island, Pak. 177 W3
Astor, Pak. 176 L12
Astorga, Sp. 144 C8
Astoria, Oreg., U.S. 108 E2
Astove Island, Seychelles 203 C17
Astra, Arg. 133 S9
Astrakhan', Russ. 157 R15
Astrolabe, Cape, Solomon Is. 217 M19
Astros, Gr. 154 K10
Astrupa, Gora, Russ. 159 D14
Astudillo, Sp. 144 C10
Asuisui, Cape, Samoa 218 L2
Asunción, Parag. 130 M10
Asunción, Punta, Arg. 133 N12
Asuncion, island, N. Mariana Is., U.S. 216 A2
Asuzudo Point, N. Mariana Is., U.S. 216 D8
Aswān, Egypt 197 E19
Aswân High Dam, Egypt 197 E19
Asyûţ, Egypt 197 D18
Ata, island, Tonga 214 K9
Ata, island, Tonga 218 H12
Atacama, Salar de, Chile 132 E8
Atacama Desert, S. Amer. 126 J4
Atafu, island, Tokelau, N.Z. 214 H10
Atakpamé, Togo 200 G11
Atalándi, Gr. 154 H11
Atalaya de Femés, peak, Canary Is. 204 P7
Atamyrat (Kerki), Turkm. 174 M11
Atapupu, Indonesia 189 M15
Atar, Mauritania 196 F6
Atarfe, Sp. 144 L11
Atascadero, Calif., U.S. 109 V5
Atascosa, river, Tex., U.S. 103 S10
Atasu, Kaz. 175 E14
Atata, island, Tonga 218 H11
Atauro, island, Timor-Leste 189 M15
Atáviros, peak, Gr. 155 N19
Atbara, river, Sudan 199 D13
Atbara, Sudan 199 D13
At-Bashy, Kyrg. 176 F12
Atchafalaya, river, La., U.S. 100 P9
Atchafalaya Bay, La., U.S. 100 Q9
Atchison, Kans., U.S. 105 S10
Ateca, Sp. 145 E13
Ath, Belg. 146 L11
Athabasca, river, Alta., Can. 82 K11
Athabasca, Alta., Can. 82 L10
Athabasca, Lake, Alta., Sask., Can. 82 J12
Athamánio, Gr. 154 F8
Athamánon, peak, Gr. 154 F8
Athboy, Ire. 143 R6
Athena, Oreg., U.S. 108 E8
Athens, Ala., U.S. 101 G15
Athens, Ga., U.S. 96 L6
Athens see Athína, Gr. 154 J12
Athens, Ohio, U.S. 99 S14
Athens, Tenn., U.S. 101 F18
Athens, Tex., U.S. 102 M13
Atherton Tableland, Austral. 210 D13
Athfālah, Saudi Arabia 172 M8
Athienou, Cyprus 160 P9
Athienou, Cyprus 160 P9
Athína (Athens), Gr. 154 J12
Athlone, Ire. 143 S5
Athol Island, Bahamas 120 B12
Athos, peak, Gr. 155 D13
Ati, Chad 197 J15
Atico, Peru 130 J4
Atikokan, Ont., Can. 83 P15
Atimoono, island, Cook Is., N.Z. 219 B15
Atina, It. 150 L10
Atiti, Afghan. 176 L8
Atitue, Fr. Polynesia, Fr. 219 P15
Atiu, island, Cook Is., N.Z. 214 K12
Atka, Alas., U.S. 110 P6
Atka, Russ. 159 F20
Atka Island, Alas., U.S. 110 P6
Atkarsk, Russ. 156 M13
Atkins, Ark., U.S. 100 F8
Atkinson, Nebr., U.S. 105 N6
Atlanta, Ga., U.S. 96 L5
Atlanta, Mich., U.S. 98 H11
Atlanta, Tex., U.S. 102 K15
Atlantic, Iowa, U.S. 105 P10
Atlantic, N.C., U.S. 96 J14
Atlantic Beach, Fla., U.S. 97 Q9
Atlantic Beach, N.C., U.S. 96 J14
Atlantic City, N.J., U.S. 94 Q10
Atlantic City, Wyo., U.S. 106 J10
Atlantic-Indian Ridge, Ind. Oc. 240 R1
Atlantis Fracture Zone, Atl. Oc. 236 J7
Atlantis II Fracture Zone, Ind. Oc. 240 N6
Atlas Mountains, Alg., Mor. 196 B9
Atlin, B.C., Can. 82 G8
'Atlit, Israel 170 L5
Atmautluak, Alas., U.S. 110 J12
Atmore, Ala., U.S. 101 N14
Atoka, Okla., U.S. 102 H12
Atoyac, Mex. 114 K11
Atrak (Etrek), river, Iran 173 B14
Atrato, river, Col. 128 D4
Atrek, river, Turkm. 174 M6
Atri, It. 150 J10
Atsumi, Japan 185 Q10
Atsunai, Japan 184 G15
Atsutoko, Japan 184 F16
Aţ Ţafīlah, Jordan 171 P6
Aţ Ţa'if, Saudi Arabia 172 L7
Attalla, Ala., U.S. 101 H16
Attapu, Laos 186 M12
Attawapiskat, river, Can. 80 G7
Attawapiskat, Ont., Can. 83 M17
At Taysīyah, plateau, Saudi Arabia 172 G9
Attent, river, Lux. 160 J9
At Tibnī, Syr. 170 F12
Attica, Ind., U.S. 99 Q8
Attica, Kans., U.S. 105 V6
Attleboro, Mass., U.S. 95 L14
Attu, Greenland, Den. 81 D21
Aţ Ţubayq, region, Saudi Arabia 172 F6
Attu Island, Alas., U.S. 110 K1
At Turbah, Yemen 172 R8
At Turbah, Yemen 172 R9
Atuel, river, Arg. 132 M8
Atuona, Fr. Polynesia, Fr. 219 M20
Atutahi, island, Cook Is., N.Z. 219 C18
Atwater, Calif., U.S. 109 S5
Atwood see Samana Cay, island, Bahamas 117 G15
Atwood, Kans., U.S. 105 R4
Atyraū, Kaz. 174 F6
Aua, Amer. Samoa, U.S. 218 M8
Auas Mountains, Namibia 194 P7
'Au'au Channel, Hawai'i, U.S. 113 G15
Aubagne, Fr. 147 Y14
Aubange, Belg. 160 K9
Aubenas, Fr. 147 W12
Aubiet, Fr. 147 X8
Aubinyà, Andorra 160 K2
Aubrac, Monts d', Fr. 147 W11
Aubry Lake, N.W.T., Can. 82 E10
Auburn, Ala., U.S. 101 L17
Auburn, Calif., U.S. 109 Q5
Auburn, Ill., U.S. 99 R5
Auburn, Ind., U.S. 99 P10
Auburn, Me., U.S. 95 G15
Auburn, N.Y., U.S. 94 J8
Auburn, Nebr., U.S. 105 R9
Auburn, Qnsld., Austral. 211 U15
Auburn, Wash., U.S. 108 C4
Auburndale, Fla., U.S. 97 U8
Aubusson, Fr. 147 U10
Auce, Latv. 141 M16
Auch, Fr. 147 X8
Auchel, Fr. 146 L10
Auckland, N.Z. 213 J19
Auckland Islands, N.Z. 214 Q7
Audience Hall, Vatican City 161 R16
Audincourt, Fr. 147 R15
Audubon, Iowa, U.S. 105 P10
Augathella, Qnsld., Austral. 211 U13
Augrabies Falls, S. Af. 202 K8
Augsburg, Ger. 148 K8
Augstisried, Switz. 160 M2
Augusta, Ark., U.S. 100 F10
Augusta, Ga., U.S. 96 L8
Augusta, It. 151 T12
Augusta, Kans., U.S. 105 U8
Augusta, Ky., U.S. 101 A18
Augusta, Me., U.S. 95 F16
Augusta, Mont., U.S. 106 C7
Augusta, Wis., U.S. 98 J3
Augusta, Golfo di, It. 151 T12
Augusta Victoria, Chile 132 E7
Augustów, Pol. 149 B17
August Town, Jam. 120 J10
Augustus, Mount, Austral. 210 F2
Augustus Downs, Qnsld., Austral. 211 R11
Aukena, island, Fr. Polynesia, Fr. 219 Q21
Auki, Solomon Is. 217 M19
Auld, Lake, Austral. 210 F5
Auletta, It. 150 M12
Äūlīeköl, Kaz. 174 C11
Aulong, island, Palau 216 P10
Auluptagel, island, Palau 216 P11
Aunuu, island, Amer. Samoa, U.S. 218 M9
Aunuu, Amer. Samoa, U.S. 218 M9
Auob, river, Namibia 202 J8
Auponhia, Indonesia 189 K15
Aur, island, Malaysia 187 U11
Auraiya, India 178 G7
Aurangabad, India 178 H9
Aurangabad, India 178 L4
Aur Atoll, Marshall Is. 216 G5
Auray, Fr. 147 R4
Aurich, Ger. 148 C6
Aurignac, Fr. 147 Y8
Aurillac, Fr. 147 V10
Aurisina, It. 150 D10
Aurora, Colo., U.S. 106 M13
Aurora, Ill., U.S. 99 N6
Aurora, Ind., U.S. 99 S10
Aurora, Minn., U.S. 104 F12
Aurora, Mo., U.S. 105 V11
Aurora, Nebr., U.S. 105 Q7
Aurukun, Qnsld., Austral. 211 P12
Aus, Namibia 202 J6
Ausa, river, It., San Marino 161 G18
Au Sable, river, Mich., U.S. 98 J11
Au Sable, Mich., U.S. 98 J12
Au Sable Point, Mich., U.S. 98 F9
Austin, Ind., U.S. 99 T9
Austin, Minn., U.S. 104 L12
Austin, Nev., U.S. 109 P9
Austin, Pa., U.S. 94 L6
Austin, Tex., U.S. 103 Q10
Austin, Lake, Austral. 210 H3
Australia 210
Australian Alps, Austral. 210 M13
Australian Capital Territory, Austral. 211 Y13
Austral Islands (Tubuai Islands), Fr. Polynesia, Fr. 219 H16
Austria, Eur. 139 V6
Austriahütte, site, Aust. 148 L10
Austvågøy, island, Nor. 140 E12
Autazes, Braz. 130 D9
Autlán, Mex. 114 H9
Autun, Fr. 147 S12
Aux Barques, Pointe, Mich., U.S. 98 K13
Auxerre, Fr. 147 R11
Auxonne, Fr. 147 S13
Auzances, Fr. 147 T10
Ava, Mo., U.S. 105 V12
Avaavaroa Passage, Cook Is., N.Z. 218 Q9
Ava Fonua'unga, bay, Tonga 218 M12
Avaha, island, Solomon Is. 217 J18
Avala, peak, Serb. & Mont. 152 F10
Avalau, island, Tuvalu 217 L22
Avallon, Fr. 147 R11
Avalon, Calif., U.S. 109 Y8
Avalon, Lake, N. Mex., U.S. 107 V14
Avalon Peninsula, Nfld. & Lab., Can. 83 M24
Ava Mata Mata Vika, bay, Tonga 218 Q7
Avanavero, Suriname 129 E15
Avanos, Turk. 168 F10
Avapeihi, Passe, Fr. Polynesia, Fr. 219 G13
Avarapa, Passe, Fr. Polynesia, Fr. 219 P14
Avarua, Cook Is., N.Z. 218 Q9
Avarua Harbour, Cook Is., N.Z. 218 Q9
Avatele, Niue, N.Z. 219 B20
Avatele Bay, Niue, N.Z. 219 B20
Avatiu, Cook Is., N.Z. 218 Q9
Avatiu Harbour, Cook Is., N.Z. 218 Q9
Avatolu, Passe, Wallis & Futuna, Fr. 218 B11
Avatoru, Fr. Polynesia, Fr. 219 K16
Āvāz, Iran 173 D17
Avdira, ruin, Gr. 155 C14
Avea, island, Fiji Is. 218 H9
Avea, Baie d', Fr. Polynesia, Fr. 219 H14
Avea, Baie d', Fr. Polynesia, Fr. 219 K23
Aveiro, Port. 144 F5
Aveiro, Braz. 130 D11
Āvej, Iran 172 C12
Avellino, It. 150 M11
Avenal, Calif., U.S. 109 U6
Avera, Fr. Polynesia, Fr. 219 B23
Avera, Fr. Polynesia, Fr. 219 K23
A. Verde, river, Arg. 133 Q9
Aversa, It. 150 M10
Aves (Bird Island), Venez. 119 J15
Aves, Islas de, Venez. 128 A9
Aves Ridge, Atl. Oc. 236 L5
Avesta, Sw. 141 K13
Avezzano, It. 150 K9

Avgó, island, Gr. 154 N11
Avgo, island, Gr. 155 P17
Aviano, It. 150 D8
Aviator Glacier, Antarctica 227 Q14
Avignon, Fr. 147 X13
Avila, Sp. 144 F10
Avilés, Sp. 144 A8
Avire, Vanuatu 218 B2
Avissawella, Sri Lanka 179 T7
Avita, Solomon Is. 217 Q23
Avlonári, Gr. 155 H13
Avoca, Iowa, U.S. 105 P9
Avon, river, Eng., U.K. 143 U12
Avon, river, Eng., U.K. 143 V11
Avon, N.C., U.S. 96 H15
Avondale, Ariz., U.S. 107 U6
Avon Downs, N. Terr., Austral. 211 S10
Avon Park, Fla., U.S. 97 U9
Avranches, Fr. 147 P6
Avsa, Gora, Russ. 159 H13
Åvsbyn, Sw. 141 F14
Avu Avu, Solomon Is. 217 P19
Awaday, W. Sahara, Mor. 196 E6
Awaji Shima, Japan 185 Q8
Āwarē, Eth. 199 G16
Awarua Bay, N.Z. 213 P15
Awa Shima, Japan 184 L12
Awat, China 180 F5
Awbārī, Şaḩrā', Lib. 197 D13
Awe, Loch, Scot., U.K. 142 L8
Aweil, Sudan 198 G11
Awini Plateau, Hawai'i, U.S. 113 K19
Awjilah, Lib. 197 D16
Awsard, W. Sahara, Mor. 196 E5
Axel Heiberg Island, Nunavut, Can. 83 B15
Axim, Ghana 200 H10
Axinim, Braz. 130 E9
Axiós, river, Gr. 154 B10
Ax-les-Thermes, Fr. 147 Z9
Axtell, Nebr., U.S. 105 Q6
Ayabe, Japan 185 P8
Ayacucho, Arg. 133 N13
Ayacucho, Peru 130 H4
Ayakkum Hu, China 180 H7
Ayaköz, Kaz. 175 E17
Ayamonte, Sp. 144 L6
Ayan, Russ. 159 H20
Ayan, Russ. 159 J15
Ayancık, Turk. 168 C10
Ayapel, Col. 128 D5
Ayaş, Turk. 168 E8
Ayat, river, Kaz. 174 C10
Ayaviri, Peru 130 J5
Aybak (Samangan), Afghan. 176 L7
Aydar Kŭl, Kaz., Uzb. 174 K12
Ayden, N.C., U.S. 96 H13
Aydere, Turkm. 174 L7
Aydın, Turk. 168 G3
Aydıncık, Turk. 168 J8
Ayerbe, Sp. 145 C14
Ayers Rock (Uluru), Austral. 210 G7
Ayeyarwady (Irrawaddy), river, Myanmar 186 F6
Ayeyarwady, Mouths of the, Myanmar 186 L5
Aykhal, Russ. 159 G15
Ay Khanom, ruin, Afghan. 176 K8
Aylesbury, Eng., U.K. 143 V13
Ayles Fiord, Nunavut, Can. 83 A16
Ayllón, Sp. 144 E11
Aylmer Lake, N.W.T., Can. 82 H12
'Ayn al 'Arab, Syr. 170 C10
'Ayn Dīwār, Syr. 170 C16
Ayní, Taj. 176 H7
'Aynūnah, Saudi Arabia 172 G5
Ayon, Ostrov, Russ. 159 C19
Ayorou, Niger 196 H10
'Ayoûn el 'Atroûs, Mauritania 196 G7
Aypolovo, Russ. 158 J11
Ayr, Qnsld., Austral. 211 S14
Ayr, Scot., U.K. 143 N9
Ayrancı, Turk. 168 H9
Ayre, Point of, Isle of Man, U.K. 143 Q9
Äyteke Bī, Kaz. 174 G10
Aytos, Bulg. 153 J17
Ayutla, Mex. 114 K11
Ayutthaya, Thai. 186 M9
Ayvacık, Turk. 168 E2
Ayvaj, Taj. 176 K7
Ayvalık, Turk. 168 E2
Āzād Shahr, Iran 173 B14
Azahar, Costa del, Sp. 145 G15
Azamgarh, India 178 G9
Azapa, Chile 132 B7
Azare, Nigeria 201 E15
Azaw, Afghan. 177 N3
A'zāz, Syr. 170 D8
Azdavay, Turk. 168 C9
Azerbaijan, Asia 167 T4
Azerbaijan, region, Iran 172 C10
Azincourt, Fr. 146 M9
Azle, Tex., U.S. 102 L11
Azmoos, Switz. 160 Q2
Azogues, Ecua. 128 K3
Azores (Açores), islands, Atl. Oc. 204 C3
Azov, Russ. 157 R10
Azov, Sea of, Russ., Ukr. 157 S9
Azov Upland, Ukr. 138 G11
Azraq, El Bahr el (Blue Nile), Sudan 199 F13
Azraq, Qaşr al, Jordan 170 M8
Aztec, N. Mex., U.S. 107 Q11
Aztec Ruins National Monument, N. Mex., U.S. 107 Q10
Azua, Dom. Rep. 117 M18
Azuaga, Sp. 144 J8
Azuero, Penínisula de, Pan. 115 P21
Azuero Peninsula see Azuero, Penínisula de, N. Amer. 80 Q9
Azul, Arg. 132 M12
Azul, Cerro, Ecua. 128 R8
Azurduy, Bol. 130 K8
Az Zabadānī, Syr. 170 J7
Az̧ Z̧āhirīyah, W. Bank 171 N5
'Azzān, Yemen 172 Q11
Az Zarqā', Jordan 170 M7
Azzel Matti, Sebkha, Alg. 196 E10
Az Zilfī, Saudi Arabia 172 H10
Az Zubayr, Iraq 172 F11

B

Ba, Fiji Is. 218 H6
Baaba, Île, New Caledonia, Fr. 218 B6
Baabda, Leb. 170 J6
Baalbeck, Leb. 170 H7
Baardheere, Somalia 199 J16
Baarn, Neth. 146 J13
Baba Burnu, Turk. 168 C7
Baba Burnu, Turk. 168 E2
Baba Dağ, Turk. 168 J4
Babadag, peak, Azerb. 169 C22
Babaeski, Turk. 168 C3
Babahoyo, Ecua. 128 K2
Babanūsah, Sudan 198 F11
Babar, island, Indonesia 189 M17
Babar, Kepulauan, Indonesia 189 M17
Babati, Tanzania 199 L14
Babayevo, Russ. 156 F9
Babayurt, Russ. 157 T15
Babe Island, Guam, U.S. 216 E10
Babeldaob see Babelthuap, island, Palau 216 N11
Babelthuap (Babeldaob), island, Palau 216 N11
Babi, island, Indonesia 188 H4
Babin Nos, Bulg., Serb. & Mont. 152 G12
Babo, Indonesia 189 K18
Baboquivari Peak, Ariz., U.S. 107 W7
Babruysk, Belarus 156 L5
Babusar Pass, Pak. 178 B4
Babushkina, Russ. 156 F11
Babuyan, island, Philippines 189 A14
Babuyan Channel, Philippines 189 B14
Babuyan Islands, Philippines 189 A13
Babylon, ruin, Iraq 172 E9
Bacaadweyn, Somalia 199 G17
Bacabal, Braz. 131 E14
Bacan, island, Indonesia 189 J16
Bacău, Rom. 153 C16
Baccarat, Fr. 147 P14
Baceno, It. 150 C3
Bachelor, Mount, Oreg., U.S. 108 H4
Bachu, China 180 F5
Back, river, Nunavut, Can. 83 G14
Bačka, region, Serb. & Mont. 152 E9
Bačka Palanka, Serb. & Mont. 152 E9
Bačka Topola, Serb. & Mont. 152 D9
Backbone Mountain, Md., U.S. 96 C10
Back Cay, Bahamas 120 E7
Bac Lieu, Vietnam 187 Q12
Bac Ninh, Vietnam 186 H12
Bacolet, Grenada 121 L23
Bacolod, Philippines 189 E14
Bacup, Eng., U.K. 143 R11
Bad, river, S. Dak., U.S. 104 L4
Badain Jaran Shamo, China 180 G11
Badajoz, Sp. 144 H7
Badalona, Sp. 145 E17
Bad Axe, Mich., U.S. 98 K13
Baddeck, N.S., Can. 83 N22
Baddo, river, Pak. 177 T4
Baden, Aust. 148 K12
Baden-Baden, Ger. 148 J6
Baderna, Croatia 152 E4
Badgah, Afghan. 176 M5
Badger, Minn., U.S. 104 E9
Bad Hersfeld, Ger. 148 F7
Bad Homburg, Ger. 148 G6
Badin, Pak. 177 W7
Bad Ischl, Aust. 148 L10
Bad Kissengen, Ger. 148 G7
Badlands, region, N. Dak., U.S. 104 G2
Badlands National Park, S. Dak., U.S. 104 L2
Bad Mergentheim, Ger. 148 H7
Badogo, Mali 196 J7
Ba Dong, Vietnam 187 Q12
Badong, China 182 K3
Badrah, Iraq 172 E10
Bad Reichenhall, Ger. 148 L10
Badr Ḩunayn, Saudi Arabia 172 K6
Bad Säckingen, Ger. 148 L5
Bad Tölz, Ger. 148 L8
Badulla, Sri Lanka 179 T8
Badupi, Myanmar 186 G4
Baengnyeongdo, island, S. Korea 182 E11
Baetic Mountains, Sp. 138 K2
Bafa Gölü, Turk. 168 G3
Bafatá, Guinea-Bissau 200 E4
Baffin Bay, Nunavut, Can. 83 D17
Baffin Bay, Tex., U.S. 103 U11
Baffin Island, Nunavut, Can. 83 E16
Bafia, Cameroon 201 H15
Bafing, river, Guinea, Mali 194 G2
Bafoulabé, Mali 196 H6
Bafoussam, Cameroon 201 H15
Bafra, Turk. 168 C11
Bafra Burnu, Turk. 168 C11
Bāft, Iran 173 G15
Baga, island, Solomon Is. 217 L15
Bagamoyo, Tanzania 199 M15
Bagana, Mount, P.N.G. 217 K14
Bagan Serai, Malaysia 187 T9
Bagansiapiapi, Indonesia 188 H6
Bagdad, Ariz., U.S. 107 S6
Bagdarin, Russ. 159 K16
Bagé, Braz. 130 Q11
Bagenalstown see Muine Bheag, Ire. 143 T6
Bages et de Sigean, Étang de, Fr. 147 Y11
Baggs, Wyo., U.S. 106 K11
Baghdād, Iraq 172 D9
Bagheria, It. 151 S9
Bāghīn, Iran 173 F15
Baghlan, Afghan. 176 L7
Baghran Khowleh, Afghan. 177 N4
Bağırpaşa Dağı, Turk. 169 F14
Bağışlı, Turk. 169 G18
Bagley, Minn., U.S. 104 F9
Bagnères-de-Bigorre, Fr. 147 Y7
Bagnères-de-Luchon, Fr. 147 Y8
Bago, Myanmar 186 K6
Bago Yoma, Myanmar 186 J6
Bagram, Afghan. 176 M8
Bagrimi, Afghan. 176 M8
Baguio, Philippines 189 B13
Bagzane, Mount, Niger 194 F5
Bahama Islands, N. Amer. 80 M9
Bahamas, N. Amer. 81 M21
Baharic-Caghag, Malta 161 J22
Bahau, Malaysia 187 U10
Bahawalnagar, Pak. 177 R11
Bahawalpur, Pak. 177 S10
Bahçe, Turk. 168 H11
Bahçesaray, Turk. 169 G17
Bäherden, Turkm. 174 L8
Bahia see Salvador, Braz. 131 H17
Bahía, Isla de la, Hond. 115 K17
Bahía Blanca, Arg. 133 N11
Bahía de Caráquez, Ecua. 128 J2
Bahia Honda Key, Fla., U.S. 97 Y9
Bahía Laura, Arg. 133 U9
Bahir Dar, Eth. 199 F14
Bahlah, Oman 173 K16
Bahraich, India 178 F8
Bahrain, Asia 167 V4
Bāhū Kalāt, Iran 173 H18
Baia de Aramă, Rom. 152 F12
Baía dos Tigres, Angola 202 F5
Baia Mare, Rom. 153 B13
Baia Sprie, Rom. 153 B13
Baïbokoum, Chad 197 K14
Bai Bung, Mui, Vietnam 187 Q11
Baicheng, China 180 F6
Băicoi, Rom. 153 E15
Baidoa see Baydhabo, Somalia 199 J16
Baie-Comeau, Que., Can. 83 N20
Baie-Mahault, Guadeloupe, Fr. 121 E14
Baihe, China 182 B13
Baihe, China 182 J2
Baikal, Lake, Russ. 166 E10
Baikha, Russ. 159 H13
Baikunthpur, India 178 J8
Baile Átha Cliath see Dublin, Ire. 143 S7
Bailén, Sp. 144 K11
Băileşti, Rom. 153 G13
Baileys Harbor, Wis., U.S. 98 H8
Bailey Town, Bahamas 120 B8
Bailique, Braz. 131 C13
Baillif, Guadeloupe, Fr. 121 G14
Bailong, river, China 180 K12
Bailundo, Angola 202 D6
Baima, China 180 K11
Bainbridge, Ga., U.S. 97 Q5
Bainet, Haiti 117 N16
Baing, Indonesia 189 N13
Bainville, Mont., U.S. 106 B13
Baiona, Sp. 144 C5
Bā'ir, Jordan 171 P8
Baird, Tex., U.S. 102 M8
Baird Inlet, Alas., U.S. 110 J12
Baird Mountains, Alas., U.S. 111 D14
Bairiki see Tarawa, Kiribati 217 G17
Bairin Youqi, China 182 A8
Bairin Zuoqi, China 181 E15
Bairnsdale, Vic., Austral. 211 Z13
Baisha, China 182 M8
Baiti, region, Nauru 217 E23
Baixo, Ilhéu de, Madeira 204 L5
Baiyin, China 180 J11
Baja, Hung. 149 N15
Baja California, peninsula, Mex. 114 B5
Bajag, India 178 J8
Bājgīrān, Iran 173 B16
Bājil, Yemen 172 Q8
Bajmok, Serb. & Mont. 152 D9
Bajo, Indonesia 189 J13
Bakchar, Russ. 158 K12
Bakel, Senegal 196 H6
Baker, Calif., U.S. 109 V11
Baker, river, Chile 133 U6
Baker, Mont., U.S. 106 D13
Baker, Nev., U.S. 109 Q13
Baker, Mount, Wash., U.S. 108 A4
Baker City, Oreg., U.S. 108 G8
Baker Foreland, Nunavut, Can. 83 H15
Baker Island, Pac. Oc. 214 G9
Baker Lake, Austral. 210 G6
Baker Lake, Nunavut, Can. 83 H14
Baker Lake, Nunavut, Can. 83 H14
Bakersfield, Calif., U.S. 109 V7
Bakhchysaray, Ukr. 157 T7
Bakhmach, Ukr. 157 N7
Bakhta, Russ. 159 H13
Bakhtegān, Daryācheh-ye, Iran 173 G14
Baki (Baku), Azerb. 169 D23
Bakırdağı, Turk. 168 G11
Bakkafjörður, Ice. 140 F4
Bakkagerði, Ice. 140 F4
Bako, Eth. 199 H14
Bakony, range, Hung. 149 M13
Baku see Baki, Azerb. 169 D23
Bakuriani, Rep. of Georgia 169 C17
Bakutis Coast, Antarctica 226 L7
Balâ, Turk. 168 E8
Balabac, island, Philippines 188 F12
Balabac, Philippines 188 F12
Balabac Strait, Malaysia, Philippines 188 F12
Balabat, F.S.M. 217 D18
Balabio, Île, New Caledonia, Fr. 218 B6
Bala Boluk, Afghan. 177 P2
Balaclava, Jam. 120 J7
Balagansk, Russ. 159 L15
Balaghat, India 178 K7
Balaghat Range, India 178 L5
Balaguer, Sp. 145 D16
Balakän, Azerb. 169 C20
Balakhna, Russ. 156 H12
Balaklava, S. Aust., Austral. 211 X10
Balaklava, Ukr. 157 T7
Balakliya, Ukr. 157 P9
Balakot, Pak. 176 M11
Balakovo, Russ. 156 M14
Balamorghab, Afghan. 176 L3
Bălan, Rom. 153 C15
Balancán, Mex. 115 J15
Balangir, India 178 K9
Balaözen, river, Kaz., Russ. 174 D5
Balashi, site, Aruba, Neth. 121 Q17
Balashov, Russ. 156 M12
Balassagyarmat, Hung. 149 K15
Balaton, lake, Hung. 149 M14
Balatonszentgyörgy, Hung. 149 M13
Balazote, Sp. 144 J12
Balbi, Mount, P.N.G. 217 J13
Balbina Reservoir, S. Amer. 126 D6
Balcarce, Arg. 133 N13
Balchik, Bulg. 153 G17
Balclutha, N.Z. 213 R16
Bald Knob, Ark., U.S. 100 F9
Bald Mountain, Nev., U.S. 109 S11
Baldwin, Fla., U.S. 97 Q8
Baldwin City, Kans., U.S. 105 T10
Baldwinsville, N.Y., U.S. 94 J8
Baldwyn, Miss., U.S. 101 H13
Baldy, Mount, Ariz., U.S. 107 T9
Baldy Peak see Baldy, Mount, Ariz., U.S. 84 K7
Balearic Islands, Sp. 145 H16
Balearic Sea, Sp. 145 G16
Baleia, Ponta da, Braz. 131 K16
Baleine Bay, St. Vincent & the Grenadines 121 J16
Balembangan, island, Malaysia 188 F12
Baleshare, island, Scot., U.K. 142 J6
Baleshwar, India 178 K11
Baley, Russ. 159 L17
Balfes Creek, Qnsld., Austral. 211 S13
Balfour Channel, Solomon Is. 217 M16
Balfour Downs, W. Aust., Austral. 211 T4
Balgazyn, Russ. 159 M14
Balgo, W. Aust., Austral. 211 S6
Balguerie, Cap, Fr. Polynesia, Fr. 219 M21
Balḩāf, Yemen 172 Q11
Bali, India 178 H3
Bali, island, Indonesia 188 M11
Bali, Selat, Indonesia 188 M11
Balıkesir, Turk. 168 E4
Balık Gölü, Turk. 168 C11
Balīkh, river, Syr. 170 D11
Balikpapan, Indonesia 188 J12
Balimo, P.N.G. 213 D18
Balingen, Ger. 148 K6
Balingian, Malaysia 187 U16
Balintang Channel, Philippines 189 A14
Bali Sea, Indonesia 188 M11
Balkanabat, Turkm. 174 L6
Balkan Mountains, Bulg. 152 H12
Balkan Peninsula, Eur. 138 J9
Balkh, Afghan. 176 K6
Balkhab, Afghan. 176 L6
Balkhash, Lake, Kaz. 166 F7
Balladonia, W. Aust., Austral. 211 X5
Ballalae, island, Solomon Is. 217 L14
Ballantyne Strait, N.W.T., Can. 82 C13
Ballarat, Vic., Austral. 211 Z12
Ballard, Lake, Austral. 210 J4
Ball Bay, Norfolk I., Austral. 217 G20
Ballenas, Bahía, Mex. 114 D6
Ballenero, Canal, Chile 133 Y8
Ballina, Ire. 143 Q4
Ballina, N.S.W., Austral. 211 W15
Ballinger, Tex., U.S. 103 N7
Ballinrobe, Ire. 143 R3
Ballinskelligs Bay, Ire. 143 U2
Ball's Pyramid, island, Austral. 214 M6
Ballycastle, N. Ire., U.K. 143 N7
Ballycroy, Ire. 143 Q3
Ballyhaise, Ire. 143 R6
Ballymena, N. Ire., U.K. 143 P7
Ballymoney, N. Ire., U.K. 143 P7
Ballysadare, Ire. 143 Q4
Ballyshannon, Ire. 143 Q5
Ballyvourney, Ire. 143 U3
Balmaceda, Chile 133 T7
Balmorhea, Tex., U.S. 103 P2
Balod, India 178 K8
Baloeri de Cristo Rey, Eq. Guinea 204 L7
Balonne, river, Qnsld., Austral. 211 V14
Balotra, India 178 G3
Balpyq Bī, Kaz. 175 G17
Balqash, Kaz. 175 F15
Balqash Köli, Kaz. 175 G15
Balrampur, India 178 F8
Balranald, N.S.W., Austral. 211 Y12
Balş, Rom. 153 F13
Balsas, river, Mex. 114 J11
Balsas, Braz. 131 F14
Balta, N. Dak., U.S. 104 E5
Balta, Ukr. 157 Q5
Baltasar Brum, Uru. 132 J13

Bălţi, Mold. 157 Q4
Baltic Plains, Eur. 138 E8
Baltic Sea, Eur. 138 E8
Baltimore, Md., U.S. 96 C13
Baltistan, region, Pak. 176 L13
Baltit, Pak. 176 K12
Baltiysk, Russ. 156 J1
Baltra, Isla, Ecua. 128 Q9
Baluchistan, region, Iran, Pak. 177 U2
Balurghat, India 178 H12
Balya, Turk. 168 E3
Balykchy (Ysyk-Köl), Kyrg. 176 E12
Balyqshy, Kaz. 174 F6
Balzers, Liech. 160 Q2
Bam, Iran 173 G16
Bama, Nigeria 201 E17
Bamaga, Qnsld., Austral. 211 N12
Bamako, Mali 196 J7
Bambari, Cen. Af. Rep. 198 H9
Bambaroo, Qnsld., Austral. 211 R13
Bamberg, Ger. 148 H8
Bamberg, S.C., U.S. 96 L9
Bamboo, Jam. 120 H8
Bamboo, W. Aust., Austral. 211 S3
Bam Co, China 180 K8
Bamenda, Cameroon 201 H15
Bamian, Afghan. 176 M6
Bamingui, Cen. Af. Rep. 198 G9
Bampūr, river, Iran 173 H17
Bampūr, Iran 173 H17
Bamy, Turkm. 174 L7
Bamyili-Beswick, N. Terr., Austral. 211 Q8
Banaba (Ocean Island), Kiribati 214 G7
Banalia, Dem. Rep. of the Congo 198 J11
Banam, Cambodia 187 P12
Banana, river, Fla., U.S. 97 T10
Banana, Kiribati 217 A23
Banana, Qnsld., Austral. 211 U14
Bananal, Ilha do, Braz. 130 G12
Bananga, India 179 T15
Bananier, Guadeloupe, Fr. 121 G14
Banaras see Varanasi, India 178 H9
Banâs, Râs, Egypt 197 E20
Banas, river, India 178 G5
Banat, region, Rom., Serb. & Mont. 152 D10
Banaz, Turk. 168 F5
Ban Ban, Laos 186 J10
Ban Bang Hin, Thai. 187 Q7
Banbridge, N. Ire., U.K. 143 Q7
Banbury, Eng., U.K. 143 U12
Banchory, Scot., U.K. 142 K11
Bancroft, Iowa, U.S. 104 M11
Banda, India 178 H6
Banda, Kepulauan, Indonesia 189 L17
Banda, Pointe, Gabon 201 M15
Banda Aceh, Indonesia 188 G3
Banda Besar, island, Indonesia 189 L17
Banda Elat, Indonesia 189 L18
Bandanaira, Indonesia 189 L17
Bandar see Machilipatnam, India 179 N8
Bandarban, Bangladesh 178 J14
Bandarbeyla, Somalia 199 F18
Bandar-e ʽAbbās, Iran 173 H15
Bandar-e Anzalī, Iran 172 B12
Bandar-e Būshehr, Iran 172 G12
Bandar-e Chārak, Iran 173 H14
Bandar-e Deylam, Iran 172 F12
Bandar-e Khoemir, Iran 173 H15
Bandar-e Māh Shahr, Iran 172 F12
Bandar-e Maqām, Iran 173 H14
Bandar-e Mollaha, Afghan. 176 L4
Bandar Seri Begawan, Brunei 188 G11
Banda Sea, Ind. Oc. 241 H17
Banda Sea, Indonesia 189 L16
Bandau, Malaysia 188 F12
Bandeira, peak, Braz. 131 L15
Bandeirante, Braz. 130 H12
Bandelier National Monument, N. Mex., U.S. 107 R12
Bandera, Arg. 132 H11
Bandera, Tex., U.S. 103 R9
Banderas Bay, N. Amer. 80 N4
Bandiagara, Mali 196 H8
Bandikui, India 178 G5
Bandırma, Turk. 168 D4
Ban Don, Vietnam 187 N13
Bandon, Oreg., U.S. 108 J1
Bändovan Burnu, Azerb. 169 E23
Bandundu, Dem. Rep. of the Congo 198 L8
Bandung, Indonesia 188 M8
Banes, Cuba 117 J13
Banff, Alta., Can. 82 M10
Banfora, Burkina Faso 200 F9
Bangalore, India 179 P6
Bangassou, Cen. Af. Rep. 198 H10
Banggai, Kepulauan, Indonesia 189 K14
Banggi, island, Malaysia 188 F12
Banggong Co, China, India 178 C7
Banghāzī (Benghazi), Lib. 197 C15
Banghiang, river, Laos 186 L12
Bangi Island, Guam, U.S. 216 D10
Bangka, island, Indonesia 189 H15
Bangka, island, Indonesia 188 K8
Bangkaru, island, Indonesia 188 H4
Bangkok see Krung Thep, Thai. 186 M9
Bangladesh, Asia 167 W9
Bangor, Me., U.S. 95 E17
Bangor Erris, Ire. 143 Q3
Bangs, Aust. 160 L2
Bangs, Tex., U.S. 103 N8
Bang Saphan, Thai. 187 P8
Bangui, Cen. Af. Rep. 198 H8
Bangui, Philippines 189 B13
Bangweulu, Lake, Zambia 202 D11
Bani, river, Mali 196 H8
Baní, Dom. Rep. 117 M19
Banihal Pass, India 177 N12
Banī Sharfā, Saudi Arabia 172 M8
Banī Walīd, Lib. 197 C14
Bāniyās, Syr. 170 F7
Banja Luka, Bosn. & Herzg. 152 F7
Banjarmasin, Indonesia 188 K11
Banjul, Gambia 196 H4
Bankä, Azerb. 169 E23
Banka, India 178 H11
Banka Banka, N. Terr., Austral. 211 R9
Banks, Bahía de, Ecua. 128 P8
Banks Island, B.C., Can. 82 K7
Banks Island, N.W.T., Can. 82 D12
Banks Islands, Vanuatu 218 B2
Banks Lake, Wash., U.S. 108 C7
Banks Peninsula, N.Z. 213 P18
Banmauk, Myanmar 186 F6
Bann, river, N. Ire., U.K. 143 P7
Bannerman Town, Bahamas 120 F6
Bannu, Pak. 177 P9
Bánovce nad Bebravou, Slovakia 149 J14
Banow, Afghan. 176 L8
Ban Phai, Thai. 186 L10
Banreaba, Kiribati 217 G17
Ban Sanam Chai, Thai. 187 R9
Banská Bystrica, Slovakia 149 J15
Banswara, India 178 J4
Bantabaré Pequeño, Eq. Guinea 204 M7
Ban Taphan, Laos 186 L12
Bantry Bay, Ire. 143 V3
Bantva, India 178 K2
Bantval, India 179 Q4
Ban Xénô, Laos 186 K11
Banzare Coast, Antarctica 227 P19
Baochang see Taibus Qi, China 182 B6
Baode, China 182 D3
Baoding, China 182 D6
Baofeng, China 182 H4
Baó Grande, Eq. Guinea 204 M8
Baoji, China 182 G1
Baojing, China 182 M2
Bao Lac, Vietnam 186 G12
Baoro, Cen. Af. Rep. 198 H8
Baoshan, China 180 N10
Baoting, China 183 U1
Baotou, China 182 C3
Baoying, China 182 J8
Bapatla, India 179 N7
Baqbaqty, Kaz. 175 H16
Baqty, Kaz. 175 F18
Baʽqūbah, Iraq 172 D10
Baquedano, Chile 132 E7
Bar, Serb. & Mont. 152 J8
Bara, Indonesia 189 K15
Bara, Sudan 198 E12
Baraawe, Somalia 199 J16
Baraboo, Wis., U.S. 98 L5
Baracoa, Cuba 117 K14
Baraga, Mich., U.S. 98 F6
Bărăganul, plain, Rom. 153 F17
Baragoi, Kenya 199 J14
Barahona, Dom. Rep. 117 M18
Bara Hoti, India 178 E7
Barak, Turk. 168 J12
Baraki, Afghan. 177 N7
Baramula, India 176 M12
Baran, India 178 H5
Baranavichy, Belarus 156 L4
Barangbarang, Indonesia 189 L13
Baranof Island, Alas., U.S. 111 M22
Baranovka, Russ. 157 N14
Barão de Melgaço, Braz. 130 J10
Barataria Bay, La., U.S. 100 R11
Barat Daya, Kepulauan, Indonesia 189 M16
Barate, Indonesia 189 N14
Baraterre, Bahamas 120 E8
Barbacena, Braz. 131 L14
Barbacoas, Col. 128 H3
Barbados, N. Amer. 81 P24
Barbados, island, N. Amer. 80 P12
Barbaria, Cap de, Sp. 145 J17
Barbastro, Sp. 145 D15
Barber, Neth. Antilles, Neth. 121 P13
Barbers Block, peak, Dominica 121 E18
Barberton, Ohio, U.S. 99 P14
Barbezieux, Fr. 147 U7
Barbourville, Ky., U.S. 101 D18
Barbuda, island, Antigua & Barbuda 119 F16
Barcaldine, Qnsld., Austral. 211 T13
Barcellona Pozzo di Gotto, It. 151 R12
Barcelona, Sp. 145 E17
Barcelona, Venez. 128 B11
Barcelos, Port. 144 D5
Barcelos, Braz. 130 C8
Barco, N.C., U.S. 96 G14
Barcoo, river, Austral. 210 G12
Barcs, Hung. 149 N13
Bärdä, Azerb. 169 D21
Barda del Medio, Arg. 133 N8
Barda Hills, India 178 J1
Bardaï, Chad 197 F14
Bardas Blancas, Arg. 132 M7
Bardawīl, Sabkhet el, Egypt 171 N2
Barddhaman, India 178 J11
Bardejov, Slovakia 149 H16
Bardoc, W. Aust., Austral. 211 W4
Bardonecchia, It. 150 E1
Bardsey Island, Wales, U.K. 143 T8
Bardstown, Ky., U.S. 101 C17
Bardwell, Ky., U.S. 100 D12
Bareilly, India 178 F7
Barentin, Fr. 147 N8
Barents Plain, Arctic Oc. 243 G13
Barents Sea, Arctic Oc. 243 D15
Barfak, Afghan. 176 L7
Barfleur, Fr. 147 N6
Barfleur, Pointe de, Fr. 147 N6
Barga, China 180 K5
Barga, It. 150 G6
Bargaal, Somalia 199 F18
Bargarh, India 178 K9
Barg-e Matal, Afghan. 176 L9
Bar Harbor, Me., U.S. 95 F18
Barhi, India 178 H10
Barhi, India 178 H7
Bari, It. 150 L14
Ba Ria, Vietnam 187 P13
Barigello, river, It. 161 G16
Barikowt, Afghan. 176 L9
Barīm (Perim), island, Yemen 172 R8
Barima, river, Guyana 129 D14
Barinas, Venez. 128 C7
Baripada, India 178 J11
Bârîs, Egypt 197 E18
Barisal, Bangladesh 178 J13
Barisan, Pegunungan, Indonesia 188 K6
Barisan Mountains see Barisan, Pegunungan, Indonesia 166 M11
Barkā', Oman 173 K16
Barka Kana, India 178 J10
Barkers, Head of, Cayman Is., U.K. 120 H2
Barkhan, Pak. 177 R8
Barkley, Lake, Ky., U.S. 101 D14
Barkly Tableland, Austral. 210 D9
Barkol, China 180 E9
Barkol Hu, China 180 E9
Barla Dağı, Turk. 168 G6
Bar-le-Duc, Fr. 147 P13
Barlee, Lake, Austral. 210 J3
Barletta, It. 150 L13
Barlinek, Pol. 148 D11
Barmer, India 178 G3
Barmouth, Wales, U.K. 143 T9
Bärnau, Ger. 148 H9
Barnaul, Russ. 158 L12
Barnegat, N.J., U.S. 94 Q11
Barnegat Light, N.J., U.S. 94 Q11
Barnes Ice Cap, Nunavut, Can. 83 E17
Barnesville, Ga., U.S. 96 M5
Barnesville, Minn., U.S. 104 G8
Barneville-Carteret, Fr. 147 N5
Barnhart, Tex., U.S. 103 P6
Barn Hill, Austral. 210 D4
Barnsdall, Okla., U.S. 102 E12
Barnsley, Eng., U.K. 143 R12
Barnstaple, Eng., U.K. 143 W9
Barnstaple Bay, Eng., U.K. 143 W9
Barnum Bay, Palau 216 Q10
Barnwell, S.C., U.S. 96 L8
Baro, Nigeria 201 G13
Baroghil Pass, Afghan., Pak. 176 K11
Baron Bluff, Virgin Islands, U.S. 120 Q2
Barora Fa, island, Solomon Is. 217 L17
Barora Ite, island, Solomon Is. 217 L17
Barpeta, India 178 G13
Barquisimeto, Venez. 128 B8
Barra, island, Scot., U.K. 142 K6
Barra, Braz. 131 G15
Barra, Ponta da, Mozambique 203 H13
Barra, Sound of, Scot., U.K. 142 K6
Barracks of Swiss Guard, Vatican City 161 P17
Barra do Bugres, Braz. 130 J10
Barra do Corda, Braz. 131 E14
Barra do São Manuel, Braz. 130 F10
Barrancabermeja, Col. 128 D5
Barrancas, Venez. 128 C12
Barrancos, Port. 144 K7
Barranqueras, Arg. 132 G13
Barranquilla, Col. 128 B5
Barranquitas, P.R., U.S. 120 N4
Barras, Braz. 131 E15
Barrax, Sp. 144 H12
Barre, Vt., U.S. 95 G13
Barreiras, Braz. 131 H14
Barreirinha, Braz. 130 D10
Barreirinhas, Braz. 131 D15
Barreiro, Port. 144 J4
Barrel Post Office, Ecua. 128 R9
Barrême, Fr. 147 W14
Barren, river, Ky., U.S. 101 D16
Barren, Nosy, Madagascar 203 F16
Barrhill, Scot., U.K. 143 P8
Barrie, Ont., Can. 83 Q18
Barrigada, Guam, U.S. 216 C11
Barrington see Santa Fe, Isla, island, Ecua. 128 Q10
Barringun, N.S.W., Austral. 211 W13
Barron, Wis., U.S. 98 H3
Barrouallie, St. Vincent & the Grenadines 121 K16
Barrow, Alas., U.S. 111 B15
Barrow, river, Ire. 143 T6
Barrow, Point, Alas., U.S. 111 B15
Barrow Canyon, Arctic Oc. 242 L5
Barrow Creek, N. Terr., Austral. 211 S8
Barrow in Furness, Eng., U.K. 143 Q10
Barrow Island, W. Aust., Austral. 211 S1
Barrow Strait, Arctic Oc. 242 P10
Barry, Ill., U.S. 99 R3
Barrytown, N.Z. 213 N17
Barshatas, Kaz. 175 E17
Barstow, Calif., U.S. 109 W10
Bar-sur-Seine, Fr. 147 Q12
Bartholomew, Bayou, Ark., La., U.S. 100 K9
Bartica, Guyana 129 D14
Bartın, Turk. 168 C8
Bartle Frere, peak, Austral. 210 D13
Bartlesville, Okla., U.S. 102 E12
Bartlett, Nebr., U.S. 105 P6
Bartlett, Tex., U.S. 103 P11
Bartolomeu Dias, Mozambique 203 G13
Barton, N. Dak., U.S. 104 E5
Barton, Vt., U.S. 95 F13
Barton Siding, S. Aust., Austral. 211 W8
Bartoszyce, Pol. 149 B16
Bartow, Fla., U.S. 97 U8
Barú, Volcán, Pan. 115 N20
Baruunharaa, Mongolia 180 C12
Baruunsuu, Mongolia 180 F12
Baruun Urt, Mongolia 181 D14
Barvas, Scot., U.K. 142 H7
Barwani, India 178 J4
Barwon, river, N.S.W., Austral. 211 W14
Barykova, Mys, Russ. 159 B21
Barysaw, Belarus 156 K5
Barysh, Russ. 156 K14
Basacato del Este, Eq. Guinea 204 M8
Basacato del Oeste, Eq. Guinea 204 M7
Basaga, Turkm. 174 M11
Basankusu, Dem. Rep. of the Congo 198 J9
Basargech'ar, Arm. 169 D19
Basaseachic Falls, N. Amer. 80 M4
Basco, Philippines 189 A14
Bascuñán, Cabo, Chile 132 H6
Basel, Switz. 150 A3
Basilan, island, Philippines 189 F14
Basilé, Eq. Guinea 204 L8
Basile, La., U.S. 100 P8
Basiliano, It. 150 D9
Basilisk Harbor, Solomon Is. 217 Q23
Basin, Wyo., U.S. 106 G10
Basingstoke, Eng., U.K. 143 W13
Basīt, Ra's al, Syr. 170 E7
Başkale, Turk. 169 G18
Baskil, Turk. 169 G13
Baskunchak, Ozero, Russ. 157 Q14
Basmat, India 178 L5
Basoko, Dem. Rep. of the Congo 198 J10
Basora, Punta, Aruba, Neth. 121 R17
Bass, Îlots de see Marotiri, Fr. Polynesia, Fr. 215 L14
Bassae, ruin, Gr. 154 K9
Bassas da India, islands, Mozambique Ch. 203 H14
Basse-Pointe, Martinique, Fr. 121 E22
Basses, Pointe des, Guadeloupe, Fr. 121 G16
Basse Terre, Trinidad & Tobago 121 Q22
Basseterre, St. Kitts & Nevis 121 B17
Basse-Terre, island, Guadeloupe, Fr. 121 F14
Basse-Terre, Guadeloupe, Fr. 121 G14
Bassett, Nebr., U.S. 105 N5
Bassett, Va., U.S. 96 G10
Bassikounou, Mauritania 196 H8
Bass Islands, Ohio, U.S. 99 N13
Bass Islands, Solomon Is. 217 N24
Bass Strait, Vic., Austral. 211 Z12
Bastak, Iran 173 H14
Bastendorf, Lux. 160 H10
Basti, India 178 G8
Bastia, Fr. 150 J4
Bastogne, Belg. 146 M13
Bastrop, La., U.S. 100 K9
Bastrop, Tex., U.S. 103 Q11
Bastuträsk, Sw. 141 G14
Basu, island, Indonesia 188 J7
Basuo see Dongfang, China 183 U1
Basupú, Eq. Guinea 204 L7
Bata, Eq. Guinea 201 K15
Bataan Peninsula, Philippines 189 C13
Batabanó, Golfo de, Cuba 116 H6
Batagay, Russ. 159 F18
Batala, India 177 P12
Batamay, Russ. 159 G18
Batan, island, Philippines 189 A14
Batang, China 180 L10
Batangafo, Cen. Af. Rep. 198 G8
Batangas, Philippines 189 C13
Batan Islands, Philippines 189 A14
Batanta, island, Indonesia 189 J17
Batavia, N.Y., U.S. 94 J6
Bataysk, Russ. 157 R11
Bates, Mount, Norfolk I., Austral. 217 F20
Batesburg, S.C., U.S. 96 L8
Batesville, Ark., U.S. 100 F9
Batesville, Ind., U.S. 99 S10
Batesville, Miss., U.S. 100 H11
Batesville, Tex., U.S. 103 S8
Batete, Eq. Guinea 204 M7
Bath, Eng., U.K. 143 V11
Bath, Jam. 120 J11
Bath, Me., U.S. 95 G16
Bath, N.Y., U.S. 94 K7
Bath, St. Kitts & Nevis 121 C18
Bathsheba, Barbados 121 K19
Bathurst, N.B., Can. 83 N21
Bathurst, N.S.W., Austral. 211 X14
Bathurst, Cape, N.W.T., Can. 82 D11
Bathurst Inlet, Nunavut, Can. 83 F13
Bathurst Island, N. Terr., Austral. 211 N7
Bathurst Island, Nunavut, Can. 83 D14
Batié, Burkina Faso 200 F9
Batiki, island, Fiji Is. 218 J7
Batista, Serra da, Braz. 131 F16
Batman, Turk. 169 G15
Batna, Alg. 196 A12
Batoicopo, Eq. Guinea 204 L7
Baton Rouge, La., U.S. 100 P10
Batouri, Cameroon 201 H17
Båtsfjord, Nor. 141 B15
Batsí, Gr. 155 J14
Battambang, Cambodia 187 N10
Batteau, Nfld. & Lab., Can. 83 K22
Batticaloa, Sri Lanka 179 S8
Battle Creek, Mich., U.S. 98 M10
Battle Creek, Mont., U.S. 106 A9
Battle Harbour, Nfld. & Lab., Can. 83 L23
Battle Mountain, Nev., U.S. 109 N9
Batu, peak, Eth. 199 G15
Batu, Kepulauan, Indonesia 188 J5

Batukelau, Indonesia 188 J11
Bat'umi, Rep. of Georgia 169 C16
Batu Pahat, Malaysia 187 V10
Batuputih, Indonesia 188 H12
Baturaja, Indonesia 188 L7
Baturité, Braz. 131 E17
Bat Yam, Israel 170 M5
Batz, Île de, Fr. 147 P3
Bau, island, Fiji Is. 218 J7
Baubau, Indonesia 189 L14
Baucau, Timor-Leste 189 M15
Bauchi, Nigeria 201 F15
Baudette, Minn., U.S. 104 E10
Baudó, Serranía de, S. Amer. 126 B2
Baugé, Fr. 147 R7
Bauges, range, Fr. 147 U14
Baun, Indonesia 189 N14
Baunatal, Ger. 148 F7
Baures, river, Bol. 130 H8
Bauru, Braz. 131 L13
Baús, Braz. 130 K11
Bautino, Kaz. 174 G5
Bautzen, Ger. 148 F11
Bavaria, region, Ger. 148 J8
Bawal, island, Indonesia 188 K9
Bawean, island, Indonesia 188 L10
Bawku, Ghana 200 F11
Baxkorgan, China 180 G8
Baxley, Ga., U.S. 97 N7
Baxoi, China 180 L9
Baxter, Minn., U.S. 104 H10
Baxter Springs, Kans., U.S. 105 V10
Bay'ah, Oman 173 J15
Bayamo, Cuba 116 K12
Bayamón, P.R., U.S. 120 M4
Bayan, Mongolia 180 E9
Bayanaūyl, Kaz. 175 D15
Bayandalay, Mongolia 180 F11
Bayanga, Cen. Af. Rep. 198 J8
Bayan Gol see Dengkou, China 182 C1
Bayan Har Shan, China 180 J9
Bayan Har Shankou, China 180 J10
Bayanhongor, Mongolia 180 E11
Bayanmönh, Mongolia 181 D13
Bayano, Lago, Pan. 115 N22
Bayan Obo, China 182 B3
Bayan Range, Afghan. 176 M5
Bayard, N. Mex., U.S. 107 V10
Bayard, Nebr., U.S. 105 P1
Bayat, Turk. 168 F6
Bayāz, Iran 173 F15
Bayboro, N.C., U.S. 96 J14
Bayburt, Turk. 169 E15
Bay City, Mich., U.S. 98 K12
Bay City, Tex., U.S. 103 S13
Baydarata Bay, Arctic Oc. 243 A14
Baydaratskaya Guba, Russ. 158 F11
Baydhabo (Baidoa), Somalia 199 J16
Bayès, Cap, New Caledonia, Fr. 218 C7
Bayeux, Fr. 147 N7
Bayfield, Wis., U.S. 98 E4
Bayghanīn, Kaz. 174 E8
Bayḩān al Qişāb, Yemen 172 Q10
Bayındır, Turk. 168 G3
Bay Islands, N. Amer. 80 P7
Bayjī, Iraq 172 C9
Baykal, Ozero, Russ. 159 L16
Baykan, Turk. 169 G16
Baykonur see Bayqongyr, Kaz. 174 G10
Baykonur Cosmodrome, Kaz. 174 G11
Baykurt, China 180 F4
Bay Minette, Ala., U.S. 101 N14
Bay of Whales, station, Antarctica 226 N11
Bayonne, Fr. 147 X5
Bayqongyr (Baykonur, Leninsk), Kaz. 174 G10
Bayramaly, Turkm. 174 M10
Bayramiç, Turk. 168 E2
Bayreuth, Ger. 148 H9
Bay St. Louis, Miss., U.S. 100 P12
Bay Springs, Miss., U.S. 100 M12
Bayt al Faqīh, Yemen 172 Q8
Bayt Laḩm (Bethlehem), W. Bank 170 M5
Baytown, Tex., U.S. 103 Q14
Baza, Sp. 144 L12
Baza'i Gonbad, Afghan. 176 K11
Bazar Dyuzi, peak, Azerb. 169 C21
Bazar-e Panjva'i, Afghan. 177 Q5
Bazar-e Taleh, Afghan. 176 L7
Bazar-Kurgan, Kyrg. 176 F10
Bazartöbe, Kaz. 174 D6
Bazas, Fr. 147 W7
Bazkovskaya, Russ. 157 P11
Bazmān, Kūh-e, Iran 173 G17
Be, Nosy, Madagascar 203 D18
Beach, N. Dak., U.S. 104 G1
Beach Haven, N.J., U.S. 94 Q11
Beachy Head, Eng., U.K. 143 W14
Beagle Bay, W. Aust., Austral. 211 R4
Béar, Cap, Fr. 147 Z11
Bearden, Ark., U.S. 100 J8
Beardmore Glacier, Antarctica 227 L13
Beardstown, Ill., U.S. 99 R4
Bear Island, Ire. 143 V2
Bear Islands see Medvezh'i Ostrova, Russ. 159 C19
Bear Lake, Idaho, Utah, U.S. 106 J8
Bear Paw Mountains, Mont., U.S. 84 C8
Bear River Range, Idaho, Utah, U.S. 106 J7
Bears Paw Mountains, Mont., U.S. 106 B9
Beasain, Sp. 144 B12
Beata, Cabo, Dom. Rep. 117 N17
Beata, Isla, Dom. Rep. 117 N17
Beata Ridge, Atl. Oc. 236 L4
Beatrice, Nebr., U.S. 105 R8
Beatrice, Cape, Austral. 210 B10
Beattock, Scot., U.K. 143 N10
Beatton River, B.C., Can. 82 J9
Beatty, Nev., U.S. 109 T10
Beau Bassin, Mauritius 205 G19
Beaucaire, Fr. 147 X12
Beauchêne Island, Falkland Is., U.K. 133 W12
Beaufort, Lux. 160 J10
Beaufort, Malaysia 188 G11
Beaufort, N.C., U.S. 96 J14
Beaufort, S.C., U.S. 96 M9
Beaufort Sea, Arctic Oc. 242 M5
Beaufort Shelf, Arctic Oc. 242 N5
Beaufort Slope, Arctic Oc. 242 N5
Beaufort West, S. Af. 202 L9
Beaugency, Fr. 147 R9
Beaumanoir, Port du, Fr. Polynesia, Fr. 219 Q17
Beaumont, Tex., U.S. 103 Q15
Beaune, Fr. 147 S13
Beausoleil, Fr. 147 X16
Beausoleil, Town Hall of, Fr. 161 C21
Beautemps Beaupré, Île, New Caledonia, Fr. 218 C8
Beauvais, Fr. 147 N9
Beauvoir, Fr. 147 S5
Beaver, Alas., U.S. 111 E17
Beaver, river, Okla., U.S. 102 E6
Beaver, Okla., U.S. 102 E7
Beaver, Oreg., U.S. 108 F2
Beaver, Utah, U.S. 107 N6
Beaver Bay, Minn., U.S. 104 F13
Beaver City, Nebr., U.S. 105 R5
Beaver Creek, Kans., U.S. 105 R4
Beaver Creek, Mont., U.S. 106 B10
Beaver Dam, Ky., U.S. 101 C15
Beaver Dam, Wis., U.S. 98 L6
Beaver Falls, Pa., U.S. 94 N3
Beaver Glacier, Antarctica 227 C19
Beaverhead, river, Mont., U.S. 106 F6
Beaverhead Mountains, Mont., U.S. 106 F6
Beaver Island, Mich., U.S. 98 G9
Beaver Lake, Ark., U.S. 100 E6
Beaverton, Oreg., U.S. 108 F3
Beawar, India 178 G4
Bebar, India 178 H1
Bebiram, Indonesia 213 B14
Beccles, Eng., U.K. 143 T16
Bečej, Serb. & Mont. 152 E10
Becerreá, Sp. 144 B7
Béchar, Alg. 196 C9
Becharof Lake, Alas., U.S. 111 L14
Beckerich, Lux. 160 J9
Beckley, W. Va., U.S. 96 E8
Beddouza, Cap, Mor. 196 B7
Bedford, Eng., U.K. 143 U13
Bedford, Ind., U.S. 99 T9
Bedford, Iowa, U.S. 105 Q10
Bedford, Pa., U.S. 94 P5
Bedford, Va., U.S. 96 F10
Bedford, Cape, Austral. 210 C13
Bedfort Point, Grenada 121 J23
Bedonia, It. 150 F5
Bedourie, Qnsld., Austral. 211 U10
Bedous, Fr. 147 Y6
Beebe, Ark., U.S. 100 G9
Beech Grove, Ind., U.S. 99 R9
Beef Island, Virgin Islands, U.K. 120 Q7
Beenleigh, Qnsld., Austral. 211 V15
Be'ér Menuḥa, Israel 171 Q5
Be'er Ora, Israel 171 R5
Beersheba see Be'ér Sheva', Israel 171 N5
Be'ér Sheva' (Beersheba), Israel 171 N5
Beetaloo, N. Terr., Austral. 211 R8
Beethoven Peninsula, Antarctica 226 F6
Beeville, Tex., U.S. 103 T10
Bega, N.S.W., Austral. 211 Z14
Bega, river, Rom. 152 D12
Bega, Canalul, Rom. 152 E10
Begejski Kanal, Serb. & Mont. 152 E10
Beggars Point, Antigua & Barbuda 121 A21
Bègles, Fr. 147 V6
Begusarai, India 178 H10
Behagle see Laï, Chad 197 K14
Behbehān, Iran 172 F12
Behring Point, Bahamas 116 E11
Behshahr, Iran 173 B14
Bei, river, China 181 N14
Bei'an, China 181 C17
Beida see Al Bayḑā', Lib. 197 B16
Beihai, China 183 S1
Beijing (Peking), China 182 D7
Beilen, Neth. 146 H14
Beiliu, China 183 R2
Beilul, Eritrea 199 E16
Beipiao, China 182 B9
Beira, Mozambique 203 G13
Beirut see Beyrouth, Leb. 170 H6
Bei Shan, China 180 F9
Beitbridge, Zimb. 202 H11
Beït ed Dîne, Leb. 170 J6
Beiuş, Rom. 152 C12
Beizhen, China 182 B10
Beja, Port. 144 K6
Beja, Tun. 196 A12
Bejaïa, Alg. 196 A11
Béjar, Sp. 144 F8
Bejestān, Iran 173 D16
Bekaa Valley, Leb. 170 J7
Bekdash see Karabogaz, Turkm. 174 J6
Békés, Hung. 149 M17
Békéscsaba, Hung. 149 M17
Bekily, Madagascar 203 J16
Bekja, island, Marshall Is. 216 K8
Bekkai, Japan 184 F16
Bekobod, Taj. 176 G8
Bekobod, Uzb. 175 L13
Bekoropoka-Antongo, Madagascar 203 H16
Bekwai, Ghana 200 H10
Bela, Pak. 177 V5
Belaga, Malaysia 188 H11
Bel Air, Mauritius 205 G20
Belalcázar, Sp. 144 J9
Belarus, Eur. 139 T9
Bela Vista, Braz. 130 L10
Belaya, river, Russ. 138 D14
Belaya, Gora, Russ. 159 C20
Belaya Glina, Russ. 157 S11
Belaya Gora, Russ. 159 E18
Belaya Kalitva, Russ. 157 Q11
Belaya Zemlya, Ostrova, Russ. 159 C13
Bełchatów, Pol. 149 F15
Belcheragh, Afghan. 176 L5
Belcher Islands, Nunavut, Can. 83 L17
Belcik, Turk. 168 E11
Belcoo, N. Ire., U.K. 143 Q5
Belderg, Ire. 143 Q3
Belding, Mich., U.S. 98 L10
Beledweyne, Somalia 199 H17
Belele, W. Aust., Austral. 211 V3
Belém, Braz. 131 D13
Belén, Arg. 132 G8
Belen, N. Mex., U.S. 107 S12
Bélep, Îles, New Caledonia, Fr. 218 B6
Bélep, Îles, New Caledonia, Fr. 214 K7
Belev, Russ. 156 L9
Belfast, Me., U.S. 95 F17
Belfast, N. Ire., U.K. 143 Q7
Belfast Lough, N. Ire., U.K. 143 P7
Belfield, N. Dak., U.S. 104 G2
Belfort, Fr. 147 R15
Belgaum, India 179 N4
Belgica Bank, Arctic Oc. 243 J15
Belgica Mountains, Antarctica 227 C16
Belgium, Eur. 139 T5
Belgodère, Fr. 150 J4
Belgorod, Russ. 157 N9
Belgrade, Mont., U.S. 106 E8
Belgrade see Beograd, Serb. & Mont. 152 F10
Belgrano II, station, Antarctica 226 E10
Belhaven, N.C., U.S. 96 H14
Belidzhi, Russ. 157 U16
Belilou see Peleliu, island, Palau 216 Q10
Belinyu, Indonesia 188 K8
Belitung (Billiton), island, Indonesia 188 K9
Belize, N. Amer. 81 P19
Belize City, Belize 115 K16
Bel'kachi, Russ. 159 H19
Bel'kovskiy, Ostrov, Russ. 159 D16
Bella Bella, B.C., Can. 82 K7
Bellac, Fr. 147 T8
Bella Coola, B.C., Can. 82 K8
Bellaire, Mich., U.S. 98 H10
Bellaire, Ohio, U.S. 99 R15
Bellaire, Tex., U.S. 103 R14
Bellary, India 179 N5
Bella Unión, Uru. 132 J13
Bella Vista, Arg. 132 G9
Bella Vista, Arg. 132 H13
Bellavista, Peru 130 F2
Belle-Anse, Haiti 117 M17
Belledonne, Chaîne de, Fr. 147 U14
Bellefontaine, Martinique, Fr. 121 F22
Bellefontaine, Ohio, U.S. 99 Q12
Bellefonte, Pa., U.S. 94 N6
Belle Fourche, S. Dak., U.S. 104 K1
Belle Fourche, river, Wyo., U.S. 106 G13
Belle Fourche Reservoir, S. Dak., U.S. 104 K1
Bellegarde, Fr. 147 Q10
Bellegarde, Fr. 147 T14
Belle Glade, Fla., U.S. 97 V10
Belle-Île, Fr. 147 R4
Belle Isle, Nfld. & Lab., Can. 83 L23
Belle Isle, Strait of, Nfld. & Lab., Can. 83 L22
Bellême, Fr. 147 Q8
Belle Plaine, Iowa, U.S. 105 N13
Belle Plaine, Minn., U.S. 104 K11
Belleville, Fr. 147 T12
Belleville, Ill., U.S. 99 T4
Belleville, Kans., U.S. 105 R7
Bellevue, Iowa, U.S. 105 N14
Bellevue, Nebr., U.S. 105 Q9
Bellevue, Ohio, U.S. 99 P13
Bellevue, Tex., U.S. 102 K10
Bellevue, Wash., U.S. 108 C4
Bellingham, Wash., U.S. 108 A4
Bellingshausen, station, Antarctica 226 C3
Bellingshausen Plain, Antarctic Oc. 244 J7
Bellingshausen Sea, Antarctica 226 H4
Bellinzona, Switz. 150 C4
Bello, Col. 128 E4
Bellona Island, Solomon Is. 217 Q18
Bellows Falls, Vt., U.S. 95 J13
Bellpat, Pak. 177 S7
Bell Peninsula, Nunavut, Can. 83 H17
Bell Point, St. Martin, Fr. 121 A14
Bell Rock (Inchcape), Scot., U.K. 142 L11
Bells, Tenn., U.S. 100 F12
Belluno, It. 150 C8
Bell Ville, Arg. 132 K11
Bellville, Tex., U.S. 103 Q12
Belmond, Iowa, U.S. 104 M11
Belmont, Grenada 121 L22
Belmont, Miss., U.S. 101 H13
Belmont, N.C., U.S. 96 J9
Belmonte, Port. 144 F7
Belmonte, Sp. 144 H12
Belmonte, Braz. 131 J16
Belmopan, Belize 115 K16
Belmullet, Ire. 143 Q3
Belogorsk, Russ. 159 K19
Belo Horizonte, Braz. 131 L14
Beloit, Kans., U.S. 105 S7
Beloit, Wis., U.S. 98 M6
Belomorsk, Russ. 158 D8
Belorado, Sp. 144 C11
Belorechensk, Russ. 157 T11
Belo-Tsiribihina, Madagascar 203 G16
Beloūsovka, Kaz. 175 D18
Beloye, Lake see Beloye, Ozero, Russ. 138 C10
Beloye More, Russ. 158 D8
Beloye Ozero, Russ. 156 F9
Belozersk, Russ. 156 F9
Belpre, Ohio, U.S. 99 S15
Belt, Mont., U.S. 106 C8
Belterra, Braz. 130 D11
Belton, S.C., U.S. 96 K7
Belton, Tex., U.S. 103 P11
Belton Lake, Tex., U.S. 103 N11
Belukha, peak, Russ. 166 F8
Belukha, Gora, Russ. 158 M12
Belush'ya Guba, Russ. 158 D10
Belvedere Courtyard, Vatican City 161 P16
Belvedere Marittimo, It. 151 P13
Belvès, Fr. 147 V8
Belvidere, Ill., U.S. 98 M6
Belvidere, S. Dak., U.S. 104 L4
Belvís de la Jara, Sp. 144 G9
Belyando, river, Austral. 210 F13
Belyy, Russ. 156 J7
Belyy, Ostrov, Russ. 158 E12
Belzoni, Miss., U.S. 100 K10
Bemaraha, plateau, Madagascar 203 G16
Bembe, Angola 202 B6
Bembibre, Sp. 144 C8
Bemidji, Minn., U.S. 104 F10
Benāb, Iran 172 B10
Benabarre, Sp. 145 D15
Benadir, region, Somalia 194 K11
Benasque, Sp. 145 C15
Benavente, Sp. 144 D9
Benavides, Tex., U.S. 103 U10
Benbecula, island, Scot., U.K. 142 J6
Bend, Oreg., U.S. 108 H5
Bendals, Antigua & Barbuda 121 B20
Bendena, Qnsld., Austral. 211 V13
Bender, Mold. 157 R5
Bender Cassim see Boosaaso, Somalia 199 F18
Bendern, Liech. 160 M2
Bendigo, Vic., Austral. 211 Z12
Bené Beraq, Israel 170 M5
Benetutti, It. 151 N4
Benevento, It. 150 M11
Bengal, Bay of, Ind. Oc. 166 K8
Bengara, Indonesia 188 H12
Bengbu, China 182 J7
Benghazi see Banghāzī, Lib. 197 C15
Benghisa Point, Malta 161 L23
Bengkalis, island, Indonesia 188 H6
Bengkalis, Indonesia 188 H6
Bengkayang, Indonesia 188 J9
Bengkulu, Indonesia 188 K6
Bengo, Baía do, Angola 202 C5
Benguela, Angola 202 D5
Benguerir, Mor. 196 B8
Beni, river, Bol. 130 H7
Beni Abbes, Alg. 196 C9
Benicarló, Sp. 145 F15
Benidorm, Sp. 145 J15
Benifaió, Sp. 145 H14
Beni Mazâr, Egypt 197 D18
Benin, Af. 195 H16
Benin, Bight of, Af. 194 J4
Benin City, Nigeria 201 H13
Beni Ounif, Alg. 196 B10
Beni Suef, Egypt 197 D18
Benitses, Gr. 154 F6
Benjamin, Tex., U.S. 102 K8
Benjamin Constant, Braz. 130 E5
Benjamín Hill, Mex. 114 C7
Benkelman, Nebr., U.S. 105 R3
Benlidi, Qnsld., Austral. 211 U13
Bennett, Ostrov, Russ. 159 C17
Bennett Peak, N. Mex., U.S. 107 Q10
Bennettsville, S.C., U.S. 96 J10
Ben Nevis, peak, Scot., U.K. 142 L8
Benneydale, N.Z. 213 K19
Bennington, Vt., U.S. 94 J12
Benoud, Alg. 196 B10
Bensbach, P.N.G. 213 E17
Bensheim, Ger. 148 H6
Benson, Ariz., U.S. 107 V8
Benson, Minn., U.S. 104 J9
Benson, N.C., U.S. 96 H12
Benson Point, Kiribati 217 B22
Bent, Iran 173 H17
Benta, Malaysia 188 G6
Bentham's, Barbados 121 J18
Bentinck Island, Myanmar 187 P7
Bentiu, Sudan 198 G12
Bentley Subglacial Trench, Antarctica 226 K10
Benton, Ark., U.S. 100 H8
Benton, Ill., U.S. 99 U6
Benton, Ky., U.S. 101 D13
Benton, La., U.S. 100 K6
Bentong, Indonesia 189 L13
Bentong, Malaysia 187 U9
Benton Harbor, Mich., U.S. 99 N9
Benton Lake, Mont., U.S. 106 C8
Bentonville, Ark., U.S. 100 E6
Bent's Old Fort National Historic Site, Colo., U.S. 107 N15

Benua, Indonesia 189 L14
Benue, river, Nigeria 201 G15
Benwee Head, Ire. 143 Q3
Benxi, China 182 C11
Beograd (Belgrade), Serb. & Mont. 152 F10
Beohari, India 178 H8
Beowawe, Nev., U.S. 109 N10
Beppu, Japan 185 R5
Beqa, island, Fiji Is. 218 J6
Bequia, island, St. Vincent & the Grenadines 119 L17
Bera Ndjoko, Congo 201 J18
Berard, F.S.M. 217 B18
Berard, Port, F.S.M. 217 B18
Berat, Albania 152 L9
Berau, Teluk, Indonesia 189 K18
Berber, Sudan 199 D13
Berbera, Somalia 199 F17
Berbérati, Cen. Af. Rep. 198 H8
Berbice, river, Guyana 129 E15
Berceto, It. 150 F5
Berchers Bay, Virgin Islands, U.K. 120 Q9
Berchtesgaden, Ger. 148 L10
Berck, Fr. 146 M9
Berdún, Sp. 145 C14
Berdyans'k, Ukr. 157 R9
Berdychiv, Ukr. 157 N5
Berea, Ky., U.S. 101 C18
Berehove, Ukr. 157 P1
Bereina, P.N.G. 213 E19
Berekua, Dominica 121 G19
Berenice, Egypt 197 E20
Berens River, Man., Can. 83 M14
Beresford, S. Dak., U.S. 104 M8
Beretău, river, Rom. 152 B12
Berezniki, Russ. 158 G9
Berga, Sp. 145 D17
Bergama, Turk. 168 E3
Bergamo, It. 150 D5
Bergara, Sp. 144 B12
Bergen, Neth. 146 H12
Bergen, Nor. 140 K9
Bergerac, Fr. 147 V8
Bergues, Fr. 146 L10
Berhala, Selat, Indonesia 188 J7
Bering, Ostrov, Russ. 159 E23
Bering Glacier, Alas., U.S. 111 K18
Bering Land Bridge National Preserve, Alas., U.S. 110 E12
Beringovskiy, Russ. 159 B21
Bering Sea, Pac. Oc. 238 B10
Bering Strait, Asia, N. Amer. 166 A12
Berja, Sp. 144 M11
Berkeley, Calif., U.S. 109 S3
Berkeley, Cabo, Ecua. 128 P7
Berkner Island, Antarctica 226 F9
Berlanga de Duero, Sp. 144 E12
Berlevåg, Nor. 141 B15
Berlin, Ger. 148 D10
Berlin, Md., U.S. 96 D15
Berlin, N.H., U.S. 95 F14
Berlin, Wis., U.S. 98 K6
Berlin, Mount, Antarctica 226 M9
Bermejito, river, Arg. 132 E11
Bermejo, river, Arg. 132 G13
Bermejo, river, Arg. 132 J8
Bermeo, Sp. 144 B12
Bermillo de Sayago, Sp. 144 E8
Bermuda Island see Main Island, Bermuda, U.K. 120 B3
Bermuda Islands, U.K., N. Amer. 80 K11
Bermuda Rise, Atl. Oc. 236 J4
Bern, Switz. 150 B2
Bernalda, It. 151 N14
Bernalillo, N. Mex., U.S. 107 S12
Bernardo de Irigoyen, Arg. 132 G15
Bernasconi, Arg. 133 N10
Bernau, Ger. 148 D10
Bernay, Fr. 147 P8
Bernburg, Ger. 148 E9
Berne, Ind., U.S. 99 Q10
Berner Alpen, Switz. 150 C2
Berneray, island, Scot., U.K. 142 J6
Berneray, island, Scot., U.K. 142 L5
Bernice, La., U.S. 100 K8
Bernie, Mo., U.S. 105 V15
Bernier Bay, Nunavut, Can. 83 E15
Bernina, Piz, It., Switz. 150 C5
Bernini's Colonnade, Vatican City 161 Q17
Beroroha, Madagascar 203 H16
Berre, Étang de, Fr. 147 X13
Berrechid, Mor. 196 B8
Berry Islands, Bahamas 116 D11
Berryville, Ark., U.S. 100 E7
Bertam, Malaysia 187 T10
Berthold, N. Dak., U.S. 104 E3
Bertholet, Cape, Austral. 210 D4
Berthoud Pass, Colo., U.S. 106 M12
Bertoua, Cameroon 201 H17
Bertraghboy Bay, Ire. 143 S3
Bertrand, Nebr., U.S. 105 Q5
Bertrange, Lux. 160 K9
Beru, island, Kiribati 214 G8
Beruniy, Uzb. 174 K9
Beruri, Braz. 130 E9
Beruwala, Sri Lanka 179 T7
Berwick, La., U.S. 100 Q9
Berwick upon Tweed, Eng., U.K. 142 M11
Berwyn, Ill., U.S. 99 N7
Berwyn, region, Wales, U.K. 143 T10
Beryslav, Ukr. 157 R7
Besalampy, Madagascar 203 F16
Besançon, Fr. 147 R14
Beserah, Malaysia 187 T10
Besham Qala, Pak. 176 M10
Besikama, Indonesia 189 N15
Beşiri, Turk. 169 G16
Besni, Turk. 168 H12
Beşparmak Dağı, Turk. 168 G3
Bessarabia, region, Mold., Ukr. 157 Q4
Bessemer, Ala., U.S. 101 J15
Bessemer, Mich., U.S. 98 F5
Bessines, Fr. 147 T9
Bestobe, Kaz. 175 C14
Bestyakh, Russ. 159 H18
Betanzos, Sp. 144 B6
Betanzos, Ría de, Sp. 144 A6
Bethanie, Namibia 202 J7
Bethany, Mo., U.S. 105 R11
Bethany, Okla., U.S. 102 G10
Bethany Beach, Del., U.S. 96 D15
Bethel, Alas., U.S. 110 J12
Bethel, Montserrat, U.K. 121 B24
Bethel Town, Jam. 120 H6
Bethesda, Md., U.S. 96 C13
Bethlehem, Pa., U.S. 94 N9
Bethlehem, S. Af. 202 K10
Bethlehem, Virgin Islands, U.S. 120 Q2
Bethlehem see Bayt Laḩm, W. Bank 170 M5
Beth-shan see Bét She'an, Israel 170 L6
Béthune, Fr. 146 L10
Betio, Kiribati 217 G17
Betong, Malaysia 188 H10
Betong, Thai. 187 S9
Betoota, Qnsld., Austral. 211 U11
Bétou, Congo 201 J19
Betpaqdala, desert, Kaz. 175 G13
Betroka, Madagascar 203 H17
Bét She'an (Beth-shan), Israel 170 L6
Betsiboka, river, Madagascar 194 M11
Bettembourg, Lux. 160 K10
Bettendorf, Iowa, U.S. 105 P14
Bettendorf, Lux. 160 H10
Bettlerjoch, pass, Aust., Liech. 160 Q3
Betul, India 178 J6
Beulah, N. Dak., U.S. 104 F3
Bevan's Town, Bahamas 120 E3
Beverley, Eng., U.K. 143 R13
Bewcastle, Eng., U.K. 143 P11
Bexhill, Eng., U.K. 143 W15
Beycesultan, ruin, Turk. 168 G5
Bey Dağı, Turk. 168 E12
Bey Dağı, Turk. 168 G11
Beykoz, Turk. 168 C5
Beyla, Guinea 200 G7
Beyneu, Kaz. 174 G7
Beypazarı, Turk. 168 E7
Beyrouth (Beirut), Leb. 170 H6
Beyşehir, Turk. 168 H7
Beyşehir Gölü, Turk. 168 G7
Beytüşşebap, Turk. 169 H17
Bezhetsk, Russ. 156 H9
Béziers, Fr. 147 Y11
Bhadarwah, India 177 N13
Bhadra, India 178 E5
Bhadrakh, India 178 K11
Bhag, Pak. 177 S6
Bhagalpur, India 178 H11
Bhakkar, Pak. 177 Q9
Bhaktapur, Nepal 178 F10
Bhamo, Myanmar 186 F7
Bhandara, India 178 K7
Bhanpura, India 178 H5
Bharatpur, India 178 F6
Bharatpur, India 178 H8
Bharuch, India 178 K3
Bhatapara, India 178 K8
Bhatinda, India 178 E5
Bhatkal, India 179 P4
Bhatpara, India 178 J12
Bhavnagar, India 178 J3
Bhawanipatna, India 178 L9
Bhera, Pak. 177 P11
Bhilai, India 178 K8
Bhilwara, India 178 H4
Bhima, river, India 178 M5
Bhimbar, Pak. 177 N11
Bhind, India 178 G6
Bhinmal, India 178 H3
Bholari, Pak. 177 W7
Bhongir, India 178 M6
Bhopal, India 178 J6
Bhubaneshwar, India 178 K10
Bhuj, India 178 H1
Bhusawal, India 178 K5
Bhutan, Asia 167 V9
Biabou, St. Vincent & the Grenadines 121 K17
Biak, island, Indonesia 189 J19
Biak, Indonesia 189 J19
Biała Podlaska, Pol. 149 E18
Białogard, Pol. 148 B12
Biały Bór, Pol. 149 B13
Białystok, Pol. 149 C17
Bianco, It. 151 R13
Biaó, peak, Eq. Guinea 204 M7
Biaora, India 178 H5
Bīārjomand, Iran 173 C15
Biaro, island, Indonesia 189 H15
Biarritz, Fr. 147 X5
Bias, Fr. 147 W6
Biau, Indonesia 189 H14
Bibala, Angola 202 E5
Bibbiena, It. 150 G7
Biberach, Ger. 148 K7
Bibi Nani, Pak. 177 R6
Bicaz, Rom. 153 C15
Bichänäk Ashyrymy, range, Arm. 169 E19
Biche, Trinidad & Tobago 121 P23
Bichvint'a, Abkhazia 169 A15
Bickleton, Wash., U.S. 108 E6
Bicknell, Ind., U.S. 99 T8
Bicknell, Utah, U.S. 107 N7
Bida, Nigeria 201 F13
Biddeford, Me., U.S. 95 H15
Bideford, Eng., U.K. 143 W9
Bieber, Calif., U.S. 108 M5
Biei, Japan 184 F14
Biel, Switz. 150 B2
Bielawa, Pol. 149 G13
Bielefeld, Ger. 148 E6
Biele Karpaty, Czech Rep., Slovakia 149 J14
Bieler See, Switz. 150 B2
Biella, It. 150 D3
Bielsa, Sp. 145 C15
Bielsko-Biała, Pol. 149 H15
Bielsk Podlaski, Pol. 149 D17
Bien Hoa, Vietnam 187 P13
Bienville, Lac, Que., Can. 83 L19
Bié Plateau, Angola 194 M6
Biescas, Sp. 145 C14
Big, river, N.W.T., Can. 82 D12
Biga, Turk. 168 D3
Bigadiç, Turk. 168 E4
Big Bay, Mich., U.S. 98 F7
Big Bay, Vanuatu 218 C1
Big Bay (Drummond Bay), Vanuatu 218 E3
Big Bell, W. Aust., Austral. 211 V3
Big Belt Mountains, Mont., U.S. 106 D8
Big Bend National Park, Tex., U.S. 103 R3
Big Blue, river, Nebr., U.S. 105 Q8
Big Bog, Minn., U.S. 104 E9
Big Canyon, river, Tex., U.S. 103 Q4
Big Creek, Calif., U.S. 109 T7
Big Cypress National Preserve, Fla., U.S. 97 W9
Big Cypress Swamp, Fla., U.S. 97 W9
Bigej, island, Marshall Is. 216 M6
Bigej Channel, Marshall Is. 216 M6
Big Falls, Minn., U.S. 104 E11
Big Fork, Minn., U.S. 104 E11
Bigfork, Minn., U.S. 104 F11
Bigfork, Mont., U.S. 106 B6
Biggar, Sask., Can. 82 M11
Biggarenn, island, Marshall Is. 216 K3
Biggerann, island, Marshall Is. 216 K2
Big Hatchet Peak, N. Mex., U.S. 107 W10
Big Hole, river, Mont., U.S. 106 E6
Big Hole National Battlefield, Mont., U.S. 106 E6
Bighorn, river, Wyo., U.S. 106 G10
Bighorn Canyon National Recreation Area, Mont., U.S. 106 F10
Bighorn Lake, Mont., U.S. 106 F10
Bighorn Mountains, Wyo., U.S. 106 F11
Bigi, island, Marshall Is. 216 K3
Big Island, Nunavut, Can. 83 H18
Big Lake, Tex., U.S. 103 N5
Big Mangrove, Bahamas 120 B8
Bigonville, Lux. 160 H9
Big Pine, Calif., U.S. 109 T8
Big Pine, Fla., U.S. 97 Y9
Big Piney, Wyo., U.S. 106 J9
Big Rapids, Mich., U.S. 98 K10
Big Sandy, Mont., U.S. 106 B9
Big Sandy, river, Wyo., U.S. 106 J9
Big Sioux, river, S. Dak., U.S. 104 L8
Big Snowy Mountains, Mont., U.S. 106 D9
Big South Fork National River and Recreation Area, Ky., Tenn., U.S. 101 E17
Big Spring, Tex., U.S. 102 M5
Big Springs, Nebr., U.S. 105 Q3
Big Stone City, S. Dak., U.S. 104 J8
Big Stone Gap, Va., U.S. 96 G7
Big Stone Lake, Minn., S. Dak., U.S. 104 J8
Big Sur, Calif., U.S. 109 U4
Big Thicket National Preserve, Tex., U.S. 103 P15
Big Timber, Mont., U.S. 106 E9
Big Trout Lake, Ont., Can. 83 M15
Big Valley Mountains, Calif., U.S. 108 M5
Big Wells, Tex., U.S. 103 S8
Big Wood, river, Idaho, U.S. 106 H5
Big Wood Cay, Bahamas 116 E11
Bihać, Bosn. & Herzg. 152 F6
Bihar Sharif, India 178 H10
Bihoro, Japan 184 F15
Bijagós, Arquipélago dos, Guinea-Bissau 200 E4
Bijapur, India 178 L7
Bijapur, India 178 M5
Bījār, Iran 172 C11
Bijeljina, Bosn. & Herzg. 152 F9
Bijie, China 180 M12
Bijire, island, Marshall Is. 216 G8
Bijnor, India 178 E6
Bikaner, India 178 F4
Bikar Atoll, Marshall Is. 216 F5
Bikeman, island, Kiribati 217 G17
Biken, island, Marshall Is. 216 H7
Bikenibeu, Kiribati 217 G18
Bikennel, island, Marshall Is. 216 L3
Bikenubati, island, Kiribati 217 F17
Bikin, Russ. 159 L21
Bikini Atoll, Marshall Is. 216 F3
Bīkkū Bīttī, peak, Lib. 197 F15
Bikoro, Dem. Rep. of the Congo 198 K8
Biläcäri, Azerb. 169 D23
Bilād Banī Bū 'Alī, Oman 173 L17
Bilaspur, India 178 J8
Biläsuvar, Azerb. 169 E22
Bila Tserkva, Ukr. 157 P5
Bilauktaung Range, Myanmar, Thai. 186 M8
Bilbao, Sp. 144 B12
Bileća, Bosn. & Herzg. 152 H8
Bilecik, Turk. 168 D5
Biłgoraj, Pol. 149 G17
Bilhorod-Dnistrovs'kyy, Ukr. 157 R5
Bilibino, Russ. 159 C20
Bilican Dağları, Turk. 169 F16
Bilin, Myanmar 186 K7
Bill, Wyo., U.S. 106 H13
Billae, island, Marshall Is. 216 H8
Bill Baileys Bank, Atl. Oc. 236 D11
Billiluna, W. Aust., Austral. 211 S6
Billings, Mont., U.S. 106 E10
Billings, Okla., U.S. 102 E11
Billings, Russ. 159 B19
Billiton see Belitung, island, Indonesia 188 K9
Billom, Fr. 147 U11
Bill Williams, river, Ariz., U.S. 107 T5
Billy Chinook, Lake, Oreg., U.S. 108 G5
Bilma, Niger 197 G13
Biloela, Qnsld., Austral. 211 U15
Bilo Gora, Croatia 152 D7
Bilohirs'k, Ukr. 157 S8
Bilopillya, Ukr. 157 N8
Biloxi, Miss., U.S. 100 P12
Biltine, Chad 197 H16
Bilto, Nor. 141 C13
Bilüü, Mongolia 180 C8
Bilzen, Belg. 146 L13
Bimini Islands, Bahamas 116 D9
Bindle, Qnsld., Austral. 211 V14
Bindloe see Marchena, Isla, island, Ecua. 128 P9
Bindura, Zimb. 202 F12
Binéfar, Sp. 145 D15
Binford, N. Dak., U.S. 104 F7
Bingara, N.S.W., Austral. 211 W14
Bingara, Qnsld., Austral. 211 V12
Bing Bong, N. Terr., Austral. 211 Q9
Bingen, Ger. 148 G6
Binger, Okla., U.S. 102 G9
Bingham, Me., U.S. 95 E16
Bingham Channel, Kiribati 217 E17
Binghamton, N.Y., U.S. 94 K9
Bingöl, Turk. 169 F15
Bingöl Dağları, Turk. 169 F16
Binhai (Dongkan), China 182 H9
Binh Khe, Vietnam 186 M14
Binh Lieu, Vietnam 186 G13
Binjai, Indonesia 188 G5
Binjai, Indonesia 188 G9
Binongko, island, Indonesia 189 L15
Bintan, island, Indonesia 188 H7
Bintuhan, Indonesia 188 L7
Bintulu, Malaysia 188 H10
Binxian, China 182 G1
Binxian, China 181 D17
Binyang, China 181 P13
Binzhou, China 182 F8
Bío-Bío, river, Chile 133 N6
Bioč, peak, Serb. & Mont. 152 H8
Bioko, island, Eq. Guinea 204 F5
Biokovo, peak, Croatia 152 H7
Bir, India 178 L5
Birāk, Lib. 197 D14
Bi'r 'Alī, Yemen 172 Q11
Birao, Cen. Af. Rep. 198 F10
Biratnagar, Nepal 178 G11
Birchip, Vic., Austral. 211 Y11
Birch Mountains, Alta., Can. 82 K11
Birch Tree Hill, Cayman Is., U.K. 120 H1
Birchwood, Alas., U.S. 111 J16
Bird City, Kans., U.S. 105 R3
Bird Island, Grenada 121 J24
Bird Island, Minn., U.S. 104 K10
Bird Island, Seychelles 205 K19
Bird Island see Aves, Isla de, Venez. 119 J15
Birdsville, Qnsld., Austral. 211 U10
Birecik, Turk. 169 H13
Bîr el 'Abd, Egypt 171 N2
Bireun, Indonesia 188 G4
Birganj, Nepal 178 G10
Bîr Ḩasana, Egypt 171 P3
Bīrjand, Iran 173 D16
Birkenhead, Eng., U.K. 143 S10
Birkirkara, Malta 161 K22
Bîrlad, river, Rom. 153 C17
Bîrlad, Rom. 153 D17
Birmingham, Ala., U.S. 101 J15
Birmingham, Eng., U.K. 143 T12
Bir Mogreïn (Fort Trinquet), Mauritania 196 D6
Birnie Island, Kiribati 214 H10
Birnin Kebbi, Nigeria 200 E12
Birni Nkonni, Niger 196 H11
Birobidzhan, Russ. 159 K20
Birong, Philippines 188 E12
Birrindudu, N. Terr., Austral. 211 R7
Birshoghyr, Kaz. 174 E9
Birsilpur, India 178 F3
Birtin, Rom. 152 C12
Birufu, Indonesia 189 L20
Biruli, Russ. 159 E14
Biryakovo, Russ. 156 F11
Birżebbuġa, Malta 161 L23
Bisa, island, Indonesia 189 J16
Bisbee, Ariz., U.S. 107 W9
Bisbee, N. Dak., U.S. 104 E6
Biscarosse et de Parentis, Lac de, Fr. 147 W6
Biscarrosse-Plage, Fr. 147 W6
Biscay, Bay of, Eur. 138 G3
Biscayne Bay, Fla., U.S. 97 X10
Biscayne National Park, Fla., U.S. 97 X10
Biscay Plain, Atl. Oc. 236 G12
Bisceglie, It. 150 L13
Bischheim, Fr. 147 P15

Biscoe Islands, Antarctica 226 E4
Biševo, island, Croatia 152 H6
Bishkek, Kyrg. 176 D11
Bisho, S. Af. 202 M10
Bishop, Calif., U.S. 109 S8
Bishop, Tex., U.S. 103 U10
Bishopville, S.C., U.S. 96 K10
Bishrī, Jabal, Syr. 170 F12
Biskra, Alg. 196 B11
Bislig, Philippines 189 F15
Bismarck, N. Dak., U.S. 104 G4
Bismarck Archipelago, P.N.G. 213 C20
Bismarck Range, P.N.G. 213 C19
Bismarck Sea, P.N.G. 213 C20
Bismil, Turk. 169 G15
Bison, S. Dak., U.S. 104 J3
Bissagos Islands see Bijagós, Arquipélago dos, Guinea-Bissau 194 G1
Bissameuttack, India 178 L9
Bissau, Guinea-Bissau 200 E4
Bissen, Lux. 160 J10
Bistcho Lake, Alta., Can. 82 J10
Bistineau, Lake, La., U.S. 100 L7
Bistreţu, Rom. 153 G13
Bistriţa, river, Rom. 153 C15
Bistriţa, Rom. 153 B14
Bitam, Gabon 201 K16
Bitburg, Ger. 160 H11
Bitlis, Turk. 169 G16
Bitola, Maced. 152 L11
Bitra Island, India 179 Q2
Bitterfontein, S. Af. 202 L7
Bitterroot, river, Mont., U.S. 106 D5
Bitterroot Range, Idaho, Mont., U.S. 84 C6
Biu, Nigeria 201 F16
Bivona, It. 151 S9
Biwa Ko, Japan 185 P9
Bixby, Okla., U.S. 102 F13
Bixessarri, Andorra 160 K2
Biyang, China 182 J5
Biysk, Russ. 158 L12
Bizerte, Tun. 197 A13
Bjelolasica, peak, Croatia 152 E5
Bjelovar, Croatia 152 D7
Bjøllånes, Nor. 140 F12
Bjørnafjorden, bay, Nor. 140 K9
Black, river, Ariz., U.S. 107 U9
Black, river, Ark., U.S. 100 F10
Black, river, Jam. 120 J7
Black, river, Mo., U.S. 105 V15
Black, river, N.Y., U.S. 94 H9
Black see Da, river, Vietnam 186 H11
Black, river, Wis., U.S. 98 J4
Blackall, Qnsld., Austral. 211 U13
Blackball, N.Z. 213 N17
Black Bay Point, Grenada 121 K22
Blackbeard Island, Ga., U.S. 97 P9
Blackbeard's Tower, Bahamas 120 B12
Black Belt, region, Ala., U.S. 85 L16
Blackburn, Eng., U.K. 143 R11
Blackburn, Mount, Alas., U.S. 111 J18
Black Canyon City, Ariz., U.S. 107 T7
Black Canyon of the Gunnison National Park, Colo., U.S. 107 N11
Black Coast, Antarctica 226 E6
Blackduck, Minn., U.S. 104 F10
Black Eagle, Mont., U.S. 106 C8
Blackfoot, Idaho, U.S. 106 H7
Blackfoot, river, Mont., U.S. 106 D6
Blackfoot Reservoir, Idaho, U.S. 106 H7
Black Forest, Ger. 148 K6
Black Hills, S. Dak., Wyo., U.S. 84 E10
Black Irtysh, river, China, Kaz. 166 F8
Black Isle, Scot., U.K. 142 J9
Black Lake, Mich., U.S. 98 H11
Blackmans, Barbados 121 K19
Black Mesa, Ariz., U.S. 107 Q8
Black Mesa, Okla., U.S. 102 E4
Blackmoor Vale, Eng., U.K. 143 W11
Black Mountain, Ky., U.S. 101 D20
Black Mountains, Ariz., U.S. 107 R4
Black Mountains, Wales, U.K. 143 U10
Black Point, Virgin Islands, U.K. 120 L11
Black Point see Kūpikipiki'o Point, Hawai'i, U.S. 112 E11
Black Point, St. Vincent & the Grenadines 121 K17
Blackpool, Eng., U.K. 143 R10
Black Range, N. Mex., U.S. 84 K8
Black River, Jam. 120 J7
Black River Bay, Jam. 120 J7
Black River Falls, Wis., U.S. 98 J4
Black Rock, Ire. 143 Q2
Black Rock, S. Amer. 126 R9
Black Rock, Trinidad & Tobago 121 N17
Black Rock Desert, Nev., U.S. 108 M7
Black Sand Beach see Kaimu Beach, Hawai'i, U.S. 113 N22
Blacksburg, Va., U.S. 96 F9
Black Sea, Asia 166 E4
Black Sea, Asia, Eur. 138 H11
Black Sea Lowland, Ukr. 138 H10
Blacks Fork, Wyo., U.S. 106 K8
Blackshear, Ga., U.S. 97 P7
Blacksod Bay, Ire. 143 Q3
Blackstone, Va., U.S. 96 F12
Blackville, S.C., U.S. 96 L9
Black Volta, river, Af. 194 H3
Blackwater, river, Ire. 143 U4
Blackwater, Qnsld., Austral. 211 T14
Blackwell, Okla., U.S. 102 E11
Blackwell, Tex., U.S. 102 M7
Blagodarnyy, Russ. 157 S13
Blagoevgrad, Bulg. 152 K12
Blagoveshchensk, Russ. 159 K19
Blain, Fr. 147 R5
Blaine, Wash., U.S. 108 A3
Blair, Nebr., U.S. 105 P9
Blair Athol, Qnsld., Austral. 211 T14
Blaj, Rom. 153 D13
Blake-Bahama Ridge, Atl. Oc. 236 J3
Blakely, Ga., U.S. 97 P4
Blakeney, Eng., U.K. 143 S15
Blake Plateau, Atl. Oc. 236 J3
Blake Point, Mich., U.S. 98 C6
Blakes, Cayman Is., U.K. 120 J4
Blanc, Cap, Mauritania 196 F4
Blanc, Cape, Tun. 194 C5
Blanc, Mont, Fr., It. 147 U15
Blanca, Costa, Sp. 145 K15
Blanca, Portella, Andorra, Fr. 160 J5
Blanca, Sierra, Tex., U.S. 103 V3
Blanca Bay, S. Amer. 126 N6
Blanca Peak, Colo., U.S. 107 P13
Blanchard, Okla., U.S. 102 G10
Blanche, Lake, Austral. 210 H11
Blanche, Pointe, Neth. Antilles, Neth. 121 C14
Blanche Channel, Solomon Is. 217 M16
Blanchisseuse, Trinidad & Tobago 121 N22
Blanchisseuse, Trinidad & Tobago 119 P17
Blanco, river, Bol. 130 J8
Blanco, river, Tex., U.S. 103 Q10
Blanco, Tex., U.S. 103 Q9
Blanco, Cape, Oreg., U.S. 108 J1
Blanding, Utah, U.S. 107 P9
Blanes, Sp. 145 D18
Blangy, Fr. 146 M9
Blankenberge, Belg. 146 K10
Blanquilla, Isla, Venez. 128 A11
Blantyre, Malawi 203 E13
Blasket Islands, Ire. 143 U2
Blaydon, Eng., U.K. 143 P12
Blaye, Fr. 147 V6
Blaze, Point, Austral. 210 B7
Blednaya, Gora, Russ. 158 D12
Blenheim, N.Z. 213 M18
Blida, Alg. 196 A11
Blidinje Jezero, Bosn. & Herzg. 152 G7
Bligh Water, Fiji Is. 218 H6
Blima, Grand Erg de, Niger 197 G14
Blind River, Ont., Can. 83 Q17
Blinman, S. Aust., Austral. 211 W10
Blitar, Indonesia 188 M10
Block Island, R.I., U.S. 95 M14
Bloemfontein, S. Af. 202 K10
Bloemhof, S. Af. 202 K10
Blois, Fr. 147 R9
Blönduós, Ice. 140 E3
Bloody Bay, Trinidad & Tobago 121 N18
Bloody Foreland, Ire. 143 N5
Bloomer, Wis., U.S. 98 H3
Bloomfield, Ind., U.S. 99 S8
Bloomfield, Iowa, U.S. 105 Q12
Bloomfield, Mo., U.S. 105 V15
Bloomfield, Nebr., U.S. 105 N7
Blooming Prairie, Minn., U.S. 104 L12
Bloomington, Ill., U.S. 99 Q6
Bloomington, Ind., U.S. 99 S8
Bloomington, Minn., U.S. 104 K11
Bloomington, Tex., U.S. 103 S12
Bloomsburg, Pa., U.S. 94 M8
Blossom, Mys, Russ. 159 B19
Blouberg, peak, S. Af. 194 P9
Blower Rock, Jam. 116 P11
Blowing Point, Anguilla, U.K. 120 R11
Blowing Point, Jam. 120 H10
Bludenz, Aust. 148 L7
Blue Earth, Minn., U.S. 104 L11
Bluefield, W. Va., U.S. 96 F8
Bluefields, Jam. 120 J6
Bluefields, Nicar. 115 M19
Bluefields Bay, Jam. 120 J6
Blue Hill, Nebr., U.S. 105 R6
Blue Hills, Turks & Caicos Is., U.K. 117 H16
Blue Hole, site, Jam. 120 J11
Bluejoint Lake, Oreg., U.S. 108 K7
Blue Lake, Calif., U.S. 108 M2
Blue Mountain, Ark., U.S. 100 G6
Blue Mountain, Oreg., U.S. 108 K8
Blue Mountain Peak, Jam. 120 J10
Blue Mountains, Jam. 120 J10
Blue Mountains, Oreg., Wash., U.S. 108 G7
Blue Nile see Azraq, El Bahr el, river, Sudan 199 F13
Blue Nile Falls see T'is Isat Fwafwatē, Eth. 199 F14
Blue Rapids, Kans., U.S. 105 R8
Blue Ridge, Ga., U.S. 96 J5
Blue Ridge, Va., N.C., U.S. 85 J18
Bluff, N.Z. 213 R15
Bluff, Utah, U.S. 107 P9
Bluff Knoll, Austral. 210 L3
Bluff Point, Austral. 210 H1
Bluffton, Ind., U.S. 99 Q10
Blumenau, Braz. 131 N13
Blunt, S. Dak., U.S. 104 K5
Bly, Oreg., U.S. 108 K5
Blyth, Eng., U.K. 143 P12
Blythe, Calif., U.S. 109 X13
Blytheville, Ark., U.S. 100 F11
Bø, Nor. 140 D12
Bø, Nor. 140 K9
Bo, Sierra Leone 200 G6
Boaco, Nicar. 115 M18
Boano, island, Indonesia 189 K16
Boardman, Ohio, U.S. 99 P16
Boatman, Qnsld., Austral. 211 V13
Boa Vista, island, Cape Verde 205 C17
Boa Vista, Braz. 130 B9
Boaz, Ala., U.S. 101 H16
Boaz Island, Bermuda, U.K. 120 B1
Bobai, China 183 S2
Bobbili, India 178 L9
Bobo Dioulasso, Burkina Faso 200 E9
Bobovdol, Bulg. 152 J12
Boby, peak, Madagascar 203 H17
Boca Chica, Dom. Rep. 117 M19
Boca Chica Key, Fla., U.S. 97 Y8
Bôca do Acre, Braz. 130 F6
Bôca do Jari, Braz. 130 D12
Bocage, Cap, New Caledonia, Fr. 218 C7
Boca Grande, Fla., U.S. 97 V8
Boca Mavaca, Venez. 128 G10
Boca Raton, Fla., U.S. 97 W10
Bocas del Toro, Pan. 115 N20
Boca Tabla, site, Neth. Antilles, Neth. 121 N13
Bocay, Nicar. 115 L18
Bochnia, Pol. 149 H16
Bocholt, Ger. 148 E5
Bocht van Hato, bay, Neth. Antilles, Neth. 121 P14
Bochum, Ger. 148 E5
Bocognano, Fr. 150 K4
Bocşa, Rom. 152 E11
Böda, Sw. 141 M14
Bodaybo, Russ. 159 J16
Bodden Bay, Cayman Is., U.K. 120 J3
Bodden Town, Cayman Is., U.K. 120 J3
Bodega Bay, Calif., U.S. 109 R2
Bodega Head, Calif., U.S. 109 R2
Bodele Depression, Chad 194 G6
Boden, Sw. 141 F14
Bodensee (Lake Constance), Aust., Ger., Switz. 148 L7
Bodī, Mongolia 180 E11
Bodi, Indonesia 189 H14
Bodkin Mill, ruin, Virgin Islands, U.S. 120 Q2
Bodmin, Eng., U.K. 143 X8
Bodmin Moor, Eng., U.K. 143 X9
Bodø, Nor. 140 E12
Bodrum, Turk. 168 H3
Bo Duc, Vietnam 187 N13
Boe, region, Nauru 217 F22
Boën, Fr. 147 U12
Boende, Dem. Rep. of the Congo 198 K9
Boeo, Capo, It. 151 S8
Boerne, Tex., U.S. 103 R9
Boeuf, river, La., U.S. 100 L9
Boffa, Guinea 200 F5
Bogalusa, La., U.S. 100 N11
Bogan, river, Austral. 210 J13
Bogantungan, Qnsld., Austral. 211 T13
Bogazi, Cyprus 160 N10
Boğazkale, Turk. 168 E10
Boğazlıyan, Turk. 168 F10
Bogdanovka, Rep. of Georgia 169 C17
Bogda Shan, China 180 E8
Bogenaga, island, Marshall Is. 216 K7
Boggabilla, N.S.W., Austral. 211 V14
Boggenadick, island, Marshall Is. 216 K7
Boggenatjen, island, Marshall Is. 216 L3
Boggerik, island, Marshall Is. 216 K3
Boggerik Passage, Marshall Is. 216 K3
Boggerlapp, island, Marshall Is. 216 K4
Boggy Peak, Antigua & Barbuda 121 B20
Bogia, P.N.G. 213 C19
Bogor, Indonesia 188 M8
Bogoroditsk, Russ. 156 L10
Bogorodsk, Russ. 156 J12
Bogotá, Col. 128 F5
Bogotol, Russ. 159 K13
Bogra, Bangladesh 178 H12
Bogué, Mauritania 196 G5
Bog Walk, Jam. 120 J9
Bo Hai, bay, China 182 E8
Bohé, Eq. Guinea 204 N7
Bohe, China 183 S2
Bohemia, region, Czech Rep. 148 H10
Bohemian Forest, Ger. 148 J9
Bohodukhiv, Ukr. 157 N8
Bohol, island, Philippines 189 E15
Bohol Sea, Philippines 189 E15
Boiaçu, Braz. 130 C8
Boim, Braz. 130 D11
Bois Blanc Island, Mich., U.S. 98 G11
Boisé, Port, New Caledonia, Fr. 218 E9
Boise, Idaho, U.S. 106 G4
Boise City, Okla., U.S. 102 E4
Bojnūrd, Iran 173 B15
Boka Kotorska, Serb. & Mont. 152 J8
Bokalijman, island, Marshall Is. 216 M7
Boké, Guinea 200 E5
Boken, island, Marshall Is. 216 G8
Boken, island, Marshall Is. 216 J8
Boken, island, Marshall Is. 216 G10
Bokenelab, island, Marshall Is. 216 G8
Bokkumaruchi, island, Marshall Is. 216 K3
Boklaplap, island, Marshall Is. 216 L8
Boknafjorden, bay, Nor. 140 L9
Boko, Congo 201 N17
Bokoluo, island, Marshall Is. 216 G7
Bokombako, island, Marshall Is. 216 G8
Bökönbaev, Kyrg. 176 E13
Bokovskaya, Russ. 157 P12
Bokpyinn, Myanmar 187 P7
Boksitogorsk, Russ. 156 F8
Boku, P.N.G. 217 K14
Bokungu, Dem. Rep. of the Congo 198 K10
Bokurdak, Turkm. 174 L8
Bol, Chad 197 J14
Bolaang, Indonesia 189 J14
Bolan Pass, Pak. 177 R6
Bolans, Antigua & Barbuda 121 B20
Bolbec, Fr. 147 N8
Boldumsaz, Turkm. 174 J9
Bole, Ghana 200 F10
Bolea, Sp. 145 C14
Bolesławiec, Pol. 148 F12
Bolgatanga, Ghana 200 F10
Bolhrad, Ukr. 157 S4
Bolivar, Mo., U.S. 105 U12
Bolivar, Tenn., U.S. 100 G12
Bolívar, Cerro, Venez. 128 D11
Bolivia, Cuba 116 H10
Bolivia, S. Amer. 127 G17
Bolkar Dağları, Turk. 168 H9
Bolkhov, Russ. 156 L8
Bollène, Fr. 147 W13
Bollnäs, Sw. 141 J13
Bollon, Qnsld., Austral. 211 V13
Bollons Tablemount, Pac. Oc. 238 R10
Bolluk Gölü, Turk. 168 G8
Bolnisi, Rep. of Georgia 169 C18
Bolobo, Dem. Rep. of the Congo 198 K8
Bologna, It. 150 F7
Bolognesi, Peru 130 G4
Bologoye, Russ. 156 G8
Bolovens Plateau, Laos 186 L12
Bolsena, It. 150 J8
Bolsena, Lago di, It. 150 J7
Bol'shaya Bicha, Russ. 158 J10
Bol'sheretsk, Russ. 159 G23
Bol'shevik, Ostrov, Russ. 159 D14
Bol'shevik Island, Russ. 166 B9
Bol'shezemel'skaya Tundra, Russ. 138 A12
Bol'shoy Begichev, Ostrov, Russ. 159 E15
Bol'shoy Lyakhovskiy, Ostrov, Russ. 159 D17
Bol'shoy Patom, Russ. 159 J17
Bol'shoy Shantar, Ostrov, Russ. 159 H20
Bolsward, Neth. 146 G13
Bolt Head, Eng., U.K. 143 Y10
Bolton, Eng., U.K. 143 R11
Bolton Point, Kiribati 217 E17
Bolu, Turk. 168 D7
Boluntay, China 180 H8
Boluo, China 183 R5
Bolvadin, Turk. 168 F6
Bolzano, It. 150 C7
Boma, Dem. Rep. of the Congo 198 L7
Bomba, Gulf of, Lib. 194 D7
Bombala, N.S.W., Austral. 211 Z13
Bombardopolis, Haiti 117 L15
Bombay see Mumbai, India 178 L3
Bombom, Ilhéu, Sao Tome and Principe 205 A21
Bomdila, India 178 F14
Bomdo, India 178 E15
Bomi, China 180 L9
Bom Jesus da Lapa, Braz. 131 H15
Bomongo, Dem. Rep. of the Congo 198 J8
Bomu, river, Cen. Af. Rep., Dem. Rep. of the Congo 198 H10
Bona, Mount, Alas., U.S. 111 J19
Bon Accueil, Mauritius 205 G20
Bonaire, island, Neth. Antilles, Neth. 118 M10
Bonang, Vic., Austral. 211 Z13
Bonanza, Utah, U.S. 106 L9
Bonao, Dom. Rep. 117 M18
Bonaparte Archipelago, Austral. 210 B5
Bonasse, Trinidad & Tobago 121 Q21
Bonavista, Nfld. & Lab., Can. 83 M24
Bonavista Bay, N. Amer. 80 G11
Bon Bon, S. Aust., Austral. 211 W9
Bondo, Dem. Rep. of the Congo 198 H10
Bondoukou, Côte d'Ivoire 200 G9
Bonds Cay, Bahamas 116 D11
Bonefish Bay, Bahamas 120 E11
Bonefish Pond, Bahamas 120 B11
Bonerate, island, Indonesia 189 M13
Bonesteel, S. Dak., U.S. 104 M6
Bonete, Cerro, Arg. 132 G7
Bongandanga, Dem. Rep. of the Congo 198 J9
Bongaree, Qnsld., Austral. 211 V15
Bongo Lava, region, Madagascar 194 N11
Bongor, Chad 197 K14
Bongos, Chaîne des, Cen. Af. Rep. 198 G9
Bonham, Tex., U.S. 102 K12
Bonifacio, Fr. 150 L4
Bonifacio, Strait of, Fr., It. 150 L4
Bonifay, Fla., U.S. 97 Q3
Bonin Islands (Ogasawara Guntō), Japan 184 K5
Bonin Trench, Pac. Oc. 238 G6
Bonita Springs, Fla., U.S. 97 W8
Bonito, Braz. 130 L10
Bonn, Ger. 148 F5
Bonners Ferry, Idaho, U.S. 106 A4
Bonne Terre, Mo., U.S. 105 T15
Bonneval, Fr. 147 Q9
Bonneville Dam, Oreg., U.S., Wash., U.S. 108 F4
Bonneville Salt Flats, Utah, U.S. 106 K5
Bonney Downs, W. Aust., Austral. 211 T3
Bonnie Rock, W. Aust., Austral. 211 W3
Bonny, Fr. 147 R10
Bonorva, It. 151 N3
Bonriki, island, Kiribati 217 G18
Bonriki, Kiribati 217 G18
Bontang, Indonesia 188 J12
Bontoc, Philippines 189 B13
Bonvouloir Islands, P.N.G. 213 E21
Bony de les Neres, Andorra 160 J3
Booby Cay, Cayman Is., U.K. 120 J2
Bookabie, S. Aust., Austral. 211 W8
Booker, Tex., U.S. 102 E7
Booker T. Washington National Monument, Va., U.S. 96 F10

Booligal, N.S.W., Austral. 211 X12
Boonah, Qnsld., Austral. 211 V15
Boonderoo, Qnsld., Austral. 211 S12
Boone, Iowa, U.S. 105 N11
Boone, N.C., U.S. 96 G8
Booneville, Ark., U.S. 100 G6
Booneville, Miss., U.S. 101 H13
Boon Point, Antigua & Barbuda 121 A20
Bööntsagaan Nuur, Mongolia 180 E10
Boonville, Ind., U.S. 99 U8
Boonville, Mo., U.S. 105 S12
Boonville, N.Y., U.S. 94 H9
Boorama, Somalia 199 F16
Boorara, Qnsld., Austral. 211 V12
Booroorban, N.S.W., Austral. 211 Y12
Boosaaso (Bender Cassim), Somalia 199 F18
Boothbay Harbor, Me., U.S. 95 G16
Boothia, Gulf of, Nunavut, Can. 83 F15
Boothia Peninsula, Nunavut, Can. 83 F15
Bootle Bay Village, Bahamas 120 E1
Booué, Gabon 201 L16
Bopeechee, S. Aust., Austral. 211 W10
Boppard, Ger. 148 G5
Boquerón, Bahía de, P.R., U.S. 120 N1
Bor, Russ. 156 H12
Bor, Serb. & Mont. 152 G11
Bor, Turk. 168 G9
Bora-Bora, island, Fr. Polynesia, Fr. 219 E15
Boracho Peak, Tex., U.S. 103 P1
Borah Peak, Idaho, U.S. 106 G6
Boran, region, Eth. 199 H15
Boran, Kaz. 175 E19
Borås, Sw. 140 M12
Borāzjān, Iran 173 G13
Borba, Port. 144 J6
Borba, Braz. 130 E9
Borborema, Planalto da, Braz. 131 F17
Borchgrevink Coast, Antarctica 227 Q14
Borçka, Turk. 169 C16
Bordeaux, Fr. 147 V6
Bordeaux Mountain, Virgin Islands, U.S. 120 N11
Borden, W. Aust., Austral. 211 Y3
Borden Island, N.W.T., Nunavut, Can. 83 B13
Borden Peninsula, Nunavut, Can. 83 E16
Bordertown, S. Aust., Austral. 211 Y11
Borðeyri, Ice. 140 E2
Bordj Flye Sainte Marie, Alg. 196 D9
Bordj le Prieur, Alg. 196 F10
Bordj Messouda, Alg. 196 C12
Bordj Omar Driss, Alg. 196 D12
Boré, Mali 196 H8
Boreas Plain, Arctic Oc. 243 H16
Borgarnes, Ice. 140 F2
Borger, Neth. 146 H14
Borger, Tex., U.S. 102 G6
Borgholm, Sw. 141 M14
Borg Massif, Antarctica 226 B12
Borgne, Lake, La., U.S. 100 Q11
Borgo Maggiore, San Marino 161 J15
Borgo San Dalmazzo, It. 150 F2
Borgosesia, It. 150 D3
Borgou, range, Benin, Nigeria 200 F12
Borhoyn Tal, Mongolia 181 E13
Borinquen, Punta, P.R., U.S. 120 M1
Borisoglebsk, Russ. 156 M12
Borisovo Sudskoye, Russ. 156 F9
Borjomi, Rep. of Georgia 169 C17
Borkou, region, Chad 197 G15
Borlänge, Sw. 141 K13
Bormio, It. 150 C6
Borneo (Kalimantan), island, Indonesia 188 J10
Bornholm, island, Den. 141 P13
Bornova, Turk. 168 F3
Boro, river, Sudan 198 G11
Boroko, Indonesia 189 J14
Boromo, Burkina Faso 200 E9
Boronga Islands, Myanmar 186 H4
Borotou, Côte d'Ivoire 200 G7
Borovichi, Russ. 156 G8
Borovo, Croatia 152 E9
Borovsk, Russ. 156 K9
Borovskoy, Kaz. 174 B11
Borroloola, N. Terr., Austral. 211 Q9
Borşa, Rom. 153 B14
Børselv, Nor. 141 C14
Borūjerd, Iran 172 D11
Boryslav, Ukr. 157 P2
Boryspil', Ukr. 157 N6
Borzya, Russ. 159 L17
Bosa, It. 151 N3
Bosanska Gradiška, Bosn. & Herzg. 152 E7
Bosanski Brod, Bosn. & Herzg. 152 E8
Bosanski Petrovac, Bosn. & Herzg. 152 F6
Boscastle, Eng., U.K. 143 X8
Boscobel, Wis., U.S. 98 L4
Bose, China 180 P12
Boseong, S. Korea 182 H13
Boshan, China 182 F7
Bosilegrad, Serb. & Mont. 152 J12
Bosna, river, Bosn. & Herzg. 152 F8
Bosnia and Herzegovina, Eur. 139 W7
Bosobolo, Dem. Rep. of the Congo 198 H9
Bōsō Hantō, Japan 185 P13
Bosporus see İstanbul Boğazi, strait, Turk. 168 C5
Bossangoa, Cen. Af. Rep. 198 G8
Bossembélé, Cen. Af. Rep. 198 H8
Bossier City, La., U.S. 100 L6
Bossut, Cape, Austral. 210 D4
Bostan, Pak. 177 R6
Bosten Hu, China 180 F7
Boston, Eng., U.K. 143 S14
Boston, Ga., U.S. 97 Q6
Boston, Mass., U.S. 95 K15
Boston Bay, Jam. 120 J11
Boston Mountains, Ark., U.S. 100 F7
Boswell, Okla., U.S. 102 J13
Botabano, Cayman Is., U.K. 120 H1
Botanic Gardens, Dominica 121 G19
Botany Bay, Austral. 210 L14
Botev, peak, Bulg. 153 J14
Botevgrad, Bulg. 153 H13
Bothnia, Gulf of, Fin., Sw. 141 H14
Boticas, Port. 144 D6
Botoşani, Rom. 153 B16
Botswana, Af. 195 P20
Bottineau, N. Dak., U.S. 104 D5
Bottle Creek, Turks & Caicos Is., U.K. 117 H17
Botwood, Nfld. & Lab., Can. 83 M23
Bouaflé, Côte d'Ivoire 200 G8
Bouaké, Côte d'Ivoire 200 G9
Bouar, Cen. Af. Rep. 198 H8
Boû Djébéha, Mali 196 G9
Bougainville, island, P.N.G. 217 K13
Bougainville, Cape, Austral. 210 B5
Bougainville, Mont, Wallis & Futuna, Fr. 218 F12
Bougainville, Mouillage de, Fr. Polynesia, Fr. 219 N17
Bougainville Strait, Solomon Is. 217 K15
Bougainville Strait, Vanuatu 218 D2
Bougouni, Mali 196 J7
Bouillante, Guadeloupe, Fr. 121 F14
Bouillon, Belg. 147 N13
Bouilly, Fr. 147 Q12
Bouira, Alg. 196 A11
Boujdour, Cape, W. Sahara, Mor. 194 E1
Boulaide, Lux. 160 H9
Boulari, Passe de, New Caledonia, Fr. 218 E8
Boulder, Colo., U.S. 106 L13
Boulder, Mont., U.S. 106 D7
Boulder City, Nev., U.S. 109 U12
Boulia, Qnsld., Austral. 211 T11
Boulogne, Fr. 147 Y8
Boulogne-sur-Mer, Fr. 146 L9
Bouloupari, New Caledonia, Fr. 218 D8
Bouna, Côte d'Ivoire 200 F9
Boundary Peak, Nev., U.S. 109 S8
Boundiali, Côte d'Ivoire 200 F8
Bountiful, Utah, U.S. 106 K7
Bounty Bay, Pitcairn I., U.K. 219 Q23
Bounty Islands, N.Z. 214 Q9
Bounty Trough, Pac. Oc. 238 Q9
Bourail, New Caledonia, Fr. 218 D7
Bouraké, New Caledonia, Fr. 218 D8
Bourayne, Port, Fr. Polynesia, Fr. 219 H14
Bourbon-Lancy, Fr. 147 S11
Bourem, Mali 196 G9
Bourganeuf, Fr. 147 U9
Bourg-en-Bresse, Fr. 147 T13
Bourges, Fr. 147 S10
Bourget, Lac du, Fr. 147 U14
Bourg-Lastic, Fr. 147 U10
Bourg-Madame, Fr. 147 Z9
Bourgneuf, Baie de, Fr. 147 S5
Bourg-St. Maurice, Fr. 147 U15
Boû Rjeïmât, Mauritania 196 F5
Bourke, N.S.W., Austral. 211 W13
Bournemouth, Eng., U.K. 143 X12
Bourscheid, Lux. 160 H10
Bousso, Chad 197 K14
Boutilimit, Mauritania 196 G5
Bouvard, Cape, Austral. 210 K2
Bovalino Marina, It. 151 R13
Boven Bolivia, Neth. Antilles, Neth. 121 Q19
Bovey, Minn., U.S. 104 F11
Bovill, Idaho, U.S. 106 D4
Bovina, Tex., U.S. 102 H4
Bowbells, N. Dak., U.S. 104 D3
Bowdle, S. Dak., U.S. 104 J5
Bowdoin, Lake, Mont., U.S. 106 B11
Bowen, Qnsld., Austral. 211 S14
Bowers Ridge, Pac. Oc. 238 C10
Bowie, Ariz., U.S. 107 V9
Bowie, Md., U.S. 96 C13
Bowie, Tex., U.S. 102 K10
Bowie Seamount, Pac. Oc. 239 C14
Bowling Green, Ky., U.S. 101 D15
Bowling Green, Mo., U.S. 105 S14
Bowling Green, Ohio, U.S. 99 P12
Bowling Green, Va., U.S. 96 E13
Bowman, N. Dak., U.S. 104 H2
Bowman Bay, Nunavut, Can. 83 G18
Bowman Glacier, Antarctica 226 K12
Bowman Island, Antarctica 227 L22
Box Butte Reservoir, Nebr., U.S. 105 N2
Box Elder Creek, Mont., U.S. 106 C10
Boxelder Creek, Mont., U.S. 106 E13
Boxing, China 182 F8
Boyabat, Turk. 168 C10
Boyang, China 182 M7
Boyarka, Russ. 159 F14
Boyce, La., U.S. 100 M8
Boyer, river, Iowa, U.S. 105 P9
Boyle, Ire. 143 R4
Boyne, river, Ire. 143 R6
Boyne City, Mich., U.S. 98 H10
Boynton Beach, Fla., U.S. 97 W10
Boyoma Falls, Dem. Rep. of the Congo 198 J11
Boysen Reservoir, Wyo., U.S. 106 H10
Bozashchy Tübegi, Kaz. 174 G6
Boz Burun, Turk. 168 D4
Bozburun, Turk. 168 H3
Bozburun Dağı, Turk. 168 H6
Bozcaada, island, Turk. 168 D2
Boz Dağ, Turk. 168 H4
Bozdoğan, Turk. 168 G4
Bozeman, Mont., U.S. 106 E8
Bozhou, China 182 H6
Bozkır, Turk. 168 H7
Bozkurt, Turk. 168 B9
Bozouls, Fr. 147 W10
Bozoum, Cen. Af. Rep. 198 G8
Bozova, Turk. 169 H13
Bozüyük, Turk. 168 E6
Bra, It. 150 F3
Brabant Island, Antarctica 226 D4
Brač, island, Croatia 152 H6
Bracadale, Loch, Scot., U.K. 142 K7
Bracciano, It. 150 K8
Bracciano, Lago di, It. 150 K8
Brackettville, Tex., U.S. 103 R7
Bračkí Kanal, Croatia 152 H6
Bracknell, Eng., U.K. 143 V13
Brad, Rom. 152 D12
Bradenton, Fla., U.S. 97 U7
Bradford, Eng., U.K. 143 R12
Bradford, Pa., U.S. 94 L5
Bradley, Ill., U.S. 99 P7
Bradley, S. Dak., U.S. 104 J7
Brady, Nebr., U.S. 105 Q4
Brady, Tex., U.S. 103 P8
Braga, Port. 144 D5
Bragado, Arg. 132 L12
Bragança, Port. 144 D7
Braham, Minn., U.S. 104 H11
Brahmanbaria, Bangladesh 178 H13
Brahmapur, India 178 L10
Brahmaputra, river, Asia 166 H9
Brahmaur, India 177 P13
Brăila, Rom. 153 E17
Brainerd, Minn., U.S. 104 H10
Braintree, Eng., U.K. 143 U15
Braintree, Mass., U.S. 95 K15
Bramsche, Ger. 148 D6
Brancaleone Marina, It. 151 S13
Branchville, S.C., U.S. 96 L9
Branco, island, Cape Verde 205 B15
Branco, river, Braz. 130 C8
Brandberg, peak, Namibia 194 N6
Brandenburg, region, Ger. 148 E10
Brandenburg, Ger. 148 D9
Brandfort, S. Af. 202 K10
Brandon, Fla., U.S. 97 U8
Brandon, Man., Can. 83 N13
Brandon, Miss., U.S. 100 L11
Brandon, S. Dak., U.S. 104 L8
Brandon Bay, Ire. 143 U2
Brandvlei, S. Af. 202 L8
Brandy Peak, Oreg., U.S. 108 K2
Branford, Fla., U.S. 97 R7
Bransby, Qnsld., Austral. 211 V11
Bransby Point, Montserrat, U.K. 121 B23
Bransfield Strait, Antarctica 226 C4
Branson, Colo., U.S. 107 Q14
Branson, Mo., U.S. 105 V12
Brantley, Ala., U.S. 101 M16
Brantley Lake, N. Mex., U.S. 107 V14
Brantôme, Fr. 147 U8
Bras d'Or Lake, N.S., Can. 83 N22
Brasil, Planalto do, Braz. 131 J14
Brasília, Braz. 131 J13
Brasília Legal, Braz. 130 E11
Braşov, Rom. 153 E15
Bras-Panon, Reunion, Fr. 205 G17
Brasstown Bald, peak, Ga., U.S. 96 J5
Brateş, Lacul, Rom. 153 E17
Bratislava (Pressburg), Slovakia 149 K13
Bratsk, Russ. 159 K15
Bratskoye Vodokhranilishche, Russ. 159 K15
Bratsk Reservoir, Russ. 166 E9
Brattleboro, Vt., U.S. 95 J13
Braţul Chilia, river, Rom. 153 E18
Braţul Sfântu-Gheorghe, river, Rom. 153 E18
Braunau, Aust. 148 K10
Braunschweig (Brunswick), Ger. 148 E8
Braunton, Eng., U.K. 143 W9
Brava, island, Cape Verde 205 E15
Brava, Costa, Sp. 145 D19
Brawley, Calif., U.S. 109 Y11
Bray, Ire. 143 S7
Bray Island, Nunavut, Can. 83 F17
Brazil, Ind., U.S. 99 S8
Brazil, S. Amer. 127 F19
Brazilian Highlands, S. Amer. 126 F9
Brazoria, Tex., U.S. 103 S13
Brazos, river, Tex., U.S. 103 P12
Brazzaville, Congo 201 M17
Brčko, Bosn. & Herzg. 152 F8
Brea, Punta, P.R., U.S. 120 P2
Breadalbane, Qnsld., Austral. 211 T11
Breakers, Cayman Is., U.K. 120 J3
Breakfast Island, Marshall Is. 216 M8
Breaux Bridge, La., U.S. 100 P9
Breaza, Rom. 153 E15
Brechin, Scot., U.K. 142 L11
Breckenridge, Colo., U.S. 106 M12
Breckenridge, Minn., U.S. 104 H8
Breckenridge, Tex., U.S. 102 L9
Brecknock, Península, Chile 133 X7
Breda, Neth. 146 K12
Bredasdorp, S. Af. 202 M8
Breezewood, Pa., U.S. 94 P5
Bregalnica, river, Maced. 152 K12
Bregenz, Aust. 148 L7
Bréhat, Île de, Fr. 147 P4
Breiðafjörður, bay, Ice. 140 E2
Breid Bay, Antarctica 227 B15
Breil-sur-Roya, Fr. 147 W16
Breisach, Fr. 147 Q15
Brejo, Braz. 131 E15
Bremen, Ga., U.S. 96 L4
Bremen, Ger. 148 C7
Bremen, Ind., U.S. 99 P9
Bremerhaven, Ger. 148 C7
Bremerton, Wash., U.S. 108 C3
Bremond, Tex., U.S. 103 N12
Brenham, Tex., U.S. 103 Q12
Brennero, It. 150 B7
Brennner Pass, Aust. 148 M8
Breno, It. 150 D6
Brentwood, Eng., U.K. 143 V14
Brentwood, N.Y., U.S. 94 N12
Brescia, It. 150 D6
Bressanone, It. 150 B7
Bressay, island, Scot., U.K. 142 D12
Bressuire, Fr. 147 S7
Brest, Belarus 156 L2
Brest, Fr. 147 Q2
Breteuil, Fr. 147 N10
Bretón, Cayo, Cuba 116 J9
Breton, Pertuis, Fr. 147 T5
Breton Islands, La., U.S. 100 Q12
Breton Sound, La., U.S. 100 Q12
Brett, Cape, N.Z. 213 H18
Breu, river, Braz., Peru 130 G5
Brevard, N.C., U.S. 96 J7
Breves, Braz. 130 D12
Brevoort Island, Nunavut, Can. 83 G19
Brewarrina, N.S.W., Austral. 211 W13
Brewer, Me., U.S. 95 F17
Brewers Bay, Virgin Islands, U.K. 120 Q6
Brewster, Kans., U.S. 105 S3
Brewster, Nebr., U.S. 105 N5
Brewster, Wash., U.S. 108 B6
Brewton, Ala., U.S. 101 N15
Bria, Cen. Af. Rep. 198 G10
Briare, Fr. 147 R10
Briatico, It. 151 Q13
Bridgend, Wales, U.K. 143 V10
Bridge Point, Bahamas 120 D5
Bridgeport, Ala., U.S. 101 G16
Bridgeport, Calif., U.S. 109 R7
Bridgeport, Conn., U.S. 94 M12
Bridgeport, Ill., U.S. 99 T7
Bridgeport, Nebr., U.S. 105 P2
Bridgeport, Tex., U.S. 102 K10
Bridgeport, W. Va., U.S. 96 C9
Bridgeport, Lake, Tex., U.S. 102 K10
Bridger Peak, Wyo., U.S. 106 K11
Bridgeton, N.J., U.S. 94 Q9
Bridgetown, Barbados 121 L18
Bridgetown, Ohio, U.S. 99 S11
Bridgetown, W. Aust., Austral. 211 Y3
Bridgewater, N.S., Can. 83 P22
Bridgton, Me., U.S. 95 G15
Bridgwater, Eng., U.K. 143 W10
Bridlington, Eng., U.K. 143 Q13
Brielle, Neth. 146 J11
Brienne-le-Château, Fr. 147 Q12
Brienza, It. 151 N12
Brienzer See, Switz. 150 B3
Brig, Switz. 150 C3
Brigantine Cays, Bahamas 120 E7
Brigham City, Utah, U.S. 106 K7
Brighton, Eng., U.K. 143 W14
Brihuega, Sp. 144 F12
Brijuni Otoci, Croatia 152 E4
Brindisi, It. 150 M15
Brinkley, Ark., U.S. 100 G10
Brinkworth, S. Aust., Austral. 211 X10
Brisbane, Qnsld., Austral. 211 V15
Bristol, Conn., U.S. 94 L12
Bristol, Eng., U.K. 143 V11
Bristol, Pa., U.S. 94 P10
Bristol, S. Dak., U.S. 104 J7
Bristol, Tenn., U.S. 101 D20
Bristol, Va., U.S. 96 G7
Bristol Bay, Alas., U.S. 111 L13
Bristol Channel, Eng., Wales, U.K. 143 W9
Bristol Lake, Calif., U.S. 109 W11
Bristol Mountains, Calif., U.S. 109 W11
Bristow, Okla., U.S. 102 F12
British Columbia, Can. 82 J8
British Isles, Ire., U.K. 143 R4
British Mountains, U.S., Can. 84 M5
British Virgin Islands, U.K., Lesser Antilles 119 E14
Britstown, S. Af. 202 L9
Britt, Iowa, U.S. 104 M11
Brittany, region, Fr. 147 Q4
Britton, S. Dak., U.S. 104 J7
Britton Hill, Fla., U.S. 97 Q3
Brive, Fr. 147 V9
Briviesca, Sp. 144 C11
Brno, Czech Rep. 149 J13
Broa, Ensenada de la, Cuba 116 G7
Broad, river, S.C., U.S. 96 J8
Broad Bay, Scot., U.K. 142 H7
Broad Haven, Ire. 143 Q3
Broadstairs, Eng., U.K. 143 V16
Broadus, Mont., U.S. 106 E12
Broadview, Sask., Can. 82 N12
Broadwater, Nebr., U.S. 105 P2
Brochet, Man., Can. 83 K13
Brocken, peak, Ger. 148 E8
Brock Island, N.W.T., Can. 83 B13
Brockport, N.Y., U.S. 94 H6
Brockton, Mass., U.S. 95 K15
Brockway, Mont., U.S. 106 C12
Brockway, Pa., U.S. 94 M5
Brodeur Peninsula, Nunavut, Can. 83 E15
Brodnica, Pol. 149 C15
Brody, Ukr. 157 N3
Brogan, Oreg., U.S. 108 H9
Broken Arrow, Okla., U.S. 102 F13
Broken Bow, Nebr., U.S. 105 P5
Broken Bow, Okla., U.S. 102 J14

Broken Bow Lake, *Okla., U.S.* **102** J14
Broken Hill, *N.S.W., Austral.* **211** X11
Broken Ridge, *Ind. Oc.* **240** M12
Brokopondo, *Suriname* **129** E16
Brønnøysund, *Nor.* **140** G11
Bronson, *Fla., U.S.* **97** S7
Bronswinkel, *Neth. Antilles, Neth.* **121** Q18
Bronte, *Tex., U.S.* **102** M7
Brookfield, *Mo., U.S.* **105** R12
Brookfield, *Wis., U.S.* **98** L7
Brookhaven, *Miss., U.S.* **100** M10
Brookings, *Oreg., U.S.* **108** L1
Brookings, *S. Dak., U.S.* **104** K8
Brooklyn, *Iowa, U.S.* **105** P12
Brooklyn Center, *Minn., U.S.* **104** J11
Brookport, *Ill., U.S.* **99** V6
Brooks, *Alta., Can.* **82** M10
Brooks Banks, *Hawai'i, U.S.* **112** M6
Brooks Range, *Alas., U.S.* **111** D14
Brooksville, *Fla., U.S.* **97** T7
Brookville, *Ind., U.S.* **99** S10
Brookville, *Pa., U.S.* **94** M4
Broome, *W. Aust., Austral.* **211** R4
Brora, *Scot., U.K.* **142** H9
Brosse, Île, *New Caledonia, Fr.* **218** E9
Brothers, *Oreg., U.S.* **108** H5
Broughton Islands, *Austral.* **210** K15
Brovary, *Ukr.* **157** N6
Browerville, *Minn., U.S.* **104** H10
Brown, Point, *Austral.* **210** J8
Brown Bay, *Virgin Islands, U.S.* **120** M11
Brownfield, *Tex., U.S.* **102** K4
Browning, *Mont., U.S.* **106** B6
Brownlee Dam, *Idaho, Oreg., U.S.* **108** G9
Browns Town, *Jam.* **116** M11
Brownstown, *Ind., U.S.* **99** T9
Browns Valley, *Minn., U.S.* **104** J8
Brownsville, *Tenn., U.S.* **100** F12
Brownsville, *Tex., U.S.* **103** X11
Brownsweg, *Suriname* **129** E16
Brownwood, *Tex., U.S.* **103** N9
Brownwood, Lake, *Tex., U.S.* **102** M9
Browse Island, *W. Aust., Austral.* **211** Q4
Brozas, *Sp.* **144** G7
Bruce, *Miss., U.S.* **100** J12
Bruce Rock, *W. Aust., Austral.* **211** X3
Bruchsal, *Ger.* **148** J6
Bruciate, river, *San Marino* **161** K16
Bruciato, *It.* **161** H14
Bruck an der Mur, *Aust.* **148** L12
Brugg, *Switz.* **150** A3
Brugge, *Belg.* **146** K11
Bruini, *India* **178** E15
Brule, river, *Wis., U.S.* **98** G6
Brumado, *Braz.* **131** J15
Brundidge, *Ala., U.S.* **101** M16
Bruneau, river, *Idaho, U.S.* **106** H4
Bruneau, *Idaho, U.S.* **106** H4
Brunei, *Asia* **167** Y12
Brunei Bay, *Brunei, Malaysia* **188** G11
Brunette Downs, *N. Terr., Austral.* **211** R9
Brunico, *It.* **150** B8
Brunner, Lake, *N.Z.* **213** N17
Brunssum, *Neth.* **146** L13
Brunswick, *Ga., U.S.* **97** P8
Brunswick *see* Braunschweig, *Ger.* **148** E8
Brunswick, *Me., U.S.* **95** G16
Brunswick, *Mo., U.S.* **105** S12
Brunswick, *Ohio, U.S.* **99** P14
Brunswick Bay, *Austral.* **210** C5
Brush, *Colo., U.S.* **106** L14
Brus Laguna, *Hond.* **115** K18
Brusque, *Braz.* **131** N13
Brussels *see* Bruxelles, *Belg.* **146** L12
Bruxelles (Brussels), *Belg.* **146** L12
Bruzual, *Venez.* **128** D8
Bryan, *Ohio, U.S.* **99** P11
Bryan, *Tex., U.S.* **103** P12
Bryan Coast, *Antarctica* **226** H6
Bryansk, *Russ.* **156** L8
Bryant, *Ark., U.S.* **100** G8
Bryant, *S. Dak., U.S.* **104** K7
Bryce Canyon National Park, *Utah, U.S.* **107** P7
Bryson City, *N.C., U.S.* **96** J6
Bryukhovetskaya, *Russ.* **157** S10
Brzeg, *Pol.* **149** F13
Brzeg Dolny, *Pol.* **149** F13
Bua, *Fiji Is.* **218** G7
Bua Bay, *Fiji Is.* **218** H7
Buache, Mount, *F.S.M.* **217** A18
Buada, region, *Nauru* **217** F23
Buada Lagoon, *Nauru* **217** F23
Buala, *Solomon Is.* **217** M18
Buariki, island, *Kiribati* **217** F17
Buariki, *Kiribati* **217** F17
Bua Yai, *Thai.* **186** L10
Bu'ayrāt al Ḩasūn, *Lib.* **197** C14
Buba, *Guinea-Bissau* **200** E4
Būbiyān, island, *Kuwait* **172** F11
Bucak, *Turk.* **168** H6
Bucakkışla, *Turk.* **168** H8
Bucaramanga, *Col.* **128** D6
Buccament Bay, *St. Vincent & the Grenadines* **121** K16
Buccaneer Archipelago, *Austral.* **210** C4
Buccaneer Point, *Bahamas* **120** B8
Buccoo Bay, *Trinidad & Tobago* **121** N17
Buchanan, *Liberia* **200** H6
Buchanan, *Mich., U.S.* **99** N9
Buchanan, Lake, *Tex., U.S.* **103** P9
Buchan Gulf, *Nunavut, Can.* **83** E17
Bucharest *see* București, *Rom.* **153** F15
Buchholz, *Ger.* **148** C8
Buchon, Point, *Calif., U.S.* **109** V5
Buchs, *Switz.* **160** N2
Buckhannon, *W. Va., U.S.* **96** D9
Buck Island, *Virgin Islands, U.S.* **120** N9
Buck Island, *Virgin Islands, U.S.* **120** Q3
Buck Island Reef National Monument, *Virgin Islands, U.S.* **120** Q3
Buckland Tableland, *Austral.* **210** G13
Buckley, *Wash., U.S.* **108** C4
Bucklin, *Kans., U.S.* **105** U5
Buckner Bay *see* Nakagusuku Wan, *Japan* **185** Y1
Bucksport, *Me., U.S.* **95** F17
Bucovina, region, *Rom., Ukr.* **153** A15
Buco Zau, *Angola* **202** A5
Bu Craa, *W. Sahara, Mor.* **196** D6
București (Bucharest), *Rom.* **153** F15
Bucyrus, *Ohio, U.S.* **99** Q13
Bud, *Nor.* **140** J10
Buda, *Tex., U.S.* **103** Q10
Budac, peak, *Rom.* **153** C15
Budalin, *Myanmar* **186** G5
Budapest, *Hung.* **149** L15
Búdardalur, *Ice.* **140** E2
Budaun, *India* **178** F7
Budd Coast, *Antarctica* **227** M21
Buddhas of Bamian, ruin, *Afghan.* **176** M6
Buddusò, *It.* **150** M4
Bude, *Eng., U.K.* **143** W9
Bude, *Miss., U.S.* **100** M10
Bude Bay, *Eng., U.K.* **143** W9
Budennovsk, *Russ.* **157** S13
Budgewoi, *N.S.W., Austral.* **211** X14
Búdir, *Ice.* **140** F4
Budjala, *Dem. Rep. of the Congo* **198** J9
Budū', Sabkhat al, *Saudi Arabia* **172** K12
Buena Esperanza, *Arg.* **132** L9
Buenaventura, *Col.* **128** F4
Buenaventura, *Mex.* **114** C8
Buenaventura Bay, *S. Amer.* **126** C2
Buena Vista, *Colo., U.S.* **107** N12
Buena Vista, *Neth. Antilles, Neth.* **121** P14
Buena Vista, *Ga., U.S.* **97** N5
Buena Vista, *Va., U.S.* **96** E10
Buena Vista Lake Bed, *Calif., U.S.* **109** V7
Buendía, Embalse de, *Sp.* **144** F12
Buenos Aires, *Arg.* **132** L13
Buenos Aires, Lago, *Arg.* **133** T7
Buenos Ayres, *Trinidad & Tobago* **121** Q21
Buen Tiempo, Cabo, *Arg.* **133** W8
Bufareh, *Indonesia* **189** K20
Buffalo, river, *Ark., U.S.* **100** E8
Buffalo, *Minn., U.S.* **104** J11
Buffalo, *Mo., U.S.* **105** U12
Buffalo, *N.Y., U.S.* **94** J5
Buffalo, *Okla., U.S.* **102** E8
Buffalo, *S. Dak., U.S.* **104** J2
Buffalo, *Tex., U.S.* **103** N13
Buffalo, *Wyo., U.S.* **106** G11
Buffalo Bill Reservoir, *Wyo., U.S.* **106** F9
Buffalo Hump, peak, *Idaho, U.S.* **106** E4
Buffalo Lake, *Tex., U.S.* **102** H5
Buffalo National River, *Ark., U.S.* **100** E8
Buff Bay, *Jam.* **120** H10
Buford, *Ga., U.S.* **96** K5
Buftea, *Rom.* **153** F15
Bug, river, *Belarus, Pol.* **138** F8
Buga, *Col.* **128** F4
Buġibba, *Malta* **161** J22
Bugio, Ilhéu do, *Madeira* **204** N4
Bugsuk, island, *Philippines* **188** F12
Bugt, *China* **181** C16
Bugul'ma, *Russ.* **156** J16
Buguruslan, *Russ.* **156** K16
Buhl, *Idaho, U.S.* **106** H5
Buhl, *Minn., U.S.* **104** F12
Buhuşi, *Rom.* **153** C16
Builth Wells, *Wales, U.K.* **143** U10
Buin, *P.N.G.* **217** K14
Buinsk, *Russ.* **156** J14
Buis-les-Baronnies, *Fr.* **147** W13
Bujalance, *Sp.* **144** K10
Bujanovac, *Serb. & Mont.* **152** J11
Bujaraloz, *Sp.* **145** E15
Bujumbura, *Burundi* **198** L12
Buka, island, *P.N.G.* **217** J13
Bukachacha, *Russ.* **159** L17
Bukama, *Dem. Rep. of the Congo* **198** N11
Bukanik, Maja, *Albania* **152** L10
Buka Passage, *P.N.G.* **217** J13
Bukavu, *Dem. Rep. of the Congo* **198** K12
Bukhara *see* Buxoro, *Uzb.* **174** L11
Bukittinggi, *Indonesia* **188** J5
Bukoba, *Tanzania* **199** K13
Bula, *Indonesia* **189** K17
Bülach, *Switz.* **150** A4
Būlaevo, *Kaz.* **175** A13
Bulan, *Philippines* **189** D14
Bulancak, *Turk.* **169** D13
Bulandshahr, *India* **178** F6
Bulanık, *Turk.* **169** F16
Bulawayo, *Zimb.* **202** G11
Buldan, *Turk.* **168** G4
Buldir Island, *Alas., U.S.* **111** M2
Bulgan, *Mongolia* **180** C11
Bulgan, *Mongolia* **180** C11
Bulgan, *Mongolia* **180** E10
Bulgaria, *Eur.* **139** W9
Buli, Teluk, *Indonesia* **189** J16
Buliluyan, Cape, *Philippines* **188** F12
Buliya, island, *Fiji Is.* **218** K7
Bullara, *W. Aust., Austral.* **211** T1
Bull Bay, *Jam.* **120** J10
Bulle, *Switz.* **150** B2
Bullenbaai, bay, *Neth. Antilles, Neth.* **121** P14
Bullfinch, *W. Aust., Austral.* **211** W3
Bullhead City, *Ariz., U.S.* **107** S4
Bull Mountains, *Mont., U.S.* **106** D10
Bulloo Downs, *Qnsld., Austral.* **211** V12
Bulloo Downs, *W. Aust., Austral.* **211** U3
Bullo River, *N. Terr., Austral.* **211** Q7
Bulls Bay, *S.C., U.S.* **96** M11
Bull Shoals Lake, *Ark., U.S.* **100** E8
Bulun, *Russ.* **159** E16
Bulung'ur, *Uzb.* **174** L12
Bumba, *Dem. Rep. of the Congo* **198** J10
Bumbat, *Mongolia* **180** D12
Bum La, *China, India* **178** F13
Buna, *Kenya* **199** J15
Bunbury, *W. Aust., Austral.* **211** X2
Bunclody (Newtownbarry), *Ire.* **143** T6
Bundaberg, *Qnsld., Austral.* **211** U15
Bundaleer, *Qnsld., Austral.* **211** V13
Bundi, *India* **178** G5
Bundooma, *N. Terr., Austral.* **211** U9
Bungalaut, Selat, *Indonesia* **188** K5
Bungku, *Indonesia* **189** K14
Bungo Suidō, *Japan* **185** S6
Bungotakada, *Japan* **185** R5
Bunia, *Dem. Rep. of the Congo* **198** J12
Bunji, *Pak.* **176** L12
Bunker, *Mo., U.S.* **105** U14
Bunkie, *La., U.S.* **100** N8
Bunnell, *Fla., U.S.* **97** S9
Buntok, *Indonesia* **188** K11
Bünyan, *Turk.* **168** F11
Bunyu, island, *Indonesia* **188** H12
Buol, *Indonesia* **189** H14
Buon Me Thuot, *Vietnam* **187** N13
Buor-Khaya Bay, *Arctic Oc.* **242** B6
Buqūm, Ḩarrat al, *Saudi Arabia* **172** L8
Bur, *Russ.* **159** J15
Bura, *Kenya* **199** K15
Burakin, *W. Aust., Austral.* **211** W3
Burang, *China* **180** K4
Burao *see* Burco, *Somalia* **199** F17
Buras, *La., U.S.* **100** R12
Buraydah, *Saudi Arabia* **172** H9
Burbank, *Calif., U.S.* **109** X8
Burco (Burao), *Somalia* **199** F17
Burdalyk, *Turkm.* **174** M11
Burdekin, river, *Austral.* **210** E13
Burdur, *Turk.* **168** G6
Burdur Gölü, *Turk.* **168** G6
Bûr Fu'ad, *Egypt* **171** N1
Burg, *Ger.* **148** E9
Burgas, *Bulg.* **153** J17
Burgaski Zaliv, *Bulg.* **153** J17
Burgasko Ezero, *Bulg.* **153** J17
Burgaw, *N.C., U.S.* **96** J12
Burgdorf, *Switz.* **150** B3
Burgerau, *Switz.* **160** P2
Burgess Hill, *Eng., U.K.* **143** W14
Burghūth, Sabkhat al, *Syr.* **170** G14
Burgos, *Sp.* **144** C11
Burgsvik, *Sw.* **141** M14
Burgundy, region, *Fr.* **147** S12
Burhaniye, *Turk.* **168** E3
Burhanpur, *India* **178** K5
Burhou, island, *Ch. Is.* **143** Y11
Burias, island, *Philippines* **189** D14
Burica, Punta, *Costa Rica, Pan.* **115** P19
Burica Point, *N. Amer.* **80** R8
Buriram, *Thai.* **186** M10
Burkburnett, *Tex., U.S.* **102** J9
Burke, *S. Dak., U.S.* **104** M6
Burke Island, *Antarctica* **226** K6
Burkesville, *Ky., U.S.* **101** D17
Burketown, *Qnsld., Austral.* **211** R11
Bur Khaybyt, *Russ.* **159** E18
Burkina Faso, *Af.* **195** G15
Burle, island, *Marshall Is.* **216** L4
Burleson, *Tex., U.S.* **102** L11
Burley, *Idaho, U.S.* **106** H5
Burlingame, *Kans., U.S.* **105** T9
Burlington, *Colo., U.S.* **106** M16
Burlington, *Iowa, U.S.* **105** Q14
Burlington, *Kans., U.S.* **105** T9
Burlington, *N.C., U.S.* **96** G10
Burlington, *Vt., U.S.* **94** F12
Burlington, *Wash., U.S.* **108** B4
Burlington, *Wis., U.S.* **98** M6
Burma *see* Myanmar, *Asia* **167** W9
Burma Road, *China* **180** N10
Burnet, *Tex., U.S.* **103** P10
Burnett Bay, *N.W.T., Can.* **82** C12
Burney, *Calif., U.S.* **108** M4
Burnham Market, *Eng., U.K.* **143** S15
Burnham on Sea, *Eng., U.K.* **143** W10
Burnie, *Tas., Austral.* **211** Y16
Burns, *Oreg., U.S.* **108** J7
Burns, *Wyo., U.S.* **106** K14
Burnside, Lake, *Austral.* **210** G5
Burns Lake, *B.C., Can.* **82** K8
Burnsville, *Minn., U.S.* **104** K11
Burnt, river, *Oreg., U.S.* **108** G8
Burnt Pine, *Norfolk I., Austral.* **217** F20
Burqin, *China* **180** D7
Burqu', Qaşr, *Jordan* **170** L10
Burray, island, *Scot., U.K.* **142** G10
Burren, region, *Ire.* **143** S3
Burrendong Reservoir, *Austral.* **210** K14
Burren Junction, *N.S.W., Austral.* **211** W14
Burriana, *Sp.* **145** G15
Burrton, *Kans., U.S.* **105** U7
Burrundie, *N. Terr., Austral.* **211** P8
Burrwood, *La., U.S.* **100** R12
Bursa, *Turk.* **168** D5
Bûr Safâga, *Egypt* **197** D19
Bûr Sa'îd (Port Said), *Egypt* **171** N1
Būr Sūdān (Port Sudan), *Sudan* **199** C14
Burt Lake, *Mich., U.S.* **98** H11
Burton, *Mich., U.S.* **98** L12
Burton, *Nebr., U.S.* **104** M5
Buru, island, *Indonesia* **189** K16
Burūm, *Yemen* **172** Q11
Burundi, *Af.* **195** K21
Burun Shibertuy, Gora, *Russ.* **159** M16
Bururi, *Burundi* **198** L12
Burwash Landing, *Yukon, Can.* **82** F7
Burwell, *Nebr., U.S.* **105** P6
Burylbaytal, *Kaz.* **175** H15
Bury St. Edmunds, *Eng., U.K.* **143** U15
Burzil Pass, *Pak.* **176** M12
Busan (Pusan), *S. Korea* **182** G14
Busanga Swamp, *Zambia* **202** E10
Buşayrah, *Syr.* **170** F13
Bushiribana, *Aruba, Neth.* **121** Q17
Bushnell, *Ill., U.S.* **99** Q4
Bushnell, *Nebr., U.S.* **105** P1
Bushy Park, *N. Terr., Austral.* **211** T8
Businga, *Dem. Rep. of the Congo* **198** H9
Bušk Blato, *Bosn. & Herzg.* **152** G7
Buşrá ash Shām, *Syr.* **170** L7
Busselton, *W. Aust., Austral.* **211** Y2
Bussière-Poitevine, *Fr.* **147** T8
Bussol', Proliv, *Russ.* **159** J23
Bussoleno, *It.* **150** E2
Bustamante, Bahía, *Arg.* **133** S9
Busuanga, island, *Philippines* **189** D13
Busu-Djanoa, *Dem. Rep. of the Congo* **198** J9
Buta, *Dem. Rep. of the Congo* **198** J10
Butare, *Rwanda* **198** K12
Butaritari, island, *Kiribati* **214** G8
Butchers Hill, *Qnsld., Austral.* **211** Q13
Bute, Island of, *Scot., U.K.* **142** M8
Butembo, *Dem. Rep. of the Congo* **198** K12
Buthidaung, *Myanmar* **186** H4
Butler, *Ala., U.S.* **101** L13
Butler, *Ga., U.S.* **96** M5
Butler, *Mo., U.S.* **105** T11
Butler, *Pa., U.S.* **94** N3
Butler Bay, *Virgin Islands, U.S.* **120** Q1
Butner, *N.C., U.S.* **96** G11
Buton, island, *Indonesia* **189** L14
Butrint, *Albania* **152** N9
Butte, *Mont., U.S.* **106** E7
Butte, *Nebr., U.S.* **104** M6
Butterworth, *Malaysia* **187** S9
Butt of Lewis, *Scot., U.K.* **142** G7
Button Bay, *Man., Can.* **83** K15
Button Islands, *Nunavut, Can.* **83** H20
Butuan, *Philippines* **189** E15
Buturlinovka, *Russ.* **157** N11
Butwal, *Nepal* **178** F9
Buulobarde, *Somalia* **199** H17
Buur Gaabo, *Somalia* **199** K16
Buurgplaatz, *Belg., Lux.* **160** G9
Buurhakaba, *Somalia* **199** J16
Buxoro (Bukhara), *Uzb.* **174** L11
Buxtehude, *Ger.* **148** C7
Buxton, *Guyana* **129** D15
Buxton, *N.C., U.S.* **96** H15
Buy, *Russ.* **156** G11
Buyanbat, *Mongolia* **180** D10
Buyant, *Mongolia* **181** D13
Buynaksk, *Russ.* **157** U15
Buyr Nuur, *Mongolia* **181** D15
Büyük Menderes, river, *Turk.* **168** G4
Buzău, river, *Rom.* **153** E16
Buzău, *Rom.* **153** E16
Buzău, Pasul, *Rom.* **153** E15
Buzaymah, *Lib.* **197** E16
Búzi, river, *Mozambique* **202** G12
Büzmeýin, *Turkm.* **174** M8
Buzul Daği, *Turk.* **169** H18
Buzuluk, *Kaz.* **174** C12
Buzuluk, *Russ.* **156** L16
Buzzards Bay, *Mass., U.S.* **95** L15
Bwokworlap, island, *Marshall Is.* **216** G11
Byahoml', *Belarus* **156** K5
Byala, *Bulg.* **153** H17
Byala Slatina, *Bulg.* **153** H13
Byam Martin, Cape, *Nunavut, Can.* **83** D17
Byam Martin Island, *Nunavut, Can.* **83** D14
Byarezina, river, *Belarus* **156** K5
Byaroza, *Belarus* **156** L3
Byblos *see* Jbail, *Leb.* **170** H6
Bydgoszcz, *Pol.* **149** C14
Byers, *Colo., U.S.* **106** M14
Byfield, *Qnsld., Austral.* **211** T15
Bykhaw, *Belarus* **156** L6
Bykovo, *Russ.* **157** P13
Bylas, *Ariz., U.S.* **107** U8
Bylot Island, *Nunavut, Can.* **83** D16
Bynum Reservoir, *Mont., U.S.* **106** B7
Byrdbreen, glacier, *Antarctica* **227** B16
Byrd Glacier, *Antarctica* **227** M14
Byrock, *N.S.W., Austral.* **211** W13
Byron, Cape, *Austral.* **210** H15
Byron, Isla, *Chile* **133** U6
Bytom, *Pol.* **149** G14
Bytów, *Pol.* **149** B13

C

C, Dome, *Antarctica* **227** M17
Caála, *Angola* **202** D6
Caazapá, *Parag.* **130** N10
Cabaiguán, *Cuba* **116** H9
Caballones, Cayo, *Cuba* **116** J10
Caballo Reservoir, *N. Mex., U.S.* **107** U11
Cabanatuan, *Philippines* **189** C13
Cabaneta, Pic de la, *Andorra, Fr.* **160** H5

Cabeza del Buey, Sp. 144 J9
Cabezas, Bol. 130 K8
Cabimas, Venez. 128 B7
Cabinda, region, Angola 202 B5
Cabinda, Angola 202 B5
Cabinet Mountains, Mont., U.S. 106 B4
Cable, Wis., U.S. 98 F3
Cabo, Braz. 131 G18
Cabo Blanco, Arg. 133 T9
Cabo Frio, Braz. 131 M15
Cabonga, Réservoir, Que., Can. 83 P19
Cabool, Mo., U.S. 105 V13
Caboolture, Qnsld., Austral. 211 V15
Caborea, Mex. 114 C6
Cabo San Lucas, Mex. 114 G7
Cabot, Ark., U.S. 100 G9
Cabot Strait, Nfld. & Lab., N.S., Can. 83 N22
Cabral, Dom. Rep. 117 M18
Cabras, Ilhéu das, Sao Tome and Principe 205 C20
Cabras Island, Guam, U.S. 216 C10
Cabrera, Dom. Rep. 117 L19
Cabrera, island, Sp. 145 H18
Cabrera Baja, Sierra de la, Sp. 144 C7
Cabrit, Îlet à, Guadeloupe, Fr. 121 G14
Cabrits, Îlet, Martinique, Fr. 121 G23
Cabrobó, Braz. 131 G16
Cabrón, Cabo, Dom. Rep. 117 L20
Čačak, Serb. & Mont. 152 G10
Caccia, Capo, It. 150 M3
Cáceres, Sp. 144 H8
Cáceres, Braz. 130 J10
Cache, river, Ark., U.S. 100 E10
Ca'Chiavello, river, San Marino 161 K16
Cachimbo, Braz. 130 G11
Cachoeira, Braz. 131 H16
Cachoeira do Sul, Braz. 130 P11
Cachoeiro do Itapemirim, Braz. 131 L15
Cacine, Guinea-Bissau 200 E4
Cacolo, Angola 202 C7
Cactus, Tex., U.S. 102 F5
Caçu, Braz. 130 K12
Caculé, Braz. 131 J15
Cacuri, Venez. 128 E10
Čadca, Slovakia 149 H14
Caddo, Okla., U.S. 102 J12
Caddo Lake, La., Tex., U.S. 100 K6
Cadena, Punta, P.R., U.S. 120 M1
Cadí, Serra del, Sp. 145 C17
Cadillac, Fr. 147 W7
Cadillac, Mich., U.S. 98 J10
Çadır Dağı, Turk. 169 G17
Cádiz, Sp. 144 M7
Cádiz, Bahía de, Sp. 144 M7
Cádiz, Golfo de, Port., Sp. 144 L6
Cadiz, Calif., U.S. 109 W11
Cadiz, Ky., U.S. 101 D14
Cadiz, Ohio, U.S. 99 Q15
Cadiz, Philippines 189 E14
Cadiz Lake, Calif., U.S. 109 X12
Caen, Fr. 147 N7
Caerdydd see Cardiff, Wales, U.K. 143 V10
Caergybi see Holyhead, Wales, U.K. 143 S9
Caernarfon Bay, Wales, U.K. 143 S9
Caerphilly, Wales, U.K. 143 V10
Caesarea, ruin, Israel 170 L5
Cafayate, Arg. 132 F9
Cagayan de Oro, Philippines 189 F15
Cagayan Islands, Philippines 189 E13
Cagayan Sulu Island, Philippines 188 F12
Cagli, It. 150 H8
Cagliari, It. 151 Q4
Cagliari, Golfo di, It. 151 Q4
Cagnes, Fr. 147 X15
Caguán, river, Col. 128 H5
Caguas, P.R., U.S. 120 N5
Caha Mountains, Ire. 143 V3
Cahir, Ire. 143 U5
Cahora Bassa, Lago de, Mozambique 202 E12
Cahore Point, Ire. 143 T7
Cahors, Fr. 147 W9
Cahul, Mold. 157 S4
Caia, Mozambique 203 F13
Caiapônia, Braz. 130 J12
Caibarién, Cuba 116 H9
Caicara, Venez. 128 D10
Caicó, Braz. 131 F17
Caicos Islands, Turks & Caicos Is., U.K. 117 J17
Caicos Passage, Bahamas, Turks & Caicos Is., U.K. 117 H16
Caijiapo, China 182 H1
Caille Island, Grenada 121 H24
Cailungo, San Marino 161 J15
Cainsville, Mo., U.S. 105 Q11
Caird Coast, Antarctica 226 D10
Cairngorm Mountains, Scot., U.K. 142 K9
Cairns, Qnsld., Austral. 211 R13
Cairo see El Qâhira, Egypt 197 C18
Cairo, Ga., U.S. 97 Q5
Cairo, Ill., U.S. 99 V5
Caixão Grande, Sao Tome and Principe 205 D20
Caja de Muertos, Isla, P.R., U.S. 120 P3
Cajamarca, Peru 130 F2
Cajàzeiras, Braz. 131 F17
Çakırgöl Dağı, Turk. 169 D14
Cakit, river, Turk. 168 H10
Çakmak, Turk. 168 F7
Çakmak Dağı, Turk. 169 E16
Cakovec, Croatia 152 C6
Çal, Turk. 168 G5
Calabar, Nigeria 201 H14
Calabash Boom, Virgin Islands, U.S. 120 N11
Calabó, Eq. Guinea 204 M7
Calabozo, Venez. 128 C9
Calabria, region, It. 138 K7
Calaburras, Punta de, Sp. 144 M9
Calacuccia, Fr. 150 K4
Calafat, Bulg. 152 G12
Calafat, Rom. 152 G12
Calahorra, Sp. 145 C13
Calais, Fr. 146 L9
Calais, Me., U.S. 95 E19
Calalaste, Sierra de, Arg. 132 F8
Calalin, island, Marshall Is. 216 G11
Calalin Channel, Marshall Is. 216 G11
Calalzo, It. 150 C8
Calama, Chile 132 D7
Calama, Braz. 130 F8
Calamar, Col. 128 B5
Calamar, Col. 128 G6
Calamian Group, Philippines 189 D13
Calamocha, Sp. 145 E13
Călan, Rom. 152 D12
Calanda, Sp. 145 E15
Calanscio, Sand Sea of, Lib. 194 E7
Calanscio, Sarīr, Lib. 194 E7
Calapan, Philippines 189 D13
Călăraşi, Rom. 153 F16
Calatayud, Sp. 145 E13
Calayan, island, Philippines 189 A13
Calbayog, Philippines 189 D15
Calcanhar, Ponta do, Braz. 131 E18
Calcasieu, river, La., U.S. 100 N7
Calcasieu Lake, La., U.S. 100 Q7
Calçoene, Braz. 130 B12
Calcutta see Kolkata, India 178 J12
Caldas da Rainha, Port. 144 G4
Caldera, Chile 132 G6
Caldera, peak, Eq. Guinea 204 M7
Çaldıran, Turk. 169 F18
Caldwell, Idaho, U.S. 106 G3
Caldwell, Kans., U.S. 105 V7
Caldwell, Tex., U.S. 103 P12
Caldy Island, Wales, U.K. 143 V8
Caledonia, Minn., U.S. 104 L13
Caledonian Canal, Scot., U.K. 142 K8
Calexico, Calif., U.S. 109 Z12
Calf of Man, cape, Isle of Man, U.K. 143 R8
Calgary, Alta., Can. 82 M10
Calheta, Azores 144 P3
Calheta, Madeira 204 M2
Calhoun, Ga., U.S. 96 K4
Calhoun City, Miss., U.S. 100 J12
Calhoun Falls, S.C., U.S. 96 K7
Cali, Col. 128 G4
Calibishie, Dominica 121 E19
Calico Rock, Ark., U.S. 100 E9
Calicut see Kozhikode, India 179 Q5
Caliente, Nev., U.S. 109 S12
California, Mo., U.S. 105 T13
California, Trinidad & Tobago 121 P22
California, U.S. 109 N4
California, Golfo de, Mex. 114 C6
California, Gulf of see California, Golfo de, N. Amer. 80 L3
California Aqueduct, Calif., U.S. 109 V6
Calilegua, Arg. 132 E10
Cälilabad, Azerb. 169 E22
Calipatria, Calif., U.S. 109 Y11
Calistoga, Calif., U.S. 109 R3
Calivigny, Grenada 121 L22
Calivigny Island, Grenada 121 L22
Callabonna, Lake, Austral. 210 H11
Callan, Ire. 143 T5
Callao, Peru 130 H3
Callaway, Nebr., U.S. 105 P5
Calliaqua, St. Vincent & the Grenadines 121 L16
Calliope, Qnsld., Austral. 211 U15
Calliope Range, Austral. 210 G15
Caloosahatchee, river, Fla., U.S. 97 V8
Caloundra, Qnsld., Austral. 211 V15
Calpe, Sp. 145 J15
Caltagirone, It. 151 T11
Caltanissetta, It. 151 T10
Çaltı Burnu, Turk. 168 C12
Calulo, Angola 202 C6
Calumet, Mich., U.S. 98 E6
Caluso, It. 150 E3
Caluula, Somalia 199 F18
Calvert, Tex., U.S. 103 P12
Calvi, Fr. 150 J4
Calvinia, S. Af. 202 L8
Calwa, Calif., U.S. 109 T6
Camabatela, Angola 202 C6
Camacupa, Angola 202 D7
Camagüey, Cuba 116 J11
Camagüey, Archipiélago de, Cuba 116 G10
Camajuaní, Cuba 116 H9
Camaná, Peru 130 J5
Camanche Reservoir, Calif., U.S. 109 R5
Camapuã, Braz. 130 K11
Câmara de Lobos, Madeira 204 M3
Camarat, Cap, Fr. 147 Y15
Çamardı, Turk. 168 G10
Camargo, Bol. 130 L7
Camargo, Okla., U.S. 102 F8
Camargue, Île de la, Fr. 147 X12
Camarón, Cape, N. Amer. 80 P8
Camarones, Arg. 133 S9
Camarones, Bahía, Arg. 133 S9
Camas, Wash., U.S. 108 F4
Camas Creek, Idaho, U.S. 106 H4
Camas Valley, Oreg., U.S. 108 J2
Ca Mau, Vietnam 187 Q12
Camballin, W. Aust., Austral. 211 R5
Cambodia, Asia 167 X11
Camborne, Eng., U.K. 143 Y8
Cambrai, Fr. 146 M11
Cambre, Sp. 144 B6
Cambria, Calif., U.S. 109 V5
Cambrian Mountains, Wales, U.K. 143 U10
Cambridge, Eng., U.K. 143 U14
Cambridge, Idaho, U.S. 106 F3
Cambridge, Jam. 116 M11
Cambridge, Mass., U.S. 95 K15
Cambridge, Md., U.S. 96 D14
Cambridge, Minn., U.S. 104 J11
Cambridge, Nebr., U.S. 105 R5
Cambridge, Ohio, U.S. 99 R14
Cambridge Bay, Nunavut, Can. 83 F13
Cambridge Downs, Qnsld., Austral. 211 S12
Cambridge Springs, Pa., U.S. 94 L3
Cambundi-Catembo, Angola 202 C7
Çam Burnu, Turk. 168 D12
Camden, Ala., U.S. 101 M14
Camden, Ark., U.S. 100 J8
Camden, Me., U.S. 95 G17
Camden, N.J., U.S. 94 P9
Camden, N.Y., U.S. 94 H9
Camden, S.C., U.S. 96 K9
Camden, Tenn., U.S. 101 E13
Camden, Tex., U.S. 103 P14
Camden Bay, Alas., U.S. 84 L4
Camden Park, St. Vincent & the Grenadines 121 L16
Camdenton, Mo., U.S. 105 T12
Çameli, Turk. 168 H5
Camerino, It. 150 H9
Cameron, Ariz., U.S. 107 R7
Cameron, La., U.S. 100 Q7
Cameron, Mo., U.S. 105 R11
Cameron, Tex., U.S. 103 P11
Cameroon, Af. 195 J18
Cameroon Mountain, Cameroon 201 J15
Cametá, Braz. 131 D13
Camiguin, island, Philippines 189 A14
Camiguin, island, Philippines 189 E15
Camilla, Ga., U.S. 97 P5
Caminha, Port. 144 D5
Camiri, Bol. 130 L8
Camirus, ruin, Gr. 155 N19
Camissombo, Angola 202 C8
Camocim, Braz. 131 D16
Camooweal, Qnsld., Austral. 211 S10
Camorta Island, India 179 S15
Campagnano di Roma, It. 150 K8
Campana, Arg. 132 L12
Campana, It. 151 P14
Campana, Isla, Chile 133 U6
Campanario, Cerro, Arg., Chile 132 M7
Campbell, Mo., U.S. 105 V15
Campbell, Cape, N.Z. 213 N18
Campbell Hill, Ohio, U.S. 99 Q12
Campbell Island, N.Z. 214 R7
Campbell Plateau, Pac. Oc. 238 R9
Campbell River, B.C., Can. 82 L7
Campbellsville, Ky., U.S. 101 C17
Campcardos, Pic de, Fr., Sp. 160 J6
Camp Crook, S. Dak., U.S. 104 J1
Campêche, Guadeloupe, Fr. 121 E15
Campeche, Mex. 115 H15
Campeche Bank, Atl. Oc. 236 K1
Campeche Bank, Mex. 115 H15
Campechuela, Cuba 116 K11
Cam Pha, Vietnam 186 H13
Campidano, plain, It. 151 P3
Campina Grande, Braz. 131 F18
Campinas, Braz. 131 M13
Campli, It. 150 J10
Campo, Cameroon 201 J15
Campo, Colo., U.S. 107 P15
Campoalegre, Col. 128 G5
Campobasso, It. 150 L11
Campofelice, It. 151 S10
Campo Gallo, Arg. 132 G11
Campo Grande, Braz. 130 L11
Campo Mourão, Braz. 130 M12
Camponi, river, Fr. Guiana, Fr. 129 F18
Campos, region, S. Amer. 126 G9
Campos, Braz. 131 L15
Camp Point, Ill., U.S. 99 R3
Campti, La., U.S. 100 M7
Camp Verde, Ariz., U.S. 107 S7
Camp Wood, Tex., U.S. 103 R7
Cam Ranh, Vietnam 187 N14
Cam Ranh, Vung, Vietnam 187 N14
Camrose, Alta., Can. 82 L10
Camsell Portage, Sask., Can. 82 J12
Camuy, P.R., U.S. 120 M2
Çan, Turk. 168 D3
Ca Na, Vietnam 187 P14
Ca Na, Mui, Vietnam 187 P14
Canaan, Trinidad & Tobago 121 N17
Canacona, India 179 N4
Canada, N. Amer. 81 F18
Canada Basin, Arctic Oc. 242 M6
Cañada de Gómez, Arg. 132 K11
Cañada Honda, Arg. 132 K8
Canada Plain, Arctic Oc. 242 L6
Canadian, river, Okla., Tex., U.S. 102 H12
Canadian, Tex., U.S. 102 F7
Canadian Shield, N. Amer. 80 E5
Çanakkale, Turk. 168 D2
Çanakkale Boğazi (Dardanelles), Turk. 168 D2
Canala, Baie de, New Caledonia, Fr. 218 D8
Canala, New Caledonia, Fr. 218 D8
Canandaigua, N.Y., U.S. 94 J7
Cananea, Mex. 114 C7
Canarias, Islas see Canary Islands, Atl. Oc. 204 C4
Canaries, St. Lucia 121 K13
Canarreos, Archipiélago de los, Cuba 116 H6
Canary Islands (Islas Canarias), Atl. Oc. 204 C4
Cañas, Costa Rica 115 N18
Canastota, N.Y., U.S. 94 J9
Canatlán, Mex. 114 F9
Canaveral, Cape, Fla., U.S. 97 T10
Canaveral National Seashore, Fla., U.S. 97 S9
Canavieiras, Braz. 131 J16
Canberra, A.C.T., Austral. 211 Y14
Canby, Calif., U.S. 108 M5
Canby, Minn., U.S. 104 K9
Cancún, Mex. 115 H17
Çandarlı, Turk. 168 F3
Çandarli Körfezi, Turk. 168 F3
Candás, Sp. 144 A9
Candé, Fr. 147 R6
Candia see Iráklio, Gr. 155 Q15
Cando, N. Dak., U.S. 104 E6
Candon, Philippines 189 B13
Canea see Haniá, Gr. 155 Q13
Cane Bay, Virgin Islands, U.S. 120 Q2
Cane Garden Bay, Virgin Islands, U.K. 120 Q6
Canelles, river, St. Lucia 121 L14
Cañete, Sp. 145 G13
Caney, Kans., U.S. 105 V9
Canfranc, Sp. 145 C14
Cangamba, Angola 202 E8
Cangas, Sp. 144 C5
Cangas del Narcea, Sp. 144 B8
Canguaretama, Braz. 131 F18
Cangwu, China 183 R3
Cangzhou, China 182 E7
Caniapiscau, river, Que., Can. 83 K19
Caniapiscau, Réservoir, Que., Can. 83 L19
Canicattì, It. 151 T10
Caniles, Sp. 144 L12
Canillo, region, Andorra 160 H4
Canillo, Andorra 160 H4
Canindé, Braz. 131 E16
Canipaan, Philippines 188 F12
Canisteo, N.Y., U.S. 94 K6
Canjáyar, Sp. 144 L12
Çankırı, Turk. 168 D9
Canna, island, Scot., U.K. 142 K7
Cannae, ruin, It. 150 L13
Cannanore, India 179 Q4
Cannelton, Ind., U.S. 99 U8
Cannes, Fr. 147 X15
Canning Hill, Austral. 210 H3
Cannonball, river, N. Dak., U.S. 104 H4
Cannon Beach, Oreg., U.S. 108 E2
Cannon Falls, Minn., U.S. 104 K12
Cannonville, Utah, U.S. 107 P7
Cann River, Vic., Austral. 211 Z13
Canoas, Braz. 130 P12
Canobie, Qnsld., Austral. 211 S11
Canoe Passage, Kiribati 217 B20
Canon City, Colo., U.S. 107 N13
Canonniers Point, Mauritius 205 F20
Canonsburg, Pa., U.S. 94 P3
Canosa di Puglia, It. 150 L13
Canouan, island, St. Vincent & the Grenadines 119 M17
Canso, Strait of, N.S., Can. 83 P22
Cantabria, Sierra de, Sp. 144 C12
Cantabrian Mountains see Cantabrica, Cordillera, Sp. 138 H2
Cantabrica, Cordillera, Sp. 144 B7
Cantalejo, Sp. 144 E10
Cantavieja, Sp. 145 F14
Canterbury, Eng., U.K. 143 V15
Canterbury Bight, N.Z. 213 P17
Can Tho, Vietnam 187 Q12
Cantiles, Cayo, Cuba 116 H7
Canto do Buriti, Braz. 131 F15
Canton see Guangzhou, China 183 R4
Canton, Ga., U.S. 96 K5
Canton, Ill., U.S. 99 Q4
Canton, Miss., U.S. 100 L11
Canton, Mo., U.S. 105 R13
Canton, N.C., U.S. 96 H7
Canton, N.Y., U.S. 94 F9
Canton, Ohio, U.S. 99 P15
Canton, Okla., U.S. 102 F9
Canton, Pa., U.S. 94 L7
Canton, S. Dak., U.S. 104 M8
Canton Lake, Okla., U.S. 102 F9
Cantù, It. 150 D4
Cantwell, Alas., U.S. 111 H17
Canumã, Braz. 130 E9
Canutama, Braz. 130 F7
Canutillo, Tex., U.S. 103 U1
Cany-Barville, Fr. 147 N8
Canyon, Tex., U.S. 102 H5
Canyon City, Oreg., U.S. 108 G7
Canyon de Chelly National Monument, Ariz., U.S. 107 R9
Canyon Ferry Lake, Mont., U.S. 106 D7
Canyon Lake, Tex., U.S. 103 Q10
Canyonlands National Park, Utah, U.S. 107 N9
Canyons of the Ancients National Monument, Colo., U.S. 107 P10
Canyonville, Oreg., U.S. 108 J3
Cao Bang, Vietnam 186 G12
Caoxian, China 182 H6
Caparra, ruin, P.R., U.S. 120 M4
Capayán, Arg. 132 H9
Cap Barbas, W. Sahara, Mor. 196 E5
Cap-Chat, Que., Can. 83 N21
Cap d'Ail, Fr. 161 F19
Cap Dorade, St. Martin, Fr. 121 B14
Cape Barren Island, Tas., Austral. 211 Y16
Cape Breton Island, N.S., Can. 83 N23

Cape Charles, Va., U.S. 96 F14
Cape Coast, Ghana 200 H10
Cape Cod Bay, Mass., U.S. 95 L16
Cape Cod National Seashore, Mass., U.S. 95 L16
Cape Coral, Fla., U.S. 97 W8
Cape Dorset, Nunavut, Can. 83 H17
Cape Fear, river, N.C., U.S. 96 K12
Cape Girardeau, Mo., U.S. 105 U16
Cape Hatteras National Seashore, N.C., U.S. 96 H15
Cape Krusenstern National Monument, Alas., U.S. 110 D12
Capel, W. Aust., Austral. 211 Y2
Capella Islands, Virgin Islands, U.S. 120 N9
Cape Lookout National Seashore, N.C., U.S. 96 J14
Cape Lookout Shoals, N.C., U.S. 96 J14
Cape May, N.J., U.S. 94 R10
Capenda-Camulembu, Angola 202 C7
Cape Palmas, Liberia 200 J7
Cape Plain, Atl. Oc. 237 T14
Cape Rodney, P.N.G. 213 E20
Cap Estate, St. Lucia 121 J14
Capesterre, Guadeloupe, Fr. 121 G16
Capesterre-Belle-Eau, Guadeloupe, Fr. 121 F15
Capestrano, It. 150 K10
Cape Town, S. Af. 202 M7
Cape Verde, Atl. Oc. 204 D3
Cape Verde Plain, Atl. Oc. 236 K10
Cape Vincent, N.Y., U.S. 94 G8
Cape York Peninsula, Qnsld., Austral. 211 P12
Cap-Haïtien, Haiti 117 L17
Capistrello, It. 150 K9
Capitan, N. Mex., U.S. 107 U13
Capitán Pablo Lagerenza, Parag. 130 K9
Capitan Peak, N. Mex., U.S. 107 T13
Capitão, Ponta, Sao Tome and Principe 205 A21
Capitol Hill, N. Mariana Is., U.S. 216 B5
Capitol Reef National Park, Utah, U.S. 107 P8
Capodistria see Koper, Slov. 152 D4
Capoeira, Corredeira, Braz. 130 F10
Cappadocia, region, Turk. 168 G9
Cappamore, Ire. 143 T4
Cap Point, St. Lucia 121 J14
Cappoquin, Ire. 143 U5
Capraia, Isola di, It. 150 H5
Capreol, Ont., Can. 83 P18
Caprera, Isola, It. 150 L4
Capri, Isola di, It. 151 N10
Capricorn Channel, Austral. 210 F15
Capricorn Group, Austral. 210 F15
Caprivi Strip, region, Namibia 202 F9
Cap Rock Escarpment, Tex., U.S. 84 K11
Captain Cook, Hawai'i, U.S. 113 M18
Captain Cook Monument, Hawai'i, U.S. 112 C5
Captain Cook Monument, Hawai'i, U.S. 113 N18
Captain Cook's Monument, Fr. Polynesia, Fr. 219 N16
Captieux, Fr. 147 W7
Captiva, Fla., U.S. 97 W8
Capua, It. 150 M10
Capucin, Cape, Dominica 121 D18
Capucin Point, Seychelles 205 P20
Capulin Volcano National Monument, N. Mex., U.S. 107 Q14
Caquetá, river, Col. 128 J7
Caracal, Rom. 153 G14
Caracaraí, Braz. 130 B9
Caracas, Venez. 128 B9
Caracol, Braz. 131 G15
Carahue, Chile 133 P6
Carajás, Serra dos, Braz. 130 E12
Caramulo, Serra do, Port. 144 F6
Caransebeş, Rom. 152 E12
Carapuse Bay, Trinidad & Tobago 121 N18
Caratasca, Laguna de, Hond. 115 K19
Caratasca Lagoon, N. Amer. 80 P8
Carauari, Braz. 130 E7
Caraúbas, Braz. 131 F17
Caravaca de la Cruz, Sp. 145 K13
Caravelas, Braz. 131 K16
Caravelle, Presqu'île la, Martinique, Fr. 121 E23
Carballiño, Sp. 144 C6
Carballo, Sp. 144 B5
Carbón, Laguna del, Arg. 133 V8
Carbonara, Capo, It. 151 Q4
Carbondale, Colo., U.S. 106 M11
Carbondale, Ill., U.S. 99 U5
Carbondale, Pa., U.S. 94 L9
Carboneras, Sp. 145 L13
Carbon Hill, Ala., U.S. 101 J14
Carbonia, It. 151 Q3
Carbonne, Fr. 147 Y8
Carcajou, Alta., Can. 82 J10
Carcans, Lac de, Fr. 147 V6
Carcasse, Cap, Haiti 117 M14
Carcassonne, Fr. 147 Y10
Carche, peak, Sp. 145 J14
Carcross, Yukon, Can. 82 G8
Cardabia, W. Aust., Austral. 211 T1
Cardamom Mountains, Cambodia 187 N10
Cardamum Island see Kadmat Island, India 179 Q3
Cardeña, Sp. 144 J10
Cárdenas, Cuba 116 G7
Cárdenas, Mex. 114 G11
Cardiff (Caerdydd), Wales, U.K. 143 V10
Cardigan (Aberteifi), Wales, U.K. 143 U9
Cardigan Bay, Wales, U.K. 143 T9
Cardona, Sp. 145 D17
Cardoso y Pinto, Eq. Guinea 204 M7
Cardwell, Qnsld., Austral. 211 R13
Carei, Rom. 152 B12
Careiro, Braz. 130 D9
Carey, Ohio, U.S. 99 P12
Carey, Lake, Austral. 210 H4
Carey Downs, W. Aust., Austral. 211 U2
Cargados Carajos Bank, Ind. Oc. 240 J7
Cargèse, Fr. 150 K3
Carhué, Arg. 132 M11
Cariati, It. 151 P14
Caribbean Sea, Atl. Oc. 236 L3
Caribou, Me., U.S. 95 B18
Caribou Mountains, N. Amer. 80 F4
Carinda, N.S.W., Austral. 211 W13
Cariñena, Sp. 145 E13
Carinhanha, Braz. 131 J15
Caripare, Braz. 131 H14
Caripito, Venez. 128 B12
Carlin, Nev., U.S. 109 N10
Carlingford Lough, Ire., U.K. 143 R7
Carlinville, Ill., U.S. 99 S4
Carlisle, Ark., U.S. 100 G9
Carlisle, Eng., U.K. 143 P10
Carlisle, Ky., U.S. 101 B18
Carlisle, Pa., U.S. 94 P7
Carlisle Bay, Barbados 121 L18
Carlisle Bay, Jam. 120 K8
Carlos, Isla, Chile 133 X7
Carlow, Ire. 143 T6
Carlsbad, Calif., U.S. 109 Y9
Carlsbad, N. Mex., U.S. 107 V14
Carlsbad, Tex., U.S. 103 N6
Carlsbad Caverns National Park, N. Mex., U.S. 107 V14
Carlsberg Ridge, Ind. Oc. 240 F7
Carlton, Minn., U.S. 104 G12
Carlyle, Ill., U.S. 99 T5
Carlyle Lake, Ill., U.S. 99 T5
Carmacks, Yukon, Can. 82 F8
Carmagnola, It. 150 E2
Carmarthen, Wales, U.K. 143 V9
Carmarthen Bay, Wales, U.K. 143 V9
Carmaux, Fr. 147 W10
Carmel-by-the-Sea, Calif., U.S. 109 T4
Carmen, Okla., U.S. 102 E9
Carmen, Isla, Mex. 114 E6
Carmen de Bolívar, Col. 128 C5
Carmen de Patagones, Arg. 133 Q11
Carmi, Ill., U.S. 99 U6
Carmona, Sp. 144 L8
Carnamah, W. Aust., Austral. 211 W2
Carnarvon, S. Af. 202 L8
Carnarvon, W. Aust., Austral. 211 U1
Carndonagh, Ire. 143 N6
Carnegie, Okla., U.S. 102 G9
Carnegie, W. Aust., Austral. 211 U5
Carnegie, Lake, Austral. 210 G4
Carnegie Ridge, Pac. Oc. 239 K19
Carney Island, Antarctica 226 M7
Carnic Alps, It. 150 C9
Car Nicobar, island, India 179 S14
Carnot, Cen. Af. Rep. 198 H8
Carnot, Cape, Austral. 210 K9
Carnsore Point, Ire. 143 U7
Caro, Mich., U.S. 98 K12
Caroço, Ilhéu, Sao Tome and Principe 205 B21
Carol City, Fla., U.S. 97 W10
Carolina, P.R., U.S. 120 M5
Carolina, Braz. 131 F13
Carolina Beach, N.C., U.S. 96 K12
Carolinas, Puntan, N. Mariana Is., U.S. 216 C8
Caroline Island, Fr. Polynesia, Fr. 215 H13
Caroline Islands, F.S.M. 214 F3
Caroline Islands, Pac. Oc. 166 J15
Caroní, river, Venez. 128 D12
Caroni Swamp, Trinidad & Tobago 121 P22
Carora, Venez. 128 B8
Carp, Nev., U.S. 109 T12
Carpathian Mountains, Eur. 138 G8
Carpathos see Kárpathos, island, Gr. 155 P18
Carpatho-Ukraine, region, Ukr. 157 P2
Carpentaria, Gulf of, Austral. 210 B10
Carpentras, Fr. 147 W13
Carpi, It. 150 F6
Carpina, Braz. 131 F18
Carpio, N. Dak., U.S. 104 E3
Carquefou, Fr. 147 R6
Carrabelle, Fla., U.S. 97 R4
Carrantuohill, peak, Ire. 143 U3
Carrara, It. 150 G5
Carrarang, W. Aust., Austral. 211 V1
Carrboro, N.C., U.S. 96 H11
Carriacou, island, Grenada 119 M17
Carrickfergus, N. Ire., U.K. 143 P7
Carrick on Shannon, Ire. 143 R5
Carrieton, S. Aust., Austral. 211 X10
Carrington, N. Dak., U.S. 104 F6
Carrión de los Condes, Sp. 144 C10
Carrizal Bajo, Chile 132 G6
Carrizo Creek, river, N. Mex., U.S. 107 Q15
Carrizo Plain National Monument, Calif., U.S. 109 V6
Carrizo Springs, Tex., U.S. 103 T7
Carrizozo, N. Mex., U.S. 107 T13
Carroll, Iowa, U.S. 105 N10
Carrollton, Ga., U.S. 96 L4
Carrollton, Ill., U.S. 99 S4
Carrollton, Ky., U.S. 101 A17
Carrollton, Mo., U.S. 105 S11
Carrollton, Tex., U.S. 102 L11
Carrot Bay, Virgin Islands, U.K. 120 R6
Carrowmore Lough, Ire. 143 Q3
Çarşamba, river, Turk. 168 H8
Çarşamba, Turk. 168 D11
Carson, N. Dak., U.S. 104 H4
Carson City, Nev., U.S. 109 Q6
Carson Sink, Nev., U.S. 109 P8
Carsonville, Mich., U.S. 98 L13
Cartagena, Col. 128 B4
Cartagena, Sp. 145 L14
Cartago, Col. 128 F4
Cartago, Costa Rica 115 N19
Carter's Cays, Bahamas 120 D3
Cartersville, Ga., U.S. 96 K4
Carthage, Ark., U.S. 100 H8
Carthage, Ill., U.S. 99 Q3
Carthage, Miss., U.S. 100 K12
Carthage, Mo., U.S. 105 V11
Carthage, N.C., U.S. 96 H11
Carthage, N.Y., U.S. 94 G9
Carthage, S. Dak., U.S. 104 L7
Carthage, Tenn., U.S. 101 E16
Carthage, Tex., U.S. 102 M15
Cartier Island, W. Aust., Austral. 211 P4
Cartwright, Nfld. & Lab., Can. 83 K22
Caruaru, Braz. 131 G17
Carúpano, Venez. 128 B12
Carutapera, Braz. 131 D14
Caruthersville, Mo., U.S. 105 W16
Carvoeiro, Braz. 130 D8
Carvoeiro, Cabo, Port. 144 G4
Cary, N.C., U.S. 96 H11
Caryapundy Swamp, Austral. 210 H11
Casablanca, Mor. 196 B8
Casa Cruz, Cape, Trinidad & Tobago 121 Q23
Casa Grande, Ariz., U.S. 107 U7
Casa Grande Ruins National Monument, Ariz., U.S. 107 U7
Casale Monferrato, It. 150 E3
Casamance, region, Senegal 196 H5
Casamanya, Pic de, Andorra 160 H3
Casanare, river, Col. 128 E7
Casarano, It. 151 N15
Cascade, Idaho, U.S. 106 F4
Cascade, Jam. 120 H6
Cascade, Mont., U.S. 106 C7
Cascade, Norfolk I., Austral. 217 F20
Cascade, Seychelles 205 P20
Cascade Bay, Norfolk I., Austral. 217 F20
Cascade Head, Oreg., U.S. 108 F2
Cascade Locks, Oreg., U.S. 108 F4
Cascade Range, U.S. 84 E3
Cascade Reservoir, Idaho, U.S. 106 F4
Cascade-Siskiyou National Monument, Oreg., U.S. 108 L3
Cascadia Basin, Pac. Oc. 239 D15
Cascavel, Braz. 130 M11
Cascina, It. 150 G6
Cascorro, Cuba 116 J11
Casere, It. 150 B8
Caserta, It. 150 M11
Cases Velles de Formentor, Sp. 145 G18
Casey, station, Antarctica 227 M21
Casey, Ill., U.S. 99 S7
Casey Bay, Antarctica 227 C19
Cashel, Ire. 143 T5
Cashmere, Wash., U.S. 108 C6
Casiguran, Philippines 189 B14
Casilda, Arg. 132 K11
Casina di Pio IV, Vatican City 161 P16
Casino Gardens, Monaco 161 D22
Casino of Monte Carlo, Monaco 161 D22
Casiquiare, river, Venez. 128 G10
Casma, Peru 130 G3
Casmalia, Calif., U.S. 109 W5
Caspar, Calif., U.S. 109 P2
Caspe, Sp. 145 E15
Casper, Wyo., U.S. 106 H12
Caspian Depression, Kaz., Russ. 166 E5
Caspian Sea, Asia 166 F5
Casquets, island, Ch. Is. 143 Y11
Cass, W. Va., U.S. 96 D10
Cass City, Mich., U.S. 98 K12
Cassel, Fr. 146 L10
Casselton, N. Dak., U.S. 104 G8
Cassiar Mountains, B.C., Can. 82 H8
Cassino, It. 150 L10
Cassis, Fr. 147 Y14
Cass Lake, Minn., U.S. 104 F10
Cassville, Mo., U.S. 105 V11
Cassville, Wis., U.S. 98 M3
Castagneto Carducci, It. 150 H6
Castanhal, Braz. 131 D13
Castaño Nuevo, Arg. 132 J7
Castara, Trinidad & Tobago 121 N18
Casteggio, It. 150 E4
Castela de Bode, Barragem do, Port. 144 G6
Castelbuono, It. 151 S10
Castel di Sangro, It. 150 L10
Castelfranco Veneto, It. 150 D8
Casteljaloux, Fr. 147 W7
Castellabate, It. 151 N11
Castellaccio, peak, San Marino 161 K15
Castellammare, Golfo di, It. 151 S9
Castellammare del Golfo, It. 151 S9
Castellaneta, It. 150 M14
Castello, It. 161 L15
Castelló de la Plana, Sp. 145 G15
Castello di Montemaggio, It. 161 K13
Castelnaudary, Fr. 147 Y9
Castelnovo ne'Monti, It. 150 F6
Castelo Branco, Port. 144 G6
Castelo de Vide, Port. 144 H6
Castelsardo, It. 150 M3
Casterton, Vic., Austral. 211 Z11
Castiglione Messer Marino, It. 150 K11
Castilhiano, Cape Verde 205 B16
Castille, region, Sp. 144 F10
Castillo de San Marcos National Monument, Fla., U.S. 97 R9
Castillon, Fr. 147 Y8
Castillos, Uru. 132 L15
Castlebar, Ire. 143 R3
Castlebay, Scot., U.K. 142 K6
Castlebridge, Ire. 143 U6
Castle Bruce, Dominica 121 F20
Castle Dale, Utah, U.S. 106 M8
Castle Douglas, Scot., U.K. 143 P9
Castlegregory, Ire. 143 U2
Castle Harbour, Bermuda, U.K. 120 B3
Castle Island, Bahamas 117 H14
Castlemaine, Vic., Austral. 211 Z12
Castle Peak, Idaho, U.S. 106 G5
Castlepollard, Ire. 143 R6
Castlerea, Ire. 143 R4
Castlereagh, river, Austral. 210 J14
Castle Roads, Bermuda, U.K. 120 B3
Castle Rock, Colo., U.S. 106 M13
Castle Rock, Wash., U.S. 108 E3
Castletownshend, Ire. 143 V3
Castlevale, Qnsld., Austral. 211 U13
Castlewood, S. Dak., U.S. 104 K8
Castres, Fr. 147 X10
Castries, Fr. 147 X12
Castries, St. Lucia 121 J14
Castries, Port, St. Lucia 121 J14
Castro, Chile 133 R6
Castro Daire, Port. 144 E6
Castro-Urdiales, Sp. 144 B11
Castro Verde, Port. 144 K5
Castrovillari, It. 151 P13
Castroville, Tex., U.S. 103 R9
Castuera, Sp. 144 J9
Çat, Turk. 169 E15
Catahoula Lake, La., U.S. 100 M8
Çatak, Turk. 169 G17
Catalan Bay, Gibraltar, U.K. 161 P23
Catalão, Braz. 131 K13
Çatalca, Turk. 168 C4
Catalina, Chile 132 F7
Catalina Point, Guam, U.S. 216 B12
Catalonia, region, Sp. 145 D17
Catamarca, Arg. 132 H9
Catanduanes, island, Philippines 189 C15
Catania, It. 151 S12
Catania, Golfo di, It. 151 T12
Catania, Piana di, It. 151 T11
Catanzaro, It. 151 Q14
Cataperdís, Pic de, Andorra, Fr. 160 G2
Catarina, Tex., U.S. 103 T8
Catarman, Philippines 189 D15
Catawba, river, N.C., S.C., U.S. 85 J18
Cat Cays, Bahamas 116 D9
Cateel, Philippines 189 F15
Catete, Angola 202 C5
Cathedral Mountain, Tex., U.S. 103 Q2
Cathedral of Monaco, Monaco 161 F21
Cathlamet, Wash., U.S. 108 E3
Catingas, region, S. Amer. 126 E7
Cat Island, Bahamas 117 E13
Cat Island see Pierrot Island, Mauritius 205 K20
Cat Island, Miss., U.S. 100 P12
Cat Lake, Ont., Can. 83 N15
Catlettsburg, Ky., U.S. 101 B20
Catlow Valley, Oreg., U.S. 108 K7
Catoche, Cape, N. Amer. 80 N7
Cato Island, Coral Sea Is. Terr., Austral. 211 U16
Catonsville, Md., U.S. 96 C13
Catria, Monte, It. 150 H8
Catriló, Arg. 132 M10
Catrimani, river, Braz. 130 C8
Catrimani, Braz. 130 C8
Catskill, N.Y., U.S. 94 K11
Catskill Mountains, N.Y., U.S. 94 K10
Cattenom, Fr. 160 L10
Cattolica Eraclea, It. 151 T9
Cauca, river, Col. 128 D5
Caucasus Mountains, Asia, Eur. 138 H13
Caucete, Arg. 132 J8
Caudry, Fr. 146 M11
Caulnes, Fr. 147 Q5
Caungula, Angola 202 C7
Cauquenes, Chile 132 M6
Caura, river, Venez. 128 E11
Caussade, Fr. 147 W9
Causse du Larzac, range, Fr. 147 X11
Cauto, river, Cuba 116 K12
Cavaillon, Fr. 147 X13
Cavalaire, Fr. 147 Y15
Cavalcante, Braz. 131 H13
Cavalese, It. 150 C7
Cavalier, N. Dak., U.S. 104 E7
Cavalla see Cavally, river, Liberia 200 H7
Cavallo, Île, Fr. 150 L4
Cavally see Cavalla, river, Côte d'Ivoire 200 H7
Cavan, Ire. 143 R6
Cave Cay, Bahamas 120 D7
Cave Creek, Ariz., U.S. 107 T7
Cave Junction, Oreg., U.S. 108 K2
Cavelle Pond, Bahamas 120 C8
Caves, Anse aux, Mauritius 205 J20
Caviana, Ilha, Braz. 131 C13
Cavignac, Fr. 147 V7
Cavo, Mount, It. 150 L8
Cavour, It. 150 E2
Çavuş Burnu, Turk. 168 J6
Çavuşçu Gölü, Turk. 168 G7
Cawker City, Kans., U.S. 105 S6
Caxias, Braz. 131 E15
Caxias, Braz. 130 E5
Caxias do Sul, Braz. 130 P12
Caxito, Angola 202 C5
Çay, Turk. 168 F6

Cayambe, peak, Ecua. 128 J3
Cayambe, Ecua. 128 J3
Cayce, S.C., U.S. 96 K9
Çaycuma, Turk. 168 C7
Çayeli, Turk. 169 D15
Cayenne, Fr. Guiana, Fr. 129 E18
Cayeux-sur-Mer, Fr. 146 M9
Cayey, P.R., U.S. 120 N4
Cayey, Sierra de, P.R., U.S. 120 N5
Çayıralan, Turk. 168 F10
Cayman Brac, Cayman Is., U.K. 116 L9
Cayman Islands, U.K., Greater Antilles 116 L8
Cayman Trench, Atl. Oc. 236 L3
Caynabo, Somalia 199 G17
Cayon, St. Kitts & Nevis 121 A17
Cay Point, Bahamas 120 C11
Cay Sal Bank, Bahamas 116 F9
Cayucos, Calif., U.S. 109 V5
Cayuga Lake, N.Y., U.S. 94 K8
Cazalla de la Sierra, Sp. 144 K8
Cazaux et de Sanguinet, Lac de, Fr. 147 W6
Cazères, Fr. 147 Y8
Cazombo, Angola 202 D9
Cazorla, Sp. 144 K11
Ceanannus Mór (Kells), Ire. 143 R6
Ceara Plain, Atl. Oc. 237 N8
Cebollar, Arg. 132 H9
Cebu, island, Philippines 189 E14
Cebu, Philippines 189 E14
Cecile Peninsula, Kiribati 217 B22
Cecina, It. 150 H6
Cedar, river, Iowa, U.S. 105 N13
Cedar Bluff Reservoir, Kans., U.S. 105 T5
Cedar Breaks National Monument, Utah, U.S. 107 P6
Cedar City, Utah, U.S. 107 P6
Cedar Creek Reservoir, Tex., U.S. 102 M12
Cedar Falls, Iowa, U.S. 105 N12
Cedar Grove, Antigua & Barbuda 121 A20
Cedar Harbour, Bahamas 120 A5
Cedar Key, Fla., U.S. 97 S6
Cedar Lake, Ind., U.S. 99 P7
Cedar Rapids, Iowa, U.S. 105 N13
Cedar River, Mich., U.S. 98 H8
Cedartown, Ga., U.S. 96 K4
Cedar Vale, Kans., U.S. 105 V8
Cedarville, Calif., U.S. 108 L6
Cedarville, Mich., U.S. 98 G11
Cedeira, Sp. 144 A6
Cedillo, Embalse de, Port., Sp. 144 G7
Cedros, Isla, Mex. 114 D5
Cedros Bay, Trinidad & Tobago 121 Q21
Cedros Trench, Pac. Oc. 239 G16
Ceel Buur, Somalia 199 H17
Ceerigaabo (Erigavo), Somalia 199 F17
Cefalù, It. 151 S10
Cegléd, Hung. 149 L15
Cehotina, river, Bosn. & Herzg., Serb. & Mont. 152 H9
Ceiba, P.R., U.S. 120 N6
Cejal, Col. 128 G9
Çekerek, river, Turk. 168 D10
Çekerek, Turk. 168 E10
Celano, It. 150 K9
Celanova, Sp. 144 C6
Celaya, Mex. 114 H11
Celebes see Sulawesi, island, Indonesia 189 K13
Celebes Basin, Ind. Oc. 241 F16
Celebes Sea, Indonesia 189 H14
Çeleken, Turkm. 174 L6
Celina, Ohio, U.S. 99 Q11
Celje, Slov. 152 D5
Cella, Sp. 145 F13
Celle, Ger. 148 D8
Celtic Sea, Ire., U.K. 143 W6
Cement, Okla., U.S. 102 H10
Çemişgezek, Turk. 169 F13
Cenderawasih, Teluk, Indonesia 189 K19
Center, N. Dak., U.S. 104 G4
Center, Tex., U.S. 102 M15
Center Hill Lake, Tenn., U.S. 101 E16
Center Point, Ala., U.S. 101 J15
Center Point, Tex., U.S. 103 Q9
Centerville, Iowa, U.S. 105 Q12
Centerville, S. Dak., U.S. 104 M8
Centerville, Tenn., U.S. 101 F14
Centerville, Tex., U.S. 103 N13
Cento, It. 150 F7
Central, Alas., U.S. 111 F18
Central, Cordillera, Dom. Rep. 117 L18
Central, Cordillera, P.R., U.S. 120 N3
Central, Cordillera, S. Amer. 126 C2
Central, Massif, Fr. 147 U10
Central African Republic, Af. 195 H19
Central America, N. Amer. 80 P7
Central Brahul Range, Pak. 177 S6
Central City, Ky., U.S. 101 C15
Central City, Nebr., U.S. 105 Q7
Central Highlands, Vietnam 186 M13
Centralia, Ill., U.S. 99 T5
Centralia, Mo., U.S. 105 S13
Centralia, Wash., U.S. 108 D3
Central Lowland, U.S. 85 F14
Central Lowlands, Austral. 210 E10
Central Makran Range, Pak. 177 U4
Central Pacific Basin, Pac. Oc. 238 J9
Central Point, Oreg., U.S. 108 K3
Central Range, P.N.G. 213 C18
Central Range, Russ. 166 C13
Central Russian Upland, Russ. 138 E11
Central Siberian Plateau, Russ. 166 C9
Central Valley, Calif., U.S. 109 N3
Centre, Ala., U.S. 101 H16
Centre de Flacq, Mauritius 205 G20
Centreville, Miss., U.S. 100 N10
Cenxi, China 183 R2
Cephalonia see Kefaloniá, Gr. 154 H7
Ceprano, It. 150 L9
Ceram, island, Indonesia 189 K17
Ceram Sea, Indonesia 189 K17
Cerasolo, It. 161 G18
Cerbère, Fr. 147 Z11
Ceres, Arg. 132 H11
Ceres, Braz. 131 J13
Cerf Island, Seychelles 203 C19
Ceriano, It. 161 G16
Cerigo see Kíthira, island, Gr. 154 N11
Cérilly, Fr. 147 S10
Çerkeş, Turk. 168 D8
Çermik, Turk. 169 G14
Cernavodă, Rom. 153 F17
Cerralvo, Isla, Mex. 114 F7
Cerredo, Torre, Sp. 144 B9
Cerreto, Monte, San Marino 161 J14
Cerrillos, Arg. 132 F9
Cerrillos, N. Mex., U.S. 107 R12
Cerro de Pasco, Peru 130 G3
Certaldo, It. 150 H6
Certers, Andorra 160 K3
Cervales, peak, Sp. 144 G9
Cervera, Sp. 145 D16
Cervera de Pisuerga, Sp. 144 B10
Cerveteri, It. 150 K8
Cervia, It. 150 F8
Cesana Torinese, It. 150 E1
Cesar, river, Col. 128 B6
Cesarò, It. 151 S11
Cesena, It. 150 G8
Cesenatico, It. 150 G8
Cēsis, Latv. 141 L17
České Budějovice, Czech Rep. 148 J11
Českomoravská Vrchovina, Czech Rep. 148 J12
Český Krumlov, Czech Rep. 148 J11
Çeşme, Turk. 168 F2
Céspedes, Cuba 116 J10
Cessnock, N.S.W., Austral. 211 X14
Cetinje, Serb. & Mont. 152 J8
Cetti Bay, Guam, U.S. 216 D10
Ceuta, Sp. 144 N9
Cévennes, range, Fr. 147 W12
Cevio, Switz. 150 C4
Ceyhan, river, Turk. 168 H11
Ceyhan, Turk. 168 H11
Ceylanpınar, Turk. 169 J14
Ceylon see Sri Lanka, Asia 179 T7
Chābahār, Iran 173 J17
Chabana, Japan 185 X2
Chablis, Fr. 147 R11
Chacachacare, island, Trinidad & Tobago 121 P21
Chacao, Canal de, Chile 133 Q6
Chachapoyas, Peru 130 F3
Chacharan, Pak. 177 S9
Chachora, India 178 H5
Chachro, Pak. 177 W9
Chaco Austral, region, S. Amer. 126 K6
Chaco Boreal, region, S. Amer. 126 H6
Chaco Culture National Historic Park, N. Mex., U.S. 107 R11
Chad, Af. 195 G19
Chad, Lake (Lac Tchad), Af. 194 G6
Chadan, Russ. 159 L13
Chadbourn, N.C., U.S. 96 K11
Chadron, Nebr., U.S. 104 M2
Chadwick, Mo., U.S. 105 V12
Chafarinas, Islas, Sp. 144 P12
Chaffee, Mo., U.S. 105 U16
Chagai, Pak. 177 S4
Chagai Hills, Pak. 177 S3
Chagda, Russ. 159 H18
Chagdo Kangri, peak, China 180 J6
Chaghcharan, Afghan. 176 M5
Chagoda, Russ. 156 F8
Chagos Archipelago, Ind. Oc. 166 M6
Chagos-Laccadive Plateau, Ind. Oc. 240 E9
Chagos Trench, Ind. Oc. 240 H9
Chaguanas, Trinidad & Tobago 121 P22
Chaguaramas, Trinidad & Tobago 121 N21
Chagyl, Turkm. 174 K7
Chahar Bagh, Afghan. 176 K5
Chahar Borj, Afghan. 176 M2
Chah-e Ab, Afghan. 176 K8
Chah-e Kerteh, Afghan. 177 P2
Chaibasa, India 178 J10
Chai-Nat, Thai. 186 L8
Chain Fracture Zone, Atl. Oc. 237 N10
Chain of Craters, Hawai'i, U.S. 113 N21
Chajarí, Arg. 132 J13
Chakar, river, Pak. 177 S7
Chakaria, Bangladesh 178 J14
Chake Chake, Tanzania 199 L15
Chakhansur, Afghan. 177 Q2
Chakwal, Pak. 177 N11
Chalais, Fr. 147 V7
Chalan Kanoa, N. Mariana Is., U.S. 216 C4
Chalan Pago, Guam, U.S. 216 C11
Chalap Dalan Range, Afghan. 177 N3
Chalbi Desert, Kenya 194 J10
Chaleur Bay, N.B., Que., Can. 83 N21
Chalhuanca, Peru 130 J4
Chaling, China 183 P4
Chalisgaon, India 178 K4
Chalkhi, Afghan. 176 L2
Chalkis see Halkída, Gr. 154 H12
Chalkyitsik, Alas., U.S. 111 E18
Chalky Mount, Barbados 121 K19
Chalky Mount, Barbados 121 K19
Challans, Fr. 147 S5
Challenger Deep, Pac. Oc. 238 H6
Challenger Fracture Zone, Pac. Oc. 239 N16
Challis, Idaho, U.S. 106 F5
Chālmeh, Iran 172 A11
Chalon, Fr. 147 S13
Châlons-sur-Marne, Fr. 147 P12
Châlus, Fr. 147 U8
Cham, Ger. 148 J9
Chama, N. Mex., U.S. 107 Q12
Chamah, peak, Malaysia 187 T9
Chaman, Pak. 177 Q5
Chaman Bid, Iran 173 B15
Chamatang, India 177 N15
Chamba, India 177 P13
Chambal, river, India 178 G5
Chamberlain, S. Dak., U.S. 104 L6
Chamberlain Lake, Me., U.S. 95 C16
Chamberlin, Mount, Alas., U.S. 111 C17
Chambers, Ariz., U.S. 107 S9
Chambersburg, Pa., U.S. 94 P6
Chambers Creek, Tex., U.S. 102 M12
Chambéry, Fr. 147 U14
Chambeshi, river, Zambia 194 M9
Chambois, Fr. 147 P7
Chamburi Kalat, Pak. 177 V4
Chamical, Arg. 132 J9
Chamizal National Memorial, Tex., U.S. 103 U2
Chamkani, Afghan. 177 N8
Ch'amo Hāyk, Eth. 199 H14
Chamoli, India 178 E7
Chamonix, Fr. 147 T15
Champagne, region, Fr. 147 Q12
Champagnole, Fr. 147 S14
Champaign, Ill., U.S. 99 R6
Champasak, Laos 186 M12
Champéry, Switz. 150 C2
Champlain, Lake, N.Y., Vt., U.S. 94 F12
Champotón, Mex. 115 J15
Chamrajnagar, India 179 Q5
Chamzinka, Russ. 156 K13
Chañaral, Chile 132 F6
Chanārān, Iran 173 B16
Chança, river, Port., Sp. 144 K6
Chandalar, river, Alas., U.S. 111 E17
Chandeleur Islands, La., U.S. 101 Q13
Chandeleur Sound, La., U.S. 100 Q12
Chandigarh, India 178 E6
Chandler, Ariz., U.S. 107 U7
Chandler, Okla., U.S. 102 G11
Chandless, river, Braz., Peru 130 G5
Chandpur, Bangladesh 178 J13
Chandrapur, India 178 L7
Chang, Ko, Thai. 187 N10
Changanacheri, India 179 R5
Changane, river, Mozambique 202 H12
Changbai Shan, China 182 B13
Chang Chenmo Range, China, India 176 M15
Changchun, China 182 A12
Changde, China 182 M3
Changhua, Taiwan, China 183 R9
Changji, China 180 E7
Chang Jiang (Yangtze), river, China 181 L13
Changjiang (Shiliu), China 183 U1
Changjin Reservoir, N. Korea 182 C13
Changle, China 183 P8
Changli, China 182 D8
Changling, China 181 E16
Changmar, China 180 J4
Changning, China 183 P4
Changping, China 182 D7
Changsha, China 182 M4
Changshan, China 182 M8
Changshu, China 182 K9
Changting, China 183 P6
Changyŏn, N. Korea 182 E12
Changzhi, China 182 F5
Changzhou, China 182 K9
Chaníon, Kólpos, Gr. 154 P12
Channapatna, India 179 Q5
Channel Country, Austral. 210 G11
Channel Islands, Calif., U.S. 109 Y7
Channel Islands, U.K. 143 Z11
Channel Islands National Park, Calif., U.S. 109 X6
Channel-Port aux Basques, Nfld. & Lab., Can. 83 N23
Channel Rock, Bahamas 116 G12
Chantada, Sp. 144 C6
Chanthaburi, Thai. 187 N10
Chantilly, Fr. 147 P10
Chantrey Inlet, Nunavut, Can. 83 G14
Chanute, Kans., U.S. 105 U9
Chão, Ilhéu, Madeira 204 N4
Chao Hu, China 182 K7
Chao Phraya, river, Thai. 186 L8
Chaoyang, China 182 B9
Chaoyang, China 183 R6
Chaozhou, China 183 R6
Chapadinha, Braz. 131 E15
Chapaev, Kaz. 174 D6
Chapak Gozar, Afghan. 176 K4
Chapala, Lago de, Mex. 114 H10
Chapala, Lake see Chapala, Lago de, N. Amer. 80 N4
Chapcha, Bhutan 178 F12
Chapel Hill, N.C., U.S. 96 H11
Chapelton, Jam. 120 J8
Chapleau, Ont., Can. 83 P17
Chapman, Ala., U.S. 101 M15
Chapman, Kans., U.S. 105 S8
Chappaquiddick Island, Mass., U.S. 95 M15
Chappell, Nebr., U.S. 105 P2
Char, India 177 N14
Chara, river, Russ. 159 J17
Chara, Russ. 159 J17
Charadai, Arg. 132 G12
Charagua, Bol. 130 K8
Charambirá, Punta, Col. 128 F3
Charcot Island, Antarctica 226 G5
Chard, Eng., U.K. 143 W11
Chardonnières, Haiti 117 M14
Charduar, India 178 F14
Chari, river, Chad 194 H6
Charikar, Afghan. 176 M8
Chariton, Iowa, U.S. 105 Q12
Chariton, river, Mo., U.S. 105 Q12
Charity, Guyana 129 D14
Chärjew see Türkmenabat, Turkm. 174 L10
Charleroi, Belg. 146 M12
Charles see Santa María, Isla, island, Ecua. 128 R9
Charles, Cape, Va., U.S. 96 F14
Charles City, Iowa, U.S. 104 M12
Charles Darwin Research Station, Ecua. 128 Q9
Charles Island, Nunavut, Can. 83 H18
Charles Mound, Ill., U.S. 98 M4
Charles Point, Austral. 210 B7
Charleston, Ill., U.S. 99 S7
Charleston, Miss., U.S. 100 H11
Charleston, Mo., U.S. 105 V16
Charleston, N.Z. 213 N17
Charleston, Oreg., U.S. 108 J1
Charleston, S.C., U.S. 96 M10
Charleston, W. Va., U.S. 96 D8
Charles Town, W. Va., U.S. 96 C12
Charlestown, Ind., U.S. 99 T10
Charlestown, St. Kitts & Nevis 121 C18
Charleville see Ráth Luirc, Ire. 143 U4
Charleville, Qnsld., Austral. 211 U13
Charleville-Mézières, Fr. 147 N12
Charlevoix, Mich., U.S. 98 H10
Charlie-Gibbs Fracture Zone, Atl. Oc. 236 F8
Charlieu, Fr. 147 T12
Charlotte, Mich., U.S. 98 M10
Charlotte, N.C., U.S. 96 J9
Charlotte, Tex., U.S. 103 S9
Charlotte Amalie, Virgin Islands, U.S. 120 M9
Charlotte Harbor, Fla., U.S. 97 V8
Charlottenberg, Sw. 140 K12
Charlottesville, Va., U.S. 96 E11
Charlotte Town see Gouyave, Grenada 121 K22
Charlottetown, P.E.I., Can. 83 N22
Charlotteville, Trinidad & Tobago 121 N18
Charlton Island, Nunavut, Can. 83 M18
Charolles, Fr. 147 T12
Charsadda, Pak. 176 M10
Chartres, Fr. 147 Q9
Chascomús, Arg. 132 M13
Chase, Kans., U.S. 105 T6
Chase City, Va., U.S. 96 F12
Chaska, Minn., U.S. 104 K11
Chassahowitzka, Fla., U.S. 97 T7
Chasseloup, Baie, New Caledonia, Fr. 218 C7
Chateaubelair, St. Vincent & the Grenadines 121 K16
Chateaubriand, Baie du, New Caledonia, Fr. 218 C9
Châteaubriant, Fr. 147 R6
Châteaudun, Fr. 147 Q9
Château-Gontier, Fr. 147 R6
Château-la-Vallière, Fr. 147 R8
Châteaulin, Fr. 147 Q3
Châteauneuf-de-Randon, Fr. 147 W11
Châteauneuf-en-Thymerais, Fr. 147 P9
Châteauneuf-sur-Loire, Fr. 147 R10
Château-Renault, Fr. 147 R8
Châteauroux, Fr. 147 S9
Château-Thierry, Fr. 147 P11
Châteauvillain, Fr. 147 Q12
Châteaux, Pointe des, Guadeloupe, Fr. 121 F16
Châtel, Fr. 147 T15
Châtelet, Belg. 146 M12
Châtellerault, Fr. 147 S8
Chatfield, Minn., U.S. 104 L12
Chatham see San Cristóbal, Isla, island, Ecua. 128 Q11
Chatham, Eng., U.K. 143 V15
Chatham, Ill., U.S. 99 R5
Chatham, Mass., U.S. 95 L16
Chatham, N.B., Can. 83 N21
Chatham, N.Y., U.S. 94 K11
Chatham, Va., U.S. 96 F10
Chatham Island, N.Z. 214 P9
Chatham Islands, N.Z. 214 P9
Chatham Rise, Pac. Oc. 238 Q9
Chatham Strait, Alas., U.S. 111 L22
Châtillon, Fr. 147 R12
Châtillon-sur-Indre, Fr. 147 S8
Chatom, Ala., U.S. 101 M13
Chatra, India 178 H10
Chatsworth, Ga., U.S. 96 J4
Chatsworth, Qnsld., Austral. 211 T11
Chattahoochee, river, Ala., Ga., U.S. 97 P4
Chattahoochee, Fla., U.S. 97 Q4
Chattanooga, Tenn., U.S. 101 G17
Chatyr-Tash, Kyrg. 176 F13
Chau Doc, Vietnam 187 P11
Chauk, Myanmar 186 H5
Chaukan Pass, India, Myanmar 178 F16
Chaumont, Fr. 147 Q13
Chaun Bay, Arctic Oc. 242 G3
Chaunskaya Guba, Russ. 159 C19
Chauny, Fr. 147 N11
Chavé, Baie, Fr. Polynesia, Fr. 219 N23
Chaves see Santa Cruz, Isla, island, Ecua. 128 Q9

Chaves, *Port.* **144** D7
Chaves, *Braz.* **131** C13
Chayek, *Kyrg.* **176** E11
Cheaha Mountain, *Ala., U.S.* **101** J16
Cheb, *Czech Rep.* **148** H9
Cheboksarskoye Vodokhranilishche, *Russ.* **156** H13
Cheboksary, *Russ.* **156** H14
Cheboygan, *Mich., U.S.* **98** G11
Chebsara, *Russ.* **156** F10
Chech, 'Erg, *Alg., Mali* **196** E9
Chechaktu, *Afghan.* **176** L4
Chechen', Ostrov, *Russ.* **157** T15
Chechnya, region, *Russ.* **157** T14
Checotah, *Okla., U.S.* **102** G13
Cheduba Island, *Myanmar* **186** J4
Cheektowaga, *N.Y., U.S.* **94** J5
Cheepie, *Qnsld., Austral.* **211** V12
Cheeyou, *Trinidad & Tobago* **121** P23
Chehalis, *Wash., U.S.* **108** D3
Chehar Borjak, *Afghan.* **177** R2
Cheju *see* Jeju, *S. Korea* **182** J13
Chekichler, *Turkm.* **174** M6
Chelan, *Wash., U.S.* **108** B6
Chelan, Lake, *Wash., U.S.* **108** B6
Chelforó, *Arg.* **133** P9
Chełm, *Pol.* **149** F18
Chełmno, *Pol.* **149** C14
Chelmsford, *Eng., U.K.* **143** V15
Chelsea, *Okla., U.S.* **102** E13
Cheltenham, *Eng., U.K.* **143** U12
Chelyabinsk, *Russ.* **158** J8
Chelyuskin, *Russ.* **159** D14
Chemillé, *Fr.* **147** S6
Chemin Grenier, *Mauritius* **205** H19
Chemnitz, *Ger.* **148** G10
Chemult, *Oreg., U.S.* **108** J4
Chemung, river, *N.Y., U.S.* **94** L7
Chenab, river, *India, Pak.* **177** R10
Cheney, *Wash., U.S.* **108** C9
Cheney Reservoir, *Kans., U.S.* **105** U7
Chengalpattu, *India* **179** Q7
Chengbu, *China* **183** P2
Chengde, *China* **182** C8
Chengdu, *China* **180** L11
Chengele, *India* **178** E15
Chenggu, *China* **182** H1
Chenghai, *China* **183** R7
Chengkou, *China* **182** J1
Ch'engkung, *Taiwan, China* **183** R10
Chenglingji, *China* **182** M4
Chengshan Jiao, cape, *China* **182** F10
Chennai (Madras), *India* **179** P7
Chenxi, *China* **182** M2
Chenzhou, *China* **183** P4
Cheom Ksan, *Cambodia* **186** M11
Cheonan, *S. Korea* **182** F13
Cheongju, *S. Korea* **182** F13
Cheorwon, *S. Korea* **182** E13
Chepén, *Peru* **130** F2
Chépénéhe, *New Caledonia, Fr.* **218** C9
Chepes, *Arg.* **132** J9
Chequamegon Bay, *Wis., U.S.* **98** F4
Cheraw, *S.C., U.S.* **96** J10
Cherbourg, *Fr.* **147** N6
Cherepovets, *Russ.* **156** F9
Chergui, Chott ech, *Alg.* **196** B10
Cherkasy, *Ukr.* **157** P6
Cherkessk, *Russ.* **157** T12
Cherlak, *Russ.* **158** K10
Chermenino, *Russ.* **156** F12
Chernaya, *Russ.* **158** E10
Chernihiv, *Ukr.* **156** M6
Cherni Vrŭkh, peak, *Bulg.* **153** J13
Chernivtsi, *Ukr.* **157** Q3
Chernobyl' *see* Chornobyl', *Ukr.* **156** M6
Chernogorsk, *Russ.* **159** L13
Chernyakhovsk, *Russ.* **156** J2
Chernyayevo, *Russ.* **159** K19
Chernyshevskiy, *Russ.* **159** H16
Cherokee, *Iowa, U.S.* **104** M9
Cherokee, *Okla., U.S.* **102** E9
Cherokees, Lake O' The, *Okla., U.S.* **102** E14
Cherokee Sound, *Bahamas* **120** B6
Cherrabun, *W. Aust., Austral.* **211** R5
Cherryfield, *Me., U.S.* **95** F18
Cherry Island *see* Anuta, *Solomon Is.* **214** J7
Cherskiy, *Russ.* **159** D19
Cherskiy Range, *Russ.* **166** C11
Cherskogo, Khrebet, *Russ.* **159** F18
Cherven Bryag, *Bulg.* **153** H13
Chervonohrad, *Ukr.* **157** N2
Cherykaw, *Belarus* **156** L6
Chesaning, *Mich., U.S.* **98** L11
Chesapeake, *Va., U.S.* **96** F14
Chesapeake Bay, *Md., Va., U.S.* **96** D14
Chesha Bay, *Arctic Oc.* **243** A17
Chesha Bay, *Russ.* **138** A11
Cheshskaya Guba, *Russ.* **158** E9
Chesht-e Sharif, *Afghan.* **176** M3
Cheshunt, *Eng., U.K.* **143** V14
Chester, *Calif., U.S.* **109** N5
Chester, *Eng., U.K.* **143** S11
Chester, *Ill., U.S.* **99** U4
Chester, *Mont., U.S.* **106** B8
Chester, *Pa., U.S.* **94** Q9
Chester, *S.C., U.S.* **96** J9
Chester, *W. Va., U.S.* **96** A9
Chesterfield, *Eng., U.K.* **143** S12
Chesterfield, Îles, *New Caledonia, Fr.* **214** K6
Chesterfield Inlet, *Nunavut, Can.* **83** H15
Chesterfield Inlet, *Nunavut, Can.* **83** H15
Chestertown, *Md., U.S.* **96** C14
Chesuncook Lake, *Me., U.S.* **95** C16
Chetamale, *India* **179** R14
Chetek, *Wis., U.S.* **98** H3
Chetlat Island, *India* **179** Q3
Chetumal, *Mex.* **115** J16
Chetumal Bay, *N. Amer.* **80** P7
Chetvertyy Kuril'skiy Proliv, *Russ.* **159** G23
Chevak, *Alas., U.S.* **110** H11
Chevanceaux, *Fr.* **147** V7
Chevelon Butte, *Ariz., U.S.* **107** S8
Cheviot Hills, *Scot., U.K.* **143** N11
Ch'ew Bahir, lake, *Eth., Kenya* **199** H14
Chewelah, *Wash., U.S.* **108** B8
Cheyenne, *Okla., U.S.* **102** G8
Cheyenne, river, *S. Dak., U.S.* **104** K3
Cheyenne, *Wyo., U.S.* **106** K13
Cheyenne Bottoms, *Kans., U.S.* **105** T6
Cheyenne Wells, *Colo., U.S.* **107** N16
Chhapra, *India* **178** G10
Chhatarpur, *India* **178** H7
Chhep, *Cambodia* **186** M12
Chhindwara, *India* **178** J6
Chhukha, *Bhutan* **178** F12
Chhung Kompong Som, bay, *Cambodia* **187** P10
Chi, river, *Thai.* **186** L11
Chiai, *Taiwan, China* **183** R9
Chiang Mai, *Thai.* **186** J8
Chiang Rai, *Thai.* **186** H8
Chiaromonte, *It.* **151** N13
Chiasso, *Switz.* **150** D4
Chiat'ura, *Rep. of Georgia* **169** B17
Chiavari, *It.* **150** F4
Chiavenna, *It.* **150** C5
Chiba, *Japan* **185** P12
Chibemba, *Angola* **202** E6
Chibia, *Angola* **202** E5
Chibougamau, *Que., Can.* **83** N19
Chiburi Shima, *Japan* **185** P6
Chicago, *Ill., U.S.* **99** N7
Chicago Heights, *Ill., U.S.* **99** P7
Chicapa, river, *Angola* **202** C8
Chichagof Island, *Alas., U.S.* **111** L22
Chichawatni, *Pak.* **177** R10
Chichén Itzá, ruin, *Mex.* **115** H16
Chichester, *Eng., U.K.* **143** W13
Chichester Range, *Austral.* **210** F3
Chichibu, *Japan* **185** P12
Chichi Jima Rettō, *Japan* **184** K5
Chickamauga, *Ga., U.S.* **96** J4
Chickamauga Lake, *Tenn., U.S.* **101** F17
Chickasaw National Recreation Area, *Okla., U.S.* **102** H11
Chickasha, *Okla., U.S.* **102** H10
Chicken Rock, *Isle of Man, U.K.* **143** R8
Chiclayo, *Peru* **130** F2
Chico, river, *Arg.* **133** S9
Chico, river, *Arg.* **133** W8
Chico, *Calif., U.S.* **109** P4
Chico, river, *Chile* **133** W8
Chicoma Mountain, *N. Mex., U.S.* **107** R12
Chicomo, *Mozambique* **202** J12
Chicopee, *Mass., U.S.* **95** K13
Chicoutimi, *Que., Can.* **83** N20
Chief Joseph Dam, *Wash., U.S.* **108** B6
Chiefland, *Fla., U.S.* **97** S7
Chieri, *It.* **150** E3
Chiesanuova, *San Marino* **161** L14
Chieti, *It.* **150** K10
Chifeng (Ulanhad), *China* **182** B8
Chignik Lagoon, *Alas., U.S.* **111** M13
Chihuahua, *Mex.* **114** D9
Chikan, *Russ.* **159** K15
Chikhachevo, *Russ.* **156** H6
Chikhli, *India* **178** K5
Chilas, *Pak.* **176** L11
Chilaw, *Sri Lanka* **179** T7
Chilca, *Peru* **130** H3
Childers, *Qnsld., Austral.* **211** U15
Childersburg, *Ala., U.S.* **101** K16
Childress, *Tex., U.S.* **102** J7
Chile, *S. Amer.* **127** P16
Chile Basin, *Pac. Oc.* **239** M20
Chilecito, *Arg.* **132** H8
Chile Rise, *Pac. Oc.* **239** P19
Chililabombwe, *Zambia* **202** D10
Chilka Lake, *India* **178** L10
Chillán, *Chile* **132** M6
Chillicothe, *Ill., U.S.* **99** P5
Chillicothe, *Mo., U.S.* **105** R11
Chillicothe, *Ohio, U.S.* **99** S13
Chillicothe, *Tex., U.S.* **102** J8
Chiloé, Isla Grande de, *Chile* **133** R6
Chiloquin, *Oreg., U.S.* **108** K4
Chilpancingo, *Mex.* **114** K11
Chiltern Hills, *Eng., U.K.* **143** V13
Chilton, *Wis., U.S.* **98** K7
Chilumba, *Malawi* **203** C13
Chilwa, Lake, *Malawi, Mozambique* **194** M10
Chimacum, *Wash., U.S.* **108** B3
Chimborazo, peak, *Ecua.* **128** K3
Chimbote, *Peru* **130** G2
Chimboy, *Uzb.* **174** J9
Chimney Rock National Historic Site, *Nebr., U.S.* **105** P1
Chimoio, *Mozambique* **202** G12
China, *Asia* **167** U9
Chinandega, *Nicar.* **115** M17
China Point, *Calif., U.S.* **109** Z8
Chinati Peak, *Tex., U.S.* **103** Q1
Chincha Alta, *Peru* **130** H3
Chincha Islands, *S. Amer.* **126** G2
Chinchilla, *Qnsld., Austral.* **211** V14
Chinchilla de Monte Aragón, *Sp.* **145** J13
Chincoteague, *Va., U.S.* **96** E15
Chincoteague Bay, *Md., U.S.* **96** D15
Chinde, *Mozambique* **203** F13
Chindwin, river, *Myanmar* **186** E5
Chingola, *Zambia* **202** D10
Chinguetti, *Mauritania* **196** F6
Chin Hills, *Myanmar* **186** G5
Chinhoyi, *Zimb.* **202** F11
Chiniot, *Pak.* **177** Q11
Chinle, *Ariz., U.S.* **107** R9
Chino, *Japan* **185** P11
Chinon, *Fr.* **147** S7
Chinook, *Mont., U.S.* **106** B9
Chinook Trough, *Pac. Oc.* **238** E10
Chino Valley, *Ariz., U.S.* **107** S6
Chinsali, *Zambia* **202** C12
Chinta, *S. Aust., Austral.* **211** W8
Chioggia, *It.* **150** E8
Chios *see* Híos, island, *Gr.* **155** H16
Chios *see* Híos, *Gr.* **155** H16
Chipata, *Zambia* **202** E12
Chipley, *Fla., U.S.* **97** Q3
Chiplun, *India* **178** M3
Chippenham, *Eng., U.K.* **143** V11
Chippewa, river, *Wis., U.S.* **98** G3
Chippewa, Lake, *Wis., U.S.* **98** G3
Chippewa Falls, *Wis., U.S.* **98** H3
Chiquián, *Peru* **130** G3
Chiquimula, *Guatemala* **115** L16
Chiquinquirá, *Col.* **128** E5
Chirchiq, *Uzb.* **175** K13
Chiredzi, *Zimb.* **202** G12
Chiricahua National Monument, *Ariz., U.S.* **107** V9
Chiricahua Peak, *Ariz., U.S.* **107** V9
Chirikof Island, *Alas., U.S.* **111** N14
Chirinda, *Russ.* **159** G14
Chiriquí, Golfo de, *Pan.* **115** P20
Chiromo, *Malawi* **203** F13
Chirpan, *Bulg.* **153** J15
Chirripo, Cerro, *Costa Rica* **115** N19
Chisasibi, *Que., Can.* **83** M18
Ch'ishan, *Taiwan, China* **183** S9
Chisholm, *Minn., U.S.* **104** F12
Chishtian Mandi, *Pak.* **177** R11
Chisimayu *see* Kismaayo, *Somalia* **199** K16
Chişinău, *Mold.* **157** R4
Chişineu Criş, *Rom.* **152** C11
Chisos Mountains, *Tex., U.S.* **103** R3
Chissioua Mtsamboro, island, *Mayotte, Fr.* **205** N17
Chistopol', *Russ.* **156** J15
Chita, *Russ.* **159** L17
Chitado, *Angola* **202** F6
Chitato, *Angola* **202** B8
Chitembo, *Angola* **202** E7
Chitipa, *Malawi* **202** C12
Chitose, *Japan* **184** G13
Chitradurga, *India* **179** P5
Chitral, *Pak.* **176** L10
Chitré, *Pan.* **115** P21
Chittagong, *Bangladesh* **178** J13
Chittaurgarh, *India* **178** H4
Chittoor, *India* **179** P6
Chitungwiza, *Zimb.* **202** F11
Chiumbe, river, *Angola* **202** C8
Chivasso, *It.* **150** E3
Chivilcoy, *Arg.* **132** L12
Chizu, *Japan* **185** P7
Chlef, *Alg.* **196** A10
Chloride, *Ariz., U.S.* **107** R5
Chobe, river, *Namibia, Zimb.* **194** N8
Choc Bay, *St. Lucia* **121** J14
Chocolate Mountains, *Calif., U.S.* **109** Y12
Choctawhatchee, river, *Fla., U.S.* **97** Q3
Choctawhatchee Bay, *Fla., U.S.* **97** Q2
Chodzież, *Pol.* **149** D13
Choele Choel, *Arg.* **133** P9
Choirokoitia, *Cyprus* **160** Q8
Choiseul, island, *Solomon Is.* **217** K15
Choiseul, *St. Lucia* **121** L13
Choiseul Sound, *Falkland Is., U.K.* **133** W12
Chojna, *Pol.* **148** D11
Chojnice, *Pol.* **149** C13
Choke Canyon Reservoir, *Tex., U.S.* **103** T10
Chokoloskee, *Fla., U.S.* **97** X9
Chokurdakh, *Russ.* **159** D18
Chola Shan, *China* **180** K10
Cholet, *Fr.* **147** S6
Cholpon-Ata, *Kyrg.* **176** D13
Choluteca, *Hond.* **115** L17
Choma, *Zambia* **202** F10
Chomutov, *Czech Rep.* **148** G10
Chon Buri, *Thai.* **187** N9
Chonchi, *Chile* **133** R6
Chone, *Ecua.* **128** J2
Chong'an, *China* **183** N7
Ch'ŏngjin, *N. Korea* **182** B14
Chong Kal, *Cambodia* **186** M10
Chongming, *China* **182** K10
Chongming Dao, *China* **182** K10
Chongqing, *China* **180** L12
Chongxin, *China* **182** G1
Chongyi, *China* **183** P5
Chonogol, *Mongolia* **181** D14
Chonos, Archipiélago de los, *Chile* **133** S6
Chornobyl' (Chernobyl'), *Ukr.* **156** M6
Chornomors'ke, *Ukr.* **157** S7
Chorregon, *Qnsld., Austral.* **211** T12
Chorrillos, *Peru* **130** H3
Chortkiv, *Ukr.* **157** P3
Ch'osan, *N. Korea* **182** C12
Chōshi, *Japan* **185** P13
Chos Malal, *Arg.* **133** N7
Chota Nagpur Plateau, *India* **166** J8
Choteau, *Mont., U.S.* **106** C7
Chotila, *India* **178** J2
Chowan, river, *N.C., U.S.* **96** G14
Chowchilla, *Calif., U.S.* **109** T6
Choybalsan, *Mongolia* **181** D14
Choyr, *Mongolia* **181** D13
Christ Church, *Barbados* **121** L19
Christchurch, *Eng., U.K.* **143** X12
Christchurch, *N.Z.* **213** P17
Christian, Point, *Pitcairn I., U.K.* **219** Q23
Christiana, *Jam.* **120** J8
Christiansburg, *Va., U.S.* **96** F9
Christiansted, *Virgin Islands, U.S.* **120** Q3
Christmas Creek, *W. Aust., Austral.* **211** R5
Christmas Island, *Austral.* **188** N8
Christmas Island *see* Kiritimati, *Kiribati* **214** G12
Christmas Lake Valley, *Oreg., U.S.* **108** J6
Christopher, *Ill., U.S.* **99** U5
Christoval, *Tex., U.S.* **103** N7
Chubb Crater *see* Nouveau-Québec, Cratère du, *Que., Can.* **83** J18
Chub Cay, *Bahamas* **116** D11
Chubut, river, *Arg.* **133** R8
Chudleigh Park, *Qnsld., Austral.* **211** S12
Chudovo, *Russ.* **156** F7
Chudskoye Ozero *see* Peipus, Lake, *Est., Russ.* **141** K17
Chugach Mountains, *Alas., U.S.* **111** J18
Chuginadak Island, *Alas., U.S.* **110** P8
Chugwater, *Wyo., U.S.* **106** J13
Chuhuyiv, *Ukr.* **157** P9
Chukai, *Malaysia* **187** T10
Chukchi Peninsula, *Russ.* **166** A12
Chukchi Plain, *Arctic Oc.* **242** J6
Chukchi Plateau, *Arctic Oc.* **242** J6
Chukchi Range, *Russ.* **166** A12
Chukchi Sea, *Arctic Oc.* **242** J3
Chukhloma, *Russ.* **156** G11
Chukotskiy Poluostrov, *Russ.* **159** A21
Chukotskoye Nagor'ye, *Russ.* **159** B20
Chula Vista, *Calif., U.S.* **109** Z10
Chumar, *India* **177** N15
Chumbicha, *Arg.* **132** H9
Chumikan, *Russ.* **159** J20
Chumphon, *Thai.* **187** P8
Chun'an, *China* **182** M8
Chuncheon, *S. Korea* **182** E13
Chungli, *Taiwan, China* **183** Q10
Chunhua, *China* **182** G2
Chunnel, tunnel, *Eng., U.K., Fr.* **143** W16
Chunya, *Tanzania* **199** M13
Chupara Point, *Trinidad & Tobago* **121** N22
Chuquibamba, *Peru* **130** J5
Chuquicamata, *Chile* **132** D7
Chur, *Switz.* **150** B5
Churachandpur, *India* **178** H14
Churchill, river, *Man., Can.* **83** K14
Churchill, *Man., Can.* **83** K15
Churchill, river, *Nfld. & Lab., Can.* **83** L21
Churchill, river, *Sask., Can.* **83** L13
Churchill, Cape, *Man., Can.* **83** K15
Churchill Falls, *Nfld. & Lab., Can.* **83** L21
Churchill Lake, *Me., U.S.* **95** C16
Churchill Lake, *Sask., Can.* **82** L12
Churchill Mountains, *Antarctica* **227** L13
Church of St. Anne, *Vatican City* **161** P17
Church of St. Stephen, *Vatican City* **161** Q15
Church Point, *La., U.S.* **100** P8
Churuguara, *Venez.* **128** B8
Chushul, *India* **177** N15
Chuska Mountains, *Ariz., N. Mex., U.S.* **107** R10
Chusovoy, *Russ.* **158** H9
Chuuk (Truk Islands), *F.S.M.* **216** Q6
Chuuk Lagoon (Truk Lagoon), *F.S.M.* **217** B15
Chuxiong, *China* **180** N11
Ciales, *P.R., U.S.* **120** M3
Cianjur, *Indonesia* **188** M8
Çiçekdağı, *Turk.* **168** E9
Cicero, *Ill., U.S.* **99** N7
Cicia, island, *Fiji Is.* **218** H9
Cidade Velha, *Cape Verde* **205** E16
Cide, *Turk.* **168** C8
Ciechanów, *Pol.* **149** D16
Ciego de Ávila, *Cuba* **116** H10
Ciempozuelos, *Sp.* **144** G11
Ciénaga, *Col.* **128** B5
Cienfuegos, *Cuba* **116** H8
Cieszyn, *Pol.* **149** H14
Cieza, *Sp.* **145** K13
Çiftlik, *Turk.* **168** G9
Cihanbeyli, *Turk.* **168** F8
Cijara, Embalse de, *Sp.* **144** H9
Çikës, Maja e, *Albania* **152** M9
Cikobia, island, *Fiji Is.* **218** F8
Cilacap, *Indonesia* **188** M9
Cilaos, *Reunion, Fr.* **205** G16
Çıldır, *Turk.* **169** D17
Çıldır Gölü, *Turk.* **169** D17
Cilician Gates, *Turk.* **168** H10
Cimarron, *Kans., U.S.* **105** U4
Cimarron, river, *Kans., Okla., U.S.* **84** J12
Cimarron, *N. Mex., U.S.* **107** Q13
Cimolais, *It.* **150** C8
Cimone, Monte, *It.* **150** G6
Cîmpina, *Rom.* **153** E15
Cîmpulung, *Rom.* **153** E14
Çınar, *Turk.* **169** H15
Cinaruco, river, *Venez.* **128** D9
Cincinnati, *Ohio, U.S.* **99** S11
Cinco Balas, Cayos, *Cuba* **116** J9
Cîndrelu, peak, *Rom.* **153** E13
Çine, *Turk.* **168** G3
Cinéma d'Eté, *Monaco* **161** B23
Cinnabar Mountain, *Idaho, U.S.* **106** H3
Cintegabelle, *Fr.* **147** Y9

Cinto, Monte, Fr. 150 J4
Cioara Doiceşti, Rom. 153 F17
Čiovo, island, Croatia 152 G6
Çırçır, Turk. 168 E12
Circle, Alas., U.S. 111 F18
Circle, Mont., U.S. 106 C12
Circleville, Ohio, U.S. 99 R13
Cirebon, Indonesia 188 M9
Cirencester, Eng., U.K. 143 V12
Ciscaucasia, region, Russ. 138 G12
Cisco, Tex., U.S. 102 M9
Cisco, Utah, U.S. 107 N9
Cisnădie, Rom. 153 D13
Cisneros, Col. 128 E5
Cistern Point, Bahamas 116 F11
Citronelle, Ala., U.S. 101 N13
Cittadella, It. 150 D7
Città di Castello, It. 150 H8
Cittanova, It. 151 R13
City of Refuge National Historic Park see Puʻuhonua o Hōnaunau National Historic Park, Hawaiʻi, U.S. 113 N18
City of Rocks National Reserve, Idaho, U.S. 106 J5
Ciucea, Rom. 152 C12
Ciudad Acuña, Mex. 114 D11
Ciudad Altamirano, Mex. 114 J11
Ciudad Bolívar, Venez. 128 C11
Ciudad Camargo, Mex. 114 E9
Ciudad Cortés, Costa Rica 115 N19
Ciudad del Carmen, Mex. 115 J15
Ciudad del Este, Parag. 130 N11
Ciudad Guayana, Venez. 128 C12
Ciudad Guerrero, Mex. 114 D8
Ciudad Guzmán, Mex. 114 H10
Ciudad Hidalgo, Mex. 115 L15
Ciudad Juárez, Mex. 114 C9
Ciudad Madero, Mex. 114 G12
Ciudad Mante, Mex. 114 G12
Ciudad Obregón, Mex. 114 D7
Ciudad Piar, Venez. 128 D12
Ciudad Real, Sp. 144 H10
Ciudad-Rodrigo, Sp. 144 F7
Ciudad Sandino, Cuba 116 H4
Ciudad Valles, Mex. 114 G12
Ciudad Victoria, Mex. 114 G12
Ciutadella de Menorca, Sp. 145 G19
Civa Burnu, Turk. 168 C11
Civita Castellana, It. 150 K8
Civitanova Marche, It. 150 H10
Civitavecchia, It. 150 K7
Civray, Fr. 147 T7
Çivril, Turk. 168 G5
Cixian, China 182 F5
Cizre, Turk. 169 H16
Clacton on Sea, Eng., U.K. 143 U15
Clair Engle Lake, Calif., U.S. 108 M3
Clairton, Pa., U.S. 94 P3
Clairview, Qnsld., Austral. 211 T14
Clam Lake, Wis., U.S. 98 F4
Clanton, Ala., U.S. 101 K15
Clare, Mich., U.S. 98 K10
Clare Island, Ire. 143 R3
Claremont, Jam. 120 H9
Claremont, N.H., U.S. 95 H13
Claremore, Okla., U.S. 102 F13
Claremorris, Ire. 143 R4
Clarence, river, N.Z. 213 N18
Clarence Island, Antarctica 226 B3
Clarence Strait, Austral. 210 A7
Clarence Town, Bahamas 117 G14
Clarendon, Ark., U.S. 100 G10
Clarendon, Tex., U.S. 102 H6
Clarie Coast, Antarctica 227 Q19
Clarinda, Iowa, U.S. 105 Q10
Clarión, Isla, Mex. 114 H4
Clarion, Iowa, U.S. 104 M11
Clarion, Pa., U.S. 94 M4
Clarion Fracture Zone, Pac. Oc. 239 H13
Clarión Island, N. Amer. 80 N2
Clark, S. Dak., U.S. 104 K7
Clark, Lake, Alas., U.S. 111 K15
Clarke Range, Austral. 210 E14
Clark Fork, Idaho, U.S. 106 B4
Clark Fork, Mont., U.S. 106 D6
Clark Mountain, Calif., U.S. 109 V11
Clarks, La., U.S. 100 L8
Clarksburg, W. Va., U.S. 96 C9
Clarksdale, Miss., U.S. 100 H10
Clarks Fork, Wyo., U.S. 106 F9
Clarkson, Nebr., U.S. 105 P8
Clarkston, Wash., U.S. 108 E9
Clarks Town, Jam. 120 H8
Clarksville, Ark., U.S. 100 F7
Clarksville, Tenn., U.S. 101 E14
Clarksville, Tex., U.S. 102 K14
Clatskanie, Oreg., U.S. 108 E3
Claude, Tex., U.S. 102 G6
Clauzetto, It. 150 C9
Claxton, Ga., U.S. 97 N8
Claxton Bay, Trinidad & Tobago 121 P22
Clay, Ky., U.S. 101 C14
Clay Center, Kans., U.S. 105 S8
Clayton, Ala., U.S. 101 M17
Clayton, Ga., U.S. 96 J6
Clayton, Idaho, U.S. 106 F5
Clayton, La., U.S. 100 M9
Clayton, N. Mex., U.S. 107 Q15
Clayton, N.Y., U.S. 94 G8
Clayton, Okla., U.S. 102 H13
Clayton Lake, Me., U.S. 95 B16
Clearbrook, Minn., U.S. 104 F9
Clear Creek, Tex., U.S. 102 K11
Clearfield, Pa., U.S. 94 M5
Clear Island, Ire. 143 V3
Clear Lake, Calif., U.S. 109 Q3
Clear Lake, Iowa, U.S. 104 M11
Clear Lake, S. Dak., U.S. 104 K8
Clear Lake, Wash., U.S. 108 B4
Clear Lake, Wis., U.S. 98 H2
Clear Lake Reservoir, Calif., U.S. 108 L5
Clearmont, Wyo., U.S. 106 F12
Clearwater, river, Alta., Sask., Can. 82 K11
Clearwater, Fla., U.S. 97 U7
Clearwater, river, Idaho, U.S. 106 D3
Clearwater, Wash., U.S. 108 C2
Clearwater Mountains, Idaho, U.S. 106 D5
Cleburne, Tex., U.S. 102 M11
Cle Elum, Wash., U.S. 108 C5
Clelles, Fr. 147 V13
Clemson, S.C., U.S. 96 K7
Clendenin, W. Va., U.S. 96 D8
Cleopatra Needle, peak, Philippines 189 E13
Clermont, Fr. 147 N10
Clermont, Qnsld., Austral. 211 T14
Clermont-Ferrand, Fr. 147 U11
Clervaux, Lux. 160 G9
Clervé, river, Lux. 160 H9
Cles, It. 150 C7
Cleveland, Miss., U.S. 100 J10
Cleveland, Ohio, U.S. 99 N14
Cleveland, Okla., U.S. 102 F12
Cleveland, Tenn., U.S. 101 G17
Cleveland, Tex., U.S. 103 Q14
Cleveland, Wis., U.S. 98 K7
Cleveland, Mount, Mont., U.S. 106 A6
Cleveland Hills, Eng., U.K. 143 Q12
Clew Bay, Ire. 143 R3
Clewiston, Fla., U.S. 97 V9
Clifden, Ire. 143 R3
Cliff, N. Mex., U.S. 107 U10
Clifton, Ariz., U.S. 107 U9
Clifton, Kans., U.S. 105 S8
Clifton, Bahamas 120 B10
Clifton, Tex., U.S. 103 N11
Clifton Forge, Va., U.S. 96 E10
Clifton Hills, S. Aust., Austral. 211 V10
Clinch, river, Tenn., U.S. 101 E19
Clingmans Dome, N.C., Tenn., U.S. 85 J17
Clint, Tex., U.S. 103 U2
Clinton, Ark., U.S. 100 F8
Clinton, Ill., U.S. 99 R6
Clinton, Ind., U.S. 99 R7
Clinton, Iowa, U.S. 105 N15
Clinton, Ky., U.S. 100 D12
Clinton, Miss., U.S. 100 L11
Clinton, Mo., U.S. 105 T11
Clinton, N.C., U.S. 96 J12
Clinton, Okla., U.S. 102 G9
Clinton, S.C., U.S. 96 K8
Clintonville, Wis., U.S. 98 J6
Clipperton, island, Pac. Oc. 215 F19
Clipperton Fracture Zone, Pac. Oc. 239 J13
Cliza, Bol. 130 K7
Cloates, Point, Austral. 210 F1
Clonakilty Bay, Ire. 143 V4
Cloncurry, river, Austral. 210 D11
Cloncurry, Qnsld., Austral. 211 S11
Cloncurry Plateau, Austral. 210 E11
Clonmany, Ire. 143 N6
Clonmel, Ire. 143 U5
Cloppenburg, Ger. 148 D6
Cloquet, Minn., U.S. 104 G12
Cloud Peak, Wyo., U.S. 106 F11
Clover, S.C., U.S. 96 J8
Cloverdale, Calif., U.S. 109 Q3
Cloverport, Ky., U.S. 101 C15
Clovis, Calif., U.S. 109 T6
Clovis, N. Mex., U.S. 107 S15
Cluj-Napoca, Rom. 153 C13
Clun, Eng., U.K. 143 U10
Cluny, Qnsld., Austral. 211 U11
Cluses, Fr. 147 T14
Clusone, It. 150 D5
Clutha, river, N.Z. 213 R16
Clyde, Kans., U.S. 105 S7
Clyde, Ohio, U.S. 99 P13
Clyde, Tex., U.S. 102 M8
Clyde, Firth of, Scot., U.K. 143 N8
Clyde Inlet, Nunavut, Can. 83 E18
Clyde River, Nunavut, Can. 83 E18
Cnossus (Knossos), ruin, Gr. 155 Q15
Coachella, Calif., U.S. 109 X11
Coachella Canal, Calif., U.S. 109 Y12
Coahoma, Tex., U.S. 102 M6
Coakley Cay, Bahamas 120 F8
Coalcomán, Mex. 114 J10
Coal Creek, N.Z. 213 Q16
Coaldale, Nev., U.S. 109 R8
Coalgate, Okla., U.S. 102 H12
Coalinga, Calif., U.S. 109 U6
Coalville, Eng., U.K. 143 T12
Coamo, P.R., U.S. 120 N4
Coari, river, Braz. 130 E8
Coari, Braz. 130 E8
Coastal Plain, U.S. 85 N12
Coast Mountains, Alas., U.S. 111 L23
Coast Mountains, B.C., Can. 82 H7
Coast Range, S. Amer. 126 A4
Coast Ranges, Calif., Oreg., U.S. 84 C3
Coats Island, Nunavut, Can. 83 H16
Coats Land, Antarctica 226 E10
Coatzacoalcos, Mex. 115 J14
Cobalt, Ont., Can. 83 P18
Cobán, Guatemala 115 L16
Cobar, N.S.W., Austral. 211 W13
Cobia, island, Fiji Is. 218 G8
Cobija, Bol. 130 G6
Coborriu, Sp. 160 L5
Cobourg Peninsula, Austral. 210 A8
Cobre, Nev., U.S. 108 M12
Cóbuè, Mozambique 203 D13
Coburg, Ger. 148 G8
Coburg Island, Nunavut, Can. 83 D16
Coca, Sp. 144 E10
Cocanada see Kakinada, India 178 M8
Cochabamba, Bol. 130 K7
Coche, Isla, Venez. 119 P14
Cochin (Kochi), India 179 R5
Cochinoca, Arg. 132 D9
Cochinos, Bahía de (Bay of Pigs), Cuba 116 H7
Cochran, Ga., U.S. 97 N6
Cochrane, Ont., Can. 83 N17
Cockburn, S. Aust., Austral. 211 X11
Cockburn Harbour, Turks & Caicos Is., U.K. 117 J17
Cockburn Town, Bahamas 120 E11
Cockburn Town, Turks & Caicos Is., U.K. 117 J18
Cocklebiddy Motel, W. Aust., Austral. 211 X6
Cockroach Island, Virgin Islands, U.S. 120 M7
Cockscomb Point, Amer. Samoa, U.S. 218 L8
Coco, river, Hond., Nicar. 115 L19
Coco, Cayo, Cuba 116 H10
Coco, Isla del, Costa Rica 115 Q17
Cocoa, Fla., U.S. 97 T9
Cocoa Island, Mauritius 205 J19
Coco Channel, India 179 P14
Coco-de-Mer Seamounts, Ind. Oc. 240 G6
Coconut Point, Amer. Samoa, U.S. 218 M7
Cocos Bay, Trinidad & Tobago 121 P23
Cocos Island, Guam, U.S. 216 E10
Cocos Island, N. Amer. 80 R7
Cocos (Keeling) Islands, Austral., Ind. Oc. 241 H13
Cocos Lagoon, Guam, U.S. 216 E10
Cocos Ridge, Pac. Oc. 239 J19
Cod, Cape, Mass., U.S. 95 L16
Coda Cavallo, Capo, It. 150 M5
Codajás, Braz. 130 D8
Codigoro, It. 150 F8
Cod Island, Nfld. & Lab., Can. 83 J21
Codlea, Rom. 153 D15
Codó, Braz. 131 E15
Codogno, It. 150 E5
Codrington, Antigua & Barbuda 119 F16
Codrington, Mount, Antarctica 227 C19
Cody, Nebr., U.S. 104 M4
Cody, Wyo., U.S. 106 F9
Coeburn, Va., U.S. 96 F7
Coen, Qnsld., Austral. 211 P12
Coëtlogon, Passe du, New Caledonia, Fr. 218 C8
Coeur d'Alene, Idaho, U.S. 106 C3
Coeur d'Alene Lake, Idaho, U.S. 106 C3
Coevorden, Neth. 146 H14
Coffeyville, Kans., U.S. 105 V9
Coffs Harbour, N.S.W., Austral. 211 W15
Cofrentes, Sp. 145 H14
Coghinas, Lago del, It. 150 M4
Cognac, Fr. 147 U7
Cogne, It. 150 D2
Cogollos, Sp. 144 D11
Cohagen, Mont., U.S. 106 C11
Cohoes, N.Y., U.S. 94 J11
Coiba, Isla de, Pan. 115 P20
Coiba Island, N. Amer. 80 R8
Coig, river, Arg. 133 V8
Coihaique, Chile 133 S7
Coimbatore, India 179 R5
Coimbra, Port. 144 F5
Coín, Sp. 144 M9
Coipasa, Salar de, Bol. 130 K6
Cojimíes, Boca de, Ecua. 128 J2
Cokato, Minn., U.S. 104 J10
Cokeville, Wyo., U.S. 106 J8
Colac, Vic., Austral. 211 Z12
Colatina, Braz. 131 L16
Colby, Kans., U.S. 105 S4
Colchester, Eng., U.K. 143 U15
Cold Bay, Alas., U.S. 110 N11
Cold Spring, Minn., U.S. 104 J10
Coldwater, Kans., U.S. 105 V5
Coldwater, Mich., U.S. 99 N10
Coldwater Creek, Tex., U.S. 102 E4
Colebrook, N.H., U.S. 95 F14
Coleman, Mich., U.S. 98 K11
Coleman, Tex., U.S. 102 M8
Coleraine, Minn., U.S. 104 F11
Coleraine, N. Ire., U.K. 143 P6
Colesberg, S. Af. 202 L9
Cole's Cave, Barbados 121 K19
Colfax, Calif., U.S. 109 Q5
Colfax, Iowa, U.S. 105 P12
Colfax, La., U.S. 100 M8
Colfax, Wash., U.S. 108 D9
Colhué Huapí, Lago, Arg. 133 S8
Colico, It. 150 C5
Colídor, Braz. 130 G11
Colihaut, Dominica 121 E18
Colima, Mex. 114 J9
Colinas, Braz. 131 E15
Colison Point, Virgin Islands, U.K. 120 R8
Coll, island, Scot., U.K. 142 L7
Colle, river, It. 161 L15
College, Alas., U.S. 111 G17
College Park, Ga., U.S. 96 L5
College Station, Tex., U.S. 103 P12
Collelongo, It. 150 K10
Collerina, N.S.W., Austral. 211 W13
Collie, W. Aust., Austral. 211 X2
Collier Bay, Austral. 210 C5
Collier Range, Austral. 210 G3
Colliers, Cayman Is., U.K. 120 J4
Colliers Point, Cayman Is., U.K. 116 L7
Collierville, Tenn., U.S. 100 G12
Collingwood, N.Z. 213 M17
Collins, Miss., U.S. 100 M12
Collins Head, Norfolk I., Austral. 217 G20
Collinson Peninsula, Nunavut, Can. 83 F14
Collinsville, Ill., U.S. 99 T4
Collinsville, Okla., U.S. 102 E13
Collinsville, Qnsld., Austral. 211 S14
Collinsville, Va., U.S. 96 G10
Collipulli, Chile 133 N6
Collonges, Fr. 147 T14
Colmar, Fr. 147 Q15
Cologne see Köln, Ger. 148 F5
Colombey-les-Belles, Fr. 147 P14
Colômbia, Braz. 131 L13
Colombia, S. Amer. 127 C15
Colombo, Sri Lanka 179 T7
Colón, Cuba 116 G8
Colón, Pan. 115 N21
Colonarie, river, St. Vincent & the Grenadines 121 K16
Colonarie, St. Vincent & the Grenadines 121 K17
Colonel Bogado, Parag. 130 N10
Colonel Hill, Bahamas 117 G14
Colonel Oviedo, Parag. 130 M10
Colonet, Cabo, Mex. 114 B5
Colonia, F.S.M. 217 D18
Colonia Dora, Arg. 132 H10
Colonial Beach, Va., U.S. 96 D13
Colonial Heights, Va., U.S. 96 F13
Colonial National Historic Park, Va., U.S. 96 F14
Colonia 25 de Mayo, Arg. 133 N8
Colonna, Capo, It. 151 Q14
Colon Ridge, Pac. Oc. 239 J18
Colonsay, island, Scot., U.K. 142 M7
Colophon, ruin, Turk. 168 G3
Colorado, river, Arg. 133 P10
Colorado, river, Tex., U.S. 103 R12
Colorado, river, U.S. 84 K5
Colorado, U.S. 106 M11
Colorado City, Ariz., U.S. 107 Q6
Colorado City, Tex., U.S. 102 M6
Colorado National Monument, Colo., U.S. 106 M10
Colorado Plateau, Ariz., U.S. 107 Q7
Colorado River Aqueduct, Calif., U.S. 109 X12
Colorado Springs, Colo., U.S. 107 N13
Colotepec, Mex. 115 L13
Colquitt, Ga., U.S. 97 P4
Colstrip, Mont., U.S. 106 E11
Columbia, Ky., U.S. 101 D17
Columbia, La., U.S. 100 L8
Columbia, Md., U.S. 96 C13
Columbia, Miss., U.S. 100 N11
Columbia, Mo., U.S. 105 S13
Columbia, N.C., U.S. 96 G14
Columbia, Pa., U.S. 94 P8
Columbia, S.C., U.S. 96 K9
Columbia, Tenn., U.S. 101 F15
Columbia, river, U.S. 84 C4
Columbia, Cape, Nunavut, Can. 83 A16
Columbia, District of, U.S. 96 C13
Columbia, Mount, Alta., B.C., Can. 82 L9
Columbia City, Ind., U.S. 99 P10
Columbia Falls, Mont., U.S. 106 B5
Columbia Mountains, B.C., Can. 82 L9
Columbia Plateau, U.S. 84 C5
Columbia Seamount, Atl. Oc. 237 R9
Columbine, Cape, S. Af. 202 M7
Columbretes, Islas, Sp. 145 G16
Columbus, Ga., U.S. 97 N4
Columbus, Ind., U.S. 99 S9
Columbus, Kans., U.S. 105 V10
Columbus, Miss., U.S. 101 J13
Columbus, Mont., U.S. 106 E9
Columbus, N. Dak., U.S. 104 D3
Columbus, N. Mex., U.S. 107 W11
Columbus, Nebr., U.S. 105 P7
Columbus, Ohio, U.S. 99 R13
Columbus, Tex., U.S. 103 R12
Columbus, Wis., U.S. 98 L6
Columbus Monument, Bahamas 120 E12
Columbus Monument, Bahamas 120 F11
Columbus Point, Trinidad & Tobago 121 P17
Colusa, Calif., U.S. 109 Q4
Colville, river, Alas., U.S. 111 C15
Colville, N.Z. 213 J19
Colville, Wash., U.S. 108 A8
Colville Channel, N.Z. 213 J19
Colville Lake, N.W.T., Can. 82 F10
Colwich, Kans., U.S. 105 U7
Comacchio, It. 150 F8
Comacchio, Valli di, It. 150 F8
Comallo, Arg. 133 Q7
Comanche, Okla., U.S. 102 J10
Comanche, Tex., U.S. 102 M9
Comandante Ferraz, station, Antarctica 226 C3
Comandante Fontana, Arg. 132 F12
Comandante Luis Piedrabuena, Arg. 133 V8
Comăneşti, Rom. 153 C16
Coma Pedrosa, Pic de, Andorra, Sp. 160 H2
Comarnic, Rom. 153 E15
Comayagua, Hond. 115 L17
Combarbalá, Chile 132 J6
Combeaufontaine, Fr. 147 R14
Combermere Bay, Myanmar 186 J4
Combles, Fr. 146 M10
Combourg, Fr. 147 Q5
Comboyne, N.S.W., Austral. 211 X15
Comerío, P.R., U.S. 120 N4
Comet, Qnsld., Austral. 211 T14
Comfort, Tex., U.S. 103 Q9

Comino (Kemmuna), island, Malta 161 H21
Cominotto, island, Malta 161 H21
Commandant Charcot Glacier, Antarctica 227 Q17
Commander Islands see Komandorskiye Ostrova, Russ. 159 E23
Commanders Bay, Aruba, Neth. 121 R17
Commerce, Ga., U.S. 96 K6
Commerce, Tex., U.S. 102 K13
Commissioner's Point, Bermuda, U.K. 120 B2
Committee Bay, Nunavut, Can. 83 F16
Commonwealth Bay, Antarctica 227 R18
Communism Peak see Qullai Ismoili Somoni, Taj. 176 H10
Como, It. 150 D4
Como, Lago di, It., Switz. 150 C4
Comodoro Rivadavia, Arg. 133 S9
Comondú, Mex. 114 E6
Comorin, Cape, India 179 S6
Comoro Islands, Mozambique Chan. 194 M11
Comoros, Af. 204 G8
Compiègne, Fr. 147 N10
Comporta, Port. 144 J5
Compostela, Mex. 114 H9
Comrat, Mold. 157 R4
Comstock Seamount, Pac. Oc. 238 D12
Cona, China 180 M8
Conakry, Guinea 200 F5
Conara Junction, Tas., Austral. 211 Z16
Conca, river, It. 161 L18
Concarneau, Fr. 147 Q3
Conceição, Braz. 131 F17
Conceição do Maú, Braz. 130 B9
Concepción, Arg. 132 G9
Concepción, Bol. 130 J8
Concepción, Chile 133 N6
Concepción del Uruguay, Arg. 132 K13
Conception, Point, Calif., U.S. 109 W5
Conception Bay, Nfld. & Lab., Can. 83 M24
Conceptión del Oro, Mex. 114 F11
Conception Island, Bahamas 117 F14
Conchas, river, N. Mex., U.S. 107 R14
Conchas Dam, N. Mex., U.S. 107 R14
Conchas Lake, N. Mex., U.S. 107 R14
Concho, Ariz., U.S. 107 T9
Concho, river, Tex., U.S. 103 N7
Conchos, river, Mex. 114 E9
Conch Point, Cayman Is., U.K. 120 H1
Con Co, Dao, Vietnam 186 K13
Conconully, Wash., U.S. 108 A6
Concord, Calif., U.S. 109 R4
Concord, Grenada 121 K22
Concord, N.C., U.S. 96 H9
Concord, N.H., U.S. 95 J14
Concordia, Arg. 132 J13
Concordia, Kans., U.S. 105 S7
Concrete, Wash., U.S. 108 A4
Condamine, Qnsld., Austral. 211 V14
Condat, Fr. 147 U10
Condé, Fr. 146 M11
Conde, S. Dak., U.S. 104 J7
Condeúba, Braz. 131 J15
Condobolin, N.S.W., Austral. 211 X13
Condom, Fr. 147 X8
Condon, Oreg., U.S. 108 F6
Concordia, station, Antarctica 227 M17
Conecuh, river, Ala., U.S. 101 M16
Conegliano, It. 150 D8
Conejos, Colo., U.S. 107 Q12
Conero, Monte, It. 150 H10
Conflict Group, P.N.G. 213 E21
Confolens, Fr. 147 T8
Congaree National Park, S.C., U.S. 96 L9
Conghua, China 183 R4
Congjiang, China 183 P1
Congo, Af. 195 K18
Congo, river, Af. 194 K6
Congo, Source of the, Dem. Rep. of the Congo 194 M8
Congo Basin, Dem. Rep. of the Congo 194 J7
Congo Canyon, Atl. Oc. 237 P14
Congo Cay, Virgin Islands, U.S. 120 M10
Congress, Ariz., U.S. 107 T6
Cónico, Cerro, Arg. 133 R7
Conil de la Frontera, Sp. 144 M8
Conn, Lough, Ire. 143 Q3
Connaught, region, Ire. 143 R4
Conneaut, Ohio, U.S. 99 N15
Connecticut, river, U.S. 95 J13
Connecticut, U.S. 94 L12
Connel, Scot., U.K. 142 L8
Connell, Wash., U.S. 108 D7
Connellsville, Pa., U.S. 94 P4
Connemara, region, Ire. 143 R3
Connersville, Ind., U.S. 99 R10
Connmara, Qnsld., Austral. 211 T12
Connors Range, Austral. 210 F14
Cononaco, Ecua. 128 J5
Conrad, Mont., U.S. 106 B7
Conroe, Tex., U.S. 103 Q14
Consdorf, Lux. 160 J10
Conselheiro Lafaiete, Braz. 131 L14
Conset Bay, Barbados 121 K20
Consolación del Sur, Cuba 116 G5
Con Son, island, Vietnam 187 Q12
Con Son, Vietnam 187 Q12
Constance, Lake see Bodensee, Aust., Ger. 148 L7
Constância dos Baetas, Braz. 130 E8
Constant, Morne, Guadeloupe, Fr. 121 G16
Constanţa, Rom. 153 F18
Constantina, Sp. 144 K8
Constantine, Alg. 196 A12
Constantinople see İstanbul, Turk. 168 C5
Constellation Inlet, Antarctica 226 H8
Constitución, Chile 132 M6
Consuegra, Sp. 144 H11
Contact, Nev., U.S. 108 L12
Contai, India 178 K11
Contamana, Peru 130 F4
Contramaestre, Cuba 116 J11
Contreras, Embalse de, Sp. 145 G13
Contreras, Isla, Chile 133 W6
Contres, Fr. 147 R9
Contrexéville, Fr. 147 Q14
Contwoyto Lake, Nunavut, Can. 82 G12
Convention Center and Auditorium, Monaco 161 D22
Conversano, It. 150 M14
Conway, Ark., U.S. 100 G8
Conway, N.H., U.S. 95 G14
Conway, S.C., U.S. 96 K11
Conway Springs, Kans., U.S. 105 U7
Conwy, Wales, U.K. 143 S9
Coober Pedy, S. Aust., Austral. 211 V9
Cook, Minn., U.S. 104 F12
Cook, S. Aust., Austral. 211 W7
Cook, Bahía, Chile 133 Y8
Cook, Baie de, Fr. Polynesia, Fr. 219 N14
Cook, Mouillage de, Fr. Polynesia, Fr. 219 P17
Cook, Mount see Aoraki, N.Z. 213 P16
Cook Bay, Vanuatu 218 G4
Cookes Peak, N. Mex., U.S. 107 V11
Cookeville, Tenn., U.S. 101 E17
Cook Ice Shelf, Antarctica 227 R16
Cook Inlet, Alas., U.S. 111 L15
Cook Island, Kiribati 217 B22
Cook Island Passage, Kiribati 217 B22
Cook Islands, N.Z., Pac. Oc. 214 J11
Cook Strait, N.Z. 213 M18
Cooktown, Qnsld., Austral. 211 Q13
Coolabah, N.S.W., Austral. 211 W13
Coolabri, Qnsld., Austral. 211 U13
Cooladdi, Qnsld., Austral. 211 V13
Coolah, N.S.W., Austral. 211 X14
Coolatai, N.S.W., Austral. 211 W14
Coolgardie, W. Aust., Austral. 211 W4
Coolidge, Ariz., U.S. 107 U7
Coolidge, Tex., U.S. 103 N12
Coolidge Dam, Ariz., U.S. 107 U8
Coonabarabran, N.S.W., Austral. 211 X14
Coonamble, N.S.W., Austral. 211 W14
Coonana, W. Aust., Austral. 211 W5
Coonbah, N.S.W., Austral. 211 X11
Coondambo, S. Aust., Austral. 211 W9
Coondapoor see Kundapura, India 179 P4
Coongoola, Qnsld., Austral. 211 V13
Coon Rapids, Iowa, U.S. 105 P10
Coon Rapids, Minn., U.S. 104 J11
Cooper, Tex., U.S. 102 K13
Cooper Creek, Austral. 210 H10
Cooper's Town, Bahamas 120 A6
Cooperstown, N. Dak., U.S. 104 F7
Cooperstown, N.Y., U.S. 94 J10
Coorow, W. Aust., Austral. 211 W2
Coosa, river, Ala., U.S. 101 H16
Coos Bay, Oreg., U.S. 108 J2
Cootamundra, N.S.W., Austral. 211 Y13
Copano Bay, Tex., U.S. 103 T11
Cope, Colo., U.S. 106 M15
Cope, Cabo, Sp. 145 L13
Copeland Island, N. Ire., U.K. 143 P8
Copenhagen see København, Den. 140 N12
Copertino, It. 151 N15
Copiapó, Chile 132 G7
Copiapó, Río, Chile 132 G6
Copinsay, island, Scot., U.K. 142 G11
Copparo, It. 150 E7
Copper, river, Alas., U.S. 111 J18
Copperas Cove, Tex., U.S. 103 P10
Copper Butte, Wash., U.S. 108 A8
Copper Center, Alas., U.S. 111 J18
Copper Harbor, Mich., U.S. 98 E7
Copper Mine Point, Virgin Islands, U.K. 120 R8
Coppolani, Mauritania 196 F5
Copulhue Pass, S. Amer. 126 M4
Coqên, China 180 K6
Coquí, P.R., U.S. 120 N4
Coquille, Oreg., U.S. 108 J2
Coquille Harbor, F.S.M. 217 A18
Coquimbo, Chile 132 J6
Corabia, Rom. 153 G14
Coracora, Peru 130 J4
Corail, Haiti 117 M15
Coral Bay, Virgin Islands, U.S. 120 N11
Coral Bay, Virgin Islands, U.S. 120 M11
Coral Gables, Fla., U.S. 97 X10
Coral Harbour, Bahamas 120 B10
Coral Harbour, Nunavut, Can. 83 H16
Coral Island see Far'ûn, Egypt 171 R5
Coral Reef National Monument, Virgin Islands, U.S. 120 N11
Coral Sea, Pac. Oc. 238 M7
Coral Sea Basin, Pac. Oc. 238 L7
Coral Sea Islands Territory, Austral. 211 R15
Coral Springs, Fla., U.S. 97 W10
Corangamite, Lake, Austral. 210 M12
Corantijn, river, Guyana, Suriname 129 E15
Corato, It. 150 L13
Corbeil-Essonnes, Fr. 147 P10
Corbières, range, Fr. 147 Y10
Corbin, Ky., U.S. 101 D18
Corby, Eng., U.K. 143 T13
Corcaigh see Cork, Ire. 143 U4
Corcoran, Calif., U.S. 109 U6
Corcovado, Golfo, Chile 133 R6
Corcubión, Sp. 144 B5
Corcyra see Kérkira, island, Gr. 154 E6
Cordele, Ga., U.S. 97 N6
Cordell, Okla., U.S. 102 G9
Cordes, Fr. 147 W9
Cordillo Downs, S. Aust., Austral. 211 U11
Córdoba, Arg. 132 J10
Córdoba, Mex. 115 J13
Córdoba, Sp. 144 K9
Córdoba, Sierras de, Arg. 132 J10
Cordouan, Île de, Fr. 147 U6
Cordova, Ala., U.S. 101 J15
Cordova, Alas., U.S. 111 K18
Corfu see Kérkira, island, Gr. 154 E6
Corguinho, Braz. 130 K11
Coria, Sp. 144 G7
Coria del Río, Sp. 144 L8
Corianino, San Marino 161 J16
Coribe, Braz. 131 H14
Corigliano Calabro, It. 151 P13
Coringa Islets, Coral Sea Is. Terr., Austral. 211 R15
Corinna, Tas., Austral. 211 Z15
Corinth see Kórinthos, Gr. 154 J11
Corinth, Grenada 121 L23
Corinth, Miss., U.S. 101 G13
Corinth, N.Y., U.S. 94 J11
Corinth Canal, Gr. 154 J11
Cork (Corcaigh), Ire. 143 U4
Cork Harbour, Ire. 143 V4
Corlay, Fr. 147 Q4
Corleone, It. 151 S9
Corleto Perticara, It. 151 N13
Çorlu, Turk. 168 C4
Cornelia, Ga., U.S. 96 K6
Cornell, Wis., U.S. 98 H3
Corner Brook, Nfld. & Lab., Can. 83 M23
Corner Seamounts, Atl. Oc. 236 H6
Corning, Ark., U.S. 100 E10
Corning, Calif., U.S. 109 P4
Corning, Iowa, U.S. 105 Q10
Corning, N.Y., U.S. 94 K7
Corno Grande, It. 150 J9
Cornwall, region, Eng., U.K. 143 X8
Cornwall, Ont., Can. 83 Q19
Cornwall, Cape, Eng., U.K. 143 Y7
Cornwallis, Port, India 179 P14
Cornwallis Island, Nunavut, Can. 83 D15
Cornwall Island, Nunavut, Can. 83 C15
Cornwall Point, Bahamas 120 C6
Coro, Venez. 128 B8
Coroatá, Braz. 131 E15
Corocoro, Bol. 130 K6
Coroico, Bol. 130 J6
Corolla, N.C., U.S. 96 G15
Coromandel Coast, India 179 Q8
Coromandel Peninsula, N.Z. 213 J19
Corona, N. Mex., U.S. 107 T13
Coronado, Calif., U.S. 109 Z9
Coronado Bay, N. Amer. 80 Q8
Coronado National Memorial, Ariz., U.S. 107 W8
Coronation Gulf, Nunavut, Can. 82 F12
Coronation Island, Antarctica 226 A4
Coronel, Chile 133 N6
Coronel Dorrego, Arg. 133 N11
Coronel Francisco Sosa, Arg. 133 P10
Coronel Pringles, Arg. 133 N11
Coronel Suárez, Arg. 133 N11
Coropuna, Nevado, Peru 130 J5
Corozal, Belize 115 J16
Corozal, Col. 128 C5
Corpus Christi, Tex., U.S. 103 U11
Corpus Christi, Lake, Tex., U.S. 103 T10
Corpus Christi Bay, Tex., U.S. 84 N12
Corral, Chile 133 P6
Corral de Almaguer, Sp. 144 G11
Corralillo, Cuba 116 G8
Corrib, Lough, Ire. 143 R3
Corrientes, Arg. 132 G13
Corrientes, Bahia de, Cuba 116 H4
Corrientes, Cabo, Col. 128 E3
Corrientes, Cabo, Cuba 116 H4
Corrientes, Cabo, Mex. 114 H9
Corrigan, Tex., U.S. 103 P14
Corrigin, W. Aust., Austral. 211 X3
Corriverton, Guyana 129 E15
Corrubedo, Cabo, Sp. 144 C5
Corry, Pa., U.S. 94 L4
Corryong, Vic., Austral. 211 Y13
Corse (Corsica), island, Fr. 150 K4
Corse, Cap, Fr. 150 H4
Corsica see Corse, island, Fr. 150 K4
Corsica, S. Dak., U.S. 104 M6
Corsicana, Tex., U.S. 102 M12
Corte, Fr. 150 K4
Cortemaggiore, It. 150 E5
Cortez, Colo., U.S. 107 P10
Cortina d'Ampezzo, It. 150 C8
Cortland, N.Y., U.S. 94 K8
Cortona, It. 150 H8
Corcubión, Ría de, Sp. 144 B5
Coruche, Port. 144 H5
Çoruh, river, Turk. 169 D15
Çorum, Turk. 168 D10
Corumbá, Braz. 130 K10
Corumbau, Ponta de, Braz. 131 K16
Corvallis, Oreg., U.S. 108 G3
Corvo, island, Azores 144 N1
Corwen, Wales, U.K. 143 T10
Coryal, Trinidad & Tobago 121 P23
Corydon, Iowa, U.S. 105 Q12
Cos see Kos, island, Gr. 155 M18
Cosenza, It. 151 P13
Coshocton, Ohio, U.S. 99 Q14
Cosmoledo, Atoll de, Seychelles 203 C17
Cosmoledo Group, Seychelles 194 L12
Cosmonaut Sea, Antarctic Oc. 245 E13
Cosmo Newberry, W. Aust., Austral. 211 V5
Cosmopolis, Wash., U.S. 108 D2
Cosne-Cours-sur-Loire, Fr. 147 R10
Cosquín, Arg. 132 J10
Cossato, It. 150 D3
Cossé-le-Vivien, Fr. 147 Q6
Costa del Silencio, Canary Is. 204 R4
Costa Rica, N. Amer. 81 Q20
Costeşti, Rom. 153 F14
Costilla, N. Mex., U.S. 107 Q13
Cotabato, Philippines 189 F15
Cotagaita, Bol. 130 L7
Coteaux, Haiti 117 M15
Côte d'Ivoire, Af. 195 H15
Côte d'Or, range, Fr. 147 S12
Cotentin, peninsula, Fr. 147 N6
Côtes-de-Fer, Haiti 117 M16
Coton, Pointe, Mauritius 205 J21
Cotonou, Benin 200 H12
Cotopaxi, peak, Ecua. 128 J3
Cotorra, Isla, Venez. 121 Q20
Cotswold Hills, Eng., U.K. 143 V11
Cottage Grove, Oreg., U.S. 108 H3
Cottbus, Ger. 148 E11
Cotter, Ark., U.S. 100 E8
Cottian Alps, Fr., It. 147 V15
Cottongarden Point, Virgin Islands, U.S. 120 Q4
Cotton Ground, St. Kitts & Nevis 121 C18
Cotton Plant, Ark., U.S. 100 G10
Cotton Valley, La., U.S. 100 K7
Cottonwood, Ariz., U.S. 107 S7
Cottonwood, Idaho, U.S. 106 D4
Cotulla, Tex., U.S. 103 T8
Coubre, Pointe de la, Fr. 147 U6
Coudersport, Pa., U.S. 94 L6
Couëron, Fr. 147 S5
Couiza, Fr. 147 Y10
Coulee City, Wash., U.S. 108 C7
Coulee Dam, Wash., U.S. 108 B7
Council, Idaho, U.S. 106 F3
Council Bluffs, Iowa, U.S. 105 P9
Council Grove, Kans., U.S. 105 T8
Courantyne, river, Guyana, Suriname 129 F15
Couronne, Cap, Fr. 147 Y13
Courtenay, B.C., Can. 82 L7
Courtenay, Fr. 147 Q10
Courtmacsherry Bay, Ire. 143 V4
Coushatta, La., U.S. 100 L7
Coutances, Fr. 147 P6
Coutras, Fr. 147 V7
Covadonga, site, Sp. 144 B9
Covarrubias, Sp. 144 D11
Cove, Oreg., U.S. 108 F8
Covelo, Calif., U.S. 109 P2
Coventry, Eng., U.K. 143 T12
Covered Market, Monaco 161 E20
Coves del Drac, Sp. 145 G19
Covilhã, Port. 144 F6
Covington, Ga., U.S. 96 L5
Covington, Ind., U.S. 99 R7
Covington, Ky., U.S. 101 A18
Covington, La., U.S. 100 P11
Covington, Okla., U.S. 102 F10
Covington, Tenn., U.S. 100 F12
Covington, Va., U.S. 96 E10
Cowal, Lake, Austral. 210 K13
Cowan, Cerro, Ecua. 128 P9
Cowan, Lake, Austral. 210 J4
Cow and Calf Islands, Myanmar 179 N15
Cow and Calves, islands, St. Vincent & the Grenadines 121 J17
Cowaramup, W. Aust., Austral. 211 Y2
Cowarie, S. Aust., Austral. 211 V10
Cowell, S. Aust., Austral. 211 X9
Coweta, Okla., U.S. 102 F13
Cowlitz, river, Wash., U.S. 108 D4
Coxim, river, Braz. 130 K11
Coxim, Braz. 130 K11
Cox's Bazar, Bangladesh 178 K14
Coyanosa Draw, Tex., U.S. 103 P3
Cozad, Nebr., U.S. 105 Q5
Cozumel, Mex. 115 H17
Cozumel, Isla, Mex. 115 H17
Cozumel Island see Cozumel, Isla, N. Amer. 80 N7
Crab Island, Mauritius 205 J20
Cradock, S. Af. 202 L10
Crafers, S. Aust., Austral. 211 Y10
Craig, Alas., U.S. 111 M23
Craig, Colo., U.S. 106 L11
Craiova, Rom. 153 F13
Cranberry Lake, N.Y., U.S. 94 G10
Cranbourne, Vic., Austral. 211 Z12
Cranbrook, B.C., Can. 82 M9
Crandon, Wis., U.S. 98 G6
Crane, Oreg., U.S. 108 J8
Crane, Tex., U.S. 103 N4
Crane Beach, Barbados 121 L20
Crane Lake, Minn., U.S. 104 E12
Craon, Fr. 147 R6
Crary Mountains, Antarctica 226 L8
Crasna, river, Rom. 152 B12
Crasna, Rom. 153 C17
Crater Lake, Oreg., U.S. 108 J4
Crater Lake National Park, Oreg., U.S. 108 J4
Craters of the Moon National Monument, Idaho, U.S. 106 H6
Crateús, Braz. 131 E16
Crato, Braz. 131 F16
Crawford, Nebr., U.S. 104 M1
Crawford, Tex., U.S. 103 N11
Crawfordsville, Ind., U.S. 99 R8
Crawfordville, Fla., U.S. 97 R5

Crazy Mountains, Mont., U.S. 106 E9
Creagorry, Scot., U.K. 142 J6
Crécy, Fr. 147 N11
Cree, river, Sask., Can. 82 K12
Creede, Colo., U.S. 107 P11
Creek Point, Bahamas 120 B10
Cree Lake, Sask., Can. 82 K12
Creeslough, Ire. 143 P5
Creighton, Nebr., U.S. 105 N7
Creil, Fr. 147 N10
Crema, It. 150 E5
Cremona, It. 150 E5
Cres, island, Croatia 152 E4
Cresbard, S. Dak., U.S. 104 J6
Crescent, Okla., U.S. 102 F10
Crescent City, Calif., U.S. 108 L1
Crescent City, Fla., U.S. 97 S8
Crescent Group, China 188 B10
Crescent Junction, Utah, U.S. 107 N9
Crescent Lake, Fla., U.S. 97 S8
Crescent Lake, Oreg., U.S. 108 J4
Cresco, Iowa, U.S. 104 M13
Crest, Fr. 147 V13
Creston, Iowa, U.S. 105 Q10
Crestview, Fla., U.S. 97 Q2
Creswell, Oreg., U.S. 108 H3
Crete see Kríti, island, Gr. 155 Q14
Crete, Nebr., U.S. 105 Q8
Crete, Sea of, Gr. 155 P13
Creus, Cap de, Sp. 145 C18
Crevasse Valley Glacier, Antarctica 226 N9
Crevillente, Sp. 145 K14
Crewe, Va., U.S. 96 F12
Crewkerne, Eng., U.K. 143 W11
Crianlarich, Scot., U.K. 142 L9
Criciúma, Braz. 130 P12
Criel-sur-Mer, Fr. 146 M9
Crimea, region, Ukr. 157 S7
Crimean Mountains see Krims'ke Hory, Ukr. 138 H11
Crinan Canal, Scot., U.K. 142 M8
Cripple Creek, Colo., U.S. 107 N13
Crisfield, Md., U.S. 96 E14
Cristalina, Braz. 131 J13
Cristóbal, Punta, Ecua. 128 Q8
Crişul Alb, river, Rom. 152 D12
Crişul Negra, river, Rom. 152 C11
Crişul Repede, river, Rom. 152 C12
Crna, river, Maced. 152 L11
Croatia, Eur. 139 V7
Crocker, Cerro, Ecua. 128 Q9
Crocker Range, Malaysia 188 G11
Crockett, Tex., U.S. 103 N13
Crocus Bay, Anguilla, U.K. 120 R11
Crocus Hill, Anguilla, U.K. 120 R11
Crofton, Nebr., U.S. 104 M7
Croisette, Cap, Fr. 147 Y13
Croisic, Pointe du, Fr. 147 R4
Croix des Bouquets, Haiti 117 M17
Croker Island, Austral. 210 A8
Cromarty Firth, Scot., U.K. 142 J9
Crompton Point, Dominica 121 E19
Crook, Colo., U.S. 106 K15
Crook, Eng., U.K. 143 P12
Crooked, river, Oreg., U.S. 108 H6
Crooked Island, Bahamas 117 G15
Crooked Island Passage, Bahamas 117 G14
Crook Point, Oreg., U.S. 108 K1
Crookston, Minn., U.S. 104 F8
Crosby, Minn., U.S. 104 H11
Crosby, N. Dak., U.S. 104 D2
Crosbyton, Tex., U.S. 102 K6
Cross City, Fla., U.S. 97 R6
Crossett, Ark., U.S. 100 K9
Crossing Rocks, Bahamas 120 C6
Cross Keys, Jam. 120 J8
Cross Plains, Tex., U.S. 102 M8
Cross Sound, Alas., U.S. 111 K21
Crossville, Tenn., U.S. 101 E17
Croswell, Mich., U.S. 98 L13
Crotone, It. 151 Q14
Crow Agency, Mont., U.S. 106 E11
Crowell, Tex., U.S. 102 J8
Crowley, La., U.S. 100 P8
Crown Haven, Bahamas 120 A5
Crown Mountain, Virgin Islands, U.S. 120 M8
Crownpoint, N. Mex., U.S. 107 R10
Crown Prince Christian Land, N. Amer. 80 A8
Croydon, Qnsld., Austral. 211 R12
Crozer, Mount, F.S.M. 217 B18
Crozet Basin, Ind. Oc. 240 N7
Crozet Islands, Ind. Oc. 204 K8
Crozet Plateau, Ind. Oc. 240 Q5
Cruces, Cuba 116 H8
Crump Island, Antigua & Barbuda 121 B21
Crump Lake, Oreg., U.S. 108 K6
Cruz, Cabo, Cuba 116 L11
Cruz Alta, Braz. 130 P11
Cruz Bay, Virgin Islands, U.S. 120 N10
Cruz del Eje, Arg. 132 J10
Cruz del Padre, Cayo, Cuba 116 G8
Cruzeiro, Ponta, Sao Tome and Principe 205 C20
Cruzeiro do Sul, Braz. 130 F4
Cruz Grande, Chile 132 H6
Crysochou Bay, Cyprus 160 P5
Crystal Caves, Bermuda, U.K. 120 B3
Crystal City, Mo., U.S. 105 T15
Crystal City, Tex., U.S. 103 S8
Crystal Falls, Mich., U.S. 98 G6
Crystal Lake, Ill., U.S. 98 M6
Crystal Mountains, Af. 194 K6
Crystal River, Fla., U.S. 97 S7
Crystal Springs, Miss., U.S. 100 M11
Csongrád, Hung. 149 M16
Csorna, Hung. 149 L13
Ctesiphon, ruin, Iraq 172 E10
Cuamba, Mozambique 203 E13
Cuando, river, Angola 202 E8
Cuangar, Angola 202 F7
Cuango, river, Angola 202 C7
Cuanza, river, Angola 202 C6
Cuauhtémoc, Mex. 114 D8
Cuba, Mo., U.S. 105 T14
Cuba, N. Amer. 81 N21
Cuba, island, N. Amer. 80 N9
Cubagua, Isla, Venez. 119 P14
Cubal, Angola 202 D6
Cubango, river, Angola 202 F7
Çubuk, Turk. 168 E8
Cuchara, Punta, P.R., U.S. 120 P3
Cuchilla de Haedo, range, Uru. 132 K13
Cuchilla Grande, range, Uru. 132 L14
Cuckold Point, Barbados 121 J19
Cucuí, Braz. 130 C7
Cúcuta, Col. 128 D6
Cudahy, Wis., U.S. 98 L7
Cuddalore, India 179 Q7
Cuddapah, India 179 P6
Cudjoehead, Montserrat, U.K. 121 B23
Cuéllar, Sp. 144 E10
Cuenca, Ecua. 128 K3
Cuenca, Sp. 144 G12
Cuenca, Serranía de, Sp. 144 F12
Cuencamé, Mex. 114 F10
Cuernavaca, Mex. 114 J11
Cuero, Tex., U.S. 103 S11
Cuevas de Altamira, Sp. 144 B10
Cuevas del Almanzora, Sp. 145 L13
Cuevo, Bol. 130 L8
Cugir, Rom. 153 D13
Cuglieri, It. 151 N3
Cuiabá, Braz. 130 J10
Cuito, river, Angola 202 F7
Cuito Cuanavale, Angola 202 E7
Çukurca, Turk. 169 H18
Cu Lao Re, island, Vietnam 186 L14
Cu Lao Thu, island, Vietnam 187 P14
Culberts Bay, Bahamas 120 B12
Culbertson, Mont., U.S. 106 B13
Culbertson, Nebr., U.S. 105 R4
Cul de Sac, river, St. Lucia 121 K14
Cul de Sac, Neth. Antilles, Neth. 121 B14
Cul de Sac, St. Martin, Fr. 121 A15
Cul-de-Sac du Marin, bay, Martinique, Fr. 121 G23
Culebra, island, P.R., U.S. 120 M7
Culebra, Sierra de la, Sp. 144 D8
Culfa, Azerb. 169 F19
Culiacán, Mex. 114 F8
Culion, island, Philippines 189 D13
Cúllar-Baza, Sp. 144 L12
Cullman, Ala., U.S. 101 H15
Culpataro, N.S.W., Austral. 211 X12
Culpeper, Va., U.S. 96 D12
Culpepper see Darwin, Isla, island, Ecua. 128 M7
Culuene, river, Braz. 130 H11
Culver, Point, Austral. 210 K5
Culverden, N.Z. 213 N17
Cumalı, Turk. 168 H3
Cumaná, Venez. 128 B11
Cumana Bay, Trinidad & Tobago 121 N23
Cumana Redhead, Trinidad & Tobago 121 N23
Cumanayagua, Cuba 116 H8
Cumberland, Ky., U.S. 101 D19
Cumberland, river, Ky., Tenn., U.S. 85 J16
Cumberland, Md., U.S. 96 C11
Cumberland, Wis., U.S. 98 G2
Cumberland, Cape, Vanuatu 218 C1
Cumberland, Lake, Ky., U.S. 101 D17
Cumberland Bay, St. Vincent & the Grenadines 121 K16
Cumberland Gap National Historic Park, Ky., Va., Tenn., U.S. 101 D19
Cumberland Island National Seashore, Ga., U.S. 97 Q8
Cumberland Islands, Austral. 210 E14
Cumberland Peninsula, Nunavut, Can. 83 F19
Cumberland Plateau, Ala., Ky., Tenn., U.S. 85 J17
Cumberland Sound, Nunavut, Can. 83 G19
Cumbernauld, Scot., U.K. 142 M9
Cumborah, N.S.W., Austral. 211 W13
Cumbrera, Cerro, Chile 133 U7
Cumbres Pass, Colo., U.S. 107 Q12
Cumbrian Mountains, Eng., U.K. 143 Q10
Cuminá, Braz. 130 D10
Cumina see Paru de Oeste, river, Braz. 130 C11
Cúmpas, Mex. 114 C7
Çumra, Turk. 168 H8
Cuna, Venez. 128 D9
Cunco, Chile 133 P6
Cunene see Kunene, river, Angola 202 F5
Cuneo, It. 150 F2
Cunnamulla, Qnsld., Austral. 211 V13
Cunningham, Lake, Bahamas 120 B11
Cunyu, W. Aust., Austral. 211 U3
Cupica, Col. 128 E3
Cupica, Golfo de, Col. 128 E3
Curaçao, island, Neth. Antilles, Neth. 119 M9
Curanilahue, Chile 133 N6
Curbur, W. Aust., Austral. 211 V2
Curcubăta, peak, Rom. 152 C12
Curecanti National Recreation Area, Colo., U.S. 107 N11
Curepipe, Mauritius 205 G20
Curiapo, Venez. 129 C13
Curicó, Chile 132 L7
Curieuse, island, Seychelles 205 M20
Curitiba, Braz. 130 N13
Curium, ruin, Cyprus 160 Q7
Curley Cut Cays, Bahamas 116 F11
Curral Velho, Cape Verde 205 C17
Curraun Peninsula, Ire. 143 R3
Current, Bahamas 120 D5
Current, river, Mo., U.S. 105 V14
Current Island, Bahamas 120 D5
Currie, Tas., Austral. 211 Y15
Currituck, N.C., U.S. 96 G14
Currituck Sound, N.C., U.S. 96 G15
Curtea de Argeş, Rom. 153 E14
Curtici, Rom. 152 D11
Curtin Springs, N. Terr., Austral. 211 U8
Curtis, Nebr., U.S. 105 Q4
Curtis Island, Kermadec Is., N.Z. 214 L9
Curuá, river, Braz. 130 F11
Curuaés, river, Braz. 130 F11
Curuçá, river, Braz. 130 E5
Curuçá, Braz. 131 C13
Cururupu, Braz. 131 D14
Curuzú Cuatiá, Arg. 132 H13
Curvelo, Braz. 131 K14
Cusco, Peru 130 H5
Cushing, Okla., U.S. 102 F11
Cusset, Fr. 147 T11
Cusson, Pointe, Que., Can. 83 J17
Custer, Mont., U.S. 106 E11
Custer, S. Dak., U.S. 104 L1
Cut, island, Indonesia 189 L18
Cut Bank, Mont., U.S. 106 B7
Cuthbert, Ga., U.S. 97 P4
Cutler Ridge, Fla., U.S. 97 X10
Cutral Có, Arg. 133 P8
Cuttack, India 178 K10
Cuvier, Cape, Austral. 210 G1
Cuvier Plateau, Ind. Oc. 241 L14
Cuxhaven, Ger. 148 B7
Cuya, Chile 132 B7
Cuyahoga Falls, Ohio, U.S. 99 P15
Cuyahoga National Park, Ohio, U.S. 99 P14
Cuyama, river, Calif., U.S. 109 W7
Cuyo Islands, Philippines 189 E13
Cuyuni, river, Guyana 129 D13
Cyclades see Kikládes, Gr. 155 L14
Cydonia see Haniá, Gr. 155 Q13
Cynthiana, Ky., U.S. 101 B18
Cyprus, Eur. 160 E6
Cyrenaica, region, Lib. 197 C16
Cyrene see Shaḩḩāt, Lib. 197 B16
Cyrus Field Bay, Nunavut, Can. 83 H19
Cythera see Kíthira, island, Gr. 154 N11
Czaplinek, Pol. 148 C12
Czech Republic, Eur. 139 U7
Częstochowa, Pol. 149 G15
Człopa, Pol. 148 D12

D

Da (Black), river, Vietnam 186 H11
Da'an, China 181 D16
Ḑab'ah, Jordan 171 N7
Dabakala, Côte d'Ivoire 200 G9
Daba Shan, China 182 J2
Dabie Shan, China 182 K6
Dabola, Guinea 200 F6
Dabqig see Uxin Qi, China 182 E2
Dąbrowa Górnicza, Pol. 149 G15
Dąbrowa Tarnowska, Pol. 149 G16
Dachau, Ger. 148 K8
Dac To, Vietnam 186 M13
Dadale, Solomon Is. 217 M18
Daday, Turk. 168 C9
Dade City, Fla., U.S. 97 T8
Dadeville, Ala., U.S. 101 K16
Dadhar, Pak. 177 S6
Dadu, river, China 180 L11
Dadu, Pak. 177 U6
Daegu, S. Korea 182 G14
Daejeon (Taejŏn), S. Korea 182 F13
Daejeong, S. Korea 182 J13
Dafeng (Dazhongji), China 182 J9
Dafní, Gr. 154 J9
Dafoe, Sask., Can. 82 M12
Dagana, Senegal 196 G5
Dagcanglhamo, China 180 K11
Dagelet see Ulleungdo, island, S. Korea 182 E15
Dagerşi, Köpetdag, Iran 173 B16
Dagö see Hiiumaa, island, Est. 141 L15
Dagupan, Philippines 189 C13
Dahab, Egypt 171 T4
Dahanu, India 178 K3
Da Hinggan Ling, China 181 E15
Dahla, Afghan. 177 Q5
Dahlak Archipelago, Eritrea 194 G10
Dahlonega, Ga., U.S. 96 K5
Dahod, India 178 J4
Dahongliutan, China 176 K15
Dai (Ndai), island, Solomon Is. 217 M19
Daigo, Japan 185 N13
Dailekh, Nepal 178 F8
Daimiel, Sp. 144 H11
Daingerfield, Tex., U.S. 102 K14
Daiō, Japan 185 Q10
Dair, Jebel ed, Sudan 194 G9
Dairen see Dalian, China 182 E10
Dairy Creek, W. Aust., Austral. 211 U2
Dai Senga Dake, Japan 184 H12
Daisetta, Tex., U.S. 103 Q15
Daitō, Japan 184 L13
Daitō Islands, Japan 184 L3
Daixian, China 182 D5
Dajabón, Dom. Rep. 117 L17
Dajarra, Qnsld., Austral. 211 S11
Dajt, Mal, Albania 152 L9
Dakar, Senegal 196 H4
Dakhla Oasis, Egypt 197 E18
Dakoank, India 179 T15
Dakoro, Niger 196 H11
Dakota City, Nebr., U.S. 105 N8
Đakovica, Serb. & Mont. 152 J10
Đakovo, Croatia 152 E8
Dákura, Nicar. 115 L19
Dala, Solomon Is. 217 M19
Dalai Nur, China 182 A7
Dalaman, river, Turk. 168 H4
Dalanzadgad, Mongolia 180 F12
Dalap, island, Marshall Is. 216 H12
Da Lat, Vietnam 187 N14
Dalbandin, Pak. 177 S4
Dalbeg, Qnsld., Austral. 211 S14
Dalby, Qnsld., Austral. 211 V15
Dale, Nor. 140 K10
Dale Country, Eng., U.K. 143 R12
Daleville, Ala., U.S. 101 N16
Dalgonally, Qnsld., Austral. 211 S11
Dalhart, Tex., U.S. 102 F4
Dali, China 182 G3
Dali, China 180 N10
Dali, Cyprus 160 P8
Dalian (Dairen), China 182 E10
Dalidag, peak, Azerb. 169 E20
Dalkhaki, Afghan. 176 L7
Dallas, Oreg., U.S. 108 G3
Dallas, Tex., U.S. 102 L12
Dall Island, Alas., U.S. 84 R7
Dalmatia, region, Croatia 152 G6
Dalmellington, Scot., U.K. 143 N9
Dal'negorsk, Russ. 159 L21
Dal'nerechensk, Russ. 159 L21
Daloa, Côte d'Ivoire 200 G8
Daltenganj, India 178 H9
Dalton, Ga., U.S. 96 J4
Dalton, Nebr., U.S. 105 P2
Dalton Highway, Alas., U.S. 111 C17
Dalupiri, island, Philippines 189 A13
Dalwhinnie, Scot., U.K. 142 K9
Daly, river, N. Terr., Austral. 211 P7
Daly Bay, Nunavut, Can. 83 H15
Daly Waters, N. Terr., Austral. 211 Q8
Daman (Damão), India 178 K3
Damanhûr, Egypt 197 C18
Damão see Daman, India 178 K3
Damar, island, Indonesia 189 J16
Damar, island, Indonesia 189 M16
Damas Cays, Bahamas 116 F9
Damascus see Dimashq, Syr. 170 J7
Damāvand, Qolleh-ye, Iran 173 C13
Damboa, Nigeria 201 E16
Dambulla, Sri Lanka 179 S7
Dame-Marie, Haiti 117 M14
Dam Ha, Vietnam 186 H13
Damietta see Dumyât, Egypt 197 C18
Daming, China 182 F6
Damīr Qābū, Syr. 170 C15
Damoh, India 178 H7
Damongo, Ghana 200 F10
Dampier, Selat, Indonesia 189 J17
Dampier Archipelago, Austral. 210 E2
Dampier Downs, W. Aust., Austral. 211 R4
Dampier Land, Austral. 210 D4
Damqawt, Yemen 173 P14
Damroh, India 178 F15
Damxung, China 180 L8
Dan, river, N.C., U.S. 96 G10
Danakil Desert, Eth. 199 E15
Da Nang, Vietnam 186 L13
Dana Point, Calif., U.S. 109 Y9
Danbury, Conn., U.S. 94 M12
Danby Lake, Calif., U.S. 109 X12
Dancheng, China 182 H6
Dancheng see Xiangshan, China 182 M10
Danco Coast, Antarctica 226 D4
Dandan, Puntan, N. Mariana Is., U.S. 216 C5
Dandong, China 182 D11
Daneborg, Greenland, Den. 81 A21
Danfeng, China 182 H3
Danforth, Me., U.S. 95 D18
Dang, river, China 180 G9
Dangara, Taj. 176 J8
Danger Islands see Pukapuka Atoll, Cook Is., N.Z. 214 J11
Dangrek Range, Thai. 186 M11
Dangriga, Belize 115 K17
Dangshan, China 182 H6
Dangtu, China 182 K8
Daniel, Wyo., U.S. 106 H9
Danilov, Russ. 156 G10
Daning, China 182 F3
Danjiangkou, China 182 J3
Danjo Guntō, Japan 185 S2
Ḑank, Oman 173 K15
Dankhar Gömpa, India 177 P15
Dankov, Russ. 156 L10
Danmark Havn, Greenland, Den. 81 A21
Dannemora, N.Y., U.S. 94 F11
Dansville, N.Y., U.S. 94 K6
Danube see Donau, Duna, Dunaj, Dunărea, Dunav, Dunay, river, Eur. 138 H9
Danube, Mouths of the, Rom. 153 E19
Danube, Source of the, Ger. 138 G6
Danube River Delta, Rom. 138 H10
Danville, Ill., U.S. 99 R7
Danville, Ky., U.S. 101 C17
Danville, Va., U.S. 96 G10

Danxian (Nada), China 183 U1
Dao, Mui, Vietnam 186 K12
Daos du Sud, Îles, New Caledonia, Fr. 218 B6
Daoxian, China 183 P3
Daphne, Ala., U.S. 101 P14
Da Qaidam, China 180 H9
Daqing, China 181 D17
Dāqūq, Iraq 172 C9
Dar'ā (Edrei), Syr. 170 L7
Dārāb, Iran 173 G14
Daraban, Pak. 177 Q9
Darabani, Rom. 153 A15
Darakht-e Yahya, Afghan. 177 Q7
Daravica, peak, Serb. & Mont. 152 J10
Ḑarbat 'Alī, Ra's, Oman 173 P14
Darbhanga, India 178 G10
Darby, Mont., U.S. 106 E5
Darby Island, Bahamas 120 D7
Dardanelle, Ark., U.S. 100 G7
Dardanelle, Lake, Ark., U.S. 100 F7
Dardanelles see Çanakkale Boğazi, strait, Turk. 168 D2
Darende, Turk. 168 G12
Dar es Salaam, Tanzania 199 M15
Darfur, region, Sudan 198 E10
Dargai, Pak. 176 M10
Darganata, Turkm. 174 K10
Dargaville, N.Z. 213 H18
Dargeçit, Turk. 169 H16
Dargun, Ger. 148 B10
Darhan, Mongolia 180 C12
Darien, Ga., U.S. 97 P8
Daringali, Solomon Is. 217 M19
Darjiling, India 178 G11
Dark Head, St. Vincent & the Grenadines 121 K16
Darling, river, N.S.W., Austral. 211 X12
Darling, Lake, N. Dak., U.S. 104 E4
Darling, Source of the, Austral. 210 H15
Darling Downs, Austral. 210 H14
Darling Range, Austral. 210 K3
Darlington, Eng., U.K. 143 Q12
Darlington, S.C., U.S. 96 K10
Darliston, Jam. 120 H6
Darlot, Lake, Austral. 210 H4
Darłowo, Pol. 148 B12
Darmstadt, Ger. 148 H6
Darnah, Lib. 197 B16
Darney, Fr. 147 Q14
Darnley, Cape, Antarctica 227 F20
Daroca, Sp. 145 E13
Daroot-Korgon, Kyrg. 176 H10
Darregueira, Arg. 133 N10
Darreh Gaz, Iran 173 B16
Darreh-ye Awd, Afghan. 176 M5
Darreh-ye Bum, Afghan. 176 M3
Darrington, Wash., U.S. 108 B5
Dar Rounga, region, Cen. Af. Rep. 194 H7
Darrouzett, Tex., U.S. 102 E7
Darsser Ort, island, Ger. 148 B10
Dartmoor, plateau, Eng., U.K. 143 X9
Dartmouth, N.S., Can. 83 P22
Daru, P.N.G. 213 E18
Darwaji-e Bala, Afghan. 177 N2
Darwha, India 178 K6
Darwin, Falkland Is., U.K. 133 W12
Darwin, N. Terr., Austral. 211 P7
Darwin, Bahía de, Ecua. 128 P10
Darwin, Isla (Culpepper), Ecua. 128 M7
Darwin, Volcán, Ecua. 128 P8
Darwin Glacier, Antarctica 227 M14
Darya Khan, Pak. 177 Q9
Das, Pak. 178 B5
Dasburg, Ger. 148 G4
Dashitou, China 182 A13
Dashkäsän, Azerb. 169 D20
Dashkuduk, Turkm. 174 K6
Dasht, river, Pak. 177 V2
Daska, Pak. 177 P12
Daşköpri, Turkm. 174 N10
Daşoguz, Turkm. 174 J9
Datça, Turk. 168 H3
Datia, India 178 G6
Datian, China 183 Q7
Datong, river, China 180 H10
Datong, China 182 C5
Datu Piang, Philippines 189 F15
Da Ty, Hon, Vietnam 187 Q14
Daud Khel, Pak. 177 P9
Daudnagar, India 178 H9
Daugava, river, Latv. 141 M17
Daugavpils, Latv. 141 M17
Daun, Ger. 160 G12
Dauphin, Man., Can. 83 N13
Dauphin Island, Ala., U.S. 101 P13
Daurada, Costa, Sp. 145 F16
Däväçi, Azerb. 169 C22
Davangere, India 179 P5
Davao, Philippines 189 F15
Davao Gulf, Philippines 189 F15
Davenport, Iowa, U.S. 105 P14
Davenport, Wash., U.S. 108 C8
Davenport Downs, Qnsld., Austral. 211 T11
Davenport Range, Austral. 210 E9
Daventry, Eng., U.K. 143 U13
David, Pan. 115 P20
David Bay, Grenada 121 J23
David City, Nebr., U.S. 105 P8
David Point, Virgin Islands, U.S. 120 N8
Davidson Mountains, Alas., U.S. 111 D18
Davis, station, Antarctica 227 G20
Davis, Calif., U.S. 109 R4
Davis, Okla., U.S. 102 H11
Davis, Mount, Pa., U.S. 94 Q4
Davis Beach, Virgin Islands, U.S. 120 Q2
Davis Dam, Ariz., Nev., U.S. 109 V12
Davis Inlet, Nfld. & Lab., Can. 83 K21
Davis Mountains, Tex., U.S. 103 P2
Davis Sea, Antarctica 227 J21
Davis Strait, Arctic Oc. 243 R16
Davlos, Cyprus 160 N10
Davos, Switz. 150 B5
Davyhurst, W. Aust., Austral. 211 W4
Dawa, river, Eth., Kenya 194 J11
Dawāsir, Wādī ad, Saudi Arabia 172 M9
Dawei, Myanmar 186 M7
Dawkah, Oman 173 N14
Dawmat al Jandal (Al Jawf), Saudi Arabia 172 F7
Dawna Range, Myanmar, Thai. 186 L7
Dawqah, Saudi Arabia 172 M7
Dawra, W. Sahara, Mor. 196 D6
Dawros Head, Ire. 143 P4
Dawson, river, Austral. 210 G14
Dawson, Ga., U.S. 97 P5
Dawson, Minn., U.S. 104 K9
Dawson, N. Dak., U.S. 104 G5
Dawson, Tex., U.S. 102 M12
Dawson, Yukon, Can. 82 E8
Dawson, Isla, Chile 133 X8
Dawson Creek, B.C., Can. 82 K9
Dawson Springs, Ky., U.S. 101 D14
Dawu, China 182 K5
Dawwah, Oman 173 L17
Dax, Fr. 147 X6
Daxing, China 182 D7
Daxinggou, China 182 A14
Daxue Mountains, China 166 H10
Daydawn, W. Aust., Austral. 211 V3
Dayong, China 182 M2
Dayr az Zawr, Syr. 170 F13
Dayr Sim'ān, Syr. 170 D8
Dayton, Ohio, U.S. 99 R11
Dayton, Tenn., U.S. 101 F17
Dayton, Tex., U.S. 103 Q14
Dayton, Wash., U.S. 108 E8
Daytona Beach, Fla., U.S. 97 S9
Dayu, China 183 Q5
Da Yunhe (Grand Canal), China 182 J8
Dayushan, island, China 183 S4
Dayville, Oreg., U.S. 108 G7
Dazhongji see Dafeng, China 182 J9
Dazkırı, Turk. 168 G5
De Aar, S. Af. 202 L9
Deadhorse, Alas., U.S. 111 C17
Deadmans Cay, Bahamas 117 G14
Deadman's Cays, Bahamas 116 F8
Dead Sea, Israel, Jordan, W. Bank 171 N6
Deadwood, S. Dak., U.S. 104 K1
Deakin, W. Aust., Austral. 211 W7
Deal, Eng., U.K. 143 V16
De'an, China 182 M6
Deán Funes, Arg. 132 J10
Dean Passage, Solomon Is. 217 R23
Dearborn, Mich., U.S. 98 M12
Dease Inlet, Alas., U.S. 111 B15
Dease Lake, B.C., Can. 82 H8
Dease Strait, Nunavut, Can. 83 F13
Death Valley, Calif., U.S. 109 U10
Death Valley, Calif., U.S. 109 T9
Death Valley National Park, Calif., U.S. 109 T9
Debar, Maced. 152 K10
Débé, Trinidad & Tobago 121 Q22
Dębica, Pol. 149 G16
Debin, Russ. 159 F20
Debir, ruin, Israel 171 N5
Dębno, Pol. 148 D11
Débo, Lake, Niger 194 G3
Debrecen, Hung. 149 L17
Debre Mark'os, Eth. 199 F14
Debuu, island, Marshall Is. 216 K4
Decatur, Ala., U.S. 101 H15
Decatur, Ga., U.S. 96 L5
Decatur, Ill., U.S. 99 R6
Decatur, Ind., U.S. 99 Q10
Decatur, Nebr., U.S. 105 N9
Decatur, Tex., U.S. 102 K11
Decazeville, Fr. 147 W10
Deccan, plateau, India 179 P5
Deception Island, Antarctica 226 C3
Dechu, India 178 G3
Decimomannu, It. 151 P4
Děčín, Czech Rep. 148 G11
Decize, Fr. 147 S11
Decorah, Iowa, U.S. 104 M13
Dedéagach see Alexandroúpoli, Gr. 155 C16
Dededo, Guam, U.S. 216 B11
Dedegöl Dağı, Turk. 168 H6
Dédougou, Burkina Faso 200 E9
Dedovichi, Russ. 156 H6
Deep, river, N. Dak., U.S. 104 E4
Deep Creek, Bahamas 120 F6
Deep Creek Lake, Md., U.S. 96 C10
Deep Creek Range, Utah, U.S. 106 L5
Deep Well, N. Terr., Austral. 211 U9
Deering, Alas., U.S. 111 E13
Deer Isle, Me., U.S. 95 G17
Deer Lodge, Mont., U.S. 106 D7
Deer Park, Wash., U.S. 108 B9
Deer River, Minn., U.S. 104 F11
Deerton, Mich., U.S. 98 F8
Deer Trail, Colo., U.S. 106 M14
Deeth, Nev., U.S. 108 M11
Defiance, Ohio, U.S. 99 P11
De Funiak Springs, Fla., U.S. 97 Q3
Deganya, Israel 170 L6
Dêgê, China 180 K10
Degeh Bur, Eth. 199 G16
Deggendorf, Ger. 148 J10
DeGrey, W. Aust., Austral. 211 S3
DeGrey, river, W. Aust., Austral. 211 S3
Deh Bīd, Iran 173 F14
Deh Khavak, Afghan. 176 L8
Dehqonobod, Uzb. 174 M12
Dehra Dun, India 178 E6
Deh Rawod, Afghan. 177 P5
Deh Shu, Afghan. 177 R3
Dehui, China 181 D17
Deim Zubeir, Sudan 198 G11
Deinkog, China 180 K9
Dej, Rom. 153 C13
Dejen, Ras, Eth. 199 E15
Dejiang, China 182 M1
De Jongs, Tanjung, Indonesia 213 D16
De Kalb, Miss., U.S. 101 K13
De Kalb, Tex., U.S. 102 K14
DeKalb, Ill., U.S. 99 N6
Dekese, Dem. Rep. of the Congo 198 L9
Dekle Beach, Fla., U.S. 97 R6
Delaford, Trinidad & Tobago 121 N18
Delamere, N. Terr., Austral. 211 Q8
De Land, Fla., U.S. 97 S9
Delano, Calif., U.S. 109 V7
Delano Peak, Utah, U.S. 107 N6
Delaport Point, Bahamas 120 B11
Delaram, Afghan. 177 P3
Delarof Islands, Alas., U.S. 110 N4
Delavan, Wis., U.S. 98 M6
Delaware, Ohio, U.S. 99 Q13
Delaware, river, U.S. 94 L9
Delaware, U.S. 96 C14
Delaware Bay, Del., N.J., U.S. 85 G20
Delaware Water Gap National Recreation Area, N.J., Pa., U.S. 94 M10
Delémont, Switz. 150 A2
De Leon, Tex., U.S. 102 M9
Delfzijl, Neth. 146 G14
Delgado, Cabo, Mozambique 203 D15
Delgany, Ire. 143 S7
Delgo, Sudan 198 C12
Delhi, India 178 F6
Delhi, La., U.S. 100 L9
Delhi, N.Y., U.S. 94 K10
Delice, river, Turk. 168 E9
Delicias, Mex. 114 D9
Deliktaş, Turk. 168 F12
Déline, N.W.T., Can. 82 F10
Delingha, China 180 H9
Delissaville, N. Terr., Austral. 211 P7
Delitzsch, Ger. 148 F9
Dell Rapids, S. Dak., U.S. 104 L8
Delmar, Del., Md., U.S. 96 D15
Delmenhorst, Ger. 148 C7
Del Norte, Colo., U.S. 107 P12
De Long Mountains, Alas., U.S. 111 D13
Deloraine, Tas., Austral. 211 Z16
Delos, ruin, Gr. 155 K15
Delphi, ruin, Gr. 154 H10
Delphi, Ind., U.S. 99 Q8
Delphos, Ohio, U.S. 99 Q11
Delray Beach, Fla., U.S. 97 W10
Del Rio, Tex., U.S. 103 R6
Delta, Colo., U.S. 107 N10
Delta, Utah, U.S. 106 M6
Delta Downs, Qnsld., Austral. 211 R11
Delta Junction, Alas., U.S. 111 G18
Deltona, Fla., U.S. 97 S9
Del Verme Falls, Eth. 199 H15
Demagiri, India 178 J14
Demanda, Sierra de la, Sp. 144 D11
Demarcation Point, Alas., U.S. 84 M5
Demba, Dem. Rep. of the Congo 198 L10
Dembéni, Comoros 205 M14
Dembī Doba, Eth. 199 G13
Demchok, India 177 N16
Demerara Plain, Atl. Oc. 236 M7
Deming, N. Mex., U.S. 107 V11
Demini, river, Braz. 130 C8
Demirci, Turk. 168 F4
Demirköprü Baraji, Turk. 168 F4
Demirköy, Turk. 168 B4
Demirtaş, Turk. 168 J7
Democratic Republic of the Congo, Af. 195 K20
Demopolis, Ala., U.S. 101 L14
Dempster Highway, Yukon, Can. 82 E9
Demta, Indonesia 213 B17
Demyansk, Russ. 156 H7
Denali see McKinley, Mount, peak, Alas., U.S. 111 H16
Denali Highway, Alas., U.S. 111 H17
Denali National Park and Preserve, Alas., U.S. 111 H16
Denali Park, Alas., U.S. 111 G17
Den Burg, Neth. 146 G12
Denekamp, Neth. 146 H14
Denges Passage, Palau 216 Q11
Dengkou (Bayan Gol), China 182 C1
Dêngqên, China 180 L9
Dengzhou, China 182 J4
Denham, W. Aust., Austral. 211 V1
Denham Springs, La., U.S. 100 P10
Den Helder, Neth. 146 H12
Denia, Sp. 145 J15
Denigomodu, region, Nauru 217 E22
Deniliquin, N.S.W., Austral. 211 Y12
Denio, Nev., U.S. 108 L8
Denis, Île, Seychelles 205 L20
Denison, Iowa, U.S. 105 N9
Denison, Tex., U.S. 102 J12
Denisovskaya, Russ. 156 E11
Denizli, Turk. 168 G4
Denmark, Eur. 139 S6
Denmark, S.C., U.S. 96 L9
Denmark, W. Aust., Austral. 211 Y3
Denmark Strait, Arctic Oc. 243 L19
Dennery, St. Lucia 121 K14
Denow, Uzb. 174 M12
Denpasar, Indonesia 188 M11
Denton, Md., U.S. 96 C14
Denton, Tex., U.S. 102 K11
D'Entrecasteaux, Point, Austral. 210 L3
D'Entrecasteaux Islands, P.N.G. 213 E21
Denver, Colo., U.S. 106 M13
Denver City, Tex., U.S. 102 L4
Deobhog, India 178 L8
Deoghar, India 178 H11
Deo Mu Gia, pass, Laos, Vietnam 186 K12
Deora, India 178 G2
Deoria, India 178 G9
Deosai Mountains, Pak. 176 L12
Deosri, India 178 G13
De Pere, Wis., U.S. 98 J7
Depoe Bay, Oreg., U.S. 108 G2
Deposit, N.Y., U.S. 94 L9
Depósito, Braz. 130 B9
Deputatskiy, Russ. 159 E18
Deqing, China 182 L9
Deqing, China 183 R3
De Queen, Ark., U.S. 100 H6
De Quincy, La., U.S. 100 P7
Dera Ghazi Khan, Pak. 177 R9
Dera Ismail Khan, Pak. 177 Q9
Dera Murad Jamali, Pak. 177 T7
Derbent, Russ. 157 U16
Derby, Eng., U.K. 143 T12
Derby, Kans., U.S. 105 U8
Derby, W. Aust., Austral. 211 R5
Derg, Lough, Ire. 143 P5
Derg, Lough, Ire. 143 S4
Dergachi, Russ. 156 M15
Dergaon, India 178 G14
Derhachi, Ukr. 157 N9
De Ridder, La., U.S. 100 N7
Derik, Turk. 169 H15
Dermott, Ark., U.S. 100 J9
Dernberg, Cape, Namibia 202 K6
Dernieres, Isles, La., U.S. 100 R10
Derravaragh, Lough, Ire. 143 R6
Derry see Londonderry, N. Ire., U.K. 143 P6
Derudeb, Sudan 199 D14
Dervaza, Turkm. 174 K8
Derventa, Bosn. & Herzg. 152 E7
Deryneia, Cyprus 160 P10
Derzhavīnsk, Kaz. 174 D12
Désappointement, Îles du, Fr. Polynesia, Fr. 219 D20
Des Arc, Ark., U.S. 100 G9
Deschutes, river, Oreg., U.S. 108 G5
Desē, Eth. 199 F15
Deseado, river, Arg. 133 T8
Desecheo, island, P.R., U.S. 117 M21
Deserta Grande, island, Madeira 204 N4
Desertas, Ilhas, Madeira 204 N4
Desert Center, Calif., U.S. 109 X12
Deshaies, Guadeloupe, Fr. 121 E14
Deshler, Nebr., U.S. 105 R7
Deskáti, Gr. 154 E9
Des Lacs, river, N. Dak., U.S. 104 E3
Desloge, Mo., U.S. 105 T15
De Smet, S. Dak., U.S. 104 K7
Des Moines, river, Iowa, U.S. 85 F13
Des Moines, Iowa, U.S. 105 P11
Des Moines, N. Mex., U.S. 107 Q14
Desna, river, Russ. 156 K7
Desnudez, Punta, Arg. 133 N12
Desolación, Isla, Chile 133 X6
De Soto, Mo., U.S. 105 T15
Des Plaines, Ill., U.S. 99 N7
Despotikó, island, Gr. 155 L14
Dessalines, Haiti 117 L16
Dessau, Ger. 148 E9
Destruction Island, Wash., U.S. 108 C2
Detmold, Ger. 148 E7
De Tour Village, Mich., U.S. 98 G11
Detroit, Mich., U.S. 98 M13
Detroit Lake, Oreg., U.S. 108 G4
Detroit Lakes, Minn., U.S. 104 G9
Detroit Seamount, Pac. Oc. 238 C8
Deva, Rom. 152 D12
Deveci Dağı, Turk. 168 E11
Develi, Turk. 168 G10
Devils, river, Tex., U.S. 103 Q6
Devilsbit Mountain, Ire. 143 T5
Devils Cataract see Raudal Yupurari, Col. 128 H7
Devils Hole, Atl. Oc. 236 E13
Devils Hole, Nev., U.S. 109 U10
Devil's Island see Diable, Île du, Fr. Guiana, Fr. 129 E18
Devils Lake, N. Dak., U.S. 104 F6
Devils Lake, N. Dak., U.S. 104 E6
Devils Paw, peak, Alas., U.S. 111 K22
Devil's Point, Bahamas 117 F13
Devil's Point, Vanuatu 218 F3
Devils Postpile National Monument, Calif., U.S. 109 S7
Devils Tower National Monument, Wyo., U.S. 106 F13
Devine, Tex., U.S. 103 S9
Devizes, Eng., U.K. 143 V12
Devon Island, Nunavut, Can. 83 D16
Devonport, Tas., Austral. 211 Z16
Devrek, Turk. 168 C7
Devrekâni, Turk. 168 C9
Devrukh, India 178 M3
Dewas, India 178 J5
Dewey, Okla., U.S. 102 E12
De Witt, Ark., U.S. 100 H9
De Witt, Iowa, U.S. 105 N14
Dexter, Me., U.S. 95 E17
Dexter, Mo., U.S. 105 V15
Dey Dey, Lake, Austral. 210 H7
Deyhūk, Iran 173 D15
Deynau, Turkm. 174 L10
Dezfūl, Iran 172 E11
Dezhou, China 182 F7
Dhaka, Bangladesh 178 H13
Dhamār, Yemen 172 Q9
Dhamtari, India 178 K8

Dhanbad, India 178 H10
D'Hanis, Tex., U.S. 103 R8
Dhanushkodi, India 179 S7
Dhar, India 178 J4
Dharan Bazar, Nepal 178 G11
Dharapuram, India 179 R6
Dharmjaygarh, India 178 J9
Dharmsala, India 177 P13
Dharwad, India 179 N4
Dhaulagiri, peak, Nepal 178 F9
Dhekelia (Eastern) Sovereign Base Area, Cyprus 160 P9
Dhenkanal, India 178 K10
Dhībān, Jordan 171 N6
Dhone, India 179 N6
Dhuburi, India 178 G12
Dhule, India 178 K4
Dhupgarh, peak, India 178 J6
Dhuusamarreeb, Somalia 199 H17
Día, island, Gr. 155 Q15
Diable, Morne au, Dominica 121 D18
Diable, Île du (Devil's Island), Fr. Guiana, Fr. 129 E18
Diablo Range, Calif., U.S. 109 S4
Diablotins, Morne, Dominica 121 E19
Diakoftó, Gr. 154 J10
Diamant, Rocher de (Diamond Rock), Martinique, Fr. 121 G22
Diamante, river, Arg. 132 L8
Diamante, Arg. 132 K12
Diamantina, river, Qnsld., Austral. 211 T11
Diamantina, Braz. 131 K15
Diamantina, Chapada, Braz. 131 H15
Diamantina Fracture Zone, Ind. Oc. 241 M13
Diamantina Lakes, Qnsld., Austral. 211 T11
Diamantino, Braz. 130 H10
Diamond Craters, Oreg., U.S. 108 J7
Diamond Harbour, India 178 J11
Diamond Head, Hawai'i, U.S. 112 E11
Diamond Mountains, Calif., U.S. 109 N6
Diamond Mountains, Nev., U.S. 109 P11
Diamond Peak, Oreg., U.S. 108 J4
Diamond Rock see Diamant, Rocher de, Martinique, Fr. 121 G22
Diamond Shoals, N.C., U.S. 96 H15
Dianbai, China 183 S2
Dian Chi, lake, China 180 N11
Dianópolis, Braz. 131 G14
Diaoyu Islands see Senkaku Shotō, China 183 P11
Diapaga, Burkina Faso 200 E12
Diavolo, Mount, India 179 Q14
Dībā al Ḩişn, U.A.E. 173 J15
Dibai, India 178 F6
Diboll, Tex., U.S. 103 N14
Dibrugarh, India 178 F15
Dibsī Faraj, Syr. 170 E10
Dickens, Tex., U.S. 102 K6
Dickinson, N. Dak., U.S. 104 G2
Dickinson Bay, Antigua & Barbuda 121 A20
Dickson, Russ. 159 E13
Dickson, Tenn., U.S. 101 E14
Dickson City, Pa., U.S. 94 M9
Dicle, Turk. 169 G14
Dicle (Tigris), river, Turk. 169 H16
Dicomano, It. 150 G7
Didimótiho, Gr. 155 B17
Didwana, India 178 F4
Die, Fr. 147 V13
Diego de Almagro, Chile 132 G7
Diego de Almagro, Isla, Chile 133 W6
Diego Ramírez, Islas, Chile 133 Y9
Diekirch, Lux. 160 H10
Diemal Find, W. Aust., Austral. 211 W3
Dien Bien, Vietnam 186 H10
Dien Chau, Vietnam 186 J12
Dieppe, Fr. 146 M8
Dieppe Bay Town, St. Kitts & Nevis 121 A17
Dierks, Ark., U.S. 100 H6
Dif, Kenya 199 J15
Diffa, Niger 197 J13
Differdange, Lux. 160 K9
Digboi, India 178 F15
Digby, N.S., Can. 83 P21
Dighton, Kans., U.S. 105 T4
Digne, Fr. 147 W14
Digoin, Fr. 147 T12
Digor, Turk. 169 D17
Digos, Philippines 189 F15
Digri, Pak. 177 W8
Digul, river, Indonesia 189 M21
Digura, island, Maldives 179 V3
Dihōk, Iraq 172 B9
Dijlah (Tigris), river, Iraq 172 E11
Dijon, Fr. 147 R13
Dika, Mys, Russ. 159 D15
Dikili, Turk. 168 E3
Díkti, Óros, Gr. 155 Q15
Dikwa, Nigeria 201 E17
Dīla, Eth. 199 H15
Dildarde Burnu, Turk. 168 J7
Dili, Timor-Leste 189 M15
Dilijan, Arm. 169 D19
Di Linh, Vietnam 187 P13
Dillenburg, Ger. 148 G6
Dilley, Tex., U.S. 103 S8
Dilling, Sudan 198 F12
Dillingham, Alas., U.S. 111 L13
Dillon, Mont., U.S. 106 F7
Dillon, S.C., U.S. 96 K11
Dillon's Bay, Vanuatu 218 G3
Dilolo, Dem. Rep. of the Congo 198 N9
Dilworth, Minn., U.S. 104 G8
Dimas, Mex. 114 F8
Dimashq (Damascus), Syr. 170 J7
Dimitrovgrad, Bulg. 153 K15
Dimitrovgrad, Russ. 156 K15
Dimitsána, Gr. 154 K9
Dimmitt, Tex., U.S. 102 H4
Dinagat, island, Philippines 189 E15
Dinajpur, Bangladesh 178 G12
Dinan, Fr. 147 Q5
Dinant, Belg. 146 M12
Dinar, Turk. 168 G5
Dīnār, Kūh-e, Iran 173 F13
Dinara, peak, Bosn. & Herzg., Croatia 152 G6
Dinara, range, Bosn. & Herzg., Croatia 152 G6
Dinaric Alps, Eur. 152 D5
Dinas Mawddwy, Wales, U.K. 143 T10
Dindigul, India 179 R6
Ding'an, China 183 U2
Dingbian, China 182 E1
Dingle, Ire. 143 U2
Dingle Bay, Ire. 143 U2
Dingli, Malta 161 L21
Dingnan, China 183 Q5
Dingo, Qnsld., Austral. 211 T14
Dingolfing, Ger. 148 K9
Dingtao, China 182 G6
Dinguiraye, Guinea 200 E6
Dingxiang, China 182 E5
Dingxing, China 182 D6
Dingzhou, China 182 E6
Dingzi Gang, bay, China 182 F9
Dinosaur, Colo., U.S. 106 L10
Dinosaur National Monument, Colo., U.S. 106 L10
Dinuba, Calif., U.S. 109 T7
Diomede Islands, Russ., U.S. 110 E11
Dion, ruin, Gr. 154 D10
Dios, P.N.G. 217 J13
Dios, Cayos de, Cuba 116 H7
Diourbel, Senegal 196 H4
Diphu Pass, India, Myanmar 186 C7
Diplo, Pak. 177 W8
Dir, Pak. 176 M10
Diré, Mali 196 H8
Dirē Dawa, Eth. 199 F16
Dírfis, Óros, Gr. 154 H12
Dirico, Angola 202 F8
Dirj, Lib. 197 C13
Dirk Hartog Island, Austral. 210 H1
Dirranbandi, Qnsld., Austral. 211 V14
Dirty Devil, river, Utah, U.S. 107 N8
Disa, India 178 H3
Disappointment, Cape, Wash., U.S. 108 E2
Disappointment, Lake, Austral. 210 F4
Discovery Bay, Austral. 210 M11
Discovery Bay, Jam. 120 H8
Discovery Tablemount, Atl. Oc. 237 U13
Disentis, Switz. 150 B4
Disney Cay, Bahamas 116 D11
Dispur, India 178 G13
Disteghil Sar, peak, Pak. 176 K12
Diu, India 178 K2
Divalak, Afghan. 177 Q3
Dīvāndarreh, Iran 172 C11
Divinhe, Mozambique 203 G13
Divinópolis, Braz. 131 L14
Diviso, Col. 128 H3
Divo, Côte d'Ivoire 200 H8
Divoúnia, island, Gr. 155 P17
Divriği, Turk. 169 F13
Diwana, Pak. 177 V6
Dixie, Idaho, U.S. 106 E4
Dixon, Calif., U.S. 109 R4
Dixon, Ill., U.S. 99 N5
Dixon, Ky., U.S. 101 C14
Dixon, Mo., U.S. 105 T13
Dixon, Mont., U.S. 106 C5
Dixon Entrance, Alas., U.S., B.C., Can. 111 N23
Dixons, Bahamas 120 E12
Diyadin, Turk. 169 E18
Diyālá, river, Iraq 172 D10
Diyarbakır, Turk. 169 G15
Dja, river, Cameroon 201 J16
Djado, Niger 197 F13
Djado, Plateau du, Niger 197 F13
Djamaa, Alg. 196 B11
Djambala, Congo 201 M17
Djanet, Alg. 196 E12
Djarrit, island, Marshall Is. 216 G12
Djelfa, Alg. 196 B11
Djénné, Mali 196 H8
Djibouti, Af. 195 G23
Djibouti, Djibouti 199 F16
Djougou, Benin 200 F11
Djoum, Cameroon 201 J16
Djúpavík, Ice. 140 E2
Djúpivogur, Ice. 140 F4
Dmitriya Lapteva, Proliv, Russ. 159 D17
Dmitriyev L'govskiy, Russ. 156 M8
Dmitrov, Russ. 156 J9
Dnepr, river, Russ. 156 J7
Dnieper see Dnipro, river, Ukr. 157 R7
Dnieper, Source of the, Russ. 138 E10
Dnieper Lowland, Belarus, Ukr. 138 F10
Dnieper Upland, Ukr. 138 G10
Dniester, river, Mold., Ukr. 157 R5
Dnipro (Dnieper), river, Ukr. 157 R7
Dniprodzerzhyns'k, Ukr. 157 Q8
Dnipropetrovs'k, Ukr. 157 Q8
Dno, Russ. 156 G6
Dnyapro, river, Belarus 156 K6
Do Ab-e Mikh-e Zarrin, Afghan. 176 L7
Doba, Chad 197 K14
Dobane, Cen. Af. Rep. 198 H10
Dobbs, Cape, Nunavut, Can. 83 H16
Doboj, Bosn. & Herzg. 152 F8
Dobre Miasto, Pol. 149 B15
Dobrich, Bulg. 153 G17
Dobruja, region, Bulg., Rom. 153 F18
Dobrush, Belarus 156 M6
Dobson, N.Z. 213 N17
Docampadó, Ensenada, Col. 128 F3
Doce, river, Braz. 131 L16
Docker River, N. Terr., Austral. 211 U7
Dock Junction, Ga., U.S. 97 P8
Doctor David Douglas Historic Monument, Hawai'i, U.S. 113 L20
Dodecanese see Dodekánissa, Gr. 155 M17
Dodekánissa (Dodecanese), Gr. 155 M17
Dodge, Nebr., U.S. 105 P8
Dodge City, Kans., U.S. 105 U5
Dodgeville, Wis., U.S. 98 L4
Dodman Point, Eng., U.K. 143 Y8
Dodoma, Tanzania 199 M14
Dodona, ruin, Gr. 154 F7
Dodson, Mont., U.S. 106 B10
Dodson, Tex., U.S. 102 H7
Doerun, Ga., U.S. 97 P5
Doetinchem, Neth. 146 J14
Dogai Coring, lake, China 180 J7
Doğanşehir, Turk. 168 G12
Dog Creek, B.C., Can. 82 L8
Dog Island, Virgin Islands, U.S. 120 N10
Dōgo, island, Japan 185 N7
Dogondoutchi, Niger 196 H10
Dog Rocks, Bahamas 116 F9
Doğruyol, Turk. 169 D17
Doğubayazıt, Turk. 169 E18
Dogwood Point, St. Kitts & Nevis 121 C18
Doha see Ad Dawḩah, Qatar 173 J13
Doi Inthanon, peak, Thai. 186 J7
Doïran, Lake see Dojransko Ezero, Maced. 152 L12
Doïránis, Límni, Gr. 154 B11
Dois Irmãos, Serra, Braz. 131 G16
Dojransko Ezero (Lake Doïran), Maced. 152 L12
Dokdo (Takeshima, Liancourt Rocks), Japan 184 M6
Dokkum, Neth. 146 G13
Dokós, island, Gr. 154 K12
Dolak (Yos Sudarso), island, Indonesia 189 M20
Doland, S. Dak., U.S. 104 K7
Dolbeau, Que., Can. 83 N19
Doldrums Fracture Zone, Atl. Oc. 236 M8
Dole, Fr. 147 S13
Dolgiy Most, Russ. 159 K14
Dolianá, Gr. 154 E7
Dolianova, It. 151 P4
Dolinsk, Russ. 159 K22
Dolly Cays, Bahamas 116 F11
Dolo Bay, Eth. 199 H16
Dolomites, range, It. 150 C7
Dolonnur see Duolun, China 182 B7
Dolores, Arg. 132 M13
Dolores, river, Colo., U.S. 107 N10
Dolores, Colo., U.S. 107 P10
Dolores, Uru. 132 L13
Dolphin, Cape, Falkland Is., U.K. 133 V12
Do Luong, Vietnam 186 J11
Dom, peak, Indonesia 213 B16
Domagnano, San Marino 161 J16
Domaniç, Turk. 168 E5
Domažlice, Czech Rep. 148 H10
Dombås, Nor. 140 J11
Doméniko, Gr. 154 E10
Domett, N.Z. 213 N18
Domeyko, Chile 132 H6
Domeyko, Cordillera, Chile 132 E7
Domfront, Fr. 147 P7
Domingitu, Neth. Antilles, Neth. 121 Q14
Dominica, N. Amer. 81 N24
Dominica, island, N. Amer. 80 N12
Dominican Republic, N. Amer. 81 N22
Dominica Passage, Lesser Antilles 119 H17
Dominion, Cape, Nunavut, Can. 83 G17
Domodossola, It. 150 C3
Domokós, Gr. 154 G10
Domoni, Comoros 205 N16
Domus de Maria, It. 151 Q3
Domuyo, Volcán, Arg. 132 M7
Dôn, river, Laos 186 L12
Don, river, Russ. 157 R10
Donaldson, Minn., U.S. 104 E8
Donaldsonville, La., U.S. 100 P10
Donalsonville, Ga., U.S. 97 Q4
Donau (Danube), river, Ger. 148 K7
Don Benito, Sp. 144 H8
Doncaster, Eng., U.K. 143 R12
Dondo, Angola 202 C6
Dondo, Indonesia 189 J14
Dondo, Mozambique 203 G13
Donegal Bay, Ire. 143 Q5
Donets'k, Ukr. 157 Q9
Donetsk, Russ. 157 Q11
Donets' Kryazh, Russ., Ukr. 157 Q10
Donets Ridge see Donets' Kryazh, Russ., Ukr. 138 G12
Donga, Nigeria 201 G15
Dong'an, China 183 P3
Dongara, W. Aust., Austral. 211 W2
Dongbei (Manchuria), region, China 181 D16
Dongfang (Basuo), China 183 U1
Dongfeng, China 182 B12
Donggou, China 182 D11
Dongguang, China 182 E7
Donghai, China 181 J16
Dong Hoi, Vietnam 186 K12
Dongkalang, Indonesia 189 J13
Dongkan see Binhai, China 182 H9
Dong Khe, Vietnam 186 G12
Dongning, China 181 D18
Dongo, Dem. Rep. of the Congo 198 J8
Dongola, Sudan 198 C12
Dongou, Congo 201 K18
Dongping, China 182 G7
Dongping, China 183 S3
Dongqiao, China 180 K7
Dongshan, China 183 R7
Dongsheng, China 182 D3
Dongtai, China 182 J9
Dongting Hu, China 182 M4
Dong Ujimqin Qi, China 181 D15
Dong Van, Vietnam 186 F11
Dongxiang, China 183 N6
Dongyztaū, Kaz. 174 F8
Doniphan, Mo., U.S. 105 V14
Dønna, island, Nor. 140 F11
Donnelly, Idaho, U.S. 106 F4
Donnellys Crossing, N.Z. 213 H18
Donner Pass, Calif., U.S. 109 Q6
Donors Hill, Qnsld., Austral. 211 R11
Donostia-San Sebastián, Sp. 145 B13
Donoússa, island, Gr. 155 L16
Donzenac, Fr. 147 V9
Doomadgee, Qnsld., Austral. 211 R10
Doon, Loch, Scot., U.K. 143 N9
Door Peninsula, Wis., U.S. 98 H8
Dora, Ala., U.S. 101 J15
Dora, N. Mex., U.S. 107 T15
Dora, Lake, Austral. 210 F4
Dorado, Playa de, P.R., U.S. 120 M4
Dorah Pass, Afghan. 176 L9
Dorchester, Eng., U.K. 143 X11
Dorchester, Cape, Nunavut, Can. 83 G17
Dordives, Fr. 147 Q10
Dordogne, river, Fr. 147 V8
Dordrecht, Neth. 146 J12
Dori, Burkina Faso 200 D11
Dório, Gr. 154 L9
Dormans, Fr. 147 P11
Dornbirn, Aust. 148 L7
Dornoch, Scot., U.K. 142 J9
Dornoch Firth, Scot., U.K. 142 J9
Dorogobuzh, Russ. 156 K7
Dorohoi, Rom. 153 A15
Dorrigo, N.S.W., Austral. 211 W15
Dorris, Calif., U.S. 108 L4
Dortmund, Ger. 148 E6
Dörtyol, Turk. 168 J11
Dörzbach, Ger. 148 H7
Dos Bahías, Cabo, Arg. 133 S9
Döşemealtı, Turk. 168 H6
Do Shakh, Afghan. 176 L6
Dos Hermanas, Sp. 144 L8
Dosso, Niger 196 J10
Dossor, Kaz. 174 F6
Dostyq, Kaz. 175 G19
Dothan, Ala., U.S. 101 N17
Douai, Fr. 146 M10
Douala, Cameroon 201 J15
Douarnenez, Fr. 147 Q3
Douarnenez, Baie de, Fr. 147 Q2
Double Island Point, Austral. 210 G15
Double Mountain Fork Brazos, river, Tex., U.S. 102 L6
Double Point, Austral. 210 D13
Doubtless Bay, N.Z. 213 H18
Doué, Fr. 147 S7
Douentza, Mali 196 H8
Douéoulou, New Caledonia, Fr. 218 C9
Douglas, Ariz., U.S. 107 W9
Douglas, Ga., U.S. 97 P7
Douglas, Isle of Man, U.K. 143 Q9
Douglas, Mich., U.S. 98 M9
Douglas, Wyo., U.S. 106 H13
Douglas, Cabo, Ecua. 128 Q7
Douglas Bay, Dominica 121 E18
Douglas Lake, Tenn., U.S. 101 E19
Douglass, Kans., U.S. 105 U8
Douglasville, Ga., U.S. 96 L4
Doullens, Fr. 146 M10
Doura, Mali 196 H7
Dourada, Serra, S. Amer. 126 G8
Dourados, Braz. 130 L11
Douro, river, Port., Sp. 144 E6
Dove Creek, Colo., U.S. 107 P10
Dover, Del., U.S. 96 C15
Dover, Eng., U.K. 143 W16
Dover, N.H., U.S. 95 J15
Dover, Ohio, U.S. 99 Q15
Dover, Strait of, Fr., U.K. 143 W16
Dover-Foxcroft, Me., U.S. 95 E17
Dowagiac, Mich., U.S. 99 N9
Dowlatabad, Afghan. 176 K4
Dowlatābād, Iran 173 G15
Dowlat Yar, Afghan. 176 M5
Downey, Calif., U.S. 109 X8
Downey, Idaho, U.S. 106 J7
Downieville, Calif., U.S. 109 P5
Downpatrick, N. Ire., U.K. 143 Q7
Downpatrick Head, Ire. 143 Q3
Downs, Kans., U.S. 105 S6
Dowshi, Afghan. 176 L7
Doxáto, Gr. 155 B13
Doylestown, Pa., U.S. 94 P10
Dōzen, island, Japan 185 P6
Drâa, Hamada du, Alg., Mor. 196 D7
Drâa, Oued, Alg., Mor. 196 C8
Drăgănești-Olt, Rom. 153 G14
Drăgășani, Rom. 153 F14
Dragon's Mouths, strait, Trinidad & Tobago 121 N21
Draguignan, Fr. 147 X15
Drain, Oreg., U.S. 108 H3
Drake, N. Dak., U.S. 104 F5
Drakensberg, range, S. Af. 202 L11
Drake Peak, Oreg., U.S. 108 K6
Dráma, Gr. 155 B13
Drammen, Nor. 140 L11
Dran, Vietnam 187 N14

Dranov, Ostrov, Rom. 153 E18
Dras, India 176 M13
Drasan, Pak. 176 K10
Drau, river, Aust. 148 M10
Drava, river, Croatia, Hung., Slov. 138 H7
Dravograd, Slov. 152 C5
Drayton, N. Dak., U.S. 104 E8
Drépano, Akrotírio, Gr. 155 E13
Dresden, Ger. 148 F10
Dreux, Fr. 147 P9
Drevsjø, Nor. 140 J12
Drew, Miss., U.S. 100 J10
Drewsey, Oreg., U.S. 108 H8
Drews Reservoir, Oreg., U.S. 108 L5
Driggs, Idaho, U.S. 106 G8
Drin, river, Albania 152 K9
Drina, river, Bosn. & Herzg., Serb. & Mont. 152 F9
Drinit, Gjiri i, Albania 152 K9
Driskill Mountain, La., U.S. 100 L7
Drøbak, Nor. 140 L11
Drobeta-Turnu Severin, Rom. 152 F12
Drogheda (Droichead Átha), Ire. 143 R7
Drohobych, Ukr. 157 P2
Droichead Átha see Drogheda, Ire. 143 R7
Droitwich, Eng., U.K. 143 U11
Drosh, Pak. 176 L10
Drouseia, Cyprus 160 P5
Drovyanoy, Russ. 158 E12
Drua, island, Fiji Is. 218 G8
Drumheller, Alta., Can. 82 M10
Drummond, Mont., U.S. 106 D6
Drummond Bay see Big Bay, Vanuatu 218 E3
Drummond Island, Mich., U.S. 98 G12
Drummond Range, Austral. 210 F13
Drumright, Okla., U.S. 102 F12
Druza, Gora, Russ. 159 F19
Dryanovo, Bulg. 153 H15
Dryden, Ont., Can. 83 N15
Dryden, Tex., U.S. 103 Q4
Drygalski Ice Tongue, Antarctica 227 P13
Drygalski Island, Antarctica 227 J21
Drygalski Mountains, Antarctica 227 B14
Dry Harbour Mountains, Jam. 120 H8
Drysdale, river, Austral. 210 C6
Dry Tortugas, islands, Fla., U.S. 85 P18
Dry Tortugas National Park, Fla., U.S. 97 Y7
Dschang, Cameroon 201 H15
Duaringa, Qnsld., Austral. 211 U14
Duarte, Pico, Dom. Rep. 117 M18
Ḑubā, Saudi Arabia 172 G5
Dubai see Dubayy, U.A.E. 173 J15
Dubăsari, Mold. 157 R5
Dubawnt, river, N.W.T., Can. 83 J13
Dubawnt Lake, Nunavut, Can. 83 H13
Dubayy (Dubai), U.A.E. 173 J15
Dubbo, N.S.W., Austral. 211 X14
Dubh Artach, Scot., U.K. 142 M6
Dublin, Ga., U.S. 96 M7
Dublin, Tex., U.S. 102 M10
Dublin (Baile Átha Cliath), Ire. 143 S7
Dublon see Tonoas, island, F.S.M. 217 C15
Dubna, Russ. 156 H9
Dubno, Ukr. 157 N3
Du Bois, Pa., U.S. 94 M5
Dubois, Idaho, U.S. 106 G7
Dubois, Wyo., U.S. 106 G9
Dubovka, Russ. 157 P13
Dubrovnik (Ragusa), Croatia 152 J8
Dubrovytsya, Ukr. 156 M4
Dubuque, Iowa, U.S. 105 N14
Duc de Gloucester, Îles, Fr. Polynesia, Fr. 219 G19
Duchesne, river, Utah, U.S. 106 L8
Duchesne, Utah, U.S. 106 L8
Duchess, Qnsld., Austral. 211 S11
Ducie Island, Pac. Oc. 215 L16
Duck, river, Tenn., U.S. 101 F15
Duck Hill, Miss., U.S. 100 J11
Ducktown, Tenn., U.S. 101 G18
Ducos, Martinique, Fr. 121 F23
Ducos, Île, New Caledonia, Fr. 218 D8
Duc Tho, Vietnam 186 J12
Dudelange, Lux. 160 K10
Dudinka, Russ. 159 F13
Dudley, Eng., U.K. 143 T11
Dudune, Île, New Caledonia, Fr. 218 D9
Duero, river, Sp. 144 E9
Dufek Coast, Antarctica 226 L12
Duffield, N. Terr., Austral. 211 U9
Duff Islands, Solomon Is. 217 N24
Dufftown, Scot., U.K. 142 J10
Dufur, Oreg., U.S. 108 F5
Dugi Otok, island, Croatia 152 G5
Dugway, Utah, U.S. 106 L6
Duifken Point, Austral. 210 B12
Duisburg, Ger. 148 E5
Duitama, Col. 128 E6
Dukla, Pol. 149 H17
Dulan (Qagan Us), China 180 J10
Dulce, river, Arg. 132 J11
Dulce, N. Mex., U.S. 107 Q11
Dulce, Golfo, Costa Rica 115 P19
Dulovo, Bulg. 153 G16
Duluth, Minn., U.S. 104 G12
Dūmā, Syr. 170 J7
Dumai, Indonesia 188 H6
Dumaran, island, Philippines 189 E13
Dumas, Ark., U.S. 100 J9
Dumas, Tex., U.S. 102 F5
Dumbarton, Scot., U.K. 142 M9
Dumbéa, New Caledonia, Fr. 218 E8
Dumfries, Scot., U.K. 143 P10
Dumka, India 178 H11
Dumoga Kecil, Indonesia 189 J15
Dumont d'Urville, station, Antarctica 227 Q18
Dumra, India 178 G10
Dumshaf Plain, Arctic Oc. 243 H19
Dumyât (Damietta), Egypt 197 C18
Dun, Fr. 147 N13
Duna (Danube), river, Hung. 149 M15
Dunaj (Danube), river, Slovakia 149 L14
Dunărea (Danube), river, Rom., Serb. & Mont. 153 F17
Dunaújváros, Hung. 149 L15
Dunav (Danube), river, Bulg., Rom., Serb. & Mont. 153 G15
Dunay (Danube), river, Rom. 153 E17
Dunbar, Qnsld., Austral. 211 Q12
Dunbar, W. Va., U.S. 96 D8
Duncan, Ariz., U.S. 107 V9
Duncan see Pinzón, Isla, island, Ecua. 128 Q9
Duncan, Okla., U.S. 102 H10
Duncan Passage, India 179 Q14
Duncans, Jam. 120 H8
Duncansby Head, Scot., U.K. 142 G10
Duncan Town, Bahamas 117 H13
Duncombe Bay, Norfolk I., Austral. 217 F20
Dundalk, Md., U.S. 96 C13
Dundalk (Dún Dealgan), Ire. 143 R7
Dundalk Bay, Ire. 143 R7
Dundas, Lake, Austral. 210 K4
Dundas Peninsula, N.W.T., Can. 83 D13
Dún Dealgan see Dundalk, Ire. 143 R7
Dundee, Scot., U.K. 142 L10
Dundee Island, Antarctica 226 C4
Dundonnell, Scot., U.K. 142 J8
Dundrennan, Scot., U.K. 143 P9
Dundrum Bay, N. Ire., U.K. 143 Q7
Dund-Urt, Mongolia 180 D12
Dund-Us see Hovd, Mongolia 180 D9
Dunedin, Fla., U.S. 97 U7
Dunedin, N.Z. 213 R16
Dunedoo, N.S.W., Austral. 211 X14
Dunes City, Oreg., U.S. 108 H2
Dunfermline, Scot., U.K. 142 M10
Dungarpur, India 178 H4
Dungarvan Harbour, Ire. 143 U5
Dungeness, Eng., U.K. 143 W15
Dungeness, Punta, Arg. 133 W9
Dungiven, N. Ire., U.K. 143 P6
Dunhua, China 182 A13
Dunhuang, China 180 G9
Dunkerque (Dunkirk), Fr. 146 L10
Dunkineely, Ire. 143 P4
Dunkirk see Dunkerque, Fr. 146 L10
Dunkirk, Ind., U.S. 99 Q10
Dunkirk, N.Y., U.S. 94 K4
Dunkwa, Ghana 200 H10
Dún Laoghaire (Kingstown), Ire. 143 S7
Dunlap, Iowa, U.S. 105 P9
Dunmanus Bay, Ire. 143 V3
Dunmanway, Ire. 143 V3
Dunmore, Pa., U.S. 94 M9
Dunmore Town, Bahamas 120 D5
Dunn, N.C., U.S. 96 H11
Dunnellon, Fla., U.S. 97 S7
Dunning, Nebr., U.S. 105 P5
Dunn's River Falls, Jam. 120 H9
Dunolly, Vic., Austral. 211 Z12
Dunsborough, W. Aust., Austral. 211 Y2
Dunseith, N. Dak., U.S. 104 E5
Dunsmuir, Calif., U.S. 108 M4
Duntroon, N.Z. 213 Q16
Dunvegan, Scot., U.K. 142 J7
Duolun (Dolonnur), China 182 B7
Dupree, S. Dak., U.S. 104 J3
Dupuyer, Mont., U.S. 106 B7
Duqm, Oman 173 M16
Duque de Caxias, Braz. 131 M15
Duque de York, Isla, Chile 133 V6
Duquesne, Pa., U.S. 94 N3
Du Quoin, Ill., U.S. 99 U5
Dura Europus, ruin, Syr. 170 G14
Durán, river, Sp. 160 K6
Durance, river, Fr. 147 W14
Durand, Wis., U.S. 98 J2
Durango, Colo., U.S. 107 P11
Durango, Mex. 114 F9
Durango, Sp. 144 B12
Durankulak, Bulg. 153 G18
Durant, Miss., U.S. 100 K11
Durant, Okla., U.S. 102 J12
Duras, Fr. 147 V7
Durazno, Uru. 132 K14
Durban, S. Af. 202 L11
Durbuy, Belg. 146 M13
Đurđevac, Croatia 152 D7
Dureji, Pak. 177 V6
Düren, Ger. 148 F5
Durg, India 178 K8
Durham, Eng., U.K. 143 P12
Durham, N.C., U.S. 96 H11
Durham, N.H., U.S. 95 J15
Durham Downs, Qnsld., Austral. 211 V11
Durlston Head, Eng., U.K. 143 X12
Ḑurmā, Saudi Arabia 172 J10
Durmitor, peak, Serb. & Mont. 138 J8
Durness, Kyle of, Scot., U.K. 142 G8
Durong, Qnsld., Austral. 211 V15
Duroy, Russ. 159 L18
Durrës, Albania 152 L9
Durrësit, Gjiri i, Albania 152 L9
Dursey Island, Ire. 143 V2
Dursunbey, Turk. 168 E4
Durtal, Fr. 147 R7
Durusu Gölü, Turk. 168 C4
Durūz, Jabal ad, Syr. 170 L8
D'Urville, Tanjung, Indonesia 213 B16
D'Urville Channel, Fiji Is. 218 J7
D'Urville Island, N.Z. 213 M18
Duşak, Turkm. 174 M9
Dûsh, Egypt 197 E18
Dushanbe, Taj. 176 H7
Dushanzi, China 180 E7
Düsseldorf, Ger. 148 F5
Dutchcap Cay, Virgin Islands, U.S. 120 M7
Dutch John, Utah, U.S. 106 K9
Dutton, Mount, Utah, U.S. 107 P7
Duvergé, Dom. Rep. 117 M17
Duwayhin, Dawḩat, Saudi Arabia 173 J13
Duyun, China 180 N12
Düzce, Turk. 168 D7
Dvina Bay, Russ. 138 B10
Dwarka, India 178 J1
Dwight, Ill., U.S. 99 P6
Dworshak Reservoir, Idaho, U.S. 106 D4
Dyat'kovo, Russ. 156 L8
Dyer, Cape, Nunavut, Can. 83 F19
Dyer Bay, N.W.T., Can. 82 C12
Dyersburg, Tenn., U.S. 100 E12
Dysart, Qnsld., Austral. 211 T14
Dzaanhushuu, Mongolia 180 D11
Dzag, Mongolia 180 D10
Dzangali, Afghan. 177 P6
Dzaoudzi, Mayotte, Fr. 205 P17
Dzavhan, river, Mongolia 180 D9
Dzerzhinsk, Russ. 156 J12
Dzhagdy, Khrebet, Russ. 159 J19
Dzhagdy Range see Dzhagdy, Khrebet, Russ. 166 D12
Dzhankoy, Ukr. 157 S8
Dzhardzhan, Russ. 159 F16
Dzharty-Rabat, Taj. 176 J11
Dzharylhach, Ostriv, Ukr. 157 S7
Dzhilandy, Taj. 176 J10
Dzhugdzhur, Khrebet, Russ. 159 H20
Dzhugdzhur Range see Dzhugdzhur, Khrebet, Russ. 166 D12
Dzhunkun, Russ. 159 H16
Działdowo, Pol. 149 C15
Dzibilchaltún, ruin, Mex. 115 H16
Dzierżoniów, Pol. 149 G13
Dzöölön, Mongolia 180 B10
Dzungarian Basin see Junggar Pendi, China 180 E7
Dzungarian Gate, China, Kaz. 175 G19
Dzvina, river, Belarus 156 J6
Dzyarzhynsk, Belarus 156 K4

E

Eads, Colo., U.S. 107 N15
Eagar, Ariz., U.S. 107 T9
Eagle, Alas., U.S. 111 F19
Eagle, Colo., U.S. 106 M11
Eagle, Mount, Virgin Islands, U.S. 120 Q2
Eagle Beach, Aruba, Neth. 121 Q16
Eagle Butte, S. Dak., U.S. 104 J4
Eagle Grove, Iowa, U.S. 105 N11
Eagle Harbor, Mich., U.S. 98 E7
Eagle Lake, Calif., U.S. 109 N5
Eagle Lake, Me., U.S. 95 B17
Eagle Lake, Tex., U.S. 103 R12
Eagle Mountain, Calif., U.S. 109 X11
Eagle Mountain, Minn., U.S. 104 F14
Eagle Mountain Lake, Tex., U.S. 102 L11
Eagle Nest Lake, N. Mex., U.S. 107 Q13
Eagle Pass, Tex., U.S. 103 S7
Eagle Peak, Calif., U.S. 108 M6
Eagle Peak, N. Mex., U.S. 107 T10
Eagle Peak, Tex., U.S. 103 V3
Eagle River, Mich., U.S. 98 E7
Eagle River, Wis., U.S. 98 G5
Eagles Mere, Pa., U.S. 94 M8
Earle, Ark., U.S. 100 G11
Earlimart, Calif., U.S. 109 U7
Earlington, Ky., U.S. 101 C14
Earp, Calif., U.S. 109 X13
Earth, Tex., U.S. 102 J4
Easky, Ire. 143 Q4
Easley, S.C., U.S. 96 J7
East Anglia, region, Eng., U.K. 143 U15
East Anglian Heights, Eng., U.K. 143 U14
East Antarctica, region, Antarctica 227 H17
East Aurora, N.Y., U.S. 94 J5
East Bay, La., U.S. 100 R12
Eastbourne, Eng., U.K. 143 W14
East Caicos, island, Turks & Caicos Is., U.K. 117 H17
East Cape, N.Z. 213 K21
East Cape, Russ. 166 A12
East Carbon, Utah, U.S. 106 M8
East Caroline Basin, Pac. Oc. 238 J6
East Channel, Marshall Is. 216 H9
East Chicago, Ind., U.S. 99 N7
East China Sea, Pac. Oc. 238 F4
East Coast Bays, N.Z. 213 J19
East Cote Blanche Bay, La., U.S. 100 Q9
East Dubuque, Ill., U.S. 98 M4
East End, Virgin Islands, U.K. 120 Q7
East End, Cayman Is., U.K. 120 J4
East End, Virgin Islands, U.S. 120 M12
East End Point, Bahamas 120 G6
East End Point, Bahamas 120 B12
East Entrance, Palau 216 L12
Easter Fracture Zone, Pac. Oc. 239 M16
Easter Island see Pascua, Isla de, Chile 215 L19
Eastern Beach, Gibraltar, U.K. 161 N23
Eastern Channel, Japan 185 Q3
Eastern Desert, Egypt 197 D19
Eastern Ghats, range, India 179 Q6
Eastern Island, Hawai'i, U.S. 112 K2
Eastern Sayan Mountains, Russ. 166 E9
Eastern Sovereign Base Area see Dhekelia Sovereign Base Area, Cyprus 160 P9
East Falkland, island, Falkland Is., U.K. 133 W12
East Fayu, island, F.S.M. 216 Q6
East Fork Bruneau, river, Idaho, U.S. 106 J4
East Fork White, river, Ind., U.S. 85 G16
East Frisian Islands, Ger. 148 B6
East Glacier Park, Mont., U.S. 106 B6
East Grand Forks, Minn., U.S. 104 F8
East Helena, Mont., U.S. 106 D7
East Indiaman Ridge, Ind. Oc. 241 L13
East Isaac, island, Bahamas 116 D10
East Jordan, Mich., U.S. 98 H10
East Lake, Mich., U.S. 98 J9
Eastland, Tex., U.S. 102 M9
East Lansing, Mich., U.S. 98 M11
Eastleigh, Eng., U.K. 143 W12
East Liverpool, Ohio, U.S. 99 Q16
East London, S. Af. 202 M10
Eastmain, river, Que., Can. 83 M19
Eastmain, Que., Can. 83 M18
Eastman, Ga., U.S. 97 N6
East Mariana Basin, Pac. Oc. 238 H7
East Millinocket, Me., U.S. 95 D17
East Moline, Ill., U.S. 99 P4
East Novaya Zemlya Trough, Arctic Oc. 243 C14
Easton, Md., U.S. 96 C14
Easton, Pa., U.S. 94 N9
East Orange, N.J., U.S. 94 N11
East Pacific Rise, Pac. Oc. 239 R16
East Pen Island, Ont., Can. 83 L16
East Peoria, Ill., U.S. 99 Q5
East Point, Ga., U.S. 96 L5
East Point, Marshall Is. 216 M9
East Point, Virgin Islands, U.S. 120 Q4
Eastpoint, Fla., U.S. 97 R4
Eastport, Me., U.S. 95 E19
East Prairie, Mo., U.S. 105 V16
East Prussia, region, Pol., Russ. 149 B16
East Ridge, Tenn., U.S. 101 G17
East St. Louis, Ill., U.S. 99 T4
East Sea see Japan, Sea of, Pac. Oc. 238 E5
East Siberian Sea, Arctic Oc. 242 G4
East Tawas, Mich., U.S. 98 J12
East Timor see Timor-Leste, Asia 167 Z14
Eastville, Va., U.S. 96 E14
East Wells, Bahamas 120 A8
Eaton, Ohio, U.S. 99 R11
Eaton Rapids, Mich., U.S. 98 M11
Eatonton, Ga., U.S. 96 L6
Eatonville, Wash., U.S. 108 D4
Eau Claire, Wis., U.S. 98 H3
Eau Claire, Lac à l', Que., Can. 83 L18
Eauripik Atoll, F.S.M. 216 Q4
Eauripik Rise, Pac. Oc. 238 J6
Ebadon, island, Marshall Is. 216 K1
Ebagoola, Qnsld., Austral. 211 Q12
Ebbw Vale, Wales, U.K. 143 V10
Ebe Khaya, Gora, Russ. 159 F15
Ebenholz, Liech. 160 P2
Eber Gölü, Turk. 168 F7
Eberswalde, Ger. 148 D10
Ebeye, island, Marshall Is. 216 N5
Ebino, Japan 185 S4
Ebinur Hu, China 180 D6
Ebjapik, island, Marshall Is. 216 N5
Eboda see 'Abda, ruin, Israel 171 P5
Eboli, It. 150 M11
Ebolowa, Cameroon 201 J16
Ebon Atoll, Marshall Is. 216 J4
Ebro, river, Sp. 145 E15
Ebro, Embalse del, Sp. 144 B11
Ebwaj, island, Marshall Is. 216 N5
Ecclesville, Trinidad & Tobago 121 Q23
Eceabat, Turk. 168 D2
Echallens, Switz. 150 B1
Echínos, Gr. 155 B14
Echo, Oreg., U.S. 108 E7
Echo Bay, N.W.T., Can. 82 F11
Echternach, Lux. 160 J11
Echuca, N.S.W., Austral. 211 Y12
Ecija, Sp. 144 L9
Eckenförde, Ger. 148 B8
Ecuador, S. Amer. 127 D14
Edah, W. Aust., Austral. 211 V3
Eday, island, Scot., U.K. 142 F10
Edcouch, Tex., U.S. 103 W10
Ed Damer, Sudan 199 D13
Ed Debba, Sudan 198 D12
Eddrachillis Bay, Scot., U.K. 142 H8
Eddystone Rocks, Eng., U.K. 143 Y9
Eddyville, Ky., U.S. 101 D13
Ede, Neth. 146 J13
Edéa, Cameroon 201 J15
Eden, N.C., U.S. 96 G10
Eden, Tex., U.S. 103 N7
Eden, Wyo., U.S. 106 J9
Edenburg, S. Af. 202 L10
Edenton, N.C., U.S. 96 G14
Édessa, Gr. 154 C9
Edessa see Şanlıurfa, Turk. 169 H13
Edgar, Nebr., U.S. 105 R7
Edgartown, Mass., U.S. 95 M15
Edgefield, S.C., U.S. 96 L8
Edgeley, N. Dak., U.S. 104 H6
Edgell Island, Nunavut, Can. 83 H19
Edgemont, S. Dak., U.S. 104 M1
Edgeøya, island, Norway 167 P7
Edgerton, Minn., U.S. 104 L9
Edgerton, Wis., U.S. 98 M6
Edgigen, island, Marshall Is. 216 K4
Edina, Mo., U.S. 105 R13
Edinburg, Tex., U.S. 103 W10

Edinburgh, Ind., U.S. 99 S9
Edinburgh, Scot., U.K. 142 M10
Edirne (Adrianople), Turk. 168 B3
Edison, Ga., U.S. 97 P4
Edison, N.J., U.S. 94 N10
Edisto, river, S.C., U.S. 96 M9
Edisto Island, S.C., U.S. 96 M10
Edithburgh, S. Aust., Austral. 211 Y10
Edjell, island, Marshall Is. 216 K4
Edmond, Okla., U.S. 102 G11
Edmonds, Wash., U.S. 108 B4
Edmonton, Alta., Can. 82 L10
Edmore, N. Dak., U.S. 104 E6
Edmundston, N.B., Can. 83 N20
Edna, Tex., U.S. 103 S12
Edolo, It. 150 C6
Edrei see Dar'ā, Syr. 170 L7
Edremit, Turk. 168 E3
Edremit Körfezi, Turk. 168 E3
Edrengiyn Nuruu, range, Mongolia 180 E10
Eduardo Castex, Arg. 132 M10
Edward, river, Austral. 210 L12
Edward, Lake, Dem. Rep. of the Congo, Uganda 198 K12
Edward River, Qnsld., Austral. 211 Q11
Edwards, Calif., U.S. 109 W8
Edwards Plateau, Tex., U.S. 103 P7
Edwardsville, Ill., U.S. 99 T4
Edward VIII Bay, Antarctica 227 D20
Edward VII Peninsula, Antarctica 226 M10
Ee, island, Cook Is., N.Z. 218 Q12
Eek, Alas., U.S. 110 K12
Eel, river, Calif., U.S. 109 N2
Éfaté (Île Vaté), Vanuatu 218 F3
Effigy Mounds National Monument, Iowa, U.S. 104 M14
Effingham, Ill., U.S. 99 S6
Eflâni, Turk. 168 C8
Efstrátios, Ágios, Gr. 155 F14
Efuenaarukosu Point, N. Mariana Is., U.S. 216 D8
Efyra, ruin, Gr. 154 F7
Egadi, Isole, It. 151 S8
Egan Range, Nev., U.S. 109 Q12
Egegik, Alas., U.S. 111 L13
Eger, Hung. 149 K16
Egeria Fracture Zone, Ind. Oc. 240 K8
Egersund, Nor. 140 M10
Egg Lagoon, Tas., Austral. 211 Y15
Egiáli, Gr. 155 L16
Eğil, Turk. 169 G14
Egilsstaðir, Ice. 140 F4
Égina (Aegina), island, Gr. 154 K12
Egina, Gr. 154 K12
Egio, Gr. 154 H9
Egiyn, river, Mongolia 180 C11
Égletons, Fr. 147 U9
Eglinton Fiord, Nunavut, Can. 83 E18
Egmont, Mount see Taranaki, Mount, N.Z. 213 L18
Eğridir, Turk. 168 G6
Eğridir Gölü, Turk. 168 G6
Eğrigöz Dağı, Turk. 168 E5
Éguzon-Chantôme, Fr. 147 T9
Egvekinot, Russ. 159 B20
Egypt, Af. 195 E21
Ehingen, Ger. 148 K7
Ehrang, Ger. 160 J12
Ehrenberg, Ariz., U.S. 107 T4
Ei, Japan 185 T4
Eiao, island, Fr. Polynesia, Fr. 215 H14
Eickelberg Seamount, Pac. Oc. 239 D14
Eidsvold, Qnsld., Austral. 211 U15
Eifel, range, Ger. 160 G11
Eigg, island, Scot., U.K. 142 K7
Eight Degree Channel, Maldives 179 S3
Eight Mile Rock, Bahamas 120 F1
Eights Coast, Antarctica 226 J6
Eighty Mile Beach, Austral. 210 E4
Eildon, Lake, Austral. 210 M12
Eil Malk see Mercherchar, island, Palau 216 P11
Einasleigh, Qnsld., Austral. 211 R12
Eindhoven, Neth. 146 K13
Einsiedeln, Switz. 150 B4
Eirik Ridge, Atl. Oc. 236 D7
Eirunepé, Braz. 130 F5
Eisch, river, Lux. 160 J9
Eischen, Lux. 160 J9
Eisenach, Ger. 148 F8
Eisenerz, Aust. 148 L11
Eisenhüttenstad, Ger. 148 E11
Eisenstadt, Aust. 149 L13
Eita, island, Kiribati 217 G17
Eita, Kiribati 217 G17
Eivissa (Ibiza), Sp. 145 H17
Ejea de los Caballeros, Sp. 145 D14
Ejin Horo Qi (Altan Xiret), China 182 D3
Ejin Qi, China 180 F11
Ejmiatsin, Arm. 169 E18
Ekalaka, Mont., U.S. 106 E13
Ekarma, island, Russ. 159 H23
Ekerem, Turkm. 174 L6
Ekeren, Belg. 146 K12
Ekiatapskiy Khrebet, Russ. 159 B20
Ekibastuz, Kaz. 175 C15
Ekonda, Russ. 159 G15
Ekström Ice Shelf, Antarctica 226 A11
Ekwan, river, Ont., Can. 83 M17
Elafonísou, Stenón, Gr. 154 N11
Elafoníssi, island, Gr. 154 M11
Elaia, Cape, Cyprus 160 N10
El 'Alamein, Egypt 197 C18
Elamanchili, India 178 M9
El 'Arîsh (Rhinocolura), Egypt 171 N3
Elása, island, Gr. 155 Q17
Elassón, Gr. 154 E10
El Astillero, Sp. 144 B11
Elat, Israel 171 R5
Elath see Ezion-geber, ruin, Jordan 171 R5
Elato Atoll, F.S.M. 216 Q5
El 'Auja see Nizzana, Israel 171 P4
El 'Auja, peak, Jordan 171 R7
Elâzığ, Turk. 169 G14
Elba, Ala., U.S. 101 M16
Elba, island, It. 150 J5
Elba, Cape (Ras Hadarba), Egypt 194 F10
El Banco, Col. 128 C5
El Barco de Ávila, Sp. 144 F9
Elbasan, Albania 152 L9
El Baúl, Venez. 128 C9
El Bayadh, Alg. 196 B10
Elbe, river, Ger. 148 C8
Elbert, Mount, Colo., U.S. 106 M12
Elberta, Mich., U.S. 98 J9
Elberton, Ga., U.S. 96 K7
Elbeuf, Fr. 147 N8
Elbistan, Turk. 168 G12
Elbląg, Pol. 149 B15
Elbow Cays, Bahamas 116 F8
Elbow Lake, Minn., U.S. 104 H9
El'brus, peak, Russ. 157 U12
El Bureij, Gaza Strip 171 N4
El Burgo de Osma, Sp. 144 D11
Elburz Mountains see Alborz, Reshteh-ye, Iran 172 B12
El Cajon, Calif., U.S. 109 Z10
El Calafate (Lago Argentino), Arg. 133 V7
El Callao, Venez. 128 D12
El Calvario, Venez. 128 C9
El Campello, Sp. 145 J14
El Campo, Tex., U.S. 103 R12
El Carmen, Arg. 132 E9
El Ceibo, Guatemala 115 K15
El Ceibo, Mex. 115 H16
El Centro, Calif., U.S. 109 Z11
El Cerro, Bol. 130 K9
Elche (Elx), Sp. 145 K14
Elchi see Wādī Mūsá, Jordan 171 Q6
El Cuyo, Mex. 115 H17
Elda, Sp. 145 J14
Elderslie, Jam. 120 H7
El'dikan, Russ. 159 G19
El Djouf, region, Mali, Mauritania 196 F7
Eldon, Iowa, U.S. 105 Q13
Eldon, Mo., U.S. 105 T12
Eldora, Iowa, U.S. 105 N12
El Dorado, Ark., U.S. 100 K8
El Dorado, Kans., U.S. 105 U8
El Dorado, Venez. 128 D12
Eldorado, Arg. 132 G15
Eldorado, Ill., U.S. 99 U6
Eldorado, Mex. 114 F8
Eldorado, Okla., U.S. 102 H8
Eldorado, Tex., U.S. 103 P6
El Dorado Springs, Mo., U.S. 105 U11
Eldoret, Kenya 199 J14
Electra, Tex., U.S. 102 J9
Electric Mills, Miss., U.S. 101 K13
Eleftheroúpoli, Gr. 155 C13
Elektrostal', Russ. 156 J10
Eléni see Makronissi, island, Gr. 155 K13
Elephant Butte Reservoir, N. Mex., U.S. 107 U11
Elephant Island, Antarctica 226 B3
Eleşkirt, Turk. 169 E17
Eleuthera Island, Bahamas 117 E13
El Faiyûm, Egypt 197 C18
El Fasher, Sudan 198 E11
El Fifi, Sudan 198 F10
Elfrida, Ariz., U.S. 107 W9
El Fuerte, Mex. 114 E8
El Galpón, Arg. 132 F10
El Gassi, Alg. 196 C11
El Gezira, region, Sudan 194 G9
Elgin, Ill., U.S. 99 N6
Elgin, N. Dak., U.S. 104 H3
Elgin, Nebr., U.S. 105 N7
Elgin, Nev., U.S. 109 S12
Elgin, Oreg., U.S. 108 F8
Elgin, Scot., U.K. 142 J10
Elgin, Tex., U.S. 103 Q11
El Gîza, Egypt 197 C18
Elgol, Scot., U.K. 142 K7
El Golea, Alg. 196 C11
Elgon, Mount, Kenya, Uganda 194 J9
El Grado, Sp. 145 D15
El Hobra, Alg. 196 C11
El Homeur, Alg. 196 C10
Eliase, Indonesia 213 D14
Elida, N. Mex., U.S. 107 T15
Elikónas (Helicon), peak, Gr. 154 H11
Elim, Alas., U.S. 111 F13
Elisabethville, Dem. Rep. of the Congo 198 N11
El Iskandarîya (Alexandria), Egypt 197 C18
Elista, Russ. 157 R13
Elizabeth, La., U.S. 100 N7
Elizabeth, N.J., U.S. 94 N11
Elizabeth, Cape, Me., U.S. 95 H16
Elizabeth City, N.C., U.S. 96 G14
Elizabeth Island, Marshall Is. 216 M8
Elizabethton, Tenn., U.S. 101 E20
Elizabethtown, Ky., U.S. 101 C16
Elizabethtown, N.C., U.S. 96 J12
Elizondo, Sp. 145 B13
El Jadida (Mazagan), Mor. 196 B8
Ełk, Pol. 149 B17
Elk, Calif., U.S. 109 Q2
Elk, river, W. Va., U.S. 96 D9
Elkader, Iowa, U.S. 104 M13
Elk City, Okla., U.S. 102 G8
Elkedra, N. Terr., Austral. 211 S9
El Kef, Tun. 196 A12
Ēl Kerē, Eth. 199 H16
El Khandaq, Sudan 198 D12
El Khârga, Egypt 197 E18
Elkhart, Ind., U.S. 99 N9
Elkhart, Kans., U.S. 105 V3
El Khnâchîch, region, Mali 196 F8
Elkhorn, river, Nebr., U.S. 105 N6
Elkhorn City, Ky., U.S. 101 C20
Elkhovo, Bulg. 153 J16
Elkin, N.C., U.S. 96 G9
Elkins, N. Mex., U.S. 107 T14
Elkins, W. Va., U.S. 96 D10
Elkland, Pa., U.S. 94 L7
Elk Mountain, Pa., U.S. 94 L9
Elk Mountain, Wyo., U.S. 106 K12
Elko, Nev., U.S. 108 M11
Elk Point, S. Dak., U.S. 104 N8
Elk River, Minn., U.S. 104 J11
Elkton, Ky., U.S. 101 D15
Elkton, Md., U.S. 96 B14
El Kûbri, Egypt 171 Q1
El Kuntilla, Egypt 171 Q4
Ellar, Sp. 160 L6
Elle, island, Marshall Is. 216 G8
Ellef Ringnes Island, Nunavut, Can. 83 B14
Ellen, Mount, Utah, U.S. 107 P8
Ellendale, N. Dak., U.S. 104 H6
Ellensburg, Wash., U.S. 108 D6
Ellep, island, Marshall Is. 216 M5
Ellep Passage, Marshall Is. 216 L4
Ellesmere, Lake, N.Z. 213 P17
Ellesmere Island, Nunavut, Can. 83 B16
Ellijay, Ga., U.S. 96 J5
Ellington, Mo., U.S. 105 U14
Ellinwood, Kans., U.S. 105 T6
Elliot Lake, Ont., Can. 83 P17
Elliott, N. Terr., Austral. 211 R8
Elliott Key, Fla., U.S. 97 X10
Ellis, Idaho, U.S. 106 F5
Ellis, Kans., U.S. 105 S5
Ellisburg, N.Y., U.S. 94 H8
Elliston, S. Aust., Austral. 211 X9
Ellisville, Miss., U.S. 100 M12
Ellon, Scot., U.K. 142 K11
Ellsworth, Kans., U.S. 105 T7
Ellsworth, Me., U.S. 95 F18
Ellsworth Land, Antarctica 226 J6
Ellsworth Mountains, Antarctica 226 H8
Elma, Wash., U.S. 108 D3
El Macao, Dom. Rep. 117 M20
Elmadağ, Turk. 168 E8
Elma Dağı, Turk. 168 E8
El Maitén, Arg. 133 Q7
Elmalı, Turk. 168 H5
El Malpais National Monument, N. Mex., U.S. 107 S10
El Mazâr, Egypt 171 N3
Elm Creek, Nebr., U.S. 105 Q5
Elm Creek, Tex., U.S. 103 S7
El Milagro, Arg. 132 J9
El Mîna, Leb. 170 H6
El Minya, Egypt 197 D18
Elmira, N.Y., U.S. 94 L7
El Morro National Monument, N. Mex., U.S. 107 S10
El Mreyyé, region, Mali, Mauritania 196 F7
Elmshorn, Ger. 148 B7
Elne, Fr. 147 Z11
El Nido, Philippines 189 E13
El Obeid (Al Ubayyiḍ), Sudan 198 E12
El Odaiya, Sudan 198 F11
Elorza, Venez. 128 D8
El Oued, Alg. 196 B12
Eloúnda, Gr. 155 Q16
Eloy, Ariz., U.S. 107 U7
El Pajuil, P.R., U.S. 120 M2
El Palito, Venez. 128 B9
El Pao, Venez. 128 C12
El Paso, Ill., U.S. 99 Q6
El Paso, Tex., U.S. 103 U1
El Pedroso, Sp. 144 K8
Elphin, Scot., U.K. 142 H8
El Portal, Calif., U.S. 109 S6
El Puerto de Santa María, Sp. 144 M8
El Qâhira (Cairo), Egypt 197 C18
El Qanṭara, Egypt 171 P1
El Qaṣr, Egypt 197 E18
El Quneitra see Al Qunayeirah, Syr. 170 K6
El Quṣeima, Egypt 171 P4
El Reno, Okla., U.S. 102 G10
El Rosario, Mex. 114 C5
Elroy, Wis., U.S. 98 K4
Elsa, Tex., U.S. 103 W10
El Salto, Mex. 114 F9
El Salvador, N. Amer. 81 Q19
Elsberry, Mo., U.S. 105 S14
El Seibo, Dom. Rep. 117 M20
El Serrat, Andorra 160 G3
El Sharana, N. Terr., Austral. 211 P8
Elsinore, Utah, U.S. 107 N7
El Sombrero, Venez. 128 C9
Elst, Neth. 146 J13
El Suweis (Suez), Egypt 171 Q1
Eltanin Bay, Antarctica 226 H6
Eltanin Fracture Zone, Pac. Oc. 239 R14
El Teleno, peak, Sp. 144 C8
Eltham, N.Z. 213 L18
El Thamad, Egypt 171 R4
El Tigre, Venez. 128 C11
El Tofo, Chile 132 H6
El'ton, Russ. 157 P14
El'ton, Ozero, Russ. 157 P14
Eltopia, Wash., U.S. 108 D7
El Toro, peak, P.R., U.S. 120 N5
El Toro, peak, Sp. 145 G20
El Ṭûr, Egypt 171 T3
El Turbio, Arg. 133 W7
Eluru, India 178 M8
Elvas, Port. 144 H7
Elven, Fr. 147 R4
Elverum, Nor. 140 K11
El Wak, Kenya 199 J15
Elwell, Lake, Mont., U.S. 106 B8
Elwood, Ind., U.S. 99 Q9
Elwood, Kans., U.S. 105 R10
Elwood, Mo., U.S. 105 R10
Elwood, Nebr., U.S. 105 Q5
Elx see Elche, Sp. 145 K14
Ely, Eng., U.K. 143 T14
Ely, Minn., U.S. 104 F12
Ely, Nev., U.S. 109 Q12
Elyria, Ohio, U.S. 99 P14
El Yunque (Anvil), peak, Cuba 117 K14
Émaé, island, Vanuatu 218 E3
Emam Saheb, Afghan. 176 K7
Émao, island, Vanuatu 218 F3
Emba, Cyprus 160 Q5
Embarcación, Arg. 132 E10
Embetsu, Japan 184 E13
Embi, Kaz. 174 E9
Embleton, Eng., U.K. 143 N12
Embrun, Fr. 147 W15
Emden, Ger. 148 C6
Emerald, Qnsld., Austral. 211 T14
Emerald Basin, Pac. Oc. 238 R8
Emerald Island, N.W.T., Can. 83 C13
Emery, Utah, U.S. 107 N8
Emet, Turk. 168 E5
Emidj, island, Marshall Is. 216 L9
Emigrant Pass, Nev., U.S. 109 N10
Emi Koussi, peak, Chad 197 G15
Emilius, Mount, It. 150 D2
Emily, Minn., U.S. 104 G11
Emin, China 180 D6
Emirau, island, P.N.G. 213 B20
Emirdağ, Turk. 168 F6
Emir Dağları, Turk. 168 F7
Emita, Tas., Austral. 211 Y16
Emmaus, Pa., U.S. 94 N9
Emmen, Neth. 146 H14
Emmetsburg, Iowa, U.S. 104 M10
Emmett, Idaho, U.S. 106 G3
Emmonak, Alas., U.S. 110 H12
Emory Peak, Tex., U.S. 103 R3
Empedrado, Arg. 132 G13
Emperor Seamounts, Pac. Oc. 238 D8
Emperor Trough, Pac. Oc. 238 D9
Empire, Mich., U.S. 98 J9
Empoli, It. 150 G6
Emporia, Kans., U.S. 105 T9
Emporia, Va., U.S. 96 F13
Emporium, Pa., U.S. 94 L5
Empress Augusta Bay, P.N.G. 217 K14
Ems, river, Ger. 148 C6
Emu Park, Qnsld., Austral. 211 T15
Ena, Japan 185 P10
Enard Bay, Scot., U.K. 142 H8
'En Boqeq, Israel 171 N6
Encamp, region, Andorra 160 H4
Encamp, Andorra 160 J3
Encarnación, Parag. 130 N10
Encinal, Tex., U.S. 103 T8
Encinitas, Calif., U.S. 109 Y9
Encino, N. Mex., U.S. 107 S13
Encino, Tex., U.S. 103 V10
Encontrados, Venez. 128 C6
Encounter Bay, Austral. 210 L10
Ende, Indonesia 189 M14
Endeavour Hill, Austral. 210 C7
Endeavour Strait, Austral. 210 A12
Enderbury Island, Kiribati 214 G10
Enderby Land, Antarctica 227 C18
Enderby Plain, Antarctic Oc. 245 E14
Enderlin, N. Dak., U.S. 104 G7
Endicott, N.Y., U.S. 94 K8
Endicott Mountains, Alas., U.S. 111 D15
Eneeldak, island, Marshall Is. 216 N8
Enengeseiru, island, F.S.M. 217 C14
Enengonomei, island, F.S.M. 217 C14
Enewetak (Eniwetok), island, Marshall Is. 216 J8
Enewetak Atoll, Marshall Is. 216 F1
Enewetak Lagoon, Marshall Is. 216 H8
Enez, Turk. 168 C2
Enfer, Pointe d', Martinique, Fr. 121 G23
Enfield, Jam. 120 H10
Enfield, N.C., U.S. 96 G13
Engaño, Cabo, Dom. Rep. 117 M21
Engaru, Japan 184 E15
Engelhard, N.C., U.S. 96 H14
Engels, Russ. 156 M14
Engenenimo, island, F.S.M. 217 C16
Enggano, island, Indonesia 188 L6
England, Ark., U.S. 100 H9
England, U.K. 143 T12
Englewood, Colo., U.S. 106 M13
Englewood, Fla., U.S. 97 V7
Englewood, Kans., U.S. 105 V5
English Channel, Eur. 138 F4
English Coast, Antarctica 226 G6
English Harbor, Kiribati 217 B20
English Harbour, Antigua & Barbuda 121 C21
English Roads, Tonga 218 J12
Enid, Okla., U.S. 102 E10
Enighed, Virgin Islands, U.S. 120 N10
Enigu, island, Marshall Is. 216 G11
Enipéas, river, Gr. 154 F10
Eniwa, Japan 184 G13
Eniwetak, island, Marshall Is. 216 M5
Eniwetak Passage, Marshall Is. 216 M5

Eniwetok see Enewetak, island, Marshall Is. 216 J8
Enjebi, island, Marshall Is. 216 G8
Enkhuizen, Neth. 146 H13
Ennadai, Nunavut, Can. 83 J13
En Nahud, Sudan 198 E11
Ennedi, range, Chad 197 G16
Ennell, Lough, Ire. 143 S5
Enngonia, N.S.W., Austral. 211 W13
Enning, S. Dak., U.S. 104 K2
Ennis, Ire. 143 T4
Ennis, Mont., U.S. 106 E7
Ennis, Tex., U.S. 102 M12
Enniscorthy, Ire. 143 T6
Enniskillen, N. Ire., U.K. 143 Q5
Ennistymon, Ire. 143 S3
Ennuebing, island, Marshall Is. 216 K4
Ennugarret, island, Marshall Is. 216 K4
Ennugenliggelap, island, Marshall Is. 216 M4
Ennumennet, island, Marshall Is. 216 K4
Ennumet, island, Marshall Is. 216 L3
Ennylabegan, island, Marshall Is. 216 N5
Enontekiö, Fin. 141 D14
Énos, Óros, Gr. 154 J7
Enriquillo, Dom. Rep. 117 N18
Enriquillo, Lago, Dom. Rep. 117 M17
Enschede, Neth. 146 J14
Ensenada, Mex. 114 B5
Ensenada, P.R., U.S. 120 N2
Enshi, China 182 L2
Ensisheim, Fr. 147 Q15
Entebbe, Uganda 199 K13
Enterprise, Ala., U.S. 101 N16
Enterprise, Miss., U.S. 101 L13
Enterprise, Oreg., U.S. 108 F9
Enterprise, Utah, U.S. 107 P5
Entinas, Punta, Sp. 144 M12
Entrada, Punta, Arg. 133 V8
Entrance Point, Bahamas 120 B8
Entre-Deux, Reunion, Fr. 205 H16
Entrepeñas, Embalse de, Sp. 144 F12
Entre Ríos, region, S. Amer. 126 L6
Entrèves, It. 150 D2
Entroncamento, Port. 144 G5
Enubuj, island, Marshall Is. 216 N5
Enugu, Nigeria 201 H14
Enumclaw, Wash., U.S. 108 C4
Enurmino, Russ. 159 A20
Envalira, Pic d', Andorra, Fr. 160 J5
Envalira, Port d', Andorra 160 J5
Envira, Braz. 130 F5
'En Yahav, Israel 171 P5
Enybor, island, Marshall Is. 216 M8
Eo, Îlot, New Caledonia, Fr. 218 C8
Eolie see Lipari, Isole, It. 151 R11
Eori, Eq. Guinea 204 N7
Eot, island, F.S.M. 217 C15
Epanomí, Gr. 154 D11
Eparit, island, F.S.M. 217 A15
Eparit, Mochun, F.S.M. 217 A15
Epéna, Congo 201 K18
Épernay, Fr. 147 P11
Épernon, Fr. 147 P9
Epeti, Roches, Fr. Polynesia, Fr. 219 M23
Ephesus, ruin, Turk. 168 G3
Ephraim, Utah, U.S. 106 M7
Ephrata, Wash., U.S. 108 C7
Epi, island, Vanuatu 218 E3
Epidavros, ruin, Gr. 154 K11
Épinal, Fr. 147 Q14
Epirus, region, Albania, Gr. 154 F7
Episkopi, Cyprus 160 Q7
Episkopi Bay, Cyprus 160 Q7
Epsilon, Qnsld., Austral. 211 V11
Epsom, Eng., U.K. 143 V14
Eptachórion, Gr. 154 D8
Épuisay, Fr. 147 R8
Epukiro, Namibia 202 H7
Epu Pel, Arg. 133 N10
Equatorial Channel, Maldives 179 X3
Equatorial Guinea, Af. 195 J17
Erbaa, Turk. 168 D11
Erçek, Turk. 169 G18
Erçek Gölü, Turk. 169 F18
Erciş, Turk. 169 F17
Erciyeş Dağı, Turk. 168 G10
Érd, Hung. 149 L15
Erdek, Turk. 168 D4
Erdemli, Turk. 168 J9
Erding, Ger. 148 K9
Ere, island, Marshall Is. 216 L3
Erebus, Mount, Antarctica 227 N13
Ereğli, Turk. 168 C7
Ereğli, Turk. 168 H9
Erei, Monti, It. 151 T11
Erenhot, China 182 A4
Eressós, Gr. 155 F16
Erétria, Gr. 154 H12
Erexim, Braz. 130 N12
Ereymentaū, Kaz. 175 C14
Erfoud, Mor. 196 C9
Erfurt, Ger. 148 F8
Ergani, Turk. 169 G14
Ergedzhey, Russ. 159 H17
Ergene, river, Turk. 168 C4
Ergun see Argun', river, China 181 B15
Ergun Youqi, China 181 B15
Ergun Zuoqi, China 181 B15
Er Hai, lake, China 180 N10
Eriboll, Scot., U.K. 142 H9
Eriboll, Loch, Scot., U.K. 142 G9
Ericht, Loch, Scot., U.K. 142 L9
Erick, Okla., U.S. 102 G7
Erie, Pa., U.S. 94 K3
Erie, Lake, Can., U.S. 85 F18
Erie Canal, N.Y., U.S. 94 J5
Erigavo see Ceerigaabo, Somalia 199 F17
Erikoússa, island, Gr. 154 E5
Erikub Atoll, Marshall Is. 216 G5
Erímanthos, Óros, Gr. 154 J9
Erimi, Cyprus 160 Q7
Erimo, Japan 184 G15
Erimo Misaki, Japan 184 G15
Erin, Tenn., U.S. 101 E14
Erin Bay, Trinidad & Tobago 121 Q21
Eriskay, island, Scot., U.K. 142 K6
Erisort, Loch, Scot., U.K. 142 H7
Erithrés, Gr. 154 J11
Eritrea, Af. 195 G22
Erkilet, Turk. 168 F10
Erlangen, Ger. 148 H8
Erlanger, Ky., U.S. 101 A17
Erldunda, N. Terr., Austral. 211 U8
Erling, Lake, Ark., U.S. 100 K7
Ermenek, Turk. 168 J8
Ermióni, Gr. 154 K11
Ermoúpoli, Gr. 155 K14
Ernabella, S. Aust., Austral. 211 U8
Ernakulam, India 179 R5
Ernée, Fr. 147 Q6
Erode, India 179 Q6
Eroj, island, Marshall Is. 216 G11
Eromanga, Qnsld., Austral. 211 U12
Er Rachidia, Mor. 196 B9
Er Rahad, Sudan 198 E12
Er Rif, range, Mor. 194 C3
Erris Head, Ire. 143 Q3
Erromango, island, Vanuatu 218 G3
Error Tablemount, Ind. Oc. 240 E6
Erskine, Minn., U.S. 104 F9
Ertai, China 180 D8
Ertis, Kaz. 175 B15
Ertis (Irtysh), river, Kaz. 175 C16
Ertix, river, China 180 D8
Erts, Andorra 160 H2
Eru, island, Marshall Is. 216 L3
Eruh, Turk. 169 H16
Erwin, N.C., U.S. 96 H11
Erwin, Tenn., U.S. 101 E20
Erzin, Russ. 159 M13
Erzincan, Turk. 169 E14
Erzurum, Turk. 169 E16
Esan Misaki, Japan 184 H13
Esashi, Japan 184 E14
Esashi, Japan 184 H12
Esbjerg, Den. 140 P11
Esbo see Espoo, Fin. 141 K16
Escalades-Engordany, region, Andorra 160 J4
Escalante, river, Utah, U.S. 107 P8
Escalante, Utah, U.S. 107 P7
Escambia, river, Fla., U.S. 97 Q1
Escanaba, river, Mich., U.S. 98 G8
Escanaba, Mich., U.S. 98 G8
Escárcego, Mex. 115 J15
Esch, Lux. 160 K9
Eschen, Liech. 160 N2
Eschnerberg, range, Liech. 160 M2
Eschwege, Ger. 148 F7
Escocesa, Bahía, Dom. Rep. 117 L19
Escondido, Calif., U.S. 109 Y10
Escudero, station, Antarctica 226 C3
Escuinapa, Mex. 114 G9
Escuintla, Guatemala 115 L15
Escuintla, Mex. 115 L15
Eséka, Cameroon 201 J15
Esenguly, Turkm. 174 M6
Eşfahan (Isfahan), Iran 173 E13
Esfandak, Iran 173 H18
Eshkamesh, Afghan. 176 K8
Eshkashem, Afghan. 176 K9
Esil, river, Kaz. 174 B12
Esil, Kaz. 174 C12
Esimi, Gr. 155 B16
Esker, Nfld. & Lab., Can. 83 L20
Eskifjörður, Ice. 140 F4
Eskilstuna, Sw. 141 L13
Eskimo Lakes, N.W.T., Can. 82 E10
Eskipazar, Turk. 168 D8
Eskişehir, Turk. 168 E6
Esla, river, Sp. 144 C9
Eslāmābād, Iran 172 D10
Eslam Qal'eh, Afghan. 176 M1
Eşler Dağı, Turk. 168 G5
Eşme, Turk. 168 F4
Esmeralda, Cuba 116 H10
Esmeralda, Qnsld., Austral. 211 R12
Esmeralda, Isla, Chile 133 U6
Esmeraldas, Ecua. 128 H2
Esmeraldas, Río, Ecua. 128 H2
Esmoriz, Port. 144 E5
Espagnol Point, St. Vincent & the Grenadines 121 J17
Espakeh, Iran 173 H17
Espalion, Fr. 147 W10
Española, Isla (Hood), Ecua. 128 R10
Espanola, N. Mex., U.S. 107 R12
Esperance, W. Aust., Austral. 211 X4
Esperance, Cape, Solomon Is. 217 N18
Esperanza, station, Antarctica 226 C4
Esperanza, Arg. 132 J11
Esperanza, P.R., U.S. 120 N6
Esperanza, Peru 130 G5
Espichel, Cabo, Port. 144 J4
Espiègle Bay, Vanuatu 218 D2
Espiel, Sp. 144 K9
Espigão Mestre, range, S. Amer. 126 G9
Espinhaço, Serra do, Braz. 131 K15
Espírito Santo see Vila Velha, Braz. 131 L16
Espiritu Santo, island, Vanuatu 218 C2
Espíritu Santo, Isla, Mex. 114 F7
Espoo (Esbo), Fin. 141 K16
Esposende, Port. 144 D5
Espuña, peak, Sp. 145 K13
Espungabera, Mozambique 202 G12
Esquel, Arg. 133 R7
Esquina, Arg. 132 J12
Essaouira, Mor. 196 B7
Essen, Belg. 146 K12
Essen, Ger. 148 E5
Essendon, Mount, Austral. 210 G4
Essequibo, river, Guyana 129 E14
Essex, Punta, Ecua. 128 R8
Essex Junction, Vt., U.S. 94 F12
Essexville, Mich., U.S. 98 K12
Essington, Port, Austral. 210 A8
Esslingen, Ger. 148 J7
Esso, Russ. 159 F22
Es Suki, Sudan 199 E13
Estaca de Bares, Punta da, Sp. 144 A7
Estacado, Llano, N. Mex., Tex., U.S. 84 K10
Estados, Isla de los (Staten Island), Arg. 133 X10
Eşţahbānāt, Iran 173 G14
Estância, Braz. 131 H17
Estancia, N. Mex., U.S. 107 S12
Estany d'Engolasters, lake, Andorra 160 J3
Estanyó, Pic de l', Andorra 160 H4
Estats, Pic d', Sp. 145 C16
Estavayer-le-Lac, Switz. 150 B2
Este, It. 150 E7
Este, Punta del, S. Amer. 126 M7
Estelí, Nicar. 115 M18
Estella (Lizarra), Sp. 145 C13
Estelline, S. Dak., U.S. 104 K8
Estelline, Tex., U.S. 102 H7
Estepona, Sp. 144 M9
Estes Park, Colo., U.S. 106 L13
Estevan, Sask., Can. 82 N12
Estherville, Iowa, U.S. 104 M10
Estill, S.C., U.S. 96 M9
Estonia, Eur. 139 R9
Estrela, Serra da, Port. 144 F6
Estrella, peak, Sp. 144 J11
Estrella Bay, Solomon Is. 217 M18
Estremoz, Port. 144 H6
Esztergom, Hung. 149 L14
Etadunna, S. Aust., Austral. 211 V10
Etal Atoll, F.S.M. 216 Q7
Étampes, Fr. 147 Q10
Étang-Sale, Reunion, Fr. 205 H15
Étaples, Fr. 146 L9
Étarik see Monument, island, Vanuatu 218 E3
Etawah, India 178 G7
Etcharai, island, Marshall Is. 216 K2
Etena, Amer. Samoa, U.S. 218 R4
Ethiopia, Af. 195 H23
Ethiopian College, Vatican City 161 Q14
Ethiopian Highlands, Eth. 194 H10
Etive, Loch, Scot., U.K. 142 L8
Etna, peak, It. 151 S11
Etna, Wyo., U.S. 106 H8
Etolikó, Gr. 154 H8
Etorofu see Iturup, island, Russ. 159 J23
Etosha Pan, Namibia 202 G6
Etoumbi, Congo 201 L17
Etowah, Tenn., U.S. 101 F18
Etrek see Atrak, river, Iran 173 B14
Ettelbruck, Lux. 160 H10
Etten, island, F.S.M. 217 B16
Etten, island, F.S.M. 217 C15
Ettlingen, Ger. 148 J6
Ettrick, N.Z. 213 Q16
Eu, Fr. 146 M9
'Eua, island, Tonga 214 K10
'Euaiki, island, Tonga 218 H12
'Euaiki, island, Tonga 218 M11
'Euakafa, island, Tonga 218 M11
Euboea see Évia, island, Gr. 155 H13
Eucla Basin, Austral. 210 J6
Eucla Motel, W. Aust., Austral. 211 W7
Euclid, Ohio, U.S. 99 N14
Eucumbene, Lake, Austral. 210 L13
Eudora, Ark., U.S. 100 K9
Eudunda, S. Aust., Austral. 211 X10
Eufaula, Ala., U.S. 101 M17
Eufaula, Okla., U.S. 102 G13
Eufaula Lake, Okla., U.S. 102 G13
Eugene, Oreg., U.S. 108 H3
Eugenia Point, N. Amer. 80 L3
Eugenio Bustos, Arg. 132 L8
Euginia, Punta, Mex. 114 D5
Eumseong, S. Korea 182 F13
Eunice, La., U.S. 100 P8
Eunice, N. Mex., U.S. 107 V15
Eupen, Belg. 146 L13
Euphrates, river, Asia 166 F3
Eupora, Miss., U.S. 100 J12
Eurardy, W. Aust., Austral. 211 V2
Eureka, Calif., U.S. 108 M1
Eureka, Ill., U.S. 99 Q5
Eureka, Kans., U.S. 105 U9
Eureka, Mont., U.S. 106 A5
Eureka, Nev., U.S. 109 P11
Eureka, Nunavut, Can. 83 B15
Eureka, S. Dak., U.S. 104 J5
Eureka, Utah, U.S. 106 L7
Eureka Springs, Ark., U.S. 100 E7
Europa, Île, Mozambique Ch. 203 H15
Europa, Picos de, Sp. 144 B9
Europa, Punta, Eq. Guinea 204 L7
Europa Point, Gibraltar, U.K. 161 R23
Eustis, Fla., U.S. 97 S8
Eutaw, Ala., U.S. 101 K14
Eutin, Ger. 148 B8
Eva Downs, N. Terr., Austral. 211 R9
Evans, Mount, Mont., U.S. 106 E6
Evanston, Ill., U.S. 99 N7
Evanston, Wyo., U.S. 106 K8
Evansville, Alas., U.S. 111 E16
Evansville, Ind., U.S. 99 U7
Evart, Mich., U.S. 98 K10
Évdilos, Gr. 155 K16
Eveleth, Minn., U.S. 104 F12
Evensk, Russ. 159 E21
Everard, Lake, Austral. 210 J9
Everard Park, S. Aust., Austral. 211 V8
Everest, Mount, China, Nepal 178 F11
Everett, Wash., U.S. 108 B4
Everglades City, Fla., U.S. 97 X9
Everglades National Park, Fla., U.S. 97 X9
Evergreen, Ala., U.S. 101 M15
Evesham, Eng., U.K. 143 U12
Évia (Euboea), island, Gr. 155 H13
Évian, Fr. 147 T14
Evora, Port. 144 J6
Évreux, Fr. 147 P8
Évros, river, Gr. 155 C16
Évros, river, Turk. 168 C3
Evrótas, river, Gr. 154 L10
Évry, Fr. 147 P10
Evrychou, Cyprus 160 P7
'Ewa, Hawai'i, U.S. 112 E11
Ewa, region, Nauru 217 E23
Ewab see Kai, Kepulauan, islands, Indonesia 189 L18
'Ewa Beach, Hawai'i, U.S. 112 E11
Ewaninga, N. Terr., Austral. 211 T8
Ewarton, Jam. 120 J9
Ewing, Nebr., U.S. 105 N6
Ewo, Congo 201 L17
Excelsior Mountains, Nev., U.S. 109 R8
Excelsior Springs, Mo., U.S. 105 S11
Executive Committee Range, Antarctica 226 L8
Exeter, Calif., U.S. 109 U7
Exeter, Eng., U.K. 143 X10
Exeter, N.H., U.S. 95 J15
Exeter Sound, Nunavut, Can. 83 F19
Exmoor, plateau, Eng., U.K. 143 W10
Exmouth, Eng., U.K. 143 X10
Exmouth, W. Aust., Austral. 211 T1
Exmouth Gulf, Austral. 210 F1
Exmouth Plateau, Ind. Oc. 241 K15
Exohí, Gr. 154 B12
Exotic Garden, Monaco 161 E20
Exploring Balavu Isles, Fiji Is. 218 H9
Exu, Braz. 131 F16
Exuma Sound, Bahamas 116 E12
Eye, Eng., U.K. 143 T15
Eyemouth, Scot., U.K. 142 M11
Eye Peninsula, Scot., U.K. 142 H7
Eyl, river, Somalia 199 G18
Eyl, Somalia 199 G18
Eymoutiers, Fr. 147 U9
Eyrarbakki, Ice. 140 F2
Eyre, Lake, Austral. 210 H10
Eyrecourt, Ire. 143 S5
Eyre North, Lake, S. Aust., Austral. 211 V10
Eyre Peninsula, Austral. 210 K9
Eyre South, Lake, Austral. 210 H10
Eysturoy, island, Faroe Is., Den. 140 J6
Ezcaray, Sp. 144 C11
Ezequiel Ramos Mexia, Embalse, Arg. 133 P8
Ezine, Turk. 168 E2
Ezion-geber (Elath), ruin, Jordan 171 R5

F

Faaa, Fr. Polynesia, Fr. 219 N15
Faaaha, Fr. Polynesia, Fr. 219 A23
Faaite, island, Fr. Polynesia, Fr. 219 E18
Faanui, Fr. Polynesia, Fr. 219 K14
Faanui, Baie de, Fr. Polynesia, Fr. 219 K14
Faaone, Fr. Polynesia, Fr. 219 P17
Faaroa, Baie de, Fr. Polynesia, Fr. 219 B23
Fabala, Guinea 200 F7
Fabens, Tex., U.S. 103 V2
Faber Lake, N.W.T., Can. 82 G11
Fabero, Sp. 144 C8
Fabriano, It. 150 H9
Facatativá, Col. 128 F5
Fachi, Niger 197 G13
Facho, Pico do, Madeira 204 L5
Facpi Point, Guam, U.S. 216 D9
Facture, Fr. 147 W6
Fada, Chad 197 G16
Fada N'Gourma, Burkina Faso 200 E11
Faddeyevskiy, Ostrov, Russ. 159 D17
Fadghamī, Syr. 170 E14
Fadian Point, Guam, U.S. 216 C11
Fadiffolu Atoll, Maldives 179 U3
Faenza, It. 150 F7
Faetano, San Marino 161 K17
Fafa, island, Tonga 218 H11
Fafe, Port. 144 D6
Fagaitua, Amer. Samoa, U.S. 218 M8
Fagaitua Bay, Amer. Samoa, U.S. 218 M8
Fagaloa Bay, Samoa 218 L4
Fagamalo, Samoa 218 K2
Fagamalo, Amer. Samoa, U.S. 218 M6
Făgăraş, Rom. 153 D14
Fagasa, Amer. Samoa, U.S. 218 M7
Fagatele Bay, Amer. Samoa, U.S. 218 N7
Fagatogo, Amer. Samoa, U.S. 218 M7
Fagernes, Nor. 140 K11
Fagnano, Lago, Chile 133 X9
Faguibine, Lake, Niger 194 G3
Fagurhólsmýri, Ice. 140 G3
Fahala, island, Maldives 179 V3
Fahefa, Tonga 218 H10
Fahie Hill, Virgin Islands, U.K. 120 Q6
Fahraj, Iran 173 G16

Faial, island, Azores 144 P3
Faibus Point, N. Mariana Is., U.S. 216 B7
Faichuk, island, F.S.M. 217 C14
Faie, Fr. Polynesia, Fr. 219 G14
Faie, Baie de, Fr. Polynesia, Fr. 219 G14
Faihava Passage, Tonga 218 L11
Faioa, island, Tonga 218 L12
Faïoa, island, Wallis & Futuna, Fr. 218 C11
Fairbanks, Alas., U.S. 111 G17
Fairborn, Ohio, U.S. 99 R12
Fairburn, Ga., U.S. 96 L5
Fairbury, Ill., U.S. 99 Q6
Fairbury, Nebr., U.S. 105 R8
Fairfax, Okla., U.S. 102 E11
Fairfax, S.C., U.S. 96 M9
Fairfield, Ala., U.S. 101 J15
Fairfield, Calif., U.S. 109 R4
Fairfield, Idaho, U.S. 106 H5
Fairfield, Ill., U.S. 99 T6
Fairfield, Iowa, U.S. 105 Q13
Fairfield, Mont., U.S. 106 C7
Fairfield, Ohio, U.S. 99 S11
Fairfield, Tex., U.S. 103 N12
Fair Haven, Vt., U.S. 94 H12
Fairhope, Ala., U.S. 101 P14
Fair Isle, Scot., U.K. 142 F11
Fairmont, Minn., U.S. 104 L10
Fairmont, W. Va., U.S. 96 C9
Fairport, Mich., U.S. 98 G8
Fairport, N.Y., U.S. 94 J7
Fairview, Mont., U.S. 106 C13
Fairview, Okla., U.S. 102 F9
Fairview, Qnsld., Austral. 211 Q12
Fairview, Tenn., U.S. 101 E15
Fairview, Utah, U.S. 106 M7
Fairweather, Mount, Alas., U.S. 111 K21
Fais, island, F.S.M. 214 F3
Faisalabad, Pak. 177 Q11
Faith, S. Dak., U.S. 104 J3
Faizabad, India 178 G8
Fajardo, P.R., U.S. 120 M6
Fajardo, P.R., U.S. 117 M23
Fakahiku, island, Tonga 218 Q6
Fakahina, island, Fr. Polynesia, Fr. 219 E20
Fakakakai, Tonga 218 P7
Fakaofu, island, Tokelau, N.Z. 214 H10
Fakarava, island, Fr. Polynesia, Fr. 219 E18
Fakel, Russ. 156 G16
Fakenham, Eng., U.K. 143 T15
Fakfak, Indonesia 189 K18
Faku, China 182 B11
Fala Ane Point, Amer. Samoa, U.S. 218 Q3
Falaise, Pointe, St. Martin, Fr. 121 B14
Falakró, Óros, Gr. 155 B13
Falamae, Solomon Is. 217 L14
Falciano, San Marino 161 G17
Falcon, Cape, Oreg., U.S. 108 E2
Falcon, Presa, Mex. 114 E12
Falconara Marittima, It. 150 H9
Falcone, Capo del, It. 150 M3
Falconer, N.Y., U.S. 94 K4
Falcon Reservoir, Tex., U.S. 103 V8
Falealupo, Samoa 218 K1
Faleasao, Amer. Samoa, U.S. 218 P3
Falefatu, island, Tuvalu 217 L23
Falelatie, Samoa 218 L3
Falelima, Samoa 218 K1
Falémé, river, Mali, Senegal 196 H6
Faleniu, Amer. Samoa, U.S. 218 M7
Falfurrias, Tex., U.S. 103 V10
Falkenberg, Sw. 140 N12
Falkensee, Ger. 148 D10
Falkirk, Scot., U.K. 142 M9
Falkland Escarpment, Atl. Oc. 237 V6
Falkland Fracture Zone, Antarctic Oc. 244 B9
Falkland Islands (Islas Malvinas), Falkland Is., U.K. 133 W12
Falkland Plateau, Atl. Oc. 237 V6
Falkland Sound, Falkland Is., U.K. 133 W12
Falknis, peak, Liech., Switz. 160 R3
Falkonéra, island, Gr. 154 M12
Falköping, Sw. 140 M12
Fallbrook, Calif., U.S. 109 Y9
Fallen Jerusalem, island, Virgin Islands, U.K. 120 R8
Fallières Coast, Antarctica 226 E5
Fallon, Nev., U.S. 109 P7
Fall River, Mass., U.S. 95 L15
Fall River Lake, Kans., U.S. 105 U9
Fall River Mills, Calif., U.S. 108 M4
Falls City, Nebr., U.S. 105 R9
Falmouth, Antigua & Barbuda 121 B21
Falmouth, Eng., U.K. 143 Y8
Falmouth, Jam. 120 H7
Falmouth, Ky., U.S. 101 A18
Falmouth, Me., U.S. 95 H16
Falmouth Harbour, Antigua & Barbuda 121 B21
False Bay, S. Af. 194 R7
False Cape, N. Amer. 80 N3
False Divi Point, India 179 N8
False Pass, Alas., U.S. 110 N11
False Point, India 178 K11
Falset, Sp. 145 E16
Falso, Cabo, Dom. Rep. 117 N17
Falso, Cabo, Mex. 114 G7
Falster, island, Den. 140 P12
Fălticeni, Rom. 153 B15
Falun, Sw. 141 K13
Famagusta see Ammochostos, Cyprus 160 P10
Fanaik, island, F.S.M. 217 D16
Fanan, island, F.S.M. 217 C16
Fanananei, Mochun, F.S.M. 217 B14
Fanangat, island, F.S.M. 217 B15
Fanannon, island, F.S.M. 217 C15
Fanapanges, island, F.S.M. 217 C14
Fanasich, island, F.S.M. 217 C14
Fanchang, China 182 K8
Fancy, St. Vincent & the Grenadines 121 J16
Fanemoch, island, F.S.M. 217 B15
Faneno, island, F.S.M. 217 B15
Fanew, island, F.S.M. 217 C15
Fanew, Mochun, F.S.M. 217 C15
Fangak, Sudan 198 G12
Fangale'ounga, Tonga 218 P7
Fangasito, island, Tonga 218 M11
Fangatau, island, Fr. Polynesia, Fr. 219 E20
Fangataufa, island, Fr. Polynesia, Fr. 219 H21
Fangcheng, China 182 J4
Fangshan, China 182 E4
Fangxian, China 182 J3
Fanning Island see Tabuaeran, Kiribati 214 F12
Fano, It. 150 G9
Fanos, island, F.S.M. 217 B15
Fanshan, China 183 N9
Fanshi, China 182 D5
Fanūdah, Saudi Arabia 172 J7
Fañunchuluyan, Bahia, N. Mariana Is., U.S. 216 B6
Fanurmot, island, F.S.M. 217 C14
Fanxian, China 182 G6
Farafangana, Madagascar 203 H17
Farâfra Oasis, Egypt 197 D18
Farah, river, Afghan. 177 P2
Farah, Afghan. 177 P2
Farallon de Medinilla, island, N. Mariana Is., U.S. 216 C2
Farallon de Pajaros, island, N. Mariana Is., U.S. 214 D4
Farallon Islands, Calif., U.S. 84 G2
Faranah, Guinea 200 F6
Farasān, Jazā'ir, Saudi Arabia 172 P8
Faraulep Atoll, F.S.M. 216 Q4
Fare, Fr. Polynesia, Fr. 219 G14
Fareara, Pointe, Fr. Polynesia, Fr. 219 Q17
Fareera, Passe, Fr. Polynesia, Fr. 219 G14
Fareham, Eng., U.K. 143 W13
Farewell, Cape see Nunap Isua, Greenland, Den. 81 D22
Farewell, Cape, N.Z. 213 M17
Farga de Moles, Sp. 160 K2
Fargo, N. Dak., U.S. 104 G8
Farg'ona, Uzb. 175 K14
Faribault, Minn., U.S. 104 K11
Faridkot, India 178 D4
Farim, Guinea-Bissau 200 E4
Farīmān, Iran 173 C16
Fariones, Punta, Canary Is. 204 P8
Farkhor, Taj. 176 K8
Farmakonísion, Gr. 155 L18
Farmersville, Tex., U.S. 102 K12
Farmerville, La., U.S. 100 K8
Farmington, Ill., U.S. 99 Q4
Farmington, Me., U.S. 95 F16
Farmington, Mo., U.S. 105 U15
Farmington, N. Mex., U.S. 107 Q10
Farmington, Utah, U.S. 106 K7
Farmville, Va., U.S. 96 F12
Farnham, N.Y., U.S. 94 K4
Fårö, island, Sw. 141 L14
Faro, Port. 144 L6
Faro, Punta del, It. 151 R12
Faroe Bank, Atl. Oc. 236 C12
Faroe-Iceland Ridge, Atl. Oc. 236 C11
Faroe Islands (Føroyar), Den. 140 J5
Farquhar, Atoll de, Seychelles 203 C19
Farrell, Pa., U.S. 94 M3
Fārs, region, Iran 173 G14
Fársala, Gr. 154 F10
Farsund, Nor. 140 M10
Fartak, Ra's, Yemen 173 P13
Far'ûn (Coral Island), Egypt 171 R5
Farwell, Tex., U.S. 102 H3
Fasā, Iran 173 G14
Fasano, It. 150 M14
Fastiv, Ukr. 157 N5
Fastnet Rock, Ire. 143 V3
Fataka (Mitre Island), Solomon Is. 214 J8
Fatato, island, Tuvalu 217 K23
Fatehabad, India 178 E5
Fatehgarh, India 178 F7
Fatehpur, India 178 G7
Fátima, Port. 144 G5
Fatsa, Turk. 168 D12
Fatu Hiva, island, Fr. Polynesia, Fr. 215 H15
Fatumanini, Passe, Wallis & Futuna, Fr. 218 B11
Fatumanongi, island, Tonga 218 P6
Fatumu, Tonga 218 J12
Faucilles, Monts, Fr. 147 Q14
Faulkton, S. Dak., U.S. 104 J6
Fauna Nui, Lac, Fr. Polynesia, Fr. 219 G14
Fauro, island, Solomon Is. 217 K15
Fauske, Nor. 140 E12
Faversham, Eng., U.K. 143 V15
Favignana, Isola, It. 151 S8
Faxaflói, bay, Ice. 140 F2
Faya-Largeau, Chad 197 G15
Fayaoué, New Caledonia, Fr. 218 C8
Fayaoué, Baie de, New Caledonia, Fr. 218 C8
Fayd, Saudi Arabia 172 H8
Fayette, Ala., U.S. 101 J14
Fayette, Miss., U.S. 100 M10
Fayette, Mo., U.S. 105 S12
Fayetteville, Ark., U.S. 100 E6
Fayetteville, N.C., U.S. 96 J11
Fayetteville, Tenn., U.S. 101 G15
Fayetteville, W. Va., U.S. 96 E8
Fazilka, India 178 E4
Fdérik, Mauritania 196 E6
Fear, Cape, N.C., U.S. 96 K12
Fécamp, Fr. 147 N8
Federal, Arg. 132 J13
Federated States of Micronesia, Pac. Oc. 214 F4
Fedorovka, Kaz. 174 B10
Fefen, island, F.S.M. 217 C15
Fehmarn, island, Ger. 148 B9
Feijó, Braz. 130 F5
Feilding, N.Z. 213 L19
Feira de Santana, Braz. 131 H16
Feixi, China 182 K7
Feke, Turk. 168 G11
Felanitx, Sp. 145 H18
Feldbach, Aust. 148 M12
Feldberg, peak, Ger. 148 K6
Feldkirch, Aust. 148 L7
Feldkirch, Aust. 160 M3
Félicité Island, Seychelles 205 M21
Felidu Atoll, Maldives 179 V3
Felipe Carrillo Puerto, Mex. 115 H17
Felixstowe, Eng., U.K. 143 U15
Fellowship, Jam. 120 J11
Fellowship, Jam. 120 J7
Feltre, It. 150 D7
Femund, lake, Nor. 140 J11
Fen, river, China 182 F4
Fena Valley Reservoir, Guam, U.S. 216 D10
Fen Country, Eng., U.K. 143 T14
Fene, Sp. 144 A6
Feneppi, island, F.S.M. 217 D15
Fengari, peak, Gr. 155 D15
Fengcheng, China 182 C11
Fengcheng, China 183 N6
Fenghuang, China 183 N2
Fengjie, China 182 K2
Fengkai, China 183 R3
Fenglin, Taiwan, China 183 R10
Fengning, China 182 C7
Fengshan, Taiwan, China 183 S9
Fengtai, China 182 J7
Fengxian, China 180 K12
Fengyüan, Taiwan, China 183 R9
Fengzhen, China 182 C5
Feni Islands, P.N.G. 213 C22
Feno, Cap de, Fr. 150 L4
Feno, Capo di, Fr. 150 K3
Fenua Fu, island, Wallis & Futuna, Fr. 218 C11
Fenualoa, island, Solomon Is. 217 P23
Fenua Roa, island, Fr. Polynesia, Fr. 219 K16
Fenxi, China 182 F4
Fenyang, China 182 F4
Feodosiya, Ukr. 157 S8
Feolin Ferry, Scot., U.K. 142 M7
Fer, Point au, La., U.S. 100 R9
Fera, island, Solomon Is. 217 M18
Ferdows, Iran 173 D16
Féres, Gr. 155 C16
Fērfēr, Eth. 199 H17
Fergana Valley, Uzb. 175 K14
Fergus Falls, Minn., U.S. 104 H9
Ferguson Seamount, Pac. Oc. 238 F9
Fergusson Island, P.N.G. 213 E21
Feridu, island, Maldives 179 U3
Ferit, island, F.S.M. 217 B16
Ferkéssédougou, Côte d'Ivoire 200 F8
Fermo, It. 150 H10
Fermont, Que., Can. 83 L20
Fermoselle, Sp. 144 E8
Fermoy, Ire. 143 U4
Fernandez Bay, Bahamas 120 E11
Fernandina, Isla (Narborough), Ecua. 128 Q7
Fernandina Beach, Fla., U.S. 97 Q8
Fernando de Noronha, S. Amer. 126 E12
Fernando de Noronha, Arquipélago de, Braz. 131 E19
Fernan Vaz see Omboué, Gabon 201 L15
Ferndale, Calif., U.S. 109 N1
Ferndale, Wash., U.S. 108 A4
Fern Grotto, Hawai'i, U.S. 112 B6
Fern Gully, Jam. 120 H9
Fernlee, Qnsld., Austral. 211 V13
Fernley, Nev., U.S. 109 P7
Ferrara, It. 150 F7
Ferrato, Capo, It. 151 P4
Ferré, Cap, Martinique, Fr. 121 G23
Ferreira do Alentejo, Port. 144 K5
Ferreira Gomes, Braz. 130 C12
Ferreñafe, Peru 130 F2
Ferret, Cap, Fr. 147 W6
Ferrette, Fr. 147 R15
Ferriday, La., U.S. 100 M9
Ferro see Hierro, island, Canary Is. 204 R3
Ferro, Ilhéu de, Madeira 204 L5
Ferrol, Sp. 144 A6
Ferrolana, Eq. Guinea 204 M6
Ferrysburg, Mich., U.S. 98 L9
Fertile, Minn., U.S. 104 F8
Fès (Fez), Mor. 196 B9
Feshi, Dem. Rep. of the Congo 198 M8
Fessenden, N. Dak., U.S. 104 F5
Festus, Mo., U.S. 105 T15
Feteşti, Rom. 153 F17
Fethiye, Turk. 168 J4
Fethiye Körfezi, Turk. 168 J4
Fetlar, island, Scot., U.K. 142 D12
Fetoa, island, Tonga 218 Q6
Fetokopunga, island, Tonga 218 Q7
Fetuna, Fr. Polynesia, Fr. 219 C23
Feuet, Lib. 196 E12
Feuilles, Rivière aux, Que., Can. 83 K19
Feurs, Fr. 147 U12
Fevzipaşa, Turk. 168 H11
Feyzabad, Afghan. 176 K9
Fez see Fès, Mor. 196 B9
Fezzan, region, Lib. 197 E13
Fianarantsoa, Madagascar 203 H17
Fichtelberg, peak, Ger. 148 G10
Fidenza, It. 150 E5
Fieberling Tablemount, Pac. Oc. 239 F15
Fields Find, W. Aust., Austral. 211 W3
Fier, Albania 152 L9
Fier-Shegan, Albania 152 L9
Fife Lake, Mich., U.S. 98 J10
Fife Ness, Scot., U.K. 142 M11
Fifth Cataract, Sudan 199 D13
Figari, Capo, It. 150 M5
Figeac, Fr. 147 W9
Fig Tree, St. Kitts & Nevis 121 C18
Figueira da Foz, Port. 144 F5
Figueres, Sp. 145 C18
Figuig, Mor. 196 B9
Fiji Islands, Pac. Oc. 214 J9
Fiji Islands Plateau, Pac. Oc. 238 L10
Filabres, Sierra de los, Sp. 144 L12
Filadelfia, Parag. 130 L9
Filchner Ice Sheet, Antarctica 226 F10
Filey, Eng., U.K. 143 Q13
Filfla, island, Malta 161 M22
Filiaşi, Rom. 153 F13
Filiátes, Gr. 154 E7
Filiatrá, Gr. 154 L9
Filicudi, Isola, It. 151 R11
Filiourí, river, Gr. 155 B15
Filipiáda, Gr. 154 F7
Filipstad, Sw. 140 K12
Fillmore, Calif., U.S. 109 W7
Fillmore, Utah, U.S. 107 N7
Filyos, river, Turk. 168 C8
Fimbul Ice Shelf, Antarctica 226 A12
Fimi, river, Dem. Rep. of the Congo 198 K8
Fiñana, Sp. 144 L12
Fındıklı, Turk. 169 C15
Findlay, Ohio, U.S. 99 P12
Findochty, Scot., U.K. 142 J10
Fineveke, Wallis & Futuna, Fr. 218 B11
Finger Lakes, N.Y., U.S. 94 K7
Fingoè, Mozambique 202 E12
Fínikas, Gr. 155 K14
Finike, Turk. 168 J5
Finisterre, Cape, Sp. 138 H2
Finke, river, N. Terr., Austral. 211 U9
Finke, N. Terr., Austral. 211 U9
Finland, Eur. 139 Q9
Finland, Minn., U.S. 104 F13
Finland, Gulf of, Est., Fin. 141 K16
Finlay, river, B.C., Can. 82 J9
Finley, N. Dak., U.S. 104 F7
Finley Cay, Bahamas 120 E5
Finnmark Plateau, Nor. 138 A8
Finnsmark-vidda, region, Nor. 141 C14
Finschhafen, P.N.G. 213 D20
Finsteraarhorn, peak, Switz. 150 C3
Fionn Loch, Scot., U.K. 142 J8
Fionnphort, Scot., U.K. 142 L7
Fiorentino, San Marino 161 K15
Fiorina, river, San Marino 161 H16
Fiorina, San Marino 161 H16
Frías, Arg. 132 H9
Firat (Euphrates), river, Turk. 169 E15
Fire Island National Seashore, N.Y., U.S. 94 N12
Firenze (Florence), It. 150 G7
Firenzuola, It. 150 G7
Firmat, Arg. 132 K11
Firminy, Fr. 147 U12
Firozabad, India 178 G6
Firoz Koh, region, Afghan. 176 M4
First Cataract, Egypt 197 E19
First Sugar Mill, Hawai'i, U.S. 112 C5
Fīrūzābād, Iran 173 G13
Fish, river, Namibia 202 J7
Fisher, river, Mont., U.S. 106 B5
Fisher, S. Aust., Austral. 211 W7
Fisher Glacier, Antarctica 227 F18
Fisher Strait, Nunavut, Can. 83 H16
Fishguard (Abergwaun), Wales, U.K. 143 U8
Fishing Cays, Bahamas 120 C10
Fish Lake, Utah, U.S. 107 N7
Fiskárdo, Gr. 154 H7
Fismes, Fr. 147 N11
Fisterra, Sp. 144 B5
Fisterra, Cabo, Sp. 144 B5
Fitchburg, Mass., U.S. 95 K14
Fitii, Fr. Polynesia, Fr. 219 G14
Fitii, Baie de, Fr. Polynesia, Fr. 219 G14
Fitiuta, Amer. Samoa, U.S. 218 N4
Fito, Mount, Samoa 218 L3
Fitri, Lac, Chad 197 J15
Fitzgerald, Alta., Can. 82 J11
Fitzgerald, Ga., U.S. 97 P6
Fitzroy, river, Qnsld., Austral. 210 F15
Fitzroy, river, W. Aust., Austral. 211 R5
Fitzroy Crossing, W. Aust., Austral. 211 R5
Fiume see Rijeka, Croatia 152 E4
Fiumicello, river, San Marino 161 J16
Fivaku, island, Maldives 179 T3
Five Island Harbour, Antigua & Barbuda 121 B20
Five Islands Village, Antigua & Barbuda 121 B20

Flagler, Colo., U.S. 106 M15
Flagstaff, Ariz., U.S. 107 S7
Flagstaff Lake, Oreg., U.S. 108 K6
Flåm, Nor. 140 K10
Flambeau, river, Wis., U.S. 98 G4
Flamborough Head, Eng., U.K. 143 Q14
Flaming Gorge National Recreation Area, Wyo., U.S. 106 K9
Flaming Gorge Reservoir, Utah, Wyo., U.S. 106 K9
Flamingo, Fla., U.S. 97 Y9
Flamingo, Teluk, Indonesia 213 C16
Flamingo Cay, Bahamas 117 G13
Flamingo Point, Bahamas 117 E13
Flanagan Island, Virgin Islands, U.S. 120 N12
Flanders, region, Belg., Fr. 146 L10
Flandreau, S. Dak., U.S. 104 L8
Flannan Isles, Scot., U.K. 142 H6
Flathead Lake, Mont., U.S. 106 B6
Flat Island, Mauritius 205 F20
Flat Island, Spratly Is. 188 E11
Flatonia, Tex., U.S. 103 R11
Flat River, Mo., U.S. 105 U15
Flattery, Cape, Austral. 210 C13
Flattery, Cape, Wash., U.S. 108 B1
Flatts Village, Bermuda, U.K. 120 B3
Flatwoods, Ky., U.S. 101 A20
Flaxton, N. Dak., U.S. 104 D3
Fleeming Channel, Bahamas 120 E5
Fleetwood, Eng., U.K. 143 R10
Flekkefjord, Nor. 140 M10
Fleming Glacier, Antarctica 226 E5
Flemingsburg, Ky., U.S. 101 B18
Flemish Cap, Atl. Oc. 236 F7
Flensburg, Ger. 148 A7
Flers, Fr. 147 P7
Fletcher Peninsula, Antarctica 226 H5
Fletcher Plain, Arctic Oc. 242 H9
Fleurance, Fr. 147 X8
Fleurier, Switz. 150 B1
Flight 93 National Memorial, Pa., U.S. 94 P4
Flinders, river, Qnsld., Austral. 211 S12
Flinders Bay, W. Aust., Austral. 211 Y2
Flinders Island, Tas., Austral. 211 Y16
Flinders Ranges, Austral. 210 J10
Flin Flon, Man., Can. 83 L13
Flint, river, Ga., U.S. 97 P5
Flint, Mich., U.S. 98 L12
Flint Hills, Kans., U.S. 105 U8
Flint Island, Fr. Polynesia, Fr. 215 J13
Flipper Point, Wake I., U.S. 216 F8
Flisa, Nor. 140 K12
Flix, Sp. 145 E15
Flixecourt, Fr. 146 M9
Flocca, river, San Marino 161 H15
Flomaton, Ala., U.S. 101 N14
Flood Range, Antarctica 226 M8
Floodwood, Minn., U.S. 104 G12
Flora, Ill., U.S. 99 T6
Flora, Ind., U.S. 99 Q9
Flora, Oreg., U.S. 108 E9
Florala, Ala., U.S. 101 N16
Florange, Fr. 147 N14
Floreana see Santa María, Isla, island, Ecua. 128 R9
Florence, Ala., U.S. 101 G14
Florence, Ariz., U.S. 107 U7
Florence, Colo., U.S. 107 N13
Florence see Firenze, It. 150 G7
Florence, Kans., U.S. 105 T8
Florence, Ky., U.S. 101 A17
Florence, Oreg., U.S. 108 H2
Florence, S.C., U.S. 96 K10
Florence, Wis., U.S. 98 G7
Florencia, Col. 128 H4
Florenville, Belg. 160 J7
Flores, island, Azores 144 N1
Flores, Guatemala 115 K16
Flores, island, Indonesia 189 M14
Flores Sea, Indonesia 189 M13
Floreşti, Mold. 157 Q4
Floresville, Tex., U.S. 103 S10
Floriano, Braz. 131 F15
Floriano Peixoto, Braz. 130 G6
Florianópolis, Braz. 131 N13
Florida, Cuba 116 J10
Florida, peninsula, N. Amer. 80 M8
Florida, P.R., U.S. 120 M3
Florida, U.S. 97 R4
Florida, Straits of, Bahamas, U.S. 80 M8
Florida Bay, Fla., U.S. 97 Y10
Florida City, Fla., U.S. 97 X10
Florida Islands, Solomon Is. 217 N18
Florida Keys, Fla., U.S. 97 Y9
Floridia, It. 151 T12
Flórina, Gr. 154 C8
Florissant, Mo., U.S. 105 S15
Florissant Fossil Beds National Monument, Colo., U.S. 107 N13
Florø, Nor. 140 J9
Flotta, island, Scot., U.K. 142 G10
Flotte, Cap de, New Caledonia, Fr. 218 D9
Floyd, N. Mex., U.S. 107 T15
Floydada, Tex., U.S. 102 J6
Flumet, Fr. 147 U14
Fly, river, P.N.G. 213 D17
Foa, island, Tonga 218 P7
Foça, Turk. 168 F2
Foča, Bosn. & Herzg. 152 H8
Focşani, Rom. 153 D16
Fofoa, island, Tonga 218 L11
Fogang, China 183 R4
Fogausa, Cape, Amer. Samoa, U.S. 218 M8
Foggia, It. 150 L12
Fogo, island, Cape Verde 205 E15
Fogo Island, Nfld. & Lab., Can. 83 L23
Fohnsdorf, Aust. 148 L11
Fokino, Russ. 156 L8
Foko Malsu, cape, F.S.M. 217 A18
Folda, bay, Nor. 140 G11
Folégandros, Gr. 155 M14
Folégandros, Gr. 155 M14
Foley, Ala., U.S. 101 P14
Foley, Minn., U.S. 104 J11
Foley Island, Nunavut, Can. 83 F17
Foligno, It. 150 J8
Folkestone, Eng., U.K. 143 W15
Folkston, Ga., U.S. 97 Q8
Follett, Tex., U.S. 102 E7
Follonica, It. 150 J6
Follonica, Golfo di, It. 150 J6
Folly Beach, S.C., U.S. 96 M10
Foloha, Tonga 218 J11
Folschette, Lux. 160 J9
Folsom, Calif., U.S. 109 Q5
Folteşti, Rom. 153 D17
Fomboni, Comoros 205 N15
Fomento, Cuba 116 H9
Fond d'Or Bay, St. Lucia 121 K14
Fond du Lac, Sask., Can. 82 J12
Fond du Lac, Wis., U.S. 98 K6
Fondi, It. 150 L9
Fongafale see Funafuti, Tuvalu 217 K24
Fono, island, F.S.M. 217 B15
Fonoifua, island, Tonga 218 Q6
Fononuk, island, F.S.M. 217 D16
Fonou, island, F.S.M. 217 C15
Fonseca, Golfo de, Hond. 115 M17
Fonseca, Gulf of see Fonseca, Golfo de, N. Amer. 80 Q7
Fontainebleau, Fr. 147 Q10
Fontana Lake, N.C., U.S. 96 J6
Fontaneda, Andorra 160 K2
Fonte Boa, Braz. 130 D7
Fontenelle Reservoir, Wyo., U.S. 106 J9
Fontenoy, Grenada 121 L22
Fontvieille, Monaco 161 F20
Fontvieille, Port of, Monaco 161 F21
Fonuafo'ou, island, Tonga 218 M12
Fonuaika, island, Tonga 218 Q6
Fonuakula, Niue, N.Z. 219 B20
Fonua'one'one, island, Tonga 218 M11
Fonua'unga, island, Tonga 218 M12
Fonuchu, island, F.S.M. 217 A15
Foping, China 182 H1
Foppolo, It. 150 D5
Forbesganj, India 178 G11
Forbes Hill, Bahamas 120 F9
Forcalquier, Fr. 147 W14
Forchheim, Ger. 148 H8
Ford, Cape, Austral. 210 B7
Fordate, island, Indonesia 213 D14
Førde, Nor. 140 K10
Ford Ranges, Antarctica 226 N9
Fords Bridge, N.S.W., Austral. 211 W12
Fordyce, Ark., U.S. 100 J8
Forécariah, Guinea 200 F5
Forel, Mont, N. Amer. 80 C10
Foreman, Ark., U.S. 100 J6
Forest, Miss., U.S. 100 L12
Forest City, Iowa, U.S. 104 M11
Forest City, N.C., U.S. 96 J8
Forest Grove, Oreg., U.S. 108 F3
Forest Home, Qnsld., Austral. 211 R12
Forest Park, Ga., U.S. 96 L5
Forest Point, Anguilla, U.K. 120 R11
Forestville, Mich., U.S. 98 K13
Forestville, Que., Can. 83 N20
Forez, Monts du, Fr. 147 U12
Forfar, Scot., U.K. 142 L10
Forgan, Okla., U.S. 102 E7
Forges-les-Eaux, Fr. 147 N9
Forks, Wash., U.S. 108 B2
Forlì, It. 150 G8
Forman, N. Dak., U.S. 104 H7
Formentera, island, Sp. 145 J17
Formiga, Braz. 131 L14
Formigas, Ilhéus, Azores 144 Q6
Formosa, Arg. 132 F13
Formosa, Braz. 131 J13
Formosa, Serra, Braz. 130 G11
Formosa do Rio Prêto, Braz. 131 G14
Føroyar see Faroe Islands, Den. 140 J5
Forrest, W. Aust., Austral. 211 W6
Forrestal Range, Antarctica 226 G10
Forrest City, Ark., U.S. 100 G10
Forrest River, W. Aust., Austral. 211 Q6
Forsayth, Qnsld., Austral. 211 R12
Forssa, Fin. 141 J15
Forst, Ger. 148 E11
Forster-Tuncurry, N.S.W., Austral. 211 X15
Forsyth, Ga., U.S. 96 M5
Forsyth, Mo., U.S. 105 V12
Forsyth, Mont., U.S. 106 D11
Fort Abbas, Pak. 177 S11
Fort Albany, Ont., Can. 83 M17
Fortaleza, Braz. 131 E17
Fort Allen, P.R., U.S. 120 N3
Fort Antoine, Monaco 161 E22
Fort Atkinson, Wis., U.S. 98 L6
Fort Benton, Mont., U.S. 106 C8
Fort Bowie National Historic Site, Ariz., U.S. 107 V9
Fort Bragg, Calif., U.S. 109 P2
Fort Caroline National Memorial, Fla., U.S. 97 Q8
Fort Charlotte, St. Lucia 121 J14
Fort Charlotte, St. Vincent & the Grenadines 121 L16
Fort Chipewyan, Alta., Can. 82 J11
Fort Cobb Reservoir, Okla., U.S. 102 G9
Fort Collins, Colo., U.S. 106 L13
Fort Davis, Tex., U.S. 103 P2
Fort Davis National Historic Site, Tex., U.S. 103 P2
Fort-de-France, Martinique, Fr. 121 F22
Fort-de-France, Baie de, Martinique, Fr. 121 F22
Fort Deposit, Ala., U.S. 101 M15
Fort Dick, Calif., U.S. 108 L2
Fort Dodge, Iowa, U.S. 105 N11
Fort Duvernette, St. Vincent & the Grenadines 121 L16
Forteau, Nfld. & Lab., Can. 83 L22
Forteau, Que., Can. 83 L22
Fortescue, river, W. Aust., Austral. 211 T3
Fortezza, It. 150 B7
Fort Fairfield, Me., U.S. 95 B18
Fort Frances, Ont., Can. 83 P14
Fort Fraser, B.C., Can. 82 K8
Fort Frederica National Monument, Ga., U.S. 97 P8
Fort Frederick, Grenada 121 L22
Fort Gaines, Ga., U.S. 97 P4
Fort Gibson, Okla., U.S. 102 F13
Fort Gibson Lake, Okla., U.S. 102 F13
Fort Good Hope, N.W.T., Can. 82 F10
Forth, Firth of, Scot., U.K. 142 M10
Fort Hall, Idaho, U.S. 106 H7
Fort Hancock, Tex., U.S. 103 V2
Fort Hope, Ont., Can. 83 N16
Fortín General Díaz, Parag. 130 M9
Fortín Infante Rivarola, Parag. 130 L8
Fortín Madrejón, Parag. 130 L9
Fortín May Alberto Gardel, Parag. 130 L8
Fortín Presidente Ayala, Parag. 130 M9
Fortín Suárez Arana, Bol. 130 K9
Fort James, Antigua & Barbuda 121 B20
Fort Jeudy, Point of, Grenada 121 L22
Fort Jones, Calif., U.S. 108 L3
Fort Kent, Me., U.S. 95 A17
Fort Klamath, Oreg., U.S. 108 K4
Fort Knox, Ky., U.S. 101 C16
Fort Laperrine see Tamanrasset, Alg. 196 F11
Fort Laramie, Wyo., U.S. 106 J13
Fort Laramie National Historic Site, Wyo., U.S. 106 J13
Fort Larned National Historic Site, Kans., U.S. 105 T5
Fort Lauderdale, Fla., U.S. 97 W10
Fort Liard, N.W.T., Can. 82 H10
Fort-Liberté, Haiti 117 L17
Fort Madison, Iowa, U.S. 105 Q14
Fort Matanzas National Monument, Fla., U.S. 97 R9
Fort McMurray, Alta., Can. 82 K11
Fort McPherson, N.W.T., Can. 82 E9
Fort Meade, Fla., U.S. 97 U8
Fort Mill, S.C., U.S. 96 J9
Fort Miribel, Alg. 196 C11
Fort Morgan, Colo., U.S. 106 L14
Fort Munro, Pak. 177 R8
Fort Myers, Fla., U.S. 97 W8
Fort Myers Beach, Fla., U.S. 97 W8
Fort Nelson, B.C., Can. 82 J9
Fort Payne, Ala., U.S. 101 H16
Fort Peck, Mont., U.S. 106 B11
Fort Peck Dam, Mont., U.S. 106 B12
Fort Peck Lake, Mont., U.S. 106 C11
Fort Pierce, Fla., U.S. 97 U10
Fort Pierre, S. Dak., U.S. 104 K5
Fort Point, Virgin Islands, U.K. 120 R8
Fort Portal, Uganda 198 J12
Fort Providence, N.W.T., Can. 82 H11
Fort Pulaski National Monument, Ga., U.S. 97 N9
Fort Raleigh National Historic Site, N.C., U.S. 96 G15
Fort Randall Dam, S. Dak., U.S. 104 M6
Fort Resolution, N.W.T., Can. 82 H11
Fortress Headquarters, Gibraltar, U.K. 161 Q22
Fort Rock, Oreg., U.S. 108 J5
Fort Royal, Guadeloupe, Fr. 121 E14
Fort St. Catherine, Bermuda, U.K. 120 A3
Fort St. John, B.C., Can. 82 K9
Fort Scaur, Bermuda, U.K. 120 B1
Fort Scott, Kans., U.S. 105 U10
Fort Scott National Historic Site, Kans., U.S. 105 U10
Fort Severn, Ont., Can. 83 L16
Fort Shevchenko, Kaz. 174 G5
Fort Simpson, N.W.T., Can. 82 H10
Fort Smith, Ark., U.S. 100 F6
Fort Smith, N.W.T., Can. 82 J11
Fort Stanwix National Monument, N.Y., U.S. 94 J9
Fort Stockton, Tex., U.S. 103 P3
Fort Sumner, N. Mex., U.S. 107 S14
Fort Sumter National Monument, S.C., U.S. 96 M10
Fort Supply, Okla., U.S. 102 E8
Fort Thompson, S. Dak., U.S. 104 L5
Fort Trinquet see Bir Mogreïn, Mauritania 196 D6
Fortuna, Calif., U.S. 109 N1
Fortuna, N. Dak., U.S. 104 D2
Fortune Hill, Bahamas 120 E12
Fortune Island see Long Cay, Bahamas 117 H14
Fort Union National Monument, N. Mex., U.S. 107 R13
Fort Union Trading Post National Historic Site, N. Dak., U.S. 104 E1
Fort Valley, Ga., U.S. 96 M5
Fort Vermilion, Alta., Can. 82 J10
Fort Walton Beach, Fla., U.S. 97 Q2
Fort Wayne, Ind., U.S. 99 P10
Fort Worth, Tex., U.S. 102 L11
Fort Yates, N. Dak., U.S. 104 H4
Fort Yukon, Alas., U.S. 111 E18
Fosforescénte, Bahía, P.R., U.S. 120 P2
Foshan, China 183 R4
Fosheim Peninsula, Nunavut, Can. 83 B16
Fossano, It. 150 F2
Fossato di Vico, It. 150 H9
Fossil, Oreg., U.S. 108 G6
Fossil Butte National Monument, Wyo., U.S. 106 J8
Fosston, Minn., U.S. 104 F9
Foster, Mount, Alas., U.S. 111 K21
Fostoria, Ohio, U.S. 99 P12
Fotuha'a, island, Tonga 218 P6
Fougères, Fr. 147 Q6
Foula, island, Scot., U.K. 142 D11
Foul Bay, Barbados 121 L20
Foulness Island, Eng., U.K. 143 V15
Foulweather, Cape, Oreg., U.S. 108 G2
Foulwind, Cape, N.Z. 213 N17
Foumban, Cameroon 201 H15
Foumbouni, Comoros 205 M14
Foundation Ice Stream, Antarctica 226 G10
Fountain, Colo., U.S. 107 N13
Fountain City, Wis., U.S. 98 J3
Fourche, Île, Lesser Antilles 119 F15
Four Corners, Wyo., U.S. 106 G14
Fourcroy, Cape, Austral. 210 A7
Fourmies, Fr. 146 M11
Four Mountains, Islands of, Alas., U.S. 110 P8
Fournaise, Piton de la, Reunion, Fr. 205 H17
Foúrni, island, Gr. 155 K17
Foúrni, Gr. 155 K17
Fourth Cataract, Sudan 199 D13
Fourup, island, F.S.M. 217 C15
Fouta Djallon, region, Guinea 200 E6
Foux, Cap-à-, Haiti 117 L15
Foveaux Strait, N.Z. 213 R15
Fowler, Colo., U.S. 107 N14
Fowler, Ind., U.S. 99 Q8
Fowler, Kans., U.S. 105 U4
Fowlers Bay, S. Aust., Austral. 211 W8
Fox, river, Ill., U.S. 99 P6
Fox, river, Wis., U.S. 98 J7
Foxe Basin, Nunavut, Can. 83 G17
Foxe Channel, Nunavut, Can. 83 H17
Foxe Peninsula, Nunavut, Can. 83 H17
Fox Glacier, N.Z. 213 P16
Fox Islands, Alas., U.S. 110 P10
Foxpark, Wyo., U.S. 106 K12
Fox Town, Bahamas 120 A5
Foyle, Lough, N. Ire., U.K. 143 P6
Foyn Coast, Antarctica 226 E4
Foz, Sp. 144 A7
Foz do Cunene, Angola 202 F5
Foz do Iguaçu, Braz. 130 M11
Fraga, Sp. 145 D15
Fram Basin, Arctic Oc. 242 H11
Framnes Mountains, Antarctica 227 E20
Fram Peak, Antarctica 227 D19
Franca, Braz. 131 L13
France, Eur. 139 U4
Francés, Cabo, Cuba 116 H4
Francés, Punta, Cuba 116 H5
Frances Lake, Yukon, Can. 82 G9
Francés Viejo, Cabo, Dom. Rep. 117 L19
Franceville, Gabon 201 L17
Francis Bay, Virgin Islands, U.S. 120 M11
Francis Case, Lake, S. Dak., U.S. 104 M6
Francisco del Oro, Mex. 114 E9
Francistown, Botswana 202 G10
Francs Peak, Wyo., U.S. 106 G9
Frankenberg, Ger. 148 F7
Frankfort, Ind., U.S. 99 Q8
Frankfort, Kans., U.S. 105 R8
Frankfort, Ky., U.S. 101 B17
Frankfort, Mich., U.S. 98 J9
Frankfurt am Main, Ger. 148 G6
Frankfurt an der Oder, Ger. 148 E11
Franklin, Ind., U.S. 99 S9
Franklin, Ky., U.S. 101 D15
Franklin, La., U.S. 100 Q9
Franklin, N.C., U.S. 96 J6
Franklin, N.H., U.S. 95 H14
Franklin, Nebr., U.S. 105 R6
Franklin, Pa., U.S. 94 M3
Franklin, Tenn., U.S. 101 F15
Franklin, Va., U.S. 96 F13
Franklin Bay, N.W.T., Can. 82 E11
Franklin D. Roosevelt Lake, Wash., U.S. 108 B8
Franklin Lake, Nev., U.S. 109 N11
Franklin Mountains, N. Amer. 80 D4
Franklin Strait, Nunavut, Can. 83 E14
Franklinton, La., U.S. 100 N11
Franklinville, N.Y., U.S. 94 K5
Frank Sound, Cayman Is., U.K. 120 J3
Frankston, Tex., U.S. 102 M13
Frantsa Iosifa, Zemlya (Franz Josef Land), Russ. 158 C12
Franz, Ont., Can. 83 P17
Franz Josef Glacier, N.Z. 213 P16
Franz Josef Land see Frantsa Iosifa, Zemlya, Russ. 158 C12
Frasca, Capo della, It. 151 P3
Fraser, river, B.C., Can. 82 L8
Fraserburg, S. Af. 202 L8
Fraserburgh, Scot., U.K. 142 J11
Fraser Island (Great Sandy Island), Austral. 210 G16
Fraser Range, W. Aust., Austral. 211 X5
Frasertown, N.Z. 213 L20

Frasin, Rom. 153 B15
Frastanz, Aust. 160 M4
Fratta, river, San Marino 161 K14
Frauenfeld, Switz. 150 A4
Frazee, Minn., U.S. 104 G9
Fredensborg, Virgin Islands, U.S. 120 Q2
Frederick, Md., U.S. 96 C12
Frederick, Okla., U.S. 102 J9
Frederick, S. Dak., U.S. 104 H6
Frederick, Mount, Austral. 210 D7
Fredericksburg, Tex., U.S. 103 Q9
Fredericksburg, Va., U.S. 96 D12
Fredericktown, Mo., U.S. 105 U15
Fredericton, N.B., Can. 83 P21
Frederikshavn, Den. 140 M11
Frederiksted, Virgin Islands, U.S. 120 R2
Fredonia, Ariz., U.S. 107 Q6
Fredonia, Kans., U.S. 105 U9
Fredonia, N.Y., U.S. 94 K4
Fredrikstad, Nor. 140 L11
Freedom, Okla., U.S. 102 E8
Freehold, N.J., U.S. 94 P11
Freeman, S. Dak., U.S. 104 M7
Freeport, Bahamas 120 F2
Freeport, Ill., U.S. 98 M5
Freeport, Me., U.S. 95 G16
Freeport, N.Y., U.S. 94 N11
Freeport, Tex., U.S. 103 S14
Freer, Tex., U.S. 103 T9
Freetown, Antigua & Barbuda 121 B21
Freetown, Bahamas 120 E2
Freetown, Jam. 120 J9
Freetown, Sierra Leone 200 G5
Freezeout Mountain, Oreg., U.S. 108 H9
Frégate, island, Seychelles 205 N21
Frégate Island, Mauritius 205 J19
Fregenal de la Sierra, Sp. 144 K7
Fréhel, Cap, Fr. 147 P5
Freiberg, Ger. 148 F10
Freiburg, Ger. 148 K5
Freidberg, Ger. 148 K8
Freirina, Chile 132 H6
Freisach, Aust. 148 M11
Freising, Ger. 148 K9
Freistadt, Aust. 148 K11
Freital, Ger. 148 F10
Fréjus, Fr. 147 X15
Fremantle, W. Aust., Austral. 211 X2
Fremont, Calif., U.S. 109 S4
Fremont, Mich., U.S. 98 L9
Fremont, Nebr., U.S. 105 P8
Fremont, Ohio, U.S. 99 P12
Fremont, river, Utah, U.S. 107 N8
Fremont Lake, Wyo., U.S. 106 H9
Fremont Mountains, Oreg., U.S. 108 J5
French Bay, Bahamas 120 F11
French Broad, river, Tenn., U.S. 101 E19
Frenchcap Cay, Virgin Islands, U.S. 120 P10
French Cays see Plana Cays, Bahamas 117 H15
French Frigate Shoals, Hawai'i, U.S. 112 M7
French Guiana, S. Amer. 127 B20
Frenchman Creek, Nebr., U.S. 105 Q3
Frenchman Flat, Nev., U.S. 109 T11
Frenchman's Cay, Virgin Islands, U.K. 120 R5
French Polynesia, Pac. Oc. 215 K14
Frenchville, Me., U.S. 95 A18
Fresh Water Bay, Barbados 121 K18
Fresh Water Lagoons, Kiribati 217 C23
Fresnay, Fr. 147 Q7
Fresnillo, Mex. 114 G10
Fresno, Calif., U.S. 109 T6
Fresno Reservoir, Mont., U.S. 106 B9
Frévent, Fr. 146 M10
Frewena, N. Terr., Austral. 211 S9
Freyung, Ger. 148 J10
Fri, Gr. 155 Q18
Fria, Guinea 200 F5
Friars Point, Miss., U.S. 100 H10
Fridtjof Nansen, Mount, Antarctica 226 K12
Friedrichshafen, Ger. 148 L7
Friend, Nebr., U.S. 105 Q7
Friesland, region, Ger., Neth. 146 G14
Frigate Bay, St. Kitts & Nevis 121 B18
Frio, river, Tex., U.S. 103 S8
Frio, Cape, S. Amer. 126 J10
Friona, Tex., U.S. 102 H4
Frisange, Lux. 160 K10
Frisco City, Ala., U.S. 101 M14
Frisian Islands, Eur. 138 E5
Frissel, Mount, Conn., U.S. 94 L12
Fritch, Tex., U.S. 102 G5
Friza, Proliv, Russ. 159 J23
Frobisher Bay, Nunavut, Can. 83 H19
Frolovo, Russ. 157 P12
Fromberg, Mont., U.S. 106 E10
Frome, Eng., U.K. 143 W11
Frome, Jam. 120 H6
Frome, Lake, S. Aust., Austral. 211 W11
Frome Downs, S. Aust., Austral. 211 W11
Frómista, Sp. 144 C10
Frontenac, Kans., U.S. 105 U10
Frontera, Mex. 114 E11
Frontera, Mex. 115 J14
Frontignan, Fr. 147 X11
Front Range, Colo., U.S. 106 L12
Frosinone, It. 150 L9
Frostburg, Md., U.S. 96 C11
Frostproof, Fla., U.S. 97 U8
Frøya, island, Nor. 140 H10
Fruita, Colo., U.S. 106 M10
Fruitland, Idaho, U.S. 106 G3
Frümsen, Switz. 160 M2
Frydendal, Virgin Islands, U.S. 120 M9
Fryeburg, Me., U.S. 95 G15
Frying Pan Shoals, N.C., U.S. 96 L13
Fu, river, China 183 N6
Fu, river, China 180 L12
Fua'amotu, Tonga 218 J11
Fua'amotu, island, Tonga 218 M11
Fuafatu, island, Tuvalu 217 K22
Fuagea, island, Tuvalu 217 L22
Fuagea, Te Ava, Tuvalu 217 K22
Fualifexe, island, Tuvalu 217 J23
Fualopa, island, Tuvalu 217 K22
Fua Mulaku, island, Maldives 179 X3
Fu'an, China 183 N9
Fucino, Piana del, It. 150 K10
Fudin, China 181 M17
Fuding, China 183 N9
Fuencaliente, Canary Is. 204 Q3
Fuencaliente, Punta de, Canary Is. 204 Q3
Fuengirola, Sp. 144 M9
Fuente de Cantos, Sp. 144 J8
Fuentesaúco, Sp. 144 E9
Fuerte Olimpo, Parag. 130 L10
Fuerteventura, island, Canary Is. 204 Q7
Fuga, island, Philippines 189 A13
Fugauvea, Passe, Wallis & Futuna, Fr. 218 B11
Fugou, China 182 H5
Fugu, China 182 D3
Fuhai, China 180 D7
Fuikbaai, bay, Neth. Antilles, Neth. 121 Q15
Fuji, peak, Japan 185 P11
Fujisawa, Japan 185 P12
Fukagawa, Japan 184 F14
Fukave, island, Tonga 218 H12
Fukuchiyama, Japan 185 P8
Fukue, Japan 185 S3
Fukue Jima, Japan 185 S2
Fukui, Japan 185 P9
Fukuoka, Japan 185 R4
Fukura, Japan 184 L12
Fukushima, Japan 184 H12
Fukushima, Japan 184 M13
Fukushima, Mount, Antarctica 227 C16
Fukuyama, Japan 185 Q7
Fulaga, island, Fiji Is. 218 K9
Fulaga Passage, Fiji Is. 218 K9
Fulda, Ger. 148 G7
Fulda, Minn., U.S. 104 L9
Fuling, China 180 L12
Fullarton, Trinidad & Tobago 121 Q21
Fullerton, Nebr., U.S. 105 P7
Fullerton Point, Antigua & Barbuda 121 B20
Fulton, Ill., U.S. 99 N4
Fulton, Ky., U.S. 100 E12
Fulton, Miss., U.S. 101 H13
Fulton, Mo., U.S. 105 S13
Fulton, N.Y., U.S. 94 H8
Fumay, Fr. 146 M12
Fumel, Fr. 147 W8
Funabashi, Japan 185 P12
Funafara, island, Tuvalu 217 L23
Funafuti, island, Tuvalu 217 K24
Funafuti (Fongafale), Tuvalu 217 K24
Funamanu, island, Tuvalu 217 K23
Funan, China 182 J6
Funangongo, island, Tuvalu 217 K23
Funchal, Madeira 204 M3
Fundo de Figueiras, Cape Verde 205 C17
Fundy, Bay of, N.B., Can., N.S. 83 P21
Funhalouro, Mozambique 203 H13
Funiya Point, N. Mariana Is., U.S. 216 E8
Funtanasupanie Point, N. Mariana Is., U.S. 216 E8
Funtua, Nigeria 201 E14
Fuping, China 182 G2
Fuqing, China 183 Q8
Furano, Japan 184 F14
Furmanov, Russ. 156 H11
Furneaux Group, Austral. 210 L16
Furqlus, Syr. 170 G8
Fürstenfeldbruck, Ger. 148 K8
Fürstenwalde, Ger. 148 E11
Fürth, Ger. 148 H8
Furth im Wald, Ger. 148 J10
Furukawa, Japan 184 L13
Fuscaldo, It. 151 P13
Fuse, Japan 185 N7
Fushan, China 182 F9
Fushun, China 182 B11
Fusio, Switz. 150 C4
Fusong, China 182 B13
Füssen, Ger. 148 L8
Futiga, Amer. Samoa, U.S. 218 M7
Futuna, island, Wallis & Futuna, Fr. 218 E11
Futuna, island, Vanuatu 218 H5
Fuwwah, Yemen 172 Q12
Fuxian, China 182 F2
Fuxin, China 182 B10
Fuya, Japan 184 L12
Fuyang, river, China 182 E6
Fuyang, China 182 J6
Fuyu, China 181 C16
Fuyun, China 180 D8
Fuzhou, China 183 P8
Füzuli, Azerb. 169 E21
Fyn, island, Den. 140 P11
Fyne, Loch, Scot., U.K. 142 M8
Fyzabad, Trinidad & Tobago 121 Q22

G

Gaalkacyo (Galcaio), Somalia 199 G17
Gabbs, Nev., U.S. 109 Q8
Gabela, Angola 202 D6
Gabert Island, F.S.M. 217 A18
Gabes, Tun. 197 B13
Gabes, Gulf of, Tun. 197 B13
Gabon, Af. 195 K18
Gaborone, Botswana 202 J10
Gabras, Sudan 198 F11
Gabriel Vera, Bol. 130 K7
Gabrovo, Bulg. 153 H15
Gackle, N. Dak., U.S. 104 G6
Gädäbäy, Azerb. 169 D19
Gadag, India 179 N5
Gadarwara, India 178 J6
Gäddede, Sw. 140 G12
Gadifuri, island, Maldives 179 V3
Gadrut, Azerb. 169 E21
Gadsden, Ala., U.S. 101 H16
Gadwal, India 179 N6
Găeşti, Rom. 153 F15
Gaeta, It. 150 L10
Gaeta, Golfo di, It. 150 M10
Gaferut, island, F.S.M. 216 P4
Gaffney, S.C., U.S. 96 J8
Gaflei, Liech. 160 P2
Gafsa, Tun. 196 B12
Gagan, island, Marshall Is. 216 K4
Gagan, P.N.G. 217 J13
Gagarin, Russ. 156 J8
Gagil-Tomil, peak, F.S.M. 217 D18
Gagnoa, Côte d'Ivoire 200 H8
Gagra, Abkhazia 169 A15
Gahi, Wallis & Futuna, Fr. 218 C11
Gahnpa, Liberia 200 G7
Gaiano, river, It. 161 L17
Gaillac, Fr. 147 X9
Gaillimh see Galway, Ire. 143 S4
Gaimán, Arg. 133 R9
Gainesville, Fla., U.S. 97 R7
Gainesville, Ga., U.S. 96 K5
Gainesville, Mo., U.S. 105 V13
Gainesville, Tex., U.S. 102 K11
Gairdner, Lake, Austral. 210 J9
Gaixian, China 182 C10
Gaja Shima, Japan 185 V3
Gakona, Alas., U.S. 111 H18
Gakuch, Pak. 176 L11
Galan, Cerro, S. Amer. 126 J5
Galap, Palau 216 M12
Galápagos Fracture Zone, Pac. Oc. 239 K14
Galápagos Islands, Pac. Oc. 215 G21
Galápagos Rift, Pac. Oc. 239 J18
Galápagos Rise, Pac. Oc. 239 L18
Galashiels, Scot., U.K. 143 N11
Galatás, Gr. 154 K12
Galateia, Cyprus 160 M10
Galaţi, Rom. 153 E17
Galatina, It. 151 N15
Galatxo, Punta del, Sp. 145 F16
Galax, Va., U.S. 96 G9
Galaxidi, Gr. 154 H10
Galbraith, Qnsld., Austral. 211 Q11
Galcaio see Gaalkacyo, Somalia 199 G17
Gáldar, Canary Is. 204 Q5
Galdhøpiggen, Nor. 140 J10
Galegu, Sudan 199 E14
Galela, Indonesia 189 H16
Galena, Alas., U.S. 111 G14
Galena, Ill., U.S. 98 M4
Galena, Kans., U.S. 105 V10
Galena Park, Tex., U.S. 103 Q14
Galeota Point, Trinidad & Tobago 121 Q23
Galera, Punta, Chile 133 P6
Galera, Punta, Ecua. 128 H2
Galera Point, Trinidad & Tobago 121 N24
Galesburg, Ill., U.S. 99 P4
Galesville, Wis., U.S. 98 K3
Galeton, Pa., U.S. 94 L6
Galets, Pointe des, Reunion, Fr. 205 F15
Gali, Abkhazia 169 B16
Galich, Russ. 156 G11
Galicia, region, Pol., Ukr. 149 G17
Galicia, region, Sp. 144 C6
Galilee, Lake, Austral. 210 F13
Galilee, Sea of, Israel 170 K6
Galina Mine, W. Aust., Austral. 211 V2
Galina Point, Jam. 120 H10
Galinoporni, Cyprus 160 M11
Galion, Ohio, U.S. 99 Q13
Galion, Baie du, Martinique, Fr. 121 E23
Galiuro Mountains, Ariz., U.S. 107 V8
Galiwinku, N. Terr., Austral. 211 P9
Gallarate, It. 150 D4
Gallatin, Mo., U.S. 105 R11
Gallatin, river, Mont., U.S. 106 E8
Gallatin, Tenn., U.S. 101 E15
Galle, Sri Lanka 179 T7
Gállego, river, Sp. 145 D14
Gallinakopf, peak, Aust., Liech. 160 P3
Gallinas, Punta, Col. 128 A7
Gallinas Peak, N. Mex., U.S. 107 T13
Gallipoli, It. 151 N15
Gallipoli, N. Terr., Austral. 211 R10
Gallipoli see Gelibolu, Turk. 168 D3
Gallipolis, Ohio, U.S. 99 S14
Gällivare, Sw. 141 E13
Gallup, N. Mex., U.S. 107 R10
Galoa, Fiji Is. 218 J6
Galt, Calif., U.S. 109 R5
Galty Mountains, Ire. 143 U5
Galva, Ill., U.S. 99 P4
Galveston, Tex., U.S. 103 R15
Galveston Bay, Tex., U.S. 103 R14
Galveston Island, Tex., U.S. 103 R14
Gálvez, Arg. 132 K11
Galwa, Nepal 178 E8
Galway (Gaillimh), Ire. 143 S4
Galway Bay, Ire. 143 S3
Gambaga, Ghana 200 F10
Gambell, Alas., U.S. 110 F10
Gambia, Af. 195 G13
Gambia, river, Gambia, Senegal 194 G1
Gambia Plain, Atl. Oc. 236 L9
Gambia Shoal, Hawai'i, U.S. 112 K2
Gambier, Îles, Fr. Polynesia, Fr. 219 Q21
Gamboma, Congo 201 L18
Gamboula, Cen. Af. Rep. 198 H7
Gamila see Tímfi, Óros, peak, Gr. 154 E7
Gamkonora, peak, Indonesia 189 H16
Gamlaha, Indonesia 189 H16
Gamleby, Sw. 141 M13
Gamperdonatal, valley, Aust. 160 P4
Gamprin, Liech. 160 M2
Gams, Switz. 160 N1
Gamua, Wallis & Futuna, Fr. 218 B11
Gan, river, China 183 P5
Gan, river, China 181 B16
Gan, island, Maldives 179 X3
Gan, island, Maldives 179 X3
Gana, river, Nigeria 194 H5
Ganado, Ariz., U.S. 107 R9
Ganado, Tex., U.S. 103 S12
Ganāveh, Iran 172 G12
Gäncä, Azerb. 169 D20
Gandajika, Dem. Rep. of the Congo 198 M10
Gandava, Pak. 177 T6
Gander, Nfld. & Lab., Can. 83 M23
Gandhinagar, India 178 J3
Gandía, Sp. 145 H15
Gang, island, Maldives 179 W3
Ganga (Ganges), river, India 178 G7
Gan Gan, Arg. 133 R8
Ganganagar, India 178 E4
Gangapur, India 178 G5
Gangawati, India 179 N5
Gangca, China 180 H10
Gangdise Range, China 166 H8
Gangdisê Shan, China 180 K5
Ganges, river, Bangladesh, India 166 J8
Ganges, Fr. 147 X11
Ganges, Mouths of the, Bangladesh, India 178 K12
Ganges Fan, Ind. Oc. 240 D11
Ganges Plain, India 166 H8
Ganggyeong, S. Korea 182 F13
Gangi, It. 151 S10
Gangneung, S. Korea 182 E14
Gangtok, India 178 F12
Gannat, Fr. 147 T11
Gannett Peak, Wyo., U.S. 106 H9
Ganongga see Ranongga, island, Solomon Is. 217 M15
Ganquan, China 182 F2
Ganseong, S. Korea 182 E14
Gantgaw, Myanmar 186 G5
Ganyu, China 182 H8
Ganyushkino, Kaz. 174 F5
Ganzhou, China 183 P5
Gao, Mali 196 H9
Gaoligong Shan, Myanmar 186 D8
Gaoping, China 182 G4
Gaotai, China 180 G10
Gaotang, China 182 F6
Gaoua, Burkina Faso 200 F9
Gaoual, Guinea 200 E5
Gaoyang, China 182 E6
Gaoyi, China 182 E5
Gaoyou Hu, China 182 J8
Gap, Fr. 147 W14
Garabil Plateau, Turkm. 174 N11
Garabogaz Bay, Turkm. 166 F5
Garabogazköl, Turkm. 174 K6
Garacad, Somalia 199 G18
Garagum, desert, Turkm. 174 K8
Garagum Canal, Turkm. 174 M10
Garaina, P.N.G. 213 D19
Garajonay, peak, Canary Is. 204 Q4
Garaliáni, Gr. 154 L9
Garanhuns, Braz. 131 G17
Garapan, N. Mariana Is., U.S. 216 B4
Garapan, Lagunan, N. Mariana Is., U.S. 216 C4
Garavuti, Taj. 176 J7
Garber, Okla., U.S. 102 E10
Garberville, Calif., U.S. 109 N2
Garbyang, India 178 E8
García de Sola, Embalse de, Sp. 144 H9
Garda, Lago di, It. 150 D6
Gardar Ridge, Atl. Oc. 236 D10
Garden City, Ga., U.S. 97 N9
Garden City, Kans., U.S. 105 U4
Garden Island Bay, La., U.S. 100 R12
Garden of the Gods, Hawai'i, U.S. 113 G14
Garden Point, N. Terr., Austral. 211 N7
Gardiner, Me., U.S. 95 G16
Gardiner, Mont., U.S. 106 F8
Gardiner, Lake, S. Aust., Austral. 211 W9
Gardiz, Afghan. 177 N8
Gardner Pinnacles, Hawai'i, U.S. 112 L6
Garessio, It. 150 F3
Garfield, Wash., U.S. 108 D9
Gargano, Promontorio del, It. 150 K12
Garhakota, India 178 H7
Garibaldi, Oreg., U.S. 108 F2
Garies, S. Af. 202 L7
Garim Island, F.S.M. 217 D18
Garissa, Kenya 199 K15
Garland, Tex., U.S. 102 L12
Garm Ab, Afghan. 177 N4
Garmisch-Partenkirchen, Ger. 148 L8
Garner, Iowa, U.S. 104 M11
Garnett, Kans., U.S. 105 T10
Garonne, river, Fr. 147 W7
Garoowe, Somalia 199 G18
Garoua, Cameroon 201 F16
Garreru, island, Palau 216 N12
Garrison, N. Dak., U.S. 104 F4

Garrison, *Utah, U.S.* **107** N5
Garron Point, *N. Ire., U.K.* **143** P7
Garrucha, *Sp.* **145** L13
Garrygala, *Turkm.* **174** L7
Garry Lake, *Nunavut, Can.* **83** G14
Garsen, *Kenya* **199** K15
Garu, *India* **178** J9
Garub, *Namibia* **202** J6
Garusuun, *Palau* **216** N11
Garut, *Indonesia* **188** M8
Garve, *Scot., U.K.* **142** J9
Garwa, *India* **178** H9
Gary, *Ind., U.S.* **99** N8
Garyarsa, *China* **180** K4
Garzón, *Col.* **128** G4
Gasa, *Bhutan* **178** F12
Gas City, *Ind., U.S.* **99** Q10
Gasconade, river, *Mo., U.S.* **105** U13
Gascony, region, *Fr.* **147** X7
Gascoyne, river, *W. Aust., Austral.* **211** U3
Gascoyne Junction, *W. Aust., Austral.* **211** U2
Gascoyne Tablemount, *Pac. Oc.* **238** P7
Gasenzen, *Switz.* **160** N1
Gashagar, *Nigeria* **201** E16
Gas Hu, *China* **180** H8
Gashua, *Nigeria* **201** E15
Gaspar Grande, island, *Trinidad & Tobago* **121** P21
Gasparillo, *Trinidad & Tobago* **121** Q22
Gaspé, *Que., Can.* **83** N21
Gaspé Peninsula, *Que., Can.* **83** N21
Gassaway, *W. Va., U.S.* **96** D9
Gaston, Lake, *N.C., Va., U.S.* **96** G12
Gastonia, *N.C., U.S.* **96** J9
Gastoúni, *Gr.* **154** J8
Gastre, *Arg.* **133** Q8
Gata, Cabo de, *Sp.* **144** M12
Gata, Cape, *Cyprus* **160** R7
Gata, Sierra de, *Sp.* **144** F8
Gataivai, *Samoa* **218** L2
Gatayake, Baie de, *Fr. Polynesia, Fr.* **219** Q20
Gatchina, *Russ.* **156** F6
Gate, *Okla., U.S.* **102** E7
Gate City, *Va., U.S.* **96** G7
Gatehouse of Fleet, *Scot., U.K.* **143** P9
Gateshead, *Eng., U.K.* **143** P12
Gates of the Arctic National Park and Preserve, *Alas., U.S.* **111** D16
Gatesville, *Tex., U.S.* **103** N10
Gateway, *Colo., U.S.* **107** N10
Gatjapar, *F.S.M.* **217** D18
Gatlinburg, *Tenn., U.S.* **101** F19
Gau, island, *Fiji Is.* **218** J7
Gausta, peak, *Nor.* **140** L10
Gautier, Pointe, *St. Lucia* **121** L14
Gavarnie, *Fr.* **147** Y7
Gavāter, *Iran* **173** J18
Gāvbandī, *Iran* **173** H14
Gavdopoúla, island, *Gr.* **155** R13
Gávdos, island, *Gr.* **155** R13
Gaviota, *Calif., U.S.* **109** W6
Gävle, *Sw.* **141** K13
Gavrilov Yam, *Russ.* **156** H10
Gávrio, *Gr.* **155** J14
Gawachab, *Namibia* **202** K7
Gawai, *Myanmar* **186** C7
Gawler, *S. Aust., Austral.* **211** Y10
Gawler Ranges, *Austral.* **210** J9
Gaxun Nur, *China* **180** F11
Gaya, *India* **178** H10
Gaya, *Niger* **196** J10
Gaya, *Nigeria* **201** E15
Gayle, *Jam.* **120** H9
Gaylord, *Mich., U.S.* **98** H11
Gaylord, *Minn., U.S.* **104** K10
Gay's Cove, *Barbados* **121** J19
Gaza *see* Ghazzah, *Gaza Strip* **171** N4
Gazak, *Afghan.* **176** L5
Gazak, *Iran* **173** G17
Gazanjyk, *Turkm.* **174** L7
Gaza Strip, occupied territory, *Asia* **171** N4
Gaziantep, *Turk.* **168** H12
Gazimağusa *see* Ammochostos, *Cyprus* **160** P10
Gazipaşa, *Turk.* **168** J7
Gazojak, *Turkm.* **174** K10
Gbadolite, *Dem. Rep. of the Congo* **198** H9
Gcuwa, *S. Af.* **202** L10
Gdańsk, *Pol.* **149** B14
Gdańsk, Gulf of, *Pol.* **138** E7
Gdov, *Russ.* **156** G5
Gdynia, *Pol.* **149** B14
Gea, island, *Marshall Is.* **216** N5
Gea Pass, *Marshall Is.* **216** N5
Geary, *Okla., U.S.* **102** G9
Gebe, island, *Indonesia* **189** J17
Gebiz, *Turk.* **168** H6
Gebze, *Turk.* **168** D5
Gedaref, *Sudan* **199** E14
Geddes, *S. Dak., U.S.* **104** M6
Gediz, river, *Turk.* **168** F3
Gediz, *Turk.* **168** F5
Gedser, *Den.* **140** P12
Geel, *Belg.* **146** K12
Geelong, *Vic., Austral.* **211** Z12
Geelvink Channel, *Austral.* **210** H1
Geesthacht, *Ger.* **148** C8
Geeveston, *Tas., Austral.* **211** Z16
Gefara, region, *Lib., Tun.* **194** D6
Géfira, *Gr.* **154** C11
Gegibu, island, *Marshall Is.* **216** L3
Gê'gyai, *China* **180** J5
Gehh, island, *Marshall Is.* **216** N5
Geidam, *Nigeria* **201** E16
Geiga, island, *Marshall Is.* **216** K1
Geilo, *Nor.* **140** K10
Geita, *Tanzania* **199** L13
Gejiu, *China* **180** P11
Gela, *It.* **151** T11
Gela, Golfo di, *It.* **151** T11
Gelam, island, *Indonesia* **188** K9
Gelasa, Selat, *Indonesia* **188** K8
Gelendzhik, *Russ.* **157** T10
Gelibolu (Gallipoli), *Turk.* **168** D3
Gellinam, island, *Marshall Is.* **216** L5
Gelsenkirchen, *Ger.* **148** E5
Gembloux, *Belg.* **146** L12
Gemena, *Dem. Rep. of the Congo* **198** J9
Gemerek, *Turk.* **168** F11
Gemlik, *Turk.* **168** D5
Gemlik Körfezi, *Turk.* **168** D5
Gemona del Friuli, *It.* **150** C9
Gemsa, *Egypt* **197** D19
Gen, river, *China* **181** B15
Genádio, *Gr.* **155** N19
Genalē, river, *Eth.* **199** H15
Genç, *Turk.* **169** F15
Geneina (Al Junaynah), *Sudan* **198** E10
General Acha, *Arg.* **133** N10
General Alvear, *Arg.* **132** L8
General Bernardo O'Higgins, station, *Antarctica* **226** C4
General Carrera, Lago, *Chile* **133** T7
General Conesa, *Arg.* **133** P10
General Eugenio A. Garay, *Parag.* **130** L8
General Güemes, *Arg.* **132** E9
General Guido, *Arg.* **132** M13
General Juan Madariage, *Arg.* **132** M13
General La Madrid, *Arg.* **133** N11
General Levalle, *Arg.* **132** L10
General Lorenzo Vintter, *Arg.* **133** Q10
General Paz, *Arg.* **132** G13
General Pico, *Arg.* **132** M10
General Pinedo, *Arg.* **132** G11
General Roca, *Arg.* **133** P8
General San Martín, *Arg.* **132** L13
General San Martín, *Arg.* **133** N10
General San Martín, *Arg.* **133** R7
General Santos, *Philippines* **189** F15
Genesee, river, *N.Y., U.S.* **94** K6
Geneseo, *Ill., U.S.* **99** P4
Geneseo, *N.Y., U.S.* **94** J6
Geneva, *Ala., U.S.* **101** N16
Geneva, *Idaho, U.S.* **106** J8
Geneva, *N.Y., U.S.* **94** J7
Geneva, *Nebr., U.S.* **105** Q7
Geneva, *Ohio, U.S.* **99** N15
Geneva *see* Genève, *Switz.* **150** C1
Geneva, Lake of *see* Léman, Lac, *Fr.* **147** T15
Genève (Geneva), *Switz.* **150** C1
Genil, river, *Sp.* **144** K9
Genisséa, *Gr.* **155** B14
Genk, *Belg.* **146** L13
Genlis, *Fr.* **147** R13
Gennargentu, Monti del, *It.* **151** N4
Genoa *see* Genova, *It.* **150** F4
Genoa, *Nebr., U.S.* **105** P7
Génolhac, *Fr.* **147** W12
Genova (Genoa), *It.* **150** F4
Genova, Golfo di, *It.* **150** G4
Genovesa, Isla (Tower), *Ecua.* **128** P10
Gent, *Belg.* **146** L11
Geographe Bay, *Austral.* **210** K2
Geographe Channel, *Austral.* **210** G1
George, river, *Que., Can.* **83** K20
George, *S. Af.* **202** M8
George, Lake, *Austral.* **210** L14
George, Lake, *Fla., U.S.* **97** S8
George, Lake, *N.Y., U.S.* **94** H11
George, Zemlya, *Russ.* **158** B12
George Bligh Bank, *Atl. Oc.* **236** D11
George Town, *Cayman Is., U.K.* **120** J1
George Town, *Malaysia* **187** S8
George Town, *Tas., Austral.* **211** Y16
Georgetown, *Del., U.S.* **96** D15
Georgetown, *Gambia* **196** H5
Georgetown, *Guyana* **129** D14
Georgetown, *Ill., U.S.* **99** R7
Georgetown, *Ky., U.S.* **101** B18
Georgetown, *Ohio, U.S.* **99** T12
Georgetown, *Qnsld., Austral.* **211** R12
Georgetown, *S.C., U.S.* **96** L11
Georgetown, *St. Vincent & the Grenadines* **121** K17
Georgetown, *Tex., U.S.* **103** P10
George-Town, *Bahamas* **120** F9
George V Coast, *Antarctica* **227** R16-R17
George VI Sound, *Antarctica* **226** F6
George Washington Birthplace National Monument, *Va., U.S.* **96** D13
George Washington Carver National Monument, *Mo., U.S.* **105** V11
George West, *Tex., U.S.* **103** T10
Georgia, *U.S.* **96** M4
Georgia, Republic of, *Asia* **167** S4
Georgia, Strait of, *B.C., Can.* **82** M8
Georgiana, *Ala., U.S.* **101** M15
Georgian Bay, *Ont., Can.* **83** Q18
Georgīevka, *Kaz.* **175** D18
Georgina, river, *Qnsld., Austral.* **211** S10
Geórgios, Ágios, *Gr.* **155** K13
Geórgios, Ágios *see* Ro, *Gr.* **155** N22
Georgiyevsk, *Russ.* **157** T13
Georgiyevskoye, *Russ.* **156** G12
Gera, *Ger.* **148** F9
Gerákion, *Gr.* **154** L10
Geral, Serra, *S. Amer.* **126** J8
Geral de Goiás, Serra, *Braz.* **131** H14
Geraldine, *Mont., U.S.* **106** C9
Geraldine, *N.Z.* **213** P17
Geraldton, *Ont., Can.* **83** N16
Geraldton, *W. Aust., Austral.* **211** W2
Gérardmer, *Fr.* **147** Q15
Gerasa *see* Jarash, *Jordan* **170** L6
Gerber, *Calif., U.S.* **109** N4
Gercüş, *Turk.* **169** H16
Gerdine, Mount, *Alas., U.S.* **84** P4
Gerede, *Turk.* **168** D8
Gereshk, *Afghan.* **177** Q4
Geretsried, *Ger.* **148** K8
Gering, *Nebr., U.S.* **105** N1
Gerlach, *Nev., U.S.* **109** N7
Gerlach, peak, *Slovakia* **138** G8
Gerlachovsky Štit, *Slovakia* **149** J16
Germantown, *Tenn., U.S.* **100** G11
Germany, *Eur.* **139** T6
Germering, *Ger.* **148** K8
Germfask, *Mich., U.S.* **98** F9
Germī, *Iran* **172** A11
Gerolakkos, *Cyprus* **160** N8
Geroliménas, *Gr.* **154** M10
Gersthofen, *Ger.* **148** K8
Gêrzê, *China* **180** K6
Gerze, *Turk.* **168** C10
Gesoa, *P.N.G.* **213** D18
Gesso, *It.* **161** L17
Getafe, *Sp.* **144** F11
Gettysburg, *Pa., U.S.* **94** Q7
Gettysburg, *S. Dak., U.S.* **104** K5
Getz Ice Shelf, *Antarctica* **226** M7
Geumpang, *Indonesia* **188** G4
Geumsan, *S. Korea* **182** G13
Geunto, Gora, *Russ.* **159** C21
Gevaş, *Turk.* **169** G17
Gex, *Fr.* **147** T14
Geylegphug, *Bhutan* **178** G13
Geyve, *Turk.* **168** D6
Ghadāmis, *Lib.* **196** C12
Ghaddūwah, *Lib.* **197** D14
Ghaghe, island, *Solomon Is.* **217** L17
Ghajn Tuffieha Bay, *Malta* **161** K21
Ghana, *Af.* **195** H16
Ghanzi, *Botswana* **202** H8
Gharandal, *Jordan* **171** Q5
Gharb, *Malta* **161** H19
Ghardaïa, *Alg.* **196** B11
Ghar Dalum, site, *Malta* **161** L23
Gharm, *Taj.* **176** H8
Gharo, *Pak.* **177** W6
Gharyān, *Lib.* **197** C13
Ghatere, *Solomon Is.* **217** M18
Ghawdex *see* Gozo, island, *Malta* **161** H20
Ghaxaq, *Malta* **161** L23
Ghazal, Bahr el, *Chad* **197** H14
Ghaziabad, *India* **178** F6
Ghazipur, *India* **178** G9
Ghazīr, *Leb.* **170** H6
Ghazni, *Afghan.* **177** N7
Ghazzah (Gaza), *Gaza Strip* **171** N4
Gheorghieni, *Rom.* **153** C15
Gherla, *Rom.* **153** C13
Ghilarza, *It.* **151** N3
Ghisonaccia, *Fr.* **150** K4
Ghormach, *Afghan.* **176** L3
Ghotki, *Pak.* **177** T8
Ghow Gardan Pass, *Afghan.* **176** M6
Ghurian, *Afghan.* **176** M2
Gia Nghia, *Vietnam* **187** N13
Gianitsá, *Gr.* **154** C10
Giannutri, Isola di, *It.* **150** K6
Gia Rai, *Vietnam* **187** Q12
Giáros, island, *Gr.* **155** K14
Giarre, *It.* **151** S12
Giba, *It.* **151** Q3
Gibara, *Cuba* **116** J12
Gibbon, *Nebr., U.S.* **105** Q6
Gibbon Point, *Anguilla, U.K.* **120** R12
Gibbonsville, *Idaho, U.S.* **106** E6
Gibb River, *W. Aust., Austral.* **211** Q6
Gibb's Hill, *Bermuda, U.K.* **120** C2
Gibeon, *Namibia* **202** J7
Gibraleón, *Sp.* **144** L7
Gibraltar, *Eur.* **160** E1
Gibraltar, *Gibraltar, U.K.* **161** P22
Gibraltar, Bay of (Bahía de Algeciras), *Gibraltar, U.K.* **161** P21
Gibraltar, Rock of, *Gibraltar, U.K.* **161** P23
Gibraltar, Strait of, *Af., Eur.* **196** A8
Gibraltar Airport, *Gibraltar, U.K.* **161** N23
Gibraltar Harbour, *Gibraltar, U.K.* **161** P22
Gibsland, *La., U.S.* **100** L7
Gibson, *W. Aust., Austral.* **211** X4
Gibson City, *Ill., U.S.* **99** Q6
Gibson Desert, *W. Aust., Austral.* **211** U5
Gidar, *Pak.* **177** T5
Giddalur, *India* **179** N6
Giddings, *Tex., U.S.* **103** Q12
Gīdolē, *Eth.* **199** H14
Gien, *Fr.* **147** R10
Giessen, *Ger.* **148** G6
Gifford, *Fla., U.S.* **97** U10
Gifford, river, *Nunavut, Can.* **83** E16
Gifhorn, *Ger.* **148** D8
Gifu, *Japan* **185** P10
Gigant, *Russ.* **157** R11
Gigha Island, *Scot., U.K.* **143** N7
Giglio, Isola del, *It.* **150** K6
Gijón, *Sp.* **144** A9
Gila, river, *Ariz., U.S.* **107** U5
Gila Bend, *Ariz., U.S.* **107** U6
Gila Bend Mountains, *Ariz., U.S.* **107** U6
Gila Cliff Dwellings National Monument, *N. Mex., U.S.* **107** U10
Gilbert, *Ariz., U.S.* **107** U7
Gilbert, *Minn., U.S.* **104** F12
Gilbert, river, *Qnsld., Austral.* **211** R12
Gilbert Islands, *Kiribati* **214** G8
Gilbert River, *Qnsld., Austral.* **211** R12
Gilbert Seamount, *Pac. Oc.* **239** C13
Gilbués, *Braz.* **131** G14
Gilchrist, *Oreg., U.S.* **108** J4
Gildford, *Mont., U.S.* **106** B9
Gilf Kebir Plateau, *Egypt* **197** E17
Gilgandra, *N.S.W., Austral.* **211** X14
Gilgit, region, *Pak.* **176** L11
Gilgit, river, *Pak.* **176** L11
Gilgit, *Pak.* **176** L11
Gill, Lough, *Ire.* **143** Q4
Gillam, *Man., Can.* **83** L14
Gillen, Lake, *Austral.* **210** G5
Gilles, Lake, *Austral.* **210** K9
Gillespie, *Ill., U.S.* **99** S4
Gillett, *Ark., U.S.* **100** H9
Gillette, *Wyo., U.S.* **106** G12
Gills Rock, *Wis., U.S.* **98** H8
Gilman, *Ill., U.S.* **99** Q7
Gilmer, *Tex., U.S.* **102** L14
Gilmore Hut, *Qnsld., Austral.* **211** U12
Gilpeppee, *Qnsld., Austral.* **211** U11
Gilroy, *Calif., U.S.* **109** T4
Gima, *Japan* **185** Y1
Gimcheon, *S. Korea* **182** F14
Gimhwa, *S. Korea* **182** E13
Gimie, Mount, *St. Lucia* **121** K14
Gimje, *S. Korea* **182** G13
Gimli, *Man., Can.* **83** N14
Gingoog, *Philippines* **189** E15
Gīnīr, *Eth.* **199** G15
Ginowan, *Japan* **185** Y1
Giohar *see* Jawhar, *Somalia* **199** J17
Gioia, Golfo di, *It.* **151** R13
Gioia del Colle, *It.* **150** M14
Gioia Tauro, *It.* **151** R13
Gióna, Óros, *Gr.* **154** H10
Gioúra, island, *Gr.* **155** F13
Giovinazzo, *It.* **150** L13
Gippsland, region, *Austral.* **210** M13
Girab, *India* **178** G2
Girard, *Kans., U.S.* **105** U10
Girard, *Pa., U.S.* **94** K3
Girardot, *Col.* **128** F5
Giresun, *Turk.* **169** D13
Girga, *Egypt* **197** D19
Gir Hills, *India* **178** K2
Giridih, *India* **178** H10
Girne *see* Keryneia, *Cyprus* **160** N8
Girolata, *Fr.* **150** J3
Girona, *Sp.* **145** D18
Gironde, river, *Fr.* **147** U6
Gisborne, *N.Z.* **213** K20
Gissi, *It.* **150** K11
Gitega, *Burundi* **198** L12
Gíthio, *Gr.* **154** M10
Giulianova, *It.* **150** J10
Giurgiu, *Rom.* **153** G15
Givet, *Fr.* **146** M12
Givors, *Fr.* **147** U13
Gizab, *Afghan.* **177** N5
Gizhduvan, *Uzb.* **174** L11
Gizo, *Solomon Is.* **217** M15
Giżycko, *Pol.* **149** B16
Gjirokastër (Argyrus), *Albania* **152** M9
Gjoa Haven, *Nunavut, Can.* **83** F14
Gjøvik, *Nor.* **140** K11
Gkreko, Cape, *Cyprus* **160** P10
Glachau, *Ger.* **148** G9
Glacier Bay, *Alas., U.S.* **111** L21
Glacier Bay National Park and Preserve, *Alas., U.S.* **111** L21
Glacier National Park, *Mont., U.S.* **106** B6
Glacier Peak, *Wash., U.S.* **108** B5
Gladewater, *Tex., U.S.* **102** L14
Gladstone, *Mich., U.S.* **98** G8
Gladstone, *Qnsld., Austral.* **211** U15
Gladstone, *S. Aust., Austral.* **211** X10
Gladwin, *Mich., U.S.* **98** K11
Glåma, river, *Nor.* **140** J11
Glasco, *Kans., U.S.* **105** S7
Glasgow, *Jam.* **120** H6
Glasgow, *Ky., U.S.* **101** D16
Glasgow, *Mo., U.S.* **105** S12
Glasgow, *Mont., U.S.* **106** B11
Glasgow, *Scot., U.K.* **142** M9
Glassboro, *N.J., U.S.* **94** Q9
Glass Buttes, *Oreg., U.S.* **108** J6
Glass Mountain, *Calif., U.S.* **108** L4
Glass Mountains, *Tex., U.S.* **103** Q3
Glazov, *Russ.* **158** G8
Glénan, Îles de, *Fr.* **147** R3
Glen Arbor, *Mich., U.S.* **98** H9
Glenariffe, *N. Ire., U.K.* **143** P7
Glenarm, *N. Ire., U.K.* **143** P7
Glenavy, *N.Z.* **213** Q17
Glenayle, *W. Aust., Austral.* **211** U4
Glenbarr, *Scot., U.K.* **143** N7
Glen Canyon Dam, *Ariz., U.S.* **107** Q7
Glen Canyon National Recreation Area, *Utah, U.S.* **107** P8
Glencoe, *Minn., U.S.* **104** K10
Glendale, *Ariz., U.S.* **107** U6
Glendale, *Calif., U.S.* **109** X8
Glendive, *Mont., U.S.* **106** C13
Glendo, *Wyo., U.S.* **106** J13
Glendo Reservoir, *Wyo., U.S.* **106** H13
Glengyle, *Qnsld., Austral.* **211** U11
Glen Innes, *N.S.W., Austral.* **211** W15
Glenmora, *La., U.S.* **100** N8
Glennallen, *Alas., U.S.* **111** H18
Glenn Highway, *Alas., U.S.* **111** J17
Glenns Ferry, *Idaho, U.S.* **106** H4
Glennville, *Ga., U.S.* **97** N8
Glenormiston, *Qnsld., Austral.* **211** T10
Glenreagh, *N.S.W., Austral.* **211** W15
Glenrock, *Wyo., U.S.* **106** H12
Glen Rose, *Tex., U.S.* **102** M10
Glenrothes, *Scot., U.K.* **142** M10
Glenroy, *W. Aust., Austral.* **211** R5
Glens Falls, *N.Y., U.S.* **94** H11

Glenties, *Ire.* **143** P5
Glen Ullin, *N. Dak., U.S.* **104** G3
Glenwood, *Ark., U.S.* **100** H7
Glenwood, *Iowa, U.S.* **105** Q9
Glenwood, *Minn., U.S.* **104** J9
Glenwood, *N. Mex., U.S.* **107** U10
Glenwood Springs, *Colo., U.S.* **106** M11
Glidden, *Wis., U.S.* **98** F4
Glina, *Croatia* **152** E6
Gliwice, *Pol.* **149** G14
Globe, *Ariz., U.S.* **107** U8
Głogów, *Pol.* **148** E12
Glorenza, *It.* **150** C6
Gloria, Puntan, *N. Mariana Is., U.S.* **216** B5
Gloria Ridge, *Atl. Oc.* **236** E7
Glorieuses, Îles, *Mozambique Ch.* **203** D17
Glossglockner, peak, *Aust.* **148** M9
Gloster, *Miss., U.S.* **100** N10
Gloucester, *Eng., U.K.* **143** V11
Gloucester, *Mass., U.S.* **95** K15
Gloucester, *N.S.W., Austral.* **211** X15
Gloucester, *P.N.G.* **213** C20
Glover Island, *Grenada* **121** L22
Gloversville, *N.Y., U.S.* **94** J10
Glubokiy, *Russ.* **157** Q11
Glubokiy, *Russ.* **157** R12
Glūbokoe, *Kaz.* **175** D18
Gmunden, *Aust.* **148** L10
Gnaraloo, *W. Aust., Austral.* **211** U1
Gniezno, *Pol.* **149** D13
Gnjilane, *Serb. & Mont.* **152** J11
Goa, *India* **179** N4
Goalpara, *India* **178** G13
Goba, *Eth.* **199** G15
Gobabis, *Namibia* **202** H7
Gobernador Duval, *Arg.* **133** N9
Gobernador Gregores, *Arg.* **133** U8
Gobi, desert, *China, Mongolia* **181** F13
Gobō, *Japan* **185** R9
Gochang, *S. Korea* **182** G13
Go Cong, *Vietnam* **187** P13
Godalming, *Eng., U.K.* **143** W13
Godavari, river, *India* **178** M8
Godavari, Mouths of the, *India* **179** N8
Goderville, *Fr.* **147** N8
Godhavn *see* Qeqertarsuaq, *Greenland, Den.* **81** C21
Godhra, *India* **178** J4
Gödöllő, *Hung.* **149** L15
Godoy Cruz, *Arg.* **132** K8
Gods, river, *Man., Can.* **83** L15
Gods Lake, *Man., Can.* **83** L14
Godthåb *see* Nuuk, *Greenland, Den.* **81** D21
Godwin Austen *see* K2, peak, *China, Pak.* **176** L13
Goes, *Neth.* **146** K11
Göfis, *Aust.* **160** M4
Gogebic, Lake, *Mich., U.S.* **98** F5
Gogebic Range, *Mich., Wis., U.S.* **85** D15
Gogland, island, *Russ.* **156** E5
Gogrial, *Sudan* **198** G11
Goianésia, *Braz.* **131** J13
Goiânia, *Braz.* **131** J13
Goikul, *Palau* **216** N12
Góis, *Port.* **144** F6
Gojōme, *Japan* **184** K12
Gojra, *Pak.* **177** Q10
Gök, river, *Turk.* **168** C10
Gokak, *India* **179** N4
Gökçeada (İmroz), island, *Turk.* **168** D2
Gökdepe, *Turkm.* **174** M8
Gökova Körfezi, *Turk.* **168** H3
Göksu, river, *Turk.* **168** G11
Göksu, river, *Turk.* **168** J9
Göksun, *Turk.* **168** G11
Golaghat, *India* **178** G14
Golan Heights, region, *Israel* **170** K6
Golbahar, *Afghan.* **176** M8
Gölbaşı, *Turk.* **168** E8
Gölbaşı, *Turk.* **168** H12
Golconda, *Nev., U.S.* **108** M9
Gölcük, *Turk.* **168** D5
Gold Beach, *Oreg., U.S.* **108** K1
Gold Coast, *Ghana* **194** J3
Gold Coast, *Qnsld., Austral.* **211** V15
Golden, *Colo., U.S.* **106** M13
Golden Bay, *N.Z.* **213** M17
Goldendale, *Wash., U.S.* **108** E5
Golden Gate, *Calif., U.S.* **109** S3
Golden Gate National Recreation Area, *Calif., U.S.* **109** R3
Golden Grove, *Jam.* **120** J11
Golden Meadow, *La., U.S.* **100** R11
Golden Ridge, *W. Aust., Austral.* **211** W4
Golden Spike National Historic Site, *Utah, U.S.* **106** K6
Goldfield, *Nev., U.S.* **109** S9
Goldsboro, *N.C., U.S.* **96** H12
Goldsmith, *Tex., U.S.* **102** M4
Goldsworthy, *W. Aust., Austral.* **211** S3
Goldthwaite, *Tex., U.S.* **103** N9
Göle, *Turk.* **169** D17
Golela, *S. Af.* **202** K12
Goleniów, *Pol.* **148** C11
Goleta, *Calif., U.S.* **109** W6
Golfito, *Costa Rica* **115** P19
Golfo Aranci, *It.* **150** M5
Goliad, *Tex., U.S.* **103** S11
Gölköy, *Turk.* **168** D12
Golmud, *China* **180** J9
Golo, river, *Fr.* **150** J4
Gölören, *Turk.* **168** G9
Golovin, *Alas., U.S.* **110** F12
Gölpazarı, *Turk.* **168** D6
Golūbovka, *Kaz.* **175** B15
Golyama Kamchiya, river, *Bulg.* **153** H16
Golyam Perelik, peak, *Bulg.* **153** K14
Goma, *Dem. Rep. of the Congo* **198** K12
Gombe, *Nigeria* **201** F15
Gombrani Island, *Mauritius* **205** J20
Gomera, island, *Canary Is.* **204** Q4
Gómez Palacio, *Mex.* **114** F10
Gonābād, *Iran* **173** D16
Gonaïves, *Haiti* **117** L16
Gonam, river, *Russ.* **159** J18
Gonam, *Russ.* **159** H19
Gonâve, Golfe de la, *Haiti* **117** L15
Gonâve, Gulf of *see* Gonâve, Golfo de la, *N. Amer.* **80** N10
Gonâve, Île de la, *Haiti* **117** M15
Gonbad-e Kāvūs, *Iran* **173** B14
Gonda, *India* **178** G8
Gonder, *Eth.* **199** E14
Gondia, *India* **178** K7
Gondomar, *Port.* **144** E5
Gönen, *Turk.* **168** D3
Gong'an, *China* **182** L4
Gongcheng, *China* **183** Q2
Gonggar, *China* **180** L7
Gongga Shan, *China* **166** H10
Gongga Shan, *China* **180** L11
Gonglee, *Liberia* **200** H7
Gongola, river, *Nigeria* **201** F16
Gongolgon, *N.S.W., Austral.* **211** W13
Gongxi, *China* **183** N6
Gongzhuling, *China* **182** A11
Góni, *Gr.* **154** E10
Gōno, river, *Japan* **185** Q6
Gōnoura, *Japan* **185** R3
Gonzales, *Calif., U.S.* **109** T4
Gonzales, *Tex., U.S.* **103** R11
González Chaves, *Arg.* **133** N12
Goodenough Island, *P.N.G.* **213** E21
Good Hope, Cape of, *S. Af.* **202** M7
Good Hope Beach, *Virgin Islands, U.S.* **120** R1
Goodhouse, *S. Af.* **202** K7
Gooding, *Idaho, U.S.* **106** H5
Goodland, *Kans., U.S.* **105** S3
Goodlands, *Mauritius* **205** F20
Goodlettsville, *Tenn., U.S.* **101** E15
Goodman, *Miss., U.S.* **100** K11
Goodman, *Wis., U.S.* **98** G6
Goodman Bay, *Bahamas* **120** B11
Goodnews Bay, *Alas., U.S.* **110** K12
Goodooga, *N.S.W., Austral.* **211** W13
Goodparla, *N. Terr., Austral.* **211** P8
Goodridge, *Minn., U.S.* **104** E9
Goodwell, *Okla., U.S.* **102** E5
Goofnuw Inlet, *F.S.M.* **217** D18
Goolgowi, *N.S.W., Austral.* **211** X12
Goomalling, *W. Aust., Austral.* **211** X3
Goondiwindi, *Qnsld., Austral.* **211** V14
Goongarrie, Lake, *Austral.* **210** J4
Goonyella, *Qnsld., Austral.* **211** T14
Goose Creek, *S.C., U.S.* **96** M10
Goose Lake, *Calif., Oreg., U.S.* **108** L6
Gora, *Russ.* **159** L17
Gora Belukha, peak, *Kaz.* **175** D20
Gorakhpur, *India* **178** G9
Goraklbad Passage, *Palau* **216** P12
Gördes, *Turk.* **168** F4
Gordion, ruin, *Turk.* **168** E7
Gordo, *Ala., U.S.* **101** K14
Gordon, *Ga., U.S.* **96** M6
Gordon, *Nebr., U.S.* **104** M3
Gordon, *Wis., U.S.* **98** F3
Gordon, Lake, *Austral.* **210** M16
Gordon Downs, *W. Aust., Austral.* **211** R6
Gordon's, *Bahamas* **117** G14
Gordonsville, *Va., U.S.* **96** E12
Goré, *Chad* **197** K14
Gore, *N.Z.* **213** R16
Gorē, *Eth.* **199** G14
Goreda, *Indonesia* **213** C15
Goree, *Tex., U.S.* **102** K8
Görele, *Turk.* **169** D13
Gorey, *Ire.* **143** T7
Gorgān, *Iran* **173** B14
Gorgona, Isla, *Col.* **128** G3
Gorgona, Isola di, *It.* **150** H5
Gorham, *N.H., U.S.* **95** F14
Gori, *Rep. of Georgia* **169** B18
Goris, *Arm.* **169** E20
Gorizia, *It.* **150** D10
Gor'kiy Reservoir *see* Gor'kovskoye Vodokhranilishche, *Russ.* **138** D11
Gor'kovskoye Vodokhranilishche, *Russ.* **156** H12
Gorlice, *Pol.* **149** H16
Görlitz, *Ger.* **148** F11
Gorman, *Tex., U.S.* **102** M9
Gorna Oryakhovitsa, *Bulg.* **153** H15
Gornja Radgona, *Slov.* **152** C6
Gornji Milanovac, *Serb. & Mont.* **152** G10
Gorno Altaysk, *Russ.* **158** L12
Gornozavodsk, *Russ.* **159** K22
Gornyak, *Russ.* **158** L11
Gorodets, *Russ.* **156** H12
Gorodishche, *Russ.* **156** L13
Goroka, *P.N.G.* **213** D19
Gorong, Kepulauan, *Indonesia* **189** L17
Gorongosa, Serra da, *Mozambique* **194** N9
Gorontalo, *Indonesia* **189** J14
Gorror, *F.S.M.* **217** D18
Gros-Morne, *Haiti* **117** L16
Gortyn, ruin, *Gr.* **155** Q14
Gorumna Island, *Ire.* **143** S3
Góry Swietokrzyskie, *Pol.* **149** F16
Gorzów Wielkopolski, *Pol.* **148** D11
Goschen Strait, *P.N.G.* **213** E21
Gosen, *Japan* **184** M12
Goseong, *S. Korea* **182** G14
Gosford, *N.S.W., Austral.* **211** X14
Goshen, *Ind., U.S.* **99** N9
Goshogawara, *Japan* **184** J12
Gosier, *Guadeloupe, Fr.* **121** F15
Goslar, *Ger.* **148** E8
Gosnel, *Ark., U.S.* **100** E11
Gospić, *Croatia* **152** F5
Gosselies, *Belg.* **146** L12
Gostivar, *Maced.* **152** K10
Göteborg, *Sw.* **140** M12
Gotha, *Ger.* **148** F8
Gothenburg, *Nebr., U.S.* **105** Q5
Gothèye, *Niger* **196** H10
Gotland, island, *Sw.* **141** M14
Goto Meer, *Neth. Antilles, Neth.* **121** Q18
Gotō Rettō, *Japan* **185** R2
Gotse Delchev, *Bulg.* **153** K13
Gotska Sandön, island, *Sw.* **141** L14
Gōtsu, *Japan* **185** Q6
Göttingen, *Ger.* **148** F7
Gouaro, Baie de, *New Caledonia, Fr.* **218** D7
Gouin, Réservoir, *Que., Can.* **83** N19
Gould, *Ark., U.S.* **100** H9
Gould Bay, *Antarctica* **226** E9
Gould Coast, *Antarctica* **226** K11
Goulding Cay, *Bahamas* **120** E12
Gouldsboro, *Me., U.S.* **95** F18
Goulvain, Cap, *New Caledonia, Fr.* **218** D7
Goumbou, *Mali* **196** H7
Goundam, *Mali* **196** G8
Gourbeyre, *Guadeloupe, Fr.* **121** G14
Gouré, *Niger* **196** H12
Gournay, *Fr.* **147** N9
Gournia, ruin, *Gr.* **155** Q16
Gouro, *Chad* **197** G15
Gouverneur, *N.Y., U.S.* **94** G9
Gouyave (Charlotte Town), *Grenada* **121** K22
Gouzon, *Fr.* **147** T10
Gove, *Kans., U.S.* **105** S4
Govena, Mys, *Russ.* **159** D22
Govenlock, *Sask., Can.* **82** N11
Gove Peninsula, *Austral.* **210** B9
Governador Valadares, *Braz.* **131** K15
Government House, *Barbados* **121** L19
Government House, *Bermuda, U.K.* **120** B2
Government House, *Monaco* **161** E21
Government Palace, *Vatican City* **161** Q15
Governor Generoso, *Philippines* **189** F15
Governor's Beach, *Gibraltar, U.K.* **161** Q23
Governor's Harbour, *Bahamas* **120** E6
Governor's Residence, *Gibraltar, U.K.* **161** P22
Govindgarh, *India* **178** H8
Govorovo, *Russ.* **159** F16
Gowanda, *N.Y., U.S.* **94** K5
Gowd-e Zereh, Dasht-e, *Afghan.* **177** R2
Gower Peninsula, *Wales, U.K.* **143** V9
Gowmal Kalay, *Afghan.* **177** P7
Gowrzanak, *Afghan.* **177** P3
Goya, *Arg.* **132** H12
Goyave, *Guadeloupe, Fr.* **121** F14
Goyaves, river, *Guadeloupe, Fr.* **121** F14
Goyaves, Îlets à, *Guadeloupe, Fr.* **121** F14
Göyçay, *Azerb.* **169** D21
Göynük, *Turk.* **168** D6
Gozha Co, *China* **180** H5
Gozo (Ghawdex), island, *Malta* **161** H20
Goz Sassulko, region, *Cen. Af. Rep., Sudan* **198** F10
Graaff-Reinet, *S. Af.* **202** L9
Grabs, *Switz.* **160** N1
Gračac, *Croatia* **152** F5
Gračanica, *Bosn. & Herzg.* **152** F8
Graceville, *Fla., U.S.* **97** Q3
Graceville, *Minn., U.S.* **104** J8
Gracias a Dios, Cabo, *Nicar.* **115** K19
Graciosa, island, *Azores* **144** P3
Graciosa, island, *Canary Is.* **204** P8
Graciosa Bay, *Solomon Is.* **217** P22
Gradaús, *Braz.* **130** F12
Graford, *Tex., U.S.* **102** L10
Grafton, *N. Dak., U.S.* **104** E7
Grafton, *N.S.W., Austral.* **211** W15
Grafton, *W. Va., U.S.* **96** C10
Grafton, *Wis., U.S.* **98** L7
Grafton, Mount, *Nev., U.S.* **109** Q12
Graham, *N.C., U.S.* **96** G11
Graham, *Ont., Can.* **83** N15
Graham, *Tex., U.S.* **102** K9
Graham, Mount, *Ariz., U.S.* **107** V9
Graham Bell, Ostrov, *Russ.* **159** C13
Graham Island, *B.C., Can.* **82** J7
Graham Island, *Nunavut, Can.* **83** C15
Graham Lake, *Me., U.S.* **95** F18
Graham Land, *Antarctica* **226** D4
Graham's Harbor, *Bahamas* **120** E11
Grahamstown, *S. Af.* **202** M10
Graian Alps, *Fr., It.* **147** U15
Grain Coast, *Liberia* **194** J2
Grajaú, *Braz.* **131** E14
Grajewo, *Pol.* **149** C17
Gramat, *Fr.* **147** V9
Grámos, Óros, *Gr.* **154** D8
Grampian Mountains, *Scot., U.K.* **142** L9
Granada, *Colo., U.S.* **107** N16
Granada, *Nicar.* **115** M18
Granada, *Sp.* **144** L11
Granadilla, *Canary Is.* **204** Q5
Gran Altiplanicie Central, plateau, *Arg.* **133** U8
Granbury, *Tex., U.S.* **102** L10
Granby, *Colo., U.S.* **106** L12
Granby, *Que., Can.* **83** P20
Granby, Mount, *Grenada* **121** K22
Gran Canaria, island, *Canary Is.* **204** R6
Gran Cayo Point, *Trinidad & Tobago* **121** Q23
Gran Chaco, region, *S. Amer.* **126** J6
Grand, river, *Mich., U.S.* **98** L10
Grand, river, *Mo., U.S.* **105** R12
Grand, river, *S. Dak., U.S.* **104** J3
Grand Anse, *Grenada* **121** L22
Grand Anse, *St. Lucia* **121** J14
Grand Anse Bay, *Grenada* **121** L22
Grand Bahama Island, *Bahamas* **116** C10
Grand Baie, *Mauritius* **205** F20
Grand Baie, *Mauritius* **205** J20
Grand Banks of Newfoundland, *Nfld. & Lab., Can.* **83** N24
Grand-Bassam, *Côte d'Ivoire* **200** H9
Grand Bay, *Dominica* **121** G19
Grand Bonum, peak, *St. Vincent & the Grenadines* **121** K16
Grand-Bourg, *Guadeloupe, Fr.* **121** G16
Grand Caicos, island, *Turks & Caicos Is., U.K.* **117** H17
Grand Caille Point, *St. Lucia* **121** K13
Grandcamp-Maisy, *Fr.* **147** N6
Grand Canal *see* Da Yunhe, *China* **182** J8
Grand Canal, *Ire.* **143** S6
Grand Canyon, *Ariz., U.S.* **107** R6
Grand Canyon, *Ariz., U.S.* **107** R7
Grand Canyon National Park, *Ariz., U.S.* **107** Q6
Grand Canyon-Parashant National Monument, *Ariz., U.S.* **107** Q5
Grand Case, *St. Martin, Fr.* **121** A14
Grand Cayman, island, *Cayman Is., U.K.* **116** L7
Grand Cess, *Liberia* **200** H7
Grand Coulee, *Wash., U.S.* **108** B7
Grand Coulee Dam, *Wash., U.S.* **108** B7
Grand Cul-de-Sac Marin, *Guadeloupe, Fr.* **121** E14
Grande, river, *Arg.* **132** M7
Grande, river, *Arg., Chile* **133** X9
Grande, river, *Bol.* **130** J8
Grande, river, *Braz.* **131** G15
Grande, river, *Braz.* **131** L13
Grande, Bahía, *Arg.* **133** V8
Grande, Boca, *Venez.* **129** C13
Grande, Cayo, *Cuba* **116** J9
Grande, Cayo, *Venez.* **118** N12
Grande, Rio, *N. Amer.* **80** M5
Grande, Salina, *Arg.* **133** N8
Grande-Anse, *Guadeloupe, Fr.* **121** E17
Grande Cayemite, island, *Haiti* **117** M15
Grande Comore, island, *Comoros* **205** M14
Grande del Norte, Río *see* Grande, Rio, *Mex.* **114** C9
Grande Montagne, *Mauritius* **205** J20
Grande Prairie, *Alta., Can.* **82** K10
Grande Riviere, *Trinidad & Tobago* **121** N23
Grande Rivière du Nord, *Haiti* **117** L17
Grande Rivière Sud Est, *Mauritius* **205** G20
Grande Ronde, river, *Oreg., U.S.* **108** E8
Grandes, Salinas, *Arg.* **132** H9
Grande-Terre, island, *Guadeloupe, Fr.* **121** E15
Grande Vigie, Pointe de la, *Guadeloupe, Fr.* **121** D15
Grandfalls, *Tex., U.S.* **103** N3
Grand Falls-Windsor, *Nfld. & Lab., Can.* **83** M23
Grandfather Mountain, *N.C., U.S.* **96** H8
Grandfield, *Okla., U.S.* **102** J9
Grand Forks, *N. Dak., U.S.* **104** F8
Grand-Gosier, *Haiti* **117** M17
Grand Harbour, *Malta* **161** K23
Grand Haven, *Mich., U.S.* **98** L9
Grand Îlet, *Guadeloupe, Fr.* **121** G14
Grand Island, *Mich., U.S.* **98** F8
Grand Island, *N.Y., U.S.* **94** J5
Grand Island, *Nebr., U.S.* **105** Q6
Grand Isle, *La., U.S.* **100** R11
Grand Junction, *Colo., U.S.* **106** M10
Grand Lake, *La., U.S.* **100** Q7
Grand Lake, *Ohio, U.S.* **99** Q11
Grand Ledge, *Mich., U.S.* **98** M11
Grand Lieu, Lac de, *Fr.* **147** S5
Grand Mal Bay, *Grenada* **121** L22
Grand Marais, *Mich., U.S.* **98** F9
Grand Marais, *Minn., U.S.* **104** F14
Grândola, *Port.* **144** J5
Grand Passage, *New Caledonia, Fr.* **218** A5
Grand Portage, *Minn., U.S.* **104** E14
Grand Portage National Monument, *Minn., U.S.* **104** E14
Grand Prairie, *Tex., U.S.* **102** L11
Grand Rapids, *Man., Can.* **83** M13
Grand Rapids, *Mich., U.S.* **98** L10
Grand Rapids, *Minn., U.S.* **104** G11
Grand Rivière, *Martinique, Fr.* **121** E22
Grand Roy, *Grenada* **121** K22
Grand Saline, *Tex., U.S.* **102** L13
Grand Staircase-Escalante National Monument, *Utah, U.S.* **107** P7
Grand Teton, *Wyo., U.S.* **106** G8
Grand Teton National Park, *Wyo., U.S.* **106** G8
Grand Traverse Bay, *Mich., U.S.* **98** H10
Grand Turk, island, *Turks & Caicos Is., U.K.* **117** J18
Grandview, *Wash., U.S.* **108** E6
Grandvilliers, *Fr.* **147** N9
Grange, *Ire.* **143** Q4
Grange, *Virgin Islands, U.S.* **120** Q3
Grange Hill, *Jam.* **120** H6
Granger, *Tex., U.S.* **103** P11

Granger, *Wash., U.S.* **108** E6
Granger, *Wyo., U.S.* **106** K9
Grangeville, *Idaho, U.S.* **106** E4
Granite, *Okla., U.S.* **102** H8
Granite, *Oreg., U.S.* **108** G8
Granite City, *Ill., U.S.* **99** T4
Granite Falls, *Minn., U.S.* **104** K9
Granite Mountains, *Calif., U.S.* **109** V10
Granite Mountains, *Wyo., U.S.* **106** H11
Granite Peak, *Mont., U.S.* **106** F9
Granite Peak, *Nev., U.S.* **108** M7
Granite Peak, *Utah, U.S.* **106** L6
Granite Peak, *W. Aust., Austral.* **211** U4
Granja, *Braz.* **131** E16
Gran Laguna Salada, *Arg.* **133** S9
Granollers, *Sp.* **145** D17
Gran Quivira *see* Salinas Pueblo Missions National Monument, site, *N. Mex., U.S.* **107** T12
Gran Sasso d'Italia, *It.* **150** J10
Grant, *Nebr., U.S.* **105** Q3
Grant, Mount, *Nev., U.S.* **109** R7
Gran Tarajal, *Canary Is.* **204** Q7
Grant City, *Mo., U.S.* **105** Q10
Grant Island, *Antarctica* **226** N8
Grant-Kohrs Ranch National Historic Site, *Mont., U.S.* **106** D6
Grant Range, *Nev., U.S.* **109** R11
Grants, *N. Mex., U.S.* **107** S11
Grantsburg, *Wis., U.S.* **98** G2
Grants Pass, *Oreg., U.S.* **108** K2
Grantville, *Ga., U.S.* **96** M4
Granville, *Fr.* **147** P6
Granville, *N. Dak., U.S.* **104** E4
Granville, *N.Y., U.S.* **94** H12
Granville Lake, *Man., Can.* **83** L13
Grão Mogol, *Braz.* **131** J15
Grapeland, *Tex., U.S.* **103** N13
Grapevine Lake, *Tex., U.S.* **102** L11
Grass Cay, *Virgin Islands, U.S.* **120** M10
Grasse, *Fr.* **147** X15
Grassholm Island, *Wales, U.K.* **143** V8
Grassmere, *Qnsld., Austral.* **211** V13
Grass Patch, *W. Aust., Austral.* **211** X4
Grass Point, *Virgin Islands, U.S.* **120** Q3
Grassrange, *Mont., U.S.* **106** D10
Grass Valley, *Calif., U.S.* **109** Q5
Grassy Bay, *Bermuda, U.K.* **120** B2
Grassy Butte, *N. Dak., U.S.* **104** F2
Grassy Key, *Fla., U.S.* **97** Y9
Graus, *Sp.* **145** C15
Grauspitz, peak, *Liech., Switz.* **160** R3
Grave, Pointe de, *Fr.* **147** U6
Gravelbourg, *Sask., Can.* **82** N12
Grave Peak, *Idaho, U.S.* **106** D5
Gravette, *Ark., U.S.* **100** E6
Gravina in Puglia, *It.* **150** M13
Gravois, Pointe-à-, *Haiti* **117** N15
Gray, *Fr.* **147** R13
Grayland, *Wash., U.S.* **108** D2
Grayling, *Alas., U.S.* **111** H13
Grayling, *Mich., U.S.* **98** J11
Grays, *Eng., U.K.* **143** V14
Grays Harbor, *Wash., U.S.* **108** D2
Grays Lake, *Idaho, U.S.* **106** H7
Grayson, *Ky., U.S.* **101** B19
Grayville, *Ill., U.S.* **99** T7
Graz, *Aust.* **148** M12
Great Artesian Basin, *Austral.* **210** G12
Great Australian Bight, *Austral.* **210** K7
Great Bacolet Bay, *Grenada* **121** L23
Great Bacolet Point, *Grenada* **121** L23
Great Bahama Bank, *Bahamas* **116** E10
Great Barrier Island, *N.Z.* **213** J19
Great Barrier Reef, *Austral.* **210** E15
Great Basin, *Nev., Utah, U.S.* **84** G5
Great Basin National Park, *Nev., U.S.* **109** Q13
Great Bay, *N.J., U.S.* **94** Q10
Great Bear Lake, *N.W.T., Can.* **82** F11
Great Bend, *Kans., U.S.* **105** T6
Great Bernera, island, *Scot., U.K.* **142** H6
Great Bird Island, *Antigua & Barbuda* **121** B21
Great Bitter Lake *see* Murrat el Kubra, Buheirat, *Egypt* **171** Q1
Great Britain, island, *U.K.* **142** M9
Great Channel, *India, Indonesia* **179** T15
Great Coco Island, *Myanmar* **186** M4
Great Courtland Bay, *Trinidad & Tobago* **121** N17
Great Crack, crater, *Hawai'i, U.S.* **113** N20
Great Crater, *Israel* **171** P5
Great Dismal Swamp, *N.C., U.S.* **96** G14
Great Divide Basin, *Wyo., U.S.* **106** J10
Great Dividing Range, *Austral.* **210** C12
Great Dog Island, *Virgin Islands, U.K.* **120** Q8
Great Driffield, *Eng., U.K.* **143** R13
Great Eastern Dunes, *Alg., Tun.* **194** D5
Greater Antilles, islands, *N. Amer.* **80** N10
Greater Khingan Range, *China* **166** E11
Greater Sunda Islands, *Indonesia* **188** K9
Great Exuma, island, *Bahamas* **120** E8
Great Fall, *Guyana* **129** E13
Great Falls, *Mont., U.S.* **106** C8
Great Falls, *S.C., U.S.* **96** K9
Great Guana Cay, *Bahamas* **116** C12
Great Guana Cay, *Bahamas* **116** F12
Great Harbour, *Virgin Islands, U.K.* **120** L11
Great Harbour Cay, *Bahamas* **116** D11
Greathead Bay, *St. Vincent & the Grenadines* **121** L16
Great Hungarian Plain (Alföld), *Hung., Serb. & Mont.* **149** M16
Great Inagua Island, *Bahamas* **117** J15
Great Indian Desert (Thar Desert), *India, Pak.* **177** T9
Great Isaac, island, *Bahamas* **116** D10
Great Karroo, region, *S. Af.* **194** Q7
Great Lake, *Bahamas* **120** F11
Great Lameshur Bay, *Virgin Islands, U.S.* **120** N11
Great Meteor Tablemount, *Atl. Oc.* **236** J9
Great Miami, river, *Ohio, U.S.* **85** G17
Great Namaland, region, *Namibia* **202** J7
Great Nicobar, island, *India* **179** T15
Great Orme's Head, *Wales, U.K.* **143** S9
Great Pedro Bluff, *Jam.* **116** N11
Great Pedro Point, *Cayman Is., U.K.* **120** J2
Great Pee Dee, river, *S.C., U.S.* **96** L11
Great Plains, *U.S.* **84** C9
Great Pond Bay, *Virgin Islands, U.S.* **120** Q3
Great Rift Valley, *Af.* **194** L9
Great River Bay, *Grenada* **121** K23
Great Ruaha, river, *Tanzania* **199** M14
Great Sacandaga Lake, *N.Y., U.S.* **94** J11
Great St. James Island, *Virgin Islands, U.S.* **120** N10
Great Sale Cay, *Bahamas* **120** D3
Great Salt Lake, *Utah, U.S.* **106** K6
Great Salt Lake Desert, *Utah, U.S.* **106** L6
Great Salt Plains Lake, *Okla., U.S.* **102** E10
Great Salt Pond, *St. Kitts & Nevis* **121** B18
Great Sand Dunes National Park, *Colo., U.S.* **107** P13
Great Sandy Desert, *Austral.* **210** E5
Great Sandy Desert, *Oreg., U.S.* **84** D4
Great Sandy Island *see* Fraser Island, *Austral.* **210** G16
Great Sitkin Island, *Alas., U.S.* **110** N5
Great Slave Lake, *N.W.T., Can.* **82** H11
Great Smoky Mountains, *N.C., Tenn., U.S.* **85** J18
Great Smoky Mountains National Park, *N.C., Tenn., U.S.* **96** H6
Great Sound, *Bermuda, U.K.* **120** C1
Great Stirrup Cay, *Bahamas* **116** D11
Great Tenasserim, river, *Myanmar* **187** N8
Great Thatch Island, *Virgin Islands, U.K.* **120** M11
Great Tobago Island, *Virgin Islands, U.K.* **120** L10
Great Victoria Desert, *Austral.* **210** H6
Great Wall, station, *Antarctica* **226** C3
Great Wall, *China* **181** H13
Great Western Dunes, *Alg.* **194** D4
Great Western Tiers, *Austral.* **210** L16
Great Yarmouth, *Eng., U.K.* **143** T16
Great Zab, river, *Turk.* **169** G18
Great Zimbabwe, ruin, *Zimb.* **202** G11
Greci, *It.* **150** L12
Gredos, Sierra de, *Sp.* **144** F9
Greece, *Eur.* **139** X8
Greece, *N.Y., U.S.* **94** H6
Greeley, *Colo., U.S.* **106** L13
Greeley, *Nebr., U.S.* **105** P6
Greely Fiord, *Nunavut, Can.* **83** B16
Green, river, *Ky., U.S.* **101** D15
Green, river, *Utah, U.S.* **106** L9
Green Bay, *Antigua & Barbuda* **121** B20
Green Bay, *Wis., U.S.* **98** H7
Green Bay, *Wis., U.S.* **98** J7
Greenbrier, river, *W. Va., U.S.* **96** E10
Greenbush, *Mich., U.S.* **98** J12
Greenbush, *Minn., U.S.* **104** E9
Green Castle, *Bahamas* **120** F6
Greencastle, *Ind., U.S.* **99** R8
Greencastle, *Pa., U.S.* **94** Q6
Green Cay, *Bahamas* **116** F11
Green Cay, *Virgin Islands, U.K.* **120** L11
Green Cay, *Virgin Islands, U.S.* **120** Q3
Green Cove Springs, *Fla., U.S.* **97** R8
Greeneville, *Tenn., U.S.* **101** E20
Greenfield, *Calif., U.S.* **109** U5
Greenfield, *Ind., U.S.* **99** R9
Greenfield, *Iowa, U.S.* **105** P10
Greenfield, *Mass., U.S.* **95** K13
Greenfield, *Mo., U.S.* **105** U11
Greenfield, *Ohio, U.S.* **99** S12
Greenfield, *Tenn., U.S.* **101** E13
Greenfield, *Wis., U.S.* **98** L7
Green Head, *Austral.* **210** J2
Green Hill, *Trinidad & Tobago* **121** N22
Green Island, *Antigua & Barbuda* **121** B21
Green Island, *Grenada* **121** J23
Green Island, *Jam.* **120** H6
Green Islands, *P.N.G.* **213** C22
Greenland, island, *N. Amer.* **80** C9
Greenland (Kalaallit Nunaat), *N. Amer.* **81** B20
Greenland Fracture Zone, *Arctic Oc.* **243** H16
Greenland Plain, *Arctic Oc.* **243** J17
Greenland Sea, *Arctic Oc.* **243** H15
Green Mountains, *Vt., U.S.* **94** J12
Green Mountains, *Wyo., U.S.* **106** J11
Greenock, *Scot., U.K.* **142** M8
Greenport, *N.Y., U.S.* **95** M13
Green River, *Utah, U.S.* **106** M9
Green River, *Wyo., U.S.* **106** K9
Greensboro, *Ala., U.S.* **101** L14
Greensboro, *Ga., U.S.* **96** L6
Greensboro, *N.C., U.S.* **96** G10
Greensburg, *Ind., U.S.* **99** S10
Greensburg, *Kans., U.S.* **105** U5
Greensburg, *Ky., U.S.* **101** C17
Greensburg, *Pa., U.S.* **94** P4
Greens Peak, *Ariz., U.S.* **107** T9
Green Turtle Cay, *Bahamas* **120** A6
Green Valley, *Ariz., U.S.* **107** V8
Greenville, *Ala., U.S.* **101** M15
Greenville, *Calif., U.S.* **109** N5
Greenville, *Fla., U.S.* **97** Q6
Greenville, *Ill., U.S.* **99** T5
Greenville, *Ky., U.S.* **101** D15
Greenville, *Liberia* **200** H7
Greenville, *Me., U.S.* **95** D16
Greenville, *Mich., U.S.* **98** L10
Greenville, *Miss., U.S.* **100** J10
Greenville, *N.C., U.S.* **96** H13
Greenville, *Ohio, U.S.* **99** R11
Greenville, *Pa., U.S.* **94** M3
Greenville, *S.C., U.S.* **96** J7
Greenville, *Tex., U.S.* **102** K12
Greenwood, *Ark., U.S.* **100** F6
Greenwood, *Ind., U.S.* **99** R9
Greenwood, *Miss., U.S.* **100** J11
Greenwood, *S.C., U.S.* **96** K7
Greer, *S.C., U.S.* **96** J7
Greers Ferry Lake, *Ark., U.S.* **100** F8
Gregory, river, *Austral.* **210** D11
Gregory, *S. Dak., U.S.* **104** M5
Gregory, Lake, *Austral.* **210** H10
Gregory Downs, *Qnsld., Austral.* **211** R10
Gregory Range, *Austral.* **210** D12
Gregory Town, *Bahamas* **120** D5
Greifswald, *Ger.* **148** B10
Greiz, *Ger.* **148** G9
Grenada, *Calif., U.S.* **108** L3
Grenada, *Miss., U.S.* **100** J11
Grenada, *N. Amer.* **81** P24
Grenada, island, *N. Amer.* **80** P12
Grenada Bay, *Grenada* **121** J23
Grenade, *Fr.* **147** X7
Grenoble, *Fr.* **147** V14
Grenora, *N. Dak., U.S.* **104** E2
Grenville, *Grenada* **121** K23
Grenville, Cape, *Austral.* **210** A12
Grenville, Point, *Wash., U.S.* **108** C2
Grenville Bay, *Grenada* **121** K23
Gresham, *Oreg., U.S.* **108** F4
Gretna, *La., U.S.* **100** Q11
Gretschins, *Switz.* **160** Q2
Grevená, *Gr.* **154** D8
Grevenmacher, *Lux.* **160** J11
Grey, Mount, *Austral.* **210** J3
Greybull, river, *Wyo., U.S.* **106** G10
Greybull, *Wyo., U.S.* **106** F10
Grey Islands, *Nfld. & Lab., Can.* **83** L23
Greylock, Mount, *Mass., U.S.* **94** K12
Grey Range, *Austral.* **210** H12
Grezzana, *It.* **150** D6
Gribanovskiy, *Russ.* **156** M11
Gridley, *Calif., U.S.* **109** P4
Grieg Point, *Kiribati* **217** B20
Griffin, *Ga., U.S.* **96** M5
Griffith, *N.S.W., Austral.* **211** Y13
Griggsville, *Ill., U.S.* **99** R3
Grimaldi Forum, *Monaco* **161** C22
Grimault, Île, *New Caledonia, Fr.* **218** D7
Grimsby, *Eng., U.K.* **143** R14
Grímsey, island, *Ice.* **140** E3
Grimshaw, *Alta., Can.* **82** K10
Grimstad, *Nor.* **140** M11
Grindelwald, *Switz.* **150** B3
Grinnell, *Iowa, U.S.* **105** P12
Grinnell Peninsula, *Nunavut, Can.* **83** C15
Grintavec, peak, *Slov.* **152** C4
Griquatown, *S. Af.* **202** K9
Grise Fiord, *Nunavut, Can.* **83** C16
Grishkino, *Russ.* **158** J12
Gris-Nez, Cap, *Fr.* **146** L9
Grisslehamn, *Sw.* **141** K14
Gródek, *Pol.* **149** C18
Groenlo, *Neth.* **146** J14
Groesbeck, *Tex., U.S.* **103** N12
Groix, Île de, *Fr.* **147** R3
Grójec, *Pol.* **149** E16
Gronau, *Ger.* **148** D5
Groningen, *Neth.* **146** G14
Groom, *Tex., U.S.* **102** G6
Groot Baai, *Neth. Antilles, Neth.* **121** B14
Groote Eylandt, *N. Terr., Austral.* **211** P10
Grootfontein, *Namibia* **202** G7
Grosio, *It.* **150** C6
Gros Islet, *St. Lucia* **121** J14
Gros Islet Bay, *St. Lucia* **121** J14
Gros-Morne, *Martinique, Fr.* **121** E22
Gros Piton, peak, *St. Lucia* **121** L13
Gros Point, *Grenada* **121** J22
Grosse Pointe, *Guadeloupe, Fr.* **121** G16
Grosseto, *It.* **150** J6
Grossvenediger, peak, *Aust.* **148** M9
Grosvenor Downs, *Qnsld., Austral.* **211** T14
Grosvenor Mountains, *Antarctica* **226** K12
Grosvenor Seamount, *Pac. Oc.* **238** G8
Gros Ventre Range, *Wyo., U.S.* **106** H8
Grotli, *Nor.* **140** J10
Groton, *S. Dak., U.S.* **104** J7
Grottaminarda, *It.* **150** M11
Grotto of Lourdes, *Vatican City* **161** Q14
Grotto of the Observatory, *Monaco* **161** F19
Grouse Creek, *Utah, U.S.* **106** J5
Grove, *Mo., U.S.* **105** V13
Grove City, *Pa., U.S.* **94** M3
Grove Hill, *Ala., U.S.* **101** M14
Grove Mountains, *Antarctica* **227** G18
Grove Place, *Virgin Islands, U.S.* **120** Q2
Grover, *Colo., U.S.* **106** K14
Grover Beach, *Calif., U.S.* **109** V5
Groves, *Tex., U.S.* **103** Q16
Groveton, *N.H., U.S.* **95** F14
Groveton, *Tex., U.S.* **103** P14
Groznyy, *Russ.* **157** T14
Grudovo, *Bulg.* **153** J17
Grudziądz, *Pol.* **149** C14
Gruinard Bay, *Scot., U.K.* **142** J8
Grundy, *Va., U.S.* **96** F7
Grundy Center, *Iowa, U.S.* **105** N12
Gruver, *Tex., U.S.* **102** F5
Gryazi, *Russ.* **156** M10
Gryazovets, *Russ.* **156** G10
Gryfino, *Pol.* **148** C11
Grygla, *Minn., U.S.* **104** E9
Guacanayabo, Golfo de, *Cuba* **116** K11
Guadalajara, *Mex.* **114** H10
Guadalajara, *Sp.* **144** F11
Guadalcanal, island, *Solomon Is.* **217** N19
Guadalcanal, *Sp.* **144** K8
Guadalquivir, river, *Sp.* **144** K9
Guadalupe, *Calif., U.S.* **109** W5
Guadalupe, *Mex.* **114** C7
Guadalupe, *Mex.* **114** G10
Guadalupe, river, *Tex., U.S.* **103** S11
Guadalupe, Isla de, *Mex.* **114** C4
Guadalupe, Sierra de, *Sp.* **144** H9
Guadalupe Island *see* Guadalupe, Isla de, *N. Amer.* **80** L2
Guadalupe Mountains, *N. Mex., U.S.* **107** V14
Guadalupe Mountains National Park, *Tex., U.S.* **102** M1
Guadalupe Peak, *Tex., U.S.* **102** M1
Guadalupita, *N. Mex., U.S.* **107** R13
Guadarrama, Sierra de, *Sp.* **144** F10
Guadeloupe, island, *Lesser Antilles* **119** H17
Guadeloupe Passage, *Lesser Antilles* **119** H16
Guadiana, river, *Port.* **144** K6
Guadiana, river, *Sp.* **144** H8
Guadiana, Bahía, *Cuba* **116** H4
Guadirikiri Cave, *Aruba, Neth.* **121** R17
Guadix, *Sp.* **144** L11
Guafo, Boca del, *Chile* **133** R6
Guafo, Isla, *Chile* **133** R5
Guai, *Indonesia* **189** K21
Guáimaro, *Cuba* **116** J11
Guainía, river, *Col.* **128** G8
Guaíra, *Braz.* **130** M11
Guajaba, Cayo, *Cuba* **116** H11
Guajará-Mirim, *Braz.* **130** G7
Guajira, Península de la, *Col.* **128** A7
Gualala, *Calif., U.S.* **109** Q2
Gualdicciolo, *San Marino* **161** J14
Gualeguay, *Arg.* **132** K12
Gualeguaychú, *Arg.* **132** K13
Gualicho, Salina, *Arg.* **133** P9
Guallatiri, Volcán, *Chile* **132** B7
Guam, island, *Pac. Oc.* **214** E4
Guamúchil, *Mex.* **114** E8
Gua Musang, *Malaysia* **187** T10
Gunal, Punta del, *Cuba* **116** J6
Guana Baai, *Neth. Antilles, Neth.* **121** B15
Guana Cay, *Bahamas* **120** C10
Guana Island, *Virgin Islands, U.K.* **120** Q7
Guanajay, *Cuba* **116** G6
Guanajuato, *Mex.* **114** H11
Guanambi, *Braz.* **131** J15
Guanapo, *Trinidad & Tobago* **121** P23
Guanare, river, *Venez.* **128** C8
Guanare, *Venez.* **128** C8
Guandacol, *Arg.* **132** H8
Guane, *Cuba* **116** H4
Guangchang, *China* **183** P6
Guangfeng, *China* **182** M8
Guanghai, *China* **183** S4
Guangning, *China* **183** R3
Guangrao, *China* **182** F8
Guangshan, *China* **182** K5
Guangshui, *China* **182** K5
Guangyuan, *China* **180** K12
Guangzhou (Canton), *China* **183** R4
Guánica, *P.R., U.S.* **120** N2
Guánica, Bahía de, *P.R., U.S.* **120** P2
Guanipa, river, *Venez.* **128** C12
Guano, Cayo, *Cuba* **116** H8
Guano Lake, *Oreg., U.S.* **108** L7
Guantánamo, *Cuba* **117** K13
Guantánamo, Bahía de, *Cuba* **117** L13
Guantanamo Bay, U.S. Naval Base, *Cuba* **117** L14
Guanyan, *China* **182** H8
Guanyang, *China* **183** P3
Guapí, *Col.* **128** G3
Guapo Bay, *Trinidad & Tobago* **121** Q21
Guaporé, river, *Bol., Braz.* **130** H9
Guara, Sierra de, *Sp.* **145** C14
Guaranda, *Ecua.* **128** K3
Guarapuava, *Braz.* **130** M12
Guaratinguetá, *Braz.* **131** M14
Guarcino, *It.* **150** K9
Guarda, *Port.* **144** F7
Guardalauaca, *Cuba* **117** J13
Guarda Mor, *Braz.* **131** K13
Guardo, *Sp.* **144** C9
Guareña, *Sp.* **144** J8
Guárico, river, *Venez.* **128** C9
Guarico, Punta, *Cuba* **117** K14
Guasave, *Mex.* **114** E8
Guascama, Punta, *Col.* **128** G3
Guasdualito, *Venez.* **128** D7
Guatemala, *Guatemala* **115** L16
Guatemala, *N. Amer.* **81** P19
Guatemala Basin, *Pac. Oc.* **239** J18
Guaviare, river, *Col.* **128** F8
Guaviare, river, *S. Amer.* **126** C4
Guayabal, *Cuba* **116** K11
Guayaguayare, *Trinidad & Tobago* **121** Q23

Guayaguayare Bay, Trinidad & Tobago 121 Q23
Guayama, P.R., U.S. 120 N4
Guayaquil, Ecua. 128 K2
Guayaquil, Gulf of, S. Amer. 126 D1
Guaymas, Mex. 114 D7
Guaynabo, P.R., U.S. 120 M4
Gûbâl, Strait of, Egypt 171 U3
Gubbio, It. 150 H8
Gubin, Pol. 148 E11
Gubkin, Russ. 157 N9
Gucheng, China 182 J3
Gudalur, India 179 Q5
Gudaut'a, Abkhazia 169 A15
Gudermes, Russ. 157 T14
Gudgeon Bay, Pitcairn I., U.K. 219 Q23
Gudur, India 179 P7
Guebwiller, Fr. 147 Q15
Guelb er Rîchât, peak, Mauritania 196 F6
Guelmim, Mor. 196 C7
Güeppí, Peru 130 C3
Guéra Massif, Chad 194 G7
Guerara, Alg. 196 B11
Guéret, Fr. 147 T9
Guernsey, island, Ch. Is. 143 Z11
Guernsey, Wyo., U.S. 106 J13
Guernsey Reservoir, Wyo., U.S. 106 J13
Gueydan, La., U.S. 100 P8
Gugegwe, island, Marshall Is. 216 M6
Guguan, island, N. Mariana Is., U.S. 216 B2
Gui, river, China 183 R2
Guía de Isora, Canary Is. 204 Q4
Guiana Highlands, S. Amer. 126 B6
Guiana Island, Antigua & Barbuda 121 B21
Guichi, China 182 L7
Guide, China 180 J11
Guienne, region, Fr. 147 W7
Guiglo, Côte d'Ivoire 200 G7
Guijá, Mozambique 202 J12
Guijuelo, Sp. 144 F8
Guildford, Eng., U.K. 143 W13
Guilford, Me., U.S. 95 E16
Guilin, China 183 Q2
Guillaume-Delisle, Lac, Que., Can. 83 L18
Guillestre, Fr. 147 V15
Guimarães, Port. 144 D6
Guimarães, Braz. 131 D15
Guin, Ala., U.S. 101 J14
Guinchos Cay, Cuba 116 G11
Guinea, Af. 195 H14
Guinea, Gulf of, Af. 194 J4
Guinea-Bissau, Af. 195 G13
Güines, Cuba 116 G6
Guingamp, Fr. 147 P4
Guiping, China 183 R2
Güira de Melena, Cuba 116 G6
Güiria, Venez. 128 B12
Guisborough, Eng., U.K. 143 Q12
Guitiriz, Sp. 144 B6
Guixi, China 183 N7
Guixian, China 183 R1
Guiyang, China 183 P4
Guiyang, China 180 N12
Gujar Khan, Pak. 177 N11
Gujranwala, Pak. 177 P12
Gujrat, Pak. 177 P11
Gulang, China 180 H11
Gulbarga, India 178 M5
Gulbene, Latv. 141 L17
Gul'cha, Kyrg. 176 G11
Gulf Islands National Seashore, Fla., U.S. 97 Q2
Gulf Islands National Seashore, Miss., U.S. 101 P13
Gulfport, Miss., U.S. 100 P12
Gulf Shores, Ala., U.S. 101 P14
Gulgong, N.S.W., Austral. 211 X14
Guling, China 182 M6
Guliston, Uzb. 175 K13
Gulitel, Mount, Palau 216 M12
Gulja see Yining, China 180 E6
Gulkana, Alas., U.S. 111 H18
Güllük, Turk. 168 H3
Gülnar, Turk. 168 J8
Gülşehir, Turk. 168 F10
Gulu, Uganda 199 J13
Gülübovo, Bulg. 153 J15
Gulya, Russ. 159 K18
Gulyantsi, Bulg. 153 G14
Guma see Pishan, China 180 G4
Gumdag, Turkm. 174 L6
Gumla, India 178 J9
Gummi, Nigeria 201 E13
Gümüşhacıköy, Turk. 168 D10
Gümüşhane, Turk. 169 D14
Gümüşören, Turk. 168 G10
Gumzai, Indonesia 189 L19
Guna, India 178 H6
Gun Bay, Cayman Is., U.K. 120 J4
Gun Cay, Bahamas 116 D9
Gun Creek, Virgin Islands, U.K. 120 Q9
Gundagai, N.S.W., Austral. 211 Y13
Gundlupet, India 179 Q5
Gündoğmuş, Turk. 168 J7
Güney, Turk. 168 G4
Gungu, Dem. Rep. of the Congo 198 L9
Gun Hill, Barbados 121 K19
Gunib, Russ. 157 U15
Gunnbjørn, peak, N. Amer. 80 B10
Gunnedah, N.S.W., Austral. 211 W14
Gunners Quoin, island, Mauritius 205 F20
Gunnewin, Qnsld., Austral. 211 U14
Gunnison, Colo., U.S. 107 N11
Gunnison, Utah, U.S. 106 M7
Gunsan, S. Korea 182 G13
Gunt, river, Taj. 176 J10
Guntersville, Ala., U.S. 101 H16
Guntersville Lake, Ala., U.S. 101 H16
Guntur, India 179 N7
Gunungsugih, Indonesia 188 L7
Guoyang, China 182 J6
Gupis, Pak. 176 L11
Gurabo, P.R., U.S. 120 N5
Gurage, peak, Eth. 194 H10
Gura Humorului, Rom. 153 B15
Gura Portiiei, strait, Rom. 153 F18
Gurban Obo, China 181 F14
Gurdaspur, India 177 P13
Gurdon, Ark., U.S. 100 J7
Güre, Turk. 168 F5
Gurer, island, Marshall Is. 216 L3
Gurguan Point, N. Mariana Is., U.S. 216 B7
Guri Dam, Venez. 128 D12
Guri i Topit, peak, Albania 152 L10
Gurimatu, P.N.G. 213 D19
Gurkovo, Bulg. 153 J15
Gurney, P.N.G. 213 E21
Gürün, Turk. 168 F12
Gurupá, Braz. 130 D12
Gurupá Island, S. Amer. 126 D8
Gurupi, river, Braz. 131 D14
Gurupi, Braz. 131 G13
Gurupi, Cape, S. Amer. 126 D9
Gurupi, Serra do, Braz. 131 E13
Gurvan Bogd Uul, range, Mongolia 180 E11
Gusau, Nigeria 201 E14
Gusev, Russ. 156 J2
Guşgy, river, Turkm. 174 N10
Guşgy, Turkm. 174 P10
Gushan, China 182 D11
Gushi, China 182 K6
Gushikawa, Japan 185 Y1
Gusikha, Russ. 159 E15
Gusinaya Bank, Arctic Oc. 243 C16
Gusinoozersk, Russ. 159 L16
Gus' Khrustal'nyy, Russ. 156 J11
Guspini, It. 151 P3
Güssing, Aust. 148 M12
Gustavia, St.-Barthélemy 119 F15
Gustine, Calif., U.S. 109 S5
Güstrow, Ger. 148 C9
Gutâiu, peak, Rom. 153 B13
Gutcher, Scot., U.K. 142 C12
Gutenberg Castle, Liech. 160 Q2
Gütersloh, Ger. 148 E6
Guthrie, Ky., U.S. 101 D15
Guthrie, Okla., U.S. 102 F11
Guthrie, Tex., U.S. 102 K7
Guthrie Center, Iowa, U.S. 105 P10
Gutian, China 183 P8
Guttenberg, Iowa, U.S. 104 M14
Güvem, Turk. 168 D8
Guwahati, India 178 G13
Guyana, S. Amer. 127 B18
Guyandotte, river, W. Va., U.S. 96 E7
Guyang, China 182 C3
Guymon, Okla., U.S. 102 E5
Guyonneau, Anse, Guadeloupe, Fr. 121 F14
Guyra, N.S.W., Austral. 211 W15
Guyuan, China 182 B6
Güzeloluk, Turk. 168 J9
Güzelyurt, Turk. 168 G9
Guzhang, China 182 M2
G'uzor, Uzb. 174 M12
Gwa, Myanmar 186 K5
Gwadar, Pak. 177 W2
Gwai, Zimb. 202 G10
Gwalior, India 178 G6
Gwanda, Zimb. 202 G11
Gwangju (Kwangju), S. Korea 182 G13
Gwardafuy, Cape, Somalia 194 G12
Gwatar Bay, Pak. 177 W1
Gweebarra Bay, Ire. 143 P4
Gweru, Zimb. 202 G11
Gwinn, Mich., U.S. 98 F7
Gwinner, N. Dak., U.S. 104 H7
Gwoza, Nigeria 201 F16
Gwydir, river, Austral. 210 J14
Gyamysh, peak, Azerb. 169 D20
Gyangzê, China 180 L7
Gyaring Co, China 180 K7
Gyaring Hu, China 180 J9
Gydan see Kolymskoye Nagor'ye, range, Russ. 159 D20
Gydanskiy Poluostrov, Russ. 158 F12
Gyda Peninsula, Russ. 166 C8
Gyêgu, China 180 K9
Gyeongju (Kyŏngju), S. Korea 182 G15
Gympie, Qnsld., Austral. 211 V15
Gyöngyös, Hung. 149 L15
Győr, Hung. 149 L14
Gypsum, Kans., U.S. 105 T7
Gyula, Hung. 149 M17
Gyumri, Arm. 169 D18
Gyzylarbat, Turkm. 174 L7
Gyzyletrek, Turkm. 174 M6
Gyzylgaya, Turkm. 174 K7
Gyzylsuw, Turkm. 174 K6
Gżira, Malta 161 K23

H

Haʻafeva, island, Tonga 218 Q6
Haag, Switz. 160 N2
Haʻakame, Tonga 218 J11
Haʻalaufuli, Tonga 218 L12
Haamaire, Baie, Fr. Polynesia, Fr. 219 K14
Haamene, Baie de, Fr. Polynesia, Fr. 219 A23
Haʻano, island, Tonga 218 P7
Haʻapai Group, Tonga 214 K10
Haapamäki, Fin. 141 H15
Haapiti, Fr. Polynesia, Fr. 219 N14
Haapsalu, Est. 141 K16
Haapu, Fr. Polynesia, Fr. 219 H14
Haarlem, Neth. 146 J12
Haʻasini, Tonga 218 J12
Haast, N.Z. 213 P15
Haast Bluff, N. Terr., Austral. 211 T8
Haava, Canal, Fr. Polynesia, Fr. 219 N20
Hab, river, Pak. 177 V6
Habahe, China 180 C7
Ḩabarūt, Oman 173 N14
Habomai, Japan 184 F16
Habomai Islands, Russ. 184 G6
Haboro, Japan 184 E13
Hachijō Jima, Japan 185 S12
Hachiman, Japan 185 P10
Hachinohe, Japan 184 J13
Hachiōji, Japan 185 P12
Hachirō Gata, Japan 184 K12
Hachita, N. Mex., U.S. 107 V10
Hacıbektaş, Turk. 168 F9
Hadarba, Ras, Sudan 199 B14
Ḩadd, Ra's al, Oman 173 K17
Haddummati Atoll, Maldives 179 W3
Hadejia, river, Nigeria 194 G5
Ḩadera, Israel 170 L5
Hadhramaut see Ḩaḑramawt, region, Yemen 166 J3
Hadīboh (Tamrida), Yemen 173 R14
Ḩadīdah, Syr. 170 D10
Hadım, Turk. 168 H7
Ḩadīthah, Iraq 172 D8
Hadja, Solomon Is. 217 P20
Hadley Bay, Nunavut, Can. 83 E13
Ha Dong, Vietnam 186 H12
Ḩaḑramawt, region, Yemen 172 Q11
Hadrian's Wall, Eng., U.K. 143 P11
Hadyach, Ukr. 157 N7
Haeju, N. Korea 182 E12
Hāʻena, Hawaiʻi, U.S. 113 M22
Haenam, S. Korea 182 H13
Ḩafar al Bāţin, Saudi Arabia 172 G10
Hafik, Turk. 168 E12
Ḩafīt, Jabal, U.A.E. 173 K15
Hafizabad, Pak. 177 P11
Hagåtña (Agana), Guam, U.S. 216 C10
Hagemeister Island, Alas., U.S. 110 L12
Hagen, Ger. 148 F6
Hagerman, N. Mex., U.S. 107 U14
Hagerman Fossil Beds National Monument, Idaho, U.S. 106 H4
Hagerstown, Md., U.S. 96 B12
Häggenås, Sw. 140 H12
Hagi, Japan 185 Q5
Ha Giang, Vietnam 186 G11
Hagia Triada, ruin, Gr. 155 R14
Hagman, Puntan, N. Mariana Is., U.S. 216 C5
Hagoi Susupe, lake, N. Mariana Is., U.S. 216 C4
Hags Head, Ire. 143 S3
Hague, Cap de la, Fr. 147 N5
Haguenau, Fr. 147 P15
Haha Jima Rettō, Japan 184 K5
Hai, Hon, Vietnam 187 Q14
Hai'an, China 182 J9
Hai'an, China 181 Q13
Haicheng, China 182 C10
Hai Duong, Vietnam 186 H12
Haifa see Ḩefa, Israel 170 K5
Haifeng, China 183 S5
Haig, W. Aust., Austral. 211 W6
Haiger, Ger. 148 G6
Haikang, China 183 T1
Haikou, China 183 T2
Haʻiku, Hawaiʻi, U.S. 113 G17
Ḩā'il, Saudi Arabia 172 H8
Hailar, China 181 C15
Hailey, Idaho, U.S. 106 G5
Hails, China 182 B1
Hailuoto, island, Fin. 141 F15
Haimen see Jiaojiang, China 182 M10
Haimen Wan, China 183 R6
Hainan, island, China 183 U2
Haines, Alas., U.S. 111 K21
Haines, Oreg., U.S. 108 G8
Haines City, Fla., U.S. 97 U8
Haines Junction, Yukon, Can. 82 G7
Hainiya Point, N. Mariana Is., U.S. 216 E8
Haiphong, Vietnam 186 H12
Haiti, N. Amer. 81 N22
Haiya, Sudan 199 D14
Haiyan, China 182 L9
Haiyan, China 180 H11
Haizhou Wan, China 182 H8
Hajdúböszörmény, Hung. 149 L17
Hajdúszoboszló, Hung. 149 L17
Hajiki Saki, Japan 184 L11
Haji Pir Pass, India, Pak. 177 N11
Ḩajjah, Yemen 172 P9
Ḩajjīābād, Iran 173 G15
Hajnáčka, Slovakia 149 K15
Hajnówka, Pol. 149 D18
Hakalau, Hawaiʻi, U.S. 113 L21
Hakamaru, island, Cook Is., N.Z. 219 B15
Hakataramea, N.Z. 213 Q16
Hakauata, island, Tonga 218 P7
Hakha, Myanmar 186 G4
Hakkari, Turk. 169 H18
Hakken San, Japan 185 Q9
Hakodate, Japan 184 H13
Hakui, Japan 185 N10
Hakupa Pass, Solomon Is. 217 J18
Hakupu, Niue, N.Z. 219 B20
Hala, Pak. 177 V7
Halaaniyaat, Juzor al (Kuria Muria Islands), Oman 173 N15
Ḩalab (Aleppo), Syr. 170 D9
Ḩalabān, Saudi Arabia 172 K9
Halachó, Mex. 115 H16
Halāliʻi Lake, Hawaiʻi, U.S. 112 C3
Halalo, Pointe, Wallis & Futuna, Fr. 218 C11
Halaʻula, Hawaiʻi, U.S. 113 K19
Halawa, Hawaiʻi, U.S. 113 K19
Hālawa, Cape, Hawaiʻi, U.S. 113 F15
Hālawa Bay, Hawaiʻi, U.S. 113 F15
Halayeb, Egypt 197 F20
Halba, Leb. 170 G7
Halban, Mongolia 180 C10
Halberstadt, Ger. 148 E8
Halcon, Mount, Philippines 189 D13
Haldwani, India 178 E7
Hale, Mich., U.S. 98 J12
Haleakalā Crater, Hawaiʻi, U.S. 113 H17
Haleakalā National Park, Hawaiʻi, U.S. 113 H18
Haleakalā Observatories, Hawaiʻi, U.S. 113 H17
Hale Center, Tex., U.S. 102 J5
Haleʻiwa, Hawaiʻi, U.S. 112 D10
Halekiʻi-Pihana Heiaus, Hawaiʻi, U.S. 113 G16
Haleyville, Ala., U.S. 101 H14
Halfeti, Turk. 168 H12
Half Moon Bay, Antigua & Barbuda 121 B21
Halfway, Oreg., U.S. 108 G9
Halgan, Cape, F.S.M. 217 A19
Halifax, N.S., Can. 83 P22
Halifax, Qnsld., Austral. 211 R13
Halifax, Va., U.S. 96 F11
Halkett, Cape, Alas., U.S. 111 B16
Hálki, island, Gr. 155 N19
Hálki, island, Gr. 155 N19
Hálki, Gr. 154 F10
Halkída (Chalkis), Gr. 154 H12
Halkidikí, peninsula, Gr. 154 D12
Hall, Aust. 148 L8
Hallandale, Fla., U.S. 97 W10
Hall Basin, Nunavut, Can. 83 A17
Hall Beach, Nunavut, Can. 83 F16
Halle, Belg. 146 L12
Halle, Ger. 148 F9
Hallein, Aust. 148 L10
Hallettsville, Tex., U.S. 103 R12
Halley, station, Antarctica 226 D10
Halliday, N. Dak., U.S. 104 F3
Hallim, S. Korea 182 J13
Hall Islands, F.S.M. 216 Q6
Hällnäs, Sw. 141 G14
Hallock, Minn., U.S. 104 E8
Hall Peninsula, Nunavut, Can. 83 H19
Halls, Tenn., U.S. 100 F12
Halls Creek, W. Aust., Austral. 211 R6
Hallstatt, Aust. 148 L10
Halmahera, island, Indonesia 189 H16
Halmahera Sea, Indonesia 189 J17
Halmeu, Rom. 152 A12
Halmstad, Sw. 140 N12
Halola, Solomon Is. 217 L14
Halsa, Nor. 140 H10
Halstead, Eng., U.K. 143 U15
Halstead, Kans., U.S. 105 U7
Haltdalen, Nor. 140 H11
Halten Bank, Atl. Oc. 236 C14
Halulu Heiau, Hawaiʻi, U.S. 113 G14
Halys see Kızılırmak, river, Turk. 168 D9
Ham, Fr. 147 N10
Hamada, Japan 185 Q6
Hamadān, Iran 172 D11
Hamaguir, Alg. 196 C9
Ḩamāh (Hamath), Syr. 170 F8
Hāmākua, region, Hawaiʻi, U.S. 113 L20
Hamamatsu, Japan 185 Q10
Hamamet, Gulf of, Tun. 194 C6
Hamar, Nor. 140 K11
Hamasaka, Japan 185 P8
Hamâta, Gebel, Egypt 197 E20
Hamath see Ḩamāh, Syr. 170 F8
Hamatombetsu, Japan 184 D14
Hamburg, Ark., U.S. 100 K9
Hamburg, Ger. 148 C8
Hamburg, Iowa, U.S. 105 Q9
Hamburg, Mo., U.S. 105 Q9
Hamburg, N.Y., U.S. 94 J5
Ḩamḑah, Saudi Arabia 172 M9
Ḩamdānah, Saudi Arabia 172 M7
Hamden, Conn., U.S. 94 M12
Hämeenlinna, Fin. 141 J16
Hamelin, W. Aust., Austral. 211 V1
Hameln, Ger. 148 E7
Hamersley Range, Austral. 210 F3
Hamhŭng, N. Korea 182 D13
Hami (Kumul), China 180 F9
Hamilton, Ala., U.S. 101 H14
Hamilton, Bermuda, U.K. 120 B2
Hamilton, Ill., U.S. 99 Q3
Hamilton, Mo., U.S. 105 R11
Hamilton, Mont., U.S. 106 D5
Hamilton, N.Y., U.S. 94 J9
Hamilton, N.Z. 213 K19
Hamilton, Ohio, U.S. 99 S11
Hamilton, Ont., Can. 83 R18
Hamilton, Scot., U.K. 142 M9
Hamilton, Tas., Austral. 211 Z16
Hamilton, Tex., U.S. 103 N10
Hamilton, Vic., Austral. 211 Z11
Hamilton, Lake, Ark., U.S. 100 H7
Hamilton Harbour, Bermuda, U.K. 120 B2
Hamilton Inlet, Nfld. & Lab., Can. 83 K22
Hamina, Fin. 141 J17

Hamirpur, India 178 G7
Hamlet, N.C., U.S. 96 J10
Hamlí, island, Gr. 155 P16
Hamlin, Tex., U.S. 102 L7
Hamm, Ger. 148 E6
Ḩammār, Hawr al, Iraq 166 G4
Hammerfest, Nor. 141 C14
Hammon, Okla., U.S. 102 G8
Hammond, Ind., U.S. 99 N7
Hammond, La., U.S. 100 P10
Hammond, Mont., U.S. 106 F13
Hammonton, N.J., U.S. 94 Q10
Hampden, N.Z. 213 Q16
Hampstead, Dominica 121 E19
Hampton, Ark., U.S. 100 J8
Hampton, Iowa, U.S. 104 M12
Hampton, S.C., U.S. 96 M9
Hampton, Va., U.S. 96 F14
Hampton Bays, N.Y., U.S. 95 N13
Hampton Butte, Oreg., U.S. 108 H6
Hampton Tableland, Austral. 210 J6
Hampyeong, S. Korea 182 G13
Ḩamrīn, Jabal, Iraq 172 D9
Hamrun, Malta 161 K23
Hams Bluff, Virgin Islands, U.S. 120 Q2
Ham Yen, Vietnam 186 G11
Han, river, China 182 K4
Hāna, Hawai'i, U.S. 113 G18
Hanahan, P.N.G. 217 J13
Hanahe, Baie, Fr. Polynesia, Fr. 219 M23
Hāna Highway, Hawai'i, U.S. 113 G18
Hanahupe, Baie, Fr. Polynesia, Fr. 219 M21
Hanaiapa, Baie, Fr. Polynesia, Fr. 219 M20
Hanaiapaoa, Baie, Fr. Polynesia, Fr. 219 M20
Hanalei, Hawai'i, U.S. 112 B5
Hanalei Bay, Hawai'i, U.S. 112 B5
Hanamaki, Japan 184 K13
Hanamalo Point, Hawai'i, U.S. 113 P18
Hanamā'ulu, Hawai'i, U.S. 112 B6
Hanamenu, Baie, Fr. Polynesia, Fr. 219 M20
Hanaoo, Fr. Polynesia, Fr. 219 N20
Hanapēpē, Hawai'i, U.S. 112 C5
Hana Teio, Fr. Polynesia, Fr. 219 N20
Hana Tetena, Fr. Polynesia, Fr. 219 N20
Hana Tuuna, Fr. Polynesia, Fr. 219 N20
Hanau, Ger. 148 G6
Hanaui, Fr. Polynesia, Fr. 219 M20
Hanawa, Japan 184 J13
Hancheng, China 182 G3
Hanchuan, China 182 L5
Hancock, Md., U.S. 96 B12
Hancock, Mich., U.S. 98 E6
Hancock, Minn., U.S. 104 J9
Handa Island, Scot., U.K. 142 H8
Handan, China 182 F5
Handsome Bay, Virgin Islands, U.K. 120 R8
Hane, Fr. Polynesia, Fr. 219 N23
Hane, Baie d', Fr. Polynesia, Fr. 219 N23
Hanford, Calif., U.S. 109 U6
Hanford Site, Wash., U.S. 108 E7
Hangayn Nuruu, range, Mongolia 180 D10
Hanggin Houqi (Xamba), China 182 C1
Hanggin Qi, China 182 C2
Hangö (Hanko), Fin. 141 K15
Hangu, China 182 D7
Hangu, Pak. 177 N9
Hangzhou, China 182 L9
Hani, Turk. 169 G15
Haniá (Canea, Cydonia), Gr. 155 Q13
Hanimadu, island, Maldives 179 T3
Ḩanish al Kabīr, Jazīrat al, Yemen 172 Q8
Hankinson, N. Dak., U.S. 104 H8
Hanko see Hangö, Fin. 141 K15
Hanksville, Utah, U.S. 107 N8
Hanle, India 177 N15
Hanna, Alta., Can. 82 M10
Hannibal, Mo., U.S. 105 R14
Hannover (Hanover), Ger. 148 D7
Hanöbukten, Sw. 141 N13
Hanoi, Vietnam 186 H12
Hanover see Hannover, Ger. 148 D7
Hanover, Kans., U.S. 105 R8
Hanover, N.H., U.S. 95 H13
Hanover, Pa., U.S. 94 Q7
Hanover, Isla, Chile 133 V6
Hanpan, Cape, P.N.G. 217 J13
Hansen Mountains, Antarctica 227 D19
Hans Lollik Island, Virgin Islands, U.S. 120 M9
Hantsavichy, Belarus 156 L4
Hanumangarh, India 178 E4
Hanuy, river, Mongolia 180 C11
Hanyang, China 182 L5
Hanzhong, China 180 K12
Hao, island, Fr. Polynesia, Fr. 219 F20
Haora, India 178 J11
Hā'ō'ū, Hawai'i, U.S. 113 H18
Hapai, Solomon Is. 217 M16
Haparanda, Sw. 141 F15
Hapatoni, Baie, Fr. Polynesia, Fr. 219 N20
Hapo, Indonesia 189 H16
Happy, Tex., U.S. 102 H5
Happy Camp, Calif., U.S. 108 L2
Happy Valley-Goose Bay, Nfld. & Lab., Can. 83 L21
Ḩaql, Saudi Arabia 172 F5
Har, Indonesia 189 L18
Ḩaraḑ, Saudi Arabia 172 K12
Ḩarad, Jabal al, Jordan 171 R6
Haradok, Belarus 156 J6
Haradzishcha, Belarus 156 L4
Haraiki, island, Fr. Polynesia, Fr. 219 E19
Haranomachi, Japan 184 M13
Harappa, ruin, Pak. 177 R11
Harare, Zimb. 202 F11
Haratini, island, Cook Is., N.Z. 219 C15
Har Ayrag, Mongolia 181 E13
Harbin, China 181 D17
Harbor Beach, Mich., U.S. 98 K13
Harbor Springs, Mich., U.S. 98 H10
Harbour Island, Bahamas 120 D5
Harbours, Bay of, Falkland Is., U.K. 133 W12
Harda, India 178 J5
Hardangerfjorden, bay, Nor. 140 K10
Hard Bargain, Bahamas 120 B5
Hardenberg, Neth. 146 H14
Harderwijk, Neth. 146 J13
Hardin, Ill., U.S. 99 S3
Hardin, Mont., U.S. 106 E11
Harding, S. Af. 202 L11
Hardman, Oreg., U.S. 108 F6
Hardwick, Ga., U.S. 96 M6
Hardy, Ark., U.S. 100 E9
Hardy, Península, Chile 133 Y9
Hardy, Pointe, St. Lucia 121 J14
Hārer, Eth. 199 G16
Hargeysa, Somalia 199 G16
Har Hu, China 180 H10
Haría, Canary Is. 204 P8
Haridwar, India 178 E6
Harihari, N.Z. 213 P16
Harij, India 178 H3
Ḩārim, Syr. 170 D8
Haripur, Pak. 177 N11
Harirud, river, Asia 173 C17
Harkány, Hung. 149 N14
Harlan, Iowa, U.S. 105 P9
Harlan, Ky., U.S. 101 D19
Harlem, Mont., U.S. 106 B10
Harlingen, Neth. 146 G13
Harlingen, Tex., U.S. 103 W11
Harlowton, Mont., U.S. 106 D9
Harmancık, Turk. 168 E5
Harmony, Minn., U.S. 104 L13
Harnai, Pak. 177 R7
Harney Basin, Oreg., U.S. 108 J7
Harney Lake, Oreg., U.S. 108 J7
Harney Peak, S. Dak., U.S. 104 L1
Harnom Point, N. Mariana Is., U.S. 216 E7
Härnösand, Sw. 141 H13
Har Nuur, Mongolia 180 D9
Haro, Sp. 144 C12
Haroldswick, Scot., U.K. 142 C12
Harpanahalli, India 179 N5
Harper, Kans., U.S. 105 V7
Harper, Liberia 200 J7
Harper Lake, Calif., U.S. 109 W9
Harpers Ferry, W. Va., U.S. 96 C12
Harput, Turk. 169 G14
Harqin, China 182 C9
Harqin Qi, China 182 B8
Ḩarrah, Yemen 172 Q12
Harrai, India 178 J7
Har Ramon, peak, Israel 171 Q4
Harran, Turk. 169 J13
Harray, Loch of, Scot., U.K. 142 G10
Harricana, river, Que., Can. 83 N18
Harriman, Tenn., U.S. 101 E18
Harrington, Wash., U.S. 108 C8
Harrington Harbour, Que., Can. 83 M22
Harrington Sound, Bermuda, U.K. 120 B3
Harris, Montserrat, U.K. 121 B24
Harris, Lake, Austral. 210 J9
Harris, Sound of, Scot., U.K. 142 J6
Harrisburg, Ark., U.S. 100 F10
Harrisburg, Ill., U.S. 99 U6
Harrisburg, Nebr., U.S. 105 P1
Harrisburg, Oreg., U.S. 108 G3
Harrisburg, Pa., U.S. 94 P7
Harrison, Ark., U.S. 100 E7
Harrison, Idaho, U.S. 106 C3
Harrison, Mich., U.S. 98 K10
Harrison, Nebr., U.S. 104 M1
Harrison, Cape, Nfld. & Lab., Can. 83 K22
Harrison Bay, Alas., U.S. 111 B16
Harrisonburg, La., U.S. 100 M9
Harrisonburg, Va., U.S. 96 D11
Harrison Point, Barbados 121 J18
Harrisonville, Mo., U.S. 105 T11
Harris Park, Scot., U.K. 142 J6
Harris Seamount, Pac. Oc. 238 D12
Harrisville, Mich., U.S. 98 J12
Harrodsburg, Ky., U.S. 101 C17
Harrogate, Eng., U.K. 143 R12
Harry S Truman Reservoir, Mo., U.S. 105 T11
Harşit, river, Turk. 169 D13
Harstad, Nor. 140 D12
Hart, Mich., U.S. 98 K9
Hart, Tex., U.S. 102 H5
Hartford, Ala., U.S. 101 N17
Hartford, Ark., U.S. 100 G6
Hartford, Conn., U.S. 95 L13
Hartford, Mich., U.S. 99 N9
Hartford, S. Dak., U.S. 104 L8
Hartford, Vt., U.S. 95 H13
Hartford, Wis., U.S. 98 L6
Hartford City, Ind., U.S. 99 Q10
Hartington, Nebr., U.S. 105 N8
Hart Lake, Oreg., U.S. 108 K6
Hartland Point, Eng., U.K. 143 W9
Hartley, Iowa, U.S. 104 M9
Hartley, Tex., U.S. 102 F4
Hart Mountain, Oreg., U.S. 108 K6
Hartselle, Ala., U.S. 101 H15
Hartshorne, Okla., U.S. 102 H13
Hartsville, S.C., U.S. 96 K10
Hartsville, Tenn., U.S. 101 E16
Hartwell, Ga., U.S. 96 K6
Hartwell Lake, Rep. of Georgia, S.C., U.S. 96 K7
Har Us Nuur, Mongolia 180 D9
Harut, river, Afghan. 177 P1
Harūz-e Bālā, Iran 173 F15
Harvard, Ill., U.S. 98 M6
Harvard, Nebr., U.S. 105 Q7
Harvest Home, Qnsld., Austral. 211 S13
Harvey, N. Dak., U.S. 104 F5
Harz, range, Ger. 148 E8
Ḩaşānah, Yemen 172 Q12
Hasan Dağı, Turk. 168 G9
Ḩasan Langī, Iran 173 H15
Hasa Plain, Saudi Arabia 166 H4
Hashaat, Mongolia 180 E12
Ḩāsik, Oman 173 N15
Hasil, island, Indonesia 189 J16
Hasilpur, Pak. 177 R10
Haskeir Island, Scot., U.K. 142 J6
Haskell, Okla., U.S. 102 F13
Haskell, Tex., U.S. 102 K8
Hassel Sound, Nunavut, Can. 83 C14
Hassi Messaoud, Alg. 196 C11
Hassi R'mel, Alg. 196 B11
Hässleholm, Sw. 141 N13
Hastings, Barbados 121 L19
Hastings, battlefield, Eng., U.K. 143 W15
Hastings, Eng., U.K. 143 W15
Hastings, Mich., U.S. 98 M10
Hastings, Minn., U.S. 104 K12
Hastings, N.Z. 213 L20
Hastings, Nebr., U.S. 105 Q6
Hasvik, Nor. 141 C13
Haswell, Colo., U.S. 107 N15
Hat see Teuaua, island, Fr. Polynesia, Fr. 219 N23
Hataedo, islands, S. Korea 182 H12
Hatay (Antioch), Turk. 168 J11
Hatch, N. Mex., U.S. 107 V11
Hatches Creek, N. Terr., Austral. 211 S9
Hatchie, river, Tenn., U.S. 100 F12
Haţeg, Rom. 152 E12
Hatgal, Mongolia 180 C11
Hatherleigh, Eng., U.K. 143 W9
Ḩāţibah, Ra's, Saudi Arabia 172 L6
Ha Tien, Vietnam 187 P11
Hatillo, P.R., U.S. 120 M2
Ha Tinh, Vietnam 186 J12
Hato Caves, Neth. Antilles, Neth. 121 P14
Hato Mayor, Dom. Rep. 117 M20
Ha Trung, Vietnam 186 H12
Hatteras, N.C., U.S. 96 H15
Hatteras, Cape, N.C., U.S. 96 H15
Hatteras Plain, Atl. Oc. 236 J4
Hattiesburg, Miss., U.S. 100 N12
Ḩaţţīyah, Jordan 171 R6
Hatton, N. Dak., U.S. 104 F7
Hatunuru, Indonesia 189 K16
Hatutu, island, Fr. Polynesia, Fr. 215 H14
Hatvan, Hung. 149 L15
Hat Yai, Thai. 187 S9
Haud, plateau, Eth. 199 G17
Haugesund, Nor. 140 L9
Haugsdorf, Aust. 148 J12
Haukeligrend, Nor. 140 L10
Haukipudas, Fin. 141 F15
Haukivesi, Fin. 141 H17
Haunanu, Pointe, Fr. Polynesia, Fr. 219 M23
Hauola Place of Refuge, Hawai'i, U.S. 112 B6
Haupt Kanal, Liech. 160 N2
Hauraki Gulf, N.Z. 213 J19
Hauser, Oreg., U.S. 108 J2
Haut, Isle au, Me., U.S. 95 G18
Hauteurs de Gâtine, Fr. 147 S6
Hauti, Fr. Polynesia, Fr. 219 K23
Hau'ula, Hawai'i, U.S. 112 D11
Havana see La Habana, Cuba 116 G6
Havana, Fla., U.S. 97 Q5
Havana, Ill., U.S. 99 Q4
Havannah, Canal de la, New Caledonia, Fr. 218 E9
Havant, Eng., U.K. 143 W13
Havasu, Lake, Ariz., Calif., U.S. 109 W13
Havel, river, Ger. 148 C10
Havelberg, Ger. 148 D9
Haveli, Pak. 177 R11
Havelock, N.C., U.S. 96 J14
Haveluloto, Tonga 218 H11
Haven, Kans., U.S. 105 U7
Haverfordwest, Wales, U.K. 143 V8
Haverhill, Eng., U.K. 143 U14
Haverhill, Mass., U.S. 95 J15
Haveri, India 179 N4
Haviland, Kans., U.S. 105 U6
Havířov, Czech Rep. 149 H14
Havlíčkův Brod, Czech Rep. 148 H12
Havre, Mont., U.S. 106 B9
Havre de Grace, Md., U.S. 96 B14
Havre-St.-Pierre, Que., Can. 83 M21
Havza, Turk. 168 D11
Hawai'i, island, Hawai'i, U.S. 113 L18
Hawai'i, U.S. 113 L17
Hawaiian Ridge, Pac. Oc. 238 G11
Hawai'i Belt Road, Hawai'i, U.S. 113 N20
Hawai'i Volcanoes National Park, Hawai'i, U.S. 113 N20
Hawarden, Iowa, U.S. 104 M8
Hawarden, Wales, U.K. 143 S10
Hawea, Lake, N.Z. 213 Q16
Ḩawf, Yemen 173 P14
Hāwī, Hawai'i, U.S. 113 K19
Hawick, Scot., U.K. 143 N11
Hawke Bay, N.Z. 213 L20
Hawker, S. Aust., Austral. 211 W10
Hawkeye Point, Iowa, U.S. 104 M9
Hawkinsville, Ga., U.S. 97 N6
Hawley, Minn., U.S. 104 G8
Hawthorne, Nev., U.S. 109 R8
Haxtun, Colo., U.S. 106 K15
Hay, river, Alta., Can. 82 J10
Hay, river, N. Terr., Austral. 211 U10
Hay, N.S.W., Austral. 211 Y12
Hayange, Fr. 147 N14
Hayes, Jam. 120 J9
Hayes, river, Man., Can. 83 L15
Hayes, S. Dak., U.S. 104 K4
Hayes, Mount, Alas., U.S. 111 G17
Hayes Center, Nebr., U.S. 105 Q4
Hayes Peninsula, N. Amer. 80 B7
Hayfork, Calif., U.S. 109 N3
Hayling Island, Eng., U.K. 143 W13
Haymā', Oman 173 M15
Haymana, Turk. 168 E8
Haynesville, La., U.S. 100 K7
Hayneville, Ala., U.S. 101 L15
Haynin, Yemen 172 P11
Hayrabolu, Turk. 168 C3
Ḩayr al Gharbī, Qaşr al, Syr. 170 H9
Ḩayr ash Sharqī, Qaşr al, Syr. 170 G11
Hay River, N.W.T., Can. 82 H11
Hays, Kans., U.S. 105 S5
Hays, Mont., U.S. 106 B10
Hay Springs, Nebr., U.S. 104 M2
Haysville, Kans., U.S. 105 U7
Haysyn, Ukr. 157 P5
Hayti, Mo., U.S. 105 W16
Hayvoron, Ukr. 157 Q5
Hayward, Calif., U.S. 109 S4
Hayward, Wis., U.S. 98 G3
Hazarajat, region, Afghan. 177 N6
Hazārān, Kūh-e, Iran 173 F15
Hazard, Ky., U.S. 101 C19
Hazar Gölü, Turk. 169 G14
Hazar Qadam, Afghan. 177 P6
Ḩaẕawẕā', Sabkhat, Saudi Arabia 172 F6
Hazebrouck, Fr. 146 L10
Hazelton, B.C., Can. 82 J8
Hazelton, N. Dak., U.S. 104 H5
Hazen, Ark., U.S. 100 G9
Hazen, N. Dak., U.S. 104 F4
Hazen, Nev., U.S. 109 P7
Ḩazeva, Israel 171 P5
Hazlehurst, Ga., U.S. 97 N7
Hazlehurst, Miss., U.S. 100 M11
Hazleton, Pa., U.S. 94 N8
Hazro, Turk. 169 G15
Healdsburg, Calif., U.S. 109 Q3
Healdton, Okla., U.S. 102 J11
Healy, Alas., U.S. 111 G17
Healy, Kans., U.S. 105 T4
Héani, Mont, Fr. Polynesia, Fr. 219 M20
Heard Island, Antarctic Oc. 245 G16
Hearne, Tex., U.S. 103 P12
Hearst, Ont., Can. 83 N17
Hearst Island, Antarctica 226 E5
Heart, river, N. Dak., U.S. 104 G4
Herat (Hirat), Afghan. 176 M2
Heath, Pointe, Que., Can. 83 M22
Heavener, Okla., U.S. 102 H14
Hebbronville, Tex., U.S. 103 U9
Heber, Ariz., U.S. 107 T8
Heber City, Utah, U.S. 106 L7
Heber Springs, Ark., U.S. 100 F9
Hebgen Lake, Mont., U.S. 106 F8
Hebi, China 182 G5
Hebrides, Sea of the, Scot., U.K. 142 L6
Hebron, N. Dak., U.S. 104 G3
Hebron, Nebr., U.S. 105 R7
Hebron see Al Khalīl, W. Bank 171 N5
Hecate Strait, B.C., Can. 82 K7
Hechi, China 181 N13
Hecho, Sp. 145 C14
Hechuan, China 180 L12
Hecla, S. Dak., U.S. 104 H7
Hecla, Cape, Nunavut, Can. 83 A16
Hectors River, Jam. 120 J11
Heddal, Nor. 140 L11
Hédé, Fr. 147 Q5
Hede see Sheyang, China 182 H9
Hede, Sw. 140 J12
He Devil Mountain, Idaho, U.S. 106 E3
Hedley, Tex., U.S. 102 H6
Hedo Misaki, Japan 185 Y2
Heel Point, Wake I., U.S. 216 F8
Heerenveen, Neth. 146 H13
Ḩefa (Haifa), Israel 170 K5
Hefei, China 182 K7
Hefeng, China 182 L2
Heflin, Ala., U.S. 101 J17
Hegang, China 181 C18
Hegura Jima, Japan 184 M10
Heicheng (Khara Khoto), ruin, China 180 F11
Heide, Ger. 148 B7
Heidelberg, Ger. 148 H6
Heidelberg, Miss., U.S. 100 M12
Heidenheim, Ger. 148 J7
Heiderscheid, Lux. 160 H9
Heihe, China 181 B17
Heilbronn, Ger. 148 J7
Heilong Jiang (Amur), river, China 181 A16
Heimaey, island, Ice. 140 G2
Heinerscheid, Lux. 160 G10
Heinola, Fin. 141 J16
Heishan, China 182 B10
Hejaz see Al Ḩijāz, region, Saudi Arabia 172 H6
Hejian, China 182 E6
Hejing, China 180 F7
Hekimhan, Turk. 168 F12

Hekla, peak, Ice. 140 F2
Hekou, China 180 P11
Helagsfjället, peak, Sw. 140 H12
Hele Islands, Solomon Is. 217 M16
Helena, Ark., U.S. 100 H10
Helena, Ga., U.S. 97 N7
Helena see Makronissi, island, Gr. 155 K13
Helena, Mont., U.S. 106 D7
Helena, Okla., U.S. 102 E9
Helengili, island, Maldives 179 U3
Helen Island, Palau 214 G2
Helen Springs, N. Terr., Austral. 211 R8
Helgoländer Bucht, Ger. 148 B6
Helicon see Elikónas, peak, Gr. 154 H11
Hell, Cayman Is., U.K. 120 H1
Hell, Nor. 140 H11
Hell-Bourg, Reunion, Fr. 205 G16
Hellespont see Çanakkale Boğazı, strait, Gr. 155 E16
Hellevoetsluis, Neth. 146 J11
Hellín, Sp. 145 J13
Hellissandur, Ice. 140 E1
Hells Canyon, Idaho, Oreg., U.S. 108 F9
Hells Canyon Dam, Idaho, Oreg., U.S. 108 F10
Hells Canyon National Recreation Area, Idaho, Oreg., U.S. 108 E9
Hell-Ville see Andoany, Madagascar 203 D18
Helmand, river, Afghan. 177 P5
Helmand, river, Afghan. 177 R2
Helmsdale, Scot., U.K. 142 H10
Helong, China 182 B14
Helper, Utah, U.S. 106 M8
Helsingborg, Sw. 140 N12
Helsingfors see Helsinki, Fin. 141 J16
Helsinki (Helsingfors), Fin. 141 J16
Hemet, Calif., U.S. 109 X10
Hemingford, Nebr., U.S. 105 N2
Hempstead, N.Y., U.S. 94 N11
Hempstead, Tex., U.S. 103 Q13
Henashi Zaki, Japan 184 J12
Henbury, N. Terr., Austral. 211 U8
Hendaye, Fr. 147 X5
Hendek, Turk. 168 D6
Henderson, Ky., U.S. 101 C14
Henderson, N.C., U.S. 96 G12
Henderson, Nev., U.S. 109 U12
Henderson, Tenn., U.S. 101 F13
Henderson, Tex., U.S. 102 M14
Henderson Island, Pac. Oc. 215 L16
Henderson Seamount, Pac. Oc. 239 G16
Hendersonville, N.C., U.S. 96 J7
Hendersonville, Tenn., U.S. 101 E15
Hengch'un, Taiwan, China 183 S9
Hengduan Shan, China 180 M10
Hengelo, Neth. 146 J14
Hengshan, China 182 E2
Hengshan, China 183 N4
Hengshui, China 182 E6
Hengxian, China 183 R1
Hengyang, China 183 N4
Heniches'k, Ukr. 157 S8
Henlopen, Cape, Del., U.S. 96 C15
Hennebont, Fr. 147 R4
Hennessey, Okla., U.S. 102 F10
Hennigsdorf, Ger. 148 D10
Henning, Minn., U.S. 104 H9
Henrietta, Tex., U.S. 102 J10
Henrietta, Ostrov, Russ. 159 C17
Henrietta Maria, Cape, Ont., Can. 83 L17
Henry, Cape, Va., U.S. 96 F14
Henryetta, Okla., U.S. 102 G12
Henry Kater Peninsula, Nunavut, Can. 83 F18
Henrys Fork, Idaho, U.S. 106 G7
Henslow, Cape, Solomon Is. 217 P19
Hentiyn Nuruu, range, Mongolia 181 C13
Heping, China 183 Q5
Heppner, Oreg., U.S. 108 F7
Hepu, China 183 S1
Hequ, China 182 D4
Herald, Ostrov, Russ. 159 A19
Herald Cays, Coral Sea Is. Terr., Austral. 211 R14
Herbault, Fr. 147 R8
Herbert, river, Austral. 210 D13
Herbert, Sask., Can. 82 N11
Hercules Dome, Antarctica 226 J11
Herdman Seamount, Atl. Oc. 237 U13
Hereford, Eng., U.K. 143 U11
Hereford, Tex., U.S. 102 H4
Hereheretue, island, Fr. Polynesia, Fr. 219 G18
Herford, Ger. 148 E7
Herington, Kans., U.S. 105 T8
Herisau, Switz. 150 A4
Hérisson, Fr. 147 T10
Heritage Range, Antarctica 226 H8
Herkimer, N.Y., U.S. 94 J10
Herlacher, Cape, Antarctica 226 L6
Herlen, river, Mongolia 181 D14
Herm, island, Ch. Is. 143 Z11
Herman, Minn., U.S. 104 J9
Hermann, Mo., U.S. 105 T14
Hermannsburg, N. Terr., Austral. 211 T8
Hermansville, Mich., U.S. 98 G7
Hermanus, S. Af. 202 M7
Hermel, Leb. 170 H7
Hermidale, N.S.W., Austral. 211 X13
Hermiston, Oreg., U.S. 108 E7
Hermit Islands, P.N.G. 213 B19
Hermleigh, Tex., U.S. 102 L6
Hermon, Mount, Leb., Syr. 170 J6
Hermosa, S. Dak., U.S. 104 L2
Hermosa, Punta, Eq. Guinea 204 L8
Hermosillo, Mex. 114 C7
Hernando, Arg. 132 K10
Hernando, Miss., U.S. 100 G11
Hernani, Sp. 145 B13
Herne, Ger. 148 E5
Herreid, S. Dak., U.S. 104 H5
Herrera, Arg. 132 H10
Herrera del Duque, Sp. 144 H9
Herrera de Pisuerga, Sp. 144 C10
Herrin, Ill., U.S. 99 U5
Herschel Island, Yukon, Can. 82 D9
Hershey, Nebr., U.S. 105 P4
Hersónissos Akrotírio, Gr. 155 P13
Hertford, Eng., U.K. 143 V14
Hertford, N.C., U.S. 96 G14
Hervás, Sp. 144 F8
Hervey Bay, Austral. 210 G15
Hervey Bay, Qnsld., Austral. 211 U15
Hervey Islands, Cook Is., N.Z. 214 K12
Herzberg, Ger. 148 E10
Hesar Range, Afghan. 176 M5
Heshui, China 182 F1
Hesperange, Lux. 160 K10
Hess Rise, Pac. Oc. 238 E9
Hettinger, N. Dak., U.S. 104 H2
Heuru, Solomon Is. 217 P20
Hexian, China 182 K8
Hexian, China 183 Q3
Hexigten Qi (Jingpeng), China 182 A7
Heyuan, China 183 R5
Heze, China 182 G6
Hialeah, Fla., U.S. 97 X10
Hiawatha, Kans., U.S. 105 R9
Hibbing, Minn., U.S. 104 F11
Hicacos, Peninsula de, Cuba 116 G7
Hickam Air Force Base, Hawai'i, U.S. 112 E11
Hickman, Ky., U.S. 100 E12
Hickmann, Arg. 132 E10
Hickory, N.C., U.S. 96 H8
Hicks Bay, N.Z. 213 K20
Hicksville, Ohio, U.S. 99 P11
Hico, Tex., U.S. 102 M10
Hidaka Sammyaku, range, Japan 184 G14
Hidalgo del Parral, Mex. 114 E9
Hienghène, New Caledonia, Fr. 218 C7
Hienghéne, Baie de, New Caledonia, Fr. 218 C7
Hierro (Ferro), island, Canary Is. 204 R3
Higgins, Tex., U.S. 102 F7
Higgins Lake, Mich., U.S. 98 J10
Higginsville, Mo., U.S. 105 S11
High Atlas, range, Mor. 194 D3
High Cay, Bahamas 120 F11
High Cliff Point, Grenada 121 J23
Highgate, Jam. 120 H10
High Island, Tex., U.S. 103 R15
Highland, Ill., U.S. 99 T5
Highland Park, Ill., U.S. 99 N7
Highlands, plateau, Scot., U.K. 142 K8
High Level, Alta., Can. 82 J10
Highmore, S. Dak., U.S. 104 K5
High Plains, U.S. 84 J10
High Point, Bermuda, U.K. 120 C1
High Point, N.C., U.S. 96 H10
High Point, N.J., U.S. 94 M10
High Red Rock, Norfolk I., Austral. 217 G20
High Rock, Bahamas 116 C10
High Rock, Bahamas 120 E3
High Springs, Fla., U.S. 97 R7
High Willhays, peak, Eng., U.K. 143 X9
Higüero, Punta, P.R., U.S. 117 M22
Higüey, Dom. Rep. 117 M20
Hiiumaa (Dagö), island, Est. 141 L15
Híjar, Sp. 145 E14
Ḩijārah, Şaḩrā' al, Iraq 172 F9
Ḩijāz, Jabal al, Saudi Arabia 172 M8
Hikari, Japan 185 R5
Hikiau Heiau, Hawai'i, U.S. 113 N18
Hiko, Nev., U.S. 109 S12
Hikueru, island, Fr. Polynesia, Fr. 219 F19
Hikurangi, peak, N.Z. 213 K20
Hikutavake, Niue, N.Z. 219 B20
Hilāl, Ras al, Lib. 194 D7
Hildesheim, Ger. 148 E7
Hilina Pali, Hawai'i, U.S. 113 N20
Hillaby, Mount, Barbados 121 K19
Hillary Coast, Antarctica 227 N14
Hill City, Kans., U.S. 105 S5
Hill City, Minn., U.S. 104 G11
Hill City, S. Dak., U.S. 104 L1
Hill Country, Tex., U.S. 103 R7
Hillman, Mich., U.S. 98 H11
Hillsboro, Ill., U.S. 99 S5
Hillsboro, Kans., U.S. 105 T8
Hillsboro, N. Dak., U.S. 104 F8
Hillsboro, N. Mex., U.S. 107 U11
Hillsboro, Ohio, U.S. 99 S12
Hillsboro, Oreg., U.S. 108 F3
Hillsboro, Tex., U.S. 102 M11
Hillsborough, Grenada 119 M17
Hillsborough, N. Ire., U.K. 143 Q7
Hillsborough Bay, Trinidad & Tobago 121 N18
Hillsdale, Mich., U.S. 99 N11
Hillside, W. Aust., Austral. 211 T3
Hillston, N.S.W., Austral. 211 X12
Hillsville, Va., U.S. 96 G9
Hillswick, Scot., U.K. 142 D11
Hilo, region, Hawai'i, U.S. 113 L21
Hilo, Hawai'i, U.S. 113 M21
Hilo Bay, Hawai'i, U.S. 113 L21
Hilton Head Island, S.C., U.S. 97 N9
Hilvan, Turk. 169 H13
Himadítida, Límni, Gr. 154 C9
Himalaya, range, Asia 166 H8
Ḩimar, Wādī al, Syr. 170 D12
Himatnagar, India 178 H3
Himeji, Japan 185 Q8
Ḩimş (Homs), Syr. 170 G8
Hinako, Kepulauan, Indonesia 188 J4
Hinche, Haiti 117 L17
Hinchinbrook Island, Alas., U.S. 111 K18
Hinchinbrook Island, Austral. 210 D13
Hinckley, Minn., U.S. 104 H12
Hindaun, India 178 G6
Hindmarsh, Lake, Austral. 210 L11
Hindu Kush, range, Afghan., Pak. 176 L8
Hines, Oreg., U.S. 108 J7
Hines Creek, Alta., Can. 82 K10
Hinesville, Ga., U.S. 97 N8
Hinganghat, India 178 K6
Hingol, river, Pak. 177 V4
Hingorja, Pak. 177 U7
Hinidan, Pak. 177 V6
Hınıs, Turk. 169 F16
Hinnøya, island, Nor. 140 D12
Hinoemata, Japan 185 N12
Hinomi Saki, Japan 185 P6
Hinthada, Myanmar 186 K5
Hinton, Okla., U.S. 102 G9
Hinton, W. Va., U.S. 96 E9
Híos (Chios), island, Gr. 155 H16
Híos (Chios), Gr. 155 H16
Hippolytushoef, Neth. 146 H12
Hirado, Japan 185 R3
Hirado Shima, Japan 185 R3
Hiranai, Japan 184 J13
Hira Se, island, Japan 185 U4
Hirat see Heart, Afghan. 176 M2
Hirata, Japan 185 P6
Hirfanlı Barajı, Turk. 168 F9
Hiroo, Japan 184 G15
Hirosaki, Japan 184 J12
Hiroshima, Japan 185 Q6
Hirson, Fr. 146 M12
Hîrşova, Rom. 153 F17
Hisarönü, Turk. 168 C7
Ḩismá, desert, Jordan, Saudi Arabia 171 S6
Ḩismá, region, Saudi Arabia 172 G5
Hispaniola, island, N. Amer. 80 N10
Ḩisyah, Syr. 170 H8
Hita, Japan 185 R5
Hitachi, Japan 185 N13
Hitadu, island, Maldives 179 W3
Hitadu, island, Maldives 179 X3
Hiti, island, Fr. Polynesia, Fr. 219 E18
Hitiaa, Fr. Polynesia, Fr. 219 N17
Hitoyoshi, Japan 185 S4
Hitra, island, Nor. 140 H10
Hiu, island, Vanuatu 218 A1
Hiva Oa, island, Fr. Polynesia, Fr. 215 H15
Hiwasa, Japan 185 R8
Hiwassee, river, Tenn., U.S. 101 G18
Hizan, Turk. 169 G17
Hjälmaren, lake, Sw. 141 L13
Hjørring, Den. 140 M11
Hkakabo Razi, peak, Myanmar 186 C7
Hlohovec, Slovakia 149 K14
Hlukhiv, Ukr. 156 M7
Hlybokaye, Belarus 156 J5
Hněvkovice, Czech Rep. 148 H11
Hnúšt'a, Slovakia 149 J15
Ho, Ghana 200 H11
Hoa Binh, Vietnam 186 H11
Hoai An, Vietnam 186 M14
Hoanib, river, Namibia 202 G5
Hoare Bay, Nunavut, Can. 83 G19
Hobart, Ind., U.S. 99 P8
Hobart, Okla., U.S. 102 H8
Hobart, Tas., Austral. 211 Z16
Hobbs, N. Mex., U.S. 107 U15
Hobbs, Mount, Austral. 210 M16
Hobbs Coast, Antarctica 226 M8
Hobe Sound, Fla., U.S. 97 V10
Hoboksar, China 180 D7
Hobot Xar see Xianghuang Qi, China 182 B5
Hobro, Den. 140 N11
Hobucken, N.C., U.S. 96 H14
Hobyo, Somalia 199 H18
Ho Chi Minh City (Saigon), Vietnam 187 P12
Hodge, La., U.S. 100 L8
Hodgenville, Ky., U.S. 101 C16
Hodgson, river, Austral. 210 C9
Hodh, region, Mauritania 194 G2
Hódmezővásárhely, Hung. 149 M16
Hodonín, Czech Rep. 149 J13
Hödrögö, Mongolia 180 C10
Hoedic, Île, Fr. 147 R4
Hoedspruit, S. Af. 202 J11
Hoeryŏng, N. Korea 182 B14
Hof, Ger. 148 G9
Höfdakaupstadur, Ice. 140 E3
Hoffman, Minn., U.S. 104 H9
Höfn, Ice. 140 G4
Hofsjökull, glacier, Ice. 140 F3
Hogansville, Ga., U.S. 96 M4
Hog Cay, Bahamas 120 F10
Hogfish Cut, Bermuda, U.K. 120 C1
Hoggar see Ahaggar, range, Alg. 196 E11
Hog Island, Grenada 121 L22
Hog Island, Va., U.S. 96 E15
Hohenems, Aust. 148 L7
Hohenwald, Tenn., U.S. 101 F14
Hohe Tauern, Aust. 148 M9
Hohhot, China 182 C4
Hohonu, island, Fr. Polynesia, Fr. 219 K17
Hoh Xil Shan, China 180 J7
Hoi An, Vietnam 186 L13
Hoisington, Kans., U.S. 105 T6
Hokatu, Fr. Polynesia, Fr. 219 N23
Hokitika, N.Z. 213 N16
Hokkaidō, island, Japan 184 G15
Hōkūkano Heiau, Hawai'i, U.S. 113 F15
Hokula, Tonga 218 P6
Hola Prystan', Ukr. 157 R7
Holbrook, Ariz., U.S. 107 S8
Holbrook, Idaho, U.S. 106 J6
Holden, Mo., U.S. 105 T11
Holden, Utah, U.S. 106 M7
Holdenville, Okla., U.S. 102 G12
Holdrege, Nebr., U.S. 105 Q5
Hole in the Wall, cape, Bahamas 120 C6
Hōlei Pali, Hawai'i, U.S. 113 N21
Holetown, Barbados 121 K18
Holguín, Cuba 116 J12
Holland, Mich., U.S. 98 M9
Hollandale, Miss., U.S. 100 K10
Holland Bay, Jam. 120 J11
Hollandsbird Island, Namibia 202 J6
Hollick-Kenyon Plateau, Antarctica 226 K8
Hollidaysburg, Pa., U.S. 94 N5
Hollis, Okla., U.S. 102 H7
Hollister, Calif., U.S. 109 T4
Hollum, Neth. 146 G13
Holly Hill, S.C., U.S. 96 L10
Holly Ridge, N.C., U.S. 96 J13
Holly Springs, Miss., U.S. 100 G12
Hollywood, Calif., U.S. 109 X8
Hollywood, Fla., U.S. 97 W10
Holman, N.W.T., Can. 82 E12
Hólmavík, Ice. 140 E2
Holme Bay, Antarctica 227 E20
Holmes Rock, Bahamas 120 E1
Holonga, Tonga 218 L12
Holopaw, Fla., U.S. 97 T9
Ḩolot Ḩaluza, desert, Israel 171 N4
Holstebro, Den. 140 N11
Holstein, Iowa, U.S. 105 N9
Holston, river, Tenn., U.S. 101 E20
Holsworthy, Eng., U.K. 143 W9
Holt, Ala., U.S. 101 K14
Holton, Kans., U.S. 105 S9
Holtville, Calif., U.S. 109 Z12
Hōlualoa, Hawai'i, U.S. 113 M18
Hōlua Slide, Hawai'i, U.S. 113 M18
Holy Cross, Alas., U.S. 111 H13
Holyhead (Caergybi), Wales, U.K. 143 S9
Holy Island, Wales, U.K. 143 S9
Holy Island (Lindisfarne), Eng., U.K. 143 N12
Holyoke, Colo., U.S. 106 L15
Holyoke, Mass., U.S. 95 K13
Hombetsu, Japan 184 F15
Hombori, Mali 196 H9
Homburg, Ger. 148 H5
Home Bay, Banaba, Kiribati 217 E20
Home Bay, Nunavut, Can. 83 F18
Homedale, Idaho, U.S. 106 G3
Homer, Alas., U.S. 111 K16
Homer, La., U.S. 100 K7
Homer, Mich., U.S. 99 N11
Homer, N.Y., U.S. 94 K8
Homerville, Ga., U.S. 97 Q7
Homestead, Fla., U.S. 97 X10
Homestead National Monument of America, Nebr., U.S. 105 R8
Homewood, Ala., U.S. 101 J15
Hominy, Okla., U.S. 102 E12
Hommalinn, Myanmar 186 E5
Homnabad, India 178 M5
Homo Bay, Vanuatu 218 D3
Homosassa Springs, Fla., U.S. 97 T7
Homs see Ḩimş, Syr. 170 G8
Homyel', Belarus 156 M6
Hōnaunau, Hawai'i, U.S. 113 N18
Honavar, India 179 P4
Honaz, Turk. 168 G5
Honda, Col. 128 E5
Hondo, Japan 185 S4
Hondo, N. Mex., U.S. 107 U13
Hondo, Tex., U.S. 103 R8
Honduras, N. Amer. 81 P20
Honduras, Golfo de, Belize, Guatemala 115 K17
Honduras, Gulf of see Honduras, Golfo de, N. Amer. 80 P7
Honea Path, S.C., U.S. 96 K7
Hønefoss, Nor. 140 K11
Honesdale, Pa., U.S. 94 L9
Honey Grove, Tex., U.S. 102 K13
Honey Lake, Calif., U.S. 109 N6
Honeyville, Utah, U.S. 106 K7
Hong (Red), river, Vietnam 186 G11
Hong'an, China 182 K5
Hong Gai, Vietnam 186 H13
Hong Hu, China 182 L4
Honghu, China 182 L4
Hongjiang, China 183 N2
Hong Kong, China 183 S5
Hongliuyuan, China 180 G9
Hongor, Mongolia 181 E14
Hongseong, S. Korea 182 F13
Hongshui, river, China 183 Q1
Hongtong, China 182 F4
Hongū, Japan 185 R9
Hongwŏn, N. Korea 182 C13
Hongze Hu, China 182 J8
Honiara, Solomon Is. 217 N18
Honiara, Solomon Is. 214 H6
Honikulu, Passe, Wallis & Futuna, Fr. 218 C11
Honiton, Eng., U.K. 143 W10
Honjō, Japan 184 K12
Honoka'a, Hawai'i, U.S. 113 K20
Honokahua, Hawai'i, U.S. 113 F16
Honokōwai, Hawai'i, U.S. 113 G15
Honolulu, Hawai'i, U.S. 112 E11
Honomanū Bay, Hawai'i, U.S. 113 G17

Honomū, Hawai'i, U.S. 113 L21
Hon Quan, Vietnam 187 P12
Honshū, island, Japan 185 P5
Honu'apo Bay, Hawai'i, U.S. 113 P20
Hood see Española, Isla, island, Ecua. 128 R10
Hood, Mount, Oreg., U.S. 108 F4
Hood River, Oreg., U.S. 108 E5
Hoodsport, Wash., U.S. 108 C3
Hoogeveen, Neth. 146 H14
Ho'okena, Hawai'i, U.S. 113 N18
Hooker, Okla., U.S. 102 E6
Hook Head, Ire. 143 U6
Ho'olehua, Hawai'i, U.S. 113 F14
Hoonah, Alas., U.S. 111 L22
Hooper, Cape, Nunavut, Can. 83 F18
Hooper Bay, Alas., U.S. 110 H11
Hoopeston, Ill., U.S. 99 Q7
Hoorn, Neth. 146 H12
Hoover, Ala., U.S. 101 J15
Hoover Dam, Ariz., Nev., U.S. 109 U12
Hopa, Turk. 169 C16
Hope, Ark., U.S. 100 J7
Hope, N. Dak., U.S. 104 G7
Hope, Cape, Nunavut, Can. 82 F12
Hope, Lake, Austral. 210 K4
Hope, Point, Alas., U.S. 84 M2
Hope Bay, Jam. 120 H10
Hopedale, Nfld. & Lab., Can. 83 K21
Hopelchén, Mex. 115 J16
Hope Mills, N.C., U.S. 96 J11
Hope Point, Myanmar 186 L7
Hopetoun, W. Aust., Austral. 211 Y4
Hope Town, Bahamas 120 B7
Hopetown, S. Af. 202 L9
Hopewell, Va., U.S. 96 F13
Hopewell Culture National Historic Park, Ohio, U.S. 99 S13
Hopewell Islands, Nunavut, Can. 83 K17
Hopkins, Mount, Ariz., U.S. 107 W8
Hopkinsville, Ky., U.S. 101 D14
Hoquiam, Wash., U.S. 108 D2
Horasan, Turk. 169 E16
Horgos, Serb. & Mont. 152 D9
Horicon, Wis., U.S. 98 L6
Horinger, China 182 C4
Horki, Belarus 156 K6
Horlick Mountains, Antarctica 226 J11
Horlivka, Ukr. 157 Q10
Ḩormak, Iran 173 F17
Hormigueros, P.R., U.S. 120 N1
Hormuz, Strait of, Iran, Oman 173 H15
Horn, Cape see Hornos, Cabo de, Chile 133 Y9
Hornavan, lake, Sw. 141 F13
Hornbeck, La., U.S. 100 M7
Hornbrook, Calif., U.S. 108 L3
Hornby Hill, Nunavut, Can. 82 F11
Horne, Îles de, Pac. Oc. 214 J9
Hornell, N.Y., U.S. 94 K6
Horn Island, Miss., U.S. 101 P13
Hornos, Cabo de (Cape Horn), Chile 133 Y9
Horodnya, Ukr. 156 M6
Horodyshche, Ukr. 157 P6
Horqin Zuoyi Houqi, China 182 A10
Horqueta, Parag. 130 M10
Horse Cave, Ky., U.S. 101 D16
Horse Creek, Wyo., U.S. 106 K13
Horsehead Lake, N. Dak., U.S. 104 G5
Horseheads, N.Y., U.S. 94 K7
Horse Mountain, N. Mex., U.S. 107 T10
Horseshoe Beach, Fla., U.S. 97 S6
Horseshoe Bend, Ark., U.S. 100 E9
Horseshoe Canyon, Utah, U.S. 107 N8
Horsham, Eng., U.K. 143 W14
Horsham, Vic., Austral. 211 Y11
Horta, Azores 144 P3
Horten, Nor. 140 L11
Horton, Kans., U.S. 105 R9
Horton, river, N.W.T., Can. 82 E11
Hoscheid, Lux. 160 H10
Hosdrug, India 179 Q4
Hoshab, Pak. 177 V3
Hoshangabad, India 178 J6
Hosingen, Lux. 160 H10
Hosmer, S. Dak., U.S. 104 J5
Hoste, Isla, Chile 133 Y9
Hosur, India 179 Q6
Hot, Thai. 186 K7
Hotan, river, China 180 F5
Hotan, China 180 G5
Hotchkiss, Colo., U.S. 107 N11
Hot Creek Range, Nev., U.S. 109 R10
Hotel de Paris, Monaco 161 D22
Hotel Hermitage, Monaco 161 D21
Hotel Métropole, Monaco 161 C22
Hotevilla, Ariz., U.S. 107 R8
Hot Springs, Ark., U.S. 100 H7
Hot Springs, Mont., U.S. 106 C5
Hot Springs, S. Dak., U.S. 104 L1
Hot Springs, Va., U.S. 96 E10
Hot Springs National Park, Ark., U.S. 100 H7
Hotspur Seamount, Atl. Oc. 237 Q8
Hot Sulphur Springs, Colo., U.S. 106 L12
Hottah Lake, N.W.T., Can. 82 G11
Hotte, Massif de la, Haiti 117 M15
Hottentot Bay, Namibia 202 J6
Houaïlou, New Caledonia, Fr. 218 D7
Houat, Île, Fr. 147 R4
Houayxay, Laos 186 H9
Houffalize, Belg. 146 M13
Houghton, Mich., U.S. 98 E6
Houlton, Me., U.S. 95 C18
Houma, China 182 G3
Houma, La., U.S. 100 Q10
Houma, Tonga 218 J11
Houma Toloa, cape, Tonga 218 J11
Hourtin, Fr. 147 V6
Houston, Minn., U.S. 104 L13
Houston, Miss., U.S. 100 J12
Houston, Mo., U.S. 105 U13
Houston, Tex., U.S. 103 Q14
Houtman Abrolhos, islands, Austral. 210 J1
Hovd (Dund-Us), Mongolia 180 D9
Hoven, S. Dak., U.S. 104 J5
Hovenweep National Monument, Utah, U.S. 107 P9
Hövsgöl, Mongolia 181 E13
Hövsgöl Nuur, Mongolia 180 C11
Howar, Wadi, Sudan 198 D11
Howard, Kans., U.S. 105 U9
Howard, S. Dak., U.S. 104 L7
Howard City, Mich., U.S. 98 L10
Howard Lake, N.W.T., Can. 82 H13
Howe, Idaho, U.S. 106 G6
Howe, Cape, Austral. 210 M14
Howe, Point, Norfolk I., Austral. 217 F20
Howland, Me., U.S. 95 E17
Howland Island, Pac. Oc. 214 G9
Ho Xa, Vietnam 186 K13
Hoxie, Ark., U.S. 100 E10
Hoxie, Kans., U.S. 105 S4
Hoy, island, Scot., U.K. 142 G10
Høyanger, Nor. 140 K10
Hoyerswerda, Ger. 148 F11
Hoyt Lakes, Minn., U.S. 104 F12
Hozat, Turk. 169 F14
Hpa-an, Myanmar 186 K7
Hradec Králové, Czech Rep. 148 G12
Hrazdan, river, Arm. 169 D18
Hrebenne, Pol. 149 G18
Hrissí, island, Gr. 155 R16
Hrissoúpoli, Gr. 155 C14
Hristianí, island, Gr. 155 N15
Hrodna, Belarus 156 K3
Hron, river, Slovakia 149 J15
Hrubieszów, Pol. 149 F18
Hsi-hseng, Myanmar 186 H7
Hsinchu, Taiwan, China 183 Q9
Hsinying, Taiwan, China 183 R9
Hsipaw, Myanmar 186 G7
Huachi, China 182 F1
Huacho, Peru 130 H3
Huade, China 182 B5
Huadian, China 182 A13
Hua Hin, Thai. 187 N8
Huahine, island, Fr. Polynesia, Fr. 219 E15
Huahine, island, Fr. Polynesia, Fr. 215 J13
Huahine, Fr. Polynesia, Fr. 219 K20
Huahine Iti, island, Fr. Polynesia, Fr. 219 H14
Huahine Nui, island, Fr. Polynesia, Fr. 219 G14
Huaibei, China 182 H7
Huaibin, China 182 J6
Huaiji, China 183 R3
Huailai, China 182 C6
Huainan, China 182 J7
Huaining, China 182 L7
Huairen, China 182 D5
Huai Yang, Thai. 187 P8
Huaiyin, China 182 J8
Huajuapan de León, Mex. 114 K12
Hualālai, peak, Hawai'i, U.S. 113 M18
Hualapai Peak, Ariz., U.S. 107 S5
Hualfín, Arg. 132 G8
Hualien, Taiwan, China 183 R10
Huallaga, river, Peru 130 F3
Huambo, Angola 202 D6
Huancané, Peru 130 J6
Huancavelica, Peru 130 H4
Huancayo, Peru 130 H4
Huang (Yellow), river, China 181 G13
Huangchuan, China 182 K6
Huanggang, China 182 L5
Huanggangliang, peak, China 182 A7
Huanghua, China 182 E7
Huangling, China 182 G2
Huangliu, China 183 U1
Huangnihe, China 182 A13
Huangquqiao, China 182 D1
Huangshan, China 182 M8
Huangshi, China 182 L5
Huangxian, China 182 E9
Huangyan, China 182 M10
Huanren, China 182 C12
Huanta, Peru 130 H4
Huantai, China 182 F8
Huánuco, Peru 130 G3
Huanxian, China 182 F1
Huara, Chile 132 C7
Huaral, Peru 130 H3
Huaraz, Peru 130 G3
Huarmey, Peru 130 G3
Huarong, China 182 L4
Huascarán, Nevado, S. Amer. 126 F2
Huasco, Chile 132 H6
Huatabampo, Mex. 114 E7
Huaura, Peru 130 H3
Huaxian, China 182 G5
Huayuan, China 182 M2
Huazhou, China 183 S2
Hubbard, Tex., U.S. 102 M12
Hubbard Lake, Mich., U.S. 98 J12
Hubbell Trading Post National Historic Site, Ariz., U.S. 107 R9
Hubli, India 179 N4
Hudiksvall, Sw. 141 J13
Hudson, Fla., U.S. 97 T7
Hudson, Mich., U.S. 99 N11
Hudson, river, N.Y., U.S. 94 L11
Hudson, N.Y., U.S. 94 K11
Hudson Bay, Can. 83 J16
Hudson Bay, Sask., Can. 83 M13
Hudson Canyon, Atl. Oc. 236 H4
Hudson Strait, Nunavut, Can. 83 H18
Hue, Vietnam 186 L13
Hu'ehu'e, Hawai'i, U.S. 113 L18
Huehuetenango, Guatemala 115 L15
Huelma, Sp. 144 K11
Huelva, Sp. 144 L7
Huerfano, river, Colo., U.S. 107 P13
Huesca, Sp. 145 D14
Huéscar, Sp. 144 K12
Huevos Monos, island, Trinidad & Tobago 121 P21
Huff, N. Dak., U.S. 104 G4
Hughenden, Qnsld., Austral. 211 S12
Hughes, Alas., U.S. 111 F15
Hughes, Ark., U.S. 100 G11
Hughes, S. Aust., Austral. 211 W7
Hughes Bay, Antarctica 226 D4
Hugli, river, India 178 J11
Hugo, Okla., U.S. 102 J13
Hugon, Île, New Caledonia, Fr. 218 D8
Hugoton, Kans., U.S. 105 V3
Hui'an, China 183 Q8
Huichang, China 183 Q6
Hŭich'ŏn, N. Korea 182 C12
Huilai, China 183 R6
Huíla Plateau, Angola 194 M6
Huimin, China 182 F7
Huinan, China 182 B12
Huinca Renancó, Arg. 132 L10
Huitong, China 183 N2
Huîtres, Baie aux, Mauritius 205 J20
Huize, China 180 N11
Huizhou, China 183 R5
Hukawng Valley, Myanmar 186 D6
Hulan, China 181 D17
Ḩulayfā', Saudi Arabia 172 H7
Hulbert, Mich., U.S. 98 F10
Hulett, Wyo., U.S. 106 F13
Hull, Ill., U.S. 99 R3
Hull Bay, Virgin Islands, U.S. 120 M9
Hulst, Neth. 146 K11
Hulu, river, China 182 F2
Hulun Nur, China 181 C15
Hulyaypole, Ukr. 157 Q9
Huma, river, China 181 A16
Huma, China 181 A16
Humacao, P.R., U.S. 120 N5
Humahuaca, Arg. 132 E9
Humaitá, Braz. 130 F8
Humansdorp, S. Af. 202 M9
Humansville, Mo., U.S. 105 U11
Ḩumar, U.A.E. 173 K14
Humbe, Angola 202 F6
Humber, river, Eng., U.K. 143 R13
Humberstone, Chile 132 C7
Humble, Tex., U.S. 103 Q14
Humboldt, Iowa, U.S. 104 M11
Humboldt, Kans., U.S. 105 U10
Humboldt, Nebr., U.S. 105 R9
Humboldt, river, Nev., U.S. 108 M9
Humboldt, Sask., Can. 82 M12
Humboldt, Tenn., U.S. 100 F12
Humboldt Bay, Calif., U.S. 108 M1
Humboldt Plain, Pac. Oc. 239 R19
Hūmedān, Iran 173 J17
Humenné, Slovakia 149 J17
Humphreys Peak, Ariz., U.S. 107 S7
Humphrys Bay, Antigua & Barbuda 121 A20
Humpty Doo, N. Terr., Austral. 211 P7
Humu'ula Saddle, Hawai'i, U.S. 113 M20
Hūn, Lib. 197 D14
Húnaflói, bay, Ice. 140 E2
Hunchun, China 182 A15
Hunedoara, Rom. 152 D12
Hunga, island, Tonga 218 L11
Hunga Ha'apai, island, Tonga 218 R5
Hunga Tonga, island, Tonga 218 R5
Hungary, Eur. 139 V8
Hungerford, N.S.W., Austral. 211 V12
Hŭngnam, N. Korea 182 D13
Hungry Bay, Bermuda, U.K. 120 B2
Hungry Horse Reservoir, Mont., U.S. 106 B6
Hungund, India 179 N5
Hunjiang, China 182 B12
Huns Mountains, Namibia 194 Q6
Hunstanton, Eng., U.K. 143 S14
Hunsrück, range, Ger. 160 K12
Hunsur, India 179 Q5
Hunt, Mongolia 180 D10
Hunter, N. Dak., U.S. 104 G8
Hunter, island, Vanuatu 214 K8
Hunter, Cape, Solomon Is. 217 P18
Hunter Islands, Tas., Austral. 211 Y15
Hunters, Bahamas 120 F2
Huntingburg, Ind., U.S. 99 T8
Huntingdon, Pa., U.S. 94 N6
Huntingdon, Tenn., U.S. 101 E13
Huntington, Ind., U.S. 99 Q10
Huntington, Oreg., U.S. 108 G9
Huntington, Tex., U.S. 103 N15
Huntington, Utah, U.S. 106 M8
Huntington, W. Va., U.S. 96 D7
Huntington Beach, Calif., U.S. 109 X8
Huntly, N.Z. 213 K19
Huntly, Scot., U.K. 142 J10
Huntsville, Ala., U.S. 101 G15
Huntsville, Ark., U.S. 100 E7
Huntsville, Mo., U.S. 105 S12
Huntsville, Tex., U.S. 103 P13
Hunucmá, Mex. 115 H16
Hunyuan, China 182 D5
Hunza, region, Pak. 176 K12
Huocheng, China 180 E6
Huolu, China 182 E5
Huon, Île, New Caledonia, Fr. 214 K7
Huong Hoa, Vietnam 186 K12
Huon Gulf, P.N.G. 213 D19
Huon Peninsula, P.N.G. 213 D19
Huoqiu, China 182 J6
Huoshan, China 182 K6
Huoxian, China 182 F4
Hupo, S. Korea 182 F14
Hurdiyo, Somalia 199 F18
Hure Qi, China 182 B10
Hurghada, Egypt 197 D19
Hurley, Wis., U.S. 98 F4
Hurmagai, Pak. 177 T4
Huron, S. Dak., U.S. 104 K7
Huron, Lake, Can., U.S. 85 D17
Huron Mountain, Mich., U.S. 98 E7
Hurtsboro, Ala., U.S. 101 L17
Húsavík, Ice. 140 E3
Huşi, Rom. 153 C17
Huslia, Alas., U.S. 111 F14
Husum, Ger. 148 B7
Hutag, Mongolia 180 C11
Hutchinson, Kans., U.S. 105 U7
Hutchinson, Minn., U.S. 104 K10
Hutch Mountain, Ariz., U.S. 107 S7
Huthi, Myanmar 186 L8
Hutland, Cayman Is., U.K. 120 H3
Huttig, Ark., U.S. 100 K8
Hutuo Ziya, river, China 182 E6
Huvadu see Suvadiva Atoll, island, Maldives 179 W3
Huxian, China 182 H2
Huy, Belg. 146 L13
Hüyük, Turk. 168 G7
Huzhou, China 182 L9
Hvammstangi, Ice. 140 E2
Hvannadalshnúkur, peak, Ice. 138 A3
Hvar (Pharus), island, Croatia 152 H6
Hvarski Kanal, Croatia 152 H6
Hveragerði, Ice. 140 F2
Hvítá, river, Ice. 140 F2
Hwange, Zimb. 202 F10
Hyannis, Mass., U.S. 95 L16
Hyannis, Nebr., U.S. 105 N3
Hyargas Nuur, Mongolia 180 C9
Hyden, W. Aust., Austral. 211 X3
Hyde Park, N.Y., U.S. 94 L11
Hyderabad, India 178 M6
Hyderabad, Pak. 177 V7
Hydra see Ídra, island, Gr. 154 L12
Hydro, Okla., U.S. 102 G9
Hyères, Fr. 147 Y14
Hyères, Îles de (Les Îles d'Or), Fr. 147 Y14
Hyesan, N. Korea 182 B13
Hyndman Peak, Idaho, U.S. 106 G5
Hyrra Banda, Cen. Af. Rep. 198 H10
Hyrynsalmi, Fin. 141 F16
Hysham, Mont., U.S. 106 D11
Hyūga, Japan 185 S5

I

Ía, Gr. 155 M15
Iaco, river, Braz. 130 G6
Iaeger, W. Va., U.S. 96 F8
Ialomiţa, river, Rom. 153 F16
Iamara, P.N.G. 213 E18
Iar Connaught, region, Ire. 143 S3
Iaşi, Rom. 153 B17
Íasmos, Gr. 155 B15
Iauaretê, Braz. 130 C6
Ibadan, Nigeria 200 G12
Ibagué, Col. 128 F5
Ibapah, Utah, U.S. 106 L5
Ibarra, Ecua. 128 H3
Ibb, Yemen 172 Q9
Iberá, Laguna, Arg. 132 H13
Iberia, Peru 130 G6
Iberian Mountains, Sp. 138 J3
Iberian Peninsula, Eur. 138 H2
Ibiapaba, Serra da, S. Amer. 126 E10
Ibipetuba, Braz. 131 G14
Ibiza see Eivissa, Sp. 145 H17
Ibiza (Ivisa), island, Sp. 145 H17
Iblei, Monti, It. 151 T11
Ibn Hani', Ra's, Syr. 170 F6
Ibo, Mozambique 203 D15
Iboperenda, Bol. 130 K8
Ibotirama, Braz. 131 H15
Ibra, Wadi, Sudan 198 F10
Ibrā', Oman 173 K16
'Ibrī, Oman 173 K15
Ibusuki, Japan 185 T4
Içá, river, Braz. 130 D6
Ica, river, Peru 130 J4
Ica, Peru 130 J4
Icacos Point, Trinidad & Tobago 121 Q21
Içana, river, Braz. 130 C6
Içana, Braz. 130 C6
İçel (Mersin), Turk. 168 J9
Iceland, Eur. 139 N3
Iceland Plateau, Arctic Oc. 243 K19
Ichchapuram, India 178 L10
Ichikawa, Japan 185 P12
Ichinohe, Japan 184 J13
Ichinomiya, Japan 185 P10
Ichinoseki, Japan 184 L13
Ichinskaya Sopka, Russ. 159 F22
Ichinskiy, Russ. 159 F22
Ichnya, Ukr. 157 N7
Ich'ŏn, N. Korea 182 E13
Icó, Braz. 131 F17
Iconium see Konya, Turk. 168 G8
Icoraci, Braz. 131 D13
Icy Cape, Alas., U.S. 111 B13
Idabel, Okla., U.S. 102 J14

Ida Grove, Iowa, U.S. 105 N9
Idah, Nigeria 201 G14
Idaho, U.S. 106 C4
Idaho City, Idaho, U.S. 106 G4
Idaho Falls, Idaho, U.S. 106 G7
Idalou, Tex., U.S. 102 K5
Idanha, Oreg., U.S. 108 G4
Idanha-a-Nova, Port. 144 G7
'Idd el Ghanam, Sudan 198 F10
Ideriyn, river, Mongolia 180 C10
Idfu, Egypt 197 E19
Idi, Indonesia 188 G4
Ídi, Óros (Psiloreítis), Gr. 155 Q14
İdil, Turk. 169 H16
Idiofa, Dem. Rep. of the Congo 198 L9
Idlib, Syr. 170 E8
Ídra (Hydra), island, Gr. 154 L12
Ídra, Gr. 154 K12
Ieper (Ypres), Belg. 146 L10
Ierápetra, Gr. 155 R16
Ierissós, Gr. 154 D12
Ieta, P.N.G. 217 J13
Ifalik Atoll, F.S.M. 216 Q4
Ife, Nigeria 201 G13
Iferouâne, Niger 196 G12
Ifjord, Nor. 141 B14
Igan, Malaysia 187 U16
Igara Paraná, river, Col. 128 J6
Igarka, Russ. 159 G13
Igatpuri, India 178 L3
Iğdır, Turk. 169 E18
Igel, Ger. 160 J11
Igikpak, Mount, Alas., U.S. 111 E15
Iglesias, It. 151 P3
Igli, Alg. 196 C9
Igloolik, Nunavut, Can. 83 F16
'Igma, Gebel el, Egypt 171 S3
Ignacio, Colo., U.S. 107 Q11
Ignalina, Lith. 141 N17
İğneada, Turk. 168 B4
İğneada Burnu, Turk. 168 B4
Igoumenítsa, Gr. 154 F7
Igra, Russ. 156 G16
Igrim, Russ. 158 G10
Iguala, Mex. 114 J11
Igualada, Sp. 145 D17
Iguatu, Braz. 131 F16
Iguazú Falls, Arg. 132 F15
Igué, Île, New Caledonia, Fr. 218 B6
Iguéla, Gabon 201 L15
Iguidi, 'Erg, Alg., Mauritania 196 D8
Iharaña (Vohemar), Madagascar 203 D18
Ihavandiffulu Atoll, Maldives 179 T3
Ihavandu, island, Maldives 179 T3
Iheya Rettō, Japan 185 X1
Iheya Shima, Japan 185 X1
Ihosy, Madagascar 203 H17
Ihu, P.N.G. 213 D19
Ii, Fin. 141 F15
Iida, Japan 185 P11
Iisalmi, Fin. 141 G16
Iittuarmiit, Greenland, Den. 81 D22
Ijevan, Arm. 169 D19
Ijill, Sebkhet, Mauritania 196 E6
IJmuiden, Neth. 146 H12
IJsselmeer, bay, Neth. 146 H13
Ijuí, Braz. 130 P11
Ijuw, region, Nauru 217 E23
Ikanbujmal, China 180 G7
Ikare, Nigeria 201 G13
Ikaría, island, Gr. 155 K16
Ikeda, Japan 184 G15
Ikela, Dem. Rep. of the Congo 198 K10
Ikhtiman, Bulg. 153 J13
Iki, island, Japan 185 R4
İkizdere, Turk. 169 D15
Ikopa, river, Madagascar 203 F17
Ikorodu, Nigeria 200 H12
Iksan, S. Korea 182 G13
Iku, island, Kiribati 217 F17
Ikuren, island, Marshall Is. 216 J8
Ilagan, Philippines 189 B14
Ilave, Peru 130 J6
Iława, Pol. 149 C15
Ilbilbie, Qnsld., Austral. 211 T14
Ilbunga, S. Aust., Austral. 211 U9
Ile, river, Kaz. 175 H16
Île-à-la-Crosse, Sask., Can. 82 L12
Ilebo, Dem. Rep. of the Congo 198 L9
Ilek, river, Kaz., Russ. 138 E14
Ilfracombe, Eng., U.K. 143 W9
Ilfracombe, Qnsld., Austral. 211 T12
Ilgaz, Turk. 168 D9
Ilgaz Dağları, Turk. 168 C9
Ilgın, Turk. 168 G7
Ílhavo, Port. 144 F5
Ilhéus, Braz. 131 J16
Ili, river, China, Kaz. 166 F7
Iliamna Lake, Alas., U.S. 111 K14
İliç, Turk. 169 F13
Ilıca, Turk. 169 E15
Iligan, Philippines 189 F15
Iliili, Amer. Samoa, U.S. 218 M7
Ili'ili'ōpae Heiau, Hawai'i, U.S. 113 F15
Ilinden, Bulg. 153 K13
Ilion, N.Y., U.S. 94 J10
'Īlio Point, Hawai'i, U.S. 113 F13
Ill, river, Aust. 160 M3
Illampu, peak, S. Amer. 126 G4
Illapel, Chile 132 J6
Illeginni, island, Marshall Is. 216 L4
Illéla, Niger 196 H11
Illichivs'k, Ukr. 157 R5
Illimani, peak, S. Amer. 126 G4
Illinois, river, Ill., U.S. 99 Q4
Illinois, river, Oreg., U.S. 108 K2
Illinois, U.S. 99 R4
Illinois Peak, Idaho, Mont., U.S. 84 C6
Illizi, Alg. 196 D12
Il'men', Ozero, Russ. 156 G7
Ilmenau, Ger. 148 G8
Ilo, Peru 130 K5
Iloilo, Philippines 189 E14
Ilorin, Nigeria 201 G13
Ilovik, island, Croatia 152 F4
Il'pyrskiy, Russ. 159 E21
Ilulissat, Greenland, Den. 81 C21
Ilwaco, Wash., U.S. 108 E2
Imabari, Japan 185 R6
Imabetsu, Japan 184 H12
I Maddock, Puntan, N. Mariana Is., U.S. 216 B6
Imaichi, Japan 185 N12
Imajō, Japan 185 P9
Imandra, Lake, Russ. 138 A9
Imarssuak Seachannel, Atl. Oc. 236 D8
Imatra, Fin. 141 H17
Imbert, Dom. Rep. 117 L18
Imese, Dem. Rep. of the Congo 198 J8
Īmī, Eth. 199 G16
Imías, Cuba 117 K14
Imieji Anchorage, Marshall Is. 216 M8
İmişli, Azerb. 169 E21
Imjun, river, N. Korea 182 D13
Imlay, Nev., U.S. 109 N8
Imlay City, Mich., U.S. 98 L12
Immarna, S. Aust., Austral. 211 W8
Immokalee, Fla., U.S. 97 W9
Imnaha, Oreg., U.S. 108 F9
Imola, It. 150 F7
Imotski, Croatia 152 H7
Imperatriz, Braz. 131 E13
Imperia, It. 150 G3
Imperial, Calif., U.S. 109 Z11
Imperial, Nebr., U.S. 105 Q3
Imperial Beach, Calif., U.S. 109 Z9
Imperial Dam, Ariz., Calif., U.S. 109 Y13
Imperial Valley, Calif., U.S. 109 Y11
Impfondo, Congo 201 K18
Imphal, India 178 H14
İmralı, island, Turk. 168 D4
İmranlı, Turk. 169 E13
Imrodj, island, Marshall Is. 216 L8
İmroz see Gökçeada, island, Turk. 168 D2
Imtān, Syr. 170 L8
Ina, Japan 185 P11
Inaccessible Island, Tristan da Cunha Is., U.K. 194 R2
I Naftan, Puntan, N. Mariana Is., U.S. 216 D5
Inamba Jima, Japan 185 R12
I-n-Amenas, Alg. 196 D12
I-n-Amguel, Alg. 196 E11
Inanwatan, Indonesia 189 K18
Inarajan, Guam, U.S. 216 D10
Inari, lake, Fin. 141 C15
Inari, Fin. 141 D15
Inca, Sp. 145 G18
Inca de Oro, Chile 132 G7
İnce Burun, Turk. 168 B10
İncekum Burnu, Turk. 168 J9
İncesu, Turk. 168 G10
Inchcape see Bell Rock, island, Scot., U.K. 142 L11
Incheon (Inch'on), S. Korea 182 F13
Inch Island, Ire. 143 P5
Inchnadamph, Scot., U.K. 142 H8
Inch'on see Incheon, S. Korea 182 F13
Incles, Port d', Andorra, Fr. 160 G5
Indalsälven, river, Sw. 138 C7
Indawgyi Lake, Myanmar 186 E6
Indefatigable see Santa Cruz, Isla, island, Ecua. 128 Q9
Independence, Calif., U.S. 109 T8
Independence, Iowa, U.S. 105 N13
Independence, Kans., U.S. 105 V9
Independence, Mo., U.S. 105 S10
Independence Mountains, Nev., U.S. 108 M10
India, Asia 167 W7
Indian, river, Fla., U.S. 97 U10
Indiana, Pa., U.S. 94 N4
Indiana, U.S. 99 R9
Indianapolis, Ind., U.S. 99 R9
Indian Harbour, Nfld. & Lab., Can. 83 K22
Indianola, Iowa, U.S. 105 P11
Indianola, Miss., U.S. 100 J10
Indianola, Nebr., U.S. 105 R4
Indian Peak, Utah, U.S. 107 N5
Indian Springs, Nev., U.S. 109 T11
Indiantown, Fla., U.S. 97 V10
Indian Town Point, Antigua & Barbuda 121 B21
Indigirka, river, Russ. 166 C11
Inđija, Serb. & Mont. 152 E10
Indio, Calif., U.S. 109 X11
Indira Point, India 179 T15
Indispensable Strait, Solomon Is. 217 N19
Indochina Peninsula, Asia 166 J11
Indomed Fracture Zone, Ind. Oc. 240 P5
Indonesia, Asia 167 Z11
Indore, India 178 J5
Indravati, river, India 178 L8
Indus, river, India, Pak. 177 W6
Indus, Mouths of the, Pak. 177 W6
Indus Fan, Ind. Oc. 240 D8
İnebolu, Turk. 168 B9
İnegöl, Turk. 168 D5
I-n-Eker, Alg. 196 E11
Ineu, Rom. 152 D11
Inez, Ky., U.S. 101 B20
Infante D. Henrique, Sao Tome and Principe 205 B21
Ingal, Niger 196 H11
Ingende, Dem. Rep. of the Congo 198 K9
Ingeniero Guillermo N. Juárez, Arg. 132 E11
Ingeniero Jacobacci, Arg. 133 Q8
Ingeniero Luiggi, Arg. 132 M10
Ingettolgoy, Mongolia 180 C11
Ingleside, Tex., U.S. 103 U11
Inglis, Fla., U.S. 97 S7
Ingolstadt, Ger. 148 J8
Ingomar, S. Aust., Austral. 211 W9
Ingraj Bazar, India 178 H11
Ingram, Tex., U.S. 103 Q8
Ingrid Christensen Coast, Antarctica 227 G19
Ingwiller, Fr. 147 P15
Inhambane, Mozambique 203 H13
Inharrime, Mozambique 203 J13
Inírida, river, Col. 128 G8
Inishannon, Ire. 143 V4
Inishbofin, island, Ire. 143 R2
Inisheer, island, Ire. 143 S3
Inishkea North, island, Ire. 143 Q2
Inishkea South, island, Ire. 143 Q2
Inishmaan, island, Ire. 143 S3
Inishmore, island, Ire. 143 S3
Inishmurray, island, Ire. 143 Q4
Inishowen Head, Ire. 143 N6
Inishshark, island, Ire. 143 R2
Inishtrahull, island, Ire. 143 N6
Inkerman, Qnsld., Austral. 211 Q11
Inland Niger Delta, Mali 196 H8
Inland Sea, Japan 185 Q6
Inn, river, Aust., Ger. 148 K10
Innamincka, S. Aust., Austral. 211 V11
Inner Brass Island, Virgin Islands, U.S. 120 M8
Inner Hebrides, Scot., U.K. 142 L7
Inner Mongolia, region, China 181 G13
Inner Sound, Scot., U.K. 142 J7
Innesowen, N.S.W., Austral. 211 W12
Innisfail, Qnsld., Austral. 211 R13
Innoko, river, Alas., U.S. 111 G14
Innsbruck, Aust. 148 L8
Inongo, Dem. Rep. of the Congo 198 K8
İnönü, Turk. 168 E6
Inoússes, island, Gr. 155 H16
Inowrocław, Pol. 149 D14
I-n-Salah, Alg. 196 D10
Insar, Russ. 156 K12
Inscription, Cape, Austral. 210 G1
Insein, Myanmar 186 K6
Insiaf, F.S.M. 217 B18
Instow, Eng., U.K. 143 W9
Inta, Russ. 158 F10
Intendente Alvear, Arg. 132 L10
Interior, S. Dak., U.S. 104 L3
International Falls, Minn., U.S. 104 E11
Interview Island, India 179 P14
Intiyaco, Arg. 132 H12
Inubō Zaki, Japan 185 P13
Inukjuak, Que., Can. 83 K18
Inuvik, N.W.T., Can. 82 E10
Inuya, river, Peru 130 G4
Inverbervie, Scot., U.K. 142 K11
Invercargill, N.Z. 213 R15
Invermoriston, Scot., U.K. 142 K9
Inverness, Fla., U.S. 97 T7
Inverness, Scot., U.K. 142 J9
Invershin, Scot., U.K. 142 J9
Inverway, N. Terr., Austral. 211 R7
Investigator Ridge, Ind. Oc. 241 H13
Investigator Strait, Austral. 210 L10
Inyokern, Calif., U.S. 109 V9
Inyo Mountains, Calif., U.S. 109 T8
Inza, Russ. 156 K13
Inzhavino, Russ. 156 M12
Inzia, river, Dem. Rep. of the Congo 198 M8
Ioánina, Gr. 154 E7
Iō Jima, Japan 185 U4
Iola, Kans., U.S. 105 U10
Ioma, P.N.G. 213 D20
Iona, Idaho, U.S. 106 G7
Iona, island, Scot., U.K. 142 L7
Ione, Calif., U.S. 109 R5
Ione, Nev., U.S. 109 Q9
Ione, Oreg., U.S. 108 F6
Ione, Wash., U.S. 108 A9
Ionia, Mich., U.S. 98 L10
Ionian Islands, Gr. 138 K8
Ionian Sea, Eur. 138 K8
Iony, Ostrov (St. Jona Island), Russ. 159 H20
Iori, river, Azerb., Rep. of Georgia 169 C20
Íos, island, Gr. 155 M15
Íos, Gr. 155 M15
Iotori Shima, Japan 185 X2
Iowa, river, Iowa, U.S. 105 P13
Iowa, U.S. 105 N10
Iowa City, Iowa, U.S. 105 P13
Iowa Falls, Iowa, U.S. 105 N12
Iowa Park, Tex., U.S. 102 J9
Ipáti, Gr. 154 G10
Ipatovo, Russ. 157 S12
Ipiales, Col. 128 H3
Ipis, island, F.S.M. 217 D16
Ipixuna, river, Braz. 130 F4
Ipixuna, Braz. 130 F5
Ipoh, Malaysia 187 T9
Iporá, Braz. 130 J12
İpsala, Turk. 168 C2
Ipswich, Eng., U.K. 143 U15
Ipswich, Jam. 120 H7
Ipswich, Qnsld., Austral. 211 V15
Ipswich, S. Dak., U.S. 104 J6
Iput', river, Russ. 156 L7
Iqaluit, Nunavut, Can. 83 H19
Iquique, Chile 132 C7
Iquitos, Peru 130 E4
Iraan, Tex., U.S. 103 P5
Iracoubo, Fr. Guiana, Fr. 129 E17
Īrafshān, Iran 173 H18
Iraio, ruin, Gr. 155 K17
Iráklia, island, Gr. 155 M15
Iráklio (Candia), Gr. 155 Q15
Iran, Asia 167 U5
Īrānshahr, Iran 173 H17
Irapuata, Mex. 114 H10
Iraq, Asia 167 T4
Irayel', Russ. 158 F9
Irazú, Volcán, Costa Rica 115 N19
Irbe Strait, Est., Latv. 141 L15
Irbid (Arbela), Jordan 170 L6
Ireland, Eur. 139 S3
Ireland, island, Ire., U.K. 143 T4
Ireland Island North, Bermuda, U.K. 120 B2
Ireland Island South, Bermuda, U.K. 120 B2
Iret', Russ. 159 F21
Irian Jaya, region, Indonesia 213 C16
Irimi, Indonesia 213 B14
Iringa, Tanzania 199 M14
Iriri, river, Braz. 130 E11
Iriru, Passe, Fr. Polynesia, Fr. 219 B23
Irish Sea, Ire., U.K. 143 S8
Irkeshtam, Kyrg. 176 G11
Irkutsk, Russ. 159 L15
Irmauw, Indonesia 189 M17
Irois Bay, Trinidad & Tobago 121 Q21
Iroise, Fr. 147 Q2
Irondequoit, N.Y., U.S. 94 H6
Iron Gate, Rom., Serb. & Mont. 138 H8
Iron Gate Dam, Rom., Serb. & Mont. 152 F12
Iron Knob, S. Aust., Austral. 211 X10
Iron Mountain, Mich., U.S. 98 G7
Iron River, Mich., U.S. 98 G6
Iron River, Wis., U.S. 98 F3
Ironton, Mo., U.S. 105 U15
Ironton, Ohio, U.S. 99 T13
Ironwood, Mich., U.S. 98 F5
Ironwood Forest National Monument, Ariz., U.S. 107 V7
Iroquois, S. Dak., U.S. 104 K7
Irō Zaki, Japan 185 Q11
Irpin', Ukr. 157 N6
Irrawaddy see Ayeyarwady, river, Myanmar 186 F6
Irsina, It. 150 M13
Irtysh, river, Russ. 158 H10
Iruña see Pamplona, Sp. 145 C13
Irvine, Ky., U.S. 101 C18
Irvine, Scot., U.K. 143 N9
Irving, Tex., U.S. 102 L11
Isabel, S. Dak., U.S. 104 J4
Isabel, Bahía, Ecua. 128 Q8
Isabela, P.R., U.S. 120 M2
Isabela, Philippines 189 F14
Isabela, Cabo, Dom. Rep. 117 K18
Isabela, Canal, Ecua. 128 Q9
Isabela, Isla (Albemarle), Ecua. 128 Q8
Isabela de Sagua, Cuba 116 G9
Isabella, Minn., U.S. 104 F13
Isabelle, Point, Mich., U.S. 98 E7
Isabel Segunda (Vieques), P.R., U.S. 120 N6
Isachsen Mountain, Antarctica 227 B15
Ísafjörður, Ice. 140 E2
Isahaya, Japan 185 S4
Isa Khel, Pak. 177 P9
Isangel, Vanuatu 218 H4
Isar, river, Ger. 148 K9
Íscar, Sp. 144 E10
Ischia, Isola d', It. 150 M10
Isdu, island, Maldives 179 W3
Ise, Japan 185 Q10
Isen Saki, Japan 185 X2
Iseo, Lago d', It. 150 D5
Isère, Pointe, Fr. Guiana, Fr. 129 E17
Isernia, It. 150 L10
Ise Wan, Japan 185 Q10
Isfahan see Eşfahan, Iran 173 E13
Isfara, Taj. 176 G9
Ishikari Wan, Japan 184 F13
Ishim, river, Russ. 158 J10
Ishim, Russ. 158 J10
Ishim Steppe, Kaz., Russ. 174 A12
Ishinomaki, Japan 184 L13
Ishinomaki Wan, Japan 184 L13
Ishioka, Japan 185 N13
Ishkuman, Pak. 176 K11
Ishpeming, Mich., U.S. 98 F7
Işık Dağı, Turk. 168 D8
Isikveren, Turk. 169 H17
Isili, It. 151 P4
Isimu, Indonesia 189 J14
Isiro, Dem. Rep. of the Congo 198 J11
Isisford, Qnsld., Austral. 211 U12
Iskandar, Uzb. 175 K13
İskenderun, Turk. 168 J11
İskilip, Turk. 168 D9
Iskŭr, river, Bulg. 153 G14
Iskushuban, Somalia 199 F18
İslâhiye, Turk. 168 H11
Islamabad see Anantnag, India 177 N12
Islamabad, Pak. 177 N11
Islamkot, Pak. 177 W9
Islamorada, Fla., U.S. 97 Y10
Isla Mujeres, Mex. 115 H17
Island Falls, Me., U.S. 95 C18
Island Lagoon, Austral. 210 J9
Island Lake, Man., Can. 83 M14
Island Park, Idaho, U.S. 106 F8
Island Park Reservoir, Idaho, U.S. 106 F7

Island Pond, *Vt., U.S.* **95** F13
Islands, Bay of, *N.Z.* **213** H18
Islas Orcadas Rise, *Atl. Oc.* **237** V9
Islay, island, *Scot., U.K.* **142** M7
Isle of Man, *Isle of Man, U.K.* **143** Q9
Isle Royale National Park, *Mich., U.S.* **98** D6
Islote Bay, *Trinidad & Tobago* **121** Q21
Ismâ'ilîya, *Egypt* **171** P1
Isna, *Egypt* **197** E19
Isoka, *Zambia* **202** C12
Isola di Capo Rizzuto, *It.* **151** Q14
Isonzo, river, *It., Slov.* **150** D9
Isparta, *Turk.* **168** G6
Ispas, *Turkm.* **174** L10
Ispikan, *Pak.* **177** V2
İspir, *Turk.* **169** D15
Israel, *Asia* **167** T3
Isrīyah, ruin, *Syr.* **170** F9
Issano, *Guyana* **129** E14
Issime, *It.* **150** D3
Issoudun, *Fr.* **147** S9
Ist, island, *Croatia* **152** F4
İstanbul (Constantinople), *Turk.* **168** C5
İstanbul Boğazi (Bosporus), *Turk.* **168** C5
Istaravshan (Ŭroteppa), *Taj.* **176** G7
Istiéa, *Gr.* **154** G11
Isto, Mount, *Alas., U.S.* **111** C18
Istokpoga, Lake, *Fla., U.S.* **97** V9
Istres, *Fr.* **147** X13
Istria, peninsula, *Croatia* **152** E4
Itabaianinha, *Braz.* **131** H17
Itabuna, *Braz.* **131** J16
Itacoatiara, *Braz.* **130** D10
Itaetê, *Braz.* **131** H16
Itaipú Dam, *Braz., Parag.* **130** M11
Itaituba, *Braz.* **130** E10
Itajaí, *Braz.* **131** N13
Italia, Monte, *Chile* **133** Y8
Italy, *Eur.* **139** W7
Itambé, Pico de, *Braz.* **131** K15
Itanagar, *India* **178** F14
Itapetinga, *Braz.* **131** J16
Itapipoca, *Braz.* **131** E16
Itasca, *Tex., U.S.* **102** M11
Itasca, Lake *see* Mississippi, Source of the, *Minn., U.S.* **104** G9
Itatupã, *Braz.* **130** C12
Itbayat, island, *Philippines* **189** A14
Itéa, *Gr.* **154** H10
Iténez, river, *Bol., Braz.* **130** H9
Itezhi-Tezhi, Lake, *Zambia* **202** E10
Ithaca *see* Itháki, island, *Gr.* **154** H7
Ithaca, *Mich., U.S.* **98** L11
Ithaca, *N.Y., U.S.* **94** K8
Itháki (Ithaca), island, *Gr.* **154** H7
Itháki (Vathý), *Gr.* **154** H7
Ítilo, *Gr.* **154** M10
Itimbiri, river, *Dem. Rep. of the Congo* **194** J7
Itiquira, river, *Braz.* **130** J10
Itō, *Japan* **185** Q12
Itoman, *Japan* **185** Y1
Itta Bena, *Miss., U.S.* **100** J11
Ittiri, *It.* **150** M3
Ittoqqortoormiit, *Greenland, Den.* **81** B22
Itu Aba Island, *Spratly Is.* **188** E11
Ituí, river, *Braz.* **130** E5
Ituiutaba, *Braz.* **131** K13
Ituni, *Guyana* **129** E14
Iturama, *Braz.* **130** K12
Iturup (Etorofu), island, *Russ.* **159** J23
Ituxi, river, *Braz.* **130** F7
Ituzaingó, *Arg.* **132** G14
Itzehoe, *Ger.* **148** B7
Iuka, *Miss., U.S.* **101** G13
Iul'tin, *Russ.* **159** B20
Ivaí, river, *Braz.* **130** M11
Ivalo, *Fin.* **141** D15
Ivangrad, *Serb. & Mont.* **152** H9
Ivanhoe, *N.S.W., Austral.* **211** X12
Ivanhoe, *W. Aust., Austral.* **211** Q6
Ivanić Grad, *Croatia* **152** D6
Ivanjica, *Serb. & Mont.* **152** G10
Ivano-Frankivs'k, *Ukr.* **157** P2
Ivanovo, *Russ.* **156** H11
Ivanteyevka, *Russ.* **156** L15
Ivatsevichy, *Belarus* **156** L3
Ivaylovgrad, *Bulg.* **153** K15
Ivdel', *Russ.* **158** G9
Ivirairai, Mont, *Fr. Polynesia, Fr.* **219** P16
Ivisa *see* Ibiza, island, *Sp.* **145** H17
Ivory Coast, *Cote dIvoire* **194** J2
Ivrea, *It.* **150** D3
Ivujivik, *Que., Can.* **83** H17
Iwadate, *Japan* **184** J12
Iwaki, *Japan* **185** N13
Iwakuni, *Japan* **185** Q6
Iwamizawa, *Japan* **184** F13
Iwanuma, *Japan* **184** L13
Iwate, *Japan* **184** K13
Iwembere Steppe, *Tanzania* **194** K9
Iwo, *Nigeria* **200** G12
Iwo Jima, *Japan* **184** L5
Ixtapa, *Mex.* **114** K10
Iyo, *Japan* **185** R6
Iž, island, *Croatia* **152** G5
Īzad Khvāst, *Iran* **173** E13
Izamal, *Mex.* **115** H16
Izberbash, *Russ.* **157** U16
Izbica, *Pol.* **149** D14
Izena Shima, *Japan* **185** X1
Izhevsk, *Russ.* **156** G16
Izhevsk, *Russ.* **158** H8
Izhma, river, *Russ.* **138** B12
Izmayil, *Ukr.* **157** S4
İzmir (Smyrna), *Turk.* **168** F3
İznik (Nicaea), *Turk.* **168** D5
İznik Gölü, *Turk.* **168** D5
Izozog, Bañados del, *S. Amer.* **126** H5
Izra', *Syr.* **170** K7
Izu Hantō, *Japan* **185** Q11
Izuhara, *Japan* **185** Q3
Izu Islands, *Japan* **166** F14
Izumo, *Japan* **185** P6
Izu Shichitō, *Japan* **185** Q12
Izu Shotō, *Japan* **184** J5
Izu Trench, *Pac. Oc.* **238** F6
Izyaslav, *Ukr.* **157** N4
Izyum, *Ukr.* **157** P9

J

Jaba, *P.N.G.* **217** K14
Jabalpur, *India* **178** J7
Jabal Zuqar, Jazīrat, *Yemen* **172** Q8
Jabbūl, *Syr.* **170** E9
Jabbūl, Sabkhat al, *Syr.* **170** E9
Jabel Abyad Plateau, *Sudan* **194** F8
Jabiru, *N. Terr., Austral.* **211** P8
Jablah, *Syr.* **170** F7
Jablaničko Jezero, *Bosn. & Herzg.* **152** G7
Jablonec, *Czech Rep.* **148** G11
Jabnoren, island, *Marshall Is.* **216** K7
Jaboatão, *Braz.* **131** G18
Jabor, *Marshall Is.* **216** M8
Jäbrayyl, *Azerb.* **169** E21
Jabuka, island, *Croatia* **152** H5
Jabwot Island, *Marshall Is.* **216** H4
Jaca, *Sp.* **145** C14
Jacareacanga, *Braz.* **130** E10
Jaciparaná, *Braz.* **130** G7
Jackman, *Me., U.S.* **95** D15
Jackpot, *Nev., U.S.* **108** L12
Jacksboro, *Tex., U.S.* **102** K10
Jackson, *Ala., U.S.* **101** M14
Jackson, *Barbados* **121** K19
Jackson, *Calif., U.S.* **109** R5
Jackson, *Ga., U.S.* **96** L5
Jackson, *La., U.S.* **100** N9
Jackson, *Mich., U.S.* **98** M11
Jackson, *Minn., U.S.* **104** L10
Jackson, *Miss., U.S.* **100** L11
Jackson, *Mo., U.S.* **105** U16
Jackson, *Ohio, U.S.* **99** S13
Jackson, *S.C., U.S.* **96** L8
Jackson, *Tenn., U.S.* **101** F13
Jackson, *Wyo., U.S.* **106** H8
Jackson, Ostrov, *Russ.* **158** C12
Jackson Bay, *N.Z.* **213** P15
Jackson Lake, *Ga., U.S.* **96** L5
Jackson Lake, *Wyo., U.S.* **106** G8
Jacksonport, *Wis., U.S.* **98** H8
Jacksonville, *Ala., U.S.* **101** J16
Jacksonville, *Ark., U.S.* **100** G9
Jacksonville, *Fla., U.S.* **97** Q8
Jacksonville, *Ill., U.S.* **99** R4
Jacksonville, *N.C., U.S.* **96** J13
Jacksonville, *Tex., U.S.* **102** M14
Jacksonville Beach, *Fla., U.S.* **97** R9
Jacmel, *Haiti* **117** M16
Jacobabad, *Pak.* **177** T7
Jacob Lake, *Ariz., U.S.* **107** Q7
Jacquinot Bay, *P.N.G.* **213** C21
Jacumba, *Calif., U.S.* **109** Z11
J.A.D. Jensen Nunatakker, peak, *N. Amer.* **80** D10
Jadraque, *Sp.* **144** E12
Jaén, *Peru* **130** F2
Jaén, *Sp.* **144** K11
Jaffa, Cape, *Austral.* **210** L10
Jaffna, *Sri Lanka* **179** R7
Jafr, Qā' al, *Jordan* **171** Q7
Jagdalpur, *India* **178** L8
Jāghir Bāzār, *Syr.* **170** C14
Jaghjagh, river, *Syr.* **170** C14
Jagodina, *Serb. & Mont.* **152** G11
Jagraon, *India* **178** D5
Jagtial, *India* **178** L6
Jaguarão, *Braz.* **130** Q11
Jahanabad, *India* **178** H10
Jahorina, peak, *Bosn. & Herzg.* **152** G8
Jahrom, *Iran* **173** G14
Jaicoa, Cordillera, *P.R., U.S.* **120** M2
Jaicós, *Braz.* **131** F16
Jaigarh, *India* **178** M3
Jaintiapur, *Bangladesh* **178** H13
Jaipur, *India* **178** G5
Jaisalmer, *India* **178** F2
Jājarm, *Iran* **173** B15
Jajpur, *India* **178** K10
Jakar, *Bhutan* **178** F13
Jakarta, *Indonesia* **188** L8
Jakeru, island, *Marshall Is.* **216** L3
Jakhau, *India* **178** H1
Jakobstad (Pietarsaari), *Fin.* **141** G15
Jal, *N. Mex., U.S.* **107** V15
Jalaihai Point, *Guam, U.S.* **216** D11
Jalalabad, *Afghan.* **176** M9
Jalal-Abad, *Kyrg.* **176** F10
Jalasjärvi, *Fin.* **141** H15
Jalaun, *India* **178** G7
Jaldak, *Afghan.* **177** P6
Jaleswar, *India* **178** K11
Jalgaon, *India* **178** K5
Jalgaon, *India* **178** K5
Jalingo, *Nigeria* **201** G16
Jalkot, *Pak.* **176** L11
Jaloklab, island, *Marshall Is.* **216** G10
Jalón, river, *Sp.* **145** E13
Jalor, *India* **178** G3
Jalpaiguri, *India* **178** G12
Jālq, *Iran* **173** G18
Jáltipan, *Mex.* **115** K14
Jaluit, island, *Marshall Is.* **216** M8
Jaluit Atoll, *Marshall Is.* **216** H4
Jaluit Lagoon, *Marshall Is.* **216** M8
Jamaame, *Somalia* **199** K16
Jamaica, *N. Amer.* **81** P21
Jamaica, island, *N. Amer.* **80** N9
Jamaica Cay, *Bahamas* **117** G13
Jamalpur, *Bangladesh* **178** H12
Jamanota, peak, *Aruba, Neth.* **121** Q17
Jaman Pass, *Afghan., Taj.* **176** J12
Jambi, *Indonesia* **188** K7
Jambusar, *India* **178** J3
James *see* San Salvador, Isla, island, *Ecua.* **128** P9
James, river, *N. Dak., U.S.* **104** G6
James, river, *S. Dak., U.S.* **104** M7
James, river, *Va., U.S.* **96** E11
James Bay, *N. Amer.* **80** G8
James Cistern, *Bahamas* **120** E6
James Point, *Bahamas* **120** D6
James Range, *Austral.* **210** F8
James Ross Island, *Antarctica* **226** C4
Jamestown, *N. Dak., U.S.* **104** G6
Jamestown, *N.Y., U.S.* **94** K4
Jamestown National Historic Site, *Va., U.S.* **96** F13
Jamestown Reservoir, *N. Dak., U.S.* **104** G6
Jammu, *India* **177** P12
Jamnagar, *India* **178** J2
Jampur, *Pak.* **177** S9
Jämsä, *Fin.* **141** J15
Jamshedpur, *India* **178** J10
Jamuna, river, *Bangladesh* **178** H12
Janaúba, *Braz.* **131** J15
Jan Bulaq, *Afghan.* **176** K6
Jand, *Pak.* **177** N10
Jandaq, *Iran* **173** D14
Jandia, peak, *Canary Is.* **204** Q7
Jandia, Punta de, *Canary Is.* **204** Q7
Jandiatuba, river, *Braz.* **130** E6
Jandola, *Pak.* **177** P8
Jan Doran, *Neth. Antilles, Neth.* **121** Q18
Janesville, *Wis., U.S.* **98** M6
Jangain, island, *P.N.G.* **217** H14
Jangaon, *India* **178** M7
Jangeru, *Indonesia* **188** K12
Jangheung, *S. Korea* **182** H13
Jangipur, *India* **178** H11
Jani Kheyl, *Afghan.* **177** P7
Janīn, *W. Bank* **170** L6
Jan Mayen, island, *Nor.* **81** A22
Jan Mayen Fracture Zone, *Arctic Oc.* **243** J18
Jan Mayen Ridge, *Arctic Oc.* **243** J19
Janów Lubelski, *Pol.* **149** F17
Jansenville, *S. Af.* **202** M9
Jan Thiel, Lagún, *Neth. Antilles, Neth.* **121** Q15
Januária, *Braz.* **131** J14
Jaora, *India* **178** H4
Japan, *Asia* **167** T14
Japan, Sea of (East Sea), *Asia* **166** F13
Japan Trench, *Pac. Oc.* **238** E6
Japtan, island, *Marshall Is.* **216** H9
Japurá, *Braz.* **130** D7
Jaquot, Pointe, *Dominica* **121** D18
Jarābulus, *Syr.* **170** C10
Jaramillo, *Arg.* **133** T9
Jaranwala, *Pak.* **177** Q11
Jarash (Gerasa), *Jordan* **170** L6
Jarbidge, river, *Idaho, U.S.* **106** J4
Jarbidge, *Nev., U.S.* **108** L11
Jardim, *Braz.* **130** L10
Jardines de la Reina, islands, *Cuba* **116** J10
Jargalant, *Mongolia* **181** D14
Jargalant, *Mongolia* **180** E10
Jarghan, *Afghan.* **176** L5
Jari, river, *Braz.* **130** C12
Jarocin, *Pol.* **149** E13
Jarosław, *Pol.* **149** G17
Jarud Qi, *China* **181** E16
Järvenpää, *Fin.* **141** J16
Jarvis Island, *Pac. Oc.* **214** G12
Järvsö, *Sw.* **141** J13
Jashpurnagar, *India* **178** J9
Jāsk, *Iran* **173** J16
Jasło, *Pol.* **149** H17
Jason Islands, *Falkland Is., U.K.* **133** V11
Jason Peninsula, *Antarctica* **226** D5
Jasonville, *Ind., U.S.* **99** S8
Jasper, *Ala., U.S.* **101** J14
Jasper, *Alta., Can.* **82** L9
Jasper, *Ark., U.S.* **100** E7
Jasper, *Fla., U.S.* **97** Q7
Jasper, *Ga., U.S.* **96** K5
Jasper, *Ind., U.S.* **99** T8
Jasper, *Tex., U.S.* **103** P15
Jastrowie, *Pol.* **149** C13
Jastrzębie-Zdrój, *Pol.* **149** H14
Jászberény, *Hung.* **149** L15
Jataí, *Braz.* **130** K12
Jati, *Pak.* **177** W7
Jatibonico, *Cuba* **116** H9
Jatobal, *Braz.* **131** E13
Jaú, river, *Braz.* **130** D8
Jauaperi, river, *Braz.* **130** C9
Jaunpur, *India* **178** G8
Java (Jawa), island, *Indonesia* **188** M9
Javari, river, *Braz., Peru* **130** E4
Java Ridge, *Ind. Oc.* **241** H15
Java Sea, *Indonesia* **188** L10
Java Trench, *Ind. Oc.* **241** H14
Jávea (Xàbia), *Sp.* **145** J15
Javhlant *see* Uliastay, *Mongolia* **180** D10
Jawa *see* Java, island, *Indonesia* **188** M9
Jawhar (Giohar), *Somalia* **199** J17
Jawi, *Indonesia* **188** J9
Jaworzno, *Pol.* **149** G15
Jay, *Okla., U.S.* **102** E14
Jaya, Puncak, *Indonesia* **213** C16
Jaya Peak, *Indonesia* **166** L16
Jayapura, *Indonesia* **189** K21
Jayawijaya, Pegunungan, *Indonesia* **189** L20
Jay Em, *Wyo., U.S.* **106** J13
Jayton, *Tex., U.S.* **102** K7
Jayuya, *P.R., U.S.* **120** N3
Jaz Mūrīan, Hāmūn-e, *Iran* **173** H16
Jbail (Byblos), *Leb.* **170** H6
Jeanerette, *La., U.S.* **100** Q9
Jeanette, Ostrov, *Russ.* **159** C17
Jean Marie River, *N.W.T., Can.* **82** H10
Jean-Rabel, *Haiti* **117** L16
Jebba, *Nigeria* **201** F13
Jebel, Bahr el (Mountain Nile), *Sudan* **199** H13
Jebri, *Pak.* **177** U5
Jebus, *Indonesia* **188** K7
Jeddah, *Saudi Arabia* **172** L7
Jedrol, island, *Marshall Is.* **216** H8
Jędrzejów, *Pol.* **149** G16
Jefferson, *Ga., U.S.* **96** K6
Jefferson, *Iowa, U.S.* **105** N10
Jefferson, river, *Mont., U.S.* **106** E7
Jefferson, *Tex., U.S.* **102** L15
Jefferson, *Wis., U.S.* **98** L6
Jefferson, Mount, *Nev., U.S.* **109** Q10
Jefferson, Mount, *Oreg., U.S.* **108** G4
Jefferson City, *Mo., U.S.* **105** T13
Jefferson City, *Tenn., U.S.* **101** E19
Jeffersonville, *Ind., U.S.* **99** T10
Jeffrey City, *Wyo., U.S.* **106** J11
Jef Jef el Kebir, desert, *Chad* **197** F15
Jega, *Nigeria* **201** E13
Jégun, *Fr.* **147** X8
Jeju (Cheju), *S. Korea* **182** J13
Jeju-Do, *S. Korea* **182** J13
Jeju Strait, *S. Korea* **182** H13
Jekyll Island, *Ga., U.S.* **97** P8
Jelbart Ice Shelf, *Antarctica* **226** A12
Jelenia Góra, *Pol.* **148** F12
Jelgava (Mitau), *Latv.* **141** M16
Jellico, *Tenn., U.S.* **101** D18
Jemaja, island, *Indonesia* **188** H8
Jember, *Indonesia* **188** M11
Jembongan, island, *Malaysia* **188** F12
Jemez Pueblo, *N. Mex., U.S.* **107** R12
Jeminay, *China* **180** D7
Jemo Island, *Marshall Is.* **216** F4
Jena, *Fla., U.S.* **97** R6
Jena, *Ger.* **148** F9
Jena, *La., U.S.* **100** M8
Jengish Chokusu (Pik Pobedy, Victory Peak), *China, Kyrg.* **176** E15
Jenkins, *Ky., U.S.* **101** C20
Jennings, *La., U.S.* **100** P8
Jenny Point, *Dominica* **121** F20
Jensen, *Utah, U.S.* **106** L9
Jensen Beach, *Fla., U.S.* **97** V10
Jens Munk Island, *Nunavut, Can.* **83** F16
Jenu, *Indonesia* **188** J9
Jeongeup, *S. Korea* **182** G13
Jeonju, *S. Korea* **182** G13
Jequié, *Braz.* **131** H16
Jequitinhonha, river, *Braz.* **131** J16
Jerantut, *Malaysia* **187** T10
Jerba Island, *Tun.* **197** B13
Jérémie, *Haiti* **117** M15
Jeremoabo, *Braz.* **131** G17
Jerez de la Frontera, *Sp.* **144** M8
Jeréz de los Caballeros, *Sp.* **144** J7
Jericho *see* Arīḥā, *W. Bank* **170** M6
Jericoacoara, Point, *S. Amer.* **126** D10
Jerid, Chott el, *Tun.* **196** B12
Jerilderie, *N.S.W., Austral.* **211** Y12
Jerimoth Hill, *R.I., U.S.* **95** L14
Jerome, *Idaho, U.S.* **106** H5
Jerramungup, *W. Aust., Austral.* **211** Y3
Jersey, island, *Ch. Is.* **143** Z11
Jersey Bay, *Virgin Islands, U.S.* **120** N10
Jersey City, *N.J., U.S.* **94** N11
Jersey Shore, *Pa., U.S.* **94** M7
Jerseyside, *Nfld. & Lab., Can.* **83** M24
Jerseyville, *Ill., U.S.* **99** S4
Jerusalem, *Israel* **170** M5
Jervis *see* Rábida, Isla, island, *Ecua.* **128** Q9
Jervis Bay, *Austral.* **210** L14
Jervis Bay Territory, *Austral.* **211** Y14
Jerzu, *It.* **151** P4
Jesenice, *Slov.* **152** C4
Jeseník, *Czech Rep.* **149** G13
Jesi, *It.* **150** H9
Jessore, *Bangladesh* **178** J12
Jesup, *Ga., U.S.* **97** P8
Jesús María, *Arg.* **132** J10
Jetmore, *Kans., U.S.* **105** T5
Jetpur, *India* **178** J2
Jewel Cave National Monument, *S. Dak., U.S.* **104** L1
Jewell, *Iowa, U.S.* **105** N11
Jewett, *Tex., U.S.* **103** N12
Jeypore, *India* **178** L8
Jezercë, Maja, *Albania* **152** J9
Jezioro Shiardwy, *Pol.* **149** B16
Jezzîne, *Leb.* **170** J6
Jhalawar, *India* **178** H5
Jhal Jhao, *Pak.* **177** V5
Jhang, *Pak.* **177** Q10
Jhansi, *India* **178** H6
Jharsuguda, *India* **178** K9
Jhatpat, *Pak.* **177** T7
Jhelum, river, *Pak.* **177** Q10
Jhelum, *Pak.* **177** P11
Jhimpir, *Pak.* **177** W7
Jhudo, *Pak.* **177** W8

Jhunjhunun, India 178 F5
Jiahe, China 183 P3
Jiaji see Qionghai, China 183 U2
Jiamusi, China 181 C18
Ji'an, China 182 C12
Ji'an, China 183 N5
Jianchang, China 182 C9
Jianchuan, China 180 N10
Jianghua, China 183 Q3
Jiangjunmiao, China 180 E8
Jiangle, China 183 P7
Jiangling, China 182 L4
Jiangmen, China 183 S4
Jiangshan, China 182 M8
Jianli, China 182 L4
Jianning, China 183 P7
Jian'ou, China 183 P8
Jianping, China 182 C9
Jianshi, China 182 L2
Jianyang, China 183 N7
Jiaohe, China 182 A13
Jiaojiang (Haimen), China 182 M10
Jiaokou, China 182 F3
Jiaonan, China 182 G9
Jiaozhou, China 182 F9
Jiaozhou Wan, China 182 G9
Jiaozuo, China 182 G5
Jiawang, China 182 H7
Jiaxian, China 182 E3
Jiaxing, China 182 L9
Jiayin, China 181 B17
Jiayu, China 182 L5
Jiayuguan, China 180 G10
Jibsh, Ra's, Oman 173 L17
Jiddat al Ḩarāsīs, desert, Oman 173 M16
Jido, India 178 E15
Jieshou, China 182 J6
Jiesjavrre, Nor. 141 C14
Jiexiu, China 182 F4
Jieyang, China 183 R6
Jiggalong, W. Aust., Austral. 211 T4
Jigüey, Bahía de, Cuba 116 H10
Jihlava, Czech Rep. 148 J12
Jijia, river, Rom. 153 B16
Jijiga, Eth. 199 G16
Jilib, Somalia 199 J16
Jilin, China 182 A12
Jiloy, Azerb. 169 D24
Jīma, Eth. 199 G14
Jimaní, Dom. Rep. 117 M17
Jimbolia, Rom. 152 D10
Jiménez, Mex. 114 E9
Jimo, China 182 F9
Jinan, China 182 F7
Jinbal, island, Marshall Is. 216 L8
Jinchang, China 180 H11
Jincheng, China 182 G4
Jindřichův Hradec, Czech Rep. 148 J11
Jinedrol, island, Marshall Is. 216 H9
Jingazhir, Taj. 176 H11
Jingbian, China 182 E2
Jingde, China 182 L8
Jingdezhen, China 182 M7
Jinggu, China 180 P10
Jinghai, China 182 D7
Jinghong, China 180 Q10
Jingle, China 182 E4
Jingmen, China 182 K4
Jingpeng see Hexigten Qi, China 182 A7
Jingpo Hu, China 181 D18
Jingxi, China 180 P12
Jingxian, China 183 P2
Jingxing, China 182 E5
Jingyu, China 182 B13
Jinhua, China 182 M9
Jinimi, island, Marshall Is. 216 H9
Jining, China 182 C5
Jining, China 182 G7
Jinja, Uganda 199 K13
Jinjiang, China 183 Q8
Jinju, S. Korea 182 G14
Jinmu Jiao, China 181 R13
Jinping, China 183 N1
Jinsha see Nantong, China 182 K9
Jinsha (Yangtze), river, China 180 N11
Jinshan, China 182 L9
Jinshi, China 182 L3
Jinxi, China 182 C9
Jinxiang, China 182 G6
Jinzhai, China 182 K6
Jinzhou, China 182 C9
Jinzhou, China 182 D10
Jiparaná, river, Braz. 130 F8
Ji-Paraná (Rondônia), Braz. 130 G8
Jipijapa, Ecua. 128 K2
Jirgatol, Taj. 176 H9
Jīroft, Iran 173 G16
Jishou, China 182 M2
Jishui, China 183 N5
Jisr ash Shughūr, Syr. 170 E7
Jiu, river, Rom. 153 G13
Jiujiang, China 182 M6
Jiuling Shan, China 182 M5
Jiulong (Kowloon), China 183 S5
Jiuquan, China 180 G10
Jiuquan Space Launch Center, China 180 G10
Jiutai, China 181 E17
Jiwani, Pak. 177 W1
Jixi, China 182 L8
Jixi, China 181 D18
Jixian, China 182 D7
Jixian, China 182 F3
Jiyuan, China 182 G4
Jīzān, Saudi Arabia 172 P8
Jizzax, Uzb. 174 L12
Joaçaba, Braz. 130 N12
João Pessoa, Braz. 131 F18
Joaquín V. González, Arg. 132 F10
Jobos, P.R., U.S. 120 P4
Jobos, Bahía de, P.R., U.S. 120 P4
Jochiwon, S. Korea 182 F13
Jodar, Sp. 144 K11
Jodhpur, India 178 G3
Joensuu, Fin. 141 G17
Joe's Hill, Kiribati 217 B23
Jōetsu, Japan 184 M11
Joeuf, Fr. 147 N14
Jogindarnagar, India 177 P14
Jogipet, India 178 M6
Johannesburg, Calif., U.S. 109 V9
Johannesburg, S. Af. 202 J10
John Day, river, Oreg., U.S. 108 G6
John Day Dam, Oreg., U.S., Wash., U.S. 108 E5
John Day Fossil Beds National Monument, Oreg., U.S. 108 G6
John D. Rockefeller Jr. Memorial Parkway, Wyo., U.S. 106 G8
John Eyre Motel, W. Aust., Austral. 211 X6
John F. Kennedy Space Center, Fla., U.S. 97 T10
John H. Kerr Reservoir, N.C., Va., U.S. 96 G12
John Martin Reservoir, Colo., U.S. 107 N15
John Millars, Bahamas 120 F6
John o'Groats, site, Scot., U.K. 142 G10
John Redmond Reservoir, Kans., U.S. 105 T9
Johns Folly Bay, Virgin Islands, U.S. 120 N11
Johnson, Kans., U.S. 105 U3
Johnsonburg, Pa., U.S. 94 M5
Johnson City, N.Y., U.S. 94 K8
Johnson City, Tenn., U.S. 101 E20
Johnson City, Tex., U.S. 103 Q9
Johnson Draw, Tex., U.S. 103 Q6
Johnsons Point, Antigua & Barbuda 121 B20
Johnston, S.C., U.S. 96 L8
Johnston, Lake, Austral. 210 K4
Johnston, Mount, Antarctica 227 F19
Johnston Atoll, Pac. Oc. 214 E10
Johnston City, Ill., U.S. 99 U6
Johnstone, Scot., U.K. 142 M9
Johnstown, N.Y., U.S. 94 J10
Johnstown, Pa., U.S. 94 P4
Johor Baharu, Malaysia 187 V11
Joigny, Fr. 147 Q11
Joinville, Braz. 131 N13
Joinville Island, Antarctica 226 C4
Jokaj, island, F.S.M. 217 F14
Jokkmokk, Sw. 141 F13
Joliet, Ill., U.S. 99 P7
Joliette, Que., Can. 83 P19
Jolo, island, Philippines 189 G14
Jolo, Philippines 189 G13
Jomda, China 180 L10
Jonesboro, Ark., U.S. 100 F10
Jonesboro, La., U.S. 100 L8
Jonesport, Me., U.S. 95 F19
Jones Sound, Nunavut, Can. 83 D16
Jonesville, La., U.S. 100 M9
Jonesville, S.C., U.S. 96 J8
Jönköping, Sw. 141 M13
Jonuta, Mex. 115 J15
Jonzac, Fr. 147 U7
Joplin, Mo., U.S. 105 V10
Joplin, Mont., U.S. 106 B8
Jordan, Asia 167 T3
Jordan, river, Jordan, W. Bank 170 M6
Jordan, Minn., U.S. 104 K11
Jordan, Mont., U.S. 106 C11
Jordan Valley, Oreg., U.S. 108 J9
Jorge Montt, Isla, Chile 133 W6
Jorhat, India 178 G15
Jorm, Afghan. 176 K9
Jörn, Sw. 141 G14
Jornada del Muerto, desert, N. Mex., U.S. 107 U12
Jorong, Indonesia 188 K11
Jørpeland, Nor. 140 L10
Jos, Nigeria 201 F14
José Batlle-y-Ordóñez, Uru. 132 L14
Joseph, Oreg., U.S. 108 F9
Joseph Bonaparte Gulf, Austral. 210 B6
Josephine Seamount, Atl. Oc. 236 H11
José Rodrigues, Braz. 130 E12
Joshimath, India 178 E7
Joshua Tree National Park, Calif., U.S. 109 X11
Josipdol, Croatia 152 E5
Jos Plateau, Nigeria 194 H5
Josselin, Fr. 147 Q4
Jost Van Dyke, island, Virgin Islands, U.K. 120 L11
Jotunheimen, range, Nor. 140 K10
Jou, Sao Tome and Principe 205 D19
Joulter Cays, Bahamas 116 D11
Joünié, Leb. 170 H6
Jourdanton, Tex., U.S. 103 S9
Joutsa, Fin. 141 H16
Joux, Lac de, Switz. 147 S14
Jovellanos, Cuba 116 G7
Joyeuse, Fr. 147 W12
J. Percy Priest Lake, Tenn., U.S. 101 E15
J. Strom Thurmond Reservoir, Ga., S.C., U.S. 96 L7
Ju, river, China 182 K3
Juana Díaz, P.R., U.S. 120 N3
Juan Aldama, Mex. 114 F10
Juan de Fuca, Strait of, Can., U.S. 84 A3
Juan de Fuca Ridge, Pac. Oc. 239 D15
Juan de Nova, Île, Mozambique Ch. 203 F16
Juan Domingo, Neth. Antilles, Neth. 121 P14
Juan Fernández, Islas, S. Amer. 126 M2
Juan José Castelli, Arg. 132 F12
Juanjuí, Peru 130 F3
Juan Stuven, Isla, Chile 133 U6
Juárez, Arg. 133 N12
Juazeiro, Braz. 131 G16
Juàzeiro do Norte, Braz. 131 F16
Juba, Sudan 199 H13
Jubany, station, Antarctica 226 C3
Jubba, Webi, Somalia 199 J16
Jubbah, Saudi Arabia 172 G8
Jubb al Jarrā', Syr. 170 G9
Juberri, Andorra 160 K2
Juby, Cape, Mor. 196 C6
Júcar, river, Sp. 145 H13
Júcaro, Cuba 116 J10
Juchitán, Mex. 115 K13
Judayyidat 'Ar'ar, Saudi Arabia 172 E8
Judenberg, Aust. 148 M11
Judge Seamount, Pac. Oc. 238 F9
Judith, river, Mont., U.S. 106 C9
Judith Basin, Mont., U.S. 106 C9
Judith Gap, Mont., U.S. 106 D9
Judsonia, Ark., U.S. 100 F9
Juegang see Rudong, China 182 K10
Juifang, Taiwan, China 183 Q10
Juigalpa, Nicar. 115 M18
Juiz de Fora, Braz. 131 L15
Julesburg, Colo., U.S. 106 K15
Juliaca, Peru 130 J6
Julia Creek, Qnsld., Austral. 211 S11
Julian, Calif., U.S. 109 Y10
Julian Alps, It., Slov. 150 C10
Jullundur, India 178 D5
Julu, China 182 F6
Jumilla, Sp. 145 J13
Jumla, Nepal 178 E8
Jumunjin, S. Korea 182 E14
Junan, China 182 G8
Juncos, P.R., U.S. 120 N5
Junction, Tex., U.S. 103 Q8
Junction, Utah, U.S. 107 N7
Junction City, Ark., U.S. 100 K8
Junction City, Kans., U.S. 105 S8
Junction City, Oreg., U.S. 108 H3
Jundah, Qnsld., Austral. 211 U12
Juneau, Alas., U.S. 111 L22
Jungar Qi, China 182 D3
Junggar Pendi (Dzungarian Basin), China 180 E7
Junglinster, Lux. 160 J10
Jungshahi, Pak. 177 W7
Juniata, river, Pa., U.S. 94 N7
Junín, Arg. 132 L11
Junín, Peru 130 H3
Junín de los Andes, Arg. 133 P7
Juniper Mountain, Oreg., U.S. 108 J6
Junlian, China 180 M12
Junnar, India 178 L4
Juno Beach, Fla., U.S. 97 V10
Juntura, Oreg., U.S. 108 H8
Jupaguá, Braz. 131 H14
Jupiter, Fla., U.S. 97 V10
Jura, island, Scot., U.K. 142 M7
Jura, Sound of, Scot., U.K. 142 M7
Juradó, Col. 128 D3
Jura Mountains, Fr., Switz. 138 G5
Jurby, Isle of Man, U.K. 143 Q9
Jurien, W. Aust., Austral. 211 W2
Juruá, river, Braz. 130 E7
Juruá, Braz. 130 D7
Juruena, river, Braz. 130 F10
Juruti, Braz. 130 D10
Justo Daract, Arg. 132 L9
Jutaí, river, Braz. 130 E6
Jutaí, Braz. 130 E6
Jutiapa, Guatemala 115 L16
Juticalpa, Hond. 115 L18
Jutland see Jylland, region, Den., Ger. 140 N11
Juventud, Isla de la (Isle of Youth), Cuba 116 J5
Juxian, China 182 G8
Juye, China 182 G6
Juzennecourt, Fr. 147 Q13
Južna Morava, river, Serb. & Mont. 152 H11
Juzzak, Pak. 177 S1
Jylland (Jutland), region, Den., Ger. 140 N11
Jyväskylä, Fin. 141 H16

K

K2 (Godwin Austen), peak, China, Pak. 176 L13
Ka‘a‘awa, Hawai‘i, U.S. 112 D11
Kaabong, Uganda 199 H13
Kaala-Gomén, New Caledonia, Fr. 218 C6
Ka‘alu‘alu Bay, Hawai‘i, U.S. 113 Q19
Kaamanen, Fin. 141 C15
Kaambooni, Somalia 199 K16
Kaambooni, Raas, Kenya, Somalia 194 K11
Kā‘anapali, Hawai‘i, U.S. 113 G15
Kaap Plateau, S. Af. 194 Q8
Kabaena, island, Indonesia 189 L14
Kabala, Sierra Leone 200 F6
Kabale, Uganda 198 K12
Kabalo, Dem. Rep. of the Congo 198 M11
Kabambare, Dem. Rep. of the Congo 198 L11
Kabara, island, Fiji Is. 218 K9
Kabarei, Indonesia 189 J17
Kabbenbock, island, Marshall Is. 216 M8
Kabinda, Dem. Rep. of the Congo 198 M10
Kabīr, river, Leb., Syr. 170 G7
Kabol (Kabul), Afghan. 176 M8
Kabong, Malaysia 188 H10
Kabongo, Dem. Rep. of the Congo 198 M11
Kabūd Gombad, Iran 173 B16
Kabul, river, Afghan. 176 M8
Kabul see Kabol, Afghan. 176 M8
Kabuli, P.N.G. 213 B19
Kabumbé, Pico, Sao Tome and Principe 205 D20
Kaburuang, island, Indonesia 189 G16
Kabwe, Zambia 202 E11
Kachīry, Kaz. 175 B15
Kachreti, Rep. of Georgia 169 C19
Kaçkar Dağı, Turk. 169 D15
Kadaingti, Myanmar 186 K7
Kadan Kyun, Myanmar 187 N7
Kadavu, island, Fiji Is. 218 K6
Kadavu Passage, Fiji Is. 218 J6
Kadé, Guinea 200 E5
Kadıköy, Turk. 168 D3
Kading, river, Laos 186 K11
Kadınhanı, Turk. 168 G7
Kadiri, India 179 P6
Kadirli, Turk. 168 H11
Kadivka, Ukr. 157 Q10
Kadmat Island (Cardamum Island), India 179 Q3
Kadoka, S. Dak., U.S. 104 L3
Kadokura Zaki, Japan 185 U4
Kadom, Russ. 156 K12
Kadoma, Zimb. 202 F11
Kadugli, Sudan 198 F12
Kaduna, Nigeria 201 F14
Kadur, India 179 P5
Kadyy, Russ. 156 G12
Kaédi, Mauritania 196 G5
Kaélé, Cameroon 201 F17
Ka‘ena Point, Hawai‘i, U.S. 112 D10
Ka‘eo, peak, Hawai‘i, U.S. 112 C3
Kaeo, N.Z. 213 H18
Kaesŏng, N. Korea 182 E13
Kāf, Saudi Arabia 172 E6
Kafar Jar Ghar Range, Afghan. 177 P6
Kafia Kingi, Sudan 198 G10
Kafiéas, Akrotírio, Gr. 155 J14
Kafue, river, Zambia 202 E10
Kafue, Zambia 202 E10
Kafuka, Japan 184 D13
Kaga, Japan 185 N9
Kaga Bandoro, Cen. Af. Rep. 198 G9
Kagan, Pak. 176 M11
Kağızman, Turk. 169 E17
Kagmar, Sudan 198 E12
Kagoshima, Japan 185 T4
Kahakuloa, Hawai‘i, U.S. 113 F16
Kahalu‘u, Hawai‘i, U.S. 112 E11
Kahalu‘u, Hawai‘i, U.S. 113 M18
Kahama, Tanzania 199 L13
Kahan, Pak. 177 S7
Kahana, Hawai‘i, U.S. 113 G15
Kahe‘a Heiau and Petroglyphs, Hawai‘i, U.S. 113 G15
Kahei Homesteads, Hawai‘i, U.S. 113 K19
Kahemba, Dem. Rep. of the Congo 198 M8
Kāhili, peak, Hawai‘i, U.S. 112 B5
Kahlotus, Wash., U.S. 108 D8
Kahnūj, Iran 173 G16
Kahoka, Mo., U.S. 105 Q13
Kaho‘olawe, island, Hawai‘i, U.S. 113 H15
Kahouanne, Îlet à, Guadeloupe, Fr. 121 E14
Kahramanmaraş, Turk. 168 H12
Kâhta, Turk. 169 H13
Kahuku, Hawai‘i, U.S. 112 D11
Kahuku, Hawai‘i, U.S. 113 P19
Kahuku Point, Hawai‘i, U.S. 112 D11
Kahului, Hawai‘i, U.S. 113 G16
Kahului Harbor, Hawai‘i, U.S. 113 G16
Kahuwa‘a (Sacred Falls), Hawai‘i, U.S. 112 D11
Kai, Kepulauan (Ewab), Indonesia 189 L18
Kaiama, Nigeria 200 F12
Kaibab Plateau, Ariz., U.S. 84 H6
Kaibara, Japan 185 Q8
Kaibito, Ariz., U.S. 107 Q8
Kaieteur Fall, Guyana 129 E14
Kaifeng, China 182 H5
Kaifu, Japan 185 R7
Kaiholena, peak, Hawai‘i, U.S. 113 P20
Kai Kecil, island, Indonesia 189 L18
Kaikoura, N.Z. 213 N18
Kailu, China 182 A9
Kailua, Hawai‘i, U.S. 112 E12
Kailua, Hawai‘i, U.S. 113 M18
Kaimana, Indonesia 213 C15
Kaimu Beach (Black Sand Beach), Hawai‘i, U.S. 113 N22
Kainji Reservoir, Nigeria 201 F13
Kaipara Harbour, N.Z. 213 J18
Kaiserslautern, Ger. 148 H6
Kaishantun, China 182 A14
Kaitaia, N.Z. 213 H18
Ka‘iwaloa Heiau and Olowalu Petroglyphs, Hawai‘i, U.S. 113 G16
Kaiwi Channel, Hawai‘i, U.S. 112 F12
Kaixian, China 182 K1
Kaiyuan, China 182 B11
Kaiyuan, China 180 P11
Kaiyuh Mountains, Alas., U.S. 111 G14
Kajaani, Fin. 141 G16
Kajabbi, Qnsld., Austral. 211 S11
Kajaki, Afghan. 177 P4
Kajaki, Band-e, Afghan. 177 P4
Kajang, Malaysia 187 U9

Kajiki, Japan 185 T4
Kaka, Sudan 199 F13
Kaka, Turkm. 174 M9
Kākā, Lae 'O, Hawai'i, U.S. 113 H16
Kakamas, S. Af. 202 K8
Kakana, India 179 S14
Kakaramea, N.Z. 213 L18
Kakdwip, India 178 J11
Kake, Alas., U.S. 111 L22
Kake, Japan 185 Q6
Kakeroma Jima, Japan 185 W3
Kākhk, Iran 173 D16
Kakhovka, Ukr. 157 R7
Kakhovka Reservoir, Ukr. 138 G11
Kakinada (Cocanada), India 178 M8
Kakogawa, Japan 185 Q8
Kakshaal Range, China, Kyrg. 176 F14
Kaktovik, Alas., U.S. 111 C18
Kakuda, Japan 184 M13
Kala, Azerb. 169 D23
Kalaallit Nunaat see Greenland, N. Amer. 81 C21
Kalabagh, Pak. 177 P9
Kalabakan, Malaysia 188 G12
Kalabo, Zambia 202 E9
Kalach, Russ. 157 N11
Kalach na Donu, Russ. 157 P12
Kalae (South Point), Hawai'i, U.S. 113 Q19
Kalafrana, Malta 161 L23
Kalahari Desert, Botswana, Namibia 202 H8
Kalāheo, Hawai'i, U.S. 112 C5
Kal'ai Khumb, Taj. 176 J9
Kalalea, Heiau o, Hawai'i, U.S. 113 Q19
Kalalua, peak, Hawai'i, U.S. 113 N21
Kalam, Pak. 176 L10
Kalama, Wash., U.S. 108 E3
Kalamáta, Gr. 154 L9
Kalamazoo, river, Mich., U.S. 98 M9
Kalamazoo, Mich., U.S. 98 M10
Kalambáka, Gr. 154 E9
Kálamos, island, Gr. 154 H7
Kalamotí, Gr. 155 J16
Kalannie, W. Aust., Austral. 211 W3
Kalao, island, Indonesia 189 M13
Kalaoa, Hawai'i, U.S. 113 M18
Kalaotoa, island, Indonesia 189 M14
Kalasin, Thai. 186 L10
Kalat see Qalat, Afghan. 177 P6
Kalat, Pak. 177 S5
Kalaupapa, Hawai'i, U.S. 113 F14
Kalaupapa National Historic Park, Hawai'i, U.S. 113 F14
Kalávrita, Gr. 154 J9
Kalawao, site, Hawai'i, U.S. 113 F15
Kalaýmor, Turkm. 174 N10
Kalay-wa, Myanmar 186 F5
Kalb, Ra's al, Yemen 172 Q11
Kälbäjär, Azerb. 169 E20
Kalbān, Oman 173 M17
Kalbarri, W. Aust., Austral. 211 V1
Kaldar, Afghan. 176 K6
Kale, Turk. 168 J5
Kalealoa, cape, Hawai'i, U.S. 112 E10
Kale Burnu, Turk. 169 D14
Kalecik, Turk. 168 E9
Kaledupa, island, Indonesia 189 L14
Kalemie, Dem. Rep. of the Congo 198 M12
Kalemyo, Myanmar 186 F5
Kalenyy, Kaz. 174 D6
Kaleybar, Iran 172 A11
Kalgoorlie, W. Aust., Austral. 211 W4
Kaliakoúda, peak, Gr. 154 G9
Kaliakra, Nos, Bulg. 153 H18
Kalianda, Indonesia 188 L8
Kalihi Wai, Hawai'i, U.S. 112 B5
Kalihi Wai Bay, Hawai'i, U.S. 112 A6
Kalí Límni, Gr. 155 P18
Kalima, Dem. Rep. of the Congo 198 K11
Kalimantan see Borneo, region, Indonesia 188 J10
Kálimnos, island, Gr. 155 L18
Kálimnos, Gr. 155 L18
Kalimpang, India 178 G11
Kaliningrad, Russ. 156 J1
Kaliningrad Oblast, Russ. 156 J2
Kalinino, Arm. 169 C18
Kalinino, Russ. 157 S10
Kalininsk, Russ. 156 M13
Kalinkavichy, Belarus 156 M5
Kalispell, Mont., U.S. 106 B5
Kalisz, Pol. 149 E14
Kalix, Sw. 141 F14
Kalkan, Turk. 168 J5
Kalkaska, Mich., U.S. 98 J10
Kallithéa, Gr. 154 J12
Kallsjön, lake, Sw. 140 H12
Kalmar, Sw. 141 N13
Kalnai, India 178 J9
Kalnik, peak, Croatia 152 D6
Kalo Chorio, Cyprus 160 Q7
Kalohi Channel, Hawai'i, U.S. 113 G14
Kaloko-Honokōhau National Historic Park, Hawai'i, U.S. 113 M18
Kaloli Point, Hawai'i, U.S. 113 M22
Kaloní, Gr. 155 F16
Kalonís, Kólpos, Gr. 155 G16
Kalpa, India 178 D6
Kalpeni Island, India 179 R3
Kalpitiya, Sri Lanka 179 S7
Kalskag, Alas., U.S. 111 J13
Kalsubai, peak, India 178 L4
Kaltag, Alas., U.S. 111 G14
Kaluga, Russ. 156 K9
Kalumburu, W. Aust., Austral. 211 Q6
Kalush, Ukr. 157 P2
Kal'ya, Russ. 158 G9
Kalyan, India 178 L3
Kalyazin, Russ. 156 H9
Kama, river, Russ. 158 H8
Kamaing, Myanmar 186 E6
Kamaishi, Japan 184 K14
Kamakal, island, Fr. Polynesia, Fr. 219 R20
Kamakou, peak, Hawai'i, U.S. 113 F15
Kamalino, Hawai'i, U.S. 112 C3
Kaman, Turk. 168 F9
Kamárai, Gr. 155 L14
Kamarān, island, Yemen 172 P8
Kama Reservoir, Russ. 138 C13
Kamariotissa, Gr. 155 D15
Kamarod, Pak. 177 T3
Kamar Zard, Afghan. 177 N2
Kambang, Indonesia 188 K6
Kambanós, Akrotírio, Gr. 155 J14
Kambove, Dem. Rep. of the Congo 198 N11
Kamchatka, Poluostrov, Russ. 159 F22
Kamchatka Peninsula see Kamchatskiy Poluostrov, Russ. 166 C13
Kamchatskiy Poluostrov, Russ. 159 E22
Kamchiya, river, Bulg. 153 H17
Kamdesh, Afghan. 176 L9
Kamehameha I Birthplace, Hawai'i, U.S. 113 J18
Kamen, Gora, Russ. 159 G14
Kaména Voúrla, Gr. 154 G11
Kamenka, Kaz. 174 C6
Kamenka, Russ. 156 L12
Kamenka, Russ. 158 E9
Kamenskiy, Russ. 157 N13
Kamensk Shakhtinskiy, Russ. 157 Q11
Kamensk Ural'skiy, Russ. 158 J9
Kamiah, Idaho, U.S. 106 D4
Kamieskroon, S. Af. 202 L7
Kamileroi, Qnsld., Austral. 211 S11
Kamiloloa, Hawai'i, U.S. 113 F14
Kamina, Dem. Rep. of the Congo 198 M10
Kamin'-Kashyrs'kyy, Ukr. 156 M3
Kaminone Shima, Japan 185 W3
Kamino Shima, Japan 185 Q3
Kamitsuki, Japan 185 R12
Kamitsushima, Japan 185 Q3
Kamiyaku, Japan 185 U4
Kamkhat Muḩaywir, ruin, Jordan 171 N7
Kamloops, B.C., Can. 82 M9
Kammuri, peak, Japan 185 Q6
Kamo, Arm. 169 D19
Kamoa Mountains, Guyana 129 G14
Kamoenai, Japan 184 F12
Kamōhio Bay, Hawai'i, U.S. 113 H16
Kamoke, Pak. 177 P12
Kamo'oloa, Hawai'i, U.S. 112 D10
Kampala, Uganda 199 K13
Kampar, Malaysia 187 T9
Kampen, Neth. 146 H13
Kamphaeng Phet, Thai. 186 L8
Kâmpóng Cham, Cambodia 187 N12
Kampong Kuala Besut, Malaysia 187 S10
Kampos, Cyprus 160 P6
Kampot, Cambodia 187 P11
Kamrau, Teluk, Indonesia 213 C15
Kamsack, Sask., Can. 83 M13
Kamsar, Guinea 200 F4
Kamuela see Waimea, Hawai'i, U.S. 113 K19
Kamui Misaki, Japan 184 F12
Kam'yanets'-Podil's'kyy, Ukr. 157 P3
Kam'yanka-Dniprovs'ka, Ukr. 157 R8
Kamyshin, Russ. 157 N13
Kamyzyak, Russ. 157 R15
Kanab, Utah, U.S. 107 Q6
Kanab Creek, Ariz., Utah, U.S. 107 Q6
Kanacea, island, Fiji Is. 218 H9
Kanaga Island, Alas., U.S. 110 N5
Kanak, river, Turk. 168 E10
Kanaláki, Gr. 154 F7
Kananga, Dem. Rep. of the Congo 198 L10
Kanapou Bay, Hawai'i, U.S. 113 H16
Kanarraville, Utah, U.S. 107 P6
Kanash, Russ. 156 J14
Kanatea, island, Tonga 218 J11
Kanawha, river, W. Va., U.S. 96 D7
Kanazawa, Japan 185 N9
Kanbalu, Myanmar 186 F6
Kanchenjunga, peak, India, Nepal 178 F11
Kanchipuram, India 179 Q7
Kandahar, Afghan. 177 Q5
Kandalaksha, Russ. 158 D8
Kandalakshskiy Zaliv, Russ. 158 D8
Kandangan, Indonesia 188 K11
Kándanos, Gr. 154 Q12
Kandersteg, Switz. 150 C3
Kandhkot, Pak. 177 T8
Kandi, Benin 200 F12
Kandi, India 178 H11
Kandiaro, Pak. 177 U7
Kandíla, Gr. 154 K10
Kandıra, Turk. 168 C6
Kandrach, Pak. 177 V5
Kandrian, P.N.G. 213 D20
Kandudu, island, Maldives 179 W3
Kandudu, island, Maldives 179 X3
Kandu-ye Bala, Afghan. 177 N5
Kandy, Sri Lanka 179 T7
Kane, Pa., U.S. 94 L5
Kane Basin, Nunavut, Can. 83 B16
Kane Fracture Zone, Atl. Oc. 236 K7
Kanengo, Note, Solomon Is. 217 P22
Kāne'ohe, Hawai'i, U.S. 112 E11
Kanevskaya, Russ. 157 S10
Kang, Afghan. 177 Q2
Kangaamiut, Greenland, Den. 81 D21
Kangal, Turk. 168 F12
Kangan, Iran 173 G13
Kangān, Iran 173 H16
Kanganpur, Pak. 177 Q12
Kangar, Malaysia 187 S8
Kangaroo Island, S. Aust., Austral. 211 Y10
Kangbao, China 182 B6
Kangding, China 180 L11
Kangean, Kepulauan, Indonesia 188 M11
Kangeeak Point, Nunavut, Can. 83 F19
Kangerlussuaq, Greenland, Den. 81 D21
Kangertittivaq, bay, N. Amer. 80 B10
Kanggava Bay, Solomon Is. 217 Q19
Kanggye, N. Korea 182 C13
Kangiqsualujjuaq, Que., Can. 83 J20
Kangiqsujuaq, Que., Can. 83 J18
Kangirsuk, Que., Can. 83 J19
Kangmar, China 180 M7
Kango, Gabon 201 K15
Kangping, China 182 B11
Kangpokpi, India 178 G14
Kangrinboqê Feng, peak, China 180 K5
Kangto, peak, China, India 178 F14
Kaniama, Dem. Rep. of the Congo 198 M10
Kaniere, N.Z. 213 N17
Kanif, F.S.M. 217 D18
Kanigiri, India 179 N7
Kanin, Poluostrov, Russ. 158 E9
Kanin Nos, Mys, Russ. 158 D9
Kanin Peninsula see Kanin, Poluostrov, Russ. 138 A11
Kanish, ruin, Turk. 168 F10
Kanita, Japan 184 J13
Kaniv, Ukr. 157 P6
Kanjarkot, site, Pak. 177 W8
Kanjiža, Serb. & Mont. 152 D10
Kankakee, Ill., U.S. 99 P7
Kankakee, river, Ill., Ind., U.S. 99 P8
Kankan, Guinea 200 F7
Kanker, India 178 K8
Kanmaw Kyun, Myanmar 187 P7
Kanmen, China 183 N10
Kannapolis, N.C., U.S. 96 H9
Kannari, Japan 184 L13
Kannauj, India 178 G7
Kano, Nigeria 201 E14
Kanokupolu, Tonga 218 H11
Kanopolis, Kans., U.S. 105 T7
Kanorado, Kans., U.S. 105 S3
Kanosh, Utah, U.S. 107 N6
Kanoya, Japan 185 T4
Kanpur, India 178 G7
Kansas, river, Kans., U.S. 105 S8
Kansas, U.S. 105 T4
Kansas City, Kans., U.S. 105 S10
Kansas City, Mo., U.S. 105 S10
Kansk, Russ. 159 K14
Kant, Kyrg. 176 D11
Kantankufri, Ghana 200 G11
Kantara Castle, Cyprus 160 N10
Kanton, island, Kiribati 214 G10
Kanuku Mountains, Guyana 129 F14
Kanye, Botswana 202 J9
Kao, island, Tonga 218 P6
Kaohsiung, Taiwan, China 183 S9
Kaoka Bay, Solomon Is. 217 N19
Kaokoland, region, Namibia 202 G5
Kaolack, Senegal 196 H4
Kaoma, Zambia 202 E9
Kapa, island, Tonga 218 M11
Kapa'a, Hawai'i, U.S. 112 B6
Kapa'au, Hawai'i, U.S. 113 K19
Kapadvanj, India 178 J3
Kapan, Arm. 169 F20
Kapanga, Dem. Rep. of the Congo 198 M10
Kapela, range, Croatia 152 E5
Kapfenberg, Aust. 148 L12
Kapıdağı, peak, Turk. 168 D4
Kapingamarangi Atoll, F.S.M. 214 G5
Kapiri Mposhi, Zambia 202 E11
Kapisillit, Greenland, Den. 81 D22
Kapiskau, river, Ont., Can. 83 M17
Kapit, Malaysia 188 H10
Kaplan, La., U.S. 100 Q8
Kapoeta, Sudan 199 H13
Kapoho Crater, Hawai'i, U.S. 113 M22
Kaposvár, Hung. 149 N14
Kappar, Pak. 177 V2
Kapuāiwa Coconut Grove, Hawai'i, U.S. 113 F14
Kapulena, Hawai'i, U.S. 113 K20
Kapunda, S. Aust., Austral. 211 X10
Kapurthala, India 178 D5
Kapuskasing, Ont., Can. 83 N17
Kapydzhik, peak, Arm. 169 F20
Kara-Balta, Kyrg. 176 E11
Karabiga, Turk. 168 D3
Karabogaz (Bekdash), Turkm. 174 J6
Karabük, Turk. 168 C8
Kara Burun, Turk. 168 J7
Karaburun, peninsula, Albania 152 M9
Karaburun, Turk. 168 F2
Karacabey, Turk. 168 D4
Karaca Dağ, Turk. 169 H14
Karacadağ, Turk. 169 H14
Karacaköy, Turk. 168 C4
Karachala, Azerb. 169 E22
Karachev, Russ. 156 L8
Karachi, Pak. 177 W6
Karad, India 178 M4
Kara Dağ, Turk. 169 H18
Kara Dağ, Turk. 168 H8
Karadag, Azerb. 169 D23
Karaginskiy, Ostrov, Russ. 159 E22
Karahallı, Turk. 168 G5
Karahüyük, Turk. 168 G7
Karaisalı, Turk. 168 H10
Karaj, Iran 172 C12
Karakeçi, Turk. 169 H14
Karakelong, island, Indonesia 189 G16
Karakoçan, Turk. 169 F14
Kara-Köl, Kyrg. 176 F10
Karakol (Przheval'sk), Kyrg. 176 E14
Karakoram Pass, China, India 176 L14
Karakoram Range, India, Pak. 176 K12
Karakul', Taj. 176 H11
Karakulino, Russ. 156 H16
Karakuwisa, Namibia 202 G8
Karam, Russ. 159 K15
Karaman, Turk. 168 H8
Karamay, China 180 D7
Karamea, N.Z. 213 M17
Karamea Bight, N.Z. 213 M17
Karamürsel, Turk. 168 D5
Karanja, India 178 K6
Karapınar, Turk. 168 H9
Kara-Say, Kyrg. 176 E14
Karasburg, Namibia 202 K7
Kara Sea, Arctic Oc. 242 C11
Karasjok, Nor. 141 C14
Karas Mountains, Namibia 194 Q7
Karasu, river, Turk. 169 E15
Karasu, river, Turk. 169 F18
Karasu, Turk. 168 C6
Karasuk, Russ. 158 K11
Karataş, Turk. 168 J10
Karatepe, Turk. 168 H11
Karathuri, Myanmar 187 P7
Karatsu, Japan 185 R4
Karatung, island, Indonesia 189 G16
Karaul, Russ. 159 F13
Karavas, Cyprus 160 N8
Karávia, island, Gr. 154 M12
Karavostasi, Cyprus 160 P7
Karavostassás, Gr. 155 M14
Karawanken, range, Slov. 152 C4
Karayazı, Turk. 169 E16
Karayün, Turk. 168 E12
Karbalā', Iraq 172 E9
Karcag, Hung. 149 L16
Kardámila, Gr. 155 H16
Kardamíli, Gr. 154 L10
Kardítsa, Gr. 154 F9
Kardiva (Karidu), island, Maldives 179 U3
Kardiva Channel, Maldives 179 U3
Kärdla, Est. 141 K15
Karesuando, Sw. 141 D14
Kargı, Turk. 168 D10
Kargil, India 176 M13
Kargilik see Yecheng, China 180 G4
Kari, Nigeria 201 F15
Kariba, Zimb. 202 F11
Kariba, Lake, Zambia, Zimb. 202 F10
Karidu see Kardiva, island, Maldives 179 U3
Kariés, Gr. 154 L10
Karikari, Cape, N.Z. 213 H18
Karimata, island, Indonesia 188 K9
Karimata, Kepulauan, Indonesia 188 K9
Karimganj, India 178 H14
Karimnagar, India 178 L7
Karimunjawa, Kepulauan, Indonesia 188 L9
Káristos, Gr. 155 J13
Karitane, N.Z. 213 Q16
Karítena, Gr. 154 K9
Karizak, Afghan. 177 P1
Karkar, island, P.N.G. 213 C19
Karkinits'ka Zatoka, Ukr. 157 S7
Karkūk (Kirkuk), Iraq 172 C9
Karlıova, Turk. 169 F15
Karlovac, Croatia 152 E5
Karlovássi, Gr. 155 J17
Karlovy Vary, Czech Rep. 148 G10
Karlshamn, Sw. 141 N13
Karlskrona, Sw. 141 N13
Karlsruhe, Ger. 148 J6
Karlstad, Minn., U.S. 104 E8
Karlstad, Sw. 140 L12
Karmala, India 178 L4
Karmir Blur, ruin, Arm. 169 E18
Karnali, river, Nepal 178 E8
Karnaphuli Reservoir, Bangladesh 178 J14
Karnes City, Tex., U.S. 103 S10
Karnobat (Polyanovgrad), Bulg. 153 J16
Karoi, Zimb. 202 F11
Karokh, Afghan. 176 M2
Karoko, Fiji Is. 218 G8
Karompa, island, Indonesia 189 M14
Karonga, Malawi 203 C13
Karonie, W. Aust., Austral. 211 W5
Karosa, Indonesia 189 K13
Karpasia Peninsula, Cyprus 160 M11
Kárpathos, Gr. 155 P18
Kárpathos (Carpathos), island, Gr. 155 P18
Kárpathos Stenón, Gr. 155 P19
Karpeníssi, Gr. 154 G9
Karperó, Gr. 154 E9
Karratha, W. Aust., Austral. 211 S2
Karre Mountains, Cen. Af. Rep. 194 H6
Karridale, W. Aust., Austral. 211 Y2
Kars, Turk. 169 D17
Kartal, Turk. 168 C5
Karumba, Qnsld., Austral. 211 R11
Kārūn, river, Iran 172 F11
Karunjie, W. Aust., Austral. 211 Q6
Karviná, Czech Rep. 149 H14
Karwar, India 179 N4
Karwi, India 178 H8
Karyaí, Gr. 155 D13
Kar'yepol'ye, Russ. 158 E9
Karynzharyk, desert, Kaz. 174 J6
Kaş, Turk. 168 J5
Kas, Sudan 198 E10

Kasai, river, *Angola, Dem. Rep. of the Congo* **194** K7
Kasaji, *Dem. Rep. of the Congo* **198** N10
Kasama, *Zambia* **202** C12
Kasane, *Botswana* **202** F9
Kasar, Ras, *Eritrea* **199** D15
Kasaragod, *India* **179** Q4
Kasari, *Japan* **185** W3
Kasari Saki, *Japan* **185** W3
Kasba Lake, *N.W.T., Nunavut, Can.* **82** J13
Kasempa, *Zambia* **202** E10
Kasenga, *Dem. Rep. of the Congo* **198** N11
Kasese, *Dem. Rep. of the Congo* **198** K11
Kasganj, *India* **178** F6
Kasha-Katuwe Tent Rocks National Monument, *N. Mex., U.S.* **107** R12
Kāshān, *Iran* **173** D13
Kashgar *see* Kashi, *China* **180** F4
Kashi (Kashgar), *China* **180** F4
Kashin, *Russ.* **156** H9
Kashira, *Russ.* **156** K9
Kashiwazaki, *Japan* **184** M11
Kashkandyow, *Afghan.* **176** K10
Kāshmar, *Iran* **173** C16
Kashmir, region, *China, India, Pak.* **176** M12
Kashmir, Vale of, *India* **176** M12
Kashmor, *Pak.* **177** T8
Kasimov, *Russ.* **156** K11
Kasiruta, island, *Indonesia* **189** J16
Kaskaskia, river, *Ill., U.S.* **99** S6
Kaskö, *Fin.* **141** H14
Kasongo, *Dem. Rep. of the Congo* **198** L11
Kasongo-Lunda, *Dem. Rep. of the Congo* **198** M8
Kaspiysk, *Russ.* **157** U15
Kaspiyskiy, *Russ.* **157** S15
Kassala, *Sudan* **199** E14
Kassándra, peninsula, *Gr.* **154** E12
Kassándra, *Gr.* **154** E12
Kassándras, Kólpos, *Gr.* **154** D12
Kassel, *Ger.* **148** F7
Kassiópi, *Gr.* **154** E6
Kasson, *Minn., U.S.* **104** L12
Kássos, island, *Gr.* **155** Q18
Kássos Stenón, *Gr.* **155** Q17
Kastamonu, *Turk.* **168** C9
Kastaniés, *Gr.* **155** A17
Kastéli *see* Kíssamos, *Gr.* **154** Q12
Kastéli, *Gr.* **155** Q15
Kastellórizon *see* Megísti, island, *Gr.* **155** N22
Kastélou, Akrotírio, *Gr.* **155** Q18
Kastoriá, *Gr.* **154** C8
Kastorías, Límni, *Gr.* **154** D8
Kasumiga Ura, lake, *Japan* **185** P13
Kasumkent, *Russ.* **157** V16
Kasur, *Pak.* **177** Q12
Katafaga, island, *Fiji Is.* **218** H9
Katahdin, Mount, *Me., U.S.* **95** D17
Katákolo, *Gr.* **154** K8
Katanga, region, *Dem. Rep. of the Congo* **198** N11
Katanga Plateau, *Dem. Rep. of the Congo, Zambia* **194** M8
Katanning, *W. Aust., Austral.* **211** Y3
Katápola, *Gr.* **155** M16
Kata Tjuta *see* Olga, Mount, peak, *Austral.* **210** G7
Katavía, *Gr.* **155** N19
Katchall Island, *India* **179** S15
Kateríni, *Gr.* **154** D10
Kates Needle, peak, *Alas., U.S., B.C., Can.* **111** L23
Katha, *Myanmar* **186** F6
Katherîna, Gebel, *Egypt* **171** T3
Katherine, river, *Austral.* **210** B8
Katherine, *N. Terr., Austral.* **211** Q8
Kathiawar, region, *India* **178** J2
Kathmandu, *Nepal* **178** F10
Kathua, *India* **177** P13
Katiu, island, *Fr. Polynesia, Fr.* **219** E18
Katlanovo, *Maced.* **152** K11
Katmai, Mount, *Alas., U.S.* **111** L14
Katmai National Park and Preserve, *Alas., U.S.* **111** L15
Káto Ahaïa, *Gr.* **154** J8
Katohau, Baie, *Fr. Polynesia, Fr.* **219** M23
Kato Lakatameia, *Cyprus* **160** P8
Káto Nevrokópi, *Gr.* **154** B12
Katoomba, *N.S.W., Austral.* **211** Y14
Katowice, *Pol.* **149** G15
Katrancık Dağı, *Turk.* **168** H6
Katrine, Loch, *Scot., U.K.* **142** M9
Katsina, *Nigeria* **201** E14
Katsumoto, *Japan* **185** R3
Katsuyama, *Japan* **185** P9
Katsuyama, *Japan* **185** Q7
Kattankudi, *Sri Lanka* **179** T8
Kattaqo'rg'on, *Uzb.* **174** L12
Kattegat, strait, *Den., Sw.* **140** N12
Katun', river, *Russ.* **158** L12
Katwe, *Uganda* **198** K12
Katwijk aan Zee, *Neth.* **146** J12
Ka'ū, region, *Hawai'i, U.S.* **113** P20
Kau, *Indonesia* **189** H16
Kaua'i, island, *Hawai'i, U.S.* **112** B5
Kaua'i Channel, *Hawai'i, U.S.* **112** C8
Kauakaiakaola Heiau, *Hawai'i, U.S.* **113** M18
Kauehi, island, *Fr. Polynesia, Fr.* **219** E18
Kaufbeuren, *Ger.* **148** K8
Kaufman, *Tex., U.S.* **102** L12
Kauhako Crater, *Hawai'i, U.S.* **113** F14
Kaukauai, *P.N.G.* **217** K14
Kaukauna, *Wis., U.S.* **98** J6
Kaukura, island, *Fr. Polynesia, Fr.* **219** E17
Ka'ula, island, *Hawai'i, U.S.* **112** D1
Ka'ula Gulch, *Hawai'i, U.S.* **113** L20
Kaulakahi Channel, *Hawai'i, U.S.* **112** B3
Ka'ū Loa Point, *Hawai'i, U.S.* **113** N18
Kaulu Paoa Heiau, *Hawai'i, U.S.* **112** B5
Kaumakani, *Hawai'i, U.S.* **112** C5
Kaumalapau, *Hawai'i, U.S.* **113** G14
Kaūmana Cave, *Hawai'i, U.S.* **113** M21
Kaumu o Kaleiho'ohie, peak, *Hawai'i, U.S.* **113** K19
Kaunakakai, *Hawai'i, U.S.* **113** F14
Kaunakakai Harbour, *Hawai'i, U.S.* **113** F14
Kaunā Point, *Hawai'i, U.S.* **113** P18
Kaunas, *Lith.* **141** N16
Kaunolū, site, *Hawai'i, U.S.* **113** H14
Kaupakulua, *Hawai'i, U.S.* **113** G17
Kaupō, *Hawai'i, U.S.* **113** H18
Ka'ūpūlehu, site, *Hawai'i, U.S.* **113** L18
Kaura-Namoda, *Nigeria* **201** E14
Kautenbach, *Lux.* **160** H9
Kautokeino, *Nor.* **141** D14
Kavacha, *Russ.* **159** D22
Kavadarci, *Maced.* **152** K11
Kavajë, *Albania* **152** L9
Kavak, *Turk.* **168** D11
Kavála (Neapolis), *Gr.* **155** C13
Kavála, Kólpos, *Gr.* **155** C13
Kavalerovo, *Russ.* **159** L21
Kavali, *India* **179** N7
Kavaratti, *India* **179** R3
Kavieng, *P.N.G.* **213** B21
Kavīr, Dasht-e (Salt Desert), *Iran* **173** D14
Kavīr-e Namak, desert, *Iran* **173** D15
Kávos, *Gr.* **154** F6
Kawagoe, *Japan* **185** P12
Kawaihae, *Hawai'i, U.S.* **113** K19
Kawaihae Bay, *Hawai'i, U.S.* **113** L19
Kawaihoa Point, *Hawai'i, U.S.* **112** C3
Kawaikini, peak, *Hawai'i, U.S.* **112** B5
Kawakawa, *N.Z.* **213** H18
Kawambwa, *Zambia* **202** C11
Kawasaki, *Japan* **185** P12
Kawasak Passage, *Palau* **216** L12
Kawe, island, *Indonesia* **189** J17
Kawela, *Hawai'i, U.S.* **112** D11
Kawela, *Hawai'i, U.S.* **113** F14
Kawela Place of Refuge, *Hawai'i, U.S.* **113** F14
Kawhia, *N.Z.* **213** K19
Kawich Peak, *Nev., U.S.* **109** R10
Kawthoung, *Myanmar* **187** Q7
Kaya, *Burkina Faso* **200** E10
Kaya, *Indonesia* **188** H12
Kayan, river, *Indonesia* **188** H12
Kayangel Islands (Ngcheangel), *Palau* **216** K12
Kayangel Passage, *Palau* **216** K12
Kayapınar, *Turk.* **169** H15
Kaycee, *Wyo., U.S.* **106** G12
Kayenta, *Ariz., U.S.* **107** Q8
Kayes, *Congo* **201** M16
Kayes, *Mali* **196** H6
Kayl, *Lux.* **160** K9
Kaymaz, *Turk.* **168** E6
Kaynar, *Turk.* **168** F11
Kaysatskoye, *Russ.* **157** N14
Kayser Gebergte, peak, *Suriname* **129** F15
Kayseri, *Turk.* **168** F10
Kazach'ye, *Russ.* **159** E17
Kazakhstan, *Asia* **167** T6
Kazakh Uplands, *Kaz.* **175** D14
Kazan, river, *Nunavut, Can.* **83** H14
Kazan', *Russ.* **156** J14
Kazan Rettō *see* Volcano Islands, *Japan* **184** L5
Kazanskaya, *Russ.* **157** P11
Kazarman, *Kyrg.* **176** F11
Kazbek, peak, *Rep. of Georgia* **169** B18
Kaz Dağı, *Turk.* **168** E3
Kāzerūn, *Iran* **173** G13
Kazi Ahmad, *Pak.* **177** V7
Kazimierz Dolny, *Pol.* **149** F17
Kazincbarcika, *Hung.* **149** K16
Kaztalovka, *Kaz.* **174** D5
Kazym Mys, *Russ.* **158** G10
Kéa (Tziá), island, *Gr.* **155** K13
Kea'au, *Hawai'i, U.S.* **113** M22
Kea'au Ranch, *Hawai'i, U.S.* **113** M22
Keadu, island, *Maldives* **179** V3
Keāhole Point, *Hawai'i, U.S.* **113** M18
Kealaikahiki, Lae 'O, *Hawai'i, U.S.* **113** H15
Kealaikahiki Channel, *Hawai'i, U.S.* **113** H15
Kealakekua, *Hawai'i, U.S.* **113** M18
Keālia, *Hawai'i, U.S.* **112** B6
Keālia, *Hawai'i, U.S.* **113** N18
Kéamu *see* Anatom, island, *Vanuatu* **218** H4
Ke'anae, *Hawai'i, U.S.* **113** G17
Keanapapa Point, *Hawai'i, U.S.* **113** G14
Kearney, *Nebr., U.S.* **105** Q6
Keauhou, *Hawai'i, U.S.* **113** M18
Keauhou Landing, *Hawai'i, U.S.* **113** N21
Ke Avainiu Pass, *Solomon Is.* **217** J18
Keawanui Bay, *Hawai'i, U.S.* **112** C3
Keban, *Turk.* **169** F13
Kebnekaise, peak, *Sw.* **141** E13
Kech, river, *Pak.* **177** V3
Keçiborlu, *Turk.* **168** G6
Kecskemét, *Hung.* **149** M15
Kediri, *Indonesia* **188** M10
Kédougou, *Senegal* **196** J6
Kędzierzyn-Koźle, *Pol.* **149** G14
Ke'ei, *Hawai'i, U.S.* **113** N18
Keele, river, *N.W.T., Can.* **82** G10
Keele Peak, *N.W.T., Yukon, Can.* **82** G9
Keeler, *Calif., U.S.* **109** U8
Keelung, *Taiwan, China* **183** Q10
Keene, *N.H., U.S.* **95** J13
Keer-weer, Cape, *Austral.* **210** B11
Keetmanshoop, *Namibia* **202** J7
Keewatin, *Minn., U.S.* **104** F11
Kefaloniá (Cephalonia), island, *Gr.* **154** H7
Kéfalos, *Gr.* **155** M18
Kefaluka, *Turk.* **168** H3
Keflavík, *Ice.* **140** F1
Kegen, *Kaz.* **175** H17
Keg River, *Alta., Can.* **82** J10
Keheili, *Sudan* **199** C13
Kehl, *Ger.* **148** J5
Keila, *Est.* **141** K16
Kéita, Bahr, *Chad* **197** K15
Keitele, lake, *Fin.* **141** H16
Keith, *S. Aust., Austral.* **211** Y11
Keith, *Scot., U.K.* **142** J10
Keith Arm, *N.W.T., Can.* **82** F10
Keithsburg, *Ill., U.S.* **99** P3
Kekaha, *Hawai'i, U.S.* **112** C4
Kékes, peak, *Hung.* **149** K16
Kekirawa, *Sri Lanka* **179** S7
Keklau, *Palau* **216** M12
Kekra, *Russ.* **159** H20
Kekri, *India* **178** G4
Kel, *Pak.* **176** M12
K'elafo, *Eth.* **199** H16
Kelai, island, *Maldives* **179** T3
Kelan, *China* **182** D4
Kelang, island, *Indonesia* **189** K16
Kelang, *Malaysia* **187** U9
Këlcyrë, *Albania* **152** M10
Kelefesia, island, *Tonga* **218** R6
Keleft, *Afghan.* **176** K5
Kelheim, *Ger.* **148** J9
Kelkit, river, *Turk.* **168** D12
Kelkit, *Turk.* **169** E14
Ke Ila, island, *Solomon Is.* **217** J18
Keller Lake, *N.W.T., Can.* **82** G10
Kellet, Cape, *N.W.T., Can.* **82** D11
Kellits, *Jam.* **120** J9
Kells *see* Ceanannus Mór, *Ire.* **143** R6
Kélo, *Chad* **197** K14
Ke Loma, island, *Solomon Is.* **217** J18
Kelowna, *B.C., Can.* **82** M9
Kelso, *Calif., U.S.* **109** W11
Kelso, *Wash., U.S.* **108** E3
Keluang, *Malaysia* **187** V10
Kelvin Seamount Cap, *Atl. Oc.* **236** H5
Kem', *Russ.* **158** D8
Kema, *Indonesia* **189** H15
Kemah, *Turk.* **169** E13
Kemaliye, *Turk.* **169** F13
Kemasik, *Malaysia* **187** T10
Kembanye, Note, *Solomon Is.* **217** Q22
Kemer, *Turk.* **168** D3
Kemer, *Turk.* **168** G4
Kemer, *Turk.* **168** J5
Kemer, *Turk.* **168** J6
Kemerovo, *Russ.* **158** K12
Kemi, river, *Fin.* **138** B8
Kemi, *Fin.* **141** F15
Kemijärvi, lake, *Fin.* **141** E15
Kemijärvi, *Fin.* **141** E15
Kemijoki, river, *Fin.* **141** D15
Kemlya, *Russ.* **156** K13
Kemmerer, *Wyo., U.S.* **106** J8
Kemmuna *see* Comino, island, *Malta* **161** H21
Kemp, Lake, *Tex., U.S.* **102** J8
Kemp Coast, *Antarctica* **227** D20
Kempendyay, *Russ.* **159** H17
Kempopla, Note, *Solomon Is.* **217** Q22
Kemp Peninsula, *Antarctica* **226** E7
Kemps Bay, *Bahamas* **116** F11
Kempsey, *N.S.W., Austral.* **211** X15
Kempten, *Ger.* **148** L7
Kenai, *Alas., U.S.* **111** K16
Kenai Fjords National Park, *Alas., U.S.* **111** K16
Kenai Peninsula, *Alas., U.S.* **111** K16
Kendal, *Eng., U.K.* **143** Q11
Kendall, *Fla., U.S.* **97** X10
Kendall, *N.S.W., Austral.* **211** X15
Kendall, *N.Y., U.S.* **94** H6
Kendall, Cape, *Nunavut, Can.* **83** H16
Kendallville, *Ind., U.S.* **99** P10
Kendari, *Indonesia* **189** K14
Kendawangan, *Indonesia* **188** K9
Kendikolu, island, *Maldives* **179** T3
Kendrapara, *India* **178** K11
Këndrevicës, Maja e, *Albania* **152** M9
Kendrick, *Idaho, U.S.* **106** D3
Kenedy, *Tex., U.S.* **103** S10
Kenema, *Sierra Leone* **200** G6
Kèngkok, *Laos* **186** L11
Kengtung, *Myanmar* **186** H8
Kenhardt, *S. Af.* **202** K8
Kenitra, *Mor.* **196** B8
Kenli, *China* **182** F8
Kenmare, *Ire.* **143** U3
Kenmare, *N. Dak., U.S.* **104** E3
Kenmore, *Scot., U.K.* **142** L9
Kennebec, river, *Me., U.S.* **95** D16
Kennebec, *S. Dak., U.S.* **104** L5
Kennebunk, *Me., U.S.* **95** H15
Kennedy, Cape *see* Canaveral, Cape, *N. Amer.* **80** M8
Kennedy Channel, *Nunavut, Can.* **83** B16
Kennedy Entrance, *Alas., U.S.* **84** Q4
Kenner, *La., U.S.* **100** Q11
Kennett, *Mo., U.S.* **105** W15
Kennewick, *Wash., U.S.* **108** E7
Keno Hill, *Yukon, Can.* **82** F8
Kenora, *Ont., Can.* **83** N14
Kenosha, *Wis., U.S.* **98** M7
Kenova, *W. Va., U.S.* **96** D7
Kent, *Ohio, U.S.* **99** P15
Kent, *Oreg., U.S.* **108** F5
Kent, *Tex., U.S.* **103** N2
Kent, *Wash., U.S.* **108** C4
Kentland, *Ind., U.S.* **99** Q7
Kenton, *Ohio, U.S.* **99** Q12
Kent Peninsula, *Nunavut, Can.* **83** F13
Kentucky, river, *Ky., U.S.* **85** H17
Kentucky, *U.S.* **101** C14
Kentucky Lake, *Ky., U.S.* **101** D13
Kentwood, *La., U.S.* **100** N10
Kentwood, *Mich., U.S.* **98** L10
Kenutu, island, *Tonga* **218** L12
Kenya, *Af.* **195** J22
Kenya, Mount, *Kenya* **199** K14
Kenya Highlands, *Kenya* **194** K10
Kēōkea, *Hawai'i, U.S.* **113** H17
Kēōkea, *Hawai'i, U.S.* **113** N18
Ke'oke'o, Pu'u o, *Hawai'i, U.S.* **113** P19
Keokuk, *Iowa, U.S.* **105** Q14
Keōmuku, *Hawai'i, U.S.* **113** G15
Keonjhargarh, *India* **178** K10
Kep, *Cambodia* **187** P11
Kepi, *Indonesia* **189** M21
Kepi i Rodonit, *Albania* **152** K9
Kępno, *Pol.* **149** F14
Kepsut, *Turk.* **168** E4
Keramotí, *Gr.* **155** C14
Keran, *Pak.* **176** M11
Kerch, *Ukr.* **157** S9
Kerchenskiy Proliv, *Russ., Ukr.* **157** S9
Kerempe Burnu, *Turk.* **168** B9
Keren, *Eritrea* **199** D15
Kerens, *Tex., U.S.* **102** M12
Kerguélen Islands, *Ind. Oc.* **240** Q8
Kerguélen Plateau, *Ind. Oc.* **240** R9
Keri, *Gr.* **154** K7
Kerikeri, *N.Z.* **213** H18
Kerinci, peak, *Indonesia* **188** K6
Kerki *see* Atamyrat, *Turkm.* **174** M11
Kerkíni, *Gr.* **154** B11
Kerkínis, Límni, *Gr.* **154** B11
Kérkira, *Gr.* **154** E6
Kérkira (Corfu, Corcyra), island, *Gr.* **154** E6
Kermadec Islands, *N.Z.* **214** L9
Kermadec Trench, *Pac. Oc.* **238** P10
Kermān, *Iran* **173** F15
Kermānshāh, *Iran* **172** D11
Kermānshāhān, *Iran* **173** F14
Kermit, *Tex., U.S.* **102** M3
Kern, river, *Calif., U.S.* **109** V7
Kernersville, *N.C., U.S.* **96** G10
Kernville, *Calif., U.S.* **109** V8
Kéros, island, *Gr.* **155** L15
Kerr, Mount, *Bahamas* **120** E11
Kerrobert, *Sask., Can.* **82** M11
Kerrville, *Tex., U.S.* **103** Q8
Kerry Head, *Ire.* **143** T2
Kershaw, *S.C., U.S.* **96** K9
Kertamulia, *Indonesia* **188** J9
Keryneia (Kyrenia, Girne), *Cyprus* **160** N8
Keryneia Range, *Cyprus* **160** N9
Keşan, *Turk.* **168** C3
Keşap, *Turk.* **169** D13
Kesennuma, *Japan* **184** L13
Keshem, *Afghan.* **176** K8
Keshīt, *Iran* **173** F16
Keshod, *India* **178** K2
Keşiş Dağı, *Turk.* **169** E14
Keskal, *India* **178** L8
Keskin, *Turk.* **168** E9
Kes'ma, *Russ.* **156** G9
Keszthely, *Hung.* **149** M13
Ketanda, *Russ.* **159** G19
Ketaun, *Indonesia* **188** K6
Ketchikan, *Alas., U.S.* **111** M23
Ketchum, *Idaho, U.S.* **106** G5
Ketchum Mountain, *Tex., U.S.* **103** N6
Keti Bandar, *Pak.* **177** X6
Kettering, *Eng., U.K.* **143** T13
Kettering, *Ohio, U.S.* **99** R11
Kettle Falls, *Wash., U.S.* **108** A8
Kettle River Range, *Wash., U.S.* **108** A8
Keul', *Russ.* **159** K15
Kewanee, *Ill., U.S.* **99** P4
Kewaunee, *Wis., U.S.* **98** J7
Keweenaw Bay, *Mich., U.S.* **98** E6
Keweenaw National Historic Park, *Mich., U.S.* **98** E6
Keweenaw Peninsula, *Mich., U.S.* **98** E7
Keweenaw Point, *Mich., U.S.* **98** E7
Key, Lough, *Ire.* **143** R5
Keyano, *Que., Can.* **83** L19
Keya Paha, river, *S. Dak., U.S.* **104** M5
Key Colony Beach, *Fla., U.S.* **97** Y9
Keyes, *Okla., U.S.* **102** E4
Keyhole Reservoir, *Wyo., U.S.* **106** F13
Key Largo, *Fla., U.S.* **97** Y10
Keyser, *W. Va., U.S.* **96** C11
Keystone, *S. Dak., U.S.* **104** L2
Keystone, *W. Va., U.S.* **96** F8
Keystone Lake, *Okla., U.S.* **84** J12
Key West, *Fla., U.S.* **97** Y8
Kežmarok, *Slovakia* **149** J16
Khabarovsk, *Russ.* **159** K21
Khābūr, river, *Syr.* **170** D14
Khada Hills, *Afghan.* **177** Q5
Khadyzhensk, *Russ.* **157** T11
Khailino, *Russ.* **159** D21
Khairpur, *Pak.* **177** S10
Khairpur, *Pak.* **177** T7
Khakhar', *Russ.* **159** H19
Khalatse, *India* **176** M14
Khalūf, *Oman* **173** L16

Khambhaliya, India 178 J1
Khambhat, Gulf of, India 178 K3
Khamgaon, India 178 K5
Khamīs Mushayţ, Saudi Arabia 172 N8
Kham Khowrki, Afghan. 177 N3
Khammouan, Laos 186 K11
Khamr, Yemen 172 P9
Khanabad, Afghan. 176 K8
Khān Abū Shāmāt, Syr. 170 J8
Khanai, Pak. 177 R6
Khanaqa, Afghan. 176 K5
Khānaqīn, Iraq 172 D10
Khān az Zābīb, Jordan 171 N7
Khanderi Island, India 178 L3
Khandwa, India 178 K5
Khandyga, Russ. 159 G18
Khanewal, Pak. 177 R10
Khangarh, Pak. 177 T10
Khaniadhana, India 178 H6
Khanka, Lake see Khanka, Ozero, China, Russ. 166 E12
Khanka, Ozero see Xingkai Hu, China, Russ. 181 D19
Khanlar, Azerb. 169 D20
Khanozai, Pak. 177 R6
Khanpur, Pak. 177 S9
Khān Shaykhūn, Syr. 170 F8
Khan Tängiri (Lord of the Sky), peak, Kaz., Kyrg. 176 E15
Khantayskoye, Ozero, Russ. 159 G13
Khanty Mansiysk, Russ. 158 H10
Khān Yūnis, Gaza Strip 171 N4
Khapalu, Pak. 176 L13
Kharabali, Russ. 157 Q15
Kharagpur, India 178 J11
Khara Khoto see Heicheng, ruin, China 180 F11
Kharan, Pak. 177 T4
Kharānaq, Iran 173 E14
Kharasavey, Mys, Russ. 158 E11
Khârga Oasis, Egypt 197 E18
Khargon, India 178 K5
Khargūsh, Taj. 176 J10
Kharian, Pak. 177 P11
Khariar, India 178 K9
Kharimkotan, island, Russ. 159 H23
Khārk, island, Iran 172 G12
Kharkiv, Ukr. 157 P9
Kharlovka, Russ. 158 D9
Kharmanli, Bulg. 153 K15
Kharovsk, Russ. 156 F10
Khartoum, Sudan 199 E13
Khartoum North, Sudan 199 E13
Kharyyalakh, Russ. 159 G15
Khasavyurt, Russ. 157 T15
Khash, river, Afghan. 177 P4
Khash, Afghan. 177 Q3
Khāsh, Iran 173 G17
Khashābiya, Jabal al, Jordan 171 Q8
Khash Desert, Afghan. 177 P2
Khashuri, Rep. of Georgia 169 C17
Khasi Hills, India 178 G13
Khaskovo, Bulg. 153 K15
Khatanga, Russ. 159 F14
Khatangskiy Zaliv, Russ. 159 E15
Khātūnīyah, Syr. 170 D15
Khatyrka, Russ. 159 C21
Khaval, Afghan. 176 L5
Khavda, India 178 H2
Khaybar, Ḩarrat, Saudi Arabia 172 J7
Khaydarkan, Kyrg. 176 G9
Khemmarat, Thai. 186 L11
Khenjan, Afghan. 176 L7
Kherson, Ukr. 157 R7
Kherwara, India 178 H4
Kheta, Russ. 159 F14
Khewari, Pak. 177 U7
Kheyrabad, Afghan. 176 K6
Khimki, Russ. 156 J9
Khipro, Pak. 177 V8
Khiri Ratthanikhom, Thai. 187 Q8
Khiwa, Uzb. 174 K9
Khizy, Azerb. 169 C22
Khlevnoye, Russ. 156 M10
Khmel'nyts'kyy, Ukr. 157 P4
Khoai, Hon, Vietnam 187 R11
Khocho, Russ. 159 H18
Khodzhakala, Turkm. 174 L7
Khojak Pass, Pak. 177 Q5
Khokhol'skiy, Russ. 156 M10
Khokhropar, Pak. 177 V9
Khok Kloi, Thai. 187 R7
Kholm, Afghan. 176 K6
Kholm, Russ. 156 H6
Kholmsk, Russ. 159 K22
Không, Laos 186 M12
Khôngxédôn, Laos 186 L12
Khon Kaen, Thai. 186 L10
Khoper, river, Russ. 156 M12
Khorāsān, region, Iran 173 C15
Khormaleq, Afghan. 177 P2
Khorol, Ukr. 157 P7
Khorramābād, Iran 172 D11
Khorugh, Taj. 176 J9
Khost, Pak. 177 R6
Khost (Khowst), Afghan. 177 N8
Khowst see Khost, Afghan. 177 N8
Khoyniki, Belarus 156 M6
Khrenovoye, Russ. 157 N11
Khromtaū, Kaz. 174 D9
Khudabad, Pak. 176 K12
Khuiala, India 178 F2
Khujand, Taj. 176 G8
Khūjayli, Uzb. 174 J9
Khulkhuta, Russ. 157 R14
Khulna, Bangladesh 178 J12
Khunjerab Pass, China, Pak. 176 K12
Khunti, India 178 J10
Khunzakh, Russ. 157 U15
Khurda, India 178 K10
Khushab, Pak. 177 P10
Khust, Ukr. 157 P2
Khuzdar, Pak. 177 T5
Khvāf, Iran 173 C17
Khvajeh Mohammad Range, Afghan. 176 K9
Khvalynsk, Russ. 156 L14
Khvor, Iran 173 D14
Khvorostyanka, Russ. 156 L15
Khvoy, Iran 172 A10
Khwazagak, Afghan. 176 M5
Khyber Pass, Afghan., Pak. 176 M9
Kia, island, Fiji Is. 218 G7
Kia, Solomon Is. 217 L17
Kiakeana Point, Hawai'i, U.S. 113 H17
Kiama, N.S.W., Austral. 211 Y14
Kiamichi, river, Okla., U.S. 102 H13
Kiana, Alas., U.S. 111 E13
Kiáto, Gr. 154 J10
Kibombo, Dem. Rep. of the Congo 198 L11
Kibwezi, Kenya 199 K14
Kičevo, Maced. 152 K10
Kickapoo, Lake, Tex., U.S. 102 K9
Kidal, Mali 196 G10
Kidnappers, Cape, N.Z. 213 L20
Kidrenen, island, Marshall Is. 216 G8
Kidrinen, island, Marshall Is. 216 J8
Kiel, Ger. 148 B8
Kiel, Wis., U.S. 98 K7
Kielce, Pol. 149 F16
Kieler Bucht, Ger. 148 A8
Kien An, Vietnam 186 H12
Kien Duc, Vietnam 187 N13
Kieta, P.N.G. 217 K14
Kiev see Kyiv, Ukr. 157 N6
Kiffa, Mauritania 196 G6
Kifissiá, Gr. 154 J12
Kifissos, river, Gr. 154 H10
Kifrī, Iraq 172 D10
Kigali, Rwanda 198 K12
Kiğı, Turk. 169 F15
Kigoma, Tanzania 198 L12
Kīhei, Hawai'i, U.S. 113 G16
Kīholo Bay, Hawai'i, U.S. 113 L18
Ki'i, Hawai'i, U.S. 112 B3
Kii Suidō, Japan 185 R8
Kikaiga Shima, Japan 185 W3
Kikiakki, Russ. 158 H12
Kikinda, Serb. & Mont. 152 D10
Kikki, Pak. 177 V2
Kikládes (Cyclades), Gr. 155 L14
Kiknur, Russ. 156 H13
Kikori, river, P.N.G. 213 D18
Kikori, P.N.G. 213 D18
Kikwit, Dem. Rep. of the Congo 198 L8
Kil, river, Pak. 177 V3
Kilafors, Sw. 141 J13
Kilakkarai, India 179 S6
Kilambe, river, Nicar. 115 L18
Kilar, India 177 N13
Kīlauea, peak, Hawai'i, U.S. 113 N21
Kīlauea, Hawai'i, U.S. 112 B6
Kīlauea Lighthouse, Hawai'i, U.S. 112 A6
Kilbeggan, Ire. 143 S5
Kilbrannan Sound, Scot., U.K. 143 N8
Kilbride, Scot., U.K. 142 K6
Kilbuck Mountains, Alas., U.S. 111 J13
Kilcar, Ire. 143 P4
Kilchoman, Scot., U.K. 142 M7
Kilcock, Ire. 143 S6
Kilcowera, Qnsld., Austral. 211 V12
Kildonan, Scot., U.K. 142 H9
Kildrummy, Scot., U.K. 142 K10
Kilgore, Nebr., U.S. 104 M4
Kilgore, Tex., U.S. 102 L14
Kılıçkaya, Turk. 169 D16
Kili Island, Marshall Is. 216 H4
Kilimanjaro, peak, Tanzania 199 L14
Kilinailau Islands, P.N.G. 217 H14
Kılınç Tepesi, Turk. 169 D13
Kilíni, Gr. 154 J8
Kilíni, Óros, Gr. 154 J10
Kilinochchi, Sri Lanka 179 S7
Kilis, Turk. 168 J12
Kiliya, Ukr. 157 S5
Kilju, N. Korea 182 C14
Kilkee, Ire. 143 T3
Kilkenny, Ire. 143 T6
Kilkís, Gr. 154 C11
Killadysert, Ire. 143 T3
Killala Bay, Ire. 143 Q4
Killarney, Lake, Bahamas 120 B11
Killary Harbour, Ire. 143 R3
Killdeer, N. Dak., U.S. 104 F2
Killeen, Tex., U.S. 103 P10
Killiniq Island, Nunavut, Can. 83 J20
Killorglin, Ire. 143 U3
Kilmaluag, Scot., U.K. 142 J7
Kilmarnock, Scot., U.K. 143 N9
Kilombero, river, Tanzania 199 M14
Kilosa, Tanzania 199 M14
Kiltan Island, India 179 Q3
Kilwa Kivinje, Tanzania 199 N15
Kim, Colo., U.S. 107 P15
Kimaam, Indonesia 189 M20
Kimball, Nebr., U.S. 105 P1
Kimball, S. Dak., U.S. 104 L6
Kimbe Bay, P.N.G. 213 C21
Kimberley, B.C., Can. 82 M9
Kimberley, S. Af. 202 K9
Kimberley, region, W. Aust., Austral. 211 R6
Kimberley, Cape, Austral. 210 C13
Kimberley Plateau, Austral. 210 C6
Kimberly, Idaho, U.S. 106 H5
Kimch'aek (Sŏngjin), N. Korea 182 C14
Kimhyŏnggwŏn, N. Korea 182 C13
Kími, Gr. 155 H13
Kímis, Akrotírio, Gr. 155 H13
Kimmirut, Nunavut, Can. 83 H19
Kimobetsu, Japan 184 G13
Kímolos, island, Gr. 155 M14
Kimovsk, Russ. 156 K10
Kimry, Russ. 156 H9
Kinabalu, peak, Malaysia 188 G12
Kinadyeng, island, Marshall Is. 216 L8
Kínaros, island, Gr. 155 L16
Kinbrace, Scot., U.K. 142 H9
Kindadal, Indonesia 189 K14
Kinder, La., U.S. 100 P7
Kindia, Guinea 200 F5
Kindu, Dem. Rep. of the Congo 198 L11
Kinel', Russ. 156 K15
Kineshma, Russ. 156 H11
King Christian IX Land, N. Amer. 80 C10
King Christian X Land, N. Amer. 80 B9
King City, Calif., U.S. 109 U5
King City, Mo., U.S. 105 R10
King Cove, Alas., U.S. 110 N11
Kingfisher, Okla., U.S. 102 F10
Kingfisher Lake, Ont., Can. 83 M15
King Frederick VI Coast, N. Amer. 80 D10
King Frederik VIII Land, N. Amer. 80 A8
King George Bay, Falkland Is., U.K. 133 W12
King George Island, Antarctica 226 C3
King George Islands, Nunavut, Can. 83 K17
King George Sound, Austral. 210 L3
King George V Memorial Hospital, Gibraltar, U.K. 161 Q23
Kingisepp, Russ. 156 F6
King Island, Alas., U.S. 110 F11
King Island, Tas., Austral. 211 Y15
King Khalid Military City, Saudi Arabia 172 G10
King Lear Peak, Nev., U.S. 108 M8
King Leopold Ranges, Austral. 210 D5
Kingman, Ariz., U.S. 107 S5
Kingman, Kans., U.S. 105 U7
King Mountain, Tex., U.S. 103 N4
Kingoonya, S. Aust., Austral. 211 W9
King Peak, Antarctica 226 J11
Kingri, Pak. 177 R8
Kings, river, Calif., U.S. 109 T7
King Salmon, Alas., U.S. 111 L14
King's Bay, Trinidad & Tobago 121 N18
Kingsbridge, Eng., U.K. 143 X10
Kingsburg, Calif., U.S. 109 T6
Kings Canyon National Park, Calif., U.S. 109 T7
Kingscote, S. Aust., Austral. 211 Y10
King Sejong, station, Antarctica 226 C3
Kingsford, Mich., U.S. 98 G7
Kingsland, Ga., U.S. 97 Q8
King's Lynn, Eng., U.K. 143 T14
Kings Mountain, N.C., U.S. 96 J8
King Sound, Austral. 210 C4
Kings Peak, Utah, U.S. 106 L8
Kingsport, Tenn., U.S. 101 D20
Kingston, Jam. 120 J10
Kingston, N.Y., U.S. 94 L11
Kingston, Norfolk I., Austral. 217 G20
Kingston, Ont., Can. 83 Q19
Kingston, Pa., U.S. 94 M8
Kingston, Tas., Austral. 211 Z16
Kingston Harbour, Jam. 120 J10
Kingston South East, S. Aust., Austral. 211 Y10
Kingston upon Hull, Eng., U.K. 143 R13
Kingstown see Dún Laoghaire, Ire. 143 S7
Kingstown, St. Vincent & the Grenadines 121 L16
Kingstown Bay, St. Vincent & the Grenadines 121 L16
Kingstree, S.C., U.S. 96 L10
Kingsville, Tex., U.S. 103 U10
King Wilhelm Land, N. Amer. 80 A9
King William Island, Nunavut, Can. 83 F14
Kiniama, Dem. Rep. of the Congo 198 N11
Kinlochewe, Scot., U.K. 142 J8
Kinmen (Quemoy), island, Taiwan, China 183 R8
Kinnear, Wyo., U.S. 106 H10
Kinniyai, Sri Lanka 179 S8
Kino, river, Japan 185 Q8
Kinsale, Montserrat, U.K. 121 B23
Kinsale, Old Head of, Ire. 143 V4
Kinshasa (Léopoldville), Dem. Rep. of the Congo 198 L7
Kinsley, Kans., U.S. 105 U5
Kinston, N.C., U.S. 96 H13
Kintore, Scot., U.K. 142 K11
Kintyre, peninsula, Scot., U.K. 143 N8
Kinvarra, Ire. 143 S4
Kinyeti, peak, Sudan 199 H13
Kinzua, Oreg., U.S. 108 G6
Kioa, island, Fiji Is. 218 G8
Kiokluk Mountains, Alas., U.S. 111 J14
Kiowa, Colo., U.S. 106 M14
Kiowa, Kans., U.S. 105 V6
Kīpahulu, Hawai'i, U.S. 113 H18
Kiparissía, Gr. 154 L9
Kiparissiakós Kólpos, Gr. 154 K9
Kipili, Tanzania 198 M12
Kipini, Kenya 199 K15
Kipnuk, Alas., U.S. 110 K11
Kirakira, Solomon Is. 217 P20
Kirá Panagiá, island, Gr. 155 F13
Kiraz, Turk. 168 G4
Kirbey, Russ. 159 G15
Kirbymoorside, Eng., U.K. 143 Q13
Kirbyville, Tex., U.S. 103 P16
Kirensk, Russ. 159 K15
Kiri, Dem. Rep. of the Congo 198 K9
Kiribati, Pac. Oc. 214 G10
Kırıkhan, Turk. 168 J11
Kırıkkale, Turk. 168 E9
Kirishi, Russ. 156 F7
Kiritimati (Christmas Island), Kiribati 214 G12
Kiriwina, island, P.N.G. 213 E21
Kırka, Turk. 168 E6
Kırkağaç, Turk. 168 E3
Kirkcaldy, Scot., U.K. 142 M10
Kirkcolm, Scot., U.K. 143 P8
Kirkenes, Nor. 141 C15
Kırkgeçit, Turk. 169 G18
Kirkjubjarklaustur, Ice. 140 G3
Kirkland, Tex., U.S. 102 J7
Kirkland Lake, Ont., Can. 83 P18
Kırklar Dağı, Turk. 169 D15
Kırklareli, Turk. 168 B3
Kirkoswald, Scot., U.K. 143 N8
Kirksville, Mo., U.S. 105 R12
Kirkuk see Karkūk, Iraq 172 C9
Kirkwall, Scot., U.K. 142 G10
Kirkwood, Mo., U.S. 105 T15
Kirn, Ger. 148 H5
Kirov, Russ. 156 K8
Kirov, Russ. 158 G8
Kirovohrad, Ukr. 157 Q6
Kirovskiy, Russ. 157 R15
Kirsanov, Russ. 156 L12
Kırşehir, Turk. 168 F9
Kirthar Range, Pak. 177 U6
Kirtland, N. Mex., U.S. 107 Q10
Kiruna, Sw. 141 E13
Kirunu, island, Marshall Is. 216 G8
Kirwan Escarpment, Antarctica 226 B12
Kirya, Russ. 156 J14
Kiryū, Japan 185 N12
Kisakata, Japan 184 K12
Kisangani (Stanleyville), Dem. Rep. of the Congo 198 J10
Kish, island, Iran 173 H14
Kishanganj, India 178 G11
Kishangarh, India 178 F2
Kishangarh, India 178 G4
Kishb, Ḩarrat al, Saudi Arabia 172 K8
Kishiga Zaki, Japan 185 U4
Kishiwada, Japan 185 Q8
Kishkeneköl, Kaz. 175 B14
Kisigo, river, Tanzania 194 L10
Kısır Dağı, Turk. 169 D17
Kiska Island, Alas., U.S. 110 M3
Kiskunfélegyháza, Hung. 149 M15
Kiskunhalas, Hung. 149 M15
Kislovodsk, Russ. 157 T12
Kismaayo (Chisimayu), Somalia 199 K16
Kiso, river, Japan 185 P10
Kíssamos (Kastéli), Gr. 154 Q12
Kissámou, Kólpos, Gr. 154 P12
Kissidougou, Guinea 200 F6
Kissimmee, river, Fla., U.S. 97 V9
Kissimmee, Fla., U.S. 97 T9
Kissimmee, Lake, Fla., U.S. 97 U9
Kistrand, Nor. 141 C14
Kisumu, Kenya 199 K13
Kisvárda, Hung. 149 K17
Kita, Mali 196 H6
Kita Daitō Jima, Japan 184 L3
Kitaibaraki, Japan 185 N13
Kita Iwo Jima, Japan 184 L5
Kitakami, Japan 184 K13
Kitakata, Japan 184 M12
Kitakyūshū, Japan 185 R4
Kitale, Kenya 199 J14
Kitami, Japan 184 F15
Kitami Sanchi, range, Japan 184 E14
Kit Carson, Colo., U.S. 107 N15
Kitchener, Ont., Can. 83 R18
Kitchener, W. Aust., Austral. 211 W5
Kíthira, Gr. 154 N11
Kíthira (Cerigo, Cythera), island, Gr. 154 N11
Kíthnos, island, Gr. 155 K13
Kíthnos, Gr. 155 K13
Kiti, Cape, Cyprus 160 Q9
Kitimat, B.C., Can. 82 K7
Kiti Point, F.S.M. 217 G14
Kitob, Uzb. 174 L12
Kitridge Point, Barbados 121 K20
Kittanning, Pa., U.S. 94 N4
Kittery, Me., U.S. 95 J15
Kittilä, Fin. 141 D14
Kittitas, Wash., U.S. 108 D6
Kitty Hawk, N.C., U.S. 96 G15
Kitwe, Zambia 202 D10
Kitzingen, Ger. 148 H7
Kiukiu, Pointe, Fr. Polynesia, Fr. 219 M20
Kiunga, P.N.G. 213 D17
Kivalina, Alas., U.S. 110 D12
Kivu, Lac, Dem. Rep. of the Congo, Rwanda 198 K12
Kiyan Saki, Japan 185 Y1
Kiyāt, Saudi Arabia 172 N8
Kıyıköy, Turk. 168 C4
Kizema, Russ. 158 F8
Kızılcahamam, Turk. 168 D8
Kızılin, Turk. 169 H13
Kızılırmak, Turk. 168 D9
Kızılırmak (Halys), river, Turk. 168 D9
Kızılliman Burnu, Turk. 168 K8
Kızıltepe, Turk. 169 H15
Kizlyar, Russ. 157 T15
Kizlyarskiy Zaliv, Russ. 157 S15
Kladno, Czech Rep. 148 H11
Klagenfurt, Aust. 148 M11

Klaipėda, Lith. 141 N15
Klaksvík, Faroe Is., Den. 140 J6
Klamath, Calif., U.S. 108 L2
Klamath, river, Calif., Oreg., U.S. 108 L2
Klamath Falls, Oreg., U.S. 108 K4
Klamath Mountains, Calif., U.S. 108 M3
Klarälven, river, Sw. 140 K12
Klatovy, Czech Rep. 148 J10
Klawer, S. Af. 202 L7
Klawock, Alas., U.S. 111 M23
Kle, Liberia 200 G6
Klein Baai, Neth. Antilles, Neth. 121 B14
Klein Bonaire, island, Neth. Antilles, Neth. 121 Q19
Kleine Berg, Neth. Antilles, Neth. 121 P14
Klekovača, Bosn. & Herzg. 152 F6
Klerksdorp, S. Af. 202 K10
Klesiv, Ukr. 156 M4
Kletskiy, Russ. 157 P12
Klichaw, Belarus 156 L5
Klickitat, Wash., U.S. 108 E5
Klin, Russ. 156 J9
Klintehamn, Sw. 141 M14
Klintsy, Russ. 156 L7
Klirou, Cyprus 160 P8
Klitoría, Gr. 154 J9
Klondike Gold Rush National Historic Park, Alas., U.S. 111 K21
Klosterneuburg, Aust. 148 K12
Klosters, Switz. 150 B5
Kluczbork, Pol. 149 F14
Klyaz'ma, river, Russ. 138 D11
Klyuchevskaya Sopka, peak, Russ. 166 C13
Knaresborough, Eng., U.K. 143 R12
Knezha, Bulg. 153 H13
Knife River, Minn., U.S. 104 G13
Knin, Croatia 152 G6
Knittlefeld, Aust. 148 L11
Knjaževac, Serb. & Mont. 152 G12
Knob, Cape, Austral. 210 L4
Knockadoon Head, Ire. 143 U5
Knokke-Heist, Belg. 146 K11
Knossos see Cnossus, ruin, Gr. 155 Q15
Knotts Island, N.C., U.S. 96 G14
Knox, Ind., U.S. 99 P8
Knox Atoll, Marshall Is. 216 H5
Knox City, Tex., U.S. 102 K7
Knox Coast, Antarctica 227 L21
Knoxville, Iowa, U.S. 105 P12
Knoxville, Tenn., U.S. 101 E18
Knud Rasmussen Land, Greenland, Den. 81 B20
Knysna, S. Af. 202 M9
Ko, Gora, Russ. 159 K21
Koba, Indonesia 188 K8
Koba, Indonesia 189 M19
Kobarid, Slov. 152 C4
Kobayashi, Japan 185 T4
Kōbe, Japan 185 Q8
København (Copenhagen), Den. 140 N12
Koblenz, Ger. 148 G5
Kobo, India 178 F15
Kobozha, Russ. 156 G8
Kobroor, island, Indonesia 189 L19
Kobryn, Belarus 156 L3
Kobu, Azerb. 169 D23
Kobuk, river, Alas., U.S. 111 E14
Kobuk, Alas., U.S. 111 E14
Kobuk Valley National Park, Alas., U.S. 111 E14
K'obulet'i, Rep. of Georgia 169 C16
Kocaeli, Turk. 168 D5
Kočani, Maced. 152 K12
Koçarlı, Turk. 168 G3
Koçbaşı Tepe, Turk. 169 F17
Koch Bihar, India 178 G12
Kochen'ga, Russ. 156 F12
Kochi see Cochin, India 179 R5
Kōchi, Japan 185 R7
Koch Island, Nunavut, Can. 83 F17
Kochkor, Kyrg. 176 E12
Koch Peak, Mont., U.S. 106 F7
Kochubey, Russ. 157 T15
Kodari, Nepal 178 F10
Koddiyar Bay, Sri Lanka 179 S8
Kodiak, Alas., U.S. 111 M15
Kodiak Island, Alas., U.S. 111 M15
Kodiak Seamount, Pac. Oc. 239 B13
Kodinar, India 178 K2
Kodinskiy, Russ. 159 J14
Kodok, Sudan 199 F13
Kodomari, Japan 184 H12
Kōes, Namibia 202 J7
Koetoi, Japan 184 D13
Kofarnihon, Taj. 176 J7
Köflach, Aust. 148 M11
Koforidua, Ghana 200 H11
Kōfu, Japan 185 P11
Koga, Japan 185 N12
Ko Gaja Shima, Japan 185 V3
Kogaluc, river, Que., Can. 83 J18
Kögart, Kyrg. 176 G11
Kogon, Uzb. 174 L11
Kohala, region, Hawai'i, U.S. 113 K19
Kohala Mountains, Hawai'i, U.S. 113 K19
Kohat, Pak. 177 N9
Koh-e Baba Range, Afghan. 176 M6
Kohima, India 178 G15
Kohistan, region, Pak. 176 L11
Kohler Glacier, Antarctica 226 L7
Kohlu, Pak. 177 R8
Kohnieh, Cambodia 187 N13
Kohtla-Järve, Est. 141 K17
Koilani, Cyprus 160 Q7
Koimbani, Comoros 205 M14
Kōje Do, S. Korea 182 G14
Ko Jima, Japan 185 S12
Kojŭ, N. Korea 182 D13
Kokas, Indonesia 189 K18
Kök-Aygyr, Kyrg. 176 F12
Kokkina, Cyprus 160 N6
Kokkola, Fin. 141 G15
Koko, Nigeria 201 E13
Koko Crater, Hawai'i, U.S. 112 E12
Koko Head, Hawai'i, U.S. 112 E12
Kokomo, Ind., U.S. 99 Q9
Kökpekti, Kaz. 175 E18
Kökshetaū, Kaz. 175 C13
Köktal, Kaz. 175 H17
Kokubu, Japan 185 T4
Kok-Yangak, Kyrg. 176 F10
Kola, island, Indonesia 189 L19
Kolachi, river, Pak. 177 T6
Kolaka, Indonesia 189 K14
Kola Peninsula, Russ. 138 A10
Kolar, India 179 P6
Kolari, Fin. 141 E14
Kolarovgrad see Shumen, Bulg. 153 H16
Kolayat, India 178 F3
Kolbano, Indonesia 189 N15
Kolbeinsey Ridge, Arctic Oc. 243 K18
Kolbio, Kenya 199 K15
Kolding, Den. 140 P11
Kolé, Vanuatu 218 C2
Kole, Dem. Rep. of the Congo 198 J11
Kole, Dem. Rep. of the Congo 198 L10
Kolekole, river, Hawai'i, U.S. 113 L21
Kolguyev, Ostrov, Russ. 158 E10
Kolguyev Island, Russ. 138 A11
Kolhapur, India 178 M4
Kolia, Wallis & Futuna, Fr. 218 E11
Koliganek, Alas., U.S. 111 K14
Kolín, Czech Rep. 148 H12
Kolkata (Calcutta), India 178 J12
Kolkhozobod, Taj. 176 J7
Kollam see Quilon, India 179 S5
Kollidam, river, India 179 R6
Kolmogorovo, Russ. 159 J13
Köln (Cologne), Ger. 148 F5
Koło, Pol. 149 E14
Koloa, island, Tonga 218 L12
Kōloa, Hawai'i, U.S. 112 C5
Kołobrzeg, Pol. 148 B12
Kolodnya, Russ. 156 K7
Kologriv, Russ. 156 G12
Kolokani, Mali 196 H7
Kolombangara, island, Solomon Is. 217 M16
Kolomna, Russ. 156 K10
Kolomyya, Ukr. 157 P3
Kolonga, Tonga 218 H12
Kolonia, F.S.M. 217 F14
Kolonodale, Indonesia 189 K14
Kolosovykh, Russ. 159 E13
Kolovai, Tonga 218 H10
Kolowr va Dah Sil, Afghan. 176 L7
Kolpashevo, Russ. 158 J12
Kolpino, Russ. 156 F6
Kol'skiy Poluostrov, Russ. 158 D9
Kolufuri, island, Maldives 179 V3
Kolumadulu Atoll, Maldives 179 V3
Kolwezi, Dem. Rep. of the Congo 198 N10
Kolyma, river, Russ. 166 B11
Kolyma Lowland, Russ. 166 B11
Kolyma Range, Russ. 166 B12
Kolymskoye Nagor'ye (Gydan), Russ. 159 E20
Kom, peak, Bulg. 152 H12
Komagane, Japan 185 P11
Komandorskiye Ostrova (Commander Islands), Russ. 159 E23
Komárno, Slovakia 149 L14
Komatsu, Japan 185 N9
Kombóti, Gr. 154 G8
Komebail Lagoon (Ngertachebeab), Palau 216 N11
Komo, island, Fiji Is. 218 J9
Komoé, river, Côte d'Ivoire 200 G9
Komodo, island, Indonesia 189 M13
Kôm Ombo, Egypt 197 E19
Komoran, island, Indonesia 189 M20
Komotiní, Gr. 155 B15
Komovi, peak, Serb. & Mont. 152 J9
Kompong Chhnang, Cambodia 187 N11
Kompong Som, Cambodia 187 P11
Kompong Speu, Cambodia 187 P11
Kompong Sralao, Cambodia 186 M12
Kompong Thom, Cambodia 187 N11
Komsomol, Kaz. 174 F7
Komsomolets, Kaz. 174 B10
Komsomolets, Ostrov, Russ. 159 C14
Komsomolets Island see Komsomolets, Ostrov, Russ. 166 B9
Komsomol'sk, Russ. 156 H10
Komsomol'skiy, Russ. 159 B19
Komsomol'sk na Amure, Russ. 159 K20
Komsomol'sk-na-Ustyurte, Uzb. 174 H8
Komusan, N. Korea 182 B14
Kona, region, Hawai'i, U.S. 113 M19
Konakovo, Russ. 156 H9
Konakpınar, Turk. 168 F12
Konawa, Okla., U.S. 102 H11
Konda, Indonesia 189 K18
Kondagaon, India 178 L8
Kondinin, W. Aust., Austral. 211 X3
Kondoa, Tanzania 199 L14
Kondol', Russ. 156 L13
Kondopoga, Russ. 158 E7
Kondoz (Kunduz), Afghan. 176 K7
Kondrovo, Russ. 156 K8
Kondukur, India 179 N7
Konduz, river, Afghan. 176 K7
Koné, New Caledonia, Fr. 218 C7
Koné, Passe de, New Caledonia, Fr. 218 C7
Köneürgench, Turkm. 174 J9
Kong, river, Laos 186 L13
Kong, Koh, Cambodia 187 P10
Kongauru, island, Palau 216 Q10
Kongiganak, Alas., U.S. 110 K12
Konginskiy Khrebet, Russ. 159 D20
Konglu, Myanmar 186 D7
Kongolo, Dem. Rep. of the Congo 198 L11
Kongor, Sudan 198 G12
Kongsberg, Nor. 140 L11
Kongsvinger, Nor. 140 K12
Kongue Falls, Gabon 201 K16
Kongwa, Tanzania 199 M14
Konibodom, Taj. 176 G8
Königswinter, Ger. 148 F5
Konin, Pol. 149 E14
Konispol, Albania 152 N9
Konjuh, peak, Bosn. & Herzg. 152 F8
Konnongorring, W. Aust., Austral. 211 X3
Konosha, Russ. 158 E7
Konotop, Ukr. 157 N7
Konqi, river, China 180 G7
Konrai, Palau 216 M12
Końskie, Pol. 149 F16
Konstantinovsk, Russ. 157 Q11
Konstanz, Ger. 148 L6
Konta, India 178 M8
Kontagora, Nigeria 201 F13
Kon Tum, Vietnam 186 M13
Konya (Iconium), Turk. 168 G8
Konza, Kenya 199 K14
Ko'oko'olau, peak, Hawai'i, U.S. 113 M20
Kookooligit Mountains, Alas., U.S. 110 F10
Kookynie, W. Aust., Austral. 211 W4
Ko'olau Range, Hawai'i, U.S. 112 D11
Koolburra, Qnsld., Austral. 211 Q12
Koonalda, S. Aust., Austral. 211 W7
Koonibba, S. Aust., Austral. 211 W8
Kootenay, river, B.C., Can. 106 A4
Kopaonik, range, Serb. & Mont. 152 H10
Kópasker, Ice. 140 E4
Kopbirlik, Kaz. 175 F16
Köpekkayası Burnu, Turk. 168 C8
Koper (Capodistria), Slov. 152 D4
Kopervik, Nor. 140 L9
Köpetdag Mountains, Turkm. 174 M8
Kopet Mountains, Iran, Turkm. 166 G5
Kopište, island, Croatia 152 H6
Koppal, India 179 N5
Koprivnica, Croatia 152 D7
Köprü, river, Turk. 168 H6
Kopstal, Lux. 160 J10
Kopylovka, Russ. 158 J12
Korab, Mal, Albania, Maced. 152 K10
K'orahē, Eth. 199 G16
Korak, island, Palau 216 N12
Korangi, Pak. 177 W6
Korba, India 178 J8
Korçë, Albania 152 M10
Korčula, island, Croatia 152 H6
Korčulanski Kanal, Croatia 152 H6
Korday, Kaz. 175 J15
Korea, peninsula, Asia 166 F12
Korea Bay, N. Korea, China 182 D11
Korea Strait, S. Korea 182 H14
Korem, Eth. 199 E15
Korenovsk, Russ. 157 S10
Korf, Russ. 159 D21
Korhogo, Côte d'Ivoire 200 F8
Kori Creek, India 177 X7
Korido, Indonesia 189 J19
Korinós, Gr. 154 D10
Korinthiakós Kólpos, Gr. 154 J10
Kórinthos (Corinth), Gr. 154 J11
Korissía, Gr. 155 K13
Kōriyama, Japan 184 M13
Korkuteli, Turk. 168 H5
Korla, China 180 F7
Kormakitis, Cyprus 160 N7
Kormakitis, Cape, Cyprus 160 N7
Körmend, Hung. 149 M13
Kornat, island, Croatia 152 G5
Koro, island, Fiji Is. 218 H7
Korolevu, Fiji Is. 218 J6
Koromiri, island, Cook Is., N.Z. 218 Q9
Koróni, Gr. 154 M9
Korónia, Límni, Gr. 154 C11
Koronída, Gr. 155 L15
Koropí, Gr. 154 J12
Koror, Palau 216 N11
Koror (Oreor), island, Palau 216 N11
Koro Sea, Fiji Is. 218 J8
Korosten', Ukr. 157 N5
Korotkova, Russ. 159 K15
Koro Toro, Chad 197 H15
Korotoyak, Russ. 157 N10
Korsnes, Nor. 140 E12
Korti, Sudan 198 D12
Kortrijk, Belg. 146 L11
Koryak Range, Russ. 166 B12
Koryakskaya Sopka, Russ. 159 F23
Koryakskoye Nagor'ye, Russ. 159 D21
Kos, Gr. 155 L18
Kos (Cos), island, Gr. 155 M18
Kō Saki, Japan 185 Q3
Kosan, N. Korea 182 D13
Kosaya Gora, Russ. 156 K9
Kościerzyna, Pol. 149 B13
Kosciusko, Miss., U.S. 100 K12
Kosciuszko, Mount, Austral. 210 L13
Koshikijima Rettō, Japan 185 T3
Köshim, river, Kaz. 174 D6
Koshk, Afghan. 176 M2
Koshk-e Kohneh, Afghan. 176 M2
Košice, Slovakia 149 J17
Kosmás, Gr. 154 L10
Koson, Uzb. 174 L11
Kosovo, region, Serb. & Mont. 152 J10
Kosovska Mitrovica, Serb. & Mont. 152 H10
Kosrae (Kusaie), island, F.S.M. 216 Q9
Kossol Passage, Palau 216 L12
Kossou, Lac de, Côte d'Ivoire 200 G8
Kosti, Sudan 199 E13
Kostino, Russ. 159 H13
Kostopil', Ukr. 157 N4
Kostroma, Russ. 156 G11
Kostromskoye Vodokhranilishche, Russ. 156 G11
Kostrzyn, Pol. 148 D11
Kostyantynivka, Ukr. 157 Q9
Koszalin, Pol. 148 B12
Kota, India 178 H5
Kotaagung, Indonesia 188 L7
Kota Baharu, Malaysia 187 S10
Kotabaru, Indonesia 188 K12
Kotabumi, Indonesia 188 L7
Kotabunan, Indonesia 189 J15
Kot Addu, Pak. 177 R9
Ko Takara Jima, Japan 185 V3
Kota Kinabalu, Malaysia 188 G11
Kota Tinggi, Malaysia 187 V11
Kotel'nich, Russ. 158 G7
Kotel'nikovo, Russ. 157 Q12
Kotel'nyy, Ostrov, Russ. 159 D16
Kotel'nyy Island, Russ. 166 B10
Köthen, Ger. 148 E9
Kotka, Fin. 141 J16
Kotlas, Russ. 158 F8
Kotlik, Alas., U.S. 110 G12
Kotooka, Japan 184 K12
Kotovs'k, Ukr. 157 Q5
Kotovsk, Russ. 156 L11
Kotri, Pak. 177 V7
Kottayam, India 179 R5
Kotto, river, Cen. Af. Rep. 198 G10
Kotu, island, Tonga 218 Q6
Kotu Group, Tonga 218 Q6
Koturdepe, Turkm. 174 L6
Kotzebue, Alas., U.S. 111 E13
Kotzebue Sound, Alas., U.S. 111 E13
Koua, New Caledonia, Fr. 218 D8
Kouakou, island, Fr. Polynesia, Fr. 219 R21
Kouango, Cen. Af. Rep. 198 H9
Koudougou, Burkina Faso 200 E10
Koufália, Gr. 154 C10
Koufoníssi, island, Gr. 155 L15
Koufoníssi, island, Gr. 155 R16
Koufós, Gr. 154 E12
Kouilou, river, Congo 201 M16
Koukdjuak, Great Plain of the, Nunavut, Can. 83 G18
Kouklia, Cyprus 160 Q6
Koúla, peak, Gr. 155 B14
Koulamoutou, Gabon 201 L16
Koulen, Cambodia 186 M11
Koulikoro, Mali 196 H7
Koumac, New Caledonia, Fr. 218 C6
Koumra, Chad 197 K15
Koungou, Mayotte, Fr. 205 P17
Kountze, Tex., U.S. 103 P15
Kourou, Fr. Guiana, Fr. 129 E18
Kouroussa, Guinea 200 F7
Koutiala, Mali 196 J8
Koutomo, Île, New Caledonia, Fr. 218 E9
Kouvola, Fin. 141 J16
Kovel', Ukr. 156 M3
Kovic, Baie, Que., Can. 83 J17
Kovin, Serb. & Mont. 152 F10
Kovrov, Russ. 156 J11
Kovur, India 179 P7
Kowanyama, Qnsld., Austral. 211 Q12
Kowloon see Jiulong, China 183 S5
Köyceğiz, Turk. 168 H4
Koyda, Russ. 158 E9
Koytendag, Turkm. 174 M12
Koyuk, Alas., U.S. 111 F13
Koyukuk, river, Alas., U.S. 111 E15
Koyukuk, Alas., U.S. 111 F14
Koyulhisar, Turk. 168 E12
Kozan, Turk. 168 H11
Kozáni, Gr. 154 D9
Kozel'sk, Russ. 156 K8
Kozhasay, Kaz. 174 E8
Kozhikode (Calicut), India 179 Q5
Kozjak, peak, Maced. 152 K11
Kozlovka, Russ. 157 N11
Kozlu, Turk. 168 C7
Kozluk, Turk. 169 G16
Koz'modem'yansk, Russ. 156 H13
Kōzu Shima, Japan 185 Q12
Kozyatyn, Ukr. 157 P5
Kpalimé, Togo 200 G11
Kra, Isthmus of, Thai. 187 Q8
Krabi, Thai. 187 R8
Kra Buri, Thai. 187 P7
Kragerø, Nor. 140 L11
Kragujevac, Serb. & Mont. 152 G10
Kraków, Pol. 149 G15
Kralendijk, Neth. Antilles, Neth. 121 Q19
Kraljevo, Serb. & Mont. 152 G10
Král'ovský Chlmec, Slovakia 149 K17
Kramators'k, Ukr. 157 Q9
Kramfors, Sw. 141 H13
Kranídi, Gr. 154 K11
Kranj, Slov. 152 C4
Krasavino, Russ. 158 F8
Kraśnik, Pol. 149 F17
Krasnoarmeysk, Kaz. 175 B13
Krasnoarmeysk, Russ. 158 H6
Krasnoarmeyskaya, Russ. 157 S10
Krasnodar, Russ. 157 S10
Krasnogorsk, Russ. 159 J22
Krasnogvardeyskoye, Russ. 157 S12
Krasnohrad, Ukr. 157 P8
Krasnokamensk, Russ. 159 L18

Krasnoslobodsk, *Russ.* **157** P13
Krasnovishersk, *Russ.* **158** G9
Krasnoyarsk, *Russ.* **159** K13
Krasnoye, *Russ.* **156** M16
Krasnyy Dolginets, *Kaz.* **174** G5
Krasnyye Baki, *Russ.* **156** H13
Krasnyy Kholm, *Russ.* **156** G9
Krasnyy Luch, *Ukr.* **157** Q10
Krasnyy Yar, *Russ.* **157** N13
Kratie, *Cambodia* **187** N12
Kraul Mountains, *Antarctica* **226** B11
Krause Lagoon Channel, *Virgin Islands, U.S.* **120** R2
Kray Lesa, *Russ.* **159** D19
Krefeld, *Ger.* **148** F5
Kremastí, *Gr.* **155** M20
Kremen, peak, *Croatia* **152** F6
Kremenchuk, *Ukr.* **157** P7
Kremenchuk Reservoir *see* Kremenchuts'ke Vodoskhovyshche, *Ukr.* **138** G10
Kremenchuts'ke Vodoskhovyshche, *Ukr.* **157** R7
Kremenets', *Ukr.* **157** N3
Krems, *Aust.* **148** K12
Kress, *Tex., U.S.* **102** J5
Kréstena, *Gr.* **154** K9
Kresty, *Russ.* **159** F13
Kretinga, *Lith.* **141** N15
Kreuzlingen, *Switz.* **150** A4
Kribi, *Cameroon* **201** J15
Krim, peak, *Slov.* **152** D4
Krims'ke Hory, *Ukr.* **157** T7
Krishna, river, *India* **179** N5
Krishnagiri, *India* **179** Q6
Krishnanagar, *India* **178** J12
Kristiansand, *Nor.* **140** M10
Kristianstad, *Sw.* **141** N13
Kristiansund, *Nor.* **140** H10
Kristinestad, *Fin.* **141** H14
Kriti (Crete), island, *Gr.* **155** Q14
Krk, island, *Croatia* **152** E4
Krnov, *Czech Rep.* **149** H13
Kroken, *Nor.* **140** G12
Krolevets', *Ukr.* **156** M7
Kromy, *Russ.* **156** M8
Krong Koh Kong, *Cambodia* **187** P10
Kronotskaya Sopka, *Russ.* **159** F22
Kronshtadt, *Russ.* **156** F6
Kroonstad, *S. Af.* **202** K10
Kropotkin, *Russ.* **157** S11
Krosno, *Pol.* **149** H17
Krosno Odrzańskie, *Pol.* **148** E11
Krotoszyn, *Pol.* **149** E13
Krstača, peak, *Serb. & Mont.* **152** H10
Krui, *Indonesia* **188** L7
Krumovgrad, *Bulg.* **153** K15
Krung Thep (Bangkok), *Thai.* **186** M9
Krupá, *Czech Rep.* **148** G10
Krupište, *Maced.* **152** K12
Krupki, *Belarus* **156** K5
Kruševac, *Serb. & Mont.* **152** G11
Krutets, *Russ.* **156** F10
Kruzof Island, *Alas., U.S.* **84** R6
Krychaw, *Belarus* **156** L6
Krylov Seamount, *Atl. Oc.* **236** L9
Krylovskaya, *Russ.* **157** R11
Krymsk, *Russ.* **157** T10
Kryvichy, *Belarus* **156** K4
Kryvyy Rih, *Ukr.* **157** Q7
Ksar el Kebir, *Mor.* **196** A8
Kuala Abang, *Brunei* **188** G11
Kuala Belait, *Brunei* **188** G11
Kuala Berang, *Malaysia* **187** T10
Kuala Dungun, *Malaysia* **187** T10
Kualakapuas, *Indonesia* **188** K11
Kuala Kerai, *Malaysia* **187** S10
Kualakurun, *Indonesia* **188** J11
Kuala Lumpur, *Malaysia* **187** U9
Kualamanjual, *Indonesia* **188** J10
Kuala Nerang, *Malaysia* **188** F6
Kualapu'u, *Hawai'i, U.S.* **113** F14
Kuala Rompin, *Malaysia* **187** U10
Kuala Terengganu, *Malaysia* **187** T10
Kualatungkal, *Indonesia* **188** J7
Kuancheng, *China* **182** C8
Kuandian, *China* **182** C11
Kuanshan, *Taiwan, China* **183** S10
Kuantan, *Malaysia* **187** T10
Kubachi, *Russ.* **157** U16
Kuban', river, *Russ.* **138** H12
Kuban Lowland, *Russ.* **138** G12
Kubbum, *Sudan* **198** F10
Kubenskoye, Ozero, *Russ.* **156** F10
Kubokawa, *Japan* **185** R6
Kubonitu, Mount, *Solomon Is.* **217** M18
Kuchaman, *India* **178** F4
Kuching, *Malaysia* **188** H9
Kuchinoerabu Jima, *Japan* **185** U4
Kuchino Shima, *Japan* **185** V3
Kuchnay Darvishan, *Afghan.* **177** Q4
Kuçovë, *Albania* **152** L9
Küçüksu, *Turk.* **169** G16
Kud, river, *Pak.* **177** U5
Kudara, *Taj.* **176** J10
Kudarebe, cape, *Aruba, Neth.* **121** Q16
Kudat, *Malaysia* **188** F12
Kudgee, *N.S.W., Austral.* **211** X11
Kudremukh, peak, *India* **179** P4
Kudu Kyuyel', *Russ.* **159** J17
Kūē'ē Ruins, *Hawai'i, U.S.* **113** P20
Kufra Oasis *see* Al Jawf, *Lib.* **197** E16
Kufstein, *Aust.* **148** L9
Kugluktuk, *Nunavut, Can.* **82** F12
Kugul'ta, *Russ.* **157** S12
Kūhak, *Iran* **173** H18
Kūhak, *Pak.* **177** U3
Kuh-e Sayyad, *Afghan.* **176** L4
Kuhgrat, peak, *Liech.* **160** N3
Kuhmo, *Fin.* **141** F16
Kui Buri, *Thai.* **187** N8
Kuikui, Lae 'O, *Hawai'i, U.S.* **113** H16
Kuikuina, *Nicar.* **115** L18
Kuiseb, river, *Namibia* **202** H6
Kuitan, *China* **183** R6
Kuito, *Angola* **202** D7
Kuiu Island, *Alas., U.S.* **84** R7
Kuivaniemi, *Fin.* **141** F15
Kuizhuang, *China* **182** D8
Kujang, *N. Korea* **182** D12
Kuji, *Japan* **184** J14
Kuju, peak, *Japan* **185** S5
Kūka'iau, *Hawai'i, U.S.* **113** K20
Kukolu, island, *Solomon Is.* **217** J18
Kukpowruk, river, *Alas., U.S.* **111** C13
Kukui, *Hawai'i, U.S.* **113** M21
Kukuihaele, *Hawai'i, U.S.* **113** K20
Kukui'ula, *Hawai'i, U.S.* **112** C5
Kuku Point, *Wake I., U.S.* **216** F7
Kula, *Serb. & Mont.* **152** E9
Kula, *Turk.* **168** F4
Kula Gangri, peak, *Bhutan, China* **178** F13
Kūlagīno, *Kaz.* **174** E6
Kula Gulf, *Solomon Is.* **217** M16
Kūlani, peak, *Hawai'i, U.S.* **113** M21
Kulaura, *Bangladesh* **178** H13
Kul'chi, *Russ.* **159** J20
Kuldīga, *Latv.* **141** M15
Kule, *Botswana* **202** H8
Kulebaki, *Russ.* **156** J11
Kulgera, *N. Terr., Austral.* **211** U8
Kulin, *W. Aust., Austral.* **211** X3
Kulkuduk, *Uzb.* **174** J10
Kullorsuaq, *Greenland, Den.* **81** C20
Kulm, *N. Dak., U.S.* **104** H6
Kulmbach, *Ger.* **148** G8
Kŭlob, *Taj.* **176** J8
Kuloy, river, *Russ.* **138** B11
Kulp, *Turk.* **169** G15
Kulu, *Turk.* **168** F8
Kūlua, Pu'u, *Hawai'i, U.S.* **113** M20
Kulumadau, *P.N.G.* **213** E21
Kulunda, *Russ.* **158** L11
Kuma, river, *Russ.* **157** S14
Kumagaya, *Japan* **185** N12
Kumai, *Indonesia* **188** K10
Kumai, Teluk, *Indonesia* **188** K10
Kumamoto, *Japan* **185** S4
Kumano, *Japan* **185** R9
Kumano Nada, *Japan* **185** R9
Kumanovo, *Maced.* **152** J11
Kuman Range, *Myanmar* **186** E7
Kumara Junction, *N.Z.* **213** N17
Kumasi, *Ghana* **200** H10
Kumawa, Pegunungan, *Indonesia* **213** C14
Kumba, *Cameroon* **201** H15
Kumbakale, *Solomon Is.* **217** K15
Kumbakonam, *India* **179** R7
Kumbe, *Indonesia* **189** M21
Kume Shima, *Japan* **185** Y1
Kumo, *Nigeria* **201** F15
Kumphawapi, *Thai.* **186** K10
Kumta, *India* **179** P4
Kumukahi, Cape, *Hawai'i, U.S.* **113** M22
Kumukh, *Russ.* **157** U15
Kumul *see* Hami, *China* **180** F9
Kumylzhenskaya, *Russ.* **157** P12
Kumzār, *Oman* **173** H15
Kunahandu, island, *Maldives* **179** W3
Kunashir, island, *Russ.* **159** K23
Kundapura (Coondapoor), *India* **179** P4
Kundar, river, *Afghan., Pak.* **177** Q8
Kundian, *Pak.* **177** P9
Kundu, *Solomon Is.* **217** M15
Kunduz *see* Kondoz, *Afghan.* **176** K7
Kunene *see* Cunene, river, *Namibia* **202** F5
Kungsbacka, *Sw.* **140** M12
Kungurtug, *Russ.* **159** M14
Kunié *see* Pins, Île des, island, *New Caledonia, Fr.* **218** E9
Kunlon, *Myanmar* **186** F7
Kunlun Mountains, *China* **166** G8
Kunlun Shan, *China* **180** H4
Kunlun Shankou, *China* **180** J9
Kunming, *China* **180** N11
Kunnamkulam, *India* **179** R5
Kunu, island, *F.S.M.* **217** B14
Kununurra, *W. Aust., Austral.* **211** Q6
Kuopio, *Fin.* **141** G16
Kupa, river, *Croatia, Slov.* **152** E6
Kupang, *Indonesia* **189** N14
Kūpikipiki'o Point (Black Point), *Hawai'i, U.S.* **112** E11
Kupino, *Russ.* **158** K11
Kupreanof Island, *Alas., U.S.* **111** M23
Kupupolo Heiau, *Hawai'i, U.S.* **112** D10
Kup''yans'k, *Ukr.* **157** P9
Kuqa, *China* **180** F6
Kür (Kura), river, *Azerb.* **169** E22
Kura, river, *Asia* **166** F5
Kurakh, *Russ.* **157** V16
Kura Lowland, *Azerb.* **169** D21
Kūrān Dap, *Iran* **173** H17
Kurashassayskiy, *Kaz.* **174** D8
Kurashiki, *Japan* **185** Q7
Kurayoshi, *Japan* **185** P7
Kurbağa Gölü, *Turk.* **168** G10
Kürchatov, *Kaz.* **175** D16
Kürdämir, *Azerb.* **169** D22
Kur Dili, cape, *Azerb.* **169** F23
Kurdistan, region, *Iran, Iraq, Turk.* **172** B9
Kurduna, *Pak.* **177** Q6
Kurduvadi, *India* **178** M4
Kŭrdzhali, *Bulg.* **153** K15
Küre, *Turk.* **168** C9
Kure, *Japan* **185** Q6
Kure Atoll (Ocean Island), *Hawai'i, U.S.* **112** K2
Kure Beach, *N.C., U.S.* **96** K12
Kuressaare, *Est.* **141** L15
Kureyka, *Russ.* **159** G13
Kurgan, *Russ.* **158** J9
Kurganinsk, *Russ.* **157** S11
Kuria Muria Islands *see* Halaaniyaat, Juzor al, *Oman* **173** N15
Kuri Bay, *W. Aust., Austral.* **211** Q5
Kurikka, *Fin.* **141** H15
Kuril Basin, *Pac. Oc.* **238** D6
Kuril Islands *see* Kuril'skiye Ostrova, *Russ.* **166** D14
Kuril'sk, *Russ.* **159** J23
Kuril'skiye Ostrova (Kuril Islands), *Russ.* **159** J23
Kuril Trench, *Pac. Oc.* **238** E7
Kurio, *Japan* **185** U4
Kurnool, *India* **179** N6
Kurobe, *Japan* **185** N10
Kuroishi, *Japan* **184** J13
Kuroiso, *Japan* **185** N12
Kuro Shima, *Japan* **185** U3
Kurshskiy Zaliv, *Lith., Russ.* **141** N15
Kursk, *Russ.* **156** M9
Kurşunlu, *Turk.* **168** D8
Kurtalan, *Turk.* **169** G16
Kurtistown, *Hawai'i, U.S.* **113** M22
Kurtoğlu Burnu, *Turk.* **168** J4
Kuru, river, *Sudan* **198** G11
Kuruçay, *Turk.* **169** E13
Kuruktag, desert, *China* **180** F7
Kuruman, *S. Af.* **202** K9
Kurume, *Japan* **185** R4
Kurunegala, *Sri Lanka* **179** T7
Kurun Uryakh, *Russ.* **159** H19
Kuşadası, *Turk.* **168** G3
Kuşadasi Körfezi, *Turk.* **168** G3
Kusaie *see* Kosrae, island, *F.S.M.* **216** Q9
Kusakaki Guntō, *Japan* **185** U3
Kus Gölü, *Turk.* **168** D4
Kushima, *Japan* **185** T5
Kushimoto, *Japan* **185** R9
Kushiro, *Japan* **184** F15
Kushnīya, *Israel* **170** K6
Kushtia, *Bangladesh* **178** H12
Kuskokwim, river, *Alas., U.S.* **111** J13
Kuskokwim Bay, *Alas., U.S.* **110** K12
Kuskokwim Mountains, *Alas., U.S.* **111** H15
Kusŏng, *N. Korea* **182** D12
Kussharo Ko, *Japan* **184** F15
Kusur, *Russ.* **157** V15
Kut, Ko, *Thai.* **187** P10
Kütahya, *Turk.* **168** E5
K'ut'aisi, *Rep. of Georgia* **169** B17
Kutanibong, *Indonesia* **188** G4
Kutch, Gulf of, *India* **178** J1
Kutchan, *Japan* **184** G13
Kutina, *Croatia* **152** E6
Kutno, *Pol.* **149** E15
Kutru, *India* **178** L7
Kutu, *Dem. Rep. of the Congo* **198** K8
Kutubdia, island, *Bangladesh* **178** J13
Kutum, *Sudan* **198** E10
Kutu-Puhi-Puhi, Pointe, *Fr. Polynesia, Fr.* **219** Q20
Kuujjuaq, *Que., Can.* **83** K19
Kuujjuarapik, *Que., Can.* **83** L18
Kuuli-Mayak, *Turkm.* **174** K6
Kuusamo, *Fin.* **141** E16
Kuvango, *Angola* **202** E6
Kuvshinovo, *Russ.* **156** H8
Kuwaé *see* Tongoa, island, *Vanuatu* **218** E3
Kuwait, *Asia* **167** U4
Kuwait *see* Al Kuwayt, *Kuwait* **172** G11
Kuybishevskiy, *Taj.* **176** J7
Kuybyshev, *Russ.* **158** K11
Kuybyshev Reservoir *see* Kuybyshevskoye Vodokhranilishche, *Russ.* **138** D13
Kuybyshevskoye Vodokhranilishche, *Russ.* **156** J15
Kuzey Anadolu Dağları, *Turk.* **168** C9
Kuznetsk, *Russ.* **156** L14
Kuzumaki, *Japan* **184** K13
Kv nangen, bay, *Nor.* **141** C13
Kvaløy, island, *Nor.* **141** D13
Kvarner, strait, *Croatia* **152** E4
Kvarnerić, strait, *Croatia* **152** F4
Kvikkjokk, *Sw.* **141** E13
Kwa, river, *Dem. Rep. of the Congo* **198** L8
Kwadak, island, *Marshall Is.* **216** M5
Kwailibesi, *Solomon Is.* **217** M19
Kwajalein, island, *Marshall Is.* **216** N5
Kwajalein Atoll, *Marshall Is.* **216** G4
Kwajalein Lagoon, *Marshall Is.* **216** L4
Kwale, *Kenya* **199** L15
Kwangju *see* Gwangju, *S. Korea* **182** G13
Kwango, river, *Angola, Dem. Rep. of the Congo* **194** L6
Kwanza, river, *Angola* **194** L6
Kwaos, *Indonesia* **189** K17
Kwekwe, *Zimb.* **202** G11
Kwenge, river, *Dem. Rep. of the Congo* **198** M8
Kwethluk, *Alas., U.S.* **110** J12
Kwidzyn, *Pol.* **149** C14
Kwigillingok, *Alas., U.S.* **110** K12
Kwilu, river, *Dem. Rep. of the Congo* **198** L8
Kwinana, *W. Aust., Austral.* **211** X2
Kwitaro, river, *Guyana* **129** F14
Kwoka, peak, *Indonesia* **189** J18
Kyaikkami, *Myanmar* **186** L7
Kyaikto, *Myanmar* **186** K6
Kyakhta, *Russ.* **159** M15
Kyaukkyi, *Myanmar* **186** J6
Kyaukme, *Myanmar* **186** G7
Kyaukphyu, *Myanmar* **186** J4
Kyauktaw, *Myanmar* **186** H4
Kybartai, *Lith.* **141** N16
Kyiv (Kiev), *Ukr.* **157** N6
Kyle, *Tex., U.S.* **103** Q10
Kyll, river, *Ger.* **160** H11
Kyllburg, *Ger.* **160** G11
Kynuna, *Qnsld., Austral.* **211** S11
Kyoga, Lake, *Uganda* **199** J13
Kyōga Misaki, *Japan* **185** P8
Kyŏngju *see* Gyeongju, *S. Korea* **182** G15
Kyŏngsŏng, *N. Korea* **182** B14
Kyōto, *Japan* **185** Q9
Kyrenia *see* Keryneia, *Cyprus* **160** N8
Kyrgyz Range, *Kaz., Kyrg.* **176** E10
Kyrgyzstan, *Asia* **167** U7
Kyshtovka, *Russ.* **158** J11
Ky Son, *Vietnam* **186** J11
Kythrea, *Cyprus* **160** N9
Kyubeyingde, *Russ.* **159** G16
Kyūroku Jima, *Japan* **184** J12
Kyushe, *Kaz.* **174** G8
Kyūshū, island, *Japan* **185** S5
Kyushu-Palau Ridge, *Pac. Oc.* **238** H5
Kyustendil, *Bulg.* **152** J12
Kyzyl, *Russ.* **159** L13
Kyzyl-Adyr, *Kyrg.* **176** E9
Kyzylkup, *Turkm.* **174** K6
Kyzyl-Kyya, *Kyrg.* **176** G10
Kyzyl-Suu, *Kyrg.* **176** E14

L

La Adela, *Arg.* **133** P10
La Almunia de Doña Godina, *Sp.* **145** E13
Laascaanood, *Somalia* **199** G17
Laasqoray, *Somalia* **199** F18
Laatzen, *Ger.* **148** D7
Lā'au Point, *Hawai'i, U.S.* **113** F13
Laayoune, *W. Sahara, Mor.* **196** D6
La Banda, *Arg.* **132** G10
La Bañeza, *Sp.* **144** C8
La Barca, *Mex.* **114** H10
La Barge, *Wyo., U.S.* **106** J9
Labasa, *Fiji Is.* **218** G7
La Baule-Escoublac, *Fr.* **147** R5
Labé, *Guinea* **200** E6
Labe, river, *Czech Rep.* **148** H12
La Belle, *Fla., U.S.* **97** V9
Labinsk, *Russ.* **157** T11
Laborie, *St. Lucia* **121** L14
Labota, *Indonesia* **189** K14
Labouheyre, *Fr.* **147** W6
Laboulaye, *Arg.* **132** L10
Labra, *Neth. Antilles, Neth.* **121** Q18
Labrador, region, *Nfld. & Lab., Can.* **83** L21
Labrador City, *Nfld. & Lab., Can.* **83** L20
Labrador Sea, *Atl. Oc.* **236** D6
Lábrea, *Braz.* **130** F7
La Brea, *Trinidad & Tobago* **121** Q21
Labrit, *Fr.* **147** W6
Labuan, island, *Malaysia* **188** G11
Labuk Bay, *Malaysia* **188** F12
Labutta, *Myanmar* **186** L5
Lac, bay, *Neth. Antilles, Neth.* **121** R19
La Calera, *Chile* **132** K6
Lacanau, *Fr.* **147** V6
Lacanau, Étang de, *Fr.* **147** V6
Lacanau-Océan, *Fr.* **147** V6
La Canourgue, *Fr.* **147** W11
La Capelle, *Fr.* **146** M11
Lacapelle-Marival, *Fr.* **147** V9
La Carolina, *Sp.* **144** J11
Lacaune, Montes de, *Fr.* **147** X10
Laccadive Sea, *India* **179** P3
Lac du Flambeau, *Wis., U.S.* **98** G5
La Ceiba, *Hond.* **115** K17
La Chambre, *Fr.* **147** U14
La Chapelle-d'Angillon, *Fr.* **147** R10
La Charité, *Fr.* **147** S10
La Châtaigneraie, *Fr.* **147** S6
La Châtre, *Fr.* **147** T9
La Chaux-de-Fonds, *Switz.* **150** B2
Lachish, ruin, *Israel* **171** N5
Lachlan, river, *Austral.* **210** K12
Lachyn, *Azerb.* **169** E20
La Ciotat, *Fr.* **147** Y14
La Citadelle, site, *Haiti* **117** L16
La Ciudad Encantada, *Sp.* **145** G13
Lackawanna, *N.Y., U.S.* **94** J5
Lac La Biche, *Alta., Can.* **82** L11
La Clayette, *Fr.* **147** T12
La Coche, island, *Guadeloupe, Fr.* **121** G14
Lacon, *Ill., U.S.* **99** P5
La Condamine, *Monaco* **161** E20
Laconia, *N.H., U.S.* **95** H14
La Conner, *Wash., U.S.* **108** B4
Lacoochee, *Fla., U.S.* **97** T8
La Cordillera, islands, *P.R., U.S.* **120** M6
La Cortinada, *Andorra* **160** H3
Lacq, *Fr.* **147** X6
Lacre Punt, *Neth. Antilles, Neth.* **121** R19
La Crosse, *Kans., U.S.* **105** T5
La Crosse, *Wash., U.S.* **108** D8
La Crosse, *Wis., U.S.* **98** K3
La Cruz, *Costa Rica* **115** M18
La Cruz, *Mex.* **114** F8
La Cumbre, Volcán, *Ecua.* **128** Q8
La Cygne, *Kans., U.S.* **105** T10
Ladakh, region, *China, India* **176** M14
Ladakh Range, *India* **176** M14
Ladd Seamount, *Hawai'i, U.S.* **112** K2

La Désirade, island, Guadeloupe, Fr. 121 E17
La Digue, island, Seychelles 205 N21
Lâdik, Turk. 168 D11
Lādīz, Iran 173 G17
Ladnun, India 178 F4
Ladoga, Lake, Russ. 138 C9
La Dogana, San Marino 161 G16
La Dorada, Col. 128 E5
Ladozhskoye Ozero (Lake Ladoga), Russ. 156 E7
Ladrillero, Golfo, Chile 133 V6
Ladron Peak, N. Mex., U.S. 107 T11
Lady Ann Strait, Nunavut, Can. 83 D16
Ladygin Yar, Russ. 159 F13
Ladysmith, S. Af. 202 K11
Ladysmith, Wis., U.S. 98 G3
Ladyzhenka, Kaz. 175 D13
Lae, P.N.G. 213 D19
Laea, Indonesia 189 L14
Lae Atoll, Marshall Is. 216 G3
Laem Ngop, Thai. 187 N10
Laerdal Tunnel, Nor. 140 K10
La Esmeralda, Venez. 128 F10
Læsø, island, Den. 140 M11
La Esperanza, Cuba 116 G5
La Esperanza, P.R., U.S. 120 M3
Lafayette, Ala., U.S. 101 K17
LaFayette, Ga., U.S. 96 K4
Lafayette, Ind., U.S. 99 Q8
Lafayette, La., U.S. 100 P8
Lafayette, Tenn., U.S. 101 E16
La Fe, Cuba 116 H4
La Fe, Cuba 116 H6
La Felguera, Sp. 144 B9
La Fère, Fr. 147 N11
La Ferme, Mauritius 205 J20
La Ferté-Macé, Fr. 147 P7
La Ferté-St.-Aubin, Fr. 147 R9
La Flèche, Fr. 147 R7
La Foa, New Caledonia, Fr. 218 D8
La Follette, Tenn., U.S. 101 E18
Laga Bor, river, Kenya 199 J15
La Gacilly, Fr. 147 R5
Lagan, river, Sw. 141 M13
Laganá, Kólpos, Gr. 154 K7
Lagash (Telloh), ruin, Iraq 172 E10
Lagdo Reservoir, Cameroon 201 G17
Laggan Bay, Scot., U.K. 143 N7
Laghouat, Alg. 196 B11
La Gineta, Sp. 145 H13
Lagoa, Azores 144 Q5
Lago Argentino see El Calafate, Arg. 133 V7
Lagodekhi, Rep. of Georgia 169 C20
Lágos, Gr. 155 B14
Lagos, Nigeria 200 H12
Lagos, Port. 144 L5
Lagos de Moreno, Mex. 114 H10
Lagosta see Lastovo, island, Croatia 152 H6
La Grand' Combe, Fr. 147 W12
La Grande, Oreg., U.S. 108 F8
La Grande 2, Réservoir de, Que., Can. 83 L18
La Grange, Ky., U.S. 101 B17
La Grange, Mo., U.S. 105 R13
La Grange, N.C., U.S. 96 H12
La Grange, Tex., U.S. 103 Q12
La Grange, Wyo., U.S. 106 J14
LaGrange, Ga., U.S. 96 M4
Lagrange, Ind., U.S. 99 N10
Lagrange, W. Aust., Austral. 211 R4
La Gran Sabana, region, Venez. 128 E12
La Grave, Fr. 147 V14
La Grulla, Tex., U.S. 103 W9
La Guaira, Venez. 128 B9
Lagua Lichan, Puntan, N. Mariana Is., U.S. 216 A6
Laguépie, Fr. 147 W9
La Guerche, Fr. 147 Q6
Lagun, Neth. Antilles, Neth. 121 N13
Laguna, N. Mex., U.S. 107 S11
Laguna Beach, Calif., U.S. 109 Y9
Laguna Blanca, Arg. 132 F13
Laguna Dam, Ariz., Calif., U.S. 109 Z13
Laguna de Perlas, Nicar. 115 M19
Laguna Grande, Arg. 133 V8
Laguna Paiva, Arg. 132 J12
Lagunas, Chile 132 C7
Lagunas, Peru 130 E3
Lagunillas, Bol. 130 K8
Lagwira, Mauritania 196 F4
Laha, China 181 C16
La Habana (Havana), Cuba 116 G6
Lahad Datu, Malaysia 188 G12
Lahaina, Hawai'i, U.S. 113 G15
Laham, Indonesia 188 J11
Lahanás, Gr. 154 C11
La Harpe, Ill., U.S. 99 Q3
Lahat, Indonesia 188 K7
Lahıc, Azerb. 169 D22
Laḩij, Yemen 172 R9
Lāhījān, Iran 172 B12
Lahi Passage, Tonga 218 H11
Lahn, river, Ger. 148 G6
Lahnstein, Ger. 148 G6
Lahontan Reservoir, Nev., U.S. 109 P7
Lahore, Pak. 177 Q12
Lahr, Ger. 148 K5
Lahri, Pak. 177 S7
Lahti, Fin. 141 J16
Laï (Behagle), Chad 197 K14
Laibin, China 183 R1
Lai Chau, Vietnam 186 G10
Lā'ie, Hawai'i, U.S. 112 D11
Laifeng, China 182 L2
L'Aigle, Fr. 147 P8
Laïka, island, Vanuatu 218 E3
Laingsburg, S. Af. 202 M8
Laird, river, N. Amer. 80 E4
Lairg, Scot., U.K. 142 H9
Laisamis, Kenya 199 J14
La Isleta, island, Canary Is. 204 Q6
Laiwu, China 182 G7
Laiyang, China 182 F9
Laizhou Wan, China 182 F8
Lajamanu, N. Terr., Austral. 211 R7
La Jara, Colo., U.S. 107 P12
Lajas, P.R., U.S. 120 N2
Lajes, Azores 144 P3
Lajes, Braz. 130 N12
Lajes das Flores, Azores 144 N1
Lajitas, Tex., U.S. 103 R2
La Jonquera, Sp. 145 C18
La Junta, Colo., U.S. 107 P15
Lakatoro, Vanuatu 218 D2
Lakaträsk, Sw. 141 F14
Lake Andes, S. Dak., U.S. 104 M6
Lake Arthur, La., U.S. 100 P8
Lakeba, island, Fiji Is. 218 J9
Lakeba Passage, Fiji Is. 218 J9
Lake Butler, Fla., U.S. 97 R7
Lake Cargelligo, N.S.W., Austral. 211 X13
Lake Charles, La., U.S. 100 P7
Lake Chelan National Recreation Area, Wash., U.S. 108 B6
Lake City, Colo., U.S. 107 P11
Lake City, Fla., U.S. 97 R7
Lake City, Iowa, U.S. 105 N10
Lake City, Mich., U.S. 98 J10
Lake City, Minn., U.S. 104 K12
Lake City, S.C., U.S. 96 L10
Lake Clark National Park and Preserve, Alas., U.S. 111 K15
Lake Coleridge, N.Z. 213 P17
Lake Crystal, Minn., U.S. 104 L10
Lake District, Eng., U.K. 143 Q10
Lake Eyre Basin, Austral. 210 G10
Lakefield, Minn., U.S. 104 L10
Lake Geneva, Wis., U.S. 98 M6
Lake Grace, W. Aust., Austral. 211 X3
Lake Harbor, Fla., U.S. 97 V9
Lake Havasu City, Ariz., U.S. 107 S4
Lake Jackson, Tex., U.S. 103 S14
Lake King, W. Aust., Austral. 211 X4
Lakeland, Fla., U.S. 97 U8
Lakeland, Ga., U.S. 97 Q6
Lake Linden, Mich., U.S. 98 E6
Lake Louise, Alta., Can. 82 M10
Lake Mead National Recreation Area, Ariz., Nev., U.S. 109 U13
Lake Meredith National Recreation Area, Tex., U.S. 102 G5
Lake Mills, Iowa, U.S. 104 M11
Lake Murray, P.N.G. 213 D17
Lake Nash, N. Terr., Austral. 211 S10
Lake Oswego, Oreg., U.S. 108 F3
Lakepa, Niue, N.Z. 219 B21
Lake Placid, N.Y., U.S. 94 G11
Lakeport, Calif., U.S. 109 Q3
Lakeport, Mich., U.S. 98 L13
Lake Preston, S. Dak., U.S. 104 K7
Lake Providence, La., U.S. 100 K10
Lake Region, Fin. 138 C9
Lake Roosevelt National Recreation Area, Wash., U.S. 108 B8
Lakeside, Nebr., U.S. 105 N2
Lakeside, Oreg., U.S. 108 H2
Lake Stewart, N.S.W., Austral. 211 V11
Lakeview, Mich., U.S. 98 L10
Lakeview, Oreg., U.S. 108 L6
Lake Village, Ark., U.S. 100 J9
Lakeville, Minn., U.S. 104 K11
Lake Violet, W. Aust., Austral. 211 V4
Lake Wales, Fla., U.S. 97 U8
Lakewood, Colo., U.S. 106 M13
Lakewood, N.J., U.S. 94 P11
Lakewood, Ohio, U.S. 99 N14
Lake Worth, Fla., U.S. 97 V10
Lakhpat, India 178 H1
Lakí, Gr. 155 L17
Lakin, Kans., U.S. 105 U3
Lakki, Pak. 177 P9
Lakkia, Cyprus 160 P8
Lakonikós Kólpos, Gr. 154 M10
Lakota, N. Dak., U.S. 104 F7
Lakselv, Nor. 141 C14
Lakshadweep, islands, India 179 R2
La Laguna, Canary Is. 204 Q5
Lala Musa, Pak. 177 P11
Lalbenque, Fr. 147 W9
L'Albera, Serra de, Sp. 145 C18
La Leonesa, Arg. 132 G13
Lalëzit, Gjiri i, Albania 152 K9
Lalībela, Eth. 199 F15
La Libertad, Ecua. 128 K2
La Libertad, Guatemala 115 K16
La Libertad, Mex. 114 C6
La Ligua, Chile 132 K6
Lalín, Sp. 144 C6
La Línea de la Concepción, Sp. 144 N9
Lalitpur, India 178 H6
Lalitpur (Patan), Nepal 178 F10
La Loche, Sask., Can. 82 K11
Lalomanu, Samoa 218 L4
Lalona, island, Tonga 218 Q7
Laluai Point, P.N.G. 217 K14
La Lune, Trinidad & Tobago 121 Q22
La Maddalena, It. 150 L4
La Madrid, Arg. 132 G9
Lamag, Malaysia 188 G12
La Malbaie, Que., Can. 83 N20
Lamalou-les-Bains, Fr. 147 X11
Lamap, Vanuatu 218 D2
Lamar, Colo., U.S. 107 N15
Lamar, Mo., U.S. 105 U11
La Marmora, Punta, It. 151 N4
La Marque, Tex., U.S. 103 R14
Lamas, Peru 130 F3
Lamas, Turk. 168 J9
La Massana, region, Andorra 160 H2
La Massana, Andorra 160 J3
Lamballe, Fr. 147 Q5
Lambaréné, Gabon 201 L15
Lambay Island, Ire. 143 S7
Lambert Glacier, Antarctica 227 F18
Lambert's Bay, S. Af. 202 L7
Lambertville, Mich., U.S. 99 N12
Lámbia, Gr. 154 J9
Lambton, Cape, N.W.T., Can. 82 E11
Lame Deer, Mont., U.S. 106 E11
Lamentin, Guadeloupe, Fr. 121 E14
La Mesa, Calif., U.S. 109 Z10
La Mesa, N. Mex., U.S. 107 V12
Lamesa, Tex., U.S. 102 L5
L'Ametlla de Mar, Sp. 145 E16
La Meyze, Fr. 147 U9
Lamía, Gr. 154 G10
Lamitan, Philippines 189 F14
Lamlam, Mount, Guam, U.S. 216 D10
Lamoille, Nev., U.S. 108 M11
Lamoni, Iowa, U.S. 105 Q11
Lamont, Wyo., U.S. 106 J11
La Montaña, region, S. Amer. 126 F3
La Mothe-Achard, Fr. 147 S5
Lamotrek Atoll, F.S.M. 216 Q5
Lamotte-Beuvron, Fr. 147 R9
LaMoure, N. Dak., U.S. 104 H7
Lampang, Thai. 186 J8
Lampasas, Tex., U.S. 103 P10
Lampertheim, Ger. 148 H6
Lampeter, Wales, U.K. 143 U9
Lamphun, Thai. 186 J8
Lamskoye, Russ. 156 L9
Lamu, Kenya 199 K15
Lamutskoye, Russ. 159 C20
Lāna'i, island, Hawai'i, U.S. 113 G14
Lāna'i City, Hawai'i, U.S. 113 G15
Lāna'ihale, peak, Hawai'i, U.S. 113 G15
Lananibot, Puntan, N. Mariana Is., U.S. 216 B7
La Nao, Cabo de, Sp. 145 J15
Lanbi Kyun, Myanmar 187 P7
Lancang, China 180 P10
Lancaster, Calif., U.S. 109 W8
Lancaster, Eng., U.K. 143 R11
Lancaster, Mo., U.S. 105 Q12
Lancaster, N.H., U.S. 95 F14
Lancaster, Ohio, U.S. 99 R13
Lancaster, Pa., U.S. 94 P8
Lancaster, S.C., U.S. 96 J9
Lancaster, Tex., U.S. 102 L12
Lancaster, Wis., U.S. 98 L4
Lancaster Sound, N. Amer. 80 C7
Lance Creek, Wyo., U.S. 106 H13
Lanciano, It. 150 K11
Landau, Ger. 148 J6
Landay, Afghan. 177 R3
Landeck, Aust. 148 L8
Lander, river, Austral. 210 E8
Lander, Wyo., U.S. 106 H10
Landerneau, Fr. 147 P3
Landivisiau, Fr. 147 P3
Land O'Lakes, Wis., U.S. 98 F5
Landor, W. Aust., Austral. 211 U2
Landquart, Switz. 150 B5
Landrum, S.C., U.S. 96 J7
Landsberg, Ger. 148 K8
Landsborough Creek, Austral. 210 F12
Land's End, cape, Eng., U.K. 143 Y7
Lands End, cape, N.W.T., Can. 82 C12
Landshut, Ger. 148 K9
Landskrona, Sw. 140 N12
Lanett, Ala., U.S. 101 K17
Langadás, Gr. 154 C11
Langádia, Gr. 154 K9
Langanes, cape, Ice. 140 E4
Langao, China 182 J2
Langar, island, F.S.M. 217 F14
Langar, Taj. 176 K10
Langdon, N. Dak., U.S. 104 E7
Langeac, Fr. 147 V11
Langenhagen, Ger. 148 D7
Langfang, China 182 D7
Langford, S. Dak., U.S. 104 J7
Langjökull, glacier, Ice. 140 F2
Langkawi, island, Malaysia 187 S8
Langlois, Oreg., U.S. 108 J1
Langøya, island, Nor. 140 D12
Langres, Fr. 147 Q13
Langres, Plateau de, Fr. 147 R12
Langsa, Indonesia 188 G5
Lang Son, Vietnam 186 G12
Lang Suan, Thai. 187 Q8
Langting, India 178 G14
Langtry, Tex., U.S. 103 R5
Langu, Thai. 187 S8
Languedoc, region, Fr. 147 X11
Lancang (Mekong), river, China 178 P10
Lankao, China 182 H5
Länkäran, Azerb. 169 F22
Lannion, Fr. 147 P4
Lano, Wallis & Futuna, Fr. 218 B11
La Noix, Fr. 161 B22
Lanouaille, Fr. 147 U8
Lansdale, Pa., U.S. 94 P9
Lansdowne, W. Aust., Austral. 211 R6
Lansdowne House, Ont., Can. 83 M16
L'Anse, Mich., U.S. 98 F6
L'Anse aux Meadows, Nfld. & Lab., Can. 83 L23
Lansing, Iowa, U.S. 104 L13
Lansing, Mich., U.S. 98 M11
Lanslebourg, Fr. 147 U15
Lanta Yai, Ko, Thai. 187 R8
Lanusei, It. 151 P4
Lanxian, China 182 E4
Lanyu (Orchid Island), Taiwan, China 183 S10
Lanzarote, island, Canary Is. 204 P7
Lanzhou, China 180 J11
Laoag, Philippines 189 B13
Lao Cai, Vietnam 186 G11
Laoha, river, China 181 F16
Laohekou, China 182 J3
Laojunmiao see Yumen, China 180 G10
La Oliva, Canary Is. 204 Q7
Laon, Fr. 147 N11
Laona, Wis., U.S. 98 G6
La Orotava, Canary Is. 204 Q5
La Oroya, Peru 130 H3
Laos, Asia 167 W10
Laoshan, China 182 G9
Laotougou, China 182 A14
Lapalisse, Fr. 147 T11
La Palma, island, Canary Is. 204 Q3
La Palma, Pan. 115 N22
La Paloma, Uru. 132 L15
La Paragua, Venez. 128 D11
La Paz, Arg. 132 J12
La Paz, Arg. 132 K8
La Paz, Bol. 130 J6
La Paz, Mex. 114 F7
La Paz, Mex. 114 G11
Lape, Te Ava i te, Tuvalu 217 J23
La Pedrera, Col. 128 J8
Lapeer, Mich., U.S. 98 L12
La Perouse Pinnacle, Hawai'i, U.S. 112 M6
La Perouse Strait, Russ., Japan 184 F5
Lâpseki, Turk. 168 D3
La Pine, Oreg., U.S. 108 H5
Lapinlahti, Fin. 141 G16
Lapithos, Cyprus 160 N8
La Place, La., U.S. 100 P10
La Plaine, Dominica 121 G20
La Plaine, Reunion, Fr. 205 G16
La Plaine des Cafres, Reunion, Fr. 205 H16
Lapland, region, Fin., Russ., Sw. 141 E13
La Plant, S. Dak., U.S. 104 J4
La Plata, Arg. 132 L13
La Plata, Md., U.S. 96 D13
La Plata, Mo., U.S. 105 R12
La Pobla de Segur, Sp. 145 C16
La Pola de Gordón, Sp. 144 B9
La Porte, Tex., U.S. 103 R14
La Porte City, Iowa, U.S. 105 N13
La Possession, Reunion, Fr. 205 G15
Lappeenranta, Fin. 141 J17
La Pryor, Tex., U.S. 103 S8
Laptev Sea, Arctic Oc. 242 C7
Lapthal, India 178 E7
Lapua, Fin. 141 H15
La Puebla de Montalbán, Sp. 144 G10
La Purísima, Mex. 114 E6
La Push, Wash., U.S. 108 B2
La Quiaca, Arg. 132 D9
L'Aquila, It. 150 K9
Lār, Iran 173 H14
Lara, Gabon 201 K16
Laracha, Sp. 144 B5
Larache, Mor. 196 A8
Laramie, river, Wyo., U.S. 106 J12
Laramie, Wyo., U.S. 106 K12
Laramie Mountains, Wyo., U.S. 106 J12
Laramie Peak, Wyo., U.S. 84 F9
Larantuka, Indonesia 189 M14
Larat, island, Indonesia 189 M18
Larche, Fr. 147 W15
Laredo, Sp. 144 B11
Laredo, Tex., U.S. 103 U8
La Réole, Fr. 147 W7
Lares, P.R., U.S. 120 M2
Largo, Fla., U.S. 97 U7
Largo, Cayo, Cuba 116 H7
Larimore, N. Dak., U.S. 104 F7
La Rioja, Arg. 132 H8
Lárissa, Gr. 154 E10
La Rivière, Reunion, Fr. 205 H15
Larkana, Pak. 177 T7
Larnaka, Cyprus 160 P9
Larnaka Bay, Cyprus 160 P9
Larnakas, Cyprus 160 N8
Larne, N. Ire., U.K. 143 P7
Larned, Kans., U.S. 105 T6
La Robla, Sp. 144 C9
La Roca de la Sierra, Sp. 144 H7
La Rocca o Guaita, San Marino 161 J15
La Roche, Fr. 147 T14
La Rochefoucauld, Fr. 147 U8
La Rochelle, Fr. 147 T6
La Roche-sur-Yon, Fr. 147 S6
Larochette, Lux. 160 J10
La Roda, Sp. 144 H12
La Romana, Dom. Rep. 117 M20
La Ronge, Sask., Can. 82 L12
Larose, La., U.S. 100 Q10
La Rousse, Fr. 161 A22
Larrimah, N. Terr., Austral. 211 Q8
Lars Christensen Coast, Antarctica 227 F20
Larsen Bay, Alas., U.S. 111 M15
Larsen Ice Shelf, Antarctica 226 E5
La Rubia, Arg. 132 J11
Laruri, India 178 G15
Larvik, Nor. 140 L11
Larvotto, peninsula, Monaco 161 B23
Larvotto, Monaco 161 B22
Larvotto Beach, Monaco 161 B22
La Sagesse Bay, Grenada 121 L23
La Sal, Utah, U.S. 107 N9
La Salle, Ill., U.S. 99 P5
Lasan, Indonesia 188 H11
Las Animas, Colo., U.S. 107 N15

La Sarre, *Que., Can.* **83** N18
Las Cabezas de San Juan, *Sp.* **144** L8
Lascahobas, *Haiti* **117** M17
Lascano, *Uru.* **132** L15
Lascelles, *Vic., Austral.* **211** Y11
La Scie, *Nfld. & Lab., Can.* **83** L23
Las Cruces, *N. Mex., U.S.* **107** V12
Las Cuevas Bay, *Trinidad & Tobago* **121** N22
La Sènia, *Sp.* **145** F15
La Serena, *Chile* **132** J6
La Seu d'Urgell, *Sp.* **145** C16
La Seyne, *Fr.* **147** Y14
Las Flores, *Arg.* **132** M12
Lash-e Joveyn, *Afghan.* **177** Q2
Las Heras, *Arg.* **132** K8
Las Heras, *Arg.* **133** T8
Lashio, *Myanmar* **186** G7
Lashkar, *India* **178** G6
Lashkar Gah, *Afghan.* **177** Q4
Lashkari Bazar, ruin, *Afghan.* **177** Q4
Lasia, island, *Indonesia* **188** H4
La Sila, range, *It.* **151** P13
Las Lomitas, *Arg.* **132** F12
Las Martinas, *Cuba* **116** H4
La Sola, island, *Venez.* **119** N15
La Solana, *Sp.* **144** H11
La Sorcière, peak, *St. Lucia* **121** K14
La Souterraine, *Fr.* **147** T9
Las Palmas, *Canary Is.* **204** Q6
La Spezia, *It.* **150** G5
Las Piedras, *P.R., U.S.* **120** N5
Las Plumas, *Arg.* **133** R9
Lassen Peak, *Calif., U.S.* **109** N4
Lassen Volcanic National Park, *Calif., U.S.* **109** N5
Lassiter Coast, *Antarctica* **226** F7
Las Tablas, *Pan.* **115** P21
Las Toscas, *Arg.* **132** H12
Lastoursville, *Gabon* **201** L16
Lastovo (Lagosta), *Croatia* **152** H6
Lastovski Kanal, *Croatia* **152** H6
Las Tunas, *Cuba* **116** J12
La Suze, *Fr.* **147** R7
Las Varillas, *Arg.* **132** K11
Las Vegas, *N. Mex., U.S.* **107** R13
Las Vegas, *Nev., U.S.* **109** U12
Lata, *Samoa* **218** K2
Latacunga, *Ecua.* **128** J3
Latady Island, *Antarctica* **226** G5
Latady Mountains, *Antarctica* **226** F7
Latakia *see* Al Lādhiqīyah, *Syr.* **170** F6
Lata Mountain, *Amer. Samoa, U.S.* **218** P4
Latehar, *India* **178** H9
La Teste, *Fr.* **147** W6
Latheron, *Scot., U.K.* **142** H10
Lathi *see* Sakao, island, *Vanuatu* **218** C2
Latiano, *It.* **150** M15
Latina, *It.* **150** L9
Lato, ruin, *Gr.* **155** Q15
La Tortuga, Isla, *Venez.* **128** B10
Latouche Treville, Cape, *Austral.* **210** D4
La Tranche-sur-Mer, *Fr.* **147** T6
La Trinité, *Martinique, Fr.* **121** E23
Latta, *S.C., U.S.* **96** K11
La Tuque, *Que., Can.* **83** P19
Latur, *India* **178** L5
Latvia, *Eur.* **139** S8
Lau Basin, *Pac. Oc.* **238** M10
Laucala, island, *Fiji Is.* **218** G8
Laufen, *Switz.* **150** A2
Laughlan Islands, *P.N.G.* **213** E22
Laughlin Peak, *N. Mex., U.S.* **107** Q14
Lau Group, *Fiji Is.* **218** H9
Lauhkaung, *Myanmar* **186** E7
Laula Katan, Puntan, *N. Mariana Is., U.S.* **216** C5
Laulau, Bahia, *N. Mariana Is., U.S.* **216** C5
Lauli‘i, *Samoa* **218** L3
Lauliituai, *Amer. Samoa, U.S.* **218** M8
Launceston, *Tas., Austral.* **211** Z16
La Unión, *Chile* **133** P6
La Unión, *Peru* **130** G3
La Unión, *Sp.* **145** K14
Laupāhoehoe, *Hawai‘i, U.S.* **113** L21
Laura *see* Majuro, island, *Marshall Is.* **216** H10
Laura, *Marshall Is.* **216** G10
Laura, *Qnsld., Austral.* **211** Q13
Laurel, *Del., U.S.* **96** D15
Laurel, *Miss., U.S.* **100** M12
Laurel, *Mont., U.S.* **106** E10
Laurel, *Nebr., U.S.* **105** N8
Laurens, *Iowa, U.S.* **104** M10
Laurens, *S.C., U.S.* **96** K8
Laurentian Fan, *Atl. Oc.* **236** G6
Laurentian Scarp, *N. Amer.* **80** H8
Laurentide Scarp, *N. Amer.* **80** G9
Lauria, *It.* **151** N12
Lau Ridge, *Pac. Oc.* **238** N10
Laurie Island, *Antarctica* **226** A5
Laurinburg, *N.C., U.S.* **96** J11
Laurium *see* Lávrio, *Gr.* **155** K13
Laurium, *Mich., U.S.* **98** E6
Laurot Islands *see* Laut Kecil, Kepulauan, *Indonesia* **188** L11
Lausanne, *Switz.* **150** C1
Laut, island, *Indonesia* **188** G8
Laut, island, *Indonesia* **188** K12
Lautaro, Volcán, *Chile* **133** U6
Lauterbourg, *Fr.* **147** P16
Laut Kecil, Kepulauan (Laurot Islands), *Indonesia* **188** L11
Lautoka, *Fiji Is.* **218** H5
Lauvi Point, *Solomon Is.* **217** P19
Lava Beds National Monument, *Calif., U.S.* **108** L4
Lavaca, river, *Tex., U.S.* **103** R12
Lavaca Bay, *Tex., U.S.* **103** S13
La Vache Bay, *Trinidad & Tobago* **121** N22
Lava Hot Springs, *Idaho, U.S.* **106** H7
Laval, *Fr.* **147** Q6
Lāvān, island, *Iran* **173** H14
Lavardac, *Fr.* **147** W7
Lavaur, *Fr.* **147** X9
L'Avedy, Cape, *P.N.G.* **217** J14
La Vega, *Dom. Rep.* **117** L18
Lavelanet, *Fr.* **147** Y9
Lavello, *It.* **150** M12
La Venta, ruin, *Mex.* **115** J14
La Verkin, *Utah, U.S.* **107** P6
Laverne, *Okla., U.S.* **102** E7
Laverton, *W. Aust., Austral.* **211** V4
La Veta, *Colo., U.S.* **107** P13
La Ville, Pointe, *St. Lucia* **121** K13
Lavina, *Mont., U.S.* **106** D10
Lavit, *Fr.* **147** X8
Lavonia, *Ga., U.S.* **96** K6
Lavoutte, Anse, *St. Lucia* **121** J14
Lavrentiya, *Russ.* **159** A21
Lávrio (Laurium), *Gr.* **155** K13
Lawa, river, *Fr. Guiana, Fr., Suriname* **129** F17
Lāwa‘i, *Hawai‘i, U.S.* **112** C5
Lawdar, *Yemen* **172** Q10
Lawena, valley, *Liech.* **160** Q2
Lawit, peak, *Indonesia* **188** H10
Lawqah, *Saudi Arabia* **172** F9
Lawra, *Ghana* **200** F10
Lawrence, *Ind., U.S.* **99** R9
Lawrence, *Kans., U.S.* **105** S10
Lawrence, *Mass., U.S.* **95** J14
Lawrenceburg, *Ind., U.S.* **99** S11
Lawrenceburg, *Tenn., U.S.* **101** G14
Lawrenceville, *Ga., U.S.* **96** L5
Lawrenceville, *Ill., U.S.* **99** T7
Lawrenceville, *Va., U.S.* **96** F12
Lawton, *Okla., U.S.* **102** H9
Lawz, Jabal al, *Saudi Arabia* **172** G5
Laylá, *Saudi Arabia* **172** L10
Layou, river, *Dominica* **121** F19
Layou, *St. Vincent & the Grenadines* **121** K16
Laysan Island, *Hawai‘i, U.S.* **112** L4
Layshi, *Myanmar* **186** E5
Layton, *Utah, U.S.* **106** K7
Laytonville, *Calif., U.S.* **109** P2
L'Azaouak, Vallée de, *Mali* **196** G11
Lázaro Cárdenas, *Mex.* **114** J10
Lazo, *Russ.* **159** F18
Leachville, *Ark., U.S.* **100** F11
Lead, *S. Dak., U.S.* **104** K1
Lead Mountain, *Me., U.S.* **95** E18
Leadore, *Idaho, U.S.* **106** F6
Leadville, *Colo., U.S.* **106** M12
Leaf, river, *N. Amer.* **80** F8
Leakesville, *Miss., U.S.* **101** N13
Leakey, *Tex., U.S.* **103** R8
Leandro N. Alem, *Arg.* **132** G14
Leane, Lough, *Ire.* **143** U3
Learmonth, *W. Aust., Austral.* **211** T1
Leava *see* Sigavé, *Wallis & Futuna, Fr.* **218** E11
Leavenworth, *Kans., U.S.* **105** S10
Leavenworth, *Wash., U.S.* **108** C5
Lebak, *Philippines* **189** F15
Lebanon, *Asia* **167** T3
Lebanon, *Ind., U.S.* **99** R9
Lebanon, *Kans., U.S.* **105** R6
Lebanon, *Ky., U.S.* **101** C17
Lebanon, region, *Leb.* **170** J6
Lebanon, *Mo., U.S.* **105** U12
Lebanon, *N.H., U.S.* **95** H13
Lebanon, *Ohio, U.S.* **99** S11
Lebanon, *Oreg., U.S.* **108** G3
Lebanon, *Pa., U.S.* **94** P8
Lebanon, *Tenn., U.S.* **101** E16
Lebap, *Turkm.* **174** K10
Le Barcarès, *Fr.* **147** Y11
Le Barp, *Fr.* **147** W6
Le Beausset, *Fr.* **147** Y14
Lebec, *Calif., U.S.* **109** W7
Lebedyn, *Ukr.* **157** N8
Le Blanc, *Fr.* **147** S8
Lebombo Mountains, *Af.* **194** P9
Le Borgne, *Haiti* **117** L16
Lębork, *Pol.* **149** B13
Le Bouscat, *Fr.* **147** V6
Lebrija, *Sp.* **144** L8
Lebu, *Chile* **133** N6
Le Cap, *New Caledonia, Fr.* **218** D7
Le Carbet, *Martinique, Fr.* **121** E22
Le Caylar, *Fr.* **147** X11
Lecce, *It.* **151** N15
Lecco, *It.* **150** D5
Lecco, Lago di, *It., Switz.* **150** D4
Le Chambon-Feugerolles, *Fr.* **147** U12
Lechang, *China* **183** Q4
Lecompte, *La., U.S.* **100** N8
Le Creusot, *Fr.* **147** S12
Ledesma, *Sp.* **144** E8
Le Diamant, *Martinique, Fr.* **121** G22
Ledong, *China* **183** U1
Le Donjon, *Fr.* **147** T11
Le Dorat, *Fr.* **147** T8
Leduck Island, *Virgin Islands, U.S.* **120** N12
Ledyanaya, Gora, *Russ.* **159** C21
Lee, *Nev., U.S.* **109** N11
Leech Lake, *Minn., U.S.* **104** G10
Leedey, *Okla., U.S.* **102** F8
Leeds, *Ala., U.S.* **101** J15
Leeds, *Eng., U.K.* **143** R12
Leeds, *N. Dak., U.S.* **104** E6
Leek, *Neth.* **146** G14
Leer, *Ger.* **148** C6
Leesburg, *Fla., U.S.* **97** T8
Leesburg, *Va., U.S.* **96** C12
Lees Summit, *Mo., U.S.* **105** S11
Lee Stocking Island, *Bahamas* **120** E8
Leesville, *La., U.S.* **100** N7
Leeuwarden, *Neth.* **146** G13
Leeuwin, Cape, *Austral.* **210** L2
Leeward Islands, *Lesser Antilles* **119** G15
Le Faou, *Fr.* **147** Q3
Lefka, *Cyprus* **160** P7
Lefkáda, *Gr.* **154** G7
Lefkáda (Leucas), island, *Gr.* **154** G7
Lefkímmi, *Gr.* **154** F6
Lefkonoiko, *Cyprus* **160** N9
Lefkoşa *see* Lefkosia, *Cyprus* **160** N8
Lefkosia (Nicosia, Lefkoşa), *Cyprus* **160** N8
Le François, *Martinique, Fr.* **121** F23
Lefroy, Lake, *Austral.* **210** J4
Legan, island, *Marshall Is.* **216** M5
Legazpi, *Philippines* **189** D14
Legges Tor, *Austral.* **210** L16
Leggett, *Calif., U.S.* **109** P2
Leghorn *see* Livorno, *It.* **150** H6
Legionowo, *Pol.* **149** D16
Legnago, *It.* **150** E7
Legnano, *It.* **150** D4
Legnica, *Pol.* **148** F12
Le Grand-Lemps, *Fr.* **147** U13
Le Grau-du-Roi, *Fr.* **147** X12
Legune, *N. Terr., Austral.* **211** Q7
Leh, *India* **176** M14
Le Havre, *Fr.* **147** N7
Lehená, *Gr.* **154** J8
Lehr, *N. Dak., U.S.* **104** H6
Lehrte, *Ger.* **148** D8
Lehua, island, *Hawai‘i, U.S.* **112** B3
Lehua, Pu‘u, *Hawai‘i, U.S.* **113** M19
Lehututu, *Botswana* **202** H8
Leiah, *Pak.* **177** Q9
Leicester, *Eng., U.K.* **143** T13
Leiden, *Neth.* **146** J12
Leigh, *N.Z.* **213** J19
Leigh Creek, *S. Aust., Austral.* **211** W10
Leikanger, *Nor.* **140** K10
Leimatu‘a, *Tonga* **218** L11
Leine, river, *Ger.* **148** E7
Leinster, region, *Ire.* **143** S6
Leipzig, *Ger.* **148** F9
Leiria, *Port.* **144** G5
Leitchfield, *Ky., U.S.* **101** C16
Leiway, *Myanmar* **186** J6
Leiyang, *China* **183** P4
Leizhou Bandao (Luichow Peninsula), *China* **183** T1
Leizhou Wan, *China* **183** T2
Le Kartala, peak, *Comoros* **205** M14
Lekeleka, island, *Tonga* **218** Q7
Lekitobi, *Indonesia* **189** K15
Leksula, *Indonesia* **189** K15
Lekunberri, *Sp.* **145** B13
Le Lamentin, *Martinique, Fr.* **121** F22
Leland, *Miss., U.S.* **100** J10
Lel'chytsy, *Belarus* **156** M5
Lele, *F.S.M.* **217** B19
Lele Harbor, *F.S.M.* **217** B19
Leleiwi Point, *Hawai‘i, U.S.* **113** M22
Lélépa, island, *Vanuatu* **218** F3
Leli, island, *Solomon Is.* **217** M20
Lelingluang, *Indonesia* **189** M17
Lelintah, *Indonesia* **189** K17
Lêliogat, Île, *New Caledonia, Fr.* **218** D9
Le Lion-d'Angers, *Fr.* **147** R6
Le Locle, *Switz.* **150** B2
Le Lorrain, *Martinique, Fr.* **121** E22
Lelystad, *Neth.* **146** H13
Le Madonie, *It.* **151** S10
Le Maire, Estrecho de, *Arg.* **133** X10
Léman, Lac (Lake of Geneva), *Fr., Switz.* **147** T15
Lemanmanu, *P.N.G.* **217** J13
Le Mans, *Fr.* **147** Q7
Le Marin, *Martinique, Fr.* **121** G23
Le Mars, *Iowa, U.S.* **104** M9
Lemei Rock, *Wash., U.S.* **108** E4
Lemesos, *Cyprus* **160** Q7
Lemgo, *Ger.* **148** E7
Lemhi, river, *Idaho, U.S.* **106** F6
Lemhi Range, *Idaho, U.S.* **106** F6
Lemieux Islands, *Nunavut, Can.* **83** G19
Lemmer, *Neth.* **146** H13
Lemmon, *S. Dak., U.S.* **104** H3
Lemmon, Mount, *Ariz., U.S.* **107** V8
Lemnos *see* Límnos, island, *Gr.* **155** E14
Le Mont-Dore, *Fr.* **147** U10
Le Montet, *Fr.* **147** T11
Lemoore, *Calif., U.S.* **109** U6
Le Morne Brabant, cape, *Mauritius* **205** H19
Le Morne Rouge, *Martinique, Fr.* **121** E22
Lemotol, bay, *F.S.M.* **217** C14
Le Moule, *Guadeloupe, Fr.* **121** E16
Lempdes, *Fr.* **147** U11
Lemsid, *W. Sahara, Mor.* **196** D6
Lena, river, *Russ.* **166** C10
Lena, river, *Russ.* **159** E16
Lena Tablemount, *Antarctic Oc.* **245** D15
Lencouacq, *Fr.* **147** W7
Lenger, *Kaz.* **175** J13
Lenghu, *China* **180** G9
Lengua de Vaca Point, *S. Amer.* **126** L4
Lenin, *Taj.* **176** J7
Leningrad *see* Sankt-Peterburg, *Russ.* **156** F6
Leningrad, *Taj.* **176** J8
Leningradskaya, *Russ.* **157** R10
Leninogorsk, *Russ.* **156** J16
Leninogorsk *see* Ridder, *Kaz.* **175** D18
Lenin Peak, *Kyrg., Taj.* **176** H10
Leninsk *see* Bayqongyr, *Kaz.* **174** G10
Leninskiy, *Russ.* **156** H13
Leninsk Kuznetskiy, *Russ.* **158** K12
Lennox, *S. Dak., U.S.* **104** M8
Lennox-King Glacier, *Antarctica* **227** L13
Lenoir, *N.C., U.S.* **96** H8
Lenoir City, *Tenn., U.S.* **101** F18
Lenora, *Kans., U.S.* **105** R5
Lenox, *Iowa, U.S.* **105** Q10
Lenox, *Mass., U.S.* **94** K12
Lens, *Fr.* **146** M10
Lensk, *Russ.* **159** J16
Lentekhi, *Rep. of Georgia* **169** B17
Lenti, *Hung.* **149** M13
Lentini, *It.* **151** T12
Lenya, *Myanmar* **187** P8
Léo, *Burkina Faso* **200** F10
Leoben, *Aust.* **148** L11
Léogâne, *Haiti* **117** M16
Leola, *S. Dak., U.S.* **104** J6
Leominster, *Mass., U.S.* **95** K14
Léon, *Fr.* **147** X6
León, *Mex.* **114** H10
León, *Nicar.* **115** M17
León, *Sp.* **144** C9
León, Montes de, *Sp.* **144** C8
Leon, *Iowa, U.S.* **105** Q11
Leon, river, *Tex., U.S.* **102** M10
Leonard, *Tex., U.S.* **102** K12
Leonard's, *Virgin Islands, U.K.* **120** Q6
Leonarisso, *Cyprus* **160** M10
Leonberg, *Ger.* **148** J6
Leonding, *Aust.* **148** K11
Leone, *Amer. Samoa, U.S.* **218** M7
Leone Bay, *Amer. Samoa, U.S.* **218** M6
Leongatha, *Vic., Austral.* **211** Z12
Leonídio, *Gr.* **154** L11
Leonora, *W. Aust., Austral.* **211** V4
Leopold and Astrid Coast, *Antarctica* **227** H21
Leopoldsburg, *Belg.* **146** K13
Léopoldville *see* Kinshasa, *Dem. Rep. of the Congo* **198** L7
Leoti, *Kans., U.S.* **105** T3
Lepanto, *Ark., U.S.* **100** F11
Lepe, *Sp.* **144** L6
Le Perthus, *Fr.* **147** Z10
Le Petit-Quevilly, *Fr.* **147** N8
Leping, *China* **182** M7
Lepontine Alps, *It., Switz.* **150** C4
Le Porge, *Fr.* **147** V6
Le Port, *Reunion, Fr.* **205** G15
Le Prêcheur, *Martinique, Fr.* **121** E21
Lepsi, *Kaz.* **175** F17
Le Puy, *Fr.* **147** V12
Ler, *Sudan* **198** G12
Lercara Friddi, *It.* **151** S10
Léré, *Chad* **197** K14
Lerida, *Qnsld., Austral.* **211** T12
Lerik, *Azerb.* **169** F22
Lerma, river, *N. Amer.* **80** N5
Lerma, *Sp.* **144** D11
Le Robert, *Martinique, Fr.* **121** F23
Léros, island, *Gr.* **155** L17
Le Roy, *N.Y., U.S.* **94** J6
LeRoy, *Kans., U.S.* **105** T9
Lerwick, *Scot., U.K.* **142** D12
Leş, *Rom.* **152** C11
Les Abymes, *Guadeloupe, Fr.* **121** E15
Le St.-Esprit, *Martinique, Fr.* **121** F23
Les Amirante, islands, *Seychelles* **205** Q20
Les Anses-d'Arlets, *Martinique, Fr.* **121** G22
Les Avirons, *Reunion, Fr.* **205** H15
Les Bons, *Andorra* **160** J3
Les Borges Blanques, *Sp.* **145** D16
Lesbos *see* Lésvos, island, *Gr.* **155** F16
Les Cayes, *Haiti* **117** M15
Les Coteaux, *Trinidad & Tobago* **121** N17
Les Ecréhou, *Ch. Is.* **143** Z12
Les Escaldes, *Andorra* **160** J3
Leshan, *China* **180** L11
Leskovac, *Serb. & Mont.* **152** H11
Les Landes, plain, *Fr.* **147** W6
Leslie, *Ark., U.S.* **100** F8
Lesmont, *Fr.* **147** Q12
Lesneven, *Fr.* **147** P3
Lesnoye, *Russ.* **156** G8
Lesosibirsk, *Russ.* **159** K13
Lesotho, *Af.* **195** Q21
Lesozavodsk, *Russ.* **159** L21
L'Esperance Rock, *Kermadec Is., N.Z.* **214** M9
Les Sables-d'Olonne, *Fr.* **147** T5
Les Saintes, islands, *Guadeloupe, Fr.* **121** G14
Lessay, *Fr.* **147** N6
Les Sept Îles, *Fr.* **147** P4
Lesser Antilles, islands, *N. Amer.* **80** N12
Lesser Caucasus, range, *Arm., Azerb., Rep. of Georgia* **169** C16
Lesser Khingan Range, *China* **166** E12
Lesser Slave Lake, *Alta., Can.* **82** K10
Lesser Sunda Islands, *Indonesia* **189** M13
Les Soeurs (The Sisters), islands, *Seychelles* **205** M21
Lesson, Point, *F.S.M.* **217** B18
Les Trois-Îlets, *Martinique, Fr.* **121** F22
Le Sueur, *Minn., U.S.* **104** K11
Lésvos (Lesbos, Mitilíni), *Gr.* **155** F16
Leszno, *Pol.* **149** E13
Le Tampon, *Reunion, Fr.* **205** H16
Letchworth, *Eng., U.K.* **143** U14
Letea, Ostrov, *Rom.* **153** E18

Le Teil, Fr. 147 W12
Lethbridge, Alta., Can. 82 N10
Lethem, Guyana 129 F14
Le Thuy, Vietnam 186 K13
Leti, Kepulauan, Indonesia 189 M16
Leticia, Col. 128 L8
Leting, China 182 D8
Letsôk-aw Kyun, Myanmar 187 P7
Leuca, It. 151 P16
Leucas see Lefkáda, island, Gr. 154 G7
Leucate, Fr. 147 Y11
Leucate, Étang de, Fr. 147 Y11
Leulumoega, Samoa 218 L3
Leuser, peak, Indonesia 188 G4
Leusoalii, Amer. Samoa, U.S. 218 P4
Levan, Utah, U.S. 106 M7
Levanger, Nor. 140 H11
Levant, Île du, Fr. 147 Y15
Levant Coast, Asia 166 F3
Levanto, It. 150 G5
Le Vauclin, Martinique, Fr. 121 F23
Levelland, Tex., U.S. 102 K4
Leveque, Cape, Austral. 210 C4
Levera Pond, Grenada 121 J23
Le Verdon-sur-Mer, Fr. 147 U6
Leverkusen, Ger. 148 F5
Levet, Fr. 147 S10
Levice, Slovakia 149 K14
Levídi, Gr. 154 K10
Levin, N.Z. 213 M19
Lévis, Que., Can. 83 P20
Lévitha, island, Gr. 155 L17
Levittown, N.Y., U.S. 94 N12
Levittown, P.R., U.S. 120 M4
Levittown, Pa., U.S. 94 P10
Levski, Bulg. 153 H14
Levuka, Fiji Is. 218 H7
Lewellen, Nebr., U.S. 105 P3
Lewes, Del., U.S. 96 C15
Lewes, Eng., U.K. 143 W14
Lewis, Kans., U.S. 105 U5
Lewis, river, Wash., U.S. 108 E4
Lewis, Isle of, Scot., U.K. 142 H6
Lewis and Clark National Historic Park, Oreg., U.S. 108 E2
Lewis and Clark Range, Mont., U.S. 106 C6
Lewisburg, Tenn., U.S. 101 F15
Lewisburg, W. Va., U.S. 96 E9
Lewis Pass, N.Z. 213 N17
Lewis Range, Austral. 210 E7
Lewis Smith Lake, Ala., U.S. 101 H14
Lewiston, Idaho, U.S. 106 D3
Lewiston, Me., U.S. 95 G16
Lewistown, Ill., U.S. 99 Q4
Lewistown, Mont., U.S. 106 C9
Lewistown, Pa., U.S. 94 N6
Lewisville, Ark., U.S. 100 J7
Lewisville Lake, Tex., U.S. 102 K11
Lexington, Ky., U.S. 101 B18
Lexington, Miss., U.S. 100 K11
Lexington, Mo., U.S. 105 S11
Lexington, N.C., U.S. 96 H10
Lexington, Nebr., U.S. 105 Q5
Lexington, Oreg., U.S. 108 F6
Lexington, Tenn., U.S. 101 F13
Lexington, Va., U.S. 96 E10
Lexington Park, Md., U.S. 96 D14
Leydsdorp, S. Af. 202 H11
Leyte, island, Philippines 189 E15
Leyte Gulf, Philippines 189 E15
Lezha, Russ. 156 G11
Lezhë, Albania 152 K9
L'gov, Russ. 156 M8
Lhasa, China 180 L8
Lhazê, China 180 L6
Lhokseumawe, Indonesia 188 G4
L'Hospitalet, Fr. 147 Z9
L'Hospitalet de Llobregat, Sp. 145 E17
Li, river, China 182 M3
Liamuiga, Mount, St. Kitts & Nevis 121 A17
Lian, river, China 183 Q4
Liancheng, China 183 Q7
Liancourt Rocks see Dokdo, Japan 184 M6
Liangbuaya, Indonesia 188 J12
Liangcheng, China 182 C4
Liangping, China 182 K1
Lianjiang, China 183 P8
Lianjiang, China 183 S2
Lianping, China 183 Q5
Lianshan, China 183 Q3
Lianxian, China 183 Q3
Lianyun, China 182 H8
Lianyungang (Xinpu), China 182 H8
Liao, river, China 182 B11
Liaocheng, China 182 F6
Liaodong Bandao, China 182 D10
Liaodong Wan, China 182 C10
Liaodun, China 180 F8
Liaoyang, China 182 C11
Liaoyuan, China 182 A12
Liaozhong, China 182 C10
Liaquatpur, Pak. 177 S9
Liard, river, N.W.T., Can. 82 H10
Liari, Pak. 177 V5
Libby, Mont., U.S. 106 B4
Libenge, Dem. Rep. of the Congo 198 H8
Liberal, Kans., U.S. 105 V4
Liberec, Czech Rep. 148 G11
Liberia, Af. 195 H14
Liberia, Costa Rica 115 N18
Liberta, Antigua & Barbuda 121 B21
Libertador General San Martín, Arg. 132 E9
Liberty, Mo., U.S. 105 S10
Liberty, N.Y., U.S. 94 L10
Liberty, S.C., U.S. 96 J7
Liberty, Tex., U.S. 103 Q14
Lib Island, Marshall Is. 216 G3
Libni, Gebel, Egypt 171 P3
Liboi, Kenya 199 K15
Libourne, Fr. 147 V7
Libreville, Gabon 201 K15
Libya, Af. 195 E9
Libyan Desert, Af. 194 E8
Libyan Plateau, Egypt, Lib. 197 C16
Licantén, Chile 132 L6
Licata, It. 151 T10
Lice, Turk. 169 G15
Lichinga, Mozambique 203 D13
Lichtenfels, Ger. 148 G8
Lichuan, China 182 L2
Lichuan, China 183 N7
Licking, river, Ky., U.S. 101 B19
Licking, Mo., U.S. 105 U13
Ličko Lešće, Croatia 152 F5
Licosa, Punta, It. 151 N11
Lida, Belarus 156 K3
Lidgerwood, N. Dak., U.S. 104 H8
Lidköping, Sw. 140 L12
Lido di Jesolo, It. 150 D8
Lido di Ostia see Lido di Roma, It. 150 L8
Lido di Roma (Lido di Ostia), It. 150 L8
Līeānī, river, Leb. 170 K6
Liechtenstein, Eur. 160 D3
Liège, Belg. 146 L13
Lieksa, Fin. 141 G17
Lienz, Aust. 148 M9
Liepāja, Latv. 141 M15
Lier, Belg. 146 K12
Liestal, Switz. 150 A3
Liffey, river, Ire. 143 S6
Lifford, Ire. 143 P5
Lifou, Île (Lifu), New Caledonia, Fr. 218 C9
Lifu see Lifou, Île, island, New Caledonia, Fr. 218 C9
Lifuka, island, Tonga 218 P7
Ligneuville, Belg. 146 M14
Ligny-en-Barrois, Fr. 147 P13
Ligurian Sea, It. 150 H4
Liha Point, Niue, N.Z. 219 B21
Lihir, island, P.N.G. 213 C21
Lihir Group, P.N.G. 213 B21
Līhu'e, Hawai'i, U.S. 112 C6
L'Îlot, island, Seychelles 205 N21
Lijeron, island, Marshall Is. 216 L7
Lijiang, China 180 M10
Likasi, Dem. Rep. of the Congo 198 N11
Likiep Atoll, Marshall Is. 216 G4
Likoma Island, Malawi 203 D13
Liku, Niue, N.Z. 219 B21
Likuone Bay, Tonga 218 L12
Likupang, Indonesia 189 H15
Lilbourn, Mo., U.S. 105 V16
L'Île-Bouchard, Fr. 147 S8
L'Île-Rousse, Fr. 150 J4
Lilian, Point, Austral. 210 H6
Lilian Point, Banaba, Kiribati 217 D20
Liling, China 183 N4
Lille, Fr. 146 L10
Lillehammer, Nor. 140 K11
Lillesand, Nor. 140 M10
Lillie Glacier, Antarctica 227 Q14
Lillooet, B.C., Can. 82 L8
Lilongwe, Malawi 202 E12
Lilo Viejo, Arg. 132 G10
Lim, river, Bosn. & Herzg., Serb. & Mont. 152 G9
Lima, Mont., U.S. 106 F7
Lima, Ohio, U.S. 99 Q11
Lima, Peru 130 H3
Lima, river, Port. 144 D5
Liman, Russ. 157 R15
Liman Beren, lake, Russ. 157 R13
Lima Reservoir, Mont., U.S. 106 F7
Limarí, Río, Chile 132 J6
Limavady, N. Ire., U.K. 143 P6
Limay, river, S. Amer. 126 N4
Limbara, Monte, It. 150 M4
Limbdi, India 178 J3
Limbé, Haiti 117 L16
Limbe, Cameroon 201 J15
Limburg, Ger. 148 G6
Limeira, Braz. 131 M13
Limenária, Gr. 155 C14
Limerick (Luimneach), Ire. 143 T4
Limestone, Me., U.S. 95 B18
Limfjorden, lake, Den. 140 N11
Limia, river, Sp. 144 D6
Limín see Thássos, Gr. 155 C14
Liminka, Fin. 141 F15
Limmen Bight, Austral. 210 B9
Límni, Gr. 154 G11
Límnos (Lemnos), island, Gr. 155 E14
Limoges, Fr. 147 U9
Limon, Colo., U.S. 106 M14
Limon, Mount, Mauritius 205 J20
Limone Piemonte, It. 150 F2
Limoux, Fr. 147 Y10
Limpopo, river, Botswana, Mozambique, S. Af. 202 H12
Limu, island, Tonga 218 Q7
Limufuafua Point, Niue, N.Z. 219 C20
Līnah, Saudi Arabia 172 G9
Lin'an, China 182 L9
Linapacan, island, Philippines 189 D13
Linares, Chile 132 M6
Linares, Mex. 114 F11
Linares, Sp. 144 K11
Linariá, Gr. 155 G14
Lincang, China 180 P10
Linchuan, China 183 N6
Lincoln, Arg. 132 L11
Lincoln, Calif., U.S. 109 Q5
Lincoln, Eng., U.K. 143 S13
Lincoln, Ill., U.S. 99 R5
Lincoln, Kans., U.S. 105 S7
Lincoln, Me., U.S. 95 E18
Lincoln, Mich., U.S. 98 J12
Lincoln, N.H., U.S. 95 G14
Lincoln, Nebr., U.S. 105 Q8
Lincoln City, Oreg., U.S. 108 F2
Lincoln Heights, Eng., U.K. 143 S13
Lincoln Island, China 188 B10
Lincoln Park, Mich., U.S. 98 M12
Lincoln Sea, N. Amer. 80 A7
Lincolnton, Ga., U.S. 96 L7
Lincolnton, N.C., U.S. 96 H8
Lind, Wash., U.S. 108 D8
Linda Downs, Qnsld., Austral. 211 T10
Lindale, Ga., U.S. 96 K4
Lindale, Tex., U.S. 102 L13
Lindau, Aust. 148 L7
Lindbergh Bay, Virgin Islands, U.S. 120 N8
Linden, Ala., U.S. 101 L14
Linden, Guyana 129 E14
Linden, Tex., U.S. 102 K15
Lindesnes, Nor. 140 M10
Lindi, Tanzania 199 N15
Lindisfarne see Holy Island, island, Eng., U.K. 143 N12
Lindo, river, Parag. 130 M10
Líndos, Gr. 155 N20
Lindsay, Calif., U.S. 109 U7
Lindsay, Mont., U.S. 106 C13
Lindsay, Okla., U.S. 102 H10
Lindsborg, Kans., U.S. 105 T7
Line Islands, Kiribati 214 G12
Linfen, China 182 F4
Lingao, China 183 T1
Lingbao, China 182 H3
Lingbi, China 182 J7
Lingchuan, China 183 P2
Lingen, Ger. 148 D6
Lingga, island, Indonesia 188 J7
Lingga, Kepulauan, Indonesia 188 J7
Lingle, Wyo., U.S. 106 J14
Lingqiu, China 181 G14
Lingshan, China 183 S1
Lingshui, China 183 V1
Lingtai, China 182 G1
Linguère, Senegal 196 G5
Lingui, China 183 Q2
Lingxian, China 183 P4
Lingyuan, China 182 C8
Linhai (Taizhou), China 182 M10
Linhares, Braz. 131 L16
Linhe, China 182 C1
Linjiang, China 182 B13
Linköping, Sw. 141 L13
Linn, Tex., U.S. 103 V10
Linnhe, Loch, Scot., U.K. 142 L8
Linqing, China 182 F6
Linquan, China 182 J6
Linru, China 182 H4
Linstead, Jam. 120 J9
Lintao, China 180 J11
Linton, Ind., U.S. 99 S8
Linton, N. Dak., U.S. 104 H5
Lintong, China 182 H2
Linxi, China 182 A8
Linxi, China 182 D8
Linxian, China 182 E3
Linyi, China 182 F7
Linyi, China 182 G8
Linz, Aust. 148 K11
Lio Matoh, Malaysia 188 H11
Lion, Golfe du, Fr. 147 Y12
Lionel Town, Jam. 120 K9
Lions, Gulf of, Fr. 138 H4
Lions Den, Zimb. 202 F11
Liot Point, N.W.T., Can. 82 D12
Liouesso, Congo 201 K17
Lipa, Philippines 189 C13
Lipari, Isola, It. 151 R11
Lipari, Isole (Eolie), It. 151 R11
Lipetsk, Russ. 156 M10
Liping, China 183 P1
Lipno, Pol. 149 D14
Līpoa Point, Hawai'i, U.S. 113 F16
Lipova, Rom. 152 D11
Lipscomb, Tex., U.S. 102 F7
Lipsí, island, Gr. 155 L17
Lipsí, Gr. 155 L17
Liptovský Mikuláš, Slovakia 149 J15
Lipu, China 183 Q2
Lipu Lekh Pass, China, India, Nepal 178 E8
Liri, river, It. 150 L10
Līsakovsk, Kaz. 174 C10
Lisala, Dem. Rep. of the Congo 198 J9
Lisboa (Lisbon), Port. 144 H4
Lisbon, N. Dak., U.S. 104 H7
Lisbon see Lisboa, Port. 144 H4
Lisbon Falls, Me., U.S. 95 G16
Lisburn, N. Ire., U.K. 143 Q7
Lisburne, Cape, Alas., U.S. 110 C12
Liscannor Bay, Ire. 143 S3
Lishu, China 182 A11
Lishui, China 182 M9
Lisianski Island, Hawai'i, U.S. 112 L3
Lisieux, Fr. 147 P8
Liski, Rom. 153 D16
Liski, Russ. 157 N10
L'Isle-sur-la-Sorgue, Fr. 147 X13
Lismore, N.S.W., Austral. 211 W15
Lismore, island, Scot., U.K. 142 L8
Lissa see Vis, island, Croatia 152 H6
Lister, Mount, Antarctica 227 N14
Listowel, Ire. 143 T3
Listowel Downs, Qnsld., Austral. 211 U13
Litang, river, China 180 M10
Litang, China 183 R1
Litang, China 180 L10
Litani, river, Fr. Guiana, Fr., Suriname 129 F17
Litchfield, Ill., U.S. 99 S5
Litchfield, Minn., U.S. 104 J10
Lit-et-Mixe, Fr. 147 W6
Lithgow, N.S.W., Austral. 211 X14
Líthino, Akrotírio, Gr. 155 R14
Lithuania, Eur. 139 S8
Litóhoro, Gr. 154 D10
Little, river, La., U.S. 100 M8
Little, river, Okla., U.S. 102 J14
Little, river, Tex., U.S. 103 P11
Little Abaco Island, Bahamas 120 A5
Little Andaman, island, India 179 R14
Little Barrier Island, N.Z. 213 J19
Little Bay, Gibraltar, U.K. 161 Q23
Little Belt Mountains, Mont., U.S. 106 D8
Little Bighorn, river, Mont., Wyo., U.S. 106 F11
Little Bighorn Battlefield National Monument, Mont., U.S. 106 E11
Little Bitter Lake see Murrat el Sughra, Buheirat, Egypt 171 Q1
Little Blue, river, Nebr., U.S. 105 R7
Little Cayman, island, Cayman Is., U.K. 116 L8
Little Chute, Wis., U.S. 98 J6
Little Coco Island, Myanmar 186 M4
Little Darby Island, Bahamas 120 D7
Little Dix Bay, Virgin Islands, U.K. 120 R8
Little Exuma, island, Bahamas 120 F9
Little Falls, Minn., U.S. 104 H10
Little Falls, N.Y., U.S. 94 J10
Littlefield, Ariz., U.S. 107 Q5
Littlefield, Tex., U.S. 102 J4
Little Fork, Minn., U.S. 104 E11
Littlefork, Minn., U.S. 104 E11
Littlehampton, Eng., U.K. 143 W13
Little Hans Lollik Island, Virgin Islands, U.S. 120 M9
Little Harbor, Bahamas 120 B7
Little Inagua Island, Bahamas 117 J16
Little Jost Van Dyke, island, Virgin Islands, U.K. 120 L11
Little London, Jam. 120 H6
Little Lost, river, Idaho, U.S. 106 G6
Little Marais, Minn., U.S. 104 F13
Little Mecatina, river, Nfld. & Lab., Que., Can. 83 L22
Little Missouri, river, S. Dak., U.S. 104 J1
Little Nicobar, island, India 179 T15
Little Powder, river, Mont., Wyo., U.S. 106 F13
Little Red, river, Ark., U.S. 100 F8
Little Rock, Ark., U.S. 100 G8
Little St. James Island, Virgin Islands, U.S. 120 N10
Little Salt Lake, Utah, U.S. 107 P6
Little San Salvador, island, Bahamas 117 E13
Little Sioux, river, Iowa, U.S. 105 N9
Little Snake, river, Colo., U.S. 106 L10
Little Sound, Cayman Is., U.K. 120 J2
Little Sound (Port Royal Bay), Bermuda, U.K. 120 C2
Little Suamico, Wis., U.S. 98 J7
Little Thatch Island, Virgin Islands, U.K. 120 R5
Little Tobago, island, Trinidad & Tobago 121 N19
Little Tobago Island, Virgin Islands, U.K. 120 L10
Littleton, Colo., U.S. 106 M13
Littleton, N.H., U.S. 95 G14
Little Wabash, river, Ill., U.S. 99 S6
Liucheng, China 183 Q1
Liuhe, China 182 B12
Liuwa Plain, Zambia 202 E9
Liuyang, China 183 N4
Liuzhai, China 180 N12
Liuzhou, China 183 Q1
Livadi, Gr. 155 L13
Livádia, Gr. 155 M18
Livadiá, Gr. 154 H11
Līvāni, Latv. 141 M17
Live Oak, Fla., U.S. 97 R7
Livermore, Calif., U.S. 109 S4
Livermore, Ky., U.S. 101 C15
Livermore, Mount, Tex., U.S. 103 P1
Liverpool, Eng., U.K. 143 S10
Liverpool, N.S., Can. 83 P22
Liverpool Bay, N.W.T., Can. 82 D11
Liverpool Range, Austral. 210 K14
Livingston, Ala., U.S. 101 L13
Livingston, Mont., U.S. 106 E8
Livingston, Tenn., U.S. 101 E17
Livingston, Tex., U.S. 103 P14
Lívingston, Guatemala 115 K16
Livingston, Lake, Tex., U.S. 103 P14
Livingstone, Zambia 202 F10
Livingston Island, Antarctica 226 C3
Livny, Russ. 156 M9
Livonia, Mich., U.S. 98 M12
Livorno (Leghorn), It. 150 H6
Livron, Fr. 147 V13
Līwā, region, U.A.E. 173 K14
Liwale, Tanzania 199 N14
Liwonde, Malawi 203 E13
Lixian, China 182 L3
Li Yubu, Sudan 198 H11
Lizard Point, Eng., U.K. 143 Y8
Lizarra see Estella, Sp. 145 C13
Ljubljana, Slov. 152 D4
Ljuboten, peak, Serb. & Mont. 152 J11

Ljusdal, Sw. 141 J13
Llaima Volcano, S. Amer. 126 N4
Llamara, Salar de, Chile 132 D7
Llandrindod Wells, Wales, U.K. 143 U10
Llanes, Sp. 144 B10
Llano, river, Tex., U.S. 103 P8
Llano, Tex., U.S. 103 P9
Llanos, region, S. Amer. 126 B4
Llanquihue, Lago, Chile 133 Q6
Llavorsí, Sp. 145 C16
Lleida, Sp. 145 D15
Llerena, Sp. 144 J8
Lleyn Peninsula, Wales, U.K. 143 T8
Llica, Bol. 130 L6
Llívia, Sp. 145 C17
Llodio, Sp. 144 B12
Llorts, Andorra 160 H3
Llosa, river, Sp. 160 K5
Lloydminster, Alta., Can. 82 L11
Llucmajor, Sp. 145 G18
Lluidas Vale, Jam. 120 J9
Llyswen, Wales, U.K. 143 U10
Ló, Ponta do, Sao Tome and Principe 205 D20
Lo, river, Vietnam 186 G11
Loa, river, Chile 132 D7
Loa, Utah, U.S. 107 N7
Loaita Island, Spratly Is. 188 E11
Lo‘alo‘a Heiau, Hawai‘i, U.S. 113 H17
Lobamba, Swaziland 203 J11
Lobatse, Botswana 202 J10
Lobaya, river, Cen. Af. Rep. 194 J6
Lobería, Arg. 133 N12
Lobería, Arg. 133 Q10
Lobikaere, island, Marshall Is. 216 G11
Lobito, Angola 202 D5
Lobitos, Peru 130 E1
Lobo, Indonesia 189 K19
Lobos, Arg. 132 L12
Lobos, Cay, Cuba 116 H11
Lobos Islands, S. Amer. 126 E1
Lobuya, Russ. 159 D19
Locana, It. 150 D2
Locarno, Switz. 150 C4
Lochcarron, Scot., U.K. 142 J8
Lochearnhead, Scot., U.K. 142 L9
Lochgilphead, Scot., U.K. 142 M8
Lochmaddy, Scot., U.K. 142 J6
Lochsa, river, Idaho, U.S. 106 D5
Lochy, Loch, Scot., U.K. 142 K8
Lockesburg, Ark., U.S. 100 H6
Lockhart, Tex., U.S. 103 Q10
Lockhart River, Qnsld., Austral. 211 P12
Lock Haven, Pa., U.S. 94 M6
Lockney, Tex., U.S. 102 J5
Lockport, N.Y., U.S. 94 J5
Lockwood Terrace, Guam, U.S. 216 C10
Locminé, Fr. 147 Q4
Locri, It. 151 R13
Lod (Lydda), Israel 170 M5
Lodeynoye Pole, Russ. 156 E8
Lodge Creek, Mont., U.S. 106 A9
Lodge Grass, Mont., U.S. 106 E11
Lodgepole, Nebr., U.S. 105 P2
Lodgepole Creek, Nebr., U.S. 105 P1
Lodhran, Pak. 177 S10
Lodi, Calif., U.S. 109 R5
Lodi, It. 150 E5
Lodja, Dem. Rep. of the Congo 198 L10
Lodwar, Kenya 199 J14
Łódź, Pol. 149 E15
Loei, Thai. 186 K9
Lofanga, island, Tonga 218 P7
Lofoten, Nor. 140 E11
Lofty Range, Austral. 210 G3
Logan, Iowa, U.S. 105 P9
Logan, Kans., U.S. 105 R5
Logan, N. Mex., U.S. 107 R15
Logan, Ohio, U.S. 99 R14
Logan, Utah, U.S. 106 J7
Logan, W. Va., U.S. 96 E7
Logan, Mount, Wash., U.S. 108 A5
Logan, Mount, Yukon, Can. 82 F7
Logansport, Ind., U.S. 99 Q9
Logansport, La., U.S. 100 L6
Logashkino, Russ. 159 D18
Logone, river, Cameroon, Chad 194 H6
Logoniégué, Burkina Faso 200 F9
Logroño, Sp. 144 C12
Loh, island, Vanuatu 218 A1
Lohardaga, India 178 J10
Loharghat, India 178 G13
Lohne, Ger. 148 D6
Loi, island, Marshall Is. 216 N5
Loi Mwe, Myanmar 186 H8
Loire, river, Fr. 147 Q10
Loire, river, Fr. 147 R6
Loíza, P.R., U.S. 120 M5
Loja, Ecua. 128 L3
Loja, Sp. 144 L10
Loji, Indonesia 189 K16
Lojjairok, island, Marshall Is. 216 N5
Lojwa, island, Marshall Is. 216 G8
Lokhwabe, Botswana 202 J8
Lokitaung, Kenya 199 H14
Loknya, Russ. 156 H6
Lokoja, Nigeria 201 G14
Lokolama, Dem. Rep. of the Congo 198 K9
Lokomo, Cameroon 201 J17
Lokoro, river, Dem. Rep. of the Congo 198 K9
Loks Land, Nunavut, Can. 83 H19
Lokuru, Solomon Is. 217 M16
Lol, river, Sudan 198 G11
Lolland, island, Den. 140 P12
Lolo Pass, Idaho, Mont., U.S. 106 D5
Lolowaï, Vanuatu 218 C2
Lom, Bulg. 153 G13
Lom, Nor. 140 J10
Lomaloma, Fiji Is. 218 H9
Lomami, river, Dem. Rep. of the Congo 198 K10
Loma Mountains, Guinea, Sierra Leone 200 F6
Lomawai, Fiji Is. 218 J5
Lombadina, W. Aust., Austral. 211 R4
Lombez, Fr. 147 X8
Lomblen, island, Indonesia 189 M14
Lombok, island, Indonesia 188 M12
Lombok, Selat, Indonesia 188 M11
Lomé, Togo 200 H11
Lomela, river, Dem. Rep. of the Congo 198 K9
Lomela, Dem. Rep. of the Congo 198 K10
Lometa, Tex., U.S. 103 N9
Lomié, Cameroon 201 J17
Lomlom, island, Solomon Is. 217 P23
Lomond, Loch, Scot., U.K. 142 M9
Lomonosov, Russ. 156 F6
Lomonosov Ridge, Arctic Oc. 242 F8
Lomphat, Cambodia 186 M13
Lompoc, Calif., U.S. 109 W5
Łomża, Pol. 149 C17
Lon, Hon, Vietnam 187 N14
Lonauli, India 178 L3
Loncoche, Chile 133 P6
Loncopué, Arg. 133 N7
London, Eng., U.K. 143 V14
London, Kiribati 217 B22
London, Ky., U.S. 101 D18
London, Ohio, U.S. 99 R12
London, Ont., Can. 83 R18
London Bridge Island, Grenada 121 J23
Londonderry, St. Lucia 121 L14
Londonderry (Derry), N. Ire., U.K. 143 P6
Londonderry, Cape, Austral. 210 B6
Londonderry, Isla, Chile 133 Y8
Londrina, Braz. 130 M12
Lone Pine, Calif., U.S. 109 T8
Lonerock, Oreg., U.S. 108 F6
Longa, river, Angola 202 C6
Long Bay, Barbados 121 L19
Long Bay, Virgin Islands, U.K. 120 R5
Long Bay, Virgin Islands, U.K. 120 R5
Long Bay, Jam. 120 H5
Long Bay, Jam. 120 K8
Long Beach, Calif., U.S. 109 X8
Long Beach, Miss., U.S. 100 P12
Long Beach, N.C., U.S. 96 K12
Long Beach, Wash., U.S. 108 D2
Longboat Key, Fla., U.S. 97 V7
Long Branch, N.J., U.S. 94 P11
Long Cay (Fortune Island), Bahamas 117 H14
Longchuan, China 183 R5
Long Creek, Oreg., U.S. 108 G7
Longdenville, Trinidad & Tobago 121 P22
Long Eaton, Eng., U.K. 143 T12
Longeau, Fr. 147 R13
Longford, Ire. 143 R5
Longglat, Indonesia 188 H12
Longhai, China 183 R7
Longhua, China 182 C7
Longido, Tanzania 199 L14
Longiram, Indonesia 188 J11
Long Island, Antigua & Barbuda 121 A21
Long Island, Bahamas 117 G14
Long Island, N.Y., U.S. 95 N13
Long Island, Nunavut, Can. 83 L17
Long Island, P.N.G. 213 C19
Long Island Sound, Conn., N.Y., U.S. 95 M13
Longjiang, China 181 C16
Longju, India 178 E14
Long Key, Fla., U.S. 97 Y10
Longkou, China 182 E9
Longlac, Ont., Can. 83 N16
Long Lake, N. Dak., U.S. 104 G5
Long Look, Virgin Islands, U.K. 120 Q7
Longmen, China 183 R5
Longmont, Colo., U.S. 106 L13
Longnan, China 183 Q5
Longnawan, Indonesia 188 H11
Longomapu, Tonga 218 L11
Long Pine, Nebr., U.S. 105 N5
Long Point, Virgin Islands, U.S. 120 N9
Long Point, Virgin Islands, U.S. 120 R2
Long Prairie, Minn., U.S. 104 H10
Longquan, China 183 N8
Long Range Mountains, N. Amer. 80 G10
Longreach, Qnsld., Austral. 211 T12
Longshan, China 182 L2
Longsheng, China 183 P2
Longs Peak, Colo., U.S. 106 L13
Longton, Qnsld., Austral. 211 S13
Longuyon, Fr. 160 L8
Longview, Tex., U.S. 102 L14
Longview, Wash., U.S. 108 E3
Longville, La., U.S. 100 P7
Longwy, Fr. 147 N13
Longxi, China 180 J12
Long Xuyen, Vietnam 187 P12
Longyan, China 183 Q7
Long'yugan, Russ. 158 G11
Lonoke, Ark., U.S. 100 G9
Lonquimay, Chile 133 N7
Lons-le-Saunier, Fr. 147 S13
Loogootee, Ind., U.S. 99 T8
Lookout, Cape, N.C., U.S. 96 J14
Lookout, Cape, Oreg., U.S. 108 F2
Lookout, Point, Austral. 210 H16
Lookout Mountain, N. Mex., U.S. 107 S10
Lookout Mountain, Tenn., U.S. 101 G17
Lookout Ridge, Alas., U.S. 111 C14
Loongana, W. Aust., Austral. 211 W6
Loop Head, Ire. 143 T2
Lop, China 180 G5
Lopatino, Russ. 156 L13
Lopatka, Cape, Russ. 166 C13
Lopatka, Mys, Russ. 159 G23
Lop Buri, Thai. 186 M9
Lopévi (Ulvéah), island, Vanuatu 218 E3
Lopez, Cap, Gabon 201 L14
Lopez Point, Calif., U.S. 109 U4
Lop Nur, China 180 G8
Lopphavet, Nor. 141 C13
Lora, Hamun-i-, Pak. 177 S4
Lorain, Ohio, U.S. 99 P14
Loraine, Tex., U.S. 102 M6
Loralai, Pak. 177 R7
Lorca, Sp. 145 K13
Lord Howe Atoll see Ontong Java Atoll, Solomon Is. 217 J18
Lord Howe Island see Tomotu Noi, Solomon Is. 217 Q22
Lord Howe Rise, Pac. Oc. 238 N8
Lord of the Sky see Khan Tängiri, peak, Kaz., Kyrg. 176 E15
Lordsburg, N. Mex., U.S. 107 V10
Lorentzweiler, Lux. 160 J10
Lorenzo, Tex., U.S. 102 K5
Loreto, Bol. 130 J7
Loreto, Mex. 114 E6
Loreto, Braz. 131 F14
Loretto, Tenn., U.S. 101 G14
Lorian Swamp, Kenya 194 J10
Lorica, Col. 128 C4
Lorient, Fr. 147 R4
Lorimers, Turks & Caicos Is., U.K. 117 H17
Loris, S.C., U.S. 96 K11
Lormes, Fr. 147 R11
Lormi, India 178 J8
Lorn, Firth of, Scot., U.K. 142 L7
Lorne, Qnsld., Austral. 211 U13
Lornel, Pointe de, Fr. 146 L9
Lörrach, Ger. 148 L5
Lorraine, region, Fr. 147 P13
Los Ángeles, Chile 133 N6
Los Alamos, N. Mex., U.S. 107 R12
Los Andes, Chile 132 K7
Los Angeles, Calif., U.S. 109 X8
Los Angeles Aqueduct, Calif., U.S. 109 V8
Losap Atoll, F.S.M. 216 Q6
Los Banos, Calif., U.S. 109 T5
Los Blancos, Arg. 132 E11
Los Cerrillos, Arg. 132 K9
Los Corrales, Sp. 144 B10
Los Cristianos, Canary Is. 204 Q4
Los Frailes, islands, Venez. 119 N14
Los Gatos, Calif., U.S. 109 S4
Losheim, Ger. 160 K12
Los Hermanos, islands, Venez. 119 N14
Lošinj, island, Croatia 152 F4
Los Lagos, Chile 133 P6
Los Llanos, Canary Is. 204 Q3
Los Loros, Chile 132 G7
Los Lunas, N. Mex., U.S. 107 S12
Los Mochis, Mex. 114 E7
Los Olmos Creek, Tex., U.S. 103 U10
Los Osos, Calif., U.S. 109 V5
Los Palacios, Cuba 116 G5
Lospalos, Timor-Leste 189 M16
Lossiemouth, Scot., U.K. 142 J10
Los Teques, Venez. 128 B9
Los Testigos, islands, Venez. 119 N15
Lostine, Oreg., U.S. 108 F9
Lost River Range, Idaho, U.S. 106 G6
Lost Trail Pass, Idaho, Mont., U.S. 106 E6
Losuia, P.N.G. 213 E21
Los Vilos, Chile 132 K6
Los Yébenes, Sp. 144 G10
Lot, river, Fr. 147 W8
Lot, F.S.M. 217 G14
Lota, Chile 133 N6
Lotagipi Swamp, Kenya 199 H14
Lot Harbor, F.S.M. 217 G14
Lotofaga, Samoa 218 L3
Lot's Wife see Sōfu Gan, island, Japan 184 K5
Lott, Tex., U.S. 103 N11
Lottin, Port, F.S.M. 217 B18
Lou, island, P.N.G. 213 B19
Louang-Namtha, Laos 186 H9
Louangphrabang, Laos 186 J10
Loubomo, Congo 201 M16
Loudéac, Fr. 147 Q4
Loudonville, Ohio, U.S. 99 Q14
Loudun, Fr. 147 S7
Loué, Fr. 147 Q7
Loufan, China 182 E4
Louga, Senegal 196 G4
Lougheed Island, Nunavut, Can. 83 C14
Louhans, Fr. 147 S13
Louisa, Ky., U.S. 101 B20
Louisburg, N.C., U.S. 96 G12
Louisburgh, Ire. 143 R3
Louisiade Archipelago, P.N.G. 213 E22
Louisiana, Mo., U.S. 105 S14
Louisiana, U.S. 100 L7
Louisiana Point, La., U.S. 100 Q6
Louis II Stadium, Monaco 161 F20
Louisville, Ga., U.S. 96 M7
Louisville, Ky., U.S. 101 B16
Louisville, Miss., U.S. 100 K12
Louisville, Nebr., U.S. 105 Q9
Louisville Ridge, Pac. Oc. 238 P10
Louis-XIV, Pointe, Que., Can. 83 L17
Louj, island, Marshall Is. 216 G8
Loukouo, Congo 201 M17
Loulan Yiji, ruin, China 180 G8
Loulay, Fr. 147 T7
Loulé, Port. 144 L5
Loup, river, Nebr., U.S. 105 P7
Loup City, Nebr., U.S. 105 P6
Lourdes, Fr. 147 Y7
Lourdes-de-Blanc-Sablon, Que., Can. 83 L22
Lousã, Port. 144 F6
Louth, Eng., U.K. 143 S14
Louth, N.S.W., Austral. 211 W12
Loutrá Eleftherón, Gr. 155 C13
Loutrá Epidsoú, Gr. 154 G11
Loutráki, Gr. 154 F12
Loutráki, Gr. 154 J11
Loutrá Smokóvou, Gr. 154 G9
Louvet Point, St. Lucia 121 K14
Louviers, Fr. 147 N8
Lovango Cay, Virgin Islands, U.S. 120 M10
Lovea, Cambodia 187 N10
Lovech, Bulg. 153 H14
Loveland, Colo., U.S. 106 L13
Loveland Pass, Colo., U.S. 106 M12
Lovell, Wyo., U.S. 106 F10
Lovelock, Nev., U.S. 109 N8
Lovere, It. 150 D5
Loving, N. Mex., U.S. 107 V14
Lovington, N. Mex., U.S. 107 U15
Low, Cape, Nunavut, Can. 83 H16
Low Cay, Bahamas 120 F11
Lowell, Mass., U.S. 95 K14
Lowell, Oreg., U.S. 108 H3
Lowell, Lake, Idaho, U.S. 106 G3
Lower Belmont Bay, Virgin Islands, U.K. 120 M11
Lower Bogue, Bahamas 120 D5
Lower Guinea, region, Af. 194 K5
Lower Hutt, N.Z. 213 M19
Lower Lake, Calif., U.S. 108 M6
Lower Lough Erne, N. Ire., U.K. 143 Q5
Lower Matecumbe Key, Fla., U.S. 97 Y10
Lower Peninsula, Mich., U.S. 85 E16
Lower Post, B.C., Can. 82 H9
Lower Red Lake, Minn., U.S. 104 F10
Lower Tunguska, river, Russ. 166 D10
Lower Valley, Cayman Is., U.K. 120 J2
Lowestoft, Eng., U.K. 143 T16
Łowicz, Pol. 149 E15
Lowital, Vanuatu 218 H4
Lowkhi, Afghan. 177 Q3
Lowman, Idaho, U.S. 106 G4
Lowville, N.Y., U.S. 94 H9
Loyal, Loch, Scot., U.K. 142 H9
Loyalty Islands, New Caledonia, Fr. 214 K7
Loyauté, Îles (Loyalty Islands), New Caledonia, Fr. 218 D9
Loyew, Belarus 156 M6
Loyola, Punta, Arg. 133 W8
Loznica, Serb. & Mont. 152 F9
Lozova, Ukr. 157 P9
Luahiwa Petroglyphs, Hawai‘i, U.S. 113 G15
Luahoko, island, Tonga 218 P7
Luama, river, Dem. Rep. of the Congo 198 L11
Luamotu, island, Tuvalu 217 L23
Luan, river, China 182 C7
Lu'an, China 182 K6
Luanco, Sp. 144 A8
Luanda, Angola 202 C5
Luang Prabang Range, Laos 186 J9
Luangwa, river, Zambia 202 E12
Luangwa, Zambia 202 E11
Luaniua, island, Solomon Is. 217 J18
Luaniva, island, Wallis & Futuna, Fr. 218 B12
Luanping, China 182 C7
Luanshya, Zambia 202 D11
Luanxian, China 182 D8
Luapula, river, Dem. Rep. of the Congo, Zambia 194 M9
Luarca, Sp. 144 A8
Luatefito, island, Tonga 218 M11
Luau, Angola 202 D8
Luba, Eq. Guinea 204 M7
Luba, Bahia de, Eq. Guinea 204 M7
Lubānas Ezers, lake, Latv. 141 M17
Lubang Island, Philippines 189 D13
Lubango, Angola 202 E5
Lubao, Dem. Rep. of the Congo 198 L11
Lubartów, Pol. 149 E17
Lübbenau, Ger. 148 E11
Lubbock, Tex., U.S. 102 K5
Lubec, Me., U.S. 95 E19
Lübeck, Ger. 148 B8
Lubero, Dem. Rep. of the Congo 198 K12
Lubéron, Montagne du, Fr. 147 X13
Lubin, Pol. 148 F12
Lublin, Pol. 149 F17
Lubliniec, Pol. 149 G14
Lubny, Ukr. 157 P7
Lubok Antu, Malaysia 188 H10
Lubuagan, Philippines 189 B13
Lubudi, Dem. Rep. of the Congo 198 N11
Lubuklinggau, Indonesia 188 K6
Lubumbashi (Elisabethville), Dem. Rep. of the Congo 198 N11
Lucas, Kans., U.S. 105 S6
Lucaya, Bahamas 120 F2
Lucca, It. 150 G6
Lucea, Jam. 120 H6
Lucedale, Miss., U.S. 101 N13
Lucena, Philippines 189 C14
Lucena, Sp. 144 L10
Lučenec, Slovakia 149 K15
Lucera, It. 150 L12
Lucerne, Lake of see Vierwaldstätter See, Switz. 150 B4

Luchegorsk, *Russ.* 159 L21
Luchuan, *China* 183 S2
Lucie, river, *Suriname* 129 F15
Lucipara, Kepulauan, *Indonesia* 189 L16
Lucira, *Angola* 202 E5
Lucknow, *India* 178 G8
Lucknow, *Qnsld., Austral.* 211 T11
Lucy Bay, *Scot., U.K.* 143 P8
Lucy Creek, *N. Terr., Austral.* 211 T9
Luda Kamchiya, river, *Bulg.* 153 H16
Ludborough, *Eng., U.K.* 143 S14
Lüdenscheid, *Ger.* 148 F6
Lüderitz, *Namibia* 202 J6
Ludhiana, *India* 178 D5
Ludington, *Mich., U.S.* 98 K9
Ludlow, *Calif., U.S.* 109 W11
Ludlow, *Vt., U.S.* 95 H13
Ludogorie, region, *Bulg.* 138 J9
Ludogorsko Plato, *Bulg.* 153 G16
Ludowici, *Ga., U.S.* 97 P8
Ludus, *Rom.* 153 C13
Ludwigsburg, *Ger.* 148 J7
Ludwigshafen, *Ger.* 148 H6
Luebo, *Dem. Rep. of the Congo* 198 L9
Luena, *Angola* 202 D8
Lufeng, *China* 183 S6
Lufilufi, *Samoa* 218 L4
Lufkin, *Tex., U.S.* 103 N14
Luga, *Russ.* 156 G6
Lugano, *Switz.* 150 D4
Luganville, *Vanuatu* 218 D2
Lugenda, river, *Mozambique* 203 D14
Lugo, *It.* 150 F7
Lugo, *Sp.* 144 B7
Lugoj, *Rom.* 152 E11
Lugovoy, *Russ.* 158 H10
Luhans'k, *Ukr.* 157 Q10
Lui, river, *China* 183 Q1
Luiana, river, *Angola* 202 F8
Luichow Peninsula *see* Leizhou Bandao, *China* 183 T1
Luimneach *see* Limerick, *Ire.* 143 T4
Luing, island, *Scot., U.K.* 142 M8
Luino, *It.* 150 D4
Luitpold Coast, *Antarctica* 226 E10
Luján, *Arg.* 132 L12
Lujor, island, *Marshall Is.* 216 G8
Lukenie, river, *Dem. Rep. of the Congo* 198 L9
Lukeville, *Ariz., U.S.* 107 V6
Lukolela, *Dem. Rep. of the Congo* 198 K8
Lukovit, *Bulg.* 153 H13
Łuków, *Pol.* 149 E17
Lukulu, *Zambia* 202 E9
Lukunor Atoll, *F.S.M.* 216 Q7
Luleå, *Sw.* 141 F14
Luleälven, river, *Sw.* 138 B8
Lüleburgaz, *Turk.* 168 C3
Lules, *Arg.* 132 G9
Lüliang Shan, *China* 182 F3
Luling, *Tex., U.S.* 103 R11
Lulonga, river, *Dem. Rep. of the Congo* 198 J9
Lulua, river, *Dem. Rep. of the Congo* 198 N10
Lulu Fakahega, peak, *Wallis & Futuna, Fr.* 218 B11
Lumajangdong Co, *China* 180 J5
Luman, *Afghan.* 177 N6
Lumbala N'guimbo, *Angola* 202 E8
Lumber City, *Ga., U.S.* 97 N7
Lumberton, *Miss., U.S.* 100 N12
Lumberton, *N.C., U.S.* 96 J11
Lumbo, *Mozambique* 203 E15
Lumbrales, *Sp.* 144 E7
Lumbres, *Fr.* 146 L9
Lumding, *India* 178 G14
Lumi, *P.N.G.* 213 C18
Lumpkin, *Ga., U.S.* 97 N4
Lumu, *Indonesia* 189 K13
Lumut, *Malaysia* 187 T9
Luna, *N. Mex., U.S.* 107 T10
Lunavada, *India* 178 J4
Lund, *Nev., U.S.* 109 Q12
Lundazi, *Zambia* 202 D12
Lundu, *Malaysia* 188 H9
Lundy Island, *Eng., U.K.* 143 W8
Lüneburg, *Ger.* 148 C8
Lüneburger Heide, region, *Ger.* 148 D8
Lunéville, *Fr.* 147 P14
Lunglei, *India* 178 J14
Lungwebungu, river, *Angola* 202 D8
Luni, river, *India* 178 G3
Luni, *India* 178 G3
Luning, *Nev., U.S.* 109 R8
Lunino, *Russ.* 156 L13
Luninyets, *Belarus* 156 M4
Luntai, *China* 180 F6
Lunyama, *Dem. Rep. of the Congo* 198 M11
Luo, river, *China* 182 G2
Luo, river, *China* 182 H4
Luobei, *China* 181 C18
Luocheng, *China* 183 Q1
Luoding, *China* 183 S3
Luohe, *China* 182 H5
Luonan, *China* 182 H3
Luoqing, river, *China* 183 Q1
Luoshan, *China* 182 K5
Luoxiao Shan, *China* 183 N5
Luoyang, *China* 182 H4
Luoyuan, *China* 183 P8
Lupanshui, *China* 180 N12
Luperón, *Dom. Rep.* 117 L18
Lupin, *Nunavut, Can.* 82 G12
Lupog, *Guam, U.S.* 216 B12
Luqa, *Malta* 161 L22
Luqu, *China* 180 J11
Luquillo, *P.R., U.S.* 120 M6
Luquillo, Sierra de, *P.R., U.S.* 120 N5
Luray, *Va., U.S.* 96 D11
Lure, *Fr.* 147 R14
Lúrio, river, *Mozambique* 203 E14
Lúrio, *Mozambique* 203 E15
Lusaka, *Zambia* 202 E11
Lusambo, *Dem. Rep. of the Congo* 198 L10
Lusancay Islands, *P.N.G.* 213 D21
Lusanga, *Dem. Rep. of the Congo* 198 L8
Lushi, *China* 182 H3
Lushnjë, *Albania* 152 L9
Lushoto, *Tanzania* 199 L15
Lüshun (Port Arthur), *China* 182 E9
Lusignan, *Fr.* 147 T7
Lusk, *Wyo., U.S.* 106 H13
Lus-la-Croix-Haute, *Fr.* 147 V14
Luso, *Port.* 144 F5
Lussac-les-Châteaux, *Fr.* 147 T8
Lustenau, *Aust.* 148 L7
Lūt, Dasht-e, *Iran* 173 E16
Lūţak, *Iran* 173 F17
Lü Tao, island, *Taiwan, China* 183 S10
Lutcher, *La., U.S.* 100 Q10
Luti, *Solomon Is.* 217 L15
Luton, *Eng., U.K.* 143 U13
Łutselk'e, *N.W.T., Can.* 82 H12
Lutsen, *Minn., U.S.* 104 F14
Luts'k, *Ukr.* 157 N3
Lützow-Holm Bay, *Antarctica* 227 B17
Luuq, *Somalia* 199 H16
Luverne, *Ala., U.S.* 101 M16
Luverne, *Minn., U.S.* 104 L9
Luvua, river, *Dem. Rep. of the Congo* 198 M11
Luxembourg, *Eur.* 160 C3
Luxembourg, *Lux.* 160 K10
Luxeuil, *Fr.* 147 R14
Luxi, *China* 182 M2
Luxi, *China* 180 N10
Luxor, *Egypt* 197 E19
Luxora, *Ark., U.S.* 100 F11
Luyi, *China* 182 H6
Luy Kalay, *Afghan.* 177 Q5
Luy Radzay, *Afghan.* 177 Q2
Luz, *Fr.* 147 Y7
Luz, *Braz.* 131 L14
Luza, *Russ.* 158 F8
Luzaide, *Fr.* 147 Y6
Luzern, *Switz.* 150 B3
Luzhai, *China* 183 Q2
Luzhou, *China* 180 M12
Luzon, island, *Philippines* 189 C14
Luzon Strait, *Philippines* 189 A13
Luzy, *Fr.* 147 S12
L'viv, *Ukr.* 157 N2
Lyady, *Russ.* 156 G6
Lyakhovskiye Ostrova, *Russ.* 159 D17
Lyaki, *Azerb.* 169 D21
Lycksele, *Sw.* 141 G13
Lycoming, *N.Y., U.S.* 94 H8
Lydda *see* Lod, *Israel* 170 M5
Lyddan Island, *Antarctica* 226 C10
Lyepyel', *Belarus* 156 K5
Lyford, *Tex., U.S.* 103 W10
Lyford Cay, *Bahamas* 120 B10
Lyme Bay, *Eng., U.K.* 143 X10
Lynch, *Ky., U.S.* 101 D20
Lynch, *Nebr., U.S.* 104 M6
Lynchburg, *Va., U.S.* 96 F11
Lynden, *Wash., U.S.* 108 A4
Lyndhurst, *S. Aust., Austral.* 211 W10
Lyndon, *W. Aust., Austral.* 211 U2
Lyndon B. Johnson National Historic Park, *Tex., U.S.* 103 Q9
Lyndonville, *Vt., U.S.* 95 F13
Lynn, *Mass., U.S.* 95 K15
Lynn Haven, *Fla., U.S.* 97 R3
Lynn Lake, *Man., Can.* 83 L13
Lynton, *W. Aust., Austral.* 211 W1
Lyon, *Fr.* 147 U13
Lyons, river, *Austral.* 210 G2
Lyons, *Ga., U.S.* 97 N7
Lyons, *Kans., U.S.* 105 T7
Lyons, *N.Y., U.S.* 94 J7
Lyons, *Nebr., U.S.* 105 P8
Lysi, *Cyprus* 160 P9
Lyskovo, *Russ.* 156 J13
Lyss, *Switz.* 150 B2
Lysychans'k, *Ukr.* 157 P10
Lytton, *B.C., Can.* 82 M8
Lyubertsy, *Russ.* 156 J9
Lyubim, *Russ.* 156 G11
Lyubimets, *Bulg.* 153 K15
Lyuboml', *Ukr.* 156 M2
Lyubotyn, *Ukr.* 157 P8
Lyubytino, *Russ.* 156 G7
Lyucha Ongokton, Gora, *Russ.* 159 G15
Lyudinovo, *Russ.* 156 L8

M

Mā'alaea, *Hawai'i, U.S.* 113 G16
Mā'alaea Bay, *Hawai'i, U.S.* 113 G16
Maale (Male), *Maldives* 179 U3
Maam Cross, *Ire.* 143 R3
Ma'ān, *Jordan* 171 Q6
Maan Ridge *see* Maanselkä, *Fin., Russ.* 138 B9
Maanselkä, range, *Fin.* 141 E16
Ma'anshan, *China* 182 K8
Maarianhamina *see* Mariehamn, *Fin.* 141 K14
Ma'arrat an Nu'mān, *Syr.* 170 E8
Maas, river, *Neth.* 146 J13
Maastricht, *Neth.* 146 L13
Ma'bar, *Yemen* 172 Q9
Mabaruma, *Guyana* 129 C14
Mabiri, Cape, *P.N.G.* 217 K14
MacAlpine Lake, *Nunavut, Can.* 83 G13
Macapá, *Braz.* 130 C12
Macaque, Morne, *Dominica* 121 F19
Macará, *Ecua.* 128 L2
Macaroni, *Qnsld., Austral.* 211 Q11
Macas, *Ecua.* 128 K3
Macau, *China* 183 S4
Macau, *Braz.* 131 E17
Macaúba, *Braz.* 130 G12
Macauley Island, *Kermadec Is., N.Z.* 214 L9
Macbride Head, *Falkland Is., U.K.* 133 W13
Macclenny, *Fla., U.S.* 97 R8
Macclesfield Bank, *Ind. Oc.* 241 D15
Macdonnell Ranges, *Austral.* 210 F8
Macedo de Cavaleiros, *Port.* 144 D7
Macedonia, *Eur.* 139 W8
Macedonia, region, *Gr.* 154 D8
Maceió, *Braz.* 131 G18
Maceió, Ponta do, *Braz.* 131 E17
Macenta, *Guinea* 200 G7
Macerata, *It.* 150 H9
Macgillycuddy's Reeks, *Ire.* 143 U2
Macgowen, Arrecife, *Ecua.* 128 R10
Mach, *Pak.* 177 R6
Machagai, *Arg.* 132 G12
Machakas, *Kenya* 199 K14
Machala, *Ecua.* 128 L2
Machanao, Mount, *Guam, U.S.* 216 A11
Machault, *Fr.* 147 N12
Machecoul, *Fr.* 147 S5
Macheng, *China* 182 K6
Macherla, *India* 179 N7
Machias, *Me., U.S.* 95 F19
Machico, *Madeira* 204 M4
Machilipatnam (Bandar), *India* 179 N8
Machiques, *Venez.* 128 B6
Machu Picchu, ruin, *Peru* 130 H5
Machynlleth, *Wales, U.K.* 143 T9
Măcin, *Rom.* 153 E17
Maçka, *Turk.* 169 D14
Mackay, *Idaho, U.S.* 106 G6
Mackay, *Qnsld., Austral.* 211 T14
Mackay, Lake, *Austral.* 210 E7
Mackenzie, river, *Austral.* 210 F14
Mackenzie, *B.C., Can.* 82 K9
Mackenzie, river, *N.W.T., Can.* 82 F10
Mackenzie Bay, *Yukon, Can.* 82 D10
Mackenzie King Island, *N.W.T., Nunavut, Can.* 83 C13
Mackenzie Mountains, *N.W.T., Yukon, Can.* 82 F9
Mackenzie Trough, *Arctic Oc.* 242 N5
Mackinac, Straits of, *Mich., U.S.* 98 G10
Mackinac Island, *Mich., U.S.* 98 G11
Mackinaw City, *Mich., U.S.* 98 G10
Macknade, *Qnsld., Austral.* 211 R13
Mačkovci, *Slov.* 152 C6
Macksville, *Kans., U.S.* 105 U6
Macksville, *N.S.W., Austral.* 211 W15
Maclear, *S. Af.* 202 L10
Macleod, Lake, *Austral.* 210 G1
Macomb, *Ill., U.S.* 99 Q4
Macomer, *It.* 151 N3
Mâcon, *Fr.* 147 T12
Macon, *Ga., U.S.* 96 M6
Macon, *Miss., U.S.* 101 K13
Macon, *Mo., U.S.* 105 R13
Macondo, *Angola* 202 D9
Macouba, *Martinique, Fr.* 121 E22
Macovane, *Mozambique* 203 H13
Macpherson, Mount, *Austral.* 210 J12
Macpherson's Strait, *India* 179 Q14
Macquarie, river, *Austral.* 210 J13
Macquarie, Port, *Austral.* 210 K15
Macquarie Island, *Austral.* 214 R6
Macquarie Ridge, *Pac. Oc.* 238 R7
Mac. Robertson Land, *Antarctica* 227 E18
Macroom, *Ire.* 143 U4
Macurijes, Punta, *Cuba* 116 J10
Macuro, *Venez.* 128 B12
Macusani, *Peru* 130 H5
Mad, river, *Calif., U.S.* 109 N2
Mādabā, *Jordan* 170 M6
Madagascar, *Af.* 195 N24
Madagascar, island, *Ind. Oc.* 194 N11
Madagascar Basin, *Ind. Oc.* 240 L6
Madagascar Plateau, *Ind. Oc.* 240 M5
Madā'in Şāliḩ, *Saudi Arabia* 172 H6
Madalai, *Palau* 216 N11
Madalena, *Azores* 144 P3
Madalena, *Sao Tome and Principe* 205 D20
Madan, *Bulg.* 153 K14
Madang, *P.N.G.* 213 C19
Madaripur, *Bangladesh* 178 J13
Madawaska, *Me., U.S.* 95 A18
Madayar, *Myanmar* 186 G6
Maddalena, Isola, *It.* 150 L4
Maddock, *N. Dak., U.S.* 104 F5
Madeira, island, *Atl. Oc.* 204 M3
Madeira, river, *Braz.* 130 E9
Madeira Islands, *Madeira* 204 C4
Madeleine, Îles de la, *Que., Can.* 83 N22
Madelia, *Minn., U.S.* 104 L10
Madeline Island, *Wis., U.S.* 98 E4
Maden, *Turk.* 169 G14
Madera, *Calif., U.S.* 109 T6
Madgaon, *India* 179 N4
Madhubani, *India* 178 G10
Madidi, river, *Bol.* 130 H6
Madill, *Okla., U.S.* 102 J12
Madimba, *Dem. Rep. of the Congo* 198 L7
Madīnat ash Sha'b, *Yemen* 172 R9
Madīnat ath Thawrah, *Syr.* 170 E11
Madīnat Zāyid, *U.A.E.* 173 K14
Madison, *Fla., U.S.* 97 Q6
Madison, *Ga., U.S.* 96 L6
Madison, *Ind., U.S.* 99 T10
Madison, *Kans., U.S.* 105 T9
Madison, *Me., U.S.* 95 F16
Madison, *Minn., U.S.* 104 J9
Madison, *N.C., U.S.* 96 G10
Madison, *Nebr., U.S.* 105 P7
Madison, *S. Dak., U.S.* 104 L8
Madison, *W. Va., U.S.* 96 E8
Madison, *Wis., U.S.* 98 L5
Madisonville, *Ky., U.S.* 101 C14
Madisonville, *Tex., U.S.* 103 P13
Madiun, *Indonesia* 188 M10
Madley, Mount, *Austral.* 210 F5
Mado Gashi, *Kenya* 199 J15
Madoi, *China* 180 J10
Madona, *Latv.* 141 L17
Madrakah, Ra's al, *Oman* 173 M16
Madras *see* Chennai, *India* 179 P7
Madras, *Oreg., U.S.* 108 G5
Madre, Laguna, *Mex., U.S.* 103 W11
Madre, Sierra, *N. Amer.* 80 P6
Madre de Dios, river, *Bol., Peru* 130 H6
Madre de Dios, Isla, *Chile* 133 V6
Madre del Sur, Sierra, *Mex.* 114 J10
Madre Lagoon *see* Madre, Laguna, *N. Amer.* 80 M5
Madre Occidental, Sierra, *Mex.* 114 D8
Madre Oriental, Sierra, *Mex.* 114 D10
Madrid, *Iowa, U.S.* 105 P11
Madrid, *Sp.* 144 F11
Madridejos, *Sp.* 144 H11
Madrid Point, *S. Amer.* 126 H4
Madriu, river, *Andorra* 160 J4
Madura, island, *Indonesia* 188 M11
Madura, *W. Aust., Austral.* 211 X6
Madura, Selat, *Indonesia* 188 M11
Madurai, *India* 179 R6
Madurantakam, *India* 179 Q7
Madyan, *Pak.* 176 M10
Maebashi, *Japan* 185 N11
Mae Hong Son, *Thai.* 186 J7
Mae Klong, river, *Thai.* 186 M8
Maentwrog, *Wales, U.K.* 143 T9
Mae Sariang, *Thai.* 186 K7
Mae Sot, *Thai.* 186 K7
Maestra, Sierra, *Cuba* 116 K12
Maeva, *Fr. Polynesia, Fr.* 219 G14
Maevatanana, *Madagascar* 203 F17
Maéwo, island, *Vanuatu* 218 C3
Mafia Island, *Tanzania* 199 M15
Maga, peak, *N. Mariana Is., U.S.* 216 B7
Magadan, *Russ.* 159 F20
Magadi, *Kenya* 199 K14
Magallanes, Estrecho de, *Chile* 133 X7
Magangué, *Col.* 128 C5
Magazine Mountain, *Ark., U.S.* 100 G7
Magdagachi, *Russ.* 159 K18
Magdalena, *Bol.* 130 H8
Magdalena, river, *Col.* 128 D5
Magdalena, *Mex.* 114 C7
Magdalena, river, *N. Amer.* 80 L3
Magdalena, *N. Mex., U.S.* 107 T11
Magdalena, Bahía, *Mex.* 114 F6
Magdalena, Isla, *Chile* 133 S6
Magdalena, Isla, *Mex.* 114 E6
Magdalena, Llano de la, *Mex.* 114 E6
Magdalena Bay, *N. Amer.* 80 M3
Magdeburg, *Ger.* 148 E9
Magdelaine Cays, *Coral Sea Is. Terr., Austral.* 211 R15
Magee, *Miss., U.S.* 100 M11
Magelang, *Indonesia* 188 M9
Magellan, Strait of, *S. Amer.* 126 R4
Magellan Rise, *Pac. Oc.* 238 J10
Magellan Seamounts, *Pac. Oc.* 238 H7
Magens Bay, *Virgin Islands, U.S.* 120 M9
Magerøya, island, *Nor.* 141 B14
Maggiòre, Lago, *It., Switz.* 150 C4
Maggotty, *Jam.* 120 J7
Magina, peak, *Sp.* 144 K11
Maglić, peak, *Bosn. & Herzg., Serb. & Mont.* 152 H8
Maglie, *It.* 151 N16
Magnitogorsk, *Russ.* 158 J8
Magnolia, *Ark., U.S.* 100 J7
Magnolia, *Miss., U.S.* 100 N10
Mago, island, *Fiji Is.* 218 H9
Magpi, Puntan, *N. Mariana Is., U.S.* 216 A5
Magude, *Mozambique* 202 J12
Magway, *Myanmar* 186 H5
Mahābād, *Iran* 172 B10
Mahabharat Range, *Nepal* 178 F8
Mahabo, *Madagascar* 203 G16
Mahad, *India* 178 M3
Mahaena, *Fr. Polynesia, Fr.* 219 N17
Mahaena, Passe de, *Fr. Polynesia, Fr.* 219 N17
Mahagi, *Dem. Rep. of the Congo* 198 J12
Mahaiatea, *Fr. Polynesia, Fr.* 219 P16
Mahajamba, Baie de la, *Madagascar* 203 E17
Mahajan, *India* 178 F4
Mahajanga, *Madagascar* 203 E17
Mahalapye, *Botswana* 202 H10
Māhān, *Iran* 173 F15
Mahana Bay, *Hawai'i, U.S.* 113 Q19
Mahanadi, river, *India* 178 K9
Mahanoro, *Madagascar* 203 G18
Mahasamund, *India* 178 K8
Mahaut, *Dominica* 121 F19
Mahavavy, river, *Madagascar* 203 F17
Mahbubnagar, *India* 178 M6
Mahd adh Dhahab, *Saudi Arabia* 172 K7

Mahdia, *Guyana* **129** E14
Mahé, island, *Seychelles* **205** P20
Mahébourg, *Mauritius* **205** G20
Mahendraganj, *India* **178** G12
Mahen dra Giri, peak, *India* **178** L9
Mahenge, *Tanzania* **199** N14
Maheno, *N.Z.* **213** Q16
Mahere Honae, island, *Fr. Polynesia, Fr.* **219** K16
Mahesana, *India* **178** H3
Mahia Peninsula, *N.Z.* **213** L20
Mahige, island, *Solomon Is.* **217** M18
Mahilyow, *Belarus* **156** K6
Mahina, *Fr. Polynesia, Fr.* **219** N16
Mahina'akaka Heiau, *Hawai'i, U.S.* **113** N22
Mahishadal, *India* **178** J11
Mahitu, island, *Fr. Polynesia, Fr.* **219** K16
Mahmud-e Raqi, *Afghan.* **176** M8
Mahmudiye, *Turk.* **168** E6
Mahnomen, *Minn., U.S.* **104** G9
Mahoba, *India* **178** H7
Māhoe, Pu'u, *Hawai'i, U.S.* **113** H17
Mahón, *Sp.* **145** G20
Mahri, *Pak.* **177** U6
Mahu, *Fr. Polynesia, Fr.* **219** K20
Mahuti, Baie de, *Fr. Polynesia, Fr.* **219** H14
Mahuva, *India* **178** K2
Maia, *Amer. Samoa, U.S.* **218** N4
Maiao, island, *Fr. Polynesia, Fr.* **219** F16
Maibong, *India* **178** G14
Maicao, *Col.* **128** B6
Maîche, *Fr.* **147** R15
Maicuru, river, *Braz.* **130** C11
Maida, *It.* **151** Q13
Maidenhead, *Eng., U.K.* **143** V13
Maiduguri, *Nigeria* **201** E16
Maigualida, Sierra, *Venez.* **128** E10
Maihar, *India* **178** H7
Maikoor, island, *Indonesia* **189** L18
Mā'ili, *Hawai'i, U.S.* **112** E10
Mailly-le-Camp, *Fr.* **147** P12
Mailsi, *Pak.* **177** R10
Main, river, *Ger.* **148** H8
Maina, island, *Cook Is., N.Z.* **218** Q11
Main Channel, *Cayman Is., U.K.* **120** H2
Mai-Ndombe, Lac, *Dem. Rep. of the Congo* **198** K8
Maine, *U.S.* **95** E15
Maine, Gulf of, *U.S.* **85** D22
Maingkwan, *Myanmar* **186** D6
Main Island (Bermuda Island), *Bermuda, U.K.* **120** B3
Mainland, island, *Scot., U.K.* **142** D12
Mainoru, *N. Terr., Austral.* **211** P9
Main Ridge, *Trinidad & Tobago* **121** N18
Maintirano, *Madagascar* **203** F16
Mainz, *Ger.* **148** G6
Maio, island, *Cape Verde* **205** D17
Maipo Volcano, *S. Amer.* **126** L4
Maiquetía, *Venez.* **128** B9
Mairenui, peak, *Fr. Polynesia, Fr.* **219** Q17
Maisí, *Cuba* **117** K15
Maisí, Punta de, *Cuba* **117** K15
Maiskhal, island, *Bangladesh* **178** K14
Maitland, *N.S.W., Austral.* **211** X15
Maitri, station, *Antarctica* **227** A14
Maíz, Islas del, *Nicar.* **115** M19
Maizuru, *Japan* **185** P8
Majene, *Indonesia* **189** K13
Majī, *Eth.* **199** H14
Majorca *see* Mallorca, island, *Sp.* **145** G19
Majuro, *Marshall Is.* **216** G12
Majuro (Laura), island, *Marshall Is.* **216** H10
Majuro Lagoon, *Marshall Is.* **216** G11
Maka'ala, Pu'u, *Hawai'i, U.S.* **113** M21
Mākaha, *Hawai'i, U.S.* **112** E10
Makakilo City, *Hawai'i, U.S.* **112** E10
Makale, *Indonesia* **189** K13
Makaleha Mountains, *Hawai'i, U.S.* **112** B6
Makalu, peak, *China, Nepal* **178** F11
Makapala, *Hawai'i, U.S.* **113** K19
Makapu Point, *Niue, N.Z.* **219** B20
Makaroa, island, *Fr. Polynesia, Fr.* **219** R20
Makarov, *Russ.* **159** J22
Makarov Basin, *Arctic Oc.* **242** H8
Makarovo, *Russ.* **159** K15
Makar'yev, *Russ.* **156** G12
Makassar *see* Ujungpandang, *Indonesia* **189** L13
Makassar Strait, *Indonesia* **188** K12
Makatea, island, *Fr. Polynesia, Fr.* **219** E17
Makawao, peak, *Hawai'i, U.S.* **113** G17
Makefu, *Niue, N.Z.* **219** B20
Make Jima, *Japan* **185** U4
Makemo, island, *Fr. Polynesia, Fr.* **219** E19
Mākena, *Hawai'i, U.S.* **113** H16
Makeni, *Sierra Leone* **200** F6
Makéone, *Vanuatu* **218** B2
Makgadikgadi Pans, *Botswana* **202** G9
Makhachkala, *Russ.* **157** U15
Makhad, *Pak.* **177** N10
Makhado, *S. Af.* **202** H11
Makhambet, *Kaz.* **174** E6
Makhfar al Buşayyah, *Iraq* **172** F10
Maki, *Indonesia* **189** K19
Makīnsk, *Kaz.* **175** C13
Makira Harbour, *Solomon Is.* **217** P20
Makiyivka, *Ukr.* **157** Q10
Makkah (Mecca), *Saudi Arabia* **172** L7
Makkovik, *Nfld. & Lab., Can.* **83** K21
Makó, *Hung.* **149** N16
Makogai, island, *Fiji Is.* **218** H7
Makokou, *Gabon* **201** K16
Mākole'ā Point, *Hawai'i, U.S.* **113** L18
Makoua, *Congo* **201** L17
Makrá, island, *Gr.* **155** N16
Makrakómi, *Gr.* **154** G10
Makrana, *India* **178** G4
Makran Coast Range, *Pak.* **177** V3
Makrinítsa, *Gr.* **154** F11
Makroníssi (Helena, Eléni), island, *Gr.* **155** K13
Mākū, *Iran* **172** A10
Makung, *Taiwan, China* **183** R8
Makunudu Atoll (Malcolm), *Maldives* **179** T3
Makura, island, *Vanuatu* **218** E3
Makurazaki, *Japan* **185** T4
Makurdi, *Nigeria* **201** G14
Mal, *Mauritania* **196** G5
Malabar Coast, *India* **179** R4
Malabo, *Eq. Guinea* **204** L7
Malabuñgan, *Philippines* **188** E12
Malacca, *Malaysia* **187** U10
Malacca, Strait of, *Indonesia, Malaysia* **188** G5
Malacky, *Slovakia* **149** K13
Malad City, *Idaho, U.S.* **106** J7
Maladzyechna, *Belarus* **156** K4
Málaga, *Col.* **128** D6
Málaga, *Sp.* **144** M10
Malagón, *Sp.* **144** H10
Malaita, island, *Solomon Is.* **217** N20
Malakal, *Palau* **216** N11
Malakal, *Sudan* **199** G13
Malakal Harbor, *Palau* **216** N11
Malakal Pass, *Palau* **216** P11
Malakanagiri, *India* **178** M8
Malakand, *Pak.* **176** M10
Malake, island, *Fiji Is.* **218** H6
Malakoff, *Tex., U.S.* **102** M13
Malakula, island, *Vanuatu* **218** D2
Malam, *F.S.M.* **217** B19
Malang, *Indonesia* **188** M10
Malanje, *Angola* **202** C6
Malans, *Switz.* **160** Q2
Malanville, *Benin* **200** E12
Malao, *Vanuatu* **218** C1
Malapo, *Tonga* **218** J11
Malapu, *Solomon Is.* **217** P23
Malar, *Pak.* **177** V4
Mälaren, lake, *Sw.* **141** L14
Malargüe, *Arg.* **132** M7
Malaspina Glacier, *Alas., U.S.* **111** K20
Malatya, *Turk.* **169** G13
Mala Vyska, *Ukr.* **157** Q6
Malawi, *Af.* **195** M22
Malawi, Lake (Lake Nyasa), *Af.* **194** M10
Malayagiri, peak, *India* **178** K10
Malaya Vishera, *Russ.* **156** G7
Malaybalay, *Philippines* **189** F15
Malāyer, *Iran* **172** D11
Malay Peninsula, *Malaysia, Thai.* **166** L10
Malaysia, *Asia* **167** Y12
Malazgirt, *Turk.* **169** F17
Malbork, *Pol.* **149** B14
Malbun, *Liech.* **160** Q3
Malcolm *see* Makunudu Atoll, island, *Maldives* **179** T3
Malcolm, *W. Aust., Austral.* **211** W4
Maldegem, *Belg.* **146** K11
Malden, *Mo., U.S.* **105** V15
Malden Island, *Kiribati* **214** H12
Maldive Islands, *Maldives* **179** U2
Maldives, *Asia* **167** Y6
Maldonado, *Uru.* **132** L14
Maldonado, Punta, *Mex.* **114** K12
Malè, *It.* **150** C6
Male *see* Maale, *Maldives* **179** U3
Maléas, Akrotírio, *Gr.* **154** M11
Male Atoll, *Maldives* **179** U3
Malebo, Pool, *Dem. Rep. of the Congo* **198** L7
Malegaon, *India* **178** K4
Malemba-Nkulu, *Dem. Rep. of the Congo* **198** M11
Malessína, *Gr.* **154** H11
Malevangga, *Solomon Is.* **217** K15
Malgobek, *Russ.* **157** T14
Malhão, Serra do, *Port.* **144** L6
Malhargarh, *India* **178** H4
Malheur, river, *Oreg., U.S.* **108** H9
Malheureux, Cape, *Mauritius* **205** F20
Malheur Lake, *Oreg., U.S.* **108** J7
Mali, *Af.* **195** G15
Mali, island, *Fiji Is.* **218** G7
Mali, river, *Myanmar* **186** D7
Mália, *Gr.* **155** Q15
Mali Drvenik, *Croatia* **152** G6
Mali Kyun, *Myanmar* **187** N7
Malili, *Indonesia* **189** K13
Malin, *Oreg., U.S.* **108** L5
Malindi, *Kenya* **199** L15
Malin Head, *Ire.* **143** N6
Malin More, *Ire.* **143** P4
Malinoa, island, *Tonga* **218** H11
Malkapur, *India* **178** K5
Malkara, *Turk.* **168** C3
Malki, *Russ.* **159** F22
Malko Tŭrnovo, *Bulg.* **153** J17
Mallacoota, *Vic., Austral.* **211** Z14
Mallawi, *Egypt* **197** D18
Mallawli, island, *Malaysia* **188** F12
Mallorca (Majorca), island, *Sp.* **145** G19
Mallow, *Ire.* **143** U4
Malmand Range, *Afghan.* **177** N3
Malmberget, *Sw.* **141** E13
Malmesbury, *S. Af.* **202** M7
Malmö, *Sw.* **140** N12
Malmok, cape, *Neth. Antilles, Neth.* **121** P18
Malo, island, *Vanuatu* **218** D2
Maloelap Atoll, *Marshall Is.* **216** G5
Maloja, *Switz.* **150** C5
Malolo, island, *Fiji Is.* **218** H5
Malone, *N.Y., U.S.* **94** F10
Maloshuyka, *Russ.* **158** E8
Måløy, *Nor.* **140** J9
Malozemel'skaya Tundra, *Russ.* **138** A11
Malpaso, peak, *Canary Is.* **204** R3
Malpelo Island, *S. Amer.* **126** C1
Malportas Pond, *Cayman Is., U.K.* **120** J3
Mäls, *Liech.* **160** Q2
Malta, *Eur.* **160** E4
Malta, island, *Malta* **161** K22
Malta, *Mont., U.S.* **106** B10
Maltahöhe, *Namibia* **202** J7
Maltese Islands, *Medit. Sea* **138** L7
Malton, *Eng., U.K.* **143** Q13
Maluku *see* Moluccas, islands, *Indonesia* **189** J16
Ma'lūlā, *Syr.* **170** J8
Malung, *Sw.* **140** K12
Maluu, *Solomon Is.* **217** M19
Malvan, *India* **179** N3
Malvern, *Ark., U.S.* **100** H8
Malvern, *Iowa, U.S.* **105** Q9
Malvern, *Jam.* **120** J7
Malvinas, Islas *see* Falkland Islands, *Falkland Is., U.K.* **133** W12
Malyn, *Ukr.* **157** N5
Malyye Karmakuly, *Russ.* **158** D11
Malyy Lyakhovskiy, Ostrov, *Russ.* **159** D17
Mamagota, *P.N.G.* **217** K14
Māmala Bay, *Hawai'i, U.S.* **112** E11
Mamalahoa Highway, *Hawai'i, U.S.* **113** L19
Mamalu Bay, *Hawai'i, U.S.* **113** H17
Mamberamo, *Indonesia* **189** K20
Mamelles, islands, *Seychelles* **205** N20
Mamer, *Lux.* **160** K9
Mameyes (Palmer), *P.R., U.S.* **120** M5
Mamfé, *Cameroon* **201** H15
Mamiña, *Chile* **132** C7
Mammoth, *Wyo., U.S.* **106** F8
Mammoth Cave National Park, *Ky., U.S.* **101** D16
Mammoth Spring, *Ark., U.S.* **100** E9
Mamoiada, *It.* **151** N4
Mamoré, river, *Bol., Braz.* **130** G7
Mamoriá, *Braz.* **130** F7
Mamou, *Guinea* **200** F6
Mamou, *La., U.S.* **100** P8
Mamoudzou, *Mayotte, Fr.* **205** P17
Mampong, *Ghana* **200** G10
Mamuju, *Indonesia* **189** K13
Man, *Côte d'Ivoire* **200** G7
Mana, river, *Fr. Guiana, Fr.* **129** E17
Mana, *Fr. Guiana, Fr.* **129** E17
Mānā, *Hawai'i, U.S.* **112** B4
Manacapuru, *Braz.* **130** D9
Manacor, *Sp.* **145** G19
Manado, *Indonesia* **189** H15
Mañagaha Island, *N. Mariana Is., U.S.* **216** B4
Managua, *Nicar.* **115** M18
Managua, Lago de, *Nicar.* **115** M18
Managua, Lake *see* Managua, Lago de, *N. Amer.* **80** Q7
Manaia, *N.Z.* **213** L18
Manakara, *Madagascar* **203** H17
Manakau, peak, *N.Z.* **213** N18
Manākhah, *Yemen* **172** Q9
Mana La, *China, India* **178** D7
Manam, island, *P.N.G.* **213** C19
Manama *see* Al Manāmah, *Bahrain* **172** H12
Manamadurai, *India* **179** R6
Mananjary, *Madagascar* **203** H17
Manantiales, *Chile* **133** W8
Manaoba, island, *Solomon Is.* **217** M19
Mānā Point, *Hawai'i, U.S.* **112** B4
Manapouri, Lake, *N.Z.* **213** Q15
Manas, *China* **180** E7
Manas Hu, *China* **180** D7
Manassas, *Va., U.S.* **96** D12
Manatí, *Cuba* **116** J12
Manatí, *P.R., U.S.* **120** M3
Manaus, *Braz.* **130** D9
Manavgat, *Turk.* **168** J6
Manawai Harbour, *Solomon Is.* **217** N20
Manbij, *Syr.* **170** D10
Manchester, *Conn., U.S.* **USNĚ2** L13
Manchester, *Eng., U.K.* **143** S11
Manchester, *Ga., U.S.* **96** M5
Manchester, *Iowa, U.S.* **105** N13
Manchester, *Ky., U.S.* **101** D19
Manchester, *N.H., U.S.* **95** J14
Manchester, *Tenn., U.S.* **101** F16
Manchhar Lake, *Pak.* **177** V6
Manchioneal, *Jam.* **120** J11
Manchuria *see* Dongbei, region, *China* **181** D16
Manchurian Plain, *China* **166** F12
Manciano, *It.* **150** J7
Mancos, *Colo., U.S.* **107** P10
Mand, river, *Iran* **173** G13
Mand, *Pak.* **177** V2
Manda, *Tanzania* **199** N13
Mandab, Bāb al, *Af., Asia* **194** G11
Mandai, *Pak.* **177** R7
Mandal, *Mongolia* **180** D12
Mandal, *Nor.* **140** M10
Mandal, *Virgin Islands, U.S.* **120** M9
Mandala, Puncak, *Indonesia* **213** C17
Mandalay, *Myanmar* **186** G6
Mandalgovĭ, *Mongolia* **180** E12
Mandalī, *Iraq* **172** D10
Mandalt *see* Sonid Zuoqi, *China* **182** A5
Mandan, *N. Dak., U.S.* **104** G4
Mandapeta, *India* **178** M8
Mandara Mountains, *Cameroon, Nigeria* **201** F16
Mandeb, Bab al, *Yemen* **172** R8
Mandel, *Afghan.* **177** N2
Mandera, *Kenya* **199** H16
Manderscheid, *Ger.* **160** G12
Mandeville, *Jam.* **120** J8
Mandi, *India* **177** P14
Mandi Burewala, *Pak.* **177** R10
Mandimba, *Mozambique* **203** E13
Mandioli, island, *Indonesia* **189** J16
Mandla, *India* **178** J7
Mándra, *Gr.* **154** J12
Mandráki, *Gr.* **155** M18
Mandritsa, *Bulg.* **153** K16
Mandritsara, *Madagascar* **203** E18
Mandsaur, *India* **178** H4
Mandu, island, *Maldives* **179** V3
Mandurah, *W. Aust., Austral.* **211** X2
Manduria, *It.* **151** N15
Mandvi, *India* **178** J1
Manfredonia, *It.* **150** L12
Manfredonia, Golfo di, *It.* **150** L13
Manga, region, *Chad, Niger* **197** H13
Manga, *Braz.* **131** J15
Mangabeiras, Chapada das, *Braz.* **131** G14
Mangaia, island, *Cook Is., N.Z.* **214** K12
Mangalia, *Rom.* **153** G18
Mangalore, *India* **179** Q4
Mangareva, island, *Fr. Polynesia, Fr.* **219** Q20
Mangarongaro, island, *Cook Is., N.Z.* **219** B17
Mangeigne, *Chad* **197** K16
Mangere, island, *Cook Is., N.Z.* **218** Q12
Manggautu, *Solomon Is.* **217** Q18
Mangghyystaū, *Kaz.* **174** H5
Manghit, *Uzb.* **174** J9
Mangnai, *China* **180** H8
Mango, island, *Tonga* **218** Q6
Mango, *Togo* **200** F11
Mangoche, *Malawi* **203** E13
Mangoky, river, *Madagascar* **203** H16
Mangole, island, *Indonesia* **189** K15
Mangqystaū Shyghanaghy, *Kaz.* **174** G5
Mangrol, *India* **178** K2
Mangrove Cay, *Bahamas* **120** D2
Manguchar, *Pak.* **177** S6
Manguinho, Ponta do, *Braz.* **131** G17
Mangum, *Okla., U.S.* **102** H8
Mangut, *Russ.* **159** M17
Manhattan, *Kans., U.S.* **105** S8
Manhattan, *Nev., U.S.* **109** R9
Mani, peninsula, *Gr.* **154** M10
Mania, river, *Madagascar* **203** G17
Maniamba, *Mozambique* **203** D13
Manica, *Mozambique* **202** G12
Manicoré, *Braz.* **130** E9
Manicouagan, Réservoir, *Que., Can.* **83** M20
Manīfah, *Saudi Arabia* **172** H12
Manifold, Cape, *Austral.* **210** F15
Manihi, island, *Fr. Polynesia, Fr.* **219** D18
Manihiki Atoll, *Cook Is., N.Z.* **214** H11
Manihiki Plateau, *Pac. Oc.* **238** L12
Manila, *Ark., U.S.* **100** F11
Manila, *Philippines* **189** C13
Manila, *Utah, U.S.* **106** K9
Manila Bay, *Philippines* **189** C13
Manily, *Russ.* **159** D21
Maningrida, *N. Terr., Austral.* **211** P9
Manini, Motus, *Fr. Polynesia, Fr.* **219** J13
Maninita, island, *Tonga* **218** M11
Manipa, island, *Indonesia* **189** K16
Manisa, *Turk.* **168** F3
Manistee, river, *Mich., U.S.* **98** J9
Manistee, *Mich., U.S.* **98** J9
Manistique, *Mich., U.S.* **98** G9
Manistique Lake, *Mich., U.S.* **98** F9
Manitoba, *Can.* **83** L14
Manitoba, Lake, *Man., Can.* **83** N13
Manitou Island, *Mich., U.S.* **98** E7
Manitou Islands, *Mich., U.S.* **98** H9
Manitowoc, *Wis., U.S.* **98** K7
Manizales, *Col.* **128** F4
Manja, *Madagascar* **203** H16
Manjra, river, *India* **178** M6
Mankato, *Kans., U.S.* **105** R7
Mankato, *Minn., U.S.* **104** L11
Manley Hot Springs, *Alas., U.S.* **111** F16
Manlleu, *Sp.* **145** D17
Manly, *Iowa, U.S.* **104** M11
Manmad, *India* **178** K4
Mann, island, *Marshall Is.* **216** M5
Manna, *Indonesia* **188** L6
Mannar, Gulf of, *India, Sri Lanka* **179** S6
Mannheim, *Ger.* **148** H6
Manning, *Iowa, U.S.* **105** P10
Manning, *N. Dak., U.S.* **104** G2
Manning, *S.C., U.S.* **96** L10
Manning, Cape, *Kiribati* **217** A23
Manning Strait, *Solomon Is.* **217** L16
Mannington, *W. Va., U.S.* **96** C9
Mann Passage, *Marshall Is.* **216** M5
Mannu, Capo, *It.* **151** N3
Manoa, *Bol.* **130** G7
Man of War Bay, *Trinidad & Tobago* **121** N18
Man-of-War Cay, *Bahamas* **117** G13
Manokotak, *Alas., U.S.* **111** L13
Manokwari, *Indonesia* **189** J19
Manono, *Dem. Rep. of the Congo* **198** M11
Manono, island, *Samoa* **218** L3
Manoron, *Myanmar* **187** P8

Mano Wan, Japan 184 M11
Man O'War Cay, Bahamas 120 B7
Man O'War Cay, Bahamas 116 C12
Manp'o, N. Korea 182 C12
Manra, island, Kiribati 214 H10
Manresa, Sp. 145 D17
Mansa, Zambia 202 D11
Mansehra, Pak. 176 M11
Mansel Island, Nunavut, Can. 83 J17
Mansfield, Ark., U.S. 100 G6
Mansfield, Eng., U.K. 143 S12
Mansfield, La., U.S. 100 L6
Mansfield, Mo., U.S. 105 V13
Mansfield, Ohio, U.S. 99 Q13
Mansfield, Pa., U.S. 94 L7
Mansfield, Vic., Austral. 211 Z12
Mansfield, Mount, Vt., U.S. 94 F12
Mansle, Fr. 147 U7
Manson, Iowa, U.S. 105 N10
Manta, Ecua. 128 J2
Mant'ap-san, peak, N. Korea 182 B14
Manteca, Calif., U.S. 109 S5
Manteo, N.C., U.S. 96 G15
Mantes-la-Jolie, Fr. 147 P9
Manti, Utah, U.S. 106 M7
Mantiqueira, Serra da, S. Amer. 126 J9
Mant Islands, F.S.M. 217 F14
Manton, Mich., U.S. 98 J10
Mantova, It. 150 E6
Mant Passage, F.S.M. 217 F14
Mantua, Cuba 116 H4
Manturovo, Russ. 156 G12
Mäntyluoto, Fin. 141 J15
Manú, Peru 130 H5
Manuae, island, Fr. Polynesia, Fr. 219 E14
Manua Islands, Amer. Samoa, U.S. 214 J10
Manuhangi, island, Fr. Polynesia, Fr. 219 F20
Manui, island, Fr. Polynesia, Fr. 219 R20
Manui, island, Indonesia 189 K14
Manukau, N.Z. 213 J19
Manulu Lagoon, Kiribati 217 B23
Manus, island, P.N.G. 213 B19
Manvers, Port, Nfld. & Lab., Can. 83 J21
Many, La., U.S. 100 M7
Manych Gudilo, Ozero, Russ. 157 R12
Manych Guidilo, Lake see Manych Guidilo, Ozero, Russ. 138 G12
Many Farms, Ariz., U.S. 107 Q9
Manzai, Pak. 177 P8
Manzanares, Sp. 144 H11
Manzanar National Historic Site, Calif., U.S. 109 T8
Manzanilla Point, Trinidad & Tobago 121 P23
Manzanillo, Cuba 116 K11
Manzanillo, Mex. 114 J9
Manzanillo Bay, Haiti 117 L17
Manzano Mountains, N. Mex., U.S. 107 S12
Manzano Peak, N. Mex., U.S. 107 S12
Manzhouli, China 181 C15
Manzil, Pak. 177 S3
Mao, Chad 197 H14
Mao, Dom. Rep. 117 L18
Maoke, Pegunungan, Indonesia 189 L20
Maoke Mountains see Maoke, Pegunungan, Indonesia 166 L16
Maoming, China 183 S2
Map, island, F.S.M. 217 C18
Mapai, Mozambique 202 H12
Mapam Yumco, lake, China 180 K5
Mapi, Indonesia 189 M21
Mapia, Kepulauan (St. David Islands), Indonesia 189 J19
Mapimí, Bolsón de, N. Amer. 80 M4
Mapleton, Iowa, U.S. 105 N9
Mapleton, Oreg., U.S. 108 H2
Mapmaker Seamounts, Pac. Oc. 238 G8
Maprik, P.N.G. 213 C18
Mapuera, river, Braz. 130 C10
Maputo, Mozambique 202 J12
Maputo, Baía de, Mozambique 202 J12
Maqat, Kaz. 174 F7
Maqellarë, Albania 152 K10
Maqnah, Saudi Arabia 172 G5
Maqshūsh, Saudi Arabia 172 K6
Maquan, river, China 180 L6
Maquela do Zombo, Angola 202 B6
Maquinchao, Arg. 133 Q8
Maquoketa, Iowa, U.S. 105 N14
Mar, Russ. 159 H16
Mar, Serra do, S. Amer. 126 K8
Mara, Guyana 129 E15
Mara, India 178 F14
Maraã, Braz. 130 D7
Maraa, Fr. Polynesia, Fr. 219 P15
Maraa, Passe de, Fr. Polynesia, Fr. 219 P15
Marabá, Braz. 131 E13
Marabo, island, Fiji Is. 218 K9
Maracá, Ilha de, Braz. 130 B12
Maracaibo, Venez. 128 B7
Maracaibo, Lago de, Venez. 128 C7
Maracaibo Basin, S. Amer. 126 A3
Maracá Island, S. Amer. 126 C8
Maracaju, Braz. 130 L11
Maracaju, Serra de, S. Amer. 126 H7
Maracanã, Braz. 131 C14
Maracay, Venez. 128 B9
Maracayo, Punta, P.R., U.S. 120 M2
Marādah, Lib. 197 D15
Maradi, Niger 196 J11
Marāghah, Sabkhat, Syr. 170 E9
Marāgheh, Iran 172 B10
Maragogipe, Braz. 131 H16
Marahuaca, Cerro, Venez. 128 F10
Marajó, Ilha de, Braz. 131 C13
Marajó Bay, S. Amer. 126 D9
Marajó Island, S. Amer. 126 D8
Marakei, island, Kiribati 214 G8
Maralal, Kenya 199 J14
Maralinga, S. Aust., Austral. 211 W8
Maramasike, island, Solomon Is. 217 N20
Marambio, station, Antarctica 226 C4
Maran, Malaysia 187 U10
Marana, Ariz., U.S. 107 V7
Maranboy, N. Terr., Austral. 211 Q8
Maranchón, Sp. 144 E12
Marand, Iran 172 A10
Marang, Malaysia 187 T10
Maranges, Sp. 160 K6
Maranhão, Barragem do, Port. 144 H6
Marano, river, It., San Marino 161 J17
Marañón, river, Peru 130 E4
Marans, Fr. 147 T6
Marargiu, Capo, It. 151 N3
Mara Rosa, Braz. 131 H13
Mărăşeşti, Rom. 153 D16
Maratea, It. 151 N12
Marathon, Fla., U.S. 97 Y9
Marathon, battle, Gr. 155 J13
Marathon, Tex., U.S. 103 Q3
Marathónas, Gr. 155 J13
Marathus see 'Amrīt, ruin, Syr. 170 G7
Maraú, Braz. 131 J16
Maravae, Solomon Is. 217 M15
Marāveh Tappeh, Iran 173 B15
Maravillas Creek, Tex., U.S. 103 Q3
Maravovo, Solomon Is. 217 N18
Maraza, Azerb. 169 D22
Marbella, Sp. 144 M9
Marble Bar, W. Aust., Austral. 211 S3
Marble Canyon, Ariz., U.S. 107 Q7
Marble Falls, Tex., U.S. 103 P10
Marburg, Ger. 148 F6
Marcel, Anse, St. Martin, Fr. 121 A14
Marceline, Mo., U.S. 105 R12
Marchena, Canal de, Ecua. 128 P10
Marchena, Isla (Bindloe), Ecua. 128 P9
Mar Chiquita, Laguna, Arg. 132 J11
Marciana, It. 150 J5
Marckolsheim, Fr. 147 Q15
Marco, Fla., U.S. 97 X8
Marcola, Oreg., U.S. 108 H3
Marcos Juárez, Arg. 132 K11
Marcus see Minami Tori Shima, island, Japan 184 L8
Marcus Baker, Mount, Alas., U.S. 111 J17
Marcy, Mount, N.Y., U.S. 94 G11
Mardan, Pak. 176 M10
Mar del Plata, Arg. 133 N13
Mardin, Turk. 169 H15
Maré, island, New Caledonia, Fr. 214 K7
Maré, Île, New Caledonia, Fr. 218 D10
Marea del Portillo, Cuba 116 L11
Marecchia, river, It. 161 H13
Marechal Taumaturgo, Braz. 130 G4
Maree, Loch, Scot., U.K. 142 J8
Marenanuka, island, Kiribati 217 F17
Marengo, Iowa, U.S. 105 P13
Marennes, Fr. 147 U6
Marettimo, Isola, It. 151 S8
Mareuil, Fr. 147 U8
Marfa, Tex., U.S. 103 Q2
Marfa, Massif de, Chad 197 J16
Margai Caka, lake, China 180 J7
Margaret River, W. Aust., Austral. 211 R6
Margarita, Isla de, Venez. 128 B11
Margat (Marghab), ruin, Syr. 170 F7
Margeride, Monts de la, Fr. 147 V11
Marghab see Margat, ruin, Syr. 170 F7
Margherita di Savoia, It. 150 L13
Marghita, Rom. 152 B12
Margow Desert, Afghan. 177 R2
Marguerite Bay, Antarctica 226 F5
Marhanets', Ukr. 157 Q8
Mari, ruin, Syr. 170 G14
Marià, Pic del, Andorra 160 H5
Maria, island, Fr. Polynesia, Fr. 219 H22
Maria, Îles, Fr. Polynesia, Fr. 214 K12
Maria Bay, Tonga 218 H11
María Elena, Chile 132 D7
Maria Islands, St. Lucia 121 L14
Mariana Islands, Pac. Oc. 166 G16
Mariana Trench, Pac. Oc. 238 H6
Mariana Trough, Pac. Oc. 238 H6
Marianna, Ark., U.S. 100 G10
Marianna, Fla., U.S. 97 Q4
Marianne, island, Seychelles 205 M21
Mariánské Lázně, Czech Rep. 148 H10
Marias, river, Mont., U.S. 106 B8
Marías, Islas, Mex. 114 G8
Marías Islands see Marías, Islas, N. Amer. 80 N4
Maria van Diemen, Cape, N.Z. 213 G17
Ma'rib, Yemen 172 P10
Maribor, Slov. 152 C6
Maricao, P.R., U.S. 120 N2
Maricopa, Ariz., U.S. 107 U7
Maricopa, Calif., U.S. 109 W7
Maridi, Sudan 198 H12
Marié, river, Braz. 130 C6
Marie Byrd Land, Antarctica 226 K7
Marie-Galante, island, Guadeloupe, Fr. 121 G16
Mariehamn (Maarianhamina), Fin. 141 K14
Mariental, Namibia 202 J7
Marietta, Ga., U.S. 96 L5
Marietta, Ohio, U.S. 99 S15
Marietta, Okla., U.S. 102 J11
Marigot, Dominica 121 E19
Marigot, Guadeloupe, Fr. 121 F14
Marigot, Haiti 117 M16
Marigot, Martinique, Fr. 121 E22
Marigot, St. Martin, Fr. 121 B14
Marigot, Baie de, St. Martin, Fr. 121 B14
Marigot Harbour, St. Lucia 121 K13
Mariiru Point, N. Mariana Is., U.S. 216 E8
Marijampolė, Lith. 141 N16
Marília, Braz. 130 L12
Marillana, W. Aust., Austral. 211 T3
Marinduque, island, Philippines 189 D14
Marine City, Mich., U.S. 98 M13
Marineland, Fla., U.S. 97 R9
Marinette, Wis., U.S. 98 H7
Maringá, Braz. 130 M12
Maringa, river, Dem. Rep. of the Congo 198 J9
Marinha Grande, Port. 144 G5
Marino, It. 150 L8
Marino, Vanuatu 218 C3
Marion, Ala., U.S. 101 L14
Marion, Ark., U.S. 100 G11
Marion, Ill., U.S. 99 U6
Marion, Ind., U.S. 99 Q10
Marion, Iowa, U.S. 105 N13
Marion, Kans., U.S. 105 T8
Marion, Ky., U.S. 101 C13
Marion, Mich., U.S. 98 K10
Marion, N.C., U.S. 96 H8
Marion, Ohio, U.S. 99 Q13
Marion, S. Dak., U.S. 104 M7
Marion, S.C., U.S. 96 K11
Marion, Va., U.S. 96 G8
Marion, Lake, S.C., U.S. 96 L10
Marion Downs, Qnsld., Austral. 211 T11
Marionville, Mo., U.S. 105 V11
Maripaviche, Venez. 128 D10
Mariposa, Calif., U.S. 109 S6
Marisa, Indonesia 189 J14
Mariscal Estigarribia, Parag. 130 L9
Maritime Alps, Fr., It. 147 W15
Maritime Museum, Bermuda, U.K. 120 B2
Maritsa, river, Eur. 138 J9
Mariupol', Ukr. 157 R9
Marivan, Iran 172 C10
Mariyets, Russ. 156 H15
Marjayoûn, Leb. 170 J6
Marka (Merca), Somalia 199 J17
Markam, China 180 L10
Markandeh, ruin, Afghan. 176 M6
Marked Tree, Ark., U.S. 100 F11
Markermeer, bay, Neth. 146 H12
Markham, Mount, Antarctica 227 L13
Markham Bay, Nunavut, Can. 83 H18
Markit, China 180 G4
Markleeville, Calif., U.S. 109 Q6
Markópoulo, Gr. 154 J7
Markovo, Russ. 159 C21
Marks, Miss., U.S. 100 H11
Marks, Russ. 156 M14
Marksville, La., U.S. 100 N8
Mark Twain Lake, Mo., U.S. 105 S13
Marlborough, Qnsld., Austral. 211 T14
Marle, Fr. 147 N11
Marlette, Mich., U.S. 98 L12
Marlin, Tex., U.S. 103 N12
Marlinton, W. Va., U.S. 96 E10
Marlow, Okla., U.S. 102 H10
Marmande, Fr. 147 W7
Marmara, island, Turk. 168 D4
Marmara Denizi, sea, Turk. 168 D4
Marmaraereğlisi, Turk. 168 C4
Marmara Gölü, Turk. 168 F4
Marmarás, Gr. 154 D12
Marmári, Gr. 155 J13
Marmaris, Turk. 168 H4
Marmarth, N. Dak., U.S. 104 H1
Marmelos, river, Braz. 130 F8
Marmet, W. Va., U.S. 96 E8
Marmolada, peak, It. 150 C7
Marmolejo, Sp. 144 K10
Marne, river, Fr. 147 P12
Marne au Rhin, Canal de la, Fr. 147 P15
Maroa, Venez. 128 G9
Maroantsetra, Madagascar 203 E18
Marobee Range, Austral. 210 K13
Maroe, Fr. Polynesia, Fr. 219 H14
Maroe, Baie de, Fr. Polynesia, Fr. 219 G14
Marokau, island, Fr. Polynesia, Fr. 219 F19
Marol, Pak. 176 M13
Maromokotro, peak, Madagascar 203 E18
Maroni, river, Fr. Guiana, Fr., Suriname 129 E17
Marónia, Gr. 155 C15
Maroochydore, Qnsld., Austral. 211 V15
Maro Reef, Hawai'i, U.S. 112 L5
Marotiri (Îlots de Bass), Fr. Polynesia, Fr. 215 L14
Maroua, Cameroon 201 F17
Maro'u Bay, Solomon Is. 217 P20
Marovoay, Madagascar 203 F17
Marpi Point, N. Mariana Is., U.S. 216 A6
Márpissa, Gr. 155 L15
Marpo, Puntan, N. Mariana Is., U.S. 216 C8
Marqaköl, lake, Kaz. 175 D19
Marquesas Fracture Zone, Pac. Oc. 239 L14
Marquesas Islands, Fr. Polynesia, Fr. 215 H14
Marquesas Keys, Fla., U.S. 97 Y8
Marquette, Mich., U.S. 98 F7
Marquis, Grenada 121 K23
Marquis, St. Lucia 121 J14
Marquis, Cape, St. Lucia 121 J14
Marquis Island, Grenada 121 K23
Marra, Jebel, Sudan 198 E10
Marrakech, Mor. 196 B8
Marra Mountains, Sudan 194 G8
Marrawah, Tas., Austral. 211 Y15
Marree, S. Aust., Austral. 211 W10
Marrero, La., U.S. 100 Q11
Marromeu, Mozambique 203 F13
Marrupa, Mozambique 203 D14
Marsa, Malta 161 K23
Marsá al Burayqah, Lib. 197 C15
Marsabit, Kenya 199 J14
Marsa Fatma, Eritrea 199 E15
Marsala, It. 151 S8
Marsalforn, Malta 161 H20
Marsaxlokk, Malta 161 L23
Marsaxlokk Bay, Malta 161 L23
Marsciano, It. 150 J8
Marseille, Fr. 147 Y13
Marsfjället, peak, Sw. 140 G12
Marshall, Alas., U.S. 110 H12
Marshall, Ark., U.S. 100 E8
Marshall, river, Austral. 210 F9
Marshall, Ill., U.S. 99 S7
Marshall, Mich., U.S. 98 M10
Marshall, Minn., U.S. 104 K9
Marshall, Mo., U.S. 105 S12
Marshall, Tex., U.S. 102 L15
Marshall Islands, Pac. Oc. 214 F8
Marshalltown, Iowa, U.S. 105 N12
Marshfield, Mo., U.S. 105 U12
Marshfield, Wis., U.S. 98 J4
Marsh Harbour, Bahamas 120 B6
Mars Hill, Me., U.S. 95 B18
Mars Hill, N.C., U.S. 96 H7
Marsh Island, La., U.S. 100 Q8
Marsland, Nebr., U.S. 105 N1
Mars-la-Tour, Fr. 147 P13
Marsugalt, island, Marshall Is. 216 K2
Mart, Tex., U.S. 103 N12
Martaban, Gulf of, Myanmar 186 L6
Martapura, Indonesia 188 K11
Martelange, Lux. 160 J8
Martha's Vineyard, island, Mass., U.S. 95 M15
Martí, Cuba 116 J11
Martigny, Switz. 150 C2
Martigues, Fr. 147 X13
Martin, S. Dak., U.S. 104 M3
Martin, Slovakia 149 J15
Martin, Tenn., U.S. 101 E13
Martin, Lake, Ala., U.S. 101 K16
Martinez, Ga., U.S. 96 L7
Martinez Lake, Ariz., U.S. 107 U4
Martinique, island, Fr., Lesser Antilles 119 K17
Martinique Passage, Lesser Antilles 119 J17
Martinsburg, W. Va., U.S. 96 C12
Martins Ferry, Ohio, U.S. 99 Q15
Martinsville, Ind., U.S. 99 S9
Martinsville, Va., U.S. 96 G10
Martos, Sp. 144 K10
Martuni, Arm. 169 E19
Martuni, Azerb. 169 E21
Maru, island, Indonesia 213 D14
Ma'ruf, Afghan. 177 Q6
Marum Volcano, Vanuatu 218 D3
Marutea, island, Fr. Polynesia, Fr. 219 E19
Marutea, island, Fr. Polynesia, Fr. 219 G22
Marvão, Port. 144 H6
Marv Dasht, Iran 173 F13
Marvel Loch, W. Aust., Austral. 211 X4
Marvine, Mount, Utah, U.S. 107 N7
Marvin Spur, Arctic Oc. 242 J10
Marwah, Afghan. 176 M3
Mary, Turkm. 174 M10
Maryborough, Qnsld., Austral. 211 U15
Maryland, U.S. 96 C12
Mary Point, Virgin Islands, U.S. 120 M11
Maryport, Eng., U.K. 143 P10
Marys, river, Nev., U.S. 108 M11
Marysvale, Utah, U.S. 107 N7
Marysville, Calif., U.S. 109 Q4
Marysville, Kans., U.S. 105 R8
Marysville, Ohio, U.S. 99 Q12
Marysville, Wash., U.S. 108 B4
Maryville, Mo., U.S. 105 R10
Maryville, Tenn., U.S. 101 F18
Marzo, Cabo, Col. 128 E3
Marzūq, Lib. 197 E14
Marzūq, Şaḩrā', Lib. 197 E13
Masada, ruin, Israel 171 N6
Masai Steppe, Tanzania 199 L14
Masallı, Azerb. 169 F22
Masalog, Puntan, N. Mariana Is., U.S. 216 B8
Masamba, Indonesia 189 K13
Masan, S. Korea 182 G14
Masasi, Tanzania 199 N15
Masaya, Nicar. 115 M18
Masbate, island, Philippines 189 D14
Masbate, Philippines 189 D14
Mascara, Alg. 196 A10
Mascarene Basin, Ind. Oc. 240 J6
Mascarene Plain, Ind. Oc. 240 K6
Mascarene Plateau, Ind. Oc. 240 H7
Masefau Bay, Amer. Samoa, U.S. 218 L8
Masein, Myanmar 186 F5
Masela, island, Indonesia 189 M17
Maseru, Lesotho 202 K10
Masescha, Liech. 160 P2
Mash'abbé Sade, Israel 171 P5
Mashhad, Iran 173 C16
Mashīz, Iran 173 F15
Mashkai, river, Pak. 177 U5
Mashkel, river, Pak. 177 T3
Mashkel, Hamun-i-, Pak. 177 T2

Mashki Chah, Pak. 177 S2
Mashuray, Afghan. 177 P7
Masi-Manimba, Dem. Rep. of the Congo 198 L8
Masin, Indonesia 189 M21
Masira see Maşīrah, Jazīrat, island, Oman 173 L17
Masira, Gulf of, Oman 166 J5
Maşīrah, Tur'at, Oman 173 L17
Maşīrah, Jazīrat (Masira), Oman 173 L17
Maşīrah, Khalīj, Oman 173 M16
Masisea, Peru 130 G4
Masjed Soleymān, Iran 172 E12
Mask, Lough, Ire. 143 R3
Maskanah (Meskéné), Syr. 170 E10
Maskelynes Islands, Vanuatu 218 E2
Maslenica, Croatia 152 F5
Maslen Nos, Bulg. 153 J17
Masoala, Presqu'île de, Madagascar 203 E18
Mason, Mich., U.S. 98 M11
Mason, Tex., U.S. 103 P8
Mason Bay, N.Z. 213 R15
Mason City, Iowa, U.S. 104 M12
Mason Hall, Trinidad & Tobago 121 N18
Masontown, Pa., U.S. 94 P3
Maspalomas, Canary Is. 204 R6
Masqaţ (Muscat), Oman 173 K16
Massa, Congo 201 M17
Massachusetts, U.S. 94 K12
Massachusetts Bay, Mass., U.S. 95 K16
Massacre, Dominica 121 F19
Massacre Bay, Amer. Samoa, U.S. 218 M7
Massafra, It. 150 M14
Massakory, Chad 197 J14
Massa Marittima, It. 150 H6
Massangena, Mozambique 202 H12
Massawa, Eritrea 199 D15
Massay, Fr. 147 S9
Mass City, Mich., U.S. 98 F6
Massena, N.Y., U.S. 94 F10
Massenya, Chad 197 J14
Masset, B.C., Can. 82 J7
Massiac, Fr. 147 V11
Massillon, Ohio, U.S. 99 P14
Massinga, Mozambique 203 H13
Masson Island, Antarctica 227 K21
Mastābah, Saudi Arabia 172 L7
Maştağa, Azerb. 169 D23
Masterton, N.Z. 213 M19
Mástiho, Akrotírio, Gr. 155 J16
Mastuj, Pak. 176 L10
Mastung, Pak. 177 R6
Mastūrah, Saudi Arabia 172 K6
Masty, Belarus 156 K3
Masuda, Japan 185 Q5
Masvingo, Zimb. 202 G11
Maşyāf, Syr. 170 F7
Mat, river, Albania 152 K9
Mataabé, Cape, Vanuatu 218 D1
Matacaw Levu, island, Fiji Is. 218 H5
Matadi, Dem. Rep. of the Congo 198 L7
Matador, Tex., U.S. 102 J6
Matagalpa, Nicar. 115 M18
Matagami, Que., Can. 83 N18
Matagorda, Tex., U.S. 103 S13
Matagorda Bay, Tex., U.S. 84 N12
Matagorda Peninsula, Tex., U.S. 103 S13
Matah see Mataso, island, Vanuatu 218 E3
Matahiva see Mataiva, island, Fr. Polynesia, Fr. 219 D17
Mataiea, Fr. Polynesia, Fr. 219 P16
Mataigou see Taole, China 182 D1
Mataiva (Matahiva), island, Fr. Polynesia, Fr. 219 D17
Matak, island, Indonesia 188 H8
Matala, Gr. 155 R14
Matalaa, Pointe, Wallis & Futuna, Fr. 218 C11
Matale, Sri Lanka 179 T7
Matam, Senegal 196 G5
Matamoros, Mex. 114 F12
Matane, Que., Can. 83 N21
Matanzas, Cuba 116 G7
Mata Point, Niue, N.Z. 219 C20
Matara, Sri Lanka 179 T7
Mataram, Indonesia 188 M12
Mataranka, N. Terr., Austral. 211 Q8
Mataró, Sp. 145 D18
Matasiri, island, Indonesia 188 L11
Mataso (Matah), island, Vanuatu 218 E3
Matatépai, Pointe, Fr. Polynesia, Fr. 219 M20
Matatiele, S. Af. 202 L11
Matatula, Cape, Amer. Samoa, U.S. 218 L9
Mataura, Fr. Polynesia, Fr. 219 K20
Mataura, Mouillage de, Fr. Polynesia, Fr. 219 K20
Matâ'utu, Wallis & Futuna, Fr. 218 B11
Matautu, Samoa 218 L3
Mata-Utu, Baie de, Wallis & Futuna, Fr. 218 B12
Matautulele Point, Amer. Samoa, U.S. 218 M7
Matauvau, Passe, Fr. Polynesia, Fr. 219 N14
Matavai, Baie de, Fr. Polynesia, Fr. 219 N16
Matavanu, Mount, Samoa 218 K2
Matavera, Cook Is., N.Z. 218 Q9
Matcha, Taj. 176 H8
Mateguá, Bol. 130 H8
Matehuala, Mex. 114 G11
Mateika, island, Tuvalu 217 L23
Mateika, Te Ava, Tuvalu 217 L23
Matelot, Trinidad & Tobago 121 N23
Matema, island, Solomon Is. 217 P22
Matera, It. 150 M13
Matese, range, It. 150 L11
Mátészalka, Hung. 149 K17
Matfors, Sw. 141 J13
Mathematicians Seamounts, Pac. Oc. 239 H17
Mather, Calif., U.S. 109 S6
Mathews, Va., U.S. 96 E14
Mathis, Tex., U.S. 103 T10
Mathráki, island, Gr. 154 E5
Mathura, India 178 F6
Mathurin Bay, Mauritius 205 J20
Mati, Philippines 189 F15
Matiere, N.Z. 213 K19
Matinicus Island, Me., U.S. 95 G17
Matira, Pointe, Fr. Polynesia, Fr. 219 L14
Matlerjoch, pass, Aust., Liech. 160 P4
Matli, Pak. 177 W7
Matlock, Eng., U.K. 143 S12
Matochkin Shar, Russ. 158 D11
Mato Grosso, Braz. 130 J9
Matopo Hills, Zimb. 194 N8
Matosinhos, Port. 144 E5
Maţraḩ, Oman 173 K16
Maţrūḩ, Egypt 197 C17
Matsu see Matsu Tao, island, Taiwan, China 183 P9
Matsubara, Japan 185 X2
Matsue, Japan 185 P6
Matsumoto, Japan 185 N11
Matsu Tao (Matsu), Taiwan, China 183 P9
Matsuyama, Japan 185 R6
Mattamuskeet, Lake, N.C., U.S. 96 H14
Mattaponi, river, Va., U.S. 96 E13
Mattawamkeag, Me., U.S. 95 D18
Matterhorn, peak, It., Switz. 150 C3
Matterhorn, peak, Nev., U.S. 108 L11
Matthew, island, Vanuatu 214 K8
Matthews Peak, Ariz., U.S. 84 J7
Matthew's Ridge, Guyana 129 D13
Matthew Town, Bahamas 117 J15
Maţţī, Sabkhat, Saudi Arabia, U.A.E. 173 K13
Mattili, India 178 L8
Mattinata, It. 150 L13
Mattoon, Ill., U.S. 99 S6
Matu, Malaysia 187 U16
Matua, Indonesia 188 K9
Matua, island, Russ. 159 H23
Matuku, island, Fiji Is. 218 K8
Matunga, island, Cook Is., N.Z. 219 B17
Matunuck, R.I., U.S. 95 M14
Matura, Trinidad & Tobago 121 P23
Matura Bay, Trinidad & Tobago 121 P23
Maturei Vavao, island, Fr. Polynesia, Fr. 219 G22
Maturín, Venez. 128 B12
Maúa, Mozambique 203 E14
Maubara, Timor-Leste 189 M15
Maubeuge, Fr. 146 M11
Maud Rise, Antarctic Oc. 244 E11
Maués, Braz. 130 D10
Maughold Head, Isle of Man, U.K. 143 Q9
Maug Islands, N. Mariana Is., U.S. 216 A2
Maui, island, Hawai'i, U.S. 113 G17
Mauke, island, Cook Is., N.Z. 214 K12
Maukme, Myanmar 186 H7
Maule, Rio, Chile 132 M6
Mauléon, Fr. 147 S6
Maullín, Chile 133 Q6
Maumee, river, Ohio, U.S. 99 P12
Maumee, Ohio, U.S. 99 N12
Maumusson, Pertuis de, Fr. 147 U6
Maun, Botswana 202 G9
Maunabo, P.R., U.S. 120 N5
Mauna Iki, peak, Hawai'i, U.S. 113 N20
Mauna Kea, peak, Hawai'i, U.S. 113 L20
Mauna Kea Adz Quarry, Hawai'i, U.S. 113 L20
Mauna Kea Observatories, Hawai'i, U.S. 113 L20
Mauna Loa, peak, Hawai'i, U.S. 113 N19
Maunaloa, Hawai'i, U.S. 113 F14
Mauna Loa Observatory, Hawai'i, U.S. 113 M20
Maunalua Bay, Hawai'i, U.S. 112 E12
Mauna Ulu, peak, Hawai'i, U.S. 113 N21
Maungapu, peak, Cook Is., N.Z. 218 P11
Maungdaw, Myanmar 186 H4
Maunoir, Lac, N.W.T., Can. 82 F11
Maupihaa (Mopelia), island, Fr. Polynesia, Fr. 219 E14
Maupin, Oreg., U.S. 108 F5
Maupiti, island, Fr. Polynesia, Fr. 219 E15
Mau Ranipur, India 178 H7
Mauren, Liech. 160 M2
Maurepas, Lake, La., U.S. 100 P10
Maures, Monts des, Fr. 147 Y15
Mauriac, Fr. 147 V10
Maurice, Lake, Austral. 210 H7
Mauritania, Af. 195 F14
Mauritius, island, Ind. Oc. 204 H9
Mauritius Trench, Ind. Oc. 240 K6
Mauron, Fr. 147 Q5
Maury Bay, Antarctica 227 P20
Maury Mountains, Oreg., U.S. 108 H6
Maury Seachannel, Atl. Oc. 236 E9
Mauston, Wis., U.S. 98 K4
Mautaro, Motu, Fr. Polynesia, Fr. 219 K21
Mautau, Pointe, Fr. Polynesia, Fr. 219 M20
Mauvezin, Fr. 147 X8
Maverick, Ariz., U.S. 107 T9
Mavinga, Angola 202 E8
Mavone, river, It. 161 G15
Mavroli, Cyprus 160 P6
Mavrovouni Mine, Cyprus 160 P7
Mawlamyine, Myanmar 186 L7
Mawlite, Myanmar 186 F5
Mawlu, Myanmar 186 F6
Mawqaq, Saudi Arabia 172 H8
Mawshij, Yemen 172 Q8
Mawson, station, Antarctica 227 E20
Mawson Coast, Antarctica 227 D20
Mawson Escarpment, Antarctica 227 F18
Mawson Peninsula, Antarctica 227 R16
Max, N. Dak., U.S. 104 F4
Maxixe, Mozambique 203 H13
Maxton, N.C., U.S. 96 J11
May, Cape, N.J., U.S. 85 G20
May, Isle of, Scot., U.K. 142 M11
Mayabandar, India 179 P14
Mayaguana Island, Bahamas 117 H16
Mayaguana Passage, Bahamas 117 H15
Mayagüez, P.R., U.S. 120 N1
Mayagüez, Bahía de, P.R., U.S. 120 N1
Mayāmey, Iran 173 C15
Mayang, China 183 N2
Mayarí, Cuba 117 K13
Mayaro Bay, Trinidad & Tobago 121 Q23
Maycock's Bay, Barbados 121 J18
Maydān Ikbiz, Syr. 170 C8
Maydh, Somalia 199 F17
Maydī, Yemen 172 P8
Mayenne, Fr. 147 Q7
Mayfa'ah, Yemen 172 Q11
Mayfield, Ky., U.S. 101 D13
Mayhill, N. Mex., U.S. 107 U13
Maykop, Russ. 157 T11
Mayluu-Suu, Kyrg. 176 F10
Mayno Gytkino, Russ. 159 C21
Mayo, Fla., U.S. 97 R6
Mayo, Trinidad & Tobago 121 P22
Mayo, Yukon, Can. 82 F8
Mayo, Cerro, Chile 133 V7
Mayo Faran, Nigeria 201 G16
Mayorga, Sp. 144 C9
Mayotte, Île de, Fr., Mozambique Ch. 203 D16
May Pen, Jam. 120 J9
Mayreau, island, St. Vincent & the Grenadines 119 M17
Maysville, Ky., U.S. 101 A18
Maysville, Mo., U.S. 105 R11
Mayumba, Gabon 201 M15
Mayville, N. Dak., U.S. 104 F8
Mayville, Wis., U.S. 98 L6
Maywood, Nebr., U.S. 105 Q4
Mazabuka, Zambia 202 F10
Mazagan see El Jadida, Mor. 196 B8
Mazagão, Braz. 130 C12
Mazamet, Fr. 147 X10
Mazar, China 180 H4
Mazara del Vallo, It. 151 S8
Mazar-e Sharif, Afghan. 176 K6
Mazari Pass, Pak. 177 S3
Mazarrón, Golfo de, Sp. 145 L13
Mazaruni, river, Guyana 129 D13
Mazatán, Mex. 114 D7
Mazatenango, Guatemala 115 L15
Mazatlán, Mex. 114 G8
Mazgirt, Turk. 169 F14
Mazıdağı, Turk. 169 H15
Mazirbe, Latv. 141 L15
Mazotos, Cyprus 160 Q9
Mazowe, Zimb. 202 F11
Mazrub, Sudan 198 E12
Mazyr, Belarus 156 M5
Mazzarino, It. 151 T10
Mazzocco, river, It. 161 K13
Mbabane, Swaziland 203 J11
Mbaïki, Cen. Af. Rep. 198 H8
Mbakaou Reservoir, Cameroon 201 H16
Mbala, Zambia 202 C12
Mbale, Uganda 199 J13
Mbalmayo, Cameroon 201 J16
Mbalo, Solomon Is. 217 P19
Mbamba Bay, Tanzania 199 N13
Mbandaka, Dem. Rep. of the Congo 198 K8
Mbang, Mount, Cameroon 201 G17
Mbang Mountains, Cameroon, Chad 194 H6
Mbanika, island, Solomon Is. 217 N18
M'banza Congo, Angola 202 B6
Mbanza-Ngungu, Dem. Rep. of the Congo 198 L7
Mbarara, Uganda 198 K12
Mbari, river, Cen. Af. Rep. 198 H10
Mbé, Cameroon 201 G16
Mbéni, Comoros 205 M14
Mbeya, Tanzania 199 N13
M'Binda, Congo 201 M16
Mbini, Eq. Guinea 201 K15
Mborokua, island, Solomon Is. 217 N17
Mbout, Mauritania 196 G6
Mbuji-Mayi, Dem. Rep. of the Congo 198 M10
Mbulo, island, Solomon Is. 217 M17
Mburucuyá, Arg. 132 G13
Mbuyuni, Tanzania 199 M14
McAlester, Okla., U.S. 102 H13
McAllen, Tex., U.S. 103 W10
McArthur River, N. Terr., Austral. 211 Q9
McCall, Idaho, U.S. 106 F4
McCamey, Tex., U.S. 103 N4
McCammon, Idaho, U.S. 106 H7
McCaysville, Ga., U.S. 96 J5
McCleary, Wash., U.S. 108 D3
McClellanville, S.C., U.S. 96 M11
McCloud, Calif., U.S. 108 M4
McColl, S.C., U.S. 96 J10
McComb, Miss., U.S. 100 N10
McConaughy, Lake, Nebr., U.S. 105 P3
McCook, Nebr., U.S. 105 R4
McCormick, S.C., U.S. 96 L7
McCrory, Ark., U.S. 100 G10
McDermitt, Nev., U.S. 108 L9
McDonald, Kans., U.S. 105 R3
McDonald Islands, Antarctic Oc. 245 G16
McDonald Peak, Mont., U.S. 106 C6
McDouall Peak, S. Aust., Austral. 211 W9
McGehee, Ark., U.S. 100 J9
McGill, Nev., U.S. 109 P12
McGrath, Alas., U.S. 111 H14
McGregor, Minn., U.S. 104 G11
McGregor, Tex., U.S. 103 N11
McGuire, Mount, Idaho, U.S. 106 E5
Mchinji, Malawi 202 E12
McIntosh, Minn., U.S. 104 F9
McIntosh, S. Dak., U.S. 104 H4
McKean Island, Kiribati 214 G10
McKeesport, Pa., U.S. 94 N3
McKees Rocks, Pa., U.S. 94 N3
McKenzie, Tenn., U.S. 101 E13
McKinlay, Qnsld., Austral. 211 S11
McKinley, Mount (Denali), Alas., U.S. 111 H16
McKinleyville, Calif., U.S. 108 M2
McKinney, Tex., U.S. 102 K12
McKinney, Lake, Kans., U.S. 105 U3
McKinnon, Wyo., U.S. 106 K9
McKittrick, Calif., U.S. 109 V6
McLaughlin, S. Dak., U.S. 104 H4
McLean, Tex., U.S. 102 G7
McLeansboro, Ill., U.S. 99 U6
McLean's Town (Self Town), Bahamas 120 E4
McLeod Bay, N.W.T., Can. 82 H12
M'Clintock Channel, Nunavut, Can. 83 E14
M'Clintock Inlet, Nunavut, Can. 83 A16
McLoughlin, Mount, Oreg., U.S. 108 K4
M'Clure Strait, N.W.T., Can. 82 C12
McMahon Line, China, India 178 F14
McMinnville, Oreg., U.S. 108 F3
McMinnville, Tenn., U.S. 101 F16
McMurdo, station, Antarctica 227 N13
McMurdo Sound, Antarctica 227 N14
McNary Dam, Oreg., Wash., U.S. 108 E7
McPherson, Kans., U.S. 105 T7
McRae, Ga., U.S. 97 N7
McVeigh, Ky., U.S. 101 C20
McVille, N. Dak., U.S. 104 F7
Mdennah, region, Alg., Mali, Mauritania 196 E8
Mdina, Malta 161 K22
Mead, Lake, Ariz., Nev., U.S. 109 U13
Meade, river, Alas., U.S. 111 C14
Meade, Kans., U.S. 105 V4
Meade Peak, Idaho, U.S. 106 J8
Meadow, Tex., U.S. 102 K4
Meadow, W. Aust., Austral. 211 V2
Meadow Lake, Sask., Can. 82 L11
Meadow Valley Wash, Nev., U.S. 109 T12
Mead Point, Anguilla, U.K. 120 R11
Mead's Bay, Anguilla, U.K. 120 R11
Meadville, Pa., U.S. 94 L3
Meandarra, Qnsld., Austral. 211 V14
Meander River, Alta., Can. 82 J10
Meares, Cape, Oreg., U.S. 108 F2
Mears, Mich., U.S. 98 K9
Meaux, Fr. 147 P10
Mebane, N.C., U.S. 96 G11
Mecca, Calif., U.S. 109 Y11
Mecca see Makkah, Saudi Arabia 172 L7
Mechanicsburg, Pa., U.S. 94 P7
Mechelen, Belg. 146 L12
Mechol, F.S.M. 217 C18
Mecitözü, Turk. 168 D10
Meck, island, Marshall Is. 216 M5
Mecklenburger Bucht, Ger. 148 B9
Mecúfi, Mozambique 203 D15
Mecula, Mozambique 203 D14
Medan, Indonesia 188 G5
Médéa, Alg. 196 A11
Medellín, Col. 128 E4
Medford, Okla., U.S. 102 E10
Medford, Oreg., U.S. 108 K3
Medford, Wis., U.S. 98 H4
Medgidia, Rom. 153 F17
Media Luna, Cayo, Cuba 116 K11
Medical Lake, Wash., U.S. 108 C8
Medicine Bow, Wyo., U.S. 106 J12
Medicine Bow Mountains, Colo., Wyo., U.S. 106 K12
Medicine Bow Peak, Wyo., U.S. 106 K12
Medicine Hat, Alta., Can. 82 N11
Medicine Lake, Mont., U.S. 106 B13
Medicine Lodge, Kans., U.S. 105 V6
Medina, N. Dak., U.S. 104 G6
Medina, N.Y., U.S. 94 H5
Medina see Al Madīnah, Saudi Arabia 172 J7
Medina, river, Tex., U.S. 103 R9
Medina, Tex., U.S. 103 R8
Medinaceli, Sp. 144 E12
Medina del Campo, Sp. 144 E9
Medina de Pomar, Sp. 144 B11
Medina de Rioseco, Sp. 144 D9
Medina Lake, Tex., U.S. 103 R9
Medina Sidonia, Sp. 144 M8
Medinipur, India 178 J11
Mednogorsk, Russ. 158 J7
Mednyy, Ostrov, Russ. 159 E23
Médoc, region, Fr. 147 V6
Mêdog, China 180 L9
Medora, N. Dak., U.S. 104 G2
Medren, island, Marshall Is. 216 H9

Medvezh'i Ostrova (Bear Islands), *Russ.* **159** C19
Medvezh'yegorsk, *Russ.* **158** D7
Medyado, island, *Marshall Is.* **216** L8
Medyai, island, *Marshall Is.* **216** L8
Meekatharra, *W. Aust., Austral.* **211** V3
Meeker, *Colo., U.S.* **106** L10
Meerut, *India* **178** F6
Meeteetse, *Wyo., U.S.* **106** G10
Mega, *Indonesia* **189** J18
Mēga, *Eth.* **199** H15
Megálo Horió, *Gr.* **155** M18
Megalópoli, *Gr.* **154** K9
Mégara, *Gr.* **154** J12
M̃égham, *Vanuatu* **218** D3
Meghri, *Arm.* **169** F20
Megiddo, *Israel* **170** L5
Megion, *Russ.* **158** H11
Megísti (Kastellórizon), *Gr.* **155** N22
Mehadia, *Rom.* **152** F12
Mehamn, *Nor.* **141** B14
Mehar, *Pak.* **177** U6
Meharry, Mount, *Austral.* **210** F3
Meherrin, river, *Va., U.S.* **96** F12
Mehetia, island, *Fr. Polynesia, Fr.* **219** F17
Mehola, *W. Bank* **170** L6
Mehrīz, *Iran* **173** E14
Mehtar Lam, *Afghan.* **176** M8
Meichang, *China* **181** L16
Meiganga, *Cameroon* **201** G17
Meighan Island, *Nunavut, Can.* **83** B14
Meigs, *Ga., U.S.* **97** Q5
Meihekou, *China* **182** B12
Meiktila, *Myanmar* **186** H6
Meiningen, *Ger.* **148** G8
Meissen, *Ger.* **148** F10
Meizhou, *China* **183** R6
Mejatto, island, *Marshall Is.* **216** K1
Mejillones, *Chile* **132** E6
Mejillones del Sur, Bahía de, *Chile* **132** E7
Mejit Island, *Marshall Is.* **216** F5
Mékambo, *Gabon* **201** K17
Mek'elē, *Eth.* **199** E15
Mekerrhane, Sebkha, *Alg.* **196** D10
Mekhtar, *Pak.* **177** R8
Mekiro, island, *Fr. Polynesia, Fr.* **219** Q20
Meknès, *Mor.* **196** B8
Mekong, river, *Asia* **166** K11
Mekong River Delta, *Vietnam* **187** Q13
Mekoryuk, *Alas., U.S.* **110** J11
Melanesia, islands, *Pac. Oc.* **214** G4
Melbourne, *Fla., U.S.* **97** T10
Melbourne, *Vic., Austral.* **211** Z12
Melbourne, Mount, *Antarctica* **227** P14
Mele, Capo, *It.* **150** G3
Mélé Bay, *Vanuatu* **218** F3
Melegnano, *It.* **150** E4
Melekeiok, *Palau* **216** N12
Melekeiok Point, *Palau* **216** N12
Melenki, *Russ.* **156** J11
Melfi, *Chad* **197** J15
Melfi, *It.* **150** M12
Melfort, *Sask., Can.* **82** M12
Melgar de Fernamental, *Sp.* **144** C10
Melide, *Sp.* **144** B6
Meligalás, *Gr.* **154** L9
Melilla, *Sp.* **144** P11
Melinka, *Chile* **133** R6
Melipilla, *Chile* **132** L6
Melita *see* Mljet, island, *Croatia* **152** J7
Melitopol', *Ukr.* **157** R8
Mellansel, *Sw.* **141** H13
Melle, *Fr.* **147** T7
Melle, *Ger.* **148** E6
Mellen, *Wis., U.S.* **98** F4
Mellieħa, *Malta* **161** J21
Mellieħa Bay, *Malta* **161** J21
Mělník, *Czech Rep.* **148** G11
Melo, *Uru.* **132** K15
Melolo, *Indonesia* **189** N13
Melos *see* Mílos, island, *Gr.* **155** M13
Melrhir, Chott, *Alg.* **196** B12
Melrose, *Minn., U.S.* **104** J10
Melrose, *W. Aust., Austral.* **211** V4
Mels, *Switz.* **150** B5
Meltaus, *Fin.* **141** E15
Melton, *Vic., Austral.* **211** Z12
Meluan, *Malaysia* **188** H10
Melun, *Fr.* **147** Q10
Melvich, *Scot., U.K.* **142** G9
Melville, *Sask., Can.* **82** N12
Melville, Lake, *Nfld. & Lab., Can.* **83** K22
Melville Bay, *N. Amer.* **80** C8
Melville Hills, *N.W.T., Nunavut, Can.* **82** E11
Melville Island, *N. Terr., Austral.* **211** N7
Melville Island, *N.W.T., Nunavut, Can.* **83** D13
Melville Peninsula, *Nunavut, Can.* **83** F16
Melvin, *Tex., U.S.* **103** N8
Melvin, Lough, *Ire., U.K.* **143** Q5
Mé Maoya, peak, *New Caledonia, Fr.* **218** D7
Memba, *Mozambique* **203** E15
Memboro, *Indonesia* **189** N13
Memmingen, *Ger.* **148** K7
Memphis, *Mo., U.S.* **105** Q13
Memphis, *Tenn., U.S.* **100** G11
Memphis, *Tex., U.S.* **102** H7
Mena, *Ark., U.S.* **100** G6
Mena, *Ukr.* **156** M7
Menahga, *Minn., U.S.* **104** G10
Menai Strait, *Wales, U.K.* **143** S9
Ménaka, *Mali* **196** H10
Menard, *Tex., U.S.* **103** P8
Menard Fracture Zone, *Pac. Oc.* **239** Q15
Menasha, *Wis., U.S.* **98** J6
Mende, *Fr.* **147** W11
Mendebo Mountains, *Eth.* **194** H10
Mendeleyev Plain, *Arctic Oc.* **242** J7
Mendeleyev Ridge, *Arctic Oc.* **242** H6
Mendeleyevsk, *Russ.* **156** H16
Mendelssohn Seamount, *Pac. Oc.* **238** G12
Mendenhall, *Miss., U.S.* **100** M11
Mendi, *P.N.G.* **213** D18
Mendī, *Eth.* **199** F14
Mendip Hills, *Eng., U.K.* **143** W11
Mendocino, *Calif., U.S.* **109** P2
Mendocino, Cape, *Calif., U.S.* **84** E2
Mendocino Fracture Zone, *Pac. Oc.* **238** E12
Mendota, *Calif., U.S.* **109** T6
Mendota, *Ill., U.S.* **99** P5
Mendoza, *Arg.* **132** K8
Menehune Ditch, *Hawai'i, U.S.* **112** B5
Meneng, region, *Nauru* **217** F23
Meneng Point, *Nauru* **217** F23
Menetés, *Gr.* **155** P18
Meng, river, *Aust.* **160** P4
Menge, island, *Marshall Is.* **216** M8
Mengen, *Turk.* **168** D7
Mengene Dağı, *Turk.* **169** G18
Menghai, *China* **180** Q10
Mengzi, *China* **180** P11
Meningie, *S. Aust., Austral.* **211** Y10
Menkere, *Russ.* **159** F17
Menno, *S. Dak., U.S.* **104** M7
Menominee, *Mich., U.S.* **98** H7
Menominee, river, *Mich., Wis., U.S.* **98** G7
Menomonee Falls, *Wis., U.S.* **98** L7
Menomonie, *Wis., U.S.* **98** H2
Menongue, *Angola* **202** E7
Menor, Mar, *Sp.* **145** K14
Menorca (Minorca), *Sp.* **145** G20
Men'shikova, Mys, *Russ.* **158** E11
Mentasta Lake, *Alas., U.S.* **111** H18
Mentawai, Kepulauan, *Indonesia* **188** K5
Mentawai Islands, *Indonesia* **166** M10
Menton, *Fr.* **147** X16
Mentor, *Ohio, U.S.* **99** N15
Menyamya, *P.N.G.* **213** D19
Menzies, *W. Aust., Austral.* **211** W4
Menzies, Mount, *Antarctica* **227** F18
Me'ona, *Israel* **170** K6
Meppel, *Neth.* **146** H13
Meppen, *Ger.* **148** D6
Mequinenza, Embalse de, *Sp.* **145** E15
Meramangye, Lake, *Austral.* **210** H8
Meramec, river, *Mo., U.S.* **105** T14
Merampit, island, *Indonesia* **189** G16
Merano, *It.* **150** C7
Meratus, Pegunungan, *Indonesia* **188** K11
Merauke, *Indonesia* **189** N21
Merca *see* Marka, *Somalia* **199** J17
Mercan Dağları, *Turk.* **169** F14
Mercara, *India* **179** Q5
Merced, *Calif., U.S.* **109** S5
Mercedario, Cerro, *S. Amer.* **126** L4
Mercedes, *Arg.* **132** H13
Mercedes, *Arg.* **132** L12
Mercedes, *Arg.* **132** L9
Mercedes, *Tex., U.S.* **103** W10
Mercedes, *Uru.* **132** K13
Merceditas, *Chile* **132** H7
Mercherchar (Eil Malk), island, *Palau* **216** P11
Mercy, Cape, *Nunavut, Can.* **83** G19
Mercy Bay, *N.W.T., Can.* **82** D12
Meredith, Cape, *Falkland Is., U.K.* **133** W11
Meredith, Lake, *Tex., U.S.* **102** G5
Mereeg, *Somalia* **199** H17
Merefa, *Ukr.* **157** P9
M̃éré Lava, island, *Vanuatu* **218** B2
Mergenevo, *Kaz.* **174** D6
Mergui Archipelago, *Myanmar* **187** N7
Meriç, river, *Turk.* **168** C2
Meriç, *Turk.* **168** C2
Mérida, *Mex.* **115** H16
Mérida, *Sp.* **144** H8
Mérida, *Venez.* **128** C7
Mérida, Cordillera de, *Venez.* **128** C7
Meriden, *Conn., U.S.* **94** M12
Meridian, *Idaho, U.S.* **106** G3
Meridian, *Miss., U.S.* **101** L13
Meridian, *Tex., U.S.* **102** M10
Mérig, island, *Vanuatu* **218** B2
Merimbula, *N.S.W., Austral.* **211** Z14
Merir, island, *Palau* **214** F2
Meritxell, *Andorra* **160** H4
Merizo, *Guam, U.S.* **216** E10
Merkel, *Tex., U.S.* **102** L7
Merkine, *Lith.* **141** P17
Meroe, ruin, *Sudan* **199** D13
Merowe, *Sudan* **199** D13
Merredin, *W. Aust., Austral.* **211** X3
Merrick Mountains, *Antarctica* **226** G7
Merrill, *Oreg., U.S.* **108** L4
Merrill, *Wis., U.S.* **98** H5
Merrillville, *Ind., U.S.* **99** P8
Merrimack, river, *N.H., U.S.* **95** J14
Merriman, *Nebr., U.S.* **104** M3
Merritt Island, *Fla., U.S.* **97** T10
Mer Rouge, *La., U.S.* **100** K9
Merryville, *La., U.S.* **100** N6
Mersch, *Lux.* **160** J10
Merseburg, *Ger.* **148** F9
Mersey River, *Eng., U.K.* **143** S10
Mersin *see* İçel, *Turk.* **168** J9
Mersing, *Malaysia* **187** U11
Merta Road, *India* **178** G4
Mertert, *Lux.* **160** J11
Merthyr Tydfil, *Wales, U.K.* **143** V10
Mértola, *Port.* **144** K6
Mertz Glacier, *Antarctica* **227** Q17
Mertz Glacier Tongue, *Antarctica* **227** R17
Mertzon, *Tex., U.S.* **103** N6
Méru, *Fr.* **147** N10
Meru, *Kenya* **199** K14
Merzifon, *Turk.* **168** D10
Merzig, *Ger.* **148** H5
Merz Seamount, *Antarctic Oc.* **244** B11
Mesa, *Ariz., U.S.* **107** U7
Mesabi Range, *Minn., U.S.* **85** C14
Mesach Mellet, region, *Lib.* **197** E13
Mesa Verde National Park, *Colo., U.S.* **107** Q10
Mescit Tepe, *Turk.* **169** D15
Meseong, island, *F.S.M.* **217** D15
Meseta, plateau, *Sp.* **138** J2
Me Shima, *Japan* **185** S2
Meskéné *see* Maskanah, *Syr.* **170** E10
Mesocco, *Switz.* **150** C4
Mesopotamia, region, *Iraq* **172** C8
Mesopotamia, *St. Vincent & the Grenadines* **121** K16
Mesquite, *Nev., U.S.* **109** T13
Mesquite, *Tex., U.S.* **102** L12
Messarás, Kólpos, *Gr.* **155** R14
Messene, ruin, *Gr.* **154** L9
Messina, *It.* **151** R12
Messina, *S. Af.* **202** H11
Messina, Stretto di, *It.* **151** R12
Messíni, *Gr.* **154** L9
Messiniakós Kólpos, *Gr.* **154** M9
Messolóngi, *Gr.* **154** H8
Mestá, *Gr.* **155** H16
Mestia, *Rep. of Georgia* **169** A17
Mestre, *It.* **150** D8
Mesudiye, *Turk.* **168** D12
Meta, river, *Venez.* **128** E8
Meta Incognita Peninsula, *Nunavut, Can.* **83** H19
Metairie, *La., U.S.* **100** Q11
Metalanim, *F.S.M.* **217** F14
Metalanim Harbor, *F.S.M.* **217** F14
Metaline Falls, *Wash., U.S.* **108** A9
Metallifere, Colline, *It.* **150** H6
Metán, *Arg.* **132** F9
Metaponto, *It.* **151** N14
Metaxádes, *Gr.* **155** B16
Meteora, ruin, *Gr.* **154** E9
Meteor Crater, *Ariz., U.S.* **107** S8
Meteor Seamount, *Atl. Oc.* **237** V14
Méthana, *Gr.* **154** K12
Methánon, island, *Gr.* **154** K12
Methóni, *Gr.* **154** M9
Metković, *Croatia* **152** H7
Metlakatla, *Alas., U.S.* **111** N24
Metlili Chaamba, *Alg.* **196** B11
Metolius, *Oreg., U.S.* **108** G5
Métoma, island, *Vanuatu* **218** A1
Metropolis, *Ill., U.S.* **99** V6
Métsovo, *Gr.* **154** E8
Metter, *Ga., U.S.* **97** N8
Mettlach, *Ger.* **160** K11
Mettur Dam, *India* **179** Q6
Metz, *Fr.* **147** P14
Meulan, *Fr.* **147** P9
Meuse, river, *Belg., Fr.* **146** M12
Mexia, *Tex., U.S.* **103** N12
Mexiana, Ilha, *Braz.* **131** C13
Mexicali, *Mex.* **114** A5
Mexican Hat, *Utah, U.S.* **107** Q9
México, *Mex.* **114** J11
Mexico, *Me., U.S.* **95** F15
Mexico, *Mo., U.S.* **105** S13
Mexico, *N. Amer.* **81** N17
Mexico, Gulf of, *N. Amer.* **80** M7
Mexico Basin, *Atl. Oc.* **236** K1
Meyanodas, *Indonesia* **213** D14
Meydan Shahr, *Afghan.* **176** M7
Meymaneh, *Afghan.* **176** L4
Meyrargues, *Fr.* **147** X13
Mezdra, *Bulg.* **153** H13
Mezen', river, *Russ.* **158** F9
Mezen', *Russ.* **158** E9
Mezen' Bay, *Russ.* **138** A11
Mezhdusharskiy, Ostrov, *Russ.* **158** E10
Mézidon-Canon, *Fr.* **147** P7
Mézin, *Fr.* **147** W7
Mezőtúr, *Hung.* **149** M16
Mezzolombardo, *It.* **150** C7
Mġarr, *Malta* **161** H20
Mġarr, *Malta* **161** K21
Miahuatlán, *Mex.* **115** K13
Miajadas, *Sp.* **144** H8
Miami, *Fla., U.S.* **97** X10
Miami, river, *N. Amer.* **80** K7
Miami, *Okla., U.S.* **102** E14
Miami, *Tex., U.S.* **102** G7
Miami Beach, *Fla., U.S.* **97** X10
Miamisburg, *Ohio, U.S.* **99** R11
Mianchi, *China* **182** H4
Mīāndowāb, *Iran* **172** B10
Miandrivazo, *Madagascar* **203** G16
Mīāneh, *Iran* **172** B11
Miani Hor, bay, *Pak.* **177** V5
Mianrud, *Pak.* **177** T3
Mianwali, *Pak.* **177** P9
Mianyang, *China* **180** L12
Miaodao, island, *China* **182** E9
Miaoli, *Taiwan, China* **183** Q9
Miarinarivo, *Madagascar* **203** G17
Miass, *Russ.* **158** J8
Michalovce, *Slovakia* **149** J17
Miches, *Dom. Rep.* **117** M20
Michigan, *U.S.* **98** F7
Michigan, Lake, *U.S.* **85** F16
Michigan City, *Ind., U.S.* **99** N8
Michurinsk, *Russ.* **156** L11
Micoud, *St. Lucia* **121** L14
Micronesia, islands, *Pac. Oc.* **214** E4
Midai, island, *Indonesia* **188** H8
Mid-Atlantic Ridge, *Atl. Oc.* **236** K7
Middelburg, *Neth.* **146** K11
Middelburg, *S. Af.* **202** L9
Middle Alkali Lake, *Calif., U.S.* **108** M6
Middle America Trench, *Pac. Oc.* **239** H18
Middle Andaman, island, *India* **179** Q14
Middle Bight, *Bahamas* **116** F11
Middlebury, *Vt., U.S.* **94** G12
Middlegate, *Norfolk I., Austral.* **217** F20
Middle Island, *St. Kitts & Nevis* **121** B17
Middle Loup, river, *Nebr., U.S.* **105** P5
Middlemarch, *N.Z.* **213** Q16
Middle Park, *Qnsld., Austral.* **211** S12
Middleport, *Ohio, U.S.* **99** S14
Middle Quarters, *Jam.* **120** J7
Middle River, *Minn., U.S.* **104** E9
Middlesboro, *Ky., U.S.* **101** D19
Middlesbrough, *Eng., U.K.* **143** Q12
Middleton, *Wis., U.S.* **98** L5
Middletown, *Conn., U.S.* **95** M13
Middletown, *N.Y., U.S.* **94** M10
Middletown, *Ohio, U.S.* **99** S11
Midelt, *Mor.* **196** B9
Midi, Canal du, *Fr.* **147** X9
Mid-Indian Basin, *Ind. Oc.* **240** H10
Mid-Indian Ridge, *Ind. Oc.* **240** G8
Midland, *Mich., U.S.* **98** K11
Midland, *S. Dak., U.S.* **104** L4
Midland, *Tex., U.S.* **102** M5
Midlothian, *Tex., U.S.* **102** L11
Mid-Pacific Mountains, *Pac. Oc.* **238** G7
Midu, island, *Maldives* **179** X3
Midway Islands, *U.S.* **112** K2
Midwest, *Wyo., U.S.* **106** H12
Midwest City, *Okla., U.S.* **102** G11
Midyat, *Turk.* **169** H16
Midžor, peak, *Bulg., Serb. & Mont.* **152** H12
Międzyrzecz, *Pol.* **148** D12
Miélan, *Fr.* **147** X7
Mielec, *Pol.* **149** G16
Miercurea Ciuc, *Rom.* **153** D15
Mieres, *Sp.* **144** B9
Miguel Calmon, *Braz.* **131** H16
Migyaunglaung, *Myanmar* **186** M7
Mihalıççık, *Turk.* **168** E7
Mijas, *Sp.* **144** M9
Mijdaḩah, *Yemen* **172** Q11
Mijek, *W. Sahara, Mor.* **196** E6
Mijikadrek, island, *Marshall Is.* **216** G8
Mikhaylovka, *Russ.* **157** N12
Mikkeli, *Fin.* **141** H16
Míkonos, island, *Gr.* **155** K15
Míkonos, *Gr.* **155** K15
Mikrí Préspa, Límni, *Gr.* **154** C8
Mikun', *Russ.* **158** F8
Mikura Jima, *Japan* **185** R12
Milaca, *Minn., U.S.* **104** H11
Miladummadulu Atoll, *Maldives* **179** T3
Milagro, *Ecua.* **128** K2
Milan *see* Milano, *It.* **150** D4
Milan, *Mo., U.S.* **105** R12
Milan, *Tenn., U.S.* **101** F13
Milano (Milan), *It.* **150** D4
Milas, *Turk.* **168** H3
Milazzo, Capo di, *It.* **151** R12
Milbank, *S. Dak., U.S.* **104** J8
Milbridge, *Me., U.S.* **95** F18
Mildenhall, *Eng., U.K.* **143** T14
Mildura, *Vic., Austral.* **211** X11
Mile, *China* **180** P11
Mile and a Quarter, *Barbados* **121** J18
Mile Gully, *Jam.* **120** J8
Mil Entrance, *F.S.M.* **217** C18
Miles, *Qnsld., Austral.* **211** V14
Miles, *Tex., U.S.* **103** N7
Miles City, *Mont., U.S.* **106** D12
Mileto, *It.* **151** R13
Miletto, Monte, *It.* **150** L11
Miletus, ruin, *Turk.* **168** G3
Mileura, *W. Aust., Austral.* **211** V3
Milford, *Del., U.S.* **96** C15
Milford, *Iowa, U.S.* **104** M10
Milford, *Mass., U.S.* **95** K14
Milford, *Nebr., U.S.* **105** Q8
Milford, *Utah, U.S.* **107** N6
Milford Bay, *Trinidad & Tobago* **121** N17
Milford Haven (Aberdaugleddau), *Wales, U.K.* **143** V8
Milford Lake, *Kans., U.S.* **105** S8
Milford Sound, *N.Z.* **213** Q15
Milgarra, *Qnsld., Austral.* **211** R11
Milgun, *W. Aust., Austral.* **211** U3
Mili Atoll, *Marshall Is.* **216** H5
Miliés, *Gr.* **154** F11
Milikapiti, *N. Terr., Austral.* **211** N7
Mililani Town, *Hawai'i, U.S.* **112** E11
Milingimbi, *N. Terr., Austral.* **211** P9
Milk, river, *Mont., U.S.* **106** B11
Milk, Wadi el, *Sudan* **198** D12
Mil'kovo, *Russ.* **159** F22
Milk River Bath, *Jam.* **120** K8
Millars Sound, *Bahamas* **120** B11
Millau, *Fr.* **147** W11
Mill City, *Oreg., U.S.* **108** G4
Milledgeville, *Ga., U.S.* **96** M6
Mille Lacs Lake, *Minn., U.S.* **104** H11
Millen, *Ga., U.S.* **96** M8
Miller, *S. Dak., U.S.* **104** K6
Millerovo, *Russ.* **157** P11
Miller Peak, *Ariz., U.S.* **107** W8
Miller Point, *Solomon Is.* **217** R24
Millersburg, *Ohio, U.S.* **99** Q14

Millers Creek, *S. Aust., Austral.* **211** W9
Millevaches, Plateau de, *Fr.* **147** U9
Milligan Cay, *St. Vincent & the Grenadines* **121** L16
Millington, *Tenn., U.S.* **100** F11
Millinocket, *Me., U.S.* **95** D17
Mill Island, *Antarctica* **227** K21
Mill Island, *Nunavut, Can.* **83** H17
Millmerran, *Qnsld., Austral.* **211** V15
Mill Reef, *Antigua & Barbuda* **121** B21
Milltown, *Mont., U.S.* **106** D6
Milltown Malbay, *Ire.* **143** T3
Millungera, *Qnsld., Austral.* **211** S11
Millville, *N.J., U.S.* **94** Q10
Milly, *Fr.* **147** Q10
Milly Milly, *W. Aust., Austral.* **211** V2
Milnor, *N. Dak., U.S.* **104** H7
Milo, river, *Guinea* **200** F7
Milo, *Me., U.S.* **95** E17
Miloli'i, *Hawai'i, U.S.* **113** P18
Milord Point, *Virgin Islands, U.S.* **120** R3
Mílos, *Gr.* **155** M13
Mílos (Melos), *Gr.* **155** M13
Milpa, *N.S.W., Austral.* **211** W11
Milparinka, *N.S.W., Austral.* **211** W11
Milton, *Fla., U.S.* **97** Q2
Milton, *Pa., U.S.* **94** M7
Milton-Freewater, *Oreg., U.S.* **108** E8
Milton Keynes, *Eng., U.K.* **143** U13
Miltonvale, *Kans., U.S.* **105** S7
Milu, island, *Marshall Is.* **216** K4
Milu Pass, *Marshall Is.* **216** K4
Milwaukee, *Wis., U.S.* **98** L7
Mimizan-Plage, *Fr.* **147** W6
Mimot, *Cambodia* **187** N12
Mims, *Fla., U.S.* **97** T9
Min, river, *China* **183** P8
Min, river, *China* **180** K11
Mina, *Nev., U.S.* **109** R8
Mina Bazar, *Pak.* **177** Q8
Minahasa, region, *Indonesia* **189** H15
Mīnā' Jabal 'Alī, *U.A.E.* **173** J15
Minamata, *Japan* **185** S4
Minami Iwo Jima, *Japan* **184** L5
Minamitane, *Japan* **185** U4
Minami Tori Shima (Marcus), *Japan* **184** L8
Minas, *Cuba* **116** J11
Minas, *Uru.* **132** L14
Mīnā' Su'ūd, *Kuwait* **172** G11
Minatitlán, *Mex.* **115** K14
Minbu, *Myanmar* **186** H5
Minco, *Okla., U.S.* **102** G10
Mindanao, island, *Philippines* **189** F15
Mindelo, *Cape Verde* **205** B15
Minden, *Ger.* **148** D7
Minden, *La., U.S.* **100** K7
Minden, *Nebr., U.S.* **105** Q6
Minden, *Nev., U.S.* **109** Q6
Mindon, *Myanmar* **186** J5
Mindoro, island, *Philippines* **189** D13
Mindoro Strait, *Philippines* **189** D13
Mindouli, *Congo* **201** M17
Mine, *Japan* **185** Q3
Mineloa, *Tex., U.S.* **102** L13
Mineral'nyye Vody, *Russ.* **157** T13
Mineral Point, *Wis., U.S.* **98** L4
Mineral Wells, *Tex., U.S.* **102** L10
Minersville, *Utah, U.S.* **107** N6
Mineyama, *Japan* **185** P8
Minfeng (Niya), *China* **180** H6
Mingäçevir, *Azerb.* **169** D21
Mingäçevir Reservoir, *Azerb.* **169** D20
Mingan, *Que., Can.* **83** M21
Mingaora, *Pak.* **176** M10
Mingenew, *W. Aust., Austral.* **211** W2
Mingin, *Myanmar* **186** G5
Minglanilla, *Sp.* **145** H13
Mingo Cay, *Virgin Islands, U.S.* **120** M10
Mingteke, *China* **180** G3
Mingteke Pass, *China, Pak.* **178** A5
Mingulay, *Scot., U.K.* **142** K5
Minho, river, *Jam.* **120** J8
Minho, river, *Port.* **144** D5
Minicoy Island, *India* **179** S3
Minidoka, *Idaho, U.S.* **106** H6
Minidoka Internment National Monument, *Idaho, U.S.* **106** H5
Minigwal, Lake, *Austral.* **210** J5
Minilya, *W. Aust., Austral.* **211** U1
Minimarg, *Pak.* **176** M12
Minjilang, *N. Terr., Austral.* **211** N8
Min'kovo, *Russ.* **156** F12
Minna, *Nigeria* **201** F13
Minneapolis, *Kans., U.S.* **105** S7
Minneapolis, *Minn., U.S.* **104** K11
Minnedosa, *Man., Can.* **83** N13
Minneola, *Kans., U.S.* **105** U5
Minneota, *Minn., U.S.* **104** K9
Minnesota, river, *Minn., U.S.* **104** K10
Minnesota, *U.S.* **104** H8
Minnewaukan, *N. Dak., U.S.* **104** E6
Miño, river, *Sp.* **144** C6
Minocqua, *Wis., U.S.* **98** G5
Minonk, *Ill., U.S.* **99** P6
Minorca *see* Menorca, island, *Sp.* **145** G20
Minot, *N. Dak., U.S.* **104** E4
Minqing, *China* **183** P8
Minsk, *Belarus* **156** K5
Minsk Mazowiecki, *Pol.* **149** E16
Minto, *N. Dak., U.S.* **104** E7
Minto, Lac, *Que., Can.* **83** K18
Minto, Mount, *Antarctica* **227** R14
Minto Inlet, *N.W.T., Can.* **82** E12
Minturno, *It.* **150** L10
Minwakh, *Yemen* **172** P11
Minxian, *China* **180** J11
Mio, *Mich., U.S.* **98** J11
Mir, *Belarus* **156** L4
Mira, *It.* **150** E8
Mira, *Port.* **144** F5
Mirabad, *Afghan.* **177** R2
Mirador, *Braz.* **131** F15
Miraflores, *Col.* **128** H7
Miragoâne, *Haiti* **117** M16
Miramar, *Arg.* **133** N13
Mirambeau, *Fr.* **147** U7
Mirambélou, Kólpos, *Gr.* **155** Q16
Miram Shah, *Pak.* **177** P8
Miran, *China* **180** G7
Miranda, river, *Braz.* **130** L10
Miranda, *Braz.* **130** L10
Miranda de Ebro, *Sp.* **144** C12
Miranda do Douro, *Port.* **144** D8
Mirandela, *Port.* **144** D7
Mirando City, *Tex., U.S.* **103** U9
Mirandola, *It.* **150** E6
Mirano, *It.* **150** D8
Mira Por Vos, island, *Bahamas* **117** H14
Mir Bacheh Kowt, *Afghan.* **176** M8
Mirbashir, *Azerb.* **169** D20
Mirbāţ, *Oman* **173** P15
Mirbāţ, Ra's, *Oman* **173** P15
Mirebalais, *Haiti* **117** M17
Mirebeau, *Fr.* **147** S7
Mirecourt, *Fr.* **147** Q14
Mirepoix, *Fr.* **147** Y9
Miri, *Malaysia* **188** G11
Miriam Vale, *Qnsld., Austral.* **211** U15
Mirik *see* Timiris, Cap, cape, *Mauritania* **196** F4
Mirim, Lagoa, *Uru.* **132** K15
Mírina, *Gr.* **155** E14
Mīrjāveh, *Iran* **173** G17
Mirnyy, station, *Antarctica* **227** J21
Mirnyy, *Russ.* **159** H16
Mirpur, *Pak.* **177** N11
Mirpur Khas, *Pak.* **177** V8
Mirpur Sakro, *Pak.* **177** W6
Mírtos, *Gr.* **155** R15
Mirzapur, *India* **178** H8
Misaki, *Japan* **185** R6
Misawa, *Japan* **184** J13
Misgar, *Pak.* **176** K12
Mish'āb, Ra's al, *Saudi Arabia* **172** G11
Mishawaka, *Ind., U.S.* **99** N9
Mi Shima, *Japan* **185** Q5
Misima, island, *P.N.G.* **213** E21
Miskitos, Cayos, *Nicar.* **115** L19
Miskitos, Costa de, *Nicar.* **115** M19
Miskolc, *Hung.* **149** K16
Misool, island, *Indonesia* **189** K17
Misquah Hills, *Minn., U.S.* **104** E14
Mişrātah, *Lib.* **197** C14
Mission, *S. Dak., U.S.* **104** M4
Mission, *Tex., U.S.* **103** W10
Mississippi, river, *U.S.* **85** K15
Mississippi, *U.S.* **100** M11
Mississippi Fan, *Atl. Oc.* **236** K2
Mississippi River, Source of the, *Minn., U.S.* **104** G9
Mississippi River Delta, *La., U.S.* **101** R13
Mississippi Sound, *Miss., U.S.* **100** P12
Mississippi State, *Miss., U.S.* **101** J13
Missoula, *Mont., U.S.* **106** D6
Missouri, river, *U.S.* **85** H14
Missouri, *U.S.* **105** T11
Missouri Valley, *Iowa, U.S.* **105** P9
Mistassini, *Que., Can.* **83** N19
Mistassini, Lac, *Que., Can.* **83** N19
Misterbianco, *It.* **151** S12
Misty Fiords National Monument, *Alas., U.S.* **111** M24
Misumi, *Japan* **185** Q5
Misurata, Cape, *Lib.* **194** D6
Mitai, *Japan* **185** S5
Mitau *see* Jelgava, *Latv.* **141** M16
Mitchell, *Ind., U.S.* **99** T9
Mitchell, *Nebr., U.S.* **105** N1
Mitchell, *Oreg., U.S.* **108** G6
Mitchell, river, *Qnsld., Austral.* **211** Q12
Mitchell, *Qnsld., Austral.* **211** V14
Mitchell, *S. Dak., U.S.* **104** L7
Mitchell, Mount, *N.C., U.S.* **96** H7
Mitchell Lake, *Ala., U.S.* **101** K15
Mitchelstown, *Ire.* **143** U4
Mithankot, *Pak.* **177** S9
Mithi, *Pak.* **177** W8
Míthimna, *Gr.* **155** F16
Mitiaro, island, *Cook Is., N.Z.* **214** K12
Mítikas, *Gr.* **154** G8
Mitilíni *see* Lésvos, island, *Gr.* **155** F16
Mitilíni (Mytilene), *Gr.* **155** G17
Mitla, *Mex.* **115** K13
Mitla Pass, *Egypt* **171** Q2
Mito, *Japan* **185** N13
Mitre, peak, *N.Z.* **213** M19
Mitre Island *see* Fataka, *Solomon Is.* **214** J8
Mitsamiouli, *Comoros* **205** L14
Mitsero, *Cyprus* **160** P8
Mitsio, Nosy, *Madagascar* **203** D18
Mitsoudjé, *Comoros* **205** M14
Mitsushima, *Japan* **185** Q3
Mittelland Canal, *Ger.* **138** F6
Mitú, *Col.* **128** H8
Mitumba Mountains, *Dem. Rep. of the Congo* **198** M11
Mitwaba, *Dem. Rep. of the Congo* **198** M11
Mityushikha, Guba, *Russ.* **158** D11
Mitzic, *Gabon* **201** K16
Miura, *Japan* **185** Q12
Mixian, *China* **182** H5
Miyake Jima, *Japan* **185** R12
Miyako, *Japan* **184** K14
Miyakonojō, *Japan* **185** T5
Miyazaki, *Japan* **185** T5
Miyazu, *Japan* **185** P8
Miyoshi, *Japan* **185** Q6
Miyun, *China* **182** C7
Mizdah, *Lib.* **197** C13
Mizen Head, *Ire.* **143** V2
Mizhi, *China* **182** E3
Mizil, *Rom.* **153** E16
Mizo Hills, *India* **178** H14
Mizusawa, *Japan* **184** K13
Mjøsa, lake, *Nor.* **140** K11
Mladá Boleslav, *Czech Rep.* **148** G11
Mladenovac, *Serb. & Mont.* **152** F10
Mława, *Pol.* **149** C15
Mlima Bénara, peak, *Mayotte, Fr.* **205** P17
Mljet (Melita), island, *Croatia* **152** J7
Mljetski Kanal, *Croatia* **152** H7
Mmabatho, *S. Af.* **202** J10
Moa, *Cuba* **117** K14
Moa, river, *Guinea, Sierra Leone* **200** G6
Moa, island, *Indonesia* **189** M16
Moab, *Utah, U.S.* **107** N9
Moaco, river, *Braz.* **130** F6
Moala, island, *Fiji Is.* **218** J8
Moanda, *Gabon* **201** L16
Moapa, *Nev., U.S.* **109** T12
Moa'ula Nui, Pu'u 'O, *Hawai'i, U.S.* **113** H16
Mobayi-Mbongo, *Dem. Rep. of the Congo* **198** H9
Mobeetie, *Tex., U.S.* **102** G7
Moberly, *Mo., U.S.* **105** S13
Mobile, river, *Ala., U.S.* **101** N14
Mobile, *Ala., U.S.* **101** P13
Mobile Bay, *Ala., U.S.* **101** P14
Mobile Point, *Ala., U.S.* **101** P14
Mobridge, *S. Dak., U.S.* **104** J5
Moca, *Dom. Rep.* **117** L18
Moca, *P.R., U.S.* **120** M1
Mocajuba, *Braz.* **131** D13
Moçambique, *Mozambique* **203** E15
Moce, island, *Fiji Is.* **218** J9
Moch, island, *F.S.M.* **217** B15
Mocha, Isla, *Chile* **133** N5
Mochenap, bay, *F.S.M.* **217** B16
Mocho Mountains, *Jam.* **120** J8
Mochonap, bay, *F.S.M.* **217** A15
Mochon Point, *N. Mariana Is., U.S.* **216** D8
Mochudi, *Botswana* **202** J10
Mocímboa da Praia, *Mozambique* **203** D15
Mocksville, *N.C., U.S.* **96** H9
Moclips, *Wash., U.S.* **108** C2
Mocoa, *Col.* **128** H4
Moctezuma, *Mex.* **114** C7
Mocuba, *Mozambique* **203** F14
Modane, *Fr.* **147** V15
Model, *Colo., U.S.* **107** P14
Modena, *It.* **150** F6
Modesto, *Calif., U.S.* **109** S5
Modica, *It.* **151** U11
Mo Duc, *Vietnam* **186** M14
Modugno, *It.* **150** M14
Moe, *Vic., Austral.* **211** Z12
Moen *see* Weno, island, *F.S.M.* **217** B15
Moengo, *Suriname* **129** E17
Moerai, *Fr. Polynesia, Fr.* **219** K23
Moerai, Baie de, *Fr. Polynesia, Fr.* **219** K23
Mogadishu *see* Muqdisho, *Somalia* **199** J17
Mogadouro, *Port.* **144** E7
Mogalo, *Dem. Rep. of the Congo* **198** J9
Mogán, *Canary Is.* **204** R5
Mogaung, *Myanmar* **186** E7
Mogi das Cruzes, *Braz.* **131** M14
Mogincual, *Mozambique* **203** E15
Mogocha, *Russ.* **159** K17
Mogoi, *Indonesia* **189** K18
Mogok, *Myanmar* **186** G6
Mogollon Rim, *Ariz., U.S.* **107** T8
Mogotes, Punta, *Arg.* **133** N13
Mohács, *Hung.* **149** N15
Mohala, *India* **178** K7
Mohall, *N. Dak., U.S.* **104** E4
Mohammad Agha, *Afghan.* **176** M8
Mohana, *India* **178** L9
Mohave, Lake, *Ariz., Nev., U.S.* **109** V12
Mohawk, river, *N.Y., U.S.* **94** J10
Mohe, *China* **181** A15
Mohéli, island, *Comoros* **205** N15
Mohelnice, *Czech Rep.* **149** H13
Mohenjo Daro, ruin, *Pak.* **177** U7
Mohill, *Ire.* **143** R5
Mohns Ridge, *Arctic Oc.* **243** G17
Mohnyin, *Myanmar* **186** E6
Mohon Peak, *Ariz., U.S.* **107** S5
Mohotani (Motane), island, *Fr. Polynesia, Fr.* **219** N21
Mohyliv-Podil's'kyy, *Ukr.* **157** Q4
Moindou, *New Caledonia, Fr.* **218** D7
Moineşti, *Rom.* **153** C16
Mo i Rana, *Nor.* **140** F12
Moirang, *India* **178** H14
Moirans, *Fr.* **147** U13
Moisie, river, *Que., Can.* **83** M20
Moissac, *Fr.* **147** W8
Moïssala, *Chad* **197** K15
Moita, *Port.* **144** J5
Mojácar, *Sp.* **145** L13
Mojados, *Sp.* **144** E10
Mojave, river, *Calif., U.S.* **109** W10
Mojave, *Calif., U.S.* **109** W8
Mojave Desert, *Calif., Nev., U.S.* **109** V10
Mojave National Preserve, *Calif., U.S.* **109** V11
Mojokerto, *Indonesia* **188** M10
Mokdale, *Indonesia* **189** N14
Mokil Atoll, *F.S.M.* **216** Q8
Mokokchung, *India* **178** G15
Mokpo, *S. Korea* **182** G13
Mol, *Belg.* **146** K13
Mola di Bari, *It.* **150** M14
Moláoi, *Gr.* **154** M11
Molat, island, *Croatia* **152** F4
Moldavia, region, *Rom.* **153** B16
Molde, *Nor.* **140** J10
Moldova, *Eur.* **139** V10
Moldova, river, *Rom.* **153** B15
Moldova Nouă, *Rom.* **152** F11
Moldoveanu, peak, *Rom.* **153** E14
Molepolole, *Botswana* **202** J10
Môle St.-Nicolas, *Haiti* **117** L15
Molesworth, *N.Z.* **213** N18
Mōlī'ele, Heiau o, *Hawai'i, U.S.* **113** Q19
Molina, *Chile* **132** L7
Molina de Aragón, *Sp.* **145** F13
Molina de Segura, *Sp.* **145** K14
Moline, *Ill., U.S.* **99** P4
Moline, *Kans., U.S.* **105** U9
Molinière Point, *Grenada* **121** K22
Molino, river, *San Marino* **161** J16
Moliterno, *It.* **151** N13
Mollendo, *Peru* **130** K5
Mollerussa, *Sp.* **145** D16
Molloy Hole, *Arctic Oc.* **243** H15
Moloa'a Bay, *Hawai'i, U.S.* **112** B6
Moloka'i, island, *Hawai'i, U.S.* **113** F14
Molokai Fracture Zone, *Pac. Oc.* **239** G14
Molopo, river, *Botswana, S. Af.* **202** J9
Moloundou, *Cameroon* **201** K17
Molsheim, *Fr.* **147** P15
Molson, *Wash., U.S.* **108** A7
Moltke, Cape, *P.N.G.* **217** K13
Molu, island, *Indonesia* **189** M17
Moluccas (Maluku), islands, *Indonesia* **189** H16
Molucca Sea, *Indonesia* **189** J15
Moma, *Mozambique* **203** F14
Moma, river, *Russ.* **159** E19
Mombasa, *Kenya* **199** L15
Mombetsu, *Japan* **184** E14
Mombetsu, *Japan* **184** G14
Momence, *Ill., U.S.* **99** P7
Momi, *Fiji Is.* **218** J5
Momote, *P.N.G.* **213** B20
Mompach, *Lux.* **160** J11
Mompós, *Col.* **128** C5
Møn, island, *Den.* **140** P12
Mona, Isla, *P.R., U.S.* **117** N21
Monach Islands, *Scot., U.K.* **142** J6
Monaco, *Eur.* **160** D3
Monaco, Port of, *Monaco* **161** D21
Monaco Railroad Station, *Monaco* **161** E20
Monaco-Ville, *Monaco* **161** F21
Monadhliath Mountains, *Scot., U.K.* **142** K9
Monaghan, *Ire.* **143** Q6
Monahans, *Tex., U.S.* **103** N3
Mona Passage, *Dom. Rep., P.R., U.S.* **117** M21
Mona Point (Monkey Point), *N. Amer.* **80** Q8
Monarch Pass, *Colo., U.S.* **107** N12
Mona Reservoir, *Utah, U.S.* **106** M7
Monari, *Afghan.* **177** P7
Moncada, *Sp.* **145** H14
Moncalieri, *It.* **150** E2
Monchegorsk, *Russ.* **158** D8
Mönchengladbach, *Ger.* **148** F5
Monchique, Serra de, *Port.* **144** L5
Moncks Corner, *S.C., U.S.* **96** L10
Monclava, *Mex.* **115** J15
Monclova, *Mex.* **114** E11
Moncton, *N.B., Can.* **83** P21
Mondego, river, *Port.* **144** F5
Mondego, Cabo, *Port.* **144** F5
Mondeodo, *Indonesia* **189** K14
Mondolfo, *It.* **150** G9
Mondoñedo, *Sp.* **144** A7
Mondorf, *Lux.* **160** K10
Mondovi, *It.* **150** F3
Mondovi, *Wis., U.S.* **98** J3
Mondragone, *It.* **150** M10
Mondy, *Russ.* **159** L15
Moneague, *Jam.* **120** H9
Monemvassía, *Gr.* **154** M11
Monessen, *Pa., U.S.* **94** P3
Monestier-de-Clermont, *Fr.* **147** V14
Monett, *Mo., U.S.* **105** V11
Monfalcone, *It.* **150** D9
Monforte, *Port.* **144** H6
Monforte, *Sp.* **144** C7
Mongalla, *Sudan* **199** H13
Mongbwalu, *Dem. Rep. of the Congo* **198** J12
Mong Cai, *Vietnam* **186** G13
Mongers Lake, *Austral.* **210** J3
Möng Hsu, *Myanmar* **186** G7
Möng Küng, *Myanmar* **186** G7
Mongmong, *Guam, U.S.* **216** C11
Möng Nawng, *Myanmar* **186** G7
Mongo, *Chad* **197** J15
Mongolia, *Asia* **167** T10
Mongolian Plateau, *China, Mongolia* **166** F11
Mongororo, *Chad* **197** J16
Mongoy, *Russ.* **159** K17
Möng Pan, *Myanmar* **186** H7
Mongton, *Myanmar* **186** H8
Mongu, *Zambia* **202** E9
Moni, *Cyprus* **160** Q8

Monier, Mount, St. Lucia 121 J14
Monistrol-sur-Loire, Fr. 147 V12
Monito, island, P.R., U.S. 117 M21
Monitor Range, Nev., U.S. 109 Q10
Monkey Point see Mona Point, N. Amer. 80 Q8
Monkira, Qnsld., Austral. 211 U11
Monmouth, Ill., U.S. 99 P4
Monmouth, Oreg., U.S. 108 G3
Mono, island, Solomon Is. 217 L14
Mono, Punta, Nicar. 115 M19
Mono Lake, Calif., U.S. 109 R7
Monólithos, Gr. 155 N19
Monomoy Island, Mass., U.S. 95 L16
Monon, Ind., U.S. 99 Q8
Monona, Iowa, U.S. 104 M13
Monongahela, river, Pa., W. Va., U.S. 94 P3
Monopoli, It. 150 M14
Monreal del Campo, Sp. 145 F13
Mon Repos, St. Lucia 121 K14
Monroe, Ga., U.S. 96 L6
Monroe, La., U.S. 100 L8
Monroe, Mich., U.S. 99 N12
Monroe, N.C., U.S. 96 J9
Monroe, Wash., U.S. 108 B4
Monroe, Wis., U.S. 98 M5
Monroe City, Mo., U.S. 105 R13
Monroe Lake, Ind., U.S. 99 S9
Monroeville, Ala., U.S. 101 M14
Monrovia, Liberia 200 H6
Monschau, Ger. 148 G4
Mönsterås, Sw. 141 M13
Montagne, Neth. Antilles, Neth. 121 Q19
Montague, Calif., U.S. 108 L3
Montague Island, Alas., U.S. 111 K17
Montalbán, Sp. 145 F14
Montalegre, Port. 144 D6
Montalto di Castro, It. 150 K7
Montana, Bulg. 153 H13
Montana, U.S. 106 D7
Montanja, Neth. Antilles, Neth. 121 Q15
Montargil, Barragem de, Port. 144 H5
Montargis, Fr. 147 Q10
Montastruc-la-Conseillère, Fr. 147 X9
Montauban, Fr. 147 X9
Montauk Point, N.Y., U.S. 95 M14
Montbard, Fr. 147 R12
Montbéliard, Fr. 147 R15
Mont Belvieu, Tex., U.S. 103 Q14
Montblanc, Sp. 145 E16
Montbrison, Fr. 147 U12
Montceau-les-Mines, Fr. 147 S12
Montchanin, Fr. 147 S12
Mont-de-Marsan, Fr. 147 X7
Montdidier, Fr. 147 N10
Mont-Dore, New Caledonia, Fr. 218 E8
Monte, river, Parag. 130 M10
Monteagle, Mount, Antarctica 227 Q14
Montebelluna, It. 150 D8
Monte Carlo, Monaco 161 C21
Monte Carlo Beach Hotel, Fr. 161 A24
Monte Carlo Country Club, Fr. 161 A23
Monte Carlo Radio and Television Station, Monaco 161 D21
Monte-Carlo Sporting Club d'Eté, Monaco 161 B23
Monte Caseros, Arg. 132 J13
Montech, Fr. 147 X8
Montecito, Calif., U.S. 109 W7
Monte Comán, Arg. 132 L8
Monte Cristi, Dom. Rep. 117 L17
Montecristo, Isola di, It. 150 K5
Monte Dinero, Arg. 133 W9
Montefiascone, It. 150 J8
Monte Giardino, San Marino 161 K16
Montego Bay, Jam. 120 H6
Montego Bay, Jam. 120 H7
Montehermoso, Sp. 144 G8
Montejunto, Serra de, Port. 144 H4
Montelicciano, It. 161 L16
Montélimar, Fr. 147 W13
Montello, Nev., U.S. 108 M12
Montemaggio, It. 161 L14
Montemarciano, It. 150 G9
Montemayor, Meseta de, Arg. 133 R9
Montemorelos, Mex. 114 F11
Montemor-o-Novo, Port. 144 J5
Montemuro, peak, Port. 144 E6
Montendre, Fr. 147 V7
Montenegro, region, Serb. & Mont. 152 H8
Montepescali, It. 150 J6
Monte Plata, Dom. Rep. 117 M19
Montepuez, Mozambique 203 D14
Monte Quemado, Arg. 132 F11
Montereau, Fr. 147 Q10
Monterey, Calif., U.S. 109 T4
Monterey, Tenn., U.S. 101 E17
Monterey Bay, Calif., U.S. 109 T4
Montería, Col. 128 C4
Monterotondo, It. 150 K8
Monterrey, Mex. 114 F11
Montesano, Wash., U.S. 108 D3
Monte San Savino, It. 150 H7
Monte Santu, Capo di, It. 151 N5
Montes Claros, Braz. 131 J15
Montescudo, It. 161 K18
Montese, It. 150 F6
Montevallo, Ala., U.S. 101 K15
Montevarchi, It. 150 H7
Montevideo, Minn., U.S. 104 K9
Montevideo, Uru. 132 L14
Monte Vista, Colo., U.S. 107 P12
Montezuma, Ga., U.S. 97 N5
Montezuma, Iowa, U.S. 105 P12
Montezuma, Kans., U.S. 105 U4
Montezuma Castle National Monument, Ariz., U.S. 107 S7
Montezuma Creek, Utah, U.S. 107 P9
Montfaucon, Fr. 147 V12
Montgenèvre, Fr. 147 V15
Montgomery, Ala., U.S. 101 L16
Montgomery, W. Va., U.S. 96 E8
Montgomery City, Mo., U.S. 105 S14
Monthey, Switz. 150 C2
Monti, It. 150 M4
Monticello, Ark., U.S. 100 J9
Monticello, Fla., U.S. 97 Q5
Monticello, Ga., U.S. 96 L6
Monticello, Ill., U.S. 99 R6
Monticello, Ind., U.S. 99 Q8
Monticello, Iowa, U.S. 105 N14
Monticello, Ky., U.S. 101 D17
Monticello, Me., U.S. 95 C18
Monticello, Minn., U.S. 104 J11
Monticello, Miss., U.S. 100 M11
Monticello, N.Y., U.S. 94 L10
Monticello, Utah, U.S. 107 P9
Montichiari, It. 150 E6
Montijo, Port. 144 J5
Montijo, Sp. 144 H7
Montilla, Sp. 144 L10
Montivilliers, Fr. 147 N7
Mont-Joli, Que., Can. 83 N20
Mont-Louis, Fr. 147 Z10
Montluçon, Fr. 147 T10
Montmarault, Fr. 147 T10
Montmédy, Fr. 160 K7
Montmirail, Fr. 147 P11
Monto, Qnsld., Austral. 211 U15
Montoro, Sp. 144 K10
Montoursville, Pa., U.S. 94 M7
Montpelier, Idaho, U.S. 106 J8
Montpelier, Jam. 120 H7
Montpelier, Ohio, U.S. 99 N11
Montpelier, Vt., U.S. 95 G13
Montpellier, Fr. 147 X12
Montpon-Ménestérol, Fr. 147 V7
Montréal, Fr. 147 Y10
Montréal, Que., Can. 83 P19
Montreal, Wis., U.S. 98 F4
Montreuil-Bellay, Fr. 147 S7
Montreux, Switz. 150 C2
Montrevault, Fr. 147 R6
Montrichard, Fr. 147 R8
Montrose, Colo., U.S. 107 N11
Montrose, Scot., U.K. 142 L11
Montsalvy, Fr. 147 V10
Montsec, Serra del, Sp. 145 D16
Montserrat, island, U.K., Lesser Antilles 119 G16
Montserrat, Monestir de, Sp. 145 D17
Monturull, Pic, Andorra, Sp. 160 K3
Monuafe, island, Tonga 218 H11
Monument, Oreg., U.S. 108 G7
Monument (Étarik), island, Vanuatu 218 E3
Monumental Buttes, Idaho, U.S. 106 C4
Monument Valley, Ariz., Utah, U.S. 107 Q9
Monveda, Dem. Rep. of the Congo 198 J9
Monywa, Myanmar 186 G5
Monza, It. 150 D4
Monze, Zambia 202 F10
Monzón, Sp. 145 D15
Moody, Tex., U.S. 103 N11
Mo'okini Heiau, Hawai'i, U.S. 113 J18
Moolawatana, S. Aust., Austral. 211 W11
Mooloogool, W. Aust., Austral. 211 U3
Moonless Mountains, Pac. Oc. 239 F14
Moora, W. Aust., Austral. 211 W2
Mooraberree, Qnsld., Austral. 211 U11
Moorcroft, Wyo., U.S. 106 G13
Moore, Okla., U.S. 102 G11
Moore, Tex., U.S. 103 S9
Moore, Lake, Austral. 210 J3
Moorea, island, Fr. Polynesia, Fr. 219 N14
Moorefield, W. Va., U.S. 96 C11
Moore Haven, Fla., U.S. 97 V9
Mooreland, Okla., U.S. 102 E8
Moore's Island, Bahamas 120 B5
Moore Town, Jam. 120 J11
Moorhead, Minn., U.S. 104 G8
Moorhead, Miss., U.S. 100 J10
Moorish Castle, Gibraltar, U.K. 161 N23
Moosehead Lake, Me., U.S. 95 D16
Moose Jaw, Sask., Can. 82 N12
Moose Lake, Minn., U.S. 104 H12
Mooselookmeguntic Lake, Me., U.S. 95 F15
Moosonee, Ont., Can. 83 N17
Mootwingee, N.S.W., Austral. 211 W11
Mopelia see Maupihaa, island, Fr. Polynesia, Fr. 219 E14
Mopti, Mali 196 H8
Moqor, Afghan. 177 P6
Moquegua, Peru 130 K5
Mor, Glen, Scot., U.K. 142 K8
Mora, Minn., U.S. 104 H11
Mora, N. Mex., U.S. 107 R13
Mora, Sw. 140 K12
Morača, river, Serb. & Mont. 152 J9
Moradabad, India 178 F6
Móra d'Ebre, Sp. 145 E16
Mora de Rubielos, Sp. 145 F14
Moraleja, Sp. 144 G7
Moraleja del Vino, Sp. 144 E9
Moran, Tex., U.S. 102 L8
Moran, Wyo., U.S. 106 G8
Morane, island, Fr. Polynesia, Fr. 219 H22
Morant Bay, Jam. 120 J11
Morant Cays, Jam. 116 N13
Morant Point, Jam. 120 J12
Morar, Loch, Scot., U.K. 142 K7
Morava, river, Czech Rep. 149 H13
Morava, river, Serb. & Mont. 152 F11
Moravia, region, Czech Rep. 149 H13
Morawhanna, Guyana 129 C14
Moray Firth, Scot., U.K. 142 J9
Morbi, India 178 J2
Morbihan, Golfe du, Fr. 147 R4
Mörbylånga, Sw. 141 N14
Morcenx, Fr. 147 W6
Mor Dağı, Turk. 169 G18
Mordovo, Russ. 156 M11
Mordyyakha, Russ. 158 F11
Moreau, river, S. Dak., U.S. 104 J2
Morebeng, S. Af. 202 H11
Morecambe, Eng., U.K. 143 R11
Morecambe Bay, Eng., U.K. 143 R10
Morehead, Ky., U.S. 101 B19
Morehead City, N.C., U.S. 96 J14
Morehouse, Mo., U.S. 105 V16
Morelia, Mex. 114 J11
Morella, Qnsld., Austral. 211 T12
Morella, Sp. 145 F15
Morena, India 178 G6
Morena, Sierra, Sp. 144 K8
Moreni, Rom. 153 E15
Moreno Valley, Calif., U.S. 109 X9
Morere, N.Z. 213 L20
Moresby Island, B.C., Can. 82 K7
Moreton, Qnsld., Austral. 211 P12
Moreton Island, Austral. 210 H16
Moreuil, Fr. 147 N10
Morez, Fr. 147 T14
Morfou, Cyprus 160 N7
Morfou Bay, Cyprus 160 N7
Morgan, S. Aust., Austral. 211 X10
Morgan, Utah, U.S. 106 K7
Morgan City, La., U.S. 100 Q9
Morganfield, Ky., U.S. 101 C14
Morgan Hill, Calif., U.S. 109 T4
Morganito, Venez. 128 E9
Morganton, N.C., U.S. 96 H8
Morgantown, W. Va., U.S. 96 C10
Morgat, Fr. 147 Q2
Morges, Switz. 150 C1
Morgex, It. 150 D2
Mori, Japan 184 G12
Moriah, Trinidad & Tobago 121 N18
Moriah, Mount, Nev., U.S. 84 G6
Moriarty, N. Mex., U.S. 107 S12
Morioka, Japan 184 K13
Moriu, Vanuatu 218 E3
Morjärv, Sw. 141 F14
Mor Khun, Pak. 176 K12
Morkoka, river, Russ. 159 G16
Morlaas, Fr. 147 Y7
Morlaix, Fr. 147 P3
Mormanno, It. 151 P13
Mormon Lake, Ariz., U.S. 107 S7
Morne-à-l'Eau, Guadeloupe, Fr. 121 E15
Morne Raquette, Dominica 121 F18
Morne Seychellois, peak, Seychelles 205 N20
Mornington, Qnsld., Austral. 211 Q11
Mornington, Isla, Chile 133 V6
Mornington Island, Qnsld., Austral. 211 Q11
Moro, Pak. 177 U7
Morocco, Af. 195 D15
Morogoro, Tanzania 199 M14
Moro Gulf, Philippines 189 F14
Morombe, Madagascar 203 H16
Mörön, Mongolia 180 C11
Morón, Arg. 132 L12
Morón, Cuba 116 H10
Morona, river, Peru 130 E3
Morondava, Madagascar 203 G16
Morón de la Frontera, Sp. 144 L9
Moroni, Comoros 205 M14
Morotai, island, Indonesia 189 H16
Moroto, Uganda 199 J13
Morovis, P.R., U.S. 120 M4
Morozovsk, Russ. 157 Q12
Morpará, Braz. 131 H15
Morpeth, Eng., U.K. 143 N12
Morrill, Nebr., U.S. 105 N1
Morrilton, Ark., U.S. 100 G8
Morrinhos, Braz. 131 K13
Morris, Ill., U.S. 99 P6
Morris, Minn., U.S. 104 J9
Morris, Okla., U.S. 102 G13
Morris Jesup, Cape, N. Amer. 80 A7
Morrison, Ill., U.S. 99 N4
Morristown, N.J., U.S. 94 N10
Morristown, N.Y., U.S. 94 F9
Morristown, S. Dak., U.S. 104 H3
Morristown, Tenn., U.S. 101 E19
Morrisville, Vt., U.S. 95 F13
Morro Bay, Calif., U.S. 109 V5
Morrosquillo, Golfo de, Col. 128 C4
Morrumbene, Mozambique 203 H13
Morshansk, Russ. 156 L11
Morsi, India 178 K6
Mortagne, Fr. 147 Q8
Mortara, It. 150 E4
Morteau, Fr. 147 S14
Morteros, Arg. 132 J11
Mortlake, Vic., Austral. 211 Z11
Mortlock Islands, F.S.M. 216 Q7
Morton, Ill., U.S. 99 Q5
Morton, Miss., U.S. 100 L12
Morton, Tex., U.S. 102 K4
Morton, Wash., U.S. 108 D4
Mortyq, Kaz. 174 D8
Moruga, Trinidad & Tobago 121 Q22
Moruroa (Mururoa), island, Fr. Polynesia, Fr. 219 H21
Morvan, Monts du, Fr. 147 S12
Morven, Qnsld., Austral. 211 U13
Morven, peak, Scot., U.K. 142 K10
Morvern, peninsula, Scot., U.K. 142 L7
Mosal'sk, Russ. 156 K8
Moscos Islands, Myanmar 186 M7
Moscow, Idaho, U.S. 106 D3
Moscow, river, Russ. 138 E11
Moscow see Moskva, Russ. 156 J9
Moscow Canal, Russ. 156 J9
Moscow University Ice Shelf, Antarctica 227 N20
Mose, Cape, Antarctica 227 P19
Mosel see Moselle, river, Ger. 148 G5
Moselle see Mosel, river, Eur. 138 G5
Moses Lake, Wash., U.S. 108 C7
Moses Lake, Wash., U.S. 108 D7
Moshi, Tanzania 199 L14
Mosinee, Wis., U.S. 98 J5
Mosjøen, Nor. 140 F12
Moskva, Taj. 176 J8
Moskva (Moscow), Russ. 156 J9
Moso, island, Vanuatu 218 F3
Mosonmagyaróvár, Hung. 149 L13
Mosquero, N. Mex., U.S. 107 R14
Mosquitia, region, Hond. 115 K18
Mosquito Coast, N. Amer. 80 Q8
Mosquito Island, Virgin Islands, U.K. 120 Q9
Mosquito Lagoon, Fla., U.S. 97 S9
Mosquitos, Golfo de los, Pan. 115 N20
Mosquitos, Gulf of see Mosquitos, Golfo de los, N. Amer. 80 Q9
Moss, Nor. 140 L11
Mossaka, Congo 201 L18
Mossburn, N.Z. 213 Q15
Mossel Bay, S. Af. 194 R7
Mossel Bay, S. Af. 202 M8
Mossendjo, Congo 201 M16
Mossgiel, N.S.W., Austral. 211 X12
Mossoró, Braz. 131 E17
Moss Point, Miss., U.S. 101 P13
Moss Town, Bahamas 120 F8
Most, Czech Rep. 148 G10
Mosta, Malta 161 K22
Mostaganem, Alg. 196 A10
Mostar, Bosn. & Herzg. 152 H7
Mostardas, Braz. 130 Q12
Mosteiros, Azores 144 Q5
Móstoles, Sp. 144 F10
Mosul see Al Mawşil, Iraq 172 C9
Mota, island, Vanuatu 218 B2
Motaba, river, Congo 201 J18
Mota del Cuervo, Sp. 144 H12
Mota Khan, Afghan. 177 N7
Motala, Sw. 141 L13
Mota Lava, island, Vanuatu 218 B2
Motane see Mohotani, island, Fr. Polynesia, Fr. 219 N21
Motherwell, Scot., U.K. 142 M9
Motihia, Motu, Fr. Polynesia, Fr. 219 K21
Moto Piti Aau, island, Fr. Polynesia, Fr. 219 K14
Motopu, Fr. Polynesia, Fr. 219 N20
Motoyoshi, Japan 184 L13
Motril, Sp. 144 M11
Motru, river, Rom. 152 F12
Motru, Rom. 152 F12
Mott, N. Dak., U.S. 104 H3
Motta Misaki, Japan 184 G12
Motu, river, N.Z. 213 K20
Motueka, N.Z. 213 M18
Motu Iti see Tupai, island, Fr. Polynesia, Fr. 219 E15
Motu Kitiu, island, Cook Is., N.Z. 218 R12
Motu Ko, island, Pukapuka, Cook Is., N.Z. 218 R2
Motu Kotawa, island, Pukapuka, Cook Is., N.Z. 218 R2
Motul, Mex. 115 H16
Motuloa, island, Tuvalu 217 L22
Motupae, island, Cook Is., N.Z. 219 C14
Motupe, Peru 130 F2
Motupena Point, P.N.G. 217 K14
Moturakau, island, Cook Is., N.Z. 218 Q11
Moturiki, island, Fiji Is. 218 J7
Motutapu, island, Cook Is., N.Z. 218 Q9
Motutapu, island, Tonga 218 H12
Motutunga, island, Fr. Polynesia, Fr. 219 E18
Motykleyka, Russ. 159 F20
Mouchard, Fr. 147 S13
Mouchoir Passage, Turks & Caicos Is., U.K. 117 J18
Moudjéria, Mauritania 196 G6
Moúdros, Gr. 155 E15
Mouila, Gabon 201 L15
Moulamein, N.S.W., Austral. 211 Y12
Mould Bay, N.W.T., Can. 83 C13
Moule a Chique, Cap, St. Lucia 121 L14
Mòulede Gaesa, Eq. Guinea 204 M7
Moulins, Fr. 147 T11
Moulins-la-Marche, Fr. 147 P8
Moulton, Ala., U.S. 101 H14
Moultrie, Ga., U.S. 97 P6
Moultrie, Lake, S.C., U.S. 96 L10
Mouly, New Caledonia, Fr. 218 C8
Mound Bayou, Miss., U.S. 100 J10
Mound City, Ill., U.S. 99 V5
Mound City, Kans., U.S. 105 T10
Mound City, Mo., U.S. 105 R10
Moundou, Chad 197 K14
Moundsville, W. Va., U.S. 96 B9
Moundville, Ala., U.S. 101 K14
Mo'unga'one, island, Tonga 218 P7
Mounlapamôk, Laos 186 M12
Mountain, Mo., U.S. 105 V13
Mountainair, N. Mex., U.S. 107 S12
Mountain Brook, Ala., U.S. 101 J15
Mountain City, Nev., U.S. 108 L10
Mountain City, Tenn., U.S. 101 D21
Mountain Home, Ark., U.S. 100 E8

Mountain Home, *Idaho, U.S.* **106** H4
Mountain Lake, *Minn., U.S.* **104** L10
Mountain Nile *see* Jebel, Bahr el, river, *Sudan* **199** H13
Mountain View, *Ark., U.S.* **100** F9
Mountain View, *Hawai'i, U.S.* **113** M21
Mountain View, *Mo., U.S.* **105** V14
Mountain View, *Wyo., U.S.* **106** K8
Mountain Village, *Alas., U.S.* **110** H12
Mount Airy, *N.C., U.S.* **96** G9
Mount Arrowsmith, *N.S.W., Austral.* **211** W11
Mount Ayr, *Iowa, U.S.* **105** Q11
Mount Barker, *W. Aust., Austral.* **211** Y3
Mount Barnett, *W. Aust., Austral.* **211** R5
Mount Bellew, *Ire.* **143** S4
Mount Carmel, *Ill., U.S.* **99** T7
Mount Carmel, *Pa., U.S.* **94** N8
Mount Cavenagh, *N. Terr., Austral.* **211** U8
Mount Cook, *N.Z.* **213** P16
Mount Coolon, *Qnsld., Austral.* **211** T14
Mount Desert Island, *Me., U.S.* **95** F18
Mount Dora, *Fla., U.S.* **97** T8
Mount Dora, *N. Mex., U.S.* **107** Q15
Mount Douglas, *Qnsld., Austral.* **211** T13
Mount Ebenezer, *N. Terr., Austral.* **211** U8
Mount Elsie, *Qnsld., Austral.* **211** S13
Mount Enterprise, *Tex., U.S.* **102** M14
Mount Gambier, *S. Aust., Austral.* **211** Z11
Mount Hagen, *P.N.G.* **213** D18
Mount Hope, *N.S.W., Austral.* **211** X13
Mount Hope, *W. Va., U.S.* **96** E8
Mount House, *W. Aust., Austral.* **211** R5
Mount Ida, *W. Aust., Austral.* **211** W4
Mount Isa, *Qnsld., Austral.* **211** S11
Mount Jewett, *Pa., U.S.* **94** L5
Mount Keith, *W. Aust., Austral.* **211** V4
Mount Lofty Ranges, *Austral.* **210** K10
Mount Magnet, *W. Aust., Austral.* **211** V3
Mount Maunganui, *N.Z.* **213** K19
Mount Molloy, *Qnsld., Austral.* **211** R13
Mount Morris, *Ill., U.S.* **99** N5
Mount Morris, *Mich., U.S.* **98** L12
Mount Mulgrave, *Qnsld., Austral.* **211** Q12
Mount Murchison, *N.S.W., Austral.* **211** W12
Mount Olive, *Miss., U.S.* **100** M11
Mount Olive, *N.C., U.S.* **96** J12
Mount Pleasant, *Iowa, U.S.* **105** Q13
Mount Pleasant, *Mich., U.S.* **98** K10
Mount Pleasant, *Tenn., U.S.* **101** F14
Mount Pleasant, *Tex., U.S.* **102** K14
Mount Rainier National Park, *Wash., U.S.* **108** D4
Mount Riddock, *N. Terr., Austral.* **211** T9
Mount Rushmore National Memorial, *S. Dak., U.S.* **104** L2
Mount St. George, *Trinidad & Tobago* **121** N18
Mount St. Helens National Volcanic Monument, *Wash., U.S.* **108** E4
Mount Sanford, *N. Terr., Austral.* **211** R7
Mount Sarah, *S. Aust., Austral.* **211** U9
Mount's Bay, *Eng., U.K.* **143** Y8
Mount Shasta, *Calif., U.S.* **108** M3
Mount Sterling, *Ill., U.S.* **99** R3
Mount Sterling, *Ky., U.S.* **101** B18
Mount Stuart, *W. Aust., Austral.* **211** T2
Mount Vernon, *Ala., U.S.* **101** N14
Mount Vernon, *Ill., U.S.* **99** T6
Mount Vernon, *Ind., U.S.* **99** U7
Mount Vernon, *Ky., U.S.* **101** C18
Mount Vernon, *Mo., U.S.* **105** V11
Mount Vernon, *N.Y., U.S.* **94** N11
Mount Vernon, *Ohio, U.S.* **99** Q13
Mount Vernon, *Oreg., U.S.* **108** G7
Mount Vernon, *Tex., U.S.* **102** K14
Mount Vernon, *W. Aust., Austral.* **211** U3
Mount Vernon, *Wash., U.S.* **108** B4
Mount Wedge, *N. Terr., Austral.* **211** T8
Mount Willoughby, *S. Aust., Austral.* **211** V9
Mount Wynne Bay, *St. Vincent & the Grenadines* **121** K16
Mount Zion, *Ill., U.S.* **99** R6
Moura, *Braz.* **130** D8
Mourão, *Port.* **144** J6
Mourne Mountains, *N. Ire., U.K.* **143** Q7
Mouroubra, *W. Aust., Austral.* **211** W3
Mouse *see* Souris, river, *N. Dak., U.S.* **104** E4
Moussoro, *Chad* **197** J14
Moutiers, *Fr.* **147** U14
Moutsamoudou, *Comoros* **205** N16
Mouzáki, *Gr.* **154** F9
Moweaqua, *Ill., U.S.* **99** R5
Mowshkheyl, *Afghan.* **177** N7
Moÿ, *Fr.* **147** N11
Moyale, *Eth.* **199** H15
Moyo, *Uganda* **199** H13
Moyobamba, *Peru* **130** F3
Moyu, *China* **180** G5
Moyynqum, desert, *Kaz.* **175** H14
Moyynty, *Kaz.* **175** F15
Mozambique, *Af.* **195** N22
Mozambique Channel, *Af.* **194** N10
Mozambique Escarpment, *Ind. Oc.* **240** N3
Mozambique Plateau, *Ind. Oc.* **240** M3
Mozarlândia, *Braz.* **130** J12
Mozdok, *Russ.* **157** T14
Mozdūrān, *Iran* **173** C17
Mozhaysk, *Russ.* **156** J8
Mozhga, *Russ.* **156** H16
Mpanda, *Tanzania* **198** M12
Mpandamatenga, *Botswana* **202** F10
Mpika, *Zambia* **202** D12
Mqabba, *Malta* **161** L22
Mrągowo, *Pol.* **149** B16
Mramani, *Comoros* **205** N16
Mrémani, *Comoros* **205** N16
Mrkojević, Zaliv, *Serb. & Mont.* **152** K9
Msaken, *Tun.* **197** B13
Msida, *Malta* **161** K23
Mstsislaw, *Belarus* **156** K6
Mt'a Didi Abuli, peak, *Rep. of Georgia* **169** C17
Mtkvari (Kura), river, *Rep. of Georgia* **169** C18
Mtsensk, *Russ.* **156** L9
Mts'khet'a, *Rep. of Georgia* **169** C18
Mtwara, *Tanzania* **199** N15
Mua, *Wallis & Futuna, Fr.* **218** E12
Mua, *Wallis & Futuna, Fr.* **218** C11
Mua, Baie de, *Wallis & Futuna, Fr.* **218** C11
Mu'a, *Tonga* **218** J12
Mualama, *Mozambique* **203** F14
Muang Bèng, *Laos* **186** H9
Muang Gnômmarat, *Laos* **186** K11
Muang Kao, *Laos* **186** M13
Muang Khamkeut, *Laos* **186** J11
Muang Khoa, *Laos* **186** H10
Muang Meung, *Laos* **186** H9
Muang Ngoy, *Laos* **186** H10
Muang Paklay, *Laos* **186** K9
Muang Phin, *Laos* **186** L12
Muang Sing, *Laos* **186** H9
Muang Xianghon, *Laos* **186** J9
Muang Xon, *Laos* **186** H10
Muar, *Malaysia* **187** V10
Muaraaman, *Indonesia* **188** K6
Muarabungo, *Indonesia* **188** J6
Muaraenim, *Indonesia* **188** K7
Muarakumpe, *Indonesia* **188** J7
Muaramawai, *Indonesia* **188** J12
Muaratewe, *Indonesia* **188** J11
Mubi, *Nigeria* **201** F16
Mucajaí, river, *Braz.* **130** B8
Muchachos, Roque de los, *Canary Is.* **204** Q3
Muchea, *W. Aust., Austral.* **211** X2
München (Munich), *Ger.* **148** K8
Muchinga Mountains, *Zambia* **202** D12
Muchkapskiy, *Russ.* **156** M12
Muchot, Puntan, *N. Mariana Is., U.S.* **216** B4
Muck, island, *Scot., U.K.* **142** K7
Muckety, *N. Terr., Austral.* **211** R8
Muckle Flugga, island, *Scot., U.K.* **142** C12
Muckle Roe, island, *Scot., U.K.* **142** D12
Muconda, *Angola* **202** D8
Mucur, *Turk.* **168** F9
Mucuripe, Ponta de, *Braz.* **131** E17
Mucusso, *Angola* **202** F8
Muda, peak, *Canary Is.* **204** Q7
Mudamuckla, *S. Aust., Austral.* **211** X9
Mudan, river, *China* **181** D18
Mudanjiang, *China* **181** D18
Mudanya, *Turk.* **168** D5
Muḑayrib, *Oman* **173** K16
Muddy Gap, *Wyo., U.S.* **106** J11
Mudgee, *N.S.W., Austral.* **211** X14
Mudhol, *India* **179** N4
Mud Lake, *Idaho, U.S.* **106** G7
Mudurnu, *Turk.* **168** D7
Mueda, *Mozambique* **203** D15
Muéo, *New Caledonia, Fr.* **218** D7
Muertos Cays, *Bahamas* **116** F9
Mufulira, *Zambia* **202** D11
Mufu Shan, *China* **182** M5
Muga, Pico de la, *Sp.* **160** K5
Muganly, *Azerb.* **169** C20
Mughalzhar Taūy, range, *Kaz.* **174** E9
Muğla, *Turk.* **168** H4
Muglad, *Sudan* **198** F11
Muglad Basin, *Sudan* **198** F11
Mugu, *Nepal* **178** E8
Mūḩ, Sabkhat al, *Syr.* **170** H10
Muḩammad, Râs, *Egypt* **171** U4
Muhammad Qol, *Sudan* **199** C14
Muḩayy, *Jordan* **171** P6
Muhembo, *Botswana* **202** F8
Mühleholz, *Liech.* **160** P2
Muhlenfels Point, *Virgin Islands, U.S.* **120** N9
Mühlhausen, *Ger.* **148** F8
Mühlig-Hofmann Mountains, *Antarctica* **227** A13
Mui Hopohoponga, cape, *Tonga* **218** J12
Muine Bheag (Bagenalstown), *Ire.* **143** T6
Muir Woods National Monument, *Calif., U.S.* **109** R3
Muisne, *Ecua.* **128** H2
Mukacheve, *Ukr.* **157** P1
Mukah, *Malaysia* **188** H10
Mukawa, *Japan* **184** G13
Mukayris, *Yemen* **172** Q10
Mukeru, *Palau* **216** N11
Mukhtadir, *Azerb.* **169** B22
Mukinbudin, *W. Aust., Austral.* **211** W3
Muko Jima Rettō, *Japan* **184** K5
Mukomuko, *Indonesia* **188** K6
Mukry, *Turkm.* **174** M12
Muktinath, *Nepal* **178** F9
Mul, *India* **178** L7
Mula, river, *India* **178** L4
Muladu, island, *Maldives* **179** T3
Mulaku Atoll, *Maldives* **179** V3
Mulâtre, Pointe, *Dominica* **121** G20
Mulazzano, *It.* **161** H18
Mulberry, *Ark., U.S.* **100** F6
Mulberry Creek, *Tex., U.S.* **102** H6
Mulchatna, river, *Alas., U.S.* **111** K14
Muldraugh, *Ky., U.S.* **101** B16
Mulegé, *Mex.* **114** D6
Mule Peak, *N. Mex., U.S.* **107** U13
Muleshoe, *Tex., U.S.* **102** J4
Mulgildie, *Qnsld., Austral.* **211** U15
Mulhacén, peak, *Sp.* **144** L11
Mülheim, *Ger.* **148** E5
Mulhouse, *Fr.* **147** R15
Muli, *China* **180** M11
Mulifanua, *Samoa* **218** L3
Muling, *China* **181** D18
Mulinu'u, Cape, *Samoa* **218** K1
Mulitapuili, Cape, *Samoa* **218** L3
Mulitefala, island, *Tuvalu* **217** J23
Mulka, *S. Aust., Austral.* **211** V10
Mull, Island of, *Scot., U.K.* **142** L7
Mull, Sound of, *Scot., U.K.* **142** L7
Mullan, *Idaho, U.S.* **106** C4
Mullen, *Nebr., U.S.* **105** N4
Mullens, *W. Va., U.S.* **96** E8
Mullet Peninsula, *Ire.* **143** Q3
Mullett Lake, *Mich., U.S.* **98** G11
Mullewa, *W. Aust., Austral.* **211** W2
Mullingar, *Ire.* **143** R6
Mullins, *S.C., U.S.* **96** K11
Mull of Galloway, cape, *Scot., U.K.* **143** Q8
Mullumbimby, *N.S.W., Austral.* **211** W15
Mulobezi, *Zambia* **202** F9
Mulroy Bay, *Ire.* **143** N5
Multan, *Pak.* **177** R9
Mulvane, *Kans., U.S.* **105** U8
Mumbai (Bombay), *India* **178** L3
Mumbwa, *Zambia* **202** E10
Mumra, *Russ.* **157** R15
Muna, island, *Indonesia* **189** L14
Muna, river, *Russ.* **159** G16
Munaba, *India* **178** G2
Munan Pass, *China, Vietnam* **186** G12
Munburra, *Qnsld., Austral.* **211** Q13
Muncie, *Ind., U.S.* **99** R10
Muncy, *Pa., U.S.* **94** M7
Munda, *Solomon Is.* **217** M16
Mundabullangana, *W. Aust., Austral.* **211** S3
Munday, *Tex., U.S.* **102** K8
Münden, *Ger.* **148** F7
Mundiwindi, *W. Aust., Austral.* **211** U3
Mundra, *India* **178** J1
Mundrabilla, *W. Aust., Austral.* **211** W6
Mundubbera, *Qnsld., Austral.* **211** U15
Mundul, *Afghan.* **176** L8
Munera, *Sp.* **144** H12
Mungana, *Qnsld., Austral.* **211** R13
Mungbere, *Dem. Rep. of the Congo* **198** J12
Mungeli, *India* **178** J8
Munger, *India* **178** H11
Mungindi, *N.S.W., Austral.* **211** W14
Munguba, *Braz.* **130** D12
Munia, island, *Fiji Is.* **218** H9
Munich *see* München, *Ger.* **148** K8
Municipal Administrative Center, *Monaco* **161** E21
Munising, *Mich., U.S.* **98** F8
Munku Sardyk, Gora, *Russ.* **159** L14
Münster, *Ger.* **148** E6
Munster, region, *Ire.* **143** U4
Muntok, *Indonesia* **188** K7
Munzur Dağları, *Turk.* **169** F14
Mu'omu'a, island, *Tonga* **218** M11
Muong Te, *Vietnam* **186** G10
Muonio, *Fin.* **141** D14
Muping, *China* **182** F10
Muqdisho (Mogadishu), *Somalia* **199** J17
Mur, river, *Aust.* **148** M10
Muradiye, *Turk.* **169** F18
Murakami, *Japan* **184** L12
Murang'a, *Kenya* **199** K14
Murashi, *Russ.* **158** G8
Murat, *Fr.* **147** V10
Murat, river, *Turk.* **169** F15
Murata, *San Marino* **161** K15
Murat Dağı, *Turk.* **168** F5
Muratlı, *Turk.* **168** C3
Muravera, *It.* **151** P4
Murazzano, *It.* **150** F3
Murça, *Port.* **144** E7
Murchison, river, *W. Aust., Austral.* **211** V2
Murcia, *Sp.* **145** K14
Mur-de-Bretagne, *Fr.* **147** Q4
Murdo, *S. Dak., U.S.* **104** L4
Mureş, river, *Rom.* **152** D11
Muret, *Fr.* **147** X9
Murfreesboro, *Ark., U.S.* **100** H7
Murfreesboro, *N.C., U.S.* **96** G13
Murfreesboro, *Tenn., U.S.* **101** F15
Murgha Kibzai, *Pak.* **177** R8
Murghob, river, *Taj.* **176** J11
Murghob, *Taj.* **176** J11
Murgoo, *W. Aust., Austral.* **211** V2
Murguz, peak, *Arm.* **169** D19
Muri, *Cook Is., N.Z.* **218** Q9
Murihiti, island, *Cook Is., N.Z.* **219** A14
Murilo Atoll, *F.S.M.* **216** Q6
Murimaora, Motu, *Fr. Polynesia, Fr.* **219** G14
Muritapua, island, *Cook Is., N.Z.* **218** Q12
Müritz, lake, *Ger.* **148** C10
Murjek, *Sw.* **141** F14
Murman Coast, *Russ.* **138** A10
Murmansk, *Russ.* **158** C9
Murmansk Rise, *Arctic Oc.* **243** D16
Muro, Capo di, *Fr.* **150** K3
Muro Lucano, *It.* **150** M12
Murom, *Russ.* **156** J11
Muroran, *Japan* **184** G13
Muros, *Sp.* **144** B5
Muros e Noia, Ría de, *Sp.* **144** B5
Muroto, *Japan* **185** R7
Muroto Zaki, *Japan* **185** R7
Murphy, *Idaho, U.S.* **106** H3
Murphy, *N.C., U.S.* **96** J6
Murphy, *N.C., U.S.* **96** J5
Murphysboro, *Ill., U.S.* **99** U5
Murrat el Kubra, Buheirat (Great Bitter Lake), *Egypt* **171** Q1
Murrat el Sughra, Buheirat (Little Bitter Lake), *Egypt* **171** Q1
Murray, river, *Austral.* **210** K11
Murray, river, *Austral.* **210** K2
Murray, *Ky., U.S.* **101** E13
Murray, Lake, *P.N.G.* **213** D17
Murray, Lake, *S.C., U.S.* **96** K8
Murray, Source of the, *Austral.* **210** L13
Murray Bridge, *S. Aust., Austral.* **211** Y10
Murray Fracture Zone, *Pac. Oc.* **238** F12
Murray River Basin, *Austral.* **210** K11
Murrayville, *Vic., Austral.* **211** Y11
Murrells Inlet, *S.C., U.S.* **96** L11
Murrenja Hill, *Austral.* **210** B7
Murrin Murrin, *W. Aust., Austral.* **211** V4
Murro di Porco, Capo, *It.* **151** T12
Murrumbidgee, river, *N.S.W., Austral.* **211** Y12
Murska Sobota, *Slov.* **152** C6
Mursko Središće, *Croatia* **152** C6
Murter, island, *Croatia* **152** G5
Murud, *India* **178** L3
Murud, Mount, *Malaysia* **188** G11
Murukta, *Russ.* **159** G14
Mururoa *see* Moruroa, island, *Fr. Polynesia, Fr.* **219** H21
Mürzzuschlag, *Aust.* **148** L12
Muş, *Turk.* **169** F16
Mûsa, Gebel (Mount Sinai), *Egypt* **171** T3
Musa Dağ, *Turk.* **168** K11
Musa Khel Bazar, *Pak.* **177** Q8
Musala, peak, *Bulg.* **153** J13
Musan, *N. Korea* **182** B14
Musandam, Ra's, *Oman* **173** H15
Musa Qal'eh, *Afghan.* **177** P4
Muşawwal, *Jordan* **171** Q6
Musaymīr, *Yemen* **172** R9
Muscat *see* Masqaţ, *Oman* **173** K16
Muscatine, *Iowa, U.S.* **105** P14
Muscle Shoals, *Ala., U.S.* **101** G14
Muse, *Okla., U.S.* **102** H14
Museum of Prehistoric Anthropology, *Monaco* **161** E20
Musgrave, Port, *Austral.* **210** A12
Musgrave Ranges, *Austral.* **210** G8
Mushie, *Dem. Rep. of the Congo* **198** L8
Musicians Seamounts, *Pac. Oc.* **238** F11
Muskegon, river, *Mich., U.S.* **98** K10
Muskegon, *Mich., U.S.* **98** L9
Muskegon Heights, *Mich., U.S.* **98** L9
Muskingum, river, *Ohio, U.S.* **99** R14
Muskogee, *Okla., U.S.* **102** F13
Muslimbagh, *Pak.* **177** R6
Muslimīyah, *Syr.* **170** D9
Musmar, *Sudan* **199** D14
Musoma, *Tanzania* **199** K13
Mussau, island, *P.N.G.* **213** B20
Mussau Islands, *P.N.G.* **213** B20
Musselburgh, *Scot., U.K.* **142** M10
Musselshell, river, *Mont., U.S.* **106** C10
Musselshell, *Mont., U.S.* **106** D10
Mussuma, *Angola* **202** E8
Mustafa-kemalpaşa, *Turk.* **168** D4
Mustahīl, *Eth.* **199** H17
Mustang, *Nepal* **178** E9
Musters, Lago, *Arg.* **133** S8
Mustique, island, *St. Vincent & the Grenadines* **119** L17
Muswellbrook, *N.S.W., Austral.* **211** X14
Mûţ, *Egypt* **197** E18
Mut, island, *Marshall Is.* **216** J8
Mut, *Turk.* **168** J8
Mutá, Ponta do, *Braz.* **131** J16
Mutalau, *Niue, N.Z.* **219** B20
Mutarara, *Mozambique* **203** F13
Mutare, *Mozambique* **202** G12
Mute, Motu, *Fr. Polynesia, Fr.* **219** J14
Muting, *Indonesia* **189** M21
Mutki, *Turk.* **169** G16
Mutnovskaya Sopka, *Russ.* **159** F23
Mutok Harbor, *F.S.M.* **217** G14
Mutoray, *Russ.* **159** J14
Mutsu, *Japan* **184** H13
Mutsu Wan, *Japan* **184** H13
Muttaburra, *Qnsld., Austral.* **211** T12
Muturi, *Indonesia* **189** K18
Mu Us Shamo (Ordos), *China* **182** D2
Muxía, *Sp.* **144** B5
Mŭynoq, *Uzb.* **174** H9
Muzaffarabad, *Pak.* **176** M11
Muzaffargarh, *Pak.* **177** R9
Muzaffarnagar, *India* **178** E6
Muzaffarpur, *India* **178** G10
Muztag, peak, *China* **180** H5
Mwaniwowo, *Solomon Is.* **217** Q21
Mwanza, *Tanzania* **199** K13
Mweka, *Dem. Rep. of the Congo* **198** L9
Mwene-Ditu, *Dem. Rep. of the Congo* **198** M10
Mwenezi, *Zimb.* **202** G11
Mweru, Lake, *Dem. Rep. of the Congo, Zambia* **194** L8
Mwinilunga, *Zambia* **202** D9
Myaksa, *Russ.* **156** G9
Myanaung, *Myanmar* **186** J5
Myanmar (Burma), *Asia* **167** W9
Mycenae, ruin, *Gr.* **154** K10

Myebon, Myanmar 186 H4
Myeik, Myanmar 187 N7
Myingyan, Myanmar 186 G6
Myitkyinā, Myanmar 186 E7
Myitta, Myanmar 186 M7
Mykolayiv, Ukr. 157 R6
Mymensingh, Bangladesh 178 H13
Mynbulaq, Uzb. 174 J10
Mynydd Preseli, peak, Wales, U.K. 143 U8
Myohaung, Myanmar 186 H4
Myoungmya, Myanmar 186 L5
Myrdal, Nor. 140 K10
Mýrdalsjökull, glacier, Ice. 140 G2
Myrhorod, Ukr. 157 P7
Myrtle Beach, S.C., U.S. 96 L11
Myrtle Creek, Oreg., U.S. 108 J3
Myrtle Grove, Fla., U.S. 97 Q1
Myrtle Point, Oreg., U.S. 108 J2
Myrtou, Cyprus 160 N7
Mysore, India 179 Q5
Mysovaya, Russ. 159 D19
Mys Shmidta, Russ. 159 B20
Mystic, Conn., U.S. 95 M14
Mystic, Iowa, U.S. 105 Q12
Mys Zhelaniya, Russ. 158 D12
Myszyniec, Pol. 149 C16
My Tho, Vietnam 187 P12
Mytilene see Mitilíni, Gr. 155 G17
Mytishchi, Russ. 156 J9
Mzé Koukoulé Bandalankoua, peak, Comoros 205 N15
Mzuzu, Malawi 202 D12

N

Na, island, F.S.M. 217 G14
Naafkopf, peak, Aust., Liech., Switz. 160 R3
Nāʻālehu, Hawaiʻi, U.S. 113 P20
Nabari, Kiribati 217 B20
Nabeina, Kiribati 217 F17
Naberezhnyye Chelny, Russ. 156 H16
Nabeul, Tun. 197 A13
Nabire, Indonesia 189 K19
Nablus see Nābulus, W. Bank 170 L6
Nabouwalu, Fiji Is. 218 H7
Nabq, Egypt 171 U4
Nābulus (Nablus), W. Bank 170 L6
Nacala, Mozambique 203 E15
Nacaome, Hond. 115 L17
Naches, Wash., U.S. 108 D5
Nachingwea, Tanzania 199 N15
Náchod, Czech Rep. 148 G12
Nachu, island, F.S.M. 217 C16
Nachvak Fiord, Nfld. & Lab., Can. 83 J20
Nacimiento, Lake, Calif., U.S. 109 V5
Našice, Croatia 152 E8
Nacogdoches, Tex., U.S. 103 N14
Nacozari Viejo, Mex. 114 C7
Nacula, island, Fiji Is. 218 H5
Nada see Danxian, China 183 U1
Nadale, island, Maldives 179 X3
Nadi, Fiji Is. 218 J5
Nadiad, India 178 J3
Nadi Bay, Fiji Is. 218 H5
Nadir, Virgin Islands, U.S. 120 N9
Nădlac, Rom. 152 D10
Nadur, Malta 161 H20
Naduri, Fiji Is. 218 G7
Nadvoitsy, Russ. 158 D8
Nadym, Russ. 158 G11
Náfpaktos, Gr. 154 H9
Náfplio, Gr. 154 K11
Nafūd ad Daḩy, desert, Saudi Arabia 172 K10
Nafūsah, Jabal, Lib. 197 C13
Nag, Pak. 177 U4
Naga, Indonesia 189 M13
Naga, Philippines 189 C14
Naga Hills, India 178 G15
Nagano, Japan 185 N11
Naganuma, Japan 184 M12
Nagaoka, Japan 184 M11
Nagaon, India 178 G14
Nagar Parkar, Pak. 177 W9
Nagasaki, Japan 185 S4
Nagato, Japan 185 Q5
Nagaur, India 178 F4
Nagēlē, Eth. 199 H15
Nagercoil, India 179 S5
Nagir, Pak. 176 K12
Nago, Japan 185 Y1
Nagorno-Karabakh, region, Azerb. 169 E20
Nagoya, Japan 185 Q10
Nagpur, India 178 K7
Nagqu, China 180 K8
Nag's Head, St. Kitts & Nevis 121 B18
Naguabo, P.R., U.S. 120 N5
Nagykanizsa, Hung. 149 M13
Naha, Japan 185 Y1
Nahanni Butte, N.W.T., Can. 82 H10
Nahari, Japan 185 R7
Nahma, Mich., U.S. 98 G8
Nahoe, Fr. Polynesia, Fr. 219 M21
Nahuei Huapí, Lago, Arg. 133 Q7
Nailaga, Fiji Is. 218 H6
Naiman Qi, China 182 B9
Nain, Nfld. & Lab., Can. 83 K21
Nāʼīn, Iran 173 E13
Nainpur, India 178 J7
Nairai, island, Fiji Is. 218 J7
Nairiri, Fr. Polynesia, Fr. 219 P16
Nairn, Scot., U.K. 142 J9
Nairobi, Kenya 199 K14
Naitaba, island, Fiji Is. 218 H9
Naitonitoni, Fiji Is. 218 J6
Najafābād, Iran 173 E13
Najd, region, Saudi Arabia 172 H8
Nájera, Sp. 144 C12
Najin (Rajin), N. Korea 182 B15
Najrān, oasis, Saudi Arabia 172 N9
Najrān, Saudi Arabia 172 N9
Naka, river, Japan 185 R7
Nakadōri Jima, Japan 185 R3
Nakagusuku Wan (Buckner Bay), Japan 185 Y1
Naka Kharai, Pak. 177 W6
Nākālele Point, Hawaiʻi, U.S. 113 F16
Nakamura, Japan 185 S6
Nakano, Japan 185 N11
Nakano Shima, Japan 185 P7
Nakano Shima, Japan 185 V3
Naka Shibetsu, Japan 184 F16
Nakatane, Japan 185 U4
Nakatombetsu, Japan 184 E14
Nakatsu, Japan 185 R5
Nakéty, New Caledonia, Fr. 218 D8
Nakfa, Eritrea 199 D15
Nakhl, Egypt 171 Q3
Nakhodka, Russ. 159 M21
Nakhon Phanom, Thai. 186 K11
Nakhon Ratchasima, Thai. 186 M10
Nakhon Sawan, Thai. 186 L8
Nakhon Si Thammarat, Thai. 187 R8
Nakina, Ont., Can. 83 N16
Nakło nad Notecią, Pol. 149 C13
Naknek, Alas., U.S. 111 L14
Nakodar, India 178 D5
Nakodu, Fiji Is. 218 H7
Nakuru, Kenya 199 K14
Nal, Pak. 177 T5
Nal'chik, Russ. 157 T13
Nalgonda, India 178 M7
Nallıhan, Turk. 168 D7
Nalogo, island, Solomon Is. 217 N22
Nālūt, Lib. 197 C13
Namaite, island, Fr. Polynesia, Fr. 219 K16
Namak, Daryācheh-ye, Iran 173 D13
Namakzar, Lake, Afghan., Iran 177 N1
Namakzār-e Shahdād, desert, Iran 173 F16
Namanga, Kenya 199 K14
Namangan, Uzb. 175 K14
Namapa, Mozambique 203 E15
Namaram, Vanuatu 218 D3
Namatanai, P.N.G. 213 C21
Nambour, Qnsld., Austral. 211 V15
Nam Can, Vietnam 187 Q11
Nam Dinh, Vietnam 186 H12
Namekagon, river, Wis., U.S. 98 G3
Namelakl Passage, Palau 216 N12
Namenalala, island, Fiji Is. 218 H7
Namgia, India 177 P15
Namib Desert, Namibia 202 H6
Namibe, Angola 202 E5
Namibia, Af. 195 P19
Namiquipa, Mex. 114 D8
Namlea, Indonesia 189 K16
Nam Ngum Dam, Laos 186 J10
Namoi, river, Austral. 210 J14
Nāmolokama Mountain, Hawaiʻi, U.S. 112 B5
Namoluk Atoll, F.S.M. 216 Q6
Namonuito Atoll, F.S.M. 216 P6
Namoren, island, Marshall Is. 216 K7
Namorik Atoll, Marshall Is. 216 H4
Nampa, Idaho, U.S. 106 G3
Nampala, Mali 196 H8
Namp'o, N. Korea 182 E12
Nampō Shotō, Japan 184 J5
Nampula, Mozambique 203 E14
Namsen, river, Nor. 140 G12
Namsê Pass, China, Nepal 178 E8
Namsos, Nor. 140 G11
Nam Tok, Thai. 186 M8
Namtsy, Russ. 159 G18
Namtu, Myanmar 186 G7
Namu Atoll, Marshall Is. 216 G4
Namuka-i-Lau, island, Fiji Is. 218 K9
Namukulu, Niue, N.Z. 219 B20
Namuli, peak, Mozambique 194 M10
Namur, Belg. 146 L12
Namutoni, Namibia 202 G7
Namwŏn, S. Korea 182 G13
Nan, river, Thai. 186 K9
Nan, Thai. 186 J9
Nanaimo, B.C., Can. 82 M8
Nānākuli, Hawaiʻi, U.S. 112 E10
Nanam, N. Korea 182 B14
Nan'an, China 183 Q8
Nanao, Japan 185 N10
Nanatsu Shima, Japan 184 M10
Nanbu, China 180 L12
Nanchang, China 182 M6
Nancheng, China 183 N6
Nanchong, China 180 L12
Nancowry Island, India 179 S15
Nancy, Fr. 147 P14
Nanda Devi, peak, India 178 E7
Nanded, India 178 L6
Nandgaon, India 178 K4
Nandurbar, India 178 K4
Nandyal, India 179 N6
Nanfeng, China 183 N6
Nanga Parbat, peak, Pak. 176 L12
Nangapinoh, Indonesia 188 J10
Nangaraun, Indonesia 188 J10
Nangatayap, Indonesia 188 J9
Nangin, Myanmar 187 P7
Nangiré, Vanuatu 218 C2
Nangis, Fr. 147 P10
Nangnim Sanmaek, range, N. Korea 182 C13
Nangong, China 182 F6
Nangtud, Mount, Philippines 189 D14
Nanij, island, Marshall Is. 216 K8
Nanjing, China 182 K8
Nanjing, China 183 R7
Nankang, China 183 P5
Nankoku, Japan 185 R7
Nan Ling, China 183 Q4
Nanliu, river, China 183 S1
Nanmatol, island, F.S.M. 217 G14
Nanmatol Islands, F.S.M. 217 G14
Nanning, China 183 R1
Nannup, W. Aust., Austral. 211 Y2
Nanortalik, Greenland, Den. 81 D22
Nanpan, river, China 180 N12
Nanping, China 183 P7
Nanri Dao, China 183 Q8
Nansan Dao, China 183 T2
Nansei Shotō see Ryukyu Islands, Japan 185 X3
Nansen Basin, Arctic Oc. 242 E10
Nansen Ridge, Arctic Oc. 242 F10
Nansen Sound, Nunavut, Can. 83 B15
Nanshan Island, Spratly Is. 188 E11
Nansio, Tanzania 199 K13
Nant, Fr. 147 X11
Nantes, Fr. 147 S6
Nanticoke, Pa., U.S. 94 M8
Nantong (Jinsha), China 182 K9
Nantou, Taiwan, China 183 R9
Nantucket, Mass., U.S. 95 M16
Nantucket Island, Mass., U.S. 95 M16
Nantucket Sound, Mass., U.S. 95 M16
Nantulo, Mozambique 203 D14
Nantwich, Eng., U.K. 143 S11
Nānuʻalele Point, Hawaiʻi, U.S. 113 G18
Nanukuloa, Fiji Is. 218 H6
Nanuku Passage, Fiji Is. 218 H8
Nanumanga, island, Tuvalu 214 H8
Nanumea, island, Tuvalu 214 H8
Nanuque, Braz. 131 K16
Nanusa, Kepulauan, Indonesia 189 G16
Nanutarra, W. Aust., Austral. 211 T2
Nanxian, China 182 M4
Nanxiong, China 183 Q5
Nanyang, China 182 J4
Nanzhang, China 182 K3
Nao Nao, island, Fr. Polynesia, Fr. 219 C23
Nao Nao, Passe, Fr. Polynesia, Fr. 219 C23
Naococane, Lac, Que., Can. 83 M19
Naomid Plain, Afghan. 177 N1
Naonao, Motu, Fr. Polynesia, Fr. 219 K16
Náousa, Gr. 154 C10
Naozhou Dao, China 183 T2
Napa, Calif., U.S. 109 R3
Nā Pali Coast, Hawaiʻi, U.S. 112 B5
Naperville, Ill., U.S. 99 N7
Napia, island, Kiribati 217 B20
Napier, N.Z. 213 L20
Napier Mountains, Antarctica 227 C19
Naples, Fla., U.S. 97 W8
Naples see Napoli, It. 150 M10
Naples, Tex., U.S. 102 K14
Napo, river, S. Amer. 126 D3
Napoleon, N. Dak., U.S. 104 H5
Napoleon, Ohio, U.S. 99 P11
Napoleonville, La., U.S. 100 Q10
Napoli (Naples), It. 150 M10
Napoli, Golfo di, It. 150 M10
Napuka, island, Fr. Polynesia, Fr. 219 D20
Nāpuʻukūlua, peak, Hawaiʻi, U.S. 113 M19
Naqoura, Leb. 170 K5
Nara, Japan 185 Q9
Nara, Mali 196 H7
Nara, river, Pak. 177 V8
Nara Canal, Pak. 177 U7
Naracoorte, S. Aust., Austral. 211 Z11
Narang, Afghan. 176 M9
Naranjito, P.R., U.S. 120 M4
Narao, Japan 185 S3
Narasannapeta, India 178 L9
Narathiwat, Thai. 187 S9
Nara Visa, N. Mex., U.S. 107 R15
Narayanganj, Bangladesh 178 H13
Narbonne, Fr. 147 Y11
Narborough see Fernandina, Isla, island, Ecua. 128 Q7
Narcondam Island, India 179 P15
Nardò, It. 151 N15
Nardoo, Qnsld., Austral. 211 R11
Narembeem, W. Aust., Austral. 211 X3
Nares Plain, Atl. Oc. 236 K5
Naretha, W. Aust., Austral. 211 W5
Narew, river, Pol. 149 C16
Narib, Namibia 202 H7
Nariva Swamp, Trinidad & Tobago 121 P23
Narlı, Turk. 168 H12
Narmada, river, India 178 J4
Narmidj, island, Marshall Is. 216 K7
Narnaul, India 178 F5
Narndee, W. Aust., Austral. 211 W3
Narngulu, W. Aust., Austral. 211 W2
Narni, It. 150 J8
Narodnaya, peak, Russ. 166 C7
Narodnaya, Gora, Russ. 158 F10
Narooma, N.S.W., Austral. 211 Z14
Narovorovo, Vanuatu 218 C3
Narowal, Pak. 177 P12
Narowlya, Belarus 156 M5
Narrabri, N.S.W., Austral. 211 W14
Narragansett Pier, R.I., U.S. 95 M14
Narrandera, N.S.W., Austral. 211 Y13
Narran Lake, Austral. 210 J13
Narrogin, W. Aust., Austral. 211 X3
Narrows, Va., U.S. 96 F9
Narsarsuaq, Greenland, Den. 81 D22
Narsinghgarh, India 178 H5
Narsipatnam, India 178 M8
Nartës, Laguna e, Albania 152 M9
Nartháki, Óros, Gr. 154 F10
Nartkala, Russ. 157 T13
Naruko, Japan 184 L13
Naruto, Japan 185 Q8
Narva, Est. 141 K17
Narvik, Nor. 140 D12
Narvskoye Vodokhranilishche, Russ. 156 F5
Nar'yan Mar, Russ. 158 E10
Naryilco, Qnsld., Austral. 211 V11
Naryn, river, Kyrg. 176 F10
Naryn, Kyrg. 176 F12
Naryn, Russ. 159 M14
Naryn Khuduk, Russ. 157 S14
Narynqol, Kaz. 175 H18
Naryn Qum, desert, Kaz. 174 E5
Näs, Sw. 140 H12
Nasarawa, Nigeria 201 G14
Nasca, Peru 130 J4
Nashua, Iowa, U.S. 104 M12
Nashua, Mont., U.S. 106 B12
Nashua, N.H., U.S. 95 J14
Nashville, Ark., U.S. 100 H6
Nashville, Ga., U.S. 97 P6
Nashville, Ill., U.S. 99 T5
Nashville, Tenn., U.S. 101 E15
Nashwauk, Minn., U.S. 104 F11
Näsijärvi, lake, Fin. 141 H15
Nasik, India 178 K4
Nasir, Sudan 199 G13
Nasirabad, India 178 G4
Naso, It. 151 R11
Nassau, island, Cook Is., N.Z. 214 J11
Nassau, Bahamas 120 B11
Nassawadox, Va., U.S. 96 E14
Nasser, Lake, Egypt 197 E19
Nässjö, Sw. 141 M13
Nastapoka Islands, Nunavut, Can. 83 K18
Nata, Botswana 202 G10
Natal, Indonesia 188 J5
Natal, Braz. 131 F18
Natal Basin, Ind. Oc. 240 L4
Natal Downs, Qnsld., Austral. 211 S13
Natalia, Tex., U.S. 103 S9
Natal'inskiy, Russ. 159 C22
Naţanz, Iran 173 D13
Natara, Russ. 159 F16
Natashquan, river, Nfld. & Lab., Que., Can. 83 L21
Natashquan, Que., Can. 83 M22
Natchez, Miss., U.S. 100 M9
Natchitoches, La., U.S. 100 M7
Natewa Bay, Fiji Is. 218 G8
National City, Calif., U.S. 109 Z10
National Museum of Fine Arts, Monaco 161 C21
Natitingou, Benin 200 F11
Natividad, Isla, Mex. 114 D5
Natividade, Braz. 131 G13
Natkyizin, Myanmar 186 M7
Natoma, Kans., U.S. 105 S6
Nattavaara, Sw. 141 E14
Natuna Besar, island, Indonesia 188 G9
Natuna Besar, Kepulauan (Bunguran Utara), Indonesia 188 G8
Natuna Islands, Indonesia 166 L11
Natuna Selatan, Kepulauan (Bunguran Selatan), Indonesia 188 H9
Natural Bridges National Monument, Utah, U.S. 107 P9
Naturaliste, Cape, Austral. 210 K2
Naturaliste Plateau, Ind. Oc. 241 M15
Naturita, Colo., U.S. 107 N10
Naturno, It. 150 C6
Naubinway, Mich., U.S. 98 G10
Naukot, Pak. 177 W8
Naungpale, Myanmar 186 J7
Nauroz Kalat, Pak. 177 S5
Nauru, Pac. Oc. 214 G7
Naushahra, India 177 N12
Naushahro Firoz, Pak. 177 U7
Nausori, Fiji Is. 218 J7
Nauta, Peru 130 E4
Nautla, Mex. 115 H13
Nauvoo, Ill., U.S. 99 Q3
Navabelitsa, Belarus 156 M6
Navadwip, India 178 J11
Navahrudak, Belarus 156 K4
Navai, Fiji Is. 218 H6
Navajo Mountain, Utah, U.S. 107 Q8
Navajo National Monument, Ariz., U.S. 107 Q8
Navajo Reservoir, N. Mex., U.S. 107 Q11
Navalmoral de la Mata, Sp. 144 G9
Navan (An Uaimh), Ire. 143 R6
Navapolatsk, Belarus 156 J5
Navarin, Cape, N. Amer. 80 P3
Navarin, Mys, Russ. 159 B21
Navarin, Cape, Russ. 166 A13
Navarino, Isla, Chile 133 Y9
Navarrenx, Fr. 147 Y6
Navasota, river, Tex., U.S. 103 N12
Navasota, Tex., U.S. 103 Q13
Navassa Island, Greater Antilles 117 M14
Navia, Sp. 144 A8
Navidad, river, Tex., U.S. 103 R12
Naviti, island, Fiji Is. 218 H5
Năvodari, Rom. 153 F18
Navoiy, Uzb. 174 L11
Navojoa, Mex. 114 E7
Navrongo, Ghana 200 F10
Navsari, India 178 K3
Navua, river, Fiji Is. 218 J6

Navua, Fiji Is. 218 J6
Nawá, Syr. 170 K7
Nawabshah, Pak. 177 V7
Nawada, India 178 H10
Nawah, Afghan. 177 P7
Nawalgarh, India 178 F5
Nawāşīf, Ḩarrat, Saudi Arabia 172 L8
Naxçıvan, region, Azerb. 169 F19
Naxçıvan, Azerb. 169 F19
Náxos, island, Gr. 155 L15
Náxos, Gr. 155 L15
Naxos, ruin, It. 151 S12
Naxxar, Malta 161 K22
Nayak, Afghan. 176 M6
Nayau, island, Fiji Is. 218 J9
Nāy Band, Iran 173 E16
Nayoro, Japan 184 E14
Nazaré, Port. 144 G5
Nazaré, Braz. 131 H16
Nazareth see Nazerat, Israel 170 L6
Nazareth, Vanuatu 218 C3
Nazareth Bank, Ind. Oc. 240 J7
Nazas, Mex. 114 F9
Nazca Ridge, Pac. Oc. 239 M20
Naze, Japan 185 W3
Nazerat (Nazareth), Israel 170 L6
Nāzīk, Iran 172 A10
Nazik Gölü, Turk. 169 F16
Nazilli, Turk. 168 G4
Nazımiye, Turk. 169 F14
Nazimovo, Russ. 159 J13
Naziya, Russ. 156 F7
Nazran', Russ. 157 U14
Nazrēt, Eth. 199 G15
Ndaga, Nigeria 201 G16
Ndai see Dai, island, Solomon Is. 217 M19
N'dalatando, Angola 202 C6
Ndélé, Cen. Af. Rep. 198 G9
Ndendé, Gabon 201 M16
Ndeni see Nendo, island, Solomon Is. 217 Q22
N'Djamena, Chad 197 J14
Ndola, Zambia 202 D11
Nduindui, Solomon Is. 217 P18
Nduindui, Vanuatu 218 C2
Nea Epidavros, Gr. 154 K11
Neagh, Lough, N. Ire., U.K. 143 P7
Neah Bay, Wash., U.S. 108 B2
Neale, Lake, Austral. 210 F7
Néa Mihanióna, Gr. 154 D11
Nea Moni, Gr. 155 H16
Néa Moudaniá, Gr. 154 D11
Neápoli, Gr. 154 D8
Neápoli, Gr. 154 M11
Neapolis see Kavála, Gr. 155 C13
Near Islands, Alas., U.S. 110 L1
Néa Zíhni, Gr. 154 B12
Neba, Île, New Caledonia, Fr. 218 B6
Nebine Creek, Austral. 210 H13
Neblina, Pico da, Braz., Venez. 130 C7
Nebraska, U.S. 105 P2
Nebraska City, Nebr., U.S. 105 Q9
Nebrodi, Monti, It. 151 S11
Nécé, New Caledonia, Fr. 218 D10
Necedah, Wis., U.S. 98 K4
Neches, river, Tex., U.S. 103 N15
Neckar, river, Ger. 148 K6
Neckarboo Range, Austral. 210 K12
Necker Island, Hawai'i, U.S. 112 M7
Necker Ridge, Pac. Oc. 238 G11
Necochea, Arg. 133 N12
Nederland, Tex., U.S. 103 Q16
Needham's Point, Barbados 121 L18
Needles, Calif., U.S. 109 W12
Neenah, Wis., U.S. 98 K6
Neftçala, Azerb. 169 E23
Nefteyugansk, Russ. 158 H11
Negaunee, Mich., U.S. 98 F7
Negeribatin, Indonesia 188 L7
Negev, region, Israel 171 P5
Negoiul, peak, Rom. 153 E14
Negomane, Mozambique 203 D14
Negombo, Sri Lanka 179 T7
Negonego, island, Fr. Polynesia, Fr. 219 F20
Negotin, Serb. & Mont. 152 G12
Negra, Laguna, Uru. 132 L15
Negre, Pic, Andorra, Sp. 160 K3
Negreira, Sp. 144 B5
Negrești-Oaș, Rom. 153 B13
Negril, Jam. 120 H5
Negritos, Peru 130 E1
Negro, river, Arg. 133 P10
Negro, river, Bol. 130 J8
Negro, river, Col., Venez. 128 G9
Negro, river, Guatemala 115 L15
Negro, river, Braz. 130 D9
Negros, island, Philippines 189 E14
Negru Vodă, Rom. 153 G17
Nehbandān, Iran 173 E17
Nehe, China 181 C16
Néhoué, Baie de, New Caledonia, Fr. 218 C6
Nehus, Cape, P.N.G. 217 J14
Neiafu, Tonga 218 L11
Neiba, Dom. Rep. 117 M17
Neiba, Bahía de, Dom. Rep. 117 M18
Neiden, Nor. 141 C15
Neiges, Piton des, Reunion, Fr. 205 G16
Neihart, Mont., U.S. 106 D8
Neijiang, China 180 L12
Neillsville, Wis., U.S. 98 J4
Neilson Reef, Pac. Oc. 239 N13
Nei Mongol Gaoyuan, region, China 182 B2
Neiqiu, China 182 F5
Neiva, Col. 128 G5
Nekoosa, Wis., U.S. 98 J5
Neksø, Den. 141 P13
Nekurandu, island, Maldives 179 T3
Nelemnoye, Russ. 159 E19
Nelidovo, Russ. 156 J7
Neligh, Nebr., U.S. 105 N7
Nel'kan, Russ. 159 H19
Nell, island, Marshall Is. 216 L4
Nellore, India 179 P7
Nell Passage, Marshall Is. 216 L3
Nelson, B.C., Can. 82 M9
Nelson, Eng., U.K. 143 R11
Nelson, river, Man., Can. 83 L14
Nelson, N.Z. 213 M18
Nelson, Nebr., U.S. 105 R7
Nelson, Nev., U.S. 109 V12
Nelson, Cape, Austral. 210 M11
Nelson, Estrecho, Chile 133 W6
Nelson House, Man., Can. 83 L13
Nelson Island, Alas., U.S. 110 J11
Nelson Lagoon, Alas., U.S. 110 N12
Nelson Reservoir, Mont., U.S. 106 B11
Néma, Mauritania 196 G7
Neman see Nemunas, river, Eur. 138 E8
Neman, Russ. 156 J2
Nembrala, Indonesia 189 N14
Neméa, Gr. 154 J10
Nemiscau, Que., Can. 83 M18
Nemrut Dagh, ruin, Turk. 169 H13
Nemrut Gölü, Turk. 169 G16
Nemunas, river, Lith. 141 N16
Nemuro, Japan 184 F16
Nemuro Strait, Japan 184 E16
Nen, river, China 181 B16
Nenagh, Ire. 143 T4
Nenana, Alas., U.S. 111 G17
Nendeln, Liech. 160 N2
Nendo (Ndeni), island, Solomon Is. 217 Q22
Nenjiang, China 181 C16
Nenom, Mochun, F.S.M. 217 B14
Neoch, islands, F.S.M. 217 D15
Neodesha, Kans., U.S. 105 U9
Neola, Utah, U.S. 106 L9
Néos, Gr. 154 D12
Neosho, river, Kans., Okla., U.S. 85 H13
Neosho, Mo., U.S. 105 V11
Nepa, Russ. 159 J15
Nepal, Asia 167 V8
Nepalganj, Nepal 178 F8
Nepean, island, Norfolk I., Austral. 217 G20
Nephi, Utah, U.S. 106 M7
Nephin, peak, Ire. 143 Q3
Nepis, Mochun, F.S.M. 217 C15
Neptune Range, Antarctica 226 G10
Nèrassol, Pic de, Fr. 160 H6
Nerchinsk, Russ. 159 L17
Nerchinskiy Zavod, Russ. 159 L18
Nerekhta, Russ. 156 H10
Neretva, river, Bosn. & Herzg., Croatia 152 H7
Neretvanski Kanal, Croatia 152 H7
Neriquinha, Angola 202 F8
Néris, Fr. 147 T10
Nerja, Sp. 144 M10
Nero Seamount, Hawai'i, U.S. 112 K2
Nerpo, Russ. 159 J17
Nerrima, W. Aust., Austral. 211 R5
Nerva, Sp. 144 K7
Nesika Beach, Oreg., U.S. 108 K1
Neskaupstadur, Ice. 140 F4
Nespelem, Wash., U.S. 108 B7
Ness, Loch, Scot., U.K. 142 J9
Ness City, Kans., U.S. 105 T5
Néstos, river, Gr. 155 B13
Netanya, Israel 170 L5
Netherdale, Qnsld., Austral. 211 S14
Netherlands, Eur. 139 T5
Netherlands Antilles, islands, Neth., Lesser Antilles 118 L9
Nettilling Lake, Nunavut, Can. 83 G18
Netzahualcóyotl, Mex. 114 J12
Neuberg, Ger. 148 J8
Neubrandenburg, Ger. 148 C10
Neuchâtel, Switz. 150 B2
Neuchâtel, Lac de, Switz. 150 B1
Neuerburg, Ger. 160 H10
Neufchâteau, Belg. 146 M13
Neufchâteau, Fr. 147 Q13
Neumagen, Ger. 148 H5
Neumayer, station, Antarctica 226 A11
Neumünster, Ger. 148 B8
Neun, river, Laos 186 H11
Neunkirchen, Aust. 148 L12
Neunkirchen, Ger. 148 H5
Neuquén, river, Arg. 133 N7
Neuquén, Arg. 133 P8
Neuruppin, Ger. 148 D10
Neuschwanstein, site, Ger. 148 L8
Neuse, river, N.C., U.S. 96 H12
Neusiedler See, Aust., Hung. 149 L13
Neuss, Ger. 148 F5
Neustadt, Ger. 148 H6
Neustrelitz, Ger. 148 C10
Neu-Ulm, Ger. 148 K7
Neuve la Habay, Belg. 160 J8
Neuvic, Fr. 147 V8
Neuwied, Ger. 148 G5
Nevada, Iowa, U.S. 105 N11
Nevada, Mo., U.S. 105 U11
Nevada, U.S. 109 Q8
Nevada, Sierra, N. Amer. 80 J2
Nevada, Sierra, Sp. 144 L11
Nevada City, Calif., U.S. 109 Q5
Nevea, Solomon Is. 217 P22
Nevel', Russ. 156 J6
Never, Russ. 159 K18
Nevers, Fr. 147 S11
Neves, Sao Tome and Principe 205 C20
Nevinnomyssk, Russ. 157 T12
Nevis, island, St. Kitts & Nevis 121 C18
Nevis, Loch, Scot., U.K. 142 K8
Nevis Peak, St. Kitts & Nevis 121 C18
Nevşehir, Turk. 168 G10
New, river, N.C., U.S. 96 J13
New, river, Va., U.S. 96 F9
New Albany, Ind., U.S. 99 T9
New Albany, Miss., U.S. 100 H12
New Amsterdam, Guyana 129 D15
Newark, Ark., U.S. 100 F9
Newark, Del., U.S. 96 B14
Newark, Eng., U.K. 143 S13
Newark, N.J., U.S. 94 N11
Newark, N.Y., U.S. 94 J7
Newark, Ohio, U.S. 99 R13
Newaygo, Mich., U.S. 98 L9
New Bedford, Mass., U.S. 95 L15
Newberg, Oreg., U.S. 108 F3
New Bern, N.C., U.S. 96 J13
Newbern, Tenn., U.S. 100 E12
Newberry, Fla., U.S. 97 R7
Newberry, Mich., U.S. 98 F10
Newberry, S.C., U.S. 96 K8
Newbiggin by the Sea, Eng., U.K. 143 N12
New Bight, Bahamas 117 F13
New Boston, Ohio, U.S. 99 T13
New Boston, Tex., U.S. 102 K15
New Braunfels, Tex., U.S. 103 R10
New Britain, Conn., U.S. 94 L12
New Britain, island, P.N.G. 213 C21
New Brunswick, Can. 83 P21
New Brunswick, N.J., U.S. 94 N10
Newburg, Mo., U.S. 105 U13
Newburgh, N.Y., U.S. 94 M11
Newburgh, Scot., U.K. 142 K11
Newbury, Eng., U.K. 143 V12
New Caledonia see Nouvelle-Calédonie, island, New Caledonia, Fr. 218 D6
New Caledonia Basin, Pac. Oc. 238 N8
New Castle, Ind., U.S. 99 R10
New Castle, Pa., U.S. 94 M3
Newcastle, Calif., U.S. 109 Q5
Newcastle, Eng., U.K. 143 P12
Newcastle, Jam. 120 J10
Newcastle, N.S.W., Austral. 211 X15
Newcastle, St. Kitts & Nevis 121 B18
Newcastle, Tex., U.S. 102 K9
Newcastle, Wyo., U.S. 106 G14
Newcastle under Lyme, Eng., U.K. 143 S11
Newcastle Waters, N. Terr., Austral. 211 R8
Newcastle West, Ire. 143 T3
New City, N.Y., U.S. 94 M11
Newdegate, W. Aust., Austral. 211 X3
New Delhi, India 178 F6
Newell, S. Dak., U.S. 104 K2
New England, N. Dak., U.S. 104 G2
New England Range, Austral. 210 J15
New England Seamounts, Atl. Oc. 236 H5
Newenham, Cape, Alas., U.S. 110 L12
Newfoundland, Island of, Nfld. & Lab., Can. 83 M23
Newfoundland and Labrador, Can. 83 K21
Newfoundland Evaporation Basin, Utah, U.S. 106 K6
New Franklin, Mo., U.S. 105 S12
New Galloway, Scot., U.K. 143 P9
New Georgia, island, Solomon Is. 217 M16
New Georgia Group, Solomon Is. 217 M16
New Georgia Sound (The Slot), Solomon Is. 217 M17
New Glasgow, N.S., Can. 83 P22
New Grant, Trinidad & Tobago 121 Q22
New Guinea, island, Indonesia, P.N.G. 166 L16
New Hampshire, U.S. 95 J14
New Hampton, Iowa, U.S. 104 M12
New Hanover, island, P.N.G. 213 B21
New Harbor, Me., U.S. 95 G17
New Haven, Conn., U.S. 94 M12
New Haven, Ind., U.S. 99 P10
New Iberia, La., U.S. 100 Q9
New Ipswich, N.H., U.S. 95 J14
New Ireland, island, P.N.G. 213 C21
New Jersey, U.S. 94 P10
Newkirk, N. Mex., U.S. 107 S14
Newkirk, Okla., U.S. 102 E11
New Lexington, Ohio, U.S. 99 R14
New Lisbon, Wis., U.S. 98 K4
New Liskeard, Ont., Can. 83 P18
New London, Conn., U.S. 95 M13
New London, Iowa, U.S. 105 Q13
New London, Wis., U.S. 98 J6
New Madrid, Mo., U.S. 105 V16
Newman, Calif., U.S. 109 S5
Newman, W. Aust., Austral. 211 T3
Newman Grove, Nebr., U.S. 105 P7
New Market, Va., U.S. 96 D11
Newmarket, Eng., U.K. 143 U14
Newmarket, Ire. 143 U3
New Martinsville, W. Va., U.S. 96 C9
New Meadows, Idaho, U.S. 106 F4
New Mexico, U.S. 107 S10
Newnan, Ga., U.S. 96 L4
New Orleans, La., U.S. 100 Q11
New Philadelphia, Ohio, U.S. 99 Q15
New Plymouth, N.Z. 213 L18
Newport, Ark., U.S. 100 F10
Newport, Eng., U.K. 143 X13
Newport, Jam. 120 J8
Newport, Ky., U.S. 101 A18
Newport, Me., U.S. 95 F17
Newport, Oreg., U.S. 108 G2
Newport, R.I., U.S. 95 M14
Newport, Tenn., U.S. 101 E19
Newport, Vt., U.S. 95 E13
Newport, Wales, U.K. 143 V10
Newport, Wash., U.S. 108 B9
Newport Beach, Calif., U.S. 109 Y8
Newport News, Va., U.S. 96 F14
New Port Richey, Fla., U.S. 97 T7
New Prague, Minn., U.S. 104 K11
New Providence, island, Bahamas 116 E11
Newquay, Eng., U.K. 143 X8
New Richmond, Wis., U.S. 98 H2
New Roads, La., U.S. 100 N9
New Rochelle, N.Y., U.S. 94 N11
New Rockford, N. Dak., U.S. 104 F6
New Ross, Ire. 143 U6
Newry, N. Ire., U.K. 143 Q7
Newry, N. Terr., Austral. 211 Q7
New Salem, N. Dak., U.S. 104 G4
New Sandy Bay, St. Vincent & the Grenadines 121 J17
New Schwabenland, region, Antarctica 226 C12
New Siberian Islands see Novosibirskiye Ostrova, Russ. 159 D16
New Smyrna Beach, Fla., U.S. 97 S9
New South Wales, Austral. 211 W13
New Springs, W. Aust., Austral. 211 U3
New Stuyahok, Alas., U.S. 111 K14
Newton, Ill., U.S. 99 S6
Newton, Iowa, U.S. 105 P12
Newton, Kans., U.S. 105 U7
Newton, Mass., U.S. 95 K14
Newton, Miss., U.S. 100 L12
Newton, Tex., U.S. 103 P16
Newton Abbot, Eng., U.K. 143 X10
Newton Stewart, Scot., U.K. 143 P9
New Town, N. Dak., U.S. 104 F3
Newtown see St. Boswells, Scot., U.K. 143 N11
Newtown, Wales, U.K. 143 T10
Newtownabbey, N. Ire., U.K. 143 P7
Newtownards, N. Ire., U.K. 143 Q7
Newtownbarry see Bunclody, Ire. 143 T6
Newtownstewart, N. Ire., U.K. 143 P6
New Ulm, Minn., U.S. 104 K10
New Waverly, Tex., U.S. 103 P13
New York, N.Y., U.S. 94 N11
New York, U.S. 94 K6
New Zealand, Pac. Oc. 214 P8
Neya, Russ. 156 G12
Neyrīz, Iran 173 G14
Neyshābūr, Iran 173 C16
Nezperce, Idaho, U.S. 106 D4
Nez Perce National Historic Park, Idaho, U.S. 106 D3
Nez Perce Pass, Idaho, Mont., U.S. 106 E5
Ngabordamlu, Tanjung, Indonesia 213 D15
Ngain, island, Marshall Is. 216 K7
Ngajangel, island, Palau 216 K12
Ngake, island, Cook Is., N.Z. 219 B14
Ngake, Pukapuka, Cook Is., N.Z. 218 Q2
Ngala, Cameroon 201 E17
Ngalkol, Palau 216 Q10
Ngamegei Passage, Palau 216 L12
Ngami, Lake, Botswana 202 G9
Ngamring, China 180 L6
Ngangla Ringco, lake, China 180 K5
Nganglong Kangri, range, China 180 J5
Nganglong Range, China 166 H8
Ngaoundéré, Cameroon 201 G16
Ngaramasch, Palau 216 R9
Ngardmau, Palau 216 M12
Ngardmau Bay, Palau 216 M12
Ngardololok, Palau 216 Q10
Ngaregur, island, Palau 216 L12
Ngarekeklav, island, Palau 216 L12
Ngaremediu, island, Palau 216 P11
Ngaruangl Passage, Palau 216 J12
Ngaruawahia, N.Z. 213 K19
Ngatangiia, Cook Is., N.Z. 218 Q9
Ngatik Atoll, F.S.M. 216 Q7
Ngauruhoe, Mount, N.Z. 213 L19
Ngcheangel see Kayangel Islands, islands, Palau 216 K12
Ngeaur see Angaur, island, Palau 216 R10
Ngemelis Islands, Palau 216 Q10
Ngerchelchuus, Mount, Palau 216 M12
Ngerchelong see Arekalong Peninsula, peninsula, Palau 216 M12
Ngeregong, island, Palau 216 Q11
Ngergoi, island, Palau 216 Q10
Ngertachebeab see Komebail Lagoon, lake, Palau 216 N11
Ngeruktabel see Urukthapel, island, Palau 216 P11
Ngesebus, island, Palau 216 Q10
Nggatokae, island, Solomon Is. 217 N17
Nggela Pile, island, Solomon Is. 217 N19
Nggela Sule, island, Solomon Is. 217 N19
Ngobasangel, island, Palau 216 P10
Ngoïla, Cameroon 201 J17
Ngoko, river, Cameroon, Congo 201 K17
Ngoring Hu, China 180 J10
Ngorongoro Crater, Tanzania 199 L14
Ngounié, river, Gabon 201 L15
Ngourti, Niger 197 H13
Nguigmi, Niger 197 H13
Nguiu, N. Terr., Austral. 211 P7
Ngukurr, N. Terr., Austral. 211 Q9
Ngulu Atoll, F.S.M. 216 Q2
Nguna, island, Vanuatu 218 E3
Nguru, Nigeria 201 E15
Nhamundá, Braz. 130 D10
Nha Trang, Vietnam 187 N14
Nhulunbuy, N. Terr., Austral. 211 P10

Niafounké, *Mali* **196** H8
Niagara, river, *N.Y., U.S.* **94** H5
Niagara, *Wis., U.S.* **98** G7
Niagara Falls, *Can., U.S.* **85** E19
Niah, *Malaysia* **188** G11
Niamey, *Niger* **196** J10
Niangara, *Dem. Rep. of the Congo* **198** H11
Niangua, river, *Mo., U.S.* **105** U12
Nianiau, Puʻu, *Hawaiʻi, U.S.* **113** G17
Nianzishan, *China* **181** C16
Nias, island, *Indonesia* **188** H4
Niau, island, *Fr. Polynesia, Fr.* **219** E17
Nibok, region, *Nauru* **217** E23
Nicaea *see* İznik, *Turk.* **168** D5
Nicaragua, *N. Amer.* **81** Q20
Nicaragua, Lago de, *Nicar.* **115** M18
Nicaragua, Lake *see* Nicar., Lago de, *N. Amer.* **80** Q8
Nicastro, *It.* **151** Q13
Nice, *Fr.* **147** X16
Nicephorium *see* Ar Raqqah, *Syr.* **170** E11
Niceville, *Fla., U.S.* **97** Q2
Nichinan, *Japan* **185** T5
Nicholas Channel, *Bahamas, Cuba* **116** F8
Nicholasville, *Ky., U.S.* **101** B18
Nicholls' Town, *Bahamas* **116** E11
Nicholson, *W. Aust., Austral.* **211** R7
Nicholson Range, *Austral.* **210** H2
Nickavilla, *Qnsld., Austral.* **211** U12
Nickerson, *Kans., U.S.* **105** T7
Nicobar Islands, *India* **179** S14
Nicopolis, ruin, *Gr.* **154** G7
Nicosia *see* Lefkosia, *Cyprus* **160** N8
Nicosia, *It.* **151** S11
Nicoya, Península de, *Costa Rica* **115** N18
Nicoya Peninsula *see* Nicoya, Península de, *N. Amer.* **80** Q8
Nida, *Lith.* **141** N15
Nidzh, *Azerb.* **169** C21
Nidzica, *Pol.* **149** C15
Niederanven, *Lux.* **160** J10
Niedere Tauern, *Aust.* **148** L11
Nienburg, *Ger.* **148** D7
Nieuw Amsterdam, *Suriname* **129** E16
Nieuw Nickerie, *Suriname* **129** E15
Nieuwpoort, *Neth. Antilles, Neth.* **121** Q15
Nieves, Pico da las, *Canary Is.* **204** R5
Nif, *F.S.M.* **217** D18
Nifiloli, island, *Solomon Is.* **217** P23
Niğde, *Turk.* **168** G10
Niger, *Af.* **195** G17
Niger, river, *Af.* **194** H5
Niger, Source of the, *Guinea* **194** H2
Niger Delta, *Nigeria* **201** J13
Nigeria, *Af.* **195** H17
Nightingale Island, *Tristan da Cunha Is., U.K.* **194** R2
Nigríta, *Gr.* **154** C12
Nihing, river, *Pak.* **177** V2
Nihiru, island, *Fr. Polynesia, Fr.* **219** E19
Nihoa, island, *Hawaiʻi, U.S.* **112** M8
Nihonmatsu, *Japan* **184** M13
Niigata, *Japan* **184** M11
Niihama, *Japan* **185** R7
Niʻihau, island, *Hawaiʻi, U.S.* **112** C3
Niimi, *Japan* **185** Q7
Nii Shima, *Japan* **185** Q12
Nijmegen, *Neth.* **146** J13
Nikalap Aru, island, *F.S.M.* **217** G13
Nikao, *Cook Is., N.Z.* **218** Q9
Nikaupara, *Cook Is., N.Z.* **218** Q11
Níkea, *Gr.* **154** F10
Nikel', *Russ.* **158** C9
Nikiboko, *Neth. Antilles, Neth.* **121** Q19
Nikítas, *Gr.* **154** D12
Nikitin Seamount, *Ind. Oc.* **240** G10
Nikolai, *Alas., U.S.* **111** H15
Nikolayevsk, *Russ.* **157** N13
Nikolayevskiy, *Russ.* **159** J19
Nikolayevsk na Amure, *Russ.* **159** J21
Nikol'sk, *Russ.* **156** K13
Nikolski, *Alas., U.S.* **110** P8
Nikol'skoye, *Russ.* **157** Q14
Nikol'skoye, *Russ.* **159** E23
Nikopol', *Ukr.* **157** Q8
Nīk Pey, *Iran* **172** B11
Niksar, *Turk.* **168** D12
Nīkshahr, *Iran* **173** H17
Nikšić, *Serb. & Mont.* **152** J8
Nikumaroro, island, *Kiribati* **214** H10
Nil, *Russ.* **159** K18
Nilandu, island, *Maldives* **179** V3
Nilandu, island, *Maldives* **179** W3
Nilandu Atoll, *Maldives* **179** V3
Nile, river, *Af.* **194** E9
Nile, Sources of the, *Burundi, Rwanda* **194** K9
Nile River Delta, *Egypt* **194** D9
Niles, *Mich., U.S.* **99** N9
Niles, *Ohio, U.S.* **99** P15
Nilgiri Hills, *India* **179** Q5
Nimach, *India* **178** H4
Nimbahera, *India* **178** H4
Nimba Mountains, *Côte d'Ivoire* **200** G7
Nimbin, *N.S.W., Austral.* **211** W15
Nîmes, *Fr.* **147** X12
Nímos, island, *Gr.* **155** M19
Nimrod Glacier, *Antarctica* **227** L13
Ninati, *Indonesia* **189** L21
Nine Degree Channel, *India* **179** S3
Ninetyeast Ridge, *Ind. Oc.* **240** K11
Ninety Mile Beach, *Austral.* **210** M13
Ninety Mile Beach, *N.Z.* **213** H18
Nineveh, ruin, *Iraq* **172** C9
Ninfas, Punta, *Arg.* **133** R10
Ningbo, *China* **182** L10
Ningcheng, *China* **182** C8
Ningde, *China* **183** P8
Ningdu, *China* **183** P6
Ningguo, *China* **182** L8
Ningshan, *China* **182** H1
Ningwu, *China* **182** D4
Ningyuan, *China* **183** P3
Ninh Binh, *Vietnam* **186** H12
Ninh Hoa, *Vietnam* **187** N14
Ninigo Group, *P.N.G.* **213** B18
Ninilchik, *Alas., U.S.* **111** K16
Niniva, island, *Tonga* **218** P6
Ninnescah, river, *Kans., U.S.* **105** U7
Ninni, island, *Marshall Is.* **216** N5
Ninnis Glacier, *Antarctica* **227** Q16
Nīnole, *Hawaiʻi, U.S.* **113** L21
Nīnole, *Hawaiʻi, U.S.* **113** P20
Ninove, *Belg.* **146** L11
Nioaque, *Braz.* **130** L10
Niobrara, river, *Nebr., U.S.* **104** M5
Nioro du Sahel, *Mali* **196** H6
Niort, *Fr.* **147** T7
Nioumachoua, *Comoros* **205** N15
Nipawin, *Sask., Can.* **82** M12
Nipe, Bahía de, *Cuba* **117** K13
Nipigon, *Ont., Can.* **83** P16
Nipigon, Lake, *Ont., Can.* **83** N16
Nipton, *Calif., U.S.* **109** V12
Niquelândia, *Braz.* **131** J13
Niquero, *Cuba* **116** K11
Nīr, *Iran* **172** B11
Nirmal, *India* **178** L6
Niš, *Serb. & Mont.* **152** H11
Nişāb, *Saudi Arabia* **172** G10
Nişāb, *Yemen* **172** Q10
Nišava, river, *Serb. & Mont.* **152** H12
Nishikō, *Japan* **185** S4
Nishine, *Japan* **184** K13
Nishinoomote, *Japan* **185** U4
Nishino Shima, *Japan* **185** P6
Nishtūn, *Yemen* **173** P13
Nissi, *Est.* **141** K16
Níssiros, island, *Gr.* **155** M18
Nisswa, *Minn., U.S.* **104** H10
Niţā', *Saudi Arabia* **172** H11
Niterói, *Braz.* **131** M15
Nitra, *Slovakia* **149** K14
Nitro, *W. Va., U.S.* **96** D8
Niuafoʻou, island, *Tonga* **214** J9
Niuatoputapu, island, *Tonga* **214** J10
Niu Aunfo Point, *Tonga* **218** H11
Niue, island, *N.Z., Pac. Oc.* **214** K10
Niulakita, island, *Tuvalu* **214** J9
Niutao, island, *Tuvalu* **214** H9
Niutoua, *Tonga* **218** H12
Niutou Shan, *China* **182** M10
Nixon, *Tex., U.S.* **103** R10
Nixon's Harbor, *Bahamas* **120** C8
Niya *see* Minfeng, *China* **180** H6
Nizamabad, *India* **178** L6
Nizamghat, *India* **178** F15
Nizam Sagar, lake, *India* **178** M6
Nizao, *Dom. Rep.* **117** M19
Nizhnekamsk, *Russ.* **156** H16
Nizhneshadrino, *Russ.* **159** J13
Nizhneudinsk, *Russ.* **159** L14
Nizhnevartovsk, *Russ.* **158** H11
Nizhneyansk, *Russ.* **159** E17
Nizhniy Baskunchak, *Russ.* **157** Q14
Nizhniy Bestyakh, *Russ.* **159** G18
Nizhniy Lomov, *Russ.* **156** L12
Nizhniy Novgorod, *Russ.* **156** J12
Nizhniy Tagil, *Russ.* **158** H9
Nizhnyaya Tunguska, river, *Russ.* **159** H13
Nizhnyaya Tura, *Russ.* **158** H9
Nizhyn, *Ukr.* **157** N6
Nizip, river, *Turk.* **168** H12
Nizip, *Turk.* **168** H12
Nizwá, *Oman* **173** K16
Nizza Monferrato, *It.* **150** F3
Nizzana (El 'Auja), *Israel* **171** P4
Njegoš, peak, *Serb. & Mont.* **152** H8
Njombe, *Tanzania* **199** N13
Nkhata Bay, *Malawi* **203** D13
Nkhotakota, *Malawi* **203** D13
Nkongsamba, *Cameroon* **201** H15
Nmai, river, *Myanmar* **186** D7
Noatak, river, *Alas., U.S.* **84** M3
Noatak, *Alas., U.S.* **111** D13
Noatak National Preserve, *Alas., U.S.* **111** D14
Nouans-les-Fontaines, *Fr.* **147** S9
Nobeoka, *Japan* **185** S5
Noblesville, *Ind., U.S.* **99** R9
Nobo, *Indonesia* **189** M14
Noboribetsu, *Japan* **184** G13
Nocera Terinese, *It.* **151** Q13
Nocona, *Tex., U.S.* **102** J10
Nodales, Bahía de los, *Arg.* **133** U9
Nodaway, river, *Mo., U.S.* **105** Q10
Nofre, Peña, *Sp.* **144** D7
Nogáles, *Mex.* **114** B7
Nogales, *Ariz., U.S.* **107** W8
Nogara, *It.* **150** E6
Nōgata, *Japan* **185** R4
Nogent-le-Rotrou, *Fr.* **147** Q8
Nogent-sur-Seine, *Fr.* **147** Q11
Noginsk, *Russ.* **156** J10
Nogoyá, *Arg.* **132** K12
Nogu Dabu, island, *P.N.G.* **217** H18
Nogueira, peak, *Port.* **144** D7
Nohar, *India* **178** E4
Noheji, *Japan* **184** J13
Nohili Point, *Hawaiʻi, U.S.* **112** B4
Nohona o Hae, peak, *Hawaiʻi, U.S.* **113** L19
Nohta, *India* **178** J7
Noia, *Sp.* **144** B5
Noire, Montagne, *Fr.* **147** X10
Noires, Montagnes, *Fr.* **147** Q3
Noirmoutier, Île de, *Fr.* **147** S5
Nojima Zaki, *Japan* **185** Q12
Noka, *Solomon Is.* **217** P22
Nokaneng, *Botswana* **202** G8
Nokia, *Fin.* **141** J15
Nok Kundi, *Pak.* **177** S2
Nokomis, *Ill., U.S.* **99** S5
Nokuku, *Vanuatu* **218** C1
Nola, *Cen. Af. Rep.* **198** H8
Noli, *It.* **150** F3
Nolinsk, *Russ.* **156** G15
Noma Misaki, *Japan* **185** T4
Nomans Land, island, *Mass., U.S.* **95** M15
Nome, *Alas., U.S.* **110** F12
Nomgon, *Mongolia* **180** F12
Nomoneas, island, *F.S.M.* **217** B15
Nomo Saki, *Japan* **185** S3
Nomuka, island, *Tonga* **218** Q6
Nomuka Group, *Tonga* **218** Q6
Nomuka Iki, island, *Tonga* **218** Q6
Nomwin Atoll, *F.S.M.* **216** Q6
Nonancourt, *Fr.* **147** P9
Nondalton, *Alas., U.S.* **111** K15
Nongjrong, *India* **178** G14
Nong Khai, *Thai.* **186** K10
Nonouti, island, *Kiribati* **214** G8
Nonpareil, *Grenada* **121** J22
Nonsuch Bay, *Antigua & Barbuda* **121** B21
Nonsuch Island, *Bermuda, U.K.* **120** B4
Nonthaburi, *Thai.* **186** M9
Nonume, *Solomon Is.* **217** Q22
Nonza, *Fr.* **150** J4
Noole, *Solomon Is.* **217** Q22
Noonan, *N. Dak., U.S.* **104** D2
Noord, *Aruba, Neth.* **121** Q16
Noordkaap, cape, *Aruba, Neth.* **121** Q17
Noordpunt, cape, *Neth. Antilles, Neth.* **121** N13
Noormarkku, *Fin.* **141** J15
Noorvik, *Alas., U.S.* **111** E13
Nóqui, *Angola* **202** B5
Nora, ruin, *It.* **151** Q4
Nora Hazel Point, *Virgin Islands, U.K.* **120** Q7
Norak, *Taj.* **176** J8
Norborne, *Mo., U.S.* **105** S11
Norcia, *It.* **150** J9
Nord, *Greenland, Den.* **81** A20
Nord, Baie du, *Mauritius* **205** J20
Nord, Pointe, *Comoros* **205** L14
Nord, Pointe, *Wallis & Futuna, Fr.* **218** E11
Nord, Pointe, *St. Martin, Fr.* **121** A15
Nordaustlandet, island, *Norway* **167** N7
Norden, *Ger.* **148** C6
Norderstedt, *Ger.* **148** C8
Nord Est, Grande Récif du, *Mayotte, Fr.* **205** N17
Nordeste, *Azores* **144** Q5
Nordfjordeid, *Nor.* **140** J10
Nordhausen, *Ger.* **148** F8
Nordhorn, *Ger.* **148** D5
Nordkapp, cape, *Nor.* **141** B14
Nordkjosbotn, *Nor.* **141** D13
Nordli, *Nor.* **140** G12
Nordoyar, island, *Faroe Is., Den.* **140** J6
Nore, river, *Ire.* **143** T5
Norfolk, *Nebr., U.S.* **105** N7
Norfolk, *Va., U.S.* **96** F14
Norfolk Island, *Austral.* **214** L7
Norfolk Ridge, *Pac. Oc.* **238** M8
Norfork Lake, *Ark., U.S.* **100** E9
Noril'sk, *Russ.* **159** F13
Normal, *Ill., U.S.* **99** Q6
Norman, *Ark., U.S.* **100** H7
Norman, river, *Austral.* **210** D11
Norman, *Okla., U.S.* **102** G11
Norman, Lake, *N.C., U.S.* **96** H9
Normanby Island, *P.N.G.* **213** E21
Normandy, region, *Fr.* **147** P6
Norman's Cay, *Bahamas* **120** G5
Norman's Pond Cay, *Bahamas* **120** E8
Normanton, *Qnsld., Austral.* **211** R11
Norman Wells, *N.W.T., Can.* **82** F10
Norna, Mount, *Austral.* **210** E11
Nornalup, *W. Aust., Austral.* **211** Y3
Ñorquincó, *Arg.* **133** Q7
Norris Lake, *Tenn., U.S.* **101** E18
Norristown, *Pa., U.S.* **94** P9
Norrköping, *Sw.* **141** L13
Norrsundet, *Sw.* **141** J13
Norseman, *W. Aust., Austral.* **211** X4
Norsk, *Russ.* **159** K19
Norsup, *Vanuatu* **218** D2
Nort, *Fr.* **147** R6
Norte, Cabo, *Braz.* **131** C13
Norte, Punta, *Arg.* **132** M13
Norte, Serra do, *Braz.* **130** G9
North, Cape, *N.S., Can.* **83** N22
North Adams, *Mass., U.S.* **94** J12
North Albanian Alps, *Albania* **152** J9
Northampton, *Eng., U.K.* **143** U13
Northampton, *Mass., U.S.* **95** K13
Northampton, *W. Aust., Austral.* **211** W2
Northampton Seamounts, *Hawaiʻi, U.S.* **112** L4
North Andaman, island, *India* **179** P14
North Aral Sea, *Kaz.* **174** G10
North Arm, *N.W.T., Can.* **82** H11
North Augusta, *S.C., U.S.* **96** L8
North Aulatsivik Island, *Nfld. & Lab., Can.* **83** J20
North Australian Basin, *Ind. Oc.* **241** J16
North Battleford, *Sask., Can.* **82** M11
North Bay, *Ont., Can.* **83** P18
North Belcher Islands, *Nunavut, Can.* **83** L17
North Bend, *Oreg., U.S.* **108** J2
North Bimini, island, *Bahamas* **120** B8
North Branch, *Minn., U.S.* **104** J12
North Branch Potomac, river, *Md., W. Va., U.S.* **96** C10
North Caicos, island, *Turks & Caicos Is., U.K.* **117** H17
North Canadian, river, *Okla., U.S.* **102** F9
North Cape, *N.Z.* **213** G18
North Cape *see* Nordkapp, *Nor.* **138** A8
North Cape, *Kiribati* **217** B20
North Carolina, *U.S.* **96** H7
North Cascades National Park, *Wash., U.S.* **108** A5
North Channel, *Mich., U.S.* **98** F12
North Channel, *N. Ire., Scot., U.K.* **143** N7
North Charleston, *S.C., U.S.* **96** M10
North Chicago, *Ill., U.S.* **98** M7
North China Plain, *China* **166** G11
Northcliffe, *W. Aust., Austral.* **211** Y3
North Comino Channel, *Malta* **161** H21
North Dakota, *U.S.* **104** F2
North Downs, *Eng., U.K.* **143** V14
North East, *Pa., U.S.* **94** K3
Northeast Cay, *Jam.* **116** P11
Northeast Pacific Basin, *Pac. Oc.* **238** D11
Northeast Pass, *Marshall Is.* **216** L8
Northeast Passage, *Solomon Is.* **217** R24
North East Point, *Cayman Is., U.K.* **116** L9
North East Point, *Kiribati* **217** B23
Northeast Point, *Bahamas* **117** G15
Northeast Point, *Jam.* **120** J11
Northeast Providence Channel, *Bahamas* **116** D12
Northeim, *Ger.* **148** E7
North Entrance, *Palau* **216** K12
Northern Cyprus, *Cyprus* **160** M8
Northern Dvina, river, *Russ.* **138** B11
Northern European Plain, *Eur.* **138** F5
Northern Ireland, *U.K.* **143** P6
Northern Karroo, region, *Lesotho, S. Af.* **194** Q7
Northern Light Lake, *Minn., U.S.* **104** E14
Northern Mariana Islands, *U.S., Pac. Oc.* **214** D4
Northern Perimeter Highway, *Braz.* **130** C10
Northern Range, *Trinidad & Tobago* **121** N22
Northern Sporades *see* Vóries Sporádes, islands, *Gr.* **155** F13
Northern Territory, *Austral.* **211** R8
Northern Uvals, *Russ.* **138** C12
Northfield, *Minn., U.S.* **104** K11
Northfield, *Vt., U.S.* **95** G13
North Fiji Islands Basin, *Pac. Oc.* **238** L9
North Fond du Lac, *Wis., U.S.* **98** K6
North Fork, *Calif., U.S.* **109** S7
North Fork Clearwater, river, *Idaho, U.S.* **106** D4
North Fork Flathead, river, *Mont., U.S.* **106** A5
North Fork Payette, river, *Idaho, U.S.* **106** F4
North Fork Red, river, *Okla., Tex., U.S.* **102** H8
North Fork Salt, river, *Mo., U.S.* **105** R13
North Friar's Bay, *St. Kitts & Nevis* **121** B18
North Frisian Islands, *Ger.* **148** A7
North Geomagnetic Pole 2005, *Nunavut, Can.* **83** B16
North Head, *N.Z.* **213** J18
North Island, *N.Z.* **213** K18
North Island, *Seychelles* **205** N19
North Korea, *Asia* **167** T12
North Lakhimpur, *India* **178** F14
North Land, islands, *Russ.* **166** B9
North Land *see* Severnaya Zemlya, *Russ.* **159** C14
North Las Vegas, *Nev., U.S.* **109** U12
North Little Rock, *Ark., U.S.* **100** G8
North Loup, river, *Nebr., U.S.* **105** N5
North Magnetic Pole 2006, *N.W.T., Can.* **83** A13
North Malosmadulu Atoll, *Maldives* **179** U3
North Manchester, *Ind., U.S.* **99** P9
North Mole, *Gibraltar, U.K.* **161** N22
North Myrtle Beach, *S.C., U.S.* **96** K12
North Naples, *Fla., U.S.* **97** W8
North Negril Point, *Jam.* **120** H5
North Olmsted, *Ohio, U.S.* **99** P14
North Palmetto Point, *Bahamas* **120** E6
North Pass, *Marshall Is.* **216** K4
North Perry, *Ohio, U.S.* **99** N15
North Pioa, peak, *Amer. Samoa, U.S.* **218** M8
North Platte, river, *Nebr., U.S.* **105** P2
North Platte, *Nebr., U.S.* **105** Q4
North Point, *Barbados* **121** J18
North Point, *Cook Is., N.Z.* **219** A14
North Point, *Mich., U.S.* **98** H12
North Point, *Seychelles* **205** N20
Northport, *Ala., U.S.* **101** K14
Northport, *Wash., U.S.* **108** A8
North Powder, *Oreg., U.S.* **108** F8
North Raccoon, river, *Iowa, U.S.* **105** P11
North Rock, *Bahamas* **120** A8
North Roe, *Scot., U.K.* **142** D12
North Ronaldsay, island, *Scot., U.K.* **142** F11
North Saskatchewan, river, *Alta., Can.* **82** L11
North Sea, *Eur.* **138** E5
North Sentinel Island, *India* **179** Q14

North Siberian Lowland, *Russ.* **166** C9
North Side, *Cayman Is., U.K.* **120** H3
North Slope, region, *Alas., U.S.* **111** C14
North Sound, *Virgin Islands, U.K.* **120** Q9
North Sound, *Cayman Is., U.K.* **120** J2
North Sound, *Ire.* **143** S3
North Sound Estates, *Cayman Is., U.K.* **120** J2
North Springfield, *Pa., U.S.* **94** K3
North Stradbroke Island, *Austral.* **210** H15
North Taranaki Bight, *N.Z.* **213** K18
North Tipalao, *Guam, U.S.* **216** C10
North Tonawanda, *N.Y., U.S.* **94** J5
North Truchas Peak, *N. Mex., U.S.* **107** R13
North Uist, island, *Scot., U.K.* **142** J6
Northumberland, Cape, *Austral.* **210** M11
Northumberland Islands, *Austral.* **210** E15
North Vanlaiphai, *India* **178** J14
North Vernon, *Ind., U.S.* **99** S10
North Walsham, *Eng., U.K.* **143** T15
Northway Junction, *Alas., U.S.* **111** H19
Northwest Angle, region, *Minn., U.S.* **104** D10
Northwest Atlantic Mid-Ocean Canyon, *Atl. Oc.* **236** D6
North West Basin, *Austral.* **210** F1
North West Bay, *Seychelles* **205** N19
North West Cape, *Austral.* **210** F1
Northwestern Hawaiian Islands, *Hawai'i, U.S.* **112** K2
Northwest Hawaiian Ridge, *Pac. Oc.* **238** F10
Northwest Pacific Basin, *Pac. Oc.* **238** E7
North West Point, *Cayman Is., U.K.* **116** L7
North West Point, *Kiribati* **217** A22
Northwest Point, *Bahamas* **120** B10
Northwest Providence Channel, *Bahamas* **116** C10
North West River, *Nfld. & Lab., Can.* **83** L21
Northwest Territories, *Can.* **82** G11
Northwich, *Eng., U.K.* **143** S11
North Wilkesboro, *N.C., U.S.* **96** G8
Northwind Escarpment, *Arctic Oc.* **242** K6
Northwind Plain, *Arctic Oc.* **242** K6
Northwind Ridge, *Arctic Oc.* **242** K6
Northwood, *Iowa, U.S.* **104** L12
Northwood, *N. Dak., U.S.* **104** F7
North York Moors, *Eng., U.K.* **143** Q13
Norton, *Kans., U.S.* **105** R5
Norton, *Va., U.S.* **96** F7
Norton Bay, *Alas., U.S.* **111** F13
Norton Shores, *Mich., U.S.* **98** L9
Norton Sound, *Alas., U.S.* **110** G12
Norvegia, Cape, *Antarctica* **226** B10
Norwalk, *Calif., U.S.* **109** X8
Norwalk, *Conn., U.S.* **94** M12
Norwalk, *Ohio, U.S.* **99** P13
Norway, *Eur.* **139** Q6
Norway, *Me., U.S.* **95** G15
Norway, *Mich., U.S.* **98** G7
Norway House, *Man., Can.* **83** M14
Norwegian Basin, *Arctic Oc.* **243** G18
Norwegian Bay, *Nunavut, Can.* **83** C15
Norwegian Sea, *Arctic Oc.* **243** G17
Norwich, *Conn., U.S.* **95** L13
Norwich, *Eng., U.K.* **143** T15
Norwich, *N.Y., U.S.* **94** K9
Norwood, *Colo., U.S.* **107** N10
Norwood, *N.C., U.S.* **96** J10
Norwood, *N.Y., U.S.* **94** F10
Norwood, *Ohio, U.S.* **99** S11
Noshiro, *Japan* **184** J12
Nosivka, *Ukr.* **157** N6
Noşratābād, *Iran* **173** F17
Noss, Isle of, *Scot., U.K.* **142** D12
Nossob, river, *Botswana, S. Af.* **202** J8
Nosy-Varika, *Madagascar* **203** G17
Noteć, river, *Pol.* **149** D13
Nótios Evvoïkós Kólpos, *Gr.* **154** H12
Noto, *It.* **151** T12
Noto, *Japan* **184** M10
Noto, Golfo di, *It.* **151** U12
Noto Hantō, *Japan* **184** M10
Notre Dame Bay, *Nfld. & Lab., Can.* **83** L23
Nottaway, river, *Que., Can.* **83** N18
Nottingham, *Eng., U.K.* **143** S13
Nottingham Island, *Nunavut, Can.* **83** H17
Nottoway, river, *Va., U.S.* **96** F13
Nouadhibou (Port Etienne), *Mauritania* **196** F4
Nouakchott, *Mauritania* **196** G5
Nouamrhar, *Mauritania* **196** F4
Nouart, *Fr.* **147** N13
Nouméa, *New Caledonia, Fr.* **218** E8
Nouna, *Burkina Faso* **200** E9
Nouveau Québec, region, *Que., Can.* **83** K19
Nouveau-Québec, Cratère du (Chubb Crater), *Que., Can.* **83** J18
Nouvelle-Calédonie (New Caledonia), island, *New Caledonia, Fr.* **218** C6
Novafeltria, *It.* **150** G8
Nova Friburgo, *Braz.* **131** M15
Nova Gorica, *Slov.* **152** D4
Nova Gradiška, *Croatia* **152** E7
Nova Iguaçu, *Braz.* **131** M14
Nova Kakhovka, *Ukr.* **157** R7
Novalukoml', *Belarus* **156** K5
Nova Mambone, *Mozambique* **203** G13
Nova Odesa, *Ukr.* **157** R6
Nova Olinda do Norte, *Braz.* **130** D9
Novara, *It.* **150** D4
Nova Scotia, *Can.* **83** P22
Nova Sofala, *Mozambique* **203** G13
Nova Xavantina, *Braz.* **130** J12
Novaya Sibir', Ostrov, *Russ.* **159** C17
Novaya Vodolaga, *Ukr.* **157** P8
Novaya Zemlya, island, *Russ.* **166** C7
Nova Zagora, *Bulg.* **153** J15
Novelda, *Sp.* **145** J14
Nové Zámky, *Slovakia* **149** K14
Novhorod-Sivers'kyy, *Ukr.* **156** M7
Novi Bečej, *Serb. & Mont.* **152** E10
Novi Ligure, *It.* **150** F4
Novi Pazar, *Bulg.* **153** H16
Novi Pazar, *Serb. & Mont.* **152** H10
Novi Sad, *Serb. & Mont.* **152** E9
Novoaleksandrovsk, *Russ.* **157** S11
Novoanninskiy, *Russ.* **157** N12
Novo Aripuanã, *Braz.* **130** E9
Novobod, *Taj.* **176** H8
Novocherkassk, *Russ.* **157** R11
Novo Cruzeiro, *Braz.* **131** K15
Novo Hamburgo, *Braz.* **130** P12
Novohrad-Volyns'kyy, *Ukr.* **157** N4
Novoĭshīmskīy, *Kaz.* **174** C12
Novokuybyshevsk, *Russ.* **156** L15
Novokuznetsk, *Russ.* **158** L12
Novolazarevskaya, station, *Antarctica* **227** A14
Novo Mesto, *Slov.* **152** D5
Novomichurinsk, *Russ.* **156** K10
Novomoskovs'k, *Ukr.* **157** Q8
Novomoskovsk, *Russ.* **156** K10
Novopokrovskaya, *Russ.* **157** S11
Novorepnoye, *Russ.* **156** M15
Novorossiysk, *Russ.* **157** T9
Novorybnoye, *Russ.* **159** F15
Novorzhev, *Russ.* **156** H6
Novoshakhtinsk, *Russ.* **157** Q11
Novosibirsk, *Russ.* **158** K12
Novosibirskiye Ostrova (New Siberian Islands), *Russ.* **159** D16
Novotitarovskaya, *Russ.* **157** S10
Novotroitsk, *Russ.* **158** J7
Novoukrayinka, *Ukr.* **157** Q6
Novouzensk, *Russ.* **157** N15
Novovolyns'k, *Ukr.* **157** N2
Novoye Ust'ye, *Russ.* **159** G20
Novozybkov, *Russ.* **156** M6
Novyy Buh, *Ukr.* **157** Q7
Novyy Port, *Russ.* **158** F11
Novyy Urengoy, *Russ.* **158** G12
Nowabad-e Ish, *Afghan.* **176** J9
Nowa Nowa, *Vic., Austral.* **211** Z13
Nowa Sól, *Pol.* **148** E12
Nowata, *Okla., U.S.* **102** E13
Now Deh, *Afghan.* **177** P2
Nowood, river, *Wyo., U.S.* **106** G11
Nowra, *N.S.W., Austral.* **211** Y14
Nowrangapur, *India* **178** L8
Nowshak, peak, *Afghan.* **176** K10
Nowshera, *Pak.* **177** N10
Nowy Sącz, *Pol.* **149** H16
Nowy Targ, *Pol.* **149** H15
Now Zad, *Afghan.* **177** P4
Noxon, *Mont., U.S.* **106** B4
Noyabr'sk, *Russ.* **158** H11
Noyon, *Fr.* **147** N10
Nozay, *Fr.* **147** R5
Nsukka, *Nigeria* **201** G14
Ntem, river, *Cameroon, Gabon* **194** J5
Ntingui, peak, *Comoros* **205** N16
Ntomba, Lac, *Dem. Rep. of the Congo* **198** K8
Ntsaouéni, *Comoros* **205** M14
Nu (Salween), river, *China* **180** N10
Nuapapu, island, *Tonga* **218** M11
Nuapapu, *Tonga* **218** L11
Nuatabu, *Kiribati* **217** F17
Nuba Mountains, *Sudan* **194** H9
Nubia, Lake, *Sudan* **198** C12
Nubian Desert, *Sudan* **199** C13
Nubledo, *Sp.* **144** A8
Nueces, river, *Tex., U.S.* **103** T9
Nueltin Lake, *Nunavut, Can.* **83** J14
Nuestra Señora, Bahía, *Chile* **132** F6
Nueva Gerona, *Cuba* **116** H6
Nueva Rosita, *Mex.* **114** E11
9 de Julio, *Arg.* **132** M11
Nuevitas, *Cuba* **116** J11
Nuevo, Bajo, *Mex.* **115** H15
Nuevo, Golfo, *Arg.* **133** R10
Nuevo Casas Grandes, *Mex.* **114** C8
Nuevo Laredo, *Mex.* **114** E11
Nuevo Rocafuerte, *Ecua.* **128** J5
Nuguria Islands, *P.N.G.* **213** C22
Nui, island, *Tuvalu* **214** H8
Nukapu, island, *Solomon Is.* **217** N22
Nukhayb, *Iraq* **172** E8
Nuku, island, *Tonga* **218** H12
Nukuaeta, island, *Wallis & Futuna, Fr.* **218** C11
Nuku'alofa, *Tonga* **218** H11
Nukubasaga, island, *Fiji Is.* **218** G9
Nukudamu, *Fiji Is.* **218** G8
Nukufetau, island, *Tuvalu* **214** H9
Nukufufulanoa, island, *Wallis & Futuna, Fr.* **218** A11
Nukufutu, island, *Wallis & Futuna, Fr.* **218** A11
Nukuhifala, island, *Wallis & Futuna, Fr.* **218** B12
Nuku Hiva, island, *Fr. Polynesia, Fr.* **215** H14
Nukuira, island, *Fiji Is.* **218** G7
Nukulaelae, island, *Tuvalu* **214** H9
Nukuloa, island, *Wallis & Futuna, Fr.* **218** A11
Nukumanu Islands, *P.N.G.* **217** H18
Nukumanu Islands, *Solomon Is.* **214** H6
Nukunono, island, *Tokelau, N.Z.* **214** H10
Nukuoro Atoll, *F.S.M.* **216** R7
Nukus, *Uzb.* **174** J9
Nukutapu, island, *Wallis & Futuna, Fr.* **218** B11
Nukutavake, island, *Fr. Polynesia, Fr.* **219** F21
Nukuteatea, island, *Wallis & Futuna, Fr.* **218** B11
Nukutipipi, island, *Fr. Polynesia, Fr.* **219** G19
Nulato, *Alas., U.S.* **111** F14
Nules, *Sp.* **145** G15
Nullagine, *W. Aust., Austral.* **211** T3
Nullarbor Plain, *Austral.* **210** J6
Num, island, *Indonesia* **189** K19
Numakawa, *Japan* **184** D13
Numan, *Nigeria* **201** F16
Numancia, Ruinas de, *Sp.* **144** D12
Numata, *Japan* **184** F13
Numata, *Japan* **185** N11
Numazu, *Japan* **185** Q11
Numbulwar, *N. Terr., Austral.* **211** P9
Num Co, *China* **180** L7
Numfoor, island, *Indonesia* **189** J19
Numila, *Hawai'i, U.S.* **112** C5
Numto, *Russ.* **158** G11
Nunap Isua (Cape Farewell), *Greenland, Den.* **81** D22
Nunavut, *Can.* **83** G14
Nuneaton, *Eng., U.K.* **143** T12
Nunivak Island, *Alas., U.S.* **110** J10
Nunligran, *Russ.* **159** A21
Nuoro, *It.* **151** N4
Nupani, island, *Solomon Is.* **217** N22
Nuquí, *Col.* **128** E3
Nura, river, *Kaz.* **175** E14
Nuremberg *see* Nürnberg, *Ger.* **148** H8
Nur Gama, *Pak.* **177** T6
Nurina, *W. Aust., Austral.* **211** W6
Nurlat, *Russ.* **156** J15
Nurmes, *Fin.* **141** G16
Nürnberg (Nuremberg), *Ger.* **148** H8
Nurpur, *Pak.* **177** Q10
Nurri, *It.* **151** P4
Nurse Cay, *Bahamas* **117** H13
Nusaybin, *Turk.* **169** H16
Nushki, *Pak.* **177** S5
Nuttal, *Pak.* **177** S7
Nutwood Downs, *N. Terr., Austral.* **211** Q9
Nu'uanu Pali Overlook, *Hawai'i, U.S.* **112** E11
Nuuk (Godthåb), *Greenland, Den.* **81** D21
Nu'ulua, island, *Samoa* **218** L4
Nuupere, Pointe, *Fr. Polynesia, Fr.* **219** N14
Nuusilaelae, island, *Amer. Samoa, U.S.* **218** N1
Nu'utele, island, *Samoa* **218** L4
Nuutele, island, *Amer. Samoa, U.S.* **218** N1
Nuuuli, *Amer. Samoa, U.S.* **218** M7
Nuweiba', *Egypt* **171** S4
Nyagan', *Russ.* **158** G10
Nyainqêntanglha Shan, *China* **180** L8
Nyala, *Sudan* **198** F10
Nyalam, *China* **180** L6
Nyamlell, *Sudan* **198** G11
Nyandoma, *Russ.* **158** E7
Nyasa, Lake *see* Malawi, Lake, *Af.* **203** D13
Nyaunglebin, *Myanmar* **186** K6
Nybergsund, *Nor.* **140** K12
Nyborg, *Den.* **140** P11
Nyborg, *Nor.* **141** C15
Nyda, *Russ.* **158** G11
Nyeri, *Kenya* **199** K14
Nyerol, *Sudan* **199** G13
Nyeying, *India* **178** F15
Nyima, *China* **180** K7
Nyingchi, *China* **180** L8
Nyíregyháza, *Hung.* **149** K17
Nykarleby, *Fin.* **141** G15
Nykøbing, *Den.* **140** P12
Nyköping, *Sw.* **141** L13
Nymagee, *N.S.W., Austral.* **211** X13
Nymphaeum *see* Pínes, Akrotírio, cape, *Gr.* **155** D13
Nyngan, *N.S.W., Austral.* **211** X13
Nyoman, river, *Belarus* **156** K3
Nyoma Rap, *India* **177** N15
Nyon, *Switz.* **150** C1
Nyong, river, *Cameroon* **201** J15
Nyons, *Fr.* **147** W13
Nysa, *Pol.* **149** G13
Nysh, *Russ.* **159** J21
Nyssa, *Oreg., U.S.* **108** H9
Nyūdō Zaki, *Japan* **184** K12
Nyuksenitsa, *Russ.* **156** E12
Nyunzu, *Dem. Rep. of the Congo* **198** M11
Nyurba, *Russ.* **159** H16
Nzega, *Tanzania* **199** L13
Nzérékoré, *Guinea* **200** G7
N'zeto, *Angola* **202** B5

O

Oacoma, *S. Dak., U.S.* **104** L5
Oahe, Lake, *N. Dak., S. Dak., U.S.* **104** J5
O'ahu, island, *Hawai'i, U.S.* **112** D10
Oak Bluffs, *Mass., U.S.* **95** M15
Oakdale, *Calif., U.S.* **109** S5
Oakdale, *La., U.S.* **100** N8
Oakes, *N. Dak., U.S.* **104** H7
Oakesdale, *Wash., U.S.* **108** C9
Oak Grove, *La., U.S.* **100** K9
Oak Harbor, *Wash., U.S.* **108** B4
Oak Hill, *Ohio, U.S.* **99** S13
Oak Hill, *W. Va., U.S.* **96** E8
Oakhurst, *Calif., U.S.* **109** S6
Oakland, *Calif., U.S.* **109** S3
Oakland, *Iowa, U.S.* **105** P9
Oakland, *Md., U.S.* **96** C10
Oakland, *Nebr., U.S.* **105** P8
Oakland, *Oreg., U.S.* **108** J3
Oakland City, *Ind., U.S.* **99** T8
Oak Lawn, *Ill., U.S.* **99** N7
Oakley, *Idaho, U.S.* **106** J5
Oakley, *Kans., U.S.* **105** S4
Oak Park, *Ill., U.S.* **99** N7
Oak Ridge, *Tenn., U.S.* **101** E18
Oakridge, *Oreg., U.S.* **108** H3
Oakvale, *S. Aust., Austral.* **211** X11
Oakwood, *Qnsld., Austral.* **211** U13
Oamaru, *N.Z.* **213** Q17
Oaro, *N.Z.* **213** N18
Oatara, island, *Fr. Polynesia, Fr.* **219** B24
Oates Coast, *Antarctica* **227** R15
Oaxaca, *Mex.* **115** K13
Ob, Gulf of, *Russ.* **166** C8
Ob', river, *Russ.* **158** G11
Oba, *Ont., Can.* **83** P17
Obama, *Japan* **185** P9
Oban, *N.Z.* **213** R15
Oban, *Qnsld., Austral.* **211** S10
Obanazawa, *Japan* **184** L13
Obando, *Col.* **128** F9
O Barco, *Sp.* **144** C7
Ob' Bank, *Arctic Oc.* **243** J15
Ob' Bay, *Antarctica* **227** R14
Obelisk, site, *Vatican City* **161** Q17
Obelisk Island, *Solomon Is.* **217** N24
Obella, island, *Marshall Is.* **216** K4
Oberdrauburg, *Aust.* **148** M10
Oberhausen, *Ger.* **148** E5
Oberlin, *Kans., U.S.* **105** R4
Oberlin, *La., U.S.* **100** P7
Oberlin, *Ohio, U.S.* **99** P14
Oberschan, *Switz.* **160** Q2
Oberursel, *Ger.* **148** G6
Obervellach, *Aust.* **148** M10
Oberwart, *Aust.* **148** L12
Obi, island, *Indonesia* **189** K16
Obi, Kepulauan, *Indonesia* **189** K16
Óbidos, *Braz.* **130** D11
Obidos, *Port.* **144** H4
Obigarm, *Taj.* **176** H8
Obihiro, *Japan* **184** G14
Obilatu, island, *Indonesia* **189** J16
Obil'noye, *Russ.* **157** Q13
Obion, *Tenn., U.S.* **100** E12
Ob-Irtysh, Source of the, *China* **166** F9
Oblachnaya, Gora, *Russ.* **159** L21
Obluch'ye, *Russ.* **159** L20
Obninsk, *Russ.* **156** K9
Obo, *Cen. Af. Rep.* **198** H11
Obome, *Indonesia* **189** K18
Oborniki, *Pol.* **149** D13
Obrenovac, *Serb. & Mont.* **152** F10
O'Brien, *Oreg., U.S.* **108** L2
Obrovac, *Croatia* **152** F5
Obruk, *Turk.* **168** G8
Obshchiy Syrt, *Russ.* **138** E13
Obskaya Guba, *Russ.* **158** F12
Obstruccíon, Fiordo, *Chile* **133** W7
Ob' Tablemount, *Ind. Oc.* **240** R4
Oca, Montes de, *Sp.* **144** C11
Ocala, *Fla., U.S.* **97** S8
Ocaña, *Col.* **128** D6
Ocaña, *Sp.* **144** G11
Occidental, Cordillera, *S. Amer.* **126** B2
Occidental, Grand Erg, *Alg.* **196** C10
Ocean Cay, *Bahamas* **116** D9
Ocean City, *Md., U.S.* **96** D15
Ocean City, *N.J., U.S.* **94** R10
Ocean Falls, *B.C., Can.* **82** K7
Ocean Island *see* Kure Atoll, *Hawai'i, U.S.* **112** K2
Ocean Island *see* Banaba, *Kiribati* **214** G7
Oceanographer Fracture Zone, *Atl. Oc.* **236** H8
Oceanographic Museum, *Monaco* **161** E21
Ocean Park, *Wash., U.S.* **108** D2
Oceanside, *Calif., U.S.* **109** Y9
Ocean Springs, *Miss., U.S.* **101** P13
Oceanview, *Guam, U.S.* **216** B11
O.C. Fisher Lake, *Tex., U.S.* **103** N7
Ocha, island, *F.S.M.* **217** D15
Ocha, Mochun, *F.S.M.* **217** D15
Och'amch'ire, *Abkhazia* **169** B16
Ochiishi, *Japan* **184** F16
Ochlockonee, river, *Ga., U.S.* **97** Q5
Ocho Rios, *Jam.* **120** H9
Ocilla, *Ga., U.S.* **97** P6
Ocmulgee, river, *Ga., U.S.* **97** N6
Ocmulgee National Monument, *Ga., U.S.* **96** M6
Ocna Mureş, *Rom.* **153** D13
Ocoa, Bahía de, *Dom. Rep.* **117** M18
Oconee, river, *Ga., U.S.* **97** N7
Oconee, Lake, *Ga., U.S.* **96** L6
Oconomowoc, *Wis., U.S.* **98** L6
Oconto, *Wis., U.S.* **98** H7
Oconto Falls, *Wis., U.S.* **98** H7
Ocracoke, *N.C., U.S.* **96** H15
Ocracoke Inlet, *N.C., U.S.* **96** J15
October Revolution Island, *Russ.* **166** B9
Ocumare del Tuy, *Venez.* **128** B10
Ōda, *Japan* **185** P6
Ŏdaejin, *N. Korea* **182** B14
Ōdate, *Japan* **184** J13
Odawara, *Japan* **185** P12

Odda, Nor. 140 K10
Odebolt, Iowa, U.S. 105 N10
Odem, Tex., U.S. 103 T11
Odemira, Port. 144 K5
Ödemiş, Turk. 168 G3
Odense, Den. 140 P11
Oder see Odra, river, Ger. 148 D11
Odesa, Ukr. 157 R6
Odessa, Mo., U.S. 105 S11
Odessa, Tex., U.S. 102 M4
Odessa, Wash., U.S. 108 C7
Odienné, Côte d'Ivoire 200 F7
O'Donnell, Tex., U.S. 102 L5
Odra see Oder, river, Pol. 148 D11
Odžaci, Serb. & Mont. 152 E9
Oecusse see Pante Macassar, Timor-Leste 189 N15
Oeiras, Braz. 131 F15
Oelrichs, S. Dak., U.S. 104 M2
Oelwein, Iowa, U.S. 104 M13
Oeno Island, Pac. Oc. 215 K16
Oenpelli, N. Terr., Austral. 211 P8
Oeta, Mount see Oíti, Óros, Gr. 154 G10
Of, Turk. 169 D15
O'Fallon Creek, Mont., U.S. 106 D13
Offenbach, Ger. 148 G6
Offenburg, Ger. 148 K6
Office of Tourism, Monaco 161 C21
Offida, It. 150 J10
Oficina Dominador, Chile 132 E7
Oficina Rica Aventura, Chile 132 D7
Ofidoúsa, island, Gr. 155 M16
Ofolanga, island, Tonga 218 P7
Ofu, island, Amer. Samoa, U.S. 218 N2
Ofu, Amer. Samoa, U.S. 218 N1
Ofu, island, Tonga 218 M12
Ōfunato, Japan 184 K14
Oga, Japan 184 K12
Ogachi, Japan 184 L13
Ogadēn, region, Eth. 199 G17
Ōgaki, Japan 185 P9
Ogallala, Nebr., U.S. 105 Q3
Ogasawara Guntō see Bonin Islands, Japan 184 K5
Ogawara Ko, Japan 184 J13
Ogbomosho, Nigeria 200 G12
Ogden, Iowa, U.S. 105 N11
Ogden, Utah, U.S. 106 K7
Ogdensburg, N.Y., U.S. 94 F9
Ogea Driki, island, Fiji Is. 218 K9
Ogea Levu, island, Fiji Is. 218 K9
Ogeechee, river, Ga., U.S. 97 N8
Ogi, Japan 184 M11
Ogilvie Mountains, Yukon, Can. 82 E8
Oglesby, Ill., U.S. 99 P6
Oglethorpe, Ga., U.S. 97 N5
Ogmore, Qnsld., Austral. 211 T14
Ognev Yar, Russ. 158 J11
Ogoja, Nigeria 201 H14
Ogoki, river, Ont., Can. 83 N16
Ogoki, Ont., Can. 83 N16
Ogooué, river, Gabon 201 L15
Ogr, Sudan 198 F11
O Grove, Sp. 144 C5
Ogulin, Croatia 152 E5
Ohau, Lake, N.Z. 213 P16
Óhi, Óros, Gr. 155 J13
O'Higgins, Lago, Chile 133 U7
Ohio, river, U.S. 85 H15
Ohio, U.S. 99 Q12
Ohonua, Tonga 218 J12
Ohrid, Maced. 152 L10
Ohrid, Lake see Ohridsko Jezero, Albania, Maced. 152 L10
Ohridsko Jezero (Lake Ohrid), Albania, Maced. 152 L10
Ōi, river, Japan 185 P11
Oiapoque, river, Fr. Guiana, Fr. 129 F18
Oiapoque, river, Braz. 130 B12
Oiapoque, Braz. 130 B12
Oil City, Pa., U.S. 94 M4
Oildale, Calif., U.S. 109 V7
Oile, Turk. 168 C5
Oilton, Okla., U.S. 102 F12
Oise, river, Fr. 147 N10
Oistins, Barbados 121 L19
Ōita, Japan 185 R5
Oíti, Óros (Mount Oeta), Gr. 154 G10
Ojika, Japan 184 L13
Ojika Jima, Japan 185 R3
Ojinaga, Mex. 114 D9
Ojiya, Japan 184 M11
Ojo de Liebre, Laguna, Mex. 114 D5
Ojos del Salado, Cerro, Arg. 132 G8
Oka, river, Russ. 156 J12
Okaba, Indonesia 189 M21
Oka-Don Plain, Russ. 138 E12
Okahandja, Namibia 202 H7
Okak Islands, Nfld. & Lab., Can. 83 J21
Okanogan, river, Can., U.S. 84 B5
Okanogan, Wash., U.S. 108 B7
Okanogan Range, Wash., U.S. 108 A6
Okara, Pak. 177 Q11
Okau, F.S.M. 217 D18
Okaukuejo, Namibia 202 G6
Okavango, river, Angola, Namibia 202 F8
Okavango Delta, Botswana 202 G9
Okaya, Japan 185 P11
Okayama, Japan 185 Q7
Okazaki, Japan 185 Q10
Okeechobee, Fla., U.S. 97 V9
Okeechobee, Lake, Fla., U.S. 97 V9
Okeene, Okla., U.S. 102 F9
Okefenokee Swamp, Fla., Ga., U.S. 97 Q7
Okemah, Okla., U.S. 102 G12
Okha, Russ. 159 H21
Okhaldhunga, Nepal 178 F10
Okhotsk, Russ. 159 G20
Okhotsk, Sea of, Russ. 159 G22
Okhtyrka, Ukr. 157 N8
Okiep, S. Af. 202 K7
Okinawa, island, Japan 185 Y2
Okinawa Shotō, Japan 185 Y1
Okino Daitō Jima, Japan 184 L3
Okino Erabu Shima, Japan 185 X2
Okino Shima, Japan 185 Q4
Okino Shima, Japan 185 S6
Oki Shotō, Japan 184 H4
Oki Shotou, Japan 185 N6
Oklahoma, U.S. 102 G8
Oklahoma City, Okla., U.S. 102 G11
Okmulgee, Okla., U.S. 102 G12
Okolona, Ky., U.S. 101 B16
Okolona, Miss., U.S. 101 J13
Okoppe, Japan 184 E14
Okoyo, Congo 201 L17
Okp'yŏng, N. Korea 182 D13
Okso' Takpochao, peak, N. Mariana Is., U.S. 216 B5
Oktyabr'sk, Kaz. 174 E8
Oktyabr'skiy, Russ. 157 Q13
Oktyabr'skiy, Russ. 158 H7
Oktyabr'skoy Revolyutsii, Ostrov, Russ. 159 D14
Ōkuchi, Japan 185 S4
Okulovka, Russ. 156 G7
Okushiri Tō, Japan 184 G12
Okwa, river, Botswana 202 H8
Okytyabr'skoye, Russ. 158 G10
Ola, Ark., U.S. 100 G7
Ólafsvík, Ice. 140 E1
Olancha Peak, Calif., U.S. 109 U8
Öland, island, Sw. 141 M14
Olary, S. Aust., Austral. 211 X11
Olathe, Kans., U.S. 105 S10
Olavarría, Arg. 132 M12
Oława, Pol. 149 F13
Olbia, It. 150 M4
Olbia, Golfo di, It. 150 M4
Old Bight, Bahamas 117 F13
Old Cork, Qnsld., Austral. 211 T11
Old Crow, Yukon, Can. 82 D9
Oldenburg, Ger. 148 C6
Old Forge, Pa., U.S. 94 M9
Old Fort Bay, Bahamas 120 B10
Oldham, Eng., U.K. 143 R11
Old Harbor, Alas., U.S. 111 M15
Old Man Bay, Cayman Is., U.K. 120 H3
Old Orchard Beach, Me., U.S. 95 H15
Old Road, Antigua & Barbuda 121 B20
Old Road Bluff, Antigua & Barbuda 121 C20
Old Road Town, St. Kitts & Nevis 121 B17
Old Stores, Cayman Is., U.K. 120 H1
Old Sugar Mill, Hawai'i, U.S. 112 D11
Old Town, Me., U.S. 95 E17
Olduvai Gorge, Tanzania 199 L14
Old Womans Point, Jam. 120 K8
Olean, N.Y., U.S. 94 K5
Olekma, river, Russ. 159 J17
Olekminsk, Russ. 159 H17
Oleksandriya, Ukr. 157 Q7
Olenegorsk, Russ. 158 D9
Olenek, river, Russ. 166 C10
Olenek, river, Russ. 159 F16
Olenek, Russ. 159 G15
Oleniy, Ostrov, Russ. 158 E12
Oléron, Île d', Fr. 147 U6
Oleśnica, Pol. 149 F13
Olga, Mount (Kata Tjuta), Austral. 210 G7
Olga Basin, Arctic Oc. 243 F14
Ölgiy, Mongolia 180 C8
Olhão da Restauração, Port. 144 L6
Olib, island, Croatia 152 F4
Olifantshoek, S. Af. 202 K8
Olimarao Atoll, F.S.M. 216 Q4
Ólimbos, Óros (Olympus), Gr. 154 D10
Olimbos, Gr. 155 P18
Olinda, Braz. 131 F18
Olio, Qnsld., Austral. 211 T12
Olite, Sp. 145 C13
Oliva, Arg. 132 K10
Olivenza, Sp. 144 J7
Olivet, Fr. 147 R9
Olivia, Minn., U.S. 104 K10
Olivo, Monte, It. 161 H17
Ölkeyek, river, Kaz. 174 E10
Olla, La., U.S. 100 M8
Olmedo, Sp. 144 E10
Olmos, Peru 130 F2
Olney, Ill., U.S. 99 T7
Olney, Tex., U.S. 102 K9
'Olomburi, Solomon Is. 217 N20
Olomouc, Czech Rep. 149 H13
Olongapo, Philippines 189 C13
Oloron, Fr. 147 Y6
Olorua, island, Fiji Is. 218 J9
Olosega, island, Amer. Samoa, U.S. 218 N2
Olosega, Amer. Samoa, U.S. 218 N2
Olotania Crater, Amer. Samoa, U.S. 218 P3
Olovyannaya, Russ. 159 L17
Olowalu, Hawai'i, U.S. 113 G16
Olpoï, Vanuatu 218 C1
Olsztyn, Pol. 149 B15
Olt, river, Rom. 153 G14
Olten, Switz. 150 A3
Olteniţa, Rom. 153 G16
Olton, Tex., U.S. 102 J5
Oltu, river, Turk. 169 D16
Oltu, Turk. 169 D16
Oluan Pi, cape, Taiwan, China 183 S9
Ólvega, Sp. 145 D13
Olympia, ruin, Gr. 154 K9
Olympia, Wash., U.S. 108 D3
Olympic National Park, Wash., U.S. 108 B3
Olympos, peak, Cyprus 160 P7
Olympus see Ólimbos, Óros, peak, Gr. 154 D10
Olympus, Mount see Ulu Dağ, Turk. 168 D5
Olympus, Mount, Wash., U.S. 108 B2
Olyutorskiy, Mys, Russ. 159 D22
Olyutorskiy, Cape, Russ. 166 B13
Olyutorskiy Zaliv, Russ. 159 D22
Ōma, Japan 184 H13
Omae Zaki, Japan 185 Q11
Ōmagari, Japan 184 K13
Omagh, N. Ire., U.K. 143 Q6
Omaha, Nebr., U.S. 105 P9
Omaha Beach, Fr. 147 N6
Omaja, Cuba 116 K12
Omak, Wash., U.S. 108 B7
Omak Lake, Wash., U.S. 108 B7
Oman, Asia 167 W4
Oman, Gulf of, Iran, Oman 173 J16
Omaok, Palau 216 Q10
Ōma Zaki, Japan 184 H13
Omba see Aoba, island, Vanuatu 218 C2
Omboué (Fernan Vaz), Gabon 201 L15
Ombu, China 180 K6
Omchak, Russ. 159 F20
Omdurman (Umm Durmān), Sudan 199 D13
Omega Gardens, Cayman Is., U.K. 120 J2
Omegna, It. 150 D3
Omelek, island, Marshall Is. 216 M5
Ometepec, Mex. 114 K12
Omihi, N.Z. 213 N17
Omin, F.S.M. 217 C18
Omodeo, Lago, It. 151 N4
Omoka, island, Cook Is., N.Z. 219 B17
Omoka, Cook Is., N.Z. 219 B17
Omolon, river, Russ. 159 D20
Omolon, Russ. 159 D20
Omoto, Japan 184 K14
Omsk, Russ. 158 K10
Omsukchan, Russ. 159 E20
Ōmu, Japan 184 E14
Omul, peak, Rom. 153 E15
Ōmuta, Japan 185 R4
Oña, Sp. 144 C11
Onaf, island, F.S.M. 217 A15
Onaga, Kans., U.S. 105 S9
Onalaska, Wis., U.S. 98 K3
Onamia, Minn., U.S. 104 H11
Onamue, island, F.S.M. 217 C14
Onancock, Va., U.S. 96 E14
Onaram, island, F.S.M. 217 C16
Onarga, Ill., U.S. 99 Q7
Onawa, Iowa, U.S. 105 N9
Onaway, Mich., U.S. 98 H11
Oncativo, Arg. 132 K10
Ondangwa, Namibia 202 F6
Ondjiva, Angola 202 F6
Ondo, Nigeria 201 G13
Ondor Sum, China 182 B5
One, Motu, Fr. Polynesia, Fr. 219 J14
One, Motu, Fr. Polynesia, Fr. 219 E14
One and Half Degree Channel, Maldives 179 W3
Oneata, island, Fiji Is. 218 J9
Onega, river, Russ. 158 E7
Onega, Russ. 158 E8
Onega, Lake see Onezhskoye Ozero, Russ. 138 C10
Onega Bay, Russ. 138 B10
Oneida, N.Y., U.S. 94 J9
Oneida, Tenn., U.S. 101 E18
Oneida Lake, N.Y., U.S. 94 J8
O'Neill, Nebr., U.S. 105 N6
Onekama, Mich., U.S. 98 J9
Onekotan, island, Russ. 159 H23
Onemak, island, Marshall Is. 216 L4
Onemak East Passage, Marshall Is. 216 L4
Onemak West Passage, Marshall Is. 216 L4
Oneonta, Ala., U.S. 101 J15
Oneonta, N.Y., U.S. 94 K10
Oneroa, island, Cook Is., N.Z. 218 Q9
Onevai, island, Tonga 218 H12
Onezhskoye Ozero, Russ. 156 E9
Ongarue, N.Z. 213 K19
Ongjin, N. Korea 182 E12
Ongniud Qi (Wudan), China 182 A8
Ongole, India 179 N7
Ongombua, Île, New Caledonia, Fr. 218 B6
Oni, Rep. of Georgia 169 B17
Onich, Scot., U.K. 142 L8
Onida, S. Dak., U.S. 104 K5
Onilahy, river, Madagascar 203 H16
Onima, Neth. Antilles, Neth. 121 Q19
Oniotto, island, Marshall Is. 216 K3
Onishika, Japan 184 E13
Onitsha, Nigeria 201 H14
Oniwaki, Japan 184 D13
Onnang, island, F.S.M. 217 C14
Ono, island, Fiji Is. 218 K6
Ōno, Japan 185 P9
Ono Channel, Fiji Is. 218 K6
Onoheha, Pass d', Fr. Polynesia, Fr. 219 N17
Ono-i-Lau, island, Fiji Is. 214 K9
Onomichi, Japan 185 Q7
Onon, Mongolia 181 C13
Onon, Mongolia 181 C13
Onon, river, Russ. 166 E11
Onsen, Japan 185 P8
Onslow, W. Aust., Austral. 211 T1
Ontario, Calif., U.S. 109 X9
Ontario, Can. 83 N16
Ontario, Oreg., U.S. 108 H9
Ontario, Lake, Can., U.S. 85 E19
Ontinyent, Sp. 145 J14
Ontonagon, Mich., U.S. 98 E5
Ontong Java Atoll (Lord Howe Atoll), Solomon Is. 217 J18
Ōnuma, Japan 184 H13
Ooa, island, Marshall Is. 216 N8
Oodnadatta, S. Aust., Austral. 211 V9
'Ō'okala, Hawai'i, U.S. 113 K21
Oologah Lake, Okla., U.S. 102 E13
Ooma, Banaba, Kiribati 217 E20
Oostende (Ostend), Belg. 146 K10
Oosterschelde, bay, Neth. 146 K11
Oostpunt, cape, Neth. Antilles, Neth. 121 Q15
'Ōpana Point, Hawai'i, U.S. 113 G17
Opava, Czech Rep. 149 H14
Opelika, Ala., U.S. 101 L17
Opelousas, La., U.S. 100 P8
Open Bay, P.N.G. 213 C21
Opheim, Mont., U.S. 106 A12
Ophir, Oreg., U.S. 108 K1
Ophthalmia Range, Austral. 210 F3
'Opihikao, Hawai'i, U.S. 113 N22
Opinaca, river, Que., Can. 83 M18
Opoa, Fr. Polynesia, Fr. 219 B23
Opochka, Russ. 156 H5
Opole, Pol. 149 G14
Oporto see Porto, Port. 144 E5
Opotiki, N.Z. 213 K20
Opp, Ala., U.S. 101 N16
Oppdal, Nor. 140 J11
Opportunity, Wash., U.S. 108 C9
Optima Lake, Okla., U.S. 102 E6
Opunake, N.Z. 213 L18
Opunohu, Baie d', Fr. Polynesia, Fr. 219 N14
Opuwo, Namibia 202 F6
Opyan, Puntan, N. Mariana Is., U.S. 216 D4
Or, river, Kaz. 174 D9
Or, Les Îles d' see Hyères, Îles de, Fr. 147 Y14
Oracabessa, Jam. 120 H9
Oracle, Ariz., U.S. 107 V8
Oradea, Rom. 152 C11
Orai, India 178 G7
Oral, Kaz. 174 C6
Oran, Alg. 196 A10
Orange, Fr. 147 W13
Orange, N.S.W., Austral. 211 X14
Orange, river, Namibia, S. Af. 202 K7
Orange, Tex., U.S. 103 Q16
Orange, Va., U.S. 96 D12
Orange, Cabo, Braz. 130 B12
Orange Bay, Jam. 120 H5
Orangeburg, S.C., U.S. 96 L9
Orange Cay, Bahamas 116 E10
Orange City, Iowa, U.S. 104 M9
Orange Grove, Tex., U.S. 103 T10
Orange Hill, St. Vincent & the Grenadines 121 J17
Orange Park, Fla., U.S. 97 R8
Orange Walk, Belize 115 J16
Oranienburg, Ger. 148 D10
Oranjemund, Namibia 202 K6
Oranjestad, Aruba, Neth. 121 Q16
Oranjestad, Neth. Antilles, Neth. 119 G15
Oraviţa, Rom. 152 E11
Orbe, Switz. 150 B1
Orbetello, It. 150 J7
Orbost, Vic., Austral. 211 Z13
Orcadas, station, Antarctica 226 A4
Orce, Sp. 144 K12
Orchard City, Colo., U.S. 107 N10
Orchid Island see Lanyu, Taiwan, China 183 S10
Orchila, Isla, Venez. 128 A10
Ord, Nebr., U.S. 105 P6
Ord, river, W. Aust., Austral. 211 Q6
Ord, Mount, Austral. 210 D5
Orderville, Utah, U.S. 107 P6
Ordes, Sp. 144 B6
Ordino, region, Andorra 160 H3
Ordino, Andorra 160 H3
Ordos see Mu Us Shamo, China 182 D2
Ordot, Guam, U.S. 216 C11
Ord River, W. Aust., Austral. 211 R7
Ordu, Turk. 168 D12
Ordubad, Azerb. 169 F20
Ordway, Colo., U.S. 107 N14
Ordzhonikidze, Ukr. 157 Q7
Oreba, island, Marshall Is. 216 K1
Örebro, Sw. 141 L13
Oregon, Ill., U.S. 99 N5
Oregon, Ohio, U.S. 99 N12
Oregon, U.S. 108 H3
Oregon Caves National Monument, Oreg., U.S. 108 L2
Oregon City, Oreg., U.S. 108 F3
Oregon Dunes National Recreation Area, Oreg., U.S. 108 H2
Orekhovo-Zuyevo, Russ. 156 J10
Orel, Russ. 156 L9
Orellana, Peru 130 F4
Orellana, Embalse de, Sp. 144 H9
Orem, Utah, U.S. 106 L7
Ore Mountains, Czech Rep., Ger. 148 G10
Ören, Turk. 168 H3
Orenburg, Russ. 158 J7
Orense see Ourense, Sp. 144 C6
Örenşehir, Turk. 168 F11
Oreor see Koror, island, Palau 216 N11
Orepuki, N.Z. 213 R15
Orestiáda, Gr. 155 A17

Oreti, river, N.Z. 213 R15
Orfanoú, Kólpos, Gr. 154 C12
Orford Ness, Eng., U.K. 143 U16
Organ Pipe Cactus National Monument, Ariz., U.S. 107 V6
Organyà, Sp. 145 C16
Orgaz, Sp. 144 G10
Orgun, Afghan. 177 P8
Orhangazi, Turk. 168 D5
Orhei, Mold. 157 Q5
Orhon, river, Mongolia 180 C12
Orick, Calif., U.S. 108 M2
Oricum see Orikon, ruin, Albania 152 M9
Orient, Wash., U.S. 108 A8
Oriental, Cordillera, S. Amer. 126 C2
Oriental, Grand Erg, Alg. 196 C11
Orientale, Baie, St. Martin, Fr. 121 B15
Oriente, Arg. 133 N12
Orihuela, Sp. 145 K14
Orikhiv, Ukr. 157 R8
Orikon (Oricum), ruin, Albania 152 M9
Orinduik, Guyana 129 E13
Orinoco, river, Venez. 128 C12
Orinoco, Source of the, S. Amer. 126 C5
Orinoco River Delta, S. Amer. 126 A6
Oristano, It. 151 N3
Oristano, Golfo di, It. 151 P3
Oriximiná, Braz. 130 D11
Orizaba, Pico de, Mex. 114 J12
Orjen, peak, Bosn. & Herzg., Serb. & Mont. 152 J8
Orkanger, Nor. 140 H11
Orkney Islands, Scot., U.K. 142 G11
Orland, Calif., U.S. 109 P4
Orlando, Fla., U.S. 97 T9
Orléans, Fr. 147 R9
Orleans, Nebr., U.S. 105 R5
Orleans, Vt., U.S. 95 F13
Ormara, Pak. 177 W4
Ormara, Ras, Pak. 177 W4
Orménio, Gr. 155 A16
Ormoc, Philippines 189 E15
Ormond Beach, Fla., U.S. 97 S9
Ormos Stomíou, Gr. 154 Q12
Örnsköldsvik, Sw. 141 H14
Orobie, Alpi, It. 150 C5
Orocovis, P.R., U.S. 120 N4
Orocué, Col. 128 F7
Orofino, Idaho, U.S. 106 D4
Oro Grande, Calif., U.S. 109 W9
Orohena, Mont, Fr. Polynesia, Fr. 219 P16
Oroluk Atoll, F.S.M. 216 Q7
Oromahana, island, Fr. Polynesia, Fr. 219 A23
Oromia, region, Eth. 199 G15
Orona, island, Kiribati 214 H10
Orono, Me., U.S. 95 E17
Oronsay, island, Scot., U.K. 142 M7
Orontes see Al 'Āş, river, Syr. 170 F7
Oropesa, Sp. 144 G9
Oropuche Lagoon, Trinidad & Tobago 121 Q22
Orós, Braz. 131 F17
Orosei, It. 151 N5
Orosei, Golfo di, It. 151 N5
Orosháza, Hung. 149 M16
Orote Peninsula, Guam, U.S. 216 C9
Oroville, Calif., U.S. 109 P4
Oroville, Wash., U.S. 108 A7
Oroville, Lake, Calif., U.S. 109 P4
Orphan Knoll, Atl. Oc. 236 F7
Orr, Minn., U.S. 104 E12
Orsa, Sw. 140 K12
Orsha, Belarus 156 K6
Orshanka, Russ. 156 H14
Orsk, Russ. 158 J8
Orsogna, It. 150 K10
Orşova, Rom. 152 F12
Orta, Turk. 168 D8
Ortaca, Turk. 168 H4
Orta Nova, It. 150 L12
Ortegal, Cabo, Sp. 144 A6
Ortepah, Afghan. 176 L4
Orthez, Fr. 147 X6
Ortigueira, Sp. 144 A6
Ortisei, It. 150 C7
Ortles, range, It. 150 C6
Ortoire, river, Trinidad & Tobago 121 Q23
Ortón, river, Bol. 130 G7
Ortona, It. 150 K11
Ortonville, Minn., U.S. 104 J8
Orto Surt, Russ. 159 H17
Orukuizu, island, Palau 216 P10
Orūmīyeh, Iran 172 B10
Orūmīyeh, Daryācheh-ye (Lake Urmia), Iran 172 B10
Orune, It. 151 N4
Oruro, Bol. 130 K7
Oruzgan, Afghan. 177 P6
Orvieto, It. 150 J8
Oryakhovo, Bulg. 153 G13
Os, river, Andorra 160 K2
Os, Sp. 160 J2
Osa, Península de, Costa Rica 115 P19
Osage, Iowa, U.S. 104 M12
Osage, river, Mo., U.S. 105 T13
Osage Beach, Mo., U.S. 105 T12
Osage City, Kans., U.S. 105 T9
Osaka, Japan 185 P10
Ōsaka, Japan 185 Q9
Osakarovka, Kaz. 175 D14
Ōsaka Wan, Japan 185 Q8
Osakis, Minn., U.S. 104 H10
Osawatomie, Kans., U.S. 105 T10
Osborne, Kans., U.S. 105 S6
Osborn Plateau, Ind. Oc. 240 J11
Oscar II Coast, Antarctica 226 D4
Osceola, Ark., U.S. 100 F11
Osceola, Iowa, U.S. 105 Q11
Osceola, Mo., U.S. 105 T11
Osceola, Nebr., U.S. 105 Q7
Oschiri, It. 150 M4
Oscoda, Mich., U.S. 98 J12
Oscura, Punta, Eq. Guinea 204 N6
Oscura Peak, N. Mex., U.S. 107 T12
Ösel see Saaremaa, island, Est. 141 L15
Osen, Nor. 140 G11
Osgood Mountains, Nev., U.S. 108 M9
Osh, Kyrg. 176 G10
Oshawa, Ont., Can. 83 Q18
Ō Shima, Japan 185 S2
Ō Shima, Japan 184 H12
Ō Shima, Japan 185 Q12
Ō Shima, Japan 185 R9
Oshkosh, Nebr., U.S. 105 P2
Oshkosh, Wis., U.S. 98 K6
Oshogbo, Nigeria 201 G13
Oshta, Russ. 156 E8
Oshwe, Dem. Rep. of the Congo 198 L9
Osijek, Croatia 152 E8
Osimo, It. 150 H9
Oskaloosa, Iowa, U.S. 105 P12
Oskarshamn, Sw. 141 M13
Öskemen (Ust' Kamenogorsk), Kaz. 175 D18
Oskoba, Russ. 159 J14
Oslo, Minn., U.S. 104 E8
Oslo, Nor. 140 L11
Osmanabad, India 178 M5
Osmancık, Turk. 168 D10
Osmaniye, Turk. 168 H11
Osnabrück, Ger. 148 D6
Osorno, Chile 133 Q6
Osorno, Sp. 144 C10
Osorno, Volcán, Chile 133 Q6
Osprey, Fla., U.S. 97 V7
Óssa, Óros, Gr. 154 E10
Ossa, Mount, Austral. 210 M16
Ossabaw Island, Ga., U.S. 97 N9
Ossabaw Sound, Ga., U.S. 97 N9
Ossa de Montiel, Sp. 144 H12
Osseo, Wis., U.S. 98 J3
Ossineke, Mich., U.S. 98 H12
Ostashkov, Russ. 156 H7
Ostend see Oostende, Belg. 146 K10
Østerdalen, valley, Nor. 140 J11
Osterholz-Scharmbeck, Ger. 148 C7
Östersund, Sw. 140 H12
Östhammar, Sw. 141 K14
Ostiglia, It. 150 E7
Ostrava, Czech Rep. 149 H14
Ostróda, Pol. 149 C15
Ostrogozhsk, Russ. 157 N10
Ostrołęka, Pol. 149 C16
Ostrov, Russ. 156 H5
Ostrowiec Świętokrzyski, Pol. 149 F16
Ostrów Mazowiecka, Pol. 149 D16
Ostrów Wielkopolski, Pol. 149 E14
O'Sullivan Dam, Wash., U.S. 108 D7
Osŭm, river, Bulg. 153 H14
Ōsumi Kaikyō, Japan 185 U4
Ōsumi Shotō, Japan 185 U4
Osuna, Sp. 144 L9
Oswego, N.Y., U.S. 94 H8
Oswestry, Eng., U.K. 143 T10
Ōta, Japan 185 N12
Otaki, N.Z. 213 M19
Otar, Kaz. 175 H16
Otare, Cerro, Col. 128 G6
Otaru, Japan 184 F13
Otavalo, Ecua. 128 H3
Otavi, Namibia 202 G7
O.T. Downs, N. Terr., Austral. 211 Q9
Oţelu Roşu, Rom. 152 E12
Otepipi, island, Fr. Polynesia, Fr. 219 L16
Othello, Wash., U.S. 108 D7
Othoní, island, Gr. 154 E5
Othris, Óros, Gr. 154 G10
Otish, Monts, Que., Can. 83 M20
Otjiwarongo, Namibia 202 G7
Otobe, Japan 184 H12
Otog Qi, China 182 D2
Otoineppu, Japan 184 E14
Otradnoye, Russ. 159 G23
Otradnyy, Russ. 156 K16
Otranto, It. 151 N16
Otranto, Strait of, Eur. 138 K8
Otsego, Mich., U.S. 98 M9
Ōtsu, Japan 184 G15
Ōtsu, Japan 185 Q9
Ōtsuchi, Japan 184 K14
Ottawa, Ill., U.S. 99 P6
Ottawa, Kans., U.S. 105 T10
Ottawa, Ohio, U.S. 99 P11
Ottawa, Ont., Can. 83 Q19
Ottawa, river, Ont., Que., Can. 83 P18
Ottawa Islands, Nunavut, Can. 83 J17
Ottenby, Sw. 141 N14
Otter Rapids, Ont., Can. 83 N17
Otter Tail Lake, Minn., U.S. 104 H9
Ottmarsheim, Fr. 147 Q15
Ottumwa, Iowa, U.S. 105 Q12
Otukpo, Nigeria 201 G14
Otutéhé, Fr. Polynesia, Fr. 219 M20
Otuzco, Peru 130 F2
Otway, Bahía, Chile 133 X7
Otway, Cape, Austral. 210 M12
Otway, Seno de, Chile 133 W7
Otztal Alps, It. 150 B6
Ou, river, China 183 N9
Ou, river, Laos 186 G10
'O'ua, island, Tonga 218 Q6
Oua, Île, New Caledonia, Fr. 218 D9
Ouachita, river, Ark., La., U.S. 100 L8
Ouachita, Lake, Ark., U.S. 100 G7
Ouachita Mountains, Ark., Okla., U.S. 85 K13
Ouaco, New Caledonia, Fr. 218 C6
Ouadane, Mauritania 196 F6
Ouadda, Cen. Af. Rep. 198 G10
Ouagadougou, Burkina Faso 200 E10
Ouahigouya, Burkina Faso 200 D10
Oualâta, Mauritania 196 G7
Oua-n-Ahaggar, Tassili, Alg. 196 F11
Ouanda Djallé, Cen. Af. Rep. 198 G10
Ouani, Comoros 205 N16
Ouargla, Alg. 196 C11
Ouarra, river, Cen. Af. Rep. 198 H11
Oubangui see Ubangi, river, Dem. Rep. of the Congo 198 J8
Oubatche, New Caledonia, Fr. 218 C6
Oudtshoorn, S. Af. 202 M8
Ouégoa, New Caledonia, Fr. 218 C6
Ouen, Île, New Caledonia, Fr. 218 E9
Ouessa, Burkina Faso 200 F10
Ouessant, Île d', Fr. 147 P2
Ouesso, Congo 201 K18
Ouest, Baie de l', Wallis & Futuna, Fr. 218 B11
Ouest, Pointe de l', Que., Can. 83 M21
Ouezzane, Mor. 196 A9
Oufrane, Alg. 196 D10
Ouinné, Baie, New Caledonia, Fr. 218 D9
Oujda, Mor. 196 B9
Oujeft, Mauritania 196 F6
Oulainen, Fin. 141 G15
Oullins, Fr. 147 U13
Oulu, river, Fin. 138 B9
Oulu (Uleåborg), Fin. 141 F15
Oulujärvi, lake, Fin. 138 C9
Oulujoki, river, Fin. 141 F15
Oulx, It. 150 E1
Oum Chalouba, Chad 197 H15
Oum Hadjer, Chad 197 J15
Oumm ed Drous Telli, Sebkhet, Mauritania 196 E6
Ounianga Kébir, Chad 197 G15
Ou Nua, Laos 186 G9
Our, river, Belg., Ger., Lux. 160 G10
Ouranópoli, Gr. 155 D13
Ouray, Colo., U.S. 107 P11
Ouray, Utah, U.S. 106 L9
Ourense (Orense), Sp. 144 C6
Ourinhos, Braz. 130 M12
Ourique, Port. 144 K5
Ouse, river, Eng., U.K. 143 Q12
Ouse, Tas., Austral. 211 Z16
Oust, Fr. 147 Y8
Outer Bailey, Atl. Oc. 236 D11
Outer Brass Island, Virgin Islands, U.S. 120 M8
Outer Hebrides, Scot., U.K. 142 J6
Outjo, Namibia 202 G6
Outokumpu, Fin. 141 G17
Out Skerries, Scot., U.K. 142 D12
Ouvéa, island, New Caledonia, Fr. 214 K7
Ouvéa, Baie d', New Caledonia, Fr. 218 C8
Ouvéa, Île (Uvéa), New Caledonia, Fr. 218 C8
Ouyen, Vic., Austral. 211 Y11
Ouzouer-le-Marché, Fr. 147 Q9
Ovacık, Turk. 168 J9
Ovaka, island, Tonga 218 M11
Ovalau, island, Fiji Is. 218 H7
Ovalle, Chile 132 J6
Ovamboland, region, Namibia 202 F6
Ovar, Port. 144 E5
Ovau, island, Solomon Is. 217 K15
Overland Park, Kans., U.S. 105 S10
Overland Village, St. Vincent & the Grenadines 121 J17
Overstrand, Eng., U.K. 143 S15
Overton, Nev., U.S. 109 T12
Overton, Tex., U.S. 102 M14
Ovgos, river, Cyprus 160 N7
Oviedo, Dom. Rep. 117 N17
Oviedo, Sp. 144 B8
Ovoot, Mongolia 181 E14
Ovruch, Ukr. 156 M5
Ow, island, F.S.M. 217 C15
Owaka, N.Z. 213 R16
Owando, Congo 201 L18
Owase, Japan 185 R9
Owatonna, Minn., U.S. 104 L11
Owbeh, Afghan. 176 M3
Owego, N.Y., U.S. 94 L8
Owel, Lough, Ire. 143 R5
Owen, Mount, N.Z. 213 M17
Owen Fracture Zone, Ind. Oc. 240 F6
Owens, river, Calif., U.S. 109 T8
Owensboro, Ky., U.S. 101 C15
Owens Lake Bed, Calif., U.S. 109 U8
Owen Stanley Range, P.N.G. 213 E20
Owensville, Mo., U.S. 105 T14
Owia, St. Vincent & the Grenadines 121 J17
Owl Creek Mountains, Wyo., U.S. 106 G10
Owo, Nigeria 201 G13
Owosso, Mich., U.S. 98 L11
Owyhee, river, Idaho, Oreg., U.S. 108 J9
Owyhee, Nev., U.S. 108 L10
Owyhee, Lake, Oreg., U.S. 108 J9
Owyhee Mountains, Idaho, U.S. 106 H3
Oxford, Ala., U.S. 101 J16
Oxford, Eng., U.K. 143 V12
Oxford, Kans., U.S. 105 V8
Oxford, Miss., U.S. 100 H12
Oxford, N.Z. 213 P17
Oxford, Nebr., U.S. 105 R5
Oxford, Ohio, U.S. 99 S11
Oxford, Pa., U.S. 94 Q8
Oxiá, island, Gr. 154 H8
Oxnard, Calif., U.S. 109 X7
Oxus see Amu Darya, river, Turkm. 174 M11
Oyem, Gabon 201 K16
Oyo, Congo 201 L18
Oyo, Nigeria 200 G12
Oyonnax, Fr. 147 T13
Oyotung, Russ. 159 D18
Oyster Bay, Jam. 120 H7
Oysterhaven, Ire. 143 V4
Oyster Pond, St. Martin, Fr. 121 B15
Oysterville, Wash., U.S. 108 D2
Oytal, Kaz. 175 J15
Oyyl, river, Kaz. 174 E7
Oyyl, Kaz. 174 E7
Özalp, Turk. 169 F18
Ozark, Ala., U.S. 101 M17
Ozark, Ark., U.S. 100 F7
Ozark, Mo., U.S. 105 V12
Ozark National Scenic Riverways, Mo., U.S. 105 U14
Ozark Plateau, Mo., Okla., U.S. 85 J13
Ozarks, Lake of the, Mo., U.S. 105 T12
Ózd, Hung. 149 K16
Özen, Kaz. 174 H6
Ozernovskiy, Russ. 159 G23
Ozernoy, Mys, Russ. 159 E22
Ozernoy, Zaliv, Russ. 159 E22
Ozery, Russ. 156 K10
Ozette Lake, Wash., U.S. 108 B2
Ozgön, Kyrg. 176 F11
Ozieri, It. 150 M4
Ozinki, Russ. 156 M15
Ozona, Tex., U.S. 103 P6
Ōzu, Japan 185 R6
Ozurget'i, Rep. of Georgia 169 C16

P

Paagoumène, New Caledonia, Fr. 218 C6
Paama, island, Vanuatu 218 E3
Paamiut, Greenland, Den. 81 D22
Paarden Bay, Aruba, Neth. 121 Q16
Paarl, S. Af. 202 M7
Pa'auhau, Hawai'i, U.S. 113 K20
Pa'auilo, Hawai'i, U.S. 113 K20
Paavola, Fin. 141 G15
Pabbay, island, Scot., U.K. 142 J6
Pabbay, island, Scot., U.K. 142 K6
Pabianice, Pol. 149 E15
Pabna, Bangladesh 178 H12
Pacaraima, Sierra, S. Amer. 126 C5
Pacasmayo, Peru 130 F2
Paceco, It. 151 S8
Pachiá, island, Gr. 155 N16
Pachino, It. 151 U12
Pachuca, Mex. 114 H12
Pachyammos, Cyprus 160 N6
Pacific-Antarctic Ridge, Antarctic Oc. 244 M9
Pacific Beach, Wash., U.S. 108 C2
Pacific City, Oreg., U.S. 108 F2
Pacific Grove, Calif., U.S. 109 T4
Pacy, Fr. 147 P9
Padam, India 177 N14
Padang, island, Indonesia 188 H6
Padang, Indonesia 188 J5
Padang Endau, Malaysia 187 U11
Padangpanjang, Indonesia 188 J5
Padangsidempuan, Indonesia 188 H5
Padangtiji, Indonesia 188 G4
Padangtikar Maya, island, Indonesia 188 J9
Paden City, W. Va., U.S. 96 C9
Paderborn, Ger. 148 E7
Padeş, peak, Rom. 152 E12
Padloping Island, Nunavut, Can. 83 F19
Padma (Ganges), river, Bangladesh 178 H12
Padmanabhapuram, India 179 S5
Padova (Padua), It. 150 E7
Padrauna, India 178 G9
Padre Island, Tex., U.S. 84 P12
Padre Island National Seashore, Tex., U.S. 103 U11
Padua see Padova, It. 150 E7
Paducah, Ky., U.S. 101 D13
Paducah, Tex., U.S. 102 J7
Paea, Fr. Polynesia, Fr. 219 P15
Paektu-san, peak, N. Korea 182 B13
Paeroa, N.Z. 213 J19
Paestum, ruin, It. 151 N11
Paeu, Solomon Is. 217 R23
Paeua, island, Fr. Polynesia, Fr. 219 K17
Pafos, Cyprus 160 Q5
Pafúri, Mozambique 202 H12
Pag, island, Croatia 152 F5
Pagadian, Philippines 189 F14
Pagai Selatan, island, Indonesia 188 K5
Pagai Utara, island, Indonesia 188 K5
Pagan, island, N. Mariana Is., U.S. 216 B2
Paganico, It. 150 J7
Pagassitikós Kólpos, Gr. 154 F11
Pagatan, Indonesia 188 K11
Page, Ariz., U.S. 107 Q7
Page, N. Dak., U.S. 104 G7
Pageland, S.C., U.S. 96 J9
Paget Island, Bermuda, U.K. 120 A4
Pagnag, China 180 K8
Pago, river, Guam, U.S. 216 C11
Pago Bay, Guam, U.S. 216 C11
Pagoda Point, Myanmar 186 L5
Pago Pago, Amer. Samoa, U.S. 218 M7
Pago Pago Harbor, Amer. Samoa, U.S. 218 M8
Pagosa Springs, Colo., U.S. 107 P11
Pagri, China 180 M7

Pagua Bay, Dominica 121 E20
Pagua Point, Dominica 121 E20
Pāhala, Hawai'i, U.S. 113 P20
Paharpur, Pak. 177 P9
Pāhoa, Hawai'i, U.S. 113 M22
Pahokee, Fla., U.S. 97 V10
Pahrump, Nev., U.S. 109 U11
Pahsimeroi, river, Idaho, U.S. 106 F6
Pahute Mesa, Nev., U.S. 109 S10
Pāi'a, Hawai'i, U.S. 113 G17
Paige, Tex., U.S. 103 Q11
Päijänne, lake, Fin. 141 H16
Paili, P.N.G. 213 E20
Pailin City, Cambodia 187 N10
Pailolo Channel, Hawai'i, U.S. 113 F16
Paine, Cerro, Chile 133 V7
Painesville, Ohio, U.S. 99 N15
Painted Desert, Ariz., U.S. 107 R7
Paint Rock, Tex., U.S. 103 N7
Paintsville, Ky., U.S. 101 B20
Paio, Motu, Fr. Polynesia, Fr. 219 K16
Païromé, New Caledonia, Fr. 218 B6
Paisley, Oreg., U.S. 108 K6
Paistunturit, Fin. 141 C14
Paita, New Caledonia, Fr. 218 E8
Paita, Peru 130 E1
Paja, Cerro, Ecua. 128 R9
Pajala, Sw. 141 E14
Pajares, Puerto de, Sp. 144 B9
Pajaro Point, Virgin Islands, U.K. 120 Q10
Pakalā, Hawai'i, U.S. 112 C5
Pakaraima Mountains, Braz. 130 A9
Pakbèng, Laos 186 H9
Pakin Atoll, F.S.M. 216 Q8
Pakistan, Asia 167 V6
Pakleni Otoci, Croatia 152 H6
Pak Nam Chumphon, Thai. 187 P8
Pakokku, Myanmar 186 G5
Pakpattan, Pak. 177 R11
Pak Phanang, Thai. 187 R8
Paks, Hung. 149 M15
Pakuru, island, F.S.M. 217 C15
Pakwach, Uganda 198 J12
Pakxan, Laos 186 J11
Pakxé, Laos 186 L12
Pal, Andorra 160 J2
Pala, Chad 197 K14
Pala, Myanmar 187 N7
Palace of Holy Office, Vatican City 161 R17
Palace of Justice, Monaco 161 E21
Palace of Monaco, Monaco 161 E21
Palace of the Tribunal, Vatican City 161 Q15
Palace Square, Monaco 161 E21
Palacios, Tex., U.S. 103 S13
Palafrugell, Sp. 145 D18
Palagruža (Pelagosa), island, Croatia 152 J6
Palaichori, Cyprus 160 P7
Palaiochóra, Gr. 154 Q12
Palaiseau, Fr. 147 P10
Palalankwe, India 179 R14
Palamás, Gr. 154 F9
Palana, Russ. 159 E21
Palanga, Lith. 141 N15
Palangkaraya, Indonesia 188 K11
Palanpur, India 178 H3
Palaoa Point, Hawai'i, U.S. 113 H14
Palapye, Botswana 202 H10
Palatka, Fla., U.S. 97 R8
Palatka, Russ. 159 F20
Palau, Pac. Oc. 214 F2
Palauk, Myanmar 187 N7
Palauli Bay, Samoa 218 L2
Palau Trench, Pac. Oc. 238 J5
Palaw, Myanmar 187 N7
Palawan, island, Philippines 188 E12
Palawan Trough, Pac. Oc. 238 J3
Palazzolo Acreide, It. 151 T11
Paldiski, Est. 141 K16
Palékastro, Gr. 155 Q17
Palel, India 178 H15
Palembang, Indonesia 188 K7
Palencia, Sp. 144 D10
Paleokastritsa, Gr. 154 E6
Palermo, Calif., U.S. 109 P4
Palermo, It. 151 R9
Palestina, Chile 132 E7
Palestina, Virgin Islands, U.S. 120 M11
Palestine, region, Asia 170 J4
Palestine, Tex., U.S. 102 M13
Paletwa, Myanmar 186 G4
Palghat, India 179 R5
Pali, India 178 G4
Palian, Thai. 187 R8
Palikir, F.S.M. 217 F14
Palikir Passage, F.S.M. 217 F13
Palinuro, Capo, It. 151 N12
Palioúri, Gr. 154 E12
Palioúri, Akrotírio, Gr. 154 E12
Palisade, Nebr., U.S. 105 R4
Paliseul, Belg. 146 M13
Palk Bay, India 179 R7
Palkonda, India 178 L9
Palk Strait, India, Sri Lanka 179 R7
Pallasovka, Russ. 157 N14
Palliser, Cape, N.Z. 213 M19
Palma, Mozambique 203 C15
Palma, Badia de, Sp. 145 G18
Palma del Río, Sp. 144 K9
Palma de Mallorca, Sp. 145 G18
Palma di Montechiaro, It. 151 T10
Palmanova, It. 150 D9
Palmares, Braz. 131 G18
Palmas, Braz. 130 N12
Palmas, Cape, Cote dIvoire, Liberia 194 J2
Palmas, Golfo di, It. 151 Q3
Palmas Altas, P.R., U.S. 120 M3
Palma Soriano, Cuba 117 K13
Palm Bay, Fla., U.S. 97 U10
Palm Beach, Aruba, Neth. 121 Q16
Palm Beach, Fla., U.S. 97 V10
Palm City, Cuba 116 H11
Palm Coast, Fla., U.S. 97 S9
Palmdale, Calif., U.S. 109 W8
Palmeira, Cape Verde 205 B17
Palmeira dos Índios, Braz. 131 G17
Palmeirinhas, Ponta das, Angola 202 C5
Palmer, Alas., U.S. 111 J17
Palmer, station, Antarctica 226 D4
Palmer see Mameyes, P.R., U.S. 120 M5
Palmer Archipelago, Antarctica 226 D3
Palmer Land, Antarctica 226 E5
Palmerston Atoll, Cook Is., N.Z. 214 K11
Palmerston North, N.Z. 213 M19
Palmer Valley, N. Terr., Austral. 211 U8
Palmerville, Qnsld., Austral. 211 Q12
Palmetto, Fla., U.S. 97 U7
Palmetto Point, Jam. 120 H10
Palmi, It. 151 R13
Palmira, Col. 128 F4
Palm Island (Prune Island), St. Vincent & the Grenadines 119 M17
Palmiste Bay, Grenada 121 K22
Palm Point, Nigeria 201 J13
Palm Springs, Calif., U.S. 109 X10
Palmyra, Mo., U.S. 105 R13
Palmyra, N.Y., U.S. 94 J7
Palmyra see Tadmur, Syr. 170 G10
Palmyra Atoll, Pac. Oc. 214 F11
Palmyras Point, India 178 K11
Palo Alto, Calif., U.S. 109 S4
Palo Alto Battlefield National Historic Site, Tex., U.S. 103 W11
Palo Duro Creek, Tex., U.S. 102 H4
Paloh, Indonesia 188 H9
Palomar Mountain, Calif., U.S. 109 Y10
Palopo, Indonesia 189 K13
Palos, Cabo de, Sp. 145 L14
Palo Seco, Trinidad & Tobago 121 Q22
Palouse, river, Wash., U.S. 108 D8
Palouse, Wash., U.S. 108 D9
Palpana, Cerro, Chile 132 D7
Palparara, Qnsld., Austral. 211 U11
Paltamo, Fin. 141 F16
Palu, Indonesia 189 J13
Palu, Turk. 169 F14
Palwal, India 178 F6
Pamiers, Fr. 147 Y9
Pamir, river, Afghan., Taj. 176 K10
Pamirs, range, Taj. 176 J10
Pamlico Sound, N.C., U.S. 96 H15
Pampa, Tex., U.S. 102 G6
Pampa del Castillo, region, Arg. 133 S8
Pampas, region, Arg. 132 M10
Pampas, Peru 130 H4
Pamplemousses, Mauritius 205 F20
Pamplona, Col. 128 D6
Pamplona (Iruña), Sp. 145 C13
Pamua, Solomon Is. 217 P20
Pamuk Imwintiati, island, F.S.M. 217 G13
Pamzal, India 176 M15
Pana, Ill., U.S. 99 S5
Panaca, Nev., U.S. 109 S12
Panacea, Fla., U.S. 97 R5
Panadura, Sri Lanka 179 T7
Panagyurishte, Bulg. 153 J14
Panahan, Indonesia 188 K10
Panaitan, island, Indonesia 188 M7
Panaji, India 179 N3
Panamá, Pan. 115 N21
Panamá, Golfo de, Pan. 115 P21
Panama, N. Amer. 81 Q21
Panama, Okla., U.S. 102 G14
Panama, Gulf of see Panamá, Golfo de, N. Amer. 80 Q9
Panama, Isthmus of, N. Amer. 80 Q9
Panama Basin, Pac. Oc. 239 J20
Panama Canal, Pan. 115 N21
Panama City, Fla., U.S. 97 R3
Panamint Range, Calif., U.S. 109 U9
Panay, island, Philippines 189 E14
Pancake Range, Nev., U.S. 109 Q11
Pančevo, Serb. & Mont. 152 F10
Pančićev Vrh, peak, Serb. & Mont. 152 H10
Pandharkawada, India 178 L6
Pandharpur, India 178 M4
Pandhurna, India 178 K6
Pandie Pandie, S. Aust., Austral. 211 U10
Paneri, India 178 G13
Panevėžys, Lith. 141 M16
Panfilovo, Russ. 157 N12
Pangai, Tonga 218 K12
Pangai, Tonga 218 P7
Pangaimoto, island, Tonga 218 L11
Pangaimotu, island, Tonga 218 H11
Pangalanes, Canal des, Madagascar 203 G18
Pangani, river, Tanzania 199 L14
Pangéo, Óros, Gr. 155 C13
Panggoe, Solomon Is. 217 L16
Pangi, Dem. Rep. of the Congo 198 L11
Pangkajene, Indonesia 189 L13
Pangkalpinang, Indonesia 188 K8
Pangnirtung, Nunavut, Can. 83 G19
Panguitch, Utah, U.S. 107 P6
Pangutaran Group, Philippines 189 F13
Panhandle, Tex., U.S. 102 G6
Panian, island, F.S.M. 217 G14
Pānī'au, peak, Hawai'i, U.S. 112 C3
Panié, Mont, New Caledonia, Fr. 218 C7
Panj, river, Afghan., Taj. 176 J9
Panj, Taj. 176 K8
Panjakent, Taj. 176 H6
Panjang, island, Indonesia 188 H9
Panjgur, Pak. 177 U3
Panjshir, river, Afghan. 176 L8
Panna, India 178 H7
Pannawonica, W. Aust., Austral. 211 T2
Pano Lefkara, Cyprus 160 P8
Pano Panagia, Cyprus 160 P6
Pano Platres, Cyprus 160 P7
Panorama Point, Nebr., U.S. USNP2 P1
Pánormos, Gr. 155 K14
Panovo, Russ. 159 J15
Panruti, India 179 Q7
Panshi, China 182 A12
Pantà de Riba-roga, Sp. 145 E15
Pantanal, wetland, Braz. 130 K10
Pantelleria, It. 151 U7
Pantelleria, Isola di, It. 151 U8
Pante Macassar (Oecusse), Timor-Leste 189 N15
Panvel, India 178 L3
Panxian, China 180 N12
Panzhihua, China 180 N11
Pao, river, Thai. 186 L10
Paola, Kans., U.S. 105 T10
Paola, Malta 161 K23
Paoli, Ind., U.S. 99 T9
Paopao, Fr. Polynesia, Fr. 219 N14
Pápa, Hung. 149 L13
Papa, Samoa 218 K1
Pāpa'aloa, Hawai'i, U.S. 113 L21
Pāpā Bay, Hawai'i, U.S. 113 P18
Pāpā Heiau, Hawai'i, U.S. 113 F15
Papai, Mount, Mauritius 205 J20
Pāpa'ikou, Hawai'i, U.S. 113 L21
Papakura, N.Z. 213 J19
Papara, Fr. Polynesia, Fr. 219 P16
Papa Stour, island, Scot., U.K. 142 D11
Papau, island, Cook Is., N.Z. 218 Q12
Papa Westray, island, Scot., U.K. 142 F10
Papeari, Fr. Polynesia, Fr. 219 P17
Papeete, Fr. Polynesia, Fr. 219 N15
Papenburg, Ger. 148 C6
Papenoo, river, Fr. Polynesia, Fr. 219 N16
Papenoo, Fr. Polynesia, Fr. 219 N16
Papetoai, Fr. Polynesia, Fr. 219 N14
Papíkio, peak, Gr. 155 B15
Pāpōhaku Beach, Hawai'i, U.S. 113 F13
Papua, Gulf of, P.N.G. 213 E19
Papua New Guinea 213 D19
Papua Passage, Cook Is., N.Z. 218 Q9
Papun, Myanmar 186 K7
Papunya, N. Terr., Austral. 211 T8
Pará, river, Braz. 131 D13
Parabel', Russ. 158 J12
Paracas Peninsula, S. Amer. 126 G2
Paracatu, Braz. 131 K14
Paracel Islands, China 188 B10
Parachilna, S. Aust., Austral. 211 W10
Parachinar, Pak. 177 N8
Parachute, Colo., U.S. 106 M10
Paraćin, Serb. & Mont. 152 G11
Paracuru, Braz. 131 E17
Paradeep see Paradwip, India 178 K11
Paradera, Aruba, Neth. 121 Q17
Paradise, Calif., U.S. 109 P4
Paradise, Grenada 121 K23
Paradise, Mich., U.S. 98 F10
Paradise, Mont., U.S. 106 C5
Paradise Bay, Malta 161 J21
Paradise Island, Bahamas 120 B11
Paradise Point, Bahamas 120 B8
Paradise Valley, Nev., U.S. 108 L9
Paradwip (Paradeep), India 178 K11
Paragould, Ark., U.S. 100 E11
Paraguá, river, Bol. 130 J9
Paragua, river, Venez. 128 E11
Paraguaipoa, Venez. 128 B6
Paraguaná, Península de, Venez. 128 A8
Paraguay, S. Amer. 127 J18
Paraguay, river, S. Amer. 126 H6
Paraíso, Mex. 115 J14
Paraíso do Tocantins, Braz. 131 G13
Parakou, Benin 200 F12
Paralakhemundi, India 178 L9
Paralimni, Cyprus 160 P10
Param, island, F.S.M. 217 F14
Paramaribo, Suriname 129 E16
Paramera, Sierra de la, Sp. 144 F9
Paramithía, Gr. 154 F7
Paramushir, island, Russ. 159 G23
Paran, Israel 171 Q5
Paranã, Braz. 131 H13
Paraná, Arg. 132 K12
Paraná, river, S. Amer. 126 L6
Paraná, Source of the, S. Amer. 126 J9
Paranaguá, Braz. 131 N13
Paranaguá Bay, S. Amer. 126 J8
Paranaíba, river, Braz. 130 K12
Paranaíba, Braz. 130 K12
Paranésti, Gr. 155 B13
Paraoa, island, Fr. Polynesia, Fr. 219 F20
Parchim, Ger. 148 C9
Pardés Hanna-Karkur, Israel 170 L5
Pardo, river, Braz. 131 J16
Pardo, river, Braz. 130 L11
Pardo, river, Braz. 131 L13
Pardoo, W. Aust., Austral. 211 S3
Pardubice, Czech Rep. 148 H12
Parea, Fr. Polynesia, Fr. 219 H14
Parece Vela, island, Japan 214 D3
Parecis, Serra dos, Braz. 130 H9
Paredes de Nava, Sp. 144 D10
Paredón, Mex. 114 F11
Parem, island, F.S.M. 217 C15
Paren', Russ. 159 D21
Parepare, Indonesia 189 K13
Párga, Gr. 154 F7
Pargny, Fr. 147 P12
Pargo, Ponta do, Madeira 204 M2
Parguera, P.R., U.S. 120 N2
Parham Peninsula, Antigua & Barbuda 121 B21
Parham Town, Virgin Islands, U.K. 120 Q7
Paria, river, Utah, U.S. 107 P7
Paria, Gulf of, Trinidad & Tobago 119 P16
Pariaguánviche, Venez. 128 C11
Paria Peninsula, S. Amer. 126 A5
Parika, Guyana 129 D14
Parikkala, Fin. 141 H17
Parima, Serra, Braz., Venez. 128 F11
Parintins, Braz. 130 D10
Paris, Ark., U.S. 100 F7
Paris, Fr. 147 P10
Paris, Ill., U.S. 99 R7
Paris, Kiribati 217 B22
Paris, Ky., U.S. 101 B18
Paris, Mo., U.S. 105 S13
Paris, Tenn., U.S. 101 E13
Paris, Tex., U.S. 102 K13
Paris Basin, Fr. 138 G4
Parisot, Fr. 147 W9
Parit Buntar, Malaysia 187 T9
Parker, Ariz., U.S. 107 T4
Parker, S. Dak., U.S. 104 M8
Parker Dam, Ariz., Calif., U.S. 109 W13
Parker Ranch, Hawai'i, U.S. 113 K19
Parkersburg, W. Va., U.S. 96 C8
Parkes, N.S.W., Austral. 211 X13
Park Falls, Wis., U.S. 98 G4
Park Forest, Ill., U.S. 99 P7
Parkin, Ark., U.S. 100 G10
Parkland, Wash., U.S. 108 C4
Park Range, Colo., U.S. 106 L12
Park Rapids, Minn., U.S. 104 G10
Park River, N. Dak., U.S. 104 E7
Parksley, Va., U.S. 96 E15
Parkston, S. Dak., U.S. 104 M7
Park Valley, Utah, U.S. 106 J6
Parlatuvier, Trinidad & Tobago 121 N18
Parma, Idaho, U.S. 106 G3
Parma, It. 150 F6
Parma, Ohio, U.S. 99 P14
Parmakan, Afghan. 177 N2
Parnaguá, Braz. 131 G14
Parnaíba, river, Braz. 131 E15
Parnaíba, Braz. 131 D16
Parnamirim, Braz. 131 F16
Parnassós, peak, Gr. 154 H10
Parnassus, N.Z. 213 N18
Párnitha, Óros, Gr. 154 J12
Párnonas, Óros, Gr. 154 L10
Pärnu, Est. 141 L16
Paromay, Russ. 159 H21
Paroo, W. Aust., Austral. 211 U3
Paropamisus Range see Sefid Kuh Mountains, Afghan. 176 M3
Páros, island, Gr. 155 L15
Páros, Gr. 155 L15
Parottee Point, Jam. 120 J7
Parowan, Utah, U.S. 107 P6
Parraburdoo, W. Aust., Austral. 211 T2
Parral, Chile 132 M6
Parras, Mex. 114 F10
Parry, Cape, N.W.T., Can. 82 E11
Parry Channel, Nunavut, Can. 83 D13
Parry Islands, N.W.T., Nunavut, Can. 83 C13
Parshall, N. Dak., U.S. 104 F3
Parsons, Kans., U.S. 105 U10
Parsons, Tenn., U.S. 101 F13
Parsons, W. Va., U.S. 96 C10
Parsons Range, Austral. 210 B9
Partanna, It. 151 S9
Parthenay, Fr. 147 S7
Partizansk, Russ. 159 M21
Paru, river, Braz. 130 C11
Paru de Oeste (Cumina), river, Braz. 130 C10
Paruru, Solomon Is. 217 P19
Parvatipuram, India 178 L9
Pasa, island, F.S.M. 217 G13
Pasadena, Calif., U.S. 109 X8
Pasadena, Tex., U.S. 103 R14
Pasado, Cabo, Ecua. 128 J2
Pasaje, Ecua. 128 L2
P'asanauri, Rep. of Georgia 169 B18
Pasarseluma, Indonesia 188 L6
Pascagoula, Miss., U.S. 101 P13
Paşcani, Rom. 153 B16
Pasco, Wash., U.S. 108 E7
Pascua, Isla de (Easter Island), Chile 215 L19
Pas de la Casa, Andorra 160 J5
Pasewalk, Ger. 148 C11
Pasighat, India 178 F15
Pasinler, Turk. 169 E16
Pasir Mas, Malaysia 187 S10
Pasley, Cape, Austral. 210 K5
Pašman, island, Croatia 152 G5
Pasni, Pak. 177 V3
Paso de Indios, Arg. 133 R8
Paso de los Toros, Uru. 132 K14
Paso Río Mayo, Arg. 133 S7
Paso Robles, Calif., U.S. 109 V5
Pasrur, Pak. 177 P12
Passau, Ger. 148 K10
Pass Christian, Miss., U.S. 100 P12
Passero, Capo, It. 151 U12
Passo Fundo, Braz. 130 P11
Passos, Braz. 131 L14
Passu Keah, island, China 188 C10
Pastavy, Belarus 156 J4
Pastaza, river, Ecua. 128 K4
Pastaza, river, Peru 130 E3
Pasto, Col. 128 H3

Pastora Peak, Ariz., U.S. 107 Q9
Pastos Bons, Braz. 131 F15
Pasuruan, Indonesia 188 M10
Patagonia, region, Arg. 133 W8
Patagonia, Ariz., U.S. 107 W8
Patan, India 178 J7
Patan see Lalitpur, Nepal 178 F10
Patanga, island, Cook Is., N.Z. 219 B18
Patani, Indonesia 189 J16
Patara Shiraki, Rep. of Georgia 169 C20
Patchogue, N.Y., U.S. 94 N12
Pate Island, Kenya 199 K15
Paterna, Sp. 145 H14
Paterson, N.J., U.S. 94 N11
Pathankot, India 177 P13
Pathein, Myanmar 186 K5
Pathfinder Reservoir, Wyo., U.S. 106 J11
Patía, river, Col. 128 G3
Patiala, India 178 E5
Patillas, P.R., U.S. 120 N5
Patio, Fr. Polynesia, Fr. 219 A23
Pati Point, Guam, U.S. 216 B12
Pativilca, Peru 130 G3
Pātkai Range, Myanmar 186 D6
Pátmos, island, Gr. 155 K17
Pátmos, Gr. 155 L17
Patna, India 178 G10
Patnos, Turk. 169 F17
Patos, Braz. 131 F17
Patos, Isla de, Venez. 121 P21
Patos de Minas, Braz. 131 K14
Patos Lagoon, S. Amer. 126 L8
Patquía, Arg. 132 H9
Pátra (Patrai), Gr. 154 J9
Patrai see Pátra, Gr. 154 J9
Patraïkós Kólpos, Gr. 154 H9
Patricio Lynch, Isla, Chile 133 U6
Patrick, Port, Vanuatu 218 H4
Patrington, Eng., U.K. 143 R14
Pattani, Thai. 187 S9
Patten, Me., U.S. 95 C18
Patterson, Calif., U.S. 109 S5
Patterson, La., U.S. 100 Q9
Patteson, Port, Vanuatu 218 B2
Patteson Passage, Vanuatu 218 C3
Patti, India 178 D5
Pattoki, Pak. 177 Q11
Patton Escarpment, Pac. Oc. 239 F16
Patu, Braz. 131 F17
Patuakhali, Bangladesh 178 J13
Patuca, river, Hond. 115 K18
Patuxent Range, Antarctica 226 H11
Patzau, Wis., U.S. 98 F2
Pátzcuaro, Mex. 114 J10
Pau, Fr. 147 Y7
Pauini, river, Braz. 130 F6
Pauini, Braz. 130 F6
Pauktaw, Myanmar 186 H4
Paulatuk, N.W.T., Can. 82 E11
Paulding, Ohio, U.S. 99 P11
Paulhaguet, Fr. 147 V11
Paulhan, Fr. 147 X11
Paulistana, Braz. 131 F16
Paulo Afonso, Braz. 131 G17
Pauls Valley, Okla., U.S. 102 H11
Paungbyin, Myanmar 186 F5
Paungde, Myanmar 186 J6
Pauni, India 178 K7
Pausania, It. 150 M4
Paʻuwela, Hawaiʻi, U.S. 113 G17
Pava, island, Tuvalu 217 J23
Pavagada, India 179 P5
Pavaiai, Amer. Samoa, U.S. 218 M7
Pavia, It. 150 E4
Pāvilosta, Latv. 141 M15
Pavlikeni, Bulg. 153 H15
Pavlodar, Kaz. 175 C16
Pavlof Volcano, Alas., U.S. 110 N12
Pavlovka, Russ. 156 L14
Pavlovo, Russ. 156 J12
Pavlovsk, Russ. 156 F6
Pavlovsk, Russ. 157 N11
Pavlovskaya, Russ. 157 S11
Pavuvu, island, Solomon Is. 217 N18
Pawarenga, N.Z. 213 H18
Pawhuska, Okla., U.S. 102 E12
Pawleys Island, S.C., U.S. 96 L11
Pawnee, Okla., U.S. 102 F11
Pawnee City, Nebr., U.S. 105 R9
Paw Paw, Mich., U.S. 98 M9
Pawtucket, R.I., U.S. 95 L14
Paxí, island, Gr. 154 F6
Paxí, Gr. 154 F6
Paxton, Ill., U.S. 99 Q7
Paxton, Nebr., U.S. 105 Q3
Payakumbuh, Indonesia 188 J6
Payer Mountains, Antarctica 227 B14
Payette, river, Idaho, U.S. 106 G3
Payette, Idaho, U.S. 106 G3
Payette Lake, Idaho, U.S. 106 F4
Payne, Lac, Que., Can. 83 J18
Paynes Find, W. Aust., Austral. 211 W3
Paynesville, Minn., U.S. 104 J10
Payong, Tanjong, Malaysia 188 G10
Paysandú, Uru. 132 K13
Payson, Ariz., U.S. 107 T7
Pazar, Turk. 169 D15
Pazar, Turk. 168 D8
Pazar, Turk. 168 E11
Pazarcık, Turk. 168 H12
Pazardzhik, Bulg. 153 J14
Pazin, Croatia 152 E4
Pčinja, river, Maced. 152 K11
Pea, river, Ala., U.S. 101 M16
Pea, Tonga 218 J11
Peabody, Kans., U.S. 105 T8
Peace, river, Alta., Can. 82 J11
Peace, river, Fla., U.S. 97 V8
Peace River, Alta., Can. 82 K10
Peach Springs, Ariz., U.S. 107 R5
Peacock Point, Wake I., U.S. 216 G8
Peak District, Eng., U.K. 143 S12
Peaked Mountain, Me., U.S. 95 B17
Peak Hill, W. Aust., Austral. 211 U3
Peale, Mount, Utah, U.S. 107 N9
Peale Island, Wake I., U.S. 216 F8
Peao, island, Kiribati 217 B20
Peard Bay, Alas., U.S. 111 B14
Pea Ridge National Military Park, Ark., U.S. 100 E6
Pearl, river, La., Miss., U.S. 85 L15
Pearl, Miss., U.S. 100 L11
Pearl and Hermes Atoll, Hawaiʻi, U.S. 112 K3
Pearl City, Hawaiʻi, U.S. 112 E11
Pearl Harbor, Hawaiʻi, U.S. 112 E11
Pearl River see Zhu, China 183 S4
Pearls Rock, Grenada 121 K23
Pearsall, Tex., U.S. 103 S9
Pearson, Ga., U.S. 97 P7
Peary Channel, Nunavut, Can. 83 B14
Peary Land, N. Amer. 80 A7
Pease, river, Tex., U.S. 102 J8
Pease Bay, Cayman Is., U.K. 120 J3
Peawanuk, Ont., Can. 83 L16
Pebane, Mozambique 203 F14
Pebas, Peru 130 D5
Pebble Island, Falkland Is., U.K. 133 V12
Peć, Serb. & Mont. 152 J10
Pecan Island, La., U.S. 100 Q8
Pechora, river, Russ. 158 F9
Pechora, Russ. 158 F10
Pechora Basin, Russ. 138 A12
Pechora Bay, Arctic Oc. 243 A16
Pechorskoy More, Russ. 158 E10
Pecos, N. Mex., U.S. 107 R13
Pecos, river, N. Mex., Tex., U.S. 84 M10
Pecos, Tex., U.S. 103 N3
Pecos National Historic Park, N. Mex., U.S. 107 R13
Pécs, Hung. 149 N14
Pedálofos, Gr. 154 D8
Peddapalli, India 178 L7
Pedder, Lake, Austral. 210 M16
Pedernales, Dom. Rep. 117 N17
Pedernales, river, Tex., U.S. 103 Q9
Pedra Azul, Braz. 131 J15
Pedra Lume, Cape Verde 205 B17
Pedras Negras, Braz. 130 H8
Pedro Afonso, Braz. 131 F13
Pedro Betancourt, Cuba 116 G7
Pedro Cays, Jam. 116 P11
Pedro de Valdivia, Chile 132 D7
Pedro Juan Caballero, Parag. 130 L10
Pedro Luro, Arg. 133 P11
Pedro Osório, Braz. 130 Q11
Pedro Point, Jam. 120 H6
Pedroso, Port. 144 E5
Pedroso, Sierra del, Sp. 144 J8
Peebles, Ohio, U.S. 99 S12
Peedamulla, W. Aust., Austral. 211 T2
Peekskill, N.Y., U.S. 94 M11
Peel, Isle of Man, U.K. 143 Q9
Peel, river, Yukon, Can. 82 E9
Pe Ell, Wash., U.S. 108 D3
Peel Sound, Nunavut, Can. 83 E15
Peetz, Colo., U.S. 106 K15
Pegasus Bay, N.Z. 213 P17
Pegeia, Cyprus 160 P5
Pego, Sp. 145 J15
Pehuajó, Arg. 132 M11
Peine, Ger. 148 D8
Peine, Pointe-à-, Dominica 121 F20
Peipus, Lake (Chudskoye Ozero), Est., Russ. 141 K17
Peixe, Braz. 131 H13
Pekalongan, Indonesia 188 M9
Pekan, Malaysia 187 U10
Pekanbaru, Indonesia 188 J6
Pekelmeer, lake, Neth. Antilles, Neth. 121 R19
Pekin, Ill., U.S. 99 Q5
Peking see Beijing, China 182 D7
Pelabuhanratu, Teluk, Indonesia 188 M8
Pelado, peak, Sp. 145 G13
Pelagosa see Palagruža, island, Croatia 152 J6
Pelahatchie, Miss., U.S. 100 L11
Pelat, Mont, Fr. 147 W15
Pelau, island, Solomon Is. 217 J18
Peleaga, peak, Rom. 152 E12
Pelée, Montagne, Martinique, Fr. 121 E22
Peleliu (Beliliou), island, Palau 216 Q10
Peleng, island, Indonesia 189 J14
Pelham, Ala., U.S. 101 K15
Pelham, Ga., U.S. 97 P5
Pelican, Alas., U.S. 111 L21
Pelican Lake, Minn., U.S. 104 E12
Pelican Point, Bahamas 120 E3
Pelican Point, Namibia 194 P6
Pelican Rapids, Minn., U.S. 104 G9
Péligre, Lac de, Haiti 117 M17
Pelikaan Punt, Neth. Antilles, Neth. 121 B14
Pelinéo, Óros, Gr. 155 H16
Pelister, peak, Maced. 152 L11
Pelješac, peninsula, Croatia 152 H7
Pella, ruin, Gr. 154 C10
Pella, Iowa, U.S. 105 P12
Pellston, Mich., U.S. 98 G10
Pelly, river, Yukon, Can. 82 G9
Pelly Bay, Nunavut, Can. 83 F15
Pelly Crossing, Yukon, Can. 82 F8
Peloponnisos, peninsula, Gr. 154 K9
Pelotas, Braz. 130 Q11
Pelusium, ruin, Egypt 171 N1
Pelvoux, Massif du, Fr. 147 V14
Pematang, Indonesia 188 J6
Pematangsiantar, Indonesia 188 H5
Pemba, Mozambique 203 D15
Pemba Bay, Mozambique 194 M11
Pemba Island, Tanzania 199 L15
Pemberton, W. Aust., Austral. 211 Y3
Pembina, N. Dak., U.S. 104 D7
Pembroke, Ga., U.S. 97 N8
Pembroke, Ont., Can. 83 Q18
Pembroke, Trinidad & Tobago 121 N18
Pembroke (Penfro), Wales, U.K. 143 V8
Pembroke Fort, Malta 161 K22
Pen, India 178 L3
Peña, Sierra de, Sp. 145 C14
Peña de Francia, Sierra de, Sp. 144 F8
Peñafiel, Sp. 144 D10
Penal, Trinidad & Tobago 121 Q22
Peñalara, peak, Sp. 144 F10
Peñalsordo, Sp. 144 J9
Penamacor, Port. 144 F7
Penambulai, island, Indonesia 189 M19
Peñaranda de Bracamonte, Sp. 144 E9
Peñarroya, peak, Sp. 145 F14
Peñarroya-Pueblonuevo, Sp. 144 J9
Peñas, Cabo de, Sp. 144 A8
Penas, Golfo de, Chile 133 T6
Peñas del Cache, peak, Canary Is. 204 P7
Pendan, Malaysia 188 H10
Pendembu, Sierra Leone 200 G6
Pender, Nebr., U.S. 105 N8
Pendleton, Oreg., U.S. 108 F7
Pend Oreille, river, Wash., U.S. 108 B9
Pend Oreille, Lake, Idaho, U.S. 106 B4
Pendra, India 178 J8
Pendroy, Mont., U.S. 106 B7
Penedo, Braz. 131 G17
Penfro see Pembroke, Wales, U.K. 143 V8
Pengcheng, China 181 H14
P'enghu Ch'üntao (Pescadores), islands, Taiwan, China 183 R9
Penglai, China 182 E9
Pengshui, China 182 L1
Penha do Tapauá, Braz. 130 E7
Peniche, Port. 144 H4
Penicuik, Scot., U.K. 142 M10
Peñíscola, Sp. 145 F15
Penmarc'h, Pointe de, Fr. 147 Q3
Penna, Punta della, It. 150 K11
Penne, It. 150 J10
Pennell Coast, Antarctica 227 R14
Penner, river, India 179 P6
Penneshaw, S. Aust., Austral. 211 Y10
Penn Hills, Pa., U.S. 94 N3
Pennine Alps, Switz. 150 C2
Pennington Gap, Va., U.S. 96 G6
Pennsylvania, U.S. 94 M3
Penn Yan, N.Y., U.S. 94 J7
Peno, Russ. 156 H7
Penobscot, river, Me., U.S. 85 C22
Penobscot Bay, Me., U.S. 95 F17
Penola, S. Aust., Austral. 211 Z11
Penonomé, Pan. 115 N21
Pénot, Mount, Vanuatu 218 D2
Penrhyn Atoll (Tongareva), Cook Is., N.Z. 214 H12
Penrith, Eng., U.K. 143 P11
Pensacola, Fla., U.S. 97 Q1
Pensacola Bay, Fla., U.S. 97 Q1
Pensacola Mountains, Antarctica 226 G11
Pentakomo, Cyprus 160 Q8
Pentecost (Île Pentecote), Vanuatu 218 D3
Pentecote, Île see Pentecost, Vanuatu 218 D3
Penticton, B.C., Can. 82 M9
Pentland Firth, Scot., U.K. 142 G10
Pentwater, Mich., U.S. 98 K9
Penuguan, Indonesia 188 K7
Penunjok, Tanjong, Malaysia 187 T10
Penwell, Tex., U.S. 103 N4
Penza, Russ. 156 L13
Penzance, Eng., U.K. 143 Y7
Penzhinskaya Guba, Russ. 159 E21
Peoples Creek, Mont., U.S. 106 B10
Peoria, Ariz., U.S. 107 U6
Peoria, Ill., U.S. 99 Q5
Pēpēʻekeo, Hawaiʻi, U.S. 113 L21
Pepillo Salcedo, Dom. Rep. 117 L17
Pepin, Lake, Minn., Wis., U.S. 98 J2
Pera, Cyprus 160 P8
Perabumulih, Indonesia 188 K7
Percival Lakes, Austral. 210 E5
Perdido, river, Ala., U.S. 101 P14
Perdido, Monte, Sp. 145 C15
Pereira, Col. 128 F4
Perelazovskiy, Russ. 157 P12
Perelyub, Russ. 156 L16
Peremul Par, island, India 179 Q2
Perenjori, W. Aust., Austral. 211 W2
Pereslavl' Zalesskiy, Russ. 156 H10
Perga, ruin, Turk. 168 H6
Pergamino, Arg. 132 L12
Perham, Minn., U.S. 104 G9
Peri, river, Turk. 169 F15
Péribonka, river, Que., Can. 83 N20
Perico, Arg. 132 E9
Perigot see Puamau, Baie, bay, Fr. Polynesia, Fr. 219 M21
Périgueux, Fr. 147 V8
Perijá, Sierra de, Col. 128 C6
Peri Lake, Austral. 210 J12
Perim see Barīm, island, Yemen 172 R8
Peristéra, island, Gr. 155 F13
Perito Moreno, Arg. 133 T7
Perkins, Okla., U.S. 102 F11
Perky, Fla., U.S. 97 Y9
Perlé, Lux. 160 J9
Perlevka, Russ. 156 M10
Perm', Russ. 158 H8
Pernambuco Plain, Atl. Oc. 237 P9
Pernik, Bulg. 152 J12
Peron, Cape, Austral. 210 K2
Peronit Burnu, Turk. 169 C15
Péronne, Fr. 146 M10
Pérouges, Fr. 147 U13
Perpetua, Cape, Oreg., U.S. 108 G2
Perpignan, Fr. 147 Z10
Perranporth, Eng., U.K. 143 X8
Perry, Fla., U.S. 97 R6
Perry, Ga., U.S. 97 N6
Perry, Iowa, U.S. 105 P11
Perry, Okla., U.S. 102 F11
Perry Island, Nunavut, Can. 83 G13
Perrysburg, Ohio, U.S. 99 N12
Perryton, Tex., U.S. 102 E6
Perryville, Alas., U.S. 111 N13
Perryville, Mo., U.S. 105 U15
Persepolis, ruin, Iran 173 F13
Perseverance Bay, Virgin Islands, U.S. 120 M8
Persian Gulf, Asia 166 G4
Pertek, Turk. 169 F14
Perth, Scot., U.K. 142 L10
Perth, W. Aust., Austral. 211 X2
Perth Basin, Ind. Oc. 241 M15
Pertoúli, Gr. 154 F8
Peru, Ill., U.S. 99 P5
Peru, Ind., U.S. 99 Q9
Peru, Nebr., U.S. 105 Q9
Peru, S. Amer. 127 E14
Peru Basin, Pac. Oc. 239 L19
Peru-Chile Trench, Pac. Oc. 239 L20
Perugia, It. 150 H8
Pervari, Turk. 169 G17
Pervomays'k, Ukr. 157 Q6
Pervomaysk, Russ. 156 K12
Pervomayskoye, Russ. 156 M14
Pervoural'sk, Russ. 158 H8
Pervyy Kuril'skiy Proliv, Russ. 159 G23
Pesaro, It. 150 G9
Pescador, Punta, Venez. 121 R21
Pescadores see P'enghu Ch'üntao, islands, Taiwan, China 183 R9
Pescara, It. 150 J10
Peschici, It. 150 K13
Peshawar, Pak. 177 N9
Peshawarun, ruin, Afghan. 177 Q2
Peshin Jan, Afghan. 177 N1
Peshkopi, Albania 152 K10
Peshtera, Bulg. 153 K14
Peshtigo, Wis., U.S. 98 H7
Pesmes, Fr. 147 R13
Pessac, Fr. 147 V6
Pessons, Pic dels, Andorra 160 J4
Pestovo, Russ. 156 G8
Pesu, India 178 G15
Petacalco, Bahía, Mex. 114 K10
Petacalco Bay see Petacalco, Bahía, N. Amer. 80 P5
Petaḥ Tiqwa, Israel 170 M5
Petal, Miss., U.S. 100 N12
Petalión, Kólpos, Gr. 155 J13
Petaluma, Calif., U.S. 109 R3
Petange, Lux. 160 K9
Petatlán, Mex. 114 K10
Petén, region, Guatemala 115 K16
Petenwell Lake, Wis., U.S. 98 J5
Peterborough, Eng., U.K. 143 T14
Peterborough, N.H., U.S. 95 J13
Peterborough, Ont., Can. 83 Q18
Peterborough, S. Aust., Austral. 211 X10
Peterhead, Scot., U.K. 142 J11
Peter I Island, Antarctica 226 J4
Petermann Ranges, Austral. 210 G7
Peter Pond Lake, Sask., Can. 82 L11
Petersburg, Alas., U.S. 111 M23
Petersburg, Ill., U.S. 99 R4
Petersburg, Ind., U.S. 99 T8
Petersburg, Tex., U.S. 102 J5
Petersburg, Va., U.S. 96 F13
Petersburg, W. Va., U.S. 96 C11
Petersfield, Jam. 120 H6
Petit Bois Island, Miss., U.S. 101 P13
Petit-Bourg, Guadeloupe, Fr. 121 F14
Petit-Canal, Guadeloupe, Fr. 121 E15
Petit Cul-de-Sac Marin, bay, Guadeloupe, Fr. 121 F15
Petite Île, Reunion, Fr. 205 H16
Petite Rivière del' Artibonite, Haiti 117 L16
Petite Terre, Îles de la, Guadeloupe, Fr. 121 F17
Petite-Terre, island, Mayotte, Fr. 205 P17
Petit-Goâve, Haiti 117 M16
Petit Gravier, Mauritius 205 J21
Petitot, river, B.C., Can. 82 H10
Petit Piton, peak, St. Lucia 121 L13
Petit Savane Point, Dominica 121 G20
Petit Trou, cape, Trinidad & Tobago 121 P17
Petoskey, Mich., U.S. 98 H10
Petra, ruin, Jordan 171 Q6
Petrich, Bulg. 153 K13
Petrified Forest National Park, Ariz., U.S. 107 S9
Petrila, Rom. 153 E13
Petrinja, Croatia 152 E6
Petro, Pak. 177 U8
Petrolândia, Braz. 131 G17
Petrolia, Calif., U.S. 109 N1
Petrolia, Tex., U.S. 102 J10
Petrolina, Braz. 131 G16

Petropavlovsk, Kaz. 175 B13
Petropavlovsk Kamchatskiy, Russ. 159 F23
Petrovac, Serb. & Mont. 152 J8
Petrovaradin, Serb. & Mont. 152 E9
Petrovgrad see Zrenjanin, Serb. & Mont. 152 E10
Petrovsk, Russ. 156 L13
Petrovsk Zabaykal'skiy, Russ. 159 L16
Petrozavodsk, Russ. 158 E7
Petukhovo, Russ. 158 J9
Pevek, Russ. 159 C19
Peyrehorade, Fr. 147 X6
Peywar Kandaw, pass, Afghan., Pak. 177 N8
Pezinok, Slovakia 149 K13
Pfaffenhofen, Ger. 148 K8
Pforzheim, Ger. 148 J6
Phaestus, ruin, Gr. 155 R14
Phaeton, Port, Fr. Polynesia, Fr. 219 P17
Phagwara, India 178 D5
Phalodi, India 178 F3
Phaltan, India 178 M4
Phan, Thai. 186 J8
Phangan, Ko, Thai. 187 Q8
Phangnga, Thai. 187 R7
Phan Ly, Vietnam 187 P14
Phan Rang, Vietnam 187 P14
Phan Thiet, Vietnam 187 P13
Pharr, Tex., U.S. 103 W10
Pharus see Hvar, island, Croatia 152 H6
Phatthalung, Thai. 187 R8
Phayao, Thai. 186 J8
Phelps, Ky., U.S. 101 C20
Phelps Lake, N.C., U.S. 96 H14
Phenix City, Ala., U.S. 101 L17
Phetchabun Range, Thai. 186 L9
Phetchaburi, Thai. 187 N8
Phiafai, Laos 186 M12
Phichai, Thai. 186 K8
Phichit, Thai. 186 L8
Philadelphia see 'Ammān, Jordan 170 M7
Philadelphia, Miss., U.S. 100 K12
Philadelphia, Pa., U.S. 94 P9
Philip, S. Dak., U.S. 104 L3
Philippeville, Belg. 146 M12
Philippi, ruin, Gr. 155 B13
Philippi, W. Va., U.S. 96 C10
Philippi Glacier, Antarctica 227 H21
Philippine Islands, Philippines 166 J13
Philippines, Asia 167 W13
Philippine Sea, Pac. Oc. 166 H14
Philippine Trench, Pac. Oc. 238 H4
Philippolis, S. Af. 202 L9
Philippopolis see Plovdiv, Bulg. 153 J14
Philippopolis see Shahbā', Syr. 170 K8
Philipsburg, Mont., U.S. 106 D6
Philipsburg, Pa., U.S. 94 N5
Philipsburg, Neth. Antilles, Neth. 121 B14
Philip Smith Mountains, Alas., U.S. 111 D17
Phillip Island, Norfolk I., Austral. 217 G20
Phillips, Tex., U.S. 102 G6
Phillips, Wis., U.S. 98 G4
Phillipsburg, Kans., U.S. 105 R5
Phillips Inlet, Nunavut, Can. 83 A15
Philomath, Oreg., U.S. 108 G3
Philpots Island, Nunavut, Can. 83 D16
Phippsburg, Colo., U.S. 106 L11
Phitsanulok, Thai. 186 K8
Phnom Penh, Cambodia 187 P11
Phoenix, Ariz., U.S. 107 U7
Phoenix, Mauritius 205 G20
Phoenix Islands, Kiribati 214 H10
Phôngsali, Laos 186 G10
Phong Tho, Vietnam 186 G10
Phraaspa, ruin, Iran 172 B11
Phrae, Thai. 186 K8
Phrao, Thai. 186 J8
Phra Thong, Ko, Thai. 187 Q7
Phrom Phiram, Thai. 186 K8
Phu Cat, Vietnam 186 M14
Phuket, Thai. 187 R7
Phuket, Ko, Thai. 187 R7
Phulabani, India 178 K9
Phulad, India 178 G4
Phu Loc, Vietnam 186 L13
Phu My, Vietnam 186 M14
Phu Quoc, Dao, Vietnam 187 Q11
Phu Rieng, Vietnam 187 P13
Phu Tho, Vietnam 186 G11
Phyarpon, Myanmar 186 L6
Piacenza, It. 150 E5
Piamafua Mountain, Amer. Samoa, U.S. 218 N2
Pianguan, China 182 D4
Pianosa, Isola, It. 150 J5
Pianosa, Isola, It. 150 K12
Pianu, island, F.S.M. 217 C14
Pianu, Mochun, F.S.M. 217 C13
Piaseczno, Pol. 149 E16
Piatra Neamţ, Rom. 153 C15
Piauí, Serra do, Braz. 131 G15
Piave, river, It. 150 D8
Piazza Armerina, It. 151 T11
Piazza del Risorgimento, It. 161 N17
Piazza Pio XII, Vatican City 161 Q17
Pibor Post, Sudan 199 G13
Picara Point, Virgin Islands, U.S. 120 M9
Picardy, region, Fr. 146 M10
Picassent, Sp. 145 H14
Picayune, Miss., U.S. 100 P11
Pichanal, Arg. 132 E10
Picher, Okla., U.S. 102 D14
Pichilemu, Chile 132 L6
Pickens, Miss., U.S. 100 K11
Pickford, Mich., U.S. 98 G11
Pickle Lake, Ont., Can. 83 N15
Pickwick Lake, Ala., Miss., Tenn., U.S. 101 G13
Pico, island, Azores 144 P3
Pico, It. 150 L9
Picos, Braz. 131 F16
Picos, Punta dos, Sp. 144 D5
Pico Truncado, Arg. 133 T9
Pictured Rocks National Lakeshore, Mich., U.S. 98 F9
Picture Gallery, Vatican City 161 N15
Picúa, Punta, P.R., U.S. 120 M5
Pidarak, Pak. 177 V3
Piedmont, Ala., U.S. 101 J17
Piedmont, region, It. 138 H5
Piedmont, Mo., U.S. 105 U15
Piedmont, region, U.S. 85 J18
Piedra, Monasterio de, Sp. 145 E13
Piedras, river, Peru 130 G5
Piedras Blancas, Point, Calif., U.S. 109 V4
Piedras Negras, Mex. 114 D11
Pieksämäki, Fin. 141 H16
Pielinen, lake, Fin. 141 G17
Pieniężno, Pol. 149 B15
Pienza, It. 150 H7
Pierce, Nebr., U.S. 105 N7
Piéria, Óros, Gr. 154 D10
Pierre, S. Dak., U.S. 104 K5
Pierrelatte, Fr. 147 W12
Pierrot Island (Cat Island), Mauritius 205 K20
Piešťany, Slovakia 149 K14
Pietarsaari see Jakobstad, Fin. 141 G15
Pieter Both, peak, Mauritius 205 G20
Pietermaritzburg, S. Af. 202 K11
Pietersburg see Polokwane, S. Af. 202 H11
Pietra-di-Verde, Fr. 150 K4
Pietrosu, peak, Rom. 153 C14
Pietrosul, peak, Rom. 153 B14
Pigailoe (West Fayu Atoll), F.S.M. 216 Q5
Pigeon, Guadeloupe, Fr. 121 F14
Pigeon, Mich., U.S. 98 K12
Pigeon Cay, Bahamas 120 B8
Pigeon Creek, Bahamas 120 F11
Pigeon Point, Trinidad & Tobago 121 N17
Piggott, Ark., U.S. 100 E11
Pigna Courtyard, Vatican City 161 N16
Pigs, Bay of see Cochinos, Bahía de, Cuba 116 H7
Pigüé, Arg. 133 N11
Piha Passage, Tonga 218 H12
Pihtipudas, Fin. 141 G15
Pi'ilanihale Heiau, Hawai'i, U.S. 113 G18
Piis-Panewu, island, F.S.M. 217 A15
Pijijiapan, Mex. 115 L14
Pikalevo, Russ. 156 F8
Pikelot, island, F.S.M. 216 Q5
Pikes Peak, Colo., U.S. 107 N13
Pikeville, Ky., U.S. 101 C20
Pikijin, island, Marshall Is. 216 L8
Piła, Pol. 149 C13
Pilão Arcado, Braz. 131 G15
Pilar, Parag. 130 N10
Pilar, Cabo, Chile 133 X6
Pilbarra Point, Vanuatu 218 G4
Pilcomayo, river, S. Amer. 126 J6
Pileni, island, Solomon Is. 217 P22
Pil'gyn, Russ. 159 B20
Pili, Gr. 154 F9
Pilibhit, India 178 F7
Pílio, Óros, Gr. 154 F11
Pilliga, N.S.W., Austral. 211 W14
Pillsbury Sound, Virgin Islands, U.S. 120 N10
Pilón, Cuba 116 L11
Pílos, Gr. 154 L9
Pilot Knob, Idaho, U.S. 106 E4
Pilot Peak, Nev., U.S. 109 R8
Pilot Point, Alas., U.S. 111 M13
Pilot Rock, Oreg., U.S. 108 F7
Pilot Station, Alas., U.S. 110 H12
Pilottown, La., U.S. 100 R12
Pilsen see Plzeň, Czech Rep. 148 H10
Pimba, S. Aust., Austral. 211 W9
Pimentel, Dom. Rep. 117 L19
Pinaki 2, island, Fr. Polynesia, Fr. 219 F21
Pinang, island, Malaysia 187 T8
Pinangah, Malaysia 188 G12
Pınarbaşı, Turk. 168 F11
Pinar del Río, Cuba 116 G5
Piñas, Ecua. 128 L2
Pinas, Arg. 132 J9
Pinckneyville, Ill., U.S. 99 U5
Pinconning, Mich., U.S. 98 K11
Pindaré, river, Braz. 131 E14
Pinders Point, Bahamas 120 F1
Pindi Bhattian, Pak. 177 P11
Pindi Gheb, Pak. 177 N10
Pindos Óros see Pindus Mountains, Gr. 154 E8
Pindus Mountains, Albania, Gr. 138 K8
Pine Barrens, region, N.J., U.S. 85 F20
Pine Bluff, Ark., U.S. 100 H9
Pine Bluffs, Wyo., U.S. 106 K14
Pine City, Minn., U.S. 104 H12
Pine Creek, N. Terr., Austral. 211 P8
Pinedale, Calif., U.S. 109 T6
Pinedale, Wyo., U.S. 106 H9
Pinega, river, Russ. 138 B11
Pinegrove, W. Aust., Austral. 211 V2
Pine Hill, N. Terr., Austral. 211 T8
Pinehill, Qnsld., Austral. 211 T13
Pine Hills, Fla., U.S. 97 T9
Pinehurst, Idaho, U.S. 106 C4
Pinehurst, N.C., U.S. 96 J10
Pine Island Bay, Antarctica 226 K7
Pine Island Glacier, Antarctica 226 J7
Pineland, Tex., U.S. 103 N15
Pinellas Park, Fla., U.S. 97 U7
Pine Point, N.W.T., Can. 82 J11
Pine Ridge, S. Dak., U.S. 104 M2
Pine River, Minn., U.S. 104 G10
Pinerolo, It. 150 E2
Pínes, Akrotírio (Nymphaeum), Gr. 155 D13
Pines, Lake O' the, Tex., U.S. 102 L14
Pinetop-Lakeside, Ariz., U.S. 107 T9
Pineville, Ky., U.S. 101 D19
Pineville, La., U.S. 100 N8
Piney Buttes, Mont., U.S. 106 C11
Ping, river, Thai. 186 L8
Pingdingshan, China 182 H5
Pingdu, China 182 F9
Pingelap Atoll, F.S.M. 216 Q8
Pingelly, W. Aust., Austral. 211 X3
Pinghe, China 183 R7
Pingjiang, China 182 M5
Pinglap, island, Marshall Is. 216 M7
Pingle, China 183 Q2
Pingli, China 182 J2
Pingliang, China 180 J12
Pinglu, China 182 D4
Pingluo, China 182 D1
Pingnan, China 183 R2
Pingquan, China 182 C8
Pingtan, China 183 Q9
P'ingtung, Taiwan, China 183 S9
Pingxiang, China 183 N5
Pingxiang, China 180 P12
Pingyang, China 183 N9
Pingyao, China 182 F4
Pingyi, China 182 G7
Pingyin, China 182 F7
Pingyuan, China 183 Q6
Pinheiro, Braz. 131 D14
Pinhel, Port. 144 F7
Pini, island, Indonesia 188 J5
Piniós, river, Gr. 154 E10
Pinjan, Indonesia 189 H13
Pinjarra, W. Aust., Austral. 211 X2
Pinlaung, Myanmar 186 H6
Pinleibu, Myanmar 186 F6
Pinnacles National Monument, Calif., U.S. 109 T5
Pinnaroo, S. Aust., Austral. 211 Y11
Pinneberg, Ger. 148 C7
Pinos, Point, Calif., U.S. 109 T4
Pinos-Puente, Sp. 144 L11
Pins, Île des (Kunié), New Caledonia, Fr. 218 E9
Pinsk, Belarus 156 M4
Pinsk Marshes, Belarus 156 M4
Pinta, Canal de, Ecua. 128 N9
Pinta, Isla (Abingdon), Ecua. 128 N9
Pintados, Chile 132 C7
Pintharuka, W. Aust., Austral. 211 W2
Pinzón, Isla (Duncan), Ecua. 128 Q9
Pioche, Nev., U.S. 109 R12
Piombino, It. 150 J6
Pioneer Fracture Zone, Pac. Oc. 239 E13
Pioneer Mountains, Mont., U.S. 106 E6
Pioneer Tablemount, Hawai'i, U.S. 112 L4
Pioner, Ostrov, Russ. 159 D14
Pionsat, Fr. 147 T10
Piotrków Trybunalski, Pol. 149 F15
Pipanaco, Salar de, Arg. 132 H9
Pipar, India 178 G4
Piparia, India 178 J6
Pipéri, island, Gr. 155 F13
Piper Peak, Nev., U.S. 109 S8
Pipe Spring National Monument, Ariz., U.S. 107 Q6
Pipestem Creek, N. Dak., U.S. 104 G6
Pipestone, Minn., U.S. 104 L8
Pipestone National Monument, Minn., U.S. 104 L8
Pipinas, Arg. 132 M13
Piplan, Pak. 177 P9
Pippu, Japan 184 F14
Piqua, Ohio, U.S. 99 R11
Piracicaba, Braz. 131 M13
Piracuruca, Braz. 131 E16
Pirae, Fr. Polynesia, Fr. 219 N16
Pirané, Arg. 132 F13
Piranhas, Braz. 130 J12
Pirapora, Braz. 131 K14
Pirássununga, Braz. 131 L13
Pireás, Gr. 154 J12
Pirgí, Gr. 155 J16
Pirgos, Gr. 154 K8
Pirimapun, Indonesia 189 M20
Pirin, range, Bulg. 153 K13
Piripiri, Braz. 131 E16
Pirmasens, Ger. 148 H5
Pirna, Ger. 148 F11
Pirogue, Guadeloupe, Fr. 121 G16
Pirojpur, Bangladesh 178 J12
Pirot, Serb. & Mont. 152 H12
Pir Panjal Range, India 177 N13
Pirsagat, river, Azerb. 169 D22
Pisa, It. 150 G6
Pisagua, Chile 132 C7
Pisamwe, island, F.S.M. 217 A15
Pisaras, island, F.S.M. 216 Q6
Piscaderabaai, bay, Neth. Antilles, Neth. 121 Q14
Pisciotta, It. 151 N12
Pisco, Peru 130 H3
Písek, Czech Rep. 148 J11
Pisemew, island, F.S.M. 217 A15
Pishan (Guma), China 180 G4
Pishin, Pak. 177 R6
Pīshīn, Iran 173 H18
Pisininin, island, F.S.M. 217 A15
Pisinun, island, F.S.M. 217 C16
Pismo Beach, Calif., U.S. 109 V5
Piso Firme, Bol. 130 H8
Pissos, Fr. 147 W6
Pissouri, Cyprus 160 Q6
Pisticci, It. 151 N13
Pistoia, It. 150 G6
Pistol River, Oreg., U.S. 108 K1
Pisz, Pol. 149 C16
Pitaga, Nfld. & Lab., Can. 83 L20
Pitanga, Braz. 130 M12
Pitav, Afghan. 176 K8
Pitcairn Island, Pac. Oc. 215 L16
Piteå, Sw. 141 F14
Piteşti, Rom. 153 F14
Pit Gorodok, Russ. 159 J13
Pithagorio, Gr. 155 K18
Pithara, W. Aust., Austral. 211 W2
Piti, Guam, U.S. 216 C10
Piti U Tai, island, Fr. Polynesia, Fr. 219 K14
Piti U Uta, island, Fr. Polynesia, Fr. 219 L14
Pitlochry, Scot., U.K. 142 L10
Piton, peak, Wallis & Futuna, Fr. 218 F11
Pitons, Anse des, St. Lucia 121 L13
Pitt, Punta, Ecua. 128 Q11
Pitti Island, India 179 R3
Pitt Island, island, N.Z. 214 P9
Pittsburg, Kans., U.S. 105 U10
Pittsburg, Tex., U.S. 102 L14
Pittsburgh, Pa., U.S. 94 N3
Pittsfield, Ill., U.S. 99 R3
Pittsfield, Mass., U.S. 94 K12
Pittsfield, Me., U.S. 95 F17
Pittston, Pa., U.S. 94 M9
Pittston Farm, Me., U.S. 95 D16
Piua Petrii, Rom. 153 F17
Piura, Peru 130 F2
Piva, river, Serb. & Mont. 152 H8
Pixian, China 182 H7
Pkulagalid, cape, Palau 216 M11
Pkulagasemieg, island, Palau 216 P11
Pkulngril, cape, Palau 216 M11
Pkurengel, cape, Palau 216 N11
Placentia Bay, Nfld. & Lab., Can. 83 M24
Placerville, Calif., U.S. 109 Q5
Placetas, Cuba 116 H9
Placida, Fla., U.S. 97 V8
Plain Dealing, La., U.S. 100 K6
Plainfield, Ind., U.S. 99 R9
Plainfield, N.J., U.S. 94 N10
Plains, Ga., U.S. 97 N5
Plains, Kans., U.S. 105 V4
Plains, Tex., U.S. 102 K4
Plainview, Minn., U.S. 104 K12
Plainview, Nebr., U.S. 105 N7
Plainview, Tex., U.S. 102 J5
Plainville, Kans., U.S. 105 S5
Plainwell, Mich., U.S. 98 M10
Plaisance, Haiti 117 L16
Pláka, Gr. 155 E15
Plakoti, Cape, Cyprus 160 M11
Plana Cays (French Cays), Bahamas 117 H15
Planken, Liech. 160 N3
Plankinton, S. Dak., U.S. 104 L6
Plano, Tex., U.S. 102 L12
Plantation, Fla., U.S. 97 W10
Plant City, Fla., U.S. 97 U8
Plaquemine, La., U.S. 100 P9
Plasencia, Sp. 144 G8
Plasstéikopf, peak, Liech. 160 Q3
Plata, Isla de la, Ecua. 128 K1
Plata, Río de la, Arg., Uru. 132 M14
Platamónas, Gr. 154 E10
Plate, River, S. Amer. 126 L6
Plateau Station, Antarctica 227 E15
Plato, Col. 128 C5
Platte, river, Mo., U.S. 105 R10
Platte, river, Nebr., U.S. 105 Q7
Platte, S. Dak., U.S. 104 M6
Platteville, Wis., U.S. 98 M4
Plattsburg, Mo., U.S. 105 S10
Plattsburgh, N.Y., U.S. 94 F12
Plattsmouth, Nebr., U.S. 105 Q9
Plauen, Ger. 148 G9
Plavsk, Russ. 156 L9
Playa Blanca, Canary Is. 204 Q7
Playa Dayaniguas, Cuba 116 H5
Playa de Guayanés, P.R., U.S. 120 N5
Playa de Guayanilla, P.R., U.S. 120 N2
Playa de Naguabo, P.R., U.S. 120 N6
Playa Girón, Cuba 116 H8
Playa Grandi, bay, Neth. Antilles, Neth. 121 N14
Playa Honda, Canary Is. 204 P7
Playas Lake, N. Mex., U.S. 107 W10
Play Ku, Vietnam 186 M13
Plaza Huincul, Arg. 133 P8
Pleasant, Lake, Ariz., U.S. 107 T6
Pleasant Bay, Bahamas 120 B10
Pleasant Grove, Utah, U.S. 106 L7
Pleasanton, Kans., U.S. 105 T10
Pleasanton, Tex., U.S. 103 S9
Pleasantville, N.J., U.S. 94 Q10
Pleasure Ridge Park, Ky., U.S. 101 B16
Pléneuf, Fr. 147 P5
Plenty, river, Austral. 210 F9
Plenty, Bay of, N.Z. 213 K20
Plentywood, Mont., U.S. 106 A13
Plesetsk, Russ. 158 E8
Plestin, Fr. 147 P3
Plétipi, Lac, Que., Can. 83 M20
Pleubian, Fr. 147 P4
Pleven, Bulg. 153 H14
Plevna, Mont., U.S. 106 D13

Pljevlja, *Serb. & Mont.* **152** H9
Ploče, *Croatia* **152** H7
Płock, *Pol.* **149** D15
Ploërmel, *Fr.* **147** Q5
Ploieşti, *Rom.* **153** E15
Plomári, *Gr.* **155** G17
Płońsk, *Pol.* **149** D15
Plouézec, *Fr.* **147** P4
Plouguerneau, *Fr.* **147** P2
Plovdiv (Philippopolis), *Bulg.* **153** J14
Plum, Pointe, *St. Martin, Fr.* **121** B13
Plummer, *Idaho, U.S.* **106** C3
Plumtree, *Zimb.* **202** G10
Plymouth, *Eng., U.K.* **143** X9
Plymouth, *Ind., U.S.* **99** P9
Plymouth, *Mass., U.S.* **95** L15
Plymouth, *Montserrat, U.K.* **121** B23
Plymouth, *N.C., U.S.* **96** H14
Plymouth, *N.H., U.S.* **95** H14
Plymouth, *Pa., U.S.* **94** M8
Plymouth, *Trinidad & Tobago* **121** N17
Plymouth, *Vt., U.S.* **94** H12
Plymouth, *Wis., U.S.* **98** K7
Plyusa, *Russ.* **156** G6
Plzeň (Pilsen), *Czech Rep.* **148** H10
Pniewy, *Pol.* **148** D12
Pô, *Burkina Faso* **200** E10
Po, river, *It.* **150** E6
Po, Foci del (Mouths of the Po), *It.* **150** E8
Po, Mouths of the *see* Po, Foci del, *It.* **150** E8
Pobeda, Gora, *Russ.* **159** E19
Pobedy, Pik *see* Jengish Chokusu, *China, Kyrg.* **176** E15
Pocahontas, *Ark., U.S.* **100** E10
Pocahontas, *Iowa, U.S.* **104** M10
Pocahontas, *Va., U.S.* **96** F8
Pocatello, *Idaho, U.S.* **106** H7
Pochep, *Russ.* **156** L7
Pochutla, *Mex.* **115** L13
Pocomoke City, *Md., U.S.* **96** D15
Poconé, *Braz.* **130** J10
Pocono Mountains, *Pa., U.S.* **94** M9
Poços de Caldas, *Braz.* **131** L13
Poddor'ye, *Russ.* **156** H6
Poděbrady, *Czech Rep.* **148** G11
Podgorica, *Serb. & Mont.* **152** J9
Podil's'ka Vysochyna, *Ukr.* **157** N3
Podkamennaya Tunguska, river, *Russ.* **159** J14
Podkamennaya Tunguska, *Russ.* **159** J13
Podol'sk, *Russ.* **156** J9
Podporozh'ye, *Russ.* **156** E8
Podravska Slatina, *Croatia* **152** D7
Podujevo, *Serb. & Mont.* **152** H11
Poggibonsi, *It.* **150** H6
Poggio Rusco, *It.* **150** E7
Poh, *Indonesia* **189** J14
P'oha, *N. Korea* **182** C14
Pōhakueaea Point, *Hawai'i, U.S.* **113** H17
Pohang, *S. Korea* **182** F15
Pohnpei (Ponape), island, *F.S.M.* **216** Q8
Pohnpei Harbor, *F.S.M.* **217** F14
Pohorje, range, *Slov.* **152** C5
Pōhue Bay, *Hawai'i, U.S.* **113** P19
Pohuerahi, peak, *Fr. Polynesia, Fr.* **219** H14
Poi, *Wallis & Futuna, Fr.* **218** E11
Poim, *Russ.* **156** L12
Poindimié, *New Caledonia, Fr.* **218** C7
Poinsett, Cape, *Antarctica* **227** M21
Point Arena, *Calif., U.S.* **109** Q2
Pointe a la Hache, *La., U.S.* **100** Q11
Pointe-à-Pitre, *Guadeloupe, Fr.* **121** F15
Pointe Michel, *Dominica* **121** G19
Pointe-Noire, *Congo* **201** N16
Pointe-Noire, *Guadeloupe, Fr.* **121** F14
Point Fortin, *Trinidad & Tobago* **121** Q21
Point Hope, *Alas., U.S.* **110** C12
Point Lake, *N.W.T., Can.* **82** G12
Point Lay, *Alas., U.S.* **111** C13
Point Pedro, *Sri Lanka* **179** R7
Point Pleasant, *N.J., U.S.* **94** P11
Point Pleasant, *W. Va., U.S.* **96** D7
Point Reyes National Seashore, *Calif., U.S.* **109** R3
Point Samson, *W. Aust., Austral.* **211** S2
Point Washington, *Fla., U.S.* **97** Q3
Po'ipū, *Hawai'i, U.S.* **112** C5
Poirino, *It.* **150** E3
Poissy, *Fr.* **147** P9
Poitiers, *Fr.* **147** T8
Poix, *Fr.* **147** N9
Pok, *F.S.M.* **217** G14
Pokataroo, *N.S.W., Austral.* **211** W14
Pokhvistnevo, *Russ.* **156** K16
Pokka, *Fin.* **141** D15
Poko, *Dem. Rep. of the Congo* **198** J11
Pola *see* Pula, *Croatia* **152** E4
Polacca, *Ariz., U.S.* **107** R8
Pola de Lena, *Sp.* **144** B8
Pola de Siero, *Sp.* **144** B9
Pola Island, *Amer. Samoa, U.S.* **218** L8
Polān, *Iran* **173** H17
Poland, *Eur.* **139** T8
Poland, *Kiribati* **217** B22
Polar Plateau, *Antarctica* **226** G12
Polatlı, *Turk.* **168** E7
Polatsk, *Belarus* **156** J5
Pol-e 'Alam, *Afghan.* **177** N7
Pol-e Khomri, *Afghan.* **176** L7
Pole Plain, *Arctic Oc.* **242** F9
Polesella, *It.* **150** E7
Policastro, Golfo di, *It.* **151** N12
Policastro Bussentino, *It.* **151** N12
Police, *Pol.* **148** C11
Police Point, *Seychelles* **205** P20
Políegos, island, *Gr.* **155** M14
Polígiros, *Gr.* **154** D12
Poligny, *Fr.* **147** S13
Polihale Heiau, *Hawai'i, U.S.* **112** B4
Polihnítos, *Gr.* **155** G16
Políkastro, *Gr.* **154** B10
Polink Point, *Jam.* **120** K9
Polis, *Cyprus* **160** P5
Polk, *Pa., U.S.* **94** M3
Pollino, Monte, *It.* **151** P13
Pollock, *S. Dak., U.S.* **104** H5
Polnovat, *Russ.* **158** G10
Poloa Bay, *Amer. Samoa, U.S.* **218** M6
Polohy, *Ukr.* **157** R9
Polokwane (Pietersburg), *S. Af.* **202** H11
Polonne, *Ukr.* **157** N4
Polson, *Mont., U.S.* **106** C5
Poltava, *Ukr.* **157** P8
Polvadera, *N. Mex., U.S.* **107** T12
Polyanovgrad *see* Karnobat, *Bulg.* **153** J16
Polyarnyy, *Russ.* **158** C9
Polynesia, islands, *Pac. Oc.* **214** D10
Polynesian Cultural Center, *Hawai'i, U.S.* **112** D11
Pom, *Indonesia* **213** B15
Pomabamba, *Peru* **130** G3
Pombal, *Port.* **144** G5
Pomene, *Mozambique* **203** H13
Pomerania, region, *Ger., Pol.* **148** C11
Pomeroy, *Ohio, U.S.* **99** S14
Pomeroy, *Wash., U.S.* **108** D9
Pomichna, *Ukr.* **157** Q6
Pomîrla, *Rom.* **153** A15
Pomona, *Calif., U.S.* **109** X9
Pomorie (Archialus), *Bulg.* **153** J17
Pomos Point, *Cyprus* **160** N6
Pompano Beach, *Fla., U.S.* **97** W10
Pompeii, ruin, *It.* **150** M11
Pompeiopolis, ruin, *Turk.* **168** J9
Pompeys Pillar National Historic Landmark, *Mont., U.S.* **106** E10
Ponape *see* Pohnpei, island, *F.S.M.* **216** Q8
Ponca City, *Okla., U.S.* **102** E11
Ponce, *P.R., U.S.* **120** N3
Ponce de Leon Bay, *Fla., U.S.* **97** X9
Ponchatoula, *La., U.S.* **100** P10
Poncin, *Fr.* **147** T13
Pond Creek, *Okla., U.S.* **102** E10
Pondicherry (Puduchcheri), *India* **179** Q7
Pondikónisí, island, *Gr.* **154** P12
Pond Inlet, *Nunavut, Can.* **83** E17
Pondosa, *Calif., U.S.* **108** M4
Ponérihouen, *New Caledonia, Fr.* **218** C7
Pones, island, *F.S.M.* **217** C16
Ponferrada, *Sp.* **144** C8
Pong, *Thai.* **186** J8
Pongara, Pointe, *Gabon* **201** K15
Pongaroa, *N.Z.* **213** M19
Pongo de Manseriche, site, *S. Amer.* **126** E2
Poniya Point, *N. Mariana Is., U.S.* **216** E7
Ponnani, *India* **179** R5
Ponoy, *Russ.* **158** D9
Pons, *Fr.* **147** U7
Ponta Delgada, *Azores* **144** Q5
Ponta do Pargo, *Madeira* **204** M2
Ponta do Sol, *Madeira* **204** M3
Ponta Grossa, *Braz.* **130** M12
Pont-à-Mousson, *Fr.* **147** P14
Ponta Porã, *Braz.* **130** L10
Pontarlier, *Fr.* **147** S14
Pontaumur, *Fr.* **147** U10
Pont-Aven, *Fr.* **147** Q3
Pontchartrain, Lake, *La., U.S.* **100** P11
Pontchâteau, *Fr.* **147** R5
Pont-d'Ain, *Fr.* **147** T13
Pont-de-Salars, *Fr.* **147** W10
Ponteareas, *Sp.* **144** C5
Pontebba, *It.* **150** C9
Pontedecimo, *It.* **150** F4
Ponte de Lima, *Port.* **144** D5
Ponte-Leccia, *Fr.* **150** J4
Pontevedra, *Sp.* **144** C5
Pontevedra, Ría de, *Sp.* **144** C5
Ponte Vedra Beach, *Fla., U.S.* **97** R9
Pontiac, *Ill., U.S.* **99** Q6
Pontiac, *Mich., U.S.* **98** M12
Pontianak, *Indonesia* **188** J9
Pontifical Academy of Sciences, *Vatican City* **161** P15
Pontinia, *It.* **150** L9
Pontivy, *Fr.* **147** Q4
Pont-l'Evêque, *Fr.* **147** N7
Pontoise, *Fr.* **147** P9
Pontotoc, *Miss., U.S.* **100** H12
Pontremoli, *It.* **150** F5
Ponts, *Sp.* **145** D16
Pontypool, *Wales, U.K.* **143** V10
Ponza, Isola di, *It.* **150** M9
Ponziane, Isole, *It.* **150** M9
Poochera, *S. Aust., Austral.* **211** X9
Poofai, Baie de, *Fr. Polynesia, Fr.* **219** K14
Poole, *Eng., U.K.* **143** X12
Poolewe, *Scot., U.K.* **142** J8
Pooncarie, *N.S.W., Austral.* **211** X11
Poopó, *Bol.* **130** K7
Poopó, Lago, *Bol.* **130** K7
Popayán, *Col.* **128** G4
Poplar, river, *Man., Can.* **83** M14
Poplar, river, *Mont., U.S.* **106** B12
Poplar, *Mont., U.S.* **106** B13
Poplar Bluff, *Mo., U.S.* **105** V15
Poplarville, *Miss., U.S.* **100** N12
Popocatépetl, peak, *Mex.* **114** J12
Popondetta, *P.N.G.* **213** E20
Popovo, *Bulg.* **153** H15
Poprad, *Slovakia* **149** J16
Porali, river, *Pak.* **177** U5
Porangahau, *N.Z.* **213** M19
Porbandar, *India* **178** J1
Porcuna, *Sp.* **144** K10
Porcupine, river, *Alas., U.S.* **111** E18
Porcupine Bank, *Atl. Oc.* **236** E11
Porcupine Mountains, *Mich., U.S.* **98** F5
Porcupine Plain, *Atl. Oc.* **236** F11
Pordenone, *It.* **150** D8
Porea, island, *Cook Is., N.Z.* **219** C14
Poreč, *Croatia* **152** E3
Porga, *Benin* **200** F11
Porgy Bay, *Bahamas* **120** B8
Pori, *Fin.* **141** J15
Porirua, *N.Z.* **213** M19
Porlamar, *Venez.* **128** B11
Pornic, *Fr.* **147** S5
Porongurup, *W. Aust., Austral.* **211** Y3
Póros, island, *Gr.* **154** K12
Póros, *Gr.* **154** K12
Porpoise Bay, *Antarctica* **227** P19
Porrentruy, *Switz.* **150** A2
Porsangen, bay, *Nor.* **141** B14
Porsuk, river, *Turk.* **168** E6
Porta, *Fr.* **160** J6
Portadown, *N. Ire., U.K.* **143** Q7
Portage, *Ind., U.S.* **99** N8
Portage, *Mich., U.S.* **99** N10
Portage, *Wis., U.S.* **98** K5
Portage la Prairie, *Man., Can.* **83** N13
Portageville, *Mo., U.S.* **105** V16
Portal, *N. Dak., U.S.* **104** D3
Port Albert, *Vic., Austral.* **211** Z13
Portalegre, *Port.* **144** H6
Portales, *N. Mex., U.S.* **107** T15
Port Alfred, *S. Af.* **202** M10
Port Allegany, *Pa., U.S.* **94** L5
Port Allen, *La., U.S.* **100** P9
Port Angeles, *Wash., U.S.* **108** B3
Port Antonio, *Jam.* **120** J11
Port-à-Piment, *Haiti* **117** M15
Port Aransas, *Tex., U.S.* **103** U11
Port Arthur *see* Lüshun, *China* **182** E9
Port Arthur, *Tex., U.S.* **103** Q16
Port Augusta, *S. Aust., Austral.* **211** X10
Port-au-Prince, *Haiti* **117** M16
Port Austin, *Mich., U.S.* **98** K13
Port Beaufort, *S. Af.* **202** M8
Port Blair, *India* **179** Q14
Port Bolivar, *Tex., U.S.* **103** R15
Portbou, *Sp.* **145** C18
Port Broughton, *S. Aust., Austral.* **211** X10
Port Burwell, *Nunavut, Can.* **83** J20
Port-Cartier, *Que., Can.* **83** M21
Port Charlotte, *Fla., U.S.* **97** V8
Port Clinton, *Ohio, U.S.* **99** N13
Port-de-Paix, *Haiti* **117** L16
Port Douglas, *Qnsld., Austral.* **211** R13
Port Eads, *La., U.S.* **100** R12
Port Edward, *S. Af.* **202** L11
Porteira, *Braz.* **130** D10
Portel, *Port.* **144** J6
Portel, *Braz.* **130** D12
Port Elizabeth, *S. Af.* **202** M10
Port Elizabeth, *St. Vincent & the Grenadines* **119** L17
Port Ellen, *Scot., U.K.* **143** N7
Porté-Puymorens, *Fr.* **160** J6
Porterdale, *Ga., U.S.* **96** L5
Porter Point, *St. Vincent & the Grenadines* **121** J16
Porterville, *Calif., U.S.* **109** U7
Porterville, *S. Af.* **202** M7
Port Esquivel, *Jam.* **120** J9
Port Etienne *see* Nouadhibou, *Mauritania* **196** F4
Port Fairy, *Vic., Austral.* **211** Z11
Port-Gentil, *Gabon* **201** L14
Port Gibson, *Miss., U.S.* **100** M10
Port Graham, *Alas., U.S.* **111** L16
Port Harcourt, *Nigeria* **201** H14
Port Hardy, *B.C., Can.* **82** L7
Port Hawkesbury, *N.S., Can.* **83** P22
Port Hedland, *W. Aust., Austral.* **211** S3
Port Heiden, *Alas., U.S.* **111** M13
Port Henry, *N.Y., U.S.* **94** G12
Porthmadog, *Wales, U.K.* **143** T9
Port Hope, *Mich., U.S.* **98** K13
Port Hope Simpson, *Nfld. & Lab., Can.* **83** L22
Port Howe, *Bahamas* **117** F13
Port Huron, *Mich., U.S.* **98** L13
Port-İliç, *Azerb.* **169** F22
Portimão, *Port.* **144** L5
Port Isabel, *Tex., U.S.* **103** W11
Port Jervis, *N.Y., U.S.* **94** M10
Port Kaiser, *Jam.* **120** K7
Port Kaituma, *Guyana* **129** D14
Port Láirge *see* Waterford, *Ire.* **143** U6
Portland, *Eng., U.K.* **143** X11
Portland, *Ind., U.S.* **99** Q10
Portland, *Me., U.S.* **95** H15
Portland, *Mich., U.S.* **98** L10
Portland, *N. Dak., U.S.* **104** F7
Portland, *Oreg., U.S.* **108** F3
Portland, *Tenn., U.S.* **101** E15
Portland, *Tex., U.S.* **103** T11
Portland, *Vic., Austral.* **211** Z11
Portland, Bill of, *Eng., U.K.* **143** X11
Portland Bight, *Jam.* **120** K9
Portland Cottage, *Jam.* **120** K9
Portland Point, *Jam.* **120** K9
Portland Rock, *Jam.* **116** P11
Port-la-Nouvelle, *Fr.* **147** Y11
Port Laoise, *Ire.* **143** S6
Port Lavaca, *Tex., U.S.* **103** S12
Port Lincoln, *S. Aust., Austral.* **211** Y9
Port Lions, *Alas., U.S.* **111** M15
Portloe, *Eng., U.K.* **143** Y8
Port Loko, *Sierra Leone* **200** F5
Port Louis, *Mauritius* **205** G20
Port-Louis, *Guadeloupe, Fr.* **121** E15
Port Macquarie, *N.S.W., Austral.* **211** X15
Port Mansfield, *Tex., U.S.* **103** V11
Port Maria, *Jam.* **120** H10
Port Mathurin, *Mauritius* **205** J20
Port-Menier, *Que., Can.* **83** M21
Port Morant, *Jam.* **120** J11
Portmore, *Jam.* **120** J10
Port Moresby, *P.N.G.* **213** E19
Portnacroish, *Scot., U.K.* **142** L8
Portnahaven, *Scot., U.K.* **143** N7
Port Neches, *Tex., U.S.* **103** Q16
Port Nelson, *Bahamas* **117** F14
Port Nolloth, *S. Af.* **202** K7
Port Norris, *N.J., U.S.* **94** R10
Porto, *Braz.* **131** E15
Porto, *Fr.* **150** K3
Porto (Oporto), *Port.* **144** E5
Porto, Golfe de, *Fr.* **150** K3
Porto Alegre, *Braz.* **130** P12
Porto Alegre, *Sao Tome and Principe* **205** E20
Porto Amboim, *Angola* **202** D5
Porto Artur, *Braz.* **130** H11
Porto Azzurro, *It.* **150** J6
Portobelo, *Pan.* **115** N21
Port O'Connor, *Tex., U.S.* **103** T12
Porto Covo, *Port.* **144** K5
Porto dos Gauchos, *Braz.* **130** G10
Porto Esperidião, *Braz.* **130** J10
Portoferraio, *It.* **150** J5
Port of Ness, *Scot., U.K.* **142** G7
Porto Franco, *Braz.* **131** F14
Port-of-Spain, *Trinidad & Tobago* **121** P22
Porto Garibaldi, *It.* **150** F8
Pórto Germenó, *Gr.* **154** J11
Porto Grande, *Braz.* **130** C12
Portogruaro, *It.* **150** D9
Portohéli, *Gr.* **154** L11
Pôrto Inglês, *Cape Verde* **205** D17
Porto Jofre, *Braz.* **130** J10
Portola, *Calif., U.S.* **109** P6
Porto Moniz, *Madeira* **204** M2
Porto Murtinho, *Braz.* **130** L10
Porto Nacional, *Braz.* **131** G13
Porto Novo, *India* **179** Q7
Porto-Novo, *Benin* **200** H12
Port Ontario, *N.Y., U.S.* **94** H8
Port Orange, *Fla., U.S.* **97** S9
Port Orchard, *Wash., U.S.* **108** C3
Porto Recanati, *It.* **150** H10
Port Orford, *Oreg., U.S.* **108** K1
Porto San Giorgio, *It.* **150** H10
Porto Santo, island, *Madeira* **204** L5
Porto Santo, *Madeira* **204** L5
Portoscuso, *It.* **151** Q3
Porto Seguro, *Braz.* **131** K16
Porto Tolle, *It.* **150** E8
Porto Torres, *It.* **150** M3
Porto-Vecchio, *Fr.* **150** L4
Porto-Vecchio, Golfe de, *Fr.* **150** L4
Porto Velho, *Braz.* **130** F8
Portoviejo, *Ecua.* **128** J2
Port Phillip Bay, *Austral.* **210** M12
Port Pirie, *S. Aust., Austral.* **211** X10
Port Royal, *Jam.* **120** J10
Port Royal, *S.C., U.S.* **97** N9
Port Royal Bay *see* Little Sound, *Bermuda, U.K.* **120** C2
Port Royal Sound, *S.C., U.S.* **97** N9
Port Said *see* Būr Sa'īd, *Egypt* **171** N1
Port St. Joe, *Fla., U.S.* **97** R4
Port St. Johns, *S. Af.* **202** L11
Port-St. Louis, *Fr.* **147** X13
Port St. Lucie, *Fla., U.S.* **97** V10
Port Salerno, *Fla., U.S.* **97** V10
Portsall, *Fr.* **147** P2
Port-Salut, *Haiti* **117** N15
Port Saunders, *Nfld. & Lab., Can.* **83** L22
Port Shepstone, *S. Af.* **202** L11
Portsmouth, *Dominica* **121** E18
Portsmouth, *Eng., U.K.* **143** W13
Portsmouth, *N.C., U.S.* **96** J14
Portsmouth, *N.H., U.S.* **95** J15
Portsmouth, *Ohio, U.S.* **99** T13
Portsmouth, *Va., U.S.* **96** F14
Port South East, *Mauritius* **205** J20
Portsoy, *Scot., U.K.* **142** J11
Port Sudan *see* Būr Sūdān, *Sudan* **199** C14
Port Sulphur, *La., U.S.* **100** Q11
Port Talbot, *Wales, U.K.* **143** V10
Port Townsend, *Wash., U.S.* **108** B3
Portugal, *Eur.* **139** W1
Portuguesa, river, *Venez.* **128** C9
Port-Vila, *Vanuatu* **218** F3
Port Vincent, *S. Aust., Austral.* **211** Y10
Port Warrender, *W. Aust., Austral.* **211** Q5
Port Washington, *Wis., U.S.* **98** L7
Porus, *Jam.* **120** J8
Porvenir, *Bol.* **130** G6
Porvenir, *Chile* **133** X8
Porvoo, *Fin.* **141** J16
Porzuna, *Sp.* **144** H10
Posadas, *Arg.* **132** G14
Poschiavo, *Switz.* **150** C5
Posio, *Fin.* **141** E16
Poso, *Indonesia* **189** J13
Posof, *Turk.* **169** C17
Possession Island, *Namibia* **202** K6
Possum Kingdom Lake, *Tex., U.S.* **102** L9
Post, *Tex., U.S.* **102** K5
Post Falls, *Idaho, U.S.* **106** C3

Postville, *Iowa, U.S.* **104** M13
Posušje, *Bosn. & Herzg.* **152** H7
Potamí, *Gr.* **155** B13
Potamós, *Gr.* **154** P11
Poteau, *Okla., U.S.* **102** G14
Poteet, *Tex., U.S.* **103** S9
Potenza, *It.* **150** M12
Poth, *Tex., U.S.* **103** S10
Potholes Reservoir, *Wash., U.S.* **108** D7
P'ot'i, *Rep. of Georgia* **169** B16
Potiskum, *Nigeria* **201** E15
Potlatch, *Idaho, U.S.* **106** C3
Pot Mountain, *Idaho, U.S.* **106** D4
Potnarvin, *Vanuatu* **218** G4
Potomac, river, *Md., Va., U.S.* **96** D13
Potosi, *Mo., U.S.* **105** T14
Potosí, *Bol.* **130** K7
Potrerillos, *Chile* **132** G7
Potsdam, *Ger.* **148** D10
Potsdam, *N.Y., U.S.* **94** F10
Pott, Île, *New Caledonia, Fr.* **218** B6
Potter, *Nebr., U.S.* **105** P1
Pottstown, *Pa., U.S.* **94** P9
Pottsville, *Pa., U.S.* **94** N8
Poudre d'Or, *Mauritius* **205** F20
Pouébo, *New Caledonia, Fr.* **218** C6
Pouembout, *New Caledonia, Fr.* **218** C7
Poughkeepsie, *N.Y., U.S.* **94** L11
Pougues, *Fr.* **147** S11
Pouilly, *Fr.* **147** R10
Poulaphouca Reservoir, *Ire.* **143** S6
Poulsbo, *Wash., U.S.* **108** C4
Poum, *New Caledonia, Fr.* **218** C6
Pouoanuu, Mont, *Fr. Polynesia, Fr.* **219** M20
Poutasi, *Samoa* **218** L3
Poutoru, *Fr. Polynesia, Fr.* **219** B23
Povai, *Fr. Polynesia, Fr.* **219** K14
Povoação, *Azores* **144** Q5
Póvoa de Varzim, *Port.* **144** D5
Povorino, *Russ.* **157** N12
Povungnituk, Baie de, *Que., Can.* **83** J17
Powder, river, *Mont., Wyo., U.S.* **106** D13
Powder, river, *Oreg., U.S.* **108** G9
Powder River, *Wyo., U.S.* **106** H11
Powell, *Wyo., U.S.* **106** F10
Powell, Lake, *Utah, U.S.* **107** Q7
Powell Butte, *Oreg., U.S.* **108** H5
Powell Point, *Bahamas* **120** F6
Powell River, *B.C., Can.* **82** M8
Powers, *Oreg., U.S.* **108** J2
Powers Lake, *N. Dak., U.S.* **104** E3
Poxoréo, *Braz.* **130** J11
Poya, *New Caledonia, Fr.* **218** D7
Poyang Hu, *China* **182** M6
Poygan, Lake, *Wis., U.S.* **98** K6
Poysdorf, *Aust.* **149** J13
Pozantı, *Turk.* **168** H10
Požarevac, *Serb. & Mont.* **152** F11
Poza Rica, *Mex.* **114** H12
Poznań, *Pol.* **149** D13
Pozo Alcón, *Sp.* **144** K12
Pozo Almonte, *Chile* **132** C7
Pozoblanco, *Sp.* **144** J9
Pozzallo, *It.* **151** U11
Pozzuoli, *It.* **150** M10
Pracana, Barragem de, *Port.* **144** G6
Pracchia, *It.* **150** G6
Prachin Buri, *Thai.* **186** M9
Prachuap Khiri Khan, *Thai.* **187** P8
Pradelles, *Fr.* **147** V12
Prado, *Braz.* **131** K16
Prague see Praha, *Czech Rep.* **148** H11
Praha (Prague), *Czech Rep.* **148** H11
Praia, *Cape Verde* **205** D16
Praia da Vitória, *Azores* **144** P4
Prainha, *Braz.* **130** D11
Prainha, *Braz.* **130** F9
Prairie City, *Oreg., U.S.* **108** G7
Prairie Dog Creek, *Kans., U.S.* **105** R4
Prairie Dog Town Fork Red, river, *Tex., U.S.* **102** H6
Prairie du Chien, *Wis., U.S.* **98** L3
Prairie Grove, *Ark., U.S.* **100** E6
Pran Buri, *Thai.* **187** N8
Praslin, island, *Seychelles* **205** M20
Praslin, *St. Lucia* **121** K14
Prasonísi, island, *Gr.* **155** P19
Pratas Island see Tungsha Tao, *Taiwan, China* **183** T6
Prato, *It.* **150** G6
Pratola Peligna, *It.* **150** K10
Prats, *Andorra* **160** H4
Prats-de-Mollo, *Fr.* **147** Z10
Pratt, *Kans., U.S.* **105** U6
Pratt Seamount, *Pac. Oc.* **239** B14
Prattville, *Ala., U.S.* **101** L15
Prazeres, *Madeira* **204** M2
Preau, *Trinidad & Tobago* **121** Q22
Précy-sous-Thil, *Fr.* **147** R12
Predazzo, *It.* **150** C7
Preguiça, *Cape Verde* **205** B15
Preguiça, *Cape Verde* **205** B17
Prehistoric Petroglyphs, ruin, *Afghan.* **176** K9
Premont, *Tex., U.S.* **103** U10
Premuda, island, *Croatia* **152** F4
Prentice, *Wis., U.S.* **98** G4
Prentiss, *Miss., U.S.* **100** M11
Prenzlau, *Ger.* **148** C10
Preobrazhenka, *Russ.* **159** J15
Preparis Island, *Myanmar* **186** M4
Preparis North Channel, *Myanmar* **186** L4
Preparis South Channel, *Myanmar* **186** M4
Přerov, *Czech Rep.* **149** H13
Prescott, *Ariz., U.S.* **107** S6
Prescott, *Ark., U.S.* **100** J7
Prescott, *Wash., U.S.* **108** E8
Presho, *S. Dak., U.S.* **104** L5
Presidencia Roca, *Arg.* **132** F12
Presidencia Roque Sáenz Peña, *Arg.* **132** G12
Presidente Dutra, *Braz.* **131** E15
Presidente Eduardo Frei, station, *Antarctica* **226** C3
Presidente Prudente, *Braz.* **130** L12
President Thiers Bank, *Pac. Oc.* **239** M13
Presidio, *Tex., U.S.* **103** R1
Prešov, *Slovakia* **149** J16
Prespa, peak, *Bulg.* **153** K14
Prespa, Lake see Prespansko Jezero, *Albania, Gr., Maced.* **152** L10
Prespansko Jezero (Lake Prespa), *Albania, Gr., Maced.* **152** L10
Presque Isle, *Me., U.S.* **95** B18
Presque Isle, *Mich., U.S.* **98** H12
Pressburg see Bratislava, *Slovakia* **149** K13
Presteigne, *Wales, U.K.* **143** U10
Preston, *Eng., U.K.* **143** R11
Preston, *Idaho, U.S.* **106** J7
Preston, *Minn., U.S.* **104** L13
Preston, *Mo., U.S.* **105** U12
Prestonsburg, *Ky., U.S.* **101** C20
Pretoria (Tshwane), *S. Af.* **202** J10
Préveza, *Gr.* **154** G7
Pribilof Islands, *Alas., U.S.* **110** L9
Priboj, *Serb. & Mont.* **152** G9
Priboj, *Serb. & Mont.* **152** J11
Příbram, *Czech Rep.* **148** H11
Price, river, *Utah, U.S.* **106** M8
Price, *Utah, U.S.* **106** M8
Price, Cape, *India* **179** P14
Prichard, *Ala., U.S.* **101** N13
Prickly Bay, *Grenada* **121** L22
Prickly Pear Cays, *Anguilla, U.K.* **120** Q10
Prickly Pear Island, *Antigua & Barbuda* **121** A21
Prickly Pear Island, *Virgin Islands, U.K.* **120** Q9
Prickly Point, *Grenada* **121** L22
Priekule, *Latv.* **141** M15
Prieska, *S. Af.* **202** L9
Priest Lake, *Idaho, U.S.* **106** B3
Priestley Glacier, *Antarctica* **227** P14
Priest River, *Idaho, U.S.* **106** B3
Prieta, Peña, *Sp.* **144** B10
Prievidza, *Slovakia* **149** J14
Prijedor, *Bosn. & Herzg.* **152** E6
Prijepolje, *Serb. & Mont.* **152** H9
Prilep, *Maced.* **152** L11
Primorsko Akhtarsk, *Russ.* **157** S10
Prince Albert, *S. Af.* **202** M8
Prince Albert, *Sask., Can.* **82** M12
Prince Albert Mountains, *Antarctica* **227** N14
Prince Albert Peninsula, *N.W.T., Can.* **82** D12
Prince Albert Sound, *N.W.T., Can.* **82** E12
Prince Alfred, Cape, *N.W.T., Can.* **82** C12
Prince Charles Island, *Nunavut, Can.* **83** F17
Prince Charles Mountains, *Antarctica* **227** F18
Prince Edward Fracture Zone, *Ind. Oc.* **240** Q3
Prince Edward Island, *Can.* **83** N22
Prince Edward Islands, *Ind. Oc.* **204** K7
Prince George, *B.C., Can.* **82** K8
Prince Gustaf Adolf Sea, *Nunavut, Can.* **83** C14
Prince Harald Coast, *Antarctica* **227** B17
Prince Kūhiō Park, *Hawai'i, U.S.* **112** C5
Prince of Wales, Cape, *Alas., U.S.* **110** E11
Prince of Wales Island, *Alas., U.S.* **111** M23
Prince of Wales Island, *Nunavut, Can.* **83** E14
Prince of Wales Island, *Qnsld., Austral.* **211** N12
Prince of Wales Strait, *N.W.T., Can.* **82** D12
Prince Olav Coast, *Antarctica* **227** B18
Prince Patrick Island, *N.W.T., Can.* **83** C13
Prince Regent Inlet, *Nunavut, Can.* **83** E15
Prince Rupert, *B.C., Can.* **82** J7
Prince Rupert Bay, *Dominica* **121** E18
Princess Anne, *Md., U.S.* **96** D14
Princess Antoinette Park, *Monaco* **161** E20
Princess Astrid Coast, *Antarctica* **227** A14
Princess Charlotte Bay, *Austral.* **210** B12
Princess Grace Hospital Center, *Monaco* **161** E19
Princess Grace Rose Garden, *Monaco* **161** F21
Princess Martha Coast, *Antarctica* **226** C11
Princess Ragnhild Coast, *Antarctica* **227** B15
Princeton, *B.C., Can.* **82** M8
Princeton, *Ill., U.S.* **99** P5
Princeton, *Ind., U.S.* **99** T7
Princeton, *Ky., U.S.* **101** D14
Princeton, *Minn., U.S.* **104** J11
Princeton, *Mo., U.S.* **105** Q11
Princeton, *N.J., U.S.* **94** P10
Princeton, *W. Va., U.S.* **96** F8
Princeville, *Hawai'i, U.S.* **112** B5
Prince William Sound, *Alas., U.S.* **111** K17
Príncipe, island, *Sao Tome and Principe* **205** A20
Príncipe da Beira, *Braz.* **130** H7
Prineville, *Oreg., U.S.* **108** G5
Pringle, *S. Dak., U.S.* **104** L1
Prior, Cabo, *Sp.* **144** A6
Prislop, Pasul, *Rom.* **153** B14
Priština, *Serb. & Mont.* **152** J11
Pritchett, *Colo., U.S.* **107** P15
Pritzwalk, *Ger.* **148** C9
Privas, *Fr.* **147** V12
Privol'noye, *Russ.* **159** G22
Privolzhsk, *Russ.* **156** H11
Privolzhskaya Vozvyshennost', *Russ.* **157** P13
Privolzhskiy, *Russ.* **156** M14
Prizren, *Serb. & Mont.* **152** J10
Probolinggo, *Indonesia* **188** M10
Proctor, *Minn., U.S.* **104** G12
Prodromi, *Cyprus* **160** P5
Progreso Limitada, *Eq. Guinea* **204** M8
Progress, station, *Antarctica* **227** G20
Progress, *Russ.* **159** K20
Prokhladnyy, *Russ.* **157** T13
Prokhod Sveti Nikola, *Bulg., Serb. & Mont.* **152** H12
Prokópi, *Gr.* **154** G12
Prokop'yevsk, *Russ.* **158** L12
Prokuplje, *Serb. & Mont.* **152** H11
Proletarsk, *Russ.* **157** R12
Promíri, *Gr.* **154** F11
Pronsfeld, *Ger.* **160** G10
Prony, *New Caledonia, Fr.* **218** E9
Prony, Baie du, *New Caledonia, Fr.* **218** E9
Propriá, *Braz.* **131** G17
Propriano, *Fr.* **150** L4
Proserpine, *Qnsld., Austral.* **211** S14
Prospect, *Barbados* **121** K18
Prospect, *Cayman Is., U.K.* **120** J2
Prospect, *Oreg., U.S.* **108** K3
Prospect Point, *Jam.* **120** K11
Prossatsáni, *Gr.* **155** B13
Prosser, *Wash., U.S.* **108** E6
Prostějov, *Czech Rep.* **149** H13
Protection, *Kans., U.S.* **105** V5
Próti, island, *Gr.* **154** L8
Provadiya, *Bulg.* **153** H17
Provence, region, *Fr.* **147** X14
Providence, *Grenada* **121** L23
Providence, *Ky., U.S.* **101** C14
Providence, *R.I., U.S.* **95** L14
Providence, Atoll de, *Seychelles* **203** C19
Providence Mountains, *Calif., U.S.* **109** W12
Providencia, Isla de, *Col.* **115** L20
Providenciales, island, *Turks & Caicos Is., U.K.* **117** H16
Provideniya, *Russ.* **159** A21
Provincetown, *Mass., U.S.* **95** K16
Provo, *Utah, U.S.* **106** L7
Prudhoe Bay, *Alas., U.S.* **84** L4
Prudhoe Bay, *Alas., U.S.* **111** C17
Prudnik, *Pol.* **149** G13
Prüm, river, *Ger.* **160** G11
Prüm, *Ger.* **148** G5
Prune Island see Palm Island, *St. Vincent & the Grenadines* **119** M17
Pruszcz Gdański, *Pol.* **149** B14
Pruszków, *Pol.* **149** E16
Prut, river, *Mold., Rom.* **153** D17
Pruzhany, *Belarus* **156** L3
Prvić, island, *Croatia* **152** E5
Prydz Bay, *Antarctica* **227** F20
Pryluky, *Ukr.* **157** N7
Pryor, *Okla., U.S.* **102** E13
Pryor Creek, *Mont., U.S.* **106** E10
Pryp'yat', river, *Ukr.* **156** M3
Przemyśl, *Pol.* **149** H18
Przheval'sk see Karakol, *Kyrg.* **176** E14
Psahná, *Gr.* **154** H12
Psará, island, *Gr.* **155** H15
Psará, *Gr.* **155** H15
Psathoúra, island, *Gr.* **155** F13
Psérimos, island, *Gr.* **155** L18
Psiloreítis see Ídi, Óros, peak, *Gr.* **155** Q14
Pskov, *Russ.* **156** G5
Pskovskoye Ozero, *Est., Russ.* **141** L17
Ptolemaïda, *Gr.* **154** D9
Ptuj, *Slov.* **152** C6
Pua, *Thai.* **186** J9
Puakō, *Hawai'i, U.S.* **113** L19
Puakonikai, *Banaba, Kiribati* **217** D20
Puamau, Baie (Perigot), *Fr. Polynesia, Fr.* **219** M21
Puán, *Arg.* **133** N11
Pua Pua, Te Ava, *Tuvalu* **217** L23
Pu'apu'a, *Samoa* **218** K2
Puaumu Nord, island, *Fr. Polynesia, Fr.* **219** Q20
Puava, Cape, *Samoa* **218** K1
Pubei, *China* **183** S1
Pucallpa, *Peru* **130** F4
Puca Urco, *Peru* **130** D5
Pucheng, *China* **182** G2
Pucheng, *China* **183** N8
Pucioasa, *Rom.* **153** E15
Puck, *Pol.* **149** A14
Pudasjärvi, *Fin.* **141** F15
Pudimoe, *S. Af.* **202** K9
Pudu, *Indonesia* **188** J6
Puduchcheri see Pondicherry, *India* **179** Q7
Pudukkottai, *India* **179** R6
Puebla, *Mex.* **114** J12
Puebla de Guzmán, *Sp.* **144** K6
Puebla de Sanabria, *Sp.* **144** D7
Pueblo, *Colo., U.S.* **107** N14
Pueblo Bonito, *N. Mex., U.S.* **107** R10
Puente-Genil, *Sp.* **144** L9
Pueo Point, *Hawai'i, U.S.* **112** C3
Pu'er, *China* **180** P10
Puerca, Punta, *P.R., U.S.* **120** N6
Puerco, river, *Ariz., U.S.* **107** S9
Puerto Acosta, *Bol.* **130** J6
Puerto Aisén, *Chile* **133** S6
Puerto América, *Peru* **130** E3
Puerto Ángel, *Mex.* **115** L13
Puerto Armuelles, *Pan.* **115** P19
Puerto Ayacucho, *Venez.* **128** E9
Puerto Ayora, *Ecua.* **128** Q9
Puerto Bahía Negra, *Parag.* **130** L10
Puerto Baquerizo Moreno, *Ecua.* **128** Q10
Puerto Barrios, *Guatemala* **115** K16
Puerto Belgrano, *Arg.* **133** N11
Puerto Berrío, *Col.* **128** E5
Puerto Cabello, *Venez.* **128** B9
Puerto Cabezas, *Nicar.* **115** L19
Puerto Carreño, *Col.* **128** E9
Puerto Chicama, *Peru* **130** F2
Puerto Coig, *Arg.* **133** V8
Puerto Colombia, *Col.* **128** B5
Puerto Cortés, *Hond.* **115** K17
Puerto Cumarebo, *Venez.* **128** B8
Puerto de la Cruz, *Canary Is.* **204** Q5
Puerto del Carmen, *Canary Is.* **204** P7
Puerto del Rosario, *Canary Is.* **204** Q7
Puerto de Luna, *N. Mex., U.S.* **107** S14
Puerto de Mazarrón, *Sp.* **145** L13
Puerto de Nutrias, *Venez.* **128** C8
Puerto Deseado, *Arg.* **133** T9
Puerto Etén, *Peru* **130** F2
Puerto Heath, *Bol.* **130** H6
Puerto Jiménez, *Costa Rica* **115** P19
Puerto La Concordia, *Col.* **128** G6
Puerto La Cruz, *Venez.* **128** B11
Puerto La Paz, *Arg.* **132** D11
Puerto Lápice, *Sp.* **144** H11
Puerto Leguízamo, *Col.* **128** J5
Puerto Limón, *Costa Rica* **115** N19
Puertollano, *Sp.* **144** J10
Puerto Lobos, *Arg.* **133** Q10
Puerto López, *Col.* **128** F6
Puerto Madryn, *Arg.* **133** R10
Puerto Maldonado, *Peru* **130** H6
Puerto Manatí, *Cuba* **116** J12
Puerto Montt, *Chile* **133** Q6
Puerto Morelos, *Mex.* **115** H17
Puerto Natales, *Chile* **133** W7
Puerto Obaldía, *Pan.* **115** N22
Puerto Padre, *Cuba* **116** J12
Puerto Páez, *Venez.* **128** E9
Puerto Peñasco, *Mex.* **114** B6
Puerto Pinasco, *Parag.* **130** L10
Puerto Pirámides, *Arg.* **133** Q10
Puerto Plata, *Dom. Rep.* **117** L18
Puerto Portillo, *Peru* **130** G4
Puerto Princesa, *Philippines* **189** E13
Puerto Real, *P.R., U.S.* **120** N1
Puerto Rico, *U.S., N. Amer.* **81** N23
Puerto Rico, island, *N. Amer.* **80** N11
Puerto Rico Trench, *Atl. Oc.* **236** L5
Puerto San Carlos, *Chile* **133** U7
Puerto San Julián, *Arg.* **133** U9
Puerto Santa Cruz, *Arg.* **133** V8
Puerto Suárez, *Bol.* **130** K10
Puerto Tres Palmas, *Parag.* **130** L10
Puerto Vallarta, *Mex.* **114** H9
Puerto Velasco Ibarra, *Ecua.* **128** R9
Puerto Villamil, *Ecua.* **128** R8
Puerto Wilches, *Col.* **128** D5
Puerto Williams, *Chile* **133** Y9
Puetton Tanapag, bay, *N. Mariana Is., U.S.* **216** B4
Pueu, *Fr. Polynesia, Fr.* **219** P17
Pueyrredón, Lago, *Arg., Chile* **133** T7
Pugachev, *Russ.* **156** L15
Puget Sound, *Wash., U.S.* **84** B4
Puhi, *Hawai'i, U.S.* **112** C6
Puigcerdà, *Sp.* **145** C17
Puig Major, peak, *Sp.* **145** G18
Puigmal d'Err, peak, *Sp.* **145** C17
Pujehun, *Sierra Leone* **200** G6
Pujiang, *China* **182** M9
Pukaki, Lake, *N.Z.* **213** P16
Pukalani, *Hawai'i, U.S.* **113** G17
Pukapuka, island, *Fr. Polynesia, Fr.* **219** D21
Pukapuka, island, *Fr. Polynesia, Fr.* **215** J15
Pukapuka Atoll (Danger Islands), *Cook Is., N.Z.* **214** J11
Pukarua, island, *Fr. Polynesia, Fr.* **219** F22
Pukch'ŏng, *N. Korea* **182** C14
Pukp'yŏng-ni, *S. Korea* **182** E14
Pula, *It.* **151** Q4
Pula (Pola), *Croatia* **152** E4
Pula, Capo di, *It.* **151** Q4
Pulap Atoll, *F.S.M.* **216** Q5
Pulaski, *N.Y., U.S.* **94** H8
Pulaski, *Tenn., U.S.* **101** G15
Pulaski, *Va., U.S.* **96** F9
Puławy, *Pol.* **149** F17
Puli, *Taiwan, China* **183** R9
Pulicat Lake, *India* **179** P7
Puliyangudi, *India* **179** S5
Puliyankulam, *Sri Lanka* **179** S7
Pull and be Damn' Point, *Virgin Islands, U.K.* **120** L11
Pullman, *Wash., U.S.* **108** D9
Pull Point, *Virgin Islands, U.S.* **120** Q3
Pulo Anna, island, *Palau* **214** F2
Pulog, Mount, *Philippines* **189** B13
Pülümür, *Turk.* **169** F14
Pulusuk, island, *F.S.M.* **216** Q5

Puluwat Atoll, F.S.M. 216 Q5
Pumpkin Creek, Mont., U.S. 106 E12
Puná, Isla, Ecua. 128 K2
Puna, region, Hawai'i, U.S. 113 N21
Punaauia, Fr. Polynesia, Fr. 219 P15
Punaauia, Pointe, Fr. Polynesia, Fr. 219 P15
Puna de Atacama, region, S. Amer. 126 J4
Punaeroa, Passe, Fr. Polynesia, Fr. 219 C23
Punakha, Bhutan 178 F12
Punalu'u, Hawai'i, U.S. 113 P20
Punan, Indonesia 188 H11
Puncak Jaya, peak, Indonesia 189 L20
Punch, India 177 N11
Pune, India 178 L4
Punitaqui, Chile 132 J6
Puno, Peru 130 J6
Punta, Cerro de, P.R., U.S. 120 N3
Punta Aguja, range, Peru 130 F1
Punta Alta, Arg. 133 N11
Punta Arenas, Chile 133 X8
Punta Coles, range, Peru 130 K5
Punta del Este, Uru. 132 L14
Punta Delgada, Arg. 133 R10
Punta Gorda, Belize 115 K16
Punta Gorda, Fla., U.S. 97 V8
Punta Negra, range, Peru 130 F1
Punta Pariñas, range, Peru 130 E1
Punta Prieta, Mex. 114 C5
Puntarenas, Costa Rica 115 N18
Punta Umbría, Sp. 144 L7
Puntland, region, Somalia 199 G18
Punto Fijo, Venez. 128 A8
Puntudo, Cerro, Arg. 133 U8
Punxsutawney, Pa., U.S. 94 M5
Puohine, Fr. Polynesia, Fr. 219 C23
Puqi, China 182 L5
Puquio, Peru 130 J4
Puranpur, India 178 F7
Purari, river, P.N.G. 213 D19
Purcell, Okla., U.S. 102 H11
Purcell Mountains, Can., U.S. 106 A4
Purdy Islands, P.N.G. 213 B19
Purgatoire, river, Colo., U.S. 107 P14
Puri, India 178 L10
Purmerend, Neth. 146 H12
Purna, river, India 178 K5
Purnia, India 178 G11
Pursat, Cambodia 187 N11
Purus, river, Braz. 130 E8
Purvis, Miss., U.S. 100 N12
Pusad, India 178 L6
Pusan see Busan, S. Korea 182 G14
Pushkin, Russ. 156 F6
Pushkino, Russ. 156 M14
Pusht-i-Rud, region, Afghan. 177 P3
Puta, Azerb. 169 D23
Putangaroa, island, Cook Is., N.Z. 219 C15
Putao, Myanmar 186 D7
Putian, China 183 Q8
Putilovo, Russ. 156 F12
Putina, Peru 130 J6
Puting, Tanjung, Indonesia 188 K10
Puto, P.N.G. 217 J13
Putorana, Plato, Russ. 159 G14
Putrachoique, Cerro, Arg. 133 R7
Puttalam, Sri Lanka 179 S7
Puttelange, Fr. 147 P15
Puttur, India 179 P7
Putumayo, river, Col. 128 K7
Putumayo, river, Ecua., Peru 128 H4
Pütürge, Turk. 169 G13
Pu'uanahulu, Hawai'i, U.S. 113 L19
Pu'uhonua o Hōnaunau National Historic Park (City of Refuge National Historic Park), Hawai'i, U.S. 113 N18
Pu'ukohola Heiau National Historic Site, Hawai'i, U.S. 113 K19
Pu'uwai, Hawai'i, U.S. 112 C3
Puwe, island, F.S.M. 217 B15
Puxian, China 182 F3
Puyallup, Wash., U.S. 108 C4
Puyang, China 182 G6
Puy de Sancy, peak, Fr. 147 U10
Puy-Guillaume, Fr. 147 U11
Puysegur Point, N.Z. 213 R14
Puzak, Hamun-e, Afghan. 177 Q2
Pweto, Dem. Rep. of the Congo 198 M12
Pya, Lake, Russ. 138 B9
P'yagina, Poluostrov, Russ. 159 F21
Pyasinskiy Zaliv, Russ. 159 E13
Pyatigorsk, Russ. 157 T13
P'yatykhatky, Ukr. 157 Q7
Pyay, Myanmar 186 J5
Pydna, battle, Gr. 154 D10
Pyeonghae, S. Korea 182 F14
Pyhäjoki, Fin. 141 G15
Pyhäselkä, lake, Fin. 141 H17
Pyinkayaing, Myanmar 186 L5
Pyinmana, Myanmar 186 J6
Pyin-U-Lwin, Myanmar 186 G6
Pymatuning Reservoir, Ohio, Pa., U.S. 99 N16
P'yŏng-sŏng, N. Korea 182 D12
P'yŏngyang, N. Korea 182 D12
Pyote, Tex., U.S. 103 N3
Pyramides, Pointe, Wallis & Futuna, Fr. 218 E11
Pyramid Lake, Nev., U.S. 109 P6
Pyramid Rock, China 188 B10
Pyramids and Sphinx, ruin, Egypt 197 C18
Pyrenees, range, Eur. 138 H4
Pýrgos, Gr. 155 R15
Pyryatyn, Ukr. 157 N7
Pytalovo, Russ. 156 H5
Pyu, Myanmar 186 J6

Q

Qabanbay, Kaz. 175 G18
Qabqa, China 180 J10
Qāḑub, Yemen 173 R14
Qaeanā, Syr. 170 J7
Qā'emābād, Iran 173 E17
Qā'emshahr, Iran 173 C13
Qagan Nur, China 182 A6
Qagan Nur, China 182 A5
Qagan Us see Dulan, China 180 J10
Qahar Youyi Houqi, China 182 B5
Qahar Youyi Zhongqi, China 182 C5
Qaidam Basin, China 166 G9
Qaidam Pendi, China 180 H9
Qairouan, Tun. 197 A13
Qala, Malta 161 H21
Qalamcheshmeh, Afghan. 177 N4
Qalansīyah, Yemen 173 R14
Qalat (Kalat), Afghan. 177 P6
Qal'at al Azzlam, ruin, Saudi Arabia 172 H5
Qal'at Bīshah, Saudi Arabia 172 M8
Qal'eh Shahr, Afghan. 176 L5
Qal'eh-ye Fath, Afghan. 177 R2
Qal'eh-ye Gaz, Afghan. 177 P4
Qal'eh-ye Now, Afghan. 176 M3
Qal'eh-ye Sarkari, Afghan. 176 L6
Qalhāt, Oman 173 K17
Qallabat, Eth. 199 E14
Qamar, Ghubbat al, Yemen 173 P13
Qamdo, China 180 L9
Qamea, island, Fiji Is. 218 G8
Qamīnis, Lib. 197 C15
Qammieh Point, Malta 161 J21
Qamystybas, Kaz. 174 G10
Qandala, Somalia 199 F18
Qapshaghay, Kaz. 175 H16
Qapshaghay Reservoir, Kaz. 175 H17
Qarabutaq, Kaz. 174 D9
Qaraghandy, Kaz. 175 E14
Qaraghayly, Kaz. 175 E15
Qarah Bagh, Afghan. 177 N7
Qaraqoynn Köli, Kaz. 175 G13
Qaratal, river, Kaz. 175 G16
Qarataū, Kaz. 175 J14
Qarataū Zhotasy, range, Kaz. 174 H13
Qaratöbe, Kaz. 174 D7
Qaraton, Kaz. 174 F7
Qaraūyl, Kaz. 175 E17
Qarazhal, Kaz. 175 F14
Qarchi Gak, Afghan. 176 K6
Qardho, Somalia 199 F18
Qarokŭl, lake, Taj. 176 H11
Qarqan, river, China 180 G7
Qarqaraly, Kaz. 175 E15
Qarqin, Afghan. 176 K5
Qarsaqbay, Kaz. 174 F12
Qarshi, Uzb. 174 L12
Qaryat al 'Ulyā, Saudi Arabia 172 H11
Qaryat az Zuwaytīnah, Lib. 197 C15
Qaşr-e Qand, Iran 173 H17
Qaşr Farāfra, Egypt 197 D17
Qaşr Ḩamām, Saudi Arabia 172 L10
Qa'ṭabah, Yemen 172 Q9
Qatar, Asia 167 V4
Qaţīnah, Buḩayrat, Syr. 170 G8
Qattara Depression, Egypt 197 C17
Qax, Azerb. 169 C20
Qāyen, Iran 173 D16
Qayghy, Kaz. 174 D11
Qaynar, Kaz. 175 E16
Qazakh, Azerb. 169 C19
Qazaly, Kaz. 174 G10
Qazaq Shyghanaghy, Kaz. 174 J6
Qazi Deh, Afghan. 176 K10
Qazimämmäd, Azerb. 169 D22
Qazvīn, Iran 172 C12
Qeissan, Sudan 199 F13
Qele Levu, island, Fiji Is. 218 G9
Qena, Egypt 197 D19
Qeqertarsuaq (Godhavn), Greenland, Den. 81 C21
Qeqertarsuatsiaat, Greenland, Den. 81 D22
Qerqertarsuaq, island, N. Amer. 80 C8
Qeshm, island, Iran 173 H15
Qeshm, Iran 173 H15
Qeysar, Afghan. 176 L4
Qianjiang, China 181 L13
Qianxian, China 182 G1
Qianyang, China 182 G1
Qianyang, China 183 N2
Qidong, China 182 K10
Qidong, China 183 P3
Qiemo, China 180 G6
Qijiaojing, China 180 E8
Qikiqtarjuaq, island, Nunavut, Can. 83 H20
Qikiqtarjuaq, Nunavut, Can. 83 F19
Qila Ladgasht, Pak. 177 T2
Qila Safed, Pak. 177 S1
Qila Saifullah, Pak. 177 R7
Qilian Shan, China 166 G9
Qimantag, range, China 180 H8
Qimen, China 182 L7
Qing, river, China 182 L3
Qingdao, China 182 G9
Qinghai Hu, China 180 H10
Qingjian, China 182 F3
Qingjiang, China 183 N6
Qingshuihe, China 182 D4
Qingtian, China 183 N9
Qingxu, China 182 E4
Qingyang, China 182 F1
Qingyuan, China 182 B12
Qingyuan, China 183 R4
Qingzhou, China 182 F8
Qinhuangdao, China 182 D9
Qin Lin, range, China 166 G11
Qin Ling, China 182 H1
Qinxian, China 182 F4
Qionghai (Jiaji), China 183 U2
Qiongshan, China 183 U2
Qiongzhou Haixia, strait, China 183 T1
Qiqian, China 181 B15
Qiqihar, China 181 C16
Qiryat Shemona, Israel 170 K6
Qishn, Yemen 173 P13
Qitai, China 180 E8
Qitaihe, China 181 D18
Qixia, China 182 F9
Qiyang, China 183 P3
Qiyl, river, Kaz. 174 D7
Qızılağac Körfäzi, Azerb. 169 F22
Qizilqum, desert, Uzb. 174 J10
Qom, river, Iran 172 D12
Qom, Iran 172 D12
Qomsheh, Iran 173 E13
Qonaqkänd, Azerb. 169 C22
Qongyrat, Kaz. 175 F15
Qo'qon, Uzb. 175 K14
Qorakŭl, Uzb. 174 L11
Qoraqalpog'iston, region, Uzb. 174 H8
Qormi, Malta 161 K22
Qosköl, Kaz. 174 E12
Qosshaghyl, Kaz. 174 F7
Qostanay, Kaz. 174 B11
Qowryah, Afghan. 177 Q4
Qrendi, Malta 161 L22
Quairading, W. Aust., Austral. 211 X3
Quakertown, Pa., U.S. 94 N9
Quamby, Qnsld., Austral. 211 S11
Quanah, Tex., U.S. 102 J8
Quan Dao Nam Du, island, Vietnam 187 Q11
Quanery, Anse, Dominica 121 F20
Quang Ngai, Vietnam 186 L14
Quang Tri, Vietnam 186 K13
Quannan, China 183 Q5
Quanshuigou, China 176 L15
Quanzhou, China 183 P3
Quanzhou, China 183 Q8
Quaraí, Braz. 130 P10
Quartier d'Orléans, St. Martin, Fr. 121 B15
Quartier du Colombier, St. Martin, Fr. 121 B14
Quartu Sant'Elena, It. 151 Q4
Quartzsite, Ariz., U.S. 107 T5
Quatre Bornes, Mauritius 205 G19
Quba, Azerb. 169 C22
Qūchān, Iran 173 B16
Qudaym, Syr. 170 G10
Queanbeyan, N.S.W., Austral. 211 Y14
Quebec, Can. 83 M20
Québec, Que., Can. 83 P20
Quebracho Coto, Arg. 132 F10
Quebradillas, P.R., U.S. 120 M2
Queen Adelaida Archipelago, S. Amer. 126 R4
Queen Alexandra Range, Antarctica 227 L13
Queen Charlotte Islands, B.C., Can. 82 J6
Queen Charlotte Sound, B.C., Can. 82 K7
Queen Elizabeth Islands, Nunavut, Can. 83 B15
Queen Elizabeth Range, Antarctica 227 L13
Queen Fabiola Mountains (Yamato Mountains), Antarctica 227 C17
Queen Ka'ahumanu Highway, Hawai'i, U.S. 113 L18
Queen Mary Coast, Antarctica 227 J21
Queen Maud Gulf, Nunavut, Can. 83 F14
Queen Maud Land, Antarctica 226 C11
Queen Maud Mountains, Antarctica 226 K12
Queensland, Austral. 211 T12
Queenstown, N.Z. 213 Q15
Queenstown, S. Af. 202 L10
Queenstown, Tas., Austral. 211 Z15
Queen Victoria's Profile, Hawai'i, U.S. 112 C6
Queets, Wash., U.S. 108 C2
Queiros, Cape, Vanuatu 218 C1
Quelimane, Mozambique 203 F14
Quellón, Chile 133 R6
Quemado, N. Mex., U.S. 107 T10
Quemado, Tex., U.S. 103 S6
Quemoy see Kinmen, island, Taiwan, China 183 R8
Quemú Quemú, Arg. 132 M10
Quequén, Arg. 133 N12
Quercy, region, Fr. 147 W9
Querétaro, Mex. 114 H11
Quesada, Costa Rica 115 N19
Queshan, China 182 J5
Quesnel, B.C., Can. 82 L8
Que Son, Vietnam 186 L13
Questa, N. Mex., U.S. 107 Q13
Quetta, Pak. 177 R6
Quetzaltenango, Guatemala 115 L15
Quezon City, Philippines 189 C13
Qufu, China 182 G7
Quibala, Angola 202 D6
Quibdó, Col. 128 E4
Quiberon, Presqu'île de, Fr. 147 R4
Quijotoa, Ariz., U.S. 107 V6
Quilá, Mex. 114 F8
Quilcene, Wash., U.S. 108 B3
Quillan, Fr. 147 Y10
Quillota, Chile 132 K6
Quilon (Kollam), India 179 S5
Quilpie, Qnsld., Austral. 211 V12
Quimilí, Arg. 132 G11
Quimper, Fr. 147 Q3
Quimperlé, Fr. 147 Q3
Quinault, river, Wash., U.S. 108 C2
Quinault, Wash., U.S. 108 C2
Quince Mil, Peru 130 H5
Quincy, Calif., U.S. 109 P5
Quincy, Fla., U.S. 97 Q5
Quincy, Ill., U.S. 99 R3
Quincy, Mass., U.S. 95 K15
Quines, Arg. 132 K9
Quinhagak, Alas., U.S. 110 K12
Qui Nhon, Vietnam 186 M14
Quinn, river, Nev., U.S. 108 L8
Quintanar de la Orden, Sp. 144 G11
Quinter, Kans., U.S. 105 S4
Quintin, Fr. 147 Q4
Quinto, Sp. 145 E14
Quintus Rocks, Bahamas 120 E5
Quipungo, Angola 202 E6
Quirindi, N.S.W., Austral. 211 X14
Quissanga, Mozambique 203 D15
Quissico, Mozambique 203 J13
Quitaque, Tex., U.S. 102 J6
Quitilipi, Arg. 132 G12
Quitman, Ga., U.S. 97 Q6
Quitman, Miss., U.S. 101 M13
Quito, Ecua. 128 J3
Quixadá, Braz. 131 E17
Qujiang, China 183 Q4
Qujing, China 180 N11
Qulan, Kaz. 175 J15
Qulandy, Kaz. 174 G9
Qulbān Banī Murrah, ruin, Jordan 171 Q8
Qullai Ismoili Somoni (Communism Peak), Taj. 176 H10
Qulsary, Kaz. 174 F7
Qundao, island, China 182 E9
Qŭnghirot, Uzb. 174 J8
Quobba, W. Aust., Austral. 211 U1
Quogue, N.Y., U.S. 95 N13
Qurayyāt, Oman 173 K16
Qŭrghonteppa, Taj. 176 J7
Quryq, Kaz. 174 H5
Qusar, Azerb. 169 C22
Quşeir, Egypt 197 D19
Qusmuryn, Kaz. 174 C11
Qusmuryn Köli, Kaz. 174 C11
Quwo, China 182 G4
Quxian, China 180 L12
Qüxü, China 180 L7
Quy Chau, Vietnam 186 J11
Quyghan, Kaz. 175 G15
Quy Hop, Vietnam 186 J11
Quzhou, China 182 F6
Quzhou, China 182 M8
Qvareli, Rep. of Georgia 169 B19
Qyzan, Kaz. 174 G6
Qyzylorda, Kaz. 174 H11

R

Raahe, Fin. 141 G15
Raas, island, Indonesia 188 M11
Raasay, island, Scot., U.K. 142 J7
Raasay, Sound of, Scot., U.K. 142 J7
Rab, island, Croatia 152 E4
Raba, Indonesia 189 M13
Rabacca, St. Vincent & the Grenadines 121 K17
Rabastens, Fr. 147 X7
Rabat see Victoria, Malta 161 H20
Rabat, Malta 161 K22
Rabat, Mor. 196 B8
Rabaul, P.N.G. 213 C21
Rabga Pass, China, Nepal 178 F11
Rabi (Rambi), island, Fiji Is. 218 G8
Rábida, Isla (Jervis), Ecua. 128 Q9
Rābigh, Saudi Arabia 172 K7
Racale, It. 151 N15
Răcari, Rom. 153 F15
Racconigi, It. 150 E2
Raccoon Cay, Bahamas 117 H13
Raccoon Point, La., U.S. 100 R10
Race, Cape, Nfld. & Lab., Can. 83 M24
Raceland, La., U.S. 100 Q10
Rachaïya, Leb. 170 J6
Rach Gia, Vietnam 187 Q11
Racine, Wis., U.S. 98 M7
Raco, Mich., U.S. 98 F10
Rădăuţi, Rom. 153 A15
Radcliff, Ky., U.S. 101 C16
Radford, Va., U.S. 96 F9
Radhanpur, India 178 H3
Radisson, Que., Can. 83 M18
Radix, Point, Trinidad & Tobago 121 Q23
Radnevo, Bulg. 153 J15
Radom, Pol. 149 F16
Radomsko, Pol. 149 F15
Radomyshl', Ukr. 157 N5
Radviliškis, Lith. 141 N16
Radwá, Jabal, Saudi Arabia 172 J6
Radzyń Podlaski, Pol. 149 E17
Rae Bareli, India 178 G8
Rae-Edzo, N.W.T., Can. 82 H11
Raeford, N.C., U.S. 96 J11
Rae Isthmus, Nunavut, Can. 83 G16
Rae Lakes, N.W.T., Can. 82 G11
Raeside, Lake, Austral. 210 H4
Raetihi, N.Z. 213 L19
Rāf, Jabal, Saudi Arabia 172 G7
Rafa', Gaza Strip 171 N4

Rafaela, *Arg.* **132** J11
Rafaï, *Cen. Af. Rep.* **198** H10
Raffadali, *It.* **151** T10
Rafḩā', *Saudi Arabia* **172** F9
Rafína, *Gr.* **155** J13
Rafsanjān, *Iran* **173** F15
Raga, *Sudan* **198** G11
Ragachow, *Belarus* **156** L6
Ragged, Mount, *Austral.* **210** K5
Ragged Island, *Bahamas* **117** H13
Ragged Island, *Me., U.S.* **95** G17
Ragged Point, *Barbados* **121** K20
Ragusa *see* Dubrovnik, *Croatia* **152** J8
Ragusa, *It.* **151** T11
Raha, *Indonesia* **189** L14
Raheb, Ras ir, *Malta* **161** K21
Rahimyar Khan, *Pak.* **177** T9
Raiatea, island, *Fr. Polynesia, Fr.* **219** E15
Raijua, island, *Indonesia* **189** N14
Rainbow Bridge National Monument, *Utah, U.S.* **107** Q8
Rainbow City, *Ala., U.S.* **101** J16
Rainbow Falls, *China* **180** L9
Rainbow Falls, *Hawai'i, U.S.* **113** M21
Rainier, *Oreg., U.S.* **108** E3
Rainier, Mount, *Wash., U.S.* **108** D4
Rainy, river, *Minn., U.S.* **104** E10
Rainy Lake, *Minn., U.S., Ont., Can.* **104** E11
Raipur, *India* **178** K8
Rairakhol, *India* **178** K9
Rairik, island, *Marshall Is.* **216** H12
Ra'īs, *Saudi Arabia* **172** K6
Raisinghnagar, *India* **178** E4
Raita Bank, *Hawai'i, U.S.* **112** L5
Raititi, Pointe, *Fr. Polynesia, Fr.* **219** K14
Raivavae (Vavitu), island, *Fr. Polynesia, Fr.* **219** J17
Raiwind, *Pak.* **177** Q12
Raja, Ujung, *Indonesia* **188** G4
Rajahmundry, *India* **178** M8
Rajampet, *India* **179** P6
Rajang, river, *Malaysia* **188** H11
Rajang, *Malaysia* **188** H10
Rajanpur, *Pak.* **177** S9
Rajapalaiyam, *India* **179** S6
Rajasthan Canal, *India* **178** F3
Rajgarh, *India* **178** F5
Rajin *see* Najin, *N. Korea* **182** B15
Rajkot, *India* **178** J2
Raj Nandgaon, *India* **178** K8
Rajpura, *India* **178** E5
Raj Samund, *India* **178** H4
Rakahanga Atoll, *Cook Is., N.Z.* **214** H11
Rakaia, *N.Z.* **213** P17
Rakaposhi, peak, *Pak.* **176** L12
Rakhiv, *Ukr.* **157** Q2
Rakhman Qaynary, *Kaz.* **175** D20
Rakhshan, river, *Pak.* **177** U4
Rakhyūt, *Oman* **173** P14
Rakiraki, *Fiji Is.* **218** H6
Rakops, *Botswana* **202** G9
Rakvere, *Est.* **141** K16
Raleigh, *Miss., U.S.* **100** M12
Raleigh, *N.C., U.S.* **96** H11
Ralik Chain, *Marshall Is.* **216** G3
Ralls, *Tex., U.S.* **102** K5
Ramah, *N. Mex., U.S.* **107** S10
Rām Allāh, *W. Bank* **170** M5
Raman, *Thai.* **187** S9
Ramanum, island, *F.S.M.* **217** B14
Ramat Gan, *Israel* **170** M5
Rambi *see* Rabi, island, *Fiji Is.* **218** G8
Rambu, *Indonesia* **189** J14
Rambutyo, island, *P.N.G.* **213** B20
Rameshki, *Russ.* **156** H9
Ramgarh, *India* **178** F2
Ram Head, *Virgin Islands, U.S.* **120** N11
Ramla, *Israel* **170** M5
Ramnagar, *India* **178** E7
Râmnicu Vâlcea, *Rom.* **153** E14
Ramona, *Calif., U.S.* **109** Y10
Ramos Island, *Solomon Is.* **217** M19
Rampart, *Alas., U.S.* **111** F16
Rampur, *India* **178** D6
Rampur, *India* **178** F7
Rampur Hat, *India* **178** H11
Ramree, *Myanmar* **186** J5
Ramree Island, *Myanmar* **186** J4
Ramsay, *Mich., U.S.* **98** F5
Ramsey Island, *Wales, U.K.* **143** V8
Ramu, *Bangladesh* **178** K14
Ramu, river, *P.N.G.* **213** C18
Ramvik, *Sw.* **141** H13
Rancagua, *Chile* **132** L7
Ranchester, *Wyo., U.S.* **106** F11
Ranchi, *India* **178** J10
Rancho Cordova, *Calif., U.S.* **109** R5
Rancione, river, *San Marino* **161** H16
Ranco, river, *San Marino* **161** H15
Ranco, Lago, *Chile* **133** P6
Randazzo, *It.* **151** S11
Randers, *Den.* **140** N11
Randolph, *Nebr., U.S.* **105** N7
Randolph, *Utah, U.S.* **106** K8
Randolph, *Vt., U.S.* **95** G13
Rangahoe, island, *Cook Is., N.Z.* **219** B13
Rangamati, *Bangladesh* **178** J14
Rangeley, *Me., U.S.* **95** E15
Rangely, *Colo., U.S.* **106** L10
Ranger, *Tex., U.S.* **102** L9
Rangiroa, island, *Fr. Polynesia, Fr.* **219** D17
Rangitaiki, river, *N.Z.* **213** K20
Rangkasbitung, *Indonesia* **188** L8
Rangkŭl, *Taj.* **176** H11
Rangoon *see* Yangon, *Myanmar* **186** K6
Rangpur, *Bangladesh* **178** G12
Rangsang, island, *Indonesia* **188** H6
Raniganj, *India* **178** J11
Ranikhet, *India* **178** E7
Ranikot, ruin, *Pak.* **177** V7
Rankin, *Tex., U.S.* **103** N5
Rankin Inlet, *Nunavut, Can.* **83** H15
Rannoch, Loch, *Scot., U.K.* **142** L9
Rann of Kutch, wetland, *India* **177** X8
Ranong, *Thai.* **187** Q7
Ranongga (Ganongga), island, *Solomon Is.* **217** M15
Rans, *Switz.* **160** P2
Ransiki, *Indonesia* **189** J19
Rantau, island, *Indonesia* **188** J6
Rantauprapat, *Indonesia* **188** H5
Rantekombola, peak, *Indonesia* **189** K13
Rantoul, *Ill., U.S.* **99** Q7
Ranwas, *Vanuatu* **218** D3
Raohe, *China* **181** C19
Raoping, *China* **183** R7
Raoul Island (Sunday), *Kermadec Is., N.Z.* **214** L9
Rapa, island, *Fr. Polynesia, Fr.* **215** L14
Rapallo, *It.* **150** F4
Rapa Passage, *Kiribati* **217** B20
Rapar, *India* **178** H2
Raper, Cape, *Nunavut, Can.* **83** E18
Rapid, river, *Minn., U.S.* **104** E10
Rapid City, *S. Dak., U.S.* **104** L2
Rapid River, *Mich., U.S.* **98** G8
Rapota, island, *Cook Is., N.Z.* **218** Q11
Rappenstein, peak, *Liech.* **160** Q3
Rápulo, river, *Bol.* **130** H7
Raquette Lake, *N.Y., U.S.* **94** G10
Raraka, island, *Fr. Polynesia, Fr.* **219** E18
Raroia, island, *Fr. Polynesia, Fr.* **219** E19
Rarotonga, island, *Cook Is., N.Z.* **214** K12
Rasa, Punta, *Arg.* **133** Q11
Ra's al 'Ayn, *Syr.* **170** C13
Ra's al Khaymah, *U.A.E.* **173** J15
Ra's an Naqb, *Jordan* **171** Q6
Rasa Point, *S. Amer.* **126** N6
Rashad, *Sudan* **198** F12
Rashîd (Rosetta), *Egypt* **197** C18
Rasht, *Iran* **172** B12
Raška, *Serb. & Mont.* **152** H10
Ras Koh Range, *Pak.* **177** S4
Raso, Cabo, *Port.* **144** J4
Rason Lake, *Austral.* **210** H5
Ra's Shamrah (Ugarit), ruin, *Syr.* **170** F6
Rasshua, island, *Russ.* **159** H23
Rasskazovo, *Russ.* **156** L11
Rasua Garhi, *Nepal* **178** F10
Ratak Chain, *Marshall Is.* **216** F5
Ratangarh, *India* **178** F4
Rathdrum, *Idaho, U.S.* **106** B3
Rathenow, *Ger.* **148** D9
Rathlin Island, *N. Ire., U.K.* **143** N7
Ráth Luirc (Charleville), *Ire.* **143** U4
Rätikon, range, *Switz.* **150** B5
Ratingen, *Ger.* **148** F5
Ratisbon *see* Regensburg, *Ger.* **148** J9
Rat Island, *Alas., U.S.* **110** M3
Rat Islands, *Alas., U.S.* **111** M2
Ratlam, *India* **178** J4
Ratnagiri, *India* **178** M3
Ratnapura, *Sri Lanka* **179** T7
Ratodero, *Pak.* **177** T7
Raton, *N. Mex., U.S.* **107** Q14
Raton Pass, *N. Mex., U.S.* **107** Q14
Rattlesnake Creek, *Oreg., U.S.* **108** K9
Rattlesnake Hills, *Wash., U.S.* **108** D6
Rattlesnake National Recreation Area, *Mont., U.S.* **106** C6
Rau, island, *Indonesia* **189** H16
Raub, *Malaysia* **187** T9
Rauch, *Arg.* **132** M12
Raudal Yupurari (Devils Cataract), *Col.* **128** H7
Raufarhöfn, *Ice.* **140** E4
Raukotaha, island, *Cook Is., N.Z.* **219** C14
Rauma, *Fin.* **141** J15
Raurkela, *India* **178** J10
Rausu, *Japan* **184** E16
Rausu Dake, *Japan* **184** E16
Ravahere, island, *Fr. Polynesia, Fr.* **219** F19
Rāvar, *Iran* **173** E15
Ravena, *N.Y., U.S.* **94** K11
Ravenna, *It.* **150** F8
Ravenna, *Nebr., U.S.* **105** Q6
Ravenna, *Ohio, U.S.* **99** P15
Ravensburg, *Ger.* **148** K7
Ravenshoe, *Qnsld., Austral.* **211** R13
Ravensthorpe, *W. Aust., Austral.* **211** X4
Ravenswood, *Qnsld., Austral.* **211** S13
Ravenswood, *W. Va., U.S.* **96** D8
Ravi, river, *Pak.* **177** Q11
Ravnina, *Turkm.* **174** M10
Rāwah, *Iraq* **172** D8
Rawaki, island, *Kiribati* **214** H10
Rawalpindi, *Pak.* **177** N11
Rawa Mazowiecka, *Pol.* **149** E15
Rawandoz, *Iraq* **172** B10
Rawḩah, *Saudi Arabia* **172** M8
Rawi, Ko, *Thai.* **187** S8
Rawicz, *Pol.* **149** F13
Rawlinna, *W. Aust., Austral.* **211** W6
Rawlins, *Wyo., U.S.* **106** J11
Rawson, *Arg.* **133** R10
Rawu, *China* **180** L9
Ray, *N. Dak., U.S.* **104** E2
Ray, Cape, *Nfld. & Lab., Can.* **83** N22
Raya, peak, *Indonesia* **188** J10
Rayachoti, *India* **179** P6
Raychikhinsk, *Russ.* **159** L19
Raydā', plain, *Saudi Arabia* **172** M11
Raymond, *Alta., Can.* **82** N10
Raymond, *Calif., U.S.* **109** S6
Raymond, *Wash., U.S.* **108** D2
Raymond Terrace, *N.S.W., Austral.* **211** X15
Raymondville, *Tex., U.S.* **103** W10
Ray Mountains, *Alas., U.S.* **84** N4
Rayne, *La., U.S.* **100** P8
Rayner Glacier, *Antarctica* **227** C18
Rayoke, island, *Russ.* **159** H23
Rayong, *Thai.* **187** N9
Raysūt, *Oman* **173** P14
Rayville, *La., U.S.* **100** L9
Raz, Pointe du, *Fr.* **147** Q2
Razelm, Lacul, *Rom.* **153** E18
Razgrad, *Bulg.* **153** G16
Razlog, *Bulg.* **153** K13
Razmak, *Pak.* **177** P8
Razo, island, *Cape Verde* **205** B15
Razzaza Lake, *Iraq* **172** E9
Ré, Île de, *Fr.* **147** T6
Re, river, *San Marino* **161** J14
Reading, *Eng., U.K.* **143** V13
Reading, *Jam.* **120** H6
Reading, *Pa., U.S.* **94** P8
Realicó, *Arg.* **132** L10
Réalmont, *Fr.* **147** X10
Ream, *Cambodia* **187** P11
Reao, island, *Fr. Polynesia, Fr.* **219** F22
Rebecca, Lake, *Austral.* **210** J4
Rebiana Sand Sea, *Lib.* **194** E7
Rebola, *Eq. Guinea* **204** L8
Rebun Tō, *Japan* **184** D13
Recey, *Fr.* **147** R12
Recherche, Archipelago of the, *Austral.* **210** K5
Rechytsa, *Belarus* **156** M6
Recife, *Braz.* **131** G18
Recife, Cape, *S. Af.* **202** M10
Récifs, Île aux, *Seychelles* **205** N21
Recklinghausen, *Ger.* **148** E5
Reconquista, *Arg.* **132** H12
Recreo, *Arg.* **132** H9
Rector, *Ark., U.S.* **100** E11
Red, river, *China, Vietnam* **166** J10
Red *see* Red River of the North, river, *Man., Can.* **83** N14
Red, river, *U.S.* **85** L14
Redang, island, *Malaysia* **187** S10
Redange sur Attert, *Lux.* **160** J9
Red Bank, *Tenn., U.S.* **101** G17
Red Bay, *Ala., U.S.* **101** H13
Red Bay, *Cayman Is., U.K.* **120** J2
Red Bluff, *Calif., U.S.* **109** N4
Red Bluff Lake, *Tex., U.S.* **102** M2
Red Butte, *Ariz., U.S.* **107** R7
Red Cliff, *St. Kitts & Nevis* **121** C18
Redcliffe, Mount, *Austral.* **210** H4
Red Cloud, *Nebr., U.S.* **105** R6
Red Deer, *Alta., Can.* **82** M10
Red Devil, *Alas., U.S.* **111** J14
Redding, *Calif., U.S.* **109** N3
Redfield, *S. Dak., U.S.* **104** K6
Red Hills, *Kans., U.S.* **105** U5
Red Hook, *Virgin Islands, U.S.* **120** N10
Redig, *S. Dak., U.S.* **104** J2
Red Lake, *Minn., U.S.* **104** F10
Red Lake, *Ont., Can.* **83** N14
Red Lake, *W. Aust., Austral.* **211** X4
Red Lake Falls, *Minn., U.S.* **104** F8
Redlands, *Calif., U.S.* **109** X9
Red Lodge, *Mont., U.S.* **106** F9
Redmond, *Oreg., U.S.* **108** H5
Red Mountian, *Mont., U.S.* **106** C7
Red Oak, *Iowa, U.S.* **105** Q10
Redon, *Fr.* **147** R5
Redonda, island, *Antigua & Barbuda* **119** G16
Redonda, Roca, *Ecua.* **128** P7
Redondo, *Port.* **144** J6
Redoubt Volcano, *Alas., U.S.* **111** K15
Red River of the North, *Minn., N. Dak., U.S.* **104** F8
Red Rock, river, *Mont., U.S.* **106** F7
Red Rocks Point, *Austral.* **210** J6
Redruth, *Eng., U.K.* **143** X8
Red Sea, *Af., Asia* **166** G2
Red Springs, *N.C., U.S.* **96** J11
Redwater, river, *Mont., U.S.* **106** C12
Red Wing, *Minn., U.S.* **104** K12
Redwood Empire, region, *Calif., U.S.* **108** L2
Redwood Falls, *Minn., U.S.* **104** K10
Redwood National Park, *Calif., U.S.* **108** L2
Ree, Lough, *Ire.* **143** R5
Reed City, *Mich., U.S.* **98** K10
Reeder, *N. Dak., U.S.* **104** H2
Reedley, *Calif., U.S.* **109** T7
Reeds, Plain of, *Vietnam* **187** P12
Reedsburg, *Wis., U.S.* **98** K4
Reedsport, *Oreg., U.S.* **108** H2
Reedville, *Va., U.S.* **96** E14
Reedy Glacier, *Antarctica* **226** K11
Reef Bay, *Virgin Islands, U.S.* **120** N11
Reef Islands, *Solomon Is.* **217** P22
Reef Islands (Rowa Islands), *Vanuatu* **218** B2
Reefton, *N.Z.* **213** N17
Reese, river, *Nev., U.S.* **109** N9
Refahiye, *Turk.* **169** E13
Reform, *Ala., U.S.* **101** J14
Refugio, *Tex., U.S.* **103** T11
Regensburg (Ratisbon), *Ger.* **148** J9
Reggane, *Alg.* **196** D10
Reggio di Calabria, *It.* **151** R12
Reggio nell'Emilia, *It.* **150** F6
Reghin, *Rom.* **153** C14
Régina, *Fr. Guiana, Fr.* **129** F18
Regina, *Sask., Can.* **82** N12
Rehoboth, *Namibia* **202** H7
Rehoboth Beach, *Del., U.S.* **96** C15
Reid, *W. Aust., Austral.* **211** W7
Reid River, *Qnsld., Austral.* **211** S13
Reidsville, *Ga., U.S.* **97** N8
Reidsville, *N.C., U.S.* **96** G10
Reigate, *Eng., U.K.* **143** W14
Reims, *Fr.* **147** N12
Reina Adelaida, Archipiélago, *Chile* **133** W6
Reindeer Lake, *Man., Sask., Can.* **83** K13
Reinga, Cape, *N.Z.* **213** G17
Reinosa, *Sp.* **144** B10
Reisdorf, *Lux.* **160** H10
Reitoru, island, *Fr. Polynesia, Fr.* **219** F19
Rekareka *see* Tehuata, island, *Fr. Polynesia, Fr.* **219** E19
Rekata Bay, *Solomon Is.* **217** L17
Reliance, *N.W.T., Can.* **82** H12
Reliance, *Wyo., U.S.* **106** K9
Remada, *Tun.* **197** C13
Remanso, *Braz.* **131** G15
Remedios, *Cuba* **116** H9
Remer, *Minn., U.S.* **104** G11
Remeshk, *Iran* **173** H16
Remich, *Lux.* **160** K11
Rémire, *Fr. Guiana, Fr.* **129** E18
Remiremont, *Fr.* **147** Q14
Remontnoye, *Russ.* **157** R13
Ren, island, *Marshall Is.* **216** K7
Rendezvous Bay, *Virgin Islands, U.S.* **120** N11
Rend Lake, *Ill., U.S.* **99** U6
Rendova, island, *Solomon Is.* **217** M16
Rendsburg, *Ger.* **148** B7
Rengat, *Indonesia* **188** J6
Reni, *Ukr.* **157** S4
Renmark, *S. Aust., Austral.* **211** X11
Rennell, island, *Solomon Is.* **217** Q19
Rennes, *Fr.* **147** Q5
Rennick Glacier, *Antarctica* **227** Q14
Reno, *Nev., U.S.* **109** P6
Renovo, *Pa., U.S.* **94** M6
Rensselaer, *Ind., U.S.* **99** P8
Renton, *Wash., U.S.* **108** C4
Renville, *Minn., U.S.* **104** K9
Repetek, *Turkm.* **174** M10
Republic, *Mich., U.S.* **98** F7
Republic, *Wash., U.S.* **108** A7
Republican, river, *Nebr., U.S.* **105** R6
Repulse Bay, *Austral.* **210** E14
Repulse Bay, *Nunavut, Can.* **83** G16
Requena, *Peru* **130** E4
Requena, *Sp.* **145** H14
Requin Bay, *Grenada* **121** L23
Reşadiye, *Turk.* **168** D12
Researcher Ridge, *Atl. Oc.* **236** L7
Reserve, *La., U.S.* **100** P10
Reserve, *N. Mex., U.S.* **107** T10
Resia, *It.* **150** B6
Resistencia, *Arg.* **132** G12
Reşiţa, *Rom.* **152** E11
Resolute, *Nunavut, Can.* **83** D15
Resolution Island, *N.Z.* **213** R14
Rest, *Jam.* **120** J8
Restinga, Punta, *Canary Is.* **204** R3
Réthimno, *Gr.* **155** Q13
Reti, *Pak.* **177** T8
Réunion, island, *Fr., Ind. Oc.* **204** H9
Reus, *Sp.* **145** E16
Reutlingen, *Ger.* **148** K7
Reva, *S. Dak., U.S.* **104** J2
Reval *see* Tallinn, *Est.* **141** K16
Revelstoke, *B.C., Can.* **82** M9
Revigny, *Fr.* **147** P13
Revillagigedo, Islas, *Mex.* **114** H5
Revillagigedo Island, *Alas., U.S.* **111** M23
Revillagigedo Islands *see* Revillagigedo, Islas, *N. Amer.* **80** N2
Revsbotn, *Nor.* **141** C14
Rewa, river, *Fiji Is.* **218** J6
Rewa, *India* **178** H8
Rexburg, *Idaho, U.S.* **106** G7
Rexford, *Mont., U.S.* **106** A5
Rexton, *Mich., U.S.* **98** F10
Rey, *Iran* **173** C13
Rey, Isla del, *Pan.* **115** N21
Rey Bouba, *Cameroon* **201** G17
Reyes, *Bol.* **130** H6
Reyes, Point, *Calif., U.S.* **84** G2
Reyhanlı, *Turk.* **168** J11
Reykjanes, cape, *Ice.* **138** A3
Reykjanes Ridge, *Atl. Oc.* **236** D9
Reykjavík, *Ice.* **140** F2
Reynosa, *Mex.* **114** F12
Rēzekne, *Latv.* **141** M17
Rgotina, *Serb. & Mont.* **152** G12
Rhaetian Alps, *Switz.* **150** C5
Rhame, *N. Dak., U.S.* **104** H2
Rheine, *Ger.* **148** D6
Rhiconich, *Scot., U.K.* **142** H8
Rhine *see* Rhein, Rhin, river, *Eur.* **138** F5
Rhine, Sources of the, *Switz.* **138** H6
Rhinelander, *Wis., U.S.* **98** G5
Rhinns of Kells, region, *Scot., U.K.* **143** P9
Rhino Camp, *Uganda* **198** J12
Rhinocolura *see* El 'Arîsh, *Egypt* **171** N3
Rhir, Cape, *Mor.* **194** D2
Rhiy di-Momī, cape, *Yemen* **173** R15
Rho, *It.* **150** D4
Rhode Island, *U.S.* **95** L14
Rhodes *see* Ródos, island, *Gr.* **155** N20
Rhodes *see* Ródos, *Gr.* **155** M20
Rhodes Peak, *Idaho, U.S.* **106** D5
Rhodope Mountains, *Bulg., Gr.* **138** J9
Rhône, river, *Fr., Switz.* **147** W12
Rhône au Rhin, Canal du, *Fr.* **147** R15
Rhum, Sound of, *Scot., U.K.* **142** K7

Rhyl, *Wales, U.K.* **143** S10
Rhynie, *Scot., U.K.* **142** K10
Riaba, *Eq. Guinea* **204** M7
Riaba, Bahia de, *Eq. Guinea* **204** M7
Riachão, *Braz.* **131** F14
Rialb, river, *Andorra* **160** G3
Riang, *India* **178** F14
Riaño, *Sp.* **144** B9
Riasi, *India* **177** N12
Riau, Kepulauan, *Indonesia* **188** J7
Riaza, *Sp.* **144** E11
Ribadeo, *Sp.* **144** A7
Ribáuè, *Mozambique* **203** E14
Ribeira Afonso, *Sao Tome and Principe* **205** D20
Ribeira Brava, *Madeira* **204** M3
Ribeira da Cruz, *Cape Verde* **205** A14
Ribeira Grande, *Azores* **144** Q5
Ribeira Grande, *Cape Verde* **205** A14
Ribeirão Prêto, *Braz.* **131** L13
Ribera, *It.* **151** S9
Riberalta, *Bol.* **130** G7
Ribes de Freser, *Sp.* **145** C17
Ribewon, island, *Marshall Is.* **216** J8
Riblah, *Syr.* **170** H8
Rib Lake, *Wis., U.S.* **98** H4
Rib Mountain, *Wis., U.S.* **98** H5
Ribniţa, *Mold.* **157** Q5
Ribnitz-Damgarten, *Ger.* **148** B9
Riccione, *It.* **150** G8
Rice Lake, *Wis., U.S.* **98** G3
Richards Bay, *S. Af.* **202** K12
Richardson Highway, *Alas., U.S.* **111** H18
Richardson Mountains, *N.W.T., Yukon, Can.* **82** E9
Richardton, *N. Dak., U.S.* **104** G3
Richey, *Mont., U.S.* **106** C13
Richfield, *Utah, U.S.* **107** N7
Richford, *Vt., U.S.* **95** E13
Rich Hill, *Mo., U.S.* **105** T11
Richland, *Ga., U.S.* **97** N4
Richland, *Mo., U.S.* **105** U13
Richland, *Oreg., U.S.* **108** G9
Richland, *Wash., U.S.* **108** E7
Richland Center, *Wis., U.S.* **98** L4
Richland Chambers Reservoir, *Tex., U.S.* **102** M13
Richlands, *Va., U.S.* **96** F8
Richland Springs, *Tex., U.S.* **103** N9
Richmond, *Calif., U.S.* **109** R3
Richmond, *Ind., U.S.* **99** R10
Richmond, *Jam.* **120** H10
Richmond, *Ky., U.S.* **101** C18
Richmond, *Me., U.S.* **95** G16
Richmond, *Mo., U.S.* **105** S11
Richmond, *N.S.W., Austral.* **211** Y14
Richmond, *Qnsld., Austral.* **211** S12
Richmond, *S. Af.* **202** L9
Richmond, *St. Vincent & the Grenadines* **121** K16
Richmond, *Tex., U.S.* **103** R13
Richmond, *Utah, U.S.* **106** J7
Richmond, *Va., U.S.* **96** E13
Richmond Hill, *Bahamas* **120** E8
Richmond Peak, *St. Vincent & the Grenadines* **121** K16
Rich Square, *N.C., U.S.* **96** G13
Richton, *Miss., U.S.* **100** N12
Richwood, *W. Va., U.S.* **96** E9
Rico, *Colo., U.S.* **107** P10
Ricobayo, Embalse de, *Sp.* **144** D8
Riḑā', *Yemen* **172** Q9
Ridanna, *It.* **150** B7
Ridder (Lenīnogorsk), *Kaz.* **175** D18
Riddle, *Idaho, U.S.* **106** J3
Riddle, *Oreg., U.S.* **108** J2
Ridgecrest, *Calif., U.S.* **109** V9
Ridgefield, *Wash., U.S.* **108** E3
Ridgeland, *S.C., U.S.* **96** M9
Ridgway, *Colo., U.S.* **107** N11
Ridgway, *Pa., U.S.* **94** M5
Riding Point, *Bahamas* **120** E3
Riding Rocks, *Bahamas* **116** D10
Riesa, *Ger.* **148** F10
Rieti, *It.* **150** K9
Rieumes, *Fr.* **147** X8
Rieupeyroux, *Fr.* **147** W10
Riez, *Fr.* **147** X14
Rifle, *Colo., U.S.* **106** M11
Rifstangi, cape, *Ice.* **138** A4
Rīga, *Latv.* **141** M16
Riga, Gulf of, *Est., Latv.* **141** L16
Rīgān, *Iran* **173** G16
Rigby, *Idaho, U.S.* **106** G7
Rigestan, desert, *Afghan.* **177** R5
Riggins, *Idaho, U.S.* **106** E4
Riglos, *Sp.* **145** C14
Rigo, *P.N.G.* **213** E20
Rigolet, *Nfld. & Lab., Can.* **83** K22
Rig Rig, *Chad* **197** H14
Riiser-Larsen Ice Shelf, *Antarctica* **226** B10
Riiser-Larsen Peninsula, *Antarctica* **227** B17
Rijeka (Fiume), *Croatia* **152** E4
Rijeka Crnojevića, *Serb. & Mont.* **152** J8
Rikitea, *Fr. Polynesia, Fr.* **219** Q20
Rikubetsu, *Japan* **184** F15
Rikuzentakata, *Japan* **184** L14
Rila, range, *Bulg.* **153** J13
Riley, *Kans., U.S.* **105** S8
Rilly, *Fr.* **147** P12
Rimā', Jabal ar, *Jordan* **170** L8
Rimah, Wādī ar, *Saudi Arabia* **172** H8
Rimatara, island, *Fr. Polynesia, Fr.* **215** K13
Rimavská Sobota, *Slovakia* **149** K15
Rimini, *It.* **150** G8
Rîmnicu Sărat, *Rom.* **153** E16
Rimouski, *Que., Can.* **83** N20
Rincón, *P.R., U.S.* **120** M1
Rincón, Bahía de, *P.R., U.S.* **120** P4
Rincon, *Neth. Antilles, Neth.* **121** Q19
Rincon, *Ga., U.S.* **97** N9
Rinconada, *Arg.* **132** D9
Rincón de la Victoria, *Sp.* **144** M10
Rincón del Bonete, Lago, *Uru.* **132** K14
Ringbu, *Nor.* **140** J11
Ringdom Gompa, *India* **176** M13
Ringdove Passage, *Solomon Is.* **217** Q23
Ringgold, *La., U.S.* **100** L7
Ringgold Isles, *Fiji Is.* **218** G9
Ringkøbing, *Den.* **140** N10
Ringling, *Okla., U.S.* **102** J10
Ringvassøy, island, *Nor.* **141** C13
Ringwood, *N. Terr., Austral.* **211** T9
Rinía, island, *Gr.* **155** K15
Rio, *Gr.* **154** H9
Riobamba, *Ecua.* **128** K3
Rio Branco, *Braz.* **130** G6
Rio Bueno, *Jam.* **120** H8
Río Bueno, *Chile* **133** P6
Rio Canario, *Neth. Antilles, Neth.* **121** P14
Río Cauto, *Cuba* **116** K12
Rio Chama, river, *N. Mex., U.S.* **107** Q12
Rio Claro, *Trinidad & Tobago* **121** Q23
Río Cuarto, *Arg.* **132** K10
Rio de Janeiro, *Braz.* **131** M15
Rio Dell, *Calif., U.S.* **109** N1
Rio do Ouro, *Sao Tome and Principe* **205** C20
Río Gallegos, *Arg.* **133** W8
Rio Grande, river, *Mex., U.S.* **84** N11
Río Grande, *Arg.* **133** X9
Rio Grande, *Braz.* **130** Q11
Rio Grande City, *Tex., U.S.* **103** W9
Rio Grande Rise, *Atl. Oc.* **237** S8
Rio Grande Wild and Scenic River, *Tex., U.S.* **103** Q4
Riohacha, *Col.* **128** B6
Rio Hondo, river, *N. Mex., U.S.* **107** U13
Riom, *Fr.* **147** U11
Río Mulatos, *Bol.* **130** K7
Río Muni, region, *Eq. Guinea* **201** K15
Rioni, river, *Rep. of Georgia* **169** B17
Rio Nuevo, *Jam.* **120** H9
Rio Peñasco, river, *N. Mex., U.S.* **107** U14
Rio Puerco, river, *N. Mex., U.S.* **107** S12
Rio Rancho, *N. Mex., U.S.* **107** S12
Rio Tejo, Foz do, *Port.* **144** J4
Río Verde, *Chile* **133** W8
Río Verde, *Mex.* **114** H11
Rio Verde, *Braz.* **130** K12
Rio Verde de Mato Grosso, *Braz.* **130** K11
Rio Vouga, Foz do, *Port.* **144** F5
Rioz, *Fr.* **147** R14
Ripley, *Calif., U.S.* **109** Y13
Ripley, *Miss., U.S.* **100** G12
Ripley, *Ohio, U.S.* **99** T12
Ripley, *Tenn., U.S.* **100** F12
Ripley, *W. Va., U.S.* **96** D8
Ripoll, *Sp.* **145** C17
Ripon, *Eng., U.K.* **143** Q12
Ripon, *Wis., U.S.* **98** K6
Risāfe *see* Ar Ruşāfah, ruin, *Syr.* **170** F11
Riscle, *Fr.* **147** X7
Rishikesh, *India* **178** E6
Rishiri Tō, *Japan* **184** D13
Rishon LeZiyyon, *Israel* **170** M5
Rising Star, *Tex., U.S.* **102** M9
Rîşnov, *Rom.* **153** E15
Rison, *Ark., U.S.* **100** H8
Risør, *Nor.* **140** L11
Rita Blanca Creek, *Tex., U.S.* **102** F4
Ritchie's Archipelago, *India* **179** Q14
Ritidian Point, *Guam, U.S.* **216** A11
Ritscher Upland, *Antarctica* **226** B11
Ritzville, *Wash., U.S.* **108** C8
Riva, river, *San Marino* **161** K16
Rivadavia, *Chile* **132** J7
Riva del Garda, *It.* **150** D6
Riva di Tures, *It.* **150** B8
Rivas, *Nicar.* **115** M18
Rive-de-Gier, *Fr.* **147** U12
Rivera, *Uru.* **132** J14
River Cess, *Liberia* **200** H7
Riverdale, *N. Dak., U.S.* **104** F4
Riverhead, *N.Y., U.S.* **95** N13
Riverina, region, *Austral.* **210** L12
Riverina, *W. Aust., Austral.* **211** W4
Riverside, *Calif., U.S.* **109** X9
Riverside, *Wash., U.S.* **108** B7
Riverside, *Wyo., U.S.* **106** K11
Riversleigh, *Qnsld., Austral.* **211** R10
Riverton, *Man., Can.* **83** N14
Riverton, *Wyo., U.S.* **106** H10
Rivesaltes, *Fr.* **147** Y10
Riviera, *Fr., It.* **138** H5
Rivière des Anguilles, *Mauritius* **205** H20
Rivière-du-Loup, *Que., Can.* **83** N20
Rivière du Rempart, *Mauritius* **205** F20
Rivière Noire, Piton de la, *Mauritius* **205** G19
Rivière-Pilote, *Martinique, Fr.* **121** F23
Rivière-Salée, *Martinique, Fr.* **121** F23
Rivne, *Ukr.* **157** N3
Rivoli, *It.* **150** E2
Riwoqê, *China* **180** L9
Riyadh *see* Ar Riyāḑ, *Saudi Arabia* **172** J10
Rize, *Turk.* **169** D15
Rizhao, *China* **182** G8
Rizokarpaso, *Cyprus* **160** M11
Rizzuto, Capo, *It.* **151** Q14
Ro, *New Caledonia, Fr.* **218** D10
Ro (Ágios Geórgios), island, *Gr.* **155** N22
Roa, *Sp.* **144** D10
Road Bay, *Anguilla, U.K.* **120** R11
Road Bay, *Virgin Islands, U.K.* **120** Q6
Road Town, *Virgin Islands, U.K.* **120** Q6
Roan Cliffs, *Colo., Utah, U.S.* **84** G7
Roanne, *Fr.* **147** T12
Roanoke, *Ala., U.S.* **101** K17
Roanoke, river, *N.C., Va., U.S.* **96** G13
Roanoke, *Va., U.S.* **96** F10
Roanoke Island, *N.C., U.S.* **96** G15
Roanoke Rapids, *N.C., U.S.* **96** G12
Roan Plateau, *Colo., U.S.* **106** M10
Roaringwater Bay, *Ire.* **143** V3
Robāţ-e Khān, *Iran* **173** D15
Robat-e Khoshk Aveh, *Afghan.* **177** P2
Robāţ-e Posht-e Bādām, *Iran* **173** D15
Robe, *S. Aust., Austral.* **211** Z10
Robersonville, *N.C., U.S.* **96** H13
Robert Glacier, *Antarctica* **227** D19
Robert Lee, *Tex., U.S.* **102** M7
Roberts, *Idaho, U.S.* **106** G7
Roberts Butte, *Antarctica* **227** Q15
Roberts Creek Mountain, *Nev., U.S.* **109** P10
Robert S. Kerr Reservoir, *Okla., U.S.* **102** G14
Roberts Mountain, *Alas., U.S.* **84** Q1
Robertsport, *Liberia* **200** G6
Robeson Channel, *Nunavut, Can.* **83** A17
Robinson, *Ill., U.S.* **99** S7
Róbinson Crusoe, Isla, *S. Amer.* **126** M2
Robinson Range, *Austral.* **210** G3
Robinson River, *N. Terr., Austral.* **211** Q10
Robinvale, *Vic., Austral.* **211** Y11
Robokaere, island, *Marshall Is.* **216** G11
Roboré, *Bol.* **130** K9
Rob Roy, island, *Solomon Is.* **217** L16
Robson, Mount, *B.C., Can.* **82** L9
Robstown, *Tex., U.S.* **103** U11
Roby, *Tex., U.S.* **102** L7
Roca Partida, Isla, *Mex.* **114** H6
Roca Partida Island *see* Roca Partida, Isla, *N. Amer.* **80** N3
Rocas, Atol das, *S. Amer.* **126** E12
Rocas Brazil, Atol das, *Braz.* **131** E18
Roccadaspide, *It.* **151** N12
Rocca San Casciano, *It.* **150** G7
Roccastrada, *It.* **150** H7
Rocha, *Uru.* **132** L15
Rochdale, *Eng., U.K.* **143** R11
Rochedo, *Braz.* **130** K11
Rochefort, *Belg.* **146** M13
Rochefort, *Fr.* **147** T6
Rochelle, *Ga., U.S.* **97** N6
Rochelle, *Ill., U.S.* **99** N5
Roche's Bluff, *Montserrat, U.K.* **121** C24
Rocheservière, *Fr.* **147** S6
Roches Noires, Mouillage des, *Fr. Polynesia, Fr.* **219** J20
Rochester, *Eng., U.K.* **143** N11
Rochester, *Eng., U.K.* **143** V15
Rochester, *Ind., U.S.* **99** P9
Rochester, *Minn., U.S.* **104** L12
Rochester, *N.H., U.S.* **95** H15
Rochester, *N.Y., U.S.* **94** J6
Rock, river, *Ill., U.S.* **99** N5
Rockall, island, *Atl. Oc.* **236** D11
Rockaway, *Oreg., U.S.* **108** F2
Rock Creek, *Mont., U.S.* **106** E9
Rock Creek Butte, *Oreg., U.S.* **108** G8
Rockdale, *Tex., U.S.* **103** P11
Rockefeller Plateau, *Antarctica* **226** L9
Rock Falls, *Ill., U.S.* **99** N5
Rockford, *Ill., U.S.* **98** M5
Rockhampton, *Qnsld., Austral.* **211** T15
Rockhampton Downs, *N. Terr., Austral.* **211** R9
Rock Hill, *S.C., U.S.* **96** J9
Rockingham, *N.C., U.S.* **96** J10
Rockingham, *W. Aust., Austral.* **211** X2
Rockingham Bay, *Austral.* **210** D13
Rock Island, *Ill., U.S.* **99** P4
Rock Lake, *N. Dak., U.S.* **104** E6
Rockland, *Me., U.S.* **95** G17
Rockland, *Mich., U.S.* **98** F6
Rocklea, *W. Aust., Austral.* **211** T2
Rockledge, *Fla., U.S.* **97** T9
Rockly Bay, *Trinidad & Tobago* **121** N17
Rockmart, *Ga., U.S.* **96** K4
Rock Port, *Mo., U.S.* **105** Q9
Rockport, *Calif., U.S.* **109** P2
Rockport, *Ind., U.S.* **99** U8
Rockport, *Tex., U.S.* **103** T11
Rock Rapids, *Iowa, U.S.* **104** M9
Rock River, *Wyo., U.S.* **106** J12
Rock Sound, *Bahamas* **120** F6
Rock Sound, *Bahamas* **120** F6
Rock Springs, *Mont., U.S.* **106** D12
Rock Springs, *Wyo., U.S.* **106** K9
Rocksprings, *Tex., U.S.* **103** Q7
Rockton, *Ill., U.S.* **98** M6
Rockville, *Ind., U.S.* **99** R8
Rockville, *Md., U.S.* **96** C13
Rockwell City, *Iowa, U.S.* **105** N10
Rockwood, *Me., U.S.* **95** D16
Rockwood, *Tenn., U.S.* **101** F18
Rocky Ford, *Colo., U.S.* **107** N14
Rocky Mount, *N.C., U.S.* **96** H12
Rocky Mount, *Va., U.S.* **96** F10
Rocky Mountain National Park, *Colo., U.S.* **106** L12
Rocky Mountains, *N. Amer.* **80** F3
Rocky Point, *Bahamas* **120** C6
Rocky Point, *Norfolk I., Austral.* **217** G20
Rocky Point, *Bahamas* **120** E11
Rodanthe, *N.C., U.S.* **96** H15
Roddickton, *Nfld. & Lab., Can.* **83** L23
Rodeo, *Arg.* **132** J7
Rodeo, *N. Mex., U.S.* **107** W10
Rodez, *Fr.* **147** W10
Rodinga, *N. Terr., Austral.* **211** U9
Ródos (Rhodes), island, *Gr.* **155** N20
Ródos (Rhodes), *Gr.* **155** M20
Rodrigues, island, *Ind. Oc.* **204** H10
Rodrigues Fracture Zone, *Ind. Oc.* **240** K7
Roebourne, *W. Aust., Austral.* **211** S2
Roebuck Bay, *Austral.* **210** D4
Roebuck Plains, *W. Aust., Austral.* **211** R4
Roermond, *Neth.* **146** K13
Roeselare, *Belg.* **146** L11
Roes Welcome Sound, *Nunavut, Can.* **83** H16
Rogagua, Lago, *Bol.* **130** H7
Rogers, *Ark., U.S.* **100** E6
Rogers, *Tex., U.S.* **103** P11
Rogers, Mount, *Va., U.S.* **96** G8
Rogers City, *Mich., U.S.* **98** H11
Rogers Lake, *Calif., U.S.* **109** W9
Rogerson, *Idaho, U.S.* **106** J5
Rogersville, *Tenn., U.S.* **101** E19
Roggan, river, *Que., Can.* **83** L18
Rogliano, *Fr.* **150** J4
Rogliano, *It.* **151** Q13
Rognan, *Nor.* **140** E12
Rogue, river, *Oreg., U.S.* **108** K2
Rogue River, *Oreg., U.S.* **108** K3
Roguron, island, *Marshall Is.* **216** G10
Rohrbach, *Aust.* **148** K10
Rohri, *Pak.* **177** T7
Rohtak, *India* **178** F5
Roi, *F.S.M.* **217** G14
Roi Anchorage, *Marshall Is.* **216** K4
Roi Et, *Thai.* **186** L11
Roi-Namur, island, *Marshall Is.* **216** K4
Rojas, *Arg.* **132** L12
Rojhan, *Pak.* **177** S8
Rojo, Cabo, *P.R., U.S.* **120** P1
Rokera, *Solomon Is.* **217** N20
Rokiškis, *Lith.* **141** M17
Rôlas, Ilhéu das, *Sao Tome and Principe* **205** E19
Rolette, *N. Dak., U.S.* **104** E5
Rolla, *Mo., U.S.* **105** T13
Rolla, *N. Dak., U.S.* **104** D5
Rolleston, *N.Z.* **213** P17
Rolleston, *Qnsld., Austral.* **211** U14
Rolletown, *Bahamas* **120** F9
Rolleville, *Bahamas* **120** E8
Rolling Fork, *Miss., U.S.* **100** K10
Rollins, *Mont., U.S.* **106** B5
Rolvsøya, island, *Nor.* **141** B14
Roma, *Qnsld., Austral.* **211** V14
Roma (Rome), *It.* **150** K8
Romain, Cape, *S.C., U.S.* **96** M11
Romaine, river, *Que., Can.* **83** M21
Roma-Los Saenz, *Tex., U.S.* **103** W9
Roman, *Rom.* **153** C16
Romanche Fracture Zone, *Atl. Oc.* **237** N11
Romanche Gap, *Atl. Oc.* **237** N10
Romang, island, *Indonesia* **189** M16
Romāni, *Egypt* **171** N1
Romania, *Eur.* **139** V9
Romanija, peak, *Bosn. & Herzg.* **152** G8
Romano, Cape, *Fla., U.S.* **97** X8
Romano, Cayo, *Cuba* **116** H11
Romanovka, *Russ.* **159** L16
Romans, *Fr.* **147** V13
Romanshorn, *Switz.* **150** A5
Romanzof, Cape, *Alas., U.S.* **84** P1
Rombo, Ilhéus do *see* Secos, Ilhéus, *Cape Verde* **205** D15
Rome, *Ga., U.S.* **96** K4
Rome *see* Roma, *It.* **150** K8
Rome, *N.Y., U.S.* **94** J9
Romilly, *Fr.* **147** Q11
Rommani, *Mor.* **196** B8
Romney, *W. Va., U.S.* **96** C11
Romny, *Ukr.* **157** N7
Romodanovo, *Russ.* **156** K13
Romorantin-Lanthenay, *Fr.* **147** R9
Romsey, *Eng., U.K.* **143** W12
Rona, island, *Scot., U.K.* **142** F7
Ronan, *Mont., U.S.* **106** C5
Roncador, Serra do, *Braz.* **130** H12
Roncador Cay, *N. Amer.* **80** P9
Ronceverte, *W. Va., U.S.* **96** E9
Ronda, *Sp.* **144** M9
Ronde, Point, *Dominica* **121** E18
Ronde Island, *Grenada* **121** H24
Rondônia *see* Ji-Paraná, *Braz.* **130** G8
Rondonópolis, *Braz.* **130** J11
Rondu, *Pak.* **176** L12
Rong, Koh, *Cambodia* **187** P10
Rong'an, *China* **183** P1
Rongcheng, *China* **182** F10
Ronge, Lac la, *N. Amer.* **80** G5
Rongelap Atoll, *Marshall Is.* **216** F3
Rongerik Atoll, *Marshall Is.* **216** F3
Rongjiang, *China* **183** P1
Rong Kwang, *Thai.* **186** J8
Rongshui, *China* **183** Q1
Rongxian, *China* **183** R2
Ronkiti, *F.S.M.* **217** G14
Ronkiti Harbor, *F.S.M.* **217** G14
Rønne, *Den.* **141** P13
Ronne Entrance, *Antarctica* **226** G6
Ronne Ice Shelf, *Antarctica* **226** F8
Ronse, *Belg.* **146** L11
Roodhouse, *Ill., U.S.* **99** S4
Roof Butte, *Ariz., U.S.* **107** Q9
Roonui, Mont, *Fr. Polynesia, Fr.* **219** Q17
Roorkee, *India* **178** E6
Roosendaal, *Neth.* **146** K12
Roosevelt, *Utah, U.S.* **106** L9
Roosevelt, Mount, *B.C., Can.* **82** J9

Roosevelt Island, Antarctica 226 M11
Roosevelt Roads Naval Station, P.R., U.S. 120 N6
Root, river, Minn., U.S. 104 L13
Roper, river, N. Terr., Austral. 211 Q9
Roper Valley, N. Terr., Austral. 211 Q9
Ropesville, Tex., U.S. 102 K4
Roquefort, Fr. 147 W7
Roques, Islas Los, Venez. 128 A10
Roquetas de Mar, Sp. 144 M12
Roraima, Mount, S. Amer. 126 B6
Røros, Nor. 140 J11
Rorschach, Switz. 150 A5
Rørvik, Nor. 140 G11
Rosa, Lake, Bahamas 117 J15
Rosa, Monte, It., Switz. 150 D3
Rosal de la Frontera, Sp. 144 K7
Rosalia, Wash., U.S. 108 C9
Rosalie, Dominica 121 F20
Rosalie Bay, Dominica 121 F20
Rosário, Braz. 131 D15
Rosario, Arg. 132 K12
Rosario, Mex. 114 G9
Rosario, Parag. 130 M10
Rosario, Cayo del, Cuba 116 H7
Rosario de la Frontera, Arg. 132 F9
Rosario de Lerma, Arg. 132 F9
Rosarno, It. 151 R13
Roscoe, S. Dak., U.S. 104 J6
Roscoe, Tex., U.S. 102 L7
Roscommon, Ire. 143 R5
Roscommon, Mich., U.S. 98 J11
Roscrea, Ire. 143 S5
Rose, Pointe de la, Martinique, Fr. 121 F23
Rose Atoll, Amer. Samoa, U.S. 214 J10
Roseau, river, Dominica 121 G19
Roseau, Dominica 121 G19
Roseau, river, Minn., U.S. 104 D8
Roseau, Minn., U.S. 104 D9
Roseau, river, St. Lucia 121 K14
Rose Belle, Mauritius 205 G20
Rosebery, Tas., Austral. 211 Z15
Rosebud, Mont., U.S. 106 D12
Rosebud, Tex., U.S. 103 P11
Rosebud Creek, Mont., U.S. 106 E12
Roseburg, Oreg., U.S. 108 J3
Rosedale, Miss., U.S. 100 J10
Rosedale, Qnsld., Austral. 211 U15
Rose Hall, Jam. 120 G7
Rose Hill, Mauritius 205 G20
Rose Island, Bahamas 120 B12
Rosenbach, Aust. 148 M10
Rosenberg, Tex., U.S. 103 R13
Rosenheim, Ger. 148 L9
Rose Peak, Ariz., U.S. 107 U9
Rosepine, La., U.S. 100 N7
Roses, Bahamas 117 G14
Roses, Sp. 145 C18
Roses, Golf de, Sp. 145 C18
Rosetown, Sask., Can. 82 M11
Rosetta see Rashîd, Egypt 197 C18
Roseville, Calif., U.S. 109 Q5
Rosholt, S. Dak., U.S. 104 H8
Rosht-Kala, Taj. 176 K9
Rosia Bay, Gibraltar, U.K. 161 Q22
Rosiclare, Ill., U.S. 99 V6
Rosignano Marittimo, It. 150 H6
Roşiori de Vede, Rom. 153 G14
Roslavl', Russ. 156 K7
Roslyatino, Russ. 156 F12
Roslyn, Wash., U.S. 108 C5
Rosporden, Fr. 147 Q3
Rosport, Lux. 160 J11
Ross, N.Z. 213 N16
Ross, Mount, N.Z. 213 M19
Ross, Point, Norfolk I., Austral. 217 G20
Rossano, It. 151 P14
Rossan Point, Ire. 143 P4
Ross Barnett Reservoir, Miss., U.S. 100 L11
Rosscarbery, Ire. 143 V3
Ross Dam, Wash., U.S. 108 A5
Rossel, Cap, New Caledonia, Fr. 218 C8
Rossel Island, P.N.G. 213 F22
Ross Ice Shelf, Antarctica 226 M12
Ross Island, Antarctica 227 N13
Ross Lake, Wash., U.S. 108 A5
Ross Lake National Recreation Area, Wash., U.S. 108 A5
Rosslare Harbour, Ire. 143 U7
Rosso, Mauritania 196 G5
Rosso, Capo, Fr. 150 K3
Ross of Mull, peninsula, Scot., U.K. 142 L7
Rossosh', Russ. 157 N10
Ross River, N. Terr., Austral. 211 T9
Ross River, Yukon, Can. 82 G8
Ross Sea, Antarctica 226 P11
Røssvatnet, lake, Nor. 140 F12
Rossville, Ill., U.S. 99 Q7
Rossville, Qnsld., Austral. 211 Q13
Rostaq, Afghan. 176 K8
Rostock, Ger. 148 B9
Rostov, Russ. 156 H10
Rostov na Donu, Russ. 157 R11
Rostrenen, Fr. 147 Q4
Roswell, Ga., U.S. 96 K5
Roswell, N. Mex., U.S. 107 U14
Rota, island, N. Mariana Is., U.S. 216 D2
Rota see Songsong, N. Mariana Is., U.S. 216 E7
Rota, Sp. 144 M7
Rotan, Tex., U.S. 102 L7
Rotenboden, Liech. 160 P2
Roth, Ger. 148 J8
Roth, Ger. 160 H10
Rothera, station, Antarctica 226 E4
Rotherham, Eng., U.K. 143 S12
Rothschild, Wis., U.S. 98 H5
Rothschild Island, Antarctica 226 F4
Roti, island, Indonesia 189 N14
Roto, N.S.W., Austral. 211 X12
Roto, Pukapuka, Cook Is., N.Z. 218 Q2
Rotondella, It. 151 N13
Rotorua, N.Z. 213 K19
Rotterdam, Neth. 146 J12
Rottumeroog, island, Neth. 146 G14
Rottumerplaat, island, Neth. 146 G14
Rotuma, island, Fiji Is. 214 J8
Roubaix, Fr. 146 L11
Rouen, Fr. 147 N8
Rouge, Baie, St. Martin, Fr. 121 B14
Rouge, Pic de la, Fr., Sp. 160 G2
Rough Point, Virgin Islands, U.K. 120 Q6
Round Island see Yalewa Kalou, Fiji Is. 218 G6
Round Island, Mauritius 205 E20
Round Island Passage, Fiji Is. 218 G6
Round Mountain, Nev., U.S. 109 Q9
Round Rock, Bahamas 120 C8
Round Rock, Tex., U.S. 103 P10
Roundstone, Ire. 143 S3
Roundup, Mont., U.S. 106 D10
Roura, Fr. Guiana, Fr. 129 E18
Rousay, island, Scot., U.K. 142 F10
Rouses Point, N.Y., U.S. 94 E12
Rouyn-Noranda, Que., Can. 83 P18
Rovaniemi, Fin. 141 E15
Rovereto, It. 150 D6
Rovieng, Cambodia 187 N11
Rovigo, It. 150 E7
Rovinj, Croatia 152 E3
Rovuma see Ruvuma, river, Tanzania 199 N15
Rowa Islands see Reef Islands, Vanuatu 218 B2
Rowd-e Lurah, river, Afghan. 177 P6
Rowena, N.S.W., Austral. 211 W14
Rowland, N.C., U.S. 96 K11
Rowley Island, Nunavut, Can. 83 F17
Roxas, Philippines 189 D14
Roxas, Philippines 189 E13
Roxboro, N.C., U.S. 96 G11
Roxborough, Trinidad & Tobago 121 N18
Roy, Mont., U.S. 106 C10
Roy, N. Mex., U.S. 107 R14
Royale, Isle, Mich., U.S. 98 D6
Royal Island, Bahamas 120 D5
Royal Oak, Mich., U.S. 99 M12
Royal Society Range, Antarctica 227 N14
Royan, Fr. 147 U6
Roy Hill, W. Aust., Austral. 211 T3
Royston, Ga., U.S. 96 K6
Roznov, Rom. 153 C16
Rrogozhinë, Albania 152 L9
Rst Bank, Arctic Oc. 243 F19
Rtishchevo, Russ. 156 M12
Rt Kamenjak, cape, Croatia 152 E4
Rua, island, Marshall Is. 216 L7
Ruacaná Falls, Angola 202 F6
Ruahara, island, Cook Is., N.Z. 219 A17
Ruapehu, Mount, N.Z. 213 L19
Ruapuke Island, N.Z. 213 R15
Ruatoria, N.Z. 213 K20
Ruawai, N.Z. 213 J18
Rub al Khali, desert, Saudi Arabia 166 H4
Rubicone, river, It. 150 G8
Rubtsovsk, Russ. 158 L11
Ruby, Alas., U.S. 111 G15
Ruby, river, Mont., U.S. 106 E7
Ruby Dome, Nev., U.S. 84 F5
Ruby Mountains, Nev., U.S. 109 N11
Rudan, Iran 173 H16
Rudbar, Afghan. 177 R2
Rudder Cut Cay, Bahamas 120 D7
Rūdnyy, Kaz. 174 C11
Rudolf, Lake see Turkana, Lake, Eth., Kenya 199 H14
Rudolph, Ostrov, Russ. 158 C12
Rudong (Juegang), China 182 K10
Rudyard, Mich., U.S. 98 F11
Rue, Fr. 146 M9
Ruffec, Fr. 147 T7
Rufiji, river, Tanzania 199 M14
Rufino, Arg. 132 L11
Rufisque, Senegal 196 H4
Rugby, N. Dak., U.S. 104 E5
Rugeley, Eng., U.K. 143 T12
Rügen, island, Ger. 148 B10
Ruggell, Liech. 160 M2
Ruhnu Saar, island, Est. 141 L16
Ruhr, river, Ger. 148 F6
Ru'i, Afghan. 176 L7
Rui'an, China 183 N9
Rui Barbosa, Braz. 131 H16
Ruiché, Eq. Guinea 204 M7
Ruidosa, Tex., U.S. 103 Q1
Ruidoso, N. Mex., U.S. 107 U13
Ruijin, China 183 P6
Ruille, Pic de, Fr. 160 G5
Ruivo, Pico, Madeira 204 M3
Ruj, peak, Bulg., Serb. & Mont. 152 H12
Rujen, peak, Bulg., Maced. 152 J12
Rukuruku Bay, Fiji Is. 218 G7
Rukwa, Lake, Tanzania 199 M13
Rule, Tex., U.S. 102 K7
Ruleville, Miss., U.S. 100 J10
Rum, island, Scot., U.K. 142 K7
Ruma, Serb. & Mont. 152 E9
Rumaylah, 'Urūq ar, Saudi Arabia 172 M10
Rumbalara, N. Terr., Austral. 211 U9
Rumbek, Sudan 198 G12
Rum Cay, Bahamas 117 F14
Rumelange, Lux. 160 K9
Rumford, Me., U.S. 95 F15
Rumia, Pol. 149 A14
Rumoi, Japan 184 F13
Rum Point, Cayman Is., U.K. 120 H2
Rum Point Channel, Cayman Is., U.K. 120 H2
Rumung, island, F.S.M. 217 C18
Runanga, N.Z. 213 N17
Runaway, Cape, N.Z. 213 K20
Runaway Bay, Jam. 120 H8
Runde, river, Zimb. 202 G12
Rundeng, Indonesia 188 H4
Rundu, Namibia 202 F8
Runge, Tex., U.S. 103 S10
Rungwa, river, Tanzania 199 M13
Rungwa, Tanzania 199 M13
Runit, island, Marshall Is. 216 H8
Running Water Draw, Tex., U.S. 102 H4
Runu, F.S.M. 217 C18
Ruo, island, F.S.M. 217 B16
Ruoqiang, China 180 G7
Rupat, island, Indonesia 188 H6
Rupert, Idaho, U.S. 106 H6
Rupert, Rivière de, Que., Can. 83 M19
Ruppert Coast, Antarctica 226 N9
Rupununi, river, Guyana 129 F14
Rurrenabaque, Bol. 130 J6
Rurutu, island, Fr. Polynesia, Fr. 219 H15
Rusanovo, Russ. 158 E10
Ruse, Bulg. 153 G15
Rushan, Taj. 176 J9
Rush City, Minn., U.S. 104 J12
Rushden, Eng., U.K. 143 U13
Rushford, Minn., U.S. 104 L13
Rush Springs, Okla., U.S. 102 H10
Rushville, Ill., U.S. 99 R4
Rushville, Ind., U.S. 99 R10
Rushville, Nebr., U.S. 104 M2
Rusk, Tex., U.S. 102 M14
Ruskin, Fla., U.S. 97 U7
Russas, Braz. 131 E17
Russell, Kans., U.S. 105 S6
Russell Cave National Monument, Ala., U.S. 101 G16
Russell Islands, Solomon Is. 217 N18
Russellville, Ala., U.S. 101 H14
Russellville, Ark., U.S. 100 F7
Russellville, Ky., U.S. 101 D15
Rüsselsheim, Ger. 148 G6
Russi, It. 150 F8
Russia, Asia 167 Q6
Russian, river, Calif., U.S. 109 Q2
Russian Fort Elizabeth, Hawai'i, U.S. 112 C5
Russian Mission, Alas., U.S. 110 H12
Russkaya Gavan', Russ. 158 D12
Russkaya Polyana, Russ. 158 K10
Rust'avi, Rep. of Georgia 169 C19
Ruston, La., U.S. 100 L8
Rutaki Passage, Cook Is., N.Z. 218 Q9
Rute, Sp. 144 L10
Ruteng, Indonesia 189 M13
Ruth, Nev., U.S. 109 P12
Rutherfordton, N.C., U.S. 96 J8
Rutland, Vt., U.S. 94 H12
Rutland Island, India 179 Q14
Rutog, China 180 J4
Ruvuma see Rovuma, river, Mozambique 203 D15
Ruwāq, Jabal ar, Syr. 170 H9
Ruwenzori, peak, Dem. Rep. of the Congo, Uganda 198 J12
Ruwer, Ger. 160 J12
Rūzaevka, Kaz. 174 C12
Ruzayevka, Russ. 156 K13
Ružomberok, Slovakia 149 J15
Rwanda, Af. 195 K21
Ryan, Okla., U.S. 102 J10
Ryan, Loch, Scot., U.K. 143 P8
Ryazan', Russ. 156 K10
Ryazhsk, Russ. 156 L10
Rybachiy, Russ. 156 J2
Rybinsk, Russ. 156 G10
Rybinskoye Vodokhranilishche, Russ. 156 G10
Rybnik, Pol. 149 H14
Rye, Colo., U.S. 107 P13
Ryegate, Mont., U.S. 106 D9
Rye Patch Reservoir, Nev., U.S. 109 N8
Ryl'sk, Russ. 156 M8
Ryōtsu, Japan 184 M11
Ryōtsu Wan, Japan 184 M11
Rypin, Pol. 149 C15
Rysy, peak, Pol., Slovakia 149 J15
Ryukyu Islands (Nansei Shotō), Japan 185 Y2
Ryukyu Trench, Pac. Oc. 238 G4
Ryzhovo, Russ. 159 E19
Rzeszów, Pol. 149 G17
Rzhev, Russ. 156 J8

S

São Marcos Bay, S. Amer. 126 D10
Sa, Thai. 186 J9
Sa'a, Solomon Is. 217 P20
Sa'ādatābād, Iran 173 G15
Saale, river, Ger. 148 G9
Saalfeld, Ger. 148 G8
Saarbrücken, Ger. 148 H5
Saaremaa (Ösel), island, Est. 141 L15
Saba, island, Neth. Antilles, Neth. 119 F15
Sab 'Ābār, Syr. 170 J9
Šabac, Serb. & Mont. 152 F9
Sabadell, Sp. 145 D17
Sabah, region, Malaysia 188 G12
Saba Island, Virgin Islands, U.S. 120 N8
Sabana, Archipiélago de, Cuba 116 G8
Sabana de La Mar, Dom. Rep. 117 L19
Sabana Grande, P.R., U.S. 120 N2
Sabanalarga, Col. 128 B5
Sabaneta, Dom. Rep. 117 L17
Sabaneta, Puntan, N. Mariana Is., U.S. 216 A5
Sabang, Indonesia 189 J13
Şabanözü, Turk. 168 D8
Sabaya, Bol. 130 K6
Şāberī, Hāmūn-e, Afghan., Iran 177 Q1
Sabetha, Kans., U.S. 105 R9
Şabḩā, Jordan 170 L7
Sabhā, Lib. 197 D14
Sabidana, Jebel, Sudan 194 F10
Sabinal, Tex., U.S. 103 R8
Sabinal, Cayo, Cuba 116 H11
Sabiñánigo, Sp. 145 C14
Sabinas Hidalgo, Mex. 114 E11
Sabine, river, La., Tex., U.S. 100 N6
Sabine, Tex., U.S. 103 Q16
Sabine Lake, La., Tex., U.S. 100 Q6
Sabinosa, Canary Is. 204 R3
Sable, Cape, Fla., U.S. 97 Y9
Sable, Cape, N.S., Can. 83 Q22
Sable, Île de, New Caledonia, Fr. 218 A6
Sable Island, N.S., Can. 83 P23
Sables, Île aux (Sandy Island), Mauritius 205 J19
Sabres, Fr. 147 W6
Sabrina Coast, Antarctica 227 N20
Sabtang, island, Philippines 189 A14
Sabugal, Port. 144 F7
Sabunçu, Azerb. 169 D23
Sabura, Pak. 177 Q6
Şabyā, Saudi Arabia 172 N8
Sabzak Pass, Afghan. 176 M3
Sabzevār, Iran 173 C15
Sacaca, Bol. 130 K7
Sacajawea Peak, Oreg., U.S. 108 F9
Sac City, Iowa, U.S. 105 N10
Sacedón, Sp. 144 F12
Săcel, Rom. 153 B14
Săcele, Rom. 153 E15
Sachigo, river, Ont., Can. 83 L15
Sachs Harbour, N.W.T., Can. 82 D11
Sacile, It. 150 D8
Sackets Harbor, N.Y., U.S. 94 G8
Saco, Me., U.S. 95 H15
Saco, Mont., U.S. 106 B11
Sacramento, river, Calif., U.S. 109 N4
Sacramento, Calif., U.S. 109 R4
Sacramento Mountains, N. Mex., U.S. 107 V13
Sacramento Valley, Calif., U.S. 84 F3
Sacred Falls see Kahuwa'a, Hawai'i, U.S. 112 D11
Sacristy and Treasury, Vatican City 161 Q16
Sada, Mayotte, Fr. 205 P17
Şa'dah, Yemen 172 P9
Sadda, Pak. 177 N8
Saddle Hill, St. Kitts & Nevis 121 C18
Saddle Mountain, Idaho, U.S. 106 G6
Saddle Mountains, Wash., U.S. 108 D6
Saddle Peak, India 179 P14
Saddle Road, Hawai'i, U.S. 113 L19
Şadh, Oman 173 N15
Sadiqabad, Pak. 177 T8
Sadiya, India 178 F15
Sadlers, St. Kitts & Nevis 121 A17
Sado, island, Japan 184 L11
Sado, river, Port. 144 J5
Sadon, Myanmar 186 E7
Sadovoye, Russ. 157 Q13
Sae Islands, P.N.G. 213 B19
Saelices, Sp. 144 G12
Şafājah, region, Saudi Arabia 172 H7
Safata Bay, Samoa 218 L3
Saffar Kalay, Afghan. 177 R3
Säffle, Sw. 140 L12
Safford, Ariz., U.S. 107 U9
Safi, Mor. 196 B7
Şāfītā, Syr. 170 G7
Safonovo, Russ. 156 K7
Safotu, Samoa 218 K2
Safranbolu, Turk. 168 C8
Saga, China 180 L6
Saga, Japan 185 R4
Sagae, Japan 184 L12
Sagaing, Myanmar 186 G6
Sagami Nada, Japan 185 Q12
Sagar, India 178 H6
Sagar, India 179 P4
Sagarejo, Rep. of Georgia 169 C19
Sage, Mount, Virgin Islands, U.K. 120 R6
Sage Creek, Mont., U.S. 106 A8
Sag Harbor, N.Y., U.S. 95 N13
Saghyz, river, Kaz. 174 E7
Saghyz, Kaz. 174 E7
Saginaw, Mich., U.S. 98 L11
Saginaw Bay, Mich., U.S. 98 K12
Saglek Bay, Nfld. & Lab., Can. 83 J20
Sagone, Fr. 150 K3
Sagone, Golfe de, Fr. 150 K3
Sagra, peak, Sp. 144 K12
Sagres, Ponta de, Port. 144 L4
Sagu, Myanmar 186 H5
Saguache, Colo., U.S. 107 N12
Sagua de Tánamo, Cuba 117 K13
Sagua la Grande, Cuba 116 G8
Saguaro National Park, Ariz., U.S. 107 V8
Sagunto-Sagunt, Sp. 145 G15
Saḩāb, Jordan 170 M7
Sahagún, Sp. 144 C9
Şaḩam, Oman 173 J15
Sahamalaza, Baie de, Madagascar 203 E17

Sahara, desert, Af. 194 F2
Sahara, Japan 184 G13
Saharan Atlas, range, Alg., Mor. 194 D4
Saharanpur, India 178 E6
Saharsa, India 178 G11
Sahel, plain, Af. 194 G3
Sahiwal, Pak. 177 P10
Sahiwal, Pak. 177 R11
Sahl Rakbah, plain, Saudi Arabia 172 K8
Sahuaripa, Mex. 114 D7
Sai, Japan 184 H13
Sai Buri, Thai. 187 S9
Saïda, Alg. 196 B10
Saïda (Sidon), Leb. 170 J6
Sa'īdābād, Iran 173 F15
Saidapet, India 179 Q7
Saidor, P.N.G. 213 C19
Saidu, Pak. 176 M10
Saignes, Fr. 147 V10
Saigon see Ho Chi Minh City, Vietnam 187 P12
SaihanTal see Sonid Youqi, China 182 A5
Saijō, Japan 185 R6
Saiki, Japan 185 S5
Sailolof, Indonesia 189 J17
Saimaa, lake, Fin. 141 H17
Saimbeyli, Turk. 168 G11
Sain, Chenal, Wallis & Futuna, Fr. 218 E12
Saindak, Pak. 177 S1
St. Abb's Head, Scot., U.K. 142 M11
St.-Agrève, Fr. 147 V12
St.-Aignan, Fr. 147 S9
St. Albans, Eng., U.K. 143 V14
St. Albans, Vt., U.S. 94 F12
St. Albans, W. Va., U.S. 96 D8
St.-Amand, Fr. 146 M11
St.-Amand-Montrond, Fr. 147 S10
St.-Amans-Soult, Fr. 147 X10
St.-Ambroix, Fr. 147 W12
St. André, Cap, Madagascar 194 M11
St.-André, Reunion, Fr. 205 G16
St. Andrew Bay, Fla., U.S. 97 R3
St. Andrews, N.Z. 213 Q17
St. Andrews, Scot., U.K. 142 L10
St. Andrews Bay, Grenada 121 K23
St. Annabaai, bay, Neth. Antilles, Neth. 121 Q14
St. Ann's Bay, Jam. 120 H9
St. Anthony, Idaho, U.S. 106 G7
St. Anthony, Nfld. & Lab., Can. 83 L23
St. Anthony's Peak, St. Kitts & Nevis 121 B18
St. Arnaud, Vic., Austral. 211 Y12
St.-Aubin-d'Aubigne, Fr. 147 Q6
St.-Aubin-du-Cormier, Fr. 147 Q6
St.-Augustin, Que., Can. 83 L22
St. Augustin Bay, Madagascar 194 P11
St. Augustine, Fla., U.S. 97 R9
St. Austell, Eng., U.K. 143 X8
St. Austell Bay, Eng., U.K. 143 X8
St.-Avold, Fr. 147 N14
St.-Barthélemy, island, Lesser Antilles 119 F15
St. Bees Head, Eng., U.K. 143 Q10
St.-Benoît, Reunion, Fr. 205 G17
St. Boswells (Newtown), Scot., U.K. 143 N11
St.-Brieuc, Fr. 147 P4
St.-Cannat, Fr. 147 X13
St. Catherine, Mount, Grenada 121 K23
St. Catherine Point, Bermuda, U.K. 120 A3
St. Catherines Island, Ga., U.S. 97 P9
St.-Cernin, Fr. 147 V10
St. Charles, Idaho, U.S. 106 J7
St. Charles, Mich., U.S. 98 L11
St. Charles, Minn., U.S. 104 L13
St. Charles, Mo., U.S. 105 S15
St. Charles' Church, Monaco 161 C22
St.-Chély-d'Apcher, Fr. 147 V11
St. Christoffelberg, peak, Neth. Antilles, Neth. 121 N13
St. Christopher see St. Kitts, island, St. Kitts & Nevis 121 A17
St. Clair, river, Mich., U.S. 98 L13
St. Clair, Mich., U.S. 98 L13
St. Clair, Mo., U.S. 105 T14
St. Clair, Lake, Can., U.S. 85 E17
St. Clair Shores, Mich., U.S. 98 M13
St.-Claude, Fr. 147 T14
St.-Claude, Guadeloupe, Fr. 121 G14
St. Clears, Wales, U.K. 143 V9
St. Cloud, Fla., U.S. 97 T9
St. Cloud, Minn., U.S. 104 J10
St. Combs, Scot., U.K. 142 J11
St. Croix, river, Me., U.S. 95 E19
St. Croix, river, Minn., Wis., U.S. 98 H1
St. Croix, island, Virgin Islands, U.S. 119 F13
St. Croix Falls, Wis., U.S. 98 G2
St. Croix Island International Historic Site, Me., U.S. 95 E19
St. Croix National Scenic Riverway, Minn., Wis., U.S. 98 G2
St. David Islands see Mapia, Kepulauan, Indonesia 189 J19
St. David's, Grenada 121 L23
St. David's Head, Wales, U.K. 143 U8
St. David's Island, Bermuda, U.K. 120 B4
St. David's Lighthouse, Bermuda, U.K. 120 A4
St. David's Point, Grenada 121 L23
St.-Denis, Fr. 147 P10
St.-Denis, Fr. 147 T6
St.-Denis, Reunion, Fr. 205 F16
St.-Dié, Fr. 147 Q15
St.-Dizier, Fr. 147 P13
Ste.-Anne, Guadeloupe, Fr. 121 F15
Ste.-Anne, Martinique, Fr. 121 G23
Ste. Dévote's Church, Monaco 161 D21
St. Edward, Nebr., U.S. 105 P7
Ste. Genevieve, Mo., U.S. 105 T15
St. Elias, Mount, Alas., U.S., Yukon, Can. 111 K19
St. Elias Mountains, Alas., U.S. 111 J19
St. Elias Mountains, B.C., Yukon, Can. 82 G7
St.-Éloy-les-Mines, Fr. 147 T10
Ste.-Luce, Martinique, Fr. 121 G23
Ste.-Marguerite, Guadeloupe, Fr. 121 E15
Ste. Marie, Cap, Madagascar 203 J16
Ste. Marie, Nosy, Madagascar 203 F18
Ste.-Marie, Guadeloupe, Fr. 121 F15
Ste.-Marie, Martinique, Fr. 121 E23
Ste.-Marie, Reunion, Fr. 205 F16
Ste.-Maxime, Fr. 147 X15
Ste.-Rose, Guadeloupe, Fr. 121 E14
Ste.-Rose, Reunion, Fr. 205 G17
Saintes, Fr. 147 U6
Ste.-Suzanna, Reunion, Fr. 205 F16
Ste. Suzanne, Fr. 147 Q7
St.-Étienne, Fr. 147 U12
St.-Étienne-du-Rouvray, Fr. 147 N8
St. Eustatius, island, Neth. Antilles, Neth. 119 G15
St.-Fargeau, Fr. 147 R11
St. Finan's Bay, Ire. 143 U2
St.-Firmin, Fr. 147 V14
St.-Florent, Golfe de, Fr. 150 J4
St.-Florentin, Fr. 147 Q11
St.-Flour, Fr. 147 V11
St. Francis, river, Ark., Mo., U.S. 85 J15
St. Francis, Kans., U.S. 105 R3
St. Francis, Me., U.S. 95 A17
St. Francis, S. Dak., U.S. 104 M4
St. Francis Bay, S. Af. 194 R8
St.-François, Guadeloupe, Fr. 121 E16
St Gallen, Switz. 150 A5
St. George, Bermuda, U.K. 120 A3
St. George, Qnsld., Austral. 211 V14
St. George, S.C., U.S. 96 L9
St. George, Utah, U.S. 107 Q5
St. George, Cape, Fla., U.S. 97 S4
St. George, Cape, P.N.G. 213 C21
St. George, Point, Calif., U.S. 108 L1
St. George Island, Alas., U.S. 110 L9
St. George Island, Fla., U.S. 97 R4
St. George's, Grenada 121 L22
St. George's Bay, Malta 161 K23
St. George's Channel, India 179 T15
St. George's Channel, Ire., U.K. 143 U7
St. George's Channel, P.N.G. 213 C21
St. George's Harbour, Grenada 121 L22
St. George's Island, Bermuda, U.K. 120 A3
St.-Germain, Fr. 147 P9
St.-Germain-des-Vaux, Fr. 147 N5
St.-Gildas, Pointe de, Fr. 147 S5
St. Giles Islands, Trinidad & Tobago 121 M18
St.-Gilles-les-Bains, Reunion, Fr. 205 G15
St.-Girons, Fr. 147 Y8
St.-Guénolé, Fr. 147 Q3
St. Helena, island, U.K., Atl. Oc. 204 G4
St. Helena, Calif., U.S. 109 R3
St. Helena Bay, S. Af. 202 L7
St. Helena Sound, S.C., U.S. 97 N10
St. Helens, Eng., U.K. 143 S11
St. Helens, Oreg., U.S. 108 E3
St. Helens, Mount, Wash., U.S. 108 E4
St. Helier, Ch. Is. 143 Z12
St.-Hillaire-du-Harcouët, Fr. 147 P6
St.-Hippolyte, Fr. 147 R15
St. Hubert, Belg. 160 H7
St.-Hyacinthe, Que., Can. 83 P20
St. Ignace, Mich., U.S. 98 G10
St. Ignatius, Mont., U.S. 106 C5
St. Ives Bay, Eng., U.K. 143 X8
St. James, Cayman Is., U.K. 120 J2
St. James, Minn., U.S. 104 L10
St. James, Mo., U.S. 105 T14
St.-Jean, Lac, Que., Can. 83 N20
St.-Jean-d'Angély, Fr. 147 U7
St.-Jean-de-Losne, Fr. 147 S13
St.-Jean-de-Luz, Fr. 147 X5
St.-Jean-de-Maurienne, Fr. 147 U14
St.-Jean-de-Monts, Fr. 147 S5
St.-Jean-Pied-de-Port, Fr. 147 Y6
St. Joe, river, Idaho, U.S. 106 C4
St. John, Kans., U.S. 105 U6
St. John, river, Me., U.S. 95 B16
St. John, N. Dak., U.S. 104 D5
St. John, N.B., Can. 83 P21
St. John, island, Virgin Islands, U.S. 120 N11
St. John, Wash., U.S. 108 D9
St. John's, Antigua & Barbuda 121 B20
St. John's, Montserrat, U.K. 121 B23
St. John's, Nfld. & Lab., Can. 83 M24
St. Johns, Ariz., U.S. 107 T9
St. Johns, river, Fla., U.S. 97 R8
St. Johns, Mich., U.S. 98 L11
St. Johnsbury, Vt., U.S. 95 F13
St. John's Church, Barbados 121 K19
St. John's Harbour, Antigua & Barbuda 121 B20
St. Jona Island see Iony, Ostrov, Russ. 159 H20
St. Jorisbaai, bay, Neth. Antilles, Neth. 121 Q15
St. Joseph, Dominica 121 F18
St. Joseph, river, Ind., U.S. 99 P10
St. Joseph, La., U.S. 100 M9
St. Joseph, Mich., U.S. 99 N9
St. Joseph, Mo., U.S. 105 R10
St. Joseph, Trinidad & Tobago 121 Q23
St. Joseph, Lake, N. Amer. 80 G7
St.-Joseph, Martinique, Fr. 121 F22
St.-Joseph, New Caledonia, Fr. 218 C8
St.-Joseph, Reunion, Fr. 205 J16
St. Joseph Bay, Fla., U.S. 97 R4
St. Joseph's Church, Fr. 161 C22
St. Julian's, Malta 161 K22
St.-Junien, Fr. 147 U8
St. Kitts (St. Christopher), island, St. Kitts & Nevis 121 A17
St. Kitts and Nevis, N. Amer. 81 N24
St.-Laurent du Maroni, Fr. Guiana, Fr. 129 E17
St. Lawrence, Barbados 121 L19
St. Lawrence, river, N. Amer. 80 G9
St. Lawrence, Tex., U.S. 103 N5
St. Lawrence, Gulf of, Atl. Oc. 236 F5
St. Lawrence, Gulf of, Que., Can. 83 N22
St. Lawrence Island, Alas., U.S. 110 G10
St. Lawrence Islands National Park, N.Y., U.S. 94 F9
St.-Leu, Reunion, Fr. 205 H15
St.-Lô, Fr. 147 P6
St. Louis, Mich., U.S. 98 L11
St. Louis, river, Minn., U.S. 104 G12
St. Louis, Mo., U.S. 105 T15
St.-Louis, Fr. 147 R15
St.-Louis, Guadeloupe, Fr. 121 G16
St.-Louis, New Caledonia, Fr. 218 E8
St.-Louis, Reunion, Fr. 205 H15
St.-Louis, Senegal 196 G4
St.-Louis du Nord, Haiti 117 L16
St.-Loup, Fr. 147 Q14
St. Lucia, N. Amer. 81 P24
St. Lucia, island, N. Amer. 80 N12
St. Lucia, Lake, S. Af. 202 K12
St. Lucia Channel, Lesser Antilles 119 K17
St.-Lys, Fr. 147 X8
St. Magnus Bay, Scot., U.K. 142 D11
St.-Maixent, Fr. 147 T7
St.-Malo, Fr. 147 P5
St.-Malo, Golfe de, Fr. 147 P5
St.-Marc, Haiti 117 L16
St.-Marc, Canal de, Haiti 117 M16
St.-Marcel, Mount, Fr. Guiana, Fr. 129 G18
St. Marie, Kaap, Neth. Antilles, Neth. 121 P13
St. Maries, Idaho, U.S. 106 C3
St. Mark Bay, Grenada 121 J22
St. Marks, Fla., U.S. 97 R5
St. Martin, island, Lesser Antilles 119 F15
St.-Martin, Fr. 147 X11
St.-Martin, Cap, Martinique, Fr. 121 E22
St. Martin's, island, Eng., U.K. 143 Y7
St. Martin's Gardens, Monaco 161 F21
St. Martinville, La., U.S. 100 P9
St. Mary's, island, Eng., U.K. 143 Y7
St. Marys, river, Fla., Ga., U.S. 97 Q8
St. Marys, Ga., U.S. 97 Q8
St. Marys, Kans., U.S. 105 S9
St. Marys, Ohio, U.S. 99 Q11
St. Marys, Pa., U.S. 94 M5
St. Marys, Tas., Austral. 211 Z16
St. Marys, Trinidad & Tobago 121 Q22
St. Marys, W. Va., U.S. 96 C8
St. Mary's Bay, Nfld. & Lab., Can. 83 M24
St. Marys City, Md., U.S. 96 D14
St. Mary's Loch, Scot., U.K. 143 N10
St.-Mathieu, Fr. 147 U8
St.-Mathieu, Pointe de, Fr. 147 Q2
St. Matthew Island, Alas., U.S. 110 H9
St. Matthews, S.C., U.S. 96 L9
St.-Maurice, river, Que., Can. 83 P19
St.-Méen-le-Grand, Fr. 147 Q5
St. Michael, Alas., U.S. 110 G12
St. Michael's Caves, Gibraltar, U.K. 161 Q23
St. Michielsbaai, bay, Neth. Antilles, Neth. 121 P14
St.-Nazaire, Fr. 147 R5
St.-Omer, Fr. 146 L10
St.-Palais, Fr. 147 Y6
St. Patrick's, Montserrat, U.K. 121 C23
St. Paul, island, Ind. Oc. 240 N10
St. Paul, Minn., U.S. 104 K12
St. Paul, Nebr., U.S. 105 P6
St.-Paul, Reunion, Fr. 205 G15
St.-Paul, Île, Ind. Oc. 204 K10
St.-Paulien, Fr. 147 V11
St. Paul Island, Alas., U.S. 110 L9
St. Paul's, St. Kitts & Nevis 121 A17
St. Pauls, N.C., U.S. 96 J11
St. Paul's Bay, Malta 161 J21
St. Paul's Bay, Malta 161 J22
St. Paul's Islands, Malta 161 J22
St. Paul's Point, Pitcairn I., U.K. 219 Q23
St.-Péray, Fr. 147 V13
St. Peter, Minn., U.S. 104 K11
St. Peter and St. Paul Rocks, Atl. Oc. 204 F2
St. Peter Port, Ch. Is. 143 Z11
St. Peter's Basilica, Vatican City 161 Q16
St. Petersburg, Fla., U.S. 97 U7
St. Petersburg see Sankt-Peterburg, Russ. 156 F6
St. Peter's Square, Vatican City 161 Q17
St.-Philippe, Reunion, Fr. 205 H17
St. Pierre, Mauritius 205 G20
St. Pierre, Trinidad & Tobago 121 N22
St.-Pierre, Martinique, Fr. 121 E22
St.-Pierre, Reunion, Fr. 205 H16
St.-Pierre and Miquelon, islands, Fr. 83 N23
St.-Pierre-de-Chignac, Fr. 147 V8
St. Pierre Island, Seychelles 203 C18
St.-Pierre-le-Moûtier, Fr. 147 S11
St. Pölten, Aust. 148 K12
St.-Pons, Fr. 147 X10
St.-Quay-Portrieux, Fr. 147 P4
St.-Quentin, Fr. 146 M11
St.-Quentin, Pointe de, Fr. 146 M9
St.-Raphaël, Fr. 147 X15
St. Rogatien Bank, Hawai'i, U.S. 112 M6
St. Roman, Monaco 161 A23
St.-Savin, Fr. 147 T8
St.-Sernin, Fr. 147 X10
St.-Servan, Fr. 147 P5
St.-Sever, Fr. 147 X6
St. Simons Island, Ga., U.S. 97 P8
St. Stanislas Bay, Kiribati 217 B22
St. Stephen, S.C., U.S. 96 L10
St. Thomas, N. Dak., U.S. 104 E7
St. Thomas, island, Virgin Islands, U.S. 120 N8
St. Thomas Bay, Virgin Islands, U.K. 120 R8
St. Thomas Harbor, Virgin Islands, U.S. 120 N9
St. Truiden, Belg. 146 L13
St. Tudwal's Islands, Wales, U.K. 143 T9
St. Veit, Aust. 148 M11
St. Vincent, Minn., U.S. 104 D8
St. Vincent, island, N. Amer. 80 P12
St. Vincent, Cape, Madagascar 194 N11
St. Vincent, Cape, Port. 138 J1
St. Vincent, Gulf, Austral. 210 K10
St. Vincent and the Grenadines, N. Amer. 81 P24
St. Vincent Island, Fla., U.S. 97 R4
St. Vincent Passage, Lesser Antilles 119 L17
St. Vith, Belg. 146 M14
St.-Vivien, Fr. 147 U6
St. Wendel, Ger. 148 H5
St. Willibrordus, Neth. Antilles, Neth. 121 P14
Saipan, island, N. Mariana Is., U.S. 216 C2
Saipan Channel, N. Mariana Is., U.S. 216 D4
Saipan Harbor, N. Mariana Is., U.S. 216 B4
Sairang, India 178 H14
Saito, Japan 185 S5
Saivomuotka, Sw. 141 D14
Sajama, Nevado, Bol. 130 K6
Sajyang Pass, China 180 N10
Sakai, Japan 185 Q8
Sakaide, Japan 185 Q7
Sakaiminato, Japan 185 P7
Sakākah, Saudi Arabia 172 F7
Saka Kalat, Pak. 177 U4
Sakakawea, Lake, N. Dak., U.S. 104 F3
Sakami, river, Que., Can. 83 M18
Sakami, Que., Can. 83 M18
Sakami, Lac, Que., Can. 83 M18
Sakania, Dem. Rep. of the Congo 198 P11
Sakao (Lathi), island, Vanuatu 218 C2
Sakarya, river, Turk. 168 D6
Sakarya, Turk. 168 D6
Sakata, Japan 184 L12
Sakçagöze, Turk. 168 H12
Sakhalin, island, Russ. 166 D13
Sakhalin, Ostrov, Russ. 159 J21
Sakhar, Afghan. 177 N5
Şäki, Azerb. 169 C21
Sakishima Shotō, Japan 184 L2
Sakon Nakhon, Thai. 186 K11
Sakrand, Pak. 177 V7
Saky, Ukr. 157 S7
Sal, island, Cape Verde 205 B17
Sal, Cay, Bahamas 116 F8
Sal, Cayo de, Venez. 118 N11
Sala, Sw. 141 K13
Sala Consilina, It. 151 N12
Salada, Laguna, Mex. 114 B5
Saladas, Arg. 132 G13
Saladillo, Arg. 132 M12
Salado, river, Arg. 132 H11
Salado, river, Arg. 132 M13
Salado, river, Arg. 132 M9
Salaga, Ghana 200 G10
Sala'ilua, Samoa 218 K2
Salal, Chad 197 H14
Salala, Sudan 199 C14
Salālah, Oman 173 P14
Salamanca, Chile 132 K7
Salamanca, Mex. 114 H11
Salamanca, N.Y., U.S. 94 K5
Salamanca, Sp. 144 E8
Salamat, Bahr, Chad 197 K15
Salamína, Gr. 154 J12
Salamis, Gr. 154 J12
Salamis, ruin, Cyprus 160 N10
Salamīyah, Syr. 170 G8
Salang Tunnel, Afghan. 176 L7
Salani, Samoa 218 L4
Salapaly Bay, Madagascar 194 P11
Salas, Sp. 144 B8
Salas de los Infantes, Sp. 144 D11
Salatiga, Indonesia 188 M9
Salavan, Laos 186 L12
Salavat, Russ. 158 J7
Salaverry, Peru 130 G2
Salawati, island, Indonesia 189 J17
Sala-y-Gómez, island, Chile 215 L19
Sala y Gómez Ridge, Pac. Oc. 239 M18
Salazie, Reunion, Fr. 205 G16
Salbris, Fr. 147 R9
Salda Gölü, Turk. 168 H5
Saldaña, Sp. 144 C10
Saldanha, S. Af. 202 M7
Sale, Vic., Austral. 211 Z13
Salebabu, island, Indonesia 189 G16

Salée, strait, Guadeloupe, Fr. 121 E15
Saleimoa, Samoa 218 L3
Salekhard, Russ. 158 F11
Salelologa, Samoa 218 K2
Salem, Ark., U.S. 100 E9
Salem, Ill., U.S. 99 T6
Salem, Ind., U.S. 99 T9
Salem, India 179 Q6
Salem, Mass., U.S. 95 K15
Salem, Mo., U.S. 105 U14
Salem, Montserrat, U.K. 121 B23
Salem, N.H., U.S. 95 J14
Salem, Ohio, U.S. 99 P15
Salem, Oreg., U.S. 108 G3
Salem, S. Dak., U.S. 104 L7
Salem, Va., U.S. 96 F10
Salem, W. Va., U.S. 96 C9
Salemi, It. 151 S9
Salerno, It. 150 M11
Salerno, Golfo di, It. 151 N11
Salez, Switz. 160 M2
Salford, Eng., U.K. 143 S11
Salgótarján, Hung. 149 K15
Salgueiro, Braz. 131 F16
Salibea, Trinidad & Tobago 121 N23
Salibia, Dominica 121 E20
Salida, Colo., U.S. 107 N12
Salies-du-Salat, Fr. 147 Y8
Şalīf, Yemen 172 P8
Salihli, Turk. 168 F4
Salihorsk, Belarus 156 L4
Salima, Malawi 203 E13
Salina, Kans., U.S. 105 T7
Salina, Utah, U.S. 107 N7
Salina, Isola, It. 151 R11
Salina Bay, Malta 161 J22
Salinas, river, Calif., U.S. 109 U5
Salinas, Calif., U.S. 109 T4
Salinas, Ecua. 128 K1
Salinas, P.R., U.S. 120 N4
Salinas, Bahía, P.R., U.S. 120 P1
Salinas Peak, N. Mex., U.S. 107 U12
Salinas Pueblo Missions National Monument (Gran Quivira), N. Mex., U.S. 107 T12
Saline, river, Ark., U.S. 100 J8
Saline, river, Kans., U.S. 105 S5
Saline Bay, Trinidad & Tobago 121 N23
Saline di Volterra, It. 150 H6
Salines, Étang des, Martinique, Fr. 121 G23
Salines, Cap de ses, Sp. 145 H18
Salines, Point, Grenada 121 L21
Salinópolis, Braz. 131 C14
Salins, Fr. 147 S14
Salisbury, Dominica 121 F18
Salisbury, Eng., U.K. 143 W12
Salisbury, Guam, U.S. 216 B12
Salisbury, Md., U.S. 96 D15
Salisbury, Mo., U.S. 105 S12
Salisbury, N.C., U.S. 96 H9
Salisbury, Ostrov, Russ. 158 C12
Salisbury Island, Nunavut, Can. 83 H17
Salisbury Plain, Eng., U.K. 143 W12
Salish Mountains, Mont., U.S. 106 B5
Şalkhad, Syr. 170 L8
Sallent, Sp. 145 D17
Sallfelden, Aust. 148 L10
Sallisaw, Okla., U.S. 102 G14
Salluit, Que., Can. 83 H18
Salmās, Iran 172 B10
Salmon, river, Idaho, U.S. 106 E5
Salmon, Idaho, U.S. 106 F6
Salmon Bank, Hawai'i, U.S. 112 K2
Salmon Gums, W. Aust., Austral. 211 X4
Salmon Peak, Tex., U.S. 103 R7
Salmon River Canyon, Idaho, U.S. 106 E5
Salmon River Mountains, Idaho, U.S. 106 F5
Salò, It. 150 D6
Salo, Fin. 141 J15
Salobelyak, Russ. 156 H14
Salome, Ariz., U.S. 107 T5
Salomon, Cap, Martinique, Fr. 121 F22
Salon, Fr. 147 X13
Salonga, river, Dem. Rep. of the Congo 198 K9
Salonica see Thessaloníki, Gr. 154 C11
Salonta, Rom. 152 C11
Salou, Cap de, Sp. 145 E16
Salpaus Ridge see Salpausselkä, Fin. 138 D9
Salpausselkä, range, Fin. 141 J16
Salqīn, Syr. 170 E8
Sal Rei, Cape Verde 205 C17
Sal'sk, Russ. 157 R12
Salsomaggiore Terme, It. 150 F5
Salt, river, Ariz., U.S. 107 U7
Salt, Sp. 145 D18
Salta, Arg. 132 F9
Saltash, Eng., U.K. 143 X9
Saltburn by the Sea, Eng., U.K. 143 Q13
Salt Cay, Bahamas 120 B12
Salt Cay, Turks & Caicos Is., U.K. 117 J18
Salt Cay, Virgin Islands, U.S. 120 M7
Salt Desert see Kavīr, Dasht-e, Iran 173 D14
Saltee Islands, Ire. 143 U6
Saltfjorden, bay, Nor. 140 E12
Salt Fork Arkansas, river, Okla., U.S. 102 E9
Salt Fork Brazos, river, Tex., U.S. 102 K6
Salt Fork Red, river, Tex., U.S. 102 H6
Saltillo, Mex. 114 F11
Salt Lake City, Utah, U.S. 106 L7
Salto, Uru. 132 J13
Salton Sea, Calif., U.S. 84 K5
Salt Range, Pak. 177 P10
Salt River, Jam. 120 K9
Salt River Bay, Virgin Islands, U.S. 120 Q2
Salt River Range, Wyo., U.S. 106 H8
Saltville, Va., U.S. 96 G8
Saluafata Harbour, Samoa 218 L4
Saluda, river, S.C., U.S. 96 K8
Saluda, S.C., U.S. 96 K8
Salûm, Egypt 197 C17
Salûm, Gulf of, Egypt, Lib. 194 D8
Saluzzo, It. 150 F2
Salvación, Bahía, Chile 133 V6
Salvador (Bahia), Braz. 131 H17
Salvador, Lake, La., U.S. 100 Q11
Salvador, Port, Falkland Is., U.K. 133 V12
Salvage Islands, Canary Is. 194 D1
Salwá, Saudi Arabia 172 J12
Salween, river, Asia 166 J10
Salyan, Azerb. 169 E22
Salyersville, Ky., U.S. 101 C19
Salzbrunn, Namibia 202 J7
Salzburg, Aust. 148 L10
Salzgitter, Ger. 148 E8
Salzwedal, Ger. 148 D8
Samaipata, Bol. 130 K8
Samalaeulu, Samoa 218 K2
Samâlût, Egypt 197 D18
Samaná, Dom. Rep. 117 L20
Samaná, Bahía de, Dom. Rep. 117 L19
Samaná, Cabo, Dom. Rep. 117 L20
Samana Cay (Atwood), Bahamas 117 G15
Samandağ, Turk. 168 K11
Samangan see Aybak, Afghan. 176 L7
Samani, Japan 184 G14
Samar, island, Philippines 189 D15
Samara, river, Russ. 138 E13
Samara, Russ. 156 K15
Samarai, P.N.G. 213 E21
Samaria Gorge, Gr. 155 Q13
Samarinda, Indonesia 188 J12
Samarqand, Uzb. 174 L12
Sāmarrā', Iraq 172 D9
Samar Sea, Philippines 189 D15
Samarskoe, Kaz. 175 D18
Samba, India 177 P12
Sambalpur, India 178 K9
Sambava, Madagascar 203 E18
Sambir, Ukr. 157 N2
Samboja, Indonesia 188 J12
Samborombón, Bahía, Arg. 132 M13
Samborombón Bay, S. Amer. 126 M7
Samburg, Russ. 158 G12
Samcheok, S. Korea 182 E14
Samdari, India 178 G3
Same, Tanzania 199 L14
Samer, Fr. 146 L9
Sámi, Gr. 154 H7
Sami, Pak. 177 V3
Samina, river, Aust., Liech. 160 N3
Saminatal, valley, Liech. 160 P3
Şāmiţah, Saudi Arabia 172 P8
Sam Lord's Castle, Barbados 121 K20
Samnangjin, S. Korea 182 G14
Samo, P.N.G. 213 C21
Samoa, Pac. Oc. 214 J10
Samoa Islands, Pac. Oc. 214 J10
Samokov, Bulg. 153 J13
Sámos, island, Gr. 155 J17
Sámos, Gr. 155 J18
Samothrace see Samothráki, island, Gr. 155 D15
Samothráki (Samothrace), island, Gr. 155 D15
Samothráki, Gr. 155 D15
Sampacho, Arg. 132 K10
Sampit, Indonesia 188 K10
Sampwe, Dem. Rep. of the Congo 198 N11
Sam Rayburn Reservoir, Tex., U.S. 103 N15
Samrong, Cambodia 186 M10
Sam Son, Vietnam 186 J12
Samson, Ala., U.S. 101 N16
Samsun, Turk. 168 C11
Samu, Indonesia 188 K11
Samui, Ko, Thai. 187 Q8
Samundri, Pak. 177 Q11
Samur, Afghan. 177 Q1
Samur, river, Russ. 157 V16
Samut Prakhan, Thai. 186 M9
Samut Songkhram, Thai. 187 N8
San, river, Cambodia 186 M13
San, Japan 185 X2
San, Mali 196 H8
San, river, Pol. 149 G17
Şan'ā' (Sanaa), Yemen 172 P9
Sana, river, Bosn. & Herzg. 152 E6
Sanaa see Şan'ā', Yemen 172 P9
San Adrián, Cabo, Sp. 144 A5
SANAE IV, station, Antarctica 226 A12
Şanāfīr, island, Saudi Arabia 172 G5
Sanaga, river, Cameroon 194 J5
San Agustín, Col. 128 G4
San Agustin, Cape, Philippines 189 F15
Sanak Islands, Alas., U.S. 110 P11
Sanām, Saudi Arabia 172 K9
San Ambrosio, Isla, S. Amer. 126 K2
Sanana, island, Indonesia 189 K15
Sanandaj, Iran 172 C11
San Andés Tuxtla, Mex. 115 J13
San Andreas, Calif., U.S. 109 R5
San Andrés, Isla de, Col. 115 M20
San Andrés del Rabanedo, Sp. 144 C9
San Andres Mountains, N. Mex., U.S. 107 U12
San Andros, Bahamas 116 E11
San Angelo, Tex., U.S. 103 N7
San Antonio, Chile 132 L6
San Antonio, N. Mex., U.S. 107 T12
San Antonio, N. Mariana Is., U.S. 216 C4
San Antonio, river, Tex., U.S. 103 S11
San Antonio, Tex., U.S. 103 R9
San Antonio, Cabo, Arg. 132 M13
San Antonio, Cabo de, Cuba 116 H4
San Antonio, Cape see San Antonio, Cabo de, N. Amer. 80 N8
San Antonio, Mount, Calif., U.S. 109 X9
San Antonio, Punta, Mex. 114 C5
San Antonio Bay, Tex., U.S. 103 T12
San Antonio de los Cobres, Arg. 132 E9
San Antonio de Ureca, Eq. Guinea 204 N7
San Antonio Missions National Historic Park, Tex., U.S. 103 R9
San Antonio Oeste, Arg. 133 Q10
Sanat, island, F.S.M. 217 C16
San Augustine, Tex., U.S. 103 N15
Sanāw, Yemen 173 N13
Sanawad, India 178 J5
San Benedetto del Tronto, It. 150 J10
San Benedicto, Isla, Mex. 114 H6
San Benedicto Island, N. Amer. 80 N3
San Benito, Tex., U.S. 103 W11
San Bernardino, Calif., U.S. 109 X9
San Bernardino Strait, Philippines 189 D15
San Bernardo, Chile 132 L7
San Blas, Mex. 114 E8
San Blas, Archipielago de, Pan. 115 N22
San Blas, Cape, Fla., U.S. 97 R4
San Blas, Punta, Pan. 115 N21
San Borja, Bol. 130 J7
San Candido, It. 150 B8
San Carlos, Arg. 132 F9
San Carlos, Ariz., U.S. 107 U8
San Carlos, Philippines 189 E14
San Carlos, Venez. 128 C7
San Carlos, Gran Caldera Volcánica de, Eq. Guinea 204 M6
San Carlos de Bariloche, Arg. 133 Q7
San Carlos de Bolívar, Arg. 132 M11
San Carlos de Río Negro, Venez. 128 G9
San Carlos Reservoir, Ariz., U.S. 107 U8
Sánchez, Dom. Rep. 117 L19
Sanchor, India 178 H3
Sanchung, Taiwan, China 183 Q10
Sanchursk, Russ. 156 H13
San Clemente, island, Calif., U.S. 109 Z8
San Clemente, Calif., U.S. 109 Y9
San Clemente, Sp. 144 H12
San Cristóbal, Arg. 132 J11
San Cristóbal, Cuba 116 G5
San Cristóbal, Dom. Rep. 117 M19
San Cristóbal, Venez. 128 D6
San Cristóbal, Isla (Chatham), Ecua. 128 Q11
San Cristobal, island, Solomon Is. 217 Q20
San Cristóbal de Las Casas, Mex. 115 K15
San Cristoforo, Monte, San Marino 161 L15
Sancti Spíritus, Cuba 116 H9
Sand, Nor. 140 L10
Sanda Island, Scot., U.K. 143 N8
Sandakan, Malaysia 188 G12
Sandal, Baie de, New Caledonia, Fr. 218 C9
San Daniele del Friuli, It. 150 C9
Sanday, island, Scot., U.K. 142 F11
Sand Bluff, Cayman Is., U.K. 120 J4
Sand Cay, India 179 Q2
Sanders, Ariz., U.S. 107 S9
Sanderson, Tex., U.S. 103 Q4
Sandersville, Ga., U.S. 96 M7
Sandes, Nor. 140 L10
Sand Hills, Nebr., U.S. 105 N3
Sandia Crest, N. Mex., U.S. 107 S12
San Diego, Calif., U.S. 109 Z9
San Diego, Tex., U.S. 103 U10
San Diego, Cabo, Arg. 133 X10
San Diego de los Baños, Cuba 116 G5
Sandıklı, Turk. 168 F6
Sand Island, Hawai'i, U.S. 112 K2
Sand Island, Solomon Is. 217 P22
Sand Island, Wis., U.S. 98 E4
Sandness, Scot., U.K. 142 D11
Sandoa, Dem. Rep. of the Congo 198 N10
Sandomierz, Pol. 149 G17
San Donà di Piave, It. 150 D8
Sandon Iwa, island, Japan 185 W3
Sandovo, Russ. 156 G9
Sandown-Shanklin, Eng., U.K. 143 X13
Sandoy, island, Faroe Is., Den. 140 J6
Sand Point, Alas., U.S. 110 N12
Sandpoint, Idaho, U.S. 106 B4
Sandray, island, Scot., U.K. 142 K6
Sandspit, B.C., Can. 82 K7
Sand Springs, Mont., U.S. 106 C11
Sand Springs, Okla., U.S. 102 F12
Sandstone, Minn., U.S. 104 H12
Sandstone, W. Aust., Austral. 211 V3
Sandur, Faroe Is., Den. 140 J6
Sandusky, Mich., U.S. 98 L13
Sandusky, Ohio, U.S. 99 P13
Sandviken, Sw. 141 K13
Sandwich, Ill., U.S. 99 N6
Sandwich Bay, Nfld. & Lab., Can. 83 K22
Sandy, Utah, U.S. 106 L7
Sandy Bay, Gibraltar, U.K. 161 P23
Sandy Bay, Jam. 120 H6
Sandy Cape, Austral. 210 G16
Sandy Cay, Virgin Islands, U.K. 120 L11
Sandy Creek, Tex., U.S. 103 R12
Sandy Ground Village, Anguilla, U.K. 120 R11
Sandy Hill Bay, Anguilla, U.K. 120 R12
Sandy Island, Grenada 121 J24
Sandy Island see Sables, Île aux, Mauritius 205 J19
Sandykgaçy, Turkm. 174 N10
Sandy Lake, Ont., Can. 83 M15
Sandy Point, Bahamas 120 C6
Sandy Point, India 179 R14
Sandy Point, Virgin Islands, U.S. 120 R1
Sandy Point Town, St. Kitts & Nevis 121 A17
Saneku, Japan 185 W3
San Esteban de Gormaz, Sp. 144 D11
San Felice Circeo, It. 150 L9
San Felipe, Chile 132 K7
San Felipe, Col. 128 G9
San Felipe, Mex. 114 B5
San Felipe, Venez. 128 B8
San Felipe, Cayos de, Cuba 116 H5
San Félix, Isla, S. Amer. 126 K2
San Fernando, Calif., U.S. 109 X8
San Fernando, Chile 132 L7
San Fernando, Mex. 114 F12
San Fernando, Sp. 144 M8
San Fernando, Trinidad & Tobago 121 Q22
San Fernando de Apure, Venez. 128 D9
San Fernando de Atabapo, Venez. 128 F9
Sanford, Fla., U.S. 97 T9
Sanford, Me., U.S. 95 H15
Sanford, N.C., U.S. 96 H11
San Francique, Trinidad & Tobago 121 Q21
San Francisco, Arg. 132 J11
San Francisco, Arg. 132 K9
San Francisco, Calif., U.S. 109 S3
San Francisco, river, N. Mex., U.S. 107 U10
San Francisco Bay, Calif., U.S. 84 G3
San Francisco de Paula, Cabo, Arg. 133 V9
San Francisco Mountain, Ariz., U.S. 84 J6
San Gabriel, Ecua. 128 H3
San Gabriel, river, Tex., U.S. 103 P11
Sangamner, India 178 L4
Sangamon, river, Ill., U.S. 99 R5
Sangan, Kuh-e, Afghan. 177 N4
Sangar, Russ. 159 G17
Sangareddi, India 178 M6
Sang Bast, Iran 173 C16
Sang Bor, Afghan. 176 M2
Sangeang, island, Indonesia 189 M13
Sang-e Masheh, Afghan. 177 N6
Sanger, Calif., U.S. 109 T7
Sanger, Tex., U.S. 102 K11
San Germán, P.R., U.S. 120 N2
Sanggan, river, China 182 D5
Sanggou Wan, China 182 F10
Sangha, river, Cameroon, Congo 201 K18
Sanghar, Pak. 177 V7
Sangihe, island, Indonesia 189 H15
Sangihe, Kepulauan, Indonesia 189 H15
San Gil, Col. 128 E6
Sangin, Afghan. 177 P4
San Giovanni, San Marino 161 K15
San Giovanni in Fiore, It. 151 Q14
San Giovanni in Persiceto, It. 150 F7
San Giovanni Valdarno, It. 150 H7
Sangkulirang, Indonesia 188 J12
Sangli, India 178 M4
Sangola, India 178 M4
Sangolquí, Ecua. 128 J3
San Gorgonio Mountain, Calif., U.S. 109 X10
Sangowo, Indonesia 189 H16
Sangre de Cristo Mountains, Colo., N. Mex., U.S. 107 P13
San Gregorio, Uru. 132 K14
Sangre Grande, Trinidad & Tobago 121 P23
Sang Sang, Nicar. 115 L18
Sangüesa, Sp. 145 C13
Sanguinet, Fr. 147 W6
Sangvor, Taj. 176 H9
Sangzhi, China 182 L2
Sanhe, China 181 B15
Sanibel Island, Fla., U.S. 97 W8
San Ignacio, Arg. 132 G14
San Ignacio, Bol. 130 J9
San Ignacio, Mex. 114 D6
Saniquellie, Liberia 200 G7
San Javier, Arg. 132 J12
San Javier, Sp. 145 K14
Sanjiang, China 183 P2
San Joaquin, river, Calif., U.S. 109 T6
San Joaquín, Bol. 130 H7
San Joaquín, Cerro, Ecua. 128 Q10
San Joaquin Valley, Calif., U.S. 84 G3
San Jon, N. Mex., U.S. 107 S15
San Jorge, Golfo, Arg. 133 T9
San Jorge Island, Solomon Is. 217 M18
San José, Costa Rica 115 N19
San José, Guatemala 115 L15
San José, Golfo, Arg. 133 Q10
San José, Laguna, P.R., U.S. 120 M5
San Jose, Calif., U.S. 109 S4
San Jose, N. Mex., U.S. 107 R13
San Jose, N. Mariana Is., U.S. 216 C4
San Jose, N. Mariana Is., U.S. 216 C8
San Jose, Isla, Mex. 114 F7
San José de Amacuro, Venez. 129 C13
San José de Jáchal, Arg. 132 J8
San José de Las Lajas, Cuba 116 G6
San José del Guaviare, Col. 128 G6
San José de Mayo, Uru. 132 L14
San José de Ocuné, Col. 128 F7
San Juan, Arg. 132 J8
San Juan, Dom. Rep. 117 M18
San Juan, P.R., U.S. 120 M4

San Juan, *Peru* 130 J4
San Juan, *Trinidad & Tobago* 121 P22
San Juan, river, *Utah, U.S.* 107 P8
San Juan, Cabezas de, *P.R., U.S.* 120 M6
San Juan, Cabo, *Arg.* 133 X10
San Juanbaai, bay, *Neth. Antilles, Neth.* 121 P13
San Juan Bautista, *Calif., U.S.* 109 T4
San Juan Bautista, *Parag.* 130 N10
San Juan Capistrano, *Calif., U.S.* 109 Y9
San Juan del Norte, *Nicar.* 115 M19
San Juan del Sur, *Nicar.* 115 M18
San Juan Islands, *Wash., U.S.* 108 A3
San Juan Mountains, *Colo., N. Mex., U.S.* 107 P11
San Juan y Martinez, *Cuba* 116 H5
San Julián, Bahía, *Arg.* 133 U9
San Julián, Gran Bajo de, *Arg.* 133 U8
San Just, Sierra de, *Sp.* 145 F14
San Justo, *Arg.* 132 J12
San Justo, *Arg.* 132 L13
Sankeshwar, *India* 179 N4
Sankt-Peterburg (St. Petersburg, Leningrad), *Russ.* 156 F6
Sankuru, river, *Dem. Rep. of the Congo* 198 L9
San Lázaro, Cabo, *Mex.* 114 E6
Şanlıurfa (Edessa), *Turk.* 169 H13
San Lorenzo, *Arg.* 132 K12
San Lorenzo, *Ecua.* 128 H3
San Lorenzo, *P.R., U.S.* 120 N5
San Lorenzo, Cabo, *Ecua.* 128 J1
San Lorenzo de El Escorial, *Sp.* 144 F10
San Lorenzo de la Parrilla, *Sp.* 144 G12
San Luis, *Arg.* 132 K9
San Luis, *Ariz., U.S.* 107 V4
San Luis, *Colo., U.S.* 107 P13
San Luis, *Cuba* 117 K13
San Luis, *Guatemala* 115 K16
San Luis, Lago de, *Bol.* 130 H8
San Luis de Palenque, *Col.* 128 E7
San Luis Obispo, *Calif., U.S.* 109 V5
San Luis Potosí, *Mex.* 114 G11
San Luis Reservoir, *Calif., U.S.* 109 T5
San Luis Río Colorado, *Mex.* 114 B6
Sanluri, *It.* 151 P3
San Marcos, *Col.* 128 C5
San Marcos, *Tex., U.S.* 103 Q10
San Marino, *Eur.* 160 D4
San Marino, river, *It., San Marino* 161 J14
San Marino, *San Marino* 161 J15
San Martín, station, *Antarctica* 226 B5
San Martín, *Arg.* 132 K8
San Martín, river, *Bol.* 130 H8
San Martín, *Col.* 128 F6
San Martin, Cape, *Calif., U.S.* 109 U4
San Martín, Lago, *Arg.* 133 U7
San Martín de los Andes, *Arg.* 133 P7
San Mateo, *Calif., U.S.* 109 S3
San Mateo, *N. Mex., U.S.* 107 S11
San Matías, Golfo, *Arg.* 133 Q10
Sanmen Wan, *China* 182 M10
Sanmenxia, *China* 182 G3
San Miguel, river, *Bol.* 130 J8
San Miguel, island, *Calif., U.S.* 109 X5
San Miguel, *El Salv.* 115 L17
San Miguel Bay, *Philippines* 189 C14
San Miguel Creek, *Tex., U.S.* 103 S9
San Miguel de Huachi, *Bol.* 130 J7
San Miguel del Monte, *Arg.* 132 M12
San Miguel de Tucumán, *Arg.* 132 G9
Sanming, *China* 183 P7
San Miniato, *It.* 150 G6
Sannat, *Malta* 161 H20
Sannicandro Garganico, *It.* 150 K12
San Nicolás, *Arg.* 132 K12
San Nicolas, island, *Calif., U.S.* 109 Y7
Sannikova, Proliv, *Russ.* 159 D17
Sannohe, *Japan* 184 J13
Sanok, *Pol.* 149 H17
San Pablo, *Philippines* 189 C13
San Pedro, *Arg.* 132 E9
San Pedro, *Arg.* 132 L12
San Pedro, river, *Ariz., U.S.* 107 V8
San Pedro, *Parag.* 130 M10
San Pedro, Sierra de, *Sp.* 144 H7
San Pedro de las Colonias, *Mex.* 114 F10
San Pedro de Macorís, *Dom. Rep.* 117 M20
San Pedro Sula, *Hond.* 115 K17
San Pietro, island, *It.* 151 N14
San Pietro, Isola di, *It.* 151 Q3
Sanpoil, river, *Wash., U.S.* 108 B7
San Quintín, *Mex.* 114 B5
San Rafael, *Arg.* 132 L8
San Rafael, *Bol.* 130 J9
San Rafael, *Calif., U.S.* 109 R3
San Rafael, Cabo, *Dom. Rep.* 117 L20
San Rafael del Yuma, *Dom. Rep.* 117 M20
San Remo, *It.* 150 G2
San Roque, *N. Mariana Is., U.S.* 216 B5
San Roque, *Sp.* 144 N9
San Saba, river, *Tex., U.S.* 103 P8
San Saba, *Tex., U.S.* 103 N9
San Salvador, *El Salv.* 115 L16
San Salvador (Watling), island, *Bahamas* 117 F14
San Salvador, Isla (Santiago, James), *Ecua.* 128 P9
San Salvador de Jujuy, *Arg.* 132 E9
San Sebastián, *P.R., U.S.* 120 M2
Sansepolcro, *It.* 150 H8
San Severo, *It.* 150 L12
Sansha, *China* 183 P9
Sanshui, *China* 183 R4
San Simeon, *Calif., U.S.* 109 V5
San Simon, *Ariz., U.S.* 107 V9
Sanski Most, *Bosn. & Herzg.* 152 F6
San Sosti, *It.* 151 P13
Sans Souci, *Trinidad & Tobago* 121 N23
Sansui, *China* 183 N1
Santa Ana, *Bol.* 130 H7
Santa Ana, *Calif., U.S.* 109 X9
Santa Ana, *El Salv.* 115 L16
Santa Ana, *Philippines* 189 B14
Santa Ana, island, *Solomon Is.* 217 Q21
Santa Anna, *Tex., U.S.* 103 N8
Santa Bárbara, *Chile* 133 N6
Santa Bárbara, *Mex.* 114 E9
Santa Bárbara, peak, *Sp.* 144 L12
Santa Barbara, island, *Calif., U.S.* 109 Y7
Santa Barbara, *Calif., U.S.* 109 W6
Santa Barbara Channel, *Calif., U.S.* 109 X6
Santa Catalina, island, *Calif., U.S.* 109 Y8
Santa Catalina, island, *Solomon Is.* 217 Q21
Santa Catalina, Gulf of, *Calif., U.S.* 109 Y8
Santa Catarina, *Sao Tome and Principe* 205 D19
Santa Catharina, *Neth. Antilles, Neth.* 121 P15
Santa Clara, *Calif., U.S.* 109 S4
Santa Clara, *Cuba* 116 H9
Santa Clara, *Oreg., U.S.* 108 H3
Santa Clotilde, *Peru* 130 D4
Santa Coloma, *Andorra* 160 J2
Santa Comba, *Sp.* 144 B5
Santa Cruz, *Neth. Antilles, Neth.* 121 N13
Santa Cruz, river, *Arg.* 133 V8
Santa Cruz, river, *Ariz., U.S.* 107 W8
Santa Cruz, *Bol.* 130 K8
Santa Cruz, island, *Calif., U.S.* 109 X6
Santa Cruz, *Calif., U.S.* 109 T4
Santa Cruz, *Canary Is.* 196 C5
Santa Cruz, *Madeira* 204 M3
Santa Cruz, *Sao Tome and Principe* 205 D20
Santa Cruz, *Braz.* 131 F18
Santa Cruz, Isla (Chaves, Indefatigable), *Ecua.* 128 Q9
Santa Cruz Cabrália, *Braz.* 131 J16
Santa Cruz da Graciosa, *Azores* 144 P3
Santa Cruz das Flores, *Azores* 144 N1
Santa Cruz de la Palma, *Canary Is.* 204 Q3
Santa Cruz del Norte, *Cuba* 116 G7
Santa Cruz del Sur, *Cuba* 116 K11
Santa Cruz de Mudela, *Sp.* 144 J11
Santa Cruz de Tenerife, *Canary Is.* 204 Q5
Santa Cruz do Sul, *Braz.* 130 P11
Santa Cruz Islands, *Solomon Is.* 214 H7
Santa Elena, *Venez.* 129 E13
Santa Elena, Cabo, *Costa Rica* 115 N18
Santa Elena Peninsula, *S. Amer.* 126 D1
Santa Eugenia, *Sp.* 144 C5
Santa Eulalia del Río, *Sp.* 145 H17
Santa Fé, *Sp.* 144 L11
Santa Fé, Canal de, *Ecua.* 128 Q10
Santa Fe, *Arg.* 132 J12
Santa Fe, *N. Mex., U.S.* 107 R12
Santa Fe, Isla (Barrington), *Ecua.* 128 Q10
Santa Helena, *Braz.* 130 E10
Santa Inés, Isla, *Chile* 133 X7
Santa Inês, *Braz.* 131 E14
Santa Isabel, *Arg.* 132 M9
Santa Isabel, *P.R., U.S.* 120 P4
Santa Isabel, island, *Solomon Is.* 217 L17
Santa Isabel, Pico de, *Eq. Guinea* 204 M7
Santa Lucía, *Arg.* 132 H12
Santa Lucía, *Arg.* 132 J8
Santa Lucía, *Cuba* 116 G5
Santa Lucía, *Uru.* 132 L14
Santa Lucia Range, *Calif., U.S.* 109 U4
Santa Luzia, *Azores* 144 P3
Santa Luzia, island, *Cape Verde* 205 B15
Santa Maddalena Vallalta, *It.* 150 B8
Santa-Manza, Golfe de, *Fr.* 150 L4
Santa Margarita, Isla, *Mex.* 114 F6
Santa Maria, island, *Azores* 144 R5
Santa Maria, *Calif., U.S.* 109 W5
Santa Maria, *Cape Verde* 205 B17
Santa Maria, *Neth. Antilles, Neth.* 121 P14
Santa Maria, *Switz.* 150 C6
Santa Maria, island, *Vanuatu* 218 B2
Santa María, *Arg.* 132 G9
Santa María, *Peru* 130 D4
Santa Maria, *Braz.* 130 D9
Santa Maria, *Braz.* 130 P11
Santa Maria, Cabo de, *Angola* 202 E5
Santa Maria, Cabo de, *Port.* 144 L6
Santa Maria, Cape, *Bahamas* 117 F13
Santa María, Cayo, *Cuba* 116 G10
Santa María, Isla (Floreana, Charles), *Ecua.* 128 R9
Santa Maria Bay, *Virgin Islands, U.S.* 120 M8
Santa Maria da Vitória, *Braz.* 131 H15
Santa María de Huerta, *Sp.* 144 E12
Santa María de Nanay, *Peru* 130 E4
Santa Maria di Leuca, Capo, *It.* 151 P16
Santa Marta, *Col.* 128 B5
Santa Martabaai, bay, *Neth. Antilles, Neth.* 121 P13
Santa Marta de Ortigueira, Ría de, *Sp.* 144 A6
Santa Marta Grande, Cabo de, *Braz.* 131 P13
Santa Monica, *Calif., U.S.* 109 X8
Santa Monica Mountains National Recreation Area, *Calif., U.S.* 109 X7
Sant Ana, *Sao Tome and Principe* 205 D20
Santana, *Madeira* 204 M3
Santana, *Braz.* 131 H15
Santana do Livramento, *Braz.* 130 P11
Santander, *Sp.* 144 B11
Santander, Bahía de, *Sp.* 144 B11
Santander Jiménez, *Mex.* 114 F12
Sant'Andrea Apostolo dello Ionio, *It.* 151 R13
Santanilla, Islas, *Hond.* 115 J19
Sant'Antioco, Isola di, *It.* 151 Q3
Sant Antoni de Portmany, *Sp.* 145 H16
Santa Olalla del Cala, *Sp.* 144 K8
Santa Paula, *Calif., U.S.* 109 X7
Santa Pola, *Sp.* 145 K14
Santaquin, *Utah, U.S.* 106 L7
Santarém, *Port.* 144 H5
Santarém, *Braz.* 130 D11
Santaren Channel, *Bahamas* 116 F9
Santa Rita, *Guam, U.S.* 216 D10
Santa Rita, *Venez.* 128 B7
Santa Rita do Weil, *Braz.* 130 D6
Santa Rosa, *Arg.* 132 K9
Santa Rosa, *Arg.* 132 M10
Santa Rosa, *Bol.* 130 G6
Santa Rosa, island, *Calif., U.S.* 109 X6
Santa Rosa, *Calif., U.S.* 109 R3
Santa Rosa, *Neth. Antilles, Neth.* 121 Q15
Santa Rosa, *Ecua.* 128 Q9
Santa Rosa, *Hond.* 115 L16
Santa Rosa, *N. Mex., U.S.* 107 S14
Santa Rosa, *Peru* 130 G5
Santa Rosa, *Peru* 130 J5
Santa Rosa, *Braz.* 130 G5
Santa Rosa, Mount, *Guam, U.S.* 216 B12
Santa Rosa and San Jacinto Mountains National Monument, *Calif., U.S.* 109 Y11
Santa Rosa Beach, *Fla., U.S.* 97 Q3
Santa Rosa Island, *Fla., U.S.* 97 Q2
Santa Rosalía, *Mex.* 114 D6
Santa Rosa Range, *Nev., U.S.* 108 L9
Santa Severina, *It.* 151 Q14
Santa Teresa, *N. Terr., Austral.* 211 T9
Santa Teresa, Embalse de, *Sp.* 144 F9
Santa Victoria, *Arg.* 132 D11
Santa Vitória do Palmar, *Braz.* 130 Q11
Santa Ynez, *Calif., U.S.* 109 W6
Santa Ynez Mountains, *Calif., U.S.* 109 W6
Sant Carles de la Ràpita, *Sp.* 145 F16
Santee, river, *S.C., U.S.* 96 L11
San Telmo Point, *N. Amer.* 80 P4
Sant'Eufemia, Golfo di, *It.* 151 Q13
Santhià, *It.* 150 E3
Santiago, island, *Cape Verde* 205 D16
Santiago, *Chile* 132 K7
Santiago, *Dom. Rep.* 117 L18
Santiago *see* San Salvador, Isla, island, *Ecua.* 128 P9
Santiago, *Pan.* 115 P20
Santiago, Punta, *Eq. Guinea* 204 N7
Santiago de Baney, *Eq. Guinea* 204 L8
Santiago de Compostela, *Sp.* 144 B5
Santiago de Cuba, *Cuba* 117 K13
Santiago del Estero, *Arg.* 132 G10
Santiago do Cacém, *Port.* 144 K5
Santiago Ixcuintla, *Mex.* 114 G9
Santiago Papasquiaro, *Mex.* 114 F9
Santiago Peak, *Tex., U.S.* 103 Q2
Santigi, *Indonesia* 189 H13
Sant Jordi, Golf de, *Sp.* 145 F16
Sant Julià de Lòria, region, *Andorra* 160 K3
Sant Julià de Lòria, *Andorra* 160 K2
Santo André, *Braz.* 131 M13
Santo Ângelo, *Braz.* 130 P11
Santo Antão, island, *Cape Verde* 205 A14
Santo António, *Cape Verde* 205 D17
Santo António, *Sao Tome and Principe* 205 A21
Santo Antônio do Içá, *Braz.* 130 D6
Santo Corazón, *Bol.* 130 K9
Santo Domingo, *Dom. Rep.* 117 M19
Santo Domingo, Cay, *Bahamas* 117 J13
Santo Domingo de Silos, *Sp.* 144 D11
Santo Domingo Pueblo, *N. Mex., U.S.* 107 R12
Santop, Mount, *Vanuatu* 218 G3
Santopitar, peak, *Sp.* 144 M10
Santoríni *see* Thíra, island, *Gr.* 155 M15
Santos, *Braz.* 131 M14
Santos, Sierra de los, *Sp.* 144 K9
Santos Dumont, *Braz.* 130 F6
Santos Plateau, *Atl. Oc.* 237 R7
Santo Tirso, *Port.* 144 E5
Santo Tomás, *Peru* 130 J5
Santo Tomás, Volcán, *Ecua.* 128 Q8
Santo Tomé, *Arg.* 132 H14
San Valentín, Monte, *Chile* 133 T6
San Vicente, *N. Mariana Is., U.S.* 216 C5
San Vicente de Alcántara, *Sp.* 144 H7
San Vicente de Barakaldo, *Sp.* 144 B12
San Vincente del Caguán, *Col.* 128 G5
Sanya, *China* 183 V1
San Ygnacio, *Tex., U.S.* 103 V8
Sanyuan, *China* 182 G2
São Bento do Norte, *Braz.* 131 E18
São Borja, *Braz.* 130 P10
São Cristóvão, *Braz.* 131 H17
São Félix do Xingu, *Braz.* 130 F12
São Filipe, *Cape Verde* 205 E15
São Francisco, river, *Braz.* 131 J15
São Francisco, Ilha de, *Braz.* 131 N13
São Gabriel, *Braz.* 130 P11
São Gabriel da Cachoeira, *Braz.* 130 C6
São Gens, peak, *Port.* 144 J6
São João da Aliança, *Braz.* 131 J13
São João da Madeira, *Port.* 144 E5
São João del Rei, *Braz.* 131 L14
São Jorge, island, *Azores* 144 P3
São José de Anauá, *Braz.* 130 C8
São José de Ribamar, *Braz.* 131 D15
São José dos Campos, *Braz.* 131 M14
São Leopoldo, *Braz.* 130 Q12
São Lourenço, Ponta de, *Madeira* 204 M4
São Lourenço do Sul, *Braz.* 130 Q12
São Luís, *Braz.* 131 D15
São Luís, Ilha de, *Braz.* 131 D15
São Mamede, Pico, *Port.* 144 H6
São Manuel *see* Teles Pires, river, *Braz.* 130 F10
São Martinho do Porto, *Port.* 144 G4
São Mateus, *Azores* 144 P3
São Mateus, *Braz.* 131 K16
São Miguel, island, *Azores* 144 Q5
São Miguel do Araguaia, *Braz.* 130 H12
Saona, Isla, *Dom. Rep.* 117 M20
Saonek, *Indonesia* 189 J17
Saoner, *India* 178 K6
São Nicolau, island, *Cape Verde* 205 B16
São Paulo, *Braz.* 131 M13
São Paulo de Olivença, *Braz.* 130 D6
São Raimundo Nonato, *Braz.* 131 G15
São Romão, *Braz.* 130 E6
São Roque, Cabo de, *Braz.* 131 F18
São Sebastião, *Azores* 144 P4
São Sebastião, Ponta, *Mozambique* 203 H13
São Sebastião Island, *S. Amer.* 126 J9
São Teotónio, *Port.* 144 K5
São Tiago, *Cape Verde* 205 D16
São Tomé, island, *Sao Tome and Principe* 205 D19
São Tomé, *Sao Tome and Principe* 205 C20
São Tomé, Cabo de, *Braz.* 131 M15
São Tomé, Pico de, *Sao Tome and Principe* 205 D20
Sao Tome and Principe, *Af.* 204 F5
Saoute, Wādī, *Syr.* 170 L9
São Vicente, island, *Cape Verde* 205 B14
São Vicente, *Madeira* 204 M3
São Vicente, Cabo de, *Port.* 144 L4
Sapanca, *Turk.* 168 D6
Sapanjang, island, *Indonesia* 188 M11
Sapele, *Nigeria* 201 H13
Sapelo Island, *Ga., U.S.* 97 P9
Sápes, *Gr.* 155 B15
Şaphane Dağı, *Turk.* 168 F5
Sapiéntza, island, *Gr.* 154 M9
Saposoa, *Peru* 130 F3
Sapphire Mountains, *Mont., U.S.* 106 D6
Sappho, *Wash., U.S.* 108 B2
Sapporo, *Japan* 184 G13
Sapri, *It.* 151 N12
Sapudi, island, *Indonesia* 188 M11
Sapulpa, *Okla., U.S.* 102 F12
Saqqez, *Iran* 172 C10
Sara Adasy, island, *Azerb.* 169 F22
Sarāb, *Iran* 172 B11
Saraburi, *Thai.* 186 M9
Saraféré, *Mali* 196 H8
Saraguro, *Ecua.* 128 L3
Sarahs, *Turkm.* 174 N9
Sarajevo, *Bosn. & Herzg.* 152 G8
Sarakhs, *Iran* 173 B17
Saranac Lake, *N.Y., U.S.* 94 G11
Saranac Lakes, *N.Y., U.S.* 94 G10
Sarandë, *Albania* 152 N9
Sarangani Islands, *Philippines* 189 G15
Sarangpur, *India* 178 J5
Saransk, *Russ.* 156 K13
Sarapul, *Russ.* 156 H16
Sarapul, *Russ.* 158 H8
Sarasota, *Fla., U.S.* 97 V7
Sarasota Bay, *Fla., U.S.* 97 V7
Saratoga, *Wyo., U.S.* 106 K11
Saratoga Springs, *N.Y., U.S.* 94 J11
Saratov, *Russ.* 156 M13
Sarāvān, *Iran* 173 G18
Sarawak, region, *Malaysia* 188 H11
Saray, *Turk.* 168 C4
Saray, *Turk.* 169 F18
Sarayköy, *Turk.* 168 G4
Sar Banader, *Afghan.* 177 R3
Sarbāz, *Iran* 173 H17
Sarbīsheh, *Iran* 173 E17
Sarcelle, Passe de la, *New Caledonia, Fr.* 218 E9
Sardar Chah, *Pak.* 177 T4
Sardegna (Sardinia), island, *It.* 151 N3
Sardinia *see* Sardegna, island, *It.* 151 N3

Sardis, *Miss., U.S.* **100 H11**
Sardis, ruin, *Turk.* **168 F4**
Sardis Lake, *Miss., U.S.* **100 H11**
Sar-e Howz, *Afghan.* **176 L4**
Sareiserjoch, *Liech.* **160 Q4**
Sar-e Pol (Sari Pol), *Afghan.* **176 L5**
Sargans, *Switz.* **160 R1**
Sargent, *Nebr., U.S.* **105 P5**
Sargodha, *Pak.* **177 P10**
Sargo Plateau, *Arctic Oc.* **242 H6**
Sarh, *Chad* **197 K15**
Sarhadd, *Afghan.* **176 K11**
Sārī, *Iran* **173 C13**
Sariá, island, *Gr.* **155 P18**
Sarigan, island, *N. Mariana Is., U.S.* **216 B2**
Sarıgöl, *Turk.* **168 G4**
Sarıkamış, *Turk.* **169 D17**
Sarina, *Qnsld., Austral.* **211 T14**
Sariñena, *Sp.* **145 D15**
Sarinleey, *Somalia* **199 J16**
Sari Pol *see* Sar-e Pol, *Afghan.* **176 L5**
Sarīr Tibasti, region, *Lib.* **197 E14**
Sariwŏn, *N. Korea* **182 E12**
Sarıyar Baraji, *Turk.* **168 E7**
Sarıyer, *Turk.* **168 C5**
Sarız, *Turk.* **168 G11**
Sarjektjåkko, peak, *Sw.* **141 E13**
Sark, island, *Ch. Is.* **143 Z11**
Sarkari Tala, *India* **178 F2**
Şarkîkaraağaç, *Turk.* **168 G7**
Şarkışla, *Turk.* **168 F11**
Şarköy, *Turk.* **168 D3**
Sarles, *N. Dak., U.S.* **104 D6**
Sarmansuyu, *Turk.* **169 G17**
Sarmi, *Indonesia* **189 K20**
Sarmiento, *Arg.* **133 S8**
Särna, *Sw.* **140 J12**
Sarnano, *It.* **150 H9**
Sarny, *Ukr.* **156 M4**
Saroma Ko, *Japan* **184 E15**
Saronikós Kólpos, *Gr.* **154 J12**
Saronno, *It.* **150 D4**
Saros Körfezi, *Turk.* **168 D3**
Sarowbi, *Afghan.* **176 M8**
Sarowbi, *Afghan.* **177 P8**
Sarpa, Ozero, *Russ.* **157 Q14**
Sar Passage, *Palau* **216 P11**
Sarqan, *Kaz.* **175 G17**
Sarracín, *Sp.* **144 C11**
Sarrebourg, *Fr.* **147 P15**
Sarreguemines, *Fr.* **147 N15**
Sarria, *Sp.* **144 B7**
Sarrión, *Sp.* **145 G14**
Sarteano, *It.* **150 J7**
Sartène, *Fr.* **150 L4**
Sarthe, river, *Fr.* **147 Q7**
Sarti, *Gr.* **155 D13**
Sarufutsu, *Japan* **184 D14**
Saruna, *Pak.* **177 V6**
Sarupsar, *India* **178 E4**
Särur, *Azerb.* **169 E19**
Sarych, Mys, *Ukr.* **157 T7**
Saryesik-Atyraū Qumy, *Kaz.* **175 G16**
Sarygamysh Köli, *Turkm., Uzb.* **174 J8**
Saryköl, *Kaz.* **174 B11**
Saryözek, *Kaz.* **175 H17**
Saryqamys, *Kaz.* **174 G7**
Saryqopa Köli, *Kaz.* **174 D11**
Sarysay, *Kaz.* **174 E9**
Saryshagan, *Kaz.* **175 G15**
Sarysū, river, *Kaz.* **175 E13**
Sary-Tash, *Kyrg.* **176 G10**
Saryzhal, *Kaz.* **175 D17**
Sasalaguan, Mount, *Guam, U.S.* **216 D10**
Sasamungga, *Solomon Is.* **217 L15**
Sasaram, *India* **178 H9**
Sasebo, *Japan* **185 R3**
Saseno *see* Sazan, island, *Albania* **152 M9**
Saskatchewan, *Can.* **82 L12**
Saskatchewan, river, *N. Amer.* **80 G5**
Saskatoon, *Sask., Can.* **82 M12**
Sason, *Turk.* **169 G16**
Sasora, *Indonesia* **189 K20**
Sasovo, *Russ.* **156 K11**
Sassafras Mountain, *S.C., U.S.* **96 J7**
Sassandra, *Côte d'Ivoire* **200 H8**
Sassari, *It.* **150 M3**
Sassnitz, *Ger.* **148 B10**
Sassofeltrio, *It.* **161 L17**
Sasstown, *Liberia* **200 H7**
Sassuolo, *It.* **150 F6**
Sasykoli, *Russ.* **158 J5**
Sasyqköl, lake, *Kaz.* **175 F18**
Sata, *Japan* **185 T4**
Satadougou Tintiba, *Mali* **196 J6**
Satala, ruin, *Turk.* **169 E14**
Sata Misaki, *Japan* **185 U4**
Satanta, *Kans., U.S.* **105 U4**
Satara, *India* **178 M4**
Sataua, *Samoa* **218 K1**
Satawal, island, *F.S.M.* **216 Q5**
Satawan Atoll, *F.S.M.* **216 Q6**
Sätbaev, *Kaz.* **174 F12**
Satbarwa, *India* **178 H9**
Satilla, river, *Ga., U.S.* **97 P6**
Satipo, *Peru* **130 H4**
Satkania, *Bangladesh* **178 J14**
Satna, *India* **178 H7**
Sato, *Japan* **185 T3**
Šator, peak, *Bosn. & Herzg.* **152 F6**
Sátoraljaújhely, *Hung.* **149 K17**
Satpura Range, *India* **178 K4**
Satteins, *Aust.* **160 M4**
Satulung, *Rom.* **153 B13**
Satu Mare, *Rom.* **152 B12**
Satun, *Thai.* **187 S8**
Satupa'itea, *Samoa* **218 L2**
Sauce, *Arg.* **132 J13**
Sauda, *Nor.* **140 L10**
Sauđárkrókur, *Ice.* **140 E3**
Saudi Arabia, *Asia* **167 U3**
Saugatuck, *Mich., U.S.* **98 M9**
Saugerties, *N.Y., U.S.* **94 L11**
Sauk Centre, *Minn., U.S.* **104 J10**
Sauk City, *Wis., U.S.* **98 L5**
Saukorem, *Indonesia* **189 J18**
Sauk Rapids, *Minn., U.S.* **104 J11**
Saulieu, *Fr.* **147 R12**
Sault Ste. Marie, *Mich., U.S.* **98 F11**
Sault Ste. Marie, *Ont., Can.* **83 P17**
Saūmalköl, *Kaz.* **174 B12**
Saumlaki, *Indonesia* **189 M17**
Saumur, *Fr.* **147 R7**
Saunders Coast, *Antarctica* **226 N10**
Saupon Point, *Guam, U.S.* **216 C11**
Saura, *Kaz.* **174 H5**
Saurimo, *Angola* **202 C8**
Sausalito, *Calif., U.S.* **109 S3**
Sauteurs, *Grenada* **121 J23**
Sauteurs Bay, *Grenada* **121 J23**
Sauveterre, *Fr.* **147 X6**
Sava, river, *Bosn. & Herzg., Croatia, Slov.* **152 F9**
Savage, *Mont., U.S.* **106 C13**
Savai'i, island, *Samoa* **218 K2**
Savalou, *Benin* **200 G12**
Savana Island, *Virgin Islands, U.S.* **120 N7**
Savane des Pétrifications, site, *Martinique, Fr.* **121 G23**
Savaneta, *Aruba, Neth.* **121 R17**
Savanna, *Ill., U.S.* **99 N4**
Savannah, *Cayman Is., U.K.* **120 J2**
Savannah, *Ga., U.S.* **97 N9**
Savannah, river, *Ga., S.C., U.S.* **96 M8**
Savannah, *Mo., U.S.* **105 R10**
Savannah, *Tenn., U.S.* **101 G13**
Savannah Bay, *Virgin Islands, U.K.* **120 Q8**
Savannah Sound, *Bahamas* **120 E6**
Savannakhét, *Laos* **186 L11**
Savanna-la-Mar, *Jam.* **120 H6**
Savanna Point, *Jam.* **120 H10**
Savaştepe, *Turk.* **168 E3**
Save, river, *Mozambique* **202 H12**
Sāveh, *Iran* **172 C12**
Savenay, *Fr.* **147 R5**
Saverne, *Fr.* **147 P15**
Savigliano, *It.* **150 F2**
Savignac-les-Églises, *Fr.* **147 V8**
Savignone, *It.* **150 F4**
Savissivik, *Greenland, Den.* **81 C20**
Savo, island, *Solomon Is.* **217 N18**
Savona, *It.* **150 F3**
Savonet, *Neth. Antilles, Neth.* **121 N13**
Savonlinna, *Fin.* **141 H17**
Savoonga, *Alas., U.S.* **110 F10**
Savukoski, *Fin.* **141 D15**
Savur, *Turk.* **169 H15**
Savusavu, *Fiji Is.* **218 G7**
Savusavu Bay, *Fiji Is.* **218 H7**
Savu Sea, *Indonesia* **189 N14**
Sawada, *Japan* **184 M11**
Sawah, *Indonesia* **188 H11**
Sawahlunto, *Indonesia* **188 J6**
Sawa-i-lau, island, *Fiji Is.* **218 H5**
Sawai Madhopur, *India* **178 G5**
Sawankhalok, *Thai.* **186 K8**
Sawatch Range, *Colo., U.S.* **107 N12**
Sawda, Jabal, *Saudi Arabia* **172 N8**
Sawdā', Jabal as, *Lib.* **197 D14**
Sawe, *Indonesia* **188 H4**
Sawi, *Thai.* **187 Q8**
Sawkanah, *Lib.* **197 D14**
Şawqirah, *Oman* **173 N15**
Şawqirah, Ghubbat, *Oman* **173 N16**
Sawtooth Mountains, *Minn., U.S.* **104 F13**
Sawtooth National Recreation Area, *Idaho, U.S.* **106 G5**
Sawtooth Range, *Idaho, U.S.* **106 G4**
Sawu, island, *Indonesia* **189 N14**
Sax, *Switz.* **160 M1**
Saxby Downs, *Qnsld., Austral.* **211 S12**
Saxony, region, *Ger.* **148 F10**
Say, *Niger* **196 J10**
Saya de Malha Bank, *Ind. Oc.* **240 H7**
Sayanogorsk, *Russ.* **159 L13**
Sayḩūt, *Yemen* **173 Q13**
Saylac, *Somalia* **199 F16**
Saynshand, *Mongolia* **181 E13**
Sayötesh, *Kaz.* **174 H6**
Sayram Hu, *China* **180 E6**
Sayre, *Okla., U.S.* **102 G8**
Sayre, *Pa., U.S.* **94 L8**
Saywūn, *Yemen* **172 P11**
Sayylyk, *Russ.* **159 E18**
Saza'i Kalan, *Afghan.* **176 L5**
Sazan (Saseno), island, *Albania* **152 M9**
Sazin, *Pak.* **176 L11**
Sbaa, *Alg.* **196 D10**
Scafell Pike, peak, *Eng., U.K.* **143 Q10**
Scalpay, island, *Scot., U.K.* **142 J7**
Scalpay, island, *Scot., U.K.* **142 K7**
Scammon Bay, *Alas., U.S.* **110 H11**
Scandia, *Kans., U.S.* **105 R7**
Scandinavia, region, *Eur.* **138 D7**
Scanzano Ionico, *It.* **151 N14**
Scapa Flow, *Scot., U.K.* **142 G10**
Scaraben, peak, *Scot., U.K.* **142 H10**
Scarba, island, *Scot., U.K.* **142 M7**
Scarborough, *Eng., U.K.* **143 Q13**
Scarborough, *Trinidad & Tobago* **121 N17**
Scarinish, *Scot., U.K.* **142 L6**
Scarp, island, *Scot., U.K.* **142 H6**
Scarriff, *Ire.* **143 T4**
Scatterbreak Channel, *Fiji Is.* **218 G8**
Šcedro, island, *Croatia* **152 H6**
Schaan, *Liech.* **160 N2**
Schaanwald, *Liech.* **160 N3**
Schefferville, *Que., Can.* **83 L20**
Schell Creek Range, *Nev., U.S.* **109 Q12**
Schellenberg, *Liech.* **160 M3**
Schenectady, *N.Y., U.S.* **94 J11**
Schertz, *Tex., U.S.* **103 R10**
Schiermonnikoog, island, *Neth.* **146 G13**
Schio, *It.* **150 D7**
Schleswig, *Ger.* **148 A7**
Schoelcher, *Martinique, Fr.* **121 F22**
Schofield, *Wis., U.S.* **98 H5**
Schofield Barracks, *Hawai'i, U.S.* **112 D10**
Schönberg, peak, *Liech.* **160 P3**
Schönebeck, *Ger.* **148 E9**
Schooner Cays, *Bahamas* **120 F6**
Schottegat, bay, *Neth. Antilles, Neth.* **121 Q14**
Schouten Islands, *P.N.G.* **213 C18**
Schrems, *Aust.* **148 J11**
Schroeder, *Minn., U.S.* **104 F13**
Schuckmannsburg, *Namibia* **202 F9**
Schulenburg, *Tex., U.S.* **103 R12**
Schull, *Ire.* **143 V3**
Schuyler, *Nebr., U.S.* **105 P8**
Schwabach, *Ger.* **148 J8**
Schwäbische Alb, *Ger.* **148 K7**
Schwäbisch Hall, *Ger.* **148 J7**
Schwaz, *Aust.* **148 L9**
Schwechat, *Aust.* **149 K13**
Schwedt, *Ger.* **148 D11**
Schweich, *Ger.* **160 J12**
Schweinfurt, *Ger.* **148 G8**
Schwerin, *Ger.* **148 C9**
Schwyz, *Switz.* **150 B4**
Sciacca, *It.* **151 S9**
Scilla, *It.* **151 R12**
Scilly, Isles of, *Eng., U.K.* **143 Y6**
Scioto, river, *Ohio, U.S.* **99 S13**
Scipio, *Utah, U.S.* **106 M7**
Scobey, *Mont., U.S.* **106 A12**
Scofield Reservoir, *Utah, U.S.* **106 M8**
Scooba, *Miss., U.S.* **101 K13**
Scotch Bonnet, cape, *St. Kitts & Nevis* **121 B18**
Scotia Sea, *Antarctic Oc.* **244 D8**
Scotland, *S. Dak., U.S.* **104 M7**
Scotland, *U.K.* **142 K9**
Scotland Neck, *N.C., U.S.* **96 G13**
Scott, Mount, *Oreg., U.S.* **108 J4**
Scott Base, station, *Antarctica* **227 N13**
Scott City, *Kans., U.S.* **105 T4**
Scott City, *Mo., U.S.* **105 U16**
Scott Coast, *Antarctica* **227 N14**
Scott Glacier, *Antarctica* **227 K21**
Scott Islands, *B.C., Can.* **82 L7**
Scott Point, *Mich., U.S.* **98 G9**
Scottsbluff, *Nebr., U.S.* **105 N1**
Scotts Bluff National Monument, *Nebr., U.S.* **105 N1**
Scottsboro, *Ala., U.S.* **101 G16**
Scottsburg, *Ind., U.S.* **99 T9**
Scottsdale, *Ariz., U.S.* **107 U7**
Scotts Head, *Dominica* **121 G19**
Scottsville, *Ky., U.S.* **101 D16**
Scottville, *Mich., U.S.* **98 K9**
Scotty's Junction, *Nev., U.S.* **109 S9**
Scranton, *Pa., U.S.* **94 M9**
Scribner, *Nebr., U.S.* **105 P8**
Scrubby Creek, *Qnsld., Austral.* **211 P12**
Scrub Island, *Anguilla, U.K.* **120 Q12**
Scunthorpe, *Eng., U.K.* **143 R13**
Scuol, *Switz.* **150 B6**
Scurdie Ness, *Scot., U.K.* **142 L11**
Scutari *see* Shkodër, *Albania* **152 K9**
Scutari, Lake *see* Skadarsko Jezero, *Albania, Serb. & Mont.* **152 J9**
Scyros *see* Skíros, island, *Gr.* **155 G13**
Sea Club, *Monaco* **161 B23**
Sea Cow Bay, *Virgin Islands, U.K.* **120 R6**
Seadrift, *Tex., U.S.* **103 T12**
Seaford, *Del., U.S.* **96 D14**
Seaford, *Eng., U.K.* **143 W14**
Seaforth, *Jam.* **120 J11**
Seaforth, Loch, *Scot., U.K.* **142 H7**
Sea Grape, *Bahamas* **120 F1**
Seagraves, *Tex., U.S.* **102 L4**
Seaham, *Eng., U.K.* **143 P12**
Sea Island, *Ga., U.S.* **97 P9**
Sea Islands, *Ga., U.S.* **85 L19**
Seal, river, *Man., Can.* **83 K14**
Seal, Cape, *S. Af.* **202 M9**
Sea Lake, *Vic., Austral.* **211 Y11**
Seal Cay, *Bahamas* **117 G13**
Seal Cays, *Turks & Caicos Is., U.K.* **117 J17**
Sealevel, *N.C., U.S.* **96 J14**
Seal Islands, *Anguilla, U.K.* **120 Q11**
Sealy, *Tex., U.S.* **103 R13**
Searchlight, *Nev., U.S.* **109 V12**
Searcy, *Ark., U.S.* **100 G9**
Searles Lake, *Calif., U.S.* **109 V9**
Seaside, *Oreg., U.S.* **108 E2**
Seaside Park, *N.J., U.S.* **94 P11**
Seaton Glacier, *Antarctica* **227 C19**
Seatons, *Antigua & Barbuda* **121 B21**
Seattle, *Wash., U.S.* **108 C4**
Sebago Lake, *Me., U.S.* **95 G15**
Sebakor, Teluk, *Indonesia* **213 C14**
Sebastian, *Fla., U.S.* **97 U10**
Sebastian, Cape, *Oreg., U.S.* **108 K1**
Sebastián Vizcaíno, Bahía, *Mex.* **114 D5**
Sebastián Vizcaíno Bay, *N. Amer.* **80 L3**
Sebastopol, *Calif., U.S.* **109 R3**
Sebatik, island, *Indonesia, Malaysia* **188 G12**
Sebeka, *Minn., U.S.* **104 G10**
Seben, *Turk.* **168 D7**
Sebeş, *Rom.* **153 D13**
Sebewaing, *Mich., U.S.* **98 K12**
Sebezh, *Russ.* **156 H5**
Şebinkarahisar, *Turk.* **169 E13**
Sebring, *Fla., U.S.* **97 U9**
Sebuyau, *Malaysia* **188 H10**
Sechura, Bahía de, *Peru* **130 F1**
Sechura Desert, *S. Amer.* **126 E1**
Secica, *Slovakia* **149 J13**
Second Cataract, *Sudan* **198 C12**
Secondigny, *Fr.* **147 S7**
Second Mesa, *Ariz., U.S.* **107 R8**
Secos, Ilhéus (Ilhéus do Rombo), *Cape Verde* **205 D15**
Secretary Island, *N.Z.* **213 Q15**
Sécure, river, *Bol.* **130 J7**
Securé, river, *S. Amer.* **126 G5**
Security, *Colo., U.S.* **107 N13**
Sedalia, *Mo., U.S.* **105 T12**
Sedan, *Fr.* **147 N12**
Sedan, *Kans., U.S.* **105 V9**
Seddon, *N.Z.* **213 N18**
Sedeh, *Iran* **173 D16**
Sedom, *Israel* **171 P6**
Sedona, *Ariz., U.S.* **107 S7**
Sedro Woolley, *Wash., U.S.* **108 A4**
Seeheim, *Namibia* **202 K7**
Sées, *Fr.* **147 P7**
Seevetal, *Ger.* **148 C8**
Seferihisar, *Turk.* **168 F2**
Sefid Kers, range, *Afghan.* **176 J9**
Sefid Kuh Mountains (Paropamisus Range), *Afghan.* **176 M3**
Seg, Lake, *Russ.* **138 C10**
Segamat, *Malaysia* **187 U10**
Segbana, *Benin* **200 F12**
Segesta, ruin, *It.* **151 S9**
Segezha, *Russ.* **158 D8**
Seghe, *Solomon Is.* **217 M16**
Ségou, *Mali* **196 H7**
Segovia, *Sp.* **144 E10**
Segré, *Fr.* **147 R6**
Seguam Island, *Alas., U.S.* **110 P7**
Séguéla, *Côte d'Ivoire* **200 G8**
Seguin, *Tex., U.S.* **103 R10**
Seguntur, *Indonesia* **188 H12**
Segura, river, *Sp.* **145 K14**
Segura, Sierra de, *Sp.* **144 K12**
Sehwan, *Pak.* **177 V7**
Seikan Submarine Tunnel, *Japan* **184 H12**
Seil, island, *Scot., U.K.* **142 L8**
Seiling, *Okla., U.S.* **102 F9**
Seinäjoki, *Fin.* **141 H15**
Seine, river, *Fr.* **147 P9**
Seine, Baie de la, *Fr.* **147 N7**
Sekerangi Passage, *Cook Is., N.Z.* **219 A17**
Sekikawa, *Japan* **184 M12**
Sekondi-Takoradi, *Ghana* **200 H10**
Sek'ot'a, *Eth.* **199 E15**
Sekseūil, *Kaz.* **174 F10**
Selah, *Wash., U.S.* **108 D6**
Selaru, island, *Indonesia* **189 M17**
Selatan, Bunguran *see* Natuna Selatan, Kepulauan, *Indonesia* **188 H9**
Selawik, *Alas., U.S.* **111 E13**
Selawik Lake, *Alas., U.S.* **111 E13**
Selayar, island, *Indonesia* **189 L13**
Selby, *Eng., U.K.* **143 R13**
Selby, *S. Dak., U.S.* **104 J5**
Selden, *Kans., U.S.* **105 S4**
Seldovia, *Alas., U.S.* **111 K16**
Selendi, *Turk.* **168 F4**
Selenga, river, *Mongolia, Russ.* **166 E10**
Selenga, river, *Russ.* **159 L16**
Selenge, river, *Mongolia* **180 C12**
Sélestat, *Fr.* **147 Q15**
Selfoss, *Ice.* **140 F2**
Selfridge, *N. Dak., U.S.* **104 H4**
Self Town *see* McLean's Town, *Bahamas* **120 E4**
Sélibaby, *Mauritania* **196 H6**
Seliger, Ozero, *Russ.* **156 H7**
Seligman, *Ariz., U.S.* **107 S6**
Selima Oasis, *Sudan* **198 C12**
Selinus, ruin, *It.* **151 S9**
Selkirk, *Scot., U.K.* **143 N10**
Selkirk Mountains, *Idaho, U.S.* **106 A3**
Sellheim, *Qnsld., Austral.* **211 S13**
Sellières, *Fr.* **147 S13**
Sells, *Ariz., U.S.* **107 V7**
Selma, *Ala., U.S.* **101 L15**
Selma, *Calif., U.S.* **109 T6**
Selma, *N.C., U.S.* **96 H12**
Selmer, *Tenn., U.S.* **101 G13**
Selongey, *Fr.* **147 R13**
Selsey Bill, *Eng., U.K.* **143 X13**
Seltz, *Fr.* **147 P16**
Selvas, region, *S. Amer.* **126 E3**
Selway, river, *Idaho, U.S.* **106 D5**
Selwyn, *Qnsld., Austral.* **211 S11**
Selwyn Mountains, *N.W.T., Yukon, Can.* **82 F9**
Selwyn Strait, *Vanuatu* **218 D3**

Semarang, Indonesia 188 M9
Sembé, Congo 201 K17
Şemdinli, Turk. 169 H19
Semenov, Russ. 156 H12
Semeru, peak, Indonesia 188 M10
Semey (Semipalatinsk), Kaz. 175 D17
Semichi Islands, Alas., U.S. 111 L2
Semiluki, Russ. 156 M10
Seminoe Dam, Wyo., U.S. 106 J11
Seminoe Reservoir, Wyo., U.S. 106 J11
Seminole, Okla., U.S. 102 G12
Seminole, Tex., U.S. 102 L4
Seminole, Lake, Fla., Ga., U.S. 97 Q4
Semipalatinsk see Semey, Kaz. 175 D17
Semipalatinsk Nuclear Test Range, Kaz. 175 D16
Semisopochnoi Island, Alas., U.S. 110 N3
Semnān, Iran 173 C14
Semporna, Malaysia 188 G12
Sen, river, Cambodia 186 M11
Seňa, Slovakia 149 J17
Senaja, Malaysia 188 F12
Senaki, Rep. of Georgia 169 B16
Sena Madureira, Braz. 130 G6
Senanga, Zambia 202 F9
Senatobia, Miss., U.S. 100 H11
Sendai, Japan 184 L13
Sendai, Japan 185 T4
Sendhwa, India 178 K4
Senduruhan, Indonesia 188 J9
Seneca, Kans., U.S. 105 R9
Seneca, Oreg., U.S. 108 H7
Seneca, S.C., U.S. 96 K6
Seneca Falls, N.Y., U.S. 94 J7
Sénégal, river, Mauritania, Senegal 196 H5
Senegal, Af. 195 G13
Senftenberg, Ger. 148 F11
Sengiley, Russ. 156 K15
Senhor do Bonfim, Braz. 131 G16
Senigallia, It. 150 G9
Senj, Croatia 152 E5
Senja, island, Nor. 140 D12
Senkaku Shotō (Diaoyu Islands), China 183 P11
Senlis, Fr. 147 N10
Senmonorom, Cambodia 187 N13
Sennar, Sudan 199 E13
Sennecey-le-Grand, Fr. 147 S13
Sennen, Eng., U.K. 143 Y7
Senneterre, Que., Can. 83 P18
Sennwald, Switz. 160 L2
Senorbì, It. 151 P4
Sens, Fr. 147 Q11
Sensuntepeque, El Salv. 115 L16
Senta, Serb. & Mont. 152 D10
Šentilj, Slov. 152 C6
Sentinel, Okla., U.S. 102 G8
Sentinel Range, Antarctica 226 H8
Senyavin Islands, F.S.M. 216 Q8
Seogwipo, S. Korea 182 J13
Seoni, India 178 J7
Seosan, S. Korea 182 F13
Seoul, S. Korea 182 E13
Sepasu, Indonesia 188 J12
Sepi, Solomon Is. 217 M18
Sepik, river, P.N.G. 213 C18
Sept-Îles, Que., Can. 83 M21
Sepúlveda, Sp. 144 E11
Sepupa, Botswana 202 G8
Sequim, Wash., U.S. 108 B3
Sequoia National Park, Calif., U.S. 109 T8
Seraing, Belg. 146 L13
Serang, Indonesia 188 L8
Serasan, island, Indonesia 188 H9
Serbia and Montenegro, Eur. 139 W8
Serdobsk, Russ. 156 L13
Serebryansk, Kaz. 175 D18
Sered', Slovakia 149 K14
Seredka, Russ. 156 G5
Şereflikoçhisar, Turk. 168 F9
Seremban, Malaysia 187 U9
Serena, Embalse la, Sp. 144 H9
Serengeti Plain, Tanzania 199 K13
Séres, Gr. 154 B12
Sergach, Russ. 156 J13
Sergeya Kirova, Ostrova, Russ. 159 D13
Sergino, Russ. 158 G10
Sergiyev Posad, Russ. 156 J9
Serian, Malaysia 188 H9
Sérifos, island, Gr. 155 L13
Sérifos, Gr. 155 L13
Sérignan, Fr. 147 Y11
Serik, Turk. 168 H6
Seringa, Serra da, Braz. 130 F12
Seriole, river, San Marino 161 L15
Serkovo, Russ. 159 G13
Sermata, island, Indonesia 189 M16
Sermata, Kepulauan, Indonesia 189 M16
Sernur, Russ. 156 H14
Seroczyn, Pol. 149 E17
Seroe Colorado, Aruba, Neth. 121 R17
Serov, Russ. 158 H9
Serowe, Botswana 202 H10
Serpa, Port. 144 K6
Serpentine Lakes, Austral. 210 H7
Serpent Island, Mauritius 205 E21
Serpent's Mouth, strait, Trinidad & Tobago 121 R21
Serpukhov, Russ. 156 K9
Serra do Navio, Braz. 130 C12
Serra Nevada de Santa Marta, S. Amer. 126 A3
Serravalle, San Marino 161 H16
Serre-Ponçon, Lac de, Fr. 147 W14
Serrera, Pic de la, Andorra, Fr. 160 G4
Serres, Fr. 147 W14
Serrezuela, Arg. 132 J9
Serrières, Fr. 147 U13
Serrinha, Braz. 131 H16
Sersale, It. 151 Q14
Sertã, Port. 144 G6
Sertão, region, S. Amer. 126 F10
Serti, Nigeria 201 G15
Serui, Indonesia 189 K19
Sérvia, Gr. 154 D9
Sesfontein, Namibia 202 G5
Sesheke, Zambia 202 F9
Sesimbra, Port. 144 J4
Sesklí, island, Gr. 155 M19
Sessa Aurunca, It. 150 L10
Sestri Levante, It. 150 F4
Sestri Ponente, It. 150 F4
Sestroretsk, Russ. 156 F6
Setana, Japan 184 G12
Sète, Fr. 147 X11
Sete Lagoas, Braz. 131 K14
Sete Quedas Falls, S. Amer. 126 J7
Sétif, Alg. 196 A11
Seto, Japan 185 P10
Setouchi, Japan 185 W3
Settat, Mor. 196 B8
Setté Cama, Gabon 201 M15
Settimo Torinese, It. 150 E3
Settlement, Marshall Is. 216 N5
Settlement, Wake I., U.S. 216 F8
Setúbal, Port. 144 J5
Setúbal, Baía de, Port. 144 J5
Seul, Lac, Ont., Can. 83 N15
Seul Choix Point, Mich., U.S. 98 G9
Sevan, Arm. 169 D19
Sevana Lich, lake, Arm. 169 D19
Sevastopol', Ukr. 157 T7
Sevelen, Switz. 160 P2
Seven Islands Bay, Nfld. & Lab., Can. 83 J20
Seven Stones, islands, Eng., U.K. 143 Y7
Severn, river, Ont., Can. 83 L16
Severn, S. Af. 202 J9
Severnaya Dvina, river, Russ. 158 F8
Severnaya Zemlya (North Land), Russ. 159 C14
Severnyy, Russ. 158 F11
Severobaykal'sk, Russ. 159 K16
Severodvinsk, Russ. 158 E8
Severo Kuril'sk, Russ. 159 G23
Severomorsk, Russ. 158 D9
Severo Sibirskaya Nizmennost', Russ. 159 F13
Sevi, Russ. 159 L13
Sevier, river, Utah, U.S. 106 M6
Sevier Desert, Utah, U.S. 106 M6
Sevier Lake, Utah, U.S. 107 N6
Sevilla, Col. 128 F4
Sevilla (Seville), Sp. 144 L8
Sevilla Nueva, site, Jam. 120 H9
Seville see Sevilla, Sp. 144 L8
Sevlievo, Bulg. 153 H14
Seward, Alas., U.S. 111 K16
Seward, Nebr., U.S. 105 Q8
Seward Peninsula, Alas., U.S. 110 F12
Sewell, Chile 132 L7
Seweweekspoortpiek, peak, S. Af. 194 Q7
Seychelles, Af. 204 F9
Seychelles Group, Seychelles 205 P20
Seydi, Turkm. 174 L10
Seydişehir, Turk. 168 H7
Seyðisfjörður, Ice. 140 F4
Seyfe Gölü, Turk. 168 F9
Seyhan, river, Turk. 168 H10
Seyhan Barajı, Turk. 168 H10
Seyitgazi, Turk. 168 E6
Seylla Glacier, Antarctica 227 E19
Seymchan, Russ. 159 E20
Seymour, Ind., U.S. 99 S9
Seymour, Iowa, U.S. 105 Q12
Seymour, Tex., U.S. 102 K8
Seymour, Vic., Austral. 211 Z12
Seymour, Wis., U.S. 98 J6
Seymour, Isla, Ecua. 128 Q9
Seyne, Fr. 147 W14
Sézanne, Fr. 147 P11
Sfakia, Gr. 155 Q13
Sfântu-Gheorghe, Ostrov, Rom. 153 E18
Sfax, Tun. 197 B13
Sferracavallo, Capo, It. 151 P5
Sfîntu Gheorghe, Rom. 153 D15
's Gravenhage (The Hague), Neth. 146 J12
Sha, river, China 183 P7
Shabla, Nos, Bulg. 153 G18
Shabwah, Yemen 172 Q11
Shache, China 180 G4
Shackleton Coast, Antarctica 227 L13
Shackleton Ice Shelf, Antarctica 227 K21
Shackleton Range, Antarctica 226 E11
Shadehill Reservoir, S. Dak., U.S. 104 H2
Shaduzup, Myanmar 186 E6
Shafter, Nev., U.S. 108 M12
Shafter, Tex., U.S. 103 Q1
Shageluk, Alas., U.S. 111 H13
Shaghan, river, Kaz. 174 F8
Shaghan, Kaz. 175 D17
Shag Rocks, S. Amer. 126 R9
Shahbā' (Philippopolis), Syr. 170 K8
Shah Bandar, Pak. 177 X7
Shahdadkot, Pak. 177 T7
Shahdadpur, Pak. 177 V7
Shahdol, India 178 J8
Shahgarh, India 178 F2
Shaḩḩāt (Cyrene), Lib. 197 B16
Shahjahanpur, India 178 F7
Shah Juy, Afghan. 177 P6
Shah Malan, Afghan. 177 Q4
Shah Maqsud Range, Afghan. 177 P5
Shahpur, India 178 M5
Shahpur, Pak. 177 P10
Shahpur Chakar, Pak. 177 V7
Shahr-e Bābak, Iran 173 F14
Shahrig, Pak. 177 R6
Shahrisabz, Uzb. 174 L12
Shāhrūd, Iran 173 C14
Shaighalu, Pak. 177 Q7
Shajapur, India 178 J5
Shakhbuz, Azerb. 169 E19
Shakhtakhty, Azerb. 169 F19
Shakhtersk, Russ. 159 J21
Shakhty, Russ. 157 Q11
Shakhun'ya, Russ. 156 G13
Shaktoolik, Alas., U.S. 111 G13
Shali, Russ. 157 U14
Shallowater, Tex., U.S. 102 K5
Shalqar, Kaz. 174 F9
Shalqar Köli, Kaz. 174 D6
Shām, Jabal ash, Oman 173 K16
Shamattawa, Man., Can. 83 L15
Shambe, Sudan 198 G12
Shamkhor, Azerb. 169 D20
Shammar, Jabal, Saudi Arabia 172 G7
Shamokin, Pa., U.S. 94 N8
Shamrock, Tex., U.S. 102 G7
Shamva, Zimb. 202 F12
Shandan, China 180 H11
Shandong Bandao, China 182 F9
Shandur Pass, Pak. 176 L10
Shangcai, China 182 J5
Shangcheng, China 182 K6
Shangchuan Dao, China 183 S4
Shangdu, China 182 B5
Shanghai, China 182 K10
Shanghang, China 183 Q6
Shangnan, China 182 H3
Shangombo, Zambia 202 F8
Shangqiu, China 182 H6
Shangrao, China 182 M7
Shangri-La (Zhongdian), China 180 M10
Shangxian, China 182 H2
Shangyi, China 182 C5
Shangyou, China 183 P5
Shaniko, Oreg., U.S. 108 G5
Shannon, Ire. 143 T4
Shannon, River, Ire. 143 T3
Shantar Islands, Russ. 166 D12
Shantarskiye Ostrova, Russ. 159 H20
Shantou (Swatow), China 183 R6
Shanxian, China 182 H6
Shanyang, China 182 H2
Shanyin, China 182 D5
Shanyincheng, China 182 D5
Shaoguan, China 183 Q4
Shaowu, China 183 N7
Shaoxing, China 182 L9
Shaoyang, China 183 N3
Shap, Eng., U.K. 143 Q11
Shapa, China 183 S3
Shapinsay, island, Scot., U.K. 142 F10
Shaqrā', Saudi Arabia 172 J10
Shaqrā', Yemen 172 R10
Shar, Kaz. 175 D17
Shār, Jabal, Saudi Arabia 172 G5
Sharan, Afghan. 177 N7
Sharâtîb, Râs, Egypt 171 T2
Sharbaqty, Kaz. 175 C16
Sharbatāt, Oman 173 N15
Sharbatāt, Ra's ash, Oman 173 N15
Sharhulsan, Mongolia 180 E12
Shari, Japan 184 E16
Sharjah, U.A.E. 173 J15
Sharkan, Russ. 156 G16
Shark Bay, W. Aust., Austral. 211 V1
Sharlawuk, Turkm. 174 L7
Sharm el Sheikh, Egypt 171 U4
Sharon, Pa., U.S. 94 M3
Sharon Springs, Kans., U.S. 105 S3
Sharpe, Lake, S. Dak., U.S. 104 L5
Sharqī, Al Jabal ash (Anti-Lebanon), Leb., Syr. 170 H7
Sharuhen, ruin, Israel 171 N4
Sharwayn, Ra's, Yemen 173 Q13
Shar'ya, Russ. 156 G13
Shashe, river, Botswana, Zimb. 202 H11
Shashi, China 182 L4
Shasta, Mount, Calif., U.S. 108 M4
Shasta Lake, Calif., U.S. 108 M4
Shatskiy Rise, Pac. Oc. 238 F7
Shatt al Arab, river, Iran, Iraq 172 F11
Shattuck, Okla., U.S. 102 F7
Shaumyan, Azerb. 169 D20
Shaumyani, Rep. of Georgia 169 C18
Shaunavon, Sask., Can. 82 N11
Shaw, Miss., U.S. 100 J10
Shawano, Wis., U.S. 98 J6
Shawinigan, Que., Can. 83 P19
Shawnee, Kans., U.S. 105 S10
Shawnee, Okla., U.S. 102 G11
Shaxian, China 183 P7
Shaybārā, island, Saudi Arabia 172 J6
Shay Gap, W. Aust., Austral. 211 S3
Shaykh 'Uthmān, Yemen 172 R9
Shayman, Taj. 176 J12
Shchekino, Russ. 156 K9
Shchigry, Russ. 156 M9
Shchūchīnsk, Kaz. 175 C13
Shebar Pass, Afghan. 176 M7
Shebekino, Russ. 157 N9
Shebelē, Wabē, Eth. 199 H16
Sheberghan, Afghan. 176 K5
Shebir, Kaz. 174 G6
Sheboygan, Wis., U.S. 98 K7
Sheboygan Falls, Wis., U.S. 98 K7
Sheelin, Lough, Ire. 143 R6
Sheep Haven, Ire. 143 N5
Sheep Mountain, Colo., U.S. 106 L11
Sheep Range, Nev., U.S. 109 T12
Sheerness, Eng., U.K. 143 V15
Shefar'am, Israel 170 K5
Sheffield, Ala., U.S. 101 G14
Sheffield, Eng., U.K. 143 S12
Sheffield, Tex., U.S. 103 P5
Sheikh Zayed Canal, Egypt 197 E18
Shekhupura, Pak. 177 Q11
Shelbina, Mo., U.S. 105 R13
Shelburne, N.S., Can. 83 Q22
Shelby, Mich., U.S. 98 K9
Shelby, Miss., U.S. 100 J10
Shelby, Mont., U.S. 106 B7
Shelby, N.C., U.S. 96 J8
Shelby, Ohio, U.S. 99 P13
Shelbyville, Ill., U.S. 99 S6
Shelbyville, Ind., U.S. 99 S9
Shelbyville, Ky., U.S. 101 B17
Shelbyville, Tenn., U.S. 101 F15
Sheldon, Iowa, U.S. 104 M9
Sheldon Point, Alas., U.S. 110 H11
Shelikhova, Zaliv, Russ. 159 E21
Shelikhov Gulf, Russ. 166 B12
Shelikof Strait, Alas., U.S. 111 L15
Shell Beach, Guyana 129 C14
Shelley, Idaho, U.S. 106 H7
Shell Lake, Wis., U.S. 98 G2
Shellman, Ga., U.S. 97 P5
Shelter Cove, Calif., U.S. 109 N1
Shelton, Nebr., U.S. 105 Q6
Shelton, Wash., U.S. 108 C3
Shemakha, Azerb. 169 D22
Shemgang, Bhutan 178 F13
Shemonaīkha, Kaz. 175 D18
Shemya Island, Alas., U.S. 111 L2
Shenandoah, Iowa, U.S. 105 Q9
Shenandoah, Pa., U.S. 94 N8
Shenandoah, Va., U.S. 96 D11
Shenandoah National Park, Va., U.S. 96 D11
Shenchi, China 182 D4
Shendam, Nigeria 201 G15
Shengxian, China 182 M9
Shenmu, China 182 D3
Shennongjia, China 182 K3
Shenqiu, China 182 J6
Shenyang, China 182 B11
Shenzhen, China 183 S5
Sheoganj, India 178 H3
Sheopur, India 178 G5
Shepetivka, Ukr. 157 N4
Shepherd, Ill., U.S. 99 R3
Shepherd Islands, Vanuatu 218 E3
Shepparton, Vic., Austral. 211 Y12
Sheppey, Isle of, Eng., U.K. 143 V15
Sherbo Island, Sierra Leone 200 G5
Sherbrooke, Que., Can. 83 P20
Sherburn, Minn., U.S. 104 L10
Shereiq, Sudan 199 C13
Sheridan, Ark., U.S. 100 H8
Sheridan, Wyo., U.S. 106 F11
Sheridan, Cape, Nunavut, Can. 83 A17
Sheringham, Eng., U.K. 143 S15
Sherkaly, Russ. 158 G10
Sherkin Island, Ire. 143 V3
Sherlovaya, Russ. 159 L17
Sherman, Tex., U.S. 102 K12
Sherman Mills, Me., U.S. 95 D18
Sherman Peak, Idaho, U.S. 84 E7
Sherobod, Uzb. 174 M12
Sherridon, Man., Can. 83 L13
's Hertogenbosch, Neth. 146 K13
Sherwood, N. Dak., U.S. 104 D4
Sherwood Forest, Eng., U.K. 143 S13
Shetland Islands (Zetland), Scot., U.K. 142 C12
Shetpe, Kaz. 174 H6
Shexian, China 182 L8
Sheyang (Hede), China 182 H9
Sheyenne, river, N. Dak., U.S. 104 F7
Sheyenne, N. Dak., U.S. 104 F6
Shiant Islands, Scot., U.K. 142 J7
Shiashkotan, island, Russ. 159 H23
Shibām, Yemen 172 P11
Shibata, Japan 184 M12
Shibecha, Japan 184 F15
Shibetsu, Japan 184 E14
Shibetsu, Japan 184 F16
Shibushi Wan, Japan 185 T5
Shicheng, China 183 P6
Shidao, China 182 F10
Shidler, Okla., U.S. 102 E12
Shiel, Loch, Scot., U.K. 142 L8
Shiel Bridge, Scot., U.K. 142 K8
Shīeli, Kaz. 174 H12
Shiguaigou, China 182 C3
Shiḩan, Yemen 173 N13
Shihezi, China 180 E7
Shijiazhuang, China 182 E5
Shikarpur, India 178 G9
Shikarpur, Pak. 177 T7
Shikine Shima, Japan 185 Q12
Shikoku, island, Japan 185 R7
Shikotan, island, Russ. 159 K23
Shikotsu Ko, Japan 184 G13
Shildon, Eng., U.K. 143 P12
Shīli, Kaz. 174 D10
Shiliguri, India 178 G11
Shilik, Kaz. 175 H17
Shiliu see Changjiang, China 183 U1

Shilka, Russ. 159 L17
Shilla, peak, India 177 P15
Shillong, India 178 G13
Shiloh National Military Park, Tenn., U.S. 101 G13
Shilou, China 182 F3
Shilovo, Russ. 156 K11
Sh'īm, Leb. 170 J6
Shimabara, Japan 185 S4
Shimada, Japan 185 Q11
Shima Hantō, Japan 185 Q10
Shimanovsk, Russ. 159 K19
Shimen, China 182 L3
Shimizu, Japan 184 F14
Shimizu, Japan 185 Q11
Shimoda, Japan 185 Q11
Shimoga, India 179 P4
Shimokoshiki, Japan 185 T3
Shimonoseki, Japan 185 R5
Shimono Shima, Japan 185 Q3
Shin, Loch, Scot., U.K. 142 H9
Shinapaaru, N. Mariana Is., U.S. 216 D8
Shināş, Oman 173 J15
Shindand, Afghan. 177 N2
Shiner, Tex., U.S. 103 R11
Shingbwiyang, Myanmar 186 D6
Shingphel, Bhutan 178 F13
Shingū, Japan 185 R9
Shinjō, Japan 184 L12
Shinkay, Afghan. 177 Q6
Shinkay Hills, Afghan. 177 P7
Shinkolobwe, Dem. Rep. of the Congo 198 N11
Shinnston, W. Va., U.S. 96 C9
Shinonoi, Japan 185 N11
Shinoússa, island, Gr. 155 M15
Shinyanga, Tanzania 199 L13
Shiono Misaki, Japan 185 R9
Shiping, China 180 P11
Ship Island, Miss., U.S. 100 P12
Shippensburg, Pa., U.S. 94 P6
Ship Rock, N. Mex., U.S. 107 Q10
Shiprock, N. Mex., U.S. 107 Q10
Shipu, China 182 M10
Shiquan, China 182 J1
Shiquanhe, China 180 J4
Shirakami Misaki, Japan 184 H12
Shirase Coast, Antarctica 226 M10
Shirase Glacier, Antarctica 227 C17
Shīrāz, Iran 173 F13
Shire, river, Malawi 203 F13
Shireet, Mongolia 181 E14
Shiren, China 182 B13
Shiretoko Misaki, Japan 184 E16
Shiriya Zaki, Japan 184 H13
Shir Khan, Afghan. 176 K7
Shīr Kūh, peak, Iran 173 E14
Shirley, Cape, Antigua & Barbuda 121 C21
Shiroishi, Japan 184 M13
Shirone, Japan 184 M11
Shirshov Ridge, Pac. Oc. 238 B9
Shishaldin Volcano, Alas., U.S. 110 N11
Shishmaref, Alas., U.S. 110 E12
Shishou, China 182 L4
Shitai, China 182 L7
Shiv, India 178 G2
Shivpuri, India 178 H6
Shivwits Plateau, Ariz., U.S. 107 R5
Shixian, China 182 A14
Shiyan, China 182 J3
Shíza, island, Gr. 154 M9
Shizhu, China 182 L1
Shizuishan, China 182 D1
Shizunai, Japan 184 G14
Shizuoka, Japan 185 Q11
Shkin, Afghan. 177 P8
Shkodër (Scutari), Albania 152 K9
Shkumbin, river, Albania 152 L9
Shmidta, Ostrov, Russ. 159 C14
Shoals, Isles of, Me., N.H., U.S. 95 J15
Shoghot, Pak. 176 L10
Sholapur, India 178 M5
Shollar, Azerb. 169 C22
Shonian Harbor, Palau 216 P11
Shonzhy, Kaz. 175 H17
Sho'rchi, Uzb. 174 M12
Shoreham by Sea, Eng., U.K. 143 W14
Shorkot, Pak. 177 Q10
Shorobe, Botswana 202 G9
Shortland, island, Solomon Is. 217 L14
Shortland Islands, Solomon Is. 217 L14
Shosambetsu, Japan 184 E13
Shoshone, Calif., U.S. 109 U10
Shoshone, Idaho, U.S. 106 H5
Shoshone, river, Wyo., U.S. 106 F10
Shoshone Falls, Idaho, U.S. 84 E6
Shoshone Lake, Wyo., U.S. 106 G8
Shoshone Mountain, Nev., U.S. 109 T10
Shoshone Mountains, Nev., U.S. 109 Q9
Shoshone Range, Nev., U.S. 109 N10
Shoshoni, Wyo., U.S. 106 H10
Shostka, Ukr. 156 M7
Shotor Khun Pass, Afghan. 176 M4
Shoval, Israel 171 N5
Shōwa, Japan 184 K12
Show Low, Ariz., U.S. 107 T9
Shpola, Ukr. 157 P6
Shreveport, La., U.S. 100 L6
Shroud Cay, Bahamas 116 E12
Shū, river, Kaz. 175 H14
Shū, Kaz. 175 H15
Shū'ab, Ra's, Yemen 173 R14
Shuangcheng, China 181 D17
Shuangchengzi, China 180 G10
Shuangliao, China 182 A11
Shuangyang, China 182 A12
Shuangyashan, China 181 C18
Shubarqudyq, Kaz. 174 E8
Shucheng, China 182 K7
Shugozero, Russ. 156 F8
Shukpa Kunzang, India 176 M15
Shule, river, China 180 G9
Shulgareh, Afghan. 176 L6
Shumagin Islands, Alas., U.S. 110 N12
Shumanay, Uzb. 174 J9
Shumen (Kolarovgrad), Bulg. 153 H16
Shumerlya, Russ. 156 J13
Shumshu, island, Russ. 159 G23
Shunchang, China 183 P7
Shungay, Kaz. 174 E4
Shungnak, Alas., U.S. 111 E14
Shuozhou, China 182 D4
Shupenzë, Albania 152 K10
Shuqualak, Miss., U.S. 101 K13
Shuraabad, Azerb. 169 C23
Shūrāb, Iran 173 D15
Shurakian, Afghan. 177 P4
Shūr Gaz, Iran 173 G16
Shurma, Russ. 156 H15
Shur Tappeh, Afghan. 176 K6
Shurugwi, Zimb. 202 G11
Shūsf, Iran 173 E17
Shūshtar, Iran 172 E11
Shuya, Russ. 156 H11
Shuyak Island, Alas., U.S. 111 L15
Shuyang, China 182 H8
Shwebo, Myanmar 186 G6
Shwedaung, Myanmar 186 J5
Shwegu, Myanmar 186 F6
Shwegyin, Myanmar 186 K6
Shweli, river, Myanmar 186 F7
Shymkent, Kaz. 175 J13
Shyngghyrlau, Kaz. 174 D7
Shyok, India 176 M15
Shyok, river, Pak. 176 L13
Sia, Indonesia 189 M19
Siafok, Hung. 149 M14
Siahan Range, Pak. 177 U4
Sialkot, Pak. 177 P12
Siantan, island, Indonesia 188 H8
Siapa, river, Venez. 128 G11
Siargao, island, Philippines 189 E15
Siátista, Gr. 154 D9
Siau, island, Indonesia 189 H15
Šiauliai, Lith. 141 M16
Sibari, It. 151 P13
Sibay, Russ. 158 J8
Šibenik, Croatia 152 G6
Siberia, region, Russ. 166 D8
Siberut, island, Indonesia 188 J5
Siberut, Selat, Indonesia 188 J5
Sibi, Pak. 177 S7
Sibidiro, P.N.G. 213 E18
Sibigo, Indonesia 188 H4
Sibiti, Congo 201 M16
Sibiu, Rom. 153 D13
Siboa, Indonesia 189 J13
Sibolga, Indonesia 188 H5
Sibsagar, India 178 F15
Sibu, Malaysia 188 H10
Sibuco, Philippines 189 F14
Sibut, Cen. Af. Rep. 198 H9
Sibutu Passage, Malaysia, Philippines 189 G13
Sibuyan, island, Philippines 189 D14
Sibuyan Sea, Philippines 189 D14
Sicasica, Bol. 130 K6
Sichon, Thai. 187 Q8
Sichuan Basin, China 166 H10
Sicié, Cap, Fr. 147 Y14
Sicilia (Sicily), island, It. 151 S10
Sicily see Sicilia, island, It. 151 S10
Sicily, Strait of, It. 151 T7
Sicuani, Peru 130 J5
Sidári, Gr. 154 E6
Sidas, Indonesia 188 J9
Siddhapur, India 178 H3
Siddipet, India 178 M6
Side, ruin, Turk. 168 J6
Síderos, Akrotírio, Gr. 155 Q17
Sîdi Barrâni, Egypt 197 C17
Sidi Bel Abbès, Alg. 196 A10
Sidi Ifni, Mor. 196 C7
Sidirókastro, Gr. 154 B12
Sidlaw Hills, Scot., U.K. 142 L10
Sidmouth, Eng., U.K. 143 X10
Sidmouth, Cape, Austral. 210 B12
Sidney, Iowa, U.S. 105 Q9
Sidney, Mont., U.S. 106 C13
Sidney, N.Y., U.S. 94 K9
Sidney, Nebr., U.S. 105 P2
Sidney, Ohio, U.S. 99 Q11
Sidney Lanier, Lake, Ga., U.S. 96 K5
Sidon see Saïda, Leb. 170 J6
Sidorovsk, Russ. 158 G12
Sidra, Gulf of, Lib. 197 C14
Siedlce, Pol. 149 E17
Siegen, Ger. 148 F6
Siemiatycze, Pol. 149 D17
Siem Pang, Cambodia 186 M12
Siem Reap, Cambodia 187 N11
Siena, It. 150 H7
Sieradz, Pol. 149 E14
Sierck, Fr. 160 L11
Sierpc, Pol. 149 D15
Sierra Blanca, Tex., U.S. 103 V3
Sierra Blanca Peak, N. Mex., U.S. 107 U13
Sierra Colorada, Arg. 133 P8
Sierra Leone, Af. 195 H14
Sierra Mojada, Mex. 114 E10
Sierra Nevada, range, Calif., U.S. 109 P5
Sierra Vista, Ariz., U.S. 107 W8
Sierre, Switz. 150 C2
Sífnos, island, Gr. 155 L14
Sigatoka, Fiji Is. 218 J5
Sigavé (Leava), Wallis & Futuna, Fr. 218 E11
Sigave, Anse de, Wallis & Futuna, Fr. 218 E11
Sigean, Fr. 147 Y10
Siġġiewi, Malta 161 L22
Sighetul Marmatiei, Rom. 153 A13
Sighişoara, Rom. 153 D14
Sighnaghi, Rep. of Georgia 169 C19
Siglufjörður, Ice. 140 E3
Signal Hill, Gibraltar, U.K. 161 P23
Signal Peak, Ariz., U.S. 107 U5
Sigourney, Iowa, U.S. 105 P13
Sigri, Gr. 155 F16
Sigüenza, Sp. 144 E12
Siguer, Pic de, Andorra, Fr. 160 G3
Siguer, Port de, Andorra, Fr. 160 G3
Siguiri, Guinea 200 E7
Sihora, India 178 J7
Sihui, China 183 R4
Siirt, Turk. 169 G16
Siis, island, F.S.M. 217 C15
Sikar, India 178 F5
Sikasso, Mali 196 J7
Sikeston, Mo., U.S. 105 V16
Sikhote Alin' Range, Russ. 166 E13
Sikinos, island, Gr. 155 M14
Sikinos, Gr. 155 M15
Sil, river, Sp. 144 C7
Silat, Indonesia 188 J10
Silba, island, Croatia 152 F4
Silchar, India 178 H14
Siler City, N.C., U.S. 96 H10
Silesia, region, Pol. 148 F13
Silet, Alg. 196 F11
Silgarhi, Nepal 178 E8
Silhouette, island, Seychelles 205 N19
Silifke, Turk. 168 J9
Siling Co, China 180 K7
Silisili, Mount, Samoa 218 K2
Silistra, Bulg. 153 G16
Silivri, Turk. 168 C4
Siljan, lake, Sw. 141 K13
Silkeborg, Den. 140 N11
Silla, Sp. 145 H14
Sillon de Talbert, Fr. 147 P4
Siloam Springs, Ark., U.S. 100 E6
Silogui, Indonesia 188 J5
Silopi, Turk. 169 H16
Silsbee, Tex., U.S. 103 P15
Silum, Liech. 160 P3
Šilutė, Lith. 141 N15
Silvan, Turk. 169 G15
Silvânia, Braz. 131 J13
Silvassa, India 178 K3
Silver Bay, Minn., U.S. 104 F13
Silver Bell, Ariz., U.S. 107 V7
Silver City, Idaho, U.S. 106 H3
Silver City, Mich., U.S. 98 E5
Silver City, N. Mex., U.S. 107 U10
Silver City, Nev., U.S. 109 Q6
Silver Creek, Oreg., U.S. 108 H6
Silver Hill, Montserrat, U.K. 121 A23
Silver Lake, Oreg., U.S. 108 J5
Silver Peak, Nev., U.S. 109 S9
Silver Plains, Qnsld., Austral. 211 P12
Silver Spring, Md., U.S. 96 C13
Silverton, Colo., U.S. 107 P11
Silverton, Oreg., U.S. 108 F3
Silverton, Tex., U.S. 102 H6
Silves, Braz. 130 D10
Silvies, river, Oreg., U.S. 108 H7
Sima, Comoros 205 N16
Simansih, Indonesia 188 K5
Simao, China 180 P10
Şīmareh, river, Iran 172 D11
Simav, river, Turk. 168 D4
Simav, Turk. 168 F5
Simbo, island, Solomon Is. 217 M15
Simcoe, Lake, Ont., Can. 83 Q18
Simdega, India 178 J9
Simeria, Rom. 152 D12
Simeulue, island, Indonesia 188 H4
Simferopol', Ukr. 157 S7
Sími, island, Gr. 155 M19
Sími, Gr. 155 M19
Simikot, Nepal 178 E8
Simi Valley, Calif., U.S. 109 X8
Simla, Colo., U.S. 106 M14
Simla, India 178 D6
Şimleu Silvaniei, Rom. 152 B12
Simms Point, Bahamas 120 B10
Simonsbaai see Simson Bay, Neth. Antilles, Neth. 121 B14
Simon's Point, Bahamas 120 F9
Simontornya, Hung. 149 M14
Simpang, Indonesia 188 J7
Simpson Desert, N. Terr., Austral. 211 U9
Simpson Peninsula, Nunavut, Can. 83 F15
Simrishamn, Sw. 141 N13
Simson Baai, Neth. Antilles, Neth. 121 B14
Simson Bay (Simsonbaai), Neth. Antilles, Neth. 121 B14
Simson Bay Lagoon, St. Martin, Fr. 121 B14
Simushir, island, Russ. 159 H23
Sinai, peninsula, Egypt 171 R3
Sinai, region, Egypt 197 C19
Sinai, Mount see Mûsa, Gebel, Egypt 171 T3
Sinai, Mount, Grenada 121 L22
Sinan, China 182 M1
Sinbang-ni, N. Korea 182 C13
Sinbaungwe, Myanmar 186 J5
Sincelejo, Col. 128 C4
Sinclair, Wyo., U.S. 106 J11
Sinclair, Lake, Ga., U.S. 96 M6
Sinclair's Bay, Scot., U.K. 142 G10
Sin Cowe Island, Spratly Is. 188 E11
Sındırgı, Turk. 168 E4
Sindoa, Mont, New Caledonia, Fr. 218 D8
Sinegorskiy, Russ. 157 Q11
Sines, Port. 144 K5
Sines, Cabo de, Port. 144 K5
Singa, Sudan 199 E13
Singapore, Asia 167 Y11
Singapore, Singapore 188 H7
Singapore Strait, Indonesia, Singapore 188 H7
Singaraja, Indonesia 188 M11
Singavi, Mont, Wallis & Futuna, Fr. 218 E11
Sing Buri, Thai. 186 M8
Singen, Ger. 148 K6
Singida, Tanzania 199 L13
Singkaling Hkāmti, Myanmar 186 E6
Singkawang, Indonesia 188 J9
Singkep, island, Indonesia 188 J7
Singleton, N.S.W., Austral. 211 X14
Sinh Ho, Vietnam 186 G10
Siniscola, It. 150 M5
Sini Vrŭkh, peak, Bulg. 153 K14
Sinj, Croatia 152 G6
Sinjai, Indonesia 189 L13
Sinjār, Iraq 172 C8
Sinkat, Sudan 199 C14
Sinkiang, region, China 180 F5
Sinnamary, Fr. Guiana, Fr. 129 E17
Sinnar, India 178 L4
Sînnicolau Mare, Rom. 152 D10
Sinó, Ponto do, Cape Verde 205 B17
Sinoe, Lacul, Rom. 153 F18
Sinop, Braz. 130 H11
Sinop (Sinope), Turk. 168 C10
Sinop Burnu, Turk. 168 B10
Sinope see Sinop, Turk. 168 C10
Sinp'o, N. Korea 182 C14
Sinsheim, Ger. 148 H6
Sintang, Indonesia 188 J10
Sint Nicolaas, Aruba, Neth. 121 R17
Sinton, Tex., U.S. 103 T11
Sinŭiju, N. Korea 182 D11
Sinzig, Ger. 148 G5
Sion, Switz. 150 C2
Siorapaluk, Greenland, Den. 81 B19
Sioux Center, Iowa, U.S. 104 M9
Sioux City, Iowa, U.S. 105 N8
Sioux Falls, S. Dak., U.S. 104 L8
Sioux Lookout, Ont., Can. 83 N15
Sioux Rapids, Iowa, U.S. 104 M10
Sipapo, Cerro, Venez. 128 E9
Siparia, Trinidad & Tobago 121 Q22
Siping, China 182 A11
Sipiwesk, Man., Can. 83 L14
Siple, Mount, Antarctica 226 M7
Siple Coast, Antarctica 226 L11
Siple Island, Antarctica 226 M7
Sipura, island, Indonesia 188 K5
Sira, India 179 P5
Siracusa (Syracuse), It. 151 T12
Şiran, Turk. 169 E14
Sirdaryo, Uzb. 175 K13
Sir Edward Pellew Group, Austral. 210 C10
Siret, river, Rom. 153 E17
Sirhān, Wādī as, Saudi Arabia 172 E6
Siri, Gebel, Egypt 194 F9
Sīrīk, Iran 173 H15
Sirik, Tanjong, Malaysia 188 H10
Sirkka, Fin. 141 D14
Sirmaur, India 178 H8
Sirna, island, Gr. 155 N17
Şırnak, Turk. 169 H17
Síros, island, Gr. 155 K14
Sirsa, India 178 E5
Sir Thomas, Mount, Austral. 210 G7
Sirur, India 178 L4
Şirvan, Turk. 169 G16
Sisak, Croatia 152 E6
Sisaket, Thai. 186 L11
Sisian, Arm. 169 E20
Siskiyou Mountains, Calif., Oreg., U.S. 108 L2
Sisophon, Cambodia 186 M10
Sisseton, S. Dak., U.S. 104 J8
Sissonne, Fr. 147 N11
Sīstān, region, Iran 173 E17
Sīstān, Daryācheh-ye, Iran 173 F17
Sister Bay, Wis., U.S. 98 H8
Sisteron, Fr. 147 W14
Sisters, Oreg., U.S. 108 G4
Sistersville, W. Va., U.S. 96 C8
Sistine Chapel, Vatican City 161 P16
Sitapur, India 178 F7
Sitges, Sp. 145 E17
Sithonía, peninsula, Gr. 154 D12
Sitía, Gr. 155 Q16
Sitian, China 180 F9
Sítio da Abadia, Braz. 131 J14
Sitka, Alas., U.S. 111 M22
Sitka National Historic Park, Alas., U.S. 111 M22
Sittard, Neth. 146 L13
Sittwe (Akyab), Myanmar 186 H4
Siufaalele Point, Amer. Samoa, U.S. 218 P3
Siufaga, Amer. Samoa, U.S. 218 P3
Siulagi Point, Amer. Samoa, U.S. 218 N3
Siuri, India 178 H11

Siuslaw, river, Oreg., U.S. 108 H2
Sivac, Serb. & Mont. 152 E9
Sivas, Turk. 168 E12
Siverek, Turk. 169 H14
Sivers'kyy Donets', river, Ukr. 157 P9
Sivrihisar, Turk. 168 E7
Sîwa, Egypt 197 D17
Siwalik Range, India, Nepal 178 C5
Siwan, India 178 G9
Sixaola, Costa Rica 115 N19
Six Feet, island, Pitcairn I., U.K. 219 Q23
Sixian, China 182 J7
Six Men's Bay, Barbados 121 J18
Sixth Cataract, Sudan 199 D13
Siyäzän, Azerb. 169 C22
Siziwang Qi, China 182 B4
Sj land, island, Den. 140 P12
Sjenica, Serb. & Mont. 152 H9
Skadarsko Jezero (Lake Scutari), Albania, Serb. & Mont. 152 J9
Skagafjördur, Ice. 140 E3
Skagen, Den. 140 M11
Skagerrak, strait, Den., Nor. 140 M11
Skagit, river, Wash., U.S. 108 B5
Skagway, Alas., U.S. 111 K21
Skála, Gr. 154 M10
Skalistyy Golets, Russ. 159 K17
Skandzoúra, island, Gr. 155 G13
Škarda, island, Croatia 152 F4
Skardu, Pak. 176 L13
Skarżysko-Kamienna, Pol. 149 F16
Skawina, Pol. 149 H15
Skeena, river, B.C., Can. 82 J8
Skegness, Eng., U.K. 143 S14
Skeleton Coast, Namibia 202 G5
Skellefteå, Sw. 141 G14
Skellefteälven, river, Sw. 141 G13
Skerries, Ire. 143 R7
Skerryvore, island, Scot., U.K. 142 L6
Skíathos, island, Gr. 154 G12
Skíathos, Gr. 154 G12
Skiatook, Okla., U.S. 102 E12
Skidmore, Tex., U.S. 103 T11
Skídra, Gr. 154 C10
Skien, Nor. 140 L11
Skierniewice, Pol. 149 E15
Skikda, Alg. 196 A12
Skipton, Eng., U.K. 143 R11
Skíros, Gr. 155 G14
Skíros (Scyros), island, Gr. 155 G13
Skive, Den. 140 N11
Skokholm Island, Wales, U.K. 143 V8
Skokie, Ill., U.S. 99 N7
Skomer Island, Wales, U.K. 143 V8
Skomv r, island, Nor. 140 E11
Skópelos, island, Gr. 154 G12
Skópelos, Gr. 154 G12
Skopin, Russ. 156 L10
Skopje, Maced. 152 K11
Skopunarfjørdur, bay, Faroe Is., Den. 140 J6
Skouriotissa, Cyprus 160 P7
Skövde, Sw. 140 L12
Skovorodino, Russ. 159 K18
Skowhegan, Me., U.S. 95 F16
Skudeneshavn, Nor. 140 L9
Skunk, river, Iowa, U.S. 105 P13
Skvyra, Ukr. 157 P5
Skye, Island of, Scot., U.K. 142 K7
Skykomish, Wash., U.S. 108 C5
Slantsy, Russ. 156 F5
Slater, Mo., U.S. 105 S12
Slatina, Rom. 153 F14
Slaton, Tex., U.S. 102 K5
Slave, river, Alta., Can. 82 J11
Slave Coast, Af. 194 J4
Slavgorod, Belarus 156 L6
Slavonia, region, Croatia 152 E7
Slavonska Požega, Croatia 152 E7
Slavonski Brod, Croatia 152 E8
Slavuta, Ukr. 157 N4
Sławno, Pol. 148 B12
Slayton, Minn., U.S. 104 L9
Sleat, Sound of, Scot., U.K. 142 K7
Sleeper Islands, Nunavut, Can. 83 K17
Sleeping Bear Dunes National Lakeshore, Mich., U.S. 98 H9
Sleepy Eye, Minn., U.S. 104 K10
Sleetmute, Alas., U.S. 111 J14
Slessor Glacier, Antarctica 226 E11
Slidell, La., U.S. 100 P11
Slide Mountain, N.Y., U.S. 94 L10
Sliema, Malta 161 K23
Slieve Aughty Mountains, Ire. 143 S4
Slieve Gamph (The Ox Mountains), Ire. 143 Q4
Sligo, Ire. 143 Q4
Sligo Bay, Ire. 143 Q4
Slippery Rock, Pa., U.S. 94 M3
Slite, Sw. 141 M14
Sliven, Bulg. 153 J16
Sljeme, peak, Croatia 152 D6
Sloan, Nev., U.S. 109 U12
Slobozia, Rom. 153 F16
Slonim, Belarus 156 L3
Slough, Eng., U.K. 143 V13
Slovakia, Eur. 139 U8
Slovenia, Eur. 139 V7
Slov"yans'k, Ukr. 157 P9
Słupsk, Pol. 149 B13
Slutsk, Belarus 156 L4
Slyudyanka, Russ. 159 L15
Smackover, Ark., U.S. 100 J8
Smallan, Pak. 177 R7
Smallwood Reservoir, Nfld. & Lab., Can. 83 L21
Smalyavichy, Belarus 156 K5
Smara, W. Sahara, Mor. 196 D6
Smederevo, Serb. & Mont. 152 F10
Smederevska Palanka, Serb. & Mont. 152 F10
Smeïda see Taoudenni, Mali 196 E8
Smerwick Harbour, Ire. 143 U2
Smethport, Pa., U.S. 94 L5
Smidovich, Russ. 158 D11
Smidovich, Russ. 159 K20
Smila, Ukr. 157 P6
Smiltene, Latv. 141 L17
Smith see Sumisu, island, Japan 184 J5
Smith, river, Mont., U.S. 106 C8
Smith Arm, N.W.T., Can. 82 F10
Smith Bay, Alas., U.S. 111 B15
Smith Bay, Nunavut, Can. 83 C16
Smith Center, Kans., U.S. 105 R6
Smithers, B.C., Can. 82 K8
Smithfield, N.C., U.S. 96 H12
Smithfield, Utah, U.S. 106 J7
Smithfield, Va., U.S. 96 F14
Smith Glacier, Antarctica 226 L7
Smith Island, Nunavut, Can. 83 J17
Smith Mountain Lake, Va., U.S. 96 F10
Smith River, B.C., Can. 82 H9
Smith River, Calif., U.S. 108 L2
Smith Sound, Nunavut, Can. 83 C16
Smithville, Tex., U.S. 103 Q11
Smoke Creek Desert, Nev., U.S. 109 N6
Smoky, river, Alta., Can. 82 L9
Smoky Bay, S. Aust., Austral. 211 X8
Smoky Hill, river, Kans., U.S. 105 T6
Smoky Hills, Kans., U.S. 105 S6
Smoky Mountains, Idaho, U.S. 106 G5
Smøla, island, Nor. 140 H10
Smolensk, Russ. 156 K7
Smolensk-Moscow Upland, Belarus, Russ. 138 E10
Smólikas, peak, Gr. 154 D8
Smolyan, Bulg. 153 K14
Smyley Island, Antarctica 226 G6
Smyrna, Del., U.S. 96 C14
Smyrna, Ga., U.S. 96 L5
Smyrna, Tenn., U.S. 101 E15
Smyrna see İzmir, Turk. 168 F3
Snaefell, peak, Isle of Man, U.K. 143 Q9
Snake, river, U.S. 84 C5
Snake, river, Yukon, Can. 82 F9
Snake City, Bahamas 120 B6
Snake Point, Anguilla, U.K. 120 Q12
Snake Range, Nev., U.S. 109 Q13
Snake River Plain, Idaho, U.S. 106 H6
Snåsa, Nor. 140 G11
Sneads, Fla., U.S. 97 Q4
Sneek, Neth. 146 G13
Sneeuberg, peak, S. Af. 194 Q8
Snezhnogorsk, Russ. 159 G13
Sněžka, peak, Czech Rep., Pol. 148 G12
Snihurivka, Ukr. 157 R7
Snina, Slovakia 149 J17
Snøhetta, peak, Nor. 140 J11
Snohomish, Wash., U.S. 108 B4
Snoqualmie, Wash., U.S. 108 C4
Snoqualmie Pass, Wash., U.S. 108 C5
Snowdon, peak, Wales, U.K. 143 S9
Snowflake, Ariz., U.S. 107 T9
Snow Hill, Md., U.S. 96 D15
Snow Hill Island, Antarctica 226 C4
Snowville, Utah, U.S. 106 J6
Snowy, river, Austral. 210 M13
Snowy Mountain, N.Y., U.S. 94 H10
Snug Corner, Bahamas 117 H15
Snuol, Cambodia 187 N12
Snyder, Okla., U.S. 102 H9
Snyder, Tex., U.S. 102 L6
Soala see Sokolo, Mali 196 H7
Soalala, Madagascar 203 F16
Soanierana-Ivongo, Madagascar 203 F18
Soap Lake, Wash., U.S. 108 C7
Soay, island, Scot., U.K. 142 K7
Sobinka, Russ. 156 J10
Sobolevo, Russ. 156 L16
Sobradinho Reservoir, S. Amer. 126 F10
Sobral, Braz. 131 E16
Soča, river, Slov. 152 C4
Sochaczew, Pol. 149 E15
Sochi, Russ. 157 T11
Society Islands, Fr. Polynesia, Fr. 219 D14
Socompa, Chile 132 E8
Socorro, Col. 128 E6
Socorro, N. Mex., U.S. 107 T12
Socorro, Tex., U.S. 103 U2
Socorro, Isla, Mex. 114 H6
Socorro Island see Socorro, Isla, N. Amer. 80 N3
Socotra see Suquṭrá, island, Yemen 173 R14
Soc Trang, Vietnam 187 Q12
Soda Lake, Calif., U.S. 109 V11
Sodankylä, Fin. 141 E15
Soda Springs, Idaho, U.S. 106 H7
Soddy-Daisy, Tenn., U.S. 101 G17
Södertälje, Sw. 141 L14
Sodiri, Sudan 198 E12
Sodo, Eth. 199 G14
Sofádes, Gr. 154 F9
Sofia see Sofiya, Bulg. 153 J13
Sofiya (Sofia), Bulg. 153 J13
Sōfu Gan (Lot's Wife), island, Japan 184 K5
Sogamoso, Col. 128 E6
Soganlı, river, Turk. 168 C8
Sognefjorden, bay, Nor. 140 K9
Sogo Nur, China 180 F11
Söğüt, Turk. 168 E6
Söğüt Gölü, Turk. 168 H5
Sogxian, China 180 K8
Sohâg, Egypt 197 D18
Sohano, P.N.G. 217 J13
Soheuksando, island, S. Korea 182 H12
Soignies, Belg. 146 L11
Soissons, Fr. 147 N11
Sojat, India 178 G4
Sokcho, S. Korea 182 E14
Söke, Turk. 168 G3
Sokhumi, Abkhazia 169 A15
Sokodé, Togo 200 F11
Sokol, Russ. 156 F10
Sokol, Russ. 159 E16
Sokol, Russ. 159 F20
Sokółka, Pol. 149 C18
Sokolo (Soala), Mali 196 H7
Sokolov, Czech Rep. 148 G9
Sokołów Podlaski, Pol. 149 D17
Sokoto, river, Nigeria 200 E12
Sokoto, Nigeria 201 E13
Sol, Costa del, Sp. 144 M10
Sol, Ponta do, Cape Verde 205 C17
Sola, Cuba 116 J11
Solander Island, N.Z. 213 R15
Solano, Punta, Col. 128 E3
Sol de Julio, Arg. 132 H10
Soldeu, Andorra 160 H4
Soldotna, Alas., U.S. 111 K16
Soledad, Calif., U.S. 109 U4
Soledad, Col. 128 B5
Solenzara, Fr. 150 K4
Solhan, Turk. 169 F15
Soligalich, Russ. 156 F11
Solikamsk, Russ. 158 G9
Solimões (Amazonas), river, Braz. 130 D7
Solingen, Ger. 148 F5
Solitary Islands, Austral. 210 J15
Sollefteå, Sw. 141 H13
Sol'lletsk, Russ. 158 J7
Solnechnogorsk, Russ. 156 J9
Solo, island, Fiji Is. 218 J7
Solok, Indonesia 188 J6
Solomon, river, Kans., U.S. 105 S7
Solomon, Kans., U.S. 105 S7
Solomon Islands, Pac. Oc. 214 H6
Solomon Sea, P.N.G. 213 D21
Solon Springs, Wis., U.S. 98 F3
Solor, island, Indonesia 189 M14
Solothurn, Switz. 150 A2
Solov'yevsk, Russ. 159 K18
Solsona, Sp. 145 D16
Šolta, island, Croatia 152 H6
Solṭānābād, Iran 173 C16
Soltan Bagh, Afghan. 177 N7
Soltan-e Bakva, Afghan. 177 P3
Sol'tsy, Russ. 156 G6
Solunska Glava, Maced. 152 K11
Soluntum, ruin, It. 151 S10
Solvay, N.Y., U.S. 94 J8
Solway Firth, Eng., Scot., U.K. 143 P10
Solwezi, Zambia 202 D10
Solyanka, Russ. 156 M16
Solyplayas, Canary Is. 204 Q7
Soma, Turk. 168 E3
Sōma, Japan 184 M13
Somain, Fr. 146 M11
Somali, region, Eth. 199 G16
Somalia, Af. 195 J24
Somali Basin, Ind. Oc. 240 G6
Somaliland, region, Somalia 199 F17
Somali Peninsula, Af. 194 H12
Somaloma, Rochers, Wallis & Futuna, Fr. 218 E11
Sombor, Serb. & Mont. 152 D9
Sombrero, island, Anguilla, U.K. 119 E15
Sombrero Channel, India 179 S15
Somers, Mont., U.S. 106 B5
Somerset, Bermuda, U.K. 120 B1
Somerset, Colo., U.S. 107 N11
Somerset, Ky., U.S. 101 D18
Somerset, Pa., U.S. 94 P4
Somerset Island, Bermuda, U.K. 120 B1
Somerset Island, Nunavut, Can. 83 E15
Somersworth, N.H., U.S. 95 H15
Somerton, Ariz., U.S. 107 V4
Somerville, Tenn., U.S. 100 G12
Somerville, Tex., U.S. 103 Q12
Someş, river, Rom. 152 B12
Sommariva, Qnsld., Austral. 211 V13
Somme, river, Fr. 146 M9
Somme, Baie de la, Fr. 146 M9
Somosomo, Fiji Is. 218 G8
Somosomo Strait, Fiji Is. 218 G8
Somuncurá, Meseta de, Arg. 133 Q9
Son, river, India 178 H10
Sŏnbong, N. Korea 182 B15
Sŏnch'ŏn, N. Korea 182 D12
Sonda, Pak. 177 W7
Sondar, India 177 N13
Sønderborg, Den. 140 P11
Sondershausen, Ger. 148 F8
Sondrio, It. 150 C5
Song, Malaysia 188 H10
Song Cau, Vietnam 186 M14
Songea, Tanzania 199 N14
Songeons, Fr. 147 N9
Songhua, river, China 181 C18
Songhua Hu, China 182 A13
Songjiang, China 182 L10
Sŏngjin see Kimch'aek, N. Korea 182 C14
Songkhla, Thai. 187 R9
Song Ma, Vietnam 186 H10
Songnim, N. Korea 182 E12
Songsong (Rota), N. Mariana Is., U.S. 216 E7
Songxi, China 183 N8
Songxian, China 182 H4
Songzi, China 182 L3
Son Ha, Vietnam 186 L14
Son Hoa, Vietnam 187 N14
Sonid Youqi (SaihanTal), China 182 A5
Sonid Zuoqi (Mandalt), China 182 A5
Sonkovo, Russ. 156 H9
Son La, Vietnam 186 H11
Sonmiani, Pak. 177 V5
Sonmiani Bay, Pak. 177 W5
Sonneberg, Ger. 148 G8
Sonoma, Calif., U.S. 109 R3
Sonora, Calif., U.S. 109 R6
Sonora, Tex., U.S. 103 P6
Sonoran Desert, Ariz., Calif., U.S. 84 K6
Sonoran Desert National Monument, Ariz., U.S. 107 U6
Sonqor, Iran 172 D11
Sonseca, Sp. 144 G10
Sonsón, Col. 128 E5
Sonsonate, El Salv. 115 L16
Sonsorol Islands, Palau 214 F2
Soperton, Ga., U.S. 97 N7
Sophia-Antipolis, Fr. 147 X15
Sopot, Pol. 149 B14
Sopron, Hung. 149 L13
Sopur, India 176 M12
Sopwer, Mochun, F.S.M. 217 A15
Sopweru, island, F.S.M. 217 A15
Sora, It. 150 L10
Sorah, Pak. 177 U7
Soran, Kaz. 175 E14
Sorazocco, San Marino 161 J16
Sorbas, Sp. 144 L12
Soresina, It. 150 E5
Sorezaru Point, Solomon Is. 217 L15
Sorgono, It. 151 N4
Sorgues, Fr. 147 W13
Sorgun, Turk. 168 E10
Soria, Sp. 144 D12
Sorkh Ab, Afghan. 177 P3
Sorkh Kowtal Temple, ruin, Afghan. 176 L7
Sørkjosen, Nor. 141 C13
Sørli, Nor. 140 G12
Sorobon, Neth. Antilles, Neth. 121 R19
Soroca, Mold. 157 Q4
Sorocaba, Braz. 131 M13
Sorol Atoll, F.S.M. 216 Q3
Sorong, Indonesia 189 J17
Soroti, Uganda 199 J13
Sørøya, island, Nor. 141 C13
Sør Rondane Mountains, Antarctica 227 B15
Sorsele, Sw. 141 F13
Sorso, It. 150 M3
Sortavala, Russ. 158 D7
Sørvágur, Faroe Is., Den. 140 J5
Sosanjaya Bay, N. Mariana Is., U.S. 216 E7
Sosanlagh Bay, N. Mariana Is., U.S. 216 E7
Sosna, Russ. 159 J15
Sosnogorsk, Russ. 158 F9
Sosnovka, Russ. 156 H14
Sosnovka, Russ. 156 H15
Sosnovka, Russ. 156 L11
Sosnovo, Russ. 156 E6
Sosnovo Ozerskoye, Russ. 159 L16
Sosnowiec, Pol. 149 G15
Soso Bay, Fiji Is. 218 K6
Sos'va, Russ. 158 G10
Sos'va, Russ. 158 H9
Soto, Neth. Antilles, Neth. 121 P13
Souanké, Congo 201 K17
Soubré, Côte d'Ivoire 200 H8
Soucis, St. Lucia 121 K14
Soudan, N. Terr., Austral. 211 S10
Souflí, Gr. 155 B16
Soufrière, peak, Guadeloupe, Fr. 121 F14
Soufrière, St. Lucia 121 K13
Soufrière Bay, St. Lucia 121 K13
Soufriere Hills, Montserrat, U.K. 121 B23
Soufrière Mountains, St. Vincent & the Grenadines 121 J16
Souillac, Fr. 147 V9
Souillac, Mauritius 205 H20
Soúnion, ruin, Gr. 155 K13
Soûr (Tyre), Leb. 170 K5
Sourdeval, Fr. 147 P6
Soure, Braz. 131 C13
Souris (Mouse), river, N. Dak., U.S. 104 E4
Sour Lake, Tex., U.S. 103 Q15
Soúrpi, Gr. 154 G11
Sousa, Braz. 131 F17
Sousel, Port. 144 H6
Sous le Vent, Îles, Fr. Polynesia, Fr. 219 E14
Sousse, Tun. 197 A13
South Africa, Af. 195 Q20
South Alligator, river, Austral. 210 B8
South Ambo Channel, Marshall Is. 216 M5
Southampton, Eng., U.K. 143 W12
Southampton, N.Y., U.S. 95 N13
Southampton, Cape, Nunavut, Can. 83 J16
Southampton Island, Nunavut, Can. 83 H16

South Andaman, island, *India* **179** Q14
South Aulatsivik Island, *Nfld. & Lab., Can.* **83** K21
South Australia, *Austral.* **211** V9
South Australian Basin, *Ind. Oc.* **241** N17
South Australian Plain, *Antarctic Oc.* **245** P17
Southaven, *Miss., U.S.* **100** G11
South Baldy, peak, *N. Mex., U.S.* **107** T11
South Bay, *Fla., U.S.* **97** V10
South Bend, *Ind., U.S.* **99** N9
South Bend, *Wash., U.S.* **108** D2
South Bimini, island, *Bahamas* **120** C8
South Boston, *Va., U.S.* **96** G11
South Branch Potomac, river, *W. Va., U.S.* **96** C11
South Caicos, island, *Turks & Caicos Is., U.K.* **117** J17
South Cape, *Fiji Is.* **218** H8
South Cape *see* Ka Lae, *Hawai'i, U.S.* **85** R16
South Carolina, *U.S.* **96** K9
South Cay, *Jam.* **116** P11
South Channel, *Marshall Is.* **216** J8
South Charleston, *W. Va., U.S.* **96** E8
South China Sea, *Asia* **166** K12
South Comino Channel, *Malta* **161** J21
South Dakota, *U.S.* **104** K2
South Downs, *Eng., U.K.* **143** W13
Southeast Indian Ridge, *Ind. Oc.* **240** P10
Southeast Pacific Basin, *Pac. Oc.* **239** Q19
Southeast Pass, *Marshall Is.* **216** M8
South East Point, *Kiribati* **217** C24
Southeast Point, *Kiribati* **217** E17
South East Range, *St. Kitts & Nevis* **121** B17
South End, *Sask., Can.* **83** L13
Southend, *Scot., U.K.* **143** N7
Southend-on-Sea, *Eng., U.K.* **143** V15
Southern Alps, *N.Z.* **213** P16
Southern Bight, *Bahamas* **116** F11
Southern Bug, river, *Ukr.* **138** G10
Southern Cross, *W. Aust., Austral.* **211** W3
Southern Indian Lake, *Man., Can.* **83** K14
Southern Pines, *N.C., U.S.* **96** J11
Southern Uplands, *Scot., U.K.* **143** N10
Southesk Tablelands, *Austral.* **210** E6
Southfield, *Jam.* **120** J7
South Fiji Islands Basin, *Pac. Oc.* **238** M9
South Fork Owyhee, river, *Idaho, Nev., U.S.* **108** L10
South Fork Shenandoah, river, *Va., U.S.* **96** D11
South Fork Solomon, river, *Kans., U.S.* **105** S5
South Friar's Bay, *St. Kitts & Nevis* **121** B18
South Fulton, *Tenn., U.S.* **100** E12
South Geomagnetic Pole, *Antarctica* **227** J16
South Georgia, island, *S. Amer.* **126** R9
South Grand, river, *Mo., U.S.* **105** T11
South Haven, *Mich., U.S.* **98** M9
South Henik Lake, *Nunavut, Can.* **83** J14
South Hill, *Va., U.S.* **96** F12
South Indian Basin, *Antarctic Oc.* **245** L15
South Island, *N.Z.* **213** Q17
South Korea, *Asia* **167** T13
South Lake Tahoe, *Calif., U.S.* **109** Q6
South Loup, river, *Nebr., U.S.* **105** P5
South Magnetic Pole, *Antarctica* **227** R19
South Male Atoll, *Maldives* **179** V3
South Malosmadulu Atoll, *Maldives* **179** U3
South Milwaukee, *Wis., U.S.* **98** L7
South Mole, *Gibraltar, U.K.* **161** P22
South Nahanni, river, *N.W.T., Can.* **82** G9
South Negril Point, *Jam.* **120** H5
South Orkney Islands, *Antarctica* **226** A4
South Ossetia, *Rep. of Georgia* **169** B18
South Palmetto Point, *Bahamas* **120** E6
South Pass, *Marshall Is.* **216** N5
South Passage, *Kiribati* **217** B22
South Pittsburg, *Tenn., U.S.* **101** G16
South Platte, river, *Colo., U.S.* **106** L14
South Point, *Barbados* **121** L19
South Point *see* Kalae, *Hawai'i, U.S.* **113** Q19
South Point, *Marshall Is.* **216** N8
South Ponte Vedra Beach, *Fla., U.S.* **97** R9
Southport, *N.C., U.S.* **96** K12
South Portland, *Me., U.S.* **95** H16
South Ronaldsay, island, *Scot., U.K.* **142** G10
South Sandwich Trench, *Antarctic Oc.* **244** D9
South San Francisco, *Calif., U.S.* **109** S3
South Saskatchewan, river, *Alta., Sask., Can.* **82** M11
South Shetland Islands, *Antarctica* **226** C3
South Shore, *Ky., U.S.* **101** A19
South Sioux City, *Nebr., U.S.* **105** N8
South Sound, *Virgin Islands, U.K.* **120** Q9
South Sound, *Ire.* **143** S3
South Sound Bluff, *Virgin Islands, U.K.* **120** Q9
South Taranaki Bight, *N.Z.* **213** L18
South Tasman Rise, *Pac. Oc.* **238** Q6
South Uist, island, *Scot., U.K.* **142** K6
Southwest Anchorage, *Virgin Islands, U.S.* **120** R2
South West Bay, *Bahamas* **120** B10
South West Bay, *Vanuatu* **218** E2
South West Cape, *Austral.* **210** M15
Southwest Cape, *Virgin Islands, U.S.* **120** R1
Southwest Cay, *Jam.* **116** P11
Southwest Indian Ridge, *Ind. Oc.* **240** Q3
Southwest Pacific Basin, *Pac. Oc.* **238** M11
Southwest Pass, *Marshall Is.* **216** M7
Southwest Passage, *Marshall Is.* **216** H7
South West Point, *Cayman Is., U.K.* **120** J1
South West Point, *Kiribati* **217** B22
South West Point, *Bahamas* **120** F11
Southwest Point, *Bahamas* **120** D6
Southwest Rift, *Hawai'i, U.S.* **113** N19
Southwest Rock, *Jam.* **116** P10
Southwold, *Eng., U.K.* **143** T16
South Yolla Bolly Mountains, *Calif., U.S.* **109** N3
Souvannakhili, *Laos* **186** L12
Souvigny, *Fr.* **147** T11
Sovata, *Rom.* **153** C14
Sovetsk, *Russ.* **156** G14
Sovetsk, *Russ.* **156** J2
Sovetskaya Gavan', *Russ.* **159** K21
Sovetskiy, *Russ.* **158** G10
Sovetskoye, *Russ.* **157** Q13
Soweto, *S. Af.* **202** J10
Sōya, *Japan* **184** D13
Sōya Misaki, *Japan* **184** D13
Soyo, *Angola* **202** B5
Spa, *Belg.* **146** L13
Spaansebaai, bay, *Neth. Antilles, Neth.* **121** Q15
Spaansewater, bay, *Neth. Antilles, Neth.* **121** Q15
Spaatz Island, *Antarctica* **226** G6
Spain, *Eur.* **139** W3
Spalatum *see* Split, *Croatia* **152** G6
Spalding, *Eng., U.K.* **143** T14
Spalding, *Nebr., U.S.* **105** P6
Spaldings, *Jam.* **120** J8
Spánda, Akrotírio, *Gr.* **154** P12
Spanish Fork, *Utah, U.S.* **106** L7
Spanish Peak, *Oreg., U.S.* **108** G6
Spanish Point, *Bermuda, U.K.* **120** B2
Spanish Rock, *Bermuda, U.K.* **120** B3
Spanish Town, *Virgin Islands, U.K.* **120** R8
Spanish Town, *Jam.* **120** J9
Spanish Wells, *Bahamas* **120** D5
Sparkman, *Ark., U.S.* **100** J8
Sparks, *Nev., U.S.* **109** P6
Sparta, *Ga., U.S.* **96** L7
Sparta *see* Spárti, *Gr.* **154** L10
Sparta, *Ill., U.S.* **99** U5
Sparta, *Tenn., U.S.* **101** F17
Sparta, *Wis., U.S.* **98** K4
Spartanburg, *S.C., U.S.* **96** J8
Spartel, Cap, *Mor.* **144** N8
Spárti (Sparta), *Gr.* **154** L10
Spartivento, Capo, *It.* **151** S13
Spearfish, *S. Dak., U.S.* **104** K1
Spearman, *Tex., U.S.* **102** F6
Speedwell Island, *Falkland Is., U.K.* **133** W12
Speightstown, *Barbados* **121** K18
Spello, *It.* **150** J8
Spelonk, *Neth. Antilles, Neth.* **121** Q19
Spencer, *Idaho, U.S.* **106** G7
Spencer, *Ind., U.S.* **99** S8
Spencer, *Iowa, U.S.* **104** M10
Spencer, *N.C., U.S.* **96** H9
Spencer, *Nebr., U.S.* **104** M6
Spencer, *W. Va., U.S.* **96** D8
Spencer, Cape, *Austral.* **210** L9
Spencer Gulf, *S. Aust., Austral.* **211** Y9
Spercheiós, river, *Gr.* **154** G10
Sperrin Mountains, *N. Ire., U.K.* **143** P6
Spétses, island, *Gr.* **154** L11
Spétses, *Gr.* **154** L11
Speyside, *Trinidad & Tobago* **121** N18
Spezand, *Pak.* **177** R6
Spicer Islands, *Nunavut, Can.* **83** F17
Spiddal, *Ire.* **143** S3
Spiess Seamount, *Antarctic Oc.* **244** C11
Spiez, *Switz.* **150** B3
Spíli, *Gr.* **155** Q14
Spilsby, *Eng., U.K.* **143** S14
Spinazzola, *It.* **150** M13
Spin Buldak, *Afghan.* **177** Q5
Spirit Lake, *Idaho, U.S.* **106** B3
Spirit Lake, *Iowa, U.S.* **104** M10
Spiro, *Okla., U.S.* **102** G14
Spišská Nová Ves, *Slovakia* **149** J16
Spitsbergen, island, *Norway* **167** N7
Spitsbergen Bank, *Arctic Oc.* **243** F16
Spitsbergen Fracture Zone, *Arctic Oc.* **243** H14
Spittal, *Aust.* **148** M10
Spittal of Glenshee, *Scot., U.K.* **142** L10
Split (Spalatum), *Croatia* **152** G6
Split Lake, *Man., Can.* **83** L14
Splügen, *Switz.* **150** C4
Spokane, river, *Wash., U.S.* **108** B8
Spokane, *Wash., U.S.* **108** C9
Spolaíta, *Gr.* **154** G8
Spoleto, *It.* **150** J8
Sposhino, *Russ.* **159** J16
Spoon, river, *Ill., U.S.* **99** P5
Spooner, *Wis., U.S.* **98** G3
Sporting Club, *Monaco* **161** D21
Spotts, *Cayman Is., U.K.* **120** J2
Sprague, river, *Oreg., U.S.* **108** K5
Sprague, *Wash., U.S.* **108** C8
Sprague Lake, *Wash., U.S.* **108** C8
Sprague River, *Oreg., U.S.* **108** K4
Spratly Island, *Spratly Is.* **188** F10
Spratly Islands, *S. China Sea* **188** E11
Spray, *Oreg., U.S.* **108** G6
Spree, river, *Ger.* **148** E11
Spremberg, *Ger.* **148** F11
Springbok, *S. Af.* **202** L7
Spring City, *Bahamas* **120** B6
Spring Creek, *W. Aust., Austral.* **211** R7
Springdale, *Ark., U.S.* **100** E6
Springdale, *Wash., U.S.* **108** B8
Springer, *N. Mex., U.S.* **107** Q14
Springfield, *Colo., U.S.* **107** P15
Springfield, *Fla., U.S.* **97** R3
Springfield, *Ill., U.S.* **99** R5
Springfield, *Ky., U.S.* **101** C17
Springfield, *Mass., U.S.* **95** L13
Springfield, *Minn., U.S.* **104** K10
Springfield, *Mo., U.S.* **105** U12
Springfield, *Ohio, U.S.* **99** R12
Springfield, *Oreg., U.S.* **108** H3
Springfield, *S. Dak., U.S.* **104** M7
Springfield, *Tenn., U.S.* **101** E15
Springfield, *Vt., U.S.* **95** H13
Spring Grove, *Minn., U.S.* **104** L13
Spring Hill, *Tenn., U.S.* **101** F15
Springhill, *La., U.S.* **100** K7
Spring Mountains, *Nev., U.S.* **109** U11
Springsure, *Qnsld., Austral.* **211** U14
Spring Valley, *Ill., U.S.* **99** P5
Spring Valley, *Minn., U.S.* **104** L12
Springview, *Nebr., U.S.* **104** M5
Springville, *N.Y., U.S.* **94** K5
Spruce Knob, *W. Va., U.S.* **96** D10
Spruce Mountain, *Nev., U.S.* **109** N12
Spruce Pine, *N.C., U.S.* **96** H7
Spulico, Capo, *It.* **151** N14
Spur, *Tex., U.S.* **102** K6
Spurn Head, *Eng., U.K.* **143** R14
Squillace, Golfo di, *It.* **151** Q14
Squinzano, *It.* **151** N15
Srebrenica, *Bosn. & Herzg.* **152** G9
Sredinnyy Khrebet, *Russ.* **159** F22
Sredne Sibirskoye Ploskogor'ye, *Russ.* **159** F14
Sredniy, *Russ.* **159** F21
Śrem, *Pol.* **149** E13
Sremska Mitrovica, *Serb. & Mont.* **152** F9
Sretensk, *Russ.* **159** L17
Sriharikota Island, *India* **179** P7
Srikakulam, *India* **178** M9
Sri Kalahasti, *India* **179** P7
Sri Lanka, *Asia* **167** Y7
Sri Lanka, island, *Ind. Oc.* **166** L8
Srinagar, *India* **176** M12
Srivardhan, *India* **178** M3
Stack Skerry, *Scot., U.K.* **142** G9
Stade, *Ger.* **148** C7
Städjan, peak, *Sw.* **140** J12
Stadlandet, *Nor.* **140** J9
Stadskanaal, *Neth.* **146** G14
Stadtallendorf, *Ger.* **148** F7
Staffa, island, *Scot., U.K.* **142** L7
Stafford, *Eng., U.K.* **143** T11
Stafford, *Kans., U.S.* **105** U6
Staithes, *Eng., U.K.* **143** Q13
Staked Plain *see* Estacado, Llano, *N. Amer.* **80** L5
Stalingrad *see* Volgograd, *Russ.* **157** P13
Stalowa Wola, *Pol.* **149** G17
Stambaugh, *Mich., U.S.* **98** G6
Stamford, *Conn., U.S.* **94** M11
Stamford, *N.Y., U.S.* **94** K10
Stamford, *Tex., U.S.* **102** L8
Stamford, Lake, *Tex., U.S.* **102** L8
Stamps, *Ark., U.S.* **100** J7
Stamsund, *Nor.* **140** E12
Stanberry, *Mo., U.S.* **105** R10
Stancomb-Wills Glacier, *Antarctica* **226** D11
Standish, *Mich., U.S.* **98** K11
Stanford, *Ky., U.S.* **101** C17
Stanford, *Mont., U.S.* **106** C9
Staniard Creek, *Bahamas* **116** E11
Stanley, *Falkland Is., U.K.* **133** W13
Stanley, *Idaho, U.S.* **106** G5
Stanley, *N. Dak., U.S.* **104** E3
Stanley, *Tas., Austral.* **211** Y15
Stanley, *Wis., U.S.* **98** H4
Stanley, Port, *Vanuatu* **218** D2
Stanleyville *see* Kisangani, *Dem. Rep. of the Congo* **198** J10
Stanovaya, *Russ.* **159** D19
Stanovoye Nagor'ye, *Russ.* **159** K16
Stanovoy Khrebet, *Russ.* **159** J18
Stanovoy Range, *Russ.* **166** D11
Stanton, *N. Dak., U.S.* **104** F4
Stanton, *Nebr., U.S.* **105** P8
Stanton, *Tex., U.S.* **102** M5
Stanwood, *Wash., U.S.* **108** B4
Staples, *Minn., U.S.* **104** H10
Stapleton, *Nebr., U.S.* **105** P4
Stara Pazova, *Serb. & Mont.* **152** F10
Staraya Russa, *Russ.* **156** G7
Stara Zagora, *Bulg.* **153** J15
Starbuck, *Minn., U.S.* **104** J9
Starbuck, *Wash., U.S.* **108** D8
Starbuck Island, *Kiribati* **214** H12
Star City, *Ark., U.S.* **100** J9
Stargard Szczeciński, *Pol.* **148** C11
Staritsa, *Russ.* **156** J8
Starke, *Fla., U.S.* **97** R8
Starkville, *Miss., U.S.* **100** J12
Starobil's'k, *Ukr.* **157** P10
Starobin, *Belarus* **156** L4
Starodub, *Russ.* **156** M7
Starogard Gdański, *Pol.* **149** B14
Starokostyantyniv, *Ukr.* **157** N4
Starorybnoye, *Russ.* **159** F14
Staroshcherbinovskaya, *Russ.* **157** R10
Starozhynets', *Ukr.* **157** Q3
Start Point, *Eng., U.K.* **143** Y10
Starve Gut Bay, *Jam.* **120** J7
Staryy Oskol, *Russ.* **157** N9
State College, *Pa., U.S.* **94** N6
Stateline, *Nev., U.S.* **109** Q6
Staten Island *see* Estados, Isla de los, *Arg.* **133** X10
Staten Island, *N.Y., U.S.* **94** N11
Statesboro, *Ga., U.S.* **97** N8
Statesville, *N.C., U.S.* **96** H9
Staunton, *Ill., U.S.* **99** S4
Staunton, *Va., U.S.* **96** E11
Stavanger, *Nor.* **140** L10
Stavropol', *Russ.* **157** S12
Stavropol' Plateau, *Russ.* **138** G13
Stavrós, *Gr.* **154** C12
Stavrós, *Gr.* **154** H7
Stavroúpoli, *Gr.* **155** B14
Stawell, *Vic., Austral.* **211** Z11
Stayton, *Oreg., U.S.* **108** G3
Steamboat Springs, *Colo., U.S.* **106** L11
Stebbins, *Alas., U.S.* **110** G12
Steele, *N. Dak., U.S.* **104** G5
Steele Point, *Virgin Islands, U.K.* **120** R5
Steels Point, *Norfolk I., Austral.* **217** F20
Steelton, *Pa., U.S.* **94** P7
Steelville, *Mo., U.S.* **105** T14
Steenbergen, *Neth.* **146** K12
Steens Mountain, *Oreg., U.S.* **108** K8
Steenwijk, *Neth.* **146** H13
Steese Highway, *Alas., U.S.* **111** F17
Stefansson Island, *Nunavut, Can.* **83** D14
Steffen, Cerro, *Arg.* **133** S7
Steg, *Liech.* **160** P3
Steinbach, *Man., Can.* **83** N14
Steinfort, *Lux.* **160** J9
Steinhatchee, *Fla., U.S.* **97** R6
Steinhort, *Liech.* **160** P3
Steinkjer, *Nor.* **140** H11
Steinsel, *Lux.* **160** J10
Stella Maris, *Bahamas* **117** F13
Stendal, *Ger.* **148** D9
Stepanakert (Xankändi), *Azerb.* **169** E20
Step'anavan, *Arm.* **169** D18
Stephen, *Minn., U.S.* **104** E8
Stephens, *Ark., U.S.* **100** J7
Stephens, Port, *Falkland Is., U.K.* **133** W11
Stephenson, *Mich., U.S.* **98** H7
Stephenson, Mount, *Antarctica* **226** F5
Stephenville, *Nfld. & Lab., Can.* **83** M23
Stephenville, *Tex., U.S.* **102** M10
Stepnogorsk, *Kaz.* **175** C14
Steps Point, *Amer. Samoa, U.S.* **218** N7
Sterling, *Colo., U.S.* **106** L15
Sterling, *Ill., U.S.* **99** N5
Sterling, *Kans., U.S.* **105** T6
Sterling, *N. Dak., U.S.* **104** G5
Sterling City, *Tex., U.S.* **102** M6
Sterling Heights, *Mich., U.S.* **98** M12
Sterling Highway, *Alas., U.S.* **111** K16
Sterlitamak, *Russ.* **158** J7
Stettiner Haff (Zalew Szczeciński), *Ger., Pol.* **148** C11
Stettler, *Alta., Can.* **82** M10
Steubenville, *Ohio, U.S.* **99** Q16
Stevenson, *Wash., U.S.* **108** E4
Stevens Point, *Wis., U.S.* **98** J5
Stevens Village, *Alas., U.S.* **111** F16
Stevensville, *Mont., U.S.* **106** D5
Steventon, *Bahamas* **120** E8
Stewart, *B.C., Can.* **82** J8
Stewart, *Nev., U.S.* **109** Q6
Stewart, Isla, *Chile* **133** Y8
Stewart Island, *N.Z.* **213** R15
Stewart Town, *Jam.* **120** H8
Steyr, *Aust.* **148** K11
Stickney, *S. Dak., U.S.* **104** L6
Stigler, *Okla., U.S.* **102** G14
Stikine, river, *B.C., Can.* **82** H8
Stiles, *Tex., U.S.* **103** N5
Stillwater, *Minn., U.S.* **104** J12
Stillwater, *Okla., U.S.* **102** F11
Stillwater Range, *Nev., U.S.* **109** P8
Stilo, *It.* **151** R13
Stilo, Punta, *It.* **151** R14
Stilwell, *Okla., U.S.* **102** F14
Štimlje, *Serb. & Mont.* **152** J10
Stinnett, *Tex., U.S.* **102** F5
Stintino, *It.* **150** M3
Štip, *Maced.* **152** K12
Stíra, *Gr.* **155** J13
Stiring-Wendel, *Fr.* **147** N15
Stirling, *Scot., U.K.* **142** M9
Stirling City, *Calif., U.S.* **109** P4
Stirling Island, *Solomon Is.* **217** L14
Stjørdalshalsen, *Nor.* **140** H11
Stobi, ruin, *Maced.* **152** K11
Stockdale, *Tex., U.S.* **103** R10

Stockerau, *Aust.* **148** K12
Stockholm, *Sw.* **141** L14
Stocking Island, *Bahamas* **120** F9
Stockport, *Eng., U.K.* **143** S11
Stocks Seamount, *Atl. Oc.* **237** Q9
Stockton, *Calif., U.S.* **109** R5
Stockton, *Ill., U.S.* **98** M4
Stockton, *Kans., U.S.* **105** S5
Stockton, *Mo., U.S.* **105** U11
Stockton Lake, *Mo., U.S.* **105** U11
Stockton-on-Tees, *Eng., U.K.* **143** Q12
Stoke on Trent, *Eng., U.K.* **143** S11
Stokes, Bahía, *Chile* **133** X7
Stokes, Mount, *N.Z.* **213** M18
Stolberg, *Ger.* **148** F4
Stolbovoy, Ostrov, *Russ.* **159** D17
Stolin, *Belarus* **156** M4
Stonehaven, *Scot., U.K.* **142** K11
Stonehenge, *Eng., U.K.* **143** W12
Stonehenge, *Qnsld., Austral.* **211** U12
Stones River National Battlefield, *Tenn., U.S.* **101** F15
Stonewall, *Miss., U.S.* **101** L13
Stonewall, *Okla., U.S.* **102** H12
Stony, river, *Alas., U.S.* **111** J14
Stony Rapids, *Sask., Can.* **82** J12
Stora Lulevatten, lake, *Sw.* **141** E13
Storavan, lake, *Sw.* **141** F13
Støren, *Nor.* **140** H11
Storkerson Bay, *N.W.T., Can.* **82** D12
Storlien, *Sw.* **140** H11
Storm Lake, *Iowa, U.S.* **105** N10
Stornoway, *Scot., U.K.* **142** H7
Storr's Lake, *Bahamas* **120** E11
Storsjön, lake, *Sw.* **140** H12
Storuman, *Sw.* **141** G13
Story, *Wyo., U.S.* **106** F11
Story City, *Iowa, U.S.* **105** N11
Stoughton, *Wis., U.S.* **98** L5
Stoyba, *Russ.* **159** K19
Strabane, *N. Ire., U.K.* **143** P6
Strahan, *Tas., Austral.* **211** Z15
Stralsund, *Ger.* **148** B10
Stranda, *Nor.* **140** J10
Strangford Lough, *N. Ire., U.K.* **143** Q8
Strangways, *S. Aust., Austral.* **211** V9
Stranorlar, *Ire.* **143** P5
Stranraer, *Scot., U.K.* **143** P8
Strasbourg, *Fr.* **147** P15
Strasburg, *N. Dak., U.S.* **104** H5
Strasburg, *Ohio, U.S.* **99** Q14
Strasburg, *Va., U.S.* **96** C11
Strassen, *Lux.* **160** K10
Strata Florida, *Wales, U.K.* **143** U9
Stratford, *Tex., U.S.* **102** F5
Stratford upon Avon, *Eng., U.K.* **143** U12
Strathalbyn, *S. Aust., Austral.* **211** Y10
Strathcona, Mount, *Antarctica* **227** K21
Strathmore, valley, *Scot., U.K.* **142** L10
Stratobowl, site, *S. Dak., U.S.* **104** L2
Stratton, *Colo., U.S.* **106** M15
Stratton, *Me., U.S.* **95** E15
Stratton, *Nebr., U.S.* **105** R3
Straubing, *Ger.* **148** J9
Strawberry Mountain, *Oreg., U.S.* **108** G7
Strawberry Reservoir, *Utah, U.S.* **106** L8
Strawn, *Tex., U.S.* **102** L9
Streaky Bay, *S. Aust., Austral.* **211** X9
Streator, *Ill., U.S.* **99** P6
Streeter, *N. Dak., U.S.* **104** G6
Streich Mound, *Austral.* **210** J5
Strelka, *Russ.* **159** F20
Streymoy, island, *Faroe Is., Den.* **140** J6
Strezhevoy, *Russ.* **158** H11
Stříbro, *Czech Rep.* **148** H10
Strickland, river, *P.N.G.* **213** D18
Strimónas, river, *Gr.* **154** C12
Stringtown, *Okla., U.S.* **102** H12
Stroma, island, *Scot., U.K.* **142** G10
Stromboli, Isola, *It.* **151** Q12
Stromeferry, *Scot., U.K.* **142** K8
Stromness, *Scot., U.K.* **142** G10
Stromsburg, *Nebr., U.S.* **105** Q7
Strömstad, *Sw.* **140** L11
Strömsund, *Sw.* **140** H12
Strongíli (Ypsilí), island, *Gr.* **155** N22
Stronsay, island, *Scot., U.K.* **142** F11
Stroud, *Eng., U.K.* **143** V11
Stroud, *Okla., U.S.* **102** F12
Stroudsburg, *Pa., U.S.* **94** N9
Strovolos, *Cyprus* **160** P8
Struga, *Maced.* **152** L10
Struma, river, *Bulg.* **153** K13
Strumica, *Maced.* **152** K12
Struy, *Scot., U.K.* **142** J9
Stryy, *Ukr.* **157** P2
Stuart, *Fla., U.S.* **97** V10
Stuart, *Nebr., U.S.* **105** N6
Stuart, *Va., U.S.* **96** G9
Stuart Island, *Alas., U.S.* **84** P2
Stuart Lake, *B.C., Can.* **82** K8
Stuart Range, *Austral.* **210** H9
Stubbs, *St. Vincent & the Grenadines* **121** L16
Stuhr, *Ger.* **148** C7
Stump Lake, *N. Dak., U.S.* **104** F7
Stumpy Point, *N.C., U.S.* **96** H15
Stung Treng, *Cambodia* **186** M12
Stupino, *Russ.* **156** K9
Sturgeon Bay, *Wis., U.S.* **98** J8
Sturgis, *Ky., U.S.* **101** C14
Sturgis, *Mich., U.S.* **99** N10
Sturgis, *S. Dak., U.S.* **104** K2
Sturt Stony Desert, *Austral.* **210** G11
Stuttgart, *Ark., U.S.* **100** H9
Stuttgart, *Ger.* **148** J7
Stykkishólmur, *Ice.* **140** E2
Suai, *Timor-Leste* **189** N15
Suakin, *Sudan* **199** C14
Suakin Archipelago, *Sudan* **194** F10
Suao, *Taiwan, China* **183** Q10
Subaşı Dağı, *Turk.* **169** G16
Subay', 'Urūq, *Saudi Arabia* **172** L9
Subei, *China* **180** G9
Subeita, ruin, *Israel* **171** P4
Subi, island, *Indonesia* **188** H9
Sublette, *Kans., U.S.* **105** U4
Subotica, *Serb. & Mont.* **152** D9
Suceava, *Rom.* **153** B15
Sučevići, *Croatia* **152** F6
Sucia, Bahía, *P.R., U.S.* **120** P1
Sücka, *Liech.* **160** P3
Sucre, *Bol.* **130** K7
Sud, Canal du, *Haiti* **117** M16
Sud, Pointe, *Comoros* **205** M14
Sud, Récif du, *Mayotte, Fr.* **205** P17
Sudak, *Ukr.* **157** T8
Sudan, *Af.* **195** G21
Sudan, *Tex., U.S.* **102** J4
Suday, *Russ.* **156** F11
Sudbury, *Ont., Can.* **83** P18
Sudd, wetland, *Sudan* **194** H9
Suddie, *Guyana* **129** D14
Sud-Est, Passe du, *Fr. Polynesia, Fr.* **219** R21
Sudeten, range, *Czech Rep., Pol.* **148** G12
Sud-Ouest, Passe du, *Fr. Polynesia, Fr.* **219** R20
Sudr, *Egypt* **171** R1
Suðuroy, island, *Faroe Is., Den.* **140** J6
Sue, river, *Sudan* **198** G11
Sueca, *Sp.* **145** H15
Suez *see* El Suweis, *Egypt* **171** Q1
Suez *see* El Suweis, *Egypt* **197** C19
Suez, Gulf of, *Egypt* **171** R1
Suez Canal, *Egypt* **171** N1
Suffolk, *Va., U.S.* **96** F14
Sugar Land, *Tex., U.S.* **103** R13
Sugar Loaf, island, *Grenada* **121** J23
Sugarloaf Key, *Fla., U.S.* **97** Y9
Suğla Gölü, *Turk.* **168** H7
Suhai Hu, *China* **180** G9
Şuḩār, *Oman* **173** J15
Sühbaatar, *Mongolia* **180** C12
Suheli Par, island, *India* **179** R3
Suhl, *Ger.* **148** G8
Şuhut, *Turk.* **168** F6
Suichang, *China* **182** M8
Suichuan, *China* **183** P5
Suide, *China* **182** E3
Suining, *China* **182** H7
Suining, *China* **183** P2
Suining, *China* **180** L12
Suippes, *Fr.* **147** P12
Suir, river, *Ire.* **143** U5
Suixi, *China* **182** H7
Suixi, *China* **183** S2
Suizhong, *China* **182** C9
Suizhou, *China* **182** K4
Sujawal, *Pak.* **177** W7
Sukabumi, *Indonesia* **188** M8
Sukadana, *Indonesia* **188** J9
Sukagawa, *Japan* **184** M13
Sūkh, *Uzb.* **175** L14
Sukhinichi, *Russ.* **156** K8
Sukhona, river, *Russ.* **156** E12
Sukhothai, *Thai.* **186** K8
Sukkur, *Pak.* **177** T7
Sukumo, *Japan* **185** S6
Sula, river, *Ukr.* **157** N7
Sula, Kepulauan, *Indonesia* **189** K15
Sulaiman Range, *Pak.* **177** R8
Sulanheer, *Mongolia* **181** F13
Sula Sgeir, island, *Scot., U.K.* **142** F7
Sulawesi (Celebes), island, *Indonesia* **189** K13
Sulei, island, *Solomon Is.* **217** M18
Sule Skerry, island, *Scot., U.K.* **142** F9
Süleymanlı, *Turk.* **168** G11
Sulima, *Sierra Leone* **200** G6
Sulina, *Rom.* **153** E19
Sullana, *Peru* **130** E2
Sulligent, *Ala., U.S.* **101** J13
Sullivan, *Ill., U.S.* **99** R6
Sullivan, *Ind., U.S.* **99** S7
Sullivan, *Mo., U.S.* **105** T14
Sulmona, *It.* **150** K10
Sulphur, *La., U.S.* **100** P7
Sulphur, *Okla., U.S.* **102** H11
Sulphur, river, *Tex., U.S.* **102** K14
Sulphur Cone, *Hawai'i, U.S.* **113** N19
Sulphur Springs, *Tex., U.S.* **102** K13
Sulphur Springs Draw, *Tex., U.S.* **102** L4
Sultan Dağları, *Turk.* **168** G7
Sultanhanı, *Turk.* **168** G9
Sultanpur, *India* **178** G8
Sulu Archipelago, *Philippines* **189** G13
Sulu Basin, *Pac. Oc.* **238** J3
Sülüklü, *Turk.* **168** F8
Sülüktü, *Kyrg.* **176** G8
Suluova, *Turk.* **168** D11
Sulu Sea, *Philippines* **189** E13
Sumampa, *Arg.* **132** H10
Sumas, *Wash., U.S.* **108** A4
Sumatra, island, *Indonesia* **166** L10
Sumaúma, *Braz.* **130** F9
Sumba, *Faroe Is., Den.* **140** J6
Sumba, island, *Indonesia* **189** N13
Sumbawa, island, *Indonesia* **188** M12
Sumbawa Besar, *Indonesia* **188** M12
Sumbawanga, *Tanzania* **198** M12
Sumbe, *Angola* **202** D5
Sumisu (Smith), island, *Japan* **184** J5
Summer Lake, *Oreg., U.S.* **108** K5
Summerland Key, *Fla., U.S.* **97** Y9
Summersville, *W. Va., U.S.* **96** D9
Summerville, *Ga., U.S.* **96** K4
Summerville, *S.C., U.S.* **96** M10
Summit, *Miss., U.S.* **100** N10
Summit Mountain, *Nev., U.S.* **109** P10
Summit Peak, *Colo., U.S.* **107** P12
Sumner, *Iowa, U.S.* **104** M13
Šumperk, *Czech Rep.* **149** H13
Sumprabum, *Myanmar* **186** D7
Sumpter, *Oreg., U.S.* **108** G8
Sumqayıt, *Azerb.* **169** D23
Sumrall, *Miss., U.S.* **100** M12
Sumter, *S.C., U.S.* **96** K10
Sumy, *Ukr.* **157** N8
Sun, river, *Mont., U.S.* **106** C7
Sunagawa, *Japan* **184** F13
Sunart, Loch, *Scot., U.K.* **142** L7
Sunbaron Roads (Tinian Harbor), *N. Mariana Is., U.S.* **216** C7
Sunburst, *Mont., U.S.* **106** A7
Sunbury, *Pa., U.S.* **94** N7
Sunbury, *Vic., Austral.* **211** Z12
Sunchales, *Arg.* **132** J11
Suncheon, *S. Korea* **182** G13
Sunch'ŏn, *N. Korea* **182** D12
Sun City, *Ariz., U.S.* **107** T6
Sunda, Selat, *Indonesia* **188** L8
Sundance, *Wyo., U.S.* **106** F13
Sundar, *Malaysia* **188** G11
Sundarbans, wetland, *Bangladesh, India* **178** J12
Sundargarh, *India* **178** J9
Sunday *see* Raoul Island, island, *Kermadec Is., N.Z.* **214** L9
Sunderland, *Eng., U.K.* **143** P12
Sundi, *Sao Tome and Principe* **205** A20
Sündiken Dağ, *Turk.* **168** E6
Sundown, *Tex., U.S.* **102** K4
Sundsvall, *Sw.* **141** J13
Sunflower, Mount, *Kans., U.S.* **105** S3
Sungaianyar, *Indonesia* **188** K12
Sungaibatu, *Indonesia* **188** J9
Sungai Kolok, *Thai.* **187** S9
Sungaipenuh, *Indonesia* **188** K6
Sungai Petani, *Malaysia* **187** S9
Sung Men, *Thai.* **186** K8
Sungurlu, *Turk.* **168** E9
Sunland Park, *N. Mex., U.S.* **107** V12
Sunnyside, *Wash., U.S.* **108** E6
Sunnyvale, *Calif., U.S.* **109** S4
Sun Prairie, *Wis., U.S.* **98** L5
Sunray, *Tex., U.S.* **102** F5
Sunset Beach, *Hawai'i, U.S.* **112** D10
Sunset Crater Volcano National Monument, *Ariz., U.S.* **107** S7
Suntar Khayata, Khrebet, *Russ.* **159** G19
Suntsar, *Pak.* **177** V2
Sunwu, *China* **181** B17
Sunyani, *Ghana* **200** G10
Suomen Ridge *see* Suomenselkä, *Fin.* **138** C9
Suomenselkä, *Fin.* **141** H15
Suonenjoki, *Fin.* **141** H16
Supai, *Ariz., U.S.* **107** R6
Superior, *Ariz., U.S.* **107** U7
Superior, *Mont., U.S.* **106** C5
Superior, *Nebr., U.S.* **105** R7
Superior, *Wis., U.S.* **98** E2
Superior, Lake, *Can., U.S.* **85** C15
Süphan Dağı, *Turk.* **169** F17
Supiori, island, *Indonesia* **213** B15
Support Force Glacier, *Antarctica* **226** G11
Supu, *Indonesia* **189** H16
Sup'ung Reservoir, *N. Korea, China* **182** C12
Suquṭrá (Socotra), island, *Yemen* **173** R14
Şūr, *Oman* **173** K17
Sur, Point, *Calif., U.S.* **109** U4
Sur, Punta, *Ecua.* **128** R9
Sura, river, *Russ.* **156** J13
Surab, *Pak.* **177** T5
Surabaya, *Indonesia* **188** M10
Sūrak, *Iran* **173** J16
Surakarta, *Indonesia* **188** M10
Suramana, *Indonesia* **189** J13
Surat, *India* **178** K3
Surat, *Qnsld., Austral.* **211** V14
Surat Thani, *Thai.* **187** Q8
Sûre, river, *Ger., Lux.* **160** J11
Sürétiméat, Mount, *Vanuatu* **218** B2
Surf City, *N.C., U.S.* **96** K13
Surgères, *Fr.* **147** T6
Surgidero de Batabanó, *Cuba* **116** G6
Surgut, *Russ.* **158** H11
Surigao, *Philippines* **189** E15
Surin, *Thai.* **186** M10
Suriname, *S. Amer.* **127** B19
Surin Nua, Ko, *Thai.* **187** Q7
Sürmene, *Turk.* **169** D14
Surprise, Île de la, *New Caledonia, Fr.* **218** A5
Surrey, *B.C., Can.* **82** M8
Sursee, *Switz.* **150** B3
Surskoye, *Russ.* **156** K14
Surt, *Lib.* **197** C14
Surtanahu, *Pak.* **177** V8
Surtsey, island, *Ice.* **140** G2
Suruç, *Turk.* **169** J13
Suruga Wan, *Japan* **185** Q11
Surulangun, *Indonesia* **188** K6
Sušac, island, *Croatia* **152** H6
Sūsah (Apollonia), *Lib.* **197** B16
Susak, island, *Croatia* **152** F4
Susaki, *Japan* **185** R7
Susamyr, *Kyrg.* **176** E11
Susanville, *Calif., U.S.* **109** N5
Suşehri, *Turk.* **169** E13
Susitna, river, *Alas., U.S.* **111** H17
Susoh, *Indonesia* **188** G4
Susquehanna, river, *Pa., U.S.* **94** N7
Susquehanna, *Pa., U.S.* **94** L9
Susques, *Arg.* **132** E9
Susubona, *Solomon Is.* **217** M18
Susuman, *Russ.* **159** F20
Susunu, *Indonesia* **213** C15
Susupe, *N. Mariana Is., U.S.* **216** C4
Susurluk, *Turk.* **168** E4
Sutak, *India* **177** N14
Sütçüler, *Turk.* **168** H6
Sutherland, *Nebr., U.S.* **105** P4
Sutherland, *S. Af.* **202** L8
Sutherlin, *Oreg., U.S.* **108** J3
Sutlej, river, *Pak.* **177** S10
Sutton, *Nebr., U.S.* **105** Q7
Sutton, river, *Ont., Can.* **83** L16
Sutton, *W. Va., U.S.* **96** D9
Sutton on Sea, *Eng., U.K.* **143** S14
Suttsu, *Japan* **184** G12
Sutwik Island, *Alas., U.S.* **111** M14
Su'u, *Solomon Is.* **217** N19
Suva, *Fiji Is.* **218** J6
Suvadiva Atoll (Huvadu), *Maldives* **179** W3
Suvorov, *Russ.* **156** K9
Suwa, *Japan* **185** P11
Suwałki, *Pol.* **149** B17
Suwannaphum, *Thai.* **186** L11
Suwannee, river, *Fla., U.S.* **85** M18
Suwannee, *Fla., U.S.* **97** S6
Suwanose Jima, *Japan* **185** V3
Suwarrow Atoll, *Cook Is., N.Z.* **214** J11
Suwayqīyah, Hawr as, *Iraq* **172** E10
Suwon, *S. Korea* **182** F13
Suyutkino, *Russ.* **157** T15
Suzhou, *China* **182** J7
Suzhou, *China* **182** K9
Suzu, *Japan* **184** M10
Suzuka, *Japan* **185** Q9
Suzu Misaki, *Japan* **184** M10
Svalbard, archipelago, *Nor.* **167** P7
Svartisen, glacier, *Nor.* **140** F12
Svatove, *Ukr.* **157** P10
Svay Rieng, *Cambodia* **187** P12
Sveg, *Sw.* **140** J12
Svendborg, *Den.* **140** P11
Sverdrup Channel, *Nunavut, Can.* **83** B15
Sverdrup Islands, *Nunavut, Can.* **83** B15
Svetac (Sveti Andrija), island, *Croatia* **152** H5
Sveti Andrija *see* Svetac, island, *Croatia* **152** H5
Svetlograd, *Russ.* **157** S12
Svetogorsk, *Russ.* **158** D7
Svilengrad, *Bulg.* **153** K16
Svir', river, *Russ.* **138** C10
Sviritsa, *Russ.* **156** E7
Svishtov, *Bulg.* **153** G15
Svobodnyy, *Russ.* **159** K19
Svolv r, *Nor.* **140** E12
Svyataya Anna Fan, *Arctic Oc.* **242** F12
Svyataya Anna Trough, *Arctic Oc.* **242** D12
Svyatoy Nos, Mys, *Russ.* **159** D17
Svyetlahorsk, *Belarus* **156** L5
Swain Reefs, *Austral.* **210** F15
Swainsboro, *Ga., U.S.* **96** M7
Swains Island, *Amer. Samoa, U.S.* **214** J10
Swakop, river, *Namibia* **202** H6
Swakopmund, *Namibia* **202** H6
Swan, river, *Austral.* **210** K2
Swan, river, *Mont., U.S.* **106** C6
Swanlinbar, *Ire.* **143** Q5
Swan Peak, *Mont., U.S.* **106** C6
Swanquarter, *N.C., U.S.* **96** H14
Swan River, *Man., Can.* **83** M13
Swansboro, *N.C., U.S.* **96** J13
Swansea (Abertawe), *Wales, U.K.* **143** V9
Swansea Bay, *Wales, U.K.* **143** V9
Swans Island, *Me., U.S.* **95** G18
Swanton, *Vt., U.S.* **94** E12
Swan Valley, *Idaho, U.S.* **106** H8
Swatow *see* Shantou, *China* **183** R6
Swaziland, *Af.* **195** Q21
Sweden, *Eur.* **139** R7
Sweeney Mountains, *Antarctica* **226** F7
Sweetgrass, *Mont., U.S.* **106** A7
Sweet Home, *Oreg., U.S.* **108** G3
Sweeting's Cay, *Bahamas* **120** E4
Sweetwater, *Tenn., U.S.* **101** F18
Sweetwater, *Tex., U.S.* **102** L7
Sweetwater, river, *Wyo., U.S.* **106** J10
Sweetwater Lake, *N. Dak., U.S.* **104** E6
Swellendam, *S. Af.* **202** M8
Swetes, *Antigua & Barbuda* **121** B21
Świdnica, *Pol.* **149** G13
Świdnik, *Pol.* **149** F17
Świdwin, *Pol.* **148** C12
Świebodzin, *Pol.* **148** E12
Świecie, *Pol.* **149** C14
Swift Current, *Sask., Can.* **82** N11
Swilly, Lough, *Ire.* **143** N5
Swindon, *Eng., U.K.* **143** V12
Swinford, *Ire.* **143** R4

Świnoujście, *Pol.* **148** B11
Switzerland, *Eur.* **139** V5
Syamzha, *Russ.* **156** F11
Syava, *Russ.* **156** G13
Sychevka, *Russ.* **156** J8
Sydney, *N.S., Can.* **83** N23
Sydney, *N.S.W., Austral.* **211** Y14
Sydney Bay, *Norfolk I., Austral.* **217** G20
Sydney Point, *Banaba, Kiribati* **217** E20
Syeri, *Indonesia* **189** K19
Syktyvkar, *Russ.* **158** F8
Sylacauga, *Ala., U.S.* **101** K16
Sylhet, *Bangladesh* **178** H13
Sylt, island, *Ger.* **148** A7
Sylva, *N.C., U.S.* **96** J6
Sylvania, *Ga., U.S.* **96** M8
Sylvania, *Ohio, U.S.* **99** N12
Sylvester, *Ga., U.S.* **97** P5
Sylvester, *Tex., U.S.* **102** L7
Sylvester, Lake, *Austral.* **210** D9
Synel'nykove, *Ukr.* **157** Q8
Synya, *Russ.* **158** F10
Syowa, station, *Antarctica* **227** B17
Syracuse *see* Siracusa, *It.* **151** T12
Syracuse, *Kans., U.S.* **105** U3
Syracuse, *N.Y., U.S.* **94** J8
Syracuse, *Nebr., U.S.* **105** Q9
Syr Darya, river, *Kaz.* **166** F6
Syria, *Asia* **167** T3
Syrian Desert, *Asia* **166** F3
Syrian Gates, *Turk.* **168** J11
Sysy Basa, *Russ.* **159** H18
Syumsi, *Russ.* **156** G15
Syutkya, peak, *Bulg.* **153** K13
Syzran', *Russ.* **156** L15
Szczecin, *Pol.* **148** C11
Szczecinek, *Pol.* **149** C13
Szczytno, *Pol.* **149** C16
Szeged, *Hung.* **149** N16
Székely, *Hung.* **149** K17
Székesfehérvár, *Hung.* **149** L14
Szekszárd, *Hung.* **149** N15
Szentes, *Hung.* **149** M16
Szolnok, *Hung.* **149** L16
Szombathely, *Hung.* **149** L13

T

Taakoka, island, *Cook Is., N.Z.* **218** Q9
Taapuna, *Fr. Polynesia, Fr.* **219** N15
Taapuna, Passe de, *Fr. Polynesia, Fr.* **219** N15
Taatioe, Mont, *Fr. Polynesia, Fr.* **219** K23
Tâba, *Egypt* **171** R5
Tabago, *P.N.G.* **217** K14
Ţābah, *Saudi Arabia* **172** H8
Tabalo, *P.N.G.* **213** B20
Tabaquite, *Trinidad & Tobago* **121** P22
Tabar Islands, *P.N.G.* **213** B21
Ţabas, *Iran* **173** D15
Ţabas, *Iran* **173** D17
Tabelbala, *Alg.* **196** C9
Tabernacle, *St. Kitts & Nevis* **121** A17
Tabernas, *Sp.* **144** L12
Tabiang, *Banaba, Kiribati* **217** D20
Tabiang, *Kiribati* **217** G17
Tabik, island, *Marshall Is.* **216** K1
Tabik Channel, *Marshall Is.* **216** K2
Tabiteuea, island, *Kiribati* **214** G8
Tabiteuea, *Kiribati* **217** G18
Tablas, island, *Philippines* **189** D14
Table, Pointe de la, *Reunion, Fr.* **205** H17
Table Mountain, *S. Dak., U.S.* **104** H1
Table Rock Lake, *Mo., U.S.* **105** V11
Tabontebike, *Kiribati* **217** E17
Tábor, *Czech Rep.* **148** J11
Tabor, *Russ.* **159** D18
Tabora, *Tanzania* **199** L13
Tabor City, *N.C., U.S.* **96** K11
Tabou, *Côte d'Ivoire* **200** H7
Tabrīz, *Iran* **172** B10
Tabu, Motu, *Fr. Polynesia, Fr.* **219** M23
Tabuaeran (Fanning Island), *Kiribati* **214** F12
Tabūk, *Saudi Arabia* **172** G6
Tabunifi, *F.S.M.* **217** D18
Taburiente, Caldera de, *Canary Is.* **204** Q3
Tacheng, *China* **180** D6
Tacloban, *Philippines* **189** D15
Tacna, *Peru* **130** K6
Tacoma, *Wash., U.S.* **108** C4
Tacuarembó, *Uru.* **132** K14
Tacutu, river, *S. Amer.* **126** C6
Tad, *Pak.* **177** V3
Tademaït, Plateau du, *Alg.* **196** D10
Tadine, *New Caledonia, Fr.* **218** D10
Tadjmout, *Alg.* **196** E11
Tadjoura, Gulf of, *Djibouti* **194** G11
Tadmur (Palmyra), *Syr.* **170** G10
Tadoule Lake, *Man., Can.* **83** K14
Tadoussac, *Que., Can.* **83** N20
Tadpatri, *India* **179** N6
Taean, *S. Korea* **182** F13
Taedong, *N. Korea* **182** C12
Taejŏn *see* Daejeon, *S. Korea* **182** F13
Taenarum *see* Ténaro, Akrotírio, *Gr.* **154** N10
Taenga, island, *Fr. Polynesia, Fr.* **219** E19
Tafahi, island, *Tonga* **214** J10
Tafalla, *Sp.* **145** C13
Tafassasset, Oued, *Alg.* **196** E12
Tafelberg, peak, *Neth. Antilles, Neth.* **121** Q15
Tafí Viejo, *Arg.* **132** G9
Tafonsak, *F.S.M.* **217** A18
Taft, *Calif., U.S.* **109** V7
Taft, *Tex., U.S.* **103** T11
Taftān, Kūh-e, *Iran* **173** G17
Taga, *Samoa* **218** L2
Taganrog, *Russ.* **157** R10
Taganrogskiy Zaliv, *Russ., Ukr.* **157** R10
Tagant, region, *Mauritania* **194** F2
Tagawa, *Japan* **185** R4
Taghaz, *Afghan.* **177** R3
Tagliamento, river, *It.* **150** C9
Tagounit, *Mor.* **196** C8
Tagtabazar, *Turkm.* **174** N10
Taguatinga, *Braz.* **131** H14
Tagula, island, *P.N.G.* **213** F22
Tagum, *Philippines* **189** F15
Tagus *see* Tajo, river, *Sp.* **144** G8
Tagus *see* Tejo, river, *Port.* **144** H5
Tahaa, island, *Fr. Polynesia, Fr.* **219** E15
Tahan, peak, *Malaysia* **187** T10
Tahanea, island, *Fr. Polynesia, Fr.* **219** E18
Tahat, Mount, *Alg.* **196** E11
Ţaherī, *Iran* **173** H13
Tahueia, Mouillage de, *Fr. Polynesia, Fr.* **219** J21
Tahgong, Puntan, *N. Mariana Is., U.S.* **216** A7
Tahi, cape, *Fr. Polynesia, Fr.* **219** K14
Tahiti, island, *Fr. Polynesia, Fr.* **219** P16
Tahlab, river, *Pak.* **177** T2
Tahlab, Dasht-i-, *Pak.* **177** S2
Tahlequah, *Okla., U.S.* **102** F14
Tahoe, Lake, *Calif., Nev., U.S.* **109** Q6
Tahoe City, *Calif., U.S.* **109** Q6
Tahoka, *Tex., U.S.* **102** K5
Taholah, *Wash., U.S.* **108** C2
Tahoua, *Niger* **196** H11
Tahtalı Dağ, *Turk.* **168** F11
Tahtalıdaği, peak, *Turk.* **168** J6
Tahuata, island, *Fr. Polynesia, Fr.* **219** N20
Tahueia, *Fr. Polynesia, Fr.* **219** K21
Tahulandang, island, *Indonesia* **189** H15
Tahuna, *Indonesia* **189** G15
Tai'an, *China* **182** G7
Taiarapu, Presqu'île de, *Fr. Polynesia, Fr.* **219** P18
Taiaro, island, *Fr. Polynesia, Fr.* **219** E18
Taibus Qi (Baochang), *China* **182** B6
Taichung, *Taiwan, China* **183** R9
Taígetos, Óros, *Gr.* **154** L10
Taigu, *China* **182** E4
Taihang Shan, *China* **182** F5
Taihape, *N.Z.* **213** L19
Taihe, *China* **183** P5
Tai Hu, *China* **182** K9
Taihu, *China* **182** L6
Taiki, *Japan* **184** G15
Tailai, *China* **181** D16
Tailem Bend, *S. Aust., Austral.* **211** Y10
Tain, *Fr.* **147** V13
Tainan, *Taiwan, China* **183** S9
Taining, *China* **183** P7
Taiof, island, *P.N.G.* **217** J13
Taipei, *Taiwan, China* **183** Q10
Taiping, *Malaysia* **187** T9
Taipingot, peak, *N. Mariana Is., U.S.* **216** E7
Tairapa, Passe, *Fr. Polynesia, Fr.* **219** K17
Taira Shima, *Japan* **185** V3
Taishan, *China* **183** S4
Taita, Mont, *Fr. Polynesia, Fr.* **219** K21
Taitao, Península de, *Chile* **133** T6
T'aitung, *Taiwan, China* **183** S10
Taivalkoski, *Fin.* **141** F16
Taiwan, China, *Asia* **167** V13
Taiwan, island, *Taiwan, China* **183** R10
Taiwan Strait, *China, Taiwan, China* **183** S8
Taiyuan, *China* **182** E4
Taizhou, *China* **182** J9
Taizhou *see* Linhai, *China* **182** M10
Ta'izz, *Yemen* **172** R9
Tajarḩī, *Lib.* **197** E14
Tajikistan, *Asia* **167** U7
Tajima, *Japan* **184** M12
Taj Mahal, site, *India* **178** G6
Tajo (Tagus), river, *Sp.* **144** G8
Tak, *Thai.* **186** K8
Taka, island, *Marshall Is.* **216** M7
Taka Atoll, *Marshall Is.* **216** F4
Takāb, *Iran* **172** C11
Takahe, Mount, *Antarctica* **226** L7
Takaiu, *F.S.M.* **217** F14
Takaka, *N.Z.* **213** M17
Takamatsu, *Japan* **185** Q7
Takamori, *Japan* **185** S5
Takaoka, *Japan* **185** N10
Takapau, *N.Z.* **213** L19
Takapoto, island, *Fr. Polynesia, Fr.* **219** D18
Takara Jima, *Japan* **185** V3
Takaroa, island, *Fr. Polynesia, Fr.* **219** D18
Takasaki, *Japan* **185** N11
Takatik, island, *F.S.M.* **217** F14
Tā-kaw, *Myanmar* **186** H7
Takayama, *Japan* **185** P10
Takefu, *Japan* **185** P9
Takengon, *Indonesia* **188** G4
Takeo, *Cambodia* **187** P11
Takeo, *Japan* **185** R4
Take Shima, *Japan* **185** U4
Takeshima *see* Dokdo, island, *Japan* **184** M6
Tākestān, *Iran* **172** C12
Taketa, *Japan* **185** S5
Takfon, *Taj.* **176** H7
Takhiatosh, *Uzb.* **174** J9
Takhtakŭpir, *Uzb.* **174** J9
Takhteh Pol, *Afghan.* **177** Q5
Taki, *P.N.G.* **217** K14
Takikawa, *Japan* **184** F13
Taklimakan Desert, *China* **166** G8
Taklimakan Shamo, *China* **180** G5
Taksimo, *Russ.* **159** K17
Takuan, Mount, *P.N.G.* **217** K14
Takua Pa, *Thai.* **187** Q7
Takum, *India* **178** F14
Takume, island, *Fr. Polynesia, Fr.* **219** E19
Takuua, island, *Cook Is., N.Z.* **219** B18
Takuua Passage, *Cook Is., N.Z.* **219** B18
Tal, *Pak.* **176** L10
Talagang, *Pak.* **177** P10
Talaimannar, *Sri Lanka* **179** S7
Talamanca, Cordillera de, *N. Amer.* **80** Q8
Talangbatu, *Indonesia* **188** L7
Talara, *Peru* **130** E1
Talas, *Kyrg.* **176** E10
Talaud, Kepulauan, *Indonesia* **189** G16
Talavera de la Reina, *Sp.* **144** G9
Talbot, Cape, *Austral.* **210** B6
Talbot Inlet, *Nunavut, Can.* **83** C16
Talbotton, *Ga., U.S.* **96** M5
Talca, *Chile* **132** M6
Talcahuano, *Chile* **132** M6
Taldora, *Qnsld., Austral.* **211** S11
Taldyqorghan, *Kaz.* **175** G17
Talhar, *Pak.* **177** W7
Talia, *S. Aust., Austral.* **211** X9
Taliabu, island, *Indonesia* **189** K15
Talihina, *Okla., U.S.* **102** H14
Tali Post, *Sudan* **198** H12
Taliwang, *Indonesia* **188** M12
Talkeetna, *Alas., U.S.* **111** H16
Talkeetna Mountains, *Alas., U.S.* **111** J17
Talladega, *Ala., U.S.* **101** J16
Tall 'Afar, *Iraq* **172** C9
Tallahassee, *Fla., U.S.* **97** Q5
Tall al Abyaḑ al 'Atiq, *Syr.* **170** D11
Tall al Aḩmar (Til Barsip), *Syr.* **170** D10
Tallapoosa, river, *Ala., U.S.* **101** L16
Tallapoosa, *Ga., U.S.* **96** L4
Tallard, *Fr.* **147** W14
Tallassee, *Ala., U.S.* **101** L16
Tall Birāk, *Syr.* **170** D14
Tall Ḩalaf, ruin, *Syr.* **170** C13
Tallinn (Reval), *Est.* **141** K16
Tall Kalakh, *Syr.* **170** G7
Tall Tamir, *Syr.* **170** D13
Tallulah, *La., U.S.* **100** L10
Tall Ya'rūbīyah, *Syr.* **170** C16
Talmont-St. Hilaire, *Fr.* **147** T5
Talnakh, *Russ.* **159** F13
Tal'ne, *Ukr.* **157** P6
Talodi, *Sudan* **198** F12
Talofofo, *Guam, U.S.* **216** D10
Talofofo Bay, *Guam, U.S.* **216** D11
Taloga, *Okla., U.S.* **102** F9
Talok, *Indonesia* **189** H13
Taloqan, *Afghan.* **176** K8
Talorha, *Mauritania* **196** F6
Talos Dome, *Antarctica* **227** Q15
Taloyoak, *Nunavut, Can.* **83** F15
Talparo, *Trinidad & Tobago* **121** P23
Talshand, *Mongolia* **180** E10
Talsi, *Latv.* **141** M16
Taltal, *Chile* **132** F7
Tama, *Iowa, U.S.* **105** N12
Tamakautonga, *Niue, N.Z.* **219** B20
Tamale, *Ghana* **200** F10
Tamana, island, *Kiribati* **214** G8
Tamanoura, *Japan* **185** S2
Tamanrasset (Fort Laperrine), *Alg.* **196** F11
Tamarin, *Mauritius* **205** G19
Tamatoa, *Fr. Polynesia, Fr.* **219** K21
Tamazunchale, *Mex.* **114** H12
Tambacounda, *Senegal* **196** H5
Tambalan, *Indonesia* **188** H11
Tambelan, Kepulauan, *Indonesia* **188** H8
Tambisan, *Malaysia* **189** G13
Tambo, *Qnsld., Austral.* **211** U13
Tambov, *Russ.* **156** L11
Tambura, *Sudan* **198** H11
Tamch, *Mongolia* **180** D9
Tamchaket, *Mauritania* **196** G6
Tame, *Col.* **128** E7
Tâmega, river, *Port.* **144** D6
Tamel Aike, *Arg.* **133** U7
Tamiahua, *Mex.* **114** H12
Tam Ky, *Vietnam* **186** L14
Tammerfors *see* Tampere, *Fin.* **141** J15
Tamotoe, Passe, *Fr. Polynesia, Fr.* **219** P17
Tampa, *Fla., U.S.* **97** U7
Tampa Bay, *Fla., U.S.* **97** U7
Tampere (Tammerfors), *Fin.* **141** J15
Tampico, *Mex.* **114** G12
Tampin, *Malaysia* **187** U10
Tampoc, river, *Fr. Guiana, Fr.* **129** F17
Tam Quan, *Vietnam* **186** M14
Tamrida *see* Hadīboh, *Yemen* **173** R14
Tamsagbulag, *Mongolia* **181** D15
Tamshiyacu, *Peru* **130** E4
Tamu, *Myanmar* **186** F5
Tamuning, *Guam, U.S.* **216** C11
Tamworth, *N.S.W., Austral.* **211** X14
Tana, river, *Fin., Nor.* **141** C15
Tana, river, *Kenya* **199** K15
Tana, *Nor.* **141** B15
Tanabe, *Japan* **185** R8
Tanacross, *Alas., U.S.* **111** H18
Tanaga Island, *Alas., U.S.* **110** N4
Tanagomba Harbor, *Solomon Is.* **217** M18
T'ana Hāyk', *Eth.* **199** F14
Tanahbala, island, *Indonesia* **188** J5
Tanahgrogot, *Indonesia* **188** K12
Tanahjampea, island, *Indonesia* **189** M13
Tanahmasa, island, *Indonesia* **188** J5
Tanahmerah, *Indonesia* **189** M21
Tanami, *N. Terr., Austral.* **211** S7
Tanami, Mount, *Austral.* **210** E7
Tanami Desert, *N. Terr., Austral.* **211** R8
Tanana, river, *Alas., U.S.* **111** G16
Tanana, *Alas., U.S.* **111** F16
Tanapag, *N. Mariana Is., U.S.* **216** B5
Tanaunella, *It.* **150** M5
Tanavuso Point, *Fiji Is.* **218** H6
Tancheng, *China* **182** H8
Tanch'ŏn, *N. Korea* **182** C14
Tăndărei, *Rom.* **153** F17
Tandil, *Arg.* **133** N12
Tandil, Sierra del, *S. Amer.* **126** M6
Tandlianwala, *Pak.* **177** Q11
Tando Adam, *Pak.* **177** V7
Tando Allahyar, *Pak.* **177** V7
Tando Bago, *Pak.* **177** W7
Tando Muhammad Khan, *Pak.* **177** W7
Tandur, *India* **178** L7
Tanega Shima, *Japan* **185** U4
Tanen Range, *Myanmar, Thai.* **186** J8
Tanezrouft, region, *Alg., Mali* **196** E9
Ţanf, Jabal aţ, *Syr.* **170** J11
Tanga, *Tanzania* **199** L15
Tangail, *Bangladesh* **178** H12
Tanga Islands, *P.N.G.* **213** C22
Tanga Langua, *Grenada* **121** J23
Tanganyika, Lake, *Af.* **194** L9
Tange Promontory, *Antarctica* **227** B19
Tanger (Tangier), *Mor.* **196** A8
Tanggu, *China* **182** D7
Tanggula Range, *China* **166** H9
Tanggula Shan, *China* **180** K7
Tanghe, *China* **182** J4
Tangi, *India* **178** L10
Tangier *see* Tanger, *Mor.* **196** A8
Tango, *Japan* **185** P8
Tangorin, *Qnsld., Austral.* **211** T12
Tangra Yumco, lake, *China* **180** K6
Tangse, *Indonesia* **188** G4
Tangshan, *China* **182** D8
Tanguisson Point, *Guam, U.S.* **216** B11
Tanimbar, Kepulauan, *Indonesia* **189** M17
Tanimbar Islands, *Indonesia* **166** L15
Tanimbili, *Solomon Is.* **217** Q23
Tanjore *see* Thanjavur, *India* **179** R6
Tanjungbalai, *Indonesia* **188** H5
Tanjungbatu, *Indonesia* **188** H12
Tanjungkarang-Telubketung, *Indonesia* **188** L7
Tanjungpandan, *Indonesia* **188** K8
Tanjungpinang, *Indonesia* **188** J7
Tanjungredep, *Indonesia* **188** H12
Tank, *Pak.* **177** P9
Ta-n-Kena, *Alg.* **196** D12
Tankovo, *Russ.* **159** J13
Tanna, island, *Vanuatu* **218** H4
Tännäs, *Sw.* **140** J12
Tannu Ola, Khrebet, *Russ.* **159** M13
Tannur, ruin, *Jordan* **171** P6
Tanobato, *Indonesia* **188** J5
Tanot, *India* **178** F2
Tânout, *Niger* **196** H12
Tanowrah, *Afghan.* **177** N2
Ţanţa, *Egypt* **197** C18
Tan-Tan, *Mor.* **196** C7
Tanumbirini, *N. Terr., Austral.* **211** Q9
Tanzania, *Af.* **195** L22
Tao, river, *China* **180** J11
Tao, Ko, *Thai.* **187** Q8
Tao'er, river, *China* **181** D16
Taojiang, *China* **182** M3
Taole (Mataigou), *China* **182** D1
Taonan, *China* **181** D16
Taongi Atoll, *Marshall Is.* **216** E4
Taos, *N. Mex., U.S.* **107** Q13
Taoudenni (Smeïda), *Mali* **196** E8
Taouz, *Mor.* **196** C9
Taoyuan, *China* **182** M3
Taoyuan, *Taiwan, China* **183** Q10
Tapa, *Est.* **141** K16
Tapachula, *Mex.* **115** L15
Tapajós, river, *Braz.* **130** E10
Tapak, island, *F.S.M.* **217** F14
Tapan, *Indonesia* **188** K6
Tapana, island, *Tonga* **218** M11
Tapanahoni, river, *Suriname* **129** F16
Tapauá, river, *Braz.* **130** E7
Tapawera, *N.Z.* **213** M17
Tapeta, *Liberia* **200** H7
Taphan Hin, *Thai.* **186** L9
Tapi, river, *India* **178** K4
Tapiche, river, *Peru* **130** F4
Tapini, *P.N.G.* **213** D19
Tapirapecó, Sierra, *Venez.* **128** G11
Tapiwa, *Banaba, Kiribati* **217** D20

Taplejung, Nepal 178 F11
Tapora, Passe, Fr. Polynesia, Fr. 219 P17
Tappahannock, Va., U.S. 96 E13
Tapu, Motu, Fr. Polynesia, Fr. 219 K13
Tapuaenuku, peak, N.Z. 213 N18
Tapuaetai, island, Cook Is., N.Z. 218 Q12
Tapuamu, Fr. Polynesia, Fr. 219 A23
Tapueraha, Passe de, Fr. Polynesia, Fr. 219 Q17
Tapul Group, Philippines 189 G13
Tapunui, island, Cook Is., N.Z. 219 A17
Tapurucuará, Braz. 130 C7
Taputapu, Cape, Amer. Samoa, U.S. 218 M6
Taputimu, Amer. Samoa, U.S. 218 N7
Ţaqah, Oman 173 P14
Taquari, river, Braz. 130 K10
Tar, river, N.C., U.S. 96 H12
Tara, Qnsld., Austral. 211 V14
Tara, Russ. 158 J10
Tara, river, Serb. & Mont. 152 H9
Tara, Hill of, Ire. 143 R6
Ţarābulus (Tripoli), Lib. 197 B13
Tarakan, island, Indonesia 188 H12
Tarakan, Indonesia 188 H12
Tarakite-iti, island, Cook Is., N.Z. 219 C14
Taranaki, Mount (Mt. Egmont), N.Z. 213 L18
Tarancón, Sp. 144 G11
Taransay, island, Scot., U.K. 142 H6
Taranto, It. 151 N14
Taranto, Golfo di, It. 151 N14
Tarapacá, Col. 128 K8
Tarapaina, Solomon Is. 217 N20
Tarapoto, Peru 130 F3
Taraqu, ruin, Afghan. 177 R1
Tarara, P.N.G. 217 K14
Tarare, Fr. 147 U12
Tarasa Dwip, island, India 179 S15
Tarascon, Fr. 147 Y9
Tarata, Peru 130 K6
Taratai, island, Kiribati 217 F17
Taratai, Kiribati 217 F17
Tarauacá, river, Braz. 130 F5
Tarauacá, Braz. 130 F5
Taravai, island, Fr. Polynesia, Fr. 219 Q20
Taravai, Fr. Polynesia, Fr. 219 Q20
Taravao, Fr. Polynesia, Fr. 219 P17
Taravao, Baie de, Fr. Polynesia, Fr. 219 P17
Taravo, river, Fr. 150 K4
Tarawa (Bairiki), Kiribati 217 G17
Tarawera, Mount, N.Z. 213 K19
Taraz, Kaz. 175 J14
Tarazit Massif, Niger 194 F5
Tarazona, Sp. 145 D13
Tarazona de la Mancha, Sp. 145 H13
Tarbagannakh, Gora, Russ. 159 G19
Tarbaghatay Zhotasy, Kaz. 175 F18
Tarbat Ness, Scot., U.K. 142 J9
Tarbert, Scot., U.K. 142 J6
Tarbert, Scot., U.K. 142 M8
Tarbes, Fr. 147 Y7
Tarboro, N.C., U.S. 96 H13
Tarbrax, Qnsld., Austral. 211 S12
Tarcoola, S. Aust., Austral. 211 W9
Tardun, W. Aust., Austral. 211 W2
Taree, N.S.W., Austral. 211 X15
Ţarfā, Ra's aţ, Saudi Arabia 172 N8
Tarfaya, Mor. 196 C6
Tarfside, Scot., U.K. 142 K10
Targhee Pass, Idaho, Mont., U.S. 106 F8
Târgu Mureş, Rom. 153 C14
Tari, P.N.G. 213 D18
Ţarīf, U.A.E. 173 K14
Tarifa, Sp. 144 N8
Tarifa, Punta de, Sp. 144 N8
Tarija, Bol. 130 L7
Tarikere, India 179 P5
Tariku-Taritatu Plain, Indonesia 189 K20
Tarim, river, China 180 F6
Tarim Basin, China 166 G8
Tarim Pendi, China 180 F5
Tarin Kowt, Afghan. 177 P5
Taritatu, river, Indonesia 213 C17
Tarkastad, S. Af. 202 L10
Tarkhankut, Mys, Ukr. 157 S7
Tarkio, Mo., U.S. 105 Q9
Tarko Sale, Russ. 158 G12
Tarkwa, Ghana 200 H10
Tarlac, Philippines 189 C13
Tarma, Peru 130 H4
Tarn, river, Fr. 147 X9
Tärnaby, Sw. 140 F12
Tarnak, river, Afghan. 177 Q5
Tarnobrzeg, Pol. 149 G17
Tarnogskiy Gorodok, Russ. 156 E12
Tarnów, Pol. 149 G16
Ţārom, Iran 173 G15
Taroom, Qnsld., Austral. 211 U14
Tarpon Springs, Fla., U.S. 97 U7
Tarpum Bay, Bahamas 120 E6
Tarpum Bay, Bahamas 120 F6
Tarquinia, It. 150 K7
Tarrabool Lake, Austral. 210 D9
Tarrafal, Cape Verde 205 B14
Tarrafal, Cape Verde 205 B15
Tarrafal, Cape Verde 205 D16
Tarragona, Sp. 145 E16
Tarraleah, Tas., Austral. 211 Z16
Tarras, N.Z. 213 Q16
Tarsia, It. 151 P13
Tarsus, Turk. 168 J10
Tarta, Turkm. 174 K6
Tartagal, Arg. 132 D10
Tartas, Fr. 147 X6
Tartu, Est. 141 K17
Ţarţūs (Tortosa), Syr. 170 G7
Taruia Passage, Cook Is., N.Z. 219 B17
Tarutao, Ko, Thai. 187 S8
Tarutung, Indonesia 188 H5
Tarvisio, It. 150 C9
Tarxien, Malta 161 K23
Tasāwah, Lib. 197 E13
Tasböget, Kaz. 174 H11
Tascosa, Tex., U.S. 102 G4
Tasek Dampar, lake, Malaysia 187 U10
Taseyevo, Russ. 159 K14
Tashanta, Russ. 158 M12
Tash Gozar, Afghan. 176 K6
Tashk, Daryācheh-ye, Iran 173 F14
Tashkent see Toshkent, Uzb. 175 K13
Tash-Kömür, Kyrg. 176 F10
Tasiilaq, Greenland, Den. 81 C22
Tasikmalaya, Indonesia 188 M9
Tasiusaq, Greenland, Den. 81 C20
Taskan, Russ. 159 F20
Taskesken, Kaz. 175 F18
Taşköprü, Turk. 168 C9
Tasman, N.Z. 213 M18
Tasman Bay, N.Z. 213 M18
Tasman Fracture Zone, Antarctic Oc. 245 N14
Tasmania, island, Austral. 210 M16
Tasmania, Austral. 211 Z15
Tasman Peninsula, Austral. 210 M16
Tasman Plain, Pac. Oc. 238 P7
Tasman Sea, Pac. Oc. 238 P7
Tăşnad, Rom. 152 B12
Taşova, Turk. 168 D11
Tassialouc, Lac, Que., Can. 83 K18
Tas Tumus, Russ. 159 G17
Tasure, Solomon Is. 217 L15
Tataacho Point, N. Mariana Is., U.S. 216 D7
Tatabánya, Hung. 149 L14
Tatafa, island, Tonga 218 P7
Tatakoto, island, Fr. Polynesia, Fr. 219 E21
Tatamba, Solomon Is. 217 M18
Tatarbunary, Ukr. 157 S5
Tatarsk, Russ. 158 K11
Tatarskiy Proliv, Russ. 159 J21
Tatar Strait, Russ. 166 D13
Tate, Ga., U.S. 96 K5
Tateyama, Japan 185 Q12
Tathlina Lake, N.W.T., Can. 82 H10
Tathlīth, Saudi Arabia 172 M9
Tatkon, Myanmar 186 H6
Tatnam, Cape, Man., Can. 83 L15
Tatry, range, Pol., Slovakia 149 J15
Tattershall, Eng., U.K. 143 S14
Tatuí, Braz. 131 M13
Tatum, N. Mex., U.S. 107 U15
Tatvan, Turk. 169 G16
Tau, island, Amer. Samoa, U.S. 218 P3
Tau, Amer. Samoa, U.S. 218 P3
Tau, island, Tonga 218 H12
Tauá, Braz. 131 F16
Tauak Passage, F.S.M. 217 F13
Tauanap, Mochun, F.S.M. 217 B14
Taubaté, Braz. 131 M14
Tauenai Channel, F.S.M. 217 G13
Tauere, island, Fr. Polynesia, Fr. 219 E20
Taugarau, island, Fr. Polynesia, Fr. 219 K18
Tauhunu, island, Cook Is., N.Z. 219 B13
Tauhunu, Cook Is., N.Z. 219 B13
Taula, island, Tonga 218 M11
Taulaga, Amer. Samoa, U.S. 218 R3
Taumako, island, Solomon Is. 217 N24
Taumarunui, N.Z. 213 L19
Taumatawhakatangihangakoauauotamateapokaiwhenuakitanatahu, peak, N.Z. 213 M19
Taum Sauk Mountain, Mo., U.S. 105 U15
Taunga, island, Tonga 218 M11
Taunggok, Myanmar 186 J5
Taunggyi, Myanmar 186 H6
Taungoo, Myanmar 186 J6
Taungup Pass, Myanmar 186 J5
Taunsa, Pak. 177 R9
Taunton, Eng., U.K. 143 W10
Taunton, Mass., U.S. 95 L15
Taupo, N.Z. 213 K19
Taupo, Lake, N.Z. 213 L19
Taupo Tablemount, Pac. Oc. 238 N7
Tauragė, Lith. 141 N16
Tauranga, N.Z. 213 K19
Taurere, Pointe, Fr. Polynesia, Fr. 219 L14
Taurus see Toros Dağları, range, Turk. 168 J8
Taūshyq, Kaz. 174 G5
Tauste, Sp. 145 D13
Tautama, island, Pitcairn I., U.K. 219 Q23
Tautau, island, Fr. Polynesia, Fr. 219 A23
Tautira, Fr. Polynesia, Fr. 219 P17
Tautu, Cook Is., N.Z. 218 Q11
Tautua, island, Cook Is., N.Z. 219 B18
Tauu Islands, P.N.G. 217 H16
Tavaerua, island, Cook Is., N.Z. 218 Q12
Tavai, Wallis & Futuna, Fr. 218 E11
Tavan Bogd Uul see Youyi Feng, peak, China, Mongolia 180 C8
Tavannes, Switz. 150 A2
Tavas, Turk. 168 G4
Tavda, Russ. 158 H9
Taverna, It. 151 Q14
Taverner Bay, Nunavut, Can. 83 G18
Tavernes, Fr. 147 X14
Tavernes de la Valldigna, Sp. 145 H15
Tavernier, Fla., U.S. 97 Y10
Taveuni, island, Fiji Is. 218 H8
Tavropoú, Límni, Gr. 154 F9
Tavşanlı, Turk. 168 E5
Tavua, Fiji Is. 218 H6
Tavu-Na-Sici, island, Fiji Is. 218 J9
Tawai, India 178 F16
Tawake, Fiji Is. 218 G8
Tawakoni, Lake, Tex., U.S. 102 L13
Tawang, India 178 F13
Tawas City, Mich., U.S. 98 J12
Tawau, Malaysia 188 G12
Tawi Tawi, island, Philippines 189 G13
Tawu, Taiwan, China 183 S9
Taxco, Mex. 114 J11
Taxkorgan, China 180 G4
Tay, Firth of, Scot., U.K. 142 L11
Tay, Loch, Scot., U.K. 142 L9
Tayan, Indonesia 188 J9
Tayandu, Kepulauan, Indonesia 189 L18
Taygonos, Poluostrov, Russ. 159 E21
Taylakova, Russ. 158 J11
Taylor, Mich., U.S. 98 M12
Taylor, Tex., U.S. 103 P11
Taylor, Mount, N. Mex., U.S. 107 S11
Taylor Glacier, Antarctica 227 N14
Taylor Highway, Alas., U.S. 111 G19
Taylors, S.C., U.S. 96 J7
Taylorsville, Miss., U.S. 100 M12
Taylorville, Ill., U.S. 99 S5
Taymā', Saudi Arabia 172 G6
Taymyr, Lake, Russ. 166 C9
Taymyr, Ozero, Russ. 159 E14
Taymyr, Poluostrov, Russ. 159 E14
Taymyr Peninsula, Russ. 166 C9
Tay Ninh, Vietnam 187 P12
Taypaq, Kaz. 174 E6
Tayshet, Russ. 159 K14
Taytay, Philippines 189 E13
Ţayyebāt, Iran 173 C17
Tayynsha (Krasnoarmeysk), Kaz. 175 B13
Taz, river, Russ. 158 G12
Taza, Mor. 196 B9
Tazawa Ko, Japan 184 K13
Tazawako, Japan 184 K13
Tazewell, Va., U.S. 96 F8
Tāzirbū, Lib. 197 E16
Tazovskiy, Russ. 158 G12
Tazovskiy Poluostrov, Russ. 158 F12
Tba P'arvani, lake, Rep. of Georgia 169 C18
T'bilisi (Tiflis), Rep. of Georgia 169 C18
Tchabal Gangdaba, range, Cameroon 201 G16
Tchad, Lac see Chad, Lake, Af. 197 J13
Tchibanga, Gabon 201 M16
Tchin-Tabaradēne, Niger 196 H11
Tczew, Pol. 149 B14
Teaehoa, Pointe, Fr. Polynesia, Fr. 219 N20
Te Afualiku, island, Tuvalu 217 J23
Teague, Tex., U.S. 103 N12
Teahupoo, Fr. Polynesia, Fr. 219 Q17
Teaiti Point, Cook Is., N.Z. 218 Q9
Teakava, island, Fr. Polynesia, Fr. 219 Q21
Te Anau, N.Z. 213 Q15
Te Anau, Lake, N.Z. 213 Q15
Teaoraereke, Kiribati 217 G17
Tearinibai, Kiribati 217 F17
Tea Tree, N. Terr., Austral. 211 T8
Teava Moa, Passe, Fr. Polynesia, Fr. 219 B24
Teavanui, Passe, Fr. Polynesia, Fr. 219 K13
Teavapiti, Passe, Fr. Polynesia, Fr. 219 B23
Teavaraa, Passe de, Fr. Polynesia, Fr. 219 P16
Teavaro, Fr. Polynesia, Fr. 219 N14
Teberda, Russ. 157 U12
Tébessa, Alg. 196 B12
Tebingtinggi, Indonesia 188 H5
Techirghiol, Rom. 153 G18
Techla, W. Sahara, Mor. 196 E5
Technití Límni Kremastón, Gr. 154 G8
Tecka, Arg. 133 R7
Tecomán, Mex. 114 J9
Tecpan, Mex. 114 K11
Tecuala, Mex. 114 G9
Tecuci, Rom. 153 D16
Tecumseh, Mich., U.S. 98 N11
Tecumseh, Nebr., U.S. 105 R9
Tecumseh, Okla., U.S. 102 G11
Teec Nos Pos, Ariz., U.S. 107 Q9
Teel, Mongolia 180 D11
Tefala, island, Tuvalu 217 L22
Tefarerii, Fr. Polynesia, Fr. 219 H14
Tefé, river, Braz. 130 E7
Tefé, Braz. 130 D7
Tefenni, Turk. 168 H5
Tegal, Indonesia 188 M9
Teglio, San Marino 161 L14
Tégua, island, Vanuatu 218 A1
Tegucigalpa, Hond. 115 L17
Teguise, Canary Is. 204 P7
Tehachapi, Calif., U.S. 109 V8
Tehachapi Mountains, Calif., U.S. 109 W8
Tehachapi Pass, Calif., U.S. 109 V8
Te Hapua, N.Z. 213 G17
Tehek Lake, Nunavut, Can. 83 H14
Tehoohaivei, Cap, Fr. Polynesia, Fr. 219 M21
Tehrān, Iran 173 C13
Tehuacán, Mex. 114 J12
Tehuantepec, Mex. 115 K13
Tehuantepec, Golfo de, Mex. 115 L14
Tehuantepec, Gulf of see Tehuantepec, Golfo de, N. Amer. 80 P6
Tehuantepec, Isthmus of see Tehuantepec, Istmo de, N. Amer. 80 P6
Tehuantepec, Istmo de, Mex. 115 K14
Tehuata (Rekareka), island, Fr. Polynesia, Fr. 219 E19
Teide, Pico de, Canary Is. 204 Q4
Teignmouth, Eng., U.K. 143 X10
Teiko, Motu, Fr. Polynesia, Fr. 219 R20
Tejen, Turkm. 174 M9
Tejenstroy, Turkm. 174 N9
Tejo (Tagus), river, Port. 144 H5
Tekamah, Nebr., U.S. 105 P9
Te Karaka, N.Z. 213 K20
Tekax, Mex. 115 H16
Tekeli, Kaz. 175 G17
Tekirdağ, Turk. 168 C3
Tekirova, Turk. 168 J6
Tekkali, India 178 L9
Tekman, Turk. 169 E16
Teknaf, Bangladesh 178 K14
Tekoa, Wash., U.S. 108 C9
Tekokota, island, Fr. Polynesia, Fr. 219 E19
Tekopua, island, Cook Is., N.Z. 218 Q12
Te Koutu Point, Cook Is., N.Z. 218 Q11
T'elavi, Rep. of Georgia 169 B19
Tel Aviv-Yafo, Israel 170 M5
Telde, Canary Is. 204 R6
Telebekelel Ngerael, Palau 216 K11
Telefomin, P.N.G. 213 C17
Telegraph Creek, B.C., Can. 82 H8
Telekitonga, island, Tonga 218 R7
Telekivavau, island, Tonga 218 Q7
Telele, island, Tuvalu 217 L23
Telén, Arg. 132 M9
Telescope Peak, Calif., U.S. 109 U9
Telescope Point, Grenada 121 K23
Teles Pires (São Manuel), river, Braz. 130 F10
Teljo, Jebel, Sudan 194 G8
Tell Atlas, Alg., Tun. 194 C4
Tell City, Ind., U.S. 99 U8
Teller, Alas., U.S. 110 F11
Tellicherry, India 179 Q4
Telloh see Lagash, ruin, Iraq 172 E10
Tell Tayinat, ruin, Turk. 168 J11
Telluride, Colo., U.S. 107 P11
Telsen, Arg. 133 R9
Telšiai, Lith. 141 N16
Telukbutun, Indonesia 188 G9
Telukdalem, Indonesia 188 J4
Teluk Intan, Malaysia 187 T9
Tema, Ghana 200 H11
Te Manga, peak, Cook Is., N.Z. 218 Q9
Tematagi, island, Fr. Polynesia, Fr. 219 H20
Tembagapura, Indonesia 189 L20
Tembenchi, Russ. 159 H14
Témbi, range, Gr. 154 E10
Temerin, Serb. & Mont. 152 E9
Temerloh, Malaysia 187 U10
Teminabuan, Indonesia 189 J18
Teminikov, Russ. 156 K12
Temirtaū, Kaz. 175 D14
Temoe (Timoe), island, Fr. Polynesia, Fr. 219 H23
Temora, N.S.W., Austral. 211 Y13
Tempe, Ariz., U.S. 107 U7
Tempio, It. 150 M4
Temple, Okla., U.S. 102 J10
Temple, Tex., U.S. 103 P11
Temple Bay, Austral. 210 B12
Temryuk, Russ. 157 S9
Temryukskiy Zaliv, Russ. 157 S9
Temse, Belg. 146 K12
Temuco, Chile 133 P6
Temuka, N.Z. 213 P17
Tena, Ecua. 128 J3
Tenali, India 179 N7
Tenao, Monaco 161 B22
Tenararo, island, Fr. Polynesia, Fr. 219 G22
Ténaro, Akrotírio (Taenarum), Gr. 154 N10
Tenarunga, island, Fr. Polynesia, Fr. 219 G22
Tenasserim, region, Myanmar 186 M7
Tenasserim, Myanmar 187 N8
Tende, Fr. 147 W16
Ten Degree Channel, India 179 R14
Tendō, Japan 184 L13
Tendürek Dağı, Turk. 169 F18
Ténéré, region, Niger 196 F12
Tenerife, island, Canary Is. 204 Q5
Tengako, island, Tuvalu 217 J24
Tengasu, island, Tuvalu 217 L22
Tengchong, China 180 N10
Te Nggano, Solomon Is. 217 R19
Tengiz, oil field, Kaz. 174 G7
Tengiz, Lake, Kaz. 166 E7
Tengiz Köli, Kaz. 175 D13
Tengxian, China 182 G7
Tengxian, China 183 R2
Tenino, Wash., U.S. 108 D3
Tenjo, Mount, Guam, U.S. 216 C10
Tenkasi, India 179 S5
Tenke, Dem. Rep. of the Congo 198 N11
Tenkiller Ferry Lake, Okla., U.S. 102 F14
Tenkodogo, Burkina Faso 200 E11

Tennant Creek, N. Terr., Austral. 211 S9
Tennessee, river, Tenn., U.S. 101 E14
Tennessee, U.S. 101 F13
Tennessee Pass, Colo., U.S. 106 M12
Tennille, Ga., U.S. 96 M7
Tenoka, island, Fr. Polynesia, Fr. 219 Q20
Ténos, Pointe, Martinique, Fr. 121 E22
Tenos see Tínos, island, Gr. 155 K15
Tenosique, Mex. 115 K15
Tensaw, river, Ala., U.S. 101 N14
Ten Sleep, Wyo., U.S. 106 G11
Ten Thousand Islands, Fla., U.S. 97 X9
Teófilo Otoni, Braz. 131 K15
Teoho Ote Papa, Pointe, Fr. Polynesia, Fr. 219 N23
Teohotepapa, Pointe, Fr. Polynesia, Fr. 219 M21
Teora, It. 150 M12
Tepa, Wallis & Futuna, Fr. 218 B11
Tepaeture, Pointe, Fr. Polynesia, Fr. 219 Q20
Tepako, Pointe, Wallis & Futuna, Fr. 218 B12
Tepa Point, Niue, N.Z. 219 B20
Tepati, Fr. Polynesia, Fr. 219 Q17
Tepé, Eq. Guinea 204 L8
Tepe, peak, Serb. & Mont. 152 J11
Tepe Musyan, ruin, Iran 172 E11
Tepic, Mex. 114 G9
Tepu, Fr. Polynesia, Fr. 219 K20
Te Puka, island, Cook Is., N.Z. 219 B13
Tepuka, island, Tuvalu 217 J22
Tepuka, Te Ava, Tuvalu 217 J22
Tepuu, Pointe, Fr. Polynesia, Fr. 219 K20
Téra, Niger 196 H9
Terae, island, Cook Is., N.Z. 219 B17
Teraina (Washington Island), island, Kiribati 214 F12
Teramo, It. 150 J10
Teratak, Indonesia 188 J9
Tercan, Turk. 169 E15
Terceira, island, Azores 144 P4
Tereai, island, Fr. Polynesia, Fr. 219 K15
Terek, river, Russ. 138 G13
Terekhovka, Belarus 156 M6
Terekli Mekteb, Russ. 157 T14
Terekty, Kaz. 175 E19
Terenos, Braz. 130 L11
Teresina, Braz. 131 E15
Terhazza, ruin, Mali 196 E8
Terihi, island, Fr. Polynesia, Fr. 219 N21
Termas de Río Hondo, Arg. 132 G9
Terme, Turk. 168 D12
Termini Imerese, It. 151 S10
Termini Imerese, Golfo di, It. 151 S10
Términos, Laguna de, Mex. 115 J15
Términos Lagoon see Términos, Laguna de, N. Amer. 80 P6
Termita, Russ. 157 S14
Termiz, Uzb. 174 M12
Termoli, It. 150 K11
Ternate, Indonesia 189 J16
Terneuzen, Neth. 146 K11
Terni, It. 150 J8
Ternitz, Aust. 148 L12
Ternopil', Ukr. 157 P3
Terrace, B.C., Can. 82 K8
Terracina, It. 150 L9
Terralba, It. 151 P3
Terrassa, Sp. 145 D17
Terrebonne Bay, La., U.S. 100 R10
Terre-de-Bas, island, Guadeloupe, Fr. 121 G14
Terre-de-Bas, Guadeloupe, Fr. 121 G14
Terre-de-Haut, island, Guadeloupe, Fr. 121 G14
Terre-de-Haut, Guadeloupe, Fr. 121 G14
Terre Haute, Ind., U.S. 99 S7
Terreiro Velho, Sao Tome and Principe 205 B21
Terrell, Tex., U.S. 102 L12
Terre Rouge, Mauritius 205 F20
Terry, Mont., U.S. 106 D12
Tersakan Gölü, Turk. 168 G8
Terschelling, island, Neth. 146 G13
Tertenia, It. 151 P4
Teru, Pak. 176 L10
Teruel, Sp. 145 F14
Teshekpuk Lake, Alas., U.S. 111 C15
Teshikaga, Japan 184 F15
Teshio, river, Japan 184 E13
Teshio, Japan 184 E13
Teshio Sanchi, Japan 184 E14
Tesiyn, river, Mongolia 180 C10
Teslić, Bosn. & Herzg. 152 F7
Teslin, Yukon, Can. 82 G8
Tesovo Netyl'skiy, Russ. 156 G6
Tessalit, Mali 196 F10
Tessaoua, Niger 196 H12
Tessenei, Eritrea 199 E14
Testa del Gargano, It. 150 K13
Tetas, Punta, Chile 132 E6
Te Tautua, Cook Is., N.Z. 219 B18
Tete, Mozambique 202 F12
Te Teko, N.Z. 213 K20
Tetepare, island, Solomon Is. 217 M16
Tetere, Russ. 159 J15
Teteven, Bulg. 153 H14
Tetford, Eng., U.K. 143 S14
Tetiaroa, island, Fr. Polynesia, Fr. 219 E16
Tetlin, Alas., U.S. 111 H19
Teton, river, Mont., U.S. 106 C8
Teton Range, Wyo., U.S. 106 G8
Tétouan, Mor. 196 A9
Tetovo, Maced. 152 K10
Tetufera, Mont, Fr. Polynesia, Fr. 219 P16
Tetutu, Pointe, Fr. Polynesia, Fr. 219 N23
Tetyushi, Russ. 156 J14
Teuaua (Hat), island, Fr. Polynesia, Fr. 219 N23
Teuco, river, Arg. 132 F12
Teulada, It. 151 Q3
Teulada, Capo, It. 151 Q3
Teuri Tō, Japan 184 E13
Teutonic College, Vatican City 161 Q16
Tevahavaha, island, Cook Is., N.Z. 219 C14
Tevai, island, Solomon Is. 217 R24
Tevaro, island, Fr. Polynesia, Fr. 219 K17
Teveiroa, island, Fr. Polynesia, Fr. 219 K13
Tevere (Tiber), river, It. 150 J8
Teverya (Tiberias), Israel 170 K6
Tewantin, Qnsld., Austral. 211 V15
Texarkana, Ark., U.S. 100 J6
Texarkana, Tex., U.S. 102 K15
Texas, U.S. 103 N4
Texas City, Tex., U.S. 103 R14
Texas Point, Tex., U.S. 103 Q16
Texel, island, Neth. 146 G12
Texhoma, Okla., U.S. 102 E5
Texico, N. Mex., U.S. 107 S15
Texline, Tex., U.S. 102 E3
Texoma, Lake, Okla., U.S. 102 J12
Texon, Tex., U.S. 103 N5
Teykovo, Russ. 156 H10
Teylan, Afghan. 176 L4
Teywarah, Afghan. 177 N4
Tezpur, India 178 G14
Tfaritiy, W. Sahara, Mor. 196 D7
Thabana Ntlenyana, peak, Lesotho 202 K11
Thabaung, Myanmar 186 K5
Thabazimbi, S. Af. 202 J10
Thaga Pass, China, India 178 D7
Thagyettaw, Myanmar 186 M7
Thai Binh, Vietnam 186 H12
Thai Hoa, Vietnam 186 J12
Thailand, Asia 167 X10
Thailand, Gulf of, Asia 166 K10
Thai Nguyen, Vietnam 186 G12
Thal, Pak. 177 N9
Thalabarivat, Cambodia 186 M12
Thal Desert, Pak. 177 Q10
Thale Luang, lake, Thai. 187 R8
Thamarīt, Oman 173 N14
Thames, River, Eng., U.K. 143 V15
Thamūd, Yemen 172 N12
Thana, Pak. 177 S3
Thandaung, Myanmar 186 J6
Thane, India 178 L3
Thanet, cape, Eng., U.K. 143 V16
Thangool, Qnsld., Austral. 211 U15
Thanh Hoa, Vietnam 186 J12
Thanh Tri, Vietnam 187 Q12
Thanjavur (Tanjore), India 179 R6
Thanlwin (Salween), river, Myanmar 186 G7
Tharabwin, Myanmar 187 N8
Thar Desert see Great Indian Desert, India, Pak. 177 T9
Thargomindah, Qnsld., Austral. 211 V12
Tharros, ruin, It. 151 N3
Tharthār Lake, Iraq 172 D9
Tha Sala, Thai. 187 Q8
Thássos, island, Gr. 155 C14
Thássos (Limín), Gr. 155 C14
Thatch Cay, Virgin Islands, U.S. 120 M10
Thaton, Myanmar 186 K7
Thatta, Pak. 177 W7
Thau, Bassin de, Fr. 147 X11
Thaungdut, Myanmar 186 F5
Thayawthadanngyi Kyun, Myanmar 187 N7
Thayer, Mo., U.S. 105 V14
Thayet, Myanmar 186 J5
The Alley, Jam. 120 K8
The Barony, Scot., U.K. 142 F10
The Baths, Virgin Islands, U.K. 120 R8
Thebes, ruin, Egypt 197 E19
Thebes see Thíva, Gr. 154 H11
The Bight, Bahamas 120 B5
The Bluff, Bahamas 120 D5
The Bottom, Neth. Antilles, Neth. 119 F15
The Brothers, islands, Bahamas 117 H13
The Brothers see Al Ikhwān, islands, Yemen 173 R14
The Caves, Qnsld., Austral. 211 T15
The Cheviot, peak, Eng., U.K. 143 N11
The Cockpit Country, Jam. 120 H7
The Cow, island, Ire. 143 V2
The Crane, Barbados 121 L20
The Dalles, Oreg., U.S. 108 F5
The Deeps, bay, Scot., U.K. 142 D12
Thedford, Nebr., U.S. 105 N4
Theebine, Qnsld., Austral. 211 V15
The Everglades, wetland, Fla., U.S. 97 X9
The Ferry Settlement, Bahamas 120 F9
The Galleries, Gibraltar, U.K. 161 N23
The Hague see 's Gravenhage, Neth. 146 J12
The Heads, cape, Oreg., U.S. 108 K1
The Isles Lagoon, Kiribati 217 B23
The Little Minch, strait, Scot., U.K. 142 J6
Thelon, river, N.W.T., Can. 83 H13
The Lynd, Qnsld., Austral. 211 R13
The Marls, islands, Bahamas 120 B6
The Minch, strait, Scot., U.K. 142 H7
The Moors, plateau, Scot., U.K. 143 P8
The Narrows, strait, Bermuda, U.K. 120 A3
The Narrows, strait, Virgin Islands, U.K., U.S. 120 M11
The Narrows, strait, Bahamas 120 B12
The Narrows, strait, St. Kitts & Nevis 121 B18
The Naze, cape, Eng., U.K. 143 U15
The North Sound, Scot., U.K. 142 F10
Theodore, Qnsld., Austral. 211 U14
Theodore Roosevelt, river, Braz. 130 F9
Theodore Roosevelt Lake, Ariz., U.S. 107 T8
Theodore Roosevelt National Park (Elkhorn Ranch Site), N. Dak., U.S. 104 F2
Theodore Roosevelt National Park (North Unit), N. Dak., U.S. 104 F2
Theodore Roosevelt National Park (South Unit), N. Dak., U.S. 104 G2
Theológos, Gr. 155 C14
The Ox Mountains see Slieve Gamph, Ire. 143 Q4
The Pas, Man., Can. 83 M13
The Pennines, range, Eng., U.K. 143 Q11
Thera, ruin, Gr. 155 N15
The Remarkables, peak, N.Z. 213 Q15
Thermaïkós Kólpos, Gr. 154 D11
Thérmo, Gr. 154 H9
Thermopolis, Wyo., U.S. 106 G10
Thermopylae, battle, Gr. 154 G10
The Rope, island, Pitcairn I., U.K. 219 Q23
The Rosses, region, Ire. 143 P5
The Salt Ponds, Jam. 120 K11
The Sisters, islands, Grenada 121 H23
The Sisters see Les Soeurs, islands, Seychelles 205 M21
The Sisters, islands, Trinidad & Tobago 121 N18
The Skerries, islands, Wales, U.K. 143 S9
The Slot see New Georgia Sound, bay, Solomon Is. 217 M17
The Smalls, islands, Wales, U.K. 143 V7
The Snares, islands, N.Z. 214 Q7
The Solent, strait, Eng., U.K. 143 X12
The Sound, Bahamas 120 A8
Thessalon, Ont., Can. 83 Q17
Thessaloníki (Salonica), Gr. 154 C11
Thessaly, region, Gr. 154 F10
The Steppes, Kaz. 174 E8
Thetford, Eng., U.K. 143 T15
The Triangle, region, Myanmar 186 D7
The Twins, S. Aust., Austral. 211 W9
The Valley, Anguilla, U.K. 120 R11
The Wash, bay, Eng., U.K. 143 S14
The Weald, region, Eng., U.K. 143 W14
The Wolds, region, Eng., U.K. 143 R13
Thíamis, river, Gr. 154 E7
Thiaucourt, Fr. 147 P13
Thibodaux, La., U.S. 100 Q10
Thief River Falls, Minn., U.S. 104 E9
Thielsen, Mount, Oreg., U.S. 108 J4
Thiene, It. 150 D7
Thiers, Fr. 147 U11
Thiès, Senegal 196 H4
Thika, Kenya 199 K14
Thímena, island, Gr. 155 K17
Thimphu, Bhutan 178 F12
Thingeyri, Ice. 140 E2
Thinkèo, Laos 186 J10
Thio, New Caledonia, Fr. 218 D8
Thíra, Gr. 155 N15
Thíra (Santoríni), island, Gr. 155 M15
Thirassía, island, Gr. 155 M15
Third Cataract, Sudan 198 C12
Thirsk, Eng., U.K. 143 Q12
Thiruvananthapuram (Trivandrum), India 179 S5
Thisted, Den. 140 N11
Thistilfjördur, bay, Ice. 140 E4
Thitu Island, Spratly Is. 188 D11
Thíva (Thebes), Gr. 154 H11
Thjórsá, river, Ice. 140 F2
Tho Chu, Dao, Vietnam 187 Q10
Thoen, Thai. 186 K8
Thohoyandou, S. Af. 202 H11
Thomas, Okla., U.S. 102 F9
Thomaston, Ga., U.S. 96 M5
Thomaston, Me., U.S. 95 G17
Thomasville, Ala., U.S. 101 M14
Thomasville, Ga., U.S. 97 Q5
Thomasville, N.C., U.S. 96 H10
Thompson, river, Iowa, U.S. 105 Q11
Thompson, Man., Can. 83 L14
Thompson Falls, Mont., U.S. 106 C4
Thompson Springs, Utah, U.S. 107 N9
Thompson Town, Jam. 120 J8
Thomson, river, Austral. 210 F12
Thomson, Ga., U.S. 96 L7
Thongwa, Myanmar 186 K6
Thonon, Fr. 147 T14
Thonze, Myanmar 186 K6
Thoreau, N. Mex., U.S. 107 S10
Thórisvatn, lake, Ice. 140 F3
Thorndale, Tex., U.S. 103 P11
Thorne Bay, Alas., U.S. 111 M23
Thornhill, Scot., U.K. 143 N9
Thornton, Colo., U.S. 106 L13
Thorntonia, Qnsld., Austral. 211 S10
Thorp, Wash., U.S. 108 D5
Thorp, Wis., U.S. 98 H4
Thorpe, Barbados 121 K18
Thórshöfn, Ice. 140 E4
Thouars, Fr. 147 S7
Thrace, region, Gr. 155 B15
Three Forks, Mont., U.S. 106 E7
Three Gorges Dam, China 182 K3
Three Kings Islands, N.Z. 213 G17
Three Lakes, Wis., U.S. 98 G6
Three Pagodas Pass, Myanmar, Thai. 186 L7
Three Points, Cape, Ghana 200 H10
Three Rivers, Mich., U.S. 99 N10
Three Rivers, Tex., U.S. 103 T10
Three Sisters, peak, Oreg., U.S. 108 H4
Three Sisters Islands, Solomon Is. 217 P20
Throckmorton, Tex., U.S. 102 K8
Throssell, Lake, Austral. 210 H5
Thuin, Belg. 146 M12
Thuir, Fr. 147 Z10
Thule Air Base, Greenland, Den. 81 C19
Thun, Switz. 150 B3
Thunder Bay, Mich., U.S. 98 H12
Thunder Bay, Ont., Can. 83 P15
Thuner See, Switz. 150 B3
Thung Song, Thai. 187 R8
Thunkar, Bhutan 178 F13
Thurles, Ire. 143 T5
Thurmont, Md., U.S. 96 C12
Thurso, Scot., U.K. 142 G10
Thurston Island, Antarctica 226 K5
Thusis, Switz. 150 B5
Thylungra, Qnsld., Austral. 211 U12
Tiamahana, Passe, Fr. Polynesia, Fr. 219 B23
Tianjin (Tientsin), China 182 D7
Tianjun, China 180 H10
Tianlin, China 180 P12
Tianmen, China 182 L4
Tianqiaoling, China 182 A14
Tian Shan, Asia 166 G7
Tianshan see Ar Horqin Qi, China 182 A9
Tianshifu, China 182 C11
Tianshui, China 180 J12
Tianshuihai, China 176 L15
Tianzhu, China 183 N1
Tiarei, Fr. Polynesia, Fr. 219 N17
Tiaret, Alg. 196 A10
Tiari, New Caledonia, Fr. 218 C6
Tiaro, Qnsld., Austral. 211 U15
Tiaro Bay, Solomon Is. 217 N18
Ti'avea, Samoa 218 L4
Tibagi, river, Braz. 130 M12
Tibati, Cameroon 201 H16
Tibé, Pic de, Guinea 200 F7
Tiber see Tevere, river, It. 150 K8
Tiber Dam, Mont., U.S. 106 B8
Tiberias see Teverya, Israel 170 K6
Tibesti Mountains, Chad 197 F15
Tibet, region, China 180 K5
Tibet, Plateau of, China 180 J6
Tibiri, Niger 196 J11
Tiboku Falls, Guyana 129 E14
Tibooburra, N.S.W., Austral. 211 W11
Tibrikot, Nepal 178 F9
Tibugá, Golfo de, Col. 128 E3
Tiburón, Isla, Mex. 114 D6
Tîchît, Mauritania 196 G7
Ticonderoga, N.Y., U.S. 94 G12
Ticul, Mex. 115 H16
Tiddim, Myanmar 186 F4
Tidjikdja, Mauritania 196 G6
Tidore, Indonesia 189 J16
Tidra, Île, Mauritania 196 F4
Tiel, Neth. 146 J13
Tiel, Senegal 196 H5
Tieling, China 182 B11
Tielongtan, China 176 L16
Tielongtan, China 180 H5
Tientsin see Tianjin, China 182 D7
Tierra Amarilla, Chile 132 G7
Tierra Amarilla, N. Mex., U.S. 107 Q12
Tierra Blanca Creek, Tex., U.S. 102 H4
Tierra del Fuego, island, S. Amer. 126 R5
Tieyon, S. Aust., Austral. 211 U8
Tiffin, Ohio, U.S. 99 P12
Tiflis see T'bilisi, Rep. of Georgia 169 C18
Tifristós, peak, Gr. 154 G9
Tifton, Ga., U.S. 97 P6
Tiga, Île, New Caledonia, Fr. 218 C10
Tiger Bay, Angola 194 N6
Tigray, region, Eth. 199 E14
Tigre, river, Ecua. 128 K4
Tigre, river, Peru 130 D3
Tigris, river, Asia 166 F4
Tigyaing, Myanmar 186 F6
Tîh, Gebel el, Egypt 171 R3
Tihamah, region, Saudia Arabia, Yemen 166 H3
Tihāmat ash Shām, range, Saudi Arabia, Yemen 172 L7
Tiheró, Gr. 155 B16
Tijuana, Mex. 114 A5
Tikamgarh, India 178 H6
Tikanlik, China 180 F7
Tikapai, island, Cook Is., N.Z. 219 B14
Tikchik Lakes, Alas., U.S. 111 K13
Tikehau, island, Fr. Polynesia, Fr. 219 D17

Tikei, island, *Fr. Polynesia, Fr.* **219** D18
Tikhoretsk, *Russ.* **157** S11
Tikhvin, *Russ.* **156** F8
Tikopia, island, *Solomon Is.* **214** J7
Tikrīt, *Iraq* **172** D9
Tiksi, *Russ.* **159** E16
Tiladummati Atoll, *Maldives* **179** T3
Til Barsip *see* Tall al Aḩmar, *Syr.* **170** D10
Tilbooroo, *Qnsld., Austral.* **211** V12
Tilburg, *Neth.* **146** K12
Til-Châtel, *Fr.* **147** R13
Tilden, *Nebr., U.S.* **105** N7
Tillabéri, *Niger* **196** H10
Tillamook, *Oreg., U.S.* **108** F2
Tillamook Head, *Oreg., U.S.* **108** E2
Tillanchang Dwip, island, *India* **179** S15
Tillia, *Niger* **196** H11
Tilloo Cay, *Bahamas* **116** C12
Tilos, island, *Gr.* **155** M18
Tilpa, *N.S.W., Austral.* **211** W12
Timan Ridge *see* Timanskiy Kryazh, *Russ.* **138** A11
Timanskiy Kryazh, *Russ.* **158** F9
Timaru, *N.Z.* **213** P17
Timashevo, *Russ.* **156** K16
Timashevsk, *Russ.* **157** S10
Timbalier Bay, *La., U.S.* **100** R11
Timbalier Island, *La., U.S.* **100** R10
Timbaúba, *Braz.* **131** F18
Timbédra, *Mauritania* **196** G7
Timber Creek, *N. Terr., Austral.* **211** Q7
Timber Lake, *S. Dak., U.S.* **104** J4
Timbío, *Col.* **128** G4
Timbuktu *see* Tombouctou, *Mali* **196** G8
Timbun Mata, island, *Philippines* **189** G13
Tímfi, Óros (Gamila), *Gr.* **154** E7
Timimoun, *Alg.* **196** C10
Timiris, Cap (Mirik), *Mauritania* **196** F4
Timiryazevskiy, *Russ.* **158** K12
Timiš, river, *Rom.* **152** E11
Timişoara, *Rom.* **152** D11
Timiti's Crack, cape, *Pitcairn I., U.K.* **219** Q23
Timmiarmiut, *Greenland, Den.* **81** D22
Timmins, *Ont., Can.* **83** P17
Timmonsville, *S.C., U.S.* **96** K10
Timms Hill, *Wis., U.S.* **98** H4
Timoe *see* Temoe, island, *Fr. Polynesia, Fr.* **219** H23
Timor, island, *Indonesia, Timor-Leste* **189** N15
Timor-Leste (East Timor), *Asia* **167** Z14
Timor Sea, *Indonesia* **189** N16
Timote, *Arg.* **132** L11
Timpanogos Cave National Monument, *Utah, U.S.* **106** L7
Timpson, *Tex., U.S.* **102** M15
Timsâh, Buheirat el (Lake Timsah), *Egypt* **171** P1
Timsah, Lake *see* Timsâh, Buheirat el, *Egypt* **171** P1
Tims Ford Lake, *Tenn., U.S.* **101** G16
Tîna, Khalîg el, *Egypt* **171** N1
Tinaca Point, *Philippines* **189** G15
Tinajo, *Canary Is.* **204** P7
Tinakula, island, *Solomon Is.* **217** P22
Tindouf, *Alg.* **196** D7
Tindouf, Sebkha de, *Alg.* **196** D8
Tineo, *Sp.* **144** B8
Tinggoa, *Solomon Is.* **217** R19
Tingmerkpuk Mountain, *Alas., U.S.* **84** M2
Tingo María, *Peru* **130** G3
Tingri, *China* **180** L6
Tinharé, Ilha de, *Braz.* **131** H16
Tinhosa Grande, island, *Sao Tome and Principe* **205** B20
Tinhosa Pequena, island, *Sao Tome and Principe* **205** B20
Tinhosas, Pedras, *Sao Tome and Principe* **205** B20
Tinian, island, *N. Mariana Is., U.S.* **216** C2
Tinian Harbor *see* Sunbaron Roads, *N. Mariana Is., U.S.* **216** C7
Tinnenburra, *Qnsld., Austral.* **211** V13
Tinogasta, *Arg.* **132** G8
Tínos, *Gr.* **155** K15
Tínos (Tenos), island, *Gr.* **155** K15
Tiñoso, Cabo, *Sp.* **145** L14
Tinrhert, Hamada de, *Alg., Lib.* **196** D12
Tinsukia, *India* **178** F15
Tintamarre, Île, *St. Martin, Fr.* **121** A15
Tintigny, *Belg.* **147** N13
Tintina, *Arg.* **132** G11
Tintinara, *S. Aust., Austral.* **211** Y11
Ti-n-Zaouâtene, *Alg.* **196** F10
Tioga, *N. Dak., U.S.* **104** E2
Tioga, *Pa., U.S.* **94** L7
Tioman, island, *Malaysia* **187** U11
Tipp City, *Ohio, U.S.* **99** R11
Tipperary, *Ire.* **143** T4
Tipperary, *N. Terr., Austral.* **211** P7
Tipton, *Calif., U.S.* **109** U7
Tipton, *Ind., U.S.* **99** Q9
Tipton, *Iowa, U.S.* **105** P14
Tipton, *Mo., U.S.* **105** T12
Tipton, *Okla., U.S.* **102** H8
Tipton, Mount, *Ariz., U.S.* **107** R5
Tiptonville, *Tenn., U.S.* **100** E12
Tiputa, *Fr. Polynesia, Fr.* **219** K16
Tiputa, Passe de, *Fr. Polynesia, Fr.* **219** K16
Tiracambu, Serra do, *Braz.* **131** E14
Tīrān, island, *Saudi Arabia* **172** G5
Tīrān, Strait of, *Egypt* **171** U4
Tirana *see* Tiranë, *Albania* **152** L9
Tiranë (Tirana), *Albania* **152** L9
Tiraspol, *Mold.* **157** R5
Ţirbīl, *Iraq* **172** E7
Tire, *Turk.* **168** G3
Tirebolu, *Turk.* **169** D13
Tiree, island, *Scot., U.K.* **142** L6
Tîrgovişte, *Rom.* **153** F15
Tîrgu Frumos, *Rom.* **153** B16
Tîrgu Jiu, *Rom.* **153** E13
Tîrgu Lăpuş, *Rom.* **153** B13
Tîrgu Neamţ, *Rom.* **153** B15
Tîrgu Ocna, *Rom.* **153** D16
Tîrgu Secuiesc, *Rom.* **153** D15
Tirich Mir, peak, *Pak.* **176** L10
Tîrna Mare, *Rom.* **152** A12
Tîrnăveni, *Rom.* **153** D13
Tírnavos, *Gr.* **154** E10
Tir Pol, *Afghan.* **176** M1
Tirso, river, *It.* **151** N3
Tiruchchendur, *India* **179** S6
Tiruchchirappalli, *India* **179** R6
Tirunelveli, *India* **179** S6
Tirupati, *India* **179** P7
Tiruppattur, *India* **179** R6
Tiruppur, *India* **179** R5
Tiruvannamalai, *India* **179** Q6
Tiryns, ruin, *Gr.* **154** K11
Tisa, river, *Serb. & Mont.* **152** D10
Tisaiyanvilai, *India* **179** S6
Tishomingo, *Okla., U.S.* **102** J12
Tisis, *Aust.* **160** M3
T'is Isat Fwafwatē (Blue Nile Falls), *Eth.* **199** F14
Tista, river, *Bangladesh, India* **178** G12
Tisza, river, *Hung.* **149** M16
Tiszafüred, *Hung.* **149** L16
Tiszaújváros, *Hung.* **149** K16
Titan Dome, *Antarctica* **226** J12
Titano, Monte, *San Marino* **161** J15
Titicaca, Lago, *Bol., Peru* **130** J6
Titikaveka, *Cook Is., N.Z.* **218** Q9
Titule, *Dem. Rep. of the Congo* **198** J11
Titusville, *Fla., U.S.* **97** T9
Titusville, *Pa., U.S.* **94** L4
Tiva, *Fr. Polynesia, Fr.* **219** A23
Tivaru, island, *Fr. Polynesia, Fr.* **219** K15
Tiverton, *Eng., U.K.* **143** W10
Tiverton, *R.I., U.S.* **95** L15
Tivoli, *Grenada* **121** K23
Tivoli, *It.* **150** K9
Tiyas, *Syr.* **170** G9
Tizimín, *Mex.* **115** H16
Tizi Ouzou, *Alg.* **196** A11
Tiznit, *Mor.* **196** C7
Tlemcen, *Alg.* **196** B10
Tmassah, *Lib.* **197** E14
Tmiet, island, *Marshall Is.* **216** L9
Toa Baja, *P.R., U.S.* **120** M4
Toachel Mlengui (West Passage), *Palau* **216** M11
Toadlena, *N. Mex., U.S.* **107** R10
Toagel Mid Passage, *Palau* **216** N11
Toahotu, *Fr. Polynesia, Fr.* **219** P17
Toamaro, island, *Fr. Polynesia, Fr.* **219** B23
Toamaro, Passe, *Fr. Polynesia, Fr.* **219** B23
Toamasina, *Madagascar* **203** F18
Toano, *Va., U.S.* **96** E13
Toataratara, Pointe, *Fr. Polynesia, Fr.* **219** L23
Toau, island, *Fr. Polynesia, Fr.* **219** E18
Toay, *Arg.* **132** M10
Tobago, island, *S. Amer.* **126** A6
Tobago, island, *Trinidad & Tobago* **119** N18
Toba Kakar Range, *Pak.* **177** Q7
Tobarra, *Sp.* **145** J13
Toba Tek Singh, *Pak.* **177** Q10
Tobermorey, *N. Terr., Austral.* **211** T10
Tobermory, *Qnsld., Austral.* **211** V12
Tobi, island, *Palau* **214** G2
Tobin, Mount, *Nev., U.S.* **109** N9
Tobi Shima, *Japan* **184** K12
Tobol, river, *Russ.* **166** E7
Toboli, *Indonesia* **189** J13
Tobol'sk, *Russ.* **158** J10
Tobolski, *Jam.* **120** H8
Tobona, island, *Solomon Is.* **217** M17
Tobruk *see* Ţubruq, *Lib.* **197** C16
Tobyl, river, *Kaz.* **174** B11
Tobyl, *Kaz.* **174** C10
Tocal, *Qnsld., Austral.* **211** T12
Tocantínia, *Braz.* **131** G13
Tocantinópolis, *Braz.* **131** F13
Tocantins, river, *Braz.* **131** D13
Toccoa, *Ga., U.S.* **96** K6
Toco, *Chile* **132** D7
Toco, *Trinidad & Tobago* **121** N23
Tocón, Punta, *P.R., U.S.* **120** P1
Toconao, *Chile* **132** E8
Tocopilla, *Chile* **132** D7
Todi, *It.* **150** J8
Todmorden, *S. Aust., Austral.* **211** V9
Todoga Saki, *Japan* **184** K14
Todos os Santos Bay, *S. Amer.* **126** G11
Todos Santos, *Mex.* **114** F7
Todos Santos, Bahía de, *Mex.* **114** B5
Tofino, *B.C., Can.* **82** M7
Tofte, *Minn., U.S.* **104** F13
Tofua, island, *Tonga* **218** P6
Toga, island, *Vanuatu* **218** A1
Tōgane, *Japan* **185** P13
Togiak, *Alas., U.S.* **110** K12
Togian, Kepulauan, *Indonesia* **189** J14
Togliatti *see* Tol'yatti, *Russ.* **156** K15
Togo, *Af.* **195** H16
Togtoh, *China* **182** C4
Togyz, *Kaz.* **174** F9
Tohatchi, *N. Mex., U.S.* **107** R10
Tohiea, Mont, *Fr. Polynesia, Fr.* **219** N14
Tohma, river, *Turk.* **168** F12
Tohopekaliga, Lake, *Fla., U.S.* **97** T9
Toi, *Japan* **184** H13
Toi, *Niue, N.Z.* **219** B20
Toibalawe, *India* **179** R14
Toili, *Indonesia* **189** J14
Toi Misaki, *Japan* **185** T5
Toiyabe Range, *Nev., U.S.* **84** G5
Tok, *Alas., U.S.* **111** H18
Tokachi Dake, *Japan* **184** F14
Tōkamachi, *Japan* **185** N11
Tokar, *Sudan* **199** D14
Tokara Kaikyō, *Japan* **185** U4
Tokara Rettō, *Japan* **185** V3
Tokarevka, *Kaz.* **175** D14
Toka Sand Cay, *Pukapuka, Cook Is., N.Z.* **218** R1
Tokat, *Turk.* **168** E11
Tŏkch'ŏn, *N. Korea* **182** D12
Tokelau, islands, *N.Z., Pac. Oc.* **214** H10
Tokerau, island, *Cook Is., N.Z.* **219** A17
Toki, *Japan* **185** P10
Toki Point, *Wake I., U.S.* **216** F8
Tokmak, *Ukr.* **157** R8
Tokmok, *Kyrg.* **176** D12
Toko, *Russ.* **159** J19
Tokomaru Bay, *N.Z.* **213** K20
Tokoro, river, *Japan* **184** F15
Tokoroa, *N.Z.* **213** K19
Toksook Bay, *Alas., U.S.* **110** J11
Toksun, *China* **180** F7
Toktar, *Afghan.* **176** L5
Toktogul, *Kyrg.* **176** E10
Tokung, *Indonesia* **188** J11
Tokuno Shima, *Japan* **185** X2
Tokunoshima, *Japan* **185** X2
Tokushima, *Japan* **185** R8
Tokuyama, *Japan* **185** R5
Tōkyō, *Japan* **185** P12
Tōkyō Wan, *Japan* **185** P12
Tol, island, *F.S.M.* **217** C14
Tôlañaro, *Madagascar* **203** J17
Tolarno, *N.S.W., Austral.* **211** X11
Tolbo, *Mongolia* **180** C8
Tolchin, Mount, *Antarctica* **226** H11
Töle Bī, *Kaz.* **175** H15
Toledo, *Iowa, U.S.* **105** N12
Toledo, *Ohio, U.S.* **99** N12
Toledo, *Oreg., U.S.* **108** G2
Toledo, *Sp.* **144** G10
Toledo, *Wash., U.S.* **108** D3
Toledo, Montes de, *Sp.* **144** H10
Toledo Bend Reservoir, *La., Tex., U.S.* **100** M6
Toli, *China* **180** D6
Toliara, *Madagascar* **203** H16
Tolitoli, *Indonesia* **189** H13
Tol'ka, *Russ.* **158** H12
Tollya, Zaliv, *Russ.* **159** D14
Tolmezzo, *It.* **150** C9
Tolo, Teluk, *Indonesia* **189** K14
Tolob, *Scot., U.K.* **142** E12
Tolosa, *Sp.* **145** B13
Toltén, *Chile* **133** P6
Tolti, *Pak.* **178** B5
Tolú, *Col.* **128** C4
Toluca, *Mex.* **114** J11
Tol'yatti (Togliatti), *Russ.* **156** K15
Tomah, *Wis., U.S.* **98** K4
Tomahawk, *Wis., U.S.* **98** H5
Tomakomai, *Japan* **184** G13
Tomanivi, peak, *Fiji Is.* **218** H6
Tomar, *Port.* **144** G5
Tomar, *Braz.* **130** C8
Tomari, *Japan* **184** H13
Tomaszów Lubelski, *Pol.* **149** G18
Tomaszów Mazowiecki, *Pol.* **149** E15
Tomatin, *Scot., U.K.* **142** K9
Tombador, Serra do, *Braz.* **130** G10
Tombe, *Solomon Is.* **217** M16
Tombigbee, river, *Ala., U.S.* **101** L13
Tombouctou (Timbuktu), *Mali* **196** G8
Tombstone, *Ariz., U.S.* **107** W8
Tombua, *Angola* **202** E5
Tomé, *Chile* **132** M6
Tomea, island, *Indonesia* **189** L15
Tomil, *F.S.M.* **217** D18
Tomil Harbor, *F.S.M.* **217** D18
Tomini, Teluk, *Indonesia* **189** J13
Tomintoul, *Scot., U.K.* **142** K10
Tomman, island, *Vanuatu* **218** E2
Tommot, *Russ.* **159** H18
Tomo, river, *Col.* **128** E8
Tomo, *New Caledonia, Fr.* **218** D8
Tomorit, Maja e, *Albania* **152** L10
Tomotu Noi (Lord Howe Island), *Solomon Is.* **217** Q22
Tompa, *Russ.* **159** K16
Tompkinsville, *Ky., U.S.* **101** D16
Tom Price, *W. Aust., Austral.* **211** T3
Tomsk, *Russ.* **158** K12
Tomsyu, *Russ.* **159** E18
Tomtor, *Russ.* **159** F17
Tomtor Tasa, Gora, *Russ.* **159** F16
Tom White, Mount, *Alas., U.S.* **111** J18
Tonalá, *Mex.* **115** K14
Tonami, *Japan* **185** N10
Tonantins, *Braz.* **130** D6
Tonasket, *Wash., U.S.* **108** A7
Tonbridge, *Eng., U.K.* **143** W14
Tønder, *Den.* **140** P11
Tondou, Massif du, *Cen. Af. Rep.* **198** G10
Tonga, *Pac. Oc.* **214** K10
Tonga, *Sudan* **198** F12
Tonga Islands, *Tonga* **214** K10
Tong'an, *China* **183** Q7
Tongareva *see* Penrhyn Atoll, island, *Cook Is., N.Z.* **214** H12
Tongariki, island, *Vanuatu* **218** E3
Tongatapu Group, *Tonga* **214** K10
Tongcheng, *China* **182** K7
Tongchuan, *China* **182** G2
Tongdao, *China* **183** P2
Tongde, *China* **180** J11
Tongeren, *Belg.* **146** L13
Tongguan, *China* **181** J13
Tonghua, *China* **182** B12
Tongjiang, *China* **181** C18
Tongliao, *China* **182** A10
Tongling, *China* **182** L7
Tonglu, *China* **182** L9
Tongo, *N.S.W., Austral.* **211** W12
Tongoa (Kuwaé), island, *Vanuatu* **218** E3
Tongoy, *Chile* **132** J6
Tongren, *China* **183** N1
Tongshi, *China* **183** U1
Tongtian, river, *China* **180** J9
Tongue, river, *Mont., U.S.* **106** E12
Tongue, *Scot., U.K.* **142** H9
Tongue, Kyle of, *Scot., U.K.* **142** G9
Tongue of the Ocean, bay, *Bahamas* **116** F11
Tongue River Reservoir, *Mont., U.S.* **106** F11
Tongxian, *China* **182** D7
Tongxin, *China* **180** H12
Tonj, *Sudan* **198** G12
Tonk, *India* **178** G5
Tonkawa, *Okla., U.S.* **102** E11
Tonkin, Gulf of, *China, Vietnam* **166** J11
Tonle Sap, lake, *Cambodia* **187** N11
Tonneins, *Fr.* **147** W7
Tonnerre, *Fr.* **147** R12
Tōno, *Japan* **184** K13
Tonoas (Dublon), island, *F.S.M.* **217** C15
Tonopah, *Nev., U.S.* **109** R9
Tønsberg, *Nor.* **140** L11
Tonto National Monument, *Ariz., U.S.* **107** U8
Tonumea, island, *Tonga* **218** R6
Tonya, *Turk.* **169** D14
Toodyay, *W. Aust., Austral.* **211** X2
Tooele, *Utah, U.S.* **106** L7
Toomaru, Mont, *Fr. Polynesia, Fr.* **219** B23
Toompine, *Qnsld., Austral.* **211** V12
Toopua, island, *Fr. Polynesia, Fr.* **219** K13
Toopua Iti, island, *Fr. Polynesia, Fr.* **219** K13
Toora Khem, *Russ.* **159** L14
Toowoomba, *Qnsld., Austral.* **211** V15
Top, Lake, *Russ.* **138** B9
Topaze, Baie, *Mauritius* **205** J20
Tope de Coroa, peak, *Cape Verde* **205** B14
Topeka, *Kans., U.S.* **105** S9
Topliţa, *Rom.* **153** C14
Topock, *Ariz., U.S.* **107** S4
Topol'čany, *Slovakia* **149** K14
Topolobampo, *Mex.* **114** E7
Toppenish, *Wash., U.S.* **108** E6
Topsail Beach, *N.C., U.S.* **96** K13
Top Springs, *N. Terr., Austral.* **211** Q8
Toquima Range, *Nev., U.S.* **109** Q9
Tor, *Sp.* **160** H1
Torbalı, *Turk.* **168** G3
Torbat-e Ḩeydarīyeh, *Iran* **173** C16
Torbat-e Jām, *Iran* **173** C17
Torbay, *Eng., U.K.* **143** X10
Torbay, *W. Aust., Austral.* **211** Y3
Torbert, Mount, *Alas., U.S.* **111** J15
Torch Lake, *Mich., U.S.* **98** H10
Töre, *Sw.* **141** F14
Torello, *It.* **161** H13
Torez, *Ukr.* **157** Q10
Torghay, river, *Kaz.* **174** E10
Torghay, *Kaz.* **174** E11
Torgo, *Russ.* **159** J17
Torhout, *Belg.* **146** L10
Torino (Turin), *It.* **150** E2
Tori Shima, *Japan* **185** Y1
Torixoreu, *Braz.* **130** J12
Torkestan Mountains, *Afghan.* **176** L4
Tornal'a, *Slovakia* **149** K16
Torneå *see* Tornio, *Fin.* **141** F15
Torneälven, river, *Sw.* **138** B8
Torneträsk, *Sw.* **141** D13
Torngat Mountains, *Nfld. & Lab., Can.* **83** J20
Tornillo, *Tex., U.S.* **103** V2
Tornimparte, *It.* **150** K9
Tornio (Torneå), *Fin.* **141** F15
Torniojoki, river, *Fin., Sw.* **141** E14
Tornquist, *Arg.* **133** N11
Tōro, *Japan* **184** F15
Toro, *Sp.* **144** D9
Toro, Cerro del, *Arg., Chile* **132** H7
Torokina, *P.N.G.* **217** K14
Törökszentmiklós, *Hung.* **149** L16
Torom, *Russ.* **159** J20
Toronto, *Kans., U.S.* **105** U9
Toronto, *Ohio, U.S.* **99** Q16

Toronto, Ont., Can. 83 Q18
Toropets, Russ. 156 H7
Tororo, Uganda 199 J13
Toros Dağı, Turk. 168 H9
Toros Dağları, Turk. 168 H7
Torquemada, Sp. 144 D10
Torrance, Calif., U.S. 109 X8
Torran Rocks, Scot., U.K. 142 M7
Torre, It. 150 M11
Torre Astura, It. 150 L8
Torre de Moncorvo, Port. 144 E7
Torredonjimeno, Sp. 144 K10
Torrejón de Ardoz, Sp. 144 F11
Torrelavega, Sp. 144 B10
Torremaggiore, It. 150 L12
Torremolinos, Sp. 144 M10
Torrens, Lake, S. Aust., Austral. 211 W10
Torrent, Sp. 145 H14
Torreón, Mex. 114 F10
Torre San Giovanni, It. 151 N15
Torres Islands, Vanuatu 218 A1
Torres Strait, Austral. 210 A12
Torres Vedras, Port. 144 H4
Torrevieja, Sp. 145 K14
Torriana, It. 161 G13
Torrijos, Sp. 144 G10
Torrington, Conn., U.S. 94 L12
Torrington, Wyo., U.S. 106 J14
Torrutj, island, Marshall Is. 216 M5
Torsby, Sw. 140 K12
Tórshavn, Faroe Is., Den. 140 J6
Tortola, island, Virgin Islands, U.K. 119 F14
Tortona, It. 150 E4
Tortosa, Sp. 145 F15
Tortosa see Ţarţūs, Syr. 170 G7
Tortosa, Cap, Sp. 145 F16
Tortue, Île de la, Haiti 117 K16
Tortuga, Isla, Ecua. 128 R9
Tortuga Island, S. Amer. 126 A5
Tortuguero, Laguna, P.R., U.S. 120 M3
Tortum, Turk. 169 E16
Ţorūd, Iran 173 C14
Torugart, Kyrg. 176 G12
Torul, Turk. 169 D14
Toruń, Pol. 149 D14
Tõrva, Est. 141 L17
Tory Island, Ire. 143 N5
Torzhok, Russ. 156 H8
Tosa del Braidal, Andorra 160 J4
Tosashimizu, Japan 185 S6
Tosa Wan, Japan 187 R7
Tosca, S. Af. 202 J9
Toscano, Arcipelago, It. 150 J6
To Shima, Japan 185 Q12
Toshka Lakes, Egypt 197 E18
Toshkent (Tashkent), Uzb. 175 K13
Tostado, Arg. 132 H11
Tosters, Aust. 160 M3
Tosu, Japan 185 R4
Tosya, Turk. 168 D9
Totana, Sp. 145 K13
Totegegie, island, Fr. Polynesia, Fr. 219 Q21
Toteng, Botswana 202 G9
Tôtes, Fr. 147 N8
Totia, island, Cook Is., N.Z. 219 C15
Totiw, island, F.S.M. 217 C15
Tot'ma, Russ. 156 F11
Totnes, Eng., U.K. 143 X10
Totness, Suriname 129 E16
Tôto, Angola 202 B6
Totokafonua, island, Tonga 218 M11
Totolom, peak, F.S.M. 217 G14
Totora, Bol. 130 K7
Totoya, island, Fiji Is. 218 K8
Tottan Hills, Antarctica 226 C11
Tottori, Japan 185 P7
Totu Tofari, island, Fr. Polynesia, Fr. 219 K14
Toubkal, Jebel, Mor. 196 C8
Toucy, Fr. 147 R11
Tougan, Burkina Faso 200 E9
Touggourt, Alg. 196 B12
Touho, New Caledonia, Fr. 218 C7
Toul, Fr. 147 P13
Touliu, Taiwan, China 183 R9
Toulon, Fr. 147 Y14
Toulouse, Fr. 147 X9
Toummo, Niger 197 F14
Toungo, Nigeria 201 G16
Touques, river, Fr. 147 P7
Touriñán, Cabo, Sp. 144 B5
Tournai, Belg. 146 L11
Tournavista, Peru 130 G4
Tournay, Fr. 147 Y7
Touros, Braz. 131 E18
Tours, Fr. 147 R8
Toury, Fr. 147 Q9
Touside, Pic, Chad 194 F6
Touwsrivier, S. Af. 202 M8
Tovarkovskiy, Russ. 156 L10
Tovuz, Azerb. 169 D19
Towada, Japan 184 J13
Towada, Japan 184 J13
Towada Ko, Japan 184 J13
Towanda, Pa., U.S. 94 L8
Tower see Genovesa, Isla, island, Ecua. 128 P10
Tower, Minn., U.S. 104 F12
Towner, N. Dak., U.S. 104 E5
Town Hall, Monaco 161 E21
Town Hill, Bermuda, U.K. 120 B3
Townsend, Mont., U.S. 106 D8
Townsend, Va., U.S. 96 F14
Townsville, Qnsld., Austral. 211 S13
Towot, Sudan 199 H13
Towraghondi, Afghan. 176 L2
Towrzi, Afghan. 177 R5
Towson, Md., U.S. 96 C13
Toyah, Tex., U.S. 103 N2
Toyahvale, Tex., U.S. 103 P2
Tōya Ko, Japan 184 G13
Toyama, Japan 185 N10
Toyama Wan, Japan 185 N10
Toyohashi, Japan 185 Q10
Toyooka, Japan 185 P8
Toyotomi, Japan 184 D13
Tozeur, Tun. 196 B12
Tqvarch'eli, Abkhazia 169 B16
Trâblous (Tripoli), Leb. 170 H7
Trabzon, Turk. 169 D14
Trachonas, Cyprus 160 N8
Tracy, Calif., U.S. 109 S4
Tracy, Minn., U.S. 104 L9
Traer, Iowa, U.S. 105 N12
Trafalgar, Cabo, Sp. 144 N8
Tráighlí see Tralee, Ire. 143 U3
Trail, B.C., Can. 82 M9
Traíra, river, Braz., Col. 128 J8
Traîtres, Baie des, Fr. Polynesia, Fr. 219 N20
Tralee (Tráighlí), Ire. 143 U3
Tralee Bay, Ire. 143 U2
Tranås, Sw. 141 M13
Trancas, Arg. 132 F9
Trang, Thai. 187 R8
Trangan, island, Indonesia 189 M18
Trangie, N.S.W., Austral. 211 X13
Tranqueras, Uru. 132 J14
Trans-Amazon Highway, Braz. 130 F9
Transantarctic Mountains, Antarctica 226 F11
Trans-Canada Highway, Can. 82 M8
Transdniestria, region, Mold. 157 R5
Transylvania, region, Rom. 152 C13
Transylvanian Alps, Rom. 152 E12
Trapani, It. 151 S8
Trapper Peak, Mont., U.S. 106 E5
Traralgon, Vic., Austral. 211 Z13
Trarza, region, Mauritania 194 F1
Trasimeno, Lago, It. 150 H8
Traun, Aust. 148 K11
Traunreut, Ger. 148 K9
Traverse, Lake, Minn., S. Dak., U.S. 104 J8
Traverse City, Mich., U.S. 98 J10
Travis, Lake, Tex., U.S. 103 Q10
Travnik, Bosn. & Herzg. 152 F7
Trayning, W. Aust., Austral. 211 X3
Trbovlje, Slov. 152 D5
Treasure Beach, Jam. 120 J7
Treasure Cay, Bahamas 120 B6
Treasurers Island, Solomon Is. 217 N24
Treasury Islands, Solomon Is. 217 L14
Třebíč, Czech Rep. 148 J12
Trebinje, Bosn. & Herzg. 152 J8
Trebisacce, It. 151 P13
Trebišov, Slovakia 149 J17
Třeboň, Czech Rep. 148 J11
Trégastel, Fr. 147 P4
Tregrosse Islets, Coral Sea Is. Terr., Austral. 211 R15
Tréguier, Fr. 147 P4
Treignac, Fr. 147 U9
Treinta-y-Tres, Uru. 132 K15
Trelew, Arg. 133 R9
Trelleborg, Sw. 140 P12
Tremadoc Bay, Wales, U.K. 143 T9
Tremblant, Mount, N. Amer. 80 H8
Tremiti, Isole, It. 150 K12
Tremonton, Utah, U.S. 106 J7
Trenary, Mich., U.S. 98 F8
Trenčín, Slovakia 149 J14
Trenque Lauquen, Arg. 132 M11
Trento, It. 150 C7
Trenton, Mich., U.S. 99 N12
Trenton, Mo., U.S. 105 R11
Trenton, N.J., U.S. 94 P10
Trenton, Nebr., U.S. 105 R4
Trenton, Tenn., U.S. 100 E12
Trepassey, Nfld. & Lab., Can. 83 M24
Tres Arroyos, Arg. 133 N12
Tres Esquinas, Col. 128 H5
Treshnish Isles, Scot., U.K. 142 L7
Três Lagoas, Braz. 130 L12
Tres Montes, Golfo, Chile 133 T6
Tres Montes, Península, Chile 133 T5
Tres Picos, Cerro, Arg. 133 R7
Tres Puntas, Cabo, Arg. 133 T9
Tres Zapotes, ruin, Mex. 115 J13
Treviso, It. 150 D8
Trevose Head, Eng., U.K. 143 X8
Trgovište, Serb. & Mont. 152 J11
Triabunna, Tas., Austral. 211 Z16
Triàngulos, Arrecifes, Mex. 115 H15
Tribulation, Cape, Austral. 210 C13
Tribune, Kans., U.S. 105 T3
Tricarico, It. 150 M13
Tricase, It. 151 N16
Trichur, India 179 R5
Trie, Fr. 147 Y7
Trier, Ger. 148 H5
Triesen, Liech. 160 Q2
Triesenberg, Liech. 160 P2
Trieste, It. 150 D10
Triglav, peak, Slov. 152 C4
Trigueros, Sp. 144 L7
Trihonida, Límni, Gr. 154 H9
Tríkala, Gr. 154 F9
Tríkeri, Gr. 154 G11
Trikomo, Cyprus 160 N10
Trikora, Puncak, Indonesia 213 C16
Trincomalee, Sri Lanka 179 S8
Třinec, Czech Rep. 149 H14
Trinidad, Bol. 130 J7
Trinidad, Calif., U.S. 108 M2
Trinidad, Colo., U.S. 107 P14
Trinidad, Cuba 116 H9
Trinidad, island, Trinidad & Tobago 119 P17
Trinidad, Golfo, Chile 133 V6
Trinidad, Isla, Arg. 133 P11
Trinidad and Tobago, N. Amer. 81 P24
Trinidad Head, Calif., U.S. 108 M1
Trinitapoli, It. 150 L13
Trinity, river, Calif., U.S. 108 M2
Trinity, river, Tex., U.S. 103 P14
Trinity, Tex., U.S. 103 P14
Trinity Bay, Nfld. & Lab., Can. 83 M24
Trinity Beach, Qnsld., Austral. 211 R13
Trinity Hills, Trinidad & Tobago 121 Q23
Trinity Islands, Alas., U.S. 111 N14
Trinity Peninsula, Antarctica 226 C4
Trinity Range, Nev., U.S. 109 N8
Trinkat Island, India 179 S15
Triolet, Mauritius 205 F20
Trion, Ga., U.S. 96 K4
Trionto, Capo, It. 151 P14
Triora, It. 150 G2
Tripoli see Trâblous, Leb. 170 H7
Tripoli see Ţarābulus, Lib. 197 B13
Trípoli, Gr. 154 K10
Tripolitania, region, Lib. 197 C13
Tripp, S. Dak., U.S. 104 M7
Tristaina, river, Andorra 160 G3
Tristaina, Pic de, Andorra, Fr. 160 G2
Tristan da Cunha Group, Atl. Oc. 204 J4
Tristan da Cunha Island, Tristan da Cunha Is., U.K. 194 R2
Tristão, Ponta do, Madeira 204 M2
Tristao, Îles, Guinea 200 E4
Trivandrum see Thiruvananthapuram, India 179 S5
Trnava, Slovakia 149 K13
Trobriand Islands, P.N.G. 213 E21
Trofors, Nor. 140 G12
Trois-Bassins, Reunion, Fr. 205 G15
Troisdorf, Ger. 148 F5
Trois Fourches, Cap des, Mor. 144 P11
Trois Pitons, Morne, Dominica 121 F19
Trois-Rivières, Guadeloupe, Fr. 121 G14
Trois-Rivières, Que., Can. 83 P20
Troisvierges, Lux. 160 G9
Troitsk, Russ. 158 J8
Troitskoye, Russ. 157 R13
Troja, Jam. 120 H9
Trojanów, Pol. 149 E17
Troll, station, Antarctica 227 B13
Trollhättan, Sw. 140 M12
Trombetas, river, Braz. 130 C10
Tromelin, island, Ind. Oc. 240 J6
Tromsø, Nor. 141 C13
Trona, Calif., U.S. 109 V9
Tronador, Monte, Arg., Chile 133 Q7
Trondheim, Nor. 140 H11
Trondheimsfjorden, Nor. 140 H11
Troodos Mountains, Cyprus 160 P7
Troon, Scot., U.K. 143 N9
Trostyanets', Ukr. 157 N8
Trou d'Eau Douce, Mauritius 205 G20
Trou Gras Point, St. Lucia 121 K14
Troumaka, St. Vincent & the Grenadines 121 K16
Troup, Tex., U.S. 102 M14
Trout Creek, Utah, U.S. 106 M5
Trout Lake, N.W.T., Can. 82 H10
Trout Lake, Ont., Can. 83 N14
Trout Peak, Wyo., U.S. 106 F9
Trout River, Nfld. & Lab., Can. 83 M23
Troy, Ala., U.S. 101 M16
Troy, Jam. 120 H7
Troy, Kans., U.S. 105 R10
Troy, Mo., U.S. 105 S14
Troy, Mont., U.S. 106 B4
Troy, N.C., U.S. 96 H10
Troy, N.Y., U.S. 94 J11
Troy, Ohio, U.S. 99 R11
Troy, Oreg., U.S. 108 E9
Troy, ruin, Turk. 168 D2
Troyes, Fr. 147 Q12
Troy Peak, Nev., U.S. 109 R11
Trübbach, Switz. 160 Q2
Trubchevsk, Russ. 156 M7
Truckee, Calif., U.S. 109 Q6
Truckee, river, Nev., U.S. 109 P6
Trujillo, Hond. 115 K18
Trujillo, Peru 130 G2
Trujillo, Venez. 128 C7
Trujillo Alto, P.R., U.S. 120 M5
Truk Islands see Chuuk, F.S.M. 216 Q6
Truk Lagoon see Chuuk Lagoon, F.S.M. 217 B15
Trumann, Ark., U.S. 100 F11
Trumbull, Mount, Ariz., U.S. 107 Q6
Truro, Eng., U.K. 143 X8
Truro, N.S., Can. 83 P22
Truth or Consequences, N. Mex., U.S. 107 U11
Trutnov, Czech Rep. 148 G12
Tryavna, Bulg. 153 H15
Trzebnica, Pol. 149 F13
Tsada, Cyprus 160 Q6
Tsagaan Bogd Uul, peak, Mongolia 180 F10
Tsagaannuur, Mongolia 180 C8
Tsagan Aman, Russ. 157 Q14
Ts'ageri, Rep. of Georgia 169 B17
Tsagveri, Rep. of Georgia 169 C17
Tsahir, Mongolia 180 D10
Tsaile, Ariz., U.S. 107 R9
Tsaka La, India 178 C7
Tsalka, Rep. of Georgia 169 C18
Tsangpo Canyon see Yarlung Zangbo Canyon, China 180 L9
Tsao see Tsau, Botswana 202 G8
Tsarevo, Bulg. 153 J17
Tsau (Tsao), Botswana 202 G8
Tschida, Lake, N. Dak., U.S. 104 G3
Tsenhermandal, Mongolia 181 D13
Tsentral'nyy, Russ. 159 G20
Tses, Namibia 202 J7
Tsetsegnuur, Mongolia 180 D9
Tsetserleg, Mongolia 180 D11
Tshabong, Botswana 202 J8
Tshane, Botswana 202 H8
Tshela, Dem. Rep. of the Congo 198 L7
Tshikapa, Dem. Rep. of the Congo 198 M9
Tshofa, Dem. Rep. of the Congo 198 L10
Tshootsha, Botswana 202 H8
Tshuapa, river, Dem. Rep. of the Congo 198 K10
Tshwane see Pretoria, S. Af. 202 J10
Tsiigehtchic, N.W.T., Can. 82 E9
Tsil'ma, river, Russ. 138 A12
Tsimlyanskoye Vodokhranilishche, Russ. 157 Q12
Tsimlyansk Reservoir, Russ. 138 F12
Tsiombe, Madagascar 203 J16
Tsipanda, Russ. 159 H19
Ts'khinvali, S. Ossetia 169 B18
Tsna, river, Russ. 156 K11
Tsnori, Rep. of Georgia 169 C20
Tsu, Japan 185 Q9
Tsubame, Japan 184 M11
Tsuchiura, Japan 185 P12
Tsugaru Kaikyō, Japan 184 H13
Tsuma, Japan 185 N7
Tsumeb, Namibia 202 G7
Tsuruga, Japan 185 P9
Tsuruga Wan, Japan 185 P9
Tsuruoka, Japan 184 L12
Tsushima, island, Japan 185 Q3
Tsutsu, Japan 185 Q3
Tsuyama, Japan 185 Q7
Tsyurupyns'k, Ukr. 157 R7
Tuahora, Pointe, Fr. Polynesia, Fr. 219 K14
Tuakau, N.Z. 213 J19
Tual, Indonesia 189 L18
Tuam, Ire. 143 R4
Tuamotu Archipelago, Fr. Polynesia, Fr. 219 D18
Tuan Giao, Vietnam 186 G10
Tuangku, island, Indonesia 188 H4
Tu'anuku, Tonga 218 L11
Tuapa, Niue, N.Z. 219 B20
Tuapse, Russ. 157 T10
Tuaran, Malaysia 188 F12
Tuasivi, Samoa 218 K2
Tuasivi, Cape, Samoa 218 K2
Tuatapere, N.Z. 213 R15
Tuauru, river, Fr. Polynesia, Fr. 219 N16
Tubac, Ariz., U.S. 107 W7
Tuba City, Ariz., U.S. 107 R7
Ţubah, Qaşr aţ, Jordan 171 N7
Tubarão, Braz. 131 P13
Tübingen, Ger. 148 J6
Tubmanburg, Liberia 200 G6
Tubou, Fiji Is. 218 J9
Ţubruq (Tobruk), Lib. 197 C16
Tubuai, island, Fr. Polynesia, Fr. 219 H16
Tubuai Islands see Austral Islands, Fr. Polynesia, Fr. 219 H16
Tucacas, Venez. 128 B9
Tucavaca, river, Bol. 130 K9
Tuckerman, Ark., U.S. 100 F10
Tucker's Town, Bermuda, U.K. 120 B3
Tuckerton, N.J., U.S. 94 Q10
Tucson, Ariz., U.S. 107 V8
Tucumcari, N. Mex., U.S. 107 S15
Tucumcari Mountain, N. Mex., U.S. 107 S15
Tucupita, Venez. 128 C12
Tucuruí, Braz. 131 E13
Tudela, Sp. 145 D13
Tuen, Qnsld., Austral. 211 V13
Tuensang, India 178 G15
Tuffé, Fr. 147 Q8
Tufi, P.N.G. 213 E20
Tufts Plain, Pac. Oc. 239 D13
Tufuone, Wallis & Futuna, Fr. 218 B11
Tufu Point, Amer. Samoa, U.S. 218 P4
Tufuvai, Tonga 218 K12
Tugela Falls, S. Af. 194 Q8
Tug Fork, Ky., W. Va., U.S. 101 C20
Tūghyl, Kaz. 175 E19
Tuguegarao, Philippines 189 B14
Tugur, Russ. 159 J20
Tui, Sp. 144 C5
Tuineje, Canary Is. 204 Q7
Tukangbesi, Kepulauan, Indonesia 189 L14
Tukao, Cook Is., N.Z. 219 A14
Tukchi, Russ. 159 H20
Tukosméra, Mount, Vanuatu 218 H4
Tūkrah, Lib. 197 C15
Tuktoyaktuk, N.W.T., Can. 82 D10
Tukums, Latv. 141 M16
Tula, Mex. 114 G11
Tula, Russ. 156 K9
Tulaghi, island, Solomon Is. 217 N19
Tulak, Afghan. 177 N3

Tulare, *Calif., U.S.* **109** U7
Tulare Lake Bed, *Calif., U.S.* **109** U6
Tularosa, *N. Mex., U.S.* **107** U12
Tulcán, *Ecua.* **128** H3
Tulcea, *Rom.* **153** E18
Tul'chyn, *Ukr.* **157** P5
Tulelake, *Calif., U.S.* **108** L4
Tuli, *Zimb.* **202** H11
Tulia, *Tex., U.S.* **102** H5
Tulit'a, *N.W.T., Can.* **82** F10
Ţulkarm, *W. Bank* **170** L5
Tullah, *Tas., Austral.* **211** Z15
Tullahoma, *Tenn., U.S.* **101** F16
Tullamore, *Ire.* **143** S5
Tullamore, *N.S.W., Austral.* **211** X13
Tulle, *Fr.* **147** V9
Tully, *Qnsld., Austral.* **211** R13
Tulsa, *Okla., U.S.* **102** F12
Tuluá, *Col.* **128** F4
Tulun, *Russ.* **159** L14
Tulu Welel, peak, *Eth.* **199** G14
Tum, *Indonesia* **189** K17
Tumacacori National Historic Park, *Ariz., U.S.* **107** W7
Tumaco, *Col.* **128** H3
Tumaco, Ensenada de, *Col.* **128** H3
Tumbes, *Peru* **130** E2
Tumby Bay, *S. Aust., Austral.* **211** X9
Tumd Youqi, *China* **182** C3
Tumd Zuoqi, *China* **182** C4
Tumen, *China* **182** A14
Tumen, river, *China, N. Korea* **182** B14
Tumeremo, *Venez.* **129** D13
Tumkur, *India* **179** P5
Tummel, Loch, *Scot., U.K.* **142** L9
Tumon Bay, *Guam, U.S.* **216** B11
Tumucumaque, Serra de, *S. Amer.* **126** C7
Tumu Mountain, *Amer. Samoa, U.S.* **218** N2
Tumu Point, *F.S.M.* **217** F13
Tumwater, *Wash., U.S.* **108** D3
Tunapuna, *Trinidad & Tobago* **121** P22
Tunas de Zaza, *Cuba* **116** J9
Tunbridge Wells, *Eng., U.K.* **143** W14
Tunceli, *Turk.* **169** F14
Tunchang, *China* **183** U1
Tundubai, *Sudan* **198** E10
Tunduma, *Tanzania* **199** N13
Tunduru, *Tanzania* **199** N14
Tundzha, river, *Bulg.* **153** J16
Tungabhadra, river, *India* **179** N6
Tunga Pass, *China, India* **178** E14
Tungkang, *Taiwan, China* **183** S9
Tungsha Ch'üntao, island, *China* **183** T6
Tungsha Tao (Pratas Island), *Taiwan, China* **183** T6
Tungua, island, *Tonga* **218** Q6
Tunguskhaya, *Russ.* **159** G17
Tunica, *Miss., U.S.* **100** G11
Tunis, *Tun.* **197** A13
Tunis, Gulf of, *Tun.* **194** C6
Tunisia, *Af.* **195** D18
Tunja, *Col.* **128** E6
Tununak, *Alas., U.S.* **110** J11
Tunuyán, *Arg.* **132** L8
Tuo, river, *China* **180** L12
Tuolumne, river, *Calif., U.S.* **109** S5
Tup, *Kyrg.* **176** D14
Tupã, *Braz.* **130** L12
Tupai (Motu Iti), island, *Fr. Polynesia, Fr.* **219** E15
Tupelo, *Miss., U.S.* **101** H13
Tupelo National Battlefield, *Miss., U.S.* **101** H13
Tupi, *Philippines* **189** F15
Tupinier, Cape, *F.S.M.* **217** B18
Tupiza, *Bol.* **130** L7
Tupper Lake, *N.Y., U.S.* **94** G10
Tüpqaraghan Tübegi, *Kaz.* **174** H6
Tupungato, Cerro, *S. Amer.* **126** L4
Túquerres, *Col.* **128** H3
Tura, *India* **178** G12
Tura, *Russ.* **159** H14
Turabah, *Saudi Arabia* **172** L8
Turakh, *Russ.* **159** E16
Turan Lowland, *Asia* **166** F6
Ţurāq al 'Ilab, range, *Syr.* **170** H10
Ţurayf, *Saudi Arabia* **172** E7
Turbaco, *Col.* **128** B5
Turbat, *Pak.* **177** V2
Turbo, *Col.* **128** D4
Turda, *Rom.* **153** C13
Turégano, *Sp.* **144** E10
Tureia, island, *Fr. Polynesia, Fr.* **219** G21
Turek, *Pol.* **149** E14
Turfan *see* Turpan, *China* **180** F8
Turghan Pass, *Afghan.* **176** K9
Türgovishte, *Bulg.* **153** H16
Turgut, *Turk.* **168** F7
Turgutlu, *Turk.* **168** F3
Turhal, *Turk.* **168** D11
Türi, *Est.* **141** K16
Turi, peak, *Fr. Polynesia, Fr.* **219** G14
Turia, river, *Sp.* **145** G14
Turiaçu, *Braz.* **131** D14
Turin *see* Torino, *It.* **150** E2
Turka, *Ukr.* **157** P2
Turkana, Lake (Lake Rudolf), *Eth., Kenya* **199** H14
Türkeli, island, *Turk.* **168** D3
Turkey, *Asia* **167** S3
Turkey, river, *Iowa, U.S.* **104** M13
Turkey, *Tex., U.S.* **102** J6
Turkey Creek, *W. Aust., Austral.* **211** R6
Türkistan, *Kaz.* **175** J13
Türkmenabat (Chärjew), *Turkm.* **174** L10
Türkmen Aylagy, *Turkm.* **174** L6
Türkmenbaşy, *Turkm.* **174** K6
Türkmenbaşy Aylagy, *Turkm.* **174** K6
Türkmen Daği, *Turk.* **168** E6
Turkmenistan, *Asia* **167** T5
Turks and Caicos Islands, *U.K., Greater Antilles* **117** J17
Turks Island Passage, *Turks & Caicos Is., U.K.* **117** J17
Turks Islands, *Turks & Caicos Is., U.K.* **117** J18
Turku (Åbo), *Fin.* **141** K15
Turkwel, river, *Kenya* **199** J14
Turlock, *Calif., U.S.* **109** S5
Turnagain, Cape, *N.Z.* **213** M19
Turner, *Mont., U.S.* **106** A10
Turner Hole, *Virgin Islands, U.S.* **120** Q4
Turnhout, *Belg.* **146** K12
Turnu Măgurele, *Rom.* **153** G14
Turnu Roşu, Pasul, *Rom.* **153** E13
Turpan (Turfan), *China* **180** F8
Turpan Depression, *China* **166** F9
Turpan Pendi, *China* **180** F8
Turquino, Pico, *Cuba* **116** K12
Tursunzoda, *Taj.* **176** J7
Turt, *Mongolia* **180** B11
Türtkül, *Uzb.* **174** K9
Turtle *see* Vatoa, island, *Fiji Is.* **218** L10
Turtle Crawls, *Cayman Is., U.K.* **120** J2
Turtle Lake, *N. Dak., U.S.* **104** F4
Turtle Mountain, *N. Dak., U.S.* **104** D5
Turtle Rocks, *Bahamas* **120** C8
Turugart Pass, *China* **180** F4
Tuscaloosa, *Ala., U.S.* **101** K14
Tuscarora, *Nev., U.S.* **108** M10
Tuscola, *Ill., U.S.* **99** R6
Tuscola, *Tex., U.S.* **102** M8
Tuscumbia, *Ala., U.S.* **101** G14
Tuskar Rock, *Ire.* **143** U7
Tuskegee, *Ala., U.S.* **101** L16
Tutak, *Turk.* **169** E17
Tutayev, *Russ.* **156** G10
Tuticorin, *India* **179** S6
Tuting, *India* **178** E15
Tutira, *N.Z.* **213** L20
Tutoko, Mount, *N.Z.* **213** Q15
Tutrakan, *Bulg.* **153** G16
Tuttle Creek Lake, *Kans., U.S.* **105** S8
Tuttlingen, *Ger.* **148** K6
Tutu, island, *Fiji Is.* **218** G7
Tutu, *Virgin Islands, U.S.* **120** N9
Tutuala, *Timor-Leste* **189** M16
Tutuila, island, *Amer. Samoa, U.S.* **218** M7
Tutumu, *Solomon Is.* **217** N19
Tuvalu, *Pac. Oc.* **214** H9
Tuvuca, island, *Fiji Is.* **218** H9
Ţuwayq, Jabal, *Saudi Arabia* **172** J10
Tuwayq Mountains, *Saudi Arabia* **166** H3
Tuxpan, *Mex.* **114** G9
Tuxpan, *Mex.* **114** H12
Tuxtla Gutiérrez, *Mex.* **115** K14
Tuyen Hoa, *Vietnam* **186** K12
Tuyen Quang, *Vietnam* **186** G11
Tuy Hoa, *Vietnam* **187** N14
Tūysarkān, *Iran* **172** D11
Tuz Gölü, *Turk.* **168** F8
Tuzigoot National Monument, *Ariz., U.S.* **107** S7
Tuzla, *Bosn. & Herzg.* **152** F8
Tuzla Gölü, *Turk.* **168** F11
Tuzluca, *Turk.* **169** E18
Tveitsund, *Nor.* **140** L11
Tver', *Russ.* **156** H8
Tvøroyri, *Faroe Is., Den.* **140** J6
Tweed Heads, *N.S.W., Austral.* **211** V15
Twentynine Palms, *Calif., U.S.* **109** X11
26 Baky Komissary, *Azerb.* **169** E23
Twin Bridges, *Mont., U.S.* **106** E7
Twin Buttes Reservoir, *Tex., U.S.* **103** N7
Twin City, *Ga., U.S.* **96** M8
Twin Falls, *Idaho, U.S.* **106** H5
Twin Peaks, *Idaho, U.S.* **106** F5
Twin Valley, *Minn., U.S.* **104** G8
Twisp, *Wash., U.S.* **108** B6
Twizel, *N.Z.* **213** P16
Two Butte Creek, *Colo., U.S.* **107** P15
Two Buttes, *Colo., U.S.* **107** P16
Two Harbors, *Minn., U.S.* **104** G13
Two Rivers, *Wis., U.S.* **98** K7
Tyab, *Iran* **173** H15
Tybee Island, *Ga., U.S.* **97** N9
Tychy, *Pol.* **149** G15
Tygda, *Russ.* **159** K19
Tyler, *Minn., U.S.* **104** K9
Tyler, *Tex., U.S.* **102** L14
Tylertown, *Miss., U.S.* **100** N11
Tymvou, *Cyprus* **160** P9
Tynda, *Russ.* **159** K18
Tyndall, *S. Dak., U.S.* **104** M7
Tyndaris, ruin, *It.* **151** R11
Tyndrum, *Scot., U.K.* **142** L8
Tynemouth, *Eng., U.K.* **143** P12
Tyonek, *Alas., U.S.* **111** J16
Tyre *see* Soûr, *Leb.* **170** K5
Tyrnyauz, *Russ.* **157** U13
Tyrol, region, *Aust., It.* **150** C6
Tyrone, *Okla., U.S.* **102** E6
Tyrone, *Pa., U.S.* **94** N5
Tyrrell, Lake, *Austral.* **210** L11
Tyrrhenian Sea, *It.* **150** L6
Tyugyuren, *Russ.* **159** E18
Tyukalinsk, *Russ.* **158** J10
Tyumen', *Russ.* **158** J9
Tywyn, *Wales, U.K.* **143** T9
Tzaneen, *S. Af.* **202** H11
Tziá *see* Kéa, island, *Gr.* **155** K13

U

U, *F.S.M.* **217** F14
Uaboe, region, *Nauru* **217** E23
Ua Huka, island, *Fr. Polynesia, Fr.* **215** H14
Ua Pu, island, *Fr. Polynesia, Fr.* **215** H14
Uaroo, *W. Aust., Austral.* **211** T2
Uatio, Île, *New Caledonia, Fr.* **218** E9
Ubá, *Braz.* **131** L15
Ubangi *see* Oubangui, river, *Congo* **201** K18
Ubauro, *Pak.* **177** T8
Ube, *Japan* **185** R5
Ubeda, *Sp.* **144** K11
Uberaba, *Braz.* **131** K13
Uberlândia, *Braz.* **131** K13
Ubierna, *Sp.* **144** C11
Ubon Ratchathani, *Thai.* **186** L11
Ubundu, *Dem. Rep. of the Congo* **198** K11
Üçajy, *Turkm.* **174** M10
Ucar, *Azerb.* **169** D21
Ucayali, river, *Peru* **130** F4
Uch, *Pak.* **177** S9
Uchiura Wan, *Japan* **184** G13
Uchiza, *Peru* **130** G3
Uchquduq, *Uzb.* **174** J11
Udachnyy, *Russ.* **159** G16
Udaipur, *India* **178** H4
Udayagiri, *India* **178** L9
Uddevalla, *Sw.* **140** M12
Uderolal, *Pak.* **177** V7
Udgir, *India* **178** L5
Udhampur, *India* **177** N12
Udine, *It.* **150** D9
Udintsev Fracture Zone, *Pac. Oc.* **238** R12
Udipi, *India* **179** P4
Udon Thani, *Thai.* **186** K10
Udot, island, *F.S.M.* **217** C15
Udskaya Guba, *Russ.* **159** J20
Udu Point, *Fiji Is.* **218** G8
Uebonti, *Indonesia* **189** J14
Ueda, *Japan* **185** N11
Uele, river, *Dem. Rep. of the Congo* **198** H10
Uelen, *Russ.* **159** A21
Uelzen, *Ger.* **148** D8
Ufa, river, *Russ.* **138** C14
Ufa, *Russ.* **158** H8
Ufra, *Turkm.* **174** K6
Ugab, river, *Namibia* **202** G6
Uganda, *Af.* **195** J21
Ugarit *see* Ra's Shamrah, ruin, *Syr.* **170** F6
Uglich, *Russ.* **156** H9
Ugljan, island, *Croatia* **152** F5
Ugljane, *Croatia* **152** G6
Uglovoye, *Russ.* **159** K19
Ugol'nyye Kopi, *Russ.* **159** B21
Ugum, river, *Guam, U.S.* **216** D10
Uherské Hradiště, *Czech Rep.* **149** J13
Uhrichsville, *Ohio, U.S.* **99** Q15
Uig, *Scot., U.K.* **142** H6
Uig, *Scot., U.K.* **142** J7
Uíge, *Angola* **202** C6
'Uiha, island, *Tonga* **218** Q7
'Uiha, *Tonga* **218** Q7
Uinta, river, *Utah, U.S.* **106** L9
Uinta Mountains, *Utah, U.S.* **106** L8
Uiseong, *S. Korea* **182** F14
Uitenhage, *S. Af.* **202** M9
Uithuizen, *Neth.* **146** G14
Ujae Atoll, *Marshall Is.* **216** G3
Ujajiivan, island, *Marshall Is.* **216** L4
Ujelang Atoll, *Marshall Is.* **216** G1
Uji Guntō, *Japan* **185** T3
Ujiie, *Japan* **185** N12
Ujjain, *India* **178** J5
Ujungpandang (Makassar), *Indonesia* **189** L13
Uke Shima, *Japan* **185** W3
Ukhiya, *Bangladesh* **178** K14
Ukhrul, *India* **178** G15
Ukhta, *Russ.* **158** F9
Ukiah, *Calif., U.S.* **109** Q2
Ukiah, *Oreg., U.S.* **108** F7
Uki Ni Masi Island, *Solomon Is.* **217** P20
Ukmergė, *Lith.* **141** N17
Ukraine, *Eur.* **139** U10
Uku, *Japan* **185** R3
Ukulahu, island, *Maldives* **179** U3
Uku Shima, *Japan* **185** R3
Ula, *Turk.* **168** H4
Ulaanbaatar (Ulan Bator), *Mongolia* **180** D12
Ulaangom, *Mongolia* **180** C9
Ulaga, *Russ.* **159** F17
Ulan Bator *see* Ulaanbaatar, *Mongolia* **180** D12
Ulan Erge, *Russ.* **157** R13
Ulanhad *see* Chifeng, *China* **182** B8
Ulanhot, *China* **181** D16
Ulan Khol, *Russ.* **157** S15
Ulansuhai Nur, *China* **182** C2
Ulan Ude, *Russ.* **159** L16
Ulaş, *Turk.* **168** F12
'Ula'ula, Pu'u, *Hawai'i, U.S.* **113** H17
Ulawa, island, *Solomon Is.* **217** N20
Ulawun, Mount, *P.N.G.* **213** C21
Uldz, river, *Mongolia* **181** C14
Uldz, *Mongolia* **181** C13
Uleåborg *see* Oulu, *Fin.* **141** F15
Uleguma, island, *Maldives* **179** T3
Ulen, *Minn., U.S.* **104** G8
Uliastay (Javhlant), *Mongolia* **180** D10
Ulingan, *P.N.G.* **213** C19
Ulithi Atoll, *F.S.M.* **216** P3
Uljin, *S. Korea* **182** F14
Uljma, *Serb. & Mont.* **152** E11
Ülken Borsyq Qumy, *Kaz.* **174** F9
Ullapool, *Scot., U.K.* **142** J8
Ulleungdo (Dagelet), island, *S. Korea* **182** E15
Ulm, *Ger.* **148** K7
Ulmarra, *N.S.W., Austral.* **211** W15
Ulsan, *S. Korea* **182** G15
Ulster, region, *Ire., U.K.* **143** Q6
Ulu, *Russ.* **159** H18
Ulubat Gölü, *Turk.* **168** D4
Uluborlu, *Turk.* **168** G6
Ulu Dağ (Mount Olympus), *Turk.* **168** D5
Ulufala Point, *Amer. Samoa, U.S.* **218** P4
Uluiutu, island, *Wallis & Futuna, Fr.* **218** A11
Ulukışla, *Turk.* **168** H9
Ulul, island, *F.S.M.* **216** Q5
Ulundi, *S. Af.* **202** K11
Ulungur Hu, *China* **180** D7
Uluru *see* Ayers Rock, peak, *Austral.* **210** G7
Ulus, *Turk.* **168** C8
Ulva, island, *Scot., U.K.* **142** L7
Ulvéah *see* Lopévi, island, *Vanuatu* **218** E3
Ulverston, *Eng., U.K.* **143** Q10
Ul'yanovsk, *Russ.* **156** K14
Ulysses, *Kans., U.S.* **105** U3
Ulytaū, range, *Kaz.* **174** E12
Uman, island, *F.S.M.* **217** C15
Uman', *Ukr.* **157** P5
Umari, *Indonesia* **189** L19
Umaria, *India* **178** J7
Umarkot, *Pak.* **177** V8
Umatac, *Guam, U.S.* **216** D10
Umatac Bay, *Guam, U.S.* **216** D10
Umatilla, river, *Oreg., U.S.* **108** F8
Umatilla, *Oreg., U.S.* **108** E7
Umba, *Russ.* **158** D8
Umboi, island, *P.N.G.* **213** C20
Umbriatico, *It.* **151** P14
Umbukul, *P.N.G.* **213** B20
Umeå, *Sw.* **141** G14
Umeälven, river, *Sw.* **141** G13
Umfors, *Sw.* **140** F12
'Umikoa, *Hawai'i, U.S.* **113** L20
Umm al Arānib, *Lib.* **197** E14
Umm al Qaywayn, *U.A.E.* **173** J15
Umm as Samīm, dry lake, *Oman, Saudi Arabia* **173** L15
Umm Bugma, site, *Egypt* **171** S2
Umm Durmān *see* Omdurman, *Sudan* **199** D13
Umm Lajj, *Saudi Arabia* **172** J6
Umm Qaşr, *Iraq* **172** F11
Umm Urūmah, island, *Saudi Arabia* **172** H5
Umnak Island, *Alas., U.S.* **110** P9
Umpqua, river, *Oreg., U.S.* **108** J2
Umred, *India* **178** K7
Umtata, *S. Af.* **202** L11
Umuahia, *Nigeria* **201** H14
Umuna, island, *Tonga* **218** L12
Una, river, *Bosn. & Herzg., Croatia* **152** E6
Unadilla, *Ga., U.S.* **97** N6
Unai Obyan, peninsula, *N. Mariana Is., U.S.* **216** D5
Unai Pass, *Afghan.* **176** M7
Unalakleet, *Alas., U.S.* **111** G13
Unalaska, *Alas., U.S.* **110** P9
Unalaska Island, *Alas., U.S.* **110** P9
'Unayzah, *Jordan* **171** Q6
'Unayzah, *Saudi Arabia* **172** H9
'Unayzah, Jabal, *Iraq, Jordan, Saudi Arabia* **170** M12
Uncía, *Bol.* **130** K7
Uncompahgre Peak, *Colo., U.S.* **107** P11
Uncompahgre Plateau, *Colo., U.S.* **107** N10
Underwood, *N. Dak., U.S.* **104** F4
Undurhaan, *Mongolia* **181** D13
Unecha, *Russ.* **156** L7
Ungama Bay, *Kenya* **194** K10
Ungava Bay, *Que., Can.* **83** J19
Ungava, Péninsule d', *Que., Can.* **83** J18
Ungava Peninsula *see* Ungava, Péninsule d', *N. Amer.* **80** F8
União da Vitória, *Braz.* **130** N12
Unije, island, *Croatia* **152** F4
Unikar, Mochun, *F.S.M.* **217** C16
Unimak Island, *Alas., U.S.* **110** N11
Unimak Pass, *Alas., U.S.* **110** N10
Unini, river, *Braz.* **130** D8
Union, *Grenada* **121** J23
Union, *Miss., U.S.* **100** L12
Union, *Mo., U.S.* **105** T14
Union, *Oreg., U.S.* **108** F8
Union, *S.C., U.S.* **96** J8
Union, island, *St. Vincent & the Grenadines* **119** M17

Unión, Bahía, *Arg.* **133** P11
Union City, *Ohio, U.S.* **99** Q11
Union City, *Pa., U.S.* **94** L3
Union City, *Tenn., U.S.* **100** E12
Union Point, *Ga., U.S.* **96** L6
Union Springs, *Ala., U.S.* **101** L16
Uniontown, *Ala., U.S.* **101** L14
Uniontown, *Pa., U.S.* **94** P3
Unionville, *Mo., U.S.* **105** Q12
Unionville, *Nev., U.S.* **109** N8
United Arab Emirates, *Asia* **167** V4
United Estates, *Bahamas* **120** E12
United Kingdom, *Eur.* **139** S4
United States, *N. Amer.* **81** K18
Unity, *Oreg., U.S.* **108** G8
University Park, *N. Mex., U.S.* **107** V12
Unnao, *India* **178** G7
Unst, island, *Scot., U.K.* **142** C12
Ünye, *Turk.* **168** D12
Unzha, *Russ.* **156** G12
Uoleva, island, *Tonga* **218** P7
Upata, *Venez.* **128** C12
Upemba, Lake, *Dem. Rep. of the Congo* **194** L8
Upernavik Kujalleq, *Greenland, Den.* **81** C20
Upham, *N. Dak., U.S.* **104** E4
Upington, *S. Af.* **202** K8
Upolu, island, *Samoa* **218** L3
'Upolu Point, *Hawai'i, U.S.* **113** J19
Upper Arlington, *Ohio, U.S.* **99** R13
Upper Bogue, *Bahamas* **120** D5
Upper Darby, *Pa., U.S.* **94** P9
Upper Guinea, region, *Af.* **194** H3
Upper Hutt, *N.Z.* **213** M19
Upper Kama Upland, *Russ.* **138** C13
Upper Klamath Lake, *Oreg., U.S.* **108** K4
Upper Lake, *Calif., U.S.* **108** L6
Upper Lough Erne, *N. Ire., U.K.* **143** Q5
Upper Manzanilla, *Trinidad & Tobago* **121** P23
Upper Missouri River Breaks National Monument, *Mont., U.S.* **106** C10
Upper Peninsula, *Mich., U.S.* **98** F6
Upper Red Lake, *Minn., U.S.* **104** E10
Upper St. Clair, *Pa., U.S.* **94** N3
Upper Sandusky, *Ohio, U.S.* **99** Q12
Uppsala, *Sw.* **141** K14
Upshi, *India* **178** C6
Upton, *Wyo., U.S.* **106** G13
'Uqayribāt, *Syr.* **170** F9
Ur, ruin, *Iraq* **172** F10
Urabá, Golfo de, *Col.* **128** D4
Urad Houqi, *China* **182** B1
Urad Qianqi, *China* **182** C2
Urad Zhongqi, *China* **182** B2
Urakawa, *Japan* **184** G14
Ural, river, *Kaz., Russ.* **166** E5
Ural, river, *Russ.* **158** J8
Uralla, *N.S.W., Austral.* **211** W15
Ural Mountains, *Russ.* **166** D7
Urana, *N.S.W., Austral.* **211** Y13
Urandangi, *Qnsld., Austral.* **211** S10
Urania, *La., U.S.* **100** M8
Uranium City, *Sask., Can.* **82** J12
Uranu, island, *F.S.M.* **217** B14
Uraricoera, river, *Braz.* **130** B8
Uraricoera, *Braz.* **130** B9
Uravan, *Colo., U.S.* **107** N10
Urawa, *Japan* **185** P12
Urbana, *Ill., U.S.* **99** R7
Urbana, *Ohio, U.S.* **99** R12
Urbandale, *Iowa, U.S.* **105** P11
Urbano Noris, *Cuba* **116** K12
Urbett, island, *Marshall Is.* **216** K7
Urbino, *It.* **150** G8
Urbión, Picos de, *Sp.* **144** D12
Urdos, *Fr.* **147** Y6
Uren', *Russ.* **156** G13
Uréparapara, island, *Vanuatu* **218** A2
Urganch, *Uzb.* **174** K9
Urgut, *Uzb.* **174** L12
Uriah, Mount, *N.Z.* **213** N17
Uribia, *Col.* **128** A6
Uriondo, *Bol.* **130** L7
Uritskoye, *Russ.* **159** H17
Urla, *Turk.* **168** F2
Urlaţi, *Rom.* **153** E15
Urlins, *Antigua & Barbuda* **121** B20
Urmia, Lake *see* Orūmīyeh, Daryācheh-ye, *Iran* **172** B10
Uroševac, *Serb. & Mont.* **152** J11
Ūroteppa *see* Istaravshan, *Taj.* **176** G7
Urt Moron, *China* **180** H8
Uruana, *Braz.* **131** J13
Uruapan, *Mex.* **114** J10
Urubamba, river, *Peru* **130** H5
Urucará, *Braz.* **130** D10
Uruçuí, *Braz.* **131** F15
Uruçuí, Serra do, *S. Amer.* **126** F9
Urugi, *Japan* **185** P10
Uruguai, river, *Braz.* **130** N11
Uruguaiana, *Braz.* **130** P10
Uruguay, *S. Amer.* **127** L19
Uruguay, river, *S. Amer.* **126** K7
Urukthapel (Ngeruktabel), island, *Palau* **216** P11
Ürümqi, *China* **180** E7
Uruno Point, *Guam, U.S.* **216** B11
Urup, island, *Russ.* **159** J23
Uryupinsk, *Russ.* **157** N12
Ürzhar, *Kaz.* **175** F18
Urzhum, *Russ.* **156** G15
Urziceni, *Rom.* **153** F16
Usa, *Japan* **185** R7
Usa, river, *Russ.* **138** A12
Uşak, *Turk.* **168** F5
Usakos, *Namibia* **202** H6
Usarp Mountains, *Antarctica* **227** Q15
Usedom, island, *Ger.* **148** B11
Useldange, *Lux.* **160** J9
Ushakova, Ostrov, *Russ.* **159** C13
Ushakovskoye, *Russ.* **159** B19
Üsharal, *Kaz.* **175** F18
Ushibuka, *Japan* **185** S4
Ushi Point, *N. Mariana Is., U.S.* **216** A8
Üshtöbe, *Kaz.* **175** G17
Ushuaia, *Arg.* **133** X9
Ushumun, *Russ.* **159** K19
Usinsk, *Russ.* **158** F10
Usman', *Russ.* **156** M10
Usol'ye Sibirskoye, *Russ.* **159** L15
Usove, *Ukr.* **156** M4
U.S. Range, *Nunavut, Can.* **83** A16
U.S.S. Arizona Memorial, *Hawai'i, U.S.* **112** E11
Ussel, *Fr.* **147** U10
Ussuri, river, *China, Russ.* **166** E12
Ussuriysk, *Russ.* **159** M21
Uster, *Switz.* **150** A4
Ustica, *It.* **151** R9
Ustica, Isola di, *It.* **151** R9
Ust' Ilimpeya, *Russ.* **159** H15
Ust' Ilimsk, *Russ.* **159** K15
Ustí nad Labem, *Czech Rep.* **148** G11
Ustka, *Pol.* **149** B13
Ust' Kamchatsk, *Russ.* **159** E22
Ust' Kamenogorsk *see* Öskemen, *Kaz.* **175** D18
Ust' Kamo, *Russ.* **159** J14
Ust' Kut, *Russ.* **159** K15
Ust' Labinsk, *Russ.* **157** S11
Ust' Maya, *Russ.* **159** G19
Ust' Mil', *Russ.* **159** H19
Ust' Nera, *Russ.* **159** F19
Ust' Olenek, *Russ.* **159** E16
Ust' Omchug, *Russ.* **159** F20
Ust' Ordynskiy, *Russ.* **159** L15
Ust' Usa, *Russ.* **158** F10
Ust' Yansk, *Russ.* **159** E17
Ust' Yudoma, *Russ.* **159** H19
Ustyurt Plateau, *Kaz., Uzb.* **174** H7
Ustyuzhna, *Russ.* **156** G9
Usu, *China* **180** E7
Usuki, *Japan* **185** R5
Usumacinta, river, *N. Amer.* **80** P6
Usvyaty, *Russ.* **156** J6
Uta, *Indonesia* **189** L19
Utah, *U.S.* **106** M6
Utah Beach, *Fr.* **147** N6
Utah Lake, *Utah, U.S.* **106** L7
Utara, Bunguran *see* Natuna Besar, Kepulauan, *Indonesia* **188** G8
Ute Creek, *N. Mex., U.S.* **107** Q14
Utete, *Tanzania* **199** M15
Uthai Thani, *Thai.* **186** L8
Uthal, *Pak.* **177** V5
Utiariti, *Braz.* **130** H10
Utica, *N.Y., U.S.* **94** J9
Utiel, *Sp.* **145** H14
Utirik Atoll, *Marshall Is.* **216** F4
Utkela, *India* **178** L9
Utnur, *India* **178** L6
Utopia, *N. Terr., Austral.* **211** T9
Utraula, *India* **178** G8
Utrecht, *Neth.* **146** J12
Utsunomiya, *Japan* **185** N12
Utta, *Russ.* **157** R14
Uttaradit, *Thai.* **186** K8
Utuado, *P.R., U.S.* **120** N3
Utuloa, *Wallis & Futuna, Fr.* **218** B11
Utupua, island, *Solomon Is.* **217** Q23
Uturoa, *Fr. Polynesia, Fr.* **219** B23
Utva, river, *Kaz.* **174** D7
Utwa, *F.S.M.* **217** B18
Uummannaq, *Greenland, Den.* **81** C21
Uusikaupunki, *Fin.* **141** J15
Uva, *Russ.* **156** G16
Uvalde, *Tex., U.S.* **103** R8
Uvarovo, *Russ.* **156** M12
Uvéa *see* Ouvéa, Île, island, *New Caledonia, Fr.* **218** C8
Uvea, island, *Wallis & Futuna, Fr.* **218** B11
Uvinza, *Tanzania* **198** L12
Uvol, *P.N.G.* **213** D21
Uvs Nuur, *Mongolia* **180** C9
Uwajima, *Japan* **185** R6
'Uwayrid, Ḩarrat al, *Saudi Arabia* **172** H6
'Uweinat, Jebel, *Sudan* **198** C11
Uxin Qi (Dabqig), *China* **182** E2
Uxmal, ruin, *Mex.* **115** H16
Uyar, *Russ.* **159** K13
Uyuni, *Bol.* **130** L7
Uyuni, Salar de, *Bol.* **130** L7
Uzbekistan, *Asia* **167** T6
Uzbel Shankou, *China, Taj.* **176** H11
Uzerche, *Fr.* **147** U9
Uzès, *Fr.* **147** W12
Uzhhorod, *Ukr.* **157** P1
Užice, *Serb. & Mont.* **152** G9
Uzlovaya, *Russ.* **156** K9
Üzümlü, *Turk.* **168** H4
Uzunköprü, *Turk.* **168** C3
Uzynköl, *Kaz.* **174** B11

V

Vaal, river, *S. Af.* **202** K10
Vaals, *Neth.* **146** L13
Vaasa, *Fin.* **141** H14
Vác, *Hung.* **149** L15
Vacaville, *Calif., U.S.* **109** R4
Vache, Île à, *Haiti* **117** N15
Vacía Talega, Punta, *P.R., U.S.* **120** M5
Vacoas, *Mauritius* **205** G20
Vadodara, *India* **178** J3
Vadsø, *Nor.* **141** C15
Vaduz, *Liech.* **160** P2
Vaduz Castle, *Liech.* **160** P2
Værøy, island, *Nor.* **140** E11
Vaga, river, *Russ.* **138** C11
Vágar, island, *Faroe Is., Den.* **140** J5
Vaghena, island, *Solomon Is.* **217** L16
Vagthus Point, *Virgin Islands, U.S.* **120** R3
Váh, river, *Slovakia* **149** J14
Vahanga, island, *Fr. Polynesia, Fr.* **219** G22
Vahitahi, island, *Fr. Polynesia, Fr.* **219** F21
Vahituri, island, *Fr. Polynesia, Fr.* **219** L17
Vaiaau, *Fr. Polynesia, Fr.* **219** B23
Vaiau, Passe, *Fr. Polynesia, Fr.* **219** Q17
Vaiden, *Miss., U.S.* **100** K11
Vaiea, *Niue, N.Z.* **219** B20
Vaiere, island, *Cook Is., N.Z.* **219** C17
Vaigalu, *Samoa* **218** L4
Vaihiria, Lac, *Fr. Polynesia, Fr.* **219** P16
Vail, *Colo., U.S.* **106** M12
Vaila, island, *Scot., U.K.* **142** D11
Vailala, *Wallis & Futuna, Fr.* **218** B11
Vailoa, *Samoa* **218** K2
Vailoatai, *Amer. Samoa, U.S.* **218** N7
Vaimalau, *Wallis & Futuna, Fr.* **218** B11
Vaini, *Tonga* **218** J11
Vaionifa, Passe, *Fr. Polynesia, Fr.* **219** P18
Vaipae, *Cook Is., N.Z.* **218** Q11
Vaipaee, *Fr. Polynesia, Fr.* **219** N23
Vaipeka, *Cook Is., N.Z.* **218** P11
Vairaatea, island, *Fr. Polynesia, Fr.* **219** F21
Vairo, *Fr. Polynesia, Fr.* **219** Q17
Vaitahu, *Fr. Polynesia, Fr.* **219** N20
Vaïtape, *Fr. Polynesia, Fr.* **219** K14
Vaitoare, *Fr. Polynesia, Fr.* **219** B23
Vaitogi, *Amer. Samoa, U.S.* **218** N7
Vaitupu, island, *Tuvalu* **214** H9
Vaitupu, *Wallis & Futuna, Fr.* **218** B11
Vai'utukakau Bay, *Tonga* **218** L11
Vaka'eitu, island, *Tonga* **218** M11
Vakfıkebir, *Turk.* **169** D14
Vakhan, region, *Afghan.* **176** K10
Vakhrushev, *Russ.* **159** J22
Vakhsh, river, *Taj.* **176** H9
Vakhtan, *Russ.* **156** G13
Valamaz, *Russ.* **156** G15
Valcheta, *Arg.* **133** Q9
Valdagno, *It.* **150** D7
Valdahon, *Fr.* **147** S14
Valdai Hills, *Russ.* **138** D10
Valdayskaya Vozvyshennost', *Russ.* **156** J7
Valdepeñas, *Sp.* **144** J11
Valderrobres, *Sp.* **145** F15
Valdes, Península, *Arg.* **133** R10
Valdez, *Alas., U.S.* **111** J18
Valdez, *Ecua.* **128** H2
Valdivia, *Chile* **133** P6
Valdivia, *Col.* **128** D4
Valdivia Fracture Zone, *Pac. Oc.* **239** P19
Val-d'Or, *Que., Can.* **83** P18
Valdosta, *Ga., U.S.* **97** Q6
Valdragone, *San Marino* **161** J15
Vale, *Oreg., U.S.* **108** H9
Valea lui Mihai, *Rom.* **152** B11
Valença, *Port.* **144** D5
Valença, *Braz.* **131** H16
Valence, *Fr.* **147** V13
Valence, *Fr.* **147** W8
Valencia, *Sp.* **145** H14
Valencia, *Venez.* **128** B9
Valencia, Golfo de, *Sp.* **145** H15
Valencia, Lake, *S. Amer.* **126** A4
Valenciennes, *Fr.* **146** M11
Valentia Island, *Ire.* **143** U2
Valentine, *Nebr., U.S.* **104** M4
Valentine, *Tex., U.S.* **103** P1
Valenza, *It.* **150** E4
Valera, *Venez.* **128** C7
Valga, *Est.* **141** L17
Valguarnera Caropepe, *It.* **151** S11
Valier, *Mont., U.S.* **106** B7
Valinco, Golfe de, *Fr.* **150** L4
Valira, river, *Andorra* **160** J3
Valira del Nort, river, *Andorra* **160** J3
Valira d'Orient, river, *Andorra* **160** H4
Valjevo, *Serb. & Mont.* **152** F9
Valka, *Latv.* **141** L17
Valkeakoski, *Fin.* **141** J15
Valkenswaard, *Neth.* **146** K13
Valkyrie Dome, *Antarctica* **227** D15
Valladolid, *Mex.* **115** H16
Valladolid, *Sp.* **144** D10
Valle de la Pascua, *Venez.* **128** C10
Valledupar, *Col.* **128** B6
Valle Fértil, Sierra del, *Arg.* **132** J8
Valle Formozo, *Sao Tome and Principe* **205** D20
Vallegrande, *Bol.* **130** K8
Vallehermoso, *Canary Is.* **204** Q4
Vallejo, *Calif., U.S.* **109** R3
Vallenar, *Chile* **132** H6
Valletta, *Malta* **161** K23
Valley Center, *Kans., U.S.* **105** U7
Valley City, *N. Dak., U.S.* **104** G7
Valley Falls, *Kans., U.S.* **105** S9
Valley Falls, *Oreg., U.S.* **108** K6
Valley Mills, *Tex., U.S.* **103** N11
Valley Station, *Ky., U.S.* **101** B16
Vallo della Lucania, *It.* **151** N12
Vallorbe, *Switz.* **150** B1
Valls, *Sp.* **145** E16
Valmeyer, *Ill., U.S.* **99** T4
Valmiera, *Latv.* **141** L17
Valmy, *Fr.* **147** P12
Valona *see* Vlorë, *Albania* **152** M9
Valozhyn, *Belarus* **156** K4
Valparaiso, *Fla., U.S.* **97** Q2
Valparaiso, *Ind., U.S.* **99** P8
Valparaíso, *Chile* **132** K6
Valparaíso, *Mex.* **114** G10
Vals, Tanjung, *Indonesia* **213** D16
Valsad, *India* **178** K3
Valüna, valley, *Liech.* **160** Q3
Valuyevka, *Russ.* **157** R13
Valuyki, *Russ.* **157** N10
Valverde, *Canary Is.* **204** R3
Valverde del Camino, *Sp.* **144** K7
Van, *Turk.* **169** G17
Van, Lake, *Turk.* **166** F4
Vana, *Solomon Is.* **217** R23
Vanadzor, *Arm.* **169** D18
Van Alstyne, *Tex., U.S.* **102** K12
Vanavana, island, *Fr. Polynesia, Fr.* **219** G21
Vanavara, *Russ.* **159** J15
Van Blommestein Meer, *Suriname* **129** E16
Van Buren, *Ark., U.S.* **100** F6
Van Buren, *Me., U.S.* **95** A18
Vanceboro, *Me., U.S.* **95** D19
Vanceboro, *N.C., U.S.* **96** H13
Vanceburg, *Ky., U.S.* **101** A19
Vancouver, *B.C., Can.* **82** M8
Vancouver, *Wash., U.S.* **108** F3
Vancouver Island, *B.C., Can.* **82** L7
Vandalia, *Ill., U.S.* **99** S5
Vandalia, *Mo., U.S.* **105** S14
Vandalia, *Ohio, U.S.* **99** R11
Vanderbilt, *Mich., U.S.* **98** H11
Vanderford Glacier, *Antarctica* **227** M20
Van Diemen, Cape, *Austral.* **210** A7
Van Diemen Gulf, *Austral.* **210** A8
Vänern, lake, *Sw.* **140** L12
Vangaindrano, *Madagascar* **203** H17
Van Gölü, *Turk.* **169** G17
Vangunu, island, *Solomon Is.* **217** M17
Vangunu, Mount, *Solomon Is.* **217** M16
Vangviang, *Laos* **186** J10
Van Horn, *Tex., U.S.* **103** N1
Vanikolo, island, *Solomon Is.* **217** R23
Vanikolo Islands, *Solomon Is.* **217** R23
Vanimo, *P.N.G.* **213** B17
Vanino, *Russ.* **159** K21
Vanj, *Taj.* **176** J9
Vankarem, *Russ.* **159** A20
Vännäs, *Sw.* **141** G14
Vannes, *Fr.* **147** R4
Van Ninh, *Vietnam* **187** N14
Vannøy, island, *Nor.* **141** C13
Vanoise, Massif de la, *Fr.* **147** U15
Vanrhynsdorp, *S. Af.* **202** L7
Vanrook, *Qnsld., Austral.* **211** R12
Vansbro, *Sw.* **140** K12
Vansittart Island, *Nunavut, Can.* **83** G16
Van Tassell, *Wyo., U.S.* **106** H14
Vanua, island, *Fiji Is.* **218** H9
Vanua Lava, island, *Vanuatu* **218** B2
Vanua Levu, island, *Fiji Is.* **218** G7
Vanua Masi, island, *Fiji Is.* **218** J9
Vanuatu, *Pac. Oc.* **214** K8
Vanua Vatu, island, *Fiji Is.* **218** J9
Vanuca, island, *Fiji Is.* **218** J6
Van Wert, *Ohio, U.S.* **99** Q11
Vao, *New Caledonia, Fr.* **218** E9
Vao, Nosy, *Madagascar* **203** F16
Varadero, *Cuba* **116** G7
Varanasi (Banaras), *India* **178** H9
Varangerfjorden, bay, *Nor.* **141** C15
Varangerhalvøya, peninsula, *Nor.* **141** B15
Varano, Lago di, *It.* **150** K12
Varas, *Afghan.* **177** N4
Varaždin, *Croatia* **152** D6
Varazze, *It.* **150** F3
Varberg, *Sw.* **140** M12
Vardar, river, *Maced.* **152** K12
Vardø, *Nor.* **141** B15
Varėna, *Lith.* **141** N17
Varennes, *Fr.* **147** N13
Varese, *It.* **150** D4
Varilhes, *Fr.* **147** Y9
Varkaus, *Fin.* **141** H16
Varna, *Bulg.* **153** H17
Varnavino, *Russ.* **156** H12
Varnenski Zaliv, *Bulg.* **153** H17
Varnensko Ezero, *Bulg.* **153** H17
Varnville, *S.C., U.S.* **96** M9
Varosha, *Cyprus* **160** P10
Varto, *Turk.* **169** F16
Vårts Järv, *Est.* **141** L17
Varungga Point, *Solomon Is.* **217** L16
Varzob, *Taj.* **176** H7
Varzy, *Fr.* **147** R11
Vasafua, island, *Tuvalu* **217** K22
Vasiliko, *Cyprus* **160** Q8
Vasil'yevo, *Russ.* **156** J14
Vaskess Bay, *Kiribati* **217** B22

Vaslui, *Rom.* **153** C17
Vassar, *Mich., U.S.* **98** L12
Vassilikí, *Gr.* **154** H7
Vassilikós, *Gr.* **154** K8
Vassilítsa, Óros, *Gr.* **154** E8
Västerås, *Sw.* **141** K13
Västervik, *Sw.* **141** M13
Vasto, *It.* **150** K11
Vasyl'kiv, *Ukr.* **157** N6
Vasyugan'ye, wetland, *Russ.* **166** E8
Vatan, *Fr.* **147** S9
Vaté, Île *see* Éfaté, *Vanuatu* **218** F3
Vatersay, island, *Scot., U.K.* **142** K6
Vathí, *Gr.* **154** H12
Vathý *see* Itháki, *Gr.* **154** H7
Vatia, *Amer. Samoa, U.S.* **218** M8
Vatia Bay, *Amer. Samoa, U.S.* **218** L8
Vatia Point, *Fiji Is.* **218** H6
Vatican City, *Eur.* **160** D4
Vatican Gardens, *Vatican City* **161** P15
Vatican Library, *Vatican City* **161** P16
Vatican Museums, *Vatican City* **161** N16
Vaticano, Capo, *It.* **151** R13
Vatican Radio, *Vatican City* **161** Q14
Vatili, *Cyprus* **160** P9
Vatnajökull, glacier, *Ice.* **140** F3
Vatneyri, *Ice.* **140** E2
Vatoa, island, *Fiji Is.* **214** K9
Vatoa (Turtle), island, *Fiji Is.* **218** L10
Vatra Dornei, *Rom.* **153** B14
Vättern, lake, *Sw.* **141** L13
Vatuki, island, *Fiji Is.* **218** G7
Vatukoula, *Fiji Is.* **218** H6
Vatulele, island, *Fiji Is.* **218** J6
Vatu Vara, island, *Fiji Is.* **218** H8
Vaughn, *Mont., U.S.* **106** C7
Vaughn, *N. Mex., U.S.* **107** S13
Vaupés, river, *Col.* **128** H7
Vauvilliers, Île, *New Caledonia, Fr.* **218** C9
Vauvilliers, Point, *F.S.M.* **217** B17
Vav, *India* **178** H3
Vavara, Motu, *Fr. Polynesia, Fr.* **219** G14
Vava'u, island, *Tonga* **218** L12
Vava'u Group, *Tonga* **214** K10
Vavitu *see* Raivavae, island, *Fr. Polynesia, Fr.* **219** J17
Vavla, *Cyprus* **160** Q8
Vavuniya, *Sri Lanka* **179** S7
Vawkavysk, *Belarus* **156** L3
Växjö, *Sw.* **141** M13
Vayegi, *Russ.* **159** C21
Vaygach, Ostrov, *Russ.* **158** E11
Veblen, *S. Dak., U.S.* **104** H7
Vecchia, river, *San Marino* **161** J16
Vedea, river, *Rom.* **153** G15
Vedeno, *Russ.* **157** U14
Veendam, *Neth.* **146** G14
Vega, island, *Nor.* **140** G11
Vega, *Tex., U.S.* **102** G4
Vega Baja, *P.R., U.S.* **120** M4
Vegadeo, *Sp.* **144** A7
Veghel, *Neth.* **146** K13
Vegorítida, Límni, *Gr.* **154** C9
Vegreville, *Alta., Can.* **82** L11
Veharnu, island, *P.N.G.* **217** H14
Veio, ruin, *It.* **150** K8
Vejer de la Frontera, *Sp.* **144** N8
Vekai, island, *Fiji Is.* **218** H9
Velarde, *N. Mex., U.S.* **107** R12
Velas, *Azores* **144** P3
Velay, Monts du, *Fr.* **147** V11
Velbert, *Ger.* **148** F5
Velden, *Aust.* **148** M10
Velé, *Wallis & Futuna, Fr.* **218** E11
Velé, Pointe, *Wallis & Futuna, Fr.* **218** E12
Velebit, range, *Croatia* **152** F5
Velenje, *Slov.* **152** C5
Veles, *Maced.* **152** K11
Velestíno, *Gr.* **154** F11
Vélez, *Col.* **128** E5
Velež, peak, *Bosn. & Herzg.* **152** H8
Vélez de la Gomera, Peñón de, *Sp.* **144** P10
Vélez-Málaga, *Sp.* **144** M10
Velhas, river, *Braz.* **131** K14
Velia, ruin, *It.* **151** N12
Velika, river, *Serb. & Mont.* **152** F11
Velika Ljubuša, peak, *Bosn. & Herzg.* **152** G7
Velika Plana, *Serb. & Mont.* **152** F10
Velikaya, river, *Russ.* **138** E9
Veliki Drvenik, island, *Croatia* **152** G6
Veliki Snežnik, peak, *Slov.* **152** D4
Veliki Troglav, peak, *Bosn. & Herzg.* **152** G6
Velikiye Luki, *Russ.* **156** J6
Velikiy Novgorod, *Russ.* **156** G7
Velikonda Range, *India* **179** N7
Veliko Tŭrnovo, *Bulg.* **153** H15
Vélingara, *Senegal* **196** H5
Velingrad, *Bulg.* **153** K13
Velizh, *Russ.* **156** J6
Vella Gulf, *Solomon Is.* **217** M15
Vella Lavella, island, *Solomon Is.* **217** L15
Velletri, *It.* **150** L9
Vellore, *India* **179** Q6
Velopoúla, island, *Gr.* **154** L12
Vel'sk, *Russ.* **158** F7
Velva, *N. Dak., U.S.* **104** F4
Vema Fracture Zone, *Atl. Oc.* **236** M7
Vema Fracture Zone, *Ind. Oc.* **240** H8
Vema Seamount, *Atl. Oc.* **237** S14
Véna, *Gr.* **155** B15
Venable Ice Shelf, *Antarctica* **226** H6
Venado Tuerto, *Arg.* **132** L11
Venango, *Nebr., U.S.* **105** Q3
Vendas Novas, *Port.* **144** J5
Vendôme, *Fr.* **147** R8
Vendôme, *Grenada* **121** K22
Veneta, Laguna, *It.* **150** E8
Venetie, *Alas., U.S.* **111** E17
Venétiko, island, *Gr.* **154** M9
Venezia (Venice), *It.* **150** E8
Venezuela, *Neth. Antilles, Neth.* **121** Q18
Venezuela, *S. Amer.* **127** B17
Venezuela, Golfo de, *Venez.* **128** B7
Vengurla, *India* **179** N3
Veniaminof, Mount, *Alas., U.S.* **111** N13
Venice, *Fla., U.S.* **97** V7
Venice *see* Venezia, *It.* **150** E8
Venice, *La., U.S.* **100** R12
Venice, Gulf of, *It.* **150** E9
Venkatapuram, *India* **178** M7
Venlo, *Neth.* **146** K14
Vennesund, *Nor.* **140** G11
Venosa, *It.* **150** M12
Venray, *Neth.* **146** K13
Vent, Îles du, *Fr. Polynesia, Fr.* **219** F16
Ventimiglia, *It.* **150** G2
Ventnor City, *N.J., U.S.* **94** Q10
Ventoso, *San Marino* **161** H15
Ventoso, Monte, *San Marino* **161** H15
Ventotene, Isola, *It.* **150** M9
Ventoux, Mont, *Fr.* **147** W13
Ventry, *Ire.* **143** U2
Ventspils, *Latv.* **141** M15
Ventuari, river, *Venez.* **128** F10
Ventura, *Calif., U.S.* **109** X7
Vénus, Pointe, *Fr. Polynesia, Fr.* **219** N16
Venus, Bahia de, *Eq. Guinea* **204** L7
Vera, *Arg.* **132** H12
Vera, *Sp.* **145** L13
Vera, Bahía, *Arg.* **133** R10
Veracruz, *Mex.* **115** J13
Veraval, *India* **178** K2
Verbania, *It.* **150** D4
Vercelli, *It.* **150** E3
Verçinin Tepesi, *Turk.* **169** D15
Verdalsøra, *Nor.* **140** H11
Verde, river, *Ariz., U.S.* **107** T7
Verde, Cape, *Senegal* **194** G1
Verde, Cay, *Bahamas* **117** H13
Verde, Península, *Arg.* **133** P11
Verdigre, *Nebr., U.S.* **105** N7
Verdigris, river, *Kans., Okla., U.S.* **85** J13
Verdun, *Fr.* **147** N13
Vereeniging, *S. Af.* **202** J10
Verga, Cap, *Guinea* **200** F4
Vergara, *Chile* **132** D7
Vergara, *Uru.* **132** K15
Vergato, *It.* **150** F6
Vergennes, *Vt., U.S.* **94** G12
Vergina, ruin, *Gr.* **154** D10
Vergt, *Fr.* **147** V8
Véria, *Gr.* **154** D10
Verín, *Sp.* **144** D7
Verkhneimbatsk, *Russ.* **159** H13
Verkhneye Penzhino, *Russ.* **159** D20
Verkhnyaya Amga, *Russ.* **159** H18
Verkhovazh'ye, *Russ.* **156** E11
Verkhov'ye, *Russ.* **156** L9
Verkhoyanskiy Khrebet, *Russ.* **159** F17
Verkhoyansk Range, *Russ.* **166** C11
Vermelharia, Ponta da, *Cape Verde* **205** B15
Vermelho, river, *Braz.* **130** J12
Vermenton, *Fr.* **147** R11
Vermilion Bay, *La., U.S.* **100** Q8
Vermilion Cliffs National Monument, *Ariz., U.S.* **107** Q7
Vermilion Lake, *Minn., U.S.* **104** F12
Vermilion Range, *Minn., U.S.* **104** F13
Vermillion, *S. Dak., U.S.* **104** M8
Vérmio, Óros, *Gr.* **154** C9
Vermont, *St. Vincent & the Grenadines* **121** K16
Vermont, *U.S.* **94** G12
Vernadsky, station, *Antarctica* **226** D4
Vernal, *Utah, U.S.* **106** L9
Verneuil, *Fr.* **147** P8
Vérno, Óros, *Gr.* **154** C8
Vernon, *Ala., U.S.* **101** J13
Vernon, *Fr.* **147** P9
Vernon, *Tex., U.S.* **102** J8
Vernonia, *Oreg., U.S.* **108** E3
Vernou, *Guadeloupe, Fr.* **121** F14
Vero Beach, *Fla., U.S.* **97** U10
Verona, *It.* **150** E6
Verona, *Miss., U.S.* **101** H13
Verraco, Punta, *P.R., U.S.* **120** P2
Versailles, *Fr.* **147** P10
Versailles, *Ky., U.S.* **101** B17
Versailles, *Mo., U.S.* **105** T12
Verte, Pointe, *Wallis & Futuna, Fr.* **218** E12
Vertientes, *Cuba* **116** J10
Verucchio, *It.* **161** G14
Verzy, *Fr.* **147** P12
Vescovato, *Fr.* **150** J4
Veselyy, *Russ.* **159** J17
Vesoul, *Fr.* **147** R14
Vesterålen, *Nor.* **140** D12
Vestfjorden, *Nor.* **140** E12
Vestfold Hills, *Antarctica* **227** G20
Vestmanna, *Faroe Is., Den.* **140** J6
Vestmannaeyjar (Westman Islands), *Ice.* **140** G2
Veststraumen Glacier, *Antarctica* **226** C11
Vestvågøy, island, *Nor.* **140** E12
Vesuvio, Monte, *It.* **150** M11
Vesuvius *see* Vesuvio, Monte, peak, *It.* **138** J7
Ves'yegonsk, *Russ.* **156** G9
Veszprém, *Hung.* **149** M14
Vétaounde, island, *Vanuatu* **218** A2
Vetapalem, *India* **179** N7
Vetavuua, island, *Fiji Is.* **218** G9
Vetluga, river, *Russ.* **138** C12
Vetralla, *It.* **150** K8
Veules-les-Roses, *Fr.* **146** M8
Vevaru, island, *Maldives* **179** V3
Vezhen, peak, *Bulg.* **153** J14
Vezirköprü, *Turk.* **168** D10
Viacha, *Bol.* **130** J6
Viana do Bolo, *Sp.* **144** C7
Viana do Castelo, *Port.* **144** D5
Vianden, *Lux.* **160** H10
Viangchan (Vientiane), *Laos* **186** K10
Viareggio, *It.* **150** G5
Viborg, *Den.* **140** N11
Vibo Valentia, *It.* **151** Q13
Vibraye, *Fr.* **147** Q8
Vic, *Sp.* **145** D17
Vic, Étang de, *Fr.* **147** X12
Vic-en-Bigorre, *Fr.* **147** X7
Vicente Guerrero, *Mex.* **114** B5
Vicenza, *It.* **150** D7
Vic-Fézensac, *Fr.* **147** X7
Vichada, river, *Col.* **128** E9
Vichuga, *Russ.* **156** H11
Vichy, *Fr.* **147** T11
Vici, *Okla., U.S.* **102** F8
Vicksburg, *Mich., U.S.* **99** N10
Vicksburg, *Miss., U.S.* **100** L10
Vicksburg National Military Park, *Miss., U.S.* **100** L10
Vicovu de Sus, *Rom.* **153** A15
Victor, Mount, *Antarctica* **227** C16
Victor Harbor, *S. Aust., Austral.* **211** Y10
Victoria, *Austral.* **211** Z12
Victoria, *B.C., Can.* **82** M8
Victoria, *Chile* **132** C7
Victoria, *Chile* **133** N6
Victoria, *Grenada* **121** J22
Victoria, *Kans., U.S.* **105** S6
Victoria, river, *N. Terr., Austral.* **211** Q7
Victoria, *Seychelles* **205** N20
Victoria, *Tex., U.S.* **103** S12
Victoria, *Va., U.S.* **96** F12
Victoria (Rabat), *Malta* **161** H20
Victoria, Lake, *Kenya, Tanzania, Uganda* **199** K13
Victoria, Mount, *Myanmar* **186** H5
Victoria, Mount, *P.N.G.* **213** E20
Victoria Falls, *Zambia, Zimb.* **202** F10
Victoria Falls, *Zimb.* **202** F10
Victoria Island, *N.W.T., Nunavut, Can.* **83** E13
Victoria Land, *Antarctica* **227** R14
Victoria River Downs, *N. Terr., Austral.* **211** Q7
Victoria Sports Centre, *Gibraltar, U.K.* **161** N23
Victoria Strait, *Nunavut, Can.* **83** F14
Victorica, *Arg.* **132** K12
Victorica, *Arg.* **132** M9
Victorin, Mount, *St. Lucia* **121** L14
Victorville, *Calif., U.S.* **109** W9
Victory Peak *see* Jengish Chokusu, *China, Kyrg.* **176** E15
Vicuña, *Chile* **132** J7
Vidalia, *Ga., U.S.* **97** N7
Vidalia, *La., U.S.* **100** M9
Videle, *Rom.* **153** F15
Vidigueira, *Port.* **144** J6
Vidin, *Bulg.* **152** G12
Vidisha, *India* **178** J6
Vidor, *Tex., U.S.* **103** Q16
Vidzy, *Belarus* **156** J4
Viedma, *Arg.* **133** Q10
Viedma, Lago, *Arg.* **133** V7
Vieille Case, *Dominica* **121** D19
Vielha, *Sp.* **145** C16
Vienna *see* Wien, *Aust.* **148** K12
Vienna, *Ga., U.S.* **97** N6
Vienna, *Ill., U.S.* **99** V6
Vienna, *W. Va., U.S.* **96** C8
Vienne, *Fr.* **147** U13
Vientiane *see* Viangchan, *Laos* **186** K10
Viento, Punta, *P.R., U.S.* **120** P5
Vieques, island, *P.R., U.S.* **120** N6
Vieques *see* Isabel Segunda, *P.R., U.S.* **120** N6
Vieques Sound, *P.R., U.S.* **120** N6
Vierge Point, *St. Lucia* **121** L14
Vierwaldstätter See (Lake of Lucerne), *Switz.* **150** B4
Vierzon, *Fr.* **147** S9
Vieste, *It.* **150** K13
Vietnam, *Asia* **167** X11
Viet Tri, *Vietnam* **186** H12
Vieux-Boucau, *Fr.* **147** X5
Vieux-Bourg, *Guadeloupe, Fr.* **121** E15
Vieux Fort, *St. Lucia* **121** L14
Vieux-Fort, *Guadeloupe, Fr.* **121** G14
Vieux-Fort, Pointe du, *Guadeloupe, Fr.* **121** G14
Vieux-Habitants, *Guadeloupe, Fr.* **121** F14
Vigan, *Philippines* **189** B13
Vigía Chico, *Mex.* **115** H17
Vignemale, Pic de, *Fr.* **147** Y7
Vigo, *Sp.* **144** C5
Vigo, Ría de, *Sp.* **144** C5
Vihari, *Pak.* **177** R10
Viipuri *see* Vyborg, *Russ.* **156** E6
Vijayawada, *India* **179** N7
Vík, *Ice.* **140** G2
Vikenara Point, *Solomon Is.* **217** M18
Vikhorevka, *Russ.* **159** K14
Vikhren, peak, *Bulg.* **153** K13
Vikna, *Nor.* **140** G11
Vila Bittencourt, *Braz.* **130** D6
Vila da Ribeira Brava, *Cape Verde* **205** B15
Vila de Moura, *Port.* **144** K6
Vila de Sagres, *Port.* **144** L4
Vila do Bispo, *Port.* **144** L4
Vila do Conde, *Port.* **144** E5
Vilafranca del Penedès, *Sp.* **145** E17
Vila Franca do Campo, *Azores* **144** Q5
Vilagarcía de Arousa, *Sp.* **144** C5
Vilalba, *Sp.* **144** B6
Vila Murtinho, *Braz.* **130** G7
Vilanculos, *Mozambique* **203** H13
Vila Nova de Gaia, *Port.* **144** E5
Vila Nova de Milfontes, *Port.* **144** K5
Vilanova i la Geltrú, *Sp.* **145** E17
Vila Real, *Port.* **144** E6
Vila-real de los Infantes, *Sp.* **145** G15
Vilar Formoso, *Port.* **144** F7
Vila Velha, *Braz.* **130** B12
Vila Velha (Espírito Santo), *Braz.* **131** L16
Vila Velha de Rodão, *Port.* **144** G6
Vilhelmina, *Sw.* **141** G13
Vilhena, *Braz.* **130** H9
Viljandi, *Est.* **141** L16
Vil'kitskogo, Proliv, *Russ.* **159** D14
Villa Ahumada, *Mex.* **114** C9
Villa Alberdi, *Arg.* **132** G9
Villa Ángela, *Arg.* **132** G12
Villa Atuel, *Arg.* **132** L8
Villablino, *Sp.* **144** B8
Villa Cañás, *Arg.* **132** L11
Villacarrillo, *Sp.* **144** K11
Villacastín, *Sp.* **144** F10
Villach, *Aust.* **148** M10
Villacidro, *It.* **151** P3
Villa Dolores, *Arg.* **132** K9
Villafranca de los Barros, *Sp.* **144** J8
Villafranca di Verona, *It.* **150** E6
Village, *Fr. Polynesia, Fr.* **219** K17
Villa Grove, *Ill., U.S.* **99** R7
Villaguay, *Arg.* **132** K12
Villa Guillermina, *Arg.* **132** H12
Villahermosa, *Mex.* **115** J14
Villa Krause, *Arg.* **132** J8
Villalba, *P.R., U.S.* **120** N3
Villalonga, *Arg.* **133** P11
Villamar, *It.* **151** P4
Villa María, *Arg.* **132** K10
Villa Martín, *Bol.* **130** L6
Villamartín, *Sp.* **144** M8
Villamontes, *Bol.* **130** L8
Villa Nueva, *Arg.* **132** K8
Villanueva, *Mex.* **114** G10
Villanueva de Córdoba, *Sp.* **144** J10
Villanueva del Fresno, *Sp.* **144** J7
Villanueva de los Infantes, *Sp.* **144** J11
Villa Ocampo, *Arg.* **132** H12
Villa Regina, *Arg.* **133** P9
Villarosa, *It.* **151** S10
Villarrica, *Chile* **133** P6
Villarrica, Lago, *Chile* **133** P6
Villarrobledo, *Sp.* **144** H12
Villasalto, *It.* **151** P4
Villasimius, *It.* **151** Q4
Villatobas, *Sp.* **144** G11
Villa Unión, *Arg.* **132** H8
Villa Unión, *Mex.* **114** G8
Villavicencio, *Col.* **128** F6
Villaviciosa, *Sp.* **144** A9
Villazón, *Bol.* **130** L7
Villedieu-les-Poêles, *Fr.* **147** P6
Villefranche, *Fr.* **147** T12
Villefranche-de-Lauragais, *Fr.* **147** X9
Villefranche-de-Rouergue, *Fr.* **147** W9
Villemaur, *Fr.* **147** Q11
Villena, *Sp.* **145** J14
Villeneuve-St. Georges, *Fr.* **147** P10
Villeneuve-sur-Lot, *Fr.* **147** W8
Ville Platte, *La., U.S.* **100** N8
Villers devant Orval, *Belg.* **160** K7
Villerupt, *Fr.* **147** N13
Villeurbanne, *Fr.* **147** U13
Villingen-Schwenningen, *Ger.* **148** K6
Villisca, *Iowa, U.S.* **105** Q10
Villupuram, *India* **179** Q7
Vilnius, *Lith.* **141** N17
Vilyuy, river, *Russ.* **166** D10
Vilyuysk, *Russ.* **159** H17
Vilyuyskoye Vodokhranilishche, *Russ.* **159** H16
Vimoutiers, *Fr.* **147** P7
Vina, *Calif., U.S.* **109** P4
Viña del Mar, *Chile* **132** K6
Vinalhaven, *Me., U.S.* **95** G17
Vinaròs, *Sp.* **145** F15
Vincennes, *Ind., U.S.* **99** T7
Vincennes Bay, *Antarctica* **227** M21
Vincent, Point, *Norfolk I., Austral.* **217** F20
Vindelälven, river, *Sw.* **141** G13
Vindeln, *Sw.* **141** G14
Vindhya Range, *India* **178** J4

Vindrey, Russ. 156 K12
Vineland, N.J., U.S. 94 Q10
Vinh, Vietnam 186 J12
Vinhais, Port. 144 D7
Vinh Chau, Vietnam 187 Q12
Vinh Long, Vietnam 187 P12
Vinita, Okla., U.S. 102 E13
Vinkovci, Croatia 152 E8
Vinnytsya, Ukr. 157 P5
Vinson Massif, Antarctica 226 H8
Vinton, Iowa, U.S. 105 N13
Vinton, La., U.S. 100 P6
Vinukonda, India 179 N7
Vipiteno, It. 150 B7
Viqueque, Timor-Leste 189 M15
Vir, island, Croatia 152 F5
Vir, Taj. 176 J10
Virac, Philippines 189 C15
Virachei, Cambodia 186 M13
Viranşehir, Turk. 169 H14
Virawah, Pak. 177 W9
Virden, Ill., U.S. 99 S5
Virden, Man., Can. 83 N13
Vire, Fr. 147 P6
Vîrfurile, Rom. 152 D12
Vírgenes, Cape, S. Amer. 126 R5
Virgin, river, Ariz., Nev., U.S. 109 T13
Virgin Gorda, island, Virgin Islands, U.K. 119 F14
Virgin Gorda Peak, Virgin Islands, U.K. 120 Q9
Virgin Islands, U.S., Lesser Antilles 119 E13
Virginia, Ill., U.S. 99 R4
Virginia, Minn., U.S. 104 F12
Virginia, U.S. 96 F10
Virginia Beach, Va., U.S. 96 F14
Virginia City, Mont., U.S. 106 E7
Virginia City, Nev., U.S. 109 Q6
Virginia Falls, N.W.T., Can. 82 H9
Virgin Islands, Lesser Antilles 119 F14
Virgin Islands National Park, Virgin Islands, U.S. 120 N11
Viroqua, Wis., U.S. 98 K3
Virovitica, Croatia 152 D7
Virrat, Fin. 141 H15
Virton, Belg. 160 K8
Virtsu, Est. 141 L16
Virú, Peru 130 G2
Virudunagar, India 179 R6
Vis (Lissa), island, Croatia 152 H6
Visalia, Calif., U.S. 109 U7
Visayan Sea, Philippines 189 D14
Visby, Sw. 141 M14
Viscount Melville Sound, Nunavut, Can. 83 D13
Višegrad, Bosn. & Herzg. 152 G9
Viseu, Port. 144 F6
Vişeu de Sus, Rom. 153 B14
Vishakhapatnam, India 178 M9
Viški Kanal, Croatia 152 H6
Viso, Monte, It. 150 F2
Viso del Marqués, Sp. 144 J11
Visp, Switz. 150 C3
Vista, Calif., U.S. 109 Y9
Vista Alegre, Braz. 130 E6
Vistula see Wisła, river, Pol. 138 F8
Vit, river, Bulg. 153 G14
Viterbo, It. 150 J8
Vitichi, Bol. 130 L7
Vitigudino, Sp. 144 E8
Viti Levu, island, Fiji Is. 218 J6
Viti Levu Bay, Fiji Is. 218 H6
Vitim, river, Russ. 166 E10
Vitim, Russ. 159 J16
Vitor, Peru 130 J5
Vitória, Braz. 130 D12
Vitória, Braz. 131 L16
Vitória da Conquista, Braz. 131 J16
Vitoria-Gasteiz, Sp. 144 C12
Vitoria Seamount, Atl. Oc. 237 R8
Vitré, Fr. 147 Q6
Vitry-le-François, Fr. 147 P12
Vitsyebsk, Belarus 156 J6
Vittangi, Sw. 141 E14
Vittorio Veneto, It. 150 D8
Vivario, Fr. 150 K4
Viveiro, Sp. 144 A7
Vivi, river, Russ. 159 H14
Vivi, Russ. 159 H14
Vivian, La., U.S. 100 K6
Viwa, island, Fiji Is. 218 H5
Vizcaíno, Desierto de, Mex. 114 D6
Vize, Turk. 168 C4
Vize, Ostrov, Russ. 159 D13
Vizianagaram, India 178 M9
Vizzini, It. 151 T11
Vjosë, river, Albania 152 M9
Vlădeasa, peak, Rom. 152 C12
Vladikavkaz, Russ. 157 U14
Vladimir, Russ. 156 J10
Vladīmīrovka, Kaz. 174 B11
Vladivostok, Russ. 159 M21
Vlasenica, Bosn. & Herzg. 152 G8
Vlasinje, Bosn. & Herzg. 152 F7
Vlieland, island, Neth. 146 G12
Vlorë (Valona), Albania 152 M9
Vlorës, Gjiri i, Albania 152 M9
Vltava, river, Czech Rep. 148 J11
Vöcklabruck, Aust. 148 K10
Vod Ab, Afghan. 176 J9
Voe, Scot., U.K. 142 D12
Vogelsberg, range, Ger. 148 G7
Voghera, It. 150 E4
Voh, New Caledonia, Fr. 218 C7
Vohemar see Iharaña, Madagascar 203 D18
Voiron, Fr. 147 U13
Voitsberg, Aust. 148 M11
Vojvodina, region, Serb. & Mont. 152 E9
Volborg, Mont., U.S. 106 E12
Volcano, Hawaiʻi, U.S. 113 N21
Volcano Islands (Kazan Rettō), Japan 184 L5
Volda, Nor. 140 J10
Volga, river, Russ. 157 R15
Volga, S. Dak., U.S. 104 K8
Volga, Source of the, Russ. 138 D10
Volga-Baltic Waterway, Russ. 156 F9
Volga-Don Canal, Russ. 157 P13
Volga River Delta, Russ. 138 G14
Volga Upland, Russ. 138 E12
Volgodonsk, Russ. 157 Q12
Volgograd (Stalingrad), Russ. 157 P13
Volgograd Reservoir see Volgogradskoye Vodokhranilishche, Russ. 138 F13
Volgogradskoye Vodokhranilishche, Russ. 157 N14
Volímes, Gr. 154 J7
Volissós, Gr. 155 H16
Volkhov, river, Russ. 138 D10
Volkhov, Russ. 156 F7
Völklingen, Ger. 148 H5
Volksrust, S. Af. 202 K11
Volna, Gora, Russ. 159 E20
Volnorez, Gora, Russ. 159 E13
Volnovakha, Ukr. 157 Q9
Volodarsk, Russ. 156 J12
Vologda, Russ. 156 F10
Vólos, Gr. 154 F11
Vol'sk, Russ. 156 M14
Volta, Lake, Ghana 200 G11
Volta, Pointe de, Wallis & Futuna, Fr. 218 F12
Voltaire, Cape, Austral. 210 B5
Volturno, river, It. 150 L10
Vólvi, Límni, Gr. 154 C12
Volx, Fr. 147 X14
Volyn-Podolian Upland, Ukr. 138 G9
Volzhsk, Russ. 156 J14
Volzhskiy, Russ. 157 P13
Vonavona, island, Solomon Is. 217 M16
Vónitsa, Gr. 154 G7
Vopnafjörður, Ice. 140 F4
Vóras, Óros, Gr. 154 C9
Vóries Sporádes (Northern Sporades), islands, Gr. 155 F13
Voring Plateau, Arctic Oc. 243 G20
Vórios Evvoïkós Kólpos, Gr. 154 H11
Vorkuta, Russ. 158 F11
Vormsi, island, Est. 141 K16
Voronezh, Russ. 156 M10
Voronin Trough, Arctic Oc. 242 D11
Vorontsovka, Russ. 159 J16
Võru, Est. 141 L17
Vorukh, Taj. 176 G9
Vosges, range, Fr. 147 P15
Voss, Nor. 140 K10
Vostochnaya, Russ. 159 E13
Vostochnyy (Vrangel'), Russ. 159 M21
Vostochnyy Sayan, Russ. 159 L14
Vostok, station, Antarctica 227 K16
Vostok Island, Fr. Polynesia, Fr. 215 H13
Votice, Czech Rep. 148 H11
Votkinsk, Russ. 156 G16
Votkinsk, Russ. 158 H8
Votlo, Vanuatu 218 E3
Voulx, Fr. 147 Q10
Voúrnios, Óros, Gr. 154 D9
Voúxa, Akrotírio, Gr. 154 P12
Vouziers, Fr. 147 N12
Vovchans'k, Ukr. 157 N9
Voyageurs National Park, Minn., U.S. 104 E11
Voyampolka, Russ. 159 E21
Voyvozh, Russ. 158 F9
Voza, Solomon Is. 217 K15
Vozhe, Ozero, Russ. 156 E10
Vozhega, Russ. 156 E10
Vozhgora, Russ. 158 F9
Voznesens'k, Ukr. 157 Q6
Vozvyshennost' Lavruska, Russ. 159 H15
Vrachíonas, peak, Gr. 154 J7
Vrahnéika, Gr. 154 J9
Vrang, Taj. 176 K10
Vrangel' see Vostochnyy, Russ. 159 M21
Vrangelya, Ostrov (Wrangel Island), Russ. 159 B19
Vranica, peak, Bosn. & Herzg. 152 G7
Vranje, Serb. & Mont. 152 J11
Vranov, Slovakia 149 J17
Vransko Jezero, Croatia 152 G5
Vratsa, Bulg. 153 H13
Vrbas, river, Bosn. & Herzg. 152 F7
Vršac, Serb. & Mont. 152 E11
Vryburg, S. Af. 202 K9
Vryheid, S. Af. 202 K11
Vuagava, island, Fiji Is. 218 K9
Vučitrn, Serb. & Mont. 152 J10
Vulcano, Isola, It. 151 R11
Vulci, ruin, It. 150 K7
Vunaniu Bay, Fiji Is. 218 J6
Vung Tau, Vietnam 187 P13
Vunindawa, Fiji Is. 218 J6
Vunisea, Fiji Is. 218 K6
Vunivutu Bay, Fiji Is. 218 G7
Vyatka, river, Russ. 138 D12
Vyatskiye Polyany, Russ. 156 H15
Vyazemskiy, Russ. 159 K21
Vyaz'ma, Russ. 156 K8
Vyazniki, Russ. 156 J11
Vyborg (Viipuri), Russ. 156 E6
Vychegda, river, Russ. 138 B12
Vychegda Lowland, Russ. 138 B12
Vyerkhnyadzvinsk, Belarus 156 J5
Vyg, Lake, Russ. 138 C10
Vyksa, Russ. 156 J11
Vylkove, Ukr. 157 S5
Vym', river, Russ. 138 B12
Vyritsa, Russ. 156 F6
Vyshniy Volochek, Russ. 156 H8
Vyškov, Czech Rep. 149 J13
Vysokaye, Belarus 156 L2
Vysokovsk, Russ. 156 J9
Vytegra, Russ. 158 E7

W

Wa, Ghana 200 F10
Waar, island, Indonesia 189 K19
Wabao, Cape, New Caledonia, Fr. 218 D10
Wabasca, river, Alta., Can. 82 K11
Wabash, river, Ill., Ind., U.S. 99 T7
Wabash, Ind., U.S. 99 Q9
Wabasha, Minn., U.S. 104 K13
Wabasso, Fla., U.S. 97 U10
Wabeno, Wis., U.S. 98 H6
Wabowden, Man., Can. 83 L14
Wabuk Point, Ont., Can. 83 L16
Waco, Tex., U.S. 103 N11
Waco Lake, Tex., U.S. 103 N11
Wad, Pak. 177 U5
Waddenzee, bay, Neth. 146 G13
Waddington, Mount, B.C., Can. 82 L8
Wadena, Minn., U.S. 104 H10
Wadena, Sask., Can. 82 M12
Wädenswil, Switz. 150 B4
Wadesboro, N.C., U.S. 96 J10
Wadeye, N. Terr., Austral. 211 P7
Wadi Halfa, Sudan 198 B12
Wādī Mūsá (Elchi), Jordan 171 Q6
Wadley, Ga., U.S. 96 M7
Wad Medani, Sudan 199 E13
Wadomari, Japan 185 X2
Wadsworth, Nev., U.S. 109 P7
Wadsworth, Ohio, U.S. 99 P14
Wadu, island, Maldives 179 T3
Waelder, Tex., U.S. 103 R11
Waeshe, Mount, Antarctica 226 M8
Wafangdian, China 182 D10
Wager Bay, Nunavut, Can. 83 G15
Wagga Wagga, N.S.W., Austral. 211 Y13
Wagin, W. Aust., Austral. 211 X3
Wagner, S. Dak., U.S. 104 M7
Wagoner, Okla., U.S. 102 F13
Wagontire Mountain, Oreg., U.S. 108 J6
Wągrowiec, Pol. 149 D13
Wahai, Indonesia 189 K17
Wahaʻula Heiau, Hawaiʻi, U.S. 113 N22
Wah Cantonment, Pak. 177 N10
Wahiawā, Hawaiʻi, U.S. 112 D11
Wahoo, Nebr., U.S. 105 P8
Wahpeton, N. Dak., U.S. 104 H8
Waħx, Ras il, Malta 161 J21
Wai, India 178 M4
Wai, Indonesia 189 K16
Wai, Koh, Cambodia 187 Q10
Waiakoa, Hawaiʻi, U.S. 113 G17
Waiʻaleʻale, peak, Hawaiʻi, U.S. 112 B5
Waialua, Hawaiʻi, U.S. 112 D10
Waialua Bay, Hawaiʻi, U.S. 112 D10
Waiʻanae Range, Hawaiʻi, U.S. 112 E10
Waiau, river, N.Z. 213 R15
Waibeem, Indonesia 189 J18
Waigama, Indonesia 189 K17
Waigeo, island, Indonesia 189 J17
Waiheʻe, Hawaiʻi, U.S. 113 G16
Waiheke Island, N.Z. 213 J19
Waikabubak, Indonesia 189 N13
Waikahalulu Bay, Hawaiʻi, U.S. 113 H16
Waikapū, Hawaiʻi, U.S. 113 G16
Waikapuna Bay, Hawaiʻi, U.S. 113 P20
Waikato, river, N.Z. 213 K19
Waikawa, N.Z. 213 R16
Waikīkī Beach, Hawaiʻi, U.S. 112 E11
Waikoloa, Hawaiʻi, U.S. 113 L19
Waikouaiti, N.Z. 213 Q16
Wailagi Lala, island, Fiji Is. 218 G9
Wailea, Hawaiʻi, U.S. 113 H16
Wailua, Hawaiʻi, U.S. 112 B6
Wailua, Hawaiʻi, U.S. 113 G17
Wailuku, river, Hawaiʻi, U.S. 113 M21
Wailuku, Hawaiʻi, U.S. 113 G16
Waimānalo Beach, Hawaiʻi, U.S. 112 E12
Waimarama, N.Z. 213 L20
Waimate, N.Z. 213 Q17
Waimea, Hawaiʻi, U.S. 112 C5
Waimea, Hawaiʻi, U.S. 112 D10
Waimea (Kamuela), Hawaiʻi, U.S. 113 K19
Waimea Canyon, Hawaiʻi, U.S. 112 B5
Wainaworasi, Solomon Is. 217 Q20
Waingapu, Indonesia 189 N13
Wainunu Bay, Fiji Is. 218 H7
Wainwright, Alas., U.S. 111 B14
Waiʻōhinu, Hawaiʻi, U.S. 113 P19
Waiohonu Petroglyphs, Hawaiʻi, U.S. 113 H18
Waiʻoli Mission, Hawaiʻi, U.S. 112 B5
Waipa, river, N.Z. 213 K19
Waipahi, N.Z. 213 R16
Waipahu, Hawaiʻi, U.S. 112 E11
Waipiʻo Bay, Hawaiʻi, U.S. 113 K20
Waipiʻo Valley, Hawaiʻi, U.S. 113 K19
Waipu, N.Z. 213 H18
Waipukurau, N.Z. 213 L19
Wairokai Harbor, Solomon Is. 217 N20
Waïsisi, Vanuatu 218 H4
Waïsisi Bay, Vanuatu 218 H4
Waitsburg, Wash., U.S. 108 E8
Wajima, Japan 184 M10
Wajir, Kenya 199 J15
Wakasa Wan, Japan 185 P9
Wakatipu, Lake, N.Z. 213 Q15
Wakaya, island, Fiji Is. 218 H7
Wakayama, Japan 185 Q8
WaKeeney, Kans., U.S. 105 S5
Wakefield, Eng., U.K. 143 R12
Wakefield, Jam. 120 H7
Wakefield, Kans., U.S. 105 S8
Wakefield, Mich., U.S. 98 F5
Wakefield, Nebr., U.S. 105 N8
Wake Forest, N.C., U.S. 96 H12
Wake Island, Wake I., U.S. 216 F8
Wakema, Myanmar 186 L5
Wakhan Mountains, Afghan. 176 K10
Wakhjir Pass, Afghan., China 176 K12
Wakkanai, Japan 184 D13
Wakuach, Lac, Que., Can. 83 K20
Wakunai, P.N.G. 217 J14
Wakuya, Japan 184 L13
Wala, New Caledonia, Fr. 218 B6
Walachia, region, Rom. 153 F14
Wałbrzych, Pol. 148 G12
Walcott, Lake, Idaho, U.S. 106 H6
Wałcz, Pol. 148 C12
Walden, Colo., U.S. 106 L12
Waldkraiburg, Ger. 148 K9
Waldo, Ark., U.S. 100 J7
Waldo Lake, Oreg., U.S. 108 H4
Waldorf, Md., U.S. 96 D13
Waldport, Oreg., U.S. 108 G2
Waldron, Ark., U.S. 100 G6
Walea, Selat, Indonesia 189 J14
Wales, Alas., U.S. 110 E11
Wales, U.K. 143 U10
Wales Island, Nunavut, Can. 83 G16
Walferdange, Lux. 160 J10
Walgreen Coast, Antarctica 226 K6
Walhalla, N. Dak., U.S. 104 D7
Walhalla, S.C., U.S. 96 J6
Walikale, Dem. Rep. of the Congo 198 K11
Walkaway, W. Aust., Austral. 211 W2
Walker, Minn., U.S. 104 G10
Walker Lake, Nev., U.S. 109 Q8
Wall, S. Dak., U.S. 104 L3
Wallabadah, Qnsld., Austral. 211 R12
Wallaby Island, Austral. 210 C11
Wallaby Plateau, Ind. Oc. 241 K14
Wallace, Idaho, U.S. 106 C4
Wallace, N.C., U.S. 96 J12
Wallace, Nebr., U.S. 105 Q4
Wallal Downs, W. Aust., Austral. 211 S3
Wallam Creek, Austral. 210 H13
Wallara, N. Terr., Austral. 211 U8
Wallaroo, S. Aust., Austral. 211 X10
Walla Walla, Wash., U.S. 108 E8
Wallibou, St. Vincent & the Grenadines 121 J16
Wallilabou, St. Vincent & the Grenadines 121 K16
Wallis, Îles, Pac. Oc. 214 J9
Wallis and Futuna, Fr., Pac. Oc. 214 J9
Wallops Island, Va., U.S. 96 E15
Wallowa, Oreg., U.S. 108 F9
Wallowa Mountains, Oreg., U.S. 108 F9
Walls, Scot., U.K. 142 D11
Wallsend, Eng., U.K. 143 P12
Walney, Isle of, Eng., U.K. 143 R10
Walnut Canyon National Monument, Ariz., U.S. 107 S7
Walnut Cove, N.C., U.S. 96 G10
Walnut Ridge, Ark., U.S. 100 E10
Walong, India 178 F16
Walsall, Eng., U.K. 143 T12
Walsenburg, Colo., U.S. 107 P13
Walsh, Colo., U.S. 107 P16
Walsrode, Ger. 148 D7
Walterboro, S.C., U.S. 96 M9
Walter F. George Reservoir, Ala., Ga., U.S. 101 M17
Walters, Okla., U.S. 102 J9
Walters Shoal, Ind. Oc. 240 M4
Walton, N.Y., U.S. 94 K9
Walvis Bay, Namibia 202 H6
Walvis Ridge, Atl. Oc. 237 S13
Walyahmoning Rock, Austral. 210 J3
Wama, Afghan. 176 M9
Wamba, river, Dem. Rep. of the Congo 198 M8
Wamba, Dem. Rep. of the Congo 198 J11
Wamego, Kans., U.S. 105 S9
Wamena, Indonesia 189 L20
Wami, river, Tanzania 199 M15
Wamsasi, Indonesia 189 K15
Wamsisi, Indonesia 189 K16
Wamsutter, Wyo., U.S. 106 K10
Wana, Pak. 177 P8
Wanaaring, N.S.W., Austral. 211 W12
Wanaka, N.Z. 213 Q16
Wanaka, Lake, N.Z. 213 Q16
Wan'an, China 183 P5
Wanapa, Neth. Antilles, Neth. 121 R19
Wanchese, N.C., U.S. 96 G15
Wanderer Bay, Solomon Is. 217 N18
Wanding, China 180 P9
Wando, S. Korea 182 H13
Wandoan, Qnsld., Austral. 211 V14

Wangal, Indonesia 213 D15
Wanganui, river, N.Z. 213 L19
Wanganui, N.Z. 213 L19
Wangaratta, Vic., Austral. 211 Y13
Wangary, S. Aust., Austral. 211 Y9
Wangdu, China 182 E6
Wangerberg, Liech. 160 Q2
Wangiwangi, island, Indonesia 189 L14
Wang Kai, Sudan 198 G12
Wangpan Yang, China 182 L10
Wangqing, China 182 A14
Wanigela, P.N.G. 213 E20
Wanione, Solomon Is. 217 P21
Wankaner, India 178 J2
Wanlaweyn, Somalia 199 J17
Wanlockhead, Scot., U.K. 143 N9
Wanning, China 183 U2
Wanow, Afghan. 177 P5
Wanxian, China 182 K1
Wanyuan, China 182 J1
Wanzai, China 183 N5
Wapakoneta, Ohio, U.S. 99 Q11
Wapato, Wash., U.S. 108 D6
Wapello, Iowa, U.S. 105 P14
Wappapello, Lake, Mo., U.S. 105 V15
Wapsipinicon, river, Iowa, U.S. 105 N13
War, W. Va., U.S. 96 F8
Waranga Basin, Austral. 210 L12
Warangal, India 178 M7
Waraseoni, India 178 K7
Waratah, Tas., Austral. 211 Z15
Warbreccan, Qnsld., Austral. 211 U12
Warburg, Ger. 148 F7
Warburton, W. Aust., Austral. 211 U6
Warden, Wash., U.S. 108 D7
Ward Hunt Island, Nunavut, Can. 83 A16
Wardija Point, Malta 161 H19
Waren, Ger. 148 C10
Waren, Indonesia 189 K19
Ware Shoals, S.C., U.S. 96 K7
Warialda, N.S.W., Austral. 211 W14
Warlubie, Pol. 149 C14
Warmbad, Namibia 202 K7
Warminster, Eng., U.K. 143 W11
Warm Springs, Ga., U.S. 96 M4
Warm Springs, Nev., U.S. 109 R10
Warm Springs, Va., U.S. 96 E10
Warm Springs Reservoir, Oreg., U.S. 108 H8
Warner Mountains, Calif., Oreg., U.S. 108 L6
Warner Robins, Ga., U.S. 96 M6
Warner Valley, Oreg., U.S. 108 K6
Waroona, W. Aust., Austral. 211 X2
Warora, India 178 K6
Warrabri, N. Terr., Austral. 211 S9
Warracknabeal, Vic., Austral. 211 Y11
Warrawagine, W. Aust., Austral. 211 S4
Warrego, river, Austral. 210 H13
Warren, Ark., U.S. 100 J8
Warren, Mich., U.S. 98 M13
Warren, Minn., U.S. 104 E8
Warren, Ohio, U.S. 99 P15
Warren, Pa., U.S. 94 L4
Warrender, Cape, Nunavut, Can. 83 D16
Warrenpoint, N. Ire., U.K. 143 Q7
Warrensburg, Mo., U.S. 105 T11
Warrenton, Ga., U.S. 96 L7
Warrenton, Oreg., U.S. 108 E2
Warrenton, S. Af. 202 K9
Warrenton, Va., U.S. 96 D12
Warri, Nigeria 201 H13
Warrina, S. Aust., Austral. 211 V9
Warrington, Eng., U.K. 143 S11
Warrington, Fla., U.S. 97 Q1
Warrnambool, Vic., Austral. 211 Z11
Warroad, Minn., U.S. 104 D9
Warsa, Indonesia 189 J19
Warsaw, Ind., U.S. 99 P9
Warsaw, N.C., U.S. 96 J12
Warsaw see Warszawa, Pol. 149 E16
Warsaw, Va., U.S. 96 E13
Warszawa (Warsaw), Pol. 149 E16
Warta, river, Pol. 148 D12
Waru, Indonesia 189 K17
Warwick, Eng., U.K. 143 U12
Warwick, Qnsld., Austral. 211 V15
Warwick, R.I., U.S. 95 L14
Wasado, peak, Indonesia 213 C15
Wasaka, Vanuatu 218 B2
Wasam, Pak. 176 K10
Wasatch Range, Utah, U.S. 106 K7
Wasco, Calif., U.S. 109 V7
Wasco, Oreg., U.S. 108 F5
Waseca, Minn., U.S. 104 L11
Washap, Pak. 177 U3
Washburn, Me., U.S. 95 B18
Washburn, N. Dak., U.S. 104 F4
Washburn, Wis., U.S. 98 F4
Washburn, Mount, Wyo., U.S. 106 F8
Washington, Neth. Antilles, Neth. 121 Q18
Washington, D.C., U.S. 96 C13
Washington, Ga., U.S. 96 L7
Washington, Ill., U.S. 99 Q5
Washington, Ind., U.S. 99 T8
Washington, Iowa, U.S. 105 P13
Washington, Kans., U.S. 105 R8
Washington, Mo., U.S. 105 T14
Washington, N.C., U.S. 96 H13
Washington, Pa., U.S. 94 P3
Washington, U.S. 108 C3
Washington, Utah, U.S. 107 Q5
Washington, Wis., U.S. 98 H8
Washington, Cape, Antarctica 227 P13
Washington, Cape, Fiji Is. 218 K6
Washington, Mount, N.H., U.S. 95 G14
Washington Court House, Ohio, U.S. 99 R12
Washington Island see Teraina, Kiribati 214 F12
Washington Island, Wis., U.S. 98 H8
Washita, river, Okla., Tex., U.S. 102 H11
Washougal, Wash., U.S. 108 F4
Washtucna, Wash., U.S. 108 D8
Washuk, Pak. 177 T4
Wasilla, Alas., U.S. 111 J16
Wasior, Indonesia 189 K19
Waskaganish, Que., Can. 83 M18
Wasserbillig, Lux. 160 J11
Waswanipi, Lac, Que., Can. 83 N18
Watampone, Indonesia 189 L13
Waterbury, Conn., U.S. 94 L12
Water Cay, Bahamas 120 E2
Water Cays, Bahamas 116 F11
Wateree Lake, S.C., U.S. 96 K9
Waterford (Port Láirge), Ire. 143 U6
Waterford Harbour, Ire. 143 U6
Water Ground, Cayman Is., U.K. 120 H1
Water Island, Virgin Islands, U.S. 120 N9
Waterloo, Ill., U.S. 99 T4
Waterloo, Iowa, U.S. 105 N12
Waterloo, N. Terr., Austral. 211 Q7
Waterloo, Trinidad & Tobago 121 P22
Waterman, Isla, Chile 133 Y8
Watersmeet, Mich., U.S. 98 F6
Waterton-Glacier International Peace Park, Mont., U.S. 106 A6
Waterton Lakes National Park, Alta., Can. 106 A6
Watertown, N.Y., U.S. 94 G9
Watertown, S. Dak., U.S. 104 K8
Watertown, Wis., U.S. 98 L6
Water Valley, Miss., U.S. 100 H12
Waterville, Kans., U.S. 105 R8
Waterville, Me., U.S. 95 F16
Waterville, Minn., U.S. 104 K11
Waterville, Wash., U.S. 108 C6
Watford, Eng., U.K. 143 V13
Watford City, N. Dak., U.S. 104 F2
Watkins Glen, N.Y., U.S. 94 K7
Watling see San Salvador, island, Bahamas 117 F14
Watling's Castle, Bahamas 120 F11
Watonga, Okla., U.S. 102 F9
Watrous, N. Mex., U.S. 107 R13
Watsa, Dem. Rep. of the Congo 198 J12
Watseka, Ill., U.S. 99 Q7
Watson, S. Aust., Austral. 211 W8
Watson Lake, Yukon, Can. 82 H9
Watsonville, Calif., U.S. 109 T4
Watt Mountain, Dominica 121 G19
Watts Bar Lake, Tenn., U.S. 101 F17
Wattwil, Switz. 150 A4
Watubela, Kepulauan, Indonesia 189 L18
Wau, P.N.G. 213 D19
Wau, Sudan 198 G11
Waubay, S. Dak., U.S. 104 J7
Wauchope, N. Terr., Austral. 211 S9
Wauchula, Fla., U.S. 97 U8
Waukarlycarly, Lake, Austral. 210 E4
Waukegan, Ill., U.S. 98 M7
Waukesha, Wis., U.S. 98 L6
Waukon, Iowa, U.S. 104 M13
Wauneta, Nebr., U.S. 105 Q3
Waupaca, Wis., U.S. 98 J6
Waupun, Wis., U.S. 98 K6
Waurika, Okla., U.S. 102 J10
Wausa, Nebr., U.S. 105 N7
Wausau, Wis., U.S. 98 H5
Wauseon, Ohio, U.S. 99 N11
Wautoma, Wis., U.S. 98 K5
Wauwatosa, Wis., U.S. 98 L7
Wave Hill, N. Terr., Austral. 211 R7
Waverly, Iowa, U.S. 104 M12
Waverly, N.Y., U.S. 94 L8
Waverly, Nebr., U.S. 105 Q8
Waverly, Ohio, U.S. 99 S13
Waverly, Tenn., U.S. 101 E14
Waverly, Va., U.S. 96 F13
Wawa, Ont., Can. 83 P17
Wāw al Kabīr, Lib. 197 E14
Waxahachie, Tex., U.S. 102 L12
Waxweiler, Ger. 160 G11
Waya, island, Fiji Is. 218 H5
Wayamli, Indonesia 189 H16
Waycross, Ga., U.S. 97 P7
Wayne, Nebr., U.S. 105 N8
Waynesboro, Ga., U.S. 96 M8
Waynesboro, Miss., U.S. 101 M13
Waynesboro, Pa., U.S. 94 Q6
Waynesboro, Tenn., U.S. 101 F14
Waynesboro, Va., U.S. 96 E11
Waynesburg, Pa., U.S. 94 P3
Waynesville, Mo., U.S. 105 U13
Waynesville, N.C., U.S. 96 H6
Waynoka, Okla., U.S. 102 E9
Wazah, Afghan. 177 N8
Wazirabad, Pak. 177 P12
Wé, New Caledonia, Fr. 218 C9
We, island, Indonesia 188 F3
Weatherford, Okla., U.S. 102 G9
Weatherford, Tex., U.S. 102 L10
Weaverville, Calif., U.S. 108 M3
Webb City, Mo., U.S. 105 V11
Weber Basin, Ind. Oc. 241 H18
Webster, Mass., U.S. 95 L14
Webster, S. Dak., U.S. 104 J7
Webster City, Iowa, U.S. 105 N11
Webster Groves, Mo., U.S. 105 T15
Webster Springs, W. Va., U.S. 96 D9
Weda, Indonesia 189 J16
Weda, Teluk, Indonesia 189 J16
Weddell Island, Falkland Is., U.K. 133 W11
Weddell Plain, Antarctic Oc. 244 E10
Weddell Sea, Antarctica 226 D7
Wedemark, Ger. 148 D7
Weed, Calif., U.S. 108 M3
Weeki Wachee, Fla., U.S. 97 T7
Weeping Water, Nebr., U.S. 105 Q9
Weert, Neth. 146 K13
Węgorzewo, Pol. 149 B16
Wei, river, China 182 H2
Wei, river, China 181 H15
Wei, river, China 180 J12
Weichang, China 182 B7
Weiden, Ger. 148 H9
Weifang, China 182 F8
Weihai, China 182 F10
Weilheim, Ger. 148 L8
Weilmoringle, N.S.W., Austral. 211 W13
Weimar, Ger. 148 F8
Weimar, Tex., U.S. 103 R12
Weinan, China 182 H2
Weinsberger Wald, Aust. 148 K11
Weipa, Qnsld., Austral. 211 P12
Weir, river, Austral. 210 H14
Weirton, W. Va., U.S. 96 B9
Weiser, river, Idaho, U.S. 106 F3
Weiser, Idaho, U.S. 106 F3
Weishan, China 182 H7
Weishan Hu, China 182 H7
Weissenburg, Ger. 148 J8
Weissenfels, Ger. 148 F9
Weiss Lake, Ala., Ga., U.S. 101 H17
Weiswampach, Lux. 160 G10
Weite, Switz. 160 Q2
Weixi, China 180 M10
Wejherowo, Pol. 149 A14
Welbourn Hill, S. Aust., Austral. 211 V9
Welch, W. Va., U.S. 96 F8
Welch Point, Cayman Is., U.K. 120 J2
Weldiya, Eth. 199 F15
Weldon, N.C., U.S. 96 G13
Welford, Qnsld., Austral. 211 U12
Weligama, Sri Lanka 179 T7
Welker Seamount, Pac. Oc. 239 C14
Welkom, S. Af. 202 K10
Wellesley Islands, Austral. 210 C11
Wellin, Belg. 146 M13
Wellington, Colo., U.S. 106 L13
Wellington, Kans., U.S. 105 V7
Wellington, N.Z. 213 M18
Wellington, Nev., U.S. 109 Q7
Wellington, Tex., U.S. 102 H7
Wellington, Isla, Chile 133 V6
Wellington, Lake, Austral. 210 M13
Wellington Bay, Nunavut, Can. 83 F13
Wells, Me., U.S. 95 H15
Wells, Minn., U.S. 104 L11
Wells, Nev., U.S. 108 M12
Wells, Tex., U.S. 103 N14
Wells, Lake, Austral. 210 G5
Wellsboro, Pa., U.S. 94 L7
Wellston, Ohio, U.S. 99 S13
Wellsville, Mo., U.S. 105 S13
Wellsville, N.Y., U.S. 94 K6
Wellsville, Ohio, U.S. 99 Q16
Wellton, Ariz., U.S. 107 U5
Wels, Aust. 148 K10
Welsh, La., U.S. 100 P7
Welshpool, Vic., Austral. 211 Z12
Welshpool, Wales, U.K. 143 T10
Wemyss Bight, Bahamas 120 F6
Wenatchee, Wash., U.S. 108 C6
Wenchang, China 183 U2
Wencheng, China 183 N9
Wenchi, Ghana 200 G10
Wendeng, China 182 F10
Wendesi, Indonesia 189 K19
Wendover, Nev., U.S. 108 M13
Wendover, Utah, U.S. 106 K5
Wengyuan, China 183 R5
Wenling, China 183 N10
Wenman see Wolf, Isla, island, Ecua. 128 M7
Weno, F.S.M. 217 B15
Weno (Moen), island, F.S.M. 217 B15
Wenshan, China 180 P11
Wensu, China 180 F5
Wentworth, N.S.W., Austral. 211 X11
Wenzhou, China 183 N9
Werdau, Ger. 148 G9
Werder, Ger. 148 E10
Werdēr, Eth. 199 G17
Weri, Indonesia 213 C14
Werris Creek, N.S.W., Austral. 211 X14
Weser, river, Ger. 148 C7
Weskan, Kans., U.S. 105 S3
Weslaco, Tex., U.S. 103 W10
Wesley, Dominica 121 E19
Wesleyville, Pa., U.S. 94 K3
Wessel Islands, Austral. 210 A9
Wessex, region, Eng., U.K. 143 W11
Wessington, S. Dak., U.S. 104 K6
Wessington Springs, S. Dak., U.S. 104 L6
Wesson, Miss., U.S. 100 M11
West, Tex., U.S. 102 M11
West Allis, Wis., U.S. 98 L7
West Antarctica, region, Antarctica 226 K9
West Bank, occupied territory, Asia 170 M6
West Bay, Cayman Is., U.K. 120 J1
West Bay, Cayman Is., U.K. 120 H1
West Bay, Fla., U.S. 97 R3
West Bay, La., U.S. 100 R12
West Bend, Wis., U.S. 98 L7
West Branch, Iowa, U.S. 105 P13
West Branch, Mich., U.S. 98 J11
Westbrook, Me., U.S. 95 H15
Westbrook, Tex., U.S. 102 M6
West Burra, island, Scot., U.K. 142 E12
Westby, Wis., U.S. 98 K4
West Caicos, island, Turks & Caicos Is., U.K. 117 J16
West Cape Howe, Austral. 210 L3
West Caroline Basin, Pac. Oc. 238 J5
West Cay, Virgin Islands, U.S. 120 M8
West Chester, Pa., U.S. 94 P9
Westcliffe, Colo., U.S. 107 N13
West Columbia, Tex., U.S. 103 R13
West Des Moines, Iowa, U.S. 105 P11
West End, Virgin Islands, U.K. 120 R5
West End, Bahamas 120 E1
West End Point, Virgin Islands, U.K. 120 L10
West End Point, Cayman Is., U.K. 116 L8
West End Village, Anguilla, U.K. 120 R11
Westerhall Bay, Grenada 121 L22
Westerhall Point, Grenada 121 L22
Westerland, Ger. 148 A7
Westerly, R.I., U.S. 95 M14
Western, river, Nunavut, Can. 83 G13
Western Australia, Austral. 211 T3
Western Beach, Gibraltar, U.K. 161 N22
Western Channel, Japan 185 Q3
Western Desert, Egypt 197 D17
Western Dvina, river, Eur. 138 E9
Western Ghats, range, India 178 L3
Western Plateau, Austral. 210 F4
Western Sahara, Af. 195 E14
Western Sayan Mountains, Russ. 166 E9
Western Soverign Base Area see Akrotiri Sovereign Base Area, Cyprus 160 Q7
Westerschelde, Neth. 146 K11
Westerville, Ohio, U.S. 99 R13
West Falkland, island, Falkland Is., U.K. 133 W11
Westfall, Oreg., U.S. 108 H8
West Fayu Atoll see Pigailoe, F.S.M. 216 Q5
Westfield, Mass., U.S. 94 L12
Westfield, N.Y., U.S. 94 K4
West Fork Poplar, river, Mont., U.S. 106 B12
West Fork Trinity, river, Tex., U.S. 102 K10
West Frankfort, Ill., U.S. 99 U6
West Frisian Islands, Neth. 146 G12
West Glacier, Mont., U.S. 106 B6
West Grand Lake, Me., U.S. 95 E18
West Helena, Ark., U.S. 100 H10
Westhope, N. Dak., U.S. 104 D4
West Ice Shelf, Antarctica 227 H21
West Indies, N. Amer. 80 N9
West Islet, Coral Sea Is. Terr., Austral. 211 T16
West Lafayette, Ind., U.S. 99 Q8
West Landing, Marshall Is. 216 G10
West Liberty, Iowa, U.S. 105 P14
West Liberty, Ky., U.S. 101 B19
Westman Islands see Vestmannaeyjar, Ice. 140 G2
West Mariana Basin, Pac. Oc. 238 H5
West Memphis, Ark., U.S. 100 G11
Westminster, Md., U.S. 96 B13
Westminster, S.C., U.S. 96 K6
West Monroe, La., U.S. 100 L8
Westmoreland, Qnsld., Austral. 211 R10
Westmorland, Calif., U.S. 109 Y11
West Nicholson, Zimb. 202 G11
Weston, Mo., U.S. 105 S10
Weston, W. Va., U.S. 96 C9
Weston Point, Kiribati 217 B20
Weston super Mare, Eng., U.K. 143 V11
West Palm Beach, Fla., U.S. 97 V10
West Passage see Toachel Mlengui, Palau 216 M11
West Plains, Mo., U.S. 105 V13
West Point, Austral. 210 K9
West Point, Ga., U.S. 96 M4
West Point, Marshall Is. 216 M7
West Point, Ky., U.S. 101 B16
West Point, Miss., U.S. 101 J13
West Point, N.Y., U.S. 94 M11
West Point, Nebr., U.S. 105 P8
West Point, Va., U.S. 96 E13
West Point Lake, Ga., U.S. 96 M4
Westport, Calif., U.S. 109 P2
Westport, Ire. 143 R3
Westport, N.Z. 213 N17
Westport, Wash., U.S. 108 D2
Westpunt, Neth. Antilles, Neth. 121 N13
Westray, island, Scot., U.K. 142 F10
Westray Firth, Scot., U.K. 142 F10
West Siberian Plain, Russ. 166 D8
West Spit, Marshall Is. 216 H7
West Union, Iowa, U.S. 104 M13
West Valley City, Utah, U.S. 106 L7
West Virginia, U.S. 96 C9

Westwego, La., U.S. 100 Q11
Westwood, Calif., U.S. 109 N5
Westwood Downs, N.S.W., Austral. 211 W11
West Wyalong, N.S.W., Austral. 211 X13
West Yellowstone, Mont., U.S. 106 F8
West York Island, Spratly Is. 188 E11
Wetar, island, Indonesia 189 M15
Wetaskiwin, Alta., Can. 82 L10
Wetumka, Okla., U.S. 102 G12
Wetumpka, Ala., U.S. 101 L16
Wetzlar, Ger. 148 G6
Wewahitchka, Fla., U.S. 97 R4
Wewak, P.N.G. 213 C18
Wewoka, Okla., U.S. 102 G12
Wexford, Ire. 143 U6
Wexford Harbour, Ire. 143 U7
Weyburn, Sask., Can. 82 N12
Weyer, Aust. 148 L11
Weymouth, Eng., U.K. 143 X11
Weymouth, Cape, Austral. 210 B12
Whakapunake, peak, N.Z. 213 K20
Whakatane, N.Z. 213 K20
Whale Cay, Bahamas 116 D11
Whale Cove, Nunavut, Can. 83 J15
Whaler Anchorage, Kiribati 217 B20
Whalsay, island, Scot., U.K. 142 D12
Whangamata, N.Z. 213 J19
Whangarei, N.Z. 213 H18
Wharton, Tex., U.S. 103 R13
Wharton Basin, Ind. Oc. 241 K13
Wheatland, Wyo., U.S. 106 J13
Wheatland Reservoir, Wyo., U.S. 106 J12
Wheaton, Minn., U.S. 104 J8
Wheeler, Tex., U.S. 102 G7
Wheeler Lake, Ala., U.S. 101 H15
Wheeler Peak, N. Mex., U.S. 107 Q13
Wheeler Peak, Nev., U.S. 84 G6
Wheeling, W. Va., U.S. 96 B9
Wheelwright, Ky., U.S. 101 C20
Whidbey, Point, Austral. 210 K9
Whiddy Island, Ire. 143 V3
Whim Creek, W. Aust., Austral. 211 S2
Whiskeytown Shasta-Trinity National Recreation Area, Calif., U.S. 108 M3
Whitby, Eng., U.K. 143 Q13
White, river, Ark., U.S. 100 H10
White, river, Colo., U.S. 106 L10
White, river, Ind., U.S. 99 T7
White, river, Nev., U.S. 109 Q12
White, river, S. Dak., U.S. 104 L5
White, S. Dak., U.S. 104 K8
White, river, Tex., U.S. 102 K6
White, Lake, Austral. 210 E7
White Bay, Virgin Islands, U.K. 120 L11
White Bird, Idaho, U.S. 106 E4
White Butte, N. Dak., U.S. 104 H2
White Cliffs, N.S.W., Austral. 211 W12
White Cloud, Mich., U.S. 98 K9
White Deer, Tex., U.S. 102 G6
Whitefish, Mont., U.S. 106 B5
Whitefish Bay, Mich., U.S. 98 F10
Whitefish Point, Mich., U.S. 98 F10
Whitefish Point, Mich., U.S. 98 F10
White Hall, Ark., U.S. 100 H9
White Hall, Ill., U.S. 99 S4
Whitehall, Mich., U.S. 98 L9
Whitehall, Mont., U.S. 106 E7
Whitehall, N.Y., U.S. 94 H12
Whitehall, Ohio, U.S. 99 R13
Whitehall, Wis., U.S. 98 J3
Whitehaven, Eng., U.K. 143 Q10
Whitehorse, Yukon, Can. 82 G8
White Horses, Jam. 120 J11
Whitehouse, Jam. 120 J6
White Island, Antarctica 227 C19
White Island, Nunavut, Can. 83 G16
White Lake, La., U.S. 100 Q8
White Mountain, Alas., U.S. 110 F12
White Mountains, Calif., U.S. 109 S8
White Mountains, N.H., U.S. 95 F14
White Mountains National Recreation Area, Alas., U.S. 111 F17
White Nile see Abyad, El Bahr el, river, Sudan 199 F13
White Pine, Mich., U.S. 98 F5
White Plains, N.Y., U.S. 94 M11
White River, S. Dak., U.S. 104 L4
Whiteriver, Ariz., U.S. 107 T9
White River Junction, Vt., U.S. 95 H13
White Salmon, Wash., U.S. 108 E5
White Sands National Monument, N. Mex., U.S. 107 U12
Whitesboro, Tex., U.S. 102 K11
Whitesburg, Ky., U.S. 101 D20
White Sea, Arctic Oc. 243 B18
White Sea-Baltic Canal, Russ. 138 B10
White Sulphur Springs, Mont., U.S. 106 D8
White Sulphur Springs, W. Va., U.S. 96 E9
Whitetail, Mont., U.S. 106 A12
Whiteville, N.C., U.S. 96 K11
Whiteville, Tenn., U.S. 100 F12
White Volta, river, Af. 194 G3
Whitewater, Mont., U.S. 106 B11
Whitewater, Wis., U.S. 98 M6
Whitewater Baldy, N. Mex., U.S. 107 U10
Whitewood, Qnsld., Austral. 211 S12
Whitewright, Tex., U.S. 102 K12
Whithorn, Scot., U.K. 143 P9
Whitman, Nebr., U.S. 105 N3
Whitman Mission National Historic Site, Wash., U.S. 108 E8
Whitmire, S.C., U.S. 96 K8
Whitmore Mountains, Antarctica 226 J10
Whitney, Lake, Tex., U.S. 102 M11
Whitney, Mount, Calif., U.S. 109 T8
Whittier, Alas., U.S. 111 K17
Wholdaia Lake, N.W.T., Can. 82 J13
Whyalla, S. Aust., Austral. 211 X10
Wialki, W. Aust., Austral. 211 W3
Wiay, island, Scot., U.K. 142 J6
Wibaux, Mont., U.S. 106 C13
Wichita, Kans., U.S. 105 U7
Wichita, river, Tex., U.S. 102 J9
Wichita Falls, Tex., U.S. 102 J9
Wichita Mountains, Okla., U.S. 102 H9
Wick, Scot., U.K. 142 H10
Wickenburg, Ariz., U.S. 107 T6
Wickepin, W. Aust., Austral. 211 X3
Wickett, Tex., U.S. 103 N3
Wickiup Reservoir, Oreg., U.S. 108 H4
Wickliffe, Ky., U.S. 100 D12
Wicklow, Ire. 143 S7
Wicklow Head, Ire. 143 T7
Wicklow Mountains, Ire. 143 T6
Wide Bay, P.N.G. 213 C21
Widnes, Eng., U.K. 143 S11
Wieleń, Pol. 148 D12
Wieluń, Pol. 149 F14
Wien (Vienna), Aust. 148 K12
Wiener Neustadt, Aust. 148 L12
Wieprz, river, Pol. 149 E17
Wiesbaden, Ger. 148 G6
Wigan, Eng., U.K. 143 R11
Wiggins, Miss., U.S. 100 N12
Wight, Isle of, Eng., U.K. 143 X12
Wigtown Bay, Scot., U.K. 143 P9
Wikieup, Ariz., U.S. 107 S5
Wil, Switz. 150 A4
Wilberforce, Cape, Austral. 210 A9
Wilbur, Wash., U.S. 108 C7
Wilburton, Okla., U.S. 102 H13
Wilcannia, N.S.W., Austral. 211 W12
Wilczek, Zemlya, Russ. 158 C12
Wildcat Peak, Nev., U.S. 109 Q10
Wildespitze, peak, Aust. 148 M8
Wildrose, N. Dak., U.S. 104 E2
Wildwood, Fla., U.S. 97 S8
Wildwood, N.J., U.S. 94 R10
Wilhelm, Mount, P.N.G. 213 C19
Wilhelm II Coast, Antarctica 227 J21
Wilhelmina Gebergte, Suriname 129 F15
Wilhelmina Mountains, S. Amer. 126 B7
Wilhelmshaven, Ger. 148 C6
Wilkes-Barre, Pa., U.S. 94 M9
Wilkes Island, Wake I., U.S. 216 F8
Wilkes Land, Antarctica 227 Q17
Wilkins Coast, Antarctica 226 E5
Willacoochee, Ga., U.S. 97 P6
Willamette, river, Oreg., U.S. 108 G3
Willapa Bay, Wash., U.S. 108 D2
Willapa Hills, Wash., U.S. 108 D3
Willard, Ohio, U.S. 99 P13
Willard, Utah, U.S. 106 K7
Willcox, Ariz., U.S. 107 V9
Willemstad, Neth. Antilles, Neth. 121 Q14
Willeroo, N. Terr., Austral. 211 Q8
William, Mount, Austral. 210 L11
William "Bill" Dannelly Reservoir, Ala., U.S. 101 L15
William Cay, Bahamas 120 E8
William Creek, S. Aust., Austral. 211 V9
Williams, Ariz., U.S. 107 S7
Williams, Calif., U.S. 109 Q4
Williams, Minn., U.S. 104 E10
Williams, W. Aust., Austral. 211 X3
Williamsburg, Ky., U.S. 101 D18
Williamsburg, Va., U.S. 96 F13
Williamsfield, Jam. 120 J8
Williams Island, Bahamas 116 E10
Williams Lake, B.C., Can. 82 L8
Williamson, W. Va., U.S. 96 E7
Williamson Glacier, Antarctica 227 M20
Williamsport, Pa., U.S. 94 M7
Williamston, N.C., U.S. 96 H13
Williamston, S.C., U.S. 96 K7
William's Town, Bahamas 120 F9
Williamstown, Ky., U.S. 101 A18
Williamstown, W. Va., U.S. 96 C8
Willikies, Antigua & Barbuda 121 B21
Willis, Tex., U.S. 103 P14
Willis Islets, Coral Sea Is. Terr., Austral. 211 R15
Williston, N. Dak., U.S. 104 E2
Williston, S.C., U.S. 96 L8
Williston Lake, B.C., Can. 82 J9
Willits, Calif., U.S. 109 P2
Willmar, Minn., U.S. 104 J10
Willoughby Bay, Antigua & Barbuda 121 B21
Willow City, N. Dak., U.S. 104 E5
Willowlake, river, N.W.T., Can. 82 G10
Willowra, N. Terr., Austral. 211 S8
Willows, Calif., U.S. 109 P4
Willow Springs, Mo., U.S. 105 V13
Wills Point, Tex., U.S. 102 L13
Wilmington, Del., U.S. 96 B14
Wilmington, Ill., U.S. 99 P7
Wilmington, N.C., U.S. 96 K12
Wilmington, Ohio, U.S. 99 S12
Wilmington, S. Aust., Austral. 211 X10
Wilmore, Ky., U.S. 101 C17
Wilmot, Ark., U.S. 100 K9
Wilmot, S. Dak., U.S. 104 J8
Wilsall, Mont., U.S. 106 E8
Wilson, Ark., U.S. 100 F11
Wilson, Kans., U.S. 105 T6
Wilson, N.C., U.S. 96 H12
Wilson, Okla., U.S. 102 J11
Wilson, Tex., U.S. 102 K5
Wilson, Mount, Colo., U.S. 107 P10
Wilson, Mount, Oreg., U.S. 108 F4
Wilson Creek, Wash., U.S. 108 C7
Wilson Hills, Antarctica 227 R15
Wilson Lake, Ala., U.S. 101 G14
Wilson Lake, Kans., U.S. 105 S6
Wilson's Creek National Battlefield, Mo., U.S. 105 V12
Wilsons Promontory, Vic., Austral. 211 Z12
Wilson Strait, Solomon Is. 217 M15
Wilton, N. Dak., U.S. 104 G4
Wiltz, river, Lux. 160 H9
Wiltz, Lux. 160 H9
Wiluna, W. Aust., Austral. 211 V4
Winamac, Ind., U.S. 99 P8
Winchester, Eng., U.K. 143 W12
Winchester, Idaho, U.S. 106 D3
Winchester, Ind., U.S. 99 R10
Winchester, Ky., U.S. 101 B18
Winchester, Tenn., U.S. 101 G16
Winchester, Va., U.S. 96 C12
Winchester Bay, Oreg., U.S. 108 H2
Wind, river, Wyo., U.S. 106 H9
Wind, river, Yukon, Can. 82 E9
Windber, Pa., U.S. 94 P5
Winder, Ga., U.S. 96 K6
Windhill Beach, Gibraltar, U.K. 161 Q23
Windhoek, Namibia 202 H7
Windom, Minn., U.S. 104 L10
Windorah, Qnsld., Austral. 211 U12
Window Rock, Ariz., U.S. 107 R10
Wind River Range, Wyo., U.S. 106 H9
Windsor, Colo., U.S. 106 L13
Windsor, Conn., U.S. 95 L13
Windsor, Eng., U.K. 143 V13
Windsor, Mo., U.S. 105 T11
Windsor, N.C., U.S. 96 G13
Windsor, Ont., Can. 83 R17
Windsor, Vt., U.S. 95 H13
Windsor Forest, Ga., U.S. 97 N9
Windward Islands, Lesser Antilles 119 L16
Windward Passage, Cuba, Haiti 117 K15
Winfield, Ala., U.S. 101 J14
Winfield, Kans., U.S. 105 V8
Wini, Indonesia 189 N15
Winifred, Mont., U.S. 106 C9
Wininen, island, F.S.M. 217 C16
Winion, Mochun, F.S.M. 217 C16
Winipirea, island, F.S.M. 217 B15
Winipiru, island, F.S.M. 217 C14
Winisk, river, Ont., Can. 83 L16
Wink, Tex., U.S. 103 N3
Winkelman, Ariz., U.S. 107 U8
Winlock, Wash., U.S. 108 D3
Winneba, Ghana 200 H10
Winnebago, Minn., U.S. 104 L11
Winnebago, Lake, Wis., U.S. 98 K6
Winnemucca, Nev., U.S. 108 M9
Winnemucca Lake, Nev., U.S. 109 N7
Winner, S. Dak., U.S. 104 M5
Winnfield, La., U.S. 100 M8
Winnibigoshish, Lake, Minn., U.S. 104 F10
Winnipeg, Man., Can. 83 N14
Winnipeg, Lake, Man., Can. 83 M14
Winnipegosis, Man., Can. 83 M13
Winnipegosis, Lake, N. Amer. 80 G5
Winnipesaukee, Lake, N.H., U.S. 95 H14
Winnsboro, La., U.S. 100 L9
Winnsboro, S.C., U.S. 96 K9
Winnsboro, Tex., U.S. 102 L14
Winona, Kans., U.S. 105 S3
Winona, Minn., U.S. 104 L13
Winona, Miss., U.S. 100 J11
Winseler, Lux. 160 H9
Winsen, Ger. 148 C8
Winslow, Ariz., U.S. 107 S8
Winslow, Me., U.S. 95 F16
Winston-Salem, N.C., U.S. 96 H10
Winter Garden, Fla., U.S. 97 T8
Winter Haven, Fla., U.S. 97 U8
Winter Park, Fla., U.S. 97 T9
Winters, Calif., U.S. 109 R4
Winters, Tex., U.S. 102 M7
Winterset, Iowa, U.S. 105 P11
Winterswijk, Neth. 146 J14
Winterthur, Switz. 150 A4
Winthrop, Me., U.S. 95 F16
Winthrop, Minn., U.S. 104 K10
Winthrop, Wash., U.S. 108 B6
Winton Heights, Bahamas 120 B12
Wippra, Ger. 148 F8
Wirrulla, S. Aust., Austral. 211 X9
Wisas, island, F.S.M. 217 C16
Wisbech, Eng., U.K. 143 T14
Wiscasset, Me., U.S. 95 G16
Wisconsin, U.S. 98 J3
Wisconsin, river, Wis., U.S. 98 J5
Wisconsin Dells, Wis., U.S. 98 K5
Wisconsin Rapids, Wis., U.S. 98 J5
Wiseman, Alas., U.S. 111 E16
Wishek, N. Dak., U.S. 104 H5
Wishram, Wash., U.S. 108 F5
Wisła, river, Pol. 149 B14
Wismar, Ger. 148 B9
Wisner, La., U.S. 100 M9
Wisner, Nebr., U.S. 105 N8
Wissembourg, Fr. 147 N16
Witchcliffe, W. Aust., Austral. 211 Y2
Witham, Eng., U.K. 143 U15
Witten, S. Dak., U.S. 104 M5
Wittenberg, Ger. 148 E10
Wittenberge, Ger. 148 D9
Wittenoom, W. Aust., Austral. 211 T3
Wittlich, Ger. 148 G5
Wittlich, Ger. 160 H12
Wittstock, Ger. 148 C10
Wittstock, Ger. 148 C9
Witu Islands, P.N.G. 213 C20
Włocławek, Pol. 149 D14
Włodawa, Pol. 149 E18
Wöbbelin, Ger. 148 C9
Woburn Bay, Grenada 121 L22
Wodonga, Vic., Austral. 211 Y13
Wohlthat Mountains, Antarctica 227 B14
Wojejairok, island, Marshall Is. 216 L4
Wojejairok Pass, Marshall Is. 216 L4
Wokam, island, Indonesia 189 L19
Wokingham, Eng., U.K. 143 V13
Wolauna, island, F.S.M. 217 G13
Wolcott, N.Y., U.S. 94 J7
Woleai Atoll, F.S.M. 216 Q4
Wolf, river, Wis., U.S. 98 H6
Wolf, Isla (Wenman), Ecua. 128 M7
Wolf, Volcán, Ecua. 128 P8
Wolf Creek, Mont., U.S. 106 D7
Wolf Creek, Oreg., U.S. 108 K2
Wolf Creek, Tex., U.S. 102 F7
Wolf Creek Pass, Colo., U.S. 107 P11
Wolfeboro, N.H., U.S. 95 H14
Wolfe City, Tex., U.S. 102 K12
Wolfen, Ger. 148 E9
Wolfenbüttel, Ger. 148 E8
Wolfforth, Tex., U.S. 102 K5
Wolf Point, Mont., U.S. 106 B12
Wolfsberg, Aust. 148 M11
Wolfsburg, Ger. 148 D8
Wollaston, Islas, Chile 133 Y9
Wollaston Lake, Sask., Can. 83 K13
Wollaston Peninsula, N.W.T., Nunavut, Can. 82 E12
Wollogorang, N. Terr., Austral. 211 R10
Wollongong, N.S.W., Austral. 211 Y14
Wolo, Indonesia 189 K13
Wolverhampton, Eng., U.K. 143 T11
Wondai, Qnsld., Austral. 211 V15
Wongan Hills, W. Aust., Austral. 211 W2
Wongawal, W. Aust., Austral. 211 U4
Wonju, S. Korea 182 F14
Wŏnsan, N. Korea 182 D13
Wonthaggi, Vic., Austral. 211 Z12
Wonti, Indonesia 213 B16
Woodall Mountain, Miss., U.S. 101 G13
Woodbine, Ga., U.S. 97 Q8
Woodbridge, Eng., U.K. 143 U15
Woodbridge, Va., U.S. 96 D13
Woodbridge Bay, Dominica 121 G19
Woodburn, N.S.W., Austral. 211 W15
Woodburn, Oreg., U.S. 108 F3
Woodbury, N.J., U.S. 94 Q9
Wood Cay, Bahamas 120 A5
Woodcock, Mount, Austral. 210 D9
Woodenbridge, Ire. 143 T7
Woodford, Grenada 121 K22
Wood Lake, Nebr., U.S. 105 N5
Woodlake, Calif., U.S. 109 U7
Woodland, Calif., U.S. 109 Q4
Woodland, Me., U.S. 95 E19
Woodland, Wash., U.S. 108 E3
Woodland Park, Colo., U.S. 106 M13
Woodlark, island, P.N.G. 213 E21
Wood River, Ill., U.S. 99 S4
Wood River, Nebr., U.S. 105 Q6
Wood River Lakes, Alas., U.S. 111 K13
Woodruff, S.C., U.S. 96 J8
Woodruff, Utah, U.S. 106 K8
Woods, Lake, Austral. 210 D8
Woods, Lake of the, Can., U.S. 85 B13
Woodsboro, Tex., U.S. 103 T11
Woodsfield, Ohio, U.S. 99 R15
Woods Hole, Mass., U.S. 95 L15
Woodstock, Qnsld., Austral. 211 S12
Woodstock, Va., U.S. 96 D11
Woodstown, N.J., U.S. 94 Q9
Woodsville, N.H., U.S. 95 G13
Woodville, Miss., U.S. 100 N9
Woodville, N.Z. 213 M19
Woodville, Tex., U.S. 103 P15
Woodward, Okla., U.S. 102 E8
Woody Head, Austral. 210 J15
Woomera, S. Aust., Austral. 211 W10
Woonsocket, R.I., U.S. 95 L14
Woonsocket, S. Dak., U.S. 104 L7
Woorabinda, Qnsld., Austral. 211 U14
Wooramel, W. Aust., Austral. 211 V1
Wooster, Ohio, U.S. 99 P14
Worbab, island, Marshall Is. 216 N5
Worcester, Eng., U.K. 143 U11
Worcester, Mass., U.S. 95 K14
Worcester, S. Af. 202 M7
Worden, Mont., U.S. 106 E10
Workai, island, Indonesia 189 M19
Workington, Eng., U.K. 143 P10
Worland, Wyo., U.S. 106 G10
Wormeldange, Lux. 160 K11
Worms, Ger. 148 H6
Worth, Lake, Tex., U.S. 102 L11
Wortham, Tex., U.S. 102 M12
Worthing, Barbados 121 L19
Worthington, Minn., U.S. 104 L9
Wosi, Indonesia 189 J16
Wotho Atoll, Marshall Is. 216 F3
Wotje Atoll, Marshall Is. 216 G5
Wotje Atoll, Marshall Is. 214 F8
Wowoni, island, Indonesia 189 L14

Wragby, Eng., U.K. 143 S13
Wrangel Island see Vrangelya, Ostrov, Russ. 159 B19
Wrangel Island, Russ. 166 A11
Wrangell, Alas., U.S. 111 M23
Wrangell, Cape, Alas., U.S. 110 K1
Wrangell Mountains, Alas., U.S. 84 P5
Wrangell-St. Elias National Park and Preserve, Alas., U.S. 111 J19
Wrangel Plain, Arctic Oc. 242 G8
Wrath, Cape, Scot., U.K. 142 G8
Wray, Colo., U.S. 106 L16
Wreck Hill, Bermuda, U.K. 120 C1
Wreck Point, S. Af. 194 Q6
Wrecks, Bay of, Kiribati 217 B23
Wrens, Ga., U.S. 96 M7
Wrexham, Wales, U.K. 143 S10
Wright, Wyo., U.S. 106 G12
Wright Brothers National Memorial, N.C., U.S. 96 G15
Wright Patman Lake, Tex., U.S. 102 K15
Wrightsville, Ga., U.S. 96 M7
Wrightsville Beach, N.C., U.S. 96 K13
Wrigley Gulf, Antarctica 226 N7
Wrocław, Pol. 149 F13
Września, Pol. 149 E13
Wu, river, China 183 N1
Wu, river, China 181 M13
Wu'an, China 182 F5
Wubin, W. Aust., Austral. 211 W2
Wubu, China 182 E3
Wuchang, China 181 D17
Wuchuan, China 182 C4
Wuchuan, China 182 M1
Wuchuan, China 183 S2
Wuda, China 182 D1
Wudan see Ongniud Qi, China 182 A8
Wudaoliang, China 180 J9
Wudi, China 182 E7
Wudinna, S. Aust., Austral. 211 X9
Wufeng, China 182 L3
Wugang, China 183 N2
Wuhai, China 182 C1
Wuhan, China 182 L5
Wuhe, China 182 J7
Wuhu, China 182 K8
Wukari, Nigeria 201 G15
Wular Lake, India 176 M12
Wulian, China 182 G8
Wuliaru, island, Indonesia 213 D14
Wum, Cameroon 201 H15
Wundowie, W. Aust., Austral. 211 X2
Wuning, China 182 M5
Wunlah, Indonesia 189 M17
Wuntho, Myanmar 186 F6
Wupatki National Monument, Ariz., U.S. 107 R7
Wuping, China 183 Q6
Wuppertal, Ger. 148 F5
Wuqi, China 182 F2
Wuqia, China 180 F4
Wuqing, China 182 D7
Wurarga, W. Aust., Austral. 211 V2
Wurung, Qnsld., Austral. 211 R11
Würzburg, Ger. 148 H7
Wushan, China 182 K2
Wusi, Vanuatu 218 C1
Wust Seamount, Atl. Oc. 237 T12
Wusuli (Ussuri), river, China 181 C19
Wutai, China 182 E5
Wutongqiao, China 180 L11
Wuvulu Island, P.N.G. 213 B18
Wuwei, China 182 K7
Wuwei, China 180 H11
Wuxi, China 182 K2
Wuxi, China 182 K9
Wuxue, China 182 L6
Wuyiling, China 181 C17
Wuyi Shan, China 183 P6
Wuyuan, China 182 C2
Wuyuan, China 182 M7
Wuzhai, China 182 D4
Wuzhen, China 182 K4
Wuzhong, China 180 H12
Wuzhou, China 183 R3
Wyandot Seamount, Atl. Oc. 237 T15
Wyandra, Qnsld., Austral. 211 V13
Wye, river, Eng., Wales, U.K. 143 U11
Wyk, Ger. 148 A7
Wylie Lake, N.C., S.C., U.S. 96 J9
Wyloo, W. Aust., Austral. 211 T2
Wymore, Nebr., U.S. 105 R8
Wynbring, S. Aust., Austral. 211 W8
Wyndham, W. Aust., Austral. 211 Q6
Wyndmere, N. Dak., U.S. 104 H8
Wynne, Ark., U.S. 100 G10
Wynnewood, Okla., U.S. 102 H11
Wynniatt Bay, N.W.T., Can. 82 E13
Wyoming, Mich., U.S. 98 L9
Wyoming, U.S. 106 H9
Wyoming Range, Wyo., U.S. 106 H8
Wyszków, Pol. 149 D16
Wytheville, Va., U.S. 96 F8
Wyville Thomson Ridge, Atl. Oc. 236 D12

X

Xaafuun, Somalia 199 F19
Xàbia see Jávea, Sp. 145 J15
Xaçmaz, Azerb. 169 C22
Xaghra, Malta 161 H20
Xaignabouri, Laos 186 J9
Xainza, China 180 K7
Xai-Xai, Mozambique 202 J12
Xalapa, Mex. 115 J13
Xalin, Somalia 199 G18
Xamba see Hanggin Houqi, China 182 C1
Xangdin Hural, China 182 A3
Xangongo, Angola 202 F6
Xankändi see Stepanakert, Azerb. 169 E20
Xánthi, Gr. 155 B14
Xanthus, ruin, Turk. 168 J4
Xapecó, Braz. 130 N11
Xapuri, Braz. 130 G6
Xarardheere, Somalia 199 H18
Xar Moron, river, China 182 A9
Xàtiva, Sp. 145 H14
Xau, Lake, Botswana 202 G9
Xayar, China 180 F6
Xèng, river, Laos 186 H10
Xenia, Ohio, U.S. 99 R12
Xépôn, Laos 186 K12
Xérxis Canal, Gr. 154 D12
Xewkija, Malta 161 H20
Xi, river, China 183 R4
Xiachuan Dao, China 183 S3
Xiajiang, China 183 N5
Xiamen (Amoy), China 183 Q7
Xi'an, China 182 H2
Xianfeng, China 182 L2
Xiang, river, China 183 P3
Xiangfan, China 182 K4
Xianghuang Qi (Hobot Xar), China 182 B5
Xiangkhoang, Laos 186 J10
Xiangning, China 182 G3
Xiangshan (Dancheng), China 182 M10
Xiangtan, China 183 N4
Xiangyin, China 182 M4
Xiangyunn, China 180 N10
Xianju, China 182 M9
Xiantao, China 182 L4
Xianyou, China 183 Q8
Xiaogan, China 182 K5
Xiao Hinggan Ling, China 181 B17
Xiaojiang, China 183 N9
Xiaoshan, China 182 L9
Xiaoyi, China 182 F4
Xiapu, China 183 P9
Xichang, China 180 M11
Xifeng, China 182 B11
Xifeng, China 182 F1
Xigazê, China 180 L7
Xilaganí, Gr. 155 C15
Xiliao, river, China 182 A10
Xilinhot, China 182 A7
Xilókastro, Gr. 154 J10
Ximiao, China 180 G10
Xin Barag Youqi, China 181 C14
Xin Barag Zuoqi, China 181 C15
Xinbin, China 182 B12
Xincai, China 182 J5
Xinfeng, China 183 Q5
Xinfeng, China 183 R5
Xinfengjiang Shuiki, China 183 R5
Xing'an, China 183 P2
Xingcheng, China 182 C9
Xinghai, China 180 J10
Xinghe, China 182 C5
Xinghua, China 182 J9
Xinghua Wan, China 183 Q8
Xingkai Hu see Khanka, Ozero, China 181 D19
Xingning, China 183 R6
Xingshan, China 182 K3
Xingtai, China 182 F5
Xingu, river, Braz. 130 D12
Xinguara, Braz. 131 F13
Xingxian, China 182 E3
Xingxingxia, China 180 F9
Xingyi, China 180 N12
Xingzi, China 182 M6
Xinhe, China 182 F6
Xinhua, China 183 N3
Xinhuang, China 183 N1
Xinhui, China 183 S4
Xining, China 180 J11
Xinji, China 182 E6
Xinjiang, China 182 G3
Xinjin, China 182 D10
Xinmin, China 182 B10
Xinning, China 183 P2
Xinpu see Lianyungang, China 182 H8
Xinshao, China 183 N3
Xinwen, China 182 G7
Xinxiang, China 182 G5
Xinxing, China 183 S3
Xinyang, China 182 K5
Xinye, China 182 J4
Xinyi, China 182 H8
Xinyi, China 183 S2
Xinyuan, China 180 E6
Xinzhou, China 182 E4
Xinzo de Limia, Sp. 144 D6
Xique Xique, Braz. 131 G15
Xishui, China 182 L6
Xiushan, China 182 M1
Xiushui, China 182 M5
Xiuyan, China 182 C11
Xiuying, China 183 T2
Xixian, China 182 J5
Xixiang, China 182 J1
Xorkol, China 180 G8
Xuan'en, China 182 L2
Xuanhan, China 182 K1
Xuanhua, China 182 C6
Xuan Loc, Vietnam 187 P13
Xuanwei, China 180 N11
Xuanzhou, China 182 L8
Xuchang, China 182 H5
Xudat, Azerb. 169 C22
Xuddur, Somalia 199 H16
Xudun, Somalia 199 G17
Xuí, Braz. 130 R11
Xulun Hoh see Zhenglan Qi, China 182 B7
Xun, river, China 183 R2
Xunke, China 181 B17
Xunwu, China 183 Q6
Xunyi, China 182 G2
Xupu, China 183 N2
Xuwen, China 183 T2
Xuyong, China 180 M12
Xuzhou, China 182 H7
Xylofagou, Cyprus 160 P10

Y

Yaak, Mont., U.S. 106 A4
Ya'an, China 180 L11
Yabbenohr, island, Marshall Is. 216 L3
Yablonovyy Khrebet, Russ. 159 L17
Yablonovyy Range, Russ. 166 E11
Yabrūd, Syr. 170 H8
Yabucoa, P.R., U.S. 120 N5
Yabucoa, Puerto, P.R., U.S. 120 N5
Yacata, island, Fiji Is. 218 H8
Yachats, Oreg., U.S. 108 G2
Yacimiento Río Turbio, Arg. 133 W7
Yacuiba, Bol. 130 L8
Yacyretá Dam, Parag. 130 N10
Yadgir, India 178 M5
Yadkin, river, N.C., U.S. 96 G9
Yadong, China 180 M7
Yadua, island, Fiji Is. 218 G6
Yafi, Indonesia 189 K21
Yagasa, island, Fiji Is. 218 K9
Yağca, Turk. 168 H6
Yaguajay, Cuba 116 H9
Yahyalı, Turk. 168 G10
Yaita, Japan 185 N12
Yakacık, Turk. 168 J11
Yakapınar, Turk. 168 J10
Yakeshi, China 181 C15
Yakima, river, Wash., U.S. 108 D6
Yakima, Wash., U.S. 108 D6
Yakishiri Jima, Japan 184 E13
Yakmach, Pak. 177 S3
Yakoma, Dem. Rep. of the Congo 198 H10
Yakossi, Cen. Af. Rep. 198 H10
Yaksha, Russ. 158 G9
Yaku Shima, Japan 185 U4
Yakutat, Alas., U.S. 111 K20
Yakutat Bay, Alas., U.S. 111 K20
Yakutsk, Russ. 159 H18
Yala, Sri Lanka 179 T8
Yala, Thai. 187 S9
Yale, Mich., U.S. 98 L13
Yale, Okla., U.S. 102 F11
Yalewa Kalou (Round Island), Fiji Is. 218 G6
Yalgoo, W. Aust., Austral. 211 V2
Yallahs, Jam. 120 J10
Yalleroi, Qnsld., Austral. 211 U13
Yallock, N.S.W., Austral. 211 X12
Yalong, river, China 180 M11
Yalova, Turk. 168 D5
Yalta, Ukr. 157 T7
Yalu, river, N. Korea, China 182 C11
Yalvaç, Turk. 168 G6
Yamada, Japan 184 K14
Yamagata, Japan 184 L12
Yamaguchi, Japan 185 Q5
Yamal, Poluostrov, Russ. 158 F11
Yamal Peninsula, Russ. 166 C8
Yamas, Indonesia 189 K21
Yamato Glacier, Antarctica 227 C16
Yamato Mountains see Queen Fabiola Mountains, Antarctica 227 C17
Yamba, N.S.W., Austral. 211 W15
Yambio, Sudan 198 H11
Yambol, Bulg. 153 J16
Yamdena, island, Indonesia 189 M17
Yamethinn, Myanmar 186 H6
Yamm, Russ. 156 G5
Yammaw, Myanmar 186 E7
Yamma Yamma, Lake, Austral. 210 G11
Yamoussoukro, Côte d'Ivoire 200 G8
Yampa, river, Colo., U.S. 106 L10
Yamzho Yumco, lake, China 180 L7
Yana, river, Russ. 166 C11
Yana, Gulf of, Arctic Oc. 242 C6
Yanagawa, Japan 185 R4
Yanai, Japan 185 R6
Yan'an, China 182 F2
Yanbu' al Baḩr, Saudi Arabia 172 J6
Yancannia, N.S.W., Austral. 211 W12
Yanchang, China 182 F3
Yancheng, China 182 J9
Yanchi, China 182 E1
Yanchuan, China 182 F3
Yandé, Île, New Caledonia, Fr. 218 B6
Yandina, Solomon Is. 217 N18
Yandoon, Myanmar 186 K6
Yangbajain, China 180 L7
Yangchun, China 183 S3
Yangi Qal'eh, Afghan. 176 J8
Yangi Qal'eh, Afghan. 176 L4
Yangjiang, China 183 S3
Yangon (Rangoon), Myanmar 186 K6
Yangquan, China 182 E5
Yangshan, China 183 Q4
Yangshuo, China 183 Q2
Yangtze see Chang Jiang, Jinsha, river, China 181 L13
Yangtze, Mouth of the, China 182 K10
Yangtze, Source of the, China 180 K7
Yangtze Gorges, China 182 K2
Yangxian, China 182 H1
Yangxin, China 182 L5
Yangyang, S. Korea 182 E14
Yangyuan, China 182 D5
Yangzhou, China 182 J8
Yanhe, China 182 M1
Yanji, China 182 A14
Yankeetown, Fla., U.S. 97 S7
Yankton, S. Dak., U.S. 104 M7
Yano-Indigirskaya Nizmennost', Russ. 159 E17
Yano-Oymyakonskoye Nagor'ye, Russ. 159 F18
Yanqi, China 180 F7
Yanshan, China 182 E7
Yanshan, China 183 N7
Yanskiy, Russ. 159 F17
Yanskiy Zaliv, Russ. 159 E17
Yantabulla, N.S.W., Austral. 211 W12
Yantai, China 182 F10
Yantra, river, Bulg. 153 H15
Yanuca, island, Fiji Is. 218 G8
Yao, Japan 185 Q9
Yaoundé, Cameroon 201 J16
Yaoxian, China 182 G2
Yap, island, F.S.M. 217 D18
Yapen, island, Indonesia 189 K19
Yapen, Selat, Indonesia 189 K19
Yapero, Indonesia 189 L20
Yap Islands, F.S.M. 216 P2
Yap Trench, Pac. Oc. 238 J5
Yaqaqa, island, Fiji Is. 218 G7
Yaqeta, island, Fiji Is. 218 H5
Yaqui, river, Mex. 114 D7
Yaquina Head, Oreg., U.S. 108 G2
Yara, Cuba 116 K12
Yaraka, Qnsld., Austral. 211 U12
Yaralıgöz, peak, Turk. 168 C9
Yaransk, Russ. 156 G14
Yardımcı Burnu, Turk. 168 J6
Yardymly, Azerb. 169 F22
Yaren, Nauru 217 F23
Yarí, river, Col. 128 H6
Yarīm, Yemen 172 Q9
Yaring, Thai. 187 S9
Yarkant, river, China 180 F5
Yarle Lakes, Austral. 210 J8
Yarlung Zangbo (Brahmaputra), river, China 180 L8
Yarlung Zangbo (Tsangpo) Canyon, China 180 L9
Yarma, Turk. 168 G8
Yarmouth, N.S., Can. 83 Q21
Yaroslavl', Russ. 156 H10
Yaroua, island, Fiji Is. 218 H9
Yarozero, Russ. 156 E10
Yarraden, Qnsld., Austral. 211 Q12
Yarraloola, W. Aust., Austral. 211 T2
Yartsevo, Russ. 156 K7
Yartsevo, Russ. 159 J13
Yarumal, Col. 128 D4
Yasawa, island, Fiji Is. 218 G6
Yasawa Group, Fiji Is. 218 H5
Yashkul', Russ. 157 R14
Yasin, Pak. 176 K11
Yasinza'i Kalay, Afghan. 177 Q4
Yasothon, Thai. 186 L11
Yasun Burnu, Turk. 168 D12
Yasur Volcano, Vanuatu 218 H4
Yata, river, Bol. 130 G7
Yatağan, Turk. 168 H4
Yatakala, Niger 196 H9
Yaté, New Caledonia, Fr. 218 E9
Yates Center, Kans., U.S. 105 U9
Yathkyed Lake, Nunavut, Can. 83 J14
Yato, Pukapuka, Cook Is., N.Z. 218 Q2
Yatsushiro, Japan 185 S4
Yauca, Peru 130 J4
Yauco, P.R., U.S. 120 N2
Yaupi, Ecua. 128 K3
Yavatmal, India 178 K6
Yaviza, Pan. 115 N22
Yawatahama, Japan 185 R6
Yawri Bay, Sierra Leone 200 G5
Yayladağı, Turk. 168 K11
Yaynangyoung, Myanmar 186 H5
Yazd, Iran 173 E14
Yazdān, Iran 173 D17
Yazılıkaya, Turk. 168 F6
Yazlıca Dağı, Turk. 169 H17
Yazman, Pak. 177 S10
Yazoo, river, Miss., U.S. 85 K15
Yazoo City, Miss., U.S. 100 K11
Ye, Myanmar 186 L7
Yebyu, Myanmar 186 M7
Yecheng (Kargilik), China 180 G4
Yecla, Sp. 145 J14
Yeeda, W. Aust., Austral. 211 R5
Yefremov, Russ. 156 L9
Yegua Creek, Tex., U.S. 103 Q12
Yeguas, Punta, P.R., U.S. 120 N5
Yei, Sudan 198 H12
Yekaterinburg, Russ. 158 H9
Yekateriny, Proliv, Russ. 159 K23
Yelabuga, Russ. 156 H16
Yela Island, P.N.G. 217 Q13
Yelan', Russ. 157 N12
Yelan Kolenovskiy, Russ. 157 N11
Yelets, Russ. 156 M10
Yélimané, Mali 196 H6
Yelizavety, Mys, Russ. 159 H21
Yell, island, Scot., U.K. 142 D12

Yellandu, India 178 M7
Yellow see Huang, river, China 181 G13
Yellow, river, Fla., U.S. 97 Q2
Yellow, Source of the, China 166 G9
Yellowknife, N.W.T., Can. 82 H11
Yellow River, Mouth of the, China 182 E8
Yellow Sea, Asia 166 G12
Yellowstone, river, Mont., U.S. 106 D11
Yellowstone Lake, Wyo., U.S. 106 F8
Yellowstone National Park, Wyo., U.S. 106 F8
Yell Sound, Scot., U.K. 142 D12
Yellville, Ark., U.S. 100 E8
Yelm, Wash., U.S. 108 D3
Yel'sk, Belarus 156 M5
Yelverton Bay, Nunavut, Can. 83 A15
Yelwa, Nigeria 201 F13
Yemanzhelinsk, Russ. 158 J8
Yemassee, S.C., U.S. 96 M9
Yemen, Asia 167 W3
Yenakiyeve, Ukr. 157 Q10
Yen Bai, Vietnam 186 G11
Yendi, Ghana 200 F11
Yeniçağa, Turk. 168 D7
Yenice, river, Turk. 168 G11
Yenice, Turk. 168 F8
Yeniceoba, Turk. 168 F8
Yenişehir, Turk. 168 D5
Yenisey, river, Russ. 166 C8
Yenisey-Angara, Source of the, Mongolia 166 F9
Yenisey Gulf, Russ. 166 C8
Yeniseysk, Russ. 159 K13
Yeniseyskiy Zaliv, Russ. 159 F13
Yen Minh, Vietnam 186 F11
Yenyuka, Russ. 159 J17
Yeola, India 178 K4
Yeongdeok, S. Korea 182 F14
Yeosu, S. Korea 182 G14
Yeovil, Eng., U.K. 143 W11
Yeppoon, Qnsld., Austral. 211 T15
Yerbogachen, Russ. 159 J15
Yerema, Russ. 159 J15
Yerevan, Arm. 169 E18
Yergeni Hills, Russ. 138 G13
Yerilla, W. Aust., Austral. 211 W4
Yerington, Nev., U.S. 109 Q7
Yerköy, Turk. 168 E9
Yermak Plateau, Arctic Oc. 243 H14
Yermo, Calif., U.S. 109 W10
Yeroḥam, Israel 171 P5
Yershov, Russ. 156 M15
Yeşilhisar, Turk. 168 G10
Yeşilırmak, river, Turk. 168 D11
Yeşilkent, Turk. 168 J11
Yeşilova, Turk. 168 H5
Yessentuki, Russ. 157 T12
Yessey, Russ. 159 G14
Yetman, N.S.W., Austral. 211 W14
Ye-u, Myanmar 186 G6
Yeu, Île d', Fr. 147 S5
Yevlax, Azerb. 169 D21
Yevpatoriya, Ukr. 157 S7
Yexian, China 182 F9
Yeysk, Russ. 157 R10
Ygatimí, Parag. 130 M11
Yi, river, China 182 G8
Yí, river, Uru. 132 K14
Yialias, river, Cyprus 160 P8
Yibin, China 180 M12
Yichang, China 182 L3
Yicheng, China 182 K4
Yichuan, China 182 F3
Yichun, China 183 N5
Yichun, China 181 C17
Yigo, Guam, U.S. 216 B11
Yijun, China 182 G2
Yilan, China 181 C18
Yildiz Dağlari, Turk. 168 B4
Yıldızeli, Turk. 168 E11
Yiliang, China 180 N11
Yinan, China 182 G8
Yinchuan, China 182 D1
Yindarlgooda, Lake, Austral. 210 J4
Yindi, W. Aust., Austral. 211 W5
Ying, river, China 181 K15
Yingcheng, China 182 K5
Yingde, China 183 R4
Yingkou, China 182 C10
Yingshan, China 182 K5
Yingshang, China 182 J6
Yingxian, China 182 D5
Yining (Gulja), China 180 E6
Yin Shan, China 182 B2
Yirga 'Alem, Eth. 199 G15
Yirol, Sudan 198 G12
Yirrkala, N. Terr., Austral. 211 P10
Yishan, China 183 Q1
Yishui, China 182 G8
Yitong, China 182 A12
Yitulihe, China 181 B15
Yiwu, China 182 M9
Yiwu, China 180 F9
Yixian, China 182 C9
Yixing, China 182 K9
Yiyang, China 182 M4
Yiyuan, China 182 G8
Ylig Bay, Guam, U.S. 216 C11
Ylivieska, Fin. 141 G15
Ÿnderbor, Kaz. 174 E6
Yoakum, Tex., U.S. 103 R11
Yobe, river, Niger, Nigeria 194 G6
Yogyakarta, Indonesia 188 M9
Yoichi, Japan 184 F13
Yokadouma, Cameroon 201 J17
Yokkaichi, Japan 185 Q9
Yoko, Cameroon 201 H16
Yokoate Shima, Japan 185 W3
Yokohama, Japan 184 H13
Yokohama, Japan 185 P12
Yokote, Japan 184 K13
Yola, Nigeria 201 F16
Yolöten, Turkm. 174 M10
Yom, river, Thai. 186 K8
Yomra, Turk. 169 D14
Yona, Guam, U.S. 216 C11
Yonago, Japan 185 P7
Yonezawa, Japan 184 M12
Yong'an, China 183 P7
Yŏngbal, N. Korea 182 B14
Yongchun, China 183 Q8
Yongdeng, China 180 H11
Yongfu, China 183 Q2
Yonggyap Pass, China, India 178 E15
Yŏngjŏ, N. Korea 182 B13
Yongkang, China 182 M9
Yongshun, China 182 M2
Yongtai, China 183 P8
Yongxin, China 183 N5
Yongxing, China 183 P4
Yongxiu, China 182 M6
Yongzhou, China 183 P3
Yonkers, N.Y., U.S. 94 N11
Yonne, river, Fr. 147 R11
York, Ala., U.S. 101 L13
York, Eng., U.K. 143 R13
York, Nebr., U.S. 105 Q7
York, Pa., U.S. 94 P7
York, S.C., U.S. 96 J8
York, Cape, Austral. 210 A12
York, Cape, N. Amer. 80 C7
Yorke Peninsula, Austral. 210 K10
Yorkton, Sask., Can. 83 N13
Yorktown, Tex., U.S. 103 S11
Yorktown, Va., U.S. 96 F14
Yoron Jima, Japan 185 X2
Yoro Shima, Japan 185 W3
Yortan Tepe, ruin, Turk. 168 F3
Yosemite National Park, Calif., U.S. 109 S7
Yoshii, river, Japan 185 Q7
Yoshkar Ola, Russ. 156 H14
Yos Sudarso see Dolak, island, Indonesia 189 M20
Yotvata, Israel 171 R5
You, river, China 180 P12
Youghal, Ire. 143 U5
Youghal Bay, Ire. 143 U5
Young, N.S.W., Austral. 211 Y13
Young, Mount, Austral. 210 C9
Young Island, Bahamas 120 E7
Young's Rock, Pitcairn I., U.K. 219 Q23
Youngstown, Ohio, U.S. 99 P16
Youth, Isle of see Juventud, Isla de la, Cuba 116 J5
Youxian, China 183 N4
Youyang, China 182 M1
Youyi Feng (Tavan Bogd Uul), peak, China, Mongolia 180 C8
Yovan, Taj. 176 J7
Yovkovo, Bulg. 153 G17
Yovo, island, P.N.G. 217 H14
Yozgat, Turk. 168 E10
Ypé Jhú, Parag. 130 M11
Ypres see Ieper, Belg. 146 L10
Ypsilanti, Mich., U.S. 98 M12
Ypsilí see Strongíli, island, Gr. 155 N22
Yreka, Calif., U.S. 108 L3
Yrghyz, river, Kaz. 174 E9
Yrghyz, Kaz. 174 E10
Ysabel Channel, P.N.G. 213 B20
Ysyk-Köl, lake, Kyrg. 176 E13
Ysyk-Köl see Balykchy, Kyrg. 176 E12
Ytterån, Sw. 140 H12
Ytyk Kyuyel', Russ. 159 G18
Yuan, river, China 182 M3
Yuan (Red), river, China 180 P11
Yuan'an, China 182 K3
Yuanbaoshan, China 182 B8
Yüanli, Taiwan, China 183 Q9
Yuanling, China 182 M2
Yuanqu, China 182 G4
Yuba, river, Calif., U.S. 109 Q4
Yuba City, Calif., U.S. 109 Q4
Yūbari, Japan 184 F14
Yuben', Taj. 176 K10
Yūbetsu, Japan 184 E15
Yucatan Channel, Cuba, Mex. 80 N7
Yucatán Peninsula, Mex. 115 H16
Yucca, Ariz., U.S. 107 S5
Yucca Flat, Nev., U.S. 109 T11
Yucca Valley, Calif., U.S. 109 X10
Yucheng, China 182 F7
Yuci, China 182 E4
Yudino, Russ. 156 J14
Yuendumu, N. Terr., Austral. 211 T8
Yueqing, China 183 N9
Yueyang, China 182 M4
Yugan, China 182 M7
Yugorenok, Russ. 159 G19
Yugorskiy Poluostrov, Russ. 158 F11
Yuhuan Dao, China 183 N10
Yukagir, Russ. 159 E17
Yukagirskoye Ploskogor'ye, Russ. 159 D19
Yukon, river, N. Amer. 80 C1
Yukon, Can. 82 F8
Yukon, Okla., U.S. 102 G10
Yukon-Charley Rivers National Preserve, Alas., U.S. 111 F18
Yukon Delta, Alas., U.S. 110 G12
Yukon Flats, Alas., U.S. 84 N4
Yukon Plateau, N. Amer. 80 D3
Yüksekova, Turk. 169 H18
Yulara, N. Terr., Austral. 211 U7
Yuleba, Qnsld., Austral. 211 V14
Yüli, Taiwan, China 183 R10
Yuli, China 180 F7
Yulin, China 182 E3
Yulin, China 183 R2
Yuma, Ariz., U.S. 107 U4
Yuma, Colo., U.S. 106 L15
Yumbi, Dem. Rep. of the Congo 198 K8
Yumen (Laojunmiao), China 180 G10
Yumenzhen, China 180 G10
Yumurtalık, Turk. 168 J10
Yunan, China 183 R3
Yunaska Island, Alas., U.S. 110 P8
Yuncheng, China 182 G3
Yungas, region, S. Amer. 126 G5
Yunhe, China 181 L16
Yunotsu, Japan 185 P6
Yunta, S. Aust., Austral. 211 X10
Yunxi, China 182 J3
Yunxian, China 182 J3
Yunxiao, China 183 R7
Yunyang, China 182 K2
Yuribey, Russ. 158 F12
Yurimaguas, Peru 130 F3
Yur'yevets, Russ. 156 H12
Yur'yev Pol'skiy, Russ. 156 H10
Yü Shan, Taiwan, China 183 R10
Yushan, China 182 M8
Yuste, Monasterio de, Sp. 144 G8
Yusufeli, Turk. 169 D16
Yutian, China 182 D7
Yutian, China 180 H5
Yuxi, China 180 P11
Yuxian, China 182 D6
Yuxian, China 182 E5
Yuza, Japan 184 L12
Yuzawa, Japan 184 K13
Yuzha, Russ. 156 H11
Yuzhno Sakhalinsk, Russ. 159 K22
Yuzhnyy, Kaz. 174 D10
Yuzhnyy, Russ. 157 S14
Yuzhnyy, Mys, Russ. 159 F21
Yverdon, Switz. 150 B1
Yvetot, Fr. 147 N8

Z

Za, river, China 180 K9
Zaanstad, Neth. 146 H12
Zabaykal'sk, Russ. 159 L17
Zabbar, Malta 161 K23
Zabīd, Yemen 172 Q8
Zābol, Iran 173 E17
Zābolī, Iran 173 H18
Zabrze, Pol. 149 G14
Zacapa, Guatemala 115 L16
Zacatecas, Mex. 114 G10
Zadar (Zara), Croatia 152 F5
Zadoi, China 180 K9
Zafóra, island, Gr. 155 N17
Zafra, Sp. 144 J7
Żagań, Pol. 148 F12
Zagorá, Gr. 154 F11
Zagora, Mor. 196 C8
Zagoria, range, Gr. 154 E7
Zagreb, Croatia 152 D6
Zagros, Kūhhā-ye (Zagros Mountains), Iran 172 D11
Zagros Mountains see Zagros, Kūhhā-ye, Iran 172 E11
Zaháro, Gr. 154 K9
Zāhedān, Iran 173 F17
Zahirabad, India 178 M6
Zahlé, Leb. 170 J7
Ẓahrān, Saudi Arabia 172 N9
Zaječar, Serb. & Mont. 152 G12
Zakamensk, Russ. 159 M15
Zakataly, Azerb. 169 C20
Zakho, Iraq 172 B9
Zakhodnyaya, river, Belarus 156 J6
Zákinthos, Gr. 154 J7
Zákinthos (Zante), island, Gr. 154 K7
Zakopane, Pol. 149 H15
Zákros, Gr. 155 Q16
Zalaegerszeg, Hung. 149 M13
Zalantun, China 181 C16
Zalău, Rom. 152 C12
Zalewo, Pol. 149 B15
Zalew Szczeciński see Stettiner Haff, Ger., Pol. 148 C11
Ẓalim, Saudi Arabia 172 K8
Zamakh, Yemen 172 P11
Zambeze see Zambezi, river, Angola, Mozambique 202 D9
Zambeze River Delta, Mozambique 203 G13
Zambezi see Zambeze, river, Zambia 202 F9
Zambezi, Zambia 202 E9
Zambezi, Source of the, Zambia 194 M8
Zambia, Af. 195 M21
Zamboanga, Philippines 189 F14
Zambrów, Pol. 149 C17
Zamindavar, region, Afghan. 177 Q3
Zamora, Ecua. 128 L3
Zamora, Sp. 144 D8
Zamość, Pol. 149 F18
Zanaga, Congo 201 M17
Zanda, China 180 K4
Zanderij, Suriname 129 E16
Zanesville, Ohio, U.S. 99 R14
Zangla, India 177 N14
Zanjān, Iran 172 C11
Zante see Zákinthos, island, Gr. 154 K7
Zanthus, W. Aust., Austral. 211 W5
Zanzibar, island, Tanzania 199 M15
Zanzibar, Tanzania 199 M15
Zaouatallaz, Alg. 196 E12
Zaoyang, China 182 K4
Zaozhuang, China 182 H7
Zapadna Morava, river, Serb. & Mont. 152 G10
Zapadnaya Dvina, Russ. 156 J7
Zapadno Sibirskaya Ravnina, Russ. 158 H11
Zapala, Arg. 133 P7
Zapata, Tex., U.S. 103 V8
Zapata, Peninsula de, Cuba 116 H7
Zapiga, Chile 132 C7
Zapiola Ridge, Atl. Oc. 237 U7
Zaporizhzhya, Ukr. 157 Q8
Zara see Zadar, Croatia 152 F5
Zara, Turk. 168 E12
Zarafshon, Uzb. 174 K11
Zarafshon Range, Taj. 176 H7
Zaragoza, Sp. 145 D14
Zarand, Iran 173 F15
Zaranj, Afghan. 177 Q2
Zarautz, Sp. 144 B12
Zaraysk, Russ. 156 K10
Zaraza, Venez. 128 C10
Zard Kūh, Iran 172 E12
Zaria, Nigeria 201 F14
Zárkos, Gr. 154 F10
Zărneşti, Rom. 153 E14
Zaruma, Ecua. 128 L2
Żary, Pol. 148 E11
Zaskar Mountains, India 177 N15
Zatish'ye, Russ. 159 D20
Zatobyl, Kaz. 174 B11
Zatoka, Ukr. 157 S5
Zavolzhsk, Russ. 156 H11
Zawiercie, Pol. 149 G15
Zāwiyat Masūs, Lib. 197 C15
Zawr, Ra's az, Saudi Arabia 172 H12
Zayaki Jangal, Pak. 177 T5
Zaysan, Kaz. 175 E19
Zaysan Köli, Kaz. 175 E19
Zayü, China 180 M9
Zdolbuniv, Ukr. 157 N3
Zealand, island, Den. 138 E6
Zebbuġ, Malta 161 H20
Zebbuġ, Malta 161 K22
Zeča, island, Croatia 152 E4
Zednes, peak, Mauritania 196 E6
Zeeland, Mich., U.S. 98 M9
Zefat, Israel 170 K6
Zeil, Mount, Austral. 210 F8
Zeist, Neth. 146 J13
Zejtun, Malta 161 L23
Zelee, Cape, Solomon Is. 217 P20
Zelenchukskaya, Russ. 157 T12
Zelenodol'sk, Russ. 156 J14
Zelenoe, Kaz. 174 E6
Zelenogorsk, Russ. 156 E6
Zelenogradsk, Russ. 156 J1
Zelenokumsk, Russ. 157 T13
Železná Ruda, Czech Rep. 148 J10
Železnik, Serb. & Mont. 152 F10
Zelzate, Belg. 146 K11
Zemetchino, Russ. 156 L12
Zemio, Cen. Af. Rep. 198 H11
Zemongo, Cen. Af. Rep. 198 G10
Zencirli, site, Turk. 168 H11
Zenica, Bosn. & Herzg. 152 F7
Zeni Su, island, Japan 185 R11
Zenobia, ruin, Syr. 170 E13
Žepče, Bosn. & Herzg. 152 F8
Zereh Depression, Afghan. 177 R2
Zerf, Ger. 160 K12
Zermatt, Switz. 150 C3
Zernez, Switz. 150 B5
Zernograd, Russ. 157 R11
Zestap'oni, Rep. of Georgia 169 B17
Zetland see Shetland Islands, islands, Scot., U.K. 142 C12
Zeya, Russ. 159 K19
Zgharta, Leb. 170 H7
Zgierz, Pol. 149 E15
Zgorzelec, Pol. 148 F11
Zhalpaqtal, Kaz. 174 D5
Zhaltyr, Kaz. 175 D13
Zhanatal, Kaz. 174 G10
Zhangaly, Kaz. 174 F5
Zhangaözen, Kaz. 174 H6
Zhanga Qazan, Kaz. 174 E5
Zhangaqorghan, Kaz. 174 H12
Zhangatas, Kaz. 175 H13
Zhangbei, China 182 C6
Zhangguangcai Ling, China 181 D18
Zhangjiakou, China 182 C6
Zhangping, China 183 Q7
Zhangpu, China 183 R7
Zhangwu, China 182 B10
Zhangye, China 180 G11
Zhangzhou, China 183 Q7
Zhangzi, China 182 G4
Zhanhua, China 182 E8
Zhanjiang, China 183 T2
Zhanyi, China 180 N11
Zhao'an, China 183 R7
Zhaoqing, China 183 R3
Zhaosu, China 180 E6
Zhaotong, China 180 M11
Zhaoxian, China 182 E6
Zhapo, China 183 S3
Zhaqsy, Kaz. 174 C12
Zharkamys, Kaz. 174 F8
Zharkent, Kaz. 175 H18
Zharma, Kaz. 175 E17
Zharmysh, Kaz. 174 H6

Zhashui, *China* **182** H2
Zhaslyk, *Uzb.* **174** H8
Zhayrang, *Kaz.* **175** F13
Zhayylma, *Kaz.* **174** D10
Zhayyq (Ural), river, *Kaz.* **174** E6
Zhdanov, *Azerb.* **169** E21
Zhecheng, *China* **182** H6
Zhelezīnka, *Kaz.* **175** B15
Zheleznodorozhnyy, *Russ.* **158** F9
Zheleznogorsk, *Russ.* **156** M8
Zheleznovodsk, *Russ.* **157** T13
Zhem, river, *Kaz.* **174** F8
Zhenba, *China* **182** J1
Zhenghe, *China* **183** N8
Zhenglan Qi (Xulun Hoh), *China* **182** B7
Zhengxiangbai Qi, *China* **182** B6
Zhengzhou, *China* **182** H5
Zhenjiang, *China* **182** K8
Zhenlai, *China* **181** D16
Zhenping, *China* **182** J2
Zhenyuan, *China* **182** G1
Zhenyuan, *China* **183** N1
Zhenyuan, *China* **180** P10
Zherdevka, *Russ.* **156** M11
Zhetiqara, *Kaz.* **174** C10
Zhexi Shuiki, *China* **183** N3
Zhezqazghan, *Kaz.* **174** F12
Zhicheng, *China* **182** L3
Zhidan, *China* **182** F2
Zhigansk, *Russ.* **159** G17
Zhigulevsk, *Russ.* **156** K15
Zhijiang, *China* **183** N2
Zhilaya Kosa, *Kaz.* **174** F6
Zhil'gur, *Russ.* **159** H18
Zhilinda, *Russ.* **159** F15
Zhlobin, *Belarus* **156** L6
Zhmerynka, *Ukr.* **157** P4
Zhob, river, *Pak.* **177** Q8
Zhob, *Pak.* **177** Q8
Zhokhova, Ostrov, *Russ.* **159** C17
Zhongba, *China* **180** L5
Zhongdian *see* Shangri-La, *China* **180** M10
Zhongning, *China* **180** H12
Zhongshan, station, *Antarctica* **227** G20
Zhongshan, *China* **183** Q3
Zhongwei, *China* **180** H12
Zhongxian, *China* **182** L1
Zhongxiang, *China* **182** K4
Zhosaly, *Kaz.* **174** G11
Zhoukou, *China* **182** J5
Zhoushan, *China* **182** L10
Zhoushan Dao, *China* **182** L10
Zhoushan Qundao, islands, *China* **182** L10
Zhovtneve, *Ukr.* **157** R6
Zhu (Pearl River), river, *China* **183** S4
Zhuanghe, *China* **182** D10
Zhucheng, *China* **182** G8
Zhuji, *China* **182** L9
Zhukovka, *Russ.* **156** L7
Zhuolu, *China* **182** C6
Zhuozhou, *China* **182** D6
Zhuozi, *China* **182** C4
Zhuozi Shan, *China* **182** C1
Zhupanovo, *Russ.* **159** F23
Zhuryn, *Kaz.* **174** E8
Zhushan, *China* **182** J2
Zhuzhou, *China* **183** N4
Zhympity, *Kaz.* **174** D6
Zhytomyr, *Ukr.* **157** N5
Zi, river, *China* **182** M3
Ziarat, *Pak.* **177** R6
Zibak, *Afghan.* **176** K9
Zibo, *China* **182** F8
Zicavo, *Fr.* **150** K4
Zichang, *China* **182** F2
Zielona Góra, *Pol.* **148** E12
Zigana Geçidi, pass, *Turk.* **169** D14
Zigar, *Taj.* **176** J8
Zigey, *Chad* **197** H14
Zigong, *China* **180** L12
Zigui, *China* **182** K3
Ziguinchor, *Senegal* **196** H4
Zile, *Turk.* **168** E11
Žilina, *Slovakia* **149** J14
Zillah, *Lib.* **197** D15
Zima, *Russ.* **159** L15
Zimbabwe, *Af.* **195** N21
Zimnicea, *Bulg.* **153** G15
Zimnicea, *Rom.* **153** G15
Zimovniki, *Russ.* **157** R12
Zinder, *Niger* **196** H12
Zinguinasso, *Côte d'Ivoire* **200** F8
Zinjibār, *Yemen* **172** R10
Zion, *Ill., U.S.* **98** M7
Zion, *St. Kitts & Nevis* **121** C18
Zion National Park, *Utah, U.S.* **107** P6
Žirje, island, *Croatia* **152** G5
Zirndorf, *Ger.* **148** H8
Zittau, *Ger.* **148** G11
Živinice, *Bosn. & Herzg.* **152** F8
Ziway Hāyk', *Eth.* **199** G15
Zixi, *China* **183** N7
Zixing, *China* **183** P4
Ziyang, *China* **182** J1
Ziyuan, *China* **183** P2
Zizhou, *China* **182** E3
Zlarin, island, *Croatia* **152** G5
Zlatoust, *Russ.* **158** J8
Zlatoustovsk, *Russ.* **159** J20
Zlín, *Czech Rep.* **149** J14
Złotów, *Pol.* **149** C13
Zmari Sar, peak, *Afghan.* **177** Q5
Zmeica, Lacul, *Rom.* **153** F18
Zmeinogorsk, *Russ.* **158** L11
Zmiyev, *Ukr.* **157** P9
Zmiyinyy, Ostriv, *Ukr.* **157** S5
Znamenka, *Kaz.* **175** D17
Znamensk, *Russ.* **156** J2
Znam'yanka, *Ukr.* **157** Q7
Znojmo, *Czech Rep.* **148** J12
Zoetermeer, *Neth.* **146** J12
Ẕofar, *Israel* **171** Q5
Zofingen, *Switz.* **150** A3
Zogang, *China* **180** L9
Zolochiv, *Ukr.* **157** N3
Zolochiv, *Ukr.* **157** N8
Zolotaya Gora, *Russ.* **159** K18
Zolotonosha, *Ukr.* **157** P6
Zomba, *Malawi* **203** E13
Zongo, *Dem. Rep. of the Congo* **198** H8
Zonguldak, *Turk.* **168** C7
Zonza, *Fr.* **150** K4
Zor Dağ, *Turk.* **169** E18
Zorkol Lake, *Afghan., Taj.* **176** J11
Zorritos, *Peru* **130** E2
Zouar, *Chad* **197** F14
Zoushi, *China* **182** M3
Zouxian, *China* **182** G7
Zrenjanin (Petrovgrad), *Serb. & Mont.* **152** E10
Zubayr, Jazā'ir az, *Yemen* **172** Q8
Zubovo, *Russ.* **156** F9
Zubtsov, *Russ.* **156** J8
Zuera, *Sp.* **145** D14
Ẓufār, region, *Oman* **173** N14
Zug, *Switz.* **150** B4
Zugdidi, *Rep. of Georgia* **169** B16
Zugspitze, peak, *Aust., Ger.* **148** L8
Zululand, region, *S. Af.* **202** K12
Žumberačka Gora, *Croatia, Slov.* **152** D5
Zumberge Coast, *Antarctica* **226** G7
Zumbo, *Mozambique* **202** E11
Zunhua, *China* **182** D8
Zuni, river, *Ariz., U.S.* **107** S9
Zuni Pueblo, *N. Mex., U.S.* **107** S10
Zunyi, *China* **180** M12
Zuoz, *Switz.* **150** C5
Zürich, *Switz.* **150** A4
Zur Kowt, *Afghan.* **177** N8
Zurrieq, *Malta* **161** L22
Zuru, *Nigeria* **201** E13
Žut, island, *Croatia* **152** G5
Zutphen, *Neth.* **146** J14
Zuwārah, *Lib.* **197** B13
Zvenyhorodka, *Ukr.* **157** P6
Zvishavane, *Zimb.* **202** G11
Zvolen, *Slovakia* **149** J15
Zvornik, *Bosn. & Herzg.* **152** F9
Zwettl, *Aust.* **148** K11
Zwickau, *Ger.* **148** G9
Zwolle, *La., U.S.* **100** M6
Zwolle, *Neth.* **146** H13
Zygi, *Cyprus* **160** Q8
Zyrya, *Azerb.* **169** D23
Zyryanka, *Russ.* **159** E19
Zyryanovo, *Russ.* **159** H13
Zyryanovsk, *Kaz.* **175** D19

Moon Index

LUNAR EQUIVALENTS
Lacus .... lake
Mare .... sea
Montes .... range
Oceanus .... ocean
Palus .... marsh
Rupes .... scarp
Sinus .... bay
Vallis .... valley
All other entries are craters.

A
Abel, 249 M18
Abulfeda, 249 K14
Aestuum, Sinus, 248 G12
Agrippa, 249 H13
Aitken, 250 K12
Albategnius, 249 K13
Al-Biruni, 250 F6
Alden, 250 L7
Aliacensis, 249 L13
Almanon, 249 K14
Alpes, Montes, 248 D12
Alpes, Vallis, 249 D13
Alphonsus, 248 K12
Altai, Rupes, 249 K14
Amundsen, 249 R13
Anaxagoras, 248 B12
Anaximenes, 248 B11
Anders, 251 M15
Anderson, 250 G12
Anguis, Mare, 249 F18
Ansgarius, 249 K19
Antoniadi, 251 P13
Apenninus, Montes, 248 G12
Apianus, 249 L13
Apollo, 251 M14
Appleton, 250 E11
Archimedes, 248 F12
Aristarchus, 248 F9
Aristillus, 249 E13
Aristoteles, 249 D14
Arnold, 249 C14
Artamonov, 250 F7
Arzachel, 248 K12
Atlas, 249 D15
Australe, Mare, 250 N7
Avicenna, 251 D18
Avogadro, 250 C12
Azophi, 249 K14

B
Baade, Vallis, 248 N8
Babbage, 248 C10
Babcock, 250 H6
Baillaud, 249 B14
Bailly, 248 Q10
Balboa, 248 F6
Balmer, 249 L18
Banachiewicz, 249 H19
Barocius, 249 M14
Barringer, 251 L15
Barrow, 249 C13
Bel'kovich, 249 B16
Bell, 251 F19
Bellingshausen, 251 P13
Belyaev, 250 F10
Berosus, 249 E17
Bettinus, 248 P11
Billy, 248 K8
Birkhoff, 251 C14
Blancanus, 248 P12
Blanchard, 251 P16
Boguslawsky, 249 Q14
Boltzmann, 251 P16
Bond, W., 249 C13
Borman, 251 M15
Bose, 251 N13
Boussingault, 249 Q14
Bragg, 251 D17
Brianchon, 251 B14
Bridgman, 250 D10
Brouwer, 251 M16
Buffon, 251 M16
Bullialdus, 248 K11
Büsching, 249 M14
Byrd, 249 B13
Byrgius, 248 L8

C
Cabannes, 251 P13
Cabeus, 248 Q12
Campbell, 250 D11
Cannizzaro, 251 C16
Cantor, 250 E8
Capuanus, 248 M11
Carnot, 251 D14
Carpatus, Montes, 248 G10
Carpenter, 248 B11
Casatus, 248 Q12
Cassini, 249 E13
Catharina, 249 K15
Caucasus, Montes, 249 E13
Chaffee, 251 M14
Chamberlin, 250 Q9
Chandler, 250 E12
Chaplygin, 250 J10
Chapman, 251 C17
Chappell, 251 D13
Charlier, 251 E16
Chebyshev, 251 M16
Chrétien, 250 N11
Clairaut, 249 N13
Clavius, 248 N12
Cleomedes, 249 F17
Cockcroft, 251 F14
Cognitum, Mare, 248 J10
Colombo, 249 K16
Compton, 250 C9
Comstock, 251 F17
Condorcet, 249 G18
Copernicus, 248 H11
Cordillera, Montes, 248 L7
Coriolis, 250 H12
Coulomb, 251 C16
Crisium, Mare, 249 G17
Crüger, 248 K7
Curie, 250 L6
Curtius, 249 P13
Cyrano, 250 K11
Cyrillus, 249 K15

D
Daedalus, 250 J12
D'Alembert, 250 D12
Dante, 251 F13
Darwin, 248 L7
Davisson, 251 M13
Debye, 251 D13
Delambre, 249 J14
DeLaRue, 249 C15
Dellinger, 250 J9
Demonax, 249 Q14
Desargues, 248 B10
De Sitter, 249 B13
Deslandres, 248 L12
Dobrovol'skij, 250 K8
Doppelmayer, 248 L9
Doppler, 251 K14
Drygalski, 248 Q11

E
Eddington, 248 F7
Einstein, 248 F6
Elvey, 251 G19
Emden, 251 C13
Endymion, 249 D15
Englehardt, 251 H14
Eötvös, 250 M9
Epidemiarum, Palus, 248 L10
Eratosthenes, 248 G12
Erro, 250 H6
Esnault-Pelterie, 251 D15
Euctemon, 249 B13
Eudoxus, 249 E14
Euler, 248 F10
Evershed, 251 E14

F
Fabricius, 249 M15
Fabry, 250 D8
Fecunditatis, Mare, 249 J17
Fermi, 250 L8
Fersman, 251 G17
Firmicus, 249 H18
Fitzgerald, 251 F13
Fizeau, 251 P15
Flammarion, 248 J12
Fleming, 250 G7
Fontenelle, 248 C12
Fowler, 251 E15
Fracastorius, 249 K15
Fra Mauro, 248 J10
Franklin, 249 E16
Freundlich, 250 F12
Frigoris, Mare, 249 D13
Furnerius, 249 M17

G
Gadomski, 251 E15
Gagarin, 250 K10
Galois, 251 K15
Gamow, 250 C11
Gärtner, 249 C14
Gassendi, 248 K9
Gauricus, 248 L12
Gauss, 249 D17
Geminus, 249 E16
Gemma Frisius, 249 L14
Gerard, 248 D8
Gerasimovich, 251 L17
Gibbs, 249 L19
Gilbert, 249 J18
Goddard, 249 G19
Goldschmidt, 249 B13
Green, 250 H8
Grimaldi, 248 J7
Grissom, 251 N15
Gruemberger, 248 P12
Gutenberg, 249 J16
Guyot, 250 G7

H
Haemus, Montes, 249 G13
Hagecius, 249 P15
Hahn, 249 E18
Hansteen, 248 K8
Hartmann, 250 H9
Hase, 249 M17
Hausen, 248 Q9
Hayn, 249 B15
Heaviside, 250 J12
Hecataeus, 249 L18
Helberg, 251 F18
Helmholtz, 249 Q15
Henyey, 251 G15
Hercules, 249 D15
Hermite, 248 A12
Herodotus, 248 F9
Herschel, J., 248 C11
Hertz, 250 G7
Hertzsprung, 251 H17
Hess, 250 N12
Hevelius, 248 H7
Heymans, 251 B14
Hilbert, 250 K7
Hipparchus, 249 J13
Hirayama, 250 J6
Houzeau, 251 K17
Hubble, 249 F19
Humboldt, 249 L18
Humboldtianum, Mare, 249 C16
Humorum, Mare, 248 L9

I
Icarus, 251 J13
Imbrium, Mare, 248 E11
Ingenii, Mare, 250 M11
Inghirami, 248 N9
Ioffe, 251 K17
Iridum, Sinus, 248 D10

J
Jackson, 251 F14
Jansky, 249 G19
Janssen, 249 N15
Jarvis, 251 M15
Joliot, 250 E6
Joule, 251 F15
Jules Verne, 250 M10
Julius Caesar, 249 H14
Jura, Montes, 248 D10

K
Kane, 249 C14
Karpinskiy, 250 B12
Kästner, 249 J19
Keeler, 250 J11
Kekulé, 251 G16
Kepler, 248 H9
Kibal'chich, 251 H15
King, 250 H8
Kircher, 248 P11
Klaproth, 248 P11
Kohlschütter, 250 G10
Kolhörster, 251 G18
Komarov, 250 F10
Kondratyuk, 250 K7
Konstantinov, 250 G11
Korolev, 251 J14
Kostinskiy, 250 G8
Kovalevskaya, 251 E16
Krafft, 248 G7
Krasovskiy, 251 H13
Kugler, 250 P9
Kurchatov, 250 E10

L
La Caille, 249 L13
Lagrange, 248 M8
Lamarck, 248 L7
Lamb, 250 N8
Lamé, 249 K18
Landau, 251 D16
Langemak, 250 J8
Langrenus, 249 J18
La Pérouse, 249 K18
Larmor, 251 F13
Lavoisier, 248 D7
Lebedev, 250 N8
Lebedinskiy, 251 H14
Leeuwenhoek, 251 L13
Legendre, 249 M18
Le Gentil, 248 Q11
Leibnitz, 250 M12
Lemaitre, 251 P14
Letronne, 248 J9
Leuschner, 251 H18
Levi-Civita, 250 L9
Licetus, 249 M13
Lilius, 249 N13
Lomonosov, 250 E7
Longomontanus, 248 N11
Lorentz, 251 E18
Lucretius, 251 J17
Lyman, 250 P12
Lyot, 249 P17

M
Mach, 251 G15
Macrobius, 249 F16
Maginus, 248 N12
Maksutov, 251 M13
Mandel'shtam, 250 H11
Manzinus, 249 P13
Marconi, 250 J10
Marginis, Mare, 249 G19
Marginis, Mare, 250 G6
Marius, 248 G8
Markov, 248 C9
Maunder, 251 K19
Maurolycus, 249 M14
Maxwell, 250 E7
McAuliffe, 251 L15
McLaughlin, 251 C17
McMath, 251 G14
McNair, 251 M15
Medii, Sinus, 248 H12
Mee, 248 N10
Meitner, 250 K7
Mendel, 251 N16
Mendeleev, 250 H9
Mercurius, 249 D16
Mersenius, 248 L9
Messala, 249 D17
Metius, 249 M15
Mezentsev, 251 B14
Michelson, 251 H17
Milankovič, 250 B12
Millikan, 250 D9
Milne, 250 M8
Minkowski, 251 N14
Minnaert, 250 P12
Mitra, 251 G14
Mohorovičić, 251 K14
Moretus, 248 P12
Mortis, Lacus, 249 D14
Moscoviense, Mare, 250 F10
Murakami, 251 L15
Mutus, 249 P14

N
Nansen, 250 B12
Nassau, 250 L12
Nectaris, Mare, 249 K15
Neper, 249 G19
Nernst, 251 D18
Neujmin, 250 L8
Newton, 248 Q12
Niepce, 251 B14
Nöther, 251 B15
Nubium, Mare, 248 K11
Numerov, 251 P13

O
Oken, 249 N17
Olbers, 248 H7
Olcott, 250 F8
Omar Khayyam, 251 C16
Onizuka, 251 M14
Oppenheimer, 251 M13
Oresme, 250 M12
Orientale, Mare, 251 L19
Orontius, 248 M12
Ostwald, 250 G8

P
Pallas, 248 H12
Palmieri, 248 L9
Papaleksi, 250 H11
Paracelsus, 250 L11
Parenago, 251 F17
Pascal, 248 B11
Paschen, 251 K16
Pasteur, 250 K7
Patsaev, 250 K9
Pauli, 250 N10

Pavlov, **250** L10
Perepelkin, **250** J8
Petavius, **249** L17
Petermann, **249** B14
Petropavlovskiy, **251** E17
Petzval, **251** P15
Phillips, **249** L18
Philolaus, **248** B12
Phocylides, **248** P9
Piccolomini, **249** L15
Pilâtre, **248** Q9
Pingré, **248** P9
Pitatus, **248** L11
Pitiscus, **249** N14
Pizzetti, **250** M8
Planck, **250** P10
Planck, Vallis, **250** P10
Plaskett, **251** B13
Plato, **248** D12
Playfair, **249** L13
Plinius, **249** G14
Plutarch, **249** F18
Poincaré, **250** N11
Poinsot, **251** B13
Polzunov, **250** F8
Poncelet, **248** B11
Pontécoulant, **249** P16
Posidonius, **249** F15
Poynting, **251** G16
Prandtl, **250** P11
Procellarum, Oceanus, **248** E8
Proclus, **249** G16
Ptolemaeus, **248** J12
Purbach, **248** L12
Putredinis, Palus, **249** F13
Pyrenaeus, Montes, **249** K16
Pythagoras, **248** B10

R

Racah, **250** K12
Raimond, **251** G14
Rayleigh, **249** E18
Razumov, **251** E17
Reinhold, **248** H11
Resnik, **251** M15
Rheita, **249** M16
Rheita, Vallis, **249** M16
Riccioli, **248** J6
Riemann, **249** D18
Riphaeus, Montes, **248** J10
Robertson, **251** F18
Roche, **250** M10
Röntgen, **251** E18
Rook, Montes, **248** L6
Roris, Sinus, **248** D9
Rosenberger, **249** P15
Rowland, **251** D13
Rozhdestvenskiy, **251** B13
Rumford, **251** L14
Russell, **248** E7

S

Sacrobosco, **249** L14
Saha, **250** J6
Scaliger, **250** L7
Scheiner, **248** P11
Schickard, **248** N9
Schiller, **248** N10
Schlesinger, **251** D15
Schliemann, **250** J10
Schlüter, **248** J6
Schneller, **251** E14
Schomberger, **249** Q13
Schrödinger, **250** Q11
Schrödinger, Vallis, **250** Q10
Schuster, **250** H10
Schwarzchild, **250** B11
Scobee, **251** L15
Scott, **249** Q13
Seares, **250** B12
Sechenov, **251** J16
Segner, **248** P10
Serenitatis, Mare, **249** F14
Seyfert, **250** F8
Sharonov, **250** G12
Shayn, **250** F12
Short, **248** Q12
Sierpinski, **250** L11
Sirsalis, **248** K8
Sklodowska, **250** L6
Smith, **251** L15
Smoluchowski, **251** B16
Smythii, Mare, **249** H19
Snellius, **249** L17
Sommerfeld, **251** C13
Somni, Palus, **249** G16
Somniorum, Lacus, **249** E15
Spencer Jones, **250** G11
Spitzbergensis, Montes, **248** E12
Spumans, Mare, **249** H18
Stebbins, **251** C14
Stefan, **251** D16
Sternberg, **251** G17
Sternfeld, **251** L15
Stevinus, **249** M16
Stiborius, **249** M15
Stöfler, **249** M13
Störmer, **250** C11
Strabo, **249** C15
Struve, **248** F7
Subbotin, **250** L9
Szilard, **250** E7

T

Taurus, Montes, **249** F16
Teneriffe, Montes, **248** D12
Theaetetus, **249** E13
Theophilus, **249** J15
Thomson, **250** L12
Tikhov, **250** C12
Timocharis, **248** F11
Tranquillitatis, Mare, **249** H15
Trumpler, **250** F12
Tsander, **251** H15
Tsiolkovskiy, **250** K9
Tycho, **248** M12

U

Undarum, Mare, **249** H18

V

Valier, **250** H12
Van de Graaff, **250** L12
Van der Waals, **250** N9
Van Rhijn, **250** D10
Van't Hoff, **251** C15
Vaporum, Mare, **249** G13
Vasco da Gama, **248** G6
Vavilov, **251** J16
Vendelinus, **249** K17
Vening Meinesz, **250** H11
Vernadskiy, **250** F9
Vesalius, **250** J7
Vestine, **250** E7
Vieta, **248** L8
Vlacq, **249** N15
Volkov, **250** K8
Volta, **248** C9
Von der Pahlen, **251** L16
Von Kármán, **250** M12
Von Neumann, **250** E11
Von Zeipel, **251** E15

W

Walther, **249** L13
Wargentin, **248** N9
Waterman, **250** L9
Wegener, **251** D17
Wells, **250** D9
Werner, **249** L13
Weyl, **251** G17
White, **251** N14
Wiechert, **250** Q12
Wiener, **250** E10
Wilhelm, **248** M11
Wilsing, **251** K15
Wilson, **248** Q11
Wrottesley, **249** L17
Wyld, **250** J6

Y

Yablochkov, **250** C10
Yamamoto, **250** C12

Z

Zach, **249** P13
Zagut, **249** L14
Zeeman, **251** Q14
Zhukovskiy, **251** H14
Zsigmondy, **251** C16
Zucchius, **248** P10

SPACECRAFT LANDING OR IMPACT SITES

Apollo 11 (Tranquillity Base) **249** H15
Apollo 12 **248** J11
Apollo 14 **248** J11
Apollo 15 **249** F13
Apollo 16 **249** J14
Apollo 17 **249** G15
Luna 2 **249** F13
Luna 5 **248** J10
Luna 7 **248** H9
Luna 8 **248** H7
Luna 9 **248** H7
Luna 13 **248** F8
Luna 15 **249** G17
Luna 16 **249** J17
Luna 17 **248** E10
Luna 18 **249** H17
Luna 20 **249** H17
Luna 21 **249** F15
Luna 23 **249** G17
Luna 24 **249** G18
Orbiter 1 **250** H11
Orbiter 2 **250** H6
Orbiter 3 **251** G19
Orbiter 5 **248** J6
Ranger 4 **251** K17
Ranger 6 **249** G14
Ranger 7 **248** J11
Ranger 8 **249** H15
Ranger 9 **248** K12
Surveyor 1 **248** J9
Surveyor 2 **248** H12
Surveyor 3 **248** J11
Surveyor 4 **248** H12
Surveyor 5 **249** H14
Surveyor 6 **248** H12
Surveyor 7 **248** M12

Printed in Verona, Italy

Acknowledgments

WORLD THEMATIC SECTION

Introduction pp. 14–15

CONSULTANTS

John Morrison
World Wildlife Fund (WWF)

GRAPHICS

ECOREGIONS: Terrestrial Ecoregions of the World were developed by D.M. Olson, E. Dinerstein, E.D. Wikramanayake, N.D. Burgess, G.V.N. Powell, E.C. Underwood, J.A. D'Amico, I. Itoua, H.E. Strand, J.C. Morrison, C.J. Loucks, T.F. Allnutt, T.H. Ricketts, Y. Kura, J.F. Lamoreux, W.W. Wettengel, P. Hedao, K.R. Kassem, World Wildlife Fund. Marine Ecoregions of the World (MEOW) were developed by the MEOW Working Group, co-chaired by The Nature Conservancy and the World Wildlife Fund (Mark Spalding, Helen Fox, Gerald Allen, Nick Davidson, Zach Ferdana, Max Finlayson, Ben Halpern, Miguel Jorge, Al Lombana, Sara Lourie, Kirsten Martin, Edmund McManus, Jennifer Molnar, Kate Newman, Cheri Recchia, James Robertson).

Structure of the Earth pp. 22–23

CONSULTANTS

Laurel M. Bybell
U.S. Geological Survey (USGS)

Robert I. Tilling
U.S. Geological Survey (USGS)

GRAPHICS

CONTINENTS ADRIFT IN TIME: Christopher R. Scotese/PALEOMAP Project
CUTAWAY OF THE EARTH: Tibor G. Tóth
TECTONIC BLOCK DIAGRAMS: Susan Sanford
PLATE TECTONICS: *National Geographic Atlas of the World,* 8th ed., Washington, D.C.: The National Geographic Society, 2005
GEOLOGIC TIME: National Geographic Books

Earth's Rocky Exterior pp. 24–25

CONSULTANTS

Jon Spencer
Arizona Geological Survey

Robert I. Tilling
U.S. Geological Survey (USGS)

GRAPHICS

ROCK CYCLE AND READING EARTH HISTORY: ChrisOrr.com and XNR Productions
GLOBAL DISTRIBUTION OF ROCK TYPES: Global distribution of surface rock from *The National Geographic Desk Reference.* Washington, D.C.: The National Geographic Society, 1999. Age of oceanic crust from Simkin et al., *This Dynamic Planet: World Map of Volcanoes, Earthquakes, Impact Craters, and Plate Tectonics,* 3rd ed. USGS, 2006

PHOTOGRAPHS

PAGE 24, (UP) R.D. Griggs, USGS; **(CT)** Sharon Johnson; **(LO)** David Muench
PAGE 25, Raymond Gehman/NGS Image Collection

Landforms pp. 26–29

CONSULTANTS

Sharon Johnson
University of California, Berkeley

Mike Slattery
Texas Christian University

GRAPHICS

FICTIONAL LANDFORMS: *National Geographic World Atlas for Young Explorers.* Washington, D.C.: The National Geographic Society, 2003
DUNES: ChrisOrr.com
RIVERS: Steven Fick/Canadian Geographic
GLACIAL LANDFORMS: Steven Fick

SATELLITE IMAGES

MISSISSIPPI RIVER DELTA: Centre National d'Etudes Spatiales (CNES)

PHOTOGRAPHS

PAGE 26, (LE) Joel Sartore/www.joelsartore.com; **(CT)** Science Photo Library/CORBIS; **(UP RT)** George F. Mobley; **(LO RT)** James D. Balog
PAGE 27, (UP LE) Wolfgang Kaehler/CORBIS; **(UP CT)** Lyle Rosbotham; **(UP RT)** Adriel Heisey; **(LO LE)** Marc Moritsch/NGS Image Collection; **(LO CT)** Peter Essick; **(LO RT)** Sam Abell, NGS
PAGE 28, (LE) Peter Essick; **(CT)** Douglas R. Grant; **(RT)** Tom and Pat Leeson
PAGE 29, (UP CT) Rob Brander; **(UP RT)** George Veni and James Jasek; **(LO LE)** Sharon Johnson; **(LO RT)** Douglas R. Grant/Parks Canada

Surface of the Earth pp. 30–31

CONSULTANTS

Peter W. Sloss
NOAA National Geophysical Data Center (NGDC)

SATELLITE IMAGES

EARTH SURFACE ELEVATIONS AND DEPTHS, A SLICE OF EARTH, AND HYPSOMETRY: Peter Sloss, NOAA National Geophysical Data Center
SNOW DEPTH AND SEA ICE: Data provided by NASA/GSFC, Don Cavalieri, Dorothy Hall, and Gene Carl Feldman
CLOUD COVER: Data provided by NASA/GISS, William B. Rossow, and Gene Carl Feldman
DAY AND NIGHT TEMPERATURE DIFFERENCE: Data provided by NASA/GSFC, Joel Susskind and Gene Carl Feldman
VEGETATION COVER : Data provided by NASA/GSFC, Compton J. Tucker, and Gene Carl Feldman

Land Cover pp. 32–33

CONSULTANTS

Paul Davis
The Global Land Cover Facility, University of Maryland

SATELLITE IMAGES

GLOBAL LAND COVER COMPOSITION: M. Hansen, R. DeFries, J.R.G. Townshend, and R. Sohlberg. 1998. "Global land cover classification at 1km spatial resolution using a classification tree approach." 1 Km Land Cover Classification Derived from AVHRR; College Park, Maryland: The Global Land Cover Facility. (Note: Data were derived from NOAA AVHRR and NASA Landsat imagery.)

PHOTOGRAPHS

PAGE 32, (UP LE) Tom and Pat Leeson/Photo Researchers; **(UP RT)** Michael Nichols/NGS Image Collection; **(LO LE)** Stephen J. Krasemann/Photo Researchers; **(LO CT LE)** Rod Planck/Photo Researchers; **(CT LE)** Jim Steinberg/Photo Researchers; **(CT RT)** Matthew C. Hansen, University of Maryland; **(LO CT RT)** Gregory G. Dimijian/Photo Researchers; **(LO RT)** Sharon Johnson
PAGE 33, (LE) Georg Gerster/Photo Researchers; **(LO CT LE)** Rod Planck/Photo Researchers; **(LE CT)** Jim Richardson; **(RT CT)** George Steinmetz; **(LO CT RT)** Steve McCurry; **(RT)** B. and C. Alexander/Photo Researchers

Climate pp. 34–37

CONSULTANTS

William Burroughs

H. Michael Mogil
Certified Consulting Meteorologist (CCM)

Vladimir Ryabinin
World Climate Research Programme

GRAPHICS

TOPOGRAPHY: ChrisOrr.com and XNR Productions
GLOBAL AIR TEMPERATURE CHANGES, 1850–2000: Reproduced by kind permission of the Climatic Research Unit.

SATELLITE IMAGES

Images originally created for the GLOBE program by NOAA's National Geophysical Data Center, Boulder, Colorado, U.S.A.
CLOUD COVER: International Satellite Cloud Climatology Project (ISCCP); National Aeronautics and Space Administration (NASA); Goddard Institute for Space Studies (GISS)
PRECIPITATION: Global Precipitation Climatology Project (GPCP); International Satellite Land Surface Climatology Project (ISLSCP)
SOLAR ENERGY: Earth Radiation Budget Experiment (ERBE); Greenhouse Effect Detection Experiment (GEDEX)
TEMPERATURE: National Center for Environmental Prediction (NCEP); National Center for Atmospheric Research (NCAR); National Weather Service (NWS)

PHOTOGRAPHS

PAGE 35, Sharon G. Johnson.

Weather pp. 38–39

CONSULTANTS

Gerry Bell
National Oceanic and Atmospheric Administration (NOAA)

H. Michael Mogil
Certified Consulting Meteorologist (CCM)

GRAPHICS

WATER CYCLE, AIR MASSES, JET STREAM, WEATHER FRONTS, CLOUD TYPES: ChrisOrr.com

SATELLITE IMAGES

HURRICANE IMAGE: NASA Goddard Space Flight Center (GSFC), data from NOAA
EL NIÑO IMAGE SEQUENCE: Courtesy Robert M. Carey, NOAA
LIGHTNING IMAGE: NASA Marshall Space Flight Center Lightning Imaging Sensor (LIS) Instrument Team, Huntsville, Alabama

Biosphere pp. 40–41

CONSULTANTS

Manuel Colunga-Garcia (Entomology), **Patrick J. Webber** (Plant Biology), **David T. Long** (Geological Sciences), **Stuart H. Gage** (Entomology), **Craig K. Harris** (Sociology)
Earth System Science Education Program, Michigan State University

Jane Robertson Vernhes
World Network of Biosphere Reserves, UNESCO

GRAPHICS

BIOSPHERE DYNAMICS: Earth Science System Education Program, Michigan State University, and ChrisOrr.com
EARTH SYSTEM DYNAMICS: Edward Gazsi
SIZE OF THE BIOSPHERE: The COMET Program and ChrisOrr.com
BIOSPHERE OVER TIME: Earth Science System Education Program, Michigan State University

SATELLITE IMAGES

BIOSPHERE FROM SPACE: SeaWiFS, NASA/Goddard Space Flight Center, Gene Carl Feldman and ORBIMAGE

Biodiversity pp. 42–43

CONSULTANTS

Craig Hilton-Taylor
International Union for Conservation of Nature and Natural Resources (IUCN)

Mike Hoffmann
Conservation International

John Morrison
World Wildlife Fund (WWF)

GENERAL REFERENCES

Conservation International: www.biodiversityhotspots.org

International Union for Conservation of Nature and Natural Resources (IUCN): www.iucnredlist.org

GRAPHICS

THE NATURAL WORLD, SPECIES DIVERSITY, AND PROJECTED BIODIVERSITY: Biodiversity. NG Maps for National Geographic Magazine, February 1999

Population pp. 44–47

CONSULTANTS

Carl Haub
Population Reference Bureau

Gregory Yetman
Center for International Earth Science Information Network (CIESIN), Columbia University

GENERAL REFERENCES

Center for International Earth Science Information Network (CIESIN), Columbia University: www.ciesin.org

International Migration, 2002. Population Division of the Department of Economic and Social Affairs of the United Nations Secretariat. New York: United Nations, 2002

Population Reference Bureau: www.prb.org

United Nations World Population Prospects: The 2004 Revision Population Database: esa.un.org/unpp

World Urbanization Prospects: The 2003 Revision. Population Division of the Department of Economic and Social Affairs of the United Nations Secretariat. New York: United Nations, 2004

GRAPHICS

POPULATION DENSITY: Center for International Earth Science Information Network (CIESIN), Columbia University, and Centro Internacional de Agricultura Tropical (CIAT), 2005. Gridded Population of the World Version 3 (GPWv3): Population Density Grids—World Population Density, 2005 [map]. Palisades, New York: Socioeconomic Data and Applications Center (SEDAC), Columbia University. Available at http://sedac.ciesin.columbia.edu/gpw. Accessed April 2006

SATELLITE IMAGES

LIGHTS OF THE WORLD: Composite image: MODIS imagery; ETOPO-2 relief; NOAA/NGDC and DMSP lights at night data

Languages pp. 48–49

CONSULTANTS

Bernard Comrie
Max Planck Institute for Evolutionary Anthropology

GRAPHICS

VOICES OF THE WORLD, HOW MANY SPEAK WHAT?, VANISHING LANGUAGES, MAJOR LANGUAGE FAMILIES TODAY: *National Geographic Atlas of the World,* 8th ed., Washington, D.C.: The National Geographic Society, 2005
EVOLUTION OF LANGUAGES: *National Geographic Almanac of Geography,* Washington, D.C.: The National Geographic Society, 2005

Religions pp. 50–51

CONSULTANTS

William M. Bodiford
University of California—Los Angeles

Todd Johnson
Center for the Study of Global Christianity, Gordon-Conwell Theological Seminary

GENERAL REFERENCES

World Christian Database: Center for the Study of Global Christianity, Gordon-Conwell Theological Seminary
www.worldchristiandatabase.org

GRAPHICS

MAJOR RELIGIONS *National Geographic Atlas of the World,* 8th ed., Washington, D.C.: The National Geographic Society, 2005

PHOTOGRAPHS

PAGE 50, (LE) Jodi Cobb, National Geographic Photographer; **(RT)** James L. Stanfield
PAGES 50–51, Tony Heiderer
PAGE 51, (LE) Thomas J. Abercrombie; **(RT)** Annie Griffiths Belt

Health and Education
pp. 52–53

CONSULTANTS

Carlos Castillo-Salgado
Pan American Health Organization (PAHO)/
World Health Organization (WHO)

George Ingram and Annababette Wils
Education Policy and Data Center

Margaret Kruk
United Nations Millennium Project and
University of Michigan School of Public Health

Ruth Levine
Center for Global Development

GENERAL REFERENCES

2004 Report on the Global AIDS Epidemic. World Health Organization and the Joint United Nations Programme on HIV/AIDS, 2004

Education Policy and Data Center: www.epdc.org

Global Burden of Disease Estimates. Geneva: World Health Organization, 2004

Human Development Report, 2005. New York: United Nations Development Programme (UNDP), 2005

UN Millennium Development Goals: www.un.org/millenniumgoals

The State of the World's Children 2006. Table 5: Education. New York: UNICEF, 2006

The World Health Report 2005. Annex table 5. Selected national health accounts indicators. Geneva: World Health Organization, 2005

World Bank list of economies, 2005. Washington, D.C.: World Bank

World Health Organization: www.who.int

Youth (15–24) and Adult (15+) Literacy Rates by Country and by Gender for 2000–2004. New York: UNESCO Institute for Statistics, 2005

GRAPHICS

ACCESS TO IMPROVED SANITATION: Adapted from *WHO Water Supply and Sanitation Monitoring Mid-Term Report, 2004.*
DEVELOPING HUMAN CAPITAL: Adapted from Human Capital Projections developed by Education Policy and Data Center.

Conflict and Terror
pp. 54–55

CONSULTANTS

Barbara Harff
U.S. Naval Academy

Monty G. Marshall
Center for Systemic Peace and Center for Global Policy,
George Mason University

Christian Oxenboll
United Nations High Commissioner for Refugees (UNHCR)

GENERAL REFERENCES

Global Statistics. Internal Displacement Monitoring Centre (iDMC). 2006: www.internal-displacement.org

Marshall, Monty G., and Ted Robert Gurr. *Peace and Conflict.* Center for International Development & Conflict Management. University of Maryland, College Park, MD: 2005

Proliferation News and Resources. Carnegie Endowment for International Peace. 2005: www.carnegieendowment.org/npp

United Nations High Commissioner for Refugees (UNHCR): www.unhcr.org

United Nations Peacekeeping: www.un.org/Depts/dpko

Economy
pp. 56–57

CONSULTANTS

William Beyers
University of Washington

Michael Finger
World Trade Organization (WTO)

Richard R. Fix
World Bank

Susan Martin
Institute for the Study of International Migration

GENERAL REFERENCES

CIA World Factbook: www.cia.gov

International Monetary Fund: www.imf.org

International Telecommunication Union: www.itu.int

International Trade Statistics, 2005. Geneva, Switzerland: World Trade Organization

UNESCO Institute for Statistics: www.uis.unesco.org

World Development Indicators, 2005, Washington, D.C.: World Bank

Note: GDP and GDP (PPP) data on this spread are from the IMF.

GRAPHICS

LABOR MIGRATION: *National Geographic Atlas of the World,* 8th ed., Washington, D.C.: The National Geographic Society, 2005

Trade
pp. 58–59

CONSULTANTS

Peter Werner and Michael Finger
World Trade Organization (WTO)

United Nations Conference on Trade
and Development (UNCTAD)

GENERAL REFERENCES

International Trade Statistics, 2005, Geneva, Switzerland: World Trade Organization

United Nations Conference on Trade and Development: www.unctad.org

World Trade Organization: www.wto.org

GRAPHICS

GROWTH OF WORLD TRADE: World Trade Organization

Food
pp. 60–61

CONSULTANTS

Freddy Nachtergaele, Sachiko Tsuji, Vincent Ngendakumana, Edward Gillin, Guy Nantel, Giulia Cimino
Food and Agriculture Organization
of the United Nations (FAO)

Birgit Meade
Economic Research Service,
U.S. Department of Agriculture (USDA)

Shahla Shapouri
Economic Research Service, U.S. Department of Agriculture
(USDA) and Food and Agriculture Organization
of the United Nations (FAO)

GENERAL REFERENCES

Food and Agriculture Organization of the United Nations (FAO) Statistics Division (agricultural data): faostat.fao.org/faostat

GRAPHICS

WORLD GRAIN PRODUCTION: *National Geographic Almanac of Geography,* Washington, D.C.: The National Geographic Society, 2005

PHOTOGRAPHS

PAGE 61, (LE) Steven L. Raymer/NGS Image Collection; (CT) Richard Olsenius/NGS Image Collection; (RT) Jim Richardson

Energy
pp. 62–63

CONSULTANTS

Connie Brooks
Sandia National Laboratories

George Douglas, Dennis Elliott, Donna Heimiller, Gary Schmitz, Thomas Stoffel
National Renewable Energy Laboratory (NREL)

Michael Grillot
U.S. Energy Information Administration

Elena Nekhaev
World Energy Council

Simon Walker
Independent Editorial and Technical Services

GENERAL REFERENCES

American Wind Energy Association. *Global Wind Energy Market Report,* 2003

Bertani, Ruggero. World Geothermal Power Generation in the Period 2001–2005. *Geothermics,* Volume 34, Number 6, December 2005, p. 651–690

BP Statistical Review of World Energy 2005

Energy Information Administration, U.S. Department of Energy: www.eia.doe.gov

National Renewable Energy Laboratory: www.nrel.gov

Power Reactor Information System. International Atomic Energy Agency: www.iaea.org/programmes/a2/index.html

Survey of Energy Resources: Biomass. World Energy Council: www.worldenergy.org

The LNG industry. Groupe International des Importateurs de Gaz Naturel Liquefie, 2004

GRAPHICS

FOSSIL FUEL EXTRACTION: ChrisOrr.com and XNR Productions

PHOTOGRAPHS

PAGE 63, (UP) Jim Richardson; (UP CT) Mark C. Burnett/Photo Researchers; (CT) Courtesy National Renewable Energy Laboratory; (LO CT) John Mead/Science Photo Library/Photo Researchers; (LO) John Mead/Science Photo Library/Photo Researchers

Minerals
pp. 64–65

CONSULTANTS

Philip Brown
University of Wisconsin—Madison

Nelson Fugate
Mineral Information Institute

W. David Menzie and J. Michael Eros
USGS Minerals Information Team

GENERAL REFERENCES

USGS Minerals Information: minerals.usgs.gov/minerals

PHOTOGRAPHS

PAGE 64, (UP LE) Philip Brown; (CT LE) Philip Brown; (LO LE) Philip Brown; (UP CT) Phillip Hayson/Photo Researchers; (CT) Mark A. Schneider/Photo Researchers; (LO CT) Steven Holt/Stockpix.com; (UP RT) Mineral Information Institute/www.mii.org; (CT RT) Russ Lappa/Photo Researchers; (LO RT) Russ Lappa/Photo Researchers;
PAGE 65, (UP LE) U.S. Geological Survey; (CT LE) E.R. Degginger/Photo Researchers; (LO LE) U.S. Geological Survey; (UP CT) U.S. Geological Survey; (CT) Mineral Information Institute/www.mii.org; (LO CT) U.S. Geological Survey; (UP RT) Kenneth W. Larsen, Courtesy Smithsonian Institution, NMNH; (CT RT) Kenneth W. Larsen, Courtesy Smithsonian Institution, NMNH; (LO RT) Philip Brown

Environmental Stresses
pp. 66–67

CONSULTANTS

Christian Lambrechts
Division of Early Warning and Assessment (DEWA),
United Nations Environment Programme (UNEP)

GENERAL REFERENCES

Acidification and eutrophication of developing country ecosystems. Swedish University of Agricultural Sciences (SLU), 2002

Centre of Documentation, Research and Experimentation on Accidental Water Pollution (Cedre): www.le-cedre.fr

EM-DAT: The OFDA/CRED International Disaster Database. Université Catholique de Louvain, Brussels, Belgium: www.em-dat.net

Energy Information Administration. U.S. Department of Energy: www.eia.doe.gov

Global Forest Resources Assessment. Forestry Department of the Food and Agriculture Organization of the United Nations, 2005

United Nations Environment Programme-World Conservation and Monitoring Program (UNEP-WCMC): www.unep-wcmc.org

GRAPHICS

HUMAN FOOTPRINT: *National Geographic Atlas of the World,* 8th ed., Washington, D.C.: The National Geographic Society, 2005

SATELLITE IMAGES

DEPLETION OF THE OZONE LAYER: Ozone Processing Team at NASA/Goddard Space Flight Center

Protected Areas
pp. 68–69

CONSULTANTS

Simon Blyth
UNEP World Conservation Monitoring
Centre (UNEP-WCMC)

UNESCO World Heritage Centre

GENERAL REFERENCES

Antarctic Protected Areas Information Archive: www.cep.aq/apa

Protected areas map and statistics produced from the World Database on Protected Areas (WDPA) in March 2006 by UNEP World Conservation Monitoring Centre (WDPA custodian) (www.unep-wcmc.org), Cambridge, UK

UNEP-WCMC: www.unep-wcmc.org

UNESCO World Heritage Centre: whc.unesco.org

PHOTOGRAPHS

PAGE 69, (UP) James P. Blair; (LO LE) Art Wolfe/Getty Images; (LO CT) Richard Nowitz/NGS Image Collection; (LO RT) Sarah Leen

Acknowledgments

Globalization
pp. 70–71

CONSULTANTS

Mary Amiti
International Monetary Fund (IMF)

Janet Pau
Global Business Policy Council, A.T. Kearney, Inc.

Shang-Jin Wei
International Monetary Fund (IMF) and National Bureau of Economic Research (NBER)

GENERAL REFERENCES

Airports Council International: www.airports.org

Amiti, Mary, and Shang-Jin Wei, 2004, "Demystifying Outsourcing." *Finance & Development*, December 2004, pp. 36–39.

Balance of Payments Statistics, 2003. Washington, D.C.: International Monetary Fund.

International Telecommunication Union: www.itu.int

"Measuring Globalization." *Foreign Policy*, May/June 2005: 52–60. Globalization Index is developed by A.T. Kearney, Inc. and Foreign Policy (Carnegie Endowment for International Peace).

World Investment Report, 2005. Geneva, Switzerland: United Nations Conference on Trade and Development.

GRAPHICS

TRANSNATIONAL CORPORATIONS: Adapted from *The Times Complete History of the World*, 6th ed. New York: Barnes & Noble Books, 2004.
EXTREMES OF GLOBALIZATION: Adapted from "Measuring Globalization." *Foreign Policy*, May/June 2005.
IMPORTS IN BUSINESS SERVICES AS A SHARE OF GDP: Adapted from Amiti, Mary, and Shang-Jin Wei, 2004, "Demystifying Outsourcing." *Finance & Development*, December 2004, pp. 36–39.

Technology and Communication
pp. 72–73

CONSULTANTS

Tim Kelly
Strategic Planning Unit, International Telecommunication Union

Sarah Parkes
Media Works Creative

GENERAL REFERENCES

International Telecommunication Union: www.itu.int

GRAPHICS

CENTERS OF TECHNOLOGICAL INNOVATION: *Human Development Report 2001*, United Nations Development Programme (source data updated by Human Development Report Office in 2006) and World Intellectual Property Organization.
MILESTONES IN TECHNOLOGY: Adapted from *Human Development Report 2001*, United Nations Development Programme.
THE DIGITAL DIVIDE: NG Maps. Source data provided by TeleGeography Research, a division of PriMetrica, Inc. (www.telegeography.com) and the International Telecommunication Union. The Fuller Projection map design is a trademark of the Buckminster Fuller Institute © 1938, 1967, and 1992. All rights reserved.

Internet
pp. 74–75

CONSULTANTS

Josh Polterock and Brad Huffaker
Cooperative Association for Internet Data Analysis (CAIDA)

GENERAL REFERENCES

Cooperative Association for Internet Data Analysis (CAIDA): www.caida.org

International Telecommunication Union: www.itu.int

GRAPHICS

All images provided by the Cooperative Association for Internet Data Analysis (CAIDA), located at the San Diego Supercomputer Center (SDSC). CAIDA is a research unit of the University of California at San Diego (UCSD). URL: www.caida.org. Sponsors of this work include CAIDA Members, Cisco Systems, Department of Homeland Security (DHS, award NBCHC-040159), National Science Foundation (NSF, awards OCI-0137121, CNS-0433668, and CCR-0311690), and WIDE. Images copyright © 2006 The Regents of the University of California.

MAPPING THE SPREAD OF A COMPUTER VIRUS: Cooperative Association for Internet Data Analysis (CAIDA) "Nyxem Virus Analysis." Copyright © 2006 The Regents of the University of California. All rights reserved. Used by permission.
GLOBAL INTERNET CONNECTIVITY: Cooperative Association for Internet Data Analysis (CAIDA) "Skitter" Internet Map, 2005. Copyright © 2005 The Regents of the University of California. All rights reserved. Used by permission.
WORLDWIDE DISTRIBUTION OF INTERNET RESOURCES: Cooperative Association for Internet Data Analysis (CAIDA) "BGP Geopolitical Analysis Visualization." Copyright © 2006 The Regents of the University of California. All rights reserved. Used by permission.

ADDITIONAL CONSULTANTS

Regional Thematic Maps

Carl Haub
Population Reference Bureau

W. David Menzie and J. Michael Eros
USGS Minerals Information Team

Freddy Nachtergaele
Food and Agriculture Organization of the United Nations (FAO)

Gregory Yetman
Center for International Earth Science Information Network (CIESIN), Columbia University

Flags and Facts

Carl Haub
Population Reference Bureau

Whitney Smith
Flag Research Center

Antarctica
pp. 222–229

Graham Bartram
The Flag Institute

Scott Borg
National Science Foundation (NSF)—Antarctic Division

Mark R. Drinkwater
European Space Agency

Kenneth Jezek
Byrd Polar Research Center, Ohio State University

Tony K. Meunier
USGS Polar Program

Whitney Smith
Flag Research Center

David G. Vaughan
Bedmap Consortium, British Antarctic Survey

Roland Warner
Antarctic Cooperative Research Centre and Australian Antarctic Division

Oceanography
pp. 232–233

Eric J. Lindstrom
National Aeronautics and Space Administration (NASA)

Keelin Kuipers
National Atmospheric and Oceanic Administration (NOAA)

Bob Molinari
NOAA

Bruce Parker
NOAA/National Ocean Service (NOS)

Richard A. Schmalz, Jr.
NOAA

Limits of the Oceans & Seas
pp. 234–235

Adam J. Kerr
International Hydrographic Management Consulting

Space
pp. 246–261

Sanjay S. Limaye and Rosalyn A. Pertzborn
Space Science and Engineering Center, University of Wisconsin—Madison

Stephen P. Maran

Robert E. Pratt
National Geographic Maps

The Moon
pp. 248–251

Paul D. Spudis
Lunar and Planetary Institute, Houston, Texas

Mars
pp. 252–253

Damond Benningfield
StarDate radio series

The Solar System
pp. 254–255

Lucy McFadden
University of Maryland, College Park

The Planets
pp. 256–257

Henry Kline
NASA Jet Propulsion Laboratory (JPL)

The Universe
pp. 258–259

Todd J. Henry
Harvard-Smithsonian Center for Astrophysics

Edmund Bertschinger
Massachusetts Institute of Technology

Donald P. Schneider
Pennsylvania State University

Marc Postman
Space Telescope Science Institute (STScI)

Christopher D. Impey
University of Arizona

R. Brent Tully
University of Hawai'i

August E. Evrard
University of Michigan

Geographic Comparisons

John Kammerer
pp. 264–265
National Geospatial-Intelligence Agency (NGA)

George Sharman
NOAA/NESDIS/NGDC

Peter H. Gleick
Pacific Institute for Studies in Development, Environment, and Security

R.L. Fisher
Scripps Institution of Oceanography

Philip Micklin
Western Michigan University

Political Entities and Status

Leo Dillon
pp. 266–269
Department of State, Office of the Geographer

Harm J. de Blij
Michigan State University

Carl Haub
Population Reference Bureau

Whitney Smith
Flag Research Center

Special Flags
pp. 270–271

Whitney Smith
Flag Research Center

Glossary
pp. 282–284

Rex Honey
University of Iowa

Bernard O. Bauer
University of Southern California

PHYSICAL AND POLITICAL MAPS

Bureau of the Census, U.S. Department of Commerce

Bureau of Land Management, U.S. Department of the Interior

Central Intelligence Agency (CIA)

National Geographic Maps

National Geospatial-Intelligence Agency (NGA)

National Park Service, U.S. Department of the Interior

Office of the Geographer, U.S. Department of State

U.S. Board on Geographic Names (BGN)

U.S. Geological Survey, U.S. Department of the Interior

PRINCIPAL REFERENCE SOURCES

Columbia Gazetteer of the World. Cohen, Saul B., ed. New York: Columbia University Press, 1998

Encarta World English Dictionary. New York: St. Martin's Press and Microsoft Encarta, 1999

Human Development Report, 2005. New York: United Nations Development Programme (UNDP), Oxford University Press, 2005

International Trade Statistics, 2005. Geneva, Switzerland: World Trade Organization

McKnight, Tom L. *Physical Geography: A Landscape Appreciation.* 5th ed. Upper Saddle River, New Jersey: Prentice Hall, 1996

National Geographic Atlas of the World, 8th ed., Washington, D.C.: The National Geographic Society, 2005

Strahler, Alan and Arthur Strahler. *Physical Geography: Science and Systems of the Human Environment.* 2nd ed., John Wiley & Sons, Inc, 2002

Tarbuck, Edward J. and Frederick K. Lutgens. *Earth: An Introduction to Physical Geology.* 7th ed. Upper Saddle River, New Jersey: Prentice Hall, 2002

World Development Indicators, 2005. Washington, D.C.: World Bank

The World Factbook 2006. Washington, D.C.: Central Intelligence Agency, 2006

The World Health Report 2005. Geneva: World Health Organization, 2001

World Investment Report, 2005. New York and Geneva: United Nations Conference on Trade and Development, 2005

Cambridge Dictionaries Online
dictionary.cambridge.org

Central Intelligence Agency
www.cia.gov

CIESIN
www.ciesin.org

Conservation International
www.conservation.org

Energy Information Agency
www.eia.doe.gov

Food and Agriculture Organization of the UN
www.fao.org

International Monetary Fund
www.imf.org

Merriam-Webster OnLine
www.m-w.com

National Aeronautics and Space Administration
www.nasa.gov

National Atmospheric and Oceanic Administration
www.noaa.gov

National Climatic Data Center
www.ncdc.noaa.gov

National Geophysical Data Center
www.ngdc.noaa.gov

National Park Service
www.nps.gov

National Renewable Energy Laboratory
www.nrel.gov

Population Reference Bureau
www.prb.org

United Nations
www.un.org

UN Conference on Trade and Development
www.unctad.org

UN Development Programme
www.undp.org

UN Educational, Cultural, and Scientific Organization
www.unesco.org

UNESCO Institute for Statistics
www.uis.unesco.org

UNEP-WCMC
www.unep-wcmc.org

UN Millennium Development Goals
www.un.org/millenniumgoals

UN Population Division
www.unpopulation.org

UN Refugee Agency
www.unhcr.org

UN Statistics Division
unstats.un.org

U.S. Board on Geographic Names
geonames.usgs.gov

U.S. Bureau of Economic Analysis
www.bea.gov

U.S. Census Bureau
www.census.gov

U.S. Geological Survey
www.usgs.gov

World Bank
www.worldbank.org

World Health Organization
www.who.int

World Trade Organization
www.wto.org

WWF
www.worldwildlife.org

SATELLITE IMAGES

CONTINENTAL SATELLITE IMAGES: NASA/Jet Propulsion Laboratory (JPL)/California Institute of Technology/Advanced Very High Resolution Radiometer (AVHRR) Project/Cartographic Applications Group (CAG)

The Cartographic Applications Group manipulated more than 500 NOAA weather satellite images acquired by the AVHRR instrument to create satellite coverages at one-kilometer resolution (one pixel of data equals one kilometer on the Earth). Using hundreds of multidate NOAA AVHRR satellite scenes and imaging in the visible and near-infrared wavelengths, the mosaics were created in a rapid fashion using semiautomated software procedures based on JPL's VICAR/IBIS image processing and GIS software.

FRONT JACKET, ANTARCTICA FROM SPACE: WorldSat International Inc., www.skyviewcafe.com, and NG Books

TITLE PAGE (PAGE 2), Peter Sloss, NOAA (National Geophysical Data Center)

PAGE 29, MISSISSIPPI RIVER DELTA: Centre National d'Etudes Spatiales (CNES)

PAGES 32–33, GLOBAL LAND COVER CLASSIFICATION AT 1KM SPATIAL RESOLUTION USING A CLASSIFICATION TREE APPROACH: M. Hansen, R. DeFries, J.R.G. Townshend, and R. Sohlberg. 1998. 1 Km Land Cover Classification Derived from AVHRR. College Park, Maryland: The Global Land Cover Facility (Note: Data was derived from NOAA AVHRR and NASA Landsat imagery.)

PAGE 34, *Images created originally for the GLOBE program by NOAA's National Geophysical Data Center, Boulder, Colorado, U.S.A.*
CLOUD COVER: International Satellite Cloud Climatology Project (ISCCP); National Aeronautics and Space Administration (NASA); Goddard Institute for Space Studies (GISS). **PRECIPITATION:** Global Precipitation Climatology Project (GPCP); International Satellite Land Surface Climatology Project (ISLSCP). **SOLAR ENERGY:** Earth Radiation Budget Experiment (ERBE); Greenhouse Effect Detection Experiment (GEDEX). **TEMPERATURE:** National Center for Environmental Prediction (NCEP); National Center for Atmospheric Research (NCAR); National Weather Service (NWS).

PAGE 38, HURRICANE IMAGE: NASA Goddard Space Flight Center (GSFC), data from NOAA

PAGE 39, EL NIÑO IMAGE SEQUENCE: Courtesy Robert M. Carey, NOAA; **LIGHTNING IMAGE:** NASA Marshall Space Flight Center Lightning Imaging Sensor (LIS) Instrument Team, Huntsville, Alabama

PAGE 40, BIOSPHERE FROM SPACE: SeaWiFS, NASA/Goddard Space Flight Center, Gene Carl Feldman and ORBIMAGE

PAGE 44, LIGHTS OF THE WORLD: Composite image: MODIS imagery; ETOPO-2 relief; NOAA/NGDC and DMSP lights at night data

PAGE 66, DEPLETION OF THE OZONE LAYER: Ozone Processing Team at NASA/Goddard Space Flight Center

PAGE 228, SURFACE ELEVATION: Byrd Polar Research Center, Ohio State University. **ICE SHEET THICKNESS:** Bedmap Project. **ICE FLOW VELOCITY:** Roland Warner, Antarctic Cooperative Research Centre and Australian Antarctic Division. **SEA ICE MOVEMENT AND WIND FLOW: SEA ICE VELOCITY DATA:** Mark R. Drinkwater and Xiang Liu, Jet Propulsion Laboratory/California Institute of Technology. **SURFACE WINDS:** Based on data from David H. Bromwich, Ohio State University, and Thomas R. Parish, University of Wyoming.

PAGES 246–247, UGC10214 ("TADPOLE GALAXY") IMAGE: NASA/Holland Ford, Johns Hopkins University; Mark Clampin and George Hartig, Space Telescope Science Institute; Garth Illingworth, University of California Observatories/Lick Observatory

PAGES 249 AND 251, CLEMENTINE TOPOGRAPHIC MAP OF THE MOON: Courtesy of the Lunar and Planetary Institute, Houston, Texas

PAGES 256 AND 257, THE PLANETS: Courtesy of NASA/JPL/Caltech

PAGE 384, ETOPO-2 relief; Digital Chart of the World

PHOTOGRAPHS

Front Jacket
(LE) Jodi Cobb/NGS Image Collection
(CT LE) Robert B. Haas/NGS Image Collection
(RT) Paul Chesley/NGS Image Collection

Interior
PAGE 24, (UP) R.D. Griggs, USGS
PAGE 24, (CT) Sharon Johnson
PAGE 24, (LO) David Muench
PAGE 25, Raymond Gehman/NGS Image Collection
PAGE 26, (LE) Joel Sartore/www.joelsartore.com
PAGE 26, (CT) Science Photo Library/CORBIS
PAGE 26, (UP RT) George F. Mobley
PAGE 26, (LO RT) James D. Balog
PAGE 27, (UP LE) Wolfgang Kaehler/CORBIS
PAGE 27, (UP CT) Lyle Rosbotham
PAGE 27, (UP RT) Adriel Heisey
PAGE 27, (LO LE) Marc Moritsch/NGS Image Collection
PAGE 27, (LO CT) Peter Essick
PAGE 27, (LO RT) Sam Abell, NGS
PAGE 28, (LE) Peter Essick
PAGE 28, (CT) Douglas R. Grant
PAGE 28, (RT) Tom and Pat Leeson
PAGE 29, (UP CT) Rob Brander
PAGE 29, (UP RT) George Veni and James Jasek
PAGE 29, (LO LE) Sharon Johnson
PAGE 29, (LO RT) Douglas R. Grant/Parks Canada
PAGE 32, (UP LE) Tom and Pat Leeson/Photo Researchers
PAGE 32, (UP RT) Michael Nichols/NGS Image Collection
PAGE 32, (LO LE) Stephen J. Krasemann/Photo Researchers
PAGE 32, (LO CT LE) Rod Planck/Photo Researchers
PAGE 32, (CT LE) Jim Steinberg/Photo Researchers
PAGE 32, (CT RT) Matthew C. Hansen, University of Maryland
PAGE 32, (LO CT RT) Gregory G. Dimijian/Photo Researchers
PAGE 32, (LO RT) Sharon Johnson
PAGE 33, (LE) Georg Gerster/Photo Researchers
PAGE 33, (LO CT LE) Rod Planck/Photo Researchers
PAGE 33, (LE CT) Jim Richardson
PAGE 33, (RT CT) George Steinmetz
PAGE 33, (LO CT RT) Steve McCurry
PAGE 33, (RT) B. and C. Alexander/PhotoResearchers
PAGE 35, Sharon Johnson
PAGE 50, (LE) Jodi Cobb/National Geographic Photographer
PAGE 50, (RT) James L. Stanfield
PAGES 50–51 Tony Heiderer
PAGE 51, (LE) Thomas J. Abercrombie
PAGE 51, (RT) Annie Griffiths Belt;
PAGE 61, (LE) Steven L. Raymer/NGS Image Collection
PAGE 61, (CT) Richard Olsenius/NGS Image Collection
PAGE 61, (RT) Jim Richardson
PAGE 63, (UP) Jim Richardson
PAGE 63, (UP CT) Courtesy National Renewable Energy Laboratory
PAGE 63, (LO CT) John Mead/Science Photo Library/Photo Researchers
PAGE 63, (LO) John Mead/Science Photo Library/Photo Researchers
PAGE 64, (UP LE) Philip Brown
PAGE 64, (CT LE) Philip Brown
PAGE 64, (LO LE) Philip Brown
PAGE 64, (UP CT) Phillip Hayson/Photo Researchers
PAGE 64, (CT) Mark A. Schneider/Photo Researchers
PAGE 64, (LO CT) Steven Holt/Stockpix.com
PAGE 64, (UP RT) Mineral Information Institute/www.mii.org
PAGE 64, (CT RT) Russ Lappa/Photo Researchers
PAGE 64, (LO RT) Russ Lappa/Photo Researchers
PAGE 65, (UP LE) U.S. Geological Survey
PAGE 65, (CT LE) E.R. Degginger/Photo Researchers
PAGE 65, (LO LE) U.S. Geological Survey
PAGE 65, (UP CT) U.S. Geological Survey
PAGE 65, (CT) Mineral Information Institute/www.mii.org
PAGE 65, (LO CT) U.S. Geological Survey
PAGE 65, (UP RT) Kenneth W. Larsen, Courtesy Smithsonian Institution, NMNH
PAGE 65, (CT RT) Kenneth W. Larsen, Courtesy Smithsonian Institution, NMNH
PAGE 65, (LO RT) Philip Brown
PAGE 69, (UP) James P. Blair
PAGE 69, (LO LE) Art Wolfe/Getty Images
PAGE 69, (LO CT) Richard Nowitz/NGS Image Collection
PAGE 69, (LO RT) Sarah Leen
PAGES 76–77, Ron Watts/CORBIS
PAGE 79, W.E. Garrett/NGS Image Collection
PAGES 122–123, Skip Brown/NGS Image Collection
PAGE 125, L. Scott Shelton
PAGES 134–135, George F. Mobley/NGS Image Collection
PAGE 137, Winfield I. Parks, Jr.
PAGES 162–163, J. Yip/Imagestate/Panoramic Images
PAGE 165, Steve McCurry/NGS Image Collection
PAGES 190–191, Beverly Joubert/NGS Image Collection
PAGE 193, David Boyer/NGS Image Collection
PAGES 206–207, Theo Allofs/CORBIS
PAGE 209, Pam Gardner/Frank Lane Picture Agency/CORBIS
PAGES 222–223, Paul A. Souders/CORBIS
PAGE 225, Maria Stenzel

KEY TO FLAGS AND FACTS

The National Geographic Society, whose cartographic policy is to recognize de facto countries, counted 192 independent nations in the spring of 2006. Within this atlas, fact boxes for independent nations, most dependencies, and U.S. states are placed on or next to regional maps that show the areas they represent. Each box includes the flag of the political entity, as well as important statistical data. Boxes for some dependencies show two flags—a local flag and the flag of the administering country. Because Paraguay and the state of Oregon have different designs on the obverse and reverse sides of their flags, their fact boxes show both sides of their flags.

The statistical data provide highlights of geography, demography, and economy. These details offer a brief overview of each entity; they present general characteristics and are not intended to be comprehensive studies. The structured nature of the text results in some generic collective or umbrella terms. The industry category, for instance, includes services in addition to traditional manufacturing sectors. Space limitations dictate the amount of information included. For example, the only languages listed for the U.S. are English and Spanish, although many others are spoken.

Fact boxes are arranged alphabetically by the conventional short forms of the country or dependency names (except for the Oceania, Islands of Africa, and Europe's Smallest Countries fact boxes, where country and dependency boxes are grouped separately). The short-form names for dependencies are followed by the name of the administering country in parentheses. The short-form names for Côte d'Ivoire, Myanmar, and Timor-Leste are followed by alternate, commonly refered to names in parentheses. The conventional long-form names of the country or dependency appear within colored stripes below the short-form names; if there are no long forms, the short forms are repeated. This policy has two exceptions: For U.S. states, nicknames are shown inside the colored stripes, and for French overseas departments, the words "Overseas Department of France" appear inside the colored stripes. These departments of France are the equivalent of states in the United States, and thus not considered dependencies.

AREA accounts for the total area of a country, U.S. state, or dependency, including all land and inland water delimited by international boundaries, intranational boundaries, or coastlines.

In the POPULATION category, the figures for U.S. state populations are from the U.S. Census Bureau's 2005 midyear estimates. Two population figures are listed for the CAPITAL and LARGEST CITY of each state. The city-proper figure, from data provided by the U.S. Census Bureau, shows the estimated number of people who lived within the incorporated city limits on July 1st of 2004. The larger metro-area figure represents the number of people who live within a U.S. Office of Management and Budget-defined metropolitan statistical area—a broader designation that includes both a city proper and the surrounding urbanized region. These July 1st, 2004 estimates are from the U.S. Census Bureau's table of Annual Estimates of the Population of Metropolitan and Micropolitan Statistical Areas. Metropolitan statistical areas and their geographic boundaries can cross state borders and are defined on the basis of population as well as other factors. Some state capitals with small populations are not defined as part of a metropolitan statistical area; in those cases, only city-proper population figures are shown.

POPULATION figures for independent nations and dependencies are mid-2005 figures from the Population Reference Bureau in Washington, D.C. Next to CAPITAL is the name of the seat of government, followed by the city's population. Capital city populations for both independent nations and dependencies are from 2003 United Nations estimates and represent the population of the city's urban agglomeration, which usually includes both city proper and adjacent suburbs. Both POPULATION and CAPITAL population figures for countries, dependencies, and U.S. states are rounded to the nearest thousand.

Under RELIGION, the most widely practiced faith appears first. "Traditional" or "indigenous" connotes beliefs of important local sects, such as Maya in Middle America. Under LANGUAGE, the most widely spoken language is listed first. Official languages are denoted using the parenthetical (official) following the language. Both RELIGION and LANGUAGE are in rank ordering, taken from the CIA World Factbook.

LITERACY generally indicates the percentage of the population above the age of 15 who can read and write. There are no universal standards of literacy, so these estimates (from the CIA World Factbook) are based on the most common definition available for a nation. LIFE EXPECTANCY (from 2005 Population Reference Bureau data) represents the average number of years a group of infants born in the same year can be expected to live if the mortality rate at each age remains constant in the future.

GDP PER CAPITA is Gross Domestic Product divided by midyear population estimates. GDP estimates for independent nations are from the UN Statistics Division and follow their methodology for data estimation (for details, see http://unstats.un.org). Estimates for dependencies are from the CIA World Factbook. All are measured in purchasers' prices (i.e., they take into account the purchasing powers of different currencies). For U.S. states, equivalent measurements to GDP on the intranational level have been used. PCPI, or Per Capita Personal INCOME, figures from the U.S. Bureau of Economic Analysis are presented; PCPI divides the total personal income of all residents of a state by the midyear population.

Individual income estimates such as GDP PER CAPITA and PCI are among the many indicators used to assess a nation's well-being. As statistical averages, they hide extremes of poverty and wealth. Furthermore, they take no account of factors that affect quality of life, such as environmental degradation, educational opportunities, and health care.

ECONOMY information for the independent nations and dependencies is divided into three general categories: Industry, Agriculture, and Exports. Because of structural limitations, only the primary industries (Ind), agricultural commodities (Agr), and exports (Exp) as listed in the CIA World Factbook are reported. Agriculture serves as an umbrella term for not only crops but also livestock, products, and fish. In the interest of conciseness, agriculture for the independent nations presents, when applicable but not limited to, three major crops, followed respectively by leading entries for livestock, products, and fish. For the other two categories, the four leading industries and export products are listed where data and space limitations allow. The information provided for each category is listed in rank order, starting with the largest by value or importance.

NA indicates that data are not available.

NATIONAL GEOGRAPHIC

Family Reference Atlas of the World

SECOND EDITION

Published by the National Geographic Society

John M. Fahey, Jr. — *President and Chief Executive Officer*

Gilbert M. Grosvenor — *Chairman of the Board*

Nina D. Hoffman — *Executive Vice President, President, Books Publishing Group*

Prepared by the Book Division

Kevin Mulroy — *Senior Vice President and Publisher*

Marianne R. Koszorus — *Design Director*

Staff for this Atlas

Carl Mehler — *Project Editor and Director of Maps*

Nicholas P. Rosenbach — *Supervisor of Map Edit*

Timothy J. Carter, Laura Exner, Steven D. Gardner, Thomas L. Gray, Joseph F. Ochlak — *Map Editors*

Matt Chwastyk, Sam Chernawsky, Gregory Ugiansky, and XNR Productions — *Map Research and Compilation*

Matt Chwastyk, Gregory Ugiansky — *Map Production Managers*

Steven D. Gardner, James Huckenpahler, Kyle T. Rector, Martin S. Walz, and XNR Productions — *Map Production*

David B. Miller — *Contributing Geographer*

Rebecca Lescaze; Principal, Carolinda E. Averitt, Laura Exner, K. M. Kostyal, Jane Sunderland — *Text Editors*

Elisabeth B. Booz, Patrick Booz, Philip Brown, William Burroughs, Carlos Castillo-Salgado, Manuel Colunga-Garcia, Byron Crape, Ellen Ficklen, Michael Finger, Richard Fix, Stuart H. Gage, Matthew C. Hansen, Craig K. Harris, Mike Hoffmann, Tim Kelly, K. M. Kostyal, Ruth Levine, Eric Lindstrom, David T. Long, Enrique Loyola-Elizondo, Stephen P. Maran, Carl Mehler, W. David Menzie, H. Michael Mogil, John Morrison, Rhea Muchow, Ted Munn, Margaret Murray, Sarah Parks, Janet Pau, Josh Polterock, Antony Shugaar, Brad Singer, Peter W. Sloss, Whitney Smith, Paul D. Spudis, Robert Tilling, Simon Walker, Patrick J. Webber, Joe Yogerst — *Contributing Writers*

Sam Chernawsky, Elizabeth B. Booz, Victoria Garrett Jones, Rhea Muchow, Joseph F. Ochlak, Anne E. Withers — *Text Researchers*

Marty Ittner, Principal; Jennifer Christiansen, Megan McCarthy, Susan K. White — *Book Design*

ChrisOrr.com, Tibor G. Tóth — *Art and Illustrations*

Dana Chivvis, Sadie Quarrier — *Photo Editors*

Abby Lepold, Meredith C. Wilcox — *Photo Assistants*

Rebecca Hinds — *Managing Editor*

R. Gary Colbert — *Production Director*

Manufacturing and Quality Control

Christopher A. Liedel — *Chief Financial Officer*

Phillip L. Schlosser — *Vice President*

John T. Dunn — *Technical Director*

Vincent P. Ryan — *Director*

Maryclare Tracy — *Manager*

Reproduction by Quad/Graphics, Alexandria, Virginia

Printed and Bound by Mondadori S.p.A., Verona, Italy

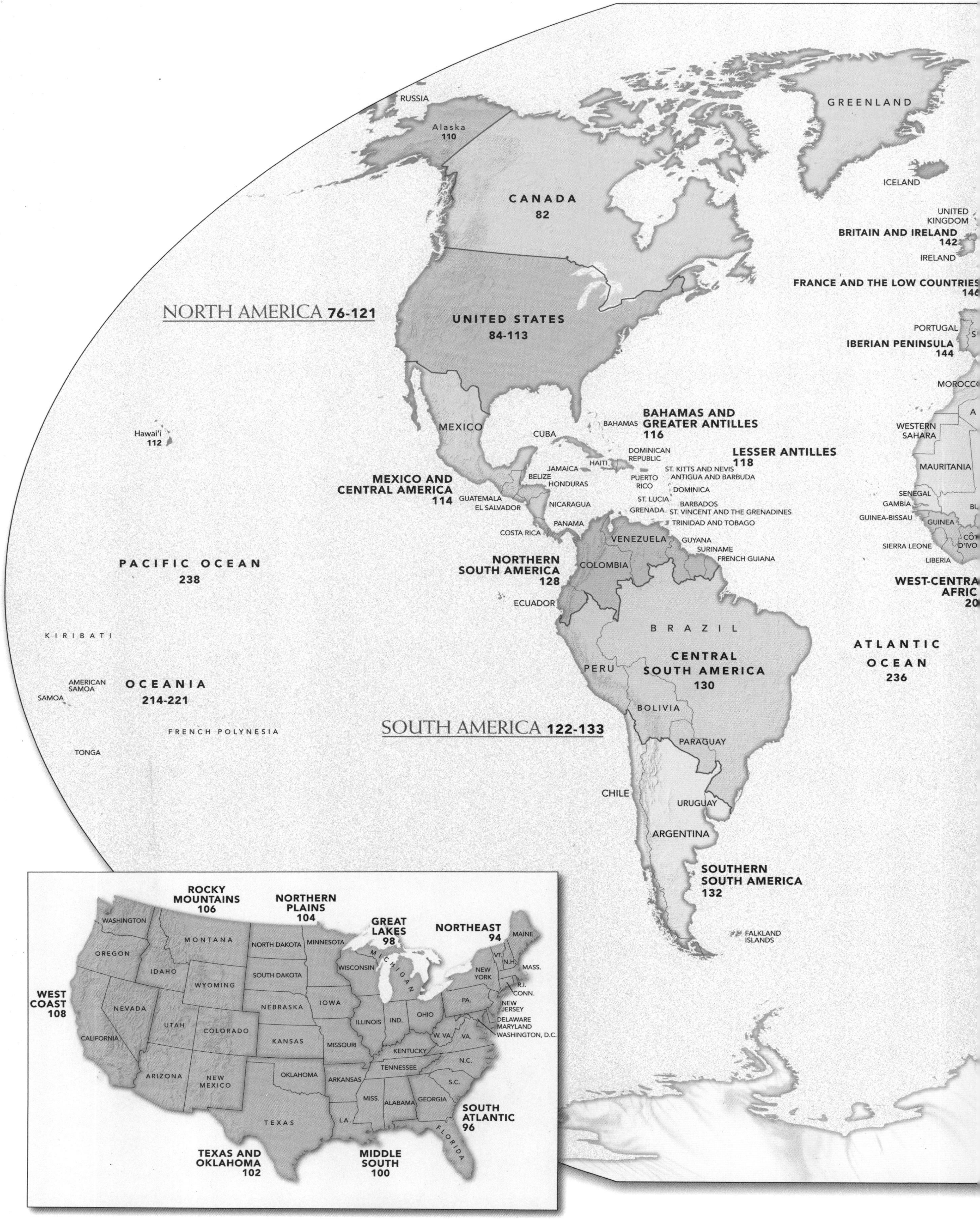

NORTH AMERICA 76-121
RUSSIA
Alaska 110
CANADA 82
GREENLAND
ICELAND
UNITED KINGDOM
BRITAIN AND IRELAND 142
IRELAND
FRANCE AND THE LOW COUNTRIES
PORTUGAL
IBERIAN PENINSULA 144
MOROCCO
UNITED STATES 84-113
MEXICO
Hawai'i 112
CUBA
BAHAMAS
BAHAMAS AND GREATER ANTILLES 116
DOMINICAN REPUBLIC
HAITI
JAMAICA
BELIZE
HONDURAS
PUERTO RICO
LESSER ANTILLES 118
ST. KITTS AND NEVIS
ANTIGUA AND BARBUDA
DOMINICA
ST. LUCIA
BARBADOS
GRENADA
ST. VINCENT AND THE GRENADINES
TRINIDAD AND TOBAGO
MEXICO AND CENTRAL AMERICA 114
GUATEMALA
EL SALVADOR
NICARAGUA
PANAMA
COSTA RICA
WESTERN SAHARA
MAURITANIA
SENEGAL
GAMBIA
GUINEA-BISSAU
GUINEA
SIERRA LEONE
LIBERIA
VENEZUELA
GUYANA
SURINAME
FRENCH GUIANA
COLOMBIA
NORTHERN SOUTH AMERICA 128
ECUADOR
PACIFIC OCEAN 238
KIRIBATI
BRAZIL
CENTRAL SOUTH AMERICA 130
PERU
BOLIVIA
ATLANTIC OCEAN 236
AMERICAN SAMOA
SAMOA
OCEANIA 214-221
FRENCH POLYNESIA
TONGA
SOUTH AMERICA 122-133
PARAGUAY
CHILE
URUGUAY
ARGENTINA
SOUTHERN SOUTH AMERICA 132
FALKLAND ISLANDS
ROCKY MOUNTAINS 106
NORTHERN PLAINS 104
GREAT LAKES 98
NORTHEAST 94
WASHINGTON
MONTANA
NORTH DAKOTA
MINNESOTA
MAINE
OREGON
MICHIGAN
VT.
N.H.
IDAHO
SOUTH DAKOTA
WISCONSIN
NEW YORK
MASS.
WYOMING
R.I.
CONN.
WEST COAST 108
NEVADA
NEBRASKA
IOWA
PA.
NEW JERSEY
UTAH
COLORADO
ILLINOIS
IND.
OHIO
DELAWARE
MARYLAND
WASHINGTON, D.C.
CALIFORNIA
KANSAS
MISSOURI
W. VA.
VA.
KENTUCKY
N.C.
TENNESSEE
ARIZONA
NEW MEXICO
OKLAHOMA
ARKANSAS
S.C.
MISS.
ALABAMA
GEORGIA
SOUTH ATLANTIC 96
TEXAS
LA.
FLORIDA
TEXAS AND OKLAHOMA 102
MIDDLE SOUTH 100